WEBSTER'S NEW WORLD® HEBREW DICTIONARY

HEBREW-ENGLISH
ENGLISH-HEBREW

HAYIM BALTSAN

HOUGHTON MIFFLIN HARCOURT
BOSTON NEW YORK

Database design and creation
by Avikam Baltsan, Tel-Aviv, Israel.

Computerized phototypesetting
by MONOLINE PRESS, Ltd., Benei Beraq, Israel.

ISBN 978-0-544-94416-9

Visit our website: hmhco.com

Library of Congress Cataloging-in-Publication Data:

Baltsan, Hayim
Webster's New World™ dictionary / by Hayim Baltsan.
p. cm.
Hebrew-English/English-Hebrew
Entry words in the Hebrew-English section appear in transliterated
form followed by the word or phrase in vernacular characters.
ISBN 978-0-671-88991-3
1. Hebrew language — Dictionaries — English 2. Hebrew
language — Transliteration into English — Dictionaries. 3. English
language — Dictionaries — Hebrew. I. Title.
PJ4833.B26 1992 91-32079
492.4'321—dc20 CIP

Printed in the United States of America

23 24 25 26 - DOC - 23 22 21 20 19

4500750382

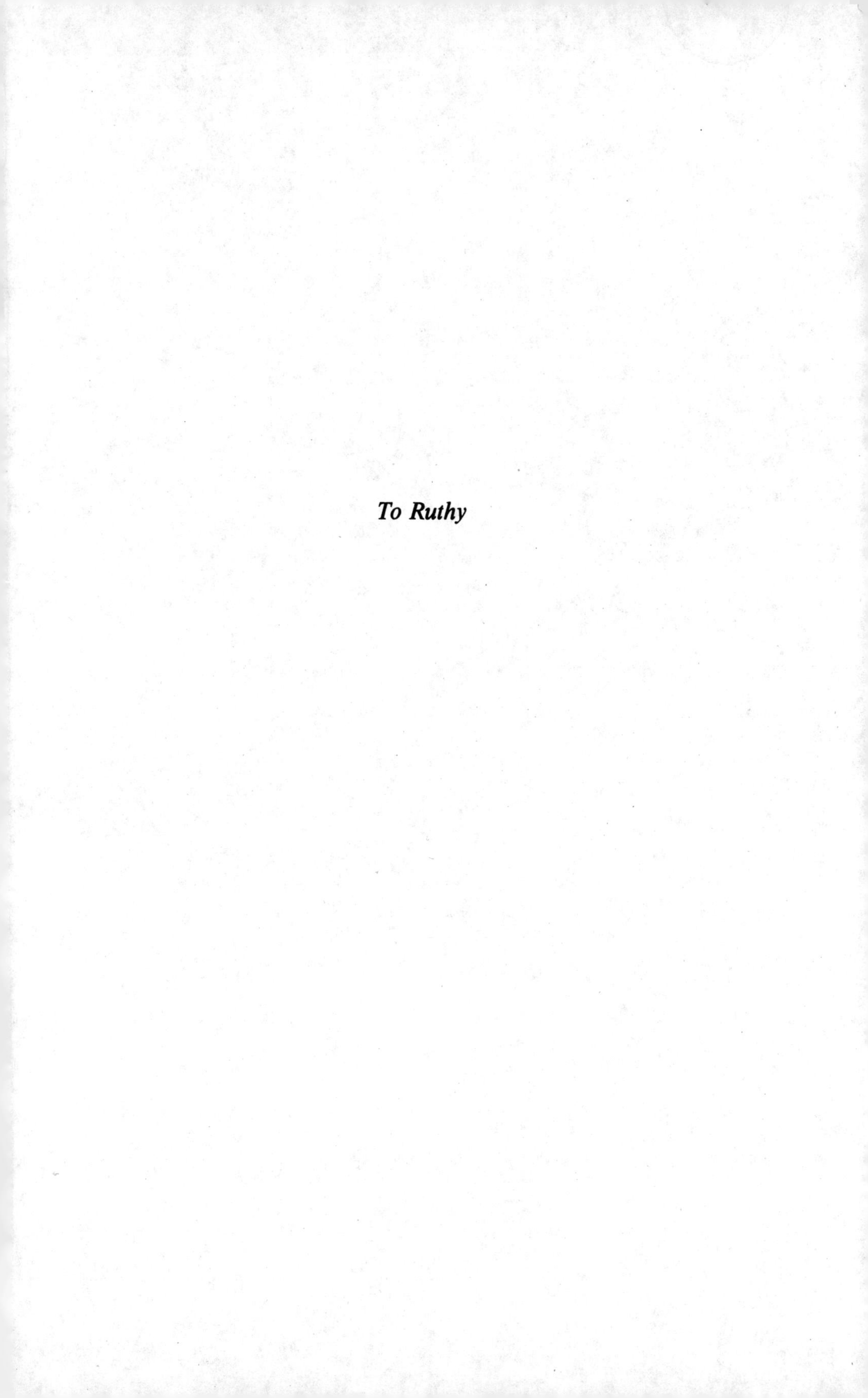

To Ruthy

TABLE OF CONTENTS

PREFACE AND ACKNOWLEDGMENTS

This is a dictionary that differs, both in structure and scope, from any other Hebrew dictionary. It has been conceived and designed with one specific purpose: to render Hebrew — a language reputed to be 'Greek' to anyone who has not invested years of study in it — accessible to all. In other words, to make it possible for everyone — even for absolute beginners not acquainted with the Hebrew alphabet — to ascertain the meaning, pronunciation, spelling or usage of any Hebrew word, name or expression in current use as easily as one would if it were Spanish, Italian, German or Swedish.

To achieve this, some departures from the traditional pattern of bilingual dictionaries were necessary. First and most conspicuously innovative of these was to present the Hebrew entry words of the Hebrew-English part of the dictionary in the Latin alphabetical order familiar to any English speaker, instead of in the normal Hebrew alphabetical order characteristic of all other Hebrew-English dictionaries. This was made possible by introducing a second innovation; that is, presenting each Hebrew word first in a phonetic transliteration using the Latin alphabet, followed by its proper Hebrew spelling. This means that it is the sound of any Hebrew word that determines where the user should look for it in the Hebrew-English part. Because we felt it was important for the user to be able to easily spell out words heard in conversation, on the radio or TV and to pronounce Hebrew equivalents found in the English-Hebrew section of this dictionary, we could not use the official Latin transliteration, as meticulously prescribed by the Hebrew Language Academy and used in road signs and maps intended for speakers of all languages. Instead, we had to devise one of our own, palatable to the ordinary English speaker, normally by no means a linguist. Furthermore, we could not be content with the normative pronunciation and usage of Hebrew words, but also had to include colloquial pronunciations and usage. For that is how the Hebrew vocabulary will most likely reach a visitor's ear. In order to accomplish this, we sometimes had to put the user's ease before normativity, and convenience before formal consistency. We applied our rules as best we could and now leave it up to the user to judge how well we accomplished our aim.

One thing needs to be emphasized. We recognize that the innovations of our transliteration system, with its minor inconsistencies, could be acceptable only so long as they are regarded as restricted specifically to this dictionary, to make it easier to use. My system could not and was never intended to be used in lieu of Hebrew's official transliteration system as prescribed by the Hebrew Language Academy. And of course it could never be considered an attempt to replace the real Hebrew alphabet, known and revered for nearly 3,000 years.

With that point cleared, let me now pass to acknowledgments due. I am indebted to many for having given me a hand, at one time or another, during the nearly 15 years it has taken to evolve the concept of this dictionary, plan its details, compile both its parts and prepare it all for print. Were I to mention all friends, colleagues, authorities and sometimes even complete strangers to whom I turned for learned advice, opinion or information, the list would have been too long. Yet, it is they, and also some of the criticisms they made, objections they raised and rectifications they proposed, that often guided me towards solutions to many of the problems encountered.

Thankful to them all, let me nevertheless confine myself to the few I owe the most to. First among them stands out the late *Abraham Even-Shushan,* Hebrew's foremost lexicographer in our time. As early as 1979, it was he who was first to give his blessing to this project, though all I had to show then were the mere idea and a few sample pages. Later, with the full draft manuscript ready, another great Hebrew linguist, *Prof. Chaim Rabin*, presided over the official approval granted to it by the highest authority in the matter, the *Council on the Teaching of Hebrew* in Jerusalem. Then, from faraway Cleveland, came an encouragement by *David B. Guralnik*, dean of American lexicographers, who recommended the book's publication to *Simon & Schuster*, by then the publishers of *Webster's New World*™ dictionaries. Last year, with the book nearly ready for printing, further encouragement came from the Vice-President of the *Hebrew Language Academy, Prof. Moshe Bar-Asher*. To all of them I stand deeply indebted.

Further thanks are due to those who assisted me in checking, editing and correcting the work after it had been completed and in advising me on putting right many details thereof. They were: *Dr. Ori Soltes* of the Cleveland Institute of Jewish Studies, *Dr. Joseph A. Reif* of Israel's Bar-Ilan University, *Mr. Raffi Moses*, and *Dr. Reuven Alberg*, formerly of Bar-Ilan University. Special thanks go also to *Mrs. Nurit Reich*, Public Consultant for Tel-Aviv Area of the Hebrew Language Academy who, with infinite patience, answered my at times almost day-by-day queries re linguistic issues demanding the latest normative rulings.

Further, let me mention my son, Artificial Intelligence Consultant *Avikam Baltsan*, who, whenever needed, rushed to my assistance, snatching time from his other, perhaps more sophisticated, projects. It is he I have to thank for the two complex databases he devised, one for the Hebrew-English section and one for the English-Hebrew, in order to render more comfortably readable the constant font changes within the text of each dictionary entry.

Last but not least, my thanks are due to those who, both in Cleveland and New York, shared with me the many and various birthpains of advancing this project and seeing it through during the nearly five years it has taken to materialize. First among those are *Dr. Victoria Neufeldt*, former Editor in Chief of *Webster's New World*, as well as *Philip Friedman* and *William Hamill*, at the time Associate Publisher and Managing Editor, respectively, of Prentice Hall General Reference.

Hayim Baltsan
May 1992

GUIDE TO THIS DICTIONARY

1. Hebrew in Latin Alphabetical Order

The most important feature of this dictionary is the exclusive consecutive order in which the Hebrew entries are ranged in the Hebrew-English part it begins with. It is not the traditional Hebrew alphabetical order, i.e., not "back to front" (in English terms), as in any other Hebrew-English dictionary, but the Latin one, familiar to any English-speaker. To achieve that, each Hebrew entry word is preceded by its English transliteration, which, alone, determines where to look for it. Hence, searching for a Hebrew word one has heard no longer requires preparatory knowledge of the Hebrew alphabet nor of its unfamiliar consecutive order. Thus, once one has sounded out and respelled the Hebrew word, one can locate it with the same ease as with a language that uses the Latin alphabet.

2. Transliteration Must Be Memorized

Becoming well acquainted with the transliteration system is therefore essential for being able to use this dictionary. This is necessary not only for locating a Hebrew entry word one wishes to know, but also to be able to pronounce properly and inflect correctly any Hebrew word learned from the second, English-Hebrew, part of this dictionary. To do this, one must thoroughly absorb the few pages of this guide.

The transliteration offered in this dictionary is an easy-to-read one and fully phonetic, yet does not require the user to assimilate any letters or signs one does not already know. Each English vowel and consonant used in the transliteration stands for only one specific sound, and each of those sounds must be memorized.

3. Letters Used in the Transliteration

Not all English letters are used in this transliteration. The vowels **i** and **u** and the consonants **c**, **q**, **w** and **x** are not used. Below are the letters used with each followed by a key word to show its pronunciation:

Vowels:	**a**	as in *far*
	e	as in *less*
	ee	as in *see*
	o	as in *more*
	oo	as in *ooze*

Consonants		
	ch	as in *chin*
	g	as in *game* or *get*
	j	as in *job*
	kh	as *ch* in the Scottish word *loch* or in the Jewish name *Chaim*
	r	is pronounced gutturally, similar to the *r* in French or German
	s	as in *safe*
	sh	as in *show*
	ts	as in *hearts* or as *tz* in *Ritz*
	y	as in *yard*
	z	as in *zero*

The remaining consonants in the system (**b, d, f, h, k, l, m, n, p, t** and **v**) are pronounced more or less as in English.

The complete transliteration is found on page xxix.

4. How to Find Combined Letters

Some Hebrew letters have no equivalents in the English alphabet. Each of these is transliterated by a digraph; i.e., two English letters combined. The digraphs used are: **ch**, **ee**, **kh**, **oo**, **sh** and **ts**. Looking in the Hebrew-English part for a word beginning with any of these combined letters, the user must remember that such combinations are allotted sections of their own. The order is strictly alphabetical:

a	**j**	**r**
b	**k**	**s**
ch	**kh**	**sh**
d	**l**	**t**
e	**m**	**ts**
ee	**n**	**v**
f	**o**	**y**
g	**oo**	**z**
h	**p**	

5. Unfamiliar Combinations of Consonants

Hebrew words, as transliterated, sometimes open with combinations of consonants (as, for example, **kf**, **tn**, etc.) that, to an English speaker, sound unfamiliar, or somewhat difficult to pronounce. Care has been taken, in such cases, to provide two forms of transliteration: one with the consonants combined (e.g., **tn**), and one with the vowel 'e' inserted between them for the ease of pronunciation. For the user's convenience, a Hebrew word like תנאי (condition) may be located in two different places, respelled one time as **tnay** and the other one as **tenay**. Equally, a Hebrew word like פסק (ruling) is available both as **psak** and **pesak**, lest the user be inclined to silence the **p**, as done in English words like *psychology* or *pneumatic*. This is a good occasion to remind the user that, in our transliteration, with the exception of digraphs coined especially for it (**ee**, **kh**, **oo**, **sh** and **ts**), every letter is pronounced as a separate sound.

6. How to Find Compound Words or Phrases

Compound words and expressions are to be found in the Hebrew-English part of the dictionary by locating alphabetically the initial component. In addition, however, they can be found by locating component-words therein as well. An expression like **tov me'od** (very good) can be found not only under **t** but also under **m**. In the latter case, however, the initial part thereof (**tov**) is enclosed in parentheses and printed in a smaller type: **(tov) me'od**.

7. Informative and Locational Entries

Where the entry looked for is no ordinary bilingual dictionary entry, but one of informational (marked ◇) or locational (marked □) character, the translation is to be found only in the entry for the full name. At the entry for the main component of a phrase, the user will find a cross-reference to the main entry. Thus, when looking for, for example,

◇ **meelkhemet ha-'atsma'oot** מלחמת העצמאות (War of Independence)

the user can expect to find the full gloss only under **m**. The entry under **a** is cross-referred to the other entry:

◇ **(meelkhemet ha)'atsma'oot** - see ◇ **meelkhemet ha-'atsma'oot.**

Similarly, when looking for, for example, the town of

□ **Petakh-Teekvah** פתח־תקוה

the user can expect to find information on its location, history, population, etc. only under **p**. The entry under **t** is cross-referred to the other entry:

□ **(Petakh) Teekvah** - see □ **Petakh-Teekvah**

8. What to Stress When Pronouncing

The stress in Hebrew falls mostly on the last syllable (as in French), whereas an English-speaking person's primary inclination is the other way round: to put the stress on the first syllable. That is why, in this dictionary, care has been taken to mark the vowel (**a**, **e**, **o**), or vowel digraph (**ee**, **oo**), in each phonetically respelled Hebrew word (or suffix) that needs stressing. Thus, in pronouncing a word, the user must stress the vowel that is underlined, e.g., **halakh**, **kelev**, **heestoreeyah**, etc. Putting the stress on the proper syllable is essential if one expects to be understood when trying to say something in Hebrew.

9. The Entry: Hebrew-English Section

(*a*) The headword: each entry opens with the transliteration of the Hebrew word, in bold type. In most cases, the headword has a *"hairline"* (|) dividing the unchangeable *"stem"* of the word from its changeable *ending*. The ending is replaced by another ending for the formation of a grammatical alternative.

(*b*) The Hebrew headword is followed by its grammatical alternatives. These include the word's *plural* (if a *noun*), *feminine gender* (if an *adjective* or *verb*) and its form in the *1st person* (if it is a *verb* in the *past tense, 3rd person, singular*). Mostly, these forms are only suffixes that need to be added to the word's unchanging *"stem"* to form such alternatives, while the changeable *ending* of the headword is dropped. The alternative, whether it is a whole word or a suffix, is preceded by an *oblique (/)* and is printed in the same bold type, only smaller. A suffix is invariably preceded by a *hyphen*.

(*c*) Then comes the word in its genuine Hebrew spelling. This, however, is not the dotted spelling characteristic of other Hebrew dictionaries. The actual use of that spelling, the so-called "*Defective*" spelling, properly dotted, is nowadays confined solely to Bible texts, prayer books, poetry and children's books. Instead, we use here the undotted ("*Plene*") spelling that is current in the press, literature and practically every field of written Hebrew in Israel and elsewhere.

(*d*) Next, printed in italics, follows an abbreviation showing the word's part of speech, according to Hebrew grammar.

(*e*) The English translation which follows consists of one or more current meanings of the word. Not meant to exhaust all possibilities, this dictionary ignores words of rare use or of unlikely occurrence. Meanings entirely different from one another are numbered separately.

(*f*) The entry normally ends with auxiliary grammatical alternatives and information. For a *noun*, the *construct case* alternative (marked *+of:* or *pl+of:*) is given, sometimes in full, but usually only as a suffix to be added to the stem of the entry word. (For an explanation of the construct case , see par. (4) on page xxv.) For a verb, alternative tenses (including the *infinitive* where the *verb* is in the *imperative* mood) are given. All are in the transliterated form and printed in a type like that of the entry word but smaller.

10. Contents of English Entry

(*a*) Headword: each entry opens with the English word or compound entered in its normal alphabetical order, letter by letter, in bold type. *Verbs* come mostly in the base form, preceded by the *preposition* **(to)**, in smaller type and between parentheses. The latter is ignored in the alphabetization.

(*b*) The English headword is followed by a Hebrew translation in the genuine Hebrew spelling (see paragraph (*c*) in section 9, above). Where the English headword has more than one meaning, additional Hebrew translations are given. Each of these is numbered and begins with the respective Hebrew word in its original spelling. Wherever needed, the Hebrew word is followed (between parentheses and in ordinary type) by a short word or hint in English, giving the particular meaning or use of the English word to which the Hebrew translation refers.

(*c*) Next , printed in italics, follows an abbreviation showing the part of speech of the Hebrew word, according to Hebrew grammar.

(*d*) Transliterated forms now follow one another in an uninterrupted sequence. First is a transliteration of the Hebrew word, in the form shown. In most cases where grammatical alternatives are given, the transliterated Hebrew word has a *hairline* (|) dividing its unchangeable *stem* from its changeable ending, which is replaced to form a grammatical alternative. The grammatical alternative is shown immediately following the transliterated Hebrew word, separated from it by an oblique line *(/)*. For a *noun*, alternatives include its *plural* and its *construct case*; for an *adjective*, its *feminine gender* form. These alternative forms are seldom full words. Mostly, they take the form of suffixes to be added to the word's unchanging *"stem"*. Suffixes are invariably preceded by a *hyphen*. For example, in the following entry

villa חווילה *nf* khaveel|ah/-ot (+*of:* -at)

khaveelah is the singular noun, *'villa'*

khaveelot is the plural noun, *'villas'*

Khaveelat is the construct case, *'(the) villa of (somebody)'*

When the English headword is a *verb*, its Hebrew translation is given in the *infinitive* form, and the grammatical alternatives include all the verb's *tenses: Past, Present* and *Future* (there are not more in Hebrew), all in full, in the *3rd person, singular, masculine*. All grammatical alternatives as above are given only in the transliterated form and are printed in the same style as the main transliteration, only a bit smaller.

11. Where to Look for What

1. *The Hebrew-English Part* — for ascertaining the meaning, correct Hebrew spelling, and grammatical alternatives of any Hebrew word that one has heard or that one already knows but wants to check up on.

2. *The English-Hebrew Part* — for learning a Hebrew word or phrase: how to pronounce it correctly and which syllable to stress; how to spell it in the Hebrew alphabet; how to form, use and pronounce correctly its various grammatical alternatives and avoid noncoordinations of gender and number in one's speech.

3. *Headwords Marked* □ in the Hebrew-English Part (labeled "Locational Entries") —

for summary data on 1250 places in Israel, each to be located by its transliterated name as colloquially pronounced. The entry contains the name in traditional Hebrew spelling as well as its transliterated Latin spelling used on road signs and in official road maps; municipal or administrative status; year of establishment; directions as to location and nearness to larger or more known places, as well as to roads and road junctions; official population figures as of December 31, 1990; and additional information as to history and characteristics of the place wherever useful.

4. *Headwords Marked* ◇ in the Hebrew-English Part (labeled "Informational Entries") — for basic information on 865 Israeli and Jewish topics of widest variety: geographic, cultural, religious, economic, social, historical, folkloristic, political, institutional, educational, etc.

5. *"Introduction to Hebrew"* (following immediately after this Guide) — for wider documentation on the language as such: its history and the miracle of its resurrection; peculiarities of its alphabet and orthography; the Hebrew system of numerals; days of the week; the Jewish calendar; international terms in Hebrew; and its distinctive features as compared with English.

6. *Pronunciation Key* (page xxviii and inside front cover) — for ascertaining, in case of any doubts, how letters and digraphs used in this transliteration read.

7. *Transliteration Alphabet* (page xxix) — for checking consecutive alphabetical order of transliterated Hebrew entries in the dictionary's Hebrew-English part.

8. *Abbreviations Used in This Dictionary* — for full texts of words or combinations of words appearing abbreviated.

INTRODUCTION TO HEBREW

1. THE HEBREW ALPHABET

The Hebrew alphabet consists of 22 consonants. In the so-called *"plene"* (full) spelling, that is in daily use, there hardly are any vowels. Consonant ו **(Vav)** acts sometimes as a vowel; ה **(Heh)** and י **(Yod)** as well as glottals א **(Alef)** and ע **('Ayeen)** act sometimes as apparent semi-vowels, but one can never be sure about their serving that way. That is why the correct pronunciation and meaning of each written Hebrew word has to be guessed from the context - which is feasible only to those who already command a large vocabulary of the language and have years of Hebrew reading behind them.

There exists, on the other hand, the so-called *"deficient"* spelling (also known as the *"pointed"* or *"dotted"* one). This format uses different combinations of dots for different vowels, and is thus not difficult to read. For technical and traditional reasons, however, *"pointed"* writing and printing is reserved only for Holy Scriptures, prayer-books and poetry. It is also used in textbooks for children and beginners as well as in literature for children in their first 3-4 years of reading. Thereafter, everyone switches to the *"plene"* (also known as *"unpointed"* or *"undotted"*) spelling where vowels are nearly nonexistent and therefore replaced by mere intelligent guessing.

Without a thorough basic knowledge of the language, then, no one can expect to be able to read Hebrew with a proper understanding of the meaning of what has been read, unless the text is *"pointed"*. In other words, unlike the situation for a learner of Spanish or Swedish, for example, who might be able to read ordinary text very soon, to read everyday Hebrew, one must know the language quite well. Normally, such knowledge can only be acquired after several months of regular study and a year or more of assiduous reading of *"pointed"* texts. Only thus may one gain a vocabulary sufficient to enable one to guess the proper vocalization of words encountered in newspapers, for instance, so that they fit the context in which they appear. Hence the need for this dictionary, to facilitate the introduction to written Hebrew.

There are also people who, perhaps having had some Hebrew schooling, might wish to try refreshing what they once knew. Others, with no background at all, might wish, out of curiosity, to form some ideas of how to read and write Hebrew or even try to speak it by means of these dictionaries.

As explained above, the main difficulty with reading *"unpointed"* Hebrew stems from the omission of letters for the vowels . It is as if we were to have to read the last nine words of the preceding sentence (underlined) respelled as stms frm th mssn f lttrs fr th vwls. We would have to guess then, by the context, whether

frm stands for from, farm or firm

mssn stands for omission, emission or mission

fr stands for for, far or fur

bng stands for being or bang.

A wide knowledge of the language is therefore required for one to be able to decide which of the many possible combinations of the few consonants involved would fit the text best.

We shall nevertheless try to formulate a number of hints as to how *"unpointed"* Hebrew reads. One must remember, though, that these are hints, not rules. Such rules have yet to be evolved.

It is incorrect to say that there are no vowels in Hebrew. In fact, there are some even in the "unpointed" spelling. Relying upon these, however, still leaves a lot to guessing, particularly since each of them may occasionally happen to be a consonant as well. That is why we shall begin with the consonants.

Consonants

Most Hebrew consonants present no problem in pronunciation,which is clear and does not vary. These are:

ג (**Geemel**) - as *g* in *get.*

ד (**Dalet**) - as *d* in *David.*

ז (**Zayeen**) - as *z* in *dozen.*

ל (**Lamed**) - as *l* in *love.*

מ (**Mem**) - as *m* in *main.*

נ (**Noon**) - as *n* in *nine.*

צ (**Tsadee**) - as *tz* in *Ritz* or German *z* in *Herz.*

ר (**Resh**) - as *r* in *road.*

Three of the above make use of an apostrophe when meant to render sounds which are not native to Hebrew, but exist in names or terms borrowed from foreign languages. They are:

ג' (**Geemel**, apostrophized) - as *j* in *job.*

ז' (**Zayeen**, apostrophized) - as *j* in *job* or *s* in *leisure.*

צ' (**Tsadee**, apostrophized) - as *ch* in *chin.*

Consonants that vary

There are four consonants, the pronunciation of which varies. The variation cannot be identified from the text in *"unpointed"* spelling. In *"pointed"* spelling, however, the variation is indicated by a dot. These are:

ב (**Bet**), which may read either **b**, as in *boy*, or **v** (**Vet**), as in *voice* (depending on whether, in *"pointed"* script, it would have been בּ or ב).

כ (**Kaf**), which may read **k**, as in *key*, or **kh** (**Khaf**), as in the Scottish *loch* or in the Jewish name *Chaim* (depending on whether, in *"pointed"* script, it would have been כּ or כ).

פ (**Peh**), which may read **p**, as in *Peter*, or **f** (**Feh**), as in *force* (depending on whether, in *"pointed"* script, it would have been פּ or פ).

ש **(Sheen)**, which may read **sh**, as in *show*, or **s (Seen)**, as in *safe* (depending on whether, in *"pointed"* script, it would have been שׁ or שׂ).

Consonants that sound alike

There are some pairs of consonants which sound alike, at least as pronounced by most Hebrew speakers, and therefore present a constant problem to the speller. This is important, since the difference in spelling engenders a change in a word's meaning. Such consonants are:

ח **(Khet)** and כ **(Khaf)**, pronounced by most Hebrew speakers as *ch* in the Scottish word *loch* and in the Jewish name *Chaim*.

ק **(Kof)** and כּ (dotted **Kaf**), described above, pronounced as *k* in *key*.

ט **(Tet)** and ת **(Tav)**, both of which are pronounced as *t* in *touch*.

ס **(Samekh)** and שׂ **(Seen)**, both of which are pronounced *s* as in *soap*.

NOTE: There actually are slight differences in pronunciation between these pairs. However, relatively few Hebrew speakers exhibit them. The majority of such purists originate from Afroasiatic - particularly Arabic-speaking - countries or families. These speakers carry into Hebrew distinctions that are fully functional in Arabic. We would advise English-speaking beginners not to attempt them.

Vowels

Modern Hebrew knows only five vowel sounds, all pronounced fully (like in Italian). They are:

a like in *far*, **e** like in *less*, **o** like in *more*, **ee** like in *feed*, **oo** like in *good*.

As said, no Hebrew letters can be regarded as pure vowels. The few consonants or semi-consonants that, at times, are used as vowels in the *"pointed"* spelling can be indentified by the diacritical signs. In the *"unpointed"* spelling, however, these particular letters are used mainly as vowels and, as such, are much more frequent. Because of the lack of diacritical signs, the reader again has to guess from the context which of two or three possible sounds each letter represents. Such vowels are:

Vav (ו).

As a vowel, ו **(Vav)** may sound **o** as in *more* or **oo** as in *food*. It would depend on whether, in *"pointed"* spelling, it were marked with a dot above it (וֹ) or with a dot in its middle (וּ).

Used as a consonant, however, it is pronounced as **va**, **ve**, or **vee** (וַ ,וֶ ,וִ or וְ) depending up on the vocalic dotting below it. In *"unpointed"* everyday spelling, when inside a word, it comes doubled (וו) and its pronunciation (whether **va**, **ve**, or **vee**) has to be guessed from the context. When opening or closing a word, the **Vav**, though consonantal, becomes single. The double וו, however, may also read **vo** וֹו or **voo** וּו, when composed of a consonant **Vav** that is followed by a second **Vav** that is a vowel for **o** or **oo**. The choice should fit the context.

Yod (י).

As a vowel, י (**Yod**) mostly vocalizes the consonant preceding it to sound **ee** as in *seed* (e.g., סיפר **seeper**, i.e., *recounted*) and sometimes **ey** pronounced as *ai* in *main* (e.g., מיתר **meytar**, i.e., *chord*). It would depend on whether, in *"pointed"* spelling, the letter were marked with one dot under it or two (סִפֵּר ,מֵיתָר).

Used as a consonant, however, **Yod** acts as the Hebrew equivalent of **y** as in *yarn*. Thus it is pronounced **ya** (יַ ,יָ), **ye** (יֶ ,יֵ ,יְ), **yee** (יִ) or **yoo** (יֻ) according to the vowel-dot under it in *"pointed"* spelling.

As we deal, however, in *"unpointed"* spelling, all we can assume, more or less, is that:

(1) At the end of a word or in its middle a **Yod** vocalizes as **ee** the consonant preceding it, e.g., גדי **ged<u>ee</u>** (kid goat), זמיר **zam<u>ee</u>r** (nightingale), or ביקש **beek<u>e</u>sh** (requested).

(2) At the beginning of a word, a **Yod** that is not followed by a vowel-letter may read **yee, ya** or **ye**, e.g., יצחק **yeets'kh<u>a</u>k** (Isaac), יזוז **yaz<u>oo</u>z** (will move), ילד **y<u>e</u>led** (small boy).

(3) In pronouncing a **Yod** that is followed by ו, the choice is mostly between **yo** (יֹו) and **yoo**(יוּ), e.g., יוסף **yos<u>e</u>f** (Joseph), מיוחד **meyookh<u>a</u>d** (particular), דיו **dy<u>o</u>** (ink).

(4) A doubling of the **Yod** (יי) in the middle of a word usually represents the consonant **y** vocalized **ya** or **yayee**: מייבש **meyab<u>e</u>sh** (dries) or גרביים **garbayeem** (socks). At the end of a word, however, such doubling stands for the composite vowel **ay**, e.g., ילדיי **yelad<u>a</u>y** (my children), בנותיי **benot<u>a</u>y** (my daughters), חיי **khay<u>a</u>y** (my life). Yet, if followed by a **final Mem** (ם), it is pronounced **ee-yee**, e.g., **tarbooteey<u>ee</u>m** (masculine plural of the adjective תרבותי **tarbut<u>ee</u>**, i.e., cultural).

Semi-consonants also Acting as Vowels

Three remaining letters have in common the fact that, in the *"unpointed"* script, they may be taken as virtual vowels at the end of a word:

Heh (ה).

ה (**Heh**) is equivalent to the English semi-consonant **h** followed by any of the following vowel sounds (see the transliteration key): **ee, e, oo, o, a**. Thus:

(1) If followed by י (**Yod**) it reads **hee**, e.g., בהיר, **bah<u>ee</u>r** (bright), תהילה **teheel<u>a</u>h** (glory); or **h<u>e</u>y**, e.g., שלהי **sheelh<u>e</u>y** (end of).

(2) Followed by a ו (**Vav**) it is pronounced **h<u>oo</u>,** e.g., הושג **hoos<u>a</u>g** (was attained); or **h<u>o</u>**, e.g., הוסיף **hos<u>ee</u>f** (added).

(3) At the beginning of a word, when not followed by a vowel letter, **Heh** can be read **ha,** e.g., הגנה **hagan<u>a</u>h** (defense), or **he**, e.g., הסכם **hesk<u>e</u>m** (agreement). Sometimes, however, it may also read **hee**, even though it is not followed by **Yod**, e.g., התכונן **heetkon<u>e</u>n** (prepared oneself), הצטדק **heets'tad<u>e</u>k** (justified oneself).

(4) In the middle of a word, the choice is mainly between **ha** and **he**, e.g., סהר **s<u>a</u>har** (moon), מהר **mah<u>e</u>r** (quickly).

(5) However, at the end of a word, the **Heh** is tantamount to **ah**, e.g., ילדה **yald<u>a</u>h**

(small girl), ספה **sapah** (couch); or to **eh**, e.g., מצפה **meetspeh** (observation point), שדה **sadeh** (field).

Alef (א).

א (**Alef**), as already noted, functions as a mere hiatus in European-based pronunciation, and often acts in lieu of vowels. Thus:

(1) Standing alone, at the beginning or in the middle of a word, it is most likely to read as **a** in *far*, e.g., אדם **adam** (human being), מאסף **me'asef** (rearguard); or as **e** in *less*, e.g., אם **em** (mother), באר **be'er** (fountain).

(2) Followed by ו (**Vav**), anywhere in the word, it is pronounced **o** as in אומר **omer** (says), מאד **me'od** (very); or **oo** as in אולם **oolam** (hall), מאומה **me'oomah** (nothing).

(3) Followed by a **Yod** (י), it reads **ee**, e.g., איבוד **eebood** (loss), ראי **re'ee** (mirror); or **ey** pronounced as the *ai* in *main*, e.g., איפה **eyfo** (where).

(4) Before a double **Yod** (יי), it reads **'ay** pronounced as the **y** in *my*, e.g., שונאיי **son'ay** (my enemies).

(5) At the end of a word the **Alef** is tantamount mostly to the vowel **a**, e.g., קרא **kara** (called), צבא **tsava** (army); or to the vowel **e**, e.g., דשא **deshe** (lawn), קורא **kore** (reader), מלא **male** (full); and, very rarely, to vowel **o**, e.g., לא **o**, (no), לקרא **leekro** (to read).

'Ayeen (ע).

ע (**'Ayeen**) is another hiatus, very much like **Alef**, which only true connoisseurs and people of Arabic-speaking extraction actually pronounce the correct way. That is, they pronounce it with a guttural inflection, of which most Hebrew-speakers are incapable. To help the user spell correctly later on, we have made a visual differentiation between these two letters in our transliteration. Instead of the ordinary apostrophe ('), which we (sometimes) use for א, we invariably transliterate the ע by an inverted one (').

As to the uses of the **'Ayeen** and hints about how it should read, when spelling is *"unpointed"*, anything said earlier about the **Alef** applies to the **'Ayeen** as well, except that:

(1) as a vowel at the end of words, the ע vocalizes as **a'** only (not as **e**), e.g., רגע **rega'** (moment), שמע **shama'** (heard).

(2) instead of termination **e'**, the **'ayeen** reads **e'a'**, e.g., יודע **yode'a'** (knows), קובע **kove'a'** (determines).

(3) instead of **o'**, the **'Ayeen** preceded by a **Vav** at the end of a word reads **o'a'**, e.g., לשמוע **leeshmo'a'** (to hear).

(4) instead of **oo'**, the **'Ayeen** preceded by a **Vav** at the end of a word reads **oo'a'**, e.g., פרוע **paroo'a'** (dissolute).

Final Letters, No Capitals

The Hebrew alphabet has no capital letters and uses none even for personal or geographical names. But it has five letters called Final Letters that take on a different shape when ending a word:

ך **(Khaf Sofeet)** replaces the **Khaf** כ (undotted **Kaf**).

ם **(Mem Sofeet)** replaces the **Mem** מ.

ן **(Noon Sofeet)** replaces the **Noon** נ.

ף **(Feh Sofeet)** replaces the **Feh** פ (undotted **Peh**).

ץ **(Tsadee Sofeet)** replaces the **Tsadee** צ.

All Final Letters are read exactly as the ones they replace. Only the first one (ך) can be vocalized and only as ךָ (**-kha**). Thus, it may read **kh** - as in (אברך) **avrekh** (married "yeshiva" scholar), שובך **shovakh** (dove-cote) - or **kha** as in (כמוך) **kamokha** (like yourself), פניך **panekha** (your face).

2. HEBREW ALPHABETICAL ORDER

Nothing is more important to a student of Hebrew, and to a beginner especially, than to master the sequence of Hebrew letters. Only thus will one be able to locate words in any Hebrew dictionary, find names and addresses in a Hebrew telephone directory or search in any type of alphabetical index. It is equally important to be able to identify each letter by its full name.

The order of Hebrew letters is as follows:

א	ב	ג	ד	ה	ו	ז
Alef	**Bet**	**Geemel**	**Dalet**	**Heh**	**Vav**	**Zayeen**

ח	ט	י	כ	ל	מ	נ
Khet	**Tet**	**Yod**	**Kaf**	**Lamed**	**Mem**	**Noon**

ס	ע	פ	צ	ק	ר	ש	ת
Samekh	**'Ayeen**	**Peh**	**Tsadee**	**Koof**	**Resh**	**Sheen**	**Tav**

To make these names easier to repeat and memorize, we may, perhaps, arrange them in pairs, one under the other, from left to right:

Alef-Bet (א־ב)
Geemel-Dalet (ג־ד)
Heh-Vav (ה־ו)
Zayeen-Khet (ז־ח)

Tet-Yod (ט־י)
Kaf-Lamed (כ־ל)
Mem-Noon (מ־נ)
Samekh-'Ayeen (ס־ע)

Peh-Tsadee (פ־צ)
Koof-Resh (ק־ר)
Sheen-Tav (ש־ת)

3. HEBREW SYSTEM OF NUMERALS

Like Latin, Hebrew has its own numerical system, dating from the time of the Second Temple, prior to the Christian Era. It is more straightforward than the Roman system, though, for it makes use not of just a few letters but of the entire alphabet. In it, each Hebrew letter takes its place consecutively, so that anyone knowing by heart the sequence should be able to master the numerical system of the letters with no difficulty. Here is how it works.

Letters from א (**Alef**) to ט (**Tet**), followed by apostrophes, stand for digits from one to nine, as follows:

א'	ב'	ג'	ד'	ה'	ו'	ז'	ח'	ט'
1	2	3	4	5	6	7	8	9

Letters from י' (**Yod**) to צ' (**Tsadee**), again apostrophized, stand for tens from 10 to 90, as follows:

י'	כ'	ל'	מ'	נ'	ס'	ע'	פ'	צ'
10	20	30	40	50	60	70	80	90

The remaining four letters, ק', ר', ש' and ת', also apostrophized, stand for the first four hundreds:

ק'	ר'	ש'	ת'
100	200	300	400

To form a figure of two digits we thus simply add the letter representing the single digit to the one representing the tens. Running from right to left, the tens number will come first and the single digit, if any, will follow to the left. Also, to allow the reader to distinguish between numerals and regular words, the last letter of any such numeral combination is preceded by quotation marks (״).

י״ב will thus be 12 and כ״ב will stand for 22

י״ג will thus be 13 and ל״ד will stand for 34

י״ח will thus be 18 and פ״ו will stand for 86

To the above procedure there are two exceptions, both in the *"teens"* group. For figures 15 and 16, instead of י״ה and י״ו, the combinations ט״ו (i.e., 9+6) for 15 and ט״ז (i.e., 9+7) for 16 are used. This is because each of the two former combinations (י״ה and י״ו) would represent, in part, God's sacrosanct name (יהוה), which the Decalogue forbids to be "uttered in vain" or, therefore, written "casually".

Figures from 100 to 499 are formed in a way similar to that used for figures under 100, except that the combination (running always from right to left), may comprise up to three letters. Thus:

while 200 is ר', 260 is ר״ס; 400 is ת' and 320 is ש״כ;

157 would be קנ״ז (100+50+7),

324 would be שכ״ד (300+20+4),

286 would be רפ״ו (200+80+6),

499 would be תצ״ט (400+90+9).

Again, it would be different (as explained above) in the case of figures ending in 15 or 16:

115 would become קט״ו (100+9+6) [instead of קי״ה (100+10+5)];

416 would become תט״ז (400+9+7) [instead of תי״ו (400+10+6)].

For figures from 499 to 999 the hundreds are composed (as in Roman numerals) by adding letters representing the additional hundreds:

500 becomes ת״ק (400+100) and so 573 becomes תקע״ג (400+100+70+3).

600 becomes ת״ר (400+200) and so 632 becomes תרל״ב (400+200+30+2).

700 becomes ת״ש (400+300) and so 747 becomes תשמ״ז (400+300+40+7).

800 becomes ת״ת (400+400) and so 861 becomes תתס״א (400+400+60+1).

900 becomes תת״ק (400+400+100) and so 954 becomes תתקנ״ד (400+400+100+50+4).

Here, too, a difference is to be noted with numerals ending in 15 or 16. Thus:

615, instead of תרי״ה (400+200+10+5), would be תרט״ו (400+200+9+6).

916, instead of תתקי״ה (400+400+100+10+6), would be תתקט״ו (400+400+100+9+7).

Thousands are counted and apostrophized in the same way as single digits except that they are separated from the rest of the figure by the word **"alafeem"**, meaning *"thousands"*. Thus,

5,000 becomes ה׳ אלפים and 900,000 - תת״ק אלפים.

16,000 - ט״ו אלפים; 17,743 - י״ז אלפים תשמ״ג and 76,450 - ע״ו אלפים ת״נ.

In everyday practice, the use of Hebrew numerals is confined to the days of the week and to designating dates of the months and the year in accordance with the Jewish Calendar. Elsewhere, everyone uses ordinary figures.

4. DAYS OF THE WEEK

Saturday, the Jewish day of rest, is called **shabat** שבת (more correctly pronounced **shabbat**) and is the original from which the English word *Sabbath* and the popular Yiddish *Shabess* derive.

The Sabbath Eve, i.e., the time between *Friday noon* and *Friday evening,* is called ערב שבת **'erev shabat**, whereas *Friday night* is referred to as ליל שבת **leyl shabat**. *Saturday night,* which to a Jew observing it represents the *Exit of the Holy Sabbath* and, to everyone in Israel, the end of the weekly rest, is called מוצאי שבת **motsa'ey shabat**.

The six working days of the week are referred to in Hebrew by their ordinal numbers, i.e., *First Day*, *Second Day*, etc. Another way of referring to them, especially in writing, is by the consecutive first six letters of the Hebrew alphabet (i.e., as if in English we were to say *A-Day*, *B-Day*, etc.). In both cases, however, one must take care that the word *Day* יום (**yom**), being a noun, should precede the ordinal (or alphabetic) numeral. Thus:

Sunday	is either	יום ראשון	**(yom reeshon)**	or	יום א׳	**(yom alef)**.
Monday	is either	יום שני	**(yom shenee)**	or	יום ב׳	**(yom bet)**.
Tuesday	is either	יום שלישי	**(yom shleeshee)**	or	יום ג׳	**(yom geemal)**.
Wednesday	is either	יום רביעי	**(yom revee'ee)**	or	יום ד׳	**(yom dalet)**.
Thursday	is either	יום חמישי	**(yom khameeshee)**	or	יום ה׳	**(yom heh)**.
Friday	is either	יום ששי	**(yom sheeshee)**	or	יום ו׳	**(yom vav)**.

5. THE JEWISH CALENDAR

While the Gregorian Calendar that is accepted worldwide governs most practical fields in Israel's everyday life — from monthly pay to budget — the Jewish Calendar preserves its place of importance as well, besides the role it plays in Jewish religious and communal life as elsewhere in the world. Its primary importance is to determine the exact dates on which Jewish holidays, days of remembrance, birthdays and bar mitzvas are celebrated. In addition, however, Israeli law formally requires every official document or item of correspondence emanating from a government office or state institution to be double-dated, i.e., to carry the Jewish Calendar date next to the Gregorian one. Furthermore, some fundamentalist groups and many religious institutions are in the habit of quoting the Jewish calendar only. It would therefore be useful to acquire some basic notions about how that calendar works.

Unlike the Gregorian Calendar (and the Roman Julian Calendar from which it stems), based on the solar year, the Jewish Calendar is based on the lunar month. A Jewish month opens with the new moon and extends over 29 or 30 days, the middle of which invariably coincides with a full moon. There are 12 months in a regular year and 13 in a leap year. The latter occurs every third or even second year (seven times in a cycle of 19 years) and the additional month it contains adjusts the lunar year to the solar one. Otherwise, should the discrepancy between the two have been allowed to persist and grow, no harmony could any longer be maintained between a holiday and the season in which it traditionally falls. In other words, Jews could find themselves celebrating Passover in autumn and observing Yom Kippur in the spring...

As is, the Jewish Year begins about the autumnal equinox and, if regular, contains the following months (listed from right to left):

אדר	שבט	טבת	כסלו	חשוון	תשרי
Adar	**Shvat**	**Tevet**	**Keeslev**	**Kheshvan**	**Teeshrey**
29	30	30	30 or 29	30 or 29	30
אלול	אב	תמוז	סיוון	אייר	ניסן
Elool	**Av**	**Tamooz**	**Seevan**	**Eeyar**	**Neesan**
29	30	29	30	29	30

In a leap year, the intercalated month, called אדר ב' **Adar Bet** and containing 29 days, is added right after **Adar** (referred to, in such a year, as אדר א' **Adar Alef,** which has 30 days).

A date according to the Jewish Calendar month is never quoted in a plain numeral. One cannot say, let alone write, **Teeshrey 27** or **Seevan 16**. The sole way to do it properly is to quote it in Jewish numerical symbols as explained above, i.e., **kaf-zayeen teeshrey** or **tet-vav seevan**. (Reminder: There are no capital letters in Hebrew.)

However, the most important and widely used item of the Jewish Calendar is the Jewish Year. The latter starts with ראש השנה Rosh Hashana - the Jewish New Year - which falls on the first day of *Tishri* א' תשרי **alef teeshrey** and ends on the 29th (last) day of *Elul* כ"ט אלול **kaf-tet elool**. As already pointed out, it governs all Jewish holidays (including Israel's *Independence Day*), days of remembrance, bar mitzvas, circumcision and marriage rituals, etc.

Jewish years are counted "since Creation", which, according to calculations based on chronological data from the Bible, is believed to have occurred in 3761 B.C.E., i.e., 5752 years ago. (Byzantine calculations by Christian theologians, on the other hand, place it in 5508 B.C.E.) In practice, however, the thousands are skipped and the Jewish year is referred to by quoting, in Jewish numerical symbols, the figure from the hundreds down. Thus, the year in which we now write is referred to as תשנ״ב **tav-sheen-noon-bet**, i.e., 400+*300+50+2=752 (not 5752).* The Jewish Calendar date for **seevan 19, 5752** would thus be י״ט סיוון תשנ״ב **yod-tet seevan tav-sheen-noon-bet**. Similarly, trying to decipher Hebrew inscriptions, one may find out from a tombstone that one's grandmother passed away on כ״ג תמוז תרפ״ז **kaf-geemal tamooz tav-resh-peh-zayeen**, i.e., *Tammuz 16, (5)687*, or from her **Ketoobah** (Ritual Marriage Certificate) that she married grandfather on כ״ה שבט תרע״א **kaf-heh shvat tav-resh-`ayeen-alef**, i.e., *Shebat 25, (5)671.*

One last thing to remember about the Jewish Calendar is that, because it is a lunar one, a Jewish date is conceived as having begun on its eve. In other words, it begins with nightfall the day before, and ends with the day's end, i.e., as soon as another evening is to begin. That is why all Jewish holiday celebrations and, of course, the Sabbath as well, begin on the evening that precedes the Jewish date.

6. INTERNATIONAL TERMS IN HEBREW

In the nearly one and a half centuries since its gradual yet spectacular resurrection as a living language, Hebrew had to cope with a most pressing task. This was the need to supply new words for the innumerable new products, instruments and concepts brought about by the industrial and scientific advancement characteristic of our age. To meet that challenge, a voluntary body of learned linguists (then called the *"Language Committee"* and reinstituted in 1953 as the official *"Hebrew Language Academy"*) has been at work since 1880 coining thousands and thousands of new words wherever required. In this process, it was mainly the "purist" tendency that prevailed. Thus, a large proportion of the new words created are indeed revivals or re-adaptations of words found in the Bible, the Talmud or extracted from other sources of Jewish learning. Equally, however, a good many new words, particularly in the fields of social and physical sciences, are Hebraicized versions of widely known international terms. Some of these are familiar to speakers of European languages. In order to recognize and assimilate them, however, there are things a newcomer to the language must know.

The revival of Hebrew, begun in the second half of the nineteenth century, developed in Central and Eastern Europe, where the German language and culture prevailed. Naturally, new words that were introduced then were based on terms as used and pronounced (even when of Greek or Latin origin) in the German language. From 1880, with the advent of Zionism and the emergence of a rich Hebrew press in Czarist Russia, and till 1917, it was mostly the Russian language that served as a source from which to borrow terms. In 1919, however, with the takeover of Palestine by Great Britain, under a mandate from the League of Nations to administer it as the future Jewish National Home to be, the era of English influence began. Although the British Mandate was abolished in 1948, with the proclamation of Israel as an independent state, the influence of English has continued ever since, on account of the constantly tightening mutual ties between Israel and the "Anglo-Saxon" world, and with the U.S.A. especially.

The historical milestones detailed above might be of some guidance to newcomers to Hebrew, whenever trying to locate or use a Hebrew word that can be expected to be part of familiar international terminology. Nineteenth-century Hebrew terms are hence likely to sound and be pronounced in the German, Russian or European way. As we approach our present times, more similarity to current English terminology might be expected, except, of course, where the "purist" tendency prevails and words of pure Hebrew origin have been coined.

In this connection, users of the English-Hebrew section of this dictionary should know that for many terms two synonyms have been struggling for public acceptance: the "purist" one and its international counterpart. In our dictionary, we offer both. Mostly, the former is offered first, for the sake of more "genuine" Hebrew. It is followed, however, by the Hebrew version of the familiar international term, even where the use of the latter is strictly colloquial. There is no rule, though, as to which one to choose and even for ourselves it is sometimes difficult to decide which synonym is more commonly accepted. That, the user will, in the end, find out by himself.

7. DISTINCTIVE FEATURES OF HEBREW

(that seem strange to an English-speaker).

(1) Hebrew is written from right to left.

(2) The Hebrew script has no capital letters at all. Consequently, there is no capitalization in Hebrew of either personal, geographic or other names.

(3) The adjective follows the noun it modifies, instead of preceding it as it does in English.

(4) In most European languages, the *genitive* case denotes ownership or some analogous relation binding two nouns: a *"possessor" noun* and a *"possessed" noun.* The *possessor noun* is inflected. In English, we call it the *possessive case* and have a choice of two ways to express it: (1) by adding the particle *'s* to the *possessor noun* (e.g., *year's* end) or, (2) by adding the preposition *of* after the *possessed noun* (e.g., end *of* the year). In Hebrew it is the latter way that is used, except that here the *possessed noun* (termed the *construct case*), instead of having the preposition *of* added, acquires a different termination and sometimes also has one of its vowels altered. It is called סמיכות (**smeekhoot**) and, to show our users how to inflect it properly, after each noun, the proper termination is indicated in this dictionary. It is given in brackets and is preceded by the abbreviation *+of*, i.e., showing the same noun's meaning in English if *of* were added to it. So, e.g., the noun אהבה, transliterated **ahav|ah/-ot** (*love/-s*), is followed by (*+of:-***at**) meaning *love of*, i.e., **ahavat**; or, e.g., ילד, transliterated **yel|ed/-adeem** (*child/-ren*), is followed by (*pl+of:* **yaldey**) meaning *children of*, i.e., **yaldey**. Where no such addition in brackets follows, or where the addition refers to the *singular* or *plural* alone, the *noun* in question is used unaltered when in the *construct* case.

(5) Unlike English, Hebrew nearly always discriminates between *masculine* and *feminine* genders. It does so not only when declining nouns but when declining adjectives or conjugating verbs as well. On the other hand, there is no *neuter* gender in Hebrew. Thus, for a beautiful *mountain* הר (**har**), marked *nm* (noun, masc.), we say הר יפה (**har yafeh**), whereas for a beautiful *hill* גבעה (**geev'ah**), marked *nf* (noun, fem.), we say גבעה יפה (**geev'ah yafah**). That is why, in this dictionary, every adjective appears in both genders, e.g., יפה is transliterated **yaf|eh/-ah**. Where the Hebrew translation of an English noun, e.g., *singer*, has two forms, one (זמר **zamar**) for a male and another (זמרת **zameret**) for a female, it is marked *nmf* (noun masc./fem.) and the transliteration takes an abbreviated

form, wherever possible: **zam|ar/-eret**. Nouns of one gender only, however, are followed by suffixes needed to form their respective plurals, e.g., סוס **soos/-eem** (*horse/-s*) or פרה **par|ah/-ot** (*cow/-s*).

(6) There is no *indefinite article* in Hebrew as there is in English for singular nouns (*a*, *an*). In Hebrew we not only say *children* (**yeladeem** ילדים) but also *child* (**yeled** ילד), and not *a child*.

(7) The *definite article*, on the other hand, is identical to the English *the*. However, it never stands by itself but invariably takes the unfamiliar form of a one-letter prefix (הַ or הֶ) added to the word (noun or adjective) to which it refers. In this dictionary it is transliterated as **ha-** or **he-** and is separated from the word itself by a *hyphen* (or by a closing *parenthesis*) which, in the Hebrew text, does not exist. הילד (*the child*) is thus transliterated **ha-yeled**, which makes it easier for the user to identify the word itself.

Two more distinctions to note about the *definite article* are:

(a) In words composed of two nouns, of which the first one is in the *construct case* (see paragraph 3 above), the definite article prefixes only the second noun. The colloquial way of adding **ha-** to **bet-sefer** (*school* or, literally, *house of the book*) is wrong. בית־הספר **bet-ha-sefer** is correct, not הבית־ספר **ha-bet-sefer**.

(b) In combinations of a noun and an adjective, the *definite article* prefixes both. Where in English we say *the beautiful girl* we must say in Hebrew הנערה היפה **ha-naarah ha-yafah**, i.e., literally, *the girl the beautiful.*

(8) In addition to the *definite article* there are quite a number of other prefixes that merge with the Hebrew word and make the latter difficult to recognize or identify. Most of those are abbreviations of prepositions or conjunctions that also exist as independent words. It is the prefixes, however, that are in general and constant use and no Hebrew text or utterance can be imagined without one or more of them. Therefore, to make it easier for the user, each such prefix, when transliterated in this dictionary, is shown separated by a *hyphen* (or by a closing *parenthesis*) from the word to which it adheres. Such prefixes are:

ו, וּ - (*and*) pronounced and transliterated **ve-**, which may change into **va-**, **vee-**, or **oo-**, depending on the consonants that follow.

ב, בּ - (*in*, *at*, *by*, *with*) pronounced and transliterated **be-**, **ba-**, **bee-**, but sometimes (see paragraph 9, below) as **ve-**, **va-**, **vee-**.

כ, כּ - an abbreviation of כמו **kemo** (*as*, *like*, *about*) pronounced and transliterated **ke-**, **ka-**, **kee-**, but sometimes (see paragraph 9, below) as **khe-**, **kha-**, **khee-**.

ל - an abbreviation of אל **el** (*to*, *towards*, *at*, *for*) pronounced and transliterated as **le-** , **la-**, **lee-**.

מ - an abbreviation of מן *meen* (*from*, *out of*) pronounced and transliterated **mee-**, me-.

ש - an abbreviation of אשר *asher* (*which*, *who*, *that*, *in order to*) pronounced and transliterated **she-**.

(9) As already explained (paragraph 7, page xvi), the pronunciation of the Hebrew letter ב (Bet) alternates between **b** and **v (Vet)** depending on whether it is dotted or not. In the same way, the pronunciation of the כ **(Kaf)** alternates between **k** and **kh** (Khaf) and of פ **(Peh)** alternates between **p** and **f (Feh)**. Thus, a reader of texts in everyday Hebrew's "unpointed" script has no written clue as to the alternative which should be

chosen. There is no way but to rely on having memorized a number of highly complicated grammatical rules one has learned at school - which most people have long forgotten. That is why, in the Hebrew-English section of our dictionary, we often give words as mispronounced, as our user is likely to hear them. However, in each case, the word's correct pronunciation is added for further guidance. In the English-Hebrew part, on the other hand, the normatively correct pronunciation appears alone in most cases. The latter is followed, wherever necessary, with a reminder in brackets (b=*v; v=b; k=kh; kh=k; p=f; f=p)* showing what the letter in question originally was, before it changed by the rules.

(10) There is no doubling of consonants in Hebrew script. Instead, the respective consonant is marked by a dot in its middle, so that the reader pronounces it doubled. (Even this is not consistent, for sometimes the dot indicates something else.) This is so, in any case, only in "pointed" script. In everyday "unpointed" script these dots are omitted just as all other pointing is. In practice, no systematic and correct doubling of consonants is detected in everyday speech. There may be exceptions, perhaps, but these are confined to an absolutely insignificant minority of specially trained and constantly supervised radio and TV announcers and to a few true connoisseurs. Our transliteration of Hebrew thus omits doubling of consonants entirely.

(11) The "*half-vowels*" **khataf-patakh** (אֲ) and **khataf-segol** (אֱ) should be "half-pronounced", but are, in fact, hardly pronounced at all by the general public. We have thus opted to ignore half-vowels altogether (except in words which, somehow, the public has learned to pronounce correctly). This dictionary is meant, above all, to enable its users to understand what ordinary people speak and to be understood more easily when users try to say anything. That consideration takes precedence over the natural wish to be lauded by connoisseurs for helping a user to a perfect pronunciation which, at this primary stage, is unlikely to be achieved, anyway.

Pronunciation Key

The letters and digraphs of the transliteration alphabet are to be pronounced as follows			Equivalent vowel point or letter in Hebrew (x signifies any Hebrew letter)

<u>Vowels</u>:

a	as in	**far**	xָ or xַ
e	as in	**less**	xֶ or xֵ
ee	as in	**see**	xִ or xִי
o	as in	**more**	xָ, xֹ or xוֹ
oo	as in	**ooze**	xֻ, וּ, or xוּ

<u>Consonants</u>:

ch	as in	chin	צ׳ or ץ׳
g	as in	game or get	ג
j	as in	job	ד׳ or ג׳
kh	as **ch** in	Scottish word **loch** or as **ch** in the common Jewish name **Chaim**	ח or כ or ך
r	is pronounced gutturally, similar to the **r** in French or German **r**		
s	as in	**safe**	ס or שׂ
sh	as in	**show**	שׁ
t	as in	**type**	ט or ת
ts	as in	**hearts** or as **tz** in **Ritz**	צ or ץ
y	as in	**yard**	י
z	as in	**zero**	ז

The remaining consonants in the system (**b, d, f, h, k, l, m, n, p, t** and **v**) are pronounced more or less as in English.

<u>Stress</u>:

Vowel *underlined* is the one to be stressed.

Transliteration Alphabet

showing in consecutive order the Latin letters and digraphs used in the transliteration and the Hebrew letter or letters each one transliterates

A	* אַ אָ הַ הָ עַ עָ
B	בּ
CH	ץ׳ צ׳
D	ד
E	* אֵ אֶ הֵ הֶ עֵ עֶ
EE	* י אִי אִ הִי הִ עִי עִ
F	ף פ
G	ג
H	ה
J	ג׳ ד׳
K	כּ ק
KH	ח כ ך
L	ל
M	מ ם
N	נ ן
O	* אוֹ אָ אֹ הוֹ הָ הֹ עוֹ עָ עֹ
OO	* וּ אוּ אֻ הוּ הֻ עוּ עֻ
P	פּ
R	ר
S	ס שׂ
SH	שׁ
T	ט ת
TS	צ ץ
V	ו וו ב
Y	י
Z	ז

*** *See page xvii of the Introduction to Hebrew for an explanation of the representation of vowels in the Hebrew writing system.***

Abbreviations Used in This Dictionary

abbr	abbreviation
acr	acronym
adj	adjective
adv	adverb
b=v	*b* replacing original *v* *
[colloq.]	colloquialism
colloq. abbr.	colloquial abbreviation
conj	conjunction
cpr	colloquial pronunciation
E.	east of (*or* eastern)
etc	et cetera
est.	established in the year
f	feminine (noun)
(f)	feminine (adj., verb or adv.)
f=p	*f* replacing original *p* *
figurat.	figurative(ly)
fut	verb in the future tense
gram.	grammar
imp	verb in the imperative mood
inf	verb in the infinitive mood
interj	interjection
Hebrew num. sys	Hebrew numerical system (explained in *Introduction to Hebrew,* pp. xx-xxii)
kh=k	*kh* replacing original *k* *
k=kh	*k* replacing original *kh* *
lit.	literally

m	masculine (noun)
(m)	masculine (adv., verb or adv.)
mf	masculine / feminine (noun)
(m/f)	masculine / feminine (adj., verb or adv.)
N.	north of (*or* northern)
npr	normative pronunciation
num	numeral
p=f	*p* replacing original *f* *
pers	person
pl or pl:	plural
Pop.	Population
pron	pronoun
prep	preposition
pres	verb in the present tense
pst	verb in the past tense
S.	south of (*or* southern)
sing or sing:	singular
synon.	synonym of ... or synonymous with...
v	verb
vi	intransitive verb
v refl	reflexive verb
t	transitive verb
v=b	*v* replacing original *b* *
W.	west of (*or* western)

* see “Consonants that vary” in “Introduction”, p. xvi, and par. (9), p. xxvi.

Note: Not listed above are abbreviations of common knowledge to any reader. Thus, if use is occasionally made of such as *music., medic., jurid., econ.* etc., our assumption is that the user will have no difficulty deciphering the meanings.

Hebrew-English

A.

transliterating Hebrew letters
A (אַ,אָ,אֶ) and **'A** (עַ,עָ,עֶ)
as well as **Ha** (הַ,הָ,הֶ).

NOTE: Most Hebrew-speakers make no distinction, in speech, between **a** = ע (**'Ayeen** - a guttural, pressed, hiatus typical of Semitic languages yet with no parallel in English) and **a** or **'a** = א (**Aleph**) - a normal hiatus which, in words grouped hereunder, should be pronounced as *a* in *father*. Thus, for the benefit of users who would not know for which of the two to look, words beginning with both **Aleph** and **'Ayeen** are grouped together. However, they are distinguished (and can be properly pronounced) by their transcriptions (**a, 'a** for **Aleph** and **'a** for **'Ayeen**).

Similarly, many Hebrew-speakers systematically swallow their **h**'s (just as some English-speakers do). A stranger to Hebrew might be looking for a word that begins in **ha** (הַ) not under **H** (where it should be; see p. 115) but under **A**. To remedy that, words beginning with **ha** (הַ) are included here with the ones beginning with **a** (אַ) and **'a** (עַ). Upon locating a word, however, the user can tell how to pronounce it correctly by the way a word is transcribed (and not necessarily the way one thought one had heard it).

a- א (*prefix*) marking *1st person, sing,* in the future tense of the Intensive **(pee'el)** and Causative **(heef'eel)** stems in Hebrew verbs.

-ah ה (suffix) **1.** marking direction or destination in nouns (equivalent to "-ward" in English e.g. **daromah** דרומה southward); **2.** expressing (poetically) desire or appeal (equivalent to "let's" in English) in 1st person, plural, using the future tense of Hebrew verbs. Thus, instead of **nelekh** נלך (we shall go) one may say **nelkhah** נלכה (let's go).

ha- -ה (prefix) the Definite Article (equivalent to "the" in English).

ha- -הֲ (*prefix*) Interrogative Particle which changes the following sentence to a question.

ha'adaf|ah/-ot העדפה *nf* preference (*+of:* **-at**).

ha'afal|ah/-ot האפלה *nf* blackout; (*+of:* **-at**).

ha'ala|'ah/-'ot העלאה **1.** *nf* promotion; **2.** *nf* raise; (*+of:* **-'at**).

ha'ala|'ah/-'ot be-dargah העלאה בדרגה *nf* promotion (in rank).

ha'alam|ah/-ot העלמה *nf* concealment; (*+of:* **-at**).

ha'alam|at/-ot mas/meeseem העלמת מס *nf* tax evasion.

ha'amad|ah/-ot העמדה *nf* setting-upright; causing to stand; placing; (*+of:* **-at**).

ha'amad|at/-ot le-deen העמדה לדין *nf* putting on trial; bringing to trial.

ha'amad|ah/-ot paneem העמדת פנים *nf* pretense.

ha'aman|ah/-ot האמנה *nf* accreditation; (*+of:* **-at**).

ha'anak|ah/-ot הענקה *nf* grant; (*+of:* **-at**).

ha'apal|ah/-ot העפלה *nf* climbing to the top; (*+of:* **-at**).

◇ **(ha)a'apalah** see ◇ **(ha)ha'apalah**.

ha'arak|ah/-ot הארקה *nf* grounding (electricity); (*+of:* **-at**).

ha'arakh|ah/-ot הארכה *nf* extension; prolongation; (*+of:* **-at**).

ha'arakh|ah/-ot הארחה *nf* lodging; accommodation; (*+of:* **-at**).

(bet/batey) ha'arakh|ah בית הארחה *nm* guest-house.

ha'arakh|ah/-ot הערכה *nf* evaluation; appreciation; (*+of:* **-at**).

ha'aram|ah/-ot הערמה *nf* evasion; tricking; (*+of:* **-at**).

ha'aram|ah 'al ha-khok הערמה על החוק *nf* evasion of the law.

ha'arats|ah/-ot הערצה *nf* admiration; (*+of:* **-at**).

ha'asak|ah/-ot העסקה *nf* employment; (*+of:* **-at**).

ha'ashar|ah/-ot העשרה *nf* enrichment; (*+of:* **-at**).

ha'atak|ah/-ot העתקה *nf* **1.** shifting; **2.** copying; (*+of:* **-at**).

ha'atakat meesmakheem העתקת מסמכים *nf* photocopying, "xeroxing".

ha'avarah/-ot העברה *nf* transfer; (*+of:* **-at**).

ha'azan|ah/-ot האזנה *nf* listening; (*+of:* **-at**).

aba (*colloq. pl* **-'eem**) אבא *nm* papa, daddy, father; (*+of:* **avee**; *v=b*).

haba|'ah/-'ot הבעה *nf* expression; (*+of:* **-'at**).

haba'at emoon הבעת אימון *nf* vote of confidence.

aba'boo'ot (*npr* **ava'boo'ot**) אבעבועות *nf pl* smallpox, variola.

aba'boo'o't (*npr* **ava'boo'ot**) **rooakh** אבעבועות רוח *nf pl* chickenpox, varicella.

(harkavat) aba'boo'ot (*npr* **ava'boo'ot**) הרכבת אבעבועות *nf* smallpox inoculation.

abeer/-ah אביר *adj* chivalrous; gallant.

abeer/-eem אביר *nm* knight; (*pl+of:* **-ey**).

abeeree/-t אבירי *adj* chivalrous, gallant.

abeeroot אבירות *nf* gallantry.

hab|eetee/-etnah הביטי *v imp f sing/pl* look! (addressing female/-s) (*inf* **lehabeet**; *pst* **heebeet**; *pres* **mabeet**; *fut* **yabeet**).

habet/habeetoo (*etc*) הבט *v imp sing pl* look! (addressing male/-s).

□ **Aboneem** see □ **Haboneem**.

□ **Aboo-Gosh** (Abu Ghosh) אבו־גוש *nm* Arab village 12 km W. of Jerusalem. Pop. 3,400.

aboov/-eem אבוב *nm* **1.** tube (inner of tire); **2.** oboe; (*pl+of:* **-ey**).

absoord/-eem אבסורד *nm* absurdity, nonsense.

absoordee/-t אבסורדי *adj* absurd.

'ad עד *prep* till, until.

'ad 'alot ha-shakhar עד עלות השחר *adv* till dawn.

'ad asher עד אשר *adv* until; till.

'ad efes makom עד אפס מקום *adv* (full) to capacity.

'ad kan עד כאן **1.** till here; **2.** thus far.

'ad kedey kakh עד כדי כך to such an extent that.

'ad kee עד כי until.

'ad koh עד כה *prep* so far; hitherto.

'ad le-kheshbon עד לחשבון *adv* on account.

'ad matay עד מתי how long? till when?

'ad 'olam עד עולם *adv* forever; to eternity.

'ad she- עד ש־ until; till.

'ad tom עד תום to the very end.

'ad ve-'ad beekhlal עד ועד בכלל *adv* until ... inclusive; including.

('adey) 'ad עדי עד *adv* forever and ever.

(be-) 'ad בעד *prep* for; in favor of.

(la-) 'ad לעד *adv* forever.

hadadee/-t הדדי *adj* mutual; reciprocal.

(agoodah) hadadeet אגודה הדדית *nf* cooperative society.

(be-haskamah) hadadeet בהסכמה הדדית *adv* in mutual agreement.

('ezrah) hadadeet עזרה הדדית *nf* mutual aid.

hadadeeyoot הדדיות *nf* reciprocity.

had|af/-fah/-aftee הדף *v* pushed; (*pres* **hodef**; *fut* **yahadof**).

hadakh|ah/-ot הדחה *nf* impeachment; dismissal; (*+of:* **-at**).

hadakhat keleem הדחת כלים *nf* washing (rinsing) dishes.

adam (*or:* **ben-adam**) אדם *nm* person; human being; (*pl:* **beney-adam**).

(agaf koakh) adam אגף כוח אדם *nm* manpower division.

(beney) adam בני אדם *nm pl* people (*pl* of **ben adam**).

(koakh) adam כוח־אדם *nm* manpower.

(tat-) adam תת־אדם *nm* sub-human.

adam|ah/-ot אדמה *nf* land; ground; (*+of:* **adm|at/-ot**).

('avodat) adamah עבודת אדמה *nf* tilling the land; cultivation of the soil.

(keevrat) adamah כברת אדמה *nf* patch of land.

(tapoo|'akh/-khey) adamah תפוח אדמה *nm* potato.

□ **Adameet** (Adamit) אדמית *nm* kibbutz (est. 1958) on Lebanese border, E. of **Rosh-Haneekrah**.

adamdam/-ah אדמדם *adj* reddish.

adaneem אדנים *nm pl* window sills; (*sing* **eden**; *pl+of:* **adney**).

adanee|t/-yot אדנית *nf* soil-filled box hung outside window sills for cultivating flowers.

◇ **adar** אדר *nm* 6th Jewish Calendar month (29 days); appr. Febr.-March.

◇ **adar alef** אדר א׳ *nm* the name of the month of Adar in a leap year, when followed by Adar Bet (30 days).

◇ **adar bet** אדר ב׳ *nm* 13th month in a Jewish leap year (that comes 6 times in 19 years, i.e. approximately every third year). Inserted between the normal Adar, which is then labelled "Adar Alef", and **Neesan**. 29 days, approx. March-April.

'ad|ar/-rah/-artee עדר *v* dug over, hoed; (*pres* **'oder**; *fut* **ya'ador**).

hadar הדר *nm* splendor; dignified behavior.

□ **Adar** *or* **Adar Ha-Karmel** see □ **Hadar** *or* **Hadar Ha-Karmel**.

(pree-) hadar פרי־הדר *nm* citrus.

hadareem הדרים *nm pl* citrus fruits.

hadas/-eem הדס myrtle (*pl+of:* **-ey**).

◇ **adasah** הדסה see ◇ **Hadasah**.

□ **Adaseem** see □ **Hadaseem**.

'adash|ah/-eem עדשה *nf* lentils.

'adash|ah/-ot עדשה *nf* lens; (*+of:* **'ad|eshet/-shot**).

'adashah kemoorah עדשה קמורה *nf* convex lens.

◇ **(nezeed) 'adasheem** see ◇ **nezeed 'adasheem**

'adashot-maga' (*npr:* **adshot** *etc*) עדשות מגע *nf pl* contact-lenses.

'adatee/-t עדתי *adj* communal; pertaining to an ethnic community.

(motsa) 'adatee מוצא עדתי *nm* ethnic (communal) origin.

(pa'ar) adatee פער עדתי *nm* inter-community gap.

'adayeen עדיין *adv* still; yet.

'adayeen lo עדיין לא *adv* not yet.

hadbak|ah/-ot הדבקה *nf* gluing; sticking; (*+of:* **-at**).
hadbar|ah/-ot הדברה *nf* extermination (of germs, insects, etc); (*+of:* **-at**).
(khom|er/-rey) hadbarah חומר־הדברה *nm* germicides; pesticides.
□ **'Adee** ('Adi) עדי *nm* communal village in Upper Galilee (est. 1980) S. of **Ramat Yokhanan**. Pop. 403.
'adee/'ada|yeem עדי *nm* ornament; jewel (*pl+of:* **-yey**).
'adeef/-ah עדיף *adj* preferable.
hadeef|ah/-ot הדיפה *nf* push; thrust; repulse; (*+of:* **-at**).
'adeefoo|t/-yot עדיפות *nf* preference; priority.
(soolam) 'adefootעדיפות סולם *nm* scale of priorities.
'adeen/-ah עדין *adj* delicate; gentle.
('eenyan) 'adeen עניין עדין *nm* a delicate matter.
(mekhaneekah) 'adeenah מכניקה עדינה *nf* precision mechanics.
(she'elah) 'adeenah שאלה עדינה *nf* a delicate question.
adeer/-ah אדיר *adj* tremendous; mighty.
(eloheem) adeereem! אלוהים אדירים! *interj* Good gracious!
adeesh/-ah אדיש *adj* indifferent; impassive.
adeesh/-ah le אדיש ל־ *adj* indifferent to.
adeesh/-ah le-gabey אדיש לגבי *adj* indifferent towards.
adeeshoot אדישות *nf* indifference; apathy.
adeev/-ah אדיב *adj* polite; courteous.
adeevoot אדיבות *nf* politeness; courtesy.
ademet אדמת *nf* rubella.
aderet/adarot אדרת overcoat; coat (*+of:* **adr|at/-ot**).
□ **Aderet** (Adderet) אדרת *nm* village in Judean hills (est 1961) 9.5 km S. of Bet Shemesh. Pop 343.
'adey 'ad עדי־עד *adv* forever and ever.
hadgam|ah/-ot הדגמה *nf* exemplification; demonstration; (*+of:* **-at**).
hadgar|ah/-ot הדגרה *nf* hatching; incubation; (*+of:* **-at**).
hadgarah/-ot melakhootee|t/-yot הדגרה מלאכותית *nf* artificial incubation.
hadgash|ah/-ot הדגשה *nf* emphasis; (*+of:* **-at**).
'adkanee/-t עדכני *adj* up-to-date.
hadlak|ah/-ot הדלקה *nf* **1.** lighting; kindling; **2.** bonfire; (*+of:* **-at**).
◇ **adlakat nerot** see ◇ **hadlakat nerot**.
◇ **'adloyad|ah/-ot** עדלאידע *nf* traditional Purim carnival held in Tel-Aviv; (*+of:* **-at**).
adm|at/-ot mereevah אדמת־מריבה *nf* disputed area.
admat nekhar אדמת ניכר *nf* foreign soil.
adm|at/-ot trasheem אדמת טרשים *nf* rocky ground.
◇ **admor/-eem** אדמו״ר *nm* (*acr of* ADonenoo, MOrenoo ve Rabenoo אדוננו, מורנו ורבנו i.e. our master, teacher and rabbi) title of a Hassidic Rabbi.
adom/adoomah אדום *adj* red.
(ha-tselav ha) adom הצלב האדום *nm* the Red Cross.
◇ **(khatsee ha-sahar ha) adom** see ◇ **khatsee ha-sahar ha-adom**.
◇ **(magen daveed) adom** see ◇ **magen daveed adom**.
adon/-eem אדון *nm* sir; master; (*pl+of:* **-ey**).
adonay אדוני *nm* God.
adonee אדוני **1.** *nm* dear sir; my master; **2.** *interj* Sir! (calling to attention).
adook/-ah אדוק *adj* pious; orthodox.
hadook/-ah הדוק *adj* tight; close.
adoomah אדומה *adj nf* red.
hadoor/-ah הדור *adj* adorned; elegant.
□ **Adorah** אדורה *nm* communal village (est. 1983) in Judean hills, 10 km W. of **Khevron** (Hebron), near **Telem**.
◇ **'adot ha-meezrakh** עדות המזרח *nf pl* Jewish communities in Israel of North-African or Asian background.
hadpasah/-ot הדפסה *nf* **1.** printing; **2.** typing; (*+of:* **-at**).
adrabah אדרבה *adv* on the contrary.
(be) hadragah בהדרגה *adv* gradually.
hadragatee/-t הדרגתי *adj* gradual.
hadran/-eem הדרן *nm* encore.
hadrat paneem הדרת פנים *nf* dignified appearence.
adreekhal/-eet אדריכל *mf* architect; (*pl:* **-eem;** *+of:* **-ey**).
ha'eem האם *conj* did not? was it not? (question-forming particle).
ha'eerah העירה *adv* to town; back to town.
ha-'emek העמק *nm* the valley colloquial way of referring to the Yizre'el Valley (see ◇ **'Emek Yeezre'el**).
ha'erev הערב *adv* tonight; this evening.
ha'et! האט! *v imp sing* masc slow down! (*inf* **leha'et;** *pst* **he'et;** *pres* **me'et;** *fut* **ya'et**).
af/apeem אף *nm* nose (p=*f*).
af אף **1.** *conj* also; even; **2.** *prep* not one; not even.
af 'al pee אף על פי although.
af 'al pee khen אף על פי כן nevertheless.
af 'al pee she- אף על פי ש־ notwithstanding that.
af (*npr:* **af lo) ekhad/akhat** אף אחד *prep m/f* nobody; not one; none.
af kee אף כי although.
af pa'am אף פעם *adv* never; not once.
◇ **af sha'al!** אף שעל! not one single step! (figurat.); opposition to even the slightest Israeli withdrawal from any part of what was Palestine.
('al) af על אף in spite of.
('eek|em/-mah/-amtee) et ha-af עיקם את האף *v* scorned; *lit.:* turned up his nose; (*pres* **me'akem** *etc; fut* **ye'akem** *etc*).

'af/-ah/-tee עף *v* **1.** flew; **2.** flying; (*pres* **'af;** *fut* **ya'oof**).

af|ah/-tah/-eetee אפה *v* baked; (*pres* **ofeh;** *fut* **yofeh**).

'af'a|f/-payeem (*p=f*) עפעף *nm* eyelid; (*pl+of:* **-pey**).

(lo hen|eed/-eedah/-adetee) 'af'af לא הניד עפעף *v* did not bat an eyelid; (*pres* **eyno meneed** *etc;* *fut* **lo yaneed** *etc*).

hafagat metakh הפגת מתח *nf* easing tension.

hafak|ah/-ot הפקה *nf* production; (*+of:* **-at**).

haf|akh/-khah/-akhtee הפך *v* **1.** overturned; upset; **2.** turned; became; (*pres* **hofekh;** *fut* **yahafokh**).

hafakh (*etc*) **le-** הפך ל turned into.

hafakhpakh/-ah הפכפך *adj* fickle; unreliable.

af'al|ah/-ot הפעלה *nf* activation; (*+of:* **-at**).

'af'apayeem עפעפיים *nm pl* eyelids.

'afar עפר *nm* **1.** dust; **2.** earth; **3.** ground.

hafar|ah/-ot הפרה *nf* violation; breach; infringement; (*+of:* **-at**).

hafar|at/-ot heskem הפרת הסכם *nf* breach of agreement.

hafar|at/-ot khok הפרת חוק *nf* infringement of the law.

hafarat nohal הפרת נוהל *nf* infringement of procedure.

hafar|at/-ot seder הפרת סדר *nf* disturbance; causing disorder.

afark|eset/-asot אפרכסת *nf* ear-piece.

afarsek/-eem אפרסק *nm* peach; (*pl+of:* **-ey**).

afarsemon/-eem אפרסמון *nm* persimmon; balsam; (*pl+of:* **-ey**).

hafats|ah/-ot הפצה *nf* **1.** distribution; **2.** dissemination; spreading; (*+of:* **-at**).

'afeefon/-eem עפיפון *nm* kite; (*pl+of:* **-ey**).

afeefyor (*npr* **apeefyor**)**/-eem** אפיפיור *nm* Pope of Rome; (*pl+of:* **-ey**).

afeek/-eem אפיק *nm* **1.** channel; **2.** river-bed; (*pl+of:* **-ey**).

□ **Afeek** (Afiq) אפיק *nm* kibbutz in S. of Golan Heights (est 1967), 6 km E. of **'En Gev**. Pop 264.

□ **Afeekeem** (Afiqim) אפיקים *nm* Highly industrialized kibbutz (founded 1924) in Jordan Valley, S. of **Tsomet Tsemakh** (Zemah Junction). Pop. 1300.

(borer) afeekeem בורר אפיקים *nm* channel-selector.

hafeekh|ah/-ot הפיכה *nf* coup d'etat; revolution; (*+of:* **-at**).

hafeekhah tseva'eet הפיכה צבאית *nf* military coup.

hafeekh|at/-ot khatser הפיכת חצר *nf* coup d'etat.

afeeloo אפילו *conj* even; even though.

□ **Afek** (Afeq) אפק *nm* kibbutz (est. 1939) 3 km E. of **Keeryat Byaleek** (Haifa area). Pop. 521.

□ **Afekah** אפקה *nm* garden-quarter in N. part of Tel-Aviv, next to T.A. University campus.

afel/-ah אפל *adj* dark; gloomy.

afel|ah/-ot אפילה *nf* darkness; dusk; (*+of:* **-at**).

hafgan|ah/-ot הפגנה *nf* demonstration; (*+of:* **-at**).

hafganatee/-t הפגנתי *adj* demonstrative.

hafgaz|ah/-ot הפגזה *nf* shelling; bombardment; (*+of:* **-at**).

hafka|'ah/-'ot הפקעה *nf* expropriation; requistion; (*+of:* **-'at**).

hafka|'at/-'ot karka' הפקעת קרקע *nf* land expropriation.

hafka|'at/-'ot mekheer/-eem הפקעת מחיר *nf* overcharging.

hafkad|ah/-ot הפקדה *nf* **1.** depositing; **2.** placing one in charge; (*+of:* **-at**).

hafkar|ah/-ot הפקרה *nf* abandonment; renunciation; (*+of:* **-at**).

hafkhad|ah/-ot הפחדה *nf* intimidation; scaring; (*+of:* **-at**).

hafkhat|ah/-ot הפחתה *nf* reduction; abatement; (*+of:* **-at**).

haflag|ah/-ot הפלגה *nf* **1.** sailing; **2.** exaggeration; **3.** superlative (Gram.); (*+of:* **-at**).

hafla|yah/-yot הפלייה *nf* discrimination; (*+of:* **-yat**).

hafle va-fele! הפלא ופלא! *interj* how wonderful!

(le) haflee להפליא *adv* splendid; splendidly.

hafna|yah/-yot הפנייה *nf* turning; referring; referral; (*+of:* **-yat**).

afood|ah/-ot אפודה *nf* vest; sweater; (*+of:* **-at**).

hafoog|ah/-ot הפוגה *nf* truce; respite; (*+of:* **-at**).

(blee) hafoogah בלי הפוגה *adv* relentlessly.

(le-lo) hafoogah ללא הפוגה *adv* incessantly.

hafookh/-ah הפוך *adj* inverted; overturned.

(kafeh) hafookh קפה הפוך *nm* a cup of coffee with abundant milk.

□ **'Afoolah** ('Afula) עפולה town (est. 1925) and main urban center of Yizre'el Valley. Located at the crossing or roads from Coastal Plain and Samaria to Lower Galilee and Jordan Valley. Pop. 27,900.

afoon|ah/-eem אפונה *nf* pea.

afoor/-ah (*npr:* **afor/-ah**) אפור *adj* gray; gloomy.

afor/-ah אפור *adj gray; gloomy.*

'afr|ah/-ot עפרה *nf* ore; (*+of:* **-at**).

hafra'|ah/-'ot הפרעה *nf* interference; (*+of:* **-at**).

hafrad|ah/-ot הפרדה *nf* separation; (*+of:* **-at**).

hafradat kokhot הפרדת כוחות *nf* disengagement (milit.).

hafrakh|ah/-ot הפרחה *nf* **1.** making bloom; **2.** spreading; (*+of:* **-at**).

hafrakhat shemamah הפרחת שממה *nf* making the desert bloom.

hafrakhat shemoo|'ah/-'ot הפרחת שמועה *nf* spreading rumors.

hafrash|ah/-ot הפרשה *nf* secretion; (*+of:* **-at**).

hafraz|ah/-ot הפרזה *nf* exaggeration; (*+of:* **-at**).

hafra|yah/-yot הפרייה *nf* fertilization (of egg); fecundation; (*+of:* **-at**).

hafrayah mal'akhooteet הפרייה מלאכותית *nf* artificial insemination.

□ **Afreedar** (Afridar) אפרידר *nf* select residential quarter of Ashkelon.
Afreekah אפריקה *nf* Africa.
(Drom-) Afreekah דרום אפריקה *nf* South-Africa.
(Tsefon-) Afreekah צפון אפריקה *nf* North-Africa.
afreeka'ee/-t אפריקאי *mf* African.
afreekanee/-t אפריקני *adj* African.
afrooree/-t אפרורי *adj* ashen; grayish.
hafsak|ah/-ot הפסקה *nf* **1.** intermission; **2.** cessation; **(+*of:* -at).**
hafsak|at/-ot 'esh הפסקת־אש *nf* cease-fire.
hafsak|at/-ot zerem הפסקת זרם *nf* power break; interruption of electric current.
afsan|a'ee (*npr:* -ay)/-a'eem אפסנאי *nm* quartermaster; storekeeper (army).
afsana'oot אפסנאות *nf* quartermastership; storekeeping (army).
afsee/-t אפסי *adj* nil; worthless; insignificant.
hafshar|ah/-ot הפשרה *nf* melting; thaw; **(+*of:* -at).**
hafshat|ah/-ot הפשטה *nf* **1.** abstraction; **2.** undressing; **(+*of:* -at).**
afta|'ah/-'ot אפתעה *nf* surprise; **(+*of:* -'at).**
hafta|'ah/-'ot הפתעה *nf* surprise; **(+*of:* -'at).**
◇ **agaf ko'akh adam** אגף כוח אדם *nm* **1.** manpower division; **2.** Israel Defence Forces Manpower Division, commonly known under its *acr.* ◇ **AKA** אכ"א.
hagla|yah/-yot הגלייה *nf* deportation; **(+*of:* -yat).**
hagmash|ah/-ot הגמשה *nf* developing flexibility **(+*of:* -at).**
'agmoomee/-t עגמומי *adj* sad; sorrowful.
'ag|ol/-'oolah עגול *adj* round; circular.
(meespar) 'agol מספר עגול *nm* round figure.
(shoolkhan) 'agol שולחן עגול *nm* round table.
agood|ah/-ot אגודה *nf* association; society; **(+*of:* -at).**
◇ **"agoodah" ("Aguda")** "אגודה" *nf [colloq.]* reference to the ◇ **Agoodat Yeesra'el** אגודת ישראל political party. (See below).
agood|ah/-ot sheetoofee|t/-yot אגודה שיתופית *nf* cooperative society.
agoodal/-eem אגודל *nm* thumb.
◇ **agoodat yeesra'el** ("Agudas Isroel") אגודת ישראל *nf* veteran right-wing strictly religious political party known outside Israel as "Agudas Isroel". Though avowedly non-Zionist for generations, it has cooperated closely with most Israeli governments and been part of the coalitions forming them.
'agoom/-ah עגום *adj* gloomy; sad.
hagoon/-ah הגון *adj* decent; honest; fair.
◇ **'agoon|ah/-ot** עגונה *nf* wife whose husband's whereabouts have for long remained unknown while no evidence could be produced to pronounce him dead. Thus, her only hope for regaining freedom to re-marry lies in a difficult procedure of having 100 Rabbis sign a joint statement pronouncing him so. **(+*of:* -at).**
'agoor/-eem עגור *nm* crane; (bird); **(*pl+of:* -ey).**
□ **'Agoor** ('Agur) עגור *nm* village on borderline between the **Shfelah** and Judean hills (est. 1950) , 4 km NW of **Tsomet ha-Elah** (HaElah Junction). Pop. 290.
'agooran/-eem עגורן *nm* crane (for lifting in construction works); **(*pl+of:* -ey).**
agor|ah/-ot אגורה *nf* **1.** Israeli coin (0.01 shekel); **(+*of:* -at); 2.** (penny worth).
□ **Agoshreem** see □ **Ha-Goshreem.**
agr|ah/-ot אגרה *nf* tax; toll; **(+*of:* -at).**
hagral|ah/-ot הגרלה *nf* lottery; **(+*of:* -at).**
agronom אגרונום *nm* agronomist; agriculturist.
agronomeeyah אגרונומיה *nf* agronomy.
hagsham|ah/-ot הגשמה *nf* implementation; fufilment; **(+*of:* -at).**
'agvanee|yah/-yot עגבנייה *nf* tomato; **(+*of:* -yat).**
(meets) 'agvaneeyot עגבניות *nm* tomato-juice.
hagzam|ah/-ot הגזמה *nf* exaggeration; **(+*of:* -at).**
aha! !אהה *interj* alas!
ahad/-ah/-etee אהד *v* sympathised; **(*pres* ohed; *fut* ye'ehad).**
ahad|ah/-ot אהדה *nf* sympathy; **(+*of:* -at).**
ahav/-ah/-tee אהב *v* loved; **(*pres* ohev; *fut* ye'ehav).**
ahav|ah/-ot אהבה *nf* love; **(+*of:* -at).**
ahavat ha-zoolat אהבת הזולת *nf* altruism.
ahavat netsakh אהבת נצח *nf* eternal love.
ahaveem אהבים *nm pl* flirtations.
(harpatk|at/-a'ot) ahaveem הרפתקת אהבים *nf* love affair.
(heetn|ah/-etah/-etee) ahaveem היתנה אהבים *v* made love; **(*pres* matneh *etc*; *fut* yatneh *etc*).**
hahee ההיא *pron f* that one (female).
aheel/-eem אהיל *nm* lampshade **(*pl+of:* -ey).**
ha-hem ההם *pron* - nm pl those.
ha-hen ההן *pron nf pl* those (females).
ahlan אהלן *interj [slang]* welcome! (Arab.).
ahlan ve-sahlan אהלן וסהלן *interj [slang]* welcome! come along! (Arab.).
hahoo' ההוא *pron nm* that one (male).
ahoov/-ah אהוב **1.** *adj* beloved; **2.** *nmf* lover; **3.** *nmf* darling **(+*of:* -at/-ey).**
◇ **AKA** אכ"א *nm* (*acr of* **Agaf Koakh Adam** אגף כוח אדם) Manpower Division (army).
haka'ah/-'ot הכאה *nf* beating; hitting; **(+*of:* -'at).**
haka|'ah/-'ot הקאה *nf* vomiting; **(+*of:* -'at).**
akadema'ee/-t אקדמאי *mf* university graduate.
◇ **('atoodah) akadema'eet** see ◇ **'atoodah akadema'eet.**
akademee/-t אקדמי *adj* academic.
akademee|yah/-yot אקדמיה *nf* academy; **(+*of:* -yat).**
ha-kadosh-borkhoo הקדוש ברוך הוא *nm* God Almighty.
'ak|af/-fah/-aftee עקף *v* circumvented; overtook; side-stepped; **(*pres* 'okef; *fut* ya'akof).**

hakaf|ah/-ot הקפה *nf* encircling; encirclement; (+*of:* **-at**).

(be) hakafah בהקפה *adv* on credit.

◇ **akafot** see ◇ **hakafot**.

hakal|ah/-ot הקלה *nf* relief; concession; (+*of:* **-at**).

'akalaton עקלתון *adj* tortuous; zigzaggy.

'akalkal/-ah עקלקל *adj* crooked; winding.

(drakheem) 'akalkalot דרכים עקלקלות *nf pl* crooked ways; roundabout ways.

hakam|ah/-ot הקמה *nf* erection; setting-up; (+*of:* **-at**).

haka'ot הקאות *nf pl* (*sing:* **haka'ah**) vomitings.

'akar/-ah עקר *adj* barren; sterile (not fertile).

'ak|ar/-rah/-artee עקר *v* **1.** removed; uprooted; **2.** left for; (*pres* **'oker**; *fut* **ya'akor**).

'akar (*etc*) **meen ha-shoresh** עקר מן השורש *v* uprooted; deracinated.

'akar (*etc*) **shen/sheenayeem** עקר שן *v* removed tooth/teeth.

'akar|ah/-ot עקרה *nf* barren woman; (+*of:* **'akeret**).

hakar|ah/-ot הכרה *nf* **1.** acquaintance; recognition; **2.** conviction; (+*of:* **-at**).

hakarah ma'amadeet הכרה מעמדית *nf* class-consciousness.

hakarah pneemeet הכרה פנימית *nf* inner conviction.

('as|ah/-tah/-eetee) hakarah עשה הכרה *v* made acquaintance; (*pres* **'oseh** *etc; fut* **ya'aseh** *etc.*).

(ba'al/-at) hakarah בעל הכרה *adj* fully aware-person.

(khas|ar/-rat) hakarah חסר הכרה *adj* unconscious.

(mee-takhat le-saf ha) hakarah מתחת לסף ההכרה *adv* subconsciously; below the threshold of consciousness; underneath one's limen.

(tat-) hakarah תת־הכרה *nm* subconscience.

hakarat ha-shetakh הכרת השטח *nf* reconnoitering; reconnaissance.

hakarat todah הכרת תודה *nf* gratefulness; gratitude.

(tat-) hakaratee/-t תת־הכרתי *adj* subconscious.

'akaroot עקרות *nf* sterility; barreness.

(kley) hakashah כלי הקשה *nm pl* percussion instruments.

'ak|ats/-tsah/-atstee עקץ *v* stung; (*pres* **'okets**; *fut* **ya'akots**).

'ak|av/-vah/-avtee עקב *v* traced; followed; (*pres* **'okev**; *fut* **ya'akov**).

'akaveesh/-eem עכביש *nm* spider; (*pl+of:* **-ey**).

(koorey) 'akaveesh קורי עכביש *nm pl* spider web.

hakdam|ah/-ot הקדמה *nf* **1.** preface; introduction; **2.** advancing; (+*of:* **-at**).

hakdash|ah/-ot הקדשה *nf* dedication; (+*of:* **-at**).

'aked|ah/-ot עקידה *nf* sacrificing one's dearest (Bibl); (+*of:* **-at**).

'akedat yeetskhak עקידת יצחק *nf* Abraham's attempted binding of his son Isaac (Bibl.).

'akeef/-ah עקיף *adj* indirect; roundabout.

'akeef|ah/-ot עקיפה *nf* overtaking (traffic); circumvention; (+*of:* **-at**).

(be) 'akeefeen בעקיפין *adv* indirectly.

'akeerah/-ot עקירה *nf* eradication (+*of:* **-at**).

'akeerat shen/sheenayeem עקירת שן/שיניים *nf* tooth/teeth extraction.

□ **Akeeryah** see □ **Ha-keeryah**.

'ak|eret/-rot bayeet עקרת בית *nf* housewife.

'akev/-eem עקב *nm* heel.

('al) akev gavoha על עקב גבוה *adv* on high heels.

'akeveem עקבים *nm pl* heels; (*sing:* **'akev**).

'akevot (*sing:* **'akev**) עקבות *nm pl* footprints.

akh/-eem אח *nm* brother; (+*of:* **akh|ee/-ey**).

akh אח *nm* fireplace.

akh אך *conj* but; yet; only.

akh khoreg אח חורג *nm* step-brother; (*pl* **akheem khorgeem**).

akh te'om אח תאום *nm* twin-brother; (*pl* **akheem te'omeem**).

akh ve-rak אך ורק *adv* only; exclusively.

hakh/hakee הך *v imp m/f sing* strike! hit! (*inf* **lehakot**; *pst* **heekah**; *pres* **makeh**; *fut* **yakeh**).

(haynoo) hakh היינו הך all the same; makes no difference.

akhad-'asar אחד עשר *num m* eleven; 11; (male persons).

akhad ha- אחד ה־ *adj m* one of the ...

akhadeem אחדים *num m pl* a few; several; some (male persons).

akhadot אחדות *num f* a few; several; some.

akh|al/-lah/-altee אכל *v* ate; (*pres* **okhel**; *fut* **yokhal**).

hakhal|ah/-ot החלה *nf* application; (+*of:* **-at**).

◇ **a-khalookah** see ◇ **(ha)khalookah**.

ha-khamah החמה *nf* the sun.

(hanets) ha-khamah הנץ החמה *nm* sunrise.

hakhan|ah/-ot הכנה *nf* preparation; (+*of:* **-at**).

ha-"khanoot" החנות *nf* **1.** *[slang]* the fly (in man's trousers); **2.** *lit* : "the store".

akhar אחר *conj* after.

'akh|ar/-rah/-artee עכר *v* disturbed; befouled; spoiled (mood); (*pres* **'okher**; *fut* **ya'kor**; *k=kh*).

akhar ha-tsohorayeem אחר הצהרים *adv* in the afternoon.

akhare|hem/-hen אחריהם/־ן *adv* pers. pron pl *m/f after them.*

akharekh|em/-en אחריכם/־ן *adv & pers.pron pl m/f* after you.

akharey אחרי *adv* after.

akharey ha-kol אחרי הכל *adv* after all.

akharey ha-tsohorayeem אחר הצהרים *adv* in the afternoon.

akharey kee-khelot ha-kol אחרי ככלות הכל *adv* ultimately.

akharey khen אחרי כן *adv* afterwards.

(karookh/krookhah) akharey כרוך אחרי *adj* attached to; attracted by.

(nat|ah/-etah/-etee) akharey נטה אחרי *v* leaned to; was inclined to follow; (*pres* **noteh** *etc; fut* **yeeteh** *etc*).

akhar kakh אחר־כך *adv* afterwards.

(le) akhar ma'aseh לאחר מעשה *adv* post factum.
(le) akhar mee-ken לאחר מכן *adv* after that.
akharon/-ah אחרון *adj* last; ultimate.
akharon akharon khaveev אחרון אחרון חביב last but not least.
(ba) akharonah באחרונה *adv* of late.
(la) akharonah לאחרונה *adv* lately.
(manah/-ot) akharon|ah/-ot מנה אחרונה *nf* dessert; course served last.
akhat אחת *num f* one.
akhat ha- אחת ה־ *num f* one of.
(ha) akhat-'esreh אחת־עשרה *adj f* the 11th.
akhat oo-le-tameed אחת ולתמיד *adv* once and for all.
(bee-nesheemah) akhat בנשימה אחת *adv* in one breath.
(yad) akhat יד אחת *nf* accord; unison.
akhav|ah/-ot אחווה *nf* brotherhood (*+of:* **-at**).
akh|az/-zah/-aztee אחז *v* held; (*pres* **okhez**; *fut* **yokhaz**).
akhaz (*etc*) **be-'emtsa'eem** אחז באמצעים *v* took measures.
hakhbad|ah/-ot הכבדה *nf* inconvenience; burden; (*+of:* **-at**).
'akhb|ar/-areem עכבר *nm* mouse (*pl+of:* **-erey**).
'akhberosh/-eem עכברוש *nm* rat (*pl+of:* **-ey**).
akhdoot אחדות *nf* unity.
hakhee הכי *adv* the most.
hakhee? הכי? *adv* is there? is it? is/was it indeed?
hakhee hakhee הכי־הכי *adj [slang]* the very best; the most.
hakhee harbeh הכי הרבה *adv* at most.
akheed/-ah אחיד *adj* uniform; homogeneous.
akheedoot אחידות *nf* uniformity.
□ **Akhee'ezer** (Ahiezer) אחיעזר *nm* village in Judean lowland (est. 1950), 3 km NW of Lod. Pop 752.
□ **Akheehood** (Ahihud) אחיהוד *nm* village in W. Galilee (est. 1950) 9 km E. of **'Ako** (Acre). Pop 446.
akheel|ah/-ot אכילה *nf* eating; (*+of:* **-at**).
(kever) akheem קבר אחים *nm* collective (fraternal) grave; mass grave.
□ **Akheesamakh** (Ahisamakh) אחיסמך *nm* village in Judean lowlands (est. 1950) 4 km E. of Ramla. Pop 677.
□ **Akheetoov** (Ahituv) אחיטוב *nm* village in N. Sharon (est. 1951), 8 km SW of **Khaderah**. Pop 483.
akheez|ah/-ot אחיזה *nf* hold; holding; (*+of:* **-at**).
(nekood|at/-ot) akheezah נקודת אחיזה *nf* foothold; lead.
akheezat 'enayeem אחיזת עיניים *nf* optical illusion; mystification.
hakhel be- החל ב־ *adv* beginning with; as of.
hakhel me- החל מ־ *adv* as from; as of;
(le) akhel לאחל *v inf* (to) wish someone; (*pst* **eekhel**; *pres* **me'akhel**; *fut* **ye'akhel**).
akhen אכן **1.** *adv* certainly; indeed; **2.** *conj* but; however.

hakhen הכן *adv* ready; prepared.
(matsav) hakhen מצב הכן *nm* standby; state of alert.
akher/-et אחר *adj* other; different.
(davar) akher דבר אחר *nm* a different matter.
akheret אחרת *adv* otherwise.
hakh'kar|ah/-ot החכרה *nf* leasing; hire; (*+of:* **-at**).
hakhlaf|ah/-ot החלפה *nf* exchange; replacement; f (*+of:* **-at**).
hakhlak|ah/-ot החלקה *nf* gliding; skiing; (*+of:* **-at**).
hakhlal|ah/-ot הכללה *nf* generalization; inclusion; (*+of:* **-at**).
hakhlam|ah/-ot החלמה *nf* recovery; convalescence; (*+of:* **-at**).
hakhlash|ah/-ot החלשה *nf* weakening; (*+of:* **-at**).
hakhlat|ah/-ot החלטה *nf* decision; resolution; (*+of:* **-at**).
(keeb|el/-lah/-altee) hakhlatah קיבל החלטה *v* adopted a resolution; took a decision; (*pres* **mekabel** *etc; fut* **yekabel** *etc*).
hakhmats|ah/-ot החמצה *nf* **1.** miss (of an opportunity); **2.** leavening; acidification.
◇ **(geeloom) akhnasah** see ◇ **geeloom hakhnasah**.
hakhna|'ah/-'ot הכנעה *nf* submissiveness; (*+of:* **-'at**).
hakhnas|ah/-ot הכנסה *nf* **1.** income; **2.** introduction; (*+of:* **-at**).
(bool/-ey) hakhnasah בול הכנסה *nm* revenue-stamp.
◇ **(geeloom) hakhnasah** גילום הכנסה *nm* payment by employer of employee's income-tax.
(me'ootey) hakhnasah מעוטי הכנסה *nm pl* people of low income.
hakhnasat orkheem הכנסת אורחים *nf* hospitality.
hakhna|yah/-yot החניה *nf* parking; (*+of:* **-yat**).
hakhnayat rekhev החניית רכב *nf* parking of a car/cars.
akhoo אחו *nm* meadow.
'akhoor/-ah עכור *adj* troubled; turbid.
akhooz/-ah אחוז *adj* seized; stricken; (*+of:* **-at**).
akhooz/-eem אחוז *nm* percent; rate; (*pl+of:* **-ey**).
◇ **akhooz ha-khaseemah** אחוז החסימה *nm* voting threshold; minimum percentage of total national vote (at Knesset elections) required for gaining a seat in the Knesset.
akhooz|ah/-ot אחוזה *nf* estate; property; (*+of:* **-at**).
□ **Akhoozah** (Ahuza) אחוזה *nf* (abbr of **Akhoozat Herbert Samuel** אחוזת הרברט סמואל) veteran residential quarter (est. 1922) of the city of Haifa located on Mt Carmel (**Karmel**).
□ **Akhoozam** (Ahuzzam) אחוזם *nm* village in **Lakheesh** area (est. 1950), 7 km S. of **Keeryat-Gat**. Pop 394.

akhor/-ayeem אחור *nm* back; backside; buttock.
(le) akhor לאחור *adv* backwards.
(me) akhor מאחור *adv* from behind.
akhorah אחורה *adv* backwards.
akhoraneet אחורנית *adv* backwards; retrospectively.
akhorayeem אחוריים *nm pl* buttocks; posterior; (*+of:* **-at**).
akhoree/-t אחורי *adj* rear; hind.
akhorey אחורי *adv* the back side of.
(me) akhorey מאחורי *adv* behind.
(me) akhorey ha-kla'eem מאחורי הקלעים *adv* behind the scenes.
(me) akhorey ha-pargod מאחורי הפרגוד *adv* behind the curtains; secretly.
akhot/akhayot אחות *nf* **1.** sister; **2.** nurse.
akh|ot/-ayot khor|eget/-got אחות חורגת *nf* step-sister.
akh|ot/-ayot ma'asee|t/-yot אחות מעשית *nf* practical nurse.
akh|ot/-ayot rakhmanee|yah/-yot אחות רחמנייה *nf* nurse.
akhot rasheet אחות ראשית *nf* head-nurse; matron.
akh|ot/-ayot te'om|ah/-ot אחות תאומה *nf* twin sister.
akhot|ee/-kha/-ekh/-o/-ah אחותי־ך־/ו־/ה *nf* my/your *m/f* his/her sister.
◻ **Akhotreem** see ◻ **Ha-khotreem**.
hakhpal|ah/-ot הכפלה *nf* **1.** multiplication; **2.** doubling; (*+of:* **-at**).
hakhra|'ah/-'ot הכרעה *nf* decision; (*+of:* **-'at**).
akhr|a'ee (*npr* **-ay**)/**-a'eet** אחראי *adj* responsible; in charge.
(ha) akhr|a'ee (*npr* **-ay**)/**-'eet** אחראי *nmf* the one in charge.
hakhraf|ah/-ot החרפה *nf* exacerbation; (*+of:* **-at**).
hakhram|ah/-ot החרמה *nf* **1.** confiscation; **2.** excommunication; (*+of:* **-at**).
akhr|av/-ay/-ayeekh אחריו־יי־/־ייך *adv* after him/me/you (*f sing*).
akhrayoot אחריות *nf* responsibility.
(be) akhrayoot באחריות *adv* **1.** guaranteed; **2.** registered (mail).
akhreet אחרית *nf* end; epilog.
◇ **akhreet ha-yameem** אחרית הימים *nf* the End of Days; Days of the Apocalypse.
akhre|ha/-kha אחריה־/ך *adv* after her/you (*m sing*).
akhrey אחרי *adv* after.
akhrey ha-kol אחרי הכול *adv* after all.
akhrey kee-khelot ha-kol אחרי ככלות הכול *adv* ultimately.
akhrey khen אחרי כן *adv* afterwards.
(karookh/krookhah) akhrey כרוך אחרי *adj* attached to; attracted by.
(nat|ah/-etah/-etee) akhrey נטה אחרי *v* leaned to; was inclined to follow; (*pres* **noteh** *etc; fut* **yeeteh** *etc*).
akhrey|hem/-hen אחריהם/־ן *adv & pers.pron pl m/f* after them.
akhreykh|em/-en אחריכם/־ן *adv & pers.pron pl m/f* after you.
akhron/-ah אחרון *adj* last; ultimate.
akhron akhron khaveev אחרון אחרון חביב last but not least.
(ba) akhronah באחרונה *adv* of late.
(la) akhronah לאחרונה *adv* lately.
(man|ah/-ot) akhron|ah/-ot מנה אחרונה *nf* dessert; course served last.
akhsan|yah/-yot אכסניה *nf* inn; guesthouse; (*+of:* **-yat**).
akhsan|yat/-yot no'ar אכסניית נוער *nf* youth hostel.
◇ **akhsharah** see ◇ **hakh'sharah**.
hakhshad|ah/-ot החשדה *nf* casting suspicion; (*+of:* **-at**).
hakhshar|ah/-ot הכשרה *nf* training; preparation; (*+of:* **-at**).
◇ **"Hakhsharah"** הכשרה *nf* process of training groups of young Jews in Diaspora for pioneering life in Israel.
hakhsharah meektso'eet הכשרה מקצועית *nf* professional training.
hakhsharat karka' הכשרת קרקע *nf* preparing ground.
'akhshav עכשיו *adv* now.
(kan ve) 'akhshav כאן ועכשיו *adv* here and now.
◇ **"(Shalom) 'Akhshav"** שלום עכשיו *nf* "Peace Now" - political movement advocating immediate and unconditional withdrawal from all "occupied territories" and entering into negotiations with PLO.
'akhshavee/-t עכשווי *adj* present; current.
hakhta|'ah/-'ot החטאה *nf* missing a target; leading astray; (*+of:* **-at**).
hakhtam|ah/-ot החתמה *nf* signing on; signing up; getting someone to sign; making one subscribe; subscription; (*+of:* **-at**).
hakhtar|ah/-ot הכתרה *nf* crowning; coronation; (*+of:* **-at**).
hakhtav|ah/-ot הכתבה *nf* dictation; (*+of:* **-at**).
akhv|ah/-ot אחווה *nf* brotherhood; (*+of:* **-at**).
◻ **Akhvah** (Ahawa) אחוה *nm* village (est. 1976) 5 km NE of **Keeryat Mal'akhee**. Pop. 129.
hakhvan|ah/-ot הכוונה *nf* guidance; directing; (*+of:* **-at**).
hakhya|'ah/-'ot החייאה *nf* resuscitation; (*+of:* **-'at**).
akhyan/-eem אחיין nmf nephew.
akhyanee|t/-yot אחיינית *nf* niece.
akhzak|ah/-ot אחזקה *nf* maintenance; (*+of:* **-at**).
hakhzakah/-ot החזקה *nf* maintenance; (*+of:* **-at**).
akhzar אכזר *nm* cruel person.
akhzaree/-t אכזרי *adj* cruel; harsh.
akhzav אכזב *adj* (masc) deceptive; disappointing.
(lo) akhzav לא אכזב *adj* - nm inexhaustible; reliable.

(nakhal) akhzav נחל אכזב *nm* winter stream; wadi.

akhzav|ah/-ot אכזבה *nf* disappointment; (*+of:* **-at**).

(nakh|al/-lah/-altee) akhzavah נחל אכזבה *v* suffered a disappointment; (*pres* **nokhel** *etc; fut* **yeenkhal** *etc*).

□ **Akhzeev** (or Tel Akhziv) אכזיב *nm* health and pleasure camp on seashore antiquities-site, 5 km N. of Nahariyya.

akhzereeyoot אכזריות *nf* cruelty.

hakh'khash|ah/-ot (*cpr* **hak'khashah**) הכחשה *nf* denial; (*+of:* **-at**).

haklat|ah/-ot הקלטה *nf* recording; taping; (*+of:* **-at**).

(seret/seertey) haklatah סרט־הקלטה *nm* recording- tape.

akleem/-eem אקלים *nm* climate.

akleemee/-t אקלימי *adj* climatic.

◇ **ha-kneset** הכנסת *nf* the Knesset — Israel's Parliament. 120 members elected (normally) once every four years by proportional vote.

□ **'Ako** ('Akko) עכו *nf* historic town of Acre, picturesque ancient harbor-city with medieval citadel, 26 km N. of Haifa. Pop. 30,300.

'ak|om (*cpr* **'akoom**)**/-oomah** עקום *adj* crooked; bent.

'akoom|ah/-ot עקומה *nf* curve (in graph); (*+of:* **-at**).

'akoor/-ah עקור *adj* uprooted.

'akoor/-eem עקור *nm* uprooted refugee; displaced person; (D.P.); (*pl+of:* **-ey**).

akoosteekah אקוסטיקה *nf* acoustics.

'akooz/-eem עכוז *nm* buttocks; posterior; (*pl+of:* **-ey**).

hakpa|'ah/-'ot הקפאה *nf* freezing; freeze; (*+of:* **-'at**).

hakpa|'at/-'ot hon הקפאת הון *nf* freezing of capital.

hakpa|'at/-'ot sakhar הקפאת שכר *nf* wage freeze.

hakpad|ah/-ot הקפדה *nf* strict observation; (*+of:* **-at**).

hakra|'ah/-'ot הקראה *nf* recitation; (*+of:* **-'at**).

hakran|ah/-ot הקרנה *nf* projection; (*+of:* **-at**).

'akra|v/-beem (*b=v*) עקרב *nm* scorpion; (*pl+of:* **-bey**).

□ **Akrayot"** see □ **Ha-Krayot**.

hakrav|ah/-ot הקרבה *nf* **1.** sacrificing; **2.** drawing near; (*+of:* **-at**).

□ **"Ha-krayot"** הקריות *nf pl [colloq.]* reference to Haifa's three seashore suburbs: **Keeryat-Khayeem, Keeryat Motskeen** and **Keeryat-Byaleek**.

akroot/-eet אקרוט *adj [slang]* devastatingly clever; extremely resourceful.

hakshakh|ah/-ot הקשחה *nf* stiffening; (*+of:* **-at**).

'akshan/-eet עקשן *nmf* stubborn, obstinate, person; (*pl:* **-eem**; *+of:* **-ey**).

'akshanee/-t עקשני *adj* obstinate; stubborn.

'akshanoo|t/-yot עקשנות *nf* stubbornness.

(be) 'akshanoot בעקשנות *adv* stubbornly.

hakshav|ah הקשבה *nf* attentive listening; (*+of:* **-at**).

aksyom|ah/-ot אקסיומה *nf* axiom.

haktan|ah/-ot הקטנה *nf* diminution; reduction; lessening; (*+of:* **-at**).

haktsa|'ah/-'ot הקצאה *nf* allotment (of shares); allocation (of funds); (*+of:* **-at**).

haktsan|ah/-ot הקצנה *nf* tendency to extremism; (*+of:* **-at**).

haktsav|ah/-ot הקצבה *nf* allocation; (*+of:* **-at**).

al אל *adv* don't; no.

al- ־אל *prefix* non-; un-; -less.

al domee אל דמי *interj* no respite; don't let off!

al-ga'at אל־געת don't touch! not to be touched!

al-keshel אל־כשל *adj* fail-proof; fool-proof.

al-kheled אל חלד *adj* stainless.

al-matakhtee/-t אל־מתכתי *adj* non-metal.

al-ma'amadee/-t אל־מעמדי *adj* classless.

al ta'eez (*npr* **ta'ez**)**/-eezee!** אל תעז ! *v imp* don't you dare! (*inf* **lo leha'eez**; *pres* **lo he'eez**; *pres* **eyno me'eez**; *fut* **lo ya'eez**).

al teedkh|of/-efee ! אל תדחוף ! *v imp* don't push! (*inf* **lo leedkhof**; *pst* **lo dakhaf**; *pres* **eyno dokhef**; *fut* **lo yeedkhof**).

al teevr|akh/-ekhee! אל תברח ! *v imp* don't run away! (*inf* **lo leevro'akh**; *pst* **lo barakh** (*b=v*); *pres* **eyno bore'akh**; *fut* **lo yeevrakh** .

al teeh|yeh/-yee! אל תהיה ! *v imp* don't you be! don't be a...; (*inf* **lo leehyot**; *pst* **lo hayah**; *pres* **eyno**; **lo yeehyeh**).

al tel|ekh/-khee! אל תלך ! *v imp* don't go! (*inf* **lo lalekhet**; *pst* **lo halakh**; *pres* **eyno holekh**; *fut* **lo yelekh**).

al teeshk|akh/-ekhee! אל תשכח ! *v imp* don't forget! don't you forget! (*inf* **lo leeshko'akh**; *pst* **lo shakhakh**; *pres* **eyno shokhe'akh**; *fut* **lo yeeshkakh** (*kh=k*)).

(sam/-ah le)al שם לאל *v* reduced to naught; frustrated; (*pres* **sam** *etc; fut* **yaseem** *etc*).

'al על *prep* on; of; including.

'al- ־על *pref* over-; super-.

'al boory|o/-ah על בוריו *adv* thorough; thoroughly.

'al da'at על דעת *prep* with the approval of.

'al da'ato shel על דעתו של *prep* with the approval of.

'al ha-perek על הפרק *prep* on the agenda.

'al gabey על גבי *prep* on; on the top of.

'al gav על גב *prep* on top of; on back of; on; upon.

'al kakh על כך for that; therefore.

'al ken על כן therefore.

'al kheshbon על חשבון *adv* on account.

'al kol paneem על כל פנים at any rate.

'al kol tsarah על כל צרה to be on the safe side.

'al korkh|o/-ah על כורחו *adv* perforce; against one's wish.

'al lo davar על לא דבר don't mention it! (standard reply to "Thanks!").

'al lo me'oomah על לא מאומה don't mention it! (reply to "Thanks!").
'al menat she- על מנת ש־ *prep* provided that.
'al nekalah על נקלה *adv* easily; with no trouble.
'al pee על פי *prep* according to.
'al pee rov על פי רוב mostly; generally.
'al peh על פה *adv* by heart; orally.
(be) 'al peh בעל פה *adv* by heart; orally.
'al peney על פני *prep* in front of.
'al peney ha-shetakh על פני השטח on the face of it; on the surface.
'al regel akhat על רגל אחת *adv* **1.** in a nutshell; in brief; **2.** in a hurry; (lit.) on one foot.
'al saf על סף *prep* on the threshold of.
'al seerton על שירטון *adv* aground.
'al semakh על סמך *prep* on the strength of.
'al she- על ש־ *prep* because.
'al shem על שם *prep* in the memory of; named after.
'al shem על שם *adj* nominal.
'al shoom על שום *prep* because; in accordance with.
'al teel|o/-ah על תילו *adv* in its place.
'al tenay על תנאי *adv* on the condition that; conditionally.
(ma'asar) 'al tenay מאסר על תנאי *nm* suspended prison sentence.
(tsav) 'al tenay צו על תנאי *nm* order nisi.
'al tenay she- על תנאי ש־ *adv* on condition that.
'al yad על יד *prep* beside; next to.
'al yedey על ידי *prep* by; through; by means of.
'al yedey kakh על ידי כך thereby.
'al yeesodee/-t על־יסודי *adj* post-primary school.
(me) 'al oo-me-'ever מעל ומעבר *adv* above and beyond.
al|ah/-ot אלה *nf* club; baton; (*+of:* **-at**).
'al|ah/-tah/-eetee עלה *v* **1.** went up; ascended; **2.** immigrated to Israel; (*pres* **'oleh;** *fut* **ya'aleh**).
'alah (*etc*) **'al (ha)'atsabeem** עלה על העצבים *v* got on one's nerves.
'alah (*etc*) **'al leeb|ee/-o/-ah** עלה על ליבי *v* occurred to (me/him/her); entered one's mind.
◇ **'alah** (*etc*) **le-torah** עלה לתורה *v* was called up to read from the Torah.
'alah 'al (ha)perek עלה על הפרק *v* came up for discussion.
'alah (*etc*) **'al seerton** עלה על שרטון *v* ran aground.
'alah (*etc*) **ba-'esh** עלה באש *v* went up in flames.
'alah (*etc*) **ba-tohoo** עלה בתוהו *v* went to naught.
'alah (*etc*) **be-da'ato/-ah** עלה בדעתו/־תה *v* occurred to him/her (etc).
'alah (*etc*) **be-yad|o/-ah** עלה בידו/־ה *v* managed; succeeded.
'al|ah (*etc*) **la-'arets** עלה לארץ *v* immigrated to Israel.
'alah (*etc*) **la-torah** עלה לתורה *v* was granted a Torah reading (at the synagogue).
'alah (*etc*) **le-regel** עלה לרגל *v* made a pilgrimage.
'alah (*etc*) **le-yeesra'el** עלה לישראל *v* emigrated to Israel.
'alah (*etc*) **mekheer** עלה מחיר *v* price went up.
ha-lah הלה *pron* that one; the one there.
hal'ah הלאה *adv* further; onward.
(gash/geshee) hal'ah! גש הלאה! *v imp sing m/f* go away! (*inf* **lageshet** *etc; pst & pres* **neegash** *etc; fut* **yeegash** *etc*).
(ve-khen) hal'ah וכן הלאה and so on; etcetera.
halokh/heelkhey nefesh הלך נפש *nm* frame of mind.
halokh/heelkhey roo'akh הלך רוח *nm* mood.
hal|akh/-khah/-akhtee הלך *v* went; (*pres* **holekh;** *fut* **yelekh**).
halakh (*etc*) **batel** הלך בטל *v* idled.
halakh (*etc*) **ba-telem** הלך בתלם *v* toed the line.
halakh (*etc*) **le-'eebood** הלך לאיבוד *v* got lost.
halakh (*etc*) **le-'olam|o/-ah** הלך לעולמו *v* passed away.
halakh (*etc*) **rakheel** הלך רכיל *v* gossiped; spread gossip.
halakh (*etc*) **sholal** הלך שולל *v* was misled; was deceived.
hal|akh/-khah ve-gad|al/-lah הלך וגדל *v* grew bigger and bigger; (*pres* **holekh ve-gadel;** *fut* **yelekh ve-yeegdal**).
halakh|ah/-ot הלכה *nf* law; rule; tradition; (*+of:* **-at**).
halakhah le-ma'aseh הלכה למעשה *nf* by rule of thumb; putting theory into practice.
(ka) halakhah כהלכה *adv* properly.
(la) halakhah להלכה *adv* theoretically; in theory.
◇ **(pesak/peeskey) halakhah** פסק הלכה *nm* decision by a rabbinical authority or court.
alakhson/-eet אלכסון *adj* diagonal.
halaloo הללו *nm pl* these.
hal|am/-mah/-amtee הלם *v* **1.** fitted; was suited to; **2.** stroke; hit; (*pres* **holem;** *fut* **yahalom**).
hal'am|ah/-ot הלאמה *nf* nationalization; (*+of:* **-at**).
(le) halan להלן *adv* following below; infra.
halan|ah/-ot הלנה *nf* providing night's lodging; putting up overnight; (*+of:* **-at**).
halanat sekhar הלנת שכר *nf* delaying payment of wages.
'alat|ah/-ot עלטה *nf* darkness; (*+of:* **-at**).
halats|ah/-ot הלצה *nf* joke; (*+of:* **-at**).
'al|av/-eha עליו/־ה on him/her.
'al|av/-eha ha-shalom עליו השלום may he/she rest in peace.
(me) 'al|av/-eha מעליו/־יה over him/her; above him/her.
'ala|y/-yeekh עלי/־יך on me/you *f*.
(me)'al|ay/-eekh מעלי/־ייך over me/you *f*; above me/you *f*.
ha-laylah הלילה *adv* tonight.
'al|az/-zah/-aztee עלז *v* rejoiced; (*pres* **'olez;** *fut* **ya'aloz**).
ha-laz הלז *pron* that one.
halbash|ah/-ot הלבשה *nf* clothing; (*+of:* **-at**).

(khanoo|t/-yot) halbashah חנות הלבשה *nf* clothing store.
aleefoo|t/-yot אליפות *nf* championship.
haleekh/-eem הליך *nm* proceeding; action; process; (*pl+of:* **-ey**).
haleekh|ah/-ot הליכה *nf* walk; march; (*+of:* **-at**).
haleekheem meeshpateeyeem הליכים משפטיים *nm pl* legal proceedings.
haleekhon הליכון *nm* walking frame for invalids.
haleekhot הליכות *nf pl* manners.
(ba) 'aleel בעליל *adv* clearly; visually.
'aleel|ah/-ot עלילה *nf* **1.** plot; **2.** frame-up; (*+of:* **-at**).
'aleel|at/-ot dam עלילת דם *nf* blood libel.
'aleelot dvareem עלילות דברים *nf pl* false accusations; trumped up charges.
aleem/-ah אלים *adj* violent.
aleemoot אלימות *nf* violence.
'aleetsoot עליצות *nf* gaiety.
'alee|yah/-yot עלייה *nf* **1.** ascent; mounting; **2.** immigration to Israel; (*+of:* **-yat**).
(ha) 'aleeyah העלייה *nf* immigration to Israel.
◇ **(ha)'aleeyah ha-sheneeyah** העלייה השניה *nf* 2nd Aliyah i.e. the immigration wave of 1904-1919.
◇ **(ha)'aleeyah ha-sheleesheet** העלייה השלישית *nf* 3rd Aliyah i.e. the immigration wave of 1919-1924.
◇ **'aleeyah 'al ha-karka'** עלייה על הקרקע *nf* settling on (new) land.
'alee|yah/-yot be-dargah עלייה בדרגה *nf* promotion.
◇ **'aleeyah bet** עלייה ב׳ *nf* the "Second Aliyah" which was the name used for the running of the British blockade (i.e. shipping Jewish immigrants "illegally" to Palestine) during the British Mandate in the years 1928-1948.
'alee|yat/-yot gag עליית גג *nf* attic.
'alee|yah/-yot le-regel עלייה לרגל *nf* pilgrimage.
'alee|yah/-yot le-torah עלייה לתורה *nf* call to read from the Torah (in synagogue).
◇ **(kleetat) 'aleeyah** קליטת עלייה *nf* absorption (integration) of immigrants.
'aleez/-ah עליז *adj* jolly; joyous; gay.
◇ **(ha)'aleezeem** העליזים *nm pl* the "gay" (homosexuals).
'aleezoot עליזות *nf* gaiety; merriment.
◇ **alef** (Aleph) אל״ף *nf* 1st letter of Hebrew alphabet, a hiatus pronounced **ah**, **eh**, **ee**, **o**, or **oo** depending on the vowel that accompanies it.
alef א׳ *num* 1 (or 1,000) in the Hebrew system of numerals.
alef-alef אל״ף־אל״ף *[colloq.] adj* A-one; first class; best quality.
alef-bet אל״ף־בי״ת *nm* alphabet.
(me) alef ve-'ad tav מאל״ף ועד תי״ו from A to Z.
(soog) alef סוג א׳ *nm* first class quality.
(yom) alef יום א׳ *nm* Sunday.
alegoree|yah/-yot אלגוריה *nf* allegory; (*+of:* **-yat**).
'al|eh/-eem עלה *nm* leaf (of tree).
'aleh needaf עלה נידף *nm* driven leaf.
'ale|hem/-hen עליהם/־הן on them *m/f*.
'alekha עליך on you *sing m*.
'alekh|em/-en עליכם/־כן on you *(pl m/f)*.
'alekh|em shalom! עליכם שלום! (return-greeting) peace to you! (to reciprocate when being greeted with "shalom 'aleykhem!", see below).
(shalom) 'alekhem! שלום עליכם (greeting) peace to you! (mostly used to greet someone on arrival or, somewhat sarcastically, when showing up late or unexpectedly).
◇ **alel** see ◇ **Halel**.
◇ **"Halel"** הלל *nm* special holiday prayer of praise.
(gam|ar/-rah et ha) halel גמר את ההלל *v* was full of praise; (*pres* **gomer** *etc; fut* **yeegmor** *etc*).
◇ **alelooyah** see ◇ **Halelooyah**.
◇ **Halelooyah (Haleluya)** הללויה "Halleluja" - praise be to God.
'alenoo עלינו on us.
(lo) 'alenoo לא עלינו may it not befall us.
halevay הלוואי *interj* if only; I wish it were.
'aleyh|em/-hen עליהם/הן on them *m/f*.
'aleykh|em/-en עליכם/־כן on you *pl m/f*.
'aleykhem shalom! עליכם שלום! (return-greeting) see **"alekhem shalom"**, above.
(shalom) 'aleykhem! שלום עליכם! (greeting) see **"shalom 'alekhem"**, above.
'aleynoo עלינו on us.
(lo) 'aleynoo לא עלינו may it not befall us.
□ **Alfey Menasheh** אלפי מנשה *nf* urban settlement (est. 1979) 12 km E. of **Kefar-Saba**. Pop 2,560.
alfon/-eem אלפון *nm* **1.** primer; **2.** alphabetic index (*pl+of:* **-ey**).
halka|'ah/-'ot הלקאה *nf* flogging; flagellation; (*+of:* **-at**).
halkham|ah/-ot הלחמה *nf* soldering; welding; (*+of:* **-at**).
alkhoot אלחוט *nm* wireless.
alkhootan/-eet אלחוטן *nmf* radio-operator.
alkhoot|ay/-a'eet אלחוטאי *nmf* radio-operator.
alkhootee/-t אלחוטי *adj* wireless.
alkohol אלכוהול *nm* alcohol.
alkoholee/-t אלכוהולי *adj* alcoholic.
'al|mah/-amot עלמה *nf* damsel; miss; (*+of:* **-mat/-mot**).
□ **'Almah** ('Alma) עלמה *nm* village in Upper Galilee (est. 1949), 9 km N. of Safed **(Tsefat)**. Pop. 594.
'almah neekhbadah עלמה נכבדה *nf* dear miss.
□ **Almagor** אלמגור *nm* village in Lower Galilee's **Korazeem** district (est. 1961), near Jordan river's estuary (into Lake Tiberias). Pop. 245.
alman/-eem אלמן *nm* widower.
alman/-ey kash אלמן קש *nm* grass-widower.

almanlah/-ot אלמנה *nf* widow; (*+of:* **almenlat/-ot**).

almanah khayah אלמנה חיה *nf* "live widow" i.e. wife deserted by a missing husband.

almavet אלמוות *nm* immortality.

(bat/benot) almavet בת אלמוות *adj (f) & nf* immortal.

(ben/bney) almavet בן אלמוות *adj (m) & nm* immortal.

almenlat/-ot kash אלמנת קש *nf* grass-widow.

□ **Almog** אלמוג *nm* kibbutz (est. 1981) next to **Tsomet Almog** (Almog Junction), 5 km W. of Dead Sea, 9 km S. of Jericho.

□ **'Almon** עלמון *nm* communal village (est. 1980) 8 km NE of Jerusalem, on road from Mount Scopus to Wadi Farakh. Pop. 224.

almonee/-t אלמוני *adj* unknown; nameless; anonymous.

(pelonee-) almonee פלוני־אלמוני *nm* "Mr. What's-his-name".

halo הלו *interj* hello! hullo!

halo הלא *adv* is it not? surely.

halokh va-shov הלוך ושוב *adv* back and forth.

halom הלום *adv* to here; hereto; hither.

alon/-eem אלון *nm* oak; (*pl+of:* **-ey**).

□ **Alon Moreh** see □ **Elon Moreh**.

□ **Alon Shevoot** (Allon Shevut) אלון שבות *nm* regional center for new settlements in **Goosh 'Etsyon**, outside Hebron. Pop. 1,490.

□ **Aloneem** (Allonim) אלונים *nm* kibbutz in N. of Yeezre'el Valley (est 1935), 5 km E. of **Keeryat Teev'on**. Pop 563.

□ **Aloney Aba** (Alloné Abba) אלוני אבא *nm* communal village (est 1948) in Lower Galilee, 5 km NE of **Keeryat Teev'on**.

□ **Aloney Yeets'khak** (**Alloné Yizhak**) אלוני יצחק *nm* youth-village (est. 1948) & school 6 km SE of **Benyameenah**. Pop. 296.

aloof/-ah אלוף *nmf* champion.

aloof/-eem אלוף *nm* Major-General.

aloof-meeshneh אלוף משנה *nm* Colonel.

aloof peekood אלוף פיקוד *nm* regional (district) commander.

(rav) aloof רב־אלוף *nm* Lieutenant-General.

(segan/-ey) aloof/-eem סגן־אלוף *nm* Lieutenant-Colonel.

(tat/-ey) aloof/-eem תת־אלוף *nm* Brigadeer-General.

'alooklah/-ot עלוקה *nf* leech; (*+of:* **-at**).

'alool/-ah עלול *adj* liable; is liable.

haloom/-ah הלום *adj* shocked; stricken.

haloom/-at ra'am הלום רעם *adj* thunderstruck.

□ **Aloomah** (Alumma) אלומה *nm* rural center (est 1965) servicing villages **Revakhah**, **Zavdee'el** and **Komemeeyoot**. Pop 503.

□ **'Aloomeem** ('Alumim) עלומים *nm* kibbutz in NW Negev (est. 1966), 3 km SW of **Tsomet Sa'ad** (Sa'ad Junction). Pop. 404.

'aloomeem עלומים *nm pl* youth.

aloomeenyoom אלומיניום *nm* aluminium; aluminum.

□ **Aloomot** (Alummot) אלומות *nf* kibbutz of the "**kvootsah**" type in Lower Galilee (est 1941), 2.5 km W. of Lake of Tiberias. Pop 250.

aloonklah/-ot אלונקה *nf* stretcher; (*+of:* **-at**).

(masa) aloonkot מסע אלונקות *nm* stretch-bearers' march (army term).

'aloolt/-yot עלות *nf* cost.

(kheshbon) 'aloot חשבון עלות *nm* cost account.

'aloov/-ah עלוב *adj* miserable; worthless.

'aloov/-at nefesh עלוב נפש *adj* wretched.

alpayeem אלפיים *num* 2,000; two thousand.

alpeelt/-yot אלפית *num* fraction 1/1000; one thousandth.

halkhanlah/-ot הלחנה *nf* composition (of music) (*+of:* **-at**).

halshanlah/-ot הלשנה *nf* denunciation; informing on: (*+of:* **-at**).

(le) altar לאלתר *adv* forthwith.

alternateevlah/-ot אלטרנטיבה *nf* alternative; (*+of:* **-at**).

altezakhen - אלטע־זאכן *[slang]* (Yiddish) **1.** *mm pl* old worn out or second-hand clothing and furniture articles; **2.** *nm* peddler of 1.

halval'ah/-'ot הלוואה *nf* loan; (*+of:* **-at**).

◇ **alva'ah mashleemah** see ◇ **halval'ah/-'ot mashleemlah/-ot**.

halvay הלוואי *interj* if only; I wish it were.

halvalyah/-yot הלוויה *nf* funeral; (*+of:* **-yat**).

'am/-eem עם *nm* nation; people; (*pl+of:* **-ey**).

'am-aratseem עם־הארצים *[colloq.] pl* of **'am ha-arets** (see below).

'am ha-arets עם הארץ **1.** *nm lit* native population; **2.** *adj & nm* ignoramus (*pl.* **'amey aratsot**).

◇ **'am ha-sefer** עם הספר *nm* (the) People of the Book (i.e the Jewish people).

◇ **'am segoolah** עם סגולה *nm* (biblical reference to the people of Israel) a unique nation; a people of distinction.

'am yeesra'el (Israel) עם ישראל *nm* the Jewish people.

(agadlat/-ot) 'am אגדת־עם *nf* folk tale.

('atslerat/-rot) 'am עצרת עם *nf* mass assembly; mass meeting.

(bet/batey) 'am בית־עם *nm* community center.

(dalat ha) 'am דלת העם *nf* the poor classes.

(koval) 'am קבל־עם *adv* in front of everyone; publicly; openly.

(koval) 'am ve-'edah קבל־עם ועדה *adv* in front of everyone; publicly; openly.

(meesh'al) 'am משאל־עם *nm* plebiscite; referendum.

(reekoodey) 'am ריקודי עם *nm pl* folk dances.

(sheer) 'am שיר־עם *nm* folk song.

(zemer) 'am זמר־עם *nm* folk song.

amlah/-ot אמה *nf* **1.** middle finger; **2.** cubit; (*+of:* **-at**).

hamlah/-tah/-eetee המה *v* roared; (*pres* **homeh**; *fut* **yehemeh**).

'am|ad/-dah/-adetee עמד *v* stood; stood up; (*pres* **'omed**; *fut* **ya'amod**).
'amad (*etc*) **'al** עמד על *v* insisted.
'amad (*etc*) **'al da'ato/-ah** עמד על דעתו/־ה *v* went on to maintain.
'amad (*etc*) **'al ha-mekakh** (**n/p meekakh**) עמד על המיקח *v* bargained.
'amad (*etc*) **'al ha-perek** עמד על הפרק *v* was due for discussion.
'amad (*etc*) **'al teev** עמד על טיב *v* realised the nature.
'amad (*etc*) **ba-meevkhan/-eem** עמד במבחן *v* stood the test.
'amad (*etc*) **ba-neesayon** עמד בניסיון *v* resisted temptation.
'amad (*etc*) **ba-perets** עמד בפרץ *v* stepped into the breach.
'amad (*etc*) **be-** עמד ב־ *v* withstood; held out.
'amad (*etc*) **be-deeboor** עמד בדיבור *v* kept his word.
'amad (*etc*) **bee-f'ney** (*f=p*) עמד בפני *v* faced; resisted.
'amad (*etc*) **ba-bekheenah/-ot** עמד בבחינה *v* passed examination.
'amad (*etc*) **le-** עמד ל־ *v* was about to -.
'amad (*etc*) **lo/lah** עמד לו *v* stood him/her in good stead.
'amad (*etc*) **mee-neged** עמד מנגד *v* kept aloof; stood by indifferently.
'amal עמל *nm* toil.
'amal kapayeem עמל כפיים *nm* manual labor.
'amal/-lah/-altee עמל *v* labored; toiled; (*pres* **'amel**; *fut* **ya'amol**).
'am|alah/-alot עמלה *nf* fee; commission; (*+of:* **-lat**).
'amamee/-t עממי *adj* popular.
(sheekoon) 'amamee שיכון עממי *nm* public housing.
'amameem עממים *nm pl* nations; ethnic groups.
am|ar/-rah/-artee אמר *v* said; (*pres* **omer**; *fut* **yomar**).
amar (*etc*) **be-leeb|o/-ah** אמר בליבו/־ה *v* thought to himself.
amar (*etc*) **noash** אמר נואש *v* gave up.
(lo) amar (*etc*) **noash** לא אמר נואש *v* never gave up.
hamar|ah/-ot המרה *nf* conversion; exchange; (*+of:* **-at**).
'amaratsoot (*npr* **'am ha-artsoot**) עם הארצות *nf* ignorance.
amargan/-eem אמרגן *nm* impresario.
amarkal/-eem אמרכל *nm* treasurer; administrator.
amat mayeem אמת מים *nf* water conduit; sewer; aqueduct.
am|at/-ot meedah אמת מידה *nf* criterion; scale; standard.
hamat|ah/-ot המתה *nf* putting to death; killing; (*+of:* **-at**).
hamatat khesed המתת חסד *nf* mercy killing; euthanasia.
ham'at|ah/-ot המעטה *nf* reducing; diminishing; (*+of:* **-at**).
(leshon) ham'atah לשון המעטה *nf* understatement.
amatl|ah/-a'ot אמתלה *nf* pretext; (*+of:* **-at**).
□ **Amatsyah** (Amazya) אמציה *nm* communal village (est 1955) in the **Lakheesh** Area 15 km NW of **Keeryat Gat**. Pop 125.
ambat אמבט *nm* bathtub.
ambat|yah/-yot אמבטיה *nf* **1.** bathroom; bath; **2.** *[colloq.]* bathtub; (*+of:* **-yat**).
(khad|ar/-rey) ambatyah חדר אמבטיה *nm* bathroom.
(tanoor) ambatyah תנור אמבטיה *nm* bathroom boiler.
amboolans/-eem אמבולנס *nm* **1.** ambulance; **2.** *[colloq.]* hearse.
□ **Amee'ad** (Ammi'ad) עמיעד *nm* kibbutz (est. 1946) in Upper Galilee, 4 km S. of **Rosh-Peenah**. Pop. 395.
ameed/-ah אמיד *adj* well to do; prosperous.
'ameed/-ah עמיד *adj* resistant; -proof.
'amed|ah/-ot עמידה *nf* stand; standing; stability; (*+of:* **-at**).
(geel ha) 'ameedah גיל העמידה *nm* middle age.
◇ **ameedar ("Amidar")** עמידר *nf* state-owned public housing company controlling 290,000 housing units of minimal standard offered for acquisition or lease to immigrants, demobbed soldiers and needy young couples.
'ameedoot עמידות *nf* resistance; resistability.
'ameel/-eem עמיל *nm* agent; commission agent.
'ameel/-ey mekhes עמיל מכס *nm* forwarding agent.
'ameelan עמילן *nm* starch.
'ameeloo|t/-yot עמילות *nf* brokerage.
ameen/-ah אמין *adj* trustworthy; credible.
□ **'Ameenadav** ('Amminadav) עמינדב *nm* village SW of Jerusalem (est. 1950), at 7 km distance from city's center. Pop. 382.
ameenoo|t/-yot אמינות *nf* authenticity; credibility.
□ **'Amee'oz** ('Ammi'oz) עמיעוז *nm* village in NW Negev (est. 1957), 4 km SW of **Tsomet Magen** (Magen Junction). Pop. 224.
□ **'Ameer** ('Amir) עמיר *nm* kibbutz in N. of the **Khoolah** Valley (est. 1939), 5 km SE of **Keeryat Shmonah**. Pop. 519.
ameer|ah/-ot אמירה *nf* saying; utterance; uttering.
□ **Ameereem** (Amirim)אמירים *nm* village (est. 1950) SW of Safed **(Tsefat)** 4 km NE of **Tsomet Khananyah**(Hananya Junction). Pop. 326 composed exclusively of vegetarians and naturalists.
'ameet/-eem עמית *nm* colleague. (*pl+of:* **-ey**).
ameetee/-t אמיתי *adj* true; genuine.
(la) ameeto shel davar לאמיתו של דבר to tell the truth.
ameetoo|t/-yot אמיתות *nf pl* veracity; truthfulness.

ameets/-ah אמיץ *adj* brave; courageous.
'amel/-ah עמל *adj* striving.
a-mekhayeh א־מחייה *adv [slang]* a real delight; invigorating.
a-metseeyeh! !א־מציאה *interj [slang]* some bargain! (ironically).
amen אמן *interj* amen.
amereek|ah/-ot אמריקה *nf* America.
amereeka'ee/-t *(cpr)* אמריקאי *nmf* American.
amereekanee/-t אמריקני *adj* American.
amfeeteatron/-eem אמפיתיאטרון *nm* amphitheater.
hamkha|'ah/-'ot המחאה *nf* money order; cheque (*+of:* **-'at**).
hamkha|'at/-'ot do'ar המחאת דואר *nf* postal money order.
hamkhash|ah/-ot המחשה *nf* concretization; visualization; realization; (*+of:* **-at**).
hamkhaz|ah/-ot המחזה *nf* dramatization; (*+of:* **-at**).
'amod/'eemdee !עמוד *v imp* stop! stand up! (*inf* **la'amod**; *pst* **'amad**; *pres* **'omed**; *fut* **ya'amod**).
'am|ok/-ookah עמוק *adj* deep.
(khareesh) 'amokחריש עמוק *nm* deep plowing; in depth; (mainly used figuratively).
hamon/-eem המון *nm* **1.** crowd; **2.** *(colloq.)* plenty.
hamon המון *card num* plenty of; a lot of.
'amood/-eem עמוד *nm* **1.** column; **2.** page.
'amood ha-kalon עמוד הקלון *nm* pillory.
'amood ha-sheedrah עמוד השידרה *nm* spinal column.
'amood/-ey tavekh עמוד תווך *nm* central pillar; main pillar.
'amood/-ey teleeyah עמוד תלייה *nm* scaffold; gallows.
('al) 'amoodeemעל עמודים *adj* the floor above ground level supported by pillars.
hamoolah/-ot המולה *nf* tumult; (*+of:* **-at**).
'amoom/-ah עמום *adj* dim; dull.
hamoom/-ah המום *adj* stunned.
amoor/-ah אמור *adj* supposed to; is said.
amoor/-ah hay|ah/-tah אמור היה *v* was supposed to.
'amoos/-ah עמוס *adj* loaded; burdened.
◇ **'amoot|ah/-ot** עמותה *nf* fellowship; society incorporated under special Israeli law for non-profit societies.
(be-dalet) amot shel בד׳ אמות של *adv* in the immediate vicinity of; (*+of:* **-at**).
ha-menookhah המנוחה *pron f* the late *(fem)*; the deceased *(fem)*.
hamra|'ah/-'ot המראה *nf* take-off; (*+of:* **-'at**).
hamrats|ah/-ot המרצה *nf* urge; legal action under summary procedure; (*+of:* **-at**).
(bakash|ah/-ot be-derekh) hamratsah בקשה בדרך המרצה *nf* application by way of motion.
hamshakh|ah/-ot המשכה *nf* continuation; (*+of:* **-at**).
hamtak|ah/-ot המתקה *nf* sweetening; (*+of:* **-at**).
hamtakat deen המתקת דין *nf* mitigation of sentence.
hamtakat mayeem המתקת מים *nf* desalination.
hamtakat ha-'onesh המתקת העונש *nf* mitigation of punishment.
hamtan|ah/-ot המתנה *nf* waiting; (*+of:* **-at**).
(khad|ar/-rey) hamtanah חדר המתנה *nm* waiting-room.
amtsa|'ah/-'ot אמצאה *nf* invention; (*+of:* **-'at**).
hamtsa|'ah/-'ot המצאה *nf* **1.** invention; **2.** delivery; (*+of:* **-'at**).
an אן *adv* where? whither?
(le) an? ?לאן *adv* where to?
ana! !אנא *interj* please!
anah? ?אנה *adv* whither? where to?
ana 'aref?! ?!אנא עארף *interj [slang] (Arab.)* what do I know?! Don't expect me to know!
'an|ah/-tah/-eetee ענה *v* answered; (*pres* **'oneh**; *fut* **ya'aneh**).
hana|'ah/-'ot הנאה *nf* pleasure; delight; (*+of:* **-'at**).
(tov|at/-ot) hana'ah טובת הנאה *nf* advantage.
(zeek|at/-ot) hana'ah זיקת הנאה *nf* privilege.
hana|'ah/-'ot הנעה *nf* propulsion; (*+of:* **-'at**).
hana'ah keedmeet הנעה קדמית *nf* front-wheel drive.
'an|ad/-dah/-adetee ענד *v* tied on; decorated; wore (jewelry); (*pres* **'oned**; *fut* **ya'anod**).
'anaf/-eem ענף *nm* branch (of tree or trade); (*pl+of:* **'anfey**).
hanaf|ah/-ot הנפה *nf* waving; brandishing; (*+of:* **-t**).
hanafat deg|el/-aleem הנפת דגל *nf* waving (displaying) flag.
'anak/-eem ענק **1.** *nm* giant; **2.** *nm* necklace; **3.** *adj (only masc sing)* gigantic.
'anakee/-t ענקי *adj* gigantic.
anakh/-eem אנך *nm* plummet; plumb line.
anakh|ah/-ot אנחה *nf* sigh (*+of:* **ankh|at/-ot**).
hanakh|ah/-ot הנחה *nf* **1.** rebate; discount; **2.** assumption; (*+of:* **-at**).
anakhee/-t אנכי *adj* vertical; perpendicular.
(kav/-eem) anakhee/-yeem קו אנכי *nm* vertical line.
anakheet אנכית *adv* vertically.
anakhnoo אנחנו *pron pl* we.
han'al|ah הנעלה *nf* **1.** putting on shoes; **2.** shoeing; shoe trade; (*+of:* **-at**).
'an|an/-aneem ענן *nm* cloud; (*pl+of:* **-eney**).
(perets) 'anan פרץ ענן *nm* cloudburst.
'ananah עננה *nf* cloudlet.
'an|aneem עננים *nm pl* (*sing:* **-an**) clouds; (*pl+of:* **-eney**).
anas/-eem אנס *nm* rapist.
an|as/-sah/-astee אנס *v* **1.** raped; **2.** compelled; (*pres* **ones**; *fut* **ye'enos**).
anasheem אנשים *nm pl* men; people; (*sing* **eesh**; *+of:* **anshey**).
anatomyah אנטומיה *nf* anatomy.
'anav/-ah עניו *adj* modest; humble; meek.
'anavah ענווה *nf* modesty; meekness; (*+of:* **'anvat**).

'anaveem ענבים *nm pl* grapes; (*sing* **'anav**; *+of:* **'eenvey**).

□ **(Keeryat) 'Anaveem** see □ **Keeryat 'Anaveem**.

(meets) 'anaveem מיץ ענבים *nm* grape juice.

andart|ah/-ot אנדרטה *nf* monument; statue (*+of:* **-at**).

andart|at/-ot zeekaron אנדרטת זיכרון *nf* memorial statue.

handasah הנדסה *nf* **1.** engineering; **2.** geometry.

handasah electroneet הנדסה אלקטרונית *nf* electronic engineering.

handasah geneteet הנדסה גנטית *nf* genetic engineering.

(kheyl) handasah חיל הנדסה *nm* engineering corps (Army).

handasat beenyan הנדסת בנין *nf* civil engineering.

handasat khashmal הנדסת חשמל *nf* electrical engineering.

handasat ma'arakhot הנדסת מערכות *nf* system engineering

handasat makhsheveem הנדסת מחשבים *nf* computer sciences; computer engineering.

handasat mekhonot הנדסת מכונות *nf* mechanical engineering.

handasat tenoo'ah הנדסת תנועה *nf* traffic engineering.

androlomoos|yah/-yot אנדרלמוסיה *nf* confusion; disorder (*+of:* **-yat**).

androgeenos/-eem אנדרוגינוס *nm* hermaphrodite.

anee אני *pron* I .

anee ma'ameen אני מאמין *nm* credo; conviction.

◇ **"anee ma'ameen"** אני מאמין *nf* "I believe" (*cpr* **"anee-mameen"**) - one of 13 basic dogmas of the Jewish faith as formulated in the XIth century by Maimonides. It asserts one's staunch belief in God and in Ultimate Redemption. Its first stanza, sung to a Hassidic tune, in the Holocaust days became a kind of hymn and, in some extermination camps, reports say, was defiantly sung by Jews on their very march to the gas chambers.

'anee/-yah עני **1.** *nmf* pauper; **2.** *adj* poor.

'anee/-yah marood/meroodah עני מרוד *nmf* poor; pauper; destitute.

'anee ve-evyon עני ואביון *nm* very poor person.

aneen/-ah אנין *adj* sensitive; delicate.

aneen/-ey da'at אנין דעת *nm* connoisseur; of sophisticated taste.

aneen/-ey ta'am אנין טעם *nm* of sophisticated taste; connoisseur.

aneenoot ha-da'at אנינות הדעת *nf* refinement; delicacy.

'aneesh|ah/-ot ענישה *nf* punishment; (*+of:* **-at**).

'aneev|ah/-ot עניבה *nf* necktie; (*+of:* **-at**).

'aneevat khenek עניבת חנק *nf* strangulation loop.

'aneeyoot עניות *nf* misery; poverty.

(deekdookey) 'aneeyoot דקדוקי עניות *nm pl* petty-mindedness; pettiness.

(la) 'aneeyoot da'at|ee/-enoo לעניות דעת in my/our humble opinion.

(te'oodat) 'aneeyoot תעודת עניות *nf* mark of incompetence.

'anef/-ah ענף *adj* extensive; widespread.

anekdot|ah/-ot אנקדוטה *nf* anecdote; joke; (*+of:* **-at**).

hanets ha-khamah הנץ החמה *nm* sunrise.

hanfash|ah/-ot (*npr* **hanpash|ah/-ot**) הנפשה *nf* animation (*+of:* **-at**).

anglee/-t אנגלי *adj* English.

anglee/-yah אנגלי *nmf* Englishman/-woman.

angleet אנגלית *nf* English (language).

angleeyah אנגליה *nf* England.

hanhag|ah/-ot הנהגה *nf* leadership; (*+of:* **-at**).

hanhal|ah/-ot הנהלה *nf* management; (*+of:* **-at**).

hanhalat kheshbonot הנהלת חשבונות *nf* accountancy; bookkeeping.

hankha|yah/-yot הנחיה *nf* directive; instruction; (*+of:* **-yat**).

ankhat revakhah אנחת רווחה *nf* sigh of relief.

hanmak|ah/-ot הנמקה *nf* argumentation; (*+of:* **-at**).

anokhee אנוכי *pron* I.

anokheeyee/-t אנוכיי *adj* selfish; egotistical.

anokheeyoot אנוכיות *nf* selfishness.

anoo אנו *pron pl* we.

anoosh/-ah אנוש *adj* severe; critical (state of illness or injury).

(khol|eh/-ah) anoosh/-ah חולה אנוש *nmf* seriously ill.

(patsoo'a'/petsoo'ah) anoosh/-ah פצוע אנוש *nmf* severely injured.

hanpak|ah/-ot הנפקה *nf* issue; (*+of:* **-at**).

hanpash|ah/-ot הנפשה *nf* animation; (*+of:* **-at**).

hansham|ah/-ot הנשמה *nf* artificial respiration; (*+of:* **-at**).

hanshamah melakhooteet הנשמה מלאכותית *nf* artificial respiration.

anshey אנשי *nm pl+of* the men/people of...

anshey roo'akh (*sing:* **eesh** *etc*) אנשי רוח *nm pl* intellectuals.

anshey shlomenoo אנשי שלומנו *nm pl* our own people; insiders.

anshey tsava (*sing* **eesh** *etc*) אנשי צבא *nm pl* military (men).

anshey tsevet (*sing* **eesh** *etc*) אנשי צוות *nm pl* members of a crew.

antee- אנטי *pref* anti-.

anteeshemee/-t אנטישמי *nmf* antisemite; adj. antisemitic.

anteeshemeeyoot אנטישמיות *nf* antisemitism.

hantsakh|ah/-ot הנצחה *nf* perpetuation; immortalization; (*+of:* **-at**).

□ **A'ogen** (or **A'ogen**) see □ **Ha-'Ogen**.

hapal|ah/-ot הפלה *nf* **1.** bringing (throwing) down; **2.** abortion; miscarriage; (*+of:* **-at**).

(erekh) apayeem ארך אפיים *adj* forbearing; patient.
apeeryon אפיריון *nm* sedan-chair.
apotrop|os/-seem (*npr* **epeetrop|os)/-seem** אפוטרופוס nmfguardian; executor.
apotropsoo|t/-yot (*npr* **epeetropsoo|t)/-yot** אפוטרופסות *nf* guardianship.
apreel אפריל *nm* April.
har/eem הר *nm* mountain; mount; (*pl+of:* **-ey**).
har/ey ga'ash הר־געש *nm* volcano.
□ **Ar Adar** see □ **Har Adar.**
□ **Ar Geelo** see □ **Har Geelo.**
□ **Ar Hertsel** see □ **Har Hertsel.**
□ **Ar Meron** see □ **Har Meron.**
□ **Ar Tabor** see □ **Har Tabor.**
har|ah/-ot הרה **1.** *adj f* pregnant; **2.** *v pres f* is pregnant; (*pst* **hartah;** *fut* **tehereh).**
hara|'ah הרעה *nf* deterioration; (*+of:* **-'at).**
◇ **Ar ha-bayeet** see ◇ **Har ha-bayeet.**
arad ארד *nm* bronze.
□ **'Arad** ערד *nf* city (est. 1961) 37 km E. of Beersheba (**Be'er Sheva'**). Pop. 15,400.
ara'ee/-t ארעי *adj* temporary; provisional.
'ar|af/-fah/-aftee ערף *v* beheaded; (*pres* **'oref;** *fut* **ya'arof).**
'araf|el/-eeleem ערפל *nm* fog; mist; (*pl+of:* **-eeley).**
ar|ag/-gah/-agtee ארג *v* wove; (*pres* **oreg;** *fut* **ye'erog).**
harag/-gah/-agtee הרג *v* killed; (*pres* **horeg;** *fut* **yaharog).**
arak ארק *nm* Arab-type brandy.
'ar|ak/-kah/-aktee ערק *v* deserted; (*pres* **'orek;** *fut* **ya'arok).**
arakah/-ot ארקה *nf* grounding (electr.); (*+of:* **-at).**
□ **Ar ha-Karmel** see □ **Har ha-Karmel.**
ar|akh/-khah/-akhtee ארך *v* lasted; (*pres* **orekh;** *fut* **ye'erakh).**
'ar|akh/-khah/-akhtee ערך *v* **1.** drew-up; **2.** edited; **3.** prepared; (*pres* **'orekh;** *fut* **ya'arokh).**
'arakh (*etc*) **heskem** ערך הסכם *v* drew up an agreement.
'arakh (*etc*) **meelkham|ah/-ot** ערך מלחמה *v* waged war.
'arakh (*etc*) **shoolkhan** ערך שולחן *v* set table.
har'al|ah/-ot הרעלה *nf* poisoning; (*+of:* **-at).**
har'al|at/-ot dam הרעלת־דם *nf* blood poisoning; toxaemia.
'ar|am/-mah/-amtee ערם *v* piled up; (*pres* **'orem;** *fut* **ya'arom).**
haram|ah/-ot הרמה *nf* lifting; raising; (*+of:* **-at).**
haramat meeshkalot הרמת משקלות *nf* weight-lifting.
haramat yadayeem הרמת ידיים *nf* show of hands.
◇ **arameet** ארמית *nf* Aramaic, ancient language which served as Jewish lingua franca between 500 BCE and 500 CE. Some of its poignant expressions and sayings are in use to this day in Rabbinical circles and in literary Hebrew.
'arar/-eem ערר *nm* objection; contestation.
'ar|ar/-erah/-artee ערר *v* contested (jurid.); (*pres* **'orer;** *fut* **ya'aror).**
hararee/-t הררי *adj* mountainous.
har|as/-sah/-astee הרס *v* demolished; destroyed; (*pres* **hores;** *fut* **yaharos).**
har'ash|ah/-ot הרעשה *nf* bombardment; (*+of:* **-at).**
harats|ah/-ot הרצה *nf* running-in (motor-car); (*+of:* **-at).**
□ **Ar ha-Tsofeem** see □ **Har ha-Tsofeem.**
ar|av/-vah/-avtee ארב *v* lurked; ambushed; (*pres* **orev;** *fut* **ye'erov).**
'ar|av/-vah/-avtee ערב *v* **1.** vouched; **2.** pleased; (*pres* **'arev;** *fut* **ya'arov).**
'arav ערב *nf* Arabia.
(artsot) 'arav ארצות ערב *nf pl* Arab countries.
(medeenot) 'arav מדינות ערב *nf pl* Arab states.
'arav|ah/-ot ערבה *nf* steppe; (*+of:* **-ot).**
□ **(ha)'Aravah** הערבה *nf* the "Aravah" Region, area of potentially reclaimable desert, stretching along the Jordanian border, from the Dead Sea to the Red Sea.
'aravee/-yah ערבי *nmf* Arab.
'aravee/-t ערבי *adj* Arab.
'araveet ערבית *nf* Arabic (language).
(geelooy) 'arayot גילוי־עריות *nm* incest.
ar|az/-zah/-aztee ארז *v* packed; (*pres* **orez;** *fut* **ye'eroz).**
arazeem (*sing* **erez**) ארזים *nm pl* cedars; (*+of:* **arzey).**
(erets ha) arazeem ארץ הארזים Land of the Cedars (i.e. Lebanon).
□ **Ar ha-Zeteem** see □ **Har ha-Zeteem.**
arba' ארבע *num f* 4 four .
arba'ah ארבעה *num m* 4; four.
arba'ah 'asar ארבעה־עשר *num m* 14; fourteen.
arba'eem ארבעים *num* 40 , forty.
(ben ha) 'arbayeem בין הערביים *adv* at dusk; twilight.
arba'-'esreh ארבע־עשרה *num f* 14, fourteen.
◇ **arba' kooshyot** ארבע קושיות *nf pl* the traditional "four questions (kashes)" chanted by the family's youngest child (or party's youngest attendant) addressed to the chief-reader of the "Haggadah" at the opening of the Passover ceremonial dinner. (The "**Seyder**").
□ **(Keeryat) Arba'** see □ **Keeryat Arba'.**
arbeh ארבה *nm* locust.
harbeh הרבה *adv* many; much.
□ **Arbel** (Arbel) ארבל **1.** Mount overlooking the Sea of Galilee 5 km NW of Tiberias; **2.** *m* village (est. 1949) in Lower Galilee's **Arbel** Valley, 4.5 km NW of TRiberias. Pop. 294.
'ardalayeem (*sing* **'ardal**) ערדליים *nm pl* galoshes; rubber shoes.
hardam|ah/-ot הרדמה *nf* anaesthetization; (*+of:* **-at).**
(khelek ha) aree חלק הארי *nm* lion's share.
◇ **aree/-t** ארי *adj & nmf* Arian.

aree/arayot ארי *nm* lion.
areelakh/-kheem אריח *nm* tile; (*pl+of:* -**khey**).
□ **Aree'el** (Ariel) אריאל *nf* new Jewish town in the heart of West Bank, 35 km E. of **Petakh-Teekvah**, off new Trans-Samaria **"Khotseh Shomron"** highway. Pop. 8,010.
areeg|ah/-ot אריגה *nf* weaving; (*+of:* -**at**).
hareeg|ah/-ot הריגה *nf* killing; manslaughter; (*+of:* -**at**).
'areek/-eem עריק *nm* deserter; (*pl+of:* -**ey**).
'areek|ah/-ot עריקה *nf* desertion; (*+of:* -**at**).
areekh/-ey nagen אריך־נגן *nm* long-play (record).
'areekh|ah/-ot עריכה *nf* editing; arraying; arranging; (*+of:* -**at**).
'areekhat-deen עריכת דין *nf* legal practice; advocacy.
'areekhat shoolkhan עריכת־שולחן *nf* laying table.
areekh|eem (*sing* **aree'akh**) אריחים *nm pl* tiles; (*pl+of:* -**ey**).
areekhoot yameem אריכות ימים *nf* longevity.
'areem ערים *nm pl* towns; cities; (*sing* **'eer**; *pl+of:* **'arey**).
'areeree/-t ערירי *adj* childless, lone.
'arees|ah/-ot עריסה *nf* cradle; crib; (*+of:* -**at**).
'areets/-ah עריץ *adj* tyrannical.
'areets/-eem עריץ *nm* tyrant; (*pl+of:* -**ey**).
'areetsoot עריצות *nf* tyranny.
areez|ah/-ot אריזה *nf* package; packaging; (*+of:* -**at**).
'arel/-eem ערל **1.** *nm & adj* uncircumcised; non-Jew; **2.** *adj* pruned (fruit).
□ **Ar'el** see □ **Har'el**.
'arem|ah/-ot ערימה *nf* pile; (*+of:* -**at**).
areshet ארשת *nf* expression; countenance.
('am ha) arets עם הארץ **1.** *nm* the native population; **2.** *nm & adj* ignoramus.
◇ **(beenyan ha) arets** see ◇ **beenyan ha-arets**.
(drom ha) arets דרום הארץ *nm* the S. part of Israel.
(ha) arets הארץ *nf* **1.** this country (i.e. Israel); **2.** the ground; the country.
(kadoor ha) arets כדור הארץ *nm* terrestrial globe.
(kan ba) arets כאן בארץ *adv* here, in this country.
(khoots la) arets חוץ לארץ *nm* abroad.
(la) arets לארץ *adv* to Israel.
(totseret ha) arets תוצרת הארץ *nf* produce of (Made in) Israel.
(yeleed/-at ha) arets יליד הארץ *nmf* native Israeli; a "Sabra".
'arev/-ah ערב *nmf* surety; guarantor.
'arev/-ah ערב *adj* agreeable; pleasant.
'arevoot *etc* see **'arvoot** etc.
harey הרי *prep* **1.** here is ...; herewith; **2.** you can see ...; **3.** in fact.
◇ **arey at mekoodeshet** see ◇ **harey at mekoodeshet**.
harey she הרי ש־ *prep* which means that...
(she) harey שהרי *prep* for it means that...
'arfeelee/-t ערפילי *adj* vague; misty.
arga|'ah ארגעה *nf* all clear; relaxation; (*+of:* -**'at**).
(ot ha) arga'ah אות הארגעה *nm* the all clear.
harga|'ah/-'ot הרגעה *nf* calming; tranquilizing; (*+of:* -**'at**).
('emtsa'ey) harga'ah אמצעי הרגעה *nm pl* tranquilizers; means of calming.
(gloollat/-ot) harga'ah גלולות הרגעה *nf pl* tranquilizer pills.
harga'at ha-rookhot הרגעת הרוחות *nf* soothing of tempers.
argaman ארגמן *nm* purple.
□ **Argaman** ארגמן *nm* village (est. 1972) in center of Jordan Valley.
hargash|ah/-ot הרגשה *nf* feeling; sensation; (*+of:* -**at**).
hargashat revakhah הרגשת רווחה *nf* feeling of relief.
arg|az/-azeem ארגז *nm* case; crate; (*pl+of:* -**ezey**).
arg|az/-ezey roo'akh ארגז רוח *nm* gable.
hargaz|ah/-ot הרגזה *nf* irritation; vexation; (*+of:* -**at**).
□ **Argenteenah** ארגנטינה *nf* Argentina.
□ **ar'hab** ארה"ב *nf* the U.S.A. (*acr of* **ARtsot-HA-Breet** ארצות הברית).
ark|ah/-ot ארכה *nf* extension; prolongation; (*+of:* -**at**).
'arka|'ah/-'ot ערכאה *nf* instance (legal); (*+of:* -**'at**).
harkav|ah/-ot הרכבה *nf* **1.** assembling; **2.** inoculation; **3.** grafting; (*+of:* -**at**).
harkavat ava'boo'ot הרכבת אבעבועות *nf* vaccination; inoculation against smallpox.
harkavat memshalah הרכבת ממשלה *nf* formation of government.
harkhak|ah/-ot הרחקה *nf* removal; distancing (*+of:* -**at**).
harkhav|ah/-ot הרחבה *nf* broadening; expansion; (*+of:* -**at**).
arkhee parkhee ארחי פרחי *nm pl* vagabonds; passers by; drifters.
arkheeyon/-eem ארכיון *nm* archive; (*pl+of:* -**ey**).
harkhek הרחק *adv* far away.
harkhek harkhek הרחק־הרחק *adv* very far away.
arkheolog/-eet ארכיאולוג *nmf* archeologist.
arkheologyah ארכיאולוגיה *nf* archeology.
(gal ha) arkoobah גל הארכובה *nm* crankshaft; (motor-car).
armon/-ot ארמון *nm* palace; castle.
harmon/-ot הרמון *nm* harem.
'armon/-eem ערמון *nm* chestnut; (*pl+of:* -**ey**).
'armonee/-t ערמוני *adj* reddish-brown.
harmonee/-t הרמוני *adj* harmonious.
harmoneek|ah/-ot הרמוניקה *nf* mouth-organ; (*+of:* -**at**).
'armonee|t ערמונית *nf* prostate; prostatic gland.
harmon|yah הרמוניה *nf* harmony (*+of:* -**yat**).
'armoomee/-t ערמומי *adj* crafty; sly.
'armoomeeyoot ערמומיות *nf* cunning.
arnak/-eem ארנק *nm* purse; bag; (*pl+of:* -**ey**).
arn|evet/-avot ארנבת *nf* hare; rabbit.
arnon|ah/-ot ארנונה *nf* property-tax; (*+of:* -**at**).

ar|okh/-ookah ארוך *adj* long; lengthy.

(lee-tvakh) arokh לטווח ארוך *adv* in the long run.

(le-'eyn) 'arokh לאין ערוך *adv* beyond comparison.

'ar|om/-oomah ערום *adj* naked; bare; nude.

aron/-ot ארון *nm pl* cupboard; closet.

aron ha-kodesh ארון הקודש *nm* the Holy Ark (in a synagogue).

aron/-ot keer ארון קיר *nm* closet; built-in cupboard.

aron/-ot meetbakh ארון מטבח *nm* kitchen cupboard.

aron ארון מתים *nm* coffin.

aroob|ah/-ot ארובה *nf* chimney; **(***+of:* **-at).**

'aroob|ah/-ot ערובה *nf* guaranty; pledge; **(***+of:* **-at).**

(ben/bat) 'aroobah בן ערובה *nmf* hostage **(***pl:* **ben|ey/-ot** *etc***).**

(makhs|an/-eney) 'aroobah מחסן־ערובה *nm* bonded warehouse.

haroog/-eem הרוג *nm* casualty; killed person; **(***pl+of:* **-ey).**

'aroog|ah/-ot ערוגה *nf* garden bed; **(***+of:* **-at).**

'arookh/-ah ערוך *adj* ready; edited.

(shoolkhan) 'arookh שולחן ערוך *nm* set table.

◇ **("shoolkhan) 'arookh"** see ◇ **"shoolkhan 'arookh".**

arookh|ah ארוכה *nf* healing; cure; **(***+of:* **-at).**

arookh|ah/-ot ארוחה *nf* meal; **(***+of:* **-at).**

arookh|ah kalah ארוחה קלה *nf* light meal; snack.

arookh|at/-ot boker ארוחת בוקר *nf* breakfast.

arookh|at/-ot 'erev ארוחת ערב *nf* supper; dinner; evening meal.

arookh|at/-ot tsohorayeem ארוחת צהריים *nf* lunch; midday meal.

'aroom/-ah ערום *adj* **1.** sly; shrewd; **2. (***npr* **'arom)** naked.

aroor/-ah ארור *adj* damned; cursed.

aroor/-ah mee she- ארור מי ש־ *interj* cursed be whoever *m/f*!

aroos/-ah ארוס **1.** *nmf* fiancé/-ée; **2.** *adj* betrothed.

haroos/-ah הרוס *adj* **1.** demolished; destroyed; **2.** (of a person) ruined; finished.

'aroots/-eem ערוץ *nm* **1.** channel (radio, tv); **2.** riverbed; **(***pl+of:* **-ey).**

◇ **(he) 'aroots ha-shenee** הערוץ השני see ◇ **'aroots shtayeem, below.**

◇ **'aroots shtayeem** ערוץ שתיים *m* "Channel Two", second television network in Israel started experimentally in 1987. Initiated by the State to become in 1992 a private fully commercial venture operating under public umbrella. Broadcasts entertainment, news and due to add commercials as well.

arooz/-ah ארוז *adj* packaged; packed.

'arpad/-eem ערפד *nm* vampire; (figurat.) bloodsucker; **(***pl+of:* **-ey).**

harpatk|ah/-a'ot הרפתקה *nf* adventure; affair; **(***+of:* **-at).**

harpatkan/-eet הרפתקן *nmf* adventurer/-ess; **(***pl+of:* **-ey).**

harpatkanoot הרפתקנות *nf* adventurism.

harpatk|at/-a'ot ahaveem (*npr* **ohaveem)** הרפתקת אהבים *nf* love-affair.

harpa|yah/-yot הרפיה *nf* relaxation; **(***+of:* **-yat).**

'arpee'akh ערפיח *nm* smog.

'arpeelee/-t (*npr* **'arfeelee/-t)** ערפילי *adj* vague; misty.

'arsal/-eem ערסל *nm* hammock; **(***pl+of:* **-ey).**

ars/-eem ארס *nm [slang]* pimp.

ars/-eet ארס *adj [slang]* extremely crafty; cunning; sly.

harsanee/-t הרסני *adj* destructive.

arsee/-t ארסי *adj* lethal; poisonous.

harsha|'ah/-'ot הרשאה *nf* license; authorization; **(***+of:* **-'at).**

harsha|'ah/-'ot הרשעה *nf* conviction (jurid); **(***+of:* **-'at).**

harsham|ah/-ot הרשמה *nf* registration; **(***+of:* **-at).**

har|tah/-eetee הרתה *v f* became pregnant; **(***pres* **harah;** *fut* **tehereh).**

harta|'ah/-'ot הרתעה *nf* deterrence; **(***+of:* **-'at).**

hartav|ah/-ot הרטבה *nf* wetting; moistening; **(***+of:* **-at).**

'arteela'ee/-t ערטילאי *adj* abstract; denuded.

arteeleryah ארטילריה *nf* artillery.

arteest/-eet ארטיסט *nmf* **1.** comedian (theatre); **2.** *(army slang)* one who tries to shirk heavier chores or responsibilities.

hartsa|'ah/-'ot הרצאה *nf* lecture; **(***+of:* **-'at).**

(oolam) hartsa'ot אולם הרצאות *nm* lecture-hall.

artsee/-t ארצי *adj* country-wide; national; terrestrial.

(eegood) artsee איגוד ארצי *nm* national federation (union).

artsot 'arav ארצות ערב *nf pl* Arab countries.

artsot ha-breet ארצות הברית *nf pl* the United States.

artsot ha-ma'arav ארצות המערב *nf pl* the Western countries.

artsot tevel ארצות תבל *nf pl* countries of the world.

◇ **(tefeelat) 'arveet** see ◇ **tefeelat 'arveet.**

'arvoo|t/-yot ערבות *nf* bail; bond.

'arvoot 'atsmeet ערבות עצמית *nf* personal bond.

'arvoot banka'eet ערבות בנקאית *nf* bank guaranty.

'arvoot hadadeet ערבות הדדית *nf* mutual bond.

(sheekhroor be) 'arvoot שחרור בערבות *nm* release on bail.

(shookhr|ar/-erah/-artee be) 'arvoot שוחרר בערבות was released on bail; **(***pres* **meshookhrar** *etc; fut* **yeshookhrar** *etc.***).**

ar|yeh/-yot אריה *nm* lion.

□ **Arzah** ארזה *nm* veteran resthouse in Jerusalem hills 7 km outside town.

harza|yah/-yot הרזיה *nf* slimming-down; reducing weight; **(***+of:* **-yat).**

has! !הס *interj* silence! hush!
has mee-lehazkeer הס מלהזכיר Mum's the word!
'as|ah/-tah/-eetee עשה *v* did; made; (*pres* **'oseh**; *fut* **ya'aseh**).
'asah (*etc*) **'atsmo/-ah** עשה עצמו *v* pretended; made oneself.
'asah (*etc*) **ba-meekhnasayeem** עשה במכנסיים **1.** *v [slang]* became utterly confused; **2.** *lit* : did it in his pants.
'asah (*etc*) **'esek** עשה עסק *v* did business.
'asah (*etc*) **hakarah** עשה הכרה *v* made acquaintance; got acquainted.
'asah (*etc*) **khayeel** עשה חיל *v* did well; made progress.
'asah (*etc*) **khayeem** עשה חיים *v [colloq.]* had a good time.
'asah (*etc*) **khesed** עשה חסד *v* did a favor.
'asah (*etc*) **seder** עשה סדר *v [colloq.]* put things in order.
'asah (*etc*) **shamot** עשה שמות *v* ravaged.
'asah (*etc*) **tsarot** עשה צרות *v* made/gave trouble.
'asah (*etc*) **tsekhok** עשה צחוק *v* made fun.
'as|ah (*etc*) **tserakh|av/-eha** עשה צרכיו *v* answered the call of nature.
hasa|'ah/-'ot הסעה *nf* transportation; (*+of:* **-'at**).
'asabeem (*npr* **'asaveem**) עשבים *nm pl* grass; (*sing:* **'esev**; *pl+of:* **'eesbey**).
'asabeem (*npr* **'asaveem**) **shoteem** עשבים שוטים *nm pl* crab grass.
(neekoosh) 'asabeem (*npr* **'asaveem**) ניכוש עשבים *nm* weeding.
as|af/-fah/-aftee אסף *v* collected; assembled; (*pres* **osef**; *fut* **ye'esof**).
□ **Asaf Harofe** אסף הרופא *nm* general hospital 13 km SE of Tel-Aviv, 3 km NE of Ramla.
asafsoof אספסוף *nm* mob; rabble; hoi polloi.
hasag|ah/-ot השגה *nf* **1.** attainment; **2.** criticism; contestation; (*+of:* **-at**).
hasagat gevool השגת גבול *nf* trespass; unethical competition.
'as|ak/-kah/-aktee עסק *v pst* dealt in; (*pres* **'osek**; *fut* **ya'asok**).
hasak|ah/-ot הסקה heating; (*+of:* **-at**).
hasakah merkazeet הסקה מרכזית *nf* central heating.
('atsey) hasakah עצי הסקה *nm pl* firewood.
hasakat maskanot הסקת מסקנות *nf* drawing conclusions.
'asakeem עסקים *nm pl* business; (*sing:* **'esek**; *pl+of:* **'eeskey**).
(anshey) 'asakeem (*sing* **eesh** *etc*) אנשי עסקים *nm pl* businessmen.
(eesh/anshey) 'asakeem איש עסקים *nm* businessman.
(eshet) 'asakeem אשת עסקים *nf* businesswoman.
hasakh|ah/-ot הסחה *nf* diversion; diverting; (*+of:* **-at**).
(pe'ool|at/-ot) hasakhah פעולת הסחה *nf* diversionary action.
hasakhat ha-da'at הסחת הדעת *nf* diverting attention; absentmindedness.
asam/-eem אסם *nm* granary; (*pl+of:* **asmey**).
'asar עשר suffix (for masc. numerals) -teen.
as|ar/-rah/-artee אסר *v* prohibited; (*pres* **oser**; *fut* **ye'esor**).
asar (*etc*) **et** אסר את *v* arrested.
'asarah עשרה *num m* 10; ten.
'asarot עשרות *nf pl* tens (*pl+of:* **'esrot**).
hasat|ah/-ot הסתה *nf* incitement; instigation; (*+of:* **-at**).
hasav|ah/-ot הסבה *nf* endorsement (of cheque or promissory note); (*+of:* **-at**).
hasavah meektso'eet הסבה מקצועית *nf* retraining for a different profession.
'asaveem עשבים *nm pl* grass; (*sing:* **'esev**; *pl+of:* **'eesbey**).
'asaveem shoteem עשבים שוטים *nm pl* crab grass.
(neekoosh) 'asaveem ניכוש עשבים *nm* weeding.
hasbar|ah/-ot הסברה *nf* information; propaganda; explanation; (*+of:* **-at**).
◊ **(merkaz) ha-hasbarah** see ◊ **merkaz ha-hasbarah**.
asbest אסבסט *nm* asbestos.
(loo|'akh/-khot) asbest לוח אסבסט *nm* asbestos sheet.
asbest galee אסבסט גלי *nm* corrugated asbestos sheets.
asbeston/-eem אסבסטון *nm* asbestos-made housing unit.
asdah/asadot אסדה *nf* craft; (*+of:* **asdat**).
asd|at/-ot nekheetah אסדת נחיתה *nf* landing craft.
aseef אסיף *nm* harvest-time.
aseemon/-eem אסימון *nm* token (in use for dialing public phones); (*pl+of:* **-ey**).
aseer/-ah אסיר *nmf* prisoner; prison inmate; captive.
aseer/-ey 'olam אסיר עולם *nm* jailed for life.
aseer/-at todah אסיר תודה *adj* ever so grateful; obliged.
◊ **aseer/-ey tseeyon** אסיר ציון *nm (lit.)* "Prisoner for Zion" i.e. any Jewish person who endured or endures imprisonment (behind the Iron curtain or in an Arab or Muslim country etc) because of having been suspected of Zionism.
'aseeree/-t עשירי *num adj m* 10th; tenth.
◊ **'aseeree le-meenyan** עשירי למניין tenth adult (aged 13 or more) Jewish male needed to achieve the quorum of ten (**meenyan** מניין) without which no Jewish public prayer can be held.
'aseeree|t/-yot עשירית *num f* 1/10; 0.1; one tenth.
'aseeree|yah/-yot עשירייה *[colloq.] num f* 10 Shekel bill.
'aseeron/-eem עשירון *num m* 1/10 (10%) of the population.
(ha) 'aseeron ha-'elyon העשירון העליון *nm* the Upper Tenth in wealth (of the population).

'asees עסיס *nm* juice; fruit juice.

'aseesee/-t עסיסי *adj* juicy.

'asee|yah/-yot עשייה *nf* deed; doing; (*+of:* **-yat**).

asef|ah/-ot אסיפה *nf* meeting; gathering; (*+of:* **-at**).

asefah klaleet אסיפה כללית *nf* general meeting.

asefah segoorah אסיפה סגורה *nf* closed session.

(peetsoots) asefah פיצוץ אסיפה *nm* breaking up a meeting.

asefat khavereem אסיפת חברים *nf* membership meeting.

aseret עשרת *num+of m* the ten of ...

□ **'Aseret** ('Aseret) עשרת *nm* rural settlement anâ regional center in Mediterranean Plain (est. 1954), 2 km E. of **Tsomet Beney Darom** (Bené Darom Junction).Pop. 700.

◇ **'aseret ha-deebrot** עשרת הדיברות *nm pl* (*sing:* **deeber**) the Ten Commandments.

◇ **'aseret yemey teshoovah** עשרת ימי תשובה *nm pl* the "Ten Days of Repentance" (from Rosh-Hashana through Yom Kippur).

hesesan/-eet הססן *nmf & adj* hesitant person; hesitating.

hasesanoot הססנות *nf* hesitation.

asfalt אספלט *nm* asphalt.

asfan/-eem אספן *nmf* collector.

hasgar|ah/-ot הסגרה *nf* extradition; (*+of:* **-at**).

'ash עש *nm* moth.

◇ **ASHAF** אש"ף *nm acr of* the Hebrew name of the so-called "Palestine Liberation Organisation" or PLO (**EErgoon le-SHeekhroor Falasteen** ארגון לשחרור פלסטין).

ashaf/-eet אשף *nmf* magician; wizard; charmer.

ashaf meetbakh אשף מטבח *nm* Master-Cook.

◇ **ashafeest/-eet** אשפיסט *[colloq.] nmf & adj* derogatory nickname for anyone (especially Israeli or Jewish) sympathizing with PLO or favoring agreement with it.

'ash|ak/-kah/-aktee עשק *v pst* exploited; subdued; (*pres* **'oshek**; *fut* **ya'ashok**).

hashak|ah/-ot השקה *nf* launching (a boat); (*+of:* **-at**).

ashakh|eem (*sing* **eshekh**) אשכים *nm pl* testicles (*pl+of:* **-ey**).

hash'al|ah/-ot השאלה *nf* lending; loaning; (*+of:* **-at**).

(be) hash'alah בהשאלה *adv* **1.** on loan; **2.** figuratively.

□ **Ashaleem** (Ashalim) אשלים *nm* kibbutz in Negev Heights (est. 1976), Pop. 47.

asham אשם *nm* guilt; blame.

(hargash|at/-ot) asham הרגשת אשם *nf* guilt feeling.

'ashan עשן *nm* smoke.

(masakh) 'ashan מסך עשן *nm* smoke-screen.

hash'ar|ah/-ot השארה *nf* leaving behind; abandonment; (*+of:* **-at**).

hash'ar|ah/-ot השערה *nf* conjecture; assumption; hypothesis; (*+of:* **-at**).

'ashashee|t/-yot עששית *nf* oil-lamp; lantern.

hash'a|yah/-yot השעיה *nf* suspension; deferment; (*+of:* **-yat**).

hashba|'ah/-'ot השבעה *nf* swearing in; invocation; (*+of:* **-'at**).

hashbakh|ah/-ot השבחה *nf* amelioration; betterment; (*+of:* **-at**).

◇ **(mas) hashbakhah** see ◇ **hetel hashbakhah**.

hashbat|ah/-ot השבתה *nf* lockout; (*+of:* **-at**).

□ **Ashdod** אשדוד *nf* new (est. 1957) harbor-town on Mediterranean seashore, 34 km S. of Tel-Aviv. Pop. 83,900.

□ **Ashdot Ya'akov** (Ashdot-Ya'aqov) אשדות יעקב *nm* twin kibbutzim in the Jordan Valley, 5 km S. of the Sea of Galilee. One (pop. 576) known as **Ashdot Ya'akov Eekhood** (Ihud) is a continuation of the original kibbutz est 1935. The other (pop 468) known as **Ashdot Ya'akov Me'ookhad** (Meuhad) is the one that in 1952 seceded from the original on idelological grounds no longer valid.

'asheer/-ah עשיר *adj* rich; wealthy.

'asheer/-eem עשיר *nm* rich or wealthy person (*pl+of:* **-ey**).

ashem/-ah אשם *adj* guilty.

ashem/-eem אשם *nm* culprit (*pl+of:* **-ey**).

asher אשר *conj & pron* which; that; who.

asher le- אשר ל- as regards; as to.

(le) asher לאשר *v inf* to confirm; (*pst* **eesher**; *pres* **me'asher**; *fut* **ye'asher**).

'asheshet עששת *nf* caries.

□ **Ashfelah** see □ **ha-shfelah**.

hashgakh|ah/-ot השגחה *nf* supervision; observation; (*+of:* **-at**).

(ha) hashgakhah ההשגחה *nf* Divine Providence.

(be) hashgakhat בהשגחת *adv* under supervision of.

(takhat) hashgakhah תחת השגחה *adv* under supervision of.

hash'ha|yah/-yot השהיה *nf* delay; suspension; (*+of:* **-yat**).

hashka|'ah/-'ot השקאה *nf* irrigation; (*+of:* **-'at**).

hashka|'ah/-'ot השקעה *nf* investment; (*+of:* **-at**).

hashkaf|ah/-ot השקפה *nf* outlook; view; (*+of:* **-at**).

(nekood|at/-ot) hashkafah נקודת השקפה *nf* point of view.

hashkaf|at/-ot 'olam השקפת עולם *nf* personal philosophy; outlook; Weltanschaung (*+of:* **-at**).

hashkam|ah/-ot השכמה *nf* early rising; (*+of:* **-at**).

ashkarah אשכרה *adv [slang] (Arab.)* plain talk.

hashka|yah/-yot השקיה *nf* irrigation; (*+of:* **-yat**).

□ **Ashkelon** (Ashqelon) אשקלון *nf* sea-shore town of Biblical fame (as Askalon) 51 km S. of Tel-Aviv. Pop. 59,700.

hashkem השכם *adv* early (in the morning).

hashkem ba-boker השכם בבוקר *adv* early in the morning.

hashkem ve-ha'arev השכם והערב *adv* day and night.

(ba-boker) hashkem בבוקר השכם *adv* early in the morning.
◇ **ashkenazee/-t** אשכנזי *adj* of Ashkenazi rite, community or ancestry, as opposed to Sephardi or Oriental rite etc.
◇ **ashkenazee/-yah** אשכנזי *nmf* Ashkenazi Jew i.e. of Central or East-European rite and ancestry, as opposed to Sephardi or Oriental Jew, i.e. one of Spanish-Portuguese rite and ancestry.
hash'khar|ah/-ot השחרה *nf* blackening; (*+of:* **-at**).
hash'khat|ah/-ot השחתה *nf* destruction; disfigurement; (*+of:* **-at**).
hash'khatat ha-meedot השחתת המידות *nf* corruption; demoralization.
ashlag (*npr* **eshlag**) אשלג *nm* potash.
□ **(meef'al ha) ashlag** see □ **meef'al ha-ashlag**.
hashlakh|ah/-ot השלכה *nf* repercussion; (*+of:* **-at**).
hashlam|ah/-ot השלמה *nf* completion; (*+of:* **-at**).
hashlam|ah/-ot השלמה *nf* resignation to.
ashla|yah/-yot אשלייה *nf* delusion; (*+of:* **-yat**).
hashla|yah/-yot השליה *nf* deluding; fooling; (*+of:* **-yat**).
ashlegan (*npr* **eshlagan**) אשלגן *nm* potassium.
ashm|ah/-ot אשמה *nf* guilt; (*+of:* **-at**).
(kofer/-et ba) ashmah כופר באשמה *v pres* pleads not guilty; denies (*pst* **kafar** *etc; fut* **yeekhpor** *etc; kh=k*).
(ketav/keetvey) ashmah כתב אשמה *nm* charge-sheet.
(modeh/-ah ba) ashmah מודה באשמה *v pres* pleads guilty; admits the charge; (*pst* **hodah** *etc; fut* **yodeh** *etc*).
(taf|al/-lah) ashmah טפל אשמה *v pst* laid blame; admitted guilt; (*pres* **tofel** *etc; fut* **yeetpol** *(p=f)*).
hashmad|ah/-ot השמדה *nf* annihilation; extermination; (*+of:* **-at**).
(makhn|eh/-ot) hashmadah מחנה השמדה *nm* extermination camp.
hashmadat 'am השמדת עם *nf* genocide.
hashman|ah/-ot השמנה *nf* putting on weight; growing fat; (*+of:* **-at**).
ashm|at/-ot shav אשמת שווא *nf* false accusation; false charge.
hashmat|ah/-ot השמטה *nf* omission; deletion; (*+of:* **-at**).
hashmats|ah/-ot השמצה *nf* defamation; (*+of:* **-at**).
('ets/'atsey) ashoo'akh עץ אשוח *nm* fir (tree).
◇ **ashoor** אשור (hist.) *nm* Assyria, ancient West-Asian empire in the Upper Tigris (on territories of today's Iraq, Kurdistan, East-Turkey) long-time foe of Biblical Israel.
ashp|ah/-atot אשפה *nf* garbage; (*+of:* **-at**).
hashpa|'ah/-'ot השפעה *nf* influence; (*+of:* **-at**).
(ba'al/-at) hashpa'ah בעל השפעה *adj* influential.
hashpal|ah/-ot השפלה *nf* humiliation; (*+of:* **-at**).
(le) ashpez לאשפז *v inf* to hospitalize; (*pst* **eeshpez**; *pres* **me'ashpez**; *fut* **ye'ashpez**).
ashr|ah/-ot אשרה *nf* visa; entry-visa; (*+of:* **-at**).
hashra|'ah/-'ot השראה *nf* inspiration; (*+of:* **-'at**).
ashra'ee (*npr* **ashray**) אשראי *nm* credit.
(meekhtav) ashra'ee (*npr* **ashray**) מכתב אשראי *nm* letter of credit.
ashray אשראי *nm* credit.
(meekht|av/-evey) ashray מכתב אשראי *nm* letter of credit.
hashra|yah/-yot השריה *nf* immersion; soaking; (*+of:* **-yat**).
ashrey אשרי *interj* blessed be...
ashrey mee אשרי מי *interj* blessed be whoever...
hashtak|ah/-ot השתקה *nf* silencing; (*+of:* **-at**).
hashtal|ah/-ot השתלה *nf* implantation; transplant; (*+of:* **-at**).
hashva|'ah/-'ot השוואה *nf* comparison; equalization; (*+of:* **-'at**).
haskal|ah/-ot השכלה *nf* education; learning; erudition; enlightenment; (*+of:* **-at**).
haskalah gevohah השכלה גבוהה *nf* higher (university) education.
haskalah teekhoneet השכלה תיכונית *nf* secondary education.
haskalah yesodeet השכלה יסודית *nf* primary education; elementary education.
haskam|ah/-ot הסכמה *nf* agreement; (*+of:* **-at**).
(be) haskamah hadadeet בהסכמה הדדית *adv* in mutual agreement.
haskar|ah/-ot השכרה *nf* leasing; hire; (*+of:* **-at**).
haskarah khodsheet השכרה חודשית *nf* monthly leasing.
haskarah khofsheet השכרה חופשית *nf* free lease (i.e. not subject to rent control).
(le) haskarah להשכרה to rent; for rent.
'askan/-eem עסקן *nm* communal or party activist; politician; (*pl+of:* **-ey**).
'askan meeflagtee עסקן מיפלגתי *nm* party worker.
(le) haskeer להשכיר *v inf* **1.** to rent; **2.** for rent; renting; (*pst* **heeskeer**; *pres* **maskeer**; *fut* **yaskeer**).
(bayeet le) haskeer בית להשכיר *nm* house for rent.
(deerah le) haskeer דירה להשכיר *nf* apartment for rent.
(kheder/khadareem le) haskeer חדר להשכיר *nm* room for rent.
askol|ah/-ot אסכולה *nf* school of thought; system; (*+of:* **-at**).
'askoon|ah/-ot עסקונה *nf* *[colloq.]* establishment; party establishment.
as|lah/-alot אסלה *nf* closed stool; lavatory seat; toilet bowl; (*+of:* **-lat**).
haslam|ah/-ot הסלמה *nf* escalation (*+of:* **-at**).
hasmakh|ah/-ot הסמכה **1.** authorization; **2.** attachment; linkage (*+of:* **-at**).
asmakht|ah/-a'ot אסמכתה *nf* reference; (*+of:* **-at**).
ason/-ot אסון *nm* disaster; accident.

ason teva' אסון טבע *nm* catastrophe.
(hemeet/-ah) ason המיט אסון *v* brought disaster; (*pres* **memeet** *etc; fut* **yameet** *etc*).
asoof/-ah אסוף *adj* collected.
asoof|ah/-ot אסופה *nf* collection; assembly; (*+of:* **-at**).
'asook/-ah עסוק *adj* busy; occupied.
asoor/-ah אסור *adj* forbidden.
asoor אסור *adv* prohibited; forbidden to.
'asoo|y/-yah עשוי *v pres & adj* **1.** done; **2.** likely to; liable to.
'asoo|y/-yah hay|ah/-tah עשוי היה *v* was likely to.
'asor/-eem עשור *nm* decade.
◇ **(ben keseh le) 'asor** see ◇ **ben keseh le-'asor**.
(la) 'asot לעשות *v inf* to do; to make; (*pst* **'asah**; *pres* **'oseh**; *fut* **ya'aseh**).
aspak|ah/-ot אספקה *nf* supply; (*+of:* **-at**).
haspak|ah/-kot הספקה *nf* supplying; supply; (*+of:* **-at**).
aspaklar|yah/-yot אספקלריה *nf* **1.** mirror; reflection; **2.** view; (*+of:* **-at**).
aspeset אספסת *nf* lucerne (plant).
hasrat|ah/-ot הסרטה *nf* filming; taking movies; (*+of:* **-at**).
(oolp|an/-eney) hasratah אולפן הסרטה *nm* film studio.
(seret/seertey) hasratah סרט הסרטה *nm* movie film.
hastarah/-ot הסתרה *nf* concealment; (*+of:* **-at**).
astrateg אסטרטג *nm* strategist.
astrateg|yah/-yot אסטרטגיה *nf* strategy (*+of:* **-yat**).
at את *pron f* you (addressing female).
at אט *adv* slowly.
at-at אט־אט *adv* little by little.
(le) 'at-le'at לאט־לאט *adv* very slowly.
atah אתה *pron m* you (addressing male).
'at|ah/-etah/-eetee עטה *v* put on; dressed in; (*pres* **'oteh**; *fut* **ya'ateh**).
'atah עתה *adv* now.
(le-'et) 'atah לעת עתה *adv* for the moment; for the time being.
(zeh) 'atah זה עתה *adv* just now.
hataf|ah/-ot הטפה *nf* sermonizing; preaching; (*+of:* **-at**).
hataf|at/-ot moosar הטפת מוסר *nf* moralizing.
hatal|ah/-ot הטלה *nf* casting; projection; throwing; (*+of:* **-at**).
hatalat ashm|ah/-ot הטלת אשמה *nf* laying the blame.
hatalat beytseem הטלת ביצים *nf* laying eggs.
hatalat eesoor הטלת איסור *nf* banning; prohibiting.
hatalat goral הטלת גורל *nf* casting lots.
hatalat mas/meeseem הטלת מס *nf* imposition of tax/-es.
hatalat moom/-eem הטלת מום *nf* maiming; mutilation.
hat'am|ah/-ot התאמה *nf* adjustment; suitabilty; (*+of:* **-at**).
(ee) hat'amah אי התאמה *nm* discrepancy; lack of harmony.
hat'am|ah/-ot הטעמה *nf* stressing; stress; (*+of:* **-at**).
□ **"A-Tanoor"** see □ **"Ha-Tanoor"**.
atar/-eem אתר *nm* site; location; (*pl+of:* **-ey**).
'atar|ah/-ot עטרה *nf* diadem; crown; (*+of:* **-at**).
hatar|ah/-ot התרה *nf* release; permission; (*+of:* **-at**).
□ **(Keekar) Atareem** see □ **Keekar Nameer**.
□ **'Atarot** ('Atarot) עטרות *nm* Jerusalem's airport located 11 km N. of the Capital.
hatash|ah/-ot התשה *nf* attrition; (*+of:* **-at**).
(meelkhemet) hatashah מלחמת התשה *nf* war of attrition.
◇ **(meelkhemet ha) atashah** see ◇ **meelkhemet ha-hatashah**.
hatav|ah/-ot הטבה *nf* **1.** bonus; favor; privilege; **2.** improvement; fringe benefit; (*+of:* **-at**).
◇ **atav|ah/-ot sotsyalee|t/-yot** see ◇ **hatav|ah/-ot sotseealee|-yot**.
◇ **hatav|ah/-ot sotsee'alee|t/-yot** הטבה סוציאלית *f lit* social benefit i.e. special privilege granted to women employees of some public institutions to work fewer hours for undiminished pay when back on the job after a pregnancy, an illness etc.
◇ **atav|at/-ot geel** see ◇ **hatav|at/-ot geel.**
hata|yah/-yot הטיה *nf* bending; deflecting; (*+of:* **-yat**).
hat'a|yah/-yot הטעיה *nf* misleading; deception; (*+of:* **-yat**).
hataz|ah/-ot התזה *nf* **1.** sprinkling; **2.** cutting off; (*+of:* **-at**).
'ateed עתיד *nm* future.
'ateed/-ah le- עתיד ל־ *adj* **1.** due to; about to **2.** *v pres* is due/about to; (*pst* **hayah 'ateed le-**; *fut* **yeehyeh 'ateed le-**).
'ateedot עתידות *nf pl* future; prospects.
(mageed/-at) 'ateedot מגיד עתידות *nm* fortune-teller.
'ateef|ah/-ot עטיפה *nf* wrapping; paper-cover; (*+of:* **-at**).
'ateek/-ah עתיק *adj* ancient.
□ **(ha-'eer) ha-'ateekah** see □ **ha-'eer ha-'ateekah**.
'ateekot עתיקות *nf pl* antiquities; antiques.
'ateeneem (*sing* **'ateen**) עטינים *nm pl* udders; (*pl+of:* **-ey**).
'ateer/-at nekhaseem עתיר נכסים *adj* wealthy; rich.
'ateer|ah/-ot עתירה *nf* petition (to a court of law); (*+of:* **-at**).
(hon) 'atek הון עתק *nm* huge amount of money.
atem אתם *pron mf pl* you (addressing several people).
aten אתן *pron f pl* you (addressing several females).

□ **'Ateret** ('Ateret) עטרת *nm* communal village (est. 1981) in SW Samaria, 10 km N. of Ramallah.

'ateret brakhot עתרת ברכות *nf* a sheaf of good wishes.

hatfal|ah/-ot התפלה *nf* desalination; (*+of:* **-at**).

hatkaf|ah/-ot התקפה *nf* attack; (*+of:* **-at**).

hatkaf|at/-ot metsakh התקפת מצח *nf* frontal attack.

hatkaf|at/-ot mena' התקפת מנע *nf* preventive attack.

(ee) hatkafah אי התקפה *nm* non-aggression.

hatkan|ah/-ot התקנה *nf* installation; installing; (*+of:* **-at**).

(demey) hatkanah דמי התקנה *nm pl* installation-fee.

atkhalah אתחלה *nf* commencement; beginning.

hatkhal|ah/-ot התחלה *nf* beginning; start; (*+of:* **-at**).

(ba) hatkhalah בהתחלה *adv* in the beginning.

◇ **atkhaltah dee-ge'oolah** אתחלתה דגאולה *(Aram.) nf* omen heralding the Jewish people's long hoped for Messianic redemption (used also figurat.).

atlas/-eem אטלס *nf* atlas; (*pl+of:* **-ey**).

□ **'Atleet** (Atlit) עתלית *nf* Carmel Coast settlement (est. 1903), 14 km S. of Haifa. Pop. 2,780.

atlet/-eet אתלט *nmf* athlete.

atletee/-t אתלטי *adj* athletic.

atleteekah אתלטיקה *nf* athletics.

atleteekah kalah אתלטיקה קלה *nf* light athletics.

hatmad|ah/-ot התמדה *nf* perseverance; (*+of:* **-at**).

(be) hatmadah בהתמדה *adv* persistently.

hatna|'ah/-'ot התנעה *nf* starting up (a machine); (*+of:* **-at**).

atom/-eem אטום *nm* atom; (*pl+of:* **-ey**).

atomee/-t אטומי *adj* atomic.

(koor/-eem) atomee/-yeem כור אטומי *nm* atomic pile.

(energyah) atomeet אנרגיה אטומית *nf* atomic energy.

aton/-ot אתון *nf* she-ass.

'atood|ah/-ot עתודה *nf* reserve.

◇ **'atoodah akadema'eet** עתודה אקדמאית *nf* Academic Reserve unit of university students granted a postonement of their active military service till after graduation.

◇ **'atooda'ee/-t** עתודאי *nmf* member of the Academic Reserve.

'atoodot עתודות *nf pl* reserves.

'atoof/-ah עטוף *adj* wrapped; enveloped.

atoom/-ah אטום *adj* **1.** opaque; impermeable; **2.** dull (figurat.).

atra|'ah/-'ot אתראה *nf* warning; (*+of:* **-'at**).

hatra'ah/-'ot התראה *nf* warning; (*+of:* **-'at**).

hatrad|ah/-ot הטרדה *nf* annoyance; molestation; (*+of:* **-at**).

hatram|ah/-ot התרמה *nf* fund-raising; collecting contributions; (*+of:* **-at**).

ats/-ah/-tee אץ *v* ran; hastened; (*pres* **ats**; *fut* **ya'oots**).

atsah lo/lah ha-derekh אצה לו/לה הדרך was/is in a hurry.

hatsa|'ah/-'ot הצעה *nf* proposition; suggestion; (*+of:* **-at**).

hatsa|'at/-'ot hakhlatah הצעת החלטה *nf* draft resolution.

hatsa|'at/-'ot khok הצעת חוק *nf* bill (legislation).

'atsab|eem (*sing:* **'atsav**) עצבים *nm pl* nerves; (*pl+of:* **-ey**).

('al|ah/-tah 'al ha) 'atsabeem עלה על העצבים *v* got on one's nerves; (*pres* **'oleh** *etc; fut* **ya'aleh** *etc*).

(heetmotetoot) 'atsabeem התמוטטות עצבים *nf* nervous breakdown.

(mereet|at/-ot) 'atsabeem מריטת עצבים *nf* nerve-racking.

(meteekh|at/-ot) 'atsabeem מתיחת עצבים *nf* nervous tension.

(rof|e/'at) 'atsabeem רופא־עצבים *nmf* neurologist.

hatsaf|ah/-ot הצפה *nf* flooding; (*+of:* **-at**).

hatsag|ah/-ot הצגה *nf* performance; show (theatrical); presentation; (*+of:* **-at**).

hatsag|ah/-ot yomee|t/-yot הצגה יומית *nf* matinee.

hatsag|at/-ot bekhorah הצגת בכורה *nf* premiere; first night.

hatsal|ah/-ot הצלה *nf* rescue; (*+of:* **-at**).

(khagor|at/-ot) hatsalah חגורת הצלה *nf* life-belt.

(pe'ool|at/-ot) hatsalah פעולת הצלה *nf* rescue action.

(seer|at/-ot) hatsalah סירת הצלה *nf* lifeboat.

(ba) 'atsaltayeem בעצלתיים *adv* lazily; very slowly.

'ats|am/-mah 'ayeen עצם עין *v* shut eye; (*pres* **'otsem** *etc; fut* **ya'atsom** *etc*).

'atsamot (*sing:* **'etsem**) עצמות *nf pl* bones.

(leshad) 'atsamot לשד עצמות *nm* marrow; bone-marrow.

(me'akh) 'atsamot מיח עצמות *nm* bone-marrow.

(mo'akh) 'atsamot מוח עצמות *nm* marrow; medulla ossium.

atsan/-eet אצן *nmf* runner (sport).

'ats|ar/-rah/-artee עצר *v* stopped; detained; (*pres* **'otser**; *fut* **ya'atsor**).

atsarah, "Atsarat Balfoor", atsaratee, (pesak-deen) atsaratee, atsarat hon see under H as normatively pronounced: **hats'harah, hats'harat balfoor, hats'haratee, (pesak-deen) hats'haratee,** and **hats'harat hon**

hatsat|ah/-ot הצתה *nf* **1.** arson; **2.** ignition (car); (*+of:* **-at**).

hatsats|ah/-ot הצצה *nf* peep; glance; (*+of:* **-at**).

hatsav|ah/-ot הצבה *nf* posting; placing; erecting; (*+of:* **-at**).

hatsba|'ah/-'ot הצבעה *nf* **1.** voting; **2.** indicating; (*+of:* **-'at**).

hatsba|'ah/-'ot be-kalpee הצבעה בקלפי *nf* balloting.

hatsba|'at/-'ot ee-emoon הצבעת אי אמון *nf* vote of no confidence.

(he'emeed/-ah le) hatsba'ah העמיד להצבעה *v* put to a vote; (*pres* **ma'ameed** *etc; fut* **ya'ameed** *etc*).

'atsbanee/-t עצבני *adj* nervous.

'atsbanoot עצבנות *nf* nervousness.

hatsda|'ah/-'ot הצדעה *nf* salute; salutation; (*+of:* **-'at**).

hatsdak|ah/-ot הצדקה *nf* justification; (*+of:* **-at**).

hatseedah! הצידה! *interj* aside! make way!

atseel/-ah אציל **1.** *adj* noble; **2.** *nmf* nobleman; aristocrat.

atseel/-at nefesh אציל־נפש *adj* of noble soul; gentle of heart.

atseelee/-t אצילי *adj* noble; gentle.

'atseer/-ah עציר *nmf* detainee.

◇ **'atseer/-ah beetkhonee/-t** עציר בטחוני *nmf* detainee under security charges.

◇ **'atseer/-ah meenhalee/-t** עציר מינהלי *nmf* detainee under administrative order.

'atseer|ah/-ot עצירה *nf* halting; stoppage; (*+of:* **-at**).

en 'atseerah (or **eyn 'atseerah**) אין עצירה *interj* no stopping.

'atseer|at/-ot peta' עצירת פתע *nf* sudden halt.

'atseeroot עצירות *nf* constipation.

'atseets/-eem עציץ *nm* flowerpot; (*pl+of:* **-ey**).

'atsel/-ah עצל *adj* lazy; indolent.

'ats|eret/-arot עצרת *nf* mass-meeting; assembly.

'ats|eret/-rot 'am עצרת עם *nf* mass assembly; mass meeting.

'atseret ha-'oom עצרת האו"ם *nf* the U.N. General Assembly.

◇ **(shemeenee) 'atseret** see ◇ **shmeenee 'atseret.**

'atsey pree (or **peree**) עצי פרי *nm pl* fruit trees; (*sing:* **'ets** *etc*).

'atsey srak (*sing* **'ets srak**) עצי סרק *nm pl* fruitless trees; not fruitbearing trees.

'atsey zayeet (*sing:* **'ets zayeet**) עצי זית *nm pl* olive trees.

hats'har|ah/-ot הצהרה *nf* declaration; statement; (*+of:* **-at**).

hats'har|ah/-ot bee-shvoo'ah הצהרה בשבועה *nf* affidavit; sworn statement.

◇ **"ats'harat** (or **hatsarat**) **balfoor"** see ◇ **hats'harat balfoor.**

hats'haratee/-t הצהרתי *adj* declarative.

(pesak-deen) hats'haratee פסק דין הצהרתי *nm* declarative judgment.

◇ **ats'har|at/-ot** (or **hatsarat**) **hon** see ◇ **hats'har|at/-ot hon.**

hatslaf|ah/-ot הצלפה *nf* lashing; (*+of:* **-at**).

hatslakh|ah/-ot הצלחה *nf* success; (*+of:* **-at**).

(be) hatslakhah בהצלחה **1.** *adv* successfully; **2.** *interj* good luck!

'atslan/-eet עצלן *nmf* sluggard; lazy.

'atslanoot עצלנות *nf* laziness; sloth.

'atsloot עצלות *nf* laziness.

hatsmad|ah/-ot הצמדה *nf* joining; linkage; (*+of:* **-at**).

◇ **atsmadah le-** see ◇ **hatsmadah le-.**

'atsma'ee/-t עצמאי *adj* independent; economically of otherwise independent.

'atsma'ee/t עצמאי *nmf* self-employed (tax-wise).

'atsma'oot עצמאות *nf* independence.

◇ **(meelkhemet ha) 'atsma'oot** see ◇ **meelkhemet ha-'atsma'oot.**

◇ **(yom ha) 'atsma'oot** see ◇ **yom ha-'atsma'oot.**

'atsmee/-t עצמי *adj* self-; own.

'atsm|ee/-ekh/-enoo/-ekhem/-ekhen עצמי־ך וכו׳ *pron* my/your (*m/f*) -self; themselves (*m/f*).

('as|ah/-tah/-eetee *etc*) **'atsmo/-ah/-ee** (*etc*) עשה עצמו *v* made him/her/my -self; pretended.

(be) 'atsm|ee/-ekhah/-ekh/-o (*etc*) בעצמי־ך וכו׳ *pron* by my/your *etc* -self.

(le) 'atsm|ee/-ekha/-ekh/-o (*etc*) לעצמי־ך וכו׳ *pron* to my/your *etc* -self.

(me) 'atsm|ee/-ekhah/-ekh/-o *etc* מעצמי־ך וכו׳ *pron* of my/your (*m/f*) *etc* own.

(nat|al/-lah 'al) 'atsmo/-ah נטל על עצמו *v* undertook upon him/her -self.

(te|'er/-'arah/-'artee le) 'atsm|o/-ah/-ee תיאר לעצמו/־ה וכו׳ *v* imagined; pictured to him/her *etc* -self (*pres* **meta'er** *etc; fut* **yeta'er** *etc*).

('arvoot) 'atsmeet ערבות עצמית *nf* personal bond.

□ **'Atsmonah** עצמונה *nm* village (est. 1982) in the S. part of the Gaza Strip settled by evacuees of Sinai's onetime **Yameet** (Yamit) town.

hatsna|'ah הצנעה *nf* concealment; hiding; (*+of:* **-'at**).

hatsnakh|ah/-ot הצנחה **1.** *nf* parachuting; (*+of:* **-at**); **2.** *[colloq.]* bringing in for a top job somebody "from above" i.e. from the outside.

hatsne'a lekhet הצנע לכת observing strict modesty.

atsool|ah/-ot אצולה *nf* aristocracy; (*+of:* **-at**).

'atsoom/-ah עצום *adj* formidable; tremendous.

atsoom|ah/-ot עצומה *nf* petition; (*+of:* **-at**).

(be-'eynayeem) 'atsoomot בעיניים עצומות *adv* blindfolded.

'atsoor/-ah עצור **1.** *v pres* is detained; **2.** *adj* detained.

'atsoov/-ah עצוב *adj* sad.

'atsor!/'eetsree! עצור! *v imp sing m/f* stop!

(tamroor) 'atsor תמרור עצור *nm* traffic-sign "stop!".

hatsrakh|ah/-ot הצרחה *nf* castling (in chess); (*+of:* **-at**).

'atsvoot עצבות *nf* sadness; melancholy.

av אב *nm* Ab, the 11th month of the Jewish year (29 days; approx. July-Aug).

av/ot אב *nm* father; (*+of:* **avee**).

◇ **av/-ot shakool/-eem** אב שכול *nm* father of a son or daughter fallen in one of nation's wars, military operations or as victim of terrorism.
◇ **(menakhem) av** see ◇ **menakhem ave.**
hav/-ee הב/הבי *v imp sing m/f* give! give me!
◇ **(teesh'ah be) 'av** see ◇ **teesh'ah be-'av.**
(tokhnee|t/-yot) av תוכנית־אב *nf* master-plan.
av|ah/-tah/-eetee אבה *v* desired; wished; (*pres* **oveh;** *fut* **yoveh**).
havah הבה *interj* let's; well, then let's ...
ava'boo'ot אבעבועות *nf pl* smallpox; variola.
ava'boo'ot roo'akh אבעבועות רוח *nf pl* chickenpox; varicella.
hava|'ah/-'ot הבאה *nf* bringing; fetching; (+*of:* **-'at**).
av|ad/-dah/-adetee אבד *v* got lost; perished; (*pres* **oved;** *fut* **yovad**).
avad 'alav ha-kelakh אבד עליו הכלח *v* got worn with age; became obsolete.
'av|ad/-dah/-adetee עבד *v* worked; (*pres* **'oved;** *fut* **ya'avod**).
'avad (*etc*) **'al|av/-eha** עבד עליו *[slang] v* bluffed him/her.
'avad (*etc*) **'al|av/-eha be-eynayeem** עבד עליו בעיניים *[slang] v* bluffed him/her shamelessly.
(la) avadon לאבדון *adv* to hell; to waste; down the drain.
av ha-'orkeem אב העורקים *nm* aorta (Anat).
avahoot אבהות *nf* fatherhood; paternity.
avak אבק *nm* dust; powder.
avak sreyfah אבק שריפה *nm* gun powder.
(sho|'ev/-'avey) avak שואב אבק *nm* vacuum cleaner.
aval אבל *conj* but; however.
havan|ah/-ot הבנה *nf* understanding; comprehension; (+*of:* **-at**).
(ee) havan|ah/-ot אי הבנה *nm* misunderstanding.
(kesh|eh/-at) havanah קשה הבנה *adj* slow-witted; slow to grasp.
avaneem (*sing:* **even**) אבנים *nf pl* stones.
(yeed|ah/-etah) avaneem יידה אבנים *v* hurled stones (*pres* **meyadeh** *etc; fut* **yeyadeh** *etc*).
(yeedooy) avaneem יידוי אבנים *nm* hurling of stones.
'avar עבר *nm* past tense (*Gram.*).
'av|ar/-rah/-artee עבר *v* passed; passed by; (*pres* **'over;** *fut* **ya'avor**).
'avar (*etc*) **'al** עבר על *v* violated; transgressed.
'avar (*etc*) **'al ha-khomer** עבר על החומר *v* went over the material; perused.
'avar (*etc*) **'aver|ah/-ot** עבר עבירה *v* committed a crime; sinned.
'avar (*etc*) **le-** עבר ל־ *v pst* went over to; switched to; moved over.
'avar pleelee עבר פלילי *v pst* criminal record.
(be) 'avar בעבר *adv* in the past.
(le-she) 'avar לשעבר **1.** *adj* ex-; former; **2.** *adv* formerly.
(zeman) 'avar זמן עבר *nm* past tense (Gram.).
havar|ah/-ot הברה *nf* syllable; (+*of:* **-at**).
◇ **avarah ashkenazeet** see ◇ **havarah ashkenazeet.**
hav'ar|ah/-ot הבערה *nf* setting fire; (+*of:* **-at**).
◇ **avarah sefaradeet** see ◇ **havarah sefaradeet.**
'avaryan/-eem עבריין *nm* delinquent; (*pl+of:* **-ey**).
'avaryanoot עבריינות *nf* delinquency.
'avaryanoot no'ar עבריינות נוער *nf* juvenile delinquency.
avatee|'akh/-kheem אבטיח *nm* water melon; (*pl+of:* **-khey**).
avats אבץ *nm* zinc.
havay הווי *nm* **1.** folklore; **2.** way of life.
havay הבאי *nm* nonsense.
(deevrey) havay דברי הבאי *nm pl* vain bragging; nonsense.
('erev/'arvey) havay ערב הווי *nm* folk-song and folk-dance party.
(tsevet) havay צוות הווי *nm* army team for unit entertainment.
'ava|yah/-yot עוויה *nf* grimace; face contortion (+*of:* **-yat**).
hava|yah/-yot הוויה *nf* existence; (+*of:* **-yat**).
(ka) havayat|o/-ah כהוויתו *adv* as it is; as it should be.
avaz/-eem אווז *nm* gander; (*pl+of:* **avzey**).
av bet-deen אב בית דין *nm* presiding judge.
◇ **avdalah** see ◇ **havdalah.**
□ **'Avdat** עבדת *nf* ruins of ancient Nabatean town in Negev, 9 km S. of **Sdeh Boker**.
avdah teekvat|o/-ah אבדה תקוותו *v* lost hope.
(le) havdeel להבדיל *v inf* to distinguish, differentiate; (*pst* **heevdeel;** *pres* **mavdeel;** *fut* **yavdeel**).
(le) havdeel להבדיל *adv* with all due difference.
'avd|ekha/-ekh (*etc*) **ha-ne'eman** עבדך הנאמן *nm* your (*m/f*) obedient servant (*m/f*).
'avdoot עבדות *nf* slavery; bondage.
aved|ah/-ot אבידה *nf* loss; (+*of:* **-at**).
avee (av) אבי *m+of* the father of.
avee avot אבי אבות *nm* **1.** the original cause of; **2.** *lit* : the grandfather of.
'avee עבי *nm* the thickness of.
(ba) 'avee ha-korah בעבי הקורה (into) the very heart of the matter.
□ **Avee'el** (Avi'el) אביאל *nm* village in Samaria (est 1949), 3 km NE of **Beenyameenah**. Pop 289.
□ **Avee'ezer** (Avi'ezer) אביעזר *nm* village in **'Adoolam** area (est 1958), 9.5 km SE of Bet Shemesh. Pop 202.
□ **Aveegdor** (Avigedor) אביגדור *nm* village (est 1950) 11 km N. of **Keeryat Gat**. Pop 377.
aveekh/-ah אביך *adj* hazy.
□ **Aveekhayeel** (Avihayil) אביחיל *nf* coop. village (est. 1932) 4 km N. of Netanyah, founded by veterans of Jewish Legion of World War I. Pop. 793.
haveel/-ah הביל *adj* humid; vaporous.
aveer אוויר *nm* air.

(do'ar) aveer דואר אוויר *nm* airmail.
(kheyl) aveer חיל אוויר *nm* air force.
(lakhats) aveer לחץ אוויר *nm* air pressure.
(meezoog) aveer מיזוג אוויר *nm* air conditioning.
(mezeg) aveer מזג אוויר *nm* weather.
(mezeg) aveer gashoom מזג אוויר גשום *nm* rainy weather.
(mezeg) aveer na'eh מזג אוויר נאה *nm* fine weather.
(mezeg) aveer no'akh מזג אוויר נוח *nm* fine weather.
(mezeg) aveer so'er מזג אוויר סוער *nm* stormy weather.
(pateesh/-ey) aveer פטיש אוויר *nm* pneumatic hammer.
(sha'af/-ah/-tee) aveer שאף אוויר *v* breathed in; (*pres* **sho'ef** *etc*; *fut* **yeesh'af** *etc*).
'aveer/-ah עביר *adj* passable; navigable.
aveerah אווירה *nf* atmosphere; (*+of:* **-at**).
aveeree/-t אוורירי *adj* air-; airy.
aveeree|yah אווירייה *nf* air force; (*+of:* **-yat**).
aveeron/-eem אווירון *nm* airplane.
'aveet עביט *nm* chamber pot.
'aveet/-ot עווית *nf* convulsion; spasm.
□ **Aveetal** (Avital) אביטל *nm* village in Yizre'el Valley (est. 1953) near Mount **Geelbo'a**', 10 km S. of **'Afoolah**. Pop 409.
aveev/-eem אביב *nm* springtime; spring.
□ **(Tel-)Aviv** see □ **Tel-Aveev**.
□ **Aveeveem** (Avivim) אביבים *nm* moshav (coop. village) in Upper Galilee (est. 1958) on Lebanese border. Pop. 327.
aveezar/-eem אביזר *nm* accessory; spare-part (*pl+of:* **-ey**).
'av|eh/-ah עבה *adj* thick.
'avel עוול *nm* injustice; wrong.
av|el/-ah אבל *adj* mournful; desolate; *nmf* mourner.
◇ **(neekhoom) aveleem** see ◇ **neekhoom aveleem**.
'aver|ah/-ot עבירה *nf* offense; contravention; sin; (*+of:* **-at**).
(sheedool lee-devar) 'averah שידול לדבר עבירה *nm* abetting; soliciting.
avk|ah (*npr* **avak|ah**)**/-ot** אבקה *nf* powder; (*+of:* **-at**).
avk|at/-ot afeeyah אבקת אפייה *nf* baking powder.
avk|at/-ot harakhah אבקת הרחה *nf* smelling powder.
avk|at/-ot keveesah אבקת כביסה *nf* laundering powder.
avk|at/-ot khalav אבקת חלב *nf* milk powder.
avk|at/-ot sookar אבקת סוכר *nf* icing/sugar powder.
avkhan|ah/-ot אבחנה *nf* diagnosis (*+of:* **-at**).
havkhan|ah/-ot הבחנה *nf* distinction; (*+of:* **-at**).
av khoreg אב חורג *nm* stepfather.
'avl|ah/-ot עוולה *nf* wrong; injustice; evil; (*+of:* **-at**).
havlag|ah/-ot הבלגה *nf* restraint; self-restraint; (*+of:* **-at**).
◇ **(ha)avlagah** see ◇ **(ha)havlagah**.
havlat|ah/-ot הבלטה *nf* emphasis; (*+of:* **-at**).
avney-derekh אבני־דרך *nf pl* milestones.
avney-khen (*sing:* **even-khen**) אבני חן *nf pl* gems; precious stones.
avney marah אבני מרה *nf pl* gallstones.
avney safah (*sing:* **even-safah**) אבני שפה *nf pl* curbstones.
'avod|ah/-ot עבודה *nf* **1.** work; labor; **2.** job; (*+of:* **-at**).
'avodah shekhorah עבודה שחורה *nf* unskilled labor.
(khad|ar/-rey) 'avodah חדר עבודה *nm* study room.
(kel|ee/-ey) 'avodah כלי עבודה *nm* tool; working tool.
(khoser) 'avodah חוסר עבודה *nm* unemployment.
(leesh|kat/-khot) 'avodah לשכת עבודה *nf* labor exchange.
(meefleget ha) 'avodah מפלגת העבודה *nf* the Labor Party; (see ◇ **meefleget ha-'avodah**).
(mekhoos|ar/-eret) 'avodah מחוסר עבודה *mf & adj* jobless; unemployed (*pl:* **mekhoosrey 'avoda**).
(menah|el/-aley) 'avodah מנהל עבודה *nm* foreman.
(sekhar) 'avodah שכר עבודה *nm* salary; wages.
(tenoo'at ha) 'avodah תנועת העבודה *nf* the Labor Movement; (see ◇ **meefleget ha-'avodah**).
'avodat adamah עבודת אדמה *nf* tilling the land; cultivation of the soil.
'avodat kapayeem עבודת כפיים *nf* manual labor.
'avodat mateh עבודת מטה *nf* staff work; teamwork.
'avodat nemaleem עבודת נמלים *nf* **1.** strenuous work; **2.** (lit.) ant-work.
'avodat perekh (*cpr* **parekh**) עבודת פרך *nf* hard labor.
'avod|at/-ot yad עבודת יד *nf* handwork; handicraft.
'avon/-ot עוון *nm* misdemeanour; sin; offense.
avokado אבוקדו *nm* avocado.
'avon pleelee עוון פלילי *nm* criminal offense.
havoo הבו *interj* let's; let us; you (addressing many) give me/us.
avood/-ah אבוד *adj* lost.
avook|ah/-ot אבוקה *nf* torch; (*+of:* **-at**).
'avoor עבור *prep* for; for the sake of.
(ba) 'avoor בעבור *adv* in consideration of; for.
'avor! עבור! *v imp* pass! keep moving!
(ka) 'avor כעבור *adv* following; at the expiration of.
avot (*sing:* **av**) אבות *nm pl* ancestors; fathers; forefathers.
(avee) avot אבי אבות *nm* **1.** forefather; **2.** (*figurat.*) the original cause of; the reason at the root of.
(ha) avot האבות *nm pl* the forefathers: Abraham, Isaac and Jacob (Bibl).

'av|ot/-ootah עבות *adj* thick; bushy.
avoteynoo אבותינו *nm pl* our forefathers.
avoy! !אבוי *interj* alas!
(oy va) avoy! !אוי ואבוי *interj* alas and alack!
havra|'ah/-'ot הבראה *nf* convalescence; **(+*of:* -'at).**
(bet/batey) havra'ah בית הבראה *nm* convalescent home: rest house.
(demey) havra'ah דמי הבראה *nm pl* vacation allowance.
havrag|ah/-ot הברגה *nf* thread (screw); **(+*of:* -at).**
havrak|ah/-ot הברקה *nf* **1.** bright idea; **2.** cabling; telegraphing; **(+*of:* -at).**
havrakh|ah/-ot הברחה *nf* smuggling; contraband; **(+*of:* -at).**
avreeree/-t אוורירי *adj* airy.
avrekh/-eem אברך *nm* married yeshiva student; **(*pl+of:* -ey).**
havshal|ah/-ot הבשלה *nf* ripening; **(+*of:* -at).**
avtakh|ah/-ot אבטחה *nf* protection; ensuring security; **(+*of:* -at).**
havtakh|ah/-ot הבטחה *nf* promise; assurance; **(+*of:* -at).**
havtakhat neesoo'eem הבטחת נישואים *nf* promise of marriage.
avtalah אבטלה *nf* unemployment; **(+*of:* -at).**
(demey) avtalah דמי אבטלה *nm pl* unemployment relief; dole.
avteepoos אבטיפוס *nm* prototype.
avzam/-eem אבזם *nm* buckle; **(*pl+of:* -ey).**
avz|ar/-areem אבזר *nm* accessory; spare part; **(*pl+of:* -erey).**
awantajee/-t אוונטג'י **1.** *nm [slang]* adventurer; **2.** *adj* adventurous.
hay|ah/-tah/-eetee היה *v* was; **(*pres* heen|enee/-kha/-o/-ah; *fut* yeehyeh).**
hayah (*etc*) be-da'at|ah/-o/-ee/-kha היה בדעתה/-ו/-י/-ך - *v* she/he/I/you had in mind; intended.
hayah (*etc*) 'al/-ay/-av/-ekha היה על *v* one/I/you (etc) should have; was supposed to.
hayah (*etc*) lee/lekha/lakh (*etc*) היה ל- לי/לך/לך *v & poss.pron.* I/you *(m/f) etc* had.
('alool/-ah) hayah (*etc*) עלול היה *v* was liable to.
(amoor/-ah) hayah (*etc*) אמור היה *v* was supposed to.
('asooy/-ah) hayah (*etc*) עשוי היה *v* was likely to.
ayal/-eem אייל *nm* stag **(*pl+of:* -ey).**
ayal|ah/-ot איילה *nf* gazelle; **(+*of:* ayelet).**
□ **Ayalon** איילון *nm* valley (known also as **'Emek Ayalon** עמק איילון) situated between the Coastal Plain and the Judean Hills. Crossed by Expressway 1.
□ **(Neteevey) Ayalon** see □ **Neteevey Ayalon.**
◇ **(Neteevey) Ayalon** see ◇ **Neteevey Ayalon.**
ha-yam הים **1.** *nm* the sea; **2.** colloquial reference to Israel's long Mediterranean waterfront in Tel-Aviv and other seaside towns.
□ **'Ayanot** ('Ayanot) עיינות *nm* educational institution (est. 1930) 3 km W. of **Nes Tseeyonah** (Ness Ziona). Classes in mechanized agriculture for boys and nursing for girls. Pop. 310.
'ayar|ah/-ot עיירה *nf* small town; **(+*of:* -at/'ayrot).**
◇ **'ayarat/'ayrot peetoo'akh** עיירת פיתוח *nf* development town i.e. any of smaller immigrant towns founded in the years 1950-1960 with the purpose of absorbing newly-arrived immigrants.
ayeh איה *adv* where.
ayeel/'eyl|eem איל *nm* ram; **(*pl+of:* -ey).**
ayeen אין *nm & adv* nothing; naught.
(me) ayeen מאין *adv* wherefrom.
(yesh me) ayeen יש מאין something out of nothing; creatio ex nihilo.
'ayeen (ע) ע"ין *nf* 16th letter of Hebrew alphabet; a guttural, pressed hiatus which has no parallel in English; is transliterated in this dictionary by '.
'ayeen 'ע numeral & adj in Hebrew numerical system (see Introduction) 70; 70th.
'ayeen/'eynayeem עין *nf* **1.** eye; **2.** spring; **3.** fountain; **(+*of:* 'eyn/-ey).**
'ayeen be-'ayeen עין בעין *adv* eye to eye.
'ayeen ha-ra' עין הרע *nf* evil eye.
(be) 'ayeen בעין *adv* **1.** in kind; **2.** visibly.
'ayeen takhat 'ayeen עין תחת עין an eye for an eye.
(be) 'ayeen tovah בעין טובה *adv* benevolently.
(be) 'ayeen yafah בעין יפה *adv* abundantly; willingly.
(blee) 'ayeen ha-ra' בלי עין הרע *adv* knock on wood!
(he'eef/-ah/he'aftee) 'ayeen העיף עין *v* threw an eye; cast a glance; **(*pres* me'eef *etc; fut* ya'eef *etc*).**
(he'el|eem/-eemah/-amtee) 'ayeen העלים עין *v* ignored; shut an eye; **(*pres* ma'aleem *etc; fut* ya'aleem *etc*).**
(ke-heref) 'ayeen כהרף עין *adv* in the twinkling of an eye.
(le-mar'eet) 'ayeen למראית עין *adv* on the face of it; seemingly.
(lo 'ats|am/-mah/-amtee) 'ayeen לא עצם עין *v* did not sleep a wink; **(*pres* 'eyno 'otsem *etc; fut* lo ya'atsom *etc*).**
(mar'eet) 'ayeen מראית עין *nf* appearance; semblance.
(tsadah) ha-'ayeen צדה העין *v pres & pst sing* the eye caught; **(*fut* tatsood *etc*).**
(tsar/-at) 'ayeen צר עין *adj* jealous; envious.
(tsaroot) 'ayeen צרות עין *nf* envy; jealousy.
'ay|eer/-areem עיר *nf* donkey foal; young ass.
'ayeet/'eyt|eem עיט *nf* vulture; **(*pl+of:* -ey).**
'ayef/-ah עייף *adj* tired.
'ayefoot עייפות *nf* fatigue; weariness.

□ **Ayelet Hashakhar** (Ayyelet haShakhar) איילת השחר *nm* kibbutz (est. 1918) and health-resort in Upper-Galilee, 8 km N. of **Rosh-Peenah**. Pop. 961.

haynoo-hakh היינו־הך all the same; makes no difference.

(de) haynoo דהיינו viz; namely.

hayo hayah/haytah היה היה *v m/f* once upon a time there was.

ayom/ayoomah איום *adj* terrible.

ayom איום *adv* terribly.

ayom ve-nora איום ונורא *adv* terribly indeed.

hayom היום *adv* today.

hayom ba-'erev היום בערב *adv* this evening; tonight.

haysher הישר *adv* directly; straight on ahead.

ayzen אייזן *adj & adv [slang]* excellent; top.

az אז *adv* then; therefore.

az mah? ?אז מה so what?

az mah be-khakh eem?! ?!אז מה בכך אם so what if ...

'az/-at nefesh עז־נפש *adj* audacious.

'az/-at paneem עז־פנים *adj* insolent; cheeky.

□ **'Azah** (Gazah) עזה *nf* historic Mediterranean town and onetime harbor and fortress of Canaanite, Philistine and Biblical fame. Gaza, as it is internationally known, is now the main town and political and administrative center of the so-called Gaza Strip, i.e. part of Palestine that in 1948 was taken over by Egypt and, following 1967 Six Day War, came under Israeli administration. Pop. 247,000 all Arab, comprises large numbers of 1948 refugees and their offsprings.

□ **(Retsoo'at) 'Azah** see □ **Retsoo'at 'Azah**.

az'ak|ah/-ot אזעקה *nf* alarm; **(**+*of:* **-at)**.

(tsefeer|at/-ot) az'akah צפירת אזעקה *nf* alarm signal.

haz'ak|ah/-ot הזעקה *nf* summoning; alert.

(ma'ar|ekhet/-khot) az'akah מערכת אזעקה *nf* alarm system.

(makh'sheer/-ey) az'akah מכשיר אזעקה *nm* alarm instrument.

(meet|kan/-eney) az'akah מיתקן אזעקה *nm* alarm apparatus.

az'ak|at/-ot emet אזעקת אמת *nf* true alarm.

az'ak|at/-ot neesayon אזעקת ניסיון *nf* alarm test.

az'ak|at/-ot shav אזעקת שווא *nf* false alarm.

az|al/-lah אזל *v* was sold out; run out; **(***pres* **ozel;** *fut* **ye'ezal)**.

hazn|ah/-ot הזנה *nf* feeding; **(**+*of:* **-at)**.

az|ar/-rah/-artee אזר *v* put in; girded; **(***pres* **ozer;** *fut* **ye'ezor)**.

azar *(etc)* **ko|'akh/-khot** אזר כוח *v* mustered strength.

'az|ar/-rah/-artee עזר *v* helped; **(***pres* **'ozer;** *fut* **ya'azor)**.

□ **'Azaryah** ('Azarya) עזריה *nm* village in the central plain (est. 1949), 5 km SE of Ramla. Pop. 485.

'az|av/-vah/-avtee עזב *v* left; abandoned; **(***pres* **'ozev;** *fut* **ya'azov)**.

azay אזי *adv* then.

haza|yah/-yot הזיה *nf* delusion; hallucination. **(**+*of:* **-yat)**.

hazaz|ah/-ot הזזה **1.** *nf* budging; sliding; shifting **(**+*of:* **-at)**; **2.** *adj* sliding; shifting.

(delet/daltot) hazazah דלת הזזה *nf* sliding door.

(khalon/-ot) hazazah חלון הזזה *nm* sliding window.

(trees/-ey) hazazah תריס הזזה *nm* sliding blind.

(halakh/-khah/-akhtee la) 'aza'zel הלך לעזאזל *v* went down the drain; went to hell; **(***pres* **holekh** *etc; fut* **yelekh** *etc***)**.

(la) 'aza'zel! !לעזאזל *interj* to hell! to hell with!

(lekh/-ee la) 'aza'zel! !לך לעזאזל *v imp sing (masc/fem) & interj* go to hell!

azeekeem אזיקים *nm pl* manacles; handcuffs; **(**+*of:* **-ey)**.

'azeev|ah/-ot עזיבה *nf* abandonment; desertion; **(**+*of:* **-at)**.

az'har|ah/-ot אזהרה *nf* warning; **(**+*of:* **-at)**.

(ot/-ot) az'harah אות אזהרה *nm* warning sign.

(sheveet|at/-ot) az'harah שביתת אזהרה *nf* warning strike.

haz'har|ah/-ot הזהרה *nf* warning; caution; **(**+*of:* **-at)**.

azkar|ah/-ot אזכרה *nf* commemoration; memorial service; **(**+*of:* **-at)**.

hazkar|ah/-ot הזכרה *nf* mentioning; reminding; **(**+*of:* **-at)**.

◇ **azkarat neshamot** see ◇ **hazkarat neshamot**.

hazman|ah/-ot הזמנה *nf* invitation; summons **(**+*of:* **-at)**.

hazmanah zoogeet הזמנה זוגית *nf* invitation for a couple.

(be) hazmanah בהזמנה *adv* (made) to order.

(le-fee) hazmanah לפי הזמנה **1.** *adj* made to order; **2.** *adv* by invitation.

(le) hazmanat להזמנת *adv* at the invitation/order of.

haznakh|ah/-ot הזנחה *nf* neglect; oversight; **(**+*of:* **-at)**.

'azoot עזות *nf* insolence.

'azoot-metsakh עזות מצח *nf* impertinence; cheek.

'azoov/-ah עזוב *adj* abandoned; deserted.

'azoov|ah/-ot עזובה *nf* desolation; desertion; **(**+*of:* **-at)**.

□ **Azor** אזור *nf* urban residential and industrial settlement (resettled 1948) 5 km SE of Tel-Aviv. Pop 7,460.

□ **Azore'a'** see □ **Ha-Zore'a'**.

azoreem (*sing:* **ezor)** אזורים *nm pl* areas; **(**+*of:* **azorey)**.

'azov!/'eezvee! !עזוב *v imp m/f* stop it! **(***inf* **la'azov;** *pst* **'azav;** *pres* **'ozev;** *fut* **ya'azov)**.

'azov otee עזוב אותי *[colloq.] v imp* leave me alone! let me go!

'azov otkha mee- עזוב אותך מ־ *[slang] v imp sing m* give up! forget about!

'azov shetooyot! עזוב שטויות *interj* don't be a fool!

(la) 'azov לעזוב *v inf* (to) leave; (to) abandon.

hazra'ah melakhooteet הזרעה מלאכותית *nf* artificial insemination.

hazrak|ah/-ot הזרקה *nf* inoculation; **(+*of:* -at)**.

hazram|ah/-ot הזרמה *nf* pouring in; causing to flow; **(+*of:* -at)**.

(ha) hazramah ההזרמה *nf* flooding with paper-money (in an inflationary economy).

□ **'Azree'el** ('Azriel) עזריאל *nm* village in Sharon (est. 1951), 7 km E. of Tel Mond. Pop. 381.

□ **'Azreekam** ('Azriqam) עזריקם *nm* village in Mediterranean Plain (est. 1950), 7 km SE of Ashdod. Pop. 501.

B.

transliterating the Hebrew consonant **Bet (ב)**

ba- ־ב *(prefix)* in the ...

ba/-'ah בא *v* came, arrived; **(*pst* ba; *fut* yavo)**.

ba/-'ah ba-yameem בא בימים *adj* elderly.

ba-'akeefeen בעקיפין *adv* indirectly.

ba-akhronah באחרונה *adv* lately; of late.

ba/-'ah 'al 'onsh|o/-ah בא על עונשו *v* met his/her punishment; **(*pst* ba *etc*; *fut* yavo *etc* *v=b*)**.

ba (*etc*) 'al sekhar|o/-ah בא על שכרו *v* got his/her remuneration/reward.

ba (*etc*) ba-yameem בא בימים *v* grew old.

ba (*etc*) bee-keshareem בא בקשרים *v* made contact; came in touch.

ba (*etc*) bee-merootsah בא במרוצה *v* came running.

ba (*etc*) be-kesher בא בקשר *v* came in touch.

ba (*etc*) be-kheshbon בא בחשבון *v* came into consideration.

bah בה *pron f* in her; about her.

bah be-sha'ah בה בשעה *adv* while; at the very time when.

(ba-khodesh ha) ba בחודש הבא *adv* next month; coming month.

ba/-'at ko'akh בא כוח *nmf* representative; attorney **(*pl:* -'ey *etc*)**.

ba (*etc*) lee/lo/lah בא לי *[slang] v* I/he/she felt like: I/she/he felt an urge.

ba (*etc*) lee-yedey heskem בא לידי הסכם *v* came to terms; reached agreement.

ba-shavoo'a ha-ba בשבוע הבא *adv* next week; coming week.

(barookh ha) ba!/-'ah! ברוך הבא! *interj m/f* welcome.

(ha) ba/-'ah הבא *adj* next.

(le-ha) ba (*npr* le-haba) להבא *adv* in the future; from now on.

(lo) ba/-'ah be-kheshbon לא בא בחשבון *v pres & adj* impossible; out of the question.

ba'al/be'aleem בעל *nm* husband; **(*pl+of:* ba'aley)**.

ba'al/-at בעל *nmf* owner; proprietor; **(*pl+of:* ba'aley)**.

ba'al/-ey 'agal|ah/-ot בעל עגלה *nm* coachman; wagon driver.

ba'al/-at bayeet בעל בית *nmf* landlord/-lady, master, host/-ess; **(*pl:* -ey bateem)**.

ba'al/-at breet בעל ברית *nmf* ally, confederate; **(*pl:* -ey breet)**.

ba'al dovor בעל־דבר *[slang] nm* the person in question.

ba'al/-at 'esek בעל עסק *nmf* business owner; **(*pl:* ba'aley 'asakeem)**.

ba'al ha-bayeet בעל הבית *nm* **1.** master; owner; **2.** host; **3.** boss; **4.** landlord.

ba'al/-at hakarah בעל הכרה *adj* fully aware person.

ba'al/-ey hon בעל הון *nm* **1.** capitalist; **2.** investor.

ba'al/-at keetsbah (*cpr* keetsvah) בעל־קיצבה *nmf* **1.** pensioner; **2.** one living on a pension or on a fixed allowance.

ba'al/-at keshareem בעל קשרים *[colloq.] nmf* well connected.

ba'al/-ey khayeem בעל־חיים *nm* animal; living creature.

ba'al/-at meektso'a בעל מקצוע *nmf* professional; a pro; **(*pl:* -ey *etc*)**.

ba'al/-ey meeshpakhah בעל משפחה *nm* family man.

ba'al/-ey melakhah בעל מלאכה *nm* craftsman; artisan.

ba'al/-at menayot (*pl:* -ey *etc*) בעל מניות shareholder.

ba'al/-at merets בעל מרץ *adj* energetic.

ba'al meroomeh בעל מרומה *nm* betrayed husband.

ba'al/-at meshek בעל משק *nmf* farm-owner; farmer.

ba'al/-at moom (*pl:* **-ey** *etc*) בעל מום **1.** *nmf* cripple; **2.** *adj* deformed.

ba'al/-at neesayon (*pl:* **-ey** *etc*) בעל ניסיון **1.** *nmf* man/woman of experience; **2.** *adj* experienced.

ba'al/-at seemkhah בעל שמחה *nmf* **1.** host/-ess; whoever gives the party; **2.** guest of honor.

ba'al tefeelah בעל תפילה *nm* (*cpr* **ba'al tefeeleh**) cantor; prayer-leader.

ba'al/-ey yekholet בעל יכולת *nm* person of means; capable.

ba'al/-tee בעל *v* (*masc. only*) had sexual intercourse; (*pres* **bo'el**; *fut* **yeev'al**; *v=b*).

ba'al|ah/-ee/-ekh בעלה *nm* (with possess. *pron* added) her/my/your husband.

ba'alat בעלת *nf* the (female) owner, mistress, boss of; proprietress.

ba-'aleel בעליל *adv* clearly; visibly.

ba'aley bateem בעלי בתים *nm pl* (*cpr* **balebateem**; *sing:* **ba'al bayeet**) landlords.

ba'aley khayeem בעלי חיים *nm pl* (*sing:* **ba'al khay**) animals; living creatures.

(tsa'ar) ba'aleykhayeem (בעלי חיים)צער *nm* **1.** pity for mistreated animals; **2.** prevention of cruelty to animals.

ba'aloo|t/-yot בעלות ownership.

(shootaf/-ah le) ba'aloot שותף לבעלות *nmf* co-owner.

ba'ar בער *nm* boor; ignorant person.

ba'ar/-ah/-tee בער *v* burned (*pres* **bo'er**; *fut* **yeev'ar**; *v=b*).

ba-areekhoot באריכות *adv* at length.

ba'aroo|t/-yot בערות *nf* illiteracy; ignorance.

ba'at/-ah/-etee בעט *v* kicked; spurned (*pres* **bo'et**; *fut* **yeev'at**; *v=b*).

ba-'atsaltayeem בעצלתיים *adv* lazily; very slowly.

ba-'avee ha-korah בעבי הקורה *adv* deeply into the matter.

ba-aveer באוויר *adv* in the air.

ba-aveer ha-patoo'akh באוויר הפתוח *adv* in the open air.

(shemeeneeyot) ba-aveer שמיניות באוויר *nf pl* doing the impossible.

ba-'avoor בעבור *adv* **1.** in consideration of; for; **2.** in retribution for.

ba'a|yah (*npr* **be'a|yah**)/**-yot** בעיה *nf* problem; difficulty; (*+of:* **-yat**).

ba'ayatee (*npr* **be'ayatee**)/**-t** בעייתי *adj* problematic.

(en) ba'ayot (*npr* **eyn be'ayot**) אין בעיות no problem; can be done.

('as|ah/-tah/-eetee) ba'ayot (*npr* **be'ayot**) עשה בעיות [*slang*] *v* made trouble (*pres* **'oseh** *etc*; *fut* **ya'aseh** *etc*).

('am|ad/-dah/-adetee) ba-bekheenah עמד בבחינה *v* passed the examination (*pres* **'omed** *etc*; *fut* **ya'amod** *etc*).

bablat בבל״ת [*slang*] *adj & adv* baloney (*acr of* **Beelbool Beytseem Le-lo Takhleet** בלבול ביצים ללא תכלית i.e. bothering someone's testicles for no reason).

(mer|ar/-erah/-artee) ba-bekhee (*npr* **bee-vkhee**) מירר בבכי *v* wept bitterly; (*pres* **memarer** *etc*; *fut* **yemarer** *etc*).

ba-boker בבוקר *adv* in the morning.

ba-boker hashkem בבוקר השכם *adv* early in the morning.

baboo|'ah/-'ot (*npr* **bavoo'ah**) בבואה *nf* reflection, image (*+of:* **-'at**).

bad/-eem בד *nm* cloth; linen; fabric (*pl+of:* **-ey**).

bad be-vad בד בבד *adv* alongside.

('al ha-) bad על הבד *adv* on the screen.

bad|ah/-etah/-eetee בדה *v* invented; concocted; thought up (*pres* **bodeh**; *fut* **yeevdeh**; *v=b*).

badad בדד *adv* alone; apart.

bad|ak/-kah/-aktee בדק *v* checked; examined (*pres* **bodek**; *fut* **yeevdok**; *v=b*).

ba-derekh בדרך *adv* on the way.

bad|ay/-a'eet בדאי *nmf* liar; fabricator.

badook/bedookah בדוק *adj* **1.** well-tested; **2.** authentic.

badooy/bedooyah בדוי *adj* imagined; imaginary; made up; fictional.

ba-'eer בעיר *adv* in town.

ba'eer/be'eerah בעיר *adj* combustible.

ba-'erev בערב *adv* in the evening.

ba-'esh באש *adv* in flames.

('al|ah/-tah) ba-'esh עלה באש *v* went up in flames (*pres* **'oleh** *etc*; *fut* **ya'aleh** *etc*).

(he'el|ah/-tah/-etee) ba-'esh העלה באש *v* set fire to (*pres* **ma'aleh** *etc*; *fut* **ya'aleh** *etc*).

bag|ad/-dah/-adetee בגד *v* **1.** betrayed; **2.** deceived (*pres* **boged**; *fut* **yeevgod**; *v=b*).

bagajneek בגאז׳ניק [*slang*] *nm* car's luggage compartment.

bag|ar/-rah/-artee בגר *v* matured (*pres* **meetbager**; *fut* **yeetbager**).

bagats בג״ץ **1.** *nm abbr.* (*acr of* **Bet deen Gavo'ah le-TSedek** בית דין גבוה לצדק) High Court of Justice; **2.** *nm* order nisi.

bagroot בגרות *nf* **1.** maturity; adulthood; **2.** matriculation

(bekheen|at/-ot) bagroot בחינת בגרות *nf* matriculation-exam.

(te'ood|at/-ot) bagroot תעודת בגרות *nf* matriculation certificate.

baheer/beheerah בהיר *adj* **1.** clear; **2.** bright; **3.** blond.

ba|hem/-hen בהם *pron pl - nmf* in them.

bak|a/-'ah/-a'tee בקע *v* broke through; penetrated (*pres* **boke'a**; *fut* **yeevka'**; *v=b*).

□ **Baka el-Garbeeye** (Baqa al-Gharbiyye) באקה אל־גארבייה *nm* Large Arab village in N. Sharon, 12 km SE of **Khaderah** (Hadera). Pop. 14,300.

bakar בקר *nm* cattle.

bakar|ah/-ot בקרה *nf* check; control (*+of:* **-at**).

bakash|ah/-ot בקשה *nf* request; petition (*+of:* **-at**).

(heeg|eesh/-eeshah/-ashtee) bakash|ah/-ot הגיש בקשה *v* petitioned; submitted petition (*pres* **mageesh** *etc; fut* **yageesh** *etc*).
bakbook/-eem בקבוק *nm* bottle (*pl+of:* **-ey**).
bakbook/-ey tav'erah בקבוק תבערה *nm* ignition bottle; "Molotov Cocktail".
bakee/bekee'ah בקי *adj* well-versed; expert.
bakh בך *pron f sing* **1.** you; **2.** in you; **3.** with you.
bakh|ah/-tah/-eetee בכה *v* wept, cried (*pres* **bokheh**; *fut* **yeevkeh**; *(v=b); kh=k*).
bakhan/-ah/-tee בחן *v* examined (*pres* **bokhen**; *fut* **yeevkhan**; *v=b*).
□ **Bakhan (Bahan)** בחן *nm* kibbutz (est. 1953) in NW Samaria , 4 km N. of **Toolkarem**. Pop. 325.
bakhar/-ah/-artee בחר *v* chose; elected (*pres* **bokher**; *fut* **yeevkhar**; *v=b*).
bakhash/-ah/-tee בחש *v* meddled; stirred; mixed (*pres* **bokhesh**; *fut* **yeevkhosh**; *v=b*).
ba-khashay בחשאי *adv* **1.** secretly; **2.** quietly; noiselessly.
ba-khatsee peh בחצי־פה *adv* half-heartedly.
ba-khazarah בחזרה *adv* back; backward; on the way back.
bakheer/bekheerah בכיר *adj* senior.
(marts|eh/-ah) bakheer/bekheerah מרצה בכיר *nmf* senior lecturer.
(pakeed/pekeedah) bakheer/bekheerah פקיד בכיר *nmf* senior official.
bakhem בכם *pron pl m nf* **1.** you; **2.** in you; **3.** with you (addressing several males, or males and females).
bakhen בכן *pron pl f* **1.** you; **2.** in you; **3.** with you (addressing several persons, all female).
(ro'eh/ro'ah) ba-kokhaveem רואה בכוכבים *nmf* astrologer; stargazer.
bakhoor/-eem בחור *nm* **1.** young fellow; **2.** fellow; guy; **3.** boyfriend (*pl+of:* **-ey**).
bakhoor ka-'erez בחור כארז *nm* a top-class guy.
bakhoor/-ey yesheevah בחור ישיבה *nm* student of a Rabbinical School; "Yeshivah"-student.
bakhoor|ah/-ot בחורה *nf* **1.** girl; **2.** lass; **3.** girlfriend (*+of:* **-at**).
bakhoorah ka-halakhah בחורה כהלכה *nf* an excellent girl.
bakhoorcheek/-eem בחורצ׳יק *[slang] nm* young lad; young chap.
ba-kol בכול *adv* in everything.
ba-kol mee-kol kol בכול מכול כול *adv* lock, stock and barrel.
ba-krav בקרב *adv* in battle.
bal בל not; don't.
bal- בל־ *(prefix)* un-, -less.
bal yeesafer/teesafer בל ייספר *adj* countless.
bal|ah/-tah/-eetee בלה *v* wore out (*pres* **baleh**; *fut* **yeevleh**; *v=b*).
bal|a'/-'ah/-a'tee בלע *v* swallowed; absorbed (*pres* **bole'a**; *fut* **yeevla'**; *v=b*).
balad|ah/-ot בלדה *nf* ballad.
(mee) bal'adey מבלעדי *adv* apart from; except.
(deer) balak דיר בלק *[slang] (Arab.) interj* beware! take care! I warn you!
bal|am/-mah/-amtee בלם *v* **1.** applied brakes; **2.** contained (*pres* **bolem**; *fut* **yeevlom**; *v=b*).
balam (*npr* **belem**) בלם brake (motor-car); (*pl:* **blameem**; *pl+of:* **beelmey**).
balam-yad בלם יד *nm* hand brake.
balagan/-eem בלגן *[slang] nm* confusion; "snafu".
balash/-eet בלש *nmf* detective (*pl:* **-eem**; *+of:* **-ey**).
bal|ash/-shah/-ashtee בלש *v* spied; did detective work (*pres* **bolesh**; *fut* **yeevlosh**; *v=b*).
balash בלאש *[slang] (Arab.) adv* nevermind, free of charge.
(seeneema) balash סינמה בלאש *[slang] (Arab.) nm* making a show of it.
bal|at/-tah/-atetee בלט *v* stood out (*pres* **bolet**; *fut* **yeevlot**; *v=b*).
balat|ah/-ot בלטה *[slang] nf* tile (*+of:* **-at**).
□ **Balata** בלטה *nm* Arab village and refugee-camp at the SE outskirts of Nablus.
ba-laylah בלילה *adv* at night.
(khakham) ba-laylah חכם בלילה *[slang]* think/-s your/himself clever (sarcastically).
balebateem בעלי בתים *nm pl [colloq.]* **1.** bosses; **2.** masters; **3.** landlords.
bal|eh/-ah בלה *adj* worn out.
balet/-eem בלט *nm* ballet.
□ **Balfooryah** בלפוריה *nm* village in Yeezre'el Valley, 2 km N. of **'Afoolah** (Afula). Pop. 257.
baloot|ah/-ot בלוטה *nf* gland (*+of:* **-at**).
balooy/blooyah בלוי *adj* worn out; sagged.
balshan/-eet בלשן *nmf* linguist (*pl+of:* **-ey**).
balshanoot בלשנות *nf* linguistics.
baloom/bloomah בלום *adj* **1.** rich; comprehensive **2.** braked.
(otsar) baloom אוצר בלום *nm* a mine of information.
bam|ah/-ot במה *nf* stage; rostrum; (*+of:* **-at**).
bama|y/-'eet במאי *nm* stage director (*pl+of:* **-'ey**).
ba-meh במה wherewith; what with.
('am|ad/-dah/-adetee) ba-meevkhan עמד (במיבחן) *v* passed the test; made it; (*pres* **'omed** *etc; fut* **ya'amod** *etc*).
ban|ah/-tah/-eetee בנה *v* built; constructed (*pres* **boneh**; *fut* **yeevneh**; *v=b*).
banalee/-t בנאלי *adj* banal.
banan|ah/-ot בננה *nf* banana (*+of:* **-at**).
bana|y/-'eem בנאי *nm* builder; mason; (*pl+of:* **-'ey**).
ba-needon בנידון in the matter under consideration.
baneem (*sing:* **ben**) בנים *nm pl* **1.** sons **2.** boys; young male persons; (*pl+of:* **beney**).
('am|ad/-dah/-adetee) ba-neesayon עמד בניסיון *v* **1.** stood the test; **2.** resisted temptation (*pres* **'omed** *etc; fut* **ya'amod** *etc*).

ba-nekhar בניכר *adv* on foreign soil.
bank/-eem בנק *nm* bank.
bank|a'ee (*npr sing* **-ay**) בנקאי *nm* banker; (*pl:* **-a'eem**; *pl+of:* **-a'ey**).
banka'ee/-t בנקאי *adj* bank; banking.
(**'arvoo|t/-yot**) **banka'ee|t/-yot** ערבות(בנקאית) *nf* bank guaranty; bank warranty.
(**reebeet**) **banka'eet** ריבית(בנקאית) *nf* bank interest rate.
bank|ay/-a'eem בנקאי *nm* banker; (*pl+of:* **-a'ey**).
banot (*sing:* **bat**) בנות *nf pl* **1.** daughters **2.** *[colloq.]* girls; young women; (*pl+of:* **benot**).
banoo בנו *pron pl mf* in us; us.
banooy/benooyah בנוי *adj* built.
(**shetakh**) **banooy** שטח בנוי *nm* built-up area.
□ **Banyas** (Banias) בניאס *nm* picturesque waterfall and nature reserve in the Golan Heights, NE of **Keeryat Shemonah**.
ba-paneem בפנים *adv* in one's face.
(**'am|ad/-dah/-adetee**) **ba-perets** עמד בפרץ *v* stepped into the breach; (*pres* **'omed** *etc; fut* **ya'amod** *etc*).
bar בר **1.** *nm* grain, cereals; **2.** *adj* open field; wild.
bar/-eem בר *nm* bar (where drinks are served).
bar/bat kayama בר־קיימא *adj* durable.
bar/bat keetsbah בר־קצבה *nmf & adj* pensionable.
bar/bat mazal בר־מזל *adj* lucky, fortunate.
◇ **bar-meetsvah** בר־מצווה *nm* **1.** "Bar-Mitzvah" - 13th birthday of a Jewish boy, on which day one is deemed to have reached maturity (from the religious point of view); **2.** a young Jewish male aged 13 or more.
bar/bat 'onsheen בר־עונשין *adj* answerable to the law.
bar/bat samkha בר־סמכא *nmf* competent; authority.
bar/bat tokef בר־תוקף *adj* valid.
(**'esev/'eesvey**) **bar** עשב בר *nm* weed.
(**perakh/peerkhey**) **bar** פרח בר *nm* field flower.
bar|a/-'ah/-atee ברא *v* created; (*pres* **bore**; *fut* **yeevra**; *v=b*).
(**tamah oo**) **barah** תמה וברה *adj f* pure and innocent.
ba-rabeem ברבים *adv* publicly.
barad ברד *nm* hail.
barak/brakeem ברק *nm* **1.** lightning; **2.** glitter; (*pl+of:* **beerkey**).
□ **Barak** ברק *nm* village (founded 1956) in Yizre'el Valley, 8 km SE of Meggido. Pop. 245.
□ **Bar'am** ברעם *nm* kibbutz (founded 1949) near Lebanese border, 5 km NE of **Tsomet Kheeram** (Hiram Junction). Pop. 431.
ba-ramah ברמה **1.** *[colloq.] adv* in the Golan Heights; **2.** *adv* aloud.
bar|ar/-erah/-artee ברר *v* selected; picked (*pres* **borer**; *fut* **yeevror**; *v=b*).
barboor/-eem ברבור *nm* swan (*pl+of:* **-ey**).
bardak ברדק *[slang] nm* upheaval; pandemonium.
baree/bree'ah בריא *adj* healthy; sound.
baree/bree'ah ve/'oo shalem/shlemah בריא ושלם *adj* safe and sound; in perfect health.
□ **Bareket** (Bareqet) ברקת *nm* village (founded 1952) 5 km 4 NE of Ben Gurion Airport. Pop. 526.
□ **Bar-Geeyora** (Bar-Giyyora) בר־גיורא *nm* village (founded 1950) and youth hostel in Judean Hills, 15 km SW of Jerusalem. Pop. 264.
□ **Barkan** ברקן *nm* village in Samaria (est 1981), 7 km W. of **Aree'el**. Pop. 425.
□ **Barkay** (Barqay) ברקאי *nm* kibbutz (founded 1947) in NE Sharon, S. of **Tsomet 'Eeron** (Iron junction). Pop. 499.
barkhash/-eem ברחש *nm* mite (*pl+of:* **-ey**).
barnash/-eem ברנש *nm* guy; fellow.
ba-reeshonah בראשונה *adv* **1.** for the first time; **2.** at first.
barookh/brookhah ברוך *adj* blessed.
barookh/brookhah ha-ba/-'ah ברוך הבא greeting of welcome (addressing male/female).
barookh/brookhah ha-neemts|a/-et ברוך הנמצא greeting *m/f* reply to **barookh ha-ba**.
barookh ha-shem ברוך השם *interj* thank God!
(**ha-kadosh**) **barookhhoo** הקדוש ברוך הוא *nm* the Holy one, blessed be He; God.
baroor/broorah ברור *adj* evident, clear.
baroor/broorah ka-shemesh ברור כשמש *adj* clear as the day.
barvaz/-eem ברווז *nm* drake; (*pl+of:* **-ey**).
barvaz|ah/-ot ברווזה *nf* duck.
barvaz 'eetona'ee ברווז עיתונאי *nm* a canard.
barzel/-eem ברזל *nm* iron.
barzel yetseekah ברזל־יציקה *nm* cast iron.
(**khoot/-ey**) **barzel** חוט ברזל *nm* wire; iron wire.
(**masakh ha**) **barzel** מסך הברזל *nm* (the) Iron Curtain.
(**meseel|at/-ot**) **barzel** מסילת ברזל *nf* railroad, railway.
bas/-eem בס *nm* bass (Music).
basar/besareem בשר **1.** meat; **2.** flesh (*+of:* **besar**).
basar va-dam בשר ודם *nm* mortal; of flesh and blood; human being.
(**merak**) **basar** מרק בשר *nm* meat soup.
(**she'er/-ey**) **basar** שאר בשר *nm* kinsman; blood relative.
basees/besees|eem בסיס *nm* **1.** basis; **2.** base (milit.); (*pl+of:* **-ey**).
basees tseva'ee בסיס צבאי *nm* military base.
ba-sefar בספר *adv* in the border district.
ba-seter בסתר *adv* in secret; secretly.
ba-sfar בספר *adv* in the border district.
ba-shavoo'a ha-ba בשבוע הבא *adv* next week.
bashel/beshelah בשל *adj* mature; ripe.
ba-shevee בשבי *adv* in captivity.
ba-sof בסוף *adv* in the end; finally.
bat/banot בת *nf* **1.** daughter; **2.** girl; young female; (*pl+of:* **benot**).

bat (followed by a numeral) ...בת *adj f* aged...
bat/benot almavet בת־אלמוות *adj f* immortal.
bat/benot 'aroobah בת־ערובה *nf* female hostage.
bat-dodah/benot dodot בת־דודה *[colloq.] nf* female cousin.
□ **Bat-Galeem** (Bat Gallim) בת־גלים *nf* popular residential quarter of downtown Haifa, on the waterfront, near the S. entrance to the city.
bat/benot khavah בת־חווה *nf* (*lit.*: daughter of Eve) woman; female.
bat/banot khor|eget/-got בת חורגת *nf* step-daughter.
bat-kol בת־קול *nf* **1.** divine voice; **2.** echo.
◇ **bat-meetsvah** בת־מצווה *nf* celebration of 12th (13th in U.S.) birthday of a Jewish girl, on which day she is deemed to have reached puberty (from religious and social point of view).
bat/benot ta'arovet בת־תערובת *nf* of mixed parentage; halfbreed (female).
□ **Bat-Shlomo** (Bat-Shelomo) בת שלמה *nf* village (est. 1889), 5 km 70 NE of **Zeekhron-Ya'akov**. Pop. 246.
□ **Batsrah (Bazera)** בצרה *nf nm* village (founded 1946) in Sharon, 4 km N. of **Tsomet Ra'ananah** (Ra'anana Junction). Pop. 412.
bat-tsekhok בת־צחוק *nf* smile.
□ **Bat-Yam** בת־ים *nf* suburban town (est. 1926) on Mediterranean seashore, 8 km S. of Tel-Aviv. Is actually the S. continuation of the latter's twin-town Jaffa **(Yafo)** and forms part of Greater Tel-Aviv. Pop. 141,300.
bat-yekheedah בת יחידה *nf* only daughter.
bat-zekooneem בת־זקונים *nf* daughter of one's old age.
bat/benot zoog בת־זוג *nf* mate; spouse; female partner.
(khevr|at/-ot) bat חברת בת *nf* subsidiary (company).
bat|akh/-khah/-akhtee בטח *v* trusted; relied on/upon (*pres* **bote'akh**; *fut* **yeevtakh**; *v=b*).
batal|ah בטלה *nf* idleness (*+of:* **-at**).
(demey) batalah דמי בטלה *nm* dole; attendance fee for unemployed; (correct term: **demey avtalah**).
(sekhar) batalah שכר בטלה *nm* dole; attendance fee for unemployed.
ba-tavekh בתווך *adv* in the middle; in the center.
ba-tekheelah בתחילה *adv* in the beginning.
batel/betelah בטל *adj* **1.** null; **2.** idle; **3.** *v pres* ceases to be binding (a law agreement).
(hal|akh/-khah/-akhtee) batel הלך בטל *v* idled; was idle (*pres* **holekh** *etc; fut* **yelekh** *etc*).
('over/-et) batel עובר בטל *nmf & adj* senile.
bateree|yah/-yot בטרייה *nf* battery (*+of:* **-yat**).
batlan/-eem בטלן *nm* idler; impractical person; (*pl+of:* **-ey**).
batlanoot בטלנות *nf* inefficiency; lack of practical approach.
('al|ah/-tah) ba-tohoo עלה בתוהו *v* went to nought (*pres* **'oleh** *etc; fut* **ya'aleh** *etc*).
batookh|ah/-ot בטוחה *nf* security; (*+of:* **-at**).
ba-tor בתור *adv* in line; in the queue.
batsal/betsaleem בצל *nm* onion; bulb (*pl+of:* **beetsley**).
batseer בציר *nm* vintage (*+of:* **betseer**).
batsek בצק *nm* dough; pastry.
batseket בצקת *nf* edema.
batsor|et/-ot בצורת *nf* drought.
ba-tsohorayeem בצהריים *adv* at noon.
ba-tsover בצובר *adv* bulk; in bulk.
(mer|ar/-erah/-artee) be-vekhee מירר בבכי *v* wept bitterly (*pres* **memarer** *etc; fut* **yemarer** *etc*).
◇ **bavel** בבל *nf* biblical Babylon (present day Iraq).
◇ **(meegdal) bavel** see ◇ **meegdal bavel**.
bayeet/bateem בית *nm* house, home (*+of:* **bet/batey**).
bayeet/bateem doo-komatee/-yeem בית דו־קומתי *nm* two-storey house.
bayeet/bateem meshootaf/-eem בית משותף *nm* condo.
bayeet/bateem rav-komatee/-yeem בית רב־קומתי *nm* multi-storied house.
◇ **bayeet reeshon** בית ראשון (hist.) *nm* the First Temple (King Solomon's) and its era (Bibl.).
◇ **bayeet shenee** בית שני (hist.) *nm* the Second Temple (destroyed in 70 C.E.) and its era.
bayeet telat-komatee בית תלת־קומתי *nm* three-storey building.
('ak|eret/-rot) bayeet עקרת בית *nf* housewife.
(ben/bat) bayeet בן בית *nmf* insider; intimate, close friend.
◇ **(ha)bayeet (ha)lavan** הבית הלבן *nm* the White House.
(khanookat ha) bayeet חנוכת הבית *nf* housewarming.
□ **(har ha) bayeet** הר הבית *nm* the Temple Mount in the Old City of Jerusalem (site of the 1st and 2nd Temples).
(khas|ar/-rat) bayeet חסר בית *adj* homeless.
(kley) bayeet כלי בית *nm pl* houseware.
(meshek) bayeet משק בית *nm* **1.** household; **2.** housework.
(shelom) bayeet שלום בית *nm* domestic peace.
(yah) bayey! יא באיי *[slang] (Arab.) interj* exclamation expressing excitement over something.
ba-yom ביום *adv* in daytime.
(bo) bayom בו ביום *adv* on the very selfsame day.
bayshan/-eet ביישן **1.** *nmf & adj* shy person, shy; **2.** *adj* ashamed.
(ha) baytah הביתה **1.** *adv* homeward; **2.** *interj* let's go home!
(hal|akh/-khah/-akhtee) ha-baytah הלך הביתה *v* went home; (*pres* **holekh** *etc; fut* **yelekh** *etc*).
baz/-eem בז *nm* falcon (*pl+of:* **-ey**).

bazah/-tah/-eetee בזה *v* despised (*pres* **baz**; *fut* **yeevzeh**; *v=b*).
bazak בזק *nm* lightning.
(bee-meheeroot ha) bazak במהירות הבזק *adv* with lightning speed.
bazelet בזלת *nf* basalt.
ba-zman בזמן *adv* on time; in time.
be- ־ב *pref* in.
be'ad בעד *prep* **1.** for; **2.** in favor of; **3.** on behalf of.
be-akhrayoot באחריות *adv* guaranteed; on the responibility of.
be-'al korkh|o/-ah בעל כורחו *adv mf* against one's will, reluctantly.
be-'al peh בעל פה *adv* by heart; orally.
◇ **(torah she) be-'al peh** see ◇ **torah she-be-'al peh**.
be'aleem (*sing:* **ba'al**) בעלים *nm pl* **1.** husbands; **2.** owners.
(ha) be'aleem (ה(בעלים *nm* owner; proprietor.
be-'am בע"מ *abbr.* (*acr of* **BE-'Eravon Moogbal**) B.M., Ltd., Inc.
(keshet) be-'anan קשת בענן *nf* rainbow.
be-'arba' 'eynayeem בארבע עיניים *adv* tete a tete; between the two of us/them.
be-'atsaltayeem (*npr* **ba-'atsaltayeem**) בעצלתיים *adv* lazily; very slowly.
be-'atsm|ah/-am/-an בעצמה *pron* by herself/themselves *mf*.
be-'atsm|ee/-ekha/-ekh/-enoo בעצמי/בעצמך/ בעצמנו *pron* by myself/yourselves (*m/f*)/ourselves.
be-'atsm|o/-ekhem/-ekhen בעצמו/בעצמכם/ בעצמכן *pron m/f* by himself/yourselves.
(mekhoon|as/-eset) be-'atsm|o/-ah מכונס בעצמו *adj* introspective.
be-'avar בעבר *adj* in the past.
be'a|yah/-yot בעיה *nf* problem; difficulty; (*+of:* **-yat**).
be'ayatee/-t בעייתי *adj* problematic.
en (*or* **eyn**) **be'ayot** אין בעיות no problem; can be done.
('as|ah/-tah/-eetee) be'ayot עשה בעיות *[slang] v* made trouble (*pres* **'oseh** *etc; fut* **ya'aseh** *etc*).
('or|er/-erah/-artee) be'a|yah/-yot עורר בעיה *v* raised a problem (*pres* **me'orer** *etc; fut* **ye'orer** *etc*).
be-'ayeen בעין *adv* actually; in kind.
be-'ayeen tovah בעין טובה *adv* benevolently.
be-'ayeen yafah בעין יפה *adv* generously, willingly.
('ayeen) be-'ayeen עין בעין *adv* eye to eye.
be'ayot בעיות *nf pl* (*sing:* **be'ayah**) problems, troubles.
be-da'at|ee/-kha/-ekh/-o/-ah בדעתי *v* it is my/your/his/her/etc intention.
('al|ah/-tah) be-da'at|ee/-o/-ah *etc* עלה בדעתו *v* it occurred to him/her/me (*pres* **'oleh** *etc; fut* **ya'aleh** *etc*).
bedal/beedley seegaree|yah/-yot בדל סיגריה *nm* cigarette butt.
be-daykanoot בדייקנות *adv* meticulously; accurately.
be-dee'avad בדיעבד *adv* **1.** post factum; **2.** as a matter of fact.
('am|ad/-dah/-adetee) be-deeboor עמד בדיבור *v* kept his/her/my word (*pres* **'omed** *etc; fut* **ya'amod** *etc*).
bedeed/-eem בדיד *nm* **1.** spade; **2.** rod (*pl+of:* **-ey**).
bedeedoot בדידות *nf* solitude, loneliness.
bedeek|ah/-ot בדיקה *nf* **1.** test; **2.** check, inspection (*+of:* **-at**).
bedeek|at/-ot dam בדיקת דם *nf* blood-test.
bedeek|at/-ot sheten בדיקת שתן *nf* urine analysis.
bedeekh|ah/-ot בדיחה *nf* anecdote; joke; (*+of:* **-at**).
be-derekh ha-teva' בדרך הטבע *adv* naturally; in the course of nature.
be-derekh klal בדרך כלל *adv* generally; as a rule.
be-dokhak בדוחק *adv* with difficulty.
□ **Bedolakh (Bedolah)** בדולח *nm* village in Gaza Strip, S. of **Kateef** Block near Egyptian border.
bedoo'ee/-t בדואי **1.** *nmf* Bedouin; **2.** *adj* pertaining to Bedouins.
bedvee/-t בדוי **1.** *nmf* Bedouin; **2.** *adj* pertaining to Bedouins.
bee- ־ב *prep* (*pref*) in, in the (used instead of be- when prefixed to a word that starts with an unvowelled consonant).
bee-brakhah (*npr* **bee-vrakhah**) בברכה **1.** with blessing; regards; **2.** yours truly.
bee-demee ha-layeel בדמי הליל *adv* in the dead of the night.
bee-demee yam|av/-ehah בדמי ימיו *adv* in the prime of his/her life.
beedood בידוד *nm* **1.** isolation; **2.** insulation.
beedoor/-eem בידור *nm* entertainment; amusement (*pl+of:* **-ey**).
bee-dvar בדבר *prep* regarding.
be-'eekar בעיקר *adv* mainly; primarily.
be-eekhoor באיחור *adv* belatedly.
be-'eekvot בעיקבות *adv* **1.** following; **2.** in the steps of.
be'eel|ah/-ot בעילה *nf* sexual intercourse; (*+of:* **-at**).
be-'een|yan/-yeney בעניין **1.** *adv* with interest; interestedly; **2.** *prep* in the matter/-s of.
bee|'er/-'arah/-'artee ביער *v* mopped up, exterminated (*pres* **meva'er**; *fut* **yeva'er**).
be-eeshon laylah באישון לילה *adv* in the middle of the night.
be-'eet|ah/-ot בעיטה *nf* kick; (*+of:* **-at**).
be-'eet|o/-ah בעיתו *adv* timely; in proper time.
(she-lo) be-'eet|o/-ah שלא בעיתו *adv* at the wrong time.
be-efes ma'aseh באפס מעשה *adv* with nothing to do.
bee-fekoodat (*f=p*) בפקודת *adv* by order of.

bee-fleeleem *(f=p)* בפלילים *adv* under criminal prosecution; criminally prosecuted.
bee-fneem בפנים *adv* inside; within.
(mee) bee-fneem מבפנים *adv* from the inside.
bee-fney בפני *prep* versus, in front of.
('am|ad/-dah/-adetee) bee-fney עמד בפני *v* **1.** faced; **2.** resisted **(***pres* **'omed** *etc; fut* **ya'amod** *etc***).**
bee-frat בפרט *adv* specially, particularly.
bee-fros בפרוס *adv* on the eve of.
bee-frotrot בפרוטרוט *adv* in detail.
beegdey khag (*sing:* **beged khag)** בגדי־חג *nm pl* **1.** Sabbath best; Sunday best; **2.** *lit* : holiday clothes.
beegdey srad בגדי־שרד *nm pl* uniform (*sing:* **beged srad).**
bee-gdolot בגדולות *adv* in a big way.
(heel|ekh/-khah/-akhtee) bee-gdolot הילך בגדולות *v* saw big; aspired to great things.
bee-glal בגלל *prep* on account of; because of.
bee-gnevah (*or:* **geneyvah)** בגניבה *adv* stealthily; furtively.
bee-gnoot בגנות *adv* in defamation of; in discreditation of.
beek'ah/beka'ot בקעה *nf* valley **(***+of:* **beek|'at/-'ot).**
□ **(ha)beek'ah** הבקעה *nf* (*lit.:* the valley) colloqial reference to the Jordan Valley.
beek|a' (or **beeke'a')/-'ah/-a'tee** ביקע *v* split, cleaved **(***pres* **mevake'a;** *fut* **yevak|a'** *(v=b)***).**
beek|er/-rah/-artee ביכר *v* preferred **(***pres* **mevaker;** *fut* **yevaker** *(v=b)***).**
beek|er/-rah/-artee ביקר *v* **1.** visited; **2.** criticized **(***pres* **mevaker;** *fut* **yevaker** *(v=b)***).**
beek|esh/-shah/-ashtee ביקש *v* **1.** requested, begged; **2.** demanded; **3.** attempted, tried **(***pres* **mevakesh;** *fut* **yevakesh** *(v=b)***).**
beekesh (*etc***) la'asot** ביקש לעשות *v* tried/wanted to do.
beekesh (*etc***) rakhameem** ביקש רחמים *v* begged for mercy.
beekesh (*etc***) reshoot** ביקש רשות *v* asked permission.
bee-ketsarah בקצרה *adv* in short.
bee-kets|eh/-ot בקצה *adv* at the edge of.
bee-kfeedah בקפידה *adv* thoroughly, meticulously.
bee-khedee בכדי *adv* in vain.
(lo) bee-khedee לא בכדי *adv* not without reason.
bee-khedey בכדי *prep* so that, in order to.
bee-khedey she- בכדי ש־ *prep* in order that, so as to.
bee-khefeefah akhat בכפיפה אחת *adv* together; side by side.
bee-khefeefoot le- בכפיפות ל־ *adv* subject to.
bee-khelal בכלל *adv* generally, in general.
bee-khelal zeh בכלל זה *adv* which includes, including.
(ve-'ad) bee-khelal ועד בכלל *adv* including (date); inclusive.
bee-khetav בכתב *adv* in writing.
bee-khevedoot בכבידות *adv* with difficulty.
bee-khevod|o/-ah oo-ve-'atsm|o/-ah בכבודו ובעצמו *adv* in person; him/her -self.
beekoor/-eem ביקור *nm* visit; **(***pl+of:* **-ey).**
beekoor/-ey bayeet ביקור בית *nm* house call (by a physician).
beekoor kholeem ביקור חולים *nm* visiting the sick.
(kartees/-ey) beekoor כרטיס ביקור *nm* visiting card.
beekoor|eem ביכורים *nm pl* first fruit harvest **(***+of:* **-ey).**
beekoosh/-eem ביקוש *nm* demand **(***pl+of:* **-ey).**
(hetse'a oo) beekoosh (*npr:* **veekoosh)** היצע וביקוש *nm & nm* supply and demand.
beekor|et/-ot ביקורת *nf* **1.** inspection; **2.** criticism; **3.** critical review.
(mat|akh/-khah/-akhtee) beekoret מתח ביקורת *v* criticized **(***pres* **mote'akh** *etc; fut* **yeemtakh** *etc***).**
(meteekhat) beekoret מתיחת ביקורת *nf* criticizing.
beekortee/-t ביקורתי *adj* critical.
bee-kreeroot בקרירות *adv* with indifference.
beekt|ah/-ot בקתה *nf* shed, hovel **(***+of:* **-at).**
bee-kvee'oot בקביעות *adv* regularly.
beel|ah/-tah/-eetee בילה *v* spent time; **(***pres* **mevaleh;** *fut* **yevaleh;** *(v=b)***).**
beelah (*etc***) ba-ne'eemeem** בילה בנעימים *v* had a good time.
beel'ad|ay/-ekha/-ayeekh/-av/-eha בלעדי without me/you (*m/f*)/him/her.
beel'adee/-t בלעדי *adj* exclusive.
beel'adey בלעדי *prep* without; apart from.
beelb|el/-elah/-altee בלבל *v* confused; mixed up **(***pres* **mevalbel;** *fut* **yevalbel;** *(v=b)***).**
beelbool/-eem בלבול *nm* disorder, confusion; **(***pl+of:* **-ey).**
beelbool/-ey mo'akh בלבול מוח *nm* (*figurat.*) confusion, headache.
beelbool/-ey rosh בלבול ראש *nm* bother; confusion.
beel|ef/-fah/-aftee בילף *v* bluffed **(***pres* **mebalef;** *fut* **yebalef).**
bee-levad בלבד *adv* only; but.
◇ **BEELOO** ביל״ו *nf* **(***hist.***)** the movement that brought the first pioneer settlers to Palestine in 1880 (mainly from Tzarist Russia, following a wave of pogroms there). Its name was the *acr of* their guiding slogan: **BEt Ya'akov, Lekhoo Ve-nelkhah!**בית יעקב לכו ונלכה! (i.e. People of Jacob, let us go!).
beeloo|y/-yeem בילוי *nm* pastime; entertainment; **(***pl+of:* **-yey).**
beelooy na'eem! בילוי נעים! *interj* have a good time!
◇ **(ha)beelooyeem** ביל״ויים **(***sing:* **Beelooyee)** members and offsprings of the **Beeloo** (Bilu) group of pioneers of the First (1880) Jewish Repatriation to Palestine (see above).
beeltee בלתי *prep* not, un-, in-.

beeltee eem בלתי אם *prep* unless.

◇ **beeltee legalee/-t** בלתי ליגלי (*hist.* colloq.) *nmf* Jewish immigrant entered into Palestine "illegally" in British Mandate days (1920-1948).

beeltee maspeek/-ah בלתי מספיק *adj* insufficient.

beeltee maspeek/-eem בלתי מספיק *[colloq.] nm* insufficient (mark).

beeltee meeflagtee/-t בלתי מפלגתי *adj* non-partisan.

beeltee me'ookhl|as/-eset בלתי מאוכלס *adj* uninhabited.

beeltee meroos|an/-enet בלתי מרוסן *adj* unbridled.

beeltee moo|kar/-keret בלתי מוכר *adj* unknown.

beeltee neesb|al/-elet בלתי נסבל *adj* intolerable.

beeltee talooy/tlooyah בלתי תלוי *adj* independent.

◇ **beeltee tsamood/tsemoodah** בלתי צמוד *adj* not linked (i.e. of a loan or investment that is not linked to any hard currency or to the C.O.L Index).

beeltee yadoo'a'/yedoo'ah בלתי ידוע *nm* unknown.

(she-en) beelt|o/-ah (*or:* **she-eyn** *etc*) שאין בלתו *adj* unique; exclusive.

bee-lvad בלבד *adv* only; but.

bee-meforash במפורש *adv* distinctly; explicitly; unequivocally.

bee-meheeroot במהירות *adv* quickly.

bee-meheeroot ha-bazak במהירות הבזק *adv* with the speed of lightning.

bee-meherah במהרה *adv* shortly; rapidly.

bee-mehoopakh במהופך *adv* upside down.

bee-mekhoovan במכוון *adv* on purpose; deliberately, intentionally.

bee-mekom (*cpr* **bee-mkom**) במקום *adv* in the place of; instead of; in lieu of.

bee-mekom|ee/-kha/-ekh/-o/-ah במקומי *adv & pron* in my/your (*m/f*)/his/her place.

bee-memootsa' בממוצע *adv* on the average; averaging.

bee-meroomaz במרומז *adv* implying; by innuendo.

bee-merootsah במרוצה *adv* running.

be-emet באמת *adv* indeed, truly.

bee-metsee'oot (*npr* **ba-mtsee'oot**) במציאות *adv* in reality.

bee-metsoraf במצורף *adv* **1.** herewith enclosed; **2.** therewith enclosed.

bee-mevookhah במבוכה *adv* in confusion.

bee-meyookhad במיוחד *adv* especially.

beemoo|y/-yeem בימוי *nm* stage-direction; (*pl+of:* **-yey**).

bee-mrootsah במרוצה *adv* running.

be-emtsa' באמצע *adv* in the middle.

be-emtsa'oot באמצעות *adv* by means of.

be-en באין *pref* in the absence of; lacking.

been|ah בינה *nf* wisdom, comprehension; (*+of:* **-at**).

(neesgav mee)beenat|ee/-o/-ah נשגב מבינתי it is beyond me/him/her to comprehend.

be-en efsharoot באין אפשרות *adv* there being no possibility; in the absence of a possibility for.

be-en mafree'a באין מפריע *adv* unhindered; with no one to hinder.

be-en 'onesh באין עונש *adv* unpunished; with no one to punish.

been|yan/-yaneem בניין *nm* building, edifice; (*pl+of:* **-yeney**).

beenyan/-eem doo-komatee/-yeem בניין דו־קומתי *nm* two-storey building.

◇ **beenyan ha-arets** בניין הארץ *nm* rebuilding the Jewish homeland.

beenyan/-eem rav-komatee/-yeem בניין רב־קומתי *nm* multi-storied building.

beenyan/-eem telat-komatee/-yeem בניין תלת־קומתי three-storey building.

(tokhnee|t/-yot) beenyan תכנית בניין *nf* construction plan.

(tokhneet) beenyan 'areem תכנית בניין ערים *nf* town planning.

be'er/-ot באר *nf* **1.** well; **2.** pit.

□ **Be'er Orah** (Be'er Ora) באר אורה *nf* youth farm (est. 1950) 20 km N. of Elat.

□ **Be'er Sheva'** (Beersheba) באר שבע *nf* Also known as Beersheba, this ancient biblical town is now the country's fourth largest city (twin-cities of Tel-Aviv excepted). It is located at 113 km S. of Tel-Aviv by road or railroad, in the middle of the Negev Desert, of which it is the administrative, cultural and industrial capital. Pop. 122,000.

□ **Be'er Toovyah** (Be'er Toviyya) באר טוביה *nm* village (est. 1887) W. of **Keeryat Mal'akhee**. Pop. 627.

□ **Be'er Ya'akov** (Be'er Ya'aqov) באר יעקב *nf* townlet (est. 1907), W. of **Tsreefeen** Army Camp. Pop. 5,730.

beerah בירה *nf* beer.

beer|ah/-ot בירה *nf* capital (*+of:* **-at**).

('eer) beerah עיר בירה *nf* capital city.

□ **Beeraneet** בירנית *nf* regional center (for pre-military youth training, fencing) in Galilee, 8 km NW of Sasa Junction.

□ **beerat ha-negev** בירת הנגב *nf* Capital of the Negev i.e. Be'er-Sheva'.

be-'eravon moogbal בעירבון מוגבל *adj* with limited liability (company); incorporated.

beerboor/-eem ברבור *nm* mumble (*pl+of:* **-ey**).

□ **Be'eree** (Be'eri) בארי *nm* kibbutz (founded 1946) in S. Negev, 8 km N. of Gaza. Pop. 717.

□ **Beereeyah** (Biriyya) ביריה *nm* village (founded 1945) in Upper Galilee, 1 km N. of Safed (**Tsefat**). Pop. 492.

□ **Beereh** (Bira, also known as **El-Beereh**) בירה *nf* Arab townlet next to Ramallah, 15 km N. of Jerusalem. Pop. approx. 28,500.

be-'erekh בערך *adv* approximately.

bee-retseefoot ברציפות *adv* continuously.

bee-retseenoot ברצינות *adv* seriously.

bee-revot ha-yameem ברבות הימים *adv* in time; as time goes by.

◇ **beerkat ha-gomel** ברכת הגומל *nf* thanksgiving prayer (on narrow escape or recovery).

◇ **beerkat ha-mazon** בירכת המזון *nf* Grace after meals.

beerkat preydah (*npr* **preedah**) בירכת פרידה *nf* bidding farewell, leave-taking; saying goodbye.

□ **Beerkat Ram** (Birkat Ram) ברכת רם *nf* natural pool in N. Golan Heights.

beerk|ayeem ברכיים *nf pl* (*sing:* **berekh**) knees (*+of:* **-ey**).

(peek) beerkayeem פיק ברכיים *nm* tottering (from fright).

be-'erom בעירום *adv* in the nude.

□ **Be'erotayeem** (Be'erotayim) בארותיים *nm* village (founded 1949) in Sharon. Pop. 342.

□ **Be'erot Yeets'khak** (Be'erot Yizhak) בארות יצחק *nm* kibbutz (founded 1949) 5 km N. of Ben-Gurion Airport. Pop. 406.

bee-rtseefoot ברציפות *adv* continuously.

bee-rtseenoot ברצינות *adv* seriously.

bee-rvot ha-yameem ברבות הימים *adv* in time; as time goes by.

beeryah (*npr* **breeyah**)/**breeyot** ברייה *nf* creature.

beeryon/-eem בריון *nm* thug, hoodlum; (*pl+of:* **-ey**).

beeryonoot בריונות *nf* hooliganism.

□ **Beer Zeyt** (Bir Zeit) ביר־זית *nm* Arab college town, 6 km N. of Ramallah. Pop. 3,500.

bees/-eem ביס *[slang] nm* small bite.

bee-sekhar (*npr* **be-sakhar**) בשכר *adv* **1.** for a fee, **2.** on account of.

bee-sekhar khodshee (*npr* **be-sakhar** *etc*) בשכר חודשי *adv* for monthly wages, for a monthly salary.

bees|em/-mah/-amtee בישם *v* perfumed; spiced; (*pres* **mevasem;** *fut* **yevasem;** *(v=b)*).

bees|er/-rah/-artee בישר *v* heralded; announced (good news); (*pres* **mevaser;** *fut* **yevaser;** *(v=b)*).

bees|es/-esah/-astee ביסס *v* based, established; (*pres* **mevases** *(v=b); fut* **yevases**).

beesh ביש *(suffix) adj* unfortunate.

beesh gada ביש גדא *nm & adj* unlucky, clumsy.

beesh-mazal ביש מזל **1.** *adj* unlucky; **2.** *nm* bad luck.

('esek) beesh עסק ביש *nm* unfortunate affair.

bee-she'at בשעת *adv* at the time of.

bee-she'at ha-dekhak בשעת הדחק *adv* in an emergency; if worse come to worst.

bee-she'at ha-tsorekh בשעת הצורך *adv* in case of need.

bee-she'at ma'aseh בשעת מעשה *adv* in the very act; at the time of doing.

bee-she'at ratson בשעת רצון *adv* at an opportune moment.

bee-shegagah בשגגה *adv* unintentionally.

bee-shekhenoot בשכנות *adv* in the neighborhood (of).

beesh|el/-lah/-altee בישל *v* **1.** cooked; **2.** cooked up, concocted (*pres* **mevashel;** *fut* **yevashel;** *(v=b)*).

bee-sheleekhoot בשליחות *adv* on a mission of; on behalf of.

bee-sheleelah בשלילה *adv* negatively; in the negative.

bee-shelemoot בשלימות *adv* entirely, fully, completely.

(dar|ash/-shah/-ashtee) bee-shelom דרש בשלום *v* greeted, sent regards; (*pres* **doresh** *etc; fut* **yeedrosh** *etc*).

bee-sheteekah בשתיקה *adv* silently.

bee-sheveel בשביל *adv* for; on behalf of.

bee-shevoo'ah בשבועה *adv* under oath.

(hats'harah) bee-shevoo'ah הצהרה בשבועה *nf* affidavit; sworn statement.

bee-shgagah בשגגה *adv* unintentionally.

bee-sh'khenoot בשכנות *adv* in the neighborhood (of).

bee-shleekhoot בשליחות *adv* on a mission of; on behalf of.

bee-shleelah בשלילה *adv* negatively, in the negative.

bee-shlemoot בשלמות *adv* entirely, fully, completely.

(dar|ash/-shah/-ashtee) bee-shlom דרש בשלום *v* greeted, sent regards; (*pres* **doresh** *etc; fut* **yeedrosh** *etc*).

beeshool/-eem בישול *nm* cooking (*pl+of:* **-ey**).

(seer/-ey) beeshool סיר בישול *nm* cooking pot.

(sefer/seefrey) beeshool ספר בישול *nm* cookbook, cooking manual.

(tanoor/-ey) beeshool תנור בישול *nm* cooking stove, cooking range.

bee-shteekah בשתיקה *adv* silently.

bee-shveel בשביל *adv* for; on behalf of.

bee-shvoo'ah בשבועה *adv* under oath.

(hats'harah) bee-shvoo'ah הצהרה בשבועה *nf* affidavit; sworn statement.

bee-skhar (*npr* **be-sakhar**) בשכר *adv* **1.** for a fee; **2.** on account of.

bee-skhar khodshee (*npr* **be-sakhar** *etc*) בשכר חודשי *adv* for monthly wages, for a monthly salary.

bee-steerah בסתירה *adv* in contradiction.

be'et בעת *adv* at the time.

be'et oo-ve-'onah akhat בעת ובעונה אחת *adv* simultaneously.

beet|akhon/-khonot ביטחון *nm* security; defense; confidence; (*+of:* **-khon**).

beetakhon 'atsmee ביטחון עצמי *nm* self-confidence.

beetakhon sadeh (*npr:* **beetkhon** *etc*) ביטחון שדה *nm* field security.

(kokhot ha)beetakhon כוחות הביטחון *nm pl* security forces.

(meesrad ha)beetakhon משרד הביטחון *nm* the Defense Ministry.

(sar ha)beetakhon שר הביטחון *nm* Minister of Defense.

(seek|at/-ot) beetakhon סיכת ביטחון *nf* safety pin.

(shetar/sheetrey) beetakhon שטר ביטחון *nm* security note.

beetan/-eem ביתן *nm* pavilion; **(***pl+of:* **-ey)**.

□ **Beetan Aharon** (Bitan Aharon) ביתן אהרן *nm* village in N. Sharon, (est 1936) 5 km N. of **Netanyah**. Nearby, picturesque small nature reserve and camping center. Pop 378.

beet|a'on/-'oneem ביטאון *nm* mouthpiece, organ; **(***+of:* **-'on/-'oney)**.

beet|e/-'ah/-etee ביטא *v* expressed **(***pres* **mevate;** *fut* **yevate;** *(v=b)***)**.

beet|el/-lah/-altee ביטל *v* cancelled, abolished **(***pres* **mevatel;** *fut* **yevatel;** *(v=b)***)**.

(khaz|ar/-rah/-artee) bee-teshoovah חזר בתשובה *v* repented; turned religious; **(***pres* **khozer** *etc; fut* **yakhzor** *etc***)**.

beet|kha/-ekh/-ee/-o/-ah *etc* בתך וכו' *nf* your *(m/f)*/ my/ his/ her *etc* ... daughter.

□ **Beetkhah (Bitha)** בטחה *nm* village (founded 1950) in W. Negev, 2 km N. of **Ofakeem**. Pop. 610.

beet'khon sadeh בטחון שדה *nm* field security.

beet'khonot בטחונות *nm pl* securities.

beetn|ah ביטנה *nf* lining **(***+of:* **-at)**.

bee-tnay בתנאי *adv* probationally; on probation.

bee-tnay she- בתנאי ש־ *adv* provided that; on condition that.

beetoo|'akh/-kheem ביטוח *nm* insurance **(***pl+of:* **-khey)**.

beetoo'akh khayeem ביטוח חיים *nm* life insurance.

beetoo'akh le'oomee ביטוח לאומי *nm* social security fund.

beetoo'akh sha'ar ביטוח שער *nm* exchange rate insurance (against inflation).

beetoo'akh zeeknah ביטוח זיקנה *nm* old age insurance.

beetool/-eem ביטול *nm* abolition, cancellation; **(***pl+of:* **-ey)**.

beetoon ביטון *nm* fortifying with concrete.

beetoo|y/-yeem ביטוי *nm* expression; **(***pl+of:* **-yey)**.

beets|a'/-'ah/-a'tee ביצע *v* executed, performed **(***pres* **mevatse'a'** *(v=b); fut* **yevatsa')**.

beets|ah/-ot ביצה *nf* marsh, swamp; **(***+of:* **-at)**.

□ **Beetsaron** ביצרון *nm* (Bizzaron) village (founded 1935) 6 km S. of Ashdod. Pop. 534.

beetsb|ets/-etsah/-atstee בצבץ *v* **1.** oozed, sprouted, **2.** protruded **(***pres* **mevatsbets;** *fut* **yevatsbets;** *(v=b)***)**.

beets|e'a'/-'ah/-a'tee ביצע *v* executed, performed **(***pres* **mevatse'a;** *fut* **yevatse'a';** *(v=b)***)**.

be-'etsem בעצם *adv* **1.** actually; **2.** during; in the very.

bee-tsemeedoot le בצמידות ל־ *adv* in adherence to; linked to.

beetsoo|'a/-'eem ביצוע *nm* performance, perpetration; carrying out; **(***pl+of:* **-'ey)**.

beetsoor/-eem ביצור *nm* fortification **(***pl+of:* **-ey)**.

beev/-eem ביב *nm* gutter, sewer **(***pl+of:* **-ey)**.

beev/-ey shofkheen ביב שופכין *nm* gutter.

bee-vrakhah *(v=b)* בברכה **1.** with blessing; regards; **2.** yours truly.

bee-yekheedoot ביחידות *adv* in private, privately.

beey|esh/-shah/-ashtee בייש *v* put to shame; **(***pres* **mevayesh** *(v=b); fut* **yevayesh)**.

be-eyn באין *pref* in the absence of; lacking.

be-eyn efsharoot באין אפשרות *adv* there being no possibility; in the absence of a possibility for.

be-eyn mafree'a באין מפריע *adv* unhindered; with no one to hinder.

be-eyn 'onesh באין עונש *adv* unpunished; with no one to punish.

beeyoom/-eem ביום *nm* staging; mise en scene; **(***pl+of:* **-ey)**.

beeyoon/-eem ביון *nm* intelligence (military service); **(***pl+of:* **-ey)**.

beeyoots/-eem ביוץ *nm* ovulation; **(***pl+of:* **-ey)**.

beeyoov/-eem ביוב *nm* sewerage; drainage; canalization; **(***pl+of:* **-ey)**.

beez|ayon/-yonot ביזיון *nm* disgrace; contempt; **(***+of:* **-yon)**.

beezbooz/-eem בזבוז *nm* waste; **(***pl+of:* **-ey)**.

bee-zeman **(***or:* **bee-zman)** בזמן *adv* while; as; at the time when.

beezoor/-eem ביזור *nm* decentralization **(***pl+of:* **-ey)**.

be-'ezrat בעזרת *adv* with the aid of.

be-'ezrat ha-shem בעזרת השם *adv* God willing; with God's help.

be-far'hesyah בפרהסיה *adv* in public; openly.

be-fashtoot *(f=p)* בפשטות *adv*; unpretentiously; simply.

be-feh male *(f=p)* בפה מלא *adv* wholeheartedly; unhesitantly; explicitly.

be-feroosh *(f=p)* בפירוש *adv* expressly.

be-fo'al *(f=p)* בפועל **1.** *adj* actual; acting; **2.** *adv*. actually; in reality.

(ma'asar) be-fo'al מאסר בפועל *nm* actual imprisonment.

be-foombee *(f=p)* בפומבי *adv* publicly; in public.

begadeem בגדים *nm pl* **(***sing:* **beged)** clothes; clothing; **(***+of:* **beegdey)**.

(khanoo|t/-yot) begadeem חנות בגדים *f* clothing store; dress shop.

be-galooy בגלוי *adv* openly: bluntly.

begap|o/-ah/-ee/-kha/-ekh בגפו/־ה/־י וכו׳ *prep & pron* by him/her/my/your *m/f* - self.
beg|ed/-adeem בגד *nm* dress; garment; garb; (*pl+of:* **beegdey**).
beged/beegdey yam בגד־ים *nm* bathing suit.
be-geder בגדר *adv* within; within the scope of.
be-geder kheedoosh בגדר חידוש *adv* (is regarded) as a novelty/innovation.
be-geder sod בגדר סוד *adv* (is regarded) as secret.
begeed|ah/-ot בגידה *nf* betrayal; (*+of:* **-at**).
be-geel בגיל at an age; at the age of.
be-geeloofeen בגילופין *adj* tipsy.
be-geen בגין on account of .
(devareem) bego דברים בגו *nm pl* there's something in it; there is a reason.
be-hadragah בהדרגה *adv* gradually; step by step.
be-haf'alah בהפעלה *adv* being set in motion.
be-hakafah בהקפה *adv* on credit.
be-hakarah בהכרה *adv* in a state of consciousness.
be-hakarah mele'ah בהכרה מלאה *adj* fully conscious.
be-hakhanah (*npr* **ba-hakhanah**) בהכנה *adv* under preparation.
behal|ah/-ot בהלה *nf* **1.** panic; alarm; **2.** haste; (*+of:* **-at**).
behalat-shav בהלת שווא *nf* false alarm.
be-halatsah (*npr* **ba-halatsah**) בהלצה *adv* jokingly.
be-hamtanah בהמתנה *adv* in waiting.
be-hanakhah (*npr* **ba-hanakhah**) בהנחה *adv* on the assumption.
be-harbeh בהרבה *adv* considerably.
be-hash'alah בהשאלה **1.** *adv* on loan; **2.** *adj* borrowed; **3.** *adv* figuratively.
be-haskamah בהסכמה *adv* in agreement.
be-haskamah hadadeet בהסכמה הדדית *adv* in mutual agreement.
(yats|a/-'ah/-atee) be-hatkafah יצא בהתקפה *v* launched an attack; (*pres* **yotse** *etc; fut* **yetse** *etc*).
hatmad|ah התמדה *nf* perseverance; (*+of:* **-at**).
be-hatslakhah בהצלחה **1.** *adv* successfully; **2.** *intj* good luck!
be-hazmanah בהזמנה **1.** *adv* to order; **2.** *adj* made to order.
be-heedoor בהידור *adv* elegantly.
beheeloo|t/-yot בהילות *nf* **1.** eagerness; **2.** haste.
beheer/at se'ar בהיר שיער *adj* fairheaded; blond.
be-heestakloot בהסתכלות *adv* under observation.
be-heezdamnoot בהזדמנות *adv* occasionally; on the occasion of.
be-hekdem בהקדם *adv* early; soon.
be-hekhlet בהחלט *adv* definitely.
be-heksher בהקשר *adv* in connection (to, with).
be-helem בהלם *adv* in a state of shock.
behem|ah/-ot בהמה *nf* animal.
behemot בהמות *nf pl* livestock.
be-hen tsedek בהן צדק *adv* honestly; on word of honor.
be-hen tseedkee בהן צדקי *adv & poss. pron* on my word of honor.
be-hesakh ha-da'at בהיסח הדעת *adv* unthinkingly, inadvertently.
be-heseg yad בהישג יד *adv* within reach.
be-heskem בהסכם *adv* in agreement.
be-het'em בהתאם *adv* accordingly.
be-het'em le- בהתאם ל־ *adv* according to.
be-heter בהיתר *adv* under license; with permission.
bek|a'/-a'eem בקע *nm* **1.** split; rift; **2.** crevice; (*pl+of:* **beek'ey**)
be-kablanoot בקבלנות *adv* **1.** piece-work; **2.** by contract.
be-kadakhtanoot בקדחתנות *adv* feverishly.
be-kaloot בקלות *adv* easily.
be-kamah (*npr* **be-khamah**) בכמה־ for how much? how much?
□ **Beka'ot** בקעות *nm* village (est. 1971) in Jordan Valley 10 km W. of Jordan river, 5 km N. of **Tsomet Beka'ot** (Beqa'ot Junction).
be-karov בקרוב *adv* shortly; soon.
be-kav ha-bree'oot בקו הבריאות *adv* in good health.
be-kav yashar בקו ישר *adv* in a straight line.
be-kavanah (*npr* **be-khavanah**) בכוונה *adv* intentionally; on purpose.
be-keem'onoot בקמעונות *adj* in retail.
be-keervat בקרבת *adv* in the vicinity of; near to.
be-keervat makom בקרבת מקום *adv* nearby.
be-keetsoor בקיצור *adv* in brief.
be-kenoot (*npr* **be-khenoot**) בכנות *adv* honestly.
be-keroov בקירוב *adv* approximately.
be-kesher בקשר *prep* in connection.
be-kesher 'eem /le- בקשר עם /ל־ **1.** *prep* in connection with/to; **2.** as regards.
bekha/bakh/bee/bo/bah בך/בי/בו/בה *pron* in you *(m/f)* / me/him/her.
be-khadrey khadareem בחדרי חדרים *adv* **1.** in utmost secrecy; **2.** in a secret place; **3.** *lit.* : in the innermost chambers.
be-khakh בכך *conj* by this; thereby.
(mah) be-khakh eem מה בכך אם it matters little if.
(shel mah) be-khakh של מה בכך *adj* of little value; of no importance.
be-khamah בכמה for how much?
be-khanayah בחניה *adv* **1.** parking; **2.** in a parking place.
be-khasoot בחסות *adv* under the auspices of.
be-khavanah בכוונה *adv* intentionally; on purpose.
be-khavod בכבוד *adv* honorably; with respect.
be-khavod rav בכבוד רב **1.** *adv* respectfully yours (concluding a letter); **2.** with great respect.

be-kha|yay/-yekha/-yayeekh בחיי־ך וכו׳ (I swear) by my/your *m/f* life.

be-khayay she בחיי ש־ I could swear that.

bekhee בכי *nm* cry; weeping.

be-khee ra' בכי רע *adv* very bad; at one's worst.

bekhee tamrooreem בכי תמרורים *nm* bitter cry.

be-khee tov בכי טוב *adv* successfully.

(mer|erah/-artee) ba-bekhee (*npr* **bee-vekhee**) מירר בבכי *v* cried bitterly; (*pres* **memarer** *etc; fut* **yemarer** *etc*).

be-kheebook yadayeem בחיבוק ידיים *adv* with folded arms; doing nothing.

bekheel|ah/-ot בחילה *nf* nausea; disgust (*+of:* **-at**).

be-kheelyon 'eynayeem בכליון עיניים *adv* with impatient yearning.

bekheenah/-ot בחינה *nf* **1.** examination; test; **2.** aspect; (*+of:* **-at**).

('am|ad/-dah/-adetee ba-)bekheenah עמד בבחינה *v* passed the examination (*pres* **'omed** *etc; fut* **ya'amod** *etc*).

be-kheenam בחינם *adv* free of charge.

bekheen|at/-ot ma'avar בחינת מעבר *nf* intermediate examination.

(mee) bekheenat מבחינת from the aspect of ...

bekheenot bagroot בחינות בגרות *nf pl* matriculation exams.

bekheer בחיר *m+of* the chosen/selected one (out of).

bekheer leebah בחיר ליבה *nm* man of her choice; her fiancé.

bekheer|ah/-ot בחירה *nf* selection; election; choice; (*+of:* **-at**).

bekheerat leebo בחירת ליבו *nf* woman of his choice; his fiancée.

◇ **bekheerot eesheeyot** בחירות אישיות *nf pl* elections on a personal (no global lists) basis.

◇ **bekheerot ezoreeyot** (*npr* **azoreeyot**) בחירות אזוריות *nf pl* regional elections (by constituencies).

◇ **bekheerot khasha'eeyot** בחירות חשאיות *nf pl* elections by secret ballot.

bekheerot la-kneset בחירות לכנסת *nf pl* elections to the Knesset.

◇ **bekheerot roobaneeyot** בחירות רובניות *nf pl* elections by majority vote (by constituencies based on the majority principle).

◇ **bekheerot yakhseeyot** בחירות יחסיות *nf pl* proportional representation

bekheeyah le-dorot בכיה לדורות *nf* a fatal mistake; a wrong that will take generations to undo.

be-kheeyoov בחיוב *adv* positively; affirmatively.

be-khefets-lev בחפץ לב *adv* willingly; with pleasure.

be-khezkat בחזקת **1.** *adv* deemed to; **2.** degree (mathemat.).

be-khoakh (*kh=k*) בכוח **1.** *adv* by force; forcibly; **2.** *adj* potential.

be-khodesh בחודש **1.** of the month (date); **2.** (*lit.*) in the month.

be-khofsheeyoot בחופשיות *adv* freely.

be-khofzah בחופזה *adv* hastily.

be-khol (*kh=k*) בכל in every; in any.

be-khol atar va-atar בכל אתר ואתר *adv* in each and every place.

be-khol derekh efshareet בכל דרך אפשרית *adv* in every possible way

be-khol 'erev בכל ערב *adv* every/each evening.

be-khol 'et בכל עת *adv* any time; at any time.

be-khol lashon בכל לשון *adv* in any language.

be-khol lashon shel bakashah בכל לשון של בקשה *adv* begging most insistently.

be-khol lev בכל לב *adv* wholeheartedly.

be-khol makom בכל מקום *adv* (in) any place; anywhere.

be-khol meekreh בכל מקרה *adv* in any case; in any event.

be-khol mekheer בכל מחיר *adv* at any price; whatever the cost.

be-khol me'od|ee/-o/-ah בכל מאודי *adv* with all my/his/her soul.

be-khol sha'ah בכל שעה *adv* at any hour; at any time.

be-khol tokef בכל תוקף *adv* most vigorously; vehemently.

be-khonenoot (*kh=k*) בכוננות *adv* on call; on stand-by; on alert.

(tam|an/-nah) be-khoob|o/-ah טמן בחובו *v* contained; (*pres* **tomen** *etc; fut* **yeetmon** *etc*).

bekhor/-ot בכור *nm* firstborn; eldest child.

bekhorah/-ot בכורה *nf* **1.** priority; **2.** seniority; **3.** birthright; (*+of:* **-at**).

(hatsagat/-ot) bekhorah הצגת בכורה *nf* premiere; first night.

(zekhoo|t/-yot) bekhorah זכות בכורה *nf* seniority right.

be-khosher (*kh=k*) בכושר *adj* in good form.

be-khoved rosh (*kh=k*) בכובד ראש *adv* seriously; in all seriousness.

□ **Beko'a'** (Beqoa') בקוע *nm* village (est. 1951) on borderline between Judea Lowland and Judea Hills , 2 km NE of **Tsomet Nakhshon** (Nahshon Junction). Pop. 415.

be-ko'akh (*npr* **be-kho'akh**) בכוח **1.** *adv* by force; forcibly; **2.** *adj* potential.

be-kol ram בקול רם *adv* aloud.

be-koshee בקושי *adv* hardly; scarcely; with difficulty.

(maspeek) be-koshee מספיק בקושי *adj* barely sufficient (school mark).

be-koved rosh (*npr* **be-khoved rosh**) בכובד ראש *adv* seriously; in all seriousness.

be-lav hakhee בלאו הכי *prep* anyway; anyhow.

belee בלי *prep* without.

(am|ar/-rah/-artee) be-leeb|o/-ah/-ee אמר בליבו *v* said to him/her/my-self; (*pres* **omer** *etc; fut* **yomar** *etc*).

be-leevyat בלוויית *adv* in company of; accompanied by.

belem (*pl:* **blameem**) בלם *nm* brake (motor-car); (*pl+of:* **beelmey**).
belem-yad בלם יד *nm* hand brake.
be-let בלית *adv* (Aramaic) in the absence of.
be-let breyrah בלית ברירה *adv* there being no alternative; with no alternative left.
be-lev בלב *adv* in the heart of.
be-lev ezor בלב אזור *adv* in the heart of an area.
be-lev ha-arets בלב הארץ *adv* in the heart of the country.
be-lev ha-'eer בלב העיר *adv* in the heart of the city.
be-lev shalem בלב שלם *adv* wholeheartedly.
be-lev yam בלב ים *adv* on the high seas.
be-lo בלא *adv* without; with no.
be-lo hakarah בלא הכרה *adj* unconscious.
be-lo hefsek בלא הפסק *adv* without interruption; uninterruptedly.
be-lo heref בלא הרף *adv* incessantly; without stop.
be-lo she בלא ש־ *adv* without that.
be-lo yod'eem בלא יודעים *adv* unknowingly; unawares.
be-mah במה with what? what with?
be-ma'amad במעמד *adv* in the presence of.
be-mafgee'a במפגיע *adv* insistently; urgently.
be-maftee'a במפתיע *adv* **1.** amazingly; surprisingly; **2.** suddenly.
be-meekreh במקרה *adv* accidentally; coincidentally.
be-meektsat במקצת *adv* somewhat.
be-meeloo'eem במילואים *adv* on army reserve duty.
('am|ad/-dah/-adetee) be-meeshpat עמד במשפט *[colloq.] v* stood trial; (*pres* **'omed** *etc; fut* **ya'amod** *etc*).
(kha|yav/-yevet) be-meeshpat חייב במשפט *adj* guilty as charged.
be-meetkaven במתכוון *adv* on purpose; intentionally.
be-merets במרץ *adv* energetically.
be-merkha'ot במרכאות *adv* in quotes; allegedly; so-to-speak.
be-meshekh במשך *adv* during.
be-meshekh ha-zman במשך הזמן *adv* in due course; in time.
be-meyshareen במישרין *adv* directly; straightforwardly.
be-mezeed במזיד *adv* deliberately.
be-mo במו *adv* with one's very; with one's own.
be-mo pee|v/-hah במו פיו *adv* with his/her own mouth.
be-mo yadav/-eha במו ידיו *adv* with his/her own hands.
be-mo'ad|o/ah במועדו *adv* on time; in his/its/her time.
be-mooda' במודע *adv* consciously.
be-mookdam במוקדם *adv* early; soon.
be-mookdam o bee-me'ookhar במוקדם או במאוחר *adv* sooner or later.
ben בין *adv* **1.** among; **2.** between.
ben- בין־ *(prefix)* inter-.
ben/baneem בן *nm* son; boy; young man; (*pl+of:* **beney**).
ben/bat בן *adj m/f* aged (followed by number of years or of month, in case of baby).
◇ **(peedyon ha) ben** see ◇ **peedyon ha-ben**.
ben/-ey adam בן אדם *nm* man; person.
ben/-ey almavet בין אלמוות *nm & adj* immortal.
ben|ah/-o/-ee/-ekh בנה/בנו/בני/בנך *nm & pref (possess. pron.)* her/his/my/your *(f)* son.
ben/-ot bayeet בן בית *nmf & adj* insider; intimate; close friend; (*pl:* **ben|ey/-ot** *etc*).
ben/-ot breet בן־ברית *nmf & adj* ally; associate; (*pl:* **ben|ey/-ot** *etc*).
ben/bat dod בן־דוד *nmf* cousin; (*pl:* **ben|ey/-ot dodeem**).
be-nakel בנקל *adv* easily.
be-nakhat בנחת *adv* gently; quietly.
□ **Ben-Amee** (Ben Ammi) בן עמי *nm* village (est. 1949) in W. Galilee, 2 km E. of **Nahareeyah**. Pop. 306.
ben/bat 'aroobah בן ערובה *nmf* hostage; (*pl:* **beney/benot** *etc*).
ben/bat geel בן־גיל **1.** *adj* of the same age; **2.** *nmf* peer.
ben/bat geel|ee/-khah/-ekh/-o/-ah בן־גילי/־ך/־ו/־ה *pron* of same age as me/you*(m/f)*/him/her.
ben ha-'arbayeem בין הערביים *nm pl* twilight; dusk.
ben ha-goyeem בין הגויים *adv* **1.** among non-Jews; **2.** amid a world of Gentile nations.
ben ha-she'ar בין השאר *adv* among other things.
ben ha-sheeteen בין השיטין *adv* between the lines.
ben ha-shoorot בין השורות *adv* between the lines.
ben ha-yeter בין היתר *adv* **1.** among the rest; **2.** among other things.
ben-gooshee/-t בין־גושי *adj* inter-bloc.
ben kakh oo-ven kakh *(v=b)* בין כך ובין כך *adv* one way or the other.
ben/bat kamah? בן כמה? *query* how old?
ben/bat keel'aeem בן כלאיים *adj & nmf* mongrel; cross-breed; (*pl:* **beney/benot** *etc*).
◇ **ben keseh le-'asor** בין כסה לעשור *adv* the seven "days of grace" between Rosh ha-Shanah and Yom Kippur.
ben/-ey khayeel בן חיל *nm* brave fellow.
ben/bat khoreen בן־חורין *nmf* freeman/free woman (*pl* **beney/benot** *etc*).
ben/bat khoreen le- בן־חורין *adj* at liberty to; free to-.
ben/bat khoreg/-et בן חורג *adj & m/f* stepson/stepdaughter; (*pl:* **ban|eem/-ot khorg|eem/-ot**).
ben koh va-khoh *(kh=k)* בין כה וכה *adv* anyway.
(meemoon) benayeem מימון־ביניים *nm* interim financing.

(peetron/-ot) benayeem פתרון־ביניים *nm* interim solution.

(taktseev/-ey) benayeem תקציב־ביניים *nm* interim budget.

(yemey ha)benayeem ימי הביניים *nm pl* the Middle Ages.

□ **Benayah** (Benaya) בניה *nm* village in seashore plain (est. 1949), 2 km S. of **Yavneh**. Pop. 337.

ben|eh/-ee ! בנה *v imp sing m/f* build! (*inf* **leevnot** *(v=b); pst* **banah**; *pres* **boneh**; *fut* **yeevneh**).

◇ **"beneh betkha"** "בנה ביתך" (*lit.*: build your own house) special Housing project sponsored by the Ministry of housing under which one is allotted land to build one's own house.

be-needon בנידון *adv* re; regarding.

be-neefrad בנפרד *adv* separately; apart.

be-neegood le- בניגוד ל־ *adv* contrary to.

be-neekhootah בניחותא *adv* at ease.

be-neemtsa בנמצא *adv* in existence; available.

benee oo-venak ביני ובינך *[slang] (Arab.)* between the two of us; between you and me.

ben-'eeronee/-t בין־עירוני *adj* interurban.

benee|yah/-yot בנייה *nf* construction; (*+of:* **-yat**).

beneeyah tromeet בנייה טרומית *nf* prefabricated construction.

(bee) beneeyah (*npr* **bee-veneeyah**) בבנייה *adv* abuilding; under construction.

◇ **(madad yoker ha)beneeyah** see ◇ **madad yoker ha-beneeyah**.

(tokhnee|t/-yot) beneeyah תוכנית בנייה *nf* building scheme; construction plan.

benenoo (or **beneynoo**) בינינו *prep & pron* between us; among us.

(she-yeesha'er) benenoo שיישאר בינינו **1.** let's keep it a secret; confidentially; **2.** (*lit.*) let it remain between us.

benenoo le-ven 'atsmenoo *(v=b)* בינינו לבין עצמנו entre nous; strictly between us.

beney adam בני אדם *nm pl* (*sing:* **ben adam**) people; human beings.

beney 'aroobah (*colloq. mispronunc.;* **'aroovah**) בני ערובה *nm pl* (*sing:* **ben-** *etc*) hostages.

□ **Beney 'Atarot** (Bené 'Atarot) בני־עטרות *nm* village (est. 1948) in Sharon, 5 km N. of Ben-Gurion Airport. Pop. 368.

□ **Beney 'Atsmon (Bené Azmon)** בני עצמון *nm* coop. village in Gaza Strip (est. 1979), 3 km SE of **Rafee'akh**. Pop. 348.

□ **Beney 'Ayeesh** (Bené 'Ayish) בני־עיש *nm* local council (est. 1958) 2 km S. of **Gederah**. Pop. 996.

□ **Beney Brak** (Bené Beraq) בני־ברק *nf* town (founded 1924) bordering on Tel-Aviv from N.E, between **Ramat-Gan** and **Petakh-Teekvah** of pronounced religious traditionalism. Pop. 116,700.

beney breet בני ברית **1.** *nm pl* (*sing:* **ben** *etc.*) l.allies. **2.** fellow-Jews.

◇ **beney breet** ("**B'nai-Brith**") בני ברית *nm* Jewish worldwide fraternal order.

□ **Beney Darom** (Bené Darom) בני דרום *nm* village (est. 1949) 4 km E. of Ashdod. Pop. 305.

□ **Beney Dror** (Bené Deror) בני דרור *nm* village in Sharon (est. 1946), 1 km E. of **Even Yehoodah**. Pop. 200.

beney ha-neooreem בני־הנעורים *nm pl* adolescents; youth.

beney no'ar בני נוער *nm pl* youth.

□ **Beney Re'em** (Bené Re'em) בני־ראם *nm* village (est. 1949) S. of Gedera. Pop. 510.

beney teesh'khoret בני תשחורת *nm pl* youngsters; young people.

□ **Beney Tseeyon** (Bené Ziyyon) בני ציון *nm* village (est. 1947) on Coastal Plain 4 km N. of **Ra'ananah**. Pop. 399.

◇ **beney yeesra'el** בני־ישראל *nm pl* (Bibl.) the Children of Israel.

◇ **beney yeesra'el (Bney Israel)** בני־ישראל *nm pl* ancient Jewish community that had been living in India and speaking the Maharati language. They differ from other Jews there in their looks, manners and rites and trace their origin to the Ten "Lost" Tribes (**'Aseret ha-Shevateem** עשרת השבטים) of Israel. Since 1950, when they numbered some 18,000, many of them emigrated to Israel where they have been successfully integrated with other immigrants.

□ **Beney Yehoodah** (Bené Yehuda) בני יהודה *nm* regional center in Golan Heights (est. 1972), 5 km NE of **'En-Gev**. Pop. 498.

ben-le'oomee/-t בינלאומי *adj* international.

(yekhaseem) ben-le'oomeeyeem יחסים בינלאומיים *nm pl* international relations.

ben/bat levayah בן־לוויה *adj & nmf* escort; companion; (*pl:* **ben|ey/-ot** *etc*).

ben/bat meen|o/-ah בן־מינו *adj* of same kind; of same sex.

ben/bat meeshpakhah בן־משפחה *nmf* relative; of the same family.

be-noakh בנוח *adv* at ease.

be-noge'a בנוגע *adv* concerning; in relation (to); in connection (with).

be-noge'a le- בנוגע ל־ **1.** *conj* as regards; **2.** *conj* concerning.

be-nokheeyoot בנוחיות *adv* comfortably.

be-nokhekhoot בנוכחות *adv* in the presence of.

be-nokhoot בנוחות *adv* comfortably.

beno le-venah *(v=b)* בינו לבינה between him and her; between lovers; between husband and wife.

benonee/-t בינוני *adj* medium; average; middle.

benoneeyoot בינוניות *nf* mediocrity.

ben... oo-ven... *(v=b)* בין... ובין... *adv* either... or ...

benokheeyoot בנוחיות*adv* comfortably.

be-nosaf le- בנוסף ל־ *adv* in addition to.

ben she- oo-ven she- *(v=b)* בין ש... ובין ש whether or -.

ben/bat she-eyn|o/-ah meen|o/-ah בן שאינו מינו *adj* of different kind; of opposite sex.

□ **Ben Shemen** (Ben Shemen) בן שמן *nm* village (est. 1911) 4 km S. of Lod. Pop. 298.

□ **(Kefar ha-No'ar) Ben Shemen** see □ **Kefar Ha-No'ar Ben Shemen.**

ben/bat ta'arovet בן־תערובת *nmf* child of mixed parentage; halfbreed (*pl:* **beney/benot** *etc*).

bentayeém בינתיים *adv* meanwhile.

ben/beney torah בן תורה *nm* learned in the torah; talmudic scholar.

ben-yabeshtee/-t בין־יבשתי *adv* inter-continental.

ben/bat yakheed/-ah בן יחיד *nm* only son/daughter.

□ **Benyameenah** (Binyamina) בנימינה town and local council (est. 1922) 7 km S. of **Zeekhron Ya'akov**. Pop. 3,390.

ben yemeen|o/-ah lee-smol|o/-ah בין ימינו לשמאלו **1.** (discerning) between one thing and the other; **2.** *(lit.)* between right and left.

□ **Ben-Zakay** בן־זכאי *nm* village (est. 1950) near the seashore, next to **Yavneh**. Pop. 433.

benzeen בנזין *nm* petrol; gasoline (Am.); benzine.

ben zeh la-zeh בין זה לזה *adv* between them: between this and that.

ben/bat zekooneem בן־זקונים *nmf* son/daughter of one's old age.

ben/bat zenooneem בן־זנונים *nmf* bastard; illegitimate son/daughter.

ben/bat zonah בן זונה *[slang]* (insult) *nmf* son/daughter of a prostitute; (*pl:* **beney zonot**).

be-'od בעוד *adv* while; after.

be-'od khodesh בעוד חודש *adv* a month from now.

be-'od mo'ed בעוד מועד *adv* while there's still time.

be-ofen she- באופן ש־ *adv* so that; in a manner that.

be-omets באומץ *adv* courageously; bravely.

be-ones באונס *adv* coerced.

be-'oz בעוז *adv* vigorously.

be-potentsyah בפוטנציה *adv* potentially; *adj* potential.

□ **Berekhyah** (Berekhya) ברכיה *nm* village (est. 1950) 3 km E. of Ashkelon. Pop. 532.

be-rashoot בראשות *adv* at the head of.

be-ratson ברצון *adv* willingly.

be-reefroof ברפרוף *adv* at a glance; superficially.

be-reetsah בריצה *adv* running.

berekh ברך *nf* knee (*pl* **beerkayeem**; *(k=kh)*).

ber|ekh/-khah/-akhtee בירך *v* greeted; blessed; (*pres* **mevarekh** *(v=b)*; *fut* **yevarekh**).

be-remez ברמז *adv* with a hint; hinting.

berer/-ah בירר *v* ascertained; cleared; (*pres* **mevarer**; *fut* **yevarer**; *(v=b)*).

beresheet (or **bresheet**) בראשית **1.** *adv* at the outset; at the beginning; **2.** *nm* the book of Genesis (Bibl.).

be-revakh ברווח *adv* profitably.

berez/brazeem ברז *nm* faucet; tap; (*pl+of:* **beerzey**).

be-rogez ברוגז *adj* angry; not on speaking terms.

be-rokh ברוך *adv* softly.

be-roo'akh ha-dvareem ברוח הדברים *adv* in the spirit of what has been said; in the spirit of things.

be-roomo shel 'olam ברומו של עולם (matters) of paramount concern.

be-rosh בראש *adv* at the head of.

be-roshem ברושם *[colloq.]* (correct: **takhat ha-roshem**) under the impression.

be-rotkheem (or **be-rotkheen**) ברותחים *adv* in boiling water.

ber|yah/-yot בריה *nf [slang]* (Yiddish) perfect housekeeper.

be-sakh בסך in the sum of.

be-sakh ha-kol בסך הכול altogether; on the whole.

be-samookh le בסמוך ל־ *adv* next to.

be-seder בסדר *adj & adv* okay; all right; in order; agreed.

be-seder gamoor בסדר גמור *adv* in perfect order.

be-seder moftee בסדר מופתי *adv* in exemplary order.

be-seemkhah בשמחה *adv* gladly; with joy.

be-seetonoot בסיטונות *adv* wholesale.

be-sever paneem yafot בסבר פנים יפות *adv* friendly; cordially (welcoming someone).

be-sha'at|o/-ah בשעתו/־ה *adv* at one time.

be-sheroot pa'eel בשירות פעיל *adv* on active (military) service.

be-shogeg בשוגג *adv* unintentionally; unintendedly.

be-shoom ofen בשום אופן *adv* in no way.

be-sod בסוד *adv* secretly; in secret.

be-sof בסוף *adv* at the end of.

be-sofo shel davar בסופו של דבר *adv* ultimately; finally.

□ **(Khevel ha) Besor** חבל הבשור *nm* the Besor District see □ **Khevel Eshkol.**

besor|ah/-ot בשורה *nf* good news; tidings (*+of:* **-at**).

"bet" ב *nf* 2nd letter of Hebrew alphabet: consonant reading **b** or **v** according to whether or not there be a dot in it were the text a dotted one.

"bet" ב׳ **1.** numeral 2 (two) in the Hebrew system of alphabetic numerology; **2.** *adj & num* 2nd (second) under the same system, used in the ordinal sense; **3.** numeral 2,000 (two thousand) (cf. Introduction, Cpt.3, p. VI) if standing alone or followed by the word אלפים (**alafeem** i.e. thousands) or by one of four Hebrew letters: ק **Koof**, ר **Resh**, ש **Sheen** or ת **Tav** (which, under that system, represent figures 100, 200, 300 and 400).

◇ **(adar) bet** see ◇ **adar bet.**

◇ **('aleeyah) Bet** see ◇ **'aleeyah bet.**
◇ **(keetah) bet** see ◇ **keetah bet.**
(yom) Bet יום ב׳ *nm* Monday.
(soog) Bet סוג ב׳ *adj* "B" quality; second-rate quality.
◇ **(sheen) bet** see ◇ **sheen bet.**
bet/batey בית *f+of* the house of (i.e. the construct case of **bayeet**).
□ **Bet Aba** בית אב״א *nm* communal village (est. 1980) half-way between **Elkanah** and **Aree'el**. Pop. 290.
be-tafkeed בתפקיד *adv* on duty.
betakh בטח *adv* certainly; surely; of course.
be-takhleet בתכלית *adv* absolutely.
□ **Bet-Alfa** בית אלפא *nm* kibbutz (est. 1922) in E. Yizre'el Valley (**'Emek Yeezre'el**). Pop. 766.
bet/batey 'almeen בית עלמין *nm* cemetery.
bet/-batey 'am בית עם *nm* community center.
□ **Bet-'Areef** (Bet Arif) בית עריף *nm* village (est. 1949) 4 km E. of Ben-Gurion Airport. Pop. 435.
□ **Bet Aryeh** בית־אריה *nm* communal village (est. 1981) 15 km SE of **Petakh-Teekvah**. Pop. 916.
be-tashloom בתשלום *adv* for a fee; against payment
□ **Bet-Berl** בית־ברל *nm* college, educational and ideological center of the Israel Labor Movement 3 km S. of **Kefar-Saba**. Pop. 327.
bet/batey boshet בית בושת *nm* brothel.
□ **Bet-Dagan** בית־דגן *nf* town (est. 1948) in the SE outskirts of Tel-Aviv. Pop. 2,150.
bet/batey deen בית־דין *nm* tribunal; court of law; rabbinical court of law.
◇ **bet-deen gavoha le-tsedek** בית דין גבוה לצדק *nm* High Court of Justice (also known by its *acr.*: BAGATS בג״ץ), one of the capacities filled by Israel Supreme Court (juridic.).
bet-deen la-'avodah בית־דין לעבודה *nm* labor-court.
bet-deen tsedek בית־דין צדק *nm* rabbinical court.
be-te'avon בתיאבון *adv* **1.** avidly; **2.** *interj* Have a pleasant meal! Bon Appetit!.
beteekhoot בטיחות *nf* safety; security.
be-teepool בטיפול *adv* being taken care of.
□ **Bet-El** (Bet-El) בית־אל *nm* communal settlement (est. 1977) 4 km NE of Ramallah. Pop. 1,350.
□ **Bet-Ela'azaree** (Bet El'azari) בית אלעזרי *nm* village (est. 1948) 3 km S. of **Tsomet Beeloo** (Bilu Junction). Pop. 405.
□ **Bet-El Bet** בית־אל ב׳ *nm* communal village (est. 1978) 4 km NE of Ramallah. Pop. 673.
be-telem בתלם *adv* with the stream.
beten בטן *nf* **1.** stomach; abdomen; belly; **2.** inner part.
('al) beten reykah על בטן ריקה *adv* on an empty stomach.
(teefoos ha) beten טיפוס הבטן *nm* typhoid fever.
be-terem בטרם *adv* prior to; before.
□ **Bet 'Ezra** (Bet-Ezra) בית עזרא *nm* village (est. 1950) on coastal plain, 10 km S. Ashdod-Ashkelon highway. Pop. 466.
bet/batey ha'arakhah בית־הארחה *nm* guesthouse.
□ **Bet ha-'Emek** (Bet Haemeq) בית העמק *nm* kibbutz in W. Galilee (est 1949), 6 km SE of **Nahareeyah**. Pop 478.
□ **Bet ha-Gadee (Bet Hagaddi)** בית־הגדי *nm* village (est. 1949) in W. Negev off the **Be'er Sheva'** road. Pop. 436.
□ **Bet ha-Levee** (Bet Halevi) בית הלוי *nm* village in Sharon (est. 1945), 3 km NE of **Tsomet ha-Sharon** (Bet Leed Junction). Pop. 268.
□ **Bet Ha-Kerem** בית־הכרם *nf* old yet fashionable residential quarter in W. part of Jerusalem, near Hebrew University **Geev'at Ram** campus, the Knesset and several luxury hotels.
bet ha-mekhokekeem בית המחוקקים *nm* the legislative assembly; the Knesset.
□ **Bet Ha-Sheetah** (Bet Hashitta) בית־השיטה *nm* kibbutz (est. 1935) in the Yizre'el Valley, 8 km NW of Bet-She'an. Pop. 1,230.
bet ha-shekhee בית־השחי *nm* armpit.
◇ **bet ha-tefootsot** (Beth Hatefutsot) בית התפוצות *nm* the Nahum Goldmann Museum of Jewish Diaspora located on Tel-Aviv University Campus (Gate 2). Uses most advanced graphic and audio-visual techniques to present 2500 years of Jewish history in communities around the world.
bet/batey havra'ah בית־הבראה *nm* resthouse; sanatorium.
□ **Bet Heelel** (Bet Hillel) בית הלל *nm* village in Upper Galilee (est. 1940), 3 km E. of **Keeryat Shmonah**. Pop. 329.
◇ **bet heelel** בית הלל *nm* a school of Talmudic thought originating some 2,000 years ago that, as opposed to **bet shamay** (see ◇ below) generally interpreted points of religious and civil law liberally.
□ **Bet-Jalah** (Bet Jala) בית ג׳אלה *nf* Christian Aratown S. of Jerusalem, 1 km W. of Bethlehem. Pop. approx. 14,000.
□ **Bet Jan** (Bet Jann) בית ג׳ן *nm* large Druze village in Upper Galilee, 10 km NE of **Karmee'el**, on slopes of Mount **Meeron**. Renown for its male population's all-out enlistment and participation in Israel's armed forces. Pop. 7,040.
bet/batey kafeh בית־קפה *nm* cafe; coffee-house.
bet/batey keeseh בית־כיסא *nm* W.C.; toilet.
bet/batey kele' בית־כלא *nm* jail.
bet/batey keneset בית־כנסת *nm* synagogue.
bet/batey keroor בית־קירור *nm* cold storage.
bet/batey kevarot בית־קברות *nm* cemetery.
□ **Bet Kamah** בית קמה *nm* kibbutz (est. 1949) in N. Negev, 20 km N. of Beersheba, on road from **Keeryat Gat**. Pop. 351.

□ **Bet Keshet** בית קשת *nm* kibbutz (est. 1944) in Lower Galilee, 5 km N. of Mount Tabor **(Har Tavor)**. Pop. 309.

□ **Bet Khanan** (Bet Hanan) בית חנן *nm* village (est. 1930) 2 km W. of **Nes-Tseeyonah**. Pop. 454.

□ **Bet Khananyah** (Bet Hananya) בית־חנניה *nm* village (est. 1950) on Coastal Plain. Pop. 267.

bet/batey kharoshet בית־חרושת *nm* factory; plant.

□ **Bet Kheelkeeyah** (Bet Hilqiyya) בית חלקיה *nm* village in the S. (est. 1963), 4 km SE of Gedera. Pop. 310.

□ **Bet Kheroot** (Bet Herut) בית חירות *nm* village (est. 1933) in N. Sharon 8 km N. of Netanya. Pop. 387.

bet/batey kholeem בית־חולים *nm* hospital.

□ **Bet-Khoron** (Bet Horon) בית־חורון *nm* communal village (est. 1977) 15 km NW of Jerusalem. Pop. 424.

□ **Bet-Lekhem** (Bet Lehem) בית־לחם *nf* historic Biblical town of Bethlehem, now mostly Christian Arab, 7 km S. of Jerusalem. Pop. approx. 44,000.

□ **Bet Lekhem ha-Gleeleet** (Bet Lehem Hagelilit) בית לחם הגלילית *nm* village (*lit.:* Galilean Betlehem) in Lower Galilee (est. 1948), 7 km NE of **Keeryat Teev'on**. Pop. 340.

bet/batey malon בית־מלון *nm* hotel.

bet/batey margo'a' בית־מרגוע *nm* resthouse; sanatorium.

◇ **bet/batey meedrash** בית־מדרש *nm* house of study for Torah-learners that is part of a traditional synagogue complex.

□ **Bet Me'eer** בית־מאיר *nm* village (est. 1950) in Judean hills, 3 km SE of **sha'ar ha-Gay** (Bab-el-Wad). Pop. 389.

bet/batey meekdash בית־מקדש *nm* **1.** temple; **2.** sanctuary.

◇ **bet ha-meekdash** בית המקדש *nm* **1.** Solomon's Temple destroyed by the Babylonians in 586 BCE; **2.** the Second Temple, built after the return of the Judeans from the Babylonian Exile and destroyed by the Romans in the year 70 C.E.

bet/batey meerkakhat בית מרקחת *nm* pharmacy; drugstore; chemist's shop.

bet/batey meeshpat בית משפט *nm* court of law.

bet (ha)meeshpat (ha)'elyon בית המשפט העליון *nm* (the) Supreme Court.

bet/batey (ha)meeshpat le-no'ar בית המשפט לנוער *nm* (the) Juvenile Court.

bet (ha)meeshpat (ha)mekhozee בית המשפט המחוזי (the) District Court.

bet/batey meeshpat (ha)shalom בית משפט השלום *nm* (the) Magistrate's Court; Justice of the Peace.

bet/batey meetbakhayeem בית מטבחיים *nm* slaughterhouse.

bet/batey megooreem בית מגורים *nm* residential building.

bet mekhes בית מכס *nm* customs house; customs station.

bet/batey melakhah בית מלאכה *nm* workshop.

bet/batey merkhats/-a'ot בית מרחץ *nm* bath house.

bet/batey neevkhareem בית נבחרים *nm* House of Representatives; Parliament; Knesset.

□ **Bet Nekhemyah** (Bet Nehemya) בית נחמיה *nm* village in central plain (est. 1950), 4 km E. of Ben Gurion Airport. Pop. 417.

be-tokef בתוקף **1.** *adj* valid; in force; **2.** *adv* vigorously.

□ **Bet 'Oozee'el** (Bet Uzziel) בית עוזיאל *nm* village in central plain (est. 1956), 7 km SE of Ramla. Pop. 268.

□ **Bet Oren** בית אורן *nm* kibbutz (est. 1939) in Carmel Mountains, 10 km S. of Haifa. Pop. 209.

□ **Bet 'Oved** (Bet 'Oved) בית עובד *nm* village (est. 1933) 5 km S. of Rishon le-Ziyyon **(Reeshon le-Tseeyon)**. Pop. 290.

□ **Bet Raban** (Bet Rabban) בית רבן *nm* religious education institute (est 1946) near **Kvootsat Yavneh**, 6 km W. of Gedera. Was onetime known as **Geev'at Vashington** (i.e. Washington Hill). Pop (pupils and staff) 600.

□ **Bet Sakhoor (Bet Sahur)** בית סאחור *nf* Arab township, predominantly Christian, in Judea hills, E. of Betlehem. Pop. 12,400.

□ **Bet Zayeet** (Bet Zayit) בית זית *nm* village in Judea hills (est 1949) 5 km W. of Jerusalem. Pop 836.

□ **Bet Zayd** (Bet Zeid) בית זייד *nf* memorial settlement (est 1943) and educational institute S. of **Keeryat Teev'on**. Pop 154.

be-tokh בתוך *adv* in; among; inside; during.

beton בטון *nm* concrete.

beton mezooyan בטון מזוין *nm* reinforced concrete; ferro-concrete.

(me'arbel/-ey) beton מערבל בטון *nm* concrete mixer.

betool|ah/-ot בתולה *nf* virgin; **(**+*of:* **-at)**.

(mazal) betoolah מזל בתולה *nm* Virgo (Zodiac).

betool|eem בתולים *nm pl* virginity; chastity **(**+*of:* **-ey)**.

betor בתור *adv* as a; in the capacity of.

betsa' בצע *nm* greed; excessive gain.

betsa' kesef בצע כסף *nm* lucre.

(ohev/-et) betsa' אוהב בצע *adj* greedy; mercenary.

(sone/-t) betsa' שונא בצע *adj* incorruptible; hater of covetousness.

be-tsa'ar בצער *adv* regrettably; with regret.

be-tsa'ar rav בצער רב *adv* with deep regret.

bets|ah/-eem ביצה *nf* egg **(**+*of:* **-at/-ey)**.

bets|ah/-eem kashah/-ot ביצה קשה *nf* hard-boiled egg.

bets|ah/-eem megoolg|elet/-alot ביצה מגולגלת *nf* soft-boiled egg.

bets|ah/-eem rak|ah/-ot ביצה רכה *nf* soft-boiled egg.

bets|ah/-eem shlook|ah/-ot ביצה שלוקה *nf* boiled egg.

(al tevalbel et ha) betseem! !אל תבלבל את הביצים *(slang, impolite)* Will you stop bothering me, please!

(en lo/lekha/lahem/lakhem) betseem /אין לו לך/להם/לכם ביצים *[slang]* he/you*(sing)*/they/you*(pl)* do(es) not have the guts; (*lit.*: testicles).

(yesh lo/lekha/lahem/lakhem) betseem /יש לו לך /להם/לכם ביצים *[slang]* he/you*(sing)*/they/you*(pl)* do(es) have the guts; (*lit.*: testicles).

be-tsav בצו *adv* by order.

be-tsavta בצוותא *adv* together; togetherness.

be-tseemtsoom בצמצום *adv* scantily; thriftily.

be-tseen'ah בצנעה *adv* in secret; privately.

bet/batey sefer בית־ספר *nm* school.

bet/batey sefer 'erev בית ספר ערב *nm* evening school; evening classes.

bet/batey sefer gavo'ah/gevoheem בית ספר גבוה *nm* school of academic status.

bet/batey sefer mamlakhtee/-yeem בית־ספר ממלכתי *nm* Government school.

bet/batey sefer meektso'ee/-yeem בית־ספר מקצועי *nm* vocational school.

bet-sefer re'alee בית־ספר ריאלי *nm* science high school.

bet/batey sefer sadeh בית ספר שדה *nm* field school.

bet/batey sefer teekhon/-eeyeem בית־ספר תיכון *nm* - secondary school; high school.

bet/batey sefer yesodee/-yeem בית־ספר יסודי *nm* elementary school; primary school.

□ **Betset** (Bezet) בצת *nm* village (est. 1949) in Upper Galilee, 8 km N. of **Nahareeyah**. Pop. 311.

◇ **bet shamay** בית שמאי *nm* a school of Talmudic thought originating some 2,000 years ago that, as opposed to **bet heelel** (see ◇ above), generally interpreted points of religious and civil law stringently.

□ **Bet-She'an** בית שאן *nf* historic town in Jordan Valley, now a development town. Pop. 13,500.

□ **Bet She'areem** (Bet She'arim) בית שערים *nm* village (est. 1936) in Yizre'el Valley, near ancient burial cave complex bearing same historic name. Pop. 381.

□ **Bet Sheekmah** (Bet Shiqma) בית־שקמה *nm* village (est. 1950) on the Coastal Plain, 5 km S. of Ashkelon. Pop. 454.

bet/batey sheemoosh בית־שימוש *nm* W.C.; toilet.

□ **Bet-Shemesh** בית שמש *nf* town (est. 1950) at the edge of the Judea Hills, 5 km of **Tsomet Sheemshon** (Shimshon Junction). Pop. 15,700.

□ **Bet Tsevee** (Bet Zevi) בית צבי *nm* educational religious center (est. 1953) incorporating a vocational school and a yeshiva S. of the Carmel Hills, near **Tsomet 'Atleet** ('Atlit Junction). Pop. 400.

be-tsoorat בצורת *adv* in the form of.

□ **Bet Yanay** (Bet Yannay) בית ינאי *nm* village on Mediterranean Coast (est. 1933), 6 km N. of Netanya. Pop. 317.

□ **Bet Yateer** (also called **Yeetaron**) בית יתיר *nm* cooperative village (est. 1979) in the Arad-Beersheba-Hebron triangle.

□ **Bet Yeets'khak** (Bet Yizhaq) בית יצחק *nm* village near Mediterranean Coast (est. 1933), 6 km N. of Netanya. Recently merged with a nearby village **Sha'ar Khefer** שער חפר (est. 1940). Joint Pop. 1,340.

□ **Bet Yehoshoo'a'** בית יהושע *nm* village (est. 1950) on Coastal Plain, 7 km S. of Netanyah. Pop. 377.

bet/batey yoldot בית יולדות *nm* maternity ward; maternity hospital.

□ **Bet Yosef** בית יוסף *nm* village in Bet She'an Valley (est. 1954). Pop. 314.

□ **Bet Zera'** (Bet Zera') בית זרע *nm* kibbutz in the Jordan Valley (est. 1927), 3 km S. of **Deganyah Alef**. Pop. 680.

bet/batey zonot בית זונות *nm* brothel; whorehouse.

be-vaday בוודאי *adv* certainly; undoubtedly: most probably.

be-vat akhat *(v=b)* בבת אחת *adv* at once; simultaneously.

be-veerkat khavereem *(v=b)* בבירכת חברים *adv* cordially yours.

be-veetkhah *(v=b)* בבטחה *adv* for sure.

be-vo ha-yom *(v=b)* בבוא היום *adv* come the day.

be-vo ha-zman *(v=b)* בבוא הזמן *adv* come the time.

be-voshet paneem *(v=b)* בבושת פנים *adv* shamefacedly; to one's disgrace.

(yad) be-yad יד ביד *adv* hand in hand.

be-yakhad ביחד *adv* together.

be-yakhas le ביחס ל־ *adv* in respect of; concerning.

be-yeekhood בייחוד *adv* especially; particularly.

be-yeter ביתר *adv* **1.** with more; **2.** in the remaining.

beyn (or **ben**) בין *prep* between; among.

beyn ha-'arbayeem בין הערביים *nm pl* twilight; dusk.

beyn ha-goyeem בין הגויים *adv* **1.** among non-Jews; **2.** amid a world of Gentile nations.

beyn ha-she'ar בין השאר *adv* among other things.

beyn ha-sheeteen בין השיטין *adv* between the lines.

beyn ha-shoorot בין השורות *adv* between the lines

beyn ha-yeter בין היתר *adv* **1.** among the rest; **2.** among other things.

beyn kakh oo-veyn-kakh *(v=b)* בין כך ובין כך *adv* one way or the other.
◇ **beyn keseh le-'asor** see ◇ **ben keseh le-'asor**.
beyn koh va-kho *(kh=k)* בין כה וכה *adv* anyway.
beyn... oo-veyn... *(v=b)* בין... ובין... *adv* either... or...
beyn she-... oo-veyn *(v=b)* **she-**... בין ...ש... ובין ש whether... or...
beyn yemeen|o/-ah lee-smol|o/-ah בין ימינו לשמאלו **1.** (discerning) between one thing and the other; **2.** *lit* between right and left.
beyn zeh la-zeh בין זה לזה *adv* between them: between this and that.
beynatayeem בינתיים *adv* meanwhile.
beynayeem ביניים *adj* interim; temporary; provisional.
(meemoon) beynayeem מימון־ביניים *nm* interim financing.
(peetron/-ot) beynayeem פתרון־ביניים *nm* interim solution.
(taktseev/-ey) beynayeem תקציב־ביניים *nm* interim budget.
(yemey ha)beynayeem ימי־הביניים *nm pl.* the Middle Ages.
beynee oo-venak ביני ובינך *[slang] (Arab.)* between the two of us; between you and me.
beynenoo (or **benenoo**) בינינו *prep & pron* between us; among us.
(she-yeesha'er) beynenoo שיישאר בינינו let's keep it a secret; confidentially.
beynenoo le-veyn 'atsmenoo *(v=b)* בינינו לבין עצמנו־ entre nous; strictly between us.
beyno le-veynah *(v=b)* בינו לבינה between him and her; between lovers; between husband and wife.
beynonee/-t בינוני *adj* medium; average; middle.
beynoneeyoot בינוניות *nf* mediocrity.
be-yod'eem (or **be-yod'een**) ביודעים *adv* knowingly.
be-yoker ביוקר *adv* dearly; expensively.
be-yosher ביושר *adv* honestly.
be-yoter ביותר *adv* most.
(sodee/-t) be-yoter סודי ביותר *adj* top-secret.
beyt, beyt- , **Beyt-** and derivatives see **bet, bet-** , **Bet-** and derivatives above.
beyts|ah/-eem ביצה *nf* egg (*+of:* **-at/-ey**).
beyts|ah/-eem kashah/-ot ביצה קשה *nf* hard-boiled egg.
beyts|ah/-eem megoolg|elet/-alot ביצה מגולגלת *nf* soft-boiled egg.
beyts|ah/-eem rak|ah/-ot ביצה רכה *nf* soft-boiled egg.
beytsah she-lo noldah ביצה שלא נולדה **1.** *lit* unborn egg yet; **2.** (*figurat.*) something too early to speak of.
beyts|ah/-eem shelook|ah/-ot ביצה שלוקה *nf* hard-boiled egg.
(al tevalbel et ha) beytseem! אל תבלבל את הביצים! *(slang, impolite)* Will you stop bothering me, please!
(eyn lo/lekha/lahem/lakhem) beytseem אין לו/לך/להם/לכם ביצים *[slang]* he/you *(sing)*/ they/you *(pl)* do(es) not have the guts; (*lit.:* testicles).
(yesh lo/lekha/lahem/lakhem) beytseem יש לו/לך/להם/לכם ביצים *[slang]* he/you *(sing)*/ they/ you *(pl)* do(es) have the guts; (*lit.:* testicles).
be-za'af בזעף *adv* furiously; angrily; in anger.
be-za'am בזעם *adv* furiously; angrily; in anger.
be-zadon בזדון *adv* maliciously; wantonly.
be-zeegzageem בזגזגים *adv* in a zigzag.
be-zeel- ha-zol בזיל הזול *adv* dirt cheap.
be-zeelzool בזלזול *adv* scornfully.
bezek בזק *nm* telecommunications.
◇ **"bezek" ("Bezeq")** "בזק" *nf* the Israel Telecommunications Corp. Ltd., a government sponsored company that has taken over Israel's telephonic services from the Ministry of Communications and been running and developing them since, as a commercial enterprise.
be-zol בזול *adv* cheap; cheaply.
bgeedah, bkhee, bkheenah, bkheerah, bkheerot and derivatives see **bekhee, bekheenah, bekheerah, bekheerot** and derivatives.
blameem (*sing:* **belem**) בלמים *nm pl* **1.** brakes; **2.** barriers; (*pl+of:* **beelmey**).
blay בלאי *nm* **1.** amortization; **2.** wear and tear; **3.** depreciation.
blee בלי *prep* without; with no.
blee 'ayeen ha-ra' בלי עין הרע *interj* knock on wood! beware of the evil eye
blee hafoogah בלי הפוגה *adv* incessantly.
blee heref בלי הרף *adv* uninterruptedly.
blee no'a' בלי נוע *adv* motionless.
blee safek בלי ספק *adv* undoubtedly.
bleel/-eem בליל *nm* mixture; concoction; (*pl+of:* **-ey**).
bleem|ah/-ot בלימה *nf* braking; stopping; (*+of:* **-at**).
bleet|ah/-ot בליטה *nf* bulge; projection; (*+of:* **-at**).
blo בלו *nm* excise (tax).
blofer/-eet בלופר *nm & adj* bluffer; cheat; liar.
blondee/-t בלונדי *nmf & adj* blond.
bloree|t/-yot בלורית *nf* mane; braid (of hair).
bnee|yah/-yot בנייה *nf* construction; (Note: pronounced **vneeyah** *etc* when preceded by suffixes **bee-** i.e. in, or **lee-** i.e. for); (*+of:* **-yat**).
bneeyah trومeet בנייה טרומית *nf* prefabricated construction.
(bee) bneeyah (*npr* **bee-vneeyah**) בבנייה *adv* abuilding; under construction.
◇ **(madad yoker ha) bneeyah** see ◇ **madad yoker ha-beneeyah**.
(tokhnee|t/-yot) bneeyah תכנית בנייה *nf* building scheme; construction plan.

bney-adam בני־אדם *nm pl* (*sing:* **ben-adam**) people; human beings.
bney 'aroobah (*colloq. mispronunc:* **'aroovah**) בני ערובה *nm pl* (*sing:* **ben-** *etc*) hostages.
□ **Bney 'Atarot** see □ **Beney 'Atarot**.
□ **Bney 'Ayeesh** see □ **Beney 'Ayeesh**.
□ **Bney Brak** see □ **Beney Brak**.
bney breet (*sing:* **ben** *etc*) בני ברית **1.** *nm pl* allies; **2.** fellow-Jews.
◇ **"bney breet"** see ◇ **"beney breet"**.
□ **Bney Darom** see □ **Beney Darom**.
bney ha-neooreem בני־הנעורים *nm pl* adolescents; youth.
beney no'ar בני נוער *nm pl* youth.
□ **Bney Re'em** see □ **Beney Re'em**.
bney teeshkhoret בני תשחורת *nm pl* youngsters.
□ **Bney Tseeyon** see □ **Beney Tseeyon**.
◇ **"bney yeesra'el"** see ◇ **"beney yeesra'el"**.
bo/ba/bee/bekha/bakh *etc*' בו/בה/בך וכו *prep & poss. pron.* in him/her/me/you *m/f etc.*
bo ba-yom בו ביום *adv* the very same day.
boded/-et בודד *adj* lone; solitary.
bo/-'ee בוא/בואי *v imp sing m/f* come! come along! (*pst & pres* **ba**; *fut* **yavo**; *(v=b)*)
bo/-'ee (*etc*) **henah** בוא/בואי הנה *v imp sing m/f* come here!
boged/-et בוגד *nmf & adj* traitor.
boged/-et בוגד *v pres* betray(s) (*pst* **bagad**; *fut* **yeevgod** *(v=b)*).
boger/-et בוגר *nmf & adj* graduate; adult; mature.
boger/-et ooneeverseetah בוגר אוניברסיטה *nmf* university graduate.
boger/-et teekhon בוגר תיכון *nmf* high school graduate.
bohen/behonot בוהן *nf* thumb; big toe.
bok/-eem בוק *nm [slang]* boor; clumsy.
boker/bekareem בוקר *nm* morning; (*pl+of:* **bokrey**).
boker boker בוקר בוקר *adv* each morning.
boker tov! בוקר טוב! *interj* Good morning!
boker tov oo-mevorakh בוקר טוב ומבורך! *interj* return greeting to **boker tov!**
(**arookh|at/-ot**) **boker** ארוחת בוקר *nf* breakfast.
(**'eeton/-ey**) **boker** עיתון בוקר *nm* morning paper.
bok|er/reem בוקר *nm* cowboy; (*pl+of:* **-rey**).
□ (**Sedeh**) **Boker** שדה בוקר see under □ **Sedeh Boker**.
bokhan/bekhaneem בוחן *nm* **1.** test; trial; **2.** quiz; (*pl+of:* **-ey**).
(**ma'azan/-ey**) **bokhan** מאזן בוחן *nm* trial balance.
bokhen/-et בוחן **1.** *nmf* tester; examiner; **2.** *adj* probing.
(**rav**) **bokhen** רב־בוחן *nm* chief tester; chief examiner.
bokher/-et בוחר *v pres* elect(s); (*pst* **bakhar**; *fut* **yeevkhor**; *(v=b)*).
bokh|er/-areem בוחר *nm* elector; voter; (*pl+of:* **-arey**).

boleshet בולשת *nf* secret police; criminal investigation branch.
bolet/-et בולט *adj* outstanding; conspicuous; *v pres* stand(s) out; (*pst* **balat**; *fut* **yeevlot**; *(v=b)*).
boo|'ah/-'ot בועה *nf* bubble; boil; blister; (*+of:* **-at**).
boobah בובה *nf [slang]* (*npr* **boobah**) doll; baby-doll.
boobah/-ot בובה *nf* doll; (*+of:* **-at**).
boobaleh בובה׳לה *[slang] nmf* darling! dear boy/girl!
bookhn|ah/-ot בוכנה *nf* piston; (*+of:* **-at**).
bookht|ah/-ot בוכטה *[slang] nf* plenty; lots of (*+of:* **-at**).
bool/-eem בול *nm* stamp; postage stamp; (*pl+of:* **-ey**).
bool/-ey do'ar בול דואר *nm* postage stamp.
bool/-ey 'ets בול עץ *nm* block of wood.
bool/-ey hakhnasah בול־הכנסה *nm* revenue stamp.
bool! בול! *interj* bull's eye! direct hit.
(**kal|a'/-'ah/-a'tee**) **bool** קלע בול *v* hit straight in the eye; (*pres* **kole'a'** *etc*; *fut* **yeekla'** *etc*).
(**pag|a'/-'ah/-a'tee**) **bool** פגע בול *v* hit the target; (*pres* **poge'a'** *etc*; *fut* **yeefga'** *etc*; *f=p*).
boola'oot בולאות *nf* stamp collecting.
boolgaree/-t בולגרי *adj* Bulgarian.
boolgaree/-yah בולגרי *nmf* Bulgarian; (people).
boolgareet בולגרית *nf* Bulgarian (the language).
(**gveenah**) **boolgareet** גבינה בולגרית *nf* white salted cheese of Balkan flavor.
boolgaryah בולגריה *nf* Bulgaria.
boolmoos בולמוס *nm* mania; strong desire.
boonker/-eem בונקר *nm* bunker.
boor/-eem בור *nm & adj m* illiterate; ignorant; boorish (*pl+of:* **-ey**).
(**sedeh**) **boor** שדה בור *nm* uncultivated field.
booreykah/-s בורקה *nf* baked filo dough; baked loaf filled with cheese, meat or spinach. Traditional favorite dish of Sephardi Jews
boorganee/-t בורגני *nmf & adj* bourgeois; *[slang]* wealthy.
boorganoot בורגנות *nf* bourgeoisie; the wealthy class.
□ **Boorgatah** (Buregeta) בורגתה *nm* village (est. 1949) in Sharon, 9 km E. of Netanya. Pop. 442.
(**'al**) **boor|yo/-yah** על בוריו *adj* thorough.
boors|ah/-ot (*npr* **boorsah**) בורסה *nf* stock-exchange; (*+of:* **-at**).
boorsah lee-neyarot 'erekh בורסה לניירות ערך *nf* securities-exchange.
boors|at/-ot yahalomeem בורסת יהלומים *nf* diamond exchange.
boosh|ah/-ot בושה *nf* shame; disgrace; (*+of:* **-at**).
booshah oo-khleemah *(kh=k)* בושה וכלימה *interj* shame on...; what a shame!
(**khas|ar/-rat**) **booshah** חסר בושה *adj* shameless.

□ **Boostan ha-Galeel** (Bustan Hagalil) בוסתן הגליל *nm* village (est. 1948) in N. Galilee, 2 km N. of Akko (Acre). Pop. 487.

bootlal/-lah בוטל *v* was cancelled; was abolished; (*pres* **mevootal**; *(v=b)*; *fut* **yevootal**).

booz בוז *nm* contempt.

booz le- ! בוז ל־ ! *interj* boo! down with! shame on ...!

bor/-ot בור *nm* pit; dungeon.

bor/-ot shofkheen בור שופכין *nm* cesspit.

bore/-t בורא *v pres* creates; (*pst* **bara**; *fut* **yeevrah** *(v=b)*).

(ha) bore הבורא *nm* the Creator; the Maker.

boreg/brageem בורג *nm* screw; (*pl+of:* **borgey**).

borer/-eem בורר *nm* **1.** arbitrator; **2.** sorter; (*pl+of:* **-ey**).

borer afeekeem בורר אפיקים *nm* channel selector (electronics).

borer makhree'a' בורר מכריע *nm* umpire.

borerootl/-yot בוררות *nf* arbitration.

borerootl khovah בוררות חובה *nf* obligatory arbitration.

(ha-kadosh) borkhoo הקדוש ברוך הוא *nm [colloq.]* God Almighty.

bos/-eem בוס *[slang] nm* boss.

bosem/bsameeem בושם *nm* perfume; scent; (*pl+of:* **bosmey**).

boser בוסר **1.** *adj* unripe (fruit, idea); **2.** *nm* fruit that is not yet ripe.

(neesoo'ey) boser נישואי בוסר *nm pl* under-age marriage.

botneem בוטנים *nm pl* (*sing:* **boten**) peanuts.

bots בוץ *nm* mud.

botsee (*npr* **bootsee**)**/-t** בוצי *adj* muddy.

boydem בוידם *[slang]* (Yiddish) *nm* attic.

bozmanee/-t בו־זמני *adj* simultaneous.

bozmaneet בו־זמנית *adv* simultaneously.

□ **Brakhah** ברכה *nm* communal settlement (est. 1983) on Mount **Greezeem**, overlooking the town of Nablus.

brakhah/-ot ברכה *nf* blessing; greeting; (*+of:* **beerlkat/-khot**; *k=kh*).

(geshem/geeshmey) brakhah גשם ברכה *nm* bountiful rain.

(ateret) brakhot עתרת ברכות *nf* a sheaf of blessings.

bram ברם *adv* yet; however.

brarah בררה *[colloq.] nf* **1.** second-rate fruits (specifically: oranges); **2.** left-overs; second-rate (also *figurat.*).

breel'akh/-kheem בריח *nm* bolt; latch; (*pl+of:* **-ey**).

breekhlah/-ot בריחה *nf* flight; escape; (*+of:* **-at**).

◇ **"(ha)breekhah"** ("Bricha") "ה"בריחה *nf* (*hist.*) the "underground railway" movement that in the years 1945-1948 gathered Jews from all over liberated Europe to ship them "illegally" to Palestine.

bree'oot בריאות *nf* health.

(meesrad ha) bree'oot משרד הבריאות *nm* Ministry of Health.

breet/-ot ברית *nf* **1.** covenant; **2.** circumcision ceremony; **3.** pact: **4.** fraternity.

◇ **breeta** בריתה *[slang] nf* reception which some parents give on occasion of the birth of a girl to parallel that of a boy's "Brith mila" (see ◇ **breet meelah** below).

□ **breet ha-mo'atsot** ברית המועצות *nf* the Soviet Union.

◇ **breet meelah** (Brith Mila) ברית מילה *nm* Jewish rite of circumcision performed at a religious and social ceremony held on the eighth day after birth of a boy.

(artsot ha) breet ארצות הברית *nf* the United States.

(ba'al/-at) breet בעל־ברית *nmf* ally.

(ben/-ey) breet בן־ברית *nm* fellow-Jew.

"(ha)breet ha-khadashah" הברית החדשה *nf* the New Testament.

(karlat/-tah/-atetee) breet כרת ברית *v* made a covenant; entered an alliance; (*pres* **koret** *etc;* *fut* **yeekhrot** *etc*).

(lookhot ha) breet לוחות הברית *nm pl* the holy tablets of the Decalogue (Bibl.).

(ha) breeyot בריות *nf pl* (*sing:* **breeyah**) the people.

brekhlah/-ot (*also pronounced:* **breykhlah/-ot**) בריכה *nf* pool; (*+of:* **-at**).

□ **Brekhat 'Amal** בריכת עמל see **"Sakhneh"**.

□ **Brekhat HaMeshoosheem** בריכת המשושים *nf* "the Hexagon Pool"- waterfall and pool surrounded by columns in the Golan Heights, 6 km NE of the Jordan estuary.

brekhat sekheeyah בריכת שחייה *nf* swimming pool.

□ **Brekhot Shelomo** בריכות שלמה *nf pl* "King Solomon's Pools" - complex of 3 large open ancient water reservoirs 4 km S. of Bethlehem.

bresheet בראשית "in the beginning" (Genesis).

(ma'aslleh/-ey) bresheet בראשית *nm* act of Creation.

brerlah/-ot (*also pronounced:* **breyrah/-ot**) ברירה *nf* choice; alternative; (*+of:* **-at**).

(en) brerah (*or:* **eyn** *etc*) אין ברירה no alternative; no choice left.

(be-let) brerah בלית ברירה in the absence of an alternative.

(let) brerah לית ברירה no alternative.

(yesh) brerah יש ברירה there is a way.

brerlat/-ot kenas ברירת קנס *nf* fine (usually for traffic offences) the payment of which dispenses one from being tried in court.

breykhlah/-ot בריכה see **brekhlah/-ot** and derivatives, above.

breyrlah/-ot ברירה see **brerlah/-ot** and derivatives, above.

brokh/-eem ברוך *[slang] nm* (Yiddish) disaster; misfortune; bad luck.

brookhah ha-ba'ah! !ברוכה הבאה (greeting) welcome! (addressing a female).

brookheem ha-ba'eem ברוכים הבאים (greeting) welcome! (addressing two persons or more persons including, at least, one male).

□ **Bror Khayeel** (Beror Hayil) ברור חיל *nm* kibbutz (est. 1948) in W. Negev 6 km NE of Sederot. Pop. 600.

brosh/-eem ברוש *nm* cypress; pine; (*pl+of:* **-ey**).

□ **Brosh** (Berosh) ברוש *nm* village (est. 1953) in W. Negev, 6 km N. of **Ofakeem**. Pop. 244.

□ **(Khevel ha)Bsor** the **Besor** District see □ **Khevel Eshkol**.

bsor|ah/-ot בשורה *nf* good news; tidings (*+of:* **-at**).

C.

See Note under CH, below.

CH.

transliterating the consonant צ׳

NOTE: Due to the fact that the letter "**c**", in English, may be read in several different ways, it is not used in the system devised here for transliterating Hebrew. One finds hereunder merely words beginning with "**ch**" that have infiltrated into Hebrew slang or colloquialisms. Hebrew words that might have begun with "**c**" as pronounced in *coming* are found in the **K.** chapter. Words beginning with the "**c**" pronounced as in *civil*, are found in the **S.** chapter.

chakh'chakh/-eem צ׳חצ׳ח *[slang] m* derogative nickname for a commonly behaving young Jew of North-African background.

chans/-eem צ׳אנס *[slang]* (Engl.) *nm* chance.

chapachool/-ah צ׳פאצ׳ול *[slang]* (Ladino) *nmf* & *adj* someone negligent and unimportant; a non-entity.

cheelee צ׳ילי *nf* Chile.

cheeleeyanee/-t צ׳יליאני *nmf & adj* Chilean.

cheek-chak צ׳יק־צ׳ק *[slang] adv* fast; in a jiffy.

(be) cheek בצ׳יק *[slang] adv* fast.

cheeps/-eem צ׳יפס *nm* French fried potato.

cheezbat/-eem צ׳יזבט *[slang] (Arab.) nm* **1.** bluff; lie; **2.** empty boast.

cheezbet/-etah/-atetee צ׳יזבט *[slang]* bluffed; told false tales (of heroism); (*pst* **mechazbet**; *fut* **yechazbet**).

chek/-eem צ׳ק *nm* check (*npr* **shek/-eem**).

cherkesee/-m צ׳רקס *nm* Circassian i.e. member of the 2,000 strong Circassian community that settled in the Galilee over a century ago in its flight from the Caucasus. Concentrated in two villages**Kafer Kana** and **Reykhaneeyeh** this Sunnite-Muslim minority is known for its loyalty to Israel; its members traditionally serve n the country's police and armed forces.

cherkeseeyah צ׳רקסייה *nf* Israeli folk dance.

choopar/-eem צ׳ופר *[slang] nm* extra grant.

choopcheek/-eem צ׳ופצ׳יק *[slang]* (Russian) **1.** protruding end of an object; **2.** *(vulgar)* penis.

D.

transliterating the Hebrew consonant ד (**Dalet**)

da'/de'ee דע *v imp s m/f* know! let it be known to you! (*pst* **yada'**; *pres* **yode'a'**; *fut* **yeda'**).

da' lekha/de'ee lakh דע לך *v imp sing m/f* take note that; let it be known that.

da'ag/-ah/-tee דאג *v* worried; took care; (*pres* **do'eg**; *fut* **yeed'ag**).

da'ag le- דאג ל־ *v* took care of; took care that.

da'akh/-a דעך *v* faded; flickered; (*pres* **do'ekh**; *fut* **yeed'akh**).

da'at דעת *nf* knowledge.

da'at kahal דעת קהל *nf* public opinion.

('al) da'at (or **da'at|ee/-o/-ah/-kha** *etc*) על דעת/־י/־ו/־ה/־ך *adv* with the (or: my/his/her/your *etc*) consent.

('alah/-tah 'al) da'at|ee/-o/-ah *etc* עלה על דעת/־י ו/־ה/־ך *v* entered my/his/her *etc* mind; occurred to me/him/her *etc*; (*pres* **'oleh** *etc*; *fut* **ya'aleh** *etc*).

('am|ad/-dah/-adetee 'al) da'ato/-ah/-ee עמד על דעתו *v* insisted; (*pres* **'omed** *etc*; *fut* **ya'amod** *etc*).

(be-hesakh ha) da'at בהיסח הדעת *adv* unthinkingly; inadvertently.

(eeb|ed/-dah 'atsm|o/-ah la) da'at איבד עצמו לדעת *v* committed suicide; (*pres* **me'abed** *etc*; *fut* **ye'abed** *etc*).

(geeloo|y/-yey) da'at גילוי דעת *nm* manifesto; public statement.

(gnevat) da'at גניבת דעת *nf* deceit; swindle.

(hayah be) da'at (or: **da'at|ee/-o/-ah/-kha**) היה בדעת/־י/־ו/־ה/־ך it was the (or: my/his/her/your *etc*) intention.

(hesakh ha) da'at היסח הדעת *nm* absentmindedness; inattention.

(kal/at) da'at קלת דעת *adj* light-headed; rash; frivolous.

(kaloot) da'at קלות דעת *nf* frivolity.

(khavat/-ot) da'at חוות דעת *nf* opinion.

(la-'aneeyoot) da'at (or: **da'at|ee/-o/-ah/-khah/-ekh** *etc*.) לעניות דעת/־י/־ו/־ה/־ך in the (or: my/his/her/your *m/f etc*) humble opinion.

(la) da'at לדעת *v inf* to know; (*pst* **yada'**; *pres* **yode'a'**; *fut* **yeda'**).

(le) da'at (or: **da'at|ee/-o/-kha/-ekh** *etc*) לדעת in the (or: my/his/her *etc*) opinion.

(mee) da'at מדעת *adv* knowingly.

(mekel/mekeelah) da'at מקל דעת *v* disregarded; did not value; (*pst* **hekel** *etc*; *fut* **yakel** *etc*).

(menee|'akh/-khah et ha) da'at מניח את הדעת *adj* satisfactory.

(nat|an/-nah et ha) da'at נתן את הדעת *v* turned attention; (*pres* **noten** *etc*; *fut* **yeeten** *etc*).

(sheekool) da'at שיקול דעת *nm* discretion.

(teroof) da'at טירוף דעת *nm* madness.

(yesh be) da'at (or: **da'atee/-o/-ah** *etc*) יש בדעת/־י/־ו/־ה/־ך it is the (or: my/his/her/your *etc*) intention.

(shak|al/-lah/-altee be) da'at|o/-ah/-ee שקל בדעתו considered; thought over; (*pres* **shokel** *etc*; *fut* **yeeshkol** *etc*).

(yats|a/-'ah mee) da'at|o/-ah יצא מדעתו *v* went mad; went out of one's mind; (*pres* **yotse** *etc*; *fut* **yetse** *etc*).

dab|er!/-ree! דבר! *v imp sing m/f* speak up! talk! (*pl m/f* **-roo!/-erna!**).

daberet דברת *nf* empty chatter.

daboor/-eem דבור *nm* wasp (*pl+of:* **-ey**).

dabran/-eet דברן *adj* talk'er; talkative.

dadeem דדים *nm pl* (sing: dad) teats; nipples; (*+of:* **dadey**).

daf/dapeem *(p=f)* דף *nm* page; sheet of paper; (*pl+of:* **dapey**).

daf khalak דף חלק *nm* **1.** blank sheet; **2.** tabula rasa (used *figurat.*).

daf|ak/-kah/-aktee ba- (or: **'al**) דפק ב־ / על *v* knocked on; (*pres* **dofek** *etc*; *fut* **yeedpok** *etc*).

dafak (*etc*) **et/oto** *etc* דפק את/אותו/־ה וכו' *v [slang]* abused, humiliated.

dafak et/otah/otan דפק את/אותה וכו' *v [slang]* laid (her); possessed sexually.

dafd|efet/-afot דפדפת *nf* writing pad.

dafnah דפנה *nf* laurel; daphne.

□ **Dafnah** (Dafna) דפנה *nm* kibbutz (est. 1939) in E. part of Upper Gallilee, 7 km NE of **Keeryat-Shmonah**. Pop. 623.

(zer/-ey) dafnah זר דפנה *nm* laurel; laurels.

dafook/defookah דפוק *[slang] adj* downtrodden; abused; battered.

dag/-eem דג *nm* fish (*pl+of:* **degey**).

dag/-ah/-tee דג *v pst.* fished; is fishing; (*pres* **dag**; *fut* **yadoog**).

dag feeleh דג־פילה *nm* fish fillet.

dag/-eem maloo'akh/melookheem דג מלוח *nm* herring.

dagah דגה *nf* fishing reserves.
dag|al/lah דגל *v* professed; (*pres* **dogel**; *fut* **yeedgol**).
dagan/deganeem דגן *nm* grain; cereals; (*pl+of:* **deegney**).
dag|ar/-rah דגר *v* **1.** hatched; **2.** *[slang]* studied hard; (*pres* **doger**; *fut* **yeedgor**).
dagdegan דגדגן *nm* clitoris.
dageem memoola'eem דגים ממולאים *nm pl* "gefilte fish" - traditional Jewish meal (stuffed fish).
(shemen) dageem שמן דגים *nm* cod-liver oil.
dagesh/degesh|eem דגש *nm* **1.** emphasis **2.** a dot in a Hebrew letter; (*pl+of:* **-ey**).
daglan/-eem דגלן *nm* standard-bearer; (*pl+of:* **-ey**).
dagool/degoolah דגול *adj* prominent; distinguished.
dagoosh/degooshah דגוש *adj* **1.** stressed; **2.** dotted (Hebrew letter).
dah|ah/-atah דהה *v* faded; (*pres* **doheh**; *fut* **yeed'heh**).
dahar/-ah/-tee דהר *v* galloped; (*pres* **doher**; *fut* **yeed'har**).
dahooy/dehooyah דהוי *adj* fading; discolored.
dak/-ah דק *adv* thin.
(remez) dak רמז דק *nm* gentle hint; slight hint.
dakah/-ot דקה *nf* minute; (*+of:* **-at**).
dakah akhat! !דקה אחת *interj* just a minute!
dak|ar/-rah/-artee דקר *v* stabbed; (*pres* **doker**; *fut* **yeedkor**).
dakh|ah/-atah/-eetee דחה *v* **1.** rejected; **2.** put off; postponed; (*pres* **dokheh**; *fut* **yeedkheh**).
dakhaf/dekhafeem דחף *nm* impulse; urge; (*pl+of:* **dakhfey**).
dakhaf/-ah/-tee דחף *v* pushed; (*pres* **dokhef**; *fut* **yeedkhof**).
dakhak/-ah/-tee דחק *v* pushed; pressed for; (*pres* **dokhek**; *fut* **yeedkhak**).
dakhak (*etc*) **bo/bah** *etc* דחק בו *v* hurried him/her *etc*; pressed him/her *etc*.
dakhak (*etc*) **et ha-kets** דחק את הקץ *v* forced the issue.
dakhak דחק *nm* **1.** congestion; **2.** (Medic.) tenesmus.
dakheel|ak/-ek דחילק *v imp m/f [colloq.] (Arab.)* please! I implore you!
dakhleel/-eem דחליל *nm* scarecrow; (*pl+of:* **-ey**).
dakhoof/dekhoofah דחוף *adj* urgent; pressing.
dakhook/dekhookah דחוק *adj* hard up; scarce.
(be-matsav) dakhook במצב דחוק *adv* in financial difficulties.
dakhooy/dekhooyah דחוי *adj* postponed.
(chek/-eem) dakhooy/dekhooyeem שיק דחוי *nm* postdated check.
dakhpor/-eem דחפור *nm* bulldozer; (*pl+of:* **-ey**).
dal/ah דל *adj* **1.** poor; **2.** scarce.
dal/-at emtsa'eem דל אמצעים *adj* short of means.
dal/-at ma'as דל מעש *adj* poor in deeds; ineffectual.
dal|ah/-tah/-eetee דלה *v* drew water; hauled up; (*pres* **doleh**; *fut* **yeedleh**).
dal|af/-fah דלף *v* leaked; dripped; (*pres* **dolef**; *fut* **yeedlof**).
dal|ak/-kah/-aktee דלק *v* **1.** burned; **2.** pursued; (*pres* **dolek**; *fut* **yeedlok**).
dalaktee/-t דלקתי *adj* inflammatory (Medic).
dalat ha-'am דלת העם *nf* the poor classes.
daled see dalet, below.
(yod) daled see yod dalet, below.
(yom) daled see (yom) dalet, below.
daleek/deleekah דליק *adj* inflammable.
daleel/deleelah דליל *adj* spare; thin.
daleket/dalakot דלקת *nf* (Medic.) inflammation.
daleket kroom ha-mo'akh דלקת קרום המוח *nf* meningitis (Medic.).
daleket prakeem דלקת־פרקים *nf* (Medic.) rheumatic fever.
daleket re'ot דלקת ריאות *nf* pneumonia (Medic.).
daleket seemponot דלקת סמפונות *nf* bronchitis (Medic.).
Dalet דל״ת 4th letter of Hebrew alphabet, equivalent to consonant **d**.
dalet ד׳ digit 4 (four) in Hebrew system of alphabetic numerology.
dalet alafeem ד׳ אלפים numeral 4,000, four thousand.
(yod) dalet - י״ד **1.** 14; fourteen; **2.** the 14th of a Jewish calendar month.
(yom) dalet יום ד׳ *nm* **1.** Wednesday; **2.** the 4th day of... (a Jewish calendar month).
daloo'akh/delookhah דלוח *adj* foul; turbid.
dalpek/-eem (*npr* **delpek**) דלפק *nm* counter (in store); (*pl+of:* **-ey**).
dalt|ee/-ekha/-ekh/-o/-ah *etc* (see **delet**) דלתי *nf & poss. pron* my/your/(*m/f*)/his/her *etc* door.
□ **Dalton** דלתון *nm* village (est. 1950) in Upper Galilee, 5 km N. of Safed (**Tsefat**). Pop. 595.
daltot דלתות *nf pl+of* the doors of... (*sing:* **delet**; *pl:* **dlatot**).
□ **Dalyah** (Daliyya) דליה *nm* kibbutz (est. 1939) 21 km NE of **Zeekhron-Ya'akov**. Pop. 892.
□ **Dalyat al Karmel** דליית אל כרמל *nm* Druze town in the Karmel Mountains, near Elyaqim-Haifa road. Pop. 10,300.
dam/-eem דם *nm* blood.
('aleelat/-ot) dam עלילת דם *nm* blood libel.
(basar va) dam בשר ודם *nm* flesh and blood; human being; mortal.
(be) dam kar דם קר *adv* in cold blood.
('eeroo|y/-yey) dam עירוי דם *nm* blood transfusion.
(ge'oolat) dam גאולת דם *nf* vendetta.
(har'al|at/-ot) dam הרעלת דם *nf* blood poisoning.
(kadooreeyot) dam כדוריות דם *nf pl* (*sing:* **kadooreet**) blood cells; corpuscles.
(keervat) dam קרבת דם *nf* blood relationship.
(kreesh/-ey) dam קריש דם *nm* blood clot.

(lakhats) dam לחץ דם *nm* blood pressure.
(makhzor ha) dam מחזור הדם *nm* blood circulation.
(motsets/-ey) dam מוצץ דם *adj* blood sucker.
(shat|at/-etah) dam שתת דם *v* bled; (*pres* **shotet** *etc; fut* **yeeshtot** *etc*).
(shkee|'at/'ot) dam שקיעת דם *nf* blood sedimentation.
(shetef/sheetfey) dam שטף דם *nf* hemorrhage.
(tsme/-'at) dam צמא דם *adj* bloodthirsty.
(zav/-at) dam זב דם *adj* bleeding.
(zov) dam זוב דם *nm* bleeding hemorrhage.
(yesh le-/lo/lah *etc*) **dam** יש ל־/לו/לה וכו' דם *[slang]* (one/he/she *etc*) has guts; has nerve.
dam|ah/-tah/-eetee דמה *v* resembled (*pres* **domeh**; *fut* **yeedmeh**).
dam|am/-emah דמם *v* remained silent; became still; (*pres* **domem**; *fut* **yeedom**).
dameem דמים *nm pl* **1.** price; **2.** money; **3.** blood; (*sing:* **dam**; *pl+of:* **demey**).
-dameem דמים *adj* bloody.
dameem, tartey mashma' דמים, תרתי משמע **1.** both in money and in blood; **2.** *lit.* : **dameem** has two meanings.
(be) dameem meroobeem בדמים מרובים *adv* at tremendous expense.
(merkhats) dameem מרחץ דמים *nm* bloodbath.
(shefeekhoot) dameem שפיכות דמים *nf* bloodshed.
('eynayeem) dam'oo עיניים דמעו *v* (eyes) shed tears.
□ **Dan** (or **Goosh Dan**) גוש דן or דן *nm* Greater Tel-Aviv area.
□ **Dan** דן *nm* kibbutz (est 1939) in E. Upper Galilee, 10 km NE of **Keeryat Shmonah**. Pop. 531.
◇ **"Dan"** "דן" *nm* bus-drivers' cooperative holding an exclusive concession for public bus transport in the city of Tel-Aviv. In neighboring cities making up the Greater Tel-Aviv area, "Dan" runs lines parallel with "Egged", the bus-drivers' cooperative that holds a virtual monopoly of public bus transportation in the entire country. (See: ◇ **"Eged"**).
dan/-ah/-tee be- דן ב־ *v* dealt with: discussed; (*pres* **dan**; *fut* **yadoon**).
dan (*etc*) **be-rotkheen** דן ברותחין *v* castigated: criticized vehemently.
dan (*etc*) **et** דן את *v* sentenced; condemned: judged.
da'on/-eem דאון *nm* glider (aircraft).
dapar/-eet דפר *nmf [slang]* (army) boor; yokel.
dar|akh/-khah/-akhtee דרך *v* **1.** stepped; **2.** bent (bow); (*pres* **dorekh**; *fut* **yeedrokh**).
dar|as/-sah/-astee דרס *v* overran; trampled; (*pres* **dores**; *fut* **yeedros**).
dar|ash/-shah/-ashtee דרש *v* demanded; (*pres* **doresh**; *fut* **yeedrosh**).
darban/-eem דרבן *nm* hedge-hog; porcupine.
dardar/-eem דרדר *nm* thorn; (*pl+of:* **-ey**).
dardas/-eem דרדס *nm* smurf (cartoon character); (*pl+of:* **-ey**).
dargah/dragot דרגה *nf* grade; degree; rank; (*+of:* **darg|at/-ot**).
(ha'ala|'ah/-'ot be) darga העלאה בדרגה *nf* promotion.
darg|at/-got sakhar דרגת שכר *nf* wage scale.
◇ **dargah yeetsoogeet** דרגה ייצוגית *nf* rank granted for representation purposes only (Army).
darkhey ha-'eekool דרכי האיכול *nf pl* digestive organs.
darkhey no'am דרכי נועם *nf pl* gentle ways.
darkhey shalom דרכי שלום *nf pl* peaceful ways.
darkon/-eem דרכון *nm* passport; (*pl+of:* **-ey**).
darom דרום *nm* S.
daroosh/drooshah דרוש *adj & v pres* required; needed; (*pres* **needrash**; *fut* **yeedaresh**).
darshan/-eem דרשן *nm* preacher; (*pl+of:* **-ey**).
darvan/-eem דרבן *nm* spur; (*pl+of:* **-ey**).
dash דש *nm* lapel.
dash/-eem ד"ש *[slang] nm acr of* **dreeshat shalom**; regards.
dash/-ah/-tee דש *v* - 1. thrashed; trampled; discussed over and over; *pres* **dash**; *fut* **yadoosh**.
dashen/deshenah דשן *adj* fertile; creamy. -
dat/-ot דת *nf* religion; faith.
(hemeer/-ah) dat המיר דת *v* converted to a different faith; (*pres* **memeer** *etc; fut* **yameer** *etc*).
(ka) dat כדת *adv* as one should; as should be.
(ka) dat ve kha-deen *(kh=k)* כדת וכדין *adv* appropriately; legally.
(kohen/kohaney) dat כהן דת *nm* priest.
datee/-t דתי *adj* religious; observant.
dateeyeem דתיים *nm pl.* religious people; strict observants.
dav|ak/-kah/-aktee דבק *v* stuck; adhered: (*pres* **davek**; *fut* **yeedbok** *(b=v)*).
davar/-eem דוור *nm* postman; (*pl+of:* **-ey**).
davar/devareem דבר *nm* **1.** word; **2.** thing; **3.** anything; (*+of:* **devar/deevrey**).
davar akher דבר אחר *nm* different matter.
davar ve-heepookho דבר והיפוכו *nm* point and counterpoint; contradiction in terms.
(af) davar אף דבר nothing; not a thing.
('al lo) davar על לא דבר don't mention it! (standard response to "todah!" !ú?ää i.e. "Thank you!").
(en) davar (*or:* **eyn** *etc*) אין דבר never mind; it doesn't matter.
(keetsooro shel) davar קיצורו של דבר to cut the story short.
(kol) davar כל דבר anything.
(la-ameeto shel) davar לאמיתו של דבר to tell the truth.
(meveen/-ey) davar מבין דבר *nm* connoisseur.
(nog|e'a/-a'at be) davar נוגע בדבר *adj & nmf* interested party.
(raglayeem le-) davar רגליים לדבר *nf pl* reason to assume; reason to believe.

(shem) davar שם דבר *nm & adj* something famous; known all over.

(shoom) davar שום דבר *nm* nothing; not a thing.

(sof) davar סוף דבר *nm* in the end; finally; epilogue.

Daveed ha-melekh דוד המלך King David (Bibl.).

(magen) daveed מגן דוד *nm* **1.** the Star of David; **2.** *(lit.) nm* shield of David.

◇ **(Magen) Daveed Adom** ◇ **Magen Daveed Adom.**

daveek/deveekah דביק *adj* sticky.

davek/devekah דבק *adj* attached; clinging to.

davka (*npr* **davka**) דווקא *adv* precisely; just.

(lav) davka לאו דווקא *adv* not necessarily.

davook/devookah דבוק *adj* glued; joined.

□ **Davrat** דברת *nm* kibbutz (est. 1946) in Yizre'el Valley, 6 km E. of Afula (**'Afoolah**). Pop. 309.

davsh|ah/-ot דוושה *nf* pedal (footboard); (*+of:* **-at**).

davshat ha-belem דוושת הבלם *nf* brake pedal.

davshat ha-matsmed דוושת המצמד *nf* clutch pedal.

day די enough.

day ve-hoter די והותר more than enough.

dayag/-eem דייג *nm* fisherman; (*pl+of:* **-ey**).

dayal/-eem דייל *nm* steward; (*pl+of:* **-ey**).

dayan/-eem דיין *nm* judge; member of a religious court or tribunal; (*pl+of:* **-ey**).

dayar/dayeret דייר *nmf* tenant; (*pl:* **dayar|eem/-ot**; *+of:* **-ey**).

dayeeg דיג *nm* fishing.

('onat ha) dayeeg עונת הדיג *nf* fishing season.

(seer|at/-ot) dayeeg סירת דיג *nf* fishing boat.

dayelet/dayalot דיילת *adj* stewardess; air-hostess.

daykan/-eet דייקן *adj* punctual.

daykanoot דייקנות *nf* punctuality.

(be) daykanoot בדייקנות *adv* punctually.

days|ah/ot דייסה *nf* **1.** porridge; **2.** *[slang]* mess; (*+of:* **-at**).

de'ah/de'ot דיעה *nf* opinion; (*+of:* **da'at**).

de'ah/de'ot kedoom|ah/-ot דיעה קדומה *nf* bias; prejudice; preconceived opinion.

(kheev|ah/-tah/-eetee) de'ah חיווה דיעה *v* expressed an opinion; (*pres* **mekhaveh** *etc; fut* **yekhaveh** *etc*).

de'ag|ah/-ot דאגה *nf* worry; concern; (*+of:* **da'ag|at/-ot**).

(khas|ar/-rat) de'agah חסר דאגה *adj* carefree.

◇ **debkah** דבקה *nf* Arab folk dance.

(be) dee'avad בדיעבד *adv* actually; as a matter of fact; post factum

deeb|ah/-ot דיבה *nf* slander; libel; defamation; (*+of:* **-at**).

(hotsa'at) deebah הוצאת דיבה *nf* libel; slandering.

(meeshpat) deebah משפט דיבה *nm* libel suit.

deeb|er/-rah/-artee דיבר *v* spoke; talked. (*pres* **medaber**; *fut* **yedaber**).

deeber (*etc*) **neekhbadot** דיבר נכבדות *v* suggested marriage; proposed marriage.

◇ **"deebook"** (**"Dybbuk"**) דיבוק *nm* a deceased person's soul believed to have penetrated another person's living body and to have taken possession of it.

deeboor/-eem דיבור *nm* speech; utterance; (*pl+of:* **-ey**).

(amad/-dah/-adetee) be-deeboor עמד בדיבור *v* kept word; kept promise; (*pres* **'omed** *etc; fut* **ya'amod** *etc*).

(heerkh|eev/-eevah/-avtee et ha) deeboor הרחיב את הדיבור *v* elaborated; discussed at length; (*pres* **markheev** *etc; fut* **yarkheev** *etc*).

(kheetookh) deeboor חיתוך דיבור *nm* diction; articulation.

(khofesh ha) deeboor חופש הדיבור *nm* freedom of speech.

(sefat) deeboor שפת דיבור *nf* vernacular; spoken language.

(yeekh|ed/-dah/-adetee et ha) deeboor ייחד את הדיבור *v* dwelt especially on ...; (*pres* **meyakhed** *etc; fut* **yeyakhed** *etc*).

deeboor|eem דיבורים *nm pl* (*sing:* **deeboor**) palavers (*pl+of:* **-ey**).

◇ **('aseret ha) deebrot** see ◇ **'aseret ha-deebrot.**

de'ee lakh דעי לך *v imp sing f* let it be known to you (addressing *sing.* fem. *pers.*).

(temeemoot) de'eem תמימות דעים *nf* unanimous opinion.

deefd|ef/-efah/-aftee דפדף *v* browsed; perused; (*pres* **medafdef**; *fut* **yedafdef**).

deegd|eg/-egah/-agtee דגדג *v* tickled; (*pres* **medagdeg**; *fut* **yedagdeg**).

deegdoog/-eem דיגדוג *nm* tickle; (*pl+of:* **-ey**).

deek|a/-'ah/-etee דיכא *v* oppressed; suppressed; (*pres* **medake**; *fut* **yedake**).

deek|a'on/-'onot דיכאון *nm* melancholy; depression.

deekdook דקדוק *nm* grammar.

deekdook|eem דקדוקים *nm pl [colloq.]* formalities; red tape; (*+of:* **-ey**).

deekdookey 'aneeyoot דקדוקי עניות *nm pl* petty-mindedness; pettiness.

deekhdookh/-eem דכדוך *nm* dejection; dismay; (*pl+of:* **-ey**).

deekhoo|y/-yeem דיחוי *nm* postponement; (*pl+of:* **-yey**).

(le-lo) deekhooy ללא דיחוי *adv* without delay.

deeklem/-emah-amtee דקלם *v* declaimed. recited; (*pres* **medaklem**; *fut* **yedaklem**).

deekloom/-eem דקלום *nm* declamation; recitation; (*pl+of:* **-ey**).

deekoo|y/-yeem דיכוי *nm* suppression; (*pl+of:* **-yey**).

deekt/-eem דיקט *nm [colloq.]* plywood; (*normat. term:* **laveed/leveedeem** לביד).

deeld|el/-elah/-altee דלדל *v* depleted; (*pres* **medaldel**; *fut* **yedaldel**).

deeldool/-eem דלדול *nm* depletion; exhaustion; (*pl+of:* **-ey**).

deel|eg/-gah-agtee דילג *v* skipped; omitted; (*pres* **medaleg**; *fut* **yedaleg**).

dee-lehalan דלהלן *adj* following; as follows.

dee-lekaman דלקמן *adj* following; as follows.

deeloog/-eem דילוג *nm* skipping; leaping over; omission (*pl+of:* **-ey**).

deem|ah/-tah/-eetee דימה *v* imagined; likened; (*pres* **medameh**; *fut* **yedameh**).

deem'ah/dema'ot דמעה *nf* tear; (*+of:* **deem|'at/-'ot**).

(heez|eel/-eelah/-altee) deem'ah הזיל דמעה *v* shed tears; (*pres* **mazeel** *etc*; *fut* **yazeel** *etc*).

□ **Deemonah** (Dimona) דימונה *nf* town (est. 1955) in E. Negev, 36 km E. of Beersheba, on road to Dead Sea. Pop. 26,000.

deemoom/-eem דימום *nm* bleeding; (*pl+of:* **-ey**).

deemooy/-eem דימוי *nm* image; (*pl+of:* **-ey**).

deemyon/-ot דמיון *nm* **1.** imagination; **2.** resemblance.

deemyonot דמיונות *nm pl* fantasies; (*sing:* **deemyon**).

deen/-eem דין *nm* judgment; law; (*pl+of:* **-ey**).

deen kedeemah דין קדימה *nm* preference.

deen ve-kheshbon דין וחשבון *nm* report; account.

('areekhat) deen עריכת־דין *nf* legal practice; advocacy.

('eevoot/-ey) deen עיוות דין *nm* miscarriage of justice.

(gezar/geezrey) deen גזר דין *nm* verdict.

(ha'amadah le) deen העמדה לדין *nf* putting on trial; bringing to justice.

(hamtakat) deen המתקת דין *nf* mitigation of sentence.

(hoo ha) deen הוא הדין *prep* the same applies.

(ka) deen כדין *adv* lawfully; as required by law.

(le) deen לדין *adv* to trial.

(let) deen ve-let dayan לית דין ולית דיין no justice and no judge.

(nat|an/-nah/-atee et ha)deen נתן את הדין *v* was brought to account; was punished.

('or|ekh/-khey) deen עורך דין *nm* lawyer; attorney-at-law; advocate.

('or|ekhet/-khot) deen עורכת דין *nf* woman lawyer.

(pesak/peeskey) deen פסק דין *nm* verdict; court decision.

(shelo ka) deen שלא כדין *adv* unlawully.

(tav|a'/-'ah/-a'tee la) deen לדין תבע *v* sued in court (*pres* **tove'a** *etc*; *fut* **yeetba'** *(b=v) etc*).

(yom ha) deen יום הדין *nm* day of judgment.

deenar/-eem דינר *nm* Dinar, the Jordanian currency unit.

deeney nefashot דיני נפשות *nm pl* capital offences.

deeney 'onsheen דיני עונשין *nm pl* penal law.

deer/-eem דיר *nm* sty; shed; (*pl+of:* **-ey**).

deer balak! דיר באלאק *v imp [slang] (Arab.)* beware! I warn you!

□ **Deer el Asad, Deer el Balakh, Deer Khana, Deer Yaseen** - see **Deir el Asad, Deir el Balakh, Deir Khana, Deir Yaseen,** below.

deer/-ey khazeereem דיר חזירים *nm* pigsty.

deer|ah/-ot דירה *nf* apartment; flat; (*+of:* **-at**).

◇ **deerah bee-dmey mafte'akh** דירה בדמי מפתח *nf* "rent-protected" apartment i.e. one the rental of which is low, being subject to the Rent Protection Law in force since 1940. Upon payment of "key-money" to the landlord, if vacant or, with landlord's consent, to the evacuating tenent, such apartment, normally available only in pre-1948 buildings,can be rented for an indefinite duration.

◇ **deerah bee-sekheeroot** דירה בשכירות *nf* rented apartment; rented flat.

◇ **deerah bee-sekheeroot khofsheet** דירה בשכירות חופשית apartment leased for "free" (i.e. uncontrolled) rental and for a limited duration.

deerah meroohetet דירה מרוהטת *nf* furnished apartment; furnished flat.

(hagbalat sekhar) deerah הגבלת שכר דירה *nf* rent control; rent restriction.

(kron/-ot) deerah קרון דירה *nm* caravan-trailer.

(sakh|ar/-rah/-artee) deerah שכר דירה *v* rented an apartment; (*pres* **sokher** *etc*; *fut* **yeeskor**; *(k=kh)*).

(sekhar) deerah שכר דירה *nm* rent.

deer|at/-ot keva דירת קבע *nf* domicile; permanent residence.

deer|at/-ot serad דירת שרד *nf* official residence; dignitary's state-provided lodging.

deerb|en/-enah/-antee דרבן *v* goaded; urged; (*pres* **medarben**; *fut* **yedarben**).

deerd|er/-erah/-artee דרדר *v* scattered; (*pres* **medarder**; *fut* **yedarder**).

deershee דרשי *v imp sing f* ask for! demand! (adressing single female); (*inf* **leedrosh**; *pst* **darash**; *pres* **doresh**; *fut* **yeedrosh**).

deershee bee-shlom דרשי בשלום *v imp* single *f* give regards to (addressing one female).

deershoo! דרשו! *v imp pl* ask for! demand! (addressing several persons including at least one male).

□ **Deeshon** (Dishon) דישון *nm* village (est. 1953) in Upper Galilee, 13 km N. of Safed (**Tsefat**). Pop. 339.

deeskee|t/-yot דיסקית *nf* **1.** disk; **2.** computer-diskette.

deeskee|t/-yot zeehooy דיסקית זיהוי *nm* identification tag.

deesk|es/-esah/-astee דיסקס *[colloq.]* - *v* discussed (*pres* **medaskes**; *fut* **yedaskes**).

deev|akh (or: **deev|e'akh)/-khah/-akhtee** דיווח *v* reported; rendered an account; (*pres* **medave'akh**; *fut* **yedavakh**).

deevoo|'akh/-kheem דיווח *nm* report; (*pl+of:* **-khey**).

deevrey defoos דברי דפוס *nm pl* printed matter; (*sing:* **devar** *etc*).

deevrey 'erekh דברי ערך *nm pl* valuables; (*sing:* **dvar** *etc*).

deevrey havay דברי הבאי *nm pl* vain talk; bragging; nonsense.

deevrey ha-yameem דברי הימים *nm pl* **1.** annals; chronicles; **2.** history.

◇ **deevrey ha-yameem** דברי הימים *nm* the Book of Chronicles (Bible).

deevrey keeshoor דברי קישור *nm pl* intermediate passages; connecting passages (literary).

deevrey ma'akhal דברי מאכל *nm pl* food items.

deeyook/-eem דיוק *nm* precision; accuracy; (*pl+of:* **-ey**).

(be) deeyook בדיוק *adv* exactly.

(see-) deeyookeem אי־דיוקים *nm pl* inaccuracies.

deeyoon/-eem דיון *nm* debate; discussion; (*pl+of:* **-ey**).

deeyoor/-eem דיור *nm* housing; (*pl+of:* **-ey**).

(peetronot) deeyoor פתרונות דיור *nm pl* housing solutions.

□ **Deezengov** (Disengoff) דיזנגוף name of two of Tel-Aviv's famous landmarks: Disengoff Street **(rekhov deezengov)** and Disengoff Square **(keekar deezengov)** making up the city's worldwide famous entertainment center and promenade.

defek דפק *nm [slang]* misfortune.

defek lo-normalee דפק לא נורמלי *nm [slang]* terrible misfortune; extremely bad luck.

degam/-eem דגם *nm* sample; pattern; mode; (*pl+of:* **deegmey**).

□ **Deganyah Alef** (Deganya A.) דגניה א׳ *nf* oldest **"kevootsah"** (a slightly different type of kibbutz, more intimate) at the S. edge of Lake Tiberias **(Keeneret)**. Est 1911. Pop. 615.

□ **Deganyah Bet** (Deganya B.) דגניה ב׳ *nf* **"kevootsah"**, (a slightly different type of kibbutz, more intimate) located next to Deganya Alef, 10 km S. of Tiberias. Est. 1920. Pop. 649.

degeer|ah/-ot דגירה *nf* hatching; incubation; (*+of:* **-at**).

deg|el/degaleem דגל *nm* flag; banner; (*pl+of:* **deegley**).

◇ **"degel ha-d'yo"** דגל הדיו *nm* (*hist.*) "The Ink-Painted Flag" - improvised Israeli flag the hoisting of which heralded the liberation of Elat in Israel's War of Independence.

(hanafat) degel/degaleem הנפת דגל *nf* hoisting of a flag; flag waving.

degem/degameem דגם *nf* sample; pattern; model; (*pl+of:* **deegmey**).

degey rekak דגי רקק *nm pl* **1.** small fish; **2.** small fry; **3.** common folk.

degey yam דגי ים *nm pl* salt-water fish; ocean fish; (*sing:* **dag-yam**).

dehaynoo דהיינו *adv* that is to say; i.e.

(man) de-hoo מן דהוא *pron* (Aramaic) someone; somebody.

deheer|ah/-ot דהירה *nf* gallop; galloping; (*+of:* **-at**).

□ **Deir el Asad** דיר אל אסד *nm* Arab town in W. Galilee, near the Acre-Safed road, next to **Karmee'el**. Pop. 5,540.

□ **Deir el Balakh** (Deir el Balah) דיר אל בלח *nf* Arab town in the Gaza Strip, 15 km S. of the Gaza-El Arish road. Pop. approx. 28,600.

□ **Deir Khana** (Deir Hanna) דיר חנא *nm* large Arab village in Lower Galilee, 10 km NW of **Tsomet Golanee** (Golani Junction). Pop. 5,460.

□ **Deir Yaseen** (Deir Yasin) דיר יאסין *nm* site of former Arab village Deir Yasin (today part of Jerusalem's **Geev'at Sha'ool** quarter) evacuated following the 1948 War.

dekeer|ah/-ot דקירה *nf* stabbing; (*+of:* **-at**).

dekeerah ba-gav דקירה בגב *nf* stab in the back.

dek|el/-aleem דקל *nm* palm tree; (*pl+of:* **deekley**).

□ **Dekel** (Deqel) דקל *nm* village in Shalom area (est. 1982), 7 km SE of Kerem Shalom, near Egyptian border. Pop. 209.

dekhak דחק *nm* emergency.

('avodot) dekhak עבודות דחק *nf pl* employment for charity's sake.

(bee-sh'at) dekhak בשעת דחק *adv* in case of emergency.

(po'el/po'aley) dekhak פועל דחק *nm* employed for charity's sake.

dekheef|ah-ot דחיפה *nf* **1.** push; **2.** impetus; (*+of:* **-at**).

dekheefoo|t/-yot דחיפות *nf* urgency.

dekhees|ah/-ot דחיסה *nf* compression; (*+of:* **-at**).

dekhee|yah/-yot דחייה *nf* **1.** postponement; **2.** rejections (*+of:* **-yat**).

(khanoot) deleekateseem חנות דליקטסים *nf* delicatessen shop.

del|ek/-akeem דלק *nm* fuel.

delet/dlatot (or, poetically: **dlatayeem**) דלת *nf* door; (*pl+of:* **daltot**).

delet/daltot hazazah דלתות הזזה *nf* sliding door.

del|et/-atayeem ne'oolah/-ot דלת נעולה *nf* locked door.

del|et/-atayeem petookh|ah/-ot דלת פתוחה *nf* open door.

del|et/-atayeem segoor|ah/-ot דלת סגורה *nf* closed door; shut door.

(defok/deefkee ba) delet! דפוק בדלת! *v imp sing m/f* knock on the door! (*pres* **dafak** *etc; fut* **yeedpok**; *etc; p=f*).

(treek|at/-ot) delet טריקת דלת *nf* slamming a door.

(neekhsey) de-lo (*npr* **de-la**) **naydey** נכסי דלא ניידי (Aramaic) *nm pl* immovable properties; real estate.

dema' דמע *nm* tears.

demamah דממה *nf* silence (*+of:* **deememat**).

dema'ot דמעות *nf pl* tears (*sing:* **deem|'ah**; *+of:* **-'at/-'ot**).

(bee) demee yam|av/-eha בדמי ימיו in the prime of his/her life.

demey דמי *nf pl+of* **1.** of the blood of; **2.** fee; allowance.

demey avtalah דמי אבטלה *nm pl* unemployment relief; dole.

demey avtakhah דמי אבטחה *nm pl* protection money; protection fee.

demey 'eravon דמי עירבון *nm pl* earnest money.

demey havra'ah דמי הבראה *nm pl* vacation allowance.

demey kedeemah דמי קדימה *nm pl* deposit; advance-payment.

demey kees דמי כיס *nm pl* pocket money.

demey khasoot דמי חסות *nm pl* "protection" fee.

demey khateemah דמי חתימה *nm pl* subscription fee.

demey keneesah דמי כניסה *nm pl* entrance fee.

demey mafteakh דמי מפתח *nm pl* "key" money.

demey peekadon דמי פיקדון *nm pl* deposit money.

demey sekheeroot דמי שכירות *nm pl* rent money.

demoo|t/-yot דמות *nf* **1.** image; **2.** figure; **3.** character.

demoo|y/-yat דמוי *adj* shaped; form.

(neekhsey) de-naydey נכסי דניידי *nm pl* (Aramaic) movable properties; chattels.

de'oo lakhem דעו לכם *v imp pl* **1.** you must/ should know; **2.** let it be known to you (*inf* **lada'at**; *pst* **yada'**; *pres* **yode'a'**; *fut* **yeda'**).

de'ot דיעות *nf pl* views; opinions; (*sing:* **de'ah**).

(hekhl|eef/-eefah/-aftee) de'ot החליף דיעות *v* exchanged views; (*pres* **makhleef** *etc; fut* **yakhleef** *etc*).

(hog|eh/-ey) de'ot הוגה דעות *nm* thinker.

(kheeloofey) de'ot (or **hakhlafat** *etc*) חילופי דעות *nm pl* exchange of opinions.

(kheelookey) de'ot חילוקי דעות *nm pl* differences of opinion; dissensions.

(le-khol ha) de'ot לכל הדעות *adv* as everyone knows.

derekh דרך *prep* through; by.

der|ekh/-akheem דרך *nf* road; way; method; (*pl+of:* **darkhey**).

('al em ha) derekh על אם הדרך *adv* at the crossroads.

(atsah lo/lah ha) derekh אצה לו/לה הדרך *v* (he/ she) was in a hurry.

(avney) derekh אבני דרך *nf pl* milestones.

(ba) derekh בדרך *adv* underway.

(keevrat) derekh כברת דרך *nf* some distance.

(preetsat) derekh פריצת דרך *nf* breakthrough.

(sal|al/-elah) derekh סלל דרך *v* paved the way; (*pres* **solel** *etc; fut* **yeeslol** *etc*).

(teeltooley) derekh טלטולי דרך *nm pl* tribulations of travel.

derekh agav דרך אגב *adv* incidentally.

derekh erets דרך ארץ *nf* **1.** respect; proper behavior; **2.** courtesy; politeness.

derekh ha-melekh דרך המלך *nf* highway; high-road.

derekh seloolah דרך סלולה *nf* the paved (i.e. the customary) way.

(be) derekh ha-teva' בדרך הטבע *adv* naturally. the natural way.

(be) derekh kelal בדרך כלל *adv* generally.

derekh kol ha-arets דרך כל הארץ *nf* the way of all flesh.

deroog|eem דרוגים *nm pl* (*sing:* **daroog**) graded (seamen); (*pl+of:* **-ey**).

devar/deevrey דבר *m+of* the word of.

(bee) devar בדבר regarding; in the matter of.

devar/deevrey emet דבר אמת *nm* word of truth.

devar/deevrey erekh דבר ערך *nm* valuable thing.

devar-mah דבר מה *nm* something.

devareem דברים *nm pl* words; things; (*sing:* **davar**; *pl+of:* **deevrey**).

(belee omer oo-) devareem בלי אומר ודברים *adv* without saying a thing.

(be-roo'akh ha) devareem ברוח הדברים in the spirit of what was said; in the spirit of things.

(geeboov) devareem גיבוב דברים *nm* verbiage; verbosity.

(zeekhron) devareem זכרון דברים *nm* protocol; memo.

devareem be-'alma דברים בעלמא *nm pl* vain talk; baloney.

devareem be-go דברים בגו there's reason for it; there's something about it.

devareem beteleem דברים בטלים *nm pl* nonsense.

devareem ka-havayatam דברים כהווייתם *nm pl* things as they really are.

devareem shel ta'am דברים של טעם *nm pl* sensible talk; talking sense.

devareem shel mah-be-kakh דברים של מה בכך *nm pl* trivialities.

devareem toveem דברים טובים *nm pl* **1.** *[slang]* goodies; **2.** good things.

(lo hayoo) devareem me-'olam לא היו דברים מעולם **1.** it is absolutely untrue; **2.** *(lit.)* these things never happened.

devash דבש *nm* honey.

(yerakh) devash ירח דבש *nm* honeymoon.

('eres) devay ערש דווי *nf* sickness-bed.

□ **Deveerah** (Devira) דבירה *nm* kibbutz (est. 1951) in N. Negev, 17 km N. of Beersheba. Pop. 421.

devekoot דביקות *nf* devotion.

devor|ah/-eem דבורה *nf* bee.

□ **Devorah** דבורה *nm* village (est. 1956) in Yizre'el Valley, 8 km SE of Afula (**'Afoolah**). Pop. 243.

deyo דיו *nm* ink.

◇ **(degel) ha'deyo** - see ◇ **degel ha-d'yo**.

◇ **(degel) ha-deyo** - see ◇ **degel ha-d'yo**.

dma'ot דמעות *nf pl* tears (*sing:* **deem'ah**; *+of:* **-'at/-'ot**).

(bee) dmee yam|av/-eha בדמי ימיו in the prime of his/her life.

dmey, dmoot, dmooy דמי see **demey, demoot, demooy**.

do דו do or c (in music).

do bemol דו במול c flat (in music).

do deeyez דו דיאז c sharp (in music).

do'ar דואר **1.** *nm* mail; post; **2.** *nm* post-office.

do'ar aveer דואר אוויר *nm* airmail.

do'ar dakhoof דואר דחוף *nm* urgent mail.

do'ar ekspres דואר אקספרס *nm* special delivery.

do'ar khaveelot דואר חבילות *nm* parcel post.

do'ar maheer דואר מהיר *nm* Express Mail Service (EMS).

do'ar na' דואר נע *nm* mobile post office.

do'ar rashoom דואר רשום *nm* registered mail.

(be) do'ar בדואר *adv* by mail.

bool/-ey do'ar בול דואר *nm* postage-stamp.

(deevrey) do'ar דברי דואר *nm pl* mail; (*sing:* **devar-do'ar**).

(ta/-'ey) do'ar תא דואר *nm* post office box; P.O.B.

(tev|at/-ot) do'ar תיבת דואר *nf* mailbox.

dod/-eem דוד **1.** *nm* uncle; **2.** *nm* (in the Bible:) beloved one; lover; (*pl+of:* **-ey**).

(ben/beney) dod/-eem בן־דוד *nm* cousin.

dod|ah/-ot דודה *nf* aunt; (*+of:* **-at**).

(bat/benot) dod|ah/-ot בת־דודה *nf [colloq.]* female cousin.

dodan/-eet דודן *nmf* cousin; (*pl:* **-eem**; *+of:* **-ey**).

dofek דופק *nm* pulse.

dofee דופי *nm* blemish; fault.

(le-lo) dofee ללא דופי *adj* blameless; irreproachable.

dofen/defaneem (also defanot) דופן *nm & nf* side; inside wall (*pl+of:* **dofnot**).

(yotse/-t) dofen יוצא דופן *adj* irregular; exceptional.

dogel/-et דוגל ב־ *v pres* advocates; professes; (*pst* **dagal**; *fut* **yeedgol**).

doger/-et דוגר *v pres* **1.** hatching; hatches; **2.** studies hard; (*pst* **dagar**; *fut* **yeedgor**).

dokh/-ot (*npr* **doo|'akh/-khot**) דו״ח (*acr of* **Deen ve-KHeshbon** דין וחשבון) *nm* **1.** report; **2.** *[slang]* traffic-ticket.

dokh/-ot (*npr* **doo|'akh/-khot**) **khanayah** דו״ח חנייה *nm* parking ticket.

(mas|ar/-rah/-artee) dokh (*npr* **doo|'akh**) מסר דו״ח *v* reported; made one's report; (*pres* **moser dokh**; *fut* **yeemsor dokh**).

(rasham/-mah/-amtee) dokh רשם דו״ח *v* handed a ticket; (*pres* **roshem**; *fut* **yeershom**).

dokhak דוחק *nm* congestion; stress.

(be) dokhak בדוחק *adv* with difficulty; hardly.

dokh|eh/-ah דוחה *adj* repulsive; rejecting.

dokh|eh/-ah דוחה *v pres* reject(s); postpone(s); (*pst* **dakhah**; *fut* **yeedkheh**).

dokhek/-et דוחק *adj* pressing.

dokhek/-et דוחק *v pres* press(es); push(es); (*pst* **dakhak**; *fut* **yeedkhak**).

dolfeen/-eem דולפין *nm* dolphin; (*pl+of:* **-ey**).

dolar/dolareem דולר *nm* dollar; U.S. Dollar.

dol|ef-et דולף **1.** *adj* leaking; **2.** *v pres* leak(s); leaks out; transpire(s); (*pst* **dalaf**; *fut* **dolef**).

□ **Dolev** דולב *nm* communal village (est. 1983) between **Bet-El** and **Modee'een** areas. Pop. 271.

dom דום *adv* still; quiet.

dom/domee/domoo דום *v imp sing (m/f) / pl* shut up! be quiet! (*pst* **nadam**; *pres* **domem**; *fut* **yeedom**)

domee דומי *nm* silence; quiet; (*+of:* **demee**).

(al) domee! !אל דומי *interj* no respite! don't let up!

dom|eh/-ah דומה *adv* it seems.

dom|eh/-ah דומה *adj* similar.

dom|eh/-ah le ־דומה ל *v pres* resemble(s); (*pst* **damah**; *fut* **yeedmeh**).

domem דומם *adj* silent.

domem/-eem דומם *nm* mineral; inanimate.

(ha-rov ha) domem הרוב הדומם *nm* (the) silent majority.

domen דומן *nm* dung; excrement.

donag דונג *nm* wax.

doo- דו *prefix* **1.** two-; **2.** bi-; **3.** ambi-; **4.** co-

doo'akh/dokhot דו״ח *nm* report.

doobar דובר *v* it has been said; it has been agreed; (*pres* **medoobar**; *fut* **yedoobar**).

doob|eem דובים *nm pl* bears (*+of:* **doobey**; *sing* **dov**).

(lo) doobeem ve-lo ya'ar לא דובים ולא יער nothing of the kind (ever happened); don't exaggerate.

doobon/-eem דובון *nm* **1.** teddy-bear; **2.** *[army slang]* warm army jacket.

dood/devadeem דוד *nm* boiler; kettle; (*pl+of:* **-ey**).

dood/-ey keetor דוד קיטור *nm* steam water heater.

dood/-ey khashmalee דוד חשמלי *nm* electric water heater.

dood/-ey shemesh דוד שמש *nm* solar water heater.

doo-'erkee/-t דו־ערכי *adj* ambivalent.

doogee|t/-yot דוגית *nm* dinghy; canoe.

doogm|ah/-a'ot דוגמה *nf* example; sample; (*+of:* **-at**).

(le) doogmah לדוגמה *adv* for instance; e.g.

(le) doogmah לדוגמה *adj* exemplary.

doogman/-eem דוגמן *nm* fashion-model; mannequin (male).

doogmanee|t/-yot דוגמנית *nf* mannequin; fashion-model (female).

(she-'en) doogmat|o/-ah שאין דוגמתו *adj* unparalleled; peerless.

doogree דוגרי *adv [slang] (Arab.)* openheartedly; frankly.

doogree/-t דוגרי *adj [slang] (Arab.)* straight; frank.

(deeb|er/-rah/-artee) doogree דיבר דוגרי *v [slang]* talked turkey; (*pres* **medaber** *etc; fut* **yedaber** *etc*).

dookas/-eem דוכס *nm* duke.

dookasee|t/-yot דוכסית *nf* duchess.

doo-keevoonee/-t דו־כיווני *adj* bi-directional.

doo-keeyoom דו־קיום *nm* co-existence.

dookhan/-eem דוכן *nm* stand; stall; pulpit; (*pl+of:* **-ey**).

doo-komatee/-t דו־קומתי *adj* two storey-; two floor-

(bayeet/bateem) doo-komatee/-yeem דו־קומתי בית *nm* two-storey house.

(otoboos/-eem) doo-komatee/-yeem דו־קומתי אוטובוס *nm* double-decker (bus).

doo-krav דו־קרב *nm* duel.

doomam דומם *adv* silently; in silence.

doo-mashma'ee/-t דו־משמעי *adj* ambiguous.

doo-mashma'oo|t/-yot דו־משמעות *nf* ambiguity.

doo-masloolee-t דו־מסלולי *adj* two-lane (road).

doo-meenee/-t דו־מיני *adj* bi-sexual.

doomeeyah דומייה *nf* silence; stillness.

doo-memadee/-t דו־מימדי *adj* bi-dimensional.

doonam/-eem דונם *nm* dunam; (*pl+of:* **-ey**).

doo-partsoofee/-t דו־פרצופי *adj* hypocritical.

doo-raglee/-t דו־רגלי *adj* two-legged.

doo-see'akh דו־שיח *nm* dialogue.

doo-seetree/-t דו־סטרי *adj* two-way.

doo-sheemooshee/-t דו־שימושי *adj* double-purpose; of double use.

doo-shenatee/- דו־שנתי *adj* bi-annual .

doo-shevoo'ee/-t דו־שבועי *adj* bi-weekly.

doo-shevoo'on/-eem דו־שבועון *nm* bi-weekly (publication).

doo-tsedadee/-t דו צדדי *adj* bilateral.

doovakh/-khah דווח *v* was reported (*pres* **medoovakh**; *fut* **yedoovakh**).

doovdevan/-eem דובדבן *nm* cherry; (*pl+of:* **-ey**).

('ets/'atsey) doovdevan עץ דובדבן *nm* cherry tree.

doovshan/-eem דובשן *nm* honey cake.

doovshanee|t/-yot דובשנית *nm* honey cookie.

□ **Dor** דור *nm* village (est. 1949) and bathing resort on Mediterranean Coast, near Carmel (**Karmel**) Hills. Pop. 219.

dor/-ot דור *nm* generation.

◇ **dor ha-meedbar** דור המדבר *nm* the Generation of the Wilderness (Bibl.) i.e. the one doomed to die out before it would reach the Promised Land.

◇ **dor ha-tekoomah** דור התקומה *nm* Revival Generation reference to Jews who, from 1880 to 1948, witnessed and/or participated in rise of independent Jewish state.

dor holekh ve-dor ba דור הולך ודור בא generations come and go.

(ba)dor ha-zeh בדור הזה in today's generation; in our generation.

(gedoley ha)dor גדולי הדור *nm pl* the great figures of this generation.

(mee) dor le-dor מדור לדור from one generation to generation.

dorey dorot דורי־דורות generation after generation.

(mee) dorey dorot מדורי דורות *adv* since time immemorial.

(yakheed/yekheedah be) dor|o/-ah יחיד בדורו *adj* unique in his/-her generation.

□ **Dorot** דורות *nm* kibbutz (est. 1941) in S. Negev, 5 km SE of Sederot (**Sderot**). Pop. 569.

(bekheeyah le) dorot בכייה לדורות *nf* a misdeed to remember.

(le) dorot לדורות *adv* for generations to come.

(pa'ar ha) dorot פער הדורות *nm* the generation gap.

doron/-ot דורון *nm* gift; present.

dov/doob|eem דוב *nm* bear; (*pl+of:* **-ey**).

dov|er/-reem דובר *nm* spokesman; (*pl+of:* **-rey**).

dover/-et emet דובר אמת *adj* telling the truth.

dov|eret/-rot דוברת *nf* spokeswoman.

□ **Dovev** דובב *nm* village (est. 1963) in Upper Galilee on the Lebanese border. Pop. 356.

dovrah/-ot דוברה raft; (*+of:* **-at**).

□ **Dovrat** see Davrat.

drakheem דרכים *nf* ways; road; (*+of:* **darkhey**; *sing:* **derekh**).

drakheem 'akalkalot דרכים עקלקלות *nf pl* crooked (roundabout) ways.

('al parashat) drakheem על פרשת דרכים *adv* at the crossroads.

(parashat) drakheem פרשת דרכים *nf* crossroads.

(shoded/-ey) drakheem שודד דרכים *nm* highway robber.

(te'oon|at/-ot) drakheem תאונת דרכים *nm* road accident.

drakon/-eem דרקון *nm* dragon (*pl+of:* **-ey**).

drama/-ot דרמה *nf* drama.

dramatee/-t דרמתי *adj* dramatic.

dreekhoot דריכות *nf* tension.

drees|ah/-ot דריסה *nf* running over; trampling (*+of:* **-at**).

dreesat regel דריסת רגל *nf* foothold.

dreesh|ah/-ot דרישה *nf* demand; request (*+of:* **-at**).

dreesh|at/-ot shalom דרישת שלום *nf* regards; compliments.

drom דרום *m+of* the South of.

drom ha-arets דרום הארץ *nm* the South of the country.

drom-afreekah דרום אפריקה *nf* South Africa.

drom afreekanee (or **afreeka'ee/-t**) דרום אפריקני *nmf & adj* South-African.

drom-amereekah דרום אמריקה *nf* South-America.

drom amereekanee (or **amereeka'ee/-t**) דרום אמריקני *nmf & adj* South-American.

drom-ma'arav דרום מערב *nm* south-west.

drom-ma'aravee/-t דרום מערבי *adj* south-western.

drom- (*npr* **dromee-**)**ma'araveet le-** דרום מערבית ל־ *adv* south-west of ...

drom-meezrakh דרום מזרח *nm* south-east.

drom- (*npr* **dromee-**)**meezrakhee/-t** דרום מזרחי *adj* south-eastern.

drom- (*npr* **dromeet-**)**meezrakheet le-** דרום מזרחית ל־ *adv* south-east of ...

dromee/-t דרומי *adj* southern.

(ha-kotev ha) dromee הקוטב הדרומי *nm* the South Pole.

dromeet le-/mee- דרומית ל־/מ־ *adv* south of.

dromeet-ma'araveet le-/mee- דרומית־מערבית ל־/מ־ *adv* south-west of.

dromeet-meezrakheet le-/mee דרומית־מזרחית ל־/מ־ *adv* south-east of.

droogeem דרוגים *nm pl* graded (seamen); (*sing:* **daroog**; *pl+of:* **droogey**).

dror דרור *nm* liberty; freedom.

(kar|a/-rah/-atee) dror קרא דרור *v* set free; liberated; (*pres* **kore**; *fut* **yeekra**).

drosh/deershee דרוש/דרשי *v imp sing m/f* ask of! demand! (*pst* **darash**; *pres* **doresh**; *fut* **yeedrosh**).

drosh/deershee bee-shlom דרוש/דרשי בשלום *v imp sing m/f* give regards to-.

dvar/deevrey דבר *m+of* the word of.

dvar/deevrey emet דבר אמת *nm* word of truth.

dvar/deevrey 'erekh דבר ערך *nm* valuable thing.

dvar-mah דבר מה *nm* something.

(bee) dvar בדבר regarding; in the matter of.

dvareem דברים *nm pl* words; things; (*sing:* **davar**; *pl+of:* **deevrey**).

dvareem be-'alma דברים בעלמא *nm pl* vain talk; baloney.

dvareem be-go דברים בגו there's reason for it; there's something about it.

dvareem beteleem דברים בטלים *nm pl* nonsense.

dvareem ka-havayatam דברים כהווייתם *nm pl* things as they really are.

dvareem shel ta'am דברים של טעם *nm pl* sensible talk; talking sense.

dvareem shel mah-be-kakh דברים של מה בכך *nm pl* trivialities.

dvareem toveem דברים טובים *nm pl* **1.** *[slang]* goodies; **2.** good things.

(blee omer oo-) dvareem בלי אומר ודברים *adv* without saying a thing.

(be-roo'akh ha) dvareem ברוח הדברים in the spirit of what was said.

(geeboov) dvareem גיבוב דברים *nm* verbiage; verbosity.

(lo hayoo) dvareem me-'olam לא היו דברים מעולם it is absolutely untrue.

(zeekhron) dvareem זכרון דברים *nm* protocol; memo.

dvash דבש *nm* honey.

(yerakh) dvash ירח דבש *nm* honeymoon.

('eres) dvay ערש דווי *nf* sickness-bed.

□ **Dveerah** see □ **Deveerah**.

dvekoot דביקות *nf* devotion.

dvor|ah/-eem דבורה *nf* bee.

□ **Dvorah** see □ **Devorah**.

d'yo (or **deyo**) דיו *nm* ink.

◇ **("degel ha) d'yo"** see ◇ **"degel ha-d'yo"**

d'yok|an/-na'ot דיוקן *nm* image; portrait.

dyota/-ot דיותה *nf* inkwell.

E.

incorporating letters **e** (אָ,אֱ), **'e** (עָ,עֶ), **he** (הֶ,הָ)

NOTE: A large proportion of Hebrew-speakers actually make no distinction between **'Ayeen** (עָ, עֶ) - a glottal consonant common to Semitic languages but with no parallel in English - and **Aleph** (אָ, אֶ), a normal hiatus. In all words grouped hereunder, these are transcribed **'e** ('Eh) or **e** (Eh) respectively, and should be pronounced as **e** in *edge* or *effort*.

For a similar reason, since many Hebrew-speakers fail to pronounce the initial letter הָ (**Heh**) we have placed words beginning with **he** (as in *helmet*, not as in *he* or *Hebrew*) with those that begin with **e**, or **'e**. However, since each word is transcribed differently, the user can ascertain its normative pronunciation.

Words beginning with **ee** or **'ee** (pronounced as in *eel* or *eerie*), or *hee* (as in *heel* or *heed*), appear in the following chapter, headed **EE**.

Heh ה *nf* fifth letter of the Hebrew alphabet, normatively pronounced like the English *h*.

Heh ה׳ **1.** digit 5 in the Hebrew system of numerals; **2.** *adj & num* the 5th day of the week i.e. Thursday or of the Jewish calendar month; 5th category of something; 5th grade at school, *etc*.

he lakh/-em/-en הא לך/לכם/לכן *v imp sing f/pl m/pl f* here, take!

he lekha הא לך *v imp sing m* **1.** here, take; **2.** Here you have... (addressing a male person, *sing*).

(yom/yemey) heh יום ה׳ *nm* Thursday.

yom heh be- יום ה׳ ב־ *nm* the 5th day of a Jewish calendar month.

he'adroo|t/-yot היעדרות *nf* absence.

◇ **he'akhzoo|t/-yot** היאחזות pioneering army settlement in an area under military occupation.

he'almoo|t/-yot היעלמות *nf* disappearance.

he'anoo|t/-yot היענות *nf* response.

he'ar|ah/-ot הערה *nf* **1.** remark; **2.** footnote; note; (*+of:* **-at**).

he'arkhoo|t/-yot היערכות *nf* deployment.

he'at|ah/-ot האטה *nf* slowdown (*+of:* **-at**).

he'avkoo|t/-yot היאבקות *nf* wrestling.

he'az|ah/-ot העזה *nf* **1.** daring; **2.** insolence; (*+of:* **-at**).

hebet/-eem היבט *nm* aspect; (*pl+of:* **-ey**).

'ed/-eem עד *nm* witness; (*pl+of:* **-ey**).

'ed/-ey haganah עד הגנה *nm* defense witness.

'ed/-ey medeenah עד מדינה *nm* state witness; state's evidence.

'ed/-ey re'eeyah עד ראייה eye-witness.

'ed/-ey sheker עד שקר *nm* false witness; perjurer.

'ed/-ey shemee'ah עד שמיעה *nm* hearsay witness.

'ed/-ey tevee'ah עד תביעה *nm* prosecution witness.

'ed|ah/-ot עדה *nf* witness (female) (*+of:* **-at**).

hed/-eem הד *nm* echo; reaction; (*pl+of:* **-ey**).

'ed|ah/-ot עדה *nf* community; congregation: (*+of:* **'ad|at/-ot**).

hedad הידד *interj* hurrah! cheers!

(kar|a/-'ah/-atee) hedad קרא הידד *v* acclaimed; (*pres* **kore** *etc; fut* **yeekra** *etc*).

edeem אדים *nm pl* vapors; fumes (*sing:* **ed**; *pl+of:* **-ey**).

hedeem הדים *nm pl* **1.** rumors; reports; **2.** echoes; (*+of:* **-ey**; *sing:* **hed**).

hedef הדף *nm* blast.

hedek הדק *nm* trigger.

eden/adaneem אדן *nm* base; pedestal (*pl+of:* **adney**).

eden/adney khalon/-ot אדן חלון *nm* window sill.

'eden עדן *nm* Eden.

(gan) 'eden גן עדן *nm* Garden of Eden.

(neeshmat|o/-ah) 'eden נשמתו עדן may he/she rest in peace.

(ta'am gan) 'eden טעם גן עדן *nm* heavenly taste.

'eder/'adareem עדר *nm* herd; flock; (*pl+of:* **adrey**).

(ro'eh ha) 'eder רועה העדר *nm* shepherd of the flock.

'edn|ah/-ot עדנה *nf* delight; pleasure (*+of:* **-at**).

'edoo|t/-yot haganah עדות הגנה *nf* defense evidence.

'edoo|t/-yot re'eeyah עדות ראייה *nf* eye-witness evidence.

'edoo|t/-yot sheker עדות שקר *nf* false evidence; perjury.

'edoo|t/-yot shemee'ah עדות שמיעה *nf* hearsay evidence.

'edoo|t/-yot tevee'ah עדות תביעה *nf* evidence for the prosecution.

(gav|ah/-tah/-eetee) 'edoo|t/-yot גבה עדות *v* took evidence (*pres* **goveh** *etc; fut* **yeegbeh** *etc; b=v*).

'edot (*npr* **'adot**) **ha-meezrakh** עדות המיזרח *nf pl* communities of Oriental (Asian, Near-Eastern, North-African) Jewish background.

hedyot/-ot הדיוט *nm* **1.** layman; **2.** simpleton.

> Attention: Words which begin with **ee**, or **'ee** (as in **eel** or **eerie**), or with **hee**, are grouped in the following chapter, headed **EE**.

he'ed|eef/-eefah/-aftee העדיף *v* preferred (*pres* **ma'adeef**; *fut* **ya'adeef**).

he'edeem/-eemah/-amtee האדים *v* flushed; reddened; (*pres* **ma'adeem**; *fut* **ya'adeem**).

he'eder העדר *nm* lack of; absence.

he'eed/-ah/he'adetee העיד *v* testified; (*pres* **me'eed**; *fut* **ya'eed**).

he'eef/-ah/he'aftee העיף *v* threw; cast; (*pres* **me'eef**; *fut* **ya'eef**).

he'eef (*etc*) העיף *v* [*slang*] fired; kicked out; ejected.

he'eef (*etc*) **'ayeen** העיף עין *v* cast a glance; threw an eye.

he'eek/he'eekah/he'aktee העיק *v* weighed heavily (*pres* **me'eek**; *fut* **ya'eek**).

he'eer/he'eerah/he'artee האיר *v* threw light on; illuminated (*pres* **me'eer**; *fut* **ya'eer**).

he'eer/he'eerah/he'artee העיר *v* **1.** awakened; **2.** remarked; (*pres* **me'eer**; *fut* **ya'eer**)

he'eets/he'eetsah/he'atstee האיץ hurried; urged; accelerated; (*pres* **me'eets**; *fut* **ya'eets**).

he|'eez (*npr* **he'ez**)/**-'ezah/-'aztee** העיז *v* dared; (*pres* **me'ez**; *fut* **ya'ez**).

he'ef|eer/-eerah/-artee האפיר *v* turned grey; (*pres* **ma'afeer**; *fut* **ya'afeeroo**).

□ **E'eksal** (Iksal) אכסל *nm* large Arab village in Lower Galilee, 2 km SE of Nazareth. Pop. 6,900.

he'el|ah/-tah/-etee העלה *v* raised; (*pres* **ma'aleh**; *fut* **ya'aleh**).

he'elah (*etc*) **'al ha-ketav** העלה על הכתב *v* put in writing.

he'elah (*etc*) **'al nes** העלה על נס *v* extolled; praised extravagantly.

he'elah (*etc*) **ba-'esh** העלה באש *v* set fire to.

he'elah (*etc*) **gerah** העלה גירה *v* ruminated; chewed its cud.

he'elah (*etc*) **khaloodah** העלה חלודה *v* rusted; got rusty.

he'elah (*etc*) **la-arets** העלה לארץ *v* brought (immigrants) to Israel.

he'el|eel/-eelah/-altee העליל *v* accused falsely; slandered; (*pres* **ma'aleel**; *fut* **ya'aleel**).

he'el|eem/-eemah/-amtee העלים *v* hid; concealed; (*pres* **ma'aleem**; *fut* **ya'aleem**).

he'eleem (*etc*) **'ayeen** העלים עין *v* ignored; shut eyes to.

he'eleem (*etc*) **hakhnasah** העלים הכנסה *v* concealed income.

he'el|eev/-eevah/-avtee העליב *v* insulted; (*pres* **ma'aleev**; *fut* **ya'aleev**).

he'em|eed/-eedah/-adetee העמיד *v* stopped; set up; (*pres* **ma'ameed**; *fut* **ya'ameed**).

he'emeed (*etc*) **le-hatsba'ah** העמיד להצבעה *v* put to vote.

he'emeed (*etc*) **le-meenyan** העמיד למניין *v* proceeded to count.

he'emeed (*etc*) **paneem** העמיד פנים *v* pretended.

he'emeed (*etc*) **et... 'al** העמיד את... על *v* drew one's attention to.

he'emeek/-ah/he'emaktee העמיק *v* deepened; descended deeply; (*pres* **ma'ameek**; *fut* **ya'ameek**).

he'emeen/-ah/he'emantee האמין *v* believed; (*pres* **ma'ameen**; *fut* **ya'ameen**).

he'emeen (*etc*) **le-** -האמין ל *v* trusted; believed (someone).

he'emeer/-ah האמיר *v* soared; went up (price); (*pres* **ma'ameer**; *fut* **ya'ameer**).

he'emees/-ah/he'emastee העמיס *v* loaded; (*pres* **ma'amees**; *fut* **ya'amees**).

he'eneek/-ah/he'enaktee העניק *v* granted; bestowed upon; (*pres* **ma'aneek**; *fut* **ya'aneek**).

he'eneesh/-ah/he'enashtee העניש *v* punished; (*pres* **ma'aneesh**; *fut* **ya'aneesh**).

he'epeel/-ah/he'epaltee העפיל *v* dared; strove towards; (*pres* **ma'apeel**; *fut* **ya'apeel**).

◇ **he'epeel** (*etc*) **la-arets** העפיל לארץ *v* succeeded in entering Palestine "illegally" (during the British Mandate period when immigration of Jews into the country was extremely restricted).

he'ereekh/-ah/he'erakhtee האריך *v* lengthened; prolonged; (*pres* **ma'areekh**; *fut* **ya'areekh**).

he'ereekh (*etc*) **yameem** האריך ימים *v* **1.** lived long; **2.** survived.

he'ereekh/-ah/he'erakhtee העריך *v* **1.** valued; estimated; **2.** appreciated; (*pres* **ma'areekh**; *fut* **ya'areekh**).

he'ereem/-ah/he'eramtee הערים **1.** tricked; cheated; **2.** piled up; (*pres* **ma'areem**; *fut* **ya'areem**).

he'ereem (*etc*) **meekhsholeem** הערים מכשולים *v* put up obstacles; made difficulties.

he'ereets/-ah/he'eratstee העריץ *v* admired; adored; (*pres* **ma'areets**; *fut* **ya'areets**).

he'eseek/-ah/he'esaktee העסיק *v* **1.** employed; **2.** kept busy; (*pres* **ma'aseek**; *fut* **ya'aseek**).

he'esheem/-ah/he'eshamtee האשים *v* accused; charged; (*pres* **ma'asheem**; *fut* **ya'asheem**).

he'esheer/-ah/he'eshartee העשיר *v* enriched; (*pres* **ma'asheer**; *fut* **ya'asheer**).

he'et/-ah/he'atetee האט *v* slowed down; (*pres* **me'et**; *fut* **ya'et**).

he'eteek/-ah/he'etaktee העתיק *v* **1.** copied; **2.** [*colloq.*] cheated (on a test); **3.** moved; (*pres* **ma'ateek**; *fut* **ya'ateek**).

he'etek/-eem העתק *nm* copy (*pl+of:* **-ey**).

he'ev|eed/-eedah/-adetee העביד *v* **1.** employed; **2.** made work; (*pres* **ma'aveed**; *fut* **ya'aveed**).

he'ev|eer/-eerah/-artee העביר *v* **1.** transferred; **2.** transported; (*pres* **ma'aveer**; *fut* **ya'aveer**).

he'eveer (*etc*) **et ha-zeman** העביר את הזמן *v* passed the time.

he'ez/-ah/he'aztee העז *v* dared; (*pres* **me'ez**; *fut* **ya'ez**).

he'ezeen/-ah/he'ezantee האזין *v* listened; (*pres* **ma'azeen**; *fut* **ya'azeen**).

efah ve-efah איפה ואיפה *f & f* double standard; discrimination.

□ **Ef'al** (Ef'al) אפעל *nf* garden guarter, parents home and convention center in SE outskirts of Ramat-Gan, across road from Zoo. Pop. 1080.

hefee'akh/-khah/hefakhtee הפיח *v* puffed up; (*pres* **mefee'akh**; *fut* **yafee'akh**).

hefeeg/-ah/hefagtee הפיג *v* eased; dispelled; (*pres* **mefeeg**; *fut* **yafeeg**).

hefeek/-ah/hefaktee הפיק *v* **1.** derived; **2.** produced; (*pres* **mefeek**; *fut* **yafeek**).

hefeek (*etc*) **to'elet** הפיק תועלת *v* profited; derived profit.

hefeets/-ah/hefatstee הפיץ *v* spread; distributed; (*pres* **mefeets**; *fut* **yafeets**).

(ha) hefekh ההפך *nm* the opposite.

(le) hefekh להפך *adv* on the contrary.

efer/afareem אפר *nm* ashes; dust.

hef|er/-erah/-artee הפר *v* contravened; violated; (*pres* **mefer**; *fut* **yafer**).

hefer (*etc*) **heskem** הפר הסכם *v* violated agreement.

hefer (*etc*) **sheveetah** הפר שביתה *v* engaged in strike-breaking.

efes/afaseem אפס *nm* zero; nought; (*pl+of:* **afsey**).

efes אפס *prep* but; however.

(ekhad-) efes (*npr* **akhat-efes**) אחד־אפס (game score) one nothing.
(me'al le) efes מעל לאפס *adv* over zero (temp.).
(mee-takhat le) efes מתחת לאפס under zero (temp.).
efes leekooyeem אפס ליקויים *adj* zero defects
hefker הפקר *nm* **1.** ownerless property; **2.** irresponsibility; lawlessness.
(shetakh/sheetkhey) hefker שטח־הפקר *nm* no-man's land.
hefkeroo|t/-yot הפקרות *nf* lawlessness; anarchy.
efo? ?איפה where?
efo she-hoo איפה שהוא *adv* somewhere
□ **Efrat** see □ **Efratah**.
□ **Efratah** אפרתה *nf* urban settlement (est 1981) in Judea hills, 6 km SW of Betlehem, 20 km S. of Jerusalem. Pop 2,420.
hefresh/-eem הפרש *nm* difference; (*pl+of:* **-ey**).
hefresheem הפרשים *nm pl* salary-differences due to a raise or to rate-of-exchange fluctuations (*sing:* **hefresh**; *pl+of:* **-ey**).
hefresheeyoot הפרשיות *nf* scale of differences.
efro|akh/-kheem אפרוח *nm* chick; fledgling.
'efron|ee/-eem עפרוני *nm* lark; (*pl+of:* **-ey**).
hefsed/-eem הפסד *nm* loss; (*pl+of:* **-ey**).
(revakh ve) hefsed רווח והפסד *nm* profit and loss.
hefsek הפסק *nm* interruption.
(le-lo) hefsek ללא הפסק *adv* without interruption.
efshar אפשר *adv* perhaps; possibly.
efshar? ?אפשר *query* may I? permit me! would you permit me?
efsharee/-t אפשרי *adj* possible; feasible.
(beeltee) efsharee/-t בלתי אפשרי *adj* (also *adv*) impossible.
efsharoo|t/-yot אפשרות *nf* possibility.
(be-en) efsharoot (*or:* **be-eyn** *etc*) באין אפשרות *adv* there being no possibility.
(meshool|al/-elet) efsharoot משולל אפשרות *adj* deprived of any possibility.
hegeh/haga|'eem הגה *nm* **1.** steering wheel; **2.** murmur; (*pl+of:* **-'ey**).
(okh|ez/-azeem be) hegeh אוחז בהגה **1.** *adj* driving; **2.** *nm* driver.
eged/agad|eem אגד *nm* bandage; (*pl+of:* **ey**).
◇ **"eged" ("Egged")** אגד Israel's largest urban and inter-urban bus company. A bus-drivers cooperative (said to be the world's largest) exercising a virtual monopoly on public bus transport throughout Israel except Greater Tel-Aviv (where there is a second cooperative bus service; see: "Dan"); Beersheba (where the city runs its own bus service); Nazareth, the Arab-populated parts of Jerusalem and territories administered since 1967 (where also Arab-run local bus services operate).
heg|ee'akh/-eekhah/-akhtee הגיח *v* burst forth; broke out; (*pres* **megee'akh**; *fut* **yagee'akh**).
heg|eef/-eefah/-aftee trees/-eem הגיף תריס *v* shut blind(s); (*pres* **megeef** *etc*; *fut* **yageef** *etc*).
heg|eev/-eevah/-avtee הגיב reacted; (*pres* **megeev**; *fut* **yageev**).
'egel/'agaleem עגל *nm* calf; (*pl+of:* **-'egley**).
'egel ha-zahav עגל הזהב *nm* the Golden Calf (Bible).
hegemon|yah/-yot הגמוניה *nf* hegemony; (*+of:* **-yat**).
heg|en/-enah/-antee הגן *v* defended (*pres* **megen**; *fut* **yagen**).
'eglah/'agalot עגלה *nf* heifer; (*+of:* **'egl|at/-ot**).
hegl|ah/-etah/-etee הגלה *v* deported; exiled; (*pres* **magleh**; *fut* **yagleh**).
'egl|at yeladeem עגלת ילדים *nf* baby carriage.
'eglon/-eem עגלון *nm* carter; coachman; wagon driver; (*pl+of:* **-ey**).
egoz/-eem אגוז *nm* nut; (*pl+of:* **ey**).
egoz/-ey pekan אגוז פקאן *nm* pecan nut.
egrof/-eem אגרוף *nm* fist; (*pl+of:* **-ey**).
egrof/-eem kamoots/kemootseem אגרוף קמוץ *nm* clenched fist.
hegyonee/-t הגיוני *adj* reasonable; logical.
ekd|akh/-akheem אקדח *nm* pistol; revolver; (*pl+of:* **-ekhey**).
ekdakh ta'oon אקדח טעון *nm* loaded gun.
hekdem הקדם *nm* earliness.
(be) hekdem בהקדם *adv* early; as soon as possible.
ekdo|'akh/-kheem אקדוח *nm* pistol; revolver; (*pl+of:* **-khey**).
ekdokhan/-eem אקדוחן *nm* gunman; (*pl+of:* **-ey**).
hek|ee/-ee'ah/-etee הקיא *v* vomited; threw up; (*pres* **mekee**; *fut* **yakee**).
hek|eem/-eemah/-amtee הקים *v* set up; erected; (*pres* **mekeem**; *fut* **yakeem**).
hek|eets/-eetsah/-atstee הקיץ *v* awakened; woke up; (*pres* **mekeets**; *fut* **yakeets**).
hekef היקף *nm* scope; perimeter; extent.
hekefee/-t היקפי *adj* peripheral.
hek|el/-elah/-altee הקל *v* eased; mitigated; (*pres* **mekel**; *fut* **yakel**).
hekel (*etc*) **rosh** הקל ראש *v* disparaged; underestimated.
(seeman/-ey) heker סימן היכר *nm* identifying mark.
hekeroo|t/-yot היכרות *nf* acquaintance.
hekesh/-eem היקש *nm* analogy.
'ekev עקב *adv* following; on account of.
ekh? ?איך how?
ekhad/akhadeem אחד *num m* 1; one.
ekhad- (*npr* **akhat-**) **efes** אחד־אפס one nothing (game score).
ekhad-ekhad אחד־אחד *adv* one by one.
ekhad le-me'ah אחד למאה *nm* one in a hundred; one percent.
('ad) ekhad עד אחד *adv* to the last.
(af) ekhad/akhat אף אחד *nmf* no-one; nobody.
(af lo) ekhad/akhat אף לא אחד *nmf* no-one; nobody; not a single one.

(be-rosh) ekhad בראש אחד *adv [slang]* of one mind.

(metoomt|am/-temet) ekhad/akhat! מטומטם אחד! *[slang]* you fool!

(peh) ekhad פה אחד *adv* unanimously.

(rega') ekhad! רגע אחד just a moment! one moment, please!

(shekhem) ekhad שכם אחד *adv* shoulder to shoulder.

ekh ha-'eenyaneem? איך העניינים? *[colloq.]* how goes it? how is everything?

ekhakhah איככה (poetical) how on earth?

hekhal/-ot היכל *nm* palace; temple.

hekhaltsoo|t/-yot היחלצות *nf* getting out of trouble; escape; volunteering.

hekhan היכן *adv* where?

hekhan she היכן ש־... there where.

hekhan she-lo היכן שלא wherever.

(me) hekhan? מהיכן? from where?

hekhb|ee/-ee'ah/-etee החביא *v* hid; (*pres* **makhbee**; *fut* **yakhbee**).

hekhd|eer/-eerah/-artee החדיר *v* inserted; caused to penetrate; (*pres* **makhdeer**; *fut* **yakhdeer**).

hekheel/-ah הכיל *v* contained; comprised; (*pres* **mekheel**; *fut* **yakheel**).

hekh|een/-eenah/-antee הכין *v* prepared (*pres* **mekheen**; *fut* **yakheen**).

hekh|eesh/-eeshah/-ashtee החיש *v* sped up; (*pres* **mekheesh**; *fut* **yakheesh**).

hekhel/-ah/heetkhaltee החל *v* began; commenced.

hekhkeem/-eemah/-amtee החכים *v* wised up; got smart; (*pres* **makhk|eem**; *fut* **yakhkeem**).

hekhk|eer/-eerah/-artee החכיר *v* leased; let; (*pres* **makhkeer**; *fut* **yakhkeer**).

hekhl|eed/-eedah/-adetee החליד *v* rusted; caused to rust; (*pres* **makhleed**; *fut* **yakhleed**).

hekhl|eef/-eefah/-aftee החליף *v* changed; replaced; (*pres* **makhleef**; *fut* **yakhleef**).

hekhl|eef (*etc*) **de'ot** החליף דעות *v* exchanged views.

hekhl|eef (*etc*) **ko'akh** החליף כוח *v* regained strength.

hekhl|eek/-eekah/-aktee החליק *v* smoothed; glided; slid; slipped; stumbled; (*pres* **makhleek**; *fut* **yakhleek**).

hekhleem/-eemah/-amtee החלים *v* recovered; (*pres* **makhleem**; *fut* **yakhleem**).

hekhl|eesh/-eeshah/-ashtee החליש weakened; (*pres* **makhleesh**; *fut* **yakhleesh**).

hekhl|eet/-eetah/-atetee החליט *v* decided; (*pres* **makhleet**; *fut* **yakhleet**).

(be) hekhlet בהחלט *adv* decidedly; absolutely.

hekhletee/-t החלטי *adj* decisive; final.

hekhleteeyoot החלטיות *nf* resoluteness.

hekhm|ee/-ee'ah/-e'tee החמיא *v* flattered; (*pres* **makhmee**; *fut* **yakhmee**).

hekhmeer/-eerah/-artee החמיר *v* **1.** aggravated; **2.** became more serious; (*pres* **makhmeer**; *fut* **takhmeer**).

hekhm|eets/-eetsah/-atstee החמיץ *v* **1.** soured; **2.** missed; failed; (*pres* **makhmeets**; *fut* **yakhmeets**).

hekhmeets (*etc*) **heezdamnoot** החמיץ הזדמנות *v* missed an opportunity.

hekhmeets (*etc*) **paneem** החמיץ פנים *v* looked sour-faced.

hekhn|ah/-etah/-etee החנה *v* parked; (*pres* **makhneh**; *fut* **yakhneh**).

hekhn|eef/-eefah/-aftee החניף *v* flattered; (*pres* **makhneef**; *fut* **yakhneef**).

hekhn|eek/-eekah/-aktee החניק *v* strangled; throttled; (*pres* **makhneek**; *fut* **yakhneek**).

ekhoo|t/-yot איכות *nf* quality.

ekhootee/-t איכותי *adj* qualitative.

ekhoz!/eekhzee! אחוז! *v imp sing (m/f)* hold! (*inf* **(le)'ekhoz**; *pst* **akhaz**; *pres* **okhez**; *fut* **yokhaz**).

hekhre'akh הכרח *nm* necessity; compulsion.

hekhr|eed/-eedah/-adetee החריד *v* terrified; (*pres* **makhreed**; *fut* **yakhreed**).

hekhr|eef/-eefah/-aftee החריף *v* grew more acute; (*pres* **makhreef**; *fut* **yakhreef**).

hekhr|eem/-eemah/-amtee החרים *v* **1.** boycotted; **2.** confiscated; (*pres* **makhreem**; *fut* **yakhreem**).

hekhr|eev/-eevah/-avtee החריב *v* destroyed; ruined; (*pres* **makhreev**; *fut* **yakhreev**).

hekhrekhee/-t הכרחי *adj* obligatory.

hekhs|eer/-eerah/-artee החסיר *v* **1.** missed; left out; **2.** subtracted; (*pres* **makhseer**; *fut* **yakhseer**).

hekh'sh|eed/-eedah/-adetee החשיד *v* threw suspicion on; (*pres* **makh'sheed**; *fut* **yakh'sheed**).

hekh'sheekh/-ah החשיך *v* darkened; night fell; (*pres* **makh'sheekh**; *fut* **yakh'sheekh**).

hekh'sh|eev/-eevah/-avtee החשיב *v* valued; esteemed; (*pres* **makh'sheev**; *fut* **yakh'sheev**).

hekh'sher/-eem הכשר *nm* legitimation; (*pl+of:* **-ey**).

◇ **ekh'sher** see ◇ **"hekh'sher"**.

ekh'shehoo איכשהו *adv* somehow.

hekht|ee/-ee'ah/-e'tee החטיא *v* missed (target); (*pres* **makhtee**; *fut* **yakhtee**).

hekht|eem/-eemah/-amtee החתים *v* signed up; got signatures; (*pres* **makhteem**; *fut* **yakhteem**).

hekht|eem (*npr* **heekh|teem**)**/-eemah/-amtee** הכתים *v* stained; sullied (*pres* **makhteem**; *fut* **yakhteem**).

hekhv|ah (*npr* **hekhev|ah**)**/-etah/-etee keedah** החווה קידה *v* took a bow; (*pres* **makhveh** *etc*; *fut* **yakhveh** *etc*).

hehkv|eer/-eerah/-artee החוויר *v* paled; (*pres* **makhveer**; *fut* **yakhveer**).

hekh|yah/-yetah/-yetee החיה *v* revived; resuscitated; (*pres* **mekhayeh**; *fut* **yekhayeh**).

hekhz|eek/-eekah/-aktee החזיק *v* held; had possession; (*pres* **makhzeek**; *fut* **yakhzeek**).

hekhzeek (*etc*) **ma'amad** החזיק מעמד *v* held out.

hekhz|eer/-eerah/-artee החזיר *v* returned; gave back; (*pres* **makhzeer**; *fut* **yakhzeer**).
hekhzer/-eem החזר *nm* refund.
ekologee/-t אקולוגי *adj* ecological.
ekonomee/-t אקונומי *adj* economic.
□ **Ekron** עקרון *nf* see **Keeryat 'Ekron**.
'ekronee/-t עקרוני *adj* fundamental; essential.
'ekroneet עקרונית *adv* on principle; in principle.
heksher/-eem הקשר *nm* connection; context; (*pl+of:* **-ey**).
(be) heksher בהקשר *adv* in connection with; in the context of.
el אל *prep* to; unto.
el/-eem אל *nm* god.
(ha) el האל *nm* God.
(dee-le) 'el דלעיל *adv* aforementioned; a/m; as above.
(le) 'el לעיל *adv* above; earlier.
ela אלא *conj* but; except; rather.
ela אלה *nf* oak (*+of:* **-at**).
el|ah/-ot אלה goddess; (*+of:* **-at**).
ela eem ken אלא אם כן unless; except if.
(mee-kan ve) elakh מכאן ואילך *adv* hereafter; from here on.
◇ **"el 'al" (El-Al)** אל־על *nf* ("To the Skies") Israel's National Airline - a government-owned company, founded in 1948. Flies to 35 destinations on four continents and employs a staff of 3,600 and a fleet of 18 Boeing airliners.
ela mah?! אלא מה ?! what else?! how else?!
ela may?! אלא מאי ?! how otherwise?!
ela mee?! אלא מי ?! who else?!
(le) 'ela oo-le-'ela לעילא ולעילא *adj* the very best.
ela she- אלא ש־ except that.
(en zeh) ela אין זה אלא could be nothing else but...
□ **Elat** אילת *nf* harbor town (est. 1949) and spa on the Red Sea near presumed site of Biblical harbor **'Etsyon-Gaver**, at Israel's southernmost point. Pop. 26,300.
□ **El'azar** (El'azar) אלעזר *nm* communal settlement (est. 1975) in Hebron Hills, 8 km SW of Bethlehem on Jerusalem-Hebron road. Pop. 267.
'elbon/-ot עלבון *nm* insult.
□ **El Daveed (El David)** אל דוד *nm* communal village (est. 1982) on slopes opposite Mount Herodion fortress, 20 km S. of Jerusalem, 5 km *nm* of **Teko'a**.
elee אלי *nm* my God.
□ **Elee'al (Eli'al)** אליעל *nm* village (est. 1968) in S. of Golan Heights, 10 km NW of **Eyn-Gev**. Pop. 241.
□ **Eleefelet** (Elifelet) אליפלט *nm* village (est. 1949) in Upper Galilee, 3 km S. of **Rosh-Peenah**. Pop. 327.
eleel/-eem אליל *nm* idol; (*pl+of:* **-ey**).
(rofe/-ey) eleel רופא אליל *nm* witch-doctor; medicine-man.
eleel|ah/-ot אלילה *nf* goddess; (*+of:* **-at**).
eleelat meen אלילת מין *nf* sex-goddess.
('avodat) eleeleem עבודת אלילים *nf* idolatry; paganism.
elee she-ba-shamayeem! אלי שבשמים ! *interj* my God in heaven!
□ **Eleeshama'** (Elishama') אלישמע *nm* village (est. 1951) 2 km S. of **Kefar-Saba**. Pop. 439.
eleh אלה *pron* these; those.
◇ **"eleh hem khayekha"** אלה הם חייך *(lit.)* "This is Your Life" - TV program to which there is an equivalent on Israel TV (see ◇ **Khayeem she-ka-'eleh** חיים שכאלה).
elef/alafeem אלף *num m* thousand; 1,000.
elef alfey אלף אלפי *num m* a thousand thousands; one million.
helekh הלך *nm* wanderer.
hel|ekh roo'akh (*npr* **hal|akh** *etc*) הלך־רוח *nm* frame of mind; mood; (*pl:* **heelkhey roo'akh**).
elektrona|y/-'eet אלקטרונאי *nmf* electronic specialist.
elektronee/-t אלקטרוני *adj* electronic.
eleetroneekah אלקטרוניקה *nf* electronics.
(tekhna'oot) elektroneekah טכנאות אלקטרוניקה *nf* electronic technology.
(tekhna|y/-'ey) elektroneekah טכנאי אלקטרוניקה *nm* electronics technician.
'elem/'alam|eem עלם *nm* young man; lad; (*pl+of:* **-ey**).
elem אלם *nm* muteness.
helem הלם *nm* shock.
□ **Eley Seenay** אלי סיני *nm* communal village est. 1982 by Sinai evacuees on sand dunes in N. part of the Gaza Strip, 4 km W. of Erez checkpost.
□ **Elkanah** (Elqana) אלקנה *nf* new town (est. 1977) in Samaria, W. of Samarian Hills, 8 km E. of **Rosh ha-'Ayeen**. Pop. 2,120.
□ **Elkosh** (Elqosh) אלקוש *nm* village (est. 1949) in Upper Galilee, 8 km W. of **Tsomet Sasa** (Sasa Junction). Pop. 250.
el nakhon אל נכון *adv* apparently; no doubt.
elo'ah אלוה *nm* God.
elohee/-t אלוהי *adj* divine.
eloheem אלוהים *nm* God.
eloheem adeereem! אלוהים אדירים ! *interj* God Almighty! Goodness Gracious!
elokeem אלוקים *nm* God (deliberately mispronounced by observant Jews, when not in prayer, instead of **eloheem** so as not to "take the name of the Lord in vain") .
□ **Elon** (Elon) אילון *nm* kibbutz (est. 1935) in W. Galilee 10 km E. of **Tsomet Rosh-ha-Neekrah** (Rosh haNikra Junction). Pop. 720.
□ **Elon-Moreh** (Elon Moré) אלון מורה *nm* communal settlement (est. 1975) on the West Bank, 10 km W. of Nablus **(Shekhem)**. Pop. 958.
eloo אלו **1**. *pron f pl* these; those; **2**. *num* some.
(see) eloo אי־אלו certain.
◇ **elool** אלול *nm* 12th month of the Jewish calendar.(29 days, approx. Aug-Sept).

□ **Elot** (Elot) אילות *nm* kibbutz (est. 1962) 5 km N. of Elat. Pop. 365.

(peh) el peh פה אל לפה *adv* face to face; (*lit.:* mouth to mouth).

□ **Elro'ee** (Elro'i) אלרואי *nm* suburb (est. 1935) of **Keeryat Teev'on**.

□ **El-Rom** אל־רום *nm* kibbutz (est. 1971) in N. sector of Golan Heights, next to Mount **Khermoneet**, 8 km from Syrian border. Pop. 263.

□ **Elyakeem** (Elyakim) אליקים *nm* village (est. 1949) 5 km SE of Yoqne'am on **Zeekhron Ya'akov-Yokne'am** road. Pop. 414.

□ **Elyakheen** (Elyakhin) אליכין *nm* village (est. 1950), 3 km S. of Hadera **(Khaderah)**. Pop. 1,670.

□ **Elyasheev** (Elyashiv) אלישיב *nm* village (est. 1951) in S. Sharon, 2 km S. of **Kefar-Saba**. Pop. 418.

'elyon/-ah עליון *adj* supreme; superior.

(ko'akh) 'elyon כוח עליון *nm* force majeure.

(me'eel) 'elyon מעיל עליון *nm* overcoat; coat.

(netseev) 'elyon נציב עליון *nm* high commissioner.

(shof|et/-teem) 'elyon/-eem שופט עליון *nm* High-Court Justice.

'elyonoot עליונות *nf* superiority.

em/eemahot אם *nf* mother.

(khalav) em (*or:* **khalev** *etc*) אם חלב *nm* mother's milk.

hem הם *pron m pl* they.

(ha) hem ההם *pron m pl* those.

em|ah אימה *nf* fright; (*+of:* **-at**).

hemah המה **1.** *pron m pl* they; **2.** *v pres* are.

◇ **em/eemahot shakool|ah/-ot** אם שכולה *nf* mother of a son or daughter fallen in one of nation's wars or from an act of terrorism.

em ha-bayeet אם הבית *nf* matron (in a hostel).

em ha-derekh אם הדרך *nf* crossroad; parting way.

□ **Em ha-Moshavot** אם המושבות *nf* "Mother of all Settlements" - petname of **Petakh-Teekvah** town, the first (est. 1878) Jewish agricultural settlement in Palestine in modern times.

emantseepatsyah (*also:* **emanseepatseeyah**) אמנציפציה *nf* emancipation.

ematay אימתי (interrogatively) *adv* when?

emat ha-tseeboor אימת הציבור *nf* stage fright.

emat mavet אימת מוות *nf* mortal fear.

'emd|ah/-ot עמדה *nf* position; stand; (*+of:* **-at**).

'emd|at/-ot mafteakh עמדת מפתח *nf* key position.

'emd|at/ot meekooakh עמדת מיקוח *nf* bargaining position.

'emd|at/-ot tatspeet עמדת תצפית *nf* observation post.

hem|eer/-eerah/-artee המיר *v* exchanged (money, goods, position); (*pres* **memeer**; *fut* **yameer**).

hemeer (*etc*) **dat** המיר דת *v* converted to another faith.

hem|eet/-eetah/-atetee המית *v* killed; deadened; (*pres* **memeet**; *fut* **yameet**).

hem|eet/-eetah/-atetee ason המיט אסון *v* brought disaster; (*pres* **memeet** *etc*; *fut* **yameet** *etc*).

hemeet (*etc*) **kalon** המיט קלון *v* disgraced; brought shame on.

'emek/'amakeem עמק *nm* valley; (*pl+of:* **'eemkey**).

□ **(ha)'emek** העמק *nm* "the Valley"- *nm* colloquial way of referring to the Yizre'el Valley (see **'Emek Yeezre'el**, below).

□ **'Emek Ayalon** עמק איילון *nm* the Ayalon Valley, see □ **Ayalon.**

□ **'Emek ha-Elah** עמק האלה *nm* the Oak Valley minor valley sandwiched between Judean Hills and the **Shfelah**, 8 km S. of Bet Shemesh.

□ **'Emek ha-Yarden** עמק הירדן *nm* the Jordan Valley 168 km long narrow valley along Jordan River, stretching from the slopes of Mount **Khermon** (Hermon) to the Dead Sea's N. shore.

□ **'Emek Khefer** עמק חפר *nm* valley in the center of the Sharon. Once a swampy area, it was reclaimed in 1939 and is today the site of many flourishing settlements.

□ **'Emek ha-Khoolah** עמק החולה *nm* valley at E. edge of Upper Galilee, with picturesque nature reserve on the site of onetime Huleh Swamps.

□ **'Emek Yeezre'el** עמק יזרעאל *nm* large and fruitful Valley of Yizre'el and the site of many flourishing settlements, mostly kibbutzim, all established in the pre-World War II era, when the valley was regarded as the classic manifestation of Jewish land reclamation.

□ **'Emek Zevooloon** עמק זבולון *nm* the Valley of Zebooloon — highly industralized valley (14 km long, 9 km wide) along Haifa Bay, stretching from Acco (Acre) in the N. to Haifa in the S.

hem hem הם הם *v pl* it's they who; they are the ones who.

emesh אמש *nm* last night.

emet/ameetot אמת *nf* truth.

(be) 'emet באמת *adv* indeed; truly.

(deevrey) emet דברי אמת *nm pl* words of truth.

(dover/-et) emet דובר אמת *adj* telling the truth.

em kol khatat אם כל חטאת *nf* the root of all evil.

em/eemahot khor|eget/-got אם חורגת *nf* step-mother.

emoon אמון *nm* confidence; trust.

(haba|'at/-'ot) emoon הבעת אמון *nf* vote of confidence.

(me'eelah be) 'emoon מעילה באמון *nf* abuse of confidence.

(nat|an/-nah/-atee) emoon/-o/-ee נתן אמון/ נו־/נה־ *v* placed one's/his/her/my confidence/ trust; (*pres* **noten** *etc*; *fut* **yeeten** *etc*).

(rakh|ash/-shah/-ashtee) emoon רחש אמון *v* had faith; had confidence; (*pres* **rokhesh** *etc; fut* **yeerkhash** *etc*).

emoon|ah/-ot אמונה *nf* faith; belief; (*+of:* **-at**).

emoon|ah/-ot tfel|ah/-ot אמונה טפלה *nf* superstition.

emooneem אמונים *nm pl* fidelity; faithfulness.

◇ **(goosh) emooneem** see ◇ **Goosh Emooneem**.

(neeshb|a'/-e'ah/-a'tee) emooneem נשבע אמונים *v* swore allegiance; (*pres* **neeshba'** *etc; fut* **yeshava'** *etc; v=b*).

(sham|ar/-rah/-artee) emooneem שמר אמונים *v* remained faithful; (*pres* **shomer** *etc; fut* **yeeshmor** *etc*).

(shevoo'at) emooneem שבועת אמונים *nf* oath of allegiance.

emor!/eemree! אמור! *v imp sing (m/f)* say! (*pst* **amar**; *pres* **omer**; *fut* **yomar**).

hemshekh/-eem המשך *nm* **1.** continuation; **2.** installment.

hemshekh yavo המשך יבוא *v & m* to be continued.

(seepoor be) hemshekheem סיפור בהמשכים *nm* a story that never ends.

hemshekheeyoo|t/-yot המשכיות continuity.

emtsa' אמצע *nm* middle.

(be) emtsa' באמצע *adv* in the middle.

emtsa|'ee/-'eem אמצעי *nm* means; measure; (*pl+of:* **-'ey**).

emtsa'ee/-t אמצעי *adj* middle.

emtsa'ee lakhats אמצעי לחץ *nm* means of pressure.

emtsa|'eem אמצעים *nm pl* means; resources; (*+of:* **-'ey**).

(akh|az/-zah/-aztee be) 'emtsa'eem אחז באמצעים *v* took measures (*pres* **okhez** *etc; fut* **yokhaz** *etc*).

(dal/-at) emtsa'eem דל אמצעים *adj* short of means.

(nak|at/-tah/-atetee) emtsa'eem נקט אמצעים *v* took measures; (*pres* **noket** *etc; fut* **yeenkot** *etc*).

(nekeet|at/-ot) emtsa'eem נקיטת אמצעים *nf* taking of measures.

(noket/-et) emtsa'eem נוקט אמצעים *v pres* is taking measures; (*pst* **nakat** *etc; fut* **yeenkot** *etc*).

emtsa'ey kheroom אמצעי חירום *nm pl* emergency measures.

emtsa'ey menee'ah אמצעי מניעה *nm pl* contraceptives.

emtsa'ey takhboorah אמצעי תחבורה *nm pl* means of transportation.

emtsa'ey tashloom אמצעי תשלום *nm pl* means of payment.

emtsa'ey teekshoret אמצעי תקשורת *nm pl* means of communication.

(be) emtsa'oot באמצעות *adv* by means of; through.

hem|yah/-yot המיה *nf* sound; cooing (of doves); (*+of:* **-yat**).

en אין (*also:* **eyn**) there is/are no/none.

hen הן **1.** *pron f pl* they; **2.** *v pres* are.

hen hen הן הן *pron f* it is they who; they are the ones (of females).

(be) 'en באין in the lack of; with no; without.

(ha) hen ההן *pron f pl* those (of female).

hen הן yes.

'en/-ey עין *nf* **1.** the eye of...; **2.** the color of...

(ke) 'en כעין *prep* like; such as.

(me) 'en מעין kind of; quasi-; such as.

(omer/omrey) hen אומר הן yesman.

hen... ve-hen... הן... והן... both... as well as...; either... or...

henah הנה to here; hither.

□ **'Enat** ('Enat) עינת *nm* kibbutz in Sharon (est. 1952), 3 km E. of **Petakh-Teekvah**. Pop. 435.

□ **'Enav** ('Enav) עינב *nm* communal settlement (est. 1981) in Samaria, 10 km SE of **Toolkarem** (Tulkarm) off main road to Nablus (**Shekhem**). Pop. 277.

(khashkhoo) 'en|av/-ay/-eha חשכו עיניו *v & nf pl* he/I/she *etc* was stunned.

(neefkekhoo) 'en|av/-ay/-eha נפקחו עיניו *v & nf pl* **1.** his/my/her etc eyes were opened; **2.** he/I/she *etc* came to realize.

'en|ay/-ekha/-ayeekh/-av/-eha *etc* עיניי/־יך/ ־ייך וכו׳ *nf & poss. pron* my/your (*m/f*)/his/her *etc* eyes.

□ **'En Ayalah** ('En Ayyala) עין איילה *nm* village (est. 1949) on Carmel (**Karmel**) Coast, 6 km N. of **Zeekhron Ya'akov**. Pop. 333.

'enayeem עיניים *nf pl* eyes (*sing:* **'ayeen**; *+of:* **'en**; *pl+of:* **'ene**).

(akheezat) 'enayeem אחיזת עיניים *nf* optical illusion.

(be) 'enayeem 'atsoomot בעיניים עצומות *adv* blindfolded.

(be-arba') 'enayeem בארבע עיניים *adv* tête-à-tête; between the two of them/you/us.

(be) sheva' 'enayeem בשבע עיניים *adv* **1.** watching most carefully; **2.** *lit* watching with seven eyes.

(kesoot) 'enayeem כסות עיניים *nf* eyewash; excuse.

(lat|ash/-shah/-ashtee) 'enayeem לטש עיניים *v* stared at; gazed at; (*pres* **lotesh** *etc; fut* **yeeltosh** *etc*).

('ov|ed/-deem 'al|av/-ekha/-ay *etc* **ba) 'enayeem** עובד עליו בעיניים *v sing/pl [slang]* he/they are just fooling him/you/me *etc*.

(pak|akh/-khah/-akhtee) 'enayeem פקח עיניים *v* opened one's eyes.

(rof|e/-'at) 'enayeem רופא עיניים *nmf* eye doctor; ophthalmologist.

(zoog/-ot) 'enayeem זוג עיניים *nm* pair of eyes.

en ba'ayot אין בעיות no problem.

□ **'En Bokek** ('En Boqeq) עין בוקק *nm* health and bathing spa on W. shore of Dead Sea. 13 km S. of **Masadah**.

en brerah אין ברירה no alternative; no choice.

en davar אין דבר never mind; doesn't matter.

□ **'En Dor** ('En Dor) עין דור *nm* kibbutz (est. 1949) in Lower Galilee, 4 km SE of Mount Tabor. Pop. 573.

henee/-'ah הניא *v* dissuaded.

hen|ee'a'/-ee'ah/-'atee הניע *v* set in motion; urged; (*pres* **menee'a'**; *fut* **yanee'a'**).

hen|ee'akh/-eekhah/-akhtee הניח *v* put at ease; calmed; (*pres* **manee'akh**; *fut* **yanee'akh**).

hen|eef/-eefah/-aftee הניף *v* swung; brandished; (*pres* **meneef**; *fut* **yaneef**).

□ **'En 'Eeron** (En 'Iron) עין עירון *nm* village (est. 1934) 2 km NW of **Karkoor** village, off the **Khaderah 'Afoolah** road. Pop. 251.

hen|ees/-eesah/-astee הניס *v* routed (*pres* **menees**; *fut* **yanees**).

hen|eev/-eevah/-avtee הניב *v* yielded (fruit); (*pres* **meneev**; *fut* **yaneev**).

energyah אנרגיה *nf* energy.

□ **'En Ganeem** עין גנים *nf* onetime village (est. 1908) that in 1950 merged with Petah-Tiqwa (**Petakh-Teekvah**) town of which it has become a residential quarter.

□ **'En Gedee** ('En Gedi) עין גדי *nm* kibbutz (est. 1953) and picturesque health and bathing resort at Biblical site on W. shore of Dead Sea, 17 km N. of Massada. Pop. 626.

□ **'En Gev** ('En Gév) עין גב *nm* kibbutz (est. 1937) and pleasure resort on E. shore of the Lake of Tiberias. Pop. 575.

□ **'En ha-Bsor** ('En Habesor) עין הבשור *nm* village in SW Negev (est. 1982), 2 km S. of **Tsomet Magen** (Magen Junction). Pop. 393.

□ **'En ha-'Emek** (En ha'Emek) עין העמק *nm* village (est. 1944) 4 km SW of **Tsomet Yokne'am** (Yoqne'am Junction). Pop. 408.

□ **'En ha-Khoresh** ('En haHoresh) עין החורש *nm* kibbutz (est. 1931) in Sharon, 6 km S. of Hadera (**Khaderah**). Pop. 805.

□ **'En ha-Meefrats** ('En haMifraz) עין המפרץ kibbutz in Haifa Bay (est. 1938), 3 km SE of Akko (Acre). Pop. 756.

□ **'En ha-Natseev** ('En haNaziv) עין הנציב *nm* kibbutz (est. 1946) in Bet-She'an Valley, 3 km S. of Bet-She'an town. Pop. 626.

□ **'En ha-Shloshah** ('En haSheloshah) עין השלושה *nm* kibbutz (est. 1950) in NW Negev opposite the Gaza Strip. Pop. 365.

□ **'En ha-Shofet** ('En haShofét) עין השופט *nm* kibbutz (est. 1937) 7 km S. of **Tsomet Yokne'am** (Yoqne'am Junction). Pop. 860.

□ **'En Hod** ('En Hod) עין הוד *nm* artists' village and art center in Carmel (**Karmel**) Hills, 4 km SE of **Tsomet 'Atleet** ('Atlit Junction). Pop. 272.

□ **'En Karmel** ('En Karmel) עין כרמל *nm* kibbutz (est. 1942) on Mediterranean Coast, opposite Carmel (**Karmel**) Hills, 4 km SE of **Tsomet 'Atleet** ('Atlit Junction). Pop. 457.

□ **'En Kerem** ('En Kerem) עין כרם *nm* picturesque residential suburb in SW Jerusalem. Encompasses a School of Agriculture (Pop. pupils & staff 173) and the Hebrew University's Hadassah Medical Center.

en khadash אין חדש no news; nothing new.

□ **'En Kharod** ('En Harod) עין חרוד *nm* kibbutz (est. 1921) in Yizre'el Valley, 15 km SE of 'Afula, off the 'Afula Bet She'an road. In 1953, following a deep ideological rift over the issue of allegiance to Moscow-style communism, the kibbutz split into two separate kibbutzim each one keeping the name "**En-Kharod**" (see below) and affiliated to a different union of kibbutzim. At present, both are affiliated to the same union (see ha-TAKAM under T).

□ **'En-Kharod-Eekhood** ('En Harod-Ihud) עין חרוד איחוד *nm* kibbutz erected after the 1953 split of above, across the road from original kibbutz. At the time affiliated with the then moderate-leftist "**Eekhood ha-Kevootsot ve-ha-Keebootseem**" union (see under EE). Pop. 711.

□ **'En-Kharod-Me'ookhad** ('En Harod-Me'uhad) עין חרוד מאוחד *nm* kibbutz on site of the original kibbutz (see above). Was affiliated (at the time of the split) with the then leftist "**ha-Keeboots ha-Me'ookhad**" (see under K). Pop. 865.

□ **'En Khatsevah** ('En Hazeva) עין חצבה *nf* large agricultural farm in the **'Aravah**, 31 km S. of Sdom.

□ **'En Khemed** (**'En Hemed**) עין חמד *nm* nature reserve and bathing resort (near historic Aqua Bella spring) in Judean Hills, 7 km E. of Jerusalem.

en lee אין לי I have none; I do not have.

en me'oomah אין מאומה there is nothing.

enosh אנוש *nm* man; human.

enooshee/-t (*npr* **enosh|ee/-t**) אנושי *adj* humane; humanitarian.

('al) enooshee/-t (*npr* **enosh|ee/-t**) על אנושי *adj* superhuman.

(beeltee) enooshee/-t (*npr* **enosh|ee/-t**) בלתי אנושי *adj* inhuman.

enoshoot אנושות *nf* mankind.

en penay אין פנאי no time to spare; no time for.

□ **'En Sareed** ('En Sarid) עין שריד *nm* village (est. 1950) in Sharon, 6 km SE of **Tsomet ha-Sharon** (haSharon Junction). Pop. 498.

en shakhar אין שחר nonsense; no truth whatsoever.

□ **'En Shemer** ('En Shemer) עין שמר *nm* kibbutz (est. 1927), 8 km NE of **Khaderah** (Hadera) on Hadera-'Afula road. Pop. 617.

ensofee/-t אינסופי *adj* endless.

hen tsedek הן צדק *nm* word of honor; parole.

entseeklopedeeyah אנציקלופדיה *nf* encyclopedia.

□ **'En Tsooreem** ('En Zurim) עין צורים *nm* kibbutz (est. 1949), 5 km S. of **Keeryat Mal'akhee**. Pop. 536.

en tsorekh אין צורך there is no need; no need to.

□ **'En Vered** ('En Wered) עין ורד *nm* village (est. 1930) in Sharon, 2 km NE of Tel-Mond. Pop. 589.

□ **'En Ya'akov** ('En Ya'aqov) עין יעקב *nm* village (est. 1950) in Upper Galilee. Pop. 347.

□ **'En Yahav** ('En Yahav) עין יהב *nm* village in the **'Aravah** (est. 1962), E. of Sdom-Eilat road, 56 km S. of Sdom. Pop. 469.

□ **'En Zeevan** ('En Ziwan) עין זיוון *nm* kibbutz (est. 1968) in Golan Heights, 5 km W. of Syrian border at **Koonetra**. Pop. 207.

en zeh mekoobal אין זה מקובל this is not customary; this is not acceptable.

en zeh/zot omer/-et אין זה אומר it does not mean.

epeelog אפילוג *nm* epilog.

epeezod|ah/-ot אפיזודה *nm* episode; **(***+of:* **-at)**.

epes עפעס *[slang]* (Yiddish) somehow.

'er/-ah ער *adj* awake; alert.

er|a'/-'ah אירע *v* happened; occurred.

her|a'/-e'ah/-a'tee הרע *v* did harm; wronged; worsened.

her|'ah/-'atah/-'etee הראה *v* showed; **(***pres* **mar'eh;** *fut* **yar'eh)**.

er|akh/-khah/-akhtee אירח *v* entertained (guests); **(***pres* **me'are'akh;** *fut* **ye'arakh)**.

'erakheem (*npr* **'arakheem)** ערכים *nm pl* values (especially moral); **(***sing:* **'erekh;** *pl+of:* **'erkey)**.

(sheenooy) 'erakheem (*npr* **'arakheem)** שינוי ערכים *nm* change of values.

'eranee/-t עירני *adj* alert.

'eranoot עירנות *nf* alertness; vigilance.

heratmoot הירתמות *nf* undertaking a task.

'er|avon/-vonot עירבון *nm* deposit; guarantee.

'eravon kaspee עירבון כספי *nm* cash deposit; cash guarantee.

(be) 'eravon moogbal בעירבון מוגבל *adj* **1.** Limited; Ltd; Inc.; **2.** *lit* : with limited liability.

her|ayon/-yonot הריון *nm* pregnancy.

(be) herayon בהריון *adj* pregnant.

heree'a/-ee'ah/-a'tee הריע *v* cheered; shouted; **(***pres* **meree'a;** *fut* **yaree'a)**.

her|ee'akh/-eekhah/-akhtee הריח *v* smelled; **(***pres* **meree'akh;** *fut* **yaree'akh)**.

her|eek/-eekah/-atee הריק *v* emptied; **(***pres* **meroken;** *fut* **yeroken)**.

her|eem/-eemah/-amtee הרים *v* raised; lifted; **(***pres* **mereem;** *fut* **yareem)**.

hereem (*etc***) rosh** הרים ראש *v* raised one's head; exalted oneself; rebelled.

her|eem (*etc***) yad** הרים יד *v* raised hand; tried to beat up.

her|eets/-eetsah/-atstee הריץ *v* dispatched; hurried; **(***pres* **mereets;** *fut* **yareets)**.

heref!/harpee! הרף! *v imp* s (*m/f*) stop! lay off!

(blee) heref בלי הרף *adv* incessantly.

(ke) heref 'ayeen כהרף עין *adv* in the twinkling of an eye.

(le-lo) heref ללא הרף *adv* constantly.

ereg ארג *nm* fabric; cloth.

hereg הרג *nm* carnage; massacre.

'erekh/'arakheem ערך *nm* **1.** value; **2.** entry (in a dictionary); **(***pl+of:* **'erkey)**.

(be) 'erekh בערך *adv* approximately.

(davar/deevrey) 'erekh דבר ערך *nm* valuable.

(kal/-at) 'erekh קל־ערך *adj* of little value.

(khas|ar/-rat) 'erekh חסר ערך *adj* worthless.

(le) 'erekh לערך *adv* approximately.

(neyar/-ot) 'erekh נייר־ערך *nm* securities.

(rav/rabat) 'erekh רב־ערך *adj* valuable; of great value.

(shev|eh/-at) 'erekh שווה־ערך *adj* equivalent; of equal value.

erekh apayeem ארך אפיים *adj* forbearing; patient.

erekh (*npr* **areekh) negen** ארך נגן *nm* long-playing gramophone record.

eres ארס *nm* poison.

'eres ערש *nf* cradle.

'eres devay ערש דווי *nf* sick-bed.

(sheer/-ey) 'eres שיר ערש *nm* lullaby.

heres הרס *nm* destruction.

heres 'atsmee הרס עצמי *nm* self-destruction.

erets/aratsot ארץ *nf* land; country; **(***pl+of:* **artsot)**.

□ **Erets** ארץ *[colloq.] nf* abbr.for **Erets Yeesra'el** (see □ below).

◇ **erets ha-arazeem** ארץ הארזים *nf* land of the Cedars (nickname for Lebanon).

erets moledet ארץ מולדת *nf* homeland; land of birth.

□ **erets yeesra'el** (Eretz Israel) ארץ ישראל *nf* Land of Israel. i.e. the territory known historically as Palestine.

◇ **erets yeesra'el ha-shlemah** ארץ ישראל השלמה *nf* Eretz Israel in its undivided integrity i.e. comprising the West Bank, the Gaza Strip and the Golan Heights.

(derekh) erets דרך ארץ *nf* good manners.

'erev/'araveem ערב **1.** *nm* evening **(***pl+of:* **'arvey)**; **2.** - *adv* on the eve of.

'erev 'erev ערב ערב *adv* every evening.

'erev havay ערב הווי *nm* folkdance and folksong party.

'erev/'arvey khag ערב חג *nm* holiday eve.

'erev rav ערב רב *nm* mob; motley crowd; riff-raff.

'erev/'arvey shabat ערב שבת *nm* Sabbath eve; (Friday evening).

'erev shabat kodesh ערב שבת קודש *nm* eve of the holy Sabbath; Friday evening.

'erev tov! ערב טוב! greeting: Good evening!

'erev tov oo-mevorakh! ערב טוב ומבורך! greeting: response to **'erev tov!**.

(arookh|at/khot) 'erev ארוחת ערב *nf* dinner; supper; evening meal.

(ba) 'erev בערב *adv* in the evening.

(be) 'erev בערב *adv* on the eve of.

(ha) 'erev הערב *adv* this evening; tonight.

('eeton/-ey) 'erev עיתון־ערב *nm* evening-paper; evening newspaper.

(khakeerat shtee va) 'erev חקירת שתי וערב *nf* cross- examination.

(leefnot) 'erev לפנות ערב *adv* towards evening.

(shetee va) 'erev שתי וערב *adv* lengthwise and crosswise; warp and woof.

erez/arazeem ארז *nm* cedar.

□ **Erez** ארז *nm* kibbutz (est. 1949) in S. part of Coastal Plain, 11 km S. of Ashkelon. Pop. 446.

'ergah ערגה *nf* nostalgia; languor.

hergel/-eem הרגל *nm* habit.

hergel/-eem neefsad/-eem הרגל נפסד *nm* wrong habit.

'erkee/-t ערכי **1.** *adj* valent (chemically); **2.** valuable (morally).

(doo-) 'erkee/-t דו ערכי *adj* ambivalent.

'erkeeyoot ערכיות *nf* **1.** valence; **2.** devotion to true values.

herkev/-eem הרכב *nm* composition.

hermetee/-t הרמטי *adj* hermetical.

hermeteet הרמטית *adv* hermetically.

'erom עירום *nm* nude.

'erom ve-'eryah עירום ועריה *nm pl* naked and bare.

(be) 'erom בעירום *adv* in the nude.

eroo|'a/-'eem אירוע *nm* event.

erooseem אירוסים *nm pl* betrothal.

'eroov עירוב *nm* encroachment; mixing.

◇ **'eroov** עירוב *nm* "Eruv" - religious legal fiction of drawing symbolic fence around a town or parts thereof so that the encompassed area may be regarded as one's "own yard". Thus, an observant Jew would be at liberty to carry things within it without that activity being considered work and desecrating the Sabbath.

□ **'Erooveen** עירובין *nm* communal village (est. 1983) in *nm* of Hebron hills, W. of Bethlehem-Hebron highway.

'eroo|y/-yeem עירוי *nm* transfusion (*pl+of:* **-yey**).

'eroo|y/-yey dam עירוי דם *nm* blood transfusion.

□ **Erodeeon** see □ **Herodeeon**.

□ **Ertseleeyah** see □ **Hertseleeyah**.

□ **Ertseleeyah-Peetoo'akh** see □ **Hertseleeyah-Peetooakh**.

'erv|ah ערווה *nf* incest; lewdness; (*+of:* **-at**).

'eryah עריה *nf* **1.** female genitals; **2.** nudity.

hesakh ha-da'at היסח הדעת *nm* absentmindedness; inattention.

(be) hesakh ha-da'at בהיסח הדעת *adv* inadvertantly; absentmindedly.

hesber/-eem הסבר *nm* explanation.

hesder/-eem הסדר *nm* arrangement; settlement.

◇ **(yesheev|at/-ot) hesder** see ◇ **yesheev|at/-ot hesder**.

hes|eek (*npr* **hees|eek**)**/-eekah/-aktee** הסיק *v* heated; burned; (*pres* **meseek**; *fut* **yaseek**).

hes|eer/-eerah/-artee הסיר *v* removed; took off; (*pres* **meseer**; *fut* **yaseer**).

hes|eet/-eetah/-atetee הסית *v* instigated; (*pres* **meseet**; *fut* **yaseet**).

hes|eet/-eetah/-atetee הסיט *v* shifted; (*pres* **meseet**; *fut* **yaseet**).

heseg/-eem הישג *nm* accomplishment; (*pl+of:* **-ey**).

(be) heseg-yad בהישג יד *adv* within reach.

(masa') hesegeem מסע הישגים *nm* show of achievements.

'esek/'asakeem עסק *nm* **1.** business; occupation; **2.** *[slang]* affair; (*pl+of:* **'eeskey**).

(ba'al/-ey) 'esek/'asakeem בעל עסק *nm* business-owner; (*f:* **-at** *etc*).

'esek beesh עסק ביש *nm* mishap; sordid affair.

'eser עשר *num f* 10; ten.

hes|ev/-ebah/-avtee *(b=v)* היסב *v* sat with; (*pres* **mesev**; *fut* **yasev**).

hesev/-eem הסב *nm* endorsement.

'esev/'asaveem עשב *nm* grass.

'esev/'eesvey bar עשב בר *nm* weed.

hesger/-eem הסגר *nm* quarantine; blockade.

esh אש *nm* fire.

('al|ah/-tah ba) 'esh עלה באש *v* went up in flames; (*pres* **'oleh** *etc*; *fut* **ya'aleh** *etc*).

(hafsak|at/-ot) esh הפסקת אש *nf* cease-fire.

(khaseen/-at) esh חסין אש *adj* fireproof.

(mekhab|eh/-ey) esh מכבה אש *nm* fireman.

□ **Eshbol** אשבול *nm* village (est. 1955) in N. Negev, 7 km NE of **Neteevot**. Pop. 278.

eshed אשד *nm* waterfall.

□ **Eshed-Keenorot** אשד כינורות *nm* central pumping station of Israel's national network of artificial irrigation. Located at the Northern edge of Lake Kinneret (**Keeneret**), 9 km *nm* of Tiberias, it raises the water 200 meters up to sea-level so that it may make its way S. and onward by gravitation.

hesh|eet/-eetah/-atetee השיט *v* set afloat; (*pres* **mesheet**; *fut* **yasheet**).

hesh|eev/-eevah/-avtee השיב *v* **1.** replied; answered; **2.** returned; (*pres* **mesheev**; *fut* **yasheev**).

hesheev (*etc*) **'al kano/-ah** השיב על כנו *v* restored.

eshel אש״ל *nm* per diem allowance (*acr* composed of initials of Hebrew words for food, drink, overnight-stay; Okhel, SHteeyah, Leenah,אוכל שתייה, לינה).

eshel/ashal|eem אשל *nm* tamarisk; (*pl+of:* **ashaley**).

□ **Eshel Ha-Nasee** (Eshel Hanasi) אשל הנשיא *nm* agricultural college(est 1952) 15 km NW of Beersheba, near **Tsomet ha-Nasee** (HaNasi Junction). Pop. (students and staff) 371.

eshet/neshot אשת *f+of* wife of.

eshet/neshot 'asakeem אשת־עסקים *nf* business- woman.

eshet-eesh אשת־איש *nf* married woman.

eshet/neshot khayeel אשת־חיל *nf* woman of valor; efficient woman.

eshet ne'oor|eem/-av/-ay אשת־נעורים *nf* wife of one's/his/my youth.
eshkol/-ot אשכול *nm* cluster.
eshkolee|t/-yot אשכולית *nm* grapefruit.
(eesh) eshkolot (*npr* ashkolot) איש אשכולות *nm* a man of multi-sided learning.
(meets) eshkoleeyot מיץ אשכוליות *nm* grapefruit juice.
eshna|v/-beem *(b=v)* אשנב *nm* **1.** hatch; porthole; **2.** window (bank); *(pl+of:* **-bey).**
eshtaked אשתקד *adv* last year.
(ka-sheleg de) 'eshtaked (*npr* eshtakad) כשלג דאשתקד *adv* (it interests me) like the snow of yesteryear.
□ **Eshta'ol** (Eshta'ol) אשתאול *nm* village (est. 1949) in Jerusalem hills, 4 km NE of **Bet-Shemesh**. Pop. 442.
(eeb|ed/-dah/-adetee) 'eshtonot/-av/-ehah/-ay איבוד עשתונות *v* lost one's (his/her/my) temper; (*pres* **me'abed'e** *etc; fut* **ye'abed** *etc*).
(ma zeh) 'eskekha?/'eskekh? מה זה עסקך? what is it, your business?!
heskem/-eem הסכם *nm* agreement; *(pl+of:* **-ey).**
('ar|akh/-khah/-akhtee) heskem ערך הסכם *v* drew up an agreement.
(ba/-'ah/-tee lee-yedey) heskem בא לידי הסכם *v* came to terms; reached agreement.
(hafar|at/-ot) heskem הפרת הסכם *nf* breach of agreement.
hesped/-eem הספד *nm* eulogy; funeral oration; *(pl+of:* **-ey).**
hespek/-eem הספק *nm* output; *(pl+of:* **-ey).**
'esreh עשרה suffix to numbers *f* ending in -teen.
(tepesh-, or teepesh-) 'esreh טפש עשרה teenage; teenager.
'esreem עשרים *num* 20; twenty.
'esronee/-t עשרוני *adj* decimal.
(sheetah) 'esroneet שיטה עשרונית *nf* decimal system.
estetee/-t אסתטי *adj* esthetic.
et את **1.** *prep* sign of the accusative case (direct object) when the object is preceded by the definite article **(ha-** ה); **2.-** *conj* et *(French)*; & *(internat.)*; and; with.
et/eeteem את *nm* shovel; spade.
'et/-eem עט *nm* pen; *(pl+of:* **-ey).**
'et/-eem kadooree/-yeem עט כדורי *nm* ballpoint pen.
'et/-eem nov|e'a/-'eem עט נובע *nm* fountain pen.
'et/'eeteem (also **'eetot)** עת *nf* time; season.
(be) 'et בעת *adv* at the time.
(be) 'et oo-ve-'onah akhat בעת ובעונה אחת *adv* simultaneously; at one and the same time.
(be-khol) 'et בכל עת *adv* any time; at all time.
(be-lo) 'et בלא עת *adv* untimely; prematurely.
(ka) 'et כעת *adv* now; right now.
(ketav/keetvey) 'et כתב עת *nm* periodical.
(le) 'et לעת *adv* at the time of.
etan/-ah איתן *adj* solid; firm; steadfast.

□ **Etan** איתן *nm* village in the **Lakheesh** area (est. 1955), 5 km S. of **Keeryat-Gat**. Pop. 348.
□ **Etaneem** (Etanim) איתנים *nm* hospital for mental diseases, 8 km W. of Jerusalem. Pop. 266.
(le) 'et 'atah לעת עתה *adv* for the time being.
etee/-t אתי *adj* ethical.
hetee'akh/-khah/-akhtee הטיח *v* spoke insolently; (*pres* **metee'akh;** *fut* **yatee'akh).**
hetee|'akh/-khah/-akhtee ashm|ah/-ot הטיח אשמה *v* accused; threw blame.
het|eel/-eelah/-altee הטיל *v* cast; threw; (*pres* **meteel;** *fut* **yateel).**
heteel *(etc)* **goral** הטיל גורל *v* drew lots.
hetees/-ah/heetastee הטיס *v* flew (an aircraft); dispatched by air; (*pres* **metees;** *fut* **yatees).**
het|eev/-eevah/-avtee הטיב *v* excelled; improved; did well; (*pres* **meteev;** *fut* **yeteev).**
heteev *(etc)* **'eem** הטיב עם *v* was good to; did good to.
hetel/-eem היטל *nm* **1.** levy;tax; **2.** projection; *(pl+of:* **-ey).**
◇ **etel 'eenoogeem** see ◇ **hetel 'eenoogeem.**
◇ **etel hashbakhah** see ◇ **hetel hashbakhah.**
(be) het'em בהתאם *adv* accordingly.
(be) het'em le- בהתאם ל- *adv* according to; in accordance with.
eten אתן *v fut* 1st pers *sing* I shall give; (*pst* **nat|an/-nah/-atee;** *pres* **noten;** *fut* **yeeten).**
heter/-eem היתר *nm* permit; license; release.
(be) heter בהיתר *adv* lawfully; openly.
hetev היטב *adv* well; thoroughly.
hetev-hetev היטב היטב *adv* most thoroughly; to the utmost.
etgar/-eem אתגר *nm* challenge; *(pl+of:* **-ey).**
hetkef/-eem התקף *nm* attack; assault; *(pl+of:* **-ey).**
hetkef/-ey lev התקף־לב *nm* heart-attack.
hetkefee/-t התקפי *adj* offensive.
hetken/-eem התקן *nm* device; *(pl+of:* **-ey).**
etkhem אתכם *accusative pron 2nd pers m pl* you (addressing males).
etkhen אתכן *accusative pron 2nd pers f pl* you (addressing females).
(me) 'et le-'et מעת לעת **1.** *adv* from time to time; **2.** *nm* 24 hours.
etmol אתמול *adv* yesterday.
etmol-sheelshom אתמול־שלשום *adv* these last few days.
etnakht|ah/-ot אתנחתה *nf* pause; intermission; *(+of:* **-at).**
etnan/-eem אתנן *nm* harlot's pay *(pl+of:* **-ey).**
etnee/-t אתני *adj* ethnic.
(motsa) etnee מוצא אתני *nm* ethnic origin.
◇ **etrog/-eem** אתרוג *nm* citron used in Sukkot holiday ritual; *(pl+of:* **-ey).**
'ets/-eem עץ *nm* **1.** tree; **2.** wood *(pl+of:* **'atsey).**
'ets/'atsey ashoo'akh עץ אשוח *nm* fir tree.
'ets/'atsey ashoor עץ אשור *nm* beechwood.
'ets/'atsey hadar עץ הדר *nm* citrus tree.
'ets lavood עץ לבוד *nm* plywood; veneer.

◇ **'ets o palee** עץ או פלי "heads or tails" formula when choosing by tossing a coin.

'ets/'atsey pree עץ פרי *nm* fruit tree.

'ets/'atsey zayeet עץ זית *nm* olive tree.

('asoo|y/-yah) 'ets עשוי עץ *adj* made of wood.

(bool/-ey) 'ets בול עץ *nm* block of wood.

(me) 'ets מעץ *adj* wooden; of wood.

'ets|ah/-ot עצה *nf* advice; (*+of:* **'atsat**).

(hees|ee/-ee'ah/-etee) 'ets|ah/-ot השיא עצה *v* gave advice; counselled.

hets|a'/-e'eem (*npr* **hetse'a**) היצע *nm* supply; offer; (*pl+of:* **-e'ey**).

hetsa' oo-veekoosh (*npr* **hetse'a** *etc*) היצע וביקוש *nm pl* supply and demand.

etsb|a'/-a'ot אצבע *nf* finger; index finger; (*pl+of:* **-e'ot**).

(lo nak|af/-fah/-aftee) etsba' לא נקף אצבע *v* didn't raise a finger; (*pres* **eyno nokef** *etc; fut* **lo yeenkof** *etc*).

etsb|a'on/-e'oneem אצבעון *nm* thimble (*pl+of:* **-e'oney**).

etsbe'onee אצבעוני *nm* Tom Thumb.

(tevee|'at/-'ot) etsba'ot טביעת אצבעות *nf* fingerprints.

hets|e'a'/-e'eem היצע *nm* supply; offer; (*+of:* **hets|a'/-e'ey**).

hetse'a' oo-veekoosh היצע וביקוש *nm pl* supply and demand.

hets|eef/-eefah/-aftee הציף *v* flooded; (*pres* **matseef**; *fut* **yatseef**).

hets|eek/-eekah/-aktee הציק *v* pestered; persecuted; (*pres* **metseek**; *fut* **yatseek**).

hets|eets/-eetsah/-atstee הציץ *v* peeped; (*pres* **metseets**; *fut* **yatseets**).

etsel אצל *prep* **1.** at; at home or buisiness of; **2.** near to; to.

◇ **"ETSEL"** אצ"ל *nm* (hist) abbr.I.Z.L. (*acr of* "Irgun Zvai Leumi" אירגון צבאי לאומי) underground military organization that fought for the liberation of Palestine from British rule (1938-1948).

'etsem/'ats|amot עצם *nf* bone; (*pl+of:* **-mot**).

'etsem/'atsameem עצם *nm* substance; object.

(be) 'etsem בעצם *adv* actually; as a matter of fact.

(shem/-ot) 'etsem שם עצם *nm* noun; (*gram.*).

(yoresh/-et) 'etser יורש עצר *nmf* heir to the throne.

'etsev עצב *nm* sorrow.

'etsev (*npr* **'atsav**)**/'atsab|eem** (*b=v*) עצב *nm* nerve; (*pl+of:* **-ey**).

etsl|ah/-am/-an אצלה/־ו/־ן *prep & pron* at her/their (*m/f*) place; with her/them (*m/f*).

etsl|ee/-enoo אצלי *prep & pron* at my/our place; with me/us.

etsl|ekha/-ekh/-ekhem/-ekhen אצלך/כם/כן *prep & pron m/f sing, m/f pl* at your place; with you.

etsl|o/-ah אצלו *prep & pron* at his/her place; with him/her.

(oved/-et) 'etsot אובד עצות *adj* perplexed; confused.

etyopee/-t אתיופי **1.** *nmf & adj* Ethiopian; **2.** Jewish immigrant from Ethiopia.

◇ **('oley) etyopeeyah** see ◇ **'oley etyopeeyah**.

ev|ah/-ot איבה *nf* enmity; hate; (*+of:* **-at**).

'eved/'avadeem עבד *nm* slave; (*pl+of:* **'avdey**).

hev|ee/-ee'ah/-e'tee הביא *v* brought; led; (*pres* **mevee**; *fut* **yavee**).

hevee (*etc*) **be-kheshbon** הביא בחשבון *v* took into account/consideration.

hevee (*etc*) **lee-yedey** הביא לידי *v* **1.** brought to; **2.** resulted in.

hev|eekh/-eekhah/-akhtee הביך *v* embarrassed.

eveel/-eem אוויל *nm* moron; stupid person; (*pl+of:* **-ey**).

eveelee/-t אווילי *adj* stupid.

hev|een/-eenah/-antee הבין *v* understood; (*pres* **meveen**; *fut* **yaveen**).

hev|ees/-eesah/-astee הביס *v* defeated; (*pres* **mevees**; *fut* **yavees**).

hev|eesh/-eeshah/-ashtee הביש *v* put to shame; (*pres* **meveesh**; *fut* **yaveesh**).

evel אבל *nm* mourning.

even/avaneem אבן *nf* stone; (*pl+of:* **avney**).

even/avney negef אבן נגף *nm* obstacle; stumbling block.

even/avney peenah אבן פינה *nm* cornerstone.

□ **Even Sapeer** (Even Sappir) אבן ספיר *nm* village (est. 1950) outside Jerusalem, 3 km SW of 'En Kerem. Pop. 453.

□ **Even Shmoo'el** (**Even Shemu'él**) אבן שמואל *nm* rural center (est. 1957) for **"Hapo'el Hameezrakhee"** (religious) settlements, 4 km from **Keeryat Gat**. Pop. 547.

even she-eyn lah hofkheen אבן שאין לה הופכין *nf* unturned (useless) stone.

even/avaneem tov|ah/-ot אבן טובה *nf* precious stone.

□ **Even Menakhem** (Even Menahem) אבן מנחם *nm* village (est. 1960) in Western Galilee, 6 km NW of **Ma'alot**. Pop. 283.

□ **Even Yehoodah** (Even Yehuda) אבן יהודה *nf* settlement (est. 1932) 8 km S. of Netanya encompassing also villages **Be'er Ganeem, Hadaseem, Tel-Tsoor** and Memorial Center (for fallen soldiers) **'En Ya'akov**. Pop. 6,490.

ever/avareem איבר *nm* limb; organ (*pl+of:* **evrey**).

ever (*npr* **evar**)**/evrey meen** איבר מין *nm* penis; genitals.

'ever/'avareem עבר *nm* side; (*pl+of:* **'evrey**).

(le) 'ever לעבר *prep* towards; in the direction of.

(me) 'ever מעבר *prep* across; beyond.

(me) 'ever la-yam מעבר לים *adv* overseas; across the sea.

(me) 'ever le-harey khoshekh מעבר להרי חושך *adv* at the end of the world.

(mee-kol) 'ever מכל עבר *adv* from all around; from everywhere.

(sefat) 'ever שפת עבר *nf* (archaic) language of the Hebrews; Hebrew.
hevdel/-eem הבדל *nm* difference; (*pl+of:* **ey**).
evoos אבוס *nm* crib; stall.
□ **'Evron** ('Evron) עברון *nm* seashore kibbutz (est. 1945) SE of Nahariyya. Pop. 682.
evyon אביון **1.** *nm* pauper; **2.** *adj* destitute.
('anee ve) evyon עני ואביון *nm* very poor; beggar.
evyonah (or **aveeyonah**) אביונה *nf* **1.** orgasm; female libido; sexual desire; **2.** caper (plant).
hevzek/-eem הבזק *nm* flash of light (*pl+of:* **-ey**).
ey?! אי?! where?!
ey la-zot אי לזאת *adv* therefore.
ey pa'am אי־פעם *adv* anytime; sometime.
ey sham אי־שם *adv* somewhere.
eyal אייל *nm* power; might; strength.
□ **Eyal** אייל *nm* kibbutz (est. 1949) in Sharon, 10 km NE of **Kefar-Saba**. Pop. 329.
(seemkhah le) eyd שמחה לאיד *nf* rejoicing over another person's calamity.
heydad הידד *interj* hurrah! cheers!
(kar|a/-'ah/-atee) heydad קרא הידד *v* acclaimed; (*pres* **kore** *etc; fut* **yeekra** *etc*).
eyfah ve-eyfah איפה ואיפה *nf & nf* double standard; discrimination.
eyfo? איפה? where?
eykh? איך? how?
eykh ha'eenyaneem? איך הענינים *[colloq.]* how goes it? how is everything?
eykhakhah איככה (poetical) how on earth?
heykhal/-ot היכל *nm* palace; temple.
heykhan היכן *adv* where?
heykhan she- היכן ש־ there where.
hekhan she-lo היכן שלא wherever.
(me) heykhan מהיכן from where.
eykh holekh? איך הולך? *[colloq.]* how goes it? how are things getting on?
eykhoo|t/-yot איכות *nf* quality.
eykhootee/-t איכותי *adj* qualitative.
(dee-le) 'eyl דלעיל *adv* aforementioned; as above.
(le) 'eyl לעיל *adv* above; earlier.
(le) 'eyla oo-le-'eyla לעילא ולעילא *adj* the very best.
(mee-kan ve) eylakh מכאן ואילך *adv* hereafter; from here on.
□ **Eylat** see □ **Elat**.
□ **Eylon** אילון see □ **Elon**.
□ **Eylot** אילות see □ **Elot**.
eym|ah אימה *nf* fright; (*+of:* **-at**).
eymat ha-tseeboor אימת הציבור *nf* stage fright.
eymatay אימתי *adv* (interrogative) when?.
eymat mavet אימת מות *nf* mortal fear.
eyn אין *adv* there is no; no.
eyn be'ayot אין בעיות no problems.
□ **'Eyn Bokek** see □ **'En Bokek**.
□ **'Eyn Dor** see □ **'En Dor**.
□ **'Eyn 'Eeron** see □ **'En 'Eeron**.
□ **'Eyn Ganeem** see □ **'En Ganeem**.
□ **'Eyn Gedee** see □ **'En Gedee**.
□ **'Eyn Gev** see □ **'En Gev**.
□ **'Eyn ha-'Emek** see □ **'En ha-'Emek**.
□ **'Eyn ha-Khoresh** see □ **'En ha-Khoresh**.
□ **'Eyn ha-Meefrats** see □ **'En ha-Meefrats**.
□ **'Eyn ha-Natseev** see □ **'En ha-Natseev**.
□ **'Eyn ha-Sheloshah** see □ **'En ha-Shloshah**.
□ **'Eyn ha-Shofet** see □ **'En ha-Shofet**.
□ **'Eyn Hod** see □ **'En Hod**.
□ **'Eyn Karmel** see □ **'En Karmel**.
□ **'Eyn Kerem** see □ **'En Kerem**.
□ **'Eyn Kharod** see □ **'En Kharod**.
□ **'Eyn Kharod-Eekhood** see □ **'En Kharod-Eekhood**.
□ **'Eyn Kharod-Me'ookhad** see □ **'En Kharod-Me'ookhad**.
□ **'Eyn Khatsevah** see □ **'En Khatsevah**.
□ **'Eyn Khemed** see □ **'En Khemed**.
□ **'Eyn Shemer** see □ **'En Shemer**.
eynsofee/-t (*npr* **eyn-sofee/-t**) אינסופי *adj* endless.
□ **'Eyn Tsooreem** see □ **'En Tsooreem**.
eyn tsorekh אין צורך *adv* there's no need to; there's no need for.
□ **'Eyn Vered** see □ **'En Vered**.
□ **'Eyn Ya'akov** see □ **'En Ya'akov**.
□ **'Eyn Yahav** see □ **'En Yahav**.
□ **'Eyn Zeevan** see □ **'En Zeevan**.
heyot she- (*or:* **ve-**) היות ש־ *conj* whereas; since.
eyr|a'/-'ah אירע *v* occurred; happened; (*pres* **meetrakhesh**; *fut* **ye'era'**).
eytan/-ah איתן *adj* solid; firm; steadfast.
□ **Eytan** see □ **'Etan**.
□ **Eytaneem** see □ **'Etaneem**.
heytev היטב *adv* well; thoroughly.
heytev heytev היטב היטב *adv* most thoroughly; to the utmost.
eyv|ah/-ot איבה *nf* enmity; hate; (*+of:* **-at**).
eyz|eh/-o איזה *pron m/f* which? what?
eyz|eh meen איזה מין what kind of.
eyz|ehoo/-ohee איזהו which one.
eyz|eh she-hoo איזה שהוא *m* any; any kind; whatever.
eyzo איזו *pron f* what? which?
eyzo she'elah?! איזו שאלה?! what a question?!
eyzor/azor|eem אזור *nm* area; sector; region: (*pl+of:* **-ey**).
eyzor meforaz אזור מפורז *nm* demilitarized zone.
eyzor/azorey megooreem אזור מגורים *nm* residential district.
eyzor/azorey metsookah אזור מצוקה *nm* poor, distressed area.
eyzor/azorey peetooakh אזור פיתוח *nm* development area.
eyzor/azorey ta'aseeyah אזור תעשייה *nm* industrial area.
eyzoree/-t (*npr* **azoree/t**) אזורי *adj* regional.
(bekheerot) eyzoreeyot (*npr* **azoreeyot**) בחירות אזוריות *nf pl* regional elections.
eyzov איזוב *nm* moss; hyssop.

eyzovey-keer אזובי קיר *nm pl* **1.** (*figurat.*) small fry; **2.** (Bibl.) the hysop that springs out between the stones of a wall.

'ez/'eez|eem עז *nf* she-goat; (*pl+of:* **-ey**).

hezeen/-ah/hezantee הזין *nf* fed; (*pres* **mezeen**; *fut* **yazeen**).

hezeez/-ah/hezaztee הזיז *v* **1.** moved; **2.** *[slang]* got things moving; (*pres* **mezeez**; *fut* **yazeez**).

hezek היזק *nm* damage.

'ezer/'azareem עזר *nm* aid; (*pl+of:* **'ezrey**).

('emtsa|'ee/-'ey) 'ezer אמצעי עזר *nm pl* auxiliary means.

(le) 'ezer לעזר of assistance.

(meshek/meeshkey) 'ezer משק עזר auxiliary farm; sideline farming.

(sefer/seefrey) 'ezer ספר עזר *nm* handbook; reference book.

ezo איזו *pron f* what? which?

ezo she'elah?! איזו שאלה?! what a question?!

ezor/azoreem אזור *nm* area; sector; region: (*pl+of:* **-ey**).

□ **Ezor Lakheesh** אזור לכיש *nm* the **Lakheesh** Area, i.e. the area of agricultural villages of the "moshav" type around the city of **Keeryat Gat**.

ezor meforaz אזור מפורז *nm* demilitarized zone.

ezor/azorey megooreem אזור מגורים *nm* residential district.

ezor/azorey metsookah אזור מצוקה *nm* poor, distressed area.

ezor/azorey peetooakh אזור פיתוח *nm* development area.

ezor/azorey ta'aseeyah אזור תעשייה *nm* industrial area.

ezoree/azoreet אזורי regional.

(bekheerot) ezoreeyot בחירות אזוריות *nf pl* regional elections.

ezov איזוב *nm* moss; hysop.

ezovey-keer אזובי קיר *nm pl* **1.** (*figurat.*) small fry; **2.** (Bibl.) the hysop that springs out of the wall.

'ezr|ah עזרה *nf* help; aid; assistance; (*+of:* **-at**).

'ezrah reeshonah עזרה ראשונה *nf* first aid.

'ezrah sotsyaleet עזרה סוציאלית *nf* social aid; social assistance.

(hosh|eet/-eetah/-atetee) 'ezrah הושיט עזרה *v* rendered assistance; (*pres* **mosheet** *etc*; *fut* **yosheet** *etc*).

(kar|a/-'ah/-atee le) 'ezrah קרא לעזרה *v* called out for help; (*pres* **kore** *etc*; *fut* **yeekra** *etc*).

ezrakh/-eet אזרח *nmf* **1.** citizen; national; **2.** civilian; (*pl+of:* **-ey**).

ezrakh/-eet khoots אזרח חוץ *nmf* foreign citizen; foreign national.

ezrakh/-eet yeesre'elee/-t אזרח ישראלי *nmf* Israeli citizen; Israeli national.

ezrakh/-eet zar/-ah אזרח זר *nmf* foreign citizen; foreign national.

ezrakhee/-t אזרחי *adj* civilian.

ezrakhoo|t/-yot אזרחות *nf* citizenship; nationality.

'ezrat nasheem עזרת נשים *nf* women's gallery (in a synagogue).

(be) 'ezrat ha-Shem בעזרת השם God willing; with the aid of God.

EE.

incorporating letters

ee (אִ,אי), **'ee** (עִ,עי) and **hee** (הִ,הי)

NOTES **1.** In this dictionary, we transliterate by **ee** (pronounced as in *eel*, *seed* or *knee*) the Hebrew vowel point **Kheereek** (אִ, אי) for which the equivalent in the International Phonetic Alphabet is i. In doing so, and departing thereby from a common practice, we have been guided by the wish to prevent the ordinary English-speaker from giving in to an instinctive inclination to read the *i* as in *item* or *bite*. That would have made an ordinary Hebrew word like **siper** סיפר sound similar to *sniper* which would be completely unrecognizable. Adopting **ee** leaves no possibility for any pronunciation other than as in *wheel* or *deed*.

2. For incorporating words beginning with עִ (**'Ayeen**) or הִ (**Heh**) with words beginning with אִ (**Alef**) see explanatory note to Chapter **E**.

ee/-yeem אי *nm* island (*pl+of:* **eeyey**).

(khatsee) ee חצי אי *nm* peninsula.

ee- אי *prefix* denoting negation; un-; not.

ee-hatkafah אי התקפה *nm* non-aggression.

ee-havan|ah/-ot אי הבנה *nm* misunderstanding.

ee-efshar אי אפשר *adv* impossible.

ee-haskamah אי־הסכמה *nm* disagreement.

ee-eymoon אי־אמון *nm* distrust; lack of confidence.

ee-heet'arvoot אי־התערבות *nf* non-interference.

ee-keeyoom אי־קיום *nm* unfulfilment.
ee-ne'eemoo|t/-yot אי־נעימות *nm* unpleasantness.
ee-sefeekah אי־ספיקה *nm* insufficiency.
ee-sefeekat ha-lev אי־ספיקת הלב *nm* coronary insufficiency.
ee-sheevyon אי־שוויון *nm* inequality.
ee-sheket אי־שקט *nm* unrest.
ee-tashloom אי־תשלום *nm* non payment.
ee-teloot אי־תלות *nm* independence.
ee-tsedek אי־צדק *nm* injustice.
ee- (mispronunciation of **ey**) אי abbr.of **ayeh** - where.
ee el|eh/-oo (mispron. of **ey-el|eh/-oo**) אי־אלה *nmf* some; certain.
ee la-zot (mispron. of **ey la-zot**) אי־לזאת *adv* on account of this/that.
ee le-kakh (*npr* **ey le-khakh**) אי לכך *adv* therefore.
hee היא *nf pron* she.
hee היא *v pres 3rd pers f* is; (*pst* **haytah**; *fut* **teehyeh**).
hee asher היא אשר it's she who.
hee hee היא היא she is the one who.
heebadloot היבדלות *nf* segregation.
eeb|ed/-dah/-adetee איבד *v* lost (*pres* **me'abed**; *fut* **ye'abed**).
eebed (*etc*) **'atsm|o/-ah la-da'at** איבד עצמו לדעת *v* committed suicide.
eebed (*etc*) **et ha-'eshtonot** איבד את העשתונות *v* lost one's temper.
eebed (*etc*) **et ha-tsafon** איבד את הצפון *v [slang]* felt lost.
'eeb|ed/-dah/-adetee עיבד *v* 1. processed; worked out; 2. arranged music; (*pres* **me'abed**; *fut* **ye'abeed**).
heeb|ee'a/-ee'ah/-a'tee הביע *v* expressed; (*pres* **mabee'a**; *fut* **yabee'a**).
heeb|eet/-eetah/-atetee הביט *v* looked at; (*pres* **mabeet**; *fut* **yabeet**).
□ **Eebleen** (I'blin) אעבלין *nm* Arab village in the W. part of Lower Galilee, 8 km E. of Qiryat Ata (**Keeryat Ata**). Pop. 7,230.
eebood איבוד *nm* loss; waste.
eebood le-da'at איבוד לדעת *nm* suicide.
(hal|akh/-khah/-akhtee le) 'eebood הלך לאיבוד *v* got lost; (*pres* **holekh** *etc*; *fut* **yelekh** *etc*).
'eebood/-eem עיבוד *nm* 1. processing; 2. music arrangement; (*pl+of:* **-ey**).
'eebood netooneem עיבוד נתונים *nm* data processing.
eed|ah/-etah/-etee אידה *v* evaporated; (*pres* **me'adeh**; *fut* **ye'adeh**).
(me) 'eedakh מאידך *conj* (Aramaic) on the other hand.
'eedan/-eem עידן *nm* era; age; epoch; (*pl+of:* **-ey**).
□ **'Eedan** (Iddan) עידן *nm* village in the Aravah (est. 1976), 8 km NE of **'En Khatsevah**.
heedard|er/-erah/-artee הידרדר *v* deteriorated; (*pres* **meedarder**; *fut* **yeedarder**).
heedarderoot הידרדרות *nf* deterioration.
heedb|eek/-eekah/-aktee הדביק *v* 1. glued 2. attained; 3. infected; (*pres* **madbeek**; *fut* **yadbeek**).
eede'al/-eem אידיאל *nm* ideal; (*pl+of:* **-ey**).
eede'alee/-t אידיאלי *adj* ideal.
heed'eeg/-ah/heed'agtee הדאיג *v* worried; bothered; (*pres* **mad'eeg**; *fut* **yad'eeg**).
heed|ee'akh/-eekhah/-akhtee הדיח *v* 1. dismissed; fired; 2. misled; 3. abetted; (*pres* **madee'akh**; *fut* **yadee'akh**).
'eedeet עידית *nf* 1. best soil; 2. best choice; first quality.
heed|ek/-kah/-aktee הידק *v* tightened; fastened; (*pres* **mehadek**; *fut* **yehadek**).
'eed|en/-nah/-antee עידן *v* pampered; indulged; (*pres* **me'aden**; *fut* **ye'aden**).
eedeologee/-t אידיאולוגי *adj* ideological.
eedeolog|yah/-yot אידיאולוגיה *nf* ideology; (*+of:* **-yat**).
heedg|eem/-eemah/-amtee הדגים *v* demonstrated; (*pres* **madgeem**; *fut* **yadgeem**).
heedg|eesh/-eeshah/-ashtee הדגיש *v* pointed out; emphasized; (*pres* **madgeesh**; *fut* **yadgeesh**).
heed|'hed/-'hadah/-'hadetee הדהד *v* echoed; resounded; (*pres* **mehad'hed**; *fut* **yehad'hed**).
heed|'heem/-'heemah/-'hamtee הדהים *v* amazed; astounded; (*pres* **mad'heem**; *fut* **yad'heem**).
'eedk|en/-enah/-antee עדכן *v* updated; (*pres* **me'adken**; *fut* **ye'adken**).
'eedkoon/-eem עדכון *nm* updating; (*pl+of:* **-ey**).
heedl|eef/-eefah/-aftee הדליף *v* 1. disclosed; divulged; 2. let leak out (a secret); (*pres* **madleef**; *fut* **yadleef**).
heedl|eek/-eekah/-aktee הדליק *v* lighted; kindled; (*pres* **madleek**; *fut* **yadleek**).
'eedood/-em עידוד *nm* encouragement; (*pl+of:* **-ey**).
'eedoon/-eem עידון *nm* refinement; (*pl+of:* **-ey**).
heedook/-eem הידוק *nm* tightening; strengthening; (*pl+of:* **-ey**).
heedook kehareem הידוק קשרים *nm* rapprochement.
'eedoor/-eem עידור *nm* hoeing; (*pl+of:* **-ey**).
heedoor הידור *nm* elegance.
(be) heedoor בהידור *adv* elegantly.
heedp|ees/-eesah/-astee הדפיס *v* printed; (*pres* **madpees**; *fut* **yadpees**).
heedr|eekh/-eekhah/-akhtee הדריך *v* guided; trained; instructed; (*pres* **madreekh**; *fut* **yadreekh**).
heef|'eel/-'eelah/-'altee הפעיל *v* activated; put in motion; (*pres* **maf'eel**; *fut* **yaf'eel**).
heefg|een/-eenah/-antee הפגין *v* demonstrated; (*pres* **mafgeen**; *fut* **yafgeen**).
heefg|eesh/-eeshah/-ashtee הפגיש *v* brought together; made meet; (*pres* **mafgeesh**; *fut* **yafgeesh**).
heefg|eez/-eezah/-aztee הפגיז *v* shelled; bombarded; (*pres* **mafgeez**; *fut* **yafgeez**).

heefk|ee'a'/-ee'ah/-a'tee הפקיע *v* requisitioned; expropriated; (*pres* **mafkee'a'**; *fut* **yafkee'a'**).

heefk|eed/-eedah/-adetee הפקיד *v* entrusted; deposited; (*pres* **mafkeed**; *fut* **yafkeed**).

heefk|eer/-eerah/-kartee הפקיר *v* abandoned; (*pres* **mafkeer**; *fut* **yafkeer**).

heefl|ee/-ee'ah/-etee הפליא *v* amazed; (*pres* **maflee**; *fut* **yaflee**).

heeflee (*etc*) **et makot|av/-eha** הפליא את מכותיו *v* gave him/her a good beating.

heefl|eeg/-eegah/-agtee הפליג **1.** sailed; **2.** exaggerated; (*pres* **mafleeg**; *fut* **yafleeg**).

heefl|eel/-eelah/-altee הפליל *v* incriminated; arraigned; (*pres* **mafleel**; *fut* **yafleel**).

heefl|eet/-eetah/-atetee הפליט *v* let slip; ejaculated; (*pres* **mafleet**; *fut* **yafleet**).

heefl|eets/-eetsah/-atstee הפליץ *[slang]* *v* farted; (*pres* **mafleets**; *fut* **yafleets**).

heefn|ah/-etah/-etee הפנה *v* directed; sent on; referred someone; (*pres* **mafneh**; *fut* **yafneh**).

heefr|eed/-eedah/-adetee הפריד *v* separated (*pres* **mafreed**; *fut* **yafreed**).

heefkh|eed/-eedah/-adetee הפחיד *v* scared; frightened; (*pres* **mafkheed**; *fut* **yafkheed**).

heefkh|eet/-eetah/-atetee הפחית *v* deducted; reduced; (*pres* **mafkheet**; *fut* **yafkheet**).

heefr|ee'a'/-ee'ah/-a'tee הפריע *v* obstructed; interfered with; (*pres* **mafree'a'**; *fut* **yafree'a'**).

heefr|eesh/-eeshah/-ashtee הפריש *v* set aside; (*pres* **mafreesh**; *fut* **yafreesh**).

heefr|eez/-eezah/-aztee הפריז *v* exaggerated; overdid; (*pres* **mafreez**; *fut* **yafreez**).

heefs|eed/-eedah/-adetee הפסיד *v* lost; (*pres* **mafseed**; *fut* **yafseed**).

heefs|eek/-eekah/-aktee הפסיק *v* ceased; stopped; interrupted; (*pres* **mafseek**; *fut* **yafseek**).

heefsh|eel/-eelah/-altee הפשיל *v* rolled up (sleeves); (*pres* **mafsheel**; *fut* **yafsheel**).

heefsh|eet/-eetah/-atetee הפשיט *v* undressed; (*pres* **mafsheet**; *fut* **yafsheet**).

eefsh|er/-erah/-artee איפשר *v* enabled; made possible; (*pres* **me'afsher**; *fut* **ye'afsher**).

heeft|ee'a'/-ee'ah/-a'tee הפתיע *v* surprised; (*pres* **maftee'a'**; *fut* **yaftee'a'**).

heeft|eer/-eerah/-artee הפטיר *v* remarked; (*pres* **mafteer**; *fut* **yafteer**).

heefts|eer/-eerah/-artee הפציר *v* implored; insisted; (*pres* **maftseer**; *fut* **yaftseer**).

heefts|eets/-eetsah/-atstee הפציץ *v* bombarded; (*pres* **maftseets**; *fut* **yaftseets**).

heegamloo|t-yot היגמלות *nf* weaning.

heegareroo|t/-yot היגררות *nf* following blindly.

heegayon היגיון *nm* logic; reasoning.

heegb|ee'ah/-eehah/-ahtee הגביה *v* raised; heightened; (*pres* **magbee'ah**; *fut* **yagbee'ah**).

heegb|eel/-eelah/-altee הגביל *v* restricted; limited; (*pres* **magbeel**; *fut* **yagbeel**).

heeg|beer/-eerah/-artee הגביר *v* increased; strengthened; (*pres* **magbeer**; *fut* **yagbeer**).

heegd|eel/-eelah/-altee הגדיל *v* increased; enlarged; (*pres* **magdeel**; *fut* **yagdeel**).

heegd|eer/-eerah/-artee הגדיר *v* defined; (*pres* **magdeer**; *fut* **yagdeer**).

heegd|eesh/-eeshah/-ashtee הגדיש *v* overdid; (*pres* **magdeesh**; *fut* **yagdeesh**).

heegdeesh (*etc*) **et ha-se'ah** הגדיש את הסאה *v* overdid it.

heeg|ee'a'/-ee'ah/-a'tee הגיע *v* arrived; reached; (*pres* **magee'a'**; *fut* **yagee'a'**).

heeg|ee'akh (*npr* **hegee'akh**)/**-eekhah/-akhtee** הגיח *v* burst forth; broke out; (*pres* **megee'akh**; *fut* **yagee'akh**).

heeg|eed/-eedah/-adetee הגיד *v* told; said; (*fut* **yageed**).

heeg|eesh/-eeshah/-ashtee הגיש *v* **1.** presented;submitted; **2.** served; supplied; (*pres* **mageesh**; *fut* **yageesh**).

heegeesh (*etc*) **bakashah** הגיש בקשה *v* petitioned; submitted a request.

heegeesh (*etc*) **heetpatroot** הגיש התפטרות *v* submitted a resignation.

heegeesh (*etc*) **tloon|ah/-ot** הגיש תלונה *v* lodged complaint.

'eeg|el/-lah/-altee עיגל *v* rounded off (figure).

heeg|er/-rah/-artee היגר *v* emigrated; left the country; (*pres* **mehager**; *fut* **yehager**).

eeg|eret/-rot איגרת *nf* letter; note.

eeg|eret/-rot aveer איגרת אוויר *nf* airletter.

eeg|eret/-rot khov איגרת חוב *nf* bond; debenture.

heegleed/-ah הגליד *v* formed a scar; cicatrized; (*pres* **magleed**; *fut* **yagleed**).

heegn|eev/-eevah/-avtee הגניב *v* smuggled in; stole into; (*pres* **magneev**; *fut* **yagneev**).

eegood/-eem איגוד *nm* union; association; (*pl+of:* **-ey**).

eegood/-eem artsee/-yeem איגוד ארצי *nm* national union; national federation.

eedood/-eem meektso'ee/-yeem איגוד מקצועי *nm* trade-union; labor union.

'eegool/-eem עיגול *nm* circle; (*pl+of:* **-ey**).

heegooy היגוי *nm* pronunciation.

heegr|eel/-eelah/-raltee הגריל *v* raffled; drew lots; (*pres* **magreel**; *fut* **yagreel**).

eegroof איגרוף *nm* boxing.

eegrot khov איגרות חוב *nf pl* debentures; bonds; (*sing:* **eegeret-khov**).

heegsh|eem/-eemah/-amtee הגשים *v* **1.** implemented; **2.** *[colloq.]* it rained (*pres* **magsheem**; *fut* **yagsheem**).

heegeeyenah היגיינה *nf* hygiene.

heegz|eem/-eemah/-amtee הגזים *v* exaggerated; (*pres* **magzeem**; *fut* **yagzeem**).

heek|ah/-tah/-etee הכה *v* beat; struck; (*pres* **makeh**; *fut* **yakeh**).

heekah (*etc*) **shor|esh/-sheem** הכה שורש *v* struck roots.

eekar/-eem איכר *nm* farmer; peasant; (*f:* **-ah/-ot**; *pl+of:* **-ey**).

'eekar/-eem עיקר *nm* essence; main thing; (*pl+of:* **-ey**).

(be) 'eekar בעיקר *adv* mainly; in the first place.

(ha) 'eekar העיקר *nm* the main thing.

(kelal ve) 'eekar כלל ועיקר *adv* at all.

(kofer/-et ba) 'eekar כופר בעיקר *nmf* **1.** heretic; **2.** contesting the main argument; doubting the whole thing.

(kol) 'eekar כל עיקר *adv* in no way.

'eekaree/-t עיקרי *adj* main; principal.

'eekaron/'ekronot עיקרון *nm* principle; (*+of:* **'ekron**).

(be) 'eekaron בעיקרון *adv* in principle.

heekb|eel/-eelah/-altee הקביל *v* drew a parallel; (*pres* **makbeel**; *fut* **yakbeel**).

heekbeel (*etc*) **et peney** הקביל את פני *v* welcomed; met on arrival; received.

heekd|eem/-eemah/-amtee הקדים *v* preceded; anticipated; (*pres* **makdeem**; *fut* **yakdeem**).

heekd|eesh/-eeshah/-ashtee הקדיש *v* devoted; dedicated; (*pres* **makdeesh**; *fut* **yakdeesh**).

heekdeesh (*etc*) **'atsmo/-ah/-ee** הקדיש עצמו *v* devoted one/him/her/my -self.

heekdeesh (*etc*) **tesoomet-lev** הקדיש תשומת־לב *v* paid/devoted attention.

heek|eef/-eefah/-aftee הקיף *v* **1.** surrounded; **2.** comprised; encompassed; (*pres* **makeef**; *fut* **yakeef**).

heek|eer/-eerah/-artee הכיר *v* **1.** recognized **2.** made acquaintance; (*pres* **makeer**; *fut* **yakeer**).

heekeer (*etc*) **tovah** הכיר טובה *v* was grateful.

eek|el/-lah/-altee עיכל *v* digested; (*pres* **me'akel**; *fut* **ye'akel**).

'eek|el/-lah/-altee עיקל *v* seized; foreclosed; (*pres* **me'akel**; *fut* **ye'akel**).

'eek|em/-mah/-amtee עיקם *v* twisted; (*pres* **me'akem**; *fut* **ye'akem**).

'eekem (*etc*) **et ha-af** עיקם את האף *v* scorned; (*lit.*) twisted the nose.

'eekesh/-et עיקש *adj* obstinate.

'eek|ev/-vah/-avtee עיכב *v* detained; delayed; (*pres* **me'akev**; *fut* **ye'akev**).

heekhb|eed/-eedah/-adetee הכביד *v* bothered; inconvenienced; (*pres* **makhbeed**; *fut* **yakhbeed**).

eekh|ed/-adah/-adetee איחד *v* united; unified; (*pres* **me'akhed**; *fut* **ye'akhed**).

heekh|'ees/-'eesah/-'astee הכעיס *v* angered; (*pres* **makh'ees**; *fut* **yakh'ees**).

heekh|'eev/-'eevah/-'avtee הכאיב *v* hurt; (*pres* **makh'eev**; *fut* **yakh'eev**).

eekh|el/-alah/-altee איחל *v* wished; congratulated.

eekher/ekhar|ah/-tee איחר *v* came late; missed; (*pres* **me'akher**; *fut* **ye'akher**).

heekhl|eel/-eelah/-altee הכליל *v* generalized; included; (*pres* **makhleel**; *fut* **yakhleel**).

heekhn|ee'a'/-ee'ah/-a'tee הכניע *v* subdued; overpowered; (*pres* **makhnee'a'**; *fut* **yakhnee'a'**).

heekhn|ees/-eesah/-astee הכניס *v* introduced; entered; (*pres* **makhnees**; *fut* **yakhnees**).

eekhood/-eem איחוד *nm* union; unification; (*pl+of:* **-ey**).

eekhooleem איחולים *nm* good wishes; (*pl+of:* **-ey**).

eekhooleem levaveeyeem איחולים לבביים *nm pl* hearty good wishes!

eekhooleem mee-kerev lev איחולים מקרב לב *nm pl* wishes from the bottom of (one's) heart.

eekhoor/-eem איחור *nm* delay; (*pl+of:* **-ey**).

(be) eekhoor באיחור *adv* late.

eekhpat איכפת concerns; touches; makes one care.

eekhpat lee/lekha/lakh/lo/lah (*etc*) איכפת לי/לך/לו וכו׳ *v* I/you(*m/f*)/he/she (*etc*) care(s).

eekhpateeyoot איכפתיות *nf* concern.

eekhpatneek/-et איכפתניק *nmf [slang]* one who does care.

heekhp|eel/-eelah/-altee הכפיל *v* **1.** doubled; **2.** multiplied; (*pres* **makhpeel**; *fut* **yakhpeel**).

heekhr|ee'a'/-ee'ah/-a'tee הכריע *v* decided; tipped the scale; (*pres* **makhree'a'**; *fut* **yakhree'a'**).

heekhr|ee'akh/-khah/-akhtee הכריח *v* forced; compelled; (*pres* **makhree'akh**; *fut* **yakhree'ah**).

heekhr|eez/-eezah/-aztee הכריז *v* announced; (*pres* **makhreez**; *fut* **yakhreez**).

eekhs|en/-enah/-antee אכסן *v* accommodated; lodged; (*pres* **me'akhsen**; *fut* **ye'akhsen**).

eekhs|en/-enah/-antee אחסן *v* stored; (*pres* **me'akhsen**; *fut* **ye'akhsen**).

heekh'sh|eel/-eelah/-altee הכשיל *v* corrupted; caused to fail; (*pres* **makh'sheel**; *fut* **yakh'sheel**).

heekh'sh|eer/-eerah/-artee הכשיר *v* **1.** prepared; **2.** made something "kosher"; (*pres* **makh'sheer**; *fut* **yakh'sheer**).

heekh'sheer (*etc*) **et ha-karka'** הכשיר את הקרקע *v* prepared the ground.

eekhsoon/-eem אכסון *nm* accommodation; putting up overnight; (*pl+of:* **-ey**).

eekhsoon אחסון *nm* storage.

heekht|eem/-eemah/-amtee הכתים *v* stained; besmirched; (*pres* **makhteem**; *fut* **yakhteem**).

heekht|eer/-eerah/-artee הכתיר *v* crowned; (*pres* **makhteer**; *fut* **yakhteer**).

heekht|eev/-eevah/-avtee הכתיב *v* dictated; (*pres* **makhteev**; *fut* **yakhteev**).

heekhz|eev/-eevah/-avtee הכזיב *v* failed; let down; (*pres* **makhzeev**; *fut* **yakhzeev**).

eekhz|ev/-evah/-avtee אכזב *v* disappointed; (*pres* **me'akhzev**; *fut* **ye'akhzev**).

heek'kh|eesh/-eeshah/-ashtee הכחיש *v* denied; (*pres* **mak'kheesh**; *fut* **yak'kheesh**).

heekl|eet/-eetah/-atetee הקליט *v* recorded; (*pres* **makleet**; *fut* **yakleet**).

eekool/-eem עיכול *nm* digestion; (*pl+of:* **ey**).

(darkhey ha) 'eekool דרכי העיכול *nm pl* digestive organs.

(ma'arekhet ha) 'eekool מערכת העיכול *nf* digestive system.

'eekool/-eem עיקול *nm* foreclosure; attachment; (*pres+of:* **-ey**).

heekon!/-ee! !היכון *v imp* s *m/f* be prepared! stand by!

'eekoor/-eem עיקור *nm* extirpation; uprooting; sterilization; (*pl+of:* **-ey**).

'eekoov/-eem עיכוב *nm* hindrance; (*pl+of:* **-ey**).

heekp|eets/-eetsah/-atstee הקפיץ *v* **1.** bounced; shocked; **2.** *[colloq.]* gave a lift by vehicle. (*pres* **makpeets;** *fut* **yakpeets**).

'eekree/-t עיקרי *adj* main; principal.

(man|ah/-ot) 'eekree|t/-yot מנה עיקרית *nf* main dish; main course; entree.

heekr|ee/-ee'ah/-etee הקריא *v* recited; read out; (*pres* **makree;** *fut* **yakree**).

heekr|ee'akh/-eekhah/-akhtee הקריח *v* grew bald; (*pres* **makree'akh;** *fut* **yakree'akh**).

heekr|een/-eenah/-antee הקרין *v* **1.** projected (on screen); **2.** radiated; (*pres* **makreen;** *fut* **yakreen**).

heekr|eets/-eetsah/-atstee הקריץ *v [slang]* got hold; unexpectedly procured; (*pres* **makreets;** *fut* **yakreets**).

heekr|eev/-eevah/-avtee הקריב *v* **1.** sacrificed; **2.** drew near; (*pres* **makreev;** *fut* **yakreev**).

heeks|eem/-eemah/-amtee הקסים *v* charmed; (*pres* **makseem;** *fut* **yakseem**).

heeksh|ah/-etah/-etee הקשה *v* **1.** hardened; **2.** made difficult; (*pres* **maksheh;** *fut* **yaksheh**).

heeksh|ee'akh/-eekhah/-akhtee הקשיח *v* stiffened; hardened; (*pres* **makshee'akh;** *fut* **yakshee'akh**).

heeksh|eev/-eevah/-avtee הקשיב *v* listened; paid attention; heeded; (*pres* **maksheev;** *fut* **yaksheev**).

heekt|een/-eenah/-antee הקטין *v* diminished; reduced; (*pres* **makteen;** *fut* **yakteen**).

heekts|eev/-eevah/-avtee הקציב *v* allocated; (*pres* **maktseev;** *fut* **yaktseev**).

'eekvee/-t עיקבי *adj* consistent; (*pl:* **-yeem/-yot**).

'eekvot עקבות *nm pl+of* footsteps of; traces of; (see **'akavot**).

(be) 'eekvot בעקבות *adv* following; in the steps of.

'eel|ah/-ot עילה *nf* **1.** cause; **2.** cause of action (legal); **3.** pretext; (*+of:* **-at**).

eelan/-ot אילן *nm* tree.

□ **Eelaneeyah** (Ilaniyya) אילנייה *nm* village in Lower Galilee, 2 km S. of **Tsomet Golanee** (Golani Junction). Better known under its historic name **Sedjerah** (סג'רה), under which it was founded in 1899. Pop. 299.

◇ **(rosh-ha-shanah la) eelanot** see ◇ **rosh-ha-shanah la-eelanot**.

'eel|at/-ot tevee'ah עילת תביעה *nf* cause of action.

heelb|een/-eenah/-antee הלבין *v* **1.** paled; whitened; **2.** turned gray (hair); (*pres* **malbeen;** *fut* **yalbeen**).

heelb|eesh/-eeshah/-ashtee הלביש *v* dressed; (*pres* **malbeesh;** *fut* **yalbeesh**).

'eelee/-t עילי *adj* upper; overhead; (*pl:* **-yeem/-yot**).

heel|'eem/-'eemah/-'amtee הלאים *v* nationalized; (*pres* **mal'eem;** *fut* **yal'eem**).

'eeleet/-ot עילית *nf* elite.

heel|'eet/-'eetah/-'atetee הלעיט *v* stuffed; (*pres* **mal'eet;** *fut* **yal'eet**).

eel|ef/-fah/-aftee אילף *v* tamed; (*pres* **me'alef;** *fut* **ye'alef**).

'eel|eg/-eget עילג *adj* tongue-tied; stuttering; (*pl:* **-geem/-got**).

heel|ekh/-khah/-akhtee הילך *v* walked; walked about; (*pres* **mehalekh;** *fut* **yehalekh**).

heelekh (*etc*) **bee-gdolot** הילך בגדולות *v* saw big; aspired to great things.

heelekh (*etc*) **eymeem** הילך אימים *v* terrorized.

ee (*npr* **ey**) **lekhakh** אי לכך *adv* therefore.

heel|el/-elah/-altee הילל *v* praised; lauded; (*pres* **mehalel;** *fut* **yehalel**).

eel|em/-emet אילם *nmf & adj* mute (*pl:* **-meem/-mot**).

eel|ets/-tsah/-atstee אילץ *v* forced; compelled; (*pres* **me'alets;** *fut* **ye'alets**).

heel|'heev/-'heevah/-'havtee הלהיב *v* excited; aroused enthusiasm; (*pres* **mal'heev;** *fut* **yal'heev**).

heelk|ah/-etah/-etee הלקה *v* flogged; whipped; (*pres* **malkeh;** *fut* **yalkeh**).

eelkakh (*npr* **ey lekhakh**) אי לכך *adv* therefore.

heelkh|eem/-eemah/-amtee הלחים *v* soldered; welded; (*pres* **malkheem;** *fut* **yalkheem**).

heelkh|een/-eenah/-antee הלחין *v* composed (music); (*pres* **malkheen;** *fut* **yalkheen**).

heelkhey roo'akh הלכי רוח *nm pl* moods (*sing:* **halakh** *etc*).

eelmale/eelmaley אלמלא /אלמלי **1.** *conj* were it not for; **2.** *conj* if.

eeloo אילו *conj* if.

(ke) eeloo כאילו *conj* as if.

heelookh/-eem הילוך *nm* **1.** gait; **2.** gear; transmission; (*pl+of:* **-ey**).

heelookheem otomateeyeem הילוכים אוטומטיים *nm pl* automatic gears.

(teyvat) heelookheem תיבת הילוכים *nf* gearbox.

heelool|ah/-ot הילולה *nm* festival; merrymaking; (*+of:* **-at**).

eelooley אילולי *conj* if it weren't for.

(be) 'eeloom shem בעילום שם *adv* incognito.

eeloots/-eem אילוץ *nm* coercion; compulsion; (*pl+of:* **-ey**).

heelsh|een/-eenah/-antee הלשין *v* informed on; denounced; (*pres* **malsheen;** *fut* **yalsheen**).

eelt|er/-erah/-artee אלתר *v* improvised; (*pres* **me'alter;** *fut* **ye'alter**).

eeltoor/-eem אלתור *nm* improvisation; (*pl+of:* **-ey**).

heelv|ah/-etah/-etee הלווה *v* lent (money) (*pres* **malveh;** *fut* **yalveh**).

eem אם *conj* if.

eem kee אם כי *conj* although.

eem ken אם כן *conj* if so.
eem yeertseh ha-shem אם ירצה השם God willing.
(ela) eem ken אלא אם כן *conj* unless; except if.
(gam) eem גם אם *conj* even if.
(zoolat) eem זולת אם *conj* except if; unless.
'eem עם *prep* with.
'eem kol zeh/zot עם כל זה *adv & conj* nevertheless; with all that *m/f*.
'eem zot עם זאת *conj* nevertheless.
(het|eev/-eevah/-avtee) 'eem היטיב עם *v* did (someone) well; did (someone) good.
(shalem/shlemah) 'eem שלם עם agreeing with.
eema/-'ot אמא Mamma; Mum; Mom.
'eemadee עימדי *prep & pers.pron* with me.
eemahee/-t אימהי *adj* motherly; maternal.
eemahoot אימהות *nf* motherhood.
eema'leh אמא'לה *nf* Mum; Mummy; Mommy; (pet-name).
□ **'Eemanooel** ('Immanu'el) עמנואל *nf* new town in Samaria Hills (est. 1983), populated by observant Jews. 15 km SW of Nablus, 25 km E. of Kefar-Sava, via the new Trans-Samaria road. Pop. 2,590.
heemanoot הימנות *nf* siding with; being counted among.
heeman'oo|t/-yot הימנעות *nf* abstention.
heemash'khoo|t/-yot הימשכות *nf* **1.** attraction to; **2.** continuation.
heemats'oot הימצאות *nf* existence; availability.
'eemdee! עמדי! *v imp sing f* stop! (addressing single female).
'eemdoo! עמדו! *v imp pl* stop! stand up! (addressing several people).
eem|ee/-kha/-ekh/-o/-ah *(etc)* אמי/־ך/־ו/־ה וכו' my/your *m/f* his/her *(etc)* mother.
heem'ees/-eesah/-astee המאיס *v* made it hateful; made one abhor; (*pres* **mam'ees;** *fut* **yam'ees**).
'eem|'em/-'amah/-'amtee עמעם *v* dimmed; (*pres* **me'am'em;** *fut* **ye'am'em**).
eem|en/-nah/-antee אימן *v* trained; (*pres* **me'amen;** *fut* **ye'amen**).
eem|et/-tah/-atetee אימת *v* confirmed; attested; (*pres* **me'amet;** *fut* **ye'amet**).
'eem|et/-tah/-atetee עימת *v* confronted; (*pres* **me'amet;** *fut* **ye'amet**).
eem|ets/-tsah/-atstee אימץ *v* adopted; embraced; (*pres* **me'amets;** *fut* **ye'amets**).
heeml|ee'akh/-eekhah/-akhtee המליח *v* salted; (*pres* **mamlee'akh;** *fut* **yamlee'akh**).
heeml|eekh/-eekhah/-akhtee המליך *v* installed as king; crowned; (*pres* **mamleekh;** *fut* **yamleekh**).
heemleet/-ah המליט *v* gave birth (mammals); laid eggs; (*pres* **mamleet;** *fut* **yamleet**).
heemleets/-eetsah/-atstee המליץ *v* recommended; (*pres* **mamleets;** *fut* **yamleets**).
eeml|el/-elah/-altee אמלל *v* made (one) miserable; (*pres* **me'amlel;** *fut* **ye'amlel**).
heem|em/-emah/-amtee הימם *v* shocked; (*pres* **mehamem;** *fut* **yehamem**).
heemnon/-eem המנון *nm* anthem (*pl+of:* **-ey**).
eemoon/-eem אימון *nm* training.
eemoon|eem אימונים *nm pl* training exercises; (*+of:* **-ey**).
(makhn|eh/-ot) eemooneem מחנה אימונים training camp.
heemoor/-eem הימור *nm* wager; bet; gamble; (*pl+of:* **-ey**).
eemoot/-eem אימות *nm* confirmation; attestation; (*pl+of:* **-ey**).
'eemoot/-eem עימות *nm* confrontation; (*pl+of:* **-ey**).
eemoots/-eem אימוץ *nm* adoption; (*pl+of:* **-ey**).
eemree! אמרי! *v imp sing f* say! tell! (addressing single female); (*pl:* **emorna!**).
heemr|ee/-ee'ah/-etee המריא *v* took off (airplane); (*pres* **mamree;** *fut* **yamree**).
heemr|eed/-eedah/-adetee המריד *v* incited to rebellion; (*pres* **mamreed;** *fut* **yamreed**).
heemr|eets/-eetsah/-atstee המריץ *v* urged; stimulated; (*pres* **mamreets;** *fut* **yamreets**).
heemsh|eekh/-eekhah/-akhtee המשיך *v* continued (*pres* **mamsheekh;** *fut* **yamsheekh**).
heemsh|eel/-eelah/-altee המשיל *v* likened; compared; (*pres* **mamsheel;** *fut* **yamsheel**).
heemsheel *(etc)* **mashal** המשיל משל *v* quoted a parable.
heemt|eek/-eekah/-aktee המתיק *v* sweetened; (*pres* **mamteek;** *fut* **yamteek**).
heemteek *(etc)* **sod** המתיק סוד *v* took counsel together.
heemt|een/-eenah/-antee המתין *v* waited; (*pres* **mamteen;** *fut* **yamteen**).
heemts|ee/-ee'ah/-etee המציא *v* **1.** invented; **2.** delivered; (*pres* **mamtsee;** *fut* **yamtsee**).
een|ah/-tah אינה *v* brought about; caused to happen.
'een|ah/-tah/-eetee עינה *v* tortured; (*pres* **me'aneh;** *fut* **ye'aneh**).
heen|ah/-o הינה *v pres* (f/m) is.
heenatkoot הינתקות *nf* severance; cutting off.
heenatsloot הינצלות *nf* rescue; escape.
'eenbal/-eem ענבל *nm* clapper; tongue of bell; (*pl+of:* **-ey**).
'eenbar ענבר *nm* amber.
heen|ee'akh/-eekhah/-akhtee הניח *v* **1.** put; **2.** laid down; **3.** let; permitted; **4.** assumed; (*pres* **manee'akh;** *fut* **yanee'akh**).
heen|'eem/-'eemah/-'amtee הנעים *v* made pleasant; agreeable; (*pres* **man'eem;** *fut* **yan'eem**).
heeneh הנה *prep* here is; behold;
heeneh hoo/hee/hem/hen הנה הוא/היא/הם/הן here he/she/they *m/f* is/are.
heenen|ee/-oo הנני *v pres* 1st pers I am/we are.
heenenee הנני here I am.
eenformatsyah אינפורמציה *nf* information.
heen|heeg/-heegah/-hagtee הנהיג *v* **1.** introduced; **2.** led; conducted; (*pres* **manheeg;** *fut* **yanheeg**).

heenkh|ah/-etah/-etee הנחה *v* directed; moderated; (*pres* **mankheh;** *fut* **yankheh**).

heenkh|eet/-eetah/-atetee הנחית *v* landed (a plane); (*pres* **mankheet;** *fut* **yankheet**).

heenkheet (*etc*) **mahaloomah/makah** הנחית מהלומה/מכה *v* inflicted a blow.

heenm|eekh/-eekhah/-akhtee הנמיך *v* lowered; (*pres* **manmeekh;** *fut* **yanmeekh**).

heenmeekh (*etc*) **toos** הנמיך טוס *v* flew at low altitude.

eenshallah אינשאללה *interj [slang] (Arab.)* God willing.

eenteleegentee/-t אינטליגנטי *adj* intelligent.

'eenoo|y/-yeem עינוי *nm* torment; torture; (*pl+of:* **-yey**).

eenteres/-eem אינטרס interest.

(neegood/-ey) eentereseem ניגוד אינטרסים *nm* conflict of interests.

heents|ee'akh/-eekhah/-akhtee הנציח *v* immortalized; perpetuated; (*pres* **mantsee'akh;** *fut* **yantsee'akh**).

'eenvey boser ענבי בוסר *nm pl* sour grapes.

'eenvey ma'akhal ענבי מאכל *nm pl* table grapes.

'een|yan/-yaneem עניין *nm* matter; interest; (*pl+of:* **-yeney**).

(be) 'eenyan בעניין *adv* **1.** with interest; **2.** in the matter of.

(le) 'eenyan לעניין *adv* concerning.

(bakhoor/-ah la) 'eenyan בחור לעניין *nmf [colloq.]* clever guy/girl.

'eenyanee/-t ענייני *adj* practical; pertinent.

(ekh ha) 'eenyaneem? (*or:* **eykh** *etc*) ?איך העניינים *[colloq.]* how's everything? how goes it?

(heeshtalsheloot ha) 'eenyaneem השתלשלות העניינים *nf* the chain of events.

(mah ha) 'eenyaneem? ?מה העניינים *[colloq.]* what's the matter?

(mafte|akh/-khot) 'eenyaneem מפתח עניינים *nm* index; table of contents.

'een|yen/-yenah/-yantee עיניין *v* aroused interest/attention; interested; (*pres* **me'anyen;** *fut* **ye'anyen**).

'eeparon/'efronot (*f=p*) עיפרון *nm* pencil; (*+of:* **'efron**).

heep|eel/-eelah/-altee הפיל *v* brought down; overthrew; (*pres* **mapeel;** *fut* **yapeel**).

heepeelah הפילה *v 3rd person f sing* miscarried.

heepn|et/-etah/-atetee היפנט *v* hypnotized; (*pres* **mehapnet;** *fut* **yehapnet**).

eepook איפוק *nm* restraint.

heepookh היפוך *nm* reverse; opposite.

heepookho shel davar היפוכו של דבר *nm* quite the contrary.

(davar ve) heepookho דבר והיפוכו *nm* a flagrant contradiction; point and counterpoint.

eepoor איפור *nm* make-up.

eepotekah/-ot איפותיקה *nf* mortgage.

(halva'ah) eepotekaeet הלוואה איפותיקאית mortgage-loan.

heepotetee/-t היפותטי *adj* hypothetical.

'eer/'areem עיר *nf* town (*pl+of:* **'arey**).

'eer/'arey beerah עיר בירה *nf* capital city.

□ **'eer ha-kodesh** עיר הקודש *nf* the Holy City (i.e. Jerusalem).

'eer/'arey peetoo'akh עיר פיתוח *nf* development town.

'eer/'arey sadeh עיר שדה *nf* provincial town.

(gan ha) 'eer גן העיר *nm* municipal park; public garden.

□ **(ha)'eer ha-'ateekah** העיר העתיקה *nf* the Old City (normally referring to the one in Jerusalem).

(rosh) 'eer ראש העיר *nm* mayor.

eer|a' (*npr* **eyr|a'**)/**-'ah** אירע *v* occurred; happened; (*pres* **meetrakhesh;** *fut* **ye'era'**).

(ha) 'eerah העירה *adv* to town; back to town.

□ **eerak** עירק *nf* Iraq.

'eerakee/-m עירקי *nm* **1.** originating from Iraq; **2.** Iraqi.

◇ **(peet|ah/-ot) 'eerakee|t/-yot** see ◇ **peet|ah/-ot 'eerakee|t/-yot.**

heerb|ah/-etah/-etee הרבה *v* multiplied; did much of (*pres* **marbeh;** *fut* **yarbeh**).

heerb|eets/-eetsah/-atstee הרביץ *v* **1.** beat up; **2.** let it go; put in; (*pres* **marbeets;** *fut* **yarbeets**).

heerbeets (*etc*) **makot** הרביץ מכות *v* gave a beating; spanked.

heerbeets (*etc*) **torah** הרביץ תורה *v* **1.** taught knowledge; **2.** gave "Torah" lessons.

'eerb|ev/-evah/-avtee ערבב *v* mixed up; confounded; (*pres* **me'arbev;** *fut* **ye'arbev**).

'eerb|el/-elah/-altee ערבל *v* mixed using a mixer; (*pres* **me'arbel;** *fut* **ye'arbel**).

'eerboov/-eem ערבוב *nm* **1.** confounding; mixing; **2.** mixture (*pl+of:* **-ey**).

'eerboov tekhoomeem ערבוב תחומים *nm* encroachment; overlapping; confusion.

'eerboov|yah/-yot ערבוביה *nf* confusion; mess; (*+of:* **-yat**).

heerd|eem/-eemah/-amtee הרדים *v* put to sleep; anesthetized; (*pres* **mardeem;** *fut* **yardeem**).

heer|'eed/-'eedah/-'adetee הרעיד *v* made tremble; (*pres* **mar'eed;** *fut* **yar'eed**).

heer'eel/-'eelah/-'altee הרעיל *v* poisoned; (*pres* **mar'eel;** *fut* **yar'eel**).

heer|'eem/-'eemah/-'amtee הרעים *v* thundered; (*pres* **mar'eem;** *fut* **yar'eem**).

heer|'eesh/-'eeshah/-'ashtee הרעיש *v* **1.** stormed; bombarded; **2.** *[colloq.]* made noises; (*pres* **mar'eesh;** *fut* **yar'eesh**).

heer'eesh (*etc*) **'olamot** הרעיש עולמות *v* made a big fuss.

'eeree|yah/-yot עירייה *nf* municipality; town-hall; (*+of:* **-yat**).

heerg|ee'a'/-ee'ah/-'atee הרגיע *v* calmed; pacified; (*pres* **margee'a';** *fut* **yargee'a'**).

heerg|eel/-eelah/-altee הרגיל *v* accustomed; (*pres* **margeel;** *fut* **yargeel**).

heerg|eesh/-eeshah/-ashtee הרגיש *v* felt; sensed; (*pres* **margeesh;** *fut* **yargeesh**).

heergeesh (*etc*) **be-ra‘** הרגיש ברע *v* felt sick.
heergeesh (*etc*) **ra‘** הרגיש רע *v* felt ill.
(lo) heergeesh (*etc*) **tov** לא הרגיש טוב *v* didn't feel well.
heerg|eez/-eezah/-aztee הרגיז *v* irritated; angered; (*pres* **margeez**; *fut* **yargeez**).
eerg|en/-enah/-antee ארגן *v* organized; arranged; (*pres* **me'argen**; *fut* **ye'argen**).
eergoon/-eem ארגון *v* organization; (*pl+of:* **-ey**).
◇ **"eergoon tseva'ee le'oomee"** אירגון צבאי לאומי *nm* Irgun Zva'i Le'umi, the "National Military Organization" also known by its acronym אצ"ל **"ETSEL"** (or IZL). It operated in Mandatory Palestine as an underground organization in the years 1938-1948 using terrorism to drive the British out of the country. Its onetime members constituted the kernel of today's Herut (**Kheroot**) Party.
◇ **(ha)eergoon** האירגון *nm* the "Irgun" - colloquial *abbr.* for "Irgun Zvai le'umi" (IZL) (see preceding entry).
‘eergool/-eem עירגול *nm* rolling (iron); (*pl+of:* **-ey**).
heer|heev/-heevah/-havtee הרהיב *v* dared; (*pres* **marheev**; *fut* **yarheev**).
heer|her/-harah/-hartee הרהר *v* mused; reflected; (*pres* **meharher**; *fut* **yeharher**).
heerhoor/-eem הרהור *nm* thought; reflection; (*pl+of:* **-ey**).
heerhoor shenee הרהור שני *nm* second thought.
heerhoorey kharatah הרהורי חרטה *nm* regrets.
heerk|eed/-eedah/-adetee הרקיד *v* led a dance; made dance; (*pres* **markeed**; *fut* **yarkeed**).
heerk|eev/-eevah/-avtee הרכיב *v* assembled; formed; (*pres* **markeev**; *fut* **yarkeev**).
heerkeev/-eevah/-avtee הרקיב *v* rotted away; (*pres* **markeev**; *fut* **yarkeev**).
heerkh|eev/-eevah/-avtee הרחיב *v* expanded; widened; (*pres* **markheev**; *fut* **yarkheev**).
heerkheev (*etc*) **et ha-deeboor** הרחיב את הדיבור *v* elaborated; discussed at length.
heerkh|eek/-eekah/-aktee הרחיק *v* **1.** went far; **2.** removed; (*pres* **markheek**; *fut* **yarkheek**).
heerkheek (*etc*) **lekhet** הרחיק לכת went too far.
‘eer|‘er/-‘arah/-‘artee ערער *v* **1.** undermined; **2.** appealed (jurid.); submitted an appeal.
‘eeronee/-t עירוני *adj* municipal; urban.
(beyn-) ‘eeronee/-t בין־עירוני *adj* inter-urban.
‘eer‘oor/-eem ערעור *nm* **1.** appeal (jurid.); **2.** undermining; (*pl+of:* **-ey**).
‘eer‘oor/-eem ezrakhee/-yeem ערעור אזרחי *nm* civil appeal.
‘eer‘oor/-eem pleelee/-yeem ערעור פלילי *nm* criminal appeal.
(heeg|eesh/-eeshah/-ashtee) ‘eer‘oor הגיש ערעור *v* brought an appeal; appealed.
(bet/batey deen le) ‘eer‘ooreem בית דין לערעורים *nm* court of appeal.
‘eeroo|y/-yey dam עירוי דם *nm* blood transfusion.
heerp|ah/-etah/-etee הרפה *v* desisted; let go;
‘eerpool/-eem ערפול *nm* obscuring.
heersh|ah/-etah/-etee הרשה *v* permitted; allowed; (*pres* **marsheh**; *fut* **yarsheh**).
heershah (*etc*) **le-‘atsm|o/-ah/-ee** הרשה לעצמו *v* allowed one/him/her/my -self.
heersh|ee'a‘/-ee‘ah/-‘atee הרשיע *v* convicted; (*pres* **marshee'a‘**; *fut* **yarshee'a‘**).
heersh|eem/-eemah/-amtee הרשים *v* impressed; (*pres* **marsheem**; *fut* **yarsheem**).
heert|ee'a‘/-ee‘ah/-‘atee הרתיע *v* deterred; (*pres* **martee'a‘**; *fut* **yartee'a‘**).
heert|ee'akh/-eekhah/-akhtee הרתיח *v* **1.** boiled (water): **2.** infuriated; (*pres* **martee'akh**; *fut* **yartee'akh**).
heertee'akh (*etc*) **et dam|o/-ah/-ee** הרתיח את דמו *v* made his/her/my blood boil.
‘eert|el/-elah/-altee ערטל *v* stripped; denuded; (*pres* **me'artel**; *fut* **ye'artel**).
‘eertool/-eem ערטול *nm* laying bare; denuding.
heerts|ah/-etah/-etee הרצה *v* lectured; (*pres* **martseh**; *fut* **yartseh**).
heerv|ee'akh/-eekhah/-akhtee הרוויח *v* profited; earned; (*pres* **marvee'akh**; *fut* **yarvee'akh**).
heesardoo|t/-yot הישרדות *nf* survival.
heesb|ee'a‘/-ee'ah/-a'tee השביע *v* sated; satisfied; (*pres* **masbee'a‘**; *fut* **yasbee'a‘**).
heesb|ee'a‘ (*etc*) **ratson** השביע רצון *v* satisfied.
heesb|eer/-eerah/-artee הסביר *v* explained; (*pres* **masbeer**; *fut* **yasbeer**).
heesd|eer/-eerah/-artee הסדיר *v* arranged; settled; (*pres* **masdeer**; *fut* **yasdeer**).
hees|ee/-ee'ah/-etee השיא *v* married off; (*pst* **masee**; *fut* **yasee**).
heesee (*etc*) **‘ets|ah/-ot** השיא עצה *v* counselled; gave advice.
hees|ee'a‘/-ee'ah/-a'tee הסיע *v* transported; (*pres* **masee'a‘**; *fut* **yasee'a‘**).
hees|ee'akh/-eekhah/-akhtee הסיח *v* deflected; diverted; (*pres* **masee'akh**; *fut* **yasee'akh**).
hees|eeg/-eegah/-agtee השיג *v* attained; reached; achieved; (*pres* **maseeg**; *fut* **yaseeg**).
hees|eek/-eekah/-aktee הסיק **1.** *v* inferred; **2.** *v* heated; burned (stove) (*pres* **maseek**; *fut* **yaseek**).
heeseek (*etc*) **maskanah/-ot** הסיק מסקנה *v* drew conclusion.
hees|‘eer/-‘eerah/-‘artee הסעיר *v* caused a storm; (*pres* **mas‘eer**; *fut* **yas‘eer**).
hees|es/-esah/-astee היסס *v* hesitated; (*pres* **mehases**; *fut* **yehases**).
heesg|eer/-eerah/-artee הסגיר *v* **1.** extradited; **2.** surrendered; (*pres* **masgeer**; *fut* **yasgeer**).
eesh/anasheem איש *nm* man; person; (*pl+of:* **anshey**).
eesh/anshey ‘asakeem איש עסקים *nm* businessman.
eesh/anshey emoon|o/-ah/-ee איש אמונו *nm* man of (his/her/my) trust; confidant.
eesh/anshey kash איש קש *nm* strawman.

eesh lo איש לא nobody did; nobody has.
eesh/anshey mada' איש מדע *nm* scientist.
eesh/anshey roo'akh איש רוח *nm* intellectual.
eesh/anshey seekhah איש שיחה *nm* interlocutor; conversationalist.
eesh/anshey seekhat|o/-ah/-ee איש שיחתו *nm* his/her/my interlocutor.
eesh/anshey sod|o/-ah/-ee איש סודו *nm* (his/her/my) confidant.
eesh/anshey tsava איש צבא *nm* soldier; military man.
eesh/anshey tseeboor איש ציבור *nm* public figure.
(en) eesh (*or:* **eyn** *etc*) אין איש there's no-one.
(eshet) eesh אשת איש *nf* married woman.
(shoom) eesh שום איש no one; nobody.
eeshah/nasheem אישה, אשה *nf* **1.** woman **2.** wife; (*+of:* **eshet/neshot, neshey**).
eeshah/nasheem nesoo|'ah/-'ot אישה נשואה *nf* married woman.
(nasa/-ta/-tee) eeshah/nasheem נשא אישה *v* (masculin only: I/you/he) married (a woman); (*pres* **nose** *etc*; *fut* **yeesa** *etc*).
heesh|'ah/-'atah/-'etee השעה suspended; (*pres* **mash'eh**; *fut* **yash'eh**).
heeshb|ee'a/-ee'ah/-'atee השביע *v* swore in; (*pres* **mashbee'a**; *fut* **yashbee'a**).
heeshb|eet/-eetah/-atetee השבית *v* **1.** disturbed; **2.** locked out; (*pres* **mashbeet**; *fut* **yashbeet**).
heeshbeet (*etc*) **seemkhah** השבית שמחה *v* put end to rejoicing.
heesh|eek/-eekah/-aktee השיק *v* launched; touched off; (*pres* **masheek**; *fut* **yasheek**).
heesh|'eel/-'eelah/-'altee השאיל *v* lent an object (not money) for temporary use; (*pres* **mash'eel**; *fut* **yash'eel**).
eeshee/-t אישי *adj* personal; private.
eesheem אישים *nm pl* personalities; (*sing:* **eesheeyoot**).
(khadal/kheedley) eesheem חדל אישים *nm* good for nothing.
heesh|'eer/-'eerah/-'artee השאיר *v* left; abandoned; (*pres* **mash'eer**; *fut* **yash'eer**).
eesheet אישית *adv* personally; in person.
(moozm|an/-enet) eesheet מוזמן אישית *adj* personally invited.
(khafatseem) eesheeyeem חפצים אישיים *nm pl* personal effects.
(zeekooyeem) eesheeyeem זיכויים אישיים *nm* tax deductibles .
eesheeyoot אישיות *nf* personality.
(peetsool ha) eesheeyoot פיצול האישיות *nm* split personality.
'eesh|en/-nah/-antee עישן *v* smoked (tobacco); (*pres* **me'ashen**; *fut* **ye'ashen**).
eesh|er/-rah/-artee אישר *v* confirmed; approved; (*pres* **me'asher**; *fut* **ye'asher**).
heeshg|ee'akh/-eekhah/-akhtee השגיח *v* supervised; took care; observed; (*pres* **mashgee'akh**; *fut* **yashgee'akh**).
heesh'|hah/-hatah/-hetee השהה *v* delayed; suspended; (*pres* **mash'heh**; *fut* **yash'heh**).
heeshk|ah/-etah/-etee השקה *v* **1.** watered; irrigated; **2.** gave to drink; (*pres* **mashkeh**; *fut* **yashkeh**).
heeshk|ee'a'/-ee'ah/-a'tee השקיע *v* invested; (*pres* **mashkee'a'**; *fut* **yashkee'a'**).
heeshk|ee'akh/-eekhah/-akhtee השכיח *v* caused to forget: (*pres* **mashkee'akh**; *fut* **yashkee'akh**).
heshk|eef/-eefah/-aftee השקיף *v* observed; looked over (*pres* **mashkeef**; *fut* **yashkeef**).
eeshk|eem/-eemah/-amtee השכים *v* got up early; (*pres* **mashkeem**; *fut* **yashkeem**).
heeshk|eet/-eetah/-atetee השקיט *v* calmed; soothed; (*pres* **mashkeet**; *fut* **yashkeet**).
heeshk|eev/-eevah/-avtee השכיב *v* **1.** put to bed; **2.** laid down; (*pres* **mashkeev**; *fut* **yashkeev**).
heesh'kh|eel/-eelah/-altee השחיל *v* threaded (needle); (*pres* **mash'kheel**; *fut* **yash'kheel**).
heesh'kh|eer/-eerah/-artee השחיר *v* blackened; (*pres* **mash'kheer**; *fut* **yash'kheer**).
heesh'kh|eet/-eetah/-atetee השחית *v* deformed; corrupted; (*pres* **mash'kheet**; *fut* **yash'kheet**).
heesh'kh|eez/-eezah/-aztee השחיז *v* sharpened; (*pres* **mash'kheez**; *fut* **yash'kheez**).
heeshl|eekh/-eekhah/-akhtee השליך *v* threw away; (*pres* **mashleekh**; *fut* **yashleekh**).
heeshl|eem/-eemah/-amtee השלים *v* **1.** made peace with; **2.** came to terms with; **3.** completed; (*pres* **mashleem**; *fut* **yashleem**).
heeshl|eesh/-eeshah/-ashtee השליש *v* **1.** tripled; **2.** entrusted; deposited for safekeeping; (*pres* **mashleesh**; *fut* **yashleesh**).
heeshl|eet/-eetah/-atetee השליט *v* enforced; (*pres* **mashleet**; *fut* **yashleet**).
heeshm|ee'a'/-ee'ah/-a'tee השמיע *v* voiced; made heard; (*pres* **mashmee'a'**; *fut* **yashmee'a'**).
heeshm|eed/-eedah/-adetee השמיד *v* wiped out; annihilated; (*pres* **mashmeed**; *fut* **yashmeed**).
heeshmeen/-eenah/-antee השמין *v* put on weight; grew fat; (*pres* **mashmeen**; *fut* **yashmeen**).
heeshm|eet/-eetah/-atetee השמיט *v* omitted (*pres* **mashmeet**; *fut* **yashmeet**).
heeshm|eets/-eetsah/-atstee השמיץ *v* defamed; libelled; (*pres* **mashmeets**; *fut* **yashmeets**).
eeshon/-eem אישון *nm* pupil of the eye; (*pl+of:* **-ey**).
(be) eeshon layeel (or **laylah**) באישון ליל *adv* in the darkness of the night.
eeshoom/-eem אישום *nm* indictment; (*pl+of:* **-ey**).
(geelyon/-ot) eeshoom גליון אישום *nm* charge list.
(ketav/keetvey) eeshoom כתב־אישום *nm* bill of indictment.

eeshoor/-eem אישור *nm* confirmation; authorisation; (*pl+of:* **-ey**).
eeshoor/-eem refoo'ee/-yeem אישור רפואי *nm* medical certificate.
heeshp|ee'a'/-ee'ah/-a'tee השפיע *v* influenced; (*pres* **mashpee'a'**; *fut* **yashpee'a'**).
heeshp|eel/-eelah/-altee השפיל *v* humiliated; (*pres* **mashpeel**; *fut* **yashpeel**).
eeshpez/-ezah/-aztee אשפז *v* hospitalized; (*pres* **me'ashpez**; *fut* **ye'ashpez**).
eeshpooz/-eem אשפוז *nm* hospitalization; (*pl+of:* **-ey**).
heeshpr|eets/-eetsah/-atstee השפריץ *[slang] v* sprinkled; sprayed; (*pres* **mashpreets**; *fut* **yashpreets**).
eeshroor/-eem אשרור *v* ratification; (*pl+of:* **-ey**).
heeshta|'ah/-'atah/-'etee השתאה *v* wondered; (*pres* **meeshta'eh**; *fut* **yeeshta'eh**).
heeshta'am|em/-emah/-amtee השתעמם *v* was bored; (*pres* **meeshta'amem**; *fut* **yeeshta'amem**).
heeshta'ash|a'/-'ah/-a'tee (*or:* **heeshta'ashe'a'** *etc*) השתעשע *v* played (with); amused oneself; was amused; (*pres* **meeshta'ashe'a'**; *fut* **yeeshta'asha'** or **yeeshta'ashe'a'**).
heeshta'b|ed/-dah/-adetee השתעבד *v* became enslaved; enslaved oneself; (*pres* **meeshta'bed**; *fut* **yeeshta'bed**).
heeshta'bdoo|t/-yot השתעבדות *nf* enslavement.
heeshtab|e'akh/-khah/-akhtee השתבח *v* prided oneself; boasted; (*pres* **meeshtabe'akh**; *fut* **yeeshtabakh**).
heeshtab|esh/-shah/-ashtee השתבש *v* went wrong; (*pres* **meeshtabesh**; *fut* **yeeshtabesh**).
heeshtab|ets/-tsah/-atstee השתבץ *v* **1.** was integrated; **2.** was dovetailed; (*pres* **meeshtabets**; *fut* **yeeshtabets**).
heeshtad|ekh/-khah/-akhtee השתדך *v* became engaged to marry as a result of matchmaking; (*pres* **meeshtadekh**; *fut* **yeeshtadekh**).
heeshtad|el/-lah/-altee השתדל *v* tried hard; endeavored; (*pres* **meeshtadel**; *fut* **yeeshtadel**).
heeshta|'el/-'alah/-'altee השתעל *v* coughed; (*pres* **meeshta'el**; *fut* **yeeshta'el**).
heeshtafsh|ef/-efah/-aftee השתפשף *v* **1.** rubbed oneself; rubbed elbows; **2.** *[slang]* was put through the mill; (*pres* **meeshtafshef**; *fut* **yeeshtafshef**).
heeshtag|a'/-'ah/-a'tee (*or:* **heeshtag|e'a'** *etc*) השתגע *v* **1.** went mad; **2.** *[slang]* wanted madly; was mad about; (*pres* **meeshtage'a'**; *fut* **yeeshtage'a'**).
heeshta|hah/-hatah/-heetee השתהה *v* was delayed; tarried; (*pres* **meeshtaheh**; *fut* **yeeshtaheh**).
heeshtak|a'/-'ah/-a'tee (*or:* **heeshtak|e'a'**) השתקע *v* settled for good; (*pres* **meeshtake'a**; *fut* **yeeshtaka'** or **yeeshtake'a'**).
heeshtak|ef/-fah/-aftee השתקף *v* was reflected; (*pres* **meeshtakef**; *fut* **yeeshtakef**).
heeshtak|en/-nah/-antee השתכן *v* **1.** settled; **2.** obtained housing; (*pres* **meeshtaken**; *fut* **yeeshtaken**).
heeshtak|er/-rah/-artee השתכר *v* got drunk; (*pres* **meeshtaker**; *fut* **yeeshtaker**).
heeshtakfoo|t/-yot השתקפות *nf* reflection.
heeshtakh|avah/-vetah/-avetee השתחווה *v* bowed; (*pres* **meeshtakhaveh**; *fut* **yeeshtakhaveh**).
heeshtakhl|el/-elah/-altee השתכלל *v* was perfected; was improved; (*pres* **meeshtakhlel**; *fut* **yeeshtakhlel**).
heeshtakhn|a'/-e'ah/-a'tee (*or:* **heeshtakhn|e'a'** *etc*) השתכנע was convinced; (*pres* **meeshtakhne'a'**; *fut* **yeeshtakhna'** or **yeeshtakhne'a'**).
heeshtakh'sh|ekh/-ekhah/-akhtee השתכשך *v* paddled; babbled; (*pres* **meeshtakh'shekh**; *fut* **yeeshtakh'shekh**).
heeshtakhv|ah (*npr* **heeshtakhavah**)**/-etah/-etee** השתחווה *v* bowed; (*pres* **meeshtakhveh**; *fut* **yeeshtakhveh**).
heshtakhr|er/-erah/-artee השתחרר *v* **1.** freed oneself; **2.** was released; was liberated; (*pres* **meeshtakhrer**; *fut* **yeeshtakhrer**).
heeshtal|em/-mah/-amtee השתלם *v* **1.** specialized; took advanced courses; **2.** paid off; was worthwhile; (*pres* **meeshtalem**; *fut* **yeeshtalem**).
heeshtal|ev/-vah/-avtee השתלב *v* integrated; intertwined; (*pres* **meeshtalev**; *fut* **yeeshtalev**).
heeshtalmoo|t/-yot השתלמות *nf* specialization course; advanced study.
◇ **(keren/karnot) heeshtalmoot** see ◇ **keren/karnot heeshtalmoot**.
heeshtalsh|el/-elah/-altee השתלשל *v* **1.** evolved; developed; **2.** hung down; (*pres* **meeshtalshel**; *fut* **yeeshtalshel**).
heeshtal|et/-tah/-atetee השתלט *v* mastered; took control of; (*pres* **meeshtalet**; *fut* **yeeshtalet**).
heeshtalsheloo|t/-yot השתלשלות *nf* development.
heeshtalsheloot ha-'eenyaneem השתלשלות העניינים *nf* (the) chain of developments.
heeshtaltoo|t/-yot השתלטות *v* taking control; seizing power; domination.
heeshtalvoo|t/-yot השתלבות *v* integration; joining in; fitting in.
heeshtam|er/-rah/-artee השתמר *v* was preserved; (*pres* **meeshtamer**; *fut* **yeeshtamer**).
heeshtam|esh/-shah/-ashtee השתמש *v* used; made use; (*pres* **meeshtamesh**; *fut* **yeeshtamesh**).
heeshtamesh (*etc*) **le-ra'ah** השתמש לרעה *v* misused.
heshtamesh (*etc*) **she-lo ka-deen** השתמש שלא כדין *v* abused.
heeshtam|et/-tah/-atetee השתמט *v* dodged; evaded; shirked; (*pres* **meeshtamet**; *fut* **yeeshtamet**).

heeshtamtoo|t/-yot השתמטות *v* evasion; dodging; shirking.

heeshtan|ah/-tah/-etee השתנה *v* changed; became different; (*pres* **meeshtaneh**; *fut* **yeeshtanah**).

heshtanoo|t/-yot השתנות *v* change; changing; alteration.

heeshtap|ekh/-khah/-akhtee השתפך *v* overflowed; spilled out; poured out effusively; (*pres* **meeshtapekh**; *fut* **yeeshtapekh**).

heeshtap|er/-rah/-artee השתפר *v* improved; bettered; (*pres* **meeshtaper**; *fut* **yeeshtaper**).

heeshtapkhoo|t/-yot השתפכות *v* outpouring; effusion.

heeshtapkhoot ha-nefesh השתפכות הנפש *nf* poetic effusions; effusive outpouring.

heeshtaproo|t/-yot השתפרות *nf* improvement.

heeshtarb|ev/-evah/-avtee השתרבב *v* was misplaced; got in somehow; (*pres* **meeshtarbev**; *fut* **yeeshtarbev**).

heeshtat|ah/-etah/-etee השתטה *v* played the fool; raved and ranted; (*pres* **meeshtateh**; *fut* **yeeshtateh**).

heeshtat|e'akh/-khah/-akhtee השתטח *v* lay down flat; prostrated oneself; (*pres* **meeshtate'akh**; *fut* **yeeshtate'akh**).

heeshtat|ef/-fah/-aftee השתתף *v* took part; participated; (*pres* **meeshtatef**; *fut* **yeeshtatef**).

heeshtat|ek/-kah/-aktee השתתק *v* **1.** fell silent; **2.** *[colloq.]* became paralyzed.

heeshtatfoo|t/-yot השתתפות *nf* participation; share.

heeshtatfoo|t/-yot be-tsa'ar השתתפות בצער *nf* condolence.

heeshtatoo|t/-yot השתטות *nf* folly; foolishness.

heeshtav|ah/-tah/-etee השתווה *v* reached equality; reached agreement; equaled; (*pres* **meeshtaveh**; *fut* **yeeshtaveh**).

heeshtav|ets/-tsah/-atstee (*npr* **heeshtab|ets** *etc*) השתבץ *v* became apoplectic with rage; (*pres* **meeshtavets**; *fut* **yeeshtavets**).

heeshtavoo|t/-yot השתוות *nf* becoming equal; measuring up to.

heeshtay|ekh/-khah/-akhtee השתייך *v* belonged to; was associated with; (*pres* **meeshtayekh**; *fut* **yeeshtayekh**).

heeshtaykhoo|t/-yot השתייכות *nf* affiliation; belonging to.

heeshtaz|ef/-fah/-aftee השתזף *v* sunbathed; tanned oneself; (*pres* **meeshtazef**; *fut* **yeeshtazef**).

heeshtazfoo|t/-yot השתזפות *v* suntanning; sunbathing.

eeshtee אשתי *nf* my wife.

heesht|eek/-eekah/-aktee השתיק *v* silenced; (*pres* **mashteek**; *fut* **yashteek**).

heesht|eel/-eelah/-altee השתיל *v* planted; transplanted; implanted (*pres* **mashteel**; *fut* **yashteel**).

heesht|een/-eenah/-antee השתין *v* urinated; (*pres* **mashteen**; *fut* **yashteen**).

heesht|eet/-eetah/-atetee השתית *v* based; founded; (*pres* **mashteet**; *fut* **yashteet**).

eesht|ekha/-o אשתך *nf* your/his wife.

eeshto shel אשתו של *nf* the wife of.

heeshtok|ek/-ekah/-aktee השתוקק *v* craved (for); yearned; (*pres* **meeshtokek**; *fut* **yeeshtokek**).

heeshtokekoo|t/-yot השתוקקות *nf* yearning; craving for.

heeshtol|el/-elah/-altee השתולל *v* raged; acted unrestrained; (*pres* **meeshtolel**; *fut* **yeeshtolel**).

heeshtoleloo|t/yot השתוללות *nf* raging; running wild.

heeshtom|em/-emah/-amtee השתומם *v* wondered; (*pres* **meeshtomem**; *fut* **yeeshtomem**).

heeshtomemoo|t/yot השתוממות *nf* bewilderment.

heeshtovev-/-evah/-avtee השתובב *v* was boisterous, naughty; (*pres* **meeshtovev**; *fut* **yeeshtovev**).

heeshtovevoo|t/yot השתובבות *nf* boisterousness; mischief.

heeshv|ah/-etah/-etee השווה *v* **1.** compared; **2.** equalized; levelled; (*pres* **mashveh**; *fut* **yashveh**).

'eesk|ah/-a'ot עסקה *nf* transaction; deal (*+of:* **-at/-ot**).

'eeskat/-ot khaveelah עסקת חבילה *nf* package-deal.

◇ **'eeskat/'eskot kombeenatsyah** עיסקת קומבינציה real-estate transaction whereby the owner (or long lease holder) of a well located building lot cedes his property right to an enterprising building contractor in exchange for future property rights to a sizable percentage of apartments in the condo apartment-building the contractor undertakes to erect.

'eeskee/-t (*npr* **'eskee**) עסקי *adj* pragmatic; businesslike.

heesk|eel/-eelah/-altee השכיל *v* succeeded; managed; (*pres* **maskeel**; *fut* **yaskeel**).

heesk|eem/-eemah/-amtee הסכים *v* agreed; (*pres* **maskeem**; *fut* **yaskeem**).

heesk|eer/-eerah/-artee השכיר *v* leased; let; (*pres* **maskeer**; *fut* **yaskeer**).

heesm|eek/-eekah/-aktee הסמיק *v* blushed; (*pres* **masmeek**; *fut* **yasmeek**).

heesm|eekh/-eekhah/-akhtee הסמיך *v* **1.** authorized; **2.** bestowed a degree; **3.** drew close; (*pres* **masmeekh**; *fut* **yasmeekh**).

heesn|ee/-ee'ah/-etee השניא *v* made hateful; made one hate; (*pres* **masnee**; *fut* **yasnee**).

eesoof/-eem איסוף *nm* collection; gathering; (*pl+of:* **-ey**).

'eesook/-eem עיסוק *nm* occupation; job; (*+of:* **-ey**).

(reepooy be-) 'eesook ריפוי בעיסוק *nm* occupational therapy.

eesoor/-eem איסור *nm* ban; prohibition; (*+of:* **-ey**).
heesoos/-eem היסוס *nm* hesitation; misgiving; (*+of:* **-ey**).
'eesoo|y/-yeem עיסוי *nm* massage; (*pl+of:* **-yey**).
heesp|eed/-eedah/-adetee הספיד *v* eulogized; (*pres* **maspeed;** *fut* **yaspeed**).
heesp|eek/-eekah/-aktee הספיק *v* managed to; sufficed; (*pres* **maspeek;** *fut* **yaspeek**).
heesr|ee'akh/-eekhah/-akhtee הסריח *v* stank; (*pres* **masree'akh;** *fut* **yasree'akh**).
heesr|eet/-eetah/-atetee הסריט *v* filmed; took movies; (*pres* **masreet;** *fut* **yasrseet**).
◇ **eesroo-khag** אסרו חג *nm* the day after Passover, Shavuot or Succot.
heesta'afoo|t/-yot הסתעפות *nf* ramification.
heesta'aroo|t/-yot הסתערות *nf* assault; storming.
heestab|ekh/-khah/-akhtee הסתבך *v* got mixed up; got involved; (*pres* **meestabekh;** *fut* **yeestabekh**).
heestab|er/-rah/-artee הסתבר *v* it became evident; (*pres* **meestaber;** *fut* **yeestaber**).
heestabkhoo|t/-yot הסתבכות *nf* involvement; entanglement.
heestabroot/-yot הסתברות *nf* probability.
heestad|er/-rah/-artee הסתדר *v* **1.** settled in; **2.** was arranged; **3.** managed; (*pres* **meestader;** *fut* **yeestader**).
heestadroo|t/-yot הסתדרות *nf* organization.
◇ **eestadroot (or heestadroot) ha-'ovdeem ha-klaleet** see ◇ **heestadroot ha-'ovdeem.**
◇ **(ha)"eestadroot"** or **(ha)"Heestadroot"** ההסתדרות *nf* the "Histadrut", colloq. *abbr.* of the full name of the General Federation of Labor see ◇ **heestadroot ha-'ovdeem.**
heesta|'er/-'arah/-'artee הסתער *v* assailed; charged; stormed; (*pres* **meesta'er;** *fut* **yeesta'er**).
heestag|el/-lah/-altee הסתגל *v* adjusted oneself; (*pres* **meestagel;** *fut* **yeestagel**).
heestag|er/-rah/-artee הסתגר *v* closeted oneself; shut oneself off; (*pres* **meestager;** *fut* **yeestager**).
heestagl|oot/-yot הסתגלות *nf* adaptation.
heestagr|oot/-yot הסתגרות *nf* seclusion.
heestak|el/-lah/-altee הסתכל *v* looked into; looked at; had a look into; (*pres* **meestakel;** *fut* **yeestakel**).
heestak|em/-mah/-amtee הסתכם *v* amounted to; summed up in; (*pres* **meestakem;** *fut* **yeestakem**).
heestak|en/-nah/-antee הסתכן *v* risked; (*pres* **meestaken;** *fut* **yeestaken**).
heestak|er/-rah/-artee השתכר *v* earned (wage); (*pres* **meestaker;** *fut* **yeestaker**).
heestakhr|er/-erah/-artee הסתחרר *v* felt dizzy; (*pres* **meestakhrer;** *fut* **yeestakhrer**).
heestakhreroo|t/-yot הסתחררות *nf* dizziness.
heestakhs|ekh/-ekhah/-akhtee הסתכסך *v* quarrelled; (*pres* **meestakhsekh;** *fut* **yeestakhsekh**).
heestakloo|t/-yot הסתכלות *nf* observation; contemplation.
(be) heestakloot בהסתכלות *adv* under observation.
(khoosh) heestakloot חוש הסתכלות *nm* sense of observation; gift for observation.
heestal|ek/-kah/-aktee הסתלק *v* got out; departed; (*pres* **meestalek;** *fut* **yeestalek**).
heestal|ek/-kee/-koo mee-kan! הסתלק מכאן! *v imp m/f sing/pl* get out of here!
heestalek (*etc*) **mee-po!** הסתלק מפה! *v imp m/f sing/pl* get out of here!
heestalkoo|t/-yot הסתלקות *nf* departure; withdrawal; passing away.
heestam|ekh/-khah/-akhtee הסתמך *v* **1.** relied; **2.** referred (*pres* **meestamekh;** *fut* **yeestamekh**).
heestam|en/-nah/-antee הסתמן *v* began to show; (*pres* **meestamen;** *fut* **yeestamen**).
heestamkhoo|t/-yot הסתמכות *nf* reliance; reference.
heestamnoo|t/-yot הסתמנות *nf* marking; sign of appearance.
heestan|en/-enah/-antee הסתנן *v* infiltrated; got through; (*pres* **meestanen;** *fut* **yeestanen**).
heestanenoo|t/-yot הסתננות *nf* **1.** infiltration; **2.** *[colloq.]* infiltration by terrorists.
heestap|ek/-kah/-aktee הסתפק *v* contained oneself with; (*pres* **meestapek;** *fut* **yeestapek**).
heestap|er/-rah/-artee הסתפר *v* took a haircut; (*pres* **meestaper;** *fut* **yeestaper**).
heestapkoot be-moo'at הסתפקות במועט *nf* frugality.
heestar|a'/-'ah/-'atee (*or:* **heestar|e'a'** *etc*) השתרע *v* stretched out; tended; spread out; (*pres* **meestare'a';** *fut* **yeestare'a'**).
heestar|ek/-kah/-aktee הסתרק *v* combed oneself (hair); (*pres* **meestarek;** *fut* **yeestarek**).
heestar|ekh/-khah/-akhtee השתרך *v* dragged along; (*pres* **meestarekh;** *fut* **yeestarekh**).
heestar|er/-erah/-artee השתרר *v* prevailed; (*pres* **meestarer;** *fut* **yeestarer**).
heestat|er/-rah/-artee הסתתר *v* hid; (*pres* **meestater;** *fut* **yeestater**).
hestatroo|t/-yot הסתתרות *nf* hiding.
heestatmoo|t/-yot הסתתמות *nf* closing; blocking up.
heestaydoo|t/-yot הסתיידות *nf* calcification.
heestaydoot ha-'orkeem הסתיידות העורקים *nf* arteriosclerosis.
heestay|e'a/-'ah/-a'tee הסתייע *v* got assistance; (*pres* **meestaye'a;** *fut* **yeestaye'a'**).
heestay|eg/-gah/-agtee הסתייג *v* dissociated oneself from; (*pres* **meestayeg;** *fut* **yeestayeg**).
heestay|em/-mah/-amtee הסתיים *v* ended; (*pres* **meestayem;** *fut* **yeestayem**).
heestaygoo|t/-yot הסתייגות *nf* reservation; demur.

heestaymoo|t/-yot הסתיימות *nf* ending; finalizing.

heest|eer/-eerah/-artee הסתיר *v* hid; concealed; (*pres* **masteer**; *fut* **yasteer**).

eestenees אסטניס *nm* fastidious person.

heester|yah/-yot היסטריה *nf* hysteria; (*+of:* **-yat**).

heestod|ed/-edah/-adetee הסתודד *v* conferred secretly; (*pres* **meestoded**; *fut* **yeestoded**).

heestoree/-t היסטורי *adj* historic.

(kedam) heestoree/-t קדם־היסטורי *adj* prehistoric.

heestoreeyah היסטוריה *nf* history.

heestov|ev/-evah/-avtee הסתובב *v* turned around; mingled; (*pres* **meestovev**; *fut* **yeestovev**).

(le) heet! !להת' *colloq. abbr.* of **le-heetra'ot!** להתראות so long! good bye! see you!

eetah איתה with her.

heet|ah/-etah/-etee הטה *v* deflected; diverted; (*pres* **mateh**; *fut* **yateh**).

heetah (*etc*) **ozen** הטה אוזן *v* lent an ear; heeded.

heetah (*etc*) **rosh** הטה ראש *v* nodded; shook head.

heetah (*etc*) **shekhem** הטה שכם *v* shouldered.

heet|'ah/-'atah/-'etee הטעה *v* led astray; misled; (*pres* **mat'eh**; *fut* **yat'eh**).

heet'ab|ah/-tah/-etee התעבה *v* thickened; (*pres* **meet'abeh**; *fut* **yeet'abeh**).

heet'abdoo|t/-yot התאבדות *nf* suicide.

heet'ab|ed/-dah/-adetee התאבד *v* committed suicide; (*pres* **meet'abed**; *fut* **yeet'abed**).

heet'ab|el/-lah/-altee התאבל *v* mourned; (*pres* **meet'abel**; *fut* **yeet'abel**).

heet'ab|en/-nah/-antee התאבן *v* was paralyzed; (*pres* **meet'aben**; *fut* **yeet'aben**).

heet'abnoot/-yot התאבנות *nf* paralysis; petrification.

heet'aboo|t/-yot התעבות *nf* condensation.

heet'aboot 'ananeem התעבות עננים *nf* thickening of clouds.

heet'ab|rah/-artee התעברה *v f* became pregnant; (*pres* **meet'aberet**; *fut* **teeta'aber**).

heet'abroo|t/-yot התעברות *nf* becoming pregnant; conception.

heet'ad|ah/-etah התאדה *v* evaporated; (*pres* **meet'adeh**; *fut* **yeet'adeh**).

heet'ad|em/-mah/-amtee התאדם *v* flushed; reddened; (*pres* **meet'adem**; *fut* **yeet'adem**).

heet'ad|en/-nah/-antee התעדן *v* became refined; indulged in luxury; (*pres* **meet'aden**; *fut* **yeet'aden**).

hee'adk|en/-enah/-antee התעדכן *v* brought (oneself) up to date; (*pres* **meet'adken**; *fut* **yee'adken**).

heet'adkenoo|t/-yot התעדכנות *nf* bringing (oneself) up to date; updating (oneself).

heet'admoo|t/-yot התאדמות *nf* reddening; flushing.

heet'adnoo|t/-yot התעדנות *nf* refinement; enjoying.

heet'adoo|t/-yot התאדות *nf* evaporation.

heet'afsh|er/-erah/-artee התאפשר *v* became possible; (*pres* **meet'afsher**; *fut* **yeet'afsher**).

heet'afsheroo|t/-yot התאפשרות *nf* emergence of a possibility.

heet'agdoo|t/-yot התאגדות *nf* union; association.

heet'ag|ed/-dah/-adnoo התאגד *v* united; amalgamated; (*pres* **meet'aged**; *fut* **yeet'aged**).

heet'ag|el/-lah/-altee התעגל *v* became round; (*pres* **meet'agel**; *fut* **yeet'agel**).

heet'agloo|t/-yot התעגלות *nf* becoming round; rounding.

heet'agr|ef/-efah/-aftee התאגרף *v* boxed; (*pres* **meet'agref**; *fut* **yeet'agref**).

heet'agrefoo|t/-yot התאגרפות *nf* boxing.

heet'ahavoo|t/-yot התאהבות *nf* falling in love.

heet'a|hev/-havah/-havtee התאהב *v* fell in love; (*pres* **meet'ahev**; *fut* **yeet'ahev**).

heet'ak|em/-mah/-amtee התעקם *v* was bent; became crooked; (*pres* **meet'akem**; *fut* **yeet'akem**).

heet'ak|esh/-shah/-ashtee התעקש *v* insisted; (*pres* **meet'akesh**; *fut* **yeet'akesh**).

heet'ak|ev/-vah/-avtee התעכב *v* was held up; was delayed; (*pres* **meet'akev**; *fut* **yeet'akev**).

eetakh איתך *conj & pron* with you (addressing *sing* females).

heetakhdoo|t/-yot התאחדות *nf* union; federation.

heet'akh|ed/-dah/-adetee התאחד *v* joined with; combined; united; (*pst* **meet'akhed**; *fut* **yeet'akhed**).

heet'akh|er/-rah/-artee התאחר *v* was late; was tardy; (*pres* **meet'akher**; *fut* **yeet'akher**).

heet'akhroo|t/-yot התאחרות *nf* delay; tardiness.

heetakhs|en/-enah/-antee התאכסן *v* stayed; lodged (as guest); (*pres* **meetakhsen**; *fut* **yeetakhsen**).

heet'akhsenoo|t/-yot התאכסנות *nf* staying; hotel accommodation.

heet'akhz|er/-erah/-artee התאכזר *v* acted/behaved cruelly; (*pres* **meet'akhzer**; *fut* **yeet'akhzer**).

heet'akhzeroo|t/-yot התאכזרות *nf* cruel treatment.

heet'akhz|ev/-evah/-avtee התאכזב *v* was disappointed; (*pres* **meet'akhzev**; *fut* **yeet'akhzev**).

heet'akhzevoo|t/-yot התאכזבות *nf* disappointment.

heet'akl|em/-emah/-amtee התאקלם *v* became acclimated; (*pres* **meet'aklem**; *fut* **yeet'aklem**).

heet'aklemoo|t/-yot התאקלמות *nf* **1.** acclimatization; **2.** *[colloq.]* getting accustomed to a new place.

heetakloo|t/-yot היתקלות *nf* encounter.

heet'akmoo|t/-yot התעקמות *nf* bending; making crooked.

heet'akshoo|t/-yot התעקשות *nf* obstinacy; stubbornness.

heet'al|ah/-tah/-etee התעלה *v* has risen; exalted; (*pres* **meet'aleh;** *fut* **yeet'aleh).**

heet'al|ef/-fah/-aftee התעלף *v* fainted; (*pres* **meet'alef;** *fut* **yeet'alef).**

heet'al|el/-elah/-altee התעלל *v* abused; maltreated; (*pres* **meet'alel;** *fut* **yeet'alel).**

heet'aleloo|t/-yot התעללות *v* outrage; abuse; maltreatment.

heet'al|em/-mah/-amtee התעלם *v* ignored; disregarded; (*pres* **met'alem;** *fut* **yeet'alem).**

het'al|es/-sah/-astee התעלס *v* made love; (*pres* **meet'ales;** *fut* **yeet'ales).**

heet'alfoo|t/-yot התעלפות *nf* fainting.

heet'alm|en/-enah/-antee התאלמן *v* became widowed; (*pres* **meet'almen;** *fut* **yeet'almen).**

heet'almenoo|t/-yot התאלמנות *v* becoming a widow; widowhood.

heet'almoo|t/-yot התעלמות *nf* disregard; ignoring.

heet'alsoo|t/-yot התעלסות *nf* love-making.

eetam איתם *conj & pers pron 3rd pers m pl nm* with them.

heet'am|ek/-kah/-aktee התעמק *v* delved deeply; (*pres* **meet'amek;** *fut* **yeet'amek).**

heet'am|el/-lah/-altee התעמל *v* exercised (gymnastics); worked up; (*pres* **meet'amel;** *fut* **yeet'amel).**

heetam|em/-emah/-amtee היתמם *v* played the innocent; (*pres* **meetamem;** *fut* **yeetamam).**

heet'am|en/-nah/-antee התאמן *v* trained; practised; (*pres* **meet'amen;** *fut* **yeet'amen).**

heet'am|et/-tah/-atetee התאמת *v* came true; was proven true; (*pres* **meet'amet;** *fut* **yeet'amet).**

heet'ame|ts/-tsah/-atstee התאמץ *v* strove; endeavored; (*pres* **meet'amets;** *fut* **yeet'amets).**

heet'amkoo|t/-yot התעמקות *nf* penetrating study; penetration.

heet'amloo|t/-yot התעמלות *nf* gymnastics; physical training; work-out.

heetamt|em/-emah/-amtee היטמטם *nf* became dumb; (*pres* **meetamtem;** *fut* **yeetamtem).**

heet'amtoo|t/-yot התאמתות *nf* verification; turning out to be true.

heet'amtsoo|t/-yot התאמצות *nf* effort; endeavor.

eetan איתן *conj & pers pron f* with them (of females).

heet'an|ah/-tah/-etee התאנה *v* persecuted; picked quarrel with; (*pres* **meet'aneh;** *fut* **yeet'aneh).**

heet'an|ah/-tah/-etee התענה *v* was tormented; tormented oneself; (*pres* **meet'aneh;** *fut* **yeet'aneh).**

heet'an|eg/-gah/-agtee התענג *v* enjoyed; derived pleasure; (*pres* **meet'aneg;** *fut* **yeet'aneg).**

eetanoo איתנו *conj & pers pron pl* with us.

heet'an|yen/-yenah/-yantee התעניין *v* took/ showed interest; (*pres* **meet'anyen;** *fut* **yeet'anyen).**

heet'anyenoo|t/-yot התעניינות *nf* interest; concern.

heet'ap|ek/-kah/-aktee התאפק *v* restrained oneself; (*pres* **meet'apek;** *fut* **yeet'apek).**

heet'ap|er/-rah/-artee התאפר *v* put on make-up; (*pres* **meet'aper;** *fut* **yeet'aper).**

heet'apkoot התאפקות *nf* restraint.

heet'aproot התאפרות *nf* putting on make-up.

heet'arb|ev/-evah/-avtee התערבב *v* got mixed up; (*pres* **meet'arbev;** *fut* **yeet'arbev).**

heet'ar|e'akh/-khah/-akhtee התארח *v* stayed as guest; (*pres* **meet'are'akh;** *fut* **yeet'are'akh).**

heet'ar|ekh/-khah/-akhtee התארך *v* **1.** dragged out; **2.** grew longer; (*pres* **meet'arekh;** *fut* **yeet'arekh).**

heet'ar|'er/-'erah/-'artee התערער *v* began to totter; (*pres* **meet'ar'er;** *fut* **yeet'ar'er).**

heet'ar|es/-sah/-astee התארס *v* became engaged /betrothed; (*pres* **meet'ares;** *fut* **yeet'ares).**

heet'ar|ev/-vah/-avtee התערב *v* **1.** interfered; **2.** intervened; **3.** bet; wagered; (*pres* **meet'arev;** *fut* **yeet'arev).**

heet'arg|en/-enah/-antee התארגן *v* got organized; organized oneself; (*pres* **meet'argen;** *fut* **yeet'argen).**

heet'arkhoo|t/-yot התארכות *nf* lengthening; prolongation.

heet'arsoo|t/-yot התארסות *nf* betrothal; engagement.

heet'arvoo|t/-yot התערבות *nf* **1.** interference; **2.** bet; wager.

heet'ar|tel/-elah/-altee התערטל *v* disrobed. stripped; (*pres* **meet'artel;** *fut* **yeet'artel).**

heet'as|ef/-fah/-aftee התאסף *v* assembled; got together; (*pres* **meet'asef;** *fut* **yeet'asef).**

heet'as|ek/-kah/-aktee התעסק *v* **1.** dealt with; **2.** engaged in; **3.** flirted with (*pres* **meet'asek;** *fut* **yeet'asek).**

heet'asfoo|t/-yot התאספות *nf* gathering; assembly.

heet'askoo|t/-yot התעסקות *nf* occupation.

heet'asl|em/-emah/-amtee התאסלם *v* converted to Islam; became a Muslim; (*pres* **meet'aslem;** *fut* **yeet'aslem).**

heet'ash|er/-rah/-artee התעשר *v* got rich; (*pres* **meet'asher;** *fut* **yeet'asher).**

heet'ashroo|t/-yot התעשרות *nf* getting rich; enrichment.

heet'at|ed/-edah/-adetee התעתד *v* prepared oneself; (*pres* **meet'ated;** *fut* **yeet'ated).**

heet'at|ef/-fah/-aftee התעטף *v* wrapped onself; (*pres* **meet'atef;** *fut* **yeet'atef).**

heet'at|esh/-'shah/-ashtee התעטש *v* sneezed; (*pres* **meet'atesh;** *fut* **yeet'atesh).**

heet'at'shoo|t/-yot התעטשות *nf* sneeze.

heet'atsb|en/-enah/-antee התעצבן *v* became nervous; became irritated; (*pres* **meet'atsben;** *fut* **yeet'atsben).**

heet'atsbenoo|t/-yot התעצבנות *nf* becoming nervous.

heet'ats|el/-lah/-altee התעצל *v* was lazy; (*pres* **meet'atsel**; *fut* **yeet'atsel**).

heet'ats|em/-mah/-amtee התעצם *v* grew strong; (*pres* **met'atsem**; *fut* **yeet'atsem**).

heet'ats|ev/-vah/-avtee התעצב *v* became sad; was grieved; (*pres* **meet'atsev**; *fut* **yeet'atsev**).

heet'atsmoo|t/-yot התעצמות *nf* expansion.

heet'atsvoo|t/-yot התעצבות *nf* saddening.

heet'av|ah/-tah/-etee התאווה *v* desired; felt an urge; (*pres* **meet'aveh**; *fut* **yeet'aveh**).

heet'hav|ah/-tah/-etee התהווה *v* emerged; was formed; (*pres* **meet'haveh**; *fut* **yeet'haveh**).

heet'av|er/-rah/-artee התעוור *v* went blind; (*pres* **meet'aver**; *fut* **yeet'aver**).

heet'avoo|t/-yot התאוות *nf* craving; urge.

heet'havoo|t/-yot התהוות *nf* formation; emergence.

heet'avr|er/-erah/-artee התאוורר *v* **1.** aired; **2.** *[colloq.]* took a walk; (*pres* **meet'avrer**; *fut* **yeet'avrer**).

heet'a|yef/-yfah/-yaftee התעייף *v* became tired; (*pres* **meet'ayef**; *fut* **yeet'ayef**).

heet'ayfoo|t/-yot התעייפות *nf* tiring; fatigue.

heet'ayfoot ha-khomer התעייפות החומר *nf* material fatigue.

heet'az|en/-nah/-antee התאזן *v* balanced; became balanced; (*pres* **meet'azen**; *fut* **yeet'azen**).

heet'az|er/-rah/-artee התאזר *v* gathered strength; (*pres* **meet'azer**; *fut* **yeet'azer**).

heet'azer (*etc*) **be-savlanoot** התאזר בסבלנות *v* gathered patience.

heet'azer (*etc*) **'oz** התאזר עוז *v* gathered courage.

heet'azr|e'akh/-ekhah/-akhtee התאזרח *v* became a citizen; naturalized; (*pres* **meet'azre'akh**; *fut* **yeet'azre'akh**).

heet'azrekhoot התאזרחות *nf* naturalization.

heetbad|ah/-etah/-etee התבדה *v* was proven false; turned out to be a lie; (*pres* **meetbadeh**; *fut* **yeetbadeh**).

heetbad|akh/-khah/-akhtee (*or:* **heetbad|e'akh** *etc*) התבדח *v* joked; jested (*pres* **meetbade'akh**; *fut* **yeetbade'akh**).

heetbad|el/-lah/-altee התבדל **1.** was secluded; **2.** segregated; kept apart; (*pres* **meetbadel**; *fut* **yeetbadel**).

heetbad|er/-rah/-artee התבדר *v* amused oneself; had fun; (*pres* **metbader**; *fut* **yeetbader**).

heetbad'khoo|t/-yot התבדחות *nf* jesting; joking; making fun.

heetbadloo|t/-yot התבדלות *nf* seclusion; segregation.

heetbadoo|t/-yot התבדות *nf* refutation.

heetbag|er/-rah/-artee התבגר *v* matured; (*pres* **meetbager**; *fut* **yeetbager**).

heetbagroot התבגרות *nf* maturation; ripening.

(geel ha) heetbagroot גיל ההתבגרות *nm* **1.** maturation age; **2.** majority.

(tekoofat ha) heetbagrot תקופת ההתבגרות *nm* maturation period.

heetbaharoo|t/-yot התבהרות *nf* brightening up; clarification.

heetba|her/-harah התבהר *v* brightened; cleared up; (*pres* **meetbaher**; *fut* **yeetbaher**).

heetbak|e'a/-'ah/-a'tee התבקע *v* burst; split open; (*pres* **meetbake'a**; *fut* **yeetbake'a**).

heetbalb|el/-elah/-altee התבלבל *v* became confused; (*pres* **meetbalbel**; *fut* **yeetbalbel**).

heetbal|et/-tah/-atetee התבלט *v* stood out; (*pres* **meetbalet**; *fut* **yeetbalet**).

heetbaloo|t/-yot התבלות *nf* wear; wear and tear.

heetbaltoo|t/-yot התבלטות *nf* prominence; conspicuousness.

heetbas|em/-mah/-amtee התבשם *v* **1.** put on scent; **2.** became tipsy; (**meetbasem**; *fut* **yeetbasem**).

heetbas|er/-rah/-artee התבשר *v* was told the (good) news; (*pres* **meetbaser**; *fut* **yeetbaser**).

heetbas|es/-esah/-astee התבסס *v* **1.** based oneself; was based on; **2.** *[colloq.]* became well established; became well to do; (*pres* **meetbases**; *fut* **yeetbases**).

heetbasesoo|t/-yot התבססות *nf* basing oneself on; consolidation.

heetbash|el/-lah/-altee התבשל *v* was cooked; cooked up; (*pres* **meetbashel**; *fut* **yeetbashel**).

heetbashloo|t/-yot התבשלות *nf* cooking; ripening.

heetbasmoo|t/-yot התבשמות *nf* putting on scent; getting tipsy.

heetbasroo|t/-yot התבשרות *nf* learning, getting the (good) news.

heetbat|e/-'ah/-etee התבטא *v* expressed oneself; expressed the opinion; (*pres* **meetbate**; *fut* **yeetbate**).

heetbatel/-lah/-altee התבטל *v* **1.** was cancelled; **2.** idled away; **3.** belittled oneself; (*pres* **meetbatel**; *fut* **yeetbatel**).

heetbatloo|t/-yot התבטלות *nf* **1.** self-disparagement; **2.** loafing.

heetbat'oo|t/-yot התבטאות *nf* expression; self-expression.

heetbats|e'a'/-'ah התבצע *v* was carried out; was executed; (*pres* **meetbatse'a'**; *fut* **yeetbatse'a'**).

heetbats|er/-rah/-artee התבצר *v* barricaded oneself; fortified oneself; (*pres* **meetbatser**; *fut* **yeetbatser**).

heetbatsroo|t/-yot התבצרות *nf* fortification; fortifying oneself.

heetba|yesh/-yshah/-yashtee התבייש *v* felt ashamed; (*pres* **meetbayesh**; *fut* **yeetbayesh**).

heetbaz|ah/-etah/-etee התבזה *v* degraded oneself; demeaned oneself; (*pres* **meetbazeh**; *fut* **yeetbazeh**).

hetbazb|ez/-ezah/-aztee התבזבז *v* was wasted, squandered; (*pres* **meetbazbez**; *fut* **yeetbazbez**).

heetbazbezoo|t/-yot התבזבזות *nf* waste; wasting.

heetbazoo|t/-yot התבזות *nf* humiliation; self-abuse.

heetb|ee'a'/-ee'ah/-a'tee הטביע *v* sank (*pres* **matbee'a'**; *fut* **yatbee'a**).

heetbee'a' (*etc*) **khotam** הטביע חותם *v* left one's mark.

heetb|eel/-eelah/-altee הטביל *v* **1.** immersed; **2.** baptized; (*pres* **matbeel**; *fut* **yatbeel**).

heetbod|ed/-edah/-adetee התבודד *v* secluded oneself; sought solitude; (*pres* **meetboded**; *fut* **yeetboded**).

heetbodedoo|t/-yot התבודדות *nf* solitude; seclusion; segregation.

heetbol|el/-elah/-altee התבולל *v* became assimilated; (*pres* **meetbolel**; *fut* **yeetbolel**).

heetboleloo|t/-yot התבוללות *nf* assimilation.

heetbon|en/-enah/-antee התבונן *v* stared; observed; (*pres* **meetbonen**; *fut* **yeetbonen**).

heetbonenoo|t/-yot התבוננות *nf* contemplation; observation.

heetbos|es/-esah/-astee התבוסס *v* rolled in; (*pres* **meetboses**; *fut* **yeetboses**).

heetboses (*etc*) **be-damo** התבוסס בדמו *v* rolled in his own blood; lay slain.

heet'da|yen/-ynah/-yantee התדיין *v* sued; conducted litigations; (*pres* **meet'dayen**; *fut* **yeet'dayen**).

heet'daynoo|t/-yot התדיינות *nf* litigation; contentiousness.

eetee אתי *conj & pers pron* with me.

eetee/-t אטי *adj* slow.

heet|ee'akh/-eekhah/-akhtee (*npr* **hetee'akh**) הטיח *v* spoke insolently; (*pst* **matee'akh**; *fut* **yatee'akh**).

heet|eef/-eefah/-aftee הטיף *v* preached; moralized; (*pres* **mateef**; *fut* **yateef**).

heet|eekh/-eekhah/-akhtee התיך *v* melted; (*pres* **mateekh**; *fut* **yateekh**).

heet|eel/-eelah/-altee הטיל *v* imposed; laid; (*pres* **mateel**; *fut* **yateel**).

heeteel (*etc*) **dofee** הטיל דופי *v* questioned; maligned.

heeteel (*etc*) **mas/meeseem** הטיל מס *v* imposed tax.

◇ **'eeteem** (**"ITIM"**) עתים *nf* Israel's cooperative national news-agency owned by the Associated Israeli Press Ltd.

heet|'eem/-'eemah/-'amtee התאים *v* fitted; matched; was suited to; corresponded; (*pres* **mat'eem**; *fut* **yat'eem**).

heet|'eem/-'eemah/-'amtee הטעים *v* emphasized; pointed out; (*pres* **mat'eem**; *fut* **yat'eem**).

(le) 'eetem לעיתים *adv* at times.

(le) 'eeteem krovot לעיתים קרובות *adv* often; at close intervals.

(le) 'eeteem mezoomanot לעיתים מזומנות *adv* at regular intervals; from time to time.

(le) 'eeteem rekhokot לעיתים רחוקות *adv* seldom; rarely; at long intervals.

(le) 'eeteem tekhoofot לעיתים תכופות *adv* often; very often.

heet|'een/-'eenah/-'antee הטעין *v* loaded; charged; (*pres* **mat'een**; *fut* **yat'een**).

heet|eer/-eerah/-artee התיר *v* **1.** allowed; **2.** undid; (*pres* **mateer**; *fut* **yateer**).

heet|eesh/-eeshah/-ashtee התיש *v* wore out; weakened; (*pres* **mateesh**; *fut* **yateesh**).

heet|eez/-eezah/-aztee התיז *v* **1.** cut off; **2.** sprinkled; (*pres* **mateez**; *fut* **yateez**).

eeter/-et איטר *nmf* left-handed person.

eet|er/-rah/-artee איתר *v* located; pinpointed; (*pres* **me'ater**; *fut* **ye'ater**).

heetga|'ah/-'atah/-'etee התגאה *v* boasted; was proud of; (*pres* **meetga'eh**; *fut* **yeetga'eh**).

heetga'ag|e'a/-'ah/-a'tee התגעגע *v* yearned; longed for; (*pres* **meetga'age'a**; *fut* **yeetga'age'a**).

heetgab|er/-rah/-artee התגבר *v* overcome; increased; (*pres* **meetgaber**; *fut* **yeetgaber**).

heetgab|esh/-shah/-ashtee התגבש *v* crystalized; became consolidated; (*pres* **meetgabesh**; *fut* **yeetgabesh**).

heetgabroo|t/-yot התגברות *nf* strengthening; surmounting.

heetgabshoo|t/-yot התגבשות *nf* consolidation; crystalization.

heetgal|ah/-tah/-etee התגלה *v* revealed oneself; turned out; was exposed; (*pres* **meetgaleh**; *fut* **yeetgaleh**).

heetgal|a'/-'ah/-'oo התגלע *v* broke out; (*pres* **meetgale'a**; *fut* **yeetgala'**).

heetgal|e'akh/-khah/-akhtee התגלח *v* shaved; (*pres* **meetgale'akh**; *fut* **yeetgale'akh**).

heetgal|em/-mah/-amtee התגלם *v* embodied; (*pres* **meetgalem**; *fut* **yeetgalem**).

heetgal|etch/-tchah/-atchtee התגלץ׳ *v* *[slang]* slipped; (*pres* **meetgaletch**; *fut* **yeetgaletch**).

heetgalg|el/-elah/-altee התגלגל *v* **1.** rolled; **2.** *[colloq.]* wandered; (*pres* **meetgalgel**; *fut* **yeetgalgel**).

heetgalmoo|t/-yot התגלמות *nf* embodiment.

heetgand|er/-erah/-artee התגנדר *v* dressed up; showed off; (*pres* **meetgander**; *fut* **yeetgander**).

heetganev/-vah/-avtee התגנב *v* stalked; moved stealthily; (*pres* **meetganev**; **yeetganev**).

heetganvoo|t/-yot התגנבות *nf* entering or leaving stealthily; stalking.

heetgar|ah/-tah/-eetee התגרה *v* teased; challenged (*pres* **meetgareh**; *fut* **yeetgareh**).

heetgar|ed/-dah/-adetee התגרד *v* scratched oneself; (*pres* **meetgared**; *fut* **yeetgared**).

heetgar|esh/-shah/-ashtee התגרש *v* divorced; (*pres* **meetgaresh**; *fut* **yeetgaresh**).

heetgaroo|t/-yot התגרות *nf* provocation.

heetgarshoo|t/-yot התגרשות *nf* divorce; divorcing.

heetgash|em/-mah/-amtee התגשם *v* materialized; came true; (*pres* **meetgashem**; *fut* **yeetgashem**).

heetgashmoo|t/-yot התגשמות *nf* materialization; incarnation.

heetgay|er/-rah/-artee התגייר *v* converted to Judaism; (*pres* **meetgayer**; *fut* **yeetgayer**).

heetgay|es/-sah/-astee התגייס *v* **1.** was drafted; enlisted (into the army); **2.** *[colloq.]*: volunteered; (*pres* **metgayes**; *fut* **yeetgayes**).

heetgayroo|t/-yot התגיירות *nf* conversion to Judaism.

heetgaysoo|t/-yot התגייסות *nf* **1.** enlistment; **2.** volunteering.

heetgol|el/-elah/-altee התגולל *v* **1.** rolled about; **2.** *[slang]* lay around; (*pres* **meetgolel**; *fut* **yeetgolel**).

heetgon|en/-enah/-antee התגונן *v* defended oneself; (*pres* **meetgonen**; *fut* **yeetgonen**).

heetgonenoo|t/-yot התגוננות *nf* self-defence.

heetgor|er/-erah/-artee התגורר *v* resided; (*pres* **meetgorer**; *fut* **yeetgorer**).

heetgoreroot/-yot התגוררות *nf* residence; dwelling.

heetgosh|esh/-eshah/-ashtee התגושש *v* wrestled; (*pres* **meetgoshesh**; *fut* **yeetgoshesh**).

heetgosheshoo|t/-yot התגוששות *nf* wrestling.

heet'hal|ekh/-khah/-akhtee התהלך *v* walked about; (*pres* **meet'halekh**; *fut* **yeet'halekh**).

heet'hal|el/-elah/-altee התהלל *v* boasted; (*pres* **meet'halel**; *fut* **yeet'halel**).

heet'hap|ekh/-khah/-akhtee התהפך *v* overturned; turned around; (*pres* **meet'hapekh**; *fut* **yeet'hapekh**).

heet'hapkhoo|t/-yot התהפכות *nf* reversal; turning over.

heet'hapkhoot ha-yotsrot התהפכות היוצרות *nf* turning things topsy-turvy.

heet'hav|ah/-tah/-etee התהווה *v* emerged; was formed; (*pres* **meet'haveh**; *fut* **yeet'haveh**).

heet'hol|el/-elah/-altee התהולל *v* roistered; got out of hand; (*pres* **meet'holel**; *fut* **yeet'holel**).

heet'holeloo|t/-yot התהוללות getting out of hand; riotousness.

heetka'aroo|t/-yot התכערות *nf* uglification; becoming ugly.

heetkab|ed/-dah/-adetee התכבד *v* was honored; had the honor; (*pres* **meetkabed**; *fut* **yeetkabed**).

heetkabdoo|t/-yot התכבדות *nf* having the honor; honoring.

heetkab|el/-lah/-altee התקבל *v* was accepted; was received; (*pres* **meetkabel**; *fut* **yeetkabel**).

heetkabloo|t/-yot התקבלות *nf* admission; acceptance; being accepted.

heetkad|em/-mah/-amtee התקדם *v* progressed; advanced; (*pres* **meetkadem**; *fut* **yeetkadem**).

heetkadmoo|t/-yot התקדמות *nf* progress; advance.

heetka|'er/-'arah/-'artee התכער *v* became ugly; (*pres* **meetka'er**; *fut* **yeetka'er**).

heetkahaloo|t/-yot התקהלות *nf* gathering; assembly.

heetka|hel/-halah/-haltee התקהל *v* gathered; assembled; (*pres* **meetkahel**; *fut* **yeetkahel**).

heetkakhashoo|t/-yot התכחשות *nf* disavowal.

heetkakh|esh/-ashah/-ashtee התכחש *v* disavowed; disowned; (*pres* **meetkakhesh**; *fut* **yeetkakhesh**).

heetkal|e'akh/-khah/-akhtee התקלח *v* took a shower; (*pres* **meetkale'akh**; *fut* **yeetkale'akh**).

heetkal|ef/-fah/-aftee התקלף *v* peeled off; (*pres* **meetkalef**; *fut* **yeetkalef**).

heetkal|es/-sah/-astee התקלס *v* mocked; derided; (*pres* **meetkales**; *fut* **yeetkales**).

heetkalfoo|t/-yot התקלפות *nf* peeling off; shedding.

heetkalk|el/-elah/-altee התקלקל *v* got spoiled; deteriorated; broke down; (*pres* **meetkalkel**; *fut* **yeetkalkel**).

heetkalkeloo|t/-yot התקלקלות deterioration; spoiling; breakdown.

heetkalsoo|t/-yot התקלסות *nf* mockery; scoffing; deriding.

heetkam|et/-tah/-atetee התקמט *v* became wrinkled; (*pres* **meetkamet**; *fut* **yeetkamet**).

heetkamtoo|t/-yot התקמטות *nf* wrinkling; shrinkage.

heetkan|e/-'ah/-e'tee התקנא *v* become envious; envied; (*pres* **meetkane'**; *fut* **yeetkane'**).

heetkan|es/-sah/-astee התכנס *v* congregated; convened; (*pres* **meetkanes**; *fut* **yeetkanes**).

heetkan'oo|t/-yot התקנאות *nf* jealousy.

heetkansoo|t/-yot התכנסות *nf* congregation; convention; gathering.

heetkap|el/-lah/-altee התקפל *v* **1.** folded-up; **2.** *[colloq.]* gave in; retreated; (*pres* **meetkapel**; *fut* **yeetkapel**).

heetkaploo|t/-yot התקפלות *nf* **1.** folding; doubling up; **2.** *[colloq.]* giving-in; retreat.

heetkarb|el/-elah/-altee התכרבל *v* wrapped oneself; (*pres* **meetkarbel**; *fut* **yeetkarbel**).

heetkar|e'akh/-khah/-akhtee התקרח *v* became bald; (*pres* **meetkare'akh**; *fut* **yeetkare'akh**).

heetkar|er/-erah/-artee התקרר *v* **1.** cooled off; **2.** *[colloq.]* caught a cold; (*pres* **meetkarer**; *fut* **yeetkarer**).

heetkareroo|t/-yot התקררות *nf* **1.** cooling off; **2.** *[slang]* a cold (illness).

heetkar|ev/-vah/-avtee התקרב *v* approached; came nearer; (*pres* **meetkarev**; *fut* **yeetkarev**).

heetkarkhoo|t/-yot התקרחות *nf* balding; becoming bald.

heetkarvoo|t/-yot התקרבות *nf* approaching; convergence; rapprochement.

heetkas|ah/-tah/-etee התכסה *v* covered oneself up; (*pres* **meetkaseh**; *fut* **yeetkaseh**).

heetkash|ah/-tah/-etee התקשה *v* **1.** found difficult; **2.** hardened; (*pres* **meetkasheh**; *fut* **yeetkasheh**).

heetkash|er/-rah/-artee התקשר *v* **1.** got in touch; **2.** *[colloq.]* telephoned; (*pres* **meetkasher**; *fut* **yeetkasher**).

heetkash|et/-tah/-atetee התקשט *v* adorned oneself; (*pres* **meetkashet**; *fut* **yeetkashet**).

heetkashoo|t/-yot התקשות *nf* hardening.
heetkasoo|t/-yot התכסות *nf* wrapping; cover.
heetkashroo|t/-yot התקשרות *nf* attachment; commitment.
heetkat|esh/-'shah/-ashtee התכתש *v* wrestled; (*pres* **meetkatesh**; *fut* **yeetkatesh**).
heetkat|ev/-vah/-avtee התכתב *v* exchanged letters; corresponded; (*pres* **meetkatev**; *fut* **yeetkatev**).
heetkats|ef/-fah/-aftee התקצף *v* became enraged; got angry; (*pres* **meetkatsef**; *fut* **yeetkatsef**).
heetkat'shoo|t/-yot התכתשות *nf* fistfight; fight.
heetkatvoo|t/-yot התכתבות *nf* correspondence; exchange of letters.
heetkav|en/-nah/-antee התכוון *v* intended; meant; (*pres* **meetkaven**; *fut* **yeetkaven**).
heetkav|ets/-'tsah/-atstee התכווץ *v* shrank; (*pres* **meetkavets**; *fut* **yeetkavets**).
heetkavtsoo|t/-yot התכווצות *nf* contraction; spasm.
heetka|yem/-ymah/-yamtee התקיים *v* **1.** took place; **2.** subsisted; **3.** existed; (*pres* **meetkayem**; *fut* **yeetkayem**).
heetk|eef/-eefah/-aftee התקיף *v* attacked; (*pres* **matkeef**; *fut* **yatkeef**).
heetk|een/-eenah/-antee התקין *v* installed; (*pres* **matkeen**; *fut* **yatkeen**).
eetkha אתך *conj & pers pron masc sing* with you (addressing male).
heetkhab|e/-'ah/-e'tee התחבא *v* hid; (*pres* **meetkhabe**; *fut* **yeetkhabe**).
heetkhab|ek/-kah/-aktee התחבק *v* hugged; embraced; (*pres* **meetkhabek**; *fut* **yeetkhabek**).
heetkhab|er/-rah/-artee התחבר *v* joined with; (*pres* **meetkhaber**; *fut* **yeetkhaber**).
heetkhab|et/-tah/-atetee התחבט *v* took pains; tried hard to solve; (*pres* **meetkhabet**; *fut* **yeetkhabet**).
heetkhab|ev/-evah/-avtee התחבב *v* endeared oneself (*pres* **meetkhabev**; *fut* **yeetkhabev**).
heetkhabevoo|t/-yot התחבבות *nf* endearing oneself; becoming popular with.
heetkhabkoo|t/-yot התחבקות *nf* embracing; hugging.
heetkhabroo|t/-yot התחברות *nf* joining; adhesion.
heetkhabtoo|t/-yot התחבטות *nf* struggle (internal); effort.
heetkhad|ed/-edah/-adetee התחדד *v* sharpened; (*pres* **meetkhaded**; *fut* **yeetkhaded**).
heetkhadedoo|t/-yot התחדדות *nf* sharpening.
heetkhadedoot yekhaseem התחדדות יחסים *nf* exacerbation of relations.
heetkhad|esh/-shah/-ashtee התחדש *v* **1.** was restored; **2.** was renewed; resumed (*pres* **meetkhadesh**; *fut* **yeetkhadesh**).
heetkhadshoo|t/-yot התחדשות renewal.
heetkhak|ekh/-'khah/-akhtee התחכך *v* **1.** scratched oneself; **2.** *[slang]* rubbed shoulders; **3.** mixed with (socially); (*pres* **meetkhakekh**; *fut* **yeetkhakekh**).
heetkhak|em/-mah/-amtee התחכם *v* **1.** outsmarted; devised means; **2.** *[colloq.]* tried to be clever; (*pres* **meetkhakem**; *fut* **yeetkhakem**).
heetkhak'khoo|t/-yot התחככות *nf* rubbing.
heetkhakmoo|t/-yot התחכמות *nf* **1.** trying to be funny; **2.** trying to outsmart.
heetkhal|ef/-fah/-aftee התחלף *v* **1.** changed into; was exchanged; **2.** *[colloq.]* changed clothes; (*pres* **meetkhalef**; *fut* **yeetkhalef**).
heetkhal|ek/-kah/-aktee התחלק *v* **1.** was divided between; **2.** slipped; (*pres* **meetkhalek**; *fut* **yeetkhalek**).
heetkhal|el/-elah/-altee התחלל *v* was desecrated; (*pres* **meetkhalel**; *fut* **yeetkhalel**).
heetkhalfoo|t/-yot התחלפות *v* change; exchange.
hetkhalkh|el/-elah/-altee התחלחל *v* was shocked; (*pres* **meetkhalkhel**; *fut* **yeetkhalkhel**).
heetkhalkoo|t/-yot התחלקות *nf* **1.** division; divisibility; **2.** slipping.
heetkham|ek/-kah/-aktee התחמק *v* evaded; shirked; slipped away; (*pres* **meetkhamek**; *fut* **yeetkhamek**).
heetkham|em/-emah/-amtee התחמם *v* warmed up; (*pres* **meetkhamem**; *fut* **yeetkhamem**).
heetkhamemoo|t/-yot התחממות *nf* warming up.
heetkhamkoo|t/-yot התחמקות *nf* evasion; shirking.
heetkhamts|en/-enah/-antee התחמצן *v* was oxidized; (*pres* **meetkhamtsen**; *fut* **yeetkhamtsen**).
heetkhan|ef/-fah/-aftee התחנף *v* fawned; ingratiated oneself; (*pres* **meetkhanef**; *fut* **yeetkhanef**).
heetkhan|ekh/-khah/-akhtee התחנך *v* was brought up; was educated; (*pres* **meetkhanekh**; *fut* **yeetkhanekh**).
heetkhan|en/-enah/-antee התחנן *v* begged; implored; (*pres* **meetkhanen**; *fut* **yeetkhanen**).
heetkhanenoo|t/-yot התחננות *v* pleading; entreating.
heetkhanfoo|t/-yot התחנפות *nf* ingratiation; flattering.
heetkhankh|en/-enah/-antee התחנחן *v* put on airs; (*pres* **meetkhankhen**; *fut* **yeetkhankhen**).
heetkhankhenoo|t/-yot התחנחנות *nf* coquetry; coquettishness.
heetkhankhoo|t/-yot התחנכות *nf* self-education.
heetkhap|er/-rah/-artee התחפר *v* dug oneself in; entrenched oneself; (*pres* **meetkhaper**; *fut* **yeetkhaper**).
heetkhap|es/-sah/-astee התחפש *v* disguised oneself; (*pres* **meetkhapes**; *fut* **yeetkhapes**).
heetkhaproo|t/-yot התחפרות *nf* entrenchment.
heetkhapsoo|t/-yot התחפשות *nf* **1.** disguise; **2.** masquerading.

heetkhar|ah/-tah/-eetee התחרה *v* competed; (*pres* **meetkhareh;** *fut* **yeetkhareh).**

heetkharb|en/-enah/-antee התחרבן *[slang] v* failed; (*pres* **meetkharben;** *fut* **yeetkharben).**

heetkharbenoo|t/-yot התחרבנות *[slang] nf* failure; disappointment.

heetkhar|et/-tah/-atetee התחרט *v* regretted; repented; changed one's mind; (*pres* **meetkharet;** *fut* **yeetkharet).**

heetkhar|esh/-shah/-ashtee התחרש *v* became deaf; (*pres* **meetkharesh;** *fut* **yeetkharesh).**

heetkharoo|t/-yot התחרות *nf* contest; competition.

heetkharshoo|t/-yot התחרשות *nf* becoming deaf.

heetkhartoo|t/-yot התחרטות *nf* contrition.

heetkhasdoot/-yot התחסדות *nf* hypocrisy.

heetkhas|ed/-dah/-adetee התחסד *v* acted hypocritically; (*pres* **meetkhased;** *fut* **yeetkhased).**

heetkhas|el/-lah/-altee התחסל *v* **1.** came to an end; **2.** was liquidated; (*pres* **meetkhasel;** *fut* **yeetkhasel).**

heetkhashb|en/-enah/-antee התחשבן *v [colloq.]* settled accounts; (*pres* **meetkhashben;** *fut* **yeetkhashben).**

heetkhashbenoo|t/-yot התחשבנות *nf* settling accounts.

heetkhash|ek/-kah/-aktee התחשק *v* felt like; had an urge for; (*pres* **meetkhashek;** *fut* **yeetkhashek).**

heetkhash|ev/-vah/-avtee התחשב *v* considered; took into account; (*pres* **meetkhashev;** *fut* **yeetkhashev).**

heetkhashm|el/-elah/-altee התחשמל *v* **1.** was electrocuted; **2.** was electrified; (*pres* **meetkhashmel;** *fut* **yeetkhashmel).**

heetkhashvoo|t/-yot התחשבות *nf* consideration.

heetkhashmeloo|t/-yot התחשמלות *nf* electrocution.

heetkhasloo|t/-yot התחסלות *nf* liquidation; self-liquidation.

heetkhat|en/-nah/-antee התחתן *v* got married; (*pres* **meetkhaten;** *fut* **yeetkhaten).**

heetkhatnoo|t/-yot התחתנות *nf* marrying; marriage.

heetkhats|ef/-fah/-aftee התחצף *v* behaved with impertinence; behaved insolently; (*pres* **meetkhatsef;** *fut* **yeetkhatsef).**

heetkhatsfoo|t/-yot התחצפות *nf* impertinence; insolence.

heetkha|yev/-yvah/-yavtee התחייב *v* undertook; pledged; (*pres* **meetkhayev;** *fut* **yeetkhayev).**

heetkhayvoo|t/-yot התחייבות *nf* undertaking; obligation.

heetkhaz|ah/-tah/-etee התחזה *v* impersonated; pretended to be; (*pres* **meetkhazeh;** *fut* **yeetkhazeh).**

heetkhaz|ek/-kah/-aktee התחזק *v* grew stronger; (*pres* **metkhazek;** *fut* **yeetkhazek).**

heetkhazkoo|t/-yot התחזקות *nf* strengthening.

heetkhazoo|t/yot התחזות *nf* impersonation.

heetkh|eel/-eelah/-altee התחיל *v* began; (*pres* **matkheel;** *fut* **yatkheel).**

heetkholel/-ah/-oo התחולל *v* occurred; broke out; (*pres* **meetkholel;** *fut* **yeetkholel).**

heetkom|em/-emah/-amtee התקומם *v* rebelled; rose against; (*pres* **meetkomem;** *fut* **yeetkomem).**

heetkomemoo|t/-yot התקוממות *nf* rebellion; uprising.

heetkon|en/-enah/-antee התכונן *v* was preparing; prepared oneself; (*pres* **meetkonen;** *fut* **yeetkonen).**

heetkonenoo|t/-yot התכוננות *nf* preparatives; preparation.

heetkot|et/-etah/-atetee התקוטט *v* quarrelled; (*pres* **meetkotet;** *fut* **yeetkotet).**

heetkotetoo|t/-yot התקוטטות *nf* quarrel; brawl.

heetlab|esh/-shah/-ashtee התלבש *v* dressed; got dressed; (*pres* **meetlabesh;** *fut* **yeetlabesh).**

heetlabesh (*etc*) **'al** התלבש על *v [slang]* determinedly took on (a task)...

heetlab|et/-tah/-atetee התלבט *v* took pains; hesitated; (*pres* **meetlabet;** *fut* **yeetlabet).**

heetlabtoo|t/-yot התלבטות *nf* struggle; hesitation.

heetlahavoot התלהבות *nf* enthusiasm; excitement; getting excited.

heetlahev/-avah/-avtee התלהב *v* was enthusiastic; (*pres* **meetlahev;** *fut* **yeetlahev).**

heetlak|akh (or **heetlak|e'akh)/-'khah/-akhtee** התלקח *v* flared up; caught fire; (*pres* **meetlake'akh;** *fut* **yeetlakakh).**

heetlakdoo|t/-yot התלכדות *nf* rallying; joining forces.

heetlak|ed/-dah/-adetee התלכד *v* rallied; joined forces; (*pres* **meetlaked;** *fut* **yeetlaked).**

heetlakh|esh/-'shah/-ashtee התלחש *v* exchanged whispers; (*pres* **meetlakhesh;** *fut* **yeetlakhesh).**

heetlak'khoo|t/-yot התלקחות *nf* flare up.

heetlakhl|ekh/-ekhah/-akhtee התלכלך *v* dirtied oneself; (*pres* **meetlakhlekh;** *fut* **yeetlakhlekh).**

heetlakhlekhoo|t/-yot התלכלכות *nf* dirtying; sullying.

heetlakhshoo|t/-yot התלחשות *nf* whisper; whispering.

heetlam|ed/-dah/-adetee התלמד *v* taught oneself; (*pres* **meetlamed;** *fut* **yeetlamed).**

eetleez/-eem אטליז *nm* butchery; butcher shop; (*pl+of:* **-ey).**

heetlon|en/-enah/-antee התלונן *v* complained; (*pres* **meetlonen;** *fut* **yeetlonen).**

heetlonenoo|t/-yot התלוננות *nf* complaining; grumbling.

heetlots|ets/-etsah/-atstee התלוצץ *v* joked; jested (*pres* **meetlotsets;** *fut* **yeetlotsets).**

heetlotsetsoo|t/-yot התלוצצות *nf* jesting; mockery.

heetma'atoot התמעטות *nf* decrease; diminution.

heetma|'et/-'atah/-'atnoo התמעט *v* diminished; became fewer; (*pres* **meetma'et;** *fut* **yeetma'et).**

heetmak|akh (or **heetmak|e'akh)/-'khah/-akhtee** התמקח *v* bargained; haggled; (*pres* **meetmake'akh;** *fut* **yeetmake'akh).**

heetmak|em/-mah/-amtee התמקם *v* settled; took up position; (*pres* **meetmakem;** *fut* **yeetmakem).**

heetmak|er/-rah/-artee התמכר *v* **1.** devoted oneself; **2.** became addicted; (*pres* **meetmaker;** *fut* **yeetmaker).**

heetmak'khoo|t/-yot התמקחות *nf* haggling.

heetmakmoo|t/-yot התמקמות *nf* taking position; localization.

hetmakroo|t/-yot התמכרות *nf* **1.** addiction; **2.** absolute devotion.

heetmal|e/-'ah/-etee התמלא *v* **1.** was filled; **2.** was fulfilled; (*pres* **meetmale;** *fut* **yeetmale).**

heetmam|esh/-shah/-ashtee התממש *v* materialized; came true; (*pres* **meetmamesh;** *fut* **yeetmamesh).**

heetmamshoo|t/-yot התממשות *nf* realization.

heetman|ah/-tah/-etee התמנה *v* was appointed; (*pres* **meetmaneh;** *fut* **yeetmaneh).**

heetmanoo|t/-yot התמנות *nf* appointment; nomination.

heetmarm|er/-erah/-artee התמרמר *v* resented; bitterly complained; (*pres* **meetmarmer;** *fut* **yeetmarmer).**

heetmarmeroo|t/-yot התמרמרות *nf* resentment; embitterment.

heetmas|ed/-dah/-adetee התמסד *v* became instituted; (*pres* **meetmased;** *fut* **yeetmased).**

heetmas|er/-rah/artee התמסר *v* **1.** devoted oneself; **2.** surrendered; **3.** (of female) gave herself to (sexually); (*pres* **meetmaser;** *fut* **yeetmaser).**

heetmasdoo|t/-yot התמסדות *nf* becoming part of the establishment; institutionalization.

heetmash|ekh/-'kha/-akhtee התמשך *v* extended; dragged out; (*pres* **meetmashekh;** *fut* **yeetmashekh).**

heetmash'khoo|t/-yot התמשכות *nf* prolongation; procrastination.

heetmasm|es/-esah/-astee התמסמס *v* melted away; fell apart; (*pres* **meetmasmes;** *fut* **yeetmasmes).**

heetmasroo|t/-yot התמסרות *nf* **1.** devotion; attachment; **2.** giving herself sexually.

heetmats|e/-'ah/-etee התמצא *v* knew one's way about; was familiar with; (*pres* **meetmatse;** *fut* **yeetmatse).**

heetmats'oot התמצאות *nf* orientation; knowing one's way about.

(khoosh) heetmats'oot חוש התמצאות *nm* sense of orientation.

heetmaz|eg/-gah/-agtee התמזג *v* blended; fused; (*pres* **meetmazeg;** *fut* **yeetmazeg).**

heetmazgoo|t/-yot התמזגות *nf* amalgamation; mixture; harmony.

heetmazmez/-ezah/-aztee התמזמז *v* **1.** wasted time; was late; **2.** *[slang]* necked; **3.** wore out; (*pres* **meetmazmez;** *fut* **yeetmazmez).**

heetmazmezoo|t/-yot התמזמזות *nf* **1.** softening; **2.** *[slang]* flirting.

heetm|eed/-eedah/-adetee התמיד *v* persisted; (*pres* **matmeed;** *fut* **yatmeed).**

heetm|een/-eenah/-antee הטמין *v* hid; (*pres* **matmeen;** *fut* **yatmeen).**

heetmod|ed/-edah/-adetee התמודד *v* confronted; contended; faced up; (*pres* **meetmoded;** *fut* **yeetmoded).**

heetmodedoo|t/-yot התמודדות *nf* confrontation; competition.

heetmog|eg/-egah/-agtee התמוגג *v* melted; dissolved with pleasure; (*pres* **meetmogeg;** *fut* **yeetmogeg).**

heetmogegoo|t/-yot התמוגגות *nf* melting (with delight), dissolving.

heetmot|et/-etah/-atetee התמוטט *v* collapsed; (*pres* **meetmotet;** *fut* **yeetmotet).**

heetmotetoo|t/-yot התמוטטות *nf* collapse.

heetmotetoot (*etc*) **'atsabeem** התמוטטות עצבים *nf* nervous breakdown.

('al saf) heetmotetoot על סף התמוטטות *adv* on the verge of breakdown.

heetn|ah/-etah/-etee התנה *v* stipulated; made it a condition; (*pres* **matneh;** *fut* **yatneh).**

heetnah (*etc*) **ahaveem** התנה אהבים *v* made love.

heetna'an|a'/-'ah/-a'tee (*or:* **heetna'an|e'a** *etc*) התנענע *v* swayed; shook; (*pres* **meetna'ane'a';** *fut* **yeetna'ane'a').**

heetna'an'oo|t/-yot התנענעות *nf* shaking; vibration.

heetna'aroo|t/-yot התנערות *v* awakening; shaking off.

heetnab|e/-'ah/-etee התנבא *v* prophesized; (*pres* **meetnabe;** *fut* **yeetnabe).**

heetnad|ef/-fah/-aftee התנדף *v* evaporated; (*pres* **meetnadef;** *fut* **yeetnadef).**

heetnad|ev/-vah/-avtee התנדב *v* volunteered; (*pres* **meetnadev;** *fut* **yeetnadev).**

heetnadn|ed/-edah/-adetee התנדנד *v* rocked; swayed; (*pres* **meetnadned;** *fut* **yeetnadned).**

heetnadvoo|t/-yot התנדבות *nf* volunteering.

heetna|'er/-'arah/-'artee התנער *v* shook off; (*pres* **meetna'er;** *fut* **yeetna'er).**

heetnagdoo|t/-yot התנגדות *nf* opposition; resistance.

('or|er/-erah/-artee) heetnagdoot עורר התנגדות *v* antagonized; (*pres* **me'orer** *etc;* *fut* **ye'orer** *etc*).

(tenoo|'at/-'ot) heetnagdoot תנועת התנגדות *nf* resistance movement.

heetnag|ed/-dah/-adetee התנגד *v* opposed; objected; (*pres* **meetnaged;** *fut* **yeetnaged).**

heetnag|esh/-shah/-ashtee התנגש *v* clashed; collided; (*pres* **meetnagesh;** *fut* **yeetnagesh).**

heetnag|ev/-vah/-avtee התנגב *v* dried oneself; (*pres* **meetnagev;** *fut* **yeetnagev).**

heetnagshoo|t/-yot התנגשות *nf* clash; collision.

heetnagvoo|t/-yot התנגבות *nf* wiping; drying oneself.

heetnahagoo|t/-yot התנהגות *nf* behavior; conduct.

heetna|heg/-hagah/-hagtee התנהג *v* behaved; (*pres* **meetnaheg;** *fut* **yeetnaheg).**

heetna|hel/-halah/-haltee התנהל *v* went on; was conducted; (*pres* **meetnahel;** *fut* **yeetnahel).**

heetnak|el/-lah/-altee התנכל *v* plotted; conspired; (*pres* **meetnakel;** *fut* **yeetnakel).**

heetnak|em/-mah/-amtee התנקם *v* avenged oneself; (*pres* **meetnakem;** *fut* **yeetnakem).**

heetnak|er/-rah/-artee התנכר *v* shunned; alienated; (*pres* **meetnaker;** *fut* **yeetnaker).**

heetnak|esh/-shah/-ashtee התנקש *v* attempted to kill; (*pres* **meetnakesh;** *fut* **yeetnakesh).**

heetnak|ez/-zah/-aztee התנקז *v* was drained; (*pres* **meetnakez;** *fut* **yetnakez).**

heetnakh|el/-alah/-altee התנחל *v* **1.** settled on land; **2.** *[colloq.]* settled in Judea, Samaria or Gaza; (*pres* **meetnakhel;** *fut* **yeetnakhel).**

heetnakhloo|t/-yot התנחלות *nf* settling (or settlement) in Judea, Samaria or Gaza areas.

heetnakh|em/-mah/-amtee התנחם *v* consoled oneself; (*pres* **meetnakhem;** *fut* **yeetnakhem).**

heetnakloo|t/-yot התנכלות *nf* plotting; scheming.

heetnakroo|t/-yot התנכרות *nf* estrangement.

heetnakshoo|t/-yot התנקשות *nf* attempt on one's life.

heetnamn|em/-emah/-amtee התנמנם *v* dozed; (*pres* **meetnamnem;** *fut* **yeetnamnem).**

heetnap|akh/-'khah/-akhtee (*or:* **heetnap|e'akh** *etc*) התנפח *v* swelled; was inflated; was boastful; (*pres* **meetnape'akh;** *fut* **yeetnape'akh).**

heetnap|el/-lah/-altee התנפל *v* attacked; assaulted; (*pres* **meetnapel;** *fut* **yeetnapel).**

heetnap|ets/-tsah/-atstee התנפץ *v* was shattered; (*pres* **meetnapets;** *fut* **yeetnapets).**

heetnapkhoo|t/-yot התנפחות *nf* swelling.

heetnaploo|t/-yot התנפלות *nf* assault; attack.

heetnas|ah/-tah/-etee התנסה *v* experienced; went through; (*pres* **meetnaseh;** *fut* **yeetnaseh).**

heetnas|e/-'ah/-etee התנשא *v* rose; was exalted; (*pres* **meetnase;** *fut* **yeetnase).**

heetnash|ef/-fah/-aftee התנשף *v* puffed; breathed heavily; (*pres* **meetnashef;** *fut* **yeetnashef).**

heetnash|ek/-kah/-aktee התנשק *v* exchanged kisses; (*pres* **meetnashek;** *fut* **yeetnashek).**

heetnashfoo|t/-yot התנשפות *nf* **1.** breathing with difficulty; **2.** regaining one's breath.

heetnashkoo|t/-yot התנשקות *nf* kissing; exchanging kisses.

heetnasoo|t/-yot התנסות *nf* experiencing; gaining experience.

heetnas'oo|t/-yot התנשאות *nf* elevation; pridefulness; haughtiness.

heetnats|akh (or: **heetnats|e'akh)/-'khah/-akhtee** התנצח *v* polemicized; exchanged arguments; (*pres* **meetnatse'akh;** *fut* **yeetnatse'akh).**

heetnats|el/-lah/-altee התנצל *v* apologized; (*pres* **meetnatsel;** *fut* **yeetnatsel).**

heetnats|er/-rah/-artee התנצר *v* converted to Christianity; (*pres* **meetnatser;** *fut* **yeetnatser).**

heetnatskhoo|t/-yot התנצחות *nf* dispute.

heetnatsloo|t/-yot התנצלות *nf* apology.

heetnatsroo|t/-yot התנצרות *nf* conversion to Christianity.

heetnav|en/-nah/-antee התנוון *v* degenerated; (*pres* **meetnaven;** *fut* **yeetnaven).**

heetnavnoo|t/-yot התנוונות *nf* degeneration; decay; atrophy.

heetnaz|er/-rah/-artee התנזר *v* abstained from; gave up; (*pres* **meetnazer;** *fut* **yeetnazer).**

heetnazroo|t/-yot התנזרות *nf* abstention from; giving up.

heetnee'a'/-'ah/-a'tee התניע *v* started up (engine); (*pres* **matnee'a';** *fut* **yatnee'a').**

heetno|'e'a'/-'a'ah/-'a'tee התנועע *v* moved; swayed; (*pres* **meetno'e'a';** *fut* **yeetno'e'a').**

heetnod|ed/-edah/-adetee התנודד *v* swayed; oscillated; (*pres* **meetnoded;** *fut* **yeetnoded).**

heetnodedoo|t/-yot התנודדות swaying; oscillating.

heetnof|ef/-efah/-aftee התנופף *v* fluttered; (*pres* **meetnofef;** *fut* **yeetnofef).**

heetnofefoo|t/-yot התנופפות *nf* waving (flag); fluttering.

heetnos|es/-esah/-astee התנוסס *v* waved; was hoisted; (*pres* **meetnoses;** *fut* **yeetnoses).**

heetnosesoo|t/-yot התנוססות *nf* flying (flag); standing out.

heetnots|ets/-etsah/-atstee התנוצץ *v* sparkled; (*pres* **meetnotsets;** *fut* **yeetnotsets).**

heetnotsetsoo|t/-yot התנוצצות *nf* gleaming; glittering.

eeto אתו *prep & pers pron* with him.

(be) 'eeto/-ah בעיתו *adv* in his/its/her proper time; in the nick of time.

(she-lo be) 'eet|o/-ah שלא בעיתו *adv* untimely; at the/his/its/her wrong time.

heet'od|ed/-edah/-adetee התעודד *v* cheered up; (*pres* **meet'oded;** *fut* **yeet'oded).**

heet'odedoo|t/-yot התעודדות *nf* encouragement; cheering up.

heet'of|ef/-efah/-aftee התעופף *v* flew about; flew off; (*pres* **meet'ofef;** *fut* **yeet'ofef).**

heet'ofefoo|t/-yot התעופפות *nf* flying.

'eeton/-eem עיתון *nm* newspaper (*pl+of:* **-ey).**

'eeton/-ey boker עיתון בוקר *nm* morning-paper.

'eeton/-ey 'erev עיתון ערב *nm* afternoon (or evening) paper.

'eetona'oot עיתונאות *nf* journalism.

'eetona'ee/-t עיתונאי *adj* journalistic.

'eetona|y/-'eet עיתונאי *nmf* newsman/ newswoman; journalist.

heet'on|en/-enah/-antee התאונן *v* complained; (*pres* **meet'onen**; *fut* **yeet'onen**).
'eetonoot עיתונות *nf* (journalistic) press.
(khofesh ha) 'eetonoot חופש העיתונות *nm* freedom of the press.
(tsal|am/-emet) 'eetonoot צלם עיתונות *nmf* press-photographer; (*pl:* **-amey** *etc*).
heetookh/-eem היתוך *nm* melting; fusion.
(koor) heetookh כור היתוך *nm* melting pot.
(nekoodat ha) heetookh נקודת ההיתוך *nf* melting point.
heetool/-eem היתול *nm* mockery; ridiculing; (*pl+of:* **-ey**).
heetoolee/-t היתולי *adj* humorous; comic.
(makhz|eh/-ot) heetoolee/-yeem מחזה היתולי *nm* comedy.
'eetoor/-eem עיטור *nm* decoration; medal; (*pl+of:* **-ey**).
◇ **'eetoor ha-'oz** עיטור העוז *nm* Medal of Valor bestowed by Israeli Army's High Command for acts of outstanding bravery.
eetoot/-eem איתות *nm* signaling; signal; (*pl+of:* **-ey**).
'eetooy עיתוי *nm* timing.
heet'or|er/-erah/-artee התעורר *v* awakened; woke up; (*pres* **meet'orer**; *fut* **yeet'orer**).
heet'oreroo|t/-yot התעוררות *nf* awakening.
heet'osh|esh/-eshah/-ashtee התאושש *v* recovered; regained strength/courage; came to oneself; (*pres* **meet'oshesh**; *fut* **yeet'oshesh**).
heet'osheshoot התאוששות *nf* recovery.
heetpa'aloo|t/-yot התפעלות *nf* admiration; excitement.
heetpa'amoo|t/-yot התפעמות *nf* excitement.
heetpa'aroo|t/-yot התפארות *nf* boasting.
heetpa|'el/-'alah/-'altee התפעל *v* was impressed; (*pres* **meetpa'el**; *fut* **yeetpa'el**).
"heetpa'el" התפעל *nm* passive and reflexive form of Hebrew verb (Gram.).
heetpa|'em/-'amah/-'amtee התפעם *v* was stirred; (*pres* **meetpa'em**; *fut* **yeetpa'em**).
heetpa|'er/-arah/-artee התפאר *v* boasted; (*pres* **meetpa'er**; *fut* **yeetpa'er**).
heetpag|er/-rah/-artee התפגר *v* **1.** died; **2.** *[slang]* croaked; (*pres* **meetpager**; *fut* **yeetpager**).
heetpagroo|t/-yot התפגרות *nf* death of an animal or of someone unworthy.
heetpak|e'a'/-'ah/-'atee התפקע *v* burst; was about to burst; (*pres* **meetpake'a'**; *fut* **yeetpake'a'**).
heetpakdoo|t/-yot התפקדות *nf* **1.** presenting oneself for census; **2.** *[colloq.]* functioning of a person.
heetpak|e'akh/-'khah/-akhtee התפכח *v* **1.** sobered up; became clever; **2.** regained sight; (*pres* **meetpake'akh**; *fut* **yeetpake'akh**).
heetpaked! !התפקד *imp* Count off! Number off!
heetpak|ed/-dah/-adetee התפקד *v* **1.** was mustered; was enumerated; **2.** *[colloq.]* functioned (of a person).
heetpakhamoo|t/-yot התפחמות *nf* carbonization; electrocution.
heetpakh|em/-mah/-amtee התפחם *v* was electrocuted, carbonized; (*pres* **meetpakhem**; *fut* **yeetpakhem**).
heetpak'khoo|t/-yot התפכחות *nf* sobering up.
heetpal|e/-'ah/-etee התפלא *v* wondered; was astonished; (*pres* **meetpale**; *fut* **yeetpale**).
heetpal|eg/-gah/-agnoo התפלג *v* split; (*pres* **meetpaleg**; *fut* **yeetpaleg**).
heetpal|el/-elah/-altee התפלל *v* prayed; (*pres* **meetpalel**; *fut* **yeetpalel**).
heetpalgoo|t/-yot התפלגות *nf* bifurcation; schism; splitting.
heetpalm|es/-esah/-astee התפלמס *v* polemicized; engaged in polemics; (*pres* **meetpalmes**; *fut* **yeetpalmes**).
heetpalmesoo|t/-yot התפלמסות *nf* polemics; disputation.
heetpals|ef/-efah/-aftee התפלסף *v* philosophized; (*pres* **meetpalsef**; *fut* **yeetpalsef**).
heetpalsefoo|t/-yot התפלספות *nf* philosophizing.
heetpalp|el/-elah/-altee התפלפל *v* quibbled; (*pres* **meetpalpel**; *fut* **yeetpalpel**).
heetpalpeloo|t/-ot התפלפלות *nf* hair-splitting dialectics.
heetpal|esh/-shah/-ashtee התפלש *v* wallowed (in the dust, in misery); (*pres* **meetpalesh**; *fut* **yeetpalesh**).
heetpal|ets/-tsah/-atstee התפלץ *v* shuddered; was paralyzed; had the jitters (*pres* **meetpalets**; *fut* **yeetpalets**).
heetpal'oo|t/-yot התפלאות *nf* amazement; surprise.
heetpalshoo|t/-yot התפלשות *nf* wallowing; rolling about.
heetpaltsoo|t/-yot התפלצות *nf* jitter; shudder.
heetpan|ah/-tah/-etee התפנה *v* **1.** vacated; **2.** found time; (*pres* **meetpaneh**; *fut* **yeetpaneh**).
heetpan|ek/-kah/-aktee התפנק *v* pampered oneself; (*pres* **meetpanek**; *fut* **yeetpanek**).
heetpankoo|t/-yot התפנקות *nf* pampering oneself.
heetpantch|er/-erah/-artee התפנצ'ר *v* *[slang]* failed; went bust; (*pres* **meetpantcher**; *fut* **yeetpantcher**).
heetpanoo|t/-yot התפנות *nf* **1.** evacuation; **2.** disengagement.
heetpar|e'a'/-'ah/-a'tee (*or:* **heetpar|a'** *etc*) התפרע *v* got wild; ran riot; (*pres* **meetpare'a'**; *fut* **yeetpare'a'**).
heetpar|ek/-kah/-aktee התפרק *v* **1.** was dismantled; **2.** relaxed; got off his chest; **3.** disarmed oneself; (*pres* **meetparek**; *fut* **yeetparek**).

heetpar|es/-sah/-astee התפרס *v* deployed; fanned out (*pres* **meetpares;** *fut* **yeetpares**).

heetpar|esh/-shah/-ashtee התפרש *v* was interpreted; (*pres* **meetparesh;** *fut* **yeetparesh**).

heetpar|ets/-tsah/-atstee התפרץ *v* burst into; became unruly; (*pres* **meetparets;** *fut* **yeetparets**).

heetpark|ed/-edah/-adetee התפרקד *v* lay on one's back; (*pres* **meetparked;** *fut* **yeetparked**).

heetparkhe'akh/-ekhah/-akhtee התפרחח *v* *[slang]* behaved like a ruffian; (*pres* **meetparkhe'akh;** *fut* **yeetparkhe'akh**).

heetparkhekhoo|t/-yot התפרחחות *nf* hooliganism.

heetparn|es/-esah/-astee התפרנס *v* earned a living; (*pres* **meetparnes;** *fut* **yeetparnes**).

heetparnesoo|t/-yot התפרנסות *nf* earning one's living; making a living.

heetpar'oo|t/-yot התפרעות *nf* riot.

heetparp|er/-erah/-artee התפרפר *v* *[slang]* **1.** shirked duty; **2.** was promiscuous (*pres* **meetparper;** *fut* **yeetparper**).

heetparperoo|t/-yot התפרפרות *nf* promiscuity; shirking one's duties.

heetpars|em/-emah/-amtee התפרסם *v* **1.** was published; **2.** became famous; earned fame; (*pres* **meetparsem;** *fut* **yeetparsem**).

heetparsemoo|t/-yot התפרסמות *nf* **1.** publication; **2.** notoriety; fame; becoming famous.

heetparsoo|t/-yot התפרסות *nf* deployment; fan-out.

heetparshoo|t/-yot התפרשות *nf* interpretation; being interpreted.

heetpartsoo|t/-yot התפרצות *nf* **1.** outbreak; eruption; **2.** *[colloq.]* burglary.

heetpash|er/-rah/-artee התפשר *v* compromised; came to terms; (*pres* **meetpasher;** *fut* **yeetpasher**).

heetpash|et/-tah/-atetee התפשט *v* **1.** undressed; **2.** spread; expanded; (*pres* **meetpashet;** *fut* **yeetpashet**).

heetpashroo|t/-yot התפשרות *nf* compromise.

heetpashtoo|t/-yot התפשטות *nf* **1.** spread; expansion; **2.** undressing.

heetpat|ah/-etah/-etee התפתה *v* was enticed; was seduced; was a fool to; (*pres* **meetpateh;** *fut* **yeetpateh**).

heetpat|akh/-'khah/-akhtee (*or:* **heetpat|e'akh** *etc*) התפתח *v* developed; progressed into; widened knowledge; (*pres* **meetpate'akh;** *fut* **yeetpate'akh**).

heetpat|el/-lah/-altee התפתל *v* wriggled; twisted; (*pres* **meetpatel;** *fut* **yeetpatel**).

heetpat|em/-mah/-amtee התפטם *v* stuffed oneself; (*pres* **meetpatem;** *fut* **yeetpatem**).

heetpat|er/-rah/-artee התפטר *v* **1.** resigned; **2.** got rid of; (*pres* **meetpater;** *fut* **yeetpater**).

heetpatkhoo|t/-yot התפתחות *nf* development; evolution.

heetpatkhootee/-t התפתחותי *adj* developmental; evolutionary.

heetpatloo|t/-yot התפתלות *nf* wriggling; winding.

heetpatmoo|t/-yot התפטמות *nf* gluttony; fattening.

heetpatoo|t/-yot התפתות *nf* succumbing.

heetpatroo|t/-yot התפטרות *nf* resignation; ridding oneself of.

(heeg|eesh/-eeshah/-ashtee) heetpatroot הגיש התפטרות *v* tended one's resignation; (*pres* **mageesh** *etc;* *fut* **yageesh** *etc*).

heetpats|el/-lah/-altee התפצל *v* split; ramified; (*pres* **meetpatsel;** *fut* **yeetpatsel**).

heetpatsloo|t/-yot התפצלות *nf* cleavage; splitting.

heetpay|es/-sah/-astee התפייס *v* reconciled oneself; (*pres* **meetpayes;** *fut* **yeetpayes**).

heetpaysoo|t/-yot התפייסות *nf* reconciliation.

heetpaz|er/-rah/-artee התפזר *v* scattered; dispersed; (*pres* **meetpazer;** *fut* **yeetpazer**).

(le) heetpazer! להתפזר! *v imp* fall out!

heetpazroo|t/-yot התפזרות *v* scattering; dispersion.

heetpor|er/-erah/-artee התפורר *v* crumbled; disintegrated; (*pres* **meetporer;** *fut* **yeetporer**).

heetporeroo|t/-yot התפוררות *nf* disintegration.

heetpots|ets/-etsah/-atstee התפוצץ *v* exploded; (*pres* **meetpotsets;** *fut* **yeetpotsets**).

heetpoot|ar/-rah/-artee התפוטר *v* *[slang]* was forced to resign; (*pres* **meetpootar;** *fut* **yeetpootar**).

heetpotsetsoo|t/-yot התפוצצות *nf* explosion.

heetr|ah/-etah/-etee התרה *v* warned; (*pres* **matreh;** *fut* **yatreh**).

heetra'an|en/-enah/-antee התרענן *v* freshened up; refreshed oneself; (*pres* **meetra'anen;** *fut* **yeetra'anen**).

heetra'anenoot התרעננות *nf* refreshment; freshing up.

heetrab|ah/-tah/-enoo התרבה *v* multiplied; increased; (*pres* **meetrabeh;** *fut* **yeetrabeh**).

heetraboo|t/-yot התרבות *nf* multiplication; proliferation.

heetra|'em/-'amah/-'amtee התרעם *v* was sore; grumbled; (*pres* **meetra'em;** *fut* **yeetra'em**).

heetrag|el/-lah/-altee התרגל *v* got used to; (*pres* **meetragel;** *fut* **yeetragel**).

heetrag|esh/-shah/-ashtee התרגש *v* was moved; was excited; (*pres* **meetragesh;** *fut* **yeetragesh**).

heetrag|ez/-zah/-aztee התרגז *v* was angered; was excited; was irritated; (*pres* **meetragez;** *fut* **yeetragez**).

heetragloo|t/-yot התרגלות *nf* accustoming oneself; habituation.

heetragshoo|t/-yot התרגשות *nf* excitement; emotion.

heetragzoo|t/-yot התרגזות *nf* irritation; anger.

heetrak|ekh/-'khah/-akhtee התרכך *v* mellowed; softened; (*pres* **meetrakekh;** *fut* **yeetrakekh**).

heetrak|em/-mah/-amtee התרקם *v* took shape; (*pres* **meetrakem**; *fut* **yeetrakem**).

heetrak|ez/-zah/-aztee התרכז *v* centered; concentrated; (*pres* **meetrakez**; *fut* **yeetrakez**).

heetrakh|ek/-kah/-aktee התרחק *v* **1.** drew away; kept distance; **2.** became estranged; kept aloof; (*pres* **meetrakhek**; *fut* **yeetrakhek**).

heetrakh|esh/-shah/-ashtee התרחש *v* occurred; happened; took place; (*pres* **meetrakhesh**; *fut* **yeetrakhesh**).

heetrakh|ets/-atsah/-atstee התרחץ *v* washed oneself; bathed.

heetrakh|ev/-vah/-avtee התרחב *v* **1.** broadened; widened; dilated; **2.** expanded; (*pres* **meetrakhev**; *fut* **yeetrakhev**).

heetrakh'koo|t/-yot התרחקות *nf* estrangement; going far.

heetrakhshoo|t/-yot התרחשות *nf* occurrence; happening.

heetrakhtsoo|t/-yot התרחצות *nf* washing oneself; bathing.

heetrakhvoo|t/-yot התרחבות expansion; broadening.

heetrak'khoo|t/-yot התרככות *nf* softening.

heetrakmoo|t/-yot התרקמות *nf* formation.

heetrakzoo|t/-yot התרכזות *nf* concentration.

'eetran/-eem עטרן *nm* tar; (*pl+of:* **-ey**).

(le) heetra'ot! להתראות *interj* (greeting) So long! Goodbye! See you later!.

heetrap|e/-'ah/-etee התרפא *v* recovered; became cured; (*pres* **meetrape**; *fut* **yeetrape**).

heetrap|ek/-kah/-aktee התרפק *v* **1.** hugged; **2.** yearned; (*pres* **meetrapek**; *fut* **yeetrapek**).

heetrap|es/-sah/-astee התרפס *v* fawned; abased oneself; (*pres* **meetrapes**; *fut* **yeetrapes**).

heetra'oo|t/-yot התראות *nf* seeing one another.

heetrapkoo|t/-yot התרפקות *nf* **1.** holding close; hugging; **2.** [*colloq.*] clinging nostalgically.

heetrap'oo|t/-yot התרפאות *nf* curing; healing.

heetrapsoo|t/-yot התרפסות *nf* abasing oneself.

hetras|ek/-kah/-aktee התרסק *v* crashed; (*pres* **meetrasek**; *fut* **yeetrasek**).

heetraskoo|t/-yot התרסקות *nf* crashing; crash.

heetrash|el/-lah/-altee התרשל *v* neglected; was negligent; (*pres* **meetrashel**; *fut* **yeetrashel**).

heetrash|em/-mah/-amtee התרשם *v* was impressed; got the impression; (*pres* **meetrashem**; *fut* **yeetrashem**).

heetrashloo|t/-yot התרשלות *nf* negligence; laxity.

heetrashmoo|t/-yot התרשמות *nf* **1.** getting an impression; **2.** impression.

heetrat|e'akh (or: **-akh**)**/-'khah/-akhtee** התרתח *v* became furious; (*pres* **meetrate'akh**; *fut* **yeetrate'akh**).

heetrat|ev/-vah/-avtee התרטב *v* got wet; became wet; (*pres* **meetratev**; *fut* **yeetratev**).

heetratkhoo|t/-yot התרתחות *nf* boiling with rage.

heetratvoo|t/-yot התרטבות *nf* becoming wet; wetting (bed).

heetrav|e'akh/-khah/-akhtee התרווח *v* felt relief; was comfortable; (*pres* **meetrave'akh**; *fut* **yeetrave'akh**).

heetravr|ev/-evah/-avtee התרברב *v* bragged; showed off; (*pres* **meetravrev**; *fut* **yeetravrev**).

heetravrevoo|t/-yot התרברבות *nf* bragging; boasting.

heetr|ee'a'/-ee'ah/-a'tee התריע *v* protested; (*pres* **matree'a'**; *fut* **yatree'a'**).

heetr|ee'akh/-eekhah/-akhtee הטריח *v* bothered; annoyed; (*pres* **matree'akh**; *fut* **yatree'akh**).

heetr|eef/-fah/-aftee הטריף [*slang*] *v* drove mad; (*pres* **matreef**; *fut* **yatreef**).

heetr|eem/-eemah/-amtee התרים *v* collected contributions; raised funds; (*pres* **matreem**; *fut* **yatreem**).

heetr|ees/-sah/-astee התריס *v* disputed; protested against; (*pres* **matrees**; *fut* **yatrees**).

eetree|yot אטריות *nf pl* noodles; (*sing:* **-yah**).

heetro'a'oot התרועעות *nf* association; becoming friends.

heetro|'e'a'/-'a'ah/-'a'tee התרועע *v* made friends with; (*pres* **meetro'e'a'**; *fut* **yeetro'e'a'**).

heetrof|ef/-efah/-aftee התרופף *v* slackened; weakened; (*pres* **meetrofef**; *fut* **yeetrofef**).

heetrofefoo|t/-yot התרופפות *nf* weakening.

heetrok|en/-nah/-antee התרוקן *v* became empty; (*pres* **meetroken**; *fut* **yeetroken**).

heetroknoo|t/-yot התרוקנות *nf* emptying; becoming empty.

heetrom|em/-emah/-amtee התרומם *v* **1.** rose; raised oneself; **2.** [*slang*] (of male) had homosexual intercourse; **3.** [*slang*] (of female) was easy to get (sexually); (*pres* **meetromem**; *fut* **yeetromem**).

heetromemoo|t/-yot התרוממות **1.** rising; **2.** exaltation.

heetrosh|esh/-eshah/-ashtee התרושש *v* was impoverished; (*pres* **meetroshesh**; *fut* **yeetroshesh**).

heetrosheshoo|t/-yot התרוששות *nf* impoverishment; pauperization.

heetrots|ets/-etsah/-atstee התרוצץ *v* run about; rushed around; (*pres* **meetrotsets**; *fut* **yeetrotsets**).

heetrotsetsoo|t/-yot התרוצצות *nf* rushing around; running about.

heetsamdoo|t/-yot היצמדות *nf* clinging.

heetsaroo|t/-yot היצרות *nf* **1.** constriction; narrowing; **2.** stenosis (medic.).

heetsb|ee'a'/-ee'ah/-a'tee הצביע *v* voted; pointed at; (*pres* **matsbee'a'**; *fut* **yatsbee'a'**).

heetsd|ee'a'/-ee'ah/-a'tee הצדיע *v* saluted; (*pres* **matsdee'a'**; *fut* **yatsdee'a'**).

heetsd|eek/-eekah/-aktee הצדיק *v* justified; approved; (*pres* **matsdeek**; *fut* **yatsdeek**).

heets|ee'a'/-ee'ah/-a'tee הציע *v* proposed; suggested; (*pres* **matsee'a'**; *fut* **yatsee'a'**).

heets|eeg/-eegah/-agtee הציג *v* placed; presented; (*pres* **matseeg**; *fut* **yatseeg**).

heets|eel/-eelah/-altee הציל *v* saved; rescued; (*pres* **matseel;** *fut* **yatseel).**

heet's|ees/-eesah/-astee התסיס *v* **1.** fomented; agitated; **2.** caused to ferment; (*pres* **mat'sees;** *fut* **yat'sees).**

heets|eet/-eetah/-atee הצית *v* set fire to; ignited; (*pres* **heetseet;** *fut* **yatseet).**

heetseev/-eevah/-avtee הציב *v* placed; put in position; (*pres* **matseev;** *fut* **yatseev).**

'eets|ev/-vah/-avtee עיצב *v* moulded; shaped; designed; (*pres* **me'atsev;** *fut* **ye'atsev).**

heets'|heev/-heevah/-havtee הצהיב *v* became yellow; yellowed; (*pres* **mats'heev;** *fut* **yats'heev).**

heets'|heer/-heerah/-hartee הצהיר *v* declared; stated; (*pres* **mats'heer;** *fut* **yats'heer).**

heetskh|eek/-eekah/-aktee הצחיק *v* made laugh; caused to laugh; (*pres* **matskheek;** *fut* **yatskheek).**

heetsl|ee'akh/-eekhah/-akhtee הצליח *v* succeeded; (*pres* **matslee'akh;** *fut* **yatslee'akh).**

heetsl|eef/-eefah/-aftee הצליף *v* sniped; whipped; (*pres* **matsleef;** *fut* **yatsleef).**

heetsm|eed/-eedah/-adetee הצמיד *v* attached; linked; (*pres* **matsmeed;** *fut* **yatsmeed).**

heetsm|ee'akh/-eekhah/-akhtee הצמיח *v* made grow; (*pres* **matsmee'akh;** *fut* **yatsmee'akh).**

heetsn|ee'a'/-ee'ah/-a'tee הצניע *v* hid; concealed; (*pres* **matsnee'a';** *fut* **yatsnee'a').**

heetsnee'a' (*etc*) **lekhet** הצניע לכת *v* behaved modestly.

heetsn|ee'akh/-eekhah/-akhtee הצניח *v* parachuted; (*pres* **matsnee'akh;** *fut* **yatsnee'akh).**

◇ **'eetsoom|eem** עיצומים *nm pl* **1.** sanctions; **2.** various forms of slow-down strikes intended to coerce employer to give in to demands (*pl+of:* **-ey).**

(be) 'eetsoom|o/-ah בעיצומו *adv* at its utmost.

(be) 'eetsoom|o/-ah shel בעיצומו של *adv* at the top of.

'eetsoor/-eem עיצור *nm* consonant; (*pl+of:* **-ey).**

'eetsoov/-eem עיצוב *nm* fashioning; shaping; (*pl+of:* **-ey).**

(be) 'eetsoov|o/-ah shel בעיצובו/־ה של *adj nmf* fashioned by ...

heetsr|eekh/-eekhah/-akhtee הצריך *v* required; necessitated; (*pres* **matsreekh;** *fut* **yatsreekh).**

heets'ta'ats|a'/-'ah/-a'tee (*or:* **heets'ta'ats|e'a'** *etc*) הצטעצע *v* toyed with; preened oneself; (*pres* **meetst'atse'a';** *fut* **yeetsta'atse'a').**

heets'ta'ats'oo|t/-yot הצטעצעות *nf* toying with.

eets'tab|ah/-a'ot אצטבה *nf* shelf; (*+of:* **-at).**

heets'taber/-rah/-arnoo הצטבר *v* piled up; accrued; (*pres* **meets'taber;** *fut* **yeets'taber).**

heets'tabroo|t/-yot הצטברות *nf* accummulation.

heets'tadek/-kah/-aktee הצטדק *v* apologized; excused oneself; justified oneself; (*pres* **meets'tadek;** *fut* **yeets'tadek).**

heets'tadkoo|t/-yot הצטדקות *nf* apology; excuse.

eets'tadyon/-eem אצטדיון *nm* stadium; (*pl+of:* **-ey).**

heets'ta|'er/-'arah/-'artee הצטער *v* felt sorry; regretted; (*pres* **meets'ta'er;** *fut* **yeets'ta'er).**

heets'ta'aroo|t/-yot הצטערות *nf* regret; feeling sorry.

heets'takh|ek/-kah/-aktee הצטחק *v* smiled; (*pres* **meets'takhek;** *fut* **yeets'takhek).**

heets'takhkoo|t/-yot הצטחקות *nf* smile; laughter.

eets'tal|ah/-ot/- אצטלה *nf* disguise; pretense; title (undeserved).

heets'tal|ek/-kah/-aktee הצטלק *v* became scarred; cicatrized; (*pres* **meets'talek;** *fut* **yeets'talek).**

heets'tal|em/-mah/-amtee הצטלם *v* was photographed; had (one's) picture taken; (*pres* **meets'talem;** *fut* **yeets'talem).**

heets'tal|ev/-vah/-avtee הצטלב *v* **1.** crossed; **2.** made the sign of the cross; (*pres* **meets'talev;** *fut* **yeets'talev).**

heets'talkoo|t/-yot הצטלקות *nf* cicatrization; scar formation.

heets'talmoo|t/-yot הצטלמות *nf* having one's picture taken; being photographed.

heets'talts|el/-elah/-altee הצטלצל *[colloq.] v* phoned one another; rang; (*pres* **meets'taltsel;** *fut* **yeets'taltsel).**

heets'taltseloo|t/-yot הצטלצלות *[colloq.] nf* phoning one another; ringing.

heets'talvoo|t/-yot הצטלבות *nf* **1.** crossing; intersection; **2.** making sign of the cross.

~**heets'tam|ek/-kah/-aktee** הצטמק *v* shrunk; shrivelled; was dried up; (*pres* **meets'tamek;** *fut* **yeets'tamek).**

heets'tamkoo|t/-yot הצטמקות *nf* shrinking.

heets'tamts|em/-emah/-amtee הצטמצם *v* confined oneself to; was reduced to; (*pres* **meets'tamtsem;** *fut* **yeets'tamtsem).**

heets'tamtsemoo|t/-yot הצטמצמות *nf* limitation; restriction.

heets'tan|e'a'/-'ah/-a'tee (*or:* **heets'tan|a'** *etc*) הצטנע *v* tried to be modest; (*pres* **meets'tane'a';** *fut* **yeets'tane'a').**

heets'tan|en/-enah/-antee הצטנן *v* caught a cold; chilled; (*pres* **meets'tanen;** *fut* **yeets'tanen).**

heets'tanenoo|t/-yot הצטננות *nf* **1.** catching cold; **2.** cooling down.

heets'tan'oo|t/-yot הצטנעות *nf* trying to be modest.

heets'tar|ef/-fah/-aftee הצטרף *v* **1.** joined; adhered; **2.** made-up; (*pres* **meets'taref;** *fut* **yeets'taref).**

heets'tar|ekh/-khah/-akhtee הצטרך *v* needed; (*pres* **meets'tarekh;** *fut* **yeets'tarekh).**

heets'tarfoo|t/-yot הצטרפות *nf* joining; siding with.
heets'tarkhoo|t/-yot הצטרכות *nf* needing; requiring.
heets'taydoo|t/-yot הצטיידות *nf* preparing oneself; equipping oneself.
heets'ta|yed/-ydah/-yadetee הצטייד *v* equipped oneself; (*pres* **meets'tayed**; *fut* **yeets'tayed**).
heets'ta|yen/-ynah/-yantee הצטיין *v* excelled; distinguished oneself; (*pres* **meets'tayen**; *fut* **yeets'tayen**).
heets'ta|yer/-yrah/-yartee הצטייר *v* was pictured; was conceived; (*pres* **meets'tayer**; *fut* **yeets'tayer**).
heets'taynoo|t/-yot הצטיינות *nf* distinction; excellence.
(be) heets'taynoot בהצטיינות *adv* with honors.
(ot/-ot) heets'taynoot אות הצטיינות *nm* medal; decoration.
(te'ood|at/-ot) heets'taynoot תעודת הצטיינות *nf* certificate of merit.
heets'tayroo|t/-yot הצטיירות *nf* image; being conceived; impression.
heets'tof|ef/-efah/-aftee הצטופף *v* crowded in; huddled together; (*pres* **meets'tofef**; *fut* **yeets'tofef**).
heets'tofefoo|t/-yot הצטופפות *nf* crowding; overcrowding; congestion.
heetv|ah/-etah/-etee התווה *v* sketched; marked; (*pres* **matveh**; *fut* **yatveh**).
heetvad|ah/-etah/-etee התוודה *v* confessed; (*pres* **meetvadeh**; *fut* **yeetvadeh**).
heetvad|a'/-'ah/-a'tee התוודע *v* became acquainted; introduced oneself; (*pres* **meetvada'**; *fut* **yeetvada'**).
heetvade'oo|t/-yot התוודעות *nf* making acquaintance.
heetvadoo|t/-yot התוודות *nf* confessing.
heetvak|akh (or **heetvak|e'akh**)/-'**khah/-akhtee** התווכח *v* argued; debated; (*pres* **meetvake'akh**; *fut* **yeetvake'akh**).
heetvak'khoo|t/-yot התווכחות *nf* arguing; disputing.
heet'ya'atsoo|t/-yot התייעצות *nf* consultation; conferring.
heet'yab|esh/-shah/-ashtee התייבש *v* dried up; was parched; (*pres* **meet'yabesh**; *fut* **yeet'yabesh**).
heet'yabshoo|t/-yot התייבשות *nf* drying up; withering.
heet'yad|ed/-edah/-adetee התיידד *v* befriended; got friendly; (*pres* **meet'yaded**; *fut* **yeet'yaded**).
heet'yadedoo|t/-yot התיידדות *nf* becoming friendly; making friends; fraternization.
heet'ya'ashoo|t/-yot התייאשות *nf* despairing.
heet'ya|'esh/-'ashah/-'ashtee התייאש *v* despaired; (*pres* **meet'ya'esh**; *fut* **yeet'ya'esh**).
heet'ya|'ets/-'atsah/-'atstee התייעץ *v* consulted; (*pres* **meet'ya'ets**; *fut* **yeet'ya'ets**).
heet'yahadoo|t/-yot התייהדות *nf* conversion to Judaism.
heet'ya|hed/-hadah/-hadetee התייהד *v* became a Jew; (*pres* **meet'yahed**; *fut* **yeet'yahed**).
heet'yak|er/-rah/-artee התייקר *v* went up (in price); became more expensive; (*pres* **meet'yaker**; *fut* **yeet'yaker**).
heet'yakhadoo|t/-yot התייחדות *nf* meeting in private; tête-á-tête.
heet'yakhadoot 'eem zeekhr|o/-ah shel התייחדות עם זיכרו של *nf* recalling the memory of (him/her).
heet'yakhamoo|t/-yot התייחמות *nf* rutting; having a period of sexual excitement.
heet'yakh|ed/-dah/-adetee התייחד *v* met in privacy; was alone with; (*pres* **meet'yakhed**; *fut* **yeet'yakhed**).
heet'yakh|em/-amah/-amtee התייחם *v* rutted; had a period of sexual excitement; (*pres* **meet'yakhem**; *fut* **yeet'yakhem**).
heet'yakh|es/-sah/-astee התייחס *v* treated; referred to; (*pres* **meet'yakhes**; *fut* **yeet'yakhes**).
heet'yakhsoo|t/-yot התייחסות *nf* reference; relation; treatment.
heet'yakroo|t/-yot התייקרות *nf* rise in price.
heet'yam|er/-rah/-artee התיימר *v* pretended; claimed; presumed; (*pres* **meet'yamer**; *fut* **yeet'yamer**).
heet'yamroo|t/-yot התיימרות *nf* pretentiousness; pretension.
heet'yap|ah/-tah/-etee התייפה *v* beautified oneself; dolled oneself up; (*pres* **meet'yapeh**; *fut* **yeet'yapeh**).
heet'yap|akh (or **heet'yap|e'akh**)/-'**khah/-akhtee** התייפח *v* cried bitterly; sobbed; (*pres* **meet'yape'akh**; *fut* **yeet'yape'akh**).
heet'yap'khoo|t/-yot התייפחות *nf* sobbing; wailing.
heet'yas|er/-rah/-artee התייסר *v* tormented oneself; (*pres* **meet'yaser**; *fut* **yeet'yaser**).
heet'yash|en/-nah/-antee התיישן *v* became obsolete; was outdated; (*pres* **meet'yashen**; *fut* **yeet'yashen**).
heet'yash|er/-rah/-artee התיישר *v* straightened out/up; (*pres* **meet'yasher**; *fut* **yeet'yasher**).
heet'yash|ev/-vah/-avtee התיישב *v* **1.** sat down; **2.** settled down; (*pres* **meet'yashev**; *fut* **yeet'yashev**).
heet'yashnoo|t/-yot התיישנות *nf* obsolescence.
(khok ha) heet'yashnoot חוק ההתיישנות *nf* law/statute of limitation.
heet'yashroo|t/-yot התיישרות *nf* straightening.
heet'yashvoo|t/-yot התיישבות *nf* settlement; settling on land.
heet'yashvoot khakla'eet התיישבות חקלאית *nf* agricultural settlement.
◇ **(ha)eet'yashvoot ha-'ovedet** see ◇ **(ha)heet'yashvoot ha-'ovedet**.
heet'yasroo|t/-yot התייסרות *nf* being chastened; torment.

heet'yat|em/-mah/-amtee התייתם *v* was orphaned; (*pres* **meet'yatem;** *fut* **yeet'yatem**).

heet'yatmoo|t/-yot התייתמות *nf* orphanhood; becoming an orphan.

heet'yats|ev/-vah/-avtee התייצב *v* reported; became stabilized; took a stand; (*pres* **meet'yatsev;** *fut* **yeet'yatsev**).

heet'yatsvoo|t/-yot התייצבות *nf* **1.** reporting for duty; **2.** stabilization.

eev|ah/-tah/-eetee איווה *v* wished; (*pres* **me'aveh;** *fut* **ye'aveh**).

'eev|ah/-tah/-etee עיווה *v* twisted; distorted; (*pres* **me'aveh;** *fut* **ye'aveh**).

heev|ah/-tah/-eetee היווה *v* constituted; consisted; formed; (*pres* **mehaveh;** *fut* **yehaveh**).

'eev|aron עיוורון *nm* blindness; (*+of:* **-ron**).

heevatsroo|t/-yot היווצרות *nf* formation.

heevd|eel/-eelah/-altee הבדיל *v* discerned; separated; (*pres* **mavdeel;** *fut* **yavdeel**).

heev'eer/-'eerah/-'artee הבעיר *v* set fire; (*pres* **mav'eer;** *fut* **yav'eer**).

heev|'eesh/-'eeshah/-'ashtee הבאיש *v* caused to stink; stank; (*pres* **mav'eesh;** *fut* **yav'eesh**).

heev'eesh (*etc*) **re'akh** הבאיש ריח *v* gave a bad name.

eevelet איוולת *nf* folly; stupidity; (his/her folly: **eevalt|o/-ah**).

heev|en/-nah/-antee היוון *v* capitalized (finance); (*pres* **mehaven;** *fut* **yehaven**).

'eev|er/-eret עיוור *nmf & adj* blind; (*pl:* **-reem/-rot**).

'eever/-et ts'va'eem עיוור צבעים *adj* color-blind.

'eev|et/-tah/-atetee עיוות *v* distorted; perverted; corrupted; (*pres* **me'avet;** *fut* **ye'avet**).

heev'|heek/-heekah/-haktee הבהיק *v* glittered; flashed; (*pres* **mav'heek;** *fut* **yav'heek**).

heev'|heel/-heelah/-haltee הבהיל *v* **1.** scared; **2.** alarmed; rushed; (*pres* **mav'heel;** *fut* **yav'heel**).

heev'|heer/-heerah/-hartee הבהיר *v* clarified; made it clear; (*pres* **mav'heer;** *fut* **yav'heer**).

heev'|hev/-havah/-havtee הבהב *v* flickered; (*pres* **mehav'hev;** *fut* **yehav'hev**).

heevk|ee'a'/-ee'ah/-a'tee הבקיע *v* broke through; (*pres* **mavkee'a';** *fut* **yavkee'a'**).

heevkh|een/-eenah/-antee הבחין *v* noticed; discerned; distinguished; (*pres* **mavkheen;** *fut* **yavkheen**).

heevl|ee'a'/-ee'a'h/-a'tee הבליע *v* skipped; concealed; (*pres* **mavlee'a';** *fut* **yavlee'a'**).

heevl|eeg/-eegah/-agtee הבליג *v* repressed one's feelings; exercised restraint; (*pres* **mavleeg;** *fut* **yavleeg**).

heevl|eet/-eetah/-atetee הבליט *v* emphasized; made conspicuous; (*pres* **mavleet;** *fut* **yavleet**).

heevoon/-eem היוון *nm* capitalization.

'eevoot/-eem עיוות *nm* distortion; iniquity; (*pl+of:* **-tey**).

'eevoot/-ey deen עיוות־דין *nm* miscarriage of justice.

◇ **'eevooteem** עיוותים *nm pl* **1.** distortions; **2.** iniquities (in labor or pay conditions).

'eevree/-t עברי *adj* Hebrew.

'eevree/-yah עברי *nmf* Hebrew; (*pl:* **-m**).

(ketav) 'eevree כתב עברי *nm* Hebrew script.

(noosakh) 'eevree נוסח עברי *nm* Hebrew version.

(deeboor) 'eevree דיבור עברי *nm* Hebrew speech; speaking Hebrew.

(teergoom) 'eevree תרגום עברי *nm* Hebrew translation.

heevr|ee/-ee'ah/-etee הבריא *v* **1.** recuperated; **2.** [*colloq.*] put on weight; (*pres* **mavree;** *fut* **yavree**).

heevr|ee'akh/-eekhah/-akhtee הבריח *v* **1.** drove off; **2.** smuggled; (*pres* **mavree'akh;** *fut* **yavree'akh**).

heevr|eeg/-eegah/-agtee הבריג *v* screwed in; threaded; (*pres* **mavreeg;** *fut* **yavreeg**).

heevr|eek/-eekah/-aktee הבריק *v* **1.** shone; **2.** polished; **3.** cabled; (*pres* **mavreek;** *fut* **yavreek**).

heevreek (*etc*) **ra'yon** הבריק רעיון *v* an idea dawned/flashed into one's mind.

heevr|eesh/-eeshah/-ashtee הבריש *v* brushed; (*pres* **mavreesh;** *fut* **yavreesh**).

'eevreet עברית *nf* Hebrew (the language).

(dab|er/-ree) 'eevreet! ! דבר עברית *v imp m/f sing* speak Hebrew!

(dover/-et) 'eevreet דובר עברית **1.** *adj* Hebrew-speaking; **2.** *nmf* Hebrew-speaker (*pl:* **dovr|ey/-ot** *etc*).

'eevret/-etah/-atetee עברת *v* Hebraicized; (*pres* **me'avret;** *fut* **ye'avret**).

'eevron ts'va'eem עיוורון צבעים *m* color-blindness; Daltonism.

eevroor איוורור *nm* ventilation; airing.

'eevroot עברות *nf* Hebraization; giving a Hebrew form to.

eevsh|ah/-ot אוושה *nf* murmur (*+of:* **-at**).

heevsh|eel/-eelah/-altee הבשיל *v* ripened; (*pres* **mavsheel;** *fut* **yavsheel**).

eevt|e'akh/-ekhah/-akhtee אבטח *v* protected; secured; (*pres* **me'avte'akh;** *fut* **ye'avte'akh**).

heevtee'akh/-ekhah/-akhtee הבטיח *v* **1.** promised; **2.** assured; (*pres* **mavtee'akh;** *fut* **yavtee'akh**).

eevtoo|'akh/-kheem איבטוח *nm* protection; securing; (*pl+of:* **-khey**).

heevz|eek/-eekah/-aktee הבזיק *v* flashed; (*pres* **mavzeek;** *fut* **yavzeek**).

ee|yem/-yemah/-yamtee איים *v* threatened; (*pres* **me'ayem;** *fut* **ye'ayem**).

eeyeem איים *nm pl* islands; (*sing:* see; *pl+of:* **eeyey**).

'ee|yen/-ynah/-yantee עיין *v* studied; read; reflected; (*pres* **me'ayen;** *fut* **ye'ayen**).

◇ **eeyar** אייר "Iyar", the 8th month of the Jewish Calendar; (29 days; approx. April-May).

eey|esh/-eshah/-ashtee אייש *v* manned; (*pres* **me'ayesh;** *fut* **ye'ayesh**).

'eeyey khoravot (*sing* **'ee** *etc*) עיי חרבות *nm pl* heaps of ruins.

'eeyey mapolet (*sing* **'ee** *etc*) עיי מפולת *nm pl* debris.

eeyoom/-eem איום *nm* threat; (*pl+of:* **-ey**).

(be-lakhats) eeyoomeemבלחץ איומים *adv* under pressure of threats; being intimidated.

eeyoom/-ey srak איום סרק *nm* empty threat.

'eeyoon/-eem עיון *nm* study; perusal; (*pl+of:* **-ey**).

(matsreekh/-ah) 'eeyoon מצריך עיון **1.** *adj* needing consideration; **2.** *v pres* needs consideration; (*pst* **heetsreekh** *etc; fut* **yatsreekh** *etc*).

'eeyoon me-khadash עיון מחדש *nf* re-consideration.

(mekhayev/-et) 'eeyoon me-khadash מחייב עיון מחדש *v pres* requires re-consideration; (*pst* **kheeyev** *etc; fut* **yekhayev** *etc*).

(yom/yemey) 'eeyoon יום עיון *nm* day-long study session.

'eeyoonee/-t עיוני *adj* theoretical; speculative.

eeyoor/-eem איור *nm* illustration; (*pl+of:* **-ey**).

'eeyoor עיור *nm* urbanization.

eeyoosh/-eem איוש *nm* manning (of staff, equipment *etc*); (*pl+of:* **-ey**).

eeyoot/-eem איות *nm* **1.** lettering; **2.** spelling; (*pl+of:* **-ey**).

'eez|avon/-vonot עיזבון *nm* legacy; estate; inheritance; (*+of:* **-von**).

(mena|hel/haley) 'eezavon מנהל עיזבון *nm* executor; administrator (of an estate).

heezda'az|a' (or: **heezda'az|e'a'**)/**-'ah/-a'tee** הזדעזע *v* was shocked, moved; (*pres* **meezda'aze'a'**; *fut* **yeeezda'aze'a'**).

heezda'az'oo|t (*npr* **heezda'z'oo|t**)/**-yot** הזדעזעות *nf* shock; shaking.

heezda|hah/-hatah/-hetee הזדהה *v* identified oneself; (*pres* **meezdaheh**; *fut* **yeezdaheh**).

heezdahamoo|t/-yot הזדהמות *v* infection.

heezda|hem/-hamah/-hamtee הזדהם *v* became infected; (*pres* **meezdahem**; *fut* **yeezdahem**).

heezdahoo|t/-yot הזדהות *nf* identification.

heezdak|ef/-fah/-aftee הזדקף *v* stood up; stood upright; (*pres* **meezdakef**; *fut* **yeezdakef**).

heezdak|en/-nah/-antee הזדקן *v* aged; grew old; (*pres* **meezdaken**; *fut* **yeezdaken**).

heezdak|ek/-ekah/-aktee הזדקק *v* needed; resorted to; (*pres* **meezdakek**; *fut* **yeezdakek**).

heezdak|ekh/-'khah/-akhtee הזדכך *v* was purified; (*pres* **meezdakekh**; *fut* **yeezdakekh**).

heezdakekhoot הזדככות *nf* purification.

heezdakekoot הזדקקות *nf* having to resort to.

heezdak|er/-rah/-artee הזדקר *v* stalled; stood out; (*pres* **meezdaker**; *fut* **yeezdaker**).

heezdakfoot הזדקפות *nf* **1.** standing upright; back stretching; **2.** erection.

heezdaknoot הזדקנות *nf* aging; growing old.

heezdakroo|t/-yot הזדקרות *nf* sticking out.

heezdam|en/-nah/-antee הזדמן *v* happened to be; occurred; (*pres* **meezdamen**; *fut* **yeezdamen**).

heezdamnoo|t/-yot הזדמנות *nf* occasion; opportunity.

(be) heezdamnoot בהזדמנות *adv* occasionally; on the occasion of.

(be-khol) heezdamnootבכל הזדמנות *adv* on every (possible) occasion.

(hekhm|eets/-eetsah/-atstee) heezdamnoot החמיץ הזדמנות *v* missed an opportunity.

(neets|el/-lah/-altee) heezdamnoot ניצל הזדמנות *v* grasped the opportunity.

heezdan|ev/-vah/-avtee הזדנב *v* trailed behind; (*pres* **meezdanev**; *fut* **yeezdanev**).

heezdang|ef/-evah/-aftee הזדנגף *v* *[slang]* went for a stroll on Tel-Aviv's popular and fashionable Dizengoff Street; (*pres* **meezdangef**; *fut* **yeezdangef**).

heezdanvoo|t/-yot הזדנבות *nf* trailing behind.

heezdar|ez/-zah/-aztee הזדרז *v* hurried; hastened; (*pres* **meezdarez**; *fut* **yeezdarez**).

heezdarzoot הזדרזות *nf* haste; hurry.

heezdav|eg/-gah/-agtee הזדווג *v* mated; copulated; (*pres* **meezdaveg**; *fut* **yeezdaveg**).

heezdavgoo|t/-yot הזדווגות *nf* mating; copulation.

heezday|en/-nah/-antee הזדיין *v* **1.** armed oneself; **2.** *[slang]* "screwed"; copulated; (*pres* **meezdayen**; *fut* **yeezdayen**).

heezdaynoo|t/-yot הזדיינות *nf* **1.** arming; armament; **2.** *[slang]* having sexual intercourse.

heezda'z|e'a'/-'ah/-a'tee (*npr* **heezda'az|e'a'** *etc*) הזדעזע *v* was shocked, moved; (*pres* **meezda'ze'a'**; *fut* **yeeezda'aze'a'**).

heezda'z'oo|t/-yot הזדעזעות *nf* shock; shaking.

heez|ee'a'/-ee'ah/-a'tee (*npr* **hez|ee'a**) הזיע *v* sweated; (*pres* **mezee'a'**; *fut* **yazee'a'**).

heez|eek/-eekah/-aktee הזיק *v* harmed; damaged; (*pres* **mazeek**; *fut* **yazeek**).

heez|eel/-eelah/-altee הזיל *v* dripped; shed; (*pres* **mazeeel**; *fut* **yazeel**).

heezeel (*etc*) **deem'ah/dema'ot** הזיל דמעה *v* shed a tear/tears.

heez|'eek/-'eekah/-'aktee הזעיק *v* alerted; (*pres* **maz'eek**; *fut* **yaz'eek**).

eez|en/-nah/-antee איזן *v* balanced; (*pres* **me'azen**; *fut* **ye'azen**).

heez'|heer/-heerah/-hartee הזהיר *v* warned; cautioned; (*pres* **maz'heer**; *fut* **yaz'heer**).

heezk|een/-eenah/-antee הזקין *v* aged; grew old; (*pres* **mazkeen**; *fut* **yazkeen**).

heezkeer/-eerah/-artee הזכיר *v* reminded; (*pres* **mazkeer**; *fut* **yazkeer**).

eezkoor/-eem אזכור *nm* reference; reminder; (*pl+of:* **-ey**).

eezmeel/-eem (*npr* **eezmel**) אזמל *nm* blade; lancet; chisel: (*pl+of:* **-ey**).

heezm|een/-eenah/-antee הזמין *v* **1.** invited; **2.** ordered; (*pres* **mazmeen**; *fut* **yazmeen**).

eezmel/-eem אזמל *nm* blade; lancet; scalpel; chisel; (*pl+of:* **-ey**).

heezn|ee'akh/-eekhah/-akhtee הזניח *v* neglected; (*pres* **maznee'akh;** *fut* **yaznee'akh**).

eezoon/-eem איזון *nm* balance; balancing; (*pl+of:* **-ey**).

heezoon/-eem היזון *nm* feeding: (*pl+of:* **-ey**).

heezoon/-eem khoz|er/-reem היזון חוזר *nm* feedback.

heezr|eek/-eekah/-aktee הזריק *v* injected; (*pres* **mazreek;** *fut* **yazreek**).

heezr|eem/-eemah/-amtee הזרים *v* poured in; caused to flow; channelled; (*pres* **mazreem;** *fut* **yazreem**).

F.

transliterating the Hebrew consonant
Feh (פ or ף)

NOTE: There are almost no pure Hebrew words that begin with the letter F. The phonetics of the classical language allow this sound only in the middle or at the end of a word or compound. In the "pointed" script a dot in the middle of the letter פ indicates its pronunciation as **p** rather than **f**. Many words of foreign origin that begin with פ reading as **f** experience a change of the **f to p** (פּ) in normative Hebrew pronunciation (e.g. *philosophy* becomes **peelosofeeyah**). Many words which in their basic form begin with **p**, when preceded by prefixes, change that sound to **f**. In such cases, the user is made aware of it by the addition, mostly in brackets, of *f=p*. Other words beginning with **f** are of diverse European origin, or slang expressions from Arabic, Yiddish or Ladino.

At the end of a word, פ has a special form (ף) called **Final Feh** (פ"ה סופית) and is always undotted and pronounced **f**. In a few words ending in **p**, however, all for foreign origin, (like e.g. **preentseep**, meaning principle), the פ remains unaltered and pronounced **p** as in the language it had been taken from (Russian).

(meedey) fa'am (*f=p*) מדי פעם *adv* every now and then.

(mee-pa'am le) fa'am (*f=p*) מפעם לפעם *adv* from time to time.

(le) fakhot (*f=p*) לפחות *adv* at least.

fakool|tah/-ot פקולטה *nf* faculty; (*+of:* **-at**).

falkhah פלחה *nf* cultivation of field crops.

fanatee/-t פנטי *adj* fanatical.

fanateeyoot פנטיות *nf* fanaticism.

(le) faneem (*f=p*) לפנים **1.** *adv* formerly; once; **2.** *adv* in front; (see **paneem**).

fantas|yah/-yot פנטסיה *nf* fantasy.

fantastee/-t פנטסטי *adj* fantastic.

fantazeeyah פנטזיה *[colloq.]nf* colorful open-air celebration in Bedouin style.

(be) far'hesyah בפרהסיה *adv* publicly; openly.

fasfoos/-eem פספוס *nm [slang]* baby; tot.

(be) fashtoot בפשטות *adv* plainly; simply; unpretentiously; (*f=p*, see **pashtoot**).

fasoolyah פסוליה *nf [slang]* beans.

◇ **"FATAKH"** (**"Fatakh"**) פת"ח *nm* PLO — main anti-Israel Arab terrorist body (*acr of* the name "Palestine Liberation Organization" in Arabic).

fashl|ah/-ot פאשלה *nf [slang]* misdeed or omission likely to bring shame.

feelosof/-eet פילוסוף *nmf* philosopher; student of philosophy.

feelosofee/-t פילוסופי *adj* philosophical.

feelosofee|yah/-yot פילוסופיה *nf* philosophy: (*+of:* **-yat**).

feenansee/-t פיננסי *adj* financial.

feenanseem פיננסים *nm pl* finance.

feerg|en/-enah/-antee פירגן *v [slang]* did not begrudge; (*pres* **mefargen;** *fut* **yefargen**).

(lo) feergen (*etc*) לא פירגן *v [slang]* begrudged.

feerm|ah/-ot פירמה *nf* firm; business; (*+of:* **-at**).

(lo le-vayesh et ha) feermah לא לבייש את הפירמה *[slang] v* not to do anything unworthy of one's name, standing, family *etc*; (*pst* **lo beeyesh** *etc;* *pres* **eyno mevayesh** *etc;* *fut* **lo yevayesh** *etc*).

feesee/-t פיסי *adj* physical.

feeseekah פיסיקה *nf* physics.

feeseeka'ee/-t פיסיקאי *nmf* physicist.

feeseekalee/-t פיסיקלי *adj* physical; of physics.

feesee'olog/-eet פיסיולוג *nmf* physiologist.

feesee'ologee/t פיסיולוגי *adj* physiological.

feesee'oterapeest/-eet פיסיותירפיסט *nmf* physiotherapist.

feesee'oterapeeyah פיסיותירפיה *nf* physiotherapy.

feesh|el/-lah/-altee פישל *v [slang]* failed; did it the wrong way; (*pres* **mefashel**; *fut* **yefashel**).

feeskalee/-t פיסקלי *adj* fiscal.

feestook/-eem פיסטוק *nm* peanut; pistachio nut.

feezee/-t פיזי *adj* physical.

feezeekah פיזיקה *nf* physics.

feezeeka'ee/-t פיזיקאי *nmf* physicist.

feezeekalee/-t פיזיקלי *adj* physical; of physics.

feezee'olog/-eet פיזיולוג *nmf* physiologist.

feezyologee/t פיזיולוגי *adj* physiological.

feezyoterapeest/-eet פיזיותירפיסט *nmf* physiotherapist.

feezyoterapeeyah פיזיותירפיה *nf* physiotherapy.

(be) feh male *(f=p)* בפה מלא *adv* expressly.

(bee) fekoodat *(f=p)* בפקודת *adv* by order of.

(lee) fekoodat *(f=p)* לפקודת *adv* at the order of.

(hafle va) fele *(f=p)* הפלא ופלא *interj* how wonderful!

felyeton/-eem פליטון *nm* feuilleton; column (in a newspaper).

(bee) feneem *(f=p)* בפנים *adv* inside.

(lee) feneem mee-shoorat ha-deen *(f=p)* לפנים משורת הדין *adv* beyond the strict letter of the law.

(mee-bee) feneem *(f=p)* מבפנים *adv* from the inside.

(bee) feney *(f=p)* בפני *adv* in the presence of; against.

(bee) feney 'atsmo/-ah *(f=p)* בפני עצמו/־ה *adv* by itself/oneself.

(mee-lee) feney *(f=p)* מלפני *adv* from; from before.

fe'odalee/-t פיאודלי *adj* feudal.

festeeval/-eem פסטיבל *nm* **1.** festival; **2.** (*figurat.*) much ado.

(le) feta' *(f=p)* לפתע *adv* all of a sudden.

(le) feta' *(f=p)* &&**peet'om** לפתע פתאום *adv* suddenly.

(sar|ad/-dah/-adetee lee) fleytah *(f=p)* שרד לפליטה *v* survived; (*pres* **sored**; *fut* **yeesrod**).

Fey פ"ה *nf* consonant פ (**Peh**) pronounced *f* when unpointed.

feyr/-eet פייר *adj [slang]* fair; just.

(be) feyroosh *(f=p)* בפירוש *adv* explicitly.

(bee) fkoodat *(f=p)* בפקודת *adv* by order of.

(lee) fkoodat *(f=p)* לפקודת *adv* at the order of.

flanel פלנל *nm* flannel.

(bee) fleeleem *(f=p)* בפלילים *adv* on trial for a criminal offense.

flegmatee/-t פלגמטי *adj* phlegmatic.

(bee) fneem *(f=p)* בפנים *adv* inside.

(lee) fneem mee-shoorat ha-deen *(f=p)* לפנים משורת הדין *adv* beyond the strict letter of the law.

(mee-bee) fneem *(f=p)* מבפנים *adv* from the inside.

(bee) fney *(f=p)* בפני *adv* in the presence of; against .

(bee) fney 'atsmo/-ah *(f=p)* בפני עצמו/־ה *adv* by itself/oneself.

(mee-lee) fney *(f=p)* מלפני *adv* from; from before.

(be) fo'al *(f=p)* בפועל **1.** *adv* actually; **2.** *adj* acting.

folklor פולקלור *nm* folklore.

fonetee/-t פונטי *adj* phonetic.

foneteekah פונטיקה *nf* phonetics.

(be) foombee (*or:* **be-foombey**; *f=p*) בפומבי *adv* publicly.

fooy! (*or:* **fooyah!**) פוי! פויה! *[slang] interj* exclamation denoting disgust.

fosfat/-eem פוספט *nm* phosphate.

foto-retsakh פוטו־רצח *nm [slang]* picture taken by an automatic camera ("Photomaton").

fotogenee/-t פוטוגני *adj* photogenic.

foonktsee|yah/-yot פונקציה *nf* function; (*+of:* **-yat**).

foonktseeyonalee/-t פונקציונלי *adj* functional.

□ **Fooreydees** (Fureidis) פרדיס *nm* large Arab village (est. 1880), on Hadera-Haifa highway, 2 km N. of **Zeekhron Ya'akov**. Pop. 6,740.

(bee) frat *(f=p)* בפרט *adv* especially; (see **prat**).

(lee) frakeem *(f=p)* לפרקים *adv* at times .

frayer/-eet פראייר *[slang] nmf* sucker.

frenk/-eet פרנק *[slang] nmf* sometimes derogatory reference to a Jew's Sephardi or Afro-Asian origin or background: (*pl:* **-eem/-eeyot**).

"Frenk-Parekh" פרנק־פארך *[slang] nm* derogatory nickname for Jew of Sephardi or Afro-Asian background.

(bee) frotrot בפרוטרוט *adv* in detail; (*f=p*, see **protrot**).

(bee) fros בפרוס *adv* on the eve of.

G.

transliterating the Hebrew consonant **Geemel** (ג)

NOTE: In this dictionary **g** is to be pronounced as in *go*, *garb*, *guy*, *get* or *geese* and never as in *gist* or *gem*.

ga'/ge'ee גע *v imp sing m/f* touch! (*inf* **laga'at**; *pst* **naga'**; *pres* **noge'a'**; *fut* **yeega'**).

ga|'ah/-atah/-'oo גאה *v* rose (tide, flow); mounted; (*pres* **go'eh**; *fut* **yeeg'eh**).

ga|'ah/-'atah/-'eetee געה *v* ailed; cried bitterly; (*pres* **go'eh**; *fut* **yeeg'eh**).

ga'agoo|'eem (*npr* **ga'goo'eem**) געגועים *nm pl* longings; yearnings; (*sing:* **ga'goo|'a**; *pl+of:* **-'ey**).

ga'al/-ah/-tee גאל *v* redeemed; (*pres* **go'el**; *fut* **yeeg'al**).

ga'ar/-ah/-tee גער *v* scolded; (*pres* **go'er**; *fut* **yeeg'ar**).

ga'ash/-ah/-tee געש *v* raged; quivered; (*pres* **go'esh**; *fut* **yeeg'ash**).

□ **Ga'ash (Ga'ash)** געש *nm* kibbutz (est. 1951) in Sharon, 10 km S. of Netanya, on the Tel-Aviv-Haifa road (Expressway 2). Pop. 538.

(har/ey) ga'ash הר געש *nm* volcano.

(al) ga'at! !אל געת *v imp* don't touch! (*pst* **naga'**; *pres* **noge'a**; *fut* **yeega'**).

(la) ga'at לגעת *v inf* to touch; touching; (*pst* **naga'**; *pres* **noge'a**; *fut* **yeega'**).

ga'av|ah/-ot גאווה *nf* pride; conceit; (*+of:* **-at**).

gab|ah/-ot גבה *nf* eyebrow; (*+of:* **-at**).

gab|ay/-a'eem גבאי *nm* treasurer of a religious institution; (*pl+of:* **-a'ey**).

(le) gab|ay/-ekha/-ayeekh/-av/-eha /לגביי־יך ־ייך *adv & poss. pron* **1.** towards me/you (*m/f*)/him/her *etc*; **2.** as far as I/you (*m/f*)/he/she etc is/are concerned.

('al) gabey על גבי *adv* on; upon; on top of.

(le) gabey לגבי *adv* regarding; about.

gabot גבות *nf pl* eyebrows; (*sing:* **gabah**).

gad|ah/-ot גדה *nf* river bank; (*+of:* **-at**).

□ **"(ha)gadah"** הגדה *nf* "the bank" - colloq. reference to the West Bank (of Jordan river); Judea and Samaria.

(beesh) gada ביש־גדא *nm & adj* clumsy; unlucky person; ne'er do well.

gad|al/-lah/-altee גדל *v* grew; increased; (*pres* **gadel**; *fut* **yeegdal**).

gadal (*etc*) **pere'** גדל פרא *v* grew wild.

gadol/gedolah גדול *adj* **1.** large; big; **2.** great; grand.

(ha-khofesh ha) gadol החופש הגדול *nm* summer (school) vacation.

◇ **(shabat ha) gadol** see ◇ **shabat ha-gadol**.

□ **Gadeesh** (Gadish) גדיש *nm* village (est. 1956) 6 km SW of **'Afoolah**. Pop. 235.

gader/gederot גדר *nf* fence; (*+of:* **geder/geedrot**).

gader khayah גדר חיה *nf* hedge.

"Gadna'" גדנ"ע *nm* premilitary youth groups; (*acr of* **Gedoodey No'ar**).

gadoosh/gedooshah גדוש *adj* congested; packed.

□ **Gadot** גדות *nm* kibbutz (est 1949) in S. part of Huleh (**Khoolah**) Valley. Pop. 433.

gafroor/-eem גפרור *nm* match.

gag/-ot גג *nm* roof; top.

gag/-ot azbest גג אסבסט *nm* asbestos-covered roof.

gag/-ot re'afeem גג רעפים *nm* tile roof.

('alee|yat/-yot) gag עליית גג *nf* attic.

(korat) gag קורת גג *nf* roof over one's head.

gagon/-eem גגון *nm* awning; roof rack; (*pl+of:* **-ey**).

ga'goo|'eem געגועים *nm pl* longings; yearnings; (*sing:* **ga'goo'a**; *pl+of:* **-'ey**).

gakhan/-ah/-tee גחן *v* leaned; inclined; (*pres* **gokhen**; *fut* **yeeg'khon**).

gakhelet/gekhaleem גחלת *nf* glowing coal.

gakhleelee|t/-yot גחלילית *nf* firefly.

gal/-eem גל *nm* **1.** wave; **2.** shaft; **3.** leap; (*pl+of:* **-ey**).

gal (*etc*) **ha-arkoobah** גל הארכובה *nm* crankshaft (motor-car).

gal|ah/-tah/-eetee גלה *v* went in exile; (*pres* **goleh**; *fut* **yeegleh**).

gal|ash/-shah/-ashtee גלש *v* run over; glided down; (*pres* **golesh**; *fut* **yeeglosh**).

gala|y/-'eem גלאי *nm* detector (electr.) (*pl+of:* **-'ey**).

□ **Gal'ed** (Gal'ed) גלעד *nm* kibbutz (est. 1945) in **Ramat Menasheh** region, 4 km S. of kibbutz Daliyya (**Dalyah**). Pop. 329.

galee/-t גלי *adj* undulating; wavy.

galeel/gleel|eem גליל *nm* **1.** cylinder; **2.** province; (*+of:* **-ey**).

(ha) galeel הגליל *nm* Galilee.

(ha) galeel (ha)'elyon הגליל העליון *nm* Upper Galilee.

(ha) galeel (ha)takhton הגליל התחתון *nm* Lower Galilee.

◇ **(meelkhemet shlom ha) galeel** see ◇ **meelkhemet shlom ha-galeel**.

(shov|er/-rey) galeem שובר גלים *nm* breakwater.

galeree|yah/-yot גלריה gallery (*+of:* **-at**).

◇ **galey tsahal ("Galey Zahal")** גלי צה"ל *m pl* Radio station operated by the Israel Army. Broadcasts round the clock entertainment, news and cultural information destined for enlisted personnel and their families but aimed equally at the general public.

galgal/-eem גלגל *nm* wheel; (*pl+of:* **-ey**).

galgal khameeshee גלגל חמישי *nm* a "fifth wheel" i.e. something entirely superfluous.
galgal/-ey kheeloots גלגל חילוץ *nm* spare wheel.
galgal khozer גלגל חוזר *nm* wheel of fortune.
galmood/-ah גלמוד *adj* solitary; lonely.
□ **Gal'on** גלאון *nm* kibbutz (est. 1946) in **Lakheesh** district, 7 km NE of Qiryat-Gat **(Keeryat-Gat)**. Pop. 418.
galoo|t/-yot גלות *nf* exile; Diaspora.
galootee/-t גלותי *adj* ghetto-like (of one's behaviour, manners or frame of mind).
galooy/glooyah גלוי *adj* overt; public.
◊ **galooyot** גלויות *nf pl* Jewish concentrations throughout the Diaspora.
◊ **(keeboots) galooyot** see ◊ **keeboots galooyot.**
◊ **(meezoog) galooyot** see ◊ **meezoog galooyot.**
galshan/-eet גלשן *nm* skier (*pl:* **-eem**; *+of:* **-ey**).
galshan/-ey roo'akh גלשן רוח *nm* air glider; hang glider.
gam גם *conj* also; too; even.
gam eem גם אם *conj* even if.
gam ken גם כן *conj* also.
gam|a/-'ah/-a'tee גמא *v* sipped; gulped; (*pres* **gome**; *fut* **yeegma**).
gamad/-ah גמד *adj* dwarflike; small of stature.
gamad/-eem גמד *nm* dwarf (*pl+of:* **-ey**).
gamal/gemal|eem גמל n camel; (*pl+of:* **-ey**).
gam|al/-lah/-altee גמל *v* reciprocated; retaliated; (*pres* **gomel**; *fut* **yeegmol**).
gam|ar/-rah/-artee גמר *v* finished; terminated; concluded (*pres* **gomer**; *fut* **yeegmor**).
gamar (*etc*) **et ha-halel** גמר את ההלל *v* had nothing but praise.
gameesh/-ah גמיש *adj* flexible; elastic.
□ **Gamla** גמלא *nf* remnants of ancient Jewish fortress in Golan Heights, site of bitter Judean resistance to Roman rule in the year 68. The excavations and restoration there are in progress 8 km S. of Ramot.
gamlah (ha)hakhlatah גמלה ההחלטה *nf* the decision has been reached.
gamoor/gemoorah גמור *adj* finished; complete; absolute.
(manooy ve) gamoor מנוי וגמור *adv* decidedly final; definitely decided.
(neemnoo ve) gamroo נמנו וגמרו *v pst pl* (they) reached a decision.
gan/-eem גן *nm* garden; (*pl+of:* **ey**).
(meseeb|at/-ot) gan מסיבת גן *nf* garden-party.
(sook|at/-ot) gan סוכת גן *nf* garden hut.
gan-'eden גן־עדן *nm* Garden of Eden; paradise.
(ta'am) gan-'eden טעם גן־עדן *nm* heavenly taste.
□ **Gan ha-Darom** גן הדרום *nm* village (est. 1953) on the Mediterranean Coast, 5 km W. of Ashdod. Pop. 328.
gan ha-'eer גן העיר *nm* city park; public garden.
□ **Gan ha-Shloshah** גן השלושה *nm* popular camping and recreation park (also known as **"Sakhneh"**) in Bet-She'an Valley, located around picturesque natural pond at the foot of Mount Geelbo'a.
□ **Gan ha-Shomron** גן השומרון *nm* village (est 1934) in W. Shomron, 3 km SW of 'Iron Junction **(Tsomet 'Eeron)**. Pop 414.
□ **Gan Khayeem** (Gan Hayyim) גן חיים *nm* village (est. 1935) in Sharon region, N. of Kefar-Sava. Pop. 310.
gan/-ey khayot גן חיות *nm* zoo.
◊ **gan/-ey khovah** גן חובה *nm* state-financed kindergarten, compulsory for children 5 years old.
◊ **gan/-eem pratee/-yeem** גן פרטי *nm* privately owned nursery school (for 3-4-year-olds).
□ **Gan Shelomo** גן שלמה *nm* kibbutz (est. 1927), 4 km S. of Rehovot **(Rekhovot)**. Pop. 403.
□ **Gan Shemoo'el** (Gan Shemu'el) גן שמואל *nm* kibbutz (est. 1921), 3 km E. of Hadera **(Khaderah)**. Pop. 1,070.
□ **Gan Shomron** see □ **Gan ha-Shomron.**
◊ **gan trom-khovah** גן טרום חובה *nm* nursery school for four-year-olds (non-compulsory).
◊ **gan trom-trom-khovah** גן טרום־טרום חובה *nm* nursery school for 2-3-year-olds (non-compulsory).
gan/-ey yarak גן ירק *nm* vegetable garden.
□ **Gan Yavneh** (Gan Yavne) גן יבנה *nm* urban settlement in the S. part of the Coastal plain, 41 km SE of Ashdod. Pop. 3,410.
gan/-ey yeladeem גן ילדים *nm* kindergarten.
□ **Gan Yosheeyah** (Gan Yoshiyya) גן יאשיה *nm* village (est. 1949) on borderline between Sharon and Shomron areas, 11 km NW of Arab town Tulkarm **(Toolkarem)**. Pop. 312.
gan|akh/-khah/-akhtee גנח *v* groaned; (*pres* **gone'akh**; *fut* **yeegnakh**).
gan|av/-vah/-avtee גנב *v* stole; (*pres* **gonev**; *fut* **yeegnov**).
gan|av/-aveem גנב *nm* thief; (*pl+of:* **-vey**).
gananoot גננות *nf* gardening.
ganan/-eem גנן *nm* gardener; (*pl+of:* **-ey**).
gan|az/-zah/-aztee גנז *v* hid; concealed; stored (*pres* **gonez**; *fut* **yeegnoz**).
gandran/-eet גנדרן *adj* dandy; coquettish.
gandranoot גנדרנות *nf* overdressing; ostentation.
□ **Gane'am** (Ganné'am) גני עם *nm* village in Sharon (est. 1934), S. of Hod ha-Sharon. Pop. 215.
gan|enet/-anot גננת *nf* kindergarten teacher (female).
gan|evet/-avot גנב *nm* thief (female).
□ **Ganey Tal** (Ganné Tal) גני טל *nm* village in Gaza Strip (est. 1979), 2 km N. of **Khan Yoones**. Pop. 350.
□ **Ganey Teekvah** (Ganné Tiqwa) גני תקוה *nf* urban settlement (est. 1953), 2 km S. of **Petakh-Teekvah**. Pop. 8,990.

□ **Ganey Yehoodah** (Ganné Yehuda) גני יהודה *nm* village (est. 1950), 4 km S. of **Petakh-Teekvah**, bordering on Tel-Aviv's posh residential suburb Savyon. Pop. 775.

□ **Ganey Yokhanan** (Ganné Yohanan) גני יוחנן *nm* village (est. 1950), 4 km SE of Rehovot. Pop. 310.

ganon/-eem גנון *nm* day nursery (for 2-3-year-olds).

□ **Ganot** (Gannot) גנות *nm* village (est. 1950) outside Tel-Aviv, next to Ganot Junction **(Tsomet Ganot)** on Expressway 1 (Tel-Aviv—Jerusalem). Pop. 380.

□ **Ganot Hadar** (Gannot Hadar) גנות הדר *nm* village (est. 1954), 3 km E. of Netanya. Pop. 76.

ganooz/gnoozah גנוז *adj* hidden; concealed.

ganza|kh/-keem גנזך *nm* archives; **(***pl+of:* **-key)**.

ga'on/ge'oneem גאון *nm* **1.** genius **2.** great rabbinical scholar; **(***+of:* **ge'on/-ey)**.

gapayeem גפיים *nm pl* limbs **(***sing:* **gaf;** *pl+of:* **gapey;** *p=f***)**.

(be) gap|o/-ah/-ee/-khah בגפו/־ה/־י/־ך *adv* alone; single; by him/her/my/your-self.

gar/-ah/-tee גר *v* resided; **(***pres* **gar;** *fut* **yagoor)**.

gar|a'/-'ah/-a'tee גרע *v* reduced; lessened; deducted; **(***pres* **gore'a;** *fut* **yeegra')**.

gar|af/-fah/-aftee גרף *v* swept; shovelled; **(***pres* **goref;** *fut* **yeegrof)**.

garaf (*etc*) **hon** גרף הון *v* made lots of money.

gar|am/-mah/-amtee גרם *v* caused; **(***pres* **gorem;** *fut* **yeegrom)**.

gar|ar/-erah/-artee גרר *v* **1.** dragged, towed; **2.** involved; **(***pres* **gorer;** *fut* **yeegror)**.

gar|as/-sah/-astee גרס *v* maintained; held opinion; **(***pres* **gores;** *fut* **yeegros)**.

garbayeem גרביים *nm pl* stockings; socks **(***sing:* **gerev;** *pl+of:* **garbey)**.

garbey meshee גרבי משי *nm pl* silk stockings.

garbey naylon גרבי ניילון *nm pl* nylon stockings.

garderobah גרדרובה *nf [colloq.]* wardrobe.

gardom/-eem גרדום *nm* scaffold; **(***pl+of:* **-ey)**.

◇ **('oley ha) gardom** see ◇ **'oley ha-gardom**.

garedet גרדת *nf* scabies (medic.).

gar'een/-eem גרעין *nm* kernel; nucleus; **(***pl+of:* **-ey)**.

◇ **gar'een** (*etc*) **heet'yashvoot'ee** גרעין התישבותי *nm* organized group of prospective settlers.

◇ **gar'een** (*etc*) **meyashev** גרעין מיישב *v* kernel of a settlement to be.

(mada'ey ha) gar'een מדעי הגרעין *nm pl* nuclear sciences.

gar'eenee/-t גרעיני *adj* nuclear.

gar'enet גרענת *nf* trachoma (medic.).

gargeer/-eem גרגיר *nm* grain; berry **(***pl+of:* **-ey)**.

gargeran/-eet גרגרן *nmf* glutton.

garg|eret/-arot גרגרת *nf* windpipe; throat.

garon/gronot גרון *nm* throat.

garoo'a/groo'ah גרוע *adj* bad; terrible.

garoo'a (*etc*) **meen/mee-** גרוע מן/מ־ *adj* worse than.

garoosh/grooshah גרוש *nmf* (also *adj*) divorced man/woman; **(***pl:* **-eem/-ot)**.

garzen/-eem גרזן *nm* hatchet; axe **(***pl+of:* **-ey)**.

gas/-ah גס *adj* coarse; vulgar; rude.

gas/-at roo'akh גס־רוח *nmf & adj* vulgar; ill-mannered.

gas|as/-esah/-astee גסס *v* agonized; was about to die; **(***pres* **goses;** *fut* **yeegsos)**.

gash!/geshee! גש! *v imp m/f sing* come here! go up! **(***inf* **lageshet;** *pst & pres* **neegash;** *fut* **yeegash)**.

gashash/-eem גשש *nm* tracker; **(***pl+of:* **-ey)**.

◇ **"(ha)gashasheem"** הגששים *[colloq.] nm pl* reference to wisecracks and excerpts made popular by one of Israel's well-known comic teams.

gashoom/geshomah גשום *adj* rainy.

(mezeg-aveer) gashoom מזג אוויר גשום *nm* rainy weather.

gasoo|t/-yot גסות *nf* rudeness; bad manners.

gasoot roo'akh גסות רוח *nf* vulgarity; rudeness.

gat גת *nf* winepress.

□ **Gat** גת *nm* kibbutz (est. 1942) 2 km N. of Keeryat-Gat (Qiryat-Gat). Pop. 539.

□ **(Keeryat) Gat** see □ **Keeryat Gat**.

gav/gabeem גב *nm* back; hind-part; **(***pl+of:* **gabey)**.

gav ha-har גב ההר *nm* hillock.

('al) gav על גב *prep* on; on top of; upon.

(dekeerah ba) gav דקירה בגב *nf* a stab in the back.

(sekheeyat) gav שחיית גב *nf* backstroke swimming.

(tarmeel/-ey) gav תרמיל גב *nm* rucksack; pack.

gav|ah/-hah/-ahtee גבה *v* grew tall **(***pres* **gavoha;** *fut* **yeegbah;** *(b=v)***)**.

gav|ah/-tah/-eetee גבה *v* collected; **(***pres* **goveh;** *fut* **yeegbeh;** *(b=v)***)**.

gavah (*etc*) **'edoo|t/-yot** גבה עדות *v* took evidence.

gavah (*etc*) **kes|ef/-afeem** גבה כסף *v* collected money.

gavah (*etc*) **khov/-ot** גבה חוב *v* collected debt.

gavah (*etc*) **mas/meeseem** גבה מס *v* collected tax.

gav|a'/-'ah/-a'tee גווע *v* expired; died; pined away; **(***pres* **gove'a;** *fut* **yeegva')**.

gav|a' (*etc*) **ba-ra'av** גווע ברעב *v* starved; was dying of hunger.

gav|al/-lah/-altee גבל *v* bordered; **(***pres* **govel;** *fut* **yeegbol;** *(b=v)***)**.

gavan/gevaneem גוון *nm* color; nuance; tinge; **(***+of:* **gon/-ey)**.

gav|ar/-rah/-artee גבר *v* overpowered; defeated; **(***pres* **gover;** *fut* **yeegbor;** *(b=v)***)**.

gavee'a/gevee'eem גביע *nm* cup; bowl; **(***+of:* **gevee|'a/-'ey)**.

gaveesh גביש *nm* crystal; **(***+of:* **gveesh/-ey)**.

gavnoon/-eem גבנון *nm* hunch; peak; **(***pl+of:* **-ey)**.

gavo'ah/gevo|hah גבוה *adj* tall; high (*pl:* **-heem/-hot**).

('al 'akev/-eem) gavo'ah/gevoheem על עקב גבוה *adv* on high heels.

(khom) gavoha חום גבוה *nm* high fever.

(pakeed/pekeedeem) gavo'ah/gevoheem פקיד גבוה *nm* senior official.

gavra raba גברא רבא (Aramaic) *nm* important person; big shot.

(kheeloofey) gavra חילופי גברא *nm pl* reshuffle; change of personnel (one person).

(ko'akh) gavra כוח גברא *nm* potency; virility.

gavree/-t גברי *adj* manly; manlike.

gavreeyoot גבריות *nf* virility; masculinity.

(kheeloofey) gavrey חילופי גברי *nm pl* reshuffle; change of personnel.

□ **Ga'ton** (Ga'ton) געתון *nm* kibbutz (est. 1940), 10 km E. of Nahariyya. Pop. 429.

gay/ge'ayot גיא *nm* valley; ravine; (*+of:* **gey**).

gayees/geysot גיס *nm* army corps; masses of troops.

gayees khameeshee גיס חמישי *nm* Fifth Column.

gaz/-eem גז *nm* gas; (*pl+of:* **-ey**).

gaz beeshool גז בישול *nm* cooking gas.

gaz khardal גז חרדל *nm* mustard gas.

gaz kheemoom גז חימום *nm* heating gas

gaz madmee'a' גז מדמיע *nm* tear-gas.

gaz/-eem ra'eel/re'eeleem גז רעיל *nm* poison gas.

(masekh|at/-ot) gaz מסיכת גז *nf* gas mask.

(matseet/metseetey) gaz מצית גז *nm* gas lighter.

gaz|al/-lah/-altee גזל *v* robbed; (*pres* **gozel**; *fut* **yeegzol**).

gaz|am/-mah/-amtee גזם *v* trimmed; (*pres* **gozem**; *fut* **yeegzom**).

gaz|ar/-rah/-artee גזר *v* cut; clipped; (*pres* **gozer**; *fut* **yeegzor**).

gazar (*etc*) **'al** גזר על *v* prohibited; forbade.

gaz|az/-ezah/-aztee גזז *v* sheared; fleeced; (*pres* **gozez**; *fut* **yeegzoz**).

gazeet גזית *nf* hewn stone.

□ **Gazeet** (Gazit) גזית *nm* kibbutz (est. 1947) in Yizre'el Valley, 5 km S. of Kefar Tavor. Pop. 630.

(even/avney) gazeet אבן גזית *nf* hewn stone block.

gazlan/-eem גזלן *nm* robber; bandit; (*pl+of:* **-ey**).

gazoz/-eem גזוז *nf* carbonated drink.

□ **Ge'ah** (Ge'a) גיאה *nm* village (est. 1949), 5 km SE of Ashkelon. Pop. 458.

□ **Ge'alyah** (Ge'alya) גאליה *nm* village (est. 1948) in Coastal Plain, 3 km W. of Rehovot (**Rekhovot**). Pop. 422.

ge'ar|ah/-ot גערה *nf* rebuke; reproof; (*+of:* **ga'r|at/-ot**).

ged|ee/-ayeem גדי *nm* kid; young goat; (*pl+of:* **-ayey**).

□ **Gederah** (Gedéra) גדרה *nf* urban township (founded in 1884 as an agricultural settlement by the "Bilu"-pioneers), 8 km SW of Rehovot. Pop. 7,780.

gedood/-eem גדוד *nm* battalion; detachment; (*pl+of:* **-ey**).

gedoodee/-t גדודי *adj* regimental.

gedool|ah גדולה *nf* greatness; (*+of:* **-at**).

gedolot גדולות *nf* great things; big deeds.

gedolot oo-netsoorot גדולות ונצורות *nm pl* tremendous things; marvels.

(heel|ekh/-khah/-akhtee bee) g'dolot הילך בגדולות *v* saw big; aspired to great things; (*pres* **mehalekh** *etc*; *fut* **yehalekh** *etc*).

ge'eh/ge'ah גאה *adj* proud; haughty.

geeben/-et גיבן *m/f & adj* hunchback.

geeb|esh/-shah/-ashtee גיבש *v* **1.** worked out; **2.** crystallized; (*pres* **megabesh**; *fut* **yegabesh**).

geeb|ev/-evah/-avtee גיבב *v* heaped; piled up; (*pres* **megabev**; *fut* **yagabev**).

geeboosh/-eem גיבוש *nm* consolidation; (*pl+of:* **-ey**).

geeboov/-eem גיבוב *nm* conglomeration; piling up; (*pl+of:* **-ey**).

geeboov devareem גיבוב דברים *nm* verbosity; verbiage.

geeboo|y/-yeem גיבוי *nm* backing; (*pl+of:* **-yey**).

geebor/-ah גיבור **1.** *nmf* hero; **2.** *adj* heroic.

□ **Geebton** (Gibbeton) גבתון *nm* suburb (est. 1933) of Rehovot (**Rekhovot**). Pop. 208.

geed|el/-lah/-altee גידל *v* reared; brought up; raised; (*pres* **megadel**; *fut* **yagadel**).

geedem/-et גידם *nmf & adj* one-armed.

□ **Geed'onah** (Gid'ona) גדעונה *nm* village (est. 1940) in Yizre'el Valley, on slope of Mount **Geelbo'a**. Pop. 119.

geedoofeem גידופים *nm pl* abuses; revilements; (*sing:* **geedoof**; *pl+of:* **-ey**).

geedool/-eem גידול *nm* growth; growing; (*pl+of:* **-ey**).

geedool/-eem mam'eer/-eem גידול ממאיר *nm* malignant tumor.

geedool 'ofot גידול עופות *nm* poultry farming.

geedool yeladeem גידול ילדים *nm* raising children.

geedool yerakot גידול ירקות *nm* growing vegetables.

geedool|eem גידולים *nm pl* crops; (*pl+of:* **-ey**).

geedoor/-eem גידור *nm* field fencing.

(yats|a/-'ah/-atee mee) geedr|o/-ah/-ee יצא מגידרו *v* lost (his/her/my) temper; (*pres* **yotse** *etc*; *fut* **yetse** *etc*).

geefoof (*npr* **geepoof**)**/-eem** גיפוף *nm* hugging; (*pl+of:* **-ey**).

geegee|t/-yot גיגית *nf* pail.

gee|hets/-hatsah/-hatstee גיהץ *nm* ironed; pressed; (*pres* **megahets**; *fut* **yegahets**).

geehoots/-eem גיהוץ *nm* ironing; pressing; (*pl+of:* **-ey**).

geekh|ah/-ot גיחה *nf* sortie; sudden onslaught; (*+of:* **-at**).

geekh|ekh/-akhah/-akhtee גיחך *v* smiled; giggled; ridiculed; (*pres* **megakhekh;** *fut* **yegakhekh**).

geekhookh/-eem גיחוך *nm* **1.** giggle; **2.** absurdity; **3.** ridiculousness; (*pl+of:* **-ey**).

geel/-eem גיל *nm* age; (*pl+of:* **-ey**).

geel גיל *nm* joy.

geel ha-'ameedah גיל העמידה *nm* middle age.

(be) geel/-eem בגיל *adv* at an age; aged.

(ha) geel ha-rakh הגיל הרך *nm* tender age.

◇ **geel ha-preeshah** גיל הפרישה *nm* retirement age (65 in Israel, although women have the option to retire at 60).

geel|ah/-tah/-eetee גילה *v* revealed; discovered; (*pres* **megaleh;** *fut* **yegaleh**).

geelah גילה *nf* gladness; joy.

□ **Geelat** (Gilat) גילת *nm* village (est. 1949) in N. Negev, 3 km NE of **Ofakeem**. Pop. 573.

geel|a'ee (*npr* **-ay**)**/-a'eem** גילאי *nm* of same age-group with; peer; aged; (*pl+of:* **-a'ey**).

geel|ay/-a'eet גילאי *nmf* of same age-group with; peer; aged; (*pl+of:* **-a'ey**).

geel|ayon/-yonot גיליון *nm* sheet; copy (of newspaper or journal); (*+of:* **-yon**).

geel|e'akh/-khah/-akhtee (*or:* **geel|akh** *etc*) גילח *v* shaved; shaved off; (*pres* **megale'akh;** *fut* **yegale'akh**).

geel|ef/-fah/-aftee גילף *v* engraved; carved; whittled; (*pres* **megalef;** *fut* **yegalef**).

□ **Geelgal** (Gilgal) גלגל *nm* kibbutz (est. 1973) in Jordan Valley, 16 km N. of Jericho, on road to Bet She'an.

geelg|el/-elah/-altee גילגל *v* **1.** rolled; **2.** brought about; **3.** *[slang]* turned over; **4.** threw around (sums of money, financial business) (*pres* **megalgel;** *fut* **yegalgel**).

geelgool/-eem גלגול *nm* **1.** rolling; **2.** *[slang]* phase; facet.

geelgool nesham|ah/-ot גלגול נשמה *nm* reincarnation.

□ **Geelo** see □ **Har Geelo**.

geeloo|'akh/-kheem גילוח *nm* shaving; shave; (*pl+of:* **-khey**).

(makhsheer/-ey) geeloo'akh מכשיר גילוח *nm* razor; shaving instrument.

(mekhon|at/-ot) geeloo'akh מכונת גילוח *nm* razor; shaver.

(mekhon|at/-ot) geeloo'akh khashmal|eet/-yot מכונת גילוח חשמלית *nf* electric shaver.

(meesh'kh|at/-ot) geeloo'akh משחת גילוח *nf* shaving cream.

(meevresh|et/-ot) geeloo'akh מברשת גילוח *nf* shaving brush.

(sakeen/-ey) geeloo'akh סכין גילוח *nm* razor blade.

geeloof/-eem גילוף *nm* carving; etching; whittling; (*pl+of:* **-ey**).

(be) geeloofeen בגילופין *adv & adj* tipsy.

geeloom/-eem גילום *nm* **1.** embodiment; **2.** grossing (income).

◇ **geeloom hakhnasah** גילום הכנסה *nm [colloq.]* payment of employee's income-tax assumed by employer.

geeloo|y-yeem גילוי *nm* discovery; uncovering; (*pl+of:* **-yey**).

geeloo|y/-yey ahadah גילוי אהדה *nm* manifestation of sympathy.

geeloo|y/-yey 'arayot גילוי עריות *nm* incest.

geeloo|y/-yey da'at גילוי דעת *nm* manifesto; public statement.

geelooy lev גילוי לב *nm* frankness; openheartedness.

(be) geelooy lev בגילוי לב *adv* openheartedly.

(be) geelooy rosh בגילוי ראש *adv* bareheaded.

geelshon/-eem גילשון *nm* air glider; hang glider; (*pl+of:* **-ey**).

geelyon/-ot eeshoom גליון אישום *nm* charge list; charge sheet.

"Geemel" גימל *nm* (Gimmel) 3rd letter of Hebrew alphabet; corresponds to English consonant **g** (pronounced as in *gave* or *gone*, not as in *vigil* or *gesture*).

Geemel ג' **1.** *num* 3 (three) in Hebrew numerical system; **2.** *ord num* 3rd (third) in Hebrew numerical system.

(yom) geemel יום ג' *nm* Tuesday (i.e. third day of the week).

(yom) geemel be- יום ג' ב־ Jewish date: 3rd day of a Jewish Calendar month; three days in....

(yod) geemel י"ג **1.** *num* 13 in Hebrew numerical system; **2.** *ord. num* the 13th (thirteenth) in Hebrew numerical system.

geemg|em/-emah/-amtee גמגם *v* stammered; (*pres* **megamgem;** *fut* **yegamgem**).

geemgoom/-eem גמגום *nm* stammer; stutter; (*pl+of:* **-ey**).

geeml|ah/-ot גמלה *nf* pension; (*+of:* **-at**).

(par|ash/-shah/-ashtee le) geemla'ot פרש לגמלאות *v* retired; (*pres* **poresh** *etc;* *fut* **yeefrosh** *(f=p) etc*).

(yats|a/-'ah/-atee le) geemla'ot יצא לגמלאות *v* retired; was pensioned (*pres* **yotse** *etc;* *fut* **yetse** *etc*).

geeml|at/-ot beetoo'akh le'oomee גמלת ביטוח לאומי *nf* social security grant.

geeml|at/-ot nekhoot (*npr* **nakhoot**) גמלת נכות *nf* disability pension.

gemnas|yah/-yot גימנסיה *nf* high school; secondary school; (*+of:* **-yat**).

geemoor/-eem גימור *nm* finish (of a product).

□ **Geemzo** (Gimzo) גימזו *nm* village (est. 1950) in Coastal Plain, 6 km SE of Lod. Pop. 450.

(be) geen בגין *prep* on account of.

geen|ah/-tah/-eetee גינה *v* denounced; condemned; blamed; (*pres* **meganeh;** *fut* **yeganeh**).

geen|ah/-ot גינה *nf* small garden; courtyard; (*+of:* **-at**).

(toot/-ey ha) geenah תות הגינה *nm* strawberry.

geen|at/-ot noy גינת נוי *nf* ornamental garden.

geen|at/-ot yarak גינת ירק *nf* vegetable garden.

□ **Geenegar** (Ginnegar) גניגר *nm* kibbutz of the **Kevootsah** type (est. 1922) in Yizre'el Valley, 2 km SE of **Meegdal ha-'Emek**. Pop. 486.

□ **Geenaton** (Ginnaton) גנתון *nm* village (est. 1949), 1 km SE of Lod town. Pop. 381.

geenooneem גינונים *nm pl* manners; (*sing:* **geenoon**; *pl+of:* **-ey**).

geenooney srak גינוני סרק *nm* mannerism; mannerisms.

geenoo|y/-yeem גינוי *nm* denunciation; condemnation; (*pl+of:* **-yey**).

□ **Geenosar** (Ginnosar) גנוסר *nm* kibbutz (est. 1937) on NW shore of Lake Tiberias (**Keeneret**). Pop. 679.

geenza|kh (*npr* **ganza|kh**)**/-keem** גינזך *nm* archives; (*pl+of:* **-key**).

geepoof/-eem גיפוף *nm* hugging (*pl+of:* **-ey**)

geepoor/-eem גיפור *nm* vulcanization; (*pl+of:* **-ey**).

geer/-eem גיר *nm* chalk; lime; (*pl+of:* **-ey**).

geeree|t/-yot גירית *nf* badger.

gereet ha-dvash גירית הדבש *nf* honey badger.

geers|ah/-a'ot גרסה *nf* version; (*+of:* **-at**).

gees/-eem גיס *nm* brother-in-law; (*pl+of:* **-ey**).

gees|ah/-ot גיסה *nf* sister-in-law; (*pl+of:* **-at**).

(me-eedakh) geesa מאידך גיסא *conj* on the other hand.

geesh|ah/-ot גישה *nf* approach; attitude; (*+of:* **-at**).

geesh|er/-rah/-artee גישר *v* bridged; (*pres* **megasher**; *fut* **yegasher**).

geeshmey berakhah (*or:* **brakhah**) גשמי ברכה *nm pl* bountiful rains; (*sing:* **geshem** *etc*).

geeshmey za'af גשמי זעף *nm pl* torrential rains.

geeshoor/-eem גישור *nm* bridging (*pl+of:* **-ey**).

geeshoosh/-eem גישוש *nm* probing; groping; feelers; (*pl+of:* **-ey**).

(kalbey) geeshoosh (*or:* **kalvey** *etc*) כלבי גישוש *nm pl* bloodhounds; (*sing:* **kelev** *etc*).

geetar|ah/-ot גיטרה *nf* guitar; (*+of:* **-at**).

□ **Geeteet** (Gittit) גתית *nm* new settlement (est. 1975) on borderline between Samaria and Jordan Valley.

geev'ah/geva'ot גבעה *nf* hill; (*+of:* **geev|'at/-'ot**).

□ **Geev'at 'Adah** (Giv'at 'Ada) גבעת עדה *nm* village (est. 1903), 8 km SE of **Zeekhron Ya'akov**. Pop. 1,310.

□ **Geev'at Brener** (Giv'at Brenner) גבעת ברנר *nm* kibbutz (est. 1928) on **Ramlah-Gederah** road, 2 km of **Tsomet Beeloo** (Bilu Junction). Pop. 1330.

□ **Geev'at Elah** (Giv'at Ela) גבעת אלה *nm* communal village in Lower Galilee (est. 1988), 5 km N. of **Meegdal ha-'Emek**. Pop. 877.

□ **Geev'at ha-Shloshah** (Giv'at Hashelosha) גבעת השלושה *nm* kibbutz (est. 1925), 2 km E. of **Petakh-Teekvah**. Pop. 440.

□ **Geev'at Khaveevah** (Giv'at Haviva) גבעת חביבה *nm* Central educational institute of kibbutzim affiliated with "**Hashomer Hatsa'eer**". 2 km S. of 'Iron Junction (**Tsomet 'Eeron**).

□ **Geev'at Khayeem Eekhood** (Giv'at Hayyim-Ihud) גבעת חיים איחוד *nm* kibbutz seceded in 1952 from kibbutz **Geev'at Khayeem** (est. 1932) located 5 km S. of **Khaderah** (Hadera) in order to pursue a more leftist political line of thought. The original rift subsided later and now both kibbutzim are affiliated with the "United Kibbutz Movement" (**TAKAM** *acr of* **ha-Tenoo'ah ha-Keebootseet ha-Me'ookhedet** התנועה הקיבוצית המאוחדת). Pop. 905.

□ **Geev'at Khayeem Me'ookhad** (Giv'at Hayyim-Me'uhad) גבעת חיים מאוחד *nm* the original kibbutz (est. 1932), now affiliated with the same "United Kibbutz Movement" (**TAKAM** *acr of* **ha-Tnoo'ah ha-Keebootseet ha-Me'ookhedet** התנועה הקיבוצית המאוחדת) as its twin-kibbutz **Geev'at Khayeem Eekhood** (גבעת חיים איחוד) that in 1952 had seceded from it. Both kibbutzim are 5 km S. of Hadera (**Khaderah**). Pop. 1,070.

□ **Geev'at Khen** (Giv'at Hen) גבעת חן *nm* village in the Sharon (est. 1933), S. of **Ra'ananah**. Pop. 288.

□ **Geev'at Ko'akh** (Giv'at Koah) גבעת כוח *nm* village (est. 1950), 5 km NE of Ben-Gurion Airport. Pop. 389.

□ **Geev'at Meekha'el** (Giv'at Micha'el) גבעת מיכאל *nm* educational institute run by the Jewish Agency, outside **Nes Tseeyonah** (Ness Ziona).

□ **Geev'at Napoleon** (Tel Djareesheh) גבעת נפוליון *nf* **1.** Ancient hill at the confluence of Ayalon brook and the Yarkon river, where borders of Tel-Aviv and Ramat Gan meet. Wrongly believed to have been erected artificially by Napoleon's army in 1799 as an elevation from which to shell Jaffa; **2.** hill near **'Ako** (Acre) with same name and similar story.

□ **Geev'at Neelee** (Giv'at Nili) גבעת נילי *nm* village (est. 1953), E. of **Zeekhron Ya'akov**. Pop. 251.

□ **Geev'at Olgah** (Giv'at Olga) גבעת אולגה *nm* Western suburb of Hadera (**Khaderah**) on the seashore, off Expressway 2, 2 km from the city.

□ **Geev'at 'Oz** (Giv'at 'Oz) גבעת עוז *nm* kibbutz (est. 1949) 2 km off Meggido Junction (**Tsomet Megeedo**), on road to Jenin (**Jeneen**). Pop. 488.

□ **Geev'at Ram** (Giv'at Ram) גבעת רם *nm* hilly sector of W. Jerusalem, beyond the Knesset, site of of the Israel Museum, the Stadium and the Hebrew University "in town" campus.

□ **Geev'at Shapeero** (Giv'at Shapiro) גבעת שפירא *nm* village (est. 1948), 4 km S. of Netanya. Pop. 109.

□ **Geev'at Shemesh** (Giv'at Shemesh) גבעת שמש *nm* educational institute for boys (est. 1954), 5 km NW of Bet Shemesh. Pop. (pupils and staff) 109.

□ **Geev'at Shmoo'el** (Giv'at Shemu'el) גבעת שמואל *nm* residential suburb (est. 1942) between **Beney-Brak** and **Petakh-Teekvah**, near Bar-Ilan **(Bar-Eelan** University, 1 km of Geha Junction **(Tsomet Geha)** Pop. 10,500.

□ **Geev'at Ye'areem** (Giv'at Ye'arim) גבעת יערים *nm* village in Judea hills (est. 1950) along road from **Tsova** to **Tsomet Sheemshon** (Shimshon Junction). Pop. 456.

□ **Geev'at Yesha'yahoo** (Giv'at Yesha'yahu) גבעת ישעיהו *nm* village in **'Adoolam** Region (est. 1958), 10 km S. of Bet Shemesh. Pop. 221.

□ **Geev'at Yo'av** (Giv'at Yo'av) גבעת יואב *nm* village (est. 1968) in Golan Heights, 5 km NE of **'Eyn-Gev**. Pop. 365.

□ **Geev'at Zayd** (Giv'at Zeid) גבעת זייד *nm* site of the impressive memorial to Alexander Zeid, pioneer-hero of Jewish self-defense in Palestine during the pre-mandate and mandate periods. Located on borderline between Yizre'el Valley and Lower Galilee.

□ **Geev'at Ze'ev** (Giv'at Ze'ev) גבעת זאב *nf* urban settlement (est. 1983) in Judean hills, 8 km SE of Ramallah. Pop. 4,780.

□ **Geev'atayeem** (Giv'atayim) גבעתיים *nf* residential town bordering on Tel-Aviv from the E., together with Ramat-Gan to its own N. and E.. Pop. 46,600.

□ **Geev'atee** (Giv'ati) גבעתי *nm* village (est. 1950), E. of Ashdod-Ashkelon road, 4 km W. of **Be'er Tooveeyah**. Pop. 438.

◇ **geev'atee** see ◇ **khateevat Geev'atee**.

geev|en/-nah/-antee גיוון *v* diversified; (*pres* **megaven**; *fut* **yegaven**).

geev'ol/-eem גבעול *nm* stalk; stem (*pl+of:* **-ey**).

□ **Geev'oleem** (Giv'olim) גבעולים *nm* village (est. 1952) in N. Negev. Pop. 232.

□ **Geev'on ha-Khadashah** (Giv'on Hahadasha) גבעון החדשה *nm* communal village in Judean Hills (est. 1980), 10 km NW of Jerusalem. Pop. 519.

geevoon/-eem גיוון *nm* tinging; tinting; (*pl+of:* **-ey**).

gee|yer/-yrah/-yartee גייר *v* converted to Judaism; (*pres* **megayer**; *fut* **yegayer**).

gee|yes/-ysah/-yastee גייס *v* mobilized; enlisted; (*pres* **megayes**; *fut* **yegayes**).

geeyoor/-eem גיור *nm* conversion to Judaism; (*pl+of:* **-ey**).

◇ **geeyoor ka-halakhah** גיור כהלכה *nm* conversion to Judaism performed in full accordance with strictly Orthodox Jewish religious law.

geeyoos/-eem גיוס *nm* mobilization; enlistment; (*pl+of:* **-ey**).

geeyoos kelalee גיוס כללי *nm* general mobilization.

geeyoos kesafeem גיוס כספים *nm* fund-raising.

geeyoos khovah גיוס חובה *nm* conscription.

(khay|av/-yevet) geeyoos חייב גיוס *nmf* conscript; subject to conscription.

(leeshkat/-ot ha) geeyoos לשכת הגיוס *nf* recruiting office.

(sarvan/-ey) geeyoos סרבן גיוס *nm* conscientious objector.

(tsav/-ey) geeyoos צו גיוס *nm* mobilization order; call-up.

geeyoret/-ot גיורת *nf* convert (female) to Judaism.

geezbar/-eet גזבר *nmf* treasurer.

geezbaroo|t/-yot גזברות *nf* treasury department.

geez'an/-eem גזען *nm* racist (*pl+of:* **-ey**).

geez'anee/-t גזעני *adj* racist.

geez'anoot גזענות *nf* racism.

geez'ee/-t גזעי *adj* **1.** thoroughbred; **2.** racial; 2. *[slang]* genuine; authentic.

geezrah/gezarot גיזרה *nf* **1.** shape; figure; waist; **2.** segment; sector; (*+of:* **geezr|at/-ot**).

gef|en/-aneem גפן *nf* vine; (*pl+of:* **gafney**).

(tsemer) gefen צמר גפן *nm* cotton; cotton-wool; absorbent cotton.

□ **Gefen** גפן *nm* village (est. 1955), 12 km E. of **Keeryat Mal'akhee**. Pop. 285.

geheenom גיהינום *nm* Hell.

geheenom 'aley adamot גיהינום עלי אדמות *nm* hell on earth.

gelem גלם *nm* crudeness; rawness.

(khom|er/-rey) gelem חומר גלם *nm* raw material.

(koop|at/-ot) gemel (*npr* **gemal**) קופת גמל *nf* provident fund.

gemar גמר *nm* end; finish; completion.

◇ **gemar khateemah tovah!** גמר חתימה טובה! **1.** well-wish used on the eve of and during **Yom Keepoor** (Day of Atonement); **2.** Lit.: "may the end (of the 10 days from Rosh Hashana to Yom Kippur) be a good seal (in the book of life for the year to come").

◇ **gemar tov!** גמר טוב! abbreviated version of above formula.

(khatsee ha) gemar חצי הגמר *nm* semi-final (sport).

(reva' ha) gemar רבע הגמר *nm* quarter-final (sport).

◇ **gemara** גמרא **1.** *nf* any volume (or study) of the **Talmood** (Talmud), the 2,000 year old corpus of Jewish canonical law; **2.** within the Talmud, that portion developed between ca 200 and 500 CE as a commentary on the Mishneh (see **meeshnah**).

gemeelah גמילה *nf* **1.** weaning; **2.** recovery treatment to cure addicts (alcohol, narcotics, smoking).

gemeeloot khasadeem גמילות חסדים *nf* doing good deeds; helping the needy.

gemeeloot khesed גמילות חסד *nf* interest-free short-term loan.

gemeeshoo|t/-yot גמישות *nf* elasticity; flexiblity.
gemer גמר *nm* end; finish; completion.
(bekheen|at/-ot) gemer בחינת גמר *nf* final exam; final examination.
(takhroo|t/-yot) gemer תחרות גמר *nf* final match; finals.
gemool/-eem גמול *nm* **1.** recompense; retribution; **2.** remuneration.
genay גנאי *nm* disgrace.
(lee) genay לגנאי *adv* to shame; notoriously.
geneez|ah/-ot גניזה *nf* storage; hiding; (*+of:* **-at**).
general/-eem גנרל *nm* general.
genev|ah/-ot גניבה *nf* theft; thievery; (*+of:* **-at**).
(bee) genevah בגניבה *adv* furtively; stealthily.
genevat da'at גניבת דעת *nf* deceit; trickery.
(bee) genoot בגנות *adv* in defamation of.
ge'ografyah גיאוגרפיה *nf* geography.
ge'onee/-t גאוני *adj* ingenious; work of genius.
ge'oneeyoot גאוניות *nf* genius.
ge'ool|ah/-ot גאולה *nf* deliverance; redemption.
◊ **(ha)ge'oolah** הגאולה *nm* the centuries-old Jewish dream of Messianic deliverance.
ge'oolat-dam גאולת דם *nf* vendetta.
□ **Ge'ooleem** (Geullim) גאולים *nm* village (est. 1936) in N. Sharon, 5 km SE of **Tsomet ha-Sharon** (Sharon Junction). Pop. 466.
□ **Ge'ooley Teyman** (Geullé Teman) גאולי תימן *nm* village (est. 1947) in N. Sharon, 6 km S. of **Tsomet Khaderah** (Hadera Junction). Pop. 297.
ge'oot גיאות *nf* **1.** prosperity; boom; **2.** high tide.
ger/-eem גר *nm* proselyte; convert to Judaism.
ger/-ey tsedek גר־צדק *nm* convert to Judaism; (*lit.*) righteous proselyte (term used by religious people).
(ha'ala|'at/-'ot) gerah העלאת גירה *nf* **1.** chewing a cud; rumination (by a cow); **2.** (disrespectfully:) useless repetition by a person.
(he'el|ah/-tah/-etee) gerah העלה גירה *v* **1.** chewed a cud; ruminated; **2.** uselessly kept on repeating (*pres* **ma'aleh** *etc; fut* **ya'aleh** *etc*).
ger|a'on/-'onot גירעון *nm* deficit; (*+of:* **geer'on**).
ger|ed/-dah/-adetee גירד *v* scratched; (*pres* **megared**; *fut* **yegared**).
gerem ma'alot גרם מעלות *nm* top of the stairs.
ger|esh/-shah/-ashtee גירש *v* expelled; threw out; (*pres* **megaresh**; *fut* **yegaresh**).
ger|esh/-shayeem גרש *nm* apostrophe (denoting abbreviation).
gerev/garb|ayeem גרב *nm* stocking; sock; (*pl+of:* **-ey**).
(kov|a'/-ey) gerev כובע־גרב *nm* knitted "stretch" cap.
germanee/-t גרמני *adj* German.
germanee/-yah גרמני *nmf* German man/woman.
germaneet גרמנית *nf* (the) German (language).
germanyah גרמניה *nf* Germany.
geroosh/-eem גירוש *nm* expulsion; deportation; (*pl+of:* **-ey**).
◊ **geroosh sefarad** גירוש ספרד *nm* the exile of Jews from Spain (1492).
geroosh|eem (or **gerousheen**) גירושים/־ין *nm pl* divorce; (*+of:* **-ey**).
geroo|y/-yeem גירוי *nm* excitation; stimulus; (*pl+of:* **-yey**).
gershayeem גרשיים *nm pl* inverted commas (to mark a Hebrew abbreviation or acronym).
gesh/geshee hal'ah! (*also:* **gash** *etc*) גש הלאה! *v imp sing m/f* go away! (*pst & pres* **neegash** *etc; fut* **yeegash** *etc*).
gesh/-ee (*etc*) **le-** גש ל־ *v imp sing m/f* go up to.
geshameem גשמים *nm pl* rains; (*sing:* **geshem**; *pl+of:* **geeshmey**).
('onat ha) geshameem עונת הגשמים *nf* the rainy season.
(yemot ha) geshameem ימות הגשמים *nf pl* the rainy days; Israeli winter.
geshee! גשי! *v imp sing f* come here! go up to! (addressing a female).
gesh|em/-ameem גשם *nm* rain; (*pl+of:* **geeshmey**).
gesh|er/-areem גשר *nm* bridge; (*pl+of:* **geeshrey**).
(rosh/rashey) gesher ראש גשר *nm* bridgehead.
□ **Gesher** גשר *nm* kibbutz (est. 1939) in Jordan Valley, 10 km S. of **Tsomet Tsemakh** (Zemah Junction), near Yarmook river, S. of its confluence with the Jordan. Pop. 563.
□ **Gesher Adam** גשר אדם *nm* Adam Bridge (formerly known as **Dameeyah** Bridge) across the Jordan, one of the 2 main crossing-points between Israel and Jordan.
□ **Gesher Allenby** גשר אלנבי *nm* Allenby Bridge across the Jordan, 10 km N. of Jericho, one of 2 main crossing-points between Israel and Jordan.
□ **Gesher ha-Zeev** (Gesher Haziv) גשר הזיו *nm* kibbutz (est. 1949) on Mediterranean Coast, 5 km N. of Nahariyya. Pop. 490.
geshoo! גשו! *v imp pl* come here! go up to! (addressing several people).
□ **Geshoor** (Geshur) גשור *nm* kibbutz (est. 1975) in S. part of Golan Heights, 3 km NW of Eli'al village.
get/geeteem גט *nm* divorce; bill of divorcement.
get|o/-a'ot גיטו *nm* ghetto.
get peetooreen גט פיטורין *nm* bill of divorcement.
gets/geetseem גץ *nm* spark.
gev/-eem גב *nm* **1.** back; **2.** (elephant's) trunk.
□ **Geva'** (Geva') גבע *nm* Kibbutz (est. 1921) in Yizre'el Valley, 10 km SE of Afula (**'Afoolah**). Pop. 605.

□ **Geva' Karmel** (Geva' Karmel) גבע כרמל *nm* village (est. 1949) on Carmel seashore, 3 km S. of Atlit (**'Atleet**). Pop. 438.
gevah/geev'hat komah גבה־קומה *adj* tall.
(khad-) gevanee/-t חד־גווני *adj* monotonous; (*npr* **khadgonee**).
(rav-) gevanee/-t רב־גווני *adj* variegated; multi-colored; (*npr* **ravgonee**).
(khad-) gevaneeyoot חד גווניות *nf* monotony; (*npr* **khadgoneeyoot**).
(rav-) gevaneeyoot רב גווניות *nf* variety; variegation; (*npr* **ravgoneeyoot**).
□ **Gevar'am** (Gevar'am) גברעם *nm* kibbutz (est. 1942) on S. Coastal Plain. 5 km E. of Mordekhay Junction (**Tsomet Mordekhay**). Pop. 278.
gevartan/-eem גברתן **1.** *adj & nm* strongman; **2.** *m* tough guy.
□ **Gevat** (Gevat) גבת *nm* kibbutz (est. 1926) in Yeezre'el Valley, 3 km E. of **Meegdal ha-'Emek**. Pop. 743.
□ **Geveem** (Gevim) גבים *nm* kibbutz (est. 1947) in S. part of coastal plain, 1.5 km S. of **Sederot**. Pop. 373.
geveen|ah/-ot גבינה *nf* cheese; (*+of:* **-at**).
geveenah boolgareet גבינה בולגרית *nf* "Bulgarian" cheese — white hard goat cheese, similar to Feta cheese.
geveenah levanah גבינה לבנה *nf* white cheese.
geveenah razah גבינה רזה *nf* lean cheese.
geveenah shmenah גבינה שמנה *nf* fat cheese.
geveenah tsefateet גבינה צפתית *nf* Safed-brand of sour cheese.
geveenah tsehoobah גבינה צהובה *nf* yellow cheese.
geveen|at/-ot kotej גבינה קוטג' *nf* cottage chese.
geveen|at/-ot kevaseem גבינת כבשים *nf* lamb-cheese.
geveeneem גבינים *nm pl* eye-brows (*sing:* **gaveen**; *pl+of:* **geveeney**).
geveer/-eem גביר *nm* rich man; (*pl+of:* **-ey**).
geveer|ah/-ot גבירה *nf* lady; matron; (*+of:* **-at**).
geveerotay ve-rabotay! גבירותי ורבותי! *interj* Ladies and gentlemen!
gevee|yah/-yot גבייה *nf* collection (of moneys or dues): (*+of:* **-yat**).
gevee|yah/-yot גוויה *nf* corpse; dead body; (*+of:* **-yat**).
gev|er/-areem גבר **1.** *nm* male; man; **2.** *[slang]* he-man; macho; (*pl+of:* **gavrey**).
gev|eret/-arot גברת *nf* Mrs.; Madam; Lady.
geveret neekhbadah גברת נכבדה Dear Madam.
geves גבס *nm* plaster; gypsum.
gevool/-ot גבול *nm* frontier; limit; boundary.
(hasag|at/-ot) gevool הסגת גבול *nf* trespassing.
(le-lo) gevool ללא גבול **1.** *adv* endlessly; with no limit; **2.** *adj* limitless.
(ma'av|ar/-rey) gevool מעבר גבול *nf* border crossing; frontier-crossing.
(maseeg/-at) gevool מסיג גבול *nmf* trespasser.
(meeshmar ha) gevool משמר הגבול *nm* frontier guard; frontier guard corps.
(haskalah) gevohah השכלה גבוהה *nf* higher (university) education.
(deeb|er/-rah/-artee) gevohah gevohah דיבר גבוהה גבוהה *v* talked in high-flown language.
□ **Gevoolot** (Gevulot) גבולות *nm* kibbutz (est. 1943) in Northern Negev, 7 km SE of Magen Junction (**Tsomet Magen**). Pop. 274.
gevoor|ah/-ot גבורה *nf* bravery; courage; valor; (*+of:* **-at**).
(heeg|ee'a/-ee'ah/-a'tee lee) gevoorot הגיע לגבורות *v* attained the age of 80.
gez גז *nm* shearing; fleece.
gez|a'/-a'eem גזע *nm* **1.** trunk; stem; **2.** race; (*pl+of:* **geez'ey**).
gezar/geezrey deen גזר דין *nm* verdict.
gezeer/-eem גזיר *nm* clipping; (*pl+of:* **-ey**).
gezel גזל *nm* robbery; plunder; loot.
gezel|ah/-ot (*or:* **gezeyl|ah/-ot**) גזילה *nf* robbery; loot; plunder; (*+of:* **-at**).
gezer גזר *nm* carrot/-s.
□ **Gezer** גזר *nm* kibbutz (est. 1945) N. of Expressway 1 (Tel-Aviv-Jerusalem), 7 km SE of Ramla. Pop. 266.
gezer|ah/-ot (*or:* **gezeyr|ah/-ot**) גזירה *nf* decree (usually harsh); (*+of:* **-at**).
gezooztr|ah/-ot גזוזטרה *nf* **1.** balcony; **2.** terrace: (*+of:* **-at**).
(bee) glal בגלל *adv* on account of.
glaleem גללים *nm pl* dung; excrements; (*sing:* **galal**; *pl+of:* **geeleley**).
gleed|ah/-ot גלידה *nf* ice cream; (*+of:* **-at**).
gleel/-eem גליל *nm* spool; roll; cylinder; (*pl+of:* **-ey**).
□ **Gleel-Yam** (Gelil Yam) גליל ים *nm* kibbutz (est. 1943) outside Herzliyya (**Hertseleeyah**) town (to its SW edge). Pop. 322.
gleem|ah/-ot גלימה *nf* cloak; gown; mantle; (*+of:* **-at**).
gleesh|ah/-ot גלישה *nf* **1.** sliding; boiling over; **2.** ski; **3.** overdraft (banking): (*+of:* **-at**).
gloof|ah/-ot גלופה *nf* block; mat; (for printing pictures); (*+of:* **-at**).
glool|ah/-ot גלולה *nf* pill; (*+of:* **-at**).
glool|ah/-ot lee-menee'at herayon גלולה למניעת הריון *nf* contraceptive pill.
glool|at/-ot harga'ah גלולת הרגעה *nf* tranquilizer.
glool|at/-ot herayon גלולת הריון *nf* contraceptive pill.
glool|at/-ot sheynah גלולת שינה *nf* sleeping pill.
gloo|yah/-yot גלויה *nf* postcard; (*+of:* **-yat**).
glooyot גלויות *adv* openly; frankly.
gmar גמר *nm* end; finish; completion.
◇ **gmar khateemah tovah!** גמר חתימה טובה! see ◇ **gemar khateemah tovah!**.
◇ **gmar tov!** גמר טוב! see ◇ **gemar tov!**

(khatsee ha) gmar חצי הגמר *nm* semi-final (sport).

(reva' ha) gmar רבע הגמר *nm* quarter-final (sport).

◇ **gmara** גמרא see ◇ **gemara.**

gmeelah גמילה *nf* **1.** weaning; **2.** recovery treatment to cure addicts (alcohol, narcotics, smoking).

gmeeloot khasadeem גמילות חסדים *nf* doing good deeds; helping the needy.

gmeeloot khesed גמילות חסד *nf* interest-free short-term loan.

gmeeshoo|t/-yot גמישות elasticity; flexiblity.

gmool/-eem גמול *nm* **1.** recompense; retribution; **2.** remuneration.

gnay גנאי *nm* disgrace.

(lee) gnay לגנאי *adv* to shame; notoriously.

gneezah/-ot גניזה *nf* storage; hiding; (*+of:* **-at**).

gnevah/-ot גניבה *nf* theft; thievery; (*+of:* **-at**).

(bee) gnevah בגניבה *adv* furtively; stealthily.

gnevat da'at גניבת דעת *nf* deceit; trickery.

(bee) gnoot בגנות *adv* in defamation of.

(davar/dvareem be) go דבר בגו there is something to it.

go'al גועל *nm* revulsion.

go'al nefesh גועל נפש *nm* disgust.

(ha) go'al nefesh הגועל נפש *nm [slang]* the very act (sexual).

go'alee/-t גועלי *[colloq.] adj* disgusting.

godel/-et גודל *v pres* grow(s); (*pst* **gadal**; *fut* **yeegdal**).

godel/gedaleem גודל *nm* size; magnitude (*pl+of:* **godley**).

go'el/-et גואל **1.** *adj* saving; redeeming; **2.** *v pres* save(s); redeem(s); (*pst* **ga'al**; *fut* **yeeg'al**).

('ad bee'at ha) go'el עד ביאת הגואל *adv* till the Messiah comes (i.e. indefinitely).

(ha) go'el הגואל *nm* the Redeemer (i.e. the Messiah).

go'esh/-et גועש **1.** *adj* stormy; **2.** *pres* **storm(s)**; (*pst* **ga'ash**; *fut* **yeeg'ash**).

gofreet גפרית *nf* sulphur; brimstone.

(esh ve) gofreet אש וגפרית *nm* **1.** hot temper; a spitfire; **2.** *lit* : fire and brimstone.

gofreetanee/-t גפריתני *adj* sulphuric.

(khoomtsah) gofreetaneet חומצה גפריתנית *nf* sulphuric acid.

◇ **(khateevat) "golanee"** see ◇ **khateevat "golanee".**

gol/-eem גול *nm [slang]* goal (soccer).

gol|ah/-ot גולה *nf* exile; place of exile.

◇ **(ha)golah** הגולה *nf* (the) Diaspora; exile.

gol|eh/-ah גולה **1.** *adj* exile; **2.** *v* is exiled; (*pst* **galah**; *fut* **yeegleh**).

golel/-elah/-altee גולל *v* unrolled; (*pres* **megolel**; *fut* **yegolel**).

gol|em/-ameem גולם *nm* boor; dummy.

golmee/-t גולמי *adj* raw; crude.

(neft) golmee נפט גולמי *nm* crude oil.

(sat|am/-mah/-amtee et ha) golel סתם את הגולל *v* put an end to (*pres* **sotem** *etc; fut* **yeestom** *etc*).

gome' גומא *nm* papyrus.

gomel/-et גומל *v pres* **1.** retaliate(s); **2.** reward(s); (*pst* **gamal**; *fut* **yeegmol**).

◇ **(beerkat ha) gomel** see ◇ **beerkat ha-gomel.**

gomleen גומלין *nm* mutuality; reciprocity.

gomleen גומלין *adj* (as a suffix) mutual.

(mees'khak/-ey) gomleen מישחק גומלין *nm* return-match.

(khad-) gonee/-t חד־גוני *adj* monotonous.

(rav-) gonee/-t רב־גוני *adj* variegated; multi-colored.

(khad-) goneeyoot חד גוניות *nf* monotony.

(rav-) goneeyoot רב גווניות *nf* variety; variegation.

gonen/-enah/-antee גונן *v* defended; protected; (*pres* **megonen**; *fut* **yegonen**).

□ **Gonen** גונן *nm* kibbutz (est. 1951) in E. part of Huleh **(Khoolah)** Valley. Pop. 467.

goof/-eem גוף *nm* **1.** body; **2.** self; **3.** person (*pl+of:* **-ey**).

goof reeshon/shenee/sheleeshee גוף ראשון/שני/שלישי *(gram.)* 1st/2nd/3rd person.

(shem/-ot ha) goof שם הגוף *nm* pronoun *(gram.)*.

goofa גופא itself; essentials.

goof|ah/-ot גופה *nf* corpse; dead body; (*+of:* **-at**).

goofanee/-t גופני *adj* corporal; bodily.

(kheenookh) goofanee חינוך גופני *nm* physical education.

(kosher) goofanee כושר גופני *nm* physical fitness.

('al) goofee ha-met על גופי המת over my dead body.

goofee|yah/-yot גופייה *nf* undershirt; (*+of:* **-yat**).

goolat ha-koteret גולת הכותרת *nf* climax; masterpiece.

goolgol|et/-ot גולגולת *nf* skull; head.

(le) goolgolet לגולגולת *adv* per head.

goom|ah/-ot גומה *nf* hole; pit.

goom|at/-ot khen גומת חן *nf* dimple.

goomee גומי *nm* rubber.

goomee-le'eesah גומי לעיסה *nm* chewing-gum.

goomkh|ah/-ot גומחה *nf* niche (*+of:* **-at**).

goor/-eem גור *nm* cub; whelp; (*pl+of:* **-ey**).

goosh/-eem גוש *nm* lump; bulk block; block; (*pl+of:* **-ey**).

◇ **goosh emooneem ("Gush Emunim")** גוש אמונים *nm* the leading movement of Jewish settlers settling all over the undivided territory of Eretz Israel (Palestine), mainly in the West Bank.

□ **Goosh 'Etsyon** (Gush Etzyon) גוש עציון *nm* cluster of Jewish settlements in the Hebron area which fell to Jordanian invasion in 1948, was wiped out then by the Jordanians and, since 1967, has been reconstructed and enlarged.

□ **Goosh Dan** (Gush Dan) גוש דן *nm* not legally defined bloc of towns and residential quarters centering around Tel-Aviv. Identical, more or less, with what is called "Greater Tel-Aviv" area.

◇ **(ha)goosh (ha)meezrakhee** הגוש המזרחי *nm* (the) Eastern Bloc.

gooshpank|ah/-ot גושפנקה *nf* seal; cachet; approval: (*+of:* **-at**).

goots/-ah גוץ *adj* short; undersized.

goovayna גוביינא *nf* **1**. collect telephone call; **2**. collection.

goozm|ah/-a'ot גוזמה *nf* exaggeration; (*+of:* **-at**).

goral/-ot גורל *nm* fate; destiny; chance.

goralee/-t גורלי *adj* fateful.

gor|ed/-dey shekhakeem גורד שחקים *nm* skyscraper.

goref/-et גורף *v pres* sweep(s); sweeps(s) away; (*pst* **garaf**; *fut* **yeegrof**).

goref (*etc*) **hon** גורף הון *v pres* make(s) lots of money.

gor|em/-meem גורם *nm* factor; cause; (*pl+of:* **-mey**).

gorem/-et גורם *adj* causing.

gorem/-et le- גורם ל־ *v pres* causes (*pst* **garam le-**; *fut* **yeegrom le-**).

goren/granot גורן *nf* barn; threshing floor.

□ **Goren** גורן *nm* village (est. 1950) in Lower Galilee, 13 km SE of **Rosh ha-Neekrah**. Pop. 405.

goses/-et גוסס *nmf & adj* moribund; dying.

goses/-et גוסס *v pres* die(s) away; agonize(s); (*pst* **gasas**; *fut* **yeegsos**).

govah/gvaheem גובה *nm* **1**. height; **2**. altitude; (*pl+of:* **gov'hey**).

gov arayot גוב אריות *nm* lions' den.

govah tseleel גובה צליל *nm* pitch.

('al ha) govah על הגובה *adv* on the level.

(mad/-ey) govah מד גובה *nm* altimeter.

gov|e'a'/-a'at גווע **1**. *v pres* die(s) away; agonize(s); (*pst* **gava'**; *fut* **yeegva'**); **2**. *adj* moribund.

gove'a' (*etc*) **ba-ra'av** גווע ברעב *v pres* is starving; is dying of hunger.

gov|eh/-eem גובה *nm* collector; (*pl+of:* **-ey**).

goveh/-ah גובה *v pres* collect(s); (*pst* **gavah**; *fut* **yeegbeh** *(b=v)*).

go|y/-yeem גוי *nm* **1**. Gentile; non-Jew; **2**. nation (Bibl); (*pl+of:* **-yey**).

goy|ah/-yot גויה *nf* gentile woman (somewhat derogatory).

(ha) goyeem הגויים *nm pl* the Gentiles; the non-Jewish world.

(beyn ha) goyeem בין הגויים *adv* amid non-Jews; amid the nations of the world.

gozal/-eem גוזל *nm* fledgling; nesting; (*pl+of:* **-ey**).

gram/-eem גרם *nm* gram; (*pl+of:* **-ey**).

grar גרר *nm* tow truck.

greed|ah/-ot גרידה *nf* **1**. abrasion; curettage; **2**. *[colloq.]* abortion; (*+of:* **-at**).

greerah/-ot גרירה *nf* towing; dragging; (*+of:* **-at**).

grees|eem גריסים *nm pl* groats; grits; (*+of:* **-ey**).

greyda גרידא *adv* merely; purely; solely.

□ **Grofeet** (Gerofit) גרופית *nm* kibbutz (est. 1966) in the **'Aravah** (arid plain) along the border with Jordan, 45 km N. of Elat **(Eylat)**. Pop. 273.

gronee/-t גרוני *adj* guttural.

groorah/-ot גרורה *nf* **1**. satellite (politic.); **2**. hypostasis of cancer (medic).

groosh/-eem גרוש *nm* **1**. onetime minor Israeli currency unit; **2**. *[colloq.]* penny.

groosh|ah/-ot גרושה *nf* divorcee; (*+of:* **-at**).

groota|'ah/-'ot גרוטאה *nf* **1**. junk; piece of junk; **2**. *[slang]* jalopy: (*+of:* **-'at**).

groota'ot גרוטאות *nf pl* scrap metal.

greesah/-ot גריסה *nf* agony; (*+of:* **-at**).

gvah/gvohat komah גבה קומה *adj* tall.

(khad-) gvanee/-t חד־גווני *adj* monotonous; (*npr* **khadgonee**).

(rav-) gvanee/-t רב־גווני *adj* variegated; multicolored; (*npr* **ravgonee**).

(khad-) gvaneeyoot חד גווניות *nf* monotony; (*npr* **khadgoneeyoot**).

(rav-) gvaneeyoot רב גווניות *nf* variety; variegation; (*npr:* **ravgoneeyoot**).

□ **Gvar'am** גברעם see □ **Gevar'am**.

gvartan/-eem גברתן **1**. *adj & nm* strongman; **2**. *m* tough guy.

□ **Gvat** (Gevat) גבת see □ **Gevat**.

gveen|ah/-ot גבינה *nf* cheese; (*+of:* **-at**).

gveenah boolgareet גבינה בולגרית *nf* "Bulgarian" cheese — white hard goat cheese, similar to Feta cheese.

gveenah levanah גבינה לבנה *nf* white cheese.

gveenah razah גבינה רזה *nf* lean cheese.

gveenah shmenah גבינה שמנה *nf* fat cheese.

gveenah tsehoobah גבינה צהובה *nf* yellow cheese.

gveenah tsfateet גבינה צפתית *nf* Safed-brand of sour cheese.

gveen|at/-ot kotej גבינה קוטג' *nf* cottage chese.

gveen|at/-ot kvaseem גבינת כבשים *nf* lamb-cheese.

gveeneem גבינים *nm pl* eye-brows (*sing:* **gaveen**; *pl+of:* **gveeney**).

gveer/-eem גביר *nm* rich man; (*pl+of:* **-ey**).

gveerah/-ot גבירה *nf* lady; matron; (*+of:* **-at**).

gveerotay ve-rabotay! גבירותי ורבותי! *interj* Ladies and gentlemen!

gvee|yah/-yot גבייה *nf* collection (of moneys or dues): (*+of:* **-yat**).

gvee|yah/-yot גווייה *nf* corpse; dead body; (*+of:* **-yat**).

gveret/gvarot גברת *nf* Mrs.; Madam; Lady.

gveret neekhbadah גברת נכבדה Dear Madam.

gvool/-ot גבול *nm* frontier; limit; boundary.

(hasag|at/-ot) gvool הסגת גבול *nf* trespassing.

(le-lo) gvool ללא גבול **1.** *adv* endlessly; with no limit; **2.** *adj* limitless.
(ma'av|ar/-rey) gvool מעבר גבול *nf* border crossing; frontier-crossing.
(maseeg/-at) gvool מסיג גבול *nmf* trespasser.
(meeshmar ha) gevool משמר הגבול *nm* frontier guard; frontier guard corps.
(haskalah) gvohah השכלה גבוהה *nf* higher (university) education.
(deeb|er/-rah/-artee) gvohah-gvohah דיבר גבוהה־גבוהה *v* talked in high-flown language.
◻ **Gvoolot** (Gevulot) גבולות see ◻ **Gevoolot**.
gvoor|ah/-ot גבורה *nf* bravery; courage; valor; **(***+of:* **-at).**
(heeg|ee'a/-ee'ah/-a'tee lee) gvoorot הגיע לגבורות *v* attained the age of 80.
gzar/geezrey deen גזר דין *nm* verdict.
gzeer/-eem גזיר *nm* clipping; **(***pl+of:* **ey).**
gzel|ah/-ot (*or:* **gzeyl|ah/-ot)** גזילה *nf* robbery; loot; plunder; **(***+of:* **-at).**
gzer|ah/-ot (*or:* **gzeyr|ah/-ot)** גזירה *nf* decree (usually harsh); **(***+of:* **-at).**
gzooztr|ah/-ot גזוזטרה *nf* **1.** balcony; **2.** terrace: **(***+of:* **-at).**

H.

transliterating the Hebrew letter **Heh** (ה)

NOTE: In everyday speech, the Hebrew letter ה is dropped by many, just as happens to the **h** in some dialect varieties of English. Therefore, the entries listed here are also found under the respective vowels following the initial **h**.

ha- ה *(prefix)* the definite article (equivalent to "the" in English).
ha- ה *(prefix)* Interrogative Particle (equivalent to: have you? is it?)
ha'adaf|ah/-ot העדפה *nf* preference; **(***+of:* **-at).**
ha'afal|ah/-ot האפלה *nf* blackout; **(***+of:* **-at).**
ha'ala|'ah/-'ot העלאה *nf* promotion; raise; **(***+of:* **-'at).**
ha'ala|'ah/-'ot be-dargah העלאה בדרגה *nf* promotion (in rank).
ha'alam|ah/-ot העלמה *nf* concealment; **(***+of:* **-at).**
ha'alam|at/-ot mas/meeseem העלמת מס *nf* tax evasion.
ha'amad|ah/-ot העמדה *nf* getting up; placing: **(***+of:* **-at).**
ha'amadah le-deen העמדה לדין *nf* bringing to trial.
ha'amad|at/-ot paneem העמדת פנים *nf* pretense.
ha'aman|ah/-ot האמנה *nf* accreditation: **(***+of:* **-at).**
ha'anak|ah/-ot הענקה *nf* grant; **(***+of:* **-at).**
ha'apal|ah/-ot העפלה *nf* **1.** venture; daring; **2.** mountaineering; **(***+of:* **-at).**
◇ **(ha)ha'apalah** ההעפלה *nf* the running of the British blockade in the Mandate period to bring Jewish immigrants "illegally" into Palestine.
ha'arak|ah/-ot הארקה *nf* grounding (electr.); **(***+of:* **-at).**
ha'arakh|ah/-ot הארכה *nf* extension; prolongation: **(***+of:* **-at).**
ha'arakh|ah/-ot הארחה *nf* lodging, accommodotion; **(***+of:* **-at).**
(bet/batey) ha'arakhahהארחה בית *nm* guest-house.
ha'arakh|ah/-ot הערכה *nf* appreciation; evaluation: **(***+of:* **-at).**
ha'aram|ah/-ot הערמה *nf* evasion; tricking; **(***+of:* **-at).**
ha'aramah (*etc*) **'al ha-khok** הערמה על החוק *nf* evasion of the law.
ha'arats|ah/-ot הערצה *nf* admiration; **(***+of:* **-at).**
ha'asak|ah/-ot העסקה *nf* employment; **(***+of:* **-at).**
ha'ashar|ah/-ot העשרה *nf* enrichment: **(***+of:* **-at).**
ha'atak|ah/-ot העתקה *nf* **1.** shifting; **2.** copying; **(***+of:* **-at).**
ha'atak|at/-ot meesmakheem העתקת מסמכים *nf* photocopying; "xeroxing".
ha'avar|ah/-ot העברה *nf* transfer; **(***+of:* **-at).**
ha'azan|ah/-ot האזנה *nf* listening; **(***+of:* **-at).**
haba|'ah/-'ot הבעה *nf* expression; **(***+of:* **-'at).**
haba'at ee-'emoon הבעת אי־אמון *nf* vote of non-confidence.
haba'at emoon הבעת אמון *nf* vote of confidence.
◇ **habeemah ("Habima")** הבימה *nf* Israel's National Theater company. Created in Moscow in 1918, it moved to Tel-Aviv, Palestine in 1925. It plays throughout the country and also toursDiaspora centers.
hab|eetee/-etnah הביטי *v imp f* sing/pl look! (addressing one/several females).
hab|et/-eetoo הבט *v imp* look *m* sing/pl (addressing one male/several persons).

□ **Haboneem** (Habonim) הבונים *nm* coop. settlement (est. 1949), 6 km S. of 'Atlit on Carmel **(Karmel)** coast. Pop. 220.

hadadee/-t הדדי *adj* mutual; reciprocal.

(agoodah) hadadeet אגודה הדדית *nf* cooperative society.

(be-haskamah) hadadeet בהסכמה הדדית *adv* in mutual agreement.

('ezrah) hadadeet עזרה הדדית *nf* mutual aid.

hadadeeyoot הדדיות *nf* reciprocity.

had|af/-fah/-aftee הדף *v* pushed; (*pres* **hadaf;** *fut* **yahadof**).

hadakh|ah/-ot הדחה *nf* **1.** impeachment; dismissal; **2.** rinsing thoroughly; (*+of:* **-at**).

hadakhat keleem הדחת כלים *nf* washing dishes.

hadar הדר *nm* splendor; dignified behavior.

□ **Hadar** הדר *nf colloq. abbr.* referring to Haifa's residential quarter **Hadar ha-Karmel** (see below).

□ **Hadar 'Am** (Hadar 'Am) הדר עם *nm* village (est 1933) in **'Emek Khefer** area, 4 km NE of Netanya. Pop. 346.

□ **Hadar ha-Karmel** (Hadar-ha-Carmel) הדר הכרמל *nf* Haifa's oldest and main residential and business area, between downtown and Mount Carmel **(Karmel)**.

(pree) hadar פרי הדר *nm* citrus.

hadar|eem הדרים *nm pl* citrus fruits; (*+of:* **-ey**).

◇ **hadasah** ("Hadassah") הדסה *nf* a network of hospitals, health-caring institutions and professional schools sponsored and operated in Israel by Hadassah Medical Association, a subsidiary of the U.S. Hadassah Zionist Women organization active in the country since 1919.

□ **Hadaseem** (Hadassim) הדסים *nm* youth-village and school SE of Netanya, off the **Mekhlaf Poleg** interchange on Expressway 2. Pop. 770 (students and staff).

hadbak|ah/-ot הדבקה *nf* gluing; sticking; (*+of:* **-at**).

hadbar|ah/-t הדברה *nf* extermination (of germs or pests): (*+of:* **-at**).

(khom|er/-rey) hadbarah חומר־הדברה *nm* germicides; pesticides.

hadeef|ah/-ot הדיפה *nf* push; thrust; repulse; (*+of:* **-at**).

□ **Hadera** see □ **Khaderah**.

hadgam|ah/-ot הדגמה *nf* exemplification; demonstration; (*+of:* **-at**).

hadgar|ah/-ot הדגרה *nf* hatching; incubation; (*+of:* **-at**).

hadgarah (*etc*) **mal'akhooteet** הדגרה מלאכותית *nf* artificial incubation.

hadgash|ah/-ot הדגשה *nf* emphasis; (*+of:* **-at**).

hadlak|ah/-ot הדלקה *nf* **1.** lighting; kindling; **2.** bonfire; (*+of:* **-at**).

◇ **hadlakat nerot** הדלקת נרות *nf* lighting Sabbath candles.

hadook/-ah הדוק *adj* tight; close.

hadoor/-ah הדור *adj* adorned; elegant.

hadpas|ah/-ot הדפסה *nf* **1.** printing; **2.** typing; (*+of:* **-at**).

hadpasah bee-mekhonah הדפסה במכונה *nf* typewriting.

(be) hadragah בהדרגה *adv* gradually.

hadragatee/-t הדרגתי *adj* gradual; gradually.

hadran הדרן *nm* encore.

hadrat paneem הדרת פנים *nf* dignified appearance.

ha'eem האם *conj* Interrogative particle; question forming particle; did not? was it not?

□ **ha-'eer ha-'ateekah** העיר העתיקה *nf* the old city. (Normally, reference is to the Old City of Jerusalem).

ha-'eerah העירה *adv* to town; back to town.

□ **ha-'Emek** העמק *nm* "the Valley " *(colloq. abbr.)* referring to the Yizre'el Valley **('Emek Yeezre'el)**.

ha'erev הערב *adv* tonight; this evening.

hafagat metakh הפגת מתח *nf* easing tension.

hafak|ah/-ot הפקה *nf* production; (*+of:* **-at**).

haf|akh/-khah/-akhtee הפך *v pst* **1.** overturned; upset; **2.** turned; became; (*pres* **hofekh;** *fut* **yahafokh**).

hafakh (*etc*) **le-** הפך ל־ *v* turned into.

hafakhpakh/-ah הפכפך *adj* unreliable; fickle.

haf'al|ah/-ot הפעלה *nf* activation; (*+of:* **-at**).

hafar|ah/-ot הפרה *nf* violation; breach; infringement; (*+of:* **-at**).

hafar|at/-ot heskem/eem הפרת הסכם *nf* breach of agreement.

hafar|at/-ot khok הפרת חוק *nf* infringement of the law.

hafar|at/-ot nohal הפרת נוהל *nf* infringement of procedure.

hafar|at/-ot seder הפרת סדר *nf* disturbing order; causing disorder.

hafats|ah/-ot הפצה *nf* **1.** distribution; **2.** dissemination; spreading; (*+of:* **-at**).

hafeekh|ah/-ot הפיכה *nf* **1.** overturning; **2.** coup d'etat; revolution; (*+of:* **-at**).

hafeekhah tseva'eet הפיכה צבאית *nf* military coup.

hafeekh|at/-ot khatser הפיכת חצר *nf* coup d'etat.

hafgan|ah/-ot הפגנה *nf* demonstration; (*+of:* **-at**).

hafgan|at/-ot mekha'ah הפגנת מחאה *nf* protest demonstration.

hafganatee/-t הפגנתי *adj* demonstrative.

hafgaz|ah/-ot הפגזה *nf* shelling; bombardment; (*+of:* **-at**).

hafka|'ah/-'ot הפקעה *nf* expropriation; attachment; requisition; (*+of:* **-'at**).

hafka|'at/-'ot kark|a'/-a'ot הפקעת קרקע *nf* land expropriation.

hafka|'at/-'ot mekheer/-eem הפקעת מחיר *nf* overcharging.

hafkad|ah/-ot הפקדה *nf* **1.** deposing; depositing; **2.** placing one in charge; (*+of:* **-at**).

hafkar|ah/-ot הפקרה *nf* abandonment; renunciation; (*+of:* **-at**).

hafkhad|ah/-ot הפחדה *nf* intimidation; scaring; (*+of:* **-at**).

hafkhat|ah/-ot הפחתה *nf* reduction; abatement; (*+of:* **-at**).

haflag|ah/-ot הפלגה *nf* **1.** sailing; **2.** exaggeration; **3.** superlative (Gram.); (*+of:* **-at**).

haflay|ah/-yot הפליה *nf* discrimination; (*+of:* **-yat**).

hafle va-fele'! (*f=p*) הפלא ופלא! *interj* how wonderful!

(le) haflee להפליא *adv* splendid; splendidly.

hafna|yah/-yot הפניה *nf* turning; referring; referral; (*+of:* **-at**).

hafoog|ah/-ot הפוגה *nf* truce; respite; (*+of:* **-at**).

(blee) hafoogah בלי הפוגה *adv* relentlessly.

(le-lo) hafoogah ללא הפוגה *adv* incessantly.

hafookh/-ah הפוך *adj* inverted; overturned.

(kafeh) hafookh קפה הפוך *nm* cup of coffee with abundant milk.

hafra|'ah/-'ot הפרעה *nf* interference (*+of:* **-'at**).

hafrad|ah הפרדה *nf* separation; (*+of:* **-at**).

hafradat kokhot הפרדת כוחות *nf* disengagement (milit).

hafrakh|ah/-ot הפרחה *nf* **1.** making bloom; **2.** spreading; (*+of:* **-at**).

hafrakhat shemamah הפרחת שממה *nf* making the desert bloom.

hafrakhat shemoo|'ah/-'ot הפרחת שמועה *nf* spreading rumors.

hafrash|ah/-shot הפרשה *nf* **1.** secretion; **2.** allocation; (*+of:* **-ot**).

hafratah הפרטה *nf* privatization.

hafray|ah/-yot הפריה *nf* impregnation; fecundation; fertilization (of egg); (*+of:* **-yat**).

hafrayah mela'khooteet הפריה מלאכותית *nf* artificial insemination.

hafraz|ah/-ot הפרזה *nf* exaggeration; (*+of:* **-at**).

hafsak|ah/-ot הפסקה *nf* **1.** intermission; **2.** cessation; (*+of:* **-at**).

hafsak|at/-ot esh הפסקת אש *nf* cease-fire.

hafsak|at/-ot zerem הפסקת זרם *nf* electric current interruption; current break.

hafshar|ah/-ot הפשרה *nf* melting; thaw; (*+of:* **-at**).

hafshat|ah/-ot הפשטה *nf* **1.** abstraction; **2.** undressing; (*+of:* **-at**).

hafta|'ah/-'ot הפתעה *nf* surprise; (*+of:* **-'at**).

(le-marbeh ha) hafta'ah למרבה ההפתעה much to one's surprise.

haftsats|ah/-ot הפצצה *nf* bombing; bombardment.

◇ **HAGA** הג"א (*acr of* **HAGAnah ezrakheet** הגנה אזרחית) *nf* civil defense.

hag|ah/-tah/-eetee הגה *v* **1.** uttered; **2.** conceived; (*pres* **hogeh**; *fut* **yehegeh**).

hagad|ah/-ot הגדה *nf* saga; tale; (*+of:* **-at**).

◇ **hagadah ("Hagadah shel Pesakh")** הגדה של פסח **1.** *nf* the "Haggadah" - the narrative of the Exodus of the Israelites from Egypt the reading of which is the main ritual of the traditional Passover "Seder" dinner; **2.** *nf* the booklet incorporating said narrative.

□ **ha-gadah** הגדה *nf* shortened reference to the West Bank.

haga|hah/-hot הגהה *nf* galley-proof; proofreading; (*+of:* **-hat**).

ha-gam הגם *conj* although.

hagan|ah/-ot הגנה *nf* defense; (*+of:* **-at**).

◇ **"Haganah"** הגנה *nf* the "Haganah" - the Jewish self-defense organization in Palestine before Israel's independance.

haganah 'atsmeet הגנה עצמית *nf* self-defense.

haganah aveereet הגנה אווירית *nf* air-defense.

(khok) haganat ha-sakhar חוק הגנת השכר *nm* law for salary protection.

haganatee/-t הגנתי *adj* defensive.

hagash|ah/-ot הגשה *nf* serving; submitting; (*+of:* **-at**).

hagav|ah/-ot הגבה *nf* reacting; (*+of:* **-at**).

hagba|hah/-hot הגבהה *nf* elevation; lifting; (*+of:* **-hat**).

hagbal|ah/-ot הגבלה *nf* limitation; restriction; (*+of:* **-at**).

hagbalat yeloodah הגבלת ילודה *nf* birth control.

hagbalat sakhar הגבלת שכר *nf* wage (salaries) control.

hagbalat sekhar deerah הגבלת שכר־דירה *nf* rent control; rent restriction.

hagbar|ah/-ot הגברה *nf* **1.** strengthening; **2.** amplification; (*+of:* **-at**).

hagdal|ah/-ot הגדלה *nf* increase; enlargement.

hagdar|ah/-ot הגדרה *nf* definition; (*+of:* **-at**).

hagdarah 'atsmeet הגדרה עצמית *nf* self-determination.

hageenoot הגינות *nf* fairness; honesty; decency.

hageer|ah/-ot הגירה *nf* migration; emigration; immigration (*+of:* **-at**).

hagla|yah/-yot הגליה *nf* deportation; (*+of:* **-yat**).

hagmash|ah/-ot הגמשה *nf* growing flexibility; becoming more flexible; (*+of:* **-at**).

hagoon/-ah הגון *adj* decent; honest.

□ **Ha-Goshreem** (Hagosherim) הגושרים *nm* kibbutz in Galilee (est. 1948), 11 km E. of **Keeryat-Shmonah**. Pop. 515.

hagral|ah/-ot הגרלה *nf* lottery; (*+of:* **-at**).

hagsham|ah/-ot הגשמה *nf* implementation; fulfilment; (*+of:* **-at**).

◇ **(le)hagshamah** להגשמה *adv* joining of a kibbutz by youth in fulfilment of pioneering or socialist ideals.

hagza|mah/-ot הגזמה *nf* exaggeration; (*+of:* **-at**).

ha-hee ההיא *pron.* that one (female).

ha-hem ההם *pron m pl* those.

ha-hen ההן *pron f pl* those (females).

◻ **Haifa** see ◻ **Kheyfah**.

haka|'ah/-'ot הכאה *nf* beating; hitting; (*+of:* **-'at**).

haka|'ah/-ot הקאה *nf* vomiting; (*+of:* **-'at**).

◇ **hakafot** הקפות *nf pl* march of Torah-scroll bearers during **Seemkhat Torah** (Yiddish: "Simches-Toireh") celebrations.

hakal|ah/-ot הקלה *nf* relief; concession; (*+of:* **-at**).

hakam|ah/-ot הקמה *nf* erection; setting-up; (*+of:* **-at**).

haka|'ot הקאות *nf pl* vomitings (*sing:* **-ah**).

hakar|ah/-ot הכרה *nf* acquaintance; recognition; (*+of:* **-at**).

◇ **hakarah ma'amadeet** הכרה מעמדית *nf* class consciousness.

hakarah peneemeet הכרה פנימית *nf* inner conviction.

('as|ah/-tah/-eetee) hakarah עשה הכרה *v* made acquaintance; (*pres* **'oseh** *etc; fut* **ya'aseh** *etc*).

(ba'al/-at) hakarah בעל הכרה *adj* fully-aware person; socially conscious.

(khas|ar/-rat) hakarah חסר הכרה *adj* unconscious.

(mee-takhat le-saf ha) hakarah מתחת לסף ההכרה *adv* subconsciously; below the threshold of consciousness.

(tat-) hakarah תת־הכרה *nf* subconsciousness.

hakarat ha-shetakh הכרת השטח *nf* reconnoitering; reconnaissance.

hakarat todah הכרת תודה *nf* gratefulness; gratitude.

(tat) hakaratee/-t תת־הכרתי *adj* subconscious.

(kley) hakashah כלי־הקשה *nm pl* percussion instruments.

hakdam|ah/-ot הקדמה *nf* **1.** preface; introduction; **2.** advancing; (*+of:* **-at**).

hakdash|ah/-ot הקדשה *nf* dedication; (*+of:* **-at**).

◻ **Ha-keeryah** (ha-Qirya) הקריה *nf* quarter in the E. part of Tel-Aviv where main Government offices are located. For its Jerusalem counterpart see ◻ **Keeryat Ben-Gooryon**, below.

hakh/hakee הך *v imp sing m/f* strike! hit!

(haynoo) hakh היינו הך all the same; makes no difference.

hakhal|ah (*npr* **hekhal|ah)/-ot** החלה *nf* application; (*+of:* **-at**).

ha-khamah החמה *nf* the sun.

(hanets) ha-khamah הנץ החמה *nm* sunrise.

hakhan|ah/-ot הכנה *nf* preparation: (*+of:* **-at**).

ha-khanoot החנות *nf [slang]* fly (trousers).

hakhbad|ah/-ot הכבדה *nf* inconvenience; burden.

hakhee הכי *adv* the most.

hakhee? הכי? *adv* is there? is it? is/was it indeed?

hakhee-hakhee הכי־הכי *adj [slang]* the very best; the most.

hakhee harbeh הכי הרבה **1.** *adv* at most; **2.** *adj* the most.

hakhel be- החל ב־ *adv* beginning with; as of.

hakhel mee- החל מ־ *adv* as from; as of.

hakhen הכן *adv* ready; prepared.

(matsav) hakhen מצב הכן *nm* standby; state of alert.

hakh'kar|ah/-ot החכרה *nf* leasing; hire: (*+of:* **-at**).

hakh'khash|ah/-ot הכחשה *nf* denial: (*+of:* **-at**).

hakhlaf|ah/-ot החלפה *nf* exchange; replacement: (*+of:* **-at**).

hakhlak|ah/-ot החלקה *nf* gliding; skiing: (*+of:* **-at**).

hakhlal|ah/-ot הכללה *nf* generalization; inclusion: (*+of:* **-at**).

hakhlam|ah/-ot החלמה *nf* recovery; convalescence; (*+of:* **-at**).

hakhlash|ah/-ot החלשה *nf* weakening; (*+of:* **-at**).

hakhlat|ah/-ot החלטה *nf* decision; resolution; (*+of:* **-at**).

(keeb|el/-lah/-altee) hakhlat|ah/-ot קיבל החלטה *v pst* adopted a resolution; made a decision; (*pres* **mekabel** *etc; fut* **yekabel** *etc*).

hakhmar|ah/-ot החמרה *nf* aggravation; (*+of:* **-at**).

hakhmat|sah/-ot החמצה *nf* **1.** miss (an opportunity); **2.** leavening; acidification; (*+of:* **-at**).

hakhna|'ah/-'ot הכנעה *nf* submissiveness; (*+of:* **-at**).

hakhnas|ah/-ot הכנסה *nf* **1.** income; **2.** introduction; (*+of:* **-at**).

(bool/-ey) hakhnasah בול הכנסה *nm* revenue stamp.

◇ **(geeloom) hakhnasah** see ◇ **geeloom hakhnasah**.

(ha'alamat) hakhnasah העלמת הכנסה *nf* tax evasion.

hakhnasat orkheem הכנסת אורחים *nf* hospitality.

hakhna|yah/-yot החניה *nf* parking; (*+of:* **-yat**).

hakhna|yat/-yot rekhev החנית רכב *nf* vehicle parking.

◻ **Ha-Khotreem** (Hahoterim) החותרים *nm* kibbutz (est. 1948), on Carmel (**Karmel**) coast, 10 km S. of Haifa. Pop. 564.

hakhpal|ah/-ot הכפלה *nf* **1.** multiplication; **2.** doubling; (*+of:* **-at**).

hakhra|'ah/-ot הכרעה decision; (*+of:* **-'at**).

hakhraf|ah/-ot החרפה *nf* exacerbation; (*pl+of:* **-at**).

hakhram|ah/-ot החרמה *nf* confiscation; excommunication; (*+of:* **-at**).

hakhshad|ah/-ot החשדה *nf* casting suspicion; (*+of:* **-at**).

hakhshar|ah/-ot הכשרה *nf* training; preparation; (*+of:* **-at**).

◇ **hakh'sharah** הכשרה *nf* special training for a pioneering life which was once obligatory for youth groups (Chalutzim) preparing to settle in Israel.

hakhsharah meektso'eet הכשרה מקצועית *nf* professional training.
hakhsharat karka' הכשרת קרקע *nf* preparing ground.
hakhta|'ah/-'ot החטאה *nf* missing target; leading astray; (*+of:* **-'at**).
hakhtam|ah/-ot החתמה *nf* signing on; signing up; getting someone to sign; (*+of:* **-at**).
hakhtar|ah/-ot הכתרה *nf* crowning; coronation; (*+of:* **-at**).
hakhtav|ah/-ot הכתבה *nf* dictation; (*+of:* **-at**).
akhv|ah/-ot אחווה *nf* brotherhood; (*+of:* **-at**).
hakhvan|ah/-ot הכוונה *nf* guidance; directing; (*+of:* **-at**).
hakhya|'ah/-'ot- החייאה *nf* resuscitation; (*+of:* **-'at**).
hakhzak|ah/-ot החזקה *nf* maintenance; (*+of:* **-at**).
hakhzar|ah/-ot החזרה *nf* return; refund; (*+of:* **-at**).
hak'khash|ah (*npr* **hakh'khash|ah**)**/-ot** הכחשה *nf* denial; (*+of:* **-at**).
haklad|ah/-ot הקלדה *nf* wordprocessing; (*+of:* **-at**).
haklat|ah/-ot הקלטה *nf* recording; taping; (*+of:* **-at**).
(seret) haklatah (seertey *etc*) סרט הקלטה *nm* recording-tape.
ha-Keneset הכנסת *nf* the Knesset, Israel's Parliament, with 120 Members, elected every four years (or less, sometimes) by proportional ballot.
hakpa|'ah/-ot הקפאה *nf* freezing; freeze; (*+of:* **-at**).
hakpa|'at/-'ot hon הקפאת הון *nf* freezing of capital.
hakpa|'at/-'ot sakhar הקפאת שכר *nf* wage freeze.
hakpad|ah/-ot הקפדה *nf* strict observation; (*+of:* **-at**).
hakra|'ah/-'ot הקראה *nf* recitation; (*+of:* **-'at**).
hakran|ah/-ot הקרנה *nf* projection: (*+of:* **-at**).
hakrav|ah/-ot הקרבה *nf* **1.** sacrificing; **2.** drawing near; (*+of:* **at**).
□ **Ha-Krayot** הקריות *nf [colloq.]* reference to Haifa's 3 seashore suburbs, NE of town; **(Keeryat-Khayeem, Keeryat Motskeen** and **Keeryat-Byaleek)**.
hak'shakh|ah/-ot הקשחה *nf* stiffening; (*+of:* **at**).
hak'shav|ah הקשבה *nf* attentive listening; (*+of:* **-at**).
haktan|ah/-ot הקטנה *nf* diminution; reduction; lessening; (*+of:* **-at**).
haktsa|'ah/-'ot הקצאה *nf* allotment (of shares); allocation (of funds); (*+of:* **-'at**).
haktsan|ah/-ot הקצנה *nf* growing tendency to extremism; exacerbation; (*+of:* **-at**).
haktsav|ah/-ot הקצבה *nf* allocation; (*+of:* **-at**).
ha-lah הלה *pron* that one; the one there.
hal'ah הלאה *adv* further; onward.
(gash/geshee) hal'ah גש הלאה *v imp sing m/f* go away!
(ve-khen) hal'ah וכן הלאה and so on; etcetera.
hal|akh/-khah/-akhtee הלך *v pst* went; (*pres* **holekh;** *fut* **yelekh**).
halakh (*etc*) **batel** הלך בטל *v pst* idled.
halakh (*etc*) **ba-telem** הלך בתלם *v pst* toed the line.
halakh (*etc*) **le-'eebood** הלך לאיבוד *v pst* got lost.
halakh (*etc*) **le-'olamo/-ah** הלך לעולמו *v pst* passed away.
halakh (*npr* **halokh)/heelkhey nefesh** הלך נפש *nm* frame of mind; mood.
halakh (*etc*) **rakheel** הלך רכיל *v pst* slandered; spread gossip.
halakh (*etc*) **sholal** הלך שולל *v pst* was misled; was deceived.
halakh (*etc*) **ve-gadal** הלך וגדל *v* grew bigger and bigger; (*pres* **holekh ve-gadel;** *fut* **yelekh ve-yeegdal**).
halakh|ah/-ot הלכה *nf* law; rule; tradition; (*+of:* **-at**).
halakhah le-ma'aseh הלכה למעשה *nf* by rule of thumb.
(ka) halakhah כהלכה *adv* properly; as one should.
(la) halakhah להלכה *adv* theoretically; in theory.
(pesak/peeskey) halakhah פסק הלכה *nm* decision by a rabbinical authority or court.
hal|am/-mah/-amtee הלם *v pst* **1.** fitted; was suited to; **2.** stroke; hit; (*pres* **holem;** *fut* **yahalom**).
hal'amah/-ot הלאמה *nf* nationalization; (*+of:* **-at**).
(le) halan להלן *adv* following below; infra.
halan|ah/-ot הלנה *nf* providing night's lodging; putting up overnight; (*+of:* **-at**).
halanat sakhar הלנת שכר *nf* delaying payment of wages.
halats|ah/-ot הלצה *nf* joke; (*+of:* **-at**).
ha-laylah הלילה *adv* tonight.
(ba-khatsot) ha-laylah בחצות הלילה *adv* at midnight.
ha-laz הלז *pron* that one.
halbash|ah הלבשה *nf* clothing; (*+of:* **-at**).
(khanoo|t/-yot) halbashah חנות הלבשה *nf* clothing store.
(deevrey) halbashah דברי הלבשה *nm pl* clothing items.
haleekh/-eem הליך *nm* proceeding; action; (*pl+of:* **-ey**).
haleekh|ah/-ot הליכה *nf* walk; march; (*pl+of:* **-ey**).
haleekheem meeshpateeyeem הליכים משפטיים *nm pl* legal proceedings.
haleekhon/-eem הליכון *nm* walking frame for invalids; (*pl+of:* **-ey**).
haleekhot הליכות *nf pl* manners.
◇ **halel** הלל *nm* the "Halel", a special God-praising prayer for holidays.

(gam|ar/-ah et ha) halel גמר את ההלל *v pst* was full of praise; (*pres* **gomer** *etc; fut* **yeegmor** *etc*).

◇ **halelooyah (Haleluya)** הללויה "Halleluja" - Praise the Lord (Psalm).

halka|'ah/-'ot הלקאה *nf* flogging; flagellation; (+*of:* **-'at**).

halka'ah 'atsmeet הלקאה עצמית *nf* self-flagellation; self-castigation; masochism.

halkham|ah/-ot הלחמה *nf* soldering; welding; (+*of:* **-at**).

halkhan|ah/-ot הלחנה *nf* composition (of music); (+*of:* **-at**).

halo הלו *interj* hello! hullo!

halo הלא *adv* is it not? surely.

halokh/heelkhey nefesh הלך נפש *nm* frame of mind; mood.

halokh va-shov הלוך ושוב *adv* back and forth.

halom הלום *adv* to here; hereto; hither.

haloom/-ah הלום *adj* shocked; stricken.

haloom/-at ra'am הלום רעם *adj* thunderstruck.

halshanah/-ot הלשנה *nf* denunclation; informing on; (+*of:* **-at**).

halva|'ah/-'ot הלוואה *nf* loan; (+*of:* **-'at**).

◇ **halva'ah mashleemah** הלוואה משלימה *nf* complementary loan i.e. supplementary mortgage (in addition to one recommended by Ministry of Housing) offered by banks to home-buyers.

halvay הלוואי *interj* if only; wish it were.

halva|yah/-ot הלוויה *nf* funeral; (+*of:* **-yat**).

ham|ah/-tah המה *v* roared; (*pres* **homeh**; *fut* **yehemeh**).

□ **Ha-Ma'peel** (HaMa'pil) המעפיל *nm* kibbutz in **'Emek Khefer** area (est 1945), 12 km NE of Netanya. Pop. 561.

hamar|ah/-ot המרה *nf* conversion; exchange; (+*of:* **-at**).

hamat|ah/-ot המתה *nf* killing; putting to death; (+*of:* **-at**).

hamatat/-ot khesed המתת חסד *nf* mercy killing; euthanasia.

ham'at|ah/-ot המעטה *nf* reducing; diminishing; (+*of:* **-at**).

(leshon) ham'atah לשון המעטה *nf* under-statement.

ha-menookhah המנוחה *pron f sing* the late; the deceased.

hamkha|'ah/-'ot המחאה *nf* money order; cheque; (+*of:* **-'at**).

hamkha'at/-'ot do'ar המחאת דואר *nf* postal money order.

hamkhash|ah/-ot המחשה *nf* concretization; visualization; realization; (+*of:* **-at**).

hamkhaz|ah/-ot המחזה *nf* dramatization; (+*of:* **-at**).

hamon/-eem המון *nm* **1.** crowd; **2.** *[colloq.]* plenty; (+*of:* **-ey**).

hamool|ah/-ot המולה *nf* tumult; (+*of:* **-at**).

hamoom/-ah המום *adj* stunned.

hamra|'ah/-'ot המראה *nf* take-off; (+*of:* **-'at**).

hamrats|ah/-ot המרצה *nf* urge; legal action under summary procedure; (+*of:* **-at**).

(bakash|ah/-ot be-derekh) hamratsah בקשה בדרך המרצה *nf* application by way of motion.

hamshakh|ah/-ot המשכה *nf* continuation; (+*of:* **-at**).

hamtak|ah/-ot המתקה *nf* sweetening; (+*of:* **-at**).

hamtakat deen המתקת דין *nf* mitigation of sentence.

hamtakat mayeem המתקת מים *nf* desalination.

hamtakat ha-'onesh המתקת העונש *nf* mitigation of punishment.

hamta|nah/-ot המתנה *nf* waiting; (+*of:* **-at**).

(khad|ar/-rey) hamtanah חדר המתנה *nm* waiting-room.

hamtsa|'ah/-'ot המצאה *nf* invention; delivery; (+*of:* **'at**).

hana'ah/-'ot הנאה *nf* pleasure; delight; (+*of:* **-'at**).

(tovat) hana'ah טובת הנאה *nf* advantage.

(zeek|at/-ot) hana'ah זיקת הנאה *nf* privilege.

hana|'ah/-'ot הנעה *nf* propulsion; (+*of:* **'at**).

hana'ah keedmeet הנעה קדמית *nf* front-wheel drive.

hanaf|ah/-ot הנפה *nf* waving; brandishing; (+*of:* **-at**).

hanafat degel/-aleem הנפת דגל *nf* waving (displaying) flag.

han'al|ah הנעלה putting on shoes; shoeing trade.

hanakh|ah/-ot הנחה *nf* **1.** rebate; discount; **2.** assumption: (+*of:* **-at**).

handasah הנדסה *nf* **1.** engineering; **2.** geometry; (+*of:* **-at**).

(kheyl) handasah חיל הנדסה *nm* engineering corps (Army).

handasah elektroneet הנדסה אלקטרונית *nf* electronic engineering.

handasah geneteet הנדסה גנטית *nf* genetic engineering.

handasat beenyan הנדסת בניין *nf* civil engineering.

handasat khashmal הנדסת חשמל *nf* electrical engineering.

handasat makhsheveem הנדסת מחשבים *nf* computer sciences; computer engineering.

handasat mekhonot הנדסת מכונות *nf* mechanical engineering.

handasat tenoo'ah הנדסת תנועה *nf* traffic engineering.

hanets ha-khamah הנץ החמה *nm* sunrise.

hanfash|ah (*npr* **hanpash|ah**)/**-ot** הנפשה *nf* animation (+*of:* **-at**).

han'hag|ah/-ot הנהגה *nf* leadership; (+*of:* **-at**).

han'hal|ah/-ot הנהלה *nf* management; (+*of:* **-at**).

han'halat kheshbonot הנהלת חשבונות *nf* bookkeeping; accountancy.

hankha|yah/-yot הנחיה *nf* directive; instruction; (+*of:* **-yat**).

hanmak|ah/-ot הנמקה *nf* argumentation; (+*of:* **-at**).

hanpak|ah/-ot הנפקה *nf* issue; (+*of:* **-at**).

hanpash|ah/-ot הנפשה *nf* animation; (*+of:* **-at**).
hansham|ah/-ot הנשמה *nf* artificial respiration; (*+of:* **-at**).
hanshamah mel'akhooteet הנשמה מלאכותית *nf* artificial respiration.
hantsakh|ah/-ot הנצחה *nf* perpetuation; immortalization; (*+of:* **-at**).
□ **Ha-'Ogen** (**Haogen**) העוגן *nm* highly industrialized kibbutz (est. 1947), NE of Netanya. Pop. 620.
□ **Ha'on** (HaOn) האון *nm* kibbutz on E. shores of Lake Tiberias (est. 1949), 3 km S. of 'En Gev. Pop. 213.
hapal|ah/-ot הפלה *nf* **1.** bringing (throwing) down; **2.** abortion; miscarriage; (*+of:* **-at**).
◇ **ha-po'el ha-meezrakhee** (**"Hapoel Hamizrahi"**) הפועל המזרחי *nf* former Religious Labor Party, now a component of **MAFDAL** the National Religious Party.
har/-eem הר *nm* mountain; mount; (*pl+of:* **-ey**).
har/-ey ga'ash הר־געש *nm* volcano.
□ **Har Adar** הר אדר *nm* urban settlement in Judea (est. 1986), 10 km NW of Jerusalem, on hill of 1967 battle fame known as **Geev'at ha-Radar** (Radar Hill) between **Keeryat 'Anaveem** and **Ma'aleh ha-Khameeshah**. Pop. 1,150.
□ **Har Geelo** הר גילה *nm* mount S. of Jerusalem, site of capital's new residential suburb neighboring **Bet-Jalah**. Pop. 340.
□ **Har Ha-bayeet** הר הבית *nm* Temple Mount in Jerusalem's Old City, beyond the Wailing Wall, site of the 1st and 2nd Temples (where the Dome of the Rock now stands).
□ **Har ha-Karmel** (Har ha-Carmel) הר הכרמל **1.** *nm* Mount Carmel which, towering over and behind Haifa, contains many picturesque residential suburbs; **2.** *nf* modern and fashionable residential part of Haifa, situated on Mount Carmel itself.
□ **Har ha-Tsofeem** (Har ha-Zofim) הר הצופים *nm* Mount Scopus overlooking Jerusalem from the NE. Site of Hebrew University's main campus.
□ **Har ha-Zeteem** (*or:* **ha-Zeyteem**) הר הזיתים *nm* Mount of Olives overlooking Jerusalem's Old City from the E. Revered by Orthodox Jews who favor it as burial ground.
□ **Har Hertsel** (Har Herzl) הר הרצל Mount Herzl National burial ground in W. of Jerusalem where Herzl, Jabotinsky and other leaders of Israel's renascence are buried.
□ **Har Kena'an** הר כנען *nm* Mount Canaan (936 *nm* altitude) outside Safed (**Tsefat**), location of some of that city's fashionable hotels and villas.
□ **Har Meron** הר מירון *nm* group of mountains in Upper-Galilee, 8 km NW of Safed (**Tsefat**).
□ **Har Tabor** הר תבור *nm* Mount Tabor; (see below, **Har Tavor**, as normatively pronunced).
□ **Har Tavor** הר תבור *nm* historical Mount Tabor, in Lower Galilee, at the center of Yizre'el Valley.
har|ah/-ot הרה **1.** *adj f* pregnant; **2.** *v pres f* is pregnant; (*pst* **hartah**; *fut* **tehereh**).
hara|'ah/-'ot הרעה *nf* deterioration; (*+of:* **-'at**).
har|ag/-gah/-agtee הרג *v* killed; (*pres* **horeg**; *fut* **yaharog**).
har'al|ah/-ot הרעלה *nf* poisoning; (*+of:* **-at**).
har'al|at/-ot dam הרעלת־דם *nf* blood poisoning; toxaemia.
haram|ah/-ot הרמה *nf* lifting; raising; (*+of:* **-at**).
haramat meeshkalot הרמת משקלות *nf* weight-lifting.
haramat yadayeem הרמת ידיים *nf* show of hands.
hararee/-t הררי *adj* mountainous.
har|as/-sah/-astee הרס *v* demolished; destroyed; (*pres* **hores**; *fut* **yaharos**).
har'ash|ah/-ot הרעשה *nf* bombardment; (*+of:* **-at**).
harats|ah/-ot הרצה *nf* running-in (motor-car); (*+of:* **-at**).
□ **(ha)'aravah** הערבה *nf* the "Aravah" Region, area of potentially reclaimable desert, stretching along the Jordanian border, from the Dead Sea to the Red Sea.
harbeh הרבה *adv* many; much.
hardam|ah/-ot הרדמה *nf* anaesthetization; (*+of:* **-at**).
hareeg|ah/-ot הריגה *nf* killing; manslaughter; (*+of:* **-at**).
harees|ah/-ot הריסה *nf* demolition.
harees|ot הריסות *nf pl* ruins (*sing:* **-ah**).
□ **Har'el** (Har'el) הראל *nm* kibbutz (est. 1948) in the hills near Jerusalem. Pop. 78.
harey הרי *prep interj* here is ...; you see ...; behold ...
◇ **harey at mekoodeshet** הרי את מקודשת beginning of wedding formula with which bridegroom addresses bride at a Jewish wedding (the **khoopah**) ceremony (*lit.:* "behold, you are consecrated..."). Equivalent to "with this ring I thee wed".
harey she- הרי ש־ *prep* which means that ...
(she) harey שהרי *prep* for it means that ...
harga'ah/-at הרגעה *nf* calming; tranquilizing.
(emtsa'ey) harga'ah הרגעה אמצעי *nm pl* tranquilizers; means of calming.
(gloolot) harga'ah גלולות הרגעה *nf pl* tranquilizer pills.
harga'at ha-rookhot הרגעת הרוחות *nf* soothing of tempers.
hargash|ah/-ot הרגשה *nf* feeling; sensation; (*+of:* **-at**).
hargash|at/-ot asham (*or:* **ashmah**) הרגשת אשם/אשמה *nf* guilty feeling
hargashat revakhah הרגשת רווחה *nf* feeling of relief.
hargaz|ah/-ot הרגזה *nf* irritating; vexing; (*+of:* **-at**).

harkav|ah/-ot הרכבה *nf* **1.** assembling; **2.** innoculation; **3.** grafting; (+*of:* **-at**).
harkavat ava'boo'ot הרכבת אבעבועות *nf* vaccination; innoculation against smallpox.
harkavat memshalah הרכבת ממשלה *nf* formation of government.
harkhak|ah/-ot הרחקה *nf* removal; distancing; (+*of:* **-at**).
harkhav|ah/-ot הרחבה *nf* broadening; expansion; (+*of:* **-at**).
harkhek הרחק *adv* far away.
harkhek-harkhek הרחק-הרחק *adv* very very far.
harmon/-ot הרמון *nm* harem; (*pl+of:* **-ey**).
harmonee/-t הרמוני *adj* harmonious.
harmonee|yah הרמוניה *nf* harmony; (+*of:* **-yat**).
haroog/-ah הרוג *adj* killed; slain.
haroog/-eem הרוג *nm* casualty; killed person; (*pl+of:* **-ey**).
haroos/-ah הרוס *adj* **1.** demolished; destroyed; **2.** (of a person) ruined; finished.
harpatk|ah/-a'ot הרפתקה *nf* adventure; affair; (+*of:* **-at**).
harpatkan/-eet הרפתקן *nmf* adventurer/-ess.
harpatkanoot הרפתקנות *nf* adventurism.
harpatk|at/-ot ahaveem הרפתקת אהבים *nf* love-affair.
harpay|ah/-yot הרפיה *nf* relaxation; (+*of:* **-yat**).
harsanee/-t הרסני *adj* destructive.
harsha|'ah/-'ot הרשעה *nf* conviction (jurid.).
harsham|ah/-ot הרשמה *nf* registration; (+*of:* **-at**).
har|tah/-eet/-eetee הרתה *v f* (she/you/I) became pregnant; (*pres* **harah;** *fut* **tahareh**).
harta|'ah/-'ot הרתעה *nf* deterrence; (+*of:* **-'at**).
hartav|ah/-ot הרטבה *nf* wetting; moistening; (+*of:* **-at**).
hartav|at/-ot laylah הרטבת לילה *nf* bedwetting.
hartsa|'ah/-'ot הרצאה *nf* lecture; (+*of:* **-'at**).
(oolam/-ey) hartsa'ot אולם הרצאות *nm* conference-hall.
harza|yah/-yot הרזיה *nf* slimming-down; reducing weight; (+*of:* **-yat**).
(makhon/mekhoneem le) harzayah מכון להרזיה *nm* slimming institute.
has! !הס *interj* silence! hush!
has mee-lehazkeer הס מלהזכיר mum's the word!
hasa|'ah/-'ot הסעה *nf* transportation; (+*of:* **-'at**).
hasag|ah/-ot הסגה *nf* **1.** encroachment; **2.** removal; (+*of:* **-at**).
hasag|ah/-ot השגה *nf* **1.** attainment; **2.** criticism; objection; (+*of:* **-at**).
hasag|at/-ot gevool הסגת גבול *nf* trespass; un-ethical competition.
hasak|ah/-ot הסקה *nf* heating; (+*of:* **-at**).
hasakah merkazeet הסקה מרכזית *nf* central heating.
('atsey) hasakah עצי הסקה *nm pl* firewood.
hasakat maskanot הסקת מסקנות *nf* drawing conclusions.

hasakh|ah/-ot הסחה *nf* diversion; diverting; (+*of:* **-at**).
(pe'ool|at/-ot) hasakhah פעולת הסחה *nf* diversionary action.
hasakh|at/-ot ha-da'at הסחת הדעת *nf* **1.** diverting attention; **2.** absentmindedness.
hasat|ah/-ot הסתה *nf* incitement; instigation; (+*of:* **-at**).
hasav|ah/-ot הסבה *nf* **1.** endorsement (of check or promissory note); **2.** transfer (lands, deeds); (+*of:* **-at**).
hasavah meektso'eet הסבה מקצועית *nf* retraining for an alternative profession.
hasbar|ah/-ot הסברה *nf* **1.** information; **2.** propaganda; (+*of:* **-at**).
◇ **(merkaz) ha-hasbarah** see ◇ **merkaz ha-hasbarah**.
hasesan/-eet הססן *nmf* **1.** hesitant person; **2.** *adj* hesitant.
hasesanoo|t-yot הססנות *nf* hesitation.
hasgar|ah/-ot הסגרה *nf* extradition; (+*of:* **-at**).
hashak|ah/-ot השקה *nf* launching (a boat); (+*of:* **-at**).
hash'al|ah/-ot השאלה *nf* lending (book *etc*); (+*of:* **-at**).
(be) hash'alah בהשאלה *adv* **1.** on loan; **2.** figuratively.
hash'ar|ah/-ot השארה *nf* leaving behind; abandonment; (+*of:* **-at**).
hash'ar|ah/-ot השערה *nf* conjecture; assumption; hypothesis; (+*of:* **-at**).
hash'ha|yah/-ot השהיה *nf* suspension; postponement; deferment; (+*of:* **-yat**).
hashba|'ah/-ot השבעה *nf* swearing in; invocation; (+*of:* **-'at**).
hashbakh|ah/-ot השבחה *nf* amelioration; betterment. (+*of:* **-at**).
hashbat|ah/-ot השבתה *nf* lockout; (+*of:* **-at**).
□ **ha-shfelah** השפלה *nf* the Judean Foothills, low hilly region in the center of the country, between Judean Hills to the E, the Coastal Plain to the W, the Samarian Hills to the N. and the N. Negev to the S.
hashgakh|ah/-ot השגחה *nf* supervision; observation. (+*of:* **-at**).
(ha) hashgakhah ההשגחה *nf* Divine Providence.
(be) hashgakhat בהשגחת *adv* under the supervision of.
(takhat) hashgakhat תחת השגחת *adv* under supervision of.
hash'ha|yah/-yot השהייה *nf* delay; suspension; (+*of:* **-yat**).
hashka|'ah/-'ot השקאה *nf* irrigation; (+*of:* **-'at**).
hashka|'ah/-'ot השקעה *nf* investment; (+*of:* **-'at**).
hashkaf|ah/-ot השקפה *nf* outlook; view; (+*of:* **-at**).
(nekood|at/-ot) hashkafah נקודת השקפה *nf* point of view.
hashkaf|at/-ot 'olam השקפת עולם *nf* personal philosophy; outlook; Weltanschauung; (+*of:* **-at**).

hashkam|ah/-ot השכמה *nf* early rising (*+of:* **-at**).

hashka|yah/-yot השקייה *nf* **1.** irrigation; watering; **2.** giving to drink. (*+of:* **-yot**).

hashkem השכם *adv* early in the morning.

hashkem ba-boker השכם בבוקר *adv* early in the morning.

hashkem ve-ha'arev השכם והערב *adv* day and night.

(ba-boker) hashkem בבוקר השכם *adv* early in the morning.

hashkhar|ah/-ot השחרה *nf* blackening; (*+of:* **-at**).

hashkhat|ah/-ot השחתה *nf* destruction; disfigurement; (*+of:* **-at**).

hashkhatat ha-meedot השחתת המידות *nf* corruption; demoralization.

hashlakh|ah/-ot השלכה *nf* repercussion; (*+of:* **-at**).

hashlam|ah/-ot השלמה *nf* completion; (*+of:* **-at**).

hashlamah 'eem השלמה עם *nf* resignation to.

hashla|yah/-yot השליה *nf* deluding; fooling; (*+of:* **-yat**).

hashmad|ah/-ot השמדה *nf* annihilation; extermination; (*+of:* **-at**).

(makhn|eh/-ot) hashmadah מחנה השמדה *nm* extermination camp.

hashmadat-'am השמדת־עם *nf* genocide.

hashman|ah/-ot השמנה *nf* putting on weight; growing fat; (*+of:* **-at**).

hashmat|ah/-ot השמטה *nf* omission; deletion; (*+of:* **-at**).

hashmats|ah/-ot השמצה *nf* defamation; (*+of:* **-at**).

hashpa|'ah/-'ot השפעה *nf* influence; (*+of:* **-at**).

(ba'al/-at) hashpa'ah בעל השפעה *adj* influential.

hashpal|ah/-ot השפלה *nf* humiliation; (*+of:* **-at**).

hashra|yah/-yot השריה *nf* immersion; soaking; (*+of:* **-yat**).

hashtak|ah/-ot השתקה *nf* silencing; (*+of:* **-at**).

hashtal|ah/-ot השתלה *nf* implantation; transplant; (*+of:* **-at**).

hashva|'ah/-'ot השוואה *nf* **1.** comparison; comparing; **2.** equalization; (*+of:* **-'at**).

haskal|ah השכלה *nf* **1.** education; learning; **2.** erudition; enlightment; (*+of:* **-at**).

haskalah gevohah השכלה גבוהה *nf* higher (university) education.

haskalah teekhoneet השכלה תיכונית *nf* secondary education.

haskalah yesodeet השכלה יסודית *nf* primary education; elementary education.

haskam|ah/-ot הסכמה *nf* agreement; (*+of:* **-at**).

(be) haskamah hadadeet בהסכמה הדדית *adv* in mutual agreement.

haskar|ah/-ot השכרה *nf* leasing; hire; (*+of:* **-at**).

◇ **haskarah khofsheet** השכרה חופשית *nf* free i.e. not subjected to the Rent Restriction Law (rent-control).

(le) haskarah להשכרה to rent; for rent.

(le) haskeer להשכיר **1.** renting; for rent; **2.** *v inf* to rent (*pst* **heeskeer**; *pres* **maskeer**; *fut* **yaskeer**).

(bayeet le) haskeer בית להשכיר *nm* house for rent.

(deer|ah/-ot le) haskeer דירה להשכיר *nf* apartment for rent.

(kheder/khadareem le) haskeer חדר להשכיר *nm* room for rent.

□ **Ha-Soleleem** (Hasolelim) הסוללים *nm* kibbutz (est. 1949) in Lower Galilee, 8 km NW of Nazareth. Pop. 261.

haspak|ah/-ot הספקה *nf* supplying; supply; (*+of:* **-at**).

hasrat|ah/-ot הסרטה *nf* filming; taking movies; (*+of:* **-at**).

(oolp|an/-eney) hasratah אולפן הסרטה *nm* film studio.

(seret/seertey) hasratah סרט הסרטה *nm* movie film.

hastar|ah/-ot הסתרה *nf* concealment; (*+of:* **-at**).

hataf|ah/-ot הטפה *nf* sermonizing; preaching; (*+of:* **-at**).

hataf|at/-ot moosar הטפת מוסר *nf* moralizing.

hatal|ah/-ot הטלה *nf* **1.** casting; projection; **2.** throwing; (*+of:* **-at**).

hatalat ashm|ah/-ot הטלה אשמה *nf* laying the blame.

hatalat betseem הטלת ביצים *nf* laying eggs.

hatalat eesoor הטלת איסור *nf* banning; prohibiting.

hatalat goral הטלת גורל *nf* casting lots.

hatalat mas/meeseem הטלת מיסים *nf* imposition of taxes.

hatal|at/-ot moom הטלת מום *nf* maiming; mutilation.

hat'am|ah/-ot התאמה *nf* adjustment; suitability; (*+of:* **-at**).

(see) hat'am|ah אי־התאמה *nf* discrepancy; lack of harmony; unsuitability; (*+of:* **-at**).

hat'am|ah/-ot הטעמה *nf* stressing; stress; (*+of:* **-at**).

□ **Ha-Tanoor** (Hatanur) התנור *nm* waterfall in Galilee near Metullah (**Metoolah**) part of a picturesque Nature Reserve.

hatar|ah/-ot התרה *nf* **1.** release; **2.** permission; (*+of:* **-at**).

hatash|ah/-ot התשה *nf* attrition; (*+of:* **-at**).

(meelkhemet) hatashah מלחמת התשה *nf* war of attrition.

◇ **(meelkhemet ha) hatashah** see ◇ **meelkhemet ha-hatashah**.

hatav|ah/-ot הטבה *nf* **1.** bonus; **2.** improvement; fringe benefit; (*+of:* **-at**).

◇ **hatav|ah/-ot sotsee'yalee|t/-yot** הטבה סוציאלית *nf (lit.)* social benefit i.e. special privilege granted to women-employees of some public institutions to work fewer hours for undiminished pay when back on the job after pregnancy, illness *etc.*

◇ **hatav|at/-ot geel** הטבת גיל *nf* age-benefit i.e. special privilege granted by some institutions to their employees allowing them, upon having reached a certain age, to work fewer hours for undiminished pay.

hatavot הטבות *nf pl* privileges; favors; fringe benefits.

hata|yah/-yot הטיה *nf* bending; deflecting; (*+of:* **-yat**).

hat'a|yah/-yot הטעיה *nf* misleading; deception; (*+of:* **-yat**).

hataz|ah/-ot התזה *nf* **1.** sprinkling; **2.** cutting off; (*+of:* **-at**).

◇ **ha-te'atron ha-kameree ("Hateatron Hakameri")** התיאטרון הקמרי *nm* the "Chamber Theater", Tel-Aviv's Municipal theatrical company, active since 1946.

◇ **ha-teekvah** התקווה *nm* "Hatikvah", the century old anthem of the Zionist movement that with proclamation of the state in 1948 became Israel's national anthem.

◇ **ha-tekheeyah ("Hatehiyah")** התחייה *nf* right-wing political party, started in 1981 by secessionists from Herut **(Kheroot)** Movement because of Israel's withdrawal from Sinai. In 1984 it was joined by **"Tsomet"** group, which later, towards the 1988 elections, separated from it. It plays leading part among three parliamentary groups intent on Israeli maintenance of full extent of its post-1967 borders.

hatfal|ah/-ot התפלה *nf* desalination; (*+of:* **-at**).

hatkaf|ah/-ot התקפה *nf* attack; (*+of:* **-at**).

hatkaf|at/-ot metsakh התקפת מצח *nf* frontal attack.

hatkaf|at/-ot mena' התקפת מנע *nf* preemptive attack.

hatkaf|at/-ot peta' התקפת פתע *nf* surprise attack.

(see) hatkafah אי־התקפה *nm* non-aggression.

hatkan|ah/-ot התקנה *nf* installation; installing; (*+of:* **-at**).

(demey) hatkanah דמי התקנה *nm pl* installation fee.

hatkhal|ah/-ot התחלה *nf* beginning; start.

(ba) hatkhalah בהתחלה *adv* in the beginning.

hatmad|ah/-ot התמדה *nf* perseverance; (*+of:* **-at**).

(be) hatmadah בהתמדה *adv* persistently.

hatna|'ah/-'ot התנעה *nf* starting up (a machine); (*+of:* **-'at**).

hatra|'ah/-'ot התראה *nf* warning; (*+of:* **-'at**).

hatrad|ah/-ot הטרדה *nf* annoyance; molestation; (*+of:* **-at**).

hatram|ah/-ot התרמה *nf* fund raising; collecting contributions; (*+of:* **-at**).

hatsa|'ah/-'ot הצעה *nf* proposition; suggestion; (*+of:* **-'at**).

hatsa|'at/-'ot 'avodah הצעת עבודה *nf* work offer.

hatsa|'at/-'ot hakhlatah הצעת החלטה *nf* draft resolution.

hatsa|'at/-'ot khok הצעת חוק *nf* bill (legislation).

hatsaf|ah/-ot הצפה *nf* flooding; (*+of:* **-at**).

hatsag|ah/-ot הצגה *nf* **1.** performance; show (theatrical); **2.** presentation; (*+of:* **-at**).

hatsag|ah/-ot yomee|t/-yot הצגה יומית *nf* matinee.

hatsag|at/-ot bkhorah הצגת בכורה *nf* premiere; first night.

hatsal|ah/-ot הצלה *nf* rescue; (*+of:* **-at**).

(khagor|at/-ot) hatsalah חגורת הצלה *nf* lifebelt.

(pe'ool|at/-ot) hatsalah פעולת הצלה *nf* rescue drive; rescue operation.

(seer|at/-ot) hatsalah סירת הצלה *nf* lifeboat.

hatsar|ah (*npr* **hats'har|ah)/-ot** הצהרה *nf* declaration; statement; (*+of:* **-at**).

hatsar|ah (*npr* **hats'har|ah)/-ot bee-shevoo'ah** הצהרה בשבועה *nf* affidavit; sworn statement.

◇ **hatsarat balfoor** see ◇ **"Hats'harat Balfoor"**.

hatsaratee (*npr* **hats'haratee)/-t** הצהרתי *adj* declarative.

(pesak/peeskey deen) hatsaratee (*npr* **hats'haratee)/-yeem** פסק־דין הצהרתי *nm* declarative judgment.

hatsat|ah/-ot הצתה *nf* **1.** arson; **2.** ignition (car); (*+of:* **-at**).

hatsats|ah/-ot הצצה *nf* peep; glance; (*+of:* **-at**).

hatsav|ah/-ot הצבה *nf* **1.** posting; placing; **2.** erecting; (*+of:* **-at**).

hatsba|'ah/-'ot הצבעה *nf* **1.** voting; **2.** indicating; (*+of:* **-'at**).

hatsba|'ah/-'ot be-kalfee (*npr* **kalpee)** הצבעה בקלפי *nf* balloting.

hatsba|'at/-'ot ee-emoon הצבעת אי־אמון *nf* vote of no confidence.

hatsba|'at/-'ot emoon הצבעת אמון *nf* vote of confidence.

(he'emeed/-ah le) hatsba'ah העמיד להצבעה *v* put to a vote; (*pres* **ma'ameed** *etc*; *fut* **ya'ameed** *etc*).

hatsda|'ah/-'ot הצדעה *nf* salute; salutation; (*+of:* **-'at**).

hatsdak|ah/-ot הצדקה *nf* justification; (*+of:* **-at**).

hatseedah! הצידה! *interj* aside! make way!

hats'har|ah/-ot הצהרה *nf* declaration; statement; (*+of:* **-at**).

hats'har|ah/-ot bee-shevoo'ah הצהרה בשבועה *nf* affidavit; sworn statement.

◇ **"Hats'harat Balfoor"** הצהרה בלפור *nf* the Balfour Declaration (Nov. 2, 1917) wherein Gt Britain expressed support for the establishment of a Jewish National Home in Palestine (which, at the time, included Trans-Jordan, i.e. what is now the Kingdom of Jordan).

hats'haratee/-t הצהרתי *adj* declarative.

(pesak/peeskey deen) hats'haratee/-yeem פסק־דין הצהרתי *nm* declarative judgment.

◇ **hats'harat hon** הצהרת הון *nf* "statement of assets" sometimes demanded from a taxpayer by income tax authorities in order to make eventual tax-evasion more difficult.

hatslaf|ah/-ot הצלפה *nf* lashing; (*+of:* **-at**).

hatslakh|ah/-ot הצלחה *nf* success; (*+of:* **-at**).

(be) hatslakhah בהצלחה **1.** *adv* successfully; **2.** *interj* (greeting) good luck!

hatsmad|ah/-ot הצמדה *nf* joining; linkage; (*+of:* **-at**).

◇ **hatsmadah le-** הצמדה ל־ *nf* linkage of Israeli currency to the C.o.L. Index, to the U.S.$ or to other hard foreign currency.

◇ **(meelkhemet) ha-'atsma'oot** see ◇ **meelkhemet ha-'atsma'oot**.

hatsna|'ah הצנעה *nf* concealment; hiding; (*+of:* **-'at**).

hatsnakh|ah/-ot הצנחה *nf* **1.** parachuting; (*+of:* **-at**); **2.** *[colloq.]* bringing in for a top job someone "from above" i.e. an outsider.

hatsne'a lekhet הצנע לכת observing strict modesty.

hatsrakh|ah/-ot הצרחה *nf* castling (in chess); (*+of:* **-at**).

hav/-ee הב/הבי *v imp sing m/f* give! give me!

havah הבה *interj* let's; well, then let's ...

havan|ah/-ot הבנה *nf* understanding; comprehension; (*+of:* **-at**).

(see) havan|ah/-ot אי הבנה *nm* misunderstanding.

(kesh|eh/-at) havanah קשה הבנה *adj* slow-witted; slow to grasp.

havar|ah/-ot הברה *nf* syllable; (*+of:* **-at**).

◇ **havarah ashkenazeet** הברה אשכנזית the Ashkenazi pronunciation of Hebrew still current in some Diaspora circles, especially religiously observant ones, and in synagogues and Yeshivas.

◇ **havarah sefaradeet** הברה ספרדית the Sephardi pronunciation of Hebrew as current in Israel which is the official pronunciation there.

hav'ar|ah/-ot הבערה *nf* setting fire; (*+of:* **-at**).

havay הווי *nm* **1.** folklore; **2.** way of life.

havay הבאי *nm* nonsense.

(deevrey) havay דברי הבאי *nm pl* vain bragging; nonsense.

('erev/'arvey) havay ערב הווי *nm* folk-song and folk-dance party.

(tsevet) havay צוות הווי *nm* army team for unit entertainments.

hava|yah/-yot הוויה *nf* existence; (*+of:* **-yat**).

(ka) havayat|o/-ah כהווייתו as it is; as it should be.

◇ **havdalah** הבדלה *nf* ceremony (*lit.:* separation) which marks the end of the Sabbath.

(le) havdeel להבדיל *v inf* to distinguish, differentiate; (*pst* **heevdeel**; *pres* **mavdeel**; *fut* **yavdeel**).

(le) havdeel להבדיל *adv* with all due difference.

haveel/-ah הביל *adj* humid; vaporous.

havhar|ah/-ot הבהרה clarification; (*+of:* **-at**).

havkhan|ah/-ot הבחנה *nf* diagnosis; diagnosing; (*+of:* **-at**).

havlag|ah/-ot הבלגה *nf* forbearance; self-restraint; (*+of:* **-at**).

◇ **(ha)havlagah** ה״הבלגה״ *nf* policy of self-restraint (in the sense of non-retaliation) proclaimed and followed in the years 1936-38 by the Jewish Agency and the "Haggana" towards the wave of incessant Arab terrorist attacks against the then 400,000-strong Jewish community in Palestine. It was bitterly criticized and opposed by the "Irgun B." and what later became the "dissident" groups of **"Etsel"** and **"Lekhee"** from which ultimately the "Herut" Party emerged.

havlat|ah/-ot הבלטה *nf* emphasis; (*+of:* **-at**).

(demey) havra'ah דמי הבראה *nm pl* vacation allowance.

havrag|ah/-ot הברגה *nf* thread (screw); (*+of:* **-at**).

havrak|ah/-ot הברקה *nf* **1.** bright idea; **2.** cabling; (*+of:* **-at**).

havrakh|ah/-ot הברחה *nf* smuggling; contraband; (*+of:* **-at**).

havshal|ah/-ot הבשלה *nf* ripening; (*+of:* **-at**).

havtakh|ah/-ot הבטחה *nf* promise; assurance; (*+of:* **-at**).

havtakh|at/-ot neesoo'een הבטחת נישואין *nf* promise of marriage.

havoo הבו *interj* **1.** let's; let us; let you; **2.** will you give.

hay|ah/-tah/-eetee היה *v* was; (*pres* **heeneh**; *fut* **yeehyeh**).

hayah be-da'at|o/-ah/-ee *etc* היה בדעתו *v pst* he/she/I *(etc)* had in mind; he/she/I *(etc)* intended.

hayah 'al/-ay/-av/-ekha *etc* היה על *v pst* I/you (*etc*) should have; I/you (*etc*) was/were supposed to.

hay|ah/-tah lee/-lekhah/-lakh *etc* היה ל־/לי *v* I/you *(etc)* had.

(amoor/-ah) hay|ah/-tah/-eetee אמור היה *v pst* was supposed to.

(asoo|y/-yah) hay|ah/-tah/-eetee *etc* עשוי היה *v pst* was likely to.

ha-yam הים *nm* "the sea" — colloquial reference to Tel-Aviv's and other shore towns' Mediterranean waterfront.

haynoo-hakh היינו הך all the same; makes no difference.

(de) haynoo דהיינו viz; namely.

hayo hay|ah/-tah היה היה *v pst* once upon a time there was.

◻ **Ha-Yogev** היוגב *nm* village in Yizre'el Valley (est. 1949), 6 km W. of 'Afula. Pop. 547.

hayom היום *adv* today.

hayom ba-'erev היום בערב *adv* this evening; tonight.

haysher היישר *adv* directly; straight on ahead.

haz'ak|ah/-ot הזעקה *nf* **1.** summoning; **2.** alert; (*+of:* **-at**).

(makhsheer/-ey) haz'akah מכשיר הזעקה *nm* alarm system.

hazan|ah/-ot/- הזנה *nf* feeding; (*+of:* **-at**).

hazay|ah/-ot הזיה *nf* delusion; hallucination; (*+of:* **-yat**).

hazaz|ah/-ot הזזה *nf* budging; sliding; shifting; (*+of:* **-at**).

(delet/daltot) hazazah דלת הזזה *nf* sliding door.

(khalon/-ot) hazazah חלון הזזה *nm* sliding window.

(trees/-ey) hazazah תריס הזזה *nm* sliding blind.

haz'har|ah/-ot הזהרה *nf* warning; caution; (*+of:* **-at**).

hazkar|ah/-ot הזכרה *nf* mentioning; reminding; (*+of:* **-at**).

◇ **hazkarat neshamot** הזכרת נשמות *nf* "Yizkor", the memorial prayer for deceased next of kin. This is held in synagogues, as part of the holiday service, right after the Torah reading has ended, on Yom Kippur,and on the last day of Succot, Passover and Shavuot.

hazman|ah/-ot הזמנה *nf* invitation; summons; (*+of:* **-at**).

hazmanah (*etc*) **zoogeet** הזמנה זוגית *nf* invitation for two.

(be) hazmanah בהזמנה *adv* (made) to order.

(le-fee) hazmanah לפי הזמנה *adv* **1.** made to order; **2.** (admission) by invitation.

(le) hazmanat להזמנת *adv* **1.** at the invitation of; **2.** by order of.

haznakh|ah/-ot הזנחה *nf* neglect; oversight; (*+of:* **-at**).

□ **Ha-Zore'a'** (Hazorea') הזורע *nm* large and highly industrialized kibbutz (est. 1936) in the Yizre'el Valley. Pop. 1,020.

□ **Ha-Zor'eem** (Hazore'im) הזורעים *nm* village (est. 1939) in **Yavne'el** lowland, Lower Galilee, 6 km SE of Tiberias. Pop. 447.

hazra'ah melakhooteet הזרעה מלאכותית *nf* artificial insemination.

hazrak|ah/-ot הזרקה *nf* innoculation; (*+of:* **-at**).

hazram|ah/-ot הזרמה *nf* pouring in; causing to flow; (*+of:* **-at**).

◇ **hazramah** ההזרמה flooding with paper-money (in an inflationary economy).

he ה *nf* fifth letter of the Hebrew alphabet. Pronounced like the English **h**.

he ה׳ *num nm* digit 5 in Hebrew alphabetic numerological system.

he lakh/-em/-en הא לך *(addressing f sing/ m pl/ f pl)* have! take! here you have.

he lekha הא לך *(addressing m sing)* have! take! here you have.

(yom) he יום ה׳ *nm* Thursday.

(yom) he be- יום ה׳ ב־ fifth day of a Jewish calendar-month.

he'ader העדר *nm* lack of; absence.

he'adroo|t/-yot היעדרות *nf* absence.

◇ **he'akhzoo|t/-yot** היאחזות *nf* pioneering army settlement in areas under military administration.

he'almoo|t/-yot היעלמות *nf* disappearance.

he'anoo|t/-yot היענות *nf* response.

he'ar|ah/-ot הערה *nf* **1.** remark; **2.** footnote; note; (*+of:* **-at**).

he'arkhoo|t/-yot היערכות *nf* deployment.

he'at|ah/-ot האטה *nf* slowdown; (*+of:* **-at**).

he'avkoo|t/-yot היאבקות *nf* wrestling.

he'az|ah/-ot העזה *nf* **1.** daring; **2.** insolence; (*+of:* **-at**).

hebet/-eem היבט *nm* aspect; (*+of:* **-ey**).

hed/-eem הד *nm* echo; reaction; (*pl+of:* **-ey**).

hedeem הדים *nm pl* rumors; reports (*+of:* **-ey**; *sing:* **hed**).

hedef הדף *nm* blast.

hedek הדק *nm* trigger.

hedyot/-ot הדיוט *nm* **1.** layman; **2.** simpleton.

> NOTE: Transliterated Hebrew words with two **e**-s separated (e.g. **e'e** or **e'e**) and therefore pronounced separately, (each as in *help* or *end*) appear first hereunder as a group. They are followed by words in which two **e**-s, undivided, form a long vowel (pronounced as in **seen**)

he'ed|eef/-eefah/-aftee העדיף preferred; (*pres* **ma'adeef**; *fut* **ya'adeef**).

he'ed|eem/-eemah/-amtee האדים *v* flushed; reddened; (*pres* **ma'adeem**; *fut* **ya'adeem**).

he'eder העדר *nm* lack of; absence (*+of:* **he'ader**).

he'eed/-ah/he'adetee העיד *v* testified; (*pres* **me'eed**; *fut* **ya'eed**).

he'eef/-ah/he'aftee העיף *v* **1.** threw; cast; **2.** *[slang]* fired; **3.** kicked out; ejected; (*pres* **me'eef**; *fut* **ya'eef**).

he'eef (*etc*) **'ayeen** העיף עין *v* threw an eye.

he'eek/-ah/he'aktee העיק *v* weighed heavy (*pres* **me'eek**; *fut* **ya'eek**).

he'eer/-ah/he'artee האיר *v* threw light on illuminated; (*pres* **me'eer**; *fut* **ya'eer**).

he'eer/-ah/he'artee העיר *v* **1.** awakened **2.** remarked; (*pres* **me'eer**; *fut* **ya'eer**).

he'eets/-ah/he'atstee האיץ *v* **1.** hurried **2.** urged; (*pres* **me'eets**; *fut* **ya'eets**).

he'eez (*npr* **he'ez**)**/-ah/he'aztee** העיז *v* dared (*pres* **me'ez**; *fut* **ya'ez**).

he'ef|eer/-ah/-artee האפיר *v* turned grey; (*pres* **ma'afeer**; *fut* **ya'afeer**).

he'el|ah/-tah/-etee העלה *v* raised; (*pres* **ma'aleh** *fut* **ya'aleh**).

he'elah (*etc*) **'al ha-ktav** העלה על הכתב *v* put in writing.

he'elah (*etc*) **'al nes** העלה על נס *v* extolled praised extravagantly.

he'elah (*etc*) **ba-'esh** העלה באש *v* set fire to.

he'elah (*etc*) **gerah** העלה גירה *v* ruminated chewed its cud.

he'elah (*etc*) **khaloodah** העלה חלודה *v* got rusty

he'elah (*etc*) **la-arets** העלה לארץ *v* brought immigrants (to Israel).

he'el|eel/-eelah/-altee העליל *v* accused falsely; slandered; (*pres* **ma'aleel**; *fut* **ya'aleel**).

he'el|eem/-ah/h-amtee העלים *v* hid; concealed; (*pres* **ma'aleem**; *fut* **ya'aleem**).

he'eleem (*etc*) **'ayeen** העלים עין *v* ignored; shut eyes to.

he'eleem (*etc*) **hakhnasah** העלים הכנסה *v* concealed income.

he'el|eev/-eevah/-avtee העליב *v* insulted; (*pres* **ma'aleev**; *fut* **ya'aleev**).

he'em|eed/-eedah/-adetee העמיד *v* stopped; set up; (*pres* **ma'ameed**; *fut* **ya'ameed**).

he'emeed (*etc*) **le-hatsba'ah** העמיד להצבעה *v* put to vote.

he'emeed (*etc*) **le meenyan** העמיד למניין *v* put to vote.

he'emeed (*etc*) **paneem** העמיד פנים *v* pretended.

he'emeed (*etc*) **otee/-oto 'al** העמיד אותי על *v* drew my/his (*etc*) attention to.

he'emeen/-eenah/-antee האמין *v* believed; (*pres* **ma'ameen**; *fut* **ya'ameen**).

he'emeen (*etc*) **be** האמין ב־ *v* believed in.

he'emeen (*etc*) **le-** האמין ל־ *v* trusted one; believed one.

he'emeer/-ah האמיר *v* soared; went up (in price) (*pres* **ma'ameer**; *fut* **ya'ameer**).

he'em|ees/-eesah/-astee העמיס *v* loaded; (*pres* **ma'mees**; *fut* **ya'amees**).

he'em|eek/-eekah/-aktee העמיק *v* deepened; descended deeply; (*pres* **ma'ameek**; *fut* **ya'ameek**).

he'en|eek/-eekah/-aktee העניק *v* granted; bestowed upon; (*pres* **ma'aneek**; *fut* **ya'aneek**).

he'en|eesh/-eeshah/-ashtee העניש *v* punished; (*pres* **ma'aneesh**; *fut* **ya'aneesh**).

he'ep|eel/-eelah/-altee העפיל *v* dared; strove upwards; (*pres* **ma'apeel**; *fut* **ya'apeel**).

◇ **he'epeel** (*etc*) **la-arets** העפיל לארץ *v* succeeded in entering Palestine "illegally" (during the British Mandate period when immigration of Jews into the country was extremely restricted).

he'er|eekh/-eekhah/-akhtee האריך *v* **1.** lengthened; **2.** prolonged; (*pres* **ma'areekh**; *fut* **ya'areekh**).

he'er|eekh (*etc*) **yameem** האריך ימים *v* lived long; survived.

he'er|eekh/-eekhah/-akhtee העריך *v* valued; estimated; (*pres* **ma'areekh**; *fut* **ya'areekh**).

he'er|eem/-eemah/-amtee הערים *v* **1.** tricked; cheated; **2.** piled up; (*pres* **ma'areem**; *fut* **ya'areem**).

he'er|eem (*etc*) **meekhsholeem** הערים מכשולים *v* put up obstacles; made difficulties.

he'er|eets/-eetsah/-atstee העריץ *v* admired; (*pres* **ma'areets**; *fut* **ya'areets**).

he'es|eek/-eekah/-aktee העסיק *v* employed; kept busy; (*pres* **ma'aseek**; *fut* **ya'aseek**).

he'esh|eem/-eemah/-amtee האשים *v* accused; charged; (*pres* **ma'asheem**; *fut* **ya'asheem**).

he'esh|eer/-eerah/-artee העשיר *v* enriched; (*pres* **ma'asheer**; *fut* **ya'asheer**).

he'et/-ah/he'atetee האט *v* slowed down; (*pres* **me'et**; *fut* **ya'et**).

he'eteek/-eekah/-aktee העתיק *v* **1.** copied; **2.** moved residence; (*pres* **ma'ateek**; *fut* **ya'ateek**).

he'et|ek/-keem העתק *nm* copy; (*pl+of*: **-key**).

he'ev|eed/-eedah/-adetee העביד *v* employed; made work; (*pres* **ma'aveed**; *fut* **ya'aveed**).

he'ev|eer/-eerah/-artee העביר *v* transferred; transported; (*pres* **ma'aveer**; *fut* **ya'aveer**).

he'eveer (*etc*) **et ha-zman** העביר את הזמן *v* passed the time.

he'ez/-ah/he'aztee העז *v* dared; (*pres* **me'ez**; *fut* **ya'ez**).

he'ez|een/-eenah/-antee האזין *v* listened; (*pres* **ma'azeen**; *fut* **ya'azeen**).

hee היא *nf pron* she.

hee היא *v pres* is; (*pst* **haytah**; *fut* **teehyeh**).

hee asher היא אשר it's she who; it's her whom.

hee hee היא היא she is the one who; it is her whom.

heebadloo|t/-yot היבדלות *nf* segregation.

heeb|eet/-eetah/-atetee הביט *v* looked (at); (*pres* **mabeet**; *fut* **yabeet**).

heedard|er/-erah/-artee הידרדר *v* deteriorated; (*pres* **meedarder**; *fut* **yeedarder**).

heedarderoot הידרדרות *nf* deterioration.

heedb|eek/-eekah/-aktee הדביק *v* **1.** glued; **2.** attained; **3.** infected; (*pres* **madbeek**; *fut* **yadbeek**).

heed|'eeg/-'eegah/-'agtee הדאיג *v* worried; bothered; (*pres* **mad'eeg**; *fut* **yad'eeg**).

heed|ek/-kah/-aktee הידק *v* tightened; fastened; (*pres* **mehadek**; *fut* **yehadek**).

heedg|eem/-eemah/-amtee הדגים *v* demonstrated; (*pres* **madgeem**; *fut* **yadgeem**).

heedg|eesh/-eeshah/-ashtee הדגיש *v* pointed out; emphasized; (*pres* **madgeesh**; *fut* **yadgeesh**).

heed'|hed/-hadah/-hadetee הדהד *v* echoed; resounded; (*pres* **mehad'hed**; *fut* **yehad'hed**).

heed'|heem/-heemah/-hamtee הדהים *v* amazed; astounded; shocked; (*pres* **mad'heem**; *fut* **yad'heem**).

heedl|eef/-eefah/-aftee הדליף *v* **1.** disclosed; divulged; **2.** made leak out (a secret); (*pres* **madleef**; *fut* **yadleef**).

heedl|eek/-eekah/-aktee הדליק *v* lighted; kindled; (*pres* **madleek**; *fut* **yadleek**).

heedook/-eem הידוק *nm* **1.** tightening; **2.** strengthening; (*pl+of*: **-ey**).

heedook kesharеem הידוק קשרים *nm* rapprochement.

heedook khagorah הידוק חגורה tightening the belt.

heedoor הידור *nm* elegance.

(be) heedoor בהידור *adv* elegantly.

heedp|ees/-eesah/-astee הדפיס *v* printed; (*pres* **madpees;** *fut* **yadpees**).

heedr|eekh/-eekhah/-akhtee הדריך *v* guided; trained; instructed; (*pres* **madreekh;** *fut* **yadreekh**).

heef|'eel/-'eelah/-'altee הפעיל *v* activated; put in motion; (*pres* **maf'eel;** *fut* **yaf'eel**).

heefg|een/-eenah/-antee הפגין *v* demonstrated; (*pres* **mafgeen;** *fut* **yafgeen**).

heefg|eesh/-eeshah/-ashtee הפגיש *v* brought together; caused to meet; (*pres* **mafgeesh;** *fut* **yafgeesh**).

heefg|eez/-eezah/-aztee הפגיז *v* shelled; bombarded; (*pres* **mafgeez;** *fut* **yafgeez**).

heefk|ee'a/-ee'ah/-a'tee הפקיע *v* requisitioned; expropriated; (*pres* **mafkee'a;** *fut* **yafkee'a**).

heefk|eed/-eedah/-adetee הפקיד *v* entrusted; deposited; (*pres* **mafkeed;** *fut* **yafkeed**).

heefk|eer/-eerah/-kartee הפקיר *v* abandoned; (*pres* **mafkeer;** *fut* **yafkeer**).

heefkh|eed/-eedah/-adetee הפחיד *v* scared; frightened; (*pres* **mafkheed;** *fut* **yafkheed**).

heefkh|eet/-eetah/-atetee הפחית *v* deducted; reduced; (*pres* **mafkheet;** *fut* **yafkheet**).

heefl|ee/-ee'ah/-etee הפליא *v* amazed; (*pres* **maflee;** *fut* **yaflee**).

heeflee (*etc*) **et makot|av/-eha** הפליא את מכותיו *v* gave him/her a good beating.

heefl|eeg/-eegah/-agtee הפליג **1.** sailed; **2.** exaggerated; (*pres* **mafleeg;** *fut* **yafleeg**).

heefl|eel/-eelah/-altee הפליל *v* incriminated; arraigned; (*pres* **mafleel;** *fut* **yafleel**).

heefl|eet/-eetah/-atetee הפליט *v* let slip; ejaculated; (*pres* **mafleet;** *fut* **yafleet**).

heefl|eets/-eetsah/-atstee הפליץ *[slang] v* farted; (*pres* **mafleets;** *fut* **yafleets**).

heefn|ah/-etah/-etee הפנה *v* directed; sent on; referred someone; (*pres* **mafneh;** *fut* **yafneh**).

heefr|ee'a'/-ee'ah/-a'tee הפריע *v* obstructed; interfered with; (*pres* **mafree'a';** *fut* **yafree'a'**).

heefr|eed/-eedah/-adetee הפריד *v* separated (*pres* **mafreed;** *fut* **yafreed**).

heefr|eekh/-eekhah/-akhtee הפריך *v* set aside; (*pres* **mafreekh;** *fut* **yafreekh**).

heefr|eesh/-eeshah/-ashtee הפריש *v* set aside; (*pres* **mafreesh;** *fut* **yafreesh**).

heefr|eez/-eezah/-aztee הפריז *v* exaggerated; overdid; (*pres* **mafreez;** *fut* **yafreez**).

heefs|eed/-eedah/-adetee הפסיד *v* lost; (*pres* **mafseed;** *fut* **yafseed**).

heefs|eek/-eekah/-aktee הפסיק *v* ceased; stopped; interrupted; (*pres* **mafseek;** *fut* **yafseek**).

heefsh|eel/-eelah/-altee הפשיל *v* rolled up (sleeves); (*pres* **mafsheel;** *fut* **yafsheel**).

heefsh|eet/-eetah/-atetee הפשיט *v* undressed; (*pres* **mafsheet;** *fut* **yafsheet**).

heeft|ee'a'/-ee'ah/-a'tee הפתיע *v* surprised; (*pres* **maftee'a';** *fut* **yaftee'a'**).

heeft|eer/-eerah/-artee הפטיר *v* remarked; (*pres* **mafteer;** *fut* **yafteer**).

heefts|eer/-eerah/-artee הפציר *v* implored; insisted; (*pres* **maftseer;** *fut* **yaftseer**).

heefts|eets/-eetsah/-atstee הפציץ *v* bombarded; (*pres* **maftseets;** *fut* **yaftseets**).

heegamloot היגמלות *nf* weaning.

heegareroo|t/-yot היגררות *nf* following blindly.

heegayon היגיון *nm* logic; reasoning.

heegb|ee'ah/-eehah/-ahtee הגביה *v* raised; heightened; (*pres* **magbee'ah;** *fut* **yagbee'ah**).

heegb|eel/-eelah/-altee הגביל *v* restricted; limited; (*pres* **magbeel;** *fut* **yagbeel**).

heeg|beer/-eerah/-artee הגביר *v* increased; strengthened; (*pres* **magbeer;** *fut* **yagbeer**).

heegd|eel/-eelah/-altee הגדיל *v* increased; enlarged; (*pres* **magdeel;** *fut* **yagdeel**).

heegd|eer/-eerah/-artee הגדיר *v* defined; (*pres* **magdeer;** *fut* **yagdeer**).

heegd|eesh/-eeshah/-ashtee הגדיש *v* overdid; (*pres* **magdeesh;** *fut* **yagdeesh**).

heegdeesh (*etc*) **et ha-se'ah** הגדיש את הסאה *v* overdid it.

heeg|ee'a'/-ee'ah/-a'tee הגיע *v* arrived; reached; (*pres* **magee'a';** *fut* **yagee'a'**).

heeg|ee'akh (*npr* **hegee'akh**)**/-eekhah/-akhtee** הגיח *v* burst forth; broke out; (*pres* **megee'akh;** *fut* **yagee'akh**).

heeg|eed/-eedah/-adetee הגיד *v* told; said; (*pres* **mageed;** *fut* **yageed**).

heeg|eesh/-eeshah/-ashtee הגיש *v* **1.** presented; submitted; **2.** served; supplied; (*pres* **mageesh;** *fut* **yageesh**).

heegeesh (*etc*) **bakashah** הגיש בקשה *v* petitioned; submitted a request.

heegeesh/-ah heetpatroot הגיש התפטרות *v* submitted one's resignation.

heegeesh (*etc*) **teloon|ah/-ot** הגיש תלונה *v* lodged a complaint.

heeg|er/-rah/-artee היגר *v* emigrated; left the country; (*pres* **mehager;** *fut* **yehager**).

heegleed/-ah הגליד *v* formed a scar; cicatrized; (*pres* **magleed;** *fut* **yagleed**).

heegm|eesh/-eeshah/-ashtee הגמיש *v* **1.** elasticized; became flexible; **2.** (*figurat.*) conceded; (*pres* **magmeesh;** *fut* **yagmeesh**).

heegn|eev/-eevah/-avtee הגניב *v* smuggled in; stole into; (*pres* **magneev;** *fut* **yagneev**).

heegooy היגוי *nm* pronunciation.

heegr|eel/-eelah/-raltee הגריל *v* raffled; drew lots; (*pres* **magreel;** *fut* **yagreel**).

heegsh|eem/-eemah/-amtee הגשים *v* **1.** implemented; **2.** *[colloq.]* it rained (*pres* **magsheem;** *fut* **yagsheem**).

heegyenah היגיינה *nf* hygiene.

heegz|eem/-eemah/-amtee הגזים *v* exaggerated; (*pres* **magzeem;** *fut* **yagzeem**).

heek|ah/-tah/-etee הכה *v* beat; struck; (*pres* **makeh;** *fut* **yakeh**).

heekah (*etc*) **shor|esh/-osheem** הכה שורש *v* struck roots.

heekb|eel/-eelah/-altee הקביל *v* drew a parallel; (*pres* **makbeel;** *fut* **yakbeel**).

heekbeel (*etc*) **et peney** הקביל את פני *v* welcomed; met on arrival; received.

heekd|eem/-eemah/-amtee הקדים *v* preceded; anticipated; (*pres* **makdeem**; *fut* **yakdeem**).

heekd|eesh/-eeshah/-ashtee הקדיש *v* devoted; dedicated; (*pres* **makdeesh**; *fut* **yakdeesh**).

heekdeesh (*etc*) **'atsm|o/-ah/-ee** הקדיש עצמו *v* devoted one/him/her/my -self.

heekdeesh (*etc*) **tesoomat-lev** הקדיש תשומת לב *v* paid/devoted attention.

heek|eef/-eefah/-aftee הקיף *v* **1.** surrounded; **2.** comprised; encompassed; (*pres* **makeef**; *fut* **yakeef**).

heek|eer/-eerah/-artee הכיר *v* **1.** recognized; **2.** made acquaintance; (*pres* **makeer**; *fut* **yakeer**).

heekeer (*etc*) **tovah** הכיר טובה *v* was grateful.

heekhb|eed/-eedah/-adetee הכביד *v* **1.** lay heavy; **2.** bothered; inconvenienced; (*pres* **makhbeed**; *fut* **yakhbeed**).

heekh|'ees/-'eesah/-'astee הכעיס *v* angered; (*pres* **makh'ees**; *fut* **yakh'ees**).

heekh|'eev/-'eevah/-'avtee הכאיב *v* hurt; (*pres* **makh'eev**; *fut* **yakh'eev**).

heekhl|eel/-eelah/-altee הכליל *v* generalized; included; (*pres* **makhleel**; *fut* **yakhleel**).

heekhn|ee'a/-ee'ah/-a'tee הכניע *v* subdued; overpowered; (*pres* **makhnee'a**; *fut* **yakhnee'a**).

heekhn|ees/-eesah/-astee הכניס *v* introduced; entered; (*pres* **makhnees**; *fut* **yakhnees**).

heekhp|eel/-eelah/-altee הכפיל *v* **1.** doubled; **2.** multiplied; (*pres* **makhpeel**; *fut* **yakhpeel**).

heekhr|ee'a'/-ee'ah/-a'tee הכריע *v* decided; tipped the scale; (*pres* **makhree'a'**; *fut* **yakhree'a'**).

heekhr|ee'akh/-eekhah/-akhtee הכריח *v* forced; compelled; (*pres* **makhree'akh**; *fut* **yakhree'ah**).

heekhr|eez/-eezah/-aztee הכריז *v* announced; (*pres* **makhreez**; *fut* **yakhreez**).

heekh'sh|eel/-eelah/-altee הכשיל *v* corrupted; caused to fail; (*pres* **makh'sheel**; *fut* **yakh'sheel**).

heekh'sh|eer/-eerah/-artee הכשיר *v* **1.** prepared; **2.** made "kosher"; (*pres* **makh'sheer**; *fut* **yakh'sheer**).

heekh'sheer (*etc*) **et ha-karka'** הכשיר את הקרקע *v* prepared the ground.

heekht|eem/-eemah/-amtee הכתים *v* stained; besmirched; (*pres* **makhteem**; *fut* **yakhteem**).

heekht|eer/-eerah/-artee הכתיר *v* crowned; (*pres* **makhteer**; *fut* **yakhteer**).

heekht|eev/-eevah/-avtee הכתיב *v* dictated; (*pres* **makhteev**; *fut* **yakhteev**).

heekhz|eev/-eevah/-avtee הכזיב *v* failed; let down; (*pres* **makhzeev**; *fut* **yakhzeev**).

heek'kh|eesh (*npr* **heekh'kh|eesh**)**/-eeshah/-ashtee** הכחיש *v* denied; (*pres* **mak'kheesh**; *fut* **yak'kheesh**).

heekl|eet/-eetah/-atetee הקליט *v* recorded; (*pres* **makleet**; *fut* **yakleet**).

heekon/-ee! היכון! *v imp sing m/f* be prepared! stand by! (*inf* **leheekon**; *pst & pres* **nakhon**; *fut* **yeekon**)

heekp|eets/-eetsah/-atstee הקפיץ *v* **1.** bounced; shocked; **2.** *[colloq.]* gave a lift by vehicle; (*pres* **makpeets**; *fut* **yakpeets**).

heekr|ee/-ee'ah/-etee הקריא *v* recited; read out; (*pres* **makree**; *fut* **yakree**).

heekr|ee'akh/-khah/-akhtee הקריח *v* grew bald; (*pres* **makree'akh**; *fut* **yakree'akh**).

heekr|een/-eenah/-antee הקרין *v* projected (on screen); radiated; (*pres* **makreen**; *fut* **yakreen**).

heekr|eets/-eetsah/-atstee הקריץ *v [slang]* got hold; unexpectedly procured; (*pres* **makreets**; *fut* **yakreets**).

heekr|eev/-eevah/-avtee הקריב *v* **1.** sacrificed; **2.** drew near; (*pres* **makreev**; *fut* **yakreev**).

heeks|eem/-eemah/-amtee הקסים *v* charmed; (*pres* **makseem**; *fut* **yakseem**).

heeksh|ah/-etah/-etee הקשה *v* hardened; made difficult; (*pres* **maksheh** *fut* **yaksheh**).

heeksh|ee'akh/-eekhah/-akhtee הקשיח *v* stiffened; hardened; (*pres* **makshee'akh**; *fut* **yakshee'akh**).

heeksh|eev/-eevah/-avtee הקשיב *v* listened; paid attention; heeded; (*pres* **maksheev**; *fut* **yaksheev**).

heekt|een/-eenah/-antee הקטין *v* diminished; reduced; (*pres* **markteen**; *fut* **yakteen**).

heekts|eev/-eevah/-avtee הקציב *v* allocated; (*pres* **maktseev**; *fut* **yaktseev**).

heelb|een/-eenah/-antee הלבין *v* **1.** paled; whitened; **2.** turned gray (hair); (*pres* **malbeen**; *fut* **yalbeen**).

heel|'eem/-'eemah/-'amtee הלאים *v* nationalized; (*pres* **mal'eem**; *fut* **yal'eem**).

heel|'eet/-'eetah/-'atetee הלעיט *v* stuffed; (*pres* **mal'eet**; *fut* **yal'eet**).

heel|ekh/-khah/-akhtee הילך *v* walked; walked about; (*pres* **mehalekh**; *fut* **yehalekh**).

heelekh (*etc*) **bee-g'dolot** הילך בגדולות *v* saw big; aspired to great things.

heelekh (*etc*) **eymeem** הילך אימים *v* terrorized.

heel|el/-elah/-altee הילל *v* praised; lauded; (*pres* **mehalel**; *fut* **yehalel**).

heelk|ah/-etah/-etee הלקה *v* flogged; whipped; (*pres* **malkeh**; *fut* **yalkeh**).

heelkh|eem/-eemah/-amtee הלחים *v* soldered; welded; (*pres* **malkheem**; *fut* **yalkheem**).

heelkh|een/-eenah/-antee הלחין *v* composed (music); (*pres* **malkheen**; *fut* **yalkheen**).

heelkhey-roo'akh הלכי רוח *nm pl* moods (*sing:* **halokh** *etc*).

heelookh/-eem הילוך *nm* **1.** gait; **2.** gear; transmission; (*pl+of:* **-ey**).

heelookheem otomateeyeem הילוכים אוטומטיים *nm pl* automatic gears.

(teyvat) heelookheem תיבת הילוכים *nf* gearbox.

heelool|ah/-ot הילולה *nm* festival; merrymaking; (*+of:* **-at**).

heelsh|een/-eenah/-antee הלשין *v* informed on; denounced; (*pres* **malsheen**; *fut* **yalsheen**).

heelv|ah/-etah/-etee הלווה *v* lent (money); (*pres* **malveh;** *fut* **yalveh).**

heemanoot הימנות *nf* **1.** siding with; **2.** being counted among.

heeman'oo|t/-yot הימנעות *nf* abstention.

heemash'khoot הימשכות *nf* **1.** attraction to; **2.** continuation.

heemats'oot הימצאות *nf* existence; availability.

heem|'ees/-'eesah/-'astee המאיס *v* made it hateful; made one abhor; (*pres* **mam'ees;** *fut* **yam'ees).**

heeml|ee'akh/-khah/-akhtee המליח *v* salted; (*pres* **mamlee'akh;** *fut* **yamlee'akh).**

heeml|eekh/-eekhah/-akhtee המליך *v* installed as king; crowned; (*pres* **mamleekh;** *fut* **yamleekh).**

heeml|eet/-ah המליט *v* gave birth (mammals); laid eggs; (*pres* **mamleet;** *fut* **yamleet).**

heeml|eets/-eetsah/-atstee המליץ *v* recommended; (*pres* **mamleets;** *fut* **yamleets).**

heem|em/-emah/-amtee הימם *v* shocked; (*pres* **mehamem;** *fut* **yehamem).**

heemnon/-eem המנון *nm* anthem (*pl+of:* **-ey).**

heemoor/-eem הימור *nm* wager; bet; gamble; (*pl+of:* **-ey).**

heemr|ee/-ee'ah/-etee המריא *v* took off (airplane); (*pres* **mamree;** *fut* **yamree).**

heemr|eed/-eedah/-adetee המריד *v* incited to rebellion; (*pres* **mamreed;** *fut* **yamreed).**

heemr|eets/-eetsah/-atstee המריץ *v* urged; stimulated; (*pres* **mamreets;** *fut* **yamreets).**

heemsh|eekh/-eekhah/-akhtee המשיך *v* continued; (*pres* **mamsheekh;** *fut* **yamsheekh).**

heemsh|eel/-eelah/-altee המשיל *v* likened; compared; (*pres* **mamsheel;** *fut* **yamsheel).**

heemsheel (*etc*) **mashal** המשיל משל *v* quoted a parable.

heemt|eek/-eekah/-aktee המתיק *v* sweetened; (*pres* **mamteek;** *fut* **yamteek).**

heemteek (*etc*) **sod** המתיק סוד *v* took sweet counsel together.

heemt|een/-eenah/-antee המתין *v* waited; (*pres* **mamteen;** *fut* **yamteen).**

heemts|ee/-ee'ah/-etee המציא *v* **1.** invented; **2.** delivered; (*pres* **mamtsee;** *fut* **yamtsee).**

heenah הינה *v pres 3rd pers f sing* is; (*pst* **haytah;** *fut* **teehyeh).**

heenakh הנך *v pres f 2nd pers sing* you are; (*pst* **hayeet;** *fut* **teehyee).**

heena|m/-n הינם *v m/f 3rd pers pl* are; (*pst* **hayoo;** *fut* **yeehyoo).**

heenatkoo|t/-yot הינתקות *nf* severance; cutting off.

heenatsloot הינצלות *nf* rescue; escape.

heen|ee'akh/-eekhah/-akhtee הניח *v* **1.** put; **2.** laid down; **3.** let; permitted; **4.** assumed; (*pres* **manee'akh;** *fut* **yanee'akh).**

heene|'eem/-'eemah/-'amtee הנעים *v* made pleasant; made agreeable; (*pres* **mane'eem;** *fut* **yane'eem).**

heeneh הנה *prep* here is; behold.

heeneh hoo/hee/hem/hen הנה הוא/היא/הם/הן here he/she/they *m/f* is/are.

heenekh (*npr* **heenakh)** הנך *v pres f 2nd pers sing* you are; (*pst* **hayeet;** *fut* **teehyee).**

heenenee הנני *v pres 1st pers sing* I am; (*pst* **hayeetee;** *fut* **ehyeh).**

heenenee הנני here I am.

heenenoo הננו *v pres 1st pers pl* we are; (*pst* **hayeenoo;** *fut* **neehyeh).**

heenenoo הננו here we are.

heen|heeg/-heegah/-hagtee הנהיג *v* **1.** introduced; **2.** led; conducted; (*pres* **man'heeg;** *fut* **yan'heeg).**

heenkha הנך *v pres m 2nd pers sing* you are; (*pst* **hayeeta;** *fut* **teehyeh).**

heenkh|ah/-etah/-etee הנחה *v* **1.** directed; **2.** moderated; (*pres* **mankheh;** *fut* **yankheh).**

heenkh|eet/-eetah/-atetee הנחית *v* **1.** landed (a plane); **2.** inflicted; (*pres* **mankheet;** *fut* **yankheet).**

heenkheet (*etc*) **mahaloomah** הנחית מהלומה *v* inflicted (a blow).

heenkheet (*etc*) **mak|ah/-ot** הנחית מכה *v* inflicted (a blow).

heenkhem/-en הנכם *v pres m/f 2nd pers pl* you are; (*pst* **hayeetem;** *fut* **teehyoo).**

heenm|eekh/-eekhah/-akhtee הנמיך *v* lowered; (*pres* **manmeekh;** *fut* **yanmeekh).**

heenmeekh (*etc*) **toos** הנמיך טוס *v* flew at low altitude.

heeno הנו *v pres 3rd pers m sing* is; (*pst* **hayah;** *fut* **yeehyeh).**

heenp|eek/-eekah/-aktee הנפיק *v* issued (shares); (*pres* **manpeek;** *fut* **yanpeek).**

heents|ee'akh/-eekhah/-akhtee הנציח *v* immortalized; perpetuated; (*pres* **mantsee'akh;** *fut* **yantsee'akh).**

heep|eel/-eelah/-altee הפיל *v* caused to fall; overthrew; (*pres* **mapeel;** *fut* **yapeel).**

heepeelah הפילה *v 3rd pers f sing* miscarried; (*pres* **mapeelah;** *fut* **tapeel).**

heepn|et/-etah/-atetee היפנט *v* hypnotized; (*pres* **mehapnet;** *fut* **yehapnet).**

heepookh/-eem היפוך *nm* reverse; opposite; (*pl+of:* **-ey).**

heepookho shel davar היפוכו של דבר *nm* quite on the contrary.

(davar ve) heepookho דבר והיפוכו *nm* a flagrant contradiction; point and counterpoint.

heepotetee/-t היפותטי *adj* hypothetical.

heepotek|ah/-ot היפותיקה *nf* mortgage (*+of:* **-at).**

(halva|'ah/-'ot) heepoteka'ee|t/-yot הלוואה היפותיקאית *nf* mortgage-loan.

heerb|ah/-etah/-etee הרבה *v* multiplied; did much of; (*pres* **marbeh;** *fut* **yarbeh).**

heerb|eets/-eetsah/-atstee הרביץ *v* **1.** beat up; **2.** let it go; **3.** put in; (*pres* **marbeets;** *fut* **yarbeets).**

heerbeets (*etc*) **makot** הרביץ מכות *v* gave a beating; spanked.

heerbeets (*etc*) **torah** הרביץ תורה *v* taught knowledge.

heerd|eem/-eemah/-amtee הרדים *v* put to sleep; anesthetized; (*pres* **mardeem**; *fut* **yardeem**).

heer|'eed/-'eedah/-'adetee הרעיד *v* made tramble; (*pres* **mar'eed**; *fut* **yar'eed**).

heer|'eel/-'eelah/-'altee הרעיל *v* poisoned; (*pres* **mar'eel**; *fut* **yar'eel**).

heer|'eem/-'eemah/-'amtee הרעים *v* thundered; (*pres* **mar'eem**; *fut* **yar'eem**).

heer|'eesh/-'eeshah/-'ashtee הרעיש *v* **1.** bombed; bombarded; **2.** *[slang]* made noises; (*pres* **mar'eesh**; *fut* **yar'eesh**).

heer'eesh (*etc*) **'olamot** הרעיש עולמות *v* made a big fuss.

heerg|ee'a'/-ee'ah/-a'tee הרגיע *v* calmed; pacified; (*pres* **margee'a'**; *fut* **yargee'a'**).

heerg|eel/-eelah/-altee הרגיל *v* accustomed; (*pres* **margeel**; *fut* **yargeel**).

heerg|eesh/-eeshah/-ashtee הרגיש *v* felt; sensed; (*pres* **margeesh**; *fut* **yargeesh**).

heergeesh (*etc*) **be-ra'** הרגיש ברע *v* felt sick.

heergeesh (*etc*) **ra'** הרגיש רע *v* felt ill.

(lo) heergeesh (*etc*) **tov** לא הרגיש טוב *v* didn't feel well.

heerg|eez/-eezah/-aztee הרגיז *v* irritated; angered; (*pres* **margeez**; *fut* **yargeez**).

heer'|heev/-heevah/-havtee הרהיב *v* dared; (*pres* **mar'heev**; *fut* **yar'heev**).

heer|her/-harah/-hartee הרהר *v* mused; reflected; (*pres* **mehar'her**; *fut* **yehar'her**).

heerhoor/-eem הרהור *nm* thought; reflection; (*pl+of*: **-ey**).

heerhoor shenee הרהור שני *nm* second thought.

heerhoorey kharatah הרהורי חרטה *nm* regrets.

heerk|eed/-eedah/-adetee הרקיד *v* led a dance; made dance; (*pres* **markeed**; *fut* **yarkeed**).

heerk|eev/-eevah/-avtee הרכיב *v* assembled; formed; (*pres* **markeev**; *fut* **yarkeev**).

heerk|eev/-eevah/-avtee הרקיב *v* rotted away; (*pres* **markeev**; *fut* **yarkeev**).

heerkh|eev/-eevah/-avtee הרחיב *v* expanded; widened; (*pres* **markheev**; *fut* **yarkheev**).

heerkheev (*etc*) **et ha-deeboor** הרחיב את הדיבור *v* elaborated; discussed at length.

heerkh|eek/-eekah/-aktee הרחיק *v* **1.** went far; **2.** removed; (*pres* **markheek**; *fut* **yarkheek**).

heerkheek (*etc*) **lekhet** הרחיק לכת *v* went too far.

heerp|ah/-etah/-etee הרפה *v* desisted; let go; (*pres* **marpeh**; *fut* **yarpeh**).

heersh|ah/-etah/-etee הרשה *v* permitted; allowed; (*pres* **marsheh**; *fut* **yarsheh**).

heershah (*etc*) **le-'atsm|o/-ah/-ee** הרשה לעצמו *v* allowed one/him/her/my -self.

heersh|ee'a'/-ee'ah/-'atee הרשיע *v* convicted; (*pres* **marshee'a'**; *fut* **yarshee'a'**).

heersh|eem/-eemah/-amtee הרשים *v* impressed; (*pres* **marsheem**; *fut* **yarsheem**).

heert|ee'a'/-ee'ah/-'atee הרתיע *v* deterred; (*pres* **martee'a'**; *fut* **yartee'a'**).

heert|ee'akh/-eekhah/-akhtee הרתיח *v* **1.** boiled (water): **2.** infuriated; (*pres* **martee'akh**; *fut* **yartee'akh**).

heertee'akh (*etc*) **et dam|o/-ah/-ee** הרתיח את דמו *v* made his/her/my blood boil.

heerts|ah/-etah/-etee הרצה *v* lectured; (*pres* **martseh**; *fut* **yartseh**).

heerv|ee'akh/-eekhah/-akhtee הרוויח *v* profited; (*pres* **marvee'akh**; *fut* **yarvee'akh**).

heesardoo|t/-yot הישרדות *nf* survival.

heesb|ee'a'/-ee'ah/-a'tee השביע *v* sated; satisfied; (*pres* **masbee'a'**; *fut* **yasbee'a'**).

heesb|ee'a' (*etc*) **ratson** השביע רצון *v* satisfied.

heesb|eer/-eerah/-artee הסביר *v* explained; (*pres* **masbeer**; *fut* **yasbeer**).

heesd|eer/-eerah/-artee הסדיר *v* arranged; settled; (*pres* **masdeer**; *fut* **yasdeer**).

hees|ee/-ee'ah/-e'tee השיא *v* married off; (*pst* **masee**; *fut* **yasee**).

heesee (*etc*) **'ets|ah/-ot** השיא עצה *v* counselled; gave advice.

hees|ee'a'/-ee'ah/-a'tee הסיע *v* transported; (*pres* **masee'a'**; *fut* **yasee'a'**).

hees|ee'akh/-eekhah/-akhtee הסיח *v* deflected; diverted; (*pres* **masee'akh**; *fut* **yasee'akh**).

hees|eeg/-eegah/-agtee השיג *v* attained; reached; achieved; (*pres* **maseeg**; *fut* **yaseeg**).

hees|eek/-eekah/-aktee הסיק *v* **1.** inferred; **2.** heated; burned; (*pres* **maseek**; *fut* **yaseek**).

heeseek (*etc*) **maskanah/-ot** הסיק מסקנה *v* drew conclusion.

hees|'eer/-'eerah/-'artee הסעיר *v* caused a storm; (*pres* **mas'eer**; *fut* **yas'eer**).

hees|es/-esah/-astee היסס *v* hesitated; (*pres* **mehases**; *fut* **yehases**).

heesg|eer/-eerah/-artee הסגיר *v* **1.** extradited; **2.** surrendered; (*pres* **masgeer**; *fut* **yasgeer**).

heesh|'ah/-'atah/-'etee השעה *v* suspended; (*pres* **mash'eh**; *fut* **yash'eh**).

heeshb|ee'a/-ee'ah/-'atee השביע *v* swore in; (*pres* **mashbee'a**; *fut* **yashbee'a**).

heeshb|eet/-eetah/-atetee השבית *v* **1.** disturbed; **2.** locked out; (*pres* **mashbeet**; *fut* **yashbeet**).

heeshbeet (*etc*) **seemkhah** השבית שמחה *v* put end to a rejoicing.

heesh|eek/-eekah/-aktee השיק *v* launched; touched off; (*pres* **masheek**; *fut* **yasheek**).

heesh|'eel/-'eelah/-'altee השאיל *v* lent an object (not money) for temporary use; (*pres* **mash'eel**; *fut* **yash'eel**).

heesh|'eer/-'eerah/-'artee השאיר *v* left; abandoned; (*pres* **mash'eer**; *fut* **yash'eer**).

heeshg|ee'akh/-eekhah/-akhtee השגיח *v* supervised; took care; observed; (*pres* **mashgee'akh**; *fut* **yashgee'akh**).

heesh'|hah/-hatah/-hetee השהה *v* delayed; suspended; (*pres* **mash'heh**; *fut* **yash'heh**).

heesh|kah/-etah/-etee השקה *v* **1.** watered; irrigated; **2.** gave to drink; (*pres* **mashkeh**; *fut* **yashkeh**).

heeshk|ee'a'/-ee'ah/-a'tee השקיע *v* invested; (*pres* **mashkee'a'**; *fut* **yashkee'a'**).

heeshk|ee'akh/-eekhah/-akhtee השכיח *v* caused to forget: (*pres* **mashkee'akh**; *fut* **yashkee'akh**).

heeshk|eef/-eefah/-aftee השקיף *v* observed; looked over (*pres* **mashkeef**; *fut* **yashkeef**).

heeshk|eem/-eemah/-amtee השכים *v* got up early; (*pres* **mashkeem**; *fut* **yashkeem**).

heeshk|eet/-eetah/-atetee השקיט *v* calmed; soothed; (*pres* **mashkeet**; *fut* **yashkeet**).

heeshk|eev/-eevah/-avtee השכיב *v* **1.** put to bed; **2.** laid down; (*pres* **mashkeev**; *fut* **yashkeev**).

heesh'kh|eel/-eelah/-altee השחיל *v* threaded (needle); (*pres* **mash'kheel**; *fut* **yash'kheel**).

heesh'kh|eer/-eerah/-artee השחיר *v* blackened; (*pres* **mash'kheer**; *fut* **yash'kheer**).

heesh'kh|eet/-eetah/-atetee השחית *v* deformed; corrupted; (*pres* **mash'kheet**; *fut* **yash'kheet**).

heesh'kh|eez/-eezah/-aztee השחיז *v* sharpened; (*pres* **mash'kheez**; *fut* **yash'kheez**).

heeshl|eekh/-eekhah/-akhtee השליך *v* threw away; (*pres* **mashleekh**; *fut* **yashleekh**).

heeshl|eem/-eemah/-amtee השלים *v* **1.** made peace with; **2.** came to terms with; **3.** completed; (*pres* **mashleem**; *fut* **yashleem**).

heeshl|eesh/-eeshah/-ashtee השליש *v* **1.** deposited; **2.** tripled (*pres* **mashleesh**; *fut* **yashleesh**).

heeshl|eet/-eetah/-atetee השליט *v* enforced; (*pres* **mashleet**; *fut* **yashleet**).

heeshm|ee'a'/-ee'ah/-a'tee השמיע *v* voiced; made heard; (*pres* **mashmee'a'**; *fut* **yashmee'a'**).

heeshm|eed/-eedah/-adetee השמיד *v* wiped out; annihilated; (*pres* **mashmeed**; *fut* **yashmeed**).

heeshm|een/-eenah/-antee השמין *v* put on weight; grew fat; (*pres* **mashmeen**; *fut* **yashmeen**).

heeshm|eet/-eetah/-atetee השמיט *v* omitted (*pres* **mashmeet**; *fut* **yashmeet**).

heeshm|eets/-eetsah/-atstee השמיץ *v* defamed; libelled; (*pres* **mashmeets**; *fut* **yashmeets**).

heeshp|ee'a'/-ee'ah/-a'tee השפיע *v* influenced; (*pres* **mashpee'a'**; *fut* **yashpee'a'**).

heeshp|eel/-eelah/-altee השפיל *v* humiliated; (*pres* **mashpeel**; *fut* **yashpeel**).

heeshpr|eets/-eetsah/-atstee השפריץ *[slang]* *v* sprinkled; sprayed; (*pres* **mashpreets**; *fut* **yashpreets**).

heeshta|'ah/-'atah/-'etee השתאה *v* wondered; (*pres* **meeshta'eh**; *fut* **yeeshta'eh**).

heeshta'am|em/-emah/-amtee השתעמם *v* was bored; (*pres* **meeshta'amem**; *fut* **yeeshta'amem**).

heeshta'ash|a'/-'ah/-a'tee (*or:* **heeshta'ash|e'a'** *etc*) השתעשע *v* played (with); amused oneself; was amused; (*pres* **meeshta'ashe'a'**; *fut* **yeeshta'ash|a'**, **yeeshta'ash|e'a'**).

heeshtab|e'akh/-khah/-akhtee (*or:* **heeshtab|akh**) השתבח *v* prided oneself; boasted; (*pres* **meeshtabe'akh**; *fut* **yeeshtab|akh, yeeshtab|e'akh**).

heeshta'b|ed/-dah/-adetee השתעבד *v* became enslaved; enslaved oneself; (*pres* **meeshta'bed**; *fut* **yeeshta'abed**).

heeshta'bdoo|t/-yot השתעבדות *nf* enslavement.

heeshtab|esh/-shah/-ashtee השתבש *v* went wrong; (*pres* **meeshtabesh**; *fut* **yeeshtabesh**).

heeshtab|ets/-tsah/-atstee השתבץ *v* **1.** was integrated; **2.** was dovetailed; (*pres* **meeshtabets**; *fut* **yeeshtabets**).

heeshtad|ekh/-khah/-akhtee השתדך *v* became engaged to marry as a result of matchmaking; (*pres* **meshtadekh**; *fut* **yeeshtadekh**).

heeshtad|el/-lah/-altee השתדל *v* tried hard; endeavored; (*pres* **meeshtadel**; *fut* **yeeshtadel**).

heeshta|'el/-'alah/-'altee השתעל *v* coughed; (*pres* **meeshta'el**; *fut* **yeeshta'el**).

heeshtafsh|ef/-efah/-aftee השתפשף *v* **1.** rubbed oneself; rubbed elbows; **2.** *[slang]* was put through the mill; (*pres* **meeshtafshef**; *fut* **yeeshtafshef**).

heeshtag|a'/-'ah/-a'tee (*or:* **heeshtag|e'a'**) השתגע *v* **1.** went mad; **2.** *[slang]* wanted madly; was mad about. (*pres* **meeshtage'a'**; *fut* **yeeshtage'a'**).

heeshta|hah/-hatah/-hetee השתהה *v* was delayed; tarried; (*pres* **meeshtaheh**; *fut* **yeeshtaheh**).

heeshtak|a'/-'ah/-a'tee (*or:* **heeshtak|e'a'**) השתקע *v* settled for good; (*pres* **meeshtake'a**; *fut* **yeeshtak'a**; also **yeeshtak|a'**, **yeeshtak|e'a'**).

heeshtak|ef/-fah/-aftee השתקף *v* was reflected; (*pres* **meeshtakef**; *fut* **yeeshtakef**).

heeshtak|en/-nah/-antee השתכן *v* **1.** settled; **2.** obtained housing; (*pres* **meeshtaken**; *fut* **yeeshtaken**).

heeshtak|er/-rah/-artee השתכר *v* got drunk; (*pres* **meeshtaker**; *fut* **yeeshtaker**).

heeshtakfoo|t/-yot השתקפות *nf* reflection.

heeshtakh|avah/-vetah/-avetee השתחווה *v* bowed; (*pres* **meeshtakhaveh**; *fut* **yeeshtakhaveh**).

heeshtakhl|el/-elah/-altee השתכלל *v* was perfected; was improved; (*pres* **meeshtakhlel**; *fut* **yeeshtakhlel**).

heeshtakhn|a'/-e'ah/-a'tee (*or:* **heeshtakhn|e'a'**) השתכנע was convinced; (*pres* **meeshtakhne'a'**; *fut* **yeeshtakhn|a'**, **yeeshtakhn|e'a'**).

heeshtakhsh|ekh/-ekhah/-akhtee השתכשך *v* paddled; babbled; (*pres* **meeshtakhshekh**; *fut* **yeeshtakhshek**).

heeshtakhv|ah/-etah/-etee השתחווה *v* bowed; (*pres* **meeshtakhveh;** *fut* **yeeshtakhveh**).

heeshtakhr|er/-erah/-artee השתחרר *v* **1.** freed oneself; **2.** was released; was liberated; (*pres* **meeshtakhrer;** *fut* **yeeshtakhrer**).

heeshtal|ev/-vah/-avtee השתלב *v* integrated; intertwined; (*pres* **meeshtalev;** *fut* **yeeshtalev**).

heeshtal|em/-mah/-amtee השתלם *v* **1.** specialized; took advanced courses; **2.** paid off; was worthwhile; (*pres* **meeshtalem;** *fut* **yeeshtalem**).

heeshtalmoo|t/-yot השתלמות *nf* specialization course; advanced study.

◇ **(keren/karnot) heeshtalmoot** see ◇ **keren/karnot heeshtalmoot**.

heeshtalsh|el/-elah/-altee השתלשל *v* **1.** evolved; developed; **2.** hung down; (*pres* **meeshtalshel;** *fut* **yeeshtalshel**).

heeshtal|et/-tah/-atetee השתלט *v* mastered; took control of; (*pres* **meeshtalet;** *fut* **yeeshtalet**).

heeshtalsheloo|t/-yot השתלשלות *nf* development.

heeshtalsheloot ha-'eenyaneem השתלשלות העניינים *nf* (the) chain of developments.

heeshtaltoo|t/-yot השתלטות *v* taking control; seizing power; domination.

heeshtalvoo|t/-yot השתלבות *v* integration; joining in; fitting in.

heeshtam|er/-rah/-artee השתמר *v* was preserved; (*pres* **meeshtamer;** *fut* **yeeshtamer**).

heeshtam|esh/-shah/-ashtee השתמש *v* used; made use; (*pres* **meeshtamesh;** *fut* **yeeshtamesh**).

heeshtamesh (*etc*) **le-ra'ah** השתמש לרעה *v* misused.

heeshtamesh (*etc*) **she-lo ka-deen** השתמש שלא כדין *v* abused.

heeshtam|et/-tah/-atetee השתמט *v* dodged; evaded; shirked; (*pres* **meeshtamet;** *fut* **yeeshtamet**).

heeshtamtoo|t/-yot השתמטות *v* evasion; dodging; shirking.

heeshtan|ah/-tah/-etee השתנה *v* changed; became different; (*pres* **meeshtaneh;** *fut* **yeeshtanah**).

heeshtanoo|t/-yot השתנות *v* change; changing; alteration.

heeshtap|ekh/-khah/-akhtee השתפך *v* overflowed; spilled out; poured out effusively; (*pres* **meeshtapekh;** *fut* **yeeshtapekh**).

heeshtap|er/-rah/-artee השתפר *v* improved; bettered; (*pres* **meshtaper;** *fut* **yeeshtaper**).

heeshtapkhoo|t/-yot השתפכות *v* outpouring; effusion.

heeshtapkhoot ha-nefesh השתפכות הנפש *nf* poetic effusions; effusive outpouring.

heeshtaproo|t/-yot השתפרות *nf* improvement.

heeshtarb|ev/-evah/-avtee השתרבב *v* was misplaced; got in somehow; (*pres* **meeshtarbev;** *fut* **yeeshtarbev**).

heeshtat|ah/-etah/-etee השתטה *v* played the fool; raved and ranted; (*pres* **meeshtateh;** *fut* **yeeshtateh**).

heeshtat|e'akh/-khah/-akhtee (*or:* **heeshtat|akh**) השתטח *v* lay down flat; prostrated oneself; (*pres* **meeshtate'akh;** *fut* **yeeshtate'akh**).

heeshtat|ef/-fah/-aftee השתתף *v* took part; participated; (*pres* **meeshtatef;** *fut* **yeeshtatef**).

heeshtat|ek/-kah/-aktee השתתק *v* **1.** fell silent; **2.** *[colloq.]* became paralyzed.

heeshtatfoo|t/-yot השתתפות *nf* participation; share.

heeshtatfoo|t/yot be-tsa'ar השתתפות בצער *nf* condolence.

heeshtatoo|t/-yot השתטות *nf* folly; foolishness.

heeshtav|ah/-tah/-etee השתווה *v* reached equality; reached agreement; equaled; (*pres* **meeshtaveh;** *fut* **yeeshtaveh**).

heeshtavoo|t/-yot השתוות *nf* becoming equal; measuring up to.

heeshtay|ekh/-khah/-akhtee השתייך *v* belonged to; was associated with; (*pres* **meeshtayekh;** *fut* **yeeshtayekh**).

heeshtaykhoo|t/-yot השתייכות *nf* affiliation; belonging to.

heeshtaz|ef/-fah/-aftee השתזף *v* sunbathed; tanned oneself; (*pres* **meeshtazef;** *fut* **yeeshtazef**).

heeshtazfoo|t/-yot השתזפות *v* suntanning; sunbathing.

heesht|eek/-eekah/-aktee השתיק *v* silenced; (*pres* **mashteek;** *fut* **yashteek**).

heesht|eel/-eelah/-altee השתיל *v* planted; transplanted; implanted (*pres* **mashteel;** *fut* **yashteel**).

heesht|een/-eenah/-antee השתין *v* urinated; (*pres* **mashteen;** *fut* **yashteen**).

heesht|eet/-eetah/-atetee השתית *v* based; founded; (*pres* **mashteet;** *fut* **yashteet**).

heeshtok|ek/-ekah/-aktee השתוקק *v* craved (for); yearned; (*pres* **meeshtokek;** *fut* **yeeshtokek**).

heeshtokekoo|t/-yot השתוקקות *nf* yearning; craving for.

heeshtol|el/-elah/-altee השתולל *v* raged; acted unrestrained; (*pres* **meeshtolel;** *fut* **yeeshtolel**).

heeshtoleloo|t/yot השתוללות *nf* raging; running wild.

heeshtom|em/-emah/-amtee השתומם *v* wondered; (*pres* **meeshtomem;** *fut* **yeeshtomem**).

heeshtomemoo|t/yot השתוממות *nf* bewilderment.

heeshtovev-/-evah/-avtee השתובב *v* was boisterous, naughty; (*pres* **meeshtovev;** *fut* **yeeshtovev**).

heeshtovevoo|t/yot השתובבות *nf* boisterousness; mischief.

heeshv|ah/-etah/-etee השווה *v* **1.** compared; **2.** equalized; levelled; (*pres* **mashveh;** *fut* **yashveh).**

heesk|eel/-eelah/-altee השכיל *v* succeeded; managed; (*pres* **maskeel;** *fut* **yaskeel).**

heesk|eem/-eemah/-amtee הסכים *v* agreed; (*pres* **maskeem;** *fut* **yaskeem).**

heesk|eer/-eerah/-artee השכיר *v* leased; let; (*pres* **maskeer;** *fut* **yaskeer).**

heesm|eek/-eekah/-aktee הסמיק *v* blushed; (*pres* **masmeek;** *fut* **yasmeek).**

heesm|eekh/-eekhah/-akhtee הסמיך *v* **1.** authorized; **2.** bestowed a degree; **3.** drew close; (*pres* **masmeekh;** *fut* **yasmeekh).**

heesn|ee/-ee'ah/-etee השניא *v* made hateful; made one hate; (*pres* **masnee;** *fut* **yasnee).**

heesoos/-eem היסוס *nm* hesitation; misgiving; (*+of:* **-ey).**

heesp|eed/-eedah/-adetee הספיד *v* eulogized; (*pres* **maspeed;** *fut* **yaspeed).**

heesp|eek/-eekah/-aktee הספיק *v* managed to; sufficed; (*pres* **maspeek;** *fut* **yaspeek).**

heesr|ee'akh/-eekhah/-akhtee הסריח *v* stank; (*pres* **masree'akh;** *fut* **yasree'akh).**

heesr|eet/-eetah/-atetee הסריט *v* filmed; took movies; (*pres* **masreet;** *fut* **yasreet).**

heesta'afoo|t/-yot הסתעפות *nf* ramification.

heesta'aroo|t/-yot הסתערות *nf* assault; storming.

heestab|ekh/-khah/-akhtee הסתבך *v* got mixed up; got involved; (*pres* **meestabekh;** *fut* **yeestabekh).**

heestab|er/-rah/-artee הסתבר *v* it became evident; (*pres* **meestaber;** *fut* **yeestaber).**

heestabkhoo|t/-yot הסתבכות *nf* involvement; entanglement.

heestabroo|t/-yot הסתברות *nf* probability.

heestad|er/-rah/-artee הסתדר *v* **1.** settled in; **2.** was arranged; **3.** managed; (*pres* **meestader;** *fut* **yeestader).**

heestadroo|t/-yot הסתדרות *nf* organization.

◇ **heestadroot ha-'ovdeem** הסתדרות העובדים *nf* Israel's General Federation of Labor, the country's largest public body, encompassing over two million members and incorporating 43 professional labor unions. True to its socialist-like ideology, it has since its foundation in 1920 built up a large system of economic enterprizes of its own known as the Labor Economy that accounts for 20% of the country's gross national product. Has its share in public health care — see ◇ **Koopat Kholeem ha-Klaleet**; in agriculture — see ◇ **(ha)TAKAM** and ◇ **Tenoo'at ha-Moshaveem**; as well as in banking, communications, sports, culture, education *etc.* Is therefore viewed by its opponents as "a state within a state".

◇ **heestadroot ha-'ovdeem ha-le'oomeet** הסתדרות העובדים הלאומית *nf* the National Federation of Labor, non-socialist parallel and opponent of the "Histadrut" advocating obligatory arbitration for settling labor disputes instead of strikes, priority of national interests over class strugglee, *etc.* Encompasses some 80,000 members and has it own health-care system (see **Koopat Kholeem Le'oomeet).**

◇ **heestadroot ha-po'el ha-meezrakhee** הסתדרות הפועל המזרחי *nf* non-socialist trade-union of religious laborers. Politically, major component of National Religious Party (◇ **MAFDAL**) while associating with the "Histadrut" in matters professional and health-care. Claims membership of 150,000, affiliation of 100 villages of "moshav" type and its own kibbutzim organized in ◇ **ha-keeboots ha-datee.**

heesta|'er/-'arah/-'artee הסתער *v* assailed; charged; stormed; (*pres* **meesta'er;** *fut* **yeesta'er).**

heestag|el/-lah/-altee הסתגל *v* adjusted oneself; (*pres* **meestagel;** *fut* **yeestagel).**

heestag|er/-rah/-artee הסתגר closeted oneself; shut oneself off; (*pres* **meestager;** *fut* **yeestager).**

heestagl|oot/-yot הסתגלות *nf* adaptation.

heestagr|oot/-yot הסתגרות *nf* seclusion.

heestak|el/-lah/-altee הסתכל *v* looked into; had a look into; (*pres* **meestakel;** *fut* **yeestakel).**

heestak|em/-mah/-amtee הסתכם *v* amounted to; summed up in; (*pres* **meestakem;** *fut* **yeestakem).**

heestak|en/-nah/-antee הסתכן *v* risked; (*pres* **meestaken;** *fut* **yeestaken).**

heestak|er/-rah/-artee השתכר *v* earned (wage); (*pres* **meestaker;** *fut* **yeestaker).**

heestakhr|er/-erah/-artee הסתחרר *v* felt dizzy; (*pres* **meestakhrer;** *fut* **yeestakhrer).**

heestakhreroo|t/-yot הסתחררות *nf* dizziness.

heestakhs|ekh/-ekhah/-akhtee הסתכסך *v* quarrelled; (*pres* **meestakhsekh;** *fut* **yeestakhsekh).**

heestakloo|t/-yot הסתכלות *nf* observation; contemplation.

(be) heestakloot בהסתכלות *adv* under observation.

(khoosh) heestakloot חוש הסתכלות *nm* sense of observation; gift for observation.

heestal|ek/-kah/-aktee הסתלק *v* got out; departed; (*pres* **meestalek;** *fut* **yeestalek).**

heestal|ek/-kee/-koo mee-kan! !הסתלק מכאן *v imp m/f sing/pl* get out of here!

heestalek *(etc)* **mee-po!** !הסתלק מפה *v imp m/f sing/pl* get out of here!

heestalkoo|t/-yot הסתלקות *nf* departure; withdrawal; passing away.

heestam|ekh/-khah/-akhtee הסתמך *v* **1.** relied; **2.** referred (*pres* **meestamekh;** *fut* **yeestamekh).**

heestam|en/-nah/-antee הסתמן *v* began to show; (*pres* **meestamen;** *fut* **yeestamen).**

heestamkhoo|t/-yot הסתמכות *nf* reliance; reference.

heestamnoo|t/-yot הסתמנות *nf* marking; sign of appearance.

heestan|en/-enah/-antee הסתנן *v* infiltrated; got through; (*pres* **meestanen**; *fut* **yeestanen**).

heestanenoo|t/-yot הסתננות *nf* **1.** infiltration; **2.** *[colloq.]* infiltration by terrorists.

heestap|ek/-kah/-aktee הסתפק *v* contained oneself with; (*pres* **meestapek**; *fut* **yeestapek**).

heestap|er/-rah/-artee הסתפר *v* took a haircut; (*pres* **meestaper**; *fut* **yeestaper**).

heestapkoot be-moo'at הסתפקות במועט *nf* frugality.

heestar|a'/-'ah/-'atee (*or:* **heestar|e'a'**) השתרע *v* stretched out; extended; spread out; (*pres* **meestare'a'**; *fut* **yeestare'a'**).

heestar|ek/-kah/-aktee הסתרק *v* combed oneself (hair); (*pres* **meestarek**; *fut* **yeestarek**).

heestar|ekh/-khah/-akhtee השתרך *v* dragged along; (*pres* **meestarekh**; *fut* **yeestarekh**).

heestar|er/-erah/-artee השתרר *v* prevailed; (*pres* **meestarer**; *fut* **yeestarer**).

heestat|er/-rah/-artee הסתתר *v* hid; (*pres* **meestater**; *fut* **yeestater**).

heestatroo|t/-yot הסתתרות *nf* hiding.

heestatmoo|t/-yot הסתתמות *nf* closing; blocking up.

heestaydoo|t/-yot הסתיידות *nf* calcification.

heestaydoot ha-'orkeem הסתיידות העורקים *nf* arteriosclerosis.

heestay|e'a/-'ah/-a'tee הסתייע *v* got assistance; (*pres* **meestaye'a**; *fut* **yeestaya'**).

heetay|eg/-gah/-agtee הסתייג *v* dissociated oneself from; (*pres* **meestayeg**; *fut* **yeestayeg**).

heestay|em/-mah/-amtee הסתיים *v* ended; (*pres* **meestayem**; *fut* **yeestayem**).

heestaygoo|t/-yot הסתייגות *nf* reservation; demurrer.

heestaymoo|t/-yot הסתיימות *nf* ending; finalizing.

heest|eer/-eerah/-artee הסתיר *v* hid; concealed; (*pres* **masteer**; *fut* **yasteer**).

heester|yah/-yot היסטריה *nf* hysteria; (+*of:* **-yat**).

heestod|ed/-edah/-adetee הסתודד *v* conferred secretly; (*pres* **meestoded**; *fut* **yeestoded**).

heestoree/-t היסטורי *adj* historic.

(kedam) heestoree/-t קדם־היסטורי *adj* prehistoric.

heestoryah היסטוריה *nf* history.

heestov|ev/-evah/-avtee הסתובב *v* turned around; mingled; (*pres* **meestovev**; *fut* **yeestovev**).

(le) heet! להת׳! *colloq. abbr.* of **le-heetra'ot** so long! good bye!

heet|ah/-etah/-etee הטה *v* deflected; diverted; (*pres* **mateh**; *fut* **yateh**).

heetah (*etc*) **ozen** הטה אוזן *v* lent an ear; heeded.

heetah (*etc*) **rosh** הטה ראש *v* nodded; shook head.

heetah (*etc*) **shekhem** הטה שכם *v* shouldered.

heet|'ah/-'atah/-'etee הטעה *v* led astray; misled; (*pres* **mat'eh**; *fut* **yat'eh**).

heet'ab|ah/-tah/-etee התעבה *v* thickened; (*pres* **meet'abeh**; *fut* **yeet'abeh**).

heet'abdoo|t/-yot התאבדות *nf* suicide.

heet'ab|ed/-dah/-adetee התאבד *v* committed suicide; (*pres* **meet'abed**; *fut* **yeet'abed**).

heet'ab|el/-lah/-altee התאבל *v* mourned; (*pres* **meet'abel**; *fut* **yeet'abel**).

heet'ab|en/-nah/-antee התאבן *v* was paralyzed; (*pres* **meet'aben**; *fut* **yeet'aben**).

heet'abnoo|t/-yot התאבנות *nf* paralysis; petrification.

heet'aboo|t/-yot התעבות *nf* condensation.

heet'aboot 'ananeem התעבות עננים *nf* thickening of clouds.

heet'ab|rah/-artee התעברה *v f* became pregnant; (*pres* **meet'aberet**; *fut* **teeta'aber**).

heet'abroo|t/-yot התעברות *nf* becoming pregnant; conception.

heet'ad|ah/-etah התאדה *v* evaporated; (*pres* **meet'adeh**; *fut* **yeet'adeh**).

heet'ad|em/-mah/-amtee התאדם *v* flushed; reddened; (*pres* **meet'adem**; *fut* **yeet'adem**).

heet'ad|en/-nah/-antee התעדן *v* became refined; indulged in luxury; (*pres* **meet'aden**; *fut* **yeet'aden**).

heet'adk|en/-enah/-antee התעדכן *v* brought (oneself) up to date; (*pres* **meet'adken**; *fut* **yeet'adken**).

heet'adkenoo|t/-yot התעדכנות *nf* bringing (oneself) up to date; updating (oneself).

heet'admoo|t/-yot התאדמות *nf* reddening; flushing.

heet'adnoo|t/-yot התעדנות *nf* refinement; enjoying.

heet'adoo|t/-yot התאדות *nf* evaporation.

heet'afsh|er/-erah/-eroo התאפשר *v* became possible; (*pres* **meet'afsher**; *fut* **yeet'afsher**).

heet'afsheroo|t/-yot התאפשרות *nf* emergence of a possibility.

heet'agdoo|t/-yot התאגדות *nf* union; association.

heet'ag|ed/-dah התאגד *v* united; amalgamated; (*pres* **meet'aged**; *fut* **yeet'aged**).

heet'ag|el/-lah/-altee התעגל *v* became round; (*pres* **meet'agel**; *fut* **yeet'agel**).

heet'agloo|t/-yot התעגלות *nf* becoming round; rounding.

heet'agr|ef/-efah/-aftee התאגרף *v* boxed; (*pres* **meet'agref**; *fut* **yeet'agref**).

heet'agrefoo|t/-yot התאגרפות *nf* boxing.

heet'ahavoo|t/-yot התאהבות *nf* falling in love.

heet'a|hev/-havah/-havtee התאהב *v* fell in love; (*pres* **meet'ahev**; *fut* **yeet'ahev**).

heet'ak|em/-mah/-amtee התעקם *v* was bent; became crooked; (*pres* **meet'akem**; *fut* **yeet'akem**).

heet'ak|esh/-shah/-ashtee התעקש *v* insisted; (*pres* **meet'akesh**; *fut* **yeet'akesh**).

heet'ak|ev/-vah/-avtee התעכב *v* was held up; was delayed; (*pres* **meet'akev;** *fut* **yeet'akev**).

heetakhdoo|t/-yot התאחדות *nf* union; federation.

heet'akh|ed/-dah/-adetee התאחד *v* joined with; combined; united; (*pst* **meet'akhed;** *fut* **yeet'akhed**).

heet'akh|er/-rah/-artee התאחר *v* was late; was tardy; (*pres* **meet'akher;** *fut* **yeet'akher**).

heet'akhroo|t/-yot התאחרות *nf* delay; tardiness.

heet'akhs|en/-enah/-antee התאכסן *v* stayed; lodged (as guest); (*pres* **meet'akhsen;** *fut* **yeet'akhsen**).

heet'akhsenoo|t/-yot התאכסנות *nf* staying; hotel accommodation.

heet'akhz|er/-erah/-artee התאכזר *v* acted/ behaved cruelly; (*pres* **meet'akhzer;** *fut* **yeet'akhzer**).

heet'akhzeroo|t/-yot התאכזרות *nf* cruel treatment.

heet'akhz|ev/-evah/-avtee התאכזב *v* was disappointed; (*pres* **meet'akhzev;** *fut* **yeet'akhzev**).

heet'akhzevoo|t/-yot התאכזבות *nf* disappointment.

heet'akl|em/-emah/-amtee התאקלם *v* became acclimated; (*pres* **meet'aklem;** *fut* **yeet'aklem**).

heet'aklemoo|t/-yot התאקלמות *nf* **1.** acclimatization; **2.** *[colloq.]* getting accustomed to a new place.

heetakloo|t/-yot היתקלות *nf* encounter.

heet'akmoo|t/-yot התעקמות *nf* bending; making crooked.

heet'akshoo|t/-yot התעקשות *nf* obstinacy; stubbornness.

heet'al|ah/-tah/-etee התעלה *v* has risen; exalted; (*pres* **meet'aleh;** *fut* **yeet'aleh**).

heet'al|ef/-fah/-aftee התעלף *v* fainted; (*pres* **meet'alef;** *fut* **yeet'alef**).

heet'al|el/-elah/-altee התעלל *v* abused; maltreated; (*pres* **meet'alel;** *fut* **yeet'alel**).

heet'aleloo|t/-yot התעללות *v* outrage; abuse; maltreatment.

heet'al|em/-mah/-amtee התעלם *v* ignored; disregarded; (*pres* **met'alem;** *fut* **yeet'alem**).

heet'al|es/-sah/-astee התעלס *v* made love; (*pres* **meet'ales;** *fut* **yeet'ales**).

heet'alfoo|t/-yot התעלפות *nf* fainting.

heet'alm|en/-enah/-antee התאלמן *v* became widowed; (*pres* **meet'almen;** *fut* **yeet'almen**).

heet'almenoo|t/-yot התאלמנות *v* becoming a widow; widowhood.

heet'almoo|t/-yot התעלמות *nf* disregard; ignoring.

heet'alsoo|t/-yot התעלסות *nf* love-making.

heet'am|ek/-kah/-aktee התעמק *v* delved deeply; (*pres* **meet'amek;** *fut* **yeet'amek**).

heet'am|el/-lah/-altee התעמל *v* exercised (gymnastics); worked up; (*pres* **meet'amel;** *fut* **yeet'amel**).

heetam|em/-emah/-amtee היתמם *v* played the innocent; (*pres* **meetamem;** *fut* **yeetamam**).

heet'am|en/-nah/-antee התאמן *v* trained; practised; (*pres* **meet'amen;** *fut* **yeet'amen**).

heet'am|et/-tah/-atetee התאמת *v* came true; was proven true; (*pres* **meet'amet;** *fut* **yeet'amet**).

heet'am|et/-tah/-atetee 'eem התעמת עם *v* contended; came to grips with; (*pres* **meet'amet 'eem;** *fut* **yeet'amet 'eem**).

heet'ame|ts/-tsah/-atstee התאמץ *v* strove; endeavored; (*pres* **meet'amets;** *fut* **yeet'amets**).

heet'amkoo|t/-yot התעמקות *nf* penetrating study; penetration.

heet'amloo|t/-yot התעמלות *nf* gymnastics; physical training; work-out.

heetamt|em/-emah/-amtee היטמטם *nf* became dumb; (*pres* **meetamtem;** *fut* **yeetamtem**).

heet'amtoo|t/-yot התאמתות *nf* verification; turning out to be true.

heet'amtsoo|t/-yot התאמצות *nf* effort; endeavor.

heet'an|ah/-tah/-etee התאנה *v* persecuted; picked quarrel with; (*pres* **meet'aneh;** *fut* **yeet'aneh**).

heet'an|ah/-tah/-etee התענה *v* was tormented; tormented oneself; (*pres* **meet'aneh;** *fut* **yeet'aneh**).

heet'an|eg/-gah/-agtee התענג *v* enjoyed; derived pleasure; (*pres* **meet'aneg;** *fut* **yeet'aneg**).

heet'an|yen/-yenah/-yantee התעניין *v* took/ showed interest; (*pres* **meet'anyen;** *fut* **yeet'anyen**).

heet'anyenoo|t/-yot התעניינות *nf* interest; concern.

heet'ap|ek/-kah/-aktee התאפק *v* restrained oneself; (*pres* **meet'apek;** *fut* **yeet'apek**).

heet'ap|er/-rah/-artee התאפר *v* put on make-up; (*pres* **meet'aper;** *fut* **yeet'aper**).

heet'apkoot התאפקות *nf* restraint.

heet'aproot התאפרות *nf* putting on make-up.

heet'arb|ev/-evah/-avtee התערבב *v* got mixed up; (*pres* **meet'arbev;** *fut* **yeet'arbev**).

heet'ar|e'akh/-khah/-akhtee התארח *v* stayed as guest; (*pres* **meet'are'akh;** *fut* **yeet'are'akh**).

heet'ar|ekh/-khah/-akhtee התארך *v* **1.** dragged out; **2.** grew longer; (*pres* **meet'arekh;** *fut* **yeet'arekh**).

heet'ar|'er/-'erah/-'artee התערער *v* began to totter; (*pres* **meet'ar'er;** *fut* **yeet'ar'er**).

heet'ar|es/-sah/-astee התארס *v* became engaged /betrothed; (*pres* **meet'ares;** *fut* **yeet'ares**).

heet'ar|ev/-vah/-avtee התערב *v* **1.** interfered; **2.** intervened; **3.** bet; wagered; (*pres* **meet'arev;** *fut* **yeet'arev**).

heet'arg|en/-enah/-antee התארגן *v* got organized; organized oneself; (*pres* **meet'argen;** *fut* **yeet'argen**).

heet'arkhoo|t/-yot התארכות *nf* lengthening; prolongation.
heet'arsoo|t/-yot התארסות *nf* betrothal; engagement.
heet'art|el/-elah/-altee התערטל *v* disrobed. stripped; (*pres* **meet'artel**; *fut* **yeet'artel**).
heet'arvoo|t/-yot התערבות *nf* **1.** interference; **2.** bet; wager.
heet'as|ef/-fah/-aftee התאסף *v* assembled; got together; (*pres* **meet'asef**; *fut* **yeet'asef**).
heet'as|ek/-kah/-aktee התעסק *v* **1.** dealt with; **2.** engaged in; **3.** flirted with (*pres* **meet'asek**; *fut* **yeet'asek**).
heet'asfoo|t/-yot התאספות *nf* gathering; assembly.
heet'askoo|t/-yot התעסקות *nf* occupation.
heet'asl|em/-emah/-amtee התאסלם *v* converted to Islam; became a Muslim; (*pres* **meet'aslem**; *fut* **yeet'aslem**).
heet'ash|er/-rah/-artee התעשר *v* got rich; (*pres* **meet'asher**; *fut* **yeet'asher**).
heet'ashroo|t/-yot התעשרות *nf* getting rich; enrichment.
heet'at|ed/-edah/-adetee התעתד *v* prepared oneself; (*pres* **meet'ated**; *fut* **yeet'ated**).
heet'at|ef/-fah/-aftee התעטף *v* wrapped onself; (*pres* **meet'atef**; *fut* **yeet'atef**).
heet'at|esh/-'shah/-ashtee התעטש *v* sneezed; (*pres* **meet'atesh**; *fut* **yeet'atesh**).
heet'at'shoo|t/-yot התעטשות *nf* sneeze.
heet'atsb|en/-enah/-antee התעצבן *v* became nervous; became irritated; (*pres* **meet'atsben**; *fut* **yeet'atsben**).
heet'atsbenoo|t/-yot התעצבנות *nf* becoming nervous.
heet'ats|el/-lah/-altee התעצל *v* was lazy; (*pres* **meet'atsel**; *fut* **yeet'atsel**).
heet'ats|em/-mah/-amtee התעצם *v* grew strong; (*pres* **meet'atsem**; *fut* **yeet'atsem**).
heet'ats|ev/-vah/-avtee התעצב *v* became sad; was grieved; (*pres* **meet'atsev**; *fut* **yeet'atsev**).
heet'atsmoo|t/-yot התעצמות *nf* expansion.
heet'atsvoo|t/-yot התעצבות *nf* saddening.
heet'av|ah/-tah/-etee התאווה *v* desired; felt an urge; (*pres* **meet'aveh**; *fut* **yeet'aveh**).
heet'hav|ah/-tah/-etee התהווה *v* emerged; was formed; (*pres* **meet'haveh**; *fut* **yeet'haveh**).
heet'av|er/-rah/-artee התעוור *v* went blind; (*pres* **meet'aver**; *fut* **yeet'aver**).
heet'avoo|t/-yot התאוות *nf* craving; urge.
heet'havoo|t/-yot התהוות *nf* formation; emergence.
heet'avr|er/-erah/-artee התאוורר *v* **1.** aired; **2.** *[colloq.]* took a walk; (*pres* **meet'avrer**; *fut* **yeet'avrer**).
heet'a|yef/-yfah/-yaftee התעייף *v* became tired; (*pres* **meet'ayef**; *fut* **yeet'ayef**).
heet'ayfoo|t/-yot התעייפות *nf* tiring; fatigue.
heet'ayfoot ha-khomer התעייפות החומר *nf* material fatigue.

heet'az|en/-nah/-antee התאזן *v* balanced; became balanced; (*pres* **meet'azen**; *fut* **yeet'azen**).
heet'az|er/-rah/-artee התאזר *v* gathered strength; (*pres* **meet'azer**; *fut* **yeet'azer**).
heet'azer (*etc*) **be-savlanoot** התאזר בסבלנות *v* gathered patience.
heet'azer (*etc*) **'oz** התאזר עוז *v* gathered courage.
heet'azr|e'akh/-ekhah/-akhtee התאזרח *v* became a citizen; naturalized; (*pres* **meet'azre'akh**; *fut* **yeet'azre'akh**).
heet'azrekhoot התאזרחות *nf* naturalization.
heetbad|ah/-etah/-etee התבדה *v* was proven false; turned out to be a lie; (*pres* **meetbadeh**; *fut* **yeetbadeh**).
heetbad|e'akh/-khah/-akhtee התבדח *v* joked; jested (*pres* **meetbade'akh**; *fut* **yeetbade'akh**).
heetbad|el/-lah/-altee התבדל **1.** was secluded; **2.** segregated; kept apart; (*pres* **meetbadel**; *fut* **yeetbadel**).
heetbad|er/-rah/-artee התבדר *v* amused oneself; had fun; (*pres* **meetbader**; *fut* **yeetbader**).
heetbad'khoo|t/-yot התבדחות *nf* jesting; joking; making fun.
heetbadloo|t/-yot התבדלות *nf* seclusion; segregation.
heetbadoo|t/-yot התבדות *nf* refutation.
heetbag|er/-rah/-artee התבגר *v* matured; (*pres* **meetbager**; *fut* **yeetbager**).
heetbagroot התבגרות *nf* maturation; ripening.
(geel ha) heetbagroot גיל ההתבגרות *nm* **1.** maturation age; **2.** majority.
(tekoofat ha) heetbagroot תקופת ההתבגרות *nm* maturation period.
heetbaharoo|t/-yot התבהרות *nf* brightening up; clarification.
heetba|her/-harah התבהר *v* brightened; cleared up; (*pres* **meetbaher**; *fut* **yeetbaher**).
heetbak|a'/-'ah/-a'tee (*or:* **heetbak|e'a'**) התבקע *v* burst; split open; (*pres* **meetbake'a'**; *fut* **yeetbake'a'**).
heetbak|esh/-shah/-ashtee התבקש *v* was asked; was requested; (*pres* **meetbakesh**; *fut* **yeetbakesh**).
heetbalb|el/-elah/-altee התבלבל *v* became confused; (*pres* **meetbalbel**; *fut* **yeetbalbel**).
heetbal|et/-tah/-atetee התבלט *v* stood out; (*pres* **meetbalet**; *fut* **yeetbalet**).
heetbaloot התבלות *nf* wear; wear and tear.
heetbaltoot התבלטות *nf* prominence; conspicuousness.
heetbas|em/-mah/-amtee התבשם *v* **1.** put on scent; **2.** became tipsy; (*pres* **meetbasem**; *fut* **yeetbasem**).
heetbas|er/-rah/-artee התבשר *v* was told the (good) news; (*pres* **meetbaser**; *fut* **yeetbaser**).
heetbas|es/-esah/-astee התבסס *v* **1.** based oneself; was based on; **2.** *[colloq.]* became well established; became well to do; (*pres* **meetbases**; *fut* **yeetbases**).

heetbasesoo|t/-yot התבססות *nf* basing oneself on; consolidation.

heetbash|el/-lah/-altee התבשל *v* was cooked; cooked up; (*pres* **meetbashel**; *fut* **yeetbashel**).

heetbashloo|t/-yot התבשלות *nf* cooking; ripening.

heetbasmoo|t/-yot התבשמות *nf* putting on scent; getting tipsy.

heetbasroo|t/-yot התבשרות *nf* learning, getting the (good) news.

heetbat|e/-'ah/-etee התבטא *v* expressed oneself; expressed the opinion; (*pres* **meetbate**; *fut* **yeetbate**).

heetbatel/-lah/-altee התבטל *v* **1.** was cancelled; **2.** idled away; **3.** belittled oneself; (*pres* **meetbatel**; *fut* **yeetbatel**).

heetbatloo|t/-yot התבטלות *nf* **1.** self-disparagement; **2.** loafing.

heetbat'oo|t/-yot התבטאות *nf* expression; self-expression.

heetbats|a'/-'ah (*or:* **heetbats|e'a'**) התבצע *v* was carried out; was executed; (*pres* **meetbatse'a'**; *fut* **yeetbatse'a'**).

heetbats|er/-rah/-artee התבצר *v* barricaded oneself; fortified oneself; (*pres* **meetbatser**; *fut* **yeetbatser**).

heetbatsroo|t/-yot התבצרות *nf* fortification; fortifying oneself.

heetba|yesh/-yshah/-yashtee התבייש *v* felt ashamed; (*pres* **meetbayesh**; *fut* **yeetbayesh**).

heetbaz|ah/-etah/-etee התבזה *v* degraded oneself; demeaned oneself; (*pres* **meetbazeh**; *fut* **yeetbazeh**).

heetbazb|ez/-ezah/-aztee התבזבז *v* was wasted, squandered; (*pres* **meetbazbez**; *fut* **yeetbazbez**).

heetbazezoo|t/-yot התבזבזות *nf* waste; wasting.

heetbazoo|t/-yot התבזות *nf* humiliation; self-abuse.

heetb|ee'a'/-ee'ah/-a'tee הטביע *v* sank (*pres* **matbee'a'**; *fut* **yatbee'a'**).

heetbee'a' (*etc*) **khotam** הטביע חותם *v* left one's mark.

heetb|eel/-eelah/-altee הטביל *v* **1.** immersed; **2.** baptized; (*pres* **matbeel**; *fut* **yatbeel**).

heetbod|ed/-edah/-adetee התבודד *v* secluded oneself; sought solitude; (*pres* **meetboded**; *fut* **yeetboded**).

heetbodedoo|t/-yot התבודדות *nf* solitude; seclusion; segregation.

heetbol|el/-elah/-altee התבולל *v* became assimilated; (*pres* **meetbolel**; *fut* **yeetbolel**).

heetboleloo|t/-yot התבוללות *nf* assimilation.

heetbon|en/-enah/-antee התבונן *v* stared; observed; (*pres* **meetbonen**; *fut* **yeetbonen**).

heetbonenoo|t/-yot התבוננות *nf* contemplation; observation.

heetbos|es/-esah/-astee התבוסס *v* rolled in; (*pres* **meetboses**; *fut* **yeetboses**).

heetboses (*etc*) **be-damo** התבוסס בדמו *v* rolled in his own blood; lay slain.

heetdaynoo|t/-yot התדיינות *nf* litigation; contentiousness.

heet|ee'akh (*npr* **hetee'akh**)/**-eekhah/-akhtee** הטיח *v* spoke insolently; (*pst* **metee'akh**; *fut* **yatee'akh**).

heet|eef/-eefah/-aftee הטיף *v* preached; moralized; (*pres* **mateef**; *fut* **yateef**).

heet|eekh/-eekhah/-akhtee התיך *v* melted; (*pres* **mateekh**; *fut* **yateekh**).

heet|eel/-eelah/-altee הטיל *v* imposed; laid; (*pres* **mateel**; *fut* **yateel**).

heeteel (*etc*) **dofee** הטיל דופי *v* questioned; maligned.

heeteel (*etc*) **mas/meeseem** הטיל מס *v* imposed tax.

heet|'eem/-'eemah/-'amtee התאים *v* fitted; matched; was suited to; corresponded; (*pres* **mat'eem**; *fut* **yat'eem**).

heet|'eem/-'eemah/-'amtee הטעים *v* emphasized; pointed out; (*pres* **mat'eem**; *fut* **yat'eem**).

heet|'een/-'eenah/-'antee הטעין *v* loaded; charged; (*pres* **mat'een**; *fut* **yat'een**).

heet|eer/-eerah/-artee התיר *v* **1.** allowed; **2.** undid; (*pres* **mateer**; *fut* **yateer**).

heet|eesh/-eeshah/-ashtee התיש *v* wore out; weakened; (*pres* **mateesh**; *fut* **yateesh**).

heet|eez/-eezah/-aztee התיז *v* **1.** cut off; **2.** sprinkled; (*pres* **mateez**; *fut* **yateez**).

heetga|'ah/-'atah/-'etee התגאה *v* boasted; was proud of; (*pres* **meetga'eh**; *fut* **yeetga'eh**).

heetga'ag|e'a (or **heetga'ag|a'**)/**-'ah/-a'tee** התגעגע *v* yearned; longed for; (*pres* **meetga'age'a**; *fut* **yeetga'age'a**).

heetgab|er/-rah/-artee התגבר *v* overcome; increased; (*pres* **meetgaber**; *fut* **yeetgaber**).

heetgab|esh/-shah/-ashtee התגבש *v* crystalized; became consolidated; (*pres* **meetgabesh**; *fut* **yeetgabesh**).

heetgabroo|t/-yot התגברות *nf* strengthening; surmounting.

heetgabshoo|t/-yot התגבשות *nf* consolidation; crystallization.

heetgal|ah/-tah/-etee התגלה *v* revealed oneself; turned out; was exposed; (*pres* **meetgaleh**; *fut* **yeetgaleh**).

heetgal|a'/-'ah/-'oo התגלע *v* broke out; (*pres* **meetgale'a**; *fut* **yeetgala'**).

heetgal|e'akh (or: **heetgal|akh**)/**-khah/-akhtee** התגלח *v* shaved; (*pres* **meetgale'akh**; *fut* **yeetgale'akh**).

heetgal|etch/-tchah/-atchtee התגלץ' *v* [*slang*] slipped; (*pres* **meetgaletch**; *fut* **yeetgaletch**).

heetgal|em/-mah/-amtee התגלם *v* embodied; (*pres* **meetgalem**; *fut* **yeetgalem**).

heetgalg|el/-elah/-altee התגלגל *v* **1.** rolled; **2.** [*colloq.*] wandered; (*pres* **meetgalgel**; *fut* **yeetgalgel**).

heetgalmoo|t/-yot התגלמות *nf* embodiment.

heetgand|er/-erah/-artee התגנדר *v* dressed up; showed off; (*pres* **meetgander**; *fut* **yeetgander**).

heetgan|ev/-vah/-avtee התגנב *v* stalked; moved stealthily; (*pres* **meetganev**; **yeetganev**).

heetganvoo|t/-yot התגנבות *nf* entering or leaving stealthily; stalking.

heetgar|ah/-tah/-eetee התגרה *v* teased; challenged (*pres* **meetgareh**; *fut* **yeetgareh**).

heetgar|ed/-dah/-adetee התגרד *v* scratched oneself; (*pres* **meetgared**; *fut* **yeetgared**).

heetgar|esh/-shah/-ashtee התגרש *v* divorced; (*pres* **meetgaresh**; *fut* **yeetgaresh**).

heetgaroo|t/-yot התגרות *nf* provocation.

heetgarshoo|t/-yot התגרשות *nf* divorce; divorcing.

heetgash|em/-mah/-amtee התגשם *v* materialized; came true; (*pres* **meetgashem**; *fut* **yeetgashem**).

heetgashmoo|t/-yot התגשמות *nf* materialization; incarnation.

heetgay|er/-rah/-artee התגייר *v* converted to Judaism; (*pres* **meetgayer**; *fut* **yeetgayer**).

heetga|yes/-ysah/-yastee התגייס *v* **1.** was drafted; enlisted (into the army); **2.** *[colloq.]* volunteered; (*pres* **metgayes**; *fut* **yeetgayes**).

heetgayroo|t/-yot התגיירות *nf* conversion to Judaism.

heetgaysoo|t/-yot התגייסות *nf* **1.** enlistment; **2.** volunteering.

heetgol|el/-elah/-altee התגולל *v* **1.** rolled about; **2.** *[slang]* lay around; (*pres* **meetgolel**; *fut* **yeetgolel**).

heetgon|en/-enah/-antee התגונן *v* defended oneself; (*pres* **meetgonen**; *fut* **yeetgonen**).

heetgonenoo|t/-yot התגוננות *nf* self-defence.

heetgor|er/-erah/-artee התגורר *v* resided; (*pres* **meetgorer**; *fut* **yeetgorer**).

heetgoreroo|t/-yot התגוררות *nf* residence; dwelling.

heetgosh|esh/-eshah/-ashtee התגושש *v* wrestled; (*pres* **meetgoshesh**; *fut* **yeetgoshesh**).

heetgosheshoo|t/-yot התגוששות *nf* wrestling.

heet'hal|ekh/-khah/-akhtee התהלך *v* walked about; (*pres* **meet'halekh**; *fut* **yeet'halekh**).

heet'hal|el/-elah/-altee התהלל *v* boasted; (*pres* **meet'halel**; *fut* **yeet'halel**).

heet'hap|ekh/-khah/-akhtee התהפך *v* overturned; turned around; (*pres* **meet'hapekh**; *fut* **yeet'hapekh**).

heet'hapkhoo|t/-yot התהפכות *nf* reversal; turning over.

heet'hapkhoot ha-yotsrot התהפכות היוצרות *nf* turning things topsy-turvy.

heet'hav|ah/-tah/-etee התהווה *v* emerged; was formed; (*pres* **meet'haveh**; *fut* **yeet'haveh**).

heet'hol|el/-elah/-altee התהולל *v* roistered; got out of hand; (*pres* **meet'holel**; *fut* **yeet'holel**).

heet'holeloo|t/-yot התהוללות getting out of hand; riotousness.

heetka'aroo|t/-yot התכערות *nf* uglification; becoming ugly.

heetkab|ed/-dah/-adetee התכבד *v* was honored; had the honor; (*pres* **meetkabed**; *fut* **yeetkabed**).

heetkabdoo|t/-yot התכבדות *nf* having the honor; honoring.

heetkab|el/-lah/-altee התקבל *v* was accepted; was received; (*pres* **meetkabel**; *fut* **yeetkabel**).

heetkabloo|t/-yot התקבלות *nf* admission; acceptance; being accepted.

heetkad|em/-mah/-amtee התקדם *v* progressed; advanced; (*pres* **meetkadem**; *fut* **yeetkadem**).

heetkadmoo|t/-yot התקדמות *nf* progress; advance.

heetka|'er/-'arah/-'artee התכער *v* became ugly; (*pres* **meetka'er**; *fut* **yeetka'er**).

heetkahaloo|t/-yot התקהלות *nf* gathering; assembly.

heetka|hel/-halah/-haltee התקהל *v* gathered; assembled; (*pres* **meetkahel**; *fut* **yeetkahel**).

heetkakhashoo|t/-yot התכחשות *nf* disavowal.

heetkakh|esh/-ashah/-ashtee התכחש *v* disavowed; disowned; (*pres* **meetkakhesh**; *fut* **yeetkakhesh**).

heetkal|e'akh/-khah/-akhtee התקלח *v* took a shower; (*pres* **meetkale'akh**; *fut* **yeetkale'akh**).

heetkal|ef/-fah/-aftee התקלף *v* peeled off; (*pres* **meetkalef**; *fut* **yeetkalef**).

heetkal|es/-sah/-astee התקלס *v* mocked; derided; (*pres* **meetkales**; *fut* **yeetkales**).

heetkalfoo|t/-yot התקלפות *nf* peeling off; shedding.

heetkalk|el/-elah/-altee התקלקל *v* got spoiled; deteriorated; broke down; (*pres* **meetkalkel**; *fut* **yeetkalkel**).

heetkalkeloo|t/-yot התקלקלות deterioration; spoiling; breakdown.

heetkalsoo|t/-yot התקלסות *nf* mockery; scoffing; deriding.

heetkam|et/-tah/-atetee התקמט *v* became wrinkled; (*pres* **meetkamet**; *fut* **yeetkamet**).

heetkamtoo|t/-yot התקמטות *nf* wrinkling; shrinkage.

heetkan|e/-'ah/-etee התקנא *v* become envious; envied; (*pres* **meetkane**; *fut* **yeetkane**).

heetkan|es/-sah/-astee התכנס *v* congregated; convened; (*pres* **meetkanes**; *fut* **yeetkanes**).

heetkan'oo|t/-yot התקנאות *nf* jealousy.

heetkansoo|t/-yot התכנסות *nf* congregation; convention; gathering.

heetkap|el/-lah/-altee התקפל *v* **1.** folded-up; **2.** *[colloq.]* gave in; retreated; (*pres* **meetkapel**; *fut* **yeetkapel**).

heetkaploo|t/-yot התקפלות *nf* folding; doubling up; giving-in; retreat.

heetkarb|el/-elah/-altee התכרבל *v* wrapped oneself; (*pres* **meetkarbel**; *fut* **yeetkarbel**).

heetkar|e'akh/-khah/-akhtee התקרח *v* became bald; (*pres* **meetkare'akh**; *fut* **yeetkare'akh**).

heetkar|er/-erah/-artee התקרר *v* **1.** cooled off; **2.** *[colloq.]* caught a cold; (*pres* **meetkarer**; *fut* **yeetkarer**).

heetkareroo|t/-yot התקררות *nf* **1**. cooling off; **2**. *[slang]* a cold (illness).

heetkar|ev/-vah/-avtee התקרב *v* approached; came nearer; (*pres* **meetkarev**; *fut* **yeetkarev**).

heetkarkhoo|t/-yot התקרחות *nf* balding; becoming bald.

heetkarvoo|t/-yot התקרבות *nf* approaching; convergence; rapprochement.

heetkas|ah/-tah/-etee התכסה *v* covered oneself up; (*pres* **meetkaseh**; *fut* **yeetkaseh**).

heetkash|eh/-tah/-etee התקשה *v* **1**. found difficult; **2**. hardened; (*pres* **meetkasheh**; *fut* **yeetkasheh**).

heetkash|er/-rah/-artee התקשר *v* **1**. got in touch; **2**. *[colloq.]* telephoned; (*pres* **meetkasher**; *fut* **yeetkasher**).

heetkash|et/-tah/-atetee התקשט *v* adorned oneself; (*pres* **meetkashet**; *fut* **yeetkashet**).

heetkashoo|t/-yot התקשות *nf* hardening.

heetkasoo|t/-yot התכסות *nf* wrapping; cover.

heetkashroo|t/-yot התקשרות *nf* attachment; commitment.

heetkat|esh/-'shah/-ashtee התכתש *v* wrestled; (*pres* **meetkatesh**; *fut* **yeetkatesh**).

heetkat|ev/-vah/-avtee התכתב *v* exchanged letters; corresponded; (*pres* **meetkatev**; *fut* **yeetkatevt**).

heetkats|ef/-fah/-aftee התקצף *v* became enraged; got angry; (*pres* **meetkatsef**; *fut* **yeetkatsef**).

heetkat'shoo|t/-yot התכתשות *nf* fistfight; fight.

heetkatvoo|t/-yot התכתבות *nf* correspondence; exchange of letters.

heetkav|en/-nah/-antee התכוון *v* intended; meant; (*pres* **meetkaven**; *fut* **yeetkaven**).

heetkav|ets/-'tsah/-atstee התכווץ *v* shrank; (*pres* **meetkavets**; *fut* **yeetkavets**).

heetkavtsoo|t/-yot התכווצות *nf* contraction; spasm.

heetka|yem/-ymah/-yamtee התקיים *v* **1**. took place; **2**. subsisted; **3**. existed; (*pres* **meetkayem**; *fut* **yeetkayem**).

heetk|eef/-eefah/-aftee התקיף *v* attacked; (*pres* **matkeef**; *fut* **yatkeef**).

heetk|een/-eenah/-antee התקין *v* installed; (*pres* **matkeen**; *fut* **yatkeen**).

heetkeen (*etc*) **takan|ah/-ot** התקין תקנה *v* made rule(s); passed regulation(s).

heetkhab|e/-'ah/-etee התחבא *v* hid; (*pres* **meetkhabe**; *fut* **yeetkhabe**).

heetkhab|ek/-kah/-aktee התחבק *v* hugged; embraced; (*pres* **meetkhabek**; *fut* **yeetkhabek**).

heetkhab|er/-rah/-artee התחבר *v* joined with; (*pres* **meetkhaber**; *fut* **yeetkhaber**).

heetkhab|et/-tah/-atetee התחבט *v* took pains; tried hard to solve; (*pres* **meetkhabet**; *fut* **yeetkhabet**).

heetkhab|ev/-evah/-avtee התחבב *v* endeared oneself (*pres* **meetkhabev**; *fut* **yeetkhabev**).

heetkhabevoo|t/-yot התחבבות *nf* endearing oneself; becoming popular with.

heetkhabkoo|t/-yot התחבקות *nf* embracing; hugging.

heetkhabroo|t/-yot התחברות *nf* joining; adhesion.

heetkhabtoo|t/-yot התחבטות *nf* struggle (internal); effort.

heetkhad|ed/-edah/-adetee התחדד *v* sharpened; (*pres* **meetkhaded**; *fut* **yeetkhaded**).

heetkhadedoo|t/-yot התחדדות *nf* sharpening.

heetkhadedoot yekhaseem התחדדות יחסים *nf* exacerbation of relations.

heetkhad|esh/-shah/-ashtee התחדש *v* **1**. was restored; **2**. was renewed; resumed (*pres* **meetkhadesh**; *fut* **yeetkhadesh**).

heetkhadshoo|t/-yot התחדשות renewal.

heetkhak|ekh/-'khah/-akhtee התחכך *v* **1**. scratched oneself; **2**. *[slang]* rubbed shoulders; **3**. mixed with (socially); (*pres* **meetkhakekh**; *fut* **yeetkhakekh**).

heetkhak|em/-mah/-amtee התחכם *v* **1**. outsmarted; devised means; **2**. *[colloq.]* tried to be clever; (*pres* **meetkhakem**; *fut* **yeetkhakem**).

heetkhak'khoo|t/-yot התחככות *nf* rubbing.

heetkhakmoo|t/-yot התחכמות *nf* **1**. trying to be funny; **2**. trying to outsmart.

heetkhal|ef/-fah/-aftee התחלף *v* **1**. changed into; was exchanged; **2**. *[colloq.]* changed clothes; (*pres* **meetkhalef**; *fut* **yeetkhalef**).

heetkhal|ek/-kah/-aktee התחלק *v* **1**. was divided between; **2**. slipped; (*pres* **meetkhalek**; *fut* **yeetkhalek**).

heetkhal|el/-elah/-altee התחלל *v* was desecrated; (*pres* **meetkhalel**; *fut* **yeetkhalel**).

heetkhalfoo|t/-yot התחלפות *v* change; exchange.

heetkhalkh|el/-elah/-altee התחלחל *v* was shocked; (*pres* **meetkhalkhel**; *fut* **yeetkhalkhel**).

heetkhalkoo|t/-yot התחלקות *nf* **1**. division; divisibility; **2**. slipping.

heetkham|ek/-kah/-aktee התחמק *v* evaded; shirked; slipped away; (*pres* **meetkhamek**; *fut* **yeetkhamek**).

heetkham|em/-emah/-amtee התחמם *v* warmed up; (*pres* **meetkhamem**; *fut* **yeetkhamem**).

heetkhamemoo|t/-yot התחממות *nf* warming up.

heetkhamkoo|t/-yot התחמקות *nf* evasion; shirking.

heetkhamts|en/-enah/-antee התחמצן *v* became oxidized; (*pres* **meetkhamtsen**; *fut* **yeetkhamtsen**).

heetkhan|ef/-fah/-aftee התחנף *v* fawned; ingratiated oneself; (*pres* **meetkhanef**; *fut* **yeetkhanef**).

heetkhan|ekh/-khah/-akhtee התחנך *v* was brought up; was educated; (*pres* **meetkhanekh**; *fut* **yeetkhanekh**).

heetkhan|en/-enah/-antee התחנן *v* begged; implored; (*pres* **meetkhanen**; *fut* **yeetkhanen**).

heetkhanenoo|t/-yot התחננות *v* pleading; entreating.

heetkhanfoo|t/-yot התחנפות *nf* ingratiation; flattering.

heetkhankh|en/-enah/-antee התחנחן *v* put on airs; (*pres* **meetkhankhen**; *fut* **yeetkhankhen**).

heetkhankhanoo|t/-yot התחנחנות *nf* coquetry; coquettishness.

heetkhankhoo|t/-yot התחנכות *nf* self-education.

heetkhap|er/-rah/-artee התחפר *v* dug oneself in; entrenched oneself; (*pres* **meetkhaper**; *fut* **yeetkhaper**).

heetkhap|es/-sah/-astee התחפש *v* disguised oneself; (*pres* **meetkhapes**; *fut* **yeetkhapes**).

heetkhaproo|t/-yot התחפרות *nf* entrenchment.

heetkhapsoo|t/-yot התחפשות *nf* **1.** disguise; **2.** masquerading.

heetkhar|ah/-tah/-eetee התחרה *v* competed; (*pres* **meetkhareh**; *fut* **yeetkhareh**).

heetkharb|en/-enah/-antee התחרבן *[slang] v* failed; (*pres* **meetkharben**; *fut* **yeetkharben**).

heetkharbenoo|t/-yot התחרבנות *[slang] nf* failure; disappointment.

heetkhar|et/-tah/-atetee התחרט *v* regretted; repented; changed one's mind; (*pres* **meetkharet**; *fut* **yeetkharet**).

heetkhar|esh/-shah/-ashtee התחרש *v* became deaf; (*pres* **meetkharesh**; *fut* **yeetkharesh**).

heetkharoo|t/-yot התחרות *nf* contest; competition.

heetkharshoo|t/-yot התחרשות *nf* becoming deaf.

heetkhartoo|t/-yot התחרטות *nf* contrition.

heetkhasdoot/-yot התחסדות *nf* hypocrisy.

heetkhas|ed/-dah/-adetee התחסד *v* acted hypocritically; (*pres* **meetkhased**; *fut* **yeetkhased**).

heetkhas|el/-lah/-altee התחסל *v* **1.** came to an end; **2.** was liquidated; (*pres* **meetkhasel**; *fut* **yeetkhasel**).

heetkhashb|en/-enah/-antee התחשבן *v* *[colloq.]* settled accounts; (*pres* **meetkhashben**; *fut* **yeetkhashben**).

heetkhashbenoo|t/-yot התחשבנות *nf* settling accounts.

heetkhash|ek/-kah/-aktee התחשק *v* felt like; had an urge for; (*pres* **meetkhashek**; *fut* **yeetkhashek**).

heetkhash|ev/-vah/-avtee התחשב *v* considered; took into account; (*pres* **meetkhashev**; *fut* **yeetkhashev**).

heetkhashm|el/-elah/-altee התחשמל *v* **1.** was electrocuted; **2.** was electrified; (*pres* **meetkhashmel**; *fut* **yeetkhashmel**).

heetkhashvoo|t/-yot התחשבות *nf* consideration.

heetkhashmeloo|t/-yot התחשמלות *nf* electrocution.

heetkhasloo|t/-yot התחסלות *nf* liquidation; self-liquidation.

heetkhat|en/-nah/-antee התחתן *v* got married; (*pres* **meetkhaten**; *fut* **yeetkhaten**).

heeetkhatnoo|t/-yot התחתנות *nf* marrying; marriage.

heetkhats|ef/-fah/-aftee התחצף *v* behaved with impertinence; behaved insolently; (*pres* **meetkhatsef**; *fut* **yeetkhatsef**).

heetkhatsfoo|t/-yot התחצפות *nf* impertinence; insolence.

heetkha|yev/-yvah/-yavtee התחייב *v* undertook; pledged; (*pres* **meetkhayev**; *fut* **yeetkhayev**).

heetkhayvoo|t/-yot התחייבות *nf* undertaking; obligation.

heetkhaz|ah/-tah/-etee התחזה *v* impersonate; pretended to be; (*pres* **meetkhazeh**; *fut* **yeetkhazeh**).

heetkhaz|ek/-kah/-aktee התחזק *v* grew stronger; (*pres* **meetkhazek**; *fut* **yeetkhazek**).

heetkhazkoo|t/-yot התחזקות *nf* strengthening.

heetkhazoo|t/-yot התחזות *nf* impersonation.

heetkh|eel/-eelah/-altee התחיל *v* began; (*pres* **matkheel**; *fut* **yatkheel**).

heetkhol|el/-elah/-altee התחולל *v* occurred; broke out; (*pres* **meetkholel**; *fut* **yeetkholel**).

heetkom|em/-emah/-amtee התקומם *v* rebelled; rose against; (*pres* **meetkomem**; *fut* **yeetkomem**).

heetkomemoo|t/-yot התקוממות *nf* rebellion; uprising.

heetkon|en/-enah/-antee התכונן *v* was preparing; prepared oneself; (*pres* **meetkonen**; *fut* **yeetkonen**).

heetkonenoo|t/-yot התכוננות *nf* preparatives; preparation.

heetkot|et/-etah/-atetee התקוטט *v* quarrelled; (*pres* **meetkotet**; *fut* **yeetkotet**).

heetkotetoo|t/-yot התקוטטות *nf* quarrel; brawl.

heetlab|esh/-shah/-ashtee התלבש *v* dressed; got dressed; (*pres* **meetlabesh**; *fut* **yeetlabesh**).

heetlab|esh (*etc*) **'al** התלבש על *v (slang)* determinedly took on.

heetlab|et/-tah/-atetee התלבט *v* **1.** took pains; **2.** hesitated; (*pres* **meetlabet**; *fut* **yeetlabet**).

heetlabtoo|t/-yot התלבטות *nf* struggle; hesitation.

heetlahavoo|t/-yot התלהבות *nf* enthusiasm; getting excited.

heetlah|ev/-havah/havtee התלהב *v* was enthusiastic; got excited; (*pres* **meetlahev**; *fut* **yeetlahev**).

heetlakdoo|t/-yot התלכדות *nf* rallying; joining forces.

heetlak|akh/-'khah/-akhtee (*or:* **heetlak|e'akh**) התלקח *v* flared up; fire; (*pres* **meetlake'akh**; *fut* **yeetlake'akh**).

heetlak|ed/-dah/-adetee התלכד *v* rallied; joined forces; (*pres* **meetlaked**; *fut* **yeetlaked**).

heetlakh'shoo|t/-yot התלחשות *nf* whisper; whispering.

heetlakh|esh/-'shah/-ashtee התלחש *v* exchanged whispers; (*pres* **meetlakhesh**; *fut* **yeetlakhesh**).

heetlak'khoo|t/-yot התלקחות *nf* flare up.

heetlakhl|ekh/-ekhah/-akhtee התלכלך *v* dirtied oneself; (*pres* **meetlakhlekh**; *fut* **yeetlakhlekh**).

heetlakhlekhoo|t/-yot התלכלכות *nf* dirtying; sullying.

heetlam|ed/-dah/-adetee התלמד *v* taught oneself; (*pres* **meetlamed**; *fut* **yeetlamed**).

heetlon|en/-enah/-antee התלונן *v* complained; (*pres* **meetlonen**; *fut* **yeetlonen**).

heetlonenoo|t/-yot התלוננות *nf* complaining; grumbling.

heetlots|ets/-etsah/-atstee התלוצץ *v* joked; jested; (*pres* **meetlotsets**; *fut* **yeetlotsets**).

heetlotsetsoo|t/-yot התלוצצות *nf* jesting; mockery.

heetma'atoot התמעטות *nf* decrease; diminution.

heetm|a'et/-'atah/-'atoo התמעט *v* diminished; became fewer; (*pres* **meetma'et**; *fut* **yeetma'et**).

heetmahm|ah/-'hah/-ahtee (*or:* **heetmahm|e'ah**) התמהמה *v* tarried; lingered; (*pres* **meetmahmeha**; *fut* **yeetmahmeha**).

heetmahm'hoo|t/-yot התמהמהות *nf* tarrying; lingering.

heetmak|akh (or: **heetmak|e'akh**)/-'**khah**/-**akhtee** התמקח *v* bargained; haggled; (*pres* **meetmake'akh**; *fut* **yeetmake'akh**).

heetmak|em/-mah/-amtee התמקם *v* settled; took up position; (*pres* **meetmakem**; *fut* **yeetmakem**).

heetmak|er/-rah/-artee התמכר *v* **1.** devoted oneself; **2.** became addicted; (*pres* **meetmaker**; *fut* **yeetmaker**).

heetmak'khoo|t/-yot התמקחות *nf* haggling.

heetmakmoo|t/-yot התמקמות *nf* taking position; localization.

heetmakroo|t/-yot התמכרות *nf* **1.** addiction; **2.** absolute devotion.

heetmal|e/-'ah/-etee התמלא *v* **1.** was filled; **2.** was fulfilled; (*pres* **meetmale**; *fut* **yeetmale**).

heetmam|esh/-shah/-ashtee התממש *v* materialized; came true; (*pres* **meetmamesh**; *fut* **yeetmamesh**).

heetmamshoo|t/-yot התממשות *nf* realization.

heetman|ah/-tah/-etee התמנה *v* was appointed; (*pres* **meetmaneh**; *fut* **yeetmaneh**).

heetmanoo|t/-yot התמנות *nf* appointment; nomination.

heetmarm|er/-erah/-artee התמרמר *v* resented; bitterly complained; (*pres* **meetmarmer**; *fut* **yeetmarmer**).

heetmarmeroo|t/-yot התמרמרות *nf* resentment; embitterment.

heetmas|ed/-dah/-adetee התמסד *v* became instituted; (*pres* **meetmased**; *fut* **yeetmased**).

heetmas|er/-rah/-artee התמסר *v* **1.** devoted oneself; surrendered; **2.** (of female person) gave herself to (sexually); (*pres* **meetmaser**; *fut* **yeetmaser**).

heetmasdoo|t/-yot התמסדות *nf* institutionalization; becoming part of the establishment.

heetmash|ekh/-'khah/-akhtee התמשך *v* extended; dragged out; (*pres* **meetmashekh**; *fut* **yeetmashekh**).

heetmash'khoo|t/-yot התמשכות *nf* prolongation; procrastination.

heetmasm|es/-esah/-astee התמסמס *v* melted away; fell apart; (*pres* **meetmasmes**; *fut* **yeetmasmes**).

heetmasroo|t/-yot התמסרות *nf* **1.** devotion; attachment **2.** giving herself sexually.

heetmats|e/-'ah/-etee התמצא *v* knew one's way about; was familiar with; (*pres* **meetmatse**; *fut* **yeetmatse**).

heetmats'oo|t/-yot התמצאות *nf* orientation.

(khoosh) heetmats'oot חוש התמצאות *nm* sense of orientation.

heetmaz|eg/-gah/-agtee התמזג *v* blended; fused; (*pres* **meetmazeg**; *fut* **yeetmazeg**).

heetmazgoo|t/-yot התמזגות *nf* amalgamation; mixture; harmony.

heetmazm|ez/-ezah/-aztee התמזמז *v* **1.** wasted time; was late; **2.** *[slang]* necked; **3.** wore out; (*pres* **meetmazmez**; *fut* **yeetmazmez**).

heetmazmezoo|t/-yot התמזמזות *nf* **1.** softening; **2.** *[slang]* flirting.

heetm|eed/-eedah/-adetee התמיד *v* persisted; (*pres* **matmeed**; *fut* **yatmeed**).

heetm|een/-eenah/-antee הטמין *v* hid; (*pres* **matmeen**; *fut* **yatmeen**).

heetmod|ed/-edah/-adetee התמודד *v* confronted; contended; faced up; (*pres* **meetmoded**; *fut* **yeetmoded**).

heetmodedoo|t/-yot התמודדות *nf* **1.** confrontation; **2.** competition.

heetmog|eg/-egah/-agtee התמוגג *v* melted; dissolved with pleasure; (*pres* **meetmogeg**; *fut* **yeetmogeg**).

heetmogegoo|t/-yot התמוגגות *nf* melting (with love); dissolving.

heetmot|et/-etah/-atetee התמוטט *v* collapsed; (*pres* **meetmotet**; *fut* **yeetmotet**).

heetmotetoo|t/-yot התמוטטות *nf* collapse.

heetmotetoot (*etc*) **'atsabeem** התמוטטות עצבים *nf* nervous breakdown.

('al saf) heetmotetoot על סף התמוטטות *adv* on the verge of breakdown.

heetn|ah/-etah/-etee התנה *v* stipulated; made it a condition; (*pres* **matneh**; *fut* **yatneh**).

heetnah (*etc*) **ahaveem** התנה אהבים *nf* made love.

heetna'an|e'a'/-'ah/-'atee התנענע *v* swayed; shook; (*pres* **meetna'ane'a'**; *fut* **yeetna'ane'a'**).

heetna'an'oo|t/-yot התנענעות *nf* shaking; vibration.

heetna'aroo|t/-yot התנערות *nf* awakening; shaking off.

heetnab|e/-ah/-etee התנבא *v* prophesized; (*pres* **meetnabe**; *fut* **yeetnabe**).

heetnad|ef/-fah/-aftee התנדף *v* evaporated; (*pres* **meetnadef**; *fut* **yeetnadef**).

heetnad|ev/-vah/-avtee התנדב *v* volunteered; (*pres* **meetnadev**; *fut* **yeetnadev**).

heetnadn|ed/-edah/-adetee התנדנד *v* **1.** docked; **2.** swayed; (*pres* **meetnadned**; *fut* **yeetnadned**).

heetnadvoo|t/-yot התנדבות *nf* volunteering.

heetna|'er/-'arah/-'artee התנער *v* shook off; (*pres* **meetna'er**; *fut* **yeetna'er**).

heetnagdoo|t/-yot התנגדות *nf* opposition; resistance.

('or|er/-erah/-artee) heetnagdoot עורר התנגדות *v* antagonized; (*pres* **me'orer** *etc*; *fut* **ye'orer** *etc*).

(tenoo|'at/-'ot) heetnagdoot תנועת התנגדות *nf* resistance movement.

heetnag|ed/-dah/-adetee התנגד *v* opposed; objected; (*pres* **meetnaged**; *fut* **yeetnaged**).

heetnag|esh/-shah/-ashtee התנגש *v* clashed; collided; (*pres* **meetnagesh**; *fut* **yeetnagesh**).

heetnag|ev/-vah/-avtee התנגב *v* dried oneself; (*pres* **meetnagev**; *fut* **yeetnagev**).

heetnagshoo|t/-yot התנגשות *nf* clash; collision.

heetnagvoo|t/-yot התנגבות *nf* wiping; drying oneself.

heetnahagoo|t/-yot התנהגות *nf* behavior; conduct.

heetna|heg/-hagah/-hagtee התנהג *v* behaved; (*pres* **meetnaheg**; *fut* **yeetnaheg**).

heetna|hel/-halah/-haltee התנהל *v* went on; was conducted; (*pres* **meetnahel**; *fut* **yeetnahel**).

heetnak|el/-lah/-altee התנכל *v* plotted; conspired; (*pres* **meetnakel**; *fut* **yeetnakel**).

heetnak|em/-mah/-amtee התנקם *v* avenged oneself; (*pres* **meetnakem**; *fut* **yeetnakem**).

heetnak|er/-rah/-artee התנכר *v* shunned; alienated; (*pres* **meetnaker**; *fut* **yeetnaker**).

heetnak|esh/-shah/-ashtee התנקש *v* attempted to kill; (*pres* **meetnakesh**; *fut* **yeetnakesh**).

heetnak|ez/-zah/-aztee התנקז *v* was drained; (*pres* **meetnakez**; *fut* **yetnakez**).

heetnakh|el/-alah/-altee התנחל *v* **1.** settled on land; **2.** *[colloq.]* settled in Judea, Samaria or in the Gaza Strip; (*pres* **meetnakhel**; *fut* **yeetnakhel**).

heetnakhloo|t/-yot התנחלות *nf* settling (or settlement) in Judea, Samaria or Gaza areas.

heetnakh|em/-amah/-amtee התנחם *v* consoled oneself; (*pres* **meetnakhem**; *fut* **yeetnakhem**).

heetnakloo|t/-yot התנכלות *nf* plotting; scheming.

heetnakroo|t/-yot התנכרות *nf* estrangement.

heetnakshoo|t/-yot התנקשות *nf* attempt on one's life.

heetnamn|em/-emah/-amtee התנמנם *v* dozed; (*pres* **meetnamnem**; *fut* **yeetnamnem**).

heetnap|akh/-khah/-akhtee (*or:* **heetnap|e'akh**) התנפח *v* swelled; was inflated; was boastful; (*pres* **meetnape'akh**; *fut* **yeetnape'akh**).

heetnap|ets/-'tsah/-atstee התנפץ *v* was shattered; (*pres* **meetnapets**; *fut* **yeetnapets**).

heetnapkhoo|t/-yot התנפחות *nf* swelling.

heetnaploo|t/-yot התנפלות *nf* assault; attack.

heetnap|el/-lah/-altee התנפל *v* attacked; assaulted; (*pres* **meetnapel**; *fut* **yeetnapel**).

heetnas|ah/-tah/-etee התנסה *v* experienced; went through; (*pres* **meetnaseh**; *fut* **yeetnaseh**).

heetnas|e/-'ah/-etee התנשא *v* rose; was exalted; boasted; (*pres* **meetnase**; *fut* **yeetnase**).

heetnash|ef/-fah/-aftee התנשף *v* puffed; breathed heavily; regained one's breath (*pres* **meetnashef**; *fut* **yeetnashef**).

heetnash|ek/-kah/-aktee התנשק *v* exchanged kisses; (*pres* **meetnashek**; *fut* **yeetnashek**).

heetnas'oo|t/-yot התנשאות *nf* elevation; pridefulness; haughtiness.

heetnashfoo|t/-yot התנשפות *nf* breathing with difficulty; regaining one's breath.

heetnashkoo|t/-yot התנשקות *nf* kissing; exchanging kisses.

heetnasoo|t/-yot התנסות *nf* experiencing; gaining experience.

heetnats|akh/-'khah/-akhtee (*or:* **heetnats|e'akh**) התנצח *v* polemicized; exchanged arguments; (*pres* **meetnatse'akh**; *fut* **yeetnatse'akh**).

heetnats|el/-lah/-altee התנצל *v* apologized; (*pres* **meetnatsel**; *fut* **yeetnatsel**).

heetnats|er/-rah/-artee התנצר *v* converted to Christianity; (*pres* **meetnatser**; *fut* **yeetnatser**).

heetnats'khoo|t/-yot התנצחות *nf* dispute.

heetnatsloo|t/-yot התנצלות *nf* apology.

heetnatsroo|t/-yot התנצרות *nf* conversion to Christianity.

heetnav|en/-nah/-antee התנוון *v* degenerated; (*pres* **meetnaven**; *fut* **yeetnaven**).

heetnavnoo|t/-yot התנוונות *nf* degeneration; decay; atrophy.

heetnaz|er/-rah/-artee התנזר *v* abstained from; gave up; (*pres* **meetnazer**; *fut* **yeetnazer**).

heetnazroo|t/-yot התנזרות *nf* **1.** abstention from; **2.** abstinence; giving up.

heetnee'a'/-'ah/-a'tee התניע *v* started up (engine); (*pres* **matnee'a'**; *fut* **yatnee'a'**).

heetno|'e'a/-'a'ah/-'a'tee התנועע *v* moved; swayed; (*pres* **meetno'e'a'**; *fut* **yeetno'e'a'**).

heetnod|ed/-edah/-adetee התנודד *v* swayed; oscillated; (*pres* **meetnoded**; *fut* **yeetnoded**).

heetnodedoo|t/-yot התנודדות *nf* swaying; oscillation.

heetnof|ef/-efah/-aftee התנופף *v* fluttered; (*pres* **meetnofef**; *fut* **yeetnofef**).

heetnofefoo|t/-yot התנופפות *nf* waving flag; fluttering.

heetnos|es/-esah/-astee התנוסס *v* waved; was hoisted; (*pres* **meetnoses**; *fut* **yeetnoses**).

heetnosesoo|t/-yot התנוססות *nf* **1.** flying (flag); **2.** standing out.

heetnots|ets/-etsah/-atstee התנוצץ *v* sparkled (*pres* **meetnotsets;** *fut* **yeetnotsets).**

heetnotsetsoo|t/-yot התנוצצות *nf* gleaming; glittering.

heet'od|ed/-edah/-adetee התעודד *v* cheered up; felt encouraged; (*pres* **meet'oded;** *fut* **yeet'oded).**

heet'odedoo|t/-yot התעודדות *nf* encouragement.

heet'of|ef/-efah/-aftee התעופף *v* **1.** flew about; **2.** flew off; (*pres* **meet'ofef;** *fut* **yeet'ofef).**

heet'ofefoo|t/-yot התעופפות *nf* flying off.

heet'on|en/-enah/-antee התאונן *v* complained; (*pres* **meet'onen;** *fut* **yeet'onen).**

heet'onenoo|t/-yot התאוננות *nf* complaining.

heetookh/-eem היתוך *nm* **1.** melting; **2.** fusion;

(koor/-ey) heetookh כור היתוך *nm* melting pot.

(nekood|at/-ot) heetookh נקודת היתוך melting point.

heetool/-eem היתול *nm* mockery; ridiculing.

heetoolee/-t היתולי *adj* humorous; comic.

(makhaz|eh/-ot) heetoolee/-yeem מחזה היתולי *nm* comedy.

heet'or|er/-erah/-artee התעורר *v* awakened; woke up; (*pres* **meet'orer;** *fut* **yeet'orer).**

heet'oreroo|t/-yot התעוררות *nf* awakening.

heet'osh|esh/-eshah/-ashtee התאושש *v* **1.** recovered; regained strength; came to oneself; **2.** regained courage; (*pres* **meet'oshesh;** *fut* **yeet'oshesh).**

heet'osheshoo|t/-yot התאוששות *nf* recovery.

heetpa'aloo|t/-yot התפעלות *nf* **1.** admiration; **2.** excitement.

heetpa'amoo|t/-yot התפעמות *nf* excitement; bewilderment.

heetpa'aroo|t/-yot התפארות *nf* boasting.

"heetpa'el" התפעל *nm* passive and reflexive form of Hebrew verb (Gram.).

heetpa|'el/-'alah/-'altee התפעל *v* was impressed; (*pres* **meetpa'el;** *fut* **yeetpa'el).**

heetpa|'em/-'amah/-'amtee התפעם *v* was stirred; (*pres* **meetpa'em;** *fut* **yeetpa'em).**

heetpa|'er/-'arah/-'artee התפאר *v* boasted: (*pres* **meetpa'er;** *fut* **yeetpa'er).**

heetpag|er/-rah/-artee התפגר *v* died; *[slang]* croaked; (*pres* **meetpager;** *fut* **yeetpager).**

heetpagroo|t/-yot התפגרות *v* death (of an animal or of an unworthy person).

heetpak|a'/-'ah/-a'tee התפקע *v* burst; was about to burst; (*pres* **meetpake'a';** *fut* **yeetpake'a').**

heetpakdoo|t/-yot התפקדות *nf* **1.** presenting oneself for census; **2.** functioning (*[colloq.]* **of a person).**

heetpak|a'/-'ah/-a'tee (*or:* **heetpak|e'a')** התפקע *v* burst; was about to burst; (*pres* **meetpake'a';** *fut* **yeetpake'a').**

heetpak|akh/-'khah/-akhtee (*or:* **heetpak|e'akh)** התפכח *v* **1.** sobered up; **2.** became clever; (*pres* **meetpake'akh;** *fut* **yeetpake'akh).**

heetpaked! התפקד! *v imp sing m* count off! number off!

heetpak|ed/-dah/-adetee התפקד *v* **1.** was mustered; **2.** *[colloq.]* functioned (of a person); (*pres* **meetpaked;** *fut* **yeetpaked).**

heetpakhamoo|t/-yot התפחמות *nf* **1.** electrocution: **2.** carbonization.

heetpakh|em/-amah/-ametee התפחם *v* was electrocuted; was carbonized; (*pres* **meetpakhem;** *fut* **yeetpakhem).**

heetpak'khoo|t/-yot התפכחות *nf* sobering up.

heetpal|e/-'ah/-etee התפלא *v* wondered; was astonished; (*pres* **meetpale;** *fut* **yeetpale).**

heetpal|eg/-gah/-agnoo התפלג *v* split; (*pres* **meetpaleg;** *fut* **yeetpaleg).**

heetpal|el/-elah/-altee התפלל *v* prayed; (*pres* **meetpalel;** *fut* **yeetpalel).**

heetpal|esh/-shah/-ashtee התפלש *v* wallowed (in the dust; in misery); (*pres* **meetpalesh;** *fut* **yeetpalesh).**

heetpal|ets/-tsah/-atstee התפלץ *v* **1.** shuddered; **2.** was paralyzed; **3.** had the jitters; (*pres* **meetpalets;** *fut* **yeetpalets).**

heetpalgoo|t/-yot התפלגות *nf* bifurcation; schism; splitting.

heetpalm|es/-esah/-astee התפלמס *v* polemicized; engaged in polemics; (*pres* **meetpalmes;** *fut* **yeetpalmes).**

heetpalmesoo|t/-yot התפלמסות *nf* polemics; disputation.

heetpal'oo|t/-yot התפלאות *nf* amazement; surprise.

heetpalp|el/-elah/-altee התפלפל *v* quibbled; (*pres* **meetpalpel;** *fut* **yeetpalpel).**

heetpalpeloo|t/-yot התפלפלות *nf* hair-splitting dialectics; casuistry.

heetpals|ef/-efah/-aftee התפלסף *v* philosophized; (*pres* **meetpalsef;** *fut* **yeetpalsef).**

heetpalsefoo|t/-yot התפלספות *nf* philosophizing.

heetpalshoo|t/-yot התפלשות *nf* rolling about.

heetpaltsoo|t/-yot התפלצות *nf* jitter; shudder.

heetpan|ah/-tah/-etee התפנה *v* **1.** vacated; **2.** found time: (*pres* **meetpaneh;** *fut* **yeetpaneh).**

heetpan|ek/-kah/-aktee התפנק *v* pampered oneself; (*pres* **meetpanek;** *fut* **yeetpanek).**

heetpankoo|t/-yot התפנקות *nf* pampering oneself.

heetpanoo|t/-yot התפנות *nf* **1.** evacuation; **2.** disengagement.

heetpantch|er/-erah/-artee התפנצ'ר *v* *[slang]* failed; went bust; (*pres* **meetpantcher;** *fut* **yeetpantcher).**

heetpar|a'/-'ah/-a'tee (*or:* **heetpar|e'a')** התפרע *v* got wild; ran riot; (*pres* **meetpare'a';** *fut* **yeetpare'a').**

heetpar|ek/-kah/-aktee התפרק *v* **1.** was dismantled; **2.** relaxed; got off his chest. **3.** disarmed oneself; (*pres* **meetparek;** *fut* **yeetparek).**

heetpar|es/-sah/-astee התפרש *v* deployed; fanned out; (*pres* **meetpares;** *fut* **yeetpares).**

heetpar|esh/-shah/-ashtee התפרש *v* was interpreted; (*pres* **meetparesh;** *fut* **yeetparesh).**

heetpar|ets/-tsah/-atstee התפרץ *v* burst into; became unruly; (*pres* **meetparets;** *fut* **yeetparets).**

heetpark|ed/-edah/-adetee התפרקד *v* lay on one's back; (*pres* **meetparked;** *fut* **yeetparked).**

heetparkhakhoo|t/-yot התפרחחות *nf* hooliganism.

heetparkh|e'akh/-ekhah/-akhtee התפרחח *v* *[slang]* behaved like a ruffian; (*pres* **meetparkhe'akh;** *fut* **yeetparkhe'akh).**

heetparn|es/-esah/-astee התפרנס *v* earned a living; (*pres* **meetparnes;** *fut* **yeetparnes).**

heetparnesoo|t/-yot התפרנסות *nf* earning one's living; making a living.

heetpar'oo|t/-yot התפרעות *v* riot.

heetparp|er/-erah/-artee התפרפר *v* *[slang]* **1.** shirked duty; **2.** was promiscuous; (*pres* **meetparper;** *fut* **yeetparper).**

heetparperoo|t/-yot התפרפרות *nf* *[slang]* promiscuity; shirking one's duties.

heetpars|em/-emah/-amtee התפרסם *v* became famous; (*pres* **meetparsem;** *fut* **yeetparsem).**

heetparsemoo|t/-yot התפרסמות *nf* gaining notoriety; fame; getting famous.

heetparsoo|t/-yot התפרשות *nf* deployment; fan-out.

heetparshoo|t/-yot התפרשות *nf* interpretation; being interpreted.

heetpartsoo|t/-yot התפרצות *nf* outbreak; eruption; *[slang]* burglary.

heetpash|er/-rah/-artee התפשר *v* compromised; came to terms; (*pres* **meetpasher;** *fut* **yeetpasher).**

heetpash|et/-tah/-atetee התפשט *v* **1.** undressed; **2.** spread; expanded; (*pres* **meetpashet;** *fut* **yeetpashet).**

heetpashroo|t/-yot התפשרות *nf* compromise.

heetpashtoo|t/-yot התפשטות *nf* **1.** spread; expansion; **2.** undressing.

heetpat|ah/-etah/-etee התפתה *v* was enticed; was seduced; was a fool to; (*pres* **meetpateh;** *fut* **yeetpateh).**

heetpat|akh/-khah/-akhtee (*or:* **heetpat|e'akh)** התפתח *v* developed; progressed into; widened knowledge; (*pres* **meetpate'akh;** *fut* **yeetpate'akh).**

heetpat|el/-lah/-altee התפתל *v* wriggled; twisted; (*pres* **meetpatel;** *fut* **yeetpatel).**

heetpat|em/-mah/-amtee התפטם *v* stuffed oneself; (*pres* **meetpatem;** *fut* **yeetpatem).**

heetpat|er/-rah/-artee התפטר *v* **1.** resigned; **2.** got rid of; (*pres* **meetpater;** *fut* **yeetpater).**

heetpat'khoo|t/-yot התפתחות *nf* development; evolution.

heetpat'khootee/-t התפתחותי *adj* developmental; evolutionary.

heetpatloo|t/-yot התפתלות *nf* wriggling; winding.

heetpatmoo|t/-yot התפטמות *nf* gluttony; fattening.

heetpatoo|t/-yot התפתות *nf* succumbing.

heetpatroo|t/-yot התפטרות *nf* resignation; ridding oneself of.

(heeg|eesh/-eesha/-ashtee) heetpatroot הגיש התפטרות *v* tended one's resignation; (*pres* **mageesh;** *fut* **yageesh).**

heetpats|el/-lah/-altee התפצל *v* split; ramified; (*pres* **meetpatsel;** *fut* **yeetpatsel).**

heetpatsloo|t/-yot התפצלות *nf* cleavage; splitting.

heetpa|yes/-ysah/-yastee התפייס *v* reconciled oneself; (*pres* **meetpayes;** *fut* **yeetpayes).**

heetpaysoo|t/-yot התפייסות *nf* reconciliation.

heetpaz|er/-rah/-artee התפזר *v* scattered; dispersed; (*pres* **meetpazer;** *fut* **yeetpazer).**

(le) heetpazer! ! להתפזר *v imp* fall out!

heetpazroo|t/-yot התפזרות *nf* scattering; dispersion.

heetpoot|ar/-rah/-artee התפוטר *v* *[slang]* was forced to resign; (*pres* **meetpootar;** *fut* **yeetpootar).**

heetpor|er/-erah/-artee התפורר *v* crumbled; disintegrated; (*pres* **meetporer;** *fut* **yeetporer).**

heetporeroo|t/-yot התפוררות *nf* desintegration.

heetpotsets/-etsah/-atstee התפוצץ *v* exploded; (*pres* **meetpotsets;** *fut* **yeetpotsets).**

heetpotsetsoo|t/-yot התפוצצות *nf* explosion.

heetr|ah/-etah/-etee התרה *v* warned; (*pres* **matreh;** *fut* **yatreh).**

heetra'anen/-enah/-antee התרענן *v* freshened up; refreshed oneself; (*pres* **meetra'anen;** *fut* **yeetra'anen).**

heetra'anenoot התרעננות *nf* refreshnent; freshing up.

heetrab|ah/-tah התרבה *v* multiplied; increased; (*pres* **meetrabeh;** *fut* **yeetrabeh).**

heetraboo|t/-yot התרבות *nf* multiplication; proliferation.

heetra|'em/-'amah/-'amtee התרעם *v* was sore; grumbled; (*pres* **meetra'em;** *fut* **yeetra'em).**

heetrag|el/-lah/-altee התרגל *v* got used to; (*pres* **meetragel;** *fut* **yeetragel).**

heetrag|esh/-shah/-ashtee התרגש *v* was moved; was excited; (*pres* **meetragesh;** *fut* **yeetragesh).**

heetrag|ez/-zah/-aztee התרגז *v* was angered; was excited; was irritated; (*pres* **meetragez;** *fut* **yeetragez).**

heetragloo|t/-yot התרגלות *nf* **1.** accustoming oneself; **2.** getting accustomed; habituation.

heetragshoo|t/-yot התרגשות *nf* excitement; emotion.

heetragzoo|t/-yot התרגזות *nf* irritation; anger.

heetrak|ekh/-'khah/-akhtee התרכך *v* mellowed; softened; (*pres* **meetrakekh**; *fut* **yeetrakekh**).

heetrak|ekh/-'khah/-akhtee התרכך *v* mellowed; (*pres* **meetrakekh**; *fut* **yeetrakekh**).

heetrak|em/-mah/-amtee התרקם *v* took shape; (*pres* **meetrakem**; *fut* **yeetrakem**).

heetrak|ez/-zah/-aztee התרכז *v* centered; concentrated; (*pres* **meetrakez**; *fut* **yeetrakez**).

heetrakhakoo|t/-yot התרחקות *nf* estrangement; going far.

heetrakhashoo|t/-yot התרחשות *nf* occurrence; happening.

heetrakhatsoo|t/-yot התרחצות *nf* washing oneself; bathing.

heetrakhavoo|t/-yot התרחבות *nf* expansion; broadening; expansion.

heetrakh|ek/-kah/-aktee התרחק *v* drew away; kept a distance; (*pres* **meetrakhek**; *fut* **yeetrakhek**).

heetrakh|esh/-shah/-ashtee התרחש *v* occurred; (*pres* **meetrakhesh**; *fut* **yeetrakhesh**).

heetrakh|ets/-atsah/-atstee התרחץ *v* washed oneself; bathed; (*pres* **meetrakhets**; *fut* **yeetrakhets**).

heetrakh|ev/-avah/-avtee התרחב *v* broadened; widened; expanded; (*pres* **meetrakhev**; *fut* **yeetrakhev**).

heetrakh'koo|t/-yot התרחקות *nf* estrangement; going far.

heetrakh'shoo|t/-yot התרחשות *nf* occurrence; happening.

heetrakh'tsoo|t/-yot התרחצות *nf* washing oneself; bathing.

heetrakh'voo|t/-yot התרחבות *nf* expansion; broadening; expansion.

heetrak'khoo|t/-yot התרככות *nf* softening.

heetrakmoo|t/-yot התרקמות *nf* formation.

heetrakzoo|t/-yot התרכזות *nf* concentration.

heetra'oo|t/-yot התראות *nf* seeing one another.

(le) heetra'ot! להתראות! (greeting) So long! See you later!

heetrap|e/-'ah/-etee התרפא *v* recovered; became cured; (*pres* **meetrape**; *fut* **yeetrape**).

heetrap|ek/-kah/-aktee התרפק *v* hugged; yearned; (*pres* **meetrapek**; *fut* **yeetrapek**).

heetrap|es/-sah/-astee התרפס *v* fawned; abased oneself; (*pres* **meetrapes**; *fut* **yeetrapes**).

heetrapkoo|t/-yot התרפקות *v* **1.** holding close; hugging; **2.** *[colloq.]* clinging nostalgically.

heetrap'oo|t/-yot התרפאות *f* curing; healing.

heetrapsoo|t/-yot התרפסות *nf* abasing oneself.

heetras|ek/-kah/-aktee התרסק *v* crashed; (*pres* **meetrasek**; *fut* **yeetrasek**).

heetrash|el/-lah/-altee התרשל *v* neglected; was negligent; (*pres* **meetrashel**; *fut* **yeetrashel**).

heetrash|em/-mah/-amtee התרשם *v* was impressed; got the impression; (*pres* **meetrashem**; *fut* **yeetrashem**).

heetrashloo|t/-yot התרשלות *nf* negligence; laxity.

heetrashmoo|t/-yot התרשמות *nf* impression.

heetraskoot|/-yot התרסקות *nf* crashing; crash.

heetrat|e'akh/-khah/-akhtee התרתח *v* became furious; (*pres* **meetrate'akh**; *fut* **yeetratakh**).

heetrat|ev/-vah/-avtee התרטב *v* got wet; became wet; (*pres* **meetratev**; *fut* **yeetratev**).

heetratkhoo|t/-yot התרתחות *nf* boiling with rage.

heetratvoo|t/-yot התרטבות *nf* **1.** wetting; becoming wet; **2.** bed wetting.

heetrav|e'akh/-khah/-akhtee התרווח *v* felt relief; was comfortable; (*pres* **meetrave'akh**; *fut* **yeetrave'akh**).

heetravr|ev/-evah/-avtee התרברב *v* bragged; showed off; (*pres* **meetravrev**; *fut* **yeetravrev**).

heetravrevoo|t/-yot התרברבות *nf* bragging; boasting.

heetr|ee'a'/-a'tee התריע *v* protested; (*pres* **matree'a'**; *fut* **yatree'a'**).

heetr|ee'akh/-eekhah/-akhtee הטריח *v* bothered; annoyed; (*pres* **matree'akh**; *fut* **yatree'akh**).

heetr|eem/-eemah/-amtee התרים *v* collected contributions; raised funds; (*pres* **matreem**; *fut* **yatreem**).

heetr|ees/-sah/-astee התריס *v* disputed; protested against; (*pres* **matrees**; *fut* **yatrees**).

heetro'a'oot התרועעות *nf* association; becoming friends.

heetro|'e'a'/-'a'ah/-'a'tee התרועע *v* made friends with; (*pres* **meetro'e'a'**; *fut* **yeetro'e'a'**).

heetrof|ef/-efah/-aftee התרופף *v* slackened; weakened; (*pres* **meetrofef**; *fut* **yeetrofef**).

heetrofefoo|t/-yot התרופפות *nf* weakening.

heetrok|en/-nah/-antee התרוקן *v* became empty; (*pres* **meetroken**; *fut* **yeetroken**).

heetroknoo|t/-yot התרוקנות *nf* emptying; becoming empty.

heetrom|em/-emah/-amtee התרומם *v* **1.** rose; raised oneself; **2.** *[slang]* (of a male) had homosexual intercourse; **3.** *[slang]* (of a female) was easy to get (sexually); (*pres* **meetromem**; *fut* **yeetromem**).

heetromemoo|t/-yot התרוממות *nf* **1.** rising; **2.** exaltation.

heetrosh|esh/-eshah/-ashtee התרושש *v* was impoverished; (*pres* **meetroshesh**; *fut* **yeetroshesh**).

heetrosheshoo|t/-yot התרוששות *v* impoverishment; pauperisation.

heetrots|ets/-etsah/-atstee התרוצץ *v* ran about; rushed around; (*pres* **meetrotsets**; *fut* **yeetrotsets**).

heetrotsetsoo|t/-yot התרוצצות *nf* rushing around; running about.

heetsamdoo|t/-yot היצמדות *nf* clinging.

heetsaroo|t/-yot היצרות *nf* **1.** constriction; narrowing; **2.** stenosis (medic.).

heetsb|ee'a'/-ee'ah/-atee הצביע *v* voted; pointed at; (*pres* **matsbee'a'**; *fut* **yatsbee'a'**).

heetsd|ee'a'/-ee'/-ah/-a'tee הצדיע *v* saluted; (*pres* **matsdee'a'**; *fut* **yatsdee'a'**).

heetsd|eek/-eekah/-aktee הצדיק *v* justified; approved; (*pres* **matsdeek**; *fut* **yatsdeek**).

heets|ee'a'/-ee'ah/-a'tee הציע *v* proposed; suggested; (*pres* **matsee'a'**; *fut* **yatsee'a'**).

heets|eeg/-eegah/-agtee הציג *v* placed; presented; (*pres* **matseeg**; *fut* **yatseeg**).

heets|eel/-eelah/-altee הציל *v* saved; rescued; (*pres* **matseel**; *fut* **yatseel**).

heet's|ees/-eesah/-astee התסיס *v* **1.** fermented; agitated; **2.** caused to ferment; (*pres* **mat'sees**; *fut* **yat'sees**).

heets|eet/-eetah/-atetee הצית *v* set fire to; ignited; (*pres* **matseet**; *fut* **yatseet**).

heets|eev/-eevah/-avtee הציב *v* placed; put in position; (*pres* **matseev**; *fut* **yatseev**).

heets'|heer/-heerah/-hartee הצהיר *v* declared; stated; (*pres* **mats'heer**; *fut* **yats'heer**).

heets'|heev/-heevah/-havtee הצהיב *v* became yellow; yellowed; (*pres* **mats'heev**; *fut* **yats'heev**).

heets'kh|eek/-eekah/-aktee הצחיק *v* made laugh; caused to laugh; (*pres* **mats'kheek**; *fut* **yats'kheek**).

heetsl|ee'akh/-eekhah/-akhtee הצליח *v* succeeded; (*pres* **matslee'akh**; *fut* **yatslee'akh**).

heetsl|eef/-eefah/-aftee הצליף *v* sniped; whipped; (*pres* **matsleef**; *fut* **yatsleef**).

heetsm|eed/-eedah/-adetee הצמיד *v* attached; linked; (*pres* **matsmeed**; *fut* **yatsmeed**).

heetsm|ee'akh/-eekhah/-akhtee הצמיח *v* made grow; (*pres* **matsmee'akh**; *fut* **yatsmee'akh**).

heetsn|ee'a'/-ee'ah/-a'tee הצניע *v* hid; concealed; (*pres* **matsnee'a'**; *fut* **yatsnee'a'**).

heetsnee'a' (*etc*) **lekhet** הצניע לכת *v* behaved modestly.

heetsn|ee'akh/-eekhah/-akhtee הצניח *v* parachuted; (*pres* **matsnee'akh**; *fut* **yatsnee'akh**).

heetsr|eekh/-eekhah/-akhtee הצריך *v* required; necessitated; (*pres* **matsreekh**; *fut* **yatsreekh**).

heets'ta'ats|e'a'/-'ah/-a'tee הצטעצע *v* toyed with; preened oneself; (*pres* **meetsta'atse'a'**; *fut* **yeetsta'atse'a'**).

heets'ta'ats'oo|t/-yot הצטעצעות *nf* toying with.

heets'tab|er/-rah/-arnoo הצטבר *v* piled up; accrued; (*pres* **meets'taber**; *fut* **yeets'taber**).

heets'tabroo|t/-yot הצטברות *nf* accummulation.

heets'tad|ek/-kah/-aktee הצטדק *v* apologized; excused oneself; justified oneself; (*pres* **meets'tadek**; *fut* **yeets'tadek**).

heets'tadkoo|t/-yot הצטדקות *nf* apology; excuse.

heets'ta|'er/-'arah/-'artee הצטער *v* felt sorry; regretted; (*pres* **meets'ta'er**; *fut* **yeets'ta'er**).

heets'ta'aroo|t/-yot הצטערות *nf* regret; feeling sorry.

heets'takh|ek/-kah/-aktee הצטחק *v* smiled; (*pres* **meets'takhek**; *fut* **yeets'takhek**).

heets'takhkoo|t/-yot הצטחקות *nf* smile; laughter.

heets'tal|ek/-kah/-aktee הצטלק *v* became scarred; cicatrized; (*pres* **meets'talek**; *fut* **yeets'talek**).

heets'tal|em/-mah/-amtee הצטלם *v* **1.** photographed; **2.** had (one's) picture taken; (*pres* **meets'talem**; *fut* **yeets'talem**).

heets'tal|ev/-vah/-avtee הצטלב *v* **1.** crossed; **2.** made the sign of the cross; (*pres* **meets'talev**; *fut* **yeets'talev**).

heets'talkoo|t/-yot הצטלקות *nf* cicatrization; scar formation.

heets'talmoo|t/-yot הצטלמות *nf* having one's picture taken; being photographed.

heets'talts|el/-elah/-altee הצטלצל *v* *[colloq.]* phoned one another; rang; (*pres* **meets'taltsel**; *fut* **yeets'taltsel**).

heets'taltseloo|t/-yot הצטלצלות *nf* **1.** *[colloq.]* phoning one another; **2.** ringing.

heets'talvoo|t/-yot הצטלבות *nf* **1.** crossing; intersection; **2.** making sign of the cross.

heets'tam|ek/-kah/-aktee הצטמק *v* shrunk; shrivelled; was dried up; (*pres* **meets'tamek**; *fut* **yeets'tamek**).

heets'tamkoo|t/-yot הצטמקות *nf* shrinking.

heets'tamts|em/-emah/-amtee הצטמצם *v* **1.** confined oneself to; **2.** was reduced to; (*pres* **meets'tamtsem**; *fut* **yeets'tamtsem**).

heets'tamtsemoo|t/-yot הצטמצמות *nf* limitation; restriction.

heets'tan|a' (or **heets'tan|e'a'**)**/-'ah/-a'tee** הצטנע *v* **1.** tried to be modest; **2.** affected modesty; (*pres* **meets'tane'a'**; *fut* **yeetstane'a'**).

heets'tan|en/-enah/-antee הצטנן *v* caught a cold; chilled; (*pres* **meets'tanen**; *fut* **yeets'tanen**).

heets'tanenoo|t/-yot הצטננות *nf* **1.** catching cold; **2.** cooling.

heets'tan'oo|t/-yot הצטנעות *nf* **1.** trying to be modest; **2.** affecting modesty.

heets'tar|ef/-fah/-aftee הצטרף *v* joined; adhered; made-up; (*pres* **meets'taref**; *fut* **yeets'tafref**).

heets'tar|ekh/-khah/-akhtee הצטרך *v* needed; (*pres* **meets'tarekh**; *fut* **yeets'tarekh**).

heets'tarfoo|t/-yot הצטרפות *nf* joining; siding with.

heets'tarkhoo|t/-yot הצטרכות *nf* needing; requiring.

heets'tav|ah/-tah/-etee הצטווה *v* was ordered; was commanded; (*pres* **meets'taveh**; *fut* **yeets'taveh**).

heets'taydoo|t/-yot הצטיידות *nf* preparing oneself; equipping oneself.

heets'ta|yed/-ydah/-yadetee הצטייד *v* equipped oneself; (*pres* **meets'tayed**; *fut* **yeets'tayed**).

heets'ta|yen/-nah/-antee הצטיין *v* excelled; distinguished oneself; (*pres* **meets'tayen**; *fut* **yeets'tayen**).

heets'ta|yer/-yrah/-yartee הצטייר *v* was pictured; was conceived; (*pres* **meets'tayer**; *fut* **yeets'tayer**).

heets'taynoo|t/-yot הצטיינות *nf* distinction; excellence.

(be) heets'taynoot בהצטיינות *adv* with honors.

(ot/-ot) heets'taynoot אות הצטיינות *nm* medal; decoration.

(te'ood|at/-ot) heets'taynoot תעודת הצטיינות *nf* certificate of merit.

heets'tayroo|t/-yot הצטיירות *nf* image; being conceived; impression.

heets'tof|ef/-efah/-aftee הצטופף *v* crowded in; huddled together; (*pres* **meets'tofef**; *fut* **yeetstofef**).

heets'tofefoo|t/-yot הצטופפות *nf* crowding; overcrowding; congestion.

heetv|ah/-etah/-etee התווה *v* sketched; marked; (*pres* **matveh**; *fut* **yatveh**).

heetvad|ah/-etah/-etee התוודה *v* confessed; (*pres* **meetvadeh**; *fut* **yeetvadeh**).

heetvad|a' (or **heetvad|e'a'**)/-**'ah/-a'tee** התוודע *v* became acquainted; introduced oneself; (*pres* **meetvade'a'**; /*fut* **yeetvade'a'**).

heetvad'oo|t/-yot התוודעות *nf* making acquaintance.

heetvadoo|t/-yot התוודות *nf* confession.

heetvak|e'akh/-'khah/-akhtee התווכח *v* argued; debated; (*pres* **meetvake'akh**; *fut* **yeetvake'kh**).

heetvak'khoo|t/-yot התווכחות *nf* arguing; disputing.

heet'ya'atsoo|t/-yot התייעצות *nf* consultation; conferring.

heet'yab|esh/-shah/-ashtee התייבש *v* dried up; was parched; (*pres* **meet'yabesh**; *fut* **yeet'yabesh**).

heet'yabshoo|t/-yot התייבשות *nf* drying up; withering.

heet'yad|ed/-edah/-adetee התיידד *v* befriended; got friendly; (*pres* **meet'yaded**; *fut* **yeet'yaded**).

heet'yadedoo|t/-yot התיידדות *nf* **1.** becoming friendly; making friends; **2.** fraternization.

heet'ya'ashoo|t/-yot התייאשות *nf* despairing.

heet'ya|'esh/-'ashah/-'ashtee התייאש *v* dispaired; (*pres* **meet'ya'esh**; *fut* **yeet'ya'esh**).

heet'ya|'ets/-'atsah/-'atstee התייעץ *v* consulted; (*pres* **meet'ya'ets** *fut* **yeet'ya'ets**).

heet'yahadoo|t/-yot התייהדות *nf* conversion to Judaism.

heet'ya|hed/-hadah/-hadetee התייהד *v* became a Jew; (*pres* **meetyahed**; *fut* **yeetyahed**).

heet'yak|er/-rah התייקר *v* went up (in price); became more expensive; (*pres* **meet'yaker**; *fut* **yeet'yaker**).

heet'yakhadoo|t/-yot (*cpr* **heet'yakhdoo|t/-yot**) התייחדות *nf* meeting in private; tête-à-tête.

heet'yakhadoot 'eem zekher/zeekhr|o/-ah shel התייחדות עם זכר/זכרו/־ה של *nf* recalling the memory of one/him/her.

heet'yakhamoo|t/-yot (*cpr* **heet'yakhmoo|t/-yot**) התייחמות *nf* rutting; having a period of sexual excitement.

heet'yakh|em/-mah/-amtee התייחם *v* rutted; had a period of sexual excitement.

heet'yakh|es/-sah/-astee התייחס *v* **1.** treated; **2.** related; **3.** referred to; (*pres* **meet'yakhes**; *fut* **yeet'yakhes**).

heet'yakhsoo|t/-yot התייחסות *nf* **1.** treatment; **2.** relation; **3.** reference.

heet'yakroo|t/-yot התייקרות *nf* rise in price.

heet'yam|er/-rah/-artee התיימר *v* pretended; claimed; presumed; (*pres* **meet'yamer**; *fut* **yeet'yamer**).

heet'yamroo|t/-yot התיימרות *nf* pretentiousness; pretension.

heet'yap|ah/-tah/-etee התייפה *v* beautified oneself; (*pres* **meet'yapeh**; *fut* **yeet'yapeh**).

heet'yap|akh/-'khah/-akhtee (*or:* **heet'yap|e'akh**) התייפח *v* cried bitterly; sobbed; (*pres* **meet'yape'akh**; *fut* **yeet'yape'akh**).

heet'yap'khoo|t/-yot התייפחות *nf* sobbing; wailing.

heet'yas|er/-rah/-artee התייסר *v* tormented oneself; (*pres* **meet'yaser**; *fut* **yeet'yaser**).

heet'yash|en/-nah/-antee התיישן *v* became obsolete; was outdated; (*pres* **meet'yashen**; *fut* **yeet'yashen**).

heet'yash|er/-rah/-artee התיישר *v* straightened out/up; (*pres* **meet'yasher**; *fut* **yeet'yasher**).

heet'yash|ev/-vah/-avtee התיישב *v* sat down; settled; (*pres* **meet'yashev**; *fut* **yeet'yashev**).

heet'yashnoo|t/-yot התיישנות *nf* obsolescence.

(khok ha) heet'yashnoot חוק ההתיישנות *nm* statute of limitations.

heet'yashroo|t/-yot התיישרות *nf* **1.** lining up. **2.** straightening oneself.

heet'yashvoo|t/-yot התיישבות *nf* settlement; settling on land.

heet'yashvoot khakla'eet התיישבות חקלאית *nf* agricultural settlement.

◇ **(ha)heet'yashvoot ha-'ovedet** ההתיישבות העובדת *nf* settlements and kibbutzim conforming to socialist ideals as defined by the "Histadrut".

heetyasroo|t/-yot התייסרות *nf* being chastened; torment.

heetyat|em/-mah/-amtee התייתם *v* was orphaned; (*pres* **meetyatem**; *fut* **yeetyatem**).

heetyats|ev/-vah/-avtee התייצב *v* reported; became stabilized; took a stand; (*pres* **meetyatsev**; *fut* **yeetyatsev**).

heetyatsvoo|t/-yot התייצבות *nf* **1.** reporting on duty; **2.** reporting to one's military unit; **3.** stabilization.

heev|ah/-tah/-eetee היווה *v* **1.** constituted; consisted; **2.** formed; (*pres* **mehaveh**; *fut* **yehaveh**).

heevatsroo|t/-yot היווצרות *nf* formation.
heevd|eel/-eelah/-altee הבדיל *v* discerned; separated; (*pres* **mavdeel**; *fut* **yavdeel**).
heev|'eer/-'eerah/-'artee הבעיר *v* set fire; (*pres* **mav'eer**; *fut* **yav'eer**).
heev|'eesh/-'eeshah/-'ashtee הבאיש *v* caused to stink; stank; (*pres* **mav'eesh**; *fut* **yav'eesh**).
heev'eesh (*etc*) **re'akh** הבאיש ריח *v* gave a bad name.
heev|en/-nah/-antee היוון *v* capitalized (finance); (*pres* **mehaven**; *fut* **yehaven**).
heev'|heek/-heekah/-haktee הבהיק *v* glittered; flashed; (*pres* **mav'heek**; *fut* **yav'heek**).
heev'|heel/-heelah/-haltee הבהיל *v* **1.** scared; **2.** alarmed; rushed; (*pres* **mav'heel**; *fut* **yav'heel**).
heev'|heer/-heerah/-hartee הבהיר *v* clarified; made it clear; (*pres* **mav'heer**; *fut* **yav'heer**).
heev'|hev/-havah/-havtee הבהב *v* flickered; (*pres* **mehav'hev**; *fut* **yehavhev**).
heevk|ee'a'/-ee'ah/-a'tee הבקיע *v* broke through; (*pres* **mavkee'a'**; *fut* **yavkee'a'**).
heevkh|een/-eenah/-antee הבחין *v* **1.** noticed; **2.** discerned; distinguished; (*pres* **mavkheen**; *fut* **yavkheen**).
heevl|ee'a'/-ee'ah/-a'tee הבליע *v* skipped; concealed; (*pres* **mavlee'a'**; *fut* **yavlee'a'**).
heevl|eeg/-eegah/-agtee הבליג *v* **1.** repressed one's feelings; **2.** exercised restraint; (*pres* **mavleeg**; *fut* **yavleeg**).
heevl|eet/-eetah/-atetee הבליט *v* emphasized; made conspicuous; (*pres* **mavleet**; *fut* **yavleet**).
heevoon/-eem היוון *nm* capitalization; (*pl+of*: **-ey**).
heevr|ee/-ee'ah/-etee הבריא *v* **1.** recuperated; **2.** *[colloq.]* put on weight; (*pres* **mavree'**; *fut* **yavree'**).
heevr|ee'akh/-eekhah/-akhtee הבריח *v* **1.** drove off; **2.** smuggled; (*pres* **mavree'akh**; *fut* **yavree'akh**).
heevr|eeg/-eegah/-agtee הבריג *v* screwed in; threaded; (*pres* **mavreeg**; *fut* **yavreeg**).
heevr|eek/-eekah/-aktee הבריק *v* **1.** shone; **2.** polished; **3.** cabled; (*pres* **mavreek**; *fut* **yavreek**).
heevreek (*etc*) **ra'ayon** הבריק רעיון *v* an idea dawned; an idea flashed into one's mind.
heevr|eesh/-eeshah/-ashtee הבריש *v* brushed; (*pres* **mavreesh**; *fut* **yavreesh**).
heevsh|eel/-eelah/-altee הבשיל *v* ripened; (*pres* **mavsheel**; *fut* **yavsheel**).
heevt|ee'akh/-eekhah/-akhtee הבטיח *v* **1.** promised; **2.** assured; (*pres* **mavtee'akh**; *fut* **yavtee'akh**).
heevz|eek/-eekah/-aktee הבזיק *nf* flashed; (*pres* **mavzeek**; *fut* **yavzeek**).
heezda'az|a' (or **heezda'az|e'a'**)/**-'ah/-a'tee** הזדעזע *v* was shocked, moved; (*pres* **meezda'aze'a'**; *fut* **yeezda'aze'a'**).
heezda'z'oo|t/-yot הזדעזעות *nf* **1.** shock; **2.** shaking.
heezda|hah/-hatah/-hetee הזדהה *v* identified oneself; (*pres* **meezdaheh**; *fut* **yeezdaheh**).
heezdahamoo|t/-yot הזדהמות *v* infection.
heezda|hem/-amah/-amtee הזדהם *v* became infected; (*pres* **meezdahem**; *fut* **yeezdahem**).
heezdahoo|t/-ot הזדהות *nf* identification.
heezdak|ef/-fah/-aftee הזדקף *v* stood up; stood upright; (*pres* **meezdakef**; *fut* **yeezdakef**).
heezdak|ek/-ekah/-aktee הזדקק *v* needed; resorted to; (*pres* **meezdakek**; *fut* **yeezdakek**).
heezdak|ekh/-'khah/-akhtee הזדכך *v* was purified; (*pres* **meezdakekh**; *fut* **yeezdakekh**).
heezdakekoo|t הזדקקות *nf* having to resort to.
heezdak|en/-nah/-antee הזדקן *v* aged; grew old; (*pres* **meezdaken**; *fut* **yeezdaken**).
heezdak|er/-rah/-artee הזדקר *v* stalled; stood out; (*pres* **meezdaker**; *fut* **yeezdaker**).
heezdakfoo|t/-yot הזדקפות *nf* erection; standing upright; back stretching.
heezdak'khoo|t/-yot הזדככות *nf* purification
heezdaknoo|t/-yot הזדקנות *nf* aging; growing old.
heezdakroo|t/-yot הזדקרות *nf* stall; stalling.
heezdam|en/-nah/-antee הזדמן *v* happened to be; occurred; (*pres* **meezdamen**; *fut* **yeezdamen**).
heezdamnoo|t/-yot הזדמנות *nf* occasion; opportunity.
(be) heezdamnoot בהזדמנות *adv* occasionally; on the occasion of.
(be-khol) heezdamnoot בכל הזדמנות *adv* on every (possible) occasion.
(hekhm|eets/-eetsah/-atstee) heezdamnoot החמיץ הזדמנות *v* missed an opportunity.
(neets|el/-lah/-altee) heezdamnoot ניצל הזדמנות *v* grasped the opportunity; (*pres* **menatsel** *etc*; *fut* **yenatsel** *etc*).
heezdan|ev/-vah/-avtee הזדנב *v* trailed behind; (*pres* **meezdanev**; *fut* **yeezdanev**).
heezdangef/-vah/-aftee הזדנגף *v [slang]* went for a stroll on Tel-Aviv's fashionable Dizengoff Street.
heezdanvoo|t/-yot הזדנבות *nf* trailing behind.
heezdar|ez/-zah/-aztee הזדרז *v* hastened; (*pres* **meezdarez**; *fut* **yeezdarez**).
heezdarzoo|t/-yot הזדרזות *nf* haste; hurry.
heezdav|eg/-gah/-agtee הזדווג *v* mated; copulated; (*pres* **meezdaveg**; *fut* **yeezdaveg**).
heezdavgoo|t/-yot הזדווגות *nf* mating; copulation.
heezday|en/-nah/-antee הזדיין *v* **1.** armed oneself; **2.** *[slang]* "screwed"; copulated; (*pres* **meezdayen**; *fut* **yeezdayen**).
heezdaynoo|t/-yot הזדיינות *nf* **1.** arming; armament; **2.** *[slang]* having sexual intercourse.
heez|ee'a'/-ee'ah/-a'tee הזיע *v* sweated; perspired; (*pres* **mazee'a'**; *fut* **yazee'a'**).
heez|eek/-eekah/-aktee הזיק *v* harmed; damaged; (*pres* **mazeek**; *fut* **yazeek**).

heez|'eek/-'eekah/-'aktee הזעיק *v* alerted; (*pres* **maz'eek;** *fut* **yaz'eek**).

heez|eel/-eelah/-altee הזיל *v* dripped; shed; (*pres* **mazeel;** *fut* **yazeel**).

heezeel (*etc*) **deem'ah/dema'ot** (*sing/pl*) הזיל דמעות *v* shed tears.

heez'|heer/-heerah/-hartee הזהיר *v* warned; (*pres* **maz'heer;** *fut* **yaz'heer**).

heezk|een/-eenah/-antee הזקין *v* aged; grew old; (*pres* **mazkeen;** *fut* **yazkeen**).

heezk|eer/-eerah/-artee הזכיר *v* reminded; (*pres* **mazkeer;** *fut* **yazkeer**).

heezm|een/-eenah/-antee הזמין *v* invited; ordered; (*pres* **mazmeen;** *fut* **yazmeen**).

heezn|ee'akh/-eekhah/-akhtee הזניח *v* neglected; (*pres* **maznee'akh;** *fut* **yaznee'akh**).

heezoon/-eem היזון *nm* feeding; (*pl+of:* **-ey**).

heezoon/-eem khozer/-zeem היזון חוזר *nm* feedback.

heezr|eek/-eekah/-aktee הזריק *v* injected; (*pres* **mazreek;** *fut* **yazreek**).

heezr|eem/-eemah/-amtee הזרים *v* poured in; caused to flow; channelled; (*pres* **mazreem;** *fut* **yazreem**).

he'anoo|t/-yot היענות *nf* response.

hebet/-eem היבט *nm* aspect; (*pl+of:* **-ey**).

hedef הדף *nm* shock.

hed|ef/-fey aveer הדף אוויר *nm* blast.

hedek/hadakeem הדק *nm* **1.** trigger; **2.** clip; (*pl+of:* **hedkey**).

(lakhats 'al ha) hedek לחץ על ההדק *v* pulled the trigger; (*pres* **lokhets** *etc; fut* **yeelkhats** *etc*).

hedyot/-ot הדיוט *nm* **1.** layman; non-professional; **2.** *[colloq.]* ignoramus; boor.

hedyot kofets be-rosh הדיוט קופץ בראש the fool always rushes to the fore.

hef|ee'akh/-eekhah/-akhtee הפיח *v* puffed up; (*pres* **mefee'akh;** *fut* **yafee'akh**).

hef|eeg/-eegah/-agtee הפיג *v* eased; dispelled; (*pres* **mefeeg;** *fut* **yafeeg**).

hef|eek/-eekah/-aktee הפיק *v* derived; produced; (*pres* **mefeek;** *fut* **yafeek**).

hefeek (*etc*) **to'elet** הפיק תועלת *v* profited; derived profit.

hef|eets/-eetsah/-atstee הפיץ *v* spread; distributed; (*pres* **mefeets;** *fut* **yafeets**).

hefekh/hafakheem היפך *nm* the opposite.

(ha) hefekh ההיפך the other way round.

(le) hefekh להיפך *adv* on the contrary.

hef|er/-erah/-artee הפר *v* contravened; violated; (*pres* **mefer;** *fut* **yafer**).

hefer (*etc*) **heskem** הפר הסכם *v* violated an agreement.

hefer (*etc*) **sheveetah** הפר שביתה *v* engaged in strike-breaking.

hefker הפקר *nm* **1.** ownerless property; **2.** irresponsiblity; lawlessness.

(shetakh/sheetkhey) hefker שטח הפקר *nm* no-man's land.

hefkeroot הפקרות *nf* **1.** lawlessness; **2.** abandon.

hefresh/-eem הפרש *nm* difference.

◇ **hefresheem** הפרשים *nm pl* salary-differences due a raise or to fluctuations in the Cost of Living Index or in the rate of exchange of the Israeli Shekel against hard currency (*sing:* **hefresh**).

hefresheeyoot הפרשיות *nf* scale of differences.

hefsed/-eem הפסד *nm* loss.

(revakh ve) hefsed רווח והפסד *nm* profit and loss.

hefsek הפסק *nm* interruption.

(le-lo) hefsek ללא הפסק *adv* without interruption.

hege'/haga'eem הגה *nm* **1.** steering wheel; **2.** murmur; (*pl+of:* **haga'ey**).

(okh|ez/-azeem be) hegeh אוחז בהגה *nm* motorist; driver.

hegee'akh/-eekhah/-akhtee הגיח *v* burst forth; broke out; (*pres* **megee'akh;** *fut* **yagee'akh**).

heg|eef/-eefah/-aftee trees/eem הגיף תריס *v* shut blind(s); (*pres* **megeef;** *fut* **yageef**).

heg|eev/-eevah/-avtee הגיב *v* reacted; (*pres* **megeev;** *fut* **yageev**).

hegemonyah (*npr* **hegmonyah**) הגמוניה *nf* hegemony.

heg|en/-enah/-antee הגן *v* defended; (*pres* **megen;** *fut* **yagen**).

hegl|ah (*cpr* **heegl|ah**)**/-etah/-etee** הגלה *v* deported; exiled; (*pres* **magleh;** *fut* **yagleh**).

hegyonee/-t הגיוני *adv* reasonable; logical.

hekdem הקדם *nm* earliness.

(be) hekdem בהקדם *adv* early; as soon as possible.

hek|ee/-ee'ah/-etee הקיא *v* vomited; threw up; (*pres* **mekee;** *fut* **yakee**).

hek|eef (*npr* **heek|eef**)**/-eefah/-aftee** הקיף *v* surrounded; comprised; (*pres* **makeef;** *fut* **yakeef**).

hek|eem/-eemah/-amtee הקים *v* set up; erected; (*pres* **mekeem;** *fut* **yakeem**).

hek|eets/-eetsah/-atstee הקיץ *v* awakened; woke up; (*pres* **mekeets;** *fut* **yakeets**).

hekef היקף *nm* **1.** scope; perimeter; **2.** extent.

hekefee/-t היקפי *adj* peripheral.

hek|el/-elah/-altee הקל *v* eased; mitigated; (*pres* **mekel;** *fut* **yakel**).

hekel (*etc*) **rosh** הקל ראש *v* disparaged; underestimated.

(seeman/-ey) heker סימן היכר *nm* identifying mark.

hekeroo|t/-yot היכרות *nf* acquaintance.

hekesh/-eem היקש *nm* analogy; (*pl+of:* **-ey**).

hekhal/-ot היכל *nm* palace; temple.

hekhal|ah/-ot החלה *nf* application; (*+of:* **-at**).

hekhaltsoo|t/-yot היחלצות *nf* **1.** getting out of trouble; escape; **2.** volunteering.

hekhan? ?היכן where?

hekhan she- -היכן ש *adv* there where.

hekhan she-lo היכן שלא *adv* wherever.

(me) hekhan מהיכן *adv* from where.

hekhb|ee/-ee'ah/-e'tee החביא *v* hid; (*pres* **makhbee**; *fut* **yakhbee**).
hekhd|eer/-eerah/-artee החדיר *v* inserted; (*pres* **makhdeer**; *fut* **yakhdeer**).
hekheel/-ah הכיל *v* contained; comprised; (*pres* **mekheel**; *fut* **yakheel**).
hekh|een/-eenah/-antee הכין *v* prepared; (*pres* **mekheen**; *fut* **yakheen**).
hekh|eesh/-eeshah/-ashtee החיש *v* sped up; (*pres* **mekheesh**; *fut* **yakheesh**).
hekh|el/-elah/-altee החל *v* began; commenced.
hekhk|eem/-eemah/-amtee החכים *v* wised up; got smart; (*pres* **makhkeem**; *fut* **yakhkeem**).
hekhk|eer/-eerah/-artee החכיר *v* leased; let; granted a long lease; (*pres* **makhkeer**; *fut* **yakhkeer**).
hekhl|eed/-ah החליד *v* rusted; caused to rust; (*pres* **makhleed**; *fut* **yakhleed**).
hekhl|eef/-eefah/-aftee החליף *v* changed; replaced; (*pres* **makhleef**; *fut* **yakhleef**).
hekhleef (*etc*) **de'ot** החליף דעות *v* exchanged views.
hekhleef (*etc*) **ko'akh** החליף כוח *v* regained strength.
hekhl|eek/-eekah/-aktee החליק *v* **1.** smoothed; **2.** glided; **3.** slid; slumped; stumbled; (*pres* **makhleek**; *fut* **yakhleek**).
hekhl|eem/-eemah/-amtee החלים *v* recovered; (*pres* **makhleem**; *fut* **yakhleem**).
hekhl|eesh/-eeshah/-ashtee החליש *v* weakened; (*pres* **makhleesh**; *fut* **yakhleesh**).
hekhl|eet/-eetah/-atetee החליט *v* decided; (*pres* **makhleet**; *fut* **yakhleet**).
(be) hekhlet בהחלט *adv* decidedly; absolutely.
hekhletee/-t החלטי *adj* decisive; final.
hekhleteeyoot החלטיות *nf* resoluteness.
hekhm|ee/-ee'ah/-etee החמיא *v* complimented; (*pres* **makhmee**; *fut* **yakhmee**).
hekhm|eets/-eetsah/-atstee החמיץ *v* **1.** missed; **2.** failed; **3.** soured; (*pres* **makhmeets**; *fut* **yakhmeets**).
hekhm|eets (*etc*) **heezdamnoot** החמיץ הזדמנות *v* missed an opportunity.
hekhm|eets (*etc*) **paneem** החמיץ פנים *v* looked sour-faced.
hekhm|eer/-eerah/-artee החמיר *v* **1.** aggravated; **2.** became more serious; (*pres* **makhmeer**; *fut* **yakhmeer**).
hekhn|ah/-etah/-etee החנה *v* parked; (*pres* **makhneh**; *fut* **yakhneh**).
hekhn|eef/-eefah/-aftee החניף *v* flattered; (*pres* **makhneef**; *fut* **yakhneef**).
hekhn|eek/-eekah/-aktee החניק *v* strangled; throttled; (*pres* **makhneek**; *fut* **yakhneek**).
hekhre'akh הכרח *nm* necessity; compulsion.
hekhr|eed/-eedah/-adetee החריד *v* terrified; (*pres* **makhreed**; *fut* **yakhreed**).
hekhreef/-eefah/-aftee החריף *v* grew more acute; (*pres* **makhreef**; *fut* **yakhreef**).
hekhr|eem/-eemah/amtee החרים *v* **1.** boycotted; **2.** confiscated; (*pres* **makhreem**; *fut* **yakhreem**).
hekhr|eesh/-eeshah/-ashtee החריש *v* **1.** remained silent; **2.** deafened; (*pres* **makhreesh**; *fut* **yakhreesh**).
hekhr|eev/-eevah/-avtee החריב *v* destroyed; ruined; (*pres* **makhreev**; *fut* **yakhreev**).
hekhrekhee/-t הכרחי *adj* obligatory.
hekhs|eer/-eerah/-artee החסיר *v* **1.** missed; left out; **2.** substracted; (*pres* **makhseer**; *fut* **yakhseer**).
hekh'sh|eed/-eedah/-adetee החשיד *v* threw suspicion on; (*pres* **makh'sheed**; *fut* **yakh'sheed**).
hekh'sheekh/-ah החשיך *v* **1.** obscured; darkened; **2.** night fell; (*pres* **makh'sheekh**; *fut* **yakh'sheekh**).
hekh'sh|eev/-eevah/-avtee החשיב *v* valued; esteemed; (*pres* **makh'sheev**; *fut* **yakh'sheev**).
hekh'sher/-eem הכשר *nm* legitimation.
◇ **"hekh'sher"** הכשר *nm* **1.** approval of food as "kosher"; **2.** rabbinical license for serving "kosher" food.
hekht|ee/-ee'ah/-etee החטיא *v* missed (target); (*pres* **makhtee**; *fut* **yakhtee**).
hekht|eem/-eemah/-amtee החתים *v* signed up; got signatures; (*pres* **makhteem**; *fut* **yakhteem**).
hekhteem/-eemah/-amtee הכתים *v* stained; sullied; (*pres* **makhteem**; *fut* **yakhteem**).
hekhv|ah/-etah/-etee keedah החווה קידה *v* took a bow (*pres* **makhveh** *etc*; *fut* **yakhveh** *etc*).
hekhv|eer/-eerah/-artee החוויר *v* paled; (*pres* **makhveer**; *fut* **yakhveer**).
hekh|yah/-yetah/-yetee החיה *v* revived; resuscitated (*pres* **mekhayeh**; *fut* **yekhayeh**).
hekhz|eek/-eekah/-aktee החזיק *v* **1.** held; **2.** had possession; (*pres* **makhzeek**; *fut* **yakhzeek**).
hekhzeek (*etc*) **ma'amad** החזיק מעמד *v* held out.
hekhz|eer/-eerah/-artee החזיר *v* returned; gave back (*pres* **makhzeer**; *fut* **yakhzeer**).
hekhzer/-eem החזר *nm* refund; (*pl+of:* **-ey**).
heksher/-eem הקשר *nm* connection; context; (*pl+of:* **-ey**).
(be) heksher shel בהקשר של *adv* in conection with.
helekh הלך *nm* wanderer.
helekh (*npr* **halokh**)/**heelkhey roo'akh** הלך רוח *nm* frame of mind; mood.
helem הלם *nm* shock.
hem הם *pers pron m pl* they.
hem hem הם הם *v pl* it is they who; they are the ones who.
(ha) hem ההם *pron nm pl* those.
hemah המה **1.** *pron m pl* they; **2.** *v pres 3rd pers pl* are.
hem|eer/-eerah/-artee המיר *v* exchanged (money, goods, position) (*pres* **memeer**; *fut* **yameer**).

hemeer (*etc*) **dat** המיר דת *v* converted to another religion.
hem|eet/-eetah/-atetee המית *v* killed; deadened; (*pres* **memeet**; *fut* **yameet**).
hem|eet/-eetah/-atetee ason המיט אסון *v* brought disaster; (*pres* **mameet** *etc*; *fut* **yameet** *etc*).
hemeet (*etc*) **kalon** המיט קלון *v* disgraced; brought shame on.
hemer/-erah/-artee המר *v* wagered; (*pres* **memer**; *fut* **yamer**).
hemshekh/-eem המשך *nm* **1.** continuation; **2.** installment.
hemshekh yavo המשך יבוא to be continued.
(seepoor be) hemshekheem סיפור בהמשכים **1.** *nm* serial; **2.** *[slang] nm* a story that never ends.
hemshekheeyoot המשכיות *nf* continuity.
hemyah המיה *nf* sound; cooing (of doves).
hen הן **1.** *pers pron f pl* they; **2.** *v pres 3rd pers f pl* are.
hen hen הן הן it is they *f* who; they *f* are the ones who.
(ha) hen ההן *pron f pl* those.
hen הן yes.
(omer/omrey) hen אומר הן *nm* yesman.
hen tsedek הן צדק *nm* word of honor; parole.
hen... ve-hen... ...הן... והן both... as well as...; either... or...
henah הנה *adv* to here; hither.
henee/-'ah הניא *v* dissuaded; (*pres* **menee**; *fut* **yanee**).
henee|'a'/-'ah/heena'tee הניע *v* set in motion; urged; (*pres* **menee'a'**; *fut* **yanee'a'**).
henee'|akh/-khah/heenakhtee הניח *v* put at ease; calmed.
hen|eed/-eedah/-adetee 'af'af הניד עפעף *v* blinked; (*pst* **meneed** *etc*; *fut* **yaneed** *etc*).
hen|eef/-eefah/-aftee הניף *v* swung; brandished; (*pres* **meneef**; *fut* **yaneef**).
hen|ees/-eesah/-astee הניס *v* routed; (*pres* **menees**; *fut* **yanees**).
hen|eev/-eevah/-avtee הניב *v* yielded (fruit); (*pres* **meneev**; *fut* **yaneev**).
her|a'/-e'ah/-a'tee הרע *v* did harm; wronged; worsened; (*pres* **mere'a**; *fut* **yare'a**).
her|'ah/-'atah/-'etee הראה *v* showed; (*pres* **mar'eh**; *fut* **yar'eh**).
heratmoot הירתמות *nf* undertaking a task.
her|ayon/-yonot הריון *nm* pregnancy; (*+of:* **-yon**).
(be) herayon בהריון *adj* pregnant.
her|ee'a'/-ee'ah/-a'tee הריע *v* cheered; shouted; (*pres* **meree'a'**; *fut* **yaree'a'**).
her|ee'akh/-eekhah/-akhtee הריח *v* smelled; (*pres* **meree'akh**; *fut* **yaree'akh**).
her|eek/-eekah/-aktee הריק *v* emptied; (*pres* **mereek**; *fut* **yareek**).
her|eem/-eemah/-amtee הרים *v* raised; lifted; (*pres* **mereem**; *fut* **yareem**).
hereem (*etc*) **rosh** הרים ראש *v* raised one's head; exalted oneself; rebelled.
hereem (*etc*) **yad** הרים יד *v* raised a hand.
hereem (*etc*) **yad 'al** הרים יד על *v* tried to beat up; raised a hand against.
hereets/-ah/heratstee הריץ *v* dispatched; hurried; (*pres* **mereets**; *fut* **yareets**).
heref!/harpee! ! הרף *v imp sing m/f* stop!.
(blee) heref בלי הרף *adv* incessantly.
(ke) heref 'ayeen כהרף עין *adv* in the twinkling of an eye.
(le-lo) heref ללא הרף *adv* constantly.
hereg הרג *nm* carnage; massacre.
heres הרס *nm* destruction.
heres 'atsmee הרס עצמי *nm* self-destruction.
hergel/-eem הרגל *nm* habit; (*pl+of:* **-ey**).
hergel/-eem neefsad/-eem הרגל נפסד *nm* wrong habit.
herkev/-eem הרכב *nm* composition.
hermetee/-t הרמטי *adj* hermetic.
hermeteet הרמטית *adv* hermetically.
□ **Herodeeon** הרודיון *nm* (*hist.*) mount in Judean Desert, 6 km SE of Bethlehem, surmounted by ruins of King Herod's fabulous fortress-retreat.
□ **Hertseleeyah** (Herzliyya) הרצליה *nf* seashore town in Sharon, halfway between Tel-Aviv and Netanya, 15 km N. of Tel-Aviv, E. of Tel-Aviv — Haifa expressway (No. 2) and railroad. Pop. 77,200.
□ **Hertseleeyah-Peetoo'akh** הרצליה פיתוח *nf* plush residential garden-city on seashore 15 km N. of Tel-Aviv and 5 km W. of **Hertseleeyah**. Favored residential area of diplomats and of immigrants and temporary residents of Anglo-Saxon background. Administratively, it is part of **Hertseleeyah** town across Tel-Aviv—Haifa expressway and railroad.
hesakh ha-da'at היסח הדעת *nm* absentmindendness; inattention.
(be) hesakh ha-da'at בהיסח הדעת inadvertantly; absentmindedly.
hesber/-eem הסבר *nm* explanation; (*pl+of:* **-ey**).
hesder/-eem הסדר *nm* arrangement; settlement; (*pl+of:* **-ey**).
◇ **(yesheev|at/-ot) hesder** see ◇ **yesheev|at/-ot hesder**.
hes|eer/-eerah/-artee הסיר *v* removed; took off; (*pres* **meseer**; *fut* **yaseer**).
hes|eet/-eetah/-atetee הסית *v* instigated; (*pres* **meseet**; *fut* **yaseet**).
hes|eet/-eetah/-atetee הסיט *v* shifted; (*pres* **meseet**; *fut* **yaseet**).
heseg/-eem הישג *nm* accomplishment; (*pl+of:* **-ey**).
(be) heseg-yad בהישג יד within reach.
(masa') hesegeem מסע הישגים *nm* show of achievements; parade of achievements.
hes|ev/-evah/-avtee היסב *v* sat with; (*pres* **mesev**; *fut* **yesev**).
hesev/-eem הסב *nm* endorsement; (*pl+of:* **-ey**).

hesger/-eem הסגר *nm* quarantine; blockade; (*pl+of:* **-ey**).

heskem/-eem הסכם *nm* agreement; (*pl+of:* **-ey**).

('ar|akh/-khah/-akhtee) heskem ערך הסכם *v* drew up an agreement; (*pres* **'orekh** *etc; fut* **ya'arokh** *etc*).

(ba/-'ah/-tee lee-yedey) heskem בא לידי הסכם *v* came to terms; reached agreement; (*pres* **ba** *etc; fut* **yavo** *etc*).

(hafar|at/-ot) heskem הפרת הסכם *nf* breach of contract; breach of agreement.

(heegee'a'/-ee'ah/-a'tee lee-kh'lal) heskem הגיע לכלל הסכם *v* came to terms; reached agreement; (*pres* **ba** *etc; fut* **yavo** *etc*).

hetee|'akh/-khah/-akhtee הטיח *v* spoke insolently; (*pres* **metee'akh;** *fut* **yatee'akh**).

hetee'akh (*etc*) **ashmah** הטיח אשמה *v* accused; threw blame.

het|eel/-eelah/-altee הטיל *v* cast; threw; (*pres* **meteel;** *fut* **yateel**).

heteel goral הטיל גורל *v* drew lots.

hetees/-ah/heetastee הטיס *v* flew (an aircraft); dispatched by air; (*pres* **metees;** *fut* **yatees**).

het|eev/-eevah/-avtee היטיב *v* excelled; improved; did well; (*pres* **meteev;** *fut* **yeteev**).

heteev (*etc*) **'eem** היטיב עם *v* was good to; did good to.

hetel/-eem היטל *nm* **1.** levy; tax; **2.** projection; (*pl+of:* **-ey**).

◇ **hetel 'eenoogeem** היטל עינוגים *nm* entertainment tax.

◇ **hetel hashbakhah** היטל השבחה *nm* special levy exacted from a real-estate owner on extra value added to one's property upon approval of a building scheme disregarding some restriction or granting exceptionally some irregular use. Is collected by local authority upon owner's making use of one's newly acquired right.

(be) het'em בהתאם accordingly.

(be) het'em le- בהתאם ל־ according to; in accordance with.

heter/-eem היתר *nm* permit; license; release; (*pl+of:* **-ey**).

hetev היטב *adv* well; thoroughly.

hetev-hetev היטב־היטב *adv* - most throughly; to the utmost.

(be) heter בהיתר lawfully; openly.

hetkef/-eem התקף *nm* attack; assault; (*pl+of:* **-ey**).

hetkef/-ey 'atsabeem התקף עצבים *nm* nervous outburst.

hetkef/-ey lev התקף לב *nm* heart-attack.

hetkefee/-t התקפי *adj* offensive.

hetken/-eem התקן *nm* device.

hets|a' (*npr* **-e'a'**)**/-e'eem** היצע *nm* supply; offer; (*pl+of:* **-e'ey**).

hetsa' (*npr* **-e'a'**) **oo-veekoosh** (*v=b*) היצע וביקוש *nm pl* supply and demand.

hetse'a' oo-veekoosh (*v=b*) היצע וביקוש *nm pl* supply and demand.

hets|eef/-eefah/-aftee הציף *v* flooded; (*pres* **metseef;** *fut* **yatseef**).

hets|eek/-eekah/-aktee הציק *v* pestered; persecuted; (*pres* **metseek;** *fut* **yatseek**).

hets|eets/-eetsah/-atstee הציץ *v* peeped; (*pres* **metseets;** *fut* **yatsets**).

hev|ee/-ee'ah/-etee הביא *v* brought; led; (*pres* **mevee;** *fut* **yavee**).

hevee (*etc*) **be-kheshbon** הביא בחשבון *v* took into account/consideration.

hevee (*etc*) **lee-yedey** הביא לידי *v* brought to; resulted in.

hev|eekh/-eekhah/-akhtee הביך *v* embarrassed; (*pres* **meveekh;** *fut* **yaveekh**).

hev|een/-eenah/-antee הבין *v* understood; (*pres* **meveen;** *fut* **yaveen**).

hev|ees/-eesah/-astee הביס *v* defeated; (*pres* **mevees;** *fut* **yavees**).

hev|eesh/-eeshah/-ashtee הביש *v* put to shame; (*pres* **meveesh;** *fut* **yaveesh**).

hevdel/-eem הבדל *nm* difference; (*pl+of:* **-ey**).

hevzek/-eem הבזק *nm* flash of light; (*pl+of:* **-ey**).

heydad! הידד! *interj* hurrah! cheers!

(kar|a/-'ah/-atee) heydad קרא הידד *v* acclaimed; (*pres* **kore** *etc; fut* **yeekra** *etc*).

heykhal/-ot היכל *nm* palace; temple.

heykhan! היכן! where?

heykhan she- היכן ש־ *adv* there where.

heykhan she-lo היכן שלא *adv* wherever.

(me) heykhan מהיכן *adv* from where.

heytev היטב *adv* well; thoroughly.

heytev-heytev היטב־היטב *adv* - most throughly; to the utmost.

heyot she- היות ש־ *conj* whereas; since.

heyot ve- היות ו־ *[colloq.] conj* whereas; since.

hez|een/-eenah/-antee הזין *nf* fed; nourished; (*pres* **mezeen;** *fut* **yazeen**).

hez|eez/-eezah/-aztee הזיז *v* **1.** moved; **2.** *[slang]* got things moving; (*pres* **mezeez;** *fut* **yazeez**).

hezek היזק *nm* damage.

ho! הו! *interj* oh! alas! woe!

hod הוד *nm* glory; splendor.

□ **Hod ha-Sharon** הוד השרון *nf* residential rural area encompassing several early-founded veteran villages N. of Petakh-Teekvah (**Ramatayeem, Magdee'el, Hadar** and **Ramat Hadar**) merged since 1951 into one Local Council. Pop. 26,000.

hod ma'alat|o/-ah הוד מעלתו/־ה *m/f* H.E. His/Her Excellency.

hod malkhoot|o/-ah הוד מלכותו/ה *m/f* H.M. His/Her Majesty.

hod|ah/-etah/-etee הודה *v* **1.** thanked; **2.** admitted; confessed; (*pres* **modeh;** *fut* **yodeh**).

hoda|'ah/-'ot הודאה *nf* admission; confession; (*+of:* **-'at**).

hoda|'ah/-'ot הודעה *nf* notification; announcement; notice; (*+of:* **-'at**).

hoda'ah mookdemet הודעה מוקדמת *nf* advance notice.

hoda|'at/-'ot peetooreem (or **petooreen**) הודעת פיטורים *nf* notice of discharge; notice of dismissal.

hoda|yah/-yot הודיה *nf* thanksgiving; (+*of:* **-yat**).

◇ **(khag ha) hodayah** see ◇ **khag ha-hodayah**.

□ **Hodayot** הודיות *nm* religious agricultural education institute (est. 1950) in Lower Galilee, 9 km W. of Tiberias.

hodee/-t הודי *adj & nmf* Indian (from India); Hindu.

hod|ee'a/-ee'ah/-a'tee הודיע *v* **1.** notified; **2.** announced; **3.** informed; (*pres* **modee'a'**; *fut* **yodee'a'**).

hodee'a' (*etc*) **me-rosh** הודיע מראש *v* notified in advance.

□ **Hodeeyah** (Hodiyya) הודיה *nm* village (est. 1949) on coastal plain, 5 km E. of Ashkelon. Pop. 368.

hona|'ah/-'ot הונאה *nf* swindle; fraud; (+*of:* **-'at**).

honee/-t הוני *adj* capital.

hoo הוא **1.** *pers pron* he; **2.** *v pres* is.

hoo hoo הוא הוא *v pres* is the one.

(ke) hoo zeh כהוא זה anything whatsoever.

(mah she) hoo מה שהוא *nm* something (of masculine or neutral gender).

hoo'ad|af/-fah/-aftee (*npr* **ho'od|af**) הועדף *v* was preferred, given preference; (*pres* **mo'odaf**; *fut* **yo'odaf**).

hoo ha-deen הוא הדין the same applies.

hoo'af/-ah/-tee הועף *v* **1.** was flown; **2.** *[slang]* was discarded; was fired; was sacked; (*pres* **moo'af**; *fut* **yoo'af**).

hoo'al|ah (*npr* **ho'ol|ah**) הועלה *v* **1.** was lifted; **2.** was raised, promoted; (*pres* **mo'oleh**; *fut* **yo'oleh**).

hoo'alah (*etc*) **la-arets** הועלה לארץ *v* was enabled to immigrate to Israel.

hoo'am/-ah/-tee הועם *v* was darkened, obscured; (*pres* **moo'am**; *fut* **yoo'am**).

hoo'am|ad (*npr* **ho'om|ad**)/**-dah/-adetee** הועמד *v* **1.** was put in place; **2.** was nominated as candidate; (*pres* **mo'omad**; *fut* **yo'omad**).

hoo'am|ak (*npr* **ho'om|ak**)/**-kah/-aktee** הועמק *v* was deepened; (*pres* **mo'omak**; *fut* **yo'omak**).

hoo'an|ak (*npr* **ho'onak**)/**-kah/-aktee** הוענק *v* was bestowed, granted; (*pres* **mo'onak**; *fut* **yo'onak**).

hoo'ar/-ah/-tee מואר *v* was *lit* up; (*pres* **moo'ar**; *fut* **yoo'ar**).

hoo'ar|akh/-khah (*npr* **ho'or|akh**) הוארך *v* was prolonged; was extended; (*pres* **moo'arakh**; *fut* **yoo'arakh**).

hoo'ar|akh (*npr* **ho'or|akh**)/**-khah/-akhtee** הוערך *v* was estimated; was evaluated; (*pres* **mo'orakh**; *fut* **yo'orakh**).

hoo'as|ak/-kah/-aktee הועסק *v* was employed; (*pres* **moo'asak**; *fut* **yoo'asak**).

hoo'at/-ah/-etee הואט *v* was slowed down; (*pres* **moo'at**; *fut* **yoo'at**).

hoo'at|ak (*npr* **ho't|ak**)/**-kah/-aktee** הועתק *v* **1.** was copied; **2.** was moved over; (*pres* **mo'tak**; *fut* **yo'tak**).

hoo'ats/-ah/-tee הואץ *v* was accelerated; was sped up; (*pres* **moo'ats**; *fut* **yoo'ats**).

hoob|a'/-'ah/-a'tee הובע *v* was expressed; (*pres* **mooba'**; *fut* **yooba'**).

ho'od|af/-fah/-aftee הועדף *v* was preferred, given preference; (*pres* **mo'odaf**; *fut* **yo'odaf**).

hoof'al/-ah/-tee הופעל *v* was activated; was started; (*pres* **moof'al**; *fut* **yoof'al**).

hoof|ar/-rah/-artee הופר *v* **1.** was violated; **2.** was cancelled; (*pres* **moofar**; *fut* **yoofar**).

hoofn|ah/-etah/-etee הופנה *v* was referred; was directed; (*pres* **moofneh**; *fut* **yoofneh**).

hoofr|a'/-e'ah/-a'tee הופרע *v* was disturbed; was interfered with; (*pres* **moofra'**; *fut* **yoofra'**).

hoofr|ah/-etah/-etee הופרה *v* was fertilized; (*pres* **moofreh**; *fut* **yoofreh**).

hoofr|akh/-ekhah הופרך *v* was refuted; was proven false; (*pres* **moofra'**; *fut* **yoofra'**).

hoofr|az/-ezah/-aztee הופרז *v* was exaggerated; (*pres* **moofraz**; *fut* **yoofraz**).

hooft|a'/-e'ah/-a'tee הופתע *v* was surprised; was taken by surprise; (*pres* **moofta'**; *fut* **yoofta'**).

hoogad lee/-lekhah/-lo/-lah הוגד לי/לך/לו/לה *v* I/you/he/she was told; (*pres* **moogad** *etc*; *fut* **yoogad** *etc*).

hoog|af/-fah/-aftee הוגף *v* was shut; was closed (door, gate, blinds); (*pres* **moogaf**; *fut* **yoogaf**).

hoog|an/-nah/-antee הוגן *v* was protected; was defended; (*pres* **moogan**; *fut* **yoogan**).

hoog|ash/-shah/-ashtee הוגש *v* **1.** was served, **2.** was brought before; (*pres* **moogash**; *fut* **yoogash**).

hoogb|ah/-ehah/-ehtee הוגבה *v* was lifted up, raised; (*pres* **moogbah**; *fut* **yoogbah**).

hoogb|al/-elah/-altee הוגבל *v* **1.** was limited; **2.** was restricted; (*pres* **moogbal**; *fut* **yoogbal**).

hoogz|am/-emah/-amtee הוגזם *v* was exaggerated; (*pres* **moogzam**; *fut* **yoogzam**).

hook|af/-fah/-aftee הוקף *v* was surrounded; (*pres* **mookaf**; *fut* **yookaf**).

hook|al/-lah/-altee הוקל *v* was eased; was alleviated, lightened; (*pres* **mookal**; *fut* **yookal**).

hook|am/-mah/-amtee הוקם *v* was established, set up, erected; (*pres* **mookam**; *fut* **yookam**).

hook|ar/-rah/-artee הוכר *v* was recognized; was acknowledged; (*pres* **mookar**; *fut* **yookar**).

hook|ash/-shah/-ashtee הוכש *v* was bitten (by snake, reptile); (*pres* **mookash**; *fut* **yookash**).

hookhakh/-ah/-tee הוכח *v* was proved; (*pres* **mookhakh**; *fut* **yookhakh**).

hookhal/-ah הוחל *v* was begun, started; (*fut* **yookhal**).

hookhal be- הוחל ב- *v* (work) has begun on...

hookh|an/-nah/-antee הוכן *v* was prepared; (*pres* **mookhan;** *fut* **yookhan).**

hookhash/-ah/-tee הוחש *v* was rushed; was accelerated; (*pres* **mookhash;** *fut* **yookhash).**

hookhb|a/-e'ah/-e'tee הוחבא *v* was hidden; (*pres* **mookhba;** *fut* **yookhba).**

hookhd|ar/-erah/-artee הוחדר *v* was inserted; was infiltrated; (*pres* **mookhdar;** *fut* **yookhdar).**

hookh'k|ar/-erah הוחכר *v* was leased; (*pres* **mookh'kar;** *fut* **yookh'kar).**

hookhm|ar/-erah/-artee הוחמר *v* was aggravated; (*pres* **mookhmar;** *fut* **yookhmar).**

hokhn|a'/-e'ah/-a'tee הוכנע *v* was subdued; was overpowered; (*pres* **mookhna';** *fut* **yookhna').**

hookhn|as/-esah/-astee הוכנס *v* was entered, brought in; (*pres* **mookhnas;** *fut* **yookhnas).**

hookhp|al/-elah/-altee הוכפל *v* **1.** was doubled; **2.** was multiplied; (*pres* **mookhpal;** *fut* **yookhpal).**

hookhp|ash/-eshah/-ashtee הוכפש *v* was pressed, trampled upon (of one's name); (*pres* **mookhpash;** *fut* **yookhpash).**

hookhr|a'/-e'ah/-a'tee הוכרע *v* was decided, outweighed; (*pres* **mookhra';** *fut* **yookhra').**

hookhr|akh/-ekhah/-akhtee הוכרח *v* was compelled; was forced; (*pres* **mookhrakh;** *fut* **yookhrakh).**

hookhs|ar/-erah/-artee הוחסר *v* **1.** was omitted; **2.** was deducted; (*pres* **mokhsar;** *fut* **yokhsar).**

hookhsh|ar/-erah/-artee הוכשר *v* **1.** was trained for; **2.** was made "kosher"; (*pres* **mookhshar;** *fut* **yookhshar).**

hookht|am/-emah/-amtee הוכתם *v* was stained; was soiled; (*pres* **mookhtam;** *fut* **yookhtam).**

hookht|am/-emah/-amtee הוחתם *v* **1.** was signed up; was made to sign; **2.** was given a subscription (*pres* **mookhtam;** *fut* **yookhtam).**

hookht|ar/-erah/-artee הוכתר *v* was crowned; (*pres* **mookhtar;** *fut* **yookhtar).**

hookhtar (*etc*) **be-hatslakhah** הוכתר בהצלחה *v* was crowned with success.

hookht|av/-evah/-avtee הוכתב *v* was dictated; (*pres* **mookhtav;** *fut* **yookhtav).**

hookn|at/-etah/-atetee הוקנט *v* was vexed, crossed, annoyed; (*pres* **mooknat;** *fut* **yooknat).**

hookr|a/-e'ah הוקרא *v* was read out; was recited; (*pres* **mookra;** *fut* **yookra).**

hookr|an/-enah הוקרן *v* **1.** was projected; **2.** was X-rayed; (*pres* **mookran;** *fut* **yookran).**

hooks|am/-emah/-amtee הוקסם *v* was fascinated, captivated, charmed; (*pres* **mooksam;** *fut* **yooksam).**

hookt|an/-enah/-antee הוקטן *v* was reduced, diminished; (*pres* **mooktan;** *fut* **yooktan).**

hool'am/-ah הולאם *v* was nationalized; (*pres* **mool'am;** *fut* **yool'am).**

hoolb|an/-ena/-antee הולבן *v* was whitened; was whitewashed (also figurat.); (*pres* **moolban;** *fut* **yoolban).**

hoolb|ash/-eshah/-ashtee הולבש *v* was dressed, dressed up; (*pres* **moolbash;** *fut* **yoolbash).**

hooledet הולדת *nf* birth (my/your*(m/f)*/his/her *etc* birth: **hooladet|ee/-kha/-ekh/-o/-ah** *etc).*

(yom/yemey) hooledet יום הולדת *nm* birthday; (my/your *(m/f)*/his/her *etc* birthday: **yom hooladet|ee/-kha/-ekh/-o/-ah** *etc*).

hoolkh|an/-enah הולחן *v* was composed (music); (*pres* **moolkhan;** *fut* **yoolkhan).**

ho'om|ak/-kah/-aktee הועמק *v* was deepened; (*pres* **mo'omak;** *fut* **yo'omak).**

hoomanee/-t הומני *adj* humane.

(megamah) hoomaneet מגמה הומנית *nf* humanities trend (in high school).

hoom|at/-tah הומת *v* was put to death, killed; (*pres* **moomat;** *fut* **yoomat).**

hoomkh|ash/-eshah הומחש *v* was tangibly demonstrated; (*pres* **moomkhash;** *fut* **yoomkhash).**

hoomkh|az/-ezah הומחז *v* was dramatized; (*pres* **moomkhaz;** *fut* **yoomkhaz).**

hoomor הומור *nm* humor.

hoomr|ats/-etsah/-atstee הומרץ *v* was urged, encouraged, stirred; (*pres* **moomrats;** *fut* **yoomrats).**

hoomsh|akh/-ekhah הומשך *v* was continued; (*pres* **moomshakh;** *fut* **yoomshakh).**

hoomsh|al/-elah/-altee הומשל *v* **1.** was likened to; **2.** installed to rule; (*pres* **moomshal;** *fut* **yoomshal).**

hoomt|ak/-ekah הומתק *v* was sweetened; (*pres* **moomtak;** *fut* **yoomtak).**

hoomts|a/-e'ah הומצא *v* **1.** was delivered; **2.** was invented; (*pres* **moomtsa;** *fut* **yoomtsa).**

hoon|af/-fah הונף *v* was hoisted; (*pres* **moonaf;** *fut* **yoonaf).**

ho'on|ak/-kah/-aktee הוענק *v* was bestowed, granted; (*pres* **mo'onak;** *fut* **yo'onak).**

hoon|akh/-khah הונח *v* was laid, put, placed; (*pres* **moonakh;** *fut* **yoonakh).**

hoonakh (*etc*) **lee/lekha/lakh/lo/lah** *etc* הונח לי/לך/לך/לו I/you*(m/f)*/he/she (*etc*) was given rest; was allowed to relax.

hoon|as/-sah/-astee הונס *v* was driven off; (*pres* **moonas;** *fut* **yoonas).**

hoonkhat/-ah הונחת *v* **1.** was landed; **2.** was brought upon; (*pres* **moonkhat;** *fut* **yoonkhat).**

hoonp|ak/-ekah הונפק *v* **1.** was issued; **2.** was extracted; **3.** was derived; (*pres* **moonpak;** *fut* **yoonpak).**

hoop|al/-lah/-altee הופל *v* **1.** was downed; **2.** was kicked down; **3.** was dropped; (*pres* **moopal;** *fut* **yoopal).**

hoor|a'/-'ah הורע *v* deteriorated; worsened; (*pres* **moora';** *fut* **yoora').**

hoor|ad/-dah/-adetee הורד *v* **1.** was brought down; **2.** was lowered; **3.** was reduced; (*pres* **moorad;** *fut* **yoorad).**

ho'or|akh/-khah הוארך *v* was prolonged; was extended; (*pres* **mo'orakh;** *fut* **yo'orakh).**

ho'or|akh/-khah/-akhtee הוערך *v* was estimated; was evaluated; (*pres* **mo'orakh**; *fut* **yo'orakh**).

hoor'ash/-ah הורעש *v* **1.** was stormed; **2.** was bombarded; was shelled; (*pres* **moor'ash**; *fut* **yoor'ash**).

hoor'al/-ah/-tee הורעל *v* was poisoned; (*pres* **moor'al**; *fut* **yoor'al**).

hoor'av/-ah/-tee הורעב *v* was starved; (*pres* **moor'av**; *fut* **yoor'av**).

hoorg|al/-elah/-altee הורגל *v* got accustomed; (*pres* **moorgal**; *fut* **yoorgal**).

hoorg|ash/-eshah/-ashtee הורגש *v* was felt; (*pres* **moorgash**; *fut* **yoorgash**).

hoorgaz/-ezah/-aztee הורגז *v* was irked; was irritated; (*pres* **moorgaz**; *fut* **yoorgaz**).

hoork|an/-enah הורכן *v* was bent; was bowed; (*pres* **moorkan**; *fut* **yoorkan**).

hoork|av/-evah הורכב *v* **1.** was composed; **2.** was assembled; **3.** was mounted; (*pres* **moorkav**; *fut* **yoorkav**).

hoorkh|ak/-ekah/-aktee הורחק *v* **1.** was removed; **2.** was dismissed; (*pres* **moorkhak**; *fut* **yoorkhak**).

hoos|ak/-kah הוסק *v* **1.** was heated; **2.** was deducted, drawn (conclusion); (*pres* **moosak**; *fut* **yoosak**).

ho'os|ak/-kah/-akhtee הועסק *v* was employed; (*pres* **mo'osak**; *fut* **yo'osak**).

hoos|am/-mah/-amtee הושם *v* was put,placed, seated; (*pres* **moosam**; *fut* **yoosam**).

hoos|ar/-rah/-artee הוסר *v* was taken off, removed; (*pres* **moosar**; *fut* **yoosar**).

hoos|ag/-gah הושג *v* was attained; (*pres* **moosag**; *fut* **yoosag**).

hoos|av/-bah/-avtee *(b=v)* הוסב *v* **1.** was endorsed; **2.** was altered, converted; (*pres* **moosav**; *fut* **yoosav**).

hoosb|ar/-erah הוסבר *v* was explained; (*pres* **moosbar**; *fut* **yoosbar**).

hoosd|ar/-erah הוסדר *v* was arranged; was set in order; (*pres* **moosdar**; *fut* **yoosdar**).

hoosg|ar/-erah/-artee הוסגר *v* **1.** was extradited; **2.** was delivered; (*pres* **moosgar**; *fut* **yoosgar**).

hoosh|ak/-kah הושק *v* was launched (boat); (*pres* **mooshak**; *fut* **yooshak**).

hoosh'al/-ah/-tee הושאל *v* was lent (a thing, not money); (*pres* **moosh'al**; *fut* **yoosh'al**).

hoosh'ar/-ah/-tee הושאר *v* was left behind; (*pres* **moosh'ar**; *fut* **yoosh'ar**).

hoosh'an/-ah/-tee הושען *v* was leaned against; (*pres* **moosh'an**; *fut* **yoosh'an**).

hooshba'/-e'ah/-a'tee הושבע *v* was sworn in; took an oath; (*pres* **mooshba'**; *fut* **yooshba'**).

hooshbat/-etah/-atetee הושבת *v* was locked out (strike); (*pres* **mooshbat**; *fut* **yooshbat**).

hoosh|'ah/-'atah/-'etee הושעה *v* **1.** was delayed, **2.** was suspended; (*pres* **moosh'eh**; *fut* **yoosh'eh**).

hoosh'|hah/-hatah/-hetee הושהה *v* was delayed; (*pres* **moosh'heh**; *fut* **yoosh'heh**).

hooshk|a'/-e'ah/-a'tee הושקע *v* was invested; (*pres* **mooshka'**; *fut* **yooshka'**).

hooshk|ah/-etah/-etee הושקה *v* **1.** was given (or made) to drink; **2.** was watered; (*pres* **mooshkeh**; *fut* **yooshkeh**).

hoosh|av/-vah/-avtee הושב *v* was returned, given back; (*pres* **mooshav**; *fut* **yooshav**).

hooshk|av/-evah/-avtee הושכב *v* was laid down; (*pres* **hooshkav**; *fut* **yooshkav**).

hooshkhal/-ah הושחל *v* was threaded, passed through; (*pres* **mooshkhal**; *fut* **yooshkhal**).

hooshkham/-ah/-tee הושחם *v* was darkened, bronzed; (*pres* **mooshkham**; *fut* **yooshkham**).

hooshkhar/-ah/-tee הושחר *v* was blackened; (*pres* **mooshkhar**; *fut* **yooshkhar**).

hooshkhat/-ah/-etee הושחת *v* **1.** was spoiled, ruined; **2.** was corrupted; (*pres* **mooshkhat**; *fut* **yooshkhat**).

hooshkhaz/-ah הושחז *v* was sharpened; was honed; (*pres* **mooshkhaz**; *fut* **yooshkhaz**).

hooshlam/-emah הושלם *v* was completed; (*pres* **mooshlam**; *fut* **yooshlam**).

hooshl|at/-etah/-atetee הושלט *v* **1.** was given dominion over; **2.** was installed; (*pres* **mooshlat**; *fut* **yooshlat**).

hooshm|a'/-e'ah/-a'tee הושמע *v* was sounded; was heard; (*pres* **mooshma'**; *fut* **yooshma'**).

hooshm|ad/-edah/-adetee הושמד *v* **1.** was destroyed; **2.** was exterminated; (*pres* **mooshmad**; *fut* **yooshmad**).

hooshm|at/-etah/-atetee הושמט *v* was omitted; was deleted; (*pres* **mooshmat**; *fut* **yooshmat**).

hooshp|a'/-e'ah/-a'tee הושפע *v* was influenced; (*pres* **mooshpa'**; *fut* **yooshpa'**).

hooshp|al/-elah/-altee הושפל *v* was humiliated; (*pres* **mooshpal**; *fut* **yooshpal**).

hooshr|ah/-etah הושרה *v* was immersed, drenched; (*pres* **mooshreh**; *fut* **yooshreh**).

hoosht|ak/-ekah/-aktee הושתק *v* was silenced; (*pres* **mooshtak**; *fut* **yooshtak**).

hoosht|al/-elah/-altee הושתל *v* **1.** was planted; **2.** was implanted; (*pres* **mooshtal**; *fut* **yooshtal**).

hoosht|at/-etah/-atetee הושתת *v* was founded; was based; (*pres* **mooshtat**; *fut* **yooshtat**).

hooshv|ah/-etah/-etee הושווה *v* **1.** was compared; **2.** was equalized; (*pres* **mooshveh**; *fut* **yooshveh**).

hoosmakh/-ekhah/-akhtee הוסמך *v* **1.** was ordained; **2.** graduated; (*pres* **moosmakh**; *fut* **yoosmakh**).

hoost|ar/-erah/-artee הוסתר *v* was concealed from; was hidden away; (*pres* **moostar**; *fut* **yoostar**).

hoosv|ah/-etah/-etee הוסווה *v* was camouflaged, hidden; (*pres* **moosveh**; *fut* **yoosveh**).

hoot|'ah/-'atah/-'etee הוטעה *v* was misled; was led astray; was deceived; (*pres* **moot'eh**; *fut* **yoot'eh**).

ho'ot|ak (*npr* **ho't|ak**)/**-kah/-aktee** הועתק *v* **1.** was copied; **2.** was moved over; (*pres* **mo'tak**; *fut* **yo'tak**).

hoot|al/-lah הוטל *v* was imposed; was thrown; (*pres* **mootal**; *fut* **yootal**).

hoot'am/-ah/-tee הותאם *v* was adapted, made to fit; (*pres* **moot'am**; *fut* **yoot'am**).

hoot'am/-ah הוטעם *v* was emphasized;was stressed; (*pres* **moot'am**; *fut* **yoot'am**).

hoot'an/-ah הוטען *v* **1.** was loaded; **2.** was imposed upon; (*pres* **moot'an**; *fut* **yoot'an**).

hoot|ar/-rah הותר *v* **1.** was untied; **2.** allowed, permitted; (*pres* **mootar**; *fut* **yootar**).

hootas/-'sah/-astee הוטס *v* was flown; (*pres* **moot'as**; *fut* **yootas**).

hoot|av/-vah הוטב *v* was improved; (*pres* **mootav**; *fut* **yootav**).

hootb|al/-elah/-altee הוטבל *v* **1.** was dipped; **2.** was baptized; (*pres* **mootbal**; *fut* **yootbal**).

hootm|an/-enah הוטמן *v* was concealed, hidden; (*pres* **mootman**; *fut* **yootman**).

hootn|ah/-etah הותנה *v* was stipulated; (*pres* **mootneh**; *fut* **yootneh**).

hootr|ad/-edah/-adetee הוטרד *v* **1.** was troubled; was disturbed; **2.** was annoyed; (*pres* **mootrad**; *fut* **yootrad**).

hoots|a/-'ah/-e'tee הוצא *v* **1.** was disbursed; was spent; **2.** was taken out; (*pres* **mootsa**; *fut* **yootsa**).

hootsa (*etc*) **le-horeg** הוצא להורג *v* was executed; was put to death.

hoots|af/-fah/-aftee הוצף *v* was flooded; (*pres* **mootsaf**; *fut* **yootsaf**).

hoots|ag/-gah/-agtee הוצג *v* **1.** was presented; was introduced; **2.** was staged; (*pres* **mootsag**; *fut* **yootsag**).

hoots|ar/-rah הוצר *v* was narrowed, straitened; (*pres* **mootsar**; *fut* **yootsar**).

hoots|at/-'tah הוצת *v* was ignited, *lit*, kindled; (*pres* **mootsat**; *fut* **yootsat**).

hootsm|ad/-edah/-adetee הוצמד *v* was linked, tied up, clutched; (*pres* **mootsmad**; *fut* **yootsmad**).

hootsn|a'/-e'ah/-a'tee הוצנע *v* was concealed, hidden; (*pres* **mootsna'**; *fut* **yootsna'**).

hootsn|akh/-ekhah/-akhtee הוצנח *v* was parachuted; (*pres* **mootsnakh**; *fut* **yootsnakh**).

hoov|a/-'ah/-e'tee הובא *v* was brought in; was carried in; (*pres* **moova**; *fut* **yoova**).

hoov|al/-lah/-altee הובל *v* was led, brought; (*pres* **mooval**; *fut* **yooval**).

hoov|an/-nah/-antee הובן *v* was understood; (*pres* **moovan**; *fut* **yoovan**).

hoov'ar/-ah הובער *v* was set on fire; was *lit*, kindled; was ignited (*pres* **moov'ar**; *fut* **yoov'ar**).

hoov|as/-sah/-astee הובס *v* was defeated; (*pres* **moovas**; *fut* **yoovas**).

hoovk|a'/-e'ah הובקע *v* was broken through; (*pres* **moovka'**; *fut* **yoovka'**).

hoovka' (*etc*) **sha'ar** הובקע שער *v* a goal has been scored.

hoovt|akh/-ekhah הובטח *v* was promised; was secured; (*pres* **moovtakh**; *fut* **yoovtakh**).

hooz|az/-ezah/-aztee הוזז *v* was shifted, moved; (*pres* **moozaz**; *fut* **yoozaz**).

hooz'ak/-ah/-tee הוזעק *v* was alerted, alarmed; (*pres* **mooz'ak**; *fut* **yooz'ak**).

□ **"Hoozayl"** (Huzayyel) "הוזייל" *nm* Beduin tribe-settlement (known also as "El-Hoozayl") at the N. entry to the Negev, off the **Keeryat Gat-Be'er Sheva'** highway. Pop. 7000.

hooz'har/-ah/-tee הוזהר *v* was warned; (*pres* **mooz'har**; *fut* **yooz'har**).

(ke) hoo zeh כהוא זה anything whatsoever.

hoozk|ar/-erah/-artee הוזכר *v* was mentioned; came up; (*pres* **moozkar**; *fut* **yoozkar**).

hoozm|an/-enah/-antee הוזמן *v* was invited; (*pres* **moozman**; *fut* **yoozman**).

hoozman (*etc*) **eesheet** הוזמן אישית *v* was invited personally.

hoozn|akh/-ekhah/-akhtee הוזנח *v* was neglected (*pres* **mooznakh**; *fut* **yooznakh**).

hoozr|am/-emah הוזרם *v* was poured; was made to flow; (*pres* **moozram**; *fut* **yoozram**).

hoozr|ak/-ekah הוזרק *v* was injected; (*pres* **moozrak**; *fut* **yoozrak**).

hora|h/-ot הורה *nf* Israeli folk-dance.

hor|ah/-tah/-etee הורה *v* directed; ordered; (*pres* **moreh**; *fut* **yoreh**).

hora'ah הוראה *sing nf* teaching (as a profession).

hora|'ah/-'ot הוראה *nf* instruction; directive; (+*of*: **-'at**).

hora|'at/-'ot keva' הוראת קבע *nf* standing order.

hora'|dah/-ot הורדה *nf* reduction; demotion; taking down; (+*of*: **-at**).

hor|eed/-eeda/-adetee הוריד *v* reduced; lowered; took down; (*pres* **moreed**; *fut* **yoreed**).

horeed meeshkal (*[colloq.]* **horeed be-meeshkal**) הוריד משקל *v* lost weight.

hor|eek/-eekah/-aktee הוריק *v* **1.** greened; **2.** *[colloq.]* emptied; (*pres* **moreek**; *fut* **yoreek**).

hor|eem הורים *nm pl* (*sing nmf* **-eh/-ah**) parents; (+*of*: **-ey**).

hor|eesh/-eeshah/-ashtee הוריש *v* bequeathed, left as inheritance; (*pres* **moreesh**; *fut* **yoreesh**).

horeg/-et הורג *v pres* kills; (*pst* **harag**; *fut* **yaharog**).

(ata/at) horeg/-et (*etc*) **otee** אתה הורג אותי *[slang]* you're killing me!...

(la) horeg להורג to death (by execution).

hor|eh/-ah הורה *nmf* parent.

◇ **hor|eh/-eem shakool/-eem** הורה שכול *nm* parent of a son or daughter fallen in one of nation's wars or as result of an act of terrorism.

horoot הורות *nf* parenthood.

horoskop/-eem הורוסקופ *nm* horoscope.

hosaf|ah/-ot הוספה *nf* increase; increment; addition; (+*of*: **-at**).

hos|eef/-eefah/-aftee הוסיף *v* added; continued; (*pres* **moseef**; *fut* **yoseef**).

hoseef (*etc*) **meeshkal** הוסיף משקל *v* put on weight.

◇ **hosha'na rabah** הושענא רבה *nm* seventh day of Succoth.

□ **Hosha'yah** (Hosha'aya) הושעיה *nm* communal settlement (est. 1981) in Lower Galilee, 1 km NE of **Tseeporee**. Pop. 335.

hosh|ee'a'/-ee'ah/-a'tee הושיע *nf* rescued; saved; (*pres* **moshee'a'**; *fut* **yoshee'a'**).

hosh|eet/-eetah/-atetee הושיט *nf* stretched out; extended; (*pres* **mosheet**; *fut* **yosheet**).

hosheet (*etc*) **ezrah** הושיט עזרה *v* rendered assistance.

hosheet (*etc*) **yad** הושיט יד *v* stretched out one's hand; lent a helping hand.

hosh|eev/-eevah/-avtee הושיב *v* placed; set; (*pres* **mosheev**; *fut* **yosheev**).

ho't|ak/-kah/-aktee הועתק *v* **1.** was copied; **2.** was moved over; (*pres* **mo'tak**; *fut* **yo'tak**).

hot|eer/-eerah/-artee הותיר *v* left; left behind; (*pres* **moteer**; *fut* **yoteer**).

hotsa|'ah/-'ot הוצאה *nf* **1.** expenditure; expense; **2.** ousting; **3.** *[colloq.]* edition; (*+of:* **-at**).

hotsa'ah le-fo'al *(f=p)* הוצאה לפועל *nf* **1.** execution (of court order); **2.** implementation.

(meesrad ha) hotsa'ah le-fo'al *(f=p)* משרד ההוצאה לפועל *nm* the office for execution of court orders.

hotsa|'ah/-ot le-horeg הוצאה להורג *nf* execution,

hotsa|'ah/-'ot le-or הוצאה לאור *nf* **1.** publishing house; **2.** publication.

hotsa'at deebah הוצאת דיבה *nf* libelling; slander.

hotsee/-ee'ah/-etee הוציא *v* **1.** took out; **2.** spent; **3.** spread; (*pres* **motsee**; *fut* **yootsee**).

hotsee (*etc*) **deebah** הוציא דיבה *v* libelled; slandered.

hotsee (*etc*) **le-fo'al** *(f=p)* הוציא לפועל *v* carried out; implemented.

hotsee (*etc*) **le-horeg** הוציא להורג *v* executed; put to death.

hotsee (*etc*) **le-or** הוציא לאור *v* published.

hotsee (*etc*) **shem ra'** הוציא שם רע *v* gave a bad name; slandered.

(le) hotsee להוציא *adv* except; excluding.

hoval|ah/-ot הובלה *nf* transportation; conveying; (*+of:* **-at**).

hov|eel/-eelah/-altee הוביל *v* **1.** transported; carried; **2.** led; (*pres* **moveel**; *fut* **yoveel**).

hoy! !הוי *interj* woe! alas!

hozal|ah/-ot הוזלה *nf* price reduction; (*+of:* **-at**).

(meevts|a'/-e'ey) hozalah מבצע הוזלה *nm* reduction sale.

hoz|eh/-ah הוזה *v pres* dreams; raves; (*pst* **hazah**; *fut* **yehezeh**).

I.

NOTE: In the transliteration system of this dictionary **i** does not appear. The vowel **i** as pronounced in *ivory, might, tissue* or *it* does not exist in Hebrew. Pronounced as in *deli* it is transliterated **ee** (as in *Tel-Aviv*, pronounced **Tel-Aveev**).

J.

NOTE: The sound represented in English by **j** has no Hebrew equivalent. It can be heard only in words borrowed from other languages (including Arabic) or in names of foreign origin (e.g. *John, Jamal, Jeanette, Jabotinsky*). Naturally, these are few and are usually defined as colloquialisms *[colloq.]* or slang *[slang]*.

jabar ג׳באר *nm [slang] (Arab.)* big hero (mostly used ironically).

jabla'ot ג׳בלאות *nm pl [slang] (Arab.)* hard-to-pass stretches of hilly territory which new army recruits must master in training exercises.

jama'ah (or **jam'ah**) ג׳מעה *nf [slang] (Arab.)* the "gang".

jamboree|yah/-yot ג׳מבורייה *[colloq.] nf* jamboree (*+of:* **-yat**).

janer/-eem ז׳אנר *nm* genre.

□ **Jatt** ג'ת *nm* Arab village in N. Samaria hills (est 1870), 9 km N. of **Toolkarem**. Pop. 5,930.
jaz/-eem ג'אז *nm* jazz.
□ **Jeebalya** ג'באליה *nf* township and refugee settlement in N. of Gaza Strip. Pop. approx. 37,135 (plus 36,060 in refugee camps).
jeegolo/-s ג'יגולו *nm* giggolo.
jeenjee/-t ג'ינג'י *nmf & adj [slang]* (Engl.: ginger) redhead; freckle-faced.
jeens/-eem ג'ינס *nm* jeans (*pl+of:* **-ey**).
(zoog) jeenseem זוג ג'ינסים *nm* a pair of jeans.
jeep/-eem ג'יפ *nm* jeep.
jeeraf|ah/-ot ג'ירפה *nf* giraffe (*+of:* **-at**).
□ **Jeneen** (Jenin) ג'נין *nf* Arab town on borderline between Yizre'el Valley and Samaria hills, 15 km E. of Netanya. Pop. 39,000.
jentel|men/-meneem ג'נטלמן *nm* gentleman.
jentelmenee/-t ג'נטלמני *adj* gentlemanly.
(be-tsoorah) jentelmeneet בצורה ג'נטלמנית *adv* in a gentleman-like manner.
jest|ah/-ot ג'סטה *nf* gesture (*+of:* **-at**).
jlob/-eem ז'לוב *[slang]* (Russian) *nm* big and threateningly strong fellow.
job/-eem ג'וב *[slang] nm* (Engl.) job; task.
jobneek/-eet ג'ובניק *[slang] m/f* derogatory army-slang definition of soldier doing a non-fighting job.
joker/-eem ג'וקר joker.
jook/-eem ג'וק *[colloq.] nm* (Russian) cockroach (*pl+of:* **-ey**).
joornal/-eem ז'ורנל *nm* magazine.
joongel/-eem ג'ונגל jungle.
(ha) joynt ה"ג'וינט" *nm* the American Joint Distribution Committee (JDC)

K.

incorporating כ and ק

ka- -כ *(prefix)* like the.
ka'ka' קעקע *nm* tattoo.
(ketov|et/-ot) ka'aka' כתובת קעקע *nf* tattooed inscription (or design).
ka'akh/ke'akheem כעך *nm* pretzel; bagel; (*pl+of:* **-ey**).
ka-amoor כאמור *conj* as said.
ka'aree|t/-yot קערית *nf* small bowl (*+of:* **-at**).
ka'arooree/-t קערורי *adj* concave.
ka'as כעס *nm* anger.
ka'as/-tee כעס *v* was angry; raged; (*pres* **ko'es**; *fut* **yeekh'as**). bn.
ka'asan/-eet כעסן *nmf & adj* quick-tempered; hothead.
ka'asher כאשר *conj* as; when.
ka'av/-ah/-avtee כאב *v* **1.** hurt; **2.** was pained by; (*pres* **ko'ev**; *fut* **yeekh'av**).
ka'avor כעבור after; following.
ka'avor khodesh כעבור חודש one month later.
ka'avor khodshayeem כעבור חודשיים two months later.
ka'avor shavoo'a כעבור שבוע a week later.
ka'avor shevoo'ayeem כעבור שבועיים a fortnight later.
ka'avor yom כעבור יום a day later.
ka'avor yomayeem כעבור יומיים *adv* two days later.
ka-zeh כזה *m* **1.** such; **2.** such a ...; **3.** as this.
ka-zot כזאת *nf* **1.** such; **2.** such a ...; **3.** as this.
ka-zotee כזאתי *nf [colloq.]* **1.** such; **2.** such a...; **3.** as this.
kabal|ah/-ot קבלה *nf* receipt; acceptance; (*+of:* **-at**).
(she|'at/-ot) kabalah שעת קבלה *nf* reception hour.
kabal|at/-ot paneem קבלת פנים *nf* **1.** reception; **2.** welcome; **3.** welcome party.
◇ **kabal|at/-ot shabat** קבלת שבת *nf* **1.** Friday evening prayer; **2.** Sabbath Eve preparations.
kabaret/-eem קברט *nm* cabaret.
kabarneet/-eem קברניט *nm* **1.** captain; skipper; **2.** leader; (*+of:* **-ey**).
kaba|y (*cpr* kaba'ee)/-'eem כבאי *nm* fireman; (*pl+of:* **-'ey**).
kabayeem קביים *nm pl* crutches; (*sing:* **kav**).
kabeenet/-eem קבינט *nm* cabinet (government).
kabeer/-ah כביר *adj* great; tremendous.
kab|el!/-lee! קבל! *v imp sing m/f* take; accept (*pst* **keebel**; *pres* **mekabel**; *fut* **yekabel**).
kabes oo-levash כבס ולבש wash & wear.
kablan/-eem קבלן *nm* contractor; (*pl+of:* **-ey**).
kablan/-ey meeshneh קבלן משנה *nm* sub-contractor.
kablanee/-t קבלני *adj* contractual; contracting.
kablanoo|t/-yot קבלנות *nf* contracting; piecework.

(be) kablanoot בקבלנות on a contractual basis; piecework.

kabran (*npr* **kavran**)**/-eem** קברן *nm* gravedigger; (*pl+of:* **-ey**).

□ **Kabree** (Kabri) כברי *nm* kibbutz (est. 1949) in W. Gallilee, 5 km E. of Nahariyya. Pop. 788.

kabtsan/-eem קבצן *nm* beggar; (*pl+of:* **-ey**).

kabtsanoot קבצנות *nf* mendicancy; begging.

kad/-eem כד *nm* pitcher; jug; (*pl+of:* **-ey**).

kad/-ah/-otee קד *v* bowed; bent; (*pres* **kad**; *fut* **yeekod**).

kad (*etc*) **keedah** קידה קד *v* took a bow; curtseyed.

kad|akh/-khah/-akhtee קדח *v* **1.** bored; drilled; **2.** was ill with fever; burned; (*pres* **kode'akh**; *fut* **yeekdakh**).

kadakhat קדחת *nf* **1.** fever; malaria; **2.** *[slang]* (you'll get) nothing.

kadakhat nesee'ah קדחת נסיעה *nf* travel fever.

kadakhat ha-sheegaron קדחת השיגרון *nf* rheumatic fever (Medic.).

kadakhat shakhat קדחת שחת *nf* hayfever (Medic.).

kadakhtanee/-t קדחתני *adj* feverish.

kadakhtanoot קדחתנות *nf* fervor; fervency.

(be) kadakhtanoot בקדחתנות feverishly.

kad|am/-mah/-amtee קדם *v* preceded; had priority over; (*pres* **kodem**; *fut* **yeekdam**).

kadar/-eem קדר *nm* potter; (*pl+of:* **ey**).

kad|ar/-rah/-artee קדר *v* became gloomy; became clouded; (*pres* **koder**; *fut* **yeekdar**).

kada'ee/-t כדאי *adj* worth; worthwhile; (*npr* **keda'ee**).

kada'eeyoot כדאיות *nf* rentability; worthwhileness; profitability.

◇ **kadee** קדי *nm* judge (under Muslim law); kadi; qadi.

kadeemah קדימה *adv* forward.

□ **Kadeemah** (Kadima) קדימה *nm* village (est. 1933) and local council in Sharon, 5 km E. of haSharon Junction (**Tsomet ha-Sharon**). Pop. 3,760.

ka-deen כדין lawfully.

◇ **kadeesh** (**"Kaddish"**) קדיש *nm* mourning prayer for deceased. According to Jewish religious law, it should be recited by sons, thrice daily, in a synagogue, for eleven months after the death of a parent.

(mee) kadmat dena מקדמת דנא *adv (Aram.)* from olden days.

kadmon/-eet קדמון *adj* ancient.

(ha-adam ha) kadmon האדם הקדמון *nm* primordial man.

kadmonee/-t קדמוני *adj* ancient.

kadmoneynoo קדמונינו *nm pl* our ancient sages.

kadmoot קדמות *nf* **1.** primacy; **2.** previous position.

(le) kadmoot|o/-ah לקדמותו back to what/how it/he/she was.

kadoom/kedoomah קדום *adj* old; ancient.

(meeshpat/-eem) kadoom/kedoomeem משפט קדום *nm* pre-conceived idea; prejudice.

□ **Kadoom** קדום *nm* former name of one of first post-1967 Jewish settlements on the West Bank. (see □ **Kedoomeem**).

kadoor/-eem כדור *nm* **1.** ball; **2.** sphere; **3.** bullet; (*pl+of:* **-ey**).

kadoor ha-arets כדור הארץ *nm* terrestrial globe.

kadoor/-eem not|ev/-veem כדור נותב *nm* tracer bullet.

kadoor/-eem shot|eh/-eem כדור שוטה *nm* stray bullet.

kadoor/-ey serak כדור סרק *nm* blank bullet.

kadooraglan/-eem כדורגלן *nm* footballer (soccer-player); (*pl+of:* **-ey**).

kadooree/-t כדורי *adj* spherical; rounded.

('et/-eem) kadooree/-yeem עט כדורי *nm* ballpoint-pen.

□ **Kadooree** כדורי *nm* short for **"Bet-Sefer Kadooree"** agricultural boarding-school in Lower Galilee, at the foot of Mount Tabor which, in the years 1937-1948, played a part in the underground training of Haganah leaders. Some of these later became leading staff officers in Israel's Army. Pop. 214.

kadooree|t/-yot כדורית *nf* ball; cell; globule; (*+of:* **-yat**).

kadooreeyot-dam כדוריות דם *nf pl* blood cells.

kadooregel כדורגל *nm* soccer; football (continental).

(takhroo|t/-yot) kadooregel תחרות כדורגל *nf* soccer match.

kadoorsal כדורסל *nm* basket ball.

(takhroo|t/-yot) kadoorsal תחרות כדורסל *nf* basket-ball game contest.

kadoorsalan/-eem כדורסלן *nm* basket-ball player; (*pl+of:* **-ey**).

kadoret כדורת *nf* bowling.

kadosh/kedoshah קדוש *adj* holy; sacred.

kadosh/kedosheem קדוש *nm* martyr who has given his/her life for Judaism (or for some cause); (*pl+of:* **-ey**).

(ha) kadosh borkhoo (*npr* **barookh hoo**) הקדוש ברוך הוא *nm* **1.** the Good Lord;; **2.** (*lit.*) the Holy One, blessed He be.

kadroo|t/-yot קדרות *nf* gloom; darkness.

ka'el|eh/-oo כאלה/ו *adj* like these; such as these.

(she) ka'el|eh/-oo שכאלה/ו *adj* as these.

ka-'et כעת right now.

ka-'et khayah כעת חיה *adv* in a year's time; a year from now (Bibl).

Kaf כ ך *nf* the 11th letter (consonant) of the Hebrew alphabet; pronounced **k** when dotted (כּ) and **kh** when undotted (כ) or in the form of Final Kaf (ך).

kaf כ' **1.** *num* 20 in the Hebrew system of numerals; **2.** *ord. num* 20th in the Hebrew system of numerals.

Kaf Sofeet כ"ף סופית *nf* form of Kaf (ך) when at end of a word.

ka|f/-pot (*p=f*) כף *nf* spoon.

ka|f/-payeem *(p=f)* כף *nf* hand.

(makh|a/-'ah/-atee) ka|f/-payeem מחא כף *v* applauded; (*pres* **mokhe kaf**; *fut* **yeemkha kaf**).

(tekee|'at/-'ot) kaf תקיעת כף *nf* handshake (in order to clinch a deal or undertake an obligation).

kaf|a/-'ah/-atee קפא *v* froze (*pres* **kofe**; *fut* **yeekpa** *(p=f)*).

kafa *(etc)* **'al ha-shemareem** קפא על השמרים *v* made no progress.

kaf|ah/-tah/-eetee כפה *v* coerced; compelled; forced; (*pres* **kofeh**; *fut* **yeekhpeh**; *kh=k; p=f*).

kaf|af/-efah/-aftee כפף *v* bent (*pres* **kofef**; *fut* **yeekhpof** *(kh=k; p=f)*).

kaf alef כ״א *num* 21; 21st.

kaf|ar/-rah/-artee כפר *v* denied; was skeptical; (*pres* **kofer**; *fut* **yeekhpor** *(kh=k; p=f)*).

kaf|at/-tah/-atetee כפת *v* tied up; bound; (*pres* **kofet**; *fut* **yeekhpot** *(kh=k; p=f)*).

kaf|ats/-tsah/-atstee קפץ *v* jumped; quickly came over; (*pres* **kofets**; *fut* **yeekpots**; *(p=f)*).

kaf-bet כ״ב *num* 22; 22nd.

kaf-dalet כ״ד *num* 24; 24th.

kafdan/-eet קפדן *adj & nmf* strict (severe) person.

kafdanoot קפדנות *nf* strictness; severity.

kafeel/kefeelah כפיל *nmf* duplicate; double; (*pl:* **-eem**; *+of:* **-ey**).

◇ **kafee|yah/-yot** כפייה traditional Arab male headgear consisting of a large square of cotton cloth (mostly white), draped and folded, held in place by a cord (**'akal**) wound around the head. (*+of:* **-yat**).

kafeh קפה *nm* **1.** coffee; **2.** cafe.

kafeh hafookh קפה הפוך *nm* coffee with abundant milk.

kafeh names קפה נמס *nm* instant coffee.

kafeh nes קפה נס *nm* instant coffee.

kafeh toorkee קפה טורקי *nm* Turkish coffee.

(bet|batey) kafeh בית קפה *nm* cafe; coffeehouse.

kaf-geemal כ״ג *num* 23; 23rd.

kaf-heh כ״ה *num* 25; 25th.

kaf-khet כ״ח *num* 28; 28th.

ka|f/-pot *(p=f)* **moznayeem** כף מאזניים *nf* scale; balance.

ka|f/-pot *(p=f)* **na'al/-ayeem** כף נעליים *nf* shoehorn.

ka|f/-pot *(p=f)* **regel/raglayeem** כף רגל *nf* sole of the foot.

kafoo/kefoo'ah קפוא *adj* frozen.

(kafeh) kafoo' קפה קפוא *nm* iced coffee.

kafoof/kefoofah כפוף *adj* bent.

kafoof le- כפוף ל־ subject to.

kafool/kefoolah כפול *adj* double.

kafooy/kafooyah כפוי *adj* forced; compelled.

kafree/-t כפרי **1.** *nmf* villager; **2.** *adj* rural; rustic.

Kafreesa'ee/-t קפריסאי *nmf & adj* Cypriot.

□ **Kafreeseen** (*cpr* **Kafreeseen**) קפריסין *nm* Cyprus.

□ **Kafr Kama** כפר כמא *nm* Circassian-Muslim village (est. 1876) in Lower Galilee, on **Kefar Tavor** - Yavne'el road, 6 km SE of Golani Junction (**Tsomet Golanee**). Pop. 2,070.

□ **Kafr Kana** (Kafr Kanna) כפר כנא *nm* Arab village in Lower Galilee, 6 km NE of Nazareth, on the Tiberias-Nazareth road. Pop. 10,700.

□ **Kafr Kara'** (Kafr Qara) כפר קרע *nm* large Arab village NE of 'Iron Junction (**Tsomet 'Eeron**). Pop. 9,160.

□ **Kafr Kasem** (Kafr Qasim) כפר קאסם *nm* large Arab village NE of **Petakh-Teekvah**. Pop. 9,970.

□ **Kafr Manda** (Kafar Manda) כפר מנדא *nm* large Arab village in Lower Galilee, at the foot of Mount **'Atsmon**. N. of **Bet Netoofah** water reservoir. Pop. 8,850.

□ **Kafr Yaseef** (Kafr Yasif) כפר יסיף *nm* large Arab township in Western Galilee, 8 km E. of Acre (**'Ako**). Pop. 6,140.

kaf-tet כ״ט *num* 29; 29th.

◇ **kaf-tet november** כ״ט נובמבר *nm* the 29th of November, anniversary of the day in 1948 on which the U.N. Assembly passed with a two-thirds majority its Resolution decreeing the partition of Palestine into two independent states: a Jewish one and an Arab one. The leaders of the Palestine Arabs and all Arab states rejected the resolution and reacted by organized anti-Jewish terrorism that soon became a declared war. The Jews saw this as their War of Independence and on May 15, 1948, with the end of the British Mandate, with hostilities at their highest and the neighboring Arab states poised to invade the country, they proclaimed the state of Israel.

kaftor/-eem כפתור *nm* button; (*pl+of:* **-ey**).

(zeeknah) kaftsah 'al|av/-eha זיקנה קפצה עליו *v* aged prematurely.

kaf vav כ״ו *num* 26; 26th.

ka|f/-pot yad/-ayeem כף יד *nf* palm of hand.

kaf zayeen כ״ז *num* 27; 27th.

kaha|h/-tah/kaheetee כהה *v* paled; darkened; fainted; (*pres* **keheh**; *fut* **yeekh'heh** *(kh=k)*).

kaha|h/-tah/kaheetee קהה *v* was blunted; wearied; (*pres* **keheh**; *fut* **yeek'heh**).

kahal קהל *nm* audience; public; (*+of:* **kehal**).

(da'at) kahal דעת קהל *nf* public opinion.

ka-halakhah כהלכה *adv* duly; as should be; in proper form.

◇ **ka-halakhah** כהלכה *adv* according to Jewish religious law.

◇ **(geeyoor) ka-halakhah** see ◇ **geeyoor ka-halakhah**.

ka-havayat|o/-ah כהווייתו/־ה *adv* as it is (*pl m/ f* **-am/-an**).

ka-henah ve-kha-henah *(kh=k)* כהנה וכהנה many times as many/much.

ka-hogen כהוגן properly; suitably.

kaka'o קקאו *nm* cocoa.

kakee קאקי *[slang] nm* excrement.

('as|ah/-tah/-eetee) kakee עשה קאקי *(vulgar colloq. unless baby-talk) v* moved one's bowels; (*pres* **'oseh etc**: *fut* **ya'aseh** *etc*).

◇ **kakh** ("Kakh") כך extremist nationalist-religious organization founded in Israel by the U.S. Jewish Defense League and modelled after it. Advocates annexation of all "territories" that had been part of former Palestine and a resettlement of all its Arab residents in neighboring Arab countries.

kakh כך so; thus.

('ad kedey) kakh עד כדי כך to such extent.

(akhar) kakh אחר כך *adv* afterwards.

('al) kakh על כך *conj* for that; therefore.

('al yedey) kakh על ידי כך *conj* thereby.

(ben) kakh oo-ven kakh *(v=b)* בין כך ובין כך one way or another; anyhow.

(kol) kakh כל כך *adv* **1.** so much; **2.** so much so;

(mah be) kakh? (*npr* **be-khakh** *(kh=k)*) מה בכך? what of it?

(mee) kakh מכך thereof; from this; from that.

(shel mah be) kakh (*npr* **be-khakh**; *kh=k*) של מה בכך *adj* trifle; of no importance.

(yesh raglayeem le) kakh יש רגליים לכך there are grounds for believing.

kakh!/kekhee! קח *v imp sing m/f* take!

kakhah ככה so; thus.

kakhah-kakhah ככה־ככה *[slang]* so-so.

kakhash כחש *nm* lie; deceit.

kakhash/-ah/-tee כחש *v* became lean; slimmed; (*pres* **kokhesh**; *fut* **yeek'khash**).

kakhol/kekhoolah כחול *adj* blue.

('ovdey ha-tsavaron ha) kakhol עובדי הצווארון הכחול *nm pl* blue-collar workers.

kakhol/kekhoolah keheh/kehah כחול־כהה *adj* dark-blue.

kakhoosh/kekhooshah כחוש *adj* lean; thin.

kaktoos/-eem קקטוס *nm* cactus; (*pl+of:* **-ey**).

kal/-ah קל *adj* light; easy.

kal/-at da'at קל דעת *adj* light-headed; rash; (*pl:* **-ey/-ot da'at**).

kal/-at 'erekh קל־ערך *adj* of little value; (*pl:* **-ey/-ot** *etc*).

kal/-at tefeesah קל תפיסה *adj* grasping; of quick perception; (*pl:* **-ey/-ot** *etc*).

kal va-khomer קל וחומר inference from minor to major; induction.

(meen ha) kal el ha-kaved מן הקל אל הכבד from the easy to the difficult; step by step.

(neshek) kal נשק קל *nm* small arms; light weapons.

kal|a/-'ah/-atee כלא *v* imprisoned; locked up; (*pres* **kole**; *fut* **yeekhla** *(kh=k)*).

kal|ah/-ot כלה *nf* **1.** bride; **2.** daughter-in-law; **3.** guest (female) of honor; (*+of:* **-at**).

(khatan ve) kalah (*npr* **khalah**) חתן וכלה *nm pl* the wedding couple; bridegroom and bride.

kal|ah/-tah/-eetee כלה *v* **1.** ran out; finished; **2.** perished; (*pres* **kaleh**; *fut* **yeekhleh** *(kh=k)*).

kal|ah/-tah/-eetee קלה *v* roasted; toasted; (*pres* **koleh**; *fut* **yeekleh**).

(atleteekah) kalah אתלטיקה קלה *nf* light athletics.

(sha'ah) kalah שעה קלה *nf* a short while.

(takhmoshet) kalah תחמושת קלה *nf* light armament.

(arookh|ah/-ot) kal|ah/-ot ארוחה קלה *nf* light meal; snack.

kal|a'/-a'eem קלע *nm* marksman; (*pl+of:* **-a'ey**).

kal|a'/-'ah/-a'tee קלע *v* **1.** shot; hit; **2.** plaited; (*pres* **kole'a'**; *fut* **yeekla'**).

kala' (*etc*) bool קלע בול *v* hit the bull's eye.

kala' (*etc*) la-matarah קלע למטרה *v* hit the target.

kal|akh/-khah/-akhtee קלח *v* flowed; (*pres* **kole'akh**; *fut* **yeeklakh**).

kalakh|at/-ot קלחת *nf* **1.** kettle; **2.** uproar.

kal|al/-elah/-altee כלל *v* included; (*pres* **kolel**; *fut* **yeekhlol** *(kh=k)*).

kalanee|t/-yot כלנית *nf* anemone.

□ **Kalansawa** (Kalansawa) קלנסווה *nm* large Arab village in Sharon, 5 km SW of **Toolkarem** Pop. 10,100.

kal|at/-tah/-atetee קלט *v* took in; absorbed; (*pres* **kolet**; *fut* **yeeklot**).

kal|at/-ot ha-'erev כלת הערב *nm* the evening's (female) guest of honor.

kal|at/-ot ha-khageegah כלת החגיגה *nf* the celebration's (female) guest of honor.

kal|at/-ot ha-meseebah כלת המסיבה *nf* the party's (female) guest of honor.

kal|at/-ot ha-pras כלת הפרס *nf* laureate; prize-winner (female).

kalbah/klavot כלבה *nf* bitch; (*+of:* **kal|bat/-vot**).

kalban (*npr* **kalvan**)**/-eem** כלבן *nm* dog-trainer; dog-keeper; (*pl+of:* **-ey**).

kalbey geeshoosh כלבי גישוש *nm pl* bloodhounds (*sing:* **kelev-geeshoosh**).

kaldan/-eet קלדן *nmf* computer operator; wordprocessing typist (*+of:* **-ey**).

kalee'a/klee'eem קליע *nm* bullet; projectile; (*pl+of:* **kelee'ey**).

kaleed/kleed|eem קליד *nm* key/-s (typewriter *etc*); (*pl+of:* **-ey**).

kaleef/kleefah קליף *adj* peelable; easy peeled.

kaleel כליל *adv* completely; entirely.

kaleel/kleelah קליל *adj* light; very light.

(mashka'ot) kaleem משקאות קלים *nm pl* soft drinks.

kal|etet/-atot קלטת *nf* cassette (audio, video *etc*).

kal|etet/-atot veede'o קלטת וידיאו *nf* video-cassette.

kalevet כלבת *nf* rabies; hydrophobia (Medic.).

(be) kaley kaloot בקלי קלות *adv* as easy as can be.

kalfan/-eet קלפן *nmf* **1.** card gambler; card shark; **2.** card addict; (*pl:* **-eem**; *+of:* **-ey**).

kal|fee (*npr* **-pee**)**/-peeyot** קלפי *nf* ballot box; poll.

(hatsba|'ah/-'ot be) kalfee הצבעה בקלפי *nf* balloting.

kalgas/-eem קלגס *nm* soldier; warrior (of an oppressive force); (*pl+of:* **ey**).

kalkal/-eem כלכל *nm* steward (on ship or plane); (*pl+of:* **-ey**).

kalkal|ah/-ot כלכלה *nf* **1.** economics; **2.** upkeep; nourishment; (*+of:* **-at**).

kalkalah קלקלה *nf* corruption; failure; disgrace.

(be) kalkalat|o/-ah/-khah/-ekh *etc* בקלקלתו/ ־ה/־ך *adv* in his/her/your (*m/f*) *etc* disgrace.

kalkelan/-eet כלכלן *nmf* economist; (*pl+of:* **-ey**).

kalkalee/-t כלכלי *adj* economic.

□ **Kalkeelyah** (Qalqilya) קלקיליה *nf* Arab town right across the so-called "Green Line" (the boundary between Israel and Jordan before 1967). 3 km E. of **Kefar Saba**. Pop. approx. 29,000.

□ **Kalmaneeyah** (Qalmaniyya) קלמניה *nm* regional center and educational institution in Sharon, 3 km N. of **Kefar Saba**.

kalmar/-eem קלמר *nm* school-box; pen-case; (*pl+of:* **-ey**).

kalon קלון *nm shame;* (*+of:* **klon|o/-ah shel** *m/f*).

('amood ha) kalon עמוד הקלון *nm* pillory.

(hem|eet/-eetah/-atetee) kalon המיט קלון *v* brought disgrace; (*pres* **memeet** *etc; fut* **yameet** *etc*).

kaloo/keloo'ah כלוא *adj* jailed; locked-up.

kaloo/keloo|eem כלוא *nm* inmate (of jail) (*pl+of:* **-ey**).

kaloo'a/keloo'|ah קלוע *adj* plaited; woven.

kaloof/keloofah קלוף *adj* peeled.

kalool/keloolah כלול *adj* included; comprised.

kaloosh/kelooshah קלוש *adj* thin; flimsy.

kaloot קלות *nf* easiness.

kaloot-da'at קלות דעת *nf* frivolity.

kaloot rosh קלות ראש *nf* levity; carelessness.

(be) kaloot בקלות *adv* easily.

(be-yeter) kaloot ביתר קלות *adv* with greater ease.

kaloot/klootah קלוט *adj* taken from; absorbed.

kaloot/klootah meen ha-aveer קלוט מן האוויר *adj* **1.** baseless; unfounded; **2.** (*lit.*) taken from the air.

kalooy/kelooyah קלוי *adj* toasted.

kaloree|yah/-yot קלוריה *nf* calory; (*+of:* **-yat**).

□ **Kalyah** קליה *nm* kibbutz (est. 1974) near the NW coast of the Dead Sea.Pop. 245.

kam/-ah/-tee קם *v* got up; stood up; rose; (*pres* **kam;** *fut* **yakoom**).

kam (*etc*) **lee-tekheeyah** קם לתחייה *v* was resurrected; came back to life.

kamah כמה *num* **1.** how many? how much? **2.** some; a few.

kamah ve-khamah (*kh=k*) כמה וכמה *num* several.

('ad) kamah she- עד כמה ש־ as far as.

('al akhat) kamah ve-khamah (*kh=k*) על אחת כמה וכמה all the more so .

(bat/benot) kamah בת כמה *query* how old is/ are? (addressing female).

(be) kamah (*npr* **be-khamah**) בכמה *query* for how much? .

(ben/beney) kamah בן כמה *query* how old is/ are? (addressing male).

(kol) kamah כל כמה despite; however; in as much as; every few.

(le) kamah (*npr* **le-khamah**) לכמה **1.** for how long? **2.** for a few;(kh=*k*).

(meedey) kamah מדי כמה *adv* **1.** *query*; how often? **2.** every few.

(pee) kamah פי כמה several times over.

(zeh) kamah khodasheem זה כמה חודשים for the last few months; several months already.

(zeh) kamah shaneem זה כמה שנים for the last few years; several years already.

(zeh) kamah shevoo'ot זה כמה שבועות for the last few weeks; several weeks already.

(zeh) kamah yameem זה כמה ימים for the last few days; several days already.

kam|ah/-'hah/-ahtee כמה *v* longed; (*pres* **kameha;** *fut* **yeekhmah**).

kamal/-lah/-altee קמל *v* withered; (*pres* **komel;** *fut* **yeekmol**).

kamats קמץ *nm* sublinear mark (ָ) serving in dotted Hebrew as vowel *a* (pronounced as in *father*) and sometimes as vowel *o* (pronounced as in *morning*).

(khataf) kamats חטף קמץ *nm* sublinear mark (ֳ) serving in dotted Hebrew as vowel *o* (pronounced as in *morning*).

kame'a'/keme'eem קמע *nf* amulet (*+of:* **keme|'a/-'ey**).

kame'ah/kemehah כמה *adj* eager; yearning.

kameree/-t קמרי *adj* chamber-.

kamo|ha/-hoo כמוה/־ו like her/him.

(she-'en) kamo|hoo/-ha שאין כמוהו/־ה *m/f* there being no one like him/her.

kamo|kha/-kh/-khem/-khen כמוך/־כם/־כן like you (*sing m/f, pl m/f*).

kamo|nee כמוני like myself.

kamo|nee/-kha כמוני־כמוך me too; the same as you.

kamoor/kemoorah קמור *adj* arched; convex.

kamoos/kemoosah כמוס *adj* secret; hidden.

(sod/-ot) kamoos/kemooseem סוד כמוס *nm* highly-guarded secret.

kamoo|t/-yot כמות *nf* quantity.

kamootee/-t כמותי *adj* quantitative.

kamoots/kemootsah קמוץ *adj* clenched.

(be-'egrof/-eem) kamoots/kemootseem באגרוף קמוץ *adv* with clenched fists.

ka-moovan (or **ke-moovan**) כמובן *adv* understandably; obviously.

kamtsan/-eet קמצן *nmf & adj* miser; stingy; (*pl:* **-eem/-eeyot**).

kamtsanoot קמצנות *nf* miserliness; stinginess.

kamtsoots/-eem קמצוץ *nm* pinch; small quantity.

kan כאן *adv* here; now.

kan ve-'akhshav כאן ועכשיו *adv* here and now.

('ad) kan עד כאן *adv* hitherto; so much; thus far.

(le) kan (*npr* **le-khan**) לכאן *adv* hereto;

(le) kan oo le-khan *(kh=k)* לכאן ולכאן *adv* in both ways; here and there.

(mee) kan מכאן *adv* from here; from this.

(mee) kan oo mee-kan מכאן ומכאן *adv* on both sides; from here and from there.

(mee) kan she- מכאן ש־ *adv* hence; from this we infer.

kan/-eem כן *nm* stand; base; **(***pl+of:* **-ey)**.

kan/-ey sheeloo'akh כן שילוח *nm* launching pad.

kan ק"נ *num* 150 (100+50) in Hebrew numerological system.

kan te'ameem ק"נ טעמים *nm pl* 150 reasons; (*figurat.*) too many pretexts.

kan|ah/-tah/-eetee קנה *v* bought; purchased; **(***pres* **koneh;** *fut* **yeekneh)**.

kanah (*etc***) et lev/leebot** קנה את לב *v* won the heart/-s.

kanah (*etc***) lo/lah/lee (***etc***) shem** קנה לו/לה/לי שם *v* **1.** acquired a reputation; **2.** gained him/her/myself a name.

kanah (*etc***) lo/lah/lee (***etc***) sheveetah** קנה לו שביתה *v* settled permanently; took a stand.

kanaf/kenafayeem כנף *nf* wing; **(***+of:* **kenaf/ kanfey)**.

(pesant|er/-rey) kanaf פסנתר כנף *nm* grand-piano; "grand".

kana'oot קנאות *nf* zeal; fanaticism.

kanar/-eem כנר *nm* violonist; **(***pl+of:* **-ey)**.

kanaree|t/-yot כנרית *nf* **1.** canary **2.** violinist (female).

kan|as/-sah/-astee קנס *v* fined; **(***pres* **kones;** *fut* **yeeknos)**.

kan|ay/-a'eet (*also:* **kan|a'ee)** קנאי *nmf* fanatic; zealot; **(***pl+of:* **-'ey)**.

ka-neer'eh (*also:* **ke-neer'eh)** כנראה *adv* apparently; as it seems.

kan|eh/-eem קנה *nm* **1.** barrel (of gun) **2.** stalk (of a plant); **(***+of:* **ken|eh/-ey)**.

kaneh ratsoots קנה רצוץ *nm* **1.** broken reed; **2.** (*figurat.*) not to be relied upon.

('ol|eh/-ah be) kaneh ekhad עולה בקנה אחד *v pres* suits; falls in line with; **(***pst* **'alah** *etc; fut* **ya'aleh** *etc***)**.

kankan/-eem קנקן *nm* jar; flask; **(***pl+of:* **-ey)**.

(ta|hah/-hatah/-heetee 'al) kankan|o/-ah תהה/תהתה על קנקנו/־ה *v* tried to make out; **(***pst* **toheh** (*etc*); *fut* **yeet'heh** *etc***)**.

(hesh|eev/-eevah/-avtee 'al) kan|o/-ah השיב/ה על כנו/ה *v* restored; reinstituted; **(***pres* **mesheev** *etc; fut* **yasheev)**.

kanooy/kenooyah קנוי *adj* bought; purchased; acquired.

□ **Kanot** כנות *nm* agricultural school for girls (est. 1952), 1 km S. of Gedera Junction **(Tsomet Gederah)**. Pop. (students & staff) 315.

kantranee/-t קנטרני *adj* quarrelsome.

kantranoot קנטרנות *nf* quarrelsomeness.

kanyan/-eet קניין *nmf* acquisitioner; buyer; **(***pl:* **-eem/-eeyot;** *+of:* **-ey)**.

kanyon/-eem (*cpr* **kanyon)** קניון *nm* mall; shopping center.

ka'oor/ke'oorah קעור *adj* concave.

ka'oos/ke'oosah כעוס *adj* angry; sore.

ka'oov/ke'oovah כאוב *adj* painful.

(be'a|yah/-yot) ke'oov|ah/-ot בעיה כאובה *nf* sore point.

kapar|ah/-ot כפרה *nf* absolution; atonement; **(***+of:* **-at)**.

kapayeem כפיים *nf pl* hands; palms; **(***sing:* **kaf)**.

('amal) kapayeem עמל כפיים *nm* manual labor.

('avod|at/-ot) kapayeem עבודת כפיים *nm* handwork; manual labor.

(makh|a/-'ah/-atee) kapayeem מחא כפיים *v* applauded; clapped hands; **(***pres* **mokhe** *etc; fut* **yeemkha** *etc***)**.

(neekyon) kapayeem נקיון כפיים *nf* incorruptibility.

(nekee/-yat) kapayeem נקי כפיים *nm* **1.** honest person; **2.** *adj* incorruptible; clean-handed.

(yegee'a') kapayeem יגיע כפיים *nm* toil of one's hands; handiwork.

kapdan (*npr* **kafdan)/-eet** קפדן *adj & nmf* strict (severe) person.

kapdanoot (*npr* **kafdanoot)** קפדנות *nf* strictness; severity.

(be) kapdanoot בקפדנות *adv* strictly; minutely.

kapee|t/-yot כפית *nf* teaspoon.

kapeetan/-eem קפיטן *nm* captain (of vessel); skipper.

kapreez|ah/-ot קפריזה *nf* caprice; whim; **(***+of:* **-at)**.

kapreezee/-t קפריזי *adj* capricious.

kaptsoneem קפצונים *nm pl [colloq.]* blanks; empty cartridges (for toy guns).

kar/-eem כר *nm* **1.** pillow; **2.** meadow; **(***pl+of:* **-ey)**.

kar/-ah קר *adj* cold; frigid.

kar/-at mezeg קר מזג *adj* cold-tempered.

kar/-at roo'akh קר־רוח *adj* composed; calm.

(be-dam) kar בדם קר *adv* in cold blood.

kar|a/-'ah/-atee קרא *v* **1.** read; recited; **2.** called; called upon; **(***pres* **kore;** *fut* **yeekra)**.

kar|ah/-tah קרה *v* happened; occurred; **(***pres* **koreh;** *fut* **yeekreh)**.

kar|ah/-tah/-eetee כרה *v* **1.** dug (hole); **2.** mined (ore); **(***pres* **koreh;** *fut* **yeekhreh** *(kh=k)***)**.

karah (*etc***) kever** כרה קבר *v* dug a grave.

karah (*etc***) ozen** כרה אוזן *v* lent an ear.

karah קרה *nf* frost; extreme cold.

kara (*etc***) dror** קרא דרור *v* set free; liberated.

kara (*etc***) heydad** קרא הידד *v* acclaimed.

kara (*etc***) teegar** קרא תיגר *v* complained bitterly against.

(sheteeyah) karah שתייה קרה *nf* cold drinks.

kara'/-'ah/-a'tee כרע *v* **1.** knelt; **2.** collapsed; **(***pres* **kore'a;** *fut* **yeekhra'** *(kh=k)***)**.

kara' (*etc***) berekh** כרע ברך *v* knelt on one's knees.

kar|a'/-'ah/-a'tee קרע *v* tore; (*pres* **kore'a**; *fut* **yeekra'**).

kara' (etc) lee-gezareem קרע לגזרים *v* tore to pieces.

◇ **kara'ee/-m** קראי *nm* member of the Karaite sect. See ◇ **kara'oot, below.**

ka-rageel כרגיל *adv* as usual; usually.

(she-lo) ka-rageel שלא כרגיל *adv* not as usual.

kar|akh/-khah/-akhtee כרך *v* **1.** bound (a book); **2.** combined; (*pres* **korekh**; *fut* **yeekrokh**).

karakh|at/-ot קרחת *nf* bald patch; bald spot.

(ba'al/-ey) karakh|at/-ot בעל קרחת *nm* bald person.

kar|am/-mah/-amtee קרם *v* crusted; covered with crust; (*pres* **korem**; *fut* **yeekrom**).

karam (etc) 'or ve-geedeem קרם עור וגידים *v* **1.** materialized; became a reality; **2.** (*lit.*) grew skin and tendons.

kar|an/-nah/-antee קרן *v* shone; radiated; (*pres* **koren**; *fut* **yeekran**).

◇ **kara'oot** קראות *nf* Karaism, Jewish sect which seceded from normative Rabbinic Judaism in the 10-th century by rejecting the Talmud. Since the establishment of the State of Israel, there has been a growing rapprochement and though the religious gap still exists, the Karaites are accepted as part of the Jewish State, forming an autonomous community.

ka-ra'ooy כראוי *adv* appropriately; properly.

kar|as/-sah/-astee קרס *v* knelt; collapsed; (*pres* **kores**; *fut* **yeekros**).

kar|at/-tah/-atee כרת *v* cut off; severed; (*pres* **koret**; *fut* **yeekhrot** *(kh=k)*).

karat (etc) breet/-ot כרת ברית *v* made a covenant; entered an alliance.

kar|ats/-tsah/-atstee קרץ *v* winked; (*pres* **korets**; *fut* **yeekrots**).

kar|av/-vah/-avtee קרב *v* approached; (*pres* **karev**; *fut* **yeekrav**).

karbolet/-ot כרבולת *nf* cock's comb; crest.

karboorator/-eem קרבורטור *[colloq.] nm* carburetor (the correct Hebrew term being: **me'ayed** מאייד).

kar|dom/-oomeem קרדום *nm* axe; (*pl+of:* -**oomey**).

kardom lakhpor bo קרדום לחפור בו *nm* an axe to grind; making a profession out of a hobby.

karee/kree'ah קריא *adj* readable; legible.

kareekatoo|rah/-ot קריקטורה *nf* cartoon; caricature.

kareekh/kreekh|eem כריך *nm* sandwich; (*+of:* -**ey**).

kareer/kreerah קריר *adj* chilly; cool.

kareesh/kreeshah קריש *adj* jellied; clotted.

kareesh/kreesh|eem כריש *nm* shark; (*pl+of:* -**ey**).

kareet/-yot כרית *nf* cushion; pillow; (*+of:* -**yat**).

kark|a'/-a'ot קרקע *nf* **1.** ground **2.** land.

(hakhsharat) kark|a'/-a'ot הכשרת קרקע *nf* preparing ground.

(heekh'sh|eer/-eerah/-artee et ha) karka' הכשיר את הקרקע *v* prepared the ground; (*pres* **makh'sheer** *etc*; *fut* **yakh'sheer** *etc*).

(komat) karka' קומת קרקע *nf* ground floor.

(peney ha) karka' פני הקרקע *nm pl* ground level; soil surface.

(tat-) karka'ee/-t תת־קרקעי *adj* subterranean; underground.

karka'ee|t/-yot קרקעית *nf* bottom.

karkhon/-eem קרחון *nm* glacier; iceberg; (*pl+of:* -**ey**).

□ **Karmee'el** (Karmi'el) כרמיאל *nf* urban settlement (est. 1964) in the Galilee, off Acre-Safed (**'Ako-Tsfat**) road. Pop. 24,200.

□ **Karmeeyah** (Karmiyya) כרמיה *nm* kibbutz in the S. part of the Coastal Plain, 7 km S. of Ashkelon. Pop. 287.

karn|af/-peem קרנף *nm* rhinoceros; (*pl+of:* -**pey**; *p=f*).

karnaval/-eem קרנבל *nm* carnival.

karnee/-t קרני *adj* hornlike; corneal.

karnee|t/-yot קרנית *nf* cornea.

□ **Karmel** כרמל *nm* Mount Carmel (**Har ha-Karmel**) Hills rising behind Haifa and stretching to the N. and to the S. parallel to the Mediterranean Coast.

□ **(Hadar ha) Karmel** see □ **Hadar ha-Karmel.**

□ **(Har ha)Karmel** see □ **Har ha-Karmel.**

□ **Karney Shomron** קרני שומרון *nm* settlement (est. 1977) in Samaria, on the new Cross Samaria (**Khotseh Shomron**) road, 15 km E. of **Kefar Saba**. Pop. 3,520.

karney rentgen קרני רנטגן *nf pl* X-rays.

karon/kronot קרון *nm* wagon; (*+of:* **kron**).

karoo'a'/kroo'ah קרוע *adj* torn.

karookh/krookhah כרוך *adj* **1.** bound; **2.** wrapped; **3.** involved.

karookh (etc) akhrey כרוך אחרי *adj* **1.** attached to; **2.** running after; attracted by.

karoosh/krooshah קרוש *adj* jellied; coagulated.

karov/krovah קרוב **1.** *adj* near; **2.** *nmf* relative (family).

karov (npr krov)/krovat meeshpakhah קרוב משפחה *nmf* family-relation; (*pl:* **krov|ey/-ot** *etc*).

karov-karov קרוב קרוב **1.** *adv* very near; **2.** *nm* close relative.

karov/krovah la-tsalakhat קרוב לצלחת *[slang] adj & adv* (*lit.:* near the plate) near to the high and mighty.

karov le-vaday קרוב לוודאי *adv* pretty sure.

karov/krovah rakhok/rekhokah קרוב רחוק *nmf* distant relative.

(be) karov בקרוב *adv* soon; shortly.

(ha) meezrakh (ha) karov המזרח הקרוב *nm* the Near East.

(mee) karov מקרוב *adv* recently; lately; from nearby.

karoz/-ot כרוז *nm* announcer; crier; herald.

karpad|ah/-ot קרפדה *nf* toad.

karpeeyon/-eem קרפיון *nm* carp (fish) (*pl+of:* -**ey**).

karsam/-eem כרסם *nm* cutter; milling cutter; (*pl+of:* **-ey**).
karsool (*npr* **karsol**)/**-ayeem** קרסול *nm* ankle; (*pl+of:* **-ey**).
◇ **(netoorey) karta** see ◇ **netoorey karta**.
(yakeerey) karta יקירי קרתא *nm pl* city notables; (*sing:* **yakeer** *etc*).
kartanee/-t קרתני *adj* parochial.
kartanoot קרתנות *nf* parochialism.
kartees/-eem כרטיס *nm* ticket; (*pl+of:* **-ey**).
kartees/-ey beekoor כרטיס ביקור *nm* visiting card.
kartees/-ey khanayah כרטיס חנייה *nm* parking voucher.
kartees/-ey kneesah כרטיס כניסה *nm* entry-ticket.
kartees/-ey neekoov כרטיס ניקוב *nm* punch-card.
karteesan/-eet כרטיסן *nmf* ticket-seller; conductor (*pl+of:* **-ey**).
karteesee|yah/-yot כרטיסייה *nf* multiple use ticket; (*+of:* **-yat**).
kartel/-eem קרטל *nm* cartel.
kart|eset/-asot כרטסת *nf* card index.
karton/-eem קרטון *nf* cardboard; (*pl+of:* **-ey**).
kartsee|t/-yot קרצית *nf* tick; (*+of:* **-yat**).
karyan/-eet קריין *nmf* announcer (radio, tv); (*pl:* **-eem/-eeyot**; *+of:* **-ey**).
karyanoot קריינות *nf* announcing; recitation.
karyer|ah/-ot קריירה *nf* career; (*+of:* **-at**).
karyereest/-eet קרייריסט *nmf* careerist; careerwoman.
kasakh כסאח *[slang]* cut down; disaster.
kas|am/-mah/-amtee קסם *v* attracted; captivated; (*pres* **kosem**; *fut* **yeeksom**).
□ **Kasb|ah/-ot** קסבה *nf* old market-place roofed by arches in an Arab town.
kasd|ah/-ot קסדה *nf* helmet; (*+of:* **-at**).
kas|efet/-afot כספת *nf* safe; safety-box.
kaset|ah/-ot קסטה *nf* cassette; (*+of:* **-at**).
kaset|at/-ot veede'o קסטת וידיאו *nf* video-cassette.
kash קש *nm* straw.
(alm|an/-enat) kash אלמן קש *nmf* straw widower/widow; (*pl:* **-eney/-enot kash**).
(eesh/anshey) kash איש קש *nm* straw man.
(kov|a'/-'ey) kash כובע קש *nm* straw hat.
kash|al/-lah/-altee כשל *v* failed; staggered; (*pres* **koshel**; *fut* **yeekashel**).
kash|ar/-eet קשר *nmf* signaller; liaison-officer; signalwoman.
kash|ar/-rah/-artee קשר *v* tied; connected; (*pres* **kosher**; *fut* **yeekshor**).
kashar (*etc*) **yekhaseem** קשר יחסים *v* established relation.
kasharoot קשרות *nf* signalling.
kashee'akh/kesheekhah קשיח *adj* hard; rigid.
kasheer/kesheerah כשיר *adj* fit; qualified; able-bodied.
kasheesh/kesheeshah קשיש *adj* elderly; aged; senior.
kasheesh (*etc*) **mee-** קשיש מ־ *adj* older than.
kashee|t/-yot קשית *nf* straw (for sipping drinks); (*[colloq.] pl* **kasheem**).
kasheh קשה *adv* hard; difficult.
kash|eh/-ah קשה *adj* hard; severe; difficult.
kasher/kesherah כשר *adj* proper; right; "Kosher".
kashoo'akh/keshookhah קשוח *adj* tough; hard.
kashoor/keshoorah קשור *adj* connected; tied.
kashoor (*etc*) **be-** קשור ב־ *adj* tied with; connected with.
ka-shoorah כשורה *adv* properly; in order.
(ha-kol) ka-shoorah הכול כשורה *adv* everything in order.
kashoov/-ah קשוב *adj* attentive.
kashot קשות *adv* harshly.
kashroot כשרות *nf* ritual fitness (of food); *[colloq.]* "Kashress" (Yiddish).
kashyoot קשיות *nf* hardness; severity.
kasoom/kesoomah קסום *adj* enchanted; bewitched.
kaspar/-eet כספר *nmf* teller (bank); (*pl+of:* **-ey**).
kaspee/-t כספי *adj* financial; pecuniary.
('er|avon/-vonot) kaspee/-yeem ערבון כספי *nm* financial guarantee.
(makhzor) kaspee מחזור כספי *nm* financial turn-over.
kaspeet כספית **1.** *nf* mercury; **2.** (*figurat.*) lively person.
kat קט *adj* tiny.
(rega') kat! רגע קט! just a second!
kat/keetot כת *nf* sect.
kat/katot קת *nf* handle; butt; haft.
kat/-ot rov|eh/-eem קת רובה *nf* rifle butt.
kat|a'/-'ah/-a'tee קטע *v* severed; interrupted; (*pres* **kote'a**; *fut* **yeekta'**).
kat|af/-fah/-aftee קטף *v* picked (fruit); (*pres* **kotef**; *fut* **yeektof**).
kat|al/-lah/-altee קטל *v* **1.** killed; **2.** (*figurat.*) strongly dissapproved.
katalog/-eem קטלוג *nm* catalog.
katan/ketanah קטן *adj* small.
(ha-masakh ha) katan המסך הקטן *nm* the small (i.e. television) screen.
◇ **(taleet) katan** see ◇ **taleet katan**.
katancheek קטנצ׳יק *[slang]* **1.** *adj m* small; **2.** *nm* little guy.
katar/-eem קטר *nm* railroad engine; train engine; (*pl+of:* **-ey**).
katastro|fah/-ot קטסטרופה *nf* catastrophe.
kat|av/-vah/-avtee כתב *v* wrote; (*pres* **kotev**; *fut* **yeekhtov** (*kh=k*)).
kat|av/-evet כתב *nmf* reporter; correspondent.
katav|ah/-ot כתבה *nf* news-report; news-dispatch.
katedr|ah/-ot קתדרה *nf* chair (university).
kateef קטיף *nm* orange-picking season; fruit-picking (*+of:* **keteef**).
□ **Kateef** (Qatif) קטיף *nm* village (est. 1977) in Gaza strip, 5 km W. of **Deer el Balakh**.

kateen/keteenah קטין **1.** *nmf* minor; **2.** *adj* under-age.
katef/ketefayeem כתף *nf* shoulder; (*pl+of:* **keetfey**).
(heet|ah/-etah/-etee) katef הטה כתף *v* shouldered; lent a hand; (*pres* **mateh** *etc; fut* **yateh** *etc*).
kategor/-eem קטיגור *nm* prosecutor; (*pl+of:* **-ey**).
kategoree/-t קטיגורי *adj* categorical.
kategor|yah/-yot קטיגוריה *nf* prosecution; (*+of:* **-yat**).
katen/ketenah קטן *v pres* grow(s) smaller; (*pst* **katan**; *fut* **yeektan**).
kat|evot/-avot כתבת *nf* woman-reporter; female correspondent.
katlanee/-t קטלני *adj* deadly; fatal; murderous.
(te'oon|ah/-ot) katlanee|t/-yot תאונה קטלנית *nf* fatal accident.
katno|'a/-'eem קטנוע *nm* motor-scooter; (*pl+of:* **-'ey**).
katnoonee/-t קטנוני *adj* petty; trivial.
katnooneeyoot קטנוניות *nf* pettiness; meanness.
katolee/-t קתולי *adj* Catholic.
katom/ketoomah כתום *adj* orange (color).
katontee me-haveen קטונתי מהבין I am at loss to understand.
katoo'a'/ketoo'ah קטוע *adj* truncated; cut; lopped off.
katoov/ketoovah כתוב *adj* written.
katoov/ketooveem כתוב *nm* Bible-passage.
katvan/-eem כתבן *nm* typist; scribe.
katvanee|t/-yot כתבנית *nf* typist (female).
katvanoot כתבנות *nf* typing.
kazeeno קזינו *nm* casino.
kats/-ah/-tee קץ *v* abhorred; loathed; (*pres* **kats**; *fut* **yakoots**).
kats|af/-fah/-aftee קצף *v* raged; was furious; (*pres* **kotsef**; *fut* **yeektsof**).
katsar/ketsarah (*also:* **katser**) קצר *adj* short; (*+of:* **ketsar/keetsrat**; *pl+of:* **keetsr|ey/-ot**).
kats|ar/-rah/-artee קצר *v* reaped; (*pres* **kotser**; *fut* **yeektsor**).
(tevakh/-eem) katsar/ketsareem טווח קצר *nm* short range.
kats|ats/-etsah/-atstee קצץ *v* chopped; cut off; (*pres* **kotsets**; *fut* **yekatsets**).
katsav/-eem קצב *nm* butcher.
kats|av/-vah/-avtee קצב *v* allotted; assigned; rationed; (*pres* **kotsev**; *fut* **yeektsov**).
katseh/ketsavot קצה *nm* end; edge; (*+of:* **ketseh/katsvey**).
(meen ha) katseh el ha-katseh מן הקצה אל הקצה from end to end.
katseen/ketseenah קצין *nmf* officer; (*+of:* **ketseen/-at**; *pl:* **-eem/-ot**; *pl+of:* **-ey**).
katseer קציר *nm* harvest; harvest season; (*+of:* **ketseer**).
katsefet קצפת *nf* whipped cream.
katseret קצרת *nf* asthma (Medic.).
katsoots/ketsootsah קצוץ *adj* chopped; cut-off.
katsoov/ketsoovah קצוב *adj* **1.** fixed; **2.** limited; rationed.
katsrah rookh|o/-ah קצרה רוחו/־ה *v* grew impatient.
katsrah yado/-ah קצרה ידו/־ה *v* was in no position.
katsran/-eem קצרן *nm* stenographer (male).
katsranee|t/-yot קצרנית *nf* stenographer (female).
katsranoot קצרנות *nf* shorthand; stenography.
□ **Katsreen** (Qatsrin) קצרין *nf* town (est. 1977) in Golan Heights, 8 km SE of **Benot Ya'akov** Jordan Bridge. Pop. 3,710.
kav/-eem קו *nm* line; (*pl+of:* **-ey**).
kav/-eem anakhee/-yeem קו אנכי *nm* vertical line.
□ **Kav ha-Mashveh** קו המשווה *nm* equator.
kav ha-rakee'a קו הרקיע *nm* skyline.
kav/-eem mafreed/-eem קו מפריד *nm* (—) dash; mark used in punctuation to indicate a break in the structure of a sentence or an appositive.
kav/-eem mekhab|er/-reem קו מחבר *nm* (-) hyphen; mark used in punctuation between parts of a compound word or between syllables of a divided word.
kav natooy קו נטוי *nm* slash line (/).
kav/-ey orekh קו אורך *nm* meridian; longitude.
kav/-ey rokhav קו רוחב *nm* parallel; latitude.
(be) kav ha-bree'oot בקו הבריאות *adv* in good health.
(mat|akh/-khah/-akhtee) kav מתח קו *v* drew a line; (*pres* **mote'akh kav**; *fut* **yeemtakh kav**).
kav|ah/-tah/-eetee כבה *v* went out; was extinguished; (*pres* **koveh**; *fut* **yeekhbeh** *(kh=k; b=v)*.
kav|a'/-'ah/-a'tee קבע *v* fixed; set up; established (*pres* **kove'a'**; *fut* **yeekba'** *(b=v)*).
kava' (*etc*) **masmerot** קבע מסמרות *v* laid down rules; established as indisputable fact.
kava' (*etc*) **seedoor/-eem** קבע סידור *v* made arrangements .
kav|al/-lah/-altee כבל *v* chained; tied down; (*pres* **kovel**; *fut* **yeekhbol** *(kh=k; b=v)*.
kav|al/-lah/-altee קבל *v* complained; (*pres* **kovel**; *fut* **yeekbol**).
kaval (*npr* **koval**) קבל *adv* in front of.
kaval (*npr* **koval**) **'am** קבל עם *adv* publicly; openly.
kavan|ah/-ot כוונה *nf* intention; intent; (*+of:* **-at**).
(be) kavanah (*npr* **be-khavanah**) **tekheelah** בכוונה תחילה *adv* with premeditation.
kavan|at/-ot zadon כוונת זדון *nf* malicious intent.
kav|ar/-rah/-artee קבר *v* buried; (*pres* **kover**; *fut* **yeekbor** *(b=v)*).
kav|ash/-shah/-ashtee כבש *v* conquered; (*pres* **kovesh**; *fut* **yeekhbosh** *(kh=k; b=v)*.
kaved/keved|eem כבד *nm* liver; (*pl+of:* **-ey**).
kaved katsoots כבד קצוץ *nm* chopped liver.

kaved/kevedah כבד *adj* heavy.
(meen ha-kal el ha) kaved מן הקל אל הכבד from what's easy to what's difficult.
kavee/-t קווי *adj* linear; lined.
kaveel/keveelah קביל *adj* acceptable.
(be) kaveem kelaleeyeem בקווים כלליים *adv* in general terms.
kaveem makbeeleem קווים מקבילים *nm pl* parallel lines.
kavees/keveesah כביס *adj* washable; launderable.
kavenet כוונת *nf* **1.** gunsight; **2.** viewfinder; **3.** guide (machine).
('al ha) kavenet על הכוונת *adv* being a target (for constant observation; for persecution).
kaveret/-arot כוורת *nf* beehive.
kavkab|eem קבקבים *nm pl* sabots; wooden shoes; (*pl+of:* **-ey**).
kavod כבוד *nm* honor; respect; (*+of:* **kevod**).
(khal|ak/-kah/-aktee) kavod חלק כבוד *v* paid one's respects; (*pres* **kholek** *etc; fut* **yakhlok** *etc*).
(pekheetoot) kavod פחיתות כבוד *nf* beneath one's dignity.
(yeer'at) kavod יראת כבוד *nf* awe; reverence.
(kol ha) kavod כל הכבוד all respect due; bravo! I take my hat off.
kavoo'a/kevoo'ah קבוע *adj* permanent; steady.
◇ **('oved/-et) kavoo'a/kevoo'ah** see ◇ **'oved/-et kavoo'a/kevoo'ah**.
kavool/kevoolah כבול *adj* **1.** chained; handcuffed; **2.** (*figurat.*) bound.
kavoor/kevoorah קבור *adj* buried.
(kan) kavoor ha-kelev כאן קבור הכלב **1.** so that's what it is all about! **2.** (*lit.*) this is where the dog is buried.
kavoosh/kevooshah כבוש *adj* occupied; conquered; pickled; canned.
kavooy/kevooyah כבוי *adj* extinct; extinguished.
kavran/-eet כוורן *nmf* apiculturist; beekeeper; (*pl:* **-eem/-eeyot**; *+of:* **-ey**).
kavran/-eem קברן *nm* gravedigger; (*pl+of:* **-ey**).
ka-yadoo'a (*also:* **ke-yadoo'a**) כידוע as is well-known; as one knows.
kayam/kayemet קיים *adj* existing.
kayam/kayemet קיים *v pres* exist(s); (*pst* **hay|ah kayam**; *fut* **yeehyeh kayam**).
ka-ya'oot כיאות *adv* properly; as befits; as should be.
kayas/-eem כייס pickpocket; (*pl+of:* **-ey**).
kayasoot כייסות *nf* pickpocketing.
kayeet קיט *nm* vacationing; summer vacation.
kayeets קיץ *nm* summer.
(khoofsh|at/-ot) kayeets חופשת קיץ *nf* summer vacation.
(neveh) kayeets נווה קיץ *nm* summer home; summer residence.
('on|at/-ot) kayeets עונת קיץ *nf* summer season.
(pagr|at/-ot) kayeets פגרת קיץ *nf* school vacation; summer vacation.

◇ **(Keren) Kayemet le-Yeesra'el** see ◇ **keren kayemet le-yeesra'el**.
kayom כיום *adv* at present; nowadays.
kaytan/-eem קייטן *nm* vacationer; (*pl+of:* **-ey**).
kaytan|ah/-ot קייטנה *nf* summer camp; summer resort; (*+of:* **-at**).
kazav/kezaveem כזב *nm* lie; falsehood; (*pl+of:* **keezvey**).
(sheker ve) kazav (*npr* **ve-khazav**)! שקר וכזב! *intj* it is a damn lie !
kaz|eh/-oo כזה *adj* such; such as this one.
(she) kaz|eh/-oo שכזה *adj (m)* like this one.
kazot כזאת *adj (f)* of such a kind; such.
(she) kazot שכזאת *adj (f)* like this one.
kazotee כזאתי *[colloq.] adj (f)* like this one; such.
ke'ar|ah/-ot קערה *nf* bowl; dish; basin; (*+of:* **ka'ar|at/-ot**).
kedam- קדם־ *(prefix)* pre-.
kedam-heestoree/-t קדם־היסטורי *adj* prehistoric.
kedày כדאי it is worthwhile.
keday/kada'eet כדאי *adj* worthwhile; worthy.
keday le- כדאי ל־ it's worth one's while.
keday she- כדאי ש־ it is worthwhile that.
(lo) keday לא כדאי *adv* it isn't worthwhile; isn't worth it.
kedayneek/-eet כדאיניק *nmf [slang]* opportunist; who's after one's own benefit.
kedeekh|ah/-ot קדיחה *nf* drilling; (*+of:* **-at**).
ke-deel'halan כדלהלן as follows.
ke-deelkaman כדלקמן as follows.
kedeem|ah/-ot קדימה *nf* preference; precedence; priority; (*+of:* **-at**).
(deen) kedeemah דין קדימה *nm* priority; precedence.
(demey) kedeemah דמי קדימה *nm pl* advance; payment; deposit.
(zekhoo|t/-yot) kedeemah זכות קדימה *nf* priority right.
keder|ah/-ot קדירה *nf* pot; (*+of:* **-at**).
kedey כדי **1.** in order to; **2.** enough to; **3.** as much as.
('ad) kedey kakh עד כדי כך to such extent, that; so much so, that.
(mee) kedey מכדי than; than required.
(tokh) kedey kakh תוך כדי כך *adv* meanwhile.
□ **Kedoomeem** (Qedumim) קדומים *nm* communal settlement in Samaria hills (est. 1977), 10 km W. of Nablus **(Sh'khem)**. Originally called **Kadoom**. Pop. 1,680.
kee כי **1.** because; **2.** if; when; that (*poetic.*).
kee 'al ken כי על כן for; since.
kee az כי אז then.
kee eem כי אם but only; except that.
('ad) kee עד כי until; until that.
(af) kee אף כי even though.
(eem) kee אם כי although.
(efes) kee אפס כי except that; but.
keeb|ah/-tah/-eetee כיבה *v* put out; extinguished; (*pres* **mekhabeh**; *fut* **yekhabeh**).

keeb|ed/-dah/-adetee כיבד *v* **1.** respected; honored; **2.** treated (guest); (*pres* **mekhabed** *(kh=k)*; *fut* **yekhabed**).

keeb|el/-lah/-altee קיבל *v* received; got; accepted; (*pres* **mekabel**; *fut* **yekabel**).

keebel (*etc*) **'al 'atsm|o/-ah** קיבל על עצמו *v* took upon him/her -self; accepted; undertook.

keebel (*etc*) **'al|av/-eha** קיבל עליו *v* took on; undertook.

keebel (*etc*) **et ha-deen** קיבל את הדין *v* accepted the judgment.

keebel (*etc*) **hakhlatah** קיבל החלטה *v* took decision; passed/adopted resolution.

keebel (*etc*) **peney** קיבל פני *v* received (someone); welcomed.

keebel (*etc*) **reshoot** קיבל רשות *v* obtained permission.

keebel (*etc*) **roshem** קיבל רושם *v* got the impression.

keebel (*etc*) **tokef** קיבל תוקף *v* came into force.

keeb|es/-sah/-astee כיבס *v* laundered; cleansed; washed; (*pres* **mekhabes**; *fut* **yekhabes** *(kh=k)*).

keeb|ets/-tsah/-atstee קיבץ *v* assembled; collected; (*pres* **mekabets**; *fut* **yekabets**).

keebets (*etc*) **nedavot** קיבץ נדבות *v* engaged in mendicancy.

keebolet קיבולת *nf* capacity; displacement.

keebood/-eem כיבוד *nm* honor; honoring; respect; (*pl+of:* **-ey**).

keebood כיבוד *nm* **1.** refreshments; treat; (for guests); **2.** sweeping (the house, floor).

keebool קיבול *nm* capacity; displacement.

(kel|ee/-ey) keebool כלי קיבול *nm* receptacle; container.

keeboos כיבוס *nm* laundering; washing.

keeboosh/-eem כיבוש *nm* conquest; (*pl+of:* **-ey**).

keeboosh ha-shemamah כיבוש השממה *nm* conquest of the desert.

(deevrey) keeboosheen דברי כיבושין *nm pl* reproof; reprimand; remonstrance.

keeboots/-eem קיבוץ *nm* gathering; (*pl+of:* **-ey**).

◇ **keeboots/-eem** קיבוץ *nm* Israeli form of agricultural (and nowadays mostly also industrial) collective farm or settlement. It is characterized by collective ownership, feeding, care and responsibility; equality in the distribution of jobs, production and a say in management; lack (or near lack) of personal property and income.

◇ **keeboots galooyot** קיבוץ גלויות *nm* Ingathering of the Exiles (i.e. of Jews from all over the world) as settlers in Israel.

◇ **(ha)keeboots ha-artsee** (Hakibbutz Ha'artzi) הקיבוץ הארצי *nm* national association of 86 kibbutzim affiliated to "Hashomer Hatzair" (◇ **ha-shomer ha-tsa'eer**) movement. As a rule, the latter ones are known to observe a more orthodox adherence to socialist and collectivist principles. Politically, most of its members support ◇ **MAPAM**.

◇ **(ha)keeboots ha-datee** הקיבוץ הדתי *nm* union of 17 religious kibbutzim affiliated with the labor section of the religious workers trade-union ◇ **ha-po'el ha-meezrakhee**.

◇ **(ha)keeboots (ha)me'ookhad** הקיבוץ - המאוחדה*nm* "the United Kibbutz" - umbrella organization that in the years 1920-1950 encompassed all kibbutzim affiliated with the **Akhdoot ha-'Avodah** אחדות העבודה party. With the latter's merger with the MAPAY party to form the Labor Party, the kibutzim of both joined in 1954 in a new umbrella organization called the Union of Kibbutzim (**Eekhood ha-Kevootsot ve-ha-Keebootseem** איחוד הקבוצות והקיבוצים). In 1980 the latter became part of today's United Kibbutz Movement התנועה הקיבוצית המאוחדת (**HA-Tenoo'ah hA-Keebootseet hA-Me'ookhedet**) known by its *acr.*: **ha-TAKAM** התק"ם.

keebootsee/-t קיבוצי *adj* **1.** collective; **2.** of a/the kibbutz or of the kibbutz movement.

('on|esh/-sheem) keebootsee/-yeem עונש קיבוצי *nm* collective punishment.

keebootsneek/-eet קיבוצניק *nmf [slang]* kibbutznik; kibbutz member.

keebooy כיבוי *nm* extinguishing; quenching.

(mekhonee|t/-yot) keebooy מכונית־כיבוי *nf* fire-engine.

keed|ah/-ot קידה *nf* bow; curtsy; (*+of:* **-at**).

(hekhv|ah/-etah/-etee) keedah החווה קידה *v* took a bow; (*pres* **makhveh**; *fut* **yakhveh**).

kee-de-ba'ee (*npr* **kee-d-va'ey**) כדבעי *adv* *(Aram.)* properly; as it should be.

keed|em/-mah/-amtee קידם *v* **1.** advanced; **2.** welcomed; (*pres* **mekadem**; *fut* **yekadem**).

keed|esh/-'shah/-ashtee קידש *v* sanctified; (*pres* **mekadesh**; *fut* **yekadesh**).

◇ **keedesh** (*etc*) **'al ha-yayeen** קידש על היין *v* chanted the "Kiddush" over a glass of wine at the opening of the festive Sabbath-Eve or Holiday-Eve dinner.

◇ **keedesh eeshah** קידש אישה *v* took a woman to wife.

keedm|ah קידמה *nf* **1.** progress; **2.** Eastern part of a country, province, territory *etc*; (*+of:* **-at**).

keedmee/-t קידמי *adj* forward; front.

(hana'ah) keedmeet הנעה קידמית *nf* front-wheel drive.

keedom|et/-ot קידומת *nf* **1.** *prefix*; **2.** area code.

keedon/-eem כידון *nm* bayonet; spear; (*pl+of:* **-ey**).

keedoo|'akh/-kheem קידוח *nm* drilling; (*pl+of:* **-ey**).

(meegd|al/-eley) keedoo'akh מגדל קידוח *nm* derrick.

◇ **keedoosh** קידוש *nm* **1.** sanctification; **2.** ceremonial Friday-night blessing chanted over wine or bread.

◇ **keedoosh ha-shem** קידוש השם *nm* martyrdom; sacrificing one's life for religious or national Jewish cause.

◇ **keedoosh levanah** קידוש לבנה *nm* special outdoor-prayer held once a month to bless the inauguration of new lunar month.

◇ **keedoosheem** (or **keedoosheen**) /קידושים קידושין *nm pl* mariage in accordance with Jewish religious law.

(khoopah ve) keedoosheen חופה וקידושין *nf* wedding ceremony in accordance with Jewish law.

keedoret (*npr* **kadoret**) כדורת *nf* bowling.

keedr|er/-erah/-artee כדרר *v* dribbled (sport); (*pres* **mekadrer**; *fut* **yekadrer**).

□ **Keedron** (Kidron) קדרון *nm* village (est. 1949) in the Coastal Plain, 2 km E. of Gedera. Pop. 718.

ke-'eeloo כאילו as if.

kee|'er/-'arah/-artee כיער *v* uglified; made ugly; (*pres* **mekha'er**; *fut* **yekha'er** *(kh=k)*).

keefoof/-eem כיפוף *nm* bend; bending; (*pl+of:* **-ey**).

keeflayeem כפליים *adv* twice; doubly; double the.

keeh|en/-hanah/-hantee כיהן *v* served; officiated; held office; (*pres* **mekhahen**; *fut* **yekhahen** *(kh=k)*).

(shemen) keek שמן קיק *nm* castor oil.

keekar/-rot כיכר *nf* **1.** square; traffic circus; **2.** loaf.

□ **Keekar Atareem** see □ **Keekar Nameer**.

keekar ha-'eer כיכר העיר *nf* town square.

keek|ar/-rot lekhem כיכר לחם *nf* loaf of bread.

□ **Keekar Nameer** (Kikar Namir) כיכר נמיר *nm* **Mordekhay Nameer** Square - *nf* tourist, entertainment and shopping center on Tel-Aviv seashore, in fashionable hotel area. Was known earlier as **"Atareem"** Square.

keeka|yon קיקיון *nm* castor-oil plant.

kee|kev/-khvah/-khavtee *(kh=k)* כיכב *v* starred (in movie or show); (*pres* **mekhakev**; *fut* **yekhakev**).

keekh|alon/-lonot כיחלון *nm* cyanosis.

keekh|ev (*npr* **keekev**)**/-vah/-avtee** כיכב *v* starred (in movie or show); (*pres* **mekhakev**; *fut* **yekhakev**).

keekhesh/-ashah/-ashtee כיחש *v* denied; lied; (*pres* **mekakhesh**; *fut* **yekakhesh**).

kee-kh'tav|o/-ah *(kh=k)* ככתבו exactly as written.

kee-kh'tavo/-ah ve-khee-leshono/-ah *(kh=k)* ככתבו וכלשונו *adv* verbatim; textually;

keekyonee/-t קיקיוני *adj* ephemeral.

kee-l'-akhar-yad כלאחר יד *adv* off-hand; unintentionally.

keelay כילי *nm* miser.

(ben/bat) keel'ayeem בן־כלאיים *nmf* mongrel; crossbreed; (*pl:* **beney/benot** *etc*).

keel|ayon כיליון *nm* ruin; annihilation; (*+of:* **-yon**).

keelayon kharoots כיליון חרוץ *nm* utter ruin.

keel|ef/-fah/-aftee קילף *v* peeled; (*pres* **mekalef**; *fut* **yekalef**).

keel|el/-elah/-altee קילל *v* cursed; (*pres* **mekalel**; *fut* **yekalel**).

keel|es/-sah/-astee קילס *v* praised; lauded; (*pres* **mekales**; *fut* **yekales**).

keelk|el/-elah/-altee קלקל *v* spoiled; damaged; perverted; (*pres* **mekalkel**; *fut* **yekalkel**).

keelk|el/-elah/-altee כלכל *v* maintained; supported; fed; (*pres* **mekhalkel**; *fut* **yekhalkel** *(kh=k)*).

keelkool/-eem קלקול *nm* spoiling; damage; malfunction; perversion; (*pl+of:* **-ey**).

keelo/-grameem קילו *nm* kilogram; (1 kg=*2.2046 Lb)*.

keelomet|er/-reem קילומטר *nm* kilometer; (1 km = *5/8 mile, 3,280.8 Feet)*.

keeloof/-eem קילוף *nm* peeling; (*pl+of:* **-ey**).

keeloo|'akh/-kheem קילוח *nm* gush; flow; (*pl+of:* **-khey**).

kee-l'-'oomat she- כלעומת ש־ *adv* just as; the same way as.

keelovat/-eem קילווט *nm* kilowatt.

keelshon/-ot קילשון *nm* pitchfork.

keelt|er/-erah/-artee קלטר *v* cultivated (plant); (*pres* **mekalter**; *fut* **yekalter**).

keelyah/kelayot כליה *nf* kidney; (*+of:* **keel|yah/-yot**).

keelyah mal'akhooteet כליה מלאכותית *nf* artificial kidney.

(hashtal|at/-ot) keelyah השתלת כליה *nf* kidney transplant.

(be) keelyon (*npr* **be-kheelyon**) **'eynayeem** בכליון עיניים *adv* impatiently.

keem'ah-keem'ah קמעה קמעה *adv* bit by bit; little by little.

keem|akhon/-khonot קימחון *nm* mildew; (*+of:* **-khan**).

keem'at כמעט *adv* almost.

keemee/-t כימי *adj* chemical.

◇ **"keemeeyah"** כימיה *nf [slang]* human chemistry i.e. taking, or not taking, a liking for one another.

keem|et/-tah/-atetee קימט *v* creased; wrinkled; (*pres* **mekamet**; *fut* **yekamet**).

keem|ets/-tsah/-atstee קימץ *v* economized; saved; (*pres* **mekamets**; *fut* **yekamets**).

keemkhee/-t קמחי *adj* flourlike; floury.

keem'ona|y (*cpr* **keem'ona|'ee**)**/-'eem** קמעונאי *nm* retailer; (*pl+of:* **-'ey**).

keem'onee/-t קימעוני *adj* retail.

(mees'khar) keem'onee מסחר קמעוני *nm* retail trade.

(be) keem'onoot בקמעונות *adv* in retail.

keemoot/-eem קימוט *nm* folding; creasing; wrinkling.

keemoots/-eem קימוץ *nm* saving; economizing; (*pl+of:* **-ey**).

keemoots|eem קימוצים *nm pl* economizings; curtailments in order to economize; (*pl+of:* **-ey**).
keemron/-eem קמרון *nm* dome; (*pl+of:* **-ey**).
keemtsoots/-eem (*npr* **kamtsoots**) קמצוץ *nm* pinch; (*pl+of:* **-ey**).
keemyah כימיה *nf* chemistry.
ke-'en כעין *adv* a sort of; a kind of.
keen|ah/-tah/-eetee כינה *v* named; called (name); nicknamed; (*pres* **mekhaneh**; *fut* **yekhaneh** (*kh=k*)).
keen|ah/-ot קינה *nf* lamentation; (*+of:* **-at**).
keen|ah/-eem כינה *nf* louse; (*pl+of:* **-ey**).
keen|'ah קנאה *nf* **1.** jealousy; **2.** envy; (*+of:* **-at**).
keen|akh/-khah/-akhtee קינח *v* wiped; (*pres* **mekane'akh**; *fut* **yekanakh**).
keenamon קינמון *nm* cinnamon.
keen|e/-'ah/-e'tee be- קינא ב־ *v* envied; (*pres* **mekane be-**; *fut* **yekane be-**).
keene' (*etc*) **le-** קינא ל־ *v* was jealous of.
keen|e'akh/-khah/-akhtee קינח *v* wiped; (*pres* **mekane'akh**; *fut* **yekane'akh**).
keeneem כינים *nm pl* lice; (*sing:* **keen|ah**; *pl+of:* **-ey**).
keeneen כינין *nm* quinine.
keen|en/-enah/-antee קינן *v* nested; dwelt; (*pres* **mekanen**; *fut* **yekanen**).
□ **Keeneret** כנרת *nf* Lake Tiberias (see □ **Yam Keeneret**).
□ **Keeneret-Moshavah** (Kinneret-Moshava) כנרת מושבה *nf* village (est. 1909) on SW coast of Lake Tiberias, 4 km NW of Zemah Junction (**Tsomet Tsemakh**). Pop. 294.
□ **(Kvootsat) Keeneret** see □ **Kvootsat Keeneret**.
□ **(Yam) Keeneret** see □ **Yam Keeneret**.
□ **(Yam) Keeneret** ים כנרת *nm* Sea of Galilee i.e. Lake Tiberias; (see □ **Yam Keeneret**).
keen|es/-sah/-astee כינס *v* convened; assembled; (*pres* **mekhanes**; *fut* **yekhanes** (*kh=k*)).
keenoo|'akh/-kheem קינוח *nm* wiping; (*pl+of:* **-khey**).
(le) keenoo'akh לקינוח *adv* for dessert.
keenoon/-eem כינון *nm* establishing; establishment.
keenoos/-eem כינוס *nm* convention; gathering; (*pl+of:* **-ey**).
keenoos/-ey kheroom כינוס חירום emergency convocation; emergency gathering.
keenoo|y/-yeem כינוי *nm* nickname; (*pl+of:* **-yey**).
keenoo|y/-yey genay כינוי גנאי *nm* derisive nickname.
keenoo|y/-yey kheebah כינוי חיבה *nm* pet-name.
keenor/-ot כינור *nm* violin.
keent|er/-erah/-artee קנטר *v* vexed; angered; annoyed; (*pres* **mekanter**; *fut* **yekanter**).
keentoor/-eem קנטור *nm* annoyance; vexation.

keen|yan/-yaneem קניין *nm* property; possession; ownership; (*pl+of:* **-yeney**).
keenyan 'adey-'ad קניין עדי עד *nm* eternal asset.
kee'oor/-eem כיעור *nm* ugliness; (*pl+of:* **-ey**).
keep|ah/-ot כיפה *nf* **1.** skullcap (worn by observant Jewish males); **2.** dome; vault; (*+of:* **-at**).
◇ **keep|ah/-ot sroogah/-ot** כיפה סרוגה *nf* crocheted skullcap - distinctive mark of modern religiously-observant male Jewish youth, mostly influenced by the "**Beney 'Akeeva**" (Akiva) youth movement.
keep|akh/-khah/-akhtee (*or:* **keep|e'akh**) קיפח *v* deprived; discriminated against; (*pres* **mekape'akh**; *fut* **yekape'akh**).
keepa'on קיפאון *nm* stagnation; (*+of:* **keef'on**; (*f=p*)).
(nekood|at/-ot) keepa'on נקודת קיפאון *nf* freezing point.
keep|el/-lah/-altee קיפל *v* folded; (*pres* **mekapel**; *fut* **yekapel**).
keepel (*etc*) **be-tokh|o/-ah** קיפל בתוכו *v* incorporated; encompassed.
keep|er/-rah/-artee ('al) כיפר על *v* atoned (for); (*pres* **mekhaper**; *fut* **yekhaper** (*kh=k*)).
keep|ets/-tsah/-atstee קיפץ *v* jumped about; skipped (*pres* **mekapets**; *fut* **yekapets**).
keepod/-eem קיפוד *nm* porcupine; hedgehog; (*pl+of:* **-ey**).
keepoo|'akh/-kheem קיפוח *nm* deprivation; discrimination; denial of rights; (*pl+of:* **-khey**).
keepool/-eem קיפול *nm* folding; pleating; (*pl+of:* **-ey**).
keepoor/-eem כיפור *nm* atonement; forgiveness; pardon (*pl+of:* **-ey**).
Keepoor כיפור *nm* Day of Atonement; "Yom Kippur".
(Yom) Keepoor יום כיפור *nm* Day of Atonement; "Yom Kippur".
(Yom ha) Keepooreem יום הכיפורים *nm* Day of Atonement; "Yom Kippur".
kee-p'shoot|o/-ah (*npr* **kee-f'shoot|o/-ah**) כפשוטו *adv* as its real meaning; as plain as it sounds; literally.
keer/-ot קיר *nm* wall.
('alon/-ey) keer קיר עלון *nm* wall-newspaper.
(ezov/azovey) keer איזוב קיר *nm* **1.** small fry; **2.** the hysop that springs out of the wall (Bibl.).
(ketovet 'al ha) keer כתובת על הקיר *nf* writing on the wall.
(loo|'akh/-khot) keer לוח קיר *nm* wall calendar.
(she'on/-ey) keer שעון קיר *nm* wall clock.
keer|ah/-ot כירה *nf* stove; range; (*+of:* **-at**).
keer|at/-ot gaz כירת גז *nf* gas range.
keerayeem כיריים *nm pl* cooking range; cooking stove.
keerayeem shel gaz כיריים של גז *nm pl* gas range.
kee-retson|kha/-ekh כרצונך *adv* as you *m/f* wish.

keerkarah/-ot כרכרה *nf* **1.** cart; buggy; **2.** light carriage; (*+of:* **-at**).
keerk|as/-aseem קרקס *nm* circus; (*pl+of:* **-ey**).
keerk|ef/-efah/-aftee קרקף *v* scalped; beheaded; (*pres* **mekarkef**; *fut* **yekarkef**).
keerk|er/-erah/-artee כרכר *v* skipped around; danced in circles; (*pres* **mekharker**; *fut* **yekarker** *(kh=k)*).
keerk|er/-erah/-artee קרקר crowed; croaked; shouted unnecessarily; (*pres* **mekarker**; *fut* **yekarker**).
keerkoor/-eem כרכור *nm* twirl; beating around the bush; (*pl+of:* **-ey**).
keerkoor/-eem קרקור *nm* **1.** undermining; shattering **2.** crowing; (*pl+of:* **-ey**).
keeroorg/-eem כירורג *nm* surgeon.
keeroorgee/-t כירורגי *adj* surgical.
keers|em/-emah/-amtee כרסם *v* nibbled; toothed (metal) (*pres* **mekharsem**; *fut* **yekharsem** *(kh=k)*).
keersoom/-eem כרסום *nm* gnawing; nibbling; etching; (*pl+of:* **-ey**).
keerts|ef/-efah/-aftee קרצף *v* scraped; curried.
kee-rtson|kha/-ekh כרצונך *adv* as you *m/f* wish.
keerv|ah/-ot קרבה *nf* proximity; nearness; (*+of:* **-at**).
(be) keervat בקרבת *adv* in the vicinity of.
(be) keervat makom בקרבת מקום *adv* nearby; in the neighbohood.
keervat meeshpakhah קרבת משפחה *nf* kinship.
keeryah/krayot קריה *nf* city; suburb; borough; (*+of:* **keeryat**).
□ **keeryah** קריה *nf* town quarter in which Government departments or other institutions or plants of a particular kind are concentrated.
□ **(Ha) keeryah** (ha-Qiryah) הקריה *nf* quarter in the Eastern part of Tel-Aviv where main Government offices are located.
□ **Keeryat 'Amal** (Qiryat Amal) קריית עמל *nf* former name of what is today a part of **Keeryat Teev'on**, see below.
□ **Keeryat 'Anaveem** (Qiryat 'Anavim) קריית ענבים *nm* kibbutz (est. 1920) of the **"Kevootsah"** type, in Judean Hills, 10 km W. of Jerusalem. Pop. 373.
□ **Keeryat Arba'** (Qiryat Arba) קריית ארבע *nf* Jewish urban settlement (est. 1968) overlooking the historic city of Hebron **(Khevron)**. Jews had been banned from Hebron since the massacre of 1929, in which the entire Jewish population there was wiped out and the centuries-old Jewish Quarter ransacked. Pop. 4,290.
□ **Keeryat Ata** (Qiryat Ata) קריית אתא *nf* town (est. 1925) in the **'Emek Zevooloon** valley, 14 km E. of Haifa. Pop. 38,900.
□ **Keeryat Ben-Gooryon** (Qiryat Ben-Gurion) קריית בן גוריון *nf* (also known as **HaKeeryah Yerooshalayeem**) a quarter in W. part of Jerusalem, next to the Knesset, where most ministries and Government offices are located.
□ **Keeryat Byaleek** (Qiryat Bialik) קריית ביאליק *nf* town (est. 1934) in **'Emek Zevooloon** (Haifa Bay), on Haifa-Acre **('Ako)** road, near Qiryat Hayyim **(Keeryat Khayeem)**. Pop. 34,900.
□ **Keeryat 'Ekron** (Qiryat 'Eqron) קריית עקרון *nf* development-town and local council (est. 1948) 2 km S. of Rehovot **(Rekhovot)**. Pop. 4,740.
□ **Keeryat Gat** קריית גת *nf* town (est. 1954) in Coastal Plain, 59 km S. of Tel-Aviv, 20 km SE of Ashkelon and 46 km N. of Beersheba. Pop. 30,000.
□ **Keeryat Khayeem** (Qiryat Hayyim) קריית חיים *nf* largest of Haifa's residential suburbs in Haifa Bay **('Emek Zevooloon)** est. 1933 as a workers' housing project. Pop. 30,000.
□ **Keeryat Mal'akhee** קריית מלאכי *nf* development-town (est. 1951) in the Coastal Plain, 10 km SE of Ashdod. Pop. 15,500.
□ **Keeryat Motskeen** (Qiryat Motskin) קריית מוצקין *nf* urban settlement (est. 1934) in Haifa Bay **('Emek Zevooloon)** on Haifa-Acre road, S. of **Keeryat Khayeem**. Pop. 32,400.
□ **Keeryat Ono** (Qiryat Ono) קריית אונו *nf* urban settlement & local council (est. 1939) E. of Ramat-Gan, 3 km S. of Geha Junction **(Tsomet Geha)**. Pop. 23,100.
□ **Keeryat Shmonah** (Qiryat Shemona) קריית שמונה *nf* development-town (est. 1949) in Upper Galilee, **Rosh-Peenah-Metoolah** road, near Lebanese border. Pop. 16,600.
□ **Keeryat Teev'on** (Qiryat Tiv'on) קריית טבעון *nf* urban settlement and local council (est. 1958) on borderline between Haifa Bay and Yizre'el Valley, 15 km SE of Haifa, on the road to Nazareth. Pop. 12,300.
□ **Keeryat Telz-Ston** (Qiryat Telz-Stone) קריית טלז־סטון *nf* religious residential settlement (est. 1975) in Judean hills; next to **(Keeryat Ye'areem)**. Pop. 1,300.
□ **Keeryat Yam** (Kiryat Yam) קריית ים *nf* residential town (est. 1946) in Haifa Bay N. of Qiryat Hayyim **(Keeryat Khayeem)**. Pop. 35,900.
□ **Keeryat Ye'areem** קריית יערים *nf* youth-village and educational center in Judean hills, (est. 1952) N. of **Aboo-Gosh** in Jerusalem area. Pop. (stud. & staff) 250.
kees/-eem כיס *nm* pocket; (*pl+of:* **-ey**).
(demey) kees דמי כיס *nm pl* pocket-money.
(ma'ot *or npr* **me'ot) kees** מעות כיס *nf pl* out-of-pocket expenses.
(panas/-ey) kees פנס כיס *nm* torch; flashlight.
(sefer/seefrey) kees ספר כיס *nm* pocket-book.
kees|ah/-tah/-eetee כיסה *v* covered; covered up; (*pres* **mekhaseh**; *fut* **yekhaseh** *(kh=k)*).
keesan/-eem כיסן *nm* stuffed pastry; (*pl+of:* **-ey**).
kees|e/-a'ot (*npr* **-'ot**) כיסא *nm* chair; (*pl+of:* **-'ot**).

kees|e/-'ot (*etc*) **galgaleem** כיסא גלגלים *nm* wheelchair.

kees|e/-'ot (*etc*) **no'akh** כיסא נוח *nm* easy chair.

(bet/-batey) keese בית כיסא *nm* lavatory; latrine; W.C.

kees|em/-meem קיסם *nm* **1.** toothpick; **2.** splinter; (*pl+of:* **-mey**).

keesey heetnagdoot כיסי התנגדות *nm pl* resistance pockets.

keesh|alon/-lonot כישלון *nm* failure; (*+of:* **-lon**).

(moo|'ad/-'edet le) keeshalon (*npr* **kheeshalon** (*kh=k*)) מועד לכישלון *adj* doomed to fail.

(nakh|al/-lah/-altee) keeshalon נחל כישלון *v* met with failure; failed; (*pres* **nokhel** *etc; fut* **yeenkhal** *etc*).

keesh|aron (*npr* **keesh|ron**)**/-ronot** כשרון *nm* talent; (*+of:* **-ron**).

(brookh/-at) keesharon (*npr* **keesh|ron**) ברוך כשרון *adj* talented; gifted; (*pl+of:* **-ey/-ot** *etc*).

(khas|ar/-at) keesharon (*npr* **keesh|ron**) חסר־כשרון *adj* untalented; (*pl+of:* **-rey/-rot** *etc*).

keesh|ef/-fah/-aftee כישף *v* bewitched; (*pres* **mekhashef**; *fut* **yekhashef**).

keesh|er/-rah/-artee קישר *v* connected; tied together; (*pres* **mekasher**; *fut* **yekasher**).

keesh|et/-tah/-atetee קישט *v* adorned; decorated; (*pres* **mekashet**; *fut* **yekashet**).

keeshk|esh/-eshah/-ashtee קשקש *v* **1.** prattled; talked nonsense; **2.** scribbled; **3.** rattled; clapped. **4.** wagged (a dog his tail); (*pres* **mekashkesh**; *fut* **yekashkesh**).

keeshkoosh/-eem קשקוש *nm* **1.** nonsense; prattle; **2.** scribbling; (*pl+of:* **-ey**).

□ **(Nakhal) Keeshon** נחל קישון *nm* small brook in Haifa Bay.

keeshoof/-eem כישוף *nm* sorcery; magic; (*pl+of:* **-ey**).

keeshoor/-eem כישור *nm* qualification; aptitude; (*pl+of:* **-ey**).

keeshoor/-eem קישור *nm* **1.** connection; **2.** tying together; (*pl+of:* **-ey**).

(deevrey) keeshoor דברי קישור *nm pl* intermediate (connecting) sentences.

(meelat/-ot) keshoor מלת קישור *nf* conjunction (*gram.*).

keeshoot/-eem קישוט *nm* ornament; decoration; (*pl+of:* **-ey**).

keeshoo'eem קישואים *nm pl* zucchini; marrows; (*sing:* **keeshoo**; *pl+of:* **-'ey**).

keeshor/-eem כישור *nm* spindle; (*pl+of:* **-ey**).

□ **Keeshor** (Kishor) כישור *nm* village (est. 1976) in Upper Galilee, 8 km S. of **Ma'alot**.

keesh|ron/-ot כשרון *nm* talent.

(brookh/-at) keeshron ברוך כשרון *adj* talented; gifted; (*pl+of:* **-ey/-ot** *etc*).

(khas|ar/-at) keeshron חסר־כשרון *adj* untalented; (*pl+of:* **-rey/-rot** *etc*).

keeshronee/-t כשרוני *adj* gifted; talented.

◇ **Keeslev (Kislev)** כסלו *nm* 3rd month of Jewish Calendar (29 or 30 days; approx. Nov-Dec).

keesoo'akh/-kheem כיסוח *nm pl* slicing down; cutting off; (*pl+of:* **-ey**).

keesoofeem כיסופים *nm pl* longings; (*sing:* **keesoof**; *pl+of:* **-ey**).

□ **Keesoofeem** (Kissufim) כיסופים *nm* kibbutz (est. 1951) in the W. Negev, 10 km NE of **Khan-Yoones** and 4 km N. of Kibbutz Nirim (**Neereem**). Pop. 387.

keesoo|y/-yeem כיסוי *nm* **1.** cover; coverage; **2.** [*colloq.*] coverage of check drawn; (*pl+of:* **-yey**).

keet|ah/-ot כיתה *nf* **1.** class; form; (in school); **2.** detachment (in army); (*+of:* **-at**).

◇ **keetah bet** (or **geemal, dalet** *etc*) (ג׳, ד׳) כיתה ב׳ 2nd (or 3rd, 4th *etc*) form/year (for 7-8, 8-9, 9-10 *etc* year-old pupils) in Israeli primary schools.

keetah (*etc*) **teepooleet** כיתה טיפולית *nm* special-care class.

keet|at/-ot ragleem כיתת רגלים *nm* infantry platoon.

keetatee/-t כיתתי *adj* sectarian.

ketateeyoot כיתתיות *nf* sectarianism; factionalism.

keet|e'a'/-a'at קיטע *nm* amputee.

keet|er/-rah/-artee כיתר *v* encircled; (*pres* **mekhater**; *fut* **yekhater** (*kh=k*)).

keeter/-rah/-artee קיטר *v* [*slang*] grumbled; kept on grumbling; (*pres* **mekater**; *fut* **yekater**).

keet'ey negeenah קטעי נגינה *nm pl* musical fragments.

keet'ey 'eetonoot קטעי עיתונות *nm pl* newspaper-cuttings; clipppings.

keetl|eg/-egah/-agtee קיטלג *v* catalogued; (*pres* **mekatleg**; *fut* **yekatleg**).

keetloog/-eem קיטלוג *nm* cataloguing; (*pl+of:* **-ey**).

keetneeyot קטניות *nf pl* legumes; (*sing:* **keetneet**).

keeton/-ot קיתון *nm* jug; pitcher.

keetonot shel shofkheen קיתונות של שופכין *nm pl* (mostly *figurat.*) heaps of refuse; heaps of garbage.

keetoo|'a'/-'eem קיטוע *nm* amputation; (*pl+of:* **'ey**).

keetoor/-eem כיתור *nm* encirclement. (*pl+of:* **-ey**).

keetoor/-eem קיטור *nm* [*slang*] constant grumbling; (*pl+of:* **-ey**).

keetoov/-eem קיטוב *nm* polarization.

keetor קיטור *nm* steam.

(onee|yat/-yot) keetor אוניית קיטור *nf* steamship.

keetreg/-egah/-agtee קיטרג *v* denounced; accused; incited against; (*pres* **mekatreg**; *fut* **yekatreg**).

keetroog/-eem קיטרוג *nm* denunciation; accusation; (*pl+of:* **-ey**).

keetsb|ah/-a'ot קצבה **1.** allowance; **2.** pension; (*+of:* **-at**).

(bar/-at) keetsbah בר קצבה *nmf & adj* pensionable.

keetsb|at/-ot nakhoot קצבת נכות *nf* disability pension.

(keetsb|at/-ot) zeeknah קצבת זקנה *nf* old age pension.

keets|er/-rah/-artee קיצר *v* shortened; abbreviated; (*pres* **mekatser**; *fut* **yekatser**).

keets|ets/-etsah/-atstee קיצץ *v* curtailed; cut-down; (*pres* **mekatsets**; *fut* **yekatsets**).

keetson/-ah קיצון *adj* extreme; ultimate.

keetsonee/-t קיצוני *adj* radical; extremist.

keetsoneeyoot קיצוניות *nf* extremism; radicalism.

keetsoor/-eem קיצור *nm* shortening; abridgment; (*pl+of:* **-ey**).

keetsoor/-ey derekh קיצור דרך *nm* shortcut.

(be) keetsoor בקיצור *adv* in short; in brief.

keetsooro shel davar קיצורו של דבר *adv* to make a long story short; in brief.

keetsoots/-eem קיצוץ *nm* cut; curtailment; (*pl+of:* **-ey**).

keetsoov/-eem קיצוב *nm* rationing; (*pl+of:* **-ey**).

keetsr|at/-ot קיצרת *adj (f)* short of.

keetsr|at/-ot komah קיצרת קומה *adj (f)* short of stature (female).

keetsr|at/-ot mo'ed קיצרת־מועד *adj (f)* short-term.

keetsr|at/-ot re'eeyah קיצרת ראייה *adj (f)* nearsighted; shortsighted.

keetsr|at/-ot re'oot קיצרת ראות *adj (f)* nearsighted; short-sighted.

keetsr|at/-ot roo'akh קיצרת רוח *adj (f)* impatient.

keetsr|at/-ot yad קיצרת יד *adj (f)* incapable; unable.

keetsv|ah (*npr* **keetsb|ah**)**/-a'ot** קיצבה **1.** allowance; **2.** pension; (*+of:* **-at**).

(bar/-at) keetsvah (*npr* **keetsbah**) בר קיצבה *nmf & adj* pensionable.

keetsv|at/-ot nekhoot (*npr* **keetsb|at/-ot nakhoot**) קיצבת נכות *nf* disability pension.

keetsv|at/-ot zeeknah (*npr* **keetsb|at** *etc*) קיצבת זיקנה *nf* old age pension.

keetvey כתבי *nm pl* the writings of.

keetvey ha-kodesh כתבי הקודש *nm pl* the Holy scriptures.

keev/-eem כיב *nm* ulcer (Medic.); (*pl+of:* **-ey**).

keev/-ey keyvah כיב קיבה *nm* stomach ulcer (Medic).

ke'ev/-eem כאב *nm* pain; (*pl+of:* **-ey**).

ke'ev/-ey beten כאב־בטן *nm* bellyache.

ke'ev/-ey garon כאב גרון *nm* sore throat.

ke'ev/-ey oznayeem כאב אוזניים *nm* earache.

ke'ev/-ey sheenayeem כאב שיניים *nm* toothache.

keev|ah/-tah/-eetee קיווה *v* hoped; (*pres* **mekaveh**; *fut* **yekaveh**).

ke'eveem כאבים *nm pl* pains; (*pl+of:* **-ey**).

(le-lo) ke'eveem ללא כאבים **1.** *adv* painlessly; **2.** *adj* painless.

keev|en/-nah/-antee כיוון *v* directed; meant; (*pres* **mekhaven** *(kh=k)*; *fut* **yekhaven**).

keev|ets/-tsah/-atstee כיווץ *v* contracted; shrank; (*pres* **mekhavets** *(kh=k)*; *fut* **yekhavets**).

ke'evey tofet כאבי תופת *nm pl* infernal pains.

keevnoon/-eem כיוונון *nm* attuning; adjustment; (*pl+of:* **-ey**).

keevoon/-eem כיוון *nm* direction; course; intention; (*pl+of:* **-ey**).

(doo-) keevoonee/-t דו־כיווני *adj* bi-directional.

(khad-) keevoonee/-t חד־כיווני *adj* one-way.

(rav-) keevoonee/-t רב־כיווני *adj* multi-directional.

keevoots/-eem כיווץ *nm* shrinking; contraction.

keevrat adamah כברת אדמה *nf* patch of land.

keevrat derekh כברת דרך *nf* some distance.

keevsah/kevasot כבשה *nf* ewe; ewe-lamb; (*+of:* **keevs|at/-ot**).

keevsat ha-rash כבשת הרש *nf* the poor man's lamb (from Biblical fable).

keevshan/-eem כבשן *nm* kiln; furnace; (*pl+of:* **keevsheney**).

◇ **keevsheney ha-hashmadah** כבשני ההשמדה *nm pl* the extermination-camp furnaces.

kee-ve-yakhol (*cpr* **keevyakhol**) כביכול **1.** *adv* as it were; **2.** *adj* so-called; so to speak.

kee'akh כיח *nm* spittle; phlegm.

kee|yef/-yefah/-yaftee כייף *v [slang]* had fun; had a good time; (*pres* **mekayef**; *fut* **yekayef**).

kee|yem/-ymah/-yamtee קיים *v* fulfilled; maintained; upheld; (*pres* **mekayem**; *fut* **yekayem**).

keeyem (*etc*) **yekhaseem** קיים יחסים *v* **1.** maintained relations with; **2.** had sexual intercourse.

ke-'eyn כעין *adv* a sort of; a kind of.

keeyoom קיום *nm* existence; fulfilment.

(doo) keeyoom דו־קיום *nm* co-existence.

(see-) keeyoom אי־קיום *nm* **1.** unfulfilment; **2.** non-existence.

(meelkhemet) keeyoom מלחמת קיום *nf* struggle for survival.

keeyor/-eem כיור *nm* washbasin; (*pl+of:* **-ey**).

keez|ez/-ezah/-aztee קיזז *v* set off; wrote off; amortized; (*pres* **mekazez**; *fut* **yekazez**).

keezooz/-eem קיזוז *nm* writing off; setting off; amortization; (*pl+of:* **-ey**).

kef/-eem כיף *nm [slang]* enjoyment; fun.

kefaf|ah/-ot כפפה *nf* glove; (*+of:* **keefef|at/-ot**).

('ala) kefak עלא כיפק *[slang] (Arab.)* terrific; the best you could wish for.

kefar/-eem כפר *nm* village; (*pl+of:* **kafrey**).

□ **Kefar Akheem** (Kefar Aḥim) כפר אחים *nm* village (est. 1949) in Coastal plain, 2 km N. of **Keeryat Mal'akhee**. Pop. 280.

□ **Kefar Aveev** (Kefar Aviv) כפר אביב *nm* village (est. 1951) in the central coastal plain, 1 km S. of **Tsomet Beney Darom** (Beney Darom Junction). Pop. 400.

□ **Kefar Avraham** כפר אברהם *nm* suburb in E. part of **Petakh-Teekvah** (originally est. 1951 as a religious village).

□ **Kefar 'Azah** (Kefar 'Azza) כפר עזה *nm* kibbutz (est. 1951) in NW Negev, 6 km E. of Gaza town, 2 km S. of Sa'ad Junction **(Tsomet Sa'ad)**. Pop. 649.

□ **Kefar Azar** כפר אז"ר *nm* village (est. 1932) E. of Ramat-Gan, 3 km N. of Mesubim Junction **(Tsomet Mesoobeem)**. Pop. 445.

□ **Kefar Barookh** (Kefar Barukh) כפר ברוך *nm* village (est. 1926) in Yizre'el Valley, 10 km NW of 'Afula. Pop. 272.

□ **Kefar Batyah** כפר בתיה *nm* youth-village (est. 1948) W. of **Ra'ananah**, comprising religious girls' school, agricultural and vocational schools. Pop. (pupils & staff) 1,000.

□ **Kefar Beeloo** (Kefar Bilu) כפר ביל"ו *nm* village (est. 1932) in central coastal plain, near Bilu Junction **(Tsomet Beeloo)**. Pop. 519.

□ **Kefar Been-Noon** (Kefar Bin Nun) כפר בן־נון *nm* village (est. 1952) off Latrun-Tel-Aviv road, 10 km SE of Ramla. Pop. 322.

□ **Kefar Bloom** (Kefar Blum) כפר בלום *nm* kibbutz (est. 1943) in the North of the **Khoolah** Valley , 6 km SE of **Keeryat Shemonah**. Pop. 672.

□ **Kefar Byaleek** (Kefar Bialik) כפר־ביאליק *nm* village on Haifa Bay, between **Keeryat Byaleek** (Bialik) and **Keeryat Ata**. Pop. 583.

□ **Kefar Danee'el** (Kefar Daniyyel) כפר דניאל *nm* village (est. 1949) on the Coastal Plain, 4 km SE of Lod town. Pop. 205.

□ **Kefar Darom** כפר דרום *nm* kibbutz (est. 1975) in the Gaza Strip, off the Gaza-**Rafee'akh** road, 3 km S. of **Deer El-Balakh**.

□ **Kefar Eleeyahoo** כפר אליהו *nm* educational center (est. 1951) of Agoodas Yeesro'el (Agudat Israel) for girls. Comprises campuses with secondary school (college), teachers' seminary, vocational school, *etc.*

□ **Kefar 'Etsyon** (Kefar 'Ezyon) כפר עציון *nm* - kibbutz (est. 1967) on site of the former village (est. 1943) destroyed by the Jordanians in the 1948 Independence War. Pop. 556.

□ **Kefar Gabeerol** (Kefar Gevirol) כפר גבירול *nm* a suburb (est. 1949) of Rehovot.

□ **Kefar Galeem** (Kefar Gallim) כפר גלים *nm* educational institution and youth-village (est. 1952) on the Carmel Coast, 6 km S. of Haifa. Pop. 368.

□ **Kefar Geed'on** (Kefar Gid'on) כפר גדעון *nm* village (est. 1923) in Yizre'el Valley, 4 km N. of 'Afula. Pop. 162.

□ **Kefar Geel'adee** (Kefar Gil'adi) כפר גלעדי *nm* kibbutz (est. 1916) in Upper Gallilee, 5 km S. of **Metoolah**. Pop. 709.

□ **Kefar Gleekson** (Kefar Glickson) כפר גליקסון *nm* kibbutz (est. 1939) 5 km E. of **Benyameenah**. Pop. 392.

□ **Kefar ha-Bapteesteem** כפר הבפטיסטים *nm* Baptist village (est. 1956) on Yarkon river, off the **Petakh-Teekvah** road. Comprises, in addition to Baptist settler community, hostel and educational institute.

□ **Kefar ha-Khoresh (Kefar haHoresh)** כפר החורש *nm* kibbutz (est. 1938) in Lower Gallilee, 2 km W. of Nazareth. Pop. 471.

□ **Kefar ha-Makabee** (Kefar haMaccabi) כפר המכבי *nm* kibbutz (est. 1936) 2 km S. of **Keeryat Ata**. Pop. 345.

□ **Kefar ha-Makabeeyah** כפר המכביה *nm* sports-center and country club at SW edge of Ramat-Gan. Site of World Maccabiah conventions.

□ **Kefar ha-Nageed** (Kefar haNagid) כפר הנגיד *nm* village (est. 1949) in Coastal Plain, 5 km W. of Rehovot. Pop. 408.

□ **Kefar ha-Nasee** (Kefar Hanasi) כפר הנשיא *nm* kibbutz (est. 1948) N. of Lake Tiberias, 4 km W. of Mahanayim Junction **(Tsomet Makhnayeem)**. Pop. 598.

□ **Kefar ha-No'ar Ben Shemen** (Kefar Hano'ar Ben-Shemen) כפר הנוער בן־שמן *nm* educational institution and youth village (est. 1906, re-est 1927) 4 km E. of Lod. Pop. (staff & pupils) 971.

□ **Kefar ha-No'ar Neetsaneem** כפר הנוער ניצנים *nm* youth-village (est. 1949) on the coastal plain, off Ashdod-Ashkelon road, near kibbutz **Neetsaneem-kvootsah**. Pop. 370.

□ **Kefar ha-No'ar ha-Datee (Kefar Hano'ar Hadatee)** כפר הנוער הדתי *nm* religious educational center (est. 1936) in Lower Galilee near Kefar Hasidim **(Kefar Khaseedeem)**. Pop. 500.

□ **Kefar ha-No'ar Yohanah Jaboteensky** כפר הנוער יוהנה ז'בוטינסקי *nm* agricultural school (est. 1948), 4 km W. of Ramla. Pop. (staff & pupils) 600.

□ **Kefar ha-Reef** (Kefar HaRif) כפר הרי"ף *nm* village (est. 1956) in Coastal Plain, 5 km NE of **Keeryat Mal'akhee**, 2 km S. of Re'em road junction. Pop. 259.

□ **Kefar ha-Ro'eh (Kefar haro'e)** כפר הרוא"ה *nm* village (est. 1933) in Sharon, 5 km of Hadera **(Khaderah)**. Pop. 973.

□ **Kefar Hes (Kefar Hess)** כפר הס *nm* village (est. 1933) in Sharon, 2 km SE of Tel-Mond. Pop. 509

□ **Kefar Khabad** (Kefar Habad) כפר חב"ד *nm* rural settlement (est. 1949) in Coastal Plain, 5 km W. of Ben Gurion Airport. Israeli center of the **Khabad** (Chabad) movement and site of several educational institutions. Pop. 3,050.

□ **Kefar Kharoov** (Kefar Haruv) כפר חרוב *nm* kibbutz (est. 1973) in the S. part of Golan Heights, 4 km SE of 'En-Gev. Pop. 281.

□ **Kefar Khaseedeem** (Kefar Hasidim) כפר חסידים *nm* village (est 1924 by Hasidim from Poland) on Haifa Bay, 6 kms S. of **Keeryat Ata**. It actually consists of two villages (see below).

□ **Kefar Khaseedeem Alef** (Kefar Hassidim Alef) כפר חסידים א *nm* village (est. 1924 by

Hasidim from Poland) on Haifa Bay, 6 km S. of **Keeryat Ata**. Pop. 446.

□ **Kefar Khaseedeem Bet** (Kefar Hasidim B) כפר חסידים ב׳ *nm* village (est. 1950) next to **Kefar Khaseedeem Alef** of which it was intended to be an extention. Pop. 200.

□ **Kefar Khayeem** (Kefar Hayyim) כפר חיים *nm* village (est. 1933) in Sharon, 4 km N. of **Tsomet ha-Sharon** road junction. Pop. 416.

□ **Kefar Kheeteem** (Kefar Hittim) כפר חיטים *nm* village (est. 1914) in Lower Galilee, 3 km NW of Tiberias. Pop. 284.

□ **Kefar Keesh** (Kefar Kisch) כפר קיש *nm* village in Lower Galilee, S. of 'Afula-Tiberias road, 3 km SE of **Kefar Tavor**. Pop. 321.

□ **Kefar Malal** (Kefar Malal) כפר מל״ל *nm* village (est. 1914) in Sharon, S. of Kefar Sava. Pop. 308.

□ **Kefar Masareek** (Kefar Masaryk) כפר מסריק *nm* kibbutz (est. 1938) in Haifa Bay, off the Haifa-Acre **(Ako)** road, 5 km S. of Acre. Pop. 652.

□ **Kefar Maymon** כפר מימון *nm* village (est. 1959) in NW part of Negev. Pop. 334.

□ **Kefar Menakhem (Kefar Menahem)** כפר מנחם *nm* kibbutz (est. 1935) in Coastal Plain, 8 km E. of **Keeryat Mal'akhee**. Pop. 590.

□ **Kefar Monash** כפר מונש *nm* village (est. 1946) in the Sharon, 3 km N. of **Tsomet ha-Sharon** junction. Pop. 413.

□ **Kefar Mordekhay** כפר מרדכי *nm* village in the Central Coastal Plain, 3 km W. of Gedera. Pop. 299.

□ **Kefar Neter** כפר נטר *nm* village (est. 1939) in Sharon, 1 km E. of autoroute 2 and of Poleg over-crossing **(Makhlef Poleg)**. Pop. 404.

□ **Kefar Peenes** (Kefar Pines) כפר פינס *nm* village (est. 1933) NE of **Pardes-Khanah**. Pop. 727.

□ **Kefar Roopeen** (Kefar Ruppin) כפר רופין *nm* kibbutz (est. 1938) in the Bet-She'an Valley, 7 km S. of Beisan **(Bet-She'an)** town. Pop. 466.

□ **Kefar Root** (Kefar Rut) כפר רות *nm* village (est. 1977) in the Ayalon Valley, 5 km N. of Mevo Khoron. Pop. 239.

□ **Kefar Rosh ha-Neekrah** (Kefar Rosh Hanikra) כפר ראש הנקרה *nm* kibbutz on Galilee coast (est. 1949), 10 km N. of Nahariyya. Pop. 570.

□ **Kefar Saba (Kefar Sava)** כפר סבא *nf* town in S. Sharon, 9 km N. of **Petakh-Teekvah**. Pop. 61,100.

□ **Kefar Seelver** (Kefar Silver) כפר סילבר *nm* agricultural school (est. 1957) E. of Ashkelon, off the Ashdod-Ashkelon road. Pop. 366.

□ **Kefar Seerkeen** (Kefar Sirkin) כפר סירקין *nm* village (est. 1936) in the E. outskirts of **Petakh-Teekvah**. Pop. 702.

□ **Kefar Shalem** כפר שלם *nf* former slum (also known as **Salameh**) in the SE part of Tel-Aviv, now gradually becoming a regular residential part of the city.

□ **Kefar Shamay** (Kefar Shammay) כפר שמאי *nm* village (est. 1949) in Upper Galilee, 3 km N. of Safed **(Tsefat)**. Pop. 322.

□ **Kele' Shatah** כלא שטה *nm* prison in the Yeezre'el Valley, off **'Afoolah-Bet-She'an** road, 2 km SW of kibbutz **Bet ha-Sheetah**.

□ **Kefar Shmoo'el** כפר שמואל *nm* village in the Coastal Plain, 6 km SE of Ramla, on the **Ramlah-Latroon** road. Pop. 341.

□ **Kefar Shmaryahoo** כפר שמריהו *nm* onetime village (est. 1937) now luxurious residential area, bordering **Hertseleeyah-Peetoo'akh** (from the E.) and abode, in particular, of foreign diplomats and residents of Anglosaxon background. Pop. 1730.

□ **Kefar Sold** (Kefar Szold) כפר סאלד *nm* kibbutz (est. 1942) in the NE part of the **Khoolah** Valley. Pop. 542.

□ **Kefar Tavor** (Kefar Tavor) כפר תבור *nm* (est. 1901) village (est. 1901 as **Meskhah** and renamed in 1909) in Lower Galilee, E. of Mount Tabor, off the 'Afula-Tiberias road. Pop. 1,010.

□ **Kefar Trooman** (Kefar Truman) כפר טרומן *nm* village (est. 1949) in the Lod area. 3 km from the Ben Gurion Airport. Pop. 321.

□ **Kefar Varboorg** (Kefar Warburg) כפר ורבורג *nm* village (est. 1939) in S. part of the Coastal Plain, 2 km SW of **Keeryat Mal'akhee**. Pop. 609.

□ **Kefar Veetkeen** (Kefar Vitkin) כפר ויתקין *nm* village (est. 1933) in Sharon, 6 km N. of Netanyah. Pop. 782.

□ **Kefar Veradeem** כפר ורדים *nm* village (est. 1983) in Upper Galilee, N. of Nahariyya. Pop. 1,510.

□ **Kefar Ya'bets** (Kefar Yabets) כפר יעבץ *nm* village (est. 1932) in Sharon, 5 km E. of Tel-Mond. Pop. 290.

□ **Kefar Yehoshoo'a'** (Kefar Yehoshu'a) כפר יהושע *nm* village (est. 1927) in the Yizre'el Valley, 5 km SE of **Keeryat Teev'on**. Pop. 555.

□ **Kefar Yekhezk'el** (Kefar Yehezquel) כפר יחזקאל *nm* village off the **'Afoolah Bet-She'an** road, 10 km SE of 'Afula. Pop. 559.

□ **Kefar Yonah** (Kefar Yona) כפר יונה *nm* rural settlement (est. 1932) in Sharon, off the **Netanyah-Toolkarem** road, 3 km E. of **Tsomet ha-Sharon** road junction. Pop. 4,600.

□ **Kefar Zeteem** (Kefar Zetim) כפר זיתים *nm* village (est. 1950) in Lower Galilee, 7 km NW of Tiberias. Pop. 321.

kefee כפי *conj* as; according to.

kefee ha-neemsar כפי הנמסר *adv* according to reports.

kefee ha-neer'eh כפי הנראה *adv* apparently.

kefee|'ah קפיאה *nf* freezing; **(+of: -'at)**.

kefee'ah 'al ha-shmareem קפיאה על השמרים *nf* resting on one's laurels; stagnation.

kefeedah קפידה *nf* meticulousness.

(bee) kefeedah בקפידה *adv* strictly; meticulously.

(bee) kefeefah (*npr* **bee-kh'feefah**) **akhat** בכפיפה אחת *adv* together.

kefeefoo|t/-yot כפיפות *nf* subordination; flexibility.

(bee) kefeefoot (*npr* **bee-kh'feefoot**) **le-** בכפיפות ל- *adv* subject to.

kefeeloo|t/-yot כפילות *nf* duplication.

kefeer|ah/-ot כפירה *nf* denial; heresy; (*+of:* **-at**).

kefeerah be-'eekar כפירה בעיקר *nf* **1.** contesting the main argument; **2.** denying the very existence of God.

kefeets/-eem קפיץ *nm* spring; coil; (*pl+of:* **-ey**).

kefeets|ah/-ot קפיצה *nf* jump; (*+of:* **-at**).

(keresh/karshey) kefeetsah קרש קפיצה *nm* springboard.

kefeets|at/-ot derekh קפיצת דרך *nf* shortcut; short distance away.

kefeetsee/-t קפיצי *adj* springy; elastic; springlike.

kefee|yah/-yot כפייה *nf* coercion; (*+of:* **-yat**).

kefeeyah dateet כפייה דתית *nf* religious coercion.

kefeeyoot tovah כפיות טובה *nf* ingratitude.

kefel כפל *nm* multiplication.

kefel-keeflayeem כפל־כיפליים *adv* many times over.

(loo'akh ha) kefel לוח הכפל *nm* multiplication table.

kef khayeem כיף חיים *[slang] nm* time of one's life.

kefoo|y/-yat tovah כפוי טובה *adj* ungrateful.

kefor כפור *nm* frost.

kefots!/keeftsee! ! קפוץ *v imp s m/f* jump! (*pst* **kafats**; *pres* **kofets**; *fut* **yeekpots**; *(p=f)*).

kefots lee! ! קפוץ לי *[slang] v imp sing m* go hang yourself! I couldn't care less.

kegon כגון *adv* e.g.: as for instance.

keheh/kehah כהה *adj* dark (shade).

keheh/kehah קהה *adj* blunt; dull.

(kakhol-) keheh כחול־כהה *adj m & nm* dark-blue.

keheelah/ot קהילה *nf* community; (*+of:* **-at**).

(va'ad ha) keheelah ועד הקהילה *nm* religious community board.

keheelatee/-t קהילתי *adj* communal.

keheelee|yah/-yot קהילייה *nf* commonwealth; community; (*+of:* **-yat**).

ke-heref 'ayeen כהרף עין *adv* in a jiffy; in the twinkling of an eye.

ke-hogen (*npr* **ka-hogen**) כהוגן *adv* properly; suitably.

ke-hoo zeh כהוא זה *adv* not a bit.

kehoon|ah/-ot כהונה *nf* **1.** office, post, rank; **2.** priesthood; **3.** tenure of office; (*+of:* **-ot**).

kehoo|t/-yot קיהות *nf* bluntness; stupor.

kehoot khoosheem קיהות חושים *nf* numbness; indolence.

(le-lo) kekhal oo-srak (*npr* **be-lo kakhal oo-ve-lo sarak**) ללא כחל ושרק *adv* unadorned.

kekhalkhal/-ah כחלחל *adj* bluish.

ke-khoot ha-sa'arah כחוט השערה *adv* by a hairbreadth.

kela'/kla'eem קלע *nm* bullet; sling.

(kaf ha) kela' כף הקלע *nm* **1.** hollow of a sling; **2.** (*figurat.*) torment; predicament.

kelakh/klakheem קלח *nm* stem; stalk; (*pl+of:* **keelkhey**).

(avad 'al|av/-eha ha) kelakh אבד עליו הקלח *adj* obsolete; out of fashion.

kelapey כלפי towards; in the direction of.

(yats|a/-'ah/-atee mee) kel|av/-eha/-ay יצא מכליו *v* lost his/her/my temper; (*pres* **yotse** *etc; fut* **yetse** *etc*).

kele' כלא *nm* prison; jail; (*pl:* **batey kele'**).

(bet/batey) kele' בית כלא *nm* prison; jail.

kelee/-m (*or:* **klee/keleem**) כלי *nm* **1.** tool; instrument; **2.** vessel.

keleem כלים *nm pl* dishes; instruments; vessels; (*sing:* **klee**; *pl+of:* **kley**).

keleem shelooveem כלים שלובים *nm pl* connected vessels.

(hadakhat) keleem הדחת כלים *nf* washing (rinsing) dishes.

(hed|ee'akh/-eekhah/-akhtee) keleem הדיח כלים *v* washed dishes; (*pres* **medee'akh**; *fut* **yadee'akh**).

(medee|'akh/-khey) keleem מדיח כלים *nm* dishwasher.

(nekhb|a/-et el ha) keleem נחבא אל הכלים *adj* self-effacing; unassuming.

(nos|e/-et) keleem נושא כלים *nmf* disciple; adjutant (*pl:* **-'ey/-'ot** *etc*).

(yats|a/-'ah/-atee meen ha) keleem יצא מן הכלים *v* lost his temper; (*pres* **yotse** *etc; fut* **yetse** *etc*).

keles קלס *nm* scorn.

(le-la'ag oo-le) keles ללעג ולקלס *adv* to scorn and derision.

kelet קלט *nm* **1.** input (computer); **2.** reception-depot for newly enlisted (Army).

kelev/klaveem כלב *nm* dog; (*pl+of:* **kalbey**; *b=v*).

kelev/kalvey bayeet כלב בית *nm* house-dog.

kelev/klaveem beytee/-yeem כלב ביתי *nm* domestic dog.

kelev/kalvey geeshoosh כלב גישוש *nm* bloodhound.

kelev/kalvey mayeem כלב מים *nm* otter.

kelev mee she- כלב מי ש־ *[slang]* under no circumstances should anyone....

kelev mee she-lo כלב מי שלא *[slang]* who the hell wouldn't?!....

kelev she-bee-klaveem! ! כלב שבכלבים *interj* son of a bitch; dirty dog!

kelev/klaveem shot|eh/-eem כלב שוטה *nm* mad dog.

kelev/kalbey shmeerah כלב שמירה *nm* watchdog.

kelev/kalvey tsayeed כלב ציד *nm* hunting dog.

kelev ze'ev כלב זאב *nm* wolfhound.

kelev/kalvey yam כלב ים *nm* seal.

kemakh/-eem קמח *nm* flour; (*pl+of:* **keemkhey**).

◇ **kemakh matsot** קמח מצות *nm* flour made of milled "Matzah" so that, during Passover, religiously observant Jews may use it for baking.

(peshoot|o/-ah) ke-mashma|'o/-'ah פשוטו כמשמעו **1.** *adj* plain; **2.** *adv* plainly.

(kharoosh/at) kemateem חרוש קמטים *adj* full of wrinkles.

kemee|hah/-hot כמיהה *nf* yearning; longing; (*+of:* **-hat**).

kemeel|ah/-ot קמילה *nf* withering; (*+of; -at*).

kemeets|ah/-ot קמיצה *nf* the fourth finger; (*+of:* **-at**).

kem|et/-ateem קמט *nm* wrinkle; crease; (*pl+of:* **keemtey**).

kemo כמו *conj* as; like.

kemokh|em/-en כמוכם/־ן like youselves *m/f*.

kemo khen כמו כן *conj* also; similarly; furthermore.

kemoorah/-ot כמורה clergy (Christian); (*+of:* **-at**).

('adash|ah/-ot) kemoor|ah/-ot עדשה קמורה *nf* convex lens.

kemot she|hoo/-hee/-hem/-hen כמות שהוא/שהיא/שהם/שהן *adj* as he/she/(it)/they *(m/f)* is/are.

kemot|o/-ah/-am/-an כמותו/־ה/־ם/־ן like him/her/them *(m/f) etc.*

(she-'eyn) kemot|o/-ah/-am/-an שאין כמותו/־ה/־ם/־ן *adj* unequalled; with no one like him/her/them *(m/f) etc.*

ken/-ah כן *adj* honest.

ken כן **1.** yes; **2.** also.

('al) ken על כן therefore.

(eem) ken אם כן if so, then...

(ela eem) ken אלא אם כן unless; provided that.

(gam) ken גם כן also; too.

(kee 'al) ken כי על כן because; since.

(le-akhar mee) ken לאחר מכן *adv* after that.

(she) ken שכן since.

(yeter-'al) ken (*npr* **yater** *etc*) יתר על כן moreover; furthermore; besides.

ken/keeneem קן *nm* nest; (*+of:* **kan/keeney**).

Kena'an כנען *nf* Canaan (Bibl).

□ **(Har) Kena'an** see □ **Har Kena'an**.

◇ **kena'anee/-t** כנעני *adj & nmf* "Canaanite", see kena'aneem, below.

◇ **kena'aneem** כנענים *nm pl* "Canaanites" - i.e. partisans of an ideology, voiced in some -intellectual and literary circles during 1945-1956, in favor of more a rigid distinction between the "Israeli nation" that is in Israel and Judaism or World Jewry at large.

ken af כן אף so even.

ke-nafsh|o/-ah/-ee/-ekhah/-ekh *etc* כנפשו/־ה/־י/־ך/־ך to his/her/my/your *m/f etc* liking.

kenas/-ot קנס *nf* fine (penalty).

ken|eh/-ah כנה *[colloq.] adj* sincere; honest.

ken|eh/-ey meedah קנה מידה *nm* scale.

ken|eh/-ey sookar קנה־סוכר *nm* sugar cane.

kenee|'ah/-'ot כניעה *nf* surrender; (*+of:* **-'at**).

ke-neer'eh (*npr* **ka-neer'eh**) כנראה *adv* apparently.

kenees|ah/-ot כניסה *nf* **1.** entry; **2.** entrance; (*+of:* **-at**).

(demey) keneesah דמי כניסה *nm pl* entrance fee.

(kartees/-ey) keneesah כרטיס כניסה *nm* entry ticket.

(reeshyon/-ot) keneesah רשיון כניסה *nm* entry permit.

(zekhoo|t/-yot) keneesah זכות כניסה *nf* right of entry.

kenee|yah/-yot קנייה *nf* purchase; buy; (*+of:* **-yat**).

(khoz|eh/-ey) keneeyah חוזה קנייה *nm* purchase contract.

(ko'akh) keneeyah כוח קנייה *nm* purchasing power.

(mas) keneeyah מס קניה *nm* purchase-tax.

ke-neged כנגד *adv* versus; as against.

ken|es/-aseem כנס *nm* congress; conference; convention; (*pl+of:* **keensey**).

kenesee|yah/-yot כנסייה *nf* church; (*+of:* **yat**).

◇ **(ha)keneset** see (ha)knesset.

(bet/batey) keneset בית כנסת *nm* synagogue.

(khav|er/-rey) keneset חבר כנסת *nm* Member of the Knesset; M.K.

ken gam כן גם so also.

kenoof|yah/-yot כנופיה *nf* gang; (*+of:* **-yat**).

kenoon|yah/-yot קנוניה *nf* conspiracy; intrigue; (*+of:* **-yat**).

kenoo|t/-yot כנות *nf* sincerity; honesty.

(be) kenoot (*npr* **be-khenoot**) בכנות *adv* honestly; sincerely.

ken yeerboo כן ירבו *interj* may there be more and more like him/her/it! (*etc*).

ken yehee ratson! כן יהי רצון! *interj* may it be God's will.

kera'/kra'eem קרע *nm* tear; breach; split; (*pl+of:* **keer'ey**).

kerakh קרח *nm* ice.

(hakhlakah 'al ha) kerakh החלקה על הקרח ice skating.

(kar/-ah ka) kerakh קר כקרח *adj* ice-cold.

kerameek|ah/-ot קרמיקה *nf* ceramics.

ker|ar/-erah/-artee קירר *v* cooled; chilled; (*pres* **mekarer;** *fut* **yekarer**).

ker|av/-vah/-avtee קירב *v* advanced; brought near; (*pres* **mekarev; fur yekarev**).

ker|e'akh/-akhat קירח *adj* bald; bald-headed.

ker|e'akh/-akhat mee-kan oo-mee-kan קירח מכאן ומכאן *adj* falling between two stools.

ke-rega' כרגע *adv* **1.** in a moment; **2.** at this minute/time.

kerekh/krakh|eem כרך *nm* volume; book; (*pl+of:* **-ey**).

kerem/krameem כרם *nm* vineyard; (*pl+of:* **karmey**).

□ **Kerem Ben-Zeemrah** (Kerem Ben Zimra) כרם בן זימרה *nm* village (est. 1949) in Upper Galilee, 8 km NW of Safed **(Tsefat)**. Pop. 302.

□ **Kerem Maharal** כרם מהר"ל *nm* village (est. 1949) in Karmel hills, 10 km N. of **Zeekhron Ya'akov**. Pop. 317.

□ **Kerem Shalom** כרם שלום *nm* kibbutz (est. 1968) in NW Negev, 7 km of **Rafee'akh**. Pop. 103.

□ **Kerem Yavneh** כרם יבנה *nf* yeshivah (est. 1954) near to kibbutz **Yavneh**, 7 km E. of Ashdod. Pop. 276.

keren/karnayeem קרן *nf* **1.** horn; **2.** ray; (*pl+of:* **karney**).

keren geemla'oot קרן גמלאות *nf* pension fund.

◇ **keren ha-yesod (Keren haYessod)** קרן היסוד the Zionist Organization's Foundation Fund an affiliation of the UJA.

◇ **keren/karnot heeshtalmoot** קרן השתלמות *nf* tax-shelter type fund formally earmarked for financing employee's study-trips or advanced studies. It is formed from tax deductions from employee's monthly paycheck plus employer's twofold (or threefold) contributions.

◇ **keren kayemet le-yeesra'el (Keren Kayemet Leisrael)** קרן קיימת לישראל *nf* the Jewish National Fund (J.N.F.), the oldest Zionist Fund, established in 1901 with the purpose of buying up uninhabited lands for settlement of new immigrants. Since the establishment of the State, having become the country's largest land-owning body (19%), it devotes its resources primarily to land reclamation and re-afforestation. Its lands are administered by ◇ **meen'hal mekarke'ey yeesra'el**.

keren/karney or קרן אור *nf* ray of light.

keren/karney leyzer קרן לייזר *nm* laser beam.

keren/karnot peetsooyeem קרן פיצויים *nf* compensation fund.

keren/karnot rekhov/-ot קרן רחוב *nf* street corner.

keren/karnot tagmooleeem קרן תגמולים *nf* combined and mutually financed employees' pension and compensation fund.

keren/kranot קרן *nf* **1.** fund; **2.** corner; (*pl+of:* **karnot**).

keren ve-reebeet קרן וריבית *nm pl* capital and interest; cost and interest.

keren ya'ar קרן יער *nf* French horn.

('al) keren ha-tsevee על קרן הצבי *adv* **1.** down the drain; a lost venture; **2.** (*lit.*) on the horn of the deer.

(mekheer/-ey ha) keren מחיר הקרן *nm* cost price.

kerer (*npr* **ker|ar**)**/-erah/-artee** קירר *v* cooled; chilled (*pres* **mekarer**; *fut* **yekarer**).

keres/-ot כרס *nf* belly; abdomen.

(svar|at/-ot) keres (*npr* **kares**) סברת כרס *nf* assumption without foundation.

keres/kraseem קרס *nm* hook; clasp.

(tselav/-ey) keres צלב־קרס *nm* swastika.

keresh/krasheem קרש *nm* plank; board; (*pl+of:* **karshey**).

keresh/karshey kefeetsah קרש קפיצה *nm* springboard.

keret קרת *nf* town; city (Bibl.).

ker|ev/-vah/-avtee קירב *v* advanced; brought near; (*pres* **mekarev**; *fut* **yekarev**).

(be) kerev בקרב *adv* among; amid; amidst.

(mee) kerev lev מקרב לב *adv* from the bottom of one's heart.

kerkhoot קירחות *nf* baldness.

keroor/-eem קירור *nm* refrigeration; cooling; chilling.

(bet/batey) keroor בית־קירור *nm* cold storage.

keroov/-eem קירוב *nm* bringing near; rapprochement.

(be) keroov בקירוב *adv* approximately.

kes כס *nm* throne; seat (poetic).

kes ha-meeshpat כס המשפט *nm* court bench; seat of judgment.

kesafeem כספים *nm pl* funds; finances; sums of money; (*sing:* **kesef**).

('eenyeney) kesafeem עניני כספים *nm pl* financial matters.

(megalgel/-et) kesafeem מגלגל כספים *[slang] v pres* handle(s) large sums of money; (*pst* **geelgel** *etc; fut* **yegalgel** *etc*).

□ **Kesalon** כסלון *nm* village (est. 1951) in Judea hills, 7 km NE of Bet-Shemesh, Pop. 231.

kes|am/-ameem קיסם *nm* **1.** toothpick; **2.** splinter; (*pl+of:* **-mey**).

kesameem קסמים *nm pl* magic charms; (*sing:* **kesem**; *pl+of:* **keesmey**).

(ma'agal) kesameem מעגל קסמים *nm* vicious circle.

kesar/-eem קיסר *nm* emperor; caesar; (*pl+of:* **-ey**).

kesaree/-t קיסרי *adj* imperial.

(neetoo|'akh/-kheem) kesaree/-yeem ניתוח קיסרי *nm* Caesarean section; (*pl+of:* **-khey**).

□ **Kesareeyah (Qesaryah)** קיסריה *nf* ruins of ancient Caesarea citadel, harbor and resort built by Herod the Great. Its reconstructed open-air amphitheatre is a popular location for concerts and other performances. Nearby, luxurious residential district with hotel and golf course has developed. 10 km N. of Hadera **(Khaderah)**. Pop. 999.

kesarketeen/-eem קסרקטין *nm* barracks; (*pl+of:* **-ey**).

kesaroo|t/-yot קיסרות *nf* empire .

kesa|yah/-yot כסיה *nf* glove; (*+of:* **-yat**).

keseel/-eem כסיל *nm* moron; simpleton; (*pl+of:* **-ey**).

◇ **(ben) kese' le-'asor** see ◇ **ben kese' le-'asor**.

kesef כסף *nm* silver.

kes|ef/-afeem כסף *nm* money; (*pl+of:* **kaspey**).

kesef katan כסף קטן *nm* **1.** small change; **2.** (fig) trifling matters.

(betsa') kesef בצע כסף *nm* lucre.

(gav|ah/-tah/-eetee) kesef גבה כסף *v* collected money; (*pres* **goveh**; *fut* **yeegbeh** *(b=v)*).

(shetar/sheetrey) kesef שטר־כסף *nm* banknote.
kes|em/-ameem קסם *nm* charm; spell; (*pl+of:* **keesmey**).
kes|et/-atot כסת *nf* featherbed; pillow; (*pl+of:* **keestot**).
kes|et/-atot קסת *nf* inkwell; (*pl+of:* **kastot**).
keshareem קשרים *nm* connections; ties; (*sing:* **kesher**; *pl+of:* **keeshrey**).
(ba/-'ah/-'tee bee) keshareem בא בקשרים *v* established contact with; (*pres* **ba** *etc; fut* **yavo** *etc*).
(ba'al/-ey) keshareem בעל קשרים *nm [slang]* well-connected person.
keshayey nesheemah קשיי נשימה *nm* breathing difficulties.
ke-she- כש־ *(prefix)* as; when; at a time when; while.
kesh|eh/-at havanah קשה הבנה *adj* slow-witted; slow to grasp; (*pl:* **-ey** *etc*).
kesh|eh/-at kheenookh קשה חינוך *adj* backward; uneducated; (*pl:* **-ey** *etc*).
kesh|eh/-at 'oref קשה עורף *adj* **1.** obstinate; **2.** *lit* stiff-necked; (*pl:* **-ey 'oref**).
kesh|eh/-at yom קשה יום *adj* depressed; unhappy; (*pl:* **-ey yom**).
kesheekhoot קשיחות *nf* rigidity; toughness.
kesheer|ah/-ot קשירה *nf* **1.** tying; **2.** plotting; (*+of:* **-at**).
kesheeroo|t/-yot כשירות *nf* fitness; worthiness; qualification.
kesheeshoot קשישות *nf* **1.** old age; **2.** seniority.
keshel כשל *nm* failure; lapse.
(al-) keshel אל־כשל *adj* foolproof.
ke-she-le-'atsm|o/-ah *(etc)* כשלעצמו *adv* per se;
ke-shem she- כשם ש־ just as.
kesh|er/-areem קשר **1.** connection; contact; **2.** conspiracy; (*pl+of:* **keeshrey**).
(be) kesher le- בקשר ל־ *adv* regarding.
(ketseen/-ey) kesher קצין קשר *nm* liaison officer.
(kheyl/-ot) kesher חיל קשר *nm* signal corps.
(meel|at/-ot) kesher מלת קשר *nf* conjunction *(gram.)*.
kesh|et/-atot קשת *nm* **1.** bow; **2.** arch; (*pl+of:* **kashtot**).
keshet be-'anan קשת בענן *nf* rainbow.
(kol tseev'ey ha) keshet כל צבעי הקשת *pl* all the colors of the rainbow.
□ **Keshet** (Qeshet) קשת *nm* village (est. 1974) in Golan Heights, 10 km E. of **Katsreen**. Pop. 354.
keshev קשב *nm* attentiveness; listening.
kesoot כסות *nf* cover; covering.
kesoot 'eynayeem כסות עיניים *nf* pretext; eye-wash; excuse.
ket|a'/-a'eem קטע *nm* excerpt; fragment; section; (*pl+of:* **keet'ey**).
(koopah) ketanah קופה קטנה *nf* petty-cash box.
ketantan/-ah קטנטן *adj* tiny; very small.

ketat|ah/-ot קטטה *nf* quarrel; squabble; (*+of:* **-at**).
ketav כתב *nm* writing; script.
ketav/keetvey eeshoom כתב אישום *nm* charge-sheet; bill of information.
ketav/keetvey 'et כתב עת *nm* periodical.
ketav/keetvey haganah כתב הגנה *nm* statement of defense.
ketav/keetvey meet'an כתב מטען *nm* bill of lading.
ketav/keetvey plaster כתב פלסטר *nm* lampoon; libelous document.
ketav/keetvey seetnah כתב שטנה *nm* indictment.
ketav/keetvey tvee'ah כתב־תביעה *nm* statement of claim; suit (legal).
ketav/keetvey yad כתב יד *nm* **1.** handwriting; **2.** manuscript.
(he'el|ah/-tah/-etee 'al ha) ketav העלה על הכתב *v* put in writing; (*pres* **ma'aleh** *etc; fut* **ya'aleh** *etc*).
ketaveem כתבים *nm pl* works; writings; (*sing:* **ktav**; *pl+of:* **keetvey**).
ketee'ah/-'ot קטיעה *nf* amputation; (*+of:* **-'at**).
keteef|ah קטיפה *nf* velvet; (*+of:* **-at**).
keteef|ah/-ot קטיפה *nf* **1.** picking (fruit); **2.** plucking (flowers); (*+of:* **-at**).
keteel|ah/-ot קטילה *nf* **1.** killing; **2.** (mostly *figurat.*) condemning, disavowing; (*+of:* **-at**).
keteen|ah/-ot קטינה *nf* female minor; (*+of:* **-at**).
keteenoot קטינות *nf* status of minor; underage.
keteev/-eem כתיב *nm* orthography; spelling.
◊ **keteev khaser** כתיב חסר *nm* "defective" spelling, i.e. spelling with no indicated vowel-letters.
◊ **keteev male** כתיב מלא *nm* "plene", "full" spelling, i.e. spelling with indicated vowel-letters.
(shegee|'at/-'ot) kteev שגיאת כתיב *nf* spelling mistake; misspelling.
keteevah כתיבה *nf* writing; (*+of:* **-at**).
◊ **keteevah va-khateemah tovah!** כתיבה וחתימה טובה! traditional Jewish New Year greeting formula for wishing Happy New Year throughout the month preceding Rosh Ha-Shanah & during the two days of the festival itself.
(mekhon|at/-ot) keteevah מכונת כתיבה *nf* typewriter.
(shoolkhan/-ot) keteevah שולחן כתיבה *nf* desk.
ketefeeyot כתפיות *nf pl* straps; shoulder loops.
ketel קטל *nm* slaughter; killing.
ketem/ketameem כתם *nm* stain; (*pl+of:* **keetmey**).
keter/ketareem כתר *nm* crown; (*pl+of:* **keetrey**).
ketonet/kotnot laylah כתונת לילה *nf* night dress; night gown.
ketonet/kotnot paseem כתונת פסים *nf* "dress of many colors"; striped gown.

◇ **ketoob|ah/-ot** כתובה *nf* marriage contract which bridegroom hands the bride at a Jewish wedding ceremony; (*+of:* **-at**).

ketoomah כתומה *adj nf* orange-colored; (*masc.:* **katom**).

□ **Ketoorah** (Qetura) קטורה *nm* kibbutz (est. 1973) on the road to Elat (**Eylat**) 10 km N. of **Yatvatah**. Pop. 177.

ketoret קטורת *nf* incense.

ketov|et/-ot כתובת *nf* **1.** address; **2.** inscription.

ketovet 'al ha-keer כתובת על הקיר *nf* writing on the wall.

ketov|et/-ot ka'aka' כתובת קעקע *nf* tattoo.

kets/keets|eem קץ *nm* end; (*pl+of:* **-ey**).

(dakhak/-ah/-tee et ha) kets דחק את הקץ *v* forced the issue; showed impatience; (*pres* **dokhek** *etc; fut* **yeedkhak** *etc*).

(mee) kets מקץ *conj* after; at the end of.

(sam/-ah/-tee) kets שם קץ *v* put an end; (*pres* **sam** *etc; fut* **yaseem** *etc*).

ketsad כיצד how; how come.

ketsar/keetsrat komah קצר קומה *adj* of short stature.

ketsar/keetsrat mo'ed קצר מועד *adj* short-term.

ketsar/keetsrat re'oot (*or:* **re'eeyah**) קצר ראות *adj* short-sighted; nearsighted.

ketsar/keetsrat ro'ee קצר רואי *adj* short-sighted; nearsighted.

ketsar/keetsrat roo'akh קצר רוח *adj* impatient; short-tempered; jittery.

ketsar/keetsrat yad קצר יד *adj m* incapable; unable.

(bee) ketsarah בקצרה *adv* in short; in brief.

(meekhnasayeem) ketsareem מכנסיים קצרים *nm pl* shorts; short pants.

ketsee/-t קיצי *adj* summer-; summery.

ketseet קיצית *adv* summerlike.

ketsef קצף *nm* **1.** foam; **2.** wrath; anger.

(shetsef) ketsef שצף קצף *nm* violent anger.

kets|er/-areem קצר *nm* **1.** short circuit (electr); **2.** *[slang]* (*figurat.*) something gone wrong.

kets|ev/-aveem קצב *nm* rhythm; (*pl+of:* **keetsbey**).

kets kol basar קץ כל בשר end of all flesh (Bibl.).

keva' קבע *nm* permanence.

-keva' קבע *(suffix) adj* permanent.

(deer|at/-ot) keva' דירת קבע *nf* domicile; permanent residence.

(hal|akh/-khah/-akhtee) keva' הלך קבע *v* was going steady; (*pres* **holekh** *etc; fut* **yelekh** *etc*).

(hora|'at/-'ot) keva' הוראת קבע *nf* standing instruction.

(khat|am/-mah/-amtee) keva' חתם קבע *v* signed on to remain in the Army professionally; joined the standing army for good; (*pres* **khotem** *etc; fut* **yakhtom** *etc*).

(pekood|at/-ot) keva' פקודת קבע *nf* standing order.

(tseva ha) keva' צבא הקבע *nm* standing (career) army.

kev|ah/-ot קיבה *nf* stomach (*+of:* **-at**).

('al) kevah rekah על קיבה ריקה *adv* on an empty stomach.

(keelkool/-ey) kevah קלקול קיבה *nm* stomach trouble; bad stomach.

kevan כיוון since; whereas.

(mee) kevan she- מכיוון ש־ *conj* since; because.

kev|el/-aleem כבל *nm* cable; chain; (*pl+of:* **kavley**).

kev|er/-areem קבר *nm* grave; tomb; (*pl+of:* **keevrey**).

kever akheem קבר אחים *nm* collective (fraternal) grave (for victims of a mass-killing).

□ **Kever Rakhel** קבר רחל *nm* Rachel's Tomb (Bibl) place of pilgrimage and historic monument at N. entry to Bethlehem.

kev|es/-aseem כבש *nm* lamb; (*pl+of:* **keevsey**).

(besar) keves בשר כבש *nm* mutton.

kev|esh/-asheem כבש *nm* gangway; ramp; gangplank; (*pl+of:* **keevshey**).

kevesh ha-matos כבש המטוס *nm* airplane ramp.

keys|am/-ameem קיסם *nm* **1.** toothpick; **2.** splinter; (*pl+of:* **-mey**).

keytsad כיצד how.

keytsee/-t קיצי *adj* summer-; summery.

keytseet קיצית *adv* summerlike.

keysar/-eem קיסר *nm* emperor; caesar; (*pl+of:* **-ey**).

keysaree/-t קיסרי *adj* imperial.

(neetoo|'akh/-kheem) keysaree/-yeem ניתוח קיסרי *nm* Caesarean section; (*pl+of:* **-khey**).

keysaroo|t/-yot קיסרות *nf* empire .

keyv|ah/-ot קיבה *nf* stomach (*+of:* **-at**).

('al) keyvah reykah על קיבה ריקה *adv* on an empty stomach.

(keelkool/-ey) keyvah קלקול קיבה *nm* stomach trouble; bad stomach.

keyvan כיוון since; whereas.

(mee) keyvan she- מכיוון ש־ *conj* since; because.

kfaf|ah/-ot כפפה *nf* glove; (*+of:* **keefef|at/-ot**).

kfar|/-eem כפר *nm* village; (*pl+of:* **kafrey**).

□ **Kfar Akheem** see □ **Kefar Akheem**, above.

□ **Kfar Aveev** see □ **Kefar Aveev**, above.

□ **Kfar Avraham** see □ **Kefar Avraham**, above.

□ **Kfar 'Azah** see □ **Kefar 'Azah**, above.

□ **Kfar Azar** see □ **Kefar Azar**, above.

□ **Kfar Barookh** see □ **Kefar Barookh**, above.

□ **Kfar Batyah** see □ **Kefar Batyah**, above.

□ **Kfar Beeloo** see □ **Kefar Beeloo**, above.

□ **Kfar Been-Noon** see □ **Kefar Been-Noon**, above.

□ **Kfar Bloom** see □ **Kefar Bloom**, above.

□ **Kfar Byaleek** see □ **Kefar Byaleek**, above.

□ **Kfar Danee'el** see □ **Kefar Danee'el**, above.

□ **Kfar Darom** see □ **Kefar Darom**, above.

□ **Kfar Eleeyahoo** see □ **Kefar Eleeyahoo**, above.
□ **Kfar 'Etsyon** see □ **Kefar 'Etsyon**, above.
□ **Kfar Gabeerol** see □ **Kefar Gabeerol**, above.
□ **Kfar Galeem** see □ **Kefar Galeem**, above.
□ **Kfar Geed'on** see □ **Kefar Geed'on**, above.
□ **Kfar Geel'adee** see □ **Kefar Geel'adee**, above.
□ **Kfar Gleekson** see □ **Kefar Gleekson**, above.
□ **Kfar ha-Bapteesteem** see □ **Kefar ha-Bapteesteem**, above.
□ **Kfar ha-Khoresh** see □ **Kefar ha-Khoresh**, above.
□ **Kfar ha-Makabee** see □ **Kefar ha-Makabee**, above.
□ **Kfar ha-Makabeeyah** see □ **Kefar ha-Makabeeyah**, above.
□ **Kfar ha-Nageed** see □ **Kefar ha-Nageed**, above.
□ **Kfar ha-No'ar Ben-Shemen** see □ **Kefar ha-No'ar Ben-Shemen**, above.
□ **Kfar ha-No'ar ha-Datee** see □ **Kefar ha-No'ar** ha-Datee, above.
□ **Kfar ha-No'ar Yohanah Jaboteensky** see □ **Kefar No'ar Yohanah Jaboteensky**Ì, above.
□ **Kfar ha-Reef** see □ **Kefar ha-Reef**, above.
□ **Kfar ha-Ro'eh** see □ **Kefar ha-Ro'eh**, above.
□ **Kfar Hes** see □ **Kefar Hes**, above.
□ **Kfar Khabad** see □ **Kefar Khabad**, above.
□ **Kfar Kharoov** see □ **Kefar Kharoov**, above.
□ **Kfar Khaseedeem Alef** see □ **Kefar Khaseedeem Alef**, above.
□ **Kfar Khaseedeem Bet** see □ **Kefar Khaseedeem Bet**, above.
□ **Kfar Khayeem** see □ **Kefar Khayeem**, above.
□ **Kfar Kheeteem** see □ **Kefar Kheeteem**, above.
□ **Kfar Keesh** see □ **Kefar Keesh**, above.
□ **Kfar Malal** see □ **Kefar Malal**, above.
□ **Kfar Masareek** see □ **Kefar Masareek**, above.
□ **Kfar Maymon** see □ **Kefar Maymon**, above.
□ **Kfar Menakhem** see □ **Kefar Menakhem**, above.
□ **Kfar Monash** see □ **Kefar Monash**, above.
□ **Kfar Mordekhay** see □ **Kefar Mordekhay**, above.
□ **Kfar Neter** see □ **Kefar Neter**, above.
□ **Kfar Peenes** see □ **Kefar Peenes**, above.
□ **Kfar Roopeen** see □ **Kefar Roopeen**, above.
□ **Kfar Root** see □ **Kefar Root**, above.
□ **Kfar Rosh ha-Neekrah** see □ **Kefar Rosh ha-Neekrah**, above.
□ **Kfar Saba** see □ **Kefar Saba**, above.
□ **Kfar Seelver** see □ **Kefar Seelver**, above.
□ **Kfar Seerkeen** see □ **Kefar Seerkeen**, above.
□ **Kfar Shalem** see □ **Kefar Shalem**, above.
□ **Kfar Shamay** see □ **Kefar Shamay**, above.
□ **Kfar Shemoo'el** see □ **Kefar Shmoo'el**, above.
□ **Kfar Shemaryahoo** see □ **Kefar Shemaryahoo**, above.
□ **Kfar Sold** see □ **Kefar Sold**, above.
□ **Kfar Tavor** see □ **Kefar Tavor**, above.
□ **Kfar Trooman** see □ **Kefar Trooman**, above.
□ **Kfar Varboorg** see □ **Kefar Varboorg**, above.
□ **Kfar Veetkeen** see □ **Kefar Veetkeen**, above.
□ **Kfar Veradeem** see □ **Kefar Veradeem**, above.
□ **Kfar Ya'bets** see □ **Kefar Ya'bets**, above.
□ **Kfar Yehoshoo'a** see □ **Kefar Yehoshoo'a**, above.
□ **Kfar Yekhezkel** see □ **Kefar Yekhezkel**, above.
□ **Kfar Yonah** see □ **Kefar Yonah**, above.
□ **Kfar Zeteem** see □ **Kefar Zeteem**, above.
kfee ha-neemsar כפי הנמסר *adv* according to reports.
kfee ha-neer'eh כפי הנראה *adv* apparently.
kfee|'ah קפיאה *nf* freezing; (*+of:* **-'at**).
kfee'ah 'al ha-shemareem קפיאה על השמרים *nf* resting on one's laurels; stagnation.
kfeedah קפידה *nf* meticulousness.
(bee) kfeedah בקפידה *adv* strictly; meticulously.
(bee) kfeefah (*npr* **bee-kh'feefah**) **akhat** בכפיפה אחת *adv* together.
kfeefoo|t/-yot כפיפות *nf* subordination; flexibility.
(bee) kfeefoot (*npr* **bee-khefeefoot**) **le-** בכפיפות ל- *adv* subject to.
kfeeloo|t/-yot כפילות *nf* duplication.
kfeer|ah/-ot כפירה *nf* denial; heresy; (*+of:* **-at**).
kfeerah be-'eekar כפירה בעיקר *nf* **1**. contesting the main argument; **2**. denying the very existence of God.
kfeets/-eem קפיץ *nm* spring; coil; (*pl+of:* **-ey**).
kfeets|ah/-ot קפיצה *nf* jump; (*+of:* **-at**).
(keresh/karshey) kfeetsah קרש קפיצה *nm* springboard.
kfeets|at/-ot derekh קפיצת דרך *nf* shortcut; short distance away.
kfeetsee/-t קפיצי *adj* springy; elastic; springlike.
kfeetsee/-t קפיצי *adj* springy; elastic; springlike.
kfee|yah/-yot כפייה *nf* coercion; (*+of:* **-yat**).
kfeeyah dateet כפייה דתית *nf* religious coercion.
kfeeyoot tovah כפיות טובה *nf* ingratitude.
kfoo|y (also kefooy)/-yat tovah כפוי טובה *adj* ungrateful.

kfor כפור *nm* frost.

kfots!/keeftsee! !קפוץ *v imp* s *m/f* jump! (*pst* **kafats;** *pres* **kofets;** *fut* **yeekpots;** *(p=f)*).

kfots lee! !קפוץ לי *[slang] v imp sing m* go hang yourself! I couldn't care less.

> Kh.
> is the combination of letters which, in this dictionary, transliterates the Hebrew consonants ח (**Khet**) and כ (**Khaf**) the pronunciation of which is nearly identical in native Hebrew speech. To an English-speaking person it sounds as the *ch* in the Scottish word *loch* or in the Jewish name *Chaim* (**Khayeem**). Thus, words beginning with that sound have been grouped in a separate chapter, under "**Kh**", which follows this chapter.

(me-akhorey ha) kla'eem מאחורי הקלעים *adv* **1.** behind the curtains; **2.** behind the scenes.

klaf קלף *nm* parchment.

klaf/-eem קלף *nm* playing card; (*pl+of:* **-ey**).

(halakh lo/lah) klaf meshage'a' הלך לו/לה קלף משגע *[colloq.] v* he/she succeeded madly; had a touch of extreme luck; (*pres* **holekh** *etc; fut* **yelekh** *etc*).

(meeskh|ak/-ekey) klafeem משחק קלפים *nm* game of cards.

□ **Klakheem** (Qelahim) קלחים *nm* village (est. 1954) in the Northern Negev, 8 km NW of **Tsomet Neteevot** (Netivot Junction). Pop. 284.

klal/-eem כלל *nm* rule; regulation; (*pl+of:* **-ey**).

klal oo-kh'lal lo *(kh=k)* כלל וכלל לא in no way; definitely not; not at all.

(be-derekh) klal בדרך כלל *adv* generally; as a rule.

(ha) klal הכלל *nm* the general public; the community.

(tovat ha) klal טובת הכלל *nf* the general good; public interest.

(yots|e/-et meen ha) klal יוצא מן הכלל *adj* exceptional; extraordinary; (*pl:* **-'eem/-'ot** *etc*).

klal|ah/-ot קללה *nf* curse; (*+of:* **keelelat**).

klalee/-t כללי *adj* general.

(ha-mateh ha) klalee המטה הכללי *nm* the General Staff.

(konsool) klalee קונסול כללי *nm* Consul General.

(mazkeer) klalee מזכיר כללי *nm* Secretary General.

(menahel) klalee מנהל כללי *nm* general manager; director general.

klaleet כללית *adv* generally; in general terms.

(asef|ah/-ot) klalee|t/-yot אסיפה כללית *nf* general meeting.

(ha-tvee'ah ha) klaleet התביעה הכללית *nf* the prosecution.

(mekheer|ah/-ot) klalee|t/-yot מכירה כללית *nf* clearance sale.

kelapey כלפי towards; in the direction of.

klasee/-t קלסי *adj* classical.

klaseekon/-eem קלסיקון *nm* classicist (*pl+of:* **-ey**).

klaster/-ey paneem קלסתר פנים *nm* features; face;

klasteron/-eem קלסתרון *nm* composite portrait for identification of suspects.

klavl|av/-abeem *(b=v)* כלבלב *nm* puppy (*pl+of:* **-abey**).

klayah כליה *nf* annihilation; disaster.

klayah (*npr* **keelyah**)**/klayot** כלייה *nm* kidney (*+of:* **keel|yat/-yot**).

(moosar) klayot מוסר כליות *nm* pangs of conscience.

klee/keleem כלי *nm* **1.** instrument; tool; **2.** vessel (*pl+of:* **kley**).

klee en khefets bo (*or:* **klee eyn** *etc*) כלי אין חפץ בו *adj* useless, unwanted thing (or person).

klee/kley hakashah כלי הקשה *nm* percussion instrument.

klee/kley keebool כלי קיבול *nm* receptacle; container.

klee/kley kheres כלי חרס *nm* pottery.

klee/kley negeenah כלי נגינה *nm* musical instrument.

klee/kley sharet כלי שרת *nm* tool; instrument.

klee|'ah/-'ot כליאה *nf* **1.** imprisonment; **2.** locking up (*+of:* **-'at**).

klee|'ah/-'ot קליעה *nf* braiding (*+of:* **-'at**).

klee|'ah/-'ot le-matarah קליעה למטרה *nf* target shooting.

kleed/-eem קליד *nm* key of a piano, typewriter *etc*; (*pl+of:* **-ey**).

kleek|ah/-ot קליקה *[colloq.] nf* clique; (*+of:* **-at**).

kleel ha-shlemoot כליל השלימות *adj* perfect; acme of perfection.

kleelat/-ot yofee כלילת יופי *adj - nf* paragon of beauty; (*m* **kleel yofee**).

kleem|ah/-ot כלימה *nf* shame; disgrace; (*+of:* **-at**).

(booshah oo) kleemah (*npr* **oo-kh'leemah**) בושה וכלימה *interj* what a shame!

kleenee/-t קליני *adj* clinical.

kleeneek|ah/-ot קליניקה *nf* clinic; (*+of:* **-at**).

kleep|ah/-ot קליפה *nf* shell; peel; skin; (*+of:* **-at**).

(kee) kleepat ha-shoom כקליפת השום *adv* **1.** valueless; worthless; **2.** (*lit.*) as a garlic peel.

kleeshe|h/-'ot קלישה *nf* **1.** cliché; pattern; **2.** cut; block for printing.

kleeshoot קלישות *nf* rootlessness; superficiality.

kleet|ah/-ot קליטה *nf* **1.** reception (of radio, t.v. *etc* broadcasts); **2.** absorption (of immigrants, newcomers, new ideas *etc*); (*+of:* **-at**).

◇ **(meesrad ha) kleetah** see ◇ **meesrad ha-kleetah**.

◇ **kleetat 'aleeyah** קליטת עליה *nf* absorption of immigrants.

◇ **kleetat khozreem** קליטת חוזרים *nf* absorption of returnees (i.e of Israelis who have resided abroad for years).

klee|yah/-yot קלייה *nf* roasting; toasting; (+*of:* **-yat**).
kleeyent/-eem קליינט *[colloq.] nm* client.
kleeyentee|t/-yot קליינטית *[colloq.] nf* female client.
kleeyentoor|ah/-ot קליינטורה *[colloq.] nf* clientele; (+*of:* **-at**).
kley 'avodah כלי עבודה *nm pl* tools; (*sing:* **klee**).
kley bayeet כלי־בית *nm pl* houseware.
kley meetah (*sing:* **klee** *etc*) כלי מיטה *nm pl* bedding; bed clothes.
kley meetbakh (*sing:* **klee** *etc*) כלי מטבח *nm pl* kitchenware.
kley rekhev (*sing:* **klee** *etc*) כלי רכב *nm pl* vehicles.
kley tayees (*sing:* **klee** *etc*) כלי טיס *nm pl* aircraft.
kley zayeen (*sing:* **klee** *etc*) כלי זין *nm pl* arms; weapons.
kley zemer (*sing:* **klee** *etc*) כלי זמר *[colloq.] nm pl* musical instruments.
klezmer/-eem קלזמר *[colloq.] nm* musician.
klomar (*or:* **kelomar**) כלומר *conj* that is to say.
klon|as/-sa'ot קלונס *nm* pole; stilt; picket.
klokel/-et קלוקל *adj* of poor quality; rotten.
klonsa'ot (*sing:* **klonas**) קלונסאות *nm pl* poles; stilts.
kloolot כלולות *nf pl* betrothal; wedding.
(leyl) kloolot ליל כלולות *nm* wedding night.
kloom כלום *nm* **1.** *[colloq.]* (incorr. use) nothing; **2.** (corr. use) something.
(lo) kloom (*npr* **khloom**) לא כלום nothing.
kloomneek/-eet כלומניק *nmf [slang]* good for nothing; nincompoop.
kloov/-eem כלוב *nm* cage; (*pl+of:* **-ey**).
klor כלור *nm* chlorine.
◇ **(ha)kneset (the Knesset)** הכנסת *nf* Israel's Parliament. 120 members elected (normally) once every four years by proportional vote.
koh כה so; thus.
('ad) koh עד כה *adv* so far; until now; to this point.
(ben) koh va-khoh (*kh=k*) בין כה וכה anyhow; anyway; meanwhile.
ko'akh/kokhot כוח *nm* force; power; strength.
ko'akh adam כוח אדם *nm* manpower.
◇ **(agaf) ko'akh adam** see ◇ **agaf ko'akh adam**.
(menahel/-et) ko'akh adam מנהל כוח אדם *nmf* manager (head) in charge of manpower.
ko'akh 'elyon כוח עליון *nm* force majeure.
ko'akh ha-koved כוח הכובד *nm* gravitation.
ko'akh ha-mesheekhah כוח המשיכה *nm* gravity.
ko'akh gavra כוח גברא *nm* sexual potency.
ko'akh keneeyah כוח קנייה *nm* purchasing power.
ko'akh mesheekhah כוח משיכה *nm* power of attraction.
ko'akh/kokhot soos כוח סוס *nm* horsepower.
◇ **(agaf) ko'akh adam** see ◇ **agaf ko'akh adam**.
(az|ar-rah/-artee) ko'akh אזר כוח *v* mustered strength; (*pres* **ozer** *etc; fut* **ye'ezor** *etc*).
(ba/-'at) ko'akh (*pl:* **-'ey** *etc*) בא כוח *nmf* **1.** holder of power of attorney; representative; **2.** Chargé d'affaires (Dipl. Corps).
(be) ko'akh (*npr* **be-kho'akh**) בכוח *adv* **1.** forcibly; by force; **2.** potentially.
(mee) ko'akh מכוח *adv* by force of; on the strength of.
(meyoop|eh/-at) ko'akh מיופה כוח *nmf* **1.** holder of a power of attorney; representative; **2.** Chargé d'Affaires (Dipl. Corps).
(yeep|ah/-tah/-eetee et) ko'akh ייפה את כוח *v* authorized; empowered; (*pres* **meyapeh** *etc; fut* **yeyapeh** *etc*).
(yeepoo|y/-yey) ko'akh ייפוי־כוח *nm* power of attorney; authorization.
(yeeshar) ko'akh יישר כוח *interj* Bravo!
ko'aleets|yah/-yot קואליציה *nf* coalition; (+*of:* **-yat**).
ko'aleetsyonee/t קואליציוני *adj* pertaining to a coalition; coalition-.
kod/-eem קוד *nm* code.
kodem קודם *adv* earlier; before.
kodem kol קודם כול *adv* first of all.
kodem le-khen קודם לכן *adv* previously; before that.
(mee) kodem מקודם *adv* before; earlier.
kodem/-et קודם *adj* previous; prior.
(kol ha) kodem zokheh כל הקודם זוכה first come, first served.
koder/-et קודר *adj* gloomy.
kod|esh/osheem קודש *nm* sanctity; holiness.
kodesh קודש *adj (suffix)* holy.
kodesh kodasheem קודש קודשים *nm* Holy of Holies.
(aron ha) kodesh ארון הקודש *nm* Holy Ark (in a synagogue).
('eer ha) kodesh עיר הקודש *nf* Holy City, i.e. Jerusalem.
('erets ha) kodesh ארץ הקודש *nf* the Holy Land, i.e. Palestine.
(keetvey ha) kodesh כתבי הקודש *nf pl* Holy Scriptures.
(kheelool ha) kodesh חילול הקודש *nm* sacrilege.
(kherdat) kodesh חרדת קודש *nf* awesome reverence.
(leshon ha) kodesh לשון הקודש *nf* the Holy Language, i.e. Hebrew.
(roo'akh ha) kodesh רוח הקודש *nm* the Holy Spirit.
(shabat) kodesh שבת קודש *nf* the Holy Sabbath.
kodkod/-eem קדקוד *nm* top of the head; vertex.
ko'ev/-et כואב **1.** *adj* hurting; aching; **2.** *v pres* hurts; aches; (*pst* **ka'av**; *fut* **yeekh'av** *(kh=k)*).
kof/-eem קוף *nm* ape; monkey; (*pl+of:* **-ey**).
kof|ah/-ot קופה *nf* female ape.
kof|ef/-efah/-aftee כופף *v* bent; (*pres* **mekofef**; *fut* **yekofef**).
kofer כופר *nm* **1.** ransom; **2.** indemnity; **3.** fine.

kofer nefesh כופר נפש *nm* ransom money.

kofer/-et כופר **1.** *v pres* contests; doubts (*pst* **kafar**; *fut* **yeekhpor**; *(kh=k; p=f)*); **2.** *nmf* skeptic; heretic.

(kofer be) 'eekar כופר בעיקר *adj* heretic; denying the existence of God.

kohel כוהל *nm* alcohol; spirt.

kohen/-et כוהן *nmf* priest/ess; (*pl:* **kohan|eem**; *+of:* **-ey**).

◇ **kohen/kohaneem** כהן *nmf* scion of the ancient biblical caste of priests in the Temple in Jerusalem. One may presume that any Jewish person bearing surnames such as Kohen, Kohn, Cohen, Cohn, Kahan, Kahane, Kogan, Kagan and many transformations or derivations of these (Katz, Katzenelson, Kaganovitch etc) is a Kohen. In various Jewish religious contexts there is some special role reserved for a Kohen. Thus, for a male, being a Kohen implies, among religiously observant Jews, a series of prerogatives and prohibitions which do not apply to other Jewish males.

kohen/kohaney dat כוהן דת *nm* priest.

kokh|av/-aveem כוכב *nm* star; (*pl+of:* **-vey**).

kokh|av/-vey kolno'a כוכב קולנוע *nm* movie-star.

□ **Kokhav ha-Shakhar** (Kokhav haShakhar) כוכב השחר *nm* agricultural settlement (est. 1975) E. of Samaria Hills, 15 km N. of Jericho, along the **Alon** road. Pop. 486.

□ **Kokhav Ya'eer** (Kokhav Ya'ir) כוכב יאיר *nm* residential settlement in E. Sharon, just over the Green Line, 9 km W. of **Toolkarem**. Pop. 3,850.

□ **Kokhav Meekha'el Sobel** (Kokhav Mikha'el Sobell) כוכב מיכאל סובל *nm* village (est. 1962) in the S. part of the Coastal Plain, 3 km S. of **Tsomet Geev'atee** road junction. Pop. 455.

kokh|av/-vey lekhet כוכב לכת *nm* planet.

kokh|av/-vey shaveet כוכב שביט *nm* comet.

kokhavee|t/-yot כוכבית *nf* asterisk (*).

kokh|evet/-avot כוכבת *nf* female movie- or stage-star.

kokhot ha-beetakhon כוחות הביטחון *nm pl* defence forces.

(hafradat) kokhot הפרדת כוחות *nf* disengagement of forces (milit.).

kokos קוקוס *nm* coconut.

kokhvanee|t/-yot כוכבנית *nf* starlet (*+of:* **-yat**).

kol כל **1.** all; **2.** every; **3.** entire.

kol-bo כל־בו **1.** *adj* all encompassing; **2.** *nm* department store.

kol davar כל דבר *nm* anything; everything.

kol deekhfeen כל דכפין *nm (Aram.)* **1.** anyone in need; **2.** *[colloq.]* anyone.

kol ekhad/akhat כל אחד/אחת *nmf* everyone; everybody.

kol ekhad ve-'ekhad כל אחד ואחד each and every one.

kol 'eekar כל עיקר *adv* in no way; at all.

kol eymat כל אימת *adv* whenever; each time.

kol ha-kavod כל הכבוד all due respect; congratulations!

◇ **kol ha-shalom** ("Kol Hashalom") "קול השלום" *nf* "The Voice of Peace", unauthorized yet tolerated privately owned piratic radio-station broadcasting entertainment programs and publicity in English from a ship near territorial waters outside Tel-Aviv.

◇ **kol needrey** כל נדרי *nf* "Kol Nidre", the opening prayer (in Aramaic) of the Day of Atonement service in synagogues on Yom Kippur Eve, with which the 24 hours of fasting and praying start.

◇ **kol yeesra'el** ("Qol Israel") קול ישראל *nm* "The Voice of Israel", identification name used by Israel radio-broadcasting services. Started by the British administration in 1936 as the "Palestine Broadcasting Service" (PBS), a tri-lingual government service, it later conveniently identified itself as "Jerusalem Calling" so to avoid using on the air the Hebrew name for Palestine ("Eretz Israel"). In 1948 it was taken over by the nascent State of Israel and identified itself as "Voice of Israel" to emphasize continuity with sporadic underground broadcasts on and off under that name since 1940. In 1965, by legislative act, it ceased to be a government service and was reorganized as a public state-sponsored radio & TV broadcasting service under the auspices of the newly created Israel Broacasting Authority (**reshoot ha-sheedoor** רשות השידור).

◇ **kol yeesra'el la-golah** "קול ישראל לגולה" *nm* "The Voice of Israel to the Diaspora", multi-lingual shortwave voice-broadcasts addressed to listeners abroad. Started in 1949 by the Jewish Agency as the "Voice of Zion to the Diaspora" (**kol tseeyon la-golah**) it became in time part of the Israel Broadcasting Authority's own services and its name was adjusted accordingly.

kol/-ot nefets קול נפץ *nm* sound of explosion.

(bat) kol בת־קול *nf* **1.** Divine Voice; **2.** echo.

(be) kol בקול *adv* aloud.

(be) kol ram בקול רם *adv* loudly.

(magbeer/-ey) kol מגביר קול *nm* **1.** loudspeaker; megaphone; **2.** amplifier.

(meyterey) kol מיתרי קול *nm pl* vocal cords.

(sham|a'/-'ah/-a'tee be) kol שמע בקול *v* heeded; obeyed; (*pres* **shome'a'** *etc*; *fut* **yeeshma'** *etc*).

(teshoovah/-ot) kol|a'at/-'ot תשובה קולעת *nf* a telling reply.

kolanee/-t קולני *adj* vociferous.

kolar/-eem קולר *nm* **1.** collar (special one used for dogs and prisoners); **2.** responsibility; (*pl+of:* **-ey**).

(tal|ah/-tah/-eetee et ha) kolar be- תלה את הקולר ־ב *v* laid the blame on; (*pres* **toleh** *etc; fut* **yeetleh** *etc*).

kol|av/-aveem קולב *nm* clothes-hanger; (*pl+of:* **-vey**).

kolbo כלבו *nm* department-store.

(bet/batey) kolbo בית כלבו *nm* department-store.

(khanoo|t/-yot) kolbo חנות כלבו *nm* department-store.

□ **Khatsor ha-Gleeleet** (Hazor haGlilit) חצור הגלילית *nf* township (est. 1953) in Upper Gallilee, 2 km N. of **Rosh-Peenah**. Pop. 7,230.

□ **Khavat Shmoo'el** (Hawwat Shemu'el) חוות שמואל *nf* experimental agricultural farm (est. 1952) dedicated to cotton-growing, 10 km N. of Bet-She'an, in the Jordan Valley.

kolboyneek/-eet כלבויניק *nmf [slang]* jack of all trades.

kol|e'a'/-a'at קולע *adj* apt; to the point; of accurate aim.

kolel כולל *adv* including.

◇ **kolel/-eem** כולל *nm* yeshiva where students, mostly married, study full-time.

kolel/-et כולל *v* **1.** *pres* **comprise(s); include(s);** (*pst* **kalal**; *fut* **yeekhlol** *(kh=k)*); **2.** *adj* comprehensive; inclusive.

(peetron) kolel פתרון כולל *nm* over-all solution.

(sekhoom) kolel סכום כולל *nm* lump sum.

kolelanee/-t כוללני *adj* all-embracing; general; comrehensive.

kolee/-t קולי *adj* vocal; sonic.

('al-) kolee/-t על־קולי *adj* supersonic.

(rav-) kolee/-t רב־קולי *adj* polyphonic.

(be) koley-kolot בקולי קולות *adv* with lots of noise; vociferously.

kolno'a קולנוע *nm* cinema; (*pl* **batey-kolno'a**).

(batey) kolno'a בתי קולנוע *nm pl* cinemas.

(kokh|av/-vey) kolno'a כוכב קולנוע *nm* filmstar; movie-star.

(kokh|evet/-avot) kolno'a כוכבת קולנוע *nf* filmstar; movie-star.

(mevak|er/-rey) kolno'a מבקר קולנוע *nm* cinema critic; movie critic.

(seret/seertey) kolno'a סרט קולנוע *nm* motion picture; movie film.

kolno'an/-eem קולנוען *nm* movie-maker.

kolno'ee/-t קולנועי *adj* cinematographic.

kolot oo-vrakeem *(v=b)* קולות וברקים *nm pl* deafening noise; thunder and lightning.

(be-rov) kolot ברוב קולות *adv* by majority vote.

kom|ah/-ot קומה *nf* **1.** floor; **2.** stature; (*+of:* **-at**).

(ba'al/-at) komah בעל קומה *adj* tall; a person of stature.

(ba'al/-at shee'oor) komah בעל שיעור קומה *adj* of moral stature.

(be) komah zkoofah בקומה זקופה *adv* upright; erect.

(gvah/geevhat) komah גבה־קומה *adj* tall.

(ketsar/keetsrat) komah קצר־קומה *adj* of short stature.

(nemookh/-at) komah נמוך־קומה *adj* of short stature.

(she'oor/-ey) komah שיעור קומה *nm* **1.** stature; **2.** degree of importance.

(zekoof/-at) komah זקוף קומה *adj* upright bearing.

(zekeefoot) komah זקיפות קומה *nf* erectness; uprightness.

komat beynayeem קומת ביניים *nf* mezzanine.

(bayeet/bateem doo-) komatee/-yeem בית דו־קומתי *nm* two-storey house.

(doo-) komatee/-t דו־קומתי *adj* of two storeys; two storied.

(otoboos/-eem doo-) komatee/-yeem אוטובוס דו־קומתי - *nm* double-decker bus.

(rav-) komatee/-yeem רב־קומתי *adj* multi-storied.

(telat-) komatee/-yeem תלת קומתי *adj* three-storied.

(melo) komat|o/-ah/-ee *etc* מלוא קומתו *nm* his/her/my *etc* full stature.

kombayn/-eem קומביין *nm* combine-harvester.

kombeenats|yah/-yot קומבינציה *[colloq.] f* combination; commercial combination; (*+of:* **yat**).

◇ **('eeskat/'eskot) kombeenatsyah** see ◇ **'eeskat/'eskot kombeenatsyah.**

kombeeneezon/-eem קומביניזון *nm* slip (lingerie); (*pl+of:* **-ey**).

komed|yah/-yot קומדיה *nf* comedy; farce; (*+of:* **yat**).

komee/-t קומי *adj* funny; comical.

komeek|a'ee/-a'eet (*npr* **komeek|ay**) קומיקאי *nmf* comedian; funny man/woman; clown.

komeekan/-eet קומיקן *nmf* comedian; funny man/woman; clown.

komeesyon/-eem קומיסיון *nm* **1.** commission; percentage of earnings; **2.** selling against a commission.

komeesyoner/-eem קומיסיונר *nm* agent working for a commission.

kom|em/-emah/-amtee קומם *v* **1.** aroused against; **2.** restored; (*pres* **mekomem**; *fut* **yekomem**).

komemeeyoot קוממיות *nf* **1.** independence; **2.** *adv* upright.

◇ **(meelkhemet ha) komemeeyoot** מלחמת הקוממיות *nf* another name for Israel's War of Independence (1947-1948) see under ◇ **meelkhemet ha-'atsma'oot.**

□ **Komemeeyoot** (Qomemiyyut) קוממיות *nm* village (est. 1950) in the Coastal Plain, 6 km NW of **Keeryat-Gat**. Pop. 388.

komer/kemareem כומר *nm* priest (Christian); (*+of:* **komrey**).

komets קומץ *nm* handful; small group.

komooneekatsyah קומוניקציה *nf* communications.

komooneezm קומוניזם *nm* communism.

(ra|v-bey) komot רב־קומות *nm* multi-storied bulding.
konan/-eem כונן *nm* diskette-drive (computers).
konanee|t/-yot כוננית *nf* bookcase; (+*of:* **-yat**).
kondeetor|yah/-yot קונדיטוריה *nf* pastry shop; (+*of:* **-yat**).
kon|eh/-ah קונה *v pres* buy(s); (*pst* **kanah**; *fut* **yeekneh**).
kon|en/-enah/-antee כונן *v* established; (*pres* **mekhonen**; *fut* **yekhonen**; *(kh=k)*).
kon|en/-anah/-antee קונן *v* lamented; (*pres* **mekonen**; *fut* **yekonen**).
konenoot/-yot כוננות *nf* **1.** alertness; **2.** "on call"; **3.** special "on call" allowance.
kones nekhaseem כונס נכסים *nm* official receiver (in bankruptcy).
kongres/-eem קונגרס *nm* congress.
◇ **(ha)kongres (ha)tseeyonee** הקונגרס הציוני *nm* (the) Zionist Congress, supreme elected authority guiding the World Zionist Movement. First convened in Basel, Switzerland, in 1897 by the founder, Dr Theodor Herzl, it has been convening regularly, every few years, in various European capitals (and, since 1951, solely in Jerusalem) to elect the movement's president and executive bodies and decide its policies.
konkoorentsyah קונקורנציה *nf [colloq.]* competition.
konkoors/-eem קונקורס *nm* contest; competitive examination; (*pl+of:* **-ey**).
konkretee/-t קונקרטי *adj* definite; concrete.
konkreteet קונקרטית *adv* in concrete (definite) terms.
konseelyoom/-eem קונסיליום *nm* medical consultation (with a specialist).
konsenzoos/-eem קונסנזוס *nm* consensus.
konsool/-eem קונסול *nm* consul; (*pl+of:* **-ey**).
konsool klalee קונסול כללי *nm* consul-general.
konsoolaree/-t קונסולרי *adj* consular.
konsool|yah/-yot קונסוליה *nf* consulate; (+*of:* **yat**).
konsteetoots|yah/-yot קונסטיטוציה *nf* constitution; (+*of:* **-yat**).
konsteetootsyonee/-t קונסטיטוציוני *adj* constitutional.
konstrookteevee/-t קונסטרוקטיבי *adj* constructive.
kontsenzoos (*npr* **konsensoos**) קונצנזוס *nm [colloq.]* consensus.
kontsert/-eem קונצרט *nm* concert; (*pl+of:* **-ey**).
koobee|yah/-yot קובייה *nf* **1.** cube; **2.** dice; (+*of:* **-yat**).
Kooboots קובוץ *nm* sublinear vowel-sign (ֻ) for "oo".
Koof (*also:* **kof**) קוף *nm* 19th letter of Hebrew Alphabet; Consonant "k" (or: "q" in the Hebrew Academy's official transliteration).
Koof (*also:* **kof**) ק' *num* 100; the 100th.
koofsa|h/-'ot קופסה *nf* box; can; (+*of:* **-at**).
(moonakh/-at be) koofsah מונח בקופסה *adv* "in the bag"; as good as in the bank.
koofsee|t/-yot קופסית *nf* small box; capsule.
koofta'ot כופתאות *nf pl* dumplings; (*sing:* **koofta'ah**).
kookee|yah/-yot קוקייה *nf* cuckoo; (+*of:* **-yat**).
kookh/-eem כוך *nm* cave; burial cave; (*pl+of:* **-ey**).
kool|ah/-am/-an/-anoo כולה/־ם/־ן/־נו all of her/them(*m/f*)/us.
kool|ee/-ekh כולי/־ך all of me/you *(f)*.
koolkh|a/-em/-en כולך/־כם/־כן all of you *sing/pl m/f*.
koolmoos/-eem קולמוס *nm* reed pen; writing quill; (*pl+of:* **-ey**).
(pleet|at/-ot) koolmoos פליטת קולמוס *nf* slip of the pen.
koom/-ee קום *v imp sing m/f* get up! (*pst & pres* **kam**; *fut* **yakoom**).
koomkoom/-eem קומקום *nm* kettle; (*pl+of:* **-ey**).
(le-kashkesh ba) koomkoom לקשקש בקומקום *[slang] v inf* talk nonsense.
koomt|ah/-ot כומתה *nf* beret; visorless cap; (+*of:* **-at**).
koomzeets/-eem קומזיץ *nm [slang]* informal get-together; campfire party.
koondas (*npr* **koondes**)/**-eem** קונדס *nm* prankster; (*pl+of:* **-ey**).
(ma'as|eh/-ey) koondas מעשה קונדס *nm* practical joke.
kondesoo|t/-yot קונדסות *nf* prank; practical jokes.
koonkhee|yah (*npr* **konkhee|yah**)/**-yot** קונכייה *nf* shell; (+*of:* **-yat**).
koontres/-eem קונטרס *nm* pamphlet; (*pl+of:* **-'ey**).
koonts/-eem קונץ *[slang] nm* trick.
koop|ah/-ot קופה *nf* box-office; cash-box; (+*of:* **-at**).
koopah ketanah קופה קטנה *nf* petty cash box.
koop|at/-ot gemel (*npr* **gemal**) קופת גמל *nf* provident fund.
(koop|at/-ot) kholeem קופת־חולים *nf* (*lit.*) sick fund; health-insurance organization.
◇ **koopat kholeem ha-klaleet** (Kupat-Holim) קופת חולים הכללית *nf* the General Health Insurance (*lit.:* Sick) Fund, a creation of the country's General Federation of Labor (Histadrut), the oldest and largest in Israel. It provides all-around health insurance to members of the Federation and their families, reaching (dependents included) some 3.4 million people — 83 percent of Israel's population. It employs, on a full time basis, a large staff of physicians, specialists and medical personnel maintaining a country-wide network of clinics and pharmacies. It also has its own hospitals and its own medical center as well as a series of rest-homes and convalescent homes.
◇ **koopat kholeem le'oomeet** ("Kupat Holim Le'umit") קופת חולים לאומית *[colloq.]*

ref. to ◇ **Koopat Kholeem le"Ovdeem Le'oomeeyeem** (see below).

◇ **koopat kholeem le-'ovdeem le'oomeeyeem** (Kupat Holim le-'Ovdim Le'umi'im) קופת חולים לעובדים לאומיים *nf* the National Health Insurance (*lit.:* Sick) Fund, an affiliation of the National Workers (non-socialist) Federation הסתדרות עובדים לאומית. Caters to members of the Federation and also to a sizeable portion of the general public. Operates own network of clinics as well as through private clinics. Takes particular interest in agricultural settlements and communities which, for ideological or political reasons, (e.g. location beyond the "Green Line"), are not affiliated with the General Federation of Labor (Histadrut). Serves a population of 300,000 people.

◇ **koopat kholeem makabee** (Kupat-Holim "Maccabi") קופת־חולים "מכבי" *nf* the Maccabi Health Insurance (*lit.:* Sick) Fund originally founded by the sports federation "Maccabi" for its own members and their families but later expanded into a fund serving a sizeable proportion of the general public. It operates on a commercial basis offering its members a choice of private clinics. Since 1987 it has also maintained its own network of pharmacies. Serves a population of 520,000 people.

◇ **koopat kholeem me'ookhedet**("Kupat-Holim Meuhedet") קופת חולים מאוחדת *nf* the United Health Insurance (*lit.:* Sick) Fund, an amalagamation of two older funds. It offers, for a monthly fee, health insurance to the general public. It also has its own clinics but ensures medical care, mainly, through a network of private clinics. It also has its own old-age and invalid-care homes. Serves a population of 250,000.

koop|at/-ot pensyah קופת פנסיה *nf* pension fund.

koop|at/-ot tagmooleen קופת תגמולין *nf* provident fund.

koopa|'ee (*npr* **koopa|y**)/**-'eem** קופאי *nm* cashier; (*pl+of:* **-'ey**).

koopa'ee|t/-yot קופאית *nf* cashier (female).

koor/-eem כור *nm* furnace; (*pl+of:* **-ey**).

koor/-eem atomee/-yeem כור אטומי *nm* atomic pile.

koor/eem gar'eenee/-yeem כור גרעיני *nm* nuclear pile.

koor/-ey heetookh כור היתוך *nm* melting pot.

koor/-eem קור *nm* web; (*pl+of:* **-ey**).

◇ **koor'an** קוראן *nm* the Koran, Islam's equivalent of the Bible.

koorey 'akaveesh קורי עכביש *nm pl* cobweb; spider web.

koorkar כורכר *nm* hard limestone ground.

koorkevan/-eem קורקבן *nm* gizzard; (*pl+of:* **-ey**).

koorn|as/-aseem קורנס *nm* sledge-hammer; (*pl+of:* **-esey**).

koors/-eem קורס *nm* course; class.

koors|ah/-ot (also/**-a'ot**) כורסה *nf* armchair; (*+of:* **-at**).

kortov קורטוב *nm* a bit; a pinch; grain.

kooryoz/-eem קוריוז *nm* queer thing; curiosity.

koos|ah/-tah/-etee כוסה *v* was covered up; (*pres* **mekhooseh**; *fut* **yekhooseh**).

koosemet כוסמת *nf* spelt; buckwheat.

kooshan/-eem קושאן *nm* land-title; immovables registration certificate.

kooshee/-m כושי *nm* Negro; black man (originally: Cushite).

kooshee|t/-yot כושית *nf* Negro woman; black woman.

koosh|yah/-yot קושיה *nf query*; question; (*+of:* **-yat**).

◇ **(arba') kooshyot** see ◇ **arba' kooshyot**.

◇ **kooskoos** קוסקוס *nm* semolina meal that is a favorite dish among Jews of North-African background.

kootn|ah/-ot כותנה *nf* cotton; (*+of:* **-at**).

kooton|et/-ot כותונת night shirt; night gown; shirt; (*+of:* **ketonet/kotnot**).

kooton|et/-not (*npr* **ketonet/kotnot**) **laylah** כותונת לילה *nf* night-gown.

kootso shel yod קוצו של יו"ד a jot; iota.

koovlan|ah/-ot קובלנה *nf* plaint; complaint; (*+of:* **-at**).

kooy|am/-mah קויים *v* was carried out; was fulfilled; (*pres* **mekooyam**; *fut* **yekooyam**).

kor קור *nm* cold.

kor roo'akh קור־רוח *nm* coolness; composure.

kor|ah/-ot קורה *nf* beam; (*+of:* **-at**).

(be-'ovee ha) korah בעובי הקורה *adv* deeply into the matter.

korakh כורח *nm* necessity; imperative.

korakh ha-metsee'oot כורח המציאות practical necessity; force of necessity.

□ **Koraneet** (Qoranit) קורנית *nm* industrial village in Western part of Upper Galilee, Tefen District, 2 km NW of **Yodpat**. Pop. 272.

korat gag קורת גג *nf* shelter; roof over one's head.

korat roo'akh קורת רוח *nf* satisfaction.

korban/-ot קורבן *nm* **1.** sacrifice; **2.** victim.

kor|e/-et (also **kor'ah**) קורא *v pres* read(s); call(s); (*pst* **kara**; *fut* **yeekra**).

kor|e/-'eem קורא *nm* reader; (*pl+of:* **-'ey**).

kor|eh/-eem כורה *nm* miner; (*pl+of:* **-ey**).

koreh/-ey nekhoshet כורה נחושת *nm* copper miner.

kor|eh/-ey pekham כורה פחם *nm* coal miner.

kor|eh/-et קורה *v pres* happen(s); it does happen; (*pst* **karah**; *fut* **yeekreh**).

kor|e'a'/-a'at קורע *v pres* tear(s); tearing; (*pst* **kara'**; *fut* **yeekra'**).

kor|e'a'/-a'at lev קורע לב *adj* heart-rending; heartbreaking.

□ **Kore'ah** קוריאה *nf* Korea.

kor|ekh/-kheem כורך *nm* bookbinder; (*pl+of:* **-khey**).
korekh/-et כורך *v pres* bind(s); combine(s); (*pst* **karakh**; *fut* **yeekrokh**).
koren/-et קורן **1.** *adj* shining; radiant; **2.** - *v pres* shine(s); radiate(s); (*pst* **karan**; *fut* **yeekran**).
korespondents|yah/-yot קורספונדנציה *nf* correspondence.
(be-'al) korkh|o/-ah *etc* בעל כורחו *adv* reluctantly; against his/her etc will.
korot קורות *nf pl* **1.** chronicles; annals; **2.** beams.
kos/-ot כוס *nm* glass.
kosee|t/-yot כוסית *nf* small glass; liqueur glass.
kosem/-et קוסם *nmf* magician; (*pl:* **kosm|eem/-ot**; *pl+of:* **-ey**).
kosem/-et קוסם *v pres* fascinate(s); enchant(s); (*pst* **kasam**; *fut* **yeeksom**).
koshee/keshayeem קושי *nm* difficulty; (*pl+of:* **-yey**).
(be) koshee בקושי *adv* hardly; with difficulty.
koshel/-et כושל **1.** *adj* inefficient; stumbling; **2.** *v pres* fail(s); stumble(s); (*pst* **kashal**; *fut* **yeekashel**).
(neehool) koshel ניהול כושל *nm* inefficient management.
kosher כושר *nm* ability.
kosher goofanee כושר גופני *nm* physical fitness.
(be) kosher (*npr* **be-khosher**) בכושר *adv* in good form.
(she|'at/-'ot) kosher שעת כושר *nf* opportunity.
kosh|er/-reem קושר *nm* plotter; (*pl+of:* **-ey**).
kosher/-et קושר *v pres* bind(s); tie(s); connect(s); (*pres* **kashar**; *fut* **yeekshor**).
kosmee/-t קוסמי *adj* cosmic.
kosmetee/-t קוסמטי *adj* cosmetic.
kosmeteekah קוסמטיקה *nf* cosmetics.
kosot-roo'akh כוסות רוח *nf pl* cupping glasses; (*sing:* **kos** *etc*).
kotbee/-t קוטבי *adj* polar; extreme.
kotej/-eem קוטג' *nm* a two-storey, one-family home; two storey villa.
(geveen|ah/-ot) kotej גבינת קוטג' *nf* cottage cheese.
kotel/ketaleem כותל *nm* wall; (*pl+of:* **kotley**).
◇ **(ha)kotel** הכותל *nm* (*colloq.abbr*) see ◇ **(ha)kotel ha-ma'aravee**.
◇ **(ha)kotel ha-ma'aravee** הכותל המערבי *nm* the Western Wall, the only relic of the Jerusalem Temple compound of 2,000 years ago, the most sacred place on earth to the Jewish people. Also known as the Wailing Wall.
□ **(ha)Kotel** הכותל *nm* the Wall, i.e. the Wailing Wall see ◇ **(ha)Kotel Ma'aravee** , above.
kot|el/-leem קוטל *nm* killer; (*pl+of:* **-ley**).
kot|el/-ley 'asaveem קוטל עשבים *nm* weed-killer.
kot|el/-ley kaneem קוטל קנים *nm* "reed cutter"; worthless person; nincompoop.
kot|el/-ley kharakeem קוטל חרקים *nm* insecticide.
kot|el/-ley peetreeyot קוטל פטריות *nm* fungicide.
koten קוטן *nm* smallness.
koter/ketareem קוטר *nm* diameter; (*pl+of:* **kotrey**).
kot|eret/-rot כותרת *nf* **1.** heading; caption; **2.** capital of a pillar.
kot|eret/-rot rashee|t/-yot כותרת ראשית *nf* headline; main headline.
(goolat ha) koteret גולת הכותרת *nf* climax; masterpiece.
kotev/ketaveem קוטב *nm* pole; axis; (*pl+of:* **-kotvey**).
(ha) kotev (ha)dromee הקוטב הדרומי *nm* the South Pole.
(ha) kotev (ha)tsefonee הקוטב הצפוני *nm* the North Pole.
kotley khazeer קותלי חזיר *nm pl* bacon.
kots/-eem קוץ *nm* thorn.
kotsee/-t קוצי *adj* thorny.
kotser קוצר *nm* shortness; brevity.
kotser roo'akh קוצר־רוח *nm* impatience.
kotser yad קוצר־יד *nm* inability; powerlessness.
kotser zeman קוצר זמן *nm* lack of time.
kotser/-et קוצר **1.** *nmf* harvester; **2.** *v pres* reap(s); (*pst* **katsar**; *fut* **yeektsor**).
kotsev/-et קוצב **1.** *nm* determinant; **2.** *v pres* allocate(s); allot(s); (*pst* **katsav**; *fut* **yeektsov**).
kots|ev/-vey lev קוצב לב *nm* pacemaker.
kotso shel yod קוצו של יוד *nm* a jot; iota.
kov|a'/-a'eem כובע *nm* hat (*pl+of:* **-'ey**).
kov|a'/-'ey gerev כובע גרב *nm* woven socklike headgear worn for protection from cold.
kov|a'/-'ey kash כובע קש *nm* straw hat.
◇ **kov|a'/-'ey tembel** כובע טמבל *nm* "Tembel"-hat considered a characteristic cap of kibbutzniks and workers and therefore popular with tourists to Israel.
koval קבל *adv* in front of.
koval 'am קבל עם *adv* publicly; openly.
(khav|ash/-shah/-ashtee) kova' חבש כובע *v* put on a hat; (*pres* **khovesh** *etc*; *fut* **yakhbosh** *etc* *b=v*).
kov'an/-eem כובען *nm* hatter; (*pl+of:* **-ey**).
koved כובד *nm* weight.
(ko'akh ha) koved כוח הכובד *nm* gravitation.
kov|esh/-sheem כובש *nm* conqueror; (*pl+of:* **-shey**).
kovesh/-et כובש *v pres* conquer(s); conquering; (*pst* **kavash**; *fut* **yeekhbosh** (*kh=k; b=v*)).
kovets/kevatseem קובץ *nm* **1.** collection; compilation; **2.** computer data-file (*pl+of:* **kovtsey**).
kozev/-et כוזב *adj* untrue; false.
kra|kh/-kheem (*npr* **-keem**; (*kh=k*)) כרך *nm* city; (*pl+of:* **-key**).
krav/-ot קרב *nm* battle.
(doo-) krav דו־קרב *nm* duel.
(sed|eh/-ot) krav שדה־קרב *nm* battlefield.

krav|ayeem קרביים *nm pl* entrails; viscera; (*pl+of:* **-ey**).

kravee/-t קרבי *adj* battle-; combat-.

(khayal/-eem) kravee/-yeem חייל קרבי *nm* combat soldier.

(nafal/-lah/-altee ba) krav נפל בקרב *v* fell in battle; (*pres* **nofel** *etc; fut* **yeepol** *etc; (p=f)*).

(neetash) krav ניטש קרב *v* fighting broke out; battle was on.

(zeer|at/-ot) krav זירת קרב *nf* battle theater.

□ **(ha)Krayot** הקריות *nf pl [colloq.]* reference to Haifa's 3 seashore residential suburbs; **Keeryat Byaleek, Keeryat Motskeen** and **Keeryat Khayeem.**

kraz|ah/-ot כרזה *nf* placard; (*+of:* **-at**).

kree קרי, קריא which should read... (i.e. giving the normative pronunciation of a word liable to be read differently due to unclear vowel structure).

kree|'ah/-'ot קריאה *nf* call (*+of:* **-'at**).

kree|'ah (*etc*) קריאה *nf* reading (books, newspapers *etc*); (*+of:* **-'at**).

kree|'ah/-'ot telefonee|t/-yot קריאה טלפונית *nf* telephone call.

(meeshkefey) kree'ah משקפי קריאה *nm pl* reading glasses.

(seeman/-ey) kree'ah סימן קריאה exclamation mark (!).

kree|'at/-'ot benayeem (*or:* **beynayeem**) קריאת ביניים *nf* interjection; heckling.

kree|'ah/-'ot קריעה *nf* tearing; rending; (*+of:* **-'at**).

◇ **kree|'ah/-'ot** קריעה *nf* symbolic act of having a piece of one's garment torn off publicly, as a sign of mourning, at the funeral of a member of one's immediate family.

kree'at takhat קריעת תחת *nf [slang]* extremely exhausting labor or effort.

◇ **kree'at shma'** קריאת שמע *nf* recital of the "shma'" credo which is the last thing an observant Jew is supposed to say before sleep.

kreekh/-eem (*npr* **kareekh**) כריך *nm* sandwich; (*pl+of:* **-ey**).

kreekh|ah/-ot כריכה *nf* binding; (*+of:* **-at**).

kreekhee|yah/-yot כריכייה *nf* bookbindery; (*+of:* **-yat**).

kreen|ah/-not קרינה *nf* radiation; irradiation; (*+of:* **-at**).

kreeroot קרירות *nf* coolness.

(bee) kreeroot בקרירות *adv* coldly; with indifference.

kreesh/-ey dam קריש דם *nm* blood-clot.

kreetee/-t קריטי *adj* critical.

kreeteek|ah/-ot קריטיקה *nf* criticism.

kreeteryon/-eem קריטריון *nm* criterion.

kreets|ah/-ot קריצה *nf* winking; blinking; (*+of:* **-at**).

kree|yah/-yot כרייה *nf* mining; digging up; (*+of:* **-yat**).

krematoryoom/-eem קרימטוריום *nm* crematorium; (*pl+of:* **-ey**).

krom כרום *nm* chrome.

kron/-ot deerah קרון דירה *nm* caravan-trailer.

kron/-ot rakevet קרון רכבת *nm* railroad car; railway-wagon.

kron/-ot sheynah קרון שינה *nm* sleeper; sleeping car; wagon-lit.

kronee/-t כרוני *adj* chronic.

kroneek|ah/-ot כרוניקה *nf* chronicle; news in brief; miscellaneous news items.

kronee|t/-yot קרונית *nf* trolley; wagonette.

kroo'eem קרואים *nm pl* guests; those invited; (*sing:* **karoo'/kroo'ah**; *pl+of:* **kroo'ey**).

kroom/-eem קרום *nm* skin membrane; crust; (*pl+of:* **-ey**).

kroom reeree קרום ריִרי *nm* mucous membrane (Medic.).

(daleket) kroom ha-mo'akh דלקת קרום המוח *nf* meningitis (Medic.).

kroov כרוב *nm* cabbage.

kroov/-eem כרוב *nm* cherub; (*pl+of:* **-ey**).

krooz/-eem כרוז *nm* proclamation; manifesto; announcement; (*pl+of:* **-ey**).

kroveem (*sing mf* **karov/krov|ah**) קרובים *nm pl* relatives; kin; (*+of:* **-at/-ey**).

krovey meeshpakhah קרובי משפחה *nm pl* relatives; kin; (*sing:* **krov** *etc*).

(le-'eeteem) krovot לעיתים קרובות *adv* often; at close intervals.

ksafeem כספים *nm pl* funds; finances; sums of money; (*sing:* **kesef**).

('eenyeney) ksafeem ענייני כספים *nm pl* financial matters.

(megalgel/-et) ksafeem מגלגל כספים *[slang] v pres* handle(s) large sums of money; (*pst* **geelgel** *etc; fut* **yegalgel** *etc*).

ksameem קסמים *nm pl* magic charms; (*sing:* **kesem**; *pl+of:* **keesmey**).

(ma'agal) ksameem מעגל קסמים *nm* vicious circle.

ksarketeen/-eem קסרקטין *nm* barracks; (*pl+of:* **-ey**).

ksa|yah/-yot כסייה *nf* glove; (*+of:* **-yat**).

kseel/-eem כסיל *nm* moron; simpleton; (*pl+of:* **-ey**).

ksoot כסות *nf* cover; covering.

ksoot 'eynayeem כסות עיניים *nf* pretext; eye-wash; excuse.

(koopah) ktanah קופה קטנה *nf* petty-cash box.

ktantan/-ah קטנטן *adj* tiny; very small.

ktat|ah/-ot קטטה *nf* quarrel; squabble; (*+of:* **-at**).

ktav כתב *nm* writing; script.

ktav/keetvey eeshoom כתב־אישום *nm* charge-sheet; bill of information.

ktav/keetvey 'et כתב עת *nm* periodical.

ktav/keetvey haganah כתב הגנה *nm* statement of defense.

ktav/keetvey meet'an כתב מטען *nm* bill of lading.

ktav/keetvey plaster כתב פלסטר *nm* lampoon; libelous document.

ktav/keetvey seetnah כתב שטנה *nm* indictment.

ktav/keetvey tvee'ah כתב־תביעה *nm* statement of claim; suit (legal).

ktav/keetvey yad כתב יד *nm* **1.** handwriting; **2.** manuscript.

(he'el|ah/-tah/-etee 'al ha) ktav העלה על הכתב *v* put in writing; (*pres* **ma'aleh** *etc; fut* **ya'aleh** *etc*).

ktaveem כתבים *nm pl* works; writings; (*sing:* **ktav**; *pl+of:* **keetvey**).

ktee'ah/-'ot קטיעה *nf* amputation; (*+of:* **-'at**).

kteef|ah קטיפה *nf* velvet; (*+of:* **-at**).

kteef|ah/-ot קטיפה *nf* **1.** picking (fruit); **2.** plucking (flowers); (*+of:* **-at**).

kteel|ah/-ot קטילה *nf* **1.** killing; **2.** (mostly *figurat.*) condemning, disavowing; (*+of:* **-at**).

kteen|ah/-ot קטינה *nf* female minor; (*+of:* **-at**).

kteenoot קטינות *nf* status of minor; underage.

kteev/-eem כתיב *nm* orthography; spelling.

◇ **kteev khaser** see keteev khaser.

◇ **kteev male** see keteev male.

(shegee|'at/-'ot) kteev שגיאת כתיב *nf* spelling mistake; misspelling.

kteevah כתיבה *nf* writing; (*+of:* **-at**).

◇ **kteevah va-khateemah tovah!** see **keteevah va-khateemah tovah!**

(mekhon|at/-ot) kteevah מכונת כתיבה *nf* typewriter.

(shoolkhan/-ot) kteevah שולחן כתיבה *nf* desk.

ktefeeyot כתפיות *nf pl* straps; shoulder loops.

ktonet/kotnot laylah כתונת לילה *nf* night dress; night shirt; night gown.

ktonet/kotnot paseem כתונת פסים *nf* "dress of many colors"; striped gown.

◇ **ktoob|ah/-ot** see ◇ **ketoob|ah/-ot**.

ktoomah כתומה *adj f* orange-colored; (*masc.:* **katom**).

□ **Ktoorah** see □ **Ketoorah**.

ktoret קטורת *nf* incense.

ktov|et/-ot כתובת *nf* **1.** address; **2.** inscription.

ktovet 'al ha-keer כתובת על הקיר *nf* writing on the wall.

ktov|et/-ot ka'aka' כתובת קעקע *nf* tattoo.

(bee) ktsarah בקצרה *adv* in short; in brief.

kvar כבר *adv* already.

(mee) kvar מכבר *adv* since long ago.

(zeh) kvar זה כבר *adv* already long ago.

kvar|ah/-ot כברה *nf* sieve.

(bet/batey) kvarot בית קברות *nm* cemetery.

kvaseem כבסים *nm pl* washing.

(gveen|at/-ot) kvaseem גבינת כבשים *nf* lamb-cheese.

kvatch/eet קוואץ' *adj & nmf [slang]* meek; softy.

kvedoot כבידות *nf* heaviness; fixing.

kvee|'ah/-'ot קביעה *nf* determination; fixing; (*+of:* **-'at**).

kveel|ah/-ot כבילה *nf* tying; binding; (*+of:* **-at**).

kveel|ah/-ot קבילה *nf* complaint; (*+of:* **-at**).

(netseev) kveelot ha-tseeboor נציב קבילות הציבור *nm* ombudsman.

kvee'oot קביעות *nf* permanence; tenure (in employment).

(bee) kvee'oot בקביעות *adv* regularly.

kvees|ah/-ot כביסה *nf* laundering; washing; (*+of:* **-at**).

(avk|at/-ot) kveesah אבקת כביסה *nm* washing powder.

(mekhon|at/-ot) kveesah מכונת כביסה *nf* washer; washing machine.

kveesh/-eem כביש *nm* road; highway; (*pl+of:* **-ey**).

kveesh/-ey agrah כביש אגרה *nm* toll road.

kveesh doo-masloolee כביש דו־מסלולי *nm* two-lane road.

kveesh doo-seetree כביש דו־סיטרי *nm* two-way road.

kveesh/-ey geeshah כביש גישה *nm* approach road; feeder line.

kveeshah כבישה *nf* canning; pickling; (*+of:* **-at**).

kvod כבוד *m+of* the honor of (way of polite reference to someone).

kvod ha- כבוד ה־ the Honorable; Esq.

kvod|o/-ah כבודו *lit;* "his/her honor" - slightly pompous, extremely polite way of addressing someone in the third person.

kvoor|ah/-ot קבורה *nf* burial; (*+of:* **-at**).

kvoorat khamor קבורת חמור *nf* **1.** contemptible burial; **2.** *lit* the burial of an ass.

kvoosheem כבושים *nm pl*; canned goods; tinned food.

kvoots|ah/-ot קבוצה *nf* **1.** group; team; **2.** squad; **3.** collection; (*+of:* **-at**).

◇ **kvootsah/-ot** קבוצה *nf* an early, small and intimate form of kibbutz, collective farm or cooperative.

(rosh/-ey) kvootsah ראש קבוצה *nm* captain of the team.

kvoots|at/-ot se'ar קווצת שיער *nf* lock; curl.

□ **Kvootsat Keeneret** (Kinneret-Qevuza) קבוצת כנרת *nf* kevootsah, i.e. an old, intimate type of kibbutz, (est. 1913) on SW coast of Lake Tiberias, between Kinneret-village and Kibbutz Deganya. Pop. 732.

□ **Kvootsat Yavneh** (Qevutsat Yavne) קבוצת יבנה *nm* kibbutz (est. 1941) of the **"kvootsah"** type, in the central part of the Coastal Plain, 5 km E. of Ashdod. Pop. 748.

kvootsatee/-t קבוצתי *adj* group-; collective.

('on|esh/-sheem) kvootsatee/-yeem עונש קבוצתי *nf* collective punishment.

kyosk/-eem קיוסק *nm* kiosk.

KH.

NOTE: The combination **kh**, in this dictionary, transliterates the Hebrew consonants ח (**Khet**) and כ (**Khaf**), the pronunciation of which is virtually identical in contemporary Hebrew speech. To an English-speaking person it sounds like the *ch* in the Scottish word *loch* or in the Jewish name *Chaim* (**Khayeem**). Thus words beginning with this sound have been grouped separately from those beginning with **K.**

Most of these words begin with ח (**Khet**), fewer with כ (**Khaf**). This is because the phonetics of the classical language require that a **Khaf**, when beginning a word, be dotted as a כּ (**Kaf**), i.e. read as **k** and not as **kh**. Preceded by some prefix, it often remains **kh**. Thus many words listed in this chapter begin with **Khaf** but with a prefix indicated in parentheses.

◇ **khabad ("Chabad")** חב"ד worldwide Hasidic movement centering around the personality of its head, the Lubavitcher Rabbi, whose residence and headquarters are in Brooklyn, New York. It has a large following in Israel, with headquarters in a township of its own, **Kefar Khabad**, near Ramla, off the old Tel-Aviv-Jerusalem road.

khabal|ah/-ot חבלה *nf* harm; sabotage; (*+of:* **-at**).

(ma'as|eh/-ey) khabalah מעשה חבלה *nm* act of sabotage.

khabash חבש *nf* Ethiopia.

◇ **('oley) khabash** see ◇ **'oley etyopeeyah**.

khabashee/-t חבשי **1.** *nmf & adj* Ethiopian; **2.** Jewish immigrant from Ethiopia.

khablan/-eem חבלן *nm* **1.** saboteur; terrorist; **2.** sapper; (*pl+of:* **-ey**).

(peegoo'a) khablanee פיגוע חבלני *nm* terrorist act; act of terrorism.

khabeebee (*npr* **khaveevee**) חביבי *[slang] interj m* dear fellow! .

khabeebtee (*npr* **khaveevatee**) חביבתי *[slang] interj f* dear girl! darling! .

khaboob! (*or:* **yah, khaboob!**) חבוב *[slang] interj m* dear fellow!

khaboor|ah/-ot חבורה *nf* bruise; (*+of:* **-at**).

khad- ־חד *num prefix* one-; mono-; single-.

khad/-ah חד *adj* sharp; shrill.

khad ve-khalak חד וחלק short and sweet.

khad|al/-lah/-altee חדל *v* ceased; stopped; (*pres* **khadel**; *fut* **yekhdal**).

khadal! kheedlee! !חדל *v imp sing m/f* stop! leave off! leave it alone!

khadal/kheedley eesheem חדל־אישים *nm & adj m* good for nothing.

khad|ar/-rah/-artee חדר *v* penetrated; pierced; (*pres* **khoder**; *fut* **yakhdor**).

khad|ar/-rey חדר *m+of* room of; -room.

khad|ar/-rey ambatyah חדר אמבטיה *nm* bathroom.

khad|ar/-rey 'avodah חדר עבודה *nm* study.

khad|ar/-rey hamtanah חדר המתנה *nm* waiting-room.

khad|ar/-rey okhel חדר אוכל *nm* dining-room.

khad|ar/-rey orkheem חדר אורחים *nm* parlor; living room; salon.

khad|ar/-rey sheynah חדר שינה *nm* bedroom.

khad|ar/-rey yeladeem חדר ילדים *nm* nursery.

khadareem חדרים *nm pl* rooms; (*sing* **kheder**; *pl+of:* **khadrey**).

khadash/-ah חדש *adj* new.

(en) khadash (*or:* **eyn** *etc*) אין חדש no news; nothing new.

(me) khadash (*or:* **mee** *etc*) מחדש *adv* anew.

('ol|eh/-eem) khadash/-eem עולה חדש *nm* new immigrant to Israel (male).

khadash|ah/-ot חדשה news; (*+of:* **-at**).

('ol|ah/-ot) khadash|ah/-ot עולה חדשה *nf* new immigrant to Israel (female).

◻ **Khadeed** (Hadid) חדיד *nm* village (est. 1949) in the Coastal Plain, 5 km NE of Lod. Pop. 457.

khadeer/-ah חדיר *adj* permeable; penetrable.

khadeer|ah/-ot חדירה *nf* penetration; (*+of:* **-at**).

khadeesh/-ah חדיש *adj* modern; up-to-date.

◻ **Khaderah** (Hadera) חדרה *nf* town (est. 1890) in N. Sharon. Pop. 45,600.

khad-gonee (*cpr* **khad-gvanee**)**/-t** חד־גוני *adj* monotonous.

khad-horee/-t חד הורי *adj* one-parent-(family).

◇ **khadj** חאג' *nm (Arab.)* title added to the name of a Muslim who has made his obligatory, once in a lifetime, pilgrimage to Mecca.

khad-mashma'ee/-t חד־משמעי *adj* unequivocal.

(ve) kha-domeh וכדומה et cetera.

khadoor/-ah חדור *adj* imbued with; inspired.

khadoo|t/-yot חדות *nf* sharpness; acuteness.

khad-pe'amee (*npr* **pa'amee**)/**-t** חד־פעמי *adj* one-time; unique.

khadranee|t/-yot חדרנית *nf* chambermaid.

(be) khadrey khadareem בחדרי חדרים *adv* in a secret place.

khadron/-eem חדרון *nm* cubicle; alcove.

khad-seetree/-t חד־סטרי *adj* one-way.

(rekhov) khad-seetree רחוב חד סטרי *nm* one-way street.

khad-shenatee/-t חד־שנתי *adj* annual; one-year-.

khad-tsedadee/-t חד־צדדי *adj* unilateral; one-sided.

khad-tsedadeeyoot חד־צדדיות *nf* bias; unilaterality.

◇ **khaf** כף *nf* 11th letter of Hebrew alphabet; consonant pronounced **kh** when not dotted; (when dotted, it is read as **k**).

◇ **khaf sofeet** (ך) *nf* form taken by the **Khaf** when it ends a word.

kha|f/-pah mee-pesha' חף מפשע *adj* innocent; guiltless.

khafaf/-efah/-aftee חפף *v* **1.** washed (hair); shampooed; **2.** was congruent (Geometry); (*pres* **khofef**; *fut* **yakhpof** *(p=f)*).

khafar/-rah/-artee חפר *v* dug; excavated; (*pres* **khofer**; *fut* **yakhpor** *(p=f)*).

khafarp|eret/-arot חפרפרת *nf* mole.

khafatseem חפצים *nm pl* things; objects; (*sing:* **khefets**; *pl+of:* **kheftsey**).

khafatseem 'eesheeyeem חפצים אישיים *nm pl* personal effects.

khafeef חפיף *[slang](Arab.) adv* bagatelle; trifling matter.

khafeef|ah/-ot חפיפה *nf* **1.** hair-wash; **2.** overlapping; (*+of:* **-at**).

khafeer|ah/-ot חפירה *nf* ditch; digging; (*+of:* **-at**).

khafees|ah/-ot חפיסה *nf* **1.** pack; package (cigarettes, chocolate); **2.** deck (of cards); (*+of:* **-at**).

khafets/-ah חפץ *adj* willing.

khaf|ets/-tsah/-atstee חפץ *v* desired (*pres* **khafets**; *fut* **yakhpots** *(p=f)*).

khafl|eh/-ot חפלה *nm [slang] (Arab.)* boisterous yet festive meal.

khafoo|y/-yat rosh חפוי ראש *adj* perplexed; ashamed.

khafoo|z/-ah חפוז *adj* hurried; hasty.

khag/-ah/-tee חג *v* circled; (*pres* **khag**; *fut* **yakhoog**).

khag/-eem חג *nm* feast; holiday; (*pl+of:* **-ey**).

(eesroo-) khag אסרו־חג *nm* morrow of a Jewish holiday.

('erev/'arvey) khag ערב חג *nm* evening beginning a Jewish holiday.

(motsa'ey) khag מוצאי חג *nm* evening ending a Jewish holiday.

khag|ag/-egah/-agtee חגג *v* celebrated; feasted; (*pres* **khogeg**; *fut* **yakhog**).

◇ **khag ha-hodayah** חג ההודיה *nm* Thanksgiving Day.

◇ **khag ha-kheroot** חג החירות *nm* the Feast of Freedom, i.e. Passover.

◇ **khag ha-matsot** חג המצות *nm* Feast of the "Matzahs", i.e. Passover (15-21 **Neesan**, approx. April).

khag ha-molad חג המולד *nm* Christmas.

◇ **khag ha-pesakh** חג הפסח *nm* "Pesach"; Passover; (15-21 **Neesan**, approx. April).

khag|ar/-rah/-artee חגר *v* **1.** put on (belt); **2.** girded (sword); (*pres* **khoger**; *fut* **yakhagor**).

◇ **khag ha-shavoo'ot** חג השבועות *nm* "Shavuot"; Pentecost; (6th **Seevan**, approx. May-June).

◇ **khag ha-sookot** חג הסוכות *nm* "Succot"; Tabernacles, also called **Khag he-Aseef** חג האסיף i.e. the Harvest (*lit.:* gathering) Festival; (15-22 **Teeshrey**, approx. Sept-Oct).

khageeg|ah/-ot חגיגה *nf* **1.** celebration; feasting; (*+of:* **-at**) ? **2.** *[slang]* a delight.

khageegee/-t חגיגי *adj* solemn; festive.

khageegeeyoot חגיגיות *nf* solemnity; festiveness.

khagoor/-ah חגור *adj* girded.

khagor/-eem חגור *nm* **1.** full pack; **2.** soldier's personal (equipment) (*pl+of:* **-ey**).

◻ **Khagor** (Hagor) חגור *nm* village (est. 1949) 5 km SE of Kefar Sava, off the **Kalkeeleeyah-Rosh ha-'Ayeen** road. Pop. 390.

khagor|ah/-ot חגורה *nf* girdle; belt; (*+of:* **-at**).

(heedook ha) khagorah הידוק החגורה *nm* tightening of the belt (*figurat.*).

khagor|at/-ot beteekhoot חגורת בטיחות *nf* safety belt (in car).

khagor|at/-ot hatsalah חגורת הצלה *nf* life-belt.

◇ **khag pooreem** חג פורים *nm* Purim; the Feast of Purim; (14-15th **Adar**, approx. March).

khag same'akh! חג שמח! *interj* Holiday Greetings! Happy Holiday!

khak/-eem ח״כ *nm acr* for "**khav|er/-rat keneset**" חבר כנסת i.e. Knesset-member; M.K. (*pl+of:* **-rey**).

khak|ah/-ot חכה *nf* fish-hook; (*+of:* **-at**).

khak|ar/-rah/-artee חקר *v* investigated; explored; studied; (*pres* **khoker**; *fut* **yakhkor**).

khakeek|ah/-ot חקיקה *nf* legislation; (*+of:* **-at**).

khakeer|ah/-ot חקירה *nf* investigation; inquiry; (*+of:* **-at**).

(va'ad|at/-ot) khakeerah ועדת חקירה *nf* commission of inquiry.

khakeer|at/-ot shetee va-'erev חקירת שתי וערב *nf* cross-examination.

(agaf ha) khakeerot אגף החקירות *nm* C.I.D. criminal investigation branch/department (police).

khak|eh/-ee! חכה! *v imp sing m/f* wait; (*inf* **lekhakot**; *pst* **kheekah**; *pres* **mekhakeh**; *fut* **yekhakeh**).

khakeh/-ee (*etc*) **rega'!** חכה רגע! *v imp sing m/f* wait a minute!

(be) khakh *(kh=k)* בכך by this; in that.

(ey le) khakh *(kh=k)* אי לכך therefore.
(mah be) khakh *(kh=k)* מה בכך what does it matter.
(shel mah be) khakh *(kh=k)* של מה בכך *adj* of little importance; unimportant.
khakla'ee/-t חקלאי *adj* agricultural; farm-.
(mesh|ek/-akeem) khakla'ee/-yeem משק חקלאי *nm* agricultural farm.
(po'el/po'aleem) khakla'ee/-yeem פועל חקלאי *nm* farm laborer.
khakla'oot חקלאות *nf* agriculture.
(torat ha) khakla'oot תורת החקלאות *nf* agronomy.
khakl|ay/-a'eet חקלאי *nmf* farmer; (*pl+of:* **-'ey**).
khakham/-ah חכם *adj* clever; wise; intelligent.
khakham ba-laylah חכם בלילה *[slang] nm* one who thinks himself clever (ironically).
(talmeed/-ey) khakham/-eem תלמיד חכם *nm* scholar (in Judaism); man of learning.
(ha) khakhameem החכמים *nm pl* our sages of old.
khakhameynoo חכמינו *nm pl* our sages of old.
khakh|ar/-rah/-artee חכר *v* leased; rented; hired; (*pres* **khokher;** *fut* **yakhkor** *(kh=k)*).
khakheer|ah/-ot חכירה *nf* lease; long-term tenancy; (*+of:* **-at**).
khakhoor/-ah חכור *adj* let; rented.
khakyan/-eet חקיין *nmf* imitator; (*pl+of:* **-ey**).
khal/-ah/-oo חל *v* **1.** became due; fell (date); **2.** applied (of a law); (*pres* **khal;** *fut* **yakhool**).
◇ **khal|ah/-ot** חלה *nf* Sabbath special bread-loaf; (*+of:* **-at**).
khal|ah/-tah/-eetee חלה *v* fell sick; was taken ill; (*pres* **kholeh;** *fut* **yekhleh**).
khal|af/-fah/-aftee חלף *v* **1.** passed; moved past; **2.** expired; vanished; (*pres* **kholef;** *fut* **yakhlof**).
khalafeem חלפים *nm pl* spare parts; (*+of:* **khelfey**).
khalak/-ah חלק *adj* smooth; blank.
(daf) khalak דף חלק *nm* **1.** blank sheet; **2.** tabula rasa; (used figurat.).
(khad ve) khalak חד וחלק *[colloq.]* clear and to the point.
(lo) khalak לא חלק *adv [colloq.]* doesn't smell good (*figurat.*).
khal|ak/-kah/-aktee 'al חלק על *v* contested; disagreed with (*pres* **kholek;** *fut* **yakhlok**).
khalak (*etc*) **kavod le-** חלק כבוד ל- *v* honored; paid respects to.
khalak (*etc*) **shevakheem** חלק שבחים *v* paid a compliment; praised.
khalaklak/-ah חלקלק *adj* slippery.
◇ **"khalakeh"** חלאקה *[slang] nf* boy's first haircut. In ultra-Orthodox Jewish circles in Israel it is done in the third year of age, at a special pilgrimage to Mount Meron (in Galilee) where haircut takes place publicly at the Lag Ba-'Omer celebrations.
khal|al/-aleem חלל *nm* fatal casualty; slain; (*pl+of:* **-eley**).
(naf|al/-lah/-altee) khal|al נפל חלל *v* fell in battle; (*pres* **nofel** *etc; fut* **yeepol** *(p=f) etc*).
khalal חלל *nm* **1.** vacuum; empty space; **2.** outer space.
khalal/-eem reyk/-eem חלל ריק *nm* empty space.
(he) khalal (ha)kheetson החלל החיצון *nm* outer space.
(tayas/-ey) khalal טייס חלל *nm* astronaut; cosmonaut.
khalalee|t/-yot חללית *nf* space-ship.
khal|am/-mah/-amtee חלם *v* dreamt; (*pres* **kholem;** *fut* **yakhalom**).
khalameesh חלמיש *nm* flint.
□ **Khalameesh** (Hallamish) חלמיש *nm* rural settlement in Samaria (est. 1977), 13 km NE of Ramallah. Was earlier known as **Neveh Tsoof.** Nearby, **Oom-Tsafa** (Umm Zaffa) Forest. Pop. 681.
khalas חלס *[slang] (Arab.)*...an end to it!
khalash/-ah חלש *adj* weak.
khal|ash/-shah/-ashtee 'al חלש על *v* commanded; reigned over (*figurat.*); (*pres* **kholesh;** *fut* **yakhlosh**).
khalashloosh/-ah חלשלוש *[slang] adj* weakling.
khal|ats/-tsah/-atstee חלץ *v* extracted; took out; (*pres* **kholets;** *fut* **yakhlots**).
khalats (*etc*) **na'al/-ayeem** חלץ נעל *v* took shoe(s) off.
khal|av/-vah/-avtee חלב *v* **1.** milked; **2.** *[slang]* pumped out; extorted; (*pres* **kholev;** *fut* **yakhlov**).
khalav חלב *nm* milk.
khalav 'ameed חלב עמיד *nm* homogenized low-fat milk.
khalav dal-shooman חלב דל-שומן *nm* low-fat milk.
khalav em חלב אם *nm* mother's milk.
khalav khamoots חלב חמוץ *nm* sour milk.
khalav male חלב מלא *nm* full milk.
khalav mefoostar חלב מפוסטר *nm* pasteurized milk.
khalav mehoomgan חלב מהומגן *nm* homogenized milk.
khalav me'ookar חלב מעוקר *nm* sterilized milk.
khalav merookaz חלב מרוכז *nm* condensed milk.
khalav razeh חלב רזה *nm* skimmed milk.
khalav taree חלב טרי *nm* fresh milk.
(avk|at/-ot) khalav אבקת חלב *nf* milk powder.
(sheveel he) khalav שביל החלב *nm* the Milky Way.
(teep|at/-ot) khalav טיפת חלב *nf* **1.** infant-care clinic; **2.** (*lit.*) a drop of milk.
(shen/sheeney) khalav שן חלב *nf* milk tooth.
khalavee/-t חלבי *adj* for milk dishes (distinction relevant for observers of "kashroot").
khalban/-eem (*npr* **khalvan**) חלבן *nm* milkman; (*pl+of:* **-ey**).
khaleef|ah/-ot חליפה *nf* suit (of clothes); costume; (*+of:* **-at**).

khaleefat ha-shabat חליפת השבת *nf* one's Sabbath clothes; Sabbath's best.
khaleefat meekhtaveem חליפת מכתבים *nf* exchange of letters; correspondence.
khaleefeen חליפין *nm pl* exchange.
(sha'ar/-ey) khaleefeen שער חליפין *nm* rate of exchange.
(sekhar) khaleefeen סחר חליפין *nm* barter.
(shtar/sheetrey) khaleefeen שטר חליפין *nm* bill of exchange.
khaleefot חליפות *adv* alternately.
khaleel/-eem חליל *nm* flute; pipe.
khaleelah חלילה *interj* God forbid!
(khas ve) khaleelah חס וחלילה *interj* God forbid!
◇ **"khaleetsah"** (**"Halitza"**) חליצה *nf* religious ceremony whereby one is freed from the obligation (conferred in the book of Leviticus) of marrying a childless brother's widow.
khalkhalah חלחלה *nf* shudder.
□ **Khalkhool** (Halhul) חלחול *nf* Arab town in Judean hills, 5 km N. of Hebron (**Khevron**), off the Hebron-Bethlehem road. Pop. approx. 14,000.
khalom/-ot חלום *nm* dream.
khalom/-ot be-hakeets חלום בהקיץ *nm* daydream.
(shag|ah/-tah/-etee ba) khalomot שגה בחלומות *v* daydreamed (*pres* **shogeh**; *fut* **yeeshgeh**).
khalomot be-aspamya חלומות באספמיא *nf pl* castles in the air; impossible dreams.
khalon/-ot חלון *nm* window.
(eden/adney) khalon אדן חלון *nm* window-sill.
khalon/-ot hazazah חלון הזזה *nf* sliding window.
khalon/-ot patoo'akh/petookheem חלון פתוח *nm* open window.
(ha) khalon patoo'akh החלון פתוח the window is open.
(saf ha) khalon סף החלון *nm* window sill.
khalood/-ah חלוד *adj* rusty.
khalood|ah חלודה *nf* rust; (*+of:* **-at**).
(he'el|ah-tah/-etee) khaloodah העלה חלודה *v* got rusty; (*pres* **ma'aleh** *etc*; *fut* **ya'aleh** *etc*).
khaloofee/-t חליפי *adj* interchangeable; substitute; alternative.
khalook/-eem חלוק *nm* dressing-gown; (*pl+of:* **-ey**).
khalook/-ah חלוק *adj* **1.** divided; **2.** disagreeing.
◇ **(ha)khalookah** החלוקה *nf* the "Chalukeh"- a system of free housing and regular handouts for subsistence which, for centuries, served as basis of the existence of a limited Jewish population in pre-Zionist Palestine. Confined to the four so-called "holy cities" (Jerusalem, Hebron, Safed and Tiberias), it was kept going by an intermittent yet steady flow of philanthropic donations collected through special emissaries sent out to Jewish communities all over the world. For centuries and well into the advent of Zionism and the British Mandate it was it that made possible for a number of communities and "landsmanschaften" of religious Jews to live at the Jewish holy places in Palestine and care for them.
khalookey nakhal חלוקי נחל *nm pl* cobblestones.
khalool/-ah חלול *adj* hollow.
khaloosh/-ah חלוש *adj* weak; feeble.
(kol 'anot) khalooshah קול ענות חלושה *nm* **1.** the tune of defeat (Bibl); **2.** a weak whispering noise.
(la) khalooteen לחלוטין *adv* absolutely.
khaloots/-ah חלוץ *nmf* pioneer; (*pl+of:* **-ey**).
khalootsee/-t חלוצי *adj* pioneering.
khalootseeyoot חלוציות *nf* pioneering; pioneering spirit.
khaltoorah/-ot חלטורה *nf [slang]* **1.** low-level art; **2.** spare-time job; moonlighting.
khalvah/-ot חלווה *nf* halvah; confection of ground sesame seeds and nuts mixed with honey.
kham/-ah חם *adj* hot.
kham/-at mezeg חם מזג *adj* hot-tempered.
(neshek) kham נשק חם *nm* firearm(s).
kham חם *nm* woman's father-in-law (my/her father-in-law: **kham|ee/-ha**).
(ha) khamah החמה *nf* (the) sun.
(hanets ha) khamah הנץ החמה *nm* sunrise.
(yemot ha) khamah ימות החמה *nm pl* sunny season; Israeli summer.
(leekooy) khamah ליקוי חמה *nm* eclipse of the sun; solar eclipse.
(be) khamah? *(kh=k)* ?בכמה for how much?
(le) khamah לכמה **1.** for how many? **2.** for a few;(kh=*k)*.
kham|ad/-dah/-adetee חמד *v* coveted; desired; (*pres* **khomed**; *fut* **yakhmod**).
khamad (*etc*) **latson** חמד לצון *v* joked; teased.
□ **Khamadeeyah** (Hamadya) חמדייה *nm* kibbutz (est. 1939) in Bet-She'an Valley, 3 km NE of Beisan (**Bet-She'an**). Pop. 440.
kham|ak/-kah/-aktee חמק *v* slipped away; (*pres* **khomek**; *fut* **yakhamok**).
khamakmak/-ah חמקמק *adj* elusive; evasive.
khamam|ah/-ot חממה *nf* hotbed; greenhouse; (*+of:* **-at**).
khamanee|t/-yot חמנית *nf* sunflower.
kham|as/-sah/-astee חמס *v* robbed; (*pres* **khomes**; *fut* **yakhmos**).
khamas חמס *nm* injustice; wrong; violence.
(za'ak/-ah/-tee) khamas זעק חמס *v* cried out for justice; (*pres* **zo'ek** *etc*; *fut* **yeez'ak** *etc*).
□ **Khamat** (Hammat) חמת *nf* ruins of ancient Biblical town excavated 2.5 km SE of Tiberias.
□ **Khamat Gader** (Hammat Gader) חמת גדר *nf* renovated hot spring spa from Roman period in S. part of Golan Heights, on **Yarmook** river.
(ma) khamat מחמת (**npr me-khamat**) *conj* on account of.
khamatsmats/-ah חמצמץ *adj* sour.

khamdan/-eet חמדן *adj* greedy; envious.
khamdanoot חמדנות *nf* greed; lustfulness.
khameem/-ah חמים *adj* warm; lukewarm.
khameemoot חמימות *nf* warmth.
◇ **khameen** חמין *nm pl* traditional Jewish Saturday noontime dish: meat-stew kept warm from Friday noon; called in Yiddish "Cholent".
khameeshah חמישה **1.** *num m* five (5); **2.** 5th (of the month).
('esreem va) khameeshah עשרים וחמישה *num m* twenty five (25).
khameeshah-'asar חמישה עשר **1.** *num m* fifteen (15); **2.** *adj* 15th (of the month).
khameeshah be- (or **le-**) חמישה ב־/ל־ *adj* the 5th (of the month).
khameeshee/-t חמישי *adj* the fifth; 5th.
(yom/yemey) khameeshee יום חמישי *nm* Thursday.
khameesh|eet/-yot חמישית *num* one fifth (1/5).
khameesheem חמישים *num* fifty (50).
khameesheey|ah/-yot חמישייה *nf* quintuplet;
khameets|ah/-ot חמיצה *nf* borsht (beet soup).
khamesh חמש *num f* five (5).
('esreem ve) khamesh עשרים וחמש *num m* twenty five (25).
khamesh-'esreh חמש עשרה *num f* fifteen (15).
◇ **khamets** חמץ *nm* any food (and primarily bread) not "kosher" for Passover.
khamood/-ah חמוד *adj* **1.** coveted; desirable; **2.** *[slang]* charming.
khamoodah (*cpr* **khamoodah**) חמודה *interj [colloq.]* darling! dear girl!
khamoodaleh חמודה'לה *interj f* dearest! my love!
khamoodee חמודי *nm [colloq.]* my darling!
khamoodon/-et חמודון *interj [colloq.] nmf* dearest! baby (lovers' slang).
khamookeem חמוקים *nm pl* curves; roundings (of woman's thighs); (*+of:* **-ey**).
khamool|ah/-ot חמולה *nf [colloq.] (Arab.)* family, clan (in a tribal society); (*+of:* **-at**).
khamoom/-ey mo'akh חמום מוח *nm & adj* hothead.
(paneem) khamoorot פנים חמורות *nf pl* grim face.
khamoor/-ah חמור *adj* serious; severe.
khamoor/-at sever חמור סבר *adj* looking grim.
khamoosh/-ah חמוש *adj* armed; (*f+of:* **-at**; *pl m+of:* **-ey**).
khamoots/-ah חמוץ *adj* sour.
khamoots-matok חמוץ מתוק *adj* bittersweet.
(melafefon/-eem) khamoots/-eem מלפפון חמוץ *nm* pickle; sour cucumber.
(paneem) khamootsot פנים חמוצות *nf pl* sour (wry) face.
□ **Khamey Zohar** (Hamey Zohar) חמי זוהר *nm pl* hot springs cure and relaxation spa and health-resort on Western coast of the Dead Sea.
khamor/-eem חמור *nm* **1.** donkey; ass; **2.** *[colloq.]* idiot; (*pl+of:* **-ey**).
khamorah/-ot חמורה *nf [slang]* idiot (female).
khamot חמות *nf* mother-in-law; wife's mother-in-law.
khamrah חמרה *nf* red loam; red-colored earth ideal for citrus-growing.
□ **Khamrah** (Hamra) חמרה *nf* village (est. 1971) in E. part of Samaria hills, on the road from Nablus (**Shekhem**) to Adam Bridge.
khamran חמרן *nm* aluminum.
khamranee/-t חמרני *adj* materialistic.
khamranoot חמרנות *nf* materialism.
khamseen/eem חמסין *nm* heat-wave; sirocco; one of year's hottest days.
◇ **khamshoosh/-eet** חמשוש *[slang] nmf* derogatory nickname used onetime for freshmen (approx. 11 y. old) entering 1st year of junior high-school (before the School Reform, see ◇ **reformah**).
khamtsan חמצן *nm* oxygen.
◇ **(ha)khamtsan shel (ha)medeenah** החמצן של המדינה *[slang] nm* (*lit.:* the country's oxygen); ironical reference to the Israeli banking system.
(mey) khamtsan מי חמצן *nm pl* hydrogen peroxide.
khan חאן *nm* old-fashioned inn in Arab or Near-Eastern tradition.
khan|ah/-tah/-eetee חנה *v* **1.** parked (car); **2.** camp; (*pres* **khoneh**; *fut* **yekhneh**).
khan|ak/-kah/-aktee חנק *v* strangled; (*pres* **khonek**; *fut* **yakhnok**).
khan|an/-enah/-antee חנן *v* **1.** endowed; **2.** pardoned (criminal); (*pres* **khonen**; *fut* **yakhon**).
khanayah/-yot חניה *nf* parking; (*+of:* **-at**).
khanayah 'al meedrakhah/-ot (*[colloq.] pron* **madrekh|ah/-ot**) חניה על מדרכה *nf* parking on the sidewalk.
khanayah asoorah חניה אסורה *nf* parking forbidden.
khanayah be-tashloom חניה בתשלום *nf* paid parking.
(doo|'akh/-khot) khanayah דו"ח חניה *nm* parking-ticket; police-report or fine for unauthorized parking.
(kartees/-ey) khanayah כרטיס חניה parking voucher.
□ **Khanee'el** (Hanni'el) חניאל *nm* village (est. 1950) in Sharon, 8 km E. of Netanya. Pop. 341.
khana|kh/-khah/-akhtee חנך *v* inaugurated; coached; (*pres* **khonekh**; *fut* **yakhnokh**).
khaneekh/-ah חניך *nmf* pupil; apprentice; (*f+of:* **-at**; *pl+of:* **-ey**).
khaneekhayeem חניכיים *nm pl* gums (of teeth).
khaneekhoot חניכות *nf* apprenticeship.
khaneek|ah/-ot חניקה *nf* strangulation; throttling; (*+of:* **-at**).
khaneen|ah/-ot חנינה *nf* amnesty; (*+of:* **-at**).

khaneet/-ot חנית *nf* spear.

(khood ha) khaneet חוד החנית *nm* spearhead.

□ **Khaneetah** (Hanita) חניתה *nf* kibbutz (est. 1938) in Upper Galilee near Lebanese border, 7 km E. of **Rosh ha-Neekrah**. Pop. 686.

khanfan/-eet חנפן *adj* flatterer.

khankan חנקן *nm* nitrogen.

khanook/-ah חנוק **1.** *adj* stifled; choked; **2.** *[colloq.] adj* terribly short of cash.

khanookah/-ot חנוכה *nf* inauguration; dedication; **(+*of:* -at)**.

◇ **khanookah** ("Hanukkah") חנוכה *nm* 8-days feast starting 25 **Keeslev** (approx. Dec.) during which candles are *lit* each evening to commemorate Maccabean victory over Greek occupiers of Judea in 165 B.C.

◇ **khanookeey|ah/-yot** חנוכייה *nf* Hanukkah candelabrum; **(+*of:* -yat)**.

khanoop|ah/-ot חנופה *nf* flattery; **(+*of:* -at)**.

khanoo|t/-yot חנות *nf* shop; store.

(ha) khanoot החנות *nf [slang]* fly (in man's trousers).

khanoo|t/-yot begadeem חנות בגדים *nf* clothes store/shop.

khanoo|t/-yot deleekateseem חנות דליקטסים *[slang] nf* delicatessen store/shop.

khanoo|t/-yot halbashah חנות הלבשה *nf* clothing store/shop.

khanoo|t/-yot kolbo חנות כלבו *nf* department-store.

khanoo|t/-yot lee-khley 'avodah *(kh=k)* חנות לכלי עבודה *nf* hardware store.

khanoo|t/-yot lee-khley bayeet *(kh=k)* חנות לכלי בית *nf* shop/store for household articles.

khanoo|t/-yot lee-khley negeenah *(kh=k)* חנות לכלי נגינה *nf* shop/store for musical instruments.

khanoo|t/-yot le-tsorkhey khashmal חנות לצורכי חשמל *nf* electric supplies and equipment store/shop.

khanoo|t/-yot le-tsorkhey kteevah חנות לצורכי כתיבה *nf* stationery store/shop.

khanoo|t/yot le-tsorkhey tseeloom חנות לצרכי צילום *nf* photographic equipment & supplies store/shop.

khanoo|t/-yot makolet חנות מכולת *nf* grocery store/shop.

khanoo|t/-yot na'alayeem חנות נעליים *nf* shoe-store.

khanoo|t/-yot perot חנות פירות *nf* fruit store/shop.

khanoo|t/-yot raheeteem חנות רהיטים *nf* furniture store/shop.

khanoo|t/-yot sefareem חנות ספרים *nf* book-store; book-shop.

khanoo|t/-yot smalot חנות שמלות *nf* store/shop for women's dresses.

khanoo|t/-yot takleeteem חנות תקליטים *nf* musical (gramophone) record & cassette store/shop.

khanoo|t/-yot yerakot חנות ירקות *nf* greengrocery.

khantareesh חנטריש *nm [slang]* **1.** no good; **2.** much ado about nothing.

khantareeshee חנטרישי *[slang] adj* false; with nothing genuine in it.

khanyon/-eem חניון *nm* **1.** car-park; parking-ground in town; **2.** camping ground; **(*pl+of:* -ey)**.

□ **Khan Yoones** חן יונס *nf* Arab town in S. part of Gaza Strip, 10 NE of border town (with Egypt) **Rafee'akh** and 23 km SW of Gaza. Pop. approx. 81,000 plus 26,225 in refugee camps.

◇ **KHAPAK** חפ״ק *nm* (*acr of* **KHavoorat Peekood Keedmeet** חבורת פיקוד קדמית) advance command group (Milit.).

(sam/-ah/-tee nafsh|o/-ah/-ee be)khap|o/-ah/-ee שם נפשו בכפו *v* risked one's (his/her/my) life; **(*pres* sam *etc; fut* yaseem *etc*)**.

khapoo|t/-yot חפות *nf* innocence.

kharah חארה *nf [slang]* **1.** excrement; shit; **2.** (*figurat.*) worst quality; bad.

khar|ah/-tah חרה *v* angered; **(*pres* khoreh; *fut* yeekhreh)**.

khar|ad/-dah/-adetee חרד *v* feared; was anxious; **(*pres* khared; *fut* yekhrad)**.

kharad|ah/-ot חרדה *nf* anxiety; **(+*of:* kherdat)**.

khara'ee/-t חראי *adj [slang]* **1.** dunglike; wrong; **2.** (sarcastically:) person in charge (wilful distortion of word **akhra'ee** i.e. responsible).

khar|ag/-gah/-agtee חרג *v* digressed; exceeded; deviated; **(*pres* khoreg; *fut* yakhrog)**.

kharak/-eem (*npr* kherek/kharakeem) חרק *nm* insect.

khar|ak/-kah/-aktee חרק *v* squeaked; gnashed; **(*pres* khorek; *fut* yakhrok)**.

kharak|eh/-ot חראקה *[slang] nf* illicit racing of stolen cars.**(*pl+of:* -ey)**.

khar|ap/-pah/-aptee חרפ *v [slang]* slept; snored; **(*pres* khorep; *fut* yakhrop)**.

kharash/-eem חרש *nm* craftsman; artisan; **(*pl+of:* -ey)**.

khar|ash/-shah/-ashtee חרש *v* **1.** ploughed; **2.** *[colloq.]* searched thoroughly for; **(*pres* khoresh; *fut* yakhrosh)**.

kharash (*etc*) mezeemot חרש מזימות *v* schemed; plotted.

kharat/-eem חרט *nm* turner; engraver; **(*pl+of:* -ey)**.

khar|at/-tah/-atetee חרט *v* engraved; turned; chiseled; **(*pres* khoret; *fut* yakhrot)**.

khar|at/-tah/-atetee חרת *v* carved; engraved; grooved; **(*pres* khoret; *fut* yakhrot)**.

kharat|ah/-ot חרטה *nf* regret; remorse; **(+*of:* -at)**.

kharatoot חרטות *nf* turnery.

khar|ats/-tsah/-atstee חרץ *v* cut; determined; decided; grooved; **(*pres* khorets; *fut* yakhrots)**.

kharats (*etc*) goral חרץ גורל *v* determined fate; sealed doom.

kharats (*etc*) **meeshpat** משפט חרץ *v* passed judgment; adjudicated.
kharats (*etc*) **lashon** חרץ לשון *v* made fun of.
khar|av/-vah/-avtee חרב *v* was ravaged; was destroyed; (*pres* **kharev**; *fut* **yekhrav**).
kharavah חרבה *nf* arid land; dryness.
kharavot חרבות *nf pl* swords; sabers; (*sing* **kherev**).
(**tseekhtsoo'akh**) **kharavot** צחצוח חרבות *nm* saber rattling.
khardal חרדל *nm* mustard.
khared/-ah חרד *adj* fearful; anxious.
khared/-eem חרד *nm* Orthodox Jew; God-fearing Jew; (*pl+of:* **-ey**).
kharedee/-t חרדי *adj* Orthodox; observant; pious.
kharee-af (*npr* **khoree-af**) חרי־אף *nm* burning anger.
khareef/-ah חריף *nm* acute; pungent.
(**mashk|eh/-a'ot**) **khareef/-eem** משקה חריף *nm* intoxicating liquor; alcoholic drink.
khareefoo|t/-yot חריפות *nf* acuteness; pungency; spiceness.
khareeg/-ah חריג *adj* exceptional; irregular.
khareeg/-eem חריג *nm* exception; (*pl+of:* **-ey**).
khareeg|ah/-ot חריגה *nf* **1.** deviation; excess; **2.** (banking) sum of overdraft allowed.
(**reebeet 'al**) **khareegah** ריבית על חריגה *nf* higher rate of interest for amounts overdrawn.
khareek|ah/-ot חריקה *nf* grinding; grating; cracking; (*+of:* **-at**).
khareek|at/-ot shen/sheenayeem חריקת שן *nf* gnashing of teeth.
khareesh חריש *nm* ploughing; ploughing season.
khareesh 'amok חריש עמוק *nm* deep ploughing (mostly used *figurat.*).
khareeshee/-t חרישי *adj* silent; soft.
khareet|ah/-ot חריטה *nf* etching; carving; turning; (*+of:* **-at**).
khareets/-eem חריץ *nm* groove; incision; slice; (*pl+of:* **-ey**).
khareetsoot חריצות *nf* diligence; skill.
kharev/-ah חרב *adj* desolate; ruined; parched.
khargol/-eem חרגול *nm* grasshopper; (*pl+of:* **-ey**).
kharon/-ot חרון *nm* anger; ire.
□ **Kharootseem** (**Haruzim**) חרוצים *nm* village (est. 1951) in Sharon, 5 km N. of Ra'anana. Pop. 624.
◇ **kharoset** חרוסת *nf* symbolic pasty food mixture served at the **Seder** (Passover dinner).
kharoshet חרושת *nf* industry; manufacture.
(**bet/batey**) **kharoshet** בית חרושת *nm* plant; factory.
kharoshtan/-eem חרושתן *nm* manufacturer; industrialist.
kharookh/-ah חרוך *adj* scorched; gutted.
kharoosh/-ah חרוש *adj* ploughed.
kharoosh/-at kemateem חרוש קמטים *adj* wrinkled completely.
kharoot/-ah חרות *v pres adj* engraved; inscribed; carved.
kharoots/-ah חרוץ *adj* diligent.
(**keelayon**) **kharoots** כיליון חרוץ *nm* utter ruin.
kharoov/-eem חרוב *nm* carob; (*pl+of:* **-ey**).
kharooz/-eem חרוז *nm* **1.** rhyme; **2.** bead; (*pl+of:* **-ey**).
kharseenah חרסינה *nf* porcelain.
kharseen|ah/-ot חרסינה *nf [slang]* ceramic tiles (for kitchen, bathroom and toilet); (*pl+of:* **-at**).
(**aree|'akh/-khey**) **kharseenah** אריח חרסינה *nm* kitchen, toilet or bathroom tile.
kharseentcheek/-eem חרסינצ׳יק *nm [slang]* construction worker skilled in laying ceramic tiles; (normative term: **ratsaf**).
kharseet חרסית *nf* red soil; clay.
khartom/-eem חרטום *nm* bow (ship); beak (of bird); (*pl+of:* **-ey**).
khartsan/-eem חרצן *nm* seed; kernel; (*pl+of:* **-ey**).
khartsee|t/-yot חרצית *nf* chrysanthemum.
khas/-ah/-tee חס *v* pitied; spared; (*pres* **khas**; *fut* **yakhoos**).
khas ve-khaleelah! חס וחלילה! *interj* God beware! God forbid!
khas ve-shalom! חס ושלום! *interj* God forbid!
khas|ah/-ot חסה *nf* lettuce; (*+of:* **-at**).
khas|ah/-tah/-eetee חסה *v* found haven; (*pres* **khoseh**; *fut* **yekheseh**).
khas|af/-fah/-aftee חשף *v* bared; uncovered; revealed; (*pres* **khosef**; *fut* **yakhsof**).
khasak|eh/-ot חסאקה *nf [slang]* surfboat; (*+of:* **-at**).
khas|akh/-khah/-akhtee חסך *v* saved; economized; spared; (*pres* **khosekh**; *fut* **yakhsokh**).
khasal! חסל! *interj* enough! stop!
khas|am/-mah/-amtee חסם *v* blocked; (*pres* **khosem**; *fut* **yakhsom**).
khasam/-eem חסם *nm* tourniquet (Medic.).
khas|ar/-rah/-artee חסר *v* lacked; missed; (*pres* **khaser**; *fut* **yekhsar**).
khas|ar/-rat חסר *adj* short of; -less.
khas|ar/-rat bayeet חסר בית *adj* homeless.
khas|ar/-rat booshah חסר בושה *adj* shameless.
khas|ar/-rat de'ag|ah/-ot חסר דאגה *adj* carefree.
khas|ar/-rat 'erekh חסר ערך *adj* worthless; valueless.
khas|ar/-rat haganah חסר הגנה *adj* defenseless.
khas|ar/-rat hakarah חסר הכרה *adj* unconscious.
khas|ar/-rat keesh|aron/-ronot חסר כשרון *adj* untalented.
khas|ar/-rat magen חסר מגן *adj* unprotected.
khas|ar/-rat mashma'oot חסר משמעות *adj* meaningless.
khas|ar/-rat matspoon חסר מצפון *adj* unscrupulous; conscienceless.
khas|ar/-rat menookhah חסר מנוחה *adj* restless.

khas|ar/-rat merets חסר מרץ *adj* unenergetic; lacking energy.
khas|ar/-rat motsa חסר מוצא *adj* desperate; hopeless.
khas|ar/-rat oneem חסר אונים *adj* powerless.
khas|ar/-rat reg|esh/-ashot חסר רגש *adj* unfeeling.
khas|ar/-rat sheenayeem חסר שיניים *adj* toothless.
khas|ar/-rat ta'am חסר טעם *adj* tasteless.
khas|ar/-rat takanah חסר תקנה *adj* beyond repair.
khas|ar/-rat takdeem חסר תקדים *adj* unprecedented.
khas|ar/-rat takhleet חסר תכלית *adj* aimless; pointless.
khas|ar/-rat teekv|ah/-ot חסר תקווה *adj* hopeless.
khas|ar/-rat to'elet חסר תועלת *adj* useless.
khas|ar/-rat yesha' חסר ישע *adj* helpless.
khas|ar/-rat yesod חסר יסוד *adj* baseless; unfounded.
khaseed/-ah חסיד *adj* devotee; fan; partisan of; (*+of:* **-at**).
◇ **khaseed/-eem** חסיד *nm* **1.** "Hussid" - partisan of the "Hassidic" movement (see **khaseedoot**, below); **2.** *nm* fervent follower; (*pl+of:* **-ey**).
khaseed|ah/-ot חסידה *nf* stork.
khaseedee/-t חסידי *adj* Hasidic.
◇ **khaseedoot** חסידות *nf* Hassidic religious movement based on attachment to a hereditary religious leader, offspring of dynasties of "Rebbe"s (Rabbis).
khaseef|ah/-ot חשיפה *nf* exposure; disrobing; (*+of:* **-at**).
khaseem|ah/-ot חסימה *nf* barring; blocking; blockage; (*+of:* **-at**).
◇ **(akhooz) khaseemah** see ◇ **akhooz khaseemah**.
khaseen/-ah חסין *adj* immune; -proof; resistant.
khaseen/-at 'esh חסין-אש *adj* fireproof.
khaseenoo|t/-yot חסינות *nf* immunity.
khaseenoot parlamentareet חסינות פרלמנטרית *nf* parliamentary immunity.
khaser/-ah חסר *adj* **1.** lacking; missing; **2.** minus (arithmet.).
◇ **(keteev) khaser** see ◇ **keteev khaser**.
khasfanee|t/-yot חשפנית *nf* stripper (female).
khasfanoo|t/-yot חשפנות *nf* striptease.
(mof|a'/-'ey) khasfanoo|t/-yot מופע חשפנות *nf* striptease show.
khash/-ah/-tee חש *v* felt; (*pres* **khash**; *fut* **yakhoosh**).
khash|ad/-adot חשד *nm* suspicion; (*pl+of:* **-dot**).
khash|ad/-dah/-adetee חשד *v* suspected; (*pres* **khoshed**; *fut* **yakhshod**).
khash|ak/-kah/-aktee חשק *v* desired; coveted; (*pres* **khoshek**; *fut* **yakhshok**).
◇ **(kheshbon/-ot) khashak** see ◇ **kheshbon/-ot khashak**.
khash|akh/-khah חשך *v* **1.** grew dim; darkened; (*pres* **khashekh**; *fut* **yekhshakh**); **2.** (referring to daylight; *3rd pers. m sing* only) it became dark (*pres* **makhsheekh**; *fut* **yakhsheekh**).
khashash/-ot חשש *nm* apprehension; misgiving.
khash|ash/-eshah/-ashtee חשש *v* feared; suspected; (*pres* **khoshesh**; *fut* **yakhshosh**).
khash|av/-vah/-avtee חשב *v* thought; (*pres* **khoshev**; *fut* **yakhshov**).
khashav/-eem חשב *nm* accountant; (*pl+of:* **-ey**).
khasha'ee/-t חשאי *adj* secret.
khasha'eeyoot חשאיות *nf* secrecy.
(ba) khasha'eeyoot בחשאיות *adv* in secrecy.
(bekheer|ah/-ot) khasha'ee|t/-yot בחירה חשאית *nf* election(s) by secret ballot.
(ba) khashay בחשאי *adv* secretly; quietly.
khashdan/-eem חשדן *nmf & adj* suspicious; suspecting; (*pl+of:* **-ey**).
khashdanoot חשדנות *nf* suspiciousness; suspicion.
khasheesh חשיש *nm* Hashish (narcotic).
khasheeshneek/-eet חשיש'ניק *[slang] nmf* drug-addict.
khasheevoo|t/-yot חשיבות *nf* importance.
khashekh|ah/-ot חשיכה *nf* darkness; (*+of:* **kheshkhat**).
(she'ot ha) khashekhah שעות החשיכה *nf pl* after dark.
khash'khoo 'eyn|av/-eha/-ekha/-ayeekh/-ay *etc* חשכו עיניו/-יה/-יך/-ייך/-יי *nm pl & v pst* his/her/your(*m/f*)/my *etc* eyes grew dim.
khashmal חשמל *nf* electricity.
◇ **(khevrat ha) khashmal** see ◇ **khevrat ha-khashmal**.
(khoot/-ey) khashmal חוט חשמל *nm* electric wire.
(zerem) khashmal (*or:* **khashmalee**) זרם חשמל *nm* electric current.
khashmal|ay/-a'eem חשמלאי *nm* electrician; (*pl+of:* **-a'ey**).
khashmalee/-t חשמלי *adj* electric.
(dood) khashmalee דוד חשמלי *nm* electric boiler; (*pl* **doodey khashmal**).
(tanoor) khashmalee תנור חשמלי *nm* electric stove; electric heater; (*pl* **tanoorey khashmal**).
(makdekh|ah/-ot) khashmalee|t/-yot מקדחה חשמלית *nf* electric drill.
khashmel|a'ee חשמלאי *[colloq.] nm* electrician; (*pl+of:* **-a'ey**).
khashmela'oot חשמלאות *nf* electrical engineering; electrical installation.
□ **Khashmona'eem** (Hashmona'im) חשמונאים *nm* urban settlement in the Modee'een area (est. 1985), resulted from union of two earlier attempted settlements on the "Green Line": **Ganey Modee'een** and **Ramat Modee'een**. Pop. 639.
khashood/-ah חשוד *adj* suspected.
khashood/-eem חשוד *nm* suspect.

khashookh/-ah חשוך *adj* **1.** dark; obscure; **2.** (*figurat.*) backward.

khashoov/-ah חשוב *adj* important.

khashoov she- חשוב ש־ *adv* it is important that...

khas'khan/-eet חסכן *adj* thrifty.

khasood/-ah חסוד *adj* hypocritical.

khasoof/-ah חשוף *adj* bare; exposed.

khasookh/-at marpe חשוך־מרפא *adj* incurable.

khasoo|t/-yot חסות *nf* protection; aegis.

(ben/bat) khasoot בן חסות *nmf* protegé/-e.

(demey) khasoot דמי־חסות *nm pl* "protection"-money; "protection"-fee.

khasoo|y/-yah חסוי *adj* "classified" (information, document).

khat|a/-'ah/-atee חטא *v* sinned; (*pres* **khote**; *fut* **yekhta**).

khata'eem חטאים *nm pl* sins; (*sing:* **khet**; *pl+of:* **khet'ey**).

khat|af/-fah/-aftee חטף *v* snatched; caught; kidnapped; (*pres* **khotef**; *fut* **yakhtof**).

khataf-kamats חטף־קמץ *nm* sublinear combined diacritic sign (ֳ) for semivowel pronounced **o**.

◇ **khataf-patakh** חטף־פתח *nm* sublinear combined diacritic sign (ֲ) indicating a short **a** in Biblical Hebrew but not distinguished in pronunciation from **patakh** in Modern Hebrew.

◇ **khataf segol** חטף סגול *nm* sublinear combined diacritic sign (ֱ) for semivowel pronounced as the short *e* of *pet*.

khat|akh/-khah/-akhtee חתך *v* cut; cut off; (*pres* **khotekh**; *fut* **yakhtokh**).

khatakh/-eem חתך *nm* incision; section; cross-section; (*pl+of:* **-ey**).

khatakh/-eem rakhav/rekhaveem חתך רחב *nm* cross-section.

khataltool/-eem חתלתול *nm* he-kitten (*pl+of:* **-ey**).

khataltool|ah/-ot חתלתולה *nf* she-kitten; (*+of:* **-at**).

khat|am/-mah/-amtee חתם *v* **1.** signed; **2.** signed up; (*pres* **khotem**; *fut* **yakhtom**).

khatam (*etc*) **keva'** חתם קבע [*colloq.*] *v* signed up to join the standing army.

khat|an/-aneem חתן *nm* **1.** bridegroom; **2.** son-in-law; **3.** guest (if a male) of honor (*pl+of:* **-ney**).

khat|an/-ney ha-'erev חתן הערב *nm* the evening's guest (male) of honor.

khat|an/-ney ha-khageegah חתן החגיגה *nm* the celebration's guest (male) of honor.

khat|an/-ney ha-meseebah חתן המסיבה *nm* the party's guest (male) of honor.

khat|an/-ney ha-pras חתן הפרס *nm* laureate (male); prize-winner.

khatan ve-kalah (*npr* **khalah**) חתן וכלה *nm pl* bridegroom and bride; the wedding couple.

(avel ben) khataneem (*or:* **avel beyn** *etc*) אבל בין חתנים *nm* (*lit.*) a mourner among grooms; a skeleton at the feast.

khat|ar/-rah/-artee חתר *v* **1.** rowed **2.** strove; **3.** undermined; (*pres* **khoter**; *fut* **yakhtor**).

khatar (*etc*) **le-** חתר ל־ *v* strove to.

khatar (*etc*) **neged/takhat** חתר נגד/תחת *v* plotted against.

khateef/-eem חטיף *nm* snack (*pl+of:* **-ey**).

khateef|ah/-ot חטיפה *nf* kidnapping; abduction; (*+of:* **-at**).

khateekh/-eem חתיך [*slang*] *nm* stunner (male); handsome man (*pl+of:* **-ey**).

khateekh|ah/-ot חתיכה *nf* **1.** piece; slice; bit; **2.** [*slang*] dish; good looker (female); beautiful woman; (*+of:* **-at**).

khateekhat... חתיכת ... *interj* [*slang*] kind of a ... (pejorative).

khateem|ah/-ot חתימה signature; (*+of:* **-at**).

(demey) khateemah דמי חתימה *nm pl* subscription fee.

◇ **(gemar) khateemah tovah!** see ◇ **gemar khateemah tovah!**

◇ **(keteevah va) khateemah tovah!** see ◇ **keteevah va-khateemah tovah!**

khateer|ah/-ot חתירה *nf* **1.** rowing; **2.** striving hard; **3.** undermining; (*+of:* **-at**).

(sekheeyat) khateerah שחיית חתירה *nf* crawl (swimming stroke).

khateev|ah/-ot חטיבה *nf* brigade; section; (*+of:* **-at**).

khateevatee/-t חטיבתי *adj* pertaining to a brigade; brigade-.

◇ **khateevat "geev'atee"** חטיבת גבעתי *nf* the Israel Defense Army's "Giv'ati" Brigade, which earned its initial fame in the 1948 War of Independence, when it withstood the onslaught of the invading Egyptian armies in the Negev.

◇ **khateevat "golanee"** חטיבת ״גולני״ *nf* brigade of the Israel army which earned its fame by its staunch defense of the country's N. borders.

khatoof/-ah חטוף *adj* **1.** quick; **2.** *nmf & adj* kidnapped; (*pl+of:* **-ey**).

(mabat/-eem) khatoof/-eem מבט חטוף *nm* quick glance.

(meetah) khatoofah מיתה חטופה *nf* sudden death.

khatookh/-ah חתוך *adj* cut.

khatool/-eem חתול *nm* cat; (*pl+of:* **-ey**).

khatool/-ey bar חתול בר *nm* wild cat.

(tseeporney) khatool ציפורני חתול *nm* marigold; calendula (flower).

khatool|ah/-ot חתולה *nf* female-cat; (*+of:* **-at**).

khatool|at/-ot meen חתולת מין *nf* sex-kitten.

khatoom/-ah חתום *adj* **1.** signed; **2.** sealed.

(he-) khatoom matah (*f* **ha-khatoomah** *etc*) החתום מטה *nmf* (the) undersigned.

khatoon|ah/-ot חתונה *nf* wedding; (*+of:* **-at**).

khatoonat ha-kesef חתונת הכסף *nf* silver wedding (anniversary).

khatoonat ha-zahav חתונת הזהב *nf* golden wedding (anniversary).

(oolam/-ey) khatoonot אולם חתונות *nm* wedding hall.

khatoov/-ah חטוב *adj* carved.

khatoovah חטובה *adj f [colloq.]* sculpturesque (female) body; body beautiful.

khatot|eret/-arot חטוטרת *nf* hunch; lump.

khatran/-eet חתרן *nmf & adj* subverter; schemer.

khatranoo|t/-yot חתרנות *nf* subversion; scheming.

khats|ah/-tah/-eetee חצה *v* **1.** crossed; **2.** divided in two; (*pres* **khotseh**; *fut* **yekhtseh**).

khatsa'eem חצאים *nm pl* halves; (*sing:* **khatsee** *or* **khetsee**; *pl+of:* **khatsa'ey**).

(la) khatsa'een לחצאין *adv* by halves; into halves.

khatsa'ee|t/-yot חצאית *nf* skirt.

khatsats חצץ *nm* gravel.

(akh|al/-lah/-altee) khatsats אכל חצץ *v* (fig) tried very hard; (*lit.:* ate gravel); (*pres* **okhel** *etc; fut* **yokhal** *etc*).

khatsav/-eem חצב *nm* squill (plant); (*pl+of:* **-ey**).

khats|av/-vah/-avtee חצב *v* hewed; chiseled; (*pres* **khotsev**; *fut* **yakhtsov**).

□ **Khatsav** (Hazav) חצב *nm* village (est. 1949) in the Coastal Plain, 4 km S. of Hadera (**Khaderah**). Pop. 612.

khatsa|yah/-yot (or **khatsee|yah/-yot**) חציה *nf* **1.** bi-section; dividing into two; **2.** crossing; (*+of:* **-at**).

(ma'av|ar/-rey) khatsayah (or **khatseeyah**) מעבר חציה *nm* pedestrian crossing.

khats|ee/-a'eem חצי *nm* half; (*pl+of:* **-a'ey**).

khats|ee/-a'ey 'ee/-yeem חצי־אי *nm* peninsula.

◇ **khatsee ha-sahar he-adom** חצי הסהר האדום *nm* "the Red Crescent" - the equivalent of the Red Cross in Muslim countries.

khatsee-sahar חצי סהר *nm* crescent; half-moon (Muslim emblem).

khatsee nekhamah חצי נחמה *nm* (colloquially: *f*) partial consolation.

khatsee-shenatee/-t חצי־שנתי *adj* semi-annual; half- yearly.

khatseel/-eem חציל *nm* eggplant; (*pl+of:* **-ey**).

khatseets|ah/-ot חציצה *nf* partition; interposition; partitioning; (*+of:* **-at**).

khatseer/-eem חציר *nm* hay grass; (*pl+of:* **-ey**).

khatseev|ah/-ot חציבה *nf* stonecutting; quarrying; digging in stony ground; (*+of:* **-at**).

khatser/-ot חצר *nf* **1.** courtyard; yard; **2.** royal court; (*+of:* **khats|ar/-rot**).

□ **Khatsereem (Hazerim)** חצרים *nm* kibbutz (est. 1946) in N. Negev, 6 km W. of Beersheba (**Be'er Sheva'**). Pop. 681.

□ **Khatsevah (Hazeva)** חצבה *nf* site of ancient Nabatean ruins near oasis in N. part of the **'Aravah**, off the road to Elat. Pop. 488.

khatsevet חצבת *nf* measles (medic.).

khatsoof/-ah חצוף *adj* arrogant; impudent.

khatsoov/-ah חצוב *adj* hewn; carved.

khatsoov|ah/-ot חצובה *nf* tripod; (*+of:* **-at**).

khatsoo|y/-yah חצוי *adj* halved; divided in two.

(be-lev) khatsooy בלב חצוי *adv* half-heartedly.

□ **Khatsor Ashdod (Hazor Ashdod)** חצור אשדוד *nm* kibbutz (est. 1946) near Mediterranean coast, 8 km SE of Ashdod. Pop. 609.

□ **Khatsor ha-Gleeleet** (Hazor haGlilit) חצור הגלילית *nf* township (est 1953) in Upper Gallilee, 2 kms N. of **Rosh-Peenah**. Pop 7,230.

khatsot חצות *nm* midnight.

(ba) khatsot ha-yom בחצות היום *adv* at midday.

◇ **(teekoon) khatsot** see ◇ **teekoon khatsot**.

khatsotsr|ah חצוצרה *nf* salpinx; Eustachian or Fallopian tube(s).

khatsotsr|ah/-ot חצוצרה *nf* trumpet; bugle; (*+of:* **-at**).

khatsotsr|at/-ot bas חצוצרת בס *nf* bass-trumpet.

khatsotsr|at/-ot ha-rekhem חצוצרת הרחם *nf* uterine tube.

khatsotsr|at/-ot ha-shema' חצוצרת השמע *nf* auditory tube.

khatsotsran/-eem חצוצרן *nm* trumpeter; bugler.

khatsran/-eet חצרן *nmf* janitor; (*pl:* **-eem**; *+of:* **-ey**).

khav/-ah/-tee חב *v* owed; was indebted.

◇ **Khavah** חוה *nf* personal name (Bibl.) Eve.

khav|ah/-ot חווה *nf* farm; (*+of:* **-at**).

(bat/benot) khavah בת־חוה *nf* daughter of Eve i.e. woman.

khav|ah/-ot khakla'ee|t/-yot חווה חקלאית *nf* agricultural farm.

khaval חבל *interj* it's a pity that...

khav|al/-lah/-altee חבל *v* wounded; injured; (*pres* **khovel**; *fut* **yakhbol** *(b=v)*).

(be) khavanah *(kh=k)* בכוונה *adv* on purpose; intentionally.

khav|ar/-rah/-artee חבר *v* associated; befriended.

khav|ash/-shah/-ashtee חבש *v* **1.** dressed; **2.** bandaged; (*pres* **khovesh**; *fut* **yakhbosh** *(b=v)*).

khavash (*etc*) **kova'** חבש כובע *v* put on a hat, headgear.

khava|'ee (*npr* **khav|ay**)**/-'eem** חוואי *nm* farmer; (*pl+of:* **-'ey**).

khav|at/-tah/-atetee חבט *v* hit; struck; (*pres* **khovet**; *fut* **yakhbot** *(b=v)*).

khav|at/-ot da'at חוות דעת *nf* opinion.

□ **Khavat ha-Shomer (Hawwat haShomer)** חוות השומר *nf* educational (religious) institution (est. 1936) in Upper Gallilee, near **Eelaneeyah** (Ilaniyya).

□ **Khavat Noy** (Hawwat Noy) חוות נוי *nf* agricultural state-farm in Sharon, near kibbutz **Ma'abarot**.

□ **Khavat Shemoo'el** (Hawwat Shemu'el) חוות שמואל *nf* experimental agricultural farm (est 1952) dedicated to cotton-growing, 10 kms N. of Bet-She'an, in the Jordan Valley.

khavat|ah/-ot חבטה *nf* blow; bang; (*+of:* **-at**).

khavats|elet/-alot חבצלת *nf* lily (plant).

□ **Khavatselet ha-Sharon** (Havazzelet haSharon) חבצלת השרון *nm* village (est. 1935) on the Mediterranean coast, 3 km N. of Netanya. Pop. 410.

khava|yah/-yot חוויה *nf* deeply felt experience; (*+of:* **-at**).

khaveel|ah/-ot חווילה *nf* villa (rarely used literary term); (*+of:* **-at**).

khaveel|ah/-ot חבילה *nf* parcel; package; (*+of:* **-at**).

('eesk|at/-ot) khaveelah עסקות חבילה *nf* package- deal.

(do'ar) khaveelot דואר חבילות *nm* parcel-post.

khavee|t/-yot חבית *nf* barrel.

khaveet|ah/-ot חביתה *nf* omelette; (*+of:* **at**).

khaveev/-ah חביב *adj* likeable; affable.

(akhron akhron) khaveev (*npr* **akharon akharon**) אחרון אחרון חביב last but not least.

khaveevatee חביבתי *nf* my dear; my darling; (addressing female).

khaveevee (*npr* **khaveevee**) חביבי *nm* my dear; my darling: (addressing male).

khaveevoot חביבות *nf* pleasantness; cordiality.

khav|er/-erah חבר *nmf* **1.** friend; pal; comrade; **2.** boyfriend/girlfriend; **3.** member (of an organization); (*f+of:* **-rat**; *pl+of:* **-rey/-rot**).

khaveree/-t חברי *adj* comradely; friendly.

(asef|at/-ot) khavereem אסיפת חברים *nf* membership meeting.

khaveroot חברות *nf* **1.** membership; **2.** comradeship; **3.** (among youngsters) boy-and-girl friendship.

khaver/-at keneset חבר־כנסת *nmf* Knesset-Member; Member of the Knesset; M.K.

(be) khavod (*kh=k*) בכבוד *adv* honorably.

(be) khavod rav (*kh=k*) בכבוד רב yours truly; yours respectfully; (polite customary formula to precede signature in a letter).

khavook/-ah חבוק *adj* embraced; clasped.

khavool/-ah חבול *adj* wounded; injured.

(mas/meesey) khaver מס־חבר *nm* membership fees.

(peenkas) khaver (*cpr* **peenkes**) פנקס־חבר *nm* membership-card; (*pl:* **peenkesey khaver**).

(profesor) khaver פרופסור חבר *nm* associate professor.

khavoor|ah/-ot חבורה *nf* gang; group; (*+of:* **-at**).

khavoosh/-ah חבוש *adj* **1.** bandaged; **2.** locked up; jailed.

khavoosheem חבושים *nm pl* quinces; (*sing:* **khavoosh**; *pl+of:* **-ey**).

khavoo|y/-yah חבוי *adj* hidden.

khavrootee/-t חברותי *adj* sociable.

kha|y/-yah חי *v pres & adj* living; alive; lively.

khay ח״י numerical *symbol* for 18 (popular good-luck numerical symbol because of its meaning: alive).

kha|y/-yah ve ka|yam/-yemet חי וקיים *adj* alive and kicking.

khayah/-yot חיה *nf* beast; animal; (*+of:* **-yot**).

(ha-roo'akh ha) khayah הרוח החיה *nf* the moving spirit.

(gader) khayah גדר חיה *nf* **1.** hedge; **2.** (*lit.:*) living fence.

khayal/-eem חייל *nm* soldier; (*pl+of:* **-ey**).

khayal (etc) be-sadeer חייל בסדיר *nm* soldier serving obligatory term of military service.

khayal (*etc*) **be-keva'** חייל בקבע *nm* soldier serving in standing army.

khayal (*etc*) **kravee** חייל קרבי *nm* combat soldier.

khayal (*etc*) **meshookhrar** חייל משוחרר *nm* ex-serviceman; one who has completed military service.

khayat/-eem חייט *nm* taylor; (*pl+of:* **-ey**).

kha|yat/-yot pere' חיית־פרא *nf* wild (untamed) animals.

kha|yat/-yot teref חיית־טרף *nf* beast of prey.

khayav/-yevet חייב *v pres adj* owes; is obliged to.

kha|yav/-eem חייב *nm* debtor; (*pl+of:* **khayvey**).

kha|yav/-yevet be-deen חייב בדין *adj* guilty as charged.

kha|yav/-yevet be-meeshpat חייב במשפט *adj* convicted by court.

kha|yav/-yevet geeyoos חייב גיוס *adj* subject to conscription.

kha|yav/-yevet meetah חייב מיתה *adj* subject to death-penalty.

kha|yay/-yekha/-yayeekh/-yav/-yehah /חיי/ חייך/חייך/חייו/חייה your *m/f* his/her *etc* life.

(be) khayay (*etc*) **she-** בחיי ש־ *adv* I swear on my life; honestly.

(be) kha|yayeekh בחייך I entreat you! for heaven's sake; (addressing single female).

khaybar חיבר *nm* zoo area in which animals roam freely.

khaydak/-eem חיידק *nm* microbe; germ; (*pl+of:* **-ey**).

khayeel/kheylot חיל *nm* force; army; (*+of:* **kheyl**).

('as|ah/-tah/-eetee) khayeel עשה חיל *v* prospered; did well; (*pres* **'oseh** *etc; fut* **ya'aseh** *etc*).

(bat/benot) khayeel בת־חיל *nf* brave girl; brave woman.

(ben/-ey) khayeel בן־חיל *nm* brave boy; fine fellow.

(eshet/neshot) khayeel אשת־חיל *nf* woman of valor.

(korot) khayeem קורות חיים *nf pl* life-story; biography; curriculum vitae.

khayeem חיים **1.** *nm pl* life; (*+of; khayey*) **2.** *v pres pl* (we/you/they) live.

◇ **"khayeem she-ka-'eleh"** חיים שכאלה *nf* Isr. TV equivalent of "This is Your Life".

('as|ah/-tah/-eetee) khayeem עשה חיים [*slang*] *v* had a good time; (*pres* **'oseh** *etc; fut* **ya'aseh** *etc*).

(ba) khayeem בחיים **1.** *adj* alive; **2.** *adv* in life.
(ba'al/-ey) khayeem בעל־חיים *nm* animal.
(beetoo'akh) khayeem ביטוח חיים *nm* life insurance.
(be'ayat) khayeem va-mavet בעיית חיים ומוות *nf* a matter of life and death.
(kef) khayeem כף חיים *nm [slang]* the good life; thrill of a lifetime.
(khedvat) khayeem חדוות חיים *nf* joy of life.
(le) khayeem! (*cpr* **le-khayeem!**) ! לחיים *interj* (toast) Cheers! To your/our/everyone's health!
(mele/-'at) khayeem מלא חיים *adj* bursting with life.
(meef'al) khayeem מפעל חיים *nm* life work.
(neesyon) khayeem נסיון חיים *nm* life experience.
(netool/-at) khayeem נטול חיים *adj* lifeless.
('oovdalt/-ot) khayeem עובדת חיים *nf* fact of life.
(orakh/orkhot) khayeem אורח חיים *nm* way of life.
(ovdan) khayeem אובדן חיים *nm* loss of life.
(ramalt/-ot) khayeem רמת חיים *nf* living standard.
(roo'akh) khayeem רוח חיים *nm* soul; breath of life.
(sam) khayeem סם חיים *nm* panacea; healing drug; elixir of life.
(seeman/-ey) khayeem סימן חיים *nm* sign of life.
(seemkhat) khayeem שמחת חיים *nf* joy of life.
(shav|ak/-kah/-aktee) khayeem le-khol khay שבק חיים לכל חי *v* passed away; died; (*pres* **shovek** *etc; fut* **yeeshbok** *(b=v) etc*).
◇ **(te'oodat) khayeem** see ◇ **te'oodat khayeem.**
(toldot) khayeem תולדות חיים *nf pl* life-story; biography; curriculum vitae.
khayeets חיץ *nm* barrier.
khayekha חייך your life (addressing single male).
(be) khayekha בחייך I entreat you! for heaven's sake! (addressing single male).
◇ **"'eleh hem khayekha"** אלה הם חייך *lit* : "This is Your Life" to which the equivalent program on Israeli TV is called: ◇ **"Khayeem She-ka-'eleh"** חיים שכאלה.
kha|yelet/-yalot חיילת *nf* woman-soldier.
kha|yelet/-yalot meshookhr|eret/-arot חיילת משוחררת *nf* ex-servicewoman; woman who has completed military service.
khayey חיי *nm pl+of* **1.** the life (lives) of ... **2.** the life-story of ...
khayey meen חיי מין *nm pl* sex-life.
khayey 'olam חיי עולם *nm pl* eternal life.
khayey 'onee חיי עוני *nm pl* life of poverty; conditions of poverty.
khayey revakhah חיי רווחה *nm pl* affluence; life of luxury; comfortable life.
khayey sha'ah חיי שעה *nm pl* fleeting moment.
(be) khayey בחיי (oath) by the life of...
(le) khayey לחיי (toast) to the life of...
□ **Khayfah** חיפה incorrect *cpr* of the name of Haifa. See *npr* □ **Kheyfah.**
khaykhanee/-t חייכני *adj* smiling; ever-smiling.
khayot adam חיות־אדם *nf* human beasts (*sing:* **khayat-adam**).
(gan/-ey) khayot גן־חיות *nm* zoo.
khaz|ah/-tah/-eetee חזה *v* foresaw; envisioned; (*pres* **khozeh**; *fut* **yekhzeh**).
◇ **KHAZAL** חז"ל *acr of* **KHAkhamenoo Zeekhronam Lee-vrakhah!** *(v=b)* i.e. our sages (of the Talmud) of blessed memory .
khazak/-ah חזק *adj* strong; robust.
khazak ve-'emats! ! חזק ואמץ *v imp* be strong and brave! (boy-scout's salute).
khazak|ah/-ot חזקה *nf* **1.** right of claim (based on possession); **2.** presumption; (*+of:* **khezkat**).
khazan/-eem חזן *nm* cantor (in synagogue); (*pl+of:* **-ey**).
khazanoot חזנות *nf* cantorial music; Jewish liturgical music.
khaz|ar/-rah/-artee חזר *v* **1.** returned; **2.** repeated; (*pres* **khozer**; *fut* **yakhzor**).
khazar (*etc*) **'al** חזר על *v* repeated; reiterated.
khazar (*etc*) **bee-teshoovah** חזר בתשובה *v* **1.** re-embraced religion; turned observant; **2.** repented.
khazar (*etc*) **bo/bah** חזר בו *v* recanted; reconsidered.
khazar/-ah ve-neeshn|ah/-etah חזר ונשנה *v* recurred; happened all over again.
khazarah חזרה *adv* back; backward.
khazar|ah/-ot חזרה *nf* **1.** return; **2.** repetition; **3.** rehearsal; (*+of:* **-at**).
(ba) khazarah בחזרה *adv* back; backward.
◇ **khazarat ha-shats** חזרת הש"ץ *nf* repeat reading of a prayer by the Cantor (alone) after the congregation reading
khaz|ay/-a'eet חזאי *nmf* weather forecaster; (*pl+of:* **-a'ey**).
khazeer/-eem חזיר *nm* **1.** pig; **2.** *interj* swine!; (*pl+of:* **-ey**).
khazeer/-ey yam חזיר־ים *nm* guinea-pig.
(besar) khazeer בשר חזיר *nm* pork.
(kotley) khazeer קותלי־חזיר *nm pl* bacon.
khazeer|ah/-ot חזירה *nf* **1.** sow; she-pig; **2.** *[colloq.] interj* dirty pig (addressing or referring to a female).
(deer/-ey) khazeereem דיר חזירים *nm* pigsty.
khazeeroo|t/-yot חזירות *nf* filthy trick; swinishness.
khazeet/-ot חזית *nf* **1.** front; facade; **2.** frontline; battlefront.
khazee|yah/-yot חזייה *nf* brassiere; bra; (*+of:* **-yat**).
khazeez/-eem חזיז *nm* petard; flash; (*pl+of:* **-ey**).
khazeret חזרת *nf* **1.** horseradish; **2.** mumps; parotitis (medic).

khazon/-ot חזון *nm* vision.
khazon neefrats חזון נפרץ *nm* usual (habitual) phenomenon.
('od) khazon la-mo'ed עוד חזון למועד time will tell; there is still a long time to wait.
□ **Khazon (Hazon)** חזון *nm* village (est. 1969) in Lower Galilee, E. of Acre-Safed **('Ako-Tsefat)** road. Pop. 469.
khazoot חזות *nf* vision; prospect.
khazoot kashah חזות קשה *nf* grim prospect.
khazootee/-t חזותי *adj* visual; optical.
(bee) khdee בכדי *adv* in vain.
(lo bee) khdee לא בכדי *adv* not without good reason.
(bee) khdey she- בכדי ש־ in order that.
kheder/khad|areem חדר room; **(+of: -ar/-rey).**
◇ **"kheder"** ("Kheyder") חדר *nm* onetime traditional primary school of a single classroom with a single "Rebeh" teaching religion all day long.
(ba) kheder בחדר *adv* in (the/his/her/etc) room.
khedv|ah/-ot חדווה *nf* joy; gaiety; **(+of: -at).**
khedvat yetseerah חדוות יצירה *nf* joy of creation.
(be) khee tov בכי טוב *adv* successfully; in the best possible manner.
(ha) khee הכי *adj* **1.** the very... **2.** the most.
(ha) khee? הכי? *query* is it? is it because?
(ha) khee ha-khee הכי הכי *[colloq.] adj* the very very.
(lo) khee לא כי it isn't that..., but.
(ve) khee וכי *query* has not there?
kheeb|ah/-ot חיבה *nf* affection; fondness; **(+of: -at).**
◇ **"kheebat tseeyon"** ("Hibat Zion") חיבת ציון (*lit.:* "Fondness for Zion") the 19th Century philanthropic movement among Jews of Eastern and Central Europe that was a precursor of Zionism and inaugurated the Jewish colonization of Palestine.
□ **Kheebat Tseeyon** (Hibbat Ziyyon) חיבת ציון *nm* village (est. 1933) 5 km S. of **Tsomet Khaderah** (Hadera Junction). Pop. 331.
kheeb|el/-lah/-altee חיבל *v* sabotaged; damaged; **(***pres* **mekhabel;** *fut* **yekhabel).**
kheeb|ek/-kah/-aktee חיבק *v* embraced; hugged; **(***pres* **mekhabek;** *fut* **yekhabek).**
kheeb|er/-rah/-artee חיבר *v* **1.** connected; joined; **2.** composed; authored; **(***pres* **mekhaber;** *fut* **yekhaber).**
kheeb|ev/-evah/-avtee חיבב *v* liked; **(***pres* **mekhabev;** *fut* **yekhabev).**
kheebook/-eem חיבוק *nm* embrace; embracing; hugging; **(***pl+of:* **-ey).**
(be) kheebook yadayeem בחיבוק ידיים *adv* with folded hands; not doing a thing.
kheeboor/-eem חיבור *nm* **1.** connection; joint; **2.** adding; addition; 2. composition; opus; **(+***of:* **-ey).**
(vav ha) kheeboor וו החיבור *nm* the letter *Vav* (ו) which, when prefixing a word, reads **ve-, va-, vee-** or **'oo** - but always means *and.*
kheed|ah/-ot חידה *nf* riddle; puzzle; **(+***of:* **-at).**
kheed|ed/-edah/-adetee חידד *v* sharpened; **(***pres* **mekhaded;** *fut* **yekhaded).**
kheed|esh/-shah/-ashtee חידש *v* renewed; renovated; **(***pres* **mekhadesh;** *fut* **yekhadesh).**
kheedon/-eem חידון *nm* quiz; **(***pl+of:* **-ey).**
kheedood/-eem חידוד **1.** spike; **2.** edge; **(***pl+of:* **-ey).**
kheeger/-et חיגר *adj* lame.
kheek|ah/-tah/-eetee חיכה *v* waited; **(***pres* **mekhakeh;** *fut* **yekhakeh).**
kheek|ah/-tah/-eetee חיקה *v* imitated; mimicked; **(***pres* **mekhakeh;** *fut* **yekhakeh).**
kheekook/-eem חיקוק **1.** enactment; **2.** carving **(***pl+of:* **-ey).**
kheekookh/-eem חיכוך *nm* friction; **(***pl+of:* **-ey).**
kheekoo|y/-yeem חיקוי *nm* imitation; mimicry; **(***pl+of:* **-yey).**
kheelazon/khelzonot חילזון *nm* snail.
kheel|ek/-kah/-aktee חילק *v* **1.** divided; **2.** distributed **(***pres* **mekhalek;** *fut* **yekhalek).**
kheel|el/-elah/-altee חילל *v* defiled; desecrated; **(***pres* **mekhalel;** *fut* **yekhalel).**
kheel|ets/-tsah/-atstee חילץ *v* rescued; **(***pres* **mekhalets;** *fut* **yekhalets).**
kheelkh|el/-elah/-altee חלחל *v* seeped; permeated; **(***pres* **mekhalkhel;** *fut* **yekhalkhel).**
kheelonee/-t חילוני *adj* secular.
kheeloof/-eem חילוף *nm* exchange; **(***pl+of:* **-ey).**
kheeloof khomareem חילוף חומרים *nm* metabolism.
(khelkey) kheeloof חלקי חילוף *nm pl* spare-parts; **(***sing:* **khelek-kheeloof).**
kheeloofee/-t חילופי *adj* commutative.
kheeloofeen חילופין *nm pl* exchange.
(zerem) kheeloofeen זרם חילופין *nm* alternating (electric) current.
kheeloofey gavree (*cpr* **gavra)** חילופי גברי *nm pl* reshuffle; personnel changes.
kheeloofey meeshm|eret/-arot חילופי משמרות *nm pl* changing of the guard.
kheelook חילוק *nm* division (arithm).
kheelookey de'ot חילוקי דעות *nm pl* differences of opinion.
kheelool shabat חילול שבת *nm* desecration of the Sabbath.
kheeloots/-eem חילוץ *nm* rescue; salvaging; **(***pl+of:* **-ey).**
(be) kheelyon 'eynayeem *(kh=k)* בכליון עיניים *adv* impatiently.
kheema'ee/-t (*npr* **keema|y/-'eet)** כימאי *nmf* chemist.
kheemee/-t (*npr* **keemee/-t)** כימי *adj* chemical.
kheem|em/-emah/-amtee חימם *v* warmed; heated; **(***pres* **mekhamem;** *fut* **yekhamem).**
kheem|esh/-shah/-ashtee חימש *v* armed; equipped; **(***pres* **mekhamesh;** *fut* **yakhamesh).**
kheemoom/-eem חימום *nm* heating; **(***pl+of:* **-ey).**

kheemoom deeratee חימום דירתי *nm* apartment-heating (each apartment to itself).

kheemoom merkazee חימום מרכזי *nm* central heating.

kheemoosh חימוש *nm* armament; arming.

kheemtsoon/-eem חמצון *nm* oxidation; (*pl+of:* **-ey**).

kheenam חינם *adv* free of charge.

(be) kheenam בחינם *adv* **1.** for no reason; **2.** free of charge.

(le) kheenam לחינם *adv* in vain.

(seen'at) kheenam שנאת חינם *nf* hatred for no reason; unjustified hatred.

kheenanee/-t חינני *adj* comely; graceful.

kheen|ekh/-khah/-akhtee חינך *v* brought up; educated; (*pres* **mekhanekh;** *fut* **yekhanekh).**

kheengah (*npr* kheengah)/-ot חינגה *nf* feast; merrymaking.

kheenookh חינוך *nm* education.

◇ **(ha)kheenookh (he)afor** החינוך האפור *nm* "grey" education *[colloq.]* - nickname given to efforts by parents in more affluent areas to supplement free compulsory public education by paying additional teachers to teach extra-curricular programs.

◇ **kheenookh khovah** חינוך חובה *nm* free ten years of school education, state-financed, compulsory in Israel for all 5-16 year olds.

◇ **kheenookh me'ooleh** חינוך מעולה *nm* excellent education.

kheenookh me'orav חינוך מעורב *nm* mixed (boys and girls together) education; coeducation.

kheenookh meyookhad חינוך מיוחד *nm* special education; (term usually used for handicapped pupils).

(kesh|eh/-at) kheenookh קשה חינוך *adj* suffering from learning disabilities.

(meesrad ha) kheenookhve-ha-tarboot משרד החינוך והתרבות *nm* Ministry of Education & Culture.

kheenookhee/-t חינוכי *adj* educational.

kheentresh/-eshah/-ashtee חינטרש *v [slang]* did something makeshift, not thoroughly; (*pres* **mekhantresh;** *fut* **yekhantresh).**

kheep|ah/-tah/-eetee חיפה *v* covered-up; (*pres* **mekhapeh;** *fut* **yekhapeh).**

kheepazon חיפזון *nm* haste; (*+of:* **khefzon).**

kheep|es/-sah/-astee חיפש *v* looked for; searched; (*pres* **mekhapes;** *fut* **yekhapes).**

kheepoos/-eem חיפוש *nm* search; (*pl+of:* **-ey).**

(tsav/-ey) kheepoos צו־חיפוש *nm* search-warrant.

kheepooshee|t/-yot חיפושית *nf* beetle; bug.

"(ha)kheepoosheeyot" החיפושיות *nf pl* "The Beatles".

kheepoo|y/-yeem חיפוי *nm* covering; covering-up; (*pl+of:* **-yey).**

◇ **Kheer** חי״ר *nm* infantry (*acr of* **kheyl ragleem** חיל רגלים).

kheerb|en/-enah/-antee חירבן *v [slang]* **1.** defecated; **2.** caused to fail; spoiled; (*pres* **mekharben;** *fut* **yekharben).**

◇ **kheereek** חיריק *nm* (abc) sublinear diacritic sign Hirik ((ִ) indicating (in dotted script) that letter over it is pronounced **ee**). So a letter is often (especially in undotted script) followed by י **(yod).**

kheerkhoor/-eem חרחור *nm* **1.** provocation; incitement; **2.** gurgle; gargle; (*pl+of:* **-ey).**

kheerkhoor/-ey meelkhamah חרחור מלחמה *nm* warmongering.

kheesakhon/kheskhonot חיסכון *nm* saving; thrift; (*+of:* **kheskhon).**

kheesaron/khesronot חיסרון *nm* **1.** lack; want of; **2.** defect; (*+of:* **khesron).**

khees|ayon/-yonot חיסיון *nm* immunity from prosecution; (*+of:* **-yon).**

khees|el/-lah/-altee חיסל *v* **1.** liquidated; **2.** *[slang]* killed (*pres* **mekhasel;** *fut* **yekhasel).**

kheesel (*etc*) חיסל *v [slang]* **1.** overcame; **2.** devoured (food).

khees|en/-nah/-antee חיסן *v* **1.** innoculated; immunized; **2.** strengthened; (*pres* **mekhasen;** *fut* **yekhasen).**

khees|er/-rah/-artee חיסר *v* deducted; subtracted; (*pres* **mekhaser;** *fut* **yekhaser).**

kheesh חיש *adv* fast; quickly.

kheesh maher חיש מהר *adv* in a jiffy.

kheeshb|en/-enah/-antee חשבן *v [colloq.]* reckoned; summed up; (*pres* **mekhashben;** *fut* **yekhashben).**

kheesh|el/-lah/-altee חישל *v* forged; moulded; (*pres* **mekhashel;** *fut* **yekhashel).**

kheesh|ev/-vah/-avtee חישב *v* calculated; estimated; (*pres* **mekhashev;** *fut* **yekhashev).**

kheeshm|el/-elah/-altee חשמל *v* **1.** electrified; (also *figurat.*); **2.** electrocuted; (*pres* **mekhashmel;** *fut* **yekhashmel).**

kheeshmool/-eem חשמול *nm* electrification; (*pl+of:* **-ey).**

kheeshool/-eem חישול *nm* forging; (*pl+of:* **-ey).**

kheeshoov/-eem חישוב *nm* reckoning; calculation; consideration; (*pl+of:* **-ey).**

(mekhon|at/-ot) kheeshoov מכונת חישוב *nf* calculating machine.

(sargel/-ey) kheeshoov סרגל חישוב *nm* slide-rule.

kheesool/-eem חיסול *nm* liquidation; (*pl+of:* **-ey).**

kheesoon/-eem חיסון *nm* **1.** immunization; inoculation; **2.** *[colloq.]* vaccination; (*pl+of:* **-ey).**

kheesoor/-eem חיסור *nm* subtraction (arithm); deduction; (*pl+of:* **-ey).**

kheesoo|y/-eem חיסוי *nm* shelter; protection; (*pl+of:* **-yey).**

kheespoos/-eem חספוס *nm* roughness; coarseness; (*pl+of:* **-ey).**

kheet|ah/-eem חיטה *nf* wheat; (*+of:* **-at).**

kheet|e/-'ah/-etee חיטא *v* cleansed; disinfected; (*pres* **mekhate;** *fut* **yekhate).**

kheet|el/-lah/-altee חיתל *v* diapered; swaddled; (*pres* **mekhatel**; *fut* **yekhatel**).

kheet|en/-nah/-antee חיתן *v* 1. married off; 2. married (performed ceremony); (*pres* **mekhaten**; *fut* **yekhaten**).

kheet|et/-etah/-atetee חיטט *v* scratched; pecked; nosed; (*pres* **mekhatet**; *fut* **yekhatet**).

kheetookh/-eem חיתוך *nm* cut; cutting; (*pl+of:* **-ey**).

kheetookh/-ey deeboor חיתוך דיבור *nm* diction; articulation.

kheetool/-eem חיתול *nm* diaper; (*pl+of:* **-ey**).

kheetool/-eem khad-pe'amee (*npr* **khad-pa'amee**)**/-yeem** חיתול חד־פעמי *nm* disposable diaper.

kheetoon/-eem חיתון *nm* marrying; marriage; (*pl+of:* **-ey**).

kheetoot/-eem חיטוט *nm* pecking; searching; (*pl+of:* **-ey**).

kheetoo|y/-yeem חיטוי *nm* disinfection; (*pl+of:* **-yey**).

kheetson/-ah חיצון *adj* outer; exterior.

(he) khalal (ha)kheetson החלל החיצון *nm* outer space.

kheetsonee/-t חיצוני *adj* exterior; external.

kheetsoneeyoot חיצוניות *nf* outward appearance.

kheev|ah/-tah/-eetee de|'ah/-'ot חיווה דעה *v* expressed opinion; (*pres* **mekhaveh** *etc*; *fut* **yekhaveh** *etc*).

kheevaron חיוורון *nm* pallor; (*+of:* **kheevron**).

kheever/-et חיוור *adj* pale.

khee|yeg/-ygah/-yagtee חייג *v* dialed; (*pres* **mekhayeg**; *fut* **yekhayeg**).

khee|yekh/-ykhah/-yakhtee חייך *v* smiled; (*pres* **mekhayekh**; *fut* **yekhayekh**).

khee|yev/-yvah/-yavtee חייב *v* 1. obligate; oblige; 2. approved of; (*pres* **mekhayev**; *fut* **yekhayev**).

kheeyev (*etc*) **kheshbon/-ot** חייב חשבון *v* charged (one's account).

kheeyoog/-eem חיוג *nm* dialing; (*pl+of:* **-ey**).

kheeyoog yasheer חיוג ישיר *nm* direct dialing.

(tsleel) kheeyoog צליל חיוג *nm* dialing tone.

kheeyookh/-eem חיוך *nm* smile; (*pl+of:* **-ey**).

kheeyookh me'ooseh חיוך מעושה *nm* feigned smile.

(ten/-ee) kheeyookh תן חיוך! *v imp sing m/f* give me a smile.

kheeyool/eem חיול *nm* recruitment; enlistment; (*pl+of:* **-ey**).

kheeyoonee/-t חיוני *adj* vital.

(tsorekh/tsrakheem) kheeyoonee/-yeem צורך חיוני *nm* vital necessity.

kheeyooneeyoot חיוניות *nf* vitality.

kheeyoov/-eem חיוב .1 *nm* 1. obligation; 2. approval; affirmation; (*pl+of:* **-ey**).

(be) kheeyoov בחיוב *adv* positively; affirmatively.

kheeyoovee! חיובי! *prep [slang]* (Army) yes!

kheeyoovee/-t חיובי *adj* positive; affirmative.

kheezayon/khezyonot חיזיון *nm* spectacle; (*+of:* **khezyon**).

kheez|ek/-kah/-aktee חיזק *v* strengthened; reinforced; (*pres* **mekhazek**; *fut* **yekhazek**).

kheez|er/-rah/-artee חיזר *v* courted; wooed; (*pres* **mekhazer**; *fut* **yekhazer**).

kheezook/-eem חיזוק *nm* 1. reinforcement; 2. corroboration (juridic.); (*pl+of:* **-ey**).

(sakhkan/-ey) kheezook שחקן חיזוק *nm* back-up player (Sport).

kheezoor/-eem חיזור *nm* courting; wooing; (*pl+of:* **-ey**).

kheezoo|y/-yeem חיזוי *nm* forecast; (*pl+of:* **-yey**).

kheezooy mezeg ha-aveer חיזוי מזג האוויר *nm* weather forecast.

(bee) khefeefah akhat בכפיפה אחת *adv* together; side by side with.

(bee) khefeefoot le- בכפיפות ל־ *adv* subject to.

khefets/khafats|eem חפץ *nm* 1. object; 2. desire; (*pl+of:* **-ey**).

(be) khefets lev בחפץ לב *adv* willingly.

(klee en) khefets bo (*or:* **klee eyn** *etc*) כלי אין חפץ בו *nm* useless; unwanted (thing or person).

(ke) kheftso|o/-ah כחפצו *adj* as he/she would have wished it.

□ **Kheftseebah** (Hefziba) חפציבה *nm* kibbutz (est. 1922) in Yizre'el Valley, at the foot of Mount Gilbo'a (**Geelbo'a**). Pop. 479.

(mekhoz) kheftso|o/-ah מחוז חפצו *nm* his/her *etc* destination/goal/aim.

khek חיק *nm* 1. bosom; lap; 2. the inside.

(be) khek בחיק in the bosom; in the midst of.

(be) khek ha-meeshpakhah בחיק המשפחה *adv* in the bosom of the family.

(be) khek ha-teva' בחיק הטבע *adv* in the bosom of nature; in the country.

kheker חקר *nm* survey; research.

kheker meevtsa'eem חקר מבצעים *nm* operations research.

khekh/kheek|eem (*k=kh*) חיך *nm* palate; (*pl+of:* **-ey**).

khel|'ah/-'ot חלאה *nf* filth; scum; (*+of:* **-'at**).

khel'at adam חלאת אדם *nf* the scum of humanity.

khel aveer חיל אוויר *nm* air force.

khel handasah חיל הנדסה *nm* engineering corps.

khel ha-yam חיל הים *nm* navy.

khel kesher חיל קשר *nm* signal corps.

khel kheemoosh חיל חימוש *nm* ordnance corps.

khelbon/-eem חלבון *nm* protein; albumen; (*pl+of:* **-ey**).

kheled חלד *nm* world.

(yemey) khel|ed/-dee/-dekha/-ekh/-do/-dah ימי חלד *nm pl* lifetime; my/your(*m/f*)/his/her lifetime.

(booshah oo) kheleemah (*kh=k*) בושה וכלימה *interj* what a shame!

khelek/khalakeem חלק *nm* part; (*pl+of:* **khelkey**).

khelek ha-aree חלק הארי *nm* lion's share.

khelek ke-khelek חלק כחלק *adv* fifty-fifty; in equal parts.

□ **Khelets** (Helez) חלץ *nm* village (est. 1950) in **Lakheesh** district, 8 km S. of Giv'ati road junction **(Tsomet Geev'atee)**. Pop. 361.

khelkah/khalakot חלקה *nf* lot; parcel; (*+of:* **khelk|at/-ot**).

khelkee/-t חלקי *adj* partial; part-time.

khelkeek/-eem חלקיק *nm* particle; (*pl+of:* **-ey**).

khelkeet חלקית *adv* partially.

('avod|ah/-ot) khelkee|t/-yot עבודה חלקית *nf* part- time work.

(meesr|ah/-ot) khelkee|t/-yot משרה חלקית *nf* part-time job.

(same'akh/smekhah be) khelk|o/-ah שמח בחלקו *adj* content with his/her lot.

khelkey חלקי *nm pl+of* parts of; (see **khelek/ khalakeem**).

khelkey kheeloof חלקי חילוף *nm pl* spare-parts.

khelev/khalaveem חלב *nm* tallow; animal fat; (*pl+of:* **khelvey**).

◇ **khelm (Chelm)** חלם *nf* mythical "city of fools" (in pre-Holocaust Poland) that served as traditional scene for funny stories about stupid people; (also pronounced **Khelem**).

khelma'ee/-t חלמאי *[colloq.]* **1.** *adj* foolish; **2.** *nmf* fool; stupid idiot.

khel matsav חיל מצב *nm* garrison.

khel meeloo'eem חיל מילואים army reserve.

khelmeet חלמית *nf* common mallow.

khel parasheem חיל פרשים *nm* cavalry.

khel ragleem חיל רגלים *nm* infantry.

khel sheeryon חיל שריון *nm* armored corps.

khel totkhaneem חיל תותחנים *nm* artillery.

khel modee'een חיל מודיעין *nm* intelligence corps.

khel meeshlo'akh חיל משלוח *nm* expeditionary force.

khelmon/-eem חלמון *nm* yolk; (*pl+of:* **-ey**).

khemd|ah/ot חמדה *nf* precious thing; delight.

khemed חמד *nm* charm; beauty.

(tsemed-) khemed צמד־חמד *nm* lovely couple (also used ironically).

□ **Khemed** (Hemed) חמד *nm* village (est. 1950) in the Coastal Plain, W. of **Reeshon le-Tseeyon**. Pop. 403.

kheml|ah/-ot חמלה *nf* pity; (*+of:* **-at**).

khen חן *nm* charm; grace.

◇ **KHEN** ח"ן *nm acr of* **Khel Nasheem** חיל נשים i.e. Women's Army Corps.

khen-khen חן־חן *interj* Thank you! (old-fashioned expression).

(af 'al pee) khen אף על פי כן nevertheless.

(akhrey) khen אחרי כן *adv* afterwards.

(even/avney) khen אבן־חן *nf* precious stone.

(ya'al|at/-ot) khen יעלת חן *nf* pretty woman.

(kemo) khen כמו כן *conj* also; *(kh=k).*

(la) khen לכן *conj* therefore; *(kh=k).*

(leefney) khen לפני כן *adv* before that; *(kh=k).*

(mats|a/-'ah/-atee) khen מצא חן *v* pleased; (*pres* **motse' khen;** *fut* **yeemtsa khen**).

(nas|a/-'ah/-atee) khen נשא חן *v* pleased; (*pres* **nose khen;** *fut* **yeesa khen**).

(oo-ve) khen ובכן *adv* consequently; then; *(kh=k).*

(ve) khen וכן *conj* as well as; and also; *(kh=k).*

(ve) khen hal'ah וכן הלאה and so on; *(kh=k).*

khenek חנק *nm* suffocation; asphyxiation.

(be) khenoot בכנות *adv* frankly; honestly; *(kh=k).*

khenvan|ee/-eem חנווני *nm* shopkeeper; (*pl+of:* **-ey**).

(lee) khe-orah לכאורה *adv* seemingly; prima facie; on the face of things.

kherbon/-ot חרבון *[slang] nm* fiasco; disaster; failure.

kheref חרף notwithstanding.

kher|ef/-fah/-aftee חרף *v* reviled; (*pres* **mekharef;** *fut* **yekharef**).

kherek/kharak|eem חרק *nm* insect; (*pl+of:* **-ey**).

kherem/kharamot חרם *nm* **1.** ban; boycott; **2.** excommunication.

(heet|eel/-eelah/-altee) kherem הטיל חרם *v* imposed a boycott; (*pres* **mateel** *etc; fut* **yateel** *etc*).

kheres/kharas|eem חרס *nm* clay; shard; (*pl+of:* **-ey**).

(klee/kley) kheres כלי־חרס *nm* pottery.

□ **Kheres** (Heres) חרס *nm* small settlement (est. 1978), 13 km SW of Nablus **(Shekhem)**.

kheresh חרש *adv* silently; secretly.

(shot|er/-rey) kheresh שוטר חרש *nm* plain-clothes detective; policeman in plain clothes.

kherev/khar|avot חרב sword; (*pl+of:* **-vot**).

□ **Kherev Le-'et** (Herev Le'et) חרב לאת *nm* village (est. 1947) in Sharon, E. of **Tsomet ha-Sharon-Khaderah** road, 4 km S. of Hadera **(Khaderah)**. Pop. 421.

kherev peefeeyot חרב פיפיות *nf* double-edged sword.

khermesh/-eem חרמש *nm* sickle; (*pl+of:* **-ey**).

(be) kheroof nefesh בחירוף־נפש *adv* risking one's life; exposing oneself to danger.

kheroom חירום *nm* emergency.

(emtsa|'ee/-'ey) kheroom אמצעי חירום *nm* emergency measure.

(khok/khookey) kheroom חוק חירום *nm* emergency law.

(matsav/-ey) kheroom מצב חירום *nm* state of emergency.

(she|'at/-'ot) kheroom שעת חירום *nf* emergency; hour of emergency.

◇ **(takanot lee-she'at) kheroom** see ◇ **takanot lee-she'at kheroom**.

kheroo|t/-yot חירות *nf* freedom; liberty.

◇ **"kheroot"** "Herut" חרות (political party) *nf* see ◇ **tenoo'at ha-kheroot**.

◇ **(khag ha) kheroot** see ◇ **khag ha-kheroot**.

◇ **(tenoo'at ha) kheroot** (or **"kheroot"**) תנועת החירות — "the Herut" right of center political party that came into being with the State of Israel. In 1965 it became the mainspring of the "Leekood" block and came to power in 1977. Originates from the underground military organization "Irgun Zva'ee Le'umi" (I.Z.L., see ◇ **Etsel**) which, in turn, grew out of Jabotinsky's Revisionist Movement in Zionism.

□ **Kheroot** (Herut) חירות *nm* village (est. 1930) 5 km N. of Kefar Sava. Pop. 435.

kherp|ah חרפה *nf* shame; (*+of:* **-ot**).

khershoot חרשות *nf* deafness.

khesed/khasadeem חסד *nm* charity; favor; (*pl+of:* **khasdey**).

khesed shel 'emet חסד של אמת *nm* paying one's last respect to deceased by attending his/her funerals.

(gemeeloot) khesed גמילות חסד *nf* short-term loan (granted as favor, without interest).

(ma'as|eh/-ey) khesed מעשה חסד *nm* act of charity.

(tsedakah va) khesed צדקה וחסד *nf & nm* charity and kindness.

kheshbon חשבון *nm* arithmetic.

kheshbon/-ot חשבון *nm* **1.** account; bank account; **2.** invoice; bill.

kheshbon/-ot 'aloo|t/-yot חשבון עלות *nm* cost-account.

◇ **kheshbon/-ot KHASHAK** חשבון חש״ק *nm acr.* for checking account: **KHeshbon SHeKeem** חשבון שיקים (banking).

kheshbon/-ot matbe'a khoots חשבון מטבע חוץ *nm* foreign currency account.

kheshbon/-ot matbe'a zar חשבון מטבע זר *nm* foreign currency account.

kheshbon nefesh חשבון נפש *nm* soul-searching.

kheshbon/-ot osh חשבון עו״ש *nm* **OSH** (*acr of* Over va-SHav עובר ושב) current account.

kheshbon/-ot 'over va-shav חשבון עובר ושב *nm* current acount.

◇ **kheshbon/-ot PATAKH** חשבון פת״ח *nm* (*acr of* **Peekdon Toshav Khoots** פקדון תושב חוץ) foreign currency account opened (in an Israeli bank) by foreign resident and therefore free to be used at will.

◇ **kheshbon/-ot PATAM** חשבון פת״ם *nm* (*acr of* **Peekdon Toshav Mekomee** פקדון תושב מקומי) foreign currency account opened by local resident and of restricted use.

kheshbon shekeem חשבון שיקים *nm* checking account.

('ad le) kheshbon עד לחשבון *adv* advance on account.

('al ha) kheshbon על החשבון *adv* on account.

(ba/-'ah/-tee be) kheshbon בא בחשבון *v* is/am *etc* can be taken into consideration; (*pres* **ba** *etc; fut* **yavo** *(v=b) etc*).

(deen/-eem ve) kheshbon/-ot דין וחשבון *nm* report; statement; account.

(hev|ee/-ee'ah/-e'tee be) kheshbon הביא בחשבון *v* took into account; took into consideration; (*pres* **mevee** *etc; fut* **yavee** *etc*).

(khee|yev/-yvah/-yavtee) kheshbon/-ot חייב חשבון *v* charged (one's) account; (*pres* **mekhayev** *etc; fut* **yekhayev** *etc*).

(lo ba be) kheshbon לא בא בחשבון *v* is out of the question.

('as|ah/-tah/-eetee) kheshbon עשה חשבון *v* tried to figure out; (*pres* **'oseh** *etc; fut* **ya'aseh** *etc*).

(pat|akh/-khah/-akhtee) kheshbon פתח חשבון *v* opened an account (*pres* **pote'akh** *etc; fut* **yeeftakh** *(f=p) etc*).

(ro|'eh/-'ey) kheshbon/-ot רואה חשבון *nm* auditor; chartered accountant.

(sag|ar/-rah/-artee) kheshbon/-ot סגר חשבון *v* closed an account; (*pres* **soger** *etc; fut* **yeesgor** *etc*).

kheshbona'oot חשבונאות *nf* accounting.

kheshbona|y/-'eet חשבונאי *nmf* accountant; (*pl+of:* **-'ey**).

kheshbona|y/-'eet moosm|akh/-ekhet חשבונאי מוסמך *nmf* certified public accountant (C.P.A.).

kheshbonee|t/-yot חשבונית *nf* invoice (serving mainly for VAT taxation purposes).

(menahel/-et) kheshbonot מנהל חשבונות *nmf* accountant.

(kheesool) kheshbonot חיסול חשבונות *nm* settling accounts (mainly used figuratively with reference to feuds in the underworld).

kheshed/khashad|ot חשד *nm* suspicion; (*pl+of:* **-dey**).

(me'orer/-et) kheshed/khashadot מעורר חשד *adj v pres* arousing suspicion; (*pst* **'orer** *etc; fut* **ye'orer** *etc*).

kheshek חשק *nm* desire; gusto; urge.

(en lee/lekha/lakh/lo/lah *etc***) kheshek** אין לי/לך/לו/לה וכו׳ חשק I/you *m/f* he/she *etc* do not feel like; (*pst* **lo hayah lee/lekha** *etc* **kheshek;** *fut* **lo yeehyeh lee/lekha** *etc* **kheshek**).

(blee) kheshek (*or:* **le-lo** *etc*) בלי/ללא חשק *adv* with no desire; unwillingly.

(yesh lee/lekha/lakh/lo/lah *etc***) kheshek** יש/לי/לך לו/לה וכו׳ חשק *[colloq.] v pres* I/you (*m/f*)/he/she *etc* feel like; (*pst* **hayah lee/lekha** *etc* **kheshek;** *fut* **yeehyeh lee/lekha** *etc* **kheshek**).

◇ **kheshvan (also called markheshvan)** חשוון *nm* 2nd month of the Jewish calendar; 29 or 30 days; approx. October-November.

◇ **khet** חי״ת (abc) *nf* 8th letter of Hebrew alphabet: guttural consonant ח pronounced **kh** (like *ch* in Scottish word *loch* or in the Jewish name *Chaim*).

khet ח׳ Hebrew numerical *symbol* for 8 or 8th.

khet/khata|'eem חטא *nm* sin; (*pl+of:* **-'ey**).

(yeer'at) khet יראת חטא *nf* piety; sin-fearing.

(bee) khetav *(kh=k)* בכתב *adv* in writing.

◇ **(torah she-bee) khetav** see ◇ **torah she-beekhtav**.

(haskalah bee-) khetav השכלה בכתב *nf* teaching by correspondence.

(kee) khetav|o/-ah ve-khee-leshon|o/-ah *(kh=k)* ככתבו וכלשונו *adj lit.* word for word.

khets/kheets|eem חץ *nm* arrow; (*pl+of:* **-ey**).

(rosh) khets ראש חץ *nm* arrowhead.

khetsee/khatsa'eem חצי *nm* half; (*pl+of:* **khats|ee/-a'ey**).

(va) khetsee וחצי and a half.

(bee) khevedoot בכבידות *adv* heavily; with difficulty.

khevel/khav|aleem חבל *nm* **1.** rope; **2.** region; district; (*pl+of:* **-ey**).

□ **khevel ha-har** חבל ההר *nm* the hilly parts of Israel.

(mesheekhat) khevel משיכת חבל *nf* tug of war.

khever חבר *nm* band; staff; league.

□ **Khever** (Hever) חבר *nm* rural center in the **Ta'anakh** area, Yeezre'el Valley.

◇ **khever ha-le'oomeem** חבר הלאומים *nm* the (onetime) League of Nations.

khever ne'emaneem חבר נאמנים *nm* board of trustees.

khever 'ovdeem חבר עובדים *nm* personnel; staff.

khever 'ozreem חבר עוזרים *nm* a staff of assistants; auxiliary staff.

khever yo'atseem חבר יועצים *nm* advisory staff; a group of advisers.

khevley leydah חבלי לידה *nm pl* birth-pangs.

khevley masheee'akh חבלי משיח *nm pl* pre-Messianic tribulations.

(lee) khevod לכבוד **1.** formula of address; to Mr/Mrs/miss; **2.** in the honor of.

(bee) khevod|o/-ah 'oo-ve-'atsm|o/-'ah בכבודו ובעצמו *adj* in person; him/her -self.

khevrah/khavarot חברה *nf* society; company; (*+of:* **khevr|at/-ot**).

(ha) khevrah החברה *nf* society.

khevrah (*etc*) **be-'am** חברה בע״מ *nf* limited company; corporation; Ltd; Inc.

(ha) khevrah (ha)gevohah החברה הגבוהה *nf* high society.

◇ **khevrah kadeesha** חברה קדישא *nf* **1.** burial society; "Hevrah Kaddisha"; **2.** *(lit.)* sacred society.

(mada'ey ha) khevrahהחברה מדעי *nm pl* social sciences.

(mankal/-ey) khevrah/khavarot מנכ״ל חברה *nm* general-manager; director-general (of a corporation).

(mena|hel/-haley) khevrah מנהל חברה *nm* company director/manager.

(nesee) khevrah נשיא חברה *nm* company president; chairman of company's board of directors.

khevrat חברת *f+of* the company of.

khevr|at/-ot bat חברת־בת *nf* subsidiary company.

khevr|at/-ot em (*or:* **ha-em**) חברת־אם ; חברת האם *nf* holding company.

(be) khevrat בחברת *adv* in the company of; accompanied by.

khevratee/-t חברתי *adj* social.

◇ **khevrat ha-khashmal** חברת החשמל *nf* the Israel Electric Corp. Ltd, a public company holding the concession on generating and supplying electric power throughout Israel. Had originally been established (1923) as the Palestine Electric Comp. Ltd., a commercial corporation holding a concession from the British Government for almost the whole of Palestine. With the emergence of the State of Israel, the corporation was renamed and its concession was renewed by the government who acquired most of its shares.

◇ **khevrat ha-'ovdeem** חברת העובדים *nf* the Workers Corporation — legal entity that is made up of and represents (at least in principle) entire membership of Histadrut. Theoretically, owns or controls everything belonging to Histadrut, i.e. a great portion of Israeli economy.

khevrayah (*cpr* **khevrayah**) חברייא *nf* group of friends/pals; "gang".

khevreh חברה *nm pl [colloq.]* group of friends/pals; "gang".

khevreman/-eem חברה'מן *[slang] nm* one of the "gang".

□ **Khevron (Hevron)** חברון *nf* historic town 36 km SW of Jerusalem in Mount Hebron area. Known internationally as Hebron and to Muslims as **"El-Khaleel"**, is first mentioned in the Bible as site where Abraham established family tomb (see □ **Me'arat ha-Makhpelah**) and later as King David's capital, before Jerusalem. Its traditional Jewish Quarter, from which Jews had been barred 1936-1967 is now being re-populated but larger part of its present Jewish population concentrates in autonomous settlement NE of the city (see □ **Keeryat Arba'**). Pop. 117,500.

khevrootee (*npr* **khavrootee**)**/-t** חברותי *adj* sociable.

□ **Kheyfah (Hefa, Haifa)** חיפה *nf* Israel's largest Mediterranean seaport, known internationally as Haifa; industrial, trade and cultural center of country's NW. Founded some 2,500 years ago at the foot of picturesque Mount Carmel **(Karmel)**, Haifa is today country's 3rd city in size, having spread to mountain's slopes (see □ **Hadar Ha-Karmel**) and top **(Har ha-Karmel)**. Pop. 245,900 comprises 22,300 Arabs, mostly Christian. Greater Haifa incorporates also 4 twin-towns on the coast ot Haifa's E. and N. (see □ **Ha-Krayot**) and one to its S. (see □ **Teerat ha-Karmel**).

kheyk חיק *nm* **1.** bosom; lap; **2.** the inside.

(be) kheyk בחיק in the bosom; in the midst of.

(be)kheyk ha-meeshpakhah בחיק המשפחה *adv* in the bosom of the family.

(be) kheyk ha-teva' בחיק הטבע *adv* in the bosom of nature; in the country.

kheyl aveer חיל אוויר *nm* air force.

kheyl handasah חיל הנדסה *nm* engineering corps.
kheyl ha-yam חיל הים *nm* navy.
kheyl kesher חיל קשר *nm* signal corps.
kheyl kheemoosh חיל חימוש *nm* ordnance corps.
kheyl matsav חיל מצב *nm* garrison.
kheyl meeloo'eem חיל מילואים *nm* army reserve.
kheyl parasheem חיל פרשים *nm* cavalry.
kheyl ragleem חיל רגלים *nm* infantry.
kheyl sheeryon חיל שריון *nm* armored corps.
kheyl totkhaneem חיל תותחנים *nm* artillery.
kheyl modee'een חיל מודיעין *nm* intelligence corps.
kheyl meeshlo'akh חיל משלוח *nm* expeditionary force.
(bee) khfeefah akhat בכפיפה אחת *adv* together; side by side with.
(bee) khfeefoot le- בכפיפות ל־ *adv* subject to.
('ad ve-'ad bee) khlal עד ועד בכלל *adv* inclusive; including.
(booshah oo) khleemah בושה וכלימה *interj* what a shame!
(be) khezkat בחזקת *adv* **1.** deemed to; tantamount to; **2.** (mathemat.) to the exponent of.
(bee) khlal בכלל *adv* generally.
(bee) khlal zeh/eleh בכלל זה *adv sing./pl.* which include(s).
(mee) khlal מכלל *adv* hence; from the fact of.
khlor כלור *nm* chlorine.
khloroform כלורופורם *nm* chloroform.
(be) kho'akh בכוח *adv* **1.** by force; **2.** potentially; (kh=*k*).
khod/khood|eem חוד *nm* point; sharp edge; (*pl+of:* **-ey**).
khoder/-et חודר *adj pres* penetrating; (*pst* **khadar;** *fut* **yakhdor**).
khod|esh/-asheem חודש *nm* month; (*pl+of:* **-shey**).
◇ **khodesh shlosh-'esreh** חודש שלוש־עשרה *nm* **1.** 13th (additional fictitious) month's salary; **2.** annual bonus.
(ba) khodesh ha-ba בחודש הבא *adv* next month.
(be-'od) khodesh בעוד חודש *adv* in a month's time.
(ka-'avor) khodesh כעבור חודש *adv* a month later; after one month.
(rosh) khodesh ראש חודש *nm* 1st day of a Jewish calendar month.
(tokh) khodesh תוך חודש *adv* within a month.
khodshayeem חודשיים *nm pl* two months.
(be-'od) khodshayeem בעוד חודשיים *adv* in two months.
(sakhar) khodshee שכר חודשי *nm* monthly salary.
khodsheet חודשית *adv* by the month.
khof/-eem חוף *nm* shore; coast; (*pl+of:* **-ey**).
khof/-ey ha-yam חוף הים *nm* seashore.
khof meevtakheem חוף מבטחים *nm* haven of refuge.
□ **(retsoo'at ha) khof** רצועת החוף *nf* (the) coastal strip.
□ **Khofeet** (Hofit) חופית *nm* village in the Sharon, on the coast, near **Kefar Veetkeen**, 6 km N. of Netanya. Pop. 886.
khofef/-et חופף **1.** *adj* overlapping; **2.** *v pres* overlaps; (*pst* **khafaf;** *fut* **yakhfof**).
khof|en/-nayeem חופן *nm* handful; (*pl+of:* **-ney**).
khof|esh/-asheem חופש *nm* **1.** freedom; liberty; **2.** *[colloq.]* vacation.
khofesh ha-deeboor חופש הדיבור *nm* freedom of speech.
khofesh ha-'eetonoot חופש העיתונות *nm* freedom of the press.
khofesh pe'oolah חופש פעולה *nm* freedom to act; freedom of action; a free hand.
(ha) khofesh (ha)gadol החופש הגדול *nm* summer (school) vacation (In Israel, normally, from end June to September 1).
khofsh|ee/-t חופשי *adj* free; at liberty to.
(matbe'a) khofshee מטבע חופשי *nm* free currency.
(meektso|'a/-'ot) khofshee/-yeem מקצוע חופשי *nm* liberal profession.
(shook) khofshee שוק חופשי *nm* free market.
(sakhar) khofshee סחר חופשי *nm* free trade.
◇ **(haskarah) khofsheet** see ◇ **haskarah khofsheet**.
(yozmah) khofsheet יוזמה חופשית *nf* free enterprise.
khofzah חופזה *nf* haste; hurry; (*+of:* **-at**).
(be) khofzah בחופזה *adv* in a hurry; hastily.
khogeg/-et חוגג **1.** *adj* celebrating; feasting; **2.** *v pres* celebrates; feasts (*pst* **khagag;** *fut* **yakhgog**).
khoger/-et חוגר *v pres* girdle(s); (*pst* **khagar;** *fut* **yakhgor**).
khog|er/-reem חוגר *nm* conscript; one liable for obligatory military service; draftee.
(peenk|as/-esey) khoger פנקס חוגר *nm* soldier's logbook.
khogl|ah/-ot חוגלה *nf* partridge; rock partridge; (*+of:* **-at**).
□ **Khoglah** (Hogla) חוגלה *nm* village (est. 1933) in the Sharon, 10 km NE of Netanya. Pop. 224.
khok/khook|eem חוק *nm* law; (*pl+of:* **-ey**).
◇ **khok haganat ha-dayar** חוק הגנת הדייר *nm* the Rent Restriction Law that, with all jurisprudence accummulated in over 50 years, is cause and basis of the entire housing regime prevailing in Israel. Originated in 1940 as a British wartime measure, it subsists to this day (mainly with regard to pre-1948 housing) making renting tenancy unprofitable to builders. It created a whole class of rent-protected tenants who cannot be ejected as long as they go on paying a token rent based on the 1940-1948 level and a class of landlords expecting nothing from their constantly decaying properties except an

eventual share in "key-money" once in a while (see ◇ **deerah bee-dmey mafte'akh**).

◇ **khok ha-shvoot** חוק השבות *nm* the Law of Return enacted at the beginning of Statehood, granting the right of repatriation and automatic Israeli citizenship to any Jewish immigrant to Israel.

◇ **khok la-haganat ha-sakhar** חוק להגנת השכר *nm* Wage Protection Law.

◇ **khok ha-heetyashnoot** חוק ההתישנות *nm* statute of limitations.

◇ **khok 'otomanee** חוק עותומני *nm* Ottoman Law, i.e. legal provisions dating from the years before 1918, when Palestine was part of the Ottoman Empire.

(hats|'at/-'ot) khok הצעת חוק *nm* bill (legislation).

(ka) khok כחוק *adv* as lawfully required; according to the law.

(medeen|at/-ot) khok מדינת חוק *nf* a state based on law.

khok|en/-aneem חוקן *nm* **1.** clyster; enema; **2.** *[slang]* proper punishment; due retribution.

khoker/-et חוקר **1.** *nmf* investigator; researcher; **2.** *v pres* investigate(s); research(es) (*pst* **khakar**; *fut* **yakhkor**).

khoker/-et mada'ee/-t חוקר מדעי *nmf* scientist; scientific researcher.

khoker/-et meeshtartee/-t חוקר משטרתי *nmf* police investigator.

khokh|eem חוחים *nm pl* thorns; (*sing:* **kho'akh**; *pl+of:* **-ey**).

khokher/-et חוכר **1.** *nmf* renter; lessee; longtime lease-holder; **2.** *v pres* leases; lease-holds; (*pst* **khakhar**; *fut* **yakhkhor**).

khokhm|ah/-ot חוכמה *nf* **1.** wisdom **2.** *[slang]* wisecrack; (*+of:* **-at**).

khol/-ot חול *nm* sand.

-khol חול־ *adj* **1.** of sand; **2.** profane; ordinary; secular.

◇ **khol ha-mo'ed** חול המועד *nm* the "intermediate" working-days during Passover and Succoth holidays (referred to in Yiddish as "Holemoyd").

(yemot ha) khol ימות החול *nm pl* working days; workdays; ordinary days.

(yom/yemey) khol ימי חול *nm* workday; ordinary day.

(mee-kodesh le) khol מקודש לחול from holy to secular; from sacred to profane.

(be) khol *(kh=k)* בכל in every; in each; at all.

(be) khol *(kh=k)* **'et** בכל עת - *adv* at all times.

(be) khol heezdamnoot *(kh=k)* בכל הזדמנות *adv* on every occasion.

(be) khol meekreh *(kh=k)* בכל מקרה *adv* in any case.

(be) khol ofen *(kh=k)* בכל אופן *adv* at any rate; anyway.

(be) khol zot *(kh=k)* בכל זאת *adv* nevertheless.

(le) khol ha-rookhot *(kh=k)* לכל הרוחות *interj* to hell! the hell with...!

(le) khol ha-shedeem! *(kh=k)* ! לכל השדים *interj* to the devil!

(le-meetah) kholah למיטה חולה *adv* **1.** (*lit.*) to a sick bed; **2.** *[slang]* into an unfortunate affair.

◇ **kholam** חולם *nm* the vowel-sign for **o** in the Hebrew script. In the dotted (vocalized) script it may take the form of a Vav with a dot (וֹ) over it (called **"Kholam male"** i.e. "a full **kholam**"); or that of a dot over the left shoulder of the consonant it follows (אֹ). In everyday undotted script it is just a Vav (ו). As such, however, it may as well signify a **shoorook** (וּ) and be read **oo** or sometimes, a Vav, and thus read **v**.

kholanee/-t חולני *adj* morbid; sickly.

kholaneeyoot חולניות *nf* morbidity.

khol|eh/-ah חולה **1.** *adj* ill; sick; **2.** *v pres* is ill; is sick; (*pst* **khalah**; *fut* **yekhleh**); **3.** *nmf* patient.

khol|eh/-eem חולה *nm* patient (Medic.).

khol|eh/-ah anoosh/-ah חולה אנוש *nmf* critically ill.

khol|eh/-at nefesh חולה נפש *nmf* mentally ill; (*pl:* **-ey/-ot** *etc*).

khol|eh/-at roo'akh חולה רוח *nmf* psychopath; (*pl:* **-ey/-ot** *etc*).

(le-meetah) kholah למיטה חולה *adv [slang]* into an unfortunate affair.

(beekoor/-ey) kholeem ביקור חולים *nm* visiting the sick.

(bet/batey) kholeem בית חולים *nm* hospital.

(koop|at/-ot) kholeem קופת־חולים *nf* health (*lit.:* sick) fund; health-insurance organization.

◇ **(koopat) kholeem** see ◇ **koopat kholeem ha-klaleet**.

◇ **(koopat) kholeem le'oomeet** see ◇ **koopat kholeem le'oomeet**.

◇ **(koopat) kholeem "makabee"** see ◇ **koopat kholeem "makabee"**.

◇ **(koopat) kholeem me'ookhedet** see ◇ **koopat kholeem me'ookhedet**.

kholeera' (*cpr* **kholera**) חולירע *nm* cholera (Medic).

□ **Kholeet** (Holit) חולית *nm* kibbutz (est. 1975) off the Gaza-**Rafee'akh** road.

kholef/-et חולף **1.** *adj* passing; fleeting; temporary; **2.** *v pres* pass(es); (*pst* **khalaf**; *fut* **yakhlof**).

khol|el/-elah/-altee חולל *v* caused; performed; (*pres* **mekholel**; *fut* **yekholel**).

kholem/-et חולם *v pres* dream(s); dreaming; (*pst* **khalam**; *fut* **yakhlom**).

kholesh/-et 'al חולש על *v pres* command(s); control(s); (*pst* **khalash**; *fut* **yakhlosh**).

kholets/-et חולץ *v pres* pull(s); take(s) off; (*pst* **khalats**; *fut* **yakhlots**).

khol|ets/-tsey pekakeem חולץ פקקים *nm* corkscrew.

kholev/-et חולב *adj v pres* milking; milk(s); (*pst* **khalav**; *fut* **yakhlov**).

(par|ah/-ot) khol|evet/-vot חולבת פרה *nf* milch cow (also used figurat.).

kholmanee/-t חולמני *adj* dreamy.

□ **Kholon** *or* **Khoolon** (Holon) חולון *nf* town originally (1933) established as a S. suburb of Tel-Aviv, has grown to be an independent town. Pop. 156,700.

kholot חולות *nm pl* sands; (*sing:* **khol**).

khom חום *nm* **1.** heat; **2.** temperature; **3.** fever.

khom gavo'ah חום גבוה *nm* high fever.

(meedot ha) khoom מידות החום *nf pl* degrees of temperature (*sing:* **meedat** *etc*).

(yesh lee/lekhah/lakh/lo/lah) khom יש לי/לך/לו/לה וכו׳ חום *v* I/you/*(m/f)*/he/she *etc* is/are running a temperature; has/have fever; (*pst* **hayah lee** *etc* **khom;** *fut* **yeehyeh lee** *etc* **khom**).

khom|ah/-ot חומה *nf* outside wall; city-wall; (*+of:* **-at**).

khomed (or **khomed shel**) חומד or חומד של *[colloq.] nm* a darling of a...

khomed/-et חומד *v pres* covet(s); lust(s) for; (*pst* **khamad;** *fut* **yakhmod**).

khomek/-et חומק *v pres* slip(s) away; (*pst* **khamak;** *fut* **yakhmok**).

khomer golmee חומר גולמי *nm* raw (unprocessed) material.

khomer ha-deen חומר הדין *adv* the fullest extent of the law.

khom|er/-oreem חומר *nm* material; stuff; substance; (*pl+of:* **-rey**).

kho|mer/-rey gelem חומר גלם *nm* raw material.

khom|er/-rey nefets חומר נפץ *nm* **1.** explosive; explosive material; **2.** explosive (used *figurat.*).

(kal va) khomer קל וחומר inferring from minor premise to major conclusion.

khomesh חומש *nm* **1.** period of five years; quinquennium; **2.** groin.

(tokhnee|t/-yot) khomesh תוכנית חומש *nf* quinquennial plan; five-year plan.

khomets חומץ *nm* vinegar.

khomets ben yayeen חומץ בן יין *nm* **1.** *lit* : vinegar originating from wine; **2.** (*figurat.*) unworthy son of a worthy father.

(khoomtsat) khomets חומצת חומץ *nf* acetic acid.

khomrah חומרה *nf* hardware (computers).

khomranoot חומרנות *nf* materialism; being materialistic.

khomree/-t חומרי *adj* economical; material.

khomreeyoot חומריות *nf* materialism.

khon|eh/-ah חונה **1.** *adj* parking; camping; **2.** *v pres* park(s); camp(s); (*pst* **khanah;** *fut* **yekhneh**).

khonek/-et חונק *v pres* strangle(s); (*pst* **khanak;** *fut* **yakhnok**).

khonekh/-et חונך *nmf* coach; trainer.

khonekh/-et חונך *v pres* **1.** inaugurate(s); **2.** tutor(s); (*pst* **khanakh;** *fut* **yakhnokh**).

(meeshpakh|ah/-ot) khon|ekhet/-khot משפחת חונכת *nf* foster family.

khon|en/-et חונן *v pres* **1.** favor(s); pity (-ies); **2.** grant(s) amnesty; **3.** bestow(s) talent (*pst* **khanan;** *fut* **yakhon**).

(be) khonenoot *(kh=k)* בכוננות *adv* stand-by.

khoob|ar/-rah/-artee חובר *v* **1.** was connected; was joined to; **2.** was authored; (*pres* **mekhoobar;** *fut* **yekhoobar**).

khood חוד *nm* point; sharp edge (*pl+of:* **-ey**).

(le) khood לחוד *adv* separately.

khoofsh|ah/-ot חופשה *nf* leave; vacation; (*+of:* **-at**).

koofshah le-lo 'tashloom חופשה ללא תשלום *nf* unpaid leave.

khoofshah shnateet חופשה שנתית *nf* annual leave.

(be) khoofshah בחופשה *adv* on leave.

khoofshat kayeets חופשת קיץ *nf* summer vacation.

khoofsh|at khag חופשת חג *nf* holiday-vacation.

khoofsh|at leemoodeem חופשת לימודים *nf* leave of study.

khoofsh|at makhalah חופשת מחלה *nf* sick-leave.

khoog/-eem חוג *nm* circle; (*pl+of:* **-ey**).

khoog leemoodeem חוג לימודים *nm* department (in a faculty, university or school).

(rosh) khoog ראש חוג *nm* department-head (in a university or school).

khoog|ah/-ot חוגה *nf* dial; telepone-dial; (*+of:* **-at**).

khook|ah/-ot חוקה *nf* constitution; (*+of:* **-at**).

khookee/-t חוקי *adj* legal.

□ **Khookok** חוקוק *nm* (Huqoq) kibbutz (est. 1945) in Lower Gallilee, 12 km NW of Tiberias (**Tveryah**). Pop. 315.

khool חו״ל (*acr of* **khoots la-'arets** חוץ לארץ) **1.** *adv* outside the country; **2.** *nm* abroad.

(be) khool בחו״ל *adv* abroad.

(le) khool לחו״ל *adv* (for, to) abroad.

(roob|o/-ah ke) khool|o/-ah רובו ככולו in his (its)/her major part; (kh=*k*).

□ **Khoolatah** (Hulata) חולתה *nm* kibbutz (est. 1946) in the Huleh (**Khoolah**) Valley. Pop. 537.

khoold|ah/-ot חולדה *nf* rat; (*+of:* **-at**).

□ **Khooldah** (Hulda) חולדה *nm* kibbutz of the **"Kevootsah"** type (est. 1907), 5 km NW of **Tsomet Nakhshon** (Nahshon Junction) in the Coastal Plain. Pop. 354.

khooleen חולין something profane or secular.

(seekh|at/-ot) khooleen שיחת חולין *nf* chat; table-talk; small-talk.

khoolsh|ah/-ot חולשה *nf* weakness; (*+of:* **-at**).

khoolsh|at ha-da'at חולשת הדעת *nf* uncertainty; moral weakness.

khoolts|ah/-ot חולצה *nf* shirt; (*+of:* **-at**).

khool|yah/-yot חוליה *nf* **1.** *lit* : link (in a chain); **2.** (fig) group; unit; (*+of:* **-yat**).

khoolyah be-sharsheret חוליה בשרשרת *nf* a link in a chain.

khool|yat/-yot beekoret (*or:* **bakarah**) חוליית ביקורת *nf* control link.

khool|yat/-yot mekhableem חולית מחבלים *nf* terrorist gang; (in Israel: referring to Arab terrorists).
(ba'aley) khoolyot בעלי חוליות *nm pl* vertebrates.
◇ **khoomash/-eem** חומש *nm* Pentateuch; one of five Pentateuch volumes; (*pl+of:* **-ey**).
khoomoos חומוס *nm* Near Eastern paste-like chick-pea dish.
khoomr|ah/-ot חומרה *nf* rigor; severity.
khoomrat ha-'aver|ah/-ot חומרת העברה *nf* the gravity of the offence.
khoomr|at ha-matsav/-eem חומרת המצב *nf* the gravity of the situation.
khoomtsah/-ot חומצה *nf* acid; (*+of:* **-at**).
khoomtsah gofreeteet חומצה גופריתית *nf* sulphuric acid.
khoomtsah khankaneet חומצה חנקנית *nf* nitric acid.
khoomtsah zarkhateet חומצה זרחתית *nf* phosphoric acid.
(netool/-at) khoomtsah נטול חומצה *adj* acid-free.
khoomtsat bor חומצת בור *nf* boric acid.
khoomtsat ha-dam חומצת הדם *nf* acidemia (Medic.).
khoomtsat khalav חומצת חלב *nf* lactic acid.
khoomtsat khomets חומצת חומץ *nf* acetic acid.
khoomtsat leemon חומצת לימון *nf* citric acid.
khoomtsat melakh חומצת מלח *nf* salicylic acid.
khoomtsat nemaleem חומצת נמלים *nf* formic acid.
khoomtsat sheten חומצת שתן *nf* uric acid.
khoop|ah/-ot חופה *nf* **1.** Jewish wedding ceremony; **2.** wedding-canopy; (*+of:* **-at**).
◇ **khoopah ve-keedoosheen** חופה וקידושין *nf & pl nm* wedding ceremony in accordance with Jewish law.
(neekhn|as/-esah/-astee le) khoopah נכנס לחופה *v* was wed; got married; (*pres* **neekhnas** *etc; fut* **yeekanes** *(k=kh) etc*).
khoop|eem (*npr* **khof|eem**) חוף *nm* shore; coast; (*pl+of:* **-ey**).
khoorb|ah/-ot חורבה *nf* ruin; (*+of:* **-at/khorvot**).
□ **Khoorfesh** (Hurfeish) חורפיש *nm* Druse village in Upper Galilee, 5 km W. of kibbutz Sasa. Pop. 3,580.
khoorsh|ah/-ot חורשה *nf* thicket; copse; small forest; (*+of:* **-at**).
□ **Khoorshat Tal** (Hurshat Tal) חורשת טל *nf* thicket of ancient oak trees 3 km E. of **Keeryat Shmonah**, near kibbutz **Ha-Goshreem**, near the Dan stream. At present, it is a nature reserve and vacationing spot.
khoosh/-eem חוש *nf* instinct; sense; (*pl+of:* **-ey**).
khoosh heetmats'oot חוש התמצאות *nm* sense of orientation.
khoosh hoomor חוש הומור *nm* sense of humor.
◇ **khoosham** חושם *nm* nickname for a fool or moron.
khooshanee/-t חושני *adj* voluptuous; sensual.
khooshaneeyoot חושניות *nf* sensuality; sensualism.
(kehoot) khoosheem קיהות חושים *nf* numbness; indolence; insensitivity.
khoot/-eem חוט *nm* **1.** thread; **2.** cord; **3.** sinew; (*pl+of:* **-ey**).
khoot/-ey barzel חוט ברזל *nm* wire.
khoot/-ey khashmal חוט חשמל *nm* electric cord; electric wire.
khoot ha-sheedrah חוט השידרה *nm* spinal cord.
khoot ma'areekh חוט מאריך *nm* extension cord.
(ke) khoot ha-sa'arah כחוט השערה *adv* by a hairbreadth.
khoot (ha) shanee חוט השני *nm* characteristic.
khoots חוץ *adv* outside; out of doors; except.
-khoots ־חוץ *adj (suffix)* **1.** foreign; **2.** outer.
khoots la-arets חוץ לארץ *nm* abroad.
khoots le- חוץ ל־ *adv* except; outside of.
khoots mee- חוץ מ־ *adv* except; apart from.
(ba) khoots בחוץ *adv* outside.
(matbe'a) khoots מטבע חוץ *nm* foreign exchange; foreign currency.
(medeeneeyoot) khoots מדיניות חוץ *nm* foreign policy.
(mee) khoots la-tekhoom מחוץ לתחום *adv* out of bounds.
(mee) khoots le- מחוץ ל־ *adv* except; from outside the.
(mee-ba) khoots מבחוץ *adv* from outside.
(meesrad ha) khoots משרד החוץ *nm* **1.** (outside U.S.:) Ministry of Foreign Affairs; Foreign Ministry; Foreign offfice; **2.** (in the U. S.) State Department.
(sar/-at ha) khoots שר החוץ *nmf* **1.** the Foreign Minister; the Minister for Foreign Affairs (outside the U.S.); **2.** The Secretary of State (in the U.S.).
(sekhar) khoots סחר חוץ *nm* foreign trade.
(totseret) khoots תוצרת חוץ *nf* imported goods; foreign produce.
ha-khootsah! !החוצה *interj* out! out you go! out with you!
khootsp|ah/-ot חוצפה *nf* insolence; effrontery; chutzpah; (*+of:* **-at**).
khor/-eem חור *nm* hole; (*pl+of:* **-ey**).
khor/-ey ha-man'ool/-eem חורי המנעול *nm* keyhole.
(mee-ba'ad le) khor ha-groosh מבעד לחור הגרוש **1.** *(lit.)* through the hole in the coin; **2.** looking solely at the financial side of it.
(ben/bat) khoreen בן־חורין **1.** *adj* free to desist; **2.** mp free man/woman.
khor|ef/-feem חורף *nm* winter.
khor|eg/-et חורג *adj* **1.** stepfather, stepmother *etc*; **2.** aberrant.
(akh/-eem) khor|eg/-geem אח חורג *nm* step-brother.
(av/-ot) khor|eg/-geem אב חורג *nm* stepfather.

(ben/baneem) khor|eg/-geem בן חורג *nm* stepson.

(akh|ot/-ayot) khor|eget/-got אחות חורגת *nf* stepsister.

(bat/banot) khor|eget/-got בת חורגת *nf* stepdaughter.

(em/eemahot) khor|eget/-got אם חורגת *nf* stepmother.

khorep/-et חורף *[slang]* (army) *v pres* sleep(s); snore(s); (*pst* **kharap;** *fut* **yakhrop**).

khoresh/-et חורש *v pres* plough(s); (*pst* **kharash;** *fut* **yakhrosh**).

khoresh/-et (*etc*) **mezeemot** חורש מזימות *v pres* plot(s) against; devise(s) evil.

□ **Khorsheem** (Horeshim) חורשים *nm* kibbutz (est. 1955) in the Sharon, 5 km SE of Kefar Sava. Pop. 223.

khorpee/-t חורפי *adj* wintry; hybernal.

khos|eh/-ah חוסה *nmf* **1.** protegé; **2.** inmate (of an institution); (*pl+of:* **-ey**).

khos|eh/-ah חוסה *v pres* take(s) refuge; find(s) shelter; (*pst* **khasah;** *fut* **yekheseh**).

khos|ekh/-ekhet חוסך **1.** *nmf* saver; economizer; (*pl+of:* **-khey**); **2.** *v pres* save(s); (*pst* **khasakh** *fut* **yakhsokh**).

khosem/-et חוסם *v pres* block(s); (*pst* **khasam;** *fut* **yakhsom**).

khos|em/-mey 'orkeem חוסם עורקים *nm* tourniquet.

khoser חוסר *nm* lack.

khoser 'avodah חוסר עבודה *nm* unemployment.

khoser bagroot חוסר בגרות *nm* immaturity.

khoser dam חוסר דם *nm* anemia.

khoser neemoos חוסר נימוס *nm* impoliteness; disrespect.

khoser emtsa'eem חוסר אמצעים *nm* lack of means.

khoser te'oom חוסר תיאום *nm* lack of coordination.

khoshekh חושך *nm* darkness.

khoshekh ve-tsalmavet חושך וצלמוות *nm pl* darkness and shadow of death.

(me-'ever le-harey) khoshekh מעבר להרי החושך *adv* at the end of the world.

khoshesh/-et חושש *nm pres* fear(s); (*pst* **khashash;** *fut* **yakhshosh**).

khosheshanee (*npr* **khoshashnee**) חוששני I'm afraid that...

khotam/-ot חותם *nm* seal; imprint.

(heetbl|ee'a/-ee'ah/-a'tee) khotam/-o/-ah הטביע/־ה חותמו/־ה left an/his/her imprint.

khote/-t חוטא **1.** *nmf* sinner; **2.** *adj* sinful.

khote/-t חוטא *v pres* sin(s); (*pres* **khata;** *fut* **yekhta**).

khotekh/-et חותך **1.** *adj* decisive; **2.** *nm* secant; **3.** *v pres* cut(s); (*pst* **khatakh;;** *fut* **yakhtokh**).

(hokhakh|ah/-ot) khot|ekhet/-khot הוכחה חותכת *nf* decisive proof.

(re'ay|ah/-yot) khot|ekhet/-khot ראיה חותכת *nf* conclusive evidence.

khotem/khatameem חוטם *nm* nose; (*pl+of:* **khotmey**).

khot|em/-meem חותם *nm* subscriber; signatory; (*pl+of:* **-mey**).

khot|em/-et חותם *v pres* sign(s) signing; (*pres* **khatam;** *fut* **yakhtom**).

khot|emet/-amot חותמת *nf* rubber-stamp.

khot|emet do'ar חותמת דואר *nf* postmark.

khot|emet goomee חותמת גומי *nf* rubber-stamp.

khot|en/-neem חותן *nm* husband's father-in-law; (*pl+of:* **-ney**).

khot|enet/-not חותנת *nf* husband's mother-in-law.

khotev/-et חוטב *v pres* cut(s) wood; (*pst* **khatav;** *fut* **yakhtov**).

khot|ev/-vey 'etseem חוטב עצים *nm* woodcutter.

khot|seh/-ah חוצה **1.** *adj* parting; crossing; **2.** *v pres* cross(es) part(s); (*pst* **khatsah;** *fut* **yekhtseh**).

□ **Khotseh Shomron** חוצה שומרון *nm* the new Trans-Samaria highway, from the so-called Green Line to the Jordan Valley.

◇ **khotvey 'etseem ve-sho'avey mayeem** חוטבי עצים ושואבי מים *nm pl* **1.** *figurat* hewers of wood and drawers of water (Joshua 9, 23); **2.** people good only for low-class manual labor.

khov/-ot חוב *nm* **1.** debt; **2.** duty.

(ba'al/-ey) khov בעל חוב *nm* debtor.

(shetar/sheetrey) khov שטר חוב *nm* promissory note.

khov|ah/-ot חובה *nf* **1.** duty; **2.** obligation; (*+of:* **-at**).

khovah חובה *adj (suffix)* obligatory; compulsory.

◇ **(gan) khovah** גן־חובה *nm* municipal kindergarten obligatory for 5 year-olds.

◇ **(gan/-ey trom) khovah** see ◇ **gan/-ey trom-khovah.**

◇ **(kheenookh) khovah** see ◇ **kheenookh khovah.**

◇ **(meel|e/-'ah/-etee) khovah** מילא חובה *v* did one's duty; (*pres* **memale** *etc;* *fut* **yemale** *etc*).

(meelveh) khovah מלווה חובה *nm* obligatory government loan.

◇ **(sheroot) khovah** see ◇ **sheroot khovah.**

(yats|a/-'ah/-atee yedey) khovah יצא ידי חובה *v* did one's duty (*pres* **yotse** *etc;* *fut* **yetse** *etc*).

khovat kavod חובת כבוד *nm* duty of honor.

khov|el/-leem חובל *nm* seaman; sailor; (*pl+of:* **-ley**).

khovel reeshon חובל ראשון *nm* first mate.

(ra|v/-bey) khov|el/-leem רב־חובל *nm* skipper; captain.

khov|eret/-rot חוברת *nf* brochure; pamphlet; booklet.

khovesh/-et חובש *nmf* medic; paramedic.

khovesh/-et חובש *v pres* **1.** bandage(s); dress(es) (a wound); **2.** put(s) on (hat); (*pst* **khavash;** *fut* **yakhbosh;** *(b=v)*).

khovev/-eem חובב *nm* amateur; (*pl+of:* **-ey**).

khovevanoot חובבנות *nf* amateurism.

(shakoo'a'/shkoo'ah be) khovot שקוע בחובות *adj* deeply in debt.

(shemeetat) khovot שמיטת חובות *nf* remission of debts; moratorium.

khoz|eh/-ah חוזה *v pres* foresee(s); visualize(s); (*pst* **khazah**; *fut* **yekhzeh**).

khoz|eh/-ah ba-kokhaveem חוזה בכוכבים *nmf* astrologer; star-gazer.

khoz|eh/-eem חוזה **1.** *nm* contract; pact; (*pl+of:* **-ey**); **2.** *nm* visionary; seer; prophet; (*pl+of:* **-ey**).

khoz|eh/-eem le-sekheeroot beeltee moogenet חוזה לשכירות בלתי מוגנת *nm* contract of uncontrolled lease.

khoz|eh/-ey sekheeroot חוזה שכירות *nm* lease contract.

◇ **khozeh ha-medeenah** חוזה המדינה *nm* the visionary who foresaw and dreamt up the establishment of the Jewish State — Dr. Theodor Herzl (1860-1904).

khozek חוזק *nm* strength.

khoz|er/-rem חוזר *nm* **1.** circular letter; **2.** returnee; repatriate; (*pl+of:* **-rey**).

khozer/-et חוזר *adj* returning; recurrent.

khozer/-et bee-teshoovah חוזר בתשובה *nmf* penitent; one who suddenly becomes very observant.

(ezoon/-eem) khoz|er/-reem היזון חוזר *nm* feedback.

(hon) khozer הון חוזר *nm* circulating capital.

(peezmon/-eem) khoz|er/-reem פזמון חוזר *nm* refrain; chorus.

◇ **(toshav/-eem) khoz|er/-reem** see ◇ **toshav/-eem khoz|er/-reem.**

(ve) khozer khaleelah וחוזר חלילה and so on; and so forth.

(be) khozkah בחוזקה *adv* violently; vehemently.

khroneek|ah/-ot כרוניקה *nf* local news; parochial news; (*+of:* **-at**).

khronee/-t כרוני *adj* chronic.

(bee) khtav *(kh=k)* בכתב *adv* in writing; (*see:* **ktav**).

(haskalah bee) khtav השכלה בכתב *nf* teaching by correspondence.

◇ **(torah she-bee) khtav** see ◇ **torah she-bee-khtav.**

(kee) khtav|o/-ah ve-khee-leshon|o/-ah *(kh=k)* ככתבו וכלשונו *adj* verbatim; word for word.

(bee) khvedoot בכבדות *adv* heavily; with difficulty.

(lee) khvod לכבוד **1.** formula of addressing; to Mr/Mrs/miss; **2.** in the honor of.

(bee) khvod|o/-ah oo-ve-'atsm|o/-'ah בכבודו ובעצמו *adj* in person; him/her -self.

L.

transliterating Hebrew letter ל (**Lamed**).

la- -ל *(prefix)* **1.** to (somewhere); **2.** to (do something); **3.** to the...

lah לה her; to her.

la'ad לעד *adv* forever.

la'ag לעג *nm* mockery; jeering.

la'ag la-rash לעג לרש *nm* mocking the poor.

la'ag/-ah/-tee לעג *v* mocked; jeered; (*pres* **lo'eg**; *fut* **yeel'ag**).

la'aganee/-t לעגני *adj* mocking; scournful.

la-akhronah לאחרונה *adv* of late; lately.

la-al לאל to naught.

(sam/-ah/-tee) le-al שם לאל *v* set at naught; (*pres* **sam** *etc*; *fut* **yaseem** *etc*).

la-ameeto shel davar לאמיתו של דבר to tell the truth.

(emet) la-ameetah אמת לאמיתה *nf* the naked truth.

la'as/-ah/-tee לעס *v* chewed; (*pres* **lo'es**; *fut* **yeel'as**).

la'asot לעשות *v inf* to do; to make; (*pst* **'asah** *pres* **'oseh**; *fut* **ya'aseh**).

(beek|esh/-shah/-ashtee) la'asot ביקש לעשות *v* tried to do; (*pres* **mevakesh** *(v=b) etc*; *fut* **yevakesh** *etc*).

la-avadon לאבדון *interj* to Hell!

la-'avod לעבוד *v inf* to work; (*pres* **'avad** *pres* **'oved**; *fut* **ya'avod**).

la-'avod (*etc*) **'al** לעבוד על *[slang] v inf* to put an air on; to mislead someone into...

la'avod (*etc*) **mefootsal** לעבוד מפוצל *[colloq.] v inf* to work with a 1-3 hour break for lunch.

la'az לעז *nm* **1.** slander; **2.** foreign (non-Hebrew) language(s).

(hots|ee/-ee'ah/-e'tee) la'az הוציא לעז *v* spoke ill of... (*pres* **motsee'** *etc*; *fut* **yotsee'**).

la-'aza'zel! !לעזאזל *interj* to Hell with; to the devil with...

(lekh/-ee) la-'aza'zel! לך לעזאזל! *interj* go to Hell! (addressing *sing m/f*).

laborant/-eet לבורנט *nmf* lab technician; laboratory assistant.

laborator|yah/-yot לבורטוריה *nf* lab; laboratory; **(+*of:* -yat)**.

◇ **ladeeno (Ladino)** לדינו *nf* Jewish-Spanish dialect the lingua franca of Sephardi Jews (equivalent to Yiddish for Ashkenazi Jews).

la-'eenyan לעניין *adv* to the point.

(bakhoor/-eem) la-'eenyan בחור לעניין *[colloq.] nm* a young man worth dealing with.

(gev|er/-areem) la-'eenyan גבר לעניין *[colloq.] nm* the right kind of fellow.

(ha-shevakh) la-el! השבח לאל! *interj* God be praised!

(todah) la-el! תודה לאל! *interj* Thank God!

◇ **lag-ba-'omer** ל״ג בעומר *nm* children's outing festival in spring, about four weeks after Passover (known in Yiddish as "Lagboymer").

laga'at לגעת *v inf* to touch; **(*pst* naga'; *pres* noge'a; *fut* yeega')**.

lag|am/-mah/-amtee לגם *v* sipped **(*pres* logem; *fut* yeelgom)**.

lageshet לגשת *v inf* to approach; to come near; **(*pst & pres* neegash; *fut* yeegash)**.

lagleganee/-t לגלגני *adj* sneering; derisive.

la-goolgolet לגולגולת *adj* per capita; per head.

la-govah לגובה *adv* upwards.

lahadam להד״ם (*acr of* **lo hayoo dvareem me-'olam** לא היו דברים מעולם) nothing of the kind; it never happened.

lahag להג *nm* prattle; chatter; nonsense talk; **(*pl+of:* -ey)**.

lahak/lehakeem להק *nm* air-squadron; **(*pl+of:* lahakey)**.

lahakah/lehakot להקה *nf* troupe; theatrical company; ensemble; **(+*of:* lahakat)**.

lahak|at/-ot yeetsoog להקת ייצוג *nf* representative troupe.

la-halakhah להלכה *adv* in theory; theoretically.

lahat להט *nm* heat; blaze; fervor.

(be) lahat בלהט *adv* with fervor.

lahat/-ah/-etee להט *v* burned; glowed; **(*pres* lohet; *fut* yeelhat)**.

lahatoot/-eem להטוט *nm* trick; **(*pl+of:* -ey)**.

lahav/lehaveem להב *nm* **1.** blade; **2.** flame **(+*of:* lahav/-ey)**.

□ **Lahav** להב *nm* kibbutz (est. 1952) in NE Negev, 13 km NE of Beersheba. Pop. 422.

□ **Lahavot ha-Bashan** להבות הבשן *nm* kibbutz (est. 1945) in **Khoolah** Valley, at the foot of Golan Hills, 10 km SE of **Keeryat Shemonah**. Pop. 457.

□ **Lahavot Khaveevah** (Lahavot Haviva) להבות חביבה *nm* kibbutz (est. 1949) 8 km SE of Hadera **(Khaderah)**. Pop. 243.

lahavyor/-eem להביור *nm* flame-thrower; **(*pl+of:* -ey)**.

lahem להם pronoun *m pl* to them.

lahen להן pronoun *f pl* to them.

lahoot/lehootah להוט *adj* eager; enthusiastic.

la-horeg (*npr* le-horeg) להורג *adv* to be executed.

(hoots|a/-'ah) la-horeg הוצא להורג *v* was executed; **(*pres* mootsa *etc*; *fut* yootsa *etc*)**.

(hotsa|'ah/-'ot) la-horeg הוצאה להורג *nf* execution.

(hots|ee/-ee'ah/-etee) la-horeg הוציא להורג *v* executed; put to death; **(*pres* motsee *etc*; *fut* yotsee *etc*)**.

lak|ah/-ot לקה *[colloq.] nf* varnish; lacquer; **(+*of:* -at)**.

lak|ah/-tah/-eetee לקה *v* was stricken; **(*pres* lokeh; *fut* yeelkeh)**.

lak|akh/-'khah/-akhtee לקח *v* took; **(*pres* loke'akh; *fut* yeekakh)**.

lakekan/-eet לקקן *nmf & adj* one with a sweet tooth.

lakh/-ah לח *adj* damp; moist.

lakh לך *pron f sing* to you; for you.

(heh) lakh הא לך here you have; take!

lakh|ad/-dah/-adetee לכד *v* captured; **(*pres* lokhed; *fut* yeelkod *(k=kh)*)**.

la-khaloofeen לחלופין *adv* alternatively.

lakhalooteen לחלוטין *adv* absolutely.

lakham/-ah/-tee לחם *v* fought; waged war; **(*pres* lokhem; *fut* yeelkhom)**.

lakhan/lekhaneem לחן *nm* tune; **(*pl+of:* lakhney)**.

lakhash/lekhasheem לחש *nm* whisper; **(*pl+of:* -lakhshey)**.

lakhash-nakhash לחש־נחש *nm* incantation; abracadabra.

(be) lakhash בלחש *adv* in a whisper; whispering.

lakhash/-ah/-tee לחש *v* whispered; **(*pres* lokhesh; *fut* yeelkhash)**.

lakhats/lekhatseem לחץ *nm* pressure; urgency; **(*pl+of:* lakhtsey)**.

lakhats (*etc*) aveer לחץ אוויר *nm* air-pressure.

lakhats (*etc*) dam לחץ דם *nm* blood-pressure.

lakhats (*etc*) neseebot (*or:* meseebot) לחץ נסיבות *nm* pressure of circumstances.

(be) lakhats בלחץ *adv* under pressure.

(emtsa|'ee/-'ey) lakhats אמצעי לחץ *nm* a means of pressure.

(mad/-ey) lakhats מד־לחץ *nm* pressure gauge.

(seer/-ey) lakhats סיר־לחץ *nm* pressure-cooker.

(takhat) lakhats תחת לחץ *adv* under pressure.

la-khatsa'een לחצאין *adv* by halves; into halves; fifty fifty.

□ **Lakheesh** (Lakhish) לכיש *nm* village (est. 1955) 10 km SE of **Keeryat-Gat** E. of the road to **Bet-Govreen**. Pop. 302.

□ **(Ezor) Lakheesh** see □ **Ezor Lakheesh**.

lakhem לכם *pronoun m pl* to you.

lakhen לכן *pronoun f pl* to you.

lakhmanee|yah/-yot לחמנייה *nf* roll (bread); **(+*of:* -yat)**.

lakhoot לחות *nf* dampness.

lakhoots/-lekhootsah לחוץ *adj* **1.** pressured; compressed; **2.** difficult.

lakhpor לחפור *v inf* to dig; (*pst* **khafar**; *pres* **khofer**; *fut* **yakhpor** *(f=p)*).

(**kardom**) **lakhpor bo** קרדום לחפור בו an ax to grind; making a profession out of it.

lakhrop לחרופ *[slang] v inf* to sleep; to snore; (*pst* **kharap**; *pres* **khorep**; *fut* **yakhrop**).

lakhshan/-eem לחשן *nm* prompter (on stage); (*pl+of:* **-ey**).

lakhtsan לחצן *nm* push-button; (*pl+of:* **-ey**).

lako'akh (or **lakoo'akh**)/**lekookhot** לקוח *nm* client.

lakooy/lekooyah לקוי *adj* defective; faulty.

lalekhet ללכת *v inf* to go; (*pst* **halakh**; *pres* **holekh**; *fut* **yelekh**).

lamah למה why.

lamah lekha/lakh *(m/f)*? למה לך? what's the use?!

lam|ad/-dah/-adetee למד *v* studied; learned; (*pres* **lomed**; *fut* **yeelmad**).

lamad (*etc*) **lekakh** למד לקח *v* learned (his) lesson.

(**kal|a'/-'ah/-a'tee**) **la-matarah** קלע למטרה *v* hit the target; (*pres* **kole'a** *etc*; *fut* **yeekla'** *etc*).

lamdan/-eet למדן *nm* diligent scholar.

lamed/lemedah למד *v pres* learn(s); infer(s); (*pres* **lamad**; *fut* **yeelmad**).

◇ **lamed** למ״ד *nm* (ל) the 12th letter of the Hebrew alphabet; consonant "L".

Lamed ל׳ *Hebrew num symbol* **1.** thirty (30); **2.** thirtieth (see Introduction).

Lamed-Alef ל״א *Hebrew num symbol* **1.** thirty-one (31); **2.** thirty-first (see Introduction).

Lamed-Bet ל״ב *Hebrew num symbol* **1.** thirty-two (32); **2.** thirty-second. (see Introduction).

Lamed Dalet ל״ד *Hebrew num symbol* **1.** thirty four (34); **2.** thirty-fourth, (see Introduction).

Lamed-Geemel ל״ג *Hebrew num symbol* **1.** thirty three (33); **2.** thirty-third, (see Introduction).

Lamed-Heh ל״ה *Hebrew num symbol* **1.** thirty five (35); **2.** thirty-fifth, (see Introduction).

Lamed-Khet ל״ח *Hebrew num symbol* **1.** thirty eight (38); **2.** thirty-eighth, (see Introduction).

Lamed-Tet ל״ט *Hebrew num symbol* **1.** thirty nine (39); **2.** thirty-ninth, (see Introduction).

Lamed-Vav ל״ו *Hebrew num symbol* **1.** thirty six (36); **2.** thirty-sixth, (see Introduction).

Lamed-Zayeen ל״ז *Hebrew num symbol* **1.** thirty seven (37); **2.** thirty-seventh, (see Introduction).

la-mo'ed למועד *adv* on time.

(**'od khazon**) **la-mo'ed** עוד חזון למועד time will tell.

la-mokaz למוכ״ז *abbr.* to the bearer; (*acr of* **Le-Moser Ktav Zeh** למוסר כתב זה).

(**eeg|eret/-rot khov**) **la-mokaz** איגרת חוב למוכ״ז *nf* bearer-bonds.

(**mena|yah/-yot**) **la-mokaz** מניה למוכ״ז *nf* bearer's share.

la-mokhorat למוחרת *adv* the next day.

lamoot למות *v inf* to die; (*pst & pres* **met**; *fut* **yamoot**).

(**nat|ah/-etah/-teetee**) **lamoot** נטה למות *v* was about to die; (*pres* **noteh** *etc*; *fut* **yeeteh** *etc*).

lamrot למרות *adv* in spite of; despite.

lamrot ha-kol למרות הכול in spite of everything.

lamrot zot למרות זאת nevertheless.

lan/-ah/-tee לן *v* stayed overnight; (*pres* **lan**; *fut* **yaloon**).

la-netsakh לנצח *adv* forever; for eternity.

lanoo לנו *pronoun* to us; for us.

la-or לאור *adv* to the light; to daylight.

(**hotsa|'ah/-'ot**) **la-or** הוצאה לאור *nf* **1.** publishing house; publishing company; **2.** publication.

(**hots|ee/-ee'ah/-etee**) **la-or** הוציא לאור *v* published; (*pres* **motsee** *etc*; *fut* **yotsee** *etc*).

(**mots|ee/-'eem**) **la-or** מוציא לאור *nm* publisher.

(**yats|a/-'ah**) **la-'or** יצא לאור *v* appeared in print; was published; (*pres* **yotse** *etc*; *fut* **yetse** *etc*).

la-orekh לאורך *adv* in length.

la-orekh ve-la-rokhav לאורך ולרוחב **1.** *lit.*: *nm* length and width; **2.** *adv nm* in every possible way.

lapeed/-eem לפיד *nm* torch; (*pl+of:* **-ey**).

◻ **Lapeedot** (Lapidot) לפידות *nm* village (est. 1978) in Upper Gallilee, 3 km SE of Ma'alot. Pop. 133.

(**hotsa|'ah/-'ot**) **la-po'al** הוצאה לפועל **1.** implementation; **2.** execution (of court order).

(**hots|ee'/-ee'ah/-e'tee**) **la-po'al** הוציא לפועל *v* implemented; carried out (*pres* **motsee'** *etc*; *fut* **yotsee'** *etc*).

la-reek לריק *adv* in vain.

(**motsee'/-eem**) **la-po'al** מוציא לפועל *nm* official who executes court orders.

la-rokhav לרוחב *adv* in width.

la-sefeerah לספירה *adv* according to the Common (Christian) Era; A.D.

lash/-ah/-tee לש *v* kneaded; (*pres* **lash**; *fut* **yaloosh**).

la-shav לשווא *adv* in vain.

lashon/leshonot לשון *nf* **1.** tongue; **2.** language; (*+of:* **leshon**).

lashon akheret לשון אחרת *adv* in other words.

lashon ha-ra' לשון הרע *nf* slander; libel.

(**be-zeh ha**) **lashon** בזה הלשון in these words.

(**tseroofey**) **lashon** צירופי לשון *nm pl* collocations; idioms; phrases.

(**ba**) **lat** בלט *adv* secretly; quietly.

lat|ash/-'shah/-ashtee לטש polished; sharpened; (*pres* **lotesh**; *fut* **yeeltosh**).

latash (*etc*) **'eynayeem** לטש עיניים *v* stared at gazed at.

latet לתת *v inf* to give; (*pst* **natan**; *pres* **noten**; *fut* **yeeten**).

◻ **Latroon** (Latrun) לטרון *nf* site of one of fiercest battles in Israel's War of Independence (1948) over a former British Police fortress that controlled the road to Jerusalem at what is now **Tsomet Latroon** (Latrun Junction), near a picturesque Trappist monastery.

latson לצון *nm* fun; prank; mockery.

(kham|ad/-dah) latson חמד לצון *v* poked fun; joked; teased; (*pres* **khomed** *etc; fut* **yakhmod** *etc*).

lav לאו no.

lav/-eem (*also:* **laveem**) לאו *nm* a religious prohibition; interdiction.

lav davka לאו דווקא *adv* not necessarily; on the contrary.

lav meforash לאו מפורש *nm* a specific, definite interdiction.

(be) lav hakhee בלאו הכי *adv* anyhow; anyway; in any case.

(be) lav mookhlat בלאו מוחלט *adv* with a categoric denial; categorically refusing.

lav|ah/-tah/-eetee לווה *v* borrowed; (*pres* **loveh**; *fut* **yeelveh**).

lavan/levanah לבן *adj* white.

(ha-bayeet ha) lavan הבית הלבן *nm* the White House.

(kakhol-) lavan כחול־לבן *adj* light blue and white the Israeli (and Jewish) national flag colors.

(selek) lavan סלק לבן *nm* turnip.

(shakhor 'al gabey) lavan שחור על גבי לבן *adv* in black and white; black on white.

(tekhelet-) lavan תכלת־לבן *adj* blue and white the Israeli (and Jewish) national flag colors.

lav|ash/-shah/-ashtee לבש *v* put on; dressed in; wore; (*pres* **lovesh**; *fut* **yeelbash** *(b=v)*).

lavash (*etc*) **tsoorah** לבש צורה *v* took the form of.

lavee/levee|'eem לביא lion; (*pl+of:* **-'ey**).

◻ **Lavee** (Lavi) לביא *nm* kibbutz (est. 1948) in Lower Galilee, 10 km W. of Tiberias. Pop. 771.

◇ **(proyekt ha) lavee** see ◇ **proyekt ha-lavee**.

la-vetakh *(v=b)* לבטח *adv* in safety; (*see:* **betakh**).

lavlav/-eem לבלב *nm* pancreas (anat.); (*pl+of:* **-ey**).

lavlar/-eem לבלר *nm* clerk; (*pl+of:* **-ey**).

lavoosh/levooshah לבוש *adj* dressed; clothed.

lavyan/-eem לוויין *nm* satellite; (*pl+of:* **-ey**).

lavyan/-ey teekshoret לוויין תקשורת *nm* communications satellite.

layeel ליל *nm* night (*poetic.*); (*+of:* **leyl**).

laylah/leylot לילה night; (*+of:* **leyl**).

laylah tov! לילה טוב! (greeting) Good night!

(aron/-ot) laylah ארון לילה *nm* bed chest; night table.

(ba) laylah בלילה *adv* at night.

(be-'eeshon) laylah באישון לילה *adv* in the dead of night.

(been) laylah בן לילה *adv* overnight.

(khatsot) laylah חצות לילה *nf* midnight.

(ha) laylah הלילה *adv* tonight.

(kooton|et/-ot) laylah (*or:* **ketonet/kotnot** *etc*) כתונת־לילה *nf* nightgown.

(khakham ba) laylah חכם בלילה *adj [slang]* clever, aren't you?!

(meeshm|eret/-arot) laylah משמרת לילה *nf* night-shift.

(mo'adon/-ey) laylah מועדון לילה *nm* night-club.

(seer/-ey) laylah סיר לילה *nm* chamber pot.

(tseepor/-ey) laylah ציפור לילה *nf* night-bird; night-owl.

(ey) la-zot אי לזאת *adv & conj* therefore.

(shom|er/-rey) laylah שומר לילה *nm* night watchman.

le- ־ל *(prefix)* **1.** to; **2.** of.

(le) akhar לאחר *adv* following; after.

le-akhar-kakh לאחר־כך *adv* afterwards; for later.

le-akhar-ma'aseh לאחר מעשה *adv* post factum.

le-akhar mee-ken לאחר מכן *adv* later on.

le'akher לאחר *v inf* to be late; (*pst* **'eekher**; *pres* **me'akher**; *fut* **ye'akher**).

le-akher/-et לאחר *adv* to someone *m/f* else.

le-akhor לאחור *adv* backwards.

le-altar לאלתר *adv* immediately.

le-an לאן (interrog.) where to?

le-at לאט *adv* slowly; slow.

le-at le-at לאט לאט *adv* very slowly.

le-at mee-day לאט מדי *adv* too slowly.

le-'atsmee לעצמי **1.** to myself; **2.** the formula for self-endorsing a cheque.

le-'atsm|o/-ah/-ekha/-ekh (*etc*) לעצמו/־ה/־ך וכו' for /to/by him/her/you (*etc*) -self.

(ke-she) le-'atsm|ee/-o/-ah/-ekha/-ekh *etc* כשלעצמי/־ו וכו' per se; by my/him/her *etc* -self.

ledah/-ot לידה *nf* birth; (*+of:* **-at**).

(khad|ar/-rey) ledah חדר לידה *nm* maternity room; delivery room.

(ma'an|ak/-key) ledah מענק לידה *nm* maternity grant.

(tseerey) ledah צירי לידה *nm pl* birth pangs.

le-deen לדין to trial.

lee לי *pron* **1.** me; **2.** to me.

lee ־ל *(prefix)* to (followed by verb or noun).

leeb|ah/-tah/-eetee ליבה *v* kindled; inflamed; (*pres* **melabeh**; *fut* **yelabeh**).

(bekheer) leebah בחיר־ליבה *nm* her heart's choice; fiancé; (*lit:* **chosen one**).

◇ **LEEBEE** לב"י *nm* the Army's "For Israel's Security" donations-fund (*acr of* **Le-ma'an Beetkhon YEEsra'el** למען ביטחון ישראל).

leeb|ee/-kha/-ekh/-o/-ah (*etc*) לבי/־ך/־ו וכו' *nm* my/your *m/f* his/her (*etc*) heart.

('alah/-tah 'al) leeb|o/-ah עלה על לבו *v* it occurred to him/her *etc*; (*pres* **'oleh** *etc; fut* **ya'aleh** *etc*).

(bekheerat) leebo בחירת לבו *nf* his beloved; his heart's choice; fiancée.

(nag|a'/-'ah el) leeb|o/-ah/-ee (*etc*) נגע אל לבו/־ה/־י he/she/I (*etc*) was touched (*figurat.*); (*pres* **noge'a'** *etc; fut* **yeega'** *etc*).

leeboon/-eem ליבון *nm* elucidation; (*pl+of:* **-ey**).

leeboo|y/-yeem ליבוי *nm* **1.** inflaming, fanning (flame); **2.** (*figurat.*) instigation; (*pl+of:* **-yey**).

le-'eenyan לעניין concerning; as regards; in the matter of.

le'ees|ah/-ot לעיסה *nf* chewing; mastication; (*+of:* **-at**).

(goomee) le'eesah גומי־לעיסה *nm* chewing-gum.

le-'eeteem לעיתים *adv* at times.

le-'eeteem krovot לעיתים קרובות *adv* often.

le-'eeteem mezoomanot לעיתים מזומנות *adv* at regular intervals.

le-'eeteem nedeerot לעיתים נדירות *adv* on rare occasions.

le-'eeteem rekhokot לעיתים רחוקות *adv* seldom.

le-'eeteem tekhoofot לעיתים תכופות *adv* quite often.

le-eet|o/-ah לאיטו *adv nmf* at his/her ease; slowly.

(oolpan/-eem) le-'eevreet אולפן לעברית *nm* Hebrew Ulpan; an intensive course for learning Hebrew.

lee-fe'ameem (*or:* **lee-f'ameem**) לפעמים *adv* sometimes.

lee-fekood|at/-ot *(f=p)* לפקודת *adv* at the order of; to the order of...

leefnay ve-leefneem לפני ולפנים *adv* in the innermost.

leefneem לפנים *adv* to the inside.

leefneem mee-shoorat ha-deen לפנים משורת הדין *adv* indulgently.

leefney לפני *adv* **1.** before; prior to; **2.** in front of.

leefney ha-sefeerah לפני הספירה *adv* **1.** before the common (Christian) Era; **2.** B.C.E. (Hebrew *abbr.* לפנה״ס used in writing only).

leefney ha-tsohorayeem לפני הצוהריים *adv* **1.** before noon; **2.** a.*m.* (Hebrew *abbr.* לפנה״צ used in writing only).

leefney khen לפני כן *adv* before that; before it.

leefney sefeerat ha-notsreem לפני ספירת הנוצרים *adv* **1.** before the Christian Era; **2.** B.C.E. (Hebrew *abbr.* לפסה״נ used in writing only).

leefney she- לפני ש־ *adv* before; before that...

◇ **leefney ha-sfeerah** לפני הספירה *adv* before the common or Christian Era; B.C.

leefnot לפנות *v inf* to turn to; to apply; (*pst* **panah**; *pres* **poneh**; *fut* **yeefneh** *(f=p)*).

leefnot boker לפנות בוקר *adv* at dawn; just before sunrise.

leefnot 'erev לפנות ערב *adv* at sunset; towards evening. .

lee-frakeem *(f=p)* לפרקים *adv* occasionally; from time to time.

leeftan/-eem לפתן *nm* compote; (*pl+of:* **-ey**).

leeg|ah/-ot ליגה *nf* league; soccer league; (*+of:* **-at**).

leegbor 'al לגבור על *v inf* to overcome; (*pst* **gavar** *etc; pres* **gover** *(v=b) etc;* **yeegbar** *etc*).

leegl|eg/-egah/-agtee לגלג *v* sneered; mocked; (*pres* **melagleg**; *fut* **yelagleg**).

leegloog/-eem ליגלוג *nm* sneer; mockery; (*pl+of:* **-ey**).

lee-gvareem לגברים for men.

lee-gvarot לגברות for women.

(heeg|ee'a/-ee'ah/-a'tee) lee-gevoorot הגיע לגבורות *v* reached the age of 80; (*pres* **magee'a** *etc; fut* **yagee'a** *etc*).

leehyot להיות *v inf* to be; (*pst* **hayah**; *pres* **heeno**; *fut* **yeehyeh**).

leehyot (*etc*) **le-'ezer** להיות לעזר *v* to be of assistance; to be of help.

leehyot (*etc*) **le-satan** להיות לשטן *v* to be an obstruction; to be in the way.

leehyot (*etc*) **nokh|e'akh** (*cpr* **nokhakh**) / **-akhat** להיות נוכח *v* to be present at.

leek|ek/-ekah/-aktee ליקק *v* licked; licked up; (*pres* **melakek**; *fut* **yelakek**).

leeker/-eem ליקר *nm* liqueur.

leek|et/-tah/-atetee ליקט *v* gathered; picked; gleaned; (*pres* **melaket**; *fut* **yelaket**).

leekh'orah לכאורה *adv* seemingly; apparently; on the face of it.

leekh'os לכעוס *v inf* to be angry; to be vexed; (*pst* **ka'as**; *pres* **ko'es**; *fut* **yeekh'as** *(k=kh)*).

(no'akh/nokhah) leekh'os נוח לכעוס *adj* irritable; irascible.

(not|eh/-ah) leekh'os נוטה לכעוס *adj* easily irritable.

leekhl|ekh/-ekhah/-akhtee לכלך *v* **1.** soiled; dirtied; **2.** *[slang]* spoiled it all; wasted. (*pres* **melakhlekh**; *fut* **yelakhlekh**).

leekhlookh/-eem לכלוך *nm* **1.** dirt; dirtying; **2.** *[slang]* good for nothing; fake; scoundrel.

le'ekhoz לאחוז *v inf* to hold; to seize; to grasp; (*pst* **akhaz**; *pres* **okhez**; *fut* **yokhaz**).

le'ekhoz (*etc*) **be-emtsa'eem** לאחוז באמצעים *v* to take measures.

lee-kheshe- לכשה־ *(prefix)* when.

lee-kheshe-yarkheev (*cpr* **leekh'she-yarkheev**) לכשירחיב *adv* when things get better (financially).

leekl|ek/-ekah/-aktee לקלק *v* licked; (*pres* **melaklek**; *fut* **yelaklek**).

leekood/-eem ליכוד *nm* consolidation; unification.

◇ **leekood** (Likkud) ליכוד *nm* right-of-the-center political bloc, that since 1977 has been the mainstay of coalitions that have formed the Israeli government. Originally, it based its power on the Herut (**kheroot**) Party supported by the Liberal Party and a few minor parties. Then, however, because of repeated deadlocks in parliamentary elections, it had to enter coalitions with its perennial adversary, the Labor Party. Meanwhile, in 1988, the cooperation between Herut and the Liberal Party became a nearly full-fledged merger. In 1990 Herut was finally able to form a government based on itself and its own associates only.

leekook/-eem ליקוק *nm* lick; licking; (*pl+of:* **-ey**).

leekoo|y/-yeem ליקוי *nm* defect; fault; (*pl+of:* **-yey**).

leekoo|y/-yey khamah ליקוי חמה *nm* solar eclipse.

leekoo|y/-yey levanah (*or:* **yare'akh**) ליקוי לבנה/ירח *nm* lunar eclipse.

leekooy me'orot ליקוי מאורות *nm* **1.** solar or lunar eclipse; **2.** fig: the people losing faith in their leaders.

leekoo|y/-yeem moosaree/-yeem ליקוי מוסרי *nm* moral deficiency.

leekoo|y/-yeem seekhlee/-yeem ליקוי שכלי *nm* mental deficiency.

(efes) leekooyeem אפס ליקויים zero defects.

leekrat לקראת *adv* towards; in anticipation of.

leekrat|ee/-kha/-ekh/-o/-ah (*etc*) לקראתי/־ך/־ו וכו׳ *adv & pron* towards me/you/(*m/f*)/him/her *etc.*

le-'el לעיל *adv* above; earlier (in a text).

(ha-neezk|ar/-eret) le-'el הנזכר לעיל *adj* the above-mentioned.

(meel) 'eyl מלעיל *nm* stress falling on penultimate syllable.

le'ela oo-le-'ela לעילא ולעילא *adv (Aram.)* beyond comparison.

leelakh/-eem לילך *nm* lilac (flower); (*pl+of:* **-ey**).

□ **Leeman** (Liman) לימן *nm* village (est. 1949) and popular camping and bathing spot on Galilee seashore, 5 km N. of Nahariyya, on road to **Rosh ha-Neekrah**. Pop. 314.

leem|ed/-dah/-adetee לימד *v* taught; (*pres* **melamed**; *fut* **yelamed**).

leemed (*etc*) **sanegoryah** לימד סניגוריה *v* defended (in court).

leemed (*etc*) **zekhoot** לימד זכות *v* argued in favor of; tried to justify.

leemed (*etc*) **khovah** לימד חובה *v* argued against; condemned.

lee-mehadreen למהדרין *adj* top-quality; for connoisseurs.

lee-merashot למראשות *adv* under one's headrest; under one's head.

leemon/-eem לימון *nm* lemon; (*pl+of:* **-ey**).

leemonad|ah/-ot לימונדה *nf* lemonade.

leemood/-eem לימוד *nm* instruction; learning; (*pl+of:* **-ey**).

(sefer/seefrey) leemood ספר לימוד *nm* textbook.

(sekhar) leemood שכר לימוד *nm* tuition; school-fees.

(sekhar) leemood moodrag שכר לימוד מודרג *nm* graduated school-fees; graded tuition.

leemoodeem לימודים *nm pl* studies; (*pl+of:* **-ey**).

leemoodeem akademeeyeem לימודים אקדמיים *nm pl* academic studies.

(khoog/-ey) leemoodeem חוג לימודים *nm* university dept.

(ma'an|ak/-key) leemoodeem מענק לימודים *nm* grant-aid for studies; scholarship.

(tokhnee|t/-yot) leemoodeem תוכנית לימודים *nf* curriculum; syllabus.

leemoodey te'oodah לימודי תעודה *nm pl* certificate studies; studying for a certificate.

leemoodey to'ar לימודי תואר *nm pl* studying for a degree.

le-'et metso לעת מצוא *adv* occasionally.

le-en לאין *adv* beyond (any possibility).

le-en 'arokh לאין ערוך *adv* beyond estimation.

le-'en gevool לאין גבול *adv* infinitely; limitless.

le-'en sefor לאין ספור *adv* innumerable; innumerably.

leen|ah/-ot לינה *nf* overnight stay; (*+of:* **-at**).

□ **Lee-on** (Li-On) לי־און *nm* rural center for settlements in the Adulam area (**Khevel 'Adoolam**), 2 km S. of ha'Ela Road Junction). Pop. 185.

leep|ef/-efah/-aftee ליפף *v* enwrapped; wound (a motor); (*pres* **melapef**; *fut* **yelapef**).

leepoof/-eem ליפוף *v* wrapping; winding; (*pl+of:* **-ey**).

leepoof/-ey mano'a/meno'eem ליפוף מנוע *nm* motor-rewiring.

◇ **leer|ah/-ot yeesre'elee|t/-yot** לירה ישראלית *nf* Israeli Pound - Israeli 1948 currency-unit, replaced in 1981 by the **Shekel** at a ratio of IL 10. equivalent to 1 Israeli Shekel. (In turn, the latter was devalued in 1986 and replaced at a ratio of 1:1000 by the New Shekel, N.S. which is thus equivalent to 10,000 onetime Israeli Pounds).

Leer|ah/-ot לירה *nf [colloq.]* abbr.for Leerah Yeesre'eleet (see **above**).

le-'erekh לערך *adv* approximately.

leerkav (*npr* **leerkov**) לרכב *v inf* to ride (an animal, bicycle, motorcycle); (*pst* **rakhav** *(kh=k)*; *pres* **rokhev**; *fut* **yeerkav**).

leerkhots לרחוץ *v inf* to wash; (*pst* **rakhats**; *pres* **rokhets**; *fut* **yeerkhots**).

leerkom לרקום *v inf* **1.** to embroider; **2.** to devise; (*pst* **rakam**; *pres* **rokem**; *fut* **yerkom**).

leerkosh לרכוש *v inf* to acquire; (*pst* **rakhash**; *pres* **rokhesh**; *fut* **yeerkosh** *(kh=k)*).

leerkov לרכב *v inf* to ride (an animal, bicycle, motorcycle); (*pst* **rakhav** *(kh=k)*; *pres* **rokhev**; *fut* **yeerkav**).

leermos לרמוס *v inf* to tread; to trample; (*pst* **ramas**; *pres* **romes**; *fut* **yeermos**).

leermoz לרמוז *v inf* to hint; to intimate; (*pst* **ramaz**; *pres* **romez**; *fut* **yeermoz**).

leer'od לרעוד *v inf* to tremble; (*pst* **ra'ad**; *pres* **ro'ed**; *fut* **yeer'ad**).

leer'ot לראות *v inf* to see; (*pst* **ra'ah**; *pres* **ro'eh**; *fut* **yeer'eh**).

leershom לרשום *v inf* to record; to note; to write; (*pst* **rasham**; *pres* **roshem**; *fut* **yeershom**).

leertom לרתום *v inf* to harness (also fig); (*pst* **ratam**; *pres* **rotem**; *fut* **yeertom**).

leerton לרטון *v inf* to grumble; (*pst* **ratan**; *pres* **roten**; *fut* **yeerton**).

leertsot לרצות *inf* to wish; to want; (*pst* **ratsah**; *pres* **rotseh**; *fut* **yeertseh**).

lee-rvakhah לרווחה *adv* widely.

(paroots/prootsah) lee-rvakhah פרוץ לרווחה *adj* widely broken into.

(patoo'akh/petookhah) lee-rvakhah פתוח לרווחה *adj* wide open.

lee-rvayah לרוויה *adv* to satiation; to one's fill.

leervot לרוות *v inf* to quench one's thirst (also fig) (*pst* **ravah**; *pres* **roveh**; *fut* **yeerveh**).

leerzot לרזות *v inf* fot grow thin; to slim; (*pst* **razah**; *pres* **marzeh**; *fut* **yeerzeh**).

leesgor לסגור *v inf* **1.** to close; **2.** to finalize; (*pst* **sagar**; *pres* **soger**; *fut* **yeesgor**).

leeshbor לשבור *v inf* to break; (*pst* **shavar**; *pres* **shover**; *fut* **yeeshbor** *(v=b)*).

leeshbot לשבות *v inf* **1.** to strike; **2.** to rest from (work); (*pst* **shavat**; *pres* **shovet**; *fut* **yeeshbot** *(v=b)*).

leeshdod לשדוד *v inf* to rob; to despoil; (*pst* **shadad**; *pres* **shoded**; *fut* **yeeshdod**).

leesh'hot לשהות *v inf* to stay; to linger; (*pst* **shahah**; *pres* **shoheh**; *fut* **yeesh'heh**).

leeshkah/leshakhot *(kh=k)* לשכה *nf* bureau; chamber; office; (*+of:* **leesh|kat/-khot**).

leesh|kat/-khot 'avodah *(kh=k)* לשכת עבודה *nf* labor exchange; employment bureau.

◇ **leeshkat ha-'eetonoot ha-memshalteet** לשכת העתונות הממשלתית *nf* Government Press Bureau (also known as Public Information Office or P.I.O.).

leeshkat (*etc*) **mees'khar** לשכת מסחר *nf* Chamber of Commerce.

leeshkat (*etc*) **modee'een** לשכת מודיעין *nf* information desk/bureau.

◇ **leeshkat reeshoom mekarke'een** לשכת רישום מקרקעין *nf* Land Registry Office (known colloquially as **Taboo**).

leeshkat (*etc*) **sar/-eem** לשכת שר *nf* ministerial bureau.

leeshkat (*etc*) **ta'asookah** לשכת תעסוקה *nf* employment exchange.

leeshkav לשכב *v inf* to lie down; (*pst* **shakhav** *(kh=k)*; *pres* **shokhev**; *fut* **yeeshkav**).

leeshkav (*etc*) **'eem** לשכב עם *v inf* **1.** to sleep with; **2.** to cohabit with; **3.** *[slang]* to lay.

leeshko'akh לשכוח *v inf* to forget; to forsake; (*pst* **shakhakh** *(kh=k)*; *pres* **shokhe'akh**; *fut* **yeeshkakh**).

leeshkol לשקול *v inf* to weigh; to ponder over; (*pst* **shakal**; *pres* **shokel**; *fut* **yeeshkol**).

leeshlo'akh לשלוח *v inf* to send; to send off; (*pst* **shalakh**; *pres* **shole'akh**; *fut* **yeeshlakh**).

leeshlol לשלול *v inf* **1.** to deny; to disapprove; to negate; **2.** to withdraw; to take away; (*pst* **shalal**; *pres* **sholel**; *fut* **yeeshlol**).

leeshlol (*etc*) **reeshayon** (*npr* **reeshyon**) לשלול רשיון *v inf* to retract driving permit; retract driving license.

lee-shmad לשמד *adv* convert to a non-Jewish faith.

leeshmo'a לשמוע *v inf* to hear; to listen; (*pst* **shama'**; *pres* **shome'a**; *fut* **yeeshma'**).

leeshmor לשמור *v inf* to guard; to observe; (*pst* **shamar**; *pres* **shomer**; *fut* **yeeshmor**).

leeshon לישון *v inf* to sleep; (*pst* **yashan**; *pres* **yashen**; *fut* **yeeshan**).

(hal|akh/-khah/-akhtee) leeshon הלך לישון *v* went to bed; (*pres* **holekh** *etc*; *fut* **yeelekh** *etc*).

(shakh|av/-vah/-avtee) leeshon שכב לישון *v* went to sleep; (*pres* **shokhev** *etc*; *fut* **yeeshkav** *etc k=kh*).

leeshpot לשפוט *v inf* to judge; to condemn; (*pst* **shafat** *(f=p)*; *pres* **shofet**; *fut* **yeeshpot**).

leeshtof לשטוף *v inf* to rinse, wash, flood; (*pst* **shataf**; *pres* **shotef**; *fut* **yeeshtof**).

leeshtok לשתוק *v inf* to be silent; (*pst* **shatak**; *pres* **shotek**; *fut* **yeshtok**).

leeshtok! לשתוק! *interj & imp* silence! shut up!

leeshtot לשתות *v inf* to drink; (*pst* **shatah**; *pres* **shoteh**; *fut* **yeeshteh**).

leeslo'akh לסלוח *v inf* to forgive; (*pst* **salakh**; *pres* **sole'akh**; *fut* **yeeslakh**).

leesmo'akh לשמוח *v inf* to rejoice; (*pst* **samakh**; *pres* **same'akh**; *fut* **yeesmakh**).

leesno לשנוא *v inf* to hate; (*pst* **sane**; *pres* **sone**; *fut* **yeesna**).

lees'od לסעוד *v inf* **1.** to eat; **2.** to succor; (*pst* **sa'ad**; *pres* **so'ed**; *fut* **yees'ad**).

leespor לספור *v inf* to count; (*pst* **safar** *(f=p)*; *pres* **sofer**; *fut* **yeespor**).

leestom לסתום *v inf* **1.** to clog, to fill; **2.** to obscure, to say vaguely; (*pres* **satam**; *pres* **sotem**; *fut* **yeestom**).

le'et לעת *adv* at the time of.

le'et 'atah לעת עתה *adv* for the time being.

le-'et metso לעת מצוא *adv* occasionally.

leet|ef/-fah/-aftee ליטף *v* **1.** caressed; **2.** patted (dog, *etc*); (*pres* **melatef**; *fut* **yelatef**).

leet|er/-reem ליטר *nm* liter = *1.0567 U.S quart.*

leet|er/-reem ליטר *nf* pound; (*pl+of:* **-rey**).

lee-tevakh/-eem arokh/arookeem (*k=kh; or:* **lee-tvakh** *etc*) לטווח ארוך *adv* for the long range.

lee-tevakh/-eem benonee/-yeem (*or:* **lee-tvakh** *etc*) לטווח בינוני *adv* for the medium range.

lee-tevakh/-eem katsar/ketsareem (*or:* **lee-tvakh** *etc*) לטווח קצר *adv* for the short range.

lee-tevakh/-eem rakhok/rekhokeem (*or:* **lee-tvakh** *etc*) לטווח רחוק *adv* for the long range.

(kam/-ah/-tee) lee-t'kheeyah קם לתחייה *v* was resurrected; came back to life; (*pres* **kam** *etc*; *fut* **yakoom** *etc*).

leetoof/-eem ליטוף *nm* caress; pat; (*pl+of:* **-ey**).

leetoosh/-eem ליטוש *nm* polish; polishing; (*pl+of:* **-ey**).

leetr|ah/-a'ot ליטרה *nf* pound; (*+of:* **-at**).

leev|ah/-tah/-eetee ליווה *v* accompanied; escorted; (*pres* **melaveh**; *fut* **yelaveh**).

le'ever לעבר *adv* towards; in the direction of.

leevl|ev/-evah/-avtee לבלב *v* blossomed; bloomed; (*pres* **melavlev**; *fut* **yelavlev**).

leevneh ליבנה *nm* birch.

('ets/'atsey) leevneh עץ ליבנה *nm* birch tree.

leevney meetah לבני מיטה *nm pl* bed-linen.

leevney shamootee לבני שמוטי *nm pl* "shamootee" bricks.
leevnot לבנות *v inf* to build; (*pst* **banah** *(b=v)*; *pres* **boneh**; *fut* **yeevneh**).
leevoo|y/-yeem ליווי *nm* **1.** escort; **2.** accompaniment (music); (*pl+of:* **-yey**).
(be) leevooy בליווי *adv* in the company of.
leevy|at khen לוויית־חן *nf* graceful addition.
(be) leevyat בלוויית *adv* accompanied by.
leevyatan/-eem לווייתן *nm* whale; (*pl+of:* **-ey**).
lee-yedey לידי *adv* **1.** to; into the hands of; **2.** in to a state of.
(he|vee/-ee'ah/-etee) lee-yedey הביא לידי *v* brought to; (*pres* **mevee** *etc*; *fut* **yavee** *etc*).
lee-yemeen לימין *adv* **1.** in support of; **2.** (also *lit*) to the right of.
le-'eyl לעיל *adv* above; earlier (in a text).
(ha-neezk|ar/-eret) le-le-'eyl הנזכר לעיל *adj* the above-mentioned.
(meel) 'eyl מלעיל *nm* stress falling on penultimate syllable.
le'eyla oo-le-'eyla לעילא ולעילא *adv (Aram.)* beyond comparison.
le-'et metso לעת מצוא *adv* occasionally.
le-eyn לאין *adv* beyond (any possibility).
le-eyn 'arokh לאין ערוך *adv* beyond estimation.
le-'eyn gvool לאין גבול *adv* infinitely; limitless.
le-'eyn sfor לאין ספור *adv* innumerable; innumerably.
le-'ezer לעזר *adv* of assistance; of help.
le-'ezrah לעזרה *adv* for help.
le-fakhot *(f=p)* לפחות *adv* at least.
le-faneem לפנים *adv* **1.** once (upon a time); **2.** in front; forward; (f=*p).*
le-fee לפי *adv* according to.
le-fee roo'akh לפי רוח *adv* according to the spirit of.
le-fee sha'ah לפי שעה *adv* for the time being; for the moment.
lefeekhakh לפיכך *conj* therefore.
le-feta' *(f=p)* לפתע *adv* suddenly.
le-feta' peet'om *(f=p)* לפתע פתאום *adv* all of a sudden.
(hots|ee/-ee'ah/-etee) le-foal (or **la-po'al**) הוציא לפועל *v* **1.** carried out; implemented; **2.** executed (court order); (*pres* **motsee** *etc*; *fut* **yotsee** *etc*).
le-gab|ay/-eykha/-ayeekh/-av/-eha (*etc*) /לגביי ־ך־ו וכו׳ regarding (towards) me/you(*m/f*)/ him/her.
le-gabey לגבי *prep* regarding; about.
legalee/-t ליגלי *adj* legal.
◇ **(beeltee) legalee/-t** see ◇ **beeltee legalee/-t**.
le-gamrey לגמרי *adv* entirely; completely.
legeem|ah/-ot לגימה *nf* sip; drink; (*+of:* **-at**).
legeeteemee/-t לגיטימי *adj* legitimate.
le-goolgolet לגולגולת *adv* per head; per capita.
legyon/-ot לגיון *nm* legion.
le-haba להבא *adv* in the future.
le-haflee להפליא **1.** *adv* splendidly; **2.** *adj* splendid.
lehakh'ees להכעיס *adv* **1.** out of spite; to anger someone; **2.** *[colloq.]* doing exactly the opposite.
lehakh'ees להכעיס *v inf* to anger; (*pres* **makh'ees**; *fut* **yakh'ees**).
lehakhnees להכניס *v inf* to introduce; to insert; (*pst* **heekhnees**; *pres* **makhnees**; *fut* **yakhnees**).
le-halakhah להלכה *adv* in theory.
le-halan להלן *adv* further on; from then on.
(ha-moozkar) le-halan (or **ha-neezkar** *etc*) הנזכר or המוזכר להלן *adj* infra; later (in a text).
lehaskeer להשכיר *v inf* to let; (*pst* **heeskeer**; *pres* **maskeer**; *fut* **yaskeer**).
lehaskeer (*etc*) **meroohat** להשכיר מרוהט *v inf* to let furnished; to lease furnished.
(bayeet/bateem) lehaskeer בית להשכיר *nm* house for rent; house to let.
(deer|ah/-ot) lehaskeer דירה להשכיר *nf* apartment for rent; flat to let.
(kheder/khadareem) lehaskeer חדר להשכיר *nm* room for rent; room to let.
lehav|ah/-ot להבה *nf* flame; (*+of:* **-at**).
(lehateel) kherem להטיל חרם *v inf* to impose a boycott on; (*pst* **heeteel** *etc*; *pres* **mateel** *etc*; *fut* **yateel** *etc*).
(lehateel *etc*) **safek** להטיל ספק *v inf* to doubt; to have doubts.
lehatsree'akh להצריח *v inf* to castle (chess) (*pst* **heetsree'akh**; *pres* **matsree'akh**; *fut* **yatsree'akh**).
□ **Lehaveem** (Lehavim) להבים *nm* settlement (est. 1985) E. of Beersheba. Pop. 250.
le-ha-yom להיום *adv* for today.
lehazkeer להזכיר *v inf* to remind; (*pst* **heezkeer**; *pres* **mazkeer**; *fut* **yazkeer**).
leheet/-eem להיט *nm* hit (song, movie, *etc*); (*pl+of:* **-tey**).
le-heet! !להת׳ *[colloq.] abbr.* of **leheetra'ot!** !להתראות - so long! see you later; Au revoir!
leheetoo|t/-yot להיטות *nf* ardor; craving.
leheetra'ot! !להתראות *interj* so long! see you later! Au Revoir!
le-hefekh להיפך *conj* on the contrary.
lehotsee להוציא *adv* excepting.
lehotsee להוציא *v inf* **1.** to take out, extract; **2.** to spend; (*pst* **hotsee**; *pres* **motsee**; *fut* **yotsee**).
le-kadmoot|o/-ah לקדמותו *adv* to what/how it *m/f* had been.
lekakh/-eem לקח *nm* lesson; moral lesson; (*pl+of:* **leek'khey**).
le-kaman לקמן *adv* further on; below (in a text).
(dee) le-kaman דלקמן *adv* that follows.
(ke-dee) le-kaman כדלקמן *adv* as follows.
lekeekh|ah/-ot לקיחה *nf* taking; (*+of:* **-at**).
le-keenoo'akh לקינוח *adv* for dessert.
lek|et/-ateem לקט *nm* compilation; collection; (*+of:* **lekte**y).
lekh/-ee לך *v imp sing m/f* go! (*pst* **halakh**; *pres* **holekh**; *fut* **yelekh**).

lekha לך *pronoun m sing* to you; for you.
lekh|ah/-ot ליחה *nf* **1.** moisture; **2.** pus; phlegm; (*+of:* **-at**).
le-khan לכאן *adv* hereto.
le-khamah (*cpr* **le-kamah**) לכמה for how many; for how long.
le-khan oo le-khan לכאן ולכאן *adv* **1.** here and there; **2.** in both directions.
le-kha-tekheelah (*cpr* **le-kha-t'kheelah**) לכתחילה *adv* initially; at first.
(mee) le-kha-tekheelah מלכתחילה *adv* from the start.
lekhayayeem לחיים *nm pl* cheeks; (*sing* **lekhee**).
le-khayeem! !לחיים *interj* (toast) cheers! to your health!
(leeshtot) le-khayeem לשתות לחיים *v inf* to toast; to drink to one's health; (*pst* **shatah** *etc; pres* **shoteh** *etc; fut* **yeeshteh** *etc*).
le-khayey לחיי *interj* (toast) to the life of...
le-khayekh|em/-en לחייכם *interj* (toast) to your *pl m/f* health.
lekh|ee/-ayayeem לחי *nf* cheek; (*pl+of:* **lekhayey**).
(steer|at/-ot) lekhee סטירת לחי *nf* slap in the face.
◇ **LEKHEE** לח"י *nf* (*acr of* **Lokhamey KHeroot YEEsra'el** לוחמי חירות ישראל the insurgent organization known as the "Stern-Gang" that fought the British throughout the years 1940 1949.
lekheed|ah/-ot לכידה *nf* capture; trapping; (*+of:* **-at**).
le-kheeloofeen (*npr* **la-khaloofeen**) לחלופין *adv* altervatively.
lekheem|ah/-ot לחימה *nf* fighting; waging war; (*+of:* **-at**).
le-kheenam לחינם *adv* in vain.
lekheesh|ah/-ot לחישה *nf* whisper; whispering; (*+of:* **-at**).
lekheets לחיץ *nm* push-button; (*pl+of:* **-ey**).
lekheets|ah/-ot לחיצה *nf* urging; pressing; (*+of:* **-at**).
lekheets|at/-ot yad לחיצת יד *nm* handshake.
lekh|em/-ameem לחם *nm* bread.
lekhem akheed לחם אחיד *nm* state-subsidized one-type bread, slightly brown.
lekhem khook|o/-ah לחם חוקו *nm* his/her daily bread.
lekhem lavan לחם לבן *nm* white bread.
lekhem paroos לחם פרוס *nm* sliced bread.
lekhem shakhor לחם שחור *nm* rye bread; brown bread; dark bread.
lekhem sheefon (*cpr* **sheepon**) לחם שיפון *nm* rye bread.
lekhem tsar לחם צר *nm* prison fare.
('ad pat) lekhem עד פת לחם *adv* to the brink of starvation.
(keek|ar/-rot) lekhem כיכר לחם *nm* loaf of bread.
(pat) lekhem פת לחם *nf* bread; slice of bread.
(proos|at/-ot) lekhem פרוסת לחם *nf* slice of bread.
(kodem) le-khen קודם לכן *adv* prior to that.
('am|ad/-dah/-adetee mee) lekhet עמד מלכת *v* stopped; (*pres* **'omed** *etc; fut* **ya'amod** *etc*).
(kokh|av/-vey) lekhet כוכב לכת *nm* planet.
(markheek/-at) lekhet מרחיק לכת *adj* far-reaching.
(sheer/-ey) lekhet שיר לכת *nm* marching tune; marching song.
le-khol ha-de'ot (*kh=k*) לכל הדעות *adv* indisputably.
le-khol ha-me'ookhar (*kh=k*) לכל המאוחר *adv* at the latest.
le-khol ha-mookdam (*kh=k*) לכל המוקדם *adv* at the earliest.
le-khol ha-pakhot (*kh=k*) לכל הפחות *adv* at least .
le-khol ha-rookhot (*kh=k*) לכל הרוחות *interj* to Hell! to the devil with ...!
le-khol ha-yoter (*kh=k*) לכל היותר *adv* at most.
le-khood לחוד *adv* separately; alone.
lekookh|ah/-ot לקוחה *nf* client (female); (*+of:* **-at**).
lel ליל *m+of* the night of.
lel ha- ליל ה- *nm* the night of.
◇ **lel ha-seder** ליל הסדר *nm* the "Seyder" night; Passover ceremonial dinner.
lel kloolot ליל כלולות *nm* wedding night; nuptial.
lel menookhah! !ליל מנוחה (greeting) Good night!
lel/-ot shabat ליל שבת *nm* (*lit.*) Sabbath Night, meaning Friday evening (when the Sabbath begins).
lel/-ot sheemooreem ליל שימורים *nm* night of vigil; watch-night.
lelee/-t לילי *adj* nightly; nocturnal.
le-lo ללא *adv* without.
le-lo deekhooy ללא דיחוי *adv* without delay.
le-lo dofee ללא דופי *adj* blameless; irreproachable.
le-lo hafoogah ללא הפוגה **1.** *adj* relentless; **2.** *adv* relentlessly.
le-lo hatslakhah ללא הצלחה **1.** *adj* unsuccessful; **2.** *adv* unsuccessfully.
le-lo hefsek ללא הפסק **1.** *adj* uninterrupted; **2.** *adv* uninterruptedly.
le-lo heref ללא הרף **1.** *adj* incessant; **2.** *adv* incessantly.
le-lo ke'eveem ללא כאבים **1.** *adj* painless; **2.** *adv* painlessly.
le-lo keevoon ללא כיוון **1.** *adj* aimless; **2.** *adv* aimlessly.
le-lo kekhal oo-srak (*npr* **oo-le-lo sarak**) ללא כחל ושרק *adj* unadorned; plain.
le-lo matarah ללא מטרה **1.** *adj* aimless; **2.** *adv* aimlessly.
le-lo pegam/-eem ללא פגם **1.** *adj* faultless; **2.** *adv* faultlessly.
le-lo ra'ash/-re'asheem ללא רעש **1.** *adj* noiseless; **2.** *adv* noiseless/-ly.

le-lo rakhameem ללא רחמים **1.** *adj* merciless; **2.** *adv* mercilessly.

le-lo rakhem ללא רחם **1.** *adj* pitiless; **2.** *adv* pitilessly; without pity.

le-lo ta'am ללא טעם **1.** *adj* tasteless; **2.** *adv* tastelessly; **3.** *adv* without any reason.

le-lo takdeem ללא תקדים **1.** *adj* unprecedented; **2.** *adv* unprecedentedly.

le-lo takhleet ללא תכלית *adv* without purpose.

le-lo takhteet ללא תחתית *adj* bottomless.

le-lo yesod ללא יסוד **1.** *adj* unfounded; baseless; **2.** *adv* with no foundation.

le-ma'lah למעלה *adv* above; up.

(yadayeem) le-ma'lah ידיים למעלה *interj* hands up!

le-ma'an למען *conj* in order that; for the sake of.

le-ma'an ha-Shem למען השם for Heaven's sake!

le-ma'an|ee/-khah/-ekh/-o/-ah למעני/־ך וכו׳ *conj & pron sing* for my/your(*m/f*)/his/her sake.

le-ma'an|enoo/-khem/-khen/-am/-an למעננו/־כם/־כן וכו׳ *conj pron pl* for our/your (*m/f*)/their *(m/f)* sake.

le-ma'aseh למעשה *adv* actually; practically.

(halakhah) le ma'aseh הלכה למעשה from theory to practice; putting theory into practice.

le-lo takanah ללא תקנה *adv* beyond repair.

le-maday למדי *adv* sufficiently; considerably.

lema'et למעט **1.** *adv* except; **2.** *v inf* to diminish; to decrease; to dwindle; (*pst* **mee'et;** *pres* **mema'et;** *fut* **yema'et**).

lemafre'a' למפרע *adv* **1.** retroactively; retrospectively; **2.** *[colloq.]* in advance.

lemakhbeer למכביר *adv* abundantly.

lemarbeh ha-hafta'ah למרבה ההפתעה *adv* to one's utmost surprise.

lemarbeh ha-pele למרבה הפלא *adv* to one's bewilderment.

lemarbeh ha-pelee'ah למרבה הפליאה *adv* to one's astonishment.

lemarbeh ha-tsa'ar למרבה הצער *adv* to one's great regret.

le-mar'eet 'ayeen למראית עין *adv* seemingly; on the face of it.

le-mar'eh למראה *adv* at the sight of.

le-margelot למרגלות *adv* at the foot of.

le-margelot ha-har למרגלות ההר *adv* at the foot of the mountain.

le-margelot ha-meetah למרגלות המיטה *adv* at the foot of the bed.

le-mashal למשל *conj* for instance; e.g.

le-matah למטה *adv* down.

lematen למתן *v inf* to moderate; to restrain; (*pst* **meeten;** *pres* **mematen;** *fut* **yematen**).

le-me'ah למאה *num* percent; in a hundred.

(ekhad/shnayeem *etc***) le-me'ah** אחד/שניים למאה one/two (*etc*) percent, in a hundred.

lemeedah/-ot למידה *nf* studying; learning; (*+of:* **-at**).

le-meesh'ee למשעי *adv* neatly; cleanly.

(merootlak/-eket) le-meetah מרותק למיטה *adj* bedridden.

◇ **lemekh** למך *[slang] nm* clumsy idiot; blundering fool.

le-meshekh למשך *adv* for the duration of.

le-meyshareem (or **le-meyshareen**) למישרים/־ין *adv* straight; smoothly.

le-mofet למופת *adj* exemplary; wonderful.

le-mokhorat (*npr* **la-mokhorat**) למוחרת *adv* the next day.

lemor לאמור as follows; in these words.

lemotar למותר *adv* needless to...

le-nafsho/-ah/-ee *etc* לנפשו/־ה/־י וכו׳ alone; by him/her/my (*etc*)-self.

le-nakhon לנכון *adv* proper.

(leemtso) le-nakhon למצוא לנכון *v inf* to think fit; (*pst* **matsa** *etc; pres* **motse** *etc; fut* **yeemtsa** *etc*).

le-neged לנגד *adv* in front of; compared with.

le-netsakh netsakheem לנצח נצחים *adv* for ever and ever.

le-nokhakh לנוכח *adv* in the face of.

le-'olam לעולם *adv* forever.

le-'olam lo לעולם לא *adv* never.

le-'olam lo 'od לעולם לא עוד *adv* never again.

le-'olam va'ed לעולם ועד *adv* for ever and ever.

(ta'oot) le-'olam khozeret טעות לעולם חוזרת errors and omissions excepted; an error tends to repeat itself.

le'om/le'oomeem לאום *nm* **1.** nation; **2.** nationality; **3.** people.

le'oomanee/-t לאומני *adj* nationalistic; chauvinistic.

le'oomanoot לאומנות *nf* nationalism; chauvinism.

le'oomat לעומת *prep* as against; compared with.

(kee) le-'oomat she- כלעומת ש־ *prep* as; just as.

le'oomee/-t לאומי *adj* national.

(beetoo'akh) le'oomee ביטוח לאומי *nm* social security; national insurance.

(doo-) le'oomee/-t דו־לאומי *adj* bi-national.

(beyn-) le'oomee/-t בין־לאומי *adj* international.

(rav-) le'oomee/-t רב־לאומי *adj* multi-national.

le'oomeeyoot לאומיות *nf* nationality.

le'oot ליאות *nf* fatigue; weariness.

(le-lo) le'oot ללא ליאות *adv* tirelessly.

le-or לאור *adv* in the light of.

le-orekh yameem לאורך ימים *adv* in the long run; for long.

(moo|'ad/-'edet) le-foor'anoot (*f=p*) מועד לפורענות *adj* bound to get in trouble.

le-ra'avah לראווה *adv* for show; for exhibition.

lerabot לרבות *adv* including.

le-ragley לרגלי *adv* on the occasion of.

(ner) le-ragley נר לרגלי *nm* guiding light; principle.

le-rega' לרגע *adv* for a moment; momentarily.

le-regel לרגל *adv* on the occasion of.

le-ro'ets לרועץ *adv* causing harm; impediment.

leseroogeen לסירוגין *adv* alternatingly; intermittently.
les|et/-atot לסת *nf* jaw.
leshad 'atsamot לשד עצמות *nm* bone marrow.
le-shanah לשנה *adv* per annum.
◇ **le-shanah tovah teekatevoo!** לשנה טובה תיכתבו! traditional well-wishing formula for the Jewish New Year. (For use with the approach of, and throughout, the festival of Rosh ha-Shanah).
◇ **le-shanah tovah teekatevoo ve-tekhatemoo!** לשנה טובה תיכתבו ותיחתמו! traditional well-wishing formula for the Jewish New Year said also during the period between Rosh haShana and the Day of Atonement (Yom Kippur).
le-shaneem לשנים *adv* for years (to come).
le-she-'avar לשעבר **1.** *adj* former; previous; onetime; **2.** *adv* formerly; previously.
le-shem לשם for; with the purpose of; for the sake of.
le-shem shamayeem לשם שמיים *adv* **1.** out of sheer idealism; **2.** for Heaven's sake.
le-shem sheenooy לשם שינוי *adv* for a change.
le-shevet o le-khesed לשבט או לחסד *adv* for good or evil; for good or for bad.
leshon ham'atah לשון המעטה *nf* understatement.
leshon ha-kodesh לשון הקודש *nf* the sacred language (i.e. Hebrew).
leshon bney adam לשון בני אדם *nf* ordinary speech.
leshon (*npr* **lashon**) **ha-ra'** לשון הרע *nf* slander.
leshon nekeyvah לשון נקבה *nf* (Gram.) feminine gender.
leshon rabeem לשון רבים *nf* (Gram.) plural.
leshon sagee nehor לשון סגי־נהור *nf* euphemism.
leshon yakheed לשון יחיד *nf* (Gram.) singular.
leshon zakhar לשון זכר *nf* (Gram.) masculine gender.
leshonee/-t לשוני *adj* lingual; linguistic.
(doo) leshonee/-t דו־לשוני *adj* bi-lingual.
(rav) leshonee/-t רב־לשוני *adj* multi-lingual.
let לית (Aramaic) there is not; there is no.
let breyrah לית ברירה there is no choice.
(be) let breyrah בלית ברירה *adv* in the absence of an alternative; for want of alternative.
let deen ve-let dayan לית דין ולית דיין (Aramaic) no justice and no judge; complete chaos.
let man de-faleeg לית מן דפליג **1.** (Aramaic) there is no objection; **2.** *(lit.)* no one can deny.
leta|'ah/-'ot לטאה *nf* lizard; **(+*of:* -'at).**
le-ta'am לטעם *adv* according to the taste of.
le-tameed לתמיד *adv* for keeps; for good.
le-te'avon! לתיאבון! (greeting) Bon appetit! Have a nice meal!
leteef|ah/-ot לטיפה *nf* pat; caress; **(+*of:* -at).**
le-teemyon לטמיון *adv* down the drain (money, investments).
leteeshat 'ayeen/'eynayem לטישת עין *nf* stare; staring at; gazing at.
le-tovah לטובה *adv* for the better.
le-tovat לטובת *adv* for the sake of.
lets/-eem לץ *nm* joker; jester.
le-tsa'aree לצערי *adv* unfortunately; to my regret.
le-tsad לצד *adv* on the side of.
le-tseeyoon לציון *adv* to mark; to point out.
(ra'ooy/re'ooyah) le-tseeyoon ראוי לציון *adj* worth mentioning.
le-tsorekh לצורך *conj* for the purpose of.
le-tsorekh ve-she-lo le-tsorekh לצורך ושלא לצורך whether needed or not.
lev/-avot לב *nm* heart.
(be) lev בלב *adv* in the heart of.
(be) lev khatsooy בלב חצוי *adv* halfheartedly.
(be) lev shalem בלב שלם *adv* wholeheartedly.
(be) lev yam בלב ים *adv* on the high seas.
(be-khefets) lev בחפץ־לב *adv* willingly.
(be-tom) lev בתום־לב *adv* in good faith; bona fide.
(geelooy) lev גילוי־לב *nm* frankness.
(gloo|y/-yat) lev גלוי־לב *adj* frank.
(hetkef/-ey) lev התקף־לב *nm* heart-attack.
(kan|ah/-tah/-eetee 'et) lev קנה את לב *v* won one's heart; **(*pres* koneh *etc; fut* yeekneh *etc*).**
(kots|ev/-vey) lev קוצב־לב *nm* pacemaker.
(makhl|at/-ot) lev מחלת־לב *nf* heart disease.
(menat|e'akh/-khey) lev מנתח לב *nm* heart-surgeon.
(morekh) lev מורך לב *nm* faintheartedness.
(needv|at/-ot) lev נדבת־לב *nf* generous gift.
(nedeevoot) lev נדיבות לב *nf* generosity.
(nog|e'a'/-a'at la) lev נוגע ללב *adj* heartrending.
(omets) lev אומץ לב *nm* courage.
(rakh/rakat) lev רך־לב *adj* cowardly.
(rekhav/rakhavat) lev רחב־לב *adj* generous.
(ro'a) lev רוע לב *nm* ill will; malice.
(sam/-ah/-tee) lev שם לב *v* paid attention; **(*pres* sam lev; *fut* yaseem lev).**
(seemat) lev שימת לב *nf* attention.
(shreeroot) lev שרירות לב *nf* arbitrariness.
(tehor/-at) lev טהור לב *adj* pure-hearted.
(tesoomet) lev תשומת לב *nf* attention.
(toov-) lev טוב לב *nm* kindness; kindheartedness.
(tov/-at) lev טוב לב *adj* kindhearted.
levad לבד *adv* alone; separately.
(bee) levad (*also pron.* **beelvad**) בלבד *adv* only; solely.
(mee) levad (*also pron.* **meelvad**) מלבד *adv* apart from; except; in addition to.
levad|ah/-o/-am/-an לבדה/־ו/־ם/־ן וכו׳ (by) her/him -self; themselves *m/f.*
leva|dee/-enoo לבדי (by) myself/ourselves.
levad|khah/-ekh/-khem/-khen לבדך/־ך/־כם/־כן by yourself *m/f*; yourselves *m/f.*
le-val לבל *conj* lest; so that not; for fear that (v=*b).*
levan|ah/-ot לבנה **1.** *nf* moon; **2.** *adj f* white.
(ha) levanah הלבנה *nf* the moon .

◇ **(keedoosh) levanah** see ◇ **keedoosh levanah**.
(gveen|ah/-ot) levan|ah/-ot גבינה לבנה white cheese.
levanban/-ah לבנבן *adj* whitish.
levaneem לבנים *nm pl* underwear; bed-linen; "whites"; (*pl+of:* **leevney**).
◇ **(Yad) le-Vaneem** see Yad le-Vaneem.
levanvan (*npr* **levanban**)**/-ah** לבנבן *adj* whitish.
levases לבסס *v inf* to base; to consolidate; (*pst* **beeses**; *pres* **mevases**; *fut* **yevases** *(b=v)*).
le-va-sof לבסוף *adv* in the end; finally.
levate'akh לבטח *v inf* to insure; to ensure; (*pst* **beete'akh**; *pres* **mevate'akh**; *fut* **yeevate'akh** *(b=v)*).
levateem לבטים *nm pl* hesitations; difficulties; (*+of:* **-ey**).
levatel לבטל *v inf* to cancel; to annul; (*pst* **beetel**; *pres* **mevatel**; *fut* **yevatel** *(b=v)*).
levaten לבטן *v inf* to reinforce with concrete; (*pst* **beeten**; *pres* **mevaten**; *fut* **yevaten** *(b=v)*).
levav/-ot לבב *nm* heart (poetic).
levavee/-t לבבי *adj* hearty; cordial.
levaveeyoot לבביות *nf* cordiality.
(ha) levay הלוואי if only...; I wish...
leva|yah/-yot לוויה *nf* funeral (*+of:* **-yat**).
(bat/bnot) levayah בת לוויה *nf* escort (female).
(ben/bney) levayah בן לוויה *nm* escort (male).
leved לבד *nm* felt.
◇ **levee/-yeem** לוי *nm* Levite i.e. scion of the Levitic tribe the task of which, in Biblical days, was to serve the Lord. Any Jewish person bearing the surname Levy, Levi, or differently spelt versions of these (or a derivative e.g. Levite, Levinson) is presumably a Levite. In Jewish ritual there is often some special role reserved for a Levite.
leveed/-eem לביד *nm* plywood; (*pl+of:* **-ey**).
leveev|ah/-ot לביבה *nf* pancake; potato pancake; (*+of:* **-at**).
(beynenoo) le-ven 'atsmenoo בינינו לבין עצמנו strictly between ourselves.
leven|ah (or **leveyn|ah**)**/-eem** לבנה *nf* brick; (*+of:* **-at**).
(beyno) le-veynah בינו לבינה between lovers; between him and her; between husband and wife.
levoosh/-eem לבוש *nm* dress; clothing.
leyade'a' ליידע *v inf* to inform; (*pst* **yeeda'**; *pres* **meyade'a'**; *fut* **yeyade'a'**).
leydah/-ot לידה *nf* birth; (*+of:* **-at**).
(khadlar/-rey) leydah חדר לידה *nm* maternity room; delivery room.
(khevley) leydah חבלי לידה *nm pl* birth pangs.
(ma'an|ak/-key) leydah מענק לידה *nm* maternity grant.
(tseerey) leydah צירי לידה *nm pl* birth pangs.
leyl ליל *nm* the night of.
leyl ha- ליל ה־ *nm* the night of the.
leyl ha-Seder ליל הסדר *nm* the "Seyder-night" (festive Passover dinner).
leyl kloolot ליל כלולות *nm* wedding night; nuptial.
leyl menookhah! ליל מנוחה! (greeting) Good night!
leyl/-ot shabat ליל שבת *nm* (*lit.*) Sabbath Night, meaning Friday evening (when the Sabbath begins).
leyl/-ot sheemooreem ליל שימורים *nm* night of vigil; watch-night.
leylee/-t לילי *adj* nightly; nocturnal.
le-yom ליום *adv* per diem; per day.
leytsan/-eem ליצן *nm* clown.
leytsanoot/-yot ליצנות *nf* merrymaking; jesting.
le-zara לזרא *adv* loathsome; repulsive.
lo לו *pron 3rd pers sing m* **1.** him; **2.** to him; **3.** for him.
lo לא *adv* no; not.
lo 'aley|noo/-khem לא עלינו *interj* may it not befall us/you; may we/you be spared something like that.
lo beekhdee לא בכדי not without good reason.
lo doobeem ve-lo ya'ar לא דובים ולא יער **1.** nothing of the sort; don't exaggerate; **2.** *(lit.)* neither bears nor forest.
lo eekhpat לא איכפת *v* it doesn't matter; (*pst* **lo hayah eekhpat**; *fut* **lo yeeyeh 'eekhpat**).
lo-eekhpateeyoot לא־איכפתיות *nf* lack of concern; nonchalance.
lo hayah/haytah shaveh/-ah לא היה שווה *v* was not worth; was not worthwhile (*pres* **lo shaveh**; *fut* **lo yeehyeh shaveh**).
lo hayah ve-lo neevra לא היה ולא נברא it never was, it never happened.
lo hayoo dvareem me-'olam לא היו דברים מעולם nothing of the kind ever happened; it is absolutely untrue.
lo khloom לא כלום nothing; not a thing.
lo kol she-ken לא כל שכן all the more so.
lo ma'al|eh/-ah ve lo moreed/-dah לא מעלה ולא מוריד **1.** makes no difference; **2.** (*lit.*) not raising and not lowering.
lo meen ha-meemna' לא מן הנמנע *v pres* it is not excluded; it is quite possible.
lo meshaneh לא משנה *v pres* (it) makes no difference; (it) doesn't matter.
lo nakhon לא נכון *adv* wrong! it isn't true.
lo nakhon/nekhonah לא נכון *adj* untrue.
lo neet|an/-enet לא ניתן *adv* not feasible.
lo normalee/-t לא נורמלי *adj* **1.** abnormal; **2.** *[slang]* extraordinary; exciting.
lo 'od 'ela לא עוד אלא *conj* not only ..., but also ...
lo sagee לא סגי *adv* not enough; it isn't enough.
lo shav|eh/-ah לא שווה **1.** *adv & v pres* it isn't worthwhile; it isn't worth it; **2.** *adj* not worthwhile; not the same.
lo ta'eem/te'eemah לא טעים *adj* not tasty; unsavory.
lo tsareekh לא צריך *adv* no need to.

lo ye'amen/te'amen לא ייאמן *adj* unbelievable; incredible.

lo yeesafer/teesafer לא ייספר *adj* countless.

lo yeetakhen/teetakhen לא ייתכן *adj* impossible; couldn't be.

lo ye'ookhar לא יאוחר *adv* at the latest; not later.

lo ye'ooman/te'ooman לא יאומן *adj* unbelievable; incredible.

lo yetoo'ar/tetoo'ar לא יתואר *adj* unimaginable.

lo yod|e'a/-a'at לא יודע *v pres* I/you/he *etc* do not know; (*pst* **lo yada'**; *fut* **lo yeda'**).

lo yootslakh/-eet לא יוצלח *nmf & adj* good for nothing.

('ad she-) lo עד שלא *prep* **1.** before; until; **2.** unless.

('adayeen) lo עדיין לא *adv* not yet.

('al) lo davar על לא דבר Don't mention it! (standard response to "Thank you"! or "Thanks"!).

(be) lo בלא *adv* without.

(be) lo hakarah בלא הכרה *adv & adj* unconscious.

(be) lo hefsek בלא הפסק *adv* without interruption.

(be) lo she- בלא ש־ without (followed by a verb).

(be) lo yod'eem בלא יודעים *adv* unknowingly; unaware.

('eem) lo אם לא' if not.

(ha) lo'? הלא? is it not...that...? isn't it that? indeed?

(le) lo ללא without; with no.

(va) lo ולא or else.

(zeh) lo kvar זה לא כבר *adv* not so long ago.

lo'a/lo'eem לוע *nm* pharynx; throat; (*pl+of:* **-'ey**).

lo'azee/-t לועזי *adj* foreign (language); non-Hebrew.

□ **Lod** (*colloq. mispronunc.* **Lood**) לוד *nf* town near Ben-Gurion Airport. Pop. 43,300 (incl. 8,990 Arabs).

lohet/-et לוהט *adj* blazing; burning.

lokham|ah/-ot לוחמה *nf* warfare; fighting; (*+of:* **-at**).

□ **Lokhamey ha-Geta'ot** (Lohamey ha-Geta'ot) לוחמי הגיטאות *nm* kibbutz on Galilee seashore, 4 km N. of Acre (**Ako**). Founded 1949 by survivors of World War II Ghetto uprisings and specializing in documentation of the Holocaust, to which the kibbutz museum is dedicated. Pop. 524.

lokhem/-et לוחם **1.** *nmf* fighter; **2.** *adj* fighting; **3.** *v pres* fight(s); (*pst* **lakham**; *fut* **yeelkhom**).

lokhsan/-eem לוכסן *nm* stroke (between figures); oblique (/); diagonal; (*pl+of:* **-ey**).

loksh/-eem לוקש *[slang] nm* salary slip; salary voucher.

lomar לומר *v inf* to say; (*pst* **amar**; *pres* **omer**; *fut* **yomar**).

(ke) lomar כלומר that is to say.

loo לו if; were it.

loo|'akh/-khot לוח *nm* **1.** bulletin; **2.** blackboard; **3.** plate; **4.** calendar; **5.** schedule.

loo'akh ha-kefel לוח הכפל *nm* multiplication table.

loo|'akh/-khot keer לוח קיר *nm* wall-calendar.

loo'akh makhsheereem לוח מכשירים *nm* instrument panel.

loo'akh mekheereem לוח מחירים *nm* price-list.

loo|'akh/-khot moda'ot לוח מודעות *nm* notice board.

loo'akh mofa'eem לוח מופעים *nm* schedule of appearances.

loo'akh sfarot לוח ספרות *nm* dial.

loo|'akh/-khot shanah לוח שנה *nm* annual calendar.

loo'akh/-khot zmaneem לוח זמנים *nm* time-table; time-schedule.

(shnat/shnot) loo'akh שנת־לוח *nf* calendar year.

□ **Lood** לוד see Lod.

lookhee|t/-yot לוחית *nf* stone-tablet; writing-tablet.

lookhot ha-breet לוחות הברית *nm pl* tablets of the Covenant, i.e. the Decalogue.

lookhsan (*npr* **lokhsan**)**/-eem** לוכסן *nm* stroke (between figures); oblique (/); diagonal; (*pl+of:* **-ey**).

lool/-eem לול *nm* hen-roost; (*pl+of:* **-ey**).

loola|'ah/-'ot לולאה *nf* **1.** hoop; tie; loop; **2.** buttonhole border; (*+of:* **-'at**).

loolan/-eem לולן *nm* poultry keeper; (*pl+of:* **-ey**).

◇ **loolav/-eem** לולב *nm* palm branch used at a synagogue ritual during Sukkot holiday; (*pl+of:* **-ey**).

loole (*or:* **looley**) לולא (לולי) *prep* were it not for; if not for.

loolyan/-eet לוליין *nmf* acrobat (*pl:* **-eem**; *+of:* **-ey**).

loolyanoot לוליינות *nf* acrobatics.

Loonah-Park לונה־פארק *nm* Luna-Park; amusement park.

□ **Loozeet** (Luzit) לוזית *nm* village (est. 1955) in the Coastal Plain, Lahish (**Lakheesh**) area, 5 km W. of ha'Ela Junction. Pop. 277.

lov|eh/ah לווה *nmf* debtor; borrower.

lov|eh/-ah לווה *v pres* borrow(s); (*pst* **lavah**; *fut* **yeelveh**).

loven לובן *nm* whiteness.

loot/-ah לוט *adj* enclosed; enveloped.

□ **Lotem** (Lotem) לוטם *nm* kibbutz (est. 1978) in Lower Galilee, 7 km SW of Hananya Junction (**Tsomet Khananyah**). Pop. 135.

M.

transliterating Hebrew consonant מ **(Mem)**

mah מה **1.** what; **2.** what?
mah... af...מה... אף... as... so is...
mah be-khakh 'eem *(kh=k)* מה בכך אם so what if...
(shel) mah be-khakh *(kh=k)* של מה בכך *adj* of little importance; trivial.
mah ben... le-ven *(v=b)* מה בין... לבין... what difference is there between ... and ...?
mah gam she- מה גם ש־ moreover; the more so.
mah ha-sha'ah? מה השעה? what time is it?
mah ma'as|ekha/-ayeekh? מה מעשיך? **1.** how are you *m/f*? **2.** what are you *m/f* doing now/ here?
mah magee'a'? מה מגיע? what do I/we owe you?
mah meeshkal|kha/-ekh? מה משקלך? how much do you *m/f* weigh? what's your *m/f* weight?
mah nafshakh? מה נפשך? let us see: one of the two...
mah neeshma'? מה נשמע? what's new? any news?
◇ **"mah neeshtanah"?** מה נשתנה? opening phrase of the "Four Questions"(in Yiddish: four Kashess) asked (usually by the youngest child) at the "Seder" on Passover Night.
mah peet'om?! מה פתאום?! why all of a sudden?!
mah sheemkha/shemekh? מה שמך? what is your *m/f* name.
mah she-en ken מה שאין כן which isn't the case...; which doesn't apply...
mah shem (or: **shem|o/-ah shel)** מה שם ...? what is the name of (or: his/her name)?
mah shlom|kha/-ekh? מה שלומך? how are you *m/f*?
mah ta'am? מה טעם? **1.** what reason is there? **2.** what sense does it make?
mah yesh? מה יש? what's the matter?
mah yesh?! מה יש?! so what?!
mah yesh lekha/lakh? מה יש לך? what's troubling you *m/f*?
mah zeh 'eesk|ekha/-ekh? מה זה עסקך? **1.** what business of yours *m/f* is it?! **2.** what do you *m/f* care?
(az) mah!? אז מה?! so what?!
(devar) mah דבר־מה *nm* something; anything.
(vee-yehee) mah - ויהי מה...and be what may!
(zeman) mah זמן־מה *nm* some time.

ma'ab|adah/-adot מעבדה *nf* laboratory; (*+of:* **-edet**).
ma'abada|tee/-t מעבדתי *adj* laboratory.
◇ **ma'abar|ah/-ot** מעברה *nf* onetime (1950-1960) immigrant transit-camp which later sometimes became a lower-class neighborhood.
□ **Ma'abarot (Ma'barot)** מעברות *nm* kibbutz (est. 1933) in Sharon, 5 km N. of haSharon Road Junction. Pop. 765.
ma'abor|et/-ot מעבורת *nf* ferryboat;
ma'aboret khalal מעבורת חלל *nf* space shuttle.
(onee|yat/-yot) ma'aboret אוניית מעבורת *nf* ferryboat.
ma'ad/-ah/-etee מעד *v* stumbled; tripped; (*pres* **mo'ed;** *fut* **yeem'ad)**.
ma'adan/-eem מעדן *nm* delicacy; delight (culinary); (*pl+of:* **-ey)**.
ma'adeem/-ah מאדים **1.** *adj* reddening; **2.** *v pres* redden(s); (*pst* **he'edeem;** *fut* **ya'adeem)**.
□ **Ma'adeem** מאדים *nm* planet Mars.
ma'ad|er (*npr* **ma'der)/-ereem** מעדר *nm* hoe; (*pl+of:* **-rey)**.
ma'afee|yah/-ot מאפייה *nf* bakery; (*+of:* **-at)**.
ma'afer|ah/-ot מאפרה *nf* ashtray; (*+of:* **-at)**.
ma'agal/-eem (*npr* **ma'gal)** מעגל *nm* circle; (*pl+of:* **ma'gley)**.
□ **Ma'agaleem** (Ma'galim) see □ **Ma'galeem**.
□ **Ma'agan (Ma'agan)** מעגן *nm* kibbutz (est. 1949) on the S. shore of Lake Tiberias (Keeneret), 1 km E. of **Tsomet Tsemakh** (Zemah Junction). Pop. 364.
□ **Ma'agan Meekha'el (Ma'agan Mikha'el)** מעגן מיכאל *nm* kibbutz (est. 1949) on Carmel seashore, at 4 km from **Zeekhron Ya'akov**. Pop. 1,120.
ma'ageel|ah/-ot מעגילה *nf* roller; mangle; (*+of:* **-at)**.
ma'ahal/-eem מאהל *nm* encampment; tented camp; (*pl+of:* **-ey)**.
ma'akav/-eem מעקב *nm* follow-up; sequence; (*pl+of:* **ma'akvey)**.
ma'ak|eh/-ot מעקה *nm* banister; parapet; railing; (*pl+of:* **-ey)**.
ma'akh/-ah/-tee מעך *v* crushed; squashed; (*pres* **mo'ekh;** *fut* **yeem'akh)**.
ma'akh|al/-aleem מאכל *nm* food; dish; (*pl+of:* **-ley)**.
ma'akh|az/-azeem מאחז *nm* **1.** grip; grasp; hold; **2.** *[colloq.]* a first stage in establishing

a new settlement in an unfriendly area; (*pl+of:* **-zey**).

ma'al/-ah/-tee מעל *v* embezzled; abused a trust; (*pres* **mo'el**; *fut* **yeem'al**).

ma'al מעל *nm* embezzlement; betrayal.

ma'alah (*npr* **ma'lah**) מעלה *adv* upwards; up.

(bet-deen shel) ma'alah (*npr* **ma'lah**) בית דין של מעלה *nm* celestial court; tribunal in Heaven.

(le) ma'alah (*npr* **le-ma'lah**) למעלה *adv* above; up; upwards.

ma'al|ah/-ot מעלה *nf* **1.** quality; **2.** step; **3.** (temperature) degree; (*+of:* **-at**).

(ram/-at) ma'alah רם מעלה *adj* high-ranking.

(reeshon/-ah be) ma'alah ראשון במעלה *adj* first in rank.

ma'alaleem מעללים *nm pl* deeds; (*sing* **ma'al|al**; *pl+of:* **-eley**).

(hod) ma'alat|o/-ah הוד מעלתו *nmf* His/Her Excellency; H.E.

ma'al|eet/-yot מעלית *nf* elevator; lift.

ma'al|eh/-ah מעלה *nm* ascent; rise; slope;

□ **Ma'aleh Adoomeem** (Ma'ale Adummim) מעלה אדומים *nf* town (est. 1982) 8 km E. of Jerusalem on Jerico road. Pop. 13,500.

□ **Ma'aleh 'Amos** (**Ma'alé Amos**) מעלה עמוס *nm* communal village Bethlehem sub-district (est. 1981), 12 km SE of **Efrata**. Pop. 251.

□ **Ma'aleh ha-Khameeshah** (**Ma'alé Hahamisha**) מעלה החמישה *nm* kibbutz (est. 1938) in Judea Hills, 10 km NW of Jerusalem, N. of **Aboo-Gosh** village. Pop. 447.

□ **Ma'aleh Efrayeem** (**Ma'lé 'Efrayim**) מעלה אפרים *nf* town (est. 1970) on the borderline between the Jordan Valley and the Samaria Hills, 13 km SW of **Gesher Adam** (Adam Bridge across Jordan). Pop. 1,430.

□ **Ma'aleh Gamla** (Ma'alé Gamla) מעלה גמלא *nm* village (est. 1977) in the Golan Heights, 6 km E. from Tiberias. Pop. É246. Nearby, the excavations of Gamla, the ancient Judean fortress which heroically resisted the Romans (68 BCE). Pop. 246.

□ **Ma'aleh Geelbo'a'** (Ma'alé Gilbo'a) מעלה גלבוע *nm* kibbutz (est. 1962) in the Bet-She'an Valley, 8 km W. of Bet-She'an. Pop. 274.

□ **Ma'aleh Meekhmas** (Ma'alé Mikhmas) מעלה מכמש *nm* communal village on Alon Highway, 10 km NE of **Neveh-Ya'akov**. Pop. 238.

(be) ma'aleh ha-derekh במעלה הדרך *adv* up the road.

(be) ma'aleh ha-geev'ah במעלה הגבעה *adv* uphill.

(be) ma'aleh ha-har במעלה ההר *adv* up the mountain.

(be) ma'aleh ha-nahar במעלה הנהר *adv* upstream.

□ **Ma'aleh Shomron** (Ma'alé Shomron) מעלה שומרון *nm* communal village (est. 1981) 12 km E. of **Kalkeeleeyah**, on the road to Nablus. Pop. 268.

□ **Ma'alot** (Ma'alot) מעלות *nf* picturesque development-town (est. 1957) in Upper Galilee, 20 km E. of Nahariyya. Forms unified local council with neighboring **Tarsheekha** (see □ **Ma'alot-Tarsheekha**).

□ **Ma'alot-Tarsheekha** (**Ma'alot-Tarshiha**) מעלות תרשיחא *nm* local council unifying the Jewish development town Ma'alot and Arab-Christian village Tarshiha. Combined pop. 10,600.

◇ **MA'AM** מע״מ *nm* (*acr of* **Mas 'Erekh Moosaf** מס ערך מוסף) V.A.T. i.e. Value Added Tax.

ma'amad/-ot מעמד *nm* status; class.

(be) ma'amad במעמד *adv* in the presence of.

(hekhz|eek/-eekah/aktee) ma'amad החזיק מעמד *v* held out; remained firm; (*pres* **makhzeeek** *etc; fut* **yakhzeek** *etc*).

ma'amadee/t מעמדי *adj* class-.

(al-) ma'amadee/-t (*or:* **'al-** *etc*) אל/על מעמדי *adj* classless.

(meelkhemet) ma'amadot מלחמת מעמדות *nf* class struggle.

ma'amar/-eem מאמר *nm* article; essay; (*pl+of:* **-ey**).

ma'amar/-eem rashee/-yeem מאמר ראשי *nm* editorial; lead article.

(be) ma'amar moosgar במאמר מוסגר *adv* in parentheses; parenthesis... unparenthesis.

ma'amas מעמס *nm* burden; load; loading capacity.

ma'am|asah/-asot מעמסה *nf* load; burden; (*+of:* **-eset/-asot**).

ma'amats/-eem מאמץ *nm* effort (*pl+of:* **-ey**).

(tos|efet/-fot) ma'amats תוספת מאמץ *nf* **1.** extra effort; **2.** extra-effort pay increment.

ma'ameen/-ah מאמין **1.** *nmf* believer; **2.** *v pres* believe(s); (*pst* **he'emeen**; *fut* **ya'ameen**).

(anee) ma'ameen/-ah אני מאמין *nm* **1.** credo; conviction; **2.** (*lit.:*) I believe.

◇ **(anee) ma'ameen** see ◇ **anee ma'ameen**.

ma'an/-eem מען *nm* address; (*+of:* **-ey**).

(le) ma'an למען *prep* for; for the sake of.

ma'an|ak/-akeem מענק *nm* grant; grant in aid; (*pl+of:* **-key**).

ma'an|ak/-key leemoodeem מענק לימודים *nm* scholarship grant.

ma'an|ak/-key leydah מענק לידה *nm* maternity grant.

ma'an|ak/-key mekh'kar מענק מחקר research scholarship; research grant.

(le) ma'an ha-shem למען השם intj for Heaven's sake.

(le) ma'an|ee/-kha/-o/-ah *etc* למעני־ך/־ו/־ה וכו׳ for my/your(*m/f*)/his/her *etc* sake.

□ **Ma'aneet** (Ma'anit) מענית *nm* kibbutz (est. 1935) NW of Mount Shomron, 4 km from 'Iron Junction (**Tsomet 'Eeron**). Pop. 550.

ma'an|eh/-eem מענה *nm* reply; response;

ma'apeel/-eem מעפיל *v pres* climb(s) to the top; (*pst* **he'epeel**; *fut* **ya'apeel**).

◇ **"ma'apeel/eem"** מעפיל *nm* "illegally" entered Jewish immigrant to Palestine under the British Mandate (1936-1948).

ma'ar|akh/-akheem מערך *nm* alignment; (*pl+of:* **-khey**).

◇ **(ha)ma'arakh** מערך *nm* (the) "Alignment", onetime political coalition between the Israel Labor Party and MAPAM.

ma'ar|akhah/-akhot מערכה *nf* **1.** act (in a play); **2.** campaign (milit. or polit.); (*+of:* **-ekhet/-khot**).

ma'ar|akhot מערכות *nf pl* systems; computerized systems; (*+of:* **-khot**).

(menat|e'akh/-akhat) ma'arakhot מנתח מערכות *nmf* systems analyst; (*pl+of:* **-khey** *etc*).

(neetoo'akh) ma'arakhot ניתוח מערכות *nm* systems analysis.

(sheedood) ma'arakhot שידוד מערכות *nm* radical reform.

ma'arav/-eem מארב *nm* ambush.

ma'arav מערב *nm* west.

(artsot ha) ma'arav ארצות המערב *nf pl* the W. lands.

(derom) ma'arav (*or:* **drom** *etc*) דרום־מערב *nm* southwest.

(medeenot ha) ma'arav מדינות המערב *nf pl* the W. states.

(tsefon) ma'arav צפון מערב *nm* northwest.

ma'aravah מערבה *adv* westward; to the W.

ma'aravee/-t מערבי *adj* W.

◇ **(kotel) ma'aravee** (*or:* **ha-kotel ha** *etc*) see ◇ **kotel ma'aravee**.

ma'araveet le- מערבית ל־ *adv* W. of.

(dromeet-) ma'araveet le- דרומית־מערבית ל־ *adv* southwest of.

(tsefoneet-) ma'araveet le- צפונית־מערבית ל־ *adv* northwest of.

ma'arbolet (*npr* **me'arbolet**) מערבולת *nf* whirlpool.

ma'arvon/-eem מערבון *nm* Western (movie); (*pl+of* **-ey**).

ma'areekh/-ah מאריך **1.** *adj* prolonging; **2.** *v pres* prolongs (*pst* **he'ereekh;** *fut* **ya'areekh**).

(kevel/kvaleem) ma'areekh/-eem כבל מאריך *nm* extension-cable; extension-cord (electric.).

(khoot/-eem) ma'areekh/-eem חוט מאריך *nm* extension cord (electric).

ma'areekh/-ah מעריך *v pres* **1.** appreciate(s); **2.** estimates; value(s); (*pst* **he'ereekh;** *fut* **ya'areekh**).

ma'areekh/-eem מעריך *nm* assessor; appraiser; (*pl+of:* **-ey**).

ma'areets/-ah מעריץ *nmf* admirer; (*pl+of:* **-ey**).

◇ **ma'areev** מעריב *nf* daily evening prayer (known in Yiddish as "Mayriv" or "Mariv").

ma'ar|ekhet/-akhot מערכת *nf* . **1.** system; **2.** editorial board; **3.** time-table.

ma'ar|ekhet/-khot 'eeton/-eem מערכת עיתון editorial board of a newspaper.

ma'arekhet ha-'eekool מערכת העיכול *nm* the digestive system.

ma'ar|ekhet/-khot keleem מערכות כלים *nf* set of instruments.

ma'ar|ekhet/-khot reev'on/-eem מערכת רבעון *nf* editorial board of a quarterly magazine.

ma'ar|ekhet/-khot shavoo'on/shvoo'oneem מערכת שבועון *nf* editorial board of a weekly publication.

ma'arekhet shnaton מערכת שנתון *nf* editorial board of a yearbook.

ma'ar|ekhet/-khot yarkhon/-eem מערכת ירחון *nf* editorial board of a monthly magazine.

(geder) ma'arekhet גדר מערכת *nm* fence that is part of a border-guarding system.

(mazkeer/-at ha) ma'arekhet מזכיר המערכת *m/f* managing editor.

ma'arkhon/-eem מערכון *nm* one-act play; (*pl+of:* **-ey**).

ma'as/-ah/-tee מאס *v* loathed; despised; (*pres* **mo'es;** *fut* **yeem'as**).

ma'as/-eem מעש *nm* deed; action; (*pl+of:* **-ey**).

□ **Ma'as** (Ma'as) מעש *nm* village (est. 1952) in the Sharon, 4 km S. of **Petakh-Teekvah**. Pop. 649.

ma'asar/-eem מאסר *nm* arrest; (*pl+of:* **-ey**).

ma'asar 'al tenay מאסר על תנאי *nm* suspended prison sentence.

ma'asar be-fo'al (*f=p*) מאסר בפועל *nm* actual prison sentence.

ma'asar 'olam מאסר עולם *nm* life imprisonment; life-sentence.

(pekood|at/-ot) ma'asar פקודת מאסר *nf* arrest warrant.

ma'asee|yah/-yot מעשייה *nf* tale; fairy-tale; (*+of:* **-yat**).

ma'as|eh/-eem מעשה *nm* **1.** deed; action; **2.** story.

ma'aseh be- מעשה ב־ the story goes...; once upon a time...

ma'as|eh/-ey bere'sheet מעשה בראשית *nm* the (act of) Creation (Genesis).

ma'as|eh/-eem megoon|eh/-eem מעשה מגונה *nm* indecent act.

ma'aseh merkavah מעשה מרכבה *nm* the complicate machinations (of forming a government).

ma'as|eh/-ey neeseem מעשה ניסים *nm* sheer miracle.

ma'aseh/-ey koondes מעשה קונדס *nm* practical joke.

ma'aseh/-ey rama'oot מעשה רמאות *nm* fraud.

ma'aseh/-ey remeeyah מעשה רמייה *nm* fraud.

ma'aseh satan מעשה שטן *nm* bad luck.

ma'aseh/-ey sdom מעשה סדום *nm* act of sodomy.

(be-efes) ma'aseh באפס מעשה *adv* with nothing to do.

(bee-sh'at) ma'aseh בשעת מעשה *adv* in the very act of...

(halakhah le) ma'aseh הלכה למעשה *adv* putting theory into practice; immediate application.

(le-akhar) ma'aseh לאחר מעשה *adv* post factum.

(seepoor ha) ma'aseh סיפור המעשה *nm* the story of how it happened.
ma'asee/-t מעשי *adj* practical.
ma'aseek/-ah מעסיק *v pres* **1.** employ(s); **2.** keep(s) busy; (*pst* **he'eseek;** *fut* **ya'aseek).**
ma'aseek/-eem מעסיק *nm* employer (*pl+of:* **-ey).**
(mas) ma'aseekeem מס מעסיקים *nm* employment tax; employers tax.
(akh|ot/-ayot) ma'as|eet/-yot אחות מעשית *nf* practical nurse.
ma'as|er/-rot מעשר *nm* tithe.
ma'asheem/-ah מאשים *v pres* accuse(s); blame(s); (*pst* **he'esheem;** *fut* **ya'asheem).**
ma'asheem/-ah מאשים *nmf* accuser; prosecutor.
ma'at|afah/-afot מעטפה *nf* envelope; (*+of:* **-efet).**
ma'ateh/-eem מעטה *nm* wrap; (*pl+of:* **-ey).**
ma'ats|amah/-amot מעצמה *nf* big power (state); (*+of:* **-emet).**
ma'atsar/-eem מעצר *nm* arrest; detention.
ma'atsar/-ey bayeet מעצר בית *nm* house arrest.
ma'atseev/-ah מעציב **1.** *adj* saddening; **2.** *v pres* sadden(s); (*pst* **he'etseev;** *fut* **ya'atseev).**
ma'ats|emet/-mot 'al מעצמת על *nf* superpower.
ma'atsor/-eem מעצור *nm* **1.** impediment; stopper; **2.** *[colloq.]* car-brakes; (*pl+of:* **-ey).**
ma'av|ak/-akeem מאבק *nm* struggle; (*pl+of:* **-key).**
ma'ava|yeem מאוויים *nm pl* longing; desire; (*+of:* **-yey).**
ma'av|ar/-areem מעבר *nm* passage; (*pl+of:* **-rey).**
ma'av|ar/-rey gvool מעבר גבול *nm* frontier crossing;
ma'av|ar/-rey khatsayah (*npr* **khatseeyah)** מעבר חצייה *nm* pedestrian crossing.
(bekheen|at/-ot) ma'avar בחינת מעבר *nf* intermediate examination.
(geel ha) ma'avar גיל המעבר *nm* transition age.
(te'ood|at/-ot) ma'avar תעודת מעבר *nf* pass; laissez-passer.
ma'aveed/-ah מעביד *v pres* **1.** employ(s); **2.** make(s) (one/people) work; (*pst* **he'eveed;** *fut* **ya'aveed).**
ma'aveed/-eem מעביד *nm* employer.
ma'ayan (*npr* **ma'yan)/-ot** מעיין *nm* spring; source.
□ **Ma'ayan Barookh** see □ **Ma'yan Barookh.**
□ **Ma'ayan Kharod** see □ **Ma'yan Kharod.**
□ **Ma'ayan Tsevee** see □ **Ma'yan Tsevee.**
ma'azan/-eem מאזן *nm* balance-sheet; (*pl+of:* **ma'azney).**
ma'az|an/-ney bokhan מאזן בוחן *nm* trial balance sheet.
ma'azeen/-ah מאזין *v pres* listen(s); (*pst* **he'ezeen;** *fut* **ya'azeen).**
ma'azeen/-eem מאזין *nm* listener; (*pl+of:* **-ey).**
□ **Ma'barot** *cpr* of the correct name □ **Ma'abarot** (see above).
mab|at/-ateem מבט *nm* look; glimpse; (*pl+of:* **-tey).**
mabat/-eem khatoof/-eem מבט חטוף *nm* quick glance.
"Mabat" (*full name:* **"Mabat la-khadashot")** מבט לחדשות *nm* the evening news program on Israeli TV.
nekood|at/-ot mabat נקודת מבט *nf* point of view.
mabeet/-ah מביט *v pres* look(s); looking; (*pst* **heebeet;** *fut* **yabeet).**
□ **Maboo'eem** (Mabbu'im) מבועים *nm* rural center (est. 1958) in NW Negev on **Bet-Kamah Neer Mosheh** road. Pop. 195.
mabool מבול *nm* flood.
mabsoot/-ah מבסוט *adj (Arab.) [slang]* pleased; contented.
mad/-ey מד־ *nm (prefix)* gauge; -meter.
mad/-ey govah מד־גובה *nm* altimeter.
mad/-ey or מד־אור *nm* light-meter.
mad|a'/-a'eem מדע *nm* science; (*pl+of:* **-'ey).**
(eesh/anshey) mada' איש מדע *nm* scientist.
madad/-eem מדד *nm* index; c.o.l. (cost of living) index.
mad|ad/-edah/-adetee מדד *v* measured; (*pres* **moded;** *fut* **yeemdod).**
madad/-ey ha-mekheereem מדד המחירים *nm* price-index.
◇ **madad ha-mekheereem la-tsarkhan** מדד המחירים לצרכן the official Consumer's Price Index, made public in Israel on the 15th of every month.
◇ **madad/-ey yoker ha-beneeyah** מדד יוקר הבנייה *nm* Construction Costs Index which usually affects the costs of housing.
madad/-ey yoker ha-meekhyah מדד יוקר המחיה *nm* cost-of-living (CoL) Index.
mada'ee/-t מדעי *adj* scientific.
madaf/-eem מדף *nm* shelf; (*pl+of:* **-ey).**
mad'an/-eet מדען *nmf* scientist; (*pl:* **-eem;** *+of:* **-ey).**
(le) maday למדי *adv* enough; sufficiently.
madbeek/-ah מדביק *adj* **1.** infectious; **2.** sticky; **3.** overtaking.
madbeek/-ah מדביק *v pres* **1.** infect(s); **2.** glue(s); **3.** overtake(s); (*pst* **heedbeek;** *fut* **yadbeek).**
madbek|ah/-ot מדבקה *nf* label; stamp hinge; sticker; (*+of:* **-at).**
madee|'akh/-khah מדיח **1.** *nmf* instigator; **2.** *v pres* 1. dismiss(es); fire(s); 2. lead(s) astray; (*pst* **heedee'akh;** *fut* **yadee'akh).**
madee|'akh (*npr* **medee|'akh)/-khey keleem** מדיח כלים *nm* dishwasher.
mad'eeg/-ah מדאיג **1.** *adj* worrying; disturbing; **2.** *v pres* worry(-s); (*pst* **heed'eeg;** *fut* **yad'eeg).**
mad|eem מדים *nm pl* uniform (clothing); (*+of:* **-ey).**
madeed/-eem מדיד *nm* gauge; caliber; calibre; (*pl+of:* **-ey).**

madeer/-ah מדיר *v pres* **1.** prohibit(s); forbid(s); **2.** keep(s) away; (*pst* **heedeer**; *fut* **yadeer**).

madeer/-ah ragl|av/-eha מדיר רגליו *v* keeps out from.

mad'ey ha-khevrah מדעי החברה *nm pl* social sciences.

mad'ey ha-makhshev מדעי המחשב *nm pl* computer sciences.

mad'ey ha-medeenah מדעי המדינה *nm pl* political science.

mad'ey ha-roo'akh מדעי הרוח *nm pl* humanities; liberal arts.

mad'ey ha-teva' מדעי הטבע *nm pl* natural sciences.

mad'ey ha-yahadoot מדעי היהדות *nm pl* Judaic studies; Jewish studies.

mad'ger|ah/-ot מדגרה *nf* incubator; (*+of:* **-at**).

madkhan/-eem מדחן *nm* parking meter; (*pl+of:* **-ey**).

madkh|ef/-afeem מדחף *nm* propeller; (*pl+of:* **-afey**).

mad|khom/-ey-khom מדחום *nm* thermometer.

madleef/-ah מדליף **1.** *nmf* informer (letting information leak out to the media); **2.** *v pres* informs; passes out information; (*pst* **heedleef**; *fut* **yadleef**).

madleek/-ah מדליק *v pres* light(s) match/candle; (*pst* **heedleek**; *fut* **yadleek**).

madleek/-ah מדליק *adj [slang]* turning one on.

madon/-eem מדון *nm* quarrel; strife.

(reev oo) madon ריב ומדון *nm pl* strife and contention.

madoo'a מדוע *adv* why.

madood/medoodah מדוד *adj* measured; gauged.

mador/medoreem מדור *nm* section (*+of:* **medor/-ey**).

madpees/-ah מדפיס *v pres* print(s); (*pst* **heedpees**; *fut* **yadpees**).

madpees/-eem מדפיס *nm* printer; (*pl+of:* **-ey**).

madp|eset/-asot מדפסת *nf* printer (computer-operated).

madreekh/-ah מדריך **1.** *nmf* instructor; guide; (*pl:* **-eem/-ot**; *nf+of:* **-at**; *pl+of:* **-ey**); **2.** *v pres* instruct(s); (*pst* **heedreekh**; *fut* **yadreekh**).

madreg|ah/-ot מדרגה *nf* stair; (*+of:* **-at**).

(be-shefel ha) madregah בשפל המדרגה *adv* in a very bad state; of a low degree.

madrekh|ah (*npr* **meedrakh|ah**) מדרכה *nf* sidewalk; (*+of:* **meedrekhet**).

(le) ma'et למעט *adv* except for.

◇ **(ha)MAFDAL** see ◇ **(ha)meeflagah ha-dateet-le'oomeet**.

maf'eel/-ah מפעיל *v pres* activate(s); (*pst* **heef'eel**; *fut* **yaf'eel**).

maf'eel/-eem מפעיל *nm* promoter; operator; activator; (*+of:* **-ey**).

(be) mafgee'a' במפגיע *adv* imperatively.

mafgeen/-ah מפגין **1.** *nmf* demonstrator (*pl+of:* **-ey**); **2.** *v pres* demonstrate(s); (*pst* **heefgeen**; *fut* **yafgeen**).

mafkee|'a'/-'ah מפקיע *v pres* **1.** overcharge(s); **2.** confiscate(s); requisition(s); (*pst* **heefkee'a**; *fut* **mafkee'a**).

mafkee|'a/-ey she'areem מפקיע שערים *nm pl* profiteer.

mafkeed/-ah מפקיד *v pres* entrust(s); deposit(s); (*pst* **heefkeed**; *fut* **yafkeed**).

mafkeed/-eem מפקיד *nm* depositor; (*pl+of:* **-ey**).

maflee/-'ah מפליא **1.** *adj & adv* amazing; **2.** *v pres* amaze(s); (*pst* **heeflee**; *fut* **yaflee**).

maflet/-eem מפלט *nm* exhaust pipe; (*pl+of:* **-ey**).

(le) mafre'a' למפרע **1.** *adv* retrospectively; **2.** *adv [colloq.]* in advance.

mafree|'a'/-'ah מפריע *v pres* disturbs; interferes; (*pst* **heefree'a'**; *fut* **yafree'a'**).

(be-en) mafree'a באין מפריע *adv* unhindered; with no one disturbing.

mafreed/-ah מפריד *adj* separating; dividing; *v pres* separate(s); (*pst* **heefreed**; *fut* **yafreed**).

(kav/-eem) mafreed/-eem קו מפריד *nm* dash (punctuation).

mafsek/-eem מפסק *nm* switch (electric. or mechanical).

◇ **(ha-se'oodah ha) mafseket** see ◇ **(ha)se'oodah (ha)mafseket**.

mafte|'akh/-khot מפתח *nm* **1.** key; **2.** index.

mafte'akh ha-'eenyaneem מפתח העניינים *nm* index; contents.

(deer|ah/-ot bee-demey) mafte'akh דירה בדמי מפתח *nf* rent-controlled apartment (subject to key-money).

(demey) mafte'akh דמי מפתח *nm pl* key-money (for admission into rent-controlled tenancy).

('emd|at/-ot) mafte'akh עמדת מפתח *nf* key position.

maftee|'a/-'ah מפתיע **1.** *adj* surprising; **2.** *v pres* surprise(s); (*pst* **heeftee'a**; *fut* **yaftee'a**).

(be) maftee'a במפתיע *adv* surprisingly.

◇ **mafteer** (*or:* **"haftarah"**) מפטיר *nm* honoring a member of the congregation called upon to chant solo a selected Bible chapter, on a Saturday or holiday, after the regular Torah reading has been concluded.

maftseets/-eem מפציץ *nm* bomber.

maftseets/-ah מפציץ *v pres* bombard(s); (*pst* **heeftseets**; *fut* **yaftseets**).

mag|a'/-a'eem מגע *nm* contact; touch; (*pl+of:* **-'ey**).

mag|a'/-a'eem meenee/-yeem מגע מיני *nm* sexual intercourse.

('ad'shot) maga' עדשות מגע *nf pl* contact-lenses.

magaf/-ayeem מגף *nm pl* boot; (*pl+of:* **-ey**).

magal/-eem מגל *nm* sickle; (*pl+of:* **-ey**).

□ **Magal** (Maggal) מגל *nm* kibbutz (est. 1953), W. of Samaria Hills, 8 km N. of Tulkarm **(Toolkarem)** on road to 'Iron Junction **(Tsomet 'Eeron)**. Pop. 473.

□ **Ma'galeem** (Ma'galim) מעגלים *nm* rural center (est. 1958) in NW Negev, 3 km from haGaddi Junction (**Tsomet Ha-gadee**). Pop. 125.

magash/-eem מגש *nm* tray; (*pl+of:* **-ey**).

◇ **MAGAV** מג"ב *nm* (*acr of* **Meeshmar ha-GVool** משמר הגבול) Israeli Police Frontier Force.

magav/-eem מגב *nm* wiper (car); (*pl+of:* **-ey**).

magbeel/-ah מגביל **1.** *adj* limiting; **2.** *v pres* limits; (*pst* **heegbeel**; *fut* **yagbeel**).

magbeer/-ah מגביר *v pres* strengthens reinforces; (*pst* **heegbeer**; *fut* **yagbeer**).

magbee|t/-yot מגבית *nf* fund-raising campaign.

(ha) magbeet המגבית *nf* the U.J.A. (United Jewish Appeal).

magber/-eem מגבר *nm* amplifier; (*pl+of:* **-ey**).

magber/-ey kol מגבר קול *nm* **1.** megaphone; **2.** loudspeaker.

□ **Magdee'el** (Magdi'el) מגדיאל *nm* onetime agricultural settlement (est. 1924) which since 1964 has become part of Hod ha-Sharon.

magdeel/-ah מגדיל *v pres* magnify/-ies; enlarge(s); (*pst* **heegdeel**; *fut* **yagdeel**).

(zekhookheet) magdeletמגדלת זכוכית *nf* magnifying glass.

magee|'a'/-'ah מגיע *v pres* arrives; reaches; is due; (*pst* **heegee'a'**; *fut* **yagee'a'**).

magee'a' le-/lee מגיע ל־ *v pres* it is owed to... (me/you/him *etc*).

magee'a' mee- מגיע מ־ *v pres* it is due from... (me/you/him *etc Pe).*

(kamah) magee'a' כמה מגיע how much; how much do I owe you?

magee|'ah/-heem מגיה *nm* proofreader.

magee|'ah/-hah מגיה *v pres* proofread(s); (*pst* **heegee'ah**; *fut* **yagee'ah**).

mageed/-ah מגיד *v pres* tell(s); (*pst* **heegeed**; *fut* **yageed**).

mageed/-at 'ateedot מגיד עתידות *nmf* fortune-teller.

mag'eel/-ah מגעיל **1.** *adj* disgusting; **2.** *v pres* disgust(s); (*pst* **heeg'eel**; *fut* **yag'eel**).

mageesh/-ah מגיש **1.** *nmf* waiter/-ress; steward(ess); **2.** *v pres* submits; brings; (*pst* **heegeesh**; *fut* **yageesh**).

mageester/-eem מגיסטר *nm* magister; (M.A., M.Sc. *etc*).

magef|ah/-ot מגפה *nf* epidemic; (*+of:* **-at**).

□ **Magen** מגן *nm* kibbutz (est. 1949) in NE Negev, 3 km S. of Magen Junction (**Tsomet Magen**). Pop. 413.

mag|en/-eeneem מגן *nm* shield; (*pl+of:* **-eeney**).

◇ **magen-daveed** מגן־דוד *nm* Star of David; (*lit.*) Shield of David.

◇ **"magen-daveed adom** מגן־דוד־אדום *nm* Israel equivalent of the Red Cross (*lit.:* Red Shield of David).

□ **Magen Sha'ool** (Magen Sha'ul) מגן שאול *nm* village (est. 1976) in the Yizre'el Valley, 10 km S. of 'Afula. Pop. 283.

mag|evet/-avot מגבת *nf* towel; (*pl+of:* **-vot**).

mag|hets/-hatseem מגהץ *nm* pressing-iron; (*colloq pron:* **megahets**); (*pl+of:* **-hatsey**).

maglev/-eem מגלב *nm* whip; (*pl+of:* **-ey**).

magletch|ah/-ot מגלצ'ה *nf [slang]* sliding board.

magref|ah/-ot מגרפה *nf* rake; trowel; (*+of:* **-at**).

magres|ah/-ot מגרסה *nf* grinding-mill; crusher; (*+of:* **-at**).

magsh|eem/-ah מגשים *v pres* fulfill(s): implement(s); (*pst* **heegsheem**; *fut* **yagsheem**).

magsheem מגשים *v pres [slang]* it rains.

□ **Magsheemeem** (Magshimim) מגשימים *nm* village (est. 1947) in Sharon, 3 km S. of **Petakh-Teekvah**. Pop. 363.

mahal|akh/-akheem מהלך *nm* **1.** move; **2.** walk; **3.** distance; **4.** gear (auto); (*pl+of:* **-khey**).

(be) mahalakh במהלך *adv* (drivers SLG) in gear.

mahalakheem otomateeyeem מהלכים אוטומטיים *nm pl* automatic gear (in cars).

mahaloom|ah/-ot מהלומה *nf* blow; (*+of:* **-at**).

mahapakh/-eem (*npr* **mahpakh/-eem**) מהפך *nm* reversal.

mahapekh|ah/-ot (*npr* **mahpekh|ah/-ot**) מהפכה *nf* revolution; upheaval; (*+of:* **-at**).

mahapkhan/-eet (*npr* **mahpkhan**) מהפכן *nmf* revolutionary.

mahapkhanee/-t (*npr* **mahpekhanee**) מהפכני *adj* revolutionary; .

mahatal|ah/-ot מהתלה *nf* farce; practical joke; (*+of:* **-at**).

mahee (*contraction of two words:* **mah hee**) מהי what is she/it?

maheer/meheerah מהיר *adj* fast; speedy.

maher מהר *adv* fast.

(kheesh) maher חיש מהר *adv* very quickly; in a jiffy.

(yoter) maher יותר מהר *adv* faster.

mahoo (*contraction of two words:* **mah hoo?**) מהו what is he/it?

mahool/meholah מהול *adj* diluted; blended.

mahoo|t/-yot מהות *nf* essence; nature.

mahootee/-t מהותי *adj* essential; substantial.

□ **Majd-el-Kroom** (Majd el Kurum) מג'ד אל־קרום *nm* large Arab village in Galilee's Bet ha-Kerem Valley, 3 km NW of **Karmee'el**. Pop. 7,680.

□ **Majdal Shams** מג'דל שאמס *nf* largest Druze township in N. of Golan Heights, located on SE slopes of Mount Hermon (**Khermon**). Pop. 6,540.

mak|ah/-ot מכה *nf* blow; stroke; (*+of:* **-at**).

(heenkheet/-ah) makah הנחית מכה *v* dealt a blow; (*pres* **mankheet makah**; *fut* **yankheet makah**).

(refoo'ah le) makah רפואה למכה *nf* anticipation of trouble; cure for anticipated ill.

◇ **"makabee" ("Maccabi")** מכבי *nf* oldest (founded in Palestine 1894) and most popular of Jewish sport-unions. Named after **Yehoodah ha-Makabee** - leader of successful Jewish uprising against Greek occupation in 165 BCE (see ◇ **khanookah**). Counts, together with its branches spread everywhere in the Jewish world, a membership of 400,000. Has its world headquarters in own quarter, **Kefar ha-Makabeeyah**, in Ramat Gan.

◇ **Makabeeyah (Maccabiah)** מכביה *nf* "Jewish Olympic Games" regarded as the most important periodic event in Jewish sports. Started in Palestine in 1932 by "Maccabi" and under its auspices, immediately won world acclaim. Since 1953 held regularly in Israel, every four years. The 13th "Bar-Mitzvah" Maccabiah (1989) enjoyed the participation of 4,500 athletes from 45 countries in 30 sport branches. The 14th is scheduled for 1993.

makaf/-eem מקף *nm* hyphen.

makak/-eem מקק *nm* cockroach; (*pl+of:* **-ey**).

makam מכ"ם *nm* radar (*acr of* **Motse Keevoon 'oo-Merkhak** (מוצא כיוון ומרחק).

makar/-eem מכר *nm* acquaintance; (*pl+of:* **-ey**).

makat/-ot mena' מכת מנע *nf* preventive blow; preemptive strike.

makat shemesh מכת שמש *nf* sunstroke.

makbeel/-ah מקביל **1.** *adj* parallel; running parallel; **2.** *v pres* run(s) parallel; (*pst* **heekbeel**; *fut* **yakbeel**).

makbeel (*etc*) **et peney** מקביל את פני *v pres* welcomes on arrival.

makbeeleem מקבילים *nm pl* parallel bars (sport).

(kaveem) makbeeleem קווים מקבילים *nm pl* parallel lines.

makde|'akh/-kheem מקדח *nm* drill bit; (*pl+of:* **-khey**).

makdekh|ah/-ot khashmal|eet/-yot מקדחה חשמלית *nf pl* electric drill.

makdem|ah/-ot (*npr:* **meekdam|ah/-ot**) מקדמה *nf* advance payment; (*+of:* **meekdem|et/-ot**).

makeef/-ah מקיף **1.** *adj* comprehensive; **2.** *v pres* comprises; encompasses; (*pst* **heekeef**; *fut* **yakeef**).

makeer/-ah מכיר *nmf* acquaintance; (*pl+of:* **-ey**).

makeer/-ah מכיר *v pres* **1.** recognizes; admits; **2.** knows; (*pst* **heekeer**; *fut* **yakeer**).

makeer (*etc*) **todah** מכיר תודה *v pres* am/are/is grateful.

mak|el/-lot מקל *nm* stick; rod.

(sookaree|yah/-yot 'al) makel סוכרייה על מקל *nf* lollypop.

makh|a/-'ah/-atee kaf/kapayeem (*p=f*) מחא כף *v* clapped hands; applauded; (*pres* **mokhe** *etc*; *fut* **yeemkha** *etc*).

makh|ah/-tah/-eetee מחה *v* **1.** protested; **2.** wiped off; (*pres* **mokheh**; *fut* **yeemkheh**).

makhak/mekhak|eem מחק *nm* eraser; (*pl+of:* **-ey**).

makhak/-ah/-tee מחק *v* erased; rubbed out; (*pres* **mokhek**; *fut* **yeemkhok**).

◇ **MAKHAL** מח"ל *acr of* **1. Meetnadvey KHoots La-arets** - מתנדבי חוץ לארץ *nm pl* the 1947-48 movement of Jewish volunteers from the Diaspora coming to aid of the Palestinian Jews in their fight for survival; **2. Meef'al ha-KHeesakhon Le-beenyan** מפעל החיסכון לבנייה *nm* the Saving for Building Program started in 1970-1973 by the Housing Ministry entitling beneficiaries to subsidized housing; **3.** Traditional balloting code-name (*acr of* **Meeflegot Kheroot ve-Leeberaleeyeem** (מפלגות חירות וליברליים) used by the **"Kheroot"** (Herut) and Liberal parties in their joint voting-list as the Likkud Bloc.

makhal/-ah/-tee מחל *v* forgave; absolved; (*pres* **mokhel**; *fut* **yeemkhol**).

makhal|ah/-ot מחלה *nf* illness; sickness; disease; (*+of:* **-at**).

(khoofshat) makhalah חופשת מחלה *nf* sick leave.

makhalat ha-nefeelah מחלת הנפילה *nf* epilepsy.

makhal|at/-ot lev מחלת־לב *nf* heart disease.

makhal|at/-ot nefesh מחלת־נפש *nf* mental disease.

makhalat yam מחלת־ים *nf* seasickness.

makhalee/-'ah מחליא **1.** *adj* sickening; **2.** *v pres* make(s) one sick; (*pst* **hekhlee**; *fut* **yakhlee**).

makhaleef/-ah מחליף **1.** *nmf* replacement; substitute; **2.** *v pres* 1. exchange(s); replace(s); (*pst* **hekhleef**; *fut* **yakhleef**).

makhaleek/-ah מחליק *v pres* **1.** smooth(s); **2.** glide(s); skate(s); (*pres* **hekheleek**; *fut* **yakhaleek**).

makhaleek|ayeem מחליקיים skates (*pl+of:* **-ey**).

makhaleesh/-ah מחליש *v pres* weaken(s); (*pst* **hekheleesh**; *fut* **yakhaleesh**).

makhalok|et/-ot מחלוקת *nf* dispute; controversy.

(sela' ha) makhaloket סלע המחלוקת *nm* bone of contention; apple of discord.

(shanooy/shnooyah be) makhaloket שנוי במחלוקת *adj* controversial; disputable.

(yeeshoov) makhaloket יישוב מחלוקת *nm* settling a dispute/controversy

makhalot zeeknah מחלות זיקנה *nf pl* gerontological (old age) diseases.

makhamat (*npr* **me-khamat**) מחמת on account of...

makhamat safek (*npr* **me-khamat**) מחמת ספק for the benefit of the doubt.

makhamee/-'ah מחמיא **1.** *adj* complimentary; **2.** *v pres* compliment(s) (*pst* **hekhemee**; *fut* **yakhamee**).

makhanak מחנק *nm* suffocation;

□ **Makhanayeem (Mahanayim)** מחניים **1.** *nm* kibbutz (founded 1892 and re-established 1939) in Upper Galilee, 3 km NE of Rosh Pina **(Rosh-Peenah)**. Pop. 432; **2.** *nm* small airfield nearby.

makhan|eh/-ah מחנה *v pres* park(s); parking; (*pst* **hekhenah**; *fut* **yakhaneh**).

makhan|eh/-ot מחנה *nm* camp.

makhan|eh/-ot 'eemooneem מחנה אימונים *nm* training camp;

makhan|eh/-ot hashmadah מחנה השמדה *nm* extermination camp;

makhan|eh/-ot reekooz מחנה ריכוז *nm* concentration camp;

makhan|eh/-ot tsava מחנה צבא *nm* army camp;

makhan|eh/-ot tsva'ee/-yeem מחנה צבאי *nm* military camp;

makhan|eh/-ot kayeets (*or:* **-kayeet**) מחנה קיץ *nm* summer camp.

makhan|eh-ot nofesh מחנה נופש *nm* recreation camp.

□ **Makhaneh Yateer** מחנה יתיר *nm* coop. village (est. 1979) located in hilly forest area, 27 km S. of Hebron (**Khevron**). Pop. 432.

makhar מחר *adv* tomorrow;

makhar/-ah/-tee מכר *v* sold; (*pres* **mokher**; *fut* **yeemkor**; *(kh=k)*).

makhar-mokhrotayeem מחר־מוחרתיים *adv* tomorrow or the day after.

makhareed/-ah מחריד *adj* terrifying; frightful.

makhareed מחריד *v pres* terrify/-ies; frighten(s); (*pst* **hekhereed**; *fut* **yakhareed**).

makhareef/-ah מחריף *adj* growing more acute; exacerbating.

makhareef/-ah מחריף *v pres* aggravate(s); exacerbate(s); (*pst* **hekhereef**; *fut* **yakhareef**).

makhareesh/-ah מחריש *adj* silent; *v pres* keep(s) silent; (*pst* **hekhereesh**; *fut* **yakhareesh**).

makhareesh (*etc*) **oznayeem** מחריש אוזניים *adj* deafening.

makharesh|ah/-ot מחרשה *nf* plough; plow; (*+of:* **-at**).

makharoz|et/-ot מחרוזת *nf* necklace; string.

makhaseh/-eem מחסה *nm* shelter; protection.

makhasheev/-ah מחשיב *v pres* value(s); attach(es) importance; (*pst* **hekhesheev**; *fut* **yakhasheev**).

(**mele'khet**) **makh'shevet** מלאכת מחשבת *nf* work of art; masterpiece.

makhat/mekhat|eem מחט *nf* needle; (*pl+of:* **-ey**).

makhat/-eem מח"ט *nm* (*acr of* **Mefaked KHateevah** מפקד חטיבה) brigadeer.

makhats מחץ *nm* shock; severe wound.

makhats מחץ *adv* SLG terribly.

(**ko'akh**) **makhats** כוח מחץ *nm* shock-troops; assault force.

(**ploog|at/-ot**) **makhats** פלוגת מחץ *nf* shock-troop.

(**rosh/-ey**) **makhats** ראש מחץ *nm* spearhead (army).

makhats/-ah/-tee מחץ *v* smashed; crushed; (*pres* **mokhets**; *fut* **yeemkhats**).

makhatseet מחצית *nf* **1.** half; **2.** half-time (sport).

makhaveer/-ah מחוויר *adj* paling; *v pres* pale(s); (*pst* **hekheveer**; *fut* **yakhaveer**).

makhav|eh/-eem מחווה *nm* **1.** index; arrow; pointer (*pl+of:* **-ey**); **2.** *erron. pronounced* (*npr* **mekhv|ah/-ot**) *nf* gesture; act.

makhaz|ay/-a'eet מחזאי *nm* dramatist; playwright.

makhaz|eh/-ot מחזה *nm* **1.** play (theatr.); **2.** sight.

makhazeh ta'too'eem מחזה תעתועים *nm* mirage.

◇ **makhazor/-eem** מחזור *nm* (in Yiddish: "makhzer") prayer-book for Jewish holidays.

makhazor/-eem מחזור *nm* **1.** cycle; **2.** graduating class; (*pl+of:* **-ey**).

makhazor ha-dam מחזור הדם *nm* blood circulation.

makhazor ha-matbe'a מחזור המטבע *nm* money in circulation.

makhazor kaspee מחזור כספי *nm* turnover; cash flow.

makhazor shenatee מחזור שנתי *nm* annual turnover.

makhzoreeyoot מחזוריות *nf* cycle; recurrence; periodicity.

(**ba**) **makhazor** במחזור *adv* in circulation;

(**yats|a/-'ah/-a'tee me-ha**) **makhazor** יצא מהמחזור went out of circulation.

(**le**) **makhbeer** למכביר *adv* abundantly.

makhb|eret/-arot מחברת *nf* copybook.

makhbes|ah/-ot (*npr* **meekhbas|ah/-ot**) מכבסה *nf* laundry; (*+of:* **meekhbes|et/-ot**).

makhbesh/-eem מכבש *nm* steamroller; press.

makhbet/-eem מחבט *nm* **1.** carpet beater; **2.** tennis racket; (*pl+of:* **-ey**).

makhbet/-ey tenees מחבט טניס *nm* tennis racket.

makhbo/-'eem מחבוא *nm* hiding-place.

(**meeskhak/-ey**) **makhbo'eem** משחק מחבואים *nm* hide-and-seek game.

makhbosh מחבוש *nm [slang]* jail; arrest.

makh'eev/-ah מכאיב *adj* painful; *v pres* pain(s) (*pst* **heekh'eev**; *fut* **yakh'eev**).

mak'hel|ah/-ot מקהלה *nf* choir; chorus; (*+of:* **-at**).

makhl|ah/-ot מחלה *nf* illness; sickness; disease; (*+of:* **-at**).

(**khoofshat**) **makhlah** חופש מחלה *nm* sick leave.

makhl|akah/-akot מחלקה *nf* **1.** section; **2.** squad; **3.** ward; (*+of:* **-eket**).

makhlakah (*etc*) **keeroorgeet** מחלקה כירורגית *nf* surgery ward.

makhlakah peneemeet מחלקה פנימית *nf* internal ward.

makhlaktee/-t מחלקתי *adj* departmental.

makhlat ha-nefeelah מחלת הנפילה *nf* epilepsy.

makhl|at/-ot lev מחלת־לב *nf* heart disease.

makhl|at/-ot nefesh מחלת־נפש *nf* mental disease.

makhlat yam מחלת־ים *nf* seasickness.

makhlatsot מחלצות *nf pl & adv* fine clothing; gala dress.

makhl|avah/-avot מחלבה *nf* dairy; (*+of:* **-evet**).

makhlee/-'ah מחליא **1.** *adj* sickening; **2.** *v pres* make(s) one sick; (*pst* **hekhlee**; *fut* **yakhlee**).

makhleef/-ah מחליף *nmf* replacement; substitute.

makhleef/-ah מחליף *v pres* **1.** exchange(s); **2.** replace(s); (*pst* **hekhleef**; *fut* **yakhleef**).

makhleek/-ah מחליק *v pres* **1.** smooth(s) **2.** glide(s); skate(s); (*pres* **hekhleek**; *fut* **yakhleek**);;

makhleek|ayeem מחליקיים *nm pl* skates (*pl+of:* **-ey**).

makhlev|ah/-ot (*npr* **makhlav|ah/-ot**) מחלבה *nf* dairy; (*+of:* **makhlevet**).

makhlok|et/-ot מחלוקת *nf* dispute; controversy;

(sela' ha) makhloket סלע המחלוקת *nm* bone of contention; apple of discord.

(shanooy/shenooyah be) makhloket שנוי במחלוקת *adj* controversial; disputable.

(yeeshoov) makhloket יישוב מחלוקת *nm* settling a dispute/controversy.

makhlot zeeknah מחלות זיקנה *nf pl* gerontological (old age) diseases.

makhma|'ah/-'ot מחמאה *nf* compliment.

makhmad leebee מחמד ליבי *nm* my darling.

makhmadee מחמדי *nm* my darling.

makhmat (*npr* **me-khamat**) מחמת on account of...

makhmat (*npr* **me-khamat**)**safek** מחמת ספק the benefit of the doubt.

makhmee/-'ah מחמיא **1.** *adj* complimentary; **2.** *v pres* compliment(s); (*pst* **hekhmee**; *fut* **yakhmee**).

makhmeer/-ah מחמיר *v pres* aggravate(s); (*pst* **hekhmeer**; *fut* **yakhmeer**).

makhmeer (*etc*) **'eem** מחמיר עם *v pres* is being harsh on; is being difficult/demanding; 2 . *v pres* is getting more serious.

makhmeer (*etc*) **ve-holekh** מחמיר והולך *v pres* is getting worse and worse.

makhnak מחנק *nm* suffocation.

makhna'oot מחנאות *nf* camping.

□ **Makhnayeem** see □ **Makhanayeem**.

makhnees/-ah מכניס **1.** *adj* profitable; paying; **2.** *v pres* put(s) in; introduce(s); **3.** *v pres* bring(s) in (financially); (*pst* **heekhnees**; *fut* **yakhnees**).

makhnees/-at orkheem מכניס אורחים *adj* hospitable.

makhn|eh/-ah מחנה *v pres* park(s); parking; (*pst* **hekhena**; *fut* **yakhneh**).

makhn|eh/-ot מחנה *nm* camp;

makhn|eh/-ot eemooneem מחנה אימונים *nm* training camp;

makhn|eh/-ot hashmadah מחנה השמדה *nm* extermination camp.

makhn|eh/-ot kayeets (*or:* **kayeet**) מחנה קיץ *nm* summer camp; summer recreation camp.

makhn|eh-ot nofesh מחנה נופש *nm* recreation camp.

makhn|eh/-ot reekooz מחנה ריכוז *nm* concentration camp;

makhn|eh/-ot tsava מחנה צבא *nm* army-camp; □ **Makhneh Yateer** see □ **Makhaneh Yateer**.

makhn|eh/-ot tseva'ee/-yeem מחנה צבאי *nm* military camp;

makhog/-eem מחוג *nm* hand (of clock or watch); (*pl+of:* **-ey**).

makhokh מחוך *nm* corset; (*pl+of:* **-ey**).

makhol/mekholot מחול *nm* dance; (*+of:* **mekhol**).

(yats|a/-'ah be) makhol יצא במחול *v* danced; started dancing; (*pst* **yotse** *etc*; *fut* **yetse** *etc*).

makhon/mekhoneem מכון *nm* institute; (*+of:* **mekhon/-ey**).

makhoor/-ah מכור *adj* **1.** sold; sold out; **2.** addicted; **3.** devoted.

makh'ov/-eem מכאוב *nm* pain; grief; (*pl+of:* **-ey**).

makhoz/mekhozot מחוז *nm* district; region; (*+of:* **mekhoz**).

makhpeer/-ah מחפיר *adj* disgracing; shameful.

makhpel|ah/-ot מכפלה *nf* product of a multiplication.

□ **(Me'arat ha) Makhpelah** see □ **Me'arat ha-Makhpelah**.

makhp|elet/-alot מכפלת *nf* hem.

makhper/-eem מחפר *nm* excavator (mechan.); (*pl+of:* **-ey**).

makhra'|ah/-ot מחראה *nf* latrine; public toilet (*+of:* **-at**).

makhree|'a'/-'ah מכריע *adj* decisive; *v pres* determined; (*pst* **heekhree'a'**; *fut* **yakhree'a'**).

(borer) makhree'a' בורר מכריע *nm* umpire.

(ha-krav ha) makhree'a' הקרב המכריע *nm* (the) decisive battle.

makhree|'akh/-khah מכריח *v pres* compel(s); force(s); (*pst* **heekhr ee'akh**; *fut* **yakhree'akh**).

makhreed/-ah מחריד **1.** *adj* terrifying; frightful; **2.** *v pres* terrif|y/-ies; frighten(s); (*pst* **hekhreed**; *fut* **yakhreed**).

makhreef/-ah מחריף **1.** *adj* growing more acute; exacerbating; **2.** *v pres* aggravate(s); exacerbate(s); (*pst* **hekhreef**; *fut* **yakhreef**).

makhreesh/-ah מחריש **1.** *adj* silent; **2.** *v pres* keep(s) silent; (*pst* **hekhreesh**; *fut* **yakhreesh**).

makhreesh/-at oznayeem מחריש אוזניים *adj* deafening.

makhresh|ah/-ot מחרשה *nf* plough; plow; (*+of:* **-at**).

makhret|ah/-ot מחרטה *nf* lathe; (*+of:* **-at**).

makhroz|et/-ot מחרוזת *nf* necklace; string.

makhsan/-eem מחסן *nm* warehouse; store; (*pl+of:* **-ey**).

makhsan/-ey 'aroobah מחסן ערובה *nm pl* bonded warehouse.

makhsana|'ee/-'eet מחסנאי *[colloq.]* *nm* storekeeper; (*pl+of:* **-'ey**).

makhsan|ay/-eem מחסנאי *nm* storekeeper; (*pl+of:* **-a'ey**).

makhsan|eet/-yot מחסנית *nf* magazine (ammunition).

makhseef/-ah מכסיף **1.** *adj* silver-haired; **2.** *v pres* gray(s); (*pst* **heekhseef**; *fut* **yakhseef**).

makhseer/-ah מחסיר *v pres* omit(s); (*pst* **hekhseer**; *fut* **yakhseer**).

makhseh/-eem מחסה *nm* shelter; protection.

□ **Makhseyah (Mahseya)** מחסיה *nm* village (est. 1950) in E. part of Judean Hills, 2 km E. of Bet-Shemesh. Pop. 241.

makh'sh|avah/-avot מחשבה *nf* thought; (+*of*: **-evet**).

(be) makh'shavah tekheelah במחשבה תחילה *adv* deliberately; with premeditation.

makh'sheel/-ah מכשיל *v pres* cause(s) to fail; (*pst* **heekh'sheel**; *fut* **yakh'sheel**).

makh'sheer/-ah מכשיר *v pres* **1.** prepare(s); train(s); **2.** makes "Kosher"; (*pst* **heekh'sheer**; *fut* **yakh'sheer**).

makh'sheer/-eem מכשיר *nm* tool; instrument; (*pl+of*: **-ey**).

makh'sheev/-ah מחשיב *v pres* value(s); attach(es) importance; (*pst* **hekh'sheev**; *fut* **yakh'sheev**).

makh'shel|ah/-ot מכשלה *nf* obstacle; ruin.

makh'sh|ev/-aveem מחשב *nm* computer; (*pl+of*: **-avey**).

makh'shev (*etc*) **eeshee** מחשב אישי *nm* P.C. personal computer.

(mad'ey ha) makh'shev מדעי המחשב *nm pl* computer sciences.

(mele'khet) makh'shevet מלאכת מחשבת *nf* work of art; masterpiece.

makh'shevon/-eem מחשבון *nm* calculator; (*pl+of*: **-ey**).

makh'shevon/-ey kees מחשבון כיס *nm* pocket calculator.

makhsof/-eem מחשוף *nm* decolletage; (*pl+of*: **-ey**).

makhsom/-eem מחסום *nm* barrier; road block; (*pl+of*: **-ey**).

makhsor/-eem מחסור *nm* want; shortage; (*pl+of*: **-ey**).

makht|eret/-arot מחתרת *nf* underground; underground movement (politic.).

makhtesh/-eem מכתש *nm* **1.** mortar; **2.** crater (geolog.).

makh'tsav|ah/-ot מחצבה *nf* quarry; (+*of*: **-at**).

makh'tsel|et/-alot מחצלת *nf* mat.

makh'ts|av/-aveem מחצב *nm* ore; mineral; (*pl+of*: **-avey**).

makh'tsev|ah/-ot מחצבה *nf* quarry; (+*of*: **-at**).

makhvat/-ot מחבת *nf* frying pan;

makhveh/-eem מחווה *nm* pointer; indicator;

makhza|y/-'ee (*cpr* **makhza|'ee/-'eem**) מחזאי *nm* playwright; (*pl+of*: **-'ey**).

makhz|eh/-ot מחזה *nm* **1.** play (theatr.); **2.** sight.

makhzeh ta'too'eem מחזה תעתועים *nm* mirage.

◇ **makhzor/-eem** see *npr* ◇ **makhazor/-eem**.

makhzor/-eem מחזור *nm* **1.** cycle; **2.** graduating class; (*pl+of*: **-ey**).

makhzor ha-dam מחזור הדם *nm* blood circulation.

makhzor ha-matbe'a מחזור המטבע *nm* money in circulation.

makhzor kaspee מחזור כספי *nm* turnover; cash flow.

makhzor shenatee מחזור שנתי *nm* annual turnover.

(ba) makhzor במחזור *adv* in circulation.

(yats|a/-'ah/-a'tee me ha) makhzor יצא מהמחזור went out of circulation.

makhzoree/-t מחזורי *adj* recurrent.

makhzoreeyoot מחזוריות *nf* cycle; recurrence; periodicity.

makle|'a'/-'eem מקלע *nm* machine-gun; (*pl+of*: **-ey**).

(tat-) makle|'a'/-'eem תת־מקלע *nm* sub-machine-gun; (*pl+of*: **-ey**).

maklet/-eem מקלט *nm* receiver; receiving-set; (*pl+of*: **-ey**).

maklet/-ey radyo מקלט רדיו *nm* radio-set; radio-receiver.

maklet/-ey televeezeeyah מקלט טלוויזיה *nm* TV-set; TV-receiver.

maklet/-ey veedyo מקלט וידאו *nm* video-tape recorder.

maklot kveesah מקלות כביסה *nm pl* clothes pegs.

(shot|er/-rey) makof שוטר מקוף *nm* beat-policeman.

makolet מכולת *nf* grocery.

(khan|oot/-yot) makolet חנות מכולת *nf* grocery-store; grocery.

makom/mekomot מקום *nm* place; location; (+*of*: **mekom**).

makom/mekomot panooy/penooyeem מקום פנוי *nm* available seat; vacant place.

makom/mekomot tafoos/tefooseem מקום תפוס *nm* occupied seat; taken place.

('ad efes) makom עד אפס מקום *adv* (full) to capacity.

('al ha) makom על המקום *adv* on the spot.

(en) makom אין מקום *nm* places; there isn't a seat left.

"(ha)makom" המקום *nm* Heaven; the Allmighty.

(ha) makom panooy המקום פנוי the seat/place is free.

(ha) makom tafoos המקום תפוס the seat/place is taken.

(ha-'eem ha) makom panooy? האם המקום פנוי? is the seat free?

(ha-'eem ha) makom tafoos? האם המקום תפוס? is the seat taken?

(mar'eh) makom מראה מקום *nm* reference.

(memale/-t) makom ממלא מקום *nmf* deputy; acting-; replacement.

makosh מכוש *nm* pick-ax.

makor/-eem מקור *nm* **1.** bird's beak; **2.** firing pin (of a rifle); (*pl+of*: **-ey**).

makor/-ot מקור *nm* **1.** source; **2.** original; (+*of*: **mekor/-ot**).

makor reeshon מקור ראשון *nm* first-hand source.

(neekoo|y/-eem ba) makor ניכוי במקור *nm* deduction at the source (of income-tax).

makot מכות *nf pl* beatings; (*sing:* **makah**).

(heeflee/-'ah) makot הפליא מכות *v* beat one up; (*pres* **maflee** *etc; fut* **yaflee** *etc*).

(heerb|eets/-eetsah/-atstee) makot הרביץ־מכות *v* gave a beating; smacked; spanked; (*pres* **marbeets etc/fut yarbeets** *etc*).

(saf|ag/-gah/-agtee) makot ספג מכות *v* took a beating; (*pres* **sofeg** *etc; fut* **yeespog** *etc p=f*).

makpeed/-ah מקפיד **1.** *adj* meticulous; exacting; **2.** *v pres* insist(s) on; was strict about; (*pst* **heekpeed;** *fut* **yakpeed**).

makpets|ah/-ot מקפצה *nf* diving board; trampoline; (*+of:* **-at**).

makree|'akh/-khah מקריח **1.** *adj* balding; **2.** *v pres* bald; (*pst* **heekree'akh;** *fut* **yakree'akh**).

makreen/-ah מקרין **1.** *adj* radiating; radiant; **2.** *v pres* radiate(s); (*pst* **heekreen;** *fut* **yakreen**).

makren/-eem מקרן *nm* projector; (*pl+of:* **-ey**).

makren/-ey shekoofeeyot מקרן שקופיות *nm* slide-projector.

makren/-ey serateem מקרן סרטים *nm* movie projector; film projector.

makseem/-ah מקסים *adj* charming; enchanting; *v pres* charm(s); enchant(s); enchant(s); (*pst* **heekseem;** *fut* **yakseem**).

makseemalee/-t מקסימלי *adj* maximal.

makseemoom מקסימום *adv* maximum; at most.

maktsef/-eem מקצף *nm* eggbeater; (*pl+of:* **-ey**).

mal/-ah/-tee מל *v* circumcized; (*pres* **mal;** *fut* **yamol**).

mal|a/-ah/-e'tee מלא *v* was filled with; (*pres* **male;** *fut* **yeemla**).

mal'ah shanah le- מלאה שנה ל־ it has been a year since.

malakh/-eem מלח *nm* sailor; (*pl+of:* **-ey**).

mala|kh/-khah/-akhtee מלך *v* reigned; ruled; (*pres* **molekh;** *fut* **yeemlokh**).

mal'akh/-eem מלאך *nm* angel; (*pl+of:* **-ey**).

mal'akhee|t/-yot מלאכית *nf [slang]* female-angel (TV character).

mal'akhootee/-t מלאכותי *adj* artificial.

(hadgarah) mal'akhooteet הדגרה מלאכותית *nf* artificial incubation.

(hafrayah) mal'akhooteet הפריה מלאכותית *nf* artificial insemination.

(hanshamah) mal'akhooteet הנשמה מלאכותית *nf* artificial respiration.

(hazra'ah) mal'akhooteet הזרעה מלאכותית *nf* artificial insemination.

malan מלאן *adv [slang]* plenty; plenty of.

malbeen/-ah מלבין *v pres* whiten(s); stand(s) out in its whiteness; (*pst* **heelbeen;** *fut* **albeen**).

malbeen/-ah מלבין *adj* whitening; shining in its whiteness.

malbeen/-ah (*etc*) **paneem** מלבין פנים *v pres* insult(s) in public.

malben/-eem מלבן *nm* rectangle; (*pl+of:* **-ey**)

◇ **"Malben"** מלבן *nf* AJDC subsidiary providing aid to elderly people in Israel.

malbenee/-t מלבני *adj* rectangular.

malboosh/-eem מלבוש *nm* dress; clothing;

male/mele'ah מלא *adj* full; ample.

male/mele'at (*npr* **mle/-'at**) **khayeem** מלא חיים *adj* lively; full of life.

(be-feh) male *(f=p)* בפה מלא *adv* expressly.

◇ **(keteev) male** see ◇ **keteev male**.

malee'akh/meleekh|eem מליח *nm* herring; (*pl+of:* **-ey**).

malgezah/-ot מלגזה *nf* lift truck; (*+of:* **-at**).

malkah/melakhot (*colloq. pron.:* **malkot**) מלכה *nf* queen.

□ **Malkeeyah** (Malkiyya) מלכיה *nm* kibbutz (est. 1949) near Lebanese border, 6 km W. of **Tsomet Ko'akh** (Ko'ah Junction). Pop. 425.

mal|kat/-khot yofee מלכת יופי־ *nf* beauty queen.

□ **Malkeeshoo'a'** מלכישוע *nm* kibbutz (est. 1976) in the **Geelbo'a** hills, S. of **Ma'aleh Geelbo'a**.

malkheen/-ah מלחין **1.** *nmf* composer (of music); **2.** *v pres* compose(s) music; (*pst* **heelkheen;** *fut* **yalkheen**).

malkh|em/-ameem מלחם *nm* soldering iron; (*pl+of* **-amey**).

malkhoo|t/-yot מלכות *nf* kingdom; realm.

(hod) malkhoot הוד מלכות *nm* royal majesty.

(hod) malkhoot|o/-ah הוד מלכותו *nmf* His/Her Majesty; H.M.

malkod|et/-ot מלכודת *nf* trap.

◇ **"malkosh"** מלקוש *nm* the spring rain (as distinguished from the autumn rain, the **"yoreh"**).

malkot מלקות *nf pl* flogging; lashing.

malmalah מלמלה *nf* muslin; fine cloth.

malon/melonot מלון *nm* hotel (*+of:* **melon**).

(bet/batey) malon בית מלון *nm* hotel.

mal'oo ... shaneem le- מלאו ... שנים ל (so and so) is ... years old.

maloo'akh/melookhah מלוח *adj* salty; salted.

(dag/-eem) maloo'akh/melookheem דג מלוח *nm* herring.

malsheen/-ah מלשין **1.** *nmf* informer; stool-pigeon; **2.** *v pres* inform(s); (*pst* **heelsheen;** *fut* **yalsheen**).

malv|eh/-ah מלווה **1.** *nmf* lender; money-lender; **2.** *v pres* lend(s) money; (*pst* **heelvah;** *fut* **yalveh**).

malveh/-eem be-reebeet מלווה בריבית *nm* **1.** loan shark; usurer; **2.** (*lit.*) lends at interest.

mamash ממש *adv* really; actually.

mamashee/-t ממשי *adj* real; actual.

mamashoot ממשות *nf* reality.

mam'eer/-ah ממאיר *adj* malignant (disease, growth).

mamlakh|ah/-ot ממלכה *nf* kingdom; (*+of:* **mamlekhet**).

◇ **(ha)mamlakhah ha-me'ookhedet** הממלכה המאוחדת *nf* the United Kingdom.

mamlakhtee/-t ממלכתי *adj* governmental; state-.

(bet/batey sefer) mamlakhtee/-yeem בית־ספר ממלכתי *nm* government-school.

mamlakhteeyoot ממלכתיות *nf* statehood.

mamon/memonot ממון *nm* big money.

mamreets/-ah ממריץ *adj* stimulating; bolstering.

mamreets/-ah ממריץ *v pres* stimulate(s); bolster(s); (*pst* **heemreets**; *fut* **yamreets**).

mamtak/-eem ממתק *nm* sweet.

mamteen/-ah ממתין **1.** *adj* waiting; **2.** *v pres* wait(s); (*pst* **heemteen**; *fut* **yamteen**).

mamteer/-ah ממטיר *v pres* rain(s); pour(s) upon; (*pst* **heemteer**; *fut* **yamteer**).

mamter|ah/-ot ממטרה *nf* sprinkler (*+of:* **-at**).

mamtsee/-'ah ממציא *v pres* **1.** invent(s); **2.** send(s); **3.** supply(ies); (*pst* **heemtsee**; *fut* **yamtsee**).

mamtsee/-'eem ממציא *nm* inventor; (*pl+of:* **-ey**).

mamzer/-ah ממזר *nmf* **1.** bastard; **2.** *[slang] adj* tricky fellow; a devil of a guy/girl.

◇ **mamzer/-et** ממזר *nmf* illegitimate child of an adulterous or incestuous union (in a strictly religious sense).

mamzeree/-t ממזרי *adj* cunning; bastardly.

man מן *nm* manna (Bibl.).

man amereeka'ee מן אמריקאי *[colloq.] nm* popcorn.

man de-hoo מן דהוא (Aramaic) *pron m* someone; somebody.

man|ah/-tah/-eetee מנה *v* counted; (*pres* **moneh**; *fut* **yeemneh**).

man|ah/-ot מנה *nf* portion; lot; (*+of:* **men|at/-ot**).

man|a'/-'ah/-a'tee מנע *v* prevented; (*pres* **mone'a**; *fut* **yeemna'**).

man|ah/-ot akharonah מנה אחרונה *nf* dessert;

man|ah/-ot 'eekareet/-yot מנה עיקרית *nf* main course; main dish.

man|ah/-ot reeshon|ah/-ot מנה ראשונה *nf* entree (at a meal).

(keeb|el/-lah/-altee) manah קיבל מנה *v pres* was reprimanded; (*pres* **makabel** *etc*; *fut* **yekabel** *etc*).

(saf|ag/-gah/-agtee) manah ספג מנה *v* got his/her *etc* comeuppance; (*prs* **sofeg** *etc*; *fut* **yeespog** *etc*; *f=p*).

mandat/-eem מנדט *nm* mandate; certificate of election.

◇ **(tekoofat ha) mandat** see ◇ **tekoofat ha-mandat**.

◇ **(bee-tekoofat ha) mandat** see ◇ **(bee)tekoofat ha-mandat**.

◇ **(bee-zeman ha) mandat** see ◇ **(bee)zeman ha-mandat**.

mandoleen|ah/-ot מנדולינה *nf* mandolin; (*+of:* **-at**).

mang|anon/-enoneem מנגנון *nm* **1.** mechanism; **2.** personnel; staff; (*+of:* **-enon/-enoney**).

mangeen|ah/-ot מנגינה *nf* tune; melody; (*+of:* **-at**).

man'heeg/-eem מנהיג *nm* leader; (*pl+of:* **-ey**).

man'heeg|ah/-ot מנהיגה *nf* leader (woman); (*+of:* **-at/-ot**).

man'heegoot/-yot מנהיגות *nf* leadership.

mankal/-eet מנכ"ל *nmf* (*acr of* **MeNahel/-et KLalee/-t** מנהל כללי) general manager; director general; executive vice-president (*pl:* **-eem**; *pl+of:* **-ey**).

mankh|eh/-ah מנחה *nmf* moderator.

mano'a'/meno|'eem מנוע *nm* engine; motor; (*+of:* **-'a'/-'ey**).

mano|'a'/-'ey (*npr* **meno|'a/-'ey**) **deezel** מנוע דיזל *nm* Diesel-engine.

(seer|at/-ot) mano'a' סירת מנוע *nf* motorboat.

mano'akh מנוח *nm* rest; quiet.

(eyn|o/-ah noten/-et) *or* **(lo noten/-et** *etc*) **mano'akh** אינו/לא נותן מנוח *v pres* incessantly bother(s); (*pst* **lo natan** *etc*; *fut* **lo yeeten** *etc*).

(ha) mano'akh המנוח *adj* the late... the deceased (male).

manof/menof|eem מנוף *nm* crane; lever; (*pl+of:* **-ey**).

manoo ve-gamroo מנו וגמרו *v pst pl* (they) ultimately decided.

manoo'a/menoo'ah מנוע *adj* barred; precluded.

man'ool/-eem מנעול *nm* lock; (*pl+of:* **-ey**).

manooy/menoo|yeem מנוי *nm* subscriber; (*pl+of:* **-yey**).

manooy ve-gamoor מנוי וגמור *adv & adj* it has been firmly decided.

(demey) manooy דמי מנוי *nm pl* subscription-fees.

manos מנוס *nm* escape; refuge.

(eyn) manos אין מנוס *adv* inevitably.

(meeshlo|'akh/-khey) manot משלוח מנות *nm* "Purim"-gift: package of food delicacies sent to friends on Purim; (known in Yiddish as "Shalekh-Munis").

ma'of מעוף *nm* **1.** flight; **2.** vision.

ma'on/me'onot מעון *nm* **1.** home; residence; **2.** hostel; (*+of:* **me'on**).

◇ **ma'on/me'onot** מעון *nm* daytime nursery (privately owned and paid for) for 2-3 year-olds.

□ **Ma'on** מעון *nm* coop. village (est. 1981) in S. Hebron hills, 12 km SE of **Keeryat-Arba'**.

ma'ookh/me'ookhah מעוך *adj* crushed; squeezed.

ma'or/me'orot מאור *nm* light; (*+of:* **me'or**).

ma'oos/me'oosah מאוס *adj* repulsive; loathsome.

ma'oz/ma'oozeem מעוז *nm* fortress; bastion.

□ **Ma'oz Khayeem (Ma'oz Hayyim)** מעוז חיים *nm* kibbutz (est. 1937) in the Bet-She'an Valley, 5 km E. of Bet-She'an proper. Pop. 574.

mapah/-ot מפה *nf* **1.** geographic map; **2.** tablecloth; **(+*of:* -at).**

mapakh nefesh מפח נפש *nm* disappointment.

mapal/-eem מפל *nm* fall; drop; **(*pl+of:* -ey).**

mapal/-ey mayeem מפל מים *nm* cascade; waterfall.

mapal/-ey metakh מפל מתח *nm* tension drop.

mapal|ah/-ot מפלה *nf* defeat; **(+*of:* -at).**

(nakh|al/-lah/-altee) mapalah/-ot נחל מפלה *v* suffered a defeat; was defeated; **(*pres* nokhel *etc; fut* yeenkhal *etc*).**

◇ **MAPAM** מפ"ם see ◇ **meefleget ha-po'aleem ha-me'ookhedet.**

mapee|t/-yot מפית *nf* napkin; serviette; **(+*of:* -yat).**

mapol|et/-ot מפולת *nf* collapse; fall.

('ee/-yey) mapolet עיי מפולת *nm* debris.

mapookhee|t/-yot מפוחית *nf* harmonica.

mar/-at מר *nmf* Mr. / Mrs.

mar/ah מר *adj* bitter.

mar/-at nefesh מר־נפש *adj* embittered.

marah מרה *nf* gall; bile.

marah shekhorah מרה שחורה *nf* melancholy; hypochondria.

(avney) marah אבני מרה *nf pl* gallstones;

(ha-teepah ha-) marah הטיפה המרה *nf* **1.** *[colloq.]* liquor; **2.** (*lit.*) the bitter drop.

(kees ha) marah כיס המרה *nm* gall-bladder.

mar|'ah/-'ot מראה *nf* mirror; **(+*of:* -'at).**

mar|ad/-dah/-adetee מרד *v* rebelled; revolted; **(*pres* mored; *fut* yeemrod).**

marak/merakeem מרק *nm* soup; **(+*of:* merak/meerkey).**

mar|akh/-khah/-akhtee מרח *v* *[slang]* **1.** smeared; performed superficially; **2.** bribed; **3.** swindled; **(*pres* more'akh; *fut* yeemrakh).**

maranan ve-rabotay! מרנן ורבותי! my learned friends!

marat מרת Mrs.

mar|at/-tah/-atetee מרט *v* plucked (hair, feathers); **(*pres* moret; *fut* yeemrot).**

marb|eh/-ah מרבה *v pres* **1.** multiplies; **2.** does too often; **(*pst* heerbah; *fut* yarbeh).**

marb|eh/-y raglayeem מרבה רגליים *nm* centipede;

(le) marbeh ha-hafta'ah למרבה ההפתעה *adv* to everyone's great surprise.

(le) marbeh ha-pele למרבה הפלא *adv* most miraculously.

(le) marbeh ha-plee'ah למרבה הפליאה *adv* to everyone's great bewilderment.

(le) marbeh ha-tsa'ar למרבה הצער *adv* to our great distress; sad to say.

marbeet מרבית *nf* most of; the major part of;

mardan/-eet מרדן *nmf* rebel.

mardanee/-t מרדני *adj* rebellious.

mardeem/-ah מרדים **1.** *adj* anesthetic; soporific; **2.** *v pres* puts one to sleep; anesthetizes; **(*pst* heerdeem; *fut* yardeem).**

(rof|e/-'ah) mardeem/-ah רופא מרדים *nmf* anesthesiologist.

mar|'eh/-'ot מראה view.

mar|'eh/-'ey makom/mekomot מראה מקום *nm* bibliographical reference.

(yef|eh/-at) mar'eh יפה מראה *adj* good-looking.

mareer/mereerah מריר *adj* bitter.

mar'eet-'ayeen מראית עין *adv* seemingly; ostensibly.

margalee|t/-yot מרגלית *nf* jewel; gem.

□ **Margaleeyot** מרגליות *nm* village (est. 1951) in Upper Galilee, near the Lebanese border, 3 km W. of **Keeryat Shmonah**. Pop. 276.

marganee|t/-yot מרגנית *nf* daisy.

margareen|ah/-ot מרגרינה *nf* margarine; **(*pl+of:* -at).**

margash מרגש *nm* disposition; feeling.

(ekh ha) margash איך המרגש *[colloq.]* how are you? how do you feel?

margelot מרגלות *nf pl* bottom of bedstead; place for the feet (in bed).

(le) margelot ha-har למרגלות ההר *adv* at the foot of the mountain.

(le) margelot ha-meetah למרגלות המיטה *adv* at the bottom of the bed.

margem|ah/-ot מרגמה *nf* mortar; mine-thrower;

margo'a מרגוע *nm* rest; repose.

(bet/batey) margo'a בית מרגוע *nm* resthouse; sanatorium.

mar'heev/-ah מרהיב *adj* resplendent.

mar'heev/-ah מרהיב *v pres* dare(s); embolden(s); **(*pst* heer'heev; *fut* yar'heev).**

mar'heev/-at 'ayeen מרהיב עין *adj* spectacular.

mar'heev/-ah (*etc*) 'oz מרהיב עוז *v pres* care(s); gather(s) the courage to.

markeev/-eem מרכיב *nm* component; **(*pl+of:* -ey).**

markeev/-ah מרכיב *v pres* assemble(s); **(*pst* heerkeev; *fut* yarkeev).**

markeev/-ah מרקיב *adj* putrid; rotting away; *v pres* rot(s) away; **(*pst* heerkeev; *fut* yarkeev).**

mar'kheek/-ah מרחיק *v pres* remove(s); rejects(s); **(*pst* heer'kheek; *fut* yarkheek).**

mar'kheek/-ah (*etc*) lekhet מרחיק לכת *v pres* go(es) far.

mar'kheek/-at lekhet מרחיק לכת *adj* far-reaching; far-fetched.

mar'kheek/-at re'oot מרחיקת ראות *adj* far sighted.

◇ **Mar'kheshvan** מרחשוון *nm* correct, original name for **kheshvan**, the 2nd Jewish Calendar month (29 or 30 days; approx. Oct. Nov.).

markol/-eem מרכול *nm* supermarket; **(*pl+of:* -ey).**

markolee|t/-yot מרכולית *nf* mini-market.

markolet מרכולת *nf* merchandise.

marneen/-ah מרנין **1.** *adj* gladdening; **2.** *v pres* gladden(s); **(*pst* heerneen; *fut* yarneen).**

marom/merom|eem מרום *nm* **1.** height; **2.** heaven; **(*pl+of:* -ey).**

mar'om/-eem מרעום *nm* fuse; **(*pl+of:* -ey).**

maroo'akh/-ah מרוח *adj* **1.** smeared; pasted; **2.** *[slang]* superficial; not genuine; inauthentic.
('anee/-yah) marood/meroodah עני מרוד *nmf* extremely poor person.
◇ **maror** מרור *nm* bitter herb tasted symbolically (to experience the bitterness of Egyptian slavery) at the ceremonial Passover dinner **(seder pesakh).**
maroo|t/-yot מרות *nf* authority; rule; mastery.
(mekabel/-et) maroot מקבל מרות *v pres* submit(s) to authority; (*pst* **keebel** *etc*; *fut* **yekabel** *etc*).
marpe מרפא *nm* healing.
marpe|'ah/-'ot (*npr* **meerpa'ah/-'ot**) מרפאה *nf* clinic.
marpedee|yah/-ot מרפדייה *nf* upholstery workshop.
marpek/-eem מרפק *nm* elbow; (*pl+of:* **-ey**).
marpekeem מרפקים *nm pl [slang]* push; influence.
Mars מרס *nm* March.
martef/-eem מרתף *nm* basement; cellar; (*pl+of:* **-ey**).
martsef|ah/-ot (*npr* **meertsaf|ah/-ot**) מרצפה *nf* tile; (*+of:* **meertsef|et/-ot**)
marts|eh/-eem מרצה *nm* lecturer; (*pl+of:* **-ey**).
marts|eh/-ah מרצה *v pres* lecture(s); (*pst* **heertsa**; *fut* **yartseh**).
marts|eh/-eem bakheer/bekheereem מרצה בכיר *nm* senior lecturer.
marts|e'a'/-e'eem מרצע *nm* awl (*pl+of:* **-e'ey**).
(yatsa ha) martse'a meen ha-sak יצא המרצע מן השק the secret is out.
marvad/-eem מרבד *nm* carpet; bedspread; (*pl+of:* **-ey**).
(bet/-batey) marze'akh בית מרזח *nm* saloon; tavern.
marzev/-eem מרזב *nm* drainpipe; (*pl+of:* **-ey**).
mas/mees|eem מס *nm* tax; (*pl+of:* **-ey**).
mas booleem מס בולים *nm* stamp duty.
◇ **mas 'erekh moosaf** מס ערך מוסף *nm* Value Added Tax (also known by its *acr.*: MA'AM i.e. V.A.T.).
mas hakhnasah מס הכנסה *nm* income tax.
◇ **mas hashbakhah** see hetel hashbakhah.
mas/-meesey khaver מס־חבר *nm* membership fee/-s.
◇ **mas keneeyah** מס־קנייה *nm* sales tax; (*lit.*) purchase tax.
◇ **mas ma'aseekeem** מס מעסיקים *nm* Tax on Employers (levied from expenditure).
◇ **mas nesee'ot** מס נסיעות *nm* Travel Tax.
◇ **mas reevkhey hon** מס רווחי הון *nm* capital gains tax.
mas rekheeshah מס רכישה *nm* tax on acquisition of immovables.
mas rekhoosh מס רכוש *nm* property tax.
mas sfatayeem מס שפתיים *nm* lip service.
◇ **mas shevakh** מס שבח *[colloq.] abbr.* of ◇ **mas shevakh mekarke'een** (see below).
◇ **mas shevakh mekarke'een** מס שבח מקרקעין *nm* tax on profit accrued through early re-sale (less than four full years after acquisition) of immovable property by private owner (not professional real-estate dealer).
(heet|eel/-eelah/-altee) mas הטיל מס *v* imposed a tax; (*pres* **mateel mas**; *fut* **yateel mas**).
(gavah/-tah/-eetee) mas גבה מס *v* collected a tax; (*pres* **goveh mas**; *fut* **yeegbeh mas** *(b=v)*).
masa/-'eem (*also:* **-ot**) משא *nm* load; burden.
masa'/-'eem (*also:* **'ot**) מסע *nm* voyage; trip (*pl+of:* **mas'ey**).
mas|a'/-'ey tselav מסע צלב *nm* crusade.
mas|ah/-ot מסה *nf* mass; (*+of:* **masat**).
mas|ah/-ot מסה *nf* essay; trial (*+of:* **masat**).
masa oo-matan משא ומתן *nm* negotiation.
(mekhonee|t/-eeyot) masa מכונית משא *nf* truck. lorry.
(onee|yat/-yot) masa אוניית משא *nf* freighter.
(rak|evet/-vot) masa רכבת משא *nf* freight-train.
masad מסד *nm* basement; basis.
□ **Masadah** (Massada) מסדה *nm* kibbutz of the **"Kevootsah"** type (est. 1937), in the Jordan Valley, 4 km S. of Lake Tiberias. Pop. 392.
□ **Masadah** מסדה restored remnants of the most famous Jewish fortress of the Second Temple era. Built by King Herod on top of a particularly steep cliff in the Judean Desert, near the Dead Sea, 17 km S. of 'En Gedi **('En Gedee)**, it became later the last stronghold of Judean rebels resisting Roman rule. The prolonged Roman siege (A.D. 71-73) ended in a mass suicide by the rebels so as to avoid captivity. Masadah has ever since been regarded as a symbol of all-out Jewish patriotism.
masa'ee|t/-yot משאית *nf* truck; lorry.
masa'ee|t/-yot haramah משאית־הרמה *nf* lifting truck.
masaj/-eem מסאז' *nm* massage.
masajeestee|t/-yot מסאז'יסטית *nf [colloq.]* masseuse.
masa|kh/-keem מסך *nm* screen; curtain; (*pl+of:* **-key**).
masakh 'ashan מסך עשן *nm* smoke screen.
masakh ha-barzel מסך הברזל *nm* the Iron Curtain.
(ha) masakh ha-katan המסך הקטן *nm* the small (i.e. television) screen.
mas|ar/-rah/-artee מסר *v* delivered; transmitted; passed (*pres* **moser**; *fut* **yeemsor**).
masar (*etc*) **dokh/-ot** (*also:* **doo'akh/dokhot**) מסר דו"ח *v* reported; made one's report.
mas|'at/-'ot nefesh משאת־נפש *nf* ideal; ultimate aspiration.
mas|ay/-a'eet מסאי *mf* essayist; essays writer.
maseeg/-ah משיג *v pres* **1.** attains; **2.** obtains (*pst* **heeseeg**; *fut* **yaseeg**).
maseeg/meseeg|at gvool מסיג גבול *nmf* trespasser (*pl:* **-ey/-ot gvool**).
maseek (*npr* **meseek**) **ha-zeyteem** מסיק הזיתים *nm* olive harvest.

maseevee/-t מסיבי *adj* massive.
masekh|ah/-ot מסיכה *nf* mask; (*+of:* **-at**).
(neshef/neeshfey) masekhot נשף מסיכות *nm* masked ball.
masekh|et/-ot מסכת *nf* **1.** pageant; **2.** web; **3.** tractate of the Talmud.
mas'ey ha-tslav מסעי הצלב *nm pl* the Crusades.
masgeer/ah מסגיר *v pres* surrenders; betrays; extradites; (*pst* **heesgeer**; *fut* **yasgeer**).
masger/-eem מסגר *nm* locksmith (*pl+of:* **-ey**).
masgeree|yah/-yot מסגרייה *nf* metal-workshop (*+of:* **at**).
masgeroot מסגרות *nf* metal-work.
mash|'abeem משאבים *nm pl* resources; (*sing:* **'av**; *pl+of:* **-'abey**; *b=v*).
mash|ah/-tah/-eetee משה *v* pulled out of the water (*pres* **mosheh**; *fut* **yeemsheh**).
mashak/eem מש"ק *nm* (*acr of* **Mefaked SHe-'eyno Katseen** מפקד שאינו קצין) non-commissioned officer; N.C.O.
mash|akh/-khah/-akhtee משך *v* pulled; dragged; drew; attracted; (*pres* **moshekh**; *fut* **yeemshokh**).
mash|akh/-khah/-akhtee משח *v* annointed; smeared; (*pres* **moshe'akh**; *fut* **yeemshakh**).
mash|al/-lah/-altee משל *v* ruled; governed; (*pres* **moshel**; *fut* **yeemshol**).
mashal/meshaleem משל *nm* **1.** fable; **2.** proverb; (*pl+of:* **meeshley**).
mashal משל *adv* as if.
(derekh) mashal דרך משל *adv* for instance; figuratively.
(le) mashal למשל *adv* for instance; e.g.
(le) mashal ve-lee-shneenah למשל ולשנינה *adv* (becoming the) laughingstock; object of ridicule.
□ **Mash'abey Sadeh** (Mash'abbé Sadé) משאבי שדה *nm* kibbutz (est. 1947) in the Negev, 25 km S. of Beersheba, 14 km N. of **Sdeh Boker**. Pop. 451.
mash|av/-aveem משב blowing; gust; (*pl+of:* **-vey**).
mash|av/-vey roo'akh משב רוח *nm* breeze; gust of wind.
mash'a|v/-beem (*b=v*) משאב *nm* source; resource; (*pl+of:* **-bey**).
mashber/-eem משבר *nm* crisis; (*pl+of:* **-ey**).
mashder/-eem משדר *nm* radio-transmitter; transmitter; (*pl+of:* **-ey**).
mashee'akh/mesheekh|eem משיח *nm* Messiah; (*pl+of:* **-ey**).
(khevley) mashee'akh חבלי משיח *nm pl* throes of the Messiah.
(yemot ha) mashee'akh ימות המשיח *nm pl* messianic era.
mashehoo משהו something.
mash'en משען *nm* support; buttress.
mash'ev|ah/-ot משאבה *nf* pump.
□ **Mash'en** (Mash'en) משען *nm* village in S. seashore plain (est. 1950), 4 km E. of Ashkelon. Pop. 565.

mash'ev|at/-ot aveer משאבת־אוויר *nf* air-pump.
mash'ev|at/-ot mayeem משאבת־מים *nf* water-pump.
mash'ev|at/-ot delek משאבת־דלק *nf* fuel-pump.
mashgee|'akh/-khah משגיח **1.** *nmf* supervisor; (*f+of:* **-khat**; *pl:* **-kheem/-khot**); **2.** *v pres* 1. notice(s); **3.** *v pres* supervise(s); (*pst* **heeshgee'akh**; *fut* **yashgee'akh**).
◇ **mashgee|'akh/-khey** משגיח כשרות *nm* "kashress" supervisor (i.e. of "kosher" slaughtering).
mashger/-eem משגר *nm* launcher; launching-pad
mashger/-ey teeleem משגר טילים *nm* rocket-launcher.
mashkanta/-'ot משכנתא *nf* mortgage; (*+of:* **-at**).
◇ **mashkanta beeltee tsemoodah** משכנתא בלתי צמודה *nf* mortgage in which neither amount of loan nor rates are linked.
◇ **mashkanta mashleemah** משכנתא משלימה *nf* complementary (second) mortgage granted by a bank to a Ministry of Housing beneficiary, obtained under that Ministry's recommendation. As a rule, the terms of such a second mortgage are less favorable than those of the first.
◇ **mashkanta/-'ot tsemood|ah/-ot** משכנתא צמודה mortgage with amount of loan and rates linked to the CoL Index or to the Index of Construction Costs.
mashka'ot משקאות *nm pl* drinks (*sing* **mashkeh**).
mashka'ot kaleem משקאות קלים *nm pl* soft drinks; (*sing:* **mashkeh kal**).
mashka'ot khareefeem משקאות חריפים *nm pl* alcoholic drinks; (*sing:* **mashkeh khareef**).
mashka'ot meshakreem משקאות משכרים *nm pl* intoxicating liquors; (*sing:* **mashkeh meshaker**).
mashk|eh/-a'ot משקה *nm* drink; beverage.
mashkeef/-eem משקיף *nm* observer.
mashkeef/-ah משקיף *v pres* look(s) on; observe(s); (*pst* **heeshkeef**; *fut* **yashkeef**).
mashkeem/-ah משכים *v pres* rise(s) early; get(s) up early; (*pst* **heeshkeem**; *fut* **yashkeem**).
mash'kheet/-ah משחית *v pres* destroy(s); deprave(s); (*pst* **heesh'kheet**; *fut* **yash'kheet**).
(kelee/keley) mash'kheet כלי־משחית deadly instrument; tool of destruction.
(onee|yat/-yot) mash'kheet אוניית משחית *nf* destroyer (ship).
mash'khet|ah/-ot (*npr* **meesh'khat|ah/-ot**) משחטה *nf* slaughterhouse; .
mash'kh|etet/-atot משחתת *nf* destroyer (ship).
mash'kh|eez/-ezet משחיז *adj* sharpening.
mash'kheez/-ah משחיז *v pres* sharpen(s); (*pst* **heesh'kheez**; *fut* **yash'kheez**).
(even) mash'khezet אבן משחזת *nf* whetstone.
mashkof/-eem משקוף *nm* lintel; (*pl+of:* **-ey**).
mashkon/-eem משכון *nm* pawn; security.

mashkona|y/-'eem משכונאי *nm* pawnbroker.
mashleem/-ah משלים *adj* complementary.
mashleem/-ah משלים *v pres* complete(s); (*pst* **heeshleem;** *fut* **yashleem**).
◇ **(halva'ah) mashleemah** see ◇ **halva'ah mashleemah.**
◇ **(mashkanta) mashleemah** see ◇ **mashkanta mashleemah,** above.
mashma' משמע *prep* meaning that; i.e.
(doo-) mashma'ee/-t דו־משמעי *adj* ambiguous.
(khad-) mashma'ee/-t חד־משמעי *adj* unequivocal.
(rav-) mashma'ee/-t רב־משמעי *adj* meaningful.
(peshoot|o/-ah ke) mashma|'o/-'ah פשוטו כמשמעו simply meaning that...
mashma'oo|t/-yot משמעות *nf* significance; meaning.
(doo-) mashma'oo|t/-yot דו־משמעות *nf* ambiguity.
(khas|ar/-rat) mashma'oot חסר משמעות *adj* meaningless.
mashma'ootee/-t משמעותי *adj* significant; meaningful.
□ **Mashmee'a' Shalom** (Mashmi'a Shalom) משמיע שלום *nm* rural settlement (est. 1949), now part of **Beney-Re'em**, 5 km NE of **Keeryat Mal'akhee.**
mashmeets/-ah משמיץ *v pres* malign(s); slander(s); (*pst* **heeshmeets;** *fut* **yashmeets**).
mashmeets/-eem משמיץ *nm* maligner; slanderer; (*pl+of:* **-ey**).
mashnek/-eem משנק *nm* choke (motor-car); throttle; (*pl+of:* **-ey**).
mashookh/meshookhah משוך *adj* **1.** pulled; **2.** drawn (of a check).
mashot/meshot|eem משוט *nm* oar; (*pl+of:* **-ey**).
mashpee|'a'/-'ah משפיע *adj* influential; *v pres* influence(s); (*pst* **heeshpee'a';** *fut* **yashpee'a'**).
mashpeel/-ah משפיל **1.** *adj* humiliating; **2.** *v pres* debase(s); lower(s); humiliate(s); (*pst* **heeshpeel;** *fut* **yashpeel**).
mashpekh/-eem משפך *nm* funnel; (*pl+of:* **-ey**).
mashrokee|t/-yot משרוקית *nf* whistle.
mashteen/-ah משתין *v pres* urinate(s); (*pst* **heeshteen;** *fut* **yashteen**).
mashtel|ah/-ot (*npr* **meeshtal|ah/-ot**) משתלה *nf* plant-nursery; seedbed; (*+of:* **meeshtelet**).
mashten|ah/-ot (*npr* **meeshtan|ah/-ot**) משתנה *nf* pissoir; urinal; (*+of:* **meeshtenet**).
mashten|ah/-ot (*npr* **meeshtan|ah/-ot**) **tseebooree|t/-yot** משתנה ציבורית *nf* public latrine.
mashvanee/-t משווני *adj* equatorial.
mashv|eh/-ah משווה **1.** *adj* equalizing; comparing; **2.** *v pres* compare(s); equalize(s); (*pst* **heeshvah;** *fut* **yashveh**).
(kav ha) mashveh קו המשווה *nm* equator.
maskan|ah/-ot מסקנה *nf* conclusion; (*+of:* **-at**).
maskeer/-ah משכיר *v pres* let(s); hire(s) out; (*pst* **heeskeer;** *fut* **yaskeer**).
maskeer/-ah משכיר *nmf* lessor; landlord.
maskhet/-eem מסחט *nm* squeezer.
maskhet|ah/-ot מסחטה *[colloq.] nf* wringer; squeezer.
maskhetat meets מסחטת מיץ *[colloq.] nf* juice squeezer.
maskhet|at/-ot yad מסחטת יד *[colloq.] nf* hand-operated wringer; hand-operated squeezer.
maskor|et/-ot משכורת *nf* salary; wage.
maskor|et/-ot khod'shee|t/-yot משכורת חודשית *nf* monthly salary; monthly wages; (Note: In Israel, there are no weekly or yearly salaries; only per month, per day or, in some fields, per hour).
maskore|t/-ot shenateet/-yot משכורת שנתית *nf* yearly wages; yearly salary; (see Note to preceding entry).
maskore|t/-ot shevoo'ee|/-yot משכורת שבועית *nf* weekly wages; weekly salary; (see Note to preceding entry).
maslool/-eem מסלול *nm* course; lane (traffic).
□ **Maslool** (Maslul) מסלול *nm* village (est. 1950) in NW Negev, 4 km N. of **Ofakeem.** Pop. 296.
(doo-) masloolee/-t דו־מסלולית *adj* two-lane; two-way.
masmer/-eem מסמר *nm* nail; (*pl+of:* **-ey**).
masmer ha-'onah מסמר העונה *nm* highlight of the season.
(kav|a'/-'ah) masmerot קבע מסמרות *v* laid down principles; (*pres* **kove'a'** *etc; fut* **yeekba'** *etc b=v*).
masnen/-eem מסנן *nm* filter.
maso paneem משוא־פנים *nm* bias; favoritism.
(le-lo) maso paneem ללא משוא־פנים *adv* without prejudice; unbiased; with no bias.
masof/mesof|eem מסוף *nm* **1.** terminal; **2.** computer-terminal; (*pl+of:* **-ey**).
masok/-eem מסוק *nm* helicopter; chopper; (*pl+of:* **-ey**).
masoo|'ah/'ot משואה *nf* beacon; fire signal; (*+of:* **-'at**).
□ **Masoo'ah** (Massu'a) משואה *nm* village (est. 1969) in the Jordan Valley. Pop. 230.
□ **Masoo'ot Yeets'khak** (Massu'ot Yizhaq) משואת יצחק *nm* village (est. 1949) in the S. seashore plain, 7 km SW of **Keeryat Mal'akhee.** Pop. 515.
masoor/mesoorah מסור *adj* **1.** devoted; dedicated; **2.** left to the discretion of.
masor/-eem משור or: מסור *nm* saw; (*pl+of:* **-ey**).
masoree|t/-yot משורית *nf* fret-saw.
masore|t/-ot מסורת *nf* tradition.
(shom|er/-rey) masoret שומר מסורת *adj* observant; tradition-guarding.
masos משוש *nm* joy; (*+of:* **mesos**).
maspeek/-ah מספיק **1.** *adj* sufficient; sufficing; **2.** *nm* passing mark (in examinations).
maspeek/-ah מספיק *v pres* suffice(s); (*pst* **heespeek;** *fut* **yaspeek**).
maspeek מספיק *adv* enough.
(beeltee) maspeek/-ah בלתי מספיק *nm* non-passing grade (in examination).

(lo) maspeek לא מספיק **1.** *adv* not enough; **2.** *adj* insufficient.

masree|'akh/-khah מסריח **1.** *adj* stinking; **2.** *v pres* stink(s); (*pst* **heesree'akh**; *fut* **yasreeakh**).

masreet/-eem מסריט **1.** *nm* movie-camera man; (*pl+of:* **-ey**); **2.** *v pres* shoot(s) movie pictures; (*pst* **heesreet**; *fut* **yasreet**).

masreg|ah/-ot מסרגה *nf* knitting needle; (*+of:* **-at**).

masrek/-ot מסרק *nm* comb.

masret|ah/-ot מסרטה *nf* movie-camera; (*+of:* **-at**).

masret|at/-ot veedyo מסרטת־וידאו *nf* video-camera.

masteek/-eem מסטיק *nm [colloq.]* chewing-gum.

◇ **masteek|ah/-ot** מסטיקה *nf* alcoholic drink (similar to anise) traditionally drunk by Sephardi Jews of Balkan background.

mastem|ah/-ot משטמה *nf* hatred; (*+of:* **-at**).

mastool/-eet מסטול *adj [slang]* **1.** drugged; **2.** drunk; tipsy.

masv|eh/-eem מסווה *nm* mask; disguise; (*pl+of:* **-ey**).

mat/-ah leepol מט ליפול *adj & v pres* tottering.

matah מטה *adv* down; downward.

(he-khatoom) matah (*or:* **ha-khatoomah** *etc*) החתום מטה *nmf & adj* the undersigned; (*pl:* **ha-khatoomeem** *etc*).

(le) matah למטה *adv* beneath; downward; lower down.

mat|a'/-a'eem מטע *nm* plantation; grove; orchard; (*pl+of* **-'ey**).

□ **Mata'** (Matta) מטע *nm* village in Judea hills (est. 1950), 8 km SE of Bet Shemesh. Pop. 295.

mat|akh/-akheem מטח *nm* salvo; (*pl+of:* **-khey**).

mat|akh/-khah/-akhtee מתח *v* stretched; extended; (*pres* **mote'akh**; *fut* **yeemtakh**).

matakh (*etc*) מתח *v [slang]* pulled one's leg.

matakh (*etc*) **beekoret** מתח ביקורת *v* criticized.

matakh (*etc*) **kav** מתח קו *v* drew a line.

matakhtee/-t מתכתי *adj* metallic.

(al-) matakhtee/-t אל־מתכתי *adj* non-metallic

matal|ah/-ot מטלה *nf* task; (*+of:* **-at**).

mat'am|eem מטעמים *nm pl* delicatessen; table delicacies; (*+of:* **-ey**).

matan מתן *nm* grant; giving.

matan reeshyon/-ot מתן רשיון granting a permit; licensing.

matan reshoot מתן רשות *nm* granting permission.

(masa oo) matan משא ומתן *nm pl* negotiations.

mat|anah/-anot מתנה *nf* gift; present; (*+of:* **-nat/-not**).

matar/metareem (*also:* **-ot**) מטר *nm* rain; rainfall; shower; (*+of:* **metar**; *pl+of:* **meetrey, meetrot**).

mat|arah/-arot מטרה *nf* goal; purpose; target; (*+of:* **-rat/-ot**).

(le-lo) matarah ללא מטרה **1.** *adj* aimless; **2.** *adv* aimlessly.

matas/-eem מטס *nm* flight (of airplanes in an air-show).

matat מתת *nf* gift.

□ **Matat** מתת *nm* village (est. 1979) in Eylon Sub-district, **'Ako** (Acco) Area, 3 km NW of Sasa.

mat'at|e/-'eem מטאטא *nm* broom.

matay מתי *adv* when.

matay she- מתי ש־ *adv [colloq.]* at the time when.

matay she-hoo מתי שהוא *adv* sometime or other.

('ad) matay עד מתי *adv* till when; how long.

(le) matay למתי *adv* for when.

(mee) matay ממתי *adv* since when.

ma'tayeem מאתיים *num* (*f pl*) two hundred; 200.

matbe|'a'/-'ot מטבע *nm* **1.** coin; **2.** currency.

matbe'a' kasheh מטבע קשה *nm* hard currency.

matbe'a' khofshee מטבע חופשי *nm* free currency.

matbe'a' khoots מטבע חוץ *nm* foreign currency.

matbe'a' yatseev מטבע יציב *nm* stable currency.

matbe'a' yeesre'elee מטבע ישראלי *nm* Israeli currency.

matbe'a' zar מטבע זר *[colloq.] nm* foreign currency.

(yeetsoov ha) matbe'a' ייצוב המטבע *nm* currency stabilization.

matben/-eem מתבן *nm* haystock; barn.

mat|eh/-ot מטה *nm* staff headquarters; HQ.

('avodat) mateh עבודת מטה *nf* staff work.

(ha) mateh (ha)klalee המטה הכללי *nm* (the) General Staff.

(rosh ha) mateh (ha)klalee ראש המטה הכללי *nm* Chief of the General Staff (normally referred to by its *acr:* **ramatkal** רמטכ״ל).

mat|'eh/-'ah מטעה *adj* deceptive; misleading.

mat|'eh/-'ah מטעה *v pres* deceive(s); mislead(s); (*pst* **heet'ah**; *fut* **yat'eh**).

mateef/-ah מטיף **1.** *nmf* preacher; **2.** *v pres* preach(es); (*pst* **heeteef**; *fut* **yateef**).

mat'eem/-ah מתאים **1.** *adj* fitting; appropriate; **2.** *v pres* fit(s); befit(s); **3.** *v pres* adjust(s); (*pst* **heet'eem**; *fut* **yat'eem**).

mat|ekhet/-akhot מתכת *nf* metal.

matematee/-t מתמטי *adj* mathematical.

matemateekah מתימטיקה *nf* mathematics.

matemateeka|'ee/-'eet (*cpr* **matemateek|ay/-'eet**) מתימטיקאי *nmf* mathematician.

mateeranee/-t מתירני *adj* permissive.

mateeranoot מתירנות *nf* permissiveness.

(tekoofat ha) mateeranoot תקופת המתירנות *nf* the Age of Permissiveness.

□ **Mateet'yahoo** מתתיהו *nm* coop. village (est. 1978) in the **Modee'een** area, NE of **Sheelat**. Pop. 218.

matkal מטכ״ל *nm* (*acr of* **Mateh Klalee** מטה כללי) General Staff.
matkheel/-ah מתחיל **1.** *nmf* beginner; **2.** *v pres* begin(s); (*pst* **heetkheel;** *fut* **yatkheel**).
matkhen|ah/-ot מטחנה *nf* mincer; (*+of:* **-at**).
matkhen|at/-ot basar מטחנת בשר *nf* meat mincer
matkon/-eem מתכון **1.** *nm* recipe; formula; **2.** prescription (Medic.); (*pl+of:* **-ey**).
matkonet מתכונת *nf* scale; form.
(ke) matkonet כמתכונת *adv* on lines similar to.
matl|eh/-eem מתלה *nm* hanger; hook.
matlee|t/-yot מטלית *nf* rag; duster.
(va'adah) matmedet ועדה מתמדת *nf* Steering Committee.
matmeed/-eem מתמיד *nm* diligent "Yeshiva" pupil.
matmeed/-ah מתמיד **1.** *adj* persistent; **2.** *v pres* persist(s); (*pst* **heetmeed;** *fut* **yatmeed**).
matmee|'ah/-hah מתמיה **1.** *adj* astonishing; strange; **2.** *v pres* astonishes; (*pst* **heetmee'ah;** *fut* **yatmee'ah**).
matmon/-eem מטמון *nm* treasure; (*pl+of:* **-ey**).
◇ **matnas/-eem** מתנ״ס *nm* (*acr of* **Mo'adon Tarboot, No'ar oo-Sport** מועדון תרבות, נוער וספורט) *nm* local youth, culture and sport community center. (*pl+of:* **-ey**).
matne|'a'/-'eem מתנע *nm* starter; self-starter.
matok/metookah מתוק *adj* sweet.
(khamoots-) matok חמוץ־מתוק *adj* bitter-sweet.
matol/metol|eem מטול *nm* projector; (*pl+of:* **-ey**).
matoo'akh/metookhah מתוח *adj* **1.** tense; **2.** stretched.
(matsav/-eem) matooakh/metookheem מצב מתוח *nm* tense situation.
matoon/metoonah מתון *adj* moderate; restrained.
matos/metoseem מטוס *nm* airplane; aircraft; (*+of:* **metos/-ey**).
matreef/-ah מטריף **1.** *adj* maddening; **2.** *v pres* drive(s) crazy; (*pst* **heetreef;** *fut* **yatreef**).
matreem/-ah מתרים **1.** *nmf* fundraiser; **2.** *v pres* collect(s) contributions; (*pst* **heetreem;** *fut* **yatreem**).
matreets|ah/-ot מטריצה *nf* matrix; (*+of:* **-at**).
matvee|yah/-yot מטווייה *nf* spinning mill; (*+of:* **-yat**).
mats|a/-'ah/-a'tee מצא *v* found; (*pres* **motse;** *fut* **yeemtsa**).
matsa (*etc*) **khen** מצא־חן *v* pleased.
matsa (*etc*) **khen be-'eyney** מצא־חן בעיני *v* pleased (someone).
matsa (*etc*) **le-nakhon** מצא לנכון *v* found it right.
mats|ah/-ot מצה *nf* "Matzos"; unleavened Passover bread; (*+of:* **-at**).
mats|a'/-a'eem מצע *nm* **1.** bedding; bed linen; **2.** political platform; (*pl+of:* **-'ey**).
matsa'eem מצעים *nm pl* bedding; bed linen.
mats'ah yad|o/-ah מצאה ידו *v* could afford.
matsat/-eem מצת *nm* spark plug; (*pl+of:* **-ey**).
mats|ats/-etsah/-atstee מצץ *v* sucked; (*pres* **motsets;** *fut* **yeemtsots**).
matsav/-eem מצב *nm* situation; state; position; (*pl+of:* **-ey**).
matsav hakhen מצב הכן *nm* stand-by; state of alert.
matsav/-ey kheroom מצב חירום *nm* state of emergency.
matsav/-eem matoo'akh/metookheem מצב מתוח *nm* tense situation.
matsav meelkhamah מצב מלחמה *nm* state of war.
matsav/-ey roo'akh מצב־רוח *nm* disposition; mood.
(kheyl) matsav חיל־מצב *nm* garrison.
(shal|at/-tah/-atetee ba) matsav שלט במצב *v* had the situation in hand; (*pres* **sholet** *etc;* *fut* **yeeshlot** *etc*).
matsavah מצבה *nf* garrison; strength.
matsbee/-'eem מצביא *nm* field-commander; (*pl+of:* **-'ey**).
matsbee|'a'/-'ah מצביע *v pres* vote(s); (*pst* **heetsbee'a';** *fut* **yatsbee'a'**).
matsbee|'a'/-'eem מצביע *nm* voter; (*pl+of:* **-'ey**).
matsber/-eem מצבר *nm* battery; accumulator; (*pl+of:* **-ey**).
matseel/-eem מציל *nm* **1.** life-guard; **2.** savior; rescuer; (*pl+of:* **-ey**).
matseel/-ah מציל *v pres* save(s); rescue(s); (*pst* **heetseel;** *fut* **yatseel**).
(ve'eyn) matseel... ...ואין מציל - and there's no one to turn to for help.
matseet/-eem מצית *nm* **1.** cigarette-lighter; **2.** arsonist.
matseet/-ah מצית *v pres* **1.** light(s); **2.** set(s) on fire; (*pst* **heetseet;** *fut* **yatseet**).
matsee|yah/-yot מצייה *nf* wafer (made of Matzah and eggs); (*+of:* **-yat**).
matsev|ah/-ot מצבה *nf* tombstone; (*+of:* **-at**).
mats'heer/-ah מצהיר *v pres* declare(s); (*pst* **heets'heer;** *fut* **yats'heer**).
mats'heev/-ah מצהיב **1.** *adj* turning yellow; **2.** *v pres* turn(s) yellow; (*pst* **heets'heev;** *fut* **yats'heev**).
mats'kheek/-ah מצחיק **1.** *adj* funny; ridiculous; **2.** *v pres* make(s) one laugh; (*pst* **heets'kheek;** *fut* **yats'kheek**).
mats'kheekan/-eet מצחיקן *nmf* jester; funnyman/-woman; prankster.
matslee|'akh/-khah מצליח **1.** *adj* successful; **2.** *v pres* succeed(s); (*pst* **heetslee'akh;** *fut* **yatslee'akh**).
□ **Matslee'akh** (Mazliah) מצליח *nm* village (est. 1950) in the central plain, 2 km S. of Ramla. Pop. (Jews of the Karaite sect) 541.
matslem|ah/-ot מצלמה *nf* camera; (*+of:* **-at**).
matslem|at/-ot veedyo מצלמת־וידיאו *nf* video-camera.
matsmed/-eem מצמד *nm* clutch (in a motor-car).

(davshat ha) matsmed דוושת המצמד *nf* clutch pedal.

matsmeed/-ah מצמיד *v pres* attaches; tie(s)-up (prices; rates); (*pst* heetsmeed; *fut* yatsmeed).

matsne|'akh/-kheem (*cpr* meetsnakh/-eem) מצנח *nm* parachute; (*pl+of:* -khey).

matsod/metsodeem מצוד *nm* hunt; comb-out; (*pl+of* -ey).

matsoots/metsootsah מצוץ *adj* sucked; sucked-in.

matsoots meen ha-'etsba' מצוץ מן האצבע *adj* 1. unfounded; invented (report); 2. (*lit.*) sucked from the finger.

□ Matsoobah see □ Matsoovah, below.

□ Matsoovah (Mazzuva) (*cpr* Matsoobah) מצובה *nm* kibbutz (est. 1940) in Western Galilee, 1 km SE of Tsomet Khaneetah (Hanita Junction). Pop. 609.

matsooy/metsooyah מצוי *adj* common; available; existing.

matsor מצור *nm* siege.

matsot מצות *nf pl* "Matzos"; unleavened bread eaten during Passover; (*sing* matsah).

(khag ha) matsot חג המצות *nm* Feast of the Matzot; i.e. Passover.

◇ (kemakh) matsot see ◇ kemakh matsot.

matspen/-eem מצפן *nm* compass.

matspoon/-eem מצפון *nm* conscience; (*pl+of:* -ey).

(ba'al/-at) matspoon בעל מצפון 1. *nmf* conscientious person; 2. *adj* scrupulous.

(khas|ar/-rat) matspoon חסר מצפון *adj* unscrupulous; conscienceless.

(mee-ta'amey) matspoon מטעמי מצפון *adv* for reasons of conscience.

(nekeef|at/-ot) matspoon נקיפת מצפון *nf* pang of conscience.

matspoonee/-t מצפוני *adj* conscientious; scrupulous.

mavdelet מבדלת *nf* room-divider; collapsible door.

mav'eer/-ah מבעיר *v pres* set(s) fire; burn(s); (*pst* heev'eer; *fut* yav'eer).

mav'eesh/-ah מבאיש *v pres* spoil(s); pollute(s); make(s) stink; (*pst* heev'eesh; *fut* yav'eesh).

mav'er/-eem מבער *nm* burner; (*pl+of:* -ey).

mavet מוות *nm* death; (*+of:* mot).

(al) mavet אלמוות *nm* immortality.

(ben/bat) mavet בן מוות *nmf* deserving death; bound to die.

mav'heel/-ah מבהיל *adj* terrifying; frightening.

mav'heel/-ah מבהיל *v pres* frighten(s); terrify(ies); (*pst* heev'heel; *fut* yav'heel).

mav'heek/-ah מבהיק 1. *adj* shiny; 2. *v pres* shine(s); (*pst* heev'heek; *fut* yav'heek).

mav'heer/-ah מבהיר 1. *adj* clarifying; 2. *v pres* clarify,-ies; (*pst* heev'heer; *fut* yav'heer).

□ Mavkee'eem (Mavqi'im) מבקיעים *nm* village in S. coastal plain, 5 km S. of Ashkelon. Pop. 137.

mavkhen|ah/-ot מבחנה *nf* test-tube; (*+of:* -at).

(teenok/-ey) mavkhenah תינוק מבחנה *nm* test-tube baby.

mavo/mevo'ot מבוא *nm* 1. entrance; 2. introduction; preface; (*+of:* mevo).

mavree|'akh/-kheem מבריח *nm* smuggler; (*pl+of:* -khey).

mavree'|akh/-khah מבריח *v pres* 1. put(s) to flight; drive(s) away; 2. smuggle(s); (*pst* heevree'akh; *fut* yavree'akh).

mavreek/-ah מבריק 1. *adj* brilliant; glowing; 2. *v pres* glitter(s); (*pst* heevreek; *fut* yavreek).

mavreg/-eem מברג *nm* screwdriver; (*pl+of:* -ey).

mavzek/-eem מבזק *nm* flashlight; (*pl+of:* -ey).

May מאי *nm* May.

(ela) may אלא מאי what else?! what else was there to expect?!

□ Ma'yan Barookh (Ma'yan Barukh) מעיין ברוך *nm* kibbutz (est. 1947) in Upper Galilee, N. of Khoolah Valley, near Lebanese border, 5 km NE of Keeryat Shmonah. Pop. 371.

□ Ma'yan Kharod מעיין חרוד *nm* springs and recreation park area in the Yizre'el Valley, at the foot of Mount Geelbo'a', near Geed'onah, 11 km SE of 'Afula.

□ Ma'yan Tsvee (Ma'yan Zevi) מעיין צבי *nm* kibbutz on Carmel (Karmel) seashore, 2 km W. of Zeekhron Ya'akov. Pop. 594.

mayeem מים *nm pl* water; (*+of:* mey).

mayeem bee-mesoorah מים במשורה *nm pl* limited quantity of water; water ration.

mayeem kareem מים קרים *nm pl* cold water.

mayeem kevedeem מים כבדים *nm pl* heavy water.

mayeem meeneraleeyeem מים מינרליים *nm pl* mineral water.

mayeem meen ha-berez מים מן הברז *nm pl* water from the tap; tap-water.

mayeem metookeem מים מתוקים *nm pl* 1. *nm pl* drinking water; potable water; fresh water; 2. (*lit.:*) sweet water (i.e. not salt water).

mayeem pshooteem מים פשוטים *nm pl* plain water.

mayeem treeyeem מיים טריים *nm pl* fresh water.

(amat ha) mayeem אמת המים *nf* aqueduct.

(ba'oo) mayeem 'ad nefesh באו מים עד נפש things have become unbearable.

(be'er) mayeem khayeem באר מים חיים well of fresh drinking water.

(hamtakat) mayeem המתקת מים *nf* water desalination.

(het|eel/-eelah/-altee) mayeem הטיל מים *v* urinated; (*pres* mateel; *fut* yateel).

(map|al/-ley) mayeem מפל מים *nm* waterfall.

(meegd|al/-eley) mayeem מגדל מים *nm* water tower.

(neteev/-ey) mayeem נתיב מים *nm* waterway.

(parash|at/-ot) mayeem פרשת מים *nm* watershed.

(peles) mayeem פלס־מים *nm* water level; spirit level.

(tokhen/-et) mayeem טוחן מים *v pres* **1.** waste(s) words; **2.** (*lit.:*) grind(s) water; (*pst* **takhan** *etc; fut* **yeetkhon** *etc*).

(tseva/tseev'ey) mayeem צבע מים *nm* watercolor.

maymeen/-ah מימין **1.** *adj* taking right turn; turning right; **2.** *v pres* take(s) right.

mayoneet מיונית *nf* mayonnaise.

maz|ag/-ga/-agtee מזג *v* poured; (*pres* **mozeg**; *fut* **yeemzog**).

mazal/-ot מזל *nm* **1.** luck; good fortune; **2.** sign of the Zodiac; **3.** constellation.

mazal te'omeem מזל תאומים *nm* Gemini.

mazal tov! !מזל טוב traditional Jewish well-wishing: congratulations! Mazeltov!

(bar/bat) mazal בר־מזל *adj* lucky; fortunate.

(beesh) mazal ביש־מזל **1.** *adj* unlucky; unfortunate; **2.** *adv* bad luck!

(le-marbeh ha) mazal למרבה המזל *adv* luckily; fortunately.

(le-ro'a' ha) mazal לרוע המזל *adv* unfortunately.

(seekhek ha) mazal שיחק המזל *adv* by a touch of luck.

(le) mazal|ee/-kha/-ekh/-oh/-ah *etc* למזלי/־ך וכו to my/your(*m/f*)/his/her *etc* good fortune.

(neetmazel) mazal|ee/-kha/-ekh/-o/-ah *etc* נתמזל מזלי/־ך וכו by a touch of my/your *etc* good fortune.

mazbal|ah/-ot (*npr* **meezbal|ah/-ot**) מזבלה *nf* garbage dump; dung hill.

mazeek/-ah מזיק **1.** *adj* harmful; **2.** *v pres* harm(s); damage(s); (*pst* **heezeek**; *fut* **yazeek**).

mazgan/-eem מזגן *nm* air-conditioner; (*pl+of:* **-ley**).

mazgan/-eem mefootsal/-eem מזגן מפוצל *nm* split-unit airconditioner.

maz'heer/-ah מזהיר **1.** *adj* brilliant; shining; **2.** *v pres* warn(s); (*pst* **heez'heer**; *fut* **yaz'heer**).

mazkal/-eet מזכ״ל *nmf abbr.* (*acr of* **MAZkeer KLalee** מזכיר כללי) secretary-general.

mazkeer/-ah מזכיר **1.** *nmf* secretary; (*f+of:* **-at**; *pl+of:* **-ey**); **2.** *v pres* remind(s); (*pst* **heezkeer**; *fut* **yazkeer**).

mazkeer ha-memshalah מזכיר הממשלה *nm* government secretary.

mazkeer klalee מזכיר כללי *nm* secretary-general.

mazkeer|ah/-ot מזכירה *nf* secretary (*+of:* **-at**; *pl+of:* **-ot**).

mazkeeroo|t/-yot מזכירות *nf* secretariat.

mazk|eret/-arot מזכרת *nm* souvenir.

(le) mazkeret למזכרת *adv* in remembrance.

□ **Mazkeret Batyah** (Mazkeret Batya) מזכרת בתיה *nf* township (est. 1883 as first agric. colony), 4 km SE of Bilu Junction (**Tsomet Beeloo**). Pop. 2,870.

mazleg/-ot מזלג *nm* fork.

mazmeen/-ah מזמין *v pres* invite(s); order(s); (*pst* **heezmeen**; *fut* **yazmeen**).

mazmer|ah/-ot מזמרה *nf pl* pruning shears.

mazon/mezonot מזון *nm* food; (*+of:* **mezon**).

◇ **(beerkat ha) mazon** see ◇ **beerkat ha-mazon**.

mazoot מזוט *nm* crude oil; heating oil.

mazor מזור *nm* healing; cure.

□ **Mazor** מזור *nm* village (est. 1949) 3 km SE of **Petakh-Teekvah**. Pop. 401.

mazrek/-eem מזרק *nm* **1.** syringe; hypodermic needle; **2.** injector; (*pl+of:* **-ey**).

me- ־מ *prep (prefix)* from; out of.

me'ah/me'ot מאה *num f* hundred; 100 (*+of:* **me'at**).

(ha) me'ah המאה *nf* century.

(le) me'ah למאה *num* per hundred; percent.

(ekhad/shnayeem etc le) me'ah אחד/שניים למאה *num.* one/two etc percent.

me'ab|ed/-deem מעבד *nm* **1.** arranger; processor; **2.** music-arranger; (*pl+of:* **-dey**).

me'abed/-et מעבד *v pres* process(es); arrange(s); (*pst* **'eebed**; *fut* **ye'abed**).

me'ab|ed/-dey tamleeleem מעבד תמלילים *nm* word-processor.

me'a|hev/-haveem מאהב *nm* lover; (*pl+of:* **-havey**).

me'a|hevet/-havot מאהבת *nf* mistress.

me'akel/-et מאכל **1.** *adj* corroding; caustic; **2.** *v pres* digest(s); (*pst* **eekel**; *fut* **ye'akel**).

me-akhar מאחר *adv* **1.** from behind; **2.** since.

me-akhar she- ־מאחר ש *adv* since; because.

me-akhar ve- ־מאחר ו *(incorr. colloq.) adv* since; because.

me'akhed/-et מאחד **1.** *adj* unifying; **2.** *v pres* unify (-ies); unite(s); (*pst* **eekhed**; *fut* **ye'akhed**).

me'akher/-et מאחר *v pres* am/are/is late; (*pst* **eekher**; *fut* **ye'akher**).

me-akhor|ay/-ayeekh/-av מאחוריי/־ך וכו from behind me/you/him *f sing.*

me-akhore|kha/-ha/-noo/-khem/-hem/-hen מאחוריך/נו וכו' from behind you/her/you/them.

me-akhorey מאחורי *prep* behind the; behind of.

me-akhorey ha-kla'eem מאחורי הקלעים *adv* behind the scenes.

me-akhorey ha-pargod מאחורי הפרגוד *adv* behind the curtain.

me'akhzev/-et מאכזב **1.** *adj* disappointing; **2.** *v pres* disappoint(s); (*pst* **eekhzev**; *fut* **ye'akhzev**).

me'al מעל *adv* from above; over.

me'al le-/la- ־מעל ל *prep* over; above of.

me-'ala|v/-y/-yeekh מעלי/־ו וכו *adv* above him/me/you (*f sing*).

ma'alef/-et מאלף **1.** *adj* instructive; **2.** *nmf* tamer; trainer (of animals); **3.** *v pres* tame(s); train(s); (*pst* **eelef**; *fut* **ye'alef**).

me-'ale|kha/-khem/-khen/-noo/-hem/-hen מעליך/־כם/־כן וכו' *adv & pron* above you *masc, sing/pl (m/f)*/us/them *(m/f)*.

me'am'em/-et מעמעם **1.** *adj* dimming; **2.** *v pres* dim(s); (*pst* **'eem'em**; *fut* **ye'am'em**).

me'am'em/-eem מעמעם *nm* dimmer (electric.).

me'am|en/-neem מאמן *nm* coach; trainer; instructor; (*pl+of:* **-ney**).
me'amen/-et מאמן *v pres* coach(es); train(s); (*pst* **eemen**; *fut* **ye'amen**).
ma'aneh/-eem מענה *nm* torturer; (*pl+of:* **-ey**).
me'aneh/-ah מענה *v pres* torture(s) pain(s); (*pst* **'eena**; *fut* **ye'aneh**).
me'an|yen/-et מעניין *adj* interesting; *v pres* interest(s); (*pst* **'eenyen**; *fut* **ye'anyen**).
me'ar|ah/-ot מערה *nf* cave; (*+of:* **-at**).
me'arakh|at/-ot מארחת *nf* hostess.
□ **Me'arat ha-Makhpelah** מערכת המכפלה *nf* cave in Hebron believed to be burial place of Patriarchs Abraham, Isaac and Jacob and Matriarchs Sara and Rebecca (Bibl.).
me'arbel/-eem מערבל *nm* mixer; (*pl+of:* **-ey**).
me'arbe|l/-ley beton מערבל בטון *nm* concrete mixer.
me'arbe|l/-ley mazon מערבל מזון *nm* food mixer.
me'ar|e'akh/-akhat מארח *v pres* play(s) host; entertain(s); (*pst* **eere'akh**; *fut* **ye'are'akh**).
me'ar|e'akh/-kheem מארח *nm* host.
me'ar'er/-et מערער **1.** *nmf* appellant; **2.** *v pres* contest(s); appeal(s); (*pst* **'eer'er**; *fut* **ye'ar'er**).
me'ashen/-et מעשן **1.** *nmf* smoker; **2.** *v pres* smoke(s); (*pst* **'eeshen**; *fut* **ye'ashen**).
me-asher מאשר *prep & conj* than.
me'asher/-et מאשר *v pres* confirm(s); (*pst* **eesher**; *fut* **ye'asher**).
me'at/-eem מעט **1.** *adv* a little; **2.** *num* few.
(kee) me'at כמעט *adv* almost.
('od) me'at עוד מעט *adv* soon; just one more bit.
me'ater/-t מאתר *v pres* locate(s); (*pst* **eeter**; *fut* **ye-ater**).
me'atsben/-et מעצבן **1.** *adj* irritating; **2.** *v pres* make(s) nervous (*pst* **'eetsben**; *fut* **ye'atsben**).
me'avrer/-eem מאוורר *nm* ventilator; (*pl+of:* **-ey**).
me'avrer/-et מאוורר *v pres* ventilate(s); air(s); (*pst* **eevrer**; *fut* **ye'avrer**).
me'avret/-et מעברת *v pres* Hebrew-izes; coins a Hebrew equivalent (for a term, a name *etc*); (*pst* **'eevret**; *fut* **ye'avret**).
me'ay|ed/-deem מאייד *nm* carburetor; vaporizor.
me'ayeem מעיים *nm pl* entrails; guts; (*sing:* **me'ee**; *pl+of:* **me'ey**).
(teefoos ha) me'ayeem טיפוס המעיים *nm* typhoid fever.
me-ayeen מאין **1.** from where? **2.** from somewhere.
me'ayem/-et מאיים *v pres* threaten(s); (*pst* **eeyem**; *fut* **ye'ayem**).
me'ayen/-et מעיין *v pres* peruse(s); (*pst* **'eeyen**; *fut* **ye'ayen**).
me'ayesh/-et מאייש *v pres* man(s); (*pst* **eeyesh**; *fut* **ye'ayesh**).
me'ayer/-et מאייר **1.** *nmf* illustrator; **2.** *v pres* illustrate(s); (*pst* **eeyer**; *fut* **ye'ayer**).
me'ayet/-et מאיית *v pres* spell(s) (letters); (*pst* **eeyet**; *fut* **ye'ayet**).
me-az מאז *adv* **1.** since; ever since; **2.** since long ago; of old.
me'azen/-et מאזן *v pres* **1.** balance(s); **2.** make(s) up; (*pst* **eezen**; *fut* **ye'azen**).
mebalef/-et (*npr* **mevalef**) מבלף *[slang] v pres* bluff(s); (*pst* **beelef**; *fut* **yevalef** *(v=b)*).
medakdek/-eem מדקדק *nmf* grammarian; (*pl+of:* **-ey**).
medakdek/-et מדקדק **1.** *v pres* strictly observe(s); (*pst* **deekdek**; *fut* **yedakdek**); **2.** *adj* meticulous; pedantic; observant.
medak|e/-'ah מדכא **1.** *adj* depressing; oppressive; **2.** *v pres* oppress(es); depress(es); (*pst* **deeke**; *fut* **yedake**).
medakhdekh/-et מדכדך *adj* depressing.
medaleg/-et מדלג *v pres* skip(s); skip(s) over; (*pst* **deeleg**; *fut* **yedaleg**).
medalel/-eem מדלל *nm* thinner (paint, *etc*); (*pl+of:* **-ey**).
medalel/-et מדלל *v pres* dilute(s); (*pst* **deelel**; *fut* **yedalel**).
medal|yah/-yot מדליה *nf* medal; (*+of:* **-yat**).
medamem/-et מדמם **1.** *adj* bleeding; **2.** *v pres* bleed(s); (*pst* **deemem**; *fut* **yedamem**).
medayek/-et מדייק **1.** *adj* punctual; **2.** *v pres* am/are/is on time; (*pst* **deeyek**; *fut* **yedayek**).
medee'|akh/-khey keleem מדיח כלים *nm* automatic dishwasher.
medeed|ah/-ot מדידה *nf* **1.** measuring; surveying; **2.** measurement; (*+of:* **-at**).
medeen|ah/-ot מדינה *nf* state; (*+of:* **-at**).
(mad'ey ha) medeenah מדעי המדינה *nm pl* humanities; liberal arts; political science.
('oved/-et) medeenah עובד מדינה *nmf* government worker.
(prakleet ha) medeenah פרקליט המדינה *nm* the Attorney General.
medeen|ay (*cpr* **medeena'ee**)**/-a'eet** מדינאי *nmf* statesman/-woman (*pl+of:* **-a'ey**).
medeena'oot מדינאות *nf* statesmanship.
medeen|at/-ot sa'ad מדינת סעד *nf* welfare-state.
medeenat yeesra'el מדינת ישראל *nf* the State of Israel.
medeenee/-t מדיני *adj* political.
medeeneeyoot מדיניות *nf* policy.
medeenot 'arav מדינות ערב *nf pl* the Arab states.
◇ **medeenot ha-'eemoot** מדינות העימות *nf pl* the "Confrontation States" i.e. Arab states opposed to the the very existence of Israel who have vowed never to make peace.
medeenot ha-goosh ha-meezrakhee מדינות הגוש המזרחי *nf pl* the Eastern Bloc states.
medeenot ha-ma'arav מדינות המערב *nf pl* the Western states.
◇ **medeenot ha-seroov** מדינות הסירוב *nf pl* the Refusal States; i.e. Arab states opposing any kind of peace with Israel.

medeenot ha-shook ha-meshootaf מדינות השוק המשותף *nf pl* the Common Market states.

('al ha) medokhah על המדוכה *adv* in search of a solution.

medook|a/-et מדוכא *adj* dejected; depressed; miserable.

medookd|ak/-eket מדוקדק *adj* precise; detailed; meticulous.

medookhd|akh/-ekhet מדוכדך *adj* dejected; depressed.

medool|al/-elet מדולל *adj* diluted.

medool|dal/-elet מדולדל *adj* depleted; sparse.

medoom|eh/-ah מדומה *adj* imaginary; simulated.

medoopl|am/-emet מדופלם *adj* certified; holding a diploma.

medoor|ah/-ot מדורה *nf* bonfire; (*+of:* **-at**).

medoor|ag (*npr* **medorag**)**/-eget** מדורג *adj* graded; gradual.

medooy|ak/-eket מדוייק *adj* accurate; exact.

medooz|ah/-ot מדוזה *nf* jelly fish; (*+of:* **-at**).

mee- ־מ *prefix* (before a word starting with an unvowelled consonant, instead of the normal **me-**) from; of; than.

mee מי who; who?

◇ **mee hoo yehoodee?** ?מי הוא יהודי who is a Jew? i.e. by what criterion should one be regarded a Jew under the Law of Return.

mee sham? ?מי שם who's there? who is it?

mee she- ־מי ש he/she who; whoever.

mee she-hay|ah/-tah/-oo מי שהיה *adj* former; ex-; formerly; who has been.

mee zeh/zo מי זה *nmf* who is it?

(et) mee את מי whom?

(ha) mee va-mee המי־ומי *nm pl* the "who's who".

(le) mee למי to whom.

(shel) mee של מי whose.

mee-ba'ad le-/la- ־מבעד ל *adv* from behind; through (window *etc*).

mee-bal'adey מבלעדי *adv* apart from; except.

mee-bayeet מבית *adv* from within; from the inside.

mee-bee-fneem מבפנים *adv* from the inside; from inside.

mee-ben מבין *adv* from among; from.

mee-be-'od מבעוד *adv* while there's still.

mee-blee מבלי *adv* without.

mee-blee meseem מבלי משים *adv* unknowingly; without noticing it; unintentionally.

meed|ah/-ot מידה *nf* measure; extent; (*+of:* **-at**).

meedah ke-neged meedah מידה כנגד מידה measure for measure.

(am|at/-ot) meedah אמת מידה *nf* standard; scale; criterion; yardstick.

(be) meedah mesooyemet במידה מסוימת *adv* to a considerable extent.

(be) meedah neekeret במידה ניכרת *adv* to a certain extent.

(be) meedah rabah במידה רבה *adv* to a great extent.

(be) meedah she- ־במידה ש *adv* to the extent to which.

(ken|eh/-ey) meedah קנה מידה *nm* measure; yardstick; scale.

(le-fee) meedah לפי מידה *adv* to measure; custom-made.

meedabek/-et מידבק *adj* **1.** contagious; **2.** sticky.

meedat ha-deen מידת הדין *nf* strict justice.

meedat ha-rakhameem מידת הרחמים *nf* leniency; merciful justice.

(be) meedat mah במידת מה *adv* to some extent.

(be-) meedat ha-yekholet (*or:* **ke-** *etc*) /במידת כמידת היכולת *adv* within the limits of one's possiblilities.

meeday מדי *adv* too

(yoter) meeday יותר מדי *adv* too much; too many.

meedbar/-eeyot מדבר *nm* desert; wilderness.

(ne'ot) meedbar נאות מדבר *nm pl* oasis.

meedbaree/-t מדברי *adj* barren; arid.

meedey מדי every; each.

meedey khodesh khod'shayeem ־מדי חודש חודשיים *adv* every one/two months.

meedey khodesh be-khod'sho מדי חודש בחודשו *adv* every month.

meedey pa'am מדי פעם *adv* each time; from time to time.

meedey shavoo'a' מדי שבוע *adv* every week; (*also:* **meedey shavoo'a' be-shavoo'a'**).

meedey yom be-yomo מדי יום ביומו *adv* every day.

meedg|am/-ameem מידגם *nm* sample; pattern; (*pl+of:* **-emey**).

meedgamee/-t מידגמי *adj* sample-.

mee-dorey dorot מדורי דורות *adv* from time immemorial.

mee-dor le-dor מדור לדור *adv* from generation to generation.

meedot מידות *nf pl* ethics; morality.

meedot ha-khom מידות החום *nf pl* hot temperatures.

meedot ha-kor מידות הקור *nf pl* cold temperatures.

(hash'khatat) meedot השחתת מידות *nf* corruption; deprivation.

◇ **(shlosh-'esreh) meedot** see ◇ **shlosh-'esreh meedot**.

(tohar) meedot טוהר מידות *nm* integrity.

(torat ha) meedot תורת המידות *nf* ethics; morality.

meedrakh מדרך *nm* foothold.

meedrakh|ah/-ot מדרכה *nf* sidewalk.

meedrakh kaf regel מדרך כף רגל as little place as would permit (or : require) the sole to tread on.

□ **Meedrakh-'Oz (Midrakh Oz)** מדרך עוז *nm* village (est. 1952) in Yizre'el Valley, 4 km NW of **Megeedo**. Pop. 436.

meedras/-eem מדרס *nm* pedal; foothold

◇ **meedrash/-eem** מדרש *nm* ("Medresh" in Yiddish) the non-legalistic part of Rabbinic literature, that mainly deals with interpretation of biblical texts, legends and traditions.

◇ **(bet/batey) meedrash** see ◇ **bet/batey meedrash.**

(bet/batey) meedrash le- בית־מדרש ל־ *nm* institute of ... studies.

meedr|ashah/-ashot מדרשה *nf* school; college; **(+*of:* -eshet).**

□ **Meedreshet Ben-Gooryon** (Midreshet Ben-Gurion) מדרשת בן־גוריון *nf* educational center established 1965 by David Ben-Gurion in heart of the Negev desert, 3 km S. of kibbutz **Sdeh-Boker**, his place of retirement. Originally named **Meedreshet Sdeh-Boker** (Sedé Boqér), it was renamed after its founder following his death. Pop. (staff and students) 629.

□ **Meedreshet Roopeen** מדרשת רופין *nf* educational institute (est. 1949) specializing in agriculture and irrigation techniques. Named after Dr. Arthur Ruppin, it is located in Sharon, 4 km N. of ha-Sharon Road Junction. Pop. 175.

□ **Meedreshet Sdeh-Boker** see □ **Meedreshet Ben-Gooryon**, above.

meedron/-eem מדרון *nm* slope; **(*pl+of:* -ey).**

meed'sha|'ah/-ot מדשאה *nf* lawn.

me'ee/me'ayeem מעי *nm* intestine; entrail **(*pl+of:* me'ey).**

me'ee 'eever מעי עיוור *nm* caecum (Anat.).

me'ee gas מעי גס *nm* colon (Anat.).

me'eed|ah/-ot מעידה *nf* stumbling; **(+*of:* -at).**

me-'eedakh geesa מאידך גיסא *adv* on the other side.

me'eek/ah מעיק **1.** *adj* oppressive; **2.** *v pres* oppress(es) **(*pst* he'eek; *fut* ya'eek).**

me'eel/-eem מעיל *nm* jacket; coat; **(*pl+of:* -ey).**

me'eel 'elyon מעיל עליון *nm* overcoat; coat.

me'eel|ah/-ot מעילה *nf* embezzlement; **(+*of:* -at).**

me'eelah be-emoon מעילה באימון *nf* abuse of confidence; breach of trust.

me-'eem מעם from.

me'eer/-ah מאיר **1.** *adj* shining; **2.** *v pres* shine(s); **(*pst* he'eer; *fut* ya'eer).**

□ **Me'eer Shefeyah** (Me'ir Shefeya) מאיר שפיה *nm* youth-village and school of agriculture (est. 1904) in S. Carmel hills, 3 km N. of **Zeekhron Ya'akov**. Pop. 371.

me'ee|t/-yot מאית *num nf* 1/100; 0.01; one hundredth.

me'eet (*npr* me'et)/-ah מאיט *v pres* slow(s) down; **(*pst* he'eet; *fut* ya'eet).**

mee'|et/-atah/-atetee מיעט *v* reduced; lessened; **(*pres* mema'et; *fut* yema'et).**

me'eets/-ah מאיץ *v pres* accelerate(s); **(*pst* he'eets; *fut* ya'eets).**

me'eets/-eem מאיץ *nm* accelerator; **(*pl+of:* -ey).**

me'eets davshat ha-delek מאיץ דוושת הדלק *nm* fuel accelerator.

me'eets/-ey khelkeekeem מאיץ חלקיקים *nm* proton accelerator.

meef'al/-eem מפעל *nm* factory; plant; **(*pl+of:* -ey).**

□ **meef'al ha-ashlag** מפעל האשלג *nm* the Dead Sea Potash Works, state-owned, one of Israel's oldest and most important industries, responsible for some of the country's largest worldwide exports: potash, brom *etc.*

◇ **meef'al ha-payees** מפעל הפיס *nm* the Israel State Lottery.

◇ **meef'al me'ooshar** מפעל מאושר *nm* new enterprise granted special tax and currency facilities under Law for Encouragement of New Investments.

meefg|a'/-a'eem מפגע *nm* nuisance; **(*pl+of:* -e'ey).**

meefg|an/-aneem מפגן *nm* demonstration; parade; **(*pl+of:* -eney).**

meefg|ash/-asheem מפגש *nm* meet; encounter **(*pl+of:* -eshey).**

meefk|ad/-adeem מיפקד *nm* **1.** parade; **2.** census; **(*pl+of:* -edey).**

meefkad ookhlooseen מיפקד אוכלוסין *nm* general population census.

meefk|adah/-adot מיפקדה *nf* headquarters; command; **(+*of:* -edet).**

meefked|et/-ot מיפקדת *nf* the headquarters of...

meeflag מיפלג *nm* Police department; **(+*of:* meeflag ha-).**

meeflag ha-no'ar מיפלג הנוער *nm* the Juvenile Department (of the Police).

meeflag|ah/-ot מפלגה *nf* political party; **(+*of:* meefleget).**

◇ **(ha)meeflagah ha-dateet-le'oomeet** המפלגה הדתית־לאומית the National Religious Party, more popularly known by its Hebrew *acr* MAFDAL מפד"ל.

(ha) meeflagah ha-leeberaleet המפלגה הליברלית *nf* the Liberal Party which, since 1988, has been part of the Leekood Bloc.

meeflagtee מפלגתי *adj* partisan; party-.

('al-)meeflagtee/-t על־מפלגתי *adj* above political parties and party-interests.

(beeltee-)meeflagtee/-t בלתי־מפלגתי *adj* non-partisan.

meefl|as/-aseem מיפלס *nm* level; **(*pl+of:* -esey).**

(doo-) meeflasee/-t דו־מיפלסי *adj* two-level-.

(rav-) meeflasee/-t רב־מיפלסי *adj* multi-level-.

meefl|at/-ateem מיפלט *nm* escape; refuge; asylum; **(*pl+of:* -etey).**

meeflatstee/-t מפלצתי *adj* monstruous.

meefleget ha- מפלגת ה־ *f (+of) the party of....*

◇ **meefleget ha-'avodah** מפלגת העבודה *nf* the Labor Party, (colloquially known also as "**Avodah**" or "**Ma'arakh**") which from 1930 to 1977 was the country's ruling party and afterwards, to mid 1990, one of the two main partners in the coalition government. In the years 1930-1967 it was widely known as **Meefleget Po'aley Erets Yeesra'el** מפלגת פועלי ארץ ישראל (Eretz Israel Workers party) and even better known by its *acr* **MAPAY** מפא״י.

◇ **meefleget ha-po'aleem ha-me'ookhedet** מפלגת הפועלים המאוחדת *nf* the United Workers Party, *[colloq.]* known by its Hebrew *acr.* **MAPAM** מפ״ם. A left-socialist Jewish-Arab party (with Jewish members being Zionists), it advocates democratic egalitarianism, collectivism in farming and enterprises, and a two-states solution to the Israel-Arab conflict. Based on ◇ **(Ha)Shomer Ha-Tsa'eer"**, ◇ **"Ha-Keeboots Ha-Me'ookhad"** (see ◇ entries), and city proletarians, it was (1968-1984) Labor Party's partner in the Alignment (◇ **"Ma'arakh"**) from which it seceded in 1988.

meefl|etset/-atsot מיפלצת *nf* monster (*pl+of:* **-etsot**).

meefn|eh/-eem מיפנה *nm* turning point; change of course.

(le) meefneh למיפנה *adv* towards a turning point.

(nekood|at/-ot) meefneh נקודת מיפנה *nf* turning point.

meefr|a'ah/-a'ot מיפרעה *nf* advance payment; payment on account; advance on salary; (*+of:* **-e'at**).

meefr|as/-aseem מפרש *nm* sail; (*pl+of:* **-esey**).

(seer|at/-ot) meefraseem סירת מפרשים *nf* sailboat.

meefraseet/-yot מיפרשית *nf* sailboat.

meefr|at/-ateem מיפרט *nm* specification; (*pl+of:* **-etey**).

meefr|ats/-atseem מפרץ *nm* bay; (*pl+of:* **-etsey**).

□ **Meefrats Kheyfah** (Haifa) מפרץ חיפה *nm* Haifa Bay.

(ha) meefrats (ha)parsee המפרץ הפרסי *nm* the Persian Gulf.

meeft|akh/-akheem מיפתח *nm* span; aperture; (*pl+of:* **-ekhey**).

meeft|an/-aneem מפתן *nm* threshold; (*pl+of:* **-eney**).

meegb|a'at/-e'ot מגבעת *nm* hat.

meegdal/-eem מיגדל *nm* tower; (*pl+of:* **meegdeley**).

□ **Meegdal** (Migdal) מגדל *nm* agricultural settlement (est. 1920) W. of Lake of Tiberias, 6 km N. of Tiberias-town. Pop. 1,100.

◇ **meegdal bavel** מגדל בבל *nm* the Tower of Babel (Bible).

□ **Meegdal ha-'Emek** (Migdal ha'Emeq) מגדל העמק *nf* development-town (est. 1953) between Yizre'el Valley and Lower Galilee, 6 km SW of Nazareth **(Natsrat)**. Pop. 17,200.

meegd|al/-eley keedoo'akh מגדל קידוח *nm* derrick.

meegd|al/-eley mayeem מגדל מים *nm* water-tower.

□ **Meegdal 'Oz** (Migdal 'Oz) מגדל עוז *nm* kibbutz (re-est 1977) in Judean hills, 3 km from **Goosh 'Etsyon** (Gush 'Ezyon), E. of **Bet-Fadjar**.

meegdalor/-eem מגדלור *nm* lighthouse; (*pl+of:* **-ey**).

meegdan/-ot מגדן *nm* confection; sweetmeat.

meegdanee|yah/-yot מגדנייה *nf* confectionery; pastry-shop; (*+of:* **-yat**).

(yotse/-t) mee-geder ha-rageel יוצא מגדר הרגיל *adj* outstanding; extraordinary.

meeg|er/-rah/-artee מיגר *v* defeated; overthrew; (*pst* **memager**; *fut* **yemager**).

meegl|ashayeem מגלשיים *nm pl* skis; (*pl+of:* **-eshey**).

meegoor/-eem מיגור *nm* defeat; overcoming; (*pl+of:* **-ey**).

meegr|a'at/-a'ot מגרעת *nf* shortcoming; defect (*pl+of:* **-e'ot**).

meegr|ash/-asheem מגרש *nm* plot of land; (*pl+of:* **-eshey**).

meegr|ash/-eshey khanayah מגרש חנייה *nm* parking lot.

meegr|ash/-eshey meeskhakheem מגרש מישחקים *nm* playground.

meegr|ash/-eshey tenees מגרש טניס n tennis court.

meegz|ar/-areem מגזר *nm* sector; section; (*pl+of:* **-erey**).

mee|her/-harah/-hartee מיהר *v* hurried; hastened; (*pres* **memaher**; *fut* **yemaher**).

meehoo? ?מי הוא (or: ?מיהו) who's he? who is it?

◇ **meehoo yehoodee?** see ◇ **mee hoo yehoodee?**

mee-kadmat dena מקדמת דנה (Aramaic) *adv* of old; from olden days.

meekakh oo-meemkar מיקח וממכר *nm pl* buying and selling; trade.

meekakh ta'oot מיקח טעות *nm* bad deal.

('am|ad/-dah/-adetee 'al ha) meekakh עמד על המיקח *v* haggled; bargained; (*pres* **'omed** *etc; fut* **ya'amod** *etc*).

('ameedah 'al ha) meekakh עמידה על המיקח *nf* haggling; bargaining.

mee-kan מכאן *adv* from here.

mee-kan ve-eylakh מכאן ואילך *adv* from here onward; from now on.

mee-karov ba/-'ah מקרוב בא *adj* of recent provenience; Johnny-come-lately.

meekb|ats/-atseem מיקבץ *nm* grouping; (*pl+of:* **-etsey**).

meekd|amah/-amot מקדמה *nf* advance payment; (*+of:* **-emet/-emot**).

meekdamee/-t מקדמי *adj* preliminary.

meekd|ash/-asheem מקדש *nm* temple; (*pl+of:* **-eshey**).

◇ **(bet ha) meekdash** בית המקדש *nm* the Jerusalem Temple (of 2,000 years ago).

◇ **(ha)meekdash** המקדש see ◇ **(bet ha)meekdash**.

meek|em/-mah/-amtee מיקם *v* located; placed; (*pres* **memakem**; *fut* **yemakem**).

mee-kerev מקרב from among; from amongst.

mee-kerev lev מקרב לב *adv* wholeheartedly.

meek|esh/-shah/-ashtee מיקש *v* mined; laid mines; (*pres* **memakesh**; *fut* **yemakesh**).

mee-kets מקץ *adv* at the end of; after.

mee-kevan מכיוון *conj* since; as; whereas.

meekhb|asah/-asot מכבסה *nf* laundry; (*+of:* **-eset/-esot**).

mee-khdey מכדי *adv* than needed for.

meekhekhol/-eem מכחול *nm* paint brush; (*pl+of:* **-ey**).

meekhla|'ah/-'ot מכלאה *nf* temporary prison; detention place or camp; (*+of:* **-'at**).

meekhlol/-eem מכלול *nm* complex.

□ **Meekhmash** see □ **Ma'aleh Meekhmas**.

□ **Meekhmoret** (Mikhmoret) מכמורת *nm* village and seaside bathing spot (est. 1945) in Sharon on the estuary of Alexander brook, 9 km N. of Netanya. Pop. 1,200.

meekhn|as/-ayeem מכנס *nm [colloq.]* "trouser".

meekhn|asayeem מכנסיים *nm pl* trousers; slacks; (*pl+of:* **-esey**).

meekhnasayeem ketsareem מכנסיים קצרים *nm pl* shorts; short pants.

(zoog/-ot) meekhnasayeem זוג מכנסיים *nm* pair of slacks; pair of trousers.

meekhnesey jeens מכנסי ג'ינס *nm pl* jeans.

mee-khoots le-/la- מחוץ ל־ *adv* except for; outside of.

meekhl|alah/-alot מכללה *nf* college; (*+of:* **-elet/-elot**).

mee-khoots la-tkhoom מחוץ לתחום *adv* **1.** out of bounds; **2.** outside the jurisdiction.

meekhr|az/-azeem מכרז *nm* tender (for contract); (*pl+of:* **-ezey**).

meekhr|eh/-ot מיכרה *nm* mine.

meekhs|ah/-ot מיכסה *nf* quota; allocation. (*+of:* **-at**).

meekhs|eh/-eem מיכסה *nm* lid; cover. (*pl+of:* **-ey**).

meekhshol/-eem מכשול *nm* obstacle. (*pl+of:* **-ey**).

(he'er|eem/-eemah/-amtee) meekhsholeem הערים מכשולים *v* put up obstacles; made difficulties; (*pres* **ma'areem** *etc; fut* **ya'areem** *etc*).

(meroots/-ey) meekhsholeem מירוץ מיכשולים *nm* obstacle race; relay race.

meekhshoor/-eem מכשור *nm* apparatus; gadgetry; (*pl+of:* **-ey**).

meekht|av/-aveem מכתב *nm* letter; (*pl+of:* **-evey**).

meekht|av/-evey ashray (*cpr* **ashra'ee**) מכתב אשראי *nm* letter of credit.

meekht|av/-evey hamlatsah מכתב המלצה *nm* letter of recommendation.

meekht|av/-evey meenooy מכתב מינוי *nm* letter of appointment.

meekht|av/-evey peetooreem (*or:* **peetooreen**) מכתב־פיטורים *nm* notice of discharge.

meekhtav/-eem rashoom/reshoomeem מכתב רשום *nm* registered (mail) letter.

meekht|av/-evey ahavah מכתב אהבה *nm* love-letter.

(khaleefat) meekhtaveem חליפת מכתבים *nf* correspondence.

(kheeloofey) meekhtaveem חילופי מכתבים *nm pl* exchange of letters.

(tev|at/-ot) meekhtaveem תיבת מכתבים *nf* letter-box; mailbox.

(neyar) meekhtaveem נייר מכתבים *nm* stationery.

meekhyah מחייה *nf* livelihood; (*+of:* **-at**).

(le) meekhyah למחיה *adv* to earn a living.

(madad yoker ha) meekhyah מדד יוקר המחיה *nm* cost of living index.

(yoker ha) meekhyah יוקר המחיה *nm* high cost of living.

meekhzoor/-eem מיחזור *nm* re-cycling.

meekl|a'/-e'eem (*npr* **makle|'a'/-e'eem**) מקלע *nm* machine-gun. (*pl+of:* **-e'ey**).

(tat-) meekla' (*npr* **tat-makle|'a'/-e'eem**) תת־מקלע *nm* sub-machine-gun; braid; (*pl+of:* **-e'ey**).

meekl|a'at/-e'ot מקלעת *nf* plait (hair); braid.

meeklakh|at/-ot מקלחת *nf* bathroom.

meeklakhon/-eem מקלחון *nm* shower stall

mee-klal מכלל *adv* hence; from the fact of...

meekl|at/ateem מיקלט *nm* **1.** shelter; refuge. **2.** air-raid shelter. (*pl+of:* **-etey**).

meekle'an/-eem (*npr* **makle|'an/-eem**) מקלען *nm* machine-gunner.

mee-klee shenee מכלי שני *adv* indirectly; from second-hand source.

meekled|et/-adot מקלדת *nf* keyboard.

mee-ko'akh מכוח *adv* by virtue of.

mee-kodem מקודם *adv* before; earlier.

mee-kol מכול of all the...; of the entire.

mee-kol 'am מכל עם of all nations.

mee-kol 'ever מכול עבר *adv* from all around; from everywhere.

mee-kol makom מכול מקום *adv* **1.** at any rate. **2.** from every spot.

mee-kol tsad מכול צד *adv* from each side.

(ba-kol) mee-kol kol בכול מכול כול *adv* lock, stock and barrel.

mee-kol va-khol מכול וכול *adv* entirely; completely.

meekoo'|akh/-kheem מיקוח *nm* bargaining.

meekood/-eem מיקוד *nm* focusing.

meekood מיקוד *nm* mail-code.

meekoom/-eem מיקום *nm* location.

meekoon מיכון *nm* mechanization.

meekoosh/-eem מיקוש *nm* minelaying.

meekpa/-eem מקפא *nm* jelly.

meekra מקרא *nm* reading matter; recitation; legend (of map).

(beekoret ha) meekra ביקורת המקרא *nf* exegesis of Biblical texts.

(ha) meekra המקרא *nm* Bible text.

meekra'ee/-t מקראי *adj* Biblical.
meekr|eh/-eem מקרה *nm* **1.** accident; chance; **2.** case.
(be) meekreh במקרה *adj* by accident; accidentally.
(be) meekreh shel במקרה של *adv* in case of.
meekree/-t מקרי *adj* accidental.
meekreeyoot מקריות *nf* chance; casualness; coincidence.
meekro- ־מיקרו *(prefix)* micro-
meekro-gal מיקרו־גל *nm* microwave-cooker.
meekts|av/-aveem מקצב *nm* beat; rhythm (*pl+of:* **-evey**).
meektso|'a'/-'ot מקצוע *nm* profession; vocation.
meektso|'a/-'ot khofshee/-eem מיקצוע חופשי *nm* liberal profession.
(ba'al/-ey) meektso'a בעל מקצוע *nm* specialist.
(eesh/anshey) meektso'a איש מקצוע *nm* a professional.
meektso'anoot מקצוענות *nf* professionalism.
meektso'ee/-t מקצועי *adj* professional.
(bet/batey-sefer) meektso'ee/-yeem בית־ספר מקצועי *nm* vocational school.
(eegood/-eem) meektso'ee/-yeem איגוד מקצועי *nm* trade-union; labor union.
(hasavah) meektso'eet הסבה מקצועית *nf* re-training for a different profession.
(seefroot) meektso'eet ספרות מקצועית *nf* pay-supplement for purchase of professional literature.
◇ **meekv|ah/-a'ot** מקוה *nf* public bath into which Orthodox Jews immerse themselves for ritual purification, as before the Sabbath or (women) after menstruation.
meekv|eh/-eem מיקווה *nm* water-reservoir; pool; confluence; (*pl+of:* **-ey**).
□ **Meekveh Yeesra'el** (Miqwe Ysra'el) מיקווה ישראל *nm* country's oldest (est. 1870) agric. school SE of Tel-Aviv, on border of Holon (**Kholon**). Staff and pupils 905.
◇ **(meel.)** ('מיל) or (.מיל) (*abbr. suffix of* **meeloo'eem** מילואים i.e. Army Reserve) equivalent to "retired" - which follows the name of any former senior army officer if one's military rank is mentioned.
(lo shav|eh/-ah) meel לא שווה מיל *adj [colloq.]* not worth a penny.
meelah מילה *nf* circumcision.
(bereet/-ot) meelah ברית מילה *nf* circumcision ceremony.
meelah/-eem מלה *nf* word; (*+of:* **-at/-ot**).
meelah be-meelah מלה במלה *adv* word for word; verbatim.
meel|at/-ot kesher מלת־קשר *nf* conjunction (Gram.).
meel|at/-ot yakhas מלת־יחס *nf* preposition (Gram.).
me-el|av/-ehah מעליו **1.** by him/her -self; **2.** of him/her -self.

meel|e/-'ah/-etee מילא *v* **1.** filled. **2.** fuflfilled; (*pres* **memale**; *fut* **yemale**).
meele (etc) akhrey (or **akhar**) (מילא אחרי) אחר *v* complied with.
meele (etc) havtakh|ah/-ot מילא הבטחה *v* kept (fulfilled) a promise.
meele (etc) khov|ah/-ot מילא חובה *v* did one's duty.
meele (etc) makom מילא מקום *v* replaced; substituted for.
meele (etc) she'elon מילא שאלון *v* filled out a questionnaire; (*pres* **memale** *etc; fut* **yemale** *etc*).
meele (etc) tafkeed/-eem מילא תפקיד *v* played the part; played a role.
meele (etc) yedey מילא ידי *v* empowered; authorized.
mee-leefney מלפני *adv* from; from before.
mee-leefney she ־מלפני ש... *adv* from before... (preceding a verb).
(mees'khak/-ey) meeleem משחק מלים *nm* pun; play on words.
(otsar) meeleem אוצר מלים *nm* vocabulary.
meeleets|yah/-yot מיליציה *nf* militia; (*+of:* **-yat**).
meel|el/-elah/-altee מילל *v* uttered; said; thought; (*pres* **memalel**; *fut* **yemalel**).
(mee) meelel?! ?! מי מילל *interj* who would have thought?!
meel'eyl מלעיל *nm* accent on penultimate syllable of word.
meelg|ah/-ot מלגה *nf* scholarship; award; (*+of:* **-at**).
meelkh|amah/-amot מלחמה *nf* war; armed struggle (also *figurat.*); (*+of:* **-emet**).
('ar|akh/-khah/-akhtee) meelkhamah ערך מלחמה *v* waged war; (*pres* **'orekh** *etc; fut* **ya'arokh** *etc*).
(kheerkhoor/-ey) meelkhamah חרחור מלחמה *nm* warmongering.
(matsav/-ey) meelkhamah מצב מלחמה *nm* state of war.
(mekharkher/-ey) meelkhamah מחרחר מלחמה *nm* warmonger.
(nekh|eh/-ey) meelkhamah נכה מלחמה *nm* disabled soldier.
(sarvan/-ey) meelkhamah סרבן מלחמה *nm* conscientious objector.
meelkhamtee/-t מלחמתי *adj* war-; belligerent; bellicose.
mee-le-kha-tekheelah מלכתחילה *adv* in advance; from the beginning; at first.
meelkhemet מלחמת *nf* (*sing +of*) the war of....
meelkhemet bazak מלחמת בזק *nf* blitzkrieg.
◇ **meelkhemet ha-'atsma'oot** מלחמת העצמאות *nf* the Israeli War of Independence which started in December 1947, while Palestine was under British rule, as an all-out Arab-Jewish guerilla war. With the end of the British Mandate on May 15, 1948 and the simultaneous proclamation of the State of Israel, the armies of Egypt, Trans-Jordan,

Syria and Iraq crossed into Palestine to join in the fighting. Thereafter, hostilities were interrupted twice by Cease-Fires imposed by the United Nations. In all, the war lasted for 20 months and ended in July 1949, after armistices had been signed with Egypt, Trans-Jordan and Syria.

◇ **meelkhemet ha-hatashah** מלחמת ההתשה *nf* the War of Attrition - a phase in the Egypt-Israel hostilities which continued from March 1969 to August 1970; the Egyptians kept on shelling heavily the then Israeli-held Western bank of the Suez canal and making incursions into it. The Israelis, in reply, bombarded, from the air, positions, towns and villages on the Egyptian-held Eastern bank. Israel emerged from that phase with nearly 700 dead and Egypt with a good part of its canal-side towns and villages virtually destroyed and deserted.

◇ **meelkhemet ha-sheekhroor** מלחמת השיחרור *nf* the War of Liberation, another name for Israel's War of Independence (see ◇ **meelkhemet ha-'atsma'oot**, above).

meelkhemet hatashah מלחמת התשה *nf* war of attrition.

meelkhemet keeyoom מלחמת קיום *nf* struggle for survival.

meelkhemet magen מלחמת מגן *nf* defensive war.

meelkhemet meetsvah מלחמת מצווה *nf* holy war; war ordained by religious authorities.

meelkh|emet/-amot 'olam מלחמת עולם *nf* world-war.

◇ **meelkhemet seenay** מלחמת סיני *nf* the 1956 Sinai War (also known as the Sinai Campaign or **Meevtsa' Kadesh** מיבצע קדש i.e. Operation Kadesh) by which Israel reacted to Egypt's blocking of the Straits of Tiran (and Israel's only Red Sea outlet, Elat). Following a four month Israeli occupation of most of Sinai, the blockade was lifted.

meelkhemet sheekhroor מלחמת שחרור *nf* war of liberation.

◇ **meelkhemet sheleg** see ◇ **meelkhemet SHLom ha-Galeel** (of which **sheleg** של״ג is acronym).

◇ **meelkhemet sheshet ha-yameem** מלחמת ששת הימים *nf* the Six-Day War (1967).

◇ **meelkhemet shlom ha-galeel** מלחמת שלום הגליל *nf* the Lebanon War (1982-1985) for which the official name was the Peace for Galilee War (**Meelkhemet SHLom ha-Galeel** מלחמת שלום הגליל).

meelkood/-eem מלכוד *nm* **1.** catch; **2.** *[colloq.]* trap (*pl+of:* **-ey**).

mee-le-ma'lah מלמעלה *adv* from above.

mee-le-ma'tah מלמטה *adv* from below.

meelm|el/-elah/-altee מלמל *v* stammered; (*pres* **memalmel**; *fut* **yemalmel**).

meelmool/-eem מלמול mumbling; uttering; (*pl+of:* **-ey**).

meelon/-eem מילון *nm* dictionary; (*pl+of:* **-ey**).

meeloo'eem מילואים *nm pl* **1.** reserve army duty; **2.** addenda; (*pl+of:* **meeloo'em**).

(kheyl) meeloo'eem חיל מילואים *nm* army reserve.

◇ **(peenk|as/-esay) meeloo'eem** see ◇ **(peenk|as/-esay)** meeloo'eem.

meeloolee/-t מילולי *adj* verbal; literal.

meelooleet מילולית *adv* literally; textually.

meelooy/-eem מילוי *nm* **1.** refill; cartridge. **2.** fulfilment; (*pl+of:* **-ey**).

meelot keeshoor מלות קישור *nf pl* intermediate passages (in a program or show).

meelra' מלרע *nm* accent on ultimate syllable of word; (Gram.).

meelt|ashah/-ashot מלטשה *nf* polishing plant; diamond polishing plant; (*+of:* **-eshet**).

mee-lvad (or **mee-levad**) מלבד *adv* except; besides.

meelv|eh/-eem (*also:* **meelv|ah/-ot**) מלווה *nm* loan.

meelveh (*etc*) **khovah** מלווה חובה *nm* obligatory government loan.

meelveh memshaltee מלווה ממשלתי *nm* government loan; state loan.

meelyard/-eem מיליארד *num nm* 1,000,000,000; billion; (*pl+of:* **-ey**).

mee-ma'al ממעל *adv* from above.

mee-matay ממתי *adv* since when?

mee-matay she- ממתי ש־ *adv [colloq.]* since the time when.

me'eymatay? ?מאימתי *adv* since when?

meemekh ממך *adv & pers.pron (f sing)* from you.

meem|en/-enah/-antee מימן *v* financed; funded; (*pres* **memamen**; *fut* **yemamen**).

meemen|ah/-ee/-oo ממנה from her/me/him.

meem|esh/-shah/-ashtee מימש *v* realized; made come true; (*pres* **memamesh**; *fut* **yemamesh**).

mee-meyla ממילא *adv* anyway; obviously.

meemkar/-eem ממכר *nm* sale.

(le) meemkar למִמכר *adv* for sale.

(mekakh oo) meemkar (*npr* **meekakh** *etc*) מיקח וממכר *nm pl* give and take; bargaining; commercial deal.

meemkha ממך *adv & pers.pron (m sing)* from you.

meemkh|atah/-atot ממחטה *nf* handkerchief; (*+of:* **-etet**).

meemlakhah/-ot (*also:* **mamlekhah** *etc*) ממלחה *nf* salt shaker; salt-cellar.

mee-mool ממול *adv* in front of; facing; opposite.

meemoon/-eem מימון *nm* financing; funding; (*pl+of:* **-ey**).

◇ **"meemoonah"** (*or:* **"meemoonah"**) מימונה *nf* popular outdoor festival celebrated by Jews of Moroccan background on the evening and day following Passover.

meemoosh/-eem מימוש *nm* realization; carrying out; fulfilment.
meemr|akh/-akheem ממרח *nm* spread; paste; (*pl+of:* **-ekhey**).
meems|ad/-adeem ממסד *nm* the Establishment; (*pl+of:* **-edey**).
meemsadee/-t ממסדי *adj* pertaining to the Establishment.
meems|ar/-areem ממסר *nm* relay (electr.); (*pl+of:* **-erey**).
meemsh|al/-aleem ממשל *nm* governing administration; (*pl+of:* **-eley**).
◇ **ha-meemshal** הממשל *nm (colloq. abbr).* reference to the Israeli administration of the territories taken over in 1967.
◇ **ha-meemshal ha-amereekanee** הממשל האמריקני *nm* the American administration; the U.S. Government.
◇ **ha-meemshal ha-yeesre'elee ba-shtakheem** הממשל הישראלי בשטחים *nm* the Israeli administration of the territories taken over in 1967.
meemt|ar/-areem ממטר *nm* shower; rain; (*pl+of:* **-erey**).
meemts|a/-a'eem ממצא *nm* finding; (*pl+of:* **-e'ey**).
meen מן *prep* out of; of; from; than.
meen ha-deen מן הדין *adv* obviously; it seems obvious.
meen ha-kal el ha-kaved מן הקל אל הכבד *adv* step by step; from the easy to the difficult.
meen ha-katseh el ha-katseh מן הקצה אל הקצה *adv* from end to end; from one end to the other.
meen ha-meenyan מן המניין *adj* regular; ordinary.
(profesor) meen ha-meenyan פרופסור מן המניין *nm* full professor.
meen ha-moten מן המותן *adj* **1.** not properly prepared; without giving thought beforehand; **2.** *lit.*: (shooting) from the hip.
meen ha-pakh el ha-pakhat מן הפח אל הפחת *adv* from bad to worse.
meen ha-ra'ooy מן הראוי *adv* it is proper; it were worthwhile.
meen ha-shoorah מן השורה *adj* ordinary; regular; rank and file.
meen ha-stam מן הסתם *adv* most probably.
meen ha-tsad מן הצד *adv* on the side.
meen ha-tsedek מן הצדק *adv* it were only just if...
meen ha-yosher מן היושר *adv* it were only fair if...
(kaloot/klootah) meen ha-aveer קלוט מן האוויר *adj* **1.** unfounded; **2.** *lit.*: recorded from the air.
(matsoots/metsootsah) meen ha-etsba' מצוץ מן האצבע *adj* false; invented; *lit.:* sucked from the finger.
(shleef|ah/-ot) meen ha-moten שליפה מן המותן *nf* **1.** irresponsible, unserious proposition or idea; **2.** (*lit.:*) drawn from the hip.
meen/-eem מין *nm* **1.** sex; **2.** gender (Gram.); **3.** sort; category.
meen nekevah מין נקבה *nm* feminine gender (Gram.).
meen tov מין טוב *nm* good quality.
meen zakhar מין זכר *nm* masculine gender (Gram.).
(le) meen למן *prep* as from; from.
(eleel|at/-ot) meen אלילת מין *nf* sex-goddess.
(ev|ar/-rey ha) meen איבר המין *nm* **1.** penis; **2.** genitalia.
(ha) meen (he)khazak המין החזק *nm* the stronger sex.
(ha) meen (ha)yafeh המין היפה *nm* the beautiful sex.
(ke) meen כמין like.
(eyzeh) meen איזה מין what kind of...?!
(khayey) meen חיי מין *nm pl* sex-life.
(seefrey) meen ספרי מין *nm pl* sex-books; porno-books.
(seertey) meen סרטי מין *nm pl* "blue" movies; porno-movies.
meen|ah/-tah/-eetee מינה *v* **1.** appointed; nominated; **2.** allotted; occasioned; (*pres* **memaneh;** *fut* **yemaneh**).
meenayeen מניין *prep* **1.** wherefrom; **2.** how?
meenayeen lekha/lakh/lakhem/lakhen מניין לך wherefrom do you (*m/f sing;m/f pl*) know?! what makes you think that...
meenee/-t מיני *adj* sexual
(doo-) meenee/-t דו־מיני *adj* bi-sexual.
meeneemalee/-t מינימלי *adj* minimal.
meeneemoom מינימום *nm* minimum.
meeneest|er/-reem מיניסטר *nm [colloq.]* cabinet minister.
(rosh shel) meeneester ראש של מיניסטר *nm [slang]* the head of a cabinet minister i.e. someone very clever.
(akhrayoot) meeneesteryaleet אחריות מיניסטריאלית ministerial responsibility.
meeneesteryon/-eem מיניסטריון *nm* ministry; (*pl+of:* **-ey**).
(shokhad) meenee שוחד מיני *nm* sexual bribery i.e. accepting sexual favors against misuse of public office.
(steey|ah/-ot) meenee|t/-yot סטייה מינית *nf* sexual perversion.
meeneeyoot מיניות *nf* sexuality.
(mag|a'/-eem) meen|ee/-yeem מגע מיני *nm* sexual intercourse.
mee-neged מנגד *prep & adv* aloof from; aside.
('am|ad/-dah/-adetee) mee-neged עמד מנגד *v* kept aloof; failed to intervene; (*pst* **'amad** *etc; fut* **ya'amod** *etc*).
meenhag/-eem מנהג *nm* custom; (*pl+of:* **-ey**).
meenhal/-eem מינהל *nm* administration; management.
meenhal 'asakeem מינהל עסקים *nm* business administration.

◇ **meenhal mekarke'ey yeesra'el** מינהל מקרקעי ישראל *nm* Israel Land Administration autonomous government body in charge of all lands that are national property or under state administration. These make up a large proportion of the land in the country and comprise, in the first place, land acquisitions that had been carried out systematically throughout the years from 1905 onward by the Jewish National Fund (see ◇ **Keren Kayemet Le-yeesra'el**); then, government lands and lands abandoned by absentees (see ◇ **neekhsey neefkadeem**). All these have been and still are leased out to applicants for housing, agriculture or other purposes for an initial period of 49 years.

meenhal tseebooree מינהל ציבורי *nm* public administration.

(ha) meenhal המינהל *nm [colloq.]* reference to the Israel Land Administration.

meen|halah/-halot מנהלה *nf* management; administration; (*+of:* **-helet**).

meenhalee/-t מינהלי *adj* administrative.

('atseer/-eem) meenhal|ee/-yeem עציר מינהלי *nm* detainee under an administrative ruling.

meen|harah/-harot מנהרה *nf* tunnel; (*+of:* **-heret**).

meenkh|ah/-ot מנחה *nf* gift; (*+of:* **-at**).

◇ **(tefeelat) meenkhah** see ◇ **tefeelat meenkhah**.

meenkhat/-eem מנחת *nm* landing ground; (*pl+of:* **-ey**).

(ben/bat) meeno בן־מינו *adj* of same sex; of same kind.

(ben/bat she-'eyn|o/-ah) meeno בן שאינו מינו *adj* of the other sex; of a different kind.

meenoo|'akh/-kheem מינוח *nm* terminology.

meenoo|y/-yeem מינוי *nm* appointment; nomination; (*pl+of:* **-yey**).

(ketav/keetvey) meenooy כתב מינוי *nm* letter of appointment.

meens|arah/-arot מנסרה *nf* sawmill; lumber mill; (*+of:* **-eret**).

meensh|ar/-areem מנשר *nm* proclamation; manifesto; (*pl+of:* **-erey**).

◇ **meenyan** מניין *nm* quorum of ten adult (aged 13 or more) males needed for a public prayer service under Jewish law.

meen|yan/-yaneem מניין *nm* count; (*pl+of:* **-yeney**).

◇ **('aseeree le) meenyan** see ◇ **'aseeree le-meenyan**.

(he'em|eed/-eedah/-adetee le) meenyan העמיד למניין *v* put to vote; obtained a counting; (*pres* **ma'ameed** *etc; fut* **ya'ameed** *etc*).

(meen ha) meenyan מן המניין *adj* ordinary; regular; rank and file.

(profes|or/-oreem meen ha) meenyan פרופסור מן המניין *nm* full professor.

(talmeed/-eem meen ha) meenyan תלמיד מן המניין *nm* regular student.

meenz|ar/-areem מנזר *nm* convent; (*pl+of:* **-erey**).

mee'oos מיאוס *nm* abhorrence; loathing.

mee'oot/-eem מיעוט *nm* minority; (*pl+of:* **-ey**).

(ben/beney) mee'ooteem בן־מיעוטים *nmf* **1.** member of an ethnic minority; **2.** *[colloq.]* Israeli Arab.

□ **Meenzar ha-Shatkaneem** מנזר השתקנים *nm* the picturesque Trappist Monastery at **Latroon** (Latrun), midway between Tel-Aviv and Jerusalem, via Expressway 1.

mee'oot she-be-mee'oot מיעוט שבמיעוט *nm* most insignificant minority.

mee-pa'am le-fa'am *(f=p)* מפעם לפעם *adv* from time to time.

mee-pe'at מפאת *adv* on account of; because of.

mee-peh le-ozen מפה לאוזן *adv* **1.** by oral tradition; **2.** confidentially; **3.** *lit.*: from mouth to ear.

mee-peney מפני *prep* because of.

mee-peney mah מפני מה *prep* on account of what? why?

mee-peney she- מפני ש־ *prep* because of.

meepoo|y/-yeem מיפוי *nm* mapping; (*pl+of:* **-yey**).

me'er|ah/-ot מארה *nf* curse; (*+of:* **-at**).

meerdaf/-eem מרדף *nm* chase; pursuit; (*pl+of:* **-ey**).

meer|'eh/-'eem מרעה *nm* pasture; (*pl+of:* **-'ey**).

(sedeh/sedot) meer'eh שדה מרעה *nm* pasture-land; grazing field.

meerk|a'/-a'eem מרקע *nm* television screen; (*pl+of:* **-e'ey**).

meerkakh|at/-ot מרקחת *nf* **1.** jam. **2.** ointment.

(bet/batey) meerkakhat בית מרקחת *nm* pharmacy; drugstore.

meerk|am/-ameem מרקם *nm* fabric; web (*pl+of:* **-emey**).

meerk|ezet/-azot מירכזת *nf* telephone-exchange (*pl+of:* **-ezot**).

meerm|ah/-ot מירמה *nf* deceit; fraud.

meermas מרמס *nm* treading underfoot; trampling.

meerp|a'ah/-a'ot מרפאה *nf* clinic; (*+of:* **-e'at/-e'ot**).

meerpes|et/-ot מרפסת *nf* balcony; verandah.

meersha'at מרשעת *nf* shrew; bitch.

meersh|am/-ameem מרשם *nm* recipe; formula; prescription; (*pl+of:* **-emey**).

meersham/-eem refoo'ee/-yeem מרשם רפואי *nm* medical prescription.

meersh|am/-emey ha-ookhlooseen מרשם האוכלוסין *nm* population register.

meersh|am/-emey ha-toshaveem מרשם התושבים *nm* population register.

meerts|efet (*npr* **marts|efet**)/**-afot** מרצפת *nm* floor tile; (*pl+of:* **-efot**).

meerv|akh/-eem מרווח *nm* clearance; span; space (*pl+of:* **-ekhey**).

mees|'adah/-'adot מסעדה *nf* restaurant; (*+of:* **-'edet**).
mees'adah (*etc*) **tseemkhoneet** מסעדה צמחונית *nm* vegetarian restaurant.
mees'af/-eem מסעף *nm* road junction.
mee-saveev מסביב *adv* around; all around.
meesb|a'ah/-a'ot מסבאה *nf* tavern; barroom; (*+of:* **-e'at/-e'ot**).
meesd|ar/-areem מסדר *nm* **1.** parade; inspection. **2.** fraternity; order; (*pl+of:* **-erey**).
meesd|ar/-erey zeehooy מסדר זיהוי *nm* identification parade.
meesderon/-ot מסדרון *nm* corridor.
◻ **meesderon yerooshalayeem** מסדרון ירושלים *nm* the onetime perilous stretch (10 km long; between km 12 and 22) of the Jerusalem-Tel-Aviv highway (Expressway 1) that passes amid Judean hills.
meeseem מיסים *nm pl* taxes; (*sing:* **mas;** *pl+of:* **meesey**).
(meshal|em/-mey) meeseem משלם מיסים *nm* taxpayer.
meesg|ad/-adeem מסגד *nm* mosque; (*pl+of:* **-edey**).
◻ **Meesgad 'Omar** מיסגד עומר *nm* Jerusalem mosque known erroneously as the "Mosque of Omar", famed in the Muslim world as "Kharam-a-Shereef" and to others as the "Dome of the Rock". Built originally of wood by the Khaleef Omar on Mount Zion, where Solomon's Temple once stood, it is today a monumental octagon-shaped building with a golden dome on top and is highly revered by Muslims everywhere.
◻ **Meesgav 'Am** (Misgav 'Am) משגב עם *nm* kibbutz (est. 1945) in Upper Galilee near Lebanese border, 4 km NW of **Keeryat-Shmonah**. Pop. 277.
◻ **Meesgav Dov** (Misgav Dov) משגב דוב *nm* village (est. 1950), 3 km W. of **Gederah**. Pop. 329.
meesg|eret/-arot מסגרת *nf* frame; framework; (*pl+of:* **-erot**).
(shed/-ah) mee-shakhat שד משחת *nmf* one devilishly clever or capable.
meesh'al/-eem משאל **1.** public opinion poll; **2.** wish; desire; (*pl+of:* **-ey**).
meesh'al/-ey 'am משאל עם *nm* referendum.
meesh'al/-ey da'at kahal משאל דעת קהל *nm* public opinion poll.
meesh|'alah/-'alot משאלה *nf* desire; request; (*+of:* **-'elet**).
◇ **"meesh'an"** (**"Mish'an"**) "משען" *nf* country-wide chain of old-age homes operated by the Histadrut for its members.
meesh'an/-eem משען *nm* support; prop; -rest; (*pl+of:* **-ey**).
meeshbets|et/-ot משבצת *nf* square (small inlay).
meeshd|ar/-areem מישדר *nm* transmission (radio; television); (*pl+of:* **-erey**).
◇ **meeshd|ar/-erey sheroot** מישדר שירות *nm* "service-broadcast" being, actually, a state-sponsored or paid-for commercial.
mee-she- מש־ (*prefix*) as soon as...
(le) meesh'ee למשעי *adv* fully; cleanly.
(megoolakh le) meesh'ee מגולח למשעי *adj* clean-shaven.
mee-shel משל *adj* belonging to...; property of...
mee-shel|ah/ -akh/-ahem/ -ahen/ -akhem/ -akhen/-anoo/-ee/-o משלה/־ך/־הם וכו' of her/your (*f sing*)/their (*m/f*)/your (*pl m/f*) our/his own.
(nofekh) mee-shel|o/-ah (*etc*) נופך משלו/־ה וכו *nm* a touch of his/her *etc* own; his/her *etc* own version.
meeshe|hoo/-hee מי שהוא or: מישהו *pron m/f* someone.
meesh|'enet/-anot משענת *nf* rest; back-rest; support.
meesh|esh/-eshah/-ashtee מישש *v* groped; touched; felt; (*pres* **memashesh;** *fut* **yemashesh**).
meeshg|al/-aleem משגל *nm* copulation; sexual intercourse; (*pl+of:* **-eley**).
meeshg|eh/-eem משגה *nm* mistake; error; (*pl+of:* **-ey**).
meeshk|a'/-a'eem משקע *nm* sediment; precipitation; (*pl+of:* **-e'ey**).
meeshka'eem משקעים *nm pl* [*colloq.*] rains.
meeshk|afayeem משקפיים *nm pl* glasses; spectacles; (*+of:* **-efey**).
meeshk|al/-aleem משקל *nm* **1.** weight; **2.** [*colloq.*] scales; (*pl+of:* **-eley**).
meeshkal (*etc*) **segoolee** משקל סגולי *nm* specific gravity.
meeshkal/-ey tarnegol משקל תרנגול *nm* bantam-weight (boxing).
(ba'al/-ey) meeshkal בעל משקל *adj* influential; carrying weight.
(hor|eed/-eedah/-adetee) meeshkal הוריד משקל *v* lost weight; (*pres* **moreed** *etc; fut* **yoreed** *etc*).
(hos|eef/-eefah/-aftee) meeshkal הוסיף משקל *v* gained weight; (*pres* **moseef** *etc; fut* **yoseef** *etc*).
('od|ef/-fey) meeshkal עודף משקל *nm* extra-weight; surplus weight.
(sheevooy) meeshkal שיווי משקל *nm* equilibrium; balance.
(shom|er/-rey) meeshkal שומר משקל *nm* weight-watcher.
(tos|efet/-afot) meeshkal תוספת משקל *nf* additional weight.
(mah) meeshkal|kha/-ekh/-o/-ah? מה משקלך/־ו/־ה? how much do/-es you (*m/f*)/he/she weigh?
(haramat) meeshkalot הרמת משקלות *nf* weight-lifting.
meeshk|an/-aneem משכן *nm* dwelling-place; residence; (*pl+of:* **-eney**).

meeshkan nesee'ey yeesra'el משכן נשיאי ישראל *nm* official residence of the Presidents of Israel.

meeshk|av/-aveem משכב *nm* bed; lying; (*pl+of:* **-evey**).

meeshk|av/-evey zakhar משכב זכר *nm* sodomy; homosexual intercourse.

(naf|al/-lah/-altee) (le)meeshkav נפל למשכב *v* became ill; (*pres* **nofel** *etc; fut* **yeepol** *etc*).

meeshkee/-t משקי *adj* economic.

meeshk|efet/-afot משקפת *nf* binoculars.

meeshkefet sadeh משקפת שדה *nf* field-glasses.

meeshkefey kree'ah משקפי קריאה *nm pl* reading glasses.

meeshkefey shemesh משקפי שמש *nm pl* sun-glasses.

meeshk|en/-enah/-antee משכן *v* pawned; pledged; (*pres* **memashken**; *fut* **yemashken**).

meeshkenot 'onee משכנות עוני *nm pl* slums.

meesh'kh|ah/-ot משחה *nf* paste; salve; (*+of:* **-at**).

meesh'kh|at/-ot geeloo'akh משחת גילוח *nf* shaving-cream.

meesh'kh|at/-ot na'alayeem משחת נעליים *nf* shoe-polish.

meesh'kh|at/-ot sheenayeem משחת שיניים *nf* tooth-paste.

meesh'kh|atah/-atot משחטה *nf* slaughter-house; (*+of:* **-etet**).

meeshkol|et/-ot משקולת *nf* weigh[illegible]ummet.

meeshkoon/-eem משכון *nm* pawning; (*pl+of:* **-ey**).

meeshlakh yad משלח יד *nm* occupation; profession; business.

meeshl|akhat/-akhot משלחת *nf* delegation; expedition; (*pl+of:* **-ekhot**).

meeshl|at/-ateem משלט *nm* strong point; stronghold; military position; (*pl+of:* **-etey**).

meeshley משלי *nm* the Book of Proverbs (Bible).

meeshlo|'akh/-kheem משלוח *nm* consignment; expedition; (*pl+of:* **-khey**).

meeshlo'akh (*etc*) **be-do'ar** משלוח בדואר *nm* sending by mail; mail parcel.

◇ **meeshlo'akh manot** משלוח מנות *nm* package of food delicacies sent to friends on Purim. (In Yiddish: "Shalekh-moonis").

(kheyl/-ot) meeshlo'akh חיל משלוח *nm* expeditionary force.

meeshma'at משמעת *nf* discipline.

meeshma'atee/-t משמעתי *adj* disciplinary.

meeshmar/-ot משמר *nm* guard.

□ **Meeshmar Ayalon** (Mishmar Ayalon) משמר אילון *nm* village (est. 1949) in the central plain, 8 km SW of Ramla. Pop. 333.

□ **Meeshmar Daveed** (Mishmar David) משמר דוד *nm* kibbutz in central lowland (est. 1948), 2 km NW of Nahshon Junction (**Tsomet Nakhshon**). Pop. 210.

□ **Meeshmar ha-'Emek (Mishmar Ha'emeq)** משמר העמק *nm* kibbutz (est 1926) in W. Yizre'el Valley, 6 kms NW of Megeedo Junction (**Tsomet Megeedo**). Pop 795.

◇ **meeshmar ha-gvool** משמר הגבול *nm* the Israeli Police Frontier Guard Force.

□ **Meeshmar ha-Negev** (Mishmar Hanegev) משמר הנגב *nm* kibbutz (est. 1946) in the Negev, 4 km N. of haNassi Junction (**Tsomet ha-Nasee**). Pop. 669.

□ **Meeshmar ha-Sharon** (Mishmar Hasharon) משמר השרון *nm* kibbutz (est. 1933) in Sharon, 6 km N. of Ha-Sharon Junction. Pop. 524.

□ **Meeshmar ha-Sheev'ah** (Mishmar Hashiv'a) משמר השבעה *nm* village (est. 1949) outside Tel-Aviv. Pop. 559.

□ **Meeshmar ha-Yarden (Mishmar Hayarden)** משמר הירדן *nm* village (est. 1889) in Upper Galilee, 3 km NW of Jordan bridge **Gesher Benot Ya'akov**. Pop. 337.

('al) meeshmar על משמר *adv* on guard of...

('al ha) meeshmar על המשמר *adv* on guard.

□ **Meeshmarot (Mishmarot)** משמרות *nm* kibbutz (est. 1933) in N. Sharon, 2 km N. of Pardes Hanna (**Pardes-Khanah**). Pop. 290.

(kheeloofey) meeshmarot חילופי משמרות *nm pl* changing the guard; change of shifts.

meeshmeret/-arot משמרת *nf* shift; watch.

□ **Meeshmeret** (Mishmeret) משמרת *nm* village (est. 1946) in Sharon, 5 km N. of Kefar-Sava. Pop. 301.

(ha) meeshmeret (ha)tse'eerah המשמרת הצעירה *nf* (the) young shift; the Young Guard.

meeshmesh/-eem משמש *nm* apricot; (*pl+of:* **-ey**).

◇ **(ha)meeshnah** המשנה *nf* the "Mishnah", a six volume collection of oral law and legal discussions compiled and finalized in written form towards 210 C.E. which forms the backbone of the Talmud (**Talmood**) compiled during the following centuries.

meeshneh משנה *adj* twice as much; double the...

-meeshneh ־משנה (*suffix*) *adj* sub-; vice-; extra-; second.

meeshneh zeheeroot משנה זהירות *nm* double care; extra care.

(aloof/-ey) meeshneh אלוף־משנה *nm* colonel (Army).

(dayar/-ey) meeshneh דייר־משנה *nm* sub-tenant.

(kablan/-ey) meeshneh קבלן־משנה *nm* sub-contractor.

(kablanoot) meeshneh קבלנות־משנה *nm* sub-contracting.

(segen/sganey) meeshneh סגן־משנה *nm* second- lieutenant.

(sekheeroot) meeshneh שכירות־משנה *nf* sublease; subtenancy.

meeshnee/-t משני *adj* secondary.

meesh'ol/-eem משעול *nm* path; lane; (*pl+of:* **-ey**).
mee shoom mah משום מה *adv* for some reason or other.
mee-shoom she- משום ש־ *conj* because of.
meeshoosh/-eem מישוש *nm* touching; feeling; (*pl+of:* **-ey**).
meeshor/-eem מישור *nm* plain (topography).
meeshpakh|ah/-ot משפחה *nf* family; (*+of:* **-at**).
meeshpakh|ah/-ot khon|ekhet/-khot משפחה חונכת *nf* adoptive family.
(ba'al/-ey) meeshpakhah/-ot בעל משפחה *nm* family-man.
(ben/bat) meeshpakhah בן־משפחה *nmf* relative; one of the family; kin; (*pl:* **ben|ey/-ot** *etc*).
(keervat) meeshpakhah קרבת משפחה *nf* kinship.
(krov/-at) meeshpakhah קרוב משפחה *nmf* relative; kin.
(shem/shmot) meeshpakhah משפחה *nm* surname; family name.
meeshpakhtee משפחתי *adj* family-; of/for the family.
meeshp|at/-ateem משפט *nm* **1.** sentence (Gram.). **2.** justice; **3.** law; **4.** trial; court-case; (*pl+of:* **-etey**).
meeshpat/-eem kadoom/kedoomeem משפט קדום *nm* prejudice; preconceived idea.
meeshpat (*etc*) **tseva'ee** משפט צבאי *nm* court-martial.
(bet/batey) meeshpat בית משפט *nm* court of law; law court.
(kes ha) meeshpat כס המשפט *nm* seat of judgment.
(khar|ats/-tsah/-atstee) meeshpat חרץ משפט *v* passed judgment; (*pres* **khorets** *etc; fut* **yakhrots** *etc*).
(kha|yav/-yevet be) meeeshpat חייב במשפט *adj* convicted.
(zakh|ah/-tah/-eetee be) meeshpat זכה במשפט *v* **1.** won a court-case; **2.** was acquitted; (*pres* **zokheh** *etc; fut* **yeezkeh** *(k=kh) etc*).
meeshpatee/-t משפטי *adj* legal; juridical.
(haleekh/-eem) meeshpatee/-yeem הליך משפטי *nm* legal proceeding.
(yo'ets/-et) meeshpatee/-t יועץ משפטי *nmf* legal adviser.
(ha) yo'ets (ha)meeshpatee היועץ המשפטי *nm* the Attorney General.
meeshpateem משפטים *nm pl* the study of law.
(tvee|'ah/-'ot) meeshpateet/-yot תביעה משפטית *nf* legal claim; legal action; suit.
meeshpetan/-eet משפטן *nm* jurist; lawyer; (*pl:* **-eem/-eeyot**).
meesht|alah/-alot משתלה *nf* plant nursery; (*+of:* **-elet**).
meeshtalet/-et משתלט *v pres* take(s) control; overpower(s) (*pst* **heeshtalet**; *fut* **yeeshtalet**).
meesht|akh/-akheem משטח *nm* surface; ground; (*pl+of:* **-ekhey**).
meesht|akh/-ekhey nekheetah משטח נחיתה *nm* landing ground.
meeshtam|et/-teem משתמט *nm* shirker; (*f:* **-etet/-tot**; *pl+of:* **-tey**).
meeshtamet/-et משתמט *v pres* shirk(s); (*pst* **heeshtamet**; *fut* **yeeshtamet**).
meesht|anah/-anot משתנה *nf* pissoir; urinal (*+of:* **-enet**).
meeshtan|ah/-ot tseebooree|t/-yot משתנה ציבורית *nf* public latrine.
meeshtan|eh/-ah משתנה **1.** *adj* changing; **2.** *v pres* change(s); (*pst* **heeshtanah**; *fut* **yeeshtaneh**).
meesht|ar/-areem משטר *nm* **1.** regime. **2.** regimen; (*pl+of:* **-erey**).
meesht|ar/-erey kheroom משטר חירום *nm* emergency regime; state of emergency.
meeshtar/-eem tsva'ee/-'eem משטר צבאי *nm* military regime.
meesht|arah/-arot משטרה *nf* police; (*+of:* **-eret/-erot**).
(mekhonee|t/-yot) meeshtarah מכונית משטרה *nf* police-car.
(takhn|at/-ot) meeshtarah תחנת משטרה *nf* police-station.
meeshtartee/-t משטרתי *adj* police-.
khok|er/-reem meeshtartee/-yeem חוקר משטרתי *nm* police investigator.
(rekhev) meeshtartee רכב משטרתי *nm* police-vehicle.
meeshteh/-eem משתה *nm* feast; banquet.
meeshtolel/-et משתולל *v pres* run(s) amok; get(s) out of hand; (*pst* **heeshtolel**; *fut* **yeeshtolel**).
meeshv|'ah/-'ot משוואה *nf* equation; (*+of:* **-'at**).
(men|at/-ot) meeskal מנת משכל *nf* I.Q.; intelligence quotient.
meesken/-ah מסכן **1.** *adj* poor; miserable; **2.** *nmf* poor, miserable person.
meeskenoot מסכנות *nf* wretchedness.
mees'khak/-eem משחק *nm* play; game; (*pl+of:* **-ey**).
mees'khak/-ey gomleen משחקי גומלין *nm* return match.
mees'khak/-ey mazal משחק מזל *nm* game of chance; game of luck.
mees'khak/-ey meeleem משחק מלים *nm* pun; play on words.
mees'khar מסחר *nm* trade; commerce.
mees'khar keem'onee מסחר קמעוני *nm* retail trade.
mees'khar seetonee מסחר סיטוני *nm* wholesale trade.
(leeshkat/leshakhot) mees'khar לשכת מסחר *nf* chamber of commerce.
mees'kharee/-t מסחרי *adj* commercial.
mees'kh|eh/-eem משחה *nm* swimming meet; swimming contest; (*pl+of:* **-ey**).
mees'khoor מסחור *nm* commercialization.
meesl|akah/-akot (*cpr* **maslekah/-ot**) מסלקה clearing house; (*+of:* **-eket**).

meesm|akh/-akheem מסמך *nm* document; (*pl+of:* **-ekhey**).

(ha'atakat) meesmakheem העתקת מסמכים *nf* xeroxing; photocopying.

meesood/-eem מיסוד *nm* institutionalization; becoming part of the establishment.

meesp|anah/-anot מספנה *nf* shipyard; dockyard; (*+of:* **-enet/-enot**).

meesp|ar/-areem מספר *nm* number; figure; (*pl+of:* **-erey**).

meespar/-eem 'ag|ol/-ooleem מספר עגול *nm* round number.

meespar khazak מספר חזק *nm [colloq.]* impressive fellow.

(metey) meespar מתי־מספר *num pl* few; just a few.

meesp|arah/-arot מספרה *nf* barber-shop; (*+of:* **-eret**).

meesparayeem מספריים *nm pl* scissors.

(zoog/-ot) meesparayeem זוג מספריים *nm* pair of scissors.

meesparee/-t מספרי *adj* numerical.

meespareet מספרית *nf [slang]* odd (naughty) kind of girl.

meesped/-eem מספד *nm* eulogy; lament; obituary; (*pl+of:* **-ey**).

meesp|er/-erah/-artee מספר *v* numbered; numerated; (*pres* **memasper**; *fut* **yemasper**).

meespo מספוא *nm* fodder.

meespoor/-eem מספור *nm* numeration.

meesr|ah/-ot משרה *nf* position; job; office; (*+of:* **-at**).

meesr|ad/-adeem משרד *nm* **1.** office; bureau; **2.** Government Ministry; Government department (*pl+of:* **-edey**).

meesr|ad/-edey adreekhaloot משרד אדריכלות *nm* architect's office.

meesrad ha-'avodah משרד העבודה *nm* Labor Ministry.

meesrad ha-beetakhon משרד הביטחון *nm* Defense Ministry.

meesrad ha-bree'oot משרד הבריאות *nm* (Public) Health Ministry.

meesrad ha-datot משרד הדתות *nm* Ministry of Religions.

meesrad ha-energyah משרד האנרגיה *nm* Ministry of Energy.

meesrad ha-kheenookh ve-ha-tarboot מישרד החינוך והתרבות *nm* Ministry of Education and Culture.

meesrad ha-khoots משרד החוץ *nm* Foreign Office; Ministry of Foreign Affairs.

meesrad ha-kleetah משרד הקליטה *nm* Ministry for the Absorption of New Immigrants.

meesrad ha-meeshpateem משרד המשפטים *nm* Ministry of Justice.

meesrad ha-meeshtarah משרד המשטרה *nm* Ministry of Police.

meesrad ha-meeskhar ve-ha-ta'aseeyah משרד המסחר והתעשייה *nm* Ministry of Trade and Industry.

meesrad ha-otsar משרד האוצר *nm* Ministry of Finance; the Treasury.

meesrad ha-pneem משרד הפנים *nm* Ministry of the Interior; the Home Office.

meesrad ha-sheekoon ve-ha-beenooy משרד השיכון והבינוי *nm* Housing and Construction Ministry.

meesrad ha-takhboorah משרד התחבורה *nm* Ministry of Transport.

meesrad ha-teekshoret משרד התקשורת *nm* Ministry of Communications.

meesrad ha-reeshooy משרד הרישוי *nm* Road Traffic Licensing Bureau.

meesr|ad/-edey 'or|ekh/-khey deen משרד עורך־דין *nm* legal office; lawyer's office; law offices.

meesrad/-eem pratee/-yeem משרד פרטי *nm* private office.

meesrad/-eem rashee/-yeem משרד ראשי *nm* main office.

meesrad ro'e|h/-y kheshbon משרד רואה־חשבון *nm* auditor's office; accountant's office.

meesr|ad/-edey teevookh משרד תיווך *nm* broker's office; brokerage agency.

(tsorkhey) meesrad צורכי משרד *nm pl* office supplies.

meesradee/-t משרדי *adj* clerical.

meestabekh מסתבך *v pres* becomes involved, entangled (*pst* **heestabekh**; *fut* **yeestabekh**).

meestaber/-et מסתבר *v pres* transpires; seems reasonable; (*pst* **heestaber** *fut* **yeestaber**).

meestaber kee/she- מסתבר כי/ש־ *adv* apparently; it seems that...

meestaken/-et מסתכן *v pres* risks; runs a risk; (*pst* **heestaken**; *fut* **yeestaken**).

◇ **meestanen/-eem** מסתנן *nm* infiltrator; terrorist.

meestanen/-et מסתנן *v pres* infiltrate(s); (*pst* **heestanen**; *fut* **yeestanen**).

meestor/-eem מסתור *nm* hideout; cache; (*pl+of:* **-ey**).

meestoreen מסתורין *nm pl* mystery.

me'et מאת *prep* by; from.

me'et le-'et מעת לעת *adv* from time to time.

me'et/me'eetah מאט *v pres* slow(s) down; (*pst* **he'eet**; *fut* **ya'eet**).

meet|ah/-ot מיטה *nf* bed; (*+of:* **-at**).

(kley) meetah כלי מיטה *nm pl* bedding.

(leevney) meetah לבני מיטה *nm pl* bedlinen.

meet|ah/-ot מיתה *nf* death; (*+of:* **-at**).

meetah khatoofah מיתה חטופה *nf* sudden death.

meet|ah/-ot meshoon|ah/-ot מיתה משונה *nf* **1.** horrible death; **2.** unnatural death.

(kha|yav/-yevet) meetah חייב מיתה *adj* deserving death.

mee-ta'am מטעם *prep* on behalf of.

meet'ab|ed/-deem מתאבד *nm* a suicide; committing suicide; (*pl+of:* **-dey**).

meet'abed/-et מתאבד *v pres* commit(s) suicide; (*pst* **heet'abed**; *fut* **yeet'abed**).

meet'ab|ek/-keem מתאבק *nm* wrestler.

meet'abek/-et מתאבק *v pres* wrestle(s); (*pst* **heet'abek;** *fut* **yeet'abek**).

meet'abel/-et מתאבל *v pres* mourn(s) (*pst* **heet'abel;** *fut* **yeet'abel**).

meet'agref/-eem מתאגרף *nm* boxer; (*pl+of:* **-ey**).

meet'agref/-et מתאגרף *v pres* box(es); (*pst* **heet'agref;** *fut* **yeet'agref**).

mee-takhat מתחת *prep* below; underneath.

mee-takhat le- מתחת ל- *prep* under; underneath.

meet'akhed/-et מתאחד *v pres* unite(s); join(s) with; (*pst* **heet'akhed;** *fut* **yeet'akhed**).

meetaltel/-et מיטלטל **1.** *adj* portable; movable; **2.** *v pres* wander(s); **3.** *v pres* is carried from place to place; (*pst* **heetaltel;** *fut* **yeetaltel**).

meet'ales/-et מתעלס *v pres* make(s) love; (*pst* **heet'ales;** *fut* **yeet'ales**).

meet'am|el/-leem מתעמל *nm* athlete; gymnast; (*pl+of:* **-ley**).

meet'amel/-et מתעמל *v pres* drill(s) do(es) physical exercises; (*pst* **heet'amel;** *fut* **yeet'amel**).

meet'an/-eem מטען *nm* luggage; cargo; (*pl+of:* **-ey**).

(ketav/keetvey) meet'an כתב־מיטען *nm* bill of lading.

(shtar/sheetrey) meet'an שטר־מיטען *nm* bill of lading.

meet'an|eh/-ah מתענה *v pres* suffer(s); torment(s) self; (*pst* **heet'anah;** *fut* **yeet'aneh**).

meet'aneg/-et מתענג *v pres* relish(es); enjoy(s); (*pst* **heet'aneg;** *fut* **yeet'aneg**).

meet'anyen/-et מתעניין *v* take(s) interest; (*pst* **heet'anyen;** *fut* **yeet'anyen**).

meet'ar/-eem מתאר *nm* outline; (*pl+of:* **-ey**).

meet'ar|e'akh/-akhat מתארח *v pres* am/ is a guest; lodge(s); (*pst* **heet'are'akh;** *fut* **yeet'are'akh**).

meet'arekh/-et מתארך *v pres* lengthen(s); (*pst* **heet'arekh;** *fut* **yeet'arekh**).

meetat nesheekah מיתת נשיקה *nf* easy, painless death.

meetat sdom מיטת סדום *nf* Procrustean bed; impossibly narrow place.

meetbag|er/-reem מתבגר *nm* adolescent; (*f:* **-eret/-rot**).

meetbager/-et מתבגר *v pres* mature(s); (*pst* **heetbager;** *fut* **yeetbager**).

meetb|akh/-akheem מטבח *nm* kitchen; (*pl+of:* **-ekhey**).

(aron/-ot) meetbakh ארון מטבח *nm* kitchen cupboard; kitchen cabinet.

(ashaf/-ey ha) meetbakh אשף המטבח *nm* master-chef.

(kley) meetbakh כלי מטבח *nm pl* kitchenware.

(bet/batey) meetbakhayeem בית מטבחיים *nm* slaughterhouse.

meetbayesh/-et מתבייש *v pres* am/is ashamed; am/is embarrassed; (*pst* **heetbayesh;** *fut* **yeetbayesh**).

meetbayet/-et מתביית **1.** *adj* homing; **2.** *v pres* home(s); (*pst* **heetbayet;** *fut* **yeetbayet**).

meetboded/-eem מתבודד *nm* hermit; recluse; (*pl+of:* **-ey**).

meetboded/-et מתבודד *v pres* keep(s) to oneself; (*pst* **heetboded;** *fut* **yeetboded**).

meetbolel/-eem מתבולל *nm* assimilationist; (*pl+of:* **-ey**).

meetbolel/-et מתבולל *v pres* become(s) assimilated; (*pst* **heetbolel;** *fut* **yeetbolel**).

meetbonen/-et מתבונן **1.** *nmf* observer; **2.** *v pres* observe(s); (*pst* **heetbonen;** *fut* **yeetbonen**).

meetdayen/-et מתדיין *v pres* engage(s) in a law-suit; (*pst* **heetdayen;** *fut* **yeetdayen**).

meetday|en/-neem מתדיין *nm* litigant; (*pl+of:* **-ney**).

meet|eg/-gah/-agtee מיתג *v* switched; (*pres* **memateg;** *fut* **yemateg**).

meet|en/-nah/-antee מיתן *v* restrained; slowed down; (*pres* **mematen;** *fut* **yematen**).

meetfal|e'akh/-akhat מתפלח *[slang] v pres* enter(s) unpermitted; is a stow away; (*pst* **heetfale'akh;** *fut* **yeetfale'akh**).

meetgal|e'akh/-akhat מתגלח *v pres* shave(s); (*pst* **heetgale'akh;** *fut* **yeetgale'akh**).

meetgal|eh/-ah מתגלה *v pres* am/are/is revealed, discovered; (*pst* **heetgalah;** *fut* **yeetgaleh**).

meetgamed/-et מתגמד *v pres* am/are/is dwarfed; (*pst* **heetgamed;** *fut* **yeetgamed**).

meetganev/-et מתגנב *v pres* slip(s) in; (*pst* **heetganev;** *fut* **yeetganev**).

meetgared/-et מתגרד *v pres* scratch(es); (*pst* **heetgared;** *fut* **yeetgared**).

meetgar|eh/-ah מתגרה *v pres* challenge(s); tease(s) (*pst* **heetgarah;** *fut* **yeetgareh**).

meetgaresh/-et מתגרש *v pres* divorce(s); (*pst* **heetgaresh;** *fut* **yeetgaresh**).

meetgayes/-et מתגייס *v pres* enlist(s); join(s); (*pst* **heetgayes;** *fut* **yeetgayes**).

meetga|yes/-yseem מתגייס *nm* draftee; military volunteer; (*pl+of:* **-ysey**).

meetgoshesh/-eem מתגושש *nm* wrestler; (*pl+of:* **-ey**).

meetgoshesh/-et מתגושש *v pres* wrestle(s); (*pst* **heetgoshesh;** *fut* **yeetgoshesh**).

meetkabed/-et מתכבד *v pres* have/has the honor; partake(s) of food offered; (*pst* **heetkabed;** *fut* **yeetkabed**).

meetkabel/-et מתקבל *v pres* am/are/is received, accepted; (*pst* **heetkabel;** *fut* **yeetkabel**).

meetkabel/-et bee-vrakhah *(v=b)* מתקבל בברכה *v pres* am/are/is welcomed; etc.

meetkabel ke-eeloo מתקבל כאילו *adv* looks as if.

meetkabes/-et מתכבס *adj* washable; launderable.

meetkabets/-et מתקבץ *v pres* gather(s); assemble(s); (*pst* **heetkabets;** *fut* **yeetkabets**).

meetkadem/-et מתקדם **1.** *adj* progressive; **2.** *v pres* advance(s); progress(es); (*pst* **heetkadem;** *fut* **yeetkadem**).

meetkale'akh/-akhat מתקלח *v pres* take(s) a shower; (*pst* **heetkale'akh;** *fut* **yeetkale'akh**).

meetkalef/-et מתקלף **1.** *adj* peeling off; shedding; **2.** *v pres* peel(s) off; shed(s); (*pst* **heetkalef;** *fut* **yeetkalef**).

meetkamet/-et מתקמט *v pres* become(s) wrinkled; (*pst* **heetkamet;** *fut* **yeetkamet**).

meetk|an/-aneem מיתקן *nm* installation; apparatus; (*pl+of:* **-eney**).

meetk|an/-eney az'akah מיתקן אזעקה *nm* alarm system.

meetkane/-t מתקנא *v pres* envy (-ies); (*pst* **heetkane;** *fut* **yeetkane**).

meetkan|e'akh/-akhat מתקנח *v pres* cleanse(s) self; (*pst* **heetkane'akh;** *fut* **yeetkane'akh**).

meetkanes/-et מתכנס *v pres* convene(s); assemble(s); (*pst* **heetkanes;** *fut* **yeetkanes**).

meetkapel/-et מתקפל **1.** *adj* folding; **2.** *v pres* fold(s); **3.** *[slang] v pres* **give(s) in; accept(s) defeat;** (*pst* **heetkapel;** *fut* **yeetkapel**).

(meetah) meetkapelet מיטה מתקפלת *nf* folding bed.

meetkar|e/-et מתקרא *v pres* call(s) oneself; (*pst* **heetkare;** *fut* **yeetkare**).

meetkar|e'akh/-akhat מתקרח *v pres* become(s) bald; (*pst* **heetkare'akh;** *fut* **yeetkare'akh**).

meetkarer/-et מתקרר *v pres* get(s) cold; (*pst* **heetkarer;** *fut* **yeetkarer**).

meetkaresh/-et מתקרשת *v pres* freeze(s); jellify (-ies); (*pst* **heetkaresh;** *fut* **yeetkaresh**).

meetkarev/-et מתקרב *v pres* approach(es); near(s); (*pst* **heetkarev;** *fut* **yeetkarev**).

meetkash|eh/-ah מתקשה *nf* **1.** harden(s) **2.** find(s) difficult; (*pst* **heetkashah;** *fut* **yeetkasheh**).

meetkasher/-et מתקשר *v pres* **1.** connect(s); **2.** *[colloq.]* phone(s) (*pst* **heetkasher;** *fut* **yeetkasher**).

meetkatesh/-et מתכתש *v pres* wrestle(s); (*pst* **heetkatesh;** *fut* **yeetkatesh**).

meetkatev/-et מתכתב *v pres* correspond(s); (*pst* **heetkatev;** *fut* **yeetkatev**).

meetkatser/-et מתקצר *v pres* become(s) shorter; (*pst* **heetkatser;** *fut* **yeetkatser**).

meetkaven/-et מתכוון *v pres* intend(s) (*pst* **heetkaven;** *fut* **yeetkaven**).

(be) meetkaven במתכוון *adv* on purpose; deliberately.

(she-lo be) meetkaven שלא במתכוון *adv* unintentionally.

meetkazez/-et מתקזז *v pres* is/are set-off, written off, amortized; (*pst* **heetkazez;** *fut* **yeetkazez**).

meetkhabe/-t מתחבא *v pres* hide(s) self; (*pst* **heetkhabe;** *fut* **yeetkhabe**).

meetkhabek/-et מתחבק *v pres* embrace(s) one another; (*pst* **heetkhabek;** *fut* **yeetkhabek**).

meetkhaber/-et מתחבר *v pres* connect(s); make(s) friends; (*pst* **heetkhaber;** *fut* **yeetkhaber**).

meetkhabet/-et מתחבט *v pres* doubt(s); cannot decide; (*pst* **heetkhabet;** *fut* **yeetkhabet**).

meetkhabev/-et מתחבב *v pres* endear(s) oneself; (*pst* **heetkhabev;** *fut* **yeetkhabev**).

meetkhadesh/-et מתחדש *adj* renewed; renovated; restored.

meetkhadesh/-et מתחדש *v pres* renew(s) oneself; renovate(s) oneself; (*pst* **heetkhadesh;** *fut* **yeetkhadesh**).

meetkhakekh/-et מתחכך *v pres* **1.** rub(s); **2.** *[slang]* rub(s) shoulders; (*pst* **heetkhakekh;** *fut* **yeetkhakekh**).

meetkhakem/-et מתחכם *v pres* try (-ies) to outsmart; (*pst* **heetkhakem;** *fut* **yeetkhakem**).

meetkhakem מתחכם **1.** *adj* trying to be clever; **2.** *nmf [slang]* "wise guy".

meetkhaleh/-ah מתחלה **1.** *adj* malingering; **2.** *nmf* malingerer; **3.** *v pres* malinger(s); (*pst* **heetkhalah;** *fut* **yeetkhaleh**).

meetkhalek/-et מתחלק *v pres* **1.** divide(s) into; **2.** slip(s); (*pst* **heetkhalek;** *fut* **yeetkhalek**).

meetkham מיתחם *nm* defined area; range; locality; (*pl+of:* **-ey**).

meetkhamek/-et מתחמק *v pres* elude(s); (*pst* **heetkhamek;** *fut* **yeetkhamek**).

meetkhamem מתחמם *v pres* warm(s) up; (*pst* **heetkhamem;** *fut* **yeetkhamem**).

meetkhanef/-et מתחנף *v pres* flatter(s); ingratiate(s) oneself; (*pst* **heetkhanef;** *fut* **yeetkhanef**).

meetkhanen/-et מתחנן *v pres* implore(s); (*pst* **heetkhanen;** *fut* **yeetkhanen**).

meetkhaper/-et מתחפר *v pres* dig(s) in; (*pst* **heetkhaper;** *fut* **yeetkhaper**).

meetkhapes/-et מתחפש *v pres* masquerade(s); (*pst* **heetkhapes;** *fut* **yeetkhapes**).

meetkhar|eh/-ah מתחרה **1.** *nmf* competitor; **2.** *adj* competing; **3.** *v pres* compete(s); (*pst* **heetkhareh;** *fut* **yeetkhareh**).

meetkharesh/-et מתחרש *v pres* become(s) deaf; (*pst* **heetkharesh;** *fut* **yeetkharesh**).

meetkharet/-et מתחרט *v pres* repent(s); change(s) one's mind; regret(s); (*pst* **heetkharet;** *fut* **yeetkharet**).

meetkhased/-et מתחסד *nmf* goody-goody; one pretending piety; (*pst* **heetkhased;** *fut* **yeetkhased**).

meetkhasel מתחסל *v pres* is being liquidated; (*pst* **heetkhasel;** *fut* **yeetkhasel**).

meetkhasen/-et מתחסן *v pres* become(s) immune; strengthen(s) oneself; (*pst* **heetkhasen;** *fut* **yeetkhasen**).

meetkhashek/-et מתחשק *adv mf [slang]* gets a yen.

meetkhatsef/-et מתחצף *v pres* get(s) cheeky; (*pst* **heetkhatsef;** *fut* **yeetkhtsef**).

meetkhazeh/-ah מתחזה **1.** *nmf* impostor; (*pl:* **-eem**; *+of:* **-ey**); **2.** *v pres* disguise(s) oneself as; impersonate(s); (*pst* **heetkhazah**; *fut* **yeetkhazeh**).

meetkomem/-et מתקומם **1.** *nmf* rebel; **2.** *v pres* revolt(s); (*pst* **heetkomem**; *fut* **yeetkomem**).

meetkonen/-et מתכונן *v pres* prepare(s); (*pst* **heetkonen**; *fut* **yeetkonen**).

meetkotet/-et מתקוטט *v pres* quarrel(s); bicker(s); (*pst* **heetkotet**; *fut* **yeetkotet**).

meetlabesh/-et מתלבש *v pres* dress(es); (*pst* **heetlabesh**; *fut* **yeetlabesh**).

meetlabesh/-et (*etc*) **'al** מתלבש על *v pres [slang]* take(s) on in all earnest.

meetlabet/-et מתלבט **1.** *adj* confused; **2.** *v pres* is confused; cannot decide; (*pst* **heetlabet**; *fut* **yeetlabet**).

meetlahet/-et מתלהט *v pres* becomes inflamed; (*pst* **heetlahet**; *fut* **yeetlahet**).

meetlahev/-et מתלהב **1.** *adj* enthusiastic; **2.** *v pres* enthuse(s); (*pst* **heetlahev**; *fut* **yeetlahev**).

meetlak|e'akh/-akhat מתלקח **1.** *adj* inflammable; **2.** *v pres* catch(es) fire; (*pst* **heetlake'akh**; *fut* **yeetlake'akh**).

meetlaked/-et מתלכד *v pres* join(s) together; (*pst* **heetlaked**; *fut* **yeetlaked**).

meetlakhesh/-et מתלחש *v pres* whisper(s) with; (*pst* **heetlakhesh**; *fut* **yeetlakhesh**).

meetlakhlekh/-et מתלכלך *v pres* get(s) dirty; dirty (-ies) oneself; (*pst* **heetlakhlekh**; *fut* **yeetlakhlekh**).

meetlamed/-et מתלמד **1.** *nmf* self-taught; **2.** *v pres* teach(es) oneself; (*pst* **heetlamed**; *fut* **yeetlamed**).

meetlav|eh/-ah מתלווה *v pres* accompany(ies); (*pst* **heetlavah**; *fut* **yeetlaveh**).

meetlonen/-et מתלונן **1.** *nmf* plaintiff; **2.** *v pres* complain(s); (*pst* **heetlonen**; *fut* **yeetlonen**).

meetlotsets/-et מתלוצץ *v pres* jest(s); poke(s) fun; (*pst* **heetlotsets**; *fut* **yeetlotsets**).

meetma'et/-et מתמעט *v pres* diminish(es); (*pst* **heetma'et**; *fut* **yeetma'et**).

meetmaked/-et מתמקד *v pres* focus(es); concentrates on; (*pst* **heetmaked**; *fut* **yeetmaked**).

meetmakem/-et מתמקם *v pres* localize(s); take(s) hold; (*pst* **heetmakem**; *fut* **yeetmakem**).

meetmaker/-et מתמכר **1.** *nmf* addict; **2.** *v pres* **1.** devote(s) oneself completely; **2.** get(s) addicted; (*pst* **heetmaker**; *fut* **yeetmaker**).

meetmakh|eh/-ah מתמחה **1.** *nmf* majoring student during specialization; (*pl+of:* **-ey**); **2.** *v pres* specialize(s); (*pst* **heetmakhah**; *fut* **yeetmakheh**).

meetmamesh/-et מתממש *v pres* come(s) true; (*pst* **heetmamesh**; *fut* **yeetmamesh**).

meetmarmer/-et מתמרמר *v pres* resent(s); (*pst* **heetmarmer**; *fut* **yeetmarmer**).

meetmaser/-et מתמסר *v pres* devote(s) self; (*pst* **heetmaser**; *fut* **yeetmaser**).

meetmashekh/-et מתמשך **1.** *adj* extensive; **2.** *v pres* extend(s); (*pst* **heetmashekh**; *fut* **yeetmashekh**).

meetmasmes/-et מתמסמס *v pres* dissolve(s); decay(s); (*pst* **heetmasmes**; *fut* **yeetmasmes**).

meetmaten/-et מתמתן *v pres* become(s) moderate; (*pst* **heetmaten**; *fut* **yeetmaten**).

meetmatse/-t מתמצא *v pres* is familiar with; (*pst* **heetmatse**; *fut* **yeetmatse**).

meetmazeg/-et מתמזג *v pres* fuse(s); blend(s); (*pst* **heetmazeg**; *fut* **yeetmazeg**).

meetmazmez/-et מתמזמז *v pres* waste(s) time; *[slang]* flirt(s); (*pst* **heetmazmez**; *fut* **yeetmazmez**).

meetmoded/-et מתמודד *v pres* take(s) on; contend(s) with; (*pst* **heetmoded**; *fut* **yeetmoded**).

meetmogeg/-et מתמוגג **1.** *adj* "melting"; **2.** *v pres* "melt(s)"; (*pst* **heetmogeg**; *fut* **yeetmogeg**).

meetmotet/-et מתמוטט collapse(s); (*pst* **heetmotet**; *fut* **yeetmotet**).

meetnabe/-t מתנבא *v pres* predicts; (*pst* **heetnabe**; *fut* **yeetnabe**).

meetnadef/-et מתנדף *v pres* evaporate(s); (*pst* **heetnadef**; *fut* **yeetnadef**).

meetnadev/-et מתנדב **1.** *nmf* volunteer; **2.** *v pres* volunteer(s); (*pst* **heetnadev**; *fut* **yeetnadev**).

◇ **meetnag|ed/-deem** מתנגד *nm* member of religious movement opposing Hasidism (**Khaseedeesm**).

meetnag|ed/-edet מתנגד **1.** *nmf* opponent; adversary; (*pl:* **-deem**; *+of:* **-dey**); **2.** *v pres* oppose(s); (*pst* **heetnaged**; *fut* **yeetnaged**).

meetnagesh/-et מתנגש *v pres* clash(es) with; (*pst* **heetnagesh**; *fut* **yeetnagesh**).

meetnaheg/-et מתנהג *v pres* behave(s); (*pst* **heetnaheg**; *fut* **yeetnaheg**).

meetnahel/-et מתנהל *v pres* is being conducted; (*pst* **heetnahel**; *fut* **yeetnahel**).

meetna'er/-et מתנער *v pres* shake(s) off; (*pst* **heetna'er**; *fut* **yeetna'er**).

meetnakel/-et מתנכל *v pres* scheme(s); (*pst* **heetnakel**; *fut* **yeetnakel**).

meetnakem/-et מתנקם *v pres* take(s) revenge; (*pst* **heetnakem**; *fut* **yeetnakem**).

meetnakesh/-et מתנקש **1.** *nmf* assailant; **2.** *v pres* attempt(s) the life; (*pst* **heetnakesh**; *fut* **yeetnakesh**).

meetnakh|el/-aleem מתנחל *nm [colloq.]* settler in West Bank or Gaza Strip settlement; (*pl+of:* **-aley**).

meetnakhel/-et מתנחל *v pres* take(s) possession; enter(s) one inheritance; (*pst* **heetnakhel**; *fut* **yeetnakhel**).

meetnashef/-et מתנשף *v pres* pant(s); gasp(s); (*pst* **heetnashef**; *fut* **yeetnashef**).

meetnashek/-et מתנשק *v pres* exchange(s) kisses; (*pst* **heetnashek**; *fut* **yeetnashek**).

meetnashem/-et מתנשם *v pres* regain(s) breath; (*pst* **heetnashem**; *fut* **yeetnashem**).

meetnatek/-et מתנתק *v pres* break(s) with; disconnect(s) oneself from; (*pst* **heetnatek**; *fut* **yeetnatek**).

meetnats|e'akh/-akhat מתנצח *v pres* polemicize(s); (*pst* **heetnatse'akh**; *fut* **yeetnatse'akh**).

meetnatsel/-et מתנצל *v pres* apologize(s); (*pst* **heetnatsel**; *fut* **yeetnatsel**).

meetnats|er/-reem מתנצר *nm* convert to Christianity; (*f:* **-eret/-rot**; *pl+of:* **-rey**).

meetnatser/-et מתנצר *v pres* turn(s) Christian; (*pst* **heetnatser**; *fut* **yeetnatser**).

meetnaven/-et מתנוון **1.** *adj* degenerate; **2.** *v pres* degenerate(s); (*pst* **heetnaven**; *fut* **yeetnaven**).

meetnazer/-et מתנזר *v pres* abstain(s) from; (*pst* **heetnazer**; *fut* **yeetnazer**).

meetnofef/-et מתנופף *v pres* wave(s); (*pst* **heetnofef**; *fut* **yeetnofef**).

meetnoses/-et מתנוסס **1.** *adj* hoisted; **2.** *v pres* is hoisted; (*pst* **heetnoses**; *fut* **yeetnoses**).

meetnotsets/-et מתנוצץ **1.** *adj* gleaming; **2.** *v pres* gleam(s); (*pst* **heetnotsets**; *fut* **yeetnotsets**).

mee-tokh מתוך *adv* out of; from the midst of.

mee-tokh she- מתוך ש־ *prep* because; since.

meetoog/-eem מיתוג *nm* switching.

meetoon/-eem מיתון *nm* **1.** moderation; **2.** economic slump.

meetpa'er/-et מתפאר *v pres* boast(s) (*pst* **heetpa'er**; *fut* **yeetpa'er**).

meetpager/-et מתפגר *v pres* die(s) (of an animal or, if of a human,derogatory); become(s) a carcass; (*pst* **heetpager**; *fut* **yeetpager**).

meetpaked/-et מתפקד *v pres* function(s); (*pst* **heetpaked**; *fut* **yeetpaked**).

meetpakh|at/-ot מטפחת *nf* scarf; handkerchief.

meetpale/-t מתפלא *v pres* wonder(s); (*pst* **heetpale**; *fut* **yeetpale**).

meetpaleg/-et מתפלג *v pres* split(s); (*pst* **heetpaleg**; *fut* **yeetpaleg**).

meetpalets/-et מתפלץ *v pres* shudder(s); (*pst* **heetpalets**; *fut* **yeetpalets**).

meetpalmes/-et מתפלמס *v pres* argue(es); (*pst* **heetpalmes**; *fut* **yeetpalmes**).

meetpalsef/-et מתפלסף *v pres* philosophize(s); (*pst* **heetpalsef**; *fut* **yeetpalsef**).

meetpan|eh/-ah מתפנה *v pres* become(s) vacant; become(s) free; (*pst* **heetpanah**; *fut* **yeetpaneh**).

meetpanek/-et מתפנק *v pres* pamper(s) oneself; (*pst* **heetpanek**; *fut* **yeetpanek**).

meetpantcher/-et מתפנצ׳ר *[slang] v pres* go(es) wrong; (*pst* **heetpantcher**; *fut* **yeetpantcher**).

meetp|arah/-arot מתפרה *nf* sewing workshop; (*+of:* **-eret/-erot**).

meetpar|e'a'/-a'at מתפרע *v pres* riot(s); (*pst* **heetpare'a'**; *fut* **yeetpare'a'**).

meetpar|e'a'/-'eem מתפרע *nm* rioter; (*pl+of:* **-'ey**).

meetparek/-et מתפרק **1.** *adj* falling apart; **2.** *v pres* fall(s) apart; (*pst* **heetparek**; *fut* **yeetparek**).

meetpares/-et מתפרש *adj* spreading out; *v pres* spread(s) out; (*pst* **heetpares**; *fut* **yeetpares**).

meetparesh/-et מתפרש *v pres* is interpreted; is construed; (*pst* **heetparesh**; *fut* **yeetparesh**).

meetparets/-et מתפרץ *v pres* erupt(s); (*pst* **heetparets**; *fut* **yeetparets**).

meetparnes/-et מתפרנס *v pres* earn(s) a living; (*pst* **heetparnes**; *fut* **yeetparnes**).

meetparper/-et מתפרפר *[slang] v pres* is promiscuous (a "butterfly"); (*pst* **heetparper**; *fut* **yeetparper**).

meetparsem/-et מתפרסם *v pres* is publicized; is published; (*pst* **heetparsem**; *fut* **yeetparsem**).

meetpasher/-et מתפשר *v pres* compromises; (*pst* **heetpasher**; *fut* **yeetpasher**).

meetpashet/-et מתפשט *v pres* **1.** undress(es); **2.** spreead(s); (*pst* **heetpashet**; *fut* **yeetpashet**).

meetpater/-et מתפטר *nm pres* **1.** resign(s); **2.** get(s) rid of; (*pst* **heetpater**; *fut* **yeetpater**).

meetpatsel/-et מתפצל *v pres* split(s); subdivide(s); (*pst* **heetpatsel**; *fut* **yeetpatsel**).

meetpazer/-et מתפזר **1.** *adj* dispersing; **2.** *v pres* disperse(s); (*pst* **heetpazer**; *fut* **yeetpazer**).

meetpoot|ar/-eem מתפוטר *[slang]* **1.** *adj* forced to resign; **2.** *v pres* am/is forced to resign; (*pst* **heetpootar**; *fut* **yeetpootar**).

meetporer/-et מתפורר **1.** *adj* desintegrating; **2.** *v pres* desintegrate(s); (*pst* **heetporer**; *fut* **yeetporer**).

meetpotsets/-et מתפוצץ *v pres* explode(s); (*pst* **heetpotsets**; *fut* **yeetpotsets**).

meetnas|eh/-ah מתנסה *v pres* experience(s); (*pst* **heetnasah**; *fut* **yeetnaseh**).

meetra'anen/-et מתרענן *v pres* freshen(s) up; (*pst* **heetra'anen**; *fut* **yeetra'anen**).

meetr|ad/-adeem מטרד *nm* nuisance; (*pl+of:* **-edey**).

meetragel/-et מתרגל *v pres* become(s) accustomed; get(s) used; (*pst* **heetragel**; *fut* **yeetragel**).

meetragesh/-et מתרגש **1.** *adj* get(s) excited; **2.** *v pres* is excited; (*pst* **heetragesh**; *fut* **yeetragesh**).

meetragez/-et מתרגז *v pres* get(s) angry; (*pst* **heetragez**; *fut* **yetragez**).

meetrakem/-et מתרקם **1.** *adj* shaping; **2.** *v pres* take(s) shape; (*pst* **heetrakem**; *fut* **yeetrakem**).

meetrakhesh/-et מתרחש *v pres* take(s) place; (*pst* **heetrakhesh**; *fut* **yeetrakhesh**).

meetrakh|ets/-atseem מתרחץ *nm* bather; (*pl+of:* **-tsey**).

meetrakhets/-et מתרחץ *v* wash(es); bath(es); (*pst* **heetrakhets**; *fut* **yeetrakhets**).

meetr|as/-aseem מתרס *nm* barricade; (*pl+of:* **-esey**).

meetrashel/-et מתרשל **1.** *adj* neglectful; **2.** *v pres* neglect(s); (*pst* **heetrashel**; *fut* **yeetrashel**).

meetratseh/-ah מתרצה *v pres* consent(s); (*pst* **heetratsah**; *fut* **yeetratseh**).

meetree|yah/-yot מטרייה *nf* umbrella; (*+of:* **-yat**).

meetromem/-et מתרומם *v pres* rise(s) up/above; (*pst* **heetromem;** *fut* **yeetromem**).

meetromem/-eem מתרומם *[slang] nm homosexual;* (*pl+of:* **-ey**).

meetromem|et/-ot מתרוממת *[slang] nf* easy lay.

meetronen/-et מתרונן *v pres* shout(s) with joy; (*pst* **heetronen;** *fut* **yeetronen**).

meets/-eem מיץ *nm* juice; (*pl+of:* **-ey**).

meets 'agvaneeyot מיץ עגבניות *nm* tomato-juice.

meets 'anaveem מיץ ענבים *nm* grape juice.

meets eshkoleeyot מיץ אשכוליות *nm* grapefruit juice.

meets/-ey perot מיץ פירות *nm* fruit juice.

meets petel מיץ פטל *nm* raspberry juice.

meets tapookheem מיץ תפוחים *nm* apple juice.

meets tapoozeem מיץ תפוזים *nm* orange juice.

meets/-eem teev'ee/-yeem מיץ טבעי *nm* natural juice.

meets|ah/-tah/-eetee מיצה *v* exhausted; (*pst* **mematseh;** *fut* **yematseh**).

meets'ad/-eem מצעד *nm* parade; (*pl+of:* **-ey**).

meets'ad ha-peezmooneem מצעד הפזמונים *nm* hit parade.

meets'ad/-eem tseva'ee/-yeem מצעד צבאי *nm* military parade.

mee-tsad מצד *adv* on the part of; on the side of.

mee-tsad ekhad מצד אחד *adv* on the one hand.

mee-tsad shenee מצד שני *adv* on the other hand.

meets'ar מצער *nm* trifle.

meetsb|a'ah/-a'ot מצבעה *nf* dye works; (*+of:* **-a'at**).

meetsbor/-eem מצבור *nm* depot; dump; (*pl+of:* **-ey**).

mee-tskhok מצחוק *adv* laughing; of laughter.

meetsn|akh/-akheem (*npr* **matsn|e'akh/-ekheem**) מצנח *nm* parachute; (*pl+of:* **-ekhey**).

meetsn|efet/-afot מצנפת *nf* headdress; turban.

meetsoo|y/-yeem מיצוי *nm* exaction; exhaustion.

□ **Meetspah** (Mizpa) מצפה *nm* village (est. 1908 as agric. colony) in Lower Galilee, 3 km W. of Tiberias. Pop. 121.

□ **meetspeem** מצפים *nm pl* a series of small-scale residential settlements established as from 1980 atop selected hills in the Galilee so as to render the area more attractive to new settlers.

◇ **meetspeh/-eem** מצפה *nm* observation-point; nascent settlement in the Galilee (see previous entry).

□ **Meetspeh Ramon** (Mizpe Ramon) מצפה רמון *nf* development township (est. 1954) and local council on NW edge of **Makhtesh Ramon** crater, impressive part of Negev Desert. Pop. 3,280.

□ **Meetspeh Shalem** (Mizpe Shalém) מצפה שלם *nm* kibbutz (est. 1978) in Judean Desert, 15 km N. of 'En Gedi (**'En Gedee**).

meetsr|akh/-akheem מצרך *nm* commodity; (*pl+of:* **-ekhey**).

meetsrakh ha-khodesh מצרך החודש *nm* sale of the month.

meetsrakh ha-shavoo'a מצרך השבוע *nm* sale of the week.

(peetsets|at/-ot) meetsrar פצצת מצרר *nf* cluster-bomb.

□ **Meetsrayeem** מצרים *nf* Egypt.

meetsree/-t מצרי *adj* Egyptian.

meetsree/-yah מצרי *nmf* Egyptian.

meetstaber/-et מצטבר **1.** *adj* accumulative; gathering; **2.** *v pres* accumulate(s); gather(s); (*pst* **heetstaber;** *fut* **yeetstaber**).

(reebeet) meetstaberet ריבית מצטברת *nf* accrued interest.

meetstadek/-et מצטדק *v pres* justify(ies) oneself; (*pres* **heetstadek;** *fut* **yeetstadek**).

meetsta'er/-et מצטער *v pres* regret(s); feel(s) sorry; (*pst* **heetsta'er;** *fut* **yeetsta'er**).

(anee) meetsta'er/-et אני מצטער *interj m/f* I'm sorry! I apologize!

meetstakhek/-et מצטחק *v pres* smile(s); (*pst* **heetstakhek;** *fut* **yeetstakhek**).

meetstalem/-et מצטלם *v pres* has one's photograph taken; (*pst* **heetstalem;** *fut* **yeetstalem**).

meetstalev/-et מצטלב *v pres* **1.** intersect(s); **2.** cross(es) one's heart; (*pst* **heetstalev;** *fut* **yeetstalev**).

meetstan|e'a'/-a'at מצטנע *v pres* affect(s) modesty; (*pst* **heetstane'a;** *fut* **yeetstane'a**).

meetstanen/-et מצטנן *v pres* catch(es) cold; (*pst* **heetstanen;** *fut* **yeetstanen**).

meetstayen/-et מצטיין **1.** *adj* distinguished; **2.** *v pres* excel(s); (*pst* **heetstayen;** *fut* **yeetstayen**).

meetstamek/-et מצטמק **1.** *adj* shrinking; **2.** *v pres* shrink(s); (*pst* **heetstamek;** *fut* **yeetstamek**).

meetstofef/-et מצטופף **1.** *adj* huddling together; **2.** *v pres* crowd(s) in; (*pst* **heetstofef;** *fut* **yeetstofef**).

meetsv|ah/-ot מצווה *nf* **1.** good deed; **2.** "mitsveh" i.e. commandment (relig.); (*+of:* **-at**).

◇ **(bar-) meetsvah** see ◇ **bar-meetsvah**.

◇ **(bat-) meetsvah** see ◇ **bat-meetsvah**.

(meelkhemet) meetsvah מלחמת מצווה *nf pres* holy war.

(seemkhat) meetsvah שמחת מצווה *nf* festivity or rejoicing with a religious basis.

◇ **(taryag) meetsvot** see ◇ **taryag meetsvot**.

(teezk|eh/-ee le) meetsvot! תזכה למצוות! *interj* well-wishing (addressing observant Jew).

meetvakh/-eem מטווח *nm* range; shooting gallery.

mee-tvakh katsar מטווח קצר *adv* from close range.

mee-tvakh rakhok מטווח רחוק *adv* from long range.

meetya'el/-et מתייעל *v pres* become(s) efficient; (*pst* **heetya'el;** *fut* **yeetya'el**).

meetya'esh/-et מתייאש *v pres* despair(s); (*pst* **heetya'esh;** *fut* **yeetya'esh**).

meetyashev/-et מתיישב *v pres* settles down; sit(s) down to; (*pst* **heetyashev;** *fut* **yeetyashev**).

meetyash|ev/-veem מתיישב *nm* settler; (*pl+of:* **-vey**).

meetyashen/-et מתיישן *v pres* become(s) obsolete; (*pst* **heetyashen;** *fut* **yeetyashen**).

meetyatsev/-et מתייצב *v pres* **1.** report(s) for duty; **2.** become(s) stabilized; (*pst* **heetyatsev;** *fut* **yeetyatsev**).

meevd|ak/-akeem מבדק *nm* test; (*pl+of:* **-ekey**).

meevdak (*etc*) **grafologee** מבדק גרפולוגי *nm* a graphologic test.

meevd|ak/-eem pseekhotekhnee/-yeem מבדק פסיכוטכני *nm* psycho-technic test; aptitude test.

meevdelet מבדלת *nf* collapsible door; room-divider.

meevdok/-eem מבדוק *nm* dry dock; (*pl+of:* **-ey**).

me-'ever מעבר *adv* beyond; across.

me-'ever la- מעבר ל־ *adv* across; beyond.

me-'ever la-daf מעבר לדף *adv* overleaf; on the verso.

me-'ever la-yam מעבר לים *adv* overseas.

me-'ever le-harey khoshekh מעבר להרי־חושך *adv* at the end of the world.

(**me-'al oo-**) **me-'ever** מעל ומעבר *adv* above and beyond.

meevkh|an/-khaneem מבחן *nm* test; exam; examination; (*pl+of:* **-eney**).

(**'am|ad/-dah/-adetee ba**) **meevkhan** עמד במבחן *v* passed the test; (*pres* **'omed** *etc;* *fut* **ya'amod** *etc*).

meevkhar/-eem מבחר *nm* selection; (*pl+of:* **-ey**).

meevn|eh/-eem מבנה *nm* structure; (*pl+of:* **-ey**).

meevr|ak/-akeem מברק *nm* telegram; cable; (*pl+of:* **-ekey**).

meevr|akah/-akot מברקה *nf* telegraph office; (*+of:* **-eket**).

meevr|eshet/-ashot מברשת *nf* brush.

meevresh|et/-ot geeloo'akh מברשת גילוח *nm* shaving-brush.

meevresh|et/-ot sheenayeem מברשת־שיניים *nm* toothbrush.

meevt|a/-a'eem מבטא *nm* pronunciation; accent; (*pl+of:* **-e'ey**).

meevta sabree (*npr* **tsabaree**) מבטא צברי *nm* native Israeli (Sabra) accent.

meevtah zar מבטא זר *nm* foreign accent.

□ **Meevtakheem** (Mivtahim) מבטחים *nm* village (est. 1950) in NW Negev, 5 km SW of Magen Road Junction. Pop. 408.

meevts|a'/-a'eem מבצע *nm* **1.** operation; performance; **2.** [*colloq.*] one-time reduction price sale; (*pl+of:* **-e'ey**).

◇ **Meevtsa' Kadesh** מיבצע קדש *nm* military operation "Kadesh" - the so-known Sinai Campaign or the Sinai War (◇ **meelkhemet seenay**). It was Israel's reaction (1965) to Egypt's having blocked the Straits of Tiran which allow access to the country's only Red Sea outlet, the port of Elat. Following a four month Israeli occupation of most of Sinai, the blockade was lifted.

(**mekheer/-ey**) **meevtsa'** מחיר מבצע *nm* special onetime reduction price.

meevtsa'ee/-t מבצעי *adj* operational; operative.

meevz|ak/-akeem מבזק *nm* flash (cabled); (*pl+of:* **-ekey**).

meeyad מייד *adv* immediately.

(**teykhef oo**) **meeyad** תיכף ומייד *adv* this very minute.

mee-yad מיד *adv* from the hand of.

mee-yad le-yad מיד ליד *adv* from hand to hand; directly.

meeyadee/-t מיידי *adj* immediate.

mee-yameem yameemah מימים ימימה *adv* every year; annually.

mee-yedey מידי *adv* from the hands of; from.

mee|yen/-yenah/-yantee מיין *v* sorted; catalogued; (*pres* **memayen;** *fut* **yemayen**).

me'eyn מעין *adj* kind of; quasi-; such as; like.

meeyoon/-eem מיון *nm* sorting; classifying.

(**khad|ar/-rey**) **meeyoon** חדר מיון *nm* **1.** sorting room; **2.** emergency room (in a hospital).

meez'ar מזער *nm* minimum.

mez'aree/-t מזערי *adj* minimal.

mee-zaveet shel מזווית של from the angle of.

meezb|alah/-alot מזבלה *nf* garbage dump; (*+of:* **-elet**).

meezb|e'akh/-ekhot מזבח *nm* altar (*+of:* **-akh**).

meez|eg/-gah/-agtee מיזג *v* blended; merged; (*pres* **memazeg;** *fut* **yemazeg**).

mee-zeh oo-mee-zeh מזה ומזה *adv* on either side; from here and there.

meezk|ar/areem מזכר *nm* memo; memorandum; (*pl+of:* **-erey**).

meezl|alah/-alot מזללה *nf* eatery (*+of:* **-elet**).

mee-zman מזמן *adv* a long time ago.

meezm|ez/-ezah/-aztee מזמז *v* **1.** wasted; **2.** [*slang*] "necked"; (*pres* **memazmez;** *fut* **yemazmez**).

meezmooz/-eem מזמוז **1.** *nm* flirting; **2.** [*slang*] "necking"; (*pl+of:* **-ey**).

meezmor/-eem מזמור *nm* hymn; song; (*pl+of:* **-ey**).

meeznon/-eem מזנון *nm* **1.** buffet (furniture); sideboard; **2.** refreshment-room.

meeznon|ay/-a'eem (*cpr* **meeznona'ee**) מזנונאי *nm* buffet attendant; (*pl+of:* **-a'ey**).

meezoog/-eem מיזוג *nm* fusion; amalgamation; blending; (*pl+of:* **-ey**).

meezoog/-ey aveer מיזוג אוויר *nm* air conditioning.

◇ **meezoog galooyot** מיזוג גלויות *nm* blending into one homogenic nation Jews repatriating from various Diaspora countries and of different backgrounds.

□ **Meezra'** (Mizra') מזרע *nm* kibbutz (est. 1923) in the Yizre'el Valley, 4 km N. of 'Afula. Pop. 861.

meezr|akah/-akot מזרקה *nf* fountain; (*+of:* -**eket**).

meezrakh מזרח *nm* E.; orient.

(ha) meezrakh (ha)karov המזרח הקרוב *nm* (the) Near East.

(ha) meezrakh (ha)rakhok המזרח הרחוק *nm* (the) Far East.

(ha) meezrakh (ha)teekhon המזרח התיכון *nm* (the) Middle East.

('adot ha) meezrakh עדות המזרח *nf pl* Jewish communities of Afro-Asian background (in Israel).

(artsot ha) meezrakh ארצות המזרח *nf pl* Eastern countries.

(drom-) meezrakh דרום־מזרח *nm* southeast.

(tsfon-) meezrakh צפון־מזרח *nm* northeast.

meezrakhee/-t מזרחי *adj* oriental; E.

◇ **(ha-goosh ha) meezrakhee** see ◇ **(ha)goosh ha-meezrakhee.**

◇ **(ha-Po'el ha) meezrakhee** see ◇ **(ha) Po'el (ha) meezrakhee.**

(dromeet-) meezrakheet le- דרומית מזרחית ל־ *adv* south-east of.

meezrakheet le- מזרחית ל־ *adv* E. of.

(tsfoneet-) meezrakheet le- צפונית מזרחית ל־ *adv* north-east of.

meezran/-eem מזרן *nm* mattress; (*pl+of:* -**ey**).

meezrekhan/-eet מזרחן *nmf* orientalist.

meezrekhanoot מזרחנות *nf* oriental studies.

meezron/-eem (*npr* **meezran**) מזרון *nm* mattress; (*pl+of:* -**ey**).

meezv|adah/-adot מזוודה *nf* suitcase; trunk; valise; (*+of:* -**edet/-edat**).

meezvadon|et/-ot מזוודונת *nf* small suitcase.

mefager/-et מפגר **1.** *adj* slow; retarded; **2.** *nmf* retarded person; **3.** *v pres* lag(s) behind; (*pst* **peeger** *(p=f)*).

mefahek/-et מפהק *v pres* yawn(s); (*pst* **peehek**; *fut* **yefahek** *(p=f)*).

mefak|e'akh/-akhat מפקח **1.** *nmf* inspector; supervisor; (*pl:* -**'kheem**; *+of:* -**'khey**); **2.** *v pres* inspect(s); supervise(s); (*pst* **peekakh** *(p=f)*; *fut* **yefakakh**).

mefak|ed/-deem מפקד *nm* commander; (*pl+of:* -**dey**).

mefaked/-et 'al מפקד על *v pres* has command over; (*pst* **peeked** *(p=f) etc*; *fut* **yefaked** *etc*).

mefakhed/-et מפחד *v pres* fear(s); (*pst* **peekhed** *(p=f)*; *fut* **yefakhed**).

mefaleg/-et מפלג *v pres* cause(s) to split; (*pst* **peeleg** *(p=f)*; *fut* **yefaleg**).

mefales/-et מפלס *v pres* pave(s) way; (*pst* **peeles** *(p=f)*; *fut* **yefales**).

□ **Mefalseem** (Mefalesim) מפלסים *nm* kibbutz (est. 1949) in S. seashore plain, 3 km W. of Gevim Junction (**Tsomet Geveem**). Pop. 421.

mefan|eh/-ah מפנה *v pres* vacate(s); (*pst* **peenah** *(p=f)*; *fut* **yefaneh**).

mefarek/-et מפרק *v pres* dismantle(s); (*pst* **perek** *(p=f)*; *fut* **yefarek**).

mefar|ek/-keem מפרק *nm* liquidator; (*pl+of:* -**key**).

mefarekh/-et מפרך *adj* hard; wearisome.

('avod|ah/-ot) mefar|ekhet/-khot עבודה מפרכת *nf* hard labor.

mefaresh/-et מפרש *v pres* interpret(s); (*pst* **peresh** *(p=f)*; *fut* **yefaresh**).

mefaret/-et מפרט *v pres* list(s) detail(s); (*pst* **peret** *(p=f)*; *fut* **yefaret**).

mefargen/-et מפרגן *v pres* am/is immune to envy; am/is not envious; (*pst* **feergen**; *fut* **yefargen**).

mefarkes/-et מפרכס *v pres* **1.** jerk(s); **2.** embellish(es); (*pst* **peerkes** *(p=f)*; *fut* **yefarkes**).

mefarnes/-eem מפרנס *nm* breadwinner; provider; (*pl+of:* -**ey**).

mefarnes/-et מפרנס *v pres* provide(s); (*pst* **peernes** *(p=f)*; *fut* **yefarnes**).

mefoon|eh/-ah מפונה **1.** *adj* ejected; evacuated; **2.** *v pres* is ejected; is evacuated; (*pst* **poonah** *(p=f)*; *fut* **yefooneh**).

mefoondr|ak/-eket מפונדרק *[slang] adj* dolled out.

mefoon|eh/-eem מפונה *nm* evacuee; (*pl+of:* -**ey**).

meforaz/-ezet מפורז **1.** *adj* demilitarized; **2.** *v pres* is demilitarized; (*pst* **poraz** *(p=f)*; *fut* **yeforaz**).

(ezor/-eem) meforaz/-eem אזור מפורז *nm* demilitarized zone.

megad|el/-leem מגדל *nm* grower; (*pl+of:* -**ley**).

megadel/-et מגדל *v pres* raise(s); (*pst* **geedel**; *fut* **yegadel**).

megad|el/-ley bakar מגדל־בקר *nm* cattle raiser.

megad|el/-ley hodeem מגדל הודים *nm* turkey raiser.

megad|el/-ley 'ofot מגדל עופות *nm* fowl raiser.

megal|eh/-ah מגלה *v pres* discover(s); (*pst* **geelah**; *fut* **yegaleh**).

megal|eh/-at keeshronot מגלה כשרונות *nmf* talent-scout.

megalem/-et מגלם *v pres* personify(-ies); impersonate(s); (*pst* **geelem**; *fut* **yegalem**).

megalgel/-et מגלגל *v pres* **1.** roll(s); keep(s) rolling; **2.** *[colloq.] v pres* transfers (*pst* **geelgel**; *fut* **yegalgel**).

megalgel (*etc*) **kesafeem** מגלגל כספים *v pres* deals in big sums of money; has all sorts of financial combinations.

megam|ah/-ot מגמה *nf* trend; tendency; (*+of:* -**at**).

megamah (*etc*) **hoomaneet** מגמה הומנית *nm* humanities trend (in high school).

megamah (*etc*) **re'aleet** מגמה ריאלית *nm* natural science trend (in high school).

megamatee/-t מגמתי *adj* tendentious; biased.

megamgem/-et מגמגם **1.** *adj* stammering; **2.** *v pres* stammers; **3.** *[slang] v pres* is not prepared to say clearly; (*pst* **geemgem**; *fut* **yegamgem**).

megared/-et מגרד *v pres* scratch(es); scrape(s); (*pst* **gered**; *fut* **yegared**).

megar|ed/-dey sh'khakeem מגרד שחקים *nm* skyscraper.

megar|eh/-ah מגרה **1.** *adj* exciting; stimulating; **2.** *v pres* excite(s); stimulate(s); (*pst* **geerah**; *fut* **yegareh**).

□ **Megadeem** (Megadim) מגדים *nm* village (est. 1949) on Carmel seashore, 2 km from 'Atlit Junction (**Tsomet Atleet**). Pop. 446.

□ **Megeedo** (Meggido) מגידו *nm* kibbutz (est. 1949) in W. of Yizre'el Valley, near Meggido Junction (**Tsomet Megeedo**). Pop. 380.

□ **(Tel) Megeedo** see □ **Tel Megeedo**.

megeel|ah/-ot מגילה *nf* scroll; (*+of:* **-at**).

◊ **(ha)megeelah** המגילה *nf* the "Meggileh" (Biblical Book of Esther) - also known as the Purim Scroll.

◊ **(ha)megeelot ha-genoozot** המגילות הגנוזות *nf pl* the "hidden scrolls" from late 2nd Temple times, discovered (in 1947 and after in caves along Dead Sea shore). Samples are exhibited in Jerusalem's Israel Museum.

megeelat/-ot yookhaseen מגילת יוחסין *nf* pedigree; family-tree chart.

meg|en/-eenah מגן *v pres* defend(s); (*pst* **hegen**; *fut* **yagen**).

meger|ah/-ot מגירה *nf* drawer; (*+of:* **-at**).

mego|hats/-hetset מגוהץ **1.** *adj* ironed; pressed; **2.** *v pres* is pressed, ironed; (*pst* **gohats**; *fut* **yegohats**).

megoob|ash/-eshet מגובש **1.** *adj* crystallized; consolidated; shaped; **2.** *v pres* is crystallized, consolidated; (*pst* **goobash**; *fut* **yegoobash**).

megood|al/-elet מגודל *adj* large; sizable.

megood|ar/-eret מגודר *adj* fenced.

megookh|akh/-ekhet מגוחך *adj* ridiculous.

megool|akh/-akhat מגולח *adj* shaven.

megool|akh/-akhat le-meesh'ee מגולח למשעי *adj* clean-shaven.

megoolgal/-elet מגולגל **1.** *adj* 1. rolled; **2.** *adj* metamorphosed; **3.** *v pres* is rolled, transposed; (*pst* **goolgal**; *fut* **yegoolgal**).

(beyts|ah/-eem) megoolg|elet/-alot ביצה מגולגלת *nf* soft-boiled egg.

megoon|eh/-ah מגונה *adj* nasty; indecent.

(ma'as|eh/-eem) megoon|eh/-eem מעשה מגונה *nm* indecent act.

megoond|ar/-eret מגונדר *adj* dolled up.

megoor|eem מגורים *nm pl* dwelling; residence; abode; (*pl+of:* **-ey**).

(bet/batey) megooreem בית מגורים *nm* residential building.

(ezor/-ey) megooreem אזור מגורים *nm* residential area.

(shekhoon|at/-ot) megooreem שכונת מגורים *nf* residential quarter.

megoosh|am/-emet מגושם *adj* coarse; crude; awkward.

megoov|an/-enet מגוון *adj* varied; diversified.

megoo|yas/-yeset מגוייס **1.** *nmf* draftee; recruit; **2.** *adj* mobilized; drafted; **3.** *v pres* is drafted, mobilized; (*pst* **gooyas**; *fut* **yegooyas**).

megoor|ad/-edet מגורד *adj* scraped; grated.

megoor|ash/-eshet (*npr* **megor|ash/-eshet**) מגורש **1.** *adj* expelled; **2.** *v pres* is expelled; (*pst* **gorash**; *fut* **yegorash**).

mehaded/-et מהדד *v pres* echo(es); resound(s); (*pst* **heeded**; *fut* **yehaded**).

mehadek/-et מהדק *v pres* tighten(s); (*pst* **heedek**; *fut* **yehadek**).

mehad|ek/-keem מהדק *nm* paper-clip; (*pl+of:* **-key**).

mehad'hed/-et מהדהד *v pres* reverberate(s); (*pst* **heed'hed**; *fut* **yehad'hed**).

(lee) mehadreen למהדרין *adv* for connoisseurs; for more demanding clients.

mehag|er/-reem מהגר *nm* emigrant; migrant; (*pl+of:* **-rey**).

mehager/-et מהגר *v pres* emigrate(s); (*pst* **heeger**; *fut* **yehager**).

meham|er/-reem מהמר *nm* gambler; (*pl+of:* **-rey**).

mehamer/-et מהמר *v pres* gamble(s); (*pst* **heemer**; *fut* **yehamer**).

mehandes/-et מהנדס *nmf* engineer; (*pl:* **-eem**; *+of:* **-ey**).

mehandes/-et bakheer/bekheerah מהנדס בכיר *nmf* senior engineer.

mehandes/-et beenyan מהנדס בניין *nmf* civil engineer; building engineer; (*pl:* **-ey** *etc*).

mehandes/-et elektroneekah מהנדס אלקטרוניקה *nmf* electronics engineer; (*pl:* **-ey** *etc*).

mehandes/-et khashmal מהנדס חשמל *nmf* electrical engineer; (*pl:* **-ey** *etc*).

mehandes/-et kheema|'ee/-'eet (*npr* **keema|y/-'eet**) מהנדס כימאי *nmf* chemical engineer.

mehandes/-et makhsheveem מהנדס מחשבים *nmf* computer engineer; (*pl:* **-ey** *etc*).

mehandes/-et mekhonot מהנדס מכונות *nmf* mechanical engineer; (*pl:* **-ey** *etc*).

mehandes/-et rashee/-t מהנדס ראשי *nmf* chief-engineer.

mehandes/-et ta'aseeyah ve-neehool מהנדס תעשייה וניהול *nmf* industrial (and management) engineer; (*pl:* **-ey** *etc*).

mehandes/-et ye'ool מהנדס ייעול *nmf* efficiency engineer; (*pl:* **-ey** *etc*).

mehapkhan/-eet (*npr* **mahpkhan/-eet**) מהפכן *nmf* revolutionary (*pl:* **-eem**; *+of:* **-ey**).

mehapkhanee/-t (*npr* **mahpkhanee/-t**) מהפכני *adj* revolutionary.

meheeroo|t/-yot מהירות *nf* speed.

(bee) meheeroot במהירות *adv* quickly.

(bee) meheeroot ha-bazak במהירות הבזק *adv* at lightning speed.

(rakevet) meheerah רכבת מהירה *nf* fast train.
me-heykhan מהיכן *adv* wherefrom; whence.
meheyman/-ah מהימן *adj* reliable; trustworthy; dependable.
meheymanoo|t/-yot מהימנות *nf* reliablity.
meherah מהרה *adv* quickly.
(bee) meherah במהרה *adv* shortly; rapidly.
mehood|ar/-eret מהודר *adj* elegant; luxurious.
mehoog|an/-enet מהוגן *adj* worthy; honest.
mehool|al/-elet מהולל *adj* famed.
mehoom|ah/-ot מהומה *nf* turmoil; confusion; panic; riot; **(**+*of:* **-at)**.
mehoomot מהומות *nf pl* riots.
(bee) mehoopakh במהופך *adv* upside down.
mehoopn|at/-etet מהופנט *adj* hypnotized.
mekabel/-et מקבל *v pres* get(s); receive(s); **(***pst* **keebel;** *fut* **yekabel)**.
mekabel **(***etc***)** **makot** מקבל מכות *v pres* get(s) a beating.
mekabel **(***etc***)** **maroot** מקבל מרות *v pres* submit(s) to authority.
mekab|el/-ley paneem/peney מקבל פנים *nm* welcomer.
mekadem/-et מקדם *v pres* advance(s); **(***pst* **keedem;** *fut* **yekadem)**.
mekad|em/-meem מקדם *nm* coefficient; factor; **(***pl+of:* **-mey)**.
mekadmey pan|av/-eha מקדמי פניו *nm pl* those coming to welcome him/her.
mekakh **(***npr* **meekakh) oo-meemkar** מיקח ומימכר *nm pl* buying and selling; trade.
mekakh ta'oot **(***npr* **meekakh)** מיקח טעות *nm* bad deal.
('am|ad/-dah/-adetee 'al ha) mekakh **(***npr* **meekakh)** עמד על המיקח *v* haggled; bargained; **(***pres* **'omed** *etc;* *fut* **ya'amod** *etc***)**.
('ameedah 'al ha) mekakh (*npr* **meekakh)** עמידה על המיקח *nf* haggling; bargaining.
mekarke'eem (also **mekarke'een**) מקרקעים or: מקרקעין *nm pl* real-estate; immovables.
◇ **(leeshkat reeshoom) mekarke'een** לשכת רישום מקרקעין *nf* Land Registry Office (known colloquially as **Taboo)**.
◇ **mekarke'ey yeesra'el** מקרקעי ישראל *nm pl* Israel's State-owned lands.
◇ **(meen'hal) mekarke'ey yeesra'el** see ◇ **meen'hal mekarke'ey yeesra'el**.
mekasher/-et מקשר *v pres* connect(s); bind(s); **(***pst* **keesher;** *fut* **yekasher)**.
mekash|er/-reem מקשר *nm* **1.** agent; contact-man; **2.** liason-officer; **(***pl+of:* **-rey)**.
mekasher sma'lee מקשר שמאלי *nm* left inside forward (soccer).
mekasher yemanee מקשר ימני *nm* right inside forward (soccer).
mekashkesh/-et מקשקש *v pres* **1.** scribble(s); **2.** *[slang]* prattle(s); chatter(s); **(***pst* **keeshkesh;** *fut* **yekashkesh)**.
mekater/-et מקטר *v pres [slang]* grumble(s); **(***pst* **keeter;** *fut* **yekater)**.

mekatser/-et מקצר *v pres* shorten(s); **(***pst* **keetser;** *fut* **yekatser)**.
mek|el/-eelah מקל *v pres* ease(s) up; alleviate(s); is lenient; **(***pst* **hekel;** *fut* **yakel)**.
mekel **(***etc***)** **da'at** מקל דעת *v pres* underestimate(s).
mekhab|eh/-ah מכבה *v pres* extinguish(es); **(***pst* **keebah;** *fut* **yekhabeh** *(k=kh)***)**.
mekhab|eh/-ey esh מכבה אש *nm* fireman.
mekhabel/-et מחבל sabotage(s); **(***pst* **kheebel;** *fut* **yekhabel)**.
mekhab|el/-leem מחבל *nm* **1.** terrorist; **2.** saboteur; **(***pl+of:* **-ley;** *nf* **-elet/-lot)**.
mekhab|er/-eret מחבר *nmf* author; **(***nm & pl:* **-reem;** *pl+of:* **-rey;** *f:* **-rot)**.
mekhaber/-et מחבר *v pres* join(s); connect(s); **(***pst* **kheeber;** *fut* **yekhaber)**.
mekhabev/-et מחבב *v pres* like(s); sympathize(s); **(***pst* **kheebev;** *fut* **yekhabev)**.
mekhableem מחבלים *nm pl* terrorists.
(khool|yat/-yot) mekhableem חוליית מחבלים *nf* group of terrorists.
me-khadash מחדש *adv* anew.
mekhaded/-eem מחדד *nm* sharpener; pencil-sharpener; **(***pl+of:* **-ey)**.
mekhadesh/-et מחדש *v pres* renovate(s); innovate(s); **(***pst* **kheedesh;** *fut* **yekhadesh)**.
mekhakeh/-ah מחכה **1.** *adj* waiting; **2.** *v pres* wait(s); expect(s); **(***pst* **kheekah;** *fut* **yekhakeh)**.
mekhakeh/-ah מחקה *v pres* imitate(s); **(***pst* **kheekah;** *fut* **yekhakeh)**.
mekhal/-eem מיכל *nm* tank; container; **(***pl+of:* **-ey)**.
mekhalee|t/-yot מיכלית *nf* tanker.
mekhal|ek/-keem מחלק *nm* **1.** distributor; newsboy; **2.** divider; **(***pl+of:* **-key)**.
mekhalek/-et מחלק *v pres* divide(s); distribute(s); **(***pst* **kheelek;** *fut* **yekhalek)**.
mekhalets/-et מחלץ *v pres* rescue(s); extricate(s); **(***pst* **kheelets;** *fut* **yekhalets)**.
me-khamat מחמת *adv* on account of.
mekhaneh/-ah מכנה *v pres* call(s); nickname(s); **(***pst* **keenah** *(k=kh);* *fut* **yekhaneh)**.
mekhaneh מכנה *nm* denominator (arithmetic).
mekhaneh meshootaf מכנה משותף *nm* common denominator.
mekhanee/-t מכני *adv* mechanical.
mekhaneekah/-ot מכניקה *nf* mechanics; **(**+*of:* **-at)**.
mekhaneekah 'adeenah מכניקה עדינה *nf* precision mechanics.
mekhan|ekh/-ekhet מחנך *nmf* educator; **(***pl:* **-kheem/-khot;** +*of:* **-khey)**.
mekhanekh/-et מחנך **1.** *adj* educative; educational; **2.** *v pres* educate(s); **(***pst* **kheenekh;** *fut* **yekhanekh)**.
mekhap|eh/-ah מחפה *v pres* cover(s); cover(s) up for; **(***pst* **kheepah;** *fut* **yekhapeh)**.
mekhapes/-et מחפש *v pres* search(es) for; **(***pst* **kheepes;** *fut* **yekhapes)**.
mekharef/-et מחרף *v pres* insult(s); vilify(ies); **(***pst* **kheeref;** *fut* **yekharef)**.

mekharef (*etc*) **nafsho/-ah** מחרף נפשו *v pres* risk(s) one's (his/her etc) life.

mekharef (*etc*) **oo-megadef** מחרף ומגדף *v pres* taunt(s) and blaspheme(s); insult(s) and abuse(s).

mekharkher/-et מחרחר *v pres* instigate(s); provoke(s); (*pst* **kheerkher**; *fut* **yekharkher**).

mekharkh|er/-arey meelkhamah מחרחר מלחמה *nm* warmonger.

mekharkh|er/-arey reev מחרחר ריב *nm* trouble-maker; instigator; one stirring up strife.

mekharsem/-et מכרסם *v pres* erode(s); nibble(s); (*pst* **keersem** *(k=kh)*; *fut* **yekharsem**).

mekharsem/-eem מכרסם *nm* rodent.

mekhaseh/-ah מכסה *v pres* cover(s); cover(s) up; (*pst* **keesah**; *fut* **yekhaseh** *(k=kh)*).

mekhaser/-et מחסר *v pres* deduct(s); subtract(s); (*pst* **kheeser**; *fut* **yekhaser**).

mekhashben/-et מחשבן *v pres [slang]* calculate(s) (*pst* **kheeshben**; *fut* **yekhashben**).

mekhashef/-et מכשף *v pres* bewitch(es); enchant(s); (*pst* **keeshef**; *fut* **yekhashef** *(k=kh)*).

mekhash|ef/-feem מכשף *nm* sorcerer; magician; wizard; (*pl+of:* **-fey**).

mekhashef|ah/-ot מכשפה *nf* witch; sorceress; (*+of:* **-at**).

(tseyd) mekhashefot ציד מכשפות *nm* witch-hunt.

mekhashev/-et מחשב *v pres* calculate(s) (*pst* **kheeshev**; *fut* **yekhashev**).

mekhash|ev/-veem (*npr* **makhsh|ev/-aveem**) מחשב *nm* computer; (*pl+of:* **makhshavey**).

(mehandes/-et) mekhashveem (*npr* **makhshaveem**) מהנדס מחשבים *nmf* computer engineer; (*pl:* **-ey** *etc*).

me-khayeel el khayeel מחיל אל חיל *adv* from one success to another; from strength yo strength.

mekha|yeh/-yah מחיה *v pres* revive(s); bring(s) life to; (*pst* **hekh'yah**; *fut* **yekhayeh**).

mekha|yeh/-yah nefashot מחיה נפשות *adj* invigorating; refreshing.

(ah-) mekhayeh! א־מחיה! *interj [slang]* wonderful!

mekhayev/-et מחייב *adj* obligatory; binding; committing.

mekhayev/-et מחייב *v pres* oblige(s); require(s); (*pst* **kheeyev**; *fut* **yekhayev**).

mekhazek/-et מחזק *v pres* strengthens; reinforce(s); (*pst* **kheezek**; *fut* **yekhazek**).

mekhazer/-et מחזר *v pres* court(s); woo(s); (*pst* **kheezer**; *fut* **yekhazer**).

mekhaz|er/-reem מחזר *nm* suitor; wooer; beau; (*pl+of:* **-rey**).

mekhazer/-et 'al ha-petakheem מחזר על הפתחים *nmf* mendicant; beggar.

(bee) mekhee-yad במחי־יד *adv* with one sweep.

mekheek|ah/-ot מחיקה *nf* erasure; erasing; (*+of:* **-at**).

mekheel/-ah מכיל *adj* containing; *v pres* contain(s); (*pst* **hekheel**; *fut* **yakheel**).

mekheel|ah/-ot מחילה **1.** pardon; forgiveness; **2.** burrow; cavern; (*+of:* **-at**).

(sleekhah oo) mekheelah! סליחה ומחילה *interj* pardon and forgiveness!

mekheen/-ah מכין **1.** *adj* preparatory; **2.** *v pres* prepare(s); (*pst* **hekheen**; *fut* **yakheen**).

mekheen|ah/-ot מכינה *nf* preparatory class; (*+of:* **-at**).

mekhee'ot kapayeem מחיאות כפיים *nf pl* applause; hand-clappings.

mekheer/-eem מחיר *nm* price; (*pl+of:* **-ey**).

mekheer/-ey (ha)keren מחיר הקרן *nm* cost-price.

mekheer/-ey meevtsa' מחיר מבצע *nm* reduced sale's price; special sale price.

mekheer/-eem moofk|a'/-a'eem מחיר מופקע *nm* exorbitant price.

mekheer/-eem moozal/-eem מחיר מוזל *nm* reduced price.

('alah/-oo' ha) mekheer/-eem עלה המחיר price(s) went up.

(tos|efet/-fot) mekheer תוספת מחיר *nf* price increase.

(yar|ad/-doo ha) mekheer/-eem ירד המחיר prices went down.

mekheer|ah/-ot מכירה *nf* sale; (*+of:* **-at**).

mekheer|ah/-ot klalee|t/-yot מכירה כללית *nf* clearance-sale.

mekheer|ah/-ot poombee|t/-yot מכירה פומבית *nf* public auction.

mekheer|at/-ot sof ha-'onah מכירת סוף העונה *nf* end-of-the-season clearance sale.

('alee|yat/-yot) mekheereem עליית מחירים *nf* rise in prices.

(hafka|'at/-'ot) mekheereem הפקעת מחירים *nf* profiteering.

(madad ha) mekheereem la-tsarkhan מדד המחירים לצרכן *nm* consumer price index.

(yereed|at/-ot) mekheereem ירידת מחירים *nf* slump in prices.

mekheeron/-eem מחירון *nm* price-list; (*pl+of:* **-ey**).

mekheets|ah/-ot מחיצה *nf* partition; room-divider; (*+of:* **-at**).

mekher מכר *nm* sale.

(rav/rabat) mekher *(b=v)* רב־מכר *nm* bestseller.

(shtar/sheetrey) mekher שטר־מכר *nm* bill of sale.

mekh|es/-aseem מכס customs; customs-duty; (*pl+of:* **meekhsey**).

('ameel/-ey) mekhes עמיל מכס *nm* forwarding agent.

(bet ha) mekhes בית המכס *nm* customs house.

(ta'areef/-ey) mekhes תעריף מכס *nm* customs-duties tariff.

mekhetsah מחצה *nf* half.

(le) mekhetsah למחצה **1.** *adv* by half; **2.** *adj (suffix)* semi-; half-.

mekhk|ar/-areem מחקר *nm* study; research; (*pl+of:* **-erey**).

mekhl|af/-afeem מחלף *nm* crossing (*pl+of:* -**efey**).

mekho|'ar/-'eret מכוער *adj* ugly.

mekhokek/-et מחוקק *v pres* legislate(s); (*pst* **khokek**; *fut* **yekhokek**).

(bet/batey) mekhokekeem בית מחוקקים *nm* parliament; legislation.

□ **Mekholah** (Mehola) מחולה *nm* village (est. 1968) in the Jordan Valley, 6 km S. of Tirat Zevi (**Teerat Tsevee**). Pop. 315.

mekholel/-et מחולל **1.** *nmf* dancer; **2.** *v pres* create(s); perform(s); (*pst* **kholel**; *fut* **yekholel**).

mekhon מכון *m+of* the institute of.

mekhon/-ey mayeem מכון מים *nm* water tower.

◇ **"Mekhon Vaytsman"** מכון ויצמן *nm* the Weizmann Institute, Israel's foremost scientific complex, a multidisciplinary center devoted to reasearch and teaching in biology, chemistry, mathematics and physics. Founded in 1934 by Prof. Chaim Weizmann, a chemist and Zionist leader, who in 1948 became the first President of Israel. Later renamed after him, it is located in the NE part of Rehovot (**Rekhovot**).

□ **"Mekhon Veengeyt"** מכון וינגייט *nm* the Wingate Institute of Physical Training, on the seashore, W. of Expreessway 2 (T.A.-Haifa), 8 km S. of Netanya. Founded 1955.

mekhon/-ey yofee מכון יופי *nm* beauty parlor.

mekhon|ah/-ot מכונה *nf* machine; (*+of:* -**at**).

mekhona'oot מכונאות *nf* mechanics; mechanical training.

mekhon|at/-ot geeloo'akh מכונת גילוח *nm* razor; safety razor.

mekhon|at/-ot geeloo'akh khashmaleet/-yot מכונת גילוח חשמלית *nf* electric razor.

mekhon|at/-ot kheeshoov מכונת חישוב *nf* calculator.

mekhon|at/-ot keteevah מכונת כתיבה *nf* typewriter.

mekhonat/-ot keteevah elektronee|t/-yot מכונת כתיבה אלקטרונית *nf* electronic typewriter.

mekhon|at/-ot keteevah kadooreet מכונת כתיבה כדורית *nf* printing ball typewriter.

mekhon|at/-ot keteevah khashmalee|t/yot מכונת כתיבה חשמלית *nf* electric typewriter.

mekhon|at/-ot keteevah yadanee|t/-yot מכונת כתיבה ידנית *nf* mechanical typewriter.

mekhon|at/-ot keveesah מכונת כביסה *nf* washing machine.

mekhon|at/-ot tefeerah מכונת תפירה *nf* sewing machine.

mekhon|at/-ot tofet מכונת תופת *nf* infernal machine.

mekhona|y/-'eem (*cpr* **mekhona|'ee**) מכונאי *nm* mechanic; (*pl+of:* -**'ey**).

mekhonee|t/-yot מכונית *nf* car; motor-car.

mekhonee|t/-yot grar מכונית גרר *nf* towing car.

mekhonee|t/-yot keebooy מכונית כיבוי *nf* fire-engine.

mekhonee|t/-yot khashmalee|t/-yot מכונית חשמלית *nf* electric car.

mekhonee|t/-yot masa' מכונית משא *nf* truck; lorry.

mekhonee|t/-yot meeshtarah מכונית משטרה *nf* police-car; police van.

mekhonee|t/-yot tender מכונית טנדר *nf* pick-up truck.

mekhonee|t/-yot tofet מכונית תופת *nf* infernal machine.

mekhonee|t/-yot tsemoodah מכונית צמודה *nf* company-car; government car (placed at official's disposal for everyday use).

mekhonen/-et מכונן **1.** *v pres* establish(es); (*pst* **konen** *(k=kh)*; *fut* **yekhonen**); **2.** *adj* founding.

mekhonen/-eem מכונן *nm* machinist; mechanic.

(asefah) mekhonenet אסיפה מכוננת *nf* statutory meeting; founding assembly.

mekhoob|ad/-edet מכובד **1.** *adj* respected; honorable; **2.** *v pres* is honored; (*pst* **koobad** *(k=kh)*; *fut* **yekhoobad**).

mekhoog|ah/-ot מחוגה *nf* calipers; compass; (*+of:* -**at**).

mekhook|am/-emet מחוכם *adj* ingenious.

mekhool|ah/-ot מכולה *nf* container; (*+of:* -**at**).

mekhool|ak/-eket מחולק **1.** *adj* divided; distributed; **2.** *v pres* is divided; (*pst* **khoolak**; *fut* **yekhoolak**).

mekhoom|ash/-asheem מחומש *nm* pentagon; (*pl+of:* -**shey**).

mekhoom|ash/-eshet מחומש *adj* fivefold.

mekhoomts|an/-enet מחומצן *adj* oxidized; bleached.

mekhoon|an/-enet מחונן **1.** *adj* gifted; **2.** *v pres* is gifted; (*pst* **khoonan**; *fut* **yekhoonan**).

mekhoon|as/-eset מכונס *v pres* is convened; congregated; (*pst* **koonas**; *fut* **yekhoonas** *(k=kh)*).

mekhoon|as/-eset be-'atsm|o/-ah מכונס בעצמו *adj* introspective.

mekhoon|eh/-ah מכונה **1.** *adj* called; nicknamed; **2.** *v pres* is called; is nicknamed; (*pst* **koonah** *(k=kh)*; *fut* **yekhooneh**).

mekhoop|al/-elet מכופל *adj* doubled; multiplied.

(kafool/kefoolah oo) mekhoop|al/-elet כפול ומכופל *adj* manifold.

mekhoop|ar/-eret מחופר *adj* dug in.

mekhoop|as/-eset מחופש *adj* disguised.

mekhoop|eh/-ah מחופה **1.** *adj* covered; **2.** *v pres* is covered (*pst* **khoopah**; *fut* **yekhoopeh**).

mekhool|al/-elet מחולל **1.** *adj* desecrated; **2.** *v pres* is desecrated; (*pst* **khoolal**; *fut* **yekhoolal**).

mekhoorb|al/-elet מכורבל *adj* crested.

mekhoorb|an/-enet מחורבן *adj [slang]* low; rotten.

mekhoos|al/-elet מחוסל *adj* liquidated; annihilated.

mekhoos|al/-elet מחוסל *v pres* is liquidated; (*pst* **khoosal**; *fut* **yekhoosal**).

mekhoos|an/-enet מחוסן **1.** *adj* immune; **2.** *v pres* is immunized; (*pst* **khoosan**; *fut* **yekhoosan**).

mekhoos|ar/-eret מחוסר *adj* **1.** deprived of; lacking; **2.** *(suffix)* -less.

mekhoos|ar/-eret 'avodah מחוסר עבודה *nmf* unemployed; jobless; (*pl:* **-rey/-ot** *etc*).

mekhoos|ar/-eret parnasah מחוסר פרנסה *adj* with no means of earning a living; (*pl:* **-rey/-rot** *etc*).

mekhoos|eh/-ah מכוסה **1.** *adj* covered; **2.** *v pres* am/is covered; (*pst* **koosah**; *fut* **yekhooseh** *(k=kh)*).

mekhoosh|al/-elet מחושל **1.** *adj* forged; **2.** *v pres* is forged; (*pst* **khooshal**; *fut* **yekhooshal**).

mekhoosh|av/-evet מחושב **1.** *adj* calculated; **2.** *v pres* is calculated; (*pst* **khooshav**; *fut* **yekhooshav**).

mekhoosp|as/-eset מחוספס *adj* rough.

mekhoot|an/-enet מחותן *nmf* relative by child's marriage; in-law; (*pl:* **-aneem**; *+of:* **-ney**).

mekhoot|ar/-eret מכותר **1.** *adj* surrounded; **2.** *v pres* is surrounded; (*pst* **kootar**; *fut* **yekhootar** *(k=kh)*).

mekhoot|av/-evet מכותב **1.** correspondent; **2.** addressee.

mekhoots|af/-efet מחוצף *adj* impertinent.

mekhoov|an/-enet מכוון *adj* **1.** calculated; **2.** intended; **3.** adjusted.

(bee) mekhoovan במכוון *adv* deliberately; intentionally; on purpose.

mekhoova|ts/-etset מכווץ **1.** *adj* shrunk; shriveled; **2.** *v pres* shrivel(s); (*pst* **koovats** *(k=kh)*; *fut* **yekhoovats**).

mekhoo|yav/-yevet מחויב *adj* obliged; *v pres* is compelled; (*pst* **khooyav**; *fut* **yekhooyav**).

mekhoo|yav/-yevet ha-metsee'oot מחויב המציאות *adj* inevitable; necessary.

mekhooz|ak/-eket מחוזק **1.** *adj* strengthened; **2.** *v pres* is reinforced; (*pst* **khoozak**; *fut* **yekhoozak**).

mekhor|ah/-ot מכורה *nf* homeland; origin; (*+of:* **-at**).

◻ **Mekhorah** (Mehora) מכורה *nm* village (est. 1975) in E. Samaria hills, 8 km NW of Mahruk Junction (**Tsomet Makhrook**). Pop. 99.

mekhoz kheftso/-ah מחוז חפצו his/her *etc* destination, goal, aim.

mekhozee/-t מחוזי *adj* regional; district-.

(bet/batey meeshpat) mekhozee/-yeem בית משפט מחוזי *nm* district court.

(shof|et/-teem) mekhozee/-yeem שופט מחוזי *nm* district-court judge.

(va'ad/ve'adeem) mekhozee/-yeem ועד מחוזי *nm* district committee.

(ve'ad|ah/-ot) mekhozee|t/-yot ועדה מחוזית *nf* district commission.

mekhv|ah/-ot מחווה *nf* gesture; (*+of:* **-at**).

mekom/-ot seter מקום סתר *nm* hidden place; hideout.

(bee) mekom במקום *adv* in lieu; instead of.

mekomee/-t מקומי *adj* local.

(mo'ets|ah/-ot) mekomee|t/-yot מועצה מקומית *nf* local council.

mekoob|al/-elet מקובל *adj* accepted; customary.

mekoob|al/-elet 'al מקובל על *adj* agreeable to; acceptable to.

(en zeh) mekoobal אין זה מקובל *adv* it is not customary.

(lo) mekoobal לא מקובל *adv* unacceptable.

mekood|ash/-eshet מקודש *v pres* is sanctified; (*pst* **koodash**; *fut* **yekoodash**).

◇ **(harey at) mekoodeshet lee!** see ◇ **harey at mekoodeshet lee!**.

mekooft|ar/-eret מכופתר *adj* buttoned up (mostly figuratively).

mekool|af/-efet מקולף *adj* peeled; shelled.

mekool|al/-elet מקולל **1.** *adj* cursed; **2.** *v pres* is cursed (*pst* **koolal**; *fut* **yekoolal**).

mekoolk|al/-elet מקולקל **1.** *adj* spoiled; adulterated; **2.** *v pres* is spoiled; is adulterated; (*pst* **koolkal**; *fut* **yekoolkal**).

mekoom|ar/-eret מקומר *adj* vaulted; convex.

mekoom|at/-etet מקומט *adj* wrinkled.

mekoop|akh/-akhat מקופח **1.** *adj* discriminated against; deprived; wronged; **2.** *v pres* is wronged; (*pst* **koopakh**; *fut* **yekoopakh**).

mekoop|al/-elet מקופל *adj* folded.

mekoor|ar/-eret מקורר *adj* cooled; refrigerated.

mekoor|av/-evet מקורב **1.** *nm* crony; (*pl:* **-aveem**; *+of:* **-vey**); **2.** *adj* close; familiar.

mekoorka'/-at מקורקע *v pres* is grounded (airman or aircraft); (*pst* **koorka'**; *fut* **yekoorka'**).

mekoorz|al/-elet מקורזל *adj* curly.

mekoorz|al/-elet se'ar מקורזל שיער *adj* curly-haired.

mekoosh|ar/-eret מקושר *v pres* is being connected, tied; (*pst* **kooshar**; *fut* **yekooshar**).

mekoosh|at/-etet מקושט **1.** *adj* adorned; **2.** *v pres* is decorated; (*pst* **kooshat**; *fut* **yekooshat**).

mekooshk|ash/-eshet מקושקש *adj [slang]* doodled; scribbled.

mekoota'/-at מקוטע *adj* fragmented; cut.

(bee) mekoota' במקוטע *adv* intermittently.

mekoots|ar/-eret מקוצר **1.** *adj* abridged; **2.** *v pres* is being abridged; (*pst* **kootsar**; *fut* **yekootsar**).

mekoots|ats/-etset מקוצץ **1.** *adj* curtailed; cut; **2.** *v pres* is being curtailed, cut; (*pst* **kootsats**; *fut* **yekootsats**).

mekoov|an/-enet מקוון *adj* on line (computer).

mekoovk|av/-evet מקווקו *adj* linear; lineal.

mekor|av/-evet מקורב *adj* favorite; familiar.

mekoree/-t מקורי *adj* original.

mekoreeyoot מקוריות *nf* originality.

melabev/-et מלבב *adj* endearing.

melafefon/-eem מלפפון *nm* cucumber; (*pl+of:* **-ey**)

melafefon *(etc)* **khamoots** מלפפון חמוץ *nm* pickle; sour cucumber.

melaked/-et מלכד **1.** *adj* consolidating; uniting; **2.** *v pres* consolidate(s); unite(s); (*pst* **leeked;** *fut* **yelaked**).

melakek/-et מלקק *v pres* lick(s); (*pst* **leekek;** *fut* **yelakek**).

melakh/-eem מלח *nm* salt; (*pl+of:* **meelkhey**).

melakh beeshool מלח בישול *nm* common salt.

(netseev) melakh נציב מלח *nm* a pillar of salt (Bible).

□ **(Yam ha) Melakh** see □ **Yam ha-Melakh.**

melakh|ah/-ot מלאכה *nf* **1.** craft; **2.** task; (*+of:* **melekhet**).

(ba'al/-ey) melakhah בעל מלאכה *nm* artisan; craftsman.

(bet/batey) melakhah בית מלאכה *nm* workshop.

melakheem מלכים *nm pl* kings; (*sing:* **melekh;** *pl+of:* **malkhey**).

(ma'adan/-ey) melakheem מעדן מלכים *nm* royal repast; great delicacy.

(se'oodat) melakheem סעודת מלכים *nf* royal feast.

melakhekh/-et מלחך *v pres* lick(s) off; lap(s) up; (*pst* **leekhekh;** *fut* **yelakhekh**).

melakhekh/-ey peenkah מלחך פנכה *nm* bootlicker; lickspit.

◇ **melamdoot** מלמדות *nf* art of teaching in East-European-style Jewish school (**"Kheyder"**).

melamed/-et מלמד *v pres* teach(es); (*pst* **leemed;** *fut* **yelamed**).

◇ **melamed** מלמד *nm* teacher of small children in a **"Kheyder"**.

melankolee/-t מלנכולי *adj* melancholic.

melaveh/-ah מלווה *nmf* escort; *v pres* escort(s); accompany(ies); (*pst* **leevah;** *fut* **yelaveh**).

melaveh/-ah מלווה *v pres* escort(s); accompany(ies); (*pst* **leevah;** *fut* **yelaveh**).

◇ **melaveh malkah** מלווה מלכה *nf* meal held on Saturday night by observant Jews to bid farewell to the outgoing Sabbath.

melay מלאי *nm* stock.

□ **Mele'ah** (Mele'a) מלאה *nm* village (est. 1956) in S. Yizre'el Valley, 4 km SE of Meggido Junction (**Tsomet Megeedo**). Pop. 304.

□ **Meleelot** (Melilot) מלילות *nm* village (est. 1953) in NW Negev, 4 km SW of haGaddi Junction (**Tsomet ha-Gadee**). Pop. 278.

melee|'ah/-'ot מליאה *nf* plenary session; (*+of:* **-'at**).

meleekhoot מליחות *nf* salinity.

meleets/-at yosher מליץ יושר *nmf* advocate; (*pl+of:* **-ey** *etc*).

meleets|ah/-ot מליצה *nf* phraseology; (*+of:* **-at**).

(le-teef'eret ha) meleetsah לתפארת המליצה *adv* for stylistic effect.

meleetsee/-t מליצי *adj* florid; rhetorical.

meleetsot nevoovot מליצות נבובות *nf pl* empty phrases.

melekh/melakheem מלך *nm* king; (*pl+of:* **malkhey**).

melekhet makhshevet מלאכת מחשבת *nf* masterpiece.

melekhet yad מלאכת יד *nf* handicraft.

melel מלל *nm* chatter; verbiage.

melet מלט *nm* cement; concrete.

melkakh|ayeem מלקחיים *nm pl* pincers; tongs; (*pl+of:* **-ey**).

melkhats|ayeem מלחציים *nm pl* pincers; vice; (*pl+of:* **-ey**).

melo מלוא *nm* plenty; the whole of.

melo ha- מלוא ה־ the full (size/content/extent *etc*).

melo komat|o/-ah/-ee/-kha/-ekh *etc* מלוא קומתו *nm* his/her/my/your *m/f etc* full height.

(kee) melo neemah כמלוא נימה *nm* a hair's breadth; not one little bit.

melodee/-t מלודי *adj* melodious.

melodee|yah/-yot מלודיה *nf* melody; (*+of:* **-yat**).

melon/-eem מלון melon; (*pl+of:* **-ey**).

melona'oot מלונאות *nf* hotelkeeping.

melona|y (*cpr* **melona|'ee**)/**-'eet** מלונאי *nm* hotelkeeper; (*pl+of:* **-ey**).

melooban/-enet מלובן *adj* white-hot; incandescent.

meloob|ash/-eshet מלובש *adj* dressed.

melook|ad/-edet מלוכד *adj* united; consolidated.

melook|ak/-eket מלוקק *adj [slang]* much too smoothed; revoltingly neat.

melookh|ah/-ot מלוכה *nf* monarchy; (*+of:* **-at**).

melookhan/-eem מלוכן *nm* monarchist; (*pl+of:* **-ey**).

melookhanee/-t מלוכני *nm* royalist; monarchist.

melookhl|akh/-ekhet מלוכלך *adj* dirty; filthy.

melookhs|an/-enet מלוכסן *adj* slanting; diagonal.

meloom|ad/-edet מלומד *adj* learned.

meloon|ah/-ot מלונה *nf* **1.** watchman's hut (vineyard or grove); **2.** kennel; (*+of:* **-at**).

meloop|af/-efet מלופף *adj* wrapped; cocooned.

melook|at/-etet מלוקט *adj* collected; compiled.

meloot|ash/-eshet מלוטש *adj* polished; honed.

meloov|eh/-ah מלווה *adj* accompanied.

meltakh|ah/-ot מלתחה *nf* wardrobe; cloakroom; (*+of:* **-at**).

meltsar/-eem מלצר *nm* waiter; (*pl+of:* **-ey**).

meltsaree|t/-yot מלצרית *nf* waitress.

meltsaroot מלצרות *nf* waiter's work; waiters trade; waiting on tables.

Mem מ *nf* 13th letter of Hebrew alphabet: consonant "m".

Mem מ *Hebrew num symbol* **1.** 40; **2.** fortieth.

Mem sofeet מ״ם סופית *nf* form "Mem" takes when ending a word: (ם).

memad/-eem ממד *nm* dimension; measure.

(doo-) memadee/-t דו־ממדי *adj* two-dimensional.

(tlat-) memadee/-t תלת־ממדי *adj* three-dimensional.

memal|e/-'ah ממלא *v pres* **1.** fill(s) **2.** fit(s); (*pst* **meele;** *fut* **yemale**).

memal|e/-ah (*also:* **-e't**) ממלא *adj* **1.** filling; **2.** fitting.

memal|e/-et makom ממלא מקום *nmf* substitute; deputy; (*pl+of:* **-ey** *etc*).

memats|eh/-ah ממצה **1.** *adj* thorough; exhaustive; **2.** *v pres* sum(s) up; (*pst* **meetsah;** *fut* **yematseh**).

memeet/-ah ממית **1.** *adj* deadly; lethal; **2.** *v pres* kill(s); deaden(s); (*pst* **hemeet;** *fut* **yameet**).

memoo|'an/-'enet ממוען **1.** *nmf* addressee; **2.** *v pres* am/is addressed; (*pst* **moo'an;** *fut* **yemoo'an**).

memook|ad/-edet ממוקד **1.** *adj* focused; **2.** *v pres* is focused; (*pst* **mookad;** *fut* **yemookad**).

memook|am/-emet ממוקם *adj* located; *v pres* am/is located; (*pst* **mookam;** *fut* **yemookam**).

memook|an/-enet ממוכן *adj* mechanized.

memook|ash/-eshet ממוקש **1.** *adj* mined (explosive); **2.** *v pres* (is) mined; (*pst* **mookash;** *fut* **yemookash**).

memool|a/-et ממולא **1.** *adj* stuffed; filled; **2.** *v pres* (is) filled; (is) fulfilled; (*pst* **moola;** *fut* **yemoola**).

(dag/-eem) memoola/-'eem דג ממולא *nm* filled fish; "Gefilte Fish".

memoolakh/-at ממולח *adj* **1.** salty; **2.** fig: sharp (of person).

memool|e (*npr* **memool|a**)**/-et** ממולא *[colloq.]* *adj* stuffed; filled.

memoom|an/-enet ממומן *v pres* (is) financed; (*pst* **mooman;** *fut* **yemooman**); *adj* financed.

memoom|ash/-eshet ממומש **1.** *adj* realized; carried out; **2.** *v pres* is being realized; is being carried out; (*pst* **moomash;** *fut* **yemoomash**).

memoon|a'/-'at ממונע *v pres* (is) motorized (*pst* **moona';** *fut* **yemoona'**).

(rekhev) memoona' רכב ממונע *nm* motorized vehicle; (used, mainly, generically).

memoon|eh/-ah ממונה **1.** *v pres* (am/is) appointed, nominated; (*pst* **moonah;** *fut* **yemooneh**); **2.** *nmf* 1. appointee; one in charge of; **3.** *nm* chargé d'affaires (Diplom. Corps).

memoorm|ar/-eret ממורמר *adj* bitter; embittered.

memoos|ad/-edet ממוסד *adj* institutionalized; accepted by the establishment.

memoosh|akh/-ekhet ממושך *adj* continuous; prolonged.

memooshk|af/-efet ממושקף *adj* *[colloq.]* bespectacled.

memooshk|an/-enet ממושכן *adj* mortgaged.

memooshma'/-at ממושמע *adj* disciplined; orderly.

memoosp|ar/-eret ממוספר **1.** *adj* numerated; numbered; **2.** *v pres* (am/is) numerated; (*pst* **moospar;** *fut* **yemoospar**).

memoot|ak/-eket ממותק *adj* sweetened.

memootsa'/-at ממוצע *adj* average; medium.

(bee) memootsa' בממוצע *adv* averaging; on the average.

(komah) memootsa'at קומה ממוצעת *nf* medium height.

memooy|an/-enet ממוין **1.** *adj* sorted; classified; **2.** *v pres* (is) sorted; (*pst* **mooyan;** *fut* **yemooyan**).

memooz|ag/-eget ממוזג *adj* air conditioned.

memr|ah/-ot מימרה *nf* saying; expression; (*+of:* **-at**).

memsh|alah/-elet ממשלה *nf* government; (*+of:* **-elet**).

(adm|at/-ot) memshalah אדמת ממשלה *nf* government land.

(harkavat) memshalah הרכבת ממשלה *nf* formation of a government.

(heetpatroot ha) memshalah התפטרות הממשלה *nf* resignation of the government.

(herkev ha) memshalah הרכב הממשלה *nm* composition of the government.

(mazkeer ha) memshalah מזכיר הממשלה *nm* the Cabinet Secretary.

(rosh ha) memshalah ראש הממשלה *nm* prime minister.

(segan rosh ha) memshalah סגן ראש הממשלה *nm* vice-premier.

(yesheev|at/-ot) memshalah ישיבת ממשלה *nf* Cabinet session.

memshaltee/-t ממשלתי *adj* state-; government-; governmental.

(pakeed/pekeedah) memshaltee/-t פקיד ממשלתי *nmf* state-official; government-official; (*+of:* **pekeed/-at** *etc; pl:* **-eem** *etc; +of:* **-ey** *etc*).

◇ **(leeshkat ha-'eetonoot ha) memshalteet** see ◇ **leeshkat ha-'eetonoot ha-memshalteet.**

◇ **MEMSI** ממס״י *nm* Hebrew *acr of* the Automobile and Tourism Club of Israel (**Mo'adon Mekhoneeyot ve-Sayaroot be-Yeesra'el** מועדון מכוניות וסיירות בישראל) equivalent of the AAA. Serves an Israeli membership of 120,000 and extends road services, on a basis of reciprocity, to visiting motorists who produce membership cards of the AAA (or other associate national auto-clubs).

(pe'ool|at/-ot) mena' פעולת מנע *nf* preventive action; preemptive action.

menagen/-et מנגן *v pres* play(s) (instrument); (*pst* **neegen;** *fut* **yenagen**).

menag|en/-neem מנגן *nm* musician; music-player; (*pl+of:* **-ney**).

mena|hel/-haleem מנהל *nmf* manager; director; (*pl+of:* **-haley**).

menahel/-et מנהל *v pres* conduct(s); manage(s); lead(s); (*pst* **neehel;** *fut* **yenahel**).

mena|hel/-haley 'asakeem מנהל עסקים *nm* business manager.

mena|hel/-haley 'avodah מנהל עבודה *nm* foreman.

mena|hel/-haley 'eezavon מנהל עיזבון *nm* administrator (of estate); executor (of will).

mena|hel/-et kheshbonot מנהל חשבונות *nm* accountant.

menahel/-et klalee/-t מנהל כללי *nmf* general manager; director general.

mena|hel/-et ko'akh adam מנהל כוח אדם *nmf* manpower manager.

mena|hel/-haley yeetsoor מנהל ייצור *nm* production manager.

menakhem/-et מנחם *v pres* console(s); (*pst* **neekhem**; *fut* **yenakhem**).

◇ **menakhem-av** מנחם אב *nm* reference (by observant Jews) to the month of Av (or Ab), 11th Jewish calendar month (30 days; approximately July-August).

□ **Menakhemyah** (Menahemya) מנחמיה *nm* rural settlement (est. 1902) and local council in the Jordan Valley, 5 km SW of Zemah Junction (**Tsomet Tsemakh**). Pop. 1,120.

menakhesh/-et מנחש *v pres* guess(es); (*pst* **neekhesh**; *fut* **yenakhesh**).

□ **Menarah** (Menara) מנרה *nm* kibbutz (est. 1943) in the hills of Upper Galilee, near the Lebanese border, 2 km W. of **Keeryat Shmonah**. Pop. 294.

men|at/-ot meeskal מנת משכל *nf* I.Q.; Intelligence Quotient.

('al) menat על מנת *adv* in order to.

menat|e'akh/-akhat מנתח *v pres* dissect(s); analyse(s); operate(s); (*pst* **neete'akh**; *fut* **yenate'akh**).

menat|e'akh/-kheem מנתח *nm* surgeon; (*pl+of:* **-khey**).

menat|e'akh/-khey lev מנתח לב *nm* heart-surgeon.

menat|e'akh/-khey ma'arakhot מנתח מערכות *nm* systems analyst.

menats|e'akh/-akhat מנצח *nmf* **1.** victor; **2.** orchestra-conductor.

menats|e'akh/-akhat 'al מנצח על *v pres* conduct(s) (orchestra); (*pst* **neetsakh 'al**; *fut* **yenatsakh 'al**).

menats|e'akh/-akhat et מנצח את *v pres* defeat(s); vanquish(es); (*pst* **neetse'akh et**; *fut* **yenatse'akh et**).

menatsel/-et מנצל *v pres* make(s) use of; exploit(s); (*pst* **neetsel**; *fut* **yenatsel**).

menats|el/-leem מנצל *nm* exploiter; (*pl+of:* **-ley**).

mena|yah/-yot מניה *nf* share (of a company); (*+of:* **-yat**).

mena|yah/-yot la-mokaz מניה למוכ"ז *nf* bearer's share.

mena|yah/-yot regeelah/-ot מניה רגילה *nf* ordinary share.

(ba'al/-at) mena|yah/-yot בעל מניה *nmf* shareholder (*pl:* **-ey** *etc*).

(shetar/-sheetrey) mena|yah/-yot שטר מניה *nm* share warrant.

(te'ood|at/-ot) mena|yah/-yot תעודת מניה *nf* share certificate.

mena|yat/-yot bkhorah מניית בכורה *nf* prefered share.

mena|yat/-yot hatavah מניית הטבה *nf* bonus share.

mena|yat/-yot meyasdeem מניית מייסדים *nf* founders share.

(hekhzer) menayot החזר מניות *nm* surrender of shares.

(peedyon) menayot פדיון מניות *nm* redemption of shares.

(soog/-ey) menayot סוג מניות *nm* class of shares.

meney oo/-vey מניה וביה *adv* instantly; spontaneously.

menee|'a'/-'ah מניע *v pres* move(s); activate(s); (*pst* **heenee'a**; *fut* **yanee'a**).

menee|'a'/-'eem מניע *nm* motive; stimulus; motor; (*pl+of:* **-ey**).

menee|'ah/-'ot מניעה *nf* prevention; impediment; (*+of:* **-'at**).

(emtsa'ey) menee'ah אמצעי מניעה *nm pl* contraceptives.

(eyn) menee'ah אין מניעה *adv* no objection; no hindrance.

(tsav/-ey) menee'ah צו מניעה *nf* injunction.

menee|'akh/-khah'et ha-da'at מניח את הדעת **1.** *adj* satisfactory; satisfying; **2.** *v* satisfy(ies); (*pst* **henee'akh** *etc*; *fut* **yanee'akh** *etc*).

menee'at te'oonot מניעת תאונות *nf* prevention of road-accidents.

meneef|ah/-ot מניפה *nf* fan; (*+of:* **-at**).

menod rosh מנוד ראש *nm* nod; shaking of the head.

menofef/-et מנופף *v pres* brandish(es); (*pst* **nofef**; *fut* **yenofef**).

menood|eh/-ah מנודה *v pres* is excommunicated, ostracized; (*pst* **noodah**; *fut* **yenoodeh**).

menoog|ad/-edet מנוגד *adj* opposed; contrary.

menook|ad/-edet מנוקד *adj* punctuated; vocalized (using Hebrew vowel-dots).

menook|av/-evet מנוקב **1.** *adj* perforated; pierced; **2.** *v pres* (is) perforated, punctured; (*pst* **nookav**; *fut* **yenookav**).

menookh|ah/-ot מנוחה *nf* rest; peacefulness; tranquillity; (*+of:* **-at**).

□ **Menookhah** (Menuha) מנוחה *nm* village (est. 1953) in **Lakheesh** district, 5 km N. of **Keeryat-Gat**. Pop. 352.

(ha) menookhah המנוחה *nf* the late (female); the deceased (female).

(khas|ar/-rat) menookhah חסר מנוחה *adj* restless.

(lel) menookhah ליל מנוחה *interj* (farewell greeting) Good night!

(motsa'ey) menookhah מוצאי מנוחה *nm pl* Saturday evening; exit of the Sabbath.

('al mey) menookhot על מי מנוחות *adv* peacefully and quietly.

menoom|ak/-eket מנומק **1.** *adj* motivated; argued; **2.** *v pres* is motivated; (*pst* **noomak**; *fut* **yenoomak**).

menoom|ar/-eret מנומר *adj* checkered.

menoom|as/-eset מנומס *adj* polite; courteous.

menoom|ash/-eshet מנומש *adj* freckled.
menoomn|am/-emet מנומנם *adj* sleepy; drowsy.
menoop|akh/-at מנופח *adj* inflated; swollen; exaggerated.
menoop|ats/-etset מנופץ *adj* broken; shattered.
(tsemer) menoopats צמר מנופץ *nm* carded wool.
menoop|eh/-ah מנופה *adj* sifted; cleaned.
menoos|ah/-ot מנוסה *nf* flight; **(+*of:* -at).**
menoosakh/-at מנוסח *v pres* is formulated, styled; **(*pst* noosakh; *fut* yenoosakh).**
menoos|eh/-ah מנוסה *adj* experienced.
menoosh|al/-elet מנושל *adj* dispossessed; *v pres* (is) dispossessed; **(*pst* nooshal; *fut* yenooshal).**
menoot|ak/-eket מנותק **1.** *adj* detached; disconnected; severed; **2.** *v pres* (am/is) detached, disconnected; severed; **(*pst* nootak; *fut* yenootak).**
menootakh/-at מנותח *v pres* (am/is) being operated on; **(*pst* nootakh; *fut* yenootakh).**
menootr|al/-elet מנוטרל **1.** *adj* neutralized; **2.** *v pres* (am/is) being neutralized; **(*pst* nootral; *fut* yenootral).**
menoots|akh/-at מנוצח *adj* defeated; vanquished; *v pres* (am/is) defeated; **(*pst* nootsakh; *fut* yenootsakh).**
menoots|al/-elet מנוצל *adj* used; exploited.
menoots|al/-elet מנוצל *v pres* (am/is) exploited, taken advantage of; **(*pst* nootsal; *fut* yenootsal).**
menooval/-elet מנוול *nmf* scoundrel.
menoovan/-enet מנוון *adj* degenerate.
menooz|al/-elet מנוזל *adj* suffering from hay-fever or chill.
menor|ah/-ot מנורה *nf* lamp; chandelier; **(+*of:* -at).**
mentah **(*npr* meentah)** מנתה *nf* mint; peppermint.
mentaleeyoot מנטליות *nf* mentality.
me'od מאוד *adv* very.
me'od-me'od מאד מאוד *adv* very-very.
(ra') me'od רע מאוד *adv* very badly.
(ra'/ra'ah) me'od רע מאוד *adj* very bad; very wicked.
(tov) me'od טוב מאוד *adv* very well.
(tov/-ah) me'od טוב מאוד *adj* very good; very nice.
(yaf|ah/-ot) me'od יפה מאוד *adj f* very beautiful (of female).
(yaf|eh/-eem) me'od יפה מאוד *adj m* very handsome (of a male).
(yafeh) me'od יפה מאוד *adv* very nicely; fine; very well.
me'oded/-et מעודד **1.** *adj* encouraging; **2.** *v pres* encourage(s); **(*pst* 'oded; *fut* ye'oded).**
me'ofef/-et מעופף **1.** *adj* flying; **2.** *v pres* fly(ies); **(*pst* 'ofef; *fut* ye'ofef).**
me-'olam מעולם *adv* never; at no time.
(lo hayoo devareem) me-'olam לא היו דברים מעולם it never happened; it is absolutely untrue.
(me-az oo) me-'olam מאז ומעולם *adv* from time immemorial.
me'on/-ot yom מעון יום *nm* day-nursery.
□ **Me'onah** (Me'ona) מעונה *nm* village (est. 1949) in Upper Galilee, 2 km W. of **Ma'alot**. Pop. 371.
me'onot מעונות *[colloq.]* dormitory; special hostel.
me'onot ha-stoodenteem מעונות הסטודנטים *nm pl* student dormitories.
me'oob|ad/-edet מעובד *adj* processed; **(*pst* "oobad; *fut* ye'oobad).**
me'oob|ak/-eket מאובק *adj* dusty.
me'oob|an/-enet מאובן *adj* petrified.
me'ooban/-eem מאובן *nm* fossil; **(*pl+of:* -ey).**
me'oob|eret/-arot מעוברת *adj f* pregnant.
◇ **(shan|ah/-eem) me'oob|eret/-arot** see ◇ **shanah me'ooberet.**
me'ood|ad **(*npr* me'od|ad)/-edet** מעודד *adj* comforted; encouraged.
me'ood|an/-enet מעודן *adj* refined.
me'oodk|an/-enet מעודכן **1.** *adj* up to date; **2.** *v pres* am/is updated; **(*pst* 'oodkan; *fut* ye'oodkan).**
me'oog|ad/-edet מאוגד *adj* organized; associated.
me'oog|al/-elet מעוגל *adj* rounded; circular.
me'oo|hav **(*npr* me'ohav)/-hevet** מאוהב *adj* in love; loving.
me'ook|al/-elet מעוקל *v pres* (is) seized, attached (by court order); **(*pst* 'ookal; *fut* ye'ookal).**
me'ook|am/-emet מעוקם **1.** *adj* bent; crooked; **2.** *v pres* is bent; **(*pst* 'ookam; *fut* ye'ookam).**
me'ook|ar/-eret מעוקר *adj* sterilized.
(khalav) me'ookar חלב מעוקר *nm* sterilized milk.
me'ook|av/-evet מעוקב *[colloq.] adj* cubic.
(met|er/-reem) me'ook|av/-eem מטר (מ"מ) מעוקב *[colloq.] nm* cubic meter (equivalent to 35.31 cubic feet).
me'ookh|ad/-edet מאוחד *adj* united; unified.
◇ **(ha-oomot ha) me'ookhadot** see ◇ **(ha)oomot ha-me'ookhadot.**
me'ookh|ar/-eret מאוחר *adj* late.
me'ookhar מאוחר *adv* late.
(bee) me'ookhar במאוחר *adv* late.
◇ **(ha-mamlakhah ha) me'ookhedet** see ◇ **(ha)mamlakhah ha-me'ookhedet,**
me'ookhl|as/-eset מאוכלס *adj* populated.
(lo) me'ookhl|as/-eset לא מאוכלס *adj* uninhabited.
me'ookhz|av/-evet מאוכזב *adj* disappointed.
me'ool|af/-efet מאולף *adj* tamed; trained.
me'ool|ats/-etset מאולץ *adj* compelled.
me'ool|eh/-ah מעולה *adj* superb.
me'ooleh מעולה **1.** *adv* excellent; **2.** *nm* "Excellent"mark (for students).
(kheenoo'kh) me'ooleh חינוך מעולה *nm* a first-class education.
me'oomah מאומה *nm* nothing.
('al lo') me'oomah על לא מאומה **1.** don't mention it! **2.** *adv* for nothing at all.

(eyn) me'oomah אין מאומה there's nothing; not a thing.
me'oom|'am/-'emet מעומעם *adj* dimmed.
me'oom|ats/-etset מאומץ *adj* **1.** strenous; **2.** adopted.
me'ooml|an/-enet מעומלן *adj* starched.
me'oon|akh/-ekhet מאונך *adj* perpendicular.
me'oon|an/-enet מעונן *adj* clouded.
me'oon|eh/-ah מעונה *adj* tortured
(kadosh/kedoshah) me'oon|eh/-ah קדוש מעונה *nmf* martyr (*pl:* **kedosheem me'ooneem**).
me'oon|yan/-yenet מעוניין *adj* interested; concerned.
me'oop|al/-elet מאופל *adj* darkened; blacked-out.
me'oop|ar/-eret מאופר *adj* made-up (face).
me'oop|as/-eset מאופס *adj* zeroed (instrument).
me'oop|ash/-eshet מעופש *adj* rotten; mouldy.
me'oor|ah/-ot מאורה *nf* den; (*+of:* **-at**).
me'oor|'ar/-'eret מעורער **1.** *adj* shaken; shattered; **2.** *v pres* (am/is) shaken, shattered; (*pst* **'oor'ar**; *fut* **ye'oor'ar**).
me'oor|av (*npr* **me'or|av**)/**-evet** מעורב *adj* involved; mixed; meddling.
me'oorb|av/-evet מעורבב *adj* mixed.
me'oor|eh/-ah מעורה *adj* rooted; integrated.
me'oorg|an/-enet מאורגן **1.** *adj* organized; **2.** *v pres* (is) being organized; (*pst* **oorgan**; *fut* **ye'oorgan**).
(pesha') me'oorgan פשע מאורגן *nm* organized crime.
me'oorp|al/-elet מעורפל *adj* vague; foggy.
me'oos|eh/-ah מעושה *adj* artificial; affected.
(kheyookh) me'ooseh חיוך מעושה *nm* artificial smile.
me'oosh|an/-enet מעושן *adj* smoked.
me'oosh|ar/-eret מאושר **1.** *adj* 1. happy; **2.** *adj* confirmed; **3.** *v pres* (is) approved; (*pst* **ooshar**; *fut* **ye'ooshar**).
◇ **(meef'al) me'ooshar** see ◇ **meef'al me'ooshar**.
me'oosh|ash/-eshet מאושש *adj* comforted; strong.
me'ooshp|az/-ezet מאושפז **1.** *adj* hospitalized; **2.** *v pres* (am/is) hospitalized; (*pst* **ooshpaz**; *fut* **ye'ooshpaz**).
me'oot|ar/-eret מעוטר *adj* **1.** adorned; **2.** decorated (medals).
me'ootey yekholet מעוטי יכולת *nm pl* **1.** of scanty means **2.** of limited capacity.
me'ootsav/-evet מעוצב *adj* shaped; moulded.
me'ootsb|an/-enet מעוצבן *adj* nervous.
me'oov|at/-etet מעוות *adj* distorted; crooked.
me'oovr|ar/-eret מאוורר *adj* ventilated; aired.
me'ooyan/-eem מעוין *nm* rhombus; diamond-shape.
me'oo|yar/-yeret מאויר *adj* illustrated.
me'ooz|an/-enet מאוזן *adj* **1.** balanced; **2.** horizontal.
me'or|a'/-a'ot מאורע *nm* event; occurrence.
◇ "המאורעות" *nm pl* usual abbrev. colloquial reference to "the Occurrences" of 1936 and 1937 in Palestine under the British Mandate, consisting of two waves of anti-Jewish terrrorist attacks, riots and violent strikes by Arab extremists led by the Jerusalem Mufti. Each lasted for several months and resulted, on one hand, in the stoppage of Jewish immigration, and on the other, in sending to Palestine a Royal Commision which, ultimately, recommended partition of the country into two states.
me'or|av/-evet מעורב *adj* involved; mixed; meddling.
(kheenookh) me'orav חינוך מעורב *nm* co-education.
(meshek) me'orav משק מעורב *nm* mixed farming.
me'or|as/-eset מאורס *adj* betrothed; fiancé/-e.
me'orer/-et מעורר *v pres* wake(s) up; stimulate(s); (*pst* **'orer**; *fut* **ye'orer**).
(sha'on/she'oneem) me'orer/-eem שעון מעורר *nm* alarm clock.
(leekooy) me'orot ליקוי מאורות *nm* **1.** obscuring; darkening; **2.** (*figurat.*) solar or lunar eclipse.
me'ot kees מעות כיס *nm pl* pocket money.
me'otet/-et מאותת *v pres* signal(s); (*pst* **otet**; *fut* **ye'otet**).
(shekheev) me-ra' שכיב מרע *nm* moribund person; fatally ill person.
mera'anen/-et מרענן *adj* refreshing; invigorating.
meragel/-et מרגל **1.** *nmf* spy; **2.** *v pres* (is) spying; (*pst* **reegel**; *fut* **yeragel**).
meragesh/-et מרגש **1.** *adj* touching; exciting; **2.** *v pres* (is) touching, exciting; (*pst* **reegesh**; *fut* **yeragesh**).
merak/meerkey basar מרק בשר *nm* meat-soup (see **marak**).
merak/meerkey 'of מרק עוף *nm* chicken-soup (see: **marak**).
merak/meerkey perot מרק פירות *nm* fruit-soup (see: **marak**).
merak/meerkey yerakot מרק ירקות *nm* vegetable-soup (see: **marak**).
merakekh/-et מרכך *v pres* soften(s); (*pst* **reekekh**; *fut* **yerakekh**).
merak|ekh/-ekhet מרכך **1.** *adj* softening; **2.** *nm* softener; (*pl+of:* **-'khey**).
merakez/-et מרכז *v pres* coordinate(s); organize(s), (*pst* **reekez**; *fut* **yerakez**).
merak|ez/-zeem מרכז *nm* coordinator; organizer; (*pl+of:* **-zey**).
merakhef/-et מרחף *v pres* hover(s); (*pst* **reekhef**; *fut* **yerakhef**).
me-rakhok מרחוק *adv* from afar.
merakhr|e'akh/-akhat מרחרח *v pres* sniff(s); (*pst* **reekhrakh**; *fut* **yerakhrakh**).
merap|e/-'ah מרפא *v pres* heal(s); (*pst* **reepe**; *fut* **yerape**).

merape/-'ey sheenayeem מרפא שיניים *nm* dental practitioner (not licensed as a doctor).
meraped/-et מרפד *v pres* pad(s); upholster(s); (*pst* **reeped**; *fut* **yeraped**).
merapet/-et מרפט *v* tatter(s); tear(s); (*pst* **reepet**; *fut* **yerapet**).
(lee) merashot למראשות *adv* under one's head; under headrest.
merasek/-et מרסק *v pres* crush(es); mince(s); (*pst* **reesek**; *fut* **yerasek**).
merasen/-et מרסן **1.** *adj* curbing; bridling; **2.** *v pres* restrain(s); rein(s); (*pst* **reesen**; *fut* **yerasen**).
merases/-et מרסס *v pres* spray(s); (*pst* **reeses**; *fut* **yerases**).
meratek/-et מרתק **1.** *adj* fascinating; **2.** *v pres* 1. fascinate(s); 2. fasten(s); link(s); (*pst* **reetek**; *fut* **yeratek**).
meratekh/-et מרתך *v pres* weld(s); solder(s); (*pst* **reetekh**; *fut* **yeratekh**).
merats|eh/ah מרצה *v pres* **1.** atone(s) for; serve(s) (prison term); **2.** appease(s); (*pst* **reetsah**; *fut* **yeratseh**).
merats|e'akh/-kheem מרצח *nm* wanton killer; murderer (*pl+of:* **-khey**).
merabee/-t מרבי *adj* maximal.
merav מרב *nm* maximum.
mered מרד *nm* mutiny; revolt.
meree מרי *nm* rebellion; disobedience.
mereed|ah/-ot מרידה *nf* revolt; rebellion; (*+of:* **-at**).
mereekh|ah/-ot מריחה *nf* **1.** smear; **2.** *[slang]* unthoroughly executed work; **3.** *[slang]* bribe; (*+of:* **-at**).
mereet|ah/-ot מריטה *nf* plucking; (*+of:* **-at**).
mereet|at/-ot 'atsabeem מריטת עצבים *nf* nerve-racking.
mereets|ah/-ot מריצה *nf* wheelbarrow; hand cart; (*+of:* **-at**).
mereev|ah/-ot מריבה *nf* quarrel; dispute; (*+of:* **-at**).
mer|ek/-akeem מרק *nm* putty; (*pl+of:* **meerkey**).
mer|ek/-kah/-aktee מירק *v* scrubbed; cleansed; (*pst* **memarek**; *fut* **yemarek**).
mer|er/-erah/-artee מירר *v* embittered; (*pst* **memarer**; *fut* **yemarer**).
merer (*etc*) **ba-bekhee** מירר בבכי *v* cry(ied) bitterly.
merets מרץ *nm* energy; zest; (his/her energy: **meerts|o/-ah**).
(ba'al/-at) merets בעל מרץ *adj* energetic.
(be) merets במרץ *adv* energetically.
(khas|ar/-rat) merets חסר מרץ *adj* languid.
('od|ef/-fey) merets עודף מרץ *nm* excess of energy; extra energy.
mereyr|ah/-ot מרירה *nf* bile; gall; (*+of:* **-at**).
merkav|ah/-ot מרכבה *nf* carriage; (*+of:* **meerkevet**).
(ma'aseh) merkavah מעשה מרכבה *nm* art of forming a government.

merk|az/-azeem מרכז **1.** *nm* center; (*pl+of:* **-ezey**); **2.** *nm* central body heading a political party or a group of bodies; caucus.
◇ **merkaz ha-hasbarah** מרכז ההסברה *nm* Government's Public Information Center.
merkazee/-t מרכזי *adj* central.
(anten|ah/-ot) merkazee|t/-yot אנטנה מרכזית *nf* central aerial (for TV reception).
(kheemoom) merkazee חימום מרכזי *nm* central heating.
(takhanah) merkazeet תחנה מרכזית *nf* central station; central bus station.
merkazee|yah/-yot מרכזייה *nf* switchboard; telephone-exchange; (*+of:* **-yat**).
merkazeeyoot מרכזיות *nf* centrality.
□ **Merkaz Shapeero** (Merkaz Shappira) מרכז שפירא *nm* regional center for settlements of **Shafeer** area in S. coastal plain (est. 1948), 5 km SW of **Keeryat Mal'akhee**. Pop. 958.
merkezan/-eet מרכזן *nmf* switchboard operator.
merk|ezet/-azot (*npr* **meerk|ezet/-azot**) מרכזת *nf* switchboard; telephone-exchange.
merkhak/-eem מרחק *nm* distance; (*pl+of:* **-ey**).
merkha'ot מרכאות *nf pl* quotation-marks; quotes.
(be) merkha'ot במרכאות *adv* in quotation marks.
merkhats/-a'ot מרחץ *nm* bath; bathing.
merkhats dameem מרחץ דמים *nm* blood-bath.
(bet/batey) merkhats בית מרחץ *nm* bath-house; public bath.
merkhav/-eem מרחב *nm* wide space; breadth; (*pl+of:* **-ey**).
merkhavee/-t מרחבי *adj* spatial; zonal.
□ **Merkhavyah-Keeboots** מרחביה קיבוץ *nm* kibbutz (est. 1911) in Yizre'el Valley - ideological center of ◇ **Ha-Shomer Ha-Tsa'eer** movement. Pop. 617.
□ **Merkhavyah-Moshav** מרחביה מושב *nm* village (est. 1922) in the Yizre'el Valley, 2 km E. of 'Afula. Pop. 277.
mero|hat/-hetet מרוהט *adj* furnished.
(deer|ah/-ot) merohetet/-ot דירה מרוהטת *nf* furnished apartment; furnished flat.
(le-haskeer) merohat להשכיר מרוהט *v inf* to rent furnished; (*pst* **heeskeer** *etc*; *fut* **yaskeer** *etc*).
(kheder/khadareem) merohat/-eem חדר מרוהט *nm* furnished room.
merok|an/-enet מרוקן *adj* drained; emptied.
merom|am/-emet מרומם *adj* elated; high.
□ **Merom Golan** מרום גולן *nm* kibbutz (est. 1967) in the Golan Heights, 5 km S. of **Koonetrah** (Syrian border-township). Pop. 429.
meromeem מרומים *nm pl* heavens.
meromem/-et מרומם *v pres* extol(s); exalt(s); (*pst* **romem**; *fut* **yeromem**).
meroob|a'/-a'at מרובע *adj* square; quadrangular.
meroob|a'/-a'eem מרובע *nm* **1.** square; **2.** *[slang]* "square".

(meeshpakh|ah/-ot) meroob|at/-ot yeladeem משפחה מרובת ילדים *nf* multi-children family.

meroob|eh/-ah מרובה *adj* numerous; frequent.

meroog|az/-ezet מרוגז *adj* annoyed; irritated.

(kheder/khadareem) meroohat/-eem חדר מרוהט *nm* furnished room.

(le-haskeer) meroohat להשכיר מרוהט *v inf* to rent furnished; (*pst* **heeskeer** *etc*; *fut* **yaskeer** *etc*).

(deer|ah/-ot) meroohetet/-ot דירה מרוהטת *nf* furnished apartment; furnished flat.

merook|az/-ezet מרוכז *adj* centered; concentrated.

merookh|ak/-eket מרוחק *adj* remote; far.

meroom|az/-ezet *adj* hinted; alluded.

(bee) meroomaz במרומז *adv* by innuendo; alluding; implying.

meroom|eh/ah מרומה *adj* cheated; deceived.

(ba'al/be'aleem) meroomeh/-eem בעל מרומה *nm* deceived husband.

meroop|ad/-edet מרופד *adj* padded; upholstered.

meroop|at/-etet מרופט *adj* shabby.

meroos|ak/-eket מרוסק *adj* mashed.

meroos|an/-enet מרוסן *adj* curbed; checked; reined in.

(lo) meroos|an/-enet לא מרוסן *adj* unrestrained; unbridled.

meroos|as/-eset מרוסס *adj* sprayed.

meroosh|a'/-a'at מרושע *adj* wicked.

meroosh|al/-elet מרושל *adj* careless; neglected.

meroosh|ash/-eshet מרושש *adj* impoverished.

meroot|ak/-eket מרותק *adj* **1.** confined; checked; **2.** absorbed; fascinated.

meroot|ak/-eket la-meetah מרותק למיטה *adj* bedridden.

meroot|akh/-ekhet מרותך *adj* welded; soldered.

meroots/-eem מירוץ *nm* race; run; (*pl+of:* **-ey**).

meroots/-ey shleekheem מירוץ שליחים *nm* relay race.

merootsah מרוצה *nf* race; run.

(bee) merootsah במרוצה *adv* running.

meroots|af/-efet מרוצף **1.** *adj* paved; floored; **2.** *v pres* (is) being paved; (*pres* **rootsaf**; *fut* **yerootsaf**).

(bee) merootsat ha-zman במרוצת הזמן *adv* in the long run.

meroots|eh/-ah מרוצה *adj* contented; satisfied.

meroovakh/-at מרווח *adj* spacious.

me-rosh מראש *adv* in advance; beforehand.

(be-todah) me-rosh בתודה מראש *adv* thanking in advance.

meroshesh/-et מרושש **1.** *adj* impoverishing; **2.** *v pres* impoverish(es); (*pst* **roshesh**; *fut* **yeroshesh**).

mesader/-et מסדר *v pres* **1.** arrange(s); fix(es); **2.** *[slang]* mislead(s); trick(s); (*pst* **seeder**; *fut* **yesader**).

mesagnen/-et מסגנן **1.** *nmf* rewrite-man/woman; **2.** *v pres* rewrite(s); (*pst* **seegnen**; *fut* **yesagnen**).

mesagseg/-et משגשג *adj* flourishing; *v pres* flourish(es); (*pst* **seegseg**; *fut* **yesagseg**).

mesakhrer/-et מסחרר *adj* dazzling; *v pres* dazzle(s); (*pst* **seekhrer**; *fut* **yesakhrer**).

mesam|e'akh/-akhat משמח *adj* gladdening; joyful; *v pres* gladden(s); (*pst* **seemakh**; *fut* **yesamakh**).

mesanen/-et מסנן *v pres* filter(s); strain(s).

mesanen|et/-ot מסננת *nf* strainer; filter.

mesanger/-et מסנגר *v pres* defend(s); plead(s) for; (*pst* **seenger**; *fut* **yesanger**).

mesanver/-et מסנוור **1.** *adj* dazzling; blinding; **2.** *v pres* blind(s); dazzle(s); (*pst* **seenver**; *fut* **yesanver**).

mesapek/-et מספק **1.** *adj* satisfying; **2.** *v pres* satisfy(ies); **3.** supply(ies); (*pst* **seepek**; *fut* **yesapek**).

mesap|er/-eret מספר **1.** *v pres* 1. tell(s); **2.** *v pres* give(s) a haircut; (*pst* **seeper**; *fut* **yesaper**); **3.** *nmf* novelist; story-teller; (*pl:* **-reem**; *+of:* **-rey**).

mes|av/-abeem מיסב *nm* bearing; (*pl+of:* **-abey**).

mesav (*etc*) **kadooree** מיסב כדורי *nm* ball-bearing.

mesa|ye'a'/-ya'at מסייע *adj* auxiliary; accessory.

mesa|ye'a'/-ya'at מסייע *v pres* assist(s); (*pst* **seeye'a'**; *fut* **yesaye'a'**).

(re'a|yah/-yot) mesa|ya'at/-y'ot ראייה מסייעת *nf* complementary evidence.

meseeb|ah/-ot מסיבה *nf* party; (*+of:* **-at**).

meseeb|at/-ot gan מסיבת גן *nf* garden-party.

meseeb|at/-ot preydah (*npr* **preedah**) מסיבת פרידה *nf* farewell-party.

meseeb|at/-ot seeyoom מסיבת סיום *nf* graduation-party.

meseebot מסיבות *nf pl* circumstances.

(be-khorakh ha) meseebot בכורח המסיבות *adv* under the circumstances; by force of events.

meseeg/-ah מסיג (*colloq. mispronunc. of* **maseeg/meseegah**) *v pres* remove(s); move(s); (*pst* **heeseeg**; *fut* **yaseeg**).

meseeg/-at gvool מסיג גבול *nmf* trespasser.

meseek ha-zeyteem מסיק הזיתים *nm* olive harvest.

meseel|ah/-ot מסילה *nf* track; rail; (*+of:* **-at**).

meseel|at/-ot barzel מסילת ברזל *nf* railroad; railway.

□ **Meseelat Tseeyon** (Mesillat Ziyyon) מסילת ציון *nm* village (est. 1950), 2 km SW of **Sha'ar Ha-Gay** (Bab el-Wad). Pop. 320.

□ **Meseelot** (Mesillot) מסילות *nm* kibbutz (est. 1938) in Bet-She'an Valley, 2 km W. of Bet-She'an. Pop. 694.

meseem/-ah 'atsm|o/-ah (*etc*) משים עצמו *v pres* pretend(s) to be.

(mee-blee) meseem מבלי משים *adv* inadvertently; unwillingly.

meseem|ah/-ot משימה *nf* task; assignment; (*+of:* **-at**).

meseer|ah/-ot מסירה *nf* **1.** delivery; handing-over; **2.** *[colloq.]* (soccer) pass; **3.** *[slang]* informing on someone; **(***+of:* **-at)**.

meseeroot מסירות *nf* devotion.

meseeroot-nefesh מסירות נפש *nf* utter devotion; devotion at life's risk.

mes|er/-areem מסר *nm* message; **(***pl+of:* **meesrey)**.

mesha'amem/-et משעמם **1.** *adj* boring; **2.** *adv m* boringly; **3.** *v pres* bore(s); **(***pst* **shee'mem;** *fut* **yesha'amem)**.

mesha'ash|e'a'/-a'at משעשע **1.** *adj* amusing; entertaining; **2.** *v pres* amuse(s); **(***pst* **sheeashe'a';** *fut* **yesha'ashe'a')**.

mesha'b|ed/-edet משעבד **1.** *adj* oppressing; enslaving; **2.** *nmf* oppressor; **(***pl+of:* **-dey)**; **3.** *v pres* oppress(es); enslave(s); **(***pst* **shee'bed;** *fut* **yesha'bed)**.

meshabesh/-et משבש *v pres* disrupt(s); spoil(s); **(***pst* **sheebesh;** *fut* **yeshabesh)**.

meshabets/-et משבץ *v pres* inlay(s); insert(s); **(***pst* **sheebets;** *fut* **yeshabets)**.

meshadekh/-et משדך *v pres* get(s) a match for; negotiate(s) a marriage; **(***pst* **sheedekh;** *fut* **yeshadekh)**.

meshadel/-et משדל *v pres* coax(es); solicit(s); **(***pst* **sheedel;** *fut* **yeshadel)**.

meshader/-et משדר *v pres* broadcast(s); **(***pst* **sheeder;** *fut* **yeshader)**.

meshag|e'a'/-a'at משגע **1.** *adj* maddening; **2.** *[slang]* fabulous; **3.** *v pres* drive(s) one mad; **(***pst* **sheege'a';** *fut* **yeshage'a')**.

(ha) meshakeem המשקים *nm pl* (*lit.:* the households) the collective farms; **(***pl+of:* **meeshkey)**.

meshakef/-et משקף **1.** *adj* reflecting; **2.** *v pres* reflect(s); **(***pst* **sheekef;** *fut* **yeshakef)**.

meshakem/-et משקם *v pres* rehabilitate(s); **(***pst* **sheekem;** *fut* **yeshakem)**.

meshaker/-et משקר *v pres* lie(s); (is) lying; **(***pst* **sheeker;** *fut* **yeshaker)**.

meshaker/-et משכר **1.** *adj* intoxicating; **2.** *v pres* intoxicate(s); **(***pst* **sheeker;** *fut* **yeshaker)**.

meshakhn|e'a'/-a'at משכנע **1.** *adj* convincing; **2.** *v pres* convince(s); **(***pst* **sheekhna';** *fut* **yeshakhne'a')**.

meshalem/-et משלם **1.** *v pres* pay(s); **(***pst* **sheelem;** *fut* **yeshalem)**; **2.** *nmf* payer.

meshal|em/-mey meeseem משלם מיסים *nm* taxpayer.

meshalshel/-eem משלשל *nm* laxative (pharmaceut.); **(***pl+of:* **-ey)**.

meshalshel/-et משלשל *v pres* **1.** lower(s); insert(s); **2.** suffer(s) from diarrhea; **(***pst* **sheelshel;** *fut* **yeshalshel)**.

meshalev/-et משלב **1.** *adj* combining; **2.** *v pres* combine(s); **(***pst* **sheelev;** *fut* **yeshalev)**.

meshamer/-et משמר **1.** *adj* preserving; preservative; **2.** *v pres* preserve(s); **(***pst* **sheemer;** *fut* **yeshamer)**.

meshamesh/-et משמש **1.** *adj* serving; **2.** *v pres* serve(s); **(***pst* **sheemesh;** *fut* **yeshamesh)**.

meshan|eh/-ah משנה *v pres* alter(s); change(s); **(***pst* **sheenah;** *fut* **yeshaneh)**.

(lo) meshaneh לא משנה *adv* doesn't matter; makes no difference.

mesharet/-et משרת *v pres* serve(s); **(***pst* **sheret;** *fut* **yesharet)**.

meshar|et/-teem משרת *nm* servant; **(***pl+of:* **-tey)**.

meshar|etet/-tot משרתת *nf* maid; woman-servant.

meshatef/-et משתף *v pres* associate(s); cut(s) one in; cooperate(s); **(***pst* **sheetef;** *fut* **yeshatef)**.

meshatef/-et pe'oolah משתף פעולה *v pres* collaborate(s).

meshat|ef/-fey pe'oolah משתף פעולה *nm* collaborator (with oppressive authorities).

meshatek/-et משתק *v pres* paralyze(s); **(***pst* **sheetek;** *fut* **yeshatek)**.

meshee משי *nm* silk.

meshee'akh tseedkenoo משיח צדקנו *nm* our true Messiah.

mesheekh|ah/-ot משיכה *nf* **1.** pulling; dragging; **2.** attraction; **3.** drawing money (from account or bank); **(***+of:* **-at)**.

(ko'akh ha) mesheekhah כוח המשיכה *nm* gravity; gravitation.

mesheekhat khevel משיכת חבל *nf* tug of war.

mesheekh|at/-ot mezoomaneem משיכת מזומנים *nf* cash drawing; withdrawing; withdrawal of cash.

mesheekhee/-t משיחי *adj* Messianic.

mesheev/-ah משיב *v pres* answer(s); respond(s); **(***pst* **hesheev;** *fut* **yasheev)**.

(ha) mesheev/-eem המשיב *nm* respondent; **(***f:* **-ah/-ot;** *nm pl+of:* **-ey)**.

mesheev/-at nefesh משיב נפש *adj* refreshing; causing satisfaction.

mesh|ek/-akeem משק *nm* **1.** economy; **2.** agricultural farm; **(***pl+of:* **meeshkey)**.

meshek bayeet משק בית *nm* housework; household.

meshek/meeshkey 'ezer משק עזר *nm* auxiliary farm (as secondary occupation).

meshek khakla'ee משק חקלאי *nm* agricultural farm.

meshek me'orav משק מעורב *nm* mixed farming.

(ba'al/-at) mesh|ek/-akeem בעל משק *nmf* farmer; farm-owner.

meshekh משך **1.** *adv* during; **2.** *nm* duration.

(be) meshekh במשך *adv* during; throughout.

(be) meshekh ha-zman במשך הזמן *adv* in due course.

(le) meshekh למשך *adv* for a duration of.

meshkee/-t (*npr* **meeshkee/-t**) משקי *adj* economic.

mesho|'ar/-'eret משוער **1.** *adj* estimated; **2.** *v pres* (is) estimated; **(***pst* **shoo'ar;** *fut* **yeshoo'ar)**.

meshoo'am|am/-emet משועמם **1.** *adj* bored; **2.** *v pres* (is) bored; **(***pst* **shoo'amam;** *fut* **yeshoo'amam)**.

meshoo'b|ad/-edet משועבד **1.** *adj* mortgaged; addicted to; enslaved; **2.** *v pres* (am/is) mortgaged; (am/is) enslaved; (*pst* **shoo'bad;** *fut* **yeshoo'bad**).

meshoob|akh/-at משובח *adj* **1.** exquisite; excellent; **2.** praiseworthy.

meshoob|ash/-eshet משובש **1.** *adj* distorted, faulty; **2.** *v pres* (is) distorted; (*pst* **shoobash;** *fut* **yeshoobash**).

meshoob|ats/-etset משובץ **1.** *adj* inlaid; **2.** *adj* chequered; **3.** *v pres* (am/is) classified, assigned; **4.** *v pres* (is) set (jewel; (*pst* **shoobats;** *fut* **yeshoobats**)).

meshoofsh|af/-efet משופשף **1.** *adj* well-worn; experienced; **2.** *[slang] mf & adj* one who's been around.

meshoog|a'/-a'at משוגע **1.** *adj* crazy; insane; **2.** *nmf* fool; (*pl:* **-a'eem/-a'ot;** *nm pl+of:* **-'ey**).

meshook|a'/-a'at משוקע *v pres* (is) immersed; (*pst* **shooka';** *fut* **yeshooka'**).

meshook|am/-emet משוקם **1.** *adj* rehabilitated; reconstructed; **2.** *v pres* (is) being rehabilitated; (*pst* **shookam;** *fut* **yeshookam**).

meshook|ats/-etset משוקץ *adj* loathsome.

meshookh|ad/-edet משוחד **1.** *adj* bribed; biased; **2.** *v pres* (am/is) bribed; (*pst* **shookhad;** *fut* **yeshookhad**).

meshookhl|al/-elet משוכלל **1.** *adj* sophisticated; improved; **2.** *v pres* (is) improved, perfected; (*pst* **shookhlal;** *fut* **yeshokhlal**).

meshookhna'/-at משוכנע **1.** *adj* convinced; **2.** *v pres* (am/is) convinced; (*pst* **shookhna';** *fut* **yshookhna'**).

meshookhr|ar/-eret משוחרר **1.** *adj* freed; liberated; released; **2.** *v pres* (is) free, released; (*pst* **shookhrar;** *fut* **yeshookhrar**).

(khayal/-eem) meshookhrar/-eem חייל משוחרר *nm* ex-serviceman; veteran; soldier who has completed his service.

(eeshah/nasheem) meshokhr|eret/-arot אישה משוחררת *nf* liberated woman.

meshool|al/-elet משולל *adj* lacking; deprived of.

meshool|al/-elet efsharoot משולל אפשרות *adj* unable to; with no possibility to.

meshoolash/-eem משולש *nm* triangle.

□ **(ha)meshoolash** המשולש *nm* "the Triangle" - colloq. reference to two alternate Arab populated areas; the "Large Triangle" and the "Small Triangle" (see below).

□ **(ha)meshoolash ha-gadol** המשולש הגדול *nm* the "Large Triangle", colloq. reference to the area marked by the three larger West Bank cities **Toolkarem**, Nablus **(Shekhem)** and Ramallah.

□ **(ha)meshoolash ha-katan** המשולש הקטן *nm* "the Small Triangle" - colloquial reference, used mainly before 1967, to three larger Arab villages (that have since grown into urban settlements) this side of the Green Line: **Teereh, Taybeh** and **Kafr Kasem.**

meshool|ash/-eshet משולש *adj* tripled; triple.

meshool|av/-evet משולב *adj* joined; combined.

(etsba') meshooleshet אצבע משולשת *nf* fig. (gesture of contempt); fico.

meshool|hav/-hevet משולהב **1.** *adj* excited; enthusiastic; **2.** *v pres* (is) enthused; (*pst* **shoolhav;** *fut* **yeshoolhav**).

◇ **meshoomad/-eem** משומד *nm* Jew who has willingly converted to another faith.

meshooman/-eem משומן *nm* octagon.

meshoom|an/-enet משומן *adj* greased; oiled.

meshoom|ar/-eret משומר *adj* canned; preserved.

meshoom|ar/-eret משומר *v pres* is being preserved; (*pst* **shoomar;** *fut* **yeshoomar**).

meshoom|ash/-'eshet משומש *adj* used; second-hand.

◇ **meshoom|edet/-adot** משומדת *nf* Jewish woman who has willingly converted to another faith.

meshoon|eh/-ah משונה *adj* strange; queer.

meshoop|a'/-a'at משופע *adj* oblique; slanting.

meshoop|a'/-a'at be- משופע ב־ *adj* abounding in; having plenty of.

meshoop|ar/-eret משופר **1.** *adj* improved; **2.** *v pres* (is) improved; (*pst* **shoopar;** *fut* **yeshoopar**).

meshoop|ats/-etset משופץ **1.** *adj* overhauled; reconditioned; **2.** *v pres* (is) overhauled, reconditioned; (*pst* **shoopats;** *fut* **yeshoopats**).

meshooryan/-eem משוריין *nm* armored vehicle; (*pl+of:* **-ey**).

meshoor|yan/-yenet משוריין **1.** *adj* armored; secured; **2.** *adj* earmarked (of a sum, fund); **3.** *v pres* (am/is) secured; **4.** *v pres* (is) earmarked (sum, fund); (*pst* **shooryan;** *fut* **yeshooryan**).

(toor/-eem) meshooryan/-eem טור משורין *nm* armored column.

meshoos|a'/-a'at משוסע *v pres* (am/is) interrupted, torn, cleft; (*pst* **shoosa';** *fut* **yeshoosa'**).

meshoosh|eh/-ah משושה *adj* hexagonal.

meshoosh|eh/-eem משושה *nm* hexagon.

meshoot|af/-efet משותף **1.** *adj* common; joint; **2.** *v pres* (is) cut in on; made party to; (*pst* **shootaf;** *fut* **yeshootaf**).

(bayeet/bateem) meshootaf/-eem בית משותף *nm* condominium; cooperative dwelling house.

meshoot|ak/-eket משותק **1.** *adj* paralyzed; **2.** *v pres* (is) paralyzed; (*pst* **shootak;** *fut* **yeshootak**).

meshoov|ak/-eket משווק *v pres* (is) being marketed; (*pst* **shoovak;** *fut* **yeshoovak**).

meshorer/-eem משורר *nm* poet (*pl+of:* **-ey**).

meshorer|et/-ot משוררת *nf* poetess.

meshosh|ah/-ot משושה *nf* antenna; aerial; (*+of:* **-at**).

meshotet/-et משוטט *v pres* prowl(s); wander(s); (*pst* **shotet**; *fut* **yeshotet**).
meshovev/-et משובב *adj* boisterous.
meshovev/-et nefesh משובב נפש *adj* refreshing; comforting.
mesoo|'af/-'efet (*npr* **meso|'af/-'efet**) מסועף ramified; branchlike.
mesoob|akh/-ekhet מסובך *adj* complex; complicated.
mesoobs|ad/-edet מסובסד **1.** *adj* subsidized; **2.** *v pres* (is) subsidized; (*pst* **soobsad**; *fut* **yesoobsad**).
mesood|ar/-eret מסודר **1.** *adj* arranged; orderly, tidy; **2.** *[colloq.] adj* financially well-off; **3.** *v pres* (is) given a job; (*pst* **soodar**; *fut* **yesoodar**).
mesood|ar/-eret ba-'avodah מסודר בעבודה *adj* holding a job; employed.
mesoof|am/-emet משופם *adj* mustached.
mesoog|al/-elet מסוגל *adj* capable of; fit for.
mesoogn|an/-enet מסוגנן *adj* stylized; re-written.
mesoog|ar/-eret מסוגר *adj* closed in; tightly closed.
(sagoor/sgoorah oo) mesoog|ar/-eret סגור ומסוגר *adj* locked and bolted.
mesook|am/-emet מסוכם *v pres* is summed-up, finalized; (*pst* **sookam**; *fut* **yesookam**).
mesook|am/-emet מסוכם *adj* summed-up; finally agreed upon.
mesook|an/-enet מסוכן *adj* dangerous.
mesookhs|akh/-ekhet מסוכסך *adj* involved in a quarrel.
mesool|ak/-edet מסולק *v pres* **1.** (is) paid-up; **2.** (is) removed; (*pst* **soolak**; *fut* **yesoolak**).
mesools|al/-elet מסולסל *adj* **1.** curled (hair); **2.** trilled (voice).
mesools|al/-elet se'ar מסולסל שיער *adj* curly.
mesoom|am/-emet מסומם **1.** *adj* drugged; **2.** *v pres* (is) drugged; (*pst* **soomam**; *fut* **yesoomam**).
mesoom|an/-enet מסומן **1.** *adj* marked; **2.** *v pres* (is) marked, earmarked; (*pst* **sooman**; *fut* **yesooman**).
mesoop|ak/-eket מסופק **1.** *adj* doubtful; **2.** *adj* supplied; **3.** *v* (is) provided; supplied; (*pst* **soopak**; *fut* **yesoopak**).
mesoop|akh/-at מסופח **1.** *adj* annexed; **2.** *v pres* (am/is) added, annexed; (*pst* **soopakh**; *fut* **yesoopakh**).
mesoop|ar/-eret מסופר **1.** *adj* narrated; told; **2.** *adj* with one's hair cut; **3.** *v pres* 1. (is) told (story); **4.** *v pres* (is) having hair cut; (*pst* **soopar**; *fut* **yesoopar**).
mesoopkanee מסופקני *v pres 1st pers sing* I doubt whether.
(mayeem bee) mesoorah מים במשורה *nm pl* water rationing; rationed water.
mesoor|ak (*npr* **mesor|ak**)/**-eket** מסורק *adj* combed.
mesoorb|al/-elet מסורבל *adj* clumsy; awkward.
mesoort|at/-etet מסורטט or משורטט *adj* **1.** drafted; **2.** crossed.
(chek/-eem) mesoortat/-eem שיק מסורטט or שיק משורטט *nm* crossed cheque.
mesoov|ag/-eget מסווג **1.** *adj* graded; classified; **2.** *v pres* (am/is) classified; (*pst* **soovag**; *fut* **yesoovag**).
mesoo|yag/-yeget מסויג *adj* reserved; restrained.
mesoo|yam/-yemet מסוים *adj* certain.
mesor|ak/-eket מסורק *adj* combed.
mesor|as/-eset מסורס *adj* distorted; castrated.
mesoratee (*npr* **masortee**)/**-t** מסורתי *adj* traditional.
met/-eem מת *nm* corpse; dead; (*pl+of:* **-ey**).
met/-ah מת **1.** *v pres* die(s); (am/is) dying; (*pst* **met**; *fut* **yamoot**); **2.** *adj* dead.
met/-ah le- (or : **la-**) מת ל־ *[colloq.] v pres* (is) "dying to..." (*pst, fut* as above).
meta'em/-et מתאם **1.** *v pres* coordinate(s); (*pst* **te'em**; *fut* **yeta'em**); **2.** *nmf* coordinator.
meta'em pe'oolot מתאם פעולות *nm* operations coordinator.
meta'er/-et מתאר *v pres* depict(s); describe(s); (*pst* **te'er**; *fut* **yeta'er**).
metaftef/-et מטפטף **1.** *v pres* drip(s); (*pst* **teeftef**; *fut* **yetaftef**); **2.** *nm [colloq.]* dropper; **3.** *adj* dripping.
metaken/-et מתקן *v pres* repair(s); mend (s); (*pst* **teeken**; *fut* **yetaken**).
metakh/-eem מתח *nm* **1.** tension; **2.** voltage.
(hafag|at/-ot) metakh הפגת מתח *nf* easing tension.
(map|al/-ley) metakh מפל מתח *nm* voltage drop.
metakhen/-et מתכן **1.** *nmf* designer; **2.** *v pres* design(s); (*pst* **teekhen**; *fut* **yetakhen**).
metakhnen/-et מתכנן **1.** *nmf* planner; **2.** *v pres* plan(s); (*pst* **teekhnen**; *fut* **yetakhnen**).
metakhnet/-et מתכנת **1.** *nmf* programmer; **2.** *v pres* program(s); (*pst* **teekhnet**; *fut* **yetakhnet**).
metaktak/-ah מתקתק *adj* sweetish.
metaktek/-et מתקתק or מטקטק *v pres* **1.** tap(s); tick(s); **2.** type(s); (*pst* **teektek**; *fut* **yetaktek**).
metaltel/-et מטלטל *v pres* fling(s); swing(s); (*pst* **teeltel**; *fut* **yetaltel**).
metalteleem (*cpr* **metalteleem**) מטלטלים *nm pl* chattels; movable property.
metalteleen מטלטלין *nm pl* personal effects.
metapel/-et מטפל **1.** *v pres* handle(s); (*pst* **teepel**; *fut* **yetapel**); **2.** *adj* handling.
metap|el/-leem מטפל *nm* therapist; attendant.
metap|elet/-lot מטפלת *nf* nursemaid.
metapes/-et מטפס *v pres* climb(s); creep(s); (*pst* **teepes**; *fut* **yetapes**).
metap|es/-seem מטפס *nm* climbing plant; creeper; (*pl+of:* **-sey**).
metargem/-eem מתרגם *nm* translator; (*pl+of:* **-ey**).
metargem/-et מתרגם *v pres* translate(s); (*pst* **teergem**; *fut* **yetargem**).

metav|ekh/-kheem מתווך *nm* mediator; agent; middleman; (*pl+of:* **-khey**).

metavekh/-et מתווך *v pres* mediate(s); (*pst* **teevekh;** *fut* **yetavekh**).

metayel/-et מטייל *v pres* tour(s); hike(s); (*pst* **teeyel;** *fut* **yetayel**).

metay|el/-leem מטייל *nm* tourist; hiker; (*pl+of:* **-ley**).

(meeney) meteekah מיני מתיקה *nm pl* assorted sweets.

meteekh|ah/-ot מתיחה *nf* **1.** stretching; **2.** *[colloq.]* practical joke; (*+of:* **-at**).

meteekhat/-ot 'atsabeem מתיחת עצבים *nf* nervous tension.

meteekhat beekoret מתיחת ביקורת *nf* criticizing.

meteekhat kav מתיחת קו *nf* drawing a line (*figurat.*).

meteekhat 'or ha-paneem מתיחת עור הפנים *nf* face lifting.

meteekhoo|t/-yot מתיחות *nf* tension.

meteekoot מתיקות *nf* sweetness.

(aron/-ot) meteem ארון מתים *nm* coffin.

(tekheeyat ha) meteem תחיית המתים **1.** *nf* resurrection of the dead; **2.** (fig) revival from disuse.

meteenoot מתינות *nf* moderation.

meteev/-ah מיטיב **1.** *adj* beneficial; **2.** *nmf* benefactor; **3.** *v pres* do(es) good to; **4.** *v pres* excel(s) in; (*pst* **heteev;** *fut* **yeteev**).

met|eg/-ageem מתג *nm* switch; (*pl+of:* **meetgey**).

met|er/-reem מטר *nm* meter; metre (equivalent to 39.37 inches or 3.281 feet).

(ha)meter (or le-meter) המטר (or למטר) *adv* per meter.

met|er/-reem koobee/-yeem מטר מעוקב *nm* cubic meter (equivalent to 35.31 cubic feet).

met|er/-reem me'ookav/-eem מטר מעוקב *[colloq.] nm* cubic meter (see **meter koobee**, above).

met|er/-reem merooba'/-'eem מטר מרובע *[colloq.] nm* square meter (see **meter ravoo'a'**, below).

meter rats מטר רץ *nm* meter length.

met|er/-reem ravoo'a/-ravoo'eem מטר רבוע *nm* square meter (equivalent to 10.76 square feet or to 1.196 square yards).

metey meespar מתי־מספר *num* just a few.

meto|'am/-'emet מתואם **1.** *adj* coordinated; **2.** *v pres* (is) coordinated; (*pst* **to'am;** *fut* **yeto'am**).

meto|'ar/-'eret מתואר **1.** *adj* described; depicted; **2.** *v pres* (is) described; (*pst* **to'ar;** *fut* **yeto'ar**).

meto|'av/-'evet מתועב *adj* despicable; abominable.

metod|ah/-ot מתודה *nf* method; (*+of:* **-at**).

metofef/-et מתופף **1.** *nmf* drummer; **2.** *v pres* beat(s) the drum; (*pst* **tofef;** *fut* **yetofef**).

metoob|al/-elet מתובל **1.** *adj* seasoned; spiced; **2.** *v pres* (is) seasoned, spiced; (*pst* **toobal;** *fut* **yetoobal**).

metoog|an/-enet מטוגן *adj* fried.

(shamenet) metookah שמנת מתוקה *nf* sweet cream.

metookhn|an/-enet מתוכנן **1.** *adj* planned; **2.** *v pres* (is) planned; (*pst* **tookhnan;** *fut* **yetookhnan**).

metookhn|at/-etet מתוכנת **1.** *adj* programmed; **2.** *v pres* (is) programmed; (*pst* **tookhnat;** *fut* **yetookhnat**).

□ **Metoolah** (Metulla) מטולה *nf* recreation township (originally est. 1896 as agricultural settlement) on Lebanese border. Pop. 820.

metoolt|al/-elet מתולתל *adj* curly.

metoomt|am/-emet מטומטם *adj* stupid; imbecile.

metoomt|am/-emet ekhad/-akhat! מטומטם אחד! *interj* you fool! you idiot!

metoon|af/-efet מטונף *adj* filthy; dirty.

metoopakh/-at מטופח *adj* well-groomed; tended.

metoop|al/-elet מטופל *adj* **1.** attended to; taken care of; **2.** burdened with.

metoop|al/-elet be- מטופל ב־ *adj* burdened with.

metoop|ash/-eshet מטופש *adj* silly; foolish.

metoorb|at/-etet מתורבת *adj* cultured; civilized; domesticated.

metoorg|am/-emet מתורגם *v pres* (is) translated; (*pst* **toorgam;** *fut* **yetoorgam**).

metoorgeman/-eet מתורגמן *nmf* interpreter.

metoosb|akh/-ekhet מתוסבך *adj* complex-ridden.

metoosht|ash/-eshet מטושטש *adj* perplexed; dazed; dim, blurred.

metootelet מטוטלת *nf* pendulum.

metor|af/-efet מטורף *adj* crazy; insane; *nmf* madman; madwoman.

metreem (*sing:* **meter**) מטרים *nm pl* meters.

metreem beneeyah מטרים בנייה *nm pl* meters to build.

metreem koobeeyeem מטרים קוביים *nm pl* cubic meters.

metreem me'ookaveem מטרים מעוקבים *[colloq.] nm pl* cubic meters.

metreem merooba'eem מטרים מרובעים *[colloq.] nm pl* square meters.

metreem revoo'eem מטרים רבועים *nm pl* square meters.

metropoleen מטרופולין *nf* metropolis.

□ **Metsadah** see □ **Masadah**.

metsaded/-et מצדד *v pres* support(s); favor(s); (*pst* **tseeded;** *fut* **yetsaded**).

metsaded/-eem מצדד *nm* supporter; partisan; (*pl+of:* **-ey**).

metsa'er/-et מצער **1.** *adj* distressing; **2.** *v pres* distress(es) pain(s); (*pst* **tsee'er;** *fut* **yetsa'er**).

metsakh מצח *nm* forehead.

◇ **METSAKH** מצ״ח *nf abbr.* Military Police, Investigation Unit (*acr of* **Meeshtarah TSva'eet KHokeret** משטרה צבאית חוקרת).

metsakh nekhooshah מצח נחושה *nm* brazen face.

('azoot) metsakh עזות מצח *nf* insolence.

(hatkafat/-ot) metsakh התקפת מצח *nf* frontal attack.

metsalem/-et מצלם *v pres* photograph(s); take(s) pictures; (*pst* **tseelem**; *fut* **yetsalem**).

metsaltsel/-et מצלצל **1.** *adj* ringing; **2.** *v pres* ring(s); (*pst* **tseeltsel**; *fut* **yetsaltsel**).

metsaltseleem מצלצלים *[colloq.] v pres 3rd pers pl* the doorbell is ringing.

metsaltseleem מצלצלים *nm pl [slang]* cash; cash-money.

metsamtsem/-et מצמצם **1.** *adj* restrictive; restricting; **2.** *v pres* restrict(s); (*pst* **tseemtsem**; *fut* **yetsamtsem**).

metsay מצאי **1.** inventory; **2.** stock.

metsee|'ah/-'ot מציאה *nf* bargain.

metseef/-ah מציף *v pres* flood(s); (*pst* **hetseef**; *fut* **yatseef**).

metseeltayeem מצלתיים *nf pl* cymbals.

metsee'oot מציאות *nf* reality.

(bee) metsee'oot במציאות *adv* in reality.

(be-khorakh ha) metsee'oot בכורח המציאות *adv* by force of realities.

(mekhoo|yav/-yevet ha) metsee'oot מחויב המציאות *adj* imperative; indispensable.

(yekar/yeekrat ha) metsee'oot יקר המציאות *adj* hard to get; rare.

metsee'ootee/-t מציאותי *adj* realistic.

metseets/-ah מציץ *v pres* peep(s); (*pst* **hetseets**; *fut* **yatseets**).

metseets/-eem מציץ *nm* Peeping Tom.

metseets|ah/-ot מציצה *nf* sucking; suction; (*+of:* **-at**).

(a) metseeyeh! א־מציאה! *interj [slang]* big bargain, indeed! (ironically).

metsoded/-et מצודד *adj* enticing.

metsoo'atsa'/-at מצועצע *adj* fancy; flamboyant.

metsood|ah/-ot מצודה *nf* fort; fortress; (*+of:* **-at**).

metsook|ah/-ot מצוקה *nf* distress; trouble; (*+of:* **-at**).

(eyzor/azorey) metsookah אזור מצוקה *nm* poor, distressed area.

metsookhtsakh/-at מצוחצח *adj* **1.** polished; shining; **2.** *[slang]* dandified.

metsool|ah/-ot מצולה *nf* depth; (*+of:* **-at**).

metsoolot yam מצולות־ים *nf pl* depths of the sea.

metsoom|ak/-eket מצומק *adj* **1.** shriveled; dried-up; **2.** *[slang]* skinny (of a person).

metsoomts|am/-emet מצומצם *adj* restricted; limited.

metsoon|an/-enet מצונן *adj* **1.** cooled; chilled; **2.** *[colloq.]* having a cold.

metsoop|eh/-ah מצופה *adj* **1.** plated; **2.** expected.

metsoopeem מצופים *nm pl* chocolate wafers.

metsoovrakh/-at מצוברח *[colloq.] adj* moody; in a bad mood; feeling low.

metsoo|yan/-yenet מצוין *adj* excellent.

metsoo|yar/-yeret מצויר *adj* drawn; painted.

metsora'/-at מצורע *nmf* leper.

metsor|af/-efet מצורף *adj* enclosed; attached.

(bee) metsoraf במצורף *adv* enclosed please find.

mevader/-et מבדר *v pres* entertain(s); distract(s); (*pst* **beeder**; *fut* **yevader** *(b=v)*).

mevade/-t מוודא *v pres* ascertain(s); (*pst* **veede**; *fut* **yevade**).

mevad|e'akh/-akhat מבדח *adj* funny; amusing.

mevager/-et מבגר *adj* making one look older.

mevaker/-et מבכר *v pres* prefers; (*pst* **beeker**; *fut* **yevaker** *(b=v)*).

mevaker/-et מבקר *v pres* **1.** visit(s); **2.** criticize(s); (*pst* **beeker**; *fut* **yevaker** *(b=v)*).

mevak|er/-reem מבקר *nm* **1.** visitor; **2.** critic; **3.** inspector; (*pl+of:* **-rey**).

mevaker/-et (*etc*) **etsel** מבקר אצל *v pres* visit(s); pay(s) visit.

mevak|er/-eret kolno'a מבקר קולנוע *nmf* film reviewer; (*pl:* **-rey** *etc*).

mevak|er/-reem seefrootee/-yeem מבקר ספרותי *nm* literary critic.

mevak|er/-eret te'atron מבקר תיאטרון *nmf* theatrical critic; (*pl:* **-rey** *etc*).

mevakesh/-et מבקש *v pres* beg(s); ask(s); request(s); (*pst* **beekesh** *(b=v)*; *fut* **yevakesh**).

(ha) mevakesh/-et המבקש *nmf* (the) petitioner.

mevalef/-et מבלף *[slang] v pres* bluff(s); (*pst* **beelef**; *fut* **yevalef** *(b=v)*)

mevas|er/-eret מבשר *v pres* herald(s); announce(s); (*pst* **beeser fyt yevaser** *(b=v)*).

mevas|er/-eret מבשר *nm* forerunner; (*pl+of:* **-rey**).

□ **Mevaseret Tseeyon** (Mevasseret Ziyyon) מבשרת ציון *nf* suburb and local council (est. 1951) atop hills outside Jerusalem, 5 km W. of the city on both sides of Freeway 1. Pop. 12,500.

mevash|el/-elet מבשל *v pres* cook(s) up; (*pst* **beeshel**; *fut* **yevashel** *(b=v)*).

mevash|elet/-lot מבשלת *nf* cook (female).

mevats|e'a'/-a'at מבצע *v pres* execute(s); carry(ies) out; (*pst* **beetsa'**; *fut* **yevatse'a'** *(b=v)*).

mevats|e'a'/-a'at מבצע *nmf* performer; executor; (*pl+of:* **-'ey**).

meveen/-ah מבין **1.** *nmf* connoisseur; **2.** *v pres* understand(s) (*pst* **heveen**; *fut* **yaveen**).

meveesh/-ah מביש *adj* shameful.

□ **Mevo Beytar** (Mevo Betar) מבוא ביתר *nm* village in Judean hills (est. 1950), 10 km SW of Jerusalem. Pop. 239.

□ **Mevo Dotan** (Mevo Dotan) מבוא דותן *nm* communal village (est. 1981) in Samaria hills, W. of Dotan Valley, 3 km S. of **Ya'bad**.

□ **Mevo Khamah** (Mevo Hamma) מבוא חמה *nm* kibbutz in S. part of the Golan Heights, 8 km NE of Zemah Junction **(Tsomet Tsemakh)**, near **Khamat Gader** hot springs. Pop. 311. □

□ **Mevo Khoron** (Mevo Horon) מבוא חורון *nm* village (est. 1974) bordering on Ayalon Valley, 5 km NE of Latrun Junction **(Tsomet Latroon)**. Pop. 346.

□ **Mevo Modee'eem** (Mevo MOdi'im) מבוא מודיעים *nm* collective village (est.1964) in the **Shfelah**, 10 km E. of Lod. Pop. 198.

mevo|hal/-helet מבוהל *adj* panicky; hasty.

□ **Mevo'ot Yam** (Mevo'ot Yam) מבואות־ים *nm* fishing- and nautical school (est. 1951), on seashore in Sharon, 10 km N. of Netanya. Pop. 700.

mevood|ad/-edet מבודד **1.** *adj* isolated; insulated; **2.** *v pres* (is) isolated, insulated; (*pst* **boodad** *(b=v)*; *fut* **yevoodad**).

mevoodakh/-at מבודח *adj* humorous; amused.

mevoog|ar/-eret מבוגר **1.** *adj* mature; aged; **2.** *nmf* adult; grown-up.

mevook|ar/-eret מבוקר *adj* controlled; visited.

mevook|ash/-eshet מבוקש *adj* wanted; sought after.

mevookh|ah/-ot מבוכה *nf* confusion; (*+of:* **-at**).

(bee) mevookhah במבוכה *adv* in a state of confusion.

mevoolb|al/-elet מבולבל **1.** *adj* mixed-up; confused; **2.** *v pres* (is) mixed-up; (*pst* **boolbal**; *fut* **yevoolbal** *(b=v)*).

mevoos|am/-emet מבושם *adj* **1.** perfumed; **2.** *[colloq.]* tipsy.

mevoos|as/-eset מבוסס *adj* established; solidly based.

mevoosh|al/-elet מבושל *adj* cooked.

mevootakh/-at מבוטח **1.** *adj* insured; **2.** *v pres* (is) insured; (*pst* **bootakh**; *fut* **yevootakh** *(b=v)*).

mevoot|al/-elet מבוטל **1.** *adj* insignificant; **2.** *adj* canceled; **3.** *v pres* (is) canceled, annulled; (*pst* **bootal** *(b=v)*; *fut* **yevootal**).

mevoot|an/-enet מבוטן **1.** *adj* concreted; cemented; **2.** *v pres* (is) cemented, concreted; (*pst* **bootan** *(b=v)*; *fut* **yevootan**).

mevoots|ar/-eret מבוצר **1.** *adj* fortified; **2.** *v pres* (is) fortified; (*pst* **bootsar**; *fut* **yevootsar** *(b=v)*).

mevoo|yal/-yelet מבויל **1.** *adj* stamped (with revenue or other stamps); **2.** - *v pres* (is) stamped (as above); (*pst* **booyal**; *fut* **yevooyal** *(b=v)*).

mevoo|yam/-yemet מבוים **1.** *adj* staged; false; **2.** *v pres* (is) staged; (*pst* **booyam** *(b=v)*; *fut* **yevooyam**).

mevor|akh/-ekhet מבורך **1.** *adj* blessed; **2.** *v pres* (is) blessed; (*pst* **borakh** *(b=v)*; *fut* **yevorakh**).

mey מי *nm pl+of* waters of...; (see: **mayeem**).

□ **Mey 'Amee** מי עמי *nm* (Me 'Ammi) village (est. 1963) in N. Samaria hills, E. of Wadi 'Ara **(Nakhal 'Eeron)**, 2 km S. of **Oom el-Fakhem**. Pop. 178.

mey khamtsan מי חמצן *nm pl* hydrogen peroxide.

mey shteeyah מי שתייה *nm pl* drinking water.

mey tehom מי תהום *nm pl* ground waters.

('al) mey menookhot על מי מנוחות *adv* peacefully and quietly.

meyabe/-t מייבא *v pres* import(s); (*pst* **yeebe**; *fut* **yeyabe**).

meyabesh/-et מייבש *v pres* dry(ies); drain(s); (*pst* **yeebesh**; *fut* **yeyabesh**).

meyab|esh/-shey keveesah מייבש כביסה *nm* laundry drier.

meyab|esh/-shey se'ar מייבש שיער *nm* hair drier.

meyade'a'/-a'at מיידע *v pres* inform(s); (*pst* **yeede'a'**; *fut* **yeyade'a'**).

meya'ets/-et מייעץ **1.** *adj* advisory; **2.** *v pres* advise(s); (*pst* **ya'ats**; *fut* **yeya'ets**).

(va'adah) meya'etset ועדה מייעצת *nf* advisory committee; advisory board.

meyag|e'a/-a'at מייגע *adj* tiring; tiresome.

meyaker/-et מייקר *v pres* increase(s) prices; raise(s) value; (*pst* **yeeker**; *fut* **yeyaker**).

meyakhed/-et מייחד *v pres* single(s) out; set(s) apart; (*pst* **yeekhed**; *fut* **yeyakhed**).

meyakhed/-et et ha-deeboor מייחד את הדיבור *v pres* (*etc*) dwells on; concentrate(s) on.

meyakhel/-et מייחל *v pres* hope(s) for; wish(es) for (*pst* **yeekhel**; *fut* **yeyakhel**).

meyakhes/-et מייחס *v pres* attribute(s); (*pst* **yeekhes**; *fut* **yeyakhes**).

meyaled/-et מיילד *nmf* obstetrician.

meyal|edet/-dot מיילדת *nf* midwife.

meyas|ed/-deem מייסד *nm* founder; founding father; (*pl+of:* **-dey**).

meyased/-et מייסד *v pres* found(s); establish(es); (*pst* **yeesed**; *fut* **yeyased**).

meyasher/-et מיישר *v pres* straighten(s); rectify(ies); (*pst* **yeesher**; *fut* **yeyasher**).

meyash|er/-rey zerem מיישר זרם *nm* rectifier (electric.).

meyasher/-et (*etc*) **hadooreem** מיישר הדורים *v pres* straighten(s) matters out.

meyalel/-et מיילל *v pres* howl(s); wail(s); (*pst* **yeelel**; *fut* **yeyalel**).

meyashev/-et מיישב *v pres* **1.** settle(s); **2.** populate(s); (*pst* **yeeshev**; *fut* **yeyashev**).

(gar'een/-eem) meyash|ev/-veem גרעין מיישב *nm* kernel of settlement in formation.

(rashoo|t/-yot) meyash|evet/-vot רשות מיישבת *nf* settling authority.

(mosadot) meyashveem מוסדות מיישבים *nm pl* settling (public) bodies.

meyatse/-t מייצא *v pres* - *v pres* export(s); (*pst* **yeetse**; *fut* **yeyatse**).

meyatseg/-et מייצג **1.** *adj* representing; representative; **2.** *v pres* represent(s); (*pst* **yeetseg**; *fut* **yeyatseg**).

meyatser/-et מייצר *v pres* produce(s); manufacture(s); (*pst* **yeetser**; *fut* **yeyatser**).

meyatsev/-et מייצב **1.** *adj* stabilizing; **2.** *v pres* stabilize(s); (*pst* **yeetsev**; *fut* **yeyatsev**).

meyda‘ מידע *nm* information.
meykham/-eem מיחם *nm* samovar.
meyla מילא *interj* so be it! nothing doing; never mind.
(mee) meyla ממילא *adv* anyway; in any case.
meymad/-eem ממד *nm* dimension; (*pl+of:* **-ey**).
meyman מימן *nm* hydrogen.
(peetsets|at/-ot) meyman פצצת מימן *nf* hydrogen bomb.
meymee/-t מימי *adj* watery.
(tat-) meymee/-t תת־מימי *adj* submarine; underwater.
meymee|yah/-yot מימייה *nf* water-bottle; canteen; (*+of:* **-yat**).
meyoo|‘ad/-‘edet מיועד **1.** *adj* destined; **2.** *v pres* (is) destined, slated; (*pst* **yoo‘ad;** *fut* **yeyoo‘ad**).
meyoo|’ash/-’eshet מיואש *adj* desperate; exasperated.
meyoob|a/-e’t מיובא *adj* imported.
meyoob|al/-elet מיובל *adj* horny; rough.
meyood|ad/-edet מיודד *adj* befriended; friend with.
meyookh|ad/-edet מיוחד **1.** *adj* special; particular; **2.** *v pres* is set aside for; (*pst* **yookhad;** *fut* **yeyookhad**).
meyookh|ad/-edet be-meen|o/-ah מיוחד במינו *adj* unique.
(bee) meyookhad במיוחד *adv* especially.
meyookh|al/-elet מיוחל *adj* hoped for.
meyookh|am/-emet מיוחם *adj* **1.** in heat (of animals); **2.** *[slang]* turned on (humans).
meyookhas/-eem מיוחס *nm* privileged person; (*pl+of:* **-ey**).
meyookh|as/-eset מיוחס *v pres* (is) attributed to; (*pst* **yookhas;** *fut* **yeyookhas**).
meyoom|an/-enet מיומן *adj* skilled; adroit.
meyoomanoo|t/-yot מיומנות *nf* skill; adroitness.
meyoop|eh/-ah מיופה **1.** *adj* embellished; **2.** *v pres* am/is authorized; (*pst* **yoopah;** *fut* **yeyoopeh**).
meyoopeh/-at ko’akh מיופה כוח *nmf* **1.** holder of power of attorney; **2.** (dipl. corps:) Chargé d’Affaires.
meyoosh|an/-enet מיושן *adj* obsolete; antiquated.
meyoosh|av/-evet מיושב *adj* **1.** populated (space); **2.** stable (person); level-headed.
meyoot|am/-emet מיותם *adj* orphaned.
meyoot|ar/-eret מיותר *adj* superfluous; redundant.
meyoots|a/-e’t מיוצא *adj* exported.
meyooza‘/-a‘at מיוזע *adj* perspiring; sweaty.
meyrav מירב *nm* the most; the major part of.
□ **Meyron** (Meron) מירון *nm* village (est. 1949) in Upper Galilee, at foot of Mount **Meeron**. Pop. 542.
(be)meyshareem (or: **be-meyshareen**) במישרים or במישרין *adv* directly.
(le) meyshareem (*or:* **le-meyshareem**) למישרים *adv* smoothly.
meyt|ar/-areem מיתר *nm* cord; (*pl+of:* **-rey**).
meytav מיטב *nm* the best of; choice; optimum.
□ **Meytav** (Metav) מיטב *nm* village in **Ta‘anakh** Region, Yizre’el Valley (est. 1954), 7 km S. of ’Afula. Pop. 340.
meytrey ha-kol מיתרי קול *nm pl* vocal cords.
meza‘az|e’a‘/-a‘at (*npr* **meza‘ze’a‘/-a‘at**) מזעזע **1.** *adj* shocking; **2.** *v pres* shock(s); (*pst* **zee‘ze’a‘;** *fut* **yeza‘ze’a‘**).
mezabel/-et מזבל *v pres* **1.** manure(s); fertilize(s); **2.** *[slang]* talk(s) high; flatter(s); (*pst* **zeebel;** *fut* **yezabel**).
mezageg/-et מזגג *v pres* glaze(s); ice(s); (*pst* **zeegeg;** *fut* **yezageg**).
mezak|eh/-ah מזכה *v pres* **1.** acquit(s); **2.** credit(s) (*pst* **zeekah;** *fut* **yezakeh**).
mezakek/-et מזקק *v pres* refine(s); distills; (*pst* **zeekek;** *fut* **yezakek**).
mezakekh/-et מזכך **1.** *adj* purifying; **2.** *v pres* purify(ies) (*pst* **zeekekh;** *fut* **yezakekh**).
mezakh/-eem מזח jetty; (*pl+of:* **meezkhey**).
mezamber/-et מזמבר *v pres* **1.** *[slang]* screw(s); **2.** *[slang]* lick(s); (*pst* **zeember;** *fut* **yezamber**).
mezamen/-et מזמן *v pres* **1.** convene(s); summon(s) together; **2.** make(s) occur; (*pst* **zeemen;** *fut* **yezamen**).
mezamer/-et מזמר *adj* **1.** singing; **2.** *v pres sing* (s); (*pst* **zeemer;** *fut* **yezamer**).
mezanek/-et מזנק *v pres* leap(s) forth; dash(es); (*pst* **zeenek;** *fut* **yezanek**).
mezanev/-et מזנב *v pres* curtail(s); attack(s) rear; (*pst* **zeenev;** *fut* **yezanev**).
mezarez/-et מזרז *v pres* hurry(ies); urge(s); goad(s); (*pst* **zeerez;** *fut* **yezarez**).
mezaveg/-et מזווג *v pres* match(es); mate(s); pair(s) off; (*pst* **zeeveg;** *fut* **yezaveg**).
mezav|eh/-eem מזווה *nm* pantry; barn; (*pl+of:* **-ey**).
mezayef/-et מזייף *v pres* forge(s); falsify(ies); (*pst* **zeeyef;** *fut* **yezayef**).
mezayen/-et מזיין *v pres* arm(s); *[slang]* fornicate(s); (*pst* **zeeyen;** *fut* **yezayen**).
meza‘a|e’a‘/-a‘at מזעזע **1.** *adj* shocking; **2.** *v pres* shock(s); (*pst* **zee‘ze’a‘;** *fut* **yeza‘ze’a‘**).
(be) mezeed במזיד *adv* willfully.
mezeeg|ah/-ot מזיגה *nf* blend; fusion; (*+of:* **-at**).
mezeem|ah/-ot מזימה *nf* intrigue; (*+of:* **-at**).
(khar|ash/-shah/-ashtee) mezeemot חרש מזימות *v* plotted against; (*pres* **khoresh** *etc;* *fut* **yakhrosh** *etc*).
(rak|am/-mah/-amtee) mezeemot רקם מזימות *v* devised evil plans against; (*pres* **rokem** *etc;* *fut* **yeerkom** *etc*).
mez|een/-ah מזין **1.** *adj* nourishing; **2.** *v pres* nourish(es) feed(s); (*pst* **hezeen;** *fut* **yazeen**).
mez|eg/-ageem מזג *nm* **1.** mixture; **2.** nature; temper; (*pl+of:* **meezgey**).
mezeg/meezgey aveer מזג אוויר *nm* weather.
mezeg aveer gashoom מזג אוויר גשום *nm* rainy weather.

mezeg aveer no'akh מזג אוויר נוח *nm* fine weather.

mezeg aveer so'er מזג אוויר סוער *nm* stormy weather.

(kar/-at) mezeg קר מזג *adj* cool-headed.

(kham/-at) mezeg חם מזג *adj* hot-tempered.

mezeh/-at ra'av מזה רעב *adj* starved; famished.

mezo|ham/-hemet מזהם **1.** *adj* filthy; infected; **2.** *v pres* (is) infected; (*pst* **zooham**; *fut* **yezooham**).

mezo|heh/-hah מזוהה *v pres* (is) identified; (*pst* **zoohah**; *fut* **yezooheh**).

mezo|heh/-hah (*etc*) **'eem** מזוהה עם *adj* identified with.

(demey) mezonot מזונות *nm pl* alimony.

mezoog|ag/-eget מזוגג *adj* glazed; iced.

mezoo|heh/-hah (*npr* **mezo|heh/hah**) מזוהה *v pres* (is) identified; (*pst* **zohah**; *fut* **yezoheh**).

mezoo|heh/-hah (*etc*) **'eem** מזוהה עם *adj* identified with.

mezook|ak/-eket מזוקק **1.** *adj* refined; distilled; **2.** *v pres* (is) refined, distilled; (*pst* **zookak**; *fut* **yezookak**).

mezook|akh/-ekhet מזוכך *adj* purified.

mezook|an/-enet מזוקן *[colloq.] adj* bearded.

mezook|eh/-ah מזוכה *adj* credited; acquitted.

mezoom|an/-enet מזומן **1.** *adj* summoned; **2.** *v pres* (is) summoned, prepared; (*pst* **zooman**; *fut* **yezooman**).

(bee) mezooman במזומן *adv* in cash.

(kesef) mezooman כסף מזומן *nm* cash.

(mookhan oo) mezooman מוכן ומזומן *adj* ready and willing.

mezoomaneem מזומנים *nm pl* cash.

(bee) mezoomaneem במזומנים *adv* in cash.

(le-'eeteem) mezoomanot לעיתים מזומנות *adv* at regular intervals.

mezoop|at/-etet מזופת **1.** *adj* tarred; asphalted; **2.** *[slang]* lousy; rotten.

mezoor|az/-ezet (*npr* **mezor|az/-ezet**) מזורז *adj* sped-up; brisk; quick.

mezoorg|ag/-eget מזורגג *[slang] adj* "bloody"; "blasted".

mezoo|yaf/-yefet מזויף *adj* false; counterfeit.

mezoo|yan/-yenet מזוין **1.** *adj* armed; **2.** *[slang]* "screwed".

(beton) mezooyan ביטון מזוין *nm* reinforced concrete; ferro-concrete.

(ma'avak/-eem) mezooyan/-eem מאבק מזוין *nm* armed struggle.

◇ **Mezooz|ah/-ot** מזוזה *nf* encased tiny parchment scroll with verses (from Deuteronomy 6:4-9 and 11:13-21) which Jews traditionally affix to doorpost of dwelling.

mezoo'z|a'/-a'at מזועזע *adj* shocked.

mezor|az/-ezet מזורז *adj* sped-up; brisk; quick.

(be) mo pee|v/-ha במו פיו *adj* with his/her (*etc*) own mouth.

(be) mo yad|av/-eha במו ידיו *adv* with his/her (*etc*) own hands.

mo'adeem le-seemkhah! !מועדים לשמחה *interj* (greeting) Happy Holiday!

(be) mo'ad|o/-ah במועדו *adv* on time; in his/her/its own time.

mo'adon/-eem מועדון *nm* club; (*pl+of:* **-ey**).

◇ **mo'adon/-ey "Tsavta"** מועדון "צוותא" *nm* chain of avant-garde theater-clubs sponsored by left-wing circles.

mo'akh/mokhot מוח *nm* brain.

mo'akh 'atsamot מוח עצמות *nm* bone-marrow; medulla ossium.

(beelbool/-ey) mo'akh בלבול מוח *nm* confusion; trouble.

(daleket kroom ha) mo'akh דלקת קרום המוח *nf* meningitis.

(khamoom/-ey) mo'akh חמום מוח *nm* hothead.

(shteef|at/-ot) mo'akh שטיפת מוח *nf* brainwashing.

(be) mo'al yad במועל יד *adv* saluting by raising one's hand.

mo'ats|ah/-ot מועצה *nf* council; (*+of:* **mo'etset**).

mo'ats|ah/-ot azoree|t/-yot מועצה אזורית *nf* regional concil.

mo'ats|ah/-ot mekomee|t/-yot מועצה מקומית *nf* local council.

□ **(breet ha) mo'atsot** ברית המועצות *nf* the (onetime) Soviet Union.

mod|ah/-ot מודה *[colloq.] nf* fashion; (*+of:* **-at**).

moda|'ah/-'ot מודעה *nf* advertisement; (*+of:* **-at**).

moda|'at/-'ot brakhah מודעת ברכה *nf* greeting advertisement.

moda|'at/-'ot evel מודעת אבל *nf* obituary notice.

(loo|'akh/-khot) moda'ot לוח מודעות *nm* notice board.

moded/-eem מודד *nm* surveyor; (*pl+of:* **-ey**).

moded/-et מודד *v pres* survey(s); measure(s); (*pst* **madad**; *fut* **yeemdod**).

modee|'a'/-'eem meeshtartee/-yeem מודיע משטרתי *nm* police informer.

modee'een מודיעין *nm pl* **1.** information; **2.** intelligence (milit.).

(kheyl) modee'een חיל מודיעין *nm* Intelligence Corps.

(leesh|kat/leshakhot) modee'een לשכת מודיעין *nm* information booth; information office.

□ **Modee'een** מודיעין *nf* remnants of the burial tombs of the Hasmonean (Maccabean) kings of ca 140-40 BCE, 12 km E. of Lod.

modeh/-ah מודה *v pres* **1.** admit(s); acknowledge(s); **2.** thank(s); (*pst* **hodah**; *fut* **yodeh**).

modernee/-t מודרני *adj* modern.

modoos/-eem מודוס *nm* mode; manner; (*pl+of:* **-ey**).

mo'ed/mo'adeem מועד *nm* **1.** term; **2.** festival; holiday; (*pl+of:* **mo'adey**).

(ba) mo'ed במועד *adv* in time; on time.

(be-'od) mo'ed בעוד מועד *adv* in good time; while there is still time.

(ketsar/keetsrat) mo'ed קצר מועד *adj* short-term.

◇ **(khol ha) mo'ed** see ◇ **khol ha-mo'ed**.

mo'eel/-ah מואיל *v pres* **1.** condescend(s); **2.** consent(s); (*pst* **ho'eel**; *fut* **yo'eel**).

mo'eel/-ah מועיל *adj* **1.** useful; **2.** *v pres* (is) of use; (*pst* **ho'eel**; *fut* **yo'eel**).

mo'el/-et מועל *v pres* misuse(s); embezzle(s); misappropriate(s); (*pst* **ma'al**; *fut* **yeem'al**).

mo'en מוען *nm* sender; addressor; (by mail).

mo'etset מועצת *nf+of* the council of...

mo'etset ha-'eer מועצת העיר *nf* town council.

mo'etset menahaleem מועצת מנהלים *nf* board of directors.

mo'etset ne'emaneem מועצת נאמנים *nf* Board of trustees.

mo'etset po'aleem מועצת פועלים *nf* Worker's Council.

mo'etset talmeedeem מועצת תלמידים *nf* students (pupils') council.

mof|a'/-a'eem מופע *nm* performance; spectacle; public appearance; (*pl+of:* **-'ey**).

(loo'akh) mofa'eem לוח מופעים *nm* table of performances.

mofee|'a'/-'ah מופיע *v pres* appear(s); make(s) appearance; (*pst* **hofee'a'**; *fut* **yofee'a'**).

mof|et/-teem מופת *nm* good example; model; (*pl+of:* **-tey**).

(le) mofet למופת *adv & adj* exemplary.

mohel/mohaleem מוהל *nm* specialist in performing the ritual of circumcision; (*pl+of:* **mohaley**).

(ha)mokaz המוכ״ז *nmf* (the) bearer (*acr of* **MOser Ketav Zeh** מוסר כתב זה).

(la) mokaz למוכ״ז *adj* bearer (bond, stock, share *etc*); to the bearer.

mok|ed/-deem מוקד *nm* focus; pyre; fire; (*pl+of:* **-dey**).

mokee|'a'/-'ah מוקיע *v pres* denounce(s); (*pst* **hokee'a'**; *fut* **yokee'a'**).

mokeer/-ah מוקיר **1.** *nmf* admirer; **2.** *v pres* admire(s); respect(s); (*pst* **hokeer**; *fut* **yokeer**).

mok|esh/-sheem מוקש *nm* mine; landmine; (*pl+of:* **-shey**).

mokhee/-t מוחי *adj* cerebral.

(sheetook) mokhee שיתוק מוחי *nm* cerebral palsy.

mokhek/-et מוחק *v pres* erase(s); wipe(s) off; (*pst* **makhak**; *fut* **yeemkhak**).

mokh|ek/-akeem (*normat. term:* **makhak/ mekhakeem**) מוחק *nm* eraser.

mokhel/-et מוחל *v pres* forgive(s); forgo(es); (*pst* **makhal**; *fut* **yeemkhol**).

mokher/-et מוכר **1.** *nmf* seller; **2.** *v pres* sell(s); (*pst* **makhar**; *fut* **yeemkor**; *(k=kh)*).

mokh|er/-reem מוכר *nm* salesman; (*pl+of:* **-rey**).

mokh|eret/-rot מוכרת *nf* saleswoman; salesgirl.

mokh|es/-seem מוכס *nm* customs-officer; (*pl+of:* **-sey**).

mokhets/-et מוחץ **1.** *adj* smashing; crushing; **2.** *v pres* smash(es); crush(es); (*pst* **makhats**; *fut* **yeemkhats**).

(le) mokhorat (*npr* **la-mokhrat**) למוחרת *adv* next day; on the following day.

(yom ha) mokhorat יום המוחרת *nm* the day after.

mokhoratayeem (*cpr* **mokhrotayeem**) מוחרתיים *nm* the day ofter tomorrow.

(sd|eh/-ot) moksheem שדה מוקשים *nm* minefield.

mol/-eem מו״ל *nm* publisher; (*acr of* **MOtsee/-'eem Le-'or** מוציא לאור).

molad/-ot מולד *nm* **1.** birth; **2.** appearance of a new moon.

(khag ha) molad חג המולד *nm* Christmas.

moledet מולדת *nf* homeland.

(erets) moledet ארץ מולדת *nf* homeland; land of birth.

□ **Moledet** מולדת *nm* village (est. 1937) in the Lower Gallilee hills, 5 km N. of **Bet ha-Sheetah**. Pop. 530.

moleed/-ah מוליד *nm* beget(s); sire(s); (*pst* **holeed**; *fut* **yoleed**).

moleekh/-ah מוליך *v pres* lead(s); conduct(s); (*pst* **holeekh**; *fut* **yoleekh**).

moleekh/-eem מוליך *nm* conductor (electric).

moleekhoot מוליכות *nf* conductivity.

(refoo'ah) mona'at רפואה מונעת *nf* preventive medicine; prophylaxis.

mon|e'a'/-a'at מונע *v pres* prevent(s); preclude(s); (*pst* **mana'**; *fut* **yeemna'**).

mon|eem (*sing:* **-eh**) מונים **1.** *nm pl* times; **2.** *-nm pl* counters (see **moneh**).

monee|t/-yot מונית *nf* taxi; cab.

◇ **monee|t/-yot ben-'eeronee|t/-yot** מונית בין־עירונית *nf* inter-urban taxi.

◇ **monee|t/-yot sheroot** מונית שירות *nf* fare-sharing taxi running parallel to an urban or inter-urban bus-line.

moneeteen מוניטין *nm pl* **1.** goodwill; **2.** reputation; fame.

(yats'oo lo/lah) moneeteen יצאו לו מוניטין *v* gained reputation; earned fame.

mon|eh/-ah מונה *v pres* count(s); (*pst* **manah**; *fut* **yeemneh**).

mon|eh/-eem מונה *nm* counter; meter; (*pl+of:* **-ey**).

monolog/-eem מונולוג *nm* monologue.

monopoleen (*cpr* **monopoleen**) מונופולין *nm* monopoly.

monotonee/-t מונוטוני *adj* monotonous.

monotoneeyoot מונוטוניות *nf* monotony.

moo|'ad/-'edet מועד *adj* forewarned; inveterate.

moo|'ad/-'edet le-foor'anoot *(f=p)* מועד לפורענות designed for trouble.

moo|'ad/-'edet le-kheeshalon *(kh=k)* מועד לכישלון *adj* doomed to fail.

('avaryan) moo'ad עבריין מועד *nm* notorious offender.

(poshe'a') moo'ad פושע מועד *nm* inveterate criminal.

moo'ad|af/-efet (*npr* **mo'od|af/-efet**) מועדף **1.** *adj* preferred; **2.** *v pres* am/is given preference; (*pst* **hoo'adaf**; *fut* **yoo'adaf**).

moo|'af/-'efet מועף *v pres* **1.** (is) flown; **2.** *[slang]* (is) thrown out; (*pst* **hoo'af**; *fut* **yoo'af**).

moo'ak|ah/-ot מועקה *nf* stress; depression; (+*of:* **-at**).

moo'am|ad (*npr* **mo'om|ad**)/**-edet** מועמד *v pres* (is) placed, put, nominated; (*pst* **hoo'amad**; *fut* **yo'amad**).

moo'am|ad (*npr* **mo'om|ad**)/**-adeem** מועמד *nm* candidate; (*pl+of:* **-dey**).

moo'am|ad (*npr* **mo'om|ad**)/**-edet le-deen** מועמד לדין *v pres* (*etc*) committed for trial.

moo|'ar/-'eret מואר **1.** *adj* lit : lighted; **2.** *v pres* (is) lit, lighted; (*pst* **hoo'ar**; *fut* **yoo'ar**).

moo'ar|akh (*npr* **mo'or|akh**)/**-ekhet** מוארך **1.** *adj* prolonged; **2.** *v pres* (is) prolonged; (is) lengthened; (*pst* **ho'orakh**; *fut* **yo'orakh**).

moo'ar|akh (*npr* **mo'or|akh**)/**-ekhet** מוערך *v pres* estimated, valued; (*pst* **ho'orakh**; *fut* **yo'orakh**).

moo'as|ak (*npr* **mo'os|ak**)/**-eket** מועסק **1.** *adj* employed; **2.** *v pres* (am/is) employed; (*pst* **ho'osak**; *fut* **yo'osak**).

moo|'at/-'etet מואט **1.** *adj* slowed-down; **2.** *v pres* (is) slowed down; (*pst* **hoo'at**; *fut* **yoo'at**).

moo|'at/-'etet מועט *adj* scarce; little.

(heestapkoot be) moo'at הסתפקות במועט *nf* frugality.

mood|a'/-a'at מודע **1.** *adj* aware; **2.** *v pres* (am/is) aware; (*pst* **hayah mooda'**; *fut* **yeehyeh mooda'**).

mo'od|af/-efet מועדף **1.** *adj* preferred; **2.** *v pres* am/is given preference; (*pst* **ho'odaf**; *fut* **yo'odaf**).

moodl|ak/-eket מודלק *adj* **1.** (*lit.*) lighted; kindled; **2.** inflamed; **3.** *v pres* (is) (lit.), lighted; (is) kindled; (*pst* **hoodlak**; *fut* **yoodlak**).

(be) mooda' במודע *adv* consciously.

mood|'ag/-'eget מודאג **1.** *adj* worried; concerned; **2.** *v pres* (am/is) worried, concerned; (*pst* **hood'ag**; *fut* **yood'ag**).

moodakh/-at מודח **1.** *adj* deposed; dismissed; **2.** *v pres* (am/is) deposed, dismissed; (*pst* **hoodakh**; *fut* **yoodakh**).

mooda'oot מודעות *nf* awareness.

moodg|am/-emet מודגם **1.** *adj* exemplified; **2.** *v pres* (is) exemplified; (*pst* **hoodgam**; *fut* **yoodgam**).

moodp|as/-eset מודפס **1.** *adj* printed; **2.** *v pres* (is) printed; (*pst* **hoodpas**; *fut* **yoodpas**).

moodr|ag/-eget מודרג *adj* graded.

(sekhar leemood) moodrag שכר לימוד מודרג *nm* graded tuition fees.

moodr|akh/-ekhet מודרך **1.** *adj* guided; **2.** *v pres* (am/is) guided; (*pst* **hoodrakh**; *fut* **yoodrakh**).

moof|'al/-'elet מופעל *v pres* (is) activated, operated; (*pst* **hoof'al**; *fut* **yoof'al**).

moof|ats/-etset מופץ **1.** *adj* spread; **2.** *v pres* (is) propagated; (*pst* **hoofats**; *fut* **yoofats**).

moofg|an/-enet מופגן **1.** *adj* manifest; **2.** *v pres* (is) demonstrated; (*pst* **hoofgan**; *fut* **yoofgan**).

moofka'/-'at מופקע **1.** *adj* overcharged; **2.** *v pres* (is) requisitioned, confiscated; (*pst* **hoofka'**; *fut* **yoofka'**).

(mekheer/-eem) moofk|a'/-a'eem מחיר מופקע *nm* exorbitant price.

moofk|ar/-eret מופקר **1.** *adj* wanton; derelict; **2.** *v pres* (is) abandoned; (*pst* **hoofkar**; *fut* **yoofkar**).

moofk|eret/-arot מופקרת *nf* whore; woman of loose character.

mofkh|at/-etet מופחת **1.** *adj* reduced; **2.** *v pres* (is) subtracted; (*pst* **hoofkhat**; *fut* **yoofkhat**).

moofl|a/-a'ah מופלא *adj* wonderful; astounding.

moofl|ag/-eget מופלג *adj* extreme; exaggerated.

(zaken/zekenah) moofl|ag/-eget זקן מופלג *nmf* very old person.

moofleh/-t מופלה **1.** *adj* discriminated against; **2.** *v pres* (is) discriminated against; (*pst* **hooflah**; *fut* **yoofleh**).

moofn|am/-emet מופנם *adj* introvert; introverted.

moofra|'/-'at מופרע **1.** *adj* disturbed; **2.** *v pres* (is) disturbed; (*pst* **hoofra'**; *fut* **yofra'**).

moofr|ad/-edet מופרד **1.** *adj* separated; **2.** *v pres* (is) separated; (*pst* **hoofrad**; *fut* **yoofrad**).

mofr|akh/-ekhet מופרך **1.** *adj* disproved; **2.** *v pres* (is) disproved; (*pst* **hoofrakh**; *fut* **yoofrakh**).

moofr|az/-ezet מופרז *adj* exaggerated.

moofreh/-t מופרה **1.** *adj* fertilized; **2.** *v pres* (is) fertilized; (*pst* **hoofrah**; *fut* **yoofreh**).

moofs|ak/-eket מופסק **1.** *adj* stopped; ceased; **2.** *v pres* (is) stopped, discontinued; (*pst* **hoofsak**; *fut* **yoofsak**).

moofsh|al/-elet מופשל *adj* rolled-up (sleeve).

moofsh|at/-etet מופשט **1.** *adj* abstract; **2.** *v pres* (is) undressed; (*pst* **hoofshat**; *fut* **yoofshat**).

moofts|ats/-etset מופצץ **1.** *adj* bombarded; **2.** *v pres* (is) bombed; (*pst* **hooftsats**; *fut* **yooftsats**).

moog/-at lev מוג־לב **1.** *nmf* coward; (*pl* **-ey**); **2.** *adj* pusillanimous; cowardly.

moog|af/-efet מוגף **1.** *adj* shut; (blinds) pulled down; **2.** *v pres* (is) shut; (*pst* **hoogaf**; *fut* **yoogaf**).

moog|an/-enet מוגן **1.** *adj* protected; **2.** *v pres* (is) protected; (*pst* **hoogan**; *fut* **yoogan**).

(dayar/-eem) moogan/-eem דייר מוגן *nm* rent-protected tenant.

(sohkh|er/-reem) moogan/-eem שוכר מוגן *nm* rent-protected lessee.

moogb|ah/-ahat מוגבה **1.** *adj* raised; **2.** *v pres* (is) raised; (is) lifted; (*pst* **hoogbah**; *fut* **yoogbah**).

moogb|al/-elet מוגבל **1.** *adj* limited; **2.** *v pres* (am/is) restricted; (*pst* **hoogbal**; *fut* **yoogbal**).

(be-'eravon) moogbal מוגבל בעירבון *adj* B.M.; of limited liability; Ltd; Inc.

moogd|al/-elet מוגדל **1.** *adj* increased; **2.** (is) enlarged; (*pst* **hoogdal**; *fut* **yoogdal**).

moogd|ar/-eret מוגדר **1.** *adj* defined; **2.** (is) defined; (*pst* **hoogdar**; *fut* **yoogdar**).

moogl|ah/-ot מוגלה *nf* pus (*+of:* **-at**).

mooglatee/-t מוגלתי *adj* purulent; suppurating.

moogmar/-eret מוגמר *adj* finished; finalized; completed.

(levarekh 'al ha) moogmar לברך על המוגמר *v inf* to celebrate completion; (*pst* **berakh** *etc*; *pres* **mevarekh** *etc*; *fut* **yevarekh** *etc b=v*)

('oovd|ah/-ot) moogm|eret/-arot עובדה מוגמרת *nf* accomplished fact; fait accompli.

moogsh|am/-emet מוגשם **1.** *adj* carried out; **2.** *v pres* is implemented; (*pst* **hoogsham**; *fut* **yoogsham**).

moogz|am/-emet מוגזם **1.** *adj* exaggerated; **2.** *v pres* (is) exaggerated; (*pst* **hoogzam**; *fut* **yoogzam**).

mook|a'/-a'at מוקע **1.** *adj* stigmatized; **2.** *v pres* (am/is) denounced, stygmatized; (*pst* **hooka'**; *fut* **yooka'**).

mook|af/-efet מוקף **1.** *adj* surrounded; **2.** *v pres* (am/is) surrounded; is encircled; (*pst* **hookaf**; *fut* **yookaf**).

mook|ar/-eret מוכר **1.** *adj* known; **2.** *v pres* (am/is) recognized; acknowledged; (*pst* **hookar**; *fut* **yookar**).

(paneem) mookarot פנים מוכרות *nf pl* familiar face(s).

mookd|am/-emet מוקדם **1.** *adj* early; **2.** *v pres* is advanced; antedated; (*pst* **hookdam**; *fut* **yookdam**).

(be) mookdam במוקדם *adv* soon; shortly; early.

(be) mookdam o bee-me'ookhar במוקדם או במאוחר *adv* sooner or later.

(le-khol ha)mookdam *(kh=k)* לכל המוקדם *adv* at the earliest.

mookd|ash/-eshet מוקדש *v pres* dedicated; consecrated; (*pst* **hookdash**; *fut* **yookdash**).

mook|eh/-ah מוכה **1.** *adj* beaten; **2.** *v pres* (am/is) beaten-up; (*pst* **hookah**; *fut* **yookeh**).

mookhakh/-at מוכח **1.** *adj* proven; **2.** *v pres* (is) proved; (*pst* **hookhakh**; *fut* **yookhakh**).

mookhan/-ah מוכן **1.** *adj* ready; ready-made; **2.** *v pres* (am/is) prepared; (*pst* **hookhan**; *fut* **yookhan**).

mookhan/-ah oo mezoom|an/-enet מוכן ומזומן *adj* prepared and ready.

(heenenee) mookhan oo mezooman הנני מוכן ומזומן **1.** (religious formula) I willingly undertake; **2.** *[colloq.]* I take it upon myself to ...

(meen ha) mookhan מן המוכן *adj* ready-made; prepared in advance.

mookh|ash/-eshet מוחש **1.** *adj* accelerated; **2.** *v pres* (am/is) rushed up; hurried; (*pst* **hookhash**; *fut* **yookhash**).

mookhashee/-t מוחשי *adj* tangible; substantial.

mookhd|ar/-eret מוחדר **1.** *adj* inserted; **2.** *v pres* (is) infused; imbued; (*pst* **hookhdar**; *fut* **yookhdar**).

mookhl|at/-etet מוחלט **1.** *adj* absolute; decisive; **2.** *v pres* (is) decided; (*pst* **hookhlat**; *fut* **yookhlat**).

mookhp|al/-elet מוכפל *v pres* **1.** (is) doubled; **2.** (is) multiplied; (*pst* **hookhpal**; *fut* **yookhpal**).

mookhr|a'/-a'at מוכרע *v pres* (is) being decided, determined; (*pst* **hookhra'**; *fut* **yookhra'**).

mookhrakh/-ah מוכרח *v pres* must; (am/is) compelled; (*pst* **hookhrakh**; *fut* **yookhrakh**).

mookh'sh|ar/-eret מוכשר **1.** *adj* capable; able; trained; **2.** *v pres* 1. (is) being made "kosher": **3.** *v pres* (am/is) being trained; (*pst* **hookh'shar**; *fut* **yookh'shar**).

mookht|am/-emet מוכתם **1.** *adj* stained; **2.** *v pres* (am/is) stained, sullied; (*pst* **hookhtam**; *fut* **yookhtam**).

mookhtar/-eem מוכתר *nm* the "Mukhtar" i.e. village headman.

mookht|ar/-eret מוכתר **1.** *adj* crowned; **2.** *v pres* (am/is) crowned; (*pst* **hookhtar**; *fut* **yookhtar**).

mookht|ar/-eret be-to'ar מוכתר בתואר **1.** *adj* bearing the title; **2.** *adj* holding a degree; **3.** having a title bestowed upon.

mookhz|ak/-eket מוחזק **1.** *adj* held; kept; **2.** *v pres* (am/is) held; (am/is) regarded; (*pst* **hookhzak**; *fut* **yookhzak**).

◇ **(ha-shtakheem ha) mookhzakeem** see ◇ **(ha)shtakheem (ha)mookhzakeem**.

mookhz|ar/-eret מוחזר **1.** *adj* returned; **2.** *v pres* (am/is) returned, given back; (*pst* **hookhzar**; *fut* **yookhzar**).

mookl|at/-etet מוקלט **1.** *adj* recorded; **2.** *v pres* (am/is) being recorded (on tape, video *etc*); (*pst* **hooklat**; *fut* **yooklat**).

(doo|'akh/-khot) mooklat/-eem דו"ח מוקלט *m* recorded account.

(deevoo|'akh/-kheem) mooklat/-eem דיווח מוקלט *m* recorded report.

(seret/srateem) mooklat/-eem סרט מוקלט *nm* recorded tape.

(kal|etet/-atot) mookl|etet/-atot קלטת מוקלטת *nf* recorded cassette.

(kaset|ah/-ot) mookl|etet/-atot קסטה מוקלטת *[colloq.] nf* recorded cassette.

(mooseekah) mookletet מוסיקה מוקלטת- *nf* recorded music.

mookp|a/-et מוקפא **1.** *adj* frozen; **2.** *v pres* (is) frozen, congealed; (*pst* **hookpa**; *fut* **yookpa**).

(okhel) mookpa אוכל מוקפא *m* frozen food.

(yerakot) mookpa'eem ירקות מוקפאים *m pl* frozen vegetables.

mookr|a/-et מוקרא **1.** *adj* read out; **2.** *v pres* (is) read out; (*pst* **hookra**; *fut* **yookra**).

mookr|an/-enet מוקרן **1.** *adj* projected; **2.** *v pres* (is) shown (on screen), x-rayed; (*pst* **hookran**; *fut* **yookran**).

mookr|av/-evet מוקרב *v pres* **1.** (am/is) sacrificed; **2.** (is) brought nearer; (*pst* **hookrav**; *fut* **yookrav**).

mooks|am/-emet מוקסם **1.** *adj* bewitched; **2.** *v pres* (am/is) charmed; (*pst* **hooksam**; *fut* **yooksam**).

mookt|an/-enet מוקטן **1.** reduced; **2.** *v pres* (is) reduced, diminished; (*pst* **hooktan**; *fut* **yooktan**).

mooktsaf/-efet מוקצף **1.** *adj* whipped up; **2.** (is) whipped up; (*pst* **hooktsaf**; *fut* **yooktsaf**).

mookts|av/-evet מוקצב **1.** *adj* allocated; **2.** *v pres* (is) allocated; (*pst* **hooktsav**; *fut* **yooktsav**).

mookts|eh/-ah מוקצה *v pres* (is) allocated; (*pst* **hooktsah**; *fut* **yooktsah**).

mooktseh mekhamat mee'oos מוקצה מחמת מיאוס *adj* loathsome; too disgusting to be touched.

mookyon/-eem מוקיון *m* clown; (*pl+of:* **-ey**).

mool מול *adv* against; opposite.

(mee) mool ממול *adv* across; opposite.

mool|'am/-emet מולאם **1.** *adj* nationalized; **2.** *v pres* (is) nationalized; (*pst* **hool'am**; *fut* **yool'am**).

moolb|ash/-eshet מולבש *v pres* (am/is) clad, dressed; (*pst* **hoolbash**; *fut* **yoolbash**).

moolkh|am/-emet מולחם *adj* - *v pres* (is) welded, soldered; (*pst* **moolkham**; *fut* **yoolkham**).

moolkh|an/-enet מולחן *v pres* (is) composed (melody); (*pst* **hoolkhan**; *fut* **yoolkhan**).

moom/-eem מום *m* deformity; defect; blemish; (*pl+of:* **-ey**).

(ba'al/-at) moom בעל מום *nmf* cripple; invalid.

(le-hateel) moom להטיל מום *v inf* to maim; (*pst* **heeteel** *etc*; *pres* **mateel** *etc*; *fut* **yateel** *etc*).

mo'om|ad/-et מועמד *adj* stood up.

moom|an/-nah/-antee מומן *v* financed; funded; (*pst* **memooman**; *fut* **yemooman**).

moom|ar/-eret מומר *nmf* baptized Jew.

moom|as/-eset מומס **1.** *adj* melted; **2.** *v pres* (is) melted; (*pst* **hoomas**; *fut* **yoomas**).

moom|at/-etet מומת *v pres* (am/is) put to death, killed; (*pst* **hoomat**; *fut* **yoomat**).

moomee|yah/-yot מומייה *nf* mummy; (*+of:* **-yat**).

moomkh|az/-ezet מומחז *adj* **1.** dramatized; **2.** *v pres* (is) dramatized; (*pst* **hoomkhaz**; *fut* **yoomkhaz**).

moomkheeyoot מומחיות *nf* **1.** expertise; **2.** specialization certificate.

moomkh|eh/-eet מומחה *nmf* specialist.

mooml|ats/-etset מומלץ **1.** *adj* recommended; **2.** *v pres* (am/is) recommended; (*pst* **hoomlats**; *fut* **yoomlats**).

moon|ah/-tah/-etee מונה *v* was appointed; (*pres* **memooneh**; *fut* **yemooneh**).

moon|af/-efet מונף **1.** *adj* hoisted; **2.** *v pres* (is) tossed, brandished; (*pst* **hoonaf**; *fut* **yoonaf**).

moonakh/-at מונח **1.** *adj* lying; **2.** *v pres* lie(s); (am/is) lying; (*pst* **hoonakh**; *fut* **yoonakh**).

moonakh/-eem מונח *m* technical term; (*pl+of:* **-ey**).

moonakh/-at be-koofsah מונח בקופסה **1.** *adj nf* secured; **2.** (*figurat.*) adv in the bag; as good as in the bank.

mooneetseepalee/-t מוניציפלי *adj* municipal.

moor|'al/-'elet מורעל **1.** *adj* poisoned; **2.** *v pres* (am/is) poisoned; (*pst* **hoor'al**; *fut* **yoor'al**).

moor|am/-emet מורם **1.** *adj* lifted; elevated: **2.** *v pres* (am/is) lifted, elevated; (*pst* **hooram**; *fut* **yooram**).

moor|'av/-'evet מורעב *v pres* (am/is) starved; (*pst* **hoor'av**; *fut* **yoor'av**).

moorg|al/-elet מורגל *v pres* accustomed; (*pst* **hoorgal**; *fut* **yoorgal**).

moorg|ash/-eshet מורגש **1.** *adj* felt; **2.** *v pres* (am/is) felt; (*pst* **hoorgash**; *fut* **yoorgash**).

moorg|az/-ezet מורגז **1.** *adj* irritated; **2.** *v pres* (is) irritated; (*pst* **hoorgaz**; *fut* **yoorgaz**).

moork|an/-enet מורכן **1.** *adj* bent; **2.** *v pres* (am/is) bent, lowered; (*pst* **hoorkan**; *fut* **yoorkan**).

moork|av/-evet מורכב *adj* complex; complicated.

moork|av/-evet mee- מורכב מ־ *v pres* (am/is) composed of; (*pst* **hoorkav** *etc*; *fut* **yoorkav** *etc*).

moorkavoo|t/-yot מורכבות *nf* complexity.

moorkh|ak/-eket מורחק *v pres* (is) removed, banished; (*pst* **hoorkhak**; *fut* **yoorkhak**).

moorkh|av/-evet מורחב **1.** *adj* enlarged; **2.** *v pres* (is) enlarged; (*pst* **hoorkhav**; *fut* **yoorkhav**).

moors|ah/-ot מורסה *nf* boil; abscess; (*+of:* **-at**).

moorsha|'/-'at מורשע **1.** *adj* convicted; **2.** *v pres* (am/is) convicted; (*pst* **hoorsha'**; *fut* **yoorsha'**).

moorsh|eh/-et מורשה *nmf* delegate; representative; *v pres* (am/is) allowed; (*pst* **hoorshah**; *fut* **yoorsheh**).

moorta|'/-'at מורתע **1.** *adj* startled; **2.** *v pres* (am/is) deterred, startled; (*pst* **hoorta'**; *fut* **yoorta'**).

moos|af/-afeem מוסף *m* supplement; (*pl+of:* **-fey**).

moosaf shel shabat (*pl* **moosafey ha-shabat**) מוסף של שבת *m* Saturday (Weekend) newspaper supplement.

('erekh) moosaf ערך מוסף *m* added value.

(mas 'erekh) moosaf מס ערך מוסף *m* V.A.T.; Value Added Tax.

moos|ag/-ageem מושג *m* notion; concept; (*pl+of:* **-'gey**).

moos|ag/-eget מושג *v pres* (is) reached, obtained; (*pst* **hoosag**; *fut* **yoosag**).

(en lee) moosag אין לי מושג I haven't the slightest idea.

(en lekha/lakh) moosag אין לך מושג you *m/f* have no idea.

moosa|kh/-keem מוסך *m* garage; (*pl+of:* **-key**).

(ba'al) moosakh בעל מוסך *m* garage-owner.

moosar מוסר *m* morals; ethics.

moosar haskel מוסר השכל *m* moral; lesson to learn.

moosar klayot מוסר כליות *m* regret; remorse.

(matee|f/-ah) moosar מטיף מוסר *v pres* moralize(s); (*pst* **heeteef** *etc*; *fut* **yateef** *etc*).

moosaree/-t מוסרי *adj* moral; ethical.

moos|at/-etet מוסט *v pres* (is) removed, deviated; (*pst* **hoosat**; *fut* **yoosat**).

moos|at/-etet מוסת **1.** *adj* incited; **2.** *v pres* (is) instigated, incited; (*pst* **hoosat**; *fut* **yoosat**).

moosb|ar/-eret מוסבר **1.** - *adj* explained; **2.** *v pres* (is) explained; (*pst* **hoosbar**; *fut* **yoosbar**).

moosd|ar/-eret מוסדר **1.** *adj* arranged; in order; **2.** *v pres* (is) arranged, organized; (*pst* **hoosdar**; *fut* **yoosdar**).

(mekom khaneeyah) moosdar מקום חנייה מוסדר *nm* organized parking lot.

mooseek|ah/-ot מוסיקה *nf* music.

mooseeka|'ee/-'eet (*npr* **mooseeka|y/-'eet**) מוסיקאי *nmf* musician.

mooseekah klaseet מוסיקה קלסית *nf* classical music.

mooseekah 'amameet מוסיקה עממית *nf* popular music.

mooseekah khaseedeet מוסיקה חסידית *nf* Hasidic music.

mooseekah le-reekoodeem מוסיקה לריקודים dance-music.

mooseekah moderneet מוסיקה מודרנית *nf* modern music.

mooseekalee/-t מוסיקלי *adj* musical.

mooseekat pop מוסיקת פופ־ *nf* pop-music.

mooseekat neshamah מוסיקת נשמה *nf* **1.** soul music; **2.** spirituals.

mooseekat reka' מוסיקת רקע **1.** background music; **2.** Muzac.

moosg|ar/-eret מוסגר *v pres* (am/is) turned over, extradited; (*pst* **hoosgar**; *fut* **yoosgar**).

(be-ma'amar) moosgar במאמר מוסגר *adv* in brackets; in parenthesis.

moosh|'al/-'elet מושאל **1.** *adj* loaned; **2.** *v pres* (am/is) loaned; (*pst* **hoosh'al**; *fut* **yoosh'al**).

mooshat/-ah מושט **1.** *adj* stretched out; floated; **2.** *v pres* (is) floated, extended; (*pst* **hooshat**; *fut* **yooshat**).

(yad/-ayeem) moosh|etet/-atot יד מושטת *nf* **1.** hand stretched out; **2.** friendly hand (*figurat.*).

mooshb|at/-etet מושבת **1.** *adj* locked out (of a workplace); **2.** *v pres* (am/is) locked out (of a workplace); (*pst* **hooshbat**; *fut* **yooshbat**).

mooshb|a'/-a'at מושבע **1.** sworn; determined; **2.** *v pres* (is) sworn in; (*pst* **hooshba'**; *fut* **yooshba'**).

(khever) mooshba'eem חבר מושבעים *m* jury (not used in the Israeli legal system).

(ohed/-et) mooshba'/-at אוהד מושבע *nmf* avowed sympathizer.

(tom|ekh/-ekhet) mooshb|a'/-a'at תומך מושבע *nmf* staunch supporter.

moosh|'heh/-'het מושהה **1.** *adj* suspended; **2.** *v pres* (am/is) suspended; (*pst* **hoosh'hah**; *fut* **yoosh'heh**).

mooshka|'/-'at מושקע **1.** invested; **2.** *pres* (is) invested; (*pst* **hooshka'**; *fut* **yooshka'**).

mooshk|an/-enah מושכן *v* was mortgaged; (*pres* **memooshkan**; *fut* **yemooshkan**).

moosh'kh|al/-elet מושחל **1.** *adj* threaded; **2.** *v pres* (is) threaded; (*pst* **hoosh'khal**; *fut* **yoosh'khal**).

moosh'kh|ar/-eret מושחר *v pres* (am/is) blackened; (*pst* **hoosh'khar**; *fut* **yoosh'khar**).

moosh'kh|at/-etet מושחת **1.** *adj* corrupted; spoiled; **2.** *v pres* (am/is) corrupted, spoiled; (*pst* **hoosh'khat**; *fut* **yoosh'khat**).

moosh'kh|az/-ezet מושחז **1.** *adj* sharpened; honed; **2.** *v pres* (is) sharpened; (is) honed; (*pst* **hoosh'khaz**; *fut* **yoosh'khaz**).

mooshl|ag/-eget מושלג *adj* covered with snow; snowed on.

mooshl|akh/-ekhet מושלך **1.** thrown out; **2.** *pres* (is) thrown; (am/is) thrown out; (*pst* **hooshlakh**; *fut* **yooshlakh**).

mooshl|am/-emet מושלם **1.** perfect; **2.** *v pres* (is) being completed; (*pst* **hooshlam**; *fut* **yooshlam**).

mooshl|at/-etet מושלט *v pres* (is) enforced; (*pst* **hooshlat**; *fut* **yooshlat**).

mooshm|a'/-a'at מושמע **1.** *adj* voiced; sounded; **2.** *v pres* (is) voiced; (is) sounded; (*pst* **hooshma'**; *fut* **yooshma'**).

mooshm|ad/-edet מושמד **1.** *adj* annihilated; **2.** *v pres* (am/is) exterminated; (*pst* **hooshmad**; *fut* **yooshmad**).

mooshm|at/-etet מושמט **1.** *adj* omitted; **2.** *v pres* (am/is) left out; (*pst* **hooshmat**; *fut* **yooshmat**).

mooshm|ats/-etset מושמץ **1.** *adj* slandered; **2.** *v pres* (am/is) slandered; slurred; (*pst* **hooshmats**; *fut* **yooshmats**).

mooshp|a'/-a'at מושפע **1.** *adj* influenced; **2.** *v pres* (am/is) influenced; (*pst* **hooshpa'**; *fut* **yooshpa'**).

mooshp|al/-elet מושפל **1.** *adj* humiliated; **2.** *v pres* (am/is) debased, humiliated; (*pst* **hooshpal**; *fut* **yooshpal**).

mooshr|ash/-eshet מושרש **1.** *adj* rooted; with roots; **2.** *v pres* (am/is) rooted; (*pst* **hoooshrash**; *fut* **yooshrash**).

mooshr|eh/-et מושרה **1.** *adj* soaked; **2.** *v pres* (is) immersed, soaked; (*pst* **hooshrah**; *fut* **yooshreh**).

moosht|ak/-eket מושתק *v pres* (am/is) silenced; (*pst* **hooshtak**; *fut* **yooshtak**).

moosht|al/-elet מושתל **1.** *adj* implanted; **2.** *v pres* (am/is) planted; is transplanted; (*pst* **hooshtal**; *fut* **yooshtal**).

moosht|an/-enet מושתן *[slang]* **1.** *adj. (lit.)* pissed on; **2.** *adj (figurat.)* negligible; unimportant; **3.** *v pres (lit.)* am/is pissed on; (*pst* **hooshtan**; *fut* **yooshtan**).

moosht|at/-etet מושתת *v* (is) based, founded on; (*pst* **hooshtat**; *fut* **yooshtat**).

mooskal/-eem reeshon/-eem מושכל ראשון *m* axiom.

moosk|am/-emet מוסכם **1.** *adj* agreed upon; **2.** *adj* conventional; **3.** *v pres* is agreed upon; (*pst* **hooskam;** *fut* **yooskam**).

mooskam she- -מוסכם ש *adv* it is agreed that.

mooskamot מוסכמות *nf pl* conventionalities.

(mored/-et be) mooskamotמורד במוסכמות *m* one who braves conventionalities; conventions.

mooslem|ee/-eet מוסלמי **1.** *nmf* Muslim; (*pl+of:* **-ey**); **2.** *adj* Islamic.

moosm|akh/-ekhet מוסמך **1.** *adj* authorized; **2.** *nmf* graduate (*pl+of:* **-ekhey**); **3.** *v pres* (am/is) entitled; (*pst* **hoosmakh;** *fut* **yoosmakh**).

moosm|akh/-ekhet le-meeshpateem מוסמך למשפטים *nmf* trained jurist.

(goof/-eem) moosmakh/-eem גוף מוסמך *m* authorized, competent body.

(gor|em/-meem) moosmakh/-eem גורם מוסמך competent factor.

(kheshbon|ay/-'eet) moosm|akh/-ekhet חשבונאי מוסמך *nmf* certified public accountant.

(meeshpetan/-eet) moosm|akh/-ekhet משפטן מוסמך *nmf* trained jurist.

(ha-mosadot ha) moosmakheem המוסדות המוסמכים the competent authorities.

mootakh/-at מוטח **1.** *adj* plastered; spoken insolently; **2.** *v pres* is thrown in one's face; (*pst* **hootakh;** *fut* **yootakh**).

moot|akh/-ekhet מותך **1.** *adj* melted; processed; **2.** *v pres* (is) melted, processed; (*pst* **hootakh;** *fut* **yootakh**).

mootal 'al מוטל על *adj* incumbent on.

moot|al/-elet מוטל *v pres* **1.** (am/is) lying, placed; **2.** (is) imposed; (*pst* **hootal;** *fut* **yootal**).

moot|al/-elet be-safek מוטל בספק *adj* doubtful; questionable.

moot|'am/-'emet מותאם **1.** *adj* fitting; appropriate; **2.** *v pres* (is) adapted; fitted; (*pst* **hoot'am;** *fut* **yoot'am**).

moot|'am/-'emet מוטעם **1.** *adj* emphasized; **2.** *v pres* (is) emphasized; (*pst* **moot'am;** *fut* **yoot'am**).

moot|'an/-'enet מוטען **1.** *adj* loaded; **2.** *v pres* (is) loaded; (*pst* **hoot'an;** *fut* **yoot'an**).

mootar מותר *adv* **1.** it is allowed; **2.** *query* is it permitted ?

moot|ar/-eret מותר **1.** *adj.* permitted; **2.** *v pres* (is) undone, permitted; (*pst* **hootar;** *fut* **yootar**).

(ha-eem) mootar lee? ?האם מותר לי may I? could I?

mootar ve-asoor מותר ואסור what's permitted and what's not.

moot|as/-eset מוטס **1.** *adj* airborne; **2.** *v pres* (am/is) flown; (*pst* **hootas;** *fut* **yootas**).

moot|ash/-eshet מותש **1.** *adj* exhausted; **2.** *v pres* (am/is) worn out; (*pst* **hootash;** *fut* **yootash**).

moot|at/-ot kenafayeem מוטת כנפיים *nf* wingspread.

mootav מוטב *adv* rather; preferably; it were better if...

moot|av/-evet מוטב *nmf* beneficiary.

mootav she-kakh מוטב שכך *adv* better this way.

(le) mootav למוטב *adv* to reform; to be reformed.

(lehakhzeer le) mootavלהחזיר למוטב *v* to restore to the right way; (*pres* **makhzeer** *etc; pst* **hekhzeer** *etc; fut* **yakhzeer** *etc*).

moot|az/-ezet מותז **1.** *adj* cut off; **2.** *v pres* (am/is) sprinkled; **3.** (is) cut off; (*pst* **hootaz;** *fut* **yootaz**).

mootb|a'/-a'at מוטבע **1.** *adj* imprinted; stamped in; **2.** *v pres* (is) sunk; **3.** *v pres* (is) impressed; (*pst* **hootba';** *fut* **yootba'**).

mootb|al/-elet מוטבל **1.** *adj* baptized; **2.** *v pres* (is) dipped; **3.** *v pres* (am/is) baptized; (*pst* **hootbal;** *fut* **yootbal**).

mootk|af/-efet מותקף **1.** *adj* attacked; assailed; **2.** *v pres* (am/is) attacked, assailed; (*pst* **hootkaf;** *fut* **yootkaf**).

mootk|an/-enet מותקן *v pres* (is) installed; (*pst* **hootkan;** *fut* **yootkan**).

mootm|an/-enet מוטמן **1.** *adj* hidden; **2.** *v pres* (is) concealed, hidden; (*pst* **hootman;** *fut* **yootman**).

mootn|a'/-a'at מותנע **1.** *adj* with the motor on; **2.** *v pres* (is) started; (*pst* **hootna';** *fut* **yootna'**).

mootn|eh/-et מותנה **1.** *adj* conditional; **2.** *v pres* (is) subject to; is stipulated that; (*pst* **hootnah;** *fut* **yootneh**).

moots|ah/-tah/-etee מוצה *v pst* has been exhausted; (*pres* **memootseh;** *fut* **yemootseh**).

moots|a'/-a'at מוצע **1.** *adj* proposed; suggested; **2.** *v pres* (is) suggested, proposed; (*pst* **hootsa';** *fut* **yootsa'**).

moots|af/-efet מוצף **1.** *adj* flooded; **2.** *v pres* (am/is) inundated; (*pst* **hootsaf;** *fut* **yootsaf**).

mootsag/-eem מוצג *m* exhibit (*pl+of:* **-ey**).

moots|ag/-eget מוצג *v pres* (am/is) presented, introduced; (*pst* **hootsag;** *fut* **yootsag**).

moots|ag/-eem meeshpatee/-eyeem *nm* court exhibit.

moots|ak/-eket מוצק *adj* solid; sturdy.

moots|al/-elet מוצל **1.** *adj* shaded; shadowed; **2.** saved; 2. *v* pres (am/is) rescued; (*pst* **hootsal;** *fut* **yootsal**).

(makom/mekomot) mootsal/-eem מקום מוצל *m* a place in the shade.

(ood/-eem) mootsal/-eem אוד מוצל *m* survivor.

moots|ar/-areem מוצר *m* produce; product (*pl+of:* **-rey**).

moots|ar/-eem mekomee/-yeem מוצר מקומי *m* local product.

moots|ar/-rey tsereekhah מוצר צריכה *m* consumer-article; (*pl* consumer goods).

moots|ar/-rey yetsoo מוצר יצוא *m* export product.

moots|ar/-rey yevoo מוצר יבוא *m* imported article; imported goods.

moots|av/-aveem מוצב *m* post (milit.); position; (*pl+of:* **-vey**).

moots|av/-evet מוצב **1**. - *adj* placed, posted; **2**. *v pres* (am/is) being placed, posted; (*pst* **hootsav**; *fut* **yootsav**).

mootsd|ak/-eket מוצדק **1**. justified; **2**. *v pres* (is) justified; (*pst* **hootsdak**; *fut* **yootsdak**).

moots'|har/-heret מוצהר **1**. declared; **2**. *v pres* (is) being declared; (*pst* **hoots'har**; *fut* **yoots'har**).

mootslakh/-at מוצלח *adj* successful.

mootsm|ad/-edet מוצמד **1**. linked; affixed; **2**. *v pres* (is) linked, affixed; (*pst* **hootsmad**; *fut* **yootsmad**).

mootsm|ad/-edet la-dolar מוצמד לדולר *adj* linked to the U.S. dollar.

mootsm|ad/-edet la-madad מוצמד למדד *adj* linked to the Index.

mootsm|ad/-edet le-madad ha-mekheereem la-tsarkhan מוצמד למדד המחירים לצרכן *adj* linked to Consumer Price Index.

mootsm|ad/-edet le-madad yoker ha-beneeyah מוצמד למדד יוקר הבניה *adj* linked to the Construction Costs Index.

mootsm|ad/-edet le-madad yoker ha-meekhyah מוצמד למדד יוקר המחיה *adj* linked to the C.O.L. index.

mootsn|a'/-a'at מוצנע **1**. *adj* discreetly hidden; **2**. *v pres* (is) being hidden; is being discreetly put out of sight; (*pst* **hootsna'**; *fut* **yootsna'**).

mootsnakh/-at מוצנח **1**. *adj* parachuted; **2**. *v pres* (am/is) parachuted; (*pst* **hootsnakh**; *fut* **yootsnakh**).

moov|an/-enet מובן **1**. *adj* understood; **2**. *v pres* (is) understood; (*pst* **hoovan**; *fut* **yoovan**).

moov|an/-enet me'el|av/-eha מובן מאליו *adj* obvious; of course.

(ka) moovan כמובן *adv* obviously.

(ke) moovan כמובן *[colloq.] adv* naturally.

moov|'ar/-'eret מובער **1**. *adj* ignited; kindled; **2**. *v pres* (is) lit; ignited; kindled; (*pst* **hoov'ar**; *fut* **yoov'ar**).

moov|as/-eset מובס **1**. *adj* defeated; **2**. *v pres* (am/is) defeated; (*pst* **hoovas**; *fut* **yoovas**).

moov|'hak/-'heket מובהק *adj* obvious; clear.

moov|'hal/-'helet מובהל **1**. *adj* frightened; **2**. *v pres* (am/is) rushed, hurried; (*pst* **hoov'hal**; *fut* **yoov'hal**).

moov'|har/-'heret מובהר **1**. *adj* clarified; **2**. *v pres* (is) clarified; (*pst* **hoov'har**; *fut* **yoov'har**).

moovk|a'/-a'at מובקע *v pres* (is) broken through, into; (*pst* **hoovka'**; *fut* **yoovka'**).

moovkh|ar/-eret מובחר *adj* selected; choice-.

moovl|a'/-a'at מובלע **1**. *adj* slurred over; **2**. *v pres* (is) eluded, slurred over; (*pst* **hoovla'**; *fut* **yoovla'**).

moovl|a'at/-a'ot מובלעת *nf* enclave; (*pl+of:* **-e'ot**).

moovrakh/-at מוברח **1**. *adj* smuggled; **2**. *v pres* (am/is) smuggled; **3**. (am/is) made to flee; (*pst* **hoovrakh**; *fut* **yoovrakh**).

moovtakh/-at מובטח **1**. *adj* assured; promised; **2**. *v pres* (is) promised, assured, secured; (*pst* **hoovtakh**; *fut* **yoovtakh**).

moovt|al/-elet מובטל **1**. *adj & nmf* unemployed; **2**. *v pres* am/is made jobless, unemployed; (*pst* **hoovtal**; *fut* **yoovtal**).

mooz|ah/-ot מוזה *[colloq.] nf* one's muse, inspiration; (*+of:* **-at**).

moozar/-ah מוזר *adj* strange; queer.

mooz|az/-ezet מוזז **1**. *adj* budged; **2**. *v pres* (is) moved, budged; (*pst* **hoozaz**; *fut* **yoozaz**).

mooz|'har/-'heret מוזהר **1**. *adj* forewarned; **2**. *v pres* (is) forewarned; (*pst* **hooz'har**; *fut* **yooz'har**).

mooz|'hav/-'hevet מוזהב *adj* gilded.

moozk|ar/-eret מוזכר **1**. *adj* mentioned; **2**. *v pres* (is) mentioned, (is) alluded to; (*pst* **hoozkar**; *fut* **yoozkar**).

moozman/-eem מוזמן *m* guest (invited); (*pl+of:* **-ey**).

moozm|an/-enet מוזמן **1**. *adj* invited; ordered; **2**. *v pres* (is) invited; (*pst* **hoozman**; *fut* **yoozman**).

mooznakh/-at מוזנח **1**. *adj* derelict; **2**. *v pres* (is) neglected, derelict; (*pst* **hooznakh**; *fut* **yooznakh**).

mor מור *m* myrrh.

mor|ah/-ot מורה *nf* teacher; (*+of:* **-at**).

mora/-'ot מורא mm fear; awe.

morad/-ot מורד *m* slope; descent.

(ba) morad במורד *adv* on the way down.

(be-) morad ha-har במורד ההר *adv* downhill; on the way down the mountain.

(ha) moral המורל *m* the morale; moral.

morash|ah/-ot מורשה *nf* heritage; legacy; (*+of:* **moreshet**).

morat roo'akh מורת רוח *nf* discontent; displeasure.

moray ve-rabotay! מורי ורבותי! *interj* my learned friends! Gentlemen! (addressing an audience).

mor|eh/-ah מורה *v pres* direct(s); order(s); (*pst* **horah**; *fut* **yoreh**).

mor|eh/-eem מורה *m* teacher; (*pl+of:* **-ey**).

mor|eh/-ah be-teekhon מורה בתיכון *[colloq.] nmf* high-school teacher.

mored/-et מורד **1**. *nmf & adj* rebel; **2**. *v pres* rebels, revolts; (*pst* **marad**; *fut* **yeemrod**).

moreed/-ah מוריד *v pres* lowers; reduces; takes down; takes off; (*pst* **horeed**; *fut* **yoreed**).

moreek/-ah מוריק *v pres* turns green; (*pst* **horeek**; *fut* **yoreek**).

moreesh/-ah מוריש **1**. *nmf* legator; testator; bestower of an inheritance; (*pl+of:* **-ey**); **2**. *v pres* bequeaths; causes to inherit; (*pst* **horeesh**; *fut* **yoreesh**).

morekh מורך *m* timidity; cowardice.

morekh lev מורך לב *m* faintheartedness.

morfyoom מורפיום *m* morphine.

mosad/-ot מוסד *m* institute; public agency; foundation; institution.

◇ **(ha) mosad** "המוסד" *nm* the "Mossad" - colloq. *abbr.* for the Israel Agency for Intelligence and Special Duties המוסד למודיעין ולתפקידים מיוחדים - a secret government service in some ways parallel to the C.I.A. in the U.S. and the equivalents to it in other countries.

mosad sagoor מוסד סגור *m* (*lit.:* closed institution); hospital for inmates.

mosadee/-t מוסדי *adj* institutional.

◇ **(ha)mosadot (ha)moosmakheem** המוסדות המוסמכים *m pl* the competent authorities; (colloq. ref. to Government and Jewish Agency departments).

◇ **mosh|av/-aveem** מושב *m* **1.** seat; **2.** form of cooperative agricultural settlement based on four principles: the land is national property; each member works personally and at one's own risk and peril; supplies, production and marketing are done solely through the Moshav's elected management; affiliation to the Histadrut's Moshav Movement **(tenoo'at ha-moshaveem** תנועת המושבים**)**; (*pl+of:* **-vey**).

◇ **mosh|av/-vey 'ovdeem** מושב עובדים *m* smallholders cooperative settlement of the "Moshav" type.

◇ **mosh|av/-aveem sheetoofee/-yeem** מושב שיתופי *m* smallholders collective settlement which, in some respects, is more similar to a kibbutz.

moshav zekeneem מושב זקנים *m* home for the aged.

◇ **(tekhoom ha) moshav** see ◇ **tekhoom ha-moshav.**

◇ **moshav|ah/-ot** מושבה *nf* onetime settlement grown into a town or township.

◇ **(tenoo'at ha) moshaveem** see ◇ **tenoo'at ha-moshaveem.**

moshavneek/-eem מושבניק *[slang] m* farmer; settler and/or member of a Moshav.

moshee|'a'/'ah מושיע **1.** *nmf & adj* savior; deliverer; **2.** *v pres* save(s); deliver(s); (*pst* **hoshee'a'**; *fut* **yoshee'a'**).

mosheet/-ah מושיט *v pres* stretches out; extends; (*pst* **hosheet**; *fut* **yosheet**).

mosheev/-ah מושיב *v pres* sits (others); settles (others); (*pst* **hosheev**; *fut* **yosheev**).

(par|at/-ot) mosheh rabenoo פרת משה רבנו *nf* (*lit.:* holy Moses cow); lady bug.

moshekh/-et מושך *v pres* **1.** pull(s) (string, rope); **2.** draw(s) (check); (*pst* **mashakh**; *fut* **yeemshokh**).

moshel/-et מושל **1.** *nmf* ruler; governor; **2.** *v pres* rules; (*pst* **mashal**; *fut* **yeemshol**).

mosh|el/-leem מושל ruler; governor; (*pl+of:* **-ley**).

moshel/-leem tsva'ee/-yeem מושל צבאי *m* military governor.

mosh'khot מושכות *nf pl* reins; (*sing:* **mosh'khah**).

mot/-ot מוט *m* bar; stick.

mot/-ot barzel מוט ברזל *m* iron bar.

(le) motar למותר *adv* needless to...; superfluous to...

motarot מותרות *m pl* luxury; luxuries.

motek/-eem מותק *[slang] m* sweetheart.

motek sheelee! מותק שלי! *[colloq.] interj* My Darling!

motel/-eem מוטל *m* motel.

mot|en/-nayeem מותן *nf* hip; (*pl+of:* **-ney**).

(meen ha) moten מן המותן *adv* from the hip (shooting, reacting).

motnayeem (*sing* **moten**) מותניים *nf pl* waist; hips; (*+of:* **motney**).

(sheenes/-sah/-astee) motnayeem שינס מותניים *v* gathered strength; (*pres* **meshanes** *etc*; *fut* **yeshanes** *etc*).

□ **Motsa** (Moza) מוצא *m* settlement outside Jerusalem, originally est. 1860 as an inn, later (1896) developed into a village and since became a residential suburb 5 km outside the city. Pop. 49.

□ **Motsa 'Eeleet** (Moza 'illit) מוצא עלית *nf* residential rural suburb (est. 1933) outside Jerusalem, 6 km W. of the city. Pop. 735.

mots|a/-a'eem מוצא **1.** *m* origin; **2.** *m* outcome; way out; (*pl+of:* **-a'ey**).

motsa 'adatee מוצא עדתי *m* community of origin.

motsa etnee מוצא אתני *m* ethnic origin.

motsa pee מוצא פי **1.** *m & possess. pron* utterance of; **2. motsa pee/-kha/-kh/-v/-hah** *etc m possess. pron* my/your *(m/f)*/his/her utterance.

motsa peh מוצא פה **1.** *m* utterance; **2. motsa pee/-kha/-kh/-v/-hah** *etc* - my/your/his/her *etc* utterance.

(be-'eyn) motsa באין מוצא *adv* there being no way out.

(khas|ar/-rat) motsa חסר מוצא *adj* hopeless; desperate; with no way out.

(nekood|at/-ot) motsa נקודת מוצא *nf* point of departure.

motsa'ey khag מוצאי חג *m pl* evening ending a Jewish holiday.

motsa'ey menookhah מוצאי מנוחה *m pl* evening ending the Sabbath rest-day; Saturday night.

motsa'ey shabat מוצאי שבת *m pl* evening ending the Sabbath; Saturday night.

mots|e/-et מוצא **1.** *nmf* finder; **2.** *adj* finding; **3.** *v pres* find(s); (*pst* **matsa**; *fut* **yeemtsa**).

motsee/-'ah מוציא *v pres* **1.** spend(s); **2.** take(s) out; (*pst* **hotsee**; *fut* **yotsee**).

motsee/-'ah la-po'al מוציא לפועל **1.** *nmf* executor; **2.** *v pres* carry(ies) out.

motsee/-'ah le-'or מוציא לאור **1.** *nmf* publisher; **2.** *v pres* publish(es); (*pst* **hotsee** *etc*; *fut* **yotsee** *etc*).

(ha) motsee oo-mevee המוציא ומביא *m* the factotum; the leading figure.

motsets/-eem מוצץ *m* baby's pacifier; (*pl+of:* **-ey**).
motsets/-et מוצץ *v pres* sucks; (*pst* **matsats**; *fut* **yeemtsots**).
motsets/-et dam מוצץ דם *nmf & adj* bloodsucker; leech.
moveel/-ah מוביל **1.** *nmf* conveyor; **2.** *adj* leading; **3.** *v pres* lead(s); carry(ies); (*pst* **hoveel**; *fut* **yoveel**).
◇ **(ha)moveel ha-artsee** המוביל הארצי *m* Israel's main water pipeline (from Lake Tiberias to the Negev).

mozayeek|ah/-ot מוזאיקה *nf* mosaic.
moz|eg/-geem מוזג *m* bartender; tavern-owner.
mozeg/-et מוזג *v pres* pour(s); fix(es) (drinks); (*pst* **mazag**; *fut* **yeemzog**).
mozn|ayeem מאזניים *m pl* scales; (*+of:* **-ey**).
(ka|f/-pot) moznayeem כף מאזניים *nf* scale (balance).
mozney tsedek מאזני צדק *m pl* just scales; accurate scales.

N.

NOTE: the Hebrew consonant נ **(Noon)**, when ending a word, takes the form of **Noon Sofeet** (ן), i.e. the "Final Noon".

na נא *interj* please! pray!
(bo/-'ee) na! בוא נא! *v imp* come! please come! (*inf* **lavo**; *pst & pres* **ba**; *fut* **yavo** *(v=b)*).
(bo/-'ee) na hena! בוא נא הנה! *v imp* come here! please, come here!
(shma'/sheem'ee) na! שמע נא! *v imp* listen! please listen! (*inf* **leeshmo'a**; *pst* **shama'**; *pres* **shome'a**; *fut* **yeeshma'**).
na'/-ah נע **1.** *adj* moving; mobile; **2.** *v pst & pres* move(s)/moved; (*fut* **yanoo'a'**).
na' va-nad נע ונד *adj & nm* vagrant; wanderer.◇ **(shva) na'** see ◇ **shva na'**.
na'al/-ayeem נעל *nf* shoe; (*pl+of:* **-ey**).
na'al/-ah/-tee נעל **1.** *v* locked; **2.** *v* wore (shoes); (*pst* **no'el**; *fut* **yeen'al**).
(kaf) na'al כף־נעל *m* shoehorn.
(khal|ats/-tsah/-atstee) na'alayeem חלץ נעליים *v* took shoes off; (*pst* **kholets** *etc*; *fut* **yakhlots** *etc*).
(khanoot/-yot) na'alayeem חנות נעליים *nf* shoe-store; shoe-shop.
(tseekhts|e'akh/-ekhah/-akhtee) na'alayeem ציחצח נעליים *v* shined shoes; (*pres* **metsakhtse'akh** *etc*; *fut* **yetakhtse'akh** *etc*).
(zoog/-ot) na'alayeem זוג נעליים *m* pair of shoes.
na'al|eh/-ah נעלה *adj* sublime; superior.
na'am/-ah/-tee נאם *v* made a speech; (*pres* **no'em**; *fut* **yeen'am**).
na'am/-ah/-tee נעם *v* pleased; (*pres* **na'eem**; *fut* **yeen'am**).
□ **Na'an** (Na'an) נען *m* kibbutz (est. 1930) 4 km E. of Rehovot **(Rekhovot)**. Pop. 1,220.
na'an|ah/-tah/-etee נענה *v* responded; was answered; (*pres* **na'aneh**; *fut* **ye'aneh**).

na'ar/ne'areem נער *m* boy; lad; (under 16) (*pl+of:* **-ey**).
na'arah/ne'arot נערה *nf* girl (under 18); (*+of:* **na'arat**).
na'arats/-ah נערץ **1.** *adj* adored; admired; **2.** *v pres* (is) adored, admired (*pst* **ne'erats**; *fut* **ye'arets**).
na'as|ah/-tah/-etee נעשה *v* became; was made; was done; (*pres* **na'aseh**; *fut* **ye'aseh**).
na'aseh ve-neeshma' נעשה ונשמע expression (Bibl.) of unwavering obedience; (*lit.*) we shall do first, then listen.
na'ats/ne'atseem נעץ *m* thumbtack; drawing-pin; (*pl+of:* **na'atsey**).
na'ats/-ah/-tee נעץ *v* thrusted; inserted; (*pres* **no'ets**; *fut* **yeen'ats**).
nad/-ah נד *v pst & pres* **1.** nodded/nods; **2.** wandered(s); **3.** deplored(s); (*fut* **yanood**).
nad|ad/-edah/-adetee נדד *v* wandered; (*pres* **noded**; *fut* **yeendod**).
nad|af/-fah/-aftee נדף *v* scented; smelled of; (*pres* **nodef**; *fut* **yeendof**).
nadam/-ah/-tee נדם *v* fell silent; (*pres* **domem**; *fut* **yeedom**).
nad|ar/-rah/-artee נדר *v* vowed; took a vow; (*pres* **noder**; *fut* **yeedor**).
nad|av/-vah/-avtee נדב *v* donated; (*pres* **menadev**; *fut* **yenadev**).
nadedah shnat/-ee/-o/-ah (*etc*) נדדה שנת־י/־ו/־ה *v* suffered (I/he/she etc) from insomnia.
nadeer/nedeerah נדיר *adj* rare.
nadeev/nedeevah נדיב *adj* generous.
◇ **(ha)nadeev ha-yadoo'a** הנדיב הידוע *nm* (*lit.:* the Well-known Benefactor) reference to

Baron Edmond James de Rothschild (1845-1934) who from 1883 onward, initiated and supported many of the first Jewish settlements in Palestine and is considered to have been the "Father of Jewish re-settlement in Palestine".

nadned|ah/-ot נדנדה *nf* swing; see-saw; (*+of:* **-at**).

nadon/-ah נדון **1.** *v* was discussed, considered; **2.** *v* was sentenced; (*pres* **nadon**; *fut* **yeedon**).

(ha) nadon (*also:* **ha-needon**) הנדון *m* re; subject under discussion.

nadosh/nedoshah נדוש *adj* threshed; banal.

nadvan/-eet נדבן *nmf* philanthropist; (*pl+of:* **-ey**).

na'eh/na'ah נאה *adj* good-looking; handsome.

na'eem/ne'eemah נעים *adj* pleasant; lovely.

na'eem me'od! נעים מאוד! *interj* customary reciprocation to being introduced: (am) very pleased (i.e. "to have met you").

(beelooy) na'eem! בילוי נעים! (greeting) Have a good time!

na'eevee/-t נאיבי *adj* naive.

na'eeveeyoot נאיביות *nf* naivete.

naf|ah/-ot נפה *nf* district; region; (*+of:* **-at**).

naf|akh/-khah/-akhtee נפח *v* **1.** blew; **2.** exhaled; (*pst* **nofe'akh**; *fut* **yeepakh** *(p=f)*).

nafakh (*etc*) **nafsh|o/-ah** *etc* נפח נפשו *v* breathed his/her *etc* last.

nafakh (*etc*) **neeshmat|o/-ah** נפח נשמתו *v* breathed his/her *etc* last.

naf|al/-lah/-altee נפל **1.** *v* fell; fell down; **2.** *v* fell in battle; (*pres* **nofel**; *fut* **yeepol** *(p=f)*).

nafal (*etc*) **'al** נפל על *v* fell in the struggle (or battle) for...

nafal (*etc*) **'al|av/-eha pakhad** נפל עליו פחד *v* was seized with fear.

nafal (*etc*) **ba-krav** נפל בקרב *v* fell in battle.

nafal (*etc*) **ba-pakh** נפל בפח *v* fell into a trap; was trapped.

nafal (*etc*) **ba-shevee** נפל בשבי *v* was taken prisoner.

nafal (*etc*) **bee-yedey** נפל בידי *v* fell into the hands of.

nafal (*etc*) **khalal** (*pl* **nafloo khalaleem**) נפל חלל *v* was killed in battle.

nafal (*etc*) **le-meeshkav** נפל למשכב *v* fell ill; was taken ill.

nafal (*etc*) **mee-** נפל מ־ **1.** *v* fell off; **2.** *v* was inferior to.

nafal (*etc*) **shadood/shedoodeem** נפל שדוד *v* was slain.

naf|ash/-shah/-ashtee נפש *v* vacationed; rested; (*pres* **nofesh**; *fut* **yeeposh** *(p=f)*).

naflah rookh|o *etc* נפלה רוחו *v* (*lit.:* his/her *etc* spirits went down); despaired; became depressed.

nafloo pan|av/-eha *etc* נפלו פניו *v* looked dejected; (*lit.*) his/her (*etc*) face fell.

nafoo'akh/nefookhah נפוח *adj* inflated; swollen.

nafool/nefoolah נפול *adj* fallen; lean (face).

nafots/nefotsah נפוץ *adj* widespread.

nafshee/-t נפשי *adj* psychic; mental; spiritual.

('al) nafsh|o/-ah/-ee *etc* על נפשו *adv* for his/her/my *etc* life.

(be) nafsh|o/-ah/-ee *etc* בנפשו **1.** *adj* vital; **2.** *adv* at his/her/my *etc* life's risk.

(ke) nafsh|o/-ah/-ee *etc* כנפשו *adv* to his/her/my *etc* liking.

(le) nafsh|o/-ah/-ee *etc* לנפשו *adv* by him-/her-/my- *etc* self; alone.

(sam/-ah/-tee) nafsh|o/-ah/-ee (*etc*) **be-khap|o/-ah/-ee** (*etc*) שם נפשו בכפו *v* risked his/her/my *etc* life; (*pres* **sam** *etc*; *fut* **yaseem** *etc*).

(shal|akh/-khah/-akhtee yad be) nafsho/-ah/-ee שלח יד בנפשו *v* took his/her/my (*etc*) life; committed suicide; (*pres* **shole'akh** *etc*; *fut* **yeeshlakh** *etc*).

naftaleen נפטלין *m* mothballs.

naftool|eem נפתולים *m pl* struggle; (*+of:* **-ey**).

nag|a'/-'ah/-a'tee נגע *v* touched; (*pres* **noge'a'**; *fut* **yeega'**).

naga' (*etc*) **'el leeb|o/-ah/-ee** *etc* (*or:* **naga' le-** *etc*) נגע אל ליבו he/she/I *etc* was touched.

naga' (*etc*) **le-** נגע ל־ *v* concerned.

nagad/-eem נגד *m* resistor; (*pl+of:* **-ey**).

nag|ad/-dah/-adetee נגד *v* contradicted; opposed; (*pres* **noged**; *fut* **yeengod**).

nagan/-eem נגן *m* musician; music-player; (*pl+of:* **-ey**).

nagar/-eem נגר *m* carpenter; (*pl+of:* **-ey**).

nagaree|yah/-yot נגרייה *nf* carpentry workshop; (*+of:* **-yat**).

nagaroot נגרות *nf* **1.** carpentry; **2.** *[colloq.]* woodwork.

nag|as/-sah/-astee נגס *v* bit; (*pres* **noges**; *fut* **yeengos**).

nageed נגיד *v fut (1st pers pl)* let's say; say; assuming.

nageed/neegeed|eem נגיד *m* **1.** governor; rector (university); **2.** very rich man; (*pl+of:* **-ey**).

nageef/negeef|eem נגיף *m* virus; (*pl+of:* **-ey**).

nagl|ah/-ot נאגלה *nf [slang]* turn (by a car or runner); (*+of:* **-at**).

nagoo'a'/negoo'ah נגוע *adj* afflicted; contaminated.

nahafokh hoo נהפוך הוא *adv* on the contrary.

nahag/-eem (*npr* **nehag/-eem**) נהג *m* driver; (*pl+of:* **-ey**).

nahag/-ah נהג *v* **1.** drove; **2.** used to...; was accustomed to ...; (*pres* **noheg**; *fut* **yeenhag**).

nahag/-ah kavod נהג כבוד *v* treated with respect.

nahagoot נהגות *nf* driving.

□ **Nahalal** נהלל *nm* smallholders village in N. of Yizre'el Valley, 7 km SE of **Keeryat Teev'on**. Since its foundation (est. 1921) it had been serving as prototype of villages of the "Moshav" type (see ◇ **moshav**). Pop.1,240.

naham/-ah/-tee נהם *v* roared; (*pres* **nohem**; *fut* **yeenham**).

nahar/neharot נהר *m* river; (*pl+of:* **naharot**).
nahar/-ah/-tee נהר *v* flocked; (*pres* **noher**; *fut* **yeenhar**).
(be-ma'aleh ha) nahar במעלה הנהר *adv* upstream.
(be-morad ha) nahar במורד הנהר *adv* downstream.
□ **Nahareeyah** (Nahariyya) נהריה *nf* town (est. 1934) and bathing resort on Mediterranean Galilee coast, 8 km N. of Acre (**'Ako**). Pop. 34,000.
naheget/nehagot נהגת *nf* woman-driver.
nahoog/nehoogah נהוג *adj* customary.
nak|a'/-'ah נקע *v* sprained; (*pres* **noke'a'**; *fut* **yeeka'**).
nak|af/-fah/-aftee נקף *v* knocked; beat; (*pres* **nokef**; *fut* **yeenkof**).
(lo) nak|af/-fah etsba' לא נקף אצבע *v* did not raise a finger.
nakam נקם *m* vengeance.
nak|am/-mah/-amtee נקם *v* avenged; (*pres* **nokem**; *fut* **yeenkom**).
nak|at/-tah/-atetee נקט *v* adopted; took; resorted to; (*pres* **noket**; *fut* **yeenkot**).
nakat (*etc*) **emtsa'eem** נקט אמצעים *v* took measures.
nak|av/-vah/-avtee נקב *v* stated explicitly; (*pres* **nokev**; *fut* **yeenkov**).
nakav (*etc*) **be-shem** נקב בשם *v* named.
nakboovee/-t נקבובי *adj* porous; permeable.
nakee/nekeeyah נקי *adj* clean; pure.
nakeek/nekeekeem נקיק *m* crevice; (*pl+of:* **-ey**).
(be) nakel בנקל *adv* easily.
nakh/-ah/-tee נח *v* rested; reposed; (*pres* **nakh**; *fut* **yanoo'akh**).
nakh/-ah נח *adj* resting.
nakh|akh/-ekhah נכח *v* attended; was present; (*pres* **nokhe'akh**; *fut* **yeehyeh nokhakh**).
nakhal/nekhaleem נחל *m* stream; ravine; (*pl+of:* **nakhaley**).
nakhal akhzav נחל אכזב *m* winter stream; wadi.
◇ **NAKHAL** נחל *m abbr.* (*acr of* **No'ar KHAlootsee Lokhem** (נוער חלוצי לוחם) elite corps in the Israel Defence Forces in which volunteers combine battle training with establishing new settlements in arid or otherwise unattractive areas.
nakhal/-ah/-tee נחל *v* inherited; got; received; sustained; (*pres* **nokhel**; *fut* **yeenkhol**).
nakhal (*etc*) **akhzavah** נחל אכזבה *v* suffered a disappointment.
nakhal (*etc*) **keeshalon** נחל כישלון *v* met with failure.
nakhal (*etc*) **mapalah** נחל מפלה *v* suffered a reverse; was defeated.
nakhal (*etc*) **neetsakhon** נחל ניצחון *v* scored a victory.
nakhal|ah/-ot נחלה *nf* possession; estate; inherited land; (*+of:* **-at**).
□ **Nakhal 'Oz** נחל עז *nm* kibbutz in N. Negev (est. 1951), 5 km SE of Gaza (**'Azah**). Pop. 490.
nakhar/-ah/-tee נחר *v* snored; (*pres* **nokher**; *fut* **yeenkhor**).
nakhash/nekhasheem נחש *m* snake.
nakhash נחש *m* guess; magic spell.
nakhat נחת *nf* contentment; gratification.
nakhat roo'akh נחת רוח *nf* satisfaction.
(be) nakhat בנחת *adv* gently; quietly.
nakhat/-ah/-etee נחת *v* landed; (*pres* **nokhet**; *fut* **yeenkhat**).
nakh|eh/-ah נכה *adj & nmf* cripple; invalid; (*+of:* **nekh|eh/-at**; *pl+of:* **-ey**).
nakh|etet/nekhatot נחתת *nf* landing-craft.
◇ **nakhla|y** (*cpr* **nakhla|'ee**)/**-'eet** נחלאי *nmf* member of Army's **Nakhal** Corps.
nakhlee'elee/-m נחליאלי *m* wagtail.
nakhon/nekhonah נכון *adj* correct; right.
nakhon נכון *adv* right you are!; right.
nakhon/nekhonah le-'akhshav נכון לעכשיו *adv* this far correct.
(el) nakhon אל נכון *adv* apparently; no doubt...
(lo) nakhon לא נכון *adv* untrue; not true; wrong.
(mats|a/-'ah/-a'tee le) nakhon מצא לנכון *v* found it right to; (*pres* **motse** *etc*; *fut* **yeemtsa** *etc*).
nakhoosh/nekhooshah נחוש *adj* determined.
nakhoot/nekhootah נחות *adj* inferior.
nakhoo|t/-yot נכות *nf* disability; infirmity; (*+of:* **nekhoo|t/-yot**).
nakhoots/nekhootsah נחוץ *adj* needed; necessary.
nakhs נאחס **1.** *adv [slang]* disgusting! **2.** - *adj [slang]* disgusting (person or matter).
nakhshol/-eem נחשול *m* torrent; wave; (*pl+of:* **-ey**).
□ **Nakhsholeem** (Nahsholim) נחשולים *nm* kibbutz on Carmel Coast (est. 1948), 4 km N. of **Zeekhron Ya'akov** interchange. Pop. 439.
□ **Nakhshon** (**Nahshon**) נחשון *nm* kibbutz in the **Shfelah** (est. 1950), 3 km E. of **Latroon**. Pop. 379.
nakhshonee/-t נחשוני *adj* daring; pioneering.
□ **Nakhshoneem** (**Nahshonim**) נחשונים *nm* kibbutz on the borderline between coastal plain and the **Shfelah** (est. 1949), 3 km S. of **Rosh ha-'Ayeen**. Pop. 249.
nakmanoot נקמנות *nf* vengefulness.
nakneek/-eem נקניק *m* sausage; (*pl+of:* **-ey**).
nakneekee|yot (*sing:* **-yah**) נקניקיות *nf pl* hot dogs; frankfurters.
nakoov/nekoovah נקוב *adj* punctured; perforated.
nakvan/-eet נקבן *nmf* card-puncher; operator of a perforating machine; (*pl+of:* **-ey**).
(ha) nal הנ"ל *adj* (*acr of:* **HA-Neezkar Le-halan**) the above-mentioned.
(ka) nal כנ"ל *adv* (*acr of:* **KA-Neezkar Le-halan**) as mentioned above.
nam/-ah/-tee נם *v* slept; *v pres* sleeps; sleeping; (*fut* **yanoom**).
namak/-ah/-tee נמק *v* rot away; (*pres* **namek**; *fut* **yeemak**).

namal/nemaleem (*npr* **namel/nemeleem**) נמל *m* harbor; port; (*+of:* **nemal/neemley**).

namel/nemeleem נמל *m* harbor; port; (*+of:* **nemal/neemley**).

names/nemasah נמס **1.** *adj* melting; **2.** *v pres* melt(s); (*pst* **namas**; *fut* **yeemas**).

(kafeh) names קפה נמס *m* instant coffee.

namer/nemereem נמר *m* tiger (*+of:* **nemer/-ey**).

namog/-ah נמוג **1.** *adj* volatile; fleeting; **2.** *v pst & pres* disappeared(s); (*inf* **leheemog**; *fut* **yeemog**).

namookh/nemookhah נמוך *adj* low; short.

nan|as/-eset ננס *nmf* dwarf; midget.

na'ool/ne'oolah נעול *adj* locked; bolted.

na'oots/ne'ootsah נעוץ *adj* stuck in; inherent.

na'or/ne'orah נאור *adj* cultured; enlightened.

na'ot/ne'otah נאות *adj* appropriate; suitable.

napakh/-eem נפח *m* locksmith; (*pl+of:* **-ey**).

napats/-eem נפץ *m* detonator; (*pl+of:* **-ey**).

narkees/-eem נרקיס *m* narcissus; (*pl+of:* **-ey**).

narkoman/-eet נרקומן *nmf* drug-addict.

narkoz|ah/-ot נרקוזה *nf* narcosis; (*+of:* **-at**).

narteek/-eem נרתיק *m* **1.** case; sheath; **2.** vagina; (*pl+of:* **-ey**).

nas/-ah/-tee נס *v* fled; escaped; (*pres* **nas**; *fut* **yanoos**).

(lo) nas leykh|o/-ah לא נס ליחו/־ה his/her capacity remains unabated.

nas|a/-'ah/-'atee נשא *v* **1.** carried; endured; **2.** married; (*pres* **nose**; *fut* **yeesa**).

nasa (*etc*) **dvar|o/-ah** נשא דברו *v* made a speech; said his/her piece.

nasa (*etc*) **eeshah** נשא אישה *v* married; took a wife.

nasa (*etc*) **khen** נשא חן *v* pleased.

nasa (*etc*) **ne'oom** נשא נאום *v* made a speech.

nasa (*etc*) **peney** נשא פני *v* showed favoritism.

nasa (*etc*) **pree/-perot** נשא פרי *v* bore fruit(s); produced results.

nasa (*etc*) **ve-nat|an/-nah** נשא ונתן *v* parleyed; negotiated.

nas|a'/-'ah/-'atee נסע *v* travelled; journeyed; (*pres* **nose'a'**; *fut* **yeesa'**).

nas|akh/-khah/-akhtee נסך *v* **1.** poured; **2.** inspired with; (*pres* **nosekh**; *fut* **yeesokh**).

nasakh (*etc*) **tardemah** נסך תרדמה *v* put to sleep.

nasa|v/-bah נסב **1.** *v pst & pres* turned to; **2.** *v* turned away; (*fut* **yeesov**).

nasee/nesee'ah נשיא *nmf* president; (*+of:* **nesee/-'at**; *pl* **-'eem**; *+of:* **-'ey**).

naseekh/neseekhah נסיך *nmf* prince(ss); (*+of:* **neseekh/-'at**; *pl* **-'eem**; *+of:* **-'ey**).

nash|af/-fah/-aftee נשף *v* blew; exhaled; (*pres* **noshef**; *fut* **yeeshof**).

nash|ak/-kah/-aktee נשק *v* kissed; (*pres* **noshek**; *fut* **yeeshak**).

nashak/-eem נשק *m* gunsmith; armorer; (*pl+of:* **-ey**).

nash|akh/-khah/-akhtee נשך *v* bit; stung; (*pres* **noshekh**; *fut* **yeeshakh**).

nash|am/-mah/-amtee נשם *v* breathed; inhaled; (*pres* **noshem**; *fut* **yeenshom**).

nasham (*etc*) **lee-revakhah** נשם לרווחה *v* breathed freely; felt great relief.

nash|ar/-rah/-artee נשר *v* **1.** fell off (leaf); **2.** dropped out from school; (*pres* **nosher**; *fut* **yeenshor**).

◊ **nashar** (*etc*) נשר *v* dropped out - colloquial term used until recently to refer to the act of an Israel-bound Jewish emigrant from the former U.S.S.R. who, once escaped from there thanks to the Israel visa, switches destination for U.S.A. or any other country outside Israel.

nash|av/-vah/-avtee נשב *v* blew; puffed; (*pres* **noshev**; *fut* **yeeshov**).

nashee/-t נשי *adj* womanly; feminine.

nasheem נשים *nf pl* (*sing:* **'eeshah**) women; (*+of:* **neshey**).

('ezrat) nasheem עזרת נשים *nf* women's gallery (in a synagogue).

(orakh) nasheem אורח נשים *m* menstruation.

(rofe/-t) nasheem רופא נשים *nmf* gynecologist (Medic.).

nasheer! (*poetic.* **nasheerah!**) נשיר *v fut 1st pers pl* let us sing!

nasheeyoot נשיות *nf* femininity.

nas|og/-ogah/nesoogotee נסוג *v* retreated; withdrew; (*pres* **nasog**; *fut* **yeesog**).

nasoo נשוא **1.** *m* predicate (Gram.); **2.** object.

nasooy/nesoo'ah נשוי *adj* married.

nasooy/nesoo'ah le- נשוי ל־ *adj* married to.

nasyoov/-eem נסיוב *m* serum; (*pl+of:* **-ey**).

nat|ah/-etah/-eetee נטה *v* turned aside; tended; (*pres* **noteh**; *fut* **yeeteh**).

natah (*etc*) **akhrey** נטה אחרי *v* tended towards; was inclined to follow.

natah (*etc*) **khesed** נטה חסד *v* favored; liked.

natah (*etc*) **lamoot** נטה למות *v* was about to die.

natah (*etc*) **ohel** נטה אוהל *v* pitched a tent.

nat|af/-fah/-aftee נטף *v* dripped; (*pres* **notef**; *fut* **yeetof**).

nat|al/-lah/-altee נטל *v* took; lifted; (*pres* **notel**; *fut* **yeetol**).

natal (*etc*) **'al 'atsm|o/-ah** נטל על עצמו *v* undertook; took upon him-/her-/my- (*etc*) self.

natal (*etc*) **reshoot** נטל רשות *v* took permission.

nat|an/-nah/-atee נתן *v* gave; allowed; let; (*pres* **noten**; *fut* **yeeten**).

natan (*etc*) **emoon** נתן אימון *v* placed one's confidence; trusted.

natan (*etc*) **et ha-da'at** נתן את הדעת *v* turned one's attention.

natan (*etc*) **et ha-deen** נתן את הדין *v* accounted for; was brought to account; was punished.

natan (*etc*) **man|ah/-ot** נתן מנה *v* gave (him/her *etc*) a comeuppance.

natan (*etc*) **reshoot** נתן רשות *v* gave permission.

natan (*etc*) **yad** נתן יד *v* lent a hand; participated.

(nas|a/-'ah ve) nat|an/-nah נשא ונתן *v* dealt; parleyed; negotiated; (*pres* **nose ve noten**; *fut* **yeesa ve-yeeten**).

□ **Natanyah** נתניה *nf* town (incorrectly pronounced colloq. name) see: □ **Netanyah**.

nat|ar/-rah/-artee נטר *v* bore a grudge; (*pres* **noter**; *fut* **yeetor**).

nat|ash/-shah/-ashtee נתש *v* evicted; ousted; (*pres* **notesh**; *fut* **yeetosh**).

nat|ash/-shah/-ashtee נטש *v* abandoned; quit; (*pres* **notesh**; *fut* **yeetosh**).

natav/-eem נתב **1.** *m* air or sea traffic controller; **2.** pilot; **3.** tracker; (*pl+of:* **-ey**).

nateekh/neteekh|eem נתיך *m* fuse; (*pl+of:* **-ey**).

nateev/neteev|eem נתיב *m* path; route; (*pl+of:* **-ey**).

natoo'a/netoo'ah נטוע *adj* planted.

natool/netoolah נטול *adj* lacking; -less.

natoon/netoonah נתון *adj* given.

natoon/netoon|eem נתון *m* datum; element; (*pl+of:* **-ey**).

natoosh/netooshah נטוש *adj* abandoned.

◇ **(rekhoosh) natoosh** see ◇ **rekhoosh natoosh**.

natooy/netooyah נטוי *adj* turned; tended.

(kav) natooy קו נטוי *m* oblique line (/).

natran נתרן *m* sodium.

nats|ar/-rah/-artee נצר *v* **1.** guarded; preserved; **2.** locked (firearm); (*pres* **notser**; *fut* **yeentsor**).

nats|ats/-etsah/-atstee נצץ *v* shone; glittered; (*pres* **notsets**; *fut* **yeentsots**).

natsee/-m נאצי *m* Nazi.

natsee/-t נאצי *adj* Nazi.

natseeg/netseeg|ah נציג *nmf* representative; (*pl* **-eem/-ot**; *+of:* **-at/-ey**).

natseev (*npr* **netseev**) **netseev|eem** נציב *m* commissioner; (*pl+of:* **-ey**).

natseev (*npr* **nesteev**) **'elyon** נציב עליון *m* high commissioner.

□ **Natseret** see □ **Natsrat**.

□ **Natseret 'Eeleet** see □ **Natsrat 'Eeleet**.

natslan/-eem נצלן *m* sponger; exploiter; (*pl+of:* **-ey**).

natslanee/-t נצלני *adj* exploitative.

natsoor נצור *adj* **1.** beleaguered; besieged; **2.** locked (firearm); on safety.

□ **Natsrat (Nazerat)** נצרת *nf* Nazareth, historic town in Lower Galilee, home of Jesus. Pop. (Christians and Muslims) 53,600.

□ **Natsrat 'Eeleet (Nazerat 'Illit)** נצרת עלית *nf* new town (est. 1957) across the road from historic Nazareth. Pop. 29,600.

natsroot נצרות *nf* Christianity.

nav|a'/-'ah/-a'tee נבע *v* derived from; stemmed out of; was due to; (*pres* **nove'a'**; *fut* **yeeba'** *(b=v)*).

navah נאווה *adj f* beautiful.

Navah נאווה popular female name.

navad/-eem נווד *nm* vagabond; vagrant; (*pl+of:* **-ey**).

navadoot נוודות *nf* vagrancy.

nav|akh/-khah/-akhtee נבח *v* barked; (*pres* **nove'akh**; *fut* **yeenbakh** *(b=v)*).

naval/nevaleem נבל *nm* scoundrel.

nav|at/-tah/-atetee נבט *v* germinated; sprouted; (*pres* **novet**; *fut* **yeenbot**; *(b=v)*).

navat/-eem נווט *nm* pilot; navigator; (*pl+of:* **-ey**).

navee/nevee|'eem נביא *nm* prophet (*f:* **-ah**).

naveh/-eem נווה *nm* dwelling; (*+of:* **neveh**).

navokh/nevokhah נבוך *adj* confused; perplexed.

navon/nevonah נבון *adj* wise.

navoov/nevoovah נבוב *adj* hollow; empty.

navran/-eem נברן *nm* rodent; field mouse; (*pl+of:* **-ey**).

na|yad/-yedet נייד **1.** *adj* mobile; movable; **2.** *nmf* wanderer.

nayadootניידות *nf* mobility.

nayakh נייח *adj* fixed; stationary.

(neekhsey de) naydey נכסי דניידי *nm pl* chattels; movable properties.

(neekhsey de-la) naydey נכסי דלא ניידי *nm pl* real estate; immovable properties.

nayedet/nayadot ניידת *nf* patrol-car.

nayedet ha-sheedoor ניידת השידור *nf* mobile broadcasting vehicle.

nayedet/nayadot meeshtarah ניידת משטרה *nf* police patrol car.

nayeret ניירת *nf* paperwork; red tape.

naz|af/-fah/-aftee נזף *v* reprimanded; (*pres* **nozef**; *fut* **yeenzof**).

naz|al/-lah/l-oo נזל *v* leaked; dripped; (*pres* **nozel**; *fut* **yeezal**).

nazeed נזיד *nm* porridge; broth; (*+of:* **nezeed**).

nazeel נזיל *adj* fluid; liquid.

nazeer/nezeer|eem נזיר *nm* monk; ascetic; (*pl+of:* **-ey**).

nazelet נזלת *nf* catarrh; cold.

nazoof נזוף *adj* reprimanded.

ne'ats|ah/-ot נאצה *nf* contempt; abuse; (*+of:* **-at**).

ne'atseem נעצים *nm pl* (*sing* **na'ats**) thumbtacks; drawing-pins.

ne'd|ar/-rah/-artee נעדר *v* was missing; was absent; (*pres* **ne'edar**; *fut* **ye'ader**).

ne'd|ar/-eret נעדר **1**. *adj* missing; absent; **2.** *nmf* absentee; (*pl:* **-areem/-arot**; *+of:* **-rey**).

ne'd|ar/-eret yekholet נעדר יכולת *adj* lacking ability; in no position.

nedav|ah/-ot נדבה *nf* donation; alms; (*+of:* **needva|t/-ot**).

nedeed|ah/-ot נדידה *nf* wandering; (*+of:* **-at**).

nedeeroot נדירות *nf* scarcity; rarity.

nedeevoo|t/-yot נדיבות *nf* generosity.

nedeev/-at lev נדיב לב *adj* generous.

ned|er/-areem נדר *nm* pledge; vow; (*pl+of:* **needrey**).

nedood|eem נדודים *nm pl* wanderings; peregrinations; (*+of:* **-ey**).

nedoodey-sheynah נדודי שינה *nm pl* insomnia.

nedoon|yah/-yot (*cpr* **nedoon|yah/-yot**) נדוניה *nf* dowry; (*+of:* **-yat**).

nee'an|e'a' (*npr* **nee'ne'a'**) /**-'ah/-a'tee** ניענע *v* nodded; shook; (*pres* **mena'ne'a'**; *fut* **yena'ne'a'**).

neeb|a/-'ah/-e'tee ניבא *v* predicted; prophesized; (*pres* **menabe**; *fut* **yenabe**).

neeb|at/-tah/-atetee ניבט *v* gazed; was seen.

neeb|el/-lah/-altee pee|v/-ha/pee ניבל פיו *v* talked obscenities; (*pres* **menabel** *etc*; *fut* **yenabel** *etc*).

neebool/-ey peh ניבול פה *nm* obscenity.

need|ah/-ot נידה *nf* Jewish woman's untouchability during menstruation (Relig.); (*+of:* **-at**).

need|ah/-etah/-etee נידה *v* cast out; banished; excommunicated; (*pres* **menadeh**; *fut* **yenadeh**).

('aleh) needaf עלה נידף *nm* fallen leaf; a driven leaf (Bibl).

needakh/-at נידח *adj* remote; out of the way.

ne'ed|ar (*npr* **ne'd|ar**) /**-rah/-artee** נעדר *v* was missing; was absent; (*pres* **ne'edar**; *fut* **ye'ader**).

ne'ed|ar/-eret (*npr* **ne'd|ar/-eret**) נעדר **1.** *adj* missing; absent; **2.** *nmf* absentee; (*pl:* **-areem/-arot**; *+of:* **-rey**).

ne'ed|ar (*npr* **ne'd|ar**) /**-eret yekholet** נעדר יכולת *adj* lacking ability; in no position.

needb|ak/-ekah/-aktee נדבק **1.** *v* stuck; adhered; **2.** caught infection; (*pres* **needbak**; *fut* **yeedabek**).

needbakh/-eem נדבך *nm* layer of bricks or stones; (*pl+of:* **-ey**).

needb|ar/-erah/-artee נדבר *v* convened; agreed; (*pres* **needbar**; *fut* **yeedaver** *(v=b)*).

need|ev/-vah/-avtee נידב *v pres* donated; contributed; (*pres* **menadev**; *fut* **yenadev**).

need'ham/-ah/-tee נדהם *v* was amazed; was stunned; (*pres* **need'ham**; *fut* **yeedahem**).

need'|ham/-hemet נדהם *adj* shocked; amazed; stunned.

needkh|ah/-etah/-etee נדחה *v* has been postponed; (*pres* **needkheh**; *fut* **yeedakheh**).

needkh|eh/-et נדחה *adj* postponed.

needkhaf/-ah/-tee נדחף *v* was pushed; pushed forth; (*pres* **needkhaf**; *fut* **yeedakhef**).

needkh|af/-efet נדחף *adj* pushed; pushing.

needkhak/-ah/-tee נדחק *v* was pressed; (*pres* **needkhak**; *fut* **yeedakhek**).

needl|ak/-ekah/-aktee נדלק *v* was lit; was ignited; (*pres* **needlak**; *fut* **yeedalek**).

needlak (*etc*) **'al** (*or:* **la-/le-**) נדלק על *[slang] v* was turned on by; was aroused by; (*pres* **needlak 'al**; *fut* **yeedalek 'al**).

needl|ak/-eket 'al (or **la-/le-**) נדלק על *[slang] adj* turned on; falling for.

needl|ah/-etah/-e'tee נדלה was heaved up; was exhausted; (*pres* **needleh**; *fut* **yeedaleh**).

(beeltee) needleh/-t בלתי נדלה *adj* inexhaustible.

needm|ah/-etah/-e'tee נדמה *v* seemed; (*pres* **nedmeh**; *fut* **yeedameh**).

needmeh נדמה *adv* seemingly; seems.

needmeh hayah ke-'eeloo נדמה היה כאילו *v* it looked as if... (*pres* **domeh** *etc*; **yeedmeh** *etc*).

needmeh lee/lekha/lakh/lo/lah *etc* נדמה לי/לך/לו וכד *v pres* seems to me/you/him/her *etc.*

(lesakhek be) needmeh lee לשחק בנדמה לי *v inf* to pretend; play "make believe".

needn|ed/-edah/-adetee נדנד *v* rocked; swung; (*pres* **menadned**; *fut* **yenadned**).

neednled (*etc*) נדנד *v [colloq.]* nagged; pestered.

neednood/-eem נדנוד *nm* rocking; swinging.

neednood (*etc*) נדנוד *nm [colloq.]* nagging; pestering.

neednood 'af'af נדנוד עפעף *nm* flick of an eyelid.

needon/-ah/-tee נידון *v* **1.** was sentenced; **2.** was debated; (*pres* **needon**; *fut* **yeedon**).

(ba/be) needon בנידון *adv* in the matter of; re; concerning.

(ha) needon הנידון *nm* re; in the matter of.

needoo|y/-yeem נידוי *nm* banishment; excommunication; ouster.

needp|as/-esah/-astee נדפס *v* was printed; (*pres* **needpas**; *fut* **yeedafes** *(f=p)*).

needr|as/-esah/-astee נדרס *v* was overrun (by vehicle); (*pres* **needras**; *fut* **yeedares**).

need|ras/-eset נדרס *adj* overrun.

needr|ash/-eshah/-ashtee נדרש *v* has been required, requested; (*pres* **needrash**; *fut* **yeedaresh**).

needr|ash/-eshet נדרש *adj* wanted; needed; required.

(pakeed) needrash פקיד נדרש *nm* "indispensable" public official (i.e. entitled to special advantages).

(askoopah) needreset אסקופה נדרסת *nf* trampled like a doormat.

◇ **(kol) needrey** see ◇ **kol needrey**.

needv|at/-ot lev נדבת לב *nf* generous gift.

ne'eel|ah/-ot נעילה *nf* locking; closing; (*+of:* **-at**).

◇ **ne'eelah ("Ne'ileh")** נעילה *nf* closing prayer in the Yom-Kippur synagogue service.

ne'eem|ah/-ot נעימה *nf* tune; melody; (*+of:* **-at**).

(beel|ah/-tah/-eetee ba) ne'eemeem בילה בנעימים *v* had a good time; (*pres* **mevaleh** *etc*; *fut* **yevaleh** *etc*).

ne'eemoo|t/-yot אי נעימות *nf* unpleasantness.

nee'er/-'arah/-'artee ניער *v* shook; stirred; (*pres* **mena'er**; *fut* **yena'er**).

◇ **neef'al** נפעל *nm* reflexive (or passive) conjugation of Hebrew verbs (Gram.).

neef'am/-ah/-tee נפעם *v* was moved; was excited; (*pres* **neef'am**; *fut* **yeepa'em** *(p=f)*).

neef'ar/-ah/-tee נפער *v* opened up; was widely opened (*pres* **neef'ar**; *fut* **yeepa'er** *(p=f)*).

neefd|ah/-etah/-etee נפדה *v* has been redeemed, ransomed, rescued; (*pres* **neefdeh**; *fut* **yeepadeh** *(p=f)*).

neefg|a'/-e'ah/-a'tee נפגע *v* was hurt; felt hurt; suffered; (*pres* **neefga'**; *fut* **yeepaga'** *(p=f)*).

neefg|a'/-a'eem נפגע *nm* casualty; (*pl+of:* **-e'ey**).

neefk|ad/-edah/-adetee נפקד *v* has been missing; was counted absent; (*pres* **neefkad**; *fut* **yeepaked** *(p=f)*).

◇ **neefkad/-eem** נפקד **1.** *nm* absentee; AWOL; **2.** legal reference to Arabs who, at the instigation of their leaders, fled Palestine during the 1948 hostilities and have been deemed "absentees" since.

◇ **(neekhsey) neefkadeem** see ◇ **neekhsey neefkadeem**.

neefkekhoo 'eyn|av/-eha/-ay/-ekha *etc* נפקחו עיניו *v 3rd pers pl pst* his/her/my/your eyes opened.

neefkhad/-ah/-etee נפחד *v* became frightened; (*pres* **neefkhad**; *fut* **yeepakhed** *(p=f)*).

neefkh|ad/-edet נפחד *adj* frightened.

neefla נפלא *adv* wonderfully; marvelously.

neefl|a/-a'ah נפלא *adj* wonderful; marvelous.

neefla'ot נפלאות *nf pl* miracles; wonders.

(neeseem ve) neefla'ot ניסים ונפלאות *nm & nf pl* miracles and wonders.

neefn|ef/-efah/-aftee נפנף *v* waved; swung; (*pres* **menafnef**; *fut* **yenafnef**).

neefnoof/-eem נפנוף *nm* waving.

neefr|a'/-e'ah/-a'tee נפרע *v* **1.** was paid up; was collected; **2.** was dishevelled (hair); (*pres* **neefra'**; *fut* **yeepara'** *(p=f)*).

neefr|ad/-edah/-adetee נפרד *v* separated; took leave; (*pres* **neefrad**; *fut* **yeepared** *(p=f)*).

neefr|ad/-edet נפרד *adj* separate; apart.

(be) neefrad בנפרד *adv* separately; apart.

neefr|ak/-ekah/-aktee נפרק *v* was unloaded, dislodged; (*pres* **neefrak**; *fut* **yeeparek** *(p=f)*).

neefr|am/-emah/-amtee נפרם *v* was ripped, undone; (*pres* **neefram**; *fut* **yeeparem**).

neefr|as/-esah/-astee נפרש *v* was spread; fanned out; (*pres* **neefras**; *fut* **yeepares** *(p=f)*).

neefr|at/-etah/-atetee נפרט *v* was changed, detailed, specified; (*pres* **neefrat**; *fut* **yeeparet** *(p=f)*).

neefr|ats/-etsah/-atstee נפרץ *v* was broken into; (*pres* **neefrats**; *fut* **yeeparets** *(p=f)*).

(khazon) neefrats חזון נפרץ *nm* a usual phenomenon.

neefs|ad/-edet נפסד *adj* harmful; corrupt.

(hergel) neefsad הרגל נפסד *nm* bad habit.

neefs|ak/-ekah/-aktee נפסק **1.** *v* stopped; was discontinued; **2.** was allocated; (*pres* **neefsak**; *fut* **yeepasek** *(p=f)*).

neefsal/-elah/-altee נפסל *v* was disqualified; (*pres* **neefsal**; *fut* **yeepasel** *(p=f)*).

neefsh|a'/-a'at נפשע *adj* sinful; criminal.

neeft|a'/-e'ah/-a'tee נפתע *v* was surprised; (*pres* **neefta'**; *fut* **yoofta'**).

neeft|ah/-etah/-etee נפתה *v* was tempted; (*pres* **neefteh**; *fut* **yeepateh** *(p=f)*).

neeft|akh/-ekhah/-akhtee נפתח *v* opened; was opened; (*pres* **neeftakh**; *fut* **yeepatakh** *(p=f)*).

neeftar/-erah/-artee נפטר *v* passed away; (*pres* **neeftar**; *fut* **yeepater** *(p=f)*).

neeftar (*etc*) **mee-** נפטר מ־ *v* got rid of.

neeft|ar/-eret נפטר *nmf* deceased person; (*pl* **-areem**; *+of:* **-erey**).

neeg|af/-fah/-aftee ניגף *v* was beaten, routed; suffered defeat.

neefts|a'/-e'ah/-a'tee נפצע *v* was wounded, injured; (*pres* **neeftsa'**; *fut* **yeepatsa'** *(p=f)*).

neeg'al/-ah/-tee נגאל *v* was redeemed, rescued, set free; (*pres* **neeg'al**; *fut* **yeega'el**).

neeg'al/-ah/-tee נגעל *v* felt disgusted, abhorred; (*pres* **neeg'al**; *fut* **yeega'el**).

neeg|ar/-rah/-artee ניגר *v* was spilled, shed.

neegar/-eret ניגר *adj* spilled.

neegash/-shah/-ashtee ניגש *v* approached; began; (*pres* **neegash**; *fut* **yeegash**).

neegash (*etc*) **yashar la-'eenyan** ניגש ישר לעניין *v* went straight to the point.

neeg|en/-nah/-antee ניגן *v* played (music); (*pres* **menagen**; *fut* **yenagen**).

neegev/-vah/-avtee ניגב *v* wiped; (*pres* **menagev**; *fut* **yenagev**).

neegl|ah/-etah/-etee נגלה *v* was revealed; was disclosed; (*pres* **neegleh**; *fut* **yeegaleh**).

neegm|ar/-erah/-artee נגמר *v* was ended; finished; (*colloq. pres* **holekh ve-neegmar**; *fut* **yeegamer**).

neegood/-eem ניגוד *nm* contrast; contradiction; (*pl+of:* **-ey**).

(be) neegood le- בניגוד ל־ *adv* contrary to; in contrast to.

neegoon/-eem ניגון *nm* melody (traditional); tune; (*pl+of:* **-ey**).

neegoov/-eem ניגוב *nm* wiping; drying; (*pl+of:* **-ey**).

neegr|ar/-erah/-artee נגרר *v* was dragged; was towed; (*pres* **neegrar**; *fut* **yeegarer**).

neegr|ar/-eret נגרר **1.** *adj* dragged; towed; **2.** *nmf* trailer.

neegz|al/-elah/-altee נגזל *v* was robbed; was despoiled; (*pres* **neegzal**; *fut* **yeegazel**).

neegz|ar/-eem נגזר *nm* derivative (*pl+of:* **-erey**).

neegz|ar/-erah/-artee נגזר *v* was derived; was decreed; was cut out; (*pres* **neegzar**; *fut* **yeegazer**).

neegz|eret/-arot נגזרת *nf* derivative.

ne'e|had/-edet נאהד *adj* was sympathized with; was liked.

ne'e|hav/-hevet נאהב **1.** *v* was loved; (prs ne'ehav; *fut* **ye'ahev**); **2.** *adj* beloved.

nee|hel/-halah/-haltee ניהל *v* directed; managed; (*pres* **menahel**; *fut* **yenahel**).

neehel (*etc*) **masa oo-matan** ניהל משא ומתן *v* conducted negotiations.

neehool/-eem ניהול *nm* management; (*pl+of:* **-ey**).

neehool masa oo-matan ניהול משא ומתן *nm* conducting negotiations.

neeh|yah/-yetah/-yetee נהיה *v* became; (*pres* **neehyeh**; *fut* **yeehyeh**).

neek|ah/-tah/-eetee ניקה *v* cleaned; (*pres* **menakeh;** *fut* **yenakeh**).

neekah/-tah/-eetee ניכה *v* deducted; discounted; (*pres* **menakeh;** *fut* **yenakeh**).

neekah (*etc*) **shtar/-ot** ניכה שטר *v* discounted a bill.

neekar/-eret ניכר *adj* substantial; noticeable; sizeable.

neek|ar/-rah/-artee ניכר *v* was recognizable; (*pres* **neekar;** *fut* **yookar**).

nee|kayon/-khyonot ניכיון *nm* deduction; discount; (+*of:* **-khyon**).

neek|ayon/-yonot ניקיון *nm* cleanness; cleanliness; (+*of:* **-yon**).

neekb|a'/-e'ah/-a'tee נקבע *v* was set; was fixed; was agreed; (*pres* **neekba';** *fut* **yeekava'** *(v=b)*).

neekbah/nekavot ניקבה *nf* tunnel; (+*of:* **neek|bat/-vot;** *(v=b)*).

neekbat roo'akh ניקבת רוח *nf* wind-tunnel.

neekb|ar/-erah/-artee נקבר *v* was buried; (*pres* **neekbar;** *fut* **yeekaver** *(v=b)*).

neekd|ash/-eshah/-ashtee נקדש *v* was sanctified; (*pres* **neekdash;** *fut* **yekoodash**).

neek|ed/-dah/-adetee ניקד *v* **1.** dotted; **2.** vocalized a Hebrew text by placing vowel-dots under and over the letters; (*pres* **menaked;** *fut* **yenaked**).

neekel ניקל *nm* **1.** nickel; **2.** *[colloq.]* chrome plate.

neek|er/-rah/-artee ניקר *v* pecked; (*pres* **menaker;** *fut* **yenaker**).

(be-meedah) neekeret במידה ניכרת *adv* to a considerable extent.

neek|ev/-vah/-avtee ניקב *v* pierced; punched; perforated; (*pres* **menakev;** *fut* **yenakev**).

neek|ez/-zah/-aztee ניקז *v* drained; (*pres* **menakez;** *fut* **yenakez**).

neekha ניחא *interj* well; so be it.

neekham/-ah/-tee ניחם *v* repented; regretted; (*pres* **neekham;** *fut* **yeenakhem**).

neekhar/-ah ניחר *adj & v 3rd pers sing m* parched (throat).

(garon/gronot) neekhar/-eem גרון ניחר *nm* parched throat.

ne'ekh|az/-zah/-aztee נאחז *v* clung to; seized; (*pres* **ne'ekhaz;** *fut* **ye'akhez**).

ne'ekh|az/-ezet נאחז *adj* holding on to; clinging to.

neekhb|ad/-ah נכבד *adj* honored, respected.

(adon/-eem) neekhbad/-eem אדון נכבד *interj m* Dear Sir.

('almah) neekhbadah עלמה נכבדה *interj f* Dear Miss.

(geveret/gevarot) neekhbad|ah/-ot גברת נכבדה *interj f* Dear Madam.

(ledaber) neekhbadot לדבר נכבדות *v inf* to propose (or discuss) marriage; (*pst* **deeber** *etc; pres* **medaber** *etc; fut* **yedaber** *etc*).

neekh|em/-emah/-amtee ניחם *v* consoled; comforted; (*pres* **menakhem;** *fut* **yenakhem**).

neekh|esh/-ashah/-ashtee ניחש *v* guessed; foretold; (*pres* **menakhesh;** *fut* **yenakhesh**).

neekhekh|ad/-edah/-adetee ניכחד *v* was exterminated; (*pres* **neekhekhad;** *fut* **yeekakhed** *(k=kh)*).

neekhl|a/-e'ah/-etee נכלא *v* was locked up; was imprisoned; (*pres* **neekhla;** *fut* **yeekala**).

neekhl|al/-elah/-altee נכלל *v* **1.** was included; **2.** was incorporated; (*pres* **neekhlal;** *fut* **yeekalel** *(k=kh)*).

neekhlal/-elet נכלל *adj & v pres* included; incorporated; comprised.

neekhl|am/-emah/-amtee נכלם *v* felt ashamed; (*pres* **neekhlam;** *fut* **yeekalem** *(k=kh)*).

neekhl|am/-emet נכלם *adj* abashed.

neekhmeroo rakh|amav/-meha/-may *etc* נכמרו רחמיו/־ה *v pl 3rd pers* he/she/I *etc* had pity on.

neekhn|a'/-e'ah/-a'tee נכנע *v* surrendered; succumbed; (*pres* **neekhna';** *fut* **yeekana'** *(k=kh)*).

neekhna'/-at נכנע *adj* submissive; docile.

neekhn|as/-esah/-astee נכנס *v* entered; came in; (*pres* **neekhnas;** *fut* **yeekanes** *(k=kh)*).

neekhn|as/-eset נכנס *adj* entering; incoming.

neekhnas (*etc*) **be-'ovee ha-korah** נכנס בעובי הקורה *v* entered into details.

neekhn|as/-esah (*etc*) **le-khoopah** נכנס לחופה got married.

neekhnas (*etc*) **le-tokef** נכנס לתוקף *v* came into force; entered into effect.

(tees|ah/-ot) neekhn|eset/-asot טיסה נכנסת *nf* incoming flight.

neekho'akh ניחוח *nm* pleasant scent.

(re'akh) neekho'akh ריח ניחוח *nm* fragrance.

neekhoom/-eem ניחום *nm* condolence; (*pl+of:* **-ey**).

◇ **neekhoom aveleem** ניחום אבלים visiting mourners to console them during **"Sheev'ah"** (i.e. the Seven Days of Mourning).

neekhoosh/-eem ניחוש *nm* guess; (*pl+of:* **-ey**).

(be) neekhoota בניחותא *adv* at ease.

neekhs|af/-efah/-aftee נכסף *v* longed for.

neekhs|af/-efet נכסף *adj* longed for; avidly awaited.

neekhsey de-lo naydee נכסי דלא ניידי *nm pl* real estate; immovable assets.

neekhsey de-naydee נכסי דניידי *nm pl* movable assets; chattels.

◇ **neekhsey neefkadeem** נכסי נפקדים *nm pl* properties of absentees i.e. of Arabs who, in the course of the 1948 hostilities, fled the territory of the newly-formed state preferring evacuation to Israeli rule. Pending a peaceful settlement (in which it is hoped that consideration will be taken also of properties abandoned by Jews who fled to Israel from Arab countries) those properties have been administered by the state ever since.

neekhsh|al/-elah/-altee נכשל *v* failed; stumbles over; (*pres* **neekhshal;** *fut* **yeekashel** *(k=kh)*).

neekhsh|al/-elet נכשל *adj* backward; lagging behind.

neekht|av/-evah/-avtee נכתב *v* was written; (*pres* **neekhtav**; *fut* **yeekatev** *(k=kh)*).

neekhv|ah/-etah/-etee נכווה *v* scalded oneself; sustained burns; (*pres* **neekhveh**; *fut* **yeekaveh** *(k=kh)*).

neekhveh/-t נכווה *adj* burnt; scalded.

neekhveh be-rotkheen נכווה ברותחים *adj* (*figurat.*) scalded with boiling water.

neekl|a'/-e'ah/-a'tee נקלע *v* **1.** was hurled into; **2.** found oneself; (*pres* **neekla'**; *fut* **yekala'**).

neekl|at/-etah/-atetee נקלט *v* was absorbed; struck root; (*pres* **neeklat**; *fut* **yeekalet**).

neeklat (*etc*) נקלט *v* **1.** (of a new immigrant:) assimilated into Israeli society; **2.** found his right place.

neekood ניקוד *nm* **1.** punctuation; **2.** dotting of Hebrew texts with vowel-dots.

neekood ניקוד *nm* (under traffic regulations) negative points on driver's personal record for traffic violations.

neekood khelkee ניקוד חלקי *nm* partial dotting of Hebrew texts (otherwise unvocalized).

neekood male ניקוד מלא *nm* full orthodox dotting of Hebrew texts.

neekoor ניכור *nm* alienation.

neekoor/-eem ניקור *nm* pecking; piercing.

neekoosh 'asaveem ניכוש עשבים *nm* weeding; punching.

neekoov/-eem ניקוב *nm* piercing; perforation; (*pl+of:* **-ey**).

(kartees/-ey) neekoov כרטיס ניקוב *nm* punch-card.

neekooy ניקוי *nm* cleaning.

neekoo|y/-yeem ניכוי *nm* deduction; discount; (*pl+of:* **-yey**).

neekoo|y/-yeem ba-makor ניכוי במקור *nm* deduction at the source (of income-tax).

neekooz/-eem ניקוז *nm* drainage; (*pl+of:* **-ey**).

neekr|a/-e'ah/-e'tee נקרא *v* was called; was read; was recited; (*pres* **neekra**; *fut* **yeekare**).

neekr|a/-e't נקרא *adj* read; readable.

neekr|a'/-e'ah/-a'tee נקרע *v* was torn; was rent; (*pres* **neekra'**; *fut* **yeekara'**).

neekr|ah/-etah/-etee נקרה *v* chanced; happened; (*pres* **neekreh**; *fut* **yeekreh**).

neekr|ah/-ot ניקרה *nf* crevice; cleft; (*+of:* **-at**).

neekyon kapayeem ניקיון כפיים *nm* integrity; incorruptibility.

neekyon shtarot נכיון שטרות *nm* discount; discounting of bills.

neel|'ag/-'eget נלעג *adj* ridiculous; ridiculed.

ne'elakh/-at נאלח *adj* infected; polluted; dirty.

ne'el|am/-emet נאלם **1.** *adj* dumbfounded; **2.** *v pres* (am/is) dumbfounded.

ne'el|am/-mah/-amtee נאלם *v* became silent; was muted; (*pres* **ne'elam**; *fut* **ye'alem**).

ne'el|am/-emet נעלם **1.** *adj* unknown; hidden; **2.** *nmf* unknown (algebr.).

ne'el|am/-mah/-amtee נעלם *v* disappeared; (*pres* **ne'elam**; *fut* **ye'alem**).

ne'el|ats/-tsah/-atstee נאלץ *v* was compelled; (*pres* **ne'elats**; *fut* **ye'alets**).

ne'el|ats/-etset נאלץ **1.** *adj* compelled; forced; **2.** *v pres* (am/is) compelled, forced; (*pst* **ne'elats**; **ye'alets**).

ne'el|av/-vah/-avtee נעלב *v* felt offended; was insulted; (*pres* **ne'elav**; *fut* **ye'alev**).

ne'el|av/-evet נעלב *adj* offended.

neelb|av/-evet נלבב *adj* good-hearted; cordial.

neel'|hav/-hevet נלהב *adj* enthusiastic.

neel'hav/-ah/-tee נלהב *v* was enthused; got excited; (*pres* **neel'hav**; *[colloq.] fut* **yeetlahev**).

□ **Neelee** (Nili) נילי *nm* communal settlement in S. Samaria (est. 1981), 10 km of Ben Gurion Airport. Pop. 329.

neelk|ad/-edah/-adetee נלכד *v* was caught; (*pres* **neelkad**; *fut* **yeelakhed** *(kh=k)*).

neelkham/-ah/-tee נלחם *v* fought; battled; (*pres* **neelkham**; *fut* **yeelakhem**).

neelkh|am/-emet נלחם *adj* fighting; *v pres* fights.

neelv|ah/-etah/-etee נלווה *v* accompanied; (*pres* **neelveh**; *fut* **yeelaveh**).

neelv|eh/-et נלווה *adj* accompanying.

neem|ah/-ot נימה *nf* note; tone; (*+of:* **-at**).

(kee-melo') neemah כמלוא נימה *adv* by a hair's breadth.

ne'eman/-eem נאמן trustee; (*pl+of:* **-ey**).

ne'em|an/-enet (*or:* **-ah**) נאמן *adj* faithful.

('avdekha ha)ne'emanעבדך הנאמן *nm* your obedient servant (addressing female: **'avdekh** *etc*).

(khever) ne'emaneemחבר נאמנים *nm* board of trustees.

ne'emanoo|t/-yot נאמנות *nf* **1.** loyalty; fidelity; **2.** trusteeship.

(keren/karnot) ne'emanoot קרן נאמנות *nf* trust fund.

ne'em|ar/-rah נאמר *v* was said; (*pres* **ne'emar**; *fut* **ye'amer**).

ne'em|ar/-eret נאמר *adj* said; told.

neem'as/-ah/-tee נמאס *v* had enough; was tired of.

neem'as (*etc*) **lee/lekha/lakh/lo/lah** נמאס לי/לך/לו/לה *v* I am /you are /he (she) is (*etc*) sick of...

neem|ek/-kah/-aktee נימק *v* argued; motivated; (*pres* **menamek**; *fut* **yenamek**).

neem|har/-heret נמהר *adj* impetuous.

neemk|ar/-erah/-artee נמכר *v* was sold; sold at; (*pres* **neemkar**; *fut* **yeemakher** *(kh=k)*).

neemk|ar/-eret נמכר *adj* sold; selling at.

neeml|akh/-ekhah/-akhtee נמלך *v* pondered; consulted; (*pres* **neemlakh**; *fut* **yeemalekh**).

neeml|akh/-ekhah/-akhtee נמלח *v* was salted; (*pres* **neemlakh**; **colloq** *fut* **yoomlakh**).

neeml|at/-etah/-atetee נמלט *v* escaped; (*pres* **neemlat**; *fut* **yeemalet**).

neeml|at/-etet נמלט *adj & nmf* fugitive; escaped.

neemn|ah/-etah/-etee נמנה *v* **1.** was counted; **2.** was numbered; (*pres* **neemneh**; *fut* **yeemaneh**).
neemnah (*etc*) **'eem** נמנה עם *v* belonged to; was one of; was counted among.
neemn|a'/-e'ah/-a'tee נמנע *v* refrained; abstained; (*pres* **neemna'** *etc; fut* **yeemana'** *etc*).
neemn|eh/-et 'eem נמנה עם *adj* counting with; counting among.
neemn|em/-emah/-amtee נימנם *v* dozed; drowsed; (*pres* **menamnem**; *fut* **yenamnem**).
neemnoo ve-gamroo נימנו וגמרו *v 3rd pers pl* (they) reached a conclusion; made up their mind.
neemnoom/-eem נימנום *nm* nap; doze; (*pl+of:* **-ey**).
neemol/-eem נימול *adj* circumcised.
neemol/-ta/-tee נימול *v* underwent circumcision; (*inf* **leheemol**; *pres* **neemol**; *fut* **yeemol**).
(ha-rakh ha) neemol הרך הנימול *nm* the baby being circumcised.
neemook נימוק *nm* reason; motive; (*pl+of:* **-ey**).
neemoos נימוס *nm* politeness.
neemoosee/-t נימוסי *adj* polite.
neemooseem נימוסים *nm pl* manners; (*+of:* **-ey**).
neemooseen נימוסין *nm pl* manners.
neemr|ats/-etset נמרץ *adj* vigorous; energetic.
neemratsot נמרצות *adv* emphatically.
neems|ar/-erah/-artee נמסר *v* **1.** was remitted; **2.** was delivered; (*pres* **neemsar**; *fut* **yeemaser**).
neems|ar/-eret נמסר *adj* handed over; reported.
(kefee ha) neemsar כפי הנמסר as it is being reported.
neemsh|ah/-etah/-etee נימשה *v* was drawn out (of the water); (*pres* **neemsheh**; *fut* **yeemasheh**).
neemsh|akh/-ekhah/-akhtee נמשך *v* **1.** was attracted; **2.** lasted; continued; (*pres* **neemshakh**; *fut* **yeemashekh**).
neemsh|akh/-ekhet נמשך **1.** *adj* continuous; continued; **2.** *v pres* continues; lasts.
neemt|akh/-ekhah/-akhtee נמתח *v* was stretched; (*pres* **neemtakh**; *fut* **yeematakh**).
neemtakh/-at נמתח **1.** *adj* elastic; **2.** *v pres* stretches.
neemtakh (*etc*) נמתח *v [slang]* was object of practical joke.
neemts|a/-e'ah/-e'tee נמצא *v* **1.** was found; **2.** was established; (*pres* **neemtsa**; *fut* **yeematse**).
neemts|a/-e't נמצא **1.** *adj* existing; available; **2.** *v pres* (*etc*) exist(s); **can be found;(am/is) to be found at.**
(barookh/brookhah ha) neemts|a/-e't! ברוך הנמצא! (greeting) response to the welcoming greeting barookh ha-ba'! ברוך הבא!.
(be) neemtsa' בנמצא *adv* available.
neen/-eem נין *nm* great-grandson; (*pl:* **-ey**).
ne'en|akh/-khah/-akhtee נאנח *v* sighed; (*pres* **ne'enakh**; *fut* **ye'anakh**).
ne'enakh/-at נאנח **1.** *adj* sighing; **2.** *v pres* sighs.
ne'en|as/-sah/-astee נאנס *v* **1.** was raped; **2.** was compelled; (*pres* **ne'enas**; *fut* **ye'anes**).
ne'en|as/-eset נאנס **1.** *adj* raped; **2.** *v pres* (am/is) raped; **3.** *v pres* (am/is) compelled.
nee'n|a'/-'ah/-a'tee (*or:* **nee'n|e'a'** *etc*) ניענע *v* nodded; shook; (*pres* **mena'ne'a'**; *fut* **yena'ne'a'**).
ne'en|eset/-asot נאנסת *nf* rape victim.
neeno|'akh/-khah נינוח *adj* relaxed.
nee'oof/-eem ניאוף *nm* adultery; fornication; (*pl+of:* **-ey**).
nee'oor ניעור *nm* shaking up.
neep|ah/-tah/-eetee ניפה *v* sifted; selected; cleaned up; (*pres* **menapeh**; *fut* **yenapeh**).
neep|akh/-khah/-akhtee (*or:* **neep|e'akh**) ניפח *v* **1.** inflated; **2.** *[colloq.]* exaggerated; (*pres* **menape'akh**; *fut* **yenape'akh**).
neep|ek/-kah/-aktee ניפק *v* issued (equipment) (emitted shares; debentures); (*pres* **menapek**; *fut* **yenapek**).
neep|ets/-tsah/-atstee ניפץ *v* smashed; shattered; (*pres* **menapets**; *fut* **yenapets**).
neepoo|'akh/-kheem ניפוח *nm* inflating; exaggerating; (*pl+of:* **-ey**).
neepoots/-eem ניפוץ *nm* shattering; (*pl+of:* **-ey**).
neepoo|y/-yeem ניפוי *nm* sifting; selection; (*pl+of:* **-yey**).
neer/-eem ניר *nm* furrow; ploughed field; (*pl+of:* **-ey**).
□ **Neer 'Akeeva** (Nir Aqiva) ניר עקיבא *nm* collective village (est. 1953) in NW Negev, 6 km NE of Netivot Junction (**Tsomet Neteevot**). Pop. 220.
□ **Neer'am** (Nir'am) נירעם *nm* kibbutz (est. 1943) in NW Negev, 2 km W. of **Sderot**. Pop. 377.
□ **Neer Baneem** (Nir Banim) ניר בנים *nm* village (est. 1954) in Lachish (**Lakheesh**) area, 7 km S. of Mal'akhi Junction (**Tsomet Mal'akhee**). Pop. 273.
□ **Neer Daveed** (Nir Dawid) ניר דוד *nm* kibbutz (originally est 1936 under the name of **Tel 'Amal** תל-עמל), 3 km W. of **Bet-She'an**. Pop. 712.
□ **Neer Eleeyahoo** (Nir Eliyyahu) ניר אליהו *nm* kibbutz (est. 1950) in Sharon, 4 km NE of Kefar-Sava. Pop. 357.
□ **Neer 'Etsyon** (**Nir Ezyon**) ניר עציון *nm* collective village (est. 1950) in Carmel hills, 4 km SE of Zikhron Ya'aqov Junction (**Tsomet Zeekhron Ya'akov**) near 'En Hod. Pop. 794.
□ **Neer Galeem** (Nir Gallim) ניר גלים *nm* village (est. 1949) in N. outskirts of **Ashdod**, near the Mediterranean shore. Pop. 513.
□ **Neer Khen** (Nir Hen) ניר ח"ן *nm* village (est. 1956) in **Lakheesh** area, 5 km W. of **Keeryat Gat**. Pop. 271.

□ **Neer Mosheh** (Nir Moshe) ניר משה *nm* village (est. 1953) in NW Negev, 4 km SE of **Sderot**. Pop. 184.

□ **Neer 'Oz** (Nir Oz) ניר עוז *nm* kibbutz (est. 1959) in NW Negev, 5 km NW of Magen Junction **(Tsomet Magen)**. Pop. 416.

□ **Neer Tsvee** (Nir Zevi) ניר צבי *nm* village (est. 1954) known earlier as the "Argentinian village", 2 km NW of Ramla. Pop. 682.

□ **Neer Yafeh** (Nir Yafe) ניר יפה *nm* village (est. 1956) in the Yizre'el Valley, 5 km E. of Meggido Junction **(Tsomet Megeedo)**. Pop. 300.

□ **Neer Yeesra'el** (Nir Yisra'el) ניר ישראל *nm* village (est. 1949) in S. seashore plain, 6 km E. of Ashkelon. Pop. 386.

□ **Neer Yeetskhak** (Nir Yizhaq) ניר יצחק *nm* kibbutz (est. 1949) in NW Negev, 8 km SW of Magen Junction **(Tsomet Magen)**. Pop. 553.

neer|'ah/-'atah/-'etee נראה *v* was seen; (*pres* **neer'eh**; *fut* **yera'eh**).

ne'er|akh/-khah/-akhtee נערך *v* **1.** was arranged; **2.** was edited; **3.** was estimated; **4.** was held; took place; (*pres* **ne'erakh**; *fut* **ye'arekh**).

ne'erakh/-ekhet נערך **1.** *adj* taking place; **2.** *v pres* (*etc*) takes place; is edited.

ne'er|am/-mah/-amtee נערם *v* was piled up; (*pres* **ne'eram**; *fut* **ye'arem**).

ne'er|am/-emet נערם **1.** *adj* piled up; **2.** *v pres* is being piled up.

neer'ash/-ah/-tee נרעש *v* **1.** was agitated; **2.** was shaken, shocked.

neer|'ash/-'eshet נרעש *adj* shaken; shocked.

neerd|af/-efah/-aftee נרדף *v* was harassed; was persecuted; (*pres* **neerdaf**; *fut* **yeradef**).

neerd|af/-efet נרדף **1.** *adj* harassed; persecuted; **2.** *v pres* (am/is) harassed, persecuted.

(shem/-ot) neerdaf/-eem שם נרדף *nm* synonym.

neerd|am/-emah/-amtee נרדם *v* fell asleep; (*pres* **neerdam**; *fut* **yeradem**).

neerd|am/-emet נרדם **1.** *adj* sleepy; asleep; **2.** *v pres* is falling asleep.

□ **Neereem** (Nirim) נירים *nm* kibbutz (est. 1946) in NW Negev, 5 km NW of **Tsomet Ma'on** (Ma'on Junction). Pop. 419.

neer|'eh/-'et נראה **1.** *adj* visible; apparent; seen; **2.** *v pres* is seen.

(ka) neer'eh כנראה *adv* as it seems.

(ke) neer'eh כנראה *adv* apparently.

neerg|a'/-e'ah/-a'tee נרגע *v* calmed down; (*pres* **neerga'**; *fut* **yeraga'**).

neerg|an/-enet נרגן *adj* grumbling.

neerg|ash/-eshah/-ashtee נרגש *v* was moved; was excited.

neerg|ash/-eshet נרגש *adj* moved; excited.

neerg|az/-ezet נרגז **1.** *adj* annoyed; upset; **2.** *v pres* is annoyed, upset; (*pst* **neergaz**; *fut* **yeetragez**).

neerk|ash/-eshah/-ashtee נרכש *v* was acquired, acquisitioned; (*pres* **neerkash**; *fut* **yerakhesh**; *(kh=k)*).

neerk|ash/-eshet נרכש **1.** *adj* acquired; **2.** *v pres* (*etc*) is acquired.

neerk|av/-evah/-avtee נרקב *v* rotted; became rotten; (*pres* **neerkav**; *fut* **yerakev**).

neerkh|av/-evet נרחב *adj* wide; spacious.

(kar) neerkhav כר נרחב *nm* ample space; ample opportunities.

neerp|a/-e'ah/-e'tee נרפא *v* recovered; was cured; (*pres* **neerpa**; *fut* **yerafe**; *(f=p)*).

neersh|am/-emah/-amtee נרשם *v* registered; was noted down; (*pres* **neersham**; *fut* **yerashem**).

neert|a'/-e'ah/-a'tee נרתע *v* recoiled; was startled; (*pres* **neerta'**; *fut* **yerata'**).

neerta'/-at נרתע **1.** *adj* recoiling; startling; **2.** *v pres* (*etc*) **recoils; startles.**

neert|av/-evah/-avtee נרטב *v* got wet; (*pres* **neertav**; *fut* **yeratev**).

neertsakh/-at נרצח *adj* murdered.

neerts|akh/-ekhah נרצח *v* was murdered; (*pres* **neertsakh**; *fut* **yeratsakh**).

nees|a/-'ah/-e'tee נישא *v* got married; (*pres* **neesa**; *fut* **yeenase**).

nees|a/-e't נישא *adj* **1.** marrying; getting married; **2.** carried.

(ram ve-) neesa רם ונישא *adj* high and mighty.

nees|ah/-tah/-eetee ניסה *v* tried; attempted; (*pres* **menaseh**; *fut* **yenaseh**).

ne'es|ah/-tah/-etee (*npr* **na'asah**) נעשה *v* **1.** was done; **2.** has become; (*pres* **na'aseh**; *fut* **ye'aseh**).

ne'es|af/-fah/-aftee נאסף *v* was collected; assembled; (*pres* **ne'esaf**; *fut* **ye'asef**).

ne'es|af/-efet נאסף **1.** *adj* assembled; collected; **2.** *v pres* is collected, assembled.

nees|akh/-khah/-akhtee ניסח *v* drafted; formulated; (*pres* **menase'akh**; *fut* **yenase'akh**).

◇ **Neesan** ניסן *nm* 7th Jewish calendar month, the month in which Passover occurs; 30 days (approximately March-April).

ne'es|ar/-rah/-artee נאסר *v* **1.** was arrested; **2.** was prohibited; (*pres* **ne'esar**; *fut* **ye'aser**).

nees'ar/-ah/-tee נסער *v* was enraged; was excited; (*pres* **nees'ar**; *fut* **yeesa'er**).

nees|'ar/-'eret נסער **1.** *adj* enraged; excited; **2.** *v pres* is enraged; is excited.

nees|ayon/-yonot ניסיון *nm* experience; (*+of:* **-yon**).

('am|ad/-dah/-adetee be) neesayon עמד בניסיון *v* stood the test; (*pres* **'omed** *etc*; *fut* **ya'amod** *etc*).

(az'ak|at/-ot) neesayon אזעקת ניסיון *nf* alarm-test.

(ba'al/-at) neesayon בעל ניסיון **1.** *adj* experienced; **2.** *nmf* person of experience.

('oved/-et be) neesayon עובד בניסיון *nmf* holder of a job during probation period.

(rakh|ash/-shah/-ashtee) neesayon רכש ניסיון *v* gained experience; **(***pres* **rokhesh** *etc; fut* **yeerkosh** *etc k=kh***)**.

(shfan/-ey) neesayon שפן ניסיון *nm* guinea pig.

(tkoof|at/-ot) neesayon תקופת ניסיון *nf* probation period.

neesb|al/-elah/-altee נסבל *v* was tolerated.

neesb|al/-elet נסבל **1.** *adj* tolerable; **2.** *v pres* is being tolerated.

(beeltee) neesb|al/elet בלתי נסבל *adj* intolerable; not to be tolerated.

neesd|ak/-ekah/-aktee נסדק *v* cracked; **(***pres* **neesdak;** *fut* **yeesadek)**.

neeseem נסים *nm pl* (sing: nes) miracles.

neeseem ve-neefla'ot נסים ונפלאות *nm pl* (fig. & mostly ironic.) wonders and miracles.

(ma'as|eh/-ey) neeseem מעשה נסים *nm* sheer miracle.

nees|er/-rah/-artee ניסר *v* sawed; sawed up; **(***pres* **menaser;** *fut* **yenaser)**.

neesg|ar/-erah/-artee נסגר *v* closed; **(***pres* **neesgar;** *fut* **yeesager)**.

neesgav/-evet נשגב *adj* sublime; exalted.

neesgav me-beenat|ee/-o/-ah נשגב מבינתי/־ו/־ה it is beyond my/his/her **(***etc***)** comprehension.

neesh'al/-ah/-altee נשאל *v* **1.** was asked; was questioned; **2.** was borrowed (an object to be returned, not money); **(***pres* **neesh'al;** *fut* **yeesha'el)**.

(ha) ne'esham/-eem הנאשם *nm* **(***f:* **ne'esh|emet/-amot)** the accused.

ne'esh|am/-emet נאשם **1.** *adj* accused of; **2.** *v pres* (am/is) accused of (*etc* below).

ne'esh|am/-mah/-amtee נאשם *v* was accused of; **(***pres* **ne'esham;** *fut* **ye'ashem)**.

neesh'an/-ah/-tee נשען *v* leaned on; got support from; **(***pres* **neesh'an;** *fut* **yeesha'en)**.

neesh'ar/-ah/-tee נשאר *v* remained; was left; **(***pres* **neesh'ar;** *fut* **yeesha'er)**.

neesh|'ar/-eret נשאר **1.** *adj* remaining; left; **2.** *v pres* **(***etc***)** remains.

neesh'av/-ah/-tee נשאב *v* was pumped; was drawn; **(***pres* **neesh'av;** *fut* **yeesha'ev)**.

neesh|'av/-evet נשאב **1.** *adj* pumped; drawn; **2.** *v pres* is pumped; is drawn.

neeshb|a'/-e'ah/-a'tee נשבע *v* swore; vowed; **(***pres* **neeshba';** *fut* **yeeshava'** *(v=b)***)**.

neeshba'/-at נשבע **1.** *adj* swearing; **2.** *v pres* swears.

neeshb|ar/-erah/-artee נשבר *v* broke; was broken; **(***pres* **neeshbar;** *fut* **yeeshaver** *(v=b)***)**.

neeshb|ar/-eret נשבר **1.** *adj* breaking; **2.** *v pres* breaks.

neeshbar lee/lo/lah נשבר לי/־ו/־ה *[colloq.]* I/he/she **(***etc***)** cannot take it any longer; had enough.

(ke-kheres ha) neeshbar כחרס הנשבר *adv* futile, like a broken shard.

neeshd|ad/-edah/-adetee נשדד *v* was robbed; **(***pres* **neeshdad;** *fut* **yeeshaded)**.

neesh|ek/-kah/-aktee נישק *v* kissed; **(***pres* **menashek;** *fut* **yenashek)**.

neesh|el/-lah/-altee נישל *v* dispossessed; dislodged; **(***pres* **menashel;** *fut* **yenashel)**.

neeshfee|yah (*npr* **neeshpee|yah)/-yot** נשפייה *nf* party (private ball); **(***+of:* **-yat)**.

neeshk|af/-efah/-aftee נשקף *v* was seen; was imminent; **(***pres* **neeshkaf;** *fut* **yeeshakef)**.

neeshk|af/-efet נשקף *adj* seen; visible; imminent.

neeshk|al/-elah/-altee נשקל *v* was weighed; was pondered; **(***pres* **neeshkal;** *fut* **yeeshakel)**.

neeshkav/-evah/-avtee נשכב *v* lay down; **(***pres* **neeshkav;** *fut* **yeeshakev)**.

neeshk|av/-evet נשכב **1.** *adj* lying down; **2.** *v pres* lies down.

neeshkhak/-ah/-tee נשחק *v* **1.** was ground to dust; **2.** was worn out; **3.** fig: was depreciated; **(***pres* **neeshkhak;** *fut* **yeeshakhek)**.

neeshl|akh/-ekhah/-akhtee נשלח was sent; was dispatched; **(***pres* **neeshlakh;** *fut* **yeeshalakh)**.

neeshl|al/-elah/-altee נשלל *v* **1.** was denied, deprived of, negated; **2.** was taken away; **(***pres* **neeshlal;** *fut* **yeeshalel)**.

neeshl|am/-emah נשלם *v* was completed; **(***pres* **neeshlam;** *colloq. fut* **yooshlam)**.

(tam/-ah- ve) neeshl|am/-emah תם ונשלם *adv* over and done with.

neeshl|at/-etah/-atetee נשלט *v* was dominated; **(***pres* **neeshlat;** *fut* **yeeshalet)**.

neeshl|at/-etet נשלט **1.** *adj* dominated; **2.** *v pres* (am/is) dominated.

neshm|a'/-e'ah/-a'tee נשמע *v* sounded; was heard; **(***pres* **neeshma';** *fut* **yeeshama')**.

(ma) neeshma'? מה נשמע? *query* what's new? what's going on?

neeshm|ad/-edah/-adetee נשמד *v* was devastated, annihilated; **(***pres* **neeshmad;** *fut* **yeeshamed)**.

neeshm|ar/-erah/-artee נשמר *v* was guarded; was careful; **(***pres* **neeshmar;** *fut* **yeeshamer)**.

neeshm|ar/-eret נשמר *adj* guarded; abstaining from.

neeshm|at/-etah/-atetee נשמט *v* was omitted; slipped from; **(***pres* **neeshmat;** *fut* **yeeshamet)**.

neeshmat|o/-ah 'eden נשמתו/־ה עדן may he/she rest in peace.

(naf|akh/-khah) neeshmat|o/-ah נפח נשמתו/־ה *v* breathed his/her last.

neeshn|ah/-etah/-etee נישנה *v* recurred; was repeated; **(***pres* **neeshneh;** *fut* **yeeshaneh)**.

(khaz|ar/-rah ve) neeshn|ah/-etah חזר ונישנה *v* happened all over again.

neeshn|eh/-et נישנה **1.** *adj* recurred; repeated; **2.** *v pres* **(***etc***) repeats itself; recurs.**

(khozer/-et ve) neeshn|eh/-et חוזר ונישנה *adj* repeating itself again and again.

neeshom/-ah/-tee נישום *v* was assessed (for taxation purposes); **(***pres* **neeshom;** *fut* **yeeshom)**.

neeshom/-ah נישום *nmf* taxpayer to be assessed; (*+of:* **-at/-ey**).

neeshool/-eem נישול *nm* dispossession; eviction.

neeshp|akh/-ekhah/-akhtee נשפך *v* was spilled; was shed; (*pres* **neeshpakh**; *fut* **yeeshafekh** *(f=p)*).

neeshp|at/-etah/-atetee נשפט *v* **1.** was tried; **2.** was sentenced; (*pres* **neeshpat**; *fut* **yeeshafet** *(f=p)*).

neeshp|at/-etet נשפט *adj* on trial; having a law-suit.

neeshpee|yah/-yot נשפייה *nf* party (private ball); (*+of:* **-yat**).

neeshtan|ah/-tah/-etee נשתנה *v* changed; became different; (*pres* **meeshtaneh**; *fut* **yeeshstaneh**).

◇ **(mah) neeshtanah?** see ◇ **mah neeshtanah?**

neeshtat|ek/-kah/-aktee נשתתק *v* calmed down; became silent; (*pres* **meeshtatek**; *fut* **yeeshtatek**).

neesk|al/-elah/-altee נסקל *v* was stoned; (*pres* **neeskal**; *fut* **yeesakel**).

neesk|ar/-erah/-artee נשכר *v* was hired; (*pres* **neeskar**; *fut* **yeesakher** *(kh=k)*).

neesk|ar/-erah/-artee נסקר *v* was surveyed; was reviewed; (*pres* **neeskar**; *fut* **yeesaker**).

(yats|a/-'ah) neesk|ar/-eret יצא נשכר got his/her reward in the end; (*pres* **yotse** *etc*; *fut* **yetse** *etc*).

neeskhar/-ah נסחר *v* was traded; was negotiated; (*pres* **neeskhar**; *fut* **yeesakher**).

neeskh|ar/-eret נסחר **1.** *adj* traded; **2.** *v pres* is traded, negotiated.

neeskh|av/-evah/-avtee נסחב *v* **1.** was dragged; was drawn along; **2.** *[colloq.]* dragged out along; (*pres* **neeskhav**; *fut* **yeesakhev**).

neeskh|av/-evet נסחב *adj* being dragged out.

neesl|akh/-ekhah/-akhtee נסלח *v* was forgiven; (*pres* **neeslakh**; *fut* **yeesalakh**).

neesl|al/-elah נסלל *v* was paved (way); (*pres* **neeslal**; *fut* **yeesalel**).

neesm|akh/-ekhah/-akhtee נסמך *v* was supported; leaned on; (*pres* **neesmakh**; *fut* **yeesamekh**).

neesm|akh/-ekhet נסמך **1.** *adj* supported by; **2.** *v pres* (*etc*) (am/is) supported by.

◇ **neesmakh** נסמך *nm (Gram)* a noun in the construct state i.e., the head noun of a compound noun phrase (as if it were followed by "of" in English).

neesoo'akh/-kheem ניסוח *nm* phrasing; wording; formulation; (*pl+of:* **-ey**).

neesoo'eem נישואים *pl* marriage; matrimony; (*+of:* **neesoo'ey**).

(taba'at) neesoo'eem טבעת נישואים *nf* wedding ring.

neesoo'ey boser נישואי בוסר *nm pl* precocious marriage.

◇ **neesoo'ey kafreeseen** נישואי קפריסין *nm pl* marriage contracted in Cyprus or anywhere outside Israel where a civil marriage can be performed. This is resorted to when a religious wedding, the only kind permitted in Israel, cannot be performed.

◇ **neesoo'ey Mekseeko** נישואי מקסיקו *nm pl* marriage contracted through proxy (obtaining registration in Mexico).

neesoo|y/-yeem ניסוי *nm* test; experiment; (*pl+of:* **-yey**).

neesooyee/-t ניסויי *adj* experimental.

neesp|ah/-etah/-etee ניספה *v* perished; met one's death; (*pres* **neespeh**; *fut* **yeesafeh** *(f=p)*).

neespah (*etc*) **ba-sho'ah** ניספה בשואה *v* perished in the Holocaust.

neespakh/-eem נספח *nm* **1.** enclosure; annex; **2.** diplomatic attaché; (*pl+of:* **-ey**).

neespakh/-eem tseva'ee/-yeem נספח צבאי *nm* Military Attahé.

neespakh/-at le-'eenyeney... ...נספח לענייני *nmf* Attaché for ... Affairs.

neesp|akh/-ekhah/-akhtee נספח *v* was added; was attached; (*pres* **neespakh**; *fut* **yeesafakh** *(f=p)*).

neesp|ar/-erah/-artee נספר *v* was counted; (*pres* **neespar**; *fut* **yeesafer** *(f=p)*).

neest|ar/-erah/-artee נסתר *v* **1.** was hidden, concealed; **2.** was refuted; (*pres* **neestar**; *fut* **yeesater**).

neest|ar/-eret נסתר *adj* hidden; unseen.

neesta|yem/-ymah/-yamtee נסתיים *v* ended; (*pres* **meestayem**; *fut* **yeestayem**).

neesyonee/-t נסיוני *adj* experimental.

neet|ak/-kah/-aktee ניתק *v* was cut off; was removed; (*pres* **neetak**; *fut* **yeenatek**).

ne'et|ak/-kah/-aktee נעתק *v* was displaced; (*pres* **ne'etak**; *fut* **ye'atek**).

neet|akh/-khah/-akhtee ניתח *v* **1.** operated (surgery); **2.** analyzed (*pres* **menate'akh**; *fut* **yenate'akh**).

neet|akh/-khah ניתך *v* poured; melted.

neet|al/-lah/-altee ניטל *v* was removed; was lilted up; (*pres* **neetal**; *fut* **yeenatel**).

neet|an/-nah ניתן *v* was given; (*pres* **neetan**; *fut* **yeenaten**).

neetan ניתן *v pres 3rd pers sing* it is feasible.

(lo) neetan לא ניתן it is not feasible; cannot be done.

neet'an/-ah/-tee נטען *v* **1.** was loaded; was charged (weapon); **2.** has been argued; (*pres* **neet'an**; *fut* **yeeta'en**).

ne'et|ar/-rah/-artee נעתר *v* granted request; agreed; (*pres* **ne'etar**; *fut* **ye'ater**).

ne'etar (*etc*) **le-** נעתר ל- *v* responded to; condescended.

ne'et|ar/-rah/-artee נעטר *v* was adorned; was crowned; (*pres* **ne'etar**; *fut* **ye'ater**).

ne'et|ar/-rah be-hatslakhah נעטר בהצלחה *v* was crowned with success.

neet|ash/-shah ניתש *v* was evicted; was ousted.

neet|ash/-eshet ניתש *adj* raging.

neetash (*etc*) **krav** ניתש קרב *nm* a battle developed; a battle raged.

neetashtesh/-ah ניטשטש *v* faded; was obliterated; (*pres* **meetashtesh;** *fut* **yeetashtesh**).

neet|'av/-'evet נתעב *adj* despicable; abominable.

neetb|a'/-e'ah/-a'tee נתבע *v* **1.** was called upon; **2.** was sued; (*pres* **neetba';** *fut* **yeetava'**).

(ha) neetb|a'/-at הנתבע *nmf* respondent; (*pl:* **-a'eem/-a'ot;** *+of:* **-e'ey**).

neet|e'akh/-khah/-akhtee ניתח *v* **1.** operated (surgery) **2.** analyzed; (*pres* **menate'akh;** *fut* **yenate'akh**).

neet|ek/-kah/-aktee ניתק *v* cut off; removed; (*pres* **menatek;** *fut* **yenatek**).

neet|er/-rah/-artee ניתר *v* hopped; bounced; (*pres* **menater;** *fut* **yenater**).

neetk|a'/-e'ah/-a'tee נתקע *v* was stuck; got stuck; (*pres* **neetka';** *fut* **yeetaka'**).

neetkab|el/-lah/-altee נתקבל *v* was received; was accepted; (*pres* **meetkabel;** *fut* **yeetkabel**).

neetk|al/-elah/-altee נתקל *v* bumped into; (*pres* **neetkal;** *fut* **yeetakel**).

neetkam|et/-tah/-atetee נתקמט *v* became wrinkled, creased; (*pres* **meetkamet;** *fut* **yeetkamet**).

neetkan|es/-sah/-astee נתכנס *v* gathered; assembled; (*pres* **meetkanes;** *fut* **yeetkanes**).

neetkas|ah/-tah/-etee נתכסה *v* was covered up; (*pres* **meetkaseh;** *fut* **yeetkaseh**).

neetkaz|ez/-ezah/-aztee נתקזז *v* was set off; (*pres* **meetkazez;** *fut* **yeetkazez**).

neetkhav|er/-rah/-artee נתחוור *v* became evident; (*pres* **meetkhaver;** *fut* **yeetkhaver**).

neetl|ah/-etah/-etee נתלה *v* was hanged; (*pres* **neetleh;** *fut* **yeetaleh**).

neetl|eh/-t נתלה **1.** *adj* hung; hanging; **2.** *v pres* is hanging; (*pst* **neetlah;** *fut* **yeetaleh**).

neetm|a'/-e'ah/-a'tee ניטמע *v* was assimilated (*pres* **neetma';** *fut* **yeetama'**).

neetm|akh/-ekhah/-akhtee נתמך *v* was supported, upheld; (*pres* **neetmakh;** *fut* **yeetamekh**).

neetmal|e/-'ah/-'etee נתמלא *v* **1.** was filled; **2.** was granted (request); (*pres* **meetmale;** *fut* **yeetmale**).

neetm|an/-enah/-antee נטמן *v* was hidden, concealed; (*pres* **neetman;** *fut* **yeetamen**).

neetmaz|eg/-gah/-agtee נתמזג *v* blended; formed a synthesis; (*pres* **meetmazeg;** *fut* **yeetmazeg**).

neetmaz|el/-lah/-altee נתמזל *v* was fortunate; was lucky; (*pres* **meetmazel;** *fut* **yeetmazel**).

neetmazel mazal|o/-ah/-ee נתמזל מזלו *v* had the good fortune.

neetoo|'akh/kheem ניתוח **1.** *nm* surgical operation; **2.** *nm* analysis; (*pl+of:* **-khey**).

neetoo'akh (*etc*) **kesaree** ניתוח קיסרי *nm* Caesarian section.

neetoo'akh ma'arakhot ניתוח מערכות *nm* systems analysis.

neetoo'akh (*etc*) **plastee** ניתוח פלסטי *nm* plastic surgery.

neetook/-eem ניתוק *nm* disconnection; breaking; disruption; (*pl+of:* **-ey**).

neetook yekhaseem ניתוק יחסים *nm* breaking off of (diplomatic) relations.

neetoots ניתוץ *nm* destruction; demolition.

neetoov/-eem ניתוב *nm* routing; tracking.

neetp|al/-elah/-altee נטפל *v* stuck to; *[slang]* pestered; (*pres* **neetpal;** *fut* **yeetapel**).

neetp|al/-elet נטפל **1.** *adj* sticking; stuck; **2.** *[slang]* pestering; **3.** *v pres [slang]* pesters.

neetp|as/-esah/-astee נתפש or: נתפס *v* **1.** was caught, seized; **2.** was perceived; (*pres* **neetpas;** *fut* **yeetafes;** (*f=p*).

neetp|as/-eset נתפס or: נתפש *adj* **1.** caught; seized; **2.** perceived.

neetr|ad/-edah/-adetee ניטרד *v* was troubled; was disturbed; (*pres* **neetrad;** *fut* **yeetared**).

neetr|af/-efah/-aftee ניטרף *v* was preyed upon, torn to pieces, devoured: (*pres* **neetraf;** *fut* **yeetaref**).

neetraf/-efet akhrey ניטרף אחרי *[colloq.] adj* mad about.

neetrak|ekh/-'khah/-akhtee נתרכך *v* softened up; (*pres* **meetrakekh;** *fut* **yeetrakekh**).

neetrash|em/-mah/-amtee נתרשם *v* got the impression; was impressed; (*pres* **meetrashem;** *fut* **yeetrashem**).

neetrosh|esh/-eshah/-ashtee נתרושש *v* was impoverished; (*pres* **meetroshesh;** *fut* **yeetroshesh**).

neetrat|e'akh/-khah/-akhtee נתרתח *v* was excited; was enraged; (*pres* **meetrate'akh;** *fut* **yeetrate'akh**).

neetr|el/-elah/-altee ניטרל *v* neutralized; (*pres* **menatrel;** *fut* **yenatrel**).

neetrool/-eem ניטרול *nm* neutralization.

neets|akh/-khah/-akhtee 'al ניצח על *v* conducted (orchestra); (*pres* **menatse'akh 'al;** *fut* **yenatsakh 'al**).

neets|akh/-khah/-akhtee et ניצח את *v* defeated; vanquished; (*pres* **menatse'akh et;** *fut* **yenatsakh et**).

neets|akhon/-khonot ניצחון *nm* victory; (*+of:* **-khon**).

(nakh|al/-lah/-altee) neetsakhon נחל ניצחון *v* scored a victory; (*pres* **nokhel** *etc; fut* **yeenkhal** *etc*).

neets|al/-lah/-altee ניצל *v* escaped; was saved; (*pres* **neetsal;** *fut* **yeenatsel**).

□ **Neetsanah (Nizzana)** ניצנה *nm* **1.** crossing-point from Israel into Egypt where S. Negev borders on Sinai; **2.** Site of excavated remnants of old Nabatean-Byzantine city.

□ **(Kefar Ha-no'ar) Neetsaneem** see □ **Kefar Ha-no'ar Neetsaneem**.

□ **Neetsaneem-kvootsah** ניצנים־קבוצה *nm* kibbutz of **"kvootsah"** type (est. 1943) on coastal plain, 7 km NE of Ashkelon. Pop. 370.

□ **Neetsaney 'Oz** (Nizzanné Oz) נצני עוז *nm* village on borderline between Sharon and Samaria (est. 1951), 3 km W. of **Toolkarem**. Pop. 348.

ne'ets|ar/-eret נעצר **1.** *adj* detained; arrested; **2.** *nmf* detainee.

ne'ets|ar/-rah/-artee נעצר *v* **1.** was arrested, detained; **2.** was stopped; (*pres* **ne'etsar**; *fut* **ye'atser**).

neets|at/-tah ניצת *v* was kindled; caught fire; (*pres* **neetsat**; *fut* **yootsat**).

neets|av/-vah/-avtee ניצב *v* stood; (*pres* **neetsav**; *fut* **yeet'yatsev**).

neets|av/-evet ניצב *adj* **1.** perpendicular; **2.** standing.

neetsav/-eem ניצב *nm* **1.** extra (in a theater); **2.** Major-General of Police.

(rav-) neetsav רב ניצב *nm* commissioner of police.

(tat/-ey) neetsav/-eem תת־ניצב *nm* Brigadeer-General of Police.

ne'ets|av/-vah/-avtee נעצב *v* felt sad; was saddened; (*pres* **ne'etsav**; *fut* **ye'atsev**).

neetse'akh/-khah/-akhtee 'al ניצח על *v* conducted (orchestra, work); (*pres* **menatse'akh 'al**; *fut* **yenatse'akh 'al**).

neets|e'akh/-khah/-akhtee et ניצח את *v* defeated; vanquished; (*pres* **menatse'akh et**; *fut* **yenatse'akh et**).

neets|el/-lah/-altee ניצל *v* made use of; utilized; exploited; (*pres* **menatsel**; *fut* **yenatsel**).

neetsel (*etc*) **heezdamnoo|t/-yot** ניצל הזדמנות *v* grasped opportunity.

neetskhee/-t נצחי *adj* eternal.

neetsl|ah/-etah/-etee נצלה was scorched; (*pres* **neetsleh**; *fut* **yeetsaleh**).

neetsl|av/-evah/-avtee נצלב *v* was crucified; (*pres* **neetslav**; *fut* **yeetsalev**).

neetsm|ad/-edah/-adetee נצמד *v* clung; adhered; (*pres* **neetsmad**; *fut* **yeetsamed**).

neetsm|ad/-edet נצמד *adj* clinging; adhering.

neetsn|ets/-etsah/-atstee נצנץ *v* flashed; gleamed; (*pres* **menatsnets**; *fut* **yenatsnets**).

neetsnets (*etc*) **ra'ayon** נצנץ רעיון *v* an idea flashed; was struck by an idea.

neetsnoots/-eem נצנוץ *nm* flash; flickering; (*pl+of*: **-ey**).

neetsod/-ah/-etee ניצוד *v* was trapped; was hunted down; (*pres* **neetsod**; *fut* **yeetsod**).

neetsol/-ah ניצול *nmf* survivor (*pl*: **-eem/-ot**; *+of*: **-at/-ey**).

◇ **neetsol/-at sho'ah** (*pl*: **neetsol/-ey/-ot** *etc*) ניצול שואה *nmf* Holocaust-survivor.

neetsoo'akh/-kheem ניצוח *nm* conducting (orchestra or operation): (*pl+of*: **-khey**).

neetsool/-eem ניצול *nm* exploitation; utilization; putting to good use; (*pl+of*: **-ey**).

neetsots/-ot ניצוץ *nm* spark.

neetsr|ah/-ot ניצרה *nf* safety-catch; safety-latch; (*+of*: **-at**).

neetsraf/-efah/-aftee נצרף *v* was refined, tested, burned; (*pres* **neetsraf**; *fut* **yeetsaref**).

neetsr|akh/-ekhah/-akhtee נצרך *v* had to; was required; (*pres* **neetsrakh**; *fut* **yeetstarekh**).

neetsrakh/-eem נצרך *adj & nmf* needy; (*pl+of*: **-ey**).

neetsr|av/-evah/-avtee נצרב *v* was seared; was scalded; (*pres* **neetsrav**; *fut* **yeetsarev**).

neev/-eem ניב *nm* idiom; dialect; (*pl+of*: **-ey**).

ne'ev|ad/-dah/-adetee נאבד *v* was lost; (*pres* **ne'evad**; *fut* **ye'aved**).

ne'ev|ad/-edet נאבד *adj* lost.

ne'evad/-dah/-adetee נעבד *v* was tilled, worked, shaped; (*pres* **ne'evad**; *fut* **ye'oobad** (*b=v*)).

ne'ev|ad/-edet נעבד *adj* worked on; tilled; processed.

ne'ev|ak/-kah/-aktee נאבק *v* struggled; wrestled; (*pres* **ne'evak**; *fut* **ye'avek**).

ne'ev|ak/-eket נאבק *adj* struggling; wrestling.

neev'al/-ah/-tee נבעל *v* had sexual intercourse; (*pres* **neev'al**; *fut* **yeeba'el**).

neev|'ar/-'eret נבער *adj* ignorant.

neev'at/-ah/-etee נבעת *v* was stricken with fear, terrified.

neev'at/-ah/-etee ha-khoots'ah נבעט החוצה was kicked out.

neevd|ak/-ekah/-aktee נבדק *v* was examined; was checked; (*pres* **neevdak**; *fut* **yeebadek** (*b=v*)).

neevd|ak/-edet נבדק **1.** *adj* checked; examined; **2.** *v pres* is checked; is examined.

neevd|al/-elah/-altee נבדל *v* differed; (*pres* **neevdal**; *fut* **yeebadel** (*b=v*)).

neevd|al/-elet נבדל *adj* separate.

neevdal נבדל *nm* offside (soccer).

neev|en/-nah/-antee ניוון *v* caused to degenerate; (*pres* **menaven**; *fut* **yenaven**).

neev|et/-tah/-atetee ניווט *v* piloted; guided; (*pres* **menavet**; *fut* **yenavet**).

neev'hal/-ah/-tee נבהל *v* became frightened; was scared; (*pres***neev'hal**; *fut* **yeebahel** (*b=v*)).

neev|hal/-helet נבהל *adj* alarmed; scared; panic-stricken.

neevk|a'/-e'ah/-a'tee נבקע *v* was split; split; (*pres* **neevka'**; *fut* **yeebaka'** (*b=v*)).

neevka'/-at נבקע **1.** *adj* splitting; **2.** *v prs* am/is splitting.

neevkh|an/-enah/-antee נבחן *v* was examined; sat for examination; (*pres* **neevkhan**; *fut* **yeebakhen** (*b=v*)).

neevkh|an/-enet נבחן *nmf* examinee; (*pl+of*: **-ey**).

neevkh|ar/-erah/-artee נבחר *v* was elected, chosen; (*pres* **neevkhar**; *fut* **yeebakher** (*b=v*)).

neevkh|ar/-eret נבחר **1.** *adj* chosen; elected; **2.** *nmf* elect (*pl*: **-areem**; *+of*: **-arey**).

(bet) neevkhareem בית נבחרים *nm* house of representatives.

neevkh|eret/-arot נבחרת *nf* selected (representative, national) team.

neevla'/-at נבלע *adj* swallowed, absorbed.

neevl|a'/-e'ah/-a'tee נבלע *v* **1.** was swallowed; **2.** got lost; (*pres* **neevla'**; *fut* **yeebala'** *(b=v)*).

neevl|am/-emah/-amtee נבלם *v* was stopped, braked, curbed; (*pres* **neevlam**; *fut* **yeebalem** *(b=v)*).

neevl|am/-emet נבלם *adj* braked, stopped, curbed.

neevn|ah/-etah/-etee נבנה *v* was built; was constructed; (*pres* **neevneh**; *fut* **yeebaneh** *(b=v)*).

neevn|eh/-et נבנה *adj* abuilding; built.

(holekh/-et ve) neevn|eh/-et הולך ונבנה *adj & v pres* (is) abuilding.

neevoon/-eem ניוון *nm* degeneration.

neevoot/-eem ניווט *nm* piloting; navigation; (*pl+of:* **-ey**).

neevr|a/-e'ah/-etee נברא *v* was created; came into being; (*pres* **neevra**; *fut* **yeebare** *(b=v)*).

(lo hayah ve-lo) neevra לא היה ולא נברא never was, never happened.

neevr|eshet/-ashot נברשת *nf* chandelier.

neevts|ar/-erah meemen|oo/-ah/-ee נבצר ממנו/־ה *v* he/she/I was unable; (*pres* **neevtsar** *etc*; *fut* **yeebatser** *etc b=v*).

neevz|eh נבזה *adj & nmf* despicable; nasty.

neevzee/-t נבזי *adj* despicable; nasty.

neevzoo|t/-yot נבזות *nf* despicable act.

neeh|yah/-yetah/-yetee נהיה *v* became.

neeh|yeh/-yet נהיה *adj & v prs* (is) becoming.

neez'ak/-ah/-tee נזעק *v* **1.** was summoned; was alerted; **2.** came in a hurry.

neez|'ak/-'eket נזעק *adj* summoned; alerted.

neez|'am/-'emet נזעם *adj* angry; sullen.

ne'ez|ar/-rah/-artee נאזר *v* gathered power; (*pres* **ne'ezar**; *fut* **ye'azer**).

ne'ez|ar/-rah/-artee נעזר *v* was assisted; (*pres* **ne'ezar**; *fut* **ye'azer**).

ne'ezar (*etc*) **'al yedey** נעזר על־ידי *v* was aided by.

ne'ezar (*etc*) **be-** נעזר ב־ *v* was assisted by.

ne'ez|av/-vah/-avtee נעזב *v* was abandoned; was left behind; (*pres* **ne'ezav**; *fut* **ye'azev**).

ne'ez|av/-evet נעזב *adj* derelict; neglected.

neez'har/-ah/-tee נזהר *v* took care; was careful to; (*pres* **neez'har**; *fut* **yeezaher**).

neez'|har/-heret נזהר *adj* careful; cautious.

neezk|ak/-ekah/-aktee נזקק *v* had to resort to; (*pres* **neezkak**; *fut* **yeezdakek**).

neezk|ak/-eket נזקק *nmf & adj* in need; needy.

neezkak/-eem נזקק *nm* person (people) in need; (*pl+of:* **-ey**).

neezk|ar/-erah/-artee נזכר *v* remembered; recalled; (*pres* **neezkar**; *fut* **yeezakher** *(kh=k)*).

neezk|ar/-eret נזכר **1.** *adj* mentioned; recalled; **2.** *v pres* (am/is) mentioned, recalled.

(ha) neezk|ar/-eret le-'eyl הנזכר לעיל *adj* above-mentioned.

(ha) neezkar/-eret le-halan הנזכר להלן *adj* mentioned below.

neezok/-ah/-tee ניזוק *v* was damaged (*pres* **neezok**; *fut* **yeenazek**).

(yats|a/-'ah/-atee) neezok יצא ניזוק *v* sustained damages; (*pres* **yotse** *etc*; *fut* **yetse** *etc*).

neezon/-ah/-tee ניזון *v* subsisted on; (*pres* **neezon**; *fut* **yeezon**).

neezr|ak/-ekah/-aktee נזרק *v* was thrown; was cast off; (*pres* **neezrak**; *fut* **yeezarek**).

neezr|ak/-eket נזרק *adj* thrown; cast off.

nefakh/-eem נפח *nm* displacement; volume; (*pl+of:* **neefkhey**).

(deeney) nefashot דיני נפשות *nm pl* capital offences.

(mekha|yeh/-yah) nefashot מחיה נפשות *adj* invigorating; refreshing.

(sakanat) nefashot סכנת נפשות *nf* mortal danger.

nefeekhoo|t/-yot נפיחות *nf* swelling.

nefeel|ah/-ot נפילה *nf* fall (*+of:* **-at**).

(makhlat) nefeelah מחלת נפילה *nf* epilepsy.

nef|el/-aleem נפל *nm* aborted foetus; (*pl+of:* **neefley**).

nefel נפל *(suffix) adj* abortive.

nef|esh/-ashot נפש *nf* soul; (*pl+of:* **-nafshot**).

('aloov/-at) nefesh עלוב נפש *adj* wretched.

('az/-at) nefesh עז נפש *adj* audacious.

(be-kheroof) nefesh בחירוף נפש *adv* at risk of life.

(go'al) nefesh גועל נפש **1.** *nm* disgust; loathing; **2.** *adj* disgusting.

(ha-go'al) nefesh "הגועל נפש" *nm [slang]* the "disgust": i.e. the sexual act itself.

(halakh/heelkhey) nefesh הלך נפש *nm* mood; frame of mind.

(kheroof) nefesh חירוף נפש *nm* risking one's life.

(kheshbon) nefesh חשבון נפש *nm* soul-searching.

(khol|eh/-at) nefesh חולה נפש *nf* mentally ill.

(kofer) nefesh כופר נפש *nm* ransom.

(la-da'at et) nefesh לדעת את נפש *v inf* "to know the heart of".

(makhl|at/-ot) nefesh מחלת נפש *nf* mental illness.

(mapakh) nefesh מפח נפש *nm* bitter disappointment.

(mar/-at) nefesh מר נפש *adj* bitter; embittered.

(mas|'at/-'ot) nefesh משאת נפש *nf* ideal.

(meseeroot) nefesh מסירות נפש *nf* utter devotion; devotion at life's risk.

(mesheev/-at) nefesh משיב נפש *adj* invigorating; refreshing.

('ogm|at/-ot) nefesh עוגמת נפש *nf* grief; sorrow; distress.

(oyev/-et be) nefesh אויב בנפש *nmf* mortal enemy.

(peekoo'akh) nefesh פיקוח נפש *nm* a matter of life and death.

(peezoor) nefesh פיזור נפש *nm* absentmindedness.

(she'at) nefesh שאט נפש *nm* contempt.

(sheevyon) nefesh שוויון נפש *nm* indifference.

(shv|eh/-at) nefesh שווה נפש *adj* indifferent.

(tseepor) nefesh ציפור נפש *nf* one's most sacred (and most vulnerable) spot.

(yedeed/-at) nefesh ידיד נפש *nmf* bosom-friend.

(yef|eh/-at) nefesh יפה נפש **1.** *nmf* high minded, refined, person; **2.** *nmf [slang]* do-gooder; over-sensitive soul.

nefets נפץ *nm* explosion.

(khom|er/-rey) nefets חומר נפץ *nm* explosive; explosive material.

(kol/-ot) nefets קול נפץ *nm* detonation; sound of explosion.

nefol|et/-ot נפולת *nf* fallout.

◇ **nefolet nemooshot** (*npr* **namoshot**) נפולת נמושות *nf* "fallout of weaklings"- derogatory reference to Israeli emigrés abroad (made by Yitzkhak Rabin, when prime-minister).

neft נפט oil; petrol.

neft golmee נפט גולמי *nm* crude oil.

(keedoo|'akh/-khey) neft קידוח נפט *nm* drilling for oil.

(kheepoosey) neft חיפושי נפט *nm* prospecting for oil.

neg|a'/-a'eem נגע *nm* plague; scourge; (*pl+of:* **neeg'ey**).

nega' ha-sameem נגע הסמים *nm* the drug-addiction plague.

(pasah) nega' פשה נגע the scourge of... spread out to.

□ **Negbah** (Negba) נגבה *nm* kibbutz (est. 1939), 12 km E. of Ashkelon. Renown for heroic resistence in 1948 Independance War to onslaught by Egypt's invading army. Pop. 677.

negd|ee/-ekha/-ekh/-o/-ah (*etc*) נגדי/־ך/־ו וכו' *adv* against me/you/(*m/f*)/him/her (*etc*).

negdee/-t נגדי *adj* opposed; contrary.

(keevoon) negdee כיוון נגדי *nm* opposite direction.

(reegool) negdee ריגול נגדי *nm* counter-espionage.

neged נגד *adv* against; contrary to.

neged ha-zerem נגד הזרם *adv* against the stream.

('ezer ke) negd|ee/-o/-ah עזר כנגדי/־ו/־ה וכו' *nm* helpmate.

(hatkaf|at/-ot) neged התקפת נגד *nf* counter-attack; counter-offensive.

(ha-tsad she-ke) neged הצד שכנגד *nm* the opposite side; the other party; opponent; adversary.

(ke) neged כנגד *adv* versus; as against.

(khat|ar/-rah/-artee) neged חתר נגד *v* plotted against; (*pres* **khoter** *etc; fut* **yakhtor** *etc*).

(la'amod mee) neged לעמוד מנגד *v inf* to keep aloof; (*pst* **'amad** *etc; pres* **'omed** *etc; fut* **ya'amod** *etc*).

(le) neged לנגד *adv* in front of; compared with.

(mee) neged מנגד *adv* aloof.

(meetkef|et/-ot) neged מתקפת נגד *nf* counter-attack; counter-offensive.

negee|'ah/-'ot נגיעה *nf* touch; connection; (*+of:* **-'at**).

negeekh|ah/-ot נגיחה *nf* ramming; goring; (*+of:* **-at**).

negeen|ah/-ot נגינה *nf* playing music; (*+of:* **-at**).

(keet'ey) negeenah קטעי נגינה *nm pl* selected musical passages.

◇ **(ha)negeenah** הנגינה *nf* (*Gram.*) accentuation; stress; (indicated in this dictionary by underline).

(klee/kley) negeenah כלי נגינה *nm* musical instrument.

(tavey) negeenah תווי נגינה *nm pl* musical score.

(teyvat) negeenah תיבת נגינה *nf* music-box.

negees|ah/-ot נגיסה *nf* bite; biting; (*+of:* **-at**).

(even/avney) negef אבן נגף *nm* stumbling block.

(areekh/-ey) negen אריך נגן **1.** *nm* long-playing record; **2.** *adj* long-playing.

□ **Negev** נגב *nm* S.; S. region.

□ **(ha)Negev** הנגב *nm* the Negev, which is Israel's largest and least populated district, stretching in triangle form southward, from center of the country to Elat.

□ **(beerat ha) negev** see □ **beerat ha-negev**.

nehag/-eem נהג *nm* driver; (*pl+of:* **-ey**).

nehedar/-eret נהדר *adj* splendid.

neheegah נהיגה *nf* driving; (*+of:* **-at**).

neheegah mona'at נהיגה מונעת *nf* preventive (i.e. more careful) driving.

(reeshyon/-ot) neheegah רשיון נהיגה *nm* driver's license; driving permit.

(she'oor/-ey) neheegah שיעור נהיגה *nm* driving lesson.

neheer|ah/-ot נהירה *nf* swarming; flocking; (*+of:* **-at**).

nehee|yah/-yot נהייה *nf* longing; following; (*+of:* **-yat**).

nehen|ah/-tah/-etee נהנה *v* enjoyed; profited; (*pres* **neheneh**; *fut* **yehaneh**).

nehen|eh/-et נהנה **1.** *adj* enjoying; profiting; **2.** *v pres* am/is enjoying, profiting.

nehp|akh/-khah/-akhtee נהפך *v* overturned; changed; turned; (*pres* **nehfakh**; *fut* **yehafekh** (*f=p*)).

neher|ag/-gah נהרג *v* was killed; (*pres* **neherag**; *fut* **yehareg**).

neher|as/-sah/-astee נהרס *v* was destroyed; was ruined; (*pres* **neheras**; *fut* **yeheres**).

□ **Nehorah** (Nehora) נהורה *nm* rural center (est. 1955) in **Lakheesh** area, 4 km W. of Plugot Junction (**Tsomet Ploogot**). Pop. 463.

nek|a'/-a'eem נקע *nm* sprain.

('al) nekalah על נקלה *adv* easily; with no difficulty.

nekam|ah/-ot נקמה *nf* revenge; retaliation; (*+of:* **neekm|at/-ot**).

nekee/-yat kapayeem נקי כפיים *adj & nmf* honest person; incorruptible; clean-handed.

nekeef|at/-ot matspoon נקיפת מצפון *nf* pang of conscience.

nekeesh|ah/-ot נקישה *nf* knock; (*+of:* **-at**).

nekeet|ah/-ot נקיטה *nf* taking; holding; (*+of:* **-at**).

nekeetat emtsa'eem נקיטת אמצעים *nf* taking measures.

nekeetat tse'adeem נקיטת צעדים *nf* taking steps.

nek|er/-areem נקר *nm* puncture; (*pl+of:* **neekrey**).

nek|ev/-aveem נקב *nm* hole; puncture; (*pl+of:* **neekvey**).

nekev|ah/-ot נקבה *nf* female; woman (coarse language); (*+of:* **-at**).

(leshon) nekevah לשון נקבה *(Gram.) nf* feminine gender.

(meen) nekevah מין נקבה *nm* feminine gender; female sex.

□ **Nekhaleem** (Nehalim) נחלים *nm* village (est. 1948), 3 km S. of **Petakh-Teekvah**. Pop. 1,480.

nekham|ah/-ot נחמה *nf* consolation; (*+of:* **-at**).

(khatsee) nekhamah חצי נחמה *nm* partial consolation.

nekhar ניכר *nm* strange (foreign) land (or lands).

(admat) nekhar אדמת ניכר *nf* foreign soil.

(ba) nekhar בניכר *adv* in a foreign land.

(yar|ad/-dah/-adetee mee) nekhas|av/-eha/-ay ירד מנכסיו/־ה/־יי *v* lost his/her/my wealth; (*pres* **yored** *etc; fut* **yered** *etc*).

nekhaseem נכסים *nm pl* (*sing:* **nekhes**) possessions; (*+of:* **neekhsey**).

('ateer/-at) nekhaseem עתיר נכסים *adj* wealthy; rich.

(kon|es/-sey) nekhaseem כונס נכסים *nm* official receiver.

nekhb|a/-e'ah/-e'tee נחבא *v* hid himself; (*pres* **nekhba**; *fut* **yekhave** *(v=b)*).

nekhb|a (*etc*) **el ha-keleem** נחבא אל הכלים *v pst* kept oneself in the background.

nekhb|a/-et el ha-keleem נחבא אל הכלים *adj* shy; diffident.

nekhb|al/-elah/-altee נחבל *v* was wounded, injured; (*pres* **nekhbal**; *fut* **yekhavel** *(v=b)*).

nekhb|ash/-eshah/-ashtee נחבש *v* **1.** was bandaged; **2.** was imprisoned; (*pres* **nekhbash**; *fut* **yekhavesh** *(v=b)*).

nekh|dah/-adot נכדה *nf* granddaughter; (*+of:* **-dat**).

nekh|eh/-ah (*npr* **nakh|eh/-eem**) נכה *adj & nmf* crippled; invalid; (*+of:* **nekh|at/-ey**).

nekh|eh/-ey meelkhamah נכה מלחמה *nm* disabled ex-servicemen.

nekh|ed/-adeem נכד *nm* grandson; grandchild; (*pl+of:* **-adey**).

nekheer|ah/-ot נחירה *nf* snore; snoring; (*+of:* **-at**).

nekheer|ayeem נחיריים *nm pl* (*sing:* **nekheer**) nostrils; (*pl+of:* **-ey**).

nekheet|ah/-ot נחיתה *nf* landing; (*+of:* **-at**).

(asd|at/-ot) nekheetah אסדת נחיתה *nf* landing craft.

(meesht|akh/-ekhey) nekheetah משטח נחיתה *nm* landing ground.

nekheetoot/-yot נחיתות *nf* inferiority.

(tasbeekh/-ey) nekheetoot תסביך נחיתות *nm* inferiority complex.

nekheetsoo|t/-yot נחיצות *nf* necessity.

nekh|es/-aseem נכס *nm* asset; property; (*pl+of:* **neekhsey**).

nekhl|ash/-eshah/-ashtee נחלש *v* weakened; (*pres* **nekhlash**; *fut* **yekhalesh**).

nekhl|ash/-eshet נחלש **1.** *adj* weakening; **2.** *v pres* weakens.

nekhl|ats/-etsah/-atstee נחלץ *v* **1.** escaped; got out; **2.** volunteered; (*pres* **nekhlats**; *fut* **yekhalets**).

nekhl|ats/-etset נחלץ **1.** *adj* volunteering; escaping; **2.** *v pres* escape(s), volunteer(s); (*pst* **nekhlats**; *fut* **yekhalets**).

nekhmad/-ah נחמד *adj* charming.

(ro|'eh/-ah) nekhokhah רואה נכוחה *v pres* sees things right; (*pst* **ra'ah** *etc; fut* **yeer'eh** *etc*).

nekhonah נכונה *adv* correctly; truly.

nekhonoot נכונות *nf* readiness; preparedness.

(metsakh) nekhooshah מצח נחושה *nm* brazen face.

nekhoo|t/-yot (*npr* **nakhoo|t/-yot**) נכות *nf* disability; infirmity.

nekhp|az/-ezah/-aztee נחפז *v* hurried; rushed; (*pres* **nekhpaz**; *fut* **yekhafez** *(f=p)*).

nekhp|az/-ezet נחפז **1.** *adj* rash; hasty; **2.** *v pres* (*etc*) rushes; precipitates.

nekhr|ad/-edah/-adetee נחרד *v* was terrified; (*pres* **nekhrad**; *fut* **yekhared**).

nekhr|ad/-edet נחרד **1.** *adj* terrified; frightened; **2.** *v pres* (*etc*) am/is terrified.

nekhr|av/-evah/-avtee נחרב *v* was ruined; was devastated; (*pres* **nekhrav**; *fut* **yekharev**).

nekhr|av/-evet נחרב **1.** *adj* ruined, devastated; **2.** *v pres* (is being) ruined, devastated.

nekhsh|al/-elet נחשל *adj* backward; primitive.

nekhshaloot נחשלות *nf* backwardness.

nekhsh|av/-evah/-avtee נחשב *v* was considered, regarded; (*pres* **nekhshav**; *fut* **yekhashev**).

nekhsh|av/-evet נחשב **1.** *adj* considered; regarded; **2.** *v pres* (am/is) considered, regarded.

(lo) nekhshav לא נחשב *adv* doesn't count; isn't taken into account.

nekht|akh/-ekhah/-akhtee נחתך *v* **1.** was cut; cut oneself; **2.** was decided; (*pres* **nekhtakh**; *fut* **yekhatekh**).

nekood|ah/-ot נקודה *nf* **1.** dot (punctuation); full stop; **2.** point; **3.** settlement; (*+of:* **-at**).

nekoodah oo-peseek נקודה ופסיק *nm pl* (;) semicolon (punctuation).

nekood|at/-ot akheezah נקודת אחיזה *nf* foothold; lead.

nekood|at/-ot hashkafah נקודת השקפה *nf* point of view; observation point.

nekood|at/-ot heetyashvoot נקודת התיישבות *nf* settlement.

nekood|at/-ot keepa'on נקודת קיפאון *nf* freezing point.

nekood|at/-ot mabat נקודת מבט *nf* point of view.

nekood|at/-ot meefneh נקודת מפנה *nf* turning point.

nekood|at/-ot motsa נקודת מוצא *nf* point of departure.

nekood|at/-ot re'oot נקודת ראות *nf* point of view.

nekood|at/-ot toorpah נקודת תורפה *nf* vulnerable spot.

nekood|at/-ot yeeshoov נקודת יישוב *nf* inhabited place.

nekoodatayeem נקודתיים *nf pl* colon (:) (punctuation).

nemal/neemley te'oofah נמל תעופה *nm* airport.

nemal|ah/-eem (*also:* **-ot**) נמלה *nf* ant; (*+of:* **-at/-ey**).

('avod|at/-ot) nemaleem עבודת נמלים *nf* **1.** strenuous work; **2.** (*lit.*) ants' work.

nemasheem נמשים *nm pl* (*sing:* **nemesh**) freckles; (*+of:* **neemshey**).

nemeekhoot נמיכות *nf* shortness; lowness.

nemek נמק *nm* necrosis (Medic.).

nemeleem נמלים *nm pl* (*sing* **namel**) harbors, ports; (*+of:* **neemley**).

nemookh/-at komah נמוך קומה *adj* short of stature.

nemooshot (*npr* **namoshot**) נמושות *nm pl* (*sing:* **namosh**) weaklings; unworthy descendants of glorious forefathers.

◇ **(nefolet) nemooshot** see ◇ **nefolet nemooshot**.

ne'o- ניאו (*prefix*) neo-

ne'on/-eem ניאון *nm* neon; neon light; fluorescent light; (*pl+of:* **-ey**).

(ha-delet) ne'oolah הדלת נעולה the door is locked.

ne'oom/-eem נאום *nm* speech; (*pl+of:* **-ey**).

(nas|a/-'ah/-a'tee) ne'oom/-eem נשא נאום made a speech; (*pres* **nose** *etc; fut* **yeesa** *etc*).

(eshet) ne'oor|av/-ay/-ekha אשת נעוריו *nf* his/my/your wife since youth.

(yemey) ne'oor|av/-eha/-ay/-ekha/-ayeekh ימי נעוריו/־ה/־ך וכו *nm pl* the days of his/her/my your *m/f* youth.

ne'oor|eem נעורים *nm pl* youth; (*+of:* **-ey**).

□ **Ne'ooreem** (Ne'urim) נעורים *nm* youth-village and education-center (est. 1953) on the Mediterranean shore, 5 km N. of Netanya. Pop. (mostly pupils) 719.

(beney ha) ne'ooreem בני הנעורים *nm pl* adolescents; youths.

ne'or/-ah/-tee ניעור *nm* awakened; (*pres* **ne'or**; *fut* **ye'or**).

ne'ot/-ah/-tee ניאות *v* consented; agreed; (*pres* **ne'ot**; *fut* **ye'ot**).

ne'ot deshe' נאות דשא *nf pl* green pastures.

□ **Ne'ot Golan (Ne'ot Golan)** נאות גולן *nm* collective village (est. 1968) in S. Golan Heights, 6 km E. of **'En-Gev**.

□ **Ne'ot ha-Keekar** (Ne'ot haKikkar) נאות הכיכר *nm* collective village (est. 1959) in the 'Aravah, S. of Dead Sea, 8 km SE of Aravah Junction **(Tsomet 'Aravah)**. Pop. 244.

ne'ot meedbar נאות מדבר *nm pl* oasis.

□ **Ne'ot Mordekhay (Ne'ot Mordekhay)** נאות מרדכי *nm* kibbutz (est. 1946) in the **Khoolah** (Huleh) Valley, 6 km SE of **Keeryat Shmonah** (Qiryat Shemona). Pop. 660.

ner/-ot נר *nm* candle.

ner le-ragley נר לרגלי *nm* guiding light.

ner/-ot neshamah נר נשמה *nm* memorial candle.

ner tameed נר תמיד *nm* eternal lamp; eternal flame.

◇ **(hadlakat) nerot** see ◇ **hadlakat nerot**.

nes/neeseem נס *nm* **1.** miracle; **2.** banner (used by army).

□ **Nes 'Ameem** (Nes Ammim) נס עמים *nm* village established (1963) by Christian idealists (with purpose of bringing Christians and Jews nearer together) W. Upper Galillee, 4 km NE of **'Ako** (Acre). Pop. 138.

□ **Nes Hareem** (Nes Harim) נס הרים *nm* village (est. 1950) in Judean hills, 7 km E. of Bet-Shemesh. Pop. 404.

nes kafeh (*also:* **kafeh nes**) נס קפה *nm* instant coffee.

□ **Nes Tseeyonah** (Nes Ziyyona) נס ציונה *nf* township (originally est 1883 as an agricultural settlement) halfway between **Reeshon** (Rishon le-Ziyyon) and Rehovot **(Rekhovot)**. Pop. 20,800.

(he'el|ah/-tah/-etee 'al) nes העלה על נס *v* commended; (*pres* **ma'aleh** *etc; fut* **ya'aleh** *etc*).

◇ **nesakh** נסח *nm* immovable property ownership certificate issued by Land-Registry **(Taboo)**.

nesee ha-medeenah נשיא המדינה *nm* the State President.

nesee/-'ey khevr|ah/-ot נשיא חברה *nm* company chairman; corporation president.

nesee|'ah נשיאה *nf* **1.** carrying of; **2.** woman-president; (*+of:* **-'at**).

nesee'ah be-'ol נשיאה בעול *nf* carrying of the burden; doing one's duty.

nesee|'ah/-'ot נסיעה *nf* voyage; trip; (*+of:* **'at**).

neseebatee/-t נסיבתי *adj* circumstantial.

neseebot נסיבות *nf pl* circumstances.

neseeg|ah/-ot נסיגה *nf* retreat; withdrawal; (*+of:* **-at**).

neseekh|ah/-ot נסיכה *nf* princess; (*+of:* **-at**).

neseekhoo|t/-yot נסיכות *nf* principality.

nesee'oot נשיאות *nf* **1.** presidium; **2.** presidency.

(mas) nesee'ot מס נסיעות *nm* travel-tax.

(sokhnoo|t/-yot) nesee'ot סוכנות נסיעות *nf* travel agency.

◇ **(yen) nesekh** see ◇ **yen nesekh**.

nesham|ah/-ot נשמה *nf* soul; (*+of:* **neeshm|at/-ot**).

(geelgool/-ey) nesham|ah/-ot גלגול נשמה *nm* transmigration of souls; metamorphosis.

◇ **(hazkarat) neshamot** see ◇ **hazkarat neshamot**.

nesheef|ah/-ot נשיפה *nf* exhalation; expiration; (*+of:* **-at**).

(kley) nesheefah כלי נשיפה *nm pl* wind instruments; woodwinds.

nesheek|ah/-ot נשיקה *nf* kiss; (*+of:* **-at**).

(meetat) nesheekah מיתת נשיקה *nf* easy, painless death.

nesheekh|ah/-ot נשיכה *nf* bite; biting; (*+of:* **-at**).

nesheem|ah/-ot נשימה *nf* breath; breathing; (*+of:* **-at**).

(bee) nesheemah akhat בנשימה אחת *adv* in one breath.

(keshayey) nesheemah קשיי נשימה *nm pl* breathing difficulties.

('otser/-et) nesheemah עוצר נשימה *adj* breathtaking.

nesheerah/-ot נשירה *nf* windfall; shedding; moulting; (*+of:* **-at**).

◇ **"nesheerah"** נשירה *nf* (*figurat.*) name given to the defection to the USA or elsewhere of emigrants from the USSR who , prior to 1990, were permitted to leave only by professing their destination as Israel.

nesh|ef/-afeem נשף *nm* (dance) ball; (*pl+of:* **neeshfey**).

neshef/neeshfey masekhot נשף מסיכות *nm* fancy-dress ball; masquerade; costume ball.

neshek נשק *nm* arms; weapons; weaponry.

neshek kal נשק קל *nm* small arms.

neshek kham נשק חם *nm* firearms.

(perook) neshek פירוק נשק *nm* disarmament.

(shveet|at/-ot) neshek שביתת נשק *nf* armistice.

neshekh נשך *nm* usury; exorbitant interest.

□ **Nesher** נשר *nm* urban settlement (est. 1925) on Haifa Bay, 6 km SE of Haifa. Pop. 11,400.

nesh|er/-areem נשר *nm* eagle; (*pl+of:* **neeshrey**).

neshey נשי *nf pl+of* the wives **(nasheem)** of.

nesoo/-'ey paneem נשוא פנים *adj* respected; imposing.

nesoo|'ah/-'ot נשואה *adj & nf* married (female).

(eeshah/nasheem) nesoo'ah/-'ot אישה נשואה *nf* married woman.

nesoret נסורת *nf* sawdust.

neta|'/-'eem נטע *nm* sapling; seedling; (*pl+of:* **neet'ey**).

neta' zar נטע זר *nm* (*figurat.*) alien corn.

□ **Neta'eem** (Neta'im) נטעים *nm* village (est. 1932) 4 km SW of **Reeshon** (Rishon leZiyyon). Pop. 227.

netakh/-eem נתח *nm* cut; piece of meat; piece; (*pl+of:* **neetkhey**).

□ **Netanyah** (Netanya) נתניה *nf* town (est. 1928) and health resort on Mediterranean coast, 30 km N. of Tel-Aviv by road and rail. Pop. 132,200.

netee|'ah/-'ot נטיעה *nf* planting; (*+of:* **-'at**).

neteekh (*npr* **nateekh**)**/-eem** נתיך fuse; (*pl+of:* **-ey**).

neteel|ah/-ot נטילה *nf* taking; receiving; (*+of:* **-at**).

◇ **neteelat yadayeem** נטילת ידיים *nf* washing of hands (religious ritual) before a meal.

neteen|ah/-ot נתינה *nf* giving; (*+of:* **-at**).

neteen|ah/-ot נתינה *nf* citizen (female) of a country; national (*f*) of a country; (*+of:* **-at**).

neteenoo|t/-yot נתינות citizenship; nationality.

neteesh|ah/-ot נטישה *nf* abandonment; (*+of:* **-at**).

neteev/-eem נתיב *nm* path; line; (*pl+of:* **-ey**).

□ **Neteev ha-'Asarah** (Netiv haAsara) נתיב העשרה *nm* village (est. 1976 in Sinai) moved 1982 to present location in S. coastal plain, 3 km SW of **Tsomet Mordekhay** (Mordekhay Junction) on Ashkelon-Gaza road. Pop. 494.

□ **Neteev ha-Gedood** (Netiv haGedud) נתיב הגדוד *nm* village (est. 1976) in Jordan Valley (West Bank), 15 km N. of Jericho.

□ **Neteev ha-Lamed-Heh** (Netiv haLamed-He) נתיב הל״ה *nm* kibbutz (est. 1949) in ha'Ela Valley **('Emek ha-'Elah)** amid Judean hills, 4 km E. of ha'Ela Junction **(Tsomet ha-'Elah)**. Pop. 382.

□ **Neteev ha-Shayarah** (Netive haShayyara) נתיב השיירה *nm* village (est. 1950) on Mediterranean coast, 4 km SE of Nahariyyah. Pop. 317.

neteevey aveer נתיבי אוויר *nm pl* airlines.

□ **Neteevey Ayalon** נתיבי אילון *pl* Tel-Aviv's trans-urban freeway connecting Expressways 1 and 2.

◇ **Neteevey Ayalon** נתיבי איילון *nf* public company sponsored by the Municipality of Tel-Aviv that is responsible for the city's trans-urban freeway and for a series of wide-scale public transportation and parking projects in Greater Tel-Aviv area.

□ **Neteevot** (Netivot) נתיבות *nf* township (est. 1956) in NW Negev, halfway between Gaza and Beersheba. Pop. 10,700.

netee|yah/-yot נטייה *nf* **1.** trend; tendency; inclination; **2.** inflection; conjugation (Gram.); (*+of:* **-yat**).

neteeyat po'al/pe'aleem נטיית פועל *nf* inflection of a verb (Gram.).

neteeyat shem/-ot נטיית שם *nf* inflection of a noun (Gram.).

net|ekh/-akheem נתך *nm* alloy; (*pl+of:* **neetkhey**).

netel נטל *nm* burden.

neto נטו *adv* net (weight, quantity).

□ **Netoo'ah** (Netu'a) נטועה *nm* village (est. 1966) in Upper Galilee near Lebanese border, 9 km NW of Hiram Junction **(Tsomet Kheeram)**. Pop. 267.

netool/-at -נטול *prefix* equivalent to the suffix "-less".

netool/-at khayeem נטול חיים *adj* lifeless.

netool/-at tseva' נטול צבע *adj* colorless.

netool/-at yesod נטול יסוד *adj* baseless; unfounded.

netoon|eem נתונים *nm pl* (*sing:* **natoon**) data; (*+of:* **-ey**).

('eebood) netooneem עיבוד נתונים *nm* data-processing.

◇ **"Netoorey Karta"** נטורי קרתא *nm pl* anti-Zionist community of ultra-orthodox Jewish religious extremists centered in Jerusalem's **Me'ah She'areem** quarter with extensions in Beney Berak and Safed.

netralee/-t נייטרלי *adj* neutral.

netraleeyoot נייטרליות *nf* neutrality.

nets/neets|eem נץ *nm* hawk; (*pl+of:* **-ey**).

nets/neets|eem poleetee/-yeem נץ פוליטי *nm* hawk (in the political sense); right-winger; (*pl+of:* **-ey**).

netsakh/-eem נצח *nm* eternity.

(la) netsakh לנצח *adv* forever.

(le) netsakh netsakheem לנצח נצחים *adv* for ever and ever.

netseeloo|t/-yot נצילות *nf* efficiency (of machine *etc*); exploitability.

netseeg/-ah (*npr* **natseeg/-ah**) נציג *nmf* representative; (*pl:* **-eem/-ot**; *+of:* **-at/-ey**).

netseegoo|t/-yot נציגות *nf* delegation; representation.

netseev/-eem נציב *nm* commissioner; governor; director; (*pl+of:* **-ey**).

netseev keveelot נציב קבילות *nm* ombudsman.

netseev mas hakhnasah נציב מס הכנסה *nm* income-tax commisioner.

netseevoo|t/-yot נציבות *nf* commission; commissionership.

netseevoot mas hakhnasah נציבות מס הכנסה *nf* income-tax commission.

netser נצר *nm* descendant; offspring.

□ **Netser Khazanee (Nezer Hazzani)** נצר חזני *nm* kibbutz (est. 1976) in Gaza strip, 5 km NE of **Khan-Yoones**. Pop. 354.

□ **Netser Serenee (Nezer Sereni)** נצר סרני *nm* -kibbutz (est. 1948) on coastal plain, 3 km E. of **Nes-Tseeyonah**. Pop. 560.

netsolet נצולת *nf* **1.** salvage; **2.** utility; profit.

nevall|ah/-ot נבלה *nf* outrage.

nevee/-'ey sheker נביא שקר *nm* false prophet.

□ **Nevateem** (Nevatim) נבטים *nm* village (est. 1946) 8 km E. of Beersheba. Pop. 532.

□ **Neveh Ateev** (Newé Ativ) נווה אטי״ב *nm* collective village in N. Golan Heights, 4 km NW of **Tsomet Mas'adah** (Mas'ada Junction). Operates Mount **Khermon** winter-sport resort.

□ **Neveh Dekaleem** (Newé Deqalim) נוה דקלים *nm* regional center in Gaza Strip (est. 1980), 1 km W. of **Khan Yoones**. Pop.1,070.

□ **Neveh Eelan** (Newé Ilan) נווה אילן *nm* collective village (est. 1971) in the Judean hills, 16 km W. of Jerusalem. Pop. 300.

□ **Neveh Efrayeem** (Newé Efrayim Monosson) נווה אפרים *nf* residential suburb outside Tel-Aviv (est. 1953) known also under its previous name of **Kefar Monosson** כפר מונוסון, 15 km E. of Tel-Aviv, 4 km NW of Ben-Gurion Airport. Pop. 2,770.

□ **Neveh Eytan** (Newé Etan) נווה איתן *nm* kibbutz (est. 1938) in Bet-She'an Valley, 3 km E. of Bet-She'an. Pop. 316.

neveh kayeets נווה קיץ *nm* summer home.

□ **Neveh Meekha'el** (Newé Mikha'el) נוה מיכאל *nm* village in **'Emek ha-Elah** Valley, at the foot of E. slopes of Judea hills (est. 1958), 9 km E. of Bet Shemesh. Incorporates (since 1983) nearby village **Rogleet** as well. Pop.296.

□ **Neveh Meevtakh (Newé Mivtah)** נווה מבטח *nm* village (est. 1950) 3 km SW of **Gederah**. Pop. 313.

□ **Neveh Oor** (Newé Ur) נווה אור *nm* kibbutz (est. 1949) in Jordan valley, 4 km S. of Gesher. Pop. 362.

□ **Neveh Tsoof** (Newé Zuf) נווה צוף *nm* village (est. 1977) in Samaria, 15 km NW of Ramallah.

□ **Neveh Yam** (Newé Yam) נווה ים *nm* kibbutz (est. 1939) on Mediterranean Coast, 2 km SW of **'Atleet**. Pop. 165.

□ **Neveh Yameen** (Newé Yamin) נווה ימין *nm* village (est. 1949) in Sharon, 1 km SE of **Kefar Saba**. Pop. 610.

□ **Neveh Yarak** (Newé Yaraq) נווה ירק *nm* village in Sharon (est. 1951), 5 km NW of **Petakh-Teekvah**. Pop. 469.

□ **Neveh Zohar** (Newé Zohar) נווה זוהר *nm* regional center and spa on Dead Sea shore, N. of Zohar Junction **(Tsomet Zohar)**.

neveekh|ah/-ot נביחה *nf* bark; barking; (*+of:* **-at**).

neveet|ah/-ot נביטה *nf* sprouting; germination; (*+of:* **-at**).

nevel נבל *nm* harp.

nevel|ah/-ot נבלה *nm* **1.** carcass; **2.** *[slang]* scoundrel; (*+of:* **neevl|at/-ot**).

nev|et/-ateem נבט *nm* sprout.

nevoo|'ah/'ot נבואה *nf* prophecy; (*+of:* **-'at**).

nevoo'ee/t נבואי *adj* prophetic.

neyar/-ot נייר *nm* paper.

neyar/-ot areezah נייר אריזה *nm* packing paper.

neyar/-ot 'ateefah נייר עטיפה *nm* wrapping paper.

neyar/-ot 'avodah נייר עבודה *nm* working paper; worksheet.

neyar 'eeton נייר עתון *nm* newsprint.

neyar/-ot 'erekh נייר ערך *nm* security (stockmarket).

neyar/-ot ha'atakah נייר העתקה *nm* copy paper.

neyar/-ot makhshev נייר מחשב *nm* computer paper.

neyar/-ot pekham נייר פחם *nm* carbon paper.

neyar/-ot taveem נייר תווים *nm* music paper.

neyar/-ot teeshoo נייר טישו *[colloq.] nm* tissue paper.

neyar/-ot too'alet נייר טואלט *nm* toilet paper.

neyar zekhookheet נייר זכוכית *nm* sandpaper.

('al ha) neyar על הנייר *adv* on paper.

(namer shel) neyar נמר של נייר *nm* paper tiger.

(pees|at/-ot) neyar פיסת נייר *nf* scrap of paper.
(boorsah lee) neyarot 'erekh בורסה לניירות ערך *nf* stock-exchange.
◇ **nezeed 'adasheem** נזיד עדשים *nm* mess of pottage (Bible, Genesis 25:34).
(bee) nezeed 'adasheem בנזיד עדשים *adv* for a song...
nezeef|ah/-ot נזיפה *nf* admonition; reprimand; (*+of:* **-at**).
nezeekeen נזיקין *nm pl* torts; damages (law).
nezeel|ah/-ot נזילה *nf* leak; leakage; (*+of:* **-at**).
nezeeloot נזילות *nf* liquidity (financ.).
nezeer|ah/-ot נזירה *nf* nun; (*+of:* **-at**).
nez|ek/-akeem נזק *nm* damage; (*pl+of:* **neezkey**).
nezem/-ameem נזם *nm* nose-ring; earring; (*pl+of:* **neezmey**).
nez|er/-areem נזר *nm* diadem; (*pl+of:* **neezrey**).
no'a נוע *nm* movement; motion.
(belee) no'a בלי נוע *adv* motionless.
no'ad/-ah/-etee נועד *v* was destined, designated; was slated; (*pres* **no'ad**; *fut* **yeyoo'ad**).
no'ad/-ah/-etee נועד *v* went; convened; assembled; (*pres* **no'ad**; *fut* **yeeva'ed** *(v=o)*).
no'akh/-nokhah נוח *adj* comfortable; easy-going; convenient.
no'akh/nokhah la-bree'ot נוח לבריות *adj* popular; amiable.
no'akh/nokhah leekh'os נוח לכעוס *adj* irritable; irrascible.
(be) no'akh בנוח *adv* at ease.
(kees|'e/-'ot) no'akh כיסא נוח *nm* easy-chair.
◇ **(teyvat) no'akh** תיבת נוח *nf* Noah's Ark (Bibl.).
no'al/-elet נואל *adj* foolish; stupid.
no'al/-ah/-tee נואל *v* was foolish to...
no'am נועם *nm* tenderness; pleasantness.
□ **No'am** (No'am) נועם *nm* village (est. 1955) in **Lakheesh** area, 6 km S. of **Keeryat-Gat**. Pop. 405.
no'am haleekhot נועם הליכות *nm* charming manners.
(be-darkhey) no'am בדרכי נועם *adv* gently; peacefully; in pleasant ways.
no'ar נוער *nm* youth; young people.
(akhsan|yat/-yot) no'ar אכסניית נוער *nf* youth hostel.
('avaryanoot) no'ar עבריינות נוער *nf* juvenile delinquency.
(beney) no'ar בני נוער *nm pl* youths; youngsters.
no'ash/-ah/-tee נואש *v* gave up hope; despaired; (*pres* **no'ash**; *[colloq.]fut* **yeetya'esh**).
no|'ash/-'eshet נואש *adj* desperate.
(am|ar/-rah/-artee) no'ash אמר נואש *v* resigned all hope; (*pres* **omer** *etc*; *fut* **yomar** *etc*).
(lo am|ar/-rah *(etc)***) no'ash** לא אמר נואש *v* never gave up; (*pres* **eyno omer** *etc*; *fut* **lo yomar** *etc*).
no'ats/-ah/-tee נועץ *v* consulted; (*pres* **no'ats**; *fut* **yeeva'ets** *(v=o)*).
no'ats/no'etset נועץ *v pres* consults; *adj* consulting.
no'az/no'ezet נועז *adj* daring.
nod/-ot נאד *nm* **1.** skin-bottle; **2.** *[slang]* fool; queer; complete idiot.
noda|'/-'ah/-a'tee נודע *v* became known; (*pres* **noda'**; *fut* **yeevada'**).
noda'/-at נודע **1.** *adj* well known; **2.** *adv* it has been learned.
noded/-et נודד **1.** *adj* wandering; **2.** *nmf* vagrant; **3.** *v pres* wanders; *nmf* vagrant; (*pst* **nadad**; *fut* **yeendod**).
no'ef/-et נואף *nmf* adulterer; adultress.
no'el/-et נועל **1.** *adj* locking; **2.** *v pres* locks; (*pst* **na'al**; *fut* **yeen'al**).
no'em/-et נואם *nmf* speaker;2. makes a speech; (*pst* **na'am**; *fut* **yeen'am**).
nof/-eem נוף *nm* landscape; scenery; (*pl+of:* **-ey**).
□ **Nof Yam** (Nof Yam) נוף־ים *nf* originally a smallholders semi-agricultural village bordering Expressway 2, it developed in the 1980s into a residential seashore district continuing northward **Hertseleeyah-Peetoo'akh** of which it is now part.
(yefeh/-at) nof יפה נוף *adj* of beautiful scenery.
nof|ef/-efah/-aftee נופף *v* waved; brandished; (*pres* **menofef**; *fut* **yenofef**).
nofekh נופך *nm* turquoise; garnet.
□ **Nofekh** נופך *nm* village (est. 1949) in Sharon. Pop. 133.
nofekh mee-shelo/-ah/-ee/-khah/-akh *etc* נופך משלו his/her/my/your *m/f etc* personal touch.
nofel/-et נופל **1.** *adj* falling; **2.** *v pres* falls; (*pst* **nafal**; *fut* **yeepol** *(p=f)*).
(lashon) nofel 'al lashon לשון נופל על לשון *nm* pun; play on words.
nofesh נופש *nm* rest; recreation.
(makhan|eh/-ot) nofesh מחנה נופש *nm* recreation camp.
nofesh/-et נופש *v pres* vacations; rests; (*pst* **nafash**; *fut [colloq.]* **yeenofesh**).
nof|esh/-sheem נופש *nmf* vacationer; (*pl+of:* **-shey**).
□ **Nogah** נוגה *nm* planet Venus.
nogdan/-eem נוגדן *nm* antibody; (*pl+of:* **-ey**).
nog|e'a'/-a'at נוגע **1.** *adj* touching; concerning; **2.** *v pres* touch(es); concern(s); (*pst* **naga'**; *fut* **yeega'**).
nog|e'a/-a'at be-davar נוגע בדבר *adj* interested party.
(be) noge'a בנוגע *adv* concerning; regarding; in connection with.
(mah be) noge'a? מה בנוגע? what about?
noged/-et נוגד **1.** - *adj* contradicting; **2.** *v pres* contradicts; (*pst* **nagad**; *fut* **yeengod**).
nog|es/-seem נוגש *nm* oppressor; (*pl+of:* **-sey**).
noges/-et נוגס *v pres* bites; (*pst* **nagas**; *fut* **yeengos**).
nohag/nehageem נוהג *nm* custom; practice; (*pl+of:* **nohogey**).

nohal/nehaleem נוהל *nm* procedure; (*pl+of:* **noholey**).

noheg/-et נוהג *v pres* **1.** drives; **2.** behaves; (*pst* **nahag**; *fut* **yeenhag**).

nokef/-et נוקף *v pres* knocks; (*pres* **nakaf**; *fut* **yeenkof**); (see: **lo nokef**, below).

(lo) nokef (*etc*) **etsba'** לא נוקף אצבע doesn't lift a finger (*figurat.*).

noket/-et emtsa'eem נוקט אמצעים *v pres* takes measures.

nokev/-et נוקב *adj* exhaustive; penetrating.

nokhakh נוכח *adv* in the face of.

(le) nokhakh לנוכח *adv* confronted with; in front of.

nokh|akh/-ekhah/-akhtee נוכח *v* realized; became convinced; (*pres* **nokhakh**; *fut* **yeevakhakh** (*v=o*)).

nokh|e'akh/-akhat נוכח **1.** *adj* present; **2.** *nmf* who's present; (*pl:* **-ekheem/-ekhot**).

nokh|e'akh/-akhat נוכח *v pres* attends; is present at; (*pst* **nakhakh**; *fut* **yeenkakh** (*k=kh*)).

nokheeyoot נוחיות *nf* **1.** [*colloq.*] bathroom and toilet; **2.** comfortability.

(be) nokheeyoot בנוחיות [*colloq.*] *adv* at ease.

nokhekhee/-t נוכחי *adj* present.

nokhekhoot נוכחות *nf* presence; attendance.

(be) nokhekhoot בנוכחות *adv* in the presence of.

nokh|el/-leem נוכל *nm* crook; swindler; (*pl+of:* **-ley**).

nokh|el/-lot נוכלת *nf* (woman) crook.

nokhoo|t/-yot נוחות *nf* comfort; convenience.

(be) nokhoot בנוחות *adv* at ease.

nokhree/-yah נוכרי *nmf* alien; foreigner.

nokhree/-t נוכרי *adj* alien; foreign.

(pe'ah/pe'ot) nokhree|t/-yot פיאה נוכרית *nf* wig; (*+of:* **pe'at**).

nokmanee/-t נוקמני *adj* vindictive.

nol|ad/-dah/-adetee נולד *v* was born; (*pres* **nolad**; *fut* **yeevaled** (*v=o*)).

(ha-rakh ha) nolad הרך הנולד *nm* the newborn.

(ra|'ah/-'atah/-eetee et ha) nolad ראה את הנולד *v* foresaw events; (*pres* **ro'eh** *etc*; *fut* **yeer'eh** *etc*).

nog|e'a/-a'at be-davar נוגע בדבר *adj* interested party.

(be) noge'a בנוגע *adv* concerning; regarding; in connection with.

(mah be) noge'a? מה בנוגע? what about?

noged/-et נוגד **1.** - *adj* contradicting; **2.** *v pres* contradicts; (*pst* **nagad**; *fut* **yeengod**).

nog|es/-seem נוגש *nm* oppressor; (*pl+of:* **-sey**).

noges/-et נוגס *v pres* bites; (*pst* **nagas**; *fut* **yeengos**).

nohag/nehageem נוהג *nm* custom; practice; (*pl+of:* **nohogey**).

nohal/nehaleem נוהל *nm* procedure; (*pl+of:* **noholey**).

noheg/-et נוהג *v pres* **1.** drives; **2.** behaves; (*pst* **nahag**; *fut* **yeenhag**).

nokef/-et נוקף *v pres* knocks; (*pres* **nakaf**; *fut* **yeenkof**); (falphabet see: **lo nokef**, below).

(lo) nokef (*etc*) **etsba'** לא נוקף אצבע doesn't lift a finger (*figurat.*).

noket/-et emtsa'eem נוקט אמצעים *v pres* takes measures.

nokev/-et נוקב *adj* exhaustive; penetrating.

nokhakh נוכח *adv* in the face of.

(le) nokhakh לנוכח *adv* confronted with; in front of.

nokh|akh/-ekhah/-akhtee נוכח *v* realized; became convinced; (*pres* **nokhakh**; *fut* **yeevakhakh** (*v=o*)).

nokh|e'akh/-akhat נוכח **1.** *adj* present; **2.** *nmf* who's present; (*pl:* **-ekheem/-ekhot**).

nokh|e'akh/-akhat נוכח *v pres* attends; is present at; (*pst* **nakhakh**; *fut* **yeenkakh** (*k=kh*)).

nokheeyoot נוחיות *nf* **1.** [*colloq.*] bathroom and toilet; **2.** comfortability.

(be) nokheeyoot בנוחיות [*colloq.*] *adv* at ease.

nokhekhee/-t נוכחי *adj* present.

nokhekhoot נוכחות *nf* presence; attendance.

(be) nokhekhoot בנוכחות *adv* in the presence of.

nokh|el/-leem נוכל *nm* crook; swindler; (*pl+of:* **-ley**).

nokh|el/-lot נוכלת *nf* (woman) crook.

nokhoo|t/-yot נוחות *nf* comfort; convenience.

(be) nokhoot בנוחות *adv* at ease.

nokhree/-yah נוכרי *nmf* alien; foreigner.

nokhree/-t נוכרי *adj* alien; foreign.

(pe'ah/pe'ot) nokhree|t/-yot פיאה נוכרית *nf* wig; (*+of:* **pe'at**).

nokmanee/-t נוקמני *adj* vindictive.

nol|ad/-dah/-adetee נולד *v* was born; (*pres* **nolad**; *fut* **yeevaled** (*v=o*)).

(ha-rakh ha) nolad הרך הנולד *nm* the newborn.

(ra|'ah/-'atah/-eetee et ha) nolad ראה את הנולד *v* foresaw events; (*pres* **ro'eh** *etc*; *fut* **yeer'eh** *etc*).

nomeenalee/-t נומינלי *adj* nominal.

noo! נו! *interj* well!; well , now...; go on!

noodneek/-eet נודניק *nmf* [*slang*] nagger; "pain in the neck"; (*pl:* **-eem/-yot**).

(telefon) noodneek טלפון נודניק *nm* [*colloq.*] repetitive telephone caller.

noog|eh/-ah נוגה *adj* sad; melancholic.

nookah/-tah/-etee נוקה *v* **1.** was cleaned, purified; **2.** (*figurat.*) was absolved; (*pres* **menookeh**; *fut* **yenookeh**).

nookah/-tah/-etee נוכה *v* has been deducted, discounted; (*pres* **menookeh**; *fut* **yenookeh**).

nook|ad/-dah/-adetee נוקד *v* was dotted, vocalized, pointed; (*pres* **menookad**; *fut* **yenookad**).

nook|av/-vah/-avtee נוקב *v* was punched, pierced, punctured; (*pres* **menookav**; *fut* **yenookav**).

nooksh|eh/-ah נוקשה *adj* tough; inflexible.

nool/-eem נול *nm* loom; (*pl+of:* **-ey**).

noom (or **noomah**)/**-ee!** נום! *v imp sing* sleep; go to sleep! (*inf* **lanoom**; *pst & pres* **nam**; *fut* **yanoom**).

◇ **noon/-eem** נון 14th letter of the Hebrew alphabet (נ) equivalent in pronunciation to Latin consonant "n". At the end of a word, Noon takes the form (ן) called "Final Noon" (noon sofeet נון סופית).

noon (נ) נון numerical *symbol*; 50; 50th.

"noon" "נון" *nm [slang]* failure; misgiving.

nur נור *nm* fire (in Talmud).

(zeekookeen dee) noor זיקוקין די־נור *nm pl* fireworks.

noor|ah/-ot נורה *nf* electric bulb; (*+of:* **-at**).

noor|ah/-tah/-etee (*npr* **norah**) נורה *v* **1.** was shot (a person); **2.** was fired (the shot); (*pres* **nooreh**; *fut* **yeeyareh**).

nooree|t/-yot נורית *nf* **1.** small electric bulb; **2.** crowfoot; buttercup (flower).

noosakh/-eem נוסח *nm* version; style; form: (*pl+of:* **-ey**).

◇ **"noosakh** (*etc*) **ashkenaz"** נוסח אשכנז *nm* the Ashkenazi version (rite) in prayer-books.

◇ **"noosakh** (*etc*) **sefarad"** נוסח ספרד *nm* the Sephardi version (rite) in prayer-books.

noosakh/-khah/-akhtee נוסח *v* was worded, formulated; (*pres* **menoosakh**; *fut* **yenoosakh**).

nooskh|ah/-a'ot נוסחה *nf* formula; version; (*+of:* **-at**).

nooskhat pla'eem (*or:* **nooskhat pele'**) נוסחת־פלאים *nf* (ironically) some miraculous formula.

nor|ah/-tah/-etee נורה *v* was shot (a person); was fired (the shot); (*pres* **nooreh**; *fut* **yeeyareh**).

nor|a/-a'ah נורא *adj* terrible.

nora נורא *adv* frightfully; terribly.

nora ve-ayom נורא ואיום *adv & adv* terrible indeed.

nora'ee/-t נוראי *adj [slang]* terrible; (sometimes used ironically).

◇ **(yameem) nora'eem** see ◇ **"yameem nora'eem"**.

□ **Nordeeyah** (Nordiyya) נורדיה *nm* collective village (est. 1948) in Sharon, 1 km SW of ha-Sharon Junction (**Tsomet ha-Sharon**). Pop. 376.

norm|ah/-ot נורמה *nf* norm; quota; (*+of:* **-at**).

normalee/-t נורמלי *adj* normal.

(lo) normalee/-t לא נורמלי *adj [slang]* (*lit.:* abnormal); "swell"; extraordinary.

normaleezatseeyah נורמליזציה *nf* normalization.

normateevee/-t נורמטיבי *adj* normative.

Norvegyah נורבגיה *nf* Norway.

norvegee/-t נורבגי *adj & nmf* Norwegian.

norvegeet נורבגית *nf* Norwegian (language).

nos|ad/-dah/-adetee נוסד *v* was founded, established; (*pres* **nosad**; *fut* **yeevased** (*v=o*)).

nos|af/-fah/-aftee נוסף *v* was added; (*pres* **nosaf**; *fut* **yeevasef** (*v=o*)).

nos|af/-efet נוסף *adj* added; additional.

nosaf 'al נוסף על *adv* in addition to.

(be) nosaf le- (*or:* **'al**) בנוסף על *adv* on the top of; in addition to.

(sha'ot) nosafot שעות נוספות *nf pl* overtime (hours).

nos|akh/-akheem נוסח *nm* version; text; form; (*pl+of:* **-khey**).

nos|e/-'eem נושא *nm* **1.** carrier; **2.** topic; **3.** subject (Gram.); (*pl+of:* **-'ey**).

nose/-t נושא *v pres* carries; (*pst* **nasa**; *fut* **yeesa**).

nos|e/-'ey geyasot נושא גייסות *nm* troop-carrier.

nos|e/-'ey keleem נושא כלים *nm* **1.** adjutant; **2.** devoted follower.

nos|e/-'ey meekhtaveem נושא מכתבים *nm* mailman.

nos|e/-'ey pree נושא פרי *adj* fruitful.

nose/-t shalom נושא שלום *adj* bringing regards; carrying a peace-message.

nos|e'a'/-a'at נוסע *v pres* travels; journeys; (*pst* **nasa'**; *fut* **yeesa'**).

nos|e'a/-a'at samooy/smoyah נוסע סמוי *nmf* stowaway.

nos|e'a/-'eem נוסע *nm* passenger; traveler; (*pl+of:* **-'ey**).

(sokhen) nose'a' סוכן נוסע *nm* traveling salesman.

(metos) nos'eem מטוס נוסעים *nm* passenger plane.

(rak|evet/-avot) nos'eem רכבת נוסעים *nm* passenger train.

□ **Nov** נוב *nm* village in S. Golan Heights (est. 1973), 2 km SW of **Ramat Magsheemeem**. Pop. 362.

novel/-et נובל **1.** *adj* withering; **2.** *v pres* withers; (*pst* **naval**; *fut* **yeebol** (*b=v*)).

novel|ah/-ot נובלה *nf* short story; novella (*+of:* **-at**).

november נובמבר *nm* November.

nover/-et נובר *v pres* pecks; nibbles; (*pst* **navar**; *fut* **yeenbor** (*b=v*)).

novet/-et נובט *v pres* buds; sprouts; (*pst* **navat**; *fut* **yeenbot** (*b=v*)).

noy נוי *nm* beauty; adornment.

(geen|at/-ot) noy גינת נוי *nf* house-garden; ornamental garden.

(peerkhey) noy פרחי נוי *nm pl* (*sing:* **perakh**) ornamental flowers.

nozef/-et נוזף *v pres* reprimands; rebukes; (*pst* **nazaf**; *fut* **yeenzof**).

noz|el/-leem נוזל *nm* liquid; (*pl+of:* **-ley**).

nozel/-et נוזל **1.** *adj* flowing; **2.** *v pres* flow(s) (*pst* **nazal**; *fut* **yeezal**).

nozlee/-t נוזלי *adj* liquid.

O.

incorporating words beginning with

o (או) **'o y** (עו) and **ho** (הו)

NOTE: **1.** The Hebrew vowel **o** is most frequently indicated by a Vav (ו) following the consonant with which it forms a syllable. In fully dotted texts it is sometimes indicated by a dot above (וֹ) and slightly to the left of the consonant letter (×). In a word where this consonant is the Alef (אוֹ), the beginning of the word will be heard as beginning with that vowel. In this section such words are spelled with **o** rather than **'o**.

Further, since most native Hebrew-speakers hardly distinguish in pronunciation between **Alef**, **'Ayeen** and **Heh**, we include in this chapter all words beginning with **o** even where these actually begin with **'Ayeen** or **Heh**. That will make it easier for the user to find such words, however pronounced, and at the same time, since they are transliterated, to pronounce each one correctly.

2. The Vav is also used to indicate the vowel **oo** (which, in a dotted text, has the dot in its middle (וּ) and not overhead (וֹ), and can therefore be clearly distinguished from). An undotted text is therefore technically ambiguous. Context and memory remove doubt in most cases.

o או or.

o... o... או ...או ... either... or...

ho! הו! *interj* oh! alas! woe!

obyekteevee/-t אובייקטיבי *adj* objective, impartial.

'od עוד *adv* more.

'od khazon la-mo'ed עוד חזון למועד time will tell.

'od pa'am עוד פעם *adv* again; please, once more, please!

'od rega'! עוד רגע! *adv* one more minute, please!.

hod הוד *nm* glory; splendor.

□ **Od ha-Sharon** see □ **Hod ha-Sharon.**

hod ma'alat|o/-ah הוד מעלתו/־ה *nmf* H.E.; His/Her Excellency.

hod malkhoot|o/-ah הוד מלכותו/־ה *nmf* H.M.; His/Her Majesty.

'od me'at עוד מעט *adv* one bit more; just one more minute.

(be) 'od בעוד *adv* **1.** while; **2.** within... (time).

(be) 'od mo'ed בעוד מועד *adv* in time; while there's still time.

(eyn) 'od אין עוד *adv* there is no more.

(kol) 'od כל עוד as long as.

(ve-lo) 'od ela ולא עוד אלא what's more, even; furthermore; not only that but...

hod|ah/-etah/-etee הודה *v* **1.** thanked; **2.** admitted; confessed; (*pres* **modeh;** *fut* **yodeh**).

hoda|'ah/-'ot הודאה *nf* admission; confession; (*+of:* **-'at**).

hoda|'ah/-'ot הודעה *nf* notification; announcement; notice; (*+of:* **-'at**).

hoda'ah mookdemet הודעה מוקדמת *nf* advance-notice.

hoda|'at/-'ot peetooreem (*or:* **peetooreen**) הודעת פיטורים *nf* notice of discharge; notice of dismissal.

hoda|yah/-'yot הודיה *nf* thanksgiving; (*+of:* **-at**).

(khag ha) hodayah חג ההודיה *nm* Thanksgiving Day.

□ **Odayot** see □ **Hodayot.**

'oded/-ah/'odadetee עודד *v* encouraged; (*pres* **me'oded;** *fut* **ye'oded**).

hodee/-m (or: **-yeem**) הודי *nm [colloq.]* turkey (fowl); (*corr. normat. term:* **tarnegol/-ey hodoo** תרנגול הודו); (*pl+of:* **-yey**).

hodee/-t הודי **1.** *adj* Indian; **2.** *nmf* Hindu.

'odee/-kha/-ekh/-o/-ah עודי/עודך/עודך/עודו וכו I/you(*m/f*)/he/she etc still...

(me)'odee/-kha/-ekh/-o/-ah מעודי/־ך/־ו never in my/your *m/f* /his/her etc life...

hod|ee'a'/-ee'ah/-a'tee הודיע *v* notified; announced; informed; (*pres* **hodee'a';** *fut* **yodee'a'**).

hodee'a (*etc*) **me-rosh** הודיע מראש *v* notified in advance.

□ **Odeeyah** see □ **Hodeeyah.**

'od|ef/-afeem עודף *nm* **1.** change (money); **2.** surplus; excess; (*pl+of:* **-fey**).

'od|ef/-fey meeshkal עודף משקל *nm* surplus weight; extra weight.

'od|ef/-fey merets עודף מרץ *nm* excess of energy.

□ **Odem** אודם *nm* collective village (est. 1975) in N. Golan Heights, 4 km S. of Mas'adah Junction **(Tsomet Mas'adah)**.

hodoo הודו *nf* India.

(tarnegol/-ey) hodoo תרנגול הודו *nm* turkey (fowl).

odot אודות about; of.

hodot הודות *adv* owing to; thanks to.

ho'eel/-ah/ho'altee הואיל *v* condescended; agreed; **(***pres* **mo'eel;** *fut* **yo'eel)**.

ho'eel ve- -הואיל ו whereas.

ho'eel/-ah/ho'altee הועיל *v* was useful to; benefited; **(***pres* **mo'eel;** *fut* **yo'eel)**.

'of/-ot עוף *nm* **1.** bird; **2.** poultry.

(merak) 'of מרק עוף *nm* chicken-soup.

hofa|'ah/-'ot הופעה *nf* appearance; **(***+of:* **-'at)**.

□ **Ofakeem** (Ofaqim) אופקים *nf* township (est. 1955) in W. Negev, 24 km W. of Beersheba and 4 km W. of Gilat Junction **(Tsomet Geelat)**. Pop. 13,700.

(rekhav/rakhvat) ofakeem רחב אופקים *adj* broad-minded.

ofan/-eem אופן *nm* wheel; **(***pl+of:* **-ey)**.

(tlat) ofan תלת אופן *nm* tricycle.

ofan|ayeem אופניים *nm pl* bicycle; **(***+of:* **-ey)**.

(rokh|ev/-evet) ofanayeem רוכב אופניים *nmf* cyclist **(***pl:* **-vey** *etc***)**.

ofano'an/-eem אופנוען *nm* motorcyclist **(***pl+of:* **-ey)**.

ofeh/ofeem אופה *nm* baker; **(***pl+of:* **ofey)**.

ofeh/ofah אופה *v pres* bakes; **(***pst* **ofah;** *fut* **yofeh)**.

ofee אופי *nm* character.

hof|ee'a'/-ee'ah/-a'tee הופיע *v* appeared; made an appearance; **(***pres* **mofee'a';** *fut* **yofee'a')**.

ofek/ofakeem אופק *nm* horizon; vista; **(***pl+of:* **ofkey)**.

(tsar/-at) ofek צר אופק narrow-minded.

(tsaroot) ofek צרות אופק *nf* narrow-mindedness.

ofel אופל *nm* darkness.

ofen/ofaneem אופן *nm* manner; mode; **(***pl+of:* **ofney)**.

(be) ofen she- -באופן ש *adv* so that; in a manner that.

(be) ofen yesodee באופן יסודי *adv* thoroughly; in a thorough manner.

(be-khol) ofen *(kh=k)* בכל אופן *adv* at any rate; in any case.

(be-shoom) ofen בשום אופן *adv* under no circumstances; in no way.

'of|er/-areem עופר *nm* fawn.

□ **'Ofer** ('Ofer) עופר *nm* village (est. 1950) in Karmel hills, 7 km W. of **Zeekhron-Ya'akov**. Pop. 265.

'oferet עופרת *nf* lead; (mineral).

ofkee/-t אופקי *adj* horizontal.

ofn|ah/-ot אופנה *nf* fashion.

ofnah khadashah אופנה חדשה *nf* new fashion.

(see ha) ofnah שיא האופנה *adj & nm* latest fashion; extremely fashionable.

ofnat ha-zrookeem אופנת הזרוקים the "hippy" fashion.

ofnat kayeets אופנת קיץ *nf* summer fashion.

ofnat khoref אופנת חורף *nf* winter fashion.

ofnatee/-t אופנתי *adj* fashionable.

ofn|ayeem (*npr* **ofan|ayeem)** אופניים *nm pl* bicycle; **(***+of:* **-ey)**.

(rokh|ev/-evet) ofnayeem (*npr* **ofanayeem)** רוכב אופניים *nmf* cyclist **(***pl:* **-vey** *etc***)**.

ofno|'a' (*npr* **ofano'a')/-'eem** אופנוע *nm* motorcycle; **(***pl+of:* **-'ey)**.

(rokh|ev/-vey) ofno'a (*npr* **ofano'a')** רוכב אופנוע *nm* motorcyclist.

ofno'an (*npr* **ofano'an)/-eem** אופנוען *nm* motorcyclist **(***pl+of:* **-ey)**.

'ofot (*sing:* **'of)** עופות *nm pl* **1.** fowl; birds; **2.** poultry.

(geedool) 'ofot גידול עופות *nm* poultry farming.

□ **Ofrah** ('Ofra) עופרה *nf* township (est. 1975) in Samaria, 7 km NE of Ramallah. Pop. 936.

ofyanee/-t אופייני *adj* typical.

ofyanee she -אופייני ש it is typical that.

'og|en/-aneem עוגן *nm* anchor; **(***pl+of:* **-ney)**.

'og|en/-ney hatsalah עוגן הצלה *nm* last resort.

'ogen/-et עוגן **1.** *adj* anchoring; mooring; **2.** *v pres* anchor(s); moor(s); **(***pst* **'agan;** *fut* **ya'agon)**.

□ **(Ha) 'Ogen** see □ **Ha-'Ogen.**

hogen/-et הוגן *adj* fair; decent.

(ka) hogen (*cpr* **ke-hogen)** כהוגן *adv* properly; well.

'ogm|at/-ot nefesh עוגמת נפש *nf* grief; sorrow.

ogoost אוגוסט *nm* August.

□ **Ohad** אוהד *nm* village (est. 1969) in W. Negev, 18 km SE of **Rafee'akh**. Pop. 202.

ohaveem אוהבים *nm pl* lovers.

ohed/ohad|eem אוהד *nm* sypathiser; **(***pl+of:* **-ey)**.

ohel/ohal|eem אוהל *nm* tent; **(***pl+of:* **-ey)**.

ohev/-et אוהב *v pres* loves; **(***pst* **ahav;** *fut* **yohav)**.

□ **Oholo** אהלו *nm* educational and convention center (est. 1951) of the Histadrut on S. shore of Lake Tiberias, near **Keeneret** village and coop. farm. Pop. (staff) 39.

ohev/-et betsa' אוהב בצע **1.** *adj* greedy; **2.** *nmf* mercenary; **(***pl:* **ohavey** *etc***)**.

ohev/-et teva' אוהב טבע *nmf* nature-lover; **(***pl:* **ohavey** *etc***)**.

hoka|'ah/-'ot הוקעה *nf* denunciation; **(***+of:* **'at)**.

hokar|ah/-ot הוקרה *nf* appreciation; esteem; **(***+of:* **-at)**.

hok|ee'a'/-ee'ah/-a'tee הוקיע *v* denounced; **(***prs* **mokee'a';** *fut* **yokee'a')**.

'okets/'okatseem עוקץ *nm* sting; **(***pl+of:* **'ooktsey)**.

o-key אוקיי *[slang]* OK; O-kay.

hokhakh|ah/-ot הוכחה *nf* proof; **(***+of:* **-at)**.

hokh|ee'akh/-eekhah/-akhtee הוכיח *v* proved; **(prs mokhee'akh;** *fut* **yokhee'akh)**.

okhel אוכל *nm* food.

okhel besaree אוכל בשרי *nm* meaty food.

okhel beytee אוכל ביתי home-made food.

okhel dee'etetee אוכל דיאטטי dietetic food.

okhel eyropee אוכל אירופי *nm* European food.

okhel kasher אוכל כשר *nm* "kosher" food.
okhel khalavee אוכל חלבי *nm* milky food.
okhel meezrakhee אוכל מזרחי *nm* Near-Eastern (*lit.:* Eastern) food.
okhel mookhan אוכל מוכן *nm* ready-made food.
okhel seenee אוכל סיני *nm* Chinese food.
okhel tseemkhonee אוכל צמחוני *nm* vegeterian food.
(khad|ar/-rey) okhel חדר אוכל *nm* dining-room.
(tsorkhey) okhel צורכי אוכל *nm pl* foodstuffs.
okhel/-et אוכל *v pres* eat(s); (*pst* **akhal**; *fut* **yokhal**).
'okh|er/-rey yeesra'el עוכר ישראל *nm* a trouble-maker for Israel (Bibl.); renegade from the Jewish cause.
okhez/-et אוחז *v pres* hold(s); (*pres* **akhaz**; *fut* **yokhaz**).
oktober אוקטובר *nm* October.
'oktsanee/-t עוקצני *adj* mordant; sarcastic.
okyanos/-eem אוקיינוס *nm* ocean.
'ol/'ool|eem עול *nm* burden; yoke; (*pl+of:* **-ey**).
'ol|ah/-ot עולה *nf* immigrant to Israel (female); (*+of:* **-at**).
'olah khadashah עולה חדשה *nf* newly arrived female immigrant.
'olal/-eem עולל *nm* baby; suckling.
'olam/-ot עולם *nm* world.
'olam ha-pesha' עולם הפשע *nm* the criminal world.
'olam oo-melo'o עולם ומלואו *nm* **1.** the whole world; **2.** a world in itself.
(ha) 'olam ha-takhton העולם התחתון *nm* the underworld.
('ad) olam עד עולם *adv* to eternity; forever.
(aseer/-ey) 'olam אסיר עולם *nm* one serving a life sentence.
(ha) 'olam ha-ba העולם הבא *nm* **1.** the world beyond; Heaven; Paradise; **2.** (*lit.*) the world to come.
(ha) 'olam ha-zeh העולם הזה *nm* this world; life on earth.
(hashkaf|at/-ot) 'olam השקפת עולם *nf* personal philosophy; outlook on the world.
(le) 'olam לעולם *adv* always; forever.
(le) 'olam lo לעולם לא *adv* never.
(le) 'olam lo 'od לעולם לא עוד *adv* never again.
(le) 'olam va-'ed לעולם ועד *adv* for ever and ever.
(lo hayoo dvareem me) 'olam לא היו דברים מעולם nothing of the kind ever happened.
(ma'asar) 'olam מאסר עולם *nm* imprisonment for life; life sentence.
(me)'olam lo... מעולם לא... *adv* never before; at no time ever.
(reebono shel) 'olam ריבונו של עולם *nm* God in heaven; Master of the Universe.
(ta'oot le)'olam khozeret טעות לעולם חוזרת errors and omissions excepted: (used in documents as *abbr. acr.* .ט.ל.ח).

'olamee/-t עולמי **1.** *adj* global; worldwide; **2.** *[slang] adj* excellent; unsurpassable.
(heer|'eesh/-'eeshah/-'ashtee) 'olamot הרעיש עולמות *v* created a fuss; (*pres* **mar'eesh** *etc; fut* **yar'eesh** *etc*).
Holand הולנד *nf* Holland.
holandee/-t הולנדי **1.** *nmf* Dutchman/ Dutchwoman; **2.** *adj* Dutch.
olar/-eem אולר *nm* pocketknife; penknife.
'ol|eh/-eem עולה *nm* immigrant to Israel; (*pl+of:* **-ey**).
'ol|eh/-ah be-kaneh ekhad עולה בקנה אחד *v pres* fits in with; (*pst* **'alah** *etc; fut* **ya'aleh** *etc*).
'ol|eh/-eem khadash/-eem עולה חדש *nm* newly arrived immigrant.
'ol|eh/-at regel עולה רגל *nm* pilgrim.
◇ **(te'ood|at/-ot)** see ◇ **te'ood|at/-ot 'oleh.**
hol|eed/-eedah/-adetee הוליד **1.** *v* begot; **2.** resulted in; (*pres* **moleed**; *fut* **yoleed**).
hol|eekh/-eekhah/-akhtee הוליך *v* led; guided; (*pres* **moleekh**; *fut* **yoleekh**).
holeekh (*etc*) **sholal** הוליך שולל *v* fooled; misled.
oleempee/-t אולימפי *adj* Olympic.
oleempyad|ah/-ot אולימפיאדה *nf* Olympic Games; (*+of:* **-at**).
holekh/-et הולך *v* goes; (*pst* **halakh**; *fut* **yelekh**).
holekh/-et batel הולך בטל *adj & nmf* idler; loafer.
holekh ba-telem הולך בתלם *v pres* toes the line; (*pst* **halakh** *etc; fut* **yelekh** *etc*).
holekh/-et ba-telem הולך בתלם *adj & nmf* conformist.
holekh/-et rakheel הולך רכיל **1.** *adj & nmf* gossiper; **2.** *v pres* gossips; (*pst* **halakh** *etc; fut* **yelekh** *etc*).
hol|ekh/-khey regel הולך רגל *nm* pedestrian.
holekh (*etc*) **ve-neevneh** הולך ונבנה **1.** *v pres* is going up; **2.** *adj* abuilding.
(eykh) holekh? ?איך הולך *[colloq.]* how goes it? how are you getting on?
(lo) holekh ba-regel לא הולך ברגל *[slang]* is not to be underrated.
(nots|ar/-'eret ve) holekh/-et (*etc*) נוצר והולך *v pres* (is) gradually developing; (*pst* **notsar ve-halakh**; *fut* **yeevatser** *(v=o)* **ve-yelekh**).
(pokhet/-et ve) holekh/-et (*etc*) פוחת והולך **1.** *adj* dwindling, diminishing; **2.** *v pres* is gradually decreasing; (*pst* **pakhat ve-halakh**; *fut* **yeefkhat ve-yelekh**).
holel/-et הולל **1.** *adj* licentious; unruly; **2.** *nmf* jester; dissolute person; (*pl+of:* **-ey**).
'ol|el/-elah/-altee עולל *v* perpetrated; committed; caused; (*pres* **me'olel**; *fut* **ye'olel**).
holeloot/-yot הוללות *nf* debauchery.
'olelot עוללות *nf pl* scraps; trivia.
holem/-et הולם **1.** *adj* suitable; appropriate; **2.** *adj* becoming; **3.** *v pres* strikes; beats; **4.** fits; suits; (*pst* **halam**; *fut* **yahalom**).
□ **'Olesh** ('Olesh) עולש *nm* village in N. part of Sharon, 8 km E. of haSharon Junction (**Tsomet ha-Sharon**). Pop. 468.

◇ **'oley etyopyah** עולי אתיופיה *nm pl* immigration waves in 1986-87 and again in 1990-91 of black-skinned Jews from Ethiopia. There, the community, dating perhaps from 1000 BCE had preserved through the ages its own brand of Judaism.

◇ **'oley ha-gardom** עולי הגרדום *nm pl* (*sing:* **'oleh** *etc*) *lit.:* "the mounters of the gallows" - reference to freedom-fighters of the Jewish resistance factions Irgun Zeva'i Leumi (**"Etsel"**) and Stern Gang (**"Lekhee"**) hanged by the British in pre-State struggle (1938-1947).

oman/-eet אומן *nmf* artist; (*pl:* **-eem/-yot**; *+of:* **-ey**).

oman|oot (*npr* **ooman|oot**)/**-yot** אומנות *nf* art.

omanootee/-t אומנותי *adj* artistic.

(teekoon) omanootee תיקון אומנותי *nm* artistic mending.

'omed/-et עומד **1.** *adj* standing; **2.** *v pres* stands; (*pst* **'amad**; *fut* **ya'amod**).

(po'al) 'omed פועל עומד *nm* (*Gram.*) intransitive verb.

(talooy/telooyah ve) 'omed/-et תלוי ועומד *adj* pending.

'om|ek/-akeem עומק *nm* depth; (*pl+of:* **-key**).

□ **Omen** אומן *nm* rural center (est. 1958) for villages of **Ta'anakh** district, 5 km E. of Meggido Junction (**Tsomet Megeedo**).

omenet/omnot אומנת *nf* nanny; governess.

omer/amareem אומר *nm* saying; speech; utterance; (*pl+of:* **eemrey**).

(blee) omer oo-dvareem בלי אומר ודברים *adv* without talk; speechlessly.

omer/-et אומר *v pres* says; (*pst* **amar**; *fut* **yomar**).

omer (*etc*) **ve-'oseh** אומר ועושה no sooner said than done.

'om|er/-areem עומר *nm* sheaf of corn; (*pl+of:* **rey**).

□ **'Omer** ('Omer) עומר *nf* fashionable residential suburb of Beersheba which originally (1949) was established as an agricultural settlement at 6 km NE of the city. Pop. 6,050.

◇ **(lag-ba) 'omer** see ◇ **lag-ba-'omer**.

◇ **(sefeerat ha) 'omer** see ◇ **sfeerat ha-'omer**.

(eyn zot) omeret אין זאת אומרת which does not mean that...

(zot) omeret זאת אומרת which means that; i.e.

'omes עומס *nm* load; burden.

(tosefet) 'omes תוספת עומס *nf* overload pay.

omets אומץ *nm* courage; audacity.

□ **Omets** (Omez) אומץ *nm* village (est. 1949) in Sharon, 6 km NW of **Toolkarem**. Pop. 222.

omets-lev אומץ לב *nm* daring; courage.

omnam אומנם indeed.

(ha) omnam? (*npr* **ha-oomnam?**) ?האומנם indeed? is that so?

homo/-'eem הומו *[slang] nm* homosexual, "gay".

homogenee/-t הומוגני *adj* homogeneous.

on/eem און *nm* strength; power.

hon הון *nm* capital; fortune.

hon 'atak (*npr* **'atek**) הון עתק *nm* fabulous wealth; fabulous sum of money.

hon khozer הון חוזר *nm* circulating capital; working capital; operating capital.

hon to'afot הון תועפות *nf* lots of money.

(ba'al/-ey) hon בעל הון *nm* capitalist; potential investor.

(gar|af/-fah/-aftee) hon גרף הון made lots of money; (*lit.*) raked in a fortune; (*pres* **goref hon**; *fut* **yeegrof hon**).

(mashkee|'a'/-'ey) hon משקיע הון *nm* capital investor.

(revakh/reevkhey) hon רווח הון *nm* capital gain.

'on|ah/-ot עונה *nf* season; (*+of:* **-at**).

(be-'et oo-ve) 'onahakhat בעת ובעונה אחת *adv* at one and the same time; simultaneously.

(masmer ha) 'onah מסמר העונה *nm* highlight of the season.

(mekheer|at/-'ot sof ha) 'onah מכירת סוף העונה *nf* end-of-season sale.

ona|'ah/-'ot אונאה *nf* deceit; (*+of:* **at**).

hon|ah/-tah/-etee הונה *v* deceived; tricked.

hona|'ah/-'ot הונאה *nf* swindle; fraud; (*+of:* **-'at**).

'onasheen עונשין *nm pl* punishment.

(bar/-at) 'onasheen בר־עונשין *adj* answerable by law.

(deeney) 'onasheen דיני עונשין *nm pl* penal laws.

◇ **'onat ha-hadareem** עונת ההדרים *nf* the citrus season (October-March).

'onat ha-kayeets עונת הקיץ *nf* the summer season.

'onat ha-khoref עונת החורף *nf* the winter season.

'onatee/-t עונתי *adj* seasonal.

'onee עוני *nm* poverty.

(meeshkenot) 'onee משכנות עוני *nm pl* slums.

(shekhoonat/-ot) 'onee שכונת עוני *nf* slum quarter.

honee/-t הוני *adj* capital.

(eyn) oneem אין אונים *adv* helplessly.

(khas|ar/-rat) oneem חסר אונים *adj* powerless; helpless.

onee|yah/-yot אונייה *nf* ship; (*+of:* **-yat**).

onee|yat/-yot keetor אוניית קיטור *nf* steamer; steamship.

onee|yat/-ot ma'boret אוניית מעבורת *nf* ferryboat.

onee|yat/-yot masa אוניית משא *nf* freighter; cargo-ship.

onee|yat/-yot nos'eem אוניית נוסעים *nf* passenger-boat.

'on|eh/-ah עונה *v pres* responds; answers; (*pst* **'anah**; *fut* **ya'aneh**).

'oneg עונג *nm* pleasure.

◇ **'oneg-shabat** עונג שבת *nm* Sabbath entertainment; reception and/or public lecture held on Sabbath.

onen/onenah/onantee אונן *v* masturbated; (*pres* **me'onen**; *fut* **ye'onen**).

onenoo|t/-yot אוננות *nf* masturbation.
ones אונס *nf* rape.
(be) ones באונס *adv* compulsively.
ones/-et אונס *v pres* **1.** compels; forces; **2.** rapes; (*pst* **anas**; *fut* **ye'enos**).
'on|esh/-asheem עונש *nm* punishment; (*pl+of:* **'onshey**).
'onesh (*etc*) **keebotsee/-yeem** עונש קיבוצי *nm* collective punishment.
'onesh (*etc*) **kvootsatee/-yeem** עונש קבוצתי *nm* collective punishment.
'on|esh/-shey mavet עונש מוות *nm* capital punishment; death sentence.
(be-'eyn) 'onesh באין עונש *adv* unpunished.
(hamtakat ha) 'onesh המתקת עונש *nf* mitigation of punishment.
'onsheen (*npr* **'onasheen**) עונשין *nm pl* punishment.
(bar/-at) 'onsheen (*npr* **'onasheen**) בר־עונשין *adj* answerable by law.
(deeney) 'onsheen (*npr* **'onasheen**) דיני עונשין *nm pl* penal laws.

Oo.
NOTE: for words beginning in **oo, 'oo, 'oo** or **hoo** (pronounced as in *oodles* or *oomph*) see next chapter.

ho'od|af/-fah/-aftee הועדף *v* was preferred, given preference; (*pres* **mo'odaf**; *fut* **yo'odaf**).
ho'ol|ah/-tah/-etee הועלה *v* was raised, promoted; (*pres* **mo'oleh**; *fut* **yo'oleh**).
ho'olah (*etc*) **la-arets** הועלה לארץ *v* was enabled to immigrate to Israel.
ho'om|ad/-dah/-adetee הועמד *v* was put, placed, nominated as candidate; (*pres* **mo'omad**; *fut* **yo'omad**).
ho'om|ak/-kah הועמק *v* was deepened; (*pres* **moo'amak**; *fut* **yoo'amak**).
ho'on|ak/-kah הוענק *v* was bestowed, granted; (*pres* **mo'onak**; *fut* **yo'onak**).
ho'or|akh/-khah/-akhtee הוארך *v* was prolonged; was extended; (*pres* **mo'orakh**; *fut* **yo'orakh**).
ho'or|akh/-khah/-akhtee הוערך *v* was estimated, evaluated; (*pres* **mo'orakh**; *fut* **yo'orakh**).
ho'os|ak/-kah/-aktee הועסק *v* was employed; (*pres* **mo'osak**; *fut* **yo'osak**).
ho'ot|ak/-kah הועתק *v* **1.** was moved over; **2.** was copied; (*pres* **mo'otak**; *fut* **yo'otak**).
ho'ov|ad/-dah/-adetee הועבד *v* was employed (**prs mo'ovad**; *fut* **yo'ovad**).
ho'ov|ar/-rah/-artee הועבר *v* was moved; was transferred; (**prs mo'ovar**; *fut* **yo'ovar**).
oper|ah/-ot אופרה *nf* opera; (*+of:* **-at**).
opera'ee/-t אופראי *adj* operatic.
operet|ah/-ot אופרטה *nf* operetta; (*+of:* **-at**).
opozeetsee|yah/-yot אופוזיציה *nf* parliamentary opposition.

opteeka|'ee (*npr* **opteeka|y**)/**-'eem** אופטיקאי *nm* optician; (*pl+of:* **-'ey**).
opteemalee/-t אופטימלי *adj* optimal.
opteemee/-t אופטימי *adj* optimistic.
opteemeeyoot אופטימיות *nf* optimism.
optsee|yah/-yot אופציה *nf* option; (*+of:* **yat**).
or/-ot אור *nm* light.
□ **Or 'Akeeva** (Or 'Aqiva) אור עקיבא *nf* industrial township (est. 1951), 2 km E. of Caesaria ruins and of fashionable residential settlement **Kesareeyah**. Pop. 8,180.
□ **Or Ha-ner** (Or haNer) אור הנר *nm* kibbutz (est. 1957) in **Lakheesh** area, 3.5 km N. of **Sderot**. Pop. 387.
or-le-yom אור ליום *adv* on the eve of...; the evening and the night preceding a certain day.
□ **Or Yehoodah** (Or Yehuda) אור יהודה *nf* township (est. 1950), 7 km SE of Tel-Aviv. Pop. 21,900.
(boker) or! בוקר אור! (greeting, answer to "boker tov!") Good morning!
(keren/karney) or קרן אור *nf* beam of light.
(le-) or לאור *adv* in the light of; in view of.
(le) or ha-yom לאור היום *adv* in daylight.
(motsee/-'eem) la-or מוציא לאור *nm* publisher.
'or/-ot עור *nm* **1.** skin; hide; **2.** leather.
(beged/beegdey) 'or בגד עור *nm* leatherwear.
(kar|am/-mah/-amtee) 'or ve-geedeem קרם עור וגידים *v* **1.** materialized; **2.** (*lit.*) grew tendons and crusted skin; (*pres* **korem** *etc*; *fut* **yeekrom** *etc*).
(meteekhat) 'or ha-paneem מתיחת עור הפנים *nf* face lifting.
(pash|at/-tah/-atetee) 'or פשט עור *v* skinned; robbed; (*pres* **poshet** *etc*; *fut* **yeefshot** *etc f=p*).
(posh|et/-tey) 'or פושט עור **1.** *nm* skinner; **2.** (*figurat.*) profiteer.
(rof|e/-'at) 'or רופא עור *nmf* dermatologist.
orah/-orot אורה *nf* **1.** light; illumination; **2.** joy; happiness.
□ **Orah** (Ora) אורה *nm* village (est. 1950), 2 km W. of Jerusalem. Pop. 388.
horah/-ot הורה *nf* Israeli folk-dance.
hor|ah/-tah/-etee הורה *v* directed; ordered; (*pres* **moreh**; *fut* **yoreh**).
hora'ah הוראה *nf* (*sing* only) teaching (as a profession).
hora|'ah/-ot הוראה *nf* instruction; directive; (*+of:* **-'at**).
hora|'at/-'ot keva הוראת קבע *nf* standing order.
horad|ah/-ot הורדה *nf* reduction; demotion; taking down; (*+of:* **-at**).
orakh/orkhot אורח *nm* manner.
orakh khayeem אורח חיים *nm* way of life.
(be) 'orakh reeshmee (*cpr* **rasmee**) באורח רשמי *adv* officially; formally.
('ov|er/-rey) orakh עובר אורח *nm* transient; passer-by.
orakhat/orkhot אורחת *nf* female guest; female visitor.

□ **Oraneem** אורנים *nm* educational center of the kibbutzim (est. 1951) 1.5 km W. of **Keeryat Teev'on**. Pop. 125.

□ **Oraneet** (Oranit) אורנית *nf* village (est. 1985), 3 km E. of **Kafr Kasem**. Pop.2,240.

ore'akh/orkh|eem אורח *nm* guest; (*pl+of:* **-ey**).

hor|eed/-eedah/-adetee הוריד *v* reduced; lowered; took down; (*pres* **mooreed**; *fut* **yoreed**).

horeed (*etc*) **meeshkal** ([*colloq.*]: **be-meeshkal**) הוריד משקל *v* lost weight.

(lo ma'aleh ve-lo) moreed לא מעלה ולא מוריד matters in no way: makes no difference.

hor|eek/-eekah/-aktee הוריק *v* **1.** greened; **2.** [*colloq.*] emptied; (*pres* **moreek**; *fut* **yoreek**).

hor|eem הורים *nm pl* (*sing nmf* **hor|eh/-ah**) parents; (*+of:* **-ey**).

hor|eesh/-eeshah/-ashtee הוריש *v* bequeathed, left as inheritance; (*pres* **moreesh**; *fut* **yoreesh**).

'or|ef/-afeem עורף *nm* **1.** neck; nape; rear; **2.** home front (military); (*pl+of:* **-fey**).

(heefnah/-etah/-etee) 'oref הפנה עורף *v* turned one's back; (*pres* **mafneh** *etc*; *fut* **yafneh** *etc*).

(kesheh/keshat) 'oref קשה עורף *adj* obstinate; stiff-necked.

(pan|ah/-tah/-eetee) 'o'ref פנה עורף *v* turned one's back; (*pres* **poneh** *etc*; *fut* **yeefneh** *etc*).

horeg/-et הורג *v pres* kills.

(atah/at) horeg/-et otee! ! אתה הורג אותי [*slang*] you're "killing me!"...

(la) horeg להורג *adv* to death by execution.

hor|eh/-ah הורה *nmf* parent.

'or|ek (*npr* **'orek**)**/-keem** עורק *nm* artery; (*pl+of:* **-key**).

'orek/-et עורק *v pres* deserts; shirks; (*pst* **'arak**; *fut* **ya'arok**).

orekh/orakheem אורך *nm* length.

orekh roo'akh אורך רוח *nm* patience.

(kav/-ey) orekh קו אורך *nm* meridian; longitude; (Geogr.).

(le) orekh לאורך *adv* in length.

(le) orekh yameem לאורך ימים *adv* for a long time.

'orekh/-et עורך **1.** *nmf* editor; **2.** *v pres* arranges; **3.** *v pres* edits; (*pst* **'arakh**; *fut* **ya'arokh**).

'orekh/-et (*etc*) **kheshbon** עורך חשבון *v pres* settles account.

'orekh/-et 'eeton/shvoo'on/yarkhon /עורך עיתון שבועון/ירחון *nmf* editor of a newspaper, weekly, monthly (*etc*).

'orekh/-et (*etc*) **seder** עורך סדר *v pres* puts in order.

◇ **'orekh/-et** (*etc*) **et ha-seder** עורך את הסדר *v* conducts the "Seder" (festive Passover dinner).

'or|ekh/-khey deen עורך דין *nm* lawyer; attorney.

'or|ekhet/-khot deen עורכת דין *nf* female lawyer.

'or|ekh/-kheem rashee/-yeem עורך ראשי *nm* chief editor; editor-in-chief.

or|en/-aneem אורן *nm* pine; pine tree; (*pl+of:* **-ney**).

'orer/-ah/'orartee עורר *v* woke up; roused; (*pres* **me'orer**; *fut* **ye'orer**).

'orer (*etc*) **be'a|yah/-yot** עורר בעיה *v* raised a problem.

'orer (*etc*) **heetnagdoot** עורר התנגדות *v* antagonized.

'orer (*etc*) **kheshed/khashadot** עורר חשד *v* aroused suspicion.

'orer (*etc*) **roshem** עורר רושם *v* gave the impression.

'orer (*etc*) **tsekhok** עורר צחוק *v* got a laugh.

orev/-et אורב *v* lurks; (*pst* **arav**; *fut* **ye'erov**).

'or|ev/-veem עורב *nm* crow; (*pl+of:* **-vey**).

orez אורז *nm* rice.

orez/-et אורז *v pres* packs; ties; (*pst* **araz**; *fut* **ye'eroz**).

orez/orzeem אורז *v* packer; (*pl+of:* **orzey**).

organee/-t אורגני *adj* organic.

(zevel) organee זבל אורגני *nm* organic fertilizer.

'orkeem עורקים *nm pl* arteries; (*sing:* **'orek**; *pl+of:* **'orkey**).

(av ha) 'orkeem אב העורקים *nm* aorta (Anat.).

(heestaydoot ha) 'orkeem הסתיידות העורקים *nf* arteriosclerosis.

orkheem אורחים *nm pl* guests; (*sing nmf:* **ore'akh/orakhat**; *pl+of:* **orkhey**).

(hakhnasat) orkheem הכנסת אורחים *nf* hospitality.

(khad|ar/-rey) orkheem חדר אורחים *nm* guestroom.

(makhnees/-at) orkheem מכניס אורחים *adj* hospitable.

(meesrad) 'orkhey deen משרד עורכי דין *nm* law-offices.

'orm|ah/-ot עורמה *nf* cunning; craftiness; (*+of:* **-at**).

horoot הורות *nf* parenthood.

horoskop/-em הורוסקופ *nm* horoscope.

□ **Orot** אורות *nm* village (est. 1952) in W. Negev, 1 km NW of **Keeryat-Mal'akhee**. Pop. 226.

'orpee/-t עורפי *adj* behind the frontline; rear-; back; occipital.

(shoorah) 'orpeet שורה עורפית *nf* rear line.

□ **Ortal** אורטל *nm* kibbutz (est. 1979) in N. of Golan Heights, 3 km SW of kibbutz **'En Zeevan**.

hosaf|ah/-ot הוספה *nf* increase; increment; addition; (*+of:* **-at**).

'os|eh/-ah עושה *v pres* does; makes; (*pst* **'asah**; *fut* **ya'aseh**).

'oseh (*etc*) **khesed** עושה חסד *v pres* does a favor, a good deed.

'oseh (*etc*) **roo'akh** עושה רוח [*colloq.*] *v pres* just makes a noise.

'oseh (*etc*) **shalom** עושה שלום *v pres* makes peace.

'oseh (*etc*) **tovah** עושה טובה *v pres* does a favor.

'oseh (*etc*) **tsarot** עושה צרות *v pres* makes trouble.

'os|eh/-ey tsarot עושה צרות *nm* trouble- maker.

'oseh (*etc*) **tserakhav** עושה צרכיו *v* eases oneself; obeys nature's call.

(omer ve) 'oseh אומר ועושה *adv* no sooner said than done.

hos|eef/-eefah/-aftee הוסיף *v* added; continued; (*pres* **moseef**; *fut* **yoseef**).

hoseef (*etc*) **meeshkal** הוסיף משקל *v* put on weight.

osef/osafeem אוסף *nm* collection; (*pl+of:* **osfey**).

'osek/-et עוסק *v pres* deals in; handles; engages in; (*pres* **'asak**; *fut* **ya'asok**).

'os|ek/-keem עוסק *nm* dealer (for legal purposes: liable to V.A.T. taxation).

'os|ek/-keem za'eer/ze'eereem עוסק זעיר *nm* minor dealer (liable to V.A.T. taxation).

(ba-meh ata/at) 'osek/-et? במה אתה עוסק? what's your (*m/f sing*) line of business?

◇ **osha'na Rabah** see ◇ **hosha'na rabah**.

hosh|ee'a'/-ee'ah/-a'tee הושיע *nf* rescued; saved; (*pres* **moshee'a'**; *fut* **yoshee'a'**).

hosh|eet/-eetah/-atetee הושיט stretched out; extended; handed; (*pres* **mosheet**; *fut* **yosheet**).

hosheet/-ah (*etc*) **ezrah** הושיט עזרה *v* rendered assistance.

hosheet/-ah (*etc*) **yad** הושיט יד *v* stretched out one's hand; lent a helping hand.

hosh|eev/-eevah/-avtee הושיב *v* placed; sat; (*pres* **mosheev**; *fut* **yosheev**).

'oshek עושק *nm* robbery; unjust gain; exploitation.

'oshek/-et עושק *v pres* exploits; subdues; (*pst* **'ashak**; *fut* **ya'ashok**).

osher אושר *nm* luck; happiness.

'osher עושר *nm* wealth; riches.

ot/-eeyot אות *nf* letter; character.

ot/-ot אות *nm* sign; decoration.

ot/-ot heetstaynoot אות הצטיינות *nm* mark of distinction; decoration; medal.

ot kalon אות קלון *nm* mark of shame.

otah אותה *pron (f sing)* **1.** her; **2.** the same.

otakh אותך *pron (f sing) sing* you.

otam אותם *pron (m pl)* **1.** them; **2.** the same.

otan אותן *pron (f pl)* them;2. the same (fem.).

otanoo אותנו *pron (mf pl)* us.

otee אותי *pron (mf sing)* me.

hot|eer/-eerah/-artee הותיר *v* left; left behind; (*pres* **moteer**; *fut* **yoteer**).

'ot|ek/-akeem עותק *nm* copy; (*pl+of:* **-key**).

'oter/-et עותר **1.** *nmf* petitioner; (*pl:* **-reem**; *+of:* **-rey**); **2.** *v pres* petitions; (*pst* **'atar**; *fut* **ya'ator**).

(day- ve) hoter די והותר *adv* more than enough; more than needed.

ot|et/-etah/-atetee אותת *v* signalled; (*pres* **me'otet**; *fut* **ye'otet**).

otkha אותך *pron (m sing)* you.

('azov) otkha me- עזוב אותך מ־ *[slang] v imp sing m* leave alone; pay no attention.

oto אוטו *nm [slang]* motor-car; automobile; (*colloq. pl:* **oto'eem**; *normat. pl:* **otomobeeleem**).

oto אותו *pron (m sing)* **1.** him; **2.** the same.

otoboos/-eem אוטובוס *nm* bus (*pl+of:* **-ey**).

otoboos (*etc*) **komatayeem** אוטובוס קומתיים *nm* double-decker (bus).

'otomanee/-t עותומני *adj* Ottoman.

(khok/khookeem) 'otomanee/-yeem חוק עותומני *nm* Ottoman Law.

otomatee/-t אוטומטי *adj* automatic.

otomateet אוטומטית *adv* automatically.

otomobeel/-eem אוטומוביל *nm* automobile.

otonomee|yah/-yot אוטונומיה *nf* autonomy.

otostrad|ah/-ot אוטוסטראדה *nf* expressway; autoroute; limited-access highway; (*+of:* **-dat**).

hotsa|'ah/-'ot הוצאה *nf* **1.** expenditure; expense; **2.** ousting; (*+of:* **-at**).

hotsa|'ah/-'ot la-or הוצאה לאור *nf* publishing house.

hotsa|'ah/-'ot la-horeg הוצאה להורג *nf* execution.

hotsa'ah la-po'al הוצאה לפועל *nf* execution (by court order); implementation.

(meesrad ha) hotsa'ah la-po'al משרד ההוצאה לפועל *nm* the execution office.

hotsa'at deebah הוצאת דיבה *nf* libel; defamation.

hotsa'at shem ra' הוצאת שם רע *nf* giving a bad name; defamation.

ots|ar/-rot אוצר *nm* treasure.

otsar meeleem אוצר מלים *nm* vocabulary.

(ha) otsar האוצר *nm* the Treasury.

(meesrad ha) otsar משרד האוצר *nm* the Ministry of Finance; the treasury.

(sar ha) otsar שר האוצר *nm* the Minister of Finance.

hots|ee/-ee'ah/-etee הוציא *v* **1.** took out; **2.** spent; **3.** spread; (*pres* **motsee**; *fut* **yotsee**).

hotsee (*etc*) **deebah** הוציא דיבה *v* libeled; slandered.

hotsee (*etc*) **la-horeg** הוציא להורג *v* executed; put to death.

hotsee (*etc*) **la-or** הוציא לאור *v* published.

hotsee (*etc*) **la-po'al** הוציא לפועל *v* carried out; implemented.

hotsee (*etc*) **shem ra'** הוציא שם רע *v* gave one a bad name; slandered.

(le) hotsee להוציא *adv* except; excluding.

'otsem עוצם *nm* strength; forcefulnees.

□ **'Otsem** ('Ozem) עוצם *nm* village (est. 1955) in **Lakheesh** area, 6 km NW of **Keeryat Gat**. Pop. 474.

'otser עוצר *nm* curfew.

'otser/-et עוצר *v pres* stops; (*pst* **'atsar**; *fut* **ya'atsor**).

'otser/-et nesheemah עוצר נשימה *adj* breathtaking.

'ots|er/-reem עוצר *nm* regent; (*pl+of:* **-rey**).

'otsm|ah/-ot עוצמה *nf* might; power; (*+of:* **-at**).

hoval|ah/-ot הובלה *nf* transportation; conveying; (*+of:* **-at**).

ovdan אובדן *nm* loss; ruin.

ovdan khayeem אובדן חיים *nm* loss of life.
ovdan khayey adam אובדן חיי אדם *nm* loss of human life.
'ovdeem עובדים *pl nm* (*sing:* **'oved**) workers; employees; (*+of:* **'ovdey**).
◇ **(heestadroot ha) 'ovdeem ha-klaleet** see ◇ **heestadroot ha-'ovdeem.**
◇ **(heestadroot ha) 'ovdeem ha-le'oomeet** see ◇ **heestadroot ha-'ovdeem ha-le'oomeet.**
(khever) 'ovdeemחבר עובדים *nm* personnel; staff.
◇ **(khevrat ha) 'ovdeem** see ◇ **khevrat ha-'ovdeem.**
(peetsooyeem le) 'ovdeem פיצויים לעובדים *nm pl* workmen's compensation.
oved/-et אובד **1.** *adj* lost; **2.** *v pres* is lost; gets lost; (*pst* **avad;** *fut* **yovad**).
oved/-et 'etsot אובד עצות *adj* perplexed; helpless.
◇ **'oved/-et kavoo'a/kvoo'ah** עובד קבוע *nmf* "permanent" worker (or employee) i.e. one who, after having held the job for some time (normally: a year or more) obtained tenure קביעות (**kvee'oot**).
'oved/-et medeenah עובד מדינה *nm* civil servant; government official.
'ov|ed/-deem sakheer/sekheereem עובד שכיר *nm* employee; wage-earner.
'oved/-et sotsyalee/-t עובד סוציאלי *nmf* social worker; (*pl:* **'ovdeem sotsee'aleem**).
'oved/-et tsahal עובד צה"ל *nmf* Army civilian employee; (*pl+of:* **'ovd|ey/-ot** *etc*).
'oved/-et עובד *v pres* works; labors; (*pst* **'avad;** *fut* **ya'avod**).
'oved/-et (*etc*) **'al** עובד על *v [slang]* is pulling (one's) leg.
'oved/-et (*etc*) **'al|ay/-ekha/-ayeekh/-av/-eha** *etc* עובד עלי/־ך/־ך/־ו/־ה *v [slang]* pulling my/your (*m/f*) /his/her leg.
'oved/-et (*etc*) **'alay/-ekha ba-'eynayeem** עובד עלי בעיניים *v* is visibly pulling my/your *etc* leg.
'ovee עובי *nm* thickness.
(neekhn|as/-esah bo) 'ovee ha-korah נכנס בעובי הקורה *v* went into details; went into the heart of the matter; (*pres* **neekhnas** *etc; fut* **yeekanes** *etc*).
hov|eel/-eelah/-altee הוביל *v* **1.** transported; carried; **2.** led; (*pres* **moveel;** *fut* **yoveel**).
'over/-et עובר *v pres* **1.** passes; **2.** transgresses; (*pst* **'avar;** *fut* **ya'avor**).
'over/-et (*etc*) **'averah** עובר עבירה *v* commits an offence.
'over/-et batel עובר בטל *adj* senile; good for nothing.
'over/-et la-sokher עובר לסוחר *adj* legal tender.
'over/-et orakh עובר אורח *adj & nmf* passer-by; transient; wayfarer; (*pl:* **'ovrey** *etc*).
'over/-reem ve-shav/-eem עובר ושב *nm* passer-by.
(kheshbon) 'over va-shav חשבון עובר ושב *nm* current bank account.
'ovesh עובש *nm* mold.
ovnayeem אובניים *nm pl* workbench; potter's wheel.
('al ha) ovnayeem על האובניים *adv* **1.** on the workbench; **2.** (*figurat.*) in the making.
'ovreem ve-shaveem עוברים ושבים *nm pl* passers by.
oy! !אוי *interj* woe! ah!
oy va-avoy! !אוי ואבוי *interj* alas! alas and alack!
hoy! !הוי *interj* woe! alas!
oyah lee! !אויה לי *interj* woe to me! alas!
oyen/-et עוין *adj* hostile.
('ed/-ah) 'oyen/-et עד עוין *nmf* hostile witness.
(eergoon) 'oyenאירגון עוין *nm* hostile organization (usual reference to PLO and subsidiaries).
oyev/oyv|eem אויב *nm* enemy; (*pl+of:* **-ey**).
oyev (*etc*) **be-nefesh** אויב בנפש *nm* mortal enemy.
'oynoo|t/-yot עוינות *nf* hostility; enmity.
'oz עוז *nm* strength; boldness.
'oz roo'akh עוז רוח *nm* courage; valor; daring.
(az|ar/-rah/-artee) 'oz אזר עוז *v* plucked up courage; (*pres* **ozer 'oz;** *fut* **ye'ezor 'oz**).
(be) 'oz בעוז *adv* vigorously.
◇ **('eetoor ha) 'oz** see ◇ **'eetoor ha-'oz.**
(heer|heev/-heevah/-havtee) 'oz הרהיב עוז *v* dared; ventured; (*pres* **marheev 'oz;** *fut* **yarheev 'oz**).
hozal|ah/-ot הוזלה *nf* price-reduction; (*+of:* **-at**).
(meevts|a'/-e'ey) hozalah מבצע הוזלה *nm* reduction sale.
hoz|eh/-ah הוזה *v pres* dreams; raves; (*pst* **hazah;** *fut* **yehezeh**).
ozel/-et אוזל *v pres* expires; runs short; is exhausted; (*pst* **azal;** *fut* **ye'ezal**).
hozeel/-eelah/-altee הוזיל *v* reduced (price); (*pres* **mozeel;** *fut* **yozeel**).
ozen/ozn|ayeem אוזן *nf* ear; (*pl+of:* **-ey**).
(heet|ah/-etah/-etee) ozen היטה אוזן *v* lent an ear; headed; (*pres* **mateh;** *fut* **yateh**).
(tof ha) 'ozen תוף האוזן *nm* ear drum.
'ozer/-et עוזר *v pres* helps; assists; (*pres* **'azar;** *fut* **ya'azor**).
'oz|er/-reem עוזר *nm* assistant; (*pl+of:* **-rey**).
'oz|eret/-rot עוזרת *nf* **1.** maid; **2.** female assistant.
'oz|eret/-rot bayeet עוזרת בית *nf* housemaid.
'ozev/-et עוזב *v pres* abandons; leaves behind; (*pst* **'azav;** *fut* **ya'azov**).
ozlat yad אוזלת יד *nf* helplessness; weakness.
oznayeem אוזניים *nf pl* (*sing:* **ozen**) ears; (*+of:* **ozney**).
(makhreesh/-at) oznayeem מחריש אוזניים *adj* deafening.
oznee|yah/-yot אוזנייה *nf* **1.** earphone; **2.** earpiece.
(zoog) ozneeyot זוג אוזניות *nm* a pair of earphones.

OO.

incorporating words beginning with
oo, **'oo** (או)**e**, **'oo** (עו) or **hoo** (הו)

oo ־ו prefixed conjunction "and" replacing the usual equivalent **ve-**, **va-** or **vee-** whenever the word (to which the *prefix* is attached) begins with an unvowelled consonant or certain vowel combinations.

hoo הוא **1**. *pers pronoun* he; **2**. *v pres* is.

hoo ha-deen הוא הדין the same applies.

hoo hoo הוא הוא *v pres* is the one.

(ke) hoo zeh כהוא זה *adv* anything whatsoever.

(mah she) hoo מה שהוא *nm* something (of masculine or unknown gender).

hoo'ad|af (*npr* **ho'od|af**)/**-fah**/**-aftee** הועדף *v* was preferred, given preference; (*pres* **mo'odaf**; *fut* **yo'odaf**).

hoo'af/**-ah**/**-tee** הועף *v* was flown; *[slang]* was discarded, sacked; (*pres* **moo'af**; *fut* **yoo'af**).

hoo'al|ah (*npr* **ho'ol|ah**)/**-tah**/**-etee** הועלה *v* was raised, promoted; (*pres* **mo'oleh**; *fut* **yo'oleh**).

hoo'alah (*etc*) **la-arets** הועלה לארץ *v* was enabled to immigrate to Israel.

hoo'am/**-ah**/**-tee** הועם *v* was darkened, obscured; (*pres* **moo'am**; *fut* **yoo'am**).

hoo'am|ad (*npr* **ho'om|ad**) /**-dah** הועמד *v* was put, placed, nominated as candidate; (*pres* **mo'omad**; *fut* **yo'omad**).

hoo'am|ak (*npr* **ho'om|ak**)/**-kah** הועמק *v* was deepened; (*pres* **moo'amak**; *fut* **yoo'amak**).

hoo'an|ak/**-kah** (*npr* **ho'on|ak** *etc*) הוענק *v* was bestowed, granted; (*pres* **mo'onak**; *fut* **yo'onak**).

hoo'ar/**-ah**/**-tee** הואר *v* was *lit* up; (*pres* **moo'ar**; *fut* **yoo'ar**).

hoo'ar|akh (*npr* **ho'or|akh**)/**-khah**/**-akhtee** הוארך *v* was prolonged; was extended; (*pres* **mo'orakh**; *fut* **yo'orakh**).

hoo'ar|akh (*npr* **ho'or|akh**)/**-khah**/**-akhtee** הוערך *v* was estimated, evaluated; (*pres* **mo'orakh**; *fut* **yo'orakh**).

hoo'as|ak (*npr* **ho'os|ak**)/**-kah**/**-aktee** הועסק *v* was employed; (*pres* **mo'osak**; *fut* **yo'osak**).

hoo'at/**-ah**/**-tee** הואט *v* was slowed down; (*pres* **moo'at**; *fut* **yoo'at**).

hoo'at|ak (*npr* **ho'ot|ak**)/**-kah**/**-aktee** הועתק *v* **1**. was moved over; **2**. was copied; (*pres* **mo'otak**; *fut* **yo'otak**).

hoo'ats/**-ah**/**-tee** הואץ *v* was accelerated, sped up; (*pres* **moo'ats**; *fut* **yoo'ats**).

hoo'av|ad (*npr* **ho'ov|ad**)/**-dah**/**-adetee** הועבד *v* was employed (**prs mo'ovad**; *fut* **yo'ovad**).

hoo'av|ar (*npr* **ho'ov|ar**)/**-rah**/**-artee** הועבר *v* was moved; was transferred; (**prs mo'ovar**; *fut* **yo'ovar**).

hoob|a'/**-'ah**/**-a'tee** הובע *v* was expressed; (*pres* **mooba'**; *fut* **yooba'**).

'oob|ad/**-dah**/**-adetee** עובד *v* **1**. was adapted; **2**. was arranged (musically); **3**. was processed; (*pres* **me'oobad**; *fut* **ye'oobad**).

'oob|ar/**-areem** עובר *nm* fetus; embryo; (*+of:* **-rey**).

ood/**-eem** אוד *nm* firebrand; (*pl+of:* **-ey**).

ood/**-eem mootsal**/**-eem** אוד מוצל *nm* (*figurat.*) survivor.

□ **Oodeem** (Udim) אודים *nm* village (est. 1947) 5 km S. of Netanya. Pop. 412.

oof! אוף! *interj* exclamation denoting one's being fed up.

'oof/**-ee!** עוף *v imp sing m/f [slang]* go away! (*inf* **la'oof**; *pst & pres* **'af**; *fut* **ya'oof**).

hoof'al/**-ah**/**-tee** הופעל *v* was activated; was started; (*pres* **moof'al**; *fut* **yoof'al**).

hoof|ar/**-rah**/**-artee** הופר *v* was violated, canceled; (*pres* **moofar**; *fut* **yoofar**).

hoofn|ah/**-etah**/**-etee** הופנה *v* was referred, directed; (*pres* **moofneh**; *fut* **yoofneh**).

hoofr|a'/**-e'ah**/**-a'tee** הופרע *v* was disturbed, interfered with; (*pres* **moofra'**; *fut* **yoofra'**).

hoofr|az/**-ezah**/**-aztee** הופרז *v* was exaggerated; (*pres* **moofraz**; *fut* **yoofraz**).

oofsh|ar/**-erah**/**-artee** אופשר *v* was made possible; (*pres* **me'oofshar**; *fut* **ye'oofshar**).

hoofta'/**-e'ah**/**-a'tee** הופתע *v* was surprised, taken by surprise; (*pres* **moofta'**; *fut* **yoofta'**).

'oog|ah/**-ot** עוגה *nf* cake; (*+of:* **-at**).

hoogad lee/**lekha**/**lakh**/**lo**/**lah** הוגד לי/לך/לו/לה I/you/he/she was told.

hoog|af/**-fah**/**-aftee** הוגף *v* was shut, closed (door, gate, blinds); (*pres* **moogaf**; *fut* **yoogaf**).

'oog|al/**-lah**/**-altee** עוגל *v* was rounded off (number, sum); (*pres* **me'oogal**; *fut* **ye'oogal**).

'oog|an/**-nah** עוגן *v* was anchored, (*figurat.*) founded; (*pres* **me'oogan**; *fut* **ye'oogan**).

hoog|an/**-nah**/**-antee** הוגן *v* was protected, defended; (*pres* **moogan**; *fut* **yoogan**).

hoog|ash/-shah הוגש *v* was served, brought before; (*pres* **moogash**; *fut* **yoogash**).

'oogav/-eem עוגב *nm* organ (music.); (*pl+of:* **-ey**).

hoogb|ah/-ehah/-ahtee הוגבה *v* was lifted up, raised; (*pres* **moogbah**; *fut* **yoogbah**).

hoogb|al/-elah/-altee הוגבל *v* was limited, restricted; (*pres* **moogbal**; *fut* **yoogbal**).

hoogb|ar/-erah/-artee הוגבר *v* was reinforced, strengthened; (*pres* **moogbar**; *fut* **yoogbar**).

oogd|ah/-ot אוגדה *nf* group (milit.) (*+of:* **-at**).

'oogee|yah/-yot עוגייה *nf* cookie; (*+of:* **-yat**).

hoogsh|am/-emah/-amtee הוגשם *v* was implemented, made to come true; (*pres* **moogsham**; *fut* **yoogsham**).

hoogz|am/-emah/-amtee הוגזם *v* was exaggerated; (*pres* **moogzam**; *fut* **yoogzam**).

hook|af/-fah/-aftee הוקף *v* was surrounded; (*pres* **mookaf**; *fut* **yookaf**).

ook|al/-lah אוכל *v* **1.** was consumed, was burned down; **2.** was digested; (*pres* **me'ookal**; *fut* **ye'ookal**).

'ook|al/-lah עוכל *v* **1.** was digested; **2.** (fig) was comprehended; (*pres* **me'ookal**; *fut* **ye'ookal**).

'ook|al/-lah עוקל *v* was seized, foreclosed; (*pres* **me'ookal**; *fut* **ye'ookal**).

hook|al/-lah הוקל *v* was eased, alleviated, lightened; (*pres* **mookal**; *fut* **yookal**).

hook|am/-mah הוקם *v* was established, set up, erected; (*pres* **mookam**; *fut* **yookam**).

'ook|ar/-rah/-artee עוקר *v* was sterilized; was castrated; (*pres* **me'ookar**; *fut* **ye'ookar**).

hook|ash/-shah/-ashtee הוכש *v* was bitten, stung (by reptile); (*pres* **mookash**; *fut* **yookash**).

ookhad/-ah אוחד *v* was united, unified; (*pres* **me'ookhad**; *fut* **ye'ookhad**).

ookh|ah/-tah אוחה *v* was stitched, joined, pieced together; (*pres* **me'ookheh**; *fut* **ye'ookheh**).

hookh|akh/-ekhah הוכח *v* was proven; (*pres* **mookhakh**; *fut* **yookhakh**).

ookhal אוכל *v fut sing 1st pers* I shall be able.

hookhal/-ah הוחל *v pst 3rd pers* was begun, started.

hookhal be- הוחל ב־ *v pst 3rd pers m sing* work has begun on...

hookhan/-ah/-tee הוכן *v* was prepared; (*pres* **mookhan**; *fut* **yookhan**).

hookhash/-ah/-tee הוחש *v* was rushed; was accelerated; (*pres* **mookhash**; *fut* **yookhash**).

hookhb|a/-e'ah/-'etee הוחבא *v* was hidden, laid up; (*pres* **mookhba**; *fut* **yookhba**).

hookhd|ar/-erah/-artee הוחדר *v* was inserted; was infiltrated; (*pres* **mookhdar**; *fut* **yookhdar**).

hookh'k|ar/-erah הוחכר *v* was let, leased; (*pres* **mookh'kar**; *fut* **yookh'kar**).

ookhl|as/-esah אוכלס *v* was populated; (*pres* **me'ookhlas**; *fut* **ye'ookhlas**).

ookhlooseen אוכלוסין *nm pl* population.

(meefk|ad/-edey) 'ookhlooseen מיפקד אוכלוסין *nm* general population census.

(meersham ha) ookhlooseen מירשם האוכלוסין *nm* population registry.

ookhloosee|yah/-yot אוכלוסייה *nf* population; (*+of:* **-yat**).

ookhlooseeyah 'oyenet אוכלוסייה עוינת *nf* hostile population.

hookhm|ar/-erah הוחמר *v* was aggravated; (*pres* **mookhmar**; *fut* **yookhmar**).

hookhn|a'/-e'ah/-a'tee הוכנע *v* was subdued; was overpowered; (*pres* **mookhna'**; *fut* **yookhna'**).

hookhn|as/-esah/-astee הוכנס *v* was entered, brought in; (*pres* **mookhnas**; *fut* **yookhnas**).

hookhp|al/-elah הוכפל *v* was doubled; multiplied; (*pres* **mookhpal**; *fut* **yookhpal**).

hookhp|ash/-eshah/-ashtee הוכפש *v* was pressed, trampled upon (of one's name); was slandered; (*pres* **mookhpash**; *fut* **yookhpash**).

hookhr|a'/-e'ah/-a'tee הוכרע *v* **1.** was decided; **2.** was outweighed; (*pres* **mookhra'**; *fut* **yookhra'**).

hookhr|akh/-ekhah/-akhtee הוכרח *v* was compelled, forced; (*pres* **mookhrakh**; *fut* **yookhrakh**).

hookhs|ar/-erah הוחסר *v* **1.** was omitted; **2.** was deducted; (*pres* **mookhsar**; *fut* **yookhsar**).

hookhsh|ar/-erah/-artee הוכשר *v* was trained for; was made "kosher"; (*pres* **mookhshar**; *fut* **yookhshar**).

hookht|am/-emah/-amtee הוחתם *v* **1.** was signed up; **2.** was made to subscribe; (**prs** **mookhtam**; *fut* **yookhtam**).

hookht|am/-emah/-amtee הוכתם *v* was stained, soiled; (*pres* **mookhtam**; *fut* **yookhtam**).

hookht|ar/-erah/-artee הוכתר *v* was crowned; (*pres* **mookhtar**; *fut* **yookhtar**).

hookhtar (*etc*) **be-hatslakhah** הוכתר בהצלחה *v* was crowned with success.

hookht|av/-evah הוכתב *v* was dictated; (*pres* **mookhtav**; *fut* **yookhtav**).

hookhz|ar/-erah/-artee הוחזר *v* has been returned; (*pres* **mookhzar**; *fut* **yookhzar**).

ookhz|av/-evah/-avtee אוכזב *v* was disappointed; (*pres* **me'ookhzav**; *fut* **ye'ookhzav**).

hookl|at/-etah/-atetee הוקלט *v* was recorded, taped; (*pres* **mooklat**; *fut* **yooklat**).

hookn|at/-etah/-atetee הוקנט *v* was vexed, crossed, annoyed; (*pres* **mooknat**; *fut* **yooknat**).

hookr|a/-e'ah הוקרא *v* was read out, recited; (*pres* **mookra**; *fut* **yookra**).

hookr|an/-enah/-antee הוקרן *v* **1.** was projected; **2.** was x-rayed; (*pres* **mookran**; *fut* **yookran**).

hooks|am/-emah/-amtee הוקסם *v* was fascinated, captivated, charmed; (*pres* **mooksam**; *fut* **yooksam**).

hookt|an/-enah/-antee הוקטן *v* was reduced, diminished; (*pres* **mooktan**; *fut* **yooktan**).

'ool/-ey yameem עול ימים *nm* youngster.

ool|af/-fah/-aftee אולף *v* was trained, tamed, domesticated; (*pres* **me'oolaf;** *fut* **ye'oolaf**).

oolam אולם *prep* but; however; nevertheleess.

oolam/ot אולם *nm* hall; parlor; (*pl+of:* **-ey**).

oolam/-ey hartsa'ot אולם הרצאות *nm* lecture hall.

oolam/-ey khatoonot אולם חתונות *nm* wedding hall.

oolam/-ey reekoodeem אולם ריקודים *nm* dancing hall.

hool'am/-ah/-tee הולאם *v* was nationalized; (*pres* **mool'am;** *fut* **yool'am**).

oolay אולי *adv* perhaps; maybe.

oolay-oolay אולי־אולי *adv* maybe, one never knows.

hoolb|an/-enah/-antee הולבן *v* **1.** was whitened; whitewashed; **2.** (fig.) was legalized (of illegal financial gains); (*pres* **moolban;** *fut* **yoolban**).

hoolb|ash/-eshah/-ashtee הולבש *v* was dressed, dressed up; (*pres* **moolbash;** *fut* **yoolbash**).

hooledet הולדת *nf* birth; (my/your*(m/f)*/his/her *etc* birth: **hooladet|ee/-khah/-ekh/-o/-ah** *etc*).

(yom/-yemey) hooledet יום הולדת *nm* birthday; (my/your*(m/f)*/his/her birthday: **yom hooladet|ee/-kha/-ekh/-o/-ah** *etc*).

oolpan/-eem אולפן *nm* studio; (*pl+of:* **-ey**).

◇ **oolpan/-eem le-'eevreet** אולפן לעברית *nm* "Ulpan" i.e. classes for intensive study of Hebrew (especially designed for new immigrants).

oolp|an/-eney haklatah אולפן הקלטה *nm* recording studio.

oolp|an/-eney hasratah אולפן הסרטה *nm* film studio.

oolp|an/-eney sheedoor אולפן שידור *nm* broadcasting studio.

oolp|an/-eney televeezeeyah אולפן טלוויזיה *nm* television studio.

oolpanee|t/-yot אולפנית *nf* summary classes (or course) of Hebrew.

hoolkh|an/-enah הולחן *v* was composed (music); (*pres* **moolkhan;** *fut* **yoolkhan**).

oolkoos/-eem אולקוס *nm* ulcer; stomach ulcer. (*pl+of:* **-ey**).

oom (*npr* **om**)/**oomeem** אום *nm* nut; screw-nut.

oom או״ם *nm* the U.N; U.N.O.; (*acr of* **ha-OOmot ha-Me'ookhadot** האומות המאוחדות) the United Nations.

('atseret ha-) oom עצרת האו״ם *nf* the U.N General Assembly.

□ **Oom el Fakhem** (Umm al Fahm) אום אל פאחם *nf* Arab township overlooking the **Wadee 'Arah** valley (**'Emek 'Eeron**) E. of **Khaderah-'Afoolah** highway. Pop. 25,400.

oomah/-mot אומה *nf* nation; (*+of:* **-at**).

ooman/-eem אומן *nm* craftsman; (*pl+of:* **-ey**).

oom|an/-nah/-antee אומן *v* was trained; (*pres* **me'ooman;** *fut* **ye'ooman**).

hoomanee/-t הומני *adj* humane.

(megamah) hoomaneet מגמה הומנית *nf* humanities cycle (of courses in high school).

oomanoo|t/-yot אומנות *nf* craftsmanship.

oom|at/-tah/-atetee אומת *v* was confirmed, verified; (*pres* **me'oomat;** *fut* **ye'oomat**).

hoom|at/-tah הומת *v* was put to death, killed; (*pres* **moomat;** *fut* **yoomat**).

(kee-le) 'oomat she- כלעומת ש־ *adv* just as...;the same way as...

(le) 'oomat לעומת *adv* compared with.

(le) 'oomat zot לעומת זאת *adv* on the other hand.

oom|ats/-tsah/-atstee אומץ *v* was adopted; (*pres* **me'oomats;** *fut* **ye'oomats**).

oomdan/-eem אומדן *nm* estimate; (*pl+of:* **-ey**).

hoomkh|ash/-eshah/-ashtee הומחש *v* was tangibly demonstrated; (*pres* **moomkhash;** *fut* **yoomkhash**).

hoomkh|az/-ezah/-aztee הומחז *v* was dramatized; (*pres* **moomkhaz;** *fut* **yoomkhaz**).

oomlal/-ah אומלל *adj & nmf* miserable; (*pl+of:* **-ey**).

ooml|al/-elah/-altee אומלל *v* was made miserable; (*pres* **me'oomlal;** *fut* **ye'oomlal**).

oomnam (*npr* **omnam**) אומנם *prep* surely; indeed.

(ha) 'oomnam? ?האומנם is it true that...? has indeed...?

hoomor הומור *nm* humor.

◇ **(ha)oomot ha-me'ookhadot** האומות המאוחדות *nf pl* the United Nations.

hoomr|ats/-etsah/-atstee הומרץ *v* was urged, encouraged, stirred; (*pres* **moomrats;** *fut* **yoomrats**).

hoomsh|akh/-ekhah/-akhtee הומשך *v* was continued; (*pres* **moomshakh;** *fut* **yoomshakh**).

hoomsh|al/-elah/-altee הומשל *v* **1.** was likened to; **2.** was installed to rule; (*pres* **moomshal;** *fut* **yoomshal**).

hoomt|ak/-ekah/-aktee הומתק *v* **1.** was sweetened; **2.** was mitigated (punishment); (*pres* **moomtak;** *fut* **yoomtak**).

oomts|ah/-ot אומצה *nf* steak; (*+of:* **-at**).

hoomts|a/-e'ah/-e'tee הומצא *v* **1.** was delivered; **2.** was invented; (*pres* **moomtsa;** *fut* **yoomtsa**).

hoon|af/-fah/-aftee הונף *v* was hoisted; (*pres* **moonaf;** *fut* **yoonaf**).

hoon|akh/-khah/-akhtee הונח *v* was laid down, put placed; (*pres* **moonakh;** *fut* **yoonakh**).

hoonakh lee/lekhah/lakh/lo/la *etc* הונח לי/לך/לך/לו I/you*(m/f)*/he/she etc was given rest, relaxed.

hoon|as/-sah/-astee הונס *v* was driven off; (*pres* **moonas;** *fut* **yoonas**).

ooneekoom/-eem אוניקום *nm [slang]* someone (or something) unique.

ooneeversalee/-t אוניברסלי *adj* universal.

ooneeverseet|ah/-a'ot אוניברסיטה *nf* university; (*+of:* **-at**).

(boger/-et) ooneeverseet|ah/-a'ot בוגר אוניברסיטה *nmf* university graduate; (*pl:* **-rey** *etc*).

ooneeverseeta'ee/-t אוניברסיטאי *adj* pertaining to a university.

hoonkhat/-ah/-etee הונחת *v* was landed; was brought upon; (*pres* **moonkhat**; *fut* **yoonkhat**).

hoonp|ak/-ekah/-aktee הונפק *v* was issued, extracted, derived; (*pres* **moonpak**; *fut* **yoonpak**).

oop|as/-sah/-astee אופס *v* was zeroed; (*pres* **me'oopas**; *fut* **ye'oopas**).

hoor|a'/-'ah הורע *v* deteriorated; worsened; (*pres* **moora'**; *fut* **yoora'**).

hoor|am/-mah/-amtee הורם *v* was raised, lifted up; (*pres* **mooram**; *fut* **yooram**).

oor|as (or|as)/-sah/-astee אורס *v* was betrothed; (*pres* **me'oras**; *fut* **ye'oras**).

□ **Ooree'el** (Uri'el) אוריאל *nf* residential quarter outside **Gederah** that developed out of a "Village for the Blind" established (1949) by "**Malben**" (Israeli subsidiary of the J.D.C.) to provide blind people and their families with housing and employment.

□ **Ooreem** (Urim) אורים *nm* kibbutz (est. 1946) in W. Negev, of the "**kevootsah**" type, 9 km W. of **Ofakeem**. Pop. 574.

hoorg|al/-elah/-altee הורגל *v* got accustomed; (*pres* **moorgal**; *fut* **yoorgal**).

hoorg|ash/-eshah/-ashtee הורגש *v* was felt; (*pres* **moorgash**; *fut* **yoorgash**).

hoorg|az/-ezah/-aztee הורגז *v* was irked, irritated; (*pres* **moorgaz**; *fut* **yoorgaz**).

hoork|an/-enah/-antee הורכן *v* was bent; was bowed; (*pres* **moorkan**; *fut* **yoorkan**).

hoork|av/-evah הורכב *v* was composed, assembled; was mounted; (*pres* **moorkav**; *fut* **yoorkav**).

(agav) oorkhah אגב אורחא *adv* incidentally; by the way.

hoorkh|ak/-ekah/-aktee הורחק *v* was removed, dismissed; (*pres* **moorkhak**; *fut* **yoorkhak**).

'oorva (*npr* **orva**) **parakh!** עורבא פרח *interj* (Aramaic) Nonsense! Sheer imagination!

oor|vah/-avot אורווה *nf* stable; (*+of:* **-vat**).

hoos|ag/-gah/-agtee הושג *v* was attained; (*pres* **moosag**; *fut* **yoosag**).

hoos|ak/-kah/-aktee הוסק *v* **1.** was heated; **2.** was deducted, drawn; (*pres* **moosak**; *fut* **yoosak**).

hoos|am/-mah/-amtee הושם *v* was put, placed, seated; (*pres* **moosam**; *fut* **yoosam**).

hoos|ar/-rah/-artee הוסר *v* was taken off, removed; (*pres* **moosar**; *fut* **yoosar**).

hoos|av/-vah/-avtee הוסב *v* was endorsed; was altered, converted; (*pres* **moosav**; *fut* **yoosav**).

hoosb|ar/-erah/-artee הוסבר *v* was explained; (*pres* **moosbar**; *fut* **yoosbar**).

hoosd|ar/-erah/-artee הוסדר *v* has been arranged, set in order; (*pres* **moosdar**; *fut* **yoosdar**).

hoosg|ar/-erah/-artee הוסגר *v* was extradited, delivered; (*pres* **moosgar**; *fut* **yoosgar**).

□ **Ooshah** (Usha) אושה *nm* kibbutz (est. 1937) in Haifa Bay, of the "**kvootsah**" type. Pop. 408.

hosh|'ah/-'atah/-'etee הושעה *v* was delayed, suspended; (*pres* **moosh'eh**; *fut* **yoosh'eh**).

hoosh|ak/-kah/-aktee הושק *v* was launched (boat); (*pres* **mooshak**; *fut* **yooshak**).

hoosh'al/-ah/-tee הושאל *v* was lent; (*pres* **moosh'al**; *fut* **yoosh'al**).

hoosh'an/-ah/-tee הושען *v* was leaned against; (*pres* **moosh'an**; *fut* **yoosh'an**).

oosh|ar/-rah/-artee אושר *v* was confirmed, approved; (*pres* **me'ooshar**; *fut* **ye'ooshar**).

hoosh'ar/-ah/-tee הושאר *v* was left, abandoned; (*pres* **moosh'ar**; *fut* **yoosh'ar**).

hoosh|av/-vah/-avtee הושב *v* was returned, given back; (*pres* **mooshav**; *fut* **yooshav**).

hooshb|a'/-e'ah/-a'tee הושבע *v* was sworn in; was made to take an oath; (*pres* **mooshba'**; *fut* **yooshba'**).

hooshb|at/-etah/-atetee הושבת *v* was locked out (strike); was frustrated; (*pres* **mooshbat**; *fut* **yooshbat**).

hoosh'|hah/-hatah/-hetee הושהה *v* was delayed, retarded; (*pres* **moosh'heh**; *fut* **yoosh'heh**).

hooshk|a'/-e'ah/-a'tee הושקע *v* was invested; (*pres* **mooshka'**; *fut* **yooshka'**).

hooshk|ah/-etah/-etee הושקה **1.** *v* was driven (or made) to drink; **2.** was irrigated; (*pres* **mooshkeh**; *fut* **yooshkeh**).

hooshk|av/-evah/-avtee הושכב *v* was laid down; (*pres* **mooshkav**; *fut* **yooshkav**).

hoosh'kh|al/-elah/-altee הושחל *v* was threaded, passed through; (*pres* **moosh'khal**; *fut* **yoosh'khal**).

hoosh'kh|am/-emah/-amtee הושחם *v* was darkened, bronzed; (*pres* **moosh'kham**; *fut* **yoosh'kham**).

hoosh'kh|ar/-erah/-artee הושחר *v* was blackened; (*pres* **moosh'khar**; *fut* **yoosh'khar**).

hoosh'kh|at/-etah/-atetee הושחת *v* was spoiled, ruined, corrupted; (*pres* **moosh'khat**; *fut* **yoosh'khat**).

hoosh'kh|az/-ezah/-aztee הושחז *v* was sharpened; was honed; (*pres* **moosh'khaz**; *fut* **yoosh'khaz**).

hooshl|am/-emah/-amtee הושלם *v* was completed; (*pres* **mooshlam**; *fut* **yooshlam**).

hooshl|at/-etah/-atetee הושלט *v* was given dominion over; was installed; (*pres* **mooshlat**; *fut* **yooshlat**).

hooshm|a'/-e'ah/-a'tee הושמע *v* was sounded; has been heard; (*pres* **mooshma'**; *fut* **yooshma'**).

hooshm|ad/-edah/-adetee הושמד *v* was exterminated; (*pres* **mooshmad**; *fut* **yooshmad**).

hooshm|at/-etah/-atetee הושמט *v* was omitted; (*pres* **mooshmat;** *fut* **yooshmat**).

hooshp|a'/-e'ah/-a'tee הושפע *v* was influenced; (*pres* **mooshpa';** *fut* **yooshpa'**).

hooshp|al/-elah/-altee הושפל *v* was humiliated; (*pres* **mooshpal;** *fut* **yooshpal**).

ooshp|az/-ezah/-aztee אושפז *v* was hospitalized; (*pres* **me'ooshpaz;** *fut* **ye'ooshpaz**).

ooshr|ar/-erah/-artee אושרר *v* was ratified; (*pres* **me'ooshrar;** *fut* **ye'ooshrar**).

hooshr|ah/-etah/-etee הושרה *v* was immersed, drenched; (*pres* **mooshreh;** *fut* **yooshreh**).

hoosht|ak/-ekah/-aktee הושתק *v* was silenced; (*pres* **mooshtak;** *fut* **yooshtak**).

hoosht|al/-elah/-altee הושתל *v* was planted, transplanted, implanted; (*pres* **mooshtal;** *fut* **yooshtal**).

hoosht|at/-etah/-atetee הושתת *v* was founded, based; (*pres* **mooshtat;** *fut* **yooshtat**).

hooshv|ah/-etah/-etee הושווה *v* was compared, equalized; (*pres* **mooshveh;** *fut* **yooshveh**).

hoosm|akh/-ekhah/-akhtee הוסמך *v* **1.** was ordained; **2.** was authorized; **3.** graduated; (*pres* **moosmakh;** *fut* **yoosmakh**).

hoost|ar/-erah/-artee הוסתר *v* was concealed from; was hidden away; (*pres* **moostar;** *fut* **yoostar**).

hoosv|ah/-etah/-etee הוסווה *v* was camouflaged, hidden; (*pres* **moosveh;** *fut* **yoosveh**).

hoot|'ah/-'atah/-'etee הוטעה *v* was misled, led astray, deceived; (*pres* **moot'eh;** *fut* **yoot'eh**).

hoot|al/-lah/-altee הוטל *v* was imposed; was thrown; (*pres* **mootal;** *fut* **yootal**).

hoot'am/-ah/-tee הותאם *v* was adapted, made to fit; (*pres* **moot'am;** *fut* **yoot'am**).

hoot'am/-ah הוטעם *v* was emphasized; (*pres* **moot'am;** *fut* **yoot'am**).

hoot'an/-ah/-tee הוטען *v* was loaded; was imposed upon; (*pres* **moot'an;** *fut* **yoot'an**).

hoot|ar/-rah/-artee הותר *v* **1.** was untied; **2.** was allowed, permitted; (*pres* **mootar;** *fut* **yootar**).

hoot|as/-'sah/-astee הוטס *v* was flown; (*pres* **mootas;** *fut* **yootas**).

hoot|av/-vah/-avtee הוטב *v* was improved; (*pres* **mootav;** *fut* **yootav**).

(taveen) oo-tekeeleen טבין ותקילין *nm pl* solid cash; good money.

hootm|an/-enah/-antee הוטמן *v* was concealed, hidden; (*pres* **mootman;** *fut* **yootman**).

hootn|ah/-etah/-etee הותנה *v* has been stipulated, agreed; (*pres* **mootneh;** *fut* **yootneh**).

hootb|al/-elah/-altee הוטבל *v* **1.** was dipped; **2.** was baptized; (*pres* **mootbal;** *fut* **yootbal**).

hootr|ad/-edah/-adetee הוטרד *v* was troubled, disturbed, annoyed; (*pres* **mootrad;** *fut* **yootrad**).

'oots/-ee lee 'etsah עוץ לי עצה *v imp* s *m/f* what would you advise me to do?

hoots|a/-'ah/-e'tee הוצא *v* was disbursed, spent, taken out; (*pres* **mootsa;** *fut* **yootsa**).

hootsa (*etc*) **la-horeg** הוצא להורג *v* was executed; was put to death.

hoots|af/-fah/-aftee הוצף *v* was flooded; (**prs mootsaf;** *fut* **yootsaf**).

hoots|ag/-gah/-agtee הוצג *v* was presented, introduced, staged; (*pres* **mootsag;** *fut* **yootsag**).

hootsar/-rah הוצר *v* was narrowed, straited; (*pres* **mootsar;** *fut* **yootsar**).

hootsat/-tah הוצת *v* was ignited, *lit*, kindled; (*pres* **mootsat;** *fut* **yootsat**).

'oots|av/-vah עוצב *v* was shaped, moulded, fashioned; (*pres* **me'ootsav;** *fut* **ye'ootsav**).

hoots|av/-vah/-avtee הוצב *v* was set up, stationed; placed; (*pres* **mootsav;** *fut* **yootsav**).

hootsm|ad/-edah/-adetee הוצמד *v* was linked, tied up, clutched; (*pres* **mootsmad;** *fut* **yootsmad**).

hootsn|a'/-e'ah/-a'tee הוצנע *v* was concealed, hidden; (*pres* **mootsna';** *fut* **yootsna'**).

hootsn|akh/-ekhah/-akhtee הוצנח *v* was parachuted, dropped from the air; (*pres* **mootsnakh;** *fut* **yootsnakh**).

hoov|a/-'ah/-e'tee הובא *v* was brought in; was carried in; (*pres* **moova;** *fut* **yoova**).

hoov|al/-lah/-altee הובל *v* was led, brought; (*pres* **mooval;** *fut* **yooval**).

hoov|an/-nah/-antee הובן *v* was understood; (*pres* **moovan;** *fut* **yoovan**).

hoov'ar/-ah/-tee הובער *v* was *lit*, kindled, ignited; (*pres* **moov'ar;** *fut* **yoov'ar**).

hoov|as/-sah/-astee הובס *v* was defeated; (*pres* **moovas;** *fut* **yoovas**).

'oovd|ah/-ot עובדה *nf* fact; (+*of:* **-at**).

'oovd|ah/-ot moogm|eret/-arot עובדה מוגמרת *nf* accomplished fact.

'oovdatee/-t עובדתי *adj* factual.

'oovdot ha-khayeem עובדות החיים *nf pl* facts of life.

(meneh) oo-veh מניה וביה *adv* instantly; in no time.

hoovk|a'/-e'ah/-a'tee הובקע *v* was broken through; (*pres* **moovka';** *fut* **yoovka'**).

hoovka' (*etc*) **sha'ar** הובקע שער *v* a goal has been scored.

oo-ve-khen (*v=b; k=kh*) ובכן and so.

(shalom) oo-vrakhah! (*v=b*) שלום וברכה! greeting; return-greeting for "Shalom".

hoovt|akh/-ekhah/-akhtee הובטח *v* was promised, secured; (*pres* **moovtakh;** *fut* **yoovtakh**).

□ **'Oozah** (Uza) עוזה *nm* village (est. 1950) S. of **Keeryat Gat**. Pop. 593.

◇ **"oozee"** ("Uzi") עוזי *nm* small Israeli-made machine-gun.

hooz|az/-ezah/-aztee הוזז *v* was shifted, moved; (*pres* **moozaz;** *fut* **yoozaz**).

hooz'ak/-ah/-tee הוזעק *v* was alerted, alarmed; (*pres* **mooz'ak;** *fut* **yooz'ak**).

□ **Oozeyl** (or: **El-Oozeyl**) see **Hoozeyl** (or: **El-Hoozeyl**).

hooz'har/-ah/-tee הוזהר *v* was warned; (*pres* **mooz'har;** *fut* **yooz'har**).

oozk|ar/-erah/-artee אוזכר *v* was mentioned; (*pres* **me'oozkar;** *fut* **ye'oozkar**).

hoozk|ar/-erah/-artee הוזכר *v* was mentioned; (*pres* **moozkar;** *fut* **yoozkar**).

hoozm|an/-enah/-antee הוזמן *v* was invited; (*pres* **moozman;** *fut* **yoozman**).

hoozman (*etc*) **eesheet** הוזמן אישית *v* was personally invited.

hoozn|akh/-ekhah/-akhtee הוזנח *v* was neglected; (*pres* **mooznakh;** *fut* **yooznakh**).

hoozr|am/-emah/-amtee הוזרם *v* was poured, made to flow; (*pres* **moozram;** *fut* **yoozram**).

hoozr|ak/-ekah הוזרק *v* was injected; (*pres* **moozrak;** *fut* **yoozrak**).

P.

corresponding to Hebrew consonant **Peh** (פ)

pa'al/-ah/-tee פעל *v* acted; (*pres* **po'el;** *fut* **yeef'al** (*f=p*)).

pa'al (*etc*) **le-ma'an** פעל למען *v* was active on behalf of; was active for.

pa'am/pe'ameem פעם **1.** *nm* one time; times; **2.** *adv* once; (*pl+of:* **pa'amey**).

(af) pa'am אף פעם *adv* never; not once.

(af) pa'am lo אף פעם לא *adv* at no time; not even once.

(ey) pa'am אי פעם *adv* at any time.

(ha) pa'am הפעם *adv* this time; one time.

(mee) pa'am le-fa'am (*f=p*) מפעם לפעם *adv* from time to time.

(meedey) pa'am מדי פעם *adv* each time.

('od) pa'am עוד פעם *adv* again, please; once more.

(shoov) pa'am שוב פעם *adv* once again.

pa'am/-ah פעם *v* (heart) beat; throbbed; (*pres* **po'em;** *fut* **yeef'am** (*f=p*)).

pa'amayeem פעמיים *adv* twice.

(khad-) pa'amee/-t חד־פעמי *adj* unique; of one-time use.

(le-sheemoosh khad-) pa'amee לשימוש חד־פעמי *adj* for one-time use.

□ **Pa'amey Tashaz** (Pa'amé Tashaz) פעמי תש״ז village in N. Negev, 10 kms E. of **Neteevot**. Pop. 307.

pa'amon/-eem פעמון *nm* bell; (*pl+of:* **-ey**).

pa'ar/pe'areem פערים *nm* gap; (*pl+of:* **pe'arey**).

(ha) pa'ar ha-'adatee הפער העדתי *nm* the inter-community gap.

pa'ar ha-dorot פער הדורות *nm* the generation gap.

pad|ah/-etah/-eetee פדה *v* redeemed; delivered; (*pres* **podeh;** *fut* **yeefdeh** (*f=p*)).

padooy/pedooyah פדוי *adj* redeemed; ransomed.

pa'eel/pe'eelah פעיל *adj* active.

(be-sheroot) pa'eel בשירות פעיל *adv* on active (military) duty.

pa'eel/-pe'eeleem פעיל *nm* activist; (*pl+of:* **pe'eeley**).

pag/-eem פג *nm* premature baby.

pag/-ah פג *v* expired; faded away; (*pres* **pag;** *fut* **yafoog**).

pag|a'/-'ah/-a'tee פגע *v* hit; hurt; (*pres* **poge'a';** *fut* **yeefga'** (*f=p*)).

paga'

(te'oon|at/-ot) paga' oo-varakh (*npr* (*v=b*) **pega' oo-vrakh**) תאונת פגע וברח *nf* "hit-and-run" accident.

pag|am/-mah/-amtee פגם *v* impaired; spoiled; (*pres* **pogem;** *fut* **yeefgom** (*f=p*)).

pag|ash/-shah/-ashtee פגש *v* met; encountered; (*pres* **pogesh;** *fut* **yeefgosh** (*f=p*)).

pagaz/pegazeem פגז *nm* cannon-shell; cannon-ball; (*+of:* **pegaz/peegzey**).

pagaz! !פגז *interj [slang]* a smasher! excellent!

pagee'a'/pegee'ah פגיע *adj* vulnerable.

pagoo'a'/pegoo'ah פגוע *adj* hurt.

pagoom/pegoomah פגום *adj* faulty; defective.

pagosh/-eem פגוש *nm* fender; bumper (of car); (*pl+of:* **-ey**).

pagr|ah/-ot פגרה *nf* vacation; (*+of:* **-at**).

(ha) pagrah הפגרה *nf* school-vacation.

pagrat ha-kayeets פגרת הקיץ *nf* summer-vacation.

pak|a'/-'ah פקע *v* expired; busted; (*pres* **poke'a;** *fut* **yeefka'** (*f=p*)).

pak'ah (*etc*) **savlanoot** פקעה סבלנות *v* lost patience; lost temper.

pak|ad/-dah/-adetee פקד *v* ordered; commanded; (*pres* **poked;** *fut* **yeefkod** (*f=p*)).

pakad/-eem פקד *nm* police-inspector; (*pl+of:* **-ey**).

(rav-)pakad רב־פקד *nm* chief-inspector (police).

pakakh/-eem פקח *nm* **1.** warden (enforcing curfew regulations); **2.** inspector (enforcing public health regulations).

pak|akh/-'khah/-akhtee 'ayeen (*or:* **'eynayeem)** פקח עין *v* opened eyes (*pres* **poke'akh** *etc; fut* **yeefkakh** *(f=p) etc*).

pakakh (*etc*) **zoog 'eynayeem** פקח זוג עיניים *v* opened a pair of astonished eyes.

pakeed/pekeedeem פקיד *nm* **1.** clerk; employee; **2.** official; (*+of:* **pekeed/-ey**).

pakeed/pekeedeem gavo'ah/gvoheem פקיד גבוה *nm* senior official.

pakeed/pekeedeem memshaltee/-yeem פקיד ממשלתי *nm* government official; government officer.

pakeed/pekeedeem needrash/-eem פקיד נדרש *nm* public official deemed "vital" i.e. entitled to privileges such as full coverage of car expenses and similar bonuses.

pa|kh/-keem פך *nm* flask; jar; (*pl+of:* **-key**).

pakh/-eem פח *nm* **1.** tin; can; **2.** pitfall; trap; (*pl+of:* **-ey**).

pakh/-ey ashpah פח אשפה *nm* dustbin; garbage-can.

pakh/-ey zevel פח זבל *nm* garbage-can.

(ba) pakh בפח *adv* in a trap.

(meen ha) pakh el ha-pakhat מן הפח אל הפחת *adv* from bad to worse.

(naf|al/-lah/-altee ba) pakh נפל בפח *v* fell into a trap; (*pres* **nofel** *etc; fut* **yeepol** *(p=f) etc*).

(tam|an/-nah/-antee) pakh טמן פח *v* set a trap; (*pres* **tomen** *etc; fut* **yeetmon** *etc*).

pakhad/pekhad|eem פחד *nm* fear; (*pl+of:* **pakhadey**).

pakhad mavet פחד מוות *nm* deadly fear.

pakhad/pekhadey shav פחד שווא *nm* unjustified fear.

(nafal) pakhad נפל פחד *v* was seized with fear. (*pres* **nofel** *etc; fut* **yeepol** *etc; (p=f)*).

pakh|ad/-adah/-adetee פחד *v* feared; (*pres* **pokhed**; *fut* **yeefkhad** *(f=p)*).

pakhakh (*npr* **pekhakh)/-eem** פחח *nm* tinsmith; sheet metal worker; (*pl+of:* **-ey**).

pakhakhoot (*npr* **pekhakhoot)** פחחות *nf* tinsmithing; sheet metal work; bodywork (in cars).

pakhakhoot (*npr* **pekhakhoot) rekhev** פחחות רכב *nf* car body repairs.

pakhat/pekhateem פחת *nm* snare; pitfall.

pakhat/-ah פחת *v* decreased; diminished; (*pres* **pokhet**; *fut* **yeefkhat**; *(f=p)*).

pakhaz ka-mayeem פחז כמים *adj* **1.** unsettled; light-headed; **2.** *lit.*: unstable like water.

pakhdan/-eet פחדן *nmf & adj* coward.

pakhdanoot פחדנות *nf* cowardice.

pakhee|t/-yot פחית *nf* **1.** tin can; **2.** small metal plate.

pakhee|t/-yot zeehooy פחית זיהוי *nf* name-plate; identification-plate; number-plate; tag.

pakhman/-eem פחמן *nm* carbon (Chemistry); (*pl+of:* **-ey**).

pakhmeyman/-eem פחמימן *nm* hydrocarbon (Chemistry); (*pl+of:* **-ey**).

pakhon/-eem פחון *nm* tin hut; tin shack; slum dwelling made of tin-plates; (*pl+of:* **-ey**).

pakhot/pekhootah פחות *adj* inferior; scanty.

pakhot פחות *adv* less; less than.

pakhot o yoter פחות או יותר *adv* more or less.

(le-khol ha) pakhot לכל הפחות *adv* at the very least.

pakhzoo|t/-yot פחזות *nf* rashness; fickle-mindedness.

pakook/pekookah פקוק *adj [slang]* corked; blocked (traffic).

pal|ash/-shah/-ashtee פלש *v* invaded; trespassed; intruded; (*pres* **polesh**; *fut* **yeeflosh** *(f=p)*).

pal|at/-tah/-atetee פלט *v* ejected; threw up; (*pres* **polet**; *fut* **yeeflot** *(f=p)*).

('ets o) palee עץ או פלי *[slang]* heads or tails (alternatives in coin-throwing); let's flip a coin!

palganoo|t/-yot פלגנות *nf* factionalism.

◇ **palmakh (Palmach)** פלמ"ח *nm* (*acr of* "**PLoogot MAKHats** פלוגות מחץ i.e. shock troops) crack-force of the Hagana (1941-1949) which played an important part in Israel's War of Independence (1947-1949) and left considerable marks on the country's folklore and poetry.

□ **Palmakheem** (Palmahim) פלמחים *nm* kibbutz (est. 1949) on Mediterranean Coast , 10 kms SW of **Reeshon Le-Tseeyon**. Pop. 473.

paltsoor/-eem (*npr* **platsoor)** פלצור *nm* lasso.

pamal|yah/-yot פמליה *nf* entourage; retinue; (*+of:* **yat**).

pamot/-eem (*cpr* **pamoot)** פמוט *nm* candlestick.

pan/-eem פן *nm* **1.** face; **2.** aspect; (*pl+of:* **peney**).

panah/-tah/-eetee פנה *v* turned; addressed oneself; (*pres* **poneh**; *fut* **yeefneh** *(f=p)*).

pan|ah/-tah (*etc*) **'oref** פנה עורף *v* turned one's back on.

panas/-eem פנס *nm* **1.** lantern; **2.** flashlight; **3.** headlight; (*pl+of:* **-ey**).

(nafloo) pan|av/-ehah נפלו פניו/־יה *v* looked dejected.

paneem פנים *nf pl (sing nm* **pan**) face; (*+of:* **pney**).

pantcher/-eem פנצ'ר *nm [slang]* **1.** puncture (tire); **2.** mishap (*figurat.*); impediment.

pantcher-makher/-eem פנצ'ר־מאכר *[slang] nm* tire-repairman; one doing tire-repairs.

paneek|ah/-ot פניקה *nf* panic; (*+of:* **-at**).

paneem el paneem פנים אל פנים *adv* face to face.

paneem khamootsot פנים חמוצות *nf pl* sour face.

paneem le-khan oo le-khan *(kh=k)* פנים לכאן ולכאן *adv* open to interpretation.

('az/-at) paneem עז פנים *adj* insolent.

(ba) paneem בפנים *adv* in the face; in one's face.

(be-sever) paneem yafot בסבר פנים יפות *adv* cordially; offering cordial reception.

(be-shoom) paneem בשום פנים *adv* by no means.

(be-voshet) paneem *(v=b)* בבושת פנים *adv* shamefacedly.

(ha'amad|at/-ot) paneem העמדת פנים *nf* pretense.

(hadrat) paneem הדרת פנים *nf* dignified appearance.

(he'em|eed/-eedah/-adetee) paneem העמיד פנים *v* pretended; (*pres* **ma'ameed** *etc; fut* **ya'ameed** *etc*).

(heesb|eer/-eerah/-artee) paneem הסביר פנים *v* showed kindness to; (*pres* **masbeer** *etc; fut* **yasbeer** *etc*).

(heelb|een/-eenah/-antee) paneem הלבין פנים *v* put to shame; (*pres* **malbeen** *etc; fut* **yalbeen** *etc*).

(kabalat/-ot) paneem קבלת פנים *nf* reception (of guests); welcome-party.

(le-lo maso') paneem ללא משוא פנים *adv* without bias.

(maso') paneem משוא פנים *nm* bias; discrimination; partiality.

(sever) paneem yafot סבר פנים יפות *nm* affability; cheerful countenance.

(klast|er/-rey) paneem קלסתר פנים *nm* physiognomy.

(nesoo/-'at) paneem נשוא פנים *adj* respected; important.

(tavey) paneem תווי פנים *nm pl* features (of face).

panooy/pnooyah פנוי *adj* **1.** vacant; free; **2.** *[colloq.]* single.

(makom/mekomot) panooy/penooyeem מקום פנוי *nm* vacant place; empty seat.

(zman) panooy זמן פנוי *nm* free time.

panter/-eem פנתר *nm* panther.

◇ **"panter/-eem"** פנתר *nm* (*colloq. ref.* to the "Black Panthers" - a sporadic movement on the Israeli political scene in the early 1970s, giving voice to the discontent of Jews of Afro-Asian background communities with the cultural and political predominance of Ashkenazi Jews.

◇ **(ha) pantereem (ha) sh'khoreem** הפנתרים השחורים *nm pl* the "Black Panthers" - see ◇ **"Panter"**, above.

pantomeem|ah/-ot פנטומימה *nf* pantomime.

pa'oor/pe'oorah פעור *adj* wide open.

pa'ot/pa'ot|ah פעוט *nmf* toddler; baby; (*pl:* **-ot**).

pa'oot/pe'ootah פעוט *adj* tiny; petty.

pa'oton/-eem פעוטון *nm* nursery; (*pl+of:* **-ey**).

par/-eem פר *nm* bull; (*pl+of:* **-ey**).

par|ah/-ot פרה *nf* cow; (*+of:* **-at**).

par|ah/-ot khol|evet/-vot פרה חולבת *nf* milch cow (mostly used figuratively).

par|a'/-'ah/-'tee פרע *v* paid up; settled payment; (*pres* **pore'a'**; *fut* **yeefra'**; *(f=p)*).

parafraz|ah/-zot פרפרזה *nf* paraphrase.

par|ak/-kah/-aktee פרק *v* unloaded; cast off; (*pres* **porek**; *fut* **yeefrok** *(f=p)*).

par|akh/-khah/-akhtee פרח *v* **1.** blossomed; bloomed; **2.** flew off; disappeared; (*pres* **pore'akh**; *fut* **yeefrakh** *(f=p)*).

par|am/-mah/-amtee פרם *v* unstitched; ripped apart; (*pres* **porem**; *fut* **yeefrom** *(f=p)*).

□ **Paran** פארן *nm* village (est. 1971) in **'Aravah** 33 km E. of **'En Yahav**. Pop. 320.

Paras פרס *nf* Persia, i.e. Iran.

par|as/-sah/-astee פרס *v* spread out; stretched; deployed; (*pres* **pores**; *fut* **yeefros** *(f=p)*).

parash/-eem פרש *nm* rider; cavalry-man; (*pl+of:* **-ey**).

par|ash/-shah/-ashtee פרש *v* retired; withdrew from; (*pres* **poresh**; *fut* **yeefrosh** *(f=p)*).

parash|ah/-eeyot פרשה *nf* affair; (*+of:* **-at**).

parashat drakheem פרשת דרכים *nf* crossroads.

parashat ha-shavoo'a פרשת השבוע *nf* Weekly Portion from the Pentateuch - one of 50 read in turn at the synagogue each Sabbath as part of morning service.

parashat ha-tvee'ah פרשת התביעה *nf* claim action.

parash|at/-ot mayeem פרשת המים *nf* watershed.

('al) parashat drakheem על פרשת דרכים *adv* at the crossroads.

par|at/-tah/-atetee פרט *v* exchanged into small change; (*pres* **poret**; *fut* **yeefrot** *(f=p)*).

par|at/-tah/- (*etc*) **'al** פרט על *v* played stringed instrument.

parat mosheh rabenoo פרת משה רבנו *nf* ladybug.

par|ats/-tsah/-'atstee פרץ *v* **1.** broke into; burgled; **2.** disrupted; burst; (*pres* **porets**; *fut* **yeefrots** *(f=p)*).

parats (*etc*) **bee-ts'khok** פרץ בצחוק *v* burst into laughter.

parats (*etc*) **bee-v'khee** (or **ba-vekhee** *(v=b)*) פרץ בבכי *v* burst into tears.

pard|es/-eem פרדס *nm* citrus grove; (*pl+of:* **-ey**).

pardesan/-eem פרדסן *nm* citrus grower; (*pl+of:* **-ey**).

□ **Pardes Khanah** (Pardes-Hanna Karkur) פרדס חנה *nm* union (since merger in 1969) of two settlements; **Pardes Khanah** (est. 1929) and **Karkoor** (est. 1913). Pop. 16,900.

pardesanoot פרדסנות *nf* citrus growing.

□ **Pardeseeyah** (Pardesiyya) פרדסיה *nm* village (est. 1942) in Sharon 3 kms S. of ha-Sharon Road Junction. Pop. 1,200.

pareekh/preekhah פריך *adj* crisp; brittle.

pareet/preeteem פריט *nm* item; entry; (*pl+of:* **-ey**).

(va'adah) pareeteteet ועדה פריטטית *nf* parity committee.

◇ **pareets/preetseem** פריץ *nm* onetime (in 19th century Poland) high and mighty Polish squire to Ghetto Jews (Yiddish: "Puretz" or "Porets").

pargee|t/-yot פרגית *nf* chicken; young hen

pargod/-eem פרגוד *nm* curtain; screen; (*pl+of:* **-ey**).

(me-akhorey ha) pargod מאחורי הפרגוד *adv* behind the scenes.

(arkhee) parkhee ארחי־פרחי *nm pl* flotsam and jetsam (*figurat.*); drifters.

parlament/-eem פרלמנט *nm* parliament.

parlamentaree/-t פרלמנטרי *adj* parliamentary.

(khaseenoot) parlamentareet חסינות פרלמנטרית *nf* parliamentary immunity.

parnas/-eem פרנס *nm* community-leader; (*pl+of:* **-ey**).

parnas|ah/-ot פרנסה *nf* livelihood; (*+of:* **-at**).

par'oh פרעה *nm* Pharaoh.

□ **Parod** פרוד *nm* kibbutz (est. 1949) in Lower Galilee, 2 kms E. of Hananyah Junction (**Tsomet Khananyah**). Pop. 338.

parodee|yah/-yot פרודיה *nf* parody; (*+of:* **-yat**).

parokh|et/-ot פרוכת *nf* curtain over doors to the Holy Torah Ark (in a synagogue).

paroo'a'/proo'ah פרוע *adj* unruly; wild.

(sey'ar) paroo'a' שיער פרוע *nm* disheveled hair; unruly hair.

paroos/proosah פרוס *adj* sliced; spread out.

(lekhem) paroos לחם פרוס *nm* sliced bread.

paroots/prootsah פרוץ *adj* broken into.

paroots/prootsah lee-revakhah פרוץ לרווחה *adj* wide open.

par'osh/-eem פרעוש *nm* flea; (*pl+of:* **-ey**).

parp|ar/-areem פרפר *nm* butterfly; (*pl+of:* **-erey**).

parp|ar/-erey laylah פרפר לילה *nm* **1.** moth (*lit.*) nocturnal butterfly; **2.** (*figurat.*) person leading active night-life.

(sekheeyat) parpar שחיית פרפר *nf* butterfly-stroke (swimming).

parper|et/-a'ot פרפרת *nf* **1.** dessert; entree; **2.** (*figurat.*) something extra.

pars|ah/-ot פרסה *nf* horse-shoe; hoof; (*+of:* **-at**).

(seevoov/-ey) parsah סיבוב פרסה *nm* U-turn.

parsee/-yah פרסי **1.** *nmf [slang]* Jew of Persian background or ancestry; **2.** *nmf* Persian.

parsee/-t פרסי *adj* Persian.

(ha-meefrats ha) parsee המפרץ הפרסי *nm* the Persian Gulf.

parshan/-eem פרשן *nm* commentator.

parshanoo|t/-yot פרשנות *nf* interpretation; commentary.

partachee/-t פרטאצ׳י *adj [slang]* incompetent; unprofessional.

parteetoor|ah/-ot פרטיטורה *nf* musical score; (*+of:* **-at**).

parteezan/-eem פרטיזן *nm* guerrrilla-fighter (in World War Two Eastern Europe); (*pl+of:* **-ey**; *f:* **-eet/-yot**).

(be-tsoorah) parteezaneet בצורה פרטיזנית *adv* in a makeshift, unprofessional manner.

partsoof/-eem פרצוף *nm* face; physiognomy; (*pl+of:* **-ey**).

(doo-) partsoofee/-t דו־פרצופי *adj* two-faced; hypocrite.

partsoofeem פרצופים *nm pl* making faces.

(doo-) partsoofeeyoot דו־פרצופיות *nf* hypocrisy.

parvah/-ot פרווה *nf* fur; (*+of:* **-at**).

(me'eel/-ey) parvah מעיל פרווה *nm* fur coat.

parvan/-eem פרוון *nm* furrier; (*pl+of:* **ey**).

parvar/-eem פרוור or: פרבר *nm suburb;* (*pl+of:* **-ey**).

pas/-eem פס *nm* **1.** stripe; **2.** rail; (*pl+of:* **-ey**).

pasah nega' פשה נגע the scourge (of...) spread.

pas|a'/-'ah/-a'tee פסע *v* paced; stepped; (*pres* **pose'a'**; *fut* **yeefsa'** (*f=p*)).

pasak/-kah/-aktee פסק *v* **1.** ceased; stopped; discontinued; **2.** ruled, decided; (*pres* **posek;** *fut* **yeefsok** (*f=p*)).

pas|akh/-khah/-akhtee פסח *v* skipped; (*pres* **pose'akh;** *fut* **yeefsakh** (*f=p*)).

pasakh (*etc*) **'al shtey ha-se'eepeem** פסח על שתי הסעיפים *v* couldn't make up one's mind; sat on the fence; vacillated.

pas|al/-lah/-altee פסל *v* disqualified; rejected; (*pres* **posel;** *fut* **yeefsol** (*f=p*)).

pas|al/-elet פסל *nmf* sculptor; (*pl:* **-aleem/-alot**).

paseevee/-t פסיבי *adj* passive.

pash|a'/-'ah/-a'tee פשע *v* sinned; committed a crime; (*pres* **poshe'a';** *fut* **yeefsha'** (*f=p*)).

pash|at/-tah/-atetee פשט *v* **1.** took off; undressed; **2.** attacked, invaded; (*pres* **poshet;** *fut* **yeefshot** (*f=p*)).

pashat (*etc*) **'or** פשט עור *v* **1.** skinned; **2.** robbed; (*pres* **poshet 'or;** *fut* **yeefshot 'or** (*f=p*)).

pashat (*etc*) **regel** פשט רגל *v* went bankrupt.

pashat (*etc*) **tsoorah ve-lavash tsoorah** פשט צורה ולבש צורה *v* changed forms.

pashat (*etc*) **yad** פשט יד *v* begged; collected alms.

pashoot/pshootah פשוט *adj* simple.

pashoot פשוט *adv* simply.

pashran/-eet פשרן **1.** *adj* compromising; **2.** *nmf* man (or woman) of compromise.

pashranee/-t פשרני *adj* compromising; of mutual understanding.

pashranoo|t/-yot פשרנות *nf* tendency to compromise.

pashtanee/-t פשטני *adj* simplistic, over-simplified.

pashteed|ah/-ot פשטידה *nf* pudding; pie; (*+of:* **-at**).

pashtoot פשטות *nf* simplicity.

(be-takhleet ha) pashtoot בתכלית הפשטות *adv* in all simplicity.

paskanee/-t פסקני *adj* indisputable.

paskanoot/-yot פסקנות *nf* indisputability.

pasook/psook|eem פסוק *nm* Bible-verse; (*pl+of:* **-ey**).

(sof) pasook סוף פסוק *nm* **1.** end of verse; **2.** full stop; an end to it.

pasool/-psoolah פסול *adj* unfit; faulty; disqualified.

pat פת *nf* loaf; piece of bread.

pat lekhem פת לחם *nf* a piece of bread.

('ad) pat lekhem עד פת לחם *adv* to the verge of starvation.

pat|akh/-khah/-akhtee פתח *v* opened; (*pres* **pote'akh**; *fut* **yeeftakh** *(f=p)*).

◇ **patakh** פתח *nm* sublinear vowel-sign **(x)** indicating the vowel **a** as in *father*.

◇ **(khataf) patakh** see ◇ **khataf-patakh**.

pat|ar/-rah/-artee פטר *v* let out; dispensed; discharged; (*pres* **poter**; *fut* **yeeftor** *(f=p)*).

patar/-rah/-artee פתר *v* solved; (*pres* **poter**; *fut* **yeeftor** *(f=p)*).

pateesh/-eem פטיש *nm* hammer; (*pl+of:* **-ey**).

pateesh/-ey aveer פטיש אוויר *nm* pneumatic hammer.

□ **Pateesh** (Pattish) פטיש *nm* village (est. 1950) in NW Negev, 6 km W. of **Ofakeem**. Pop. 607.

patent/-eem פטנט *nm* **1.** patent; **2.** *[colloq.]* device.

patetee/-t פתטי *adj* pathetic.

patolog/-eem פתולוג *nm* pathologist.

patologee/-t פתולוגי *adj* pathological.

patoo'akh/ptookhah פתוח *adj* open.

(ha-khalon) patoo'akh החלון פתוח *v* the window is open.

(ha sha'ar) patoo'akh השער פתוח *v* the gate is open.

patoor/ptoorah פטור *adj* exempt.

patos פתוס *nm* pathos.

patpetan/-eet פטפטן *adj & nmf* prattler; chatterbox.

patreeot/-eem פטריוט *nm* patriot.

patreeotee/-t פטריוטי *adj* patriotic.

patrol/-eem פטרול *nm* patrol.

patron/-eem פטרון *nm* patron; guardian; (*pl+of:* **-ey**).

pats|a'/-'ah/-a'tee פצע *v* wounded; injured; (*pres* **potse'a'**; *fut* **yeeftsa'** *(f=p)*).

pats|ah/-tah/-eetee peh פצה פה *v* opened one's mouth; (*pres* **potseh**; *fut* **yeeftseh peh** *(f=p)*).

patsats/-eem פצץ *nm* detonator; (*pl+of:* **-ey**).

"patsats" פצץ *nm [slang]* a "smasher".

patseefeest/-eem פציפיסט *nmf* pacifist.

patsoo'a'/ptsoo'ah פצוע *adj* wounded; injured.

patsoor/ptsoorah פצור *adj* filed; notched.

patsyent/-eet פציינט *nmf* (doctor's) patient.

payees פיס *nm* lottery-ticket.

◇ **(meef'al ha) payees** see ◇ **meef'al ha-payees.**

paysanee/-t פייסני *adj* conciliatory.

paysanoot פייסנות *nf* appeasement; conciliation.

paytan/-eem פייטן *nm* poet; liturgical poet; (*pl+of:* **-ey**).

paz פז **1.** *nm* fine gold; **2.** *adj (+of)* golden; of gold.

paz|al/-lah/-altee פזל *v* ogled; squinted; eyed; (*pres* **pozel**; *fut* **yeefzol**; *(f=p)*).

◇ **PAZAM** פז"ם *nm abbr.Army slang* (*acr of* **Perek Zman Meeneemalee**); minimal time of service required for officer's advancement to a higher rank.

pazeez/pzeezah פזיז *adj* impetuous; rash.

pazran/-eet פזרן *adj* lavish spender.

pazranoot פזרנות *nf* lavishness.

peh/peeyot פה *nm* mouth.

peh ekhad פה אחד *adv* unanimously.

peh el peh פה אל פה **1.** *adv* face to face; **2.** *lit* : mouth to mouth.

(ba-khatsee) peh בחצי פה *adv* half-heartedly.

(be-'al) peh בעל־פה *adv* by heart; orally.

(be) peh (*npr* **feh** *(f=p)*) **male** בפה מלא *adv* without hesitation.

(be-khol) peh *(kh=k)* בכל פה *adv* greedily.

(leefto'akh) peh la-satan לפתוח פה לשטן *v inf* **1.** invite misfortune; **2.** (*lit.*) open one's mouth to the devil; (*pst* **patakh** *etc*; *pres* **pote'akh** *etc*; *fut* **yeeftakh** *etc f=p*).

(mee) peh el peh מפה אל פה *adv* to overflowing.

(mee) peh le-ozen מפה לאוזן *adv* secretly.

(motsa) peh מוצא פה *nm* utterance.

(neebool) peh ניבול פה *nm* obscene language.

(pat|akh/-khah/-akhtee et ha) peh פתח את הפה *v* opened one's mouth (*figurat.*) (*pres* **pote'akh** *etc*; *fut* **yeeftakh** *etc f=p*).

pats|ah/-tah/-eetee peh פצה פה *v* dared to speak; (*pres* **potseh** *etc*; *fut* **yeeftseh** *etc f=p*).

(peetkhon) peh פיתחון פה *nm* pretext.

(pleet|at/-ot) peh פליטת פה *nf* slip of the tongue.

(steem|at/-ot) peh סתימת פה *nf* shutting people's mouth; denying the right of free speech.

pe|'ah/-'ot פיאה *nf* **1.** wig; **2.** side locks worn by very religious Jews (*pl:* **pe'ot**).

pe'ah nokhreet פיאה נוכרית *nf* wig.

pe'altan/-et פעלתן *nmf* active person; activist.

pe'altanoo|t/-yot פעלתנות *nf* intense activity; activism.

pedagog/-eem פדגוג *nm* educator; pedagogue.

pedagogee/-t פדגוגי *adj* pedagogical.

pedagogyah פדגוגיה *nf* education; pedagogy.

□ **Pedayah** (Pedaya) פדיה *nm* village (est. 1951) 7 km S. of Ramla on secondary road to Jerusalem. Pop. 424.

pedeekyoor פדיקור *nm* pedicure.

pedoot פדות *nf* redemption; delivery.

□ **Pedooyeem** (Peduyim) פדויים *nm* village (est. 1950) in NW Negev, 2 km N. of **Ofakeem**. Pop. 313.

pee פי **1.**...times; -fold; multiplied; **2.** the mouth (**peh**) of.

pee kamah פי כמה *adv* manyfold.

pee kamah ve-khamah *(kh=k)* פי כמה וכמה *adv* several times over.

pee ha-taba'at פי הטבעת *nm* anus.

pee shloshah פי שלושה *num* threefold; triply; (*colloq. incorr. use:* **pee shalosh**).

pee shnayeem פי שניים *num* twice; double; (*colloq. incorr. use:* **pee shtayeem**).

(af 'al) pee אף על פי *conj* although; notwithstanding.

(af 'al) pee khen *(kh=k)* אף על פי כן *conj* nevertheless.

(af 'al) pee she- אף על פי ש־ *conj* although; in spite of the fact that.

('al) pee על פי *conj* according to.

('al) pee rov על פי רוב *adv* mainly; mostly.

◇ **(veetameen) pee** see ◇ **veetameen pee**.

peey|ah/-yot פייה *nf* mouthpiece; aperture; (*+of:* **yat**).

pee'an|akh (or: **pee'an|e'akh)/-khah/-akhtee** פיענח *v* deciphered; (*pres* **mefa'ane'akh** *(f=p)*; *fut* **yefa'ane'akh**).

pee'anoo'akh פיענוח *nm* deciphering.

peedyon/-ot פדיון *nm* **1.** proceeds; **2.** delivery sale (cash).

◇ **"peedyon"** פדיון *nm* a Hassid's contribution to the upkeep of his Rabbi's "court".

◇ **peedyon ha-ben** פדיון הבן *nm* "Redeeming one's first-born" ceremony held in synagogue on or after the 30th day from the birth of a first-born son.

pe'eeloo|t/-yot פעילות *nf* activity.

pe'eem|ah/-ot פעימה *nf* beat; stroke; (*+of:* **at**).

(kherev) peefeeyot) חרב פיפיות *nf* two-edged sword.

peeg|er/-rah/-artee פיגר *v* fell behind; lagged; (*pres* **mefager**; *fut* **yefager** *(f=p)*).

peegoo|'a'/-'eem פיגוע *nm* hit; blow; (*pl+of:* **-'ey**).

peegoo|'a'/-'eem (*etc*) **khablanee/-yeem** פיגוע חבלני *nm* terrorist act; act of terrorism.

peegoom/-eem פיגום *nm* scaffolding; (*pl+of:* **-ey**).

peegoor/-eem פיגור *nm* lag; arrears (of payment); (*pl+of:* **-ey**).

peegoor (*etc*) **seekhlee** פיגור שכלי *nm* mental retardation.

peegoor (*etc*) **sveevatee** פיגור סביבתי *nm* environmental retardation.

peegyon/-ot פגיון *nm* bayonet; dagger.

pee|hek/-hakah/-haktee פיהק *v* yawned; (*pres* **mefahek** *(f=p)*; *fut* **yefahek**).

peehook/-eem פיהוק *nm* yawn; (*pl+of:* **ey**).

peejam|ah/-ot פיג'מה *nf* pajamas; pyjamas; (*+of:* **-at**).

peek/-eem פיק land-measure; approx. cubit; 1/1,000 of metric dunum; 1.77778 cubic feet.

peek beerkayeem פיק ברכיים *nm* trembling (knees) with fear.

peek|adon/-donot פיקדון *nm* deposit; (*+of:* **-don**).

(dmey) peekadon דמי פיקדון *pl* deposit charge; deposit money.

peek|akh/-'khah/-akhtee פיקח *v* supervised; (*pres* **mefake'akh**; *fut* **yefakakh** *(f=p)*).

peekakhon פיכחון *nm* sobriety.

pekantee/-t פיקנטי *adj* piquant.

peek|e'akh/-akhat פיכח *adj* sober.

peek|e'akh/-'kheet פיקח *adj* clever.

peek|e'akh/-'khah/-akhtee פיקח *v* supervised; (*pres* **mefake'akh**; *fut* **yefakakh** *(f=p)*).

peek|ed/-dah/-adetee פיקד *v* commanded; (*pres* **mefaked**; *fut* **yefaked** *(f=p)*).

peekh|et/-atah/-atetee פיחת *v* devalued; (*pres* **mefakhet**; *fut* **yefakhet** *(f=p)*).

peekhoot/-eem פיחות *nm* devaluation; (*pl+of:* **-ey**).

peek'khee/-t פיקחי *adj* intelligent; clever.

peek'khoo't פיקחות *nf* intelligence; cleverness.

peekneek/-eem פיקניק *nm* picnic.

peekoo'akh פיקוח *nm* control; supervision; inspection.

peekoo'akh nefesh פיקוח נפש *nm* a matter of life and death; saving an endangered life.

(be) peekoo'akh (*npr* **be-feekoo'akh**) בפיקוח *adv & adj* controlled; rationed.

peekood/-eem פיקוד *nm* command.

(aloof ha) peekood אלוף הפיקוד *nm* regional (district) commander.

peekood/-eem פיקוד *nm [colloq.]* subordinate; (*pl+of:* **-ey**).

peekp|ek/-aktee פיקפק *v* doubted; (*pres* **mefakpek** *(f=p)*; *fut* **yefakpek**).

peekpook/-eem פקפוק *nm* doubt; hesitation; (*pl+of:* **ey**).

(le-lo) peekpook ללא פקפוק *adv* without hesitation.

peel/-eem פיל *nm* elephant; (*pl+of:* **-ey**).

(shen) peel שן פיל *nf* ivory.

peel|eg/-gah/-agtee פילג *v* divided; caused a split; (*pres* **mefaleg**; *fut* **yefaleg** *(f=p)*).

peel|egesh/-agsheem פילגש *nf* mistress; kept woman; concubine; (*pl+of:* **-agshey**).

peelel/-elah/-altee פילל *v* thought; supposed.

(mee) peelel? מי פילל? who would have thought?

peel|es/-sah/-astee פילס *v* paved the way; leveled; (*pres* **mefales** *(f=p)*; *fut* **yefales**).

peeloog/-eem פילוג *nm* division; split; (*pl+of:* **-ey**).

peeloos/-eem פילוס *nm* clearance (of road); construction (of road).

peelpel/-leem פילפל *nm* pepper; (*pl+of:* **-ey**).

peelpool/-eem פלפול *nm* hairsplitting argumentation; (*pl+of:* **-ey**).

peelpooleesteek|ah/-ot פילפוליסטיקה *nf* sophistical casuistry (*+of:* **-at**).

peem|ah/-ot פימה *nf* double chin; (*+of:* **-at**).

peen/-eem פין *nm* pin; (*pl+of:* **-ey**).

peen פין *nm* penis.

peen|ah/-ot פינה *nf* corner; (*+of:* **-at**).

peen|ah/-tah/-eetee פינה *v* vacated; (*pres* **mefaneh**; *fut* **yefaneh** *(f=p)*).

(even/avney) peenah אבן פינה *nf* cornerstone.

peen|ek/-kah/-aktee פינק *v* pampered; spoiled; (*pres* **mefanek**; *fut* **yefanek** *(f=p)*).

peenkah/-a'ot פינכה *nf* plate; platter; (*+of:* **-at**).

(melakh|ekh/-akhey) peenkah מלחך פינכה *adj & nmf* bootlicker.

peenkas/-eem (*cpr* **peenkes**) פנקס *nm* notebook; ledger; register; (*pl+of:* **-ey**).

peenk|as/-esey khaver פנקס חבר *nm* membership-card; membership booklet.

peenk|as/-esey khoger פנקס חוגר *nm* enlisted man's (or woman's) service book.

◇ **peenk|as/-esey meeloo'eem** פנקס מילואים *nm* army reserve personal service booklet.

peenk|as/-esey sheroot פנקס שירות *nm* service logbook.

(mena|hel/-haley) peenkaseem מנהל פנקסים *nm* bookkeeper.

(neehool) peenkaseem ניהול פנקסים *nm* bookkeeping.

peenkesan/-eet פנקסן *nmf* bookkeeper.

peenkesanoot פנקסנות *nf* bookkeeping.

peenkesanoot kfoolah פנקסנות כפולה *nf* **1.** double-entry bookkeeping; **2.** double bookkeeping (*figurat.*).

peenook/-eem פינוק *nm* pampering; (*pl+of:* **-ey**).

peenoo|y/-yeem פינוי *nm* eviction; clearing; removal; (*pl+of:* **-yey**).

(tsav/-ey) peenooy צו פינוי *nm* eviction order.

peepee פיפי *nm baby-talk & slang for* **1.** urinating, **2.** penis.

(kherev) peepeeyot (*npr* **peefeeyot**) חרב פיפיות *nf* two-edged sword.

peerameed|ah/-ot פירמידה *nf* pyramid; (*+of:* **-at**).

peerdah/pradot פרדה *nf* mare; (*+of:* **peerd|at/-ot**).

peerkhakh/-eem פרחח *nm* hoodlum; ruffian; monster; (*pl+of:* **-ey**).

peerkhakhee|t/-yot פרחחית *nf* floozie.

peerkhonee/-t פרחוני *adj* flowery.

peerkoos/-eem פרכוס *nm* spasm; adornment; (*pl+of:* **-ey**).

peern|es/-esah/-astee פירנס *v* supported; sustained; (*pres* **mefarnes** (*f=p*); *fut* **yefarnes**).

peerp|er/-erah/-artee פירפר *v* quivered; (*pres* **mefarper** (*f=p*); *fut* **yefarper**).

peerpoor/-eem פרפור *nm* quiver; spasm; (*pl+of:* **-ey**).

peers|em/-emah/-amtee פירסם *v* published; publicized; (*pres* **mefarsem** (*f=p*); *fut* **yefarsem**).

peersom|et/-mot פרסומת *nf* publicity.

peersoom/-eem פרסום *nm* publication; (*pl+of:* **-ey**).

peertsah/pratsot פרצה *nf* breach; gap; (*+of:* **peertsat**).

peeryon/-ot פריון *nm* productivity.

peerzool/-eem פרזול *nm* household fittings; (*pl+of:* **-ey**).

pees|ah/-ot פיסה *nf* piece; strip; (*+of:* **-at**).

pees|at/-ot neyar פיסת נייר *nf* scrap of paper.

pees|e'akh/-akhat פיסח **1.** *adj* lame; **2.** *nmf* lame person.

pees|ek/-kah/-aktee פישק *v* opened (legs) wide apart; straddled; (*pres* **mefasek**; *fut* **yefasek** (*f=p*)).

pees|el/-lah/-altee פיסל *v* carved; sculpture; (*pres* **mefasel** (*f=p*); *fut* **yefasel**).

peesgah/pesagot פסגה *nf* summit; (*+of:* **peesg|at/-ot**).

(ve'eed|at/-ot) peesgah ועידת פיסגה *nf* summit conference.

peesher/-eet פישר *[slang]* **1.** *nmf* youngster; **2.** *lit* too young to control own urination.

peesh|er/-rah/-artee פישר *v* mediated; compromised; (*pres* **mefasher** (*f=p*); *fut* **yefasher**).

peesh|et/-tah/-atetee פישט *v* simplified; streamlined; (*pres* **mefashet** (*f=p*); *fut* **yefashet**).

peeshp|ash/-asheem פישפש *nm* wicket; (*pl+of:* **-eshey**).

peeshpesh/-eem פישפש *nm* bug; (*pl+of:* **-ey**).

peeshp|esh/-eshah/-ashtee פישפש *v* examined; searched; (*pres* **mefashpesh** (*f=p*); *fut* **yefashpesh**).

peeshtan/-eem פשתן *nm* linen; flax.

peeshoot/-eem פישוט *nm* simplification; (*pl+of:* **-ey**).

peesk|ah/-a'ot פיסקה *nf* paragraph; (*+of:* **-at/-ot**).

peeslon/-eem פסלון *nf* statuette; figurine; (*pl+of:* **-ey**).

peesook/-eem פיסוק *nm* punctuation; (*pl+of:* **-ey**).

peesook/-eem פישוק *nm* divarication; straddling; (*pl+of:* **-ey**).

(be)peesook raglayeem (*npr:* **be-feesook** *etc*) בפישוק רגלים *adv* with legs wide apart.

peesool/-eem פיסול *nm* sculpture; (*pl+of:* **-ey**).

peestoor פיסטור *nm* pasteurization; (*pl+of:* **-ey**).

peet|ah/-ot פיתה *nf* oriental style bread loaf (flat and mostly round); (*+of:* **-at**).

peet|ah/-etah/-eetee פיתה *v* seduced; (*pres* **mefateh** (*f=p*); *fut* **yefateh**).

◇ **peet|ah/-ot 'eerakee|t/-yot** פיתה עירקית *nf* Iraqi-type "**peetah**" (flat bread-loaf).

peetooreem פיטורים *nm pl* dismissal; discharge; firing.

(hoda|'at/-'ot) peetooreem (or: **peetooreen**) הודעת פיטורים *nf* notice of dismissal, of discharge.

(peetsooyey) peetooreem (or **peetooreen**) פיצויי פיטורים *nm pl* severance-pay.

(get) peetooreen גט פיטורין *nm* letter of divorcement; divorce.

peetooy/-eem פיתוי *nm* temptation; seduction; (*pl+of:* **yey**).

peetp|et/-etah/-atetee פטפט *v* prattled; chattered; (*pres* **mefatpet** (*f=p*); *fut* **yefatpet**).

peetpoot/-eem פטפוט *nm* prattle; chatter; (*pl+of:* **-ey**).

peetpootey beytseem פתפותי ביצים *nm* confusion; nonsense-talk.

peetree|yah/-yot פיטרייה *nf* mushroom; fungus; (*+of:* **yat**).

peetr|el/-elah/-altee פיטרל *v* patrolled; (*pres* **mefatrel** (*f=p*); *fut* **yefatrel**).

peetronot deeyoor פתרונות דיור *nm pl* (*sing:* **peetron**) housing solutions.

peetrool/-eem פיטרול *nm* patrolling; (*pl+of:* **-ey**).

peets|ah/-ot פיצה *nf* pizza; (*+of:* **-at**).

peets|ah/-tah/-eetee פיצה *v* indemnified; compensated; (*pres* **mefatseh** *(f=p); fut* **yefatseh**).

peets|akh/-khah/-akhtee פיצח *v* cracked; split; (*pres* **mefatse'akh** *(f=p); fut* **yefatsakh**).

peets|el/-lah/-altee פיצל *v* split; (*pres* **mefatsel** *(f=p); fut* **yefatsel**).

peets|ets/-etsah/-atstee פיצץ *v* blew up; (*pres* **mefotsets** *(f=p); fut* **yefotsets**).

peetsets|at/-ot gaz madmee'a פצצת גז מדמיע *nf* teargas bomb.

peetsets|at/-ot meen פצצת מין *nf* sex bomb, "bombshell".

peetsets|at/-ot serakhon פצצת סירחון *nf* stink bomb.

peetsets|at/-ot tav'erah פצצת תבערה *nf* incendiary bomb.

peetsets|at/-ot zman פיצצת זמן *nf* time-bomb.

peetsoo|'akh/-kheem פיצוח *nm* cracking; splitting; (*pl+of:* **-khey**).

peetsool/-eem פיצול *nm* splitting; (*pl+of:* **-ey**).

peetsool ha-eesheeyoot פיצול האישיות *nm* split personality.

peetsoots/-eem פיצוץ *nm* explosion; (*pl+of:* **-ey**).

peetsoots asefah פיצוץ אסיפה *nm* breaking up a meeting.

peetsoo|y/-yeem פיצוי *nm* compensation; indemnification; (*pl+of:* **-yey**).

peetsooyeem le-'ov|ed/-deem פיצויים לעובד *nm pl* workman's compensation.

peetsooyey peetooreem (or **peetooreen**) פיצויי פיטורים *nm pl* severence-pay.

peetspon/-et פצפון **1.** *adj* tiny; **2.** *nmf* little one.

(be-mo) pee|v/-ha במו פיו *adv* with his/her very mouth.

(mootsa) pee|v/-ha מוצא פיו *nm* promise; word; utterance.

(neeb|el/-ah) pee|v/-ha ניבל פיו *v* talked obscenely; (*pres* **menabel** *etc; fut* **yenabel** *etc*).

peeyakh פיח *nm* soot.

pee|yes/-ysah/-yastee פייס *v* appeased; consoled; (*pres* **mefayes** *(f=p); fut* **yefayes**).

peeyoos/-eem פיוס *nm* conciliation; appeasement; (*pl+of:* **-ey**).

peeyoot/-eem פיוט *nm* poetry; liturgical poem; (*pl+of:* **-ey**).

peeyootee/-t פיוטי *adj* lyrical; poetic.

peez|em/-mah/-amtee פיזם *v* hummed; (*pres* **mefazem** *(f=p); fut* **yefazem**).

peez|er/-rah/-artee פיזר *v* squandered; (*pres* **mefazer** *(f=p); fut* **yefazer**).

peez|ez/-ezah/-aztee פיזז *v* jumped about; danced; (*pres* **mefazez** *(f=p); fut* **yefazez**).

peezmon/-eem פזמון *nm* tune; pop-song; *[slang]* (ironically) pretext; (*pl+of:* **-ey**).

peezmon khozer פזמון חוזר *nm* refrain; chorus.

(meets'ad/-ey) peezmoneem מצעד פזמונים *nm* hit parade.

peezmona|y (*cpr* **peezmona|'ee**)/**-'eem** פזמונאי *nm* songwriter; (*pl+of:* **-'ey**).

peezoor/-eem פיזור *nm* disbanding; dispersal; (*pl+of:* **-ey**).

peezoor nefesh פיזור נפש *nm* absent-mindedness.

peg|a'/-a'eem פגע *nm* mishap; accident; (*pl+of:* **peeg'ey**).

pega' oo-vrakh *(v=b)* פגע וברח *v imp* hit and run.

(te'oon|at/-ot) pega' oo-vrakh תאונת פגע וברח *nf* "hit-and-run" accident.

pegam/-eem פגם *nm* defect; blemish; (*pl+of:* **-ey**).

(le-lo) pegam ללא פגם **1.** *adv* faultlessly; **2.** *adj* faultless.

pegee|'ah/-'ot פגיעה *nf* hit; blow; (*+of:* **'at**).

pegeem|ah/-ot פגימה *nf* defect; flaw; (*+of:* **-at**).

pegee'oot פגיעות *nf* vulnerability.

pegeesh|ah/-ot פגישה *nf* meeting; (*+of:* **-at**).

peg|er/-areem פגר *nm* carcass; cadaver; (*pl+of:* **peegrey**).

pe'eem|ah/-ot פעימה *nf* beat; stroke; (*+of:* **at**).

peka|'at/-'ot פקעת *nf* coil; bulb; tube.

pekak/-eem פקק *nm* cork; stopper; (*pl+of:* **ey**).

pekak פקק *nm [slang]* one capable (or supposed) to fill any vacancy that opens up.

pekak/-ey tenoo'ah פקק a traffic jam.

(khol|ets/-tsey) pekakeem חולץ פקקים *nm* cork extractor; corkscrew.

pekee|'ah/-'ot פקיעה *nf* expiration; (*+of:* **-'at**).

pekee|'at/-'ot tokef פקיעת תוקף *nf* expiration; abolition.

pekeed/-ey ha-shoomah פקיד השומה *nm* assessment officer; income-tax assessor.

pekeed|ah/-ot פקידה *nf* female employee, clerk, office-worker; (*+of:* **-at**).

pekeedoot פקידות *nf* **1.** office-work; **2.** officialdom.

pekeedootee/-t פקידותי *adj* clerical.

□ **Pekee'een ha-Khadashah** (Peqi'in ha-Hadasha) פקיעין החדשה *nm* village (est. 1955) in Upper Galilee, 5 km SE of **Ma'alot-Tarsheekha**. Pop. 205.

pekham/-eem פחם *nm* coal; (*+of:* **pakh|am/-mey**).

(neyar/-ot) pekham נייר פחם *nm* carbon-paper.

pekhat/-eem פחת *nm* amortisation; depreciation.

pekheetoot kavod פחיתות כבוד *nf* something beneath one's dignity.

pekood|ah/-ot פקודה *nf* order; (*+of:* **-at**).

pekood|at/-ot keva' פקודת קבע *nf* standing order.

pekood|at/-ot ma'asar פקודת מאסר *nf* warrant of arrest.

pekood|at/-ot yom פקודת יום *nf* order of the day.

(bee) pekoodat (*npr* **bee-fkoodat**) בפקודת *adv* by order of.

pekoodeem פקודים *nm pl* (*sing:* **pakood**) subordinates; (*pl+of:* **-ey**).

pelakh/plakheem פלח *nm* slice; segment; (*pl+of:* **peelkhey**).
pele/pla'eem פלא *nm* wonder; miracle; (*pl+of:* **peel'ey**).
(be-orakh) pele באורח פלא *adv* miraculously.
pele pla'eem! ! פלא פלאים *interj* what a wonder! (ironically).
(seer/-ey) pele סיר פלא *nm* wonder pan; wonder pot.
(yeled/-yaldey) pele ילד פלא *nm* child prodigy.
peled פלד *(suffix) adj* steel-; made of steel.
peleg/plageem פלג *nm* faction; political faction; (*+of:* **plag/palgey**).
pelekh/plakheem פלך *nm* **1.** spindle; **2.** district; region.
peles/plaseem פלס *nm* scale; meter; (*pl+of:* **peelsey**).
peles mayeem פלס מים *nm* spirit-level.
pen פן *prep* lest.
penay פנאי *nm* spare time; leisure.
(en) penay אין פנאי no time to spare.
(she|'at/-'ot ha) penay שעת הפנאי *nf* leisure time; moment of leisure.
peneem ha ־פנים ה *nm* the inside of; the interior.
◇ **(meesrad ha) peneem** see ◇ **meesrad ha-peneem**.
(sar ha) peneem שר הפנים *nm* the Minister of the Interior; the Home secretary.
peneemah פנימה *adv* inward.
peneemee/-m פנימי *nm [colloq.]* tire's inner tube.
peneemee/-t פנימי *adj* internal.
(rof|e/-'ah) peneemee/-t רופא פנימי *nmf* specialist in internal Medicine.
(hakarah) peneemeet הכרה פנימית *nf* inner conviction.
(makhlakah) peneemeet מחלקה פנימית *nf* internal ward.
peneemee|yah/-yot פנימייה *nf* boarding school; dormitory; (*+of:* **-yat**).
peneen|ah/-eem פנינה *nf* pearl; (*+of:* **-at**).
peneetseeleen פניצילין *nm* penicilin.
peney פני *nf pl+of* the face of; the surface of.
peney ha-dvareem פני הדברים *nf pl* the face of things; appearances.
peney ha-'eer (or **ha-keheelah**) פני העיר *nm pl* dignitaries (of the town or community).
peney ha-karka' פני הקרקע *nf pl* ground level; soil surface.
peney ha-shetakh פני השטח *nf pl* surface .
('al) peney על פני *adv* on; more then.
peney ha-yam פני הים *nf pl* sea-level.
(keeb|el/-lah/-altee) peney קיבל פני *v* welcomed; met; received; (*pres* **mekabel** *etc; fut* **yekabel** *etc*).
(keed|em/-mah/-amtee) peney קידם פני *v* welcomed; received; met; (*pres* **mekadem** *etc; fut* **yekadem** *etc*).
(mee) peney מפני *prep* because of.
(mee) peney mah? ?מפני מה why? on what account?
(mee) peney she- ־מפני ש *prep* because of.
(nas|a/-'ah/-a'tee) peney נשא פני *v* favored; (*pres* **nose** *etc; fut* **yeesa** *etc*).
penseeyon/-eem פנסיון *nm* boarding-house.
pens|yah/-yot פנסיה *nf* pension; (*+of:* **-yat**).
pe'ool|ah/-ot פעולה *nf* act; action; (*+of:* **-at**).
(khofesh) pe'oolah חופש פעולה *nm* freedom of action.
(sdeh/sdot) pe'oolah שדה פעולה *nm* field of activity.
(sheetoof) pe'oolah שיתוף פעולה *nm* cooperation.
(meshatef/-et) pe'oolah משתף פעולה *v pres* cooperates; collaborates; (*pres* **sheetef** *etc; fut* **yeshatef** *etc*).
(meshatef/-fey) pe'oolah משתף פעולה *nm* collaborator (with oppressive authorities).
(meta|'em/-'amey) pe'oolah מתאם פעולה *nm* coordinator of operations.
◇ **pe'ool|at/-ot tagmool** פעולת תגמול *nf* **1.** reprisal operation; **2.** Israeli forces' reprisal operation for act of terrorism.
pe'ooton/-eem (*npr* **pa'oton**) פעוטון *nm* nursery (*pl+of:* **-ey**).
pera'ee/-t פראי *adj* wild.
(shveet|ah/-ot) pera'ee|t/-yot שביתה פראית *nf* wildcat strike.
per|ak/-kah/-aktee פירק *v* dismantled; undid; (*pres* **mefarek** *(f=p); fut* **yefarek**).
(daleket) perakeem דלקת פרקים *nf* rheumatoid arthritis (Medic.).
(rashey) perakeem ראשי פרקים *nm pl* outline.
perakh/prakheem פרח *nm* **1.** flower; **2.** cadet; (*pl+of:* **peerkhey**).
perakh/peerkhey bar פרח בר *nm* wild flower.
perakh/peerkhey tayees פרח טיס *nm* air cadet.
pera'on/peer'onot פירעון *nm* payment; (*+of:* **peer'on**).
pera'ot פרעות *nf pl* pogrom; riots.
pera'oo|t/-yot פראות *nf* savagery.
per|ash/-shah/-ashtee פירש *v* interpreted; (*pres* **mefaresh** *(f=p); fut* **yefaresh**).
per|at/-tah/-atetee פירט *v* detailed; gave details of: (*pres* **mefaret** *(f=p); fut* **yefaret**).
peratee/-t פרטי *adj* private.
(gan/-eem) peratee/-yeem גן פרטי *nm* privately-owned nursery school (for 3-4 years old).
(mekhonee|t/-yot) peratee|t/-yot מכונית פרטית *nf* private car.
(oto) peratee אוטו פרטי *nm* private car.
(shem/-ot) peratee/-yeem שם פרטי *nm* first name.
perat|eem פרטים *nm pl* details; items; (*sing:* **perat**; *pl+of:* **-ey**).
(peertey) perateem פרטי פרטים *nm pl* full details; (*npr* **pratey** *etc*).
per|az/-rah/-aztee פירז *v* demilitarized; (*pres* **mefarez** *(f=p); fut* **yefarez**).
□ **Perazon** see □ **Prazon**

perateeyoot פרטיות *nf* privacy.

per|e'/-a'eem פרא *nm* wild person; savage; (*pl+of:* **peer'ey**).

pere פרא *(suffix) adj* wild.

pere/peer'ey adam פרא אדם *nm* savage; wild person.

(gad|al/-lah/-altee) pere' גדל פרא *v* grew wild; (*pres* **gadel** *etc; fut* **yeegdal** *etc*).

per|ed/pradeem פרד *nm* mule; (*pl+of:* **peerdey**).

peree hadar פרי הדר *nm* citrus fruit.

peree ma'alal|av/-eha *etc* פרי מעלליו/־יה *nm* fruits of his/her *etc* own doings.

(nas|a/-'ah) peree נשא פרי *v* bore fruit; (*pres* **nose** *etc; fut* **yeesa** *etc*).

pereek|ah/-ot פריקה *nf* unloading; (*+of:* **-at**).

pereekh|ah/-ot פריחה *nf* bloom; flourishing; (*+of:* **at**).

perees|ah/-ot פריסה *nf* **1.** deployment (of armed forces); **2.** slicing (bread); (*+of:* **-at**).

pereesh|ah/-ot פרישה *nf* retirement; (*+of:* **-at**).

pereeshoot פרישות *nf* abstinence.

pereet|ah/-ot פריטה *nf* **1.** getting change (money); **2.** playing percussion instrument (*+of:* **-at**).

pereets|ah/-ot פריצה burglary; (*+of:* **-at**).

pereets|at/-ot derekh פריצת דרך *nf* breakthrough.

pereets|at/-ot geder פריצת גדר *nf* transgression.

pereetsoo|t/-yot פריצות *nf* licentiousness.

pereeyodee/-t פריודי *adj* periodic.

pereg/prageem פרג *nm* poppy; (*pl+of:* **peergey**).

per|ek (*npr* **per|ak**)**/-kah/-aktee** פירק *v* dismantled; undid; (*pres* **mefarek** *(f=p); fut* **yefarek**).

perek/prakeem פרק *nm* **1.** chapter; section; **2.** joint; knuckle; (*pl+of:* **peerkey**).

perek bee-fney 'atsmo פרק בפני עצמו *adv* a chapter in itself.

perek ha-yad פרק היד *nm* knuckle of the hand.

('al ha) perek על הפרק *adv* on the agenda.

('al|ah/-tah 'al ha) perek עלה על הפרק *v* came up for discussion; (*pres* **'oleh** *etc; fut* **ya'aleh** *etc*).

('am|ad/-dah 'al ha) perek עמד על הפרק *v* was due for discussion; (*pres* **'omed** *etc; fut* **ya'amod** *etc*).

perekh פרך *nm* oppression; oppressive work.

('avodat) perekh עבודת פרך *nf* hard labor.

per|esh (*npr* **per|ash**)**/-shah/-ashtee** פירש *v* interpreted; (*pres* **mefaresh** *(f=p); fut* **yefaresh**).

per|et/-tah/-atetee פירט *v* detailed; gave details; (*pres* **mefaret** *(f=p); fut* **yefaret**).

perets פרץ *nm* breach; breakthrough.

perets 'anan פרץ ענן *nm* cloudburst.

('am|ad/-dah/-adetee ba) perets עמד בפרץ *v* stepped into the breach; (*pres* **'omed** *etc; fut* **ya'amod** *etc*).

per|ez (*npr* **per|az**)**/-zah/-aztee** פירז *v* demilitarized; (*pres* **mefarez** *(f=p); fut* **yefarez**).

peroo|'a'/-'at sey'ar פרוע שיער *adj* dishevelled; unkempt.

perood/-eem פירוד *nm* discord.

perook/-eem פירוק *nm* **1.** dismantling; **2.** winding up of a company, business *etc.*

perook neshek פירוק נשק *nm* disarmament.

(be) perook (*npr* **be-ferook**) בפירוק *adv* in process of being wound up.

peroor/-eem פירור *nm* crumb; bread-crumb; (*pl+of:* **-ey**).

peroos|ah/-ot פרוסה *nf* slice; bread-slice; (*+of:* **-at**).

peroos|at/-ot lekhem פרוסת לחם *nf* slice of bread.

peroosh/-eem פירוש *nm* commentary; meaning; (*pl+of:* **-ey**).

peroot/-eem פירוט *nm* list; details; (*pl+of:* **-ey**).

peroot|ah/-ot פרוטה *nf* **1.** 1/1000 of the onetime Israeli Pound; **2.** (fig) penny.

(af) perootah אף פרוטה not one penny!

(lo shav|eh/-ah) perootah לא שווה פרוטה *adj* not worth a penny.

peroots|ah/-ot פרוצה *nf* hooker; prostitute; (*+of:* **at**).

perooz/-eem פירוז *nm* demilitarization (*pl+of:* **-ey**).

perot פירות *nm pl* fruits (*sing:* **pree**).

(khanoot) perot חנות פירות *nf* fruit-shop; fruit-store.

(merak/meerkey) perot מרק פירות *nm* fruit soup.

perspekteev|ah/-ot פרספקטיבה *nf* perspective.

□ **Pesagot** פסגות *nm* communal village in Judea hills (est. 1981), 1 km E. of Ramallah. Pop. 536.

pesak/-eem פסק *nm* ruling; verdict; (*pl+of:* **peeskey**).

pesak/peeskey deen פסק דין *nm* sentence; verdict; judgment.

◇ **pesak/peeskey halakhah** פסק הלכה *nm* decision by a rabbinical authority or court.

◇ **pesakh** פסח *nm* Passover, Jewish holiday, celebrated in commemoration of the deliverance of the Israelites from slavery in Egypt and their 40 year-long march to the Promised Land of Israel (Exodus 12). Throughout Passover, starting on the 14th of Nisan (approx. March-April) Jews are permitted to eat, instead of bread, Matzah only. Passover is also called the Festival of Liberty (**Khag ha-Kheroot** חג החירות) and the Spring Festival (**Khag he-Aveev** חג האביב).

◇ **(seder) pesakh** see ◇ **seder pesakh**.

pesee|'ah/-'ot פסיעה *nf* step; pacing; (*+of:* **-'at**).

peseek/-eem פסיק *nm* comma; (punctuation).

(nekoodah oo) peseek (*npr* **oo-fseek**; *f=p*) נקודה ופסיק *nm pl* semicolon (punctuation).

peseek|ah/-ot פסיקה *nf* court-ruling; jurisprudence; (*+of:* **-at**).

peseekh|ah/-ot פסיחה *nf* skipping (*+of:* **-at**).

peseekhah 'al shtey ha-se'eepeem פסיחה על שתי הסעיפים *nf* vacillation; wavering.

peseel|ah/-ot פסילה *nf* disqualification; (*+of:* **-at**).

peseemee/-t פסימי *adj* pessimistic.
peseemeeyoot פסימיות *nf* pessimism.
pesek-zman פסק זמן *nm* time out; short intermission in a sports competition, between halves.
pesel/psaleem פסל *nm* statue; (*pl+of:* **peesley**).
peseyfas פסיפס *nm* mosaic.
pesha'/psha'eem פשע *nm* crime; (*pl+of:* **peesh'ey**).
pesha' me'oorgan פשע מאורגן *nm* organized crime.
(kha|f/-pah mee) pesha' *(f=p)* חף מפשע *adj* guiltless; innocent.
('olam ha) pesha' עולם הפשע *nm* the world of crime.
(shootaf/-ah la) pesha' שותף לפשע *adj & nmf* accessory to a crime.
peshar|ah/-ot פשרה *nf* compromise; (*+of:* **-at**).
peshat פשט *nm* plain meaning.
peshee|'ah/-'ot פשיעה *nf* delinquency; (*+of:* **-'at**).
pesheet|ah/-ot פשיטה *nf* **1.** raid; **2.** stripping; **3.** spread; (*+of:* **-at**).
pesheet|at/-ot 'or פשיטת עור *nf* skinning; profiteering.
pesheet|at/-ot regel פשיטת רגל *nf* bankruptcy.
pesheet|at yad פשיטת יד *nf* begging; mendicancy.
pesher פשר *nm* meaning; significance.
pesher davar פשר דבר *nm* (the) meaning thereof.
peshoot|o/-ah ke-mashma|'o/-'ah פשוטו כמשמעו *adj* **1.** plain; **2.** *adv* plainly.
pesolet פסולת *nf* rubbish; refuse.
pesool פסול *nm* defect; flaw.
◇ **pesool/-at kheetoon** פסול-חתון *nmf* single or couple who may not be married under Rabbinical law (*e.g.* a Cohen with a divorcée or a **"mamzer"** with anyone who is not a **"mamzer"** or a **"mamzeret"**); (*pl:* **-ey** *etc*).
peta' פתע *(suffix) adj* sudden; surprise.
(hatkaf|at/-ot) peta' התקפת פתע *nf* surprise attack.
(le) peta' (*npr* **le-feta'**) לפתע *adv* suddenly; all of a sudden.
petakh/ptakheem פתח *nm* doorway; opening; (*pl+of:* **peetkhey**).
petakh teekvah פתח תקווה *nm* gleam of hope.
□ **Petakh Teekvah** (Petakh Tiqva) פתח תקווה *nf* town (est. 1878 as first Jewish agric. settlement) 10 km NE of Tel-Aviv. Pop. 144,000.
□ **Petakhyah** (Petahya) פתחיה *nm* village (est. 1951), 6 km S. of Ramlah. Pop. 435.
petameem פטמים *nm pl* fattened fowl or livestock; (*sing:* **petam**; *pl+of:* **-ey**).
petay|ah/-yot פתיה *nf* silly female; simple-minded female; (*+of:* **yat**).
pet|ee/-ayeem פתי *nm* fool; simpleton.
peteekh|ah/-ot פתיחה *nf* opening; (*+of:* **-at**).
peteekhoo|t/-yot פתיחות *nf* open-mindedness.
peteel/-eem פתיל *nm* **1.** thread; wick; **2.** lamp wick; **3.** fuse; (*pl+of:* **-ey**).
peteelee|yah/-yot פתילייה *nf* kerosene cooker; (*+of:* **yat**).
petek/ptakeem פתק *nm* note; slip of paper; (*pl+of:* **peetkey**).
petel פטל *nm* raspberry.
(meets/-ey) petel מיץ פטל *nm* raspberry juice.
pet|en/-aneem פתן *nm* cobra (*pl+of:* **peetney**).
(ha-delet) petookhah הדלת פתוחה the door is open.
petor/-eem פטור *nm* exemption; tax-remission; (*pl+of:* **ey**).
petrozeel|yah פטרוזיליה *nf* parsley; (*+of:* **-yat**).
pets|a'/-a'eem פצע *nm* wound; injury; (*pl+of:* **peets'ey**).
pets|a'/-a'eem anoosh/-eem פצע אנוש *nm* fatal or serious wound or injury.
pets|a'/-a'eem sheetkhee/-yeem פצע שטחי *nm* surface wound.
□ **Petsa'el** (Peza'el) פצאל *nm* village (est. 1970) in the Jordan Valley, 10 km SW of Adam Bridge across Jordan, by Alon highway. Pop. 295.
petsats|ah/-ot פצצה *nf* bomb; (*+of:* **peetsets|at/-ot**).
"petsatsah" פצצה *nf [slang]* a "looker", "dish", "bombshell" (woman of "smashing" looks or sex-appeal).
petsatsat gaz madmee'a (*npr* **peetsetsat** *etc*) פצצת גז מדמיע *nf* tear-gas bomb.
petsatsat meen (*npr* **peetsetsat** *etc*) פצצת מין *nf* sex-bomb; "bombshell".
petsats|at/-ot tav'erah (*npr* **peetsetsat** *etc*) פצצת תבערה *nf* incendiary bomb.
petsats|at/-ot zman (*npr* **peetsetsat** *etc*) פצצת זמן *nf* time bomb.
petsee|'ah/-'ot פציעה *nf* wounding; (*+of:* **-'at**).
petseer|ah/-ot פצירה *nf* file (tool for cutting and smoothing); (*+of:* **-at**).
pezeel|ah/-ot פזילה *nf* squint; ogling; (*+of:* **-at**); strabismus (Medic).
pezeezoo|t/-yot פזיזות *nf* rashness; impulsiveness.
◇ **pezoor|ah/-ot** פזורה *nf* diaspora; population of a nation living outside its homeland; (*+of:* **-at**).
◇ **pey** פ"א *nf* 17th letter of hebrew Alphabet (פּ), a consonant pronounced (in a dotted text) **p** if dotted (פּ) and **ph** (i.e. **f**) when not dotted (פ). In undotted texts no such differentiation is possible so that the choice between reading it **p** or *f* would depend on context or memory.
Pey פ' **1.** *num* 80; **2.** the 80th.
◇ **pey sofeet** פ"א סופית shape Pey takes when ending a word (ף), where it is invariably pronounced **ph** (which we transliterate as **f**).
pladah/-ot פלדה *nf* steel. (*+of:* **at**).
(tsemer) pladah צמר פלדה *nm* steel-wool.
(yar|ad/-dah/-adetee) pla'eem ירד פלאים *v* declined greatly; (*pres* **yored** *etc*; *fut* **yered** *etc*).

plastee/-t פלסטי *adj* plastic.
(neetoo|'akh/-kheem) plastee/-yeem ניתוח פלסטי *nm* plastic surgery.
plaster פלסתר *adj* deceitful; shame; fraudulent.
(ktav/keetvey) plaster כתב פלסתר *nm* libellous writing; lampoon.
platsoor/-eem פלצור *nm* lasso.
plee|'ah/-'ot פליאה *nf* marvel; wonder; (*+of:* **-at**).
pleelee/-t פלילי *adj* criminal; penal.
('avar) pleelee עבר פלילי *nm* criminal record.
('avon/-ot) pleelee/-yeem עוון פלילי *nm* criminal offence.
pleeleem פלילים *nm pl* criminal acts; criminal action.
(bee) pleeleem (*npr* **bee-fleeleem**) בפלילים *adv* criminally prosecuted.
pleesh|ah/-ot פלישה *nf* intrusion; invasion; (*+of:* **-at**).
pleet|ah/-ot פליטה *nf* ejection; exhaust; (*+of:* **at**).
(tseenor/-ot) pleetah צינור פליטה *nm* exhaust-pipe.
pleetat/-ot koolmos פליטת קולמוס *nf* slip of the pen.
pleetat/-ot peh פליטת פה *nf* slip of the tongue.
pleez פליז *nm* brass.
pleyt|ah פליטה *nf* escape; survivors; (*+of:* **-at**).
(sar|ad/-dah/-adetee lee) pletah (*npr* **lee-fletah**) שרד לפליטה *v* survived; (*pres* **sored** *etc; fut* **yeesrod** *etc*).
(she'ereet ha) pleytah פארית הפליטה *nf* surviving remnants; what was left of.
◇ **(she'ereet ha) pleytah** see ◇ **she'ereet ha-pleytah.**
plonee/-t almonee/-t פלוני אלמוני *nmf* John Doe; Mr. / Mrs. "what's his/her name".
plonter פלונטר *nm [slang]* mess.
ploogah/-ot פלוגה *nf* army-company; group; squad; (*+of:* **at**).
ploogatee/-t פלוגתי *adj* of an army-company.
ploogt|ah/-ot פלוגתא *nf* controversy; dissension; (*+of:* **at**).
ploos פלוס *prep* plus.
pnay פנאי *nm* spare time; leisure.
(eyn) pnay אין פנאי no time to spare.
(she|'at/-'ot ha) pnay שעת הפנאי *nf* leisure time; moment of leisure.
pneem ha פנים ה־ *nm* the inside of; the interior.
◇ **(meesrad ha) pneem** see ◇ **meesrad ha-peneem.**
(sar ha) pneem שר הפנים *nm* the Minister of the interior; the Home secretary.
pneemah פנימה *adv* inward.
pneemee/-m פנימי *nm [colloq.]* tire's inner tube.
pneemee/-t פנימי *adj* internal.
(rof|e/-'ah) pneemee/-t רופא פנימי *nmf* specialist in internal medicine.
(hakarah) pneemeet הכרה פנימית *nf* inner conviction.
(makhlakah) pneemeet מחלקה פנימית *nf* internal ward.
pneemee|yah/-yot פנימייה *nf* boarding school; (*+of:* **-yat**).
pneen|ah/-eem פנינה *nf* pearl; (*+of:* **-at**).
pney פני *nf pl+of* the face of; the surface of.
pney ha-dvareem פני הדברים *nf pl* the face of things; appearances.
pney ha-'eer (or **ha-keheelah**) פני העיר *nm pl* dignitaries (of the town or community).
pney ha-karka' פני הקרקע *nf pl* ground level; soil surface.
pney ha-shetakh פני השטח *nf pl* surface.
('al) pney על פני *adv* on; more then.
pney ha-yam פני הים *nf pl* sea-level.
(keeb|el/-lah/-altee) pney קיבל פני *v* welcomed; met; received; (*pres* **mekabel** *etc; fut* **yekabel** *etc*).
(keed|em/-mah/-amtee) pney קידם פני *v* welcomed; received; met; (*pres* **mekadem** *etc; fut* **yekadem** *etc*).
(mee) pney מפני *prep* because of.
(mee) pney mah? ?מפני מה *query* why? on what account?
(mee) pney she- מפני ש־ *prep* because of.
(nas|a/-'ah/-a'tee) pney נשא פני *v* favored; (*pres* **nose** *etc; fut* **yeesa** *etc*).
poh פה *adv* here.
poh va-sham פה ושם *adv* here and there.
(lekh/-ee mee) poh לך מפה *v imp sing m/f* get out of here! (*inf* **lalekhet** *etc; pst* **halakh** *etc; pres* **holekh** *etc; fut* **yelekh** *etc*).
(mee) poh מפה *adv* from here; herefrom.
po'al/pe'aleem פועל *nm* (Gram.) verb; (*pl+of:* **po'oley**).
po'al kap|av/-eha/-ay *etc* פועל כפיו/־ה *nm* of his/her/my *etc* own doing.
po'al 'omed פועל עומד *nm* (Gram.) intransitive verb.
◇ **po'aley tseeyon** (Poalei Zion) פועלי ציון *nm* "Workers for Zion", worldwide Jewish Socialist (Marxist) Party which originated in Eastern Europe (1906). Its Palestine subsidiary (since 1919) **"Akhdoot ha-'Avodah"** אחדות העבודה later (1930) merged with **"ha-Po'el ha-Tsa'eer"** הפועל הצעיר (Palestine subsidiary of ◇ **Tse'eerey Tseeyon**), to form the "Eretz Israel Workers Party" (**Meefleget Poaley Erets Yeesra'el** מפלגת פועלי ארץ ישראל). The latter, known by its acronym **MAPAY** (מפא"י), fortwith became the major force in the country's politics for many years.
po'al yotse פועל יוצא *nm* **1.** (Gram.) transitive verb; **2.** outcome; result.
(hotsa'ah la) po'al הוצאה לפועל *nf* **1.** implementation; **2.** execution (under court-order).
(hots|ee/-ee'ah/-etee la) po'al הוציא לפועל *v* executed; implemented; (*pres* **motsee** *etc; fut* **yotsee** *etc*).
(hotsee *etc* **el ha) po'al** הוציא אל הפועל *v* executed; implemented.

(to'ar ha) po'al תואר הפועל *nm* (Gram.) adverb.

po'el/-et פועל *v pres* functions; operates; activates; (*pst* **pa'al**; *fut* **yeef'al** *(f=p)*).

(va'ad) po'el ועד פועל *nm* executive committee .

(ha-va'ad ha) po'el הוועד הפועל *nm* **1.** the Exective Committee; **2.** *[colloq.]* the Executive Council of the General Federation of Labor (Histadrut).

po'el/po'aleem פועל *nm* worker; laborer; (*pl+of:* **po'aley**).

po'el/po'aley dkhak פועל דחק *nm* worker employed under relief-employment scheme.

◇ **ha-Po'el ha-Meezrakhee** הפועל המזרחי *nf* former Religious Labor Party, now a component of ◇ **MAFDAL**, the National Religious Party.

po'el/po'aleem khakla'ee/-yeem פועל חקלאי *nm* farm-laborer.

po|'el/-'aleem shakhor/sh'khoreem פועל שחור *nm* manual laborer.

po'em|ah/-ot פואמה *nf* poem; (*+of:* **-at**).

pokhet/-et פוחת **1.** *adj* dwindling; **2.** *v pres* dwindles; (*pst* **pakhat**; *fut* **yeefkhat** *(f=p)*).

pokhet/-et ve-holekh/-et פוחת והולך **1.** *adj* constantly dwindling; **2.** *v pres* constantly decreases, diminishes; (*pres* **pakhat ve-halakh**; *fut* **yeefkhat ve-yelekh** *(f=p)*).

po'elet/po'alot פועלת *nf* female worker.

pokh|ez/-azeem פוחז *nm & adj* reckless, irresponsible person.

pol/-eem פול *nm* horse-bean; bean.

polanee/-t פולני/ת *adj* Polish.

polanee/-yah פולני/־ה *nmf* Pole.

polaneet פולנית *nf* Polish (language).

polanyah פולניה *nf* Poland.

poleen פולין *nf* Poland (the more traditional term in use).

poleep/-eem פוליפ *nm* adenoid; (*pl+of:* **-ey**).

polees|ah/-ots פוליסה *nf* (insurance) policy; (*+of:* **-at**).

polees|at/-ot beetoo'akh פוליסת ביטוח *nf* insurance policy.

poleetee/-t פוליטי *adj* political.

poleeteekah/-ot פוליטיקה *nf* policy; politics.

poleeteeka'ee/-t פוליטיקאי *nmf* politician.

poleetoor|ah/-ot פוליטורה *nf* furniture polish; (*+of:* **-at**).

poleetoorcheek/-eem פוליטורצ'יק *[colloq.] nm* furniture polisher.

polesh/-et פולש **1.** *adj* intruding; **2.** *nmf* intruder; invader; (*pl+of:* **polshey**).

polesh/-et פולש *v pres* intrudes; invades; (*pst* **palash**; *fut* **yeeflosh** *(f=p)*).

poobleetseest/-eem פובליציסט *nm* writer on public affairs.

poodel/-eem פודל *nm* poodle.

poodr|ah/-ot פודרה *nf* face powder; (*+of:* **-at**).

pookh פוך *nm* kohl (cosmetic preparation used in Orient for eye-makeup).

pookhlats/-eem פוחלץ *nm* stuffed carcass of animal or bird; (*pl+of:* **-ey**).

poolkhan/-eem פולחן *nm* ritual; cult; (*pl+of:* **-ey**).

poolkhanee/-t פולחני *adj* ritual; cultic; of worship.

poolmoos/-eem פולמוס *nm* polemic.

poolmoosee/-t פולמוסי *adj* polemical.

poombee/-t פומבי *adj* public; overt.

(be) poombee (*npr* **be-foombee**) בפומבי *adv* publicly; openly.

(mekheer|ah/-ot) poombee|t/-yot מכירה פומבית *nf* auction-sale; public auction.

poomee|t/-yot פומית *nf* mouth piece (telephone-receiver).

poompee|yah/-yot פומפייה *nf* grater; (*+of:* **-yat**).

poond|ak/-akeem פונדק *nm* inn; tavern; (*pl+of:* **-ekey**).

poonsh פונש *nm* punch.

poopeek/-eem פופיק *nm [slang]* navel.

poor/-eem פור *nm* lot.

(nafal ha) poor נפל הפור the lots have been cast; (*pres* **nofel** *etc*; *fut* **yeepol** *(p=f) etc*).

poor'anoo|t/-yot פורענות *nf* calamity; misfortune.

(moo|'ad/-'edet le) poor'anoot (*npr* **le-foor'anoot** *(f=p)*); מועד לפורענות *adj* designed for trouble; inviting trouble.

◇ **pooreem** (*also:* **pooreem**) פורים *nm* the Purim holiday; Feast of Esther; (approx in March).

(khag) pooreem חג פורים *nm* the Purim holiday.

(shooshan) pooreem שושן פורים the 2nd day of the Purim holiday.

poorkan/-eem פורקן *nm* vent; relief; (*pl+of:* **-ey**).

(nat|an/-nah/-atee) poorkan נתן פורקן *v* gave vent; (*pres* **noten** *etc*; *fut* **yeeten** *etc*).

poorsam/-emah/-amtee פורסם *v* was publicized, published; (*pres* **mefoorsam** *(f=p)*; *fut* **yefoorsam**).

poosht/-eet פושט *[slang] nmf* irresponsible youngster.

poostemah/-mot פוסטמה *[slang] nmf & adj* a pain in the neck.

pot|ar/-rah/-artee פוטר *v* was fired; was discharged; (*pres* **mefootar** *(f=p)*; *fut* **yefootar**).

pootsah/-tah/-etee פוצה *v* was indemnified; (*pres* **mefootseh** *(f=p)*; *fut* **yefootseh**).

pootsal/-lah/-altee פוצל *v* was split; (*pres* **mefootsal** *(f=p)*; *fut* **yefootsal**).

poots|ats/-etsah/-atstee פוצץ *v* was exploded, blown up; (*pres* **mefootsats** *(f=p)*; *fut* **yefootsats**).

popoolaree/-t פופולרי *adj* popular.

▫ **Porat** פורת *nm* village (est. 1950) in Sharon, 7 km SE of haSharon Road Junction, near **Kefar Yabets**. Pop. 447.

por|e'a/-'eem פורע *nm* rioter; hooligan; (*pl+of:* **-'ey**).

por|e'a/-a'at sey'ar/-ot פורע שיער *v pres* dishevels hair; (*pst* **para'** *etc*; *fut* **yeefra'** *etc* *f=p*).

□ **Poreeyah 'Eeleet** (Poriyya 'Illit) פוריה עלית *nf* urban settlement (est. 1955) in Lower Gallilee, 6 km S. of Tiberias. Pop. 646.

□ **Poreeyah Kefar 'Avodah** (Poriyya Kefar Avoda) פוריה כפר עבודה *nm* village (est. 1949) in Lower Gallilee, 4 km NW of Zemah Junction (**Tsomet Tsemakh**). Pop. 152.

□ **Poreeyah Neveh 'Oved** (Poriyya Newe Oved) פוריה נווה־עובד *nf* urban settlement (est. 1949) in Lower Gallilee, 5 km S. of Tiberias. Pop. 718.

por|er/-erah/-artee פורר *v* crumbled; broke up; (*pres* **meforer** *(f=p)*; *fut* **yeforer**).

porets/-et פורץ *v pres* through; erupts; (*pst* **parats**; *fut* **yeefrots** *(f=p)*).

(seret/seertey) porno סרט פורנו *nm* porno movie; blue movie.

pornografee/-t פורנוגרפי *adj* pornographic.

por|ets/-tseem פורץ *nm* burglar; (*pl+of:* **-tsey**).

por|ets/-tsey geder פורץ גדר *nm* transgreessor.

posek/-et פוסק *v pres* **1.** decides; **2.** discontinues; (*pst* **pasak**; *fut* **yeefsok** *(f=p)*).

pos|ek/-keem פוסק *nm* arbiter; rabbinic authority; (*pl+of:* **-key**).

pos|ek/-key halakhah פוסק הלכה *nm* setter of rules.

(beeltee) posek/-et בלתי פוסק *adj* incessant; uninterrupted.

posh|e'a/-a'at פושע **1.** *adj* sinful; criminal; **2.** *v pres* sins; commits crime; (*pst* **pasha'**; *fut* **yeefsha'** *(f=p)*).

posh|e'a/-'eem פושע *nm* criminal; (*pl+of:* **-'ey**).

poshe'a moo'ad פושע מועד *nm m* inveterate criminal.

posh|e'a/-'ey meelkhamah פושע מלחמה *nm* war-criminal.

posher/-et פושר *adj* lukewarm; tepid.

poshet/-et פושט *pres* **1.** takes off; undresses; **2.** raids; **3.** spreads; (*pst* **pashat**; *fut* **yeefshot** *(f=p)*).

poshet (*etc*) **'or** פושט עור **1.** *nm* skinner; profiteer; **2.** *pres* skins; profiteers.

poshet/-et (*etc*) **regel** פושט רגל *v pres* goes bankrupt.

posh|et/-tey regel פושט רגל *nm* bankrupt.

poshet/-et (*etc*) **tsoorah** פושט צורה *v pres* alters one's own appearence.

poshet (*etc*) **tsoorah ve-lovesh tsoorah** פושט צורה ולובש צורה *v pres* undergoes metamorphosis.

posh|et/-tey yad פושט יד *nm* beggar; mendicant.

(mayeem) poshreem מים פושרים *nm pl* lukewarm water.

poshreen פושרין *nm pl* tepid water; lukewarm water.

(be) potentseeyah בפוטנציה **1.** *adj* potential; **2.** *adv* potentially.

poter/-et פוטר *v pres* **1.** exempts; **2.** dismisses; frees; (*pst* **patar**; *fut* **yeeftor** *(f=p)*).

poter/-et פותר *v pres* solves; (*pst* **patar**; *fut* **yeeftor** *(f=p)*).

potkhan/-eem פותחן *nm* can-opener; (*pl+of:* **-ey**).

pots|ets/-etsah/-atstee פוצץ *v* blew up; (*pres* **mefotsets** *(f=p)*; *fut* **yefotsets**).

pozah/-ot פוזה *nf* pose; (*+of:* **at**).

pra'ee/-t פראי *adj* wild.

(shveet|ah/-ot) pra'ee|t/-yot שביתה פראית *nf* wildcat strike.

(daleket) prakeem דלקת פרקים *nf* rheumatic fever (Medic.).

(rashey) prakeem ראשי פרקים *nm pl* outline.

prakheem פרחים *nm pl* plowers (*sing:* **perakh**; *pl+of:* **peerkhey**).

prakleet/-eem פרקליט *nm* lawyer; attorney; (*pl+of:* **-ey**).

prakleet/-at ha-medeenah פרקליט המדינה *nm* state Attorney; the Attorney General.

prakleet/-tat ha-mekhoz פרקליט המחוז *nmf* district Attorney.

prakteek|ah/-ot פרקטיקה *nf* practice.

prakteekah prateet פרקטיקה פרטית *nf* **1.** private practice; **2.** right of a State- or public-employed physician to attend private patients.

pra'oot/-yot פראות *nf* savagery.

pra'ot פרעות *nf pl* pogrom.

pras/-eem פרס *nm* prize; premium; award; (*pl+of:* **-ey**).

prat/-eem פרט *nm* detail; (*pl+of:* **-ey**).

prat פרט *nm* private person; individual.

prat le- פרט ל־ *adv* with the exception of.

(khofesh ha) prat חופש הפרט *nm* individual freedom; freedom of the individual.

(tseen'at ha) prat צנעת הפרט *nm* a person's privacy.

(zekhooyot ha) prat זכויות הפרט *nf pl* individual rights.

□ **Prat** פרת *nm* the river Euphrates.

pratee/-t פרטי *adj* private.

(gan/-eem) pratee/-yeem גן פרטי *nm* privately-owned nursery school (for 3-4-year-olds).

(mekhonee|t/-yot) pratee|t/-yot מכונית פרטית *nf* private car.

(oto) pratee אוטו פרטי *nm* private car.

(shem/-ot) pratee/-yeem שם פרטי *nm* first name.

prateem פרטים *nm pl* details; items; (*sing:* **prat**; *pl+of:* **-ey**).

(peertey) prateem פרטי פרטים *nm pl* full details; (*npr* **pratey**).

prateeyoot פרטיות *nf* privacy.

□ **Prazon** (Perazon) פרזון *nm* village (est. 1953) in **Ta'anakh** district of Yîzre'el Valley, 8 km S. of 'Afula (**'Afoolah**). Pop. 316.

pree/-perot פרי *nm* fruit.

pree hadar פרי־הדר *nm* citrus fruit.

pree ma'alal|av/-eha *etc* פרי מעלליו/־יה *nm* fruits of his/her *etc* own doings.

(nas|a/-'ah/'atee) pree נשא פרי *v* bore fruit; (*pres* **nose** *etc*; *fut* **yeesa** *etc*).

preed|ah/-ot פרידה *nf* parting; farewell; separation; (+*of:* -**at**).

(beer|kat/-khot) preedah בירכת פרידה *nf* bidding farewell; saying goodbye; taking leave.

(meseeb|at/-ot) preedah מסיבת פרידה *nf* farewell-party.

preek|ah/-ot פריקה *nf* unloading; (+*of:* -**at**).

preekh|ah/-ot פריחה *nf* bloom; flourishing; (+*of:* **at**).

preemeeteevee/-t פרימיטיבי *adj* primitive.

◇ **preemoos/-eem** פרימוס *nm* **1.** oil-cooker; **2.** *[colloq.]* nickname for Piper-planes used in 1948 war by "Hagana".

preentseep/-eem פרינציפ *nm* a principle; a matter of principle.

preentseepyonee/-t פרינציפיוני *adj* which is a matter of principle.

preentseepyoneet פרינציפיונית *adv* in principle.

prees|ah/-ot פריסה *nf* **1.** deployment (of armed forces); **2.** slicing (bread); (+*of:* -**at**).

preesh|ah/-ot פרישה *nf* retirement; (+*of:* -**at**).

preeshoot פרישות *nf* abstinence.

preet|ah/-ot פריטה *nf* **1.** getting change (money); **2.** playing percussion instrument (+*of:* -**at**).

preets|ah/-ot פריצה burglary; (+*of:* -**at**).

preets|at/-ot derekh פריצת דרך *nf* breakthrough.

preets|at/-ot geder פריצת גדר *nf* transgression.

preetsoo|t/-yot פריצות *nf* licentiousness.

preeveelegee|yah/-yot פריבילגיה *nf* privilege; (+*of:* **yat**).

preyd|ah (*npr* **preed|ah**)**/-ot** פרידה *nf* parting; farewell; separation; (+*of:* -**at**).

(beer|kat/-khot) preydah (*npr* **preed|ah**) בירכת פרידה *nf* bidding farewell; saying goodbye; taking leave.

(meseeb|at/-ot) preydah (*npr* **preed|ah**) מסיבת פרידה *nf* farewell-party.

prodookteevee/-t פרודוקטיבי *adj* fruitful; productive.

profesoor|ah/-ot פרופסורה *nf* *[colloq.]* professorship.

profes|or/-oreem פרופסור *nm* professor; prof.

profesor-khaver פרופסור חבר *nm* associate-professor.

profesor meen ha-meenyan פרופסור מן המניין *nm* full professor.

profesoree|t/-yot פרופסורית *nf* woman-professor.

progreseevee/-t פרוגרסיבי *adj* progressive.

proletaree/-t פרולטרי *adj* proletarian.

proletaryon/-eem פרולטריון *nm* proletariat.

prolog/-eem פרולוג *nf* prologue.

proo|'a'/-'at se'ar פרועת שיער *adj* dishevelled; unkempt.

proos|ah/-ot פרוסה *nf* slice; bread-slice; (+*of:* -**at**).

proos|at/-ot lekhem פרוסת לחם *nf* slice of bread.

proot|ah/-ot פרוטה *nf* **1.** 1/1000 of the onetime Israeli Pound; **2.** (fig) penny.

(af) prootah אף פרוטה not one penny!

(lo shav|eh/-ah) prootah לא שווה פרוטה *adj* not worth a penny.

proots|ah/-ot פרוצה *nf* hooker; prostitute; (+*of:* **at**).

proports|yah/-yot פרופורציה *nf* proportion; (+*of:* **yat**).

prospekt/-eem פרוספקט *nm* prospectus.

protekts|yah/-yot פרוטקציה *nf [colloq.]* "pull"; connections for obtaining favors from officialdom.

protestantee/-t פרוטסטנטי *adj* Protestant.

protez|ah/-ot פרותזה *nf* **1.** artificial limb; **2.** dental plate; (+*of:* -**at**).

protrot פרוטרוט *nm* **1.** small change; **2.** details.

protsedoor|ah/-ot פרוצדורה *nf* procedure; (+*of:* -**at**).

proveents|yah/-yot פרובינציה *nf* **1.** province; **2.** small town area; (+*of:* -**yat**).

proveentsyal/-eet פרובינציאל *nmf* small-town person; one with a parochial mentality.

proveentsyalee/-t פרובינציאלי *adj* provincial; parochial.

provokateevee/-t פרובוקטיבי *adj* provocative; daring; challenging.

provokats|yah/-yot פרובוקציה *nf* provocation; (+*of:* -**yat**).

proyekt/-eem פרויקט *nm* project.

◇ **proyekt ha-lavee** פרויאקט הלביא *nm* popular project for Israel Air Industries to embark upon manufacturing a new top-of-the-line military aircraft of their own conception and design. It was ultimately shelved in 1988, for economic reasons, after successful flights of two prototypes. A single technology demonstrator still remains flying.

proz|ah/-ot פרוזה *nf* prose; (+*of:* -**at**).

proza'ee/-t פרוזאי *adj* prosaic.

prozdor/-eem פרוזדור *nm* corridor; (*pl+of:* -**ey**).

□ **"prozdor yerooshaayeem"** פרוזדור ירושלים *nm* "The Jerusalem Corridor" - area with hills on both sides of last stretch of 22 km beginning at **Sha'ar ha-Gay** שער הגיא (in Arabic, **Bab-El-Wad**) of the Tel-Aviv Jerusalem highway (Expressway 1). In 1948 hostilities, this stretch proved most vital to the Capital's defense and cost many lives.

psak/-eem פסק *nm* ruling; verdict; (*pl+of:* **peeskey**).

psak/peeskey deen פסק דין *nm* sentence; verdict; judgment.

psak/peeskey halakhah פסק הלכה *nm* decision (or verdict) by rabbinical court or authority.

psant|er/-reem פסנתר *nm* piano; (*pl+of:* -**rey**).

psant|er/-rey kanaf פסנתר כנף *nm* grand-piano; "grand".

psantran/-eet פסנתרן *nmf* pianist; (*pl:* -**eem/-eeyot**; +*of:* -**ey**).

psedoneem/-eem פסידונים *nm* pseudonym; pen-name.

psee|'ah/-'ot פסיעה *nf* step; pacing; (+*of:* -'at).
pseek/-eem פסיק *nm* comma; (punctuation).
(nekoodah oo) pseek (*npr* **oo-fseek**; *f=p*) נקודה ופסיק *nm* semicolon (punctuation).
pseek|ah/-ot פסיקה *nf* court-ruling; jurisprudence; (+*of:* -at).
pseekh|ah/-ot פסיחה *nf* skipping (+*of:* -at).
pseekhah 'al shtey ha-se'eepeem פסיחה על שתי הסעיפים *nf* vacillation; wavering.
pseekhee/-t פסיכי **1.** *adj* psychotic; **2.** *nmf [slang]* loony.
pseekhee'at|or/-reem פסיכיאטור *nm [colloq.]* psychiatrist; (*pl+of:* -rey).
pseekhee'atreyah פסיכיאטריה *nm* psychiatry.
pseekho'analeez|ah/-ot פסיכו־אנליזה *nf* psychoanalysis.
pseekholog/-eet פסיכולוג *nmf* psychologist.
pseekhologyah kleeneet פסיכולוגיה קלינית *nf* clinical psychology (Medic.).
pseekhologyah sheemoosheet פסיכולוגיה שימושית *nf* applied psychology (Medic.).
pseekhopat/-eet פסיכופט *nmf* psychopath; psychotic; psycho.
pseekhotekhnee/-t פסיכו־טכני *adj* psychotechnical.
pseekhoz|ah/-ot פסיכוזה *nf* psychosis; (+*of:* -at).
pseel|ah/-ot פסילה *nf* disqualification; (+*of:* -at).
pseydo- פסידו *prefix* pseudo-
pseydoneem/-eem פסידונים *nf* pseudonym.
pseyfas פסיפס *nm* mosaic.
pshar|ah/-ot פשרה *nf* compromise; (+*of:* -at).
pshat פשט *nm* plain meaning.
pshee|'ah/-'ot פשיעה *nf* delinquency; (+*of:* -'at).
psheet|ah/-ot פשיטה *nf* **1.** raid; **2.** stripping; **3.** spread; (+*of:* -at).
psheet|at/-ot 'or פשיטת עור *nf* skinning; profiteering.
psheet|at/-ot regel פשיטת רגל *nf* bankruptcy.
psheet|at yad פשיטת יד *nf* begging; mendicancy.
pshoot|o/-ah ke-mashma|'o/-'ah פשוטו כמשמעו *adj* **1.** plain; **2.** *adv* plainly.
psolet פסולת *nf* rubbish; refuse.
psool פסול *nm* defect; flaw.
◇ **psool/-at kheetoon** see ◇ **pesool/-at kheetoon.**
□ **Ptakhyah** see □ **Petakhyah.**
ptameem פטמים *nm pl* fattened fowl or livestock; (*sing:* **ptam**; *pl+of:* -ey).
ptay|ah/-yot פתיה *nf* silly female; simple-minded female; (+*of:* yat).
pteekh|ah/-ot פתיחה *nf* opening; (+*of:* -at).
pteekhoot/-yot פתיחות *nf* open-mindedness.
pteel/-eem פתיל *nm* **1.** thread; **2.** fuse; (*pl+of:* -ey).
pteeleeyah/-yot פתילייה *nf* kerosene cooker; (+*of:* -yat).
(ha-delet) ptookhah הדלת פתוחה the door is open.
ptor/-eem פטור *nm* exemption; tax-remission; (*pl+of:* -ey).
ptsatsah/-ot פצצה *nf* bomb; (+*of:* **peetsets|at/-ot**).
"ptsatsah" פצצה *[slang] nf* a "looker" , "dish" (i.e. female of "smashing" looks or sex-appeal).
ptsatsat gaz madmee'a (*npr* **peetsetsat** *etc*) פצצת גז מדמיע *nf* tear-gas bomb.
ptsatsat meen (*npr* **peetsetsat** *etc*) פצצת מין *nf* sex-bomb;" bombshell".
ptsats|at/-ot tav'erah (*npr* **peetsetsat** *etc*) פצצת תבערה *nf* incendiary bomb.
ptsats|at/-ot zman (*npr* **peetsetsat** *etc*) פצצת זמן *nf* time bomb.
ptsee|'ah/-'ot פציעה *nf* wounding; (+*of:* -'at).
ptseer|ah/-ot פצירה *nf* file (tool for cutting and smoothing); (+*of:* -at).
pzeel|ah/-ot (+*of:* -at) פזילה *nf* squint; ogling; strabismus (Medic.).
pzeezoo|t/-yot פזיזות *nf* rashness; impulsiveness.
◇ **pzoor|ah/-ot** see ◇ **pezoorah.**

Q.

NOTE: The Hebrew Language Academy, official authority on the Hebrew language, has (in its Rules for Transliteration of Hebrew Script into Latin Script, Official Gazette, 1957) ruled that the Latin letter **Q** is the proper transliteration of the Hebrew letter **Koof** (ק), also known as **Kof**. This is followed in Israel when transliterating geographic and personal names, scientific terminology, etc. The practical purpose it serves is to distinguish words spelled with **Koof** (ק) from words spelled with **Kaf** (כ). This is useful to people who write Hebrew and read it fluently.

In practice, a person listening to everyday speech would find it nearly impossible to tell **Koof** (ק) from **Kaf** (כ). Thus in this dictionary, devised for beginners, we do not follow the Academy.

In our transliteration we do not use the letter **Q** at all. Instead, we use **K** both for **Kaf** (כּ) and **Koof** (ק). However, every entry is offered in Hebrew letters as well, so users who know the Hebrew alphabet can discern proper spelling. Place names are followed in brackets by official transliterations, i.e. as appearing in road maps and on road signs.

R.

transliterating Hebrew consonant **Resh** (ר)

ra' רע *adv* bad; badly.
ra'/ra'ah רע *adj* bad; malicious.
ra' me'od רע מאד *adv* very bad; very badly.
ra'/ra'ah me'od רע מאד *adj* extremely malicious; very bad.
('ayeen ha) ra' עין הרע *nf* evil eye.
(heerg|eesh/-eeshah/-ashtee) ra' הרגיש רע *v* didn't feel well; (*pres* **margeesh** *etc; fut* **yargeesh** *etc*).
(heergeesh *etc* **be) ra'** הרגיש ברע *v* fell sick.
(lashon ha) ra' לשון הרע *nf* slander; libel.
(re'akh/rekhot) ra'/ra'eem ריח רע *nm* bad odor; stench.
(shem) ra' שם רע *nm* evil repute; defamation.
(shoresh ha) ra' שורש הרע *nm* the root of the evil.
(yetser ha) ra' יצר הרע *nm* evil inclination; evil nature.
ra'ah/ra'atah/ra'eetee ראה *v* saw; (*pres* **ro'eh**; *fut* **yeer'eh**).
ra|'ah (*etc*) **et ha-nolad** ראה את הנולד *v* **1.** foresaw events; **2.** (*lit.*) saw what is to be born.
ra|'ah/-'ot רעה *nf* calamity; (*+of:* **-'at**).
ra'ah kholah רעה חולה *nf* a sore evil.
ra'ad/re'adeem רעד *nm* tremor; (*pl+of:* **ra'adey**).
ra'ad/-ah/-etee רעד *v* trembled; (*pres* **ro'ed**; *fut* **yeer'ad**).
ra'al/re'aleem רעל *nm* poison.
ra'am/re'ameem רעם *nm* thunder; (*pl+of:* **ey**).
ra'am/-ah/-tee רעם *v* thundered; (*pres* **ro'em**; *fut* **yeer'am**).
ra'amah/re'amot רעמה *nf* mane; (*+of:* **-at**).
ra'anan/-ah רענן *adj* fresh; flourishing.
□ **Ra'ananah** (Ra'anana) רעננה *nm* urban settlement (est. 1921) in Sharon, bridging **Hertseleeyah** to its W. and **Kefar Saba** to its E. Pop. 53,600.
ra'ananoot רעננות *nf* freshness.
ra'ash/re'asheem רעש *nm* noise; (*pl+of:* **-ey**).
ra'ash רעש *nm* earthquake.
(le-lo) ra'ash ללא רעש **1.** *adv* noiselessly; **2.** *adj* noiseless.
ra'ash/-ah/-tee רעש *v* **1.** made noise; **2.** raged; (*pres* **ro'esh**; *fut* **yeer'ash**).
ra'av רעב *nm* hunger; starvation.
(gav|a'/-'ah/-a'tee ba) ra'av גווע ברעב *v* was dying of hunger; (*pres* **gove'a'** *etc; fut* **yeegva'** *etc*).
(maskor|et/-ot) ra'av משכורת רעב *nf* starvation wage; starvation-pay.
(mez|eh/-at) ra'av מזה רעב *nmf & adj* starved by famine.
ra'av/-ah/-tee רעב *v* starved; famished; (*pres* **ra'ev**; *fut* **yeer'av**).
ra'av (*etc*) **le-lekhem** רעב ללחם *v* was hungry for bread i.e. lacked means of subsistence.
ra'av|ah ראווה *nf* show; display; (*+of:* **-at**).
(khalon/-ot) ra'avah חלון ראווה *nm* show-window.
(le) ra'avah לראווה *adv* for show; exhibition.
ra'avtanee/-t ראוותני *adj* exhibitionist.
ra'avtanoot ראוותנות *nf* exhibitionism.
◇ **Hosha'na Raba** הושענא רבא *nm* seventh day of the Succot festival.
rabanan רבנן *nm pl* the Sages of the Talmud.
rabaneet רבנית *nf* Rabbi's wife.
rabanoot רבנות *nf* rabbinate.
◇ **(ha)rabanoot ha)rasheet** הרבנות הראשית *nf* Chief Rabbinate, State-recognized authority for Jewish religious matters, governing network of Jewish rabbinical courts with jurisdiction over matters pertaining to personal status of Jews and especially to their marital status.
rabatee/-t רבתי *adj* **1.** capital (letter); **2.** Great; Greater (town).
rabeem רבים **1.** *nm pl* many; **2.** *nm* (Gram.) plural.
(ba) rabeem ברבים *adv* publicly; in public.
(leshon) rabeem לשון רבים *nf* (Gram.) plural.
(rashoot ha) rabeem רשות הרבים *nf* public domain.
(tsarat) rabeem צרת רבים *nf* a sorrow shared by many.
◇ **rabee-yanooka** רבי־ינוקא *nm* child-rabbi, i.e. a Hassidic Rabbi who inherited his position before having reached age 13.
(le) rabot לרבות *adv* including.
rabotay רבותי intj *m pl* Gentlemen!
(gveerotay ve) rabotay !גבירותי ורבותי! *interj nm pl* Ladies and Gentlemen!

(maranan ve) rabotay מרנן ורבותי *nm pl* My learned friends!
rad|ah/-etah/-eetee רדה *v* tyrannized; (*pres* **rodeh**; *fut* **yeerdeh**).
rad|af/-fah/-aftee רדף *v* chased; pursued; (*pres* **rodef**; *fut* **yeerdof**).
radeeyat|or/-oreem רדיאטור *nm* radiator.
radyo רדיו *nm* **1.** radio; **2.** *[colloq.]* radio set.
tekhna'oot radyo טכנאות רדיו *nf* radio-technics.
(tekhn|ay/-a'ey) radyo טכנאי רדיו *nm* radio-technician.
(sheedoor/-ey) radyo שידור רדיו *nm* radio broadcast; radio transmission.
radood/redoodah רדוד *adj* **1.** shallow; **2.** (*figurat.*) superficial.
radoom/redoomah רדום *adj* sleepy; asleep.
ra'ev/re'evah רעב **1.** *adj* hungry; **2.** *v pres* starves; (*pst* **ra'av**; *fut* **yeer'av**).
raf|eh/-ah רפה *adj* weak.
□ **Rafee'akh** (Rafiah) רפיח *nf* Arab township (Arabic: Rafah) on Egyptian border, at S. end of Gaza Strip. Pop. 45,355 (plus 36,000 in refugee camps)
rafooy/refooyah רפוי *adj* slack; lax.
rafr|efet/-afot רפרפת *nf* pudding.
rafsood|ah/-ot רפסודה *nf* ferry; raft; (+*of*: **-at**).
raftan/-eet רפתן *nmf* dairy farmer.
rag|ash/-shah/-ashtee רגש *v* agitated; (*pres* **rogesh**; *fut* **yeergosh**).
rag|az/-zah/-aztee רגז *v* was angry; (*pres* **rogez**; *fut* **yeergaz**).
rageel/regeelah רגיל *adj* usual; ordinary.
rageel/regeelah le- -רגיל ל *v pres* is used to; is accustomed to; (*pres* **hayah** *etc*; *fut* **yeehyeh** *etc*).
(beeltee) rageel/regeelah (*or*: **lo** *etc*) בלתי רגיל *adj* unusual.
(ka) rageel כרגיל *adv* as usual; usually.
(she-lo) rageel שלא רגיל *adv* not as usual; unusually.
rageesh/regeeshah רגיש *adj* sensitive; touchy.
ragl|ayeem רגליים *nf pl* legs; feet; (*sing*: **regel**; *pl+of*: **-ey**).
raglayeem la-davar רגליים לדבר *pl* reasons to assume; reasons to believe.
(marb|eh/-ey) raglayeem מרבה רגליים *nm* centipede.
(peesook) raglayeem פישוק רגליים *nm* straddle; standing with legs apart.
(yesh) raglayeem le-khakh יש רגליים לכך there's a reason to it; there are reasons to believe it.
raglee רגלי *adv* on foot.
raglee/-m רגלי *nm* infantry-man.
(keet|at/-ot) ragleem כיתת רגלים *nf* infantry squad.
(kheyl) ragleem חיל רגלים *nm* infantry.
(le) ragley לרגלי *prep* on account of; in view of.
ragoo'a'/regoo'ah רגוע *adj* relaxed; tranquil.
ragshan/-eet רגשן *adj & nmf* sentimentalist.
ragshanee/-t רגשני *adj* sentimental; emotional.
ragshanoo|t/-yot רגשנות *nf* sentimentality.
ragzan/-eet רגזן *adj* bad-tempered; irate.
□ **Rahat** רהט *nf* Bedouin township (est. 1980) 26 km N. of **Be'er Sheva'**, located across road from kibbutz **Shooval**. Being first Israeli experiment in settling nomads permanently on land, it consists of 24 separate independent sections, each allotted to a different Bedouin tribe. Pop. 20,400.
raheet/-eem (*cpr* **reheet/-eem**) רהיט *nm* furniture item; piece of furniture (*pl+of*: **-ey**).
rahoot/rehootah רהוט *adj* fluent
rak רק *prep* only.
rak rega' רק רגע *interj* just a minute.
rak rega' kat! !רק רגע קט *interj* just a little moment; just a second!
(akh ve) rak אך ורק *conj* solely; exclusively.
rak|ah/-ot רקה *nf* temple (physiol.); (+*of*: **-at**).
rak|a'/-'ah/-a'tee רקע *v* **1.** stamped; **2.** hammered out (metal); (*pres* **roke'a'**; *fut* **yeerka'**).
raka' (*etc*) **be-raglav** (*etc*) רקע ברגליו *v* stamped with one's foot.
rak|ad/-dah/-adetee רקד *v* danced; (*pres* **roked**; *fut* **yeerkod**).
rak|ak/-ekah/-aktee רקק *v* spit; (*pres* **rokek**; *fut* **yeerkok**).
◇ **RAKAKH** רק"ח *nf* (*acr.* of: **Resheemah Komooneesteet KHadashah** רשימה קומוניסטית חדשה i.e. the New Communist List) abbr.name (for elections) of the Israel Communist Party previously known as **MAKEE** (*acr of* **Meeflagah Komooneesteet Yesre'eleet** מפלגה קומוניסטית ישראלית). Is further known as **KHADASH**, *acr of* **KHAzeet Demokrateet le-SHalom** חזית דימוקרטית לשלום i.e. Democratic Peace Front.
rak|akh/-khah/-akhtee רקח *v* compounded; concocted; mixed; (*pres* **roke'akh**; *fut* **yeerkakh**).
rak|am/-mah/-amtee רקם *v* embroidered; (*pres* **rokem**; *fut* **yeerkom**).
rakam (*etc*) **mezeem|ah/-ot** רקם מזימה *v* schemed; devised evil plan.
rak|av/-vah/-avtee רקב *v* decayed; rot; (*[colloq.]* *pres* **neerkav**; *fut* **yerakev**).
rakav רקב *nm* decay; decayed matter.
rakav/-eem רכב *nm* coachman; (*pl+of*: **-ey**).
rakaz/-eem רכז *nm* organizer; coordinator; (*pl+of*: **-ey**).
rakdan/-eem רקדן *nm* dancer; (*pl+of*: **-ey**).
rakdanee|t/-yot רקדנית *nf* dancer (female); danseuse.
rakee'a'/rekee|'eem רקיע *nm* heaven; sky; (*pl+of*: **-'ey**).
(ba) rakee'a' ha-shveeee ברקיע השביעי *adv* in the seventh heaven; happy to the utmost.
(kav/-ey ha) rakee'a' קו הרקיע *nm* skyline.
rakekhet רככת *nf* rickets (Medic.).
raket|ah/-ot רקיטה *nf* rocket; (+*of*: *-at*).
◇ **rakevel** רכבל *nm* funicular; cable-car. Exists in Israel in four places: (**1**) in Haifa, to

carry commuters between Downtown and residential areas on Mount Carmel **(Karmel)**; (**2**) in the Golan Heights, to carry gliders to Mount Hermon **(Khermon)** slopes to practice ski and wintersports; (**3**) in **Rosh Ha-Neekrah** to the seaside mountain top from which Lebanon can be viewed across the border; (**4**) at Mount **Masadah**, to convey sightseers to the top of the ancient fortress mount.

rakevet/-avot רכבת *nf* train.

rakevet *(etc)* **ekspres** רכבת אקספרס *nf* express train.

rak|evet *(etc)* **masa** רכבת משא *nf* freight train.

rakevet *(etc)* **meheerah** רכבת מהירה *nf* fast train.

rakevet *(etc)* **nos'eem** רכבת נוסעים *nf* passenger-train.

◇ **rakevet** *(etc)* **parvareem** רכבת פרברים *nf* suburbian commuters train for Greater Tel-Aviv area, building of which, along ◇ **Neteevey Ayalon** freeway, started in 1991. Scheduled to go into operation in 1993.

rakevet *(etc)* **regeelah** רכבת רגילה *nf* regular train; ordinary train.

rakevet *(etc)* **takhteet** רכבת תחתית *nf* subway; underground train; metro.

(kron/-ot) rakevet קרון רכבת *nm* railway-car.

rake|zet/-azot רכזת *nf* organizer (female); coordinator.

rakh/rakah *(k=kh)* רך *adj* soft.

rakh/rakat lev רך-לב *adj* **1.** soft-hearted; **2.** timid; fearful.

(ha) rakh ha-nolad הרך הנולד *nm* the newborn.

(geel) rakh גיל רך *nm* tender age.

rakhak/-ah/-tee רחק *v* kept far away; departed; *(pres* **rakhok**; *fut* **yeerkhak**).

rakhameem רחמים *nm pl* pity; mercy; compassion; (*+of:* **rakhmey**).

(beek|esh/-shah/-ashtee) rakhameem ביקש רחמים *v* asked for mercy; *(pres* **mevakesh** *etc; fut* **yevakesh** *etc v=b)*.

(le-lo) rakhameem ללא רחמים **1.** *adj* merciless; **2.** *adv* without pity; mercilessly.

(meedat ha) rakhameem מידת הרחמים *nf* leniency; clemency.

rakh|an/-nah/-antee רכן *v* bowed; *(pres* **rokhen**; *fut* **yeerkon** *(k=kh))*.

rakh|as/-sah/-astee רכס *v* buttoned; fastened; *(pres* **rokhes**; *fut* **yeerkos** *(k=kh))*.

rakhash/rekhasheem רחש *nm* murmur; whisper; wish; (*pl+of:* **rakhashey**).

rakhash/-ah/-tee רחש *v* **1.** felt; **2.** murmured; *(pres* **rokhesh**; *fut* **yeerkhash**).

rakhash *(etc)* **emoon** רחש אמון *v* felt confidence; had faith.

rakh|ash/-shah/-ashtee רכש *v* acquired; *(pres* **rokhesh**; *fut* **yeerkosh** *(k=kh))*.

rakhash *(etc)* **neesayon** רכש ניסיון *v* gained experience.

rakhashey lev רחשי לב *nm pl* heartfelt wishes.

rakhats/-ah/-tee רחץ *v* washed; bathed; *(pres* **rokhets**; *fut* **yeerkhats**).

rakhats *(etc)* **be-neekyon kap|av/-eha** רחץ בניקיון כפיו *v* washed one's hands; denied responsibility.

rakhav/rekhavah רחב *adj* wide; broad.

(khatakh/-eem) rakhav/rekhaveem חתך רחב *nm* cross-section.

rakh|av/-vah/-avtee רכב *v* rode; *(pres* **rokhev**; *fut* **yeerkav** *(k=kh))*.

rakhav/-ah/-tee רחב *v* widened; expanded; (*[colloq.] pres* **meetrakhev**; *fut* **yeerkhav**).

(khoog/-eem) rakhav/rekhaveem חוג רחב *nm* wide circle.

(meegzar/-eem) rakhav/rekhaveem מיגזר רחב *nm* wide sector.

(hal|akh/-khah/-akhtee) rakheel הלך רכיל *v* gossiped; slandered; *(pres* **holekh** *etc; fut* **yelekh** *etc)*.

rakh|efet/-afot רחפת *nf* hovercraft.

rakhel/rekheleem רחל *nf* ewe; sheep; (*pl+of:* **-ey**).

rakh|em/-ameel רחם! *v imp sing m/f* have mercy; have pity; (*inf* **lerakhem**; *pst* **reekhem**; *pres* **merakhem**; *fut* **yerakhem**).

(le-lo) rakhem ללא רחם *adv* without mercy; pitilessly.

(lo yad|a'/-'ah/-a'tee) rakhem לא ידע רחם *v* knew no mercy; *(pres* **eyno yode'a'** *etc; fut* **lo yeda'** *etc)*.

rakhlan/-eet רכלן *nmf & adj* gossipmonger; gossiper (*pl+of:* **-ey**).

rakhman/-eet רחמן *nmf & adj* merciful, compassionate (person); (*pl+of:* **-ey**).

(akh/-eem) rakhman/-eem אח רחמן *nm* male-nurse.

(akh|ot/-ayot) rakhmanee|yah/-yot אחות רחמניה *nf* nurse.

rakhmanoot רחמנות *nf* mercy; compassion.

(neekhmeroo) rakham|av/-eha נכמרו רחמיו/יה *v* had pity on; *(pres* **neekhmareem** *etc; fut* **yeekamroo** *etc k=kh)*.

rakhmey shamayeem רחמי שמיים *nm pl* heavenly mercy.

rakhok/rekhokah רחוק *adj* far; distant.

rakhok רחוק *adv* far; far away.

rakhok rakhok רחוק רחוק *adv* very far away.

(ha-meezrakh ha) rakhok המזרח הרחוק *nm* the Far East.

(karov/krovah) rakhok/rekhokah קרוב רחוק *nmf* distant relative; (*pl* **kroveem rekhokeem**).

(me) rakhok מרחוק *adv* from afar.

rakhoom/rekhoomah רחום *adj* merciful; compassionate.

rakhoon/rekhoonah רכון *adj* bent; bending.

rakhoots/rekhootsah רחוץ *adj* washed.

rakhoov/rekhoovah רכוב *adj* mounted; riding.

rakhrookhee/-t רכרוכי **1.** *adj* softish; unstable; **2.** *[slang] nmf* softie.

rakhrookheeyoot רכרוכיות *nf* softishness; instability.

rakhts|ah/-ot רחצה *nf* bathing; washing; (*+of:* **-at**).

rakhv|ah (*npr* **rekhav|ah**)/**-ot** רחבה *nf* square; place (in a city); (*+of:* **rakhavat**).

rakhvoo|t (*npr* **rakhavoo|t**)/**-yot** רחבות *nf* largesse; comfort; luxury.

rakoo|t/-yot רכות *nf* softness; tenderness.

rakoov/rekoovah רקוב *adj* rotten.

ram/-ah רם *adj* **1.** high; lofty; **2.** loud.

ram/-at dereg רם דרג *adj* high ranking; of high rank.

(be-kol) ram בקול רם *adv* aloud; loudly.

□ **Ramah** (Rama) רמה *nm* large Arab rural settlement, 6 km E. of Karmi'el (**Karmee'el**). Pop. (predominantly Christian) 6,010.

ram|ah/-ot רמה *nf* **1.** level; **2.** elevation; height; (*+of:* **-at**).

ramah seekhleet רמה שכלית *nf* intelligence level.

(ba) ramah ברמה *adv* loudly; openly.

□ **(ha)Ramah** הרמה *nf* (*lit.:* "the height") colloquial reference to **Ramat ha-Golan** the Golan Heights.

□ **Ramalah** (Ramallah) ראמאללה *nf* Arab town in Judean hills, 13 km N. of Jerusalem. Pop. 29,200.

rama'oo|t/-yot רמאות *nf* swindle; deceit; fraud.

(ma'as|eh/-ey) rama'oot מעשה רמאות *nm* fraudulous act; swindle.

ram|as/-sah/-astee רמס *v* trampled; (*pres* **romes**; *fut* **yeermos**).

□ **Ramat Aveev** (Ramat-Aviv) רמת אביב *nf* one of Tel-Aviv's more recently built residential areas, located N. of Yarkon river, around Tel-Aviv University Campus.

□ **Ramat Daveed** (Ramat David) רמת דוד *nm* kibbutz (est. 1926) in Yizre'el Valley, 3 km W. of **Meegdal ha-'Emek**. Pop. 369.

□ **Ramat Ef'al** (Ramat Ef'al) רמת אפעל *nf* residential garden-suburb SE of Ramat-Gan, 1 km S. of **Sheeba (Tel-ha-Shomer)** Hospital complex. Pop. 2,730.

□ **Ramat Gan** רמת־גן *nf* twin-city of Tel-Aviv, having **Giv'atayeem** to its S. and **Beney Berak** to its N., all three bordering on the metropolis from the E. Pop. 119,500.

□ **Ramat Hadar** רמת הדר *nf* onetime agricultural settlement (est. 1938), now part of **Hod ha-Sharon**. Pop. 276.

□ **Ramat Hadasah** רמת הדסה *nm* educational institute and boarding-school for Youth-Aliyah youngsters (est. 1948). Pop. 400.

□ **Ramat ha-Golan** (Golan Heights) רמת הגולן *nf* elevated region in the N. part of Israel bordering on: **1.** Mount **Khermon** (Hermon) (N.); **2. Rookan** river (E.); **3. Yarmook** river (S.); **4. Khoolah** (Chuleh) Valley and Lake Tiberias (Sea of Galilee) (W.). In 1983 the territory, under Israeli rule since 1967, was decreed by the Knesset to be part of Israel.

□ **Ramat ha-Khayal** (Ramat haHayyal) רמת החייל *nf* - residential suburb of Tel-Aviv located on NE side of the town, between Zahala (**Tsahalah**) and **Sheekoon Dan**.

□ **Ramat ha-Kovesh** רמת הכובש *nm* kibbutz (est. 1932) 5 km N. of **Kefar Saba**. Pop. 635.

□ **Ramat ha-Nadeev** (Ramat haNadiv) רמת הנדיב *nf* memorial park (est. 1954) between **Zeekhron Ya'akov** and **Benyameenah** centering around the grave of Baron Edmond James de Rothschild (1845-1934) promoter and patron of Jewish resettlement of Palestine.

□ **Ramat ha-Sharon** רמת השרון *nf* urban settlement (est. 1931) 15 km N. of Tel-Aviv, bordering on **Hertseleeyah**. Pop. 36,900.

□ **Ramat ha-Shofet** (Ramat haShofet) רמת השופט *nm* kibbutz (est. 1941), 6 km S. of Yokne'am Junction (**Tsomet Yokne'am**). Pop. 708.

ramat/-mot khayeem רמת חיים *nf* living standard.

□ **Ramat Khen** רמת חן *nf* residential garden-suburb on the SE side of Tel-Aviv forming part of Ramat-Gan proper.

□ **Ramat Magsheemeem** (Ramat Magshimim) רמת מגשימים *nm* cooperative settlement (est. 1968) in Golan Heights, 7 km E. of Eli'el (**Elee'el**). Pop. 387.

□ **Ramat Peenkas** רמת פנקס *nf* residential suburb outside Tel-Aviv on **Geha** road SE of Mesubim Junction (**Tsomet Mesoobeem**). Pop. 556.

□ **Ramat Rakhel** (Ramat Rahél) רמת רחל *nm* kibbutz (est. 1926) outside Jerusalem, SE of the city on the road to Bethlehem. Pop. 311.

□ **Ramat Razee'el** (Ramat Razi'el) רמת רזיאל *nm* village in Judean hills (est. 1948), 7 km E. of Shimshon Junction (**Tsomet Sheemshon**). Pop. 318.

□ **Ramat Tsvee** (Ramat Zevi) רמת צבי *nm* village in Lower Galilee, 4 km N. of **'En Kharod**. Pop. 353.

□ **Ramat Yeeshay** (Ramat Yishay) רמת ישי *nm* village (est. 1925) 4 km E. of **Keeryat Teev'on**. Pop. 2,450.

□ **Ramat Yokhanan** (Ramat Yohanan) רמת יוחנן *nm* kibbutz (est. 1932) in Haifa Bay, 2 km SE of **Keeryat Ata**. Pop. 649.

◇ **ramatkal/-eem** רמטכ"ל *nm* (*acr of* **Rosh ha-MAteh ha-KLalee** ראש המטה הכללי) Chief of General Staff; (*pl+of:* **-ey**).

rama|y/-'eet רמאי *nmf* liar; crook; (*pl:* **-'eem/-'eeyot**; *+of:* **-'ey**).

ram|az/-zah/-aztee רמז *v* hinted; (*pres* **romez**; *fut* **yeermoz**).

ramkol/-eem רמקול *nm* loudspeaker; (*pl+of:* **-ey**).

□ **Ramlah** (Ramla) רמלה *nf* historic town between the lowlands and Coastal Plain, 15 km E. of Tel-Aviv. Pop. 47,900.

ramla'ee/-t רמלאי *nmf* resident of Ramla.

□ **Ram On** רם און *nm* village (est. 1960) in Ta'anakh sector of Yizre'el Valley, 8 km SE of **Megeedo**. Pop. 339.

ramoos/remoosah רמוס *adj* downtrodden; trampled.

□ **Ramot** רמות **1.** *nf* new large and rapidly developing residential suburb in NE Jerusalem; **2.** *nm* village (est. 1970) in the Golan Heights, 2 km E. of Lake Tiberias, 7 km N. of kibbutz **'En Gev**. Pop. 406.

□ **Ramot ha-Shaveem** (Ramot haShavim) רמות השבים *nm* village (est. 1933) in Sharon, 1 km S. of Ra'anana Road Junction. Pop. 755.

□ **Ramot Me'eer** (Ramot Me'ir) רמות מאיר *nm* village (est. 1949 and re-est 1969), 4 km SE of Rehovot **(Rekhovot)**. Pop. 229.

□ **Ramot Menasheh** (Ramot Menashe) רמות מנשה *nm* kibbutz (est. 1948), 10 km NE of **Zeekhron Ya'akov**. Pop. 601.

□ **Ramot Naftalee** (Ramot Naftali) רמות נפתלי *nm* village (est. 1945) in Upper Galilee, 10 km S. of **Keeryat Shmonah**. Pop. 354.

ramzor/-eem רמזור *nm* traffic-light; **(***pl+of:* **-ey)**.

□ **Ranen** (Rannen) רנן *nm* village (est. 1950) in NW Negev, 2 km N. of **Ofakeem**. Pop. 344, mostly Karaites.

ra'oo'a'/re'oo'ah רעוע *adj* unstable; decrepit; delapidated.

ra'ool/re'oolah רעול *adj* veiled.

ra'ooy/re'ooyah ראוי *adj* worthy.

(ka) ra'ooy כראוי *adv* appropriately; properly.

(meen ha) ra'ooy מן הראוי *adv* it were proper if...

rapad/-eem רפד *nm* upholsterer; **(***pl+of:* **-ey)**.

◇ **raport/-eem** רפורט *nm [colloq.]* **1.** traffic ticket; **2.** police report for a traffic offense; **3.** municipal ticket for unlawful or unpaid-for parking.

rapsod|yah/-yot רפסודיה *nf* rhapsody; **(***+of:* **yot)**.

rash רש *nm & adj* pauper.

(keevsat ha) rash כיבשת הרש *nf* "poor man's lamb" (*figurat.*) alluding to Bible story (II Samuel, Ch. 12).

(la'ag la) rash לעג לרש *nm* mocking the poor (*figurat.*).

rasha'/resha|'eet רשע *nmf* villain; **(***pl:* **-'eem;** *+of:* **reesh'ey)**.

rash|am/-mah/-amtee רשם *v* noted down; registered; **(***pres* **roshem;** *fut* **yeershom)**.

rasham/-eem רשם *nm* registrar; **(***pl+of:* **-ey)**.

rasham **(***etc***) dokh (***npr* **doo'akh)** רשם דו״ח *v* wrote out a traffic-ticket.

rasha|y/-eet רשאי *adj* entitled; allowed; free to.

rashee/-t ראשי *adj* main; chief.

(ma'amar/-eem) rashee/-yeem מאמר ראשי *nm* editorial.

(meesrad/-eem) rashee/-yeem משרד ראשי *nm* main office.

('or|ekh/-kheem) rashee/-yeem עורך ראשי *nm* editor-in-chief; **(***pl+of:* **-khey)**.

◇ **(rav/raban|eem) rashee/-yeem** see rav rashee.

(kot|eret/-rot) rashee|t/-yot כותרת ראשית *nf* headline; main headline.

◇ **(ha-rabanoot ha) rasheet** see ◇ **(ha)rabanoot ha-rasheet**, above.

rashey prakeem ראשי פרקים *nm pl* chapter headings; gist.

rashey tevot ראשי תיבות *nm pl* initials (for abbreviations); acronym.

rashlan/-eet רשלן **1.** *adj* negligent; slovenly; **2.** *nmf* negligent, slovenly person.

rashlanee/-t רשלני *adj* careless; slovenly.

rashlanoo|t/-yot רשלנות *nf* negligence; carelessness.

rashoom/reshoomah רשום *adj* registered; noted.

(do'ar) rashoom דואר רשום *nm* registered mail.

(meekhtav/-eem) rashoom/-reshoomeem מכתב רשום *nm* registered letter.

rashoot ראשות *nf* leadership; heading.

(be) rashoot בראשות *adv* at the head of...

rashoo|t/-yot רשות *nf* **1.** authority; **2.** domain.

rashoo|t/-yot mekomee|t/-yot רשות מקומית *nf* local authority; municipality.

(ha) rashoot ha-meyashevet הרשות המיישבת *nf* the settlement (land) authority.

(ha) rashoot ha-moosmekhet הרשות המוסמכת *nf* the competent authority.

rasmee/-t (*npr* **reeshmee/-t)** רשמי *adj* official.

(be-orakh) rasmee (*npr* **reeshmee)** באורח רשמי *adv* officially; formally.

rasmeet (*npr* **reeshmeet)** רשמית *adv* officially.

rasmeeyoot (*npr* **reeshmeeyoot)** רשמיות *nf* officialism; formality.

rat|akh/-khah/-akhtee רתח *v* boiled; **(***pres* **rote'akh;** *fut* **yeertakh)**.

ratakh/-eem רתך *nm* welder; solder; **(***pl+of:* **-ey)**.

ratakhoot רתכות *nf* welding; soldering.

rat|am/-mah/-amtee רתם *v* harnessed; **(***pres* **rotem;** *fut* **yeertom)**.

rat|an/-nah/-antee רטן *v* grumbled; **(***pres* **roten;** *fut* **yeerton)**.

ratoo'akh/retookhah רתוח *adj* boiled.

ratook/retookah רתוק *adj* linked; chained.

ratoom/retoomah רתום *adj* harnessed.

ratoov/retoovah (*npr* **rat|ov/retoobah)** רטוב *adj* wet.

◇ **rats ("Ratz")** רצ *nf* Civil Rights and Peace Movement, left of the center political party advocating self-determination for Palestinian Arabs and two-states solution to Israeli-Arab conflict as well as separation between State and religion.

rats/-ah/-tee רץ *v* run; **(***pres* **rats;** *fut* **yaroots)**.

rats/-ah רץ **1.** *nmf* runner; **2.** *adj* running.

(meter) rats מטר רץ *adj* per meter length.

rats|ah/-tah/-eetee רצה *v* wanted; wished; **(***pres* **rotseh;** *fut* **yeertseh)**.

ratsaf/-eem רצף *nm* floor-layer; floor-tiler.

rats|akh/-khah/-akhtee רצח *v* murdered; (*pres* **rotse'akh;** *fut* **yeertsakh**).
ratseef/retseef|eem רציף *nm* quay; pier; platform; wharf; (*pl+of:* **-ey**).
ratskhanee/-t רצחני *adj* murderous.
ratson/retsonot רצון *nm* will; desire. (*+of:* **retson**).
ratson tov רצון טוב *nm* good will.
(be) ratson ברצון *adv* willingly; gladly; with pleasure.
(heesb|ee'a'/-ee'ah/-a'tee) ratson השביע רצון *v* satisfied; (*pres* **masbee'a'** *etc; fut* **yasbee'a'** *etc*).
(me) ratson מרצון *adv* voluntarily; of one's own free will.
(sva'/sve'at) ratson שבע רצון *adj* satisfied; content.
(svee'at) ratson (*or:* **svee'oot** *etc*) שביעת / שביעות רצון *nf* satisfaction; contentment.
ratsoof/retsoofah רצוף *adj* **1.** enclosed; attached; **2.** continuous; non-stop; successive.
(la'avod) ratsoof (*or:* **'oved** *etc*) לעבוד רצוף *v inf* to work (or *v pres:* works, working) non-stop i.e. with no afternoon break; (*pst* **'avad** *etc; fut* **ya'avod** *etc*).
ratsoots/retsootsah רצוץ *adj* **1.** *[colloq.]* exhausted; **2.** crushed; downtrodden.
(kaneh) ratsoots קנה רצוץ *nm* **1.** *lit* : broken reed; **2.** (*figurat.*) something not to be relied upon.
ratsooy/retsooyah רצוי *adj* desirable; welcome.
(lo) ratsooy/retsooyah (*or:* **beeltee** *etc*) לא /בלתי רצוי *adj* unwanted; unwelcome.
(ore'akh/orakhat) ratsooy/retsooyah אורח רצוי *nmf* welcome guest.
ratsyonalee/-t רציונלי *adj* rational; reasonable.
rav/-ah/-tee רב *v* quarreled; (**prs rav;** *fut* **yareev**).
rav/rabaneem (*b=v*) רב *nm* Rabbi; (*pl+of:* **rabaney**).
◇ **rav/raban|eem rashee/-yeem** (*b=v*) רב ראשי *nm* Chief Rabbi, heading the hierarchy of Rabbis in a country where there are Jewish communities organized under Rabbinic leadership. In Israel, there are two Chief-Rabbis, filling jointly and equally the Chief Rabbinate. One leads Jews of the Ashkenazi Rite and the other, (holding the traditional title of **Reeshon le-Tseeyon** ראשון לציון i.e. "the First in Zion"), leads Jews of the Sephardi Rite. Both stand for re-election by a body of Religious Councils every five years.
rav- ־רב (*prefix*) multi-; chief-; (*pl* **rabey** (*b=v*)).
rav-aloof רב־אלוף *nm* lieutenant-general.
rav-bokhen רב־בוחן *nm* chief-examiner; chief-tester.
rav-gvanee/-t (*npr:* **ravgonee/-t**) רב גוני *adj* multi-colored; variegated.
ravgvaneeyoot (*npr:* **ravgoneeyoot**) רב־גוניות *nf* variety; variegation.
rav-khovel רב־חובל *nm* skipper; captain (of a boat); (*pl* **rabey** (*b=v*) **khovleem**).
rav-kalay רב־כלאי *nm* chief-warden.
rav-kolee/-t רב־קולי *adj* polyphonic.
rav-komatee/-t רב־קומתי *adj* multi-storied.
rav-komot רב־קומות *nm* multi-storied building; (*pl* **rabey** (*b=v*) **komot**).
rav-mashma'ee/-t רב־משמעי *adj* meaningful.
rav/rabey mekher (*b=v*) רב־מכר *nm* bestseller.
rav-oman רב־אמן *nm* maestro; (*pl* **rabey** (*b=v*) **omaneem**).
rav-pakad רב פקד *nm* Police-superintendent.
rav/rabat roshem (*b=v*) רב־רושם *adj* impressive; most impressive.
rav-samal רב־סמל *nm* first sergeant; sergeant-major; (*pl* **rabey** (*b=v*) **samal'eem**).
rav-seren רב־סרן *nm* major (Army); (*pl* **rabey** (*b=v*) **sraneem**).
rav-sheemooshee/-t רב־שימושי *adj* multi-purpose.
rav-shlabee/-t רב שלבי *adj* multi-stage.
rav-shnatee/-t רב־שנתי *adj* perennial (Botan.).
rav-tabakheem רב־טבחים *nm* arch-murderer; (**rabey** (*b=v*) **tabakheem**).
rav-todot! !רב־תודות *interj* many thanks! thank you so much!
rav-toor|ay/-a'eet רב־טוראי *nmf* corporal (Army).
rav-tsedadee/-t רב־צדדי *adj* multi-lateral.
('erev) rav ערב־רב *nm* mob; motley crowd; riff-raff.
rav|ah/-tah/-eetee רבה *v* multiplied; increased; (*pres* **rav;** *fut* **yeerbeh** (*b=v*)).
ravah/-tah/-eetee רווה *v* was saturated; had enough; (*pres* **raveh;** *fut* **yeervah**).
ravah (*etc*) **nakhat** רווה נחת *v* derived pleasure.
ravak/-eem רווק *nm* bachelor; (*pl+of:* **-ey**).
ravak|ah/-ot רווקה *nf* bachelorette; spinster; unmarried woman; (*+of:* **-at**).
rav|akh/-khah רווח *v* prevailed (opinion); circulated (rumor); (*pres* **rove'akh;** *fut* **yeervakh**).
ravakh (*etc*) **lo/la/-** *etc* רווח לו/לה וכו *v* (he/she/etc) felt relief.
ravakoot רווקות *nf* bachelorhood; spinsterhood; being unmarried.
rav|ats/-tsah/-atstee רבץ *v* **1.** lay down; **2.** *[slang]* overstayed; stayed too long.
rav|eh/-ah רווה *adj* well-watered.
raveed/reveed|eem רביד *nm* necklace; chain; (*pl+of:* **-ey**).
raveets רביץ *[colloq.] nm* layer of cement plaster applied on expanded metal (XPM).
ravoo'a'/revoo'ah רבוע *adj* square; quadrate.
(met|er/-reem) ravoo'a'/revoo'eem מטר רבוע *nm* square meter; (approx. 10 sq. feet).
ravooy/revooyah רווי *adj* saturated; resonant.
ravrevan/-eet רברבן **1.** *nmf* vaunter; **2.** *adj* boastful.
ravrevanoot רברבנות *nf* boastfulness.
ra'|yah/-yot רעיה *nf* wife; spouse; (*+of:* **-yat**).
ra'yat|ee/-kha/-o רעיתי/־תך/־תו *nf* my/your/his wife.

ra'yon/-ot רעיון *nm* idea; thought.

(neetsnets) ra'yon ניצנץ רעיון *v* an idea flashed; (*pres* **menatsnets** *etc; fut* **yenatsnets** *etc*).

ra'yonee/-t רעיוני *adj* ideological; rational.

raz/-eem רז *nm* mystery; secret; (*pl+of:* **-ey**).

raz|ah/-tah/-eetee רזה *v* slimmed; lost weight; (*pres* **razeh**; *fut* **yeerzeh**).

(gveenah) razah גבינה רזה *nf* cheese from skimmed milk.

raz|eh/-ah רזה *adj* thin; skinny.

(khalav) razeh חלב רזה *nm* skimmed milk.

re|'a'/-'eem רע *nm* friend; companion.

re|'ah/-'ot ריאה *nf* lung (Anat.); (*+of:* **-'at**).

re'ad|ah/-ot רעדה *nf* tremor; shivering; (*+of:* **ra'adat**).

re'afeem רעפים *nm pl* tiles; roofing tiles; (*sing:* **ra'af**).

(gag/-ot) re'afeem גג רעפים *nm* tile roof.

re'akts|yah/-yot ריאקציה *nf* reaction; extreme "rightism" (politically) (*+of:* **yat**).

re'akh/rekhot ריח *nm* odor; smell; scent.

re'akh neekho'akh ריח ניחוח *nm* fragrance.

re'akh ra' ריח רע *nm* bad odor.

(heev|'eesh/-'eeshah/-'ashtee) re'akh הבאיש ריח *v* gave bad name; (*pres* **mav'eesh** *etc; fut* **yav'eesh** *etc*).

re'al|ah/-ot רעלה *nf* veil (worn by Muslim women); (*+of:* **ra'al|at/-ot**).

re'alee/-t ריאלי **1.** *adj* real; **2.** *nm* school with science course of study.

(bet-sefer) re'alee בית ספר ריאלי *nm* science high-school.

(megamah) re'aleet מגמה ריאלית *nf* natural science trend (in high school).

re'a|yah/-yot ראיה *nf* proof; evidence; (*+of:* **-yat**).

re'a|yah/-yot mesa|ya'at/-ye'ot ראיה מסייעת *nf* corroborating evidence.

re'ayon/ra'ayonot ראיון *nm* interview (*+of:* **ra'ayon**).

redeedoo|t/-yot רדידות *nf* **1.** shallowness; **2.** (*figurat.*) superficiality.

redeef|ah/-fot רדיפה *nf* pursuit; (*+of:* **-at**).

redeefat betsa' רדיפת בצע *nf* greed; lucre.

redeefot רדיפות *nf pl* persecutions; (*sing:* **redeefah**).

ree'anoon ריענון *nm* freshening up; refreshing.

reeb|ah/-ot ריבה *nf* jam; (*+of:* **-at**).

reebeet ריבית *nf* interest (on money borrowed or invested).

reebeet banka'eet ריבית בנקאית *nf* bank interest rate.

reebeet be'ad khareegah (*[colloq.]* **reebeet khareegah**) ריבית בעד חריגה *nf* increased rate of interest applied to overdraft exceeding approved ceiling.

reebeet de-reebeet ריבית דריבית *nf* compound interest.

reebeet meetstaberet ריבית מצטברת *nf* accrued interest.

reebeet ketsootsah ריבית קצוצה *nf* exhorbitant rate of interest.

(lav|ah/-tah/-eetee be) reebeet לווה בריבית *v* borrowed against interest; (*pres* **loveh** *etc; fut* **yeelveh** *etc*).

(le-lo) reebeet ללא ריבית *adj & adv* interest-free; without interest.

(malv|eh/-ah be) reebeet מלווה בריבית *v pres* lends against interest; (*pst* **heelvah** *etc; fut* **yalveh** *etc*).

(malv|eh/-eem be) reebeet מלווה בריבית *nm* usurer; loan shark.

reebo/-'ot ריבוא *nm* myriad; 10,000.

reebon/-eem ריבון *nm* sovereign; (*pl+of:* **-ey**).

reebon ha-'olameem! ריבון העולמים! *interj* God! (*lit.:* Sovereign of the worlds).

reebonee/-t ריבוני *adj* sovereign.

reebono shel 'olam! ריבונו של עולם! **1.** *interj* for God's sake! **2.** *nm* Master of the Universe!

reebonoot/-yot ריבונות *nf* sovereignty.

reebooy ריבוי *nf* increase; plentitude.

reech-rach/-eem ריץ׳־רץ׳ *[slang] nm* zipper.

re'ee/mar'ot ראי *n (sing m, pl f)* mirror.

re'eed|ah/-ot רעידה *nf* tremor; shaking; trembling; (*+of:* **-at**).

re'eedat/-ot adamah רעידת אדמה *nf* earthquake.

□ **Re'eem** (Re'im) רעים *nm* kibbutz in NW Negev (est. 1949), near Gaza Strip. Pop. 328.

re'eem ahooveem רעים אהובים *nf pl* beloved friends.

(seekh|at/-ot) re'eem שיחת רעים *nf* friendly talk; talk between friends.

(takhroot) re'eem תחרות רעים *nf* friendly match.

re'eeno'a' ראינוע *nm* cinema (used before sound was added to films, now called **kolno'a**).

re'ee|yah/-yot ראייה *nf* sight; eyesight; (*+of:* **-yat**).

('ed/-at) re'eeyah עד ראייה *nmf* eyewitness; (*pl:* **'ed|ey/-ot** *etc*).

(ketsar/keetsrat) re'eeyah קצר־ראייה *adj* short-sighted; nearsighted.

(kotser) re'eeyah קוצר ראייה *nf* shortsightedness; nearsightedness.

(sdeh) re'eeyah שדה ראייה *nm* field of vision.

re'eeyat ha-nolad ראיית הנולד **1.** *nf* foresight; **2.** *lit.* seeing what is to be born.

reefr|ef/-efah/-aftee רפרף *v* fluttered; hovered; (*pres* **merafref**; *fut* **yerafref**).

reefroof/-eem רפרוף *nm* fluttering; hovering; (*pl+of:* **-ey**).

(be) reefroof ברפרוף *adv* at a glance; superficially.

reefyon/-ot רפיון *nf* slackness; feebleness.

reeg'ee/-t רגעי *adj* momentary.

reeg|el/-lah/-altee ריגל *v* spied; (*pres* **meragel**; *fut* **yeragel**).

reegool/-eem ריגול *nm* espionage; spying; (*pl+of:* **-ey**).

reegool negdee ריגול נגדי *nm* counter-espionage.

reegoosh/-eem ריגוש *nm* emotion; excitement; (*pl+of:* **-ey**).
reegshee/-t רגשי *nm* emotional; sentimental.
reehoot/-eem ריהוט *nm* **1.** furnishing; **2.** *[colloq.]* furniture; (*pl+of:* **-ey**).
(la) reek לריק *adv* in vain.
reeka'/-'ah/-a'tee ריקע *v* hammered out; flattened (metal); (*pres* **merake'a'**; *fut* **yerake'a'**).
reekavon ריקבון *nm* rot; decay; (*+of:* **reekvon**).
reek|ekh/-'khah/-akhtee ריכך *v* softened; softened up; (*pres* **merakekh**; *fut* **yerakekh**).
reek|ez/-zah/-aztee ריכז *v* concentrated; (*pres* **merakez**; *fut* **yerakez**).
reekh|ef/-afah/-aftee ריחף *v* **1.** hovered; **2.** was imminent; (*pres* **merakhef**; *fut* **yerakhef**).
reekh|el/-lah/-altee ריכל *v* gossiped; (*pres* **merakhel**; *fut* **yerakhel**).
reekh|em/-amah/-amtee ריחם *v* pitied; (*pres* **merakhem**; *fut* **yerakhem**).
reekhoof/-eem ריחוף *nm* hovering; flying; (*pl+of:* **-ey**).
reekhook/-eem ריחוק *nm* remoteness; (*pl+of:* **-ey**).
(be) reekhook makom בריחוק מקום *adv* at a distance.
reekhr|e'akh/-ekhah/-akhtee ריחרח *v* sniffed; snooped; (*pres* **merakhre'akh**; *fut* **yerakhre'akh**).
reekoo|'a'/-'eem ריקוע *nm* **1.** hammering out; flattening (metal); **2.** thin metal sheet.
reekmah/rekamot ריקמה **1.** *nf* embroidery; **2.** *nf* tissue (Anat.); texture; structure (*+of:* **reekm|at/-ot**).
reekood/-eem ריקוד *nm* dance; (*pl+of:* **-ey**).
reekood/-ey 'am ריקוד עם *nm* folk dance.
reekookh/-eem ריכוך *nm* softening; softening up; (*pl+of:* **-ey**).
reekooz/-eem ריכוז *nm* concentration; (*pl+of:* **-ey**).
(makhan|eh/-ot) reekooz מחנה ריכוז *nm* concentration-camp.
reekoozee/-t ריכוזי *adj* centralized.
reemah/-tah/-eetee רימה *v* cheated; swindled; (*pres* **merameh**; *fut* **yerameh**).
reemah רימה *nf* grave-worm; (*+of:* **-at**).
reemon/-eem רימון *nm* **1.** pomegranate; **2.** grenade; (*pl+of:* **-ey**).
reemon/-ey yad רימון יד *nm* hand-grenade.
□ **Reemoneem** (Rimmonim) רימונים *nm* communal settlement (est. 1977) in SE Samaria hills. Pop. 240.
reen|ah/-ot רינה *nf* song; music; (*+of:* **-at**).
□ **Reenatyah** (Rinnatya) רנתיה *nm* village (est. 1949) 5 km SE of **Petakh Teekvah**. Pop. 361 43.
reen|en/-enah/-antee רינן *v* **1.** gossiped; **2.** sang for joy; (*pres* **meranen**; *fut* **yeranen**).
reenenoo kee (*or:* **she-**) רוננו כי /ש- *v 3rd pers. pl* there has been a rumor around that (*pres* **meraneneem kee**; *fut* **yeranenoo kee**).

reep|ah/-tah/-eetee ריפה *v* weakened; relaxed; (*pres* **merapeh**; *fut* **yerapeh**).
reepah (*etc*) **et yedey** ריפה את ידי *v* discouraged; (*pres* **merapeh** *etc*; *fut* **yerapeh** *etc*).
reep|e/-'ah/-e'tee ריפא *v* cured; (*pres* **merape**; *fut* **yerape**).
reep|ed/-dah/-adetee ריפד *v* padded; upholstered; (*pres* **meraped**; *fut* **yeraped**).
reepood/-eem ריפוד *nm* upholstery; padding; (*pl+of:* **-ey**).
reepoo|y/-yeem ריפוי *nm* cure; healing; (*pl+of:* **-yey**).
reepooy be-'eesook ריפוי בעיסוק *nm* occupational therapy (Medic.).
reer/-eem ריר *nm* spit; mucus.
reeree/-t ריריי *adj* mucous.
(kroom) reeree קרום רירי *nm* mucous membrane (Medic).
reeree|t/-yot רירית *nf* mucosa (Medic.).
rees|eem ריסים *nm* eyelashes; (*sing:* **rees**; *pl+of:* **-ey**).
rees|ek/-kah/-aktee ריסק *v* crushed; smashed; (*pres* **merasek**; *fut* **yerasek**).
rees|en/-nah/-antee ריסן *v* restrained; curbed; (*pres* **merasen**; *fut* **yerasen**).
rees|es/-esah/-astee ריסס *v* sprayed; pulverized; (*pres* **merases**; *fut* **yerases**).
reeshayon see *npr* reeshyon.
reeshmee/-t רשמי *adj* official; (*cpr* **rasmee**).
reeshmeet רשמית *adv* officially.
reeshmeeyoot רשמיות *nf* official behavior; formality (*cpr* **rasmeeyoot**).
□ **Reeshon** ראשון *nm [colloq.]* short name for □ **Reeshon le-Tseeyon**. See below.
reeshon/-ah ראשון *adj* first.
reeshon/-ah ba-ma'alah ראשון במעלה *adj* of first rank.
□ **Reeshon le-Tseeyon** (Rishon leZiyyon) ראשון לציון *nf* town (since 1950; est. 1882 as one of first Jewish agric. settlements) in central coastal plain, 8 km SE of Tel-Aviv. Pop. 139,500.
(goof) reeshon גוף ראשון *nm* 1st person (Gram.).
◇ **(ha)reeshon le-tseeyon** ("Rishon le-Zion") הראשון לציון *nm* "the First One in Zion" - traditional honorary title bestowed since 1708 on the Chief Rabbi of Sephardic Jewish communities in Palestine and held today by Israel's Chief Rabbi of Sephardi Rite.
(mee-klee) reeshon מכלי ראשון *adv* from a first-hand source.
(mee-makor) reeshon ממקור ראשון *adv* from a first-hand source.
(mooskal) reeshon מושכל ראשון *nm* axiom.
(samal) reeshon סמל ראשון *nm* staff-sergeant (army).
(to'ar) reeshon תואר ראשון *nm* bachelor's degree.
(yom/yemey) reeshon יום ראשון *nm* Sunday.
reeshonah ראשונה *adv* in the first place.
(ba) reeshonah בראשונה *adv* at first; in the beginning.
('ezrah) reeshonah עזרה ראשונה *nf* first aid.

(la) reeshonah לראשונה *adv* for the first time.

(man|ah/-ot) reeshon|ah/-ot מנה ראשונה *nf* appetizer (at a meal); first course.

reeshool/-eem רישול *nm* negligence; slovenliness; (*pl+of:* **-ey**).

reeshoom/-eem רישום *nm* **1.** registration; **2.** sketch; (*pl+of:* **-ey**).

reeshoosh/-eem רישוש *nm* impoverishment.

reesh'oo|t/-yot רשעות *nf* malice; wickedness.

reeshoo|y/-yeem רישוי *nm* licensing.

(meesrad ha) reeshooy משרד הרישוי *nm* driving licensing office.

□ **Reeshpon** (Rishpon) רשפון *nm* village in Sharon (est. 1936), 2 km N. of **Hertseleeyah**. Location of national network of aerials for radio-communication. Pop. 543.

reeshr|esh/-eshah/-ashtee רישרש *v* rustled; (*pres* **merashresh;** *fut* **yerashresh**).

reeshroosh/-eem רישרוש *nm* rustle; (*pl+of:* **-ey**).

reeshtee|t/-yot רשתית *nf* retina; reticulum.

reeshyon/-ot רשיון *nm* permit; license.

(matan) reeshyon מתן רשיון *nm* granting of permit (or of license).

(shleel|at/-ot) reeshyon שלילת רשיון *nf* withdrawal of (driver's) license; cancelling of permit.

reeshyon/-ot neheegah רשיון נהיגה *nm* driving license; driving permit.

reesook/-eem ריסוק *nm* crushing.

reesoon/-eem ריסון curbing; bridling; reining in.

reesoos/-eem ריסוס *nm* spraying.

reetch-ratch/-eem ריץ׳־רץ׳ *[slang] nm* zipper.

reet|ek/-kah/-aktee ריתק *v* enthralled; tied up; (*pres* **meratek;** *fut* **yeratek**).

reet|ekh/-khah/-akhtee ריתך *v* welded; soldered (*pres* **meratekh;** *fut* **yeratekh**).

reet|esh/-shah/-ashtee ריטש *v* **1.** retouched (photgr.); **2.** crushed to death; (*pres* **meratesh** *fut* **yeratesh**).

reet|et/-etah/-atetee ריטט *v* quivered; trembled; (*pres* **meratet;** *fut* **yeratet**).

reetmah/retamot ריתמה *nf* harness; (*+of:* **reetm|at/-ot**).

reetmee/-t ריתמי *adj* rhythmical.

reetmoos/-eem ריתמוס *nm* rhythm; (*pl+of:* **-ey**).

reetook/-eem ריתוק *nm* clamping; chaining; linking; (*pl+of:* **-ey**).

◇ **(tsav/-ey) reetook** see ◇ **tsav/-ey reetook**.

reetookh/-eem ריתוך *nm* welding; soldering; (*pl+of:* **-ey**).

reetoon/-eem ריטון *nm* grumbling; (*pl+of:* **-ey**).

reetoosh/-eem ריטוש *nm* **1.** retouching (photogr.); **2.** tearing (a body) to pieces.

reets|ah/-ot ריצה *nf* run; running; (*+of:* **-at**).

reets|ah/-tah/-eetee ריצה *v* **1.** served (sentence); **2.** atoned; (*pres* **meratseh;** *fut* **yeratseh**).

(be) reetsah בריצה *adv* running.

reets|ef/-fah/-aftee ריצף *v* paved (floor); tiled; (*pres* **meratsef;** *fut* **yeratsef**).

reetsoof/-eem ריצוף *nm* tiling; paving; (*pl+of:* **-ey**).

reetsooy ריצוי *nm* **1.** serving (sentence); **2.** appeasing.

reetspah/retsafot (*f=p*) רצפה *nf* floor; (*+of:* **reetsp|at/-ot**).

reev/-eem ריב *nm* quarrel; dispute.

reev|ah/-tah/-eetee ריווה *v* quenched; watered; (*pres* **meraveh;** *fut* **yeraveh**).

reev|ah/-ot ריבה *nf* girl; lass; damsel; (*+of:* **-at**).

reev'on/-eem רבעון *nm* **1.** quarter (of year); **2.** quarterly (magazine); (*pl+of:* **-ey**).

ree'|yen/-yenah/-yantee ראיין *v* interviewed; (*pres* **mera'yen;** *fut* **yera'yen**).

refaf|ah/-ot רפפה *nf* lattice work; shutter; (*+of:* **reefef|at/-ot**).

refa'eem רפאים *nm pl* ghosts.

(roo|'akh/-khot) refa'eem רוח רפאים *nm* ghost.

ref|et/-atot רפת *nf* barn; cowshed; (*pl+of:* **reeftot**).

refoo|'ah/-'ot רפואה *nf* medical science; medicine; (*+of:* **-'at**).

refoo'ah mona'at רפואה מונעת *nf* preventive medicine.

refoo'ah shleymah! !רפואה שלמה *interj* (wishing one a speedy and/or) complete recovery.

(fakoolt|ah/-ot lee) refoo'ah פקולטה לרפואה *nf* medical faculty.

(ketseen/-at) refoo'ah קצין רפואה *nmf* medical officer.

(kheyl) refoo'ah חיל רפואה *nm* medical corps (Army).

refoo'an/-eet רפואן *nmf* medical worker.

refoo'ee/-t רפואי *adj* medical.

(eeshoor/-eem) refoo'ee/-yeem אישור רפואי *nm* medical certificate; (*pl+of:* **-ey**).

(teepool) refoo'ee טיפול רפואי *nm* medical treatment; medical care.

reform|ah/-ot רפורמה *nf* reform; (*+of:* **-at**).

◇ **(ha)reformah** הרפורמה *nf* "the Reform", *[colloq.]* reference to the reform introduced in Israeli public schools, early in the seventies, according to which high schools begin from Grade 7 (Intermediate Division Grades 7-9, Senior Division Grades 10-12). This system (of a 6-year Primary School and a 6-year High School) replaces the earlier 8-year Primary and 4-year High School. About 60% of schools are part of the Reform.

◇ **reformee/-t** רפורמי *adj* reform; pertaining to the Reform Judaism movement.

reg|a'/-a'eem רגע *nm* minute; moment; (*pl+of:* **-reeg'ey**).

rega'! !רגע *interj* Just a minute!

rega' ekhad! !רגע אחד *interj* Just one minute! One moment, please...

rega' kat! !רגע קט *interj* Just a second!

(been) rega' בן־רגע *adv* instantly; in a moment.

(ka) rega' כרגע *adv* right now; at this moment.

(le) rega' לרגע **1.** *adv* for a moment; **2.** *adj* momentarily.

('od) rega'! !עוד רגע *interj & adv* one more moment.

◇ **(shalosh) regaleem** see ◇ **shalosh regaleem.**

□ **Regaveem** (Regavim) רגבים *nm* kibbutz in Menashe Heights **(Ramot Menasheh)**, 3 km E. of **Geev'at-'Adah**. Pop. 296.

□ **Regbah** (Regba) רגבה *nm* coop. agric. & industr. village (est. 1946) on Galilee Coast of Mediterranean, 3 km S. of Nahariyya. Pop. 611.

regee|'ah/-'ot רגיעה *nf* rest; relaxation; **(***+of:* **-'at).**

◇ **"regeelah"** רגילה *nf* (army slang) regular four-day leave to which an IDF soldier is entitled once every 3 months.

(rakevet) regeelah רכבת רגילה *nf* regular train.

regeeshoo|t/-yot רגישות *nf* sensitivity; touchiness.

regel/ragl|ayeem רגל *nf* leg; foot; **(***pl+of:* **-ey).**

regel/regel רגל *nf* foot/feet (measure).

('al|ah/-tah/-eetee le) regel עלה לרגל *v* made a pilgrimage; **(***pres* **oleh** *etc; fut* **ya'aleh** *etc***).**

('al) regel akhat על רגל אחת **1.** *adv* in brief; in a hurry; **2.** (*lit.*) on one foot.

('alee|yah/-yot le) regel עלייה לרגל *nf* pilgrimage.

(ba) regel ברגל *adv* on foot; walking.

(dreesat) regel דריסת רגל *nf* foothold.

(hol|ekh/-ekhet) regel הולך רגל *nmf* pedestrian; **(***pl:* **-ey** *etc***).**

(kaf/kapot) regel/raglayeem כף רגל *nf* sole of the foot.

(le) regel לרגל *adv* on the occasion of; in connection with.

(meedrakh kaf) regel מדרך כף רגל *nm* foothold; as much as foot's sole treads on.

(poshet/-et) regel פושט רגל *nmf* bankrupt.

(psheet|at/-ot) regel פשיטת רגל *nf* **1.** bankruptcy; **2.** (*figurat.*) final failure.

reg|esh/-ashot רגש *nm* feeling; **(***pl+of:* **reegshot).**

(khas|ar/-rat) regesh חסר רגש *adj* heartless; unfeeling; indifferent.

reg|ev/-aveem רגב *nm* clod; divot of earth; **(***pl+of:* **reegvey).**

reheeteem (*npr* **raheeteem)** רהיטים *nm pl* **(***sing:* **raheet)** furniture; **(***+of:* **reheetey).**

rek/reykah ריק *adj* empty; (for derivatives of rek see reyk).

reka' רקע *nm* background.

(degey) rekak דגי רקק *nm* **1.** small fish; **2.** (*figurat.*) small fry.

rekam ריקם *adv* empty-handed.

rekanoo|t/-yot ריקנות *nf* emptiness.

□ **Rekhan** (Rehan) ריחן *nm* collective village (est. 1977) in Jenin Sub-district.

□ **Rekhaseem** (Rekhasim) רכסים *nm* urban settlement in S. side of Haifa Bay, 5 km NW of **Keeryat Teev'on**, near **Kefar Khaseedeem**. Pop. 4,190.

rekhav/rakhavat ofakeem רחב אופקים *adj* broad-minded.

rekhav/rakhavat yadayeem רחב ידיים *adj* spacious.

rekhayeem ריחיים *nm pl* **1.** a pair of grindstones; **2.** *figurat.*: heavy burden.

rekheeloo|t/-yot רכילות *nf* gossip.

rekheesh|ah/-ot רכישה *nf* acquisition; **(***+of:* **-at).**

rekheev|ah/-ot רכיבה *nf* riding; ride; **(***+of:* **-at).**

rekhel|ah/-ot רחלה *nf* ewe; sheep; **(***+of:* **-at).**

rekhem רחם *nm* womb; uterus.

rekh|es/-aseem רכס *nm* ridge **(***pl+of:* **reekhsey).**

rekhesh רכש *nm* procurement of equipment or arms.

rekh|ev/-aveem רכב *nm* vehicle; **(***pl+of:* **reekhbey;** *b=v***).**

rekhev memoona' רכב ממונע *nm* motorized vehicle.

(klee/kley) rekhev כלי רכב *nm* vehicle.

(pekhakhoot) rekhev פחחות רכב *nf* car-body repairs.

(reeshyon) rekhev רשיון רכב *nm* car registration (document).

◇ **rekhev tsamood** רכב צמוד *adv* (with) car attached (i.e. use of own or company-car at employer's expense).

(le-'eeteem) rekhokot לעיתים רחוקות *adv* seldom; at rare intervals.

rekhoosh רכוש *nm* property.

◇ **rekhoosh natoosh** רכוש נטוש *nm* lands abandoned by Arabs who fled country during 1948-49 war that have been administered since by **Meen'hal Mekarke'ey Yeesra'el** the Israel Lands Administration.

(mas) rekhoosh מס רכוש *nm* property tax.

rekhooshanee/-t רכושני *adj* capitalistic.

rekhooshanoot רכושנות *nf* capitalism.

rekhov/-ot רחוב *nm* street.

(keren) rekhov קרן רחוב *nm* street-corner.

□ **Rekhovot** (Rehovot) רחובות *nf* town (originally est 1880 as agr. settlement) in central plain 20 km S. of Tel-Aviv. Home of Weizmann Institute of Science. Pop. 80,300.

rektor/-eem רקטור *nm* rector.

remees|ah/-ot רמיסה *nf* trampling; **(***+of:* **-at).**

remee|yah/-yot רמייה *nf* deceit; fraud; **(***+of:* **-yat).**

(ma'as|eh/-ey) remeeyah מעשה רמייה *nm* fraudulent act.

remeez|ah/-ot רמיזה *nf* hint; indication; **(***+of:* **-at).**

rem|es/-aseem רמש *nm* creeper; reptile; insect; **(***pl+of:* **reemsey).**

rem|ez/-azeem רמז *nm* hint; intimation; innuendo; **(***pl+of:* **reemzey).**

remez dak רמז דק *nm* slight hint; gentle hint.

(be) remez ברמז *adv* giving to understand.

(keren/karney) rentgen קרן רנטגן *nm* X-ray.

(sheekoof/-ey) rentgen שיקוף רנטגן *nm* X-ray examination.

(shekef/sheekfey) rentgen שקף רנטגן *nm* X-ray picture transparency.

re'oot ראות *nf* visibility.

re'oot lekooyah ראות לקויה *nf* bad visibility.

re'oot רעות *nf* friendship; comradeship.

re'oot roo'akh רעות רוח *nf* vanity; futility.

(kee) re'oot 'eyn|av/-eha *(etc)* כראות עיניו/־יה as he/she/etc sees fit.

(ketsar/keetsrat) re'oot קצר ראות *adj* short-sighted; nearsighted.

(lee-fee) re'oot 'eyn|av/-'eha לפי ראות עיניו/־יה at his/her/etc discretion.

(markheek/-at) re'oot מרחיק ראות *adj* far-sighted.

(nekood|at/-ot) re'oot נקודת ראות *nf* point of view.

(rekhok/-at) re'oot רחוק ראות *adj* far-sighted.

reorganeezats|yah/-yot ריאורגניזציה *nf* reorganization.

re'ot ריאות *nf pl* **(***sing:* **re'ah)** lungs.

(daleket) re'ot דלקת ריאות *nf* pneumonia (Medic).

repertoo'ar/-eem רפרטואר *nm* repertoire; repertory.

reportaj|ah/-ot רפורטאז׳ה *nf* **1.** press report; **2.** news-reporting; **(***+of:* **-at)**.

reporter/-eet רפורטר *nmf* reporter.

reprodooktsyah/-yot רפרודוקציה *nf* reproduction (of painting) **(***+of:* **-yat)**.

resees/-eem רסיס *nm* splinter; fragment; **(***pl+of:* **-ey)**.

resek רסק *nm* mash; sauce.

resen רסן *nm* bridle; restraint.

(shloo|'akh/-khat) resen שלוח־רסן *adj* unbridled; unrestraind.

(reemon/-ey) reses רימון רסס *nm* fragmentation grenade.

"Resh" ריי״ש *nf* 20th letter of Hebrew alphabet: consonant **r**.

"Resh" ר׳ *num symbol* **1.** 200; **2.** 200th.

resha רישא *nm* first part; of a phrase or of a paragraph; beginning.

resha' רשע *nm* evil; wickedness.

□ **Reshafeem** (Reshafim) רשפים *nm* kibbutz (est. 1948) in **Bet-She'an** Valley, 2 km SW of Bet-She'an proper. Pop. 476.

reshamkol/-eem רשמקול *nm* tape-recorder (audio).

resheem|ah/-ot רשימה *nf* **1.** list; **2.** essay; **(***+of:* **-at)**.

resheet ראשית *nf* beginning.

resheet davar ראשית דבר *adv* it all began with.

resheet kol ראשית כול *adv* first of all; to begin with.

(be) resheet בראשית *adv* in the beginning; at the outset.

(ma'as|eh/-ey be) resheet מעשה בראשית *nm* **1.** pioneering work; **2.** The Creation.

(mee-be) resheet מבראשית *adv* anew; from the beginning.

resh|et/-atot רשת *nf* **1.** net; **2.** network; **(***pl+of:* **reeshtot)**.

(reshet/reeshtot) sheevook רשת שיווק *nf* chain of stores.

reshoomot רשומות *nf pl* records.

◇ **"reshoomot"** (**"Reshumot"**) רשומות *nm* Israel's "Official Gazette".

reshoo|t/-yot רשות *nf* **1.** permission; **2.** authority; **3.** domain.

(beekesh/-shah/-ashtee) reshoot ביקש רשות *v* asked permission; **(***pres* **mevakesh** *etc; fut* **yevakesh** *etc v=b***)**.

(bee) reshoot ברשות *adv* with permision; with the permission of.

(keeb|el/-lah/-altee) reshoot קיבל רשות *v* was granted permission; obtained permission; **(***pres* **mekabel** *etc; fut* **yekabel** *etc***)**.

(nat|al/-lah/-altee) reshoot נטל רשות *v* took permission; **(***pres* **notel** *etc; fut* **yeetol** *etc***)**.

(nat|an/-nah/-atee) reshoot נתן רשות *v* gave permission; **(***pres* **noten** *etc; fut* **yeeten** *etc***)**.

reshoot ha-rabeem רשות הרבים *nf* public domain; public property.

reshoot ha-yakheed רשות היחיד *nf* private domain; private property.

reshoo|t (*npr* **rashoo|t)/-yot mekomee|t/-yot** רשות מקומית *nf* local authority; municipality.

(ha) reshoot (*npr* **rashoot) ha-meyashevet** הרשות המיישבת *nf* the settlement (land) authority.

(ha) reshoot (*npr* **rashoot) ha-moosmekhet** הרשות המוסמכת *nf* the competent authority.

□ **Retameem** (Retamim) רתמים *nm* keebootz in Negev, 3 km NW of **Reveeveem**.

retee|'ah/-'ot רתיעה *nf* recoil; rebounding; **(***+of:* **-'at)**.

reteekh|ah/-ot רתיחה *nf* **1.** boiling; **2.** rage; **(***+of:* **-at)**.

(nekoodat ha) reteekhah נקודת הרתיחה *nf* boiling-point.

reteem|ah/-ot רתימה *nf* harnessing; tie-up; **(***+of:* **-at)**.

reteen|ah/-ot רטינה *nf* grumbling; **(***+of:* **-at)**.

reteevoo|t/-yot רטיבות *nf* wetness; moisture.

retee|yah/-yot רטייה *nf* patch; bandage; **(***+of:* **-yat)**.

retet רטט *nm* quiver; vibration.

retoree/-t רטורי *adj* rhetorical.

retroakteevee/-t רטרואקטיבי *adj* retroactive; retrospective.

rets|akh/-seekhot רצח *nm (pl nf)* murder.

(foto) retsakh פוטו רצח *nm [slang]* express-photo.

retseefoo|t/-yot רציפות *nf* consecutiveness; continuity.

(bee) retseefoot ברציפות *adv* continuously.

retseekh|ah/-ot רציחה murdering; **(***+of:* **-at)**.

retseenee/-t רציני *adj* serious.

retseenoo|t/-yot רצינות *nf* seriousness; gravity.

(bee) retseenoot ברצינות *adv* seriously.

rets|ef/-afeem רצף *nm* continuity; **(***pl+of:* **reetsfey)**.

retson/-ot רצון *m+of* the wish of; the will of.
(kee) retson כרצון in accordance with the wish of...
retsonee/-t רצוני *adj* voluntary; arbitrary.
(kee) retson|ee/-kha/-ekh/-o/-ah כרצוני/־נך/־נר/־נה as I/you(*m/f*)/he/she wish.
retsoo|'ah/-'ot רצועה *nf* strip; strap; (*+of:* **-'at**).
□ **(ha)retsoo'ah** הרצועה *nf [colloq.]* "the strip" i.e. the Gaza Strip.
□ **Retsoo'at 'Azah** רצועת עזה *nf* the Gaza Strip.
□ **Retsoo'at ha-khof** רצועת החוף *nf* the Coastal Strip.
rev|a'/-a'eem רבע *nm* quarter; 1/4; (*pl+of:* **reev'ey**).
reva' ha-gmar רבע הגמר *nm* quarter final (sport).
reva' shnatee/-t רבע שנתי *adj* quarterly.
(pakhot) reva' פחות רבע *adv* a quarter to... (telling time).
(va) reva' ורבע *adv* a quarter past...(telling time).
□ **Revadeem** (Revadim) רבדים *nm* kibbutz (est. 1948) NE of Re'em Junction **(Tsomet Re'em)**. Pop. 375.
revakh/-eem רווח *nm* **1.** profit; **2.** interval; (*pl+of:* **reevkhey**).
revakh/reevkhey hon רווח הון *nm* capital gain.
revakh ve-hefsed רווח והפסד *nm pl* profit and loss.
(be) revakh ברווח *adv* profitably.
revakhah רווחה *nf* comfort; relief; well-being.
(khayey) revakhah חיי רווחה *nm pl* life of abundance.
(medeen|at/-ot) revakhah מדינת רווחה *nf* welfare state.
(nash|am/-mah/-amtee lee) revakhah נשם לרווחה *v* breathed with relief; (*pres* **noshem** *etc; fut* **yeenshom** *etc*).
(paroots/prootsah lee) revakhah פרוץ לרווחה *adj* **1.** wide open; **2.** widely broken into.
(bee) revakhah ברווחה *adj* comfortably.
(lee) revakhah לרווחה *adv* **1.** widely; **2.** with a feeling of relief.
revav/-eem רבב *nm* stain; fleck; grease-spot.
revav|ah/-ot רבבה *nf* myriad; 10,000; (*+of:* **reevev|at/-ot**).
reva|yah/-yot רוויה *nf* saturation; satiation.
□ **Revayah** (Rewaya) רויה *nm* village (est. 1952) in Bet-She'an Valley, 6 km SE of Bet-She'an proper. Pop. 214.
□ **Revakhah** (Rewaha) רוחה *nm* village (est. 1953), 4 km NW of Plugot Junction **(Tsomet Ploogot)**. Pop. 460.
(lee) revayah לרוויה *adv* to saturation; to one's fill.
revee'a' רביע *num nm* quarter.
(lee-shleesh ve-lee) revee'a' לשליש ולרביע *adj* in parts; partially.
(soos/-ey) revee'ah סוס־רביעה *nm* stallion.
revee'ee/-t רביעי *ord num nmf* fourth; 4th.
(yom/yemey) revee'ee יום רביעי *nm* Wednesday.
revee'ee|yah/-yot רביעייה *nf* **1.** quartet (Music); **2.** quadruplet; (*+of:* **yat**).
□ **Reveeveem** (Revivim) רביבים *nm* kibbutz (est. 1943) in N. Negev, 25 km S. of Be'er Sheba **(Be'er Sheva')**. Pop. 630.
revee|yah/-yot רבייה *nf* procreation; reproduction; (*+of:* **-yat**).
rey|akh/-khot ריח *nm* smell; (see also **re'akh**).
reyakh neekho'akh ריח ניחוח *nm* fragrance.
reyk/-ah ריק *adj* empty.
(khalal) reyk חלל ריק *nm* vacuum; empty space.
reyka ריקא *nm* good for nothing; bum.
reykam ריקם *adv* with nothing; empty-handed.
reykanoo|t/-yot ריקנות *nf* **1.** emptiness; **2.** (*figurat.*) vanity.
□ **Reykhan** see □ **Rekhan**.
reysha רישא *nm* first part (of a phrase or of a paragraph); beginning.
rezerv|ah/-ot רזרבה *nf* reserve; (*+of:* **-at**).
rezervee/-t רזרבי *adj* spare; reserve.
ro'a' רוע *nm* badness; malice.
ro'a'/-lev רוע־לב *nm* malice; wickedness.
(le) ro'a' ha-mazal לרוע המזל *adv* unfortunately.
rodan/-eem רודן *nm* dictator; tyrant; (*pl+of:* **-ey**).
rodanee/-t רודני *adj* dictatorial; tyrannical.
rodanoo|t/-yot רודנות *nf* dictatorship; tyranny.
□ **Ro'ee** (Ro'i) רועי *nm* village (est. 1976) in E. of Mount Samaria, 3 km N. of **Beka'ot**.
ro'eh/ro'ah רואה **1.** *v pres* sees; (*pst* **ra'ah;** *fut* **yeer'eh**); **2.** *nmf* seer/-ess.
ro'eh/ro'ah ba-kokhaveem רואה בכוכבים *nmf* astrologer.
ro'eh/ro'ey kheshbon רואה חשבון *nf* auditor.
ro'eh/ro'ah (*etc*) nekhokhah רואה נכוחה *v pres* sees things right.
ro'eh/ro'at shekhorot רואה שחורות **1.** *adj* pessimistic; **2.** *nmf* pessimist.
ro'eh/ro'ah רועה **1.** *nmf* shepherd/ess; (*pl+of:* **ro'ey**); **2.** *adj* grazing; **3.** *v pres* grazes; (*pst* **ra'ah;** *fut* **yeer'eh**).
ro'eh/ro'at ha-'eder רועה העדר *nm* shepherd of the flock.
ro'eh rookhanee רועה רוחני *nm* spiritual leader; pastor.
ro'eh/ro'ey tson רועה צאן shepherd.
ro'eh/ro'ey zonot רועה זונות *nm* pimp.
ro'esh/-et רועש **1.** *adj* noisy; **2.** *v pres* makes a noise; (*pst* **ra'ash;** *fut* **yar'eesh**).
(le) ro'ets לרועץ *adv* causing harm; impediment.
(meesrad) ro'eh kheshbon משרד רואה חשבון *nm* auditing office.
rof|e/-'ah רופא *nmf* physician; (*pl* **-'eem/-'ot;** *pl+of:* **-'ey**).
rofe/-t af-ozen-garon רופא אף אוזן גרון *nmf* ear-nose-throat doctor; laryngologist.
rof|e/-'ey eleel רופא אליל *nm* witch-doctor.
rofe/-t 'eynayeem רופא עיניים *nmf* ophthalmologist.

rof|e/-'ah klalee/-t רופא כללי *nmf* general practitioner.
rofe/-t nasheem רופא נשים *nmf* gynecologist.
rofe/-t 'or רופא עור *nmf* dermatologist.
rof|e/-'ah pneemee/-t רופא פנימי *nmf* internist.
rofe/-t sheenayeem רופא שיניים *nmf* dentist; dental surgeon.
rof|e/-'ah toran/-eet רופא תורן *nmf* physician on duty.
rof|e/-t yeladeem רופא ילדים *nmf* pediatrician.
rofef/-et רופף *adj* weak; flimsy; shaky.
rof|ef/-efah/-aftee רופף *v* weakened; slackened; shook; (*pres* **merofef**; *fut* **yerofef**).
rog|e'a'/-a'at רוגע **1.** *adj* calm; relaxed; **2.** *v pres* relaxes; (*pst* **raga'**; *fut* **yeraga'**).
rogez רוגז *nm* anger.
(be) rogez ברוגז *adv [colloq.]* not on speaking terms; angry.
rogez/-et רוגז *adj* angry; sore.
rogez/-et רוגז *v pres* is angry; (*pst* **ragaz**; *fut* **yeergoz**).
□ **Rogleet** (Rogelit) רוגלית *nm* village (est. 1958) in Judean hills, 9 km S. of Bet-Shemesh. Pop. 320.
rok רוק *nm* spit; saliva.
rok|akhat/-'khot רוקחת *nf* female pharmacist; female druggist.
rok|e'akh/-'kheem רוקח *nm* pharmacist; druggist; (*pl+of:* **rok'khey**).
rokem/-et רוקם **1.** *nmf* embroiderer; **2.** *v pres* embroiders; (*pst* **rakam**; *fut* **yeerkom**).
rokem (*etc*) **mezeemot** רוקם מזימות **1.** *v pres* schemes; plots; **2.** *adj* schemer; plotter.
rok|en/-nah/-antee רוקן *v* emptied; (*pres* **meroken**; *fut* **yeroken**).
rokh רוך *nm* tenderness; softness.
rokhak רוחק *nm* distance; remoteness.
rokhav/rekhaveem רוחב *nm* width; latitude; (*pl+of:* **rakhvey**).
rokhav lev רוחב לב *nm* generosity; wisdom.
(kav/-ey) rokhav קו רוחב latitude; parallel (Geogr.).
(la-orekh ve-la) rokhav לאורך ולרוחב *adv* through (its) length and breadth.
rokh|el/-leem רוכל *nm* peddler; hawker; (*pl+of:* **rokhley**).
rokhesh/-et רוחש *v pres* **1.** feels; **2.** whispers; (*pst* **rakhash**; *fut* **yeerkhosh**).
rokhesh/-et רוכש *v* acquires; (*pst* **rakhash**; *fut* **yeerkosh** *(k=kh)*).
rokhev/-et רוכב rides; (*pst* **rakhav**; *fut* **yeerkav** *(k=kh)*).
rokh|ev/-veem רוכב *nm* rider; (*pl+of:* **rokhvey**).
(rokh|ev/-vey) ofanayeem רוכב אופניים *nm* cyclist.
rokh|ev/-vey ofano'a' רוכב אופנוע *nm* motorcyclist.
rokhloot רוכלות *nf* peddling; hawking.
rokhsan/-eem רוכסן *nm* zipper; slide fastener; (*pl+of:* **-ey**).
rok'khoot רוקחות *nf* pharmaceuticals.

rom רום *nm* altitude (*+of:* **room**).
roma רומא *nf* Rome.
roma'ee/-m רומאי *nm* Roman.
(ha)roma'eem רומאים *nm pl* "the Romans" - *[colloq.]* reference to Romans in antiquity who subjugated the State of Judea and destroyed the Second Temple in 70 CE.
romakh/remakheem רומח *nm* lance; (*pl+of:* **romkhey**).
roman/-eem רומן *nm* **1.** love-affair; romance; **2.** novel.
romantee/-t רומאנטי *adj* romantic.
romee/-t רומי *adj* Roman.
romeet רומית *nf* Latin (language).
rom|em/-emah/-amtee רומם *v* raised; extolled; (*pres* **meromem**; *fut* **yeromem**).
romemoot רוממות *nf* **1.** majesty; **2.** superiority.
(hod) romemoot|o/-ah/-kha/-ekh הוד רוממותו/־ה *nmf* His/Her/Your (*m/f*) Majesty.
ron רון *nm* music; song.
ron|en/-enah/-antee רונן *v* sang; chanted; (*pres* **meronen**; *fut* **yeronen**).
roo|'akh/-khot רוח *nf* **1.** wind; **2.** spirit.
roo'akh ha-kodesh רוח הקודש *nm* the Holy Spirit; divine inspiration.
roo'akh khayeem רוח חיים *nf* breath of life; soul.
roo'akh/-khot refa'eem רוח רפאים *nf* ghost; phantom.
roo'akh shetoot רוח שטות *nf* spirit of foolishness.
(ava'boo'ot) roo'akh אבעבועות רוח *nf pl* chickenpox; varicella (Medic.).
(anshey) roo'akh אנשי רוח *nm pl* (*sing:* **eesh** *etc*) men of spirit; intellectuals.
(be) roo'akh ברוח *adv* in the spirit of.
(be) roo'akh ha-dvareem ברוח הדברים *adv* in the spirit of what has been said (or agreed upon).
(be) roo'akh tovah ברוח טובה *adv* in good spirit; amicably; amiably.
(galshan/-ey) roo'akh גלשן רוח *nm* hang-glider.
(gas/-at) roo'akh גס־רוח *adj* vulgar.
(ha) roo'akh ha-khayah הרוח החיה *nf* the moving spirit.
(halokh/heelkhey) roo'akh הלך רוח *nm* mood; state of mind.
(kar/-at) roo'akh קר־רוח *adj* composed; calm.
(ketsar/keetsrat) roo'akh קצר רוח *adj* impatient.
(khol|eh/-at) roo'akh חולה רוח n nmf&adj insane; mentally deranged.
(kor) roo'akh קור רוח *nm* coolness; composure.
(korat) roo'akh קורת רוח *nf* satisfaction.
(kosot) roo'akh כוסות רוח *nf pl* cupping glasses.
(kotser) roo'akh קוצר רוח *nm* impatience.
(le-fee) roo'akh לפי רוח *adv* in the spirit of; to the liking of.
(mad'ey ha) roo'akh מדעי הרוח *nm pl* humanities; liberal arts.

(mats|av/-vey) roo'akh מצב־רוח *nm* **1.** mood; disposition; **2.** *[colloq.]* bad mood.

(morat) roo'akh מורת רוח *nf* resentment; discontent.

(naflah) roo|'akh/-khee/-kho/-khah נפלה רוח/ ־י the/my/his/her *(etc)* spirit sank; despaired.

(nakhat) roo'akh נחת־רוח *nf* contentment; pleasure.

(orekh) roo'akh אורך רוח *nm* patience.

('os|eh/-ah) roo'akh עושה רוח *v pres [slang]* exaggerates (*figurat.*); makes "big noise"; (*lit.*) makes wind; (*pst* **'asah** *etc; fut* **ya'aseh** *etc*).

('oz) roo'akh עוז רוח *nm* courage; daring.

(re'oot) roo'akh רעות רוח *nf* vanity; futility.

(she'ar) roo'akhשאר רוח *nm* high intelligence; noble spirit.

(takhn|at/-ot) roo'akh טחנת רוח *nf* windmill.

roob|o/-ah ke-khool|o/-ah *(kh=k)* רובו ככולו *nm* the major (overwhelming) part.

roogz|ah/-ot רוגזה *nf* wrath; anger; (*+of:* **-at**).

□ **Rookhamah** (Ruhama) רוחמה *nm* kibbutz (est. 1944) 15 km SE of **Sderot** (Sederot), where S. coastal plain borders the Negev. Pop. 596.

rookhanee/-t רוחני *adj* spiritual.

rookhaneeyoot רוחניות *nf* spirituality.

(katsrah) rookh|o/-ah/-ee קצרה רוחו/־ה/־י *v pst nf sing* grew impatient; (*pres* **ketserah** *etc; fut* **teektsar** *etc*).

rookhot רוחות *nf pl* (*sing:* **roo'akh**) spirits; winds.

(le-khol ha) rookhot! לכל הרוחות! *interj* to Hell! to Hell with!

roosee/-t רוסי *adj* Russian.

roosee/-yah רוסי *nmf* **1.** Russian; **2.** *[colloq.]* Jewish immigrant from the USSR.

rooseet רוסית *nf* Russian (the language).

roosyah רוסיה *nf* Russia.

rosh/rash|eem ראש *nm* head; top; topman; (*pl+of:* **-ey**).

rosh be-rosh ראש בראש *adv [slang]* seeing eye to eye.

rosh/rashey 'eer/-'areem ראש עיר *nm* mayor.

rosh/rashey gesher ראש גשר *nm* bridgehead.

□ **Rosh ha-'Ayeen** (Rosh ha'Ayin) ראש העין *nf* township (est. 1950), 4 km E. of **Petakh-Teekvah**. Pop. 12,100.

rosh/rashey khets ראש חץ *nm* spearhead.

rosh khodesh ראש חודש *nm* 1st day of a Jewish (lunar) month.

rosh/rashey khoog/-eem ראש חוג *nm* department-head (in a university).

rosh/rashey kvootsah ראש קבוצה *nm* Team-Captain (Sport).

rosh ha-mateh ha-klalee ראש המטה הכללי *nm* Chief of the General Staff (Army).

rosh ha-memshalah ראש הממשלה *nm* the Prime-Minister.

rosh ha-mo'atsah ראש המועצה *nm* Chairman of (Local) Council.

rosh memshalah ראש ממשלה *nm* prime-minister; (*pl:* **rashey memshalot**).

rosh mo'atsah mekomeet ראש מועצה מקומית *nm* chairman of local council; (*pl:* **rashey mo'etsot mekomeeyot**).

◇ **rosh ha-shanah ("Rosh ha-Shana")** ראש השנה *nm* Jewish New Year festival (approx. mid-September).

◇ **rosh-ha-shanah la-eelanot** ראש השנה לאילנות *nm* New Year Festival for Trees. Better known as **"Too bee-Shvat"**, traditional children's holiday of tree-planting, occurring on the 15th day of **Shvat** (Jan.-Feb.).

□ **Rosh ha-Neekrah** ראש הנקרה *nf* picturesque hilltop on Mediterranean coast that has been serving as frontier-crossing point into Lebanon since 1918.

□ **Rosh Peenah** (Rosh Pinna) ראש פינה *nm* semi-urban settlement (est. 1882), 4 km E. of Safed (**Tsefat**). Pop. 1,660.

□ **Rosh Tsooreem** (Rosh Zurim) ראש צורים *nm* kibbutz (est. 1969) in Judean hills, 8 km SW of Bethlehem. Pop. 269.

◇ **rosh/rashey yesheev|ah/-ot** ראש ישיבה *nm* Head of a "Yeshiva".

(ba) rosh oo-va-reeshonah *(v=b)* בראש ובראשונה *adv* first of all.

(be) rosh בראש *adv* at the head of.

(be) rosh ekhad בראש אחד *adv* eye to eye.

(beelbool/-ey) rosh בלבול ראש *nm* bother; confusion.

(be-geelooy) rosh בגילוי ראש *adv* bare-headed (forbidden to observant Jewish males).

(be-khoved) rosh בכובד ראש *adv* seriously; in earnest.

(het|ee'akh/-eekhah/-akhtee) rosh ba-kotel הטיח ראש בכותל *v* banged one's head against a stone wall; (*pres* **metee'akh** *etc; fut* **yatee'akh** *etc*).

(hek|el/-elah/-altee) rosh הקל ראש *v* disparaged; underestimated; (*pres* **mekel** *etc; fut* **yakel** *etc*).

(kaloot) rosh קלות ראש *nf* levity; carelessness.

(ke'ev/-ey) rosh כאב ראש *nm* headache.

(khaf|af/-efah/-aftee et ha) rosh חפף את הראש *v* washed (hair) shampooed; (*pres* **khofef** *etc; fut* **yakhfof** *etc*).

(khafeef|at/-ot) rosh חפיפת ראש *nf* hair-wash; shampooing.

(khafoo|y/-yat) rosh חפוי ראש *adj* perplexed; ashamed.

(koved) rosh כובד ראש *nm* gravity; seriousness.

(me) rosh מראש *adv* in advance; beforehand.

(shom|er/-rey) rosh שומר ראש *nm* bodyguard.

(yash|av/-vah/-avtee) rosh ישב ראש *v* chaired; presided; (*pres* **yoshev** *etc; fut* **yeshev** *etc*).

(yosh|ev/-vey) rosh יושב ראש *nmf* chairman; chairperson; (*f:* **-evet/-vot** *etc*).

(yoshev) rosh ha-kneset יושב ראש הכנסת *nm* Speaker of the Knesset.

roshem/reshameem רושם *nm* impression; mark; (*pl+of:* **reeshmey**).

roshem metsooyan רושם מצוין *nm* excellent impression.

roshem tov רושם טוב *nm* good impression.

('os|eh/-ah) roshem עושה רושם *v pres* makes an impression; (*pst* **'asah** *etc; fut* **ya'aseh** *etc*).

('or|er/-erah/-artee) roshem עורר רושם *v* created an impression; (*pres* **me'orer** *etc; fut* **ye'orer** *etc*).

(keebel/-lah/-altee) roshem קיבל רושם *v* got the impression; (*pres* **mekabel** *etc; fut* **yekabel** *etc*).

(rav/rabat) roshem *(b=v)* רב רושם *adj* impressive; most impressive.

roshem/-et רושם *v pres* notes; registers; (*pst* **rasham;** *fut* **yeershom**).

roshesh/-eshah/-ashtee רושש *v* impoverished; (*pres* **meroshesh;** *fut* **yeroshesh**).

rotats|yah/-yot רוטציה *nf* **1.** rotation; **2.** alternation in a public office; (*+of:* **-yat**).

rot|e'akh/-akhat רותח **1.** *adj* boiling; **2.** *v pres* boils; (*pst* **ratakh;** *fut* **yeertakh**).

rotem/-et רותם *v pres* harnesses; (*pst* **ratam;** *fut* **yeertom**).

rotev/retaveem רוטב *nm* sauce; gravy; (*pl+of:* **rotvey**).

(dan/-ah/-tee be) rot'kheen דן ברותחין *v* **1.** vehemently criticized; **2.** severely punished; (*pres* **dan** *etc; fut* **yadoon** *etc*).

(neekhv|ah/-etah/-etee be) rot'kheen נכווה ברותחין *v pst* **1.** (*lit.:*) got scalded with boiling water **2.** (*figurat.*) learned one's lesson once; (*pres* **neekhveh** *etc; fut* **yeekaveh** *etc k=kh*).

rots|eh/-ah רוצה *v pres* wishes; desires; (*pst* **ratsah;** *fut* **yeertseh**).

rots|e'akh/-akhat רוצח **1.** *nmf* murderer; (*pl:* **-kheem/-khot;** *+of:* **-khey**); **2.** *v pres* murders; (*pst* **ratsakh;** *fut* **yeertsakh**).

rots|ets/-etsah/-atstee רוצץ *v* crushed; shattered; (*pres* **merotsets;** *fut* **yerotsets**).

rov רוב *nm* majority.

rov khelkee רוב חלקי *nm* partial majority.

rov khookee רוב חוקי *nm* quorum; legitimate majority.

rov kolot רוב קולות *nm* majority of votes.

rov roob|o/-bah רוב רובו *nm* the absolute majority of.

rov makhree'a' רוב מכריע *nm* overwhelming majority.

(al pee) rov על פי רוב *adv* mostly.

(be) rov meekreem ברוב מקרים *adv* in most cases.

(ha) rov ha-domem הרוב הדומם *nm* the silent majority.

(la) rov לרוב *adv* mostly; generally.

rova'/reva'eem רובע *nm* quarter (of a town); (*pl+of:* **rov'ey**).

rov|a'/-'ey megooreem רובע מגורים *nm* residential quarter.

rova' ha-zonot רובע הזונות *nm* redlight district.

(ha) rova' ha-yehoodee הרובע היהודי *nm* the Jewish quarter.

rov|a'ee (*npr* **-ay**)**/-a'eem** רובאי *nm* rifleman; (*pl+of:* **-a'ey**).

rov|eh/-eem רובה *nm* rifle; (*pl+of:* **-ey**).

roveh mekhoodan רובה מכודן *nm* bayoneted rifle.

roveh ta'oon רובה טעון *nm* loaded rifle.

rov|e'akh/-akhat רווח *adj* current; prevailing.

rove|'akh/-akhat רווח *v pres* prevails; (*pst* **ravakh;** *fut* **yeervakh**).

roved/-revadeem רובד *nm* layer; stratum; (*pl+of:* **rovdey**).

rovets/-et רובץ *v pres* sits; lies; broods; (*pst* **ravats;** *fut* **yeerbats** *(b=v)*).

roze'n/-et רוזן *nmf* count/-ess; (*pl+of:* **rozney**).

S.

incorporating **Samekh** (ס) and **Seen** (שׂ)

NOTE: The Hebrew letter ש has pronunciations visually distinguished only in a dotted spelling. Marked with a dot over its left shoulder (שׂ), it is called **Seen** and is pronounced as the **s** in *so*, *sister* or *this*. **Samekh** (ס) is pronounced similarly. So we intermix the transliterations of words beginning with **Seen** and **Samekh** in the same chapter. Words should be sought according to the phonetical sound at their beginning, rather than their Hebrew spelling. (The correct spelling is indicated, of course, in the Hebrew letters for each entry.)

The letter (ש), however, if not marked at all, or if marked with a dot over its right shoulder, (שׁ) is called **Sheen** and pronounced **sh** (as in *shallow*, *bashful* or *wish*). In this dictionary transliterations of words beginning with **Sh** are found in the following chapter.

sa! se'ee! ! שאי ! שא *v imp m/f sing* carry! take! (*inf* **laset**; *pst* **nasa**; *pres* **nose**; *fut* **yeesa**).

sa'! se'ee! ! סעי ! סע *v imp m/f sing* drive on! (*inf* **leenso'a'**; *pst* **nasa'**; *pres* **nose'a'**; *fut* **yeesa'**).

sa'ad/se'adeem סעד *nm* support; assistance; welfare.

(leeshk|at/-ot) sa'ad לשכת סעד *nf* welfare bureau; social aid bureau.

(maskoret) sa'ad משכורת סעד *nf* low pay (i.e. equivalent to social aid allowance).

(medeenat) sa'ad מדינת סעד *nf* welfare state.

(meesrad ha) sa'ad משרד הסעד *nf* Ministry of Social Welfare.

□ **Sa'ad** (Saad) סעד *nm* kibbutz (est. 1947) in NW Negev, 7 km NW of **Neteevot**. Pop. 689.

sa'ad/-ah/-etee סעד *v* had a meal (dined, lunched *etc*); (*pres* **so'ed**; *fut* **yees'ad**).

sa'ar סער *nm* tempest; storm.

sa'ar/-ah/-tee סער *v* raged; stormed; (*pres* **so'er**; *fut* **yees'ar**).

□ **Sa'ar** (Sa'ar) סער *nm* kibbutz (est. 1948), 2 km N. of Nahariyya, on Galilee Coast of Mediterranean. Pop. 299.

sa'arah/se'arot שערה *nf* a hair; (*+of:* **sa'ar|at/-ot**).

(ke-khoot ha) sa'arah כחוט השערה *adv* by a hair's breadth.

sa'arot seyvah שערות שיבה *nf pl* gray hair.

sab|a/-eem סבא *nm [colloq.]* grandpa; (*pl+of:* **-ey**).

sababah סבבה *adv [slang]* excellent; very good.

sabal/-eem סבל *nm* porter; (*pl+of:* **-ey**).

sabaloot סבלות *nf* porterage.

sabon/-eem סבון *nm* soap; (*pl+of:* **-ey**).

sabr|a/-es סברה *nm [colloq.]* Israel- or Palestine-born Jew.

sabt|a/-ot סבתא *nf [colloq.]* granny; grandma.

sada'oot שדאות *nf* outdoor orientation.

sadar/-eem סדר *nm* typesetter; (*+of:* **ey**).

sadar/-ey defoos סדר דפוס *nm* typesetter.

sad|eh/-ot שדה *nm* field (*+of:* **sdeh/sdot**).

(bet-sefer) sadeh בית־ספר שדה *nm* field school.

('eer/'arey) sadeh עיר־שדה *nf* provincial town.

(toot/-ey) sadeh תות־שדה *nm* strawberry.

sadeen/sdeeneem סדין *nm* bed sheet; (*+of:* **sdeen/-ey**).

sadeen khashmalee סדין חשמלי *nm* electric bed sheet.

sadeer/sdeerah סדיר *adj* regular.

(sheroot) sadeer שירות סדיר *nm* regular (obligatory) military service.

(tsava) sadeer צבא סדיר *nm* regular army (composed of draftees).

sadn|ah/-ot סדנה *nf* workshop (*+of:* **-at**).

sadook/sedookah סדוק *adj* cracked.

sadran/-eet סדרן *nmf* usher; steward; (*pl:* **-eem/-eeyot**; *+of:* **-ey**).

se'eef (*npr* **se'eef)/se'eefeem** סעיף *nm* paragraph; article; (*+of:* **se'eef/-ey**).

sa'eer/se'eerah שעיר *adj* hairy.

sa'eer la-'azazel שעיר לעזאזל *nm* scapegoat.

saf/seep|eem *(p=f)* סף *nm* threshold; sill; (*pl+of:* **-ey**).

saf/seepey khalon/-ot *(p=f)* סף חלון *nm* window sill.

('al) saf על סף *adv* on the threshold of; about to.

(mee-takhat le) saf ha-hakarah מתחת לסף ההכרה *adv* underneath one's awareness; subconsciously.

saf|ah/-ot שפה *nf* **1.** language; **2.** shore; (*+of:* **sfat**).

safah/sfatayeem שפה *nf* lip; (*+of:* **sfat/seeftot**).

(even/avney) safah אבני־שפה *nf* curbstone.

(meen ha) safah oo-lekhoots מן השפה ולחוץ *adv* lip-service; hypocritically.

saf|ad/-dah/-adetee ספד *v* mourned; eulogized; (*pres* **sofed**; *fut* **yeespod** *(p=f)*).

saf|ag/-gah/-agtee ספג *v* absorbed; (**prs sofeg**; *fut* **yeespog** *(p=f)*).

saf|ak/-kah/-aktee kapayeem ספק כפיים *v* clapped hands (in sorrow); (*pres* **sofek** *etc*; *fut* **yeespok** *etc p=f*).

safam/sefameem שפם *nm* moustache; (*+of:* **sefam/-ey**).

saf|ar/-rah/-artee ספר *v* counted; (*pres* **sofer**; *fut* **yeespor** *(p=f)*).

safek/sefekot ספק *nm* doubt.

(be) safek בספק **1.** *adv* in doubt; **2.** *adj* doubtful; doubting.

(blee) safek בלי ספק *adv* no doubt; undoubtedly.

(en) safek אין ספק *v pres* there's no doubt; (*pres* **lo hayah safek**; *fut* **lo yeehyeh safek**).

(heet|eel/-eelah/-altee) safek הטיל ספק *v* doubted; questioned; (*pres* **mateel** *etc*; *fut* **yateel** *etc*).

(le-lo) safek ללא ספק *adv* undoubtedly.

(moot|al/-elet be) safek מוטל בספק *adj* doubtful; problematic.

(tsel shel) safek צל של ספק *nm* shadow of a doubt.

safkan/-eet ספקן *nmf & adj* skeptic; (*pl+of:* **-ey**).

safoog/sefoogah ספוג *adj* steeped in; permeated.

safoor/sefoorah ספור *adj* counted; numbered.

safran/-eet ספרן *nmf* librarian; (*pl:* **-eem/-eeyot**; *pl+of:* **-ey**).

safroot (*npr* **seefroot**) ספרות *nf* literature.

◇ **safroot meektso'eet** see ◇ **seefroot meektso'eet**.

safroot (*npr* **seefroot**) **to'evah** ספרות תועבה *nf* pornography.

safroot (*npr* **seefroot**) **yafah** ספרות יפה *nf* fiction.

safs|al/-aleem ספסל *nm* bench; (*pl+of:* **-eley**).

safs|ar/-areem ספסר *nm* profiteer; speculator; (*pl+of:* **-erey**).

safsaroo|t/-yot ספסרות *nf* profiteering.

□ **Safsoofah** ספסופה see □ **Seefsoofah**.

sag|ad/-dah/-adetee סגד *v* worshipped; (*pres* **soged**; *fut* **yeesgod**).

sag|ar/-rah/-artee סגר **1.** *v* closed; shut; (*pres* **soger**; *fut* **yeesgor**); **2.** *v [colloq.]* finalized; concluded (deal); got it settled.
sagee/segee'ah שגיא *adj* sublime; great.
sagee סגי *adv* enough.
sagee nehor סגי־נהור **1.** *adj (euphemism)* with plenty of light i.e. blind; **2.** *nm* blind person.
(leshon) sagee nehor לשון סגי נהור *nf* **1.** euphemism; **2.** the opposite of what it is said (as in **sagee nehor**).
(lo) sagee לא סגי **1.** *adv* not enough; **2.** *v pres* isn't enough.
sagfan/-eet סגפן *adj & nmf* ascetic; (*pl+of:* **-ey**).
sagol/segoolah סגול *adj* violet.
sagoor/segoorah סגור *adj* closed; shut.
(ha-sha'ar) sagoor השער סגור *nm* the gate is closed.
sagreer סגריר *nm* bad weather.
(yom/yemey) sagreer יום סגריר *nm* rainy day.
sagreeree/-t סגרירי *adj* rainy.
sahar סהר *nm* moon (poetic).
(khatsee) sahar חצי סהר *nm* half-moon; crescent (emblem of Islam).
◇ **(ha)sahar he-adom** הסהר האדום *nm* the Red Crescent (Muslim parallel to the Red Cross).
saharooree/-t סהרורי *adj* moonstruck.
sak/-eem שק *nm* sack; bag; (*pl+of:* **-ey**).
sakan|ah/-ot סכנה *nf* danger; (*+of:* **-at**).
sakanat klayah סכנת כליה *nf* danger of extinction.
sakanat mavet סכנת מוות *nf* mortal danger.
sakanat nefashot סכנת נפשות *nf* mortal peril; danger to life.
sak|ar/-rah/-artee סקר *v* surveyed; (*pres* **soker**; *fut* **yeeskor**).
sakeek/-eem שקיק *nm* small-size paperbag or envelope; (*pl+of:* **-ey**).
sakeen/-eem סכין *nm* knife; (*pl+of:* **-ey**).
sakeen/-ey geeloo'akh סכין גילוח *nm* shaving-blade; razor-blade.
sakee|t/-yot שקית *nf* (paper or plastic) bag.
(le)sakel לסכל *v inf* to frustrate; to stultify; (*pst* **seekel**; *pres* **mesakel**; *fut* **yesakel**).
(le)sakem לסכם *v inf* to sum up; (*pst* **seekem**; *pres* **mesakem**; *fut* **yesakem**).
sakh/-ah/-tee שח *v* told; (*pres* **sakh**; *fut* **yasee'akh**).
sakh/sekhoom|eem סך *nm* amount; sum; (*pl+of:* **-ey**).
sakh ha-kol סך הכול *nm* total; total sum; total amount.
(ba) sakh בסך *adv* in orderly procession.
(be) sakh בסך *adv* in the amount (sum) of...; amounting to (sum).
(be) sakh ha-kol בסך הכול *adv* in all; altogether amounting to.
sakh|ah/-tah/-eetee שחה *v* swam; (*pres* **sokheh**; *fut* **yeeskheh**).
sakhah (*etc*) **neged ha-zerem** שחה נגד הזרם *v* **1.** (*lit.*) swam against the flow; **2.** (*figurat.*) stood up against accepted ideas.
sakhaf סחף *nm* erosion.
sakhaf/-ah/-tee סחף *v* **1.** swept; **2.** eroded; (*pres* **sokhef**; *fut* **yeeskhaf**).
sakhar סחר *nm* trade; (*+of:* **sekhar**).
sakhar/-ah/-tee סחר *v* traded; (*pres* **sokher**; *fut* **yeeskhar**).
sakh|ar/-rah/-tee שכר *v* hired; rented; (*pres* **sokher**; *fut* **yeeskor** *(k=kh)*).
sakhar שכר *nm* pay; (*+of:* **sekhar**).
sakhar hogen שכר הוגן *nm* fair salary.
sakhar kavoo'a' שכר קבוע *nm* fixed salary.
sakhar khodshee שכר חודשי *nm* monthly salary.
sakhar memootsa' שכר ממוצע *nm* average salary.
sakhar mooskam שכר מוסכם *nm* agreed-upon salary.
sakhar shevoo'ee שכר שבועי *nm* weekly salary.
sakhar shnatee שכר שנתי *nm* annual salary.
sakhar yomee שכר יומי daily salary.
sakhat/-ah/-etee סחט *v* **1.** wrung; **2.** extorted; (*pres* **sokhet**; *fut* **yeeskhat**).
sakhav/-ah/-tee סחב *v* dragged; carried along; (*pres* **sokhev**; *fut* **yeeskhav**).
sakhav (*etc*) סחב *v [slang]* stole.
sakheer/sekheerah סחיר *adj* negotiable.
sakheer/sekheer|ah שכיר **1.** *nmf* wage-earner; hireling; (*pl:* **-eem**; *+of:* **-ey**); **2.** *adj* salaried; paid.
('oved/-et) sakheer/sekheerah עובד שכיר *nmf* paid hand; salaried worker.
sakhevet סחבת *nf* red-tape; procrastination.
sakhkan/-eem שחקן **1.** actor; player; **2.** player (in sport); (*pl+of:* **-ey**).
sakhkan/-ey kheezook שחקן חיזוק *nm* a player, often foreign, added to a team's roster to strengthen it.
sakhkanee|t/-yot שחקנית *nf* actress.
sakh|ek/-kee! שחק! שחקי! *imp sing m/f* play! (*pst* **seekhek**; *pres* **mesakhek**; *fut* **yesakhek**).
(le) sakhek לשחק *v inf* to play; (*pst* **seekhek**; *pres* **mesakhek**; *fut* **yesakhek**).
sakhlav/-eem סחלב *nm* orchid; (*pl+of:* **-ey**).
◻ **Sakhneh** סחנה *nf* natural pool in Bet-She'an Valley (also called: **Brekhat 'Amal** בריכת עמל), in center of picturesque camping and recreation park Gan ha-Shloshah, 14 km E. of **'Afoolah**.
◻ **Sakhneen** (Sakhnin) סחנין *nf* Arab township in Lower Galilee, 6 km S. of **Karmee'el**. Pop. 16,300.
sakhoor/sekhoorah שכור *adj* rented; hired.
sakhoot/sekhootah סחוט *adj* exhausted; squeezed out.
sakhsekhan/-eet סכסכן *nmf & adj* trouble-maker; quarrelsome; (*pl+of:* **-ey**).
saksekhanoo|t/-yot סכסכנות *nf* quarrelsomeness.
sakhtan/-eet סחטן *nmf* extortionist; (*pl+of:* **-ey**).
sakhtanoo|t/-yot סחטנות *nf* extortionism; blackmail.

sakhyan/-eet שחיין *nmf* swimmer; (*pl+of:* **-ey**).
sakoom/-eem סכו"ם *nm* cutlery; tableware; (*acr of* **SAkeeneem, Kapot OO-Mazlegot** ,סכינים, כפות ומזלגות i.e. knives, spoons and forks).
sakran/-eet סקרן *nmf & adj* curious, inquisitive person; (*pl+of:* **-ey**).
sakranoo|t/-yot סקרנות *nf* curiosity.
sal/-eem סל *nm* basket; (*pl+of:* **-ey**).
sal/-ey meetsrakheem סל מצרכים *nm* commodities basket.
sal|ad/-dah/-adetee סלד *v* shrank from; abhorred; (*pres* **soled**; *fut* **yeeslod**).
sal|akh/-khah/-akhtee סלח *v* forgave; (*pres* **sole'akh**; *fut* **yeeslakh**).
sal|al/-elah/-altee סלל *v* paved way; (*pres* **solel**; *fut* **yeeslol**).
salal (*etc*) **derekh/drakheem** סלל דרך *v* paved the way.
salat/-eem סלט *nm* salad.
salat perot סלט פירות *nm* fruit salad.
salat tekheenah סלט טחינה *nm* "tahina" salad; thick sesame oil salad.
salat yerakot סלט ירקות *nm* vegetable salad.
sal'ee/-t סלעי *adj* rocky.
salkhan/-eet סלחן *adj* forgiver; forgiving.
salkhanoot סלחנות *nf* leniency; tolerance.
salmon סלמון *nm* salmon.
salon/-eem סלון *nm* drawing room; salon.
(reekoodeem) saloneeyeem ריקודים סלוניים *nm pl* ball room dances (as opposed to folk dances).
salool/seloolah סלול *adj* paved.
salseel|ah/-ot סלסילה *nf* small basket; (*+of:* **-at**).
sam/-eem סם *nm* drugs; poison; (*pl+of:* **-ey**).
sam/-ah/-tee שם *v* laid; placed; put; (*pres* **sam**; *fut* **yaseem**).
sam (*etc*) **kets** שם קץ *v* put an end.
sam khayeem סם חיים *nm* elixir of life; healing drug.
sam (*etc*) **le-al** שם לאל *v* reduced to naught.
sam (*etc*) **lev** שם לב *v* paid attention.
sam mardeem סם מרדים *nm* narcotic.
sam mavet סם מוות *nm* deadly poison.
sam/-ah (*etc*) **nafsh|o/-ah be-khap|o/-ah** שם נפשו בכפו *v* endangered his/her own life.
sam|akh/-khah/-akhtee שמח *v* rejoiced; was glad; (*pres* **same'akh**; *fut* **yeesmakh**).
samakh (*etc*) **be-khelk|o/-ah/-ee** שמח בחלקו *v* was happy/rejoiced with what he/she/I has/have.
sam|akh/-khah/-akhtee סמך *v* relied on (*pres* **somekh**; *fut* **yesmokh**).
samakh (*etc*) **yad|o/-ah/-ee** סמך ידו *v* approved.
samal/-eem סמל *nm* sergeant; petty-officer; (*pl+of:* **-ey**).
samal meevtsa'eem סמל מבצעים *nm* operations sergeant.
samal reeshon סמל ראשון *nm* staff sergeant.
samal toran סמל תורן *nm* duty non-com; duty sergeant.

(rav) samal רב-סמל *nm* sergeant-major; (*pl:* **rabey-samaleem**).
samankal/-eet סמנכ"ל *nmf* deputy director general (*acr of* **Sgan Menahel KeLalee** סגן מנהל כללי).
samatokh|ah/-ot סמטוחה *nf [slang]* (Russian) big noise; scandal.
same'akh/semekhah שמח **1.** *adj* glad; happy; **2.** *v pres* glad; (*pst* **samakh**; *fut* **yeesmakh**).
same'akh/semekhah be-khelk|o/-ah שמח בחלקו *adj* contented with what he/she has.
(khag) same'akh! !חג שמח *interj* (greeting) Happy Holiday!
sameekh/semeekhah סמיך *adj* thick; dense.
sameem סמים *nm pl* (sing: sam) drugs; narcotics.
(nega' ha) sameem נגע הסמים *nm* the plague of drug-addiction .
"Samekh" (ס) סמ"ך *nm* 15th letter of Hebrew Alphabet: consonant "S".
"Samekh" 'ס *numer. symbol* sixty; 60; 60th.
◇ **samekh tet/-eet** ס"ט *adj acr of* **sefaradee tahor** ספרדי טהור i.e. "pure Sephardi" which some Sephardi Jews would add after their surname thus emphasizing that they are of pure Spanish-Jewish stock.
sam|elet/-alot סמלת *nm* female sergeant; petty-officer (female).
sameman/-eem סממן *nm* ingredient; spice.
(bar/bat) samkha בר-סמכא *adj* authority.
samkhoo|t/-yot סמכות *nf* authority; competence.
samkhootee/-t סמכותי *adj* authoritative.
samookh/semookhah סמוך *adj* close; neighboring.
samookh oo-vatoo'akh (*v=b*) סמוך ובטוח *adj* absolutely certain.
(be) samookh le- -בסמוך ל *adv* next to...
samooy/smooyah סמוי unseen; concealed.
(nos|e'a'/-a'at) samooy/smooyah נוסע סמוי *nmf* stowaway.
(shootaf/-ah) samooy/smooyah שותף סמוי *nmf* silent partner.
sandak/-eem סנדק godfather; (*pl+of:* **-ey**).
sandal/-eem סנדל *nm* sandal.
sandlar/-eem סנדלר *nm* shoemaker; cobbler; (*pl+of:* **-ey**).
sandlaree|yah/-yot סנדלרייה *nf* shoemaker's workshop; (*+of:* **-yot**).
sandlaroot סנדלרות *nf* shoemaking; shoemaker's trade.
san|e/-'ah/-'etee שנא *v* hated; (*pres* **sone**; *fut* **yeesna**).
sanegor/-eet סניגור *nmf* **1.** counsel for the defense; **2.** defender (in a trial or argument).
sanegor|yah/-yot סניגוריה *nf* defense (in a trial); (*+of:* **-yat**).
(leem|ed/-dah/-adetee) sanegoryah לימד סניגוריה *v* defended; stood up for; (*pres* **melamed** *etc*; *fut* **yelamed** *etc*).
◇ **sanhedreen** סנהדרין *nm* synod of Jewish scholars acting as a court of law (100 B.C.E 425 C.E.).

sanktseeyah/-yot סנקציה *nf* sanction; (*+of:* **-yat**).

◇ **sanktseeyot** סנקציות *nf [colloq.]* pressure-measures applied by workers or employees to get acceptance of their demands, short of going on a formal strike.

sanoo/senoo'ah שנוא *adj* hated.

santeemet|er (*npr* **senteemet|er**)**/-reem** סנטימטר *nm* centimeter.

santer/-eem סנטר *nm* chin.

sanvereem סנוורים *nm pl* blindness.

sap|ah/-ot ספה *nf* couch; sofa; (*+of:* **-at**).

sapak/-eem ספק *nm* supplier; provider; (*pl+of:* **-ey**).

sapan/-eem ספן *nm* seaman; (*pl+of:* **-ey**).

sapanoot ספנות *nf* shipping.

sapar/-eem ספר *nf* barber; hairdresser; (*pl+of:* **-ey**).

saparee|t/-yot ספרית *nf* hair-stylist (female).

saparoot ספרות *nf* hair-dressing.

◇ **sapeekhes** ספיחס *nm* **1.** *[slang]* traditional first-time haircut (for boys aged 3); **2.** (derisively:) fresh haircut.

sapeer ספיר *nm* sapphire.

□ **Sapeer** (Sappir) ספיר *nm* area supply center in **Aravah**, 8 km SW of **'En-Yahav**, serving settlements **Paran**, **Khatsevah** (Hazeva), **Tsofar** (Zofar) and **'En-Yahav**. Pop. 325.

sar/-ah/-tee סר *v* **1.** paid a visit; **2.** turned away; (*pres* **sar**; *fut* **yasoor**).

sar/-at ta'am סר־טעם *adj* vulgar; of bad taste.

sar ve-za'ef סר וזעף *adj* sullen and dejected.

sar/-eem שר *nm* government minister; cabinet minister; (*+of:* **-at**).

sar|ah/-ot שרה *nf* government minister; cabinet-minister (female); (*+of:* **-at**).

sar/-ah belee teek שר בלי תיק *nmf* minister without portfolio.

sar/-at (ha)'avodah שר העבודה *nmf* Minister of Labor.

sar/-at (ha)beenooy ve-ha-sheekoon שר הבינוי והשיכון *nmf* Minister of Construction and Housing.

sar/-at (ha)beetakhon שר הביטחון *nmf* Minister of Defense (*lit.:* Security).

sar/-at (ha)bree'oot שר הבריאות *nmf* Minister of Health.

sar (ha)datot שר הדתות *nm* Minister of Religious Affairs.

sar/-at (ha)khakla'oot שר החקלאות *nmf* Minister of Agriculture.

sar/-at (ha)kheenookh ve-(ha)tarboot שר החינוך והתרבות *nmf* Minister of Education and Culture.

sar/at (ha)khoots שר החוץ *nmf* Foreign Minister.

sar/-at (ha)kleetah שר הקליטה *nmf* Minister of Absorption (of new immigrants).

sar/-at (ha)kalkalah ve-ha-teekhnoon שר הכלכלה והתכנון *nmf* Minister of Economy and Planning.

sar/-at (ha)meeshpateem שר המשפטים *nmf* Minister of Justice.

sar/-at (ha)meeskhar ve-(ha)ta'aseeyah שר המסחר והתעשייה *nmf* Minister of Trade and Industry.

sar/-at (ha)otsar שר האוצר *nmf* Minister of Finance (*lit.:* Treasury).

sar/-at (ha)peneem שר הפנים *nmf* Minister of the Interior; Home Secretary.

sar/-at (ha)takhboorah שר התחבורה *nmf* Minister of Transportation.

sar/-at (ha)teekshoret שר התקשורת *nmf* Minister of Communications.

sar|ad/-dah/-adetee שרד *v* remained; escaped; (*pres* **sored**; *fut* **yeesrod**).

sarad (*etc*) **lee-fleytah** שרד לפליטה *v* survived; was left over.

sar|af/-fah/-aftee שרף *v* burned; set fire to; burned down; (*pres* **soref**; *fut* **yeesrof**).

yen saraf (*[colloq.]* **yayeen** *etc*) יין שרף *nm* brandy; gin; arak.

sar|ag/-gah/-agtee סרג *v* knitted; (*pres* **soreg**; *fut* **yeesrog**).

sar|ak/-kah/-aktee סרק *v* combed; (also *figurat.*); (*pres* **sorek**; *fut* **yeesrok**).

sar|akh/-khah/-akhtee סרח *v* sinned; (*pres* **sore'akh**; *fut* **yeesrakh**).

sar|ar/-erah שרר *v* prevailed; reigned; (*pres* **sorer**; *fut* **yeesror**).

sarar (*etc*) **khoshekh** שרר חושך *v* it was very dark; (*pres* **sorer** *etc*; *fut* **yeesror** *etc*).

sarar (*etc*) **sheket** שרר שקט *v* it was quiet; (*pres* **sorer** *etc*; *fut* **yeesror** *etc*).

sar|at/-tah/-atetee שרט *v* scratched; (*pres* **soret**; *fut* **yeesrot**).

sarbal/-eem סרבל *nm* overall; (*pl+of:* **-ey**).

sardeen/-eem סרדין *nm* sardine; (*pl+of:* **ey**).

sareed/sreed|eem שריד *nm* remnant; survivor; (*pl+of:* **-ey**).

□ **Sareed** (Sarid) שריד *nm* kibbutz (est. 1926) in Yizre'el Valley, 2 km SW of **Meegdal ha-'Emek**. Pop. 703.

sareeg/sreeg|eem סריג *nm* lattice; lattice-work; (*pl+of:* **-ey**).

sarees/-eem סריס *nm* eunuch; castrated male.

sar'efet סרעפת *nf* diaphragm (Anat.).

sar|etet/-atot שרטת *nf* scratch.

saroo'a'/sroo'ah שרוע *adj* stretched out.

saroo'akh/srookhah סרוח *adj* stretched out.

saroof/sroofah שרוף *adj* **1.** burnt; burnt out; **2.** *[colloq.]* ardent; devotee, partisan (of a party, ideology, sport *etc*).

saroog/sroogah סרוג *adj* knitted.

sarook/srookah סרוק *adj* combed.

(tsemer) sarook צמר סרוק *nm* combed wool.

sargel/-eem סרגל *nm* ruler; straight edge; (*pl+of:* **-ey**).

sargel/-ey kheeshoov סרגל־חישוב *nm* slide-rule.

sarkastee/-t סרקסטי *adj* sarcastic.

sarsoor/-eem סרסור *nm* **1.** middleman; broker; **2.** procurer; pimp; (*pl+of:* **-ey**).

sarsoor (*etc*) **lee-devar 'averah** סרסור לדבר עבירה *nm* panderer; procurer; pimp.

sartan/-eem סרטן *nm* **1.** crab; **2.** cancer.

(makhalat ha) sartan מחלת הסרטן *nf* the cancer disease.

sartanee/-t סרטני *adj* cancerous.

(geedool/-eem) sartanee/-yeem גידול סרטני *nm* cancerous growth.

sartat/-eem סרטט or: שרטט *nm* draftsman; (*pl+of:* **-ey**).

sart|etet/-atot סרטטת or: שרטטת *nf* draftswoman.

sarvan/-eem סרבן *nm* obstinate person; refuser; (*pl+of:* **-ey**).

sarvan/-ey geeyoos סרבן גיוס *nm* conscientious objector (to being drafted).

sarvan/-ey meelkhamah סרבן מלחמה *nm* conscientious objector (to war).

sas/-ah/-tee שש *v* rejoiced; was glad to; (*pres* **sas**; *fut* **yasees**).

□ **Sasa** סאסא geogr *nm* kibbutz (est. 1949) in Upper Galilee, near **Tsomet Kheeram** (Hiram Junction). Pop. 431.

sason/sesonot ששון *nm* joy (*+of:* **seson**).

sason ve-seemkhah! !ששון ושמחה **1.** *interj* What a joy! **2.** (*lit.*) joy and happiness!

sat|ah/-etah/-eetee סטה *v* turned away; deviated; (*pres* **soteh**; *fut* **yeesteh**).

sat|am/-mah/-amtee סתם *v* **1.** filled (hole, tooth, mouth); **2.** was vague about; (*pres* **sotem**; *fut* **yeestom**).

satam (*etc*) **et ha-golel** סתם את הגולל *v* put an end to.

satam (*etc*) **et ha-peh** סתם את הפה *v* shut (his/her *etc* mouth).

satan שטן *nm* **1.** Satan; **2.** accuser; opposer; **3.** obstacle.

(al teeft|akh/-ekhee) peh la-satan אל תפתח פה לשטן *v imp* let's not invite misfortune.

(leehyot le) satan להיות לשטן *v inf* to be an obstacle; to be an obstruction.

(ma'aseh) satan מעשה שטן bad luck.

sat|ar/-rah/-artee סטר *v* slapped; (*pres* **soter**; *fut* **yeestor**).

sat|ar/-rah/-artee סתר *v* refuted; contradicted; (*pres* **soter**; *fut* **yeestor**).

satat/-eem סתת *nm* stonemason; (*pl+of:* **-ey**).

satatoot סתתות *nf* stonecutting.

sateer|ah/-ot סטירה *nf* satire; (*+of:* **-at**).

sateereekan/-eem סטיריקן *nm* satirist.

satoom/stoomah סתום *adj* **1.** corked; closed; obturated; **2.** vague; unintelligible.

"satoom/stoomah" סתום *adj [slang]* thick-headed.

sav/-eem סב *nm* old man; grandfather; ancestor; (*pl+of:* **-ey**).

sav/savah שב *adj* gray-haired.

sav|a/-eem (*[colloq.]* **saba/-'eem**) סבא *nm* grandfather.

sav|a'/-'ah/-'atee שבע *v* had enough; was satiated; (*pres* **save'a'**; *fut* **yeesba'**; *(b=v)*).

sav|al/-lah/-altee סבל *v* suffered; tolerated; (*pres* **sovel**; *fut* **yeeesbol**; *(b=v)*).

sav|ar/-rah/-artee סבר *v* thought; supposed; considered; (*pres* **sover**; *fut* **yeesbor**; *(b=v)*).

savar/-eem סבר *nm* stevedore; (*pl+of:* **-ey**).

sav|av/-evah/-avtee סבב *v* circled; turned around; rotated; (*pres* **sovev**; *fut* **yeesov**).

save'a'/seve'ah שבע *adj* saturated; glutted.

saveel/seveelah סביל *adj* tolerable; passive.

saveer/seveerah סביר *adj* reasonable.

saveev סביב *adv* round; around.

saveev-saveev סביב־סביב *adv* round about; round and round.

(mee) saveev מסביב *adv* around.

savlan/-eet סבלן *adj* patient; tolerant; (*pl:* **-eem**).

savlanee/-eet סבלני *adj* patient; tolerant (*pl* **-eem/-eeyot**).

savlanoot סבלנות *nf* patience.

(pak'ah) savlanoot|o/-ah/-ee פקעה סבלנותו/־ה *v f & nf* lost his/her/my patience; (*pres* **poka'at** *etc*; *fut* **teefka'** *etc*).

savoor סבור *v pres* believes; is of the opinion; (*pres* **savar**; *fut* **yeesbor**; *(b=v)*).

savyon/-eem סביון *nm* groundsel; yellow weed; (*pl+of:* **-ey**).

□ **Savyon** סביון *nf* fashionable residential suburb of Tel-Aviv and **Petakh-Teekvah** (est. 1954) in central coastal plain, 2 km SW of **Petakh-Teekvah**, 20 km E. of Tel-Aviv. Pop. 2,510.

sawa-sawa סאוה־סאוה *[slang] (Arab.)* together; with one another.

sayad/-eem סייד *nm* plasterer; whitewasher; (*pl+of:* **-ey**).

sayaf/-eem סייף *nm* swordsman; fencer; (*pl+of:* **-ey**).

sayaf|eet/-ot סייפית *nf* fencer (woman).

sayeef סיף *nm* **1.** sword; **2.** fencing (Sports).

sayar/-eem סייר *nm* scout; (*pl+of:* **-ey**).

sayaroot סיירות *nf* reconnaissance.

sayeret/sayarot סיירת *nf* **1.** reconnaissance patrol; **2.** cruiser (navy).

sayfan/-eem סייפן *nm* gladiolus; (*pl+of:* **-ey**).

□ **Sdeh Boker**, **Sdeh Daveed** *etc* for names of places beginning with **Sdeh** - see □ **Sedeh Boker**, **Sedeh Daveed** *etc* names of places beginning with **Sedeh**. (Similarly, look for names of places beginning with **Sedey**).

sdeh/sdot krav שדה קרב *nm* battleground; battlefield.

sdeh/sdot meer'eh שדה מרעה *nm* pasture land; grazing field.

sdeh/sdot moksheem שדה מוקשים *nm* minefield.

sdeh/sdot pe'oolah שדה פעולה *nm* field of activity.

sdeh/sdot re'eeyah שדה ראייה *nm* field of vision.

sdeh/sdot te'oofah שדה תעופה *nm* airfield.

sder|ah/-ot שדרה *nf* alley; (*+of:* **-at**).
sderot שדרות *nf pl* boulevard.
□ **Sderot** see □ **Sederot**, below.
□ **Sdey Avraham, Sdey Khemed, Sdey Troomot** i.e. names of places beginning with **"Sdey"** - see □ **Sedey Avraham, Sedey Khemed, Sedey Troomot** *etc.* (Similarly, look for names of places beginning with **Sedeh**).
□ **Sdom** see □ **Sedom**, below.
◇ **sdom va-'amorah** see ◇ **sedom va-'amorah**, below.
(ma'as|eh/-ey) sdom מעשה סדום *nm* act of sodomy.
(meetat) sdom מיטת סדום *nf* Procrustean bed; painfully uncomfortable bed.
□ **Sdot Meekhah** see □ **Sedot Meekhah**, below.
□ **Sdot Yam** see □ **Sedot Yam**, below.
se'ar שיער *nm* hair; (*+of:* **s'ar**).
(beheer/-at) se'ar בהיר שיער *adj* blond; fair-haired.
(kvoots|at/-ot) se'ar קבוצת שיער *nf* lock; curl.
(mekoorz|al/-elet) se'ar מקורזל שיער *adj* curly.
(mesools|al/-elet) se'ar מסולסל שיער *adj* wavy-haired; with undulated hair.
se'ar|ah/-ot סערה *nf* storm; (*+of:* **sa'ar|at/-ot**).
se'arah (*npr* **sa'arah**)**/se'arot** שערה *nf* a hair; (*+of:* **sa'ar|at/-ot**).
(ke-khoot ha) se'arah (*npr* **sa'arah**) כחוט השערה *adv* by a hairbreadth.
sebev/svaveem (*npr* **sevev** *etc*) סבב *nm [slang]* round.
□ **Sedeh Boker** (Sedé Boqer) שדה בוקר *nm* kibbutz (est. 1953) in Negev hills, 40 km S. of Beersheba. Became famous when David Ben-Gurion settled there on his retirement from public life (1953) and later willed it as burial place for his wife, Pola, and himself. Pop. 372.
□ **Sedeh Daveed** (Sedé Dawid) שדה דוד *nm* village (est. 1955) in **Lakheesh** District, 8 km SW of **Keeryat-Gat**. Pop. 392.
□ **Sedeh Eelan** (Sedé Ilan) שדה אילן *nm* village (est. 1949) in Lower Galilee, 3 km SE of Golani Junction **(Tsomet Golanee)**. Pop. 341.
□ **Sedeh Elee'ezer** (Sedé Eli'ezer) שדה אליעזר *nm* village (est. 1952) in Upper Galilee, W. of Yesod ha-Ma'lah Junction **(Tsomet Yesood ha-Ma'alah)**. Pop. 328.
□ **Sedeh Eleeyahoo** (Sedé Eliyahu) שדה אליהו *nm* kibbutz (est. 1939) in Bet-She'an Valley, 6 km S. of Bet-She'an proper. Pop. 654.
sedeh/sedot krav שדה קרב *nm* battleground; battlefield.
sedeh/sedot meer'eh שדה מרעה *nm* pasture land; grazing field.
sedeh/sedot moksheem שדה מוקשים *nm* minefield.
□ **Sedeh Mosheh** (Sedé Moshe) שדה משה *nm* village (est. 1956) in **Lakheesh** District, 2 km E. of **Keeryat Gat**. Pop. 252.
□ **Sedeh Nakhoom** (Sedé Nahum) שדה נחום *nm* kibbutz (est. 1937) in Bet-She'an Valley, 2 km NW of Bet-She'an proper. Pop. 330.
□ **Sedeh Neetsan** (Sedé Nizzan) שדה ניצן *nm* village (est. 1973) in Eshkol District of W. Negev, 5 km SE of Gvulot Junction **(Tsomet Gevoolot)**. Pop. 248.
□ **Sedeh Nekhemyah** (Sedé Nehemya) שדה נחמיה *nm* kibbutz (est. 1940) in N. **Khoolah** Valley, 5 km E. of **Keeryat Shmonah**. Pop. 407.
□ **Sedeh 'Oozeeyahoo** (Sedé Uziyyahu) שדה עוזיהו *nm* village (est. 1950) in central coastal plain, 5 km SE of Ashdod. Pop. 623.
sedeh/sedot pe'oolah שדה פעולה *nm* field of activity.
sedeh/sedot re'eeyah שדה ראייה *nm* field of vision.
sedeh/sedot te'oofah שדה תעופה *nm* airfield.
□ **Sedeh Tsevee** (Sedé Zevi) שדה צבי *nm* village (est. 1953) in N. Negev, 4 km W. of **Tsomet Bet-Kamah** (Bet-Kama Junction). Pop. 260.
□ **Sedeh Varboorg** (Sedé Warburg) שדה ורבורג *nm* village (est. 1938) in Sharon, 2 km N. of **Kefar Saba**. Pop. 453.
□ **Sedeh Ya'akov** (Sedé Ya'aqov) שדה יעקב *nm* village (est. 1927) in W. Yizre'el Valley, 2 km SE of **Keeryat Teev'on**. Pop. 717.
□ **Sedeh Yeets'khak** (Sedé Yizhaq) שדה יצחק *nm* village (est. 1952) 7 km SE of Hadera Road Junction). Pop. 480.
□ **Sedeh Yo'av** (Sedé Yo'av) שדה יואב *nm* kibbutz (est. 1956), 2 km SE of Giv'ati Junction **(Tsomet Geev'atee)**. Pop. 273.
sedek/sdakeem סדק *nm* crack; split; (*pl+of:* **seedkey**).
sed|er/-areem סדר *nm* order; arrangement; (*pl+of:* **seedrey**).
◇ **seder pesakh** סדר פסח *nm* Passover "Seyder" (ceremonial festival dinner).
seder yom סדר יום *nm* agenda.
('as|ah/-tah/-eetee) seder עשה סדר *v* put things in order; (*pres* **'oseh** *etc; fut* **ya'aseh** *etc*).
(be) seder בסדר *adv* OK; all right; in order.
(be) seder gamoor בסדר גמור *adv* in perfect order; absolutely OK.
(be) seder moftee בסדר מופתי *adv* in exemplary order.
(see-) seder/sdareem אי־סדר *nm* disorder.
◇ **(leyl ha) seder** see ◇ **lel ha-seder**.
seder|ah/-ot שדרה *nf* alley; (*+of:* **-at**).
sederot שדרות *nf pl* boulevard.
□ **Sederot** שדרות *nf* township (est. 1951) in NW Negev, 14 km S. of Ashkelon. Pop. 10,000.
□ **Sedey Avraham** (Sedey Avraham) שדי אברהם *nm* village (est. 1982) in Beersheba sub-district, 10 km SW of Magen Road Junction).

□ **Sedey Khemed** (Sedey Hemed) שדי חמד *nm* village in Sharon, 1 km SE of Kefar Sava. Pop. 283.

□ **Sedey Troomot** (Sedey Terumot) שדי תרומות *nm* village (est. 1951) in Bet-She'an Valley, 6 km S. of Bet-She'an proper. Pop. 411.

□ **Sedom** (Sodom) סדום center of Dead Sea Potash Works, at S. end of Dead Sea, 13 km NE of 'Arava Junction **(Tsomet ha-'Aravah)**.

◇ **sedom va-'amorah** סדום ועמורה *nf* Sodom and Gomorrah, Biblical towns proverbial for their wickedness (Genesis 18,19).

(ma'as|eh/-ey) sedom מעשה סדום *nm* act of sodomy.

(meetat) sedom מיטת סדום *nf* Procrustean bed; painfully uncomfortable bed.

□ **Sedot Meekhah** (Sedot Mikha) שדות מיכה *nm* village (est. 1955), 7 km S. of Bet-Shemesh. Pop. 326.

□ **Sedot Yam** שדות ים *nm* kibbutz (est. 1940) in N. Sharon on Mediterranean coast, 5 km N. of Hadera **(Khaderah)**. Pop. 625.

see/-'eem שיא record; peak; maximum; (*pl+of:* **-'ey**).

see|'ah/-'ot סיעה *nf* faction; group; (*+of:* **-'at**).

see|'akh/-kheem שיח *nm* bush; shrub; (*pl+of:* **-khey**).

see'akh שיח *nm* conversation; talk.

(doo-) see'akh דו־שיח *nm* dialogue.

(rav-) see'akh רב־שיח *nm* discussion (mostly public) with several participants; symposium.

see'atee/-t סיעתי *adj* factional.

seeb|ah/-ot סיבה *nf* reason; cause; (*+of:* **-at**).

seebatee/-t סיבתי *adj* causal.

seebeet סיבית *nf* chipboard.

seeb|ekh/-khah/-akhtee סיבך *v* complicated; messed up; (*pres* **mesabekh**; *fut* **yesabekh**).

seeb|en/-nah/-antee סיבן *v* **1.** soaped; **2.** *[slang]* fooled; (*pres* **mesaben**; *fut* **yesaben**).

seeb|ev/-evah/-avtee סיבב *v* twisted round; surrounded; (*colloq. pres* **mesovev** *(v=b)*; *fut* **yesovev**).

seebookh/-eem סיבוך *nm* complication; entanglement; (*pl+of:* **-ey**).

seeboon/-eem סיבון *nm* **1.** soaping; **2.** *[slang]* hoax; (*pl+of:* **-ey**).

seeboov/-eem סיבוב *nm* round; tour; (*pl+of:* **-ey**).

seeboov shenee סיבוב שני *nm* second round (in war or sports).

seeboovee/-t סיבובי *adj* circular; rotative; rotational.

seedan סידן *nm* calcium (Chem.).

seed|er/-rah/-artee סידר *v* arranged; put in order; (*pres* **mesader**; *fut* **yesader**).

seeder (*etc*) **et** סידר את *v [slang]* "fixed" someone; played a practical joke on.

seedood/-eem שידוד *nm* ploughing; harrowing; (*pl+of:* **-ey**).

seedood ma'arakhot (*npr* **sheedood**) שידוד מערכות *nm* radical reform; reshuffle.

seedoor/-eem סידור *nm* arrangement; (*pl+of:* **-ey**).

◇ **seedoor** (*or:* **"seedoor tefeelah"**) סידור־תפילה *nm* every-day prayer-book.

seedooree/-t סידורי *adj* ordinal; consecutive.

seedrah/sedarot סידרה *nf* series; soap-opera (TV); (*+of:* **-at**).

se'eef/-eem סעיף *nm* article; paragraph; (*pl+of:* **-ey**).

(pas|akh/-khah/-akhtee 'al shtey ha) se'eepeem פסח על שתי הסעיפים *v* sat on the fence; vacillated; (*pres* **pose'akh** *etc; fut* **yeefsakh** *etc f=p*).

(pseekhah 'al shetey ha) se'eepeem פסיחה על שתי הסעיפים *nf* vacillation; wavering.

seeflon/-eem ספלון *nm* small cup; (*pl+of:* **-ey**).

seefon/-eem סיפון *nm* syphon; (*pl+of:* **-ey**).

seefrah/sfarot ספרה *nf* figure; digit; (*+of:* **seefr|at/-ot**).

seefree|yah/-yot ספרייה *nf* library; (*+of:* **-yat**).

seefr|er/-erah/-artee ספרר *v* numbered; numerated; (*pres* **mesafrer**; *fut* **yesafrer**).

seefron/-eem ספרון *nm* booklet; (*pl+of:* **-ey**).

seefroor/-eem ספרור *nm* numeration; numbering.

seefroo|t/-yot ספרות *nf* literature.

seefroot meektso'eet ספרות מקצועית *nf* professional literature.

◇ **seefroot meektso'eet** ספרות מקצועית *nf* **1.** *nf* professional literature; **2.** *nm* emolument added to monthly salary for purchase of professional publications.

seefroot yafah ספרות יפה *nf* fiction.

seefrootee/-t ספרותי *adj* literary.

□ **Seefsoofah** (Sifsufa) ספסופה *nm* village (est. 1949) in Upper Gallilee, 3 km N. of Miron Junction **(Tsomet Meeron)**. Pop. 438.

◇ **seeftakh/-eem** סיפתח *nm [slang]* first cash-earning (or sale) of the day (regarded as good omen).

seegar|ah/-ot סיגרה *nf* cigar; (*+of:* **-at**).

seegaree|yah/-yot סיגרייה *nf* cigarette; (*+of:* **-yat**).

(bedal/beedley) seegaree|yah/-yot בדל סיגרייה *nm* cigarette butt.

(khafees|at/-ot) seegareeyot חפיסת סיגריות *nf* pack of cigarettes.

seeg|el/-lah/-altee סיגל *v* adjusted; adapted; (*pres* **mesagel**; *fut* **yesagel**).

seegn|en/-enah/-antee סיגנן *v* rewrote; corrected style; re-styled; (*pres* **mesagnen**; *fut* **yesagnen**).

seegnon/-eem סגנון *nm* style; (*pl+of:* **-ey**).

seegnonee/-t סגנוני *adj* stylish; pertaining to style.

seegool/-eem סיגול *nm* adaption at; adjustment.

seegs|eg/-egah/-agtee שיגשג *v* flourished; thrived.

seegsoog/-eem שגשוג *nm* boom; prosperity; (*pl+of:* **-ey**).

seek|ah/-ot סיכה *nf* pin; clip; (*+of:* **-at**).

seek|at/-ot beetakhon סיכת ביטחון *nf* safety-pin.

seek|el/-lah/-altee סיכל *v* frustrated; upset; (*pres* **mesakel;** *fut* **yesakel**).

seek|el/-lah/-altee סיקל *v* cleared (field) of stones; (*pres* **mesakel;** *fut* **yesakel**).

seek|em/-mah/-amtee סיכם *v* summed up; (*pres* **mesakem;** *fut* **yesakem**).

seek|en/-nah/-antee סיכן *v* endangered; risked; (*pres* **mesaken;** *fut* **yesaken**).

seek|er/-rah/-artee סיקר *v* covered (journalistically); (*pres* **mesaker;** *fut* **yesaker**).

seekh|ah/-ot שיחה *nf* **1.** talk; conversation; **2.** telephone-call; (*+of:* **-at**).

seekhah (*etc*) **'al shem** שיחה על שם *nf* "person to person" telephone call.

seekh|ah/-ot beyn-'eeronee|t/-yot שיחה בין־עירונית *nf* inter-urban call; trunk-call.

seekh|ah/-ot eeshee|t/-yot שיחה אישית *nf* personal conversation; personal call.

seekh|ah/-ot le-khool שיחה לחו"ל *nf* telephone-call to outside the country.

seekh|ah/-ot mekomee|t/-yot שיחה מקומית *nf* local call.

seekh|ah/-ot pratee|t/-yot שיחה פרטית *nf* private conversation; private call.

seekh|ah/-ot transatlantee|t/-yot שיחה טראנסאטלנטית *nf* Trans-Atlantic call; overseas call.

seekh|ah/-ot yesheer|ah/-ot שיחה ישירה *nf* direct call; direct conversation.

seekh|ah/-ot סיכה *nf* lubrication; greasing; (*+of:* **-at**).

seekh|at/-ot goovayna (*npr* **goovyana**) שיחת גוביינא *nf* collect-call.

seekh|at/-ot ha-yom שיחת היום *nf* topic of the day.

seekh|at/-ot khooleen שיחת חולין *nf* small talk; chat; table-talk.

seekh|at/-ot khoots שיחת חוץ *nf* outside call.

seekh|at/-ot re'eem שיחת רעים *nf* friendly talk.

(eesh/anshey) seekhah איש שיחה *nm* interlocutor; conversationalist.

(ben/bat) seekhat|ee/-o/-ah *etc* בן/בת שיחתי/־ו/־ה *nmf* my/his/her *etc.* interlocutor.

seekh|ek/-akah/-aktee שיחק *v* played; (*pres* **mesakhek;** *fut* **yesakhek**).

seekhek (*etc*) **otah** שיחק אותה *v [slang]* scored a success.

seekhlee/-t שכלי *adj* mental.

(peegoor) seekhlee פיגור שכלי *nm* mental retardation.

seekhletanee/-t שכלתני *adj* rationalist; intellectual.

seekhloo|t/-yot סכלות *nf* stupidity.

seekhon/-eem שיחון *nm* coversation manual; (*pl+of:* **-ey**).

seekhr|er/-erah/-artee סחרר *v* turned one's head; (*pres* **mesakhrer;** *fut* **yesakhrer**).

seekhroor/-eem סחרור *nm* spin; (*pl+of:* **-ey**).

seekhs|ekh/-ekhah/-akhtee סיכסך *v* fomented quarrel; instigated; (*pres* **mesakhsekh;** *fut* **yesakhsekh**).

seekhsookh/-eem סכסוך *nm* quarrel; dispute; (*pl+of:* **-ey**).

(yeesh|ev/-vah/-avtee) seekhsookh יישב סכסוך *v* settled a dispute; (*pres* **meyashev** *etc; fut* **yeyashev** *etc*).

(yeeshoov) seekhsookh יישוב סכסוך *nm* settling a dispute.

seekool/-eem סיכול *nf* frustration; (*pl+of:* **-ey**).

seekool/-eem סיקול *nf* clearing of stones (a field); (*pl+of:* **-ey**).

seekoom/-eem סיכום *nm* summing-up; summary; conclusion; (*pl+of:* **-ey**).

seekoor/-eem סיקור *nm* coverage (journalistic); (*pl+of:* **-ey**).

seekoo|y/-yeem סיכוי *nm* prospect; chance.

(meyrav ha) seekooyeem מירב הסיכויים *nm* most prospects; major chance.

(torat ha) seekooyeem תורת הסיכויים *nf* laws of chance.

seekr|en/-enah/-antee סיקרן *v* intrigued; arouse curiosity; (*pres* **mesakren;** *fut* **yesakren**).

seel|ef/-fah/-aftee סילף *v* distorted; twisted; (*pres* **mesalef;** *fut* **yesalef**).

seel|ek/-kah/-aktee סילק *v* **1.** removed; **2.** paid up; (*pres* **mesalek;** *fut* **yesalek**).

seelek (*etc*) **khov/-ot** סילק חוב *v* repaid a debt.

seelkhee lee! סלחי לי! *interj* Pardon me! (addressing female).

seelo סילו *nm* silo.

seelon/-eem סילון *nm* jet; stream; (*pl+of:* **-ey**).

seelon/-ey mayeem סילון מים *nm* water-jet.

(khoog ha) seelon חוג הסילון *nm* jet set.

(metos/-ey) seelon מטוס סילון *nm* jet airplane.

seelonee/-t סילוני *adj* jet-; jet-like.

□ **Seeloo'an** (Silwan) סילואן *nm* Arab village in SE Jerusalem, outside the Old City wall. Site of the one-time Jewish village **Kefar ha-Sheelo'akh** כפר השילוח (est. 1984) evacuated in 1948. Back in the news by end 1991 following Jewish attemps buy back and re-settle former Jewish houses there.

seeloof/-eem סילוף *nm* distortion; (*pl+of:* **-ey**).

seelook/-eem סילוק *nm* **1.** removal; **2.** payment.

seelook/-ey yad סילוק־יד *nm* dispossession.

(kheshbon) seelookeen חשבון סילוקין *nm* clearing account (banking).

seels|el/-elah/-altee סילסל *v* **1.** waved (hair); **2.** trilled (voice); (*pres* **mesalsel;** *fut* **yesalsel**).

seelsool tmeedee סלסול תמידי *nm* permanent wave.

seem/-ee! שים! *v imp sing m/f* put! place! (*pst & pres* **sam;** *fut* **yaseem**).

seem|akh/-khah/-akhtee שימח *v* gladdened; (*pres* **mesame'akh;** *fut* **yesamakh**).

seeman/-eem סימן *nm* sign; mark; (*pl+of:* **-ey**).

seeman/-ey heker סימן היכר *nm* recognition-mark.

seeman/-ey khayeem סימן חיים *nm* sign of life.

seeman/-ey kree'ah סימן קריאה *nm* exclamation mark (!).

seeman/-ey she'elah סימן שאלה *nm* question mark (?).

(be) seeman tov! בסימן טוב! *interj* Good omen! Good luck!

seemaney zeeknah סימני זקנה *nm pl* signs of old age; symptoms of old age.

seemat lev שימת לב *nf* attention.

seem|e'akh/-khah/-akhtee שימח *v* gladdened; (*pres* **mesame'akh;** *fut* **yesame'akh).**

seem|el/-lah/-altee סימל *v* symbolized; (*pres* **mesamel;** *fut* **yesamel).**

seem|em/-emah/-amtee סימם *v* drugged; (*pres* **mesamem;** *fut* **yesamem).**

seem|en/-nah/-antee סימן *v* marked; earmarked; designated; (*pres* **mesamen;** *fut* **yesamen).**

seemfon (*npr* **seempon)/-ot** סימפון *nm* bronchial tube (Anat.).

(daleket) seemfonot דלקת סמפונות *nf* bronchitis (Medic.).

seemfon|yah/-yot סימפוניה *nf* symphony; (+*of:* **-yat).**

seemkhah/smakhot שמחה *nf* **1.** joy; **2.** happy occasion (wedding *etc*); (+*of:* **seemkh|at/-ot).**

seemkhah le-'eyd שמחה לאיד *nf* rejoicing over another's calamity.

(ba'al/-at) seemkhah בעל שמחה *nmf* **1.** host (-ess) giving party or banquet; **2.** guest of honor; (*pl:* **-ey/-ot** *etc*).

(be) seemkhah בשמחה *adv* gladly.

(heeshb|eet/-eetah/-atetee) seemkhah השבית שמחה *v* spoiled the party; (*pres* **mashbeet** *etc;* *fut* **yashbeet** *etc*).

(mo'adeem le) seemkhah! מועדים לשמחה! *interj* (greeting) Joyous Holiday!

◇ **seemkhat bet ha-sho'evah** שמחת בית השואבה *nf* Feast of Water-Drawing (dating from the time of the 2nd Temple), held in Jerusalem during Succot.

seemkhat meetsvah שמחת מצווה *nf* celebration of religious character.

◇ **seemkhat torah ("Simchas Toira")** שמחת־תורה *nm* "Rejoicing of the Torah" holiday that ends the Jewish Holiday Season in autumn, coming at the end of Succot. The main events are a procession with Torah scrolls and reading its last and first passages to complete and rebegin its annual cycle.

seemlah/smalot שמלה *nf* dress; gown; (+*of:* **seeml|at/-ot).**

seemlat khoopah שמלת חופה *nm* bridal gown; wedding dress.

seemlee/-t סמלי *adj* symbolic.

seemleeyoot סמליות *nf* symbolism.

seemool/-eem סימול *nm* symbolization.

seemooltanee/-t סימולטאני *adj* simultaneous.

seemooltaneet סימולטאנית *adv* simultaneously.

seemoom/-eem סימום *nm* drugging; (*pl+of:* **-ey).**

seemoon/-eem סימון *nm* marking; earmarking; (*pl+of:* **-ey).**

seempatee/-t סימפאתי *adj* nice; pleasant; lovable.

seempat|yah/-yot סימפאתיה *nf* sympathy; (+*of:* **-yat).**

seempon/-ot סמפון *nm* bronchial tube (Anat.).

(daleket) seemponot דלקת סמפונות *nf* bronchitis (Medic.).

seemt|ah/-'ot סמטה *nf* alley; side-street; (+*of:* **-at).**

◇ **"seen"** (שׂ) שי״ן 21st letter of Hebrew Alphabet; consonant **S** (in dotted script this is only when dot is placed over its left side).

□ **Seen** סין *nf* China.

seen|'ah/-'ot שנאה *nf* hatred; hate; (+*of:* **-at).**

seenar (*cpr* **seenor)/-eem** סינר *nm* apron; (*pl+of:* **seenerey).**

seen'at kheenam שנאת חינם *nf* blind hatred; unreasoning hatred.

seen'at mavet שנאת מוות *nf* deadly hate.

□ **Seenay** סיני *nm* **1.** Sinai peninsula; **2.** Mount Sinai.

seenee/-t סיני *adj* Chinese.

seenee/-m סיני *nm* Chinaman

seeneet סינית **1.** *nf* Chinese (language); **2.** *nf* Chinese woman (*pl* **seeneeyot).**

seen|en/-enah/-antee סינן *v* **1.** filtered; strained; **2.** quipped; (*pres* **mesanen;** *fut* **yesanen).**

seenoon/-eem סינון *nm* filtration; filtering; (*pl+of:* **-ey).**

seenor/-eem סינור *[colloq.] nm* apron; (*pl+of:* **-ey).**

seenver/-erah/-artee סנוור *v* blinded; dazzled; (*pres* **mesanver;** *fut* **yesanver).**

seenvoor/-eem סנוור *nm* blinding; dazzling; (*pl+of:* **-ey).**

seep|akh/-khah/-akhtee סיפח *v* annexed; (*pres* **mesape'akh;** *fut* **yesapakh).**

seep|e'akh/-khah/-akhtee סיפח *v* annexed; (*pres* **mesape'akh;** *fut* **yesape'akh).**

seep|ek/-kah/-aktee סיפק *v* supplied; provided;furnished; (*pres* **mesapek;** *fut* **yesapek).**

(lo hayah) seepek לא היה סיפק *v* there was not time enough; (*pres* **eyn** *etc;* *fut* **lo yeehyeh** *etc*).

seep|er/-rah/-artee סיפר *v* **1.** told; narrated; **2.** gave a haircut; (*pres* **mesaper;** *fut* **yesaper).**

seepoo|'akh/-kheem סיפוח *nm* annexation; (*pl+of:* **khey).**

seepook/-eem סיפוק *nm* satisfaction.

seepoon/-eem סיפון *nm* deck (ship); (*pl+of:* **-ey).**

seepoor/-eem סיפור *nm* story; (*pl+of:* **-ey).**

seepooreem סיפורים *interj* just stories!...

seepoorey ma'aseeyot סיפורי מעשיות *nm pl* tales; fairy-tales.
seepoorey yeladeem סיפורי ילדים *nm pl* children's stories.
seeporet סיפורת *nf* fiction; narrative literature.
seer/-eem סיר *nm* pot; (*pl+of:* **-ey**).
seer/-ey lakhats סיר־לחץ *nm* pressure-cooker.
seer/-ey laylah סיר־לילה *nm* chamber pot.
seer/-ey pele' סיר־פלא *nm* wonder pan; wonder pot.
seer|ah/-ot סירה *nf* boat; (*+of:* **-at**).
seerakhon (*npr* **seerkhon**) סירחון *nm* stench; stink; (*+of:* **seerkhon**).
seer|at/-ot dayeeg סירת־דיג *nf* fishing boat.
seer|at/-ot hatsalah סירת הצלה *nf* lifeboat.
seer|at/-ot mano'a' סירת מנוע *nf* motorboat.
seer|at/-ot meefras סירת מפרש *nf* sailboat.
seer|at/-ot meeshmar סירת משמר *nf* patrol boat.
seerbool/-eem סרבול *nm* heavy-handedness; red-tape; making things dificult.
seeren|ah/-ot סירנה *nf* siren; (*+of:* **-at**).
seerkhon/-ot סרחון *nm* stench; stink.
seerop/-eem סירופ *nm* syrup; (*pl+of:* **-ey**).
seers|er/-rah/-artee סירסר *v* mediated; (*pres* **mesarser**; *fut* **yesarser**).
seersoor/-eem סירסור *nm* middleman; pimp; procurer; (*pl+of:* **-ey**).
seert|et/-etah/-atetee סירטט *v* sketched; drew; (*pres* **mesartet**; *fut* **yesartet**).
seertey porno סרטי פורנו *nm* porno movies; (*sing:* **seret**).
seertey to'evah סרטי תועבה *nm* "blue" movies; (*sing:* **seret to'evah**).
seerton/-eem סרטון *nm* film strip; (*pl+of:* **-ey**).
seerton שרטון *nm* sandbank.
('al|ah/-tah/-eetee 'al) seerton עלה על שרטון *nm* ran aground; (*pres* **'oleh** *etc; fut* **ya'aleh** *etc*).
seertoot/-eem סרטוט *nm* draft; drawing; (*pl+of:* **-ey**).
seesm|ah/-a'ot סיסמה *nf* slogan; password; (*+of:* **-at**).
se'et שאת *nf* **1.** swelling; **2.** dignity.
(be-yeter) se'et ביתר שאת *adv* even more so.
seet|et/-etah/-atetee סיתת *v* dressed stones; (*pres* **mesatet**; *fut* **yesatet**).
seetn|ah/-ot שטנה *nf* denunciation; slander; (*+of:* **-at**).
(ketav/keetvey) seetnah כתב שטנה *nm* lampoon; indictment.
seeton|ay/-a'eem סיטונאי *nm* wholesaler; (*pl+of:* **-a'ey**).
seetonoot (*or:* **seetona'oot**) סיטונות *nf* wholesale- trade.
(be) seetonoot בסיטונות *adv* wholesale.
seetoo'ats|yah/-yot סיטואציה *nf* situation.
seetoot/-eem סיתות *nm* stone-cutting; stone dressing; (*pl+of:* **-ey**).
(doo) seetree/-t דו־סיטרי *adj* two-way -.
(khad) seetree/-t חד־סיטרי *adj* one-way-.

□ **Seetreeyah** (Sitriyya) סיתריה *nm* village (est. 1949) in central coastal plain, 3 km NW of Bilu Junction (**Tsomet Beeloo**). Pop. 391.
seev/-eem סיב *nm* fiber; (*pl+of:* **-ey**).
◇ **seevan (Sivan)** סיון *nm* 9th Jewish Calendar month; 30 days; approx. May-June.
seevee/-t סיבי *adj* fibrous.
seev|eg/-gah/-agtee סיווג *v* graded; classified. (*pres* **mesaveg**; *fut* **yesaveg**).
seevoog/-eem סיווג *nm* grading; classification; (*pl+of:* **-ey**).
see|ya' (or: **see|ye'a'**)/**-y'ah/-ya'tee** סייע *v* aided; assisted; (*pres* **mesaye'a'**; *fut* **yesaye'a'**).
seey|ed/-edah/-adetee סייד *v* plastered; whitewashed; (*pres* **mesayed**; *fut* **yesayed**).
seey|em/-emah/-amtee סיים *v* concluded; ended; (*pres* **mesayem**; *fut* **yesayem**).
seey|er/-erah/-artee סייר *v* toured; (*pres* **mesayer**; *fut* **yesayer**).
seeyom|et/-ot סיומת *nf* suffix.
seeyoo'a' סיוע *nm* assistance; aid.
seeyood/-eem סיוד *nm* plastering; whitewashing; (*pl+of:* **-ey**).
seeyoof/-eem סיוף *nm* fencing (sport); (*pl+of:* **-ey**).
seeyoom/-eem סיום *nm* concluding; ending; (*pl+of:* **-ey**).
seeyoor/-eem סיור *nm* tour; reconnaissance; (*pl+of:* **-ey**).
seeyoot/-eem סיוט *nm* nightmare; (*pl+of:* **-ey**).
sefakh/sfakheem ספח *nm* coupon; addendum; (*pl+of:* **seefkhey**).
sefar ספר *nm* frontier zone.
(yeeshoov/-ey) sefar יישוב ספר *nm* border settlement.
sefarad ספרד *nf* Spain.
◇ **(geroosh) sefarad** see ◇ **geroosh sefarad**.
◇ **(noosakh) sefarad** see ◇ **noosakh sefarad**.
sefaradee/-m ספרדי *nm* **1.** Jew of Sephardi Rite or background; **2.** Spaniard.
sefaradee/-t ספרדי *adj* **1.** Sephardi; Spanish-Jewish; **2.** Spanish.
sefaradeet ספרדית *nf* Spanish (the language).
sefat deeboor שפת דיבור *nf* vernacular; spoken language.
sefat em שפת אם *nf* mother tongue.
sefat 'ever שפת עבר *nf* the Hebrew language (poetical archaism).
sefat ha-yam שפת הים *nf* **1.** beachside; **2.** coastline.
sefatayeem שפתיים *pl* (*sing:* **safah**) lips; (*pl+of:* **seeftot**).
(mas) sefatayeem מס שפתיים *nm* lip service.
sefeen|ah/-ot ספינה *nf* boat; ship; (*+of:* **-at**).
sefeer|ah/-ot ספירה *nf* count; (*+of:* **-at**).
(la) sefeerah לספירה A.D.; Common or Christian Era.
◇ **(leefney ha) sefeerah** see ◇ **leefney ha-sfeerah**.
◇ **sefeerat ha-'omer** see ◇ **sfeerat ha-'omer**.
sefeerat melay ספירת מלאי *nf* stock-taking; inventory count.

sef|el/-aleem ספל *nm* cup; (*pl+of:* **seefley**).

sef|er/-areem ספר *nm* book; (*pl+of:* **seefrey**).

sefer/seefrey 'ezer ספר־עזר *nm* reference book.

sefer ha-sefareem ספר הספרים *nm* "the Book of Books" i.e. the Bible.

sefer/seefrey kees ספר כיס *nm* pocket-book.

sefer/seefrey leemood ספר לימוד *nm* textbook.

sefer/seefrey sheerah ספר שירה *nm* book of poetry.

sefer/seefrey torah ספר תורה *nm* Torah scroll; Pentateuch scroll.

('am ha) sefer עם הספר *nm* the People of the Book- i.e. the Jewish People.

(bet/batey) sefer בית־ספר *nm* school.

(bet/batey) sefer 'eeronee/-yeem בית־ספר עירוני *nm* municipal school.

(bet/batey) sefer gavo'ah/gvoheem בית־ספר גבוה *nm* college; university.

(bet/batey) sefer le-van|eem/-ot (*v=b*) בית־ספר לבנים/לבנות *nm* school for boys/girls.

(bet/batey) sefer memshaltee/-yeem בית־ספר ממשלתי *nm* government school.

(bet/batey) sefer teekhon/-eeyeem בית־ספר תיכון *nm* secondary (high) school.

(bet/batey) sefer yesodee/-yeem בית־ספר יסודי *nm* elementary (grammar) school.

sefor! seefree! ספור! ספרי! *v imp sing m/f* count! please, count! (*inf* **leespor**; *pst* **safar**; *pres* **sofer**; *fut* **yeespor** (*p=f*)).

(le-en) sefor לאין־ספור *adj* countless.

segan/-eet סגן *nmf* deputy; assistant; vice-.

segan/-ey aloof/-eem סגן אלוף *nm* lieutenant-colonel.

segan nasee סגן נשיא *nm* vice-president.

segan rosh ha-memshalah סגן ראש הממשלה *nm* vice-premier; deputy prime-minister.

segan/-ey sar/-eem סגן שר *nm* vice-minister; deputy-minister.

seganoo|t/-yot סגנות *nf* lieutenancy; deputation.

segel סגל *nm* staff; personnel.

segel deeplomatee סגל דיפלומטי *nm* Diplomatic Corps.

segen/sgan|eem סגן *nm* **1.** 1st lieutenant (Army) **2.** deputy (hierarchy); (*pl+of:* **-ey**).

segen/sganey meeshneh סגן משנה *nm* 2nd lieutenant.

seger/sgareem סגר *nm* shutter.

□ **Segev** שגב *nm* rural settlement (est. 1973) in Lower Galilee, 8 km SE of Ahihud Junction (**Tsomet Akheehood**). Pop. 53.

◇ **segol ("Segol")** סגול *nm* vowel "EH" (pronounced as in "ten") in dotted Hebrew script in form of 3 sublinear dots (x̣).

◇ **(khataf) segol** see ◇ **Khataf Segol**.

segool|ah/-ot סגולה *nf* **1.** virtue; **2.** quality; chracteristic; **3.** remedy; (*+of:* **-at**).

□ **Segoolah** (Segula) סגולה *nm* village (est. 1953) in **Lakheesh** District, 6 km N. of **Keeryat-Gat**. Pop. 275.

◇ **('am) segoolah** see ◇ **'am segoolah**.

(kee) segoolah neged כסגולה נגד *adv* as a remedy against.

(yekheedey) segoolah יחידי סגולה *nm pl* outstanding people; people of unique distinction.

segoolee/-t סגולי *adj* specific.

(meeshkal) segoolee משקל סגולי *nm* specific gravity.

segor! seegree! סגור! סגרי! *v imp sing m/f* close! shut! (*inf* **leesgor**; *pst* **sagar**; *pres* **soger**; *fut* **yeesgor**).

seker/skareem סקר *nm* survey; (*pl+of:* **seekrey**).

sekhakh סכך *nm* freshly cut branches with leaves, for roofing a "Succah".

sekhakh|ah/-ot סככה *nf* shed; (*+of:* **-at**).

sekhar סחר *nm+of* trade of.

sekhar (*npr* **sakhar**) שכר *nm* remuneration.

sekhar 'avodah שכר עבודה *nm* wages; salary.

sekhar batalah שכר בטלה *nm* dole; attendance fee (for unemployed).

sekhar deerah שכר דירה *nm* rent.

sekhar deerah moogan שכר דירה מוגן *nm* controlled rent.

sekhar khaleefeen סחר־חליפין *nm* barter.

sekhar (*npr* **sakhar**) **khodshee** שכר חודשי *nm* monthly salary.

sekhar leemood שכר לימוד *nm* tuition fee.

sekhar leemood moodrag שכר־לימוד מודרג *nm* graded school fees.

sekhar sofreem שכר סופרים *nm* royalties; author's fee.

sekhar teerkhah שכר טירחה *nm* fee.

◇ **sekhar yesod** שכר יסוד *nm* basic pay i.e. not including various emoluments and allowances.

(bee) sekhar בשכר [*colloq.*] *adv* **1.** for a fee (*npr* **be-sakhar**); **2.** on account of.

(bee) sekhar (*npr* **be-sakhar**) **khodshee** בשכר חודשי *adv* **1.** for a monthly salary; for monthly wages; **2.** [*colloq.*] *adv nm* for monthly rent (*correct:* **bee-sekheeroot khodsheet**).

(bee) sekhar khofshee בשכר חופשי *adv* [*colloq.*] against free (uncontrolled) rent (*correct:* **bee-sekheeroot khofsheet**).

(darg|at/-ot ha) sekhar (*npr* **ha-sakhar**) דרגת השכר *nf* wage scale.

(hagdalat) sekhar (*npr* **sakhar**) הגדלת שכר *nf* salary increase; increased pay.

(hakpa'at) sekhar (*npr* **sakhar**) הקפאת שכר *nf* wage freeze.

(halanat) sekhar (*npr* **sakhar**) הלנת שכר *nf* holding back wages.

(horad|at/-ot) sekhar (*npr* **sakhar**) הורדת השכר *nf* reduction in salary; reduced wages.

(khok le-haganat ha) sekhar (*npr* **sakhar**) חוק להגנת השכר *nm* Wage Protection Law.

sekharkhar/-ah סחרחר *adj* dizzy.

(yatsa) sekhar|o/-ah be-hefsed|o/-ah יצא שכרו בהפסדו/ה *v* **1.** *lit* his/her loss exceeded his/her profit; **2.** did not prove worthwhile (*pres* **yotse** *etc*; *fut* **yetse** *etc*).

sekhav|ah/-ot סחבה *nf* rug; mop; (*+of:* **-at**).

(blo|y/-yey) sekhavot בלויי־סחבות *nm pl* worn-out rag.
sekheer/-at שכיר *nmf+of* hireling of.
sekheer/-ey 'et שכיר־עט *nm* hack-writer; hired journalist.
sekheer/-ey kherev שכיר חרב *nm* mercenary.
sekheer|ah/-ot שכירה *nf* hiring; renting; leasing; (*+of:* **-at**).
sekheeroo|t/-yot שכירות *nf* lease; rent.
sekheeroot khodsheet שכירות חודשית *nf* monthly rent; rent payable by the month.
sekheeroot meeshneh שכירות משנה *nf* sublease; subtenancy.
sekheeroot moogenet שכירות מוגנת *nf* rent-protected tenancy.
(deerah bee) sekheerootדירה בשכירות *nf* rented apartment; rented flat.
(bee) sekheeroot khofsheet בשכירות חופשית against free (uncontrolled) rent.
(demey) sekheeroot דמי שכירות *nm pl* rent.
(khoz|eh/-ey) sekheeroot חוזה שכירות *nm* contract of lease.
(khozeh lee) sekheerootbeeltee moogenet חוזה לשכירות בלתי מוגנת *nf* contract of unprotected lease.
sekheet|ah/-ot סחיטה *nf* extortion; (*pl+of:* **-at**).
sekheev|ah/-ot סחיבה *nf* dragging; pulling; *[slang]* pinching; pilfering; (*+of:* **-at**).
sekhee|yah/-yot שחייה *nf* swimming; (*+of:* **-yat**).
(breykh|at/-ot) sekheeyah בריכת שחייה *nf* swimming pool.
(leemood/-ey) sekheeyah לימוד שחייה *nf* swimming instruction.
(she'oor/-ey) sekheeyah שיעור שחייה *nm* swimming lesson.
(takhroo|t/-yot) sekheeyah תחרות שחייה *nf* swimming contest.
sekheeyat gav שחיית גב *nf* back-stroke (swimming).
sekheeyat khateerah שחיית חתירה *nf* crawl-stroke (swimming).
sekheeyat parpar שחיית פרפר *nf* butterfly-stroke (swimming).
sekhel שכל *nm* intelligence; cleverness.
(be) sekhel בשכל *adv* intelligently; cleverly.
(ha) sekhel ha-yashar השכל הישר *nm* common sense.
sekher/sekhareem סכר *nm* dam; (*pl+of:* **seekhrey**).
sekher שכר *nm* charter.
sekher-mekher שכר־מכר *[colloq.] nm* hire-purchase; (correct legal term: **meekakh agav sekheeroot** מיקח אגב שכירות).
(tees|at/-ot) sekher טיסת שכר *nf* charter-flight.
sekhoom/-eem סכום *nm* sum; (*pl+of:* **-ey**).
sekhoom kolel סכום כולל *nm* total amount.
sekhog סחוג *nm* spicy Yemenite sauce.
sekhor-sekhor סחור סחור *adv* round about; round and round.
sekhor|ah/-ot סחורה *nf* merchandise; (*+of:* **-at**).
sekhoos סחוס *nm* cartilage.
sekhvee שכווי *nm* rooster; cock.
sel|a'/-a'eem סלע *nm* rock; cliff; (*pl+of:* **sal'ey**).
selek סלק *nm* beet.
selek lavan סלק לבן *nm* turnip.
selek sookar סלק סוכר *nm* sugar beet.
selekteevee/-t סלקטיבי *adj* selective.
◊ **selektsee|yah/-yot** סלקציה *nf* **1.** selection; **2.** reference to daily "selections" carried out by the Nazis in Holocaust death-camps of those relegated to immediate extermination; (*+of:* **-yat**).
semadar סמדר *nm* (Semadar) blossom.
semakh! seemkhee! שמח ! שמחי ! *v imp sing m/f* rejoice! be glad!; (*inf* **leesmo'akh**; *pst* **samakh**; *pres* **same'akh**; *fut* **yeesmakh**).
('al) semakh על סמך *adv* on grounds of; on the basis of.
semeekhah/-ot שמיכה *nf* blanket; (*+of:* **-at**).
semeekhoo|t/-yot סמיכות *nf* **1.** density; **2.** proximity.
semeekhoot ha-parasheeyot סמיכות הפרשיות *nf* juxtaposition.
semel/smaleem סמל *nm symbol*; token; (*pl+of:* **seemley**).
semel (*etc*) **mees'kharee** סמל מסחרי־ *nm* trade-mark.
semol שמאל *nm* left (hand, side).
(mekasher) semalee מקשר שמאלי *nm* left inside forward (soccer).
seneelee/-t סנילי *adj* senile.
seneeleeyoot סניליות *nf* senility.
□ **Seneer** see □ **Sneer**, below.
sensatsee|yah/-yot סנסציה *nf* sensation; (*+of:* **-yat**).
se'ood/-eem סיעוד *nm* nursing (profession).
se'ood|ah/-ot סעודה *nf* banquet; meal; (*+of:* **-at**).
◊ **(ha)se'oodah ha-mafseket** הסעודה המפסקת *nf* final meal before Yom Kippur or **Teesh'ah be-Av** fasting.
se'oodat melakheem סעודת מלכים *nf* royal feast.
◊ **se'oodat shabat** סעודת שבת *nf* Friday night "Sabbath Dinner".
se'orah/-eem שעורה *nf* barley; (*+of:* **-at**).
se'orah ba-'ayeen שעורה בעין *nf* stye (in the eye).
september ספטמבר *nm* September.
(beegdey) serad בגדי שרד *nm pl* official uniform.
(deer|at/-ot) serad דירת שרד *nm* official residence; state-provided lodging.
serak סרק *(suffix) adj* futile; idle; pointless.
('atsey) serak עצי סרק *nm* barren (fruitless) trees.
(eeyoom/-ey) serak איום סרק *nm* empty threat.
(geenooney) serak גינוני סרק *nm pl* pretentious manners.
(kadoor/-ey) serak כדור סרק *nm* blank bullet.
(veekoo|'akh/-khey) serak ויכוח סרק *nm* futile, fruitless debate.

serakhon (*npr* **seerkhon**)/**-ot** סירחון *nm* stench; stink.

serar|ah/-ot שררה *nf* rule; power; authority; (*+of:* **-at**).

(ahavat) serarah אהבת שררה *nf* lust for power.

seref|ah/-ot שריפה *nf* fire; (*+of:* **-at**).

(avak) serefah אבק שריפה *nm* gunpowder.

seren/sran|eem סרן *nm* **1.** captain (Army); **2.** axle; (*pl+of:* **-ey**).

(rav/rabey) seren/sraneem רב־סרן *nm* major (Army).

serenad|ah/-ot סרנדה *nf* serenade; (*+of:* **-at**).

ser|es/-sah/-astee סירס *v* **1.** distorted; **2.** castrated; (*pres* **mesares;** *fut* **yesares**).

seret/srateem סרט *nm* **1.** film; **2.** ribbon; **3.** tape; (*pl+of:* **seertey**).

seret/seertey haklatah סרט הקלטה *nm* recording tape.

seret/seertey hasratah סרט הסרטה *nm* movie film.

seret/seertey kolno'a' סרט קולנוע *nm* movie; motion picture.

seret/seertey tseeloom סרט צילום *nm* roll of film.

seret/seertey veedyo סרט וידיאו *nm* video cassette.

serev/-vah/-avtee סירב *v* refused; declined; (*pres* **mesarev;** *fut* **yesarev**).

serokh/-eem שרוך *nm* lace; shoestring; (*pl+of:* **-ey**).

◇ **(keepah) seroogah** see ◇ **keepah sroogah**.

(le) seroogeen לסירוגין *adv* intermittently.

seroos/-eem סירוס *nm* **1.** distortion; **2.** castration.

seroov/-eem סירוב *nm* refusal; (*pl+of:* **-ey**).

(be) seroov mookhlat בסירוב מוחלט *adv* with a flat refusal.

◇ **(medeenot ha) seroov** see ◇ **medeenot ha-seroov**.

(neetkal/-elah/-altee be) seroov נתקל בסירוב *v* met with refusal; (*pres* **neetkal** *etc;* *fut* **yeetakel** *etc*).

◇ **"seroovnik"/-eem** סירובניק *nm [slang]* "Refusenik"; Soviet Jew whose application to emigrate to Israel has been refused.

◇ **serteefeekat/-eem** סרטיפיקט *nm* "Certificate" - notorious and hard to get permit that, throughout the British Mandate period, was needed for immigrating to Palestine.

seter/stareem סתר *nm* secrecy; secret hiding.

-seter סתר *(suffix) adj* secret.

(ba) seter בסתר *adv* secretly.

(mekom/-ot) seter מקום סתר *nm* hidden place; secret retreat.

sev|a'/-e'at ratson שבע רצון *adj* pleased; content.

sevakh/-eem סבך *nm* complication; tangle; brambles; (*pl+of:* **seevkhey**).

sevakh|ah/-ot סבכה *nf* grill; grate; shed; (*+of:* **-at**).

sevar|ah/-ot סברה *nf* version; supposition; (*+of:* **-at**).

sevarat/-ot keres (*npr* **kares**) סברת־כרס *nf* baseless assumption.

seve'at ratson שבעת רצון *adj f* pleased; satisfied (see **seva' ratson**, above).

sevee'at ratson שביעת־רצון *nf* contentment; satisfaction.

seveeloo|t/-yot סבילות *nf* tolerance; passivity.

sevee'oot שביעות *nf* satisfaction; contentment.

sevee'oot ratson שביעות רצון *nf* satisfaction; contentment.

seveeroo|t/-yot סבירות *nf* **1.** reasonableness; **2.** probability.

seveeroot gevohah סבירות גבוהה *nf* high probability.

seveeroot nemookhah סבירות נמוכה *nf* low probability.

seveev|ah/-ot סביבה *nf* environment; neighborhood; (*+of:* **-at**).

seveevatee/-t סביבתי *adj* environmental.

(peegoor) seveevatee פיגור סביבתי *nm* environmental retardation.

seveevon/-eem סביבון *nm* spinning top—standard Chanukkah toy.

sevel/seevlot סבל *nm* suffering; endurance.

sever סבר *nm* countenance.

sever paneem סבר פנים *nm* affability.

(be) sever paneem yafot בסבר פנים יפות *adv* cordially; friendly.

(khamoor/-at) sever חמור סבר *adj* grim-faced.

sevev/svaveem סבב *nm [slang]* round.

sevooranee (*or:* **savoornee**) סבורני *v pres* I believe; I think; I consider.

seyfa סיפא (Aramaic) *nm* concluding section of a paragraph.

seyv|ah שיבה *nf* gray hair; old age; (*+of:* **-at**).

seyvah tovah שיבה טובה *nf* aging happily; aging gracefully.

('ad zeeknah ve) seyvah עד זיקנה ושיבה *adv* till old age.

(se'ar/sa'arot) seyvah שער שיבה *nmf* gray hair.

sfar ספר *nm* frontier zone.

(ba) sfar בספר *adv* in a near-the-border area.

(yeeshoov/-ey) sfar יישוב ספר *nm* border settlement.

sfarad ספרד *nf* Spain.

◇ **(geroosh) sfarad** see ◇ **geroosh sefarad**.

◇ **(noosakh) sfarad** see ◇ **noosakh sefarad**.

sfaradee/-m ספרדי *nm* **1.** Jew of Sephardi Rite or background; **2.** Spaniard.

sfaradee/-t ספרדי *adj* **1.** Sephardi; Spanish-Jewish; **2.** Spanish.

sfaradeet ספרדית *nf* Spanish (language).

sfardeeyah/-yot ספרדייה *nf* **1.** Sephardi Jewish woman; **2.** Spanish woman.

(loo'akh) sfarot לוח ספרות *nm* dial.

sfat deeboor שפת דיבור *nf* vernacular; spoken language.

sfat em שפת אם *nf* mother tongue.

sfat 'ever שפת עבר *nf* the Hebrew language (poetic archaism).

sfat ha-yam שפת הים *nf* **1.** beachside; seashore; **2.** coastline.

sfatayeem שפתיים *nf pl* (*sing:* **safah**) lips; (*pl+of:* **seeftot**).

(mas) sfatayeem מס שפתיים *nm* lip service.

sfaton/-eem שפתון *nm* lipstick; (*pl+of:* **-ey**).

sfeder (*npr* **sveder**)**/-eem** סוודר *nm* sweater; pullover.

sfeeg|ah/-ot ספיגה *nf* absorption; (*+of:* **-ot**).

sfeek|ah/-ot ספיקה *nf* **1.** flow; **2.** clapping; **3.** sufficiency; (*+of:* **-at**).

(see-) sfeekah אי־ספיקה *nm* insufficiency; (*+of:* **-at**).

(see-) sfeekat ha-lev אי ספיקת הלב *nm* coronary insufficiency (Medic.).

sfeen|ah/-ot ספינה *nf* boat; ship; (*+of:* **-at**).

sfeer|ah/-ot ספירה *nf* count; (*+of:* **-at**).

(la) sferah לספירה A.D.; Common or Christian Era.

◇ **(leefney ha) sfeerah** see ◇ **leefney ha-sfeerah**.

◇ **sfeerat ha-'omer** ספירת העומר *nf* evening-prayer recited daily to count 49 days from 2nd day of Passover to **Shavoo'ot**.

sfeerat melay ספירת מלאי *nf* stock-taking; inventory count.

sfoor|eem/-ot ספורים *adj pl* counted; few.

sfog/-eem ספוג *nm* sponge.

sfor! seefree! ספור ! ספרי ! *v imp sing m/f* count! please, count! (*inf* **leespor**; *pst* **safar**; *pres* **sofer**; *fut* **yeespor** *(p=f)*).

(le-en) sfor לאין־ספור *adj* countless.

sgalgal/-ah סגלגל *adj* oval; rotund.

sgan/-eet סגן *nmf* deputy; assistant; vice-.

sgan/-ey aloof/-eem סגן אלוף lieutenant-colonel.

sgan nasee סגן ־נשיא *nm* vice-president.

sgan rosh ha-memshalah סגן ראש הממשלה *nm* vice-premier; deputy prime-minister.

sgan/-ey sar/-eem סגן שר *nm* vice-minister; deputy-minister.

sganoo|t/-yot סגנות *nf* lieutenancy; deputation.

sgeed|ah/-ot סגידה *nf* worship; (*+of:* **-at**).

sgeer|ah/-ot סגירה *nf* closure; (*+of:* **-at**).

sgool|ah/-ot סגולה *nf* **1.** characteristic; **2.** remedy; (*+of:* **-at**).

◇ **('am) sgoolah** see ◇ **'am segoolah**.

(yekheedey) sgoolah יחידי סגולה *nm pl & adj pl* outstanding people.

sgoolee/-t סגולי *adj* specific.

(meeshkal) sgoolee משקל סגולי *nm* specific gravity.

(asef|at/-ot) sgoor|ah/-ot אסיפה סגורה *nf* closed meeting.

(yesheev|ah/-ot) sgoorah ישיבה סגורה *nf* closed session.

sgor! seegree! סגור ! סגרי ! *v imp sing m/f* close! shut! (*inf* **leesgor**; *pst* **sagar**; *pres* **soger**; *fut* **yeesgor**).

> **Sh**
> is a sound for which the Hebrew alphabet uses one letter, the consonant ש **Sheen**. Words beginning with **sh** will thus be found in the next chapter.

skandal/-eem סקנדל *nm* scandal.

skeel|ah/-ot סקילה *nf* stoning to death (ancient form of punishment); (*+of:* **-at**).

skeer|ah/-ot סקירה *nf* review; survey; glance; (*+of:* **-at**).

skeets|ah/-ot סקיצה *nf* sketch; (*+of:* **-at**).

skeptee/-t סקפטי *adj* sceptic; sceptical.

s'khakh סכך *nm* freshly cut branches with leaves for roofing a "Succah".

s'khakh|ah/-ot סככה *nf* shed; (*+of:* **-at**).

s'khar סחר *nm+of* trade of.

s'khar (*npr* **sakhar**) שכר *nm* remuneration.

s'khar 'avodah שכר עבודה *nm* wages; salary.

s'khar batalah שכר בטלה *nm* dole; attendance fee (for unemployed).

s'khar deerah שכר־דירה *nm* rent.

s'khar deerah moogan שכר־דירה מוגן *nm* controlled rent.

s'khar khaleefeen סחר־חליפין *nm* barter.

s'khar (*npr* **sakhar**) **khodshee** שכר חודשי *nm* monthly salary.

s'khar leemood שכר לימוד *nm* tuition fee.

s'khar leemood moodrag שכר לימוד מודרג *nm* graded school fees.

s'khar sofreem שכר סופרים *nm* royalties; author's fee.

s'khar teerkhah שכר טירחה *nm* fee.

s'khar yesod שכר יסוד *nm* basic pay.

(bee) s'khar בשכר *adv* **1.** (*npr* **be-sakhar**) for a fee; **2.** on account of.

(bee) s'khar (*npr* **be-sakhar**) **khodshee** בשכר חודשי *adv* **1.** for a monthly salary; for monthly wages; **2.** *adv [colloq.]* for a monthly rent (see **s'kheeroot khodsheet**).

(bee) s'khar khofshee בשכר חופשי *adv [colloq.]* against free (uncontrolled) rent see **s'kheeroot khofsheet**).

(darg|at/-ot ha)s'khar (*npr* **sakhar**) דרגת השכר *nf* wage scale.

(hagdalat) s'khar (*npr* **sakhar**) הגדלת שכר *nf* salary increase; increased pay.

(hakpa'at) s'khar (*npr* **sakhar**) הקפאת שכר *nf* wage freeze.

(halanat) s'khar (*npr* **sakhar**) הלנת שכר *nf* holding back wages.

(horad|at/-ot) s'khar (*npr* **sakhar**) הורדת השכר *nf* reduction in salary; reduced wages.

◇ **(khok la-haganat ha) s'khar (or sakhar)** see ◇ **khok la-haganat ha-sakhar**.

s'kharkhar/-ah סחרחר *adj* dizzy.

s'kharkhoret סחרחורת *nf* dizziness.

(ba/ba'ah 'al) s'khar|o/-ah בא/־ה על שכרו/־ה *v pst & pres* got his/her remuneration; (*fut* **yavo** *etc*).

(yatsa) s'khar|o/-ah be-hefsed|o/-ah יצא שכרו בהפסדו/ה *v* **1.** *lit* his/her loss exceeded his/her profit; **2.** did not prove worthwhile; (*pres* **yotse'** *etc; fut* **yetse'** *etc*).

s'khav|ah/-ot סחבה *nf* rug; mop; (*+of:* **-at**).

(bloy/-yey) s'khavot בלוי־סחבות *nm pl* worn-out rag.

s'kheer/-at שכיר *mf+of* hireling of.

s'kheer/-ey 'et שכיר עט *nm* hack-writer; hired journalist.

s'kheer/-ey kherev שכיר חרב *nm* mercenary.

s'kheer|ah/-ot שכירה *nf* hiring; renting; leasing; (*+of:* **-at**).

s'kheeroo|t/-yot שכירות *nf* lease; rent.

s'kheeroot khodsheet שכירות חודשית *nf* monthly rent; rent payable by the month.

s'kheeroot meeshneh שכירות משנה *nf* sublease; subtenancy.

s'kheeroot khofsheet שכירות חופשית *nf* free (uncontrolled) rent.

s'kheeroot moogenet שכירות מוגנת *nf* rent-protected tenancy.

(deerah bee) s'kheeroot דירה בשכירות *nf* rented apartment; rented flat.

(demey) s'kheeroot דמי שכירות *nm pl* rent.

(khoz|eh/-ey) s'kheeroot חוזה שכירות *nm* contract of lease.

(khozeh lee) s'kheeroot beeltee moogenet חוזה לשכירות בלתי־מוגנת *nf* contract of unprotected lease.

s'kheet|ah/-ot סחיטה *nf* extortion; (*pl+of:* **-at**).

s'kheev|ah/-ot סחיבה **1.** *nf* dragging; pulling; **2.** *nf [slang]* pinching; pilfering; (*+of:* **-at**).

s'khee|yah/-yot שחייה *nf* swimming; (*+of:* **-yat**).

(breykh|at/-ot) s'kheeyah בריכת שחייה *nf* swimming pool.

(leemood/-ey) s'kheeyah לימוד שחייה *nf* swimming instruction.

(shee'oor/-ey) s'kheeyah שיעור שחייה *nm* swimming lesson.

(takhroo|t/-yot) s'kheeyah תחרות שחייה *nf* swimming contest.

s'kheeyat gav שחיית גב *nf* back-stroke (swimming).

s'kheeyat khateerah שחיית חתירה *nf* crawl-stroke (swimming).

s'kheeyat parpar שחיית פרפר *nf* butterfly-stroke (swimming).

s'khoog סחוג *nm* spicy Yemenite sauce.

s'khoom/-eem סכום *nm* sum; (*pl+of:* **-ey**).

s'khoom kolel סכום כולל *nm* total amount.

s'khor-s'khor סחור סחור *adv* round about; round and round.

s'khor|ah/-ot סחורה *nf* merchandise; (*+of:* **-at**).

s'khoos סחוס *nm* cartilage.

slakh! seelkhee! סלח! סלחי! *v imp sing m/f* forgive! (*inf* **leeslo'akh;** *pst* **salakh;** *pres* **sole'akh;** *fut* **yeeslakh**).

slakh/seelkhee lee סלח לי! סלחי לי! *v imp sing m/f* please, forgive me!

sleed|ah/-ot סלידה *nf* aversion; disgust; (*+of:* **-at**).

sleekhah! סליחה! *interj* pardon! I beg your pardon.

◇ **sleekhot** סליחות *nf pl* past-midnight prayers held nightly before and after Rosh-haShanah, and on special occasions i.e. fast days.

sleel/-eem סליל *nm* spool; (*pl+of:* **-ey**).

sleelah סלילה *nf* paving; (*+of:* **-at**).

sleng סלנג *nm* slang.

(ba-derekh ha) sloolah בדרך הסלולה *adv* **1.** the customary way; **2.** *lit* : taking the paved path.

smadar סמדר *nm* (Semadar) blossom.

smakh! seemkhee! שמח! שמחי! *v imp sing m/f* rejoice! be glad!; (*inf* **leesmo'akh;** *pst* **samakh;** *pres* **same'akh;** *fut* **yeesmakh**).

('al) smakh על סמך *adv* on grounds of; on the basis of.

smalee/-t שמאלי *adj* **1.** left; left-handed; **2.** leftist.

(mekasher) smalee מקשר שמאלי *nm* left inside forward (soccer).

smalot שמלות *nf pl* (*sing:* **seemlah**) dresses; (*+of:* **seemlot**).

smartoot/-eem סמרטוט *nm* rag; cloth.

smartootar/-eem סמרטוטר *nm* junkman; scrap-dealer; (*pl+of:* **-ey**).

smartootee/-t סמרטוטי *adj [slang]* rotten.

smeekhah/-ot שמיכה *nf* blanket; (*+of:* **-at**).

smeekhoo|t/-yot סמיכות *nf* **1.** density; **2.** proximity.

smeekhoot ha-parasheeyot סמיכות הפרשיות *nf* juxtaposition.

smeekhoot le-rabanoot סמיכות לרבנות *nf* ordination as Rabbi.

smoking/-eem סמוקינג *nm* tuxedo; dinner jacket.

smol שמאל *nm* left (hand, side).

smolah שמאלה *adv* **1.** keep left; **2.** to the left of.

smolanee/-t שמאלני *adj* leftist.

smolanoot שמאלנות *nf* leftism.

sna|'ee/-'eem סנאי *nm* squirrel; (*pl+of:* **-'ey**).

snapeer/-eem סנפיר *nm* fin; bilge keel; (*pl+of:* **-ey**).

sneh סנה *nm* thornbush.

sneef/-eem סניף *nm* branch (of company, bank, organization); (*pl+of:* **-ey**).

□ **Sneer** (Senir) שניר *nm* kibbutz (est. 1967) in **Khoolah** Valley, 2 km E. of kibbutz Dan. Pop. 278.

snok|eret/-arot סנוקרת *nm* punch; sock.

snoonee|t/-yot סנונית *nf* swallow (bird); (*+of:* **-yat**).

sod/-ot סוד *nm* secret.

(be) sod בסוד *adv* secretly; confidentially.

sod|ah/-ot סודה *nf* soda.

sodee/-t סודי *adj* secret; clandestine.

sodee/-t be-yoter סודי ביותר *adj* top secret.

sodeeyoot סודיות *nf* secrecy.

(eesh/anshey) sodo/-dah אנשי סודו *nm* his/her confidant; man of trust.

so'en/-et סואן *adj* bustling.

so'er/-et סוער **1.** *adj* stormy; turbulent; **2.** *v pres* rages; storms; (*pst* **sa'ar;** *fut* **yees'ar**).

sof/-eem סוף *nm* end; (*pl+of:* **-ey**).

sof davar סוף דבר **1.** *adv* in the end; finally; **2.** *nm* epilogue.

sof pasook סוף פסוק *nm* **1.** end quote; **2.** *[slang]* and that is that.

sof/-ey shavoo'a' סוף שבוע *nm* weekend.

sof sof סוף סוף *adv* at last; anyway.

(ba) sof בסוף *adv* in the end.

(eyn) sof אין־סוף **1.** *nm* infinite; **2.** *adv* endlessly.

(le-va) sof לבסוף *adv* in the end.

sofee/-t סופי *adj* final.

sofeet סופית *adv* finally.

sofer/-et סופר *v* counts; (*pst* **safar;** *fut* **yeespor** *(p=f)*).

sof|er/-reem סופר *nm* writer; author; scribe; (*pl+of:* **sofrey**).

sof|eret/-rot סופרת *nf* authoress; woman-writer.

◇ **sof|er/-rey stam** סופר סת״ם *nm* religious scribe copying on parchment scrolls, in print-type letters, the complete text of the Torah (Pentateuch) as well as, on smaller slips of parchment, texts for placement in **Mezoozah** containers and phylactery boxes. **STaM** is an *acr of* **Seefrey-torah, Tefeeleen** (phylacteries), **Mezoozot** ספרי־תורה, תפילין, מזוזות.

(be) sofo shel davar בסופו של דבר *adv* ultimately.

soged/-et סוגד *v pres* worships; (*pst* **sagad;** *fut* **yeesgod**).

soger/-et סוגר *v pres* closes; (*pst* **sagar;** *fut* **yeesgor**).

sograyeem סוגריים *nm pl* brackets; parentheses; (Gram.).

(bet/batey) sohar בית־סוהר *nm* prison.

soher/-et סוהר *nmf* prison guard; (*pl:* **sohar|eem/-ot**).

soker/-et סוקר *v pres* reviews; scrutinizes; (*pres* **sakar;** *fut* **yeeskor**).

sokh|akh/-ekhah/-akhtee (*or:* **sokhe'akh**) שוחח *v* chatted; discussed; (*pres* **mesokhe'akh;** *fut* **yesokhakh**).

sokhekh/-eem סוכך *nm* parasol; sunshade; (*pl+of:* **ey**).

sokh|en/-neem סוכן *nm* agent; (*pl+of:* **-ney**).

sokhen/-et khasha'ee/-t סוכן חשאי *nmf* secret agent.

sokhen nose'a' סוכן נוסע *nm* travelling salesman.

sokhen/-et zar/-ah סוכן זר *nmf* foreign agent.

sokh|enet/-not סוכנת *nf* **1.** agent (female); **2.** housekeeper.

sokh|er/-areem סוחר *nm* merchant; (*pl+of:* **arey**).

sokher/-et be- סוחר ב־ *v pres* trades in; deals in; (*pres* **sakhar;** *fut* **yees'khor**).

sokher/-et שוכר *v pres* leases; rents; (*pst* **sakhar;** *fut* **yeeskor;** *(k=kh)*).

sokh|er/-reem שוכר *nm* hirer; lessee; tenant; (*pl+of:* **rey**).

◇ **sokher/-et moog|an/-enet** שוכר מוגן *nm* tenant protected under Rent Restriction laws.

('over/-et la) sokher עובר לסוחר *adj* accepted as legal tender.

(tsee ha) sokher צי הסוחר *nm* merchant fleet.

sokhnoo|t/-yot סוכנות *nf* agency.

◇ **sokhnoot** (or **ha-sokhnoot**) סוכנות or הסוכנות *nf (colloq. abbr.)* see ◇ **(ha)sokhnoot ha-yehoodeet.**

sokhnoot khadashot סוכנות חדשות *nf* news-agency; news-service.

sokhnoot yedee'ot סוכנות ידיעות *nf* news-agency; news-service.

◇ **(ha)sokhnoot ha-yehoodeet** הסוכנות היהודית *nf* the Jewish Agency i.e. the worldwide body whose purpose is repatriation of Jews to their homeland: Palestine. Organized in Zurich in 1929 under a League of Nations Mandate, it worked with the World Zionist Organization towards creating a Jewish State in Palestine and was internationally regarded as the prospective government of that state. Since the proclamation of the State of Israel in 1948 it has confined its activities to handling immigration, fundraising and financing successful absorption of immigrants into Israel.

sokhnoot nesee'ot סוכנות נסיעות *nf* travel agency.

solan/-eet סולן *nmf* soloist; (*pl:* **-eem/-eeyot;** *pl+of:* **-ey**).

soled/-et סולד *v pres* resents; shrinks from; (*pst* **salad;** *fut* **yeeslod**).

(af) soled אף סולד *nm* pug nose.

soleedareeyoot סולידאריות *nf* solidarity.

soleedee/-t סולידי *adj* solid.

solelah/-ot סוללה *nf* battery; (*+of:* **-at**).

solelah neet'enet סוללה נטענת *nf* rechargeable battery.

soler סולר *nm* diesel oil; heating oil.

solet סולת *nf* fine flour.

(kemakh) solet קמח סולת *nf* fine flour.

solo סולו *adv* solo.

somekh/-et סומך *v pres* relies on; (*pres* **samakh;** *fut* **yeesmokh**).

son|e'/-'eem שונא *nm* enemy; (*pl+of:* **-'ey**).

sone'/-t שונא *v pres* hates; (*pst* **sane';** *fut* **yeesna'**).

sone'/-t betsa' שונא בצע *adj* incorruptible; *lit.:* lucre-hating.

son|e'/-'ey yeesra'el שונא ישראל *nm* antisemite; Jew-hater.

soobseed|yah/-yot סובסידייה *nf* subsidy; (*+of:* **-yat**).

soodar/-eem סודר *nm* scarf; shawl; (*pl+of:* **-ey**).

soof סוף *nm* reed; bulrush.

□ **(Yam) Soof** see □ **Yam Soof.**

soof|ah/-ot סופה *nf* gale; storm.

soofganee|yah/-yot סופגנייה *nf* doughnut; standard pastry for Hanukkah.

soog/-eem סוג *nm* category; class; (*pl+of:* -'**ey**).
soog alef/bet/geemal *etc* סוג א'/ב'/ג' *adv* **1.** a/b/c *etc* quality; **2.** 1st/2nd/3rd *etc* class.
soog alef-alef סוג אלף־אלף *[colloq.] adj* top quality.
soog|yah/-yot סוגיה *nf* problem; (*+of:* **-yat**).
sook|ah/-ot סוכה *nf* booth; shed;
◇ **sook|ah/-ot** סוכה *nf* "Sukkah" - makeshift shed erected at Sukkot by each Jewish household. In it the festival is celebrated, to commemorate the flimsy structures that sheltered the Israelites during their 40-year wandering in the desert, from Egypt to the Promised Land. (*+of:* **-at**).
sook|am/-mah/-amtee סוכם *v* was summed up; was ageed upon; (*pres* **mesookam**; *fut* **yesookam**).
sookar/-eem סוכר *nm* sugar; (*pl+of:* **-ey**).
(kneh/-kney) sookar קנה סוכר *nm* sugar cane.
(selek) sookar סלק סוכר *nm* sugar beet.
sookaree|yah/-yot סוכרייה *nf* candy; sweet; (*+of:* **-yat**).
sookaree|yah/-yot 'al makel סוכרייה על מקל *nf* lollypop.
sookat gan סוכת גן *nf* garden-hut.
sookeret סוכרת *nf* diabetes (Medic).
◇ **sookot** סוכות *nm* "Sukkot" ("Sukkos" in Yiddish) Feast of Tabernacles (15-22 **Teeshrey**, sometime in October, 5 days after Yom Kippur). Throughout the festival, an observant Jew eats and spends time in a specially built shed called a **Sookah** (see above).
◇ **(khag ha) sookot** see ◇ **khag ha-sookot**.
sookrazeet סוכרזית *nm* synthetic sweetener.
sool|ak/-kah/-aktee סולק *v* was removed; was gotten rid of (*pres* **mesoolak**; *fut* **yesoolak**).
soolam/-ot סולם *nm* **1.** ladder; **2.** scale.
soolam 'adeefooyot סולם עדיפויות *nm* scale of priorities.
◇ **soolkh|ah/-ot** סולחה *(Arab.) nf* traditional (originally among Arabs) peace-making ceremony ending a feud between persons, families, tribes or communities (usually by agreeing upon some sort of compensation).
sooltan/-eem סולטן *nm* Sultan.
sool|yah/-yot סוליה *nf* sole; (*+of:* **-yat**).
sooma' סומא *nm* blind man.
(ke) sooma ba-aroobah כסומא בארובה *adv* blindfolded; like a blind man inside a chimney.
soom|am/-emah/-amtee סומם *v* was drugged; (*pres* **mesoomam**; *fut* **yesoomam**).
soom|an/-nah/-antee סומן *v* was marked; (*pres* **mesooman**; *fut* **yesooman**).
soomsoom סומסום *nm* sesame (Botan.).
soonee/-t סוני *adj* Sunni; pertaining to the Sunni sect in Islam.
soonee/-t סוני *nm* Sunni; follower of the Sunni rite in Islam.
soop|ar/-rah/-artee סופר *v* **1.** was told; **2.** was given a haircut; (*pres* **mesoopar**; *fut* **yesoopar**).
soor/-ee el|ay/-av/-eha *etc* סור אלי/־יו/־יה *v imp sing m/f* come in to see me/him/her *etc*; (*inf* **lasoor** *etc*; *pst & pres* **sar** *etc*; *fut* **yasoor** *etc*).
soor/-ee ha-tseedah סור הצידה *v imp sing m/f* step aside!
sooree/-t סורי *adj* Syrian.
sooree/-m סורי *nm* Syrian.
□ **sooryah** סוריה *nf* Syria.
◇ **sooryah ha-gedolah** סוריה הגדולה *nf* Greater Syria traditional dream of Arab nationalists for a Greater Syria to comprise also Israel, Jordan, Lebanon and, perhaps, Iraq.
soos/-ey revee'ah סוס רביעה *nm* stallion.
(ko'akh/kokhot) soos כוח־סוס *nm* horsepower; H.P.
sooverenee/-t סוברני *adj* sovereign.
soreg/-et סורג *v* knits; plaits; (*pst* **sarag**; *fut* **yeesrog**).
sor|eg/-geem סורג *nm* grid; bars; (*pl+of:* **-gey**).
sorer/-et סורר *adj* unruly; rebellious.
sotsyalee/-t סוציאלי *adj* social.
('oved/-et) sotsyalee/-t עובד סוציאלי *nmf* social worker; (*pl:* **'ovd|eem/-ot** *etc*).
('ezrah) sotsyaleet עזרה סוציאלית *nf* social aid; welfare.
sotsyaleezm סוציאליזם *nm* socialism.
sotsyaleest/-eet סוציאליסט *nmf* socialist.
sotsyaleestee/-eet סוציאליסטי *adj* socialist.
sotsyolog/-eet סוציולוג *nmf* sociologist.
sotsyologee/-t סוציולוגי *adj* sociological.
sova' שובע *nm* satiety; plenty.
(la) sova' לשובע *adv* (eat) to one's full.
(zolel ve) sove' זולל וסובא *adj* glutton and drunkard.
sovel/-et סובל *v pres* suffers; (*pst* **saval**; *fut* **yeesbol** *(b=v)*).
sovev/-ah/-vavtee סובב *v* circled; twisted around; (*pres* **mesovev**; *fut* **yesovev**).
sovlanee/-t סובלני *adj* tolerant.
sovlanoot סובלנות *nf* tolerance.
sovyetee/-t סובייטי *adj* Soviet.
soyah סויה *nf* soya.
◇ **spanyoleet** ספניולית *nf* Judeo-Spanish; Ladino-the "Lingua franca" of Jews of the Sephardi (Spanish) rite.
spetseefee/-t ספציפי *adj* specific.
sport/-eem ספורט *nm* sport.
sport|ay/-a'eem ספורטאי *nm* sportsman; athlete; (*pl+of:* **-a'ey**).
sporta'ee|t/-yot ספורטאית *nf* sportswoman; woman athlete.
sporteevee/-t ספורטיבי *adj* sporty; sportive.
(beegdey) srad בגדי שרד *nm pl* official uniform.
(deer|at/-ot) srad דירת שרד *nm* official residence; state-provided lodging.
srak סרק *(suffix) adj* futile; idle; pointless.
('atsey) srak עצי סרק *nm* barren (fruitless) trees.
(eeyoom/-ey) srak איום סרק *nm* empty threat.
(geenooney) srak גינוני סרק *nm pl* pretentious manners.
(kadoor/-ey) srak כדור סרק *nm* blank bullet.

(veekoo|'akh/-khey) srak ויכוח סרק *nm* futile, fruitless debate.

srar|ah/-ot שררה *nf* rule; power; authority; **(**+*of:* **-at)**.

(ahavat) srarah אהבת שררה *nf* lust for power.

srateem (*sing:* **seret)** סרטים *nm pl* **1.** films; movies; **2.** bands; tapes; **(***pl+of:* **sertey)**.

(makren/-ey) srateem מקרן סרטים *nm* movie projector; film projector.

sreek|ah/-ot סריקה *nf* combing; search of an area; (+*of:* **-at)**.

sreetah/-ot סריטה *nf* scratch; (+*of:* **-at)**.

sref|ah/-ot שריפה *nf* fire; (+*of:* **-at)**.

(avak) srefah אבק שריפה *nm* gunpowder.

srokh/-eem שרוך *nm* lace; shoestring; (*pl+of:* **-ey)**.

◇ **(keep|ah/-ot) sroog|ah/-ot** see ◇ **keepah sroogah**.

staglan/-eet סתגלן *nmf* opportunist.

staglanoot סתגלנות *nf* opportunism; knack for adjustment.

staj סטאז' *nf* **1.** training (for practicing law); **2.** internship (for physicians).

stajer/-eet סטז'ר *nmf* newly-graduated lawyer doing one's clerkship or physician doing one's internship.

stam סתם *adv* merely; mere; with no particular reason.

stam kakh סתם כך *adv* with no particular reason

(kakhah) stam ככה־סתם *adv* just like that.

(meen ha) stam מן הסתם *adv* probably.

◇ **(sof|er/-rey) stam** see ◇ **sof|er/-rey stam**, above.

stamee/-t סתמי *adj* vague; neutral.

standartee/-t סטנדרטי *adj* standard.

stanee/-t שטני *adj* diabolical.

stav/-eem סתיו *nm* autumn.

stavee/-t סתוי *adj* autumnal.

steem|ah/-ot סתימה *nf* **1.** obstruction; **2.** traffic jam; (+*of:* **-at)**.

steem|ah/-ot ba-shen סתימה בשן *nf* dental filling.

steer|ah/-ot סתירה *nf* contradiction; (+*of:* **-at)**.

steer|ah/-ot סטירה *nf* slap.

(bee) steerah בסתירה *adv* in contradiction to.

steerat/-ot lekhee סטירת לחי *nf* slap in the face.

stee|yah/-yot סטייה *nf* deviation; aberration; (+*of:* **yat)**.

stee|yah/-yot meenee|t/-yot סטייה מינית *nf* sexual deviation; perversion.

steereelee/-t סטרילי *adj* sterile.

stereeleezats|yah/-yot סטריליזציה *nf* sterilization.

steryo סטריאו *nm* stereo.

steyk/-eem סטייק *nm* steak.

stoodent/-eet סטודנט *nmf* university-student.

stsen|ah/-ot סצינה *nf [colloq.]* scene; (+*of:* **-at)**.

sva'/sve'at ratson שבע רצון *adj* pleased; content.

svakh/-eem סבך *nm* complication; tangle; brambles; (*pl+of:* **seevkhey)**.

svakh|ah/-ot סבכה *nf* grill; grate; shed; (+*of:* **-at)**.

svar|ah/-ot סברה *nf* version; supposition; (+*of:* **-at)**.

svarat/-ot keres (*npr* **kares)** סברת כרס *nf* baseless assumption.

sve'at ratson שבעת רצון *adj f* pleased; satisfied (see **sva' ratson**, above).

sveder/-eem סוודר *nm* sweater; pullover.

svee'at ratson (also: **svee'oot** *etc*) שביעת רצון or: שביעות־רצון *nf* contentment; satisfaction.

sveeloo|t/-yot סבילות *nf* passivity; tolerance.

svee'oot שביעות *nf* satisfaction; contentment.

svee'oot ratson שביעות רצון *nf* satisfaction; contentment.

sveeroo|t/-yot סבירות *nf* **1.** reasonableness; **2.** probability.

sveeroot gvohah סבירות גבוהה *nf* high probability.

sveeroot nemookhah סבירות נמוכה *nf* low probability.

sveev|ah/-ot סביבה *nf* environment; neighborhood; (+*of:* **-at)**.

sveevatee/-t סביבתי *adj* environmental.

(peegoor) sveevatee פיגור סביבתי *nm* environmenental retardation.

sveevon/-eem סביבון *nm* spinning top — standard Chanukkah (**Hanookah**) toy.

svooranee סבורני *v pres* I believe; I think; I consider.

syag/-eem סייג *nm* restriction; limitation; (*pl+of:* **-ey)**.

syakh/-eem סייח *nm* foal; colt; (*pl+of:* **-ey)**.

SH.

Note: **Sh** is a sound for which the Hebrew alphabet has a single letter, ש **(Sheen)**. In dotted Hebrew script, **Sheen** is either undotted or dotted over its right side (שׁ) and can thus be distinguished from **Seen** (שׂ), which is dotted over its left side and pronounced **S** (as in *sorry* or *system*). In everyday undotted script, no distinction is visible. As a convenience, then, we have grouped all Hebrew words beginning with **Sh** hereunder separately from those beginning with **S**.

sha|'ah/-'ot שעה *nf* hour; (*+of:* **she|'at/-'ot**).

sha|'ah/-'atah/-'eetee שעה *v* paid heed; (*pres* **sho'eh**; *fut* **yeesh'eh**).

sha'ah kalah שעה קלה *nf* a while; a few moments.

(be) sha'ah she בשעה ש־ *adv* while; when.

(be) sha'ah tovah! בשעה טובה! (greeting) Good luck!

(le-fee) sha'ahלפי שעה *adv* for the time being.

(mah ha) sha'ah? מה השעה? what time is it?

sha'af/-ah/-tee שאף *v* aspired; (*pres* **sho'ef**; *fut* **yeesh'af**).

sha'af (*etc*) **aveer** שאף אוויר *v* breathed in.

sha'ag/-ah/-tee שאג *v* roared; (*pres* **sho'eg**; *fut* **yeesh'ag**).

sha'al/-ah/-tee שאל *v* asked; borrowed; (*pres* **sho'el**; *fut* **yeesh'al**).

sha'al/she'aleem שעל *nm* step; (*pl+of:* **sha'ley**).

◇ **(af) sha'al** see ◇ **af sha'al**.

□ **Sha'al** (Sha'al) שעל *nm* coop. village (est. 1967) in the Golan Heights, 4 km W. of **Ramat Magsheemeem**.

□ **Sha'alveem** (Sha'alvim) שעלבים *nm* kibbutz in Ayalon Valley (est. 1951), 4 km NW of Latrun Junction **(Tsomet Latroon)**. Pop. 979.

sha'am שעם *nm* cork.

sha'an (*npr* **she'an**)/**-eem** שען *nm* watchmaker.

sha'anan/-ah שאנן *adj* serene; tranquil.

sha'ananoot שאננות *adj* serenity; tranquillity; nonchalance.

sha'ar/she'areem שער *nm* **1.** gate; **2.** rate of exchange; market-price; **3.** goal (soccer); (*pl+of:* **sha'arey**).

□ **Sha'ar Efrayeem** (Sha'ar Efrayim) שער אפרים *nm* village (est. 1953) on the so-called "Green Line", 3 km W. of **Toolkarem**. Pop. 342.

□ **Sha'arey Teekvah** (Sha'aré Tiqwa) שערי תקוה *nm* communal village in Samaria hills (est. 1983), 1 km W. of **Elkanah**, 7 km E. of **Rosh ha-'Ayeen**. Pop. 1,160.

□ **Sha'ar ha-Amakeem** (Sha'ar Ha'amakim) שער העמקים *nm* kibbutz (est. 1935), 1 km NE of **Keeryat Teev'on**. Pop. 627.

□ **Sha'ar ha-Golan** (Sha'ar ha Golan) שער הגולן *nm* kibbutz in Jordan Valley, 2 km SE of Zemah Junction **(Tsomet Tsemakh)**. Pop. 623.

□ **Sha'ar ha-Gay** שער הגיא *nm* entrance to valley in Judean hills (known widely also by its Arabic name **Bab-el-Wad**) through which the road passes from the coastal plain to Jerusalem. Scene of fierce 1947/8 battles over the control of the T.A.-Jerusalem highway (now Expressway 1), lifeline to the Capital.

□ **Sha'ar Menasheh** שער מנשה *nm* settlement for housing aged people and Holocaust survivors (est. 1949) by "Malben" (a J.D.C. Israel subsidiary), 3 km S. of 'Iron Junction **(Tsomet 'Eeron)**. Pop. 1,080.

sha'ar/-ey khaleefeen שער חליפין *nm* rate of exchange.

(ha) sha'ar patoo'akh השער פתוח the gate is open.

(ha) sha'ar sagoor השער סגור the gate is closed.

(heefk|ee'a'/-ee'ah/-a'tee) sha'ar/-ey הפקיע שער *v* raised the price of... (*pres* **mafkee'a'** *etc*; *fut* **yafkee'a'** *etc*).

(heevk|ee'a'/-ee'ah/-a'tee) sha'ar/she'areem הבקיע שער *v pst* scored a goal (soccer); (*pres* **mavkee'a'** *etc*; *fut* **yavkee'a'** *etc*).

sha'arooree|yah/-yot שערורייה *nf* scandal; (*+of:* **-yat**).

sha'ashoo|'a'/-'eem שעשוע *nm* play; distraction; (*pl+of:* **-'ey**).

('eeskey) sha'ashoo'eem עסקי שעשועים *nm pl* show-business.

sha'at/-ah/-etee שעט *v* trampled; (*pres* **sho'et**; *fut* **yeesh'at**).

sha'atayeem (*npr* **she'atayeem**) שעתיים *nf pl* two hours; a couple of hours.

◇ **sha'atnez** שעטנז *nm* mixture of linen and wool forbidden by Bible (Leviticus 19:19; Deuter.22:11) and under Rabbinical Law, to be woven, sewn or worn together.

sha'av/-ah/-tee שאב *v* drew; obtained; (*pres* **sho'ev**; *fut* **yeesh'av**).

sha'avah שעווה *nf* wax; (*+of:* **-at**).

sha'avaneet/-yot שעוונית *nf* oil cloth; linoleum.
shabab שבאב *nm [slang]* "the gang"; "the boys".
◇ **SHABAK** שב"ך *nm acr.* for **SHeroot Beetakhon Klalee** שרות בטחון כללי see ◇ **Sheen-Bet**.
shabat/-ot שבת *nf* Saturday; Sabbath.
◇ **"Shabat ha-Gadol"** שבת הגדול *nf* the last Saturday before Passover.
shabat kodesh שבת קודש *nf* the holy Sabbath.
shabat shalom! !שבת שלום customary pre-Sabbath and Sabbath greeting (both for greeter and greeted).
('erev/-'arvey) shabat/-ot ערב שבת *nm* Friday evening; eve of the Sabbath.
◇ **(kabalat) shabat** קבלת שבת *nf* **1.** Friday evening prayer; **2.** preparing for the Sabbath.
(kheelool) shabat חילול שבת *nm* desecration of the Sabbath.
(leyl/-ot) shabat ליל שבת *nm* Friday evening (Sabbath eve).
(moosaf/-eem shel) shabat מוסף של שבת *nm* weekend newspaper supplement (available Friday mornings).
(motsa'ey) shabat מוצאי שבת *nm pl* **1.** Saturday evening; **2.** (*lit.*) exit of the Sabbath.
◇ **('oneg) shabat** see ◇ **'oneg-shabat**.
◇ **(se'oodat/-ot) shabat** see ◇ **se'oodat/-ot shabat**.
◇ **(tefeelat) shabat** see ◇ **tefeelat shabat**.
(tset ha) shabat צאת השבת *nm* Saturday at nightfall; *(lit.)* exit of the Sabbath.
shabaton/-toneem שבתון *nm* work stoppage; rest from work; general strike; (*pl+of:* **-toney**).
(shenat/-ot) shabaton שנת שבתון *nf* Sabbatical year.
shablonah/-ot שבלונה *nf* stereotype; mold; (*+of:* **-at**).
shablonee/-t שבלוני *adj* trivial; trite.
shablool/-eem שבלול *nm* snail; (*pl+of:* **-ey**).
shabtay שבתאי *nm* Saturn (planet).
shad/-ayeem שד *nm* breast (of women); (*pl+of:* **shdey**).
shadad/-edah/-adetee שדד *v* robbed; pillaged; (*pres* **shoded**; *fut* **yeeshdod**).
shadar/-eem שדר *nm* broadcaster; announcer; (*pl+of:* **-ey**).
shadareet/-yot שדרית *nf* woman-broadcaster/announcer.
shaday שדי *nm* God; Almighty; (used in prayers).
shadayeem שדיים *nm pl* (*sing* **shad**) breasts (of women); (*+of:* **shdey**).
shadkhan/-eet שדכן *nmf* marriage broker; matchmaker; (*pl:* **-eem/-eeyot**; *pl+of:* **-ey**).
shadkhanoot/-yot שדכנות *nf* matchmaking; marriage brokerage.
□ **Shadmot Dvorah** (Shadmot Devora) שדמות דבורה *nm* village (est. 1939) in Lower Galilee, on road to Yavne'el, NE of **Kefar Tavor**. Pop. 366.
shadood/shedoodah שדוד **1.** *adj* robbed; pillaged; **2.** killed (by murderers).
shadoof/shedoofah שדוף *adj* blighted; scorched; empty.
shadran/-eet שדרן *nmf* broadcaster; (*pl+of:* **-ey**).
sha'elet שעלת *nf* whooping cough; (Medic.).
shafah/-ot שאפה *nf [slang] (Arab.)* beautiful girl.
shafa'/-'ah/-a'tee שפע *v* abounded; flowed; (*pres* **shofe'a'**; *fut* **yeeshpa'** *(p=f)*).
shafa' (etc) kheeyookheem שפע חיוכים *v* was all smiles.
shafakh/-khah/-akhtee שפך *v* poured; spilled; (*pres* **shofekh**; *fut* **yeeshpokh** *(p=f)*).
shafakh (etc) et leebo /-ah *etc* שפך את לבו *v* poured out his/her etc heart.
shafal/shefalah שפל *adj* mean; base.
shafan/shefaneem שפן *nm* rabbit; (*pl+of:* **-ey**).
shafat/-tah/-atetee שפט *v* tried; judged; sentenced; (*pres* **shofet**; *fut* **yeeshpot** *(p=f)*).
shafel/shefelah שפל *v pres* is humiliated, subdued; (*pst* **shafal**; *fut* **yeeshpal** *(p=f)*).
shafar/-rah/-artee שפר *v* was good, pleasing; (*pres* **shofer**; *fut* **yeeshpor** *(p=f)*).
□ **Shafeer** (Shafir) שפיר *nm* village in the **Shfelah** (est. 1949), 4 km SW of **Keeryat Mal'akhee**. Pop. 294.
shafoot/shefootah שפוט *adj* condemned; tried.
shafooy/shefooyah שפוי *adj* **1.** sound of mind; sane; **2.** sober; reasonable.
shagah/-tah/-eetee שגה *v* erred; made a mistake; (*pres* **shogeh**; *fut* **yeeshgeh**).
shagoor/shegoorah שגור *adj* routine; fluent.
shagreer/-eem שגריר *nm* ambassador; (*pl+of:* **-ey**).
shagreerah/-ot שגרירה *nf* ambassadress; (*+of:* **-at**).
shagreer (etc) meyookhad שגריר מיוחד *nm* envoy extraordinary.
shagreeroot/-yot שגרירות *nf* embassy.
shahah/-atah/-eetee שהה *v* stayed; lingered; (*pres* **shoheh**; *fut* **yeesh'heh**).
shaka'/-'ah/-a'tee שקע *v* sank; settled; (*pres* **shok'e'a'**; *fut* **yeeshka'**).
shaka' (etc) be-khovot שקע בחובות *v* sank deeply in debts.
(ha-shemesh) shak'ah השמש שקעה *v* the sun set.
shakad/-dah/-adetee שקד *v* concentrated; was diligent; (*pres* **shoked**; *fut* **yeeshkod**).
shakal/-lah/-altee שקל *v* weighed; considered; (*pres* **shokel**; *fut* **yeeshkol**).
shakal (etc) be-da'to/-ah/-ee *etc* שקל בדעתו *v* he/she/I *etc* was considering.
shakak/-ekah/-aktee שקק *v* bustled; (*pres* **shokek**; *fut* **yeeshkok**).
shakak (etc) khayeem שקק חיים *v* was full of life.
shakat/-tah/-atetee שקט *v* calmed down; (*pres* **shaket**; *fut* **yeeshkot**).

shakdan/-eet שקדן *nmf & adj* diligent, studious person.

shakdanoot שקדנות *nf* diligence; perseverence.

shaked/shked|eem שקד *nm* almond; (*pl+of:* **-ey**).

shaket/sheketah שקט *adj* quiet.

shakh ש״ח *nm* New Shekel; N.S.; (*acr of* **shekel khadash** ; שקל חדש *pl* **shkaleem khadasheem**).

shakhaf/sh'khafeem שחף *nm* seagull; (*pl+of:* **shakhafey**).

shakhak/sh'khak|eem שחק *nm* heaven; (*pl+of:* **shakhakey**).

shakhak/-ah/-tee שחק *v* crushed; pulverized; (*pres* **shokhek**; *fut* **yeeshkhok**).

shakh|akh/-ekhah/-akhtee שכח forgot; (*pres* **shokhe'akh**; *fut* **yeeshkakh**; *(k=kh)*).

shakh|akh/-ekhah/-shakotee שכך *v* subsided; quieted down; (*pres* **shakh**; *fut* **yashokh**).

shakh|an/-nah/-antee שכן *v* dwelt; (*pres* **shokhen**; *fut* **yeeshkon**; *(k=kh)*).

shakhar שחר *nm* **1.** dawn; **2.** meaning; sense.

('ad 'alot ha) shakhar עד עלות השחר *adv* till dawn; till sunrise.

(ayelet ha) shakhar איילת השחר *nf* dawn; morning star.

('eem) shakhar עם שחר *adv* at dawn.

(eyn) shakhar אין שחר nonsense; no truth whatever.

(khas|ar/-rat) shakhar חסר שחר *adj* absurd; senseless.

shakh|ar/-rah/-artee שחר *v* took interest in; (*pres* **shokher**; *fut* **yeeshkhar**).

shakhareet שחרית *nf* daily morning prayer.

shakhat שחת *nm* hay; fodder.

('arem|at/-ot) shakhat ערימת שחת *nf* haystack.

(shed/-ah mee)shakhat שד משחת *nmf* a "devil" of a person; someone extremely clever or mischievous.

shakhat/-ah/-etee שחט *v* slaughtered; (*pres* **shokhet**; *fut* **yeeshkhot**).

shakh|av/-vah/-avtee שכב *v* lay; lay down; (*pres* **shokhev**; *fut* **yeeshkav**; *(k=kh)*).

shakhav (*etc*) **'eem** שכב עם *v* slept with.

shakhav (*etc*) **leeshon** שכב לישון *v* went to bed.

shakhee'akh/-sh'kheekhah שכיח *adj* usual; frequent.

shakhefet שחפת *nf* tuberculosis (Medic.).

shakhen/shekhen|ah שכן *nmf* neighbor; (*pl:* **-eem/-ot**; *+of:* **-at/-ey**).

shakhen/shekhenah שכן *adj* neighboring.

shakhl|ah/-ot שחלה *nf* ovary; (*+of:* **-at**).

shakhlav/-eem שחלב *nm* orchid; (*pl+of:* **-ey**).

shakhmat שחמט *nm* chess.

shakhmata|y/-'eem שחמטאי *nm* chess-player; (*pl+of:* **ey**).

shakhook/shekhookah שחוק *adj* worn; tattered.

shakhoom/shekhoomah שחום *adj* dark-brown.

shakhoon/shekhoonah שחון *adj* parched; rainless; hot and dry.

shakhoot/shekhootah שחוט *adj* slaughtered.

shakhor/shekhorah שחור *adj* black.

shakhor 'al-gabey lavan שחור על־גבי לבן *adj* black on white.

shakhor mee-sh'khor שחור משחור *adv* blacker than black.

(panter/-eem) shakhor/shekhoreem פנתר שחור *nm* member of the "Black Panthers" movement (see ◇ **pantereem shekhoreem**)

(po'el/-po'aleem) shakhor/shekhoreem פועל שחור *nm* unskilled laborer.

(shook) shakhor שוק שחור *nm* black market.

(yom) shakhor יום שחור *nm* black letter day; day of misfortunes.

shakhreet שחרית *nf* daily morning prayer.

shakhtsan/-eet שחצן *nmf* insolent, arrogant person.

shakhtsanoot שחצנות *nf* arrogance; insolence.

shakhvanee|t/-yot שכבנית *[slang] nf* whore.

shakna|y (*npr* **sakna|y**)**/-'eem** שקנאי *nm* pelican; (*pl+of:* **-'ey**).

shakoo'a'/shekoo'ah שקוע *adj* immersed; absorbed (mentally); sunk.

shakood/shekoodah שקוד *adj* diligent; studious.

shakoof/shekoofah שקוף *adj* transparent.

shakool/-ah שכול *adj* bereaved of offspring; bereft of child.

◇ **(av/-ot) shakool/-eem** see ◇ **av shakool**.

◇ **(em/eemahot) shakool|ah/-ot** see ◇ **em shakoolah**.

shakool/shekoolah שקול *adj* balanced; poised.

◇ **(hor|eh/-eem) shakool/-eem** see ◇ **hor|eh/-eem shakool/-eem**.

shakran/-eet שקרן *nmf* liar; (*pl+of:* **-ey**).

◇ **"shakshookah"** שקשוקה *nf* popular North African dish: tomato slices fried in eggs.

shal|af/-fah/-aftee שלף *v* drew out (sword or weapon);unsheathed (*pres* **sholef**; *fut* **yeeshlof**).

shal|akh/-khah/-akhtee שלח *v* sent; dispatched; (*pres* **shole'akh**; *fut* **yeeshlakh**).

◇ **shalakh et 'amee!** ! שלח את עמי *v imp sing m* (slogan) Let my people go!

shalakh (*etc*) **yad** שלח יד *v* raised hand against; embezzled.

shalakh (*etc*) **yad be-nafsh|o/-ah** *etc* שלח יד בנפשו/־ה *v* committed suicide.

shalal שלל *nm* **1.** booty; **2.** abundance; (*+of:* **shlal**).

shal|al/-elah/-altee שלל *v* **1.** disapproved; negated; **2.** deprived; (*pres* **sholel**; *fut* **yeeshlol**).

shalam/-eem שלם *nm* paymaster (Army); (*pl+of:* **-ey**).

shalat (*also:* **shelat-rakhok**) שלט רחוק *nm* remote control device (for TV-set).

shal|at/-tah/-atetee שלט *v* ruled; controlled; mastered; (*pres* **sholet**; *fut* **yeeshlot**).

shalat (*etc*) **ba-matsav** שלט במצב *v* had situation in hand; had in control.

shalat (*etc*) **be-rookh|o/-ah/-etc** שלט ברוחו *v* controlled him/her etc -self; mastered his/her/etc temper.

shalav/shlab|eem *(b=v)* שלב *nm* **1.** stage; phase; **2.** rung of ladder; **(***pl+of:* **-ey).**
shald|ag/-ageem שלדג *nm* kingfisher; **(***pl+of:* **-egey).**
shalee'akh/shelee|kheem שליח *nm* **1.** emissary; messenger; **2.** an Israeli representing an Israeli institution or political party abroad; **(+***of:* **-akh/-khey).**
shaleesh/-eem שליש *nm* adjutant.
shaleeshoot שלישות *nf* adjutancy.
shaleet/-eem שליט *nm* ruler; **(***pl+of:* **-ey).**
shalekhet שלכת *nf* shedding of the tree leaves.
('aley) shalekhet עלי שלכת *nm* fallen leaves.
(be) shalekhet בשלכת *adj* defoliating; losing leaves (in autumn).
shalem/shlemah שלם *adj* whole; complete.
shalem/shlemah 'eem שלם עם *adj* fully in agreement with.
(baree/bree'ah) ve-shalem/shlemah בריא ושלם *adj* safe and sound.
(be-lev) shalem בלב שלם *adv* wholeheartedly.
shalev/shlevah שליו *adj* quiet; serene.
shalgon/-eem שלגון *nm* ice-cream cone; ice-cream brick; **(***pl+of:* **-ey).**
shal|hevet/-havot שלהבת *nf* flame.
shalmon|eem שלמונים *nm pl* bribe; **(***pl+of:* **-ey).**
shalom שלום *nm* peace; well-being; **(+***of:* **shlom).**
shalom! !שלום (greeting) Hello! Goodbye!
◇ **"shalom 'akhshav"** שלום עכשיו *nf* "Peace Now" protest movement advocating immediate negotiations with PLO to resolve Arab-Israeli conflict and withdrawal from all occupied territories.
shalom 'al|ekha!/-ayeekh שלום עליך/־יך (greeting) *sing m/f* peace be with you!
shalom 'aleykhem! !שלום עליכם (greeting) *sing & pl* greetings to you ! Peace be with you !
shalom lekha/lakh! !שלום לך/לך (greeting) *sing m/f* Goodbye to you!
shalom oo-vrakhah! *(v=b)* !שלום וברכה (greeting) customary response to "Shalom!"; (*lit.*) peace and blesssing!
shalom rav! !שלום רב (greeting) much peace (to you!).
('al|av/-eha ha) shalom עליו/עליה השלום may he/she rest in peace.
('aleykhem) shalom! !עליכם שלום response to **shalom 'aleykhem!**
(dreesh|at/-ot) shalom דרישת שלום *nf* regards (from or to someone).
(khas ve) shalom! !חס ושלום *interj* Heaven forbid!
(nose/-t) shalom נושא שלום *adj* bringing regards; carrying a peace message.
('os|eh/-ah) shalom עושה שלום **1.** *nmf* peacemaker; **2.** *adj* making peace; **3.** *v pres* makes peace; **(***pst* **'asah** *etc; fut* **ya'aseh** *etc).*
(shabat) shalom! !שבת שלום (greeting) a Sabbath of peace!
(shabat) shalom oo-mevorakh! !שבת שלום ומבורך (return-greeting) a peaceful and blessed Sabath!
(shof|et/-tey) shalom שופט שלום *nm* justice of the peace; magistrate.
shaloo'akh/shelookhah שלוח *adj* sent; dispatched.
shaloof/sheloofah שלוף *adj* unsheathed; drawn.
shalosh שלוש *num f* three; (3).
◇ **shalosh regaleem** שלוש רגלים *nm pl* the three "Pilgrimage Festivals": Passover, Pentecost and Tabernacles (in Hebrew: **pesakh** פסח, **shavoo'ot** שבועות, **sookot** סוכות).
shalpookhee|t/-yot שלפוחית *nf* vesicle.
shalpookheet ha-sheten שלפוחית השתן *nf* bladder.
shalshel|et/-a'ot שלשלת *nf* chain.
shalshelet yookhaseen שלשלת יוחסין *nf* family tree; pedigree; genealogy.
shalter/-eem שאלטר *nm [colloq.]* switch (Electr.).
shalv|ah/-ot שלווה *nf* quiet; serenity; **(+***of:* **-at).**
(taf|as/-sah/-astee) shalvah תפס שלווה *v* took a rest; **(***pres* **tofes** *etc; fut* **yeetpos** *etc p=f).*
□ **Shalvah** (Shalva) שלווה *nm* village (est. 1952) in **Lakheesh** District, 4 km S. of **Keeryat Gat.** Pop. 465.
sham שם *adv* there.
(ey) sham אי־שם *adv* somewhere.
(mee)sham? ?מי שם *query* who's there?
(poh va) sham פה ושם *adv* here and there.
shamah שמה *adv* **1.** to there; **2.** *[colloq.]* there.
sham|a'/-'ah/-a'tee שמע *v* heard; **(***pres* **shome'ea';** *fut* **yeeshma').**
shama' *(etc)* **be-kol** שמע בקול *v* heeded; obeyed.
sham|am/-emah **(***npr:* **shamem)** שמם *v* was laid waste; was desolate; **(***pres* **shomem;** *fut* **yesham).**
sham|an/-nah/-antee שמן *v* grew fat; **(***pres* **shamen;** *fut* **yeeshman).**
shama'oo|t/-yot שמאות *nf* assessing; evaluating.
sham|ar/-rah/-artee שמר *v* **1.** guarded; kept; **2.** observed; **(***pres* **shomer;** *fut* **yeeshmor).**
shamar *(etc)* **emooneem** שמר אמונים *v* remained faithful.
shamash/-eem שמש *nm* attendant; sexton; janitor; **(***pl+of:* **-ey).**
◇ **(ha)shamash** השמש *nm* the candle used to light candles each evening of Hanukkah.
sham|at/-tah/-atetee שמט *v* dropped; abandoned; **(***pres* **shomet;** *fut* **yeeshmot).**
sham|ay/-a'eem שמאי assessor; valuator; **(***pl+of:* **-a'ey).**
◇ **(bet) shamay** see ◇ **bet shamay.**
shamayeem שמיים *nm pl* sky; **(+***of:* **shmey).**
(keepat ha)shamayeem כיפת השמיים *nf* sky; dome of Heaven.
(la) shamayeem לשמיים *adv* towards the sky.
(le-shem) shamayeem לשם שמיים *adv* for the sake of Heaven i.e. unselfishly.

(rakhamey) shamayeem רחמי שמיים *nm pl* Heaven's mercy.

(shomoo) shamayeem! שומו שמיים! *interj* Oh! Heavens!

(takhat keepat ha) shamayeem תחת כיפת השמיים *adv* under the open sky, i.e. with no roof over one's head.

(yeer'at) shamayeem יראת שמיים *nf* fear of God.

(yere/-'at) shamayeem ירא שמיים *adj* God-fearing.

shamaymee/-t שמימי *adj* heavenly; celestial.

shameer שמיר *nm* flint; emery.

□ **Shameer** (Shamir) שמיר *nm* kibbutz (est. 1944) in **Khoolah** Valley, 9 km SE of **Keeryat Shmonah**. Pop. 541.

shameesh/shmeeshah שמיש *adj* serviceable; usable.

shamen/shmenah שמן *adj* fat; plump.

sham|enet/-anot שמנת *nf* cream (sour).

shamenet metookah שמנת מתוקה *nf* cream; sweet cream.

shamnoonee/-t שמנוני *adj* greasy; slightly oily.

shamoor/shemoorah שמור *adj* reserved; guarded; kept.

shamoot/shemootah שמוט *adj* turned aside; dislocated.

(leevney) shamootee לבני שמוטי *nf* "Shamootee" bricks a type of fireproof bricks.

(tapoozey) shamootee תפוזי שמוטי *nm pl* oranges of the "Shamootee" variety

shamot שמות *nf pl* devastation; havoc.

('as|ah/-tah/-eetee) shamot עשה שמות *v* devastated; created havoc; (*pres* **'oseh** *etc; fut* **ya'aseh** *etc*).

shampanyah שמפניה *nf* champagne.

shampoo/-'eem שמפו *nm* shampoo.

shamran/-eet שמרן *nmf* conservative.

shamranee/-t שמרני *adj* conservative.

(meefleget ha) shamraneem מפלגת השמרנים *nf* the Conservative Party (in England).

shamranoo|t/-yot שמרנות *nf* conservatism.

shan|ah/-eem שנה *nf* year; (*+of:* **shn|at/-ot**).

◇ **shanah me'ooberet** שנה מעוברת *nf* leap year (that has 13 lunar Jewish calendar months).

shanah tovah! שנה טובה! (greeting) Happy New Year! (Rosh-ha-Shana eve greeting).

(ba) shanah she-'avrah בשנה שעברה *nf* last year.

(ha) shanah השנה *adv* this year.

(ha) shanah ha-ba'ah השנה הבאה *nf* next year.

(le) shanah לשנה *adv* **1.** per annum; **2.** for a year's time.

◇ **(le)shanah tovah teekatevoo!** see ◇ **le-shanah tovah teekatevoo!**

◇ **(le)shanah tovah tekhatemoo!** see ◇ **le-shanah tovah teekatevoo ve-tekhatemoo!**

(loo|'akh/-khot) shanah לוח שנה *nm* calendar.

(mal'ah) shanah מלאה שנה *v* it has been a year.

◇ **(rosh ha) shanah** see ◇ **rosh ha-shanah.**

(tokh) shanah תוך שנה *adv* within a year.

(yom ha) shanah יום השנה *nm* **1.** anniversary; **2.** jahrzeit (**"Yortsayt"**).

shana|y/-'eem שנאי *nm* transformer (Electr.); (*pl+of:* **-'ey**).

(mal'oo lo/la/lee *etc...*) **shaneem** מלאו לו/לה/לי... שנים he/she/I etc is/am ... years old.

shanee שני *nm* scarlet; crimson.

(khoot ha) shanee חוט השני *nm* basic thread; principal motif.

shaneet שנית *nf* scarlet fever; (Medic.).

shanen/-ee le-'atsm|ekha/-ekh שנן לעצמך! *v imp sing m/f* **1.** (*lit.*) repeat to yourself! **2.** do remember, please! (*pst* **sheenen** *etc; pres* **meshanen** *etc; fut* **yeshanen** *etc*).

shanoon/shenoonah שנון *adj* sharp-witted; clever, witty.

shanooy/shenooyah be-makhloket שנוי במחלוקת *adj* controversial.

shans|ah/-ot שאנסה *nf [colloq.]* chance.

sha'on שאון *nm* noise; (*+of:* **she'on**).

sha'on/she'oneem שעון *nm* **1.** clock; **2.** watch; (*pl+of:* **-ey**).

sha'on (*etc*) **deegeetalee** שעון דיגיטלי *nm* digital watch.

sha'on me'orer שעון מעורר *nm* alarm clock.

sha'ool/she'oolah שאול *adj* borrowed.

sha'oon/she'oonah שעון *adj* leaning; leaned against.

sha'oov/she'oovah שאוב *adj* derived; drawn (water).

sha'ot nosafot שעות נוספות *nf* overtime hours; (*sing:* **sha'ah nosefet**).

shapa'at שפעת *nf* influenza; flu; grippe.

shapeer/-ah שפיר **1.** *adj* fine; good; **2.** *adv* well.

shapoodeem (*sing:* **shapood**) שפודים *nm pl* **1.** skewers; spits; **2.** *[colloq.]* knitting needles; (*pl+of:* **-ey**).

shar/-ah/-tee שר *v* sang; (*pres* **shar**; *fut* **yasheer**).

shar|ah/-tah/-eetee שרה *v* soaked; (*pres* **shoreh**; *fut* **yeeshreh**).

shar|ak/-kah/-aktee שרק *v* whistled; (*pres* **shorek**; *fut* **yeeshrok**).

sharat/-eem שרת *nm* janitor; attendant (in a public institution).

sharav שרב *nm* heat wave; **"khamseen"**.

shareer/shreerah שריר *adj* firm; subsisting; in force.

shareer/shreerah ve-ka|yam/-yemet שריר וקיים *adj* firm and abiding.

(klee/kley) sharet כלי שרת *nm* tool.

□ **Sharon** שרון *nm* central district of Israel stretching from Mediterranean Coast 14-20 km East to "Green Line", and from the Carmel hills in the N. 80 km S. to the **Yarkon** River.

□ **Sharonah** שרונה *nm* village (est. 1938) in Lower Galilee, 5 km NE of Kefar Tabor. Pop. 411.

sharooy/sherooyah שרוי *adj* **1.** living; **2.** drenched.

sharsh|eret/-arot (*also:* **-era'ot**) שרשרת *nf* chain.

□ **Sharsheret** שרשרת *nm* village (est. 1951) in NW Negev, 2 km S. of **Neteevot**. Pop. 306.

sharveet/-eem שרביט *nm* baton; sceptre; (*pl+of:* **-ey**).

sharvool/-eem שרוול *nm* sleeve; (*pl+of:* **-ey**).

◇ **shashleek (or sheeshleek)** ששליק *nm [colloq.]* shish-kebab.

shasoo'a'/shesoo'ah שסוע *adj* cleft; split.

shastom/-eem שסתום *nm* valve; (*pl+of:* **-ey**).

shat/-ah שט *adj* sailing; rowing.

shat/-ah/-etee שט *v* sailed; rowed; (*pres* **shat**; *fut* **yashoot**).

□ **(Kele') Shatah** see □ **Kele' Shatah**.

shat|ah/-etah/-eetee שתה *v* drank; (*pres* **shoteh**; *fut* **yeeshteh**).

shatah (*etc*) **le-khayeem** שתה לחיים *v* toasted (wirh a drink).

shat|af/-fah/-aftee שטף *v* washed away; rinsed; (*pres* **shotef**; *fut* **yeeshatef**).

shat|ak/-kah/-aktee שתק *v* kept silent; (*pres* **shotek**; *fut* **yeeshtok**).

shat|akh/-khah/-akhtee שטח *v* laid out; extended; (*pres* **shote'akh**; *fut* **yeeshtakh**).

shat|al/-lah/-altee שתל *v* planted seedling; (*pres* **shotel**; *fut* **yeeshtol**).

shat|at/-etah/-atetee שתת *v* flowed; dripped; (*pres* **shotet**; *fut* **yeeshtot**).

shatat (*etc*) **dam** שתת דם *v* bled.

shatee'akh/sheteekheem שטיח *nm* carpet; (*pl+of:* **-ey**).

shatee'akh (*etc*) **parsee/-yeem** שטיח פרסי *nm* Persian rug; Persian carpet.

shatkan/-eet שתקן *adj* silent; reticent.

□ **(meenzar ha) shatkaneem** see □ **meenzar ha-shatkaneem**.

shatkanoot שתקנות *nf* reticence.

shatoo'akh/shetookhah שטוח *adj* flat.

shatoof/shetoofah שטוף *adj* **1.** flooded; **2.** addicted to.

shatool/shetoolah שתול *adj* planted.

shatooy/shetooyah שתוי *adj* drunk; intoxicated.

shatyan/-eet שתיין *nmf* drunkard.

shav/-ah/-tee שב *v* returned; came back; (*pres* **shav**; *fut* **yashoov**).

shav (*etc*) **lee-tekheeyah** שב לתחייה *v pres* was resurrected; came back to life.

(kheshbon 'over va) shav חשבון עובר ושב *nm* current bank account.

shav שווא **1.** *adv* in vain; **2.** *nm* lie; false.

(az'ak|at/-ot) shav אזעקת שווא *nm* false alarm.

(la) shav לשווא *adv* in vain.

(meeksam) shav מקסם שווא *nm* illusion.

(shemoo|'at/-'ot) shav שמועת שווא *nf* false rumor.

(shevoo|'at/-'ot) shav שבועת שווא *nf* false oath; perjury.

shav|ah/-tah/-eetee שבה *v* captured; (*pres* **shoveh**; *fut* **yeeshbeh** (*b=v*)).

shav|ak/-kah/-aktee khayeem שבק חיים *v* passed away; (*pres* **shovek** *etc*; *fut* **yeeshbok** *etc b=v*).

shav|ar/-rah/-artee שבר *v* broke; (*pres* **shover**; *fut* **yeeshbor** (*b=v*)).

shav|at/-tah/-atetee שבת *v* went on strike; ceased work; (*pres* **shovet**; *fut* **yeeshbot** (*b=v*)).

shavats שבץ *nm* apoplexy.

shav|eh/-ah שווה **1.** *v pres* is equal; is worth; (*pst* **shavah**; *fut* **yeeshveh**) **2.** *adj* worth; equal.

shaveh be-shaveh שווה בשווה *adv* in equal shares.

shav|eh/-ah le-khol (*kh=k*) **nefesh** שווה לכל נפש *adj* suitable for everyone.

(lo) shav|eh/-ah לא שווה *v pres* isn't worth it; isn't worthwhile.

(lo) shav|eh/-ah prootah לא שווה פרוטה *adj* not worth a penny.

(ha-tsad ha) shaveh הצד השווה *nm* common characteristic; analogy.

shaveer/sheveerah שביר *adj* breakable; fragile.

(kokh|av/-vey) shaveet כוכב שביט *nm* comet.

□ **Shavey Shomron** (Shave' Shomeron) שבי שומרון *nm* communal settlement (est. 1978) in Samarian hills, 10 km NW of Nablus (**Shekhem**). Pop. 476.

□ **Shavey Tseeyon** (Shave' Ziyyon) שבי ציון *nm* coop. village (est. 1938) on Galilee Coast, 2 km S. of Nahariyya. Pop. 672.

shavoo|'a'/-'ot שבוע *nm* week; (*+of:* **shvoo|'a'/-'ot**).

shavoo'a' tov! שבוע טוב! (greeting) a good week! - traditional greeting used on Saturday evening, on the threshold of a new week.

shavoo'a' tov oo-mevorakh! שבוע טוב ומבורך! (return-greeting) a good and blessed week! - customary reply to "**shavoo'a' tov!**".

(ba) shavoo'a' ha-ba' בשבוע הבא *adv* next week.

(ha) shavoo'a' השבוע *adv* this week; this very week.

(ha) shavoo'a' she-'avar השבוע שעבר *nm* last week.

(ka-'avor) shavoo'a' כעבור שבוע *adv* a week later.

(tokh) shavoo'a' תוך שבוע *adv* within a week; within one week.

shavoo'ot שבועות **1.** *nm pl* weeks; **2.** *nm* the Pentecost holiday.

◇ **(khag ha) shavoo'ot** see ◇ **khag ha-shavoo'ot**.

shavoor/shevoorah שבור *adj* broken.

shavooy/shevooyah שבוי *nm* prisoner; captive; (*+of:* **shevoo|y/-yat**; *pl+of:* **-yey/-yot**).

shavsh|evet/-avot שבשבת *nf* weather vane; vane.

shay שי *nm* gift.

sha|yakh/-yekhet שייך **1.** *adj* belonging; **2.** *v pres* belongs to.

shayakh (*etc*) **le-** שייך ל- *v pres* belongs to *[colloq.] pst* **heeshtayekh le-**; *fut* **yeeshtayekh le-**).

(zeh lo) shayakh זה לא שייך *adj* does not apply here; doesn't belong.

shayar|ah/-ot שיירה *nf* caravan; convoy; (*+of:* **shayeret**).

shaykhoo|t/-yot שייכות *nf* belonging; appurtenance; connection.

(en la-zeh kol) shaykhoot אין לזה כל שייכות it has no connection whatever.

shayeesh שיש *nm* marble.

shayeet שיט *nm* sailing; rowing; (*+of:* **sheyt**).

(klee/kley) shayeet כלי שיט *nm* sea-craft.

shay|etet/-atot שייטת *nf* flotilla.

shazoof/shezoofah שזוף *adj* tanned; sunburned.

shazoor/shezoorah שזור *adj* interwoven; intertwined.

□ **Shdemah** (Shedema) שדמה *nm* village (est. 1954) in Coastal Plain, 4 km NW of **Gederah**. Pop. 209.

shdool|ah/-ot שדולה *nm* lobby (politics); (*+of:* **-at**).

she- -ש (prefixed relative pronoun) which; that; who.

('ad) she- -עד ש *(prefix)* until; till such time.

(af) she- -אף ש *(prefix)* although.

(af 'al pee) she- -אף על פי ש *(prefix)* notwithstanding that; although.

('al) she- -על ש *(prefix)* because; on account of.

(bee-khdey) she- -בכדי ש *(prefix)* in order that.

(ela) she- -אלא ש *(prefix)* but; however.

(heykhan) she- -היכן ש *(prefix)* where; wherever.

(ke) she- -כש *(prefix)* when.

(keyvan) she- -כיוון ש *(prefix)* since; for.

(leefney) she- -לפני ש *(prefix)* before (time).

(lee-khe) she- -לכש *(prefix)* when.

(mee) she- -משׁ *(prefix)* as soon as.

(mee-kedey) she- -מכדי ש *(prefix)* than needed for.

(mee-kevan) she- -מכיוון ש *(prefix)* because; for the reason that.

(mee-leefney) she- -מלפני ש *(prefix)* prior to; from before.

(mee-peney) she- -מפני ש *(prefix)* because.

(mee-shoom) she- -משום ש *(prefix)* because; on account of.

she'aftan/-eet שאפתן *adj & nmf* ambitious (person).

she'aftanoo|t/-yot שאפתנות *nf* ambition.

she'ag|ah/-ot שאגה *nf* roar; (*+of:* **sha'agat**).

she'an/-eem שען *nm* watchmaker; (*pl+of:* **-ey**).

she'anoot שענות *nf* watchmaking.

she'ar שאר *nm* remainder.

she'ar roo'akh שאר רוח *nm* excellence; nobility; inspiration.

(beyn ha) she'ar בין השאר *adv* inter alia; among other things.

(hafka|'at/-'ot) she'areem הפקעת שערים *nf* profiteering; overcharging.

(mafkee|'a'/-'ey) she'areem מפקיע שערים *nm* profiteer.

□ **(Me'ah) She'areem** see □ **Me'ah She'areem**.

□ **She'ar Yashoov** (She'ar Yashuv) שאר ישוב *nm* village (est. 1940) in N. of **Khoolah** Valley, 7 km E. of **Keeryat Shmonah**. Pop. 255.

she'at nefesh שאט נפש *nm* disgust.

she|'at/-'ot שעת... *nf* the hour of...

she'at kheroom שעת חירום *nf* emergency.

she'at kosher שעת כושר *nf* opportunity; propitious time.

(bee) she'at בשעת *adv* **1.** (*lit.*) in the hour of; during; **2.** at the time of.

(bee) she'at ha-dekhak בשעת הדחק *adv* in case of extreme need.

(bee) she'at ha-penay בשעת הפנאי *adv* in a moment of leisure.

(bee) she'at ha-tsorekh בשעת הצורך *adv* if need be.

(bee) she'at ma'aseh בשעת מעשה *adv* on the spot; in the very act of.

she-'avar שעבר *adj* last; past.

(le) she-'avar לשעבר *adj & adv* former; formerly; previously.

(ba-shavoo'a) she-'avar בשבוע שעבר *adv* last week.

(ha-shanah) she-'avrah השנה שעברה *nf* last year.

shed/-eem שד *nm* demon; devil; (*pl+of:* **-ey**).

shed|ah/-ot שדה *nm* female demon; she-devil; (*+of:* **-at**).

shed/-ah mee-shakhat שד משחת *nmf* a "devil" of a person; someone devilishly energetic or crafty.

□ **Shedemah** see □ **Shdemah**.

shedool|ah/-ot שדולה *nm* lobby (politics); (*+of:* **-at**).

sheder/shdareem שדר *nm* message.

shee'abood/-eem שעבוד *nm* mortgage; pledge; bondage.

shee'am|em/-emah/-amtee שעמם *v* bored; (*pres* **mesha'amem**; *fut* **yesha'amem**).

shee'amoom/-eem שעמום *nm* boredom; (*pl+of:* **-ey**).

shee'arookh שערוך *nm* revaluation.

shee'ash|a' (or: **shee'ash|e'a'**)/**-'ah/-a'tee** שיעשע *v* amused; (*pres* **mesha'ashe'a'**; *fut* **yesha'ashe'a'**).

sheeb|e'akh/-khah/-akhtee שיבח *v* praised; lauded; extolled; (*pres* **meshabe'akh**; *fut* **yeshabe'akh**).

shee'bed/-dah/-adetee שעבד *v* mortgaged; bonded; (*pres* **mesha'bed**; *fut* **yesha'bed**).

sheeber/-eem שיבר *nm [colloq.]* master water-tap; main faucet.

sheeb|esh/-shah/-ashtee שיבש *v* disrupted; (*pres* **meshabesh**; *fut* **yeshabesh**).

sheeb|ets/-tsah/-atstee שיבץ *v* adjusted; laid in; filled in; (*pres* **meshabets**; *fut* **yeshabets**).

□ **Sheeboleem** (Shibbolim) שבלים *nm* village in the NW Negev, 3 km S. of ha-Gaddi Junction (**Tsomet ha-Gadee**). Pop. 279.

sheebol|et/-eem שיבולת *nf* ear of corn; spike; (*pl+of:* **-ey**).
sheebol|et/-ot שיבולת *nf* shibboleth; current (of river) vortex; (*pl+of:* **-ey**).
sheebolet-shoo'al שיבולת שועל *nf* oats.
sheeboosh/-eem שיבוש *nm* disruption; distortion; blunder; error; (*pl+of:* **-ey**).
sheeboots/-eem שיבוץ *nm* setting; grading; interweaving; (*pl+of:* **-ey**).
sheed|ah/-ot שידה *nf* dresser; (*+of:* **-at**).
sheed|afon שידפון *nm* blight.
sheed|ekh/-khah/-akhtee שידך *v* matched; brought together (*pres* **meshadekh;** *fut* **yeshadekh**).
sheed|el/-lah/-altee שידל *v* coaxed; persuaded; solicited; (*pres* **meshadel;** *fut* **yeshadel**).
sheed|er/-rah/-artee שידר *v* broadcast; (*pres* **meshader;** *fut* **yeshader**).
sheedookh/-eem שידוך *nm* match; marriage-combination (*pl+of:* **-ey**).
sheedool/-eem שידול *nm* persuasion; coaxing; (*pl+of:* **-ey**).
sheedool (*etc*) **lee-dvar 'averah** שידול לדבר עבירה *nm* abetting; instigating to commit a crime.
sheedool (*etc*) **lee-znoot** שידול לזנות *nm* soliciting (prostitution).
sheedoor/-eem שידור *nm* broadcast; (*pl+of:* **-ey**).
sheedoor (*etc*) **khozer** שידור חוזר *nm* re-broadcast.
sheedoor/-ey radyo שידור רדיו *nm* radio broadcast.
sheedoor/-ey televeezyah שידור טלוויזיה *nm* television broadcast.
(nay|edet/-adot) sheedoor ניידת שידור *nf* mobile broadcasting unit.
(rashoot ha) sheedoor רשות השידור *nm* Israel Broadcasting Authority.
(takhan|at/-ot) sheedoor תחנת שידור *nf* broadcasting station.
sheedoorey yeesra'el שידורי ישראל *nm pl* Israel broadcasting transmissions.
('amood ha) sheedrah עמוד השידרה *nm* spinal column.
(khoot ha) sheedrah חוט השידרה *nm* spinal cord.
◇ **shee'eem** שיעים *nm pl* (*sing:* **Shee'ee**) Shiites Muslim sect particularly dominant in Iran, Syria, and Lebanon.
she'eel|ah/-ot שאילה *nf* borrowing; (*+of:* **-at**).
she'eelt|ah/-ot שאילתה *nf* interpellation; (*+of:* **-at**).
shee|'er/-'arah/-'artee שיער *v* surmised; assumed; (*pres* **mesha'er;** *fut* **yesha'er**).
she'eev|ah/-ot שאיבה *nf* drawing (pumping) water from a well; deriving; (*+of:* **-at**).
sheef|'ah שפעה *nf* plenty, multitude (*+of:* **-'ot**).
sheefkhah/shfakhot שפחה *nf* maid; female slave; (*+of:* **-t**).
sheefloo|t/-yot שפלות *nf* baseness; meanness.
sheepoot/-eem שיפוט *nm* jurisdiction.
sheepootee/-t שיפוטי *adj* judicial; jurisdictional.
sheefsh|ef/-efah/-aftee שיפשף *v* rubbed; scrubbed; (*pres* **meshafshef/-fut yeshafshef**).
sheefshoof שפשוף *nm* **1.** rubbing; abrasion; **2.** *[slang]* being put through the mill (in the Army);.
sheeg|a'/-'ah/-a'tee שיגע *v* drove mad; (*pres* **meshage'a';** *fut* **yeshaga'**).
sheeg|a'on/-'onot שיגעון *nm* madness.
sheega'on שיגעון *adv* *[slang]* something wonderfully exciting.
sheegaron שיגרון *nm* rheumatism (Medic.).
(kadakhat ha) sheegaron קדחת השיגרון *nf* rheumatic fever.
sheeg|e'a'/-'ah/-a'tee שיגע *v* drove mad; (*pres* **meshage'a';** *fut* **yeshage'a'**).
sheeg|er/-rah/-artee שיגר *v* dispatched; sent; (*pres* **meshager;** *fut* **yeshager**).
sheegoo|'a'/-'eem שיגוע *nm* driving one mad; (*pl+of:* **-'ey**).
sheegoor/-eem שיגור *nm* launching; sending; (*pl+of:* **-ey**).
sheegrah/-ot שגרה *nf* routine; (*+of:* **-at**).
sheegratee/-t שגרתי *adj* routine; habitual.
shee|hek/-hakah/-haktee שיהק *v* hiccoughed; (*pres* **meshahek;** *fut* **yeshahek**).
sheehook/-eem שיהוק *nm* hiccough; hiccup; (*pl+of:* **-ey**).
sheek|a'/-e'ah/-a'tee (*also:* **sheek|e'a'**) שיקע *v* immersed; inserted; (*pres* **meshake'a';** *fut* **yeshaka', yeshake'a'**).
sheekaron שיכרון *nm* intoxication; inebriation; (*+of:* **sheekhron;** *(kh=k)*).
sheek|ef/-fah/-aftee שיקף *v* reflected; (*pres* **meshakef;** *fut* **yeshakef**).
sheek|ekh/-'khah/-akhtee שיכך *v* calmed; appeased; (*pres* **meshakekh;** *fut* **yeshakekh**).
sheek|em/-mah/-amtee שיקם *v* rehabilitated; restored; (*pres* **meshakem;** *fut* **yeshakem**).
sheek|en/-nah/-antee שיכן *v* housed; provided housing; (*pres* **meshaken;** *fut* **yeshaken**).
sheek|er/-rah/-artee שיקר *v* lied; deceived; (*pres* **meshaker;** *fut* **yeshaker**).
sheek|er/-rah/-artee שיכר *v* made one drink; intoxicated; (*pres* **meshaker;** *fut* **yeshaker**).
sheek|ets/-tsah/-atstee שיקץ *v* abhorred; detested; (*pres* **meshakets;** *fut* **yeshakets**).
sheekh|ed/-adah/-adetee שיחד *v* bribed; (*pres* **meshakhed;** *fut* **yeshakhed**).
sheek'kh|ah/-ot שיכחה *nf* oblivion; forgetfulness; (*+of:* **-at**).
sheekhlool/-eem שכלול *nm* improvement; perfection; (*pl+of:* **-ey**).
sheekhmeeyah/-ot שכמייה *nf* cape (garment).
sheekhn|a'/-e'ah/-a'tee שיכנע *v* convinced; (*pres* **meshakhne'a';** *fut* **yeshakhne'a'**).
sheekhnoo|'a'/-'eem שיכנוע *nm* persuasion; (*pl+of:* **-'ey**).
sheekhood/-eem שיחוד *nm* bribing; (*pl+of:* **-ey**).

sheekhpool/-eem שכפול *nm* mimeographing; duplicating; (*pl+of:* **-ey**).

(mekhon|at/-ot) sheekhpool מכונת שכפול *nf* duplicating machine.

sheekhr|er/-erah/-artee שחרר *v* freed; liberated; (*pres* **meshakhrer;** *fut* **yeshakhrer**).

sheekhroor/-eem שחרור *nm* liberation; (*pl+of:* **-ey**).

◇ **(meelkhemet ha) sheekhroor** see ◇ **meelkhemet ha-sheekhroor.**

sheekhroot שכרות *nf* drunkenness; addiction to liquor.

sheekhsh|ekh/-ekhah/-akhtee שיכשך *v* splashed; stirred; (*pres* **meshakhshekh;** *fut* **yeshakhshekh**).

sheekht|ev/-evah/-avtee שכתב *v* rewrote; (*pres* **meshakhtev;** *fut* **yeshakhtev**).

sheekhtoov/-eem שכתוב *nm* rewrite; (*pl+of:* **-ey**).

sheekhvah/sh'khavot שיכבה *nf* **1.** layer; **2.** social stratum; (*+of:* **sheekhvat**).

sheekhz|er/-erah/-artee שחזר *v* reconstructed; restored; (*pres* **meshakhzer;** *fut* **yeshakhzer**).

sheekhzoor/-eem שחזור *nm* reconstruction; (*pl+of:* **-ey**).

sheekm|ah/-eem שקמה *nf* sycamore; (*+of:* **-at**).

sheekoof/-eem שיקוף *nm* reflection; (*pl+of:* **-ey**).

sheekoof/-ey rentgen שיקוף רנטגן *nm* X-ray picture.

sheekoofee|t (*npr* **shkoofee|t**)**/-yot** שקופית *nf* slide (photographic transparency).

(makren/-ey) sheekoofeeyot (*npr* **shkoofeeyot**) מקרן שקופיות *nm* slide projector.

sheekookh/-eem שיכוך *nm* calming; appeasing.

sheekool/-eem שיקול *nm* consideration; (*pl+of:* **-ey**).

sheekool/-eem שיכול *nm* bereavement of offspring.

sheekool da'at שיקול דעת *nm* discretion.

sheekoom/-eem שיקום *nm* rehabilitation; (*pl+of:* **-ey**).

sheekoon/-eem שיכון *nm* **1.** housing; **2.** housing project; **3.** housing quarter.

◇ **"sheekoon 'amamee"** שיכון עממי *nm* **1.** "Popular Housing" project housing scheme; **2.** housing type.

◇ **"sheekoon beneh-betkha"** see ◇ **"beneh-betkha".**

◇ **sheekoon 'oleem** שיכון עולים *nm* "Immigrant Housing" project (or housing type).

◇ **"sheekoon oo-feetoo'akh"** (**"Shikun u-Fitu'akh"**) "שיכון ופיתוח" *nm* Government's major housing company.

◇ **"sheekoon 'ovdeem"** (**"Shikun Ovdim"**) "שיכון עובדים" *nm* Histadrut's main housing company.

sheekoon/-eem tseebooree/-yeem שיכון ציבורי *nm* public housing.

◇ **sheekoon mefooneem** שיכון מפונים *nm* housing project for slum evacuees.

(meesrad ha-beenooy ve-ha) sheekoon משרד הבינוי והשיכון *nm* Ministry of Construction and Housing.

(sar ha-beenooy ve-ha) sheekoon שר הבינוי והשיכון *nm* the Minister of Construction and Housing.

sheekooneem שיכונים *nm pl* popular housing project areas.

sheekoots/-eem שיקוץ *nm* abomination; (*pl+of:* **-ey**).

sheekoo|y/-yeem שיקוי *nm* drink; beverage; (*pl+of:* **-yey**).

sheekor/-eem שיכור **1.** *nm* drunkard; (*pl+of:* **-ey**); **2.** *adj* drunken; drunk.

sheeks|ah/-ot שיקצה *nf* **1.** non-Jewish girl; **2.** girl of non-Jewish apperance.

sheeksh|ek/-ekah/-aktee שיקשק *v* fluttered; (*pres* **meshakshek;** *fut* **yeshakshek**).

sheekshook/-eem שקשוק *nm* clatter; (*pl+of:* **-ey**).

□ **Sheelat** (Shilat) שילת *nm* village (est. 1977) in Ayalon Valley, 3 km SE of **Mevo-Modee'een.** Pop. 283.

she'el|ah/-ot שאלה *nf* question; *query*; (*+of:* **-at**).

she'elah 'adeenah שאלה עדינה *nf* delicate question.

(eyzo) she'elah! איזו שאלה! *interj* what a question!

(ot ha) she'elah אות השאלה *nm* question-mark.

(seeman/-ey) she'elah סימן שאלה *nm* question-mark.

sheel|akh/-khah/-akhtee (*also:* **sheel|e'akh**) שילח *v* sent away; dismissed; (*pres* **meshale'akh;** *fut* **yeshale'akh**).

she'elat tam שאלת תם *nm* naive question; simpleton's wondering.

sheeldah שילדה *nf* chassis; frame (of car) .

sheel|em/-mah/-amtee שילם *v* paid; (*pres* **meshalem;** *fut* **yeshalem**).

(nakam ve) sheelem נקם ושילם *nm* vengeance; retribution.

sheel|ev/-vah/-avtee שילב *v* combined; (*pres* **meshalev;** *fut* **yeshalev**).

◇ **"sheelgeeyah"** "שלגייה" *nf* "Snow-White".

sheel|hev/-havah/-havtee שלהב *v* incited; inflamed; (*pres* **meshalhev;** *fut* **yeshalhev**).

□ **Sheelo** (Shillo) שילה *nm* settlement (est. 1979) in Samarian Hills on site of ancient Biblical city with same name, 3 km E. of **Ma'aleh Levonah.** Pop. 673+.

she'elon/-eem שאלון *nm* questionnaire; (*pl+of:* **-ey**).

(meel|e/-'ah/-e'tee) she'elon מילא שאלון *v* filled out a questionnaire.

sheeloo|'akh/-kheem שילוח *nm* **1.** launching; **2.** exile; dismissal; (*pl+of:* **-khey**).

(kan/-ey) sheeloo'akh כן שילוח *nm* launching pad; launching ramp; (milit.).

sheeloomeem שילומים *nm pl* (*sing:* **sheeloom**) reparations; retribution; (*pl+of:* **-ey**).

◊ **(ha)sheeloomeem** השילומים *nm pl* reparations paid by Germany to Israel in the years 1952-1962 as token-compensation for the Holocaust.

sheeloosh/-eem שילוש *nm* tripling; (*pl+of:* **-ey**).

sheeloot/-eem שילוט *nm* posting signs; (*pl+of:* **-ey**).

sheeloov/-eem שילוב *nm* folding; combining into; (*pl+of:* **-ey**).

sheelsh|el/-elah/-altee שילשל *v* **1.** dropped into (e.g. a letter into a mailbox); **2.** was seized with diarrhea; (*pres* **meshalshel**; *fut* **yeshalshel**).

sheelshom שלשום *nm* the day before yesterday.

(temol) sheelshom תמול שלשום *adv* not so long ago; a few days ago.

(lo kee-temol) sheelshom לא כתמול שלשום *adv* not as it used to be; not as formerly.

sheelshool/-eem שלשול *nm* diarrhea (Medic.); (*pl+of* **-ey**).

sheelton/-ot שלטון *nm* rule; authority; government.

(ha) sheeltonot השלטונות *nm pl* the authorities.

sheelyah/shelayot שלייה *nf* placenta (Medic.); (*+of:* **sheel|yat/-yot**).

sheem|en/-nah/-antee שימן *v* oiled; greased; (*pres* **meshamen**; *fut* **yeshamen**).

sheem|er/-rah/-artee שימר *v* preserved; (*pres* **meshamer**; *fut* **yeshamer**).

sheem|esh/-shah/-ashtee שימש *v* served; (*pres* **meshamesh**; *fut* **yeshamesh**).

sheemoor/-eem שימור *nm* preservation; conservation.

sheemooreem שימורים *nm pl* canned food; preserved food; (*+of:* **-ey**).

(leyl/-ot) sheemooreem ליל שימורים *nm* vigil; watchnight; night of staying awake.

sheemoosh/-eem שימוש *nm* use; (*pl+of:* **-ey**).

sheemoosh (*etc*) **she-lo ka-deen** שימוש שלא כדין *nm* unlawful use.

(bet/batey) sheemoosh בית שימוש *nm* latrine; W.C.; privy.

sheemooshee/-t שימושי *adj* useful; practical; serviceable.

(doo-) sheemooshee/-t דו־שימושי *adj* of double use; dual-purpose.

(rav-) sheemooshee/-t רב־שימושי *adj* multi-purpose.

(balshanoot) sheemoosheet בלשנות שימושית *nf* applied linguistics.

(p'seekhologyah) sheemoosheet פסיכולוגיה שימושית *nf* applied psychology.

sheemshah/shmashot שמשה *nf* windowpane; (*+of:* **sheemsh|at/-ot**).

sheemshee|yah/-yot שמשייה *nf* parasol; sunshade; (*+of:* **-yat**).

sheemtsah שמצה *nf* disgrace; derision.

(paroo'a'/proo'ah le) sheemtsah פרוע לשמצה *adj* unruly; undisciplined.

(yadoo'a'/yedoo'ah le) sheemtsah ידוע לשמצה *adj* notorious; infamous.

◊ **sheen** (שי״ן) ש **1.** *nf* 21st letter of Hebrew alphabet; **2.** *nm* letter pronounced "sh" when dotted over its right shoulder or not dotted at all, in a dotted text.

◊ **sheen** ש׳ numer. symbol: 300; the 300th.

◊ **sheen bet** (שי״ן בי״ת) ש״ב *abbr. nm* (*acr.* for **"SHeroot Beetakhon"** שירות ביטחון) Israel's secret State Security Service.

sheen|ah/-tah/-eetee שינה *v* altered; changed; (*pres* **meshaneh**; *fut* **yeshaneh**).

sheenayeem שיניים *nf pl* (*sing:* **shen**) teeth; (*+of:* **sheeney**).

sheenayeem totavot שיניים תותבות *nf pl* (*sing:* **shen totevet**) false teeth; dentures.

(ke'ev/-ey) sheenayeem כאב שיניים *nm* toothache.

(khas|ar/-rat) sheenayeem חסר שיניים *adj* toothless.

(meeshkh|at/-ot) sheenayeem משחת שיניים *nf* toothpaste.

(meevresh|et/-ot) sheenayeem מברשת שיניים *nf* toothbrush.

(merap|e/-'ey) sheenayeem מרפא שיניים *nm* dental practitioner (not a university graduate).

(nat|an/-nah/-atee ba) sheenayeem נתן בשיניים *v* [*slang*] knocked (one's) teeth out; (mainly *figurat.*); (*pres* **noten** *etc*; *fut* **yeeten** *etc*).

(rof|e/-t) sheenayeem רופא שיניים *nmf* dentist.

(tekhn|ay) sheenayeem (*or:* **tekhna'|ee/-'ey** *etc*) טכנאי שיניים *nm* dental technician.

sheenanee|t/-yot שיננית *nf* dental hygienist.

sheen|en/-enah/-antee שינן *v* inculcated; memorized; (*pres* **meshanen**; *fut* **yeshanen**).

sheen|es/-sah/-astee motn|av/-eha/-ay שינס מותניו *v* gathered strength; made effort; (*pres* **meshanes** *etc*; *fut* **yeshanes** *etc*).

sheenoo|'a'/-'eem שינוע *nm* cargo-handling; (*pl+of:* **'ey**).

sheenoo|y/-yeem שינוי *nm* change; alteration; (*pl+of:* **-yey**).

◊ **sheenooy** (**"Shinui"**) שינוי *nf* left-of-center political party (in Knesset since 1977), Dovish, non-socialist.

sheenooy 'arakheem שינוי ערכים *nm* change of values; revaluation.

sheenooy le-ra'ah שינוי לרעה *nm* deterioration; change for the worse.

sheenooy le-tovah שינוי לטובה *nm* improvement; change for the better.

sheenooy shem שינוי שם *nm* change of name.

(le-lo) sheenooy ללא שינוי **1.** *adv* without change; **2.** *adj* unchanged.

(le-shem) sheenooy לשם שינוי *adv* for a change.

shee'ool/-eem שיעול *nm* cough; (*pl+of:* **-ey**).

shee'oor/-eem שיעור *nm* **1.** lesson; **2.** proportion, extent; (*pl+of:* **-ey**).

shee'oor/-ey 'eevreet שיעור עברית *nm* Hebrew lesson.

shee'oor komah שיעור קומה *nm* stature.

shee'oor/-ey s'kheeyah שיעור שחייה *nm* swimming lesson.

(keeb|el/-lah/-altee) shee'oor קיבל שיעור *v* **1.** was given a lesson; **2.** (*figurat.*) was taught a lesson (*pres* **mekabel** *etc; fut* **yekabel** *etc*).

(nat|an/-nah/-atee) shee'oor נתן שיעור *v* gave a lesson; (*pres* **noten** *etc; fut* **yeeten** *etc*).

(le) shee'oo|reem (*or:* **-reen**) לשיעורין *adv* in rates; in installments.

(ma'arekhet) shee'ooreem מערכת שיעורים *nf* curriculum.

sheep|er/-rah/-artee שיפר *v* improved; (*pres* **meshaper;** *fut* **yeshaper**).

sheep|ets/-tsah/-atstee שיפץ *v* overhauled; renovated; (*pres* **meshapets;** *fut* **yeshapets**).

sheepon שיפון *nm* rye.

(lekhem) sheepon לחם שיפון *nm* rye bread.

sheepoo|'a'/-'eem שיפוע *nm* slope; (*pl+of:* **-'ey**).

sheepoor/-eem שיפור *nm* improvement; (*pl+of:* **-ey**).

sheepoots/-eem שיפוץ *nm* overhaul; refurbishing; renovation; (*pl+of:* **ey**).

sheer/-eem שיר *nm* song; verse; (*pl+of:* **-ey**).

sheer/-ey 'am שיר עם *nm* folk-song.

sheer/-ey 'eres שיר ערש *nm* lullaby.

she'er/-eem שאר *nm* relative (*pl+of:* **-ey**).

she'er/-ey basar שאר בשר *nm* kinsman; next of kin; blood relative.

sheer|ah/-ot שירה *nf* **1.** poetry; **2.** singing; (*+of:* **-at**).

sheerah be-tseeboor שירה בציבור *nf* community singing.

sheerb|ev/-evah/-avtee שרבב *v* interpolated; stuck out; (*pres* **mesharbev;** *fut* **yesharbev**).

sheerboov/-eem שרבוב *nm* interpolation; (*pl+of:* **-ey**).

she'er|eem שארים *nm pl* surviving next of kin; (*+of:* **-ey**).

she'eree|t/-yot שארית *nf* remnant; rest.

she'ereet ha-pleytah שארית הפליטה *nf* remnant; what has been spared.

◇ **she'ereet ha-pleytah** שארית הפליטה *nf* generic term that was in use immediately after the Holocaust with regard to the few Jews (some 100,000) who survived, out of six million deportees.

sheeron/-eem שירון *nm* song book; (*pl+of:* **-ey**).

sheeryen/-yenah/-yantee שריין *v* secured; reserved (*pres* **mesharyen;** *fut* **yesharyen**).

sheeryon/-eem שריון *nm* armor; armored forces; (*pl+of:* **-ey**).

(Kheyl ha) sheeryon חיל השריון *nm* the Tank Corps (Army).

sheeryon|ay/-a'eet שריונאי *nmf* soldier serving in an armored unit (Army).

sheeryonee|t/-yot שריונית *nf* armored car; (*pl+of:* **-yot**).

sheeryoon/-eem שריון *nm* **1.** armoring; **2.** securing; (*pl+of:* **-ey**).

shees|a'/-'ah/-a'tee שיסע *v* **1.** interrupted a speaker; **2.** tore to pieces; (*pres* **meshase'a';** *fut* **yeshasa'**).

shees|ah/-tah/-eetee שיסה *v* incited; instigated; set on; (*pres* **meshaseh;** *fut* **yeshaseh**).

sheeshah/shesh שישה/שש *num m/f* six; (*m+of:* **sheshet**).

sheeshee/-t שישי *adj* sixth.

sheeshee be- שישי ב־ *adj* the sixth of... (name of the month).

sheeshee le-khodesh ששי לחודש *nm* the sixth of the month.

(yom/yemey) sheeshee יום שישי *nm* Friday.

sheesheem שישים *num* 60; sixty.

sheeshee|t/-yot שישית *nf* 1/6; one sixth.

sheeshee|yah/-yot שישייה *nf* **1.** sextet; set of 6; **2.** sextuplets; (*+of:* **-yat**).

sheesoo|'a'/-'eem שיסוע *nm* **1.** tearing to pieces; **2.** interrupting; (*pl+of:* **-'ey**).

sheesooy/-eem שיסוי *nm* instigation; fomenting; setting on; (*pl+of:* **-ey**).

sheetah/-ot שיטה *nf* method; system; (*+of:* **-tat**).

sheet|ah/-etah/-teetee שיטה *v* **1.** mocked; teased; **2.** made a fool of; (*pres* **meshateh;** *fut* **yeshateh**).

sheet|afon/-fonot שיטפון *nm* flood; (*+of:* **sheetfon**).

sheetatee/-t שיטתי *adj* systematic; methodical.

sheetateeyoot שיטתיות *nf* methodicalness.

sheet|ef/-fah/-aftee שיתף *v* **1.** associated; **2.** let participate; (*pres* **meshatef;** *fut* **yeshatef**).

sheet|ek/-kah/-aktee שיתק *v* paralyzed; silenced; (*pres* **meshatek;** *fut* **yeshatek**).

sheetkhee/-t שטחי *adj* superficial.

sheetkheeyoot שטחיות *nf* superficiality; shallowness.

sheetoof/-eem שיתוף *nm* participation; association; (*pl+of:* **-ey**).

sheetoof (*etc*) **pe'oolah** שיתוף פעולה *nm* cooperation; collaboration.

(be) sheetoof 'eem בשיתוף עם *adv* in cooperation with; with the collaboration of.

sheetoofee/-t שיתופי *adj* collective; cooperative.

(moshav/-eem) sheetoofee/-yeem מושב שיתופי *nm* cooperative village.

(agood|ah/-ot) sheetoofee|t/-yot אגודה שיתופית *nf* cooperative society.

sheetook/-eem שיתוק *nm* paralysis; (*pl+of:* **-ey**).

sheetook mokhee שיתוק מוחי *nm* cerebral palsy (Medic.).

sheetook yeladeem שיתוק ילדים *nm* polio; infantile paralysis; (Medic.).

sheev|ah/-ot שיבה *nf* return; (*+of:* **-at**).

sheevah/-tah/-eetee שיווה *v* visualized; (*pres* **meshaveh;** *fut* **yeshaveh**).

◇ **(zekhoot ha)sheevah** see ◇ **zekhoot ha-sheevah**.

sheev'ah/sheva' שבעה/שבע *num m/f* seven; 7; (*m+of:* **sheev'at**).

◇ **(yash|av/-vah/-avtee) sheev'ah** see ◇ **yash|av/-vah/-avtee sheev'ah**.

◇ **sheev'ah** שבעה *nm* "Seven Days of Mourning" obligatory for nearest relatives of deceased (wife or husband, parents, children, brothers, sisters). During the "**sheev'ah**" mourners sit together (on low seats) at deceased's last domicile and receive visitors who come to express condolences.

(ha)sheev'ah-'asar/shva'-'esreh השבעה עשר/ השבע עשרה *adj m/f* the 17th.

sheev'atayeem שבעתיים *adv* sevenfold; seven times.

sheev'eem שבעים *num* 70; seventy.

(ha) sheev'eem השבעים *adj num* the 70th.

(deeb|er/-rah/-artee be) sheevkh|o/-ah/-ee דיבר בשבחו/־ה *v* praised him/her/me *etc.*

sheev|ek/-kah/-aktee שיווק *v* marketed; (*pres* **meshavek**; *fut* **yeshavek**).

sheevook/-eem שיווק *nm* marketing; (*pl+of:* **-ey**).

(reshet/reeshtot) sheevook רשת שיווק *nf* marketing network; chainstore.

sheevooy/-eem שיווי *nm* equalization; parity.

sheevoo|y/-yey meeshkal שיווי משקל *nm* equilibrium; poise.

sheevooy zkhooyot שיווי זכויות *nm* equality of rights; parity.

□ **Sheevtah** (Subeita) שבטה *nm* ruins of ancient Nabatean city in Negev, 13 km S. of **Sedeh Boker**.

sheevtee/-t שבטי *adj* tribal.

sheevyon/-eem שוויון *nm* equality.

seevyon nefesh שוויון נפש *nm* indifference.

sheevyon zekhooyot שוויון זכויות *nm* equality of rights.

(be) sheevyon nefesh בשוויון נפש *adv* indifferently.

(see) sheevyon אי שוויון *nm* inequality.

sheevyonee/-t שוויוני *adj* egalitarian.

sheevyoneeyoot שוויוניות *nf* egalitarianism.

shee|yef/-yefah/-aftee שייף *v* filed; smoothed; (*pres* **meshayef**; *fut* **yeshayef**).

shee|yekh/-yekhah/-yakhtee שייך *v* attributed; (*pres* **meshayekh**; *fut* **yeshayekh**).

she-'en beelt|o/-ah שאין בלתו/־ה *adj* unequalled; that has no equal.

she-'en doogmat|o/-ah שאין דוגמתו *adj* unlike; that has no par.

she-'en ha-da'at sovalt|o/-ah שאין הדעת סובלתו *adj* intolerable.

she-'en kamo|hoo/-hah שאין כמוהו/־ה *adj* that has nothing like it (him/her).

she-'en kemot|o/-ah שאין כמותו/־ה *adj* unequalled.

(even) she-'en lah hofkheen אבן שאין לה הופכין *nf* unturned (i.e. useless) stone.

shee|yet/-yetah/-yatetee שייט *v* cruised; navigated; (*pres* **meshayet**; *fut* **yeshayet**).

sheeyookh/-eem שיוך *nm* attribution; (*pl+of:* **-ey**).

sheeyoor/-eem שיור *nm* remainder; (*pl+of:* **-ey**).

sheeyoof/-eem שיוף *nm* filing; smoothing; (*pl+of:* **-ey**).

sheeyoot/-eem שיוט *nm* cruising; navigating; (*pl+of:* **-ey**).

(teel/-ey) sheeyoot טיל שיוט *nm* cruise missile.

sheezoof/-eem שיזוף *nm* sunbathing; tanning; (*pl+of:* **-ey**).

shefa' שפע *nm* abundance.

(be) shefa' בשפע *adv* abundantly; plentifully.

('eedan ha) shefa' עידן השפע *nm* the age of abundance.

(keren ha) shefa' קרן השפע *nf* cornucopia - the legendary horn of plenty.

(tekoofat ha) shefa' תקופת השפע *nf* the age of plenty.

shefekh/shefakheem שפך *nm* estuary; heap; (*pl+of:* **sheefkhey**).

shefel שפל *nm* depression; low tide.

□ **Shefer** שפר *nm* village (est. 1950) in Upper Galilee 3 km NE of Hananya Junction (**Tsomet Khananyah**). Pop. 231.

shefof|eret/-arot שפופרת *nf* tube.

(be-kheymah) shefookhah בחימה שפוכה *adv* furiously.

shegag|ah/-ot שגגה *nf* inadvertent mistake; unintended offence.

(bee) shegagah בשגגה *adv* unintentionally.

shegee|'ah/-'ot שגיאה *nf* error; mistake; (*+of:* **-'at**).

shegee|'at/-'ot keteev שגיאת כתיב *nf* spelling error.

she-hee שהיא (or, as a *suffix:* ־שהי) *sing f* **1.** some; **2.** whatever.

(eyzo) she-hee איזושהי *sing f* some; any kind of.

(kemot) she-hee כמות שהיא as she/it is.

shehee|yah/-yot שהייה *nf* sojourn; stay; (*+of:* **-yat**).

she-hem/-hen שהם *pronoun plus suffix pl m/f* who are; which are.

(eleh/eloo) she-hem אלה/אלו שהם/ן *pl m/f* some.

(kemot) she-hem/-hen כמות שהם/הן *pl m/f* as they are.

she-hoo/-hee שהוא (or, as a suffix:****** ־שהו) *pronoun sing m/f* **1.** some; **2.** who is; **3.** whatever.

(eyzeh) she-hoo איזשהו *sing m* some.

(kemot) she-hoo כמות שהוא as is; as he/it is.

(mah) she-hoo מה שהוא (or, contracted spelling: משהו) *sing m* something.

(matay) she-hoo מתי שהוא *adv* sometime; whenever.

shek/-eem שיק *nm* cheque.

shek/-eem eeshee/-yeem שיק אישי *nm* personal cheque.

shek/-eem mesoortat/-eem שיק מסורטט *nm* crossed cheque (not to be endorsed over to anyone else).

sheka'/sheka'eem שקע *nm* **1.** depression; **2.** socket; outlet (electric.); (*pl+of:* **sheek'ey**).

sheka'arooree/-t שקערורי *adj* concave.

shekeed|ah/-ot שקידה *nf* diligence; (*+of:* **-at**).

(bee) shekeedah בשקידה *adv* dilligently.

shekeefoo|t/-yot שקיפות *nf* transparency.

shekeel|ah/-ot שקילה *nf* weighing; (*+of:* **-at**).

◇ **shekel /shkaleem** שקל *nm* the Shequel, Israeli currency unit that in 1968 replaced the previous unit called Israel Pound or Israel Lira. In turn, the Shequel, too, was replaced, as of January 1, 1986, by the New Shekel (see next entry: ◇ **shekel khadash**).

◇ **shekel/shkaleem khadash/-eem** שקל חדש *nm* the New Shequel, Israel's currency unit since Jan. 1986, equivalent to U.S.$ 0.42 (according to May 1992 exchange-rate).

◇ **"shekem"** שקם *nm* army chainstores and canteens; (parallel to the PX in the U.S. army and to the NAAFFI in the UK).

she-kamo|kha/-kh שכמוך *interj...* that you *m/f* are!

she-ken שכן *prep* for; since.

sheker/shkareem שקר *nm* lie; falsehood. (*pl+of:* **sheekrey**).

('ed/-ey) sheker עד שקר *nm* false witness.

('ed|at/-ot) sheker עדת שקר *nf* false witness (female).

('edoo|t/-yot) sheker עדות שקר *nf* false testimony; perjury.

(neeshb|a'/-e'ah/-a'tee la) sheker נשבע לשקר *v* swore falsely; perjured; (*pres* **neeshba'** *etc; fut* **yeeshava'** *etc v=b*).

(nevee/-'ey) sheker נביא שקר *nm* false prophet.

(nevoo|'at/-'ot) sheker נבואת שקר *nf* false prophecy.

(shevoo|'at/-'ot) sheker שבועת שקר *nf* perjury; false oath.

sheket שקט **1.** *nm* silence; calm; **2.** *interj* quiet, please!

(see-) sheket אי־שקט *nm* unrest.

◻ **Shekhanyah** (Sekhanya) שכניה *nm* industrial village (est. 1977) in Upper Galilee's **Tefen** district, 2 km N. of **Yodfat**. Pop. 144.

shekhar שיכר *nm* beer; ale.

shekharkhar/-ah שחרחר *adj* dark-tanned; swarthy; blackish.

shekharkhor|et/-ot שחרחורת *nf* good-looking brunette.

shekheek|ah/-ot שחיקה *nf* grinding; pulverization; (*+of:* **-at**).

shekheekat ha-sakhar שחיקת השכר *nf* erosion of purchasing power of wages.

(bet ha) shekhee בית השחי *nm* armpit.

shekheekhoo|t/-yot שכיחות *nf* frequency.

shekheen שחין *nm* boils.

(ha)shekheenah השכינה *nf* heavenly spirit.

shekheet|ah/-ot שחיטה *nf* **1.** slaughter; **2.** slaughtering in compliance with Jewish ritual; (*+of:* **-at**).

shekheetoo|t/-yot שחיתות *nf* corruption; demoralization.

shekheev|ah/-ot שכיבה **1.** lying; reclining; **2.** cohabitation; (*+of:* **-at**).

(bee) shekheevah בשכיבה *adv* lying down.

◇ **shekheev me-ra'** שכיב מרע *nm* fatally ill; moribund.

(tsava'at) shekheevme-ra' צוואת שכיב מרע *nm* a dying person's last will.

shekhem שכם *nm* shoulder; (*+of:* **shekhem/sheekhmey**).

◻ **Shekhem** see ◻ **Sh'khem**.

(heet|ah/-etah/-etee) shekhem הטה שכם *v* shouldered; (*pres* **mateh** *etc; fut* **yateh** *etc*).

shekhem ekhad שכם אחד *adv* shoulder to shoulder.

shekhenoot שכנות *nf* vicinity; neighborhood.

(bee) shekhenoot בשכנות *adv* in proximity of; nearby.

(yakhasey) shekhenoot יחסי שכנות *nm pl* neighborly relations.

shekho|'akh/-khah שחוח *adj* stooped; with bent head.

shekhoon|ah/-ot שכונה *nf* neighborhood; quarter; district; residential area.

shekhoon|at/-ot 'onee שכונת עוני *nf* slum district; slum area.

shekhoonatee/-t שכונתי *adj* neighborhood; area-

(ha) shekhoonot השכונות *nf pl* suburbia.

('avod|ah/-ot) shekhor|ah/-ot עבודה שחורה *nf* unskilled labor.

(marah) shekhorah מרה שחורה *nf* hypochondria; melancholy.

◇ **(ha-pantereem ha) shekhoreem** see ◇ **panter**.

(ro'eh/ro'at) shekhorot רואה שחורות *adj & nmf* pessimistic; pessimist.

(taleet) she-koolahtekhelet טלית שכולה תכלת *nf* **1.** paragon of virtue (used ironically); **2.** (*lit.*) a prayer-shawl of purest blue.

shel של *prep* of; belonging to.

(be) shel בשל *prep* on account of.

(mee) shel משל *adj* belonging to.

shelah שלה *poss. pron.* her; hers.

shelahe|m/-n שלהם *poss. pron.* their; theirs (*m/f*).

shelakh/-em/-en שלך *poss. pron.* your; yours; (*sing f / pl m/f*).

shelanoo שלנו *poss. pron.* our; ours.

shela|v/-beem (*b=v*) שלב *nm* **1.** rung of ladder; **2.** step; stage; (*pl+of:* **-bey**).

sheled/shladeem שלד *nm* a skeleton; (*pl+of:* **sheeldey**).

shelee שלי *poss. pron.* my; mine.

shelee|'akh/-khey שליח *m+of* emissary of; messenger of.

◇ **shelee|'akh/-khey tseeboor** שליח ציבור *nm* **1.** cantor; one who leads prayer service in synagogue; **2.** public servant.

(meroots/-ey) sheleekheem מרוץ שליחים *nm* relay race.

sheleekhoo|t/-yot שליחות *nf* **1.** mission; **2.** errand.

sheleesh/-eem שליש *num m* **1.** 1/3; one third; third part; **2.** trimester.

(lee) sheleesh ve-lee-revee'a' לשליש ולרביע *adv* partially; in bits and pieces.

sheleeshee/-t שלישי *adj & num* third; 3rd.
(goof) sheleeshee גוף שלישי *nm* third person (Gram.).
(to'ar) sheleeshee תואר שלישי *nm* PhD degree.
(tsad) sheleeshee צד שלישי *nm* third party (to a deal, court-action or contract).
(yom/yemey) sheleeshee יום שלישי *nm* Tuesday.
sheleeshee|yah/-yot שלישייה *nf* triplets; 3; trio; (*+of:* **yat**).
shelee|tah/-tot שליטה *nf* control; command; proficiency.
(ba'al/-ey) sheleetah בעל שליטה *nm* main shareholder (in a corporate body).
(refoo'ah) shelemah! רפואה שלמה! Have a complete recovery! (said to someone in ill health or injured).
shelemoo|t/-yot שלימות *nf* integrity; totality; perfection.
shelkha שלך *poss. pron. 2nd pers masc sing* your, yours .
shel mah be-khakh *(kh=k)* של מה בכך *adj* of no importance; trifle.
shelo שלו *poss. pron.* his.
she-lo be-'eet|o/-ah שלא בעתו *adv* untimely; at the wrong time.
she-lo be-khavanah *(kh=k)* שלא בכוונה *adv* unintentionally.
she-lo ka-deen שלא כדין *adv* unlawfully.
(heeshtam|esh/-shah/-ashtee) she-lo ka-deen השתמש שלא כדין *v* made unlawful use; abused; (*pres* **meeshtamesh** *etc; fut* **yeeshtamesh** *etc*).
shelom שלום *m+of* the peace **(shalom)** of...
shelom bayeet שלום בית *nm* domestic peace; peace of the household.
◇ **(meelkhemet) shelom ha-galeel** see ◇ **meelkhemet shlom ha-galeel**.
□ **Shelomee** see □ **Shlomee**.
(mah) shelom|kha/-ekh? מה שלומך? **1.** (*query* & greeting) *sing m/f* How do you do? **2.** (*lit.*) how's your health?
Shelomo שלמה Hebrew version of the name Salomon.
sheloo|'akh/-khat resen שלוח רסן *adj* unbridled; unrestrained.
(beytsah/-eem) shelook|ah/-ot ביצה שלוקה *nf* hardboiled egg.
shelookh|ah/-ot שלוחה *nf* extension; branch; subsidiary.
□ **Shelookhot** see □ **Shlookhot**.
shelooleet/-yot שלולית *nf* puddle.
sheloov/-at zro'a' שלוב זרוע *adj* arm-in-arm.
shelosh שלוש *num prefix* tri-
shelosh-'esreh שלוש-עשרה *num f* 13; thirteen.
sheloshah שלושה *num m* 3; three.
sheloshah 'asar שלושה-עשר *num m* 13; thirteen.
(ha) sheloshah-'asar/shelosh-'esreh השלושה-עשר *adj & num m/f* the 13th; the thirteenth.
◇ **(khodesh) shelosh-'esreh** see ◇ **khodesh shelosh-'esreh**.
(pee) sheloshah פי שלושה *adv* threefold.
shelosheem שלושים *num* 30; thirty.
(ha) shelosheem ba-khodesh השלושים בחודש *nm* ths 30th of the month.
◇ **(yom ha) shelosheem** see ◇ **yom ha-shlosheem**.
shem/-ot שם *nm* name.
shem davar שם דבר *nm* something well-known; renowned.
shem/-ot 'etsem שם עצם *nm* noun (Gram.).
shem/-ot goof שם גוף *nm* pronoun (Gram.).
shem/-ot meeshpakhah שם משפחה *nm* surname; family name.
shem/-ot neerdaf/-eem שם נרדף *nm* synonym.
shem/-ot pratee/-yeem שם פרטי *nm* first name.
shem ra' שם רע *nm* bad name; evil repute.
shem/-ot to'ar שם תואר *nm* adjective (Gram.).
shem tov שם טוב *nm* good name; reputation.
('al) shem על שם **1.** *adv* in the memory of; **2.** *adj* nominal.
(barookh ha) shem! ברוך השם! *interj* thank God! God be praised!
(be-'ezrat ha) shem בעזרת השם *adv* with God's help.
(be) shem בשם *nm* in the name of; on behalf of.
(be-'eeloom) shem בעילום שם *adv* incognito.
(eem yeertseh ha) shem אם ירצה השם *adv* God willing; with the grace of God.
(ha) shem השם *nm* God; the Almighty.
(ha) shem yeetbarakh השם יתברך *nm* God, blessed be He.
◇ **('al keedoosh ha) shem** see ◇ **keedoosh ha-shem**.
◇ **(keedoosh ha) shem** see ◇ **keedoosh ha-shem**.
(mena|yah/-yot 'al) shem מניה על שם *nf* nominal share.
(nak|av/-vah/-avtee be) shem נקב בשם *v* named; (*pres* **nokev** *etc; fut* **yeenkov** *etc*).
(seekh|ah/-ot 'al) shem שיחה על שם *nf* person-to- person call.
(sheenooy) shem שינוי שם *nm* change of name.
(hotsa'at) shem ra' הוצאת שם רע *nf* slander; libel; giving a bad name.
(hots|ee/-ee'ah/-e'tee) shem ra' הוציא שם רע *v* gave a bad name; slandered; (*pres* **motsee** *etc; fut* **yotsee** *etc*).
(kanah/-tah/-eetee) shem קנה שם *v* acquired a reputation.
(ke) shem she- כשם ש- just as...
(kheelool ha) shem חילול השם *nm* sacrilege; profanation.
(le) shem לשם for the purpose of; in order to.
(le shem) shamayeem לשם שמיים *adv* unselfishly; for an ideal.
(le-ma'an ha) shem למען השם *adv* for Heaven's sake.
shema שמא *prep* perhaps.
shema'! sheem'ee! (*npr* **sheem'eel**) שמע! שמעי! *v imp sing m/f* listen! (*inf* **leeshmo'a'**; *pst* **shama'** *pres* **shome'a'**; *fut* **yeeshma'**).

shema' na! sheem'ee (*npr* **sheem'ee**) **na!** !שמע נא ! שמעי נא *v* will you *m/f* listen, please!

◇ **shema' yeesra'el!** see ◇ **shma' yeesra'el!**

◇ **(kree'at) shema'!** see ◇ **kree'at shma'!**

shemad שמד *nm* a Jew's baptism; forced apostasy.

shemam|ah/-ot שממה *nf* desolation; wilderness; (*+of:* **sheemem|ot/-ot**).

shemanman/-ah שמנמן *adj* plump; fattish.

shemashot שמשות *nf pl* **1.** (*sing:* **sheemshah**) windowpanes; **2.** suns (*sing:* **shemesh**).

(beyn ha) shemashot בין השמשות *adv* twilight; dusk.

shemee/-t שמי *adj* Semitic.

shemee/-t שמי *adj* nominal.

shemee|'ah/-'ot שמיעה *nf* hearing.

('edoo|t/-yot) shemee'ah עדות שמיעה *nf* hearsay evidence.

shemee'atee/-t שמיעתי *adj* auditory; aural.

shemeenee/-t שמיני *adj & num* 8th; eighth.

◇ **shemeenee 'atseret** see ◇ **shmeenee 'atseret.**

shemeenee|t/-yot שמינית *nf* (fraction) 1/8; one eighth.

shemeeneet she-bee-shmeenet שמינית שבשמינית *nf lit* : 1/8; infinitesimal part.

shemeeneeyot ba-aveer שמיניות באויר *nf pl* doing the impossible.

shemeer|ah/-ot שמירה *nf* **1.** guarding; **2.** guard duty; (*+of:* **-at**).

(kelev/kalbey) shemeerah כלב־שמירה *nm* watchdog.

◇ **shemeetah** see ◇ **shmeetah.**

◇ **(shnat ha) shemeetah** see ◇ **shnat ha-shmeetah.**

shemeetat khovot שמיטת חובות *nf* remission of debts.

shemen/shmaneem שמן *nm* oil (*pl+of:* **shamney**).

shemen dageem שמן דגים *nm* fish oil; cod liver oil.

shemen keek שמן קיק *nm* castor oil.

shemen/shamney ma'akhal שמן מאכל *nm* edible oil.

shemen/shamney seekhah (*cpr* **seekah**) שמן סיכה *nm* lubricating oil.

shemen zayeet שמן זית *nm* olive oil.

shemesh/shmashot שמש *nf* sun.

(baroor/broorah ka) shemesh ברור כשמש *adj* clear as day.

(mak|at/-ot) shemesh מכת שמש *nf* sunstroke.

(meeshkefey) shemesh משקפי שמש *nm pl* sunglasses.

(shekee'at ha) shemesh שקיעת השמש *nf* sunset.

(zereekhat ha) shemesh זריחת השמש *nf* sunrise.

shemets שמץ *nm* a bit; a particle.

shemets davar שמץ דבר *nm* however little.

shemon|ah/-eh שמונה *num m/f* 8; eight.

shemon|ah/-eh 'asar/'esreh שמונה־עשר/ שמונה־עשרה *adj & num m/f* 18; eighteen.

shemoneem שמונים *num* 80; eighty.

(ha) shemoneem השמונים *adj & num* 80th; of eighty.

(yovel ha) shemoneem יובל השמונים *nm* eightieth anniversary.

shemoneh שמונה *num f* 8; eight.

shemoneh-'esreh שמונה־עשרה *num f* 18; eighteen.

◇ **"shemoneh-'esreh"** see ◇ **"shmoneh-'esreh".**

shemoo|'ah/-'ot שמועה *nf* rumor; (*+of:* **-'at**).

(mee-pee ha) shemoo'ah מפי השמועה *adv* from hearsay; according to rumor.

shemoo|'at/-'ot shav שמועת שווא *nf* false rumor.

shemoor|ah/-ot שמורה *nf* reservation (*+of:* **-at**).

shemoor|at/-ot teva' שמורת טבע *nf* nature preserve.

shen/sheenayeem שן *nf* tooth; (*pl+of:* **sheeney**).

shen/sheenayeem tot|evet/-avot שן תותבת *nf* false tooth; denture.

shen/sheeney beenah שן בינה *nm* wisdom tooth.

shen/sheeney khalav שן חלב *nm* milk tooth.

shen peel שן פיל *nm* ivory.

('akar/-rah/-artee) shen/sheenayeem עקר שן *v* extracted a tooth; (*pres* **'oker** *etc; fut* **ya'akor** *etc*).

('akeerat) shen/sheenayeem עקירת שן *nf* tooth extraction.

(meegdal) shen מגדל שן *nm* ivory tower.

(steem|at/-ot) shen/sheenayeem סתימת שן *nf* dental filling.

(yats|a/-'ah/-tee be) shen va-'ayeen יצא בשן ועין *v* barely escaped; (*pres* **yotse** *etc; fut* **yetse** *etc*).

shenee/-yah שני *adj num* second; 2nd.

(goof) shenee גוף שני *nm* 2nd person (Gram.).

(mee-klee) shenee מכלי שני *adv* indirectly; from second-hand source.

◇ **(seder) shenee** see ◇ **seder shenee.**

(to'ar) shenee תואר שני *nm* Master's degree.

(le-mashal ve-lee) sheneenah למשל ולשנינה *adv* **1.** to become an object of derision; **2.** to be made a proverb and a byword.

sheneenoo|t/-yot שנינות *nf* sarcasm; wit.

sheneet שנית *adv* secondly; again.

sheneeyah/-yot שנייה *nf* second; 1/60 of a minute; (*+of:* **-yat**)

sheneeyah שניה *adj & num f* 2nd; (*m:* **shenee**).

◇ **(ha-'aleeyah ha) sheneeyah** see ◇ **(ha)'aleeyah ha-shneeyah.**

(heezdamnoot) sheneeyah הזדמנות שנייה *nf* second chance.

sheney שני *num m* 2; two.

sheneym-'asar שנים עשר *num m* 12; twelve.

(ha) sheneym-'asar השנים־עשר *adj & num m* 12th; twelfth.

shen'hav שנהב *nm* ivory.

she'ol שאול *nf* hell.

she'ool (*npr* **shee'ool**) שיעול *nm* cough.

she'oor (*npr* **shee'oor**) /**-eem** שיעור *nm* lesson; (*pl+of:* **-ey**).
she'oor (*npr* **shee'oor**)/**-ey bayeet** שיעור בית *nm* homework.
she'oor (*npr* **shee'oor**)/**-ey 'eevreet** שיעור עברית *nm* Hebrew lesson.
she'oor (*npr* **shee'oor**)/**-ey negeenah** שיעור נגינה *nm* music lesson.
she'oor (*npr* **shee'oor**)/**-ey neheegah** שיעור נהיגה *nm* driving lesson.
she'oor (*npr* **shee'oor**)/**-eem pratee/-yeem** שיעור פרטי *nm* private lesson.
she'oor (*npr* **shee'oor**)/**-ey s'kheeyah** שיעור שחייה *nm* swimming lesson.
(keeb|el/-lah/-altee) she'oor (*npr* **shee'oor**) קיבל שיעור *v* **1.** was given a lesson; **2.** (*figurat.*) was taught a lesson (*pres* **mekabel** *etc; fut* **yekabel** *etc*).
(nat|an/-nah/-atee) she'oor (*npr* **shee'oor**) נתן שיעור *v* gave a lesson; (*pres* **noten** *etc; fut* **yeeten** *etc*).
(ma'arekhet) she'ooreem (*npr* **shee'ooreem**) מערכת שיעורים *nf* curriculum.
she'ot kabalah שעות קבלה *nf pl* reception hours.
(bee) she'ot ha-'erev בשעות הערב *adv* in the evening.
(bee) she'ot ha-khashekhah בשעות החשיכה *adv* after dark.
(bee) she'ot ha-laylah בשעות הלילה *adv* at night.
(bee) she'ot ha-yom בשעות היום *adv* in daytime.
sher|esh/-shah/-ashtee שירש *v* eradicated; uprooted; (*pres* **mesharesh**; *fut* **yesharesh**).
sher|et/-tah/-atetee שירת *v* served; (*pres* **mesharet**; *fut* **yesharet**).
sherets/shrats|eem שרץ *nm* reptile; creeping thing; (*pl+of:* **-ey**).
◇ **sheroot beetakhon** שירות ביטחון *nm* Israel's secret State Security. Known more by its two-letter *acr* ש"ב **"SHeen-Bet"** (שי"ן-בי"ת).
sheroot/-eem שירות *nm* service; (*pl+of:* **-ey**).
◇ **sheroot ha-ta'asookah** שירות התעסוקה *nm* the (Israeli Government's) employment service.
◇ **sheroot khovah** שירות חובה *nm* compulsory military service (conscription) for men (18-21) and women (18-20).
◇ **sheroot sadeer** שירות סדיר *nm* obligatory (*lit.:* regular) military service.
sheroot ta'asookah שירות תעסוקה *nm* employment office.
(be) sheroot pa'eel בשירות פעיל *adv* on active (military) service.
◇ **(monee|t/-yot) sheroot** see ◇ **monee|t/-yot sheroot**.
(peenkas) sheroot פנקס שירות *nm* military service log-booklet.
(ha) sherooteem השירותים *nm* (the) "services" i.e.; restrooms, lavatory, W.C.
shesek שסק *nm* loquat (fruit).
shesh שש *num f* 6; six.
shesh-'esreh שש-עשרה *num f* 16; sixteen.
('esreem va) shesh עשרים ושש *num f* 26; twenty six.
shet שת *nm* buttocks.
(khasoof/-at) shet חשוף שת *adj* with bare buttocks.
shetakh/-eem שטח *nm* area; surface; (*pl+of:* **sheetkhey**).
shetakh banooy שטח בנוי *nm* built-up area.
shetakh hefker שטח הפקר *nm* no-man's land.
('al peney ha) shetakh על פני השטח *adv* on the surface.
sheteh! shtee! שתה! שתי! *v imp sing m/f* drink! will you drink! (*pst* **shatah**; *fut* **yeeshteh**).
shetee שתי *nm* warp (in a loom).
shetee va-'erev שתי וערב *adv* crosswise; length and breadth.
(khakeer|at/-ot) shetee va-'erev חקירת שתי וערב *nf* cross-examination.
sheteef|ah/-ot שטיפה *nf* rinsing; washing away; (*+of:* **-at**).
sheteef|at/-ot mo'akh שטיפת מוח *nf* brain-washing.
sheteek|ah/-ot שתיקה *nf* silence; reticence; (*+of:* **-at**).
sheteel/-eem שתיל *nm* seedling; (*pl+of:* **-ey**).
sheteel|ah/-ot שתילה *nf* planting; (*+of:* **-at**).
shetee|yah/-yot שתייה *nf* **1.** drinking; **2.** drink; (*+of:* **-yat**).
sheteeyah karah שתייה קרה *nf* cold drinks.
shetef שטף *nm* flow; fluency.
shetef/sheetfey dam שטף דם *nm* hemorrhage.
(ba) shetakh בשטח *adv* in the field.
(be) shetef בשטף *adv* fluently.
shetem 'esreh שתים-עשרה *num f* 12; twelve.
sheten/shtaneem שתן *nm* urine.
(bedeek|at/-ot) sheten בדיקת שתן *nf* urinalysis.
(shalpookheet ha) sheten שלפוחית השתן *nf* bladder.
shetey שתי *num f* 2; two (preceding a feminine noun).
□ **Shetoolah** see □ **Shtoolah**.
□ **Shetooleem** see □ **Shtooleem**.
shetoo|t/-yot שטות *nf* folly; nonsense.
(dvar) shetoot דבר שטות *nf* folly; nonsense; stupid, trifling matter.
(ma'aseh) shetoot מעשה שטות *nm* folly; act of foolishness.
(roo'akh) shetoot רוח שטות *nm* a spirit of foolishness.
shetooyot! שטויות! *nf pl* (*sing:* **shtoot**) nonsense! rubbish!
('azov/'eezvee) shetooyot! עזוב שטויות! *v imp sing m/f* enough with this nonsense!
shetsef-ketsef שצף קצף *nm* violent anger.
(be) shetsef-ketsef בשצף קצף *adv* in flowing fury; in violent anger.
shev/-ee! שב! שבי! *v imp sing m/f* sit down! (*inf* **lashevet**; *pst* **yashav**; *pres* **yoshev**; *fut* **yeshev**).
sheva' שבע *num f* 7; seven.

(be) sheva' 'eynayeem בשבע עיניים *adv* **1.** carefully; with utmost attention; **2.** (*lit.*) with 7 eyes.

◇ **sheva** see ◇ **shva**.

◇ **sheva na'** see ◇ **shva na'**.

◇ **sheva nakh** see ◇ **shva nakh**.

sheva'ee/-t שוואי *adj* unvoweled (consonant) i.e. with a silent Shva under it (in dotted script).

sheva'-esreh שבע־עשרה *num f* 17; seventeen.

shevakh/-eem שבח *nm* praise; (*pl+of:* **sheevkhey**).

(ha) shevakh la-'el! !השבח לאל **1.** thank Heaven; **2.** (*lit.*) God be praised!

(mas) shevakh מס שבח *nm* land-sale tax; real-estate sale tax.

(tseeyoon le) shevakh ציון לשבח *nm* **1.** commendation; **2.** mention in dispatches (Army).

shevakheem שבחים *nm pl* (*sing:* **shevakh**) praises; (*+of:* **sheevkhey**).

shevareem שברים *nm pl* (*sing:* **shever**) fraction; (*pl+of:* **sheevrey**).

shevareem שוורים *nm pl* (*sing:* **shor**) oxen, bulls (*pl+of:* **shorey**).

shevat שבט *nm* 5th Jewish Calendar month (approx. Jan.-Feb.); 30 days.

shevav/-eem שבב *nm* splinter; chip; (*pl+of:* **-ey**).

('eebood) shevavee עיבוד שבבי *nm* chipwork.

sheveel !שבי *v imp sing f* sit down! (addressing female); (*inf* **lashevet**; *pst* **yashav**; *pres* **yoshev**; *fut* **yeshev**).

shevee שבי *nm* captivity.

shevee'ee/-t שביעי *adj & num* 7th; seventh.

◇ **shevee'ee shel pesakh** see ◇ **shvee'ee shel pesakh**.

shevee'ee|t/-yot שביעית *nf* 1/7; one seventh.

(ba) shevee בשבי *adv* in captivity.

(naf|al/-lah/-altee ba) shevee נפל בשבי *v* was taken prisoner; (*pres* **nofel** *etc; fut* **yeepol** *etc p=f*).

sheveel/-eem שביל *nm* pathway; (*pl+of:* **-ey**).

sheveel ha-zahav שביל הזהב *nm* the golden mean.

sheveel he-khalav שביל החלב *nm* the Milky Way.

shevees/-eem שביס *nm* hairnet; woman's head-ornament; (*pl+of:* **-ey**).

sheveet|ah/-ot שביתה *nf* strike; (*+of:* **-at**).

sheveet|ah/-ot peer'ee|t (*cpr* **pra'ee|t**)/**-yot** שביתה פראית *nf* wildcat strike.

(hef|er/-erah/-artee) sheveetah הפר שביתה *v* engaged in strike-breaking; (*pres* **mefer** *etc; fut* **yafer** *etc*).

(mef|er/-eerey) sheveetah מפר שביתה *nm* strike-breaker; "blackleg"; "scab".

sheveet|at/-ot שביתת *f+of* strike of...

sheveet|at/-ot az'harah שביתת אזהרה *nf* warning-strike.

sheveet|at/-ot he'atah שביתת האטה *nf* slow-down strike.

sheveet|at/-ot neshek שביתת נשק *nf* armistice; truce.

sheveet|at/-ot ra'av שביתת רעב *nf* hunger-strike.

sheveet|at/-ot shevet שביתת שבת *nf* sit-down strike.

sheveev/-eem שביב *nm* spark; (*pl+of:* **-ey**).

sheveev shel teekvah שביב של תקווה *nm* spark of hope.

shevee|yah/-yot שבייה *nf* capturing; taking prisoner; (*+of:* **-yat**).

shev|eh/-at 'erekh שווה ערך *adj* equivalent; equal in value.

shev|eh/-at nefesh שווה נפש *adj* indifferent.

shev|eh/-at zekhooyot שווה זכויות *adj* of equal rights.

shever שבר *nm* **1.** fracture; **2.** hernia (Medic.).

shev|er/-areem שבר *nm* fraction; fragment; (*pl+of:* **sheevrey**).

shever 'anan שבר ענן *nm* cloudburst.

shev|et/-ateem שבט *nm* **1.** tribe; **2.** sceptre; **3.** whip; (*pl+of:* **sheevtey**).

(le) shevet o le-khesed לשבט או לחסד *adv* for good or for bad.

shevet akheem שבת אחים *nm* **1.** fraternal togetherness; **2.** *lit* : sitting together like brothers.

(shveetat/-ot) shevet שביתת שבת *nf* sit-down strike.

shevoo|'a' שבוע *m+of* the week of...

shevoo|'ah/-ot שבועה *nf* oath; (*+of:* **-'at**).

(hats'har|ah/-ot bee) shvoo'ah הצהרה בשבועה *nf* affidavit; sworn statement.

shevoo|'at/-'ot emooneem שבועת אמונים *nf* oath of allegiance; oath of office.

shevoo|'at/-'ot shav שבועת שווא *nf* false oath; perjury.

shevoo|'at/-'ot sheker שבועת שקר *nf* perjury.

shevoo'ayeem שבועיים *nm pl* fortnight; two weeks.

shevoo'ee/-t שבועי *adj* weekly.

(sakhar) shevoo'ee שכר שבועי *nm* weekly salary.

shevoo'on/-eem שבועון *nm* weekly (magazine); (*pl+of:* **-ey**).

(doo-) shevoo'on דו־שבועון *nm* bi-weekly.

shevoot שבות *nf* **1.** repatriation; return; **2.** captivity.

◇ **(khok ha) shevoot** see ◇ **khok ha-shvoot**.

▫ **Shevoot 'Am** see ▫ **Shvoot 'Am**.

shevoo|y/-yey meelkhamah שבוי מלחמה *nm* prisoner of war.

sheygets/shekotseem שייגץ *[colloq.] nm* **1.** non-Jewish youngster; **2.** *[slang]* cheeky fellow or young Jew with a non-Jewish appearance.

sheykh/-eem שיך *nm* Sheik, head of an Arab family, tribe or village.

(yah) sheykh! !יא שיך *[colloq.] (Arab.) interj* dear chap; dear fellow!

sheynah שינה *nf* sleep; (*+of:* **shnat**).

(kadoor/-ey) sheynah כדור שינה *nm* sleeping pill.
(khad|ar/-rey) sheynah חדר שינה *nm* bedroom.
(nedoodey) sheynah נדודי שינה *nm pl* insomnia.
shezeef/-eem שזיף *nm* plum (*pl+of:* **-ey**).
shezeer|ah/-ot שזירה *nf* interweaving; twisting.
□ **Shezor (Shezor)** שזור *nm* village (est. 1953) in Lower Galilee, 9 km NE of **Karmee'el**. Pop. 262.
shfan/-ey neesayon שפן ניסיון *nm* guinea-pig.
shfakheem שפכים *nm pl* (*sing:* **shefekh**) sewage; slops; (*pl+of:* **sheefkhey**).
shfanee|yah/-yot שפנייה *nf* rabbit hutch; (*+of:* **-yat**).
□ **Shfar'am** (Shefar'am or Shefa Amr) שפרעם *nm* mixed (Christian, Muslim, Druse, Jewish) township in Lower Galilee, 4 km E. of **Keeryat Ata**. Pop. 20,900.
□ **Shfayeem** (Shefayim) שפיים *nm* kibbutz (est. 1935) on Sharon Coast, 5 km N. of **Hertseleeyah**. Pop. 741.
shfeekhah/-ot שפיכה *nf* spilling (*+of:* **-at**).
shfeekhoot dameem שפיכות דמים *nf* bloodshed.
shfeetah/-ot שפיטה *nf* (law) trying; judging; sentencing.
◇ **(shoomah lefee meytav ha) shfeetah** see ◇ **shoomah lefee meytav ha-shfeetah**.
shfeeyoot שפיות *nf* sanity.
shfelah/-ot שפלה *nf* lowland; (*+of:* **-at**).
□ **(ha)shfelah** השפלה *nf* "the lowlands", hilly area in center of Israel, 100 km long and 20-40 km wide, stretching between Judean Hills to E. and Coastal Plain to W, from Samaria Mountains to N, to the Negev to S.
shfof|eret/-arot שפופרת *nf* tube.
(be-kheymah) shfookhahשפוכה בחימה *adv* furiously.
shgag|ah/-ot שגגה *nf* inadvertent mistake; unintended offence.
(bee) shgagah בשגגה *adv* unintentionally.
shgee|'ah/-'ot שגיאה *nf* error; mistake; (*+of:* **-'at**).
shgee|'at/-'ot keteev שגיאת כתיב *nf* spelling error.
shka'arooree/-t שקערורי *adj* concave.
shkedeeyah/-yot שקדייה *nf* almond-tree.
shkee|'ah/-'ot שקיעה *nf* sinking; decline; (*+of:* **'at**).
(ha) shkee'ah השקיעה *nf* sunset.
shkee|'at/-'ot dam שקיעת דם *nf* blood sedimentation (Medic.).
shkee'at ha-shemesh שקיעת השמש *nf* sunset.
shkeed|ah/-ot שקידה *nf* diligence; (*+of:* **-at**).
(bee) shkeedah בשקידה *adv* diligently.
shkeefoo|t/-yot שקיפות *nf* transparency.
shkeel|ah/-ot שקילה *nf* weighing; (*+of:* **-at**).
sh'khak|eem שחקים *nm pl* heavens; skies; (*+of:* **-ey**).
(gor|ed/-dey) sh'khakeem גורד שחקים *nm* skyscraper.
□ **Sh'khanyah** see □ **Shekhanyah**.
sh'kharkhar/-ah שחר *adj* dark-tanned; swarthy; blackish.
sh'kharkhor|et/-ot שחרחורת *nf* good-looking brunette.
sh'kheek|ah/-ot שחיקה *nf* grinding; pulverization; (*+of:* **-at**).
sh'kheekat ha-sakhar שחיקת השכר *nf* erosion of purchasing power of wages.
sh'kheekhoo|t/-yot שכיחות *nf* frequency.
sh'kheen שחין *nm* boils.
(ha) sh'kheenah השכינה *nf* heavenly spirit.
sh'kheet|ah/-ot שחיטה *nf* **1.** slaughter; **2.** kosher slaughtering i.e. in compliance with Jewish law; (*+of:* **-at**).
sh'kheetoo|t/-yot שחיתות *nf* corruption; demoralization.
sh'kheev|ah/-ot שכיבה **1.** lying; reclining; **2.** cohabitation; (*+of:* **-at**).
(bee) sh'kheevah בשכיבה ad lying down.
□ **Sh'khem** (Shekhem or Nablus) שכם *nf* historic Biblical town and at present the country's largest and most important Arab and Muslim center. Pop. 124,700, also includes a small number of Arab Christians and a Samaritan community over 2,600 years old.
sh'khem ekhad שכם אחד *adv* shoulder to shoulder.
sh'khenoot שכנות *nf* vicinity; neighborhood.
(bee) sh'khenoot בשכנות *adv* in proximity of; nearby.
(yakhasey) sh'khenootשכנות יחסי *nm pl* neighborly relations.
sh'kho|'akh/-khah שחוח *adj* stooped; with bent head.
sh'khoon|ah/-ot שכונה *nf* neighborhood; quarter; district; residential area.
sh'khoon|at/-ot 'onee שכונת עוני *nf* slum district; slum area.
shkoonatee/-t שכונתי *adj* neighborhood; area-
(ha) sh'khoonot השכונות *nf pl* suburbia.
('avod|ah/-ot) sh'khor|ah/-ot עבודה שחורה *nf* unskilled labor.
(marah) sh'khorah מרה שחורה *nf* hypochondria; melancholy.
◇ **(ha-pantereem ha) sh'khoreem** see ◇ **(ha)pantereem ha-sh'khoreem**.
shlager/-eem שלאגר *[slang] nm* a hit.
shlash|ah/-ot שלשה *nf* trio; group of three.
shlat שלט *nm* remote control device for TV set (*colloq. abbr. of* **shelat rakhok**).
shla|v/-beem (*b=v*) שלב *nm* **1.** rung of ladder; **2.** step; stage; (*pl+of:* **-bey**).
(ro'eh/ro'at) sh'khorot רואה שחורות *adj & nmf* pessimistic; pessimist.
(rav-) shlabee/-t רב־שלבי *adj* multi-stage.
shlee|'akh/-khey שליח *m+of* emissary of; messenger of.

◇ **shlee|'akh/-khey tseeboor** שליח ציבור *nm* **1.** cantor; one who leads prayer service in synagogue; **2.** public servant.

shleef|ah/-ot שליפה *nf* unsheathing; drawing (out); (*+of:* **-at**).

shleef|ah/-ot meen ha-moten שליפה מן המותן *nf* drawing from the hip.

(meroots/-ey) shleekheem מרוץ שליחים *nm* relay race.

shleekhoo|t/-yot שליחות *nf* **1.** mission; **2.** errand.

(bee) shleekhoot בשליחות *adv* on a mission.

(yats|a/-'ah/-'atee bee) shleekhoot יצא בשליחות *v* left on a mission; (*pres* **yotse** *etc; fut* **yestse** *etc*).

shleel|ah/-ot שלילה *nf* **1.** negation; denial; **2.** deprivation; (*+of:* **-at**).

(bee) shleelah בשלילה *adv* negatively; in the negative.

shleelat reeshyon שלילת רשיון *nf* withdrawal of license.

shleelat zekhoo|t/-ooyot שלילת זכות *nf* denial of right.

shleelee שלילי *nm* unsatisfactory mark in school.

shleelee! !שלילי negative! no! (Army slang).

shleelee/-t שלילי *adj* negative.

shleesh/-eem שליש *num m* **1.** 1/3; one third; third part; **2.** trimester.

(lee) shleesh ve-lee-revee'a' לשליש ולרביע *adv* partially; in bits and pieces.

shleeshee/-t שלישי *adj & num* third; 3rd.

◇ **(beetoo'akh tsad) shleeshee** see ◇ **beetoo'akh tsad shleeshee**.

(goof) shleeshee גוף שלישי *nm* third person (Gram.).

(to'ar) shleeshee תואר שלישי *nm* PhD degree.

(tsad) shleeshee צד שלישי *nm* third party (to a deal, court-action or contract).

(yom/yemey) shleeshee יום שלישי *nm* Tuesday.

◇ **(ha-'aleeyah ha) shleesheet** see ◇ **(ha)'aleeyah ha-shleesheet**.

sleeshee|yah/-yot שלישייה *nf* triplets; 3; trio; (*+of:* **yat**).

shlee|tah/-tot שליטה *nf* control; command; proficiency.

(ba'al/-ey) shleetah בעל שליטה *nm* main shareholder (in a corporate body).

(.efoo'ah) shlemah! רפואה שלמה! Have a complete recovery! (said to someone in ill health or injured).

shlemoo|t/-yot שלמות *nf* integrity; totality; perfection.

◇ **shlemoot ha-arets** שלמות הארץ *nf* "country's integrity" - dogma of partisans of an undivided Eretz-Israel, i.e. that Israel consist of full territory of former Palestine.

(bee) shlemoot בשלמות *adv* fully; completely.

shlom שלום *.m+of* the peace **(shalom)** of...

shlom bayeet שלום בית *nm* domestic peace; peace of the household.

(drosh/deershee bee) shlom דרוש בשלום *v imp sing m/f* give my regards to...

◇ **(meelkhemet) shlom ha-galeel** see ◇ **meelkhemet shlom ha-galeel**.

□ **Shlomee** (Shelomi) שלומי *nf* township (est. 1949) on Galilee Coast, 4 km SE of **Rosh ha-Neekrah**. Pop. 2,460.

(anshey) shlomenoo אנשי שלומנו *nm pl* our own people; insiders.

(mah) shlom|kha/-ekh? מה שלומך? **1.** (*query & greeting*) *sing m/f* How do you do? **2.** (*lit.*) how's your health?

shloo|'akh/-khat resen שלוח רסן *adj* unbridled; unrestrained.

shlook/-eem שלוק *nm [slang]* (Yiddish) sip; gulp.

(beytsah/-eem) shlook|ah/-ot ביצה שלוקה *nf* hardboiled egg.

shlookh|ah/-ot שלוחה *nf* extension; branch; subsidiary.

□ **Shlookhot** (Sheluhot) שלוחות *nm* kibbutz (est. 1949) in Bet-She'an Valley, 3 km SE of Bet-She'an proper. Pop. 564.

shlooleet/-yot שלולית *nf* puddle.

shloomee'el (npr shloomee'el) שלומיאל *nm* sad sack; ne'er do well.

shloomee'elee/-t שלומיאלי *adj* clumsy; ill-starred.

shloomper/-eet שלומפר *[slang] adj* untidy; negligent person.

shloov/-at zro'a' שלוב זרוע *adj* arm-in-arm.

shlosh שלוש *(prefix)* tri-

shlosh-'esreh שלוש־עשרה *num f* 13; thirteen.

◇ **shlosh-'esreh meedot** שלוש־עשרה מידות 13 attributes characterizing God (according to Exodus 34: 6-7).

shloshah שלושה *num m* 3; three.

shloshah 'asar שלושה־עשר *num m* 13; thirteen.

(ha) shloshah-'asar/shlosh-'esreh השלושה־עשר *adj & num m/f* the 13th; the thirteenth.

(khodesh) shlosh-'esreh חודש שלוש־עשרה *nm* **1.** 13th month; **2.** annual extra-salary bonus.

(pee) shloshah פי שלושה *adv* threefold.

shlosheem שלושים *num* 30; thirty.

(ha) shlosheem ba-khodesh השלושים בחודש *nm* the 30th of the month.

◇ **(yom ha) shlosheem** see ◇ **yom ha-shlosheem**.

shma'! sheem'ee! (cpr sheem'ee!) !שמע ! שמעי *v imp sing m/f* listen! (*inf* **leeshmo'a'**; *pst* **shama'** *pres* **shome'a'**; *fut* **yeeshma'**).

shma' na! sheem'ee (cpr sheem'ee!) na! שמע נא! שמעי נא! *v* will you *m/f* listen, please!

◇ **shma' yeesra'el!** "Shma Yisroel!" שמע ישראל! , the opening words "Hear Oh Israel!" of the fundamental Jewish credo that has become the traditional formula for identifying oneself with Judaism.

◇ **(kree'at) shma'!** see ◇ **kree'at shma'!**

shmad שמד *nm* a Jew's baptism; forced apostasy.

(yats|a/-'ah/-tee lee) shmad יצא לשמד *v* deserted the Jewish faith; (*pres* **yotse** *etc; fut* **yetse** *etc*).
shmam|ah/-ot שממה *nf* desolation; wilderness; (*+of:* **sheemem|at/-ot**).
(hafrakhat ha) shmamah הפרחת השממה *nf* reclamation; making the desert bloom.
(keeboosh ha) shmamahהשממה כיבוש *nm* conquest of the wilderness (desert).
shmanman/-ah שמנמן *adj* plump; fattish.
shmareem שמרים *nm pl* yeast.
shmartaf/-eem שמרטף *nm* babysitter.
shmashot שמשות *nf pl* **1.** (*sing:* **sheemshah**) windowpanes; **2.** suns (*sing:* **shemesh**).
(beyn ha) shmashot בין השמשות *adv* twilight; dusk.
shmee|'ah/-'ot שמיעה *nf* hearing.
('edoo|t/-yot) shmee'ah עדות שמיעה *nf* hearsay evidence.
shmee'atee/-t שמיעתי *adj* auditory; aural.
shmeenee/-t שמיני *adj & num* 8th; eighth.
◇ **shmeenee 'atseret** שמיני עצרת *nm* last day (outside Israel the day before last) of the Sukkot holiday.
shmeeneest/-eet שמיניסט *[slang] nmf* student in his/her last high school year.
shmeenee|t/-yot שמינית *nf* (fraction) 1/8; one eighth.
shmeeneet she-bee-shmeeneet שמינית שבשמינית *nf* (*lit.*) 1/8; infinitesimal part.
shmeeneeyot ba-aveer שמיניות באוויר *nf pl* doing the impossible.
shmeer|ah/-ot שמירה *nf* **1.** guarding; **2.** guard duty; (*+of:* **-at**).
(kelev/kalbey) shmeerah כלב שמירה *nm* watchdog.
◇ **shmeetah** שמיטה *nf* fallow year; sabbatical year.
◇ **(shnat ha) shmeetah** see ◇ **shnat ha-shmeetah**.
shmeetat khovot שמיטת חובות *nf* remission of debts.
shmegegeh שמגגה *[slang] nm* stupid, impractical and worthless person.
(lee) shm|o/-ah לשמו *adv* for the sake of the thing in itself; unselfishly.
shmon|ah/-eh שמונה *num m/f* 8; eight.
shmon|ah/-eh 'asar/'esreh שמונה־עשר/שמונה־עשרה *num m/f & adj* 18; eighteen.
shmoneem שמונים *num* 80; eighty.
(ha) shmoneem השמונים *adj & num* the 80th; the eightieth; of eighty.
(yovel ha) shmoneemיובל השמונים *nm* eightieth anniversary.
shmoneh שמונה *num f* 8; eight.
shmoneh-'esreh שמונה־עשרה *num f* 18; eighteen.
◇ **"shmoneh-'esreh"** שמונה עשרה "the 18 Benedictions" - the central part of each of an observant Jew's 3 daily prayers, to be recited standing.
shmoo|'ah/-'ot שמועה *nf* rumor; (*+of:* **-'at**).
(mee-pee ha) shmoo'ah מפי השמועה *adv* from hearsay; according to rumor.
shmoo|'at/-'ot shav שמועת שווא *nf* false rumor.
shmoor|ah/-ot שמורה reservation; (*+of:* **-at**).
shmoorat/-ot teva שמורת טבע *nf* nature preserve.
◇ **shnat ha-shmeetah** שנת השמיטה *nf* fallow (sabbatical) year recurring every seventh year.
shnat/shnot loo'akh שנת לוח *nf* calendar year.
shnatayeem שנתיים *nf pl* two years.
shnatee/-t שנתי *adj* annual; yearly.
(doo-) shnatee/-t דו־שנתי *adj* bi-annual.
(khad-) shnatee/-t חד־שנתי *adj* annual; for one year.
(khatsee-) shnatee/-t חצי שנתי *adj* semi-annual; half-yearly.
(makhzor/-eem) shnatee/-yeem מחזור שנתי *nm* annual turnover.
(rav-) shnatee/-t רב־שנתי *adj* perennial.
(reva'-) shnatee/-t רבע שנתי *adj* quarterly.
(tlat-) shnatee/-t תלת־שנתי *adj* triennial.
(nadedah) shnat|o/-ah/-ee *etc* נדדה שנתו/־ה/־י *v* couldn't sleep.
shnaton/-eem שנתון *nm* **1.** yearbook; **2.** age-group (army, school *etc*); (*pl+of:* **-ey**).
◇ **shnat tash-noon** (or **tash-noon alef/ bet/geemal** *etc*) תש"נ/תשנ"א/תשנ"ב/תשנ"ג *nf* Jewish calendar year 750/751/752/753 (actually 5750/5751/5752/5753) *etc.* (See in INTRODUCTION TO HEBREW section explaining mechanism of Jewish chronology).
shnayeem שניים *num m* two; (when preceding a plural noun: **shney**).
(pee) shnayeem פי שניים *adv* double; twice as many.
(le-mashal ve-lee) shneenah למשל ולשנינה *adv* **1.** to become an object of derision; **2.** (*lit.*) (to make one) become a proverb and a byword.
shneenoo|t/-yot שנינות *nf* sarcasm; wit.
shneeyah/-yot שנייה *nf* second; 1/60 of a minute; (*+of:* **-yat**).
shneeyah שניה *adj & num f* 2nd; (*m:* **shenee**).
◇ **(ha-'aleeyah ha)shneeyah** see ◇ **(ha)'aleeyah ha-shneeyah**.
(heezdamnoot) shneeyahשניה הזדמנות *nf* second chance.
shney שני *num m* 2; two.
shneym-'asar שנים־עשר *num m* 12; twelve.
(ha) shneym-'asar השנים־עשר *num m* the 12th; twelfth.
shnorer/-eet שנורר *[colloq.] nm* schnorrer; one who solicits contributions.
shnor|er/-erah/-artee שנורר *v* s schnorred; solicited contributions; (*pres* **meshnorer**; *fut* **yeshnorer**).
shnoreroo|t/-yot שנוררות *nf* schnorring; begging; living on handouts.
she'on/-ey keer שעון קיר *nm* wall clock.
she'on/-ey yad שעון יד *nm* wrist watch.
she'oo'eet שעועית *nf* bean; beans.

(merak) she'oo'eet מרק שעועית *nf* bean-soup.

sho|'ah/-'ot שואה *nf* catastrophe; (*+of:* **-'at**).

◇ **(ha)sho'ah** השואה *nf* the Holocaust, i.e. resolute campaign for total extermination of the Jewish people carried out by Nazi Germany in the years 1939-1945. As a result, 6,000,000 Jews (one third of the Jews in the world at that time and about 90 percent of the Jews of Europe) were exterminated.

◇ **(neesp|ah/-etah/-oo ba) sho'ah** see ◇ **neesp|ah/-etah/-oo ba-sho'ah**.

◇ **(yom ha)sho'ah ve-ha-gvoorah** see ◇ **yom ha-sho'ah ve-ha-gvoorah**.

shod שוד *nm* robbery; hold-up.

shod drakheem שוד דרכים *nm* highway robbery.

shod mezooyan שוד מזוין *nm* armed robbery.

shoded/-eem שודד *nm* bandit; robber; (*pl+of:* **-ey**).

shoded/-ey drakheem שודד דרכים *nm* highway robber.

shoded/-ey yam שודד ים *nm* pirate.

shoded/-et שודד *v pres* robs; (*pst* **shadad**; *fut* **yeeshdod**).

shoded|et/-ot שודדת *nf* woman-bandit.

sho'el/-et שואל **1.** *v pres* asks; (*pst* **sha'al**; *fut* **yeesh'al**); **2.** *nmf* inquirer; (*pl:* **sho'al|eem/-ot**; *+of:* **-ey**).

sho|'er/-'areem שוער *nm* **1.** gatekeeper; doorkeeper; **2.** goalkeeper (soccer).

sho'ev/-et שואב *v pres* draws, pumps (water); derives (information); (*pst* **sha'av**; *fut* **yeesh'av**).

sho|'ev/-'avey avak שואב אבק *nm* vacuum cleaner.

sho|'ev/-'avey mayeem שואב מים *nm* water-drawer.

◇ **(khotvey 'etseem ve)sho'avey mayeem** see ◇ **khotvey 'etseem ve-sho'avey mayeem**.

□ **Sho'evah** (Sho'eva) שואבה *nm* village in the Judean hills, 6 km E. of **Sha'ar ha-Gay**. Pop. 318.

(even) sho'evet אבן שואבת *nf* lodestone; magnet; (mostly used figuratively).

shof|e'a'/-a'at שופע *adj* abundant; flowing.

(khazeh) shofe'a' חזה שופע *nf* abundant breasts.

◇ **shofar/-ot** שופר *nm* the shofar i.e. a ram's horn used in synagogue rituals.

(tekee|'ah/-'ot ba) shofar תקיעה בשופר *nf* blowing the shofar.

(tekee|'at/-'ot) shofar תקיעת שופר *nf* shofar blowing.

shofekh/-et שופך *v pres* spills; (*pst* **shafakh**; *fut* **yeeshpokh**; *(p=f)*).

shof|et/-teem שופט *nm* judge; (*pl+of:* **-tey**).

shofet/-et שופט *v pres* judges; (*pst* **shafat**; *fut* **yeeshpot** *(p=f)*).

shofet/-et 'elyon/-ah שופט עליון *nmf* Justice; Supreme Court Judge.

shofet/-et mekhozee/-t שופט מחוזי *nmf* District Court Judge.

shofet/-et shalom שופט שלום *nmf* Justice of the Peace; magistrate.

(beev/-ey) shofkheen ביב שופכין *nm* gutter.

(bor/-ot) shofkheen בור שופכין *nm* cesspit; cesspool.

shoft|eem שופטים *nm pl* judges (*sing:* **shofet**; *+of:* **-ey**).

shog|eh/-ah שוגה *v pres* **1.** errs; blunders; **2.** staggers; (*pst* **shagah**; *fut* **yeeshgeh**).

shog|eh/-ah שוגה *adj* erring; one who indulges in day-dreaming.

(be) shogeg בשוגג *adv* unintentionally.

shok/-ayeem שוק *nm* leg; thigh; (*pl+of:* **-ey**).

shok/-eem שוק *nm* shock.

(keeb|el/-lah/-altee) shok קיבל שוק *v* got a shock; (*pres* **mekabel** *etc*; *fut* **yekabel** *etc*).

shok|e'a'/-a'at שוקע **1.** *adj* sinking; **2.** *v pres* sinks; (*pst* **shaka'**; *fut* **yeeshka'**).

□ **Shokedah** (Shoqeda) שוקדה *nm* village (est. 1957) in NW Negev, 6 km W. of **Neteevot**. Pop. 176.

shoket שוקת *nf* trough; basin.

(leefney) shoket shvoorah לפני שוקת שבורה *adv* before a broken basin i.e. (*figurat.*) with all hopes gone.

shokhad שוחד *nm* bribe.

shokh|et/-ateem שוחט *nm* ritual i.e. kosher slaughterer (of poultry and cattle) according to Jewish law.

shokhet/-et שוחט *v pres* slaughters; (*pst* **shakhat**; *fut* **yeesh'khot**).

shokhev/-et שוכב *v pres* lies (down); (*pst* **shakhav**; *fut* **yeeshkav** *(k=kh)*).

shokolad/-eem שוקולד *nm* chocolate.

sholal שולל *adj* stray; confused.

(hal|akh/-khah/-akhtee) sholal הלך שולל was misled; went astray; (*pres* **holekh** *etc*; *fut* **yelekh** *etc*).

(hol|eekh/-eekhah/-akhtee) sholal הוליך שולל *v* led astray; misled; (*pres* **moleekh** *etc*; *fut* **yoleekh** *etc*).

sholef/-et שולף *v pres* draws out; unsheathes; (*pst* **shalaf**; *fut* **yeeshlof**).

sholel/-et שולל *v pres* **1.** negates; **2.** condemns; disapproves.

shom|e'a'/-'eem שומע *nm* listener; (*pl+of:* **-'ey**).

shom|e'a'/-a'at שומע *v pres* listens; hears; (*pst* **shama'**; *fut* **yeeshma'**).

shomem/-ah שומם *adj* desolate; uninhabited.

shomen שומן *nm* excess of fatness.

shom|er/-reem שומר *nm* watchman; (*pl+of:* **-rey**).

shomer/-et emooneem שומר אמונים *v pres* stays faithful; (*pst* **shamar** *etc*; *fut* **yeeshmor** *etc*).

shomer/-rey laylah שומר לילה *nm* night-watchman.

shomer/-eret masoret שומר מסורת *adj & nmf* observant; tradition-guarding; (*pl:* **-rey** *etc*).

shom|er/-rey rosh שומר ראש *nm* bodyguard.

"(Ha)shomer" השומר *nf* organization of Jewish watchmen in the pre-Mandate era. Between 1909 and 1920, its members kept guard defending Jewish settlements scattered throughout Palestine and their heroic exploits earned some of them a legendary halo. It is regarded as the precursory of the Haganah.

◇ **"(ha)shomer ha-tsa'eer"** ("Hashomer Hatzair") השומר הצעיר *nf* left-wing Zionist youth movement with branches all over Israel, Western Europe, North and South America. Advocates achievement of Zionist ideals by each youth's personal "self-realization" through joining a kibbutz and becoming part of Hakibbutz Ha'artzi (◇ **(ha)keeboots ha-artsee**).

□ **Shomerah** שומרה *nm* village (est. 1949) in Upper Galilee, near Lebanese border, 12 km E. of Hanita Junction **(Tsomet Khaneetah)**. Pop. 261.

□ **Shomrat** (Shomerat) שומרת *nm* village (est. 1948) on Galilee Coast, 4 N. of Acre. Pop. 439.

□ **Shomron** שומרון *nf* Samaria, district that stretches from Jordan Valley in E. to Coastal Plain in W. and from Bet-She'an Valley in N. to **Levonah** (Labboon) Valley in S. Under Israeli administration since 1967.

shon|eh/-ah שונה **1.** *adj* different; **2.** *v pres* differs; (*pst* **hayah shoneh**; *fut* **yeeshtaneh**).

shonee שוני *nm* difference; variance; variety.

shonot שונות *nm pl* miscellaneous.

shomron|ee/-eem שומרוני *nm* Samaritan (*pl+of:* **-ey**).

◇ **(ha)shomroneem** השומרונים *nm pl* Samaritans - a small, tightly organized community of descendants of ancient Samaritans who have resided in the country since the fall of the Israelite Kingdom to Babylonians in 586 BCE. Their present population numbers some 540 people, half of whom live in an autonomous quarter of Nablus (near Mount **Greezeem**, revered by them). The other half live in an area of Holon **(Kholon)** near Tel-Aviv in growing assimilation with general Jewish population.

□ **Shoo'afat** (Shu'fat) שועפט *nf* fashionable, mainly Christian, suburb of North Jerusalem, beyond Mount Scopus.

shoo'al/-eem שועל *nm* fox; (*pl+of:* **-ey**).

(sheebolet) shoo'al שיבולת שועל *nm* oats.

shook/shvakeem שוק *nm* market; market-place; (*pl+of:* **shookey**).

shook khofshee שוק חופשי *nm* free market.

shook shakhor שוק שחור *nm* black market.

(ha) shook ha-meshootaf השוק המשותף *nm* the Common Market.

shool|am/-mah שולם *v* was paid-up; (*pres* **meshoolam**; *fut* **yeshoolam**).

shool|ayeem שוליים *nm pl* edge; margins; (*pl+of:* **-ey**).

shoolayeem שוליים (*suffix*) *adj* marginal.

shoolee/-t שולי *adj* marginal.

shooley שולי *nm pl+of* the margins of.

(be) shooley בשולי *adj* at the end of; at the bottom of.

shoolkhan/-ot שולחן *nm* table.

shoolkhan 'arookh שולחן ערוך *nm* set table.

◇ **"shoolkhan 'arookh"** שולחן ערוך *nm* 15th Century codification that became the prevailing code of Jewish religious observance; ("Shulchen-Orech" in Yiddish).

shoolkhan/-ot kteevah שולחן כתיבה *nm* desk.

('ar|akh/-khah/-tee) shoolkhan ערך שולחן *v* set table; (*pres* **'orekh** *etc*; *fut* **ya'arokh** *etc*).

('areekhat) shoolkhan עריכת שולחן *nf* setting the table.

(tenees) shoolkhan טניס שולחן *nm* table-tennis; ping-pong.

shooll|yah/-yot שוליה *nm* apprentice; (*+of:* **-yat**).

shoom שום **1.** not any; none; **2.** *nm* garlic.

shoom davar שום דבר nothing; not a thing.

shoom eesh שום איש no one; nobody.

shoom makom שום מקום nowhere.

('al) shoom על שום *adv* because; in accordance with.

(be) shoom ofen בשום אופן *adv* in no way.

(be) shoom paneem בשום פנים *adv* by no means; under no circumstances.

(kee-kleepat ha) shoom כקליפת השום *adv* not worth anything at all; valueless.

(mee) shoom משום kind of.

(mee) shoom mah משום מה for some reason.

(mee) shoom she- משום ש־ because.

shoom|ah/-ot שומה *nf* assessment; valuation; (*+of:* **-ot**).

(pekeed ha)shoomah פקיד השומה *nm* assessment officer; income tax assessor.

◇ **shoomah lefee meytav ha-shfeetah** שומה לפי מיטב השפיטה *nf* discretionary income-tax assessment of tax-payer who has failed to submit yearly income report.

shooman/-eem שומן *nm* fat; (*pl+of:* **-ey**).

shoon|ah/-tah/-etee שונה *v* was altered; was changed; (*pres* **meshooneh**; *fut* **yeshooneh**).

shoomshoom (*cpr* **soomsoom**) **/-eem** שומשום *nm* sesame **(plant)**.

shoop|ar/-rah/-artee שופר *v* was improved; (*pres* **meshoopar**; *fut* **yeshoopar**).

shoor|ah/-ot שורה *nf* **1.** line; row; **2.** rank; **3.** series; (*+of:* **-at**).

(be) shoorah בשורה *adv* in line; lined up.

(ka) shoorah כשורה *adv* properly.

(lo ka) shoorah לא כשורה *adv* not in order; not as should be.

(meen ha) shoorah מן השורה *adj* ordinary; regular; rank and file.

◇ **shoorook (Shuruk)** שורוק *nm* letter **Vav** (וּ) with dot in center indicating that it is a vowel pronounced **oo**.

(ve) shoot ושות *abbr.* **(ve-shootafav)** -... and associates.

shoot|af/-fah/-tee שותף *v* was associated, made partner; (*pres* **meshootaf**; *fut* **yeshootaf**).

shootaf/-eem שותף *v* partner; associate; (*pl+of:* **-ey**).

shoot|af/-ah le-ba'aloot שותף לבעלות *nmf* co-owner.

shootaf/-ah le-pesha' שותף לפשע *nmf* accessory to a crime.

shootaf/-ah le-kheder שותף לחדר *nmf* room mate.

shootafoo|t/-yot שותפות *nf* partnership; cooperation.

shoov/-ee! שובי ! *v imp sing m/f* come back! (*inf* **lashoov**; *pst & pres* **shav**; *fut* **yashoov**).

shoov שוב *adv* again.

shoov pa'am שוב פעם *[slang] adv* once more; once again.

shoov ve-shoov שוב ושוב *adv* again and again.

□ **Shoovah** (Shuva) שובה *nm* village (est. 1950) in NW Negev, E. of Sa'ad Junction (**Tsomet Sa'ad**). Pop. 387.

shooval/-eem (*npr* **shovel/shvaleem**) שובל **1.** *nm* train (of dress); **2.** wake (of ship, aircraft); (*pl+of:* **-ey**).

□ **Shooval** see □ **Shoval**, below.

shor/shvareem שור *nm* ox; bull; (*pl+of:* **-ey**).

shorek/-et שורק *v pres* whistles (*pst* **sharak**; *fut* **yeeshrok**).

shor|esh/-asheem שורש *nm* root; (*pl+of:* **-shey**).

□ **Shoresh** שורש *nm* coop. village (est. 1948) 5 km SE of **Sha'ar ha-Gay** (Bab-el-Wad). Pop. 173.

('ak|ar/-rah/-artee meen ha) shoresh עקר מן השורש *v* uprooted; deracinated; (*pres* **'oker** *etc*; *fut* **ya'akor** *etc*).

('akeerah meen ha) shoresh עקירה מן השורש *nf* uprooting; eradication.

(heek|ah/-tah/-etee) shor|esh/-osheem הכה שורש *v* struck a root; (*pres* **makeh** *etc*; *fut* **yakeh** *etc*).

shorshee/-t שורשי *adj* deeply rooted.

shorsheeyoot שורשיות *nf* deeprootedness.

Shosh שוש abbr.of the common female name **"Shoshanah"** (Rose, Lily).

shoshan/-eem שושן *nm* lily; (*pl+of:* **-ey**).

shoshan|ah/-eem שושנה *nf* rose; (*+of:* **-at**).

Shoshanah שושנה common feminine name (*abbr.* **Shosh; Shoshee**).

□ **Shoshanat ha-'Amakeem** (Shoshannat ha'Amaqim) שושנת העמקים *nm* rural and urban settlement (est. 1951) in Sharon, N. of Netanya, near **Khavatselet ha-Sharon**. Pop. 719.

shosh|elet/-alot שושלת *nf* dynasty.

shoshveen/-eem שושבין *nm* best man; usher (at a wedding); (*pl+of:* **-ey**).

shoshveen|ah/-ot שושבינה *nf* bridesmaid; (*+of:* **-at**).

shot/-eem שוט *nm* whip; (*pl+of:* **-at**).

shot|eh/-ah שותה *v pres* drinks; (*pst* **shatah**; *fut* **yeeshteh**).

shot|eh/-ah שוטה *adj & nmf* stupid; fool.

(kadoor/-eem) shot|eh/-eem כדור שוטה *nm* stray bullet.

(kelev/klaveem) shot|eh/-eem כלב שוטה *nm* mad dog.

(khaseed/-eem) shot|eh/-eem חסיד שוטה *nm* blindly and foolishly over-zealous partisan.

shotef/-et שוטף *v pres* rinses; washes away; (*pst* **shataf**; *fut* **yeeshtof**).

shotef/-et שוטף **1.** *adj* fluent; current; **2.** *adv* fluently.

(geshem) shotef גשם שוטף *nm* torrential rain.

shotek/-et שותק **1.** *adj* taciturn; silent; **2.** *v pres* keeps silent; (*pres* **shatak**; *fut* **yeeshtok**).

shot|er/-reem שוטר *nm* policeman; (*pl+of:* **-rey**).

shot|er/-rey kheresh שוטר חרש *nm* plain-clothesman; plain-clothes detective.

shot|er/-rey makof שוטר מקוף *nm* beat policeman.

shoter/-et tenoo'ah שוטר תנועה *nmf* traffic policeman/policewoman.

shot|eret/-rot שוטרת *nf* policewoman.

shot|et/-etah/-atetee שוטט *v* wandered; roamed; (*pres* **meshotet**; *fut* **yeshotet**).

shotetoo|t/-yot שוטטות *nf* loitering; vagrancy.

(halokh va) shov הלוך ושוב *adv* back and forth.

shovakh/-eem שובך *nm* dovecote.

□ **Shoval** שובל *nm* kibbutz (est. 1946) in N. Negev, 4 km SW of Bet-Kama Junction (**Tsomet Bet-Kamah**). Pop 555.

shov|av/-evah שובב *adj* naughty; unruly.

shovee שווי *nm* value; worth.

shoveeneest/-eem שוביניסט *nm* chauvinist.

shovel/shvaleem שובל **1.** *nm* train (of dress); **2.** wake (of ship, aircraft); (*pl+of:* **-ey**).

shov|er/-reem שובר *nm* voucher; receipt; (*pl+of:* **-rey**).

shover/-et שובר *v pres* breaks; (*pst* **shavar**; *fut* **yeeshbor** *(b=v)*).

shov|er/-rey galeem שובר גלים *nm* breakwater.

shovet/-et שובת *v pres* strikes; ceases work; (*pst* **shavat**; *fut* **yeeshbot** *(b=v)*).

shov|et/-teem שובת *nm* striker; (*pl+of:* **-tey**).

shovevoo|t/-yot שובבות *nf* naughtiness; mischief; lightheadedness.

shpakhtel/-eem שפאכטל *[colloq.] nm* spatula.

shrafra|f/-peem שרפרף *nm* stool; (*pl+of:* **-pey**).

shravee/-t שרבי *adj* hot and dry (weather).

shravrav/-eem שרברב *nm* plumber; (*pl+of:* **-ey**).

shravravoot שרברבות *nf* plumbing.

◇ **Shraga** שרגא Hebrew (Aramaic in origin) counterpart of Yiddish name **Fayvel** (Feivel).

shreek|ah/-ot שריקה *nf* whistle; (*+of:* **kat**).

shreer/-eem שריר *nm* muscle; (*pl+of:* **-ey**).

shreeree/-t שרירי *adj* muscular.

shreeroo|t/-yot שרירות *nf* stubbornness; obstinacy.

shreeroot lev שרירות לב *nf* arbitrariness.

shreerootee/-t שרירותי *adj* arbitrary.

shtadlan/-eem שתדלן *nm* interceder; mediator; lobbyist; (*pl+of:* **-ey**).

shtadlanoo|t/-yot שתדלנות *nf* intercession; mediation; lobbying.

◇ **(ha)shtakheem** see ◇ **(ha)shtakheem ha-mookhzakeem**

◇ **(ha)shtakheem ha-mookhzakeem** השטחים המוחזקים *nm pl* territories under Israeli rule since 1967: West Bank (Samaria and parts of Judea), Gaza Strip and Golan Heights.

shtaltan/-eet שתלטן *adj* domineering.

shtaltanoot שתלטנות *nf* drive to domineer.

shtants/-eem שטאנץ *[colloq.] nm* **1.** casting form; mold; **2.** (*figurat.*) prototype.

shtar/-ot שטר *nm* bill; (*pl+of:* **sheetrey**).

shtar/sheetrey beetakhon שטר ביטחון *nm* security note.

shtar/sheetrey boreroot שטר בוררות *nm* arbitration agreement.

shtar/sheetrey kesef שטר כסף *nm* banknote.

shtar/sheetrey khaleefeen שטר חליפין *nm* bill of exchange.

shtar/sheetrey khov שטר חוב *nm* promissory note.

shtar/sheetrey meet'an שטר מטען *nm* bill of lading.

shtar/sheetrey mekher שטר מכר *nm* bill of sale; deed of sale.

shtar she-lo koobad שטר שלא כובד *nm* unhonored promissory note.

(neek|ah/-tah/-eetee) shtar ניכה שטר *v* discounted a bill; (*pres* **menakeh** *etc; fut* **yenakeh** *etc*).

(neekhyon) shtarot נכיון שטרות *nm* discount; bill discounting.

shtayeem שתיים *num f* 2; two.

(akhat oo) shtayeem אחת ושתיים *adv* at once.

(holekh 'al) shtayeem הולך על שתיים *nm & adj* two-legged walker i.e. bi-ped human.

(pee) shtayeem פי שתיים *adv* twice; double.

shteh! shtee! ! שתה ! שתי *v imp sing m/f* drink! will you drink! (*inf* **leeshtot**; *pst* **shatah**; *pres* **shoteh**; *fut* **yeeshteh**).

shtee שתי *nm* warp (in a loom).

shtee va-'erev שתי וערב *adv* crosswise; length and breadth.

(khakeer|at/-ot) shtee va-'erev חקירת שתי וערב *nf* cross-examination.

shteef|ah/-ot שטיפה *nf* rinsing; washing away; (*+of:* **-at**).

shteef|at/-ot mo'akh שטיפת מוח *nf* brainwashing.

shteek|ah/-ot שתיקה *nf* silence; reticence; (*+of:* **-at**).

(bee) shteekah בשתיקה *adv* silently.

shteel/-eem שתיל *nm* seedling; (*pl+of:* **-ey**).

shteel|ah/-ot שתילה *nf* planting; (*+of:* **-at**).

shtee|yah/-yot שתייה *nf* **1.** drinking; **2.** drink; (*+of:* **-yat**).

shteeyah karah שתייה קרה *nf* cold drink.

(demey) shteeyah דמי שתייה *nm pl* ti; service charge.

(mey) shteeyah מי שתייה *nm pl* drinking water.

shteker/-eem שטקר *[slang] nm* plug; jack; (electr.).

shtem 'esreh שתים־עשרה *num f* 12; twelve.

(ha) shtem-'esreh שתים־עשרה *adj & num f* 12th; twelfth.

shtey שתי *num f* 2; two (when preceding a feminine noun).

shtok! sheetkee! ! שתוק ! שתקי *v imp sing m/f* shut up! keep silent! (*inf* **leeshtok**; *pst* **shatak**; *pres* **shotek**; *fut* **yeeshtok**).

□ **Shtoolah** (Shetula) שתולה *nm* village (est. 1969) in Upper Galilee, 9 km NE of **Ma'alot**. Pop. 214.

□ **Shtooleem** (Shetulim) שתולים *nm* village (est. 1950) in Central Coastal Plain, 3 km SE of Ashdod. Pop. 555.

shtoo|t/-yot שטות *nf* folly; nonsense.

(dvar) shtoot דבר שטות *nf* folly; nonsense; stupid, trifling matter.

(ma'aseh) shtoot מעשה שטות *nm* folly; act of foolishness.

(roo'akh) shtoot רוח שטות *nm* a spirit of foolishness.

shtooyot! ! שטויות *nf pl* (*sing:* **shtoot**) nonsense! rubbish!

('azov/'eezvee) shtooyot! ! עזוב שטויות *v imp sing m/f* enough with this nonsense!

shtroodel/-eem שטרודל *[colloq.] nm* strudel.

◇ **shva (Shva)** שווא *nm* usually silent sublinear Hebrew diacritic sign ( ); (see **shva na'** *or* **shva nakh, below**).

shva'-esreh שבע־עשרה *num f* 17; seventeen.

Shva Na' שווא נע *nm* Mobile Shva i.e. that forms a syllable with the voweled consonant following it.

Shva Nakh שווא נח *nm* Quiescent Shva i.e. that closes a syllable.

shva'ee/-t שוואי *adj* unvoweled (consonant) i.e. with a Shva under it (in dotted script).

(ra'ooy/re'ooyah lee)shvakh ראוי לשבח *adj* commendable.

(tseeyoon/-eem lee) shvakh (*npr* **le-shevakh**) ציון לשבח *nm* commendation.

shvakheem שבחים *nm pl* (*sing:* **shevakh**) praises; (*+of:* **sheevkhey**).

shvareem שברים *nm pl* (*sing:* **shever**) fraction; (*pl+of:* **sheevrey**).

shvareem שוורים *nm pl* (sing: shor) oxen, bulls (*pl+of:* **shorey**).

shvat שבט *nm* 5th Jewish Calendar month (approx. Jan.-Feb.); 30 days.

shvav/-eem שבב *nm* splinter; chip; (*pl+of:* **-ey**).

('eebood) shvavee עיבוד שבבי *nm* chipwork.

shv|eh/-at 'erekh שווה ערך *adj* equivalent; equal in value.

shv|eh/-at nefesh שווה נפש *adj* indifferent.

shv|eh/-at zekhooyot שווה זכויות *adj* of equal rights.

shvee! ! שבי *v imp sing f* sit down! (addressing female); (*inf* **lashevet**; *pst* **yashvah**; *pres* **yoshevet**; *fut* **teshev**).

shvee שבי *nm* captivity.
shvee'ee/-t שביעי *adj & num* 7th; seventh.
◇ **shvee'ee shel pesakh** שביעי של פסח *nm* the 7th (and 2nd festive) day of Passover holiday; (outside Israel there is also an 8th day so that, altogether, there are four festive days: the first two and the last two).
shvee'ee|t/-yot שביעית *nf* 1/7; one seventh.
shveel/-eem שביל *nm* pathway; (*pl+of:* **-ey**).
shveel ha-zahav שביל הזהב *nm* the golden mean.
shvee he-khalav שביל החלב *nm* the Milky Way.
(bee) shveel בשביל *prep* for; on behalf of; for the sake of.
shveer|ah/-ot שבירה *nf* breaking; disruption; (*+of:* **-at**).
shveeroo|t/-yot שבירות *nf* fragility; brittleness.
shvees/-eem שביס *nm* hairnet; woman's head-ornament; (*pl+of:* **-ey**).
shveet|ah/-ot שביתה *nf* strike; (*+of:* **-at**).
shveet|ah/-ot peer'ee|t (*cpr* **pra'ee|t)/-yot** שביתה פראית *nf* wildcat strike.
(hefer/-ah/hefartee) shveetah הפר שביתה *v* engaged in strike-breaking; (*pres* **mefer** *etc; fut* **yafer** *etc*).
(kan|ah/-tah/-eetee) shveetah קנה שביתה *v pst* got a hold; (*pres* **koneh** *etc; fut* **yeekneh** *etc*).
(mef|er/-eerey) shveetah מפר שביתה *nm* strike-breaker; "blackleg"; "scab".
shveet|at/-ot שביתת *f+of* strike of...
shveet|at/-ot az'harah שביתת אזהרה *nf* warning-strike.
shveet|at/-ot he'atah שביתת האטה *nf* slow-down strike.
shveet|at/-ot neshek שביתת נשק *nf* armistice; truce.
shveet|at/-ot ra'av שביתת רעב *nf* hunger-strike.
shveet|at/-ot shevet שביתת שבת *nf* sit-down strike.
shveetser/-eet שוויצר *[slang] nmf* show-off; eager beaver.
shveev/-eem שביב *nm* spark; (*pl+of:* **-ey**).
shveev teekvah שביב תקווה *nm* spark of hope.
shvee|yah/-yot שבייה *nf* capturing; taking prisoner; (*+of:* **yat**).
shvoo'a' ha- -שבוע ה *m+of* the week of...
shvoo|'ah/-ot שבועה *nf* oath; (*+of:* **-'at**).
(hats'har|ah/-ot bee)shvoo'ah הצהרה בשבועה *nf* affidavit; sworn statement.
shvoo|'at/-'ot emooneem שבועת אמונים *nf* oath of allegiance; oath of office.
shvoo|'at/-'ot shav שבועת שווא *nf* false oath; perjury.
shvoo|'at/-'ot sheker שבועת שקר *nf* perjury.
shvoo'ayeem שבועיים *nm pl* fortnight; two weeks.
shvoo'ee/-t שבועי *adj* weekly.
(sakhar) shvoo'ee שכר שבועי *nm* weekly salary.
shvoo'on/-eem שבועון *nm* weekly (magazine); (*pl+of:* **-ey**).
(doo-) shvoo'on דו־שבועון *nm* bi-weekly.
shvoot שבות *nf* **1.** repatriation; return; **2.** captivity.
◇ **(khok ha)shvoot** see ◇ **khok ha-shvoot**.
□ **Shvoot 'Am** (Shevut Am) שבות־עם *nm* dwindling residue of once intensely active transit-camp for new immigrants in Sharon which was then also known as the **Bet-Leed "Ma'abarah"** (transit-camp).
shvoo|y/-yey meelkhamah שבוי מלחמה *nm* prisoner of war.
shyar|eem שיירים *nm pl* remnants; leftovers; (*pl+of:* **-ey**).

T.

incorporating **Tet** (ט) and **Tav** (ת)

NOTE: In this dictionary **t** combined with **s** as **ts** is also used to transliterate the Hebrew consonant צ **(Tsadee)**. The pronunciation of this is similar, if not identical, to the *tz* combination in *Ritz*. Thus, words beginning with **ts** (i.e. with צ) are found grouped in a separate chapter that follows this one, headed **Ts.**

ta|/-'eem תא *nm* cell; (*pl+of:* **-'ey**).
ta|'/-'ey do'ar תא דואר *nm* Post Office Box; P.O.B.
ta'ah/ta'atah/ta'eetee תעה *v* went astray; (*pres* **to'eh**; *fut* **yeet'eh**).
ta'ah/ta'atah/ta'eetee טעה *v* erred; made a mistake; (*pres* **to'eh**; *fut* **yeet'eh**).
tahah/tahatah/taheetee תהה *v* wondered; (*pres* **toheh**; *fut* **yeet'heh**).
ta'ageed/-eem תאגיד *nm* corporation; (*pl+of:* **-ey**).

ta'alool/-eem תעלול *nm* hoax; trick; (*pl+of:* **-ey**).
tahaleekh/-eem תהליך *nm* process; (*pl+of:* **-ey**).
tahalookh|ah/-ot תהלוכה *nf* procession; (*+of:* **-at**).
ta'aloom|ah/-ot תעלומה *nf* mystery; enigma; (*+of:* **-at**).
ta'am/-ah/-tee תאם *v* fitted; matched; (*pres* **to'em**; *fut* **yeet'am**).
ta'am/-ah/-tee טעם *v* tasted; (*pres* **to'em**; *fut* **yeet'am**).
ta'am/te'ameem טעם *nm* **1.** taste; **2.** justification; reason; (*pl+of:* **ta'amey**).
ta'am gan-'eden טעם גן-עדן *nm* **1.** delicious; very tasty; **2.** (*lit.*) taste of heaven.
(aneen/-at) ta'am אנין טעם *adj* connoisseur; of delicate taste.
(dvareem shel) ta'am דברים של טעם *nm pl* sensible words.
(khas|ar/-rat) ta'am חסר טעם *adj* tasteless; lacking taste.
(le) ta'am לטעם *adv* according to the taste of.
(le-lo) ta'am ללא טעם *adv* **1.** tastelessly; **2.** without any reason.
(le-lo) ta'am ve-rey'akh ללא טעם וריח *adv* with neither taste nor smell.
(mah) ta'am? מה טעם? what is the reason?
(mee) ta'am מטעם on behalf of.
(toov) ta'am טוב־טעם *nm* exquisite taste.
(le) ta'am|ee/-khah/-ekh/-o/-ah *etc* לטעמי/־ך/־ו/־ה *adv* according to my/your(*m/f*)/his/her *etc* taste.
(mee) ta'amey matspoon מטעמי מצפון *nf* for reasons of conscience.
ta'amlan/-eet תעמלן *nmf* propagandist; agitator; (*pl:* **-eem**; *+of:* **-ey**).
ta'amoolah תעמולה *nf* propaganda; (*+of:* **-at**).
ta'amoolatee/-t תעמולתי *adj* propagandist.
ta'an/-ah/-tee טען *v* claimed; argued; (*pres* **to'en**; *fut* **yeet'an**).
ta'an (*etc*) **/-'et** טען *v* loaded.
ta'anah/-ot טענה *nf* claim; argument; (*+of:* **-at**).
ta'anee|t/-yot תענית *nf* fast (not eating or drinking).
ta'aneet tseeboor תענית ציבור *nf* public fast.
ta'an|eh/-ee תענה *v fut (used as imp) sing m/f* answer! reply! (*inf* **la'anot**; *pst* **'anah**; *pres* **'oneh**).
ta'anoog/-ot תענוג *nm* pleasure; delight.
ta'ar/te'areem תער *nm* razor; (*pl+of:* **ta'arey**).
ta'areef/-eem תעריף *nm* tariff; price-list; fees; (*pl+of:* **-ey**).
ta'areekh/-eem תאריך *nm* date; (*pl+of:* **-ey**).
ta'areekhon/-eem תאריכון *nm* date-stamp; (*pl+of:* **-ey**).
ta'arookh|ah/-ot תערוכה *nf* exhibition; fair; (*+of:* **-at**).
ta'arov|et/-ot תערובת *nf* mixture.
(ben/bat) ta'arovet בן/בת תערובת *nmf* halfbreed.
(neesoo'ey) ta'arovet נישואי תערובת *nm pl* mixed marriage.

◇ **ta'as** תעש *nm [colloq.]* abbr.reference (dating from the Hagana's underground days) to Israel's defense-arms industry.
ta'as|eh/-see! תעשה! תעשי! *v fut (used as imp) sing m/f* do! make! (*inf* **la'asot**; *pst* **'asah**; *pres* **'oseh**)
ta'aseek/-ee תעסיק *v fut (used as imp) sing m/f* **1.** employ! (someone); **2.** keep (someone) busy! (*inf* **leha'aseek**; *pst* **he'eseek**; *pres* **ma'aseek**).
ta'asee|yah/-yot תעשייה *nf* industry; manufacture; (*+of:* **-yat**).
(meesrad ha-meeskhar ve-ha) ta'aseeyah משרד המסחר והתעשייה *nm* Ministry of Commerce and Industry.
(sar ha-meeskhar ve-ha) ta'aseeyah שר המסחר והתעשייה *nm* Minister of Commerce and Industry.
ta'aseeyan/-eem תעשיין *nm* manufacturer; industrialist; (*pl+of:* **-ey**).
ta'aseeyatee/-t תעשייתי *adj* industrial.
ta'asook|ah/-ot תעסוקה *nf* occupation; employment; (*+of:* **-at**).
(leeshkat) ta'asookah לשכת תעסוקה *nf* employment office.
◇ **(sheroot ha) ta'asookah** see ◇ **sheroot ha-ta'asookah**.
ta'ateek/-eem תעתיק *nm* transliteration; transcription; (*+of:* **-ey**).
ta'ateek/-ee תעתיק *v fut (used as imp) sing m/f* copy! (*inf* **leha'ateek**; *pst* **he'eteek**; *pres* **ma'ateek**).
ta'atoo|'a'/-'eem תעתוע *nm* mischief; illusion; deception; (*pl+of:* **-'ey**).
(khazon/-ot) ta'atoo'eem חזון תעתועים *nm* mirage.
(makhz|eh/-ot) ta'atoo'eem מחזה תעתועים *nm* illusionary vision.
ta'av|ah/-ot תאווה *nf* passion; desire; (*+of:* **-at**).
ta'avat betsa' תאוות בצע *nf* lust for money; greed.
ta'avat besareem תאוות בשרים *nf* carnal desire; sexual lust.
ta'avoor|ah תעבורה *nf* traffic; (*+of:* **-at**).
□ **Tabah** (Taba) טאבה *nf* narrow stretch of desert on borderline between Israel and Egypt, which after 1967, as part of Eilat, developed into a fashionable international spa and bathing resort. With signing of the Egyptian-Israeli peace-treaty, a claim on it was raised by Egypt and it became a bone of contention between the two countries. In 1988, through international arbitration, Taba, together with its Israeli-built luxury hotel, was transferred to Egypt, which agreed to purchase the hotel and facilitate its continued patronage by Israeli tourist clientele.
taba|'at/-'ot טבעת *nf* ring.
taba'at khenek טבעת חנק *nf* choking ring.
tab|a'at/-'ot neesoo'eem טבעת נישואים *nf* wedding ring.
tab|a'at/-'ot zahav טבעת זהב *nf* golden ring.

(pee ha) taba'at פי הטבעת *nm* anus (Anat.).
tabak טבק *nm* tobacco.
tabakh/-eet טבח *nmf* cook; chef; (*pl:* **-eem**; *nmf:* **-ey**).
(rav) tabakheem רב־טבחים *nm* arch-murderer.
tabee|'a'/-'ee תביע *v fut (used as imp) sing m/f* express! give expression! (*inf* **lehabee'a'**; *pst* **heebee'a'**; *pres* **mabee'a'**).
◇ **taboo** טאבו *nm [colloq.]* (relic of Turkish rule) Land Registry Office. (Legal term: **leeshkat reeshoom mekarke'een** לשכת רישום מקרקעין).
taboo טאבו *nm & adj* taboo; lie; forbidden; not to be mentioned.
taboor/-eem טבור navel; hub; (*pl+of:* **-ey**).
tadeer/tedeerah תדיר *adj* frequent.
tadeer תדיר *adv* frequently; often.
tadhemah תדהמה *nf* stupefaction; (*+of:* **-at**).
tadleek/-ee! תדליק! *v fut (used as imp) sing m/f* light it! (*inf* **lehadleek**; *pst* **heedleek**; *pres* **madleek**).
tadleek/-ee (*etc*) **et ha-khashmal!** תדליק את החשמל! *v fut (used as imp) sing m/f* switch on the electricity!
tadleek/-ee (*etc*) **et ha-or!** תדליק את האור! *v fut (used as imp) sing m/f* put on, the light!
tadmee|t/-yot תדמית *nf* image.
tadpees/-ee תדפיס *v fut (used as imp) sing m/f* print! type! (*inf* **lehadpees**; *pst* **heedpees**; *pres* **madpees**).
tadpees/-eem תדפיס *nm* reprint; offprint; (*pl+of:* **-ey**).
tadreekh/-ee תדריך *v fut (used as imp) sing m/f* instruct! guide! (*inf* **lehadreekh**; *pst* **heedreekh**; *pres* **madreekh**).
tadreekh/-eem תדריך *nm* briefing; directions; (*pl+of:* **-ey**).
ta'ee/-t תאי *adj* cellular.
ta'eem/te'eemah טעים *adj* tasty.
(lo) ta'eem/te'eemah לא טעים *adj* untasty; unsavory.
ta'eet תאית *nf* cellulose.
ta'eez (*npr* **ta'ez**)/**-ee!** תעיז! *v fut (used as imp) sing m/f* dare! just dare! (*inf* **leha'ez**; *pst* **he'ez**; *pres* **me'ez**).
(al) ta'eez (*npr* **ta'ez**)/**-ee!** אל תעיז! *v fut (used as imp) sing m/f* don't you dare! (*inf* **lo leha'ez**; *pst* **lo he'ez**; *pres* **eyno me'ez**).
ta'ev/te'evah תאב *v pres* craves; longs for.
taf טף *nm* children; kids.
taf (*npr:* **tav**) (ת) תי"ו 22nd letter of Hebrew alphabet; consonant **t**.
taf (*npr* **tav**) ת *num symbol* 400; four hundred.
taf|akh/-khah/-akhtee טפח *v pres* slapped; stroked; patted; (*pres* **tofe'akh**; *fut* **yeetpakh**; *(p=f)*).
tafakh (*etc*) **'al ha-shekhem** טפח על השכם *v* patted on the back.
taf|akh/-khah/-akhtee תפח *v* swelled up; (*pres* **tofe'akh**; *fut* **yeetpakh** *(p=f)*).
taf|al/-lah/-altee טפל *v* imputed; ascribed; (*pres* **tofel**; *fut* **yeetpol** *(p=f)*).
taf|ar/-rah/-artee תפר *v* sew; stitched; (*pres* **tofer**; *fut* **yeetpor** *(p=f)*).
taf|as/-sah/-astee תפס *v* **1.** seized; grasped; **2.** caught; **3.** realized; (*pres* **tofes**; *fut* **yeetpos**; *(p=f)*).
tafel/tfelah תפל *adj* tasteless; untasty.
tafel/tfelah טפל *adj* subordinate; without importance.
tafkeed/-eem תפקיד *nm* role; function; job; (*pl+of:* **-ey**).
(be) tafkeed בתפקיד *adv* on duty.
(meel|e/-'ah/-e'tee) tafkeed מילא תפקיד *v* played a part; (*pres* **memale** *etc*; *fut* **yemale** *etc*).
tafnee/-t/-yot תפנית *nf* turn; half-turn; change of course.
tafnook|eem תפנוקים *nm pl* (*sing:* **tafnook**) pampering; indulgence; (*pl+of:* **-ey**).
tafoo'akh/tfookhah תפוח *adj* swollen.
tafoor/tfoorah תפור *adj* sewn.
taf'oor|ah/-ot תפאורה *nf* decoration; setting, scenery (theatric.); (*+of:* **-at**).
tafoos/tfoosah תפוס *adj* occupied; engaged.
tafran/-eet תפרן *adj [slang]* penniless. (*pl:* **-eem**; *+of:* **-ey**).
tafreet/-eem תפריט *nm* menu; (*pl+of:* **-ey**).
tafsan/-eem טפסן *nm* scaffolding erector; (*pl+of:* **-ey**).
◇ **taf-sheen-noon-bet**, ◇ **taf-sheen-noon-geemel**, ◇ **taf-sheen-samekh**, **taf-sheen-samekh-daled** *etc* (as colloq. pronounced) - see *npr* ◇ **tav-sheen-noon-bet**, ◇ **tav-sheen-noon-geemel**, ◇ **tav-sheen-samekh**, ◇ **tav-sheen-samekh-dalet** *etc.*
taftaf|ah/-ot טפטפה *nf* Israeli water-saving irrigation-device for vegetable-gardens and grass.
taft|efet/-afot טפטפת *nf* dropper.
tag/-eem תג *nm* tag; badge; insignia; (*pl+of:* **-ey**).
tagar/-eem תגר *nm* trader; merchant; (*pl+of:* **-ey**).
taglee|t/-yot תגלית *nf* discovery.
tagmool/-eem תגמול *nm* reprisal; retribution; (*pl+of:* **-ey**).
◇ **(pe'ool|at/-ot) tagmool** see ◇ **pe'ool|at/-ot tagmool**.
tagmooleem (*or:* **tagmooleen**) תגמולים/־ין *nm pl* gratuities; compensations; pension.
(keren/kranot) tagmooleem קרן תגמולים *nf* pension fund.
(koop|at/-ot) tagmooleem קופת תגמולים *nf* provident fund.
tagmooleen תגמולין *nm pl* gratuities; compensations; pensions.
tagran/-eet תגרן *nmf & adj* peddler; haggler; (*pl+of:* **-ey**).
tahah/tahatah/taheetee תהה *v* wondered; (*pres* **toheh**; *fut* **yeet'heh**).
tahah (*etc*) **'al kankan|o/-ah/-ee** תהה על קנקנו/־ה/־י *v* examined his(its)/her/my *etc* nature.
tahaleekh/-eem תהליך *nm* process; (*pl+of:* **-ey**).

tahalookh|ah/-ot תהלוכה *nf* procession; (*+of:* **-at**).
tahpookh|ah/-ot תהפוכה *nf* deceit; perversion; distortion; (*+of:* **-at**).
tahpookhot goral תהפוכות גורל *nf pl* vagaries of fate.
tahor/tehorah טהור *adj* clean; pure.
tak|a'/-'ah/-a'tee תקע **1.** *[slang]* struck (blow); flashed; **2.** blew (horn); (*pres* **toke'a'**; *fut* **yeetka'**).
tak|af/-fah/-aftee תקף *v* assailed; attacked; (*pres* **tokef**; *fut* **yeetkof**).
◇ **(ha)TAKAM** התק"ם *nm* the United Kibbutz Movement (*acr of* **ha-Tenoo'ah ha-Keebootseet ha-Me'ookhedet** התנועה הקיבוצית המאוחדת). Largest national kibbutz association encompassing 175 of them i.e. all kibbutzim except 86 affiliated to ◇ **ha-keeboots ha-artsee** and 17 affiliated to ◇ **ha-keeboots ha-datee**.
takal|ah/-ot תקלה *nf* mishap; obstacle; (*+of:* **-at**).
takan|ah/-ot תקנה *nf* **1.** amendment; **2.** regulation (*+of:* **-at**).
(khas|ar/-rat) takanah חסר־תקנה *adj* irremediable; irreparable.
(le-lo) takanah ללא תקנה *adv* beyond repair.
takanot lee-she'at kheroom תקנות לשעת חירום *nf* Emergency Regulations - set of regulations originally enacted by the British Mandate authorities in the years 1936-1946 to meet war needs and combat terrorism. Part of those regulations remain in force as of 1992 to combat Arab terrorism.
takanon/-eem תקנון *nm* by-laws; constitution; (*pl+of:* **-ey**).
takanot תקנות *nf pl* (*sing:* **takanah**) regulations; by-laws.
takanot lee-she'at kheroom תקנות לשעת חירום *nf pl* emergency regulations.
takbool/-eem תקבול *nm* cash-entry; intake; receipt (cash); (*pl+of:* **-ey**).
takdeem/-eem תקדים *nm* precedent; (*pl+of:* **-ey**).
(khas|ar/-rat) takdeem חסר תקדים *adj* unprecedented.
takdeem/-ee! תקדים! *v fut (used as imp) sing m/f* advance! make it earlier! (*inf* **lehakdeem**; *pst* **heekdeem**; *fut* **yakdeem**).
takeef/-ah תקיף *adj* forceful; mighty.
takeef/-ee! תקיף *v fut (used as imp) sing m/f* encircle! surround! (*inf* **lehakeef**; *pst* **heekeef**; *pres* **makeef**).
takeefoot תקיפות *nf* firmness; resolve.
takeen/tekeenah תקין *adj* regular; normal; in working condition.
takef/tekefah תקף *adj* valid.
takel/-eem תקל *nm [slang]* mishap; accident; malfunction; misunderstanding.
takhan/-ah/-tee טחן *v* milled; ground; (*pres* **tokhen**; *fut* **yeetkhon**).
takhan|ah/-ot טחנה *nf* mill; (*+of:* **-at**).
takhan|ah/-ot תחנה *nf* station; stop; (*+of:* **-at**).
takhan|ah merkazeet תחנה מרכזית *nf* central (bus) station.
takhan|at/-ot delek תחנת דלק *nf* gas station; petrol station; filling station.
takhan|at/-ot kemakh טחנת קמח *nf* flour mill.
takhan|at/-ot meeshtarah תחנת משטרה *nf* police station; police precinct.
takhan|at/-ot moneeyot תחנת מוניות *nf* taxi-station; taxicab stop.
takhan|at/-ot otoboos/-eem תחנת אוטובוס *nf* bus stop; bus station.
takhan|at/-ot rakevet תחנת רכבת *nm* railroad stop; railway station.
takhan|at/-ot roo'akh טחנת רוח *nf* windmill.
takhanat/-ot sheedoor תחנת שידור *nf* broadcasting station.
takhan|at/-ot taksee תחנת טקסי *nf* taxi-station; taxicab stop.
takhat תחת **1.** *adv* under; beneath; instead; **2.** *nm [colloq.]* buttock; rump.
takhat lakhats תחת לחץ *adv* under pressure.
(kree'at) takhat קריעת תחת *nf [slang]* inhumanly tiring effort.
(mee) takhat le- מתחת ל־ *adv* under; beneath.
takhav טחב *nm* dampness.
takhav/-ah/-tee תחב *v* inserted; pushed; (*pres* **tokhev**; *fut* **yeetkhov**).
takhbeeb (*npr* **takhbeev**) **/-eem** תחביב *nm* hobby; (*pl+of:* **-ey**).
takhbeer/-eem תחביר *nm* syntax (Gram.).
takhbeev/-eem תחביב *nm* hobby; (*pl+of:* **-ey**).
takhbool|ah/-ot תחבולה *nf* trick; device; (*+of:* **-at**).
takhboor|ah תחבורה *nf* transport; communication; (*+of:* **-at**).
(emtsa|'ee/-'ey) takhboorah אמצעי תחבורה *nm* means of transportation.
(meesrad ha) takhboorah משרד התחבורה *nm* Ministry of Transport.
(sar ha) takhboorah שר התחבורה *nm* Minister of Transport.
takhbosh|et/-shot תחבושת *nf* bandage.
takheen/-ee! תכין! *v fut (used as imp) sing m/f* prepare! will you prepare! (*inf* **lehakheen**; *pst* **hekheen**; *pres* **mekheen**).
takhekhan/-eet תככן *nmf* plotter; intriguer.
takhekhanoot תככנות *nf* intriguing; quarrel-mongering.
takhleef/-eem תחליף *nm* substitute; (*pl+of:* **-ey**).
takhleef/-ee! תחליף!! *v fut (used as imp) sing m/f* will you please change! change! (*pst* **hekhleef**; *pres* **makhleef**; *inf* **lehakhleef**).
takhleefee/-t תחליפי *adj* alternative.
takhleet/-yot תכלית *nf* purpose; final end; final purpose.
takhleet/-ee! תחליט *v fut (used as imp) sing m/f* make up your mind! will you decide! (*inf* **lehakhleet**; *pst* **hekhleet**; *pres* **makhleet**).
(be) takhleet בתכלית *adv* absolutely; definitely.

takhles! ! תכלית *[slang]* (Yiddish) *interj* come to the point! Let's be practical!

(khas|ar/-rat) takhleet חסר תכלית *adj* aimless; pointless.

takhleetee/-t תכליתי *adj* intentional; purposeful.

takhleeteeyoot תכליתיות *nf* purposefulness.

takhloo|'ah/-'ot תחלואה *nf* incidence of diseases; morbidity; **(***+of:* **-'at)**.

takhloof|ah/-ot תחלופה *nf* natural replacement; new growth; **(***+of:* **-at)**.

takhmeets/-eem תחמיץ *nm* marinade **(***pl+of:* **-ey)**.

(al *or* **bal) takhmeets/-ee** ! אל תחמיץ *v fut (used as imp) sing m/f [colloq.]* don't miss! don't omit! **(***inf* **lo lehakhmeets;** *pst* **lo hekhmeets;** *pres* **eyno makhmeets)**.

takhmoshet תחמושת *nf* ammunition.

takhmots|et/-ot תחמוצת *nf* oxide; (Chem.).

(doo-) takhmotset דו־תחמוצת *nf* dioxide (Chem.).

takhn|ah/-ot (*npr* **takhan|ah/-ot)** תחנה *nf* station; stop; **(***+of:* **-at)**.

takhnah (*npr* **takhanah) merkazeet** תחנה מרכזית *nf* central (bus) station.

takhn|at/-ot (*npr* **takhan|ah/-ot) delek** תחנת דלק *nf* gas station; petrol station; filling station.

takhn|at/-ot (*npr* **takhan|ah/-ot) kemakh** טחנת קמח *nf* flour mill.

takhn|at/-ot (*npr* **takhan|ah/-ot) meeshtarah** תחנת משטרה *nf* police station; police precinct.

takhn|at/-ot (*npr* **takhan|ah/-ot) moneeyot** תחנת מוניות *nf* taxi-station; taxicab stop.

takhn|at/-ot (*npr* **takhan|ah/-ot) otoboos/-eem** תחנת אוטובוס *nf* bus stop; bus station.

takhn|at/-ot (*npr* **takhan|ah/-ot) rakevet** תחנת רכבת *nm* railroad stop; railway station.

takhn|at/-ot (*npr* **takhan|ah/-ot) roo'akh** טחנת רוח *nf* windmill.

takhnat/-ot (*npr* **takhan|ah/-ot) sheedoor** תחנת שידור *nf* broadcasting station.

takhn|at/-ot taksee (*npr* **takhan|ah/-ot** *etc***)** תחנת טקסי *nf* taxi-station; taxicab stop.

takhnees/ee תכניס *v fut (used as imp) sing m/f* **1.** take in! **2.** introduce! **3.** insert! **(***inf* **lehakhnees;** *pst* **heekhnees;** *pres* **makhnees)**.

takhnoon|eem תחנונים *nm pl* supplications; **(***pl+of:* **-ey)**.

takhol/tekhoolah תכולה *adj* light-blue; sky-blue.

takhoo'akh/tekhookhah תחוח *adj* loose (soil).

takhoof/tekhoofah תכוף *adj* urgent; hurried.

takhoof תכוף *adv* urgent.

takhoon/tekhoonah טחון *adj* ground; milled.

takhposet/-ot תחפושת *nf* disguise; costume.

takhkeer/-eem תחקיר *nm* investigation; **(***pl+of:* **-ey)**.

takhk|or/-eree תחקור *v fut (used as imp) sing m/f* will you investigate! will you research! **(***inf* **lakhkor;** *pst* **khakar;** *pres* **khoker)**.

takhr|ah (*npr* **takhar|ah)/-ot** תחרה *nf* lace; **(***+of:* **-at)**.

takhree|'akh/-khee! ! תכריח *v fut (used as imp) sing m/f* will you force! compel! **(***inf* **lehakhree'akh;** *pst* **heekhree'akh;** *pres* **makhree'akh)**.

takhreekh|eem תכריכים *nm pl* shrouds; **(***pl+of:* **-ey)**.

takhreem/-ee (*npr* **takhareem/-ee)** תחרים *v fut (used as imp) sing m/f* confiscate! sequestrate! **(***inf* **lehakhareem;** *pst* **hekhereem;** *pres* **makhareem)**.

takhreem/-eem תחרים *nm* lace; **(***pl+of:* **-ey)**.

takhreet/-eem תחריט *nm* etching; **(***pl+of:* **-ey)**.

takhreez/-ee! ! תכריז *v fut (used as imp) sing m/f* will you declare!; **(***inf* **lehakhreez;** *pst* **heekhreez** *pres* **makhreez)**.

takhroo|t/-yot (*npr* **takharoo|t/-yot)** תחרות *nf* **1.** competition; rivalry; **2.** contest; match.

takhroot (*etc***) gmar** תחרות גמר *nf* final match; final contest.

takharoot (*etc***) re'eem** תחרות רעים *nf* friendly match.

takhroot (*etc***) s'kheeyah** תחרות שחייה *nf* swimming contest.

takhseer/-ee תחסיר *v fut (used as imp)* deduct! skip! **(***inf* **lehakhseer;** *pst* **hekhseer;** *pres* **makhseer)**.

takhsees/-eem תכסיס *nm* trick; 1. manoever; stratagem.

takhseesan/-eet תכסיסן *nmf* tactician.

takhseesee/-t תכסיסי *adj* tactical.

takhsheer/-eem תכשיר *nm* preparation; article; **(***pl+of:* **-ey)**.

takhsheev/-eem תחשיב *nm* estimate; calculation; **(***pl+of:* **-ey)**.

takhsh|ov/-evee! ! תחשוב *v fut (used as imp) sing m/f* think! just think! **(***inf* **lakhshov;** *pst* **khashav;** *pres* **khoshev)**.

takhtee/-t תחתי *adj* lower.

takhteet/-yot תחתית *nf* **1.** bottom; **2.** saucer.

(be) takhteet ha-madregah בתחתית המדרגה *adv* at the bottom of the scale.

(be) takhteet ha-soolam בתחתית הסולם *adv* at the bottom of the ladder (*figurat.*).

(khaveet le-lo) takhteet חבית ללא תחתית *nm* bottomless barrel (mostly figurat.).

□ **(Khayfah) Takhteet** חיפה תחתית *nf* Downtown Haifa.

(le-lo) takhteet ללא תחתית *adj* bottomless.

(rakevet) takhteet רכבת תחתית *nf* subway; underground; metro.

□ **(Tveryah) Takhteet** טבריה תחתית *nf* Downtown Tiberias.

takhteev/-eem תכתיב *nm* **1.** dictate; **2.** dictation; **(***pl+of:* **-ey)**.

takhteev/-ee! ! תכתיב *v fut (used as imp) sing m/f* will you please dictate! dictate, please! **(***inf* **lehakhteev;** *pst* **heekhteev;** *pres* **makhteev)**.

takhton/-ah תחתון *adj* lower; lowest.

('olam) takhton עולם תחתון *nm* underworld.

takhton|eem תחתונים *nm pl* underpants; (*pl+of:* **-ey**).

takhzeek/-ee! תחזיק! *v fut (used as imp) sing m/f* keep! hold! (*inf* **lehakhzeek**; *pst* **hekhzeek**; *pres* **makhzeek**).

takhzeer/-ee! תחזיר! *v fut (used as imp) sing m/f* give back! will you return! (*inf* **lehakhzeer**; *pst* **hekhzeer**; *pres* **makhzeer**).

(le) takhzek לתחזק *v inf* to maintain (provide maintenance); (*pst* **teekhzek**; *pres* **metakhzek**; *fut* **yetakhzek**).

takhzook|ah תחזוקה *nf* maintenance; (*+of:* **-at**).

takleet/-eem תקליט *nm* gramophone-record; (*pl+of:* **-ey**).

takleet/-ee! תקליט! *v fut (used as imp) sing m/f* record! will you record! (*inf* **lehakleet**; *pst* **heekleet**; *pres* **makleet**).

(khanoo|t/-yot) takleeteem חנות תקליטים *nf* records and cassettes store.

takleetee|yah/-yot תקליטייה *nf* phonograph records collection; (*+of:* **-at**).

takoo'a'/tekoo'ah תקוע *adj* stuck; stuck in.

takree|t/-yot תקרית *nf* incident.

◇ **taksheer** תקשי״ר *nm abbr.* (*acr.:* **TAKnon SHEroot** תקנון שירות) Israeli Civil Service Code.

taksheev/-ee! תקשיב! *v fut (used as imp) sing m/f* listen! (*inf* **lehaksheev**; *pst* **heeksheev**; *pres* **maksheev**).

takt טקט *nm* tact.

taktee/-t טקטי *adj* tactical.

taktseer/-eem תקציר *nm* synopsis; summary; abstract; (*pl+of:* **-ey**).

taktseev/-eem תקציב *nm* budget; (*pl+of:* **-ey**).

taktseevee/-t תקציבי *adj* budgetary.

takoom/-ee! תקום! *v fut (used as imp) sing m/f* get up! stand up! (*inf* **lakoom**; *pst & pres* **kam**).

tal/telaleem טל *nm* dew; (*pl+of:* **telaley**).

□ **Tal Shakhar** טל שחר *nm* village (est. 1948) 3 km SW of Nahshon Junction (**Tsomet Nakhshon**). Pop. 396.

□ **Tal El** (Tal El) טל אל *nm* communal settlement (est. 1980) in W. Galilee, 2 km NE of Ahihud Junction (**Tsomet Akheehood**). Pop. 273.

□ **Tal Or** טל אור *nf* agric. farm in N. Negev, 12 km NW of **Ofakeem**.

tal|ah/-tah/-eetee תלה *v* hung; hanged; (*pres* **toleh**; *fut* **yeetleh**).

talah (*etc*) **teekvot** תלה תקוות *v* pinned hopes on.

tal|ash/-shah/-ashtee תלש *v* tore; tore off; (*pres* **tolesh**; *fut* **yeetlosh**).

talbeesh/-ee תלביש *v fut (used as imp) sing m/f* dress (someone else)! (*pst* **heelbeesh**; *pres* **malbeesh**; *inf* **lehalbeesh**).

taleh טלה *nm* lamb.

◇ **taleet/-ot** טלית *nf* "Taless", Jewish prayer shawl.

◇ **taleet katan** טלית קטן *nm* short fringed shawl which observant male Jews wear under shirt; (Yiddish: "Talis koten").

◇ **taleet oo-tfeeleen** טלית ותפילין *nf & nm pl* prayer shawl and phylacteries, an observant Jewish male's obligatory attire (phylacteries only on weekdays) at morning prayer.

◇ **taleet she-koolah tekhelet** טלית שכולה תכלת *nf* **1.** (*figurat.*) an all-blue taleet; **2.** ironic reference to someone who is not altogether a paragon of virtue.

talmeed/-ah תלמיד *nmf* pupil; student; (*pl+of:* **-ey**).

talmeed/-ey khakham/-eem תלמיד חכם *nm* scholar; learned person (in Jewish religious studies).

talmeed/-ah meen ha-meenyan תלמיד מן המניין *nm* regular student (in a University).

talmeed/-ah meetstayen/-et תלמיד מצטיין *nm* outstanding pupil.

(mo'etset ha-) talmeedeem מועצת התלמידים *nf* pupils' council.

□ **Talmey El'azar** (Talmé El'azar) תלמי אלעזר *nm* village (est. 1952) in N. Sharon, 2 km S. of **Pardes Khanah**. Pop. 258.

□ **Talmey Eleeyahoo** (Talmé Eliyyahu) תלמי אליהו *nm* village (est. 1970) in Eshkol District, NW Negev, 4 km S. of Gevulot Junction (**Tsomet Gvoolot**). Pop. 265.

□ **Talmey Beeloo** (Talmé Bilu) תלמי ביל״ו *nm* village (est. 1953) in N. Negev, 4 km E. of Hageddi Junction (**Tsomet Ha-Gedee**). Pop. 296.

□ **Talmey Yafeh** (Talmé Yafe) תלמי יפה *nm* coop. village (est. 1950) in the S. of Coastal Plain, 5 km SE of Ashkelon. Pop. 135.

□ **Talmey Yekhee'el** (**Talmé Yehi'el**) תלמי יחיאל *nm* - village (est. 1949) in Coastal plain, 3 km N. of **Keeryat Mal'akhee**. Pop. 366.

□ **Talmey Yosef** (Talmé Yosef) תלמי יוסף *nm* village in Shalom district, 10 km SW of Gevulot Junction (**Tsomet Gvoolot**) where it was transferred in 1982, after original settlement, founded in Yamit (**Yameet**) district in 1977, had been ceded to Egypt).

◇ **talmood** (**Talmud**) תלמוד *nm* the 2000-year old compendium of Jewish law, legends and morals.

◇ **talmood torah** תלמוד תורה *nm* **1.** elementary Jewish religious school; **2.** study of the Torah.

talool/tloolah תלול *adj* steep.

taloosh/tlooshah תלוש *adj* detached; alienated.

talooy/tlooyah תלוי *adj* **1.** depending; hanging; **2.** pending; sub-judice.

talooy/tlooyah be- תלוי ב- *v pres* depends on; depending on.

talooy תלוי *adv* it depends; it would depend...

(beeltee) talooy/tlooyah בלתי תלוי *adj* independent.

taltal/-eem תלתל *nm* curl; (*pl+of:* **-ey**).

talyan/-eem תליין *nm* hangman; executioner; (*pl+of:* **-ey**).

talyon/-eem תליון *nm* pendant.

tam/-ah תם *v* ended; was completed; (*pres* **tam**; *fut* **yeetam** *or* **yeetom**).
tam/-ah תם *adj* **1.** flawless; **2.** naive.
tam/-ah ve-neeshl|am/-emah תם ונשלם *v pst m/f* has been fully completed; (*pres m/f* **tam/-ah ve-neeshl|am/-emet**; *fut* **yeetam ve-yooshlam**).
tam|ah/-'hah/-ahtee תמה *v* wondered; (*pres* **tameha**; *fut* **yeetmah**).
tamah oo-barah (*npr* **oo-varah**) תמה וברה *adj f* pure and innocent.
tam|akh/-khah/-akhtee תמך *v* supported; (*pres* **tomekh**; *fut* **yeetmokh**).
taman/-nah/-antee טמן *v* hid; (*pres* **tomen**; *fut* **yeetmon**).
taman (*etc*) **pakh** טמן פח *v* set a trap.
tam|an/-nah (*etc*) **yad|o/-ah ba-tsalakhat** טמן ידו בצלחת *v lit* : hid one's hand in one's pocket, i.e. sat idle.
tamar/temar|eem תמר *nm* palmtree; (*pl+of:* **-ey**).
tame'/teme'ah טמא *adj* impure; defiled.
tameed תמיד *adv* always.
(akhat oo-le) tameed אחת ולתמיד *adv* once and for all; once and forever.
(le) tameed לתמיד *adv* forever; for good.
(ner) tameed נר תמיד *nm* eternal lamp; memorial candle.
tameem/temeemah תמים *adj* naive.
tameer/temeerah תמיר *adj* erect; tall.
tameer/temeerah טמיר *adj* secret; confidential.
tame'ah/temehah תמה *adj* astonished; surprised; (*pst* **tamah**; *fut* **yeetmah**).
tamkheer/-eem תמחיר *nm* cost accounting.
tamkheeran/-eet תמחירן *nmf* cost-accountant; (*pl+of:* **-ey**).
tamkhooy תמחוי *nm* soup kitchen.
tamleel/-eem תמליל *nm* text; libretto; wording; (*pl+of:* **-ey**).
(me'ab|ed/-dey) tamleeleem מעבד תמלילים *nm* word-processor.
tamleets/-ee! תמליץ! *v fut (used as imp) sing m/f* will you recommend! (*inf* **lehamleets**; *pst* **heemleets**; *pres* **mamleets**).
tamloogeem תמלוגים *nm pl* (*sing:* **tamloog**) royalties; royalty rights; (*pl+of:* **-ey**).
tamnoon/-eem תמנון *nm* octopus; (*pl+of:* **-ey**).
tamoo'ah/temoohah תמוה *adj* strange; surprising.
tamoon/temoonah טמון *v pres & adj* hidden; concealed.
◇ **Tamooz** תמוז *nm* 10th Jewish calendar month (approx. June-July) 29 days.
tamreets/-eem תמריץ *nm* incentive; (*pl+of:* **-ey**).
tamrook|eem תמרוקים *nm pl* cosmetics; (*pl+of:* **-ey**).
tamroor/-eem תמרור *nm* traffic sign; signpost; road sign.
tamroor "atsor" תמרור עצור *nm* "stop!" sign (traffic).
tamrooreem תמרורים *nm pl* bitterness.
(bekhee) tamrooreem בכי תמרורים *nm* bitter crying.
tamseer/-eem תמסיר *nm* handout; communique; (*pl+of:* **-ey**).
tamtsee/-'ee! תמציא! *v fut (used as imp) sing m/f* will you supply ! will you deliver! (*inf* **lehamtsee'**; *pst* **heemtsee'**; *pres* **mamtsee'**).
tamtsee|t/-yot תמצית *nf* essence; summary.
tamtseetee/-t תמציתי *adj* concise; essential.
tan/-eem תן *nm* jackal.
◇ **tana'eem** תנאים *nm pl* (*sing:* **tana**) Mishnaic scholars quoted in the Talmud.
◇ **TANAKH** תנ"ך *nm* Hebrew Bible; the Old Testament (name being *acr of* **Torah, Nevee'eem, Ketooveem** תורה נביאים,כתובים).
tanakhee/-t תנ"כי *adj* biblical.
tandoo טנדו *adv* two together.
taneen/-eem תנין *nm* crocodile; (*pl+of:* **-ey**).
tank/-eem טנק *nm* tank; (*pl+of:* **-ey**).
tankeest/-eem טנקיסט *nm* soldier in tank crew.
tanmeekh/-ee תנמיך *v fut (used as imp) sing m/f* lower! will you please lower! (*inf* **lehanmeekh**; *pst* **heenmeekh**; *pres* **manmeekh**).
tanoor/-eem תנור *nm* stove; oven; furnace; (*pl+of:* **-ey**).
tanoor/-ey afeeyah תנור אפייה *nm* oven; baking oven.
tanoor/-ey ambatyah תנור אמבטיה *nm* bathroom stove; bathroom boiler.
tanoor/-ey beeshool תנור בישול *nm* cooking stove; cooking range.
tanoor/-ey gaz תנור גז *nm* gas stove.
tanoor/-ey hasakah תנור הסקה *nm* heater; heating stove.
tanoor/-eem khashmalee/-yeem תנור חשמלי *nm* electric heater; electric stove.
tanoor/-ey kheemoom תנור חימום *nm* heater.
tanoor/-ey meekro-gal תנור מיקרוגל *nm* microwave cooker.
□ **Tantoorah** טנטורה *nm* (see □ **Dor**).
ta'oon/te'oonah טעון *adj* **1.** loaded (weapon); **2.** requiring; in need of.
ta'oon/te'oonah teepool טעון טיפול *v pres* requires attention; needs to be dealt with.
(ekdakh) ta'oon טעון *nm* loaded gun.
(roveh) ta'oon רובה טעון *nm* loaded rifle.
ta'oo|t/-yot טעות *nf* mistake.
ta'oot le-'olam khozeret טעות לעולם חוזרת errors and omissions excepted.
(meekakh) ta'oot מיקח טעות *nm* bad bargain; purchase by mistake.
(teekoon) ta'oot תיקון טעות *nm* correction.
tapeel/-ee! תפיל! *v fut (used as imp) sing m/f* **1.** (warning) careful, it may fall! **2.** (order) let it fall! (*inf* **lehapeel**; *pst* **heepeel**; *pres* **mapeel**).
tapeel/-eem טפיל *nm & adj* parasite; (*pl+of:* **-ey**).
tapoo|'akh/-kheem תפוח *nm* apple; (*pl+of:* **-khey**).
tapoo|'akh/-khey adamah תפוח אדמה *nm* potato.
tapoo|'akh/-khey zahav תפוח זהב *nm* orange.
tapood/-eem תפוד *nm* potato; (*pl+of:* **-ey**).

(meets/-ey) tapookheem מיץ תפוחים *nm* apple juice.

tapookhey 'ets תפוחי עץ *nm pl* apples; *(lit.)* tree-apples.

tapooz/-eem תפוז *nm* orange; (*pl+of:* **-ey**).

(meets/-ey) tapoozeem מיץ תפוזים *nm* orange juice.

tapoozey shamootee תפוזי שמוטי *nm* orange of the "Shamootee" variety.

□ **Ta'oz** (Ta'oz) תעוז *nm* village (est. 1950) in Interior Plain **(Shefelah)** , 4 km NW of Shimshon Junction **(Tsomet Sheemshon)**. Pop. 420.

tar/-ah תר *v* toured; (*pres* **tar**; *fut* **yatoor**).

tar|af/-fah/-aftee טרף *v* **1.** devoured; ravaged; **2.** shuffled (cards); (*pres* **toref**; *fut* **yeetrof**).

tar|ak/-kah/-aktee טרק *v* slammed (door); (*pres* **torek**; *fut* **yeetrok**).

tar|akh/-khah/-akhtee טרח *v* labored; took trouble; (*pres* **tore'akh**; *fut* **yeetrakh**).

tar|am/-mah/-amtee תרם *v* donated; contributed; (*pres* **torem**; *fut* **yeetrom**).

tarash/-eem טר"ש *nm* (*acr.* of: **Tooray ReeSHon** טוראי ראשון PFC (army); private first class.

tarashee|t/-yot טרש"ית *[slang] nf* (*acr.* of: **Toora'eet ReeSHonah** טוראית ראשונה private first class (female).

tarbeets/-ee! ! תרביץ *v fut (used as imp) sing m/f* go on! beat (one) up! (*pst* **heerbeets**; *pres* **marbeets**; *inf* **leharbeets**).

(al) tarbeets/-ee! ! אל תרביץ *v fut (used as imp) sing m/f* don't beat!

tarboot/-yot תרבות *nf* culture.

tarbootee/-t תרבותי *nf* cultured; cultural.

tardan/-eet טרדן **1.** *adj* bothersome; **2.** *nmf* bothersome person; (*pl+of:* **-ey**).

tardemah/-ot תרדמה *nf* deep sleep; torpor.

(nas|akh/-khah/-akhtee) tardemah נסך תרדמה *v* cast deep sleep; made fall asleep; (*pres* **nosekh** *etc*; *fut* **yeesokh** *etc*).

taree/treeyah טרי *adj* fresh.

tareem/-ee תרים *v fut (used as imp) sing m/f* lift! raise! (*pst* **hereem**; *pres* **mereem**; *inf* **lehareem**).

◇ **taref/trefah** טרף *adj* **1.** non-kosher; (food or act); **2.** forbidden to observant Jews; **3.** (*figurat.*) against the law.

tar'elah תרעלה *nf* poison; (*+of:* **-at**).

tareshet טרשת *nf* sclerosis (Medic.).

tareshet ha-'orkeem טרשת העורקים *nf* arteriosclerosis (Medic.).

targeel/-ee תרגיל *v fut (used as imp) sing m/f* get (someone) used! (*inf* **lehargeel**; *pst* **heergeel**; *pres* **margeel**).

targeel/-eem תרגיל *nm* **1.** exercise; **2.** *[slang]* trick played on someone; (*pl+of:* **-ey**).

targeel/-'ey hasakhah תרגיל הסחה *nm* diversionary exercise; diversionary tactics.

targeesh/-ee! ! תרגיש *v fut (used as imp) sing m/f* please feel! will you sense! (*inf* **lehargeesh**; *pst* **heergeesh**; *pres* **margeesh**).

targem/-ee! ! תרגם *v fut (used as imp) sing m/f* translate, please!! (*inf* **letargem**; *pst* **teergem**; *pres* **metargem**).

targoom/-eem תרגום *nm* translation; translated version; (*pl+of:* **-ey**).

tarkeev/-eem תרכיב *nm* serum; vaccine; (*pl+of:* **-ey**).

tarkeev/-ee! ! תרכיב *v fut (used as imp) sing m/f* **1.** give a lift! take for a ride! **2.** mount (a part)! (*inf* **leharkeev**; *pst* **heerkeev**; *pres* **markeev**).

tarkeez/-eem תרכיז *nm* concentrate; (*pl+of:* **-ey**).

tarkheev/-ee! ! תרחיב *imp sing m/f* please enlarge! widen please! (*inf* **leharkheev**; *pst* **heerkheev** *pres* **markheev**).

tarmeel/-eem תרמיל *nm* **1.** bag; knapsack; **2.** cartridge-case (milit.).

tarmeel/-ey tsad תרמיל צד *nm* rucksack; pack.

tarmee|t/-yot תרמית *nf* fraud; deceit.

tarnegol/-eem תרנגול *nm* cock; rooster; (*pl+of:* **-ey**).

tarnegol/-ey hodoo תרנגול הודו *nm* turkey.

(meeshkal) tarnegol משקל תרנגול *nm* bantamweight.

tarnegol|et/-ot תרנגולת *nf* hen; chicken.

tar'om|et/-ot תרעומת *nf* grudge.

tarood/troodah טרוד *adj* busy; preoccupied.

□ **Taroom** (Tarum) תרום *nm* village (est. 1950) in Interior Plain **(Shfelah)** , 3 km NW of Shimshon Junction **(Tsomet Sheemshon)**. Pop. 344.

tarsees/-eem תרסיס *nm* spray; (*pl+of:* **-ey**).

tarsheem/-ee! ! תרשים *v fut (used as imp) sing m/f* will you impress! (*pst* **heersheem**; *pres* **marsheem**; *inf* **leharsheem**).

tarsheem/-eem תרשים *nm* chart; graph; sketch; (*pl+of:* **-ey**).

tartey-mashma' תרתי משמע **1.** *adv* with double meaning; ambiguously; **2.** *adj* ambiguous; having two different meanings.

(dameem) tartey mashma' דמים תרתי משמע both money and blood; compensation plus punishment.

taryag תרי"ג *num symbol:* 613 (**tav** i.e. 400 + **resh** i.e. 200 + **yod** i.e. 10 + **geemal** i.e. 3).

◇ **taryag meetsvot** תרי"ג מיצוות *nf pl* 613 precepts contained in the Torah which an observant Jew strives to fulfil and which form the foundation of **halakhah**(Jewish religious law).

tarzan/-eem טרזן *nm* dandy.

tas/-ah/-tee טס *v* flew (by airplane); (*pres* **tas**; *fut* **yatoos**).

tas/-eem טס *nm* tray; platter; (*pl+of:* **-ey**).

tasas/-eem תסס *nm* light sparkling soda-drink. (*pl+of:* **-ey**).

tasbeekh/-eem תסביך *nm* complex (Psycholog.); (*pl+of:* **-ey**).

tasbeekh/-ey 'elyonoot תסביך עליונות *nm* superiority complex (Psycholog.).

tasbeekh/-ey nekheetoot תסביך נחיתות *nm* inferiority complex (Psycholog.).

tasbeer/-ee! !תסביר *v fut (used as imp) sing m/f* explain! (*inf* **lehasbeer**; *pst* **heesbeer**; *pres* **masbeer**).

tasgeer/-ee! !תסגיר *v fut (used as imp) sing m/f* hand over! extradite! (*pst* **heesgeer**; *pres* **masgeer**; *fut* **yasgeer**).

tash/-ah/-tee תש *v* weakened; became exhausted; (*pres* **tash**; *fut* **yeetash**).

tash|ash/-eshah/-ashtee תשש *v* weakened; (*pres* **tash**; *fut* **yeetash**).

tashash kokh|o/-ah/-ee תשש כוחו/־ה/־י he, she, I (*etc*) has/have no power left; cannot cope any longer.

tashbets/-eem תשבץ *nm* crossword puzzle; (*pl+of:* **-ey**).

tash'eer/-ee תשאיר *v fut (used as imp) sing m/f* leave behind! abandon! (*inf* **lehash'eer**; *pst* **heesh'eer**; *pres* **mash'eer**).

tashkeef/-eem תשקיף *nm* forecast; prospectus (at the stock-exchange); (*pl+of:* **-ey**).

◇ **"tashleekh" ("Tashlich")** תשליך *nf* open-air religious ritual (held on 1st day of Rosh ha-Shanah) of "throwing one's sins" into a river or sea.

tashleekh/-ee! !תשליך *v fut (used as imp) sing m/f* throw! throw away!; (*inf* **lehashleekh**; *pst* **heeshleekh**; *pres* **mashleekh**).

tashleel/-eem תשליל *nm* negative; (*pl+of:* **-ey**).

tashleem/-ee! !תשלים *v fut (used as imp) sing m/f* **1.** you will complete! you will end! **2.** make peace; (*inf* **lehashleem**; *pst* **heeshleem**; *pres* **mashleem**).

tashleem/-ee 'eem ha-'oovdah! תשלים עם העובדה! *v fut (used as imp) sing m/f* you have to accept the fact.

tashleet/-ee! !תשליט *v fut (used as imp) sing m/f* will you enforce! (*inf* **lehashleet**; *pst* **heeshleet**; *pres* **mashleet**).

tashleet (*etc***) seder!** !תשליט סדר *v fut (used as imp) sing m/f* will you enforce order! please enforce order!

tashloom/-eem תשלום *nm* payment; (*pl+of:* **-ey**).

(be) tashloom בתשלום *adv* for a fee; against payment.

(le) tashloom לתשלום *nm* for payment; to pay.

(emtsa'ey) tashloom אמצעי תשלום *nm pl* means of payment.

tashmeesh ha-meetah (*or:* **tashmeesh**) תשמיש המיטה *nm* **1.** coitus; sexual intercourse; **2.** (*lit.*) use of the bed (term used in observant circles).

tashmeeshey kedooshah תשמישי קדושה *nm pl* ritual articles.

◇ **tash-nab** (or **-nav**) תשנ״ב *nf acr of* Jewish year **tav-sheen-noon-bet** (or **vet**) i.e. (5)752 (1991/92); (digit 5 marking millenium is usually skipped).

◇ **tash-nad** (or **tash-noon-dalet**) תשנ״ד *nf acr of* Jewish year **av-sheen-noon-dalet** i.e. (5)754 (1993/94); (digit 5 marking millenium is usually skipped).

◇ **tash-noon** תש״ן *nf acr* for the Jewish year tav-sheen-noon (5)750 (1989/90); (digit 5 marking millenium is usually skipped).

◇ **tash-noon-geemel** (or **tash-nag**) תשנ״ג *nf acr* for the Jewish year tav-sheen-noon-geemel (5)753 (1992/93). (digit 5 marking millenium is usually skipped).

tashoosh/teshooshah תשוש *adj* exhausted.

tashoov/-ee! !תשוב *v fut (used as imp) sing m/f* come back! will you come back! (*pst & pres* **shav**; *inf* **lashoov**).

tashreer/-eem תשריר *nm* validation; (*pl+of:* **-ey**).

tashtee|t/-yot תשתית *nf* base; infra-structure.

taskeel/-ee lehaveen! !תשכיל להבין *v fut (used as imp) sing m/f* try to understand! get it into your mind! (*pst* **heeskeel** *etc*; *pres* **maskeel** *etc*; *inf* **lehaskeel** *etc*).

taskeem/-ee! !תסכים *v fut (used as imp) sing m/f* will you agree! please agree! (*pst* **heeskeem**; *pres* **maskeem**; *inf* **lehaskeem**).

taskeem/-ee she- תסכים ש־ *v fut (used as imp) sing m/f* you'll agree that...

taskeer/-eem תסקיר *nm* survey; report; (*pl+of:* **-ey**).

taskeet/-eem תסכית *nm* radio-play; (*pl+of:* **-ey**).

tasreet/-eem תשריט *nm* drawing; town-planning scheme; (*pl+of:* **-ey**).

tasreet/-ee תסריט *v fut (used as imp) sing m/f* take a movie picture! take a video shot! (*inf* **lehasreet**; *pst* **heesreet**; *pres* **masreet**).

tasreet/-eem תסריט *nm* scenario; movie-script; (*pl+of:* **-ey**).

tasreet|ay/-a'eet תסריטאי *nmf* script-writer; scenario writer; (*pl+of:* **-a'ey**).

tasteer/-ee! !תסתיר *v fut (used as imp) sing m/f* hide! cover up! (*inf* **lehasteer**; *pst* **heesteer!** *pres* **masteer**).

tat- תת־ *(prefix) adj* under-; sub-

tat-adam תת־אדם *nm* subhuman.

tat-aloof/-eem תת־אלוף *nm* brigadier-general; (*pl+of:* **-ey**).

tat-hakarah תת־הכרה *nf* the subconscious.

tat-hakaratee/-t תת־הכרתי *adj* subconscious.

tat-karka'ee/-t תת־קרקעי *adj* subterranean.

tat-makle|'a'/-'eem תת־מקלע *nm* submachinegun; (*pl+of:* **-'ey**).

tat-meekl|a'/-a'eem תת־מקלע *nm* submachinegun; (*pl+of:* **-e'ey**).

tat-meymee/-t תת־מימי *adj* submarine; underwater.

tat-sar/-eem תת־שר *nm* deputy cabinet minister; vice-minister; (*pl+of:* **ey**).

tat-teeknee/-t תת־תיקני *adj* substandard.

tat-tezoonah תת־תזונה *nf* undernourishment; malnutrition.

tats'heer/-eem תצהיר *nm* affidavit; sworn statement.

tats'heer/-ee! !תצהיר *v fut (used as imp) sing m/f* will you declare! state! (*inf* **lehats'heer**; *pst* **heets'heer**; *pres* **mats'heer**).

tatsloom/-eem תצלום *nm* photograph; (*pl+of:* **-ey**).

tatspeet/-yot תצפית *nf* observation; expectation.

('emdat/-ot) tatspeet עמדת תצפית *nf* observation post.

(meegd|al/-eley) tatspeet מגדל תצפית *nm* observation tower.

◇ **tav** (*cpr* **Taf**) (תי״ו) ת *nf* 22nd letter of Hebrew alphabet; consonant "t".

◇ **tav** (*cpr* **Taf**) 'ת *num symbol* : 400.

tav/-eem תו *nm* mark; musical note; (*pl+of:* **-ey**).

(me-alef ve-'ad) tav מאל״ף ועד תי״ו from "A" to "Z".

tav|ah/-tah/-eetee טווה *v* spun (thread); (*pres* **toveh**; *fut* **yeetveh**).

tav|a'/-'ah/-a'tee טבע *v* drowned; (*pres* **tove'a'**; *fut* **yeetba'** (*b=v*)).

tav|a'/-'ah/-a'tee תבע *v* demanded; urged; (*pres* **tove'a'**; *fut* **yeetba'** (*b=v*)).

tav-a' (*etc*) **le-deen** תבע לדין *v* sued (in court).

(tsafra) tava צפרא טבא (greeting) Good morning! (old fashioned Aram.).

tav|akh/-khah/-akhtee טבח *v* slaughtered; (*pres* **tove'akh**; *fut* **yeetbakh** (*b=v*)).

tav|al/-lah/-altee טבל *v* dipped; immersed; (*pres* **tovel**; *fut* **yeetbol** (*b=v*)).

tavas/-eem טווס *nm* peacock; (*pl+of:* **-ey**).

tavee/-'ee! !תביא *v fut (used as imp) sing m/f* **1.** bring! bring over! **2.** *[slang]* give me! pass on! (*inf* **lehavee**; *pst* **hevee**; *pres* **mevee**).

tav|eem תווים *nm pl* **1.** musical score; **2.** lines; features; (*pl+of:* **-ey**).

taveen/-ee! !תבין *v fut (used as imp) sing m/f* please understand! will you understand! (*inf* **lehaveen**; *pst* **heveen**; *pres* **meveen**).

taveen oo-tekeeleen טבין ותקילין *m pl* solid cash; good money.

tavee|t/-yot תווית *nf* label.

('amood/-ey) tavekh עמוד תווך *nm* central pillar.

(ba) tavekh בתווך *adv* in the middle; in the center.

tav'er|ah/-ot תבערה *nf* fire; conflagration; (*+of:* **-at**).

(peetsets|at/-ot) tav'erah פצצת תבערה *nf* incendiary bomb.

tavey (*sing* **tav**) **negeenah** תווי נגינה *nm pl* musical score.

tavey paneem תווי פנים *nm pl* features (of a face).

tavl|ah/-a'ot טבלה *nf* plate; table; (*+of:* **-at**).

tavleeg/-ee! !תבליג *v fut (used as imp) sing m/f* forebear! restrain yourself! (*inf* **lehavleeg**; *pst* **heevleeg**; *pres* **mavleeg**).

tavleen/-eem תבלין *nm* spice; seasoning; (*pl+of:* **-ey**).

tavleet/-ee! !תבליט *v fut (used as imp) sing m/f* stress! emphasize! (*inf* **lehavleet**; *pst* **heevleet**; *pres* **mavleet**).

tavleet/-eem תבליט *nm* relief; (*pl+of:* **-ey**).

tavlee|t/-yot טבלית *nf* tablet.

tavnee|t/-yot תבנית *nf* form; pattern; format.

tavoo'a'/tvoo'ah טבוע *adj* **1.** sunk; **2.** imprinted.

tavool/tvoolah טבול *adj* dipped; immersed.

tavreeg/-ee! !תבריג *v fut (used as imp) sing m/f* screw it on! screw it in! (not fig); (*inf* **lehavreeg**; *pst* **heevreeg**; *pres* **mavreeg**).

tavreeg/-eem תבריג *nm* thread; screw-thread; (*pl+of:* **-ey**).

tavroo|'ah תברואה *nf* sanitation; (*+of:* **-'at**).

tavroo'an/-eet תברואן *nmf* sanitation-officer; (*pl+of:* **-ey**).

tavsheel/-eem תבשיל *nm* dish; cooked food; (*pl+of:* **-ey**).

◇ **tav-sheen-noon** תש״ן *nf* Jewish calendar year (5)750 1989/90 (digit 5 marking millenium is usually skipped). Also known by its *acr* **tash-noon**.

◇ **tav-sheen-noon-bet** (or-**vet**) תשנ״ב *nf* Jewish calendar year (5)752 - 1991/92 (digit 5 marking millenium is usually skipped). Also known by its partial *acr* **tash-noon-bet** (or **vet**) as well as by its full *acr* **tashnab** (or **tashnav**).

◇ **tav-sheen-noon-dalet** תשנ״ד *nf* Jewish calendar year (5)754 1993/94 - (digit 5 marking millenium is usually skipped). Also known by its *acr* **tash-nad**.

◇ **tav-sheen-noon-geemel** תשנ״ג *nf* the Jewish calendar year (5)753 - 1992/93 (digit 5 marking millenium is usually skipped). Also known by its *acr* **tash-nag**.

◇ **tav-sheen-samekh** תש״ס - *nf* Jewish calendar year (5)760 - 1999/2000 - (digit 5 marking millenium is usually skipped). Also known by its *acr* **tashas**.

◇ **tav-sheen-samekh-dalet** תשס״ד - *nf* Jewish calendar year (5)764 - 2003/04 - (digit 5 marking millenium is usually skipped). Also known by its partial *acr* **tash-samekh-dalet**.

◇ **tav-sheen-samekh-tet** תשס״ט *nf* Jewish calendar year (5)769 2008/09 - (digit 5 marking millenium is usually skipped). Also known by its *acr* **tash-sat**.

tavtee'akh/-khee! !תבטיח *v fut (used as imp) sing m/f* promise! (*inf* **lehavtee'akh**; *pst* **heevtee'akh**; *pres* **mavtee'akh**).

tayakh/-eem טייח *nm* plasterer; (*pl+of:* **-ey**).

tayar/-eem תייר *nm* tourist; (*pl+of:* **-ey**).

tayaroot תיירות *nf* tourism.

tayas/-eem טייס *nm* flier; pilot; (*pl+of:* **-ey**).

tayas/-ey khalal טייס חלל *nm* astronaut.

tayas/-ey krav טייס קרב *nm* fighter-pilot.

□ **Taybeh** (Tayiba) טייבה *nf* Arab township in Sharon, 6 km E. of **Toolkarem**. Pop. 21,200.

tayeel תייל *nm* barbed wire.

tayees טיס *nm* flying; aviation.

(kley) tayees כלי טיס *nm pl* aircraft.

tayeesh/tyasheem תיש *nm* goat.

tayelet/tayalot טיילת *nf* promenade.

tayeret/tayarot תיירת *nf* woman-tourist.

tayeset/tayasot טייסת *nf* **1.** air-squadron; **2.** lady-pilot.
tazkeek/-eem תזקיק *nm* distillate; (*pl+of:* **-ey**).
tazkeer/-ee! תזכיר! *v fut (used as imp) sing m/f* remind! will you remind! (*pst* **heezkeer**; *pres* **mazkeer**; *inf* **lehazkeer**).
tazkeer/-eem תזכיר *nm* memorandum; (*pl+of:* **-ey**).
tazmeen/-ee! תזמין! *v fut (used as imp) sing m/f* invite! order! will you order! (*inf* **lehazmeen**; *pst* **heezmeen**; *pres* **mazmeen**).
tazreek/-ee! תזריק! *v fut (used as imp) sing m/f* inject! innoculate! (*pst* **heezreek**; *pres* **mazreek**; *inf* **lehazreek**).
tazreem/-ee! תזרים! *v fut (used as imp) sing m/f* pour! cause to flow! discharge! (*inf* **lehazreem**; *pst* **heezreem**; *pres* **mazreem**).
tazreem/-eem תזרים *nm* flow; (*pl+of:* **-ey**).
te'al|ah/-ot תעלה *nf* canal; (*+of:* **-at**).
◇ **te'alat ha-yameem** תעלת הימים *nf* projected canal between Mediterranean and Dead Sea which was dropped for lack of funds and due to political opposition.
□ **Te'alat Soo'ets** תעלת סואץ *nf* Suez Canal.
(kan) te'ameem ק״ן טעמים *nm pl* too many pretexts.
□ **Te'ashoor** (Te'ashur) תאשור *nf* village (est. 1953) in NW Negev, 6 km NE of **Ofakeem**. Pop. 184.
te'atralee/-t תיאטרלי *adj* theatrical.
te'atron/-eem תיאטרון *nm* theater; (*pl+of:* **-ey**).
te'avon תיאבון *nm* appetite.
(be) te'avon בתיאבון (greeting) Bon Appetit! Have a pleasant meal!
(le) te'avon לתיאבון *adv* as much as one pleases.
ted|er/-areem תדר *nm* frequency (electr., radio).
tedeeroot תדירות *nf* frequency.
tee'akh טיח *nm* plaster.
teeb|el/-lah/-altee תיבל *v* spiced; seasoned; flavored; (*pst* **metabel**; *fut* **yetabel**).
teeboo|'a'/-'eem טיבוע *nf* sinking; (*pl+of:* **-'ey**).
teebool/-eem טיבול *nm* dipping.
□ **Teed'har** (Tidhar) תדהר *nm* village (est. 1953) in NW Negev, 7 km N. of **Ofakeem**. Pop. 190.
teedkhaf/-ee! תדחף! *v fut (used as imp) sing m/f* push! push on!
tazooz/-ee! תזוז! *v fut (used as imp) sing m/f* move! (*pst & pres* **zaz**; *inf* **lazooz**).
(al) tazooz/-ee (etc)! אל תזוז! *v fut (used as imp) sing m/f* don't move! (*pst & pres* **lo zaz**; *inf* **lo lazooz**).
(al) teedkhaf/-ee! אל תדחף! *v fut (used as imp) sing m/f* don't push! stop pushing! (*pst* **lo dakhaf**; *pres* **eyno dokhef**; *inf* **lo leedkhof**).
teedl|ek/-ekah/-aktee תדלק *v* refueled; (*pres* **metadlek**; *fut* **yetadlek**).
teedlook/-eem תדלוק *nm pl* refueling; (*pl+of:* **-ey**).
teedr|ekh/-ekhah/-akhtee תדרך *v* briefed; directed; (*pres* **metadrekh**; *fut* **yetadrekh**).
teedrookh/-eem תדרוך *nm* briefing; (*pl+of:* **-ey**).
tee|'ed/-'adah תיעד *v* documented; (*pres* **meta'ed**; *fut* **yeta'ed**).
te'eem|ah/-ot טעימה *nf* tasting; (*+of:* **-at**).
te'een|ah/-ot טעינה *nf* charging; loading; (*+of:* **-at**).
tee|'es/-'asah/-te'astee תיעש *v* industrialized; (*pres* **meta'es**; *fut* **yeta'es**).
tee|'ev/-'avah/te'avtee תיעב *v* abhorred; loathed; (*pres* **meta'ev**; *fut* **yeta'ev**).
te'ee|yah/-yot תעייה *nf* straying; wandering.
teef|'el/-'alah/-'altee תפעל *v* operated; put into operation; (*pres* **metaf'el**; *fut* **yetaf'el**).
teef'eret תפארת *nf* splendor; glory.
teefk|ed/-edah/-adetee תפקד *v* functioned; (*pres* **metafked**; *fut* **yetafked**).
teefkood/-eem תפקוד *nm* functioning (*pl+of:* **-ey**).
teefloo|t/-yot תפלות *nf* tastelessness; lewdness.
teefoof/-eem תיפוף *nm* drumming.
teef'ool/-eem תפעול *nm* operation; putting into operation; (*pl+of:* **-ey**).
teefoos טיפוס *nf* typhus (Medic.).
teefoos ha-beharot טיפוס הבהרות *nm* eruptive typhoid; exanthematous typhoid; (Medic.).
teefoos ha-beten טיפוס הבטן *nm* typhoid fever; (Medic.).
teefoos ha-me'ayeem טיפוס המעיים *nm* abdominal typhus (Medic.).
□ **Teefrakh** (Tifrah) תפרח *nm* village (est. 1949) in N. Negev, 3 km W. of **Tsomet ha-Nasee** (haNassi Junction). Pop. 952.
teeftef/-efah/-aftee טיפטף *v* dripped; (*pres* **metaftef**; *fut* **yetaftef**).
teeftoof/-eem טפטוף *nm* dripping; (*pl+of:* **-ey**).
teefzor|et/-ot תפזורת *nf* bulk.
(be) teefzoret בתפזורת - *adv* as bulk; in bulk; unpackaged cargo.
(kar|a/-'ah/-a'tee) teegar (*cpr* **tagar**) קרא תגר *v* complained; protested; (*pres* **kore** *etc; fut* **yeekra** *etc*).
teegb|er/-erah/-artee תגבר *v* reinforced; (*pres* **metagber**; *fut* **yetagber**).
teegbor|et/-ot תגבורת *nf* reinforcement.
teeg|en/-nah/-antee טיגן *v* fried; (*pres* **metagen**; *fut* **yetagen**).
teegoon/-eem טיגון *nm* frying; (*pl+of:* **-ey**).
teegr|ah/-ot תגרה *nf* skirmish; tussle; (*+of:* **-at**).
teegr|at/-ot yadayeem תגרת ידיים *nf* fist fight.
tee|her/-harah/-hartee טיהר *v* **1.** purified; **2.** purged; (*pres* **metaher**; *fut* **yetaher**).
teehoor (*cpr* **tehoor**)**/-eem** טיהור *nm* **1.** purge; **2.** cleaning; (*pl+of:* **-ey**).
teeh|yeh/-yee תהיה *v fut (used as imp) sing m/f* be! you will be! (*inf* **leehyot**; *pst* **hayah**; *pres* **heeno**).
teek/-eem תיק *nm* **1.** briefcase; file; folder; **2.** ministerial portfolio; (*pl+of:* **-ey**).
teek/-ey ha-... תיק ה־... *nm* the ministerial portofolio of...
(sar/-ah blee) teek שר בלי תיק *nmf* minister without portofolio.

teek|akh/-'khee תיקח *v fut (used as imp) sing m/f* take! (*inf* **lakakhat**; *pst* **lakakh**; *pres* **loke'akh**).

teekan/-eem תיקן *nm* cockroach; (*pl+of:* **-ey**).

teekb|a'/-e'ee תקבע *v fut (used as imp) sing m/f* will you fix, decide, determine (*pst* **kava'** *(v=b)*; *pres* **kove'a'**; *fut* **yeekba'**).

teek|en/-nah/-antee תיקן *v* repaired; mended; (*pres* **metaken**; *fut* **yetaken**).

teekhk|er/-erah/-artee תחקר *v* investigated; de-briefed; (*pres* **metakhker**; *fut* **yetakhker**).

teekhkoom/-eem תחכום *nm* sophistication; intricacy; (*pl+of:* **-ey**).

teekhkoor/-eem תחקור *nm* de-briefing; investigation; (*pl+of:* **-ey**).

teekhn|en/-enah/-antee תכנן *v* planned out; (*pres* **metakhnen**; *fut* **yetakhnen**).

teekhn|et/-etah/-atetee תכנת *v* programmed; (*pres* **metakhnet**; *fut* **yetakhnet**).

teekhnoon/-eem תכנון *nm* planning; (*pl+of:* **-ey**).

teekhnoot/-eem תכנות *nm* programming; (*pl+of:* **-ey**).

teekhon/-ah תיכון *adj* middle; intermediate.

teekhon/-eem תיכון *nm [colloq.]* secondary school; high-school; (*pl+of:* **-ey**).

(bet/batey-sefer) teekhon/-eem בית־ספר תיכון *nm* secondary school; high school.

(bog|er/-eret) teekhon בוגר תיכון *nmf* high-school graduate; (*pl+of:* **-rey/-rot**).

(ha-meezrakh ha) teekhon המזרח התיכון *nm* the Middle East.

(ha-yam ha) teekhon הים התיכון *nm* the Mediterranean Sea.

teekhonee/-t תיכוני *adj* middle; secondary (education).

teekhoneest/-eet תיכוניסט *nmf [colloq.]* high-school student.

teekhoom/-eem תיחום *nm* demarcation; delimitation; (*pl+of:* **-ey**).

teekhoon/-eem תיכון *nm* design; (*pl+of:* **-ey**).

teekhtov|et/-ot תכתובת *nf* exchange of letters; correspondence.

teekhzek/-ekah/-aktee תחזק *v* supplied maintenance; (*pres* **metakhzek**; *fut* **yetakhzek**).

teekhzook/-eem תחזוק *nm* maintenance; (*pl+of:* **-ey**).

teeknee/-t תקני *adj* standard; normal.

(tat-) teeknee/-t תת־תקני *adj* substandard.

teekn|eh/-ee תקנה *v fut (used as imp) sing m/f* buy! (*pst* **kanah**; *pres* **koneh**; *inf* **leeknot**).

teekoon/-eem תיקון *nm* repair; (*pl+of:* **-ey**).

teekoon omanootee תיקון אמנותי *nm* artistic mending.

◇ **teekoon khatsot** תיקון חצות synagogue midnight prayer mourning the destruction of the Temple. Nowadays, it is recited almost solely in Jerusalem, by extreme devotees congregating at weekday midnights in front of the Wailing Wall.

teekoon ta'oot תיקון טעות *nm* correction.

(ke) teekoon|o/-ah כתיקונו/־ה *adv - nmf* properly; correctly.

teekr|ah/-ot תקרה *nf* **1.** ceiling; **2.** ceiling (in *figurat.* or economic sense) (*+of:* **-at**).

teekrovet תקרובת *nf* refreshments.

teekshor|et/-ot תקשורת *nf* communications.

(meesrad ha) teekshoret משרד התקשורת *nm* Ministry of Communications.

(sar/-at ha) teekshoret שר התקשורת *nmf* Minister of Communications.

teekt|ek/-ekah/-aktee תיקתק or: טיקטק *[colloq.]* *v* ticked (watch, clock); (*pres* **metaktek**; *fut* **yetaktek**).

teekt|ek/-ekah/-aktee טיקטק *[colloq.] v* typed (on typewriter, computer keyboard); (*pres* **metaktek**; *fut* **yetaktek**).

teektook/-eem תקתוק *[colloq.] nm* ticking (clock); (*pl+of:* **-ey**).

teektook/-eem טקטוק *[colloq.] nm* typing; typerwriting; (*pl+of:* **-ey**).

teektook (*etc*) **bee-mekhonah** טקטוק במכונה *[colloq.] nm* typewriting.

teektsoov/-eem תקצוב *nm* budgeting; (*pl+of:* **-ey**).

teekv|a' (*npr* **teekb|a'**)/**-e'ee** תקבע *v fut (used as imp) sing m/f* will you fix, decide, determine (*pst* **kava'**; *pres* **kove'a'**; *fut* **yeekba'**).

teekv|ah/-ot תקווה *nf* hope; (*+of:* **-at**).

(shveev/-ey) teekvah שביב תקווה *nm* one bit of hope.

(zeek/-ey) teekvah זיק תקווה *nm* spark of hope.

◇ **(ha)teekvah** see ◇ **ha-teekvah**.

(avdah) teekvah אבדה תקווה *v* gone was the hope; hope was lost.

(khas|ar/-rat) teekvah חסר תקווה *adj* hopeless.

(avdah) teekvat|ee/-khah/-ekh/-o/-ah אבדה תקוותי *v pst* gone was my/your (*m/f*)/his/her hope; (*pres* **ovedet** *etc*; *fut* **tovad** *etc*).

(tal|ah/-tah/-eetee) teekvot תלה תקוות *v* he/she/I pinned hopes on... (*pres* **toleh** *etc*; *fut* **yeetleh** *etc*).

teel/-eem טיל *nm* rocket; missile; (*pl+of:* **-ey**).

teel/-ey katyooshah טיל קטיושה *nm* "Katyusha" (Russian-made) rocket.

teelbosh|et/-shot תלבושת *nf* dress; costume.

teelboshet akheedah תלבושת אחידה *nf* uniform.

teeley teeleem shel תילי תילים של *nm pl* heaps and heaps of...

teelgr|ef/-efah/-aftee טילגרף *v* telegraphed; cabled; (*pres* **metalgref**; *fut* **yetalgref**).

teelf|en (*npr* **teelpe|n**)/**-enah/-antee** טילפן *v* phoned; telephoned; (*pres* **metalpen**; *fut* **yetalpen** *(p=f)*).

('omed/et 'al) teel|o/-ah עומד על תילו *v pres* stands in its place (*pst* **'amad** *etc*; *fut* **ya'amod** *etc*).

teelp|en/-enah/-antee טילפן *v* phoned; telephoned; (*pres* **metalpen**; *fut* **yetalpen**).

teeltan/-eem תלתן *nm* clover (Botan.).

('al|eh/-ey) teeltan עלה תלתן clover-leaf.

teelt|el/-elah/-altee טילטל *v* moved; carried; (*pres* **metaltel**; *fut* **yetaltel**).
teeltool/-eem טלטול *nm* moving; wandering; peregrination.
teeltooley derekh טלטולי דרך *nm pl* tribulations of travel.
teelyon/-eem (*[colloq.]*: **talyon/-eem**) תליון *nm* pendant; medallion; (*pl+of:* **-ey**).
te|'em/-'amah/-'amtee תיאם *v* coordinated; (*pres* **meta'em**; *fut* **yeta'em**).
teem|ahon תימהון *nm* amazement; (*+of:* **-hon**).
teemhonee/-t תמהוני *adj* queer; eccentric.
□ **Teemna'** (Timna') תמנע *nf* site of Israel's 3,000 year old copper mines 25 km N. of Elat, which, after some twenty years of not very profitable exploitation, were abandoned in 1976 and now serve as a tourist attraction and amusement park.
teemn|a'/-e'ee תמנע *v fut (used as imp) sing m/f* will you prevent! (*pst* **mana'**; *fut* **yeemna'**).
teemookheen תימוכין *nm pl* backing; support.
□ **Teemoreem** (Timmorim) תמורים *nm* coop. village (est. 1954) in the central Coastal Plain, 1 km S. of Mal'akhi Junction (**Tsomet Mal'akhee**). Pop 313.
□ **Teemrat** (Timrat) תמרת *nm* communal settlement (est. 1981) in Lower Galilee, 4 km NW of **Meegdal ha-'Emek**. Pop 981.
teemren/-enah/-antee תמרן *v* maneuvered; (*pres* **metamren**; *fut* **yetamren**).
teemron/-eem תמרון *nm* maneuver; stratagem; (*pl+of:* **-ey**).
teemroon/-eem תמרון *nm* maneuvering; tactics; (*pl+of:* **-ey**).
teemsakh/-eem תמסח *nm* crocodile; (*pl+of:* **-ey**).
teemsor|et/-ot תמסורת *nf* transmission.
teemt|em/-emah/-amtee טימטם *v* dulled; stupefied; (*pres* **metamtem**; *fut* **yetamtem**).
teemts|a/-e'ee ! תמצא *v fut (used as imp) sing m/f* find! (*inf* **leemtso**; *pst* **matsa**; *pres* **motse**).
teemts|et/-etah/-atetee תמצת *v* summed up; condensed; (*pres* **metamtset**; *fut* **yetamtset**).
teemtsoot/-eem תמצות *nm* condensation; summarizing; (*pl+of:* **ey**).
(yar|ad/-dah le) teemyon ירד לטמיון *v* went down the drain; (*pres* **yored** *etc*; *fut* **yered** *etc*).
teen טין *nm* silt; clay.
teenah/-ot טינה *nf* grudge; (*+of:* **-at**).
teen|ah/-tah/-eetee תינה *v* recounted; told troubles; (*pres* **metaneh**; *fut* **yetaneh**).
te'en|ah/-eem תאנה *nf* fig (*pl+of:* **-at**).
teen|ef/-fah/-aftee טינף *v* dirtied; (*pres* **metanef**; *fut* **yetanef**).
teengodet תנגודת *nf* resistance; body-resistance.
teenof|et/-ot טינופת *nf* filth.
teenok/-ot תינוק *nm* baby; infant; (*pl+of:* **et**).
teenok/-ot mavkhenah תינוק מבחנה *nm* test-tube baby.
teenok|et/-ot תינוקת *nf* baby-girl; infant-girl.
teenoof/-eem טינוף *nm* dirtying; (*pl+of:* **-ey**).
tee'ood/-eem תיעוד *nm* documentation.
teep-top טיפ־טופ *adj [colloq.]* tiptop.
teep-teepah טיפ־טיפה *adv [colloq.]* a little; just a drop.
teepah/-ot טיפה *nf* drop; (*+of:* **-at**).
(ha) teepah ha-marah הטיפה המרה *nf* liquor.
teep|akh/-khah/-akhtee טיפח *v* nursed; cultivated; fostered (*pres* **metape'akh**; *fut* **yetapakh**).
teep|at/-ot khalav טיפת חלב *nf* infant care center.
teep|e'akh/-khah/-akhtee טיפח *v* nursed; cultivated; fostered (*pres* **metape'akh**; *fut* **yetapakh**).
teepeen teepeen טיפין טיפין *adv* drop by drop.
teep|el/-lah/-altee טיפל *v* handled; tackled; (*pres* **metapel**; *fut* **yetapel**).
teep|es/-sah/-astee טיפס *v* climbed; (*pres* **metapes**; *fut* **yetapes**).
teep|esh/-shah טיפש *nmf & adj* stupid; fool; (*pl:* **-sheem/-shot**).
teepesh-'esreh טיפש־עשרה *adj* teenage; teenager.
(geel ha) teepesh-'esreh גיל הטיפש־עשרה *nm* the teenage years.
teepoo|'akh/-kheem טיפוח *nm* nursing; cultivation; (*pl+of:* **-khey**).
(te'oon/-ey) teepoo'akh טעון טיפוח *adj* requiring special care.
◇ **(te'ooney) teepoo'akh** see ◇ **te'ooney teepoo'akh**, below.
(ben/bat) teepookheem בן/בת טיפוחים *nmf* pampered favorite (*pl:* **bney** *etc*).
teepool/-eem טיפול *nm* treatment; handling; (*pl+of:* **-ey**).
teepool refoo'ee טיפול רפואי *nm* medical care.
(be) teepool בטיפול *adv* being taken care of.
(te'oon/-at) teepool טעון טיפול *adj* in need of care (*pl:* **-ey** *etc*).
teepoos/-eem טיפוס *nm* **1.** type; **2.** *[slang]* person (unfavorably); (*pl+of:* **-ey**).
(av-) teepoos אב־טיפוס *nm* prototype.
teepoosee/-t טיפוסי *adj* typical.
teepshee/-t טיפשי *adj* stupid; foolish.
teepshee טיפשי *adv* it is stupid to.
teepshon/-et טיפשון *nmf [slang]* silly little fool.
teepshoo|t/-yot טיפשות *nf* stupidity; folly.
te|'er (*npr* **te'ar**) **/-'arah/-'artee** תיאר *v* described; depicted; (*pres* **meta'er**; *fut* **yeta'er**).
te'er (*etc*) **le-'atsm|o/-ah/-ee** *etc* תיאר לעצמו *v* imagined; (*pres* **meta'er** *etc*; *fut* **yeta'er** *etc*).
□ **Teerah** (Tira) טירה *nf* large Arab township, 7 km N. of **Kefar Saba**. Pop. 13,700.
teer|ah/-ot טירה *nf* fortress; castle; (*+of:* **-at**).
teeras תירס *nm* corn.
□ **Teerat ha-Karmel** (Tirat haKarmel) טירת הכרמל *nf* urban settlement (est. 1949) on Carmel Coast, 6 km S. of Downtown Haifa. Pop. 15,000.

□ **Teerat Shalom** (Tirat Shalom) טירת שלום *nf* agric. suburb (est. 1931) of **Nes-Tseeyonah**.
□ **Teerat Tsvee** (Tirat Zevi) טירת צבי *nm* kibbutz (est. 1937), 3 km S. of Bet She'an. Pop. 740.
□ **Teerat Yehoodah** (Tirat Yehuda) טירת יהודה *nm* - village (est. 1949), 5 km NE of Ben-Gurion Airport. Pop. 482.
teer|'eh/-'ee! תראה! *v fut (used as imp) sing m/f* look! (*inf* **leer'ot**; *pst* **ra'ah**; *pres* **ro'eh**).
teergel/-elah/-altee תרגל *v* trained; drilled; (*pres* **metargel**; *fut* **yetargel**).
teergem/-emah/-amtee תרגם *v* translated; interpreted; (*pres* **metargem**; *fut* **yetargem**).
teergol|et/-ot תרגולת *nf* drill; series of exercises.
teergool/-eem תרגול *nm* training; drill; exercise; (*pl+of:* **-ey**).
teergoom/-eem תרגום *nm* translation; translating; (*pl+of:* **-ey**).
teerkh|ah/-ot טירחה *nf* bother; trouble; endeavor; (*+of:* **-at**).
(sekhar) teerkhah שכר טירחה *nm* fee.
teerkov|et/-ot תרכובת *nf* composition.
teeron/-eet טירון *nmf* **1.** recruit; **2.** novice; (*pl:* **-eem**; *+of:* **-ey**).
teeronoo|t/-yot טירונות *nf* basic training (milit.); novitiate.
(be) teeronoot בטירונות *adv* doing one's basic military training.
teerosh תירוש *nm* must; new must; new wine.
□ **Teerosh** (Tirosh) תירוש *nm* (est. 1955) in **Lakheesh** District, 10 km E. of Re'em Junction (**Tsomet Re'em**). Pop. 303.
teerter/-erah/-artee טירטר *v* rattled; harassed; (*pres* **metarter**; *fut* **yetarter**).
teertoor/-eem טרטור *nm* rattle; harassment (*pl+of:* **-ey**).
teesah/-ot טיסה *nf* flight; (*+of:* **-at**).
teesah neekhneset טיסה נכנסת *nf* incoming flight.
teesah yotset טיסה יוצאת *nf* outgoing flight.
teesan/-eem טיסן *nm* **1.** kite; **2.** flying model.
teesat/-ot sekher טיסת שכר *nf* charter flight.
teesbokh|et/-ot תסבוכת *nf* mix-up; complication.
teesg|or/-eree תסגור *v fut (used as imp) sing m/f* close! shut! (*inf* **leesgor**; *pst* **sagar**; *pres* **soger**).
teesh'ah/tesha' תשעה/תשע *num m/f* nine.
teesh'ah-'asar תשעה־עשר *num m* 19; nineteen.
◇ **teesh'ah be-av ("Tishebov")** תשעה באב *nm* the Ninth of Ab (Yiddish: Tisheboov) fast day (approx. July-August) to commemorate destruction of the 1st (586 BCE) and the 2nd (70 CE) Temples and loss of national homeland.
teesha|'er/-'aree! תישאר! *v fut (used as imp) sing m/f* stay! will you remain! (*inf* **leheesha'er**; *pst* **neesh'ar**; *pres* **neesh'ar**).
teesh'al/-ee! תשאל! *v fut (used as imp) sing m/f* ask! demand! (*inf* **leesh'ol**; *pst* **sha'al**; *pres* **sho'el**).
teesh'af/-ee! תשאף! *v fut (used as imp) sing m/f* aspire! (*inf* **leesh'of**; *pst* **sha'af**; *pres* **sho'ef**).
teesh'af/-ee (*etc*) **aveer!** תשאף אוויר! *v fut (used as imp) sing m/f* breath in!
teeshav|a'/-'ee! תישבע! *v fut (used as imp) sing m/f* swear! (*inf* **leheeshava'**; *pst* **neeshba'**; *pres* **neeshba'** *(v=b)*).
teeshbakhot תשבחות *nf pl* panegyric; words of praise.
teeshboots/-eem תשבוץ *nm* posting; grading; (*pl+of:* **-ey**).
teeshdor|et/-ot תשדורת *nf* broadcast dispatch; message.
teesh'eem תשעים *num* 90; ninety.
teeshk|akh/-ekhee! תשכח! *v fut (used as imp) sing m/f* forget! (*inf* **leeshko'akh**; *pst* **shakhakh**; *pres* **shokhe'akh** *(kh=k)*).
teeshk|av/-evee! תשכב! *v fut (used as imp) sing m/f* lie down! (*inf* **leeshkav**; *pst* **shakhav**; *pres* **shokhev** *(kh=k)*).
(beney) teeshkhoret בני תשחורת *nm pl* the younger generation.
teeshl|akh/-ekhee! תשלח! *v fut (used as imp) sing m/f* send! dispatch! (*inf* **leeshlo'akh**; *pst* **shalakh**; *pres* **shole'akh**).
teeshlov|et/-ot תשלובת *nf* complex (Econ.); gearing engagement.
teeshm|a'/-e'ee! תשמע! *v fut (used as imp) sing m/f* listen! hear! (*inf* **leeshmo'a'**; *pst* **shama'**; *pres* **shome'a'**).
teesh'ool/-eem תשאול *nm* interrogation; (*pl+of:* **-ey**).
teeshp|okh/-ekhee תשפוך *v fut (used as imp) sing m/f* pour! pour out! spill! shed! (*inf* **leeshpokh**; *pst* **shafakh**; *pres* **shofekh** *(f=p)*).
teeshpokh|et/-ot תשפוכת *nf* spill-out.
◇ **teeshrey** תשרי *nm* Tishre, 1st Jewish calendar month (approx Sep-Oct); 30 days.
teeshtesh/-eshah/-ashtee טישטש *v* covered up; blurred; obliterated; (*pres* **metashtesh**; *fut* **yetashtesh**).
teeshtesh *etc* טישטש *v [slang]* got one confused.
teesht|of/-efee תשטוף *v fut (used as imp) sing m/f* wash away! rinse! (*inf* **leeshtof**; *pst* **shataf**; *pres* **shotef**).
teeshtoosh/-eem טשטוש *nm* blotting; blurring; (*pl+of:* **-ey**).
teesm|akh/-ekhee! תשמח! *v fut (used as imp) sing m/f* rejoice! be glad! (*inf* **leesmo'akh**; *pst* **samakh**; *pres* **same'akh**).
teesmon|et/-ot תסמונת *nf* syndrome (Medic.).
teespor|et/-ot תספורת *nf* haircut.
teesrok|et/-ot תסרוקת *nf* hairdo; coiffure.
teet טיט *nm* clay; soil.
teet|e/-'ah/-e'tee טאטא *v* swept (with broom); (*pres* **meta'te**; *fut* **yeta'te**).
teetsrokhet תצרוכת *nf* consumption.
(mootsar/-ey) teetsrokhet מוצר תצרוכת *nm pl* consumer goods.

teetstar|ekh/-khee תצטרך *v fut (used as imp) sing m/f* you will have to! (*inf* **leheetstarekh**; *pst* **heetstarekh**; *pres* **meetstarekh**).

teev טיב *nm* quality.

teev me'ooleh טיב מעולה *nm* superior quality.

('am|ad/-dah/-etee) 'al teev עמד על טיב *v* realized the nature of; (*pres* **'omed** *etc*; *fut* **ya'amod** *etc*).

teev'ee/-t טבעי *adj* natural.

(be-godel) teev'ee בגודל טבעי *adj* life-size; full-size.

teev'eeyoot טבעיות *nf* naturalness.

teevekh/-khah/-akhtee תיווך *v* mediated; interceded; (*pres* **metavekh**; *fut* **yetavekh**).

□ **Teev'on** (Tiv'on) טבעון *nf* see **Keeryat Teev'on**.

teev'on|ee/-t טבעוני *nm & adj* naturalist (*pl* **-eeyeem/-eeyot**).

teev'onoot טבעונות *nf* naturalism, vegetarianism.

teevookh/-eem תיווך *nm* mediation; intercession; (*pl+of:* **-ey**).

(meesr|ad/-edey) teevookh משרד תיווך *nm* brokerage agency.

teeyakh/-yekhah/-yakhtee (or: **tee|ye'akh**) טייח *v* plastered; coated; (*pres* **metaye'akh**; *fut* **yetayakh** or: **yetaye'akh**)).

tee|yek/-ykah/-yaktee תייק *v* filed (records *etc*); (*pres* **metayek**; *fut* **yetayek**).

tee|yel/-yelah/-yaltee טייל *v* strolled; took a walk; took a trip; (*pres* **metayel**; *fut* **yetayel**).

teeyook/-eem תיוק *nm* filing (of papers, *etc*).

teeyool/-eem טיול *nm* promenade; excursion; trip; (*pl+of:* **-ey**).

teeyoor/-eem תיור *nm* touring; sightseeing; (*pl+of:* **-ey**).

◇ **teezk|eh/-ee le-meetsvot!** תזכה למצוות! (greeting) be blessed with good deeds!

teezk|or/-eree! תזכור! *v fut (used as imp) sing m/f* remember! (*inf* **leezkor**; *pst* **zakhar** *(kh=k)*; *pres* **zokher**).

teezkor|et/-ot תזכורת *nm* reminder; memo.

teezmen/-enah/-antee תזמן *v* timed; (*pres* **metazmen**; *fut* **yetazmen**).

teezmer/-erah/-artee תזמר *v* orchestrated; (*pres* **metazmer**; *fut* **yetazmer**).

teezmoon/-eem תזמון *nm* timing; (*pl+of:* **-ey**).

teezmoor/-eem תזמור *nm* orchestration; scoring; (*pl+of:* **-ey**).

teezmor|et/-ot תזמורת *nf* orchestra.

teezmoret feelharmoneet תזמורת פילהרמונית *nf* philharmonic orchestra.

teezmoret kamereet תזמורת קאמרית *nf* chamber-music orchestra.

teezmortee/-t תזמורתי *adj* orchestral.

□ **Tefakhot (Tefahot)** טפחות *nm* village (est. 1980) in Lower Galilee, 2 km NE of **Tsalmon** water reservoir.

tefakhot טפחות *nf pl* roof (poetical).

(mee-masad ve-'ad ha) tefakhot ממסד ועד טפחות *adv* from foundation to roof i.e. from top to bottom.

tefeekhoo|t/-yot תפיחות *nf* swelling.

tefeel|ah/-ot תפילה *nf* prayer; (*+of:* **-at**).

◇ **tefeelat 'arveet** תפילת ערבית *nf* evening prayer (**ma'areev** מעריב).

◇ **tefeelat meenkhah** תפילת מנחה *nf* afternoon prayer service

◇ **tefeelah be-tseeboor** תפילה בציבור *nf* public prayer which, under Jewish law, is only recited with at least than 10 Jewish males aged 13 or over present.

(ba'al) tefeelah בעל תפילה *nm* cantor; hazan; one who leads public prayer.

◇ **(seedoor/-ey) tefeelah** see ◇ **seedoor/-ey tefeelah**.

tefeelat shabat תפילת שבת *nf* the Sabbath (including Friday night) prayers.

tefeeleen תפילין *nm pl* phylacteries.

◇ **(taleet oo) tefeeleen** see ◇ **taleet oo-tefeeleen**.

tefeer|ah/-ot תפירה *nf* sewing; (*+of:* **-at**).

(mekhon|at/-ot) tefeerah מכונת תפירה *nf* sewing machine.

tefees|ah/-ot תפיסה *nf* **1.** grasp; seizure; **2.** conception; point of view; (*+of:* **-at**).

(kal/-at) tefeesah קל תפיסה *adj* easy-grasping.

(meheer/-at) tefeesah מהיר תפיסה *adj* of quick perception.

(emoon|ah/-ot) tefel|ah/-ot אמונה טפלה *nf* superstition.

tefer/tfareem תפר *nm* seam; stitch; (*pl+of:* **teefrey**).

tefes/tfaseem תפס *nm* clip; catch; (*pl+of:* **teefsey**).

tefook|ah/-ot תפוקה *nf* production; output; (*+of:* **-at**).

tefoots|ah/-ot תפוצה *nf* circulation (of newspaper or magazine); (*+of:* **-at**).

◇ **(ha)tefootsot** התפוצות *nf pl* the Diaspora i.e. Jewish communities outside Israel.

tegoovah/-ot תגובה *nf* reaction; reacting (*+of:* **-at**).

teh תה *nm* tea.

teheel|ah/-ot תהילה *nf* fame; glory; (*+of:* **-at**).

teheeleem תהלים *nm* the Book of Psalms (Bible).

tehee|yah/-yot תהייה *nf* **1.** amazement; wondering; **2.** regret; (*+of:* **-yat**).

tehom/-ot תהום *nf* abyss.

(mey) tehom מי תהום *nm pl* ground-water.

tehomee/-t תהומי *adj* abysmal; bottomless.

tehoodah/-ot תהודה *nf* resonance; (*+of:* **-at**).

tehor/-at lev טהר לב *adj* pure-hearted.

tek|a'/-a'eem תקע *nm* plug (Electr.).

tek|en/-aneem תקן *nm* norm; list; standard; (*pl+of:* **teekney**).

tek|er/-areem תקר *nm* puncture; flat tire; (*pl+of:* **teekrey**).

tek|es/-aseem טקס *nm* ceremony; (*pl+of:* **teeksey**).

tekee|'ah/-'ot תקיעה *nf* blowing of horn or "Shofar" (*+of:* -'**at**).

◇ **tekee'ah be-shofar** תקיעה בשופר *nf* blowing "Shofar" (ram's horn) that is part of Rosh ha-Shana morning prayer (unless it falls on Sabbath) and also signals ending Yom Kippur fast. It is further done (mainly by Near Eastern Jews) to give solemnity to certain rare acts or occasions.

◇ **tekee|'at/-'ot kaf** תקיעת כף *nf* handshake (to seal a deal or to make a promise).

tekee|'at/-'ot shofar תקיעת שופר *nf* blowing the "**Shofar**" (see ◇ **tekee'ah be-shofar**, above).

tekeef|ah/-ot תקיפה *nf* assault; attack; (*+of:* -**at**).

tekhakh|eem תככים *nm pl* intrigues; (*+of:* -**ey**).

tekheefoot תכיפות *nf* urgency; frequency.

tekheek|ah/-ot תחיקה *nf* legislation; (*+of:* -**at**).

tekheel|ah תחילה **1.** *adv* at first; first; **2.** *nf* beginning; (*+of:* -**at**).

(ba) tekheelah בתחילה *adv* at first; in the beginning.

(be-khavanah) tekheelah בכוונה תחילה *adv* with premeditation.

(be-makhshavah) tekheelah במחשבה תחילה *adv* deliberately.

(le-kha) tekheelah לכתחילה *adv* in the beginning; at first.

(mee-le-kha) tekheelah מלכתחילה *adv* from the start.

tekheelatee/-t תחילתי *adj* initial.

tekheenah (or **takheenah**) טחינה *nf* thick sesame oil paste.

(salat) tekheenah סלט טחינה *nm* "**takheenah**" salad, popular beginning of an Arab-style meal.

tekheen|ah/-ot טחינה *nf* milling; grinding; crushing; (*+of:* -**at**).

tekheen|ah/-ot תחינה *nf* supplication; litany.

tekheenatee תחינתי *nf* my request; my supplication.

tekheeyah תחייה *nf* revival; resurrection; (*+of:* -**yat**).

(kam/-ah/-tee lee) tekheeyah קם לתחייה *v* was resurrected; (*pres* **kam** *etc; fut* **yakoom** *etc*).

(shav/-ah/-tee lee) tekheeyah שב לתחייה *v* came back to life; (*pres* **shav** *etc; fut* **yashoov** *etc*).

◇ **(Ha) tekheeyah** see ◇ **Ha-Tekheeyah**.

◇ **tekheeyat ha-meteem** תחית המתים *nf* Resurrection of the Dead belief in an apocalyptic resurrection on Day of Judgment and coming of the Messiah.

tekhef תיכף *adv* immediately; at once.

tekhef oo-mee-yad תיכף ומייד *adv* immediately; instantly.

tekhelet תכלת *nf* light-blue; azure.

◇ **tekhelet-lavan** תכלת לבן *adj* blue and white colors of Jewish (and Israeli) national flag.

(shmey) tekhelet שמי תכלת *nm pl* blue skies.

◇ **(taleet she-koolah) tekhelet** see ◇ **taleet she-koolah tekhelet.**

tekh|es/-aseem טכס *nm* ceremony; (*pl+of:* **teekhsey**).

tekhn|a'ee (*npr* **tekhn|ay**) /-**a'eem** טכנאי *nmf* technician; (*pl+of:* -**a'ey**).

tekhn|ay/-a'ey elektroneekah טכנאי אלקטרוניקה *nmf* electronics technician.

tekhn|ay/-a'ey metoseem טכנאי מטוסים *nm* aircraft technician.

tekhn|ay/-a'ey radyo טכנאי רדיו *nm* radio technician.

tekhn|ay/-a'ey rekhev טכנאי רכב *nm* motor vehicle mechanic.

tekhn|ay/-a'ey sheenayeem טכנאי שיניים *nm* dental technician.

tekhn|ay/-a'ey televeezyah טכנאי טלוויזיה *nm* TV- technician.

tekhna'oot טכנאות *nf* technology.

tekhnee/-t טכני *adj* technical.

◇ **tekhneeyon** (**Technion**) הטכניון *nm* the Israeli Institute of Technology in Haifa. The country's oldest scientific institution and school of engineering.

tekhneek|ah/-ot טכניקה *nf* technique; technics.

tekhol טחול *nm* spleen.

(le-'eeteem) tekhoofot לעיתים תכופות *adv* often; frequently.

tekhool|ah/-ot תחולה *nf* incidence (of a law); inception; (*+of:* -**at**).

tekhool|ah/-ot תכולה *nf* content; capacity; (*+of:* -**at**).

tekhoom/-eem תחום *nm* **1.** limit; boundary; **2.** zone; sphere; (*pl+of:* -**ey**).

◇ **tekhoom ha-moshav** תחום המושב *nm* "Pale" (in pre-revolutionary Czarist Russia) limited zone in which Jews were allowed to reside.

(mee-khoots la) tekhoom מחוץ לתחום **1.** *adv* out of bounds; **2.** *adv* "beyond the Pale".

tekhoon|ah/-ot תכונה *nf* **1.** trait; characteristic; **2.** preparation; (*+of:* -**at**).

tekhoonah rabah תכונה רבה *nf* extensive preparation.

tekhoosh|ah/-ot תחושה *nf* feeling; (*+of:* -**at**).

tekhoreem טחורים *nm pl* piles; hemorrhoids.

□ **Teko'a'** (Teqo'a) תקוע *nm* village (est. 1970) at edge of Judean Desert, 2 km SW of Herodeon. Pop. 474.

tekoofat ha-'even תקופת האבן *nf* the Stone Age.

tekoofat ha-heetbagroot תקופת ההתבגרות *nf* maturation age; adolescence.

◇ **tekoofat ha-mandat** תקופת המנדט *nf* the "Mandate Days" i .e. the years during which Palestine was under British rule. They began with country's conquest by British troops in 1918 and continued from April 1920 to May 15, 1948 under a Mandate from the League of Nations (the precursor of the U.N) to administer it with the purpose of establishing a Jewish National Home there.

tekoofat ha-mateeranoot תקופת המתירנות *nf* the Age of permissiveness.

tekoofat ha-shefa' תקופת השפע *nf* the Age of abundance.

◇ **tekoofat ha-sho'ah** תקופת השואה the Holocaust period (1939-1945).

◇ **tekoofat ha-tsena'** תקופת הצנע *nf* the Austerity Period i.e. years 1951-54 when young state of Israel had to enforce strict austerity on its suddenly tripled population.

tekoofat tseenoon תקופת צינון *nf* cooling-off period.

tekoomah תקומה *nf* **1.** recovery; **2.** resurrection (*figurat.*); (*+of:* **-at**).

□ **Tekoomah** (Tequma) תקומה *nm* village (est. 1949) in S. coastal plain, 3 km NW of Netivot Junction (**Tsomet Neteevot**). Pop. 345.

◇ **(dor ha) tekoomah** see ◇ **dor ha-tekoomah**.

tel/teeleem תל *nm* hill.

□ **Tel 'Adasheem** (Tel Adashim) תל עדשים village (est. 1913) in Yizre'el Valley, 5 km N. of 'Afula. Pop. 399.

□ **Telaleem** (Telalim) טללים *nm* village (est. 1978) in Negev, 3 km SE of Mash'abim Junction (**Tsomet Mash'abeem**). Pop. 89.

□ **Telameem** (Telamim) תלמים village *nm* (est. 1950) in **Lakheesh** District 10 km S. of Giv'ati Junction (**Tsomet Geev'atee**). Pop. 463.

□ **Tel-Asher** תל־אשר *nm* village NW of **Hertseleeyah**.

□ **Tel 'a-Shomer** see □ **Tel ha-Shomer**, below.

telat- ־תלת *(prefix) adj* tri-; three-

telat-memadee/-t תלת־מימדי *adj* three-dimensional.

telat-ofan תלת־אופן *nm* tricycle.

telat-shenatee/-t תלת־שנתי *adj* triennial.

□ **Tel-Aviv** תל־אביב *[colloq.]* name of Israel's largest metropolis, the correct legal name for which, since its merger with its mother-town Jaffa in 1949 , is "Tel-Aviv-Yafo" (see next entry).

□ **Tel-Aveev-Yafo** (Tel-Aviv-Yafo) תל־אביב־יפו *nf* (colloquially referred to as Tel-Aviv) is Israel's main metropolis. Founded 1909 as a residential garden-suburb on seaside sands outside 3,000 year old harbor-town Jaffa (**Yafo**). with which it is now merged. Though population, including that of Jaffa, hardly surpasses 339,400, T.-A. functions as commercial, financial, cultural, artistic and administrative heart of Greater Tel-Aviv area (Tel-Aviv **Rabatee** תל־אביב רבתי see next entry)..

□ **Tel-Aviv Rabatee** תל־אביב רבתי *nf* Greater Tel-Aviv area, encompassing five residential towns together with Tel-Aviv-Yafo proper: **Ramat-Gan, Bney-Brak** (Beney Berak), **Geev'atayeem** (Giv'atayim), **Kholon** (Holon), and **Bat-Yam**. Total pop. over 1,200,000 people.

tela|y/-'eem טלאי *nm* patch; (*pl+of:* **-ey**).

telay 'al gabey telay טלאי על גבי טלאי *adv* botching; clumsy repair.

teleeloo|t/-yot תלילות *nf* steepness.

teleesh|ah/-ot תלישה *nf* picking; tearing off.

teleeshoo|t/-yot תלישות *nf* alienation; lack of roots.

telee|yah/-yot תלייה *nf* hanging; (*+of:* **-yat**).

('amood/-ey) teleeyah עמוד תלייה *nm* scaffold; gallows.

teloon|ah/-ot תלונה *nf* complaint; (*+of:* **-at**).

□ **Tel ha-Shomer** תל־השומר *nm* residential area (est. 1934) in SE Ramat-Gan near **Kefar Azar**, (onetime known as Tel-Litwinsky) centering around **Sheeba** (Shiba) Hospital and Medical Center .

□ **Tel Katseer (Tel Qazir)** תל קציר *nm* kibbutz near SW coast of Lake Tiberias (est. 1949), 4 km E. of Zemah Junction (**Tsomet Tsemakh**). Pop. 396.

□ **Tel-Khanan** (Tel-Hanan) תל־חנן *nm* residential quarter (est. 1948) of Nesher settlement, Haifa Bay, 5 km SE of Haifa.

□ **Tel-Khay** (Tel-Hay) תל־חי *nf* memorial ground in Upper Gallilee, 2 km N. of **Keeryat-Shmonah**, to a village of pioneers that existed there from 1893 until raided and destroyed in 1920 by a gang of anti-Jewish desperadoes from Syria. The heroic resistence put up by the settlers, led by Josef Trumpeldor who fell in the battle, became one of the cherished sagas of Jewish persistence in recovering the nation's homeland. Memorial grounds, part of kibbutz **Kefar Geel'adee**, comprise reconstructed quarters and an arms museum.

□ **Tel Megeedo** (Tel Meggido) תל מגידו *nm* site of excavations about 1 km NE of kibbutz Meggido. Remnants are of fortress-palace complexes, mostly from the time of Kings Solomon and Ahab.

□ **Tel-Mond** תל־מונד *nf* rural settlement (est. 1929) in Sharon, 7 km N. of **Kefar Saba**. Pop. 3,490.

□ **Tel-Tsoor** (Tel Zur) תל־צור *nf* one-time village (est. 1922) now a residential quarter of **Even Yehoodah**.

□ **Tel-Yeets'khak (Tel Yizhak)** תל־יצחק *nm* kibbutz (est. 1938) in Sharon, 3 km SE of **Poleg** Crossing. Pop. 627.

□ **Tel Yosef** תל־יוסף *nm* kibbutz (est. 1921) in Yizre'el Valley, near **'En Kharod**. Pop. 508.

telefon/-eem טלפון *nm* telephone; phone; (*pl+of:* **-ey**).

telefon|ay/-a'eet טלפונאי *nmf* telephone operator.

telefoneest/-eet טלפוניסט *nmf [colloq.]* telephone operator.

telefoneet טלפונית *adv* by telephone.

telegraf טלגרף *nm* telegraph.

telegram|ah/-ot טלגרמה *nf* telegram; cable.

tel|ekh/-khee! ! תלך *v fut (used as imp) sing m/f* go! (*inf* **lalekhet**; *pst* **halakh**; *pres* **holekh**).

(al) tel|ekh/-khee! ! אל תלך *v fut (used as imp) sing m/f* don't go!

tel|em/-ameem תלם *nm* furrow; (*pl+of:* **talmey**).

(hal|akh/-khah/-akhtee ba) telem הלך בתלם *v* toed the line; (*pres* **holekh** *etc; fut* **yelekh** *etc*).

televeez|yah/-yot טלוויזיה *nf* television; (*+of:* **-yat**).

(kokh|av/-evet) televeezyah כוכב טלוויזיה *nmf* television star.

(maklet/-ey) televeezyah מקלט טלוויזיה *nm* television set.

(seedr|at/-ot) televeezyah סידרת טלוויזיה television series.

(sheedoor/-ey) televeezyah שידור טלוויזיה *nm* television broadcast.

◇ **televeezyah bee-khvaleem** טלוויזיה בכבלים *f* cable television supplied all over Israel to paying subscribers by concessionaires, one per each area.

televeezyonee/-t טלוויזיוני *adj* television-

teloon|ah/-ot תלונה *nf* complaint; (*+of:* **-at**).

(heegeesh/-ah/heegashtee) teloonah הגיש תלונה *v* lodged a complaint; (*pres* **mageesh** *etc; fut* **yageesh** *etc.*).

teloosh/-eem תלוש *nm* coupon; (*pl+of:* **-ey**).

teloot תלות *nf* dependence.

(ee-) teloot אי־תלות *nf* independence.

tema|her/-haree תמהר *v fut (used as imp) sing m/f* hurry! (*inf* **lemaher**; *pst* **meeher**; *pres* **memaher**).

(al) tema|her/-haree אל תמהר *v fut (used as imp) sing m/f* don't hurry! (*inf* **lo lemaher**; *pst* **lo meeher**; *pres* **eyno memaher**; *fut* **lo yemaher**).

temareem תמרים *nm pl* (*sing:* **tamar**) dates; (*pl+of:* **teemrey**).

tembel/-eet טמבל *nmf [slang]* fool; dumbbell.

tembel/-eet shekmot|kha/-ekh! טמבל שכמותך! *nmf [slang]* you fool!

(al teeh|yeh/-yee) tembel/-eet! אל תהיה טמבל! *v fut (used as imp) sing m/f* don't be a fool.

(kov|a'/-a'ey) tembel כובע טמבל *nm* peaked cap considered by some as typically Israeli.

temeedee/-t תמידי *adj* constant; permanent.

temee|hah/-hot תמיהה *nf* astonishment; wondering; (*+of:* **-hat**).

temeekh|ah/-ot תמיכה *nf* support; (*+of:* **-at**).

temeemoo|t/-yot תמימות *nf* innocence; naivete.

temeemoo|t/-yot de'eem תמימות דעים *nf* similarity of opinions; unanimity.

temees|ah/-ot תמיסה *nf* solution (physical); (*+of:* **-at**).

temol-sheelshom תמול שלשום *adv* formerly; not so long ago.

(lo kee) tmol sheelshom לא כתמול שלשום *adv* not the way it used to be.

temoon|ah/-ot תמונה *nf* picture; image; (*+of:* **-at**).

temoor|ah/-ot תמורה *nf* **1.** change; **2.** counter-value; consideration (jurid.); (*+of:* **-at**).

(le-lo) temoor|ah ללא תמורה *adv* free; asking nothing in exchange.

temoorat תמורת *adv* in exchange for.

temoot|ah/-ot תמותה *nf* mortality; (*+of:* **-at**).

temperament/-eem טמפרמנט *nm* temper.

ten/-ee! ! תני ! תן *v fut (used as imp) sing m/f* give! (*inf* **latet**; *pst* **natan**; *pres* **noten**).

ten/-ee (etc) kheeyookh! תן/תני חיוך *v fut (used as imp) sing m/f* give a smile!

ten/-ee (etc) lee! (etc) ! תן לי *v fut (used as imp) sing m/f* give me!

◇ **tena'eem** תנאים *nm pl* traditional Jewish betrothal ceremony.

tena|y/-a'eem תנאי *nm* condition (*pl+of:* **-a'ey**).

('al) tenay על תנאי *adv* on the condition; conditionally.

(bee)tenay she- בתנאי ש־ *adv* provided that...; on condition that...

◇ **(tsav 'al) tenay** see ◇ **tsav 'al tenay**.

tender/-eem טנדר *nm* van; tender; pick-up truck.

tenees טניס *nm* tennis; lawn-tennis.

tenees shoolkhan טניס שולחן *nm* table tennis; ping-pong.

(makhbet/-ey) tenees מחבט טניס *nm* tennis racket.

(meegr|ash/-eshey) tenees מגרש טניס *nm* tennis court.

(na'aley) tenees נעלי טניס *nm pl* tennis shoes.

tenoo|'ah/-'ot תנועה *nf* **1.** movement; swing; **2.** vowel; **3.** political (or social) movement; (*+of:* **-'at**).

tenoo|'ah/-'ot ketan|ah/-ot תנועה קטנה *nf* short vowel (Gram.).

tenoo|'at/-'ot ha- תנועת ה־ *nf* movement of...

◇ **tenoo'at ha-'Avodah** תנועת העבודה *nf* Israeli Labor Movement see ◇ **meefleget ha-'avodah**.

◇ **tenoo'at ha-kheroot** תנועת החירות *nm* right of center political party that came into being with the State of Israel. In 1965 it became the mainspring of the "**Leekood**" ("Likud") block and came to power in 1977. Originates from the underground military organization "Irgun Zva'ee Le'umi" (I.Z.L., see ◇ **Etsel**) which, in turn, grew out of Jabotinsky's Revisionist movement in Zionism, before that.

tenoo|'at/-'ot mekha'ah תנועת מחאה *nf* protest movement.

◇ **tenoo'at ha-moshaveem** תנועת המושבים *nf* organization of "Moshav"-type (smallholders cooperative settlement) villages.

tenoof|ah/-ot תנופה *nf* momentum; (*+of:* **-at**).

tenookh/-eem תנוך *nm* lobe; (*pl+of:* **-ey**).

tenookh|ah/-ot תנוחה *nf* position of the body; (*+of:* **-at**).

tenoom|ah/-ot תנומה *nf* nap; slumber; (*+of:* **-at**).

tenoov|ah/-ot תנובה *nf* crop; yield; (*+of:* **-at**).

◇ **tenoovah** ("Tnuvah") תנובה *nf* **1.** Histadrut"s major complex for cooperative marketing and distribution of farm produce from kibbutzim and "moshav"-type villages; **2.** small eating-place selling dairy products supplied by "Tnuvah".

□ **Tenoovot** (Tenuvot) תנובות *nm* village (est. 1952) in Sharon, 6 km E. of haSharon Road Junction. Pop. 471.

te'om/-ah תאום *adj & nmf* twin.

(akh/-eem) te'om/-eem אח תאום *nm* twin brother.

(akh|ot/-ayot) te'om|ah/-ot אחות תאומה *nf* twin sister.

te'om|eem/-ot תאומים *nmf pl* twins.

(mazal) te'omeem מזל תאומים *nm* Gemini (Zodiac).

te'ood|ah/-ot תעודה *nf* certificate; testimony; **(**+*of:* **-at).**

te'oodat 'aneeyoot תעודת עניות *nf* a mark of incompetence.

te'ood|at/-ot bagroot תעודת בגרות *nf* matriculation certificate.

te'ood|at/-ot gemer (*or:* **gmar)** תעודת גמר *nf* graduation certificate.

◇ **te'ood|at/-ot kashroot** תעודת כשרות *nf* certificate of "Kashrut" (issued by Rabbinate to restaurants, hotels *etc*).

◇ **te'ood|at/-ot khayeem** תעודת חיים *nf* official certificate confirming the fact of one's being alive (required from time to time from beneficiaries of a lifetime pension from abroad).

te'ood|at/-ot ma'avar תעודת מעבר *nf* laissez-passer; pass.

◇ **te'oodat/-ot 'oleh** תעודת עולה *nf* "New Immigrant's Card" issued by Ministry of Absorption to new arrivals who wish to settle in Israel under Law of Return. It entitles them to immediate Israeli citizenship as well as to a number of bonuses including initial accommodation, assistance in the study of Hebrew, subsequent housing, tax exemptions, aid in finding employment, social care, *etc*.

◇ **te'ood|at/-ot zehoot** תעודת זהות *nf* Identity Card (obligatory for any resident of Israel over age 18).

te'oofah תעופה *nf* aviation; flying.

(nemal/neemley) te'oofah נמל תעופה *nm* airport.

(sedeh/sedot) te'oofah שדה תעופה *nm* airfield.

te'oom/-eem תיאום *nm* coordination; **(***pl+of:* **-ey).**

(khoser) te'oom חוסר תיאום *nm* lack of coordination.

te'oon/-eem טיעון *nm* argumentation.

te'oon/-at teepool טעון טיפול *adj* in need of care (*pl:* **-ey** *etc*).

te'oon|ah/-ot תאונה *nf* accident; **(**+*of:* **-at).**

te'oonah/-ot katlanee|t/-yot תאונה קטלנית *nf* fatal accident.

te'oon|at/-ot 'avodah תאונת עבודה *nf* work accident.

te'oon|at/-ot drakheem תאונת דרכים *nf* road accident.

te'oonat paga' oo-varakh *(v=b)* תאונת פגע וברח *nf* hit and run accident.

◇ **te'ooney teepoo'akh** טעוני טיפוח *nm pl* reference to socially-disadvantaged school students (coming mainly from poor families of a North African or Middle Eastern origin) who receive assistance in order to enjoy equal learning opportunities with others.

te'oor/-eem תיאור *nm* description; **(***pl+of:* **-ey).**

te'oots|ah/-ot תאוצה *nf* acceleration; **(**+*of:* **-at).**

te'ooz|ah/-ot תעוזה *nf* daring; courage; **(**+*of:* **-at).**

te'or|yah/-yot תיאוריה *nf* theory; **(**+*of:* **-yat).**

tered תרד *nm* spinach.

ter|ed/-dee! !תרד! תרדי *v fut (used as imp) sing m/f* get off! get down! **(***inf* **laredet;** *pst* **yarad;** *pres* **yored).**

teref טרף *nm* prey.

(kha|yat/-yot) teref חיית טרף *nf* beast of prey.

terem טרם *adv* **1.** before; **2.** not yet.

(be) terem בטרם *adv* prior to; before.

(be) terem 'et בטרם עת *adv* prematurely.

ter|ets/-tsah/-atstee תירץ *v* motivated; explained; tried to justify; **(***pres* **metarets;** *fut* **yetarets).**

termee/-t תרמי *adj* thermal.

termos/-eem תרמוס *nm* thermos; vacuum-bottle.

teroof/-eem טירוף *nm* folly; madness **(***pl+of:* **-ey).**

teroots/-eem תירוץ *nm* excuse; pretext; **(***pl+of:* **-ey).**

teror טירור *nm* terrorism.

teroreest/-eet טירוריסט *nmf [colloq.]* terrorist.

terpenteen טרפנטין *nm* turpentine.

(al) tesab|ekh/-khee אל תסבך *v fut (used as imp) sing m/f* don't complicate things! **(***inf* **lo lesabekh;** *pst* **lo seebekh;** *pres* **eyno mesabekh;** *fut* **lo yesabekh).**

tesad|er/-ree תסדר *v fut (used as imp) sing m/f* arrange! **(***inf* **lesader;** *pst* **seeder;** *pres* **mesader).**

tesal|ek/-ee תסלק *v fut (used as imp) sing m/f* remove! **(***inf* **lesalek;** *pst* **seelek;** *pres* **mesalek).**

tesap|er/-ree תספר *v fut (used as imp) sing m/f* **1.** tell! tell the story! **2.** cut (hair)! **(***inf* **lesaper;** *pst* **seeper;** *pres* **mesaper).**

tesees|ah/-ot תסיסה *nf* **1.** fermentation; **2.** (*figurat.*) agitation; unrest; **(**+*of:* **-at).**

tesha' תשע *nf num* 9; nine.

tesha'-'esreh תשע־עשרה *num f* 19; nineteen.

(ha) tesha'-'esreh התשע־עשרה *adj & num f* 19th; nineteenth.

('esreem, shlosheem, arba'eem *etc* **va)tesha'** עשרים, שלושים, ארבעים ותשע *num f* 29, 39, 49; twenty, thirty, forty *etc* nine.

(ha-'esreem *etc* **va)tesha'** העשרים ותשע *adj & num* 29th; twenty *etc* -ninth.

teshee'ee/-t תשיעי *adj & num* 9th; ninth.

teshee'ee|t/-yot תשיעית *num f* 1/9; ninth (part).

tesheeshoo|t/-yot תשישות *nf* weakness; exhaustion.

tesh|er/-areem תשר *nm* tip; present; gift; (*pl+of:* **teeshrey**).

tesh|ev/-vee! !תשבי !תשב *v imp sing m/f* sit down! sit! (*pst* **yashav** *pres* **yoshev**; *inf* **lashevet**).

teshoo|'ah/-'ot תשועה *nf* deliverance; salvation; (*+of:* **-'at**).

teshook|ah/-ot תשוקה *nf* desire; passion; (*+of:* **-at**).

teshoo'ot תשואות *nf pl* cheers; cheering; applause.

teshoo'ot so'arot תשואות סוערות *nf pl* stormy applause.

teshoor|ah/-ot תשורה gift; present; (*+of:* **-at**).

teshoov|ah/-ot תשובה *nf* **1.** answer; reply; **2.** repentance; **3.** non-religious person's re-embracement of religion.

◇ **('aseret yemey) teshoovah** see ◇ **'aseret yemey teshoovah.**

(ba'al/-ey) teshoovah בעל תשובה *nm* repentant sinner.

(khaz|ar/-rah/-artee bee) teshoovah חזר בתשובה *v* repented; turned religious; (*pres* **khozer** *etc*; *fut* **yakhzor** *etc*).

(khoz|er/-reem bee) teshoovah חוזר בתשובה *nm* repentant sinner; non-religious person's re-embracing religion.

tesoo|'ah/-'ot תשואה *nf* yield (financial); (*+of:* **-'at**).

tesoom|ah/-ot תשומה *nf* input; assignment; (*+of:* **-at**).

tesoomat (*npr* **tesoomet**) **lev** תשומת לב *nf* attention; attentiveness.

('or|er/-erah/-artee) tesoomat lev עורר תשומת לב *v* aroused attention; (*pres* **me'orer** *etc*; *inf* **le'orer** *etc*).

test/-eem טסט *nm [slang]* test.

Tet (טת) ט *nf* 9th letter of Hebrew Alphabet; consonant "t".

Tet 'ט *num. symbol 9.*

◇ **tet be-av** see ◇ **Teesh'ah be-av.**

◇ **tet-vav** ט״ו *num. symbol* (15) (fifteen) composed of letters **Tet** (=ט9) and **Vav** (=ו6) instead of **Yod** (=י10) and **Heh** (=ה5), since the latter two form together the word **yah** יה which is one of the Divine Names that "must not be uttered in vain".

◇ **tet-zayeen** ט״ז *num. symbol* sixteen (16) composed of **Tet** (=ט9) and **Zayeen** (=ז7) instead of the
Yod (=י10) and **Vav** (=ו6) since combination **Yod-Vav** (י״ו) would form part of the Divine Name that "must not be uttered in vain".

(la) tet לתת *v inf* to give; (*pst* **natan** *pres* **noten**; *fut* **yeeten**).

(la) tet (*etc*) **poorkan** לתת פורקן *v inf* to give vent.

(la) tet (*etc*) **shekhem** לתת שכם *v inf* to give a hand.

◇ **(samekh-) tet** see ◇ **samekh-tet.**

tetsoog|ah/-ot תצוגה *nf* display; exhibit; (*+of:* **gat**).

teva' טבע *nm* nature.

(ason/-ot) teva' אסון טבע *nm* natural disaster.

(be-derekh ha) teva' בדרך הטבע *adv* naturally; the natural way.

(mad'ey ha) teva' מדעי הטבע *nm pl* natural sciences.

(meen) teva' she-ka-zeh מין טבע שכזה *nm [slang]* some character!

(ohev/-et) teva' אוהב טבע *adj* nature-loving.

(ohev/-ohavey) teva' אוהב טבע *nm* nature lover.

(shmoor|at/-ot) teva' שמורת טבע *nf* nature reserve.

tev|ah/-ot תיבה *nf* **1.** box; chest; **2.** word; **3.** musical bar; (*+of:* **-at**).

tevakh טבח *nm* massacre.

tevakh/-eem טווח *nm* range; distance.

(aroo|key/-khot) tevakh ארוכי טווח *adj* long-range.

(keetsrey/-ot) tevakh קצרי טווח *adj* short-range.

(lee) tevakh arokh לטווח ארוך *adv* in the long run.

(lee) tevakh katser לטווח קצר **1.** *adv* in the short run; **2.** *adj* short range.

(lee) tevakh rakhok לטווח רחוק **1.** *adv* at long distance; **2.** *adj* long-range.

tevalool (*cpr* **tavlool**)/**-eem** תבלול *nm* cataract; (*pl+of:* **-ey**).

◇ **tev|at/-ot do'ar** תיבת־דואר *nf* **1.** private letter-box or mail box into which mail is delivered for addressee; **2.** public mail box into which letters are droppped for mailing; **3.** *(incorrect colloquial use)* Post Office box; P.O. box (for which correct term is **ta/ ta'ey do'ar** but confusion is due to Hebrew acronyms in use (ת״ד or .ת.ד) which do not fit here.

tev|at-heelookheem תיבת הילוכים *nf* gearbox.

tev|at/-ot meekhtaveem תיבת מכתבים *nf* letterbox; mailbox.

tev|at/-ot neegeenah תיבת נגינה *nf* music box.

◇ **tevat no'akh** תיבת נוח *nf* Noah's ark.

tevay/-eem תוואי *nm* outline; construction-plan; (*pl+of:* **-a'ey**).

tevee|'ah/-'ot תביעה *nf* demand; claim; (*+of:* **-'at**).

tevee|'ah/-'ot meeshpatee|t/-yot תביעה משפטית *nf* legal claim.

('ed/-ey ha) tevee'ah עד תביעה *nm* prosecution witness.

(ha) tevee'ah ha-klaleet התביעה הכללית *nf* the prosecution.

(ketav/keetvey) tevee'ah כתב תביעה *nm* statement of claim.

(parashat ha) tevee'ah פרשת התביעה *nf* statement of claim (in a civil case).

tevee|'ah/-'ot טביעה *nf* drowning; (*+of:* **-'at**).

tevee'at 'ayeen טביעת עין *nf* perceptiveness; deep insight.

tevee|'at/-'ot etsba'ot טביעת אצבעות *nf* fingerprints.

teveel|ah/-ot טבילה *nf* **1.** dipping; **2.** baptism (*+of:* **-at**).

tevee|yah/-yot טוויה *nf* spinning (thread); (*+of:* **-yat**).

(galgal) teveeyah גלגל טוויה *nm* spinning wheel.

tevel תבל *nf* universe.

('ad ketsot) tevel עד קצות תבל *adv* to the end of the world.

(artsot) tevel ארצות תבל *nf pl* countries of the world.

□ **Teveryah** see □ **Tveryah.**

◇ **tevet** טבת *nm* 4th Jewish Calendar month (approx. Dec.-Jan.). 29 days.

tevoo|'ah/-'ot תבואה *nf* grain crop; (*+of:* **-'at**).

tevoon|ah/-ot תבונה *nf* wisdom; understanding; (*+of:* **-at**).

tevoonat kapayeem תבונת כפיים *nf* handicraft.

tevoos|ah/-ot תבוסה *nf* defeat; (*+of:* **-at**).

tevoosanoot תבוסנות *nf* defeatism.

tevoostan/-eet תבוסתן *nmf* defeatist (*pl:* **eem/-eeyot**; *+of:* **-ey**).

tevoostanoot תבוסתנות *nf* defeatism.

tevot (*sing:* **teyvah**) תיבות *nf pl* **1.** boxes; **2.** words; **3.** bars (music).

tevot pree hadar תיבות פרי הדר *nf pl* citrus-fruit boxes.

(rashey) tevot ראשי תיבות *nm pl* initials of words; abbreviations; acronyms.

tey תה *nm* tea.

teykoo תיקו *nm* stalemate; draw (sport).

Teyman תימן *nf* Yemen.

teymanee/-m תימני *nm* Yemenite; Jew of Yemenite background.

teymanee/-t תימני *adj* Yemenite.

teymanee|yah/-yot תימנייה *nf* Yemenite (woman or girl); (*+of:* **-at**).

teyv|ah/-ot תיבה *nf* **1.** box; chest; **2.** word; **3.** musical bar; (*+of:* **-at**).

teyv|at/-ot do'ar see ◇ **tev|at/-ot do'ar.**

teyv|at-heelookheem תיבת הילוכים *nf* gearbox.

teyv|at/-ot meekhtaveem תיבת מכתבים *nf* letterbox; mailbox.

teyv|at/-ot neegeenah תיבת נגינה *nf* music box.

◇ **teyvat no'akh** see ◇ **tevat no'akh.**

teyvot (*sing:* **teyvah**) תיבות *nf pl* **1.** boxes; **2.** words; **3.** bars (music).

teyvot pree hadar תיבות פרי הדר *nf pl* citrus-fruit boxes.

(rashey) teyvot ראשי תיבות *nm pl* initials of words; abbreviations; acronyms.

tez|ah/-ot תיזה *nf* thesis.

tezoon|ah/-ot תזונה *nf* nutrition; nourishment; (*+of:* **-at**).

(tat-) tezoonah תת־תזונה *nf* undernourishment; malnutrition.

tezoonatee/-t תזונתי *adj* nutritional.

tezooz|ah/-ot תזוזה *nf* shift; displacement; motion; (*+of:* **-at**).

tfadal/-ee! !תפאדל *nmf [slang] (Arab.)* please! welcome! be my guest!

□ **Tfakhot** see □ **Tefakhot.**

tfakhot טפחות *nf pl* roof (poetical).

(mee-masad ve-'ad ha) tfakhot ממסד ועד טפחות *adv* from foundation to roof i.e. from top to bottom.

tfeekhoo|t/-yot תפיחות *nf* swelling.

tfeel|ah/-ot תפילה *nf* prayer; (*+of:* **-at**).

◇ **tfeelah be-tseeboor** see ◇ **tefeelah be-tseeboor.**

(ba'al) tfeelah בעל תפילה *nm* cantor; hazan; one who leads public prayer.

◇ **(seedoor/-ey) tfeelah** see ◇ **seedoor/-ey tefeelah.**

tfeelat shabat תפילת שבת *nf* the Sabbath (including Friday night's) prayers.

tfeeleen תפילין *nm pl* phylacteries.

◇ **(taleet oo) tfeeleen** see ◇ **taleet oo-tefeeleen.**

tfeerah/-ot תפירה *nf* sewing; (*+of:* **-at**).

(mekhon|at/-ot) tfeerah מכונת תפירה *nf* sewing machine.

tfees|ah/-ot תפיסה *nf* **1.** grasp; seizure; **2.** conception; point of view; (*+of:* **-at**).

(kal/-at) tfeesah קל־תפיסה *adj* easy-grasping.

(meheer/-at) tfeesah מהיר תפיסה *adj* of quick perception.

(emoon|ah/-ot) tfel|ah/-ot אמונה טפלה *nf* superstition.

tfook|ah/-ot תפוקה *nf* production; output; (*+of:* **-at**).

tfoots|ah/-ot תפוצה *nf* circulation (of newspaper or magazine); (*+of:* **-at**).

◇ **(ha)tfootsot** see ◇ **ha-tefootsot.**

tkee|'ah/-'ot תקיעה *nf* blowing of horn or **"Shofar"** (*+of:* **-'at**).

◇ **tkee'ah be-shofar** see ◇ **tekee'ah be-shofar.**

tkee|'at/-'ot kaf תקיעת כף *nf* handshake (to seal a deal or to make a promise).

tkee|'at/-'ot shofar תקיעת שופר *nf* blowing **"Shofar"** (see **tekee'ah be-shofar**).

tkeef|ah/-ot תקיפה *nf* assault; attack; (*+of:* **-at**).

tkhakh|eem תככים *nm pl* intrigues; (*+of:* **-ey**).

tkheefoot תכיפות *nf* urgency; frequency.

tkheek|ah/-ot תחיקה *nf* legislation; (*+of:* **-at**).

tkheel|ah תחילה **1.** *adv* at first; first; **2.** *nf* beginning; (*+of:* **-at**).

'(ba) tkheelah בתחילה *adv* at first; in the beginning.

(be-khavanah) tkheelah בכוונה תחילה *adv* with premeditation.

(be-makhshavah) tkheelah במחשבה תחילה *adv* deliberately.

(le-kha) tkheelah לכתחילה *adv* in the beginning; at first.

(mee-le-kha) tkheelah מלכתחילה *adv* from the start.

tkheelatee/-t תחילתי *adj* initial.

"tkheenah" טחינה *nf* thick sesame oil paste.

(salat) tkheenah סלט טחינה *nm* **"takheenah"** salad, popular entry to an Arab-style meal.
tkheen|ah/-ot טחינה *nf* milling; grinding; crushing; (*+of:* **-at**).
tkheen|ah/-ot תחינה *nf* supplication; litany.
tkheenatee תחינתי *nf* my request; my supplication.
tkheeyah תחייה *nf* revival; resurrection; (*+of:* **-yat**).
(kam/-ah/-tee lee) tkheeyah קם לתחייה *v* was resurrected; (*pres* **kam** *etc; fut* **yakoom** *etc*).
(shav/-ah/-tee lee) tkheeyah שב לתחייה *v* came back to life; (*pres* **shav** *etc; fut* **yashoov** *etc*).
◇ **"(Ha)tkheeyah"** see ◇ **"Ha-Tkheeyah"**.
◇ **tkheeyat ha-meteem** see ◇ **tekheeyat ha-meteem**.
tkhelet תכלת *nf* light-blue; azure.
◇ **tkhelet-lavan** see ◇ **tekhelet-lavan**.
(shmey) tkhelet שמי תכלת *nm pl* blue skies.
◇ **(taleet she-koolah) tkhelet** see ◇ **taleet she-koolah tekhelet**.
tkhol טחול *nm* spleen.
(le-'eeteem) tkhoofot לעיתים תכופות *adv* often; frequently.
tkhool|ah/-ot תחולה *nf* incidence (of a law); inception; (*+of:* **-at**).
tkhool|ah/-ot תכולה *nf* content; capacity; (*+of:* **-at**).
tkhoom/-eem תחום *nm* **1.** limit; boundary; **2.** zone; sphere; (*pl+of:* **-ey**).
◇ **tkhoom ha-moshav** see ◇ **tekhoom ha-moshav**.
(mee-khoots la) tkhoom מחוץ לתחום *adv* out of bounds.
tkhoon|ah/-ot תכונה *nf* **1.** trait; characteristic; **2.** preparation; (*+of:* **-at**).
tkhoonah rabah תכונה רבה *nf* extensive preparation.
tkhoosh|ah/-ot תחושה *nf* feeling; (*+of:* **-at**).
tkhoreem טחורים *nm pl* piles; hemorrhoids.
tkoof'ah/-ot תקופה *nf* era; period; (*+of:* **-at**).
tkoofat ha-'even תקופת האבן *nf* the Stone Age.
tkoofat ha-heetbagroot תקופת ההתבגרות *nf* maturation age; adolescence.
◇ **tkoofat ha-mandat** see ◇ **tekoofat ha-mandat**.
tkoofat ha-mateeranoot תקופת המתירנות *nf* the Age of permissiveness.
tkoofat ha-shefa' תקופת השפע *nf* the Age of abundance.
◇ **tkoofat ha-sho'ah** see ◇ **tekoofat ha-sho'ah**.
tkoofat tseenoon תקופת צינון *nf* cooling-off period.
◇ **tkoofat ha-tsena'** see ◇ **tekoofat ha-tsena'**.
tkoomah תקומה *nf* **1.** recovery; **2.** resurrection (*figurat.*); recovery; (*+of:* **-at**).
□ **Tkoomah** see □ **Tekoomah**.
◇ **(dor ha) tkoomah** see ◇ **dor ha-tekoomah**.
□ **Tlaleem** see □ **Telaleem**.
□ **Tlameem** see □ **Telameem**.
tlat- ־תלת *(prefix) adj* tri-; three-
tlat-memadee/-t תלת־מימדי *adj* three-dimensional.
tlat-ofan תלת־אופן *nm* tricycle.
tlat-shnatee/-t תלת־שנתי *adj* triennial.
tlay/-tla'eem טלאי *nm* patch; (*pl+of:* **-ey**).
tlay 'al gabey tlay טלאי על־גבי טלאי *adv* botching; clumsy repair.
tleeloo|t/-yot תלילות *nf* steepness.
tleesh|ah/-ot תלישה *nf* picking; tearing off.
tleeshoo|t/-yot תלישות *nf* alienation; lack of roots.
tlee|yah/-yot תלייה *nf* hanging; (*+of:* **-yat**).
('amood/-ey) tleeyah עמוד תלייה *nm* scaffold; gallows.
tloon|ah/-ot תלונה *nf* complaint; (*+of:* **-at**).
(heeg|eesh/-eeshah/-ashtee) tloonah הגיש תלונה *v* lodged a complaint; (*pres* **mageesh** *etc; fut* **yageesh** *etc.*).
tloosh/-eem תלוש *nm* coupon; (*pl+of:* **-ey**).
tloot תלות *nf* dependence.
(ee-) tloot אי־תלות *nf* independence.
tmareem תמרים *nm pl* (*sing:* **tamar**) dates; (*pl+of:* **teemrey**).
tmeedee/-t תמידי *adj* constant; permanent.
tmee|hah/-hot תמיה *nf* astonishment; wondering; (*+of:* **-hat**).
tmeekh|ah/-ot תמיכה *nf* support; (*+of:* **-at**).
tmeemoo|t/-yot תמימות *nf* innocence; naiveté.
tmeemoo|t/-yot de'eem תמימות דעים *nf* similarity of opinions; unanimity.
tmees|ah/-ot תמיסה *nf* solution (physical); (*+of:* **-at**).
tmol-sheelshom תמול שלשום *adv* formerly; not so long ago.
(lo kee) tmol sheelshom לא כתמול שלשום *adv* not the way it used to be.
tmoon|ah/-ot תמונה *nf* picture; image; (*+of:* **-at**).
tmoor|ah/-ot תמורה *nf* **1.** change; **2.** counter-value; consideration (jurid.); (*+of:* **-at**).
(le-lo) tmoor|ah ללא תמורה *adv* free; asking nothing in exchange.
tmoorat תמורת *adv* in exchange for.
tmoot|ah/-ot תמותה *nf* mortality; (*+of:* **-at**).
◇ **tna'eem** see ◇ **tena'eem**.
tna|y/-a'eem תנאי *nm* condition (*pl+of:* **-a'ey**).
('al) tnay על תנאי *adv* on the condition; conditionally.
(bee) tnay she- ־בתנאי ש *adv* provided that...; on condition that...
◇ **(tsav 'al) tnay** see ◇ **tsav 'al tenay**.
tnoo|'ah/-'ot תנועה *nf* **1.** movement; swing; **2.** vowel; **3.** political (or social) movement; (*+of:* **-'at**).
tnoo|'ah/-'ot ketan|ah/-ot תנועה קטנה *nf* short vowel (Gram.).
tnoo|'at/-'ot ha- ־תנועת ה *nf* the movement of...
◇ **tnoo'at ha-'avodah** see ◇ **tenoo'at ha-'avodah**.

◇ **tnoo'at ha-kheroot** see ◇ **tenoo'at ha-kheroot**.

tnoo|'at/-'ot mekha'ah תנועת מחאה *nf* protest movement.

◇ **tnoo'at ha-moshaveem** see ◇ **tenoo'at ha-moshaveem**.

tnoof|ah/-ot תנופה *nf* momentum; (*+of:* **-at**).

tnookh/-eem תנוך *nm* lobe; (*pl+of:* **-ey**).

tnookh|ah/-ot תנוחה *nf* body position; (*+of:* **-at**).

tnoom|ah/-ot תנומה *nf* nap; slumber; (*+of:* **-at**).

tnoov|ah/-ot תנובה *nf* crop; yield; (*+of:* **-at**).

◇ **tnoovah** see ◇ **tenoovah**.

□ **Tnoovot** see □ **Tenuvot**.

(hon) to'afot הון תועפות *nm* tremendous amount of money.

to'altee/-t תועלתי *adj* useful; utilitarian.

to'an|ah/-ot תואנה *nf* pretext (*+of:* **-at**).

to'ar/te'areem תואר *m* **1.** title; degree; **2.** appearance; form; (*pl+of:* **to'orey**).

to'ar ha-po'al תואר הפועל *nm* adverb (Gram.).

to'ar reeshon תואר ראשון *nm* **1.** (*lit.*) 1st Degree; **2.** Bachelor's Degree; B.A., B.Sc. (*etc*).

to'ar shenee תואר שני *nm* **1.** (*lit.*) 2nd degree; **2.** Master's degree; M.A.; M.Sc. (*etc*).

to'ar shleeshee תואר שלישי *nm* **1.** (*lit.*) 3rd degree; **2.** Doctor's degree; Ph.D.

(shem/-ot) to'ar שם תואר *nm* adjective (Gram.).

(yef|eh/-at) to'ar יפה תואר *adj* good-looking; beautiful; handsome.

tod|ah/-ot תודה *nf* thanks; thankfulness; (*+of:* **-at**).

todah! תודה! *interj* thanks! thank you!

todah la-'el! תודה לאל! *interj* thank God!

todah rabah! תודה רבה! *interj* thanks very much!

(aseer/-at) todah אסיר תודה *adj* ever so grateful.

(be) todah me-rosh בתודה מראש *adv* thanking in advance.

(hakarat) todah הכרת תודה *nf* gratefulness; gratitude.

(makeer/-ah) todah מכיר תודה *v pres* is grateful; (*pst* **heekeer** *etc*; *fut* **yakeer** *etc.*).

toda|'ah/-'ot תודעה *nf* awareness; (*+of:* **-'at**).

toda'ah yehoodeet תודעה יהודית *nf* Jewish consciousness; Jewish awareness.

(zerem ha) toda'ah זרם התודעה *nm* stream of consciousness.

(rav) todot רב תודות many thanks!

to'eh/to'ah תועה **1.** *adj* straying; lost; **2.** *v pres* strays; (*pst* **ta'ah**; *fut* **yeet'eh**).

to'eh/to'ah טועה **1.** *adj* erroneous; mistaken; **2.** *v pres* errs; is mistaken; (*pst* **ta'ah**; *fut* **yeet'eh**).

to'elet תועלת *nf* use; usefulness; utility.

(hef|eek/-eekah/-aktee) to'elet הפיק תועלת *v* derived profit; made use; (*pres* **mefeek** *etc*; *fut* **yafeek** *etc*).

(khas|ar/-rat) to'elet חסר תועלת *adj* useless; of no use.

to'|em/-ameem תואם *nm [colloq.]* (*abbr. of* **to'em** IBM) IBM compatible personal computer; (*pl+of:* **-amey**).

to'em/-et תואם *v pres* fits; corresponds to; (*pst* **ta'am**; *fut* **yeet'am**).

to'ev|ah/-ot תועבה *nf* shameful vice; obscenity; abomination; (*+of:* **-at**).

(seefroot) to'evah ספרות תועבה *nf* pornography.

(seret/seertey) to'evah סרט תועבה *nm* porno-movie; "blue" movie.

tof/toop|eem תוף *nm* drum; (*pl+of:* **-ey**).

tof ha-ozen תוף האוזן *nm* ear-drum (Anat.).

tofa|'ah/-'ot תופעה *nf* phenomenon.

tof|e'akh/-akhat תופח *v pres* swells; puffs up; (*pst* **tafakh**; *fut* **yeetpakh** (*p=f*)).

(kemakh) tofe'akh me-'elav קמח תופח מאליו *nm* self-rising flour.

tofee טופי *nm* toffee.

tofef/-aftee תופף *v* drummed; (*pres* **metofef**; *fut* **yetofef**).

tofel/-et ashmah טופל אשמה *v pres* imputes; charges; (*pst* **tafal** *etc*; *fut* **yeetpol** (*p=f*) *etc*).

tofer/-et תופר *v pres* sews; (*pst* **tafar**; *fut* **yeetpor** (*p=f*)).

tof|eret/-rot תופרת *nf* seamstress; dressmaker.

tofes/tfaseem טופס *nm* printed form; copy (of book or booklet); (*pl+of:* **tofsey**).

(mal|e/-'ee) tofes! מלא טופס! *v imp sing m/f* fill out a form; (see: **meele tofes**).

(meel|e/-'ah/-etee) tofes מילא טופס *v* filled out a form; (*pres* **memale** *etc*; *fut* **yemale** *etc*).

tofet תופת *nm* **1.** Hell; inferno; **2.** Tophet (Bibl.).

(ke'evey) tofet כאבי תופת *nm pl* infernal pains.

(mekhon|at/-ot) tofet מכונת־תופת *nf* infernal machine; explosive device.

tohar טוהר *nm* purity.

tohar ha-meedot טוהר המידות *nm* integrity.

tohar/-ah/-tee טוהר *v* was purified; was purged; (*pres* **metohar**; *fut* **yetohar**).

tohoo תוהו *nm* nothingness; desolation; vain.

tohoo va-vohoo תוהו ובוהו *nm pl* chaos; disorder.

('al|ah/-tah ba) tohoo עלה בתוהו *v* failed; went to naught; (*pres* **'oleh** *etc*; *fut* **ya'aleh** *etc*).

◇ **tohorah** טהרה *nf* **1.** purity; **2.** cleansing of corpse prior to burial.

tok|e'a'/-a'at תוקע *v pres* **1.** trumpets; blows; **2.** *[slang]* bring up unexpectedly (in a conversation); (*pst* **taka'**; *fut* **yeetka'**).

toke'a' ba-shofar תוקע בשופר *nm* "Shofar" blower.

tokef/tekafeem תוקף *nm* validity; (*pl+of:* **tokfey**).

(bar/bat) tokef בר/בת־תוקף *adj* valid; effective.

(be) tokef בתוקף *adv* in force.

(be-khol) tokef בכל תוקף *adv* most vigorously; vehemently.

(keeb|el/-lah/-altee) tokef קיבל תוקף *v* came into force; (*pres* **makabel** *etc*; *fut* **yekabel** *etc*).

(paka') tokef פקע תוקף *v* expired (validity); (*pres* **poke'a'** *etc; fut* **yeefka'** *etc f=p*).

(pekee'at) tokef פקיעת תוקף *nf* expiration; abolition.

tok|ef/-feem תוקף *nm* assailant; attacker; (*pl+of:* **-fey**).

tokef/-et תוקף **1.** *adj* assailing; **2.** *v pres* assails; attacks; (*pres* **takaf;** *fut* **yeetkof**).

tokfan/-eet תוקפן *nmf* aggressor; (*pl+of:* **-ey**).

tokfanee/-t תוקפני *adj* aggressive.

tokfanoot/-yot תוקפנות *nf* **1.** aggression; **2.** aggressiveness.

tokh תוך **1.** *adv* within; **2.** *nm* interior; contents.

tokh תוך *(prefix)* intra-

tokh kedey תוך כדי *adv* while; during.

tokh khodesh / shanah / shavoo'a' / shevoo'ayeem תוך חודש/שנה/שבוע/שבועיים within a month/year/week/fortnight.

(be) tokh בתוך **1.** in; inside; among **2.** during; within.

(le) tokh לתוך into.

(mee) tokh מתוך out of.

tokhakh|ah/-ot תוכחה *nf* rebuke; reproof; (*+of:* **-at**).

tokhelet תוחלת *nf* expectation; hope.

□ **Tokhelet** (Tohelet) תוחלת *nm* village (est. 1951) in Coastal Plain, 2 km SE of Bet-Dagan Road Junction). Pop. 310.

tokhelet khayeem תוחלת חיים *nf* life expectancy.

(le-lo) tokhelet ללא תוחלת *adv* without hope; hopelessly.

tokhen/tekhaneem תוכן *nm* content; (*pl+of:* **tokhney**).

tokh|en/-aneem טוחן *nm* miller.

tokhen/-et טוחן *v pres* grinds; mills; crushes; (*pst* **takhan;** *fut* **yeetkhan**).

tokhen/-et mayeem טוחן מים *v pres [colloq.]* keeps on repeating self.

tokh|enet/-anot טוחנת *nf* **1.** molar tooth; **2.** miller's wife.

tokhnee|t/-yot תוכנית *nf* plan; program.

tokhnee|t/-yot av תוכנית אב *nf* master-plan.

tokhnee|t/-yot beenyan תוכנית בניין *nf* construction plan.

tokhnee|t/-yot bneeyah תוכנית בנייה *nf* building scheme.

tokhnee|t/-yot beenyan 'areem תוכנית בניין ערים *nf* town-planning scheme.

tokhnee|t/-yot khomesh תוכנית חומש *nm* Five-Year Plan.

tokhnee|t/-yot leemoodeem תוכנית לימודים *nf* curriculum.

tokhnee|yah/-yot תוכנייה *nf* program (leaf or booklet) of concert, theater performance, *etc.*

tokpan (*npr* **tokfan**)/**-eet** תוקפן *nmf* aggressor; (*pl+of:* **-ey**).

tokpanee (*npr* **tokfanee**)/**-t** תוקפני *adj* aggressive.

tokpanoot (*npr* **tokfan|oot**) תוקפנות *nf* **1.** aggression; **2.** aggressiveness.

(neekhnas/-esah) le-tokp|o/-ah נכנס לתוקפו *v* entered into effect; (*pres* **neekhnas** *etc; fut* **yeekanes** *etc k=kh*).

tola|'at/-'eem תולעת *nf* worm.

◇ **tola'at ya'akov** תולעת יעקב *nf* "that worm, Jacob"- reference to unjustified inferiority complex of the Jewish people (Bibl.).

tolad|ah/-ot תולדה *nf* result; consequence; (*+of:* **toledet**).

tolar/-eem תול"ר *nm abbr.* (*acr of* **TOtakh Le-lo Reta'** (תותח לא רתע)) recoilless gun.

toldot תולדות *nf pl+of* history of; outcome of.

toldot khayeem תולדות חיים *nf pl* curriculum vitae; biography.

tom תום *nm* **1.** completion; **2.** simplicity; naiveté.

tom-lev תום לב *nm* good faith.

(be) tom lev בתום לב *adv* in good faith; bona fide.

tombon/-eem טומבון *nm [colloq.]* fender.

tomekh/-et תומך *v pres* supports; (*pst* **tamakh;** *fut* **yeetmokh**).

tom|ekh/-kheem תומך *nm* supporter; partisan; (*pl+of:* **khey**).

tomen/-et טומן *v pres* hides; conceals; (*pst* **taman;** *fut* **yeetmon**).

tomen/-et (*etc*) **be-khoob|o/-ah** טומן בחובו *v pres* holds in store (*figurat.*).

('atsey) tomer עצי תומר *nm* palm-tree; date-palm.

□ **Tomer** תומר *nm* village (est. 1978) in Jordan Valley, 3 km S. of **Patsa'el**. Pop.248.

ton/-eem טון *nm* tone.

ton|ah/-ot טונה *nf* ton.

(neyar) too'alet נייר טואלט *nm [colloq.]* toilet paper.

◇ **too-bee-shvat** ט"ו בשבט *nm* Arbor-Day tree-planting and outing holiday (primarily for school-children) to mark approach of spring; held on 15th of **Shevat** (approx. Jan.-Feb.).

too'ar/-ah/-tee (*npr:* **to'ar** *etc*) תואר *v* was described, portrayed; (*pst* **meto'ar;** *fut* **yeto'ar**).

toofeen|eem תופינים *nm pl* cookies; (*pl+of:* **-ey**).

toog|ah תוגה *nf* grief; sadness; (*+of:* **-at**).

took|ee תוכי *nm* parrot; (*pl+of:* **-ey**).

□ **Toolkerem** (Tulkarm) טול כרם *nf* Arab town across Green Line from Sharon, 16 km E. of Netanya. Pop. 44,800.

toom|'ah/'ot טומאה *nf* impurity; defilement; (*+of:* **at**).

(le) toom|o/-ah לתומו *adv* innocently; in good faith.

toomtoom/-eet טומטום *nmf [slang]* **1.** stupid; dumb; **2.** hermaphrodite.

tooneesa'ee (*npr* **tooneesa'ee**)/**-t** טוניסאי *nmf & adj* Tunisian.

tooneeseeyah תוניסיה *nf* Tunisia.

toop|al/-lah/-altee טופל *v* was attended to; was dealt with; (*pres* **metoopal;** *fut* **yetoopal**).

(ekdakh) toopee אקדח תופי *nm* revolver.

toop|eem תופים *nm pl* (*sing* **tof**) drums; (*+of:* **-ey**).

(be) toopeem oo-vee-mekholot בתופים ובמחולות *adv* **1.** *lit* : with drums and dances; **2.** (*figurat.*) with a big noise; most willingly.

toor/-eem טור *nm* column; (*pl+of:* **-ey**).

toor/-eem meshooryan/-eem טור משוריין *nm* armored column.

(ba'al/-at) toor בעל טור *nmf* columnist.

toor|ay/-a'eem טוראי *nm* private; common soldier; (*pl+of:* **-a'ey**).

tooray reeshon טוראי ראשון *nm* private first class (Pfc) lance-corporal; (*abbr:* **tarash**).

tooree/-t טורי *adj* arranged in a row.

(bayeet/bateem) tooree/-yeem בית טורי *nm* single-storied row house.

(doo-) tooree/-t דו־טורי *adj* **1.** arranged in two columns; **2.** double-breasted (jacket).

tooree|yah/-yot טורייה *nf* wide hoe.

toorg|am/-emah/-amtee תורגם *v* was translated; (*pres* **metoorgam**; *fut* **yetoorgam**).

toorgeman/-eet תורגמן *nmf* translator; interpreter; (*pl+of:* **-ey**).

toorkee/-t טורקי *adj* Turkish.

toorkee/-yah טורקי *nmf* Turk/Turkish woman.

(kafeh) toorkee קפה טורקי *nm* Turkish coffee.

toorkyah טורקיה *nf* Turkey.

toorp|ad/-edah/-adetee טורפד *v* was torpedoed (actually or figuratively); (*pres* **metoorpad**; *fut* **yetoorpad**).

toorpah תורפה *nf* weakness; frailty; (*+of:* **-at**).

(nekood|at/-ot) toorpah נקודת תורפה *nf* vulnerable point; Achilles heel.

toos/-ee טוס טוסי *v imp sing m/f* fly! (*pst & pres* **tas**; *fut* **yatoos**).

toosh/-eem טוש *nm* **1.** India ink; **2.** felt-tip pen.

toosheeyah תושייה *nf* resourcefulness; (*+of:* **-yat**).

□ **Toosheeyah** (Tushiyya) תושייה *nm* rural center (est. 1958) in NW Negev, 5 km NW of **Neteevot**. Pop. 415.

toot/-eem תות *nm* berry; (*pl+of:* **-ey**).

toot ha-geenah תות הגינה *nm* strawberry.

toot-sadeh תות שדה *nm* strawberry.

tootey bar תותי בר *nm pl* wild berries.

toov טוב *nm* goodness.

.oov lev טוב לב *nm* kind-heartendness; kindness.

toov ta'am טוב טעם *nm* exquisite taste.

(kol) toov! כל טוב ! (greeting) all the best!

(mee-kol) toov מכל טוב the best of everything.

□ **Tooval** (Tuval) תובל *nm* industrial village (est. 1978), 6 km NW of **Karmee'el**. Pop. 112.

tooveem (or **tooveen**) טובים or: טובין *nm pl* goods.

tor/-eem תור *nm* queue; line; turn.

(ba) tor בתור *adv* in the queue; in line.

(be) tor בתור *adv* as; in capacity of.

(mee-khoots la) tor מחוץ לתור *adv* out of turn.

tor|ah/-ot תורה *nf* **1.** (s) the Torah; the Pentateuch; Mosaic Law; **2.** theory; (*+of:* **-at**).

◇ **torah she-be-'al peh** תורה שבעל פה *nf* the Oral Law; i.e. the Talmud as distinct from the Written Law (**torah she-bee-khtav**) i.e the Pentateuch. At its origin, before codified, it was transmitted orally.

◇ **'alah** (*etc*) **le-torah** עלה לתורה *v* was called up to read from the Torah.

◇ **torah she-bee-khtav** (*kh=k*) תורה שבכתב *nf* the Written Law, i.e. the Bible.

◇ **('al|ah/-tah/-eetee le) torah** see ◇ **'alah** (*etc*) **le-torah**.

(ben/beney) torah בן־תורה *nm* learned in the Torah; scholar.

(heerb|eets/-eetsah/-atstee) torah הרביץ תורה *v* taught knowledge; (*pres* **marbeets** *etc*; *fut* **yarbeets** *etc*).

◇ **(seemkhat) torah** see ◇ **Seemkhat Torah**.

(sefer/seefrey) torah ספר תורה *nm* the Scrolls of the Law.

(talmood) torah תלמוד תורה **1.** study of the Torah; **2.** elementary religious school.

toran/-eet תורן *nmf* person on duty; (*pl+of:* **-ey**).

(katseen) toran קצין תורן *nm* duty-officer.

(rof|e/-'ah) toran/-eet רופא תורן *nmf* physician on duty.

(samal) toran סמל תורן *nm* NCO on duty; petty-officer on duty.

toranee/-t תורני *adj* learned in Torah.

toranoot/-yot תורנות *nf* duty by roster; turn at duty.

(be) toranoot בתורנות *adv* on duty; taking one's turn.

torashah/-ot תורשה *nf* heredity; (*+of:* **-at**).

torashtee/-t תורשתי *adj* hereditary.

torashteeyoot תורשתיות *nf* hereditary nature.

torat ha- תורת ה־ *f+of* the theory of...

torat ha-khakla'oot תורת החקלאות *nf* agronomy.

torat ha-meedot תורת המידות *nf* ethics.

torat ha-yakhseeyoot (*npr* **yakhasoot**) תורת היחסיות *nf* the theory of relativity.

(be) torat בתורת *adv* as; in the capacity of...

tordanee/-t טורדני *adj* tiresome; nagging.

tordanoo|t/-yot טורדנות *nf* wearisomeness.

tor|eh/-ee! ! תורה *v fut (used as imp) sing m/f* will you direct! please, order! (*inf* **lehorot**; *pst* **horah**; *pres* **moreh**).

toreed/-ee! ! תוריד *v fut (used as imp) sing m/f* bring down! take down! (*inf* **lehoreed**; *pst* **horeed**; *pres* **moreed**).

tor|em/-meem תורם *nm* donor; contributor (*pl+of:* **-mey**).

torem/-et תורם *v pres* donates; contributes; (*pst* **taram**; *fut* **yeetrom**).

toren/traneem תורן *nm* mast; (*pl+of:* **torney**).

tosafot תוספות *nf pl* free additions to a restaurant meal (salads, sauce etc).

toseef/-ee! ! תוסיף *v fut (used as imp) sing m/f* add! (*inf* **lehoseef**; *pst* **hoseef**; *pres* **moseef**).

tos|efet/-afot תוספת *nf* addition; supplement; (*pl+of:* **-fot**).
tosefet ma'amats תוספת מאמץ *nf* **1.** extra-effort; **2.** additional effort bonus.
(tosefet) meeshkal תוספת משקל *nf* additional weight; extra-weight; overweight.
tos|efet/-fot mekheer תוספת מחיר *nf* additional price; extra-pay.
tos|efet/-fot 'omes תוספת עומס *nf* overload; over exertion supplement.
tos|efet/-fot sakhar תוספת שכר *nf* salary increment.
tos|efet/-fot yoker תוספת יוקר *nf* cost of living allowance.
toseftan תוספתן *nm* appendix (Medic.).
toses/-et תוסס *adj* seething; bubbling; active.
toshav/-eem תושב *nm* resident; inhabitant; (*pl+of:* **toshvey**).
(meersham ha) toshaveem מרשם התושבים *nm* population register.
◇ **toshav/-eem khoz|er/-reem** תושב חוזר *nm* Israeli returnee from residence abroad.
tosheev/-ee! תושיב! *vt fut (used as imp) sing m/f* seat (someone)! put (someone)! (*inf* **lehosheev**; *pst* **hosheev**).
tosh|evet/-avot תושבת *nf* female resident; female inhabitant.
totakh/-eem תותח *nm* artillery-gun; (*pl+of:* **totkhey**).
tot|av/-evet תותב *adj* artificial; inserted.
tot|efet/-afot טוטפת *nf* phylactery.
('ayeen) totevet עין תותבת *nf* artificial eye.
(regel/raglayeem) tot|evet/-vot רגל תותבת *nf* artificial leg.
(shen/sheenayeem) tot|evet/-vot שן תותבת *nf* false tooth; denture.
totkhan/-eem תותחן *nm* gunner; artillery-man; (*pl+of:* **-ey**).
(kheyl) totkhaneem חיל התותחנים *nm* Artillery Corps.
tots|a'ah/-a'ot תוצאה *nf* result; outcome; (*+of:* **-'at**).
totsa|'ah/-'ot sofee|t/-yot תוצאה סופית *nf* final result.
(nat|an/-nah/-atee) totsa'ot נתן תוצאות *v* produced results; (*pres* **noten** *etc; fut* **yeeten** *etc*).
tots|ar/-eem תוצר *nm* product; (*pl+of:* **-ey**).
totsee/-'ee! תוציא! *v fut (used as imp) sing m/f [colloq.]* take out! (*inf* **lehotsee**; *pst* **hotsee**; *pres* **motsee**).
tots|eret/-arot תוצרת *nf* produce; product.
totseret ha-arets תוצרת הארץ *nf* locally made; Made in Israel.
totseret khoots תוצרת חוץ *nf* foreign-made goods; imported goods.
tov טוב *adv* well; all right.
tov me'od טוב מאוד *adv* very good; very well.
tov-tov טוב־טוב *adv* thoroughly.
tov/-ah טוב *adj* good.
tov/-ah le- טוב ל־ *adj* good for... suitable for...
tov/-ah me'od טוב מאוד *adj* very good.
tov/-ah yoter טוב יותר *adj* better.
(be-seeman) tov בסימן טוב (greeting) Good omen! Good luck!
('erev) tov! ערב טוב! (greeting) Good evening!
('erev) tov oo-mevorakh! ערב טוב ומבורך! (return-greeting) Good evening!
(ha) tov be-yoter הטוב ביותר *adj* the best; the very best.
(laylah) tov! לילה טוב! (greeting) Good night!
(mazal) tov! מזל טוב! (greeting) Mazeltov! Good luck! Congratulations!
(roshem) tov רושם טוב *nm* good impression.
(shavoo'a) tov! שבוע טוב! Good Week! (greeting to use on Saturday evenings as a new week begins).
(shavoo'a) tov oo-mevorakh! שבוע טוב ומבורך! Good and blessed week! (return-greeting to **shavoo'a' tov!**).
(shem) tov שם טוב *nm* (one's) good name.
(yeehyeh) tov! יהיה טוב! *[colloq.]* it'll be alright! no need to worry!
(yom/-yameem) tov/-eem יום טוב *nm* holiday; feast.
(zakhoor/zekhoorah la) tov זכור לטוב *adj* (he/she) of blessed memory! bless his /her memory!
tovah/-ot טובה *nf* favor (*+of:* **-at**).
(be-roo'akh) tovah ברוח טובה *adv* amicably; with plenty of goodwill.
(be-sha'ah) tovah בשעה טובה **1.** (greeting) good luck! **2.** (*lit.*) (greeting) in a propitious moment.
(even/-avaneem) tov|ah/-ot אבן טובה *nf* precious stone.
◇ **(gemar khateemah) tovah!** see ◇ **gemar khateemah tovah!**
(kefeeyoot) tovah כפיות טובה *nf* ingratitude.
(kefooy/-at) tovah כפוי טובה *adj* ungrateful.
(khateemah) tovah! חתימה טובה (greeting) Happy New Year! (in use on the eve of Yom Kippur).
◇ **(kteevah va-khateemah) tovah!** see ◇ **keteevah va-khateemah tovah!**
(le) tovah לטובה *adv* for the better.
◇ **(le-shanah) tovah!** see ◇ **le-shanah tovah!**
(nesee'ah) tovah! נסיעה טובה! (farewell wish) Bon voyage!
('os|eh/-ah) tovah עושה טובה *v pres* does a favor; (*pst* **'asah** *etc; fut* **ya'aseh** *etc*).
(seyvah) tovah שיבה טובה *nf* aged gracefully; ripe old age.
(shanah) tovah! שנה טובה! (greeting) New Year Greetings!
(sheenooy le) tovah שינוי לטובה *nm* improvement; change for the better.
toval|ah/-ot תובלה *nf* transportation; forwarding; (*+of:* **-at**).
(khevr|at/-ot) tovalah חברת תובלה *nf* forwarding company.

(metos/-ey) tovalah מטוס תובלה *nm* cargo plane.
tov'an|ah/-ot תובענה *nf* claim; (*+of:* **-at**).
tovat ha-klal טובת הכלל *nf* the public good.
tov|at/-ot hana'ah טובת הנאה *nf* benefit; goodwill (as compensation).
(le) tovat לטובת *adv* for the benefit of.
(le) tovat|ah/-ee/-kha/-ekh/-o לטובתה/־י/־ך/־ך/־ו *adv & poss.pron sing* for her/my/your(*m/f*)/his *etc* benefit.
tov|e'a'/-a'at תובע *v* claims; demands; (*pst* **tava'**; *fut* **yeetba'** *(b=v)*).
tov|e'a'/-'eem תובע *nm* claimant; prosecutor; (*f* **tov|a'at/-'ot**).
(ha) tove'a' ha-klalee התובע הכללי *nm* Public Prosecutor; Attorney General.
traged|yah/-yot טרגדיה *nf* tragedy; (*+of:* **-yat**).
tragee/-t טראגי *adj* tragic.
trakleen/-eem טרקלין *nm* drawing-room; parlor; (*pl+of:* **-ey**).
traktor/-eem טרקטור *nm* tractor.
traktoreest/-eem טרקטוריסט *nm* tractor driver.
tranzeestor/-eem טרנזיסטור *nm [colloq.]* transistor-radio.
(adm|at/-ot) trasheem אדמת טרשים *nf* rocky land.
treek|ah/-ot טריקה *nf* slamming; (*+of:* **-at**).
treek|at/-ot delet טריקת דלת *nf* slamming a door.
trees/-eem תריס *nm* shutter; blind; (*pl+of:* **-ey**).
treeseem meetkapleem תריסים מתקפלים *nm pl* folding blinds.
treesey hazazah תריסי הזזה *nm pl* sliding blinds.
(heeg|eef/-eefah/-aftee) treeseem הגיף תריסים *v* shut blinds; (*pres* **megeef** *etc*; *fut* **yageef** *etc*).
treeyoot טריות *nf* freshness; novelty.
treez טריז *nm* wedge.
(tak|a'/-'ah/-a'tee) treez תקע טריז *v* entered a wedge; (*pres* **toke'a'** *etc*; *fut* **yeetka'** *etc*).
tref|ah/-ot טריפה *nf* non-kosher food.
tremp/-eem טרמפ *nm [colloq.]* hitchhike.
trey-'asar תרי־עשר *nm* Book of the Twelve Minor Prophets (Hosea to Malachi).
treysar/-eem תריסר *nm* dozen (*pl+of:* **-ey**).
trom- טרום *(prefix)* pre-; ante-
◇ **(gan/-ey) trom-khovah** see ◇ **gan/-ey trom khovah**.
◇ **(gan/-ey) trom-trom khovah** see ◇ **gan/-ey trom-trom khovah**.
tromee (*npr* **tromee**)**/-t** טרומי *adj* prefabricated.
(beneeyah) tromeet בנייה טרומית *nf* prefabricated construction.
troo|'ah/-'ot תרועה *nf* **1.** ovation; cheers; **2.** blowing of trumpet; (*+of:* **-'at**).
troof|ah/-ot תרופה *nf* remedy; medicine.
troof|at/-ot pele' תרופת־פלא *nf* miracle-drug.
troomee/-t תרומי *adj* distinguished; supreme.
(meedot) troomeeyot מידות תרומיות *nf* supreme qualities (of person).

troon|yah/-yot טרוניה *nf* grievance; grudge; (*+of:* **yat**).
troot|ah/-ot טרוטה *nf* trout; (*+of:* **-at**).
tropee/-t טרופי *adj* tropical.

> **Ts**
> is the transliteration of the Hebrew letter **Tsadee** (צ). Words beginning with **Tsadee** (pronounced **ts**) are grouped in a separate chapter following this one.

tvakh/-eem טווח *nm* range; distance.
(aroo|key/-khot) tvakh ארוכי טווח *adj* long-range.
(keetsrey/-ot) tvakh קצרי טווח *adj* short-range.
(lee) tvakh arokh לטווח ארוך *adv* in the long run.
(lee) tvakh katser לטווח קצר **1.** *adv* in the short run; **2.** *adj* short range.
(lee) tvakh rakhok לטווח רחוק **1.** *adv* at long distance; **2.** *adj* long-range.
tvalool/-eem תבלול *nm* cataract; (*pl+of:* **-ey**).
tvay/-eem תוואי *nm* outline; construction-plan; (*pl+of:* **-a'ey**).
tvee|'ah/-'ot תביעה *nf* demand; claim; (*+of:* **-'at**).
tvee|'ah/-'ot meeshpatee|t/-yot תביעה משפטית *nf* legal claim.
('ed/-ey ha) tvee'ah עד תביעה *nm* prosecution witness.
(ha) tvee'ah ha-klaleet התביעה הכללית *nf* the prosecution.
(ktav/keetvey) tvee'ah כתב תביעה *nm* statement of claim.
(parashat ha) tvee'ah פרשת התביעה *nf* statement of claim (in a civil case).
tvee|'ah/-'ot טביעה *nf* drowning; (*+of:* **-'at**).
tvee'at 'ayeen טביעת עין *nf* perceptiveness; deep insight.
tvee|'at/-'ot etsba'ot טביעת אצבעות *nf* fingerprints.
tveel|ah/-ot טבילה *nf* **1.** dipping; **2.** baptism (*+of:* **-at**).
tvee|yah/-yot טווייה *nf* spinning (of thread); (*+of:* **-yat**).
(galgal) tveeyah גלגל טווייה *nm* spinning wheel.
□ **Tveryah** טבריה *nf* (Tiberias/Teverya) historic town and spa on E. shore of **Yam Keeneret** (also known as Sea of Galilee or Lake Tiberias). Pop. 33,400.
tvoo|'ah/-'ot תבואה *nf* grain crop; (*+of:* **-'at**).
tvoon|ah/-ot תבונה *nf* wisdom; understanding; (*+of:* **-at**).
tvoonat kapayeem תבונת כפיים *nf* handicraft.
tvoos|ah/-ot תבוסה *nf* defeat; (*+of:* **-at**).
tvoosanoot תבוסנות *nf* defeatism.
tvoostan/-eet תבוסתן *nmf* defeatist (*pl:* **eem/-eeyot**; *+of:* **-ey**).
tvoostanoot תבוסתנות *nf* defeatism.
tyoot|ah/-ot טיוטה *nf* rough draft (*+of:* **-at**).

TS.

transliterating words beginning with **Tsadee (צ)**

tsa'ad/tse'adeem צעד *nm* step; (*pl+of:* **tsa'adey**).
tsa'ad/-ah/-etee צעד *v* paced; marched; (*pres* **tso'ed;** *fut* **yeets'ad**).
(be) tsa'adey tsav בצעדי צב **1.** *adv* at a snail's pace; extremely slow; **2.** (*lit.*) at a turtle's pace.
tsa'ak/-ah/-tee צעק *v* shouted; yelled; (*pres* **tso'ek;** *fut* **yeets'ak**).
tsa'akan/-eet צעקן *nmf* shouter; yeller.
tsa'akanee/-t צעקני *adj* vociferous; noisy.
tsa'ar צער *nm* sorrow.
tsa'ar ba'aley khayeem צער בעלי חיים *m* pity for (maltreated) animals, i.e. the need for kindness to animals.
(be) tsa'ar בצער *adv* regretfully.
(be) tsa'ar rav בצער רב *adv* with utmost regret.
(heeshtatfoot be) tsa'ar השתתפות בצער *nf* condolence; condolences.
(le-marbeh ha) tsa'ar למרבה הצער *adv* to one's deep regret.
(le) tsa'ar|ee/-khah/-ekh/-o/-ah לצערי/־ך/־ך/־ו/־ה to my/your(*m/f*)/his/her utmost regret.
tsa'atsoo|'a'/-'eem צעצוע *nm* toy; (*pl+of:* **-'ey**).
tsab|a' (*cpr* **tsaba'ee**) **/-a'eem** צבע *nm* painter; house-painter.
tsaba'oot צבעות *nf* house-painting.
◇ **tsabar/-eet** צבר *nmf* **1.** "Sabra" native-born Israeli; **2.** "Sabra" Jew born in Israel or in what was called Palestine before 1948.
tsabaree (*cpr* **sabree**)**/-t** צברי *adj* Sabra-
(meevta') tsabaree (*or:* **tsabree**) מבטא צברי *nm* native (Sabra) accent.
tsabreeyoot צבריות *nf* the native Israeli character; the traits of a "sabra".
tsad/-ah/-etee צד *v* hunted; caught; (*pres* **tsad;** *fut* **yatsood**).
tsad/tsedadeem צד *nm* side; party; (*pl+of:* **tseedey**).
tsad shleeshee צד שלישי *nm* third party.
('al ha) tsad ha- tov be-yoter על הצד הטוב ביותר *adv* the best posible way.
(ba) tsad בצד *adv* on the side; apart.
(be) tsad בצד *adv* **1.** beside; **2.** on the side of.
(ha) tsad ha-shaveh הצד השווה *nm* analogy; common characteristic.
(le) tsad לצד *adv* on the side of; beside.
(mee) tsad מצד *adv* on the part of; on behalf of.
(mee) tsad ekhad מצד אחד *adv* on one hand; on one side.
(mee) tsad shenee מצד שני *adv* on the other hand; on the other side.
(meen ha) tsad מן הצד *adv* on the side.
(meet'an/-ey) tsad מיטען צד *nm* side-mine i.e. a mine laid beside the road that is made to explode when passed by.
tsadah ha-'ayeen צדה העין *v pst & pres* the eye caught.
tsad|ak/-kah/-tee צדק *v* was right; was just; (*pres* **tsodek;** *fut* **yeetsdak**).
◇ **TSADAL** צד"ל *nm* the South-Lebanon Army (*acr of* **TSeva Drom Levanon** צבא דרום לבנון).
◇ **tsadee** (צד"י) צ *nf* 19th letter of the Hebrew alphabet (colloq. called **Tsadeek**) pronounced **ts** (like *tz* in *Ritz*). At the end of a word, this letter takes a different form (ץ) called "Final Tsadee".
◇ **tsadee** צ' *num symbol* for 90; ninety (in Hebrew numerical system).
◇ **tsadee sofeet** צד"י סופית *nf* "Final Tsadee" i.e. the form a Tsadee takes (ץ) when ending a word.
◇ **tsadeek/-eem** צדיק *nm* righteous man; Hasidic Rabbi; (*pl+of:* **-ey**).
tsadeek/-ey ha-dor צדיק הדור *nm* the saint (i.e righteous figure of his generation).
tsadeket צדקת *nf* a righteous woman.
◇ **tsadeek gadol** צדיק גדול *nm* **1.** a great righteous Rabbi; **2.** (ironically) one affecting pose of being extremely honest and just.
tsadkanee/-t צדקני *adj* over-pious; pretentiously righteous; hypocrite.
tsadkanoot (*or:* **tseedkanoot**) צדקנות *nf* self-justification; hypocrisy.
tsa'eef/tse'eef|eem צעיף *nm* veil; (*pl+of:* **-ey**).
tsa'eer/tse'eer|ah צעיר **1.** *nmf* young man/woman (*pl:* **-eem;** *+of:* **-ey**); **2.** *adj* young.
tsaf/-ah/-tee צף *v* floated; (*pres* **tsaf;** *fut* **yatsoof**).
tsaf/-ah צף *adj* floating; afloat.
tsaf|ar/-rah/-artee צפר *v* hooted; sounded the siren; (*pres* **tsofer;** *fut* **yeetspor;** *(p=f)*).
tsafedet (*npr* **tsapedet**) צפדת *nf* tetanus (Medic.).
tsafon צפון *nm* North.

(eeb|ed/-dah/-adetee et ha) tsafon איבד את הצפון *[colloq.] v* was disturbed, disoriented, disconcerted; (*pres* **me'abed** *etc; fut* **ye'abed** *etc*).

tsafonah צפונה *adv* northward.

tsafoof/tsefoofah צפוף *adj* crowded.

tsafoon/tsefoonah צפון *adj* hidden.

tsafooy/tsefooyah צפוי *adj* expected; anticipated.

tsafra tava! צפרא טבא! (greeting) Good morning! (archaic).

□ **Tsafreereem** (Zafririm) צפרירים *nm* village (est. 1958) in **'Adoolam** district, 3 km S. of haElah Junction (**Tsomet ha-Elah**). Pop. 203.

tsafts|afah/-afot צפצפה *nf* poplar; (*+of:* **-efet**).

tsaftsef/-ee! צפצף! *[colloq.] imp sing m/f* **1.** don't give a damn! disregard! **2.** (*lit.*) whistle! (*inf* **letsaftsef**; *pst* **tseeftsef**; *pres* **metsaftsef**; *fut* **yetsaftsef**).

tsaftsef|ah/-ot צפצפה *nf* whistle.

□ **Tsafreeyah** (Zafriyya) צפריה *nm* village (est. 1949) 4 km W. of Ben-Gurion Airport. Pop. 619.

tsag/-eem צג *nm* computer screen; monitor.

◇ **TSAHAL** (ZAHAL) צה״ל *nm* I.D.F. i.e. Israel Defense Forces (*acr of* **TSeva HAganah Le-yeesra'el** צבא הגנה לישראל).

□ **Tsahalah** (Zahala) צהלה *nf* garden suburb outside Tel-Aviv, NE of the city.

tsahalee/-t צה״לי *adj* pertaining to the Israel Defense Forces.

tsahevet צהבת *nf* jaundice; (Medic.).

tsahov/tsehoobah צהוב *adj* yellow.

tsakh/-ah צח *adj* **1.** fresh (air, complexion); **2.** pure (language).

tsakhak/-ah/-tee צחק *v* laughed; (*pres* **tsokhek**; *fut* **yeets'khak**).

tsakhan|ah/-ot צחנה *nf* stink; stench; (*+of:* **-at**).

tsakhee'akh/tsekheekhah צחיח *adj* parched.

tsakhoo|t/-yot צחות *nf* purity; clearness.

tsakhor/tsekhorah צחור *adj* white.

tsakhot צחות *adv* fluently; perfectly; eloquently.

tsalah/-tah/-eetee צלה *v* grilled; roasted; (*pres* **tsoleh**; *fut* **yeetsleh**).

tsal|a'/-'ah/-a'tee צלע *v* limped; (*pres* **tsole'a'**; *fut* **yeetsla'**).

tsalaf/-eem צלף *nm* sniper; (*pl+of:* **-ey**).

tsal|af/-fah/-aftee צלף *v* sniped; (*pres* **tsolef**; *fut* **yeetslof**).

tsal|akh/-khah/-akhtee צלח *v* crossed (river); (*pres* **tsole'akh**; *fut* **yeetslakh**).

tsalakh|at/-ot צלחת *nf* **1.** saucer; plate; **2.** pocket (Biblic. style, obsolete).

(karov/krovah la) tsalakhat קרוב לצלחת *adj [slang]* **1.** near to the source of distribution; **2.** (*lit.*) near the saucer.

tsalakh|at/-ot me'ofef|et/-ot צלחת מעופפת *nf* flying saucer.

tsal|al/-elah/-altee צלל *v* dived; (*pres* **tsolel**; *fut* **yeetslol**).

tsalam/-eem צלם *nm* photographer; cameraman; (*pl+of:* **-ey**).

tsalam/-ey 'eetonoot צלם עיתונות *nm* press-photographer.

tsalash/-eem צל״ש *nm abbr.* (*acr of* **TSeeyoon Le-SHevakh**) commendation.

tsal|av/-vah/-avtee צלב *v* crucified; (*pres* **tsolev**; *fut* **yeetslov**).

tsalban/-eem צלבן *nm* crusader; (*pl+of:* **-ey**).

tsalbanee/-t צלבני *adj* crusader-; crusading.

(tkoofat ha) tsalbaneem תקופת הצלבנים *nf* the Crusader Era.

tsal|eket/-akot צלקת *nf* scar.

tsal|emet/-mot צלמת *nf* woman-photographer.

tsalemet 'eetonoot צלמת עתונות *nf* woman press-photographer.

tsalkhah dark|o/-ah/-ee *etc* צלחה דרכו/־ה/־י *v* he/she/I succeeded.

tsalmanee|yah/-yah/-yot צלמנייה **1.** *nf* photo-studio; **2.** *[erron. colloq.] nf* (correct term **matslem|ah/-ot**) camera (*+of:* **yat**).

tsalmavet צלמוות *nm* shadow of death; great darkness.

(be-gey) tsalmavet בגיא צלמוות *adv* in the Valley of the Shadow of Death (Bibl.).

(khoshekh ve) tsalmavet חושך וצלמוות *nm pl* darkness and the shadow of death.

tsalool/tseloolah צלול *adj* **1.** clear (air, water); **2.** sound (mind, conscience).

tsaloov/tseloovah צלוב *adj* crucified.

tsalooy/tselooyah צלוי *adj* grilled; roasted.

tsalyan/-eem צליין *nm* pilgrim (*pl+of:* **-ey**).

tsam/-ah/-tee צם *v* fasted; (*pres* **tsam**; *fut* **yatsoom**).

tsamah צמא *nm* thirst.

tsam|a/-'ah/-e'tee צמא *v* felt thirsty; (*pres* **tsame**; *fut* **yeetsma**).

tsam|ah/-ot צמה *nf* tress; lock of hair; woman's long hair; (*+of:* **-at**).

tsam|akh/-khah/-akhtee צמח *v* grew; (*pres* **tsome'akh**; *fut* **yeetsmakh**).

tsame/tseme'ah צמא *adj* thirsty.

tsameed/tsemeed|eem צמיד *nm* bracelet; (*pl+of:* **-ey**).

tsameeg (*npr* **tsemeeg**)**/tsemeeg|eem** צמיג *nm* automobile tire; (*pl+of:* **-ey**).

tsameret צמרת *adj* (*figurat.*) best; chosen; prime-

tsam|eret/-arot צמרת *nf* tree-top; summit; (*pl+of:* **-rot**).

tsameret ha- צמרת ה־ *f+of* (*figurat.*) the elite of .. the cream of...

tsamood/tsemoodah צמוד *adj* **1.** attached; linked; joined; **2.** *[colloq.]* linked (price or pay) to the US Dollar or to the C.O.L. Index.

tsamood le- צמוד ל־ *adv* linked to (currency or index).

◇ **(rekhev) tsamood** see ◇ **rekhev tsamood**.

tsamtsam/-eem צמצם *nm* diaphragm (Photogr.).

tsan|akh/-khah/-tee צנח *v* **1.** dropped; fell; **2.** parachuted; (*pres* **tsone'akh**; *fut* **yeetsnakh**).

tsan|eret/-arot צנרת *nf* tubing; pipe system (plumbing); (*pl+of:* **rot**).

tsankhan/-eem צנחן *nm* parachutist; paratrooper; (*pl+of:* **-ey**).

(kheyl ha) tsankhaneem חיל הצנחנים *nm* the Paratroop Corps.

tsanoo'a'/tsenoo'ah צנוע *adj* modest.

tsanoom/tsenoomah צנום *adj* skinny.

tsar/-ah צר *adj* narrow.

tsar/-ah/-tee צר *v* besieged; beleaguered; (*pres* **tsar;** *fut* **yatsoor**).

tsar/-at 'ayeen צר עין *adj* envious; covetous.

tsar lee צר לי *v* I am sorry; I feel sorry.

tsar/-at mo'akh צר מוח *adj* narrow-minded.

(ha) tsar הצר *nm* (poetic) the enemy; foe.

tsar|ah/-ot צרה *nf* trouble; misfortune.

tsarah tseroorah צרה צרורה *nf* infinite trouble; endless trouble.

('al kol) tsarah על כל צרה to be on the safe side; in any event.

tsar|af/-fah/-aftee צרף *v* refined; tested in flame; (*pres* **tsoref;** *fut* **yeetsrof**).

tsar|akh/-khah/-akhtee צרח *v* shrieked; yelled; (*pres* **tsore'akh;** *fut* **yeetsrakh**).

tsar|akh/-khah/-akhtee צרך *v* consumed; (*pres* **tsorekh;** *fut* **yeetsrokh**).

tsar|am/-mah/-amtee צרם *v* grated (on ears); (*pres* **tsorem;** *fut* **yeetsrom**).

tsar|at/-ot rabeem צרת רבים *nf* shared sorrow; common misery.

tsarat rabeem khatsee nekhamah צרת רבים חצי נחמה (proverb) sorrow shared is sorrow halved; (i.e. misery loves company).

tsarav/-vah/-avtee צרב *v* scorched; burned; (*pres* **tsorev;** *fut* **yeetsrov**).

tsareekh צריך *adv* it is necessary; what's needed is...

(lo) tsareekh לא צריך *adv* no need; it isn't necessary.

tsareekh/tsereekhah צריך *v pres* must; needs; (*pst* **hayah tsareekh;** *fut* **yeehyeh tsareekh**).

tsareekh she- צריך ש־ *adv* there's need that...

tsaredet צרדת *nf* hoarseness.

tsarevet צרבת *nf* pyrosis; heartburn (Medic.).

tsarkhan/-eem צרכן *nm* consumer; (*pl+of:* **-ey**).

tsarkhan/-eet צרחן *nmf* screamer; shrieker; yeller.

tsarkhanee|yah/-yot צרכנייה *nf* co-op store; grocery co-op; (*+of:* **-yat**).

tsarkhanoot צרכנות **1.** *nf* consumers (as a body); consumption; **2.** *nf* consumer-awareness.

(kol) tsaroo'a' ve-khol *(kh=k)* **zav** כל צרוע וכל זב *nm* riff-raff.

tsarood/tseroodah צרוד *adj* hoarse; husky-voiced.

tsaroof/tseroofah צרוף *adj* pure; refined.

tsaroo|t/-yot צרות *nf* narrowness.

tsaroot 'ayeen צרות עין *nf* envy; jealousy.

tsaroot mokheen צרות מוחין *nf* narrow-mindedness.

tsaroot ofek צרות אופק *nf* narrow-mindedness.

tsarot צרות *nf pl* (*sing:* **tsarah**) troubles; calamities.

('as|ah/-tah/-eetee) tsarot עשה צרות *v* made trouble; gave trouble.

(be) tsarot בצרות *adv* in trouble.

('os|eh/-ah) tsarot עושה צרות *nmf* trouble-maker.

tsartsar (*cpr* **tsratsar**)/**tseertsar|eem** צרצר *nm* cricket; (*pl+of:* **-ey**).

tsats/-ah/-tee צץ *v* sprang forth; appeared; (*pres* **tsats;** *fut* **yatsoots**).

tsav/-eem צב *nm* tortoise; turtle.

tsav/-eem צו *nm* decree; order; warrant; (*pl+of:* **-ey**).

◇ **tsav/-ey 'al tnay** צו על תנאי *nm* order nisi by Israeli Supreme Court sitting as High Court of Justice (juridic.).

tsav/-ey geeyoos צו גיוס *nm* mobilization order.

tsav/-ey kheepoos צו חיפוש *nm* search warrant.

tsav/-ey kheroom צו חירום *nm* emergency order.

tsav ma'atsar צו מעצר *nm* warrant of arrest; detention-order.

tsav/-ey menee'ah צו מניעה *nm* injunction.

tsav/-ey peenooy צו פינוי *nm* eviction order.

◇ **tsav/-ey reetook** צו ריתוק *nm* "Attachment Order" issued upon request by a court to prevent vital worker from participating in a public utility strike (juridic.).

(be-tsa'adey) tsav בצעדי צב *adv* at a snail's pace; (*lit.*) at a turtle's pace.

tsav|a/-'ah/-atee צבא *v* congregated; (*pres* **tsove;** *fut* **yeetsba** *(b=v)*).

tsava/tseva'ot צבא *nm* army; (*+of:* **tseva/tseev'ot**).

tsava sadeer צבא סדיר *nm* regular army of soldiers in obligatory service.

(eesh/anshey) tsava איש צבא *nm* military man.

(makhn|eh/-ot) tsava מחנה צבא *nm* army camp.

(yots|e/-'ey) tsava יוצא צבא *nm* person subject to conscription.

tsav|a'/-'ah/-a'tee צבע *v* painted (*pres* **tsove'a';** *fut* **yeetsba'** *(b=v)*).

tsav|ah/-tah/-eetee צבה *v* swelled; puffed; (*pres* **tsoveh;** *fut* **yeetsbeh** *(b=v)*).

tsava|'ah/-ot צוואה *nf* will; testament; (*+of:* **-at**).

(keeyoom) tsava'ah קיום צוואה *nm* probate.

tsava'at shekheev me-ra' צוואת שכיב מרע *nf* dying person's last will and testament.

tsav|akh/-khah/-akhtee צווח *v* yelled; (*pres* **tsove'akh;** *fut* **yeetsvakh**).

tsav|ar/-rah/-artee צבר *v* amassed; accumulated; (*pres* **tsover;** *fut* **yeetsbor** *(b=v)*).

tsavar צוואר *nm* neck; nape.

tsavar bakbook צוואר בקבוק *nm* bottleneck.

('ad) tsavar עד צוואר *adv* up to one's neck.

(neerd|af/-efah/-aftee 'al) tsavar נרדף על צוואר *v* was mercilessly persecuted.

tsav|aron/-roneem צווארון *nm* collar; (*pl+of:* **-roney**).

tsavaron kakhol צווארון כחול *nm* blue collar.

tsavaron lavan צווארון לבן *nm* white-collar.

('avaryaney ha) tsavaron ha-lavan עבריייני הצווארון הלבן *nm pl* white-collar offenders.

('ovdey ha) tsavaron ha-lavan עובדי הצווארון הלבן *nm pl* white-collar workers.

tsav|at/-tah/-atetee צבט *v* pinched; (*pres* **tsovet**; *fut* **yeetsbot** *(b=v)*).

tsavo'a'/tsevo|'eem צבוע *nm* hyena; striped hyena (*pl+of:* **-ey**).

tsavoo'a'/tsevoo'ah צבוע **1.** *adj* painted; **2.** *nmf* hypocrite.

tsavta צוותא *nf* team; togetherness.

(be) tsavta בצוותא *adv* together.

◇ **(mo'adon/-ey) "tsavta"** see ◇ **mo'adon/-ey "tsavta"**.

tsayad/-eem צייד *nm* hunter; (*pl+of:* **-ey**).

tsayar/-eem צייר *nm* painter (artist); (*pl+of:* **-ey**).

tsayeed ציד *nm* hunting; game (*+of:* **tseyd**).

(rov|eh/-ey) tsayeed רובה ציד *nm* shotgun.

tsa|yer/-yree! צייר! *v imp sing m/f* paint! (*inf* **letsayer**; *pst* **tseeyer**; *pres* **metsayer**; *fut* **yetsayer**).

tsa|yeret/-yarot ציירת *nf* woman painter.

tsaytan/-eet צייתן *adj* obedient.

tsaytanoot צייתנות *nf* obedience.

tse/-'ee צא! *v imp sing m/f* get out! out! (*inf* **latset**; *pst* **yatsa**; *pres* **yotse**; *fut* **yetse**).

tse'ad|ah/-ot צעדה *nm* march; (*+of:* **tsa'ad|at/-ot**).

tsedadee/-t צדדי *adj* lateral; side-

(doo-) tsedadee/-t דו־צדדי *adj* bi-lateral.

(khad-) tsedadee/-t חד־צדדי *adj* one-sided; unilateral.

(rav-) tsedadee/-t רב־צדדי *adj* multilateral; versatile.

tsedadeem צדדים *nm pl* (sing: tsad) sides; (*+of:* **tseedey**).

(khad-) tsedadeeyoot חד־צדדיות *nf* bias; one-sidedness.

(rav-) tsedadeeyoot רב־צדדיות *nf* versatility; multi-lateralness.

tsedafeem צדפים *nm pl* (*sing:* **tsedef**) shells (*pl+of:* **tseedfey**).

tsedak|ah/-ot צדקה *nf* **1.** charity; **2.** justice; right; (*+of:* **tseedk|at/-ot**).

(noten/-et) tsedakah נותן צדקה *v pres* gives to charity; (*pst* **natan** *etc*; *fut* **yeeten** *etc*).

('oseh/-ah) tsedakah עושה צדקה *v pres* does justice; (*pst* **'asah** *etc*; *fut* **ya'aseh** *etc*).

tsedek צדק **1.** *nm* justice; (*+of:* **tseedkat**); **2.** *nm* planet Jupiter.

◇ **(bet-meeshpat gavoha le) tsedek** see ◇ **bet-meeshpat gavoha le-tsedek**.

(ger/-at) tsedek גר־צדק *nmf* convert to Judaism (*pl:* **-ey** *etc*).

(hen) tsedek הן צדק *nm* word of honor.

(meen ha) tsedek מן הצדק it is only just.

tsee/-yeem צי *nm* fleet.

tsee adeer צי אדיר *nm* armada.

tsee ha-sokher צי הסוחר *nm* merchant fleet.

tseeboor ציבור *nm* public.

(anshey) tseeboor אנשי ציבור *nm pl* (*sing:* **eesh** *etc*) public figures.

(bree'oot ha) tseeboor בריאות הציבור *nm* public health.

(eesh/-anshey) tseeboor איש ציבור *nm* public figure.

(eymat ha) tseeboor אימת הציבור *nf* stage fright.

(sheerah be) tseeboor שירה בציבור *nf* community singing.

(sheroot la) tseeboor שירות לציבור *nm* public service.

(shlee|'akh/-khey) tseeboor שליח ציבור *nm* **1.** cantor; **2.** public servant.

◇ **(tefeelah be) tseeboor** see ◇ **tefeelah be-tseeboor**.

(tsorkhey) tseeboor צורכי ציבור *nm pl* public needs; social work.

(yakhsey) tseeboor יחסי ציבור *nm pl* public relations.

(yedoo|'ah/-'ot ba) tseeboor ידועה בציבור *nf* reputed wife; common-law wife.

tseebooree/-t ציבורי *adj* public.

(meen'hal) tseebooree מינהל ציבורי *nm* public administration.

(sheekoon/-eem) tseebooree/-yeem שיכון ציבורי *nm* public housing project.

(makhra|'ah/-'ot) tseeboore|et/-yot מחראה ציבורית *nf* public latrine.

(mashten|ah/-ot) tseeboore|et/-yot (*correct:* **meeshtanah**) משתנה ציבורית *nf* public urinal.

(ha) tseedah! הצידה! *interj* aside! make way!

tseed|ed/-edah/-adetee צידד *v* sided with... (*pres* **metsaded**; *fut* **yetsaded**).

tseedkanee/-t צדקני *adj* righteous; pious (also ironical).

tseedook/-eem צידוק *nm* justification; (*pl+of:* **-ey**).

tse'ee! צאי! *v imp sing nf* get out! (*inf* **latset**; *pst* **yatsa**; *pres* **yotse**; *fut* **yetse**).

tse'eed|ah/-ot צעידה *nf* marching; stepping; (*+of:* **-at**).

tsee|'er/-'arah/-'artee ציער *v* pained; caused grief; (*pres* **metsa'er**; *fut* **yetsa'er**).

tse'eer|ah/-ot צעירה *nf* young girl; young woman.

(ha-meeshmeret ha) tse'eerah המשמרת הצעירה *nf* the young guard.

◇ **Tse'eerey Tseeyon** ("Tze'irei Tzion") צעירי ציון *m pl* Zionist Labor Party (Socialist but not Marxist) originating in Czarist Russia as "the Young of Zion". Its subsidiary in Palestine, re-named **"Ha-Po'el ha-Tsa'eer"** (Young Laborer) adopted a Social-Democratic ideology and, in 1930, merged with **"Akhdoot ha-'Avodah"** creating the "Eretz Israel Workers Party" (**"MAPAY"**

מפא״י) becoming the major force in the country's politics for many years.

tseefts|ef/-efah/-aftee ציפצף *v* whistled; (*pres* **metsaftsef;** *fut* **yetsaftsef**).

tseeftsef (*etc*) **'al** ציפצף על *v [colloq.]* flaunted; disregarded; ignored.

tseeftsoof/-eem צפצוף *nm* whistling; chirping; (*pl+of:* **-ey**).

tseeftsoof/-eem 'al צפצוף על *nm [colloq.]* flaunting.

tseekhkook/-eem צחקוק *nm* chuckle; giggle; (*pl+of:* **-ey**).

tseekhts|akh/-ekhah/-akhtee (*or:* **tseekhtse'akh**) ציחצח *v* polished; burnished (*pres* **metsakhtse'akh;** *fut* **yetsakhtse'akh**).

tseekhtse'akh (*etc*) **na'alayeem** ציחצח נעליים *v* shined shoes.

tseekhtse'akh (*etc*) **sheenayeem** ציחצח שיניים *v* brushed teeth.

tseekhtsoo|'akh/-kheem צחצוח *nm* polishing.

tseekhtsoo'akh (*etc*) **kharavot** צחצוח חרבות *nm* saber-rattling.

□ **Tse'eleem** (**Ze'elim**) צאלים kibbutz (est. 1947) in W. Negev, 12 km SE of Magen Junction (**Tsomet Magen**). Pop. 452.

tseeleend|er/-reem צילינדר *nm* **1.** cylinder; **2.** top-hat.

tseel|em/-mah/-amtee צילם *v* photographed; (*pres* **metsalem;** *fut* **yetsalem**).

tseeloom/-eem צילום *nm* photo; photograph; snapshot; (*pl+of:* **-ey**).

(**seret/seertey**) **tseeloom** סרט צילום *nm* roll of film.

tseelts|el/-elah/-altee צילצל *v* rang; (*pres* **metsaltsel;** *fut* **yetsaltsel**).

tseeltsool/-eem צלצול *nm* **1.** ring; **2.** sound; (*pl+of:* **-ey**).

tseem|a'on/-'onot צימאון *nm* thirst; (*+of:* **-'on**).

tseem|e'akh/-khah/-akhtee צימח *v* grew; (*pres* **metsame'akh;** *fut* **yetsame'akh**).

tseemkhee|yah/-yot צמחייה *nf* vegetation; flora; (*+of:* **-yat**).

tseemkhonee/-t צמחוני *nmf & adj* vegetarian.

tseemkhonoot צמחונות *nf* vegetarianism.

tseemts|em/-emah/-amtee צימצם *v* reduced; restricted; (*pres* **metsamtsem;** *fut* **yetsamtsem**).

tseemtsoom/-eem צמצום *nm* reduction; curtailment; economy; (*pl+of:* **-ey**).

(**be**) **tseemtsoom** בצמצום *adv* thriftily; scantily.

tseen|ah צינה *nf* chill; (*+of:* **-at**).

tseen|'ah צנעה *nf* privacy; secrecy; modesty; (*+of:* **-'at**).

(**be**) **tseen'ah** בצנעה *adv* privately; secretly.

tseen'at ha-prat צנעת הפרט *nf* privacy of the individual (juridic.).

tseenee/-t ציני *adj* cynical.

tseeneekan/-eet ציניקן *nmf* cynic; (*pl+of:* **-ey**).

tseeneeyoot ציניות *nf* cynicism.

tseen|en/-enah/-antee צינן *v* cooled; chilled; (*pres* **metsanen;** *fut* **yetsanen**).

tseenok צינוק *nm* **1.** lock-up; prison-cell; **2.** solitary confinement.

tseenoon/-eem צינון *nm* cooling; chilling; (*pl+of:* **-ey**).

(**tekoof|at/-ot**) **tseenoon** תקופת צינון *nf* cooling-off period.

tseenor/-ot צינור *nm* **1.** pipe; tube; **2.** pipeline; channel.

tseenor/-ot pleetah צינור פליטה *nm* exhaust-pipe.

tseents|enet/-anot צנצנת *nf* jar.

tseenz|er/-erah/-artee צנזר *v* censored; (*pres* **metsanzer;** *fut* **yetsanzer**).

tseenzoor/-eem צנזור *nm* censoring; censorship; (*pl+of:* **-ey**).

tseep|ah/-tah/-eetee ציפה *v* **1.** expected; **2.** coated; (*pres* **metsapeh;** *fut* **yetsapeh**).

tseep|ah/-ot ציפה *nf* case; blanket cover; pillow-case; (*+of:* **-at**).

tseep|eet/-ot ציפית *nf* pillow-case.

tseepee|yah/-yot ציפייה *nf* expectation; anticipation; (*+of:* **yat**).

tseepoo|y/-yeem ציפוי *nm* coating; sheeting; (*pl+of:* **yey**).

tseepor/-eem ציפור *nf* bird; (*pl+of:* **-ey**).

tseepor nefesh ציפור נפש *nf* one's most sacred and vulnerable spot.

□ **Tseeporee** (**Zippori**) צפורי village in Lower Galilee, 4 km NW of Nazareth. Pop. 340.

tseepor|en/-neem ציפורן *nm* carnation; (*pl+of:* **-ney**).

tseepor|nayeem ציפורניים *nm pl* (sing: -en) fingernails; (*pl+of:* **-ney**).

tseeporney khatool ציפורני חתול *nm* marigold; hen-and-chickens (flower).

tseer/-eem ציר *nm* **1.** envoy; **2.** axis; **3.** pole; (*pl+of:* **-ey**).

(**ha**) **tseer ha-dromee** הציר הדרומי *nm* the South Pole.

(**ha**) **tseer ha-tsefonee** הציר הצפוני *nm* the North Pole.

tseer'ah/tsera'ot צרעה *nf* hornet.

tseer|eem צירים *nm pl* (*sing* **tseer**) birth pangs; (*pl+of:* **-ey**).

tseerey leydah צירי לידה *nm pl* birth pangs.

tseeroo|t/-yot צירות *nf* legation (Diplom.).

tseerts|er/-erah/-artee צירצר *v* chirped; (*pres* **metsartser;** *fut* **yetsartser**).

tseertsoor/-eem צרצור *nm* chirping; (*pl+of:* **-ey**).

tseetat|ah/-ot ציטטה *nf* citation; quotation; (*+of:* **-at**).

tseet|et/-etah/-atetee ציטט *v* cited; quoted; (*pres* **metsatet;** *fut* **yetsatet**).

tseetoot/-eem ציטוט *nm* citation; quotation; (*pl+of:* **-ey**).

tseetoot/-eem ציתות *nm* listening-in.

tseets/-eem ציץ *nm* sprout; blossom; (*pl+of:* **-ey**).

tse'etsa/-'eem צאצא *nm* descendant; scion; offspring; (*pl+of:* **ey**).

tseetsee/-m ציצי *nm [slang]* tit; woman's breast.

◇ **tseetsee|t/-yot** ציציות *nf* **1.** corner fringes of prayer shawl **(taleet)**; **2.** small prayer shawl-like undergarment worn by observant Jewish men.

tseev|ah/-tah/-eetee ציווה *v* ordered; (*pres* **metsaveh**; *fut* **yetsaveh**).

tseeveeleezatsee|yah/-yot ציוויליזציה *nf* civilisation.

tseev'ey ha-keshet צבעי הקשת *nm pl* colors of the rainbow.

tseev'onee/-m צבעוני *nm* tulip (flower).

tseev'onee/-t צבעוני *adj* colored.

tseevoo|y/-yeem ציווי *nm* **1.** imperative (Gram.) **2.** order; command; (*pl+of:* **-ey**).

tseevyon/-eem צביון *nm* character; nature (*pl+of:* **-ey**).

tsee|yed/-yedah/-yadetee צייד *v* equipped; (*pres* **metsayed**; *fut* **yetsayed**).

tsee|yen/-yenah/-yantee ציין *v* marked; observed; (*pres* **metsayen**; *fut* **yetsayen**).

tsee|yer/-yerah/-yartee צייר *v* painted; drew; (*pres* **metsayer**; *fut* **yetsayer**).

tsee|yet/-yetah/yatetee ציית *v* heeded; obeyed; (*pres* **metsayet**; *fut* **yetsayet**).

tsee|yets/-yetsah/-yatstee צייץ *v* twittered; chirped; (*pres* **metsayets**; *fut* **yetsayets**).

◇ **tseeyon (Zion)** ציון *nf* Biblical name of elevation "Mount Zion" in Jerusalem's old City on which Solomon's Temple (and the Second Temple that followed it) once stood.

□ **(Har) Tseeyon** see □ **Har Tseeyon**.

◇ **(khovevey) tseeyon** see ◇ **khovevey tseeyon**.

◇ **(po'aley) tseeyon** see ◇ **po'aley tseeeyon**.

□ **(Reeshon) le-Tseeyon** see □ **Reeshon le-Tseeyon**.

◇ **(ha-reeshon le) tseeyon** see ◇ **ha-reeshon le-tseeyon**.

◇ **(tse'eerey) tseeyon** see ◇ **tse'eerey tseeyon**.

tseeyonee/-t ציוני **1.** *adj* Zionist; **2.** *nmf* Zionist.

◇ **tseeyonoot** ציונות *nf* Zionism, worldwide Jewish movement striving towards the repatriation of Jews to their onetime homeland, Eretz Israel (known until 1948 as Palestine). Activated Political Zionism began in 1886, led by Dr. Theodor Herzl, a Viennese dramatist and journalist. Systematically promoting Jewish Immigration to Palestine, it attained a first goal in 1917 with England's Balfour Declaration supporting the creation of a Jewish National Home in Palestine. In 1922, Great Britain was indeed entrusted by the League of Nations with a Mandate over Palestine with that aim in view. Zionism came nearer to its goal in 1948 with the proclamation of an independent Jewish State, Israel, in a part of Palestine. In the 40 years since, the Jewish State has continued to grow; as of 1990, nearly 1/3 of the Jewish people lives in Israel the government of which, in cooperation with the Jewish Agency, actively encourages more and more Jews to come and settle there.

"tseeyonoot" ציונות *nf [slang]* "Zionist talk" - i.e. incorrigibly idealistic and bombastic verbiage.

tseeyood ציוד *nm* equipment.

tseeyoon/-eem ציון *nm* **1.** remark; notation; **2.** mark (at school) (*pl+of:* **-ey**).

tseeyoon/-eem le-shevakh ציון לשבח *nm* commendation; mention in military dispatches.

tseeyoor/-eem ציור *nm* drawing; painting.

tseeyooree/-t ציורי *adj* picturesque.

tseeyoot/-eem ציות *nf* obedience.

tseeyoots/-eem ציוץ *nm* chirping.

tsefa'/tsfa'eem צפע *nm* viper; poisonous snake; (*pl+of:* **tseef'ey**).

tsefarde|'a'/-'eem צפרדע *nf* frog; (*pl+of:* **-'ey**).

□ **Tsefat** (Zefat) צפת *nf* Safed, historic 2,000 year old city in Lower Galilee on a slope of Mount Canaan **(Har Kena'an)**. Pop. 19,300.

tsefeefoo|t/-yot צפיפות *nf* **1.** crowding; **2.** density.

tsefeer|ah/-ot צפירה *nf* siren; blowing of a car horn; (*+of:* **-at**).

tsefeer|at/-ot arga'ah צפירת ארגעה *nf* all-clear siren.

tsefeer|at/-ot az'akah צפירת אזעקה *nf* alarm signal.

tsefon-ma'arav צפון־מערב *nm* northwest.

tsefon-meezrakh צפון־מזרח *nm* northeast.

tsefonee/-t צפוני *adj* N.

tsefonee/-yeem צפוני *nm* northerner.

tsefoneet-ma'araveetle- צפונית־מערבית ל־ *adv* northwest of...

tsefoneet-mezrakheet le- צפונית־מזרחית ל־ *adv* northeast of...

tsehav|hav/-hevet צהבהב *adj* yellowish.

(gveenah) tsehoobah גבינה צהובה *nf* yellow (hard) cheese.

tsekheekhoot צחיחות *nf* aridity; dryness.

tsekhok/-eem צחוק *nm* laugh; laughter; mockery.

('as|ah/-tah/-eetee) tsekhok עשה צחוק *v* made fun; (*pres* **'oseh** *etc*; *fut* **ya'aseh** *etc*).

(bat-) tsekhok בת־צחוק *nf* smile.

(bee) tsekhok בצחוק *adv* jokingly.

(heetgalg|el/-elah/-altee mee) tsekhok התגלגל מצחוק *v* was rolling with laughter; (*pres* **meetgalgel** *etc*; *fut* **yeetgalgel** *etc*).

(heetpak|e'a'/-'ah/-a'tee mee) tsekhok (*or:* **heetpaka'** *etc*) התפקע מצחוק *v* rolled with laughter; (*pres* **meetpake'a'** *etc*; *fut* **yeetpake'a'** *etc*).

(lee) tsekhok לצחוק *adv* laughing stock.

('or|er/-erah/-artee) tsekhok עורר צחוק *v* aroused laughter; caused a laugh; (*pres* **me'orer** *etc*; *fut* **ye'orer** *etc*).

tsel/-aleem צל *nm* shadow; (*pl+of:* **tseeleley**).

□ **Tselafon** (Zelafon) צלפון *nm* village 2 km SE of Nahshon Junction **(Tsomet Nakhshon)**. Pop. 477.

tsel shel safek צל של ספק *nm* shadow of a doubt.

(be) tsel korat בצל קורת *adv* under the roof of; enjoying the hospitality of .

tsel|a'/-a'ot צלע *nf* rib; **(***pl+of:* **tsal'ot)**.

tselalee|t/-yot צללית *nf* silhouette.

tselav/-eem צלב *nm* cross; **(***pl+of:* **-ey)**.

tselav/-ey keres צלב קרס *nm* swastika.

(ha) tselav he-'adom הצלב האדום *nm* the Red Cross.

(mas|a'/-'ey) tselav מסע צלב *nm* crusade.

(mas'ey ha) tselav מסעי הצלב *nm pl* the Crusades.

(nos'ey ha) tselav נושאי הצלב *nm pl* the Crusaders.

tselee צלי *nm* grill.

tselee|'ah/-'ot צליעה *nf* limping; **(***+of:* **-'at)**.

tselee/-'esh צלי אש *nm* roasted on fire.

tseleef|ah/-ot צליפה *nf* sniping; **(***+of:* **-at)**.

tseleekh|ah/-ot צליחה *nf* crossing (river); **(***+of:* **-at)**.

tseleelah/-ot צלילה *nf* diving; **(***+of:* **-at)**.

tseleel/-eem צליל *nm* sound; **(***pl+of:* **-ey)**.

tseleel kheeyoog צליל חיוג *nm* dial tone.

(gon ha) tseleel גון הצליל *nm* timbre.

(govah ha) tseleel גובה הצליל *nm* pitch.

('otsmat ha) tseleel עוצמת הצליל *nm* loudness; amplitude.

(maftseets/-ey) tseleelah מפציץ צלילה *nm* dive-bomber.

tseleeloot צלילות *nf* clarity; lucidity; clearness.

tseleeloot ha-da'at צלילות הדעת *nf* clear-mindedness; lucidity.

tseleeloot ha-kol צלילות הקול *nf* sonority of voice; clearness of voice.

tseleeloot ha-makhshavah צלילות המחשבה *nf* lucidity of thinking.

tseleevah/-ot צליבה *nf* crucifying; crucifixion; **(***+of:* **-at)**.

tselee|yah/-yot צלייה *nf* roasting; **(***+of:* **yat)**.

tselem demoot adam צלם דמות אדם *nm* likeness of a human being.

tselem eloheem צלם אלוהים *nm* **1.** likeness of God; **2.** *(lit.)* God's image.

tselof|akh/-akheem צלופח *nm* eel; **(***pl+of:* **-khey)**.

tselofan צלופן *nm* cellophane.

tselokhee|t/-yot צלוחית *nf* vial; flagon; fiask.

tselooloyd צלולויד *nm* celluloid.

tselsyoos צלסיוס *nm* Celsius.

(ma'alot) tselsyoos מעלות צלסיוס *nf pl* degrees Celsius (Centigrade).

□ **Tsemakh (Zemah)** צמח *nm* regional industrial center at the S. edge of Lake Tiberias serving kibbutzim around the lake and as crossroads to those in the Jordan Valley and the Golan Heights.

tsemakh/-eem צמח *nm* plant; **(***pl+of:* **tseemkhey)**.

tsemakh/tseemkhey bar צמח בר *nm* wild plant; weed.

tsemarmoret צמרמורת *nf* shivers; shuddering.

(tseme/-'at) da'at צמא דעת *adj* thirsty for knowledge.

tseme/-'at dam צמא דם *adj* bloodthirsty.

tseme/-'at teheelah צמא תהילה *adj* thirsty for glory.

tsem|ed/-adeem צמד *nm* couple; **(***pl+of:* **tseemdey)**.

tsemed-khemed צמד־חמד *nm* **1.** lovely couple; **2.** (ironically) a hell of a couple.

tsemeedoo|t/-yot צמידות *nf* coupling; linkage.

(bee) tsemeedoot le- בצמידות ל־ *adv* linked to... in linkage with.

tsemeeg/-eem צמיג *nm* automobile tire; **(***pl+of:* **-ey)**.

tsemeegoo|t/-yot צמיגות *nf* viscosity; stickiness.

tsemeetoot צמיתות *nf* perpetuity; beyond reclaim.

(lee) tsemeetoot לצמיתות *adv* for good; for eternity.

tsement צמנט *[colloq.] nm* cement.

tsemer צמר *nm* wool.

tsemer-gefen צמר גפן *nm* cotton.

tsemer menoopats צמר מנופץ *nm* carded wool.

tsemer pladah צמר־פלדה *nm* steel-wool.

tsemer sarook צמר סרוק *nm* combed wool; carded wool.

tsemer sla'eem צמר סלעים *nm* rock wool.

tsemer zekhookheet צמר זכוכית *nm* glass-wool.

◇ **"tsemoodeem"** צמודים *nm pl* **(***sing:* **tsamood)** *[colloq.]* securities linked to the U.S dollar or to the Israeli Cost of Living Index.

tsena' צנע *nm* austerity.

◇ **(tkoofat ha) tsena'** see ◇ **tekoofat ha-tsena'**.

tseneef/-eem צניף *nm* turban; head-dress; **(***pl+of:* **-ey)**.

tseneekh|ah/-ot צניחה *nm* parachute jump; **(***+of:* **-at)**.

tseneekhah khofsheet צניחה חופשית *nm* free parachute jump.

tseneemeem צנימים *nm pl* **(***sing:* **tsaneem)** biscuits; toast; rusk; **(***+of:* **tseneemey)**.

(lee) tseneeneem לצנינים *adv* being an eyesore; a pain in the neck.

tsenee'oot צניעות *nf* **1.** modesty; **2.** chastity.

tsenon/-eem צנון *nm* radish.

tsenoonee|t/-yot צנונית *nm* small radish.

tsenovar/-eem (*or:* **ts'nobar** *etc***)** צנובר *nm* pine cone; cinnobar.

tsenzoor|ah/-ot צנזורה *nf* censorship.

tsenzor/-eem צנזור *nm* censor.

tse'oo! צאו! *v imp nm pl* get out! (addressing several people); **(***inf* **latset;** *pst* **yatsa;** *pres* **yotse;** *fut* **yetse)**.

tseratsar/tseertsar|eem צרצר *nm* cricket; **(***pl+of:* **-ey)**.

tsereedoo|t/-ooyot צרידות *nf* hoarseness.

tsereef/-eem צריף *nm* shack; hut; (*pl+of:* **-ey**).
tsereef/-ey asbest צריף אסבסט *nm* asbestos-shack.
tsereef/-ey 'ets צריף עץ *nm* wooden shack.
□ **Tsereefeen** see Tsreefeen.
tsereekh|ah/-ot צריחה *nf* scream; yell; (*+of:* **-at**).
tsereekh|ah/-ot צריכה *nf* consumption of goods; (*+of:* **-at**).
tsereev|ah/-ot צריבה *nf* cauterization; staining of wood (*+of:* **-at**).
tser|ef/-fah/-aftee צירף *v* added; combined; (*pres* **metsaref**; *fut* **yetsaref**).
tseroof/-eem צירוף *nm* combination; (*pl+of:* **-ey**).
tseroof/-ey lashon צירוף לשון *nm* idiom; phrase.
(tsarah) tseroorah צרה צרורה *nf* great trouble.
tseror/-ot צרור *nm* bundle; parcel.
tset צאת *nf* exit of...
tset ha-shabat צאת השבת *nf* Saturday at nightfall; (*lit.*) exit of the Sabbath.
tsev|a'/-a'eem צבע *nm* **1.** paint; **2.** color; (*pl+of:* **tseev'ey**).
(khas|ar/-rat) tseva' חסר צבע *adj* colorless.
(netool/-at) tseva' נטול צבע *adj* colorless.
◇ **tseva haganah le-yeesra'el** צבא הגנה לישראל *nm* Israel Defence Forces; I.D.F.; the Israeli Army.
tseva ha-keva' צבא הקבע *nm* the standing (career) army.
tseva'ee/-t צבאי *adj* military; army.
(basees/bseeseem) tseva'ee/-yeem בסיס צבאי *nm* military base. (*+of:* **besees/-ey**).
(bet/batey deen) tseva'ee/-yeem בית־דין צבאי *nm* military court.
(makhan|eh/-ot) tseva'ee/-yeem מחנה צבאי *nm* military camp; army camp.
(meeshtar) tseva'ee משטר צבאי *nm* martial law.
tsevakh|ah/-ot צווחה *nf* yell; (*+of:* **-at**).
tsevat/-ot צבת *nf* pliers; tongs.
tsev|ee/-a'eem צבי *nm* deer; stag; antelope; (*pl+of:* **-a'ey**).
('al keren ha) tsevee על קרן הצבי *adv* down the drain; a lost venture; (*lit.*) on the horns of a deer.
('erets ha) tsevee ארץ הצבי *nf* Eretz Israel; (*lit.*) Land of the Deer.
(ha) tsevee Yeesra'el הצבי ישראל *nm* poetical reference to the Jewish people.
tseveer|ah/-ot צבירה *nf* accumulation (*+of:* **-at**).
tseveet|ah/-ot צביטה *nf* pinch; pinching; (*+of:* **-at**).
tseveetah (*etc*) **ba-lev** צביטה בלב *nf* a heart pain.
tsevee|yah/-yot צבייה *nf* gazelle.
□ **Tseveeyah** (Zeviyya) צבייה *nm* kibbutz (est. 1979) in Lower Galilee, 5 km SE of **Karmee'el**.
tsev|et/-ateem צוות *nm* crew; team; staff; (*pl+of:* **tseevtey**).

(eesh/-anshey) tsevet איש צוות *nm* crew member; staff member.
tseydah צידה *nf* provision.
tseydanee|t/-yot צידנית *nf* picnic hamper.
◇ **tseyreh** צירה (**x**)sublinear vowel in "dotted" Hebrew script that is sometimes pronounced as the **a** in *face* and sometimes as the **e** in *get*.
tsfarde|'a'/-'eem צפרדע *nf* frog; (*pl+of:* **-'ey**).
□ **Tsfat** see □ **Tsefat**.
tsfeefoo|t/-yot צפיפות *nf* **1.** crowding; **2.** density.
tsfeer|ah/-ot צפירה *nf* siren; blowing of a car horn; (*+of:* **-at**).
tsfeer|at/-ot arga'ah צפירת ארגעה *nf* all-clear siren.
tsfeer|at/-ot az'akah צפירת אזעקה *nf* alarm signal.
tsfon-ma'arav צפון־מערב *nm* northwest.
tsfon-meezrakh צפון־מזרח *nm* northeast.
tsfonee/-t צפוני *adj* N.
tsfonee/-yeem צפוני *nm* northerner.
tsfoneet-ma'araveet le- צפונית־מערבית ל־ *adv* northwest of...
tsfoneet-mezrakheet le- צפונית־מזרחית ל־ *adv* northeast of...
ts'kheekhoot צחיחות *nf* aridity; dryness.
ts'khok/-eem צחוק *nm* laugh; laughter; mockery.
('as|ah/-tah/-eetee) ts'khok עשה צחוק *v* made fun; (*pres* **'oseh** *etc*; *fut* **ya'aseh** *etc*).
(bat-) ts'khok בת־צחוק *nf* smile.
(bee) ts'khok בצחוק *adv* jokingly.
(heetgalg|el/-elah/-altee mee) ts'khok התגלגל מצחוק *v* was rolling with laughter; (*pres* **meetgalgel** *etc*; *fut* **yeetgalgel** *etc*).
(heetpak|e'a'/-'ah/-a'tee mee) ts'khok התפקע מצחוק *v* rolled with laughter; (*pres* **meetpake'a'** *etc*; *fut* **yeetpake'a'** *etc*).
(lee) ts'khok לצחוק *adv* laughing stock.
('or|er/-erah/-artee) ts'khok עורר צחוק *v* aroused laughter; caused a laugh; (*pres* **me'orer** *etc*; *fut* **ye'orer** *etc*).
tslaleem צללים *nm pl* (*sing* **tsel**) shadows; (*+of:* **tseeleley**).
tslalee|t/-yot צללית *nf* silhouette.
tslav/-eem צלב *nm* cross; (*pl+of:* **-ey**).
tslav/-ey keres צלב קרס *nm* swastika.
(ha) tslav he-'adom הצלב האדום *nm* the Red Cross.
(mas|a'/-'ey) tslav מסע צלב *nm* crusade.
(mas'ey ha) tslav מסעי הצלב *nm pl* the Crusades.
(nos'ey ha) tslav נושאי הצלב *nm pl* the Crusaders.
tslee צלי *nm* grill.
tslee|'ah/-'ot צליעה *nf* limping; (*+of:* **-'at**).
tslee-'esh צלי אש *nm* roasted on fire.
tsleef|ah/-ot צליפה *nf* sniping; (*+of:* **-at**).
tsleekh|ah/-ot צליחה *nf* crossing (river); (*+of:* **-at**).
tsleel|ah/-ot צלילה *nf* diving; (*+of:* **-at**).
tsleel/-eem צליל *nm* sound; (*pl+of:* **-ey**).
tsleel kheeyoog צליל חיוג *nm* dial tone.
(gon ha) tsleel גון הצליל *nm* timbre.

(govah ha) tsleel גובה הצליל *nm* pitch.
('otsmat ha) tsleel עוצמת הצליל *nm* loudness; amplitude.
(maftseets/-ey) tsleelah מפציץ צלילה *nm* dive-bomber.
tsleeloot צלילות *nf* clarity; lucidity; clearness.
tsleeloot ha-da'at צלילות הדעת *nf* clear-mindedness; lucidity.
tsleeloot ha-kol צלילות הקול *nf* sonority of voice; clearness of voice.
tsleeloot ha-makhshavah צלילות המחשבה *nf* lucidity of thinking.
tsleevah/-ot צליבה *nf* crucifying; crucifixion; **(**+*of:* **-at).**
tslee|yah/-yot צלייה *nf* roasting; **(**+*of:* **yat).**
tslof|akh/-akheem צלופח *nm* eel **(***pl*+*of:* **-khey).**
tslokhee|t/-yot צלוחית *nf* vial; flagon; fiask.
tsmarmoret צמרמורת *nf* shivers; shuddering.
(tsme/-'at) da'at צמא דעת *adj* thirsty for knowledge.
tsme/-'at dam צמא דם *adj* bloodthirsty.
tsme/-'at teheelah צמא תהילה *adj* thirsty for glory.
tsmeedoo|t/-yot צמידות *nf* coupling; linkage.
(bee) tsmeedoot le- בצמידות ל־ *adv* linked to... in linkage with.
tsmeegoo|t/-yot צמיגות *nf* viscosity; stickiness.
tsmeetoot צמיתות *nf* perpetuity; beyond reclaim.
(lee) tsmeetoot לצמיתות *adv* for good; for eternity.
◇ **"tsmoodeem"** see ◇ **"tsemoodeem".**
tsneef/-eem צניף *nm* turban; head-dress; **(***pl*+*of:* **-ey).**
tsneekh|ah/-ot צניחה *nm* parachute jump; **(**+*of:* **-at).**
tsneekhah khofsheet צניחה חופשית *nm* free parachute jump.
tsneemeem צנימים *nm pl* **(***sing:* **tsaneem)** biscuits; toast; rusk; **(**+*of:* **tsneemey).**
(lee) tsneeneem לצנינים *adv* being an eyesore; a pain in the neck.
tsnee'oot צניעות *nf* **1.** modesty; **2.** chastity.
tsnon/-eem צנון *nm* radish.
tsnoonee|t/-yot צנונית *nm* small radish.
tsnovar **(***cpr* **tsnobar)/-eem** צנובר *nm* pine cone; cinnobar.
tso|'ah/-'ot צואה *nf* excrement; dung; **(**+*of:* **-'at).**
tso'anee/-yah צועני *nmf* Gypsy.
tso'anee/-t צועני *adj* Gypsy.
tsodek/-et צודק **1.** *adj* just; **2.** *v pres* is right; he's/she's right.
tso'ed/-et צועד **1.** *nmf* marcher; **2.** *v pres* marches **(***pst* **tsa'ad;** *fut* **yeets'ad).**
tso'ek/-et צועק *v pres* shouts; yells; **(***pst* **tsa'ak;** *fut* **yeets'ak).**
tso|'er/-'areem צוער *nm* cadet; **(***pl*+*of:* **-'arey).**
tsof|ah/-ot צופה *nf* girl scout; **(**+*of:* **-at).**
□ **Tsofar** (Zofar) צופר *nm* village (est. 1968) in the **'Aravah**, 20 km S. of **'En Yahav**. Pop. 211.
tsofar/-eem צופר *nm* horn; car-horn.
tsof|eem צופים *nm pl* **(***sing:* **tsofeh)** scouts; boy-scouts; **(**+*of:* **-ey).**
□ **(Har ha) Tsofeem** see □ **Har ha-Tsofeem.**
□ **Tsofeet** (Zofit) צופית *nm* village (est. 1930) outside **Kefar Saba**, 2 km N. of the township. Pop. 359.
□ **Tsofeeyah** (Zofiyya) צופיה *nm* closed institution (est. 1955) for delinquent girls. Located on seaside of Coastal Plain, 2 km SW of **Yavneh.**
tsofeeyoot צופיות *nf* scouting.
tsof|eh/-ah צופה *v pres* views; watches; **(***pst* **tsafah;** *fut* **yeetspeh** *(p=f)***).**
tsof|eh/-eem צופה **1.** *nm* spectator; **2.** boy scout; **(***pl*+*of:* **-ey).**
tsof|ef/-efah/-aftee צופף *v* condensed; crowded in; **(***pres* **metsofef;** *fut* **yetsofef).**
tsofen צופן *nm* code; cipher.
tsofen/-et צופן *v pres* holds in store; hides; **(***pst* **tsafan;** *fut* **yeetspon** *(p=f)***).**
□ **Tsohar (Zohar)** צוהר *nm* regional supply center (est. 1973) for **Khevel ha-Besor** settlements **('Amee'oz, Meevtakheem, Ohad, Sedeh Neetsan, Talmey Eleeyahoo and Yesha')** in SE Negev. Pop. 299.
tsohol|ah צהלה *nf* rejoicing; merriment; **(**+*of:* **-at).**
tsohor|ayeem צהריים *nm* **1.** noon; **2.** *[colloq.]* lunch; **(**+*of:* **-ey).**
tsohorayeem toveem! צהריים טובים! (greeting) Good afternoon!
(akhar ha) tsohorayeem אחר־הצהריים *adv* afternoon; p.*m.*
(akhrey ha) tsohorayeem אחרי הצהריים *adv* in the afternoon.
(arookh|at/-ot) tsohorayeem ארוחת צהריים *nf* lunch; luncheon.
(ba) tsohorayeem בצהריים *adv* at noon.
(leefney ha) tsohorayeem לפני הצהריים *adv* before noon; a.*m.*
(be) tsohorey yom בצהרי יום *adv* at midday.
tsol צול *nm [colloq.]* inch.
tsol|e'a'/-a'at צולע **1.** *adj* limping; **2.** *v pres* limps; **(***pst* **tsala';** *fut* **yeetsla').**
tsolelan/-eem צוללן *nm* diver; **(***pl*+*of:* **-ey).**
tsolel|et/-ot צוללת *nf* submarine.
(.. az anee) tsolelet! אז אני צוללת! *[slang]*... then, I must be a submarine! (something incredible).
tsom/-mot צום *nm* fast.
tsom keepoor צום כיפור *nm* "Yom Kippur" fasting.
◇ **tsom teesh'ah be-av** צום תשעה באב *nm* **teesh'ah be-av** i.e. 9th of Av (Yiddish: "Tisheboov") fasting (see ◇ **teesh'ah be-av).**
tsom|e'akh/-akhat צומח **1.** *adj* growing; **2.** *v pres* grows; **(***pst* **tsamakh;** *fut* **yeetsmakh).**
(ha) tsome'akh הצומח *nm* flora.
tsomet/tsemateem צומת *nm* road-junction; **(***pl*+*of:* **tsomtey).**
tson צאן *nm pl* flocks (of sheep or goats).

tson barzel צאן ברזל *nm pl* assets of permanent value.

tsonen/-et צונן *adj* cool; chilling; (used also *figurat*).

tsoof/-eem צוף *nm* **1.** nectar (in flowers) **2.** light drink (taste of honey).

tsook/-eem צוק *nm* reef; (*+of:* **-ey**).

tsoor/-eem צור *nm* rock; fortress.

□ **Tsoor Hadasah** צור הדסה *nm* regional centre (est. 1960) in Judean hills, 10 km SW of Jerusalem, 4 km W. of **Mevo Betar**. Pop. 246.

□ **Tsoor Mosheh** (Zur Moshe) צור משה *nm* village (est. 1937) in Sharon, 3 km SE of haSharon Road Junction. Pop. 492.

□ **Tsoor Natan** צור נתן *nm* coop. village (est. 1966) 3 km N. of **Kokhav-Ya'eer**, 8 km S. of **Toolkarem**. Pop. 203.

◇ **tsoor yeesra'el** צור ישראל *nm* God, Rock of Israel.

tsoor|ah/-ot צורה *nf* form; shape; (*+of:* **-at**).

(be) tsoorat בצורת *adv* in the form of...

(lav|ash/-shah/-ashtee) tsoorah לבש צורה *v* took the form of...; (*pres* **lovesh** *etc; fut* **yeelbash** *etc b=v*).

(pash|at/-tah/-atetee) tsoorah ve lavash (*etc*) **tsoorah** פשט צורה ולבש צורה *v* transformed oneself into..; changed appearences.

□ **Tsooree'el** (Zuri'el) צוריאל *nm* village (est. 1950) in Upper Galilee 3 km E. of **Ma'alot -Tarsheekhah**. Pop. 252.

□ **Tsooreet** (Zurit) צורית *nm* communal settlement (est. 1980) in Lower Galilee, 5 km SE of **Karmee'el**. Pop. 256.

tsootseek/-eet צוציק *nmf [slang]* ragamuffin; youngster.

□ **Tsor'ah** (Zor'a) צרעה *nm* kibbutz (est. 1948) on borderline between **Shfelah** and Judean hills, 2 km NW of Bet Shemesh. Pop. 941.

tsor|e'akh/-akhat צורח **1.** *v pres* screams; yells; **2.** *adj* screaming; yelling; (*pst* **tsarakh;** *fut* **yeetsrakh**).

tsor|ef/-feem צורף *nm* goldsmith; silversmith; (*pl+of:* **-fey**).

tsorekh/tserakheem צורך *nm* need; necessity; (*pl+of:* **tsorkhey**).

tsorekh/tserakheem kheeyoonee/-yeem צורך חיוני *nm* vital need.

tsor|ekh/-khey ha-sha'ah צורך השעה *nm* demand of the hour.

(en) tsorekh אין צורך *adv* no need; you needn't...

(le) tsorekh לצורך *adv* for the purpose of.

(le) tsorekh ve-she-lo le-tsorekh לצורך ושלא לצורך *adv* whether needed or not.

(yesh) tsorekh יש צורך *v pres* there is need that...; it is necessary; (*pst* **hayah** *etc;* **yeehyeh** *etc*).

tsorekh/-et צורך *v pres* consumes; (*pst* **tsarakh;** *fut* **yeetsrokh**).

tsorem/-et צורם **1.** *adj* grating; raucous; **2.** *v pres* grates; (*pst* **tsaram;** *fut* **yeetsrom**).

tsorer/-eem צורר *nm* oppressor; (*pl+of:* **-ey**).

tsorer yeesra'el צורר ישראל *nm* Jew-hater.

tsorev/-et צורב **1.** *adj* scorching; burning; **2.** *v pres* scorches; (*pst* **tsarav;** *fut* **yeetsrov**).

tsorfat (*npr* **tsarfat**) צרפת *nf* France.

tsorfatee/-t (*npr* **tsarfatee/-t**) צרפתי *adj* French.

tsorfatee/-yah (*npr* **tsarfatee/-yah**) צרפתי *nmf* Frenchman/Frenchwoman.

tsorfateet (*npr* **tsarfateet**) צרפתית *nf* French (language).

tsorkhey okhel צורכי אוכל *nm pl* foodstuffs.

tsorkhey shabat צורכי שבת *nm pl* needs in preparation for the Sabbath.

tsorkhey tseeboor צורכי ציבור *nm pl* public needs; social work.

(khanoo|t/-yot le) tsorkhey khashmal חנות לצורכי חשמל *nf* electrical supplies store.

(khanoo|t/-yot le) tsorkhey kteevah חנות לצורכי כתיבה *nf* stationery store.

(khanoo|t/-yot le) tsorkhey tseeloom חנות לצורכי צילום *nf* photographic equipment and supplies store.

tsot|et/-etah/-atetee צותת *v* listened in; overheard; (*pres* **metsotet;** *fut* **yetsotet**).

□ **Tsova** (Zova) צובה *nm* kibbutz (est. 1948) in Judean hills, 6 km E. of **Ramat Razee'el**. Pop. 473.

tsover/-et צובר *v pres* amasses; accumulates; (*pst* **tsavar;** *fut* **yeetsbor** *(b=v)*).

(ba) tsover בצובר *adv* in bulk.

('asah/-tah/-eetee) tsrakh|av/-eha/-ay *etc* עשה צרכיו *v* eased nature; relieved him/her/my self *etc*; (*pres* **'oseh** *etc; fut* **ya'aseh** *etc*).

tsratsar/tseertsar|eem צרצר *nm* cricket; (*pl+of:* **-ey**).

tsreedoo|t/-yot צרידות *nf* hoarseness.

tsreef/-eem צריף *nm* shack; hut; (*pl+of:* **-ey**).

tsreef/-ey asbest צריף אסבסט *nm* asbestos-shack.

tsreef/-ey 'ets צריף עץ *nm* wooden shack.

□ **Tsreefeen** (Zerifin) צריפין *nm* largest military base in Coastal Plain, 3 km NE of Ramla. Originally built by advancing British forces in World War I, under name of Sarafend, it became one of main British bases in the Middle East throughout British rule and especially during World War II.

tsreekh|ah/-ot צריחה *nf* scream; yell; (*+of:* **-at**).

tsreekh|ah/-ot צריכה *nf* consumption of goods; (*+of:* **-at**).

tsreev|ah/-ot צריבה *nf* cauterization; staining of wood (*+of:* **-at**).

(tsarah) tsroorah צרה צרורה *nf* great trouble.

□ **Tsroofah** (**Zerufa**) צרופה *nm* village on Carmel coast, (est. 1949), 6 km S. of 'Atlit Interchange. Pop. 396.

tsror/-ot צרור *nm* bundle; parcel.

◇ **tsva haganah le-yeesra'el** see ◇ **tseva haganah le-yeesra'el**.

tsva ha-keva' צבא הקבע *nm* the standing (career) army.

tsva'ee/-t צבאי *adj* military; army.

(basees/bseeseem) tsva'ee/-yeem בסיס צבאי *nm* military base. **(**+*of:* **bsees/-ey).**

(bet/batey deen) tsva'ee/-yeem בית־דין צבאי *nm* military court.

(makhan|eh/-ot) tsva'ee/-yeem מחנה צבאי *nm* military camp; army camp.

(meeshtar) tsva'ee משטר צבאי *nm* martial law.

tsvakh|ah/-ot צווחה *nf* yell; **(**+*of:* **-at).**

tsvat/-ot צבת *nf* pliers; tongs.

tsvee/tsva'eem צבי *nm* deer; stag; antelope; **(***pl+of:* **tsva'ey).**

('al keren ha) tsvee על קרן הצבי *adv* down the drain; a lost venture; (*lit.*) on the horns of a deer.

(erets ha) tsvee ארץ הצבי *nf* Eretz Israel; *(lit.)* Land of the Deer.

(ha) tsvee Yeesra'el הצבי ישראל *nm* poetical reference to the Jewish people.

tsver|ah/-ot צבירה *nf* accumulation **(**+*of:* **-at).**

tsveet|ah/-ot צביטה *nf* pinch; pinching; **(**+*of:* **-at).**

tsveetah (*etc*) **ba-lev** צביטה בלב *nf* a heart pain.

tsvee|yah/-yot צבייה *nf* gazelle.

□ **Tsveeyah** see □ **Tseveeyah**.

U.

NOTE: In this dictionary, the Hebrew vowels **Shoorok** (וּ) and **Kooboots** (ֻx) are rendered by **oo** as in **food** or **fool**. **U** is not used at all.

V.

NOTE: The consonant **v** - as pronounced in the English words *value*, *velvet* or *void* - has two equivalents in the Hebrew alphabet:

1. Vet ב, the undotted version of **Bet** בּ **(b)** as in *baby* and, in dotted texts, with a central dot בּ (that is absent from **Vet**). The letter is therefore ambiguous in an undotted text where it can be guessed correctly only from its context.

2. Vav ו, which is ambiguous as well since it may also represent the vowels **o** and **oo**. In dotted texts these two vowels are clearly indicated by their dots: וֹ and וּ respectively, but not in everyday undotted spelling. In the latter, therefore, the **Vav** mostly appears doubled. There are exceptions, however (at the beginning and end of words), where the context helps.

va'ad/ve'ad|eem ועד *nm* committee; **(***pl+of:* **-ey).**

◇ **(ha)va'ad ha-po'el** הועד הפועל *nm* the Executive Committee (usually referring to the Executive Committee of the Histadrut General Federation of Labor).

va'ad|ah/-ot (*cpr:* **ve'ad|ah)** ועדה *nf* commission; committee; **(**+*of:* **-at).**

va'adah matmedet ועדה מתמדת *nf* steering committee.

va'adah meya'etset ועדה מייעצת *nf* advisory committee; consultative committee.

va'ad|ah/-ot pareetetee|t-yot ועדה פריטטית *nf* parity committee.

va'ad|at/-ot kabalah ועדת קבלה *nf* reception committee; admissions committee.

va'ad|at/-ot khakeerah ועדת חקירה *nf* commission of inquiry.

(oy) va-avoy! אוי ואבוי! *interj* woe to me! alas and alack.

(basar) va-dam בשר ודם *nm* flesh and blood; mortal.

vada'oo|t/-yot ודאות *nf* certainty.

(be) vada'oot בוודאות *adv* with certainty.

vad|ay/-a'eet ([*colloq.*]*:* **vada'ee)** ודאי *adj* certain.

(be) vaday בוודאי *adv* certainly.

(karov le) vaday קרוב לוודאי *adv* almost certainly.

vadee/-yot ואדי *nm* wadi (dry watercourse); ravine.

(boker) va-'erev בוקר וערב *adv* day and night; mornings and evenings.

(shtee) va-'erev שתי וערב **1.** *adv* crosswise; **2.** *nm* length and breadth; warp and woof.

(hafle) va-fele *(f=p)* הפלא ופלא *interj* (sometimes ironically) how wonderful!

◇ **(keteevah) va-khateemah tovah!** see ◇ **keteevah va-khateemah tovah!**

(kal) va-khomer קל וחומר *adv* so much the more; inference from major to minor.

va-lo ולא or else...

vals/-eem ואלס *nm* waltz.

vaneel וניל *nm* vanilla.

□ **Vardon** (Wardon) ורדון *nm* - rural center (est. 1968) in **Lakheesh** district, 5 km N. of **Keeryat Gat**, serving settlements **Segoolah**, **Menookhah** and **Nakhalah**. Pop. 56.

varod/vroodah ורוד *adj* pink.

vasal/-eem וסל *nm* vassal.

vasat/-eem וסת *nm* regulator; control; (*pl+of:* **-ey**).

vasat/-ey neegood וסת ניגוד *nm* contrast control (on a TV-set).

vasat/-ey 'otsmah וסת עוצמה *nm* volume control (in an audio-set).

vasat/-ey tseleel וסת צליל *nm* tone control (in an audio-set).

(halokh) va-shov הלוך ושוב *adv* back and forth.

(be) vat akhat *(v=b)* בבת אחת *adv* at once; simultaneously.

(tohoo) va-vohoo תוהו ובוהו *nm* chaos; disorder.

vav/-eem וו *nm* hook; (*pl+of:* **-ey**).

◇ **vav/-eem** ו (וי"ו) *nm* 6th letter in the Hebrew alphabet. **1.** Unless dotted in middle (וּ) or above (וֹ), its pronunciation is equivalent to English consonant *v* as in *velvet* or *victory*. If text is undotted, it is normally doubled (וו) to distinguish it from וֹ and וּ except when opening or closing a word; **2.** Dotted in its middle, (וּ) is equivalent to the combined vowel *oo*, as in *fool* or *food;* **3.** Dotted above, (וֹ), it is equivalent to the vowel *o*, (as in *most* or *gold*).

(kaf-) vav *(etc)* כ"ו *numer. symbol* for 26 (**Kaf**=20 plus **vav**=6 makes 26).

◇ **(tet-) vav** see ◇ **tet-vav**.

(yom/yemey) vav יום ו' *nm* the 6th Day i.e. Friday.

vay וי *interj* woe (denoting grief or pain).

vay lee/lekha/lakh/lo/lah וי לי/לך/לך/לו/לה *interj & pers.pron* woe to me/you(*m/f*)/him/her *etc.*

va-yehee ויהי *v* (Bibl. form of past tense) and it came to pass...; (*normative pst* **hayah**; *pres* **heeno**; *fut* **yeehyeh**).

ve- ו *(prefix) conj* and; (Note: **ve-** may become **va-** or **vee-** or even **oo-** depending on the phonological structure of the syllable which follows it. In colloquial Hebrew rules are ignored by many who pronounce the conjunction invariably **ve**).

ve-'ad bee-khlal ועד בכלל **1.** *adv* inclusive; **2.** *adv* including.

ve'ad|ah/-ot (*npr:* **va'ad|ah**) ועדה *nf* commission; committee; (*+of:* **-at**).

ve-dal וד"ל *abbr.* (*acr.* for **VE-DAy Le-khakeema bee-remeeza** (ודי לחכימא ברמיזא) "A word to the wise is sufficient".

ve-day ודי and that is it! ...and enough with it!

ve-day le-khakeema bee-remeeza ודי לחכימא ברמיזא *(Aram.)* A word to the wise is sufficient.

veed|e/-'ah/-e'tee וידא *v* made sure; ascertained; (*pres* **mevade**; *fut* **yevade**).

veede'o וידאו *nm* video.

(makhsheer/-ey) veede'o מכשיר וידיאו *nm* video-tape recorder.

(maklet/-ey) veede'o מקלט וידיאו *nm* video-set.

(seefree|yat/-yot) veede'o סיפריית וידיאו video-teque; videotape lending library.

(seret/seertey) veede'o סרט וידיאו *nm* video-tape.

veedoo|y/-yeem וידוי *nm* confession; (*pl+of:* **-yey**).

ve'eed|ah/-ot ועידה *nf* conference; (*+of:* **-at**).

ve'eed|at/-ot peesgah ועידת פסגה *nf* summit meeting.

veekoo|'akh/-kheem ויכוח *nm* discussion; debate; (*pl+of:* **-khey**).

veekoo|'akh/-kheem so|'er/-'areem ויכוח סוער *nm* stormy debate.

veekoo|'akh/-khey srak ויכוח סרק *nm* futile (fruitless) discussion.

veelon/-ot וילון *nm* curtain.

(khazak) ve-'emats! חזק ואמץ! (greeting) be strong and brave! (traditional Israeli boy-scout salute taken from the Bible).

veeralee/-t ויראלי *adj* viral.

veeroos/-eem וירוס *nm* virus; (*pl+of:* **-ey**).

veertoo'oz/-eem וירטואוז *nm* virtuoso.

vees|et/-tah/-atetee ויסת *v* adjusted; regulated; (*pres* **mevaset**; *fut* **yevaset**).

veesher/-eem וישר *nm [colloq.]* car's windshield wiper; (normative term is **mag|ev/-veem** מגב).

veesoot/-eem ויסות *nm* regulation; (*pl+of:* **-ey**).

veetameen/-eem ויטמין *nm* vitamin.

◇ **"veetameen pee"** ויטמין פי *nm [slang]* "Vitamin P." - (**P** for **protekts|yah/-yot**) "connections"; pulling of strings; use/abuse of influence.

veet|er/-rah/-artee ויתר *v* conceded; gave way; renounced; (*pres* **mevater**; *fut* **yevater**).

veetoor/-eem ויתור *nm* concession; disclaimer; renunciation; (*pl+of:* **-ey**).

(mee-kan) ve-'eylakh מכאן ואילך *adv* from now on; from here onward.

ve-'eyn matseel ואין מציל *adv* with no one to turn to for help.

vee-yehee mah! ויהי מה! and be what may!

veez|ah/-ot ויזה *nf* visa; (*+of:* **-at**).

veez|at/-ot ma'avar ויזת מעבר *nf* transit visa.
(hal|akh/-khah *etc*) **ve-gadal** הלך וגדל *v* grew constantly; (*pres* **holekh ve-godel**; *fut* **yelekh ve-yeegdal**).
(holekh/-et) ve-gadel/'oo-gdelah הולך וגדל *v pres* grows incessantly.
(manooy) ve-gamoor מנוי וגמור *adj* it is firmly decided.
(neemnoo) ve-gamroo נמנו וגמרו *v pst* it was discussed and decided.
ve-gomer'וגו' or: וגומר etcetera; and so on.
(hashkem) ve-ha'arev השכם והערב *adv* morning and evening.
(hen)... ve-hen... ...הן...והן as well as...
(day) ve-hoter די והותר *adv* more than needed; more than enough.
ve-kha-domeh *(kh=k)* וכדומה and the like.
ve-kha-yotse be-'eleh *(kh=k)* וכיוצא באלה and everything emerging therefrom.
ve-kha-yotse bo/bah *(kh=k)* וכיוצא בו/בה and anything similar to it/him/her.
ve-khen ...וכן and also...; and equally.
ve-khen hal'ah וכן הלאה *adv* and so forth.
ve-kho 'וכו *abbr.* **(ve-khooleh)** etcetera.
ve-khooleh וכולי etcetera.
ve-khooleh ve-khooleh וכולי וכולי (or, in *abbr.* form, 'וכו' וכו i.e. etcetera etcetera; and so on and on.
(ahlan) ve-sahlan אהלן וסהלן (greeting) *[slang]* welcome! be my guest! (from Arabic).
velad/-ot ולד *nm* infant; newborn.
(tam) ve-neeshlam תם ונשלם *adv* over and done with.
(tal'ooy/telooyah) ve-'omed/-et תלוי ועומד *adj* pending; sub-judice.
veradrad/-ah ורדרד *adj* pinkish; rosy.
□ **Veradeem** see □ **Vradeem**.
(akh) ve-rak אך ורק *adv* only; exclusively; solely.
ver|ed/-adeem ורד *nm* rose; rosebush; (*pl+of:* **-ey**).
□ **Vered ha-Galeel** ורד הגליל *nf* large farm and camping ground (est. 1961) 13 km N. of Tiberias.
□ **Vered Yereekho** ורד יריחו *nm* communal settlement (est. 1980) in Judean Desert, 4 km SE of Jericho, 2 km NW of **Nabee Moosah** (believed by Muslims to be the burial place of Moses). Pop. 210.
vereed/-eem וריד *nm* vein; (*pl+of:* **-ey**).
(le-tokh ha) vereed (*npr* **vareed**) לתוך הווריד **1.** *adj* intravenous; **2.** *adv* intravenously.
veset וסת *nm* menstruation.
(baree/bree'ah) ve-shalem/'oo-shlemah בריא ושלם *adj* safe and sound.
veshet ושט *nm* esophagus; gullet.
(halokh) ve-shoov (*npr* **va-shov**) הלוך ושוב *adv* back and forth.
(la) vetakh לבטח *adv* in safety.
vetek וותק *nm* tenure; seniority.
vetereenar/-eem וטרינר veterinary.
vetereenaree/-t וטרינרי *adj* veterinary.
veto/-'eem וטו *nm* veto.
vlad/-ot ולד *nm* infant; newborn.
voolgaree/-t וולגרי *adj* vulgar.
voosvoos/-eet ווס־ווס *[slang] nmf* Yiddish-speaker (as Ashkenazi or European Jews are sometimes derisively nicknamed by Jews of Afro-Asian descent).
□ **Vradeem** ורדים *nm* educational institution (est. 1935) of **"Ha-Shomer ha-Tsa'eer"** kibbutzim, 10 km S. of Netanya.
vradrad/-ah ורדרד *adj* pinkish; rosy.
(bee) vrakhah *(v=b)* בברכה *adv* with kind regards (complimentary closing of letter).
vreed/-eem וריד vein; (*pl+of:* **-ey**).
(le-tokh ha)vreed לתוך הווריד **1.** *adj* intravenous; **2.** *adv* intravenously.

W.

Note: There is no **W** (pronounced as in *well*) in normal, unpretentious Hebrew. Those insisting on pronouncing it, when transliterated, do so only in words or names which are of non-Hebrew origin, e.g. English (*Washington* **ושינגטון**, *weekend* **ויקאנד**) or Arabic (*wadi* **ואדי**). However, most Israelis pronounce these words **Vasheengton, veekend** and **vadee**.

X.

Note: This sound is not found in Hebrew as a single consonant. It is therefore not used at all in our transliteration.

Y.

transliterating the Hebrew letter **Yod** (י) in its function as a consonant (as in *youth, you, yield*).

yah יא *interj [slang]* oh, you!

yah ba'yeh! יא באיה! *interj [slang] (Arab.)* exclamation expressing excitement.

ya sheykh! יא שיך! *interj [slang] (Arab.)* dear fellow! chief! boss!

yah יה God (one of the Divine names appearing only in prayers).

Ya'akov יעקוב *nm* Jacob.

◇ **(tola'at) Ya'akov** see ◇ **tola'at Ya'akov**.

ya'ad/ye'adeem יעד *nm* objective; target; (*pl+of:* **-ey**).

□ **Ya'ad** יעד *nm* collective industrial village (est. 1974) in Lower Galilee, N. of **Bet Netoofah Valley**, 8 km SW of **Karmee'el**. Pop. 298.

ya'alat/-ot khen יעלת חן *nm* pretty woman; belle.

ya'an יען *adv* because; since.

ya'an kee יען כי *adv* because; on account of.

ya'ar/ye'arot יער *nm* forest; (*pl+of:* **ya'arot**).

□ **Ya'ar ha-Kedosheem** יער הקדושים *nm* "Martyrs Forest" - large forest planted in Jerusalem hills, 4 km S. of **Sha'ar ha-Gay** (overlooking Freeway 1) as memorial to the numerous Jewish communities which perished in the Holocaust.

□ **Ya'ar Hertsel** יער הרצל *nm* (Herzl Forest) large forest planted (beginning in 1908) in the **Shfelah**, SE of Ben Shemen, in memory of Dr Theodor Herzl, the founder of active political Zionism.

(lo doobeem ve-lo) ya'ar לא דובים ולא יער **1.** flat denial; nothing of the kind! **2.** *lit* neither bears nor forest!

□ **Ya'arah** (Ya'ara) יערה *nm* village est 1950 in W. Upper Gallilee, 8 km SE of **Rosh ha-Neekrah**. Pop. 325.

ya'aran/-eem יערן *nm* forester; (*pl+of:* **-ey**).

ya'aranoot יערנות *nf* forestry.

ya'ats/-ah/-tee יעץ *v* advised; (*pres* **meya'ets**; *fut* **yeya'ets**).

yab|ashah/-ashot יבשה *nf* dry land; (*+of:* **-eshet**).

yabashtee/-t יבשתי *adj* continental.

(beyn-) yabashtee/-t בין־יבשתי *adj* inter-continental.

yabayeh! (*correct:* **ya ba'yeh!**) יאבאיה! *interj [slang] (Arab.)* Oh, God! expression of excitement.

yab|elet/-alot יבלת *nf* corn; callus; wart.

yab|eshet/-ashot יבשת *nf* continent; mainland.

yableet יבלית *nf* Bermuda grass.

yad/-ayeem יד *nf* hand; (*pl+of:* **yedey**).

yad יד *nf* memorial; monument.

yad akhat יד אחת *nf* accord; unison.

□ **Yad Avshalom** יד אבשלום *nm* "Absalom's Monument"; ancient tomb traditionally taken to be a monument to King David's treacherous son, outside Jerusalem's Old City Walls.

□ **Yad Beenyameen** (Yad Binyamin) יד בנימין *nm* - educational center (est. 1962) 4 km SE of **Gederah**. Pop. 443.

yad be-yad יד ביד *adv* hand in hand.

□ **Yad ha-Shemonah** (Yad haShemona) יד השמונה *nm* small coop. settlement (est. 1971) in Judean hills, 3 km W. of **Aboo Gosh**. Pop. 80.

yad kmootsah יד קמוצה *nf* (*lit.*) clenched hand; stinginess.

□ **Yad Kennedy** יד קנדי *nm* memorial site (est. 1966) to President John F. Kennedy, located in Jerusalem hills, near **'Ameenadav** village.

□ **Yad Khanah** (Yad Hanna) יד חנה *nm* kibbutz (est. 1950) on very edge of Green Line, where Samaria and Sharon districts meet, 2 km NW of **Toolkarm**. Known as sole kibbutz whose members embrace doctrine of Communism. Pop. 128.

□ **Yad Khanah Me'ookhad** יד חנה מאוחד *nm* (Yad Hanna Me'uhad) kibbutz next to **Yad Khanah** from which it seceded in 1953 when the latter embraced communism.

yad khazakah יד חזקה *nf* strong hand (normally used to describe policy or attitude).

yad khofsheet יד חופשית *nf* free hand; carte blanche.

◇ **Yad la-Baneem** see *npr* ◇ **Yad la-Vaneem**.

◇ **Yad la-Vaneem** יד לבנים *nm* "Memorial to the Sons" - institution existing in every major Israeli town, dedicated to commemorating those fallen in wars fought for survival of the state.

yad/-ayeem moosh|etet/-atot יד מושטת *nf* helping hand; hand stretched out.

□ **Yad Mordekhay** יד מרדכי *nm* kibbutz (est. 1943) in S. of Coastal Plain, 10 km S. of Ashkelon. Pop. 718.

□ **Yad Natan** יד נתן *nm* village (est. 1953) in the **Shefelah**, 6 km NW of Plugot Junction **(Tsomet Ploogot)**. Pop. 275.

yad petookhah יד פתוחה *nf* open hand; generosity.

□ **Yad Rambam** יד רמב"ם *nm* village (est. 1955) in the Shfelah, 5 km SE of Ramla proper. Pop. 540.

□ **Yad va-Shem** יד ושם *nm* national memorial to the 6,000,000 Jews who perished in the Holocaust. Its museum, memorial halls and archives are housed in a compound erected by "**Yad va-Shem** Commemoration Authority" set up under a law of 1953.

('al) yad על יד *adv* near; next to.

('avodat/-ot) yad עבודת יד *nf* handwork; handicraft.

(bee-mekhee) yad במחי יד *adv* with one sweep.

(be-heseg) yad בהישג יד *adv* within reach.

(belem) yad בלם יד *nm* car hand-brake.

(be-mo'al) yad במועל יד *adv* by raising one's hand (in salute).

(her|eem/-eemah/-amtee) yad הרים יד *v* raised a hand; (*pres* **mereem yad;** *fut* **yareem yad**).

(hosh|eet/-eetah/-atetee) yad הושיט יד *v* extended helping hand; (*pres* **mosheet yad;** *fut* **yosheet yad**).

(kaf/kapot) yad/-ayeem *(p=f)* כף יד *nf* palm.

(ke) yad כיד *adv* according to the ability of.

(ke) yad ha-melekh כיד המלך *adv* royally.

(kee-le-akhar) yad כלאחר יד *adv* off-hand.

(kotser) yad קוצר יד *nm* shorthandedness; incapacity.

(ketav/keetvey) yad כתב יד *nm* **1.** handwriting; **2.** manuscript.

(le) yad ליד *adv* near; next to; under the auspices of .

(lekheets|at/-ot) yad לחיצת יד *nf* handshake.

(mee) yad מיד *adv* **1.** immediately; **2.** from the hand of.

(mee) yad le-yad מיד ליד *adv* changing hands; from hand to hand.

(meeshlo'akh) yad משלוח־יד *nm* occupation; profession.

(melekhet) yad מלאכת יד *nf* handicraft.

(nat|an/-nah/-atee) yad נתן יד *v* **1.** lent a hand; **2.** participated; (*pres* **noten** *etc; fut* **yeeten** *etc*).

(ozlat) yad אוזלת יד *nf* incapacity; exhaustion; weakness.

(pash|at/-tah/-atetee) yad פשט יד *v* begged for alms; (*pres* **poshet** *etc; fut* **yeefshot** *etc f=p*).

(posh|et/-tey) yad פושט יד *nm* beggar; mendicant; (*f:* **-et yad**).

(psheet|at/-ot) yad פשיטת יד *nf* mendicancy; begging for alms.

(sam|akh/-khah/-akhtee) yad סמך יד *v* authorized; supported; (*pres* **somekh** *etc; fut* **yeesmokh** *etc*).

(seelook) yad סילוק יד *nm* dispossession.

(shal|akh/-khah/-akhtee) yad שלח יד *v* misappropriated; embezzled; (*pres* **shole'akh yad;** *fut* **yeeshlakh yad**).

(shalakh *etc*) **yad be-naf|sho/-shah** *etc* שלח יד בנפשו *v* committed suicide.

(she'on/-ey) yad שעון יד *nm* wristwatch.

(taman/-nah/-antee) yad be-tsalakhat טמן יד בצלחת *nm* **1.** sat idle; remained impassive; **2.** *lit* kept hand in pocket; (*pres* **tomen** *etc; fut* **yeetmon** *etc*).

yad|ah/-o/-ee/-kha/-ekh ידה/ידו/ידי/ידך/ידך *f & poss.pron* her/his/my/your *m/f etc* hand.

yad|a'/-'ah/-a'tee ידע *v* knew; (*pres* **yode'a';** *fut* **yeda'**).

yada' (*etc*) **et** ידע את *v* had sexual intercourse with (Biblical expression).

yada' (*etc*) **nefesh** ידע נפש *v* knew the heart of; understood; sympathized.

yad|ah/-etah/-eetee even/avaneem ידה אבן *v* threw stone.

yad'an/-eet ידען *nmf* connoisseur.

yadanee/-t ידני *[colloq.] adj* manual.

yadaneet ידנית *[colloq.] adv* manually; by hand.

(be-mo) yad|av/-eha/-ay *etc* במו ידיו *adv* with his/her/my very own hands.

(haram|at/-ot) yadayeem הרמת ידיים *nf* show of hands.

(neteelat) yadayeem נטילת ידיים *nf* washing hands (before a meal).

(rekhav/rakhvat) yadayeem רחב ידיים *adj* spacious.

(teegr|at/-ot) yadayeem תגרת ידיים *nf* fist fight.

yadeed/yededeem ידיד *nm* friend; (*+of:* **yedeed/-ey**).

yadee|t/-yot ידית *nf* handle.

yad|o/-ah/-ee (*etc*) **'al ha-'elyonah** ידו על העליונה has the upper hand.

yad|o/-ah/-ee (*etc*) **'al ha-takhtonah** ידו על התחתונה *v* is at a disadvantage.

(katsrah) yad|o/-ah/-ee *etc* קצרה ידו־ה/ *v* **1.** was in no position; **2.** (*lit.*) his hand was too short; (*pres* **ketsarah** *etc; fut* **teektsar** *etc*).

(meel|e/-'ah/-etee) et yad|o/-ah/-ee *etc* מילא את ידו *v* empowered; authorized.

(sam|akh/-khah/-akhtee) yad|o/-ah/-ee סמך ידו *v* gave his/her/my (*etc*) approval.

(yesh la'al) yad|o/-ah/-ee יש לאל ידו *v* can afford; is/am able to.

yadoo'a'/yedoo'ah ידוע *adj* known; well known.

◇ **(ha-nadeev ha) yadoo'a'** see ◇ **(ha)nadeev ha-yadoo'a'**.

(ka) yadoo'a' כידוע *adv* as known.

ya'eh/ya'ah יאה *adj* proper; fitting.

ya|'eh/-'eem יעה *nm* shovel; spade; scoop (*pl+of:* **-'ey**).

ya'eel/ye'eelah יעיל *adj* efficient.

ya'el/ye'eleem יעל *nm* ibex; mountain goat.

□ **Ya'el** יעל *nm* (Ya'el) rural center in Ta'anakh region, 6 km S. of **'Afoolah**.

ya'en/ye'en|eem יען *nm* ostrich (*pl+of:* **-ey**).

□ **Yafeet** (Yafit) יפית *nm* village (est. 1980) in the S. of Jordan Valley, 3 km S. of ruins of **Alexandreeyon (Keren Sarteba)** hilltop fortress.

yaf|eh/-ah יפה *adj* beautiful; handsome.

yaf|eh/-ah me'od יפה מאד *adj* very beautiful.

yafeh me'od יפה מאד *adv* very well; very nice.

(seefroot) yafah ספרות יפה *nf* fiction; good literature.

□ **Yafo** (*npr* **Yafo**) יפו *nf* Jaffa, 3,000 year-old harbor-town which is now part of Tel-Aviv-Yafo.

yag|a'/-'ah/-a'tee יגע *v* labored; toiled; (*pres* **yage'a'**; *fut* **yeega'**).

yage'a'/yege'ah יגע *adj* exhausted; weary.

('ayef ve) yage'a עייף ויגע *adj* dead tired.

□ **Yagel** יגל *nm* village (est. 1950) 2 km W. of Ben Gurion Airport. Pop. 402.

yagon/yegoneem יגון *nm* sorrow; grief; (*+of:* **yegon/-ey**).

□ **Yagoor** (Yagur) יגור *nm* kibbutz (est. 1922) in Haifa Bay, 12 km SE of Haifa. Pop. 1360.

yahadoot יהדות *nf* **1.** Judaism; **2.** Jewishness; **3.** Jewry.

yahalom/-eem יהלום *nm* diamond; (*pl+of:* **-ey**).

yahaloman/-eem יהלומן *nm* diamond-dealer; (*pl+of:* **-ey**).

□ **Yahel** יהל *nm* kibbutz (est. 1976) in the **'Aravah**, 70 km N. of Elat.

yak|ad/-dah/-adetee יקד *v* burned; blazed; (*pres* **yoked**; *fut* **yeekad**).

yakar/-yekarah יקר *adj* dear; expensive.

yakeenton/-eem יקינתון *nm* hyacinth (flower).

yakeer/-ah יקיר **1.** *adj* beloved; dearest; **2.** *nmf* dear one.

□ **Yakeer** (Yaqqir) יקיר *nm* communal village (est. 1981) 25 km E. of **Petakh Teekvah**. Pop. 351.

yakeeratee יקירתי *nf* my dear one! my darling! (addressing female).

◇ **yakeer/-at yerooshalayeem** (or: **Tel-Aviv, Haifa** *etc*) יקיר ירושלים / תל־אביב / וכו׳ / *nmf* honorary title of Distinguished Citizen bestowed yearly by municipalities of Jerusalem, Tel-Aviv *etc* on meritorious residents who have reached high age.

yakeer|ay/-otay יקיריי *nmf* my dear ones!

yakeeree יקירי *nm* my dear one! darling! (addressing male).

yakeerey karta יקירי קרתא *nm pl* city notables.

yakhad יחד *adv* together.

yakhad 'eem יחד עם *adv* together with.

(be) yakhad ביחד *adv* together.

yakhas/yekhaseem יחס *nm* relation; (*pl+of:* **yakhsey**).

(be) yakhas le- ביחס ל־ *adv* in respect of; concerning.

(meelat/-lot) yakhas מלת יחס *nm* (Gram.) preposition.

yakhsan/-eet יחסן *nmf* **1.** of good descent; **2.** snob; who puts on airs.

yakhasee/-t יחסי *adj* relative; commensurate.

yakhaseet יחסית *adv* relatively; comparatively.

yakhaseeyoot יחסיות *nf* relativity.

(torat ha) yakhasoot תורת היחסות *nf* the Theory of Relativity.

(bekheerot) yakhaseeyot בחירות יחסיות *nf pl* proportional representation (in elections).

yakhasey enosh יחסי אנוש *nm pl* human relations.

yakhasey shekhenoot יחסי שכינות *nm pl* neighborly relations.

yakhasey tseeboor יחסי ציבור *nm pl* public relations.

yakheed/yekheedah יחיד *adj* single; singular.

yakheed/yekheedah be-dor|o/-ah יחיד בדורו *adj* unique in his/her generation.

yakheed/yekheedah be-meen|o/-ah יחיד במינו *adj* unique; one of his/her/its kind.

(ben/bat) yakheed/yekheedah בן/בת יחיד/ה *nmf* only son/daughter.

(leshon) yakheed לשון יחיד *nf* Gram. singular.

(reshoot ha) yakheed רשות היחיד *nf* private domain.

□ **Yakheenee** (Yakhini) יכיני *nm* village (est. 1950) in NW Negev, 4 km 34 S. of **Sderot** township. Pop. 437.

yakhef/yekhefah יחף *adj* barefoot.

yakhfan/-eet יחפן *nmf* ragamuffin (*pl+of:* **-ey**).

yakhol/yekholah יכול *v pres* can; is able; (*pst* **yakhol hayah**; *fut* **yookhal**).

yakhol leehyot יכול להיות could be; possibly.

(kee-ve) yakhol כביכול *adv* so to speak; as it were.

(kol-) yakhol/yekholah כל יכול *adj* omnipotent.

yakhsan/-eet יחסן *nmf* **1.** of good descent; **2.** snob; who puts on airs.

yakhsee/-t (*npr* **yakhasee/-t**) יחסי *adj* relative; commensurate.

yakhseet (*npr* **yakhaseet**) יחסית *adv* relatively; comparatively.

yakhseeyoot יחסיות *nf* relativity.

(torat ha) yakhseeyoot (*npr* **yakhasoot**) תורת היחסיות *nf* the Theory of Relativity.

(bekheerot) yakhseeyot (*npr* **yakhaseeyot**) בחירות יחסיות *nf pl* proportional representation (in elections).

yakhsey (*npr* **yakhasey**) **enosh** יחסי אנוש *nm pl* human relations.

yakhsey (*npr* **yakhasey**) **sh'khenoot** יחסי שכינות *nm pl* neighborly relations.

yakhsey (*npr* **yakhasey**) **tseeboor** יחסי ציבור *nm pl* public relations.

yakht|ah/-ot יאכטה *nf* yacht (*+of:* **-at**).

yakhtsan/-eet יחצ״ן *nmf* P.R. man/woman; Public relations man/woman (*acr of* **YAKHasey TSeeboor** יחסי־ציבור).

□ **Yakoom** (Yaqum) יקום *nm* kibbutz (est. 1947) in Sharon, 10 km N. of **Hertseleeyah**. Pop. 456.

yakran/-eet יקרן *adj & nmf* one whose prices are high; high-priced; expensive.

yallah! !יאללה *interj [slang] (Arab.)* yallah! let's go! come on! go on!

yal|dah/-adet/-adetee ילדה *v pst f sing/pl* gave birth; (*pres* **yoledet**; *fut* **teled**).

yaldah/yeladot ילדה *nf* girl; small girl; (*+of:* **yald |at/-ot**).

yaldat pele ילדת פלא *nf* child prodigy (girl).

yaldon ילדון *nm [slang]* boy; young brat.

yaldonet ילדונת *nf* little girl (pet name).

yaldoot ילדות *nf* childhood.

yaldootee/-t ילדותי *adj* childish.

yaldooteeyoot ילדותיות *nf* childishness.

yaleed/yeleedah יליד *nmf* native; (*+of:* **yeleed/ -at**).

yalkoot/-eem ילקוט *nm* **1.** bag; satchel; **2.** anthology; (*pl+of:* **-ey**).

yam/-eem ים *nm* sea.

□ **Yam Keeneret** ים כנרת *nm* Sea of Kinneret, (know also as Sea of Galilee and Lake of Tiberias), Israel's largest (4 billion cubic meters) body of sweet water. A harp-shaped natural lake in N. Jordan Valley, it is located 212 *m.* below sea-level and covers 170 square km. Its shores provide some of country's most picturesque scenery and recreation spots.

□ **Yam ha-Melakh** ים המלח *nm* (*lit.:* Salt Sea) Dead Sea, lowest place on earth (398 *m* below-sea-level), 80 km long, covering 1,000 square km. It also forms a 15 km wide (at its largest) boundary between Israel and Jordan.

□ **Yam Soof** ים סוף *nm* Red Sea.

□ **(Bat) Yam** see □ **Bat-Yam.**

(be-lev) yam בלב ים *adv* on high seas.

(ha) yam ha-adree'atee הים האדריאטי *nm* Adriatic Sea.

(ha) yam ha-baltee הים הבלטי *nm* Baltic Sea.

(ha) yam ha-'ege'ee הים האגאי *nm* Aegean Sea.

(ha) yam ha-kaspee הים הכספי *nm* Caspian Sea.

(ha) yam ha-lavan הים הלבן *nm* White Sea.

(ha) yam ha-shakhor הים השחור *nm* Black Sea.

(ha) yam ha-teekhon הים התיכון *nm* Mediterranean Sea.

(ha) yam ha-tsfoonee הים הצפוני *nm* North Sea.

(khazeer/-ey) yam חזיר ים *nm* guinea-pig.

(khof ha) yam חוף הים *nm* seashore.

(makhlat) yam מחלת ים *nf* sea-sickness; nausea.

(me-'ever le) yam מעבר לים *adv* overseas.

(pney ha) yam פני הים *nf pl* sea-level.

(sfat ha) yam שפת הים *nf* coastline.

(shoded/-ey) yam שודד ים *nm* pirate.

(yor|ed/-dey) yam יורד ים *nm* seafarer.

(ze'ev ha) yam זאב הים *nm* sea-wolf; hake (fish).

yam|ah/-mot ימה *nf* lake; (*+of:* **-at**).

yama'oot ימאות *nf* seamanship.

(bee-d'mee) yam|av/-eha בדמי ימיו *adv* in the prime of his/her life.

yam|ay/-a'eem (*cpr* **yam|a'ee**) ימאי *nm* seaman; (*pl+of:* **-a'ey**).

(mee) yam|av/-ay/-eha/-ekha lo (*etc*) מימיו לא וכו' never has/have he/I/she/you (*etc*)...

yamee/-t ימי *adj* maritime; naval.

yameem ימים **1.** *nm pl* (*sing* **yam** ים) seas; (*pl+of* **yamey**); **2.** *nm pl* (*sing* **yom** יום) days; (*pl+of:* **yemey**).

◇ **yameem nora'eem** ימים נוראים *nm pl* "Ten Days of Awe" (for repentance) from Rosh ha-Shana through Yom Kippur.

◇ **(akhreet ha) yameem** see ◇ **akhreet ha-yameem.**

(areekhoot) yameem אריכות ימים *nf* longevity; long life.

(ba/-'ah ba) yameem בא בימים *adj* getting old; elderly; advanced in age.

(bee-revot ha) yameem ברבות הימים *adv* in time; as time goes by.

(deevrey ha) yameem דברי הימים *nm pl* **1.** annals; history; **2.** (Bibl.) Book of Chronicles.

(he'er|eekh/-eekhah/-akhtee) yameem האריך ימים *v* went on to live; lived long; (*pres* **ma'areekh** *etc; fut* **ya'areekh** *etc*).

(le-orekh) yameem לאורך ימים *adv* in the long run; for long.

(mee) yameem yameemah מימים ימימה *adv* each year; annually.

('ool/-ey) yameem עול ימים *nm* youngster.

◇ **(ta'alat ha) yameem** see ◇ **te'alat ha-yameem.**

yameen ימין *nm* **1.** right (hand); **2.** the (political) Right; (*+of:* **yemeen**).

yameen oo-smol ימין ושמאל *adv* right and left.

yan|ak/-kah/-aktee ינק *v* **1.** sucked; **2.** *figurat* absorbed; (*pres* **yonek**; *fut* **yeenak**).

yanoo'ar ינואר *nm* January.

yanooka ינוקא *nm* babe; child;

◇ **(rabee-) yanooka** see ◇ **rabee-yanooka.**

□ **Yanoov** (Yanuv) ינוב *nm* village (est. 1950) in the Sharon, 5 km SE of **Tsomet ha-Sharon** (haSharon Junction). Pop. 335.

yanshoof/-eem ינשוף *nm* owl; (*pl+of:* **-ey**).

ya'oot/ye'ootah יאות *adj* proper; befitting.

(ka) ya'oot כיאות *adv* properly.

yar|ah/-tah/-eetee ירה *v* shot; fired; (*pres* **yoreh**; *fut* **yeereh**).

yar|ad/-dah/-adetee ירד *v* descended; came down; (*pres* **yored**; *fut* **yered**).

◇ **"yarad"** (*etc*) ירד *v figurat* emigrated from Israel (*lit.:* descended, went down).

yarad (*etc*) **le-kha|yey/-yay/-yav/-yeha** ירד לחיי/לחייו/לחייה *v* made one's/my/his/her life miserable; tormented; persecuted.

yarad (*etc*) **le-teemyon** ירד לטמיון *v* went down the drain.

yarad (*etc*) **pla'eem** ירד פלאים *v* went down (diminished, decreased) considerably.

yarad (*etc*) **mee-nekhas|av/-eha** *etc* ירד מנכסיו/ה *v* lost all his/her etc wealth.

yar|ak/-kah/-aktee ירק *v* spat; (*pres* **yorek;** *fut* **yeerak**).

yarak/yerakot ירק *nm* vegetable.

(gan/-ey) yarak גן ירק *nm* vegetable garden.

yar|ash/-shah/-tee ירש *v* inherited (*pres* **yoresh;** *fut* **yeerash**).

□ **Yarden** ירדן *nm* Jordan river - largest water-stream in Israel (250 km long) feeding both Sea of Galilee and Dead Sea as well as Israel's artificial irrigation lifeline (Jordan-Negev Pipeline). It serves, from Gesher-Naharayeem southward, as Israel's border with the Kingdom of Jordan.

□ **(Beek'at ha) Yarden** see □ **'Emek ha-Yarden.**

□ **('Emek ha) Yarden** see □ **'Emek ha-Yarden.**

□ **(mamlekhet) yarden** see □ **mamlekhet yarden.**

□ **Yardenah** (Yardena) ירדנה *nm* village (est. 1952) in Jordan Valley, 10 km NE of Bet-She'an. Pop. 338.

yare/yere'ah ירא *adj* fearful.

yar|e/-'ah ירא *v* feared; (*pres* **yare;** *fut* **yeera**).

yare'akh/yerekh|eem ירח *nm* moon; (*pl+of:* **-ey**).

yareev/yereeveem יריב *nm* opponent; adversary; rival; (*+of:* **yereev/-ey**).

yarekh/yerekhayeem ירך *nf* hip; thigh; loin; (*pl+of:* **yarkhey**).

yarkan/-eem ירקן *nm* greengrocer; (*pl+of:* **-ey**).

yar|khatayeem ירכתיים *nm pl* **1.** stern (in a ship); **2.** remote corner; (*pl+of:* **-ketey;** *(k=kh)*).

□ **Yarkheev** (Yarhiv) ירחיב *nm* village (est. 1949) on Green Line, 5 km E. of **Kefar Saba**, 4 km S. of **Kalkeeleeyah** (Qalqilya). Pop. 436.

(lee-kh'she) yarkheev לכשירחיב *adv* when things get better (financially).

yarkhon/-eem ירחון *nm* monthly (magazine); (*pl+of:* **-ey**).

□ **Yarkon** (Yarqon) ירקון *nm* **Yarkon** river, a winding brook, 30 km long, starting beyond **Petakh Teekvah**, with estuary into Mediterranean just N. of the center of Tel-Aviv. Serves the the city as a landmark and demarcation-line between the town "proper" and its "across the Yarkon" **(me-'ever la-yarkon)** residential areas to which 3 bridges serve as sole connections.

□ **Yarkonah** (Yarqona) ירקונה *nm* village (est. 1932) in Sharon, 4 km S. of **Kefar Saba**. Pop. 150.

yarod ירוד *nm* cataract (Medic.).

yarood/yeroodah ירוד *adj* low; reduced.

yas|ad/-dah/-adetee יסד *v* founded; established; (*pres* **meyased;** *fut* **yeyased**).

yash י"ש *nm abbr.* (*acr.* of: **yeyn saraf** יין שרף) brandy.

yashan/yeshanah ישן **1.** *adj* old (object); **2.** *adj* old (person) see **zaken/zekenah.**

yashan/yeshanah noshan/-ah ישן נושן *adj* very old; ancient.

yash|an/-nah/-antee ישן *v* slept; (*pres* **yashen;** *fut* **yeeshan**).

yashar/yesharah ישר *adj* straight; honest.

yashar ישר *adv* straight; directly.

yashar ve-la-'eenyan ישר ולעניין *adv* straight to the point.

(neeg|ash/-shah/-ashtee) yashar la-'eenyan ניגש ישר לעניין *v* went straight to the point; (*pres* **neegash** *etc;* *fut* **yeegash** *etc*).

(ha-sekhel ha) yashar השכל הישר *nm* common sense.

yash|av/-vah/-avtee ישב *v* sat; (*pres* **yoshev;** *fut* **yeshev**).

yashav (*etc*) **'al ha-medokhah** ישב על המדוכה *v* was searching for a solution.

yashav (*etc*) **be-deen** ישב בדין *v* sat in court.

yashav (*etc*) **be-rosh** ישב בראש *v* presided; chaired.

◇ **yashav** (*etc*) **"sheev'ah"** ישב שבעה *v* "sat" in observance of "7 days of mourning" (see ◇ **sheev'ah**).

yasheer/yesheerah ישיר *adj* direct; through.

(kheeyoog) yasheer חיוג ישיר *nm* direct dialing (telephone).

(otoboos) yasheer אוטובוס ישיר *nm* direct (non-stop) bus to destination-point.

(zerem) yasheer זרם ישיר *nm* direct current (Electr.).

yasheesh/yesheesh|ah ישיש *nmf* old man/woman; (*pl:* **-eem;** *+of:* **-ey**).

yashen/yeshenah ישן **1.** *adj* asleep; sleeping; **2.** *v pres* sleeps; (*pst* **yashan;** *fut* **yeeshan**).

yashoov/yeshoovah ישוב *adj* seated.

□ **Yashresh** ישרש *nm* village (est. 1950) 3 km S. of Ramla. Pop. 367.

yashvan/-eem ישבן *nm* behind; buttocks; (*pl+of:* **-ey**).

yashvan/-eet ישבן *nmf* capable of persistence and learning.

yasmeen/-eem יסמין *nm* jasmine (flower).

yas'oor/-eem יסעור *nm* shearwater; puffin (bird); (*pl+of:* **-ey**).

□ **Yas'oor** (Yas'ur) יסעור *nm* kibbutz (est. 1949) in W. Galilee, 10 km E. of Acre (**'Ako**), 2 km S. of Ahihud Junction (**Tsomet Akheehood**). Pop. 350.

yated/yetedot יתד *nm* peg; wedge; stake.

□ **Yated** יתד *nm* village (est. 1980) in Shalom district, 9 km SW of **Kerem Shalom**.

yater 'al ken יתר על כן *adv* furthermore; moreover.

yatmoot יתמות *nf* orphanhood.

yatom/yetom|ah יתום *nmf* orphan; (*pl:* **-eem/-ot;** *+of:* **-ey**).

yatoosh (*cpr* **yeetoosh**) **/-eem** יתוש *nm* mosquito; (*pl+of:* **-ey**).

yats|a/-'ah/-atee יצא *v* went out; left; came out; (*pres* **yotse;** *fut* **yetse**).

yatsa (*etc*) **bee-shleekhoot** יצא בשליחות *v* left on a mission.
yatsa (*etc*) **be-shalom** יצא בשלום *v* got out safe and sound; came out unscathed and sound.
yatsa (*etc*) **be-shen va-'ayeen** יצא בשן ועין *v* came out by the skin of one's teeth; suffered serious losses.
yatsa (*etc*) **le-geemla'ot** יצא לגמלאות *v* retired; was pensioned.
yatsa (*etc*) **le-khool** יצא לחו"ל *v* went abroad.
yatsa (*etc*) **le-'or** יצא לאור *v* appeared in print; was published.
yatsa (*etc*) **la-po'al** יצא לפועל *v* was carried out; was executed.
yatsa (*etc*) **mee-da'at|o/-ah/-ee** *etc* יצא מדעתו *v* went out of his/her/my (*etc*) mind.
yatsa (*etc*) **mee-geedr|o/-ah/-ee** *etc* יצא מגדרו *v* **1.** went out of his/her/my (*etc*) way; **2.** burst out.
yatsa (*etc*) **mee-kel|av/-eha/-ay** *etc* יצא מכליו *v* lost his/her/my (*etc*) temper.
yatsa (*etc*) **neezok/-ah** יצא ניזוק *v* sustained damage.
yatsa (*etc*) **skhar|o/-ah/-ee be-hefsed|o/-ah/-ee** יצא שכרו בהפסדו *v* his/her/my gain wasn't worth the candle; his/her/my loss exceeded the profit.
yatsa (*etc*) **yedey khovah** יצא ידי חובה *v* did his/her/my duty.
yatsa (*etc*) **zak|ay/-a'eet** יצא זכאי *v* was acquitted.
yats|ak/-kah/-aktee יצק *v* **1.** poured; **2.** cast; (*pres* **yotsek**; *fut* **yeetsok**).
yats'anee|t/-yot יצאנית *nf* hooker; streetwalker; prostitute.
yats|ar/-rah/-artee יצר *v* created; (*pres* **yotser**; *fut* **yeetsor**).
yatsee'a'/yetsee|'eem יציע *nm* balcony (in theater); (*pl+of:* **-'ey**).
□ **Yatseets** (Yaziz) יציץ *nm* village (est. 1950) 7 km S. of Ramla. Pop. 349.
yatseev/yetseevah יציב *adj* firm; stable.
(matbe'a) yatseev מטבע יציב *nm* stable currency.
yatseevoo|t/-yot יציבות *nf* stability.
yatsook/yetsookah יצוק *adj* cast; poured.
yats'oo lo/-lah/-lee (*etc*) **moneeteen** יצאו לו/לה מוניטין *v* gained a reputation; earned fame.
yatsran/-eem יצרן *nm* manufacturer; producer.
Yavan יוון *nf* Greece.
yav|ash/-shah/-ashtee יבש *v* dried; dried out; (*pres* **yavesh**; *fut* **yeebash** (*b=v*)).
□ **Yavne'el** יבנאל *nm* large rural settlement (est. 1901) in Lower Galilee 10 km SW of Tiberias. Pop. 1,700.
□ **Yavneh** (Yavne) יבנה *nf* township (est. 1949) in the central part of the coastal plain, 8 km SW of Rehovot (**Rekhovot**). Pop. 22,700.
yavo'! יבוא! *v imp* come in!
(hemshekh) yavo המשך יבוא to be continued; continuation follows.
□ **Yavor** יבור *nf* large farm (est. 1952) in Lower Galilee, 2 km SE of Ahihud Junction (**Tsomet Akheehood**).
yayeen/yeynot יין *nm* wine; (*+of:* **yeyn**).
yaz|am/-mah/-amtee יזם *v* initiated; prompted; (*pres* **yozem**; *fut* **yeezom**).
yazam/-eem יזם *nm* initiator; promoter; (*pl+of:* **-ey**).
□ **Ye'af** (Ye'af) יעף *nm* rural supply center (est. 1968) in Sharon, 10 km SE of Netanya. Pop. 29.
yeda' ידע *nm* know-how; knowledge.
yedee|'ah/-'ot ידיעה *nf* **1.** news; **2.** knowledge; (*+of:* **-'at**).
yedee'at ha-arets ידיעת הארץ *nf* geography of Israel.
yedeed (*npr* **yadeed**) **/yedee|eem** ידיד *nm* friend; (*pl+of:* **-ey**).
yedeed/-ey nefesh ידיד נפש *nmf* bosom-friend.
yedeed|ah/-ot ידידה *nf* girlfriend; (*+of:* **-at**).
□ **Yedeedah** (Yedida) ידידה *nm* special education establishment (est. 1960) in Jerusalem hills, half way between **Aboo-Gosh** village and kibbutz **Ma'aleh ha-Khameeshah**. Pop. 124.
yedeedoo|t/-yot ידידות *nf* friendship.
yedeedootee/-t ידידותי *adj* friendly; amiable.
□ **Yedeedyah** (Yedidya) ידידיה *nm* village (est. 1935) in Sharon, 3 km N. of haSharon Road Junction). Pop. 397.
yedee'on/-eem ידיעון *nm* bulletin; (*pl+of:* **-ey**).
yedee'ot ידיעות *nf pl* (*sing:* **yedee'ah**) news.
(sheroot/-ey) yedee'ot שירות ידיעות *nm* news-service.
(sokhnoo|t/-yot) yedee'ot סוכנות ידיעות *nf* news-agency.
yedey (*pl:* **yadayeem**) ידי *nm pl+of* the hands of...
('al) yedey על ידי *prep* by: by means of: through.
('al) yedey kakh על ידי כך *adv* thereby; by that.
(lee) yedey לידי *prep* to; into the hands of; into a position of.
(meel|e/-'ah/-e'tee) yedey מילא ידי *v* empowered; authorized; (*pres* **memale** *etc*; *fut* **yemale** *etc*).
(reep|ah/-ptah/-eetee) yedey ריפה ידי *v* discouraged; (*pres* **merapeh** *etc*; *fut* **yerapeh** *etc*).
yedoo'ah be-tseeboor ידועה בציבור *nf* reputed wife; common-law wife.
yeeb|esh/-shah/-ashtee ייבש *v* dried; (*pres* **meyabesh**; *fut* **yeyabesh**).
yeeb|ev/-evah/-avtee יבב *v* sobbed; whimpered; (*pres* **meyabev**; *fut* **yeyabev**).
yeeboo ייבוא *nm* importation.
yeeboo khozer ייבוא חוזר *nm* reimportation.
yeeboosh/-eem *nm* drying; drainage.
yeed|ah/-etah/-eetee יידה *v* hurled; threw; (*pres* **meyadeh**; *fut* **yeyadeh**).
yeedah (*etc*) **avaneem** יידה אבנים *v* threw stones.

yeedeesh יידיש or אידיש *nf* Yiddish, German-like language that has been, and partly still is, the lingua franca of East European Jews and their descendants in other countries.

yeedeesha'ee/-t יידישאי or אידישאי *adj* of, or pertaining to, Yiddish.

yeedeeshee/-t יידישי or אידישי *adj [colloq.]* of, or pertaining to, Yiddish.

yeedeesheest/-eet יידישיסט or אידישיסט *nmf* **1.** devotee of Yiddish; **2.** partisan of Yiddishism.

yeedeesheez|em/-meem יידישיזם or אידישיזם *nm* **1.** Yiddish phrase, word or idiom; **2.** ideology advocating the hegemony of Yiddish as the national tongue of the Jewish people.

yeedooy יידוי *nf* hurling; throwing.

yeedooy avaneem יידוי אבנים *nf* stone throwing.

yee|'el/-'alah/-'altee ייעל *v* rendered efficient; (*pres* **meya'el**; *fut* **yeya'el**).

ye'eeloo|t/-yot יעילות *nf* efficiency.

□ **Yeef'at** (Yif'at) יפעת *nm* kibbutz (est. 1952) in Yizre'el Valley, near **Meegdal ha-'Emek**. Pop. 820.

□ **Yeeftakh** (Yiftah) יפתח *nm* kibbutz (est. 1948) in Upper Galilee, 9 km S. of **Keeryat Shmonah**. Pop. 536.

yeek|er/-rah/-artee ייקר *v* increased prices; (*pres* **meyaker**; *fut* **yeyaker**).

yeekh|ed/-adah/-adetee ייחד *v* singled out; set apart; (*pres* **meyakhed**; *fut* **yeyakhed**).

yeekhed (*etc*) **et ha-deeboor** ייחד את הדיבור *v* dwelt on; discussed.

yeekh|el/-alah/-altee ייחל *v* hoped for; waited; (*pres* **meyakhel**; *fut* **yeyakhel**).

yeekhes ייחס *v* attributed; (*pres* **meyakhes**; *fut* **yeyakhes**).

yeekhood ייחוד *nm* uniqueness; setting up.

(be) yeekhood בייחוד *adv* especially.

yeekhoodee/-t ייחודי *adj* exclusive.

yeekhoom/-eem ייחום *nm* **1.** sexual heat (in animals); **2.** *[slang]* sexual excitement (in humans).

yeekhoos/-eem ייחוס *nm* **1.** attribution; **2.** pedigree; lineage.

yeekoor/-eem ייקור *nm* **1.** rise of prices; **2.** endearment.

yeel|el/-elah/-altee יילל *v* howled; lamented; (*pres* **meyalel**; *fut* **yeyalel**).

□ **Yeenon** (Yinnon) ינון *nm* village (est. 1952) in **Shfelah**, 2 km S. of Re'em Junction (**Tsomet Re'em**). Pop. 549.

yee'ool ייעול *nm* improving efficiency.

yeep|ah/-tah/-eetee ייפה *v* beautified; adorned; (*pres* **meyapeh**; *fut* **yeyapeh**).

yeepah (*etc*) **ko'akh** ייפה כוח *v* **1.** authorized; empowered; **2.** gave power of attorney to; (*pres* **meyapeh** *etc*; *fut* **yeyapeh** *etc*).

yeepooy/-eem ייפוי *nm* beautification.

yeepoo|y/-yey ko'akh ייפוי כוח *nm* power of attorney.

yeer|'ah יראה *nf* fright; fear; (*+of:* **-at**).

yeer'at kavod יראת כבוד *nf* awe; respect.

yeer'at khet יראת חטא *nf* fear of sin.

yeer'at shamayeem יראת שמיים *nf* fear of God.

□ **Yeer'on** (Yir'on) יראון *nm* kibbutz (est. 1949) in Upper Gallilee, near Lebanese border. Pop. 341.

(eem) yeertseh ha-Shem אם ירצה השם God willing; by the grace of God.

(bal) yeesafer בל ייספר *adj* countless.

(lo) yeesafer לא ייספר *adj* countless.

yees|ed/-dah/-adetee ייסד *nf* founded; established; (*pres* **meyased**; *fut* **yeyased**).

yees|em/-mah/-amtee יישם *v* applied; put to use; (*pres* **meyasem**; *fut* **yeyasem**).

yees|er/-rah/-artee ייסר *v* chastized; rebuked; (*pres* **meyaser**; *fut* **yeyaser**).

yeeshar ko'akh! יישר כוח! (greeting) bravo! you were good, indeed! excellent performance!

□ **Yeesh'ee** (Yish'i) ישעי *nm* village (est. 1950) 2 km W. of Bet-Shemesh. Pop. 448.

yeesh|er/-rah/-artee יישר *v* straightened; (*pres* **meyasher**; *fut* **yeyasher**).

yeesh|ev/-vah/-avtee יישב *v* populated; settled; (*pres* **meyashev**; *fut* **yeyashev**).

yeeshev (*etc*) **seekhsookh** יישב סכסוך *v* settled a dispute.

yeeshoor/-eem יישור *nm* rectification; straightening; (*pl+of:* **-ey**).

yeeshoor karka' יישור קרקע *nm* leveling ground.

yeeshoor sheenayeem יישור שיניים *nm* orthodontics.

yeeshoov/-eem יישוב *nm* settlement; (*pl+of:* **-ey**).

yeeshoov da'at יישוב דעת *nm* presence of mind.

yeeshoov seekhsookh/-eem יישוב סכסוך *nm* settling a dispute.

yeeshoov/-ey sfar יישוב ספר *nm* frontier settlement.

◇ **(ha)yeeshoov** היישוב *nm* "the Yishuv", name by which Palestine's Jewish population was referred to in the pre-State era.

(nekood|at/-ot) yeeshoov נקודת יישוב *nf* inhabited place.

yeesoom/-eem יישום *nm* realization; application; putting into practice; (*pl+of:* **-ey**).

yeesoor|eem ייסורים *nm pl* tribulations; sufferings; (*+of:* **-ey**).

yeesra'el ישראל **1.** *nm* Israel (the nation); **2.** *nf* Israel (the State).

◇ **(erets) yeesra'el** see ◇ **erets yeesra'el**.

◇ **(erets) yeesra'el ha-shlemah** see ◇ **erets yeesra'el ha-shlemah**.

yeesre'elee/-t ישראלי *mf & adj* Israeli.

(ezrakh/-eet) yeesre'lee/-t אזרח ישראלי *mf* Israeli citizen; Israeli national.

(matbe'a') yeesre'lee מטבע ישראלי *nm* Israeli currency.

yeetakhen ייתכן *conj* perhaps.

(lo) yeetakhen לא ייתכן *adv* impossible; couldn't be.

yeet|aron/-ronot (*npr* **yeetron/-ot**) יתרון *nm* advantage.

□ **Yeetav** (Yitav) ייט״ב *nm* kibbbutz (est. 1970) in Jordan Valley, 10 km NW of Jericho.

yeetr|ah/-ot ייתרה *nf* remainder; surplus; rest; balance; (*+of:* **-at**).

yeetron/-ot יתרון *nm* advantage.

yeets|e/-'ah/-etee ייצא *v* exported; (*pres* **meyatse**; *fut* **yeyatse**).

yeets|eg/-gah/-agtee ייצג *v* represented; (*pres* **meyatseg**; *fut* **yeyatseg**).

yeets|ev/-vah/-avtee ייצב *v* stabilized; (*pres* **meyatsev**; *fut* **yeyatsev**).

yeets'har יצהר *nm* pure olive oil; pure vegetable oil.

yeetsoo ייצוא **1.** exportation; exporting; **2.** *[colloq.]* export (correct term: **yetsoo**).

yeetsoog/-eem ייצוג *nm* representation.

yeetsoogee/-t ייצוגי *adj* representative.

◇ **(dargah) yeetsoogeet** see ◇ **dargah yeetsoogeet**.

yeetsoor/-eem ייצור *nm* manufacturing; production.

(peeryon ha) yeetsoor פריון הייצור *nm* productivity.

yeetsoov/-eem ייצוב *nm* stabilization.

yeetsoov ha-matbe'a' ייצוב המטבע *nm* currency stabilization.

yeevoo (*npr* **yeeboo**) ייבוא *nm* importation.

◇ **"yeezkor"** יזכור *nf* "Yizkor" - memorial prayer for deceased relatives (recited in synagogue on Yom Kippur, Shavuot and last day of Succot and Passover).

□ **Yeezre'am** (Yizre'am) יזרעם *nm* seed-growing farm (est. 1954) in NW Negev, 3 km NW of **Tsomet Neteevot** (Netivot Junction).

□ **Yeezre'el** (Yizre'el) יזרעאל *nm* kibbutz (est. 1948) in Yizre'el Valley, 6 km SE of **'Afoolah**. Pop. 490.

□ **('Emek) Yeezre'el** see □ **'Emek Yeezre'el**.

yef|at/-ot mar'eh יפת מראה **1.** *nf* (a) beauty; **2.** *adj* beautiful; goodlooking; (applicable to females only).

yef|eh/-at nefesh יפה נפש *adj & nmf* **1.** high-minded; gentle; **2.** sarcastic reference to a disgruntled (leftist) intellectual; (*pl:* **-ey** *etc*).

yef|eh/-at nof יפה נוף *adj* of beautiful scenery.

yefehf|eh/-eeyah יפהפה *adj* beautiful.

yefehfee|yah/-yot יפהפייה *nf* belle; beauty (female).

yefey ha-nefesh יפי הנפש *nm pl* **1.** those of "gentle soul"; **2.** sarcastic reference to disgruntled, leftist intelligentsia; (*sing:* **yef|eh/-at** *etc*).

yega' יגע *nm* toil; exertion.

yegee'a' kapayeem יגיע כפיים *nm* laboring with one's hands; handiwork.

yegee|'ah/-'ot יגיעה *nf* toil; pain; (*+of:* **'at**).

yehe/tehe יהא *v fut sing m/f* let there be; be it.

yehee/tehee יהי *v fut sing m/f* let there be; be it.

□ **Yehood** (Yehud) יהוד *nf* town (est. 1948) in central coastal plain, 5 km N. of Ben Gurion Airport. Pop. 16,200.

yehood|ee/-eem יהודי *nm* Jew; (*pl+of:* **-ey**).

yehoodee/-t יהודי *adj* Jewish.

yehoodee/-yah יהודי *nmf* Jew.

◇ **(mee hoo) yehoodee?** see ◇ **mee hoo yehoodee?**

◇ **(ha-sokhnoot ha) yehoodeet** see ◇ **(ha)sokhnoot ha-yehoodeet**.

(toda'ah) yehoodeet תודעה יהודית *nf* Jewish consciousness; awareness of being a Jew.

yehoodee|yah/-yot יהודייה *nf* Jewish woman.

yehoodon/-eem יהודון *nm* Jewboy (derisively); Jew as referred to by antisemites.

yekar יקר *nm* honor; worthiness.

yekar/yeekrat ha-metsee'oot יקר המציאות *adj* rare; scarce.

yekar|ah/-ot יקרה *adj - nf* (*m:* **yakar**) dear; expensive.

◇ **yek|eh/-eet** יקה **1.** *nmf [colloq.]* German-born Jew; **2.** *adj* punctual, pedantic (reputed characteristics of German Jews).

yekeets|ah/-ot יקיצה *nf* awakening; (*+of:* **-at**).

◇ **yekeets|ah/-ot** יקיצה *nf* the telephonic "wake up call" automatic service (in Israel: dial 174 or 175).

yek|ev/-aveem יקב *nm* wine cellar; wine press; (*pl+of:* **yeekvey**).

yekhaseem benle'oomeeyeem יחסים בינלאומיים *nm pl* international relations.

(kash|ar/-rah/-artee) yekhaseem קשר יחסים *v* established relations; (*pres* **kosher** *etc; fut* **yeekshor** *etc*).

(heetkhadedoot) yekhaseem התחדדות יחסים *nf* exacerbation.

(neetook) yekhaseem ניתוק יחסים *nm* severance of relations.

(kee|yem/-yemah/-yamtee) yekhaseem קיים יחסים **1.** - *v* maintained relations with; **2.** had sexual intercourse.

□ **Yekhee'am** (Yehi'am) יחיעם *nm* kibbutz (est. 1946) in Upper Galilee, 12 km W. of Nahariyya. Pop. 479.

yekheed|ah/-ot יחידה *nf* unit; (*+of:* **-at**).

yekheed|ah/-ot kravee|t/-yot יחידה קרבית *nf* fighting unit; combat unit.

(bat) yekheedah בת יחידה *nf* only daughter.

yekheed|ee/-ah יחידי *adj* singular; alone.

(lee) yekheedeem ליחידים *adv* in retail.

yekheedey segoolah יחידי סגולה *pl & adj pl* outstanding people; people who are one in a million.

yekheedoot יחידות *nf* singularity; uniqueness.

(bee) yekheedoot ביחידות *adv* in private; privately.

yekoom יקום *nm* universe.

yekholet יכולת *nf* ability, capability.

('ad ketseh gevool ha) yekholet עד קצה גבול היכולת *adv* to exhaustion; to the very limit of one's capacity.

(ba'al/-at) yekholet בעל יכולת *nmf* person with potential; man of means.

(ba'aley) yekholet בעלי יכולת *nm pl* people with means.

(meed|at/-ot ha) yekholet מידת היכולת *nf* potential.

(me'ootey) yekholet מעוטי יכולת *adj pl & nm pl* people without means.

(ne'd|ar/-rat) yekholet נעדר יכולת *adj* lacking ability; in no position to...

yelad|eem/-ot ילדים *nmf pl* (*sing:* **yeled/yaldah**) children; (*+of:* **yald|ey/-ot**).

('egl|at/-ot) yeladeem עגלת ילדים *nf* baby-carriage.

(gan/ey) yeladeem גן ילדים *nm* kindergarten.

(geedool) yeladeem גידול ילדים *nm* raising children.

(khad|ar/-rey) yeladeem חדר ילדים *nm* nursery; children's room.

(meeshpakh|ah/-ot brookhat/-ot) yeladeem משפחה ברוכת ילדים *nf* family with many children.

(rof|e/-'at or *(npr)* **/-et) yeladeem** רופא ילדים *nmf* pediatrician.

(seepoorey) yeladeem סיפורי ילדים *nm pl* children's stories.

(sheetook) yeladeem שיתוק ילדים *nm* polio infantile paralysis; (Medic.).

yelal|ah/-ot יללה *nf* howl; wail; (*+of:* **-at**).

yel|ed/-adeem ילד *nm* child; small boy; (*pl+of:* **yaldey**).

yeled/yaldey pele' ילד פלא *nm* wonder boy; child prodigy.

yeleed/-ah יליד *nmf* native; (*nf+of:* **-at**; *nm & pl* **-ey**).

yeleed/-ey ha-arets יליד הארץ *nm & adj* "Sabra": native-born Israeli.

yelood|ah/ot ילודה *nf* birthrate; (*+of:* **-at**).

(hagbalat ha) yeloodah הגבלת הילודה *nf* birth-control.

yemam|ah/-ot יממה *nf* 24 hour period; (*+of:* **-at**).

yemanee/-t ימני **1.** *adj* right; **2.** *nmf & adj* political rightist.

(mekasher) yemanee מקשר ימני *nm* right inside forward (Soccer).

yemeen (*npr* **yameen**) ימין *nm* **1.** right (hand); **2.** the (political) Right; (*+of:* **yemeen**).

yemeen (*npr* **yameen**) **oo-smol** ימין ושמאל *adv* right and left.

◻ **Yemeen Ord** (Yemin Orde) ימין אורד *nm* youth village & religious educational center (est. 1952) in S. Carmel hills, near **'En Hod** village.

yemeenah (*cpr* **yameenah**) ימינה *adv* to the right; keep right!

(lee) yemeen|ee/-o/-ah (*etc*) לימיני/־ו/־ה וכו' **1.** *adv* to my/his/her (*etc*) right; **2.** in my/his/her (*etc*) support.

yemey ha-beynayeem ימי הביניים *nm pl* the Middle Ages.

yemey kedem ימי קדם *nm pl* ancient times.

yemey ne'oor|ay/-av/-eha (*etc*) ימי נעוריי/־יו/־יה *nm pl* days of my/his/her (*etc*) youth.

◇ **('aseret) yemey teshoovah** see ◇ **'aseret yemey teshoovah.**

(bee) yemey kheroom בימי חירום *adv* in times of emergency.

yemot ימות *nm pl+of* (*sing:* **yom**) days (alternative and more commonly used plural is **yameem**; *+of:* **yemey**).

yemot ha-g'shameem ימות הגשמים *nm pl* rainy season; Israeli winter.

yemot ha-khamah ימות החמה *nm pl* sunny season; Israeli summer.

yemot ha-khol ימות החול *nm pl* weekdays; working days.

yemot ha-mashee'akh ימות המשיח *nm pl* the Messianic Era; days to come.

yen saraf יין שרף *nm* brandy.

◇ **yen nesekh** יין נסך *nm* wine prohibited to a strictly observant Jew because of having been served by a non-Jew and therefore having possibly served for a libation to false gods.

yeneek|ah/-ot יניקה *nf* sucking; suction; (*+of:* **-at**).

yenot יינות *nm pl* (*sing:* **yayeen**) wine.

ye'ood/-eem ייעוד *nm* mission; vocation; assignment; (*pl+of:* **-ey**).

ye'ool (*npr* **yee'ool**) ייעול *nm* improving efficiency.

ye'oosh ייאוש *nm* despair.

yerakh/-eem ירח *nm* month; (*pl+of:* **yarkhey**).

yerakh dvash ירח דבש *nm* honeymoon.

yerakot ירקות *nm pl* (*sing:* **yarak**) vegetables; greenery.

(geedool/-ey) yerakot גידול ירקות *nm* growing vegetables.

(khanoot) yerakot חנות ירקות *nf* greengrocery.

(merak/meerkey) yerakot מרק ירקות *nm* vegetable soup.

yerakrak/-ah ירקרק *adj* greenish.

yeret/-tah/-atetee יירט *v* intercepted; forced down (plane); (*pres* **meyaret**; *fut* **yeyaret**).

yere/-'at shamayeem ירא שמיים *adj* Godfearing.

yeree ירי *nm* shooting; (*+of:* **yeree**).

yeree|'ah/-'ot יריעה *nf* sheet; length of cloth; (*+of:* **-'at**).

yereed|ah/-ot ירידה *nf* descent; drop; (*+of:* **-at**).

◇ **(ha)"yereedah"** ירידה *nf* emigration of Jews from Israel to elsewhere that is viewed by some as a form of desertion.

yereek|ah/-ot יריקה *nf* spitting; (*+of:* **-at**).

◻ **Yereekho** (Yeriho) יריחו *nf* Biblical Jericho, historic town at S. edge of the Jordan Valley, present population of which is mostly Muslim. Pop. 17,900.

yereevoo|t/-yot ירִיבות *nm* rivalry; opposition.

yeree|yah/yot ירִייה *nf* shot; shooting; (*+of:* **yat**).

yerek ירק *nm* vegetable; green plant.

yerekhayeem ירכיים *nf pl* (*sing:* **yarekh**) thighs; loins; (*pl+of:* **yarkhey**).

(agan ha) yerekhayeem אגן הירכיים *nm* pelvis.

yeeret (*npr* **yer|et)/-tah/-atetee** יירט *v* intercepted; forced down (plane); (*pres* **meyaret;** *fut* **yeyaret**).

□ **Yerokham** (Yeroham) ירוחם *nf* township (est. 1951) in Negev hills, on edge of the desert, 25 km S. of Beershcba. Pop. 6,160.

yeroosh|ah/-ot ירושה *nf* inheritance; heritage; estate; (*+of:* **-at**).

□ **Yerooshalayeem** (Yerushalayim) ירושלים *nf* eternal Jerusalem, Holy City to many creeds, one of the oldest cities in the world. Capital of ancient Israel and Judea from the time of King David until the destruction of the Second Temple in 70 C.E., it was proclaimed Capital of Israel in 1950. It contains the seat of the President, the Government and the Knesset. Pop. 524,500 of which 146,300 are non-Jews.

yeroot/-eem יירוט *nm* interception (of airplanes). (*pl+of:* **-ey**).

yesh יש there is; there are.

yesh be-da'at/-ee/-khah/-ekh/-o/-ah יש בדעת/י/ך it is my/your(*m/f*)/his/her (*etc*) intention.

yesh brerah יש ברירה there is an alternative.

yesh lah/lakh/lakhem/lakhen יש לה/לך/לו/ לכם/לכן she/you(*m/f*)/he/you (*pl m/f*)/they(*m/f*) have.

> *Note: Hebrew has no verb "to have" and the above (meaning literally: there is for me, for you, etc.) is the usual alternative to it.*

yesh la-el yad|o/-ah/-ee (*etc*) יש לאל ידו/־ה/־י it is in his/her/my (*etc*) power to...

yesh lee/lekha/lakh/lo/lah יש לי/לך/לו/לה I/you (*sing m/f*)/he/she have (see *above Note*).

yesh omreem יש אומרים there are people who say; some people say.

yesh tsorekh יש צורך *v pres* there is need that; it is necessary; (*pres* **hayah** *etc; fut* **yeehyeh** *etc*).

yesh va-yesh יש ויש **1.** there is enough and to spare; **2.** there are all kinds of people.

(mah) yesh? מה יש? what's the matter? what do you want?

(mah) yesh lekha/lakh/lo/lah? מה יש לך/לך/ לו/לה? *query* what's the matter with you(*m/f*)/him/her? what's troubling you(*m/f*)/him/her (*etc*)?

□ **Yesha'** (Yesha') ישע *nm* village (est. 1957) in NW Negev, 5 km SW of Magen Junction (**Tsomet Magen**). Pop. 219.

□ **Yesha'** (Yesha') יש"ע *nf acr of* **Yeehoodah** יהודה (Judea), **Shomron** שומרון (Samaria) and **'Azah** עזה (Gazah Strip). Collective name for territories under Israeli rule since 1967 that were not decreed by the Knesset (as East-Jerusalem and the Golan Heights were) parts of Israel.

yesheemon/-eem ישימון *nm* wasteland; desert.

◇ **yesheev|ah/-ot** ישיבה *nf* **1.** session; sitting; **2.** "Yeshivah"; traditional Rabbinical school: (*+of:* **-at**).

yesheev|ah/-ot sgoor|ah/-ot ישיבה סגורה *nf* closed session.

(rosh/-ey) yesheev|ah/-ot ראש ישיבה *nm* headmaster of a "Yeshivah" (Rabbinical school).

◇ **yesheev|at/-ot hesder** ישיבת הסדר *nf* new type of Israeli Rabbinical School differing from traditional "Yeshivah". Its pupils do not avail thesemselves of exemption from military service to which "Yeshivah"-students and professional Torah-learners are entitled under law. On the contrary, they form their own combat units in the army and endeavor to serve with distinction.

yesheev|at/-ot ha-kneset ישיבת הכנסת *nf* Knesset session.

yesheev|at/-ot han'halah ישיבת הנהלה *nf* board meeting.

yesheev|at/-ot melee'ah ישיבת מליאה *nf* plenary meeting; plenary session.

yesheev|at/-ot memshalah ישיבת ממשלה *nf* Cabinet session.

yesheev|at/-ot mo'atsah ישיבת מועצה *nf* Council meeting

yesheev|at/-ot va'ad ישיבת ועד *nf* committee session; committee meeting.

yesheev|at/-ot va'adah ישיבת ועדה *nf* commission meeting.

yeshn|am/-an ישנם/־ן/ *v pres pl m/f* there are (*m/f*).

yeshn|o/-ah ישנו/־ה/ *v pres sing m/f* there is (*m/f*).

yeshoo|'ah/-'ot ישועה *nf* rescue; salvation; (*+of:* **-'at**).

yeshoo|'ot ve-nekhamot ישועות ונחמות *nf pl* **1.** salvations and solaces; **2.** *[colloq.]* exaggerated promises.

yeshoo|t/-yot ישות *nf* entity.

yesod/-ot יסוד *nm* basis; foundation.

□ **Yesood ha-Ma'alah** (Yesud haMa'ala) יסוד המעלה *nm* village (est. 1883) in **Khoolah** Valley, 6 km N. of **Gesher Benot Ya'akov** bridge across Jordan. Pop. 799.

('al) yesod על יסוד *conj* on the basis of...

◇ **(keren ha) yesod** see ◇ **keren ha-yesod**.

(khas|ar/-rat) yesod חסר יסוד *adj* unfounded; lacking any foundation.

(le-lo) yesod ללא יסוד *adv* without foundation.

(netool/-at) yesod נטול יסוד *adj* unfounded; baseless; lacking foundation.

◇ **(sekhar) yesod** see ◇ **sekhar yesod**.

yesodee/-t יסודי *adj* **1.** elementary; **2.** thorough.

('al) yesodee/-t על־יסודי *adj* post-primary.

(be-ofen) yesodee באופן יסודי *adv* thoroughly; in a thorough manner.

(bet/batey sefer) yesodee/-yeem בית ספר יסודי *nm* elementary (primary) school.

(neekooy) yesodee ניקוי יסודי *nm* thorough cleaning.

yesodeeyoot יסודיות *nf* thoroughness.

□ **Yesodot** יסודות *nm* collective village (est. 1948) in the Shefelah, 5 km W. of Nahshon Junction **(Tsomet Nakhshon)**. Pop. 331.

yeter יתר *adj (suffix)* over-

(ha) yeter היתר *nm* the rest; excess.

yeter (*npr* **yater**) **'al ken** יתר על כן *adv* furthermore; moreover.

(be) yeter kaloot ביתר קלות *adv* more easily.

(be) yeter se'et ביתר שאת *adv* even more so.

(ben ha) yeter בין היתר *adv* inter alia; among other things.

(zekhoo|t/-yot) yeter זכות יתר *nf* privilege.

(bet/-batey) yetomeem בית יתומים *nm* orphanage.

yetsee|'ah/-'ot יציאה *nf* exit; going out; (*+of:* **-'at**).

yetseek|ah/-ot יציקה *nf* casting (of metal, *etc*); (*+of:* **-at**).

(barzel) yetseekah ברזל יציקה *nm* cast iron.

(bet/-batey) yetseekah בית יציקה *nf* foundry.

yetseer/-eem יציר *nm* product; creation; (*pl+of:* **-ey**).

yetseer/-ey kap|av/-eha/-ay יציר כפיו/־ה/־י *nm* work of one's own hands.

yetseer|ah/-ot יצירה **1.** *nf* creation; **2.** *nf* work (of art, literature etc); (*+of:* **-at**).

(khedvat) yetseerah חדוות יצירה *nf* joy of creation; creativity.

yetseerateeyoot יצירתיות *nf* creativity.

yetseev|ah/-ot יציבה *nf* posture; carriage; (*+of:* **-at**).

yetseevoot (*npr* **yatseevoot**) יציבות *nf* stability.

yets|er/-areem יצר *nm* instinct; (*pl+of:* **yeetsrey**).

yetser ha-ra' יצר הרע *nm* evil nature; evil inclination.

yetsoo יצוא *nm* export.

yetsoo khozer יצוא חוזר *nm* re-export.

yetsoo samooy יצוא סמוי *nm* concealed export.

yetsoo|'a'/-'eem יצוע *nm* couch; bed; (*pl+of:* **-'ey**).

yetsoo'an/-eem יצואן *nm* exporter; (*pl+of:* **-ey**).

◇ **yetsoo'an meetstayen** יצואן מצטיין *nm* "Outstanding Exporter": honorary title from the Israel Ministry of Trade and Industry accorded to exporter whose exports exceed a certain amount.

yetsoor/-eem יצור *nm* creature; (*pl+of:* **-ey**).

yetsoor/-eem enoosheee/-yeem יצור אנושי *nm* human being.

yevanee/-t יווני *adj* Greek.

yevanee/-yah יווני *nmf* Greek (man / woman).

yevaneet יוונית *nf* Greek (language).

yevav|ah/-ot יבבה *nf* lamentation; (*+of:* **yeevev|at/-ot**).

yevoo/-'eem יבוא *nm* import.

◇ **yevoo eeshee** יבוא אישי *nm* personal import i.e. ordered directly from supplier abroad (not through an importer) which entitles one to certain tax-duty advantages.

yevoo'an/-eem יבואן *nm* importer; (*pl+of:* **-ey**).

yevool/-eem יבול *nm* crop; (*pl+of:* **-ey**).

□ **Yevool** (Yevul) יבול *nm* village (est. 1980) in Shalom district, 6 km SE of **Kerem Shalom**.

yeza' יזע *nm* **1.** sweat; **2.** (*figurat.*) hard work.

◇ **yod/-een** יו״ד (י) *nf* 10th letter of Hebrew alphabet (also called **"Yood"**) serving as vowel for **ee** or **ey** and as consonant **y**.

◇ **yod** י׳ **1.** *num. symbol* 10; ten; **2.** *adj & num* 10th; tenth.

yod יוד *nm* iodine.

yod-alef י״א **1.** *num. symbol* 11; eleven; **2.** *adj & num* 11th; eleventh.

yod-bet י״ב **1.** *num. symbol* 12; twelve; **2.** *adj & num* 12th; twelfth.

yod-dalet (*cpr* **daled**) י״ד **1.** *num. symbol* 14; fourteen; **2.** *adj & num* 14th fourteenth.

□ **Yodfat** (Yodefat) יודפת *nm* collective village (est. 1960) in Lower Galilee 13 km SW of **Tsomet Akheehood** (Ahihud Junction), N. of **Bet-Netoofah** Valley. Pop. 247.

yod-geemal י״ג **1.** *num. symbol* 13; thirteen; **2.** *adj & num* 13th; thirteenth.

yod-khet י״ח **1.** *num. symbol* 18; eighteen; **2.** *adj & num* 18th; eighteenth.

yod-tet י״ט **1.** *num. symbol* 19; nineteen; **2.** *adj & num* 19th; nineteenth.

yod-zayeen י״ז **1.** *num. symbol* 17; seventeen; **2.** *adj & num* 17th; seventeenth.

(kotso shel) yod קוצו של יו״ד *nm* a jot; iota (*lit.:* the serif of a Yod).

yod|e'a'/-a'at יודע *v pres* knows; (*pst* **yada'**; *fut* **yeda'**).

yod|e'a'/-'ey davar יודע דבר **1.** *adj* knowledgeable; **2.** *nm* connoisseur.

yod|e'a'/-a'at nefesh יודע נפש *v pres* knows the heart; understands; (*pst* **yada'** *etc; fut* **yeda'** *etc*).

(be) yod'een ביודעין *adv* knowingly.

(be-lo) yod'een בלא יודעין *adv* unknowingly.

yo'ets/yo'ats|eem יועץ *nm* adviser; counsellor; (*pl+of:* **-ey**).

yo'ets/-et meeshpatee/-t יועץ משפטי *nmf* legal adviser.

(ha) yo'ets ha-meeshpatee היועץ המשפטי *nm* the Attorney-General.

yofee יופי *nm* beauty; (*+of:* **yefee**).

yofee! יופי! *interj* excellent! fine! OK!

(mal|kat/-khot) yofee מלכת יופי *nf* beauty queen.

(mekhon/-ey) yofee מכון יופי *nm* beauty parlor.

yogoort/-eem יוגורט *nm* yoghurt.

yoker יוקר *nm* dearness; expensiveness.

yoker ha-meekhyah יוקר המחיה *nm* high cost of living; cost of living.

(be) yoker ביוקר *adv* dearly.

◇ **(madad) yoker ha-bneeyah** see ◇ **madad yoker ha-beneeyah.**

◇ **(madad) yoker ha-meekhyah** see ◇ **madad yoker ha-meekhyah.**

(tos|efet/-fot) yoker תוספת יוקר *nf* cost of living increment.

(megeelat) yokhaseen מגילת יוחסין *nf* pedigree; family tree; family register; genealogy.

(shalshelet) yokhaseen שלשלת יוחסין *nf* family tree; pedigree; genealogy.

□ **Yokne'am (Yoqne'am)** יקנעם *nm* village (est. 1935) on borderline between the Yizre'el Valley and the Carmel Hills. Pop. 787.

□ **Yokne'am 'Eeleet** (Yoqne'am Illit) יקנעם עלית *nf* - town(est. 1949) on borderline between Yizre'el Valley and Carmel Hills. Originated as transit-camp for new immigrants, developed into a town. Pop. 6,220.

yol|edet/-dot יולדת *nf* woman who has just given birth to a child.

(bet/-batey) yoldot בית יולדות *nm* maternity-ward.

yom/yameem יום *nm* day; (*pl+of:* **yemey**).

yom/yemey alef יום א׳ *nm* Sunday.

yom/yemey bet יום ב׳ *nm* Monday.

yom/-yemey dalet (*cpr* **daled**) יום ד׳ *nm* Wednesday.

yom/-yemey 'eeyoon יום עיון *nm* study day;

yom/-yemey geemal יום ג׳ *nm* Tuesday.

◇ **yom ha-'atsma'oot** יום העצמאות *nm* Independence Day celebrated on 5th of Sivan **(Seevan)** throughout Israel and by official Israeli and Zionist institutions abroad. However, there are circles and occasions abroad, where celebrations connected with the anniversary of Israel's independence are held also according to the Gregorian calendar, i.e. on May 15.

◇ **yom ha-kadeesh ha-klalee** יום הקדיש הכללי *nm* "General Kaddish Day" set by Jewish religious authorities for saying "Kaddish" (see ◇ **kadeesh**) in remembrance of relatives (close and distant) perished in the Holocaust on dates unknown, as well as a day of general mourning for all six million victims. It is held and observed, mainly in orthodox circles, on the 10th day of Tevet (approx. December) which, earlier, had been a day of fasting in remembrance of the siege of Biblical Jerusalem by Babilonians begun on that Hebrew date (586 BCE).

yom ha-keepooreem יום הכפורים *nm* Day of Atonement; Yom Kippur.

◇ **yom ha-shlosheem** יום השלושים *nm* 30th day after passing away of someone i.e. day marking end of a month of mourning.

yom ha-mokhorat יום המחרת *nm* the day after; the morrow.

◇ **yom ha-sho'ah** יום השואה *nm colloq. abbr.* of **yom ha-zeekaron la-sho'ah ve-la-gevoorah** יום הזיכרון לשואה ולגבורה i.e. Remembrance Day for Victims of the Holocaust and for the Heroes of the Jewish Resistence. Israel's official mourning- and commemoration-day for the six million Jews perished in the Holocaust. Held yearly on the last day of Nissan (approx. April) which was the Jewish calendar date on which the uprising of the Warsaw Ghetto broke out in 1943.

◇ **yom ha-zeekar'on** יום הזיכרון *nm* Remembrance-Day for the fallen in Israel's wars for survival held on the 4th day of Iyar **(Yeeyar)**, which is the eve of Independence Day celebrated on the fifth day of Yeeyar.

yom/yemey hey יום ה׳ *nm* Thursday.

yom/yemey hooledet יום הולדת *nm* birthday.

yom keepoor יום כיפור *nm* Yom Kippur; Day of Atonement; (Held on the 10th day of Teeshrey; approx.Sept.-Oct.).

yom/yemey khameeshee יום חמישי *nm* Thursday.

yom/yemey khol יום חול *nm* weekday.

yom/yemey reeshon יום ראשון *nm* Sunday.

yom/yemey revee'ee יום רביעי *nm* Wednesday.

yom/yemey shabat יום שבת *nm* Saturday.

yom shakhor יום שחור *nm* "black" day; day of misfortunes.

yom/yemey shanah יום שנה *nm* anniversary.

yom/yemey sheeshee יום שישי *nm* Friday.

yom/yemey shenee יום שני *nm* Monday.

yo/yemey shleeshee יום שלישי *nm* Tuesday.

yom/yameem tov/-eem יום טוב *nm* holiday; feast day.

yom va-laylah יום ולילה *adv* day and night.

yom/yemey vav יום ו׳ *nm* Friday.

yom-yom יום־יום *adv* day by day; daily.

yom-yomayeem יום־יומיים *adv* a day or two; a couple of days.

yom-yomee/-t יום־יומי *adj* daily; ordinary.

yom/yemey zeekaron יום זיכרון *nm* memorial day.

(ba) yom ביום *adv* in daytime.

(bee-she'ot ha) yom בשעות היום *adv* during the day.

(bo-ba) yom בו־ביום *adv* on the very same day.

(ka-'avor) yom כעבור יום *adv* a day later.

(kesh|eh/-at) yom קשה יום *adj* miserable; depressed.

(meedey) yom מדי יום *adv* each day; daily.

(meedey) yom be-yomo מדי יום ביומו *adv* every single day.

(me'on/-ot) yom מעון יום *nm* day nursery.

(pekood|at/-ot) yom פקודת יום *nf* order of the day.

yomam va-laylah יומם ולילה *adv* by day and by night.

yoman/-eem יומן *nm* diary; (*pl+of:* **-ey**).

yoman|ay (*cpr* **yomana'ee**) **/a'eem** יומנאי *nm* desk-sergeant; (in a police station).

yomayeem יומיים *nm pl* two days.

yomayeem-shloshah יומיים־שלושה *nm pl* a couple of days.

(be-'od) yomayeem בעוד יומיים *adv* within the next two days; by the day after tomorrow.

yomee/-t יומי *adj* **1.** daily; **2.** daytime-

(ka'avor) yomayeem כעבור יומיים *adv* two days later.

(hatsag|ah/-ot) yomeet הצגה יומית *nf* matinee.

yomon/-eem יומון *nm* daily (newspaper) (*pl+of:* **-ey**).

yomr|ah/-ot יומרה *nf* pretense; pretentiousness; (*+of:* **-at**).

yomranee/-t יומרני *adj* ambitious; pretentious.

yon|ah/-eem יונה *nf* pigeon; dove; (*+of:* **-at/-ey**).

"yonah" (*etc*) יונה *nf* "dove" (politically).

□ **Yonatan** יונתן *nm* collective village (est. 1975) in Golan Heights, 4 km W. of Tel Peres.

yonee/-t "יוני" *adj* dovish (politically).

yon|ek/-keem יונק *nm* mammal; (*pl+of:* **-key**).

yonek/-et יונק *v pres* sucks; (*pst* **yanak**; *fut* **yeenak**)

◇ **yood/-een** see ◇ **yod/-een**.

◇ **yood** see ◇ **yod**.

yood-alef י״א **1.** *num.symbol* 11; eleven; **2.** *adj & num* 11th; eleventh.

yood-bet י״ב **1.** *num. symbol* 12; twelve; **2.** *adj & num* 12th; twelfth.

yood-dalet (*cpr* **daled**) י״ד **1.** *num. symbol* 14; fourteen; **2.** *adj & num*; 14th; fourteenth.

yood-geemal י״ג **1.** *num. symbol* 13; thirteen; **2.** *adj & num* 13th; thirteenth.

yood-khet י״ח **1.** *num. symbol* 18; eighteen; **2.** *adj & num* 18th; eighteenth.

yood-tet י״ט **1.** *num. symbol* 19; nineteen; **2.** *adj & num* 19th; nineteenth.

yood-zayeen י״ז **1.** *num. symbol* 17; seventeen; **2.** *adj & num* 17th; seventeenth.

(kotso shel) yood קוצו של יו״ד *nm* a jot; iota.

yookr|ah/-ot יוקרה *nf* prestige; (*+of:* **-at**).

Yoolee יולי *nm* July.

yoomr|ah/-ot יומרה *nf* pretense; pretentiousness; (*+of:* **-at**).

yoomranee/-t יומרני *adj* ambitious; pretentious.

Yoonee יוני *nm* June.

yooreedee/-t יורידי *adj* legal; juridical.

yootah יוטה *nf [colloq.]* jute; burlap.

(lo) yootslakh/-eem לא־יוצלח *nmf & adj* ne'er do well; a failure.

yooval/-eem יובל *nm* stream; brook; (*pl+of:* **-ey**).

□ **Yooval** (Yuval) יובל *nm* village (est. 1952) in Upper Gallilee, 4 km NE of **Keeryat Shmonah**, near Lebanese border. Pop. 318.

□ **Yoovaleem** יובלים *nm* village (est. 1982) in Lower Galilee, 2 km NE of Segev. Pop. 747.

yor/-eem יו״ר *nmf* (*acr of* **YOshev/-et Rosh** יושב ראש) chairman; chairperson.

◇ **Yoram** יורם masculine first name.

◇ **"Yoram/-eem"** "יורם" *[slang]* nickname for young man or youngster who is diligent, orderly, disciplined and polite or in any other way too much of a "square".

yor|eh/-ah יורה *v pres* shoots; (*pst* **yarah**; *fut* **yeereh**).

(ha) yoreh היורה *nm* first autumn rain after long rainless Israeli summer.

yored/-et יורד *v pres* descends; goes down; (*pst* **yarad**; *fut* **yered**).

◇ **"yor|ed/-deem"** יורד *nm* emigrant from Israel to elsewhere, or Israeli who extends his/her sojourn abroad beyond a reasonable period required by studies, job, family or business arrangements.

yor|ed/-dey yam יורד ים *nm* seafarer.

yor|esh/-sheem יורש *nmf* heir.

yoresh/-et 'etser יורש עצר *nmf* heir/-ess to the throne.

□ **Yosheevyah** (Yoshivya) יושיביה *nm* village (est. 1950) in NW Negev, 3 km N. of **Neteevot** township. Pop. 236.

yoshen יושן *nm* oldness; age.

yosher יושר honesty; integrity; equity; fairness.

(be) yosher ביושר *adv* equitably; honestly; fairly.

(meen ha) yosher מן היושר *adv* it were only fair; in fairness.

(meleets/-at) yosher מליץ יושר *nmf* advocate; defender.

yoshev/-et יושב *adj* sitting; seated; *v pres* sits (*pst* **yashav**; *fut* **yeshev**).

yoshev/-et rosh יושב ראש *v pres* chairs; presides; (*pst* **yashav** *etc*; *fut* **yeshev** *etc*).

yosh|ev/-evet rosh יושב ראש *nmf* chairman,chairwoman; chairperson; (*pl:* **-vey rosh**).

yoter יותר *adv* more.

yoter mee- יותר מ־ *adv* more than.

yoter mee-day יותר מדי *adv* too much; more than enough.

yoter tov/-ah יותר טוב *adj* better.

yoter tov יותר טוב *adv* better.

(be) yoter ביותר *adv* to the utmost; most.

(le-khol ha) yoter לכל היותר *adv* at most.

(pakhot o) yoter פחות או יותר *adv* more or less.

yots|e/-et יוצא *v pres* departs; goes out; (*pst* **yatsa**; *fut* **yetse**).

yots|e/-et dofen יוצא דופן *adj* odd; exception.

yots|e/-et mee-geder ha-rageel יוצא מגדר הרגיל *adj* extraordinary.

yots|e/-et meen ha-klal יוצא מן הכלל **1.** *adj* exceptional; **2.** *nmf* exception.

yots|e/-'ey tsava יוצא צבא *nm* person subject to conscription.

(do'ar) yotse דואר יוצא *nm* outgoing mail.

(ka) yotse bo/-bah כיוצא בה/בו similarly; in similar cases.

(ka) yots|e/-'ey be-eleh כיוצא באלה like these.

(po'al) yotse פועל יוצא *nm* transitive verb (Gram.).

(ve-kha) yotse bo/bah וכיוצא בו/בה *adv m/f* and similarly; and in similar cases.

(ve-ka) yotse be-'eleh וכיוצא באלה and similarly.

yotser/-et יוצר *v pres* creates; (*pst* **yatsar**; *fut* **yeetsor**).

yots|er/-reem יוצר *nm* creator; author; (*pl+of:* **-rey**).

(tees|ah/-ot) yots|et/-'ot טיסה יוצאת *nf* outgoing flight.

(zekhoo|t/-yot) yotsreem זכות יוצרים *nf* copyright.

□ **Yotvatah** (Yotvata) יטבתה *nm* kibbutz (est. 1951) in **'Aravah** 40 km N. of Elat, on road to that city. Pop. 543.

yov|el/-lot יובל *nm* jubilee.

yovesh יובש *nm* dryness.

yozem/-et יוזם **1.** *nmf* initiator; (*pl m+of:* **yozmey**); **2.** *v pres* initiates; (*pst* **yazam**; *fut* **yeezom**).

yozm|ah/-ot יוזמה *nf* initiative; resourcefulness; (*+of:* **-at**).

Z.

transliterating the Hebrew letter **Zayeen** (ז)

za'/-ah/-tee זע *v* budged; moved.

za'af זעף *nm* wrath; anger; (my/his/her anger: **za'p|ee/-o/-ah** *(p=f)*.

(be) za'af בזעף *adv* angrily.

(geeshmey) za'af גשמי זעף *nm pl* (*sing:* **geshem**) torrential rains.

za'af/-ah/-tee זעף *v* raged; was angry : (*pres* **za'ef**; *fut* **yeez'af**).

za'ak/-ah/-tee זעק *v* cried out; (*pres* **zo'ek**; *fut* **yeez'ak**).

za'ak (*etc*) **khamas** זעק חמס *v* complained bitterly.

za'ak|ah/-ot (*npr* **ze'ak|ah/-ot**) זעקה *nf* outcry; (*+of:* **-at/-ot**).

za'am זעם *nm* rage; anger.

(be) za'am בזעם *adv* angrily; with anger.

za'am/-ah/-tee זעם *v* was angry; (*pres* **zo'em**; *fut* **yeez'am**).

za'atoot/-eem זאטוט *nm* youngster; brat; *imp*; (*pl+of:* **-ey**).

za'azoo|'a'/-'eem זעזוע *nm* shock; (*pl+of:* **-'ey**).

(bol|em/-mey) za'azoo'eem בולם זעזועים *nm* shock-absorber.

zaban/-eem זבן *nm* salesman; vendor; (*pl+of:* **-ey**).

zabanee|t/-yot זבנית *nf* salesgirl; saleswoman.

zadon זדון *nm* malice; (*+of:* **zedon**).

(be) zadon בזדון *adv* maliciously; with malice aforethought.

za'eer/ze'eerah זעיר *adj* minuscule; tiny; minor.

(sar ve) za'ef סר וזעף *adj (m)* sullen and displeased.

zagag/-eem זגג *nm* glazier (*pl+of:* **-ey**).

zahar/-ah/-tee זהר *v* shone; glittered; (*pres* **zoher**; *fut* **yeez'har**).

zahav זהב *nm* gold; (*+of:* **zehav**).

('egel ha) zahav עגל הזהב *nm* the Golden Calf (Bibl.).

(shveel ha) zahav שביל הזהב *nm* the Golden Mean.

(tab|a'at/-'ot) zahav טבעת זהב *nf* golden ring.

(tapoo|'akh/-khey) zahav תפוח זהב *nm* orange (fruit).

zaheer/zeheerah זהיר *adj* cautious; careful.

zahoov/zehoovah זהוב *adj* gilded; golden.

zahoov/zehoov|eem זהוב *nm* gold coin; gulden; guilder; (*pl+of:* **-ey**).

zak|af/-fah/-aftee זקף *v* straightened up; (*pres* **zokef**; *fut* **yeezkof**).

zakaf (*etc*) **'al ha-kheshbon** זקף על החשבון *v* debited; charged the account.

zak|an/-nah/-antee זקן *v* aged; grew old; (*pres* **zaken**; *fut* **yazkeen**).

zakan/zekaneem זקן *nm* beard; (*+of:* **zkan/-ey**).

zak|ay/-a'eet זכאי *adj* **1.** innocent; acquitted; **2.** entitled to; deserving.

(yats|a/-'ah/-a'tee) zaka|y/-'eet יצא זכאי *v* was acquitted; (*pres* **yotse** *etc*; *fut* **yetse** *etc*).

zakeef/zekeef|eem זקיף *nm* sentry; guard; (*pl+of:* **-ey**).

zaken/zekeneem זקן *nm* old man; elder; (*+of:* **zeekney**).

zaken/zekenah זקן *adj* old; aged.

zaken/zekenah moofl|ag/-eget זקן מופלג *nmf & adj* extremely old.

zakh/zakah *(k=kh)* זך *adj* limpid; pure; clear.

zakh|ah/-tah/-eetee זכה *v* won; (*pres* **zokheh**; *fut* **yeezkeh** *(k=kh)*).

zakhal/zekhaleem זחל *nm* larva; (*pl+of:* **zakhley**).

zakh|al/-lah/-altee זחל *v* crept; crawled (*pres* **zokhel**; *fut* **yeezkhal**).

zakh|ar/zekhareem זכר *nm* male; (*pl+of:* **zeekhrey**).

zakh|ar/-rah/-tee זכר *v* remembered; recalled; (*pres* **zokher**; *fut* **yeezkor** *(k=kh)*).

(leshon) zakhar לשון זכר *nm* masculine gender (Gram.).

(meen) zakhar מין זכר *nm* masculine sex; masculine gender (Gram).

(meeshkav) zakhar משכב זכר *nm* pederasty; sodomy.

zakhoor/zekhoorah זכור *adj* remembered; memorable.

zakhoor (*etc*) **la-tov** זכור לטוב *nm* of blessed memory.

zakhoor lee/lekha/lakh/lo/lah (*etc*) זכור לי/לך/לו/לה I/you(*m/f*)/he/she (*etc*) seem to recall.

zakoof/zekoofah זקוף *adj* erect; straight.

zakook/zekookah זקוק **1.** *adj* needy; in need; **2.** *v pres* needs (*pst* **neezkak**; *fut [colloq.]* **yeezdakek**).

zal ז"ל *abbr.* (*acr of* **zeekhron|o/-ah lee-vrakhah** זכרונו/־ה לברכה) the late; of blessed memory.

zal|ag/-gah/-agtee זלג *v* dripped; (*pres* **zoleg**; *fut* **yeezlog**).

zal|al/-elah/-altee זלל *v* gorged oneself; ate greedily; (*pres* **zolel**; *fut* **yeezlol**).

zamam/-emah/-amtee זמם *v* schemed; (*pres* **zomem**; *fut* **yazom**).

zamar/-eem זמר mr singer (male); songster; (*pl+of:* **-ey**).

zam|ar/-eret 'am זמר עם *nmf* folk-singer.

zamar/-ey pop זמר פופ *nm* pop-singer (male).

zameen/zemeenah זמין *adj* available.

zameer/zemeer|eem זמיר *nm* nightingale; (*pl+of:* **-ey**).

zam|eret/-arot זמרת *nf* singer (female); songstress.

zam|eret/-rot 'am זמרת עם *nf* folk-singer (female).

zam|eret/-rot pop זמרת פופ *nf* pop-singer (female).

zamzam/-eem זמזם *nm* buzzer; (*pl+of:* **-ey**).

zan/-ah/-tee זן *v* fed; (*pres* **zan**; *fut* **yazoon**).

zan/-eem זן *nm* breed; species; (*pl+of:* **-ey**).

zan|akh/-khah/-akhtee זנח *v* abandoned; neglected; (*pres* **zone'akh**; *fut* **yeeznakh**).

zanav/zenavot זנב *nm* tail; butt; (*pl+of:* **zenav/zenavot**).

zan|ay/-a'eem זנאי *nm* fornicator; (*pl+of:* **-a'ey**).

zanee'akh/zeneekhah זניח *adj* negligible.

□ **Zano'akh** (Zanoah) זנוח *nm* village (est. 1950) in Judean Hills, 3 km S. of Bet Shemesh. Pop. 315.

zanz|onet/-anot זנזונת *nf* precocious hooker; young prostitute; young harlot.

za'oom/ze'oomah זעום *adj* scarce.

zar/-ah זר *adj* strange; foreign.

zar/-eem זר *nm* stranger; foreigner.

(matbe'a') zar מטבע *nm* foreign currency.

(meevta') zar מבטא זר *nm* foreign accent.

(neta') zar נטע זר *nm* alien corn (figurat.).

(sokh|en/-neem) zar/-eem סוכן זר *nm* foreign agent.

(le) zara לזרא *adv* loathsome; repulsive.

zar|ah/-tah/-eetee זרה *v* fanned out; sprinkled; (*pres* **zoreh**; *fut* **yeezreh**).

zarah (*etc*) **melakh** זרה מלח *v* poured salt on wounds (*figurat.*).

zar|a'/-'ah/-a'tee זרע *v* sowed; seeded; (*pres* **zore'a'**; *fut* **yeezra'**).

zar|ak/-kah/-aktee זרק *v* threw; (*pres* **zorek**; *fut* **yeezrok**).

zar|akh/-khah/-akhtee זרח *v* shone (the sun); (*pres* **zore'akh**; *fut* **yeezrakh**).

zar|am/-mah זרם *v* flowed; (*pres* **zorem**; *fut* **yeezrom**).

zarboovee|t/-yot זרבובית *nf* spout of a kettle.

□ **Zar'eet** (Zar'it) זרעית *nm* village (est. 1967) in Upper Galilee.

zareez/zreezah זריז *adj* alert; agile.

zarkor/-eem זרקור *nm* projector; searchlight.

(ha shemesh) zarkhah השמש זרחה *v* the sun was shining; (*pres* **zorakhat**; *fut* **teezrakh**).

zarkhan זרחן *nm* phosphorus.

zarnook/-eem זרנוק *nm* hose; tube; (*pl+of:* **-ey**).

zaroo'a'/zeroo'ah זרוע *adj* sown; seeded.

zarook/zerookah זרוק **1.** *adj* thrown out; derelict; **2.** *[colloq.] nmf* hippie.

zaroo|t/-yot זרות *nf* estrangement; strangeness.

zav/-ah זב *v pres* drips; trickles; (*pst* **zav**; *fut* **yazoov**).

zav/-ah זב *adj* dripping; trickling.

zav/-at dam זב דם *adj* bleeding.

(kol tsaroo'a ve-khol) zav כל צרוע וכל זב *nm pl* riff-raff; all kinds of riff-raff.

(erets) zavat khalav oo-dvash ארץ זבת חלב ודבש *nf* "land flowing with milk and honey" (Bibl.).

□ **Zavdee'el** (Zavdi'el) זבדיאל *nm* village (est. 1950) in South, 5 km NW of **Keeryat Gat**. Pop. 381.

zavee|t/-yot זווית *nf* angle; corner.

(keren) zaveet קרן זווית *nf* dark corner.

(mee) zaveet shel מזווית של *adv* from the angle of...

zaveetan/-eem זוויתן *nm* angle-bar; angle-iron; (*pl+of:* **-ey**).

zaveetee/-t זוויתי *adj* angular.

◇ **zayeen** (ז) ז"ין 7th letter of Hebrew alphabet: consonant **Z** pronounced as in *zero* or *zebra*.

◇ **zayeen** 'ז **1.** *num. symbol* 7; seven; **2.** *adj & num* 7th; seventh.

zayeen זין *nm [slang]* penis.

(klee/kley) zayeen כלי זין *nm* weapon.

zayeet/zeyteem זית *nm* **1.** olive; **2.** olive-tree; (*pl+of:* **-ey**).

(ke) zayeet כזית *adj* a small quantity; (*lit.:* as big as an olive).

zayfan/-eem זייפן *nm* forger; faker; (*pl+of:* **-ey**).

zaz/-ah/-tee זז *v pres* moved; budged; (*pres* **zaz**; *fut* **yazooz**).

zaz/-ah זז *adj* moving; budging.

za'azoo|'a'/-'eem זעזוע *nm* shock; (*pl+of:* **-'ey**).

zbaleh זבאלה *nm [slang] (Arab.)* **1**. (*lit.*: dung); **2**. bad quality merchandise; **3**. bad company.
zbeng זבנג *interj [slang]* bang.
zdonee/-t זדוני *adj* malicious.
ze'ah זיעה *nf* sweat; (*+of:* **ze'at**).
ze'ak|ah/-ot זעקה *nf* outcry; (*+of:* **za'ak|at/-ot**).
zedonee/-t זדוני *adj* malicious.
zee'azoo|'a (*npr* **za'azoo|'a'**)**/-'eem** זעזוע *nm* shock; (*pl+of:* **-'ey**).
zeebel/-lah/-altee זיבל *v* fertilized; (*pres* **mezabel**; *fut* **yezabel**).
zeebel (*etc*) זיבל *v [slang]* told a pack of lies.
zeebool/-eem זיבול *nm* fertilizing.
"zeebooleem" זיבולים *nm pl [slang]* blah-blah.
zeebooreet זיבורית **1**. *nf* poor soil; **2**. *nf figurat.* worst quality.
zeeft זיפת *[slang] nm & adv (Arab.)* no-good; bad.
zeeftee/-t זיפתי *[slang] adj* very bad (disposition, work, health *etc*).
zeefzeef זיפזיף *nm* coarse sand (used in construction for making mortar, mixing concrete *etc*).
zeeg|eg/-egah/-agtee זיגג *v* glazed (installed glass panes); (*pres* **mezageg**; *fut* **yezageg**).
zeegoog/-eem זיגוג *nm* glazing (installing glass panes); (*pl+of:* **-ey**).
zeegzag/-eem זיגזג *nm* zigzag.
(be) zeegzageem בזיגזגים *adv* (moving) in zigzags.
zee|hah/-hatah/-heetee זיהה *v* identified; (*pres* **mezaheh**; *fut* **yezaheh**).
zee|hem/-hamah/hamtee זיהם *v* infected; polluted; (*pres* **mezahem**; *fut* **yezahem**).
zeehoom/-eem זיהום *nm* infection (Medic.); pollution; (*pl+of:* **-ey**).
zeehoo|y/-yeem זיהוי *nm* identification; (*pl+of:* **-yey**).
(meesd|ar/-erey) zeehooy מיסדר זיהוי *nm* identification parade; police line-up.
(pakhee|t/-yot) zeehooy פחית זיהוי *nm* identification disk.
zeek/-eem זיק *nm* spark; flash; (*pl+of:* **-ey**).
zeekah/-tah/-eetee זיכה *v* **1**. acquitted; **2**. credited; **3**. favored; (*pres* **mezakeh**; *fut* **yezakeh**).
zeek|ah/-ot זיקה *nf* link; inclination; connection; (*+of:* **-at**).
zee|karon/-khronot *(kh=k)* זיכרון memory; recollection; (*+of:* **-khron**).
('atseret) zeekaron עצרת זיכרון *nf* memorial assembly.
(ba'al/-at) zeekaron בעל זיכרון *nf* of retentive memory.
(bool/-ey) zeekaron בול זיכרון *nm* commemorative stamp.
(matsev|et/-ot) zeekaron מצבת זיכרון *nm* memorial; monument.
◇ **(yom ha) zeekaron** see ◇ **yom ha-zeekaron**.
◇ **(yom ha) zeekaron la-sho'ah ve-la-gevoorah** see ◇ **yom ha-sho'ah**.
zee|kayon/-khyonot *(kh=k)* זיכיון *nm* concession; (*+of:* **zeekhyon**).
□ **Zeekeem** (Ziqim) זיקים *nm* kibbutz (est. 1949) in South, 3 km S. of Ashkelon. Pop. 359.
zeekee|t/-yot זיקית *nf* chameleon.
zeekf|ah (*cpr* **zeekp|ah**)**/-ot** זיקפה *nf* erection (sexual); (*+of:* **-at**).
□ **Zeekhron** זכרון *nf colloq. reference to* □ **Zeekhron Ya'akov** see below.
□ **Zeekhron Ya'akov** (Zikhron Ya'aqov) זכרון יעקב *nf* township and vacationing spot (est. 1882 as agr. settlement) in S. Carmel hills overlooking sea. Pop. 6,510.
zeekhron|o/-ah lee-vrakhah *(v=b)* זכרונו לברכה of blessed memory.
zeekhronot זכרונות *nm pl* (*sing:* **zeekaron**) memories; memoires; reminiscences.
zeekn|ah זיקנה *nf* old age; (*+of:* **-at**).
zeeknah kaftsah 'al|av/-ehah זיקנה קפצה עליו *v* he/she aged prematurely; (*pres* **kofetset** *etc*; *fut* **teekpots** *etc p=f*).
('ad) zeeknah ve-seyvah עד זיקנה ושיבה *adv* until a ripe old age.
(beetoo'akh) zeeknah ביטוח זיקנה *nm* old-age insurance.
(makhl|at/-ot) zeeknah מחלת זיקנה *nf* geriatric diseases (Medic.).
(seeman/-ey) zeeknah סימן זיקנה *nm* sign of old age; symptom of old age.
zeekook/-eem זיקוק *nm* distillation; refining.
(bet/batey) zeekook בית־זיקוק *nm* refinery; oil-refinery. (In Israel, two: one in Haifa Bay, one in Ashdod).
zeekookeen dee-noor זיקוקין די־נור *nm pl* fireworks.
zeekoo|y/-yeem זיכוי *nm* **1**. acquittal (in trial); **2**. crediting; (account, taxation) (*pl+of:* **-yey**).
zeekooy be-meeshpat זיכוי במשפט *nm* acquittal (in a trial).
zeekoo|y/-yeem eeshee/-yeem זיכוי אישי *nm* tax deduction.
zeekp|ah/-ot זיקפה *nf* erection (sexual); (*+of:* **-at**).
zeel ha-zol זיל הזול *nm* extreme cheapness; greatly reduced prices.
(be) zeel ha-zol בזיל הזול *adv* dirt cheap.
zeelz|el/-elah/-altee זילזל *v* neglected; belittled (*pres* **mezalzel**; *fut* **yezalzel**).
zeelzool/-eem זילזול *nm* contempt; scorn; (*pl+of:* **-ey**).
zeem|ah/-ot זימה *nf* **1**. prostitution; lechery; **2**. incest; (*+of:* **-at**).
zeem|en/-nah/-antee זימן *v* convened; invited; (*pres* **mezamen**; *fut* **yezamen**).
zeem|er/-rah/-artee זימר *v* sang; (*pres* **mezamer**; *fut* **yezamer**).
zeemoon/-eem זימון *nm* summons; convocation; (*pl+of:* **-ey**).
zeemr|ah זימרה *nf* singing; (*+of:* **-at**).

zeemrah be-tseeboor זימרה בציבור *nf* community singing.

□ **Zeemrat** (Zimrat) זימרת *nm* village (est. 1957) in NW Negev. Pop. 328.

zeemz|em/-emah/-amtee זימזם *v* hummed; buzzed; (*pres* **mezamzem**; *fut* **yezamzem**).

zeemzoom/-eem זמזום *nm* buzzing; humming; (*pl+of:* **-ey**).

zeen|ek/-kah/-aktee זינק *v* leaped; sprung forth; (*pres* **mezanek**; *fut* **yezanek**).

zeen|ev/-vah זינב *v* curtailed; docked; pursued; (*pres* **mezanev**; *fut* **yezanev**).

zeenook/-eem זינוק *nm* **1.** leap; jump; **2.** start (in sport contests) (*pl+of:* **-ey**).

(ot ha) zeenook אות הזינוק *nm* starting signal.

zeep|et/-tah/-atetee זיפת *v* pitched; asphalted; tarred; (*pres* **mezapet**; *fut* **yezapet**).

zeepoot/-eem זיפות *nm* pitching; asphalting; tarring; (*pl+of:* **-ey**).

zeer|ah/-ot זירה *nf* arena; (*+of:* **-at**).

zeer|at/-ot ha-krav זירת הקרב *nf* theater of operations; battlefield area.

zeev זיו *nm* radiance.

ze'ev/-eem זאב *nm* wolf; (*pl+of:* **-ey**).

ze'ev/-ey yam זאב־ים *nm* sea-wolf; hake (fish).

zeevah זיוה *nf* popular feminine first name.

zeev|ah זיבה *nf* gonorrhea; (*+of:* **-at**).

□ **Zeevan** see **'En Zeevan**.

zeev|eg/-gah/-agtee זיווג *v* matched; paired; (*pres* **mezaveg**; *fut* **yezaveg**).

zeevoog/-eem זיווג *nf* match; matchmaking; (*pl+of:* **-ey**).

zee|yef/-yefah/-yaftee זייף *v* forged; counterfeited; (*pres* **mezayef**; *fut* **yezayef**).

zee|yen/-yenah/-yantee זיין *v* **1.** armed **2.** *[slang]* had sexual intercourse with; screwed; (*pres* **mezayen**; *fut* **yezayen**).

zeeyoof/-eem זיוף *nm* forgery; (*pl+of:* **-ey**).

zeeyoon/-eem זיון *nm* **1.** arming; armament; **2.** reinforcing concrete; **3.** *[slang]* lay; sexual intercourse; (*pl+of:* **-ey**).

zee'z|a'/-'ah/-a'tee זיעזע *v* shocked; (*pres* **meza'ze'a'**; *fut* **yeza'ze'a'**).

zefek/zefakeem זפק *nm* goiter; struma; (*pl+of:* **zeefkey**).

zefet זפת *nm* tar; pitch.

zeh/zo (or **/zot**) זה *pronoun m/f* this; this one.

zeh 'atah זה עתה *[colloq.] adv* just now.

zeh/zo et zeh/zo זה את זה *adv* one another; each other.

zeh kvar זה כבר *adv* a long time ago.

zeh lo kvar זה לא כבר *adv* not so long ago.

zeh lo shayakh זה לא שייך *v pres* it has no bearing; it does not matter.

zeh mee-zeh זה מזה *adv* from each other; one from the other.

(ba) zeh בזה *adv* herewith.

(be) zeh ha-lashon בזה הלשון *adv* in these words.

('eem kol) zeh/-zot עם כל זה *adv* with all that; nevertheless.

(ka) zeh/zot כזה such.

(ke-hoo) zeh כהוא זה *adv* not one bit.

(mah) zeh/zot? מה זה? what's that *m/f*?

(mah) zeh peet'om? מה זה פתאום? why all of a sudden?

(mee) zeh/zot? מי זה? מי זאת? who is it *m/f*? who's that *m/f*?

zehavhav/-ah זהבהב *adj* golden-brown; golden.

zeheh/zehah זהה *adj* identical.

zeheeroot זהירות *nf* **1.** caution; **2.** *interj* attention! careful!

(meeshneh) zeheeroot משנה זהירות *nf* double care; extra care.

zehoo זהו *m* this is; this is it.

zehoo zeh זהו זה *m* this is that; that's it!

zehoot זהות *nf* identity.

(te'oo|dat/-ot) zehoot תעודת זהות *nf* identity card.

zekan ha- זקן ה־ *m+of* chief; head of; (*pl+of:* **zeekney**).

zekankan/-eem זקנקן *nm* small (sparse) beard.

zekeefah/-ot זקיפה *nf* standing upright; straightening oneself out; (*+of:* **-at**).

zekeefah le-khovah זקיפה לחובה *nf* debiting.

zekeefah lee-zekhoot זקיפה לזכות *nf* crediting.

zekeefoot komah זקיפות קומה *nm* uprightness; (also figurat.).

zeken|ah/-ot זקנה *nf* old woman; (*+of:* **-at**).

zekentee זקנתי *nf* my grandmother.

□ **Zekharyah** (Zekharya) זכריה *nm* village (est. 1950) on **Bet-Shemesh - Bet Govreen** road. Pop. 401.

zekheel|ah/-ot זחילה *nf* crawling; (*+of:* **-at**).

zekhee|yah/-yot זכייה *nf* gain; win; (*+of:* **yat**).

zekher זכר *nm* remembrance; reminder.

(eyn) zekher אין זכר not a trace; nothing to remind.

(le) zekher לזכר in memory of.

zekhookhee|t/-yot זכוכית *nf* glass; glasswork.

zekhookheet magdelet זכוכית מגדלת *nf* magnifying glass.

(neyar) zekhookheet נייר זכוכית *nm* sand paper.

(tsemer) zekhookheet צמר זכוכית *nm* glass wool.

zekhoo|t/-yot זכות *nf* right; privilege.

zekhoo|t/-yot bekhorah זכות בכורה *nf* seniority right.

zekhoo|t/-yot kedeemah זכות קדימה *nf* priority right.

zekhoo|t/-yot kneesah זכות כניסה *nf* right of entry.

zekhoo|t/-yot yeter זכות יתר *nf* privilege.

zekhoo|t/-yot yotsreem זכות יוצרים *nf* copyright.

(bee) zekhoot בזכות *adv* **1.** by right; by right of; **2.** thanks to.

(lee) zekhoot לזכות *adv* in favor of; to the credit of.

◇ **zekhoot ha-sheevah** זכות השיבה *nf* the PLO claim that, as a condition to accepting some kind of peace with Israel, all refugees who left

Palestine in 1948 and/or their descendants should be granted an optional "Right of Return".

(**leem|ed/-dah/-adetee**) **zekhoot** לימוד זכות *v* defended; pleaded the case of; (*pst* **melamed** *etc; fut* **yelamed** *etc*).

(**le-khaf**) **zekhoot** לכף זכות *adv* in favor; towards making allowances.

zekhooyot זכויות *nf pl* (*sing:* **zekhoot**) rights.

zekhooyot ha-'ezrakh זכויות האזרח *nm pl* (*sing:* **zekhoot** *etc*) civil rights.

zekhooyot ha-prat זכויות הפרט *nm pl* (*sing:* **zekhoot** *etc*) personal rights.

(**sheevooy**) **zekhooyot** שיווי זכויות *nm* parity of rights; equal rights.

(**sheveh/shvat**) **zekhooyot** שווה זכויות *adj* of equal rights.

(**be-komah**) **zekoofah** בקומה זקופה *adv* upright; erect.

(**bat-**) **zekooneem** בת זקונים *nf* youngest daughter; "daughter of one's old age".

(**ben-**) **zekooneem** בן־זקונים *nm* youngest son; "son of one's old age".

zeleel|ah/-ot זלילה *nf* gluttony; voraciousness; (*+of:* **-at**).

zeman/-eem זמן *nm* time; (*pl+of:* **-ey**).

zeman 'ateed זמן עתיד *nf* future tense (Gram.).

zeman 'avar זמן עבר *nm* past tense (Gram.).

◇ **zeman ha-mandat** (*or:* **zman** *etc*) זמן המנדט *nm* time of the Mandate, see ◇ **tekoofat ha-mandat**.

zeman hoveh זמן הווה *nm* present tense (Gram.).

zeman-mah זמן־מה *nm* some time.

zeman panooy זמן פנוי *nm* free time.

(**ba**) **zeman** בזמן *adv* on time; in time.

(**bee**) **zeman she-** בזמן ש־ *adv* while; as; at a time when.

(**bee-merootsat ha**) **zeman** במרוצת הזמן *adv* as time goes on; with time.

(**bo ba**) **zeman** בו־בזמן *adv* at the very same time.

(**dey**) **zeman** די זמן *nm* time enough.

(**mee**) **zeman** מזמן *adv* for some time; since the time; since long ago.

(**pesek**) **zeman** פסק זמן *nm* time out (in sporting events).

zemanee/-t זמני *adj* temporary; provisional.

zeman|eem זמנים *nm pl* (*sing:* **zeman**) times; (*+of:* **-ey**).

(**loo|'akh/-khot**) **zemaneem** לוח זמנים *nm* timetable.

zemeenoo|t/-yot זמינות *nf* availability.

zemer זמר *nm* song.

(**klee/kley**) **zemer** כלי־זמר *nm* musical instrument.

(**kley**)**zemer** (*cpr* **klezmer/-eem**) כליזמר or: כלי־זמר *nmf* musician.

zemor|ah/-ot זמורה *nf* branch; twig; sprout; (*+of:* **-at**).

□ **Zemorot** see Zmorot.

zenoot זנות *nf* prostitution.

(**sheedool lee**) **zenoot** שידול לזנות *nm* soliciting.

zer/-eem זר *nm* wreath (*pl+of:* **-ey**).

zer/-ey dafnah זר דפנה *nm* laurel.

zer|a'/-a'eem זרע *nm* seed; (*pl+of:* **zar'ey**).

(**mee**) **zera'** מזרע *adv* of ... origin; from the seed of; offspring of.

□ **Zerakhyah** see □ **Zrakhyah**.

zeree|'ah/-'ot זריעה *nf* sowing; (*+of:* **-'at**).

zereek|ah/-ot זריקה *nf* **1.** injection; **2.** throwing; (*+of:* **-at**).

zereekh|ah/-ot זריחה *nf* sunrise; (*+of:* **-at**).

zereemah/-ot זרימה *nf* flow; flowing; (*+of:* **-at**).

zereezoo|t/-yot זריזות *nf* agility; alertness.

zerem/zrameem זרם *nm* current; stream; (*pl+of:* **zeermey**).

zerem ha-toda'ah זרם התודעה *nm* stream of consciousness.

zerem khashmal זרם חשמל *nm* electric current.

zerem kheeloofeen זרם חילופין *nm* alternating current; A.C.

zerem khalash זרם חלש *nm* low voltage.

zerem yasheer זרם ישיר *nm* direct current; D.C.

(**meyash|er/-rey**) **zerem** מיישר זרם *nm* rectifier.

(**neged ha**) **zerem** נגד הזרם *adv* against the stream.

zeret זרת *nf* **1.** little finger; **2.** span.

zer|ez/-zah/-aztee זירז *v* hurried; sped up; (*pres* **mezarez**; *fut* **yezarez**).

zero|'a'/-'ot זרוע *nf* arm.

□ **Zeroo'ah** see □ **Zroo'ah**.

(**ofnat ha**)**zerookeem** אופנת הזרוקים *nf* the hippie fashion; the hippie fad.

zerooz/-eem זירוז *nm* urging; speeding up; (*pl+of:* **-ey**).

□ **Zetan** זיתן *nm* village (est. 1950) in the **Shfelah**, 4 km N. of town of Lod. Pop. 578.

zeva|'ah/-'ot זוועה *nf* horror; (*+of:* **zav'at**).

zeva'atee (*npr* **zav'atee**)**/-t** זוועתי *adj* horrible.

zev|el/-aleem זבל *nm* garbage; dung; manure; (*pl+of:* **zeevley**).

zev|el/-aleem kheemee (*npr* **keemee**)**/-yeem** זבל כימי *nm* chemical fertilizer.

zev|el/-aleem organee/-yeem זבל אורגני *nm* organic fertilizer.

(**pakh/-ey**) **zevel** פח זבל *nm* garbage-can; dustbin.

zevoov/-eem זבוב *nm* fly (insect); (*pl+of:* **-ey**).

zevoovon/-eem זבובון *nm* gnat; small fly; (*pl+of:* **-ey**).

zeyt|eem זיתים *nm pl* (*sing:* **zayeet**) olives; (*+of:* **-ey**).

□ (**Har ha**) **Zeyteem** see □ **Har ha-Zeyteem**.

(**meseek ha**) **zeyteem** מסיק הזיתים *nm* olive harvest.

zgoogee/-t זגוגי *adj* glassy; translucent.

zgoogee|t/-yot זגוגית *nf* glass sheet.

zift/-eem (i pronounced as in *this*) זיפת *(Arab.) [slang]* **1.** *nm* no-good; bad; **2.** *adv* unhappy, unhappily, bad.

ziftee/-t (i pronounced as in *this*) זיפתי *(Arab.) adj [slang]* bad.

zkan ha- זקן ה־ *m+of* chief; head of; (*pl+of:* **zeekney**).

zkankan/-eem זקנקן *nm* small (sparse) beard.

zkeefah/-ot זקיפה *nf* standing upright; staightening oneself out; (*+of:* **-at**).

zkeefah le-khovah זקיפה לחובה *nf* debiting.

zkeefah lee-zkhoot זקיפה לזכות *nf* crediting.

zkeefoot komah זקיפות קומה *nm* uprightness; (also used *figurat.*).

zken|ah/-ot זקנה *nf* old woman; (*+of:* **-at**).

zkentee זקנתי *nf* my grandmother.

zkhee|yah/-yot זכייה *nf* gain; win; (*+of:* **yat**).

zkheel|ah/-ot זחילה *nf* crawling; (*+of:* **-at**).

zkhookheet/-yot זכוכית *nf* glass.

zkhoo|t/-yot זכות *nf* right; privilege.

zkhoo|t/-yot bekhorah זכות בכורה *nf* seniority right.

zkhoo|t/-yot kedeemah זכות קדימה *nf* priority right.

zkhoo|t/-yot kneesah זכות כניסה *nf* right of entry.

zkhoo|t/-yot yeter זכות יתר *nf* privilege.

zkhoo|t/-yot yotsreem זכות יוצרים *nf* copyright.

(bee) zkhoot בזכות *adv* **1.** by right; by right of; **2.** thanks to.

(lee) zkhoot לזכות *adv* in favor of; to the credit of.

(leem|ed/-dah/-adetee) zkhoot לימוד זכות *v* defended; pleaded the case of; (*pst* **melamed** *etc; fut* **yelamed** *etc*).

(le-khaf) zkhoot לכף זכות *adv* in favor; towards making allowances.

zkhooyot זכויות *nf pl* (*sing:* **zkhoot**) rights.

zkhooyot ha-'ezrakh זכויות האזרח *nm pl* (*sing:* **zkhoot** *etc*) civil rights.

zkhooyot ha-prat זכויות הפרט *nm pl* (*sing:* **zkhoot** *etc*) personal rights.

(sheevooy) zkhooyot שיווי זכויות *nm* parity of rights; equal rights.

(sheveh/shvat) zkhooyot שווה זכויות *adj* of equal rights.

(be-komah) zkoofah בקומה זקופה *adv* upright; erect.

(bat-) zkooneem בת זקונים *nf* youngest daughter; "daughter of one's old age".

(ben-) zkooneem בן־זקונים *nm* youngest son; "son of one's old age".

zleel|ah/-ot זלילה *nf* gluttony; voraciousness; (*+of:* **-at**).

zman/-eem זמן *nm* time; (*pl+of:* **-ey**).

zman 'ateed זמן עתיד future tense (Gram.).

zman 'avar זמן עבר *nm* past tense (Gram.).

zman hoveh זמן הווה *nm* present tense (Gram.).

zman-mah זמן מה *nm* some time.

zman panooy זמן פנוי *nm* free time.

(ba) zman בזמן *adv* on time; in time.

(bee) zman she- בזמן ש־ *adv* while; as; at a time when.

(bee-m'rootsat ha) zman במרוצת הזמן *adv* as time goes on; with time.

(bo ba) zman בו־בזמן *adv* at the very same time.

(dey) zman די זמן *nm* time enough.

(mee) zman מזמן *adv* for some time; since the time; since long ago.

(pesek) zman פסק זמן *nm* time out (in sporting events).

zmanee/-t זמני *adj* temporary; provisional.

zman|eem זמנים *nm pl* (*sing:* **zman**) times; (*+of:* **-ey**).

(loo|'akh/-khot) zmaneem לוח זמנים *nm* timetable.

zmeenoo|t/-yot זמינות *nf* availability.

zmor|ah/-ot זמורה *nf* branch; twig; sprout; (*+of:* **-at**).

□ **Zmorot** (Zemorot) זמורות *nm* vineyard farm (est. 1955) in S., 10 km NE of Ashkelon.

znoot זנות *nf* prostitution.

(sheedool lee) znoot שידול לזנות *nm* soliciting.

zo (also: **zot**; *[colloq.]*: **zoo**) זו *pron f* this; that; this one; that one.

(ka) zo (*also:* **ka-zoo**) כזו *adj f* like this one; like that one.

zohar זוהר *nm* glow; glamor.

□ **Zohar** זוהר *nm* village (est. 1950) in **Lakheesh** district, 8 km W. of **Keeryat-Gat**. Pop. 375.

(na'ar|at/-ot) zohar נערת זוהר *nf* glamor girl.

zoher/-et זוהר **1.** *adj* glamorous; shining; **2.** *v pres* shines; radiates; (*pst* **zahar**; *fut* **yeez'har**).

zokh|eh/-ah זוכה **1.** *v pres* wins; (*pst* **zakhah**; *fut* **yeezkeh**; *(k=kh)*); **2.** *nmf* winner; (*+of:* **-at/-ey**).

zokhel/-et זוחל **1.** *v pres* creeps; crawls; (*pst* **zakhal**; *fut* **yeezkhol**); **2.** *adj* creeping; crawling.

zokh|el/-aleem זוחל *nm* reptile; creeper; (*pl+of:* **-aley**); (Zoology).

(peekhoot/-eem) zokh|el/-aleem פיחות זוחל *nm* creeping devaluation; (Econ.).

zol/-ah זול *adj* cheap.

(be) zol בזול *adv* cheap; cheaply.

zolel/-et זולל *v pres* overeats; gluttonizes; (*pst* **zalal**; *fut* **yeezlol**).

zolelan/-eet זוללן *nmf & adj* glutton.

zon|ah/-ot זונה *nf* prostitute; harlot; hooker; whore; (*+of:* **-at**).

(bet/batey) zonot בית זונות *nm* brothel; whorehouse.

(ro|'eh/-'ey) zonot רועה זונות *nm* pimp.

(rova' ha) zonot רובע הזונות *nm* red-light district.

zoo (also **zo** *or* **zot**) זו **1.** *pron f* this; this one; that one; **2.** *v pres f* is; this is.

zoo ha-derekh זו הדרך this is the way (to follow); this is the right course.

zoog/-ot זוג *nm* **1.** pair; **2.** couple.

(bat/benot) zoog בת־זוג *nf* spouse; female partner; mate.

(ben/beney) zoog בן־זוג *nm* spouse; male partner; mate.

zoogat|ee/-kha/-o זוגתי־ך־ו *nf & poss.pron* my/your/his wife.

zoogee/-t זוגי *adj* dual; even.

(hazman|ah/-ot) zoogee|t/-yot הזמנה זוגית *nf* dual invitation.

zoo|ham/-hamah/-hamtee זוהם *v* was polluted; was contaminated; (*pres* **mezoham**; *fut* **yezooham**).

zooham|ah/-ot זוהמה *nf* filth; (*+of:* **-at**).

zook|ah/-tah/-etee זוכה **1.** *v* was acquitted; **2.** was credited; (*pres* **mezookeh**; *fut* **yezookeh**).

zoolat זולת *prep* except; else.

zoolat eem זולת אם *prep* except if...; unless.

(ahavat ha) zoolat אהבת הזולת *nf* altruism.

zoolat|ee/-kha/-o זולתי וכו׳ *prep & poss.pron* except me/you/him.

zoot|a/-ot זוטא *adj* small; minor; mini-.

zootar/-eem זוטר *nm* junior.

zootar/-eet זוטר *adj* junior.

zootot זוטות *nf pl* (*sing:* **zoota**) trifles; bagatelles.

zot (*also:* **zo** *or* **zoo**) זאת *pron f* this one; this.

zot hee זאת היא this is.

zot omeret זאת אומרת that is; i.e.

(be-khol) zot בכל זאת *adv* nevertheless; notwithstanding.

('eem) zot עם זאת *adv* however; nevertheless.

(en) zot ela אין זאת אלא only meaning that; meaning nothing but...

(ha) zot הזאת *adj f* this one.

(ka) zot כזאת *adj f* like this one; such.

(mah) zot omeret?! מה זאת אומרת?! (*query* & expression of outrage) what does it mean?! what does this mean?! What is this?!

(ha) zotee (*npr* **ha-zot**) הזאתי *[colloq.] adj* this one;that one.

(ka) zotee (*npr* **ka-zot**) כזאתי *[colloq.] adj* like this one; such.

zov dam זוב דם *nm* bleeding; hemorrhage.

□ **Zrakhyah** (Zerakhya) זרחיה *nm* village (est. 1950) in **Lakheesh** district, 10 km N. of **Keeryat-Gat**. Pop. 438.

zree|'ah/-'ot זריעה *nf* sowing; (*+of:* **-'at**).

zreek|ah/-ot זריקה *nf* **1.** injection; **2.** throwing; (*+of:* **-at**).

zreekh|ah/-ot זריחה *nf* sunrise; (*+of:* **-at**).

zreemah/-ot זרימה *nf* flow; flowing; (*+of:* **-at**).

zreezoo|t/-yot זריזות *nf* agility; alertness.

zro|'a'/-'ot זרוע *nf* arm.

□ **Zroo'ah** (Zeru'a) זרועה *nm* village (est. 1953) in N. Negev. Pop. 260.

(ofnat ha) zrookeem אופנת הזרוקים *nf* the hippie fashion; the hippie fad.

zva|'ah/-'ot זוועה *nf* horror; (*+of:* **zav'at**).

zva'atee (*npr* **zav'atee**)**/-t** זוועתי *adj* horrible.

zvoov/-eem זבוב *nm* fly (insect); (*pl+of:* **-ey**).

zvoovon/-eem זבובון *nm* gnat; small fly; (*pl+of:* **-ey**).

English-Hebrew

A.

A,a Hebrew having no vowels, the English "A" is transliterated as אָ (Aleph) when pronounced as in "bar" and as אֶ or איי when pronounced as in "able".

a אחד/אחת *nmf* ekhad/akhat.

(what) a איזה מין eyzeh meen.

(such) a אחד/אחת כזה *nmf* ekhad/akhat ka-zeh/zo (*or:* zot).

A to Z מאלף ועד תיו me-alef ve-'ad tav.

(taken) aback מופתע *adj* mooft|a'/-a'at.

(to) abandon 1. לנטוש *inf* leentosh; *pst* natash; *pres* notesh; *fut* yeentosh; **2.** להפקיר (renounce ownership) *inf* lehafkeer; *pst* heefkeer; *pres* mafkeer; *fut* yafkeer.

abandoned 1. נטוש *adj* natoosh/netooshah; **2.** מופקר (derelict) *adj* moofk|ar/-eret.

abandonment 1. נטישה *nf* neteesh|ah/-ot (+*of:* -at); **2.** התמסרות (devotion) *nf* heetmasroo|t/-yot.

(to) abase 1. להשפיל *inf* lehashpeel; *pst* heeshpeel; *pres* mashpeel; *fut* yashpeel; **2.** לבזות (humiliate) *inf* levazot; *pst* beezah; *pres* mevazeh; *fut* yevazeh.

abasement השפלה *nf* hashpal|ah/-ot (+*of:* -at).

abashed נכלם *adj* neekhl|am/-emet.

(to) abate להפחית *inf* lehafkheet; *pst* heefkheet; *pres* mafkheet; *fut* yafkheet.

abatement 1. הפחתה *nf* hafkhat|ah/-ot (+*of:* -at); **2.** ניכוי (deduction) *nm* neekooy/-eem (*pl+of:* -ey).

abbey מנזר *nm* meenz|ar/-areem (*pl+of:* -erey).

(to) abbreviate לקצר *inf* lekatser; *pst* keetser; *pres* mekatser; *fut* yekatser.

abbreviation 1. קיצור *nm* keetsoor/-eem (*pl+of:* -ey); **2.** ראשי תיבות (acronym) *nm pl* rashey tevot.

ABC 1. אלף־בית *nm* alef-bet; **2.** א״ב *nm acr* alef-bet.

(to) abdicate להתפטר (resign) *inf* leheetpater; *pst* heetpater; *pres* meetpater; *fut* yeetpater.

abdomen 1. בטן *nf* bet|en/-aneem (*pl+of:* beetney); **2.** כרס (belly) *nf* keres/kreseem (*pl+of:* kresey).

(to) abduct לחטוף *inf* lakhatof; *pst* khataf; *pres* khotef; *fut* yakhatof.

abduction חטיפה *nf* khateef|ah/-ot (+*of:* -at).

aberration עיוות *nm* 'eevoot/-eem (*pl+of:* -ey).

(to) abet 1. לסייע לדבר עבירה *inf* lesaye'a' lee-dvar 'averah; *pst* seeya' *etc*; *pres* mesaye'a' *etc*; yesaye'a' *etc*; **2.** להסית לדבר עבירה (incite to commit) *inf* lehaseet lee-dvar 'averah; *pst* heseet *etc*; *pres* meseet *etc*; *fut* yaseet *etc*.

abeyance השהיה *nf* hash'ha|yah/-yot (+*of:* -yat).

(to hold in) abeyance להשהות *inf* lehash'hot; *pst* heesh'hah; *pres* mash'heh; *fut* yash'heh.

(to) abhor לתעב *inf* leta'ev; *pst* te'ev; *pres* meta'ev; *fut* yeta'ev.

abhorrence תיעוב *nm* te'oov/-eem (*pl+of:* -ey).

(to) abide לשמור אמונים *inf* leeshmor emooneem; *pst* shamar *etc*; *pres* shomer *etc*; *fut* yeeshmor *etc*.

(to) abide by לקיים *inf* lekayem; *pst* keeyem; *pres* mekayem; *fut* yekayem.

ability יכולת *nf* yekholet.

abject בזוי *adj* bazooy/bezooyah.

(to) abjure להתכחש ל־ *inf* leheetkakhesh le-; *pst* heetkakhesh le-; *pres* meetkakhesh le-; *fut* yeetkakhesh le-.

ablaze בלהבות *adj & adv* be-lehavot.

able 1. מסוגל *adj* mesoog|al/-elet; **2.** מוכשר (capable) *adj* mookhsh|ar/-eret.

(to be) able להיות מסוגל *inf* leehyot mesoog|al/elet; *pst* hayah *etc*; *pres* mesoogal; *fut* yeehyeh *etc*.

able-bodied כשיר *adj* kasheer/kesheerah.

abloom בפריחה *adv* bee-freekhah (*f=p*).

abnegation ויתור *nm* veetoor/-eem (*pl+of:* -ey).

abnormal 1. לא־נורמלי *adj* lo-normalee/-t; **2.** סוטה (pervert) *adj & nmf* sot|eh/-ah.

aboard 1. על סיפון *adv* 'al seepoon; **2.** על גבי (on top of) *adv* 'al gabey.

(to go) aboard לעלות על סיפון *inf* la'alot 'al seepoon; *pst* 'alah *etc*; *pres* 'oleh *etc*; *fut* ya'aleh *etc*.

abode מעון *nm* ma'on/me'onot (+*of:* me'on).

(to) abolish לבטל *inf* levatel; *pst* beetel (*b=v*); *pres* mevatel; *fut* yevatel.

abolition ביטול *nm* beetool/-eem (*pl+of:* -ey).

abominable מתועב *adj* meto|'av/-'evet.

(to) abort 1. להפיל (a fetus) *inf* lehapeel; *pst* heepeel; *pres* mapeel; *fut* yapeel; **2.** לעצור (project, operation) *inf* la'atsor; *pst* 'atsar; *pres* 'otser; *fut* ya'atsor.

abortion הפלה *nf* hapal|ah/-ot (+*of:* -at).

(to) abound לשפוע *inf* leeshpo'a'; *pst* shafa' (*f=p*); *pres* shofe'a'; *fut* yeeshpa'.

(to) abound with לשרוץ *inf* leeshrots; *pst* sharats; *pres* shorets; *fut* yeeshrots.

about (concerning) אודות odot.

about (near) בסביבות bee-sveevot.

about (time) בערך be-'erekh.

(to be) about להימצא בסביבה *inf* leheematse ba-sveevah; *pst & pres* neemtsa *etc*; *fut* yeematse *etc*.

above 1. למעלה *adv* le-ma'lah; **2.** מעל (on top of) *adv* me-'al.

(from) above 1. מלמעלה *adv* mee-le-ma'lah; **2.** ממעל (from higher up) *adv* mee-ma'al.

above all מעל לכל *adv* me'al la-kol.

above-mentioned 1. הנזכר לעיל *adj* ha-neezk|ar/-eret le-'eyl; **2.** הנ"ל (a/m) *nmf* ha-nal (*acr of* 1).

abrasive 1. מלטש *nm* melat|esh/-'sheem (*pl+of:* -'shey); **2.** *adj* melatesh/-et.

abreast זה בצד זה *nmf* zeh/zo be-tsad zeh/zo.

(to) abridge לקצר *inf* lekatser; *pst* keetser; *pres* mekatser; *fut* yekatser.

abridgment תקציר *nm* taktseer/-eem (*pl+of:* -ey).

abroad 1. בחוץ לארץ *adv* be-khoots la-arets; **2.** בחו"ל (*acr of* 1) be-khool.

(to go) abroad לצאת לחו"ל *inf* latset le-khool; *pst* yatsa *etc*; *pres* yotse *etc*; *fut* yetse *etc*.

(to) abrogate לבטל *inf* levatel; *pst* beetel *(b=v)*; *pres* mevatel; *fut* yevatel.

abrupt 1. פתאומי *adj* peet'omee/-t; **2.** תלול (steep) *adj* talool/teloolah.

abscess 1. מורסה *nf* moors|ah/-ot (*+of:* -at); **2.** כיב (canker) *nm* keev/-eem (*pl+of:* -ey).

(to) abscond 1. להימלט *inf* leheemalet; *pst & pres* neemlat; *fut* yeemalet; **2.** לברוח (flee) *inf* leevro'akh; *pst* barakh *(b=v)*; *pres* bore'akh; *fut* yeevrakh.

absence היעדרות *nf* he'adroo|t/-yot.

(leave of) absence חופשה ללא תשלום *nf* khoofsh|ah/-ot le-lo tashloom.

absence of mind היסח הדעת *nm* hesakh ha-da'at.

absent נעדר *adj* ne'd|ar/-eret.

(to) absent oneself להיעדר *inf* lehe'ader; *pst & pres* ne'dar; *fut* ye'ader.

absentee נפקד *nm* neefk|ad/-adeem (*pl+of:* -edey).

absentee landlord בעל־בית נפקד *nm* ba'al-bayeet neefkad.

absent-minded מפוזר *adj* mefooz|ar/-eret.

absolute 1. מוחלט *adj* mookhl|at/-etet; **2.** החלטי (definitive) *adj* hekhletee/-t.

absolutely בהחלט *adv* be-hekhlet.

absolution 1. מחילה *nf* mekheel|ah/-ot (*+of:* -at); **2.** כפרת עוונות (expiation) *nf* kaparat 'avonot.

(to) absolve 1. לפטור מחטא *inf* leeftor me-khet; *pst* patar *(p=f) etc*; *pres* poter *etc*; *fut* yeeftor *etc*; **2.** לפטור מעונש (acquit) *inf* leeftor me-'onesh; *pst* patar *(p=f) etc*; *pres* poter *etc*; *fut* yeeftor *etc*.

(to) absorb 1. לספוג *inf* leespog; *pst* safag *(f=p)*; *pres* sofeg; *fut* yeespog; **2.** לקלוט (take in) *inf* leeklot; *pst* kalat; *pres* kolet; *fut* yeeklot.

absorbent סופג *adj & nmf* sofeg/-et.

absorbing מרתק *adj* meratek/-et.

absorption 1. ספיגה *nf* sfeeg|ah/-ot (*+of:* -at); **2.** קליטה (reception) *nf* kleet|ah/-ot (*+of:* -at).

(Ministry of Immigrant) Absorption 1. המשרד לקליטת העליה *nm* ha-meesrad lee-kleetat ha-'aleeyah; **2.** משרד הקליטה *(colloq. abbr.)* *nm* meesrad ha-kleetah.

(to) abstain להימנע *inf* leheemana'; *pst* neemna'; *fut* yeemana'.

abstention הימנעות *nf* heeman'oo|t/-yot.

abstinence התנזרות *nf* heetnazroo|t/-yot.

abstract 1. מופשט *adj* moofsh|at/-etet; **2.** אבסטראקטי *adj* abstraktee/-t; **3.** תמצית *nf* tamtsee|t/-yot.

(in the) abstract 1. להלכה *adv* la-halakhah; **2.** באופן מופשט (theoretically) *adv* be-ofen moofshat.

abstraction הפשטה *nf* hafshat|ah/-ot (*+of:* -at).

absurd אבסורדי *adj* absoordee/-t.

absurdity אבסורד *nm* absoord/-eem.

abundance שפע *nm* shefa'.

abundant שופע *adj* shof|e'a'/-a'at.

abuse 1. התעללות *nf* heet'aleloo|t/-yot; **2.** שימוש לרעה (misuse) *nm* sheemoosh/-eem le-ra'ah.

(to) abuse 1. להשתמש לרעה (misuse) *inf* leheeshtamesh le-ra'ah; *pst* heeshtamesh *etc*; *pres* meeshtamesh *etc*; *fut* yeeshtamesh *etc*; **2.** לגדף (insult) *inf* legadef; *pst* geedef; *pres* megadef; *fut* yegadef.

abusive פוגע *adj* pog|e'a/-a'at.

abyss תהום *nf* tehom/-ot.

academic אקדמי *adj* akademee/-t.

academy אקדמיה *nf* akadem|yah/-yot (*+of:* -yat).

(to) accede 1. להסכים *inf* lehaskeem; *pst* heeskeem; *pres* maskeem; *fut* yaskeem; **2.** להיכנס לתפקיד (enter upon office) *inf* leheekanes le-tafkeed; *pst & pres* neekhnas *(kh=k) etc*; *fut* yeekanes *etc*.

(to) accelerate 1. להחיש *inf* lehakheesh; *pst* hekheesh; *pres* mekheesh; *fut* yakheesh; **2.** לזרז (hasten) *inf* lezarez; *pst* zerez; *pres* mezarez; *pres* yezarez; **3.** להאיץ (speed up) *inf* leha'eets; *pst* he'eets; *pres* me'eets; *fut* ya'eets.

acceleration 1. תאוצה *nf* te'oots|ah/-ot (*+of:* -at); **2.** החשה (speeding) *nf* hekhash|ah-ot (*+of:* -at).

accelerator מאיץ *nm* me'eets/-eem (*pl+of:* -ey).

accent 1. מבטא *nm* meevta/-'eem (*pl+of:* -'ey); **2.** הדגש (emphasis) *nm* hedgesh/-eem (*pl+of:* -ey).

(to) accentuate להדגיש *inf* lehadgeesh; *pst* heedgeesh; *pres* madgeesh; *fut* yadgeesh.

(to) accept 1. לקבל *inf* lekabel; *pst* keebel; *pres* mekabel; *fut* yekabel; **2.** להסכים (agree) *inf* lehaskeem; *pst* heeskeem; *pres* maskeem; *fut* yaskeem.

acceptable 1. מקובל mekoob|al/-elet; **2.** קביל (jurid.) *adj* kaveel/keveelah.

acceptance 1. קבלה *nf* kabal|ah (*+of:* -at); **2.** הסכמה (agreement) *nf* haskam|ah/-ot (*+of:* -at).

access גישה *nf* geesh|ah/-ot (*+of:* -at).

accessible נגיש *adj* nageesh/negeeshah.

accessories 1. אבזרים *nm pl* avz|areem (*+of:* -erey); **2.** אביזרים *[colloq.]* *nm pl* aveez|areem (*sing:* aveez|ar; *+of:* -rey).

accessory 1. מסייע (to a crime) *nmf & adj* (aiding) mesa|ye'a'/-ya'at; **2.** אבזר (machine part) *nm* avz|ar/-areem (*+of:* -erey).

accident 1. תאונה *nf* te'oon|ah/-ot (*+of:* -at); **2.** מקרה (coincidence) *nm* meekr|eh/-eem (*pl+of:* -ey).

(by) accident במקרה *adv* be-meekreh.

accidental מקרי *adj* meekree/-t.

accidentally במקרה *adv* be-meekreh.

acclaim תשואות *nf* teshoo'ot.

(to) acclaim לקבל בתשואות *inf* lekabel bee-teshoo'ot; *pst* keebel *etc; pres* mekabel *etc; fut* yekabel *etc.*

acclamation תרועת רצון *nf* troo|'at/-'ot ratson.

(to) acclimate, (to) acclimatize 1. לאקלם *vt* le'aklem; *pst* eeklem; *pres* me'aklem; *fut* ye'aklem; **2.** להתאקלם *v rfl inf* leheet'aklem; *pst* heet'aklem; *pres* meet'aklem; *fut* heet'aklem.

(to) accommodate 1. להתאים (adapt) *inf* lehat'eem; *pst* heet'eem; *pres* mat'eem; *fut* yat'eem; **2.** לארח (entertain) *inf* le'are'akh; *pst* erakh; *pres* me'are'akh; *fut* ye'are'akh; **3.** לאכסן (lodge) *inf* le'akhsen; *pst* eekhsen; *pres* me'akhsen; *fut* ye'akhsen.

(to) accommodate oneself להסתגל *inf* leheestagel; *pst* heestagel; *pres* meestagel; *fut* yeestagel.

accommodation 1. אכסון (quartering) *nm* eekhsoon/-eem (*pl+of:* -ey); **2.** התאמה (adjustment) *nf* hat'am|ah/-ot (*+of:* -at).

accompaniment ליווי *nm* leevoo|y/-yeem (*pl+of:* -yey).

accompanist מלווה *nmf* melav|eh/-ah (*pl:* -eem/ -ot).

(to) accompany ללוות *inf* lelavot; *pst* leevah; *pres* melaveh; *fut* yelaveh.

accomplice שותף לפשע *nmf* shootaf/-ah (*pl:* -eem/ -ot) le-fesha' *(f=p)*.

(to) accomplish להשיג *inf* lehaseeg; *pst* heeseeg; *pres* maseeg; *fut* yaseeg.

accomplished מושלם *adj* mooshl|am/-emet.

accomplishment הישג *nm* heseg/-eem (*pl+of:* -ey).

accord 1. תיאום *nm* te'oom/-eem (*pl+of:* -ey); **2.** הסכמה (agreement) *nf* haskam|ah/-ot (*+of:* -at).

(of one's own) accord מרצונו שלו *adv* me-retson|o/-ah shel|o/-ah *(m/f)*.

(in) accord with בתיאום עם *adv* be-te'oom 'eem.

accordance תיאום *nm* te'oom/-eem (*pl+of:* -ey).

(in) accordance with בהתאם ל־ *adv* be-het'em le-

according לפי lefee.

according (to) לדברי *adv* le-deevrey.

accordion אקורדיון *nm* akordyon/-eem.

account חשבון *nm* kheshbon/-ot.

(on no) account בשום אופן be-shoom ofen.

(on one's own) account על אחריותו שלו *adv* 'al akhrayoot|o/-ah shel|o/-ah *(m/f)*.

(to) account לתת את הדין *inf* latet et ha-deen; *pst* natan *etc; pres* noten *etc; fut* yeeten *etc.*

(on) account of בגלל *prep* beeglal.

accountable אחראי *adj* akhra'ee/-t.

accountancy, accounting 1. הנהלת חשבונות *nf* hanhalat kheshbonot; **2.** חשבונאות *nf* kheshbona'oot.

accountant מנהל חשבונות *nmf* menahel/-et kheshbonot.

accounting ניהול חשבונות *nm* neehool kheshbonot.

(to) accredit 1. להסמיך *inf* lehasmeekh; *pst* heesmeekh; *pres* masmeekh; *fut* yasmeekh; **2.** למנות (appoint) *inf* lemanot; *pst* meenah; *pres* memaneh; *fut* yemaneh.

(to) accrue 1. להצטבר (accummulate) *inf* leheetstaber; *pst* heetstaber; *pres* meetstaber; *fut* yeetstaber; **2.** לצמוח (grow) *inf* leetsmo'akh; *pst* tsamakh; *pres* tsome'akh; *fut* yeetsmakh.

(to) accummulate לצבור *inf* leetsbor; *pst* tsavar *(v=b); pres* tsover; *fut* yeetsbor.

accummulation צבירה *nf* tseveer|ah/-ot (*+of:* -at).

accuracy 1. דיוק *nm* deeyook/-eem (*pl+of:* -ey); **2.** דייקנות (punctuality) *nf* daykanoo|t/-yot.

accurate מדויק *adj* medooy|ak/-eket.

accusation האשמה *nf* ha'asham|ah/-ot (*+of:* -at).

(to) accuse להאשים *inf* leha'asheem; *pst* he'esheem; *pres* ma'asheem; *fut* ya'asheem.

accused נאשם *nmf* ne'esh|am/-emet (*pl:* -ameem/ -amot).

(to) accustom להרגיל *inf* lehargeel; *pst* heergeel; *pres* margeel; *fut* yargeel.

(to) accustom oneself להתרגל *inf* leheetragel; *pst* heetragel; *pres* meetragel; *fut* yeetragel.

accustomed מורגל *adj* moorg|al/-elet.

ace 1. אס (in cards) *[slang] nm* as/-eem; **2.** אלוף (in sports) *nm* aloof/-eem (*pl+of:* -ey); *nf* aloof|ah/-ot (*+of:* -at); **3.** מומחה (specialist) *nm* moomkh|eh/ -eem (*pl+of:* -ey).

acetate אצטט *nm* atsetat/-eem.

acetylene אצטילן *nm* atseteelen.

ache כאב *nm* ke'ev/-eem (*pl+of:* -ey).

(head) ache כאב ראש *nm* ke'ev/-ey rosh.

(tooth) ache כאב שיניים *nm* ke'ev/-ey sheenayeem.

(to) achieve 1. להגשים *inf* lehagsheem; *pst* heegsheem; *pres* magsheem; *fut* yagsheem; **2.** להשיג (attain) *inf* lehaseeg; *pst* heeseeg; *pres* maseeg; *fut* yaseeg.

achievement הישג *nm* heseg/-eem (*pl+of:* -ey).

acid 1. חומצה *nf* khoomts|ah/-ot (*+of:* -at); **2.** חמוץ (sour) *adj* khamoots/-ah.

(to) acknowledge 1. להכיר *inf* lehakeer; *pst* heekeer; *pres* makeer; *fut* yakeer; **2.** להודות (admit) *inf* lehodot; *pst* hodah; *pres* modeh; *fut* yodeh.

acknowledgement הכרה *nf* hakar|ah/-ot (*+of:* -at).

acknowledgement of delivery אישור מסירה *nm* eeshoor/-ey meseerah.

acknowledgement of receipt אישור קבלה *nm* eeshoor/-ey kabalah.

acme שיא *nm* see/-'eem (*pl+of:* -'ey).

acne פצעוני־בגרות *nm pl* peets'oney bagroot.

acorn אצטרובל *nm* eetstroobal/-eem (*pl+of:* -ey).

acoustic אקוסטי *adj* akoostee/-t.

acoustics 1. תורת הקול *nf* torat ha-kol; **2.** אקוסטיקה *nf* akoosteekah.

(to) acquaint 1. להכיר *inf* lehakeer; *pst* heekeer; *pres* makeer; *fut* yakeer; **2.** להציג (introduce) *inf* lehatseeg; *pst* heetseeg; *pres* matseeg; *pres* yatseeg.

acquaintance 1. היכרות (knowledge) *nf* hekeroo|t/ -yot; **2.** מכיר (person) *nmf* makeer/-ah.

(to) acquiesce להסכים בשתיקה *inf* lehaskeem bee-shteekah; *pst* heeskeem *etc; pres* maskeem *etc; fut* yaskeem *etc.*

acquiescence 1. הסכמה בשתיקה *nf* haskam|ah/-ot bee-shteekah; **2.** השלמה (reconciliation) *nf* hashlam|ah/-ot (*+of:* -at).

(to) acquire לרכוש *inf* leerkosh; *pst* rakhash *(kh=k)*; *pres* rokhesh; *fut* yeerkosh.

acquisition רכישה *nf* rekheesh|ah/-ot (*+of:* -at).

(to) acquit 1. לזכות בדין *nf* lezakot be-deen; *pst* zeekah *etc*; *pres* mezakeh *etc*; *fut* yezakeh *etc*; **2.** לסלק חוב (settle debt) *inf* lesalek khov; *pst* seelek *etc*; *pres* mesalek *etc*; *fut* yesalek *etc*.

acquittal זיכוי *nm* zeekoo|y/-yeem (*pl+of:* -yey).

acrid צורב *adj* tsorev/-et.

acrobat לוליין *nmf* loolyan/-eet (*pl:* -eem/-eeyot; *pl+of:* -ey).

acrobatic אקרובטי *adj* akrobatee/-t.

acrobatics 1. לוליינות *nf* loolyanoot; **2.** אקרובטיקה *nf* akroobateek|ah/-ot (*+of:* -at).

acronym ראשי תיבות *nm pl* rashey teyvot.

across 1. ממול (opposite) *adv* mee-mool; **2.** דרך (through) *prep* derekh; **3.** מעבר (beyond) *prep* me'ever; **4.** לרוחב (through its breadth) *adv* le-rokhav.

act 1. מעשה *nm* ma'aseh/-eem (*pl+of:* -ey); **2.** פעולה (deed) *nf* pe'ool|ah/-ot (*+of:* -at); **3.** מערכה (in a play) *nf* ma'arakh|ah/-ot.

(to) act 1. לשחק *inf* lesakhek; *pst* seekhek; *pres* mesakhek; *fut* yesakhek; **2.** לפעול (do) *inf* leef'ol; *pst* pa'al *(p=f)*; *pres* po'el; *fut* yeef'al.

acting משחק *nm* meeskhak.

action פעולה *nf* pe'ool|ah/-ot (*+of:* -at).

(to) activate לתפעל *inf* letaf'el; *pst* teef'el; *pres* metaf'el; *fut* yetaf'el.

active פעיל *adj* pa'eel/pe'eelah.

activist אקטיביסט *nmf* akteeveest/-eet.

activity פעילות *nf* pe'eeloo|t/-yot.

actor שחקן sakhkan/-eem (*pl+of:* -ey).

actress שחקנית *nf* sakhkanee|t/-yot.

actual ממשי *adj* mamashee/-t.

actuality 1. מציאות *nf* metsee'oot; **2.** ממשות (reality) *nf* mamashoo|t/-yot.

actually למעשה *adv* le-ma'aseh.

actuary אקטואר *nm* aktoo'ar/-eem (*pl+of:* -ey).

(to) actuate 1. לתפעל *inf* letaf'el; *pst* teef'el; *pres* metaf'el; *fut* yetaf'el; **2.** להניע (move) *inf* lehanee'a'; *pst* henee'a'; *pres* menee'a'; *fut* yanee'a'.

acuity חריפות *nf* khareefoo|t/-yot.

acumen מהירות תפיסה *nf* meheeroot tfeesah.

acupuncture אקופונקטורה *nf* akoopoonktoorah.

acute חריף *adj* khareef/-ah.

acuteness חריפות *nf* khareefoo|t/-yot.

adage פיתגם *nm* peetgam/-eem (*pl+of:* -ey).

adamant עיקש *adj* 'eekesh/-et.

(to) adapt 1. להתאים *inf* lehat'eem; *pst* heet'eem; *pres* mat'eem; *fut* yat'eem; **2.** לסגל (fit) *inf* lesagel; *pst* seegel; *pres* mesagel; *fut* yesagel.

adaptation 1. סיגול *nm* seegool; **2.** עיבוד (processing) *nm* 'eebood/-eem (*pl+of:* -ey).

(to) add להוסיף *inf* lehoseef; *pst* hoseef; *pres* moseef; *fut* yoseef.

addict מתמכר *nmf* meetmaker/-et.

(drug) addict מכור לסמים *nmf & adj* makhoor/mekhoorah le-sameem.

addiction התמכרות *nf* heetmakroo|t/-yot.

addition 1. חיבור (mathem.) *nm* kheeboor; **2.** תוספת (supplement) *nf* tos|efet/-afot.

address 1. כתובת *nf* ketov|et/-ot; **2.** מען (mail-) ma'an/-eem (*pl+of:* -ey).

(to) address להפנות *inf* lehafnot; *pst* heefnah; *pres* mafneh; *fut* yafneh.

addressee ממוען *adj* memoo|'an/-'enet.

adept 1. מיומן *adj* meyoom|an/-enet; **2.** בר־סמכא (expert) *nmf* bar/bat samkha.

adequate 1. מספיק *adj* masp|eek/-eket; **2.** מניח את הדעת (acceptable) *adj* menee|akh/-khah et ha-da'at.

(to) adhere 1. להצטרף *inf* leheetstaref; *pst* heetstaref; *pres* meetstaref; *fut* yeetstaref; **2.** לדבוק (cling) *inf* leedbok; *pst* davak *(v=b)*; *pres* davek; *fut* yeedbak.

adherence הצטרפות *nf* heetstarfoo|t/-yot.

adhesive מדביק *nm* madbeek/-eem.

adieu להתראות leheetra'ot!

adjacent סמוך *adj* samookh/smookhah.

adjective שם תואר *nm* shem/-ot to'ar.

(to) adjoin 1. לגבול *inf* leegbol; *pst* gaval *(v=b)*; *pres* govel; *fut* yeegbol; **2.** לצרף (add) *inf* letsaref; *pst* tseref; *pres* metsaref; *fut* yetsaref.

(to) adjourn לדחות *inf* leedkhot; *pst* dakhah; *pres* dokheh; *fut* yeedkheh.

adjournment דחייה *nf* dekhee|yah/-yot (*+of:* -yat).

(to) adjudge לפסוק *inf* leefsok; *pst* pasak; *(p=f) pres* posek; *fut* yeefsok.

(to) ad-lib לאלתר *inf* le'alter; *pst* eelter; *pres* me'alter; *fut* ye'alter.

(to) administer לנהל *inf* lenahel; *pst* neehel; *pres* menahel; *fut* yenahel.

administration 1. ניהול *nm* neehool; **2.** מינהל (management) *nm* meenhal/-eem (*pl+of:* -ey).

administrator 1. מנהל *nmf* menahel/-et; **2.** אמרכל (also treasurer) *nm* amarkal/-eem (*pl+of:* -ey).

admirable ראוי להערצה *adj* ra'ooy/re'ooyah le-ha'aratsah.

(to) admire להעריץ *inf* leha'areets; *pst* he'ereets; *pres* ma'areets; *fut* ya'areets.

admirer מעריץ *nmf* ma'areets/-ah.

admissible קביל *adj* kaveel/kveelah.

admission 1. כניסה *nf* knees|ah/-ot (*+of:* -at); **2.** הודאה (acknowledgement) *nf* hoda|'ah/-'ot (*+of:* -'at).

(to) admit 1. לתת להיכנס (let enter) *inf* latet leheekanes; *pst* natan *etc*; *pres* noten *etc*; *fut* yeeten *etc*; **2.** להודות (acknowledge) *inf* lehodot; *pst* hodah; *pres* modeh; *fut* yodeh.

admittance רשות כניסה *nf* reshoot keneesah.

admixture ערבוב *nm* 'eerboov/-eem (*pl+of:* -ey).

(to) admonish להזהיר *inf* lehaz'heer; *pst* heez'heer; *pres* maz'heer; *fut* yaz'heer.

admonition אזהרה *nf* az'har|ah/-ot (*+of:* -at).

ado מהומה *nf* mehoom|ah/-ot (*+of:* -at).

adolescence התבגרות *nf* heetbagroo|t/-yot.

adolescent מתבגר *nmf* meetbager/-et.

(to) adopt לאמץ *inf* le'amets; *pst* eemets; *pres* me'amets; *fut* ye'amets.

adoption אימוץ *nm* eemoots/-eem (*pl+of:* -ey).
adoration הערצה *nf* ha'arats|ah/-ot (+*of:* -at).
(to) adore להעריץ *inf* leha'areets; *pst* he'ereets; *pres* ma'areets; *fut* ya'areets.
(to) adorn לקשט *inf* lekashet; *pst* keeshet; *pres* mekashet; *fut* yekashet.
adornment קישוט *nm* keeshoot/-eem (*pl+of:* -ey).
adroit זריז *adj* zareez/zreezah.
adroitness זריזות *nf* zreezoot.
adult 1. בוגר *nmf & adj* boger/-et; **2.** מבוגר (grown up) *nmf & adj* mevoog|ar/eret
(to) adulterate 1. לזייף *inf* lezayef; *pst* zeeyef; *pres* mezayef; *fut* yezayef; **2.** למהול (dilute) *inf* leemhol; *pst* mahal; *pres* mohel; *fut* yeemhal.
adulterer נואף *nm* no|'ef/-'afeem (*pl+of:* -'afey).
adultery ניאוף *nm* nee'oof/-eem (*pl+of:* -ey).
adultress מנאפת *nf* mena|'efet/-'afot.
advance התקדמות *nf* heetkadmoo|t/-yot.
(to) advance להתקדם *inf* leheetkadem; *pst* heetkadem; *pres* meetkadem; *fut* yeetkadem.
advancement 1. קידום *nm* keedoom/-eem (*pl+of:* -ey); **2.** התקדמות (progress) *nf* heetkadmoo|t/-yot.
advantage יתרון *nm* yeetron/-ot.
(to take) advantage לנצל *inf* lenatsel; *pst* neetsel; *pres* menatsel; *fut* yenatsel.
advantageous כדאי *adj* keda'ee/-t.
adventure הרפתקה *nf* harpatk|ah/-a'ot (+*of:* -at).
adventure |r/-ss - הרפתקן *nmf* harpatkan/-eet.
adventurous הרפתקני *adj* harpatkanee/-t.
adversary 1. מתנגד *nmf* meetnaged/-et; **2.** בר־פלוגתא (opponent) *nmf* bar/bat ploogta.
adverse 1. נוגד *adj* noged/-et; **2.** מנוגד (contrary) *adj* menoog|ad/-edet.
adversity 1. אסון *nm* ason/-ot; **2.** מצוקה (distress) *nf* metsook|ah/-ot (+*of:* -at).
(to) advertise לפרסם *inf* lefarsem; *pst* peersem; *(p=f) pres* mefarsem; *fut* yefarsem.
advertisement מודעה *nf* mod|a'ah/-a'ot (+*of:* -a'at/-'ot).
advertiser מפרסם *nmf* mefarsem/-et (*pl:* -eem; +*of:* -ey).
advertising פרסום *nm* peersoom/-eem (*pl+of:* -ey).
advice 1. עצה *nf* 'ets|ah/-ot (+*of:* 'atsat); **2.** הודעה (notice) *nf* hoda|'ah/-'ot (+*of:* -'at).
(to) advise 1. לייעץ *inf* leya'ets; *pst* ya'ats; *pres* meya'ets; *fut* yeya'ets; **2.** להודיע (inform) *inf* lehodee'a'; *pst* hodee'a'; *pres* modee'a'; *fut* yodee'a'.
adviser, advisor יועץ *nm* yo'ets/yo'atseem (*pl+of:* yo'atsey).
advocate 1. עורך־דין (attorney) *nmf* 'orekh/-et deen (*pl:* 'orkh|ey/-ot *etc*); **2.** סניגור (defense counsel) *nmf* sanegor/-eet (*pl:* -eem; +*of:* -ey).
(to) advocate 1. לסנגר *inf* lesanger; *pst* seenger; *pres* mesanger; *fut* yesanger; **2.** להמליץ (recommend) *inf* lehamleets; *pst* heemleets; *pres* mamleets; *fut* yamleets.
aerial 1. משושה *nf* meshosh|ah/-ot (+*of:* -at); **2.** אנטנה (antenna) *nf* anten|ah/-ot (+*of:* -at).
aeroplane, airplane 1. מטוס *nm* matos/metos|eem (*pl+of:* -ey); **2.** אווירון (aircraft) *nm* aveeron/-eem (*pl+of:* -ey).
aesthetic אסתטי *adj* estetee/-t.
afar למרחוק *adv* le-me-rakhok.
(from) afar ממרחקים *adv* mee-merkhakeem.
affable חביב *adj* khaveev/-ah.
affair פרשה *nf* parash|ah/-eeyot (*also:* -ot).
(love) affair פרשת אהבים *nf* parash|at/-eeyot (*also:* -ot) ahaveem.
(to) affect 1. להשפיע *inf* lehashpee'a'; *pst* heeshpee'a'; *pres* mashpee'a'; *fut* yashpee'a'; **2.** לפגוע (hurt) *inf* leefgo'a'; *pst* paga' *(p=f)*; *pres* poge'a'; *fut* yeefga'.
affectation העמדת פנים *nf* ha'amad|at/-ot paneem.
affected מעושה *adj* me'oos|eh/-ah.
affection חיבה *nf* kheeb|ah/-ot (+*of:* -at).
affectionate מגלה חביבות *adj* megal|eh/-ah khaveevoot.
affidavit תצהיר *nm* tats'heer/-eem (*pl+of:* -ey).
(to) affiliate להתחבר *inf* leheetkhaber; *pst* heetkhaber; *pres* meetkhaber; *fut* yeetkhaber.
affiliation התחברות *nf* heetkhabroo|t/-yot.
affinity משיכה טבעית *nf* mesheekhah teev'eet.
(to) affirm 1. לקבוע *inf* leekbo'a'; *pst* kava' *(v=b)*; *pres* kove'a'; *fut* yeekba'; **2.** להצהיר (declare) *inf* lehats'heer; *pst* heets'heer; *pres* mats'heer; *fut* yats'heer; **3.** לאשר (confirm) *inf* le'asher; *pst* eesher; *pres* me'asher; *fut* ye'asher.
affirmation הודעה *nf* hoda'|ah/-ot (+*of:* -at).
affirmative חיובי *adj* kheeyoovee/-t.
(to) affix להדביק *inf* lehadbeek; *pst* heedbeek; *pres* madbeek; *fut* yadbeek.
(to) affix one's signature 1. לחתום (sign) *inf* lakhatom; *pst* khatam; *pres* khotem; *fut* yakhatom; **2.** להטביע חותמת (seal) *inf* lehatbee'a' khotemet; *pst* heetbee'a' *etc*; *pres* matbee'a' *etc*; *fut* yatbee'a' *etc*.
(to) afflict לצער *inf* letsa'er; *inf* tsee'er; *pres* metsa'er; *fut* yetsa'er.
(to be) afflicted להתענות *inf* leheet'anot; *pst* heet'anah; *pres* meet'aneh; *fut* yeet'aneh.
affliction עינוי *nm* 'eenooy/-eem.
affluent שופע *adj* shof|e'a'/-a'at
(to) affront להעליב *inf* leha'aleev; *pst* he'eleev; *pres* ma'aleev; *fut* ya'aleev.
afire בוער *adj* bo'er/-et.
afloat צף *adj* tsaf/-ah.
afoot ברגל *adv* ba-regel.
aforesaid 1. האמור לעיל *adj* ha-amoor/-ah le-'eyl; **2.** הנ״ל ha-nal *adj* (*acr of* ha-neezk|ar/-eret le-'eyl).
afraid נפחד *adj* neefkh|ad/-edet.
afresh מחדש *adv* me-khadash.
African 1. אפריקני *adj* afreekanee/-t; **2.** אפריקאי *[colloq.] nmf* afreeka'ee/-t.
after 1. אחר *adv* akhar; **2.** אחרי *adv* akharey.
after all 1. אחרי ככלות הכול *adv* akharey keekhlot ha-kol; **2.** בסופו של דבר (in the end) *adv* be-sofo shel davar.
after effect תוצאה שלאחר מעשה *nf* totsa|'ah/-'ot she-le-akhar ma'ase.
(day) after tomorrow מחרתיים *nm* mokhoratayeem.
aftermath תוצאה *nf* totsa|'ah/-'ot (+*of:* -'at).
afternoon אחר הצהריים akhar ha-tsohorayeem.

aftertaste טעם לוואי *nm* ta'am/-ey levay.
afterwards לאחר מכן *adv* le-akhar mee-ken.
again 1. שוב *adv* shoov; **2.** עוד פעם *adv* 'od pa'am.
again and again שוב ושוב *adv adv* shoov va-shoov.
(never) again לעולם לא עוד *adv* le-'olam lo 'od.
against נגד *prep* neged.
age גיל *nm* geel/-eem (*pl+of:* -ey).
(of) age לבגרות le-vagroot *(v=b).*
(to) age להזקין *inf* lehazkeen; *pst* heezkeen; *pres* mazkeen; *fut* yazkeen.
(under) age קטין *adj* kateen/keteenah.
aged ... years בן ... שנים *adj* ben/bat... shaneem.
ageless נצחי *adj* neetskhee/-t.
agency סוכנות *nf* sokhnoo|t/-yot.
(Jewish) Agency 1. הסוכנות היהודית *nf* ha-sokhnoot ha-yehoodeet; **2.** הסוכנות *(colloq. abbr.) nf* ha-sokhnoot.
agent סוכן *nmf* sokhen/-et.
(secret) agent סוכן חשאי *nmf* sokhen/-et khasha'ee/-t.
agglomeration הצטברות *nf* heetstabroo|t/-yot.
(to) aggravate להחמיר *inf* lehakhmeer; *pst* hekhmeer; *pres* makhmeer; *fut* yakhmeer.
aggregate 1. מקבץ *nm* meekb|ats/-atseem (*pl+of:* -etsey); **2.** אגרגט *nm* agregat/-eem.
(to) aggregate לקבץ *inf* lekabets; *pst* keebets; *pres* mekabets; *fut* yekabets.
aggression תוקפנות *nf* tokfanoo|t/-yot.
aggressive תוקפני *adj* tokfanee/-t.
aggressor תוקפן *nm* tokfan/-eem (*pl+of:* -ey).
aggrieved נפגע *adj* neefg|a'/-a'at.
aghast נדהם *adj* need|ham/-hemet.
agile זריז *adj* zareez/zreezah.
agility זריזות *nf* zreezoo|t/-yot.
(to) agitate להתסיס *inf* lehat'sees; *pst* heet'sees; *pres* mat'sees; *fut* yat'sees.
agitation הסתה *nf* hasat|ah/-ot (*+of:* -at).
agitator מסית *nmf* meseet/-ah (*pl:* -eem; *+of:* -ey).
aglow 1. לוהט *adj* lohet/-et; **2.** בלהט *adv* be-lahat.
ago 1. לפני־כן leefney-khen; **2.** לפנים *adv* lefaneem.
(long) ago מזמן *adv* mee-zman.
(years) ago לפני שנים *adv* leefney shaneem.
(to) agonize להתענות *inf* leheet'anot; *pst* heet'anah; *pres* meet'aneh; *fut* yeet'aneh.
agony ייסורים *nm pl* yeesoor|eem (*pl+of:* -ey).
agrarian 1. אגררי *adj* agraree/-t; **2.** חקלאי *adj* khakla'ee/-t.
(to) agree להסכים *inf* lehaskeem; *pst* heeskeem; *pres* maskeem; *fut* yaskeem.
agreeable נעים *adj* na'eem/ne'eemah.
agreement הסכם *nm* heskem/-eem (*pl+of:* -ey).
agricultural חקלאי *adj* khakla'ee/-t.
agriculture חקלאות *nf* khakla'oot.
agriculturist חקלאי *nm* khakla|y/-'eem (*f* -'eet/-'eeyot; *pl+of:* -'ey).
agronomy אגרונומיה *nf* agronomyah.
aground על שרטון *adv* 'al seerton.
ahead קדימה *adv* kadeemah.
(to get) ahead להתקדם *inf* leheetkadem; *pst* heetkadem; *pres* meetkadem; *fut* yeetkadem.
(to go) ahead להתחיל בפעולה *inf* lehatkheel be-fe'oolah; *pst* heetkheel *etc; pres* matkheel *etc; fut* yatkheel *etc.*
ahead of time לפני המועד *adv* leefney ha-mo'ed.
aid 1. עזרה *nf* 'ezr|ah/-ot (*+of:* -at); **2.** סיוע (assistance) *nm* seeyoo'a'.
(first) aid עזרה ראשונה *nf* 'ezrah reeshonah.
(first-)aid station תחנת עזרה ראשונה *nf* takhan|at/-ot 'ezrah reeshonah.
aide-de-camp שליש *nm* shaleesh/-eem (*pl+of:* -ey).
aide-memoire זכרון דברים *nm* zeekhron dvareem.
(to) ail לכאוב *inf* leekh'ov; *pst* ka'av *(k=kh); pres* ko'ev; *fut* yeekh'av.
ailment מחלה *nf* makhal|ah/-ot (*+of:* -at).
aim מטרה *nf* matar|ah/-ot (*+of:* -at).
(to) aim 1. לשאוף *inf* leesh'of; *pst* sha'af; *pres* sho'ef; *fut* yeesh'af; **2.** לכוון אל (weapon) *inf* lekhaven el; *pst* keeven el *(k=kh); pres* mekhaven el; *fut* yekhaven el.
aimless חסר תכלית *adj* khas|ar/-rat takhleet.
aimlessly ללא מטרה *adv* le-lo matarah.
air אוויר *nm* aveer.
(in the) air בטיסה *adv* be-teesah.
(on the) air בשידור *adv* be-sheedoor.
(open) air תחת כיפת השמיים *adv* takhat keepat ha-shamayeem.
airborne מוטס *adj* moot|as/-eset.
airbrakes מעצורי אוויר *nm pl* ma'atsorey aveer.
airconditioner מזגן *nm* mazg|an/-aneem (*pl+of:* -eney).
airconditioning מיזוג אוויר *nm* meezoog aveer.
aircraft כלי־טיס *nm* klee/kley tayees.
aircraft carrier נושאת מטוסים *nf* nos|et/-'ot metoseem.
airfield שדה תעופה *nm* sdeh/sdot te'oofah.
airline נתיבי אוויר *nm pl* neteevey aveer.
airmail דואר אוויר *nm* do'ar aveer.
airman 1. אווירא׳ *nm* aveera|y/-'eem (*pl+of:* -'ey); **2.** איש חיל אוויר (airforce man) *nm* eesh/anshey kheyl aveer.
airplane 1. מטוס *nm* matos/metoseem (*+of:* metos/-ey); **2.** אווירון (aircraft) *nm* aveeron/-eem (*pl+of:* -ey).
airport נמל תעופה *nm* nemal/neemley te'oofah.
airtight אטום *adj* atoom/-ah.
airy מאוורר *adj* me'oovr|ar/-eret.
ajar פתוח למחצה *adj* patoo'akh/petookhah le-mekhtsah.
alarm אזעקה *nf* az'ak|ah/-ot (*+of:* -at).
alarm clock שעון מעורר *nm* sha'on/she'oneem me'orer/-eem.
alarm system מערכת אזעקה *nf* ma'ar|ekhet/-khot az'akah.
album אלבום *nm* alboom/-eem (*pl+of:* -ey).
albumen, albumin חלבון *nm* khelbon/-eem (*pl+of:* -ey).
alcohol 1. כוהל *nm* kohal; **2.** אלכוהול *nm* alkohol.
alcoholic 1. שתיין כרוני *nmf* shatyan/-eet kronee/-t; **2.** אלכוהולי *adj* alkoholee/-t.
alcove קובה *nf* koob|ah/-ot (*+of:* -at).
alderman חבר מועצת העיר *nmf* khav|er/-rat mo'etset ha'eer.

ale 1. שיכר *nm* shekhar; **2.** בירה כהה וחריפה (dark bitter beer) *nf* beerah kehah va-khareefah.
alert 1. עירני *adj* 'eranee/-t; **2.** אות אזעקה (alarm) *nm* ot/-ot az'akah.
(on the) alert על המשמר *adv* 'al ha-meeshmar.
alfalfa אספסת *nf* aspeset.
algebra אלגברה *nf* algebrah
alias המתכנה *adj* ha-meetkan|eh/-et.
alibi 1. אליבי aleebee; **2.** תירוץ *nm* teroots/-eem (*pl+of:* -ey).
alien 1. זר (stranger) *adj & nmf* zar/-ah; **2.** נוכרי *nmf* nokhree/-yah; **3.** נוכרי *adj* nokhree/-t.
(to) alienate 1. להרחיק *inf* leharkheek; *pst* heerkheek; *pres* markheek; *fut* yarkheek; **2.** להתנכר (ignore) *inf* leheetnaker; *pst* heetnaker; *pres* meetnaker; *fut* yeetnaker.
(to) alight 1. לרדת *inf* laredet; *pst* yarad; *pres* yored; *fut* yered; **2.** לנחות (land) *inf* leenkhot; *pst* nakhat; *pres* nokhet; *fut* yeenkhat.
(to) align להיערך *inf* lehe'arekh; *pst & pres* ne'erakh; *fut* ye'arekh.
alignment מערך *nf* ma'ar|akh/-akheem (*pl+of:* -khey).
(the) Alignment המערך *nm* ha-ma'arakh, Israel's onetime political block (1968-1985) with the United Workers Party.
alike בצורה דומה *adv* be-tsoorah domah.
alimony מזונות *nm pl* mezonot.
alive 1. חי *adj* khay/-ah; **2.** בחיים *adv* ba-khayeem.
alive with שורץ *adj* shorets/-et.
all כל *num* kol.
(not at) all לגמרי לא le-gamrey lo.
(nothing at) all שום דבר shoom davar.
(once and for) all אחת ולתמיד akhat oo-le-tameed.
all at once בבת אחת *adv* be-vat akhat.
all over תם ונשלם *adj* tam/-ah ve-neeshl|am/-emah.
all right בסדר be-seder.
all told בסך הכול be-sakh ha-kol.
(to) allay להרגיע *inf* lehargee'a'; *pst* heergee'a'; *pres* margee'a'; *fut* yargee'a'.
allegation טענה *nf* ta'an|ah/te'anot (*+of:* -at).
(to) allege 1. לטעון (claim) *inf* leet'on; *pst* ta'an; *pres* to'en; *fut* yeet'an; **2.** להאשים (accuse) *inf* leha'asheem; *pst* he'esheem; *pres* ma'asheem; *fut* ya'asheem.
allegiance נאמנות *nf* ne'emanoo|t/-yot.
allegory אלגוריה *nf* alegor|yah/-yot.
allergy אלרגיה *nf* alerg|yah/-yot (*+of:* -yat).
(to) alleviate 1. לרכך (soften) *inf* lerakekh; *pst* reekekh; *pres* merakekh; *fut* yerakekh; **2.** להקל (ease) *inf* lehakel; *pst* hekel; *pres* mekel; *fut* yakel.
alley סמטה *nf* seemt|ah/-a'ot (*+of:* -at).
(blind) alley סמטה ללא מוצא *nf* seemtah le-lo motsa.
alliance ברית *nf* breet/-ot.
allied בעל־ברית *adj* ba'al/-at (*pl:* -ey/-ot) breet.
alligator תנין *nm* taneen/-eem (*pl+of:* -ey).
(to) allot להקצות *inf* lehaktsot; *pst* heektsah; *pres* maktseh; *fut* yaktseh.
(to) allow 1. להרשות (permit) *inf* leharshot; *pst* heershah; *pres* marsheh; *fut* yarsheh; **2.** להקציב (allocate) *inf* lehaktseev; *pst* heektseev; *pres* maktseev; *fut* yaktseev.
allowance 1. הקצבה (allocation) *nf* haktsav|ah/-ot (*+of:* -at); **2.** קצבה (pension) *nf* keetsb|ah/-a'ot (*+of:* -at).
(monthly) allowance קצבה חודשית *nf* keetsbah khodsheet.
(to make) allowance להביא בחשבון *inf* lehavee be-kheshbon; *pst* hevee *etc*; *pres* mevee *etc*; *fut* yavee *etc*.
alloy 1. נתך *nm* net|ekh/-akheem (*pl+of:* neetkhey); **2.** סגסוגת *nf* sagsog|et/-ot.
(to) allude לרמוז *inf* leermoz; *pst* ramaz; *pres* romez; *fut* yeermoz.
(to) allure לפתות *inf* lefatot; *pst* peetah *(p=f)*; *pres* mefateh; *fut* yefateh.
allurement פיתוי *nm* peetoo|y/-yeem (*pl+of:* -yey).
alluring מפתה *adj* mefat|eh/-ah.
allusion רמז *nm* rem|ez/-azeem (*pl+of:* reemzey).
ally בעל־ברית *nmf* ba'al/-at (*pl:* -ey/-ot) breet.
(to) ally oneself לבוא בברית *inf* lavo bee-vreet *(v=b)*; *pst & pres* ba *(b=v) etc*; *fut* yavo *etc*.
almanac ספר שנה *nm* sefer/seefrey shanah.
almighty כול־יכול *adj* kol-yakhol/yekholah.
(the) Almighty 1. הקדוש ברוך הוא *nm* ha-kadosh barookh hoo; **2.** *cpr* ha-kadosh borkhoo.
almond שקד *nm* shaked/shkedeem (*pl+of:* shkedey).
almost כמעט *adv* keem'at.
alms צדקה *nf* tsedak|ah/-ot (*+of:* tseedkat).
alms box קופת צדקה *nf* koop|at/-ot tsedakah.
aloft כלפי מעלה *adv* kelapey ma'lah.
alone לבד *adv* levad.
(all) alone לגמרי לבד *adv* legamrey levad.
(to let) alone לעזוב לנפשו *inf* la'azov le-nafsh|o/-ah *(m/f)*; *pst* 'azav *etc*; *pres* 'ozev *etc*; *fut* ya'azov *etc*.
along לאורך *adv* le-orekh.
(all) along מלכתחילה *adv* mee-le-kha-tekheelah
(to carry) along לקחת אתו *inf* lakakhat eet|o/-ah *(m/f)*; *pst* lakakh *etc*; *pres* loke'akh *etc*; *fut* yeekakh *etc*.
(to get) along להסתדר *inf* leheestader; *pst* heestader; *pres* meestader; *fut* yeestader.
(to go) along להצטרף *inf* leheetstaref; *pst* heetstaref; *pres* meetstaref; *fut* yeetstaref.
alongside לצד *adv* letsad.
along the coast לאורך החוף *adv* le-orekh ha-khof.
along with יחד עם *adv* yakhad 'eem.
aloof אדיש *adj* adeesh/-ah.
aloofness התבדלות *nf* heetbadloo|t/-yot.
aloud בקול *adv* be-kol.
alphabet אלף־בית *nm* alef-bet.
already כבר *adv* kvar.
also 1. גם *conj* gam; **2.** כמו כן *prep* kemo-khen.
altar מזבח *nm* meezb|e'akh/-akhot (*+of:* -akh/-ekhot).
(to) alter לשנות *inf* leshanot; *pst* sheenah; *pres* meshaneh; *fut* yeshaneh.
alteration שינוי *nm* sheenoo|y/-yeem (*pl+of:* -yey).
(to) alternate לפעול לסירוגין *inf* leef'ol le-seroogeen; *pst* pa'al *etc*; *pres* po'el *etc*; *fut* yeeef'al *etc*.

alternately בזה אחר זה *adv* ba-zeh akhar zeh.

alternating current זרם חילופין *nm* zerem kheeloofeen.

alternative 1. אלטרנטיבה *nf* alternateev|ah/-ot; **2.** חלופה *nf* khaloof|ah/-ot.

although 1. על אף אשר *conj* 'al af asher; **2.** אף על פי *conj* af-'al-pee.

alto אלט *nm* alt/-eem.

altogether בסך הכול be-sakh hakol.

altruist 1. אלטרואיסטי *adj* altroo'eestee/-t; **2.** אלטרואיסט *nmf* altroo'eest/-eet; **3.** דואג לזולת *adj* do'eg/-et la-zoolat.

aluminum 1. אלומיניום *nm* aloomeenyoom; **2.** חמרן *nm* khamran.

alumnus, -na 1. בוגר אוניברסיטה *nmf* boger/-et ooneeverseetah; **2.** חניך לשעבר *nmf* khaneekh/-ah le-she-'avar.

always 1. תמיד *adv* tameed; **2.** לעולם (forever) *adv* le-'olam.

a.m. 1. לפני הצהריים *adv* leefney ha-tsohorayeem; **2.** לפנה"צ (*acr of* 1) *adv* leefney ha-tsohorayeem.

amalgam 1. מסג *nm* mes|eg/-ageem; **2.** תצרופת (synthesis) *nf* teetsrof|et/-ot.

(to) amalgamate לצרוף לאחד *inf* leetsrof le-ekhad; *pst* tsaraf *etc; pres* tsoref *etc; fut* yeetsrof *etc.*

(to) amass 1. לצבור (accummulate) *inf* leetsbor; *pres* tsavar *(v=b); pres* tsover; *fut* yeetsbor; **2.** לערום (heap) *inf* la'arom; *pst* 'aram; *pres* 'orem; *fut* ya'arom.

amateur חובב *nmf* khovev/-et.

amateurish חובבני *adj* khovevanee/-t.

(to) amaze 1. להפליא *inf* lehaflee; *pst* heeflee; *pres* maflee; *fut* yaflee; **2.** להפתיע (surprise) *inf* lehaftee'a'; *pst* heeftee'a'; *pres* maftee'a'; *fut* yaftee'a'.

amazement תימהון *nm* teem|ahon/-honot (*+of:* -hon).

amazing מדהים *adj* madheem/-ah.

ambassador, -dress שגריר *nmf* shagreer/-ah.

amber ענבר *nm* 'eenbar.

ambient 1. סובב *adj* sovev/-et; **2.** מקיף (comprehensive) *adj* makeef/-ah.

ambiguity כפל משמעות *nm* kefel mashma'oo|t/-yot.

ambiguous דו־משמעי *adj* doo-mashma'ee/-t.

ambition 1. שאפתנות *nf* she'aftanoo|t/-yot; **2.** יומרה (pretension) *nf* yoomr|ah/-ot (*+of:* -at).

ambitious שאפתן *nmf & adj* she'aftan/-eet.

ambivalent דו־ערכי *adj* doo-'erkee/-t.

(to) amble לצעוד בנחת *inf* leets'od be-nakhat; *pst* tsa'ad *etc; pres* tso'ed *etc; fut* yeets'ad *etc.*

ambulance אמבולנס *nm* amboolans/-eem (*pl+of:* -ey).

ambulatory נייד *adj* nayad/nayedet.

ambush מארב *nm* ma'ar|av/-aveem (*pl+of:* -vey).

(to) ambush לתקוף ממארב *inf* leetkof mee-ma'arav; *pst* takaf *etc; pres* tokef *etc; fut* yeetkof *etc.*

ameba אמבה *nf* ameb|ah/-ot (*+of:* -at).

(to) ameliorate להיטיב *inf* leheyteev; *pst* heyteev; *pres* meyteev; *fut* yeyteev.

amelioration 1. הטבה (betterment) *nf* hatav|ah/-ot (*+of:* -at); **2.** שיפור (improvement) *nm* sheepoor/-eem (*pl+of:* -ey).

amen אמן amen.

(to) amend לתקן *inf* letaken; *pst* teeken; *pres* metaken; *fut* yetaken.

amendment 1. תיקון לחוק (of law) *m* teekoon/-eem le-khok; **2.** תיקון להצעה (of proposal) *nm* teekoon/-eem le-hatsa'ah.

(to make) amends for לכפר על *inf* lekhaper 'al; *pst* keeper *(k=kh)* 'al; *pres* mekhaper 'al; *fut* yekhaper 'al.

amenity נוחות *nf* nokhoo|t/-yot.

American אמריקני *nmf & adj* amereekanee/-t.

amethyst אחלמה *nf* akhlam|ah/-eem (*pl+of:* -ey).

amiable 1. מסביר פנים *adj* masbeer/-at paneem; **2.** חביב (agreeable) *adj* khaveev/-ah.

amicable 1. ידידותי (friendly) *adj* yedeedootee/-t; **2.** חברי (comradely) *adj* khaveree/-t.

amid, amidst 1. בתוך be-tokh; **2.** בקרב (among) *prep* be-kerev.

amiss 1. מוטעה *adj* moot|'eh/-'et; **2.** שלא כשורה (wrong) *adv* she-lo ka-shoorah.

(to take) amiss להיעלב *inf* lehe'alev; *pst & pres* ne'elav; *fut* ye'alev *etc.*

ammonia 1. אמוניה *nf* amonyah; **2.** אמוניאק *nm* amonyak.

ammunition תחמושת *nf* takhmoshet.

amnesia 1. מחלת השכחה *nf* makhlat ha-sheekhekhah; **2.** אמנסיה *nf* amnes|yah/-yot (*+of:* -yat).

amnesty חנינה כללית *nf* khaneenah klaleet.

among, amongst 1. בין ben; **2.** בתוך (in middle of) *prep* be-tokh; **3.** בקרב (amid) *prep* be-kerev.

amorous עוגב *adj* 'ogev/-et.

amorphous חסר צורה *adj* khas|ar/-rat tsoorah.

amortization 1. פחת *nm* pekhat; **2.** בלאי (wear) *nm* blay; **3.** אמורטיזאציה *nf* amorteezatsyah.

(to) amortize לנכות פחת *inf* lenakot pekhat; *pst* neekah *etc; pres* menakeh *etc; fut* yenakeh *etc.*

amount 1. סכום (sum) *nm* sekhoom/-eem (*pl+of:* -ey); **2.** כמות (quantity) *nf* kamoo|t/-yot; **3.** שיעור (dose) *nm* shee'oor/-eem (*pl+of:* -ey).

(to) amount להסתכם *inf* leheestakem; *pst* heestakem; *pres* meestakem; *fut* yeestakem.

amphitheater אמפיתאטרון *nm* amfeete'atron/-eem (*pl+of:* -ey).

ample 1. די *adj* day; **2.** מספק *adj* mesapek/-et.

(to) amplify 1. להגביר (intensify) *inf* lehagbeer; *pst* heegbeer; *pres* magbeer; *fut* yagbeer; **2.** להרחיב (enlarge) *inf* leharkheev; *pst* heerkheev; *pres* markheev; *fut* yarkheev.

amplitude 1. מלוא *nm* melo; **2.** מלוא גודל (full size) *nm* melo godel.

(to) amputate לקטוע *inf* leekto'a'; *pst* kata'; *pres* kote'a'; *fut* yeekta'.

amputation קטיעה *nf* ketee'ah/-ot (*+of:* -at).

amputee קיטע *nmf* keet|e'a'/-a'at.

amulet קמיע *nm* kame'a'/kme'ot.

(to) amuse 1. לבדר *inf* levader; *pst* beeder *(b=v)*; *pres* mevader; *fut* yevader; **2.** לשעשע (delight) *inf* lesha'she'a'; *pst* shee'ashe'a'; *pres* mesha'she'a'; *fut* yesha'she'a'.

(to) amuse oneself להשתעשע *inf* leheeshta'she'a'; *pst* heeshta'she'a'; *pres* meeshtashe'a'; *fut* yeeshta'she'a'.

amusement 1. בידור *nm* beedoor/-eem (*pl+of:* -ey); **2.** שעשוע (delight) *nm* sha'shoo|'a'/-'eem (*pl+of:* -'ey).

amusing 1. מהנה *adj* mehan|eh/-ah; **2.** משעשע (entertaining) *adj* mesha'sh|e'a/-a'at.

an אחד *nmf* ekhad/akhat.

anachronism אנכרוניזם *nm* anakhroneezm/-eem.

anal אנאלי *adj* analee/-t.

analogous מקביל *adj* makbeel/-ah.

analogy 1. אנלוגיה *nf* analog|yah/-yot (*+of:* -yat); **2.** הקבלה (parallel) *nf* hakbal|ah/-ot (*+of:* -at).

analysis 1. ניתוח *nm* neetoo'|akh/-kheem (*pl+of:* -khey); **2.** אנליזה *nf* analeez|ah/-ot (*+of:* -at).

analyst מנתח *nm* menat|e'akh/-akhat (*pl* -kheem/-khot).

(systems) analyst מנתח מערכות *nmf* menat|e'akh/-akhat ma'arakhot (*pl:* -khey *etc*).

(to) analyze לנתח *inf* lenate'akh; *pst* neetakh; *pres* menate'akh; *fut* yenate'akh.

anarchist אנרכיסט *nmf* anarkheest/-eet.

anarchy 1. אנרכיה *nf* anarkh|yah/-yot (*+of:* -yat); **2.** תוהו ובוהו (chaos) *nm pl* tohoo va-vohoo.

anathema חרם *nm* kherem/kharamot.

anatomy אנטומיה *nf* anatom|yah/-yot (*+of:* -yat).

ancestor אבי אבות *nm* avee avot.

ancestral נחלת אבות *nf* nakhalat avot.

ancestry ייחוס אבות *nm* yeekhoos avot.

anchor עוגן 'og|en/-aneem (*pl+of:* -ney).

(to drop) anchor להשליך עוגן *inf* lehashleekh 'ogen; *pst* heeshleekh *etc*; *pres* mashleekh *etc*; *fut* yashleekh *etc*.

anchorage מעגן *nm* ma'ag|an/-aneem (*pl+of:* -ney).

anchovy אנשובי anshovee.

ancient קדום *adj* kadoom/kedoomah.

(the) ancients הקדמונים *nm pl* ha-kadmoneem.

ancillary משני *adj* meeshnee/-t.

and 1. ־ו ve-, va-, oo-; **2.** וכן ve-khen; **3.** את (& in a business name) et.

and so forth 1. וכולה ve-khooleh; **2.** וכו׳ (abbr) ve-khooleh ve-khooleh.

anecdote 1. בדיחה *nf* bedeekhah/-ot (*+of:* -at); **2.** אנקדוטה *nf* anekdotah/-ot.

anemia אנמיה *nf* anem|yah/-yot (*+of:* -yat).

anesthetic 1. מרדים *adj* mardeem/-ah; **2.** סם מרדים (anaesthetic drug) *nm* sam/-eem mardeem/-eem.

anew מחדש *adv* me-khadash.

angel מלאך *nm* mal'akh/-eem (*pl+of:* -ey).

angelic 1. כרובי *adj* kroovee/-t; **2.** מלאכי *adj* mal'akhee/-t; **3.** צדקני (rightous) *adj* tseedkanee/-t.

anger 1. זעם *nm* za'am; **2.** כעס *nm* ka'as.

angina 1. אנגינה *nf* angeenah/-ot (*+of:* -at); **2.** דלקת הגרון (throat inflammation) *nf* daleket/-akot ha-garon.

angina pectoris 1. אנגינה פקטוריס *nf* angeenah pektorees; **2.** תעוקת הלב *nf* te'ookat ha-lev.

angle 1. זווית *nf* zavee|t/-yot; **2.** נקודת מבט (viewpoint) *nf* nekood|at/-ot mabat.

angler דייג חכה *nm* dayag khakah.

Anglican אנגליקני *adj* angleekanee/-t.

Anglo-Saxon אנגלו־סקסי *nmf & adj* anglo-saksee/-t.

angry 1. כועס *adj* ko'es/-et; **2.** זועם (irate) *adj* zo'em/-et.

anguish כאב־לב *nm* ke'ev/-ey lev.

angular זוויתי *adj* zaveetee/-t.

animal 1. בעל חיים *nm* ba'al/-ey khayeem; **2.** בהמה *nf* behem|ah/-ot (*+of:* -at); **3.** בהמי *adj* bahamee/-t.

animal magnetism משיכה פיסית *nf* mesheekhah feeseet.

animate ער *adj* 'er/-ah.

(to) animate 1. להכניס רוח חיים *inf* lehakhnees roo'akh khayeem; *pst* heekhnees *etc*; *pres* makhnees *etc*; *fut* yakhnees *etc*; **2.** להמריץ (bolster) *inf* lehamreets; *pst* heemreets; *pres* mamreets; *fut* yamreets; **3.** להנפיש (cartoon) *inf* lehanpeesh; *pst* heenpeesh; *pres* manpeesh; *fut* yanpeesh.

animated cartoon סרט הנפשה *nm* seret/seertey hanpashah (*cpr* hanfashah).

animation 1. עירנות *nf* 'eranoo|t/-yot; **2.** אנימציה *nf* aneematsyah.

animosity טינה *nf* teen|ah/-ot (*+of:* -at).

anise אניסון *nm* aneeson.

ankle קרסול *nm* kars|ol/-oolayeem (*pl+of:* -ooley).

annals 1. דברי הימים *nm pl* deevrey ha-yameem; **2.** תולדות *nf pl* toladot.

annex 1. נספח *nm* neesp|akh/-akheem (*pl+of:* -ekhey); **2.** אגף (wing) *nm* aga|f/-peem (*p=f; pl+of:* -pey).

(to) annex לספח *inf* lesape'akh; *pst* seepakh; *pres* mesape'akh; *fut* yesapakh.

annexation סיפוח *nm* seepoo|'akh/-kheem (*pl+of:* -khey).

(to) annihilate 1. להשמיד *inf* lehashmeed; *pst* heeshmeed; *pres* mashmeed; *fut* yashmeed; **2.** לחסל (liquidate) *inf* lekhasel; *pst* kheesel; *pres* mekhasel; *fut* yekhasel.

annihilation 1. השמדה *nf* hashmad|ah/-ot (*+of:* -at); **2.** חיסול (liquidation) *nm* kheesool/-eem (*pl+of:* -ey).

anniversary 1. יום השנה *nm* yom/yemey ha-shanah; **2.** יובל (jubilee) *nm* yov|el/-lot.

(to) annotate לרשום פרשנות שוליים *inf* leershom parshanoot shoolayeem; *pst* rasham *etc*; *pres* roshem *etc*; *fut* yeershom *etc*.

annotation פרשנות שוליים *nf* parshanoot shoolayeem.

(to) announce להכריז *inf* lehakhreez; *pst* heekhreez; *pres* makhreez; *fut* yakhreez.

announcement 1. הכרזה *nf* hakhrazah/-ot (*+of:* -at); **2.** הודעה (notice) *nf* hoda|'ah/-'ot (*+of:* -'at).

announcer קריין *nmf* karyan/-eet.

(to) annoy להטריד *inf* lehatreed; *pst* heetreed; *pres* matreed; *fut* yatreed.

annoyance 1. מטרד *nm* meetr|ad/-adeem (*pl+of:* -edey); 2. הטרדה (nuisance) *nf* hatrad|ah/-ot (*+of:* -at).

annual 1. שנתי *adj* shnatee/-t; 2. שנתון (yearbook) *nm* shnaton/-eem (*pl+of:* -ey).

annuity 1. קצבה שנתית *nf* keetsb|ah/-ot shnatee|t/-yot; 2. הכנסה שנתית (yearly income) *nf* hakhnas|ah/-ot shnatee|t/-yot.

(to) annul לבטל *inf* levatel; *pst* beetel *(b=v)*; *pres* mevatel; *fut* yevatel.

annulment ביטול *nm* beetool/-eem (*pl+of:* -ey).

(to) anoint למשוח *inf* leemsho'akh; *pst* mashakh; *pres* moshe'akh; *fut* yeemshakh.

anomalous 1. חריג *adj* khareeg/-ah; 2. לא תקין (irregular) *adj* lo takeen/-tkeenah.

anomaly 1. חריגה *nf* khareeg|ah/-ot (*+of:* -at); 2. אנומליה *nf* anomal|yah/-yot (*+of:* -yat).

anonymous 1. אלמוני *adj* almonee/-t; 2. אנונימי *adj* anoneemee/-t.

another 1. אחר *adj* akher/-et; 2. נוסף (additional) *adj* nos|af/-efet.

another one עוד אחד *adj* 'od ekhad/akhat.

answer תשובה *nf* teshoovah/-ot (*+of:* -at).

(to) answer 1. לענות *inf* la'anot; *pst* 'anah; *pres* 'oneh; *fut* ya'aneh; 2. להשיב (reply) *inf* lehasheev; *pst* hesheev; *pres* mesheev; *fut* yasheev.

(to) answer for לשאת באחריות *inf* laset be-akhrayoot; *pst* nasa *etc*; *pres* nose *etc*; *fut* yeesa *etc*.

(to) answer to לענות על הצורך *inf* la'anot 'al ha-tsorekh; *pst* 'anah *etc*; *pres* 'oneh *etc*; *fut* ya'aneh *etc*.

ant נמלה *nf* nemal|ah/-eem (*pl+of:* neemley).

antacid נוגד חומצות (chemical) *nm* nog|ed/-dey khoomtsot.

antagonism 1. יריבות *nf* yereevoo|t/-yot; 2. ניגוד קוטבי (total opposition) *nm* neegood kotbee; 3. אנטגוניזם *nm* antagoneezm.

antagonist יריב *nmf* yareev/yereevah.

(to) antagonize לעורר התנגדות *inf* le'orer heetnagdoot; *pst* 'orer *etc*; *pres* me'orer *etc*; *fut* ye'orer *etc*.

antarctic אנטארקטי *adj* antarktee/-t.

antecedent קודם *adj* kodem/-et.

antechamber פרוזדור *nm* prozdor/-eem (*pl+of:* -ey).

antelope 1. דישון *nm* deeshon/-eem (*pl+of:* -ey); 2. אנטילופה *nf* anteelop|ah/-ot (*+of:* -at).

antenna 1. מחוש (feeler) *nm* makhosh/mekhosh|eem (*pl+of:* -ey); 2. אנטנה (radio, TV) *nf* anten|ah/-ot (*+of:* -at); 3. משושה (aerial) *nf* meshosh|ah/-ot (*+of:* -at).

anterior קדמי *adj* keedmee/-t.

anteroom חדר המתנה *nm* khad|ar/-rey hamtanah.

anthem המנון *nm* heemnon/-eem (*pl+of:* -ey).

(national) anthem 1. המנון לאומי *nm* heemnon le'oomee; 2. "התקווה" (Israel's national anthem) *nf* "ha-teekvah".

anthology אנתולוגיה *nf* antolog|yah/-yot (*+of:* -yat).

anthrax פחמת *nf* pakhemet.

anthropology 1. תורת האדם *nf* torat he-adam; 2. אנתרופולוגיה *nf* antropologyah.

antiaircraft 1. אנטי־אווירי *adj* antee-averee/-t; 2. נון־מם *adj* (*acr of* Neged Metoseem) noon-mem.

antibiotic 1. אנטי־ביוטי *adj* antee-beeyotee/-t; 2. תרופה אנטיביוטית (antibiotic drug) *nf* troof|ah/-ot antee-beeyotee|t/-yot.

antibody נוגדן *nm* nogdan/-eem (*pl+of:* -ey).

(to) anticipate לצפות מראש *inf* leetspot me-rosh; *pst* tsafah *(f=p) etc*; *pres* tsofeh *etc*; *fut* yeetspeh *etc*.

anticipation ציפייה *nf* tseepee|yah/-yot (*+of:* -yat).

antics תעלולים *nm pl* ta'alool|eem (*pl+of:* -ey).

antidote 1. סם־נגד *nm* sam/-ey neged; 2. אנטידוט *nm* anteedot/-eem.

antiglare מונע סנוור *nm & adj* mone'a' seenvoor.

antipathy סלידה *nf* sleedah/-ot (*+of:* -at).

antiquarian 1. סוחר עתיקות (antiques dealer) *nmf* sokh|er/-eret (*pl:* -arey) 'ateekot; 2. סוחר בספרים משומשים (second-hand books dealer) *nmf* sokher/-et bee-sfareem meshoomasheem.

antiquary 1. חוקר עתיקות (researcher) *nmf* khok|er/-eret (*pl:* -rey) 'ateekot; 2. אספן עתיקות (collector) *nm* asfan/-ey 'ateekot.

antiquated מיושן *adj* meyoosh|an/-enet.

antique 1. עתיק *adj* 'ateek/-ah; 2. עתיקות *nf pl* 'ateekot; 3. שריד עתיקות (relic) *nm* sreed/-ey 'ateekot.

antique dealer סוחר עתיקות *nm* sokh|er/-eret (*pl:* -arey) 'ateekot.

antiquity 1. קדמוניות *nf* kadmoneeyoot; 2. קדמונות *nf* kadmonoot.

antisemite אנטישמי *adj* anteeshemee/-t.

antiseptic 1. חומר חיטוי *nm* khom|er/-rey kheetooy; 2. מחטא (disinfectant) *nm* mekhat|e/-'eem (*pl+of:* -'ey).

antisocial 1. אנטי־חברתי *adj* antee-khevratee/-t; 2. אלמנט אנטי־סוציאלי (antisoc. element) *nm* element/-eem antee-sotsyalee/-yeem.

anti-Soviet אנטי־סובייטי *adj* antee-sovyetee/-t.

antithesis 1. היפוך *nm* heepookh/-eem (*pl+of:* -ey); 2. אנטיתזה antee-tez|ah/-ot (*+of:* -at).

antler קרן צבי *nf* keren/karney ts'vee.

antonym היפוכו של דבר *nm* heepookho shel davar.

anvil סדן *nm* sad|an/-aneem (*pl+of:* -ney).

anxiety חרדה kharad|ah/-ot (*+of:* kherdat).

anxious 1. חושש *adj* khoshesh/-et; 2. משתוקק *adj* meeshtokek/-et.

any 1. כלשהו *nmf* kolshe|hoo/-hee; 2. איזשהו *nmf* eyzeshehoo/eyzoshehee.

(in) any case 1. בכל מקרה be-khol meekreh; 2. מכל מקום mee-kol makom.

any more 1. עוד 'od; 2. יותר yoter.

anybody 1. מישהו *nmf* meeshe|hoo/-hee; 2. כל אחד (everyone) *nmf* kol ekhad/akhat.

anyhow בכל אופן *adv* be-khol ofen.

anyone 1. מישהו *nmf* meeshe|hoo/-hee; 2. כל אחד (everyone) *nmf* kol ekhad/akhat.

anything משהו *nm* mashehoo.

anything you wish כל אשר תרצה kol asher teerts|eh/-ee.

anyway 1. בכל אופן *adv* be-khol *(kh=k)* ofen; 2. בכל מקרה (in any case) *adv* be-khol *(kh=k)*

meekreh; 3. בכל צורה (in any form) *adv* be-khol *(kh=k)* tsoorah.
anywhere, any place 1. בכל מקום (in) *adv* be-khol *(kh=k)* makom; **2.** לכל מקום (to) *adv* le-khol *(kh=k)* makom.
aorta אב העורקים *nm* av ha-'orkeem.
apace מהר *adv* maher
apart 1. לחוד *adv* le-khood; **2.** בנפרד *adv* be-neefrad.
apartheid 1. אפארטהייד *nm* apart'hayd; **2.** הפרדה גזעית (racial segregation) *nf* hafradah geez'eet.
apartment דירה *nf* deer|ah/-ot (+*of:* -at).
(furnished) apartment דירה מרוהטת *nf* deer|ah/-ot mero|hetet/-hatot.
apartment building בית דירות *nf* bet/batey deerot.
apathetic 1. אדיש *adj* adeesh/-ah; **2.** אפאתי *adj* apatee/-t.
apathy 1. אדישות (indifference) *nf* adeeshoot; **2.** אפאתיה *nf* apat|yah/-yot (+*of:* -yat).
ape קוף *nm* kof/-eem (*pl+of:* -ey).
(to) ape לחקות *inf* lekhakot; *pst* kheekah; *pres* mekhakeh; *fut* yekhakeh.
aperitif אפריטיף *nm* apereeteef/-eem.
aperture 1. פתח *nm* petakh/-eem (*pl+of:* peetkhey); **2.** חריר *nm* khareer/-eem (*pl+of:* -ey).
apex 1. קדקוד *nm* kodkod/-eem (*pl+of:* -ey); **2.** שיא (peak) *nm* see/-'eem (*pl+of:* -ey).
aphorism 1. אימרה (saying) *nf* eemrah/-ot (+*of:* -at); **2.** פתגם (proverb) *nm* peetgam/-eem (*pl+of:* -ey)
aphrodisiac 1. מעורר תשוקה *adj* me'orer/-et teshookah; **2.** סם מגרה חשק (drug exciting sexual desire) *nm* sam/-eem megar|eh/-ey kheshek.
apiece 1. כל אחד *adv* kol ekhad/akhat; **2.** ליחידה *adv* lee-yekheedah.
aplomb ביטחון עצמי *nm* beetakhon 'atsmee.
Apocalypse אחרית הימים *nf* akhareet ha-yameem.
Apocrypha הספרים החיצוניים *nm pl* ha-sfareem ha-kheetsoneeyeem.
apogee שיא *nm* see/-'eem (*pl+of:* -'ey).
apolitical אפוליטי *adj* apoleetee/-t.
apologetically בהצטדקות *adv* be-heetstadkoot.
(to) apologize 1. להתנצל *inf* leheetnatsel; *pst* heetnatsel; *pres* meetnatsel; *fut* yeetnatsel; **2.** להצטדק (justify oneself) *inf* leheetstadek; *pst* heetstadek; *pres* meetstadek; *fut* yeetstadek.
apology התנצלות *nf* heetnatsloo|t/-yot.
apoplexy שבץ *nm* shavats
apostle 1. מבשר *nm* mevas|er/-reem (*pl+of:* -rey); **2.** שליח *nm* shalee'akh/shlee|kheem (+*of:* -'akh/ -khey).
apostrophe גרש *nm* geresh.
apothecary רוקח *nmf* rok|e'akh/-akhat (*pl:* -'kheem/ -'khot; +*of:* -'khey).
(to) appal להחריד *inf* lehakhreed; *pst* hekhreed; *pres* makhreed; *fut* yakhreed.
appalling מחריד *adj* makhreed/-ah.
appallingly בצורה מחרידה *adv* be-tsoorah makhreedah.
apparatus מתקן *nm* meetk|an/-aneem (*pl+of:* -eney).
apparel רכוש *nm* rekhoosh.
apparent גלוי *adj* galooy/glooyah.
apparently כנראה *adv* ka-neer'eh.
apparition הופעה *nf* hofa|'ah/-'ot (+*of:* -'at).
appeal 1. קריאה לתמיכה (plea for support) *nf* kree|'ah/-'ot lee-tmeekhah; **2.** משיכה (attraction) *nf* mesheekh|ah/-ot (+*of:* -at); **3.** ערעור (in court) *nm* 'eer'oor/-eem (*pl+of:* -ey).
(United Jewish) Appeal המגבית היהודית המאוחדת *nf* ha-magbeet ha-yehoodeet ha-me'ookhedet.
(to) appeal 1. לבקש (request) *inf* levakesh; *pst* beekesh *(b=v)*; *pres* mevakesh; *fut* yevakesh; **2.** לצודד (attract) *inf* letsoded; *pst* tsoded; *pres* metsoded; *fut* yetsoded; **3.** לערער (in court) *inf* le'ar'er; *pst* 'eer'er; *pres* me'ar'er; *fut* ye'ar'er.
(to) appear 1. להופיע *inf* lehofee'a'; *pst* hofee'a'; *pres* mofee'a'; *fut* yofee'a'; **2.** להיראות (seem) *inf* lehera'ot; *pst* neer'ah; *pres* neer'eh; *fut* yera'eh.
appearance 1. הופעה *nf* hofa|'ah/-'ot (+*of:* -'at); **2.** מראה (look) *nm* mar'eh.
(to) appease 1. לפייס *inf* lefayes; *pst* peeyes *(p=f)*; *pres* mefayes; *fut* yefayes; **2.** להרגיע (calm) *inf* lehargee'a'; *pst* heergee'a'; *pres* margee'a'; *fut* yargee'a'.
appeasement פיוס *nm* peeyoos/-eem (*pl+of:* -ey).
(to) append לצרף *inf* letsaref; *pst* tseref; *pres* metsaref; *fut* yetsaref.
appendage תוספת *nf* tos|efet/-afot (*pl+of:* -fot).
appendicitis 1. דלקת התוספתן *nf* daleket ha-toseftan; **2.** אפנדיציט *nm* apendeetseet.
appendix 1. תוספתן (anatomy) *nm* toseftan; **2.** נספח (supplement) *nm* neesp|akh/-akheem (*pl+of:* -ekhey).
(to) appertain להשתייך *inf* leheeshtayekh; *pst* heeshtayekh; *pres* meeshtayekh; *fut* yeeshtayekh.
appetite 1. תיאבון *nm* te'avon (+*of:* ta'avon); **2.** חשק (desire) *nm* kheshek.
appetizer מנה ראשונה *nf* manah reeshonah.
appetizing מגרה תיאבון *adj* megar|eh/-ah te'avon.
(to) applaud למחוא כף *inf* leemkho kaf; *pst* makha kaf; *pres* mokhe kaf; *fut* yeemkha kaf.
applause מחיאות כפיים *nf pl* mekhee'ot kapayeem.
apple תפוח *nm* tapoo|akh/-kheem (*pl+of:* -khey).
apple of the eye בבת עין *nf* bavat 'ayeen.
apple pie עוגת תפוחים *nf* 'oog|at/-ot tapookheem.
apple tree עץ תפוח *nm* 'ets/'atsey tapoo'akh.
applejack שיכר תפוחים *nm* shekhar tapookheem.
applesauce רסק תפוחים *nm* resek tapookheem.
appliance מכשיר *nm* makhsheer/-eem (*pl+of:* -ey).
applicable ישים *adj* yaseem/yeseemah.
applicant 1. מבקש *nmf* mevakesh/-et; **2.** עותר (petitioner) *nmf* 'oter/-et.
application 1. בקשה *nf* bakash|ah/-ot (+*of:* -at); **2.** עתירה (petition) *nf* 'ateer|ah/-ot (+*of:* -at); **3.** שקידה (diligence) *nf* shekeed|ah (+*of:* -at); **4.** יישום (use) *nm* yeesoom/-eem (*pl+of:* -ey).
application form טופס בקשה *nm* tof|es/-sey bakashah.
applied sciences מדעים שימושיים *nm* mada'/-eem sheemooshee/-yeem.

(to) apply 1. לבקש *inf* levakesh; *pst* beekesh *(b=v); pres* mevakesh; *fut* yevakesh; **2.** לעתור (petition) *inf* la'ator; *pst* 'atar; *pres* 'oter; *fut* ya'ator; **3.** להחיל (refer,render applicable) *inf* lehakheel; *pst* hekheel; *pres* mekheel; *fut* yakheel; **4.** למרוח (spread) *inf* leemro'akh; *pst* marakh; *pres* more'akh; *fut* yeemrakh; **5.** ליישם (put to use) *inf* leyasem; *pst* yeesem; *pres* meyasem; *fut* yeyasem.

(to) appoint 1. למנות *inf* lemanot; *pst* meenah; *pres* memaneh; *fut* yemaneh; **2.** לקבוע (determine) *inf* leekbo'a'; *pst* kava' *(v=b)*; *pres* kove'a'; *fut* yeekba'.

appointed 1. קבוע *adj* kavoo'a'/kvoo'ah; **2.** ממונה *adj* memoon|eh/-ah.

appointment 1. מינוי *nm* meenooy/-eem (*pl+of:* -ey); **2.** פגישה (meeting) *nf* pegeesh|ah/-ot (*+of:* -at).

apportionment 1. מינון *nm* meenoon/-eem (*pl+of:* -ey); **2.** קיצוב (rationing) *nm* keetsoov/-eem (*pl+of:* -ey).

appraisal 1. אומדן *nm* oomdan/-eem (*pl+of:* oomdeney); **2.** אומד *nm* omed.

(to) appraise 1. לאמוד *inf* le'emod; *pst* amad; *pres* omed; *fut* ye'emod; **2.** להעריך (estimate) *inf* leha'areekh; *pst* he'ereekh; *pres* ma'areekh; *fut* ya'areekh.

appreciably במידה ניכרת *adv* be-meedah neekeret.

(to) appreciate 1. להעריך *inf* leha'areekh; *pst* he'ereekh; *pres* ma'areekh; *fut* ya'areekh; **2.** להחשיב (value) *inf* lehakhsheev; *pst* hekhsheev; *pres* makhheev; *fut* yakhsheev

appreciation 1. הערכה *nf* ha'arakh|ah/-ot (*+of:* -at); **2.** הוקרה (esteem) *nf* hokar|ah/-ot (*+of:* -at).

(to) apprehend 1. לעצור (detain) *inf* la'atsor; *pst* 'atsar; *pres* 'otser; *fut* ya'atsor; **2.** לאסור (arrest) *inf* le'esor; *pst* asar; *pres* oser; *fut* ye'esor.

apprehensive 1. מהיר תפיסה *adj* meheer/-at tefeesah; **2.** חושש (hesitant) *adj* khoshesh/-et.

apprehensively תוך חשש *adv* tokh khashash.

apprentice 1. שוליה *nm* shool|yah/-yot (*+of:* -yat); **2.** חניך (trainee) *nmf* khaneekh/-ah.

apprenticeship חניכות *nf* khaneekhoo|t/-yot.

approach גישה *nf* geesh|ah/-ot (*+of:* -at).

(to) approach 1. לגשת (draw near) *inf* lageshet; *pst & pres* neegash; *fut* yeegash; **2.** להתקרב (come near) *inf* leheetkarev; *pst* heetkarev; *pres* meetkarev; *fut* yeetkarev.

approachable נוח לגישה *adj* no'akh/nokhah legeeshah.

approaching מתקרב *adj* meetkarev/-et.

approbation 1. אישור *nm* eeshoor/-eem (*pl+of:* -ey); **2.** היתר (license) *nm* heter/-eem (*pl+of:* -ey).

appropriate 1. הולם (befitting) *adj* holem/-et; **2.** מתאים (suitable) *adj* mat'eem/-ah.

(to) appropriate 1. לרכוש (acquire) *inf* leerkosh; *pst* rakhash *(kh=k)*; *pres* rokhesh; *fut* yeerkosh; **2.** להקצות (allot) *inf* lehaktsot; *pst* heektsah; *pres* maktseh; *fut* yaktseh.

appropriately כיאות *adv* ka-ya'oot.

appropriation הקצבה *nf* haktsav|ah/-ot (*+of:* -at).

approval 1. אישור (confirmation) *nm* eeshoor/-eem (*pl+of:* -ey); **2.** הסכמה (consent) *nf* haskam|ah/-ot (*+of:* -at).

(to) approve 1. לאשר (ratify) *inf* le'asher; *pst* eesher; *pres* me'asher; *fut* ye'asher; **2.** לחייב (favor) *inf* lekhayev; *pst* kheeyev; *pres* mekhayev; *fut* yekhayev.

approvingly בחיוב *adv* be-kheeyoov.

approximate משוער *adj* mesho|'ar/-'eret.

(to) approximate לשער *inf* lesha'er; *pst* shee'er; *pres* mesha'er; *fut* yesha'er.

approximately בערך *adv* be-'erekh.

approximation אומדן משוער *nm* oomdan/-eem mesho|'ar/-eem.

apricot משמש *nm* meeshmesh/-eem (*pl+of:* -ey).

April אפריל *nm* apreel.

April Fools Day האחד באפריל *[colloq.] nm* ha-'ekhad be-apreel.

apron סינר *nm* seen|ar/-areem (*pl+of:* -rey).

apropos 1. בהקשר של *adv* be-heksher shel; **2.** דרך אגב *adv* derekh agav.

apt 1. כשיר *adj* kasheer/kesheerah; **2.** מתאים (suitable) *adj* mat'eem/-ah.

aptitude 1. כשרון *nm* keeshron/-ot; **2.** חריצות (diligence) *nf* khareetsoot.

aptly בכשרון *adv* be-kheeshron *(kh=k)*.

aquamarine 1. כצבע מי הים *adj* ke-tseva' mey ha-yam; **2.** כחול־ירקרק (greenish-blue) *adj* kakhol/kekhoolah yerakr|ak/-eket.

aquarium אקווריון *nm* akvaryon/-eem (*pl+of:* -ey).

aquatics משחקי מים *nm pl* mees'khakey mayeem.

aqueduct מוביל מים *nm* moveel/-ey mayeem.

aquiline נשרי *adj* neeshree/-t.

Arab 1. ערבי,־ה *nmf* 'arvee/-yah (*pl:* -m/-yot; *+of:* 'arveeyey); **2.** ערבי,־ת *adj* 'aravee/-t.

Arabia ערב *nf* 'arav.

Arabian Nights אלף לילה ולילה (Thousand-and-one Nights) *nm* elef laylah ve-laylah.

Arabic ערבית (language) *nf* 'araveet.

arbitrarily בשרירות *adv* bee-shreeroot.

arbitrary שרירותי *adj* shreerootee/-t.

arbitration בוררות *nf* boreroo|t/-yot.

arbitrator בורר *nm* borer/-eem (*pl+of:* -ey).

arc קשת *nf* kesh|et/-atot (*pl+of:* kashtot).

arc light מנורת קשת *nf* menor|at/-ot keshet.

arc welding הלחמת קשת *nf* halkham|at/-ot keshet.

arcade 1. מעבר מקומר *nm* ma'avar mekoomar; **2.** פסז׳ *nm* pasaj/-eem.

arch 1. קשת *nf* kesh|et/-atot (*pl+of:* kashtot); **2.** שער מקושת *nm* sha'ar/she'areem mekooshat/-eem.

archer קשת *nm* kashat/-eem (*pl+of:* -ey).

archaeology, archeology ארכיאולוגיה *nf* arkhe'ologyah.

archaic 1. ארכאי *adj* arkha'ee/-t; **2.** עתיק *adj* 'ateek/-ah.

archbishop ארכיבישוף *nm* arkheebeeshof.

archduke ארכידוכס *nmf* arkheedook|as/-seet.

arch-enemy שונא בנפש *nm* son|e/-'eem ba-nefesh.

archetype אבטיפוס *nm* avteepoos.

architect 1. אדריכל *nmf* adreekhal/-eet; **2.** ארדיכל *nmf* ardeekhal/-eet; **3.** ארכיטקט *nmf* arkheetekt/-eet.

architectural, architectonic ארכיטקטוני *adj* arkheetektonee/-t.
architecture 1. אדריכלות *nf* adreekhaloot; **2.** ארדיכלות *nf* ardeekhaloot; **3.** ארכיטקטורה *nf* arkheetektoor|ah (*+of:* -at).
archives 1. גנזך *nm* ganza|kh/-keem (*k=kh; pl+of:* -key); **2.** בית־גנזים *nm* bet/batey genazeem.
archway קימור *nm* keemoor/-eem (*pl+of:* -ey)
ardent נלהב *adj* neel|hav/-hevet.
ardently בהתלהבות *adv* be-heetlahavoot.
ardor להט *nm* lahat.
arduous מאומץ *adj* me'oom|ats/-etset.
arduously במאמצים *adv* be-ma'amatseem.
area אזור *nm* eyzor/azor|eem (*pl+of:* -ey).
area manager מנהל אזורי *nm* mena|hel/-haleem azoree/-yeem.
area of disagreement 1. תחום מחלוקת *nm* tekhoom/-ey makhaloket; **2.** שטח מריבה (disputed area) *nm* shetakh/sheetkhey mereevah.
arena זירה *nf* zeer|ah/-ot (*+of:* -at).
Argentina ארגנטינה *nf* argenteenah.
(to) argue 1. להתווכח *inf* leheetvake'akh; *pst* heetvakakh; *pres* meetvake'akh; *fut* yeetvakakh; **2.** לנמק (give reasons) *inf* lenamek; *pst* neemek; *pres* menamek; *fut* yenamek.
argument 1. ויכוח *nm* veekoo|'akh/-kheem (*pl+of:* -khey); **2.** נימוק (reason) *nm* neemook/-eem (*pl+of:* -ey).
argumentative פולמוסי *adj* poolmoosee/-t.
aria אריה *nf* ar|yah/-yot (*+of:* -yat).
arid 1. יבש (dry) *adj* yavesh/yeveshah; **2.** צחיח (barren) *adj* tsakhee'akh/tsekheekhah.
aridity 1. יובש (dryness) *nm* yovesh; **2.** צחיחות (barrenness) *nf* tsekheekhoo|t/-yot.
aright כראוי *adv* ka-ra'ooy.
(to) arise 1. לקום (get up) *inf* lakoom; *pst & pres* kam; *fut* yakoom; **2.** לנבוע (stem) *inf* leenbo'a'; *pst* nava' *(v=b); pres* nove'a'; *fut* yeenba'.
aristocracy 1. אצולה (class) *nf* atsool|ah/-ot (*+of:* -at); **2.** אצילות (quality) *nf* atseeloot; **3.** אריסטוקרטיה *nf* areestokratee|yah/-yot (*+of:* -yat).
aristocrat אציל *nmf* atseel/-ah (*+of:* -at; *pl+of:* -ey).
aristocratic 1. אריסטוקרטי *adj* areestokratee/-t; **2.** אצילי *adj* atseelee/-t.
arithmetic 1. תורת החשבון *nf* torat ha-kheshbon; **2.** אריתמטיקה *nf* areetmeteekah.
arithmetically לפי כללי החשבון *adv* lefee klaley ha-kheshbon.
ark תיבה *nf* teyv|ah/-ot (*+of:* -at).
(holy) ark ארון הקודש *nm* aron/-ot ha-kodesh.
(Noah's) ark תיבת נוח *nf* teyvat no'akh.
Ark of the Covenant ארון הברית *nm* aron ha-breet.
arm זרוע *nf* zro'|a/-ot.
arm in arm שלוב־זרוע *adj* shloov|at zro'a' (*pl:* -ey/ -ot *etc*).
(to) arm לחמש *inf* lekhamesh; *pst* kheemesh; *pres* mekhamesh; *fut* yekhamesh.
arm rest מסעד לזרוע *nm* mees'ad/-eem la-zro'a'.
armament חימוש *nm* kheemoosh/-eem (*pl+of:* -ey).
armchair כורסה *nf* koors|ah/-a'ot (*+of:* -at).
armed 1. חמוש *adj* khamoosh/-ah; **2.** מזוין *adj* mezooy|an/-enet.
armed forces 1. כוחות מזוינים *nm pl* kokhot mezooyaneem; **2.** צבא (army) *nm* tsava/tseva'ot (*pl+of:* tseev'ot).
armed robbery שוד מזוין *nm* shod mezooyan.
armed services שירותי הביטחון *nm pl* sherootey ha-beetakhon.
armistice שביתת נשק *nf* shveet|at/-ot neshek.
armor שריון *nm* sheeryon/-eem (*pl+of:* -ey).
armored car רכב משוריין *nm* rekh|ev/aveem meshooryan/-eem.
armpit בית השחי *nm* bet ha-shekhee.
arms נשק *nm* neshek.
army צבא *nm* tsava/tseva'ot (*pl+of:* tseev'ot).
(Israel Defence) Army 1. צבא הגנה לישראל *nm* tseva haganah le-yeesra'el; **2.** צה״ל (*acr of* 1, equivalent to IDF) *nm* tsahal.
army corps גיס *nm* gayees/gyasot (*pl+of:* geysot).
aroma ניחוח *adj* neekho|'akh/-kheem (*pl+of:* -khey).
aromatic ארומטי *adj* aromatee/-t.
around סביב *adv* saveev (*also:* sveev).
(to) arouse 1. לעורר *inf* le'orer; *pst* 'orer; *pres* me'orer; *fut* ye'orer; **2.** להניע (move) *inf* lehanee'a'; *pst* henee'a'; *pres* menee'a'; *fut* yanee'a
(to) arraign 1. להעמיד לדין *inf* leha'ameed le-deen; *pst* he'emeed *etc*; *pres* ma'ameed *etc*; *fut* ya'ameed *etc*; **2.** להאשים (accuse) *inf* leha'asheem; *pst* he'esheem; *pres* ma'asheem; *fut* ya'asheem.
(to) arrange 1. לסדר *inf* lesader; *pst* seeder; *pres* mesader; *fut* yesader; **2.** להסדיר (regulate) *inf* lehasdeer; *pst* heesdeer; *pres* masdeer; *fut* yasdeer.
arrangement 1. סידור *nm* seedoor/-eem (*pl+of:* -ey); **2.** הסדר (settlement) *nm* hesder/-eem (*pl+of:* -ey).
array היערכות *nm* he'arkhoo|t/-yot.
(to) array לערוך *inf* la'arokh; *pst* 'arakh; *pres* 'orekh; *fut* ya'arokh.
arrears 1. פיגורים *nm pl* peegooreem; **2.** חובות רובצים (floating debts) *nm pl* khovot rovtseem
arrest 1. מאסר *nm* ma'as|ar/-areem (*pl+of:* -rey); **2.** מעצר (detention) *nm* ma'ats|ar/-areem (*pl+of:* -rey).
(to) arrest 1. לאסור *inf* le'esor; *pst* asar; *pres* oser; *fut* ye'esor; **2.** לעצור (stop, detain) *inf* la'atsor; *pst* 'atsar; *pres* 'otser; *fut* ya'atsor.
arrival 1. בוא *nm* bo; **2.** הופעה *nf* hofa|'ah/-'ot (*+of:* -'at).
(to) arrive 1. להגיע (reach) *inf* lehagee'a'; *pst* heegee'a'; *pres* magee'a'; *fut* yagee'a'; **2.** לבוא (come) *inf* lavo; *pst & pres* ba (*b=v*); *fut* yavo; **3.** להופיע (appear) *inf* lehofee'a'; *pst* hofee'a'; *pres* mofee'a'; *fut* yofee'a'.
arrogance שחצנות *nf* shakhtsanoo|t/-yot.
arrogant שחצן *adj* shakhtsan/-eet.
arrow חץ *nm* khets/kheets|eem (*pl+of:* -ey).
arsenal מחסן נשק *nm* makhs|an/-eney neshek.
arsenic זרניך *nm* zarneekh.
arson הצתה *nf* hatsat|ah/-ot (*+of:* -at).
arsonist מצית *nm* matseet/-eem (*pl+of:* -ey).

art 1. אמנות *nf* omanoo|t/-yot; **2.** מיומנות (skill) *nf* meyoomanoo|t/-yot.
artery עורק 'or|ek/keem (*pl+of:* -key).
artful ערמומי *adj* 'armoomee/-t.
artichoke 1. חורשף *nm* khoorsh|af/-afeem (*pl+of:* -efey); **2.** ארטישוק *nm* arteeshok/-eem.
article מאמר (press) *nm* ma'am|ar/-areem (*pl+of:* -rey).
article (of law) סעיף *nm* se'eef/-eem (*pl+of:* -ey).
article (of merchandise) פריט preet/-eem (*pl+of:* -ey).
articulate מובע ברורות *adj* moob|a'/-a'at brooroٍt.
(to) articulate להביע *inf* lehabee'a'; *pst* heebee'a'; *pres* mabee'a'; *fut* yabee'a'.
articulation 1. חיתוך דיבור *nm* kheetookh/-ey deeboor; **2.** מפרק (joint) *nm* meefr|ak/-akeem (*pl+of:* -ekey).
artifact דבר מלאכותי *nm* davar/dvareem mel'akhootee/-yeem.
artifice תחבולה *nf* takhbool|ah/-ot (*+of:* -at).
artificial מלאכותי mal'akhootee/-yeem.
artillery חיל התותחנים *nf* kheyl ha-totkhaneem.
artisan 1. בעל־מלאכה *nm* ba'al/-ey melakhah; **2.** אומן (craftsman) ooman/-eem (*pl+of:* -ey).
artist 1. אמן *nmf* oman/-eet; **2.** שחקן (stage, film) *nmf* sakhkan/-eet (*pl:* -eem/-eeyot; *+of:* -ey); **3.** צייר (painter) *nmf* tsa|yar/-yeret (*pl:* -yareem; *+of:* -yarey).
artistic אמנותי *adj* omanootee/-t.
artistically בצורה אמנותית be-tsoorah omanooteet.
(master of) arts מוסמך למדעי הרוח *nmf* moosm|akh/-ekhet le-mad'ey ha-rooakh.
as 1. כמו *adv* kemo; **2.** כפי *adv* kefee; **3.** כשם *adv* keshem.
(the same) as ממש כמו *adv* mamash kemo.
as far עד כמה *adv* 'ad kamah.
as for אשר ל־ asher le-.
as if כאילו ke'eeloo.
as long as כל עוד kol 'od.
as much ככל ke-khol.
as well 1. גם כן gam ken; **2.** כמו כן (also) kemo khen.
as yet 1. עדיין *adv* 'adayeen; **2.** בינתיים (meanwhile) *adv* beynatayeem.
asbestos אזבסט *nm* asbest.
(to) ascend 1. לעלות (go up) *inf* la'alot; *pst* 'alah; *pres* 'oleh; *fut* ya'aleh; **2.** לטפס (climb) *inf* letapes; *pst* teepes; *pres* metapes; *fut* yetapes.
ascension 1. עלייה *nf* 'alee|yah/-yot (*+of:* -at); **2.** התרוממות (rising) *nf* heetromemoo|t/-yot.
ascent 1. עלייה *nf* 'alee|yah/-ot (*+of:* -yat); **2.** טיפוס (climbing) *nm* teepoos.
(to) ascertain לוודא *inf* levade; *pst* veede; *pres* mevade; *fut* yevade.
ascetic סגפני *adj* sagfanee/-t.
(to) ascribe לייחס *inf* leyakhes; *pst* yeekhes; *pres* meyakhes; *fut* yeyakhes.
ash אפר *nm* efer.
ashamed 1. מבויש *adj* mevooy|ash/-eshet; **2.** מתבייש *adj* meetbayesh/-et.

(to be) ashamed להתבייש *inf* leheetbayesh; *pst* heetbayesh; *pres* meetbayesh; *fut* yeetbayesh.
ashore על החוף *adv* 'al ha-khof.
(to go) ashore לעלות לחוף *inf* la'alot la-khof; *pst* 'alah *etc*; *pres* 'oleh *etc*; *fut* ya'aleh *etc*.
ashtray מאפרה *nf* ma'afer|ah/-ot (*+of:* -at).
Asiatic 1. אסייני *nmf & adj* aseeyanee/-t; **2.** אסייתי *[colloq.] nmf & adj* aseeyatee/-t.
aside הצידה *adv* ha-tseedah.
(to) ask לשאול *inf* leesh'ol; *pst* sha'al; *pres* sho'el; *fut* yeesh'al.
(to) ask for 1. לבקש *inf* levakesh; *pst* beekesh *(b=v)*; *pres* mevakesh; *fut* yevakesh; **2.** לתבוע (demand) *inf* leetbo'a'; *pst* tava' *(v=b)*; *pres* tove'a'; *fut* yeetba'.
askance בעקיפין *adv* ba-'akeefeen.
(to look) askance להסתכל בחשדנות *inf* leheestakel be-khashdanoot; *pst* heestakel *etc*; *pres* meestakel *etc*; *fut* yeestakel *etc*.
asleep רדום *adj* radoom/redoomah.
(to fall) asleep להירדם *inf* leheradem; *pst & pres* neerdam; *fut* yeradem.
asparagus אספרג *nm* aspereg.
aspect היבט *nm* hebet/-eem (*pl+of:* -ey)
asphalt אספלט *nm* asfalt.
aspiration שאיפה *nf* she'eef|ah/-ot (*+of:* -at)
(to) aspire לשאוף *inf* leesh'of; *pst* sha'af; *pres* sho'ef; *fut* yeesh'af.
aspirin אספירין *nm* aspeereen/-eem.
ass 1. חמור (donkey) *nm* khamor/-eem (*pl+of:* -ey); **2.** עכוז (buttocks) *nm* 'akooz/-eem (*pl+of:* -ey).
(to) assail 1. להתנפל *inf* leheetnapel; *pst* heetnapel; *pres* meetnapel; *fut* yeetnapel; **2.** לתקוף (attack) *inf* leetkof; *pst* takaf; *pres* tokef; *fut* yeetkof
assailant תוקף *nm* tok|ef/-feem (*pl+of:* -fey).
assassin רוצח *nmf* rots|e'akh/-akhat (*pl:* -kheem/-khot).
(to) assassinate לרצוח *inf* leertso'akh; *pst* ratsakh; *pres* rotse'akh; *fut* yeertsakh.
assassination רצח *nm* rets|akh/-eekhot.
assault 1. תקיפה *nf* tekeef|ah/-ot (*+of:* -at); **2.** התנפלות *nf* heetnaploo|t/-yot.
(to) assault 1. להתנפל *inf* leheetnapel; *pst* heetnapel; *pres* meetnapel; *fut* yeetnapel; **2.** לתקוף (attack) *inf* leetkof; *pst* takaf; *pres* tokef; *fut* yeetkof.
(to) assay לבדוק *inf* leevdok; *pst* badak *(b=v)*; *pres* bodek; *fut* yeevdok.
(to) assemble 1. להרכיב (parts) *inf* leharkeev; *pst* heerkeev; *pres* markeev; *fut* yarkeev; **2.** לאסוף (collect) *inf* le'esof; *pst* asaf; *pres* osef; *fut* ye'esof.
assembly 1. אסיפה (meeting) *nf* asef|ah/-ot (*+of:* -at); **2.** כינוס (ingathering) *nm* keenoos/-eem (*pl+of:* -ey).
(the General) Assembly העצרת הכללית *nf* ha-'atseret ha-klaleet.
assent הסכמה *nf* haskam|ah/-ot (*+of:* -at).
(to) assert 1. לטעון *inf* leet'on; *pst* ta'an; *pres* to'en; *fut* yeet'an; **2.** לעמוד על שלו *inf* la'amod 'al shelo; *pst* 'amad *etc*; *pres* 'omed *etc*; *fut* ya'amod *etc*.
(to) assert oneself להתבלט *inf* leheetbalet; *pst* heetbalet; *pres* meetbalet *etc*; *fut* yeetbalet.
assertion טענה *nf* ta'anah/te'anot (*+of:* ta'an|at/-ot).

(to) assess 1. לשום (for tax) *inf* lashoom; *pst & pres* sham; *fut* yashoom; **2.** לאמוד (estimate) *inf* le'emod; *pst* amad; *pres* omed; *fut* ye'emod.

assessment שומה *nf* shoom|ah/-ot (*+of:* -at).

asset נכס *nm* nekh|es/-aseem (*pl+of:* neekhsey).

assets 1. נכסים *nm pl* nekhaseem (*pl+of:* neekhsey); **2.** רכוש (property) *nm* rekhoosh; **3.** אקטיב *nm* akteev/-eem.

(personal) assets נכסים אישיים *nm pl* nekhaseem eesheeyeem.

assiduous מתמיד *adj* matmeed/-ah.

(to) assign 1. למנות (appoint) *inf* lemanot; *pst* meenah; *pres* memaneh; *fut* yemaneh; **2.** להעביר (transfer) *inf* leha'aveer; *pst* he'eveer; *pres* ma'aveer; *fut* ya'aveer; **3.** לייחס (ascribe) *inf* leyakhes; *pst* yeekhes; *pres* meyakhes; *fut* yeyakhes.

assignment 1. משימה (task) *nf* meseem|ah/-ot (*+of:* -at); **2.** מינוי (appointment) *nm* meenooy/-eem (*pl+of:* -ey).

(to) assimilate 1. לאכל *vt inf* le'akel; *pst* eekel; *pres* me'akel; *fut* ye'akel; **2.** להיטמע *vi inf* leheetama'; *pst & pres* neetma'; *fut* yeetama'.

assimilation התבוללות *nf* heetboleloot.

(to) assist לסייע *inf* lesaye'a'; *pst* seeye'a'; *pres* mesaye'a'; *fut* yesaye'a'.

assistance 1. עזרה (help) *nf* 'ezr|ah (*+of:* -at); **2.** סיוע (aid) *nm* seeyoo'a'.

assistant עוזר *nmf* 'ozer/-et.

associate שותף *nmf* shoot|af/-efet (*pl+of:* -afey).

(to) associate לשתף *inf* leshatef; *pst* sheetef; *pres* meshatef; *fut* yeshatef.

association 1. התאחדות heet'akhdoo|t/-yot; **2.** שותפות (partnership) *nf* shoot|afoot/-fooyot.

(to) assort למיין *inf* lemayen; *pst* meeyen; *pres* memayen; *fut* yemayen.

assorted מסוגים שונים mee-soogeem shoneem.

assortment מבחר *nm* meevkhar/-eem (*pl+of:* -ey).

(to) assume להניח *inf* lehanee'akh; *pst* heenee'akh; *pres* manee'akh; *fut* yanee'akh.

assumption הנחה *nf* hanakhah/-ot (*+of:* -at).

assurance 1. הבטחה *nf* havtakh|ah/-ot (*+of:* -at); **2.** ביטוח *nm* beetoo|'akh/-kheem (*pl+of:* -khey)

(to) assure 1. להבטיח (pledge) *inf* lehavtee'akh; *pst* heevtee'akh; *pres* mavtee'akh; *fut* yavtee'akh; **2.** לבטח (insure) *inf* levate'akh; *pst* beetakh (*b=v*); *pres* mevate'akh; *fut* yevatakh.

assuredly בבטחה *adv* be-veetkhah.

asterisk כוכבית *nf* kokhavee|t/-yot.

astigmatism אסטיגמטיות *nf* asteegmateeyoot.

(to) astonish להתמיה *inf* lehatmeeha; *pst* heetmeeha; *pres* matmeeha; *fut* yatmeeha.

astonishing מתמיה *adj* matmee|ha/-hah.

astonishment 1. תימהון *nm* teem|ahon/-honot (*+of:* -hon); **2.** השתוממות (amazement) *nf* heeshtomemoo|t/-yot.

(to) astound להדהים *inf* lehad'heem; *pst* heed'heem; *pres* mad'heem; *fut* yad'heem.

astray שולל *adv* sholal.

(to go) astray לתעות *inf* leet'ot; *pst* ta'ah; *pres* to'eh; *fut* yeet'eh.

(to lead) astray להתעות *inf* lehat'ot; *pst* heet'ah; *pres* mat'eh; *fut* yat'eh.

astride בפישוק *adv* be-feesook (*f=p*).

astrology אסטרולוגיה *nf* astrologyah.

astronaut 1. אסטרונאוט *nm* astrona'oot/-eem; **2.** טייס חלל *nm* tayas/-ey khalal.

astronomer אסטרונום *nm* astronom/-eem (*pl+of:* -ey).

astronomy אסטרונומיה *nf* astronomyah.

astrophysics אסטרופיסיקה *nf* astrofeeseekah.

astute חריף *adj* khareef/-ah.

asunder לחלקים *adv* la-khalakeem.

(to tear) asunder לקרוע לגזרים *inf* leekro'a' lee-gezareem; *pst* kara' *etc*; *pres* kore'a' *etc*; *fut* yeekra' *etc*.

asylum מקלט *nm* meekl|at/ateem (*pl+of:* -etey).

(orphan) asylum בית־יתומים *nm* bet/batey yetomeem.

at 1. אצל *prep* etsel; **2.** ־ב (*prefix*) be-.

at last סוף סוף *adv* sof sof.

at once מיד *adv* meeyad.

at work בעבודה *adv* ba-'avodah.

atheist אתאיסט *nmf* ate'eest/-eet.

athlete אתלט *nm* atlet/-eem (*pl+of:* -ey).

athletic אתלטי *adj* atletee/-t.

athletics אתלטיקה *nf* atleteekah.

Atlantic 1. האוקיינוס האטלאנטי (Atlantic Ocean) mm ha-okyanos ha-atlantee; **2.** אטלאנטי *adj* atlantee/-t.

atlas אטלס *nm* atlas/-eem (*pl+of:* -ey).

atmosphere 1. אטמוספירה *nf* atmosferah/-ot (*+of:* -at); **2.** אווירה *nf* aveer|ah/-ot (*+of:* -at).

atmospheric אטמוספרי *adj* atmosferee/-t.

atom אטום atom/-eem (*pl+of:* -ey).

atomic אטומי *adj* atomee/-t.

atomic energy אנרגיה אטומית *nf* energyah atomeet.

atomic pile כור גרעיני *nm* koor/-eem gar'eenee/-yeem.

(to) atone לכפר *inf* lekhaper; *pst* keeper; *pres* mekhaper; *fut* yekhaper.

atonement 1. כיפור *nm* keepoor/-eem (*pl+of:* -ey); **2.** כפרה *nf* kaparah/-ot (*+of:* -at).

(Day of) Atonement יום כיפור *nm* yom keepoor.

atrocious אכזרי *adj* akhzaree/-t.

atrocity 1. אכזריות *nf* akhzereeyoot; **2.** מעשה אכזריות (act of) *nm* ma'as|eh/-ey akhzereeyoot.

(to) attach 1. לקשר (connect) *inf* lekasher; *pst* keesher; *pres* mekasher; *fut* yekasher; **2.** לייחס (ascribe) *inf* leyakhes; *pst* yeekhes; *pres* meyakhes; *fut* yeyakhes.

attachment 1. התקשרות (commitment) *nf* heetkashroo|t/-yot; **2.** נאמנות (devotion) *nf* ne'emanoo|t/-yot; **3.** עיקול (seizure) *nm* 'eekool/-eem (*pl+of:* -ey).

attack התקפה hatkaf|ah/-ot (*+of:* -at).

(to) attack 1. לתקוף *inf* leetkof; *pst* takaf; *pres* tokef; *fut* yeetkof; **2.** להתקיף *inf* lehatkeef; *pst* heetkeef; *pres* matkeef; *fut* yatkeef.

attacker תוקף *nm* tok|ef/-feem (*pl+of:* -fey).

(to) attain להשיג *inf* lehaseeg; *pst* heeseeg; *pres* maseeg; *fut* yaseeg.

attainment השגה hasag|ah/-ot (*+of:* -at).

attempt ניסיון *nm* nees|ayon/-yonot (*+of:* -yon).
(to) attempt לנסות *inf* lenasot; *pst* neesah; *pres* menaseh; *fut* yenaseh.
attempt on the life of התנקשות בחיי *nf* heetnakshoo|t/-yot be-khayey.
(to) attend 1. להיות נוכח *inf* leehyot nokhe'akh; *pst* nakhakh; *pres* nokhe'akh; *fut* yeehyeh nokhe'akh; **2.** לטפל *inf* letapel; *pst* teepel; *pres* metapel; *fut* yetapel.
attendance נוכחות *nf* nokhekhoot.
attendant 1. שרת *nm* sharat/-eem (*pl+of:* -ey); **2.** שמש (janitor) *nm* shamash/-eem (*+of:* -ey); **3.** מטפלת (nursemaid) *nf* metap|elet/-lot.
attention תשומת־לב *nf* tesoomet lev.
(to pay) attention לשים לב *inf* laseem lev; *pst & pres* sam lev; *fut* yaseem lev.
attentive קשוב *adj* kashoov/-ah.
(to) attest לאשר *inf* le'asher; *pst* eesher; *pres* me'asher; *fut* ye'asher.
attic עליית־גג *nf* 'alee|yat/-yot gag.
attire לבוש *nm* levoosh.
attitude 1. יחס *nm* yakhas/yekhaseem (*pl+of:* -ey); **2.** עמדה (position) *nf* 'emd|ah/-ot (*+of:* -at); **3.** גישה (approach) *nf* geesh|ah/-ot (*+of:* -at).
attorney בא־כוח *nmf* ba/-'at ko'akh (*pl:* -'ey *etc*).
(district) attorney תובע מחוזי *nmf* tov|e'a'/-a'at mekhozee/-t.
(power of) attorney ייפוי־כוח *nm* yeepoo|y/-yey ko'akh.
attorney-at-law 1. עורך־דין (advocate) *nmf* 'orekh/-et (*pl:* 'orkh|ey/-ot) deen; **2.** פרקליט (counsel) *nmf* prakleet/-ah (*+of:* -at).
attorney general 1. התובע הכללי *nm* ha-tove'a' ha-klalee; **2.** היועץ המשפטי (legal adviser) *nm* ha-yo'ets ha-meeshpatee.
(to) attract 1. להסב תשומת־לב (attention) *inf* lehasev tesoomet lev; *pst* hesev *etc*; *pres* mesev *etc*; *fut* yasev *etc*; **2.** למשוך (draw) *inf* leemshokh; *pst* mashakh; *pres* moshekh; *fut* yeemshokh.
attraction 1. משיכה *nf* mesheekhah/-ot (*+of:* -at); **2.** כוח משיכה (gravitation) *nm* ko'akh mesheekhah.
attractive מושך *adj* moshekh/-et.
attractiveness חינניות *nf* kheenaneeyoot.
attribute תכונה *nf* tekhoon|ah/-ot (*+of:* -at).
attrition התשה *nf* hatash|ah/-ot (*+of:* -at).
(War of) Attrition מלחמת ההתשה *nf* meelkhemet ha-hatashah.
auburn חום־זהוב *adj* khoom/-ah zahov/zehoobah (*b=v*).
auction מכירה פומבית *nf* mekheer|ah/-ot poombee|t/-yot.
audacious אמיץ *adj* ameets/-ah.
audacity תעוזה *nf* te'ooz|ah/-ot (*+of:* -at).
audible נשמע *adj* neeshm|a'/-a'at.
audience 1. קהל (public) *nm* kahal; **2.** ריאיון re'ayon/ra'ayonot (*+of:* ra'yon).
audio-visual אור־קולי *adj* or-kolee/-t.
audit ביקורת חשבונות *nf* beekoret kheshbonot.
(to) audit לבקר חשבונות *inf* levaker kheshbonot; *pst* beeker (*b=v*) *etc*; *pres* mevaker *etc*; *fut* yevaker *etc*.
audition אודיציה *nf* odeets|yah/-yot (*+of:* -yat).
auditor רואה־חשבון *nm* ro|'eh/-'ey kheshbon.
auditorium אודיטוריום *nm* odeetoryoom/-eem.
auger מקדח *nm* makde|'akh/-kheem (*pl+of:* -khey).
aught משהו mashehoo.
(to) augment להגדיל *inf* lehagdeel; *pst* heegdeel; *pres* magdeel; *fut* yagdeel.
augur מגיד עתידות *nmf* mageed/-at 'ateedot.
(to) augur 1. לראות מראש (foresee) *inf* leer'ot me-rosh; *pst* ra'ah *etc*; *pres* ro'eh *etc*; *fut* yeer'eh *etc*; **2.** לנבא (foretell) *inf* lenabe; *pst* neeba; *pres* menabe; *fut* yenabe.
(to) augur ill לנבא רעות *inf* lenabe ra'ot; *pst* neeba *etc*; *pres* menabe *etc*; *fut* yenabe *etc*.
August אוגוסט *nm* ogoost.
aunt דודה *nf* dod|ah/-ot (*+of:* -at).
auspices חסות *nf* khasoo|t/-yot.
auspicious מבטיח *adj* mavtee|'akh/-khah.
austere קפדני *adj* kapdanee/-t.
austerity צנע *nm* tsena'.
Austrian 1. אוסטרי *adj* ostree/-t; **2.** אוסטרי *nmf* ostree/-t.
authentic אותנטי *adj* otentee/-t.
author מחבר *nm* mekhab|er/-eret (*pl:* -reem/-rot; *+of:* -rey).
authoritative מוסמך *adj* moosm|akh/-ekhet.
authority 1. שלטון *nm* sheelton/-ot; **2.** סמכות (competence) *nf* samkhoo|t/-yot; **3.** אוטוריטה *nf* otoreet|ah/-ot (*+of:* -at).
(to) authorize 1. להסמיך *inf* lehasmeekh; *pst* heesmeekh; *pres* masmeekh; *fut* yasmeekh; **2.** לאשר (confirm) *inf* le'asher; *pst* eesher; *pres* me'asher; *fut* ye'asher; **3.** להרשות (allow) *inf* leharshot; *pst* heershah; *pres* marsheh; *fut* yarsheh.
auto 1. אוטו *nm* oto/otomobeeleem; **2.** אוטויים *[colloq.] pl* otoyeem; **3.** מכונית *nf* mekhonee|t/-yot.
autocrat שליט יחיד *nmf* shaleet/-ah yakheed/yekheedah.
autograph 1. אוטוגרף *nm* otograf/-eem (*pl+of:* -ey); **2.** חתימה למזכרת *nf* khateem|ah/-ot le-mazkeret.
automatic אוטומאטי *adj* otomatee/-t.
automatically 1. אוטומאטית *adv* otomateet; **2.** באופן אוטומאטי *adv* be-ofen otomatee.
automobile מכונית *nf* mekhonee|t/-yot.
autonomous אוטונומי *adj* otonomee/-t.
autonomy אוטונומיה *nf* otonom|yah/-yot (*+of:* -yat).
autopsy ניתוח שלאחר המוות *nm* neetoo|'akh/-kheem shele-akhar ha-mavet.
autumn סתיו *nf* stav/-eem (*pl+of:* -ey).
autumnal סתווי *adj* stavee/-t.
auxiliary מסייע *adj* mesa|ye'a'/-ya'at.
avail תועלת *nf* to'elet.
(of no) avail 1. ללא תועלת *adv* le-lo to'elet; **2.** חסר תועלת *adj* khas|ar/-rat to'elet.
(to) avail להועיל *inf* leho'eel; *pst* ho'eel; *pres* mo'eel; *fut* yo'eel.
(to) avail oneself of להפיק תועלת *inf* lehafeek to'elet; *pst* hefeek *etc*; *pres* mefeek *etc*; *fut* yafeek *etc*.
available מצוי *adj* matsooy/metsooyah.

avalanche מפולת *nf* mapol|et/-ot.
avarice קמצנות *nf* kamtsanoot.
avaricious קמצן *adj* kamtsan/-eet.
(to) avenge לנקום *inf* leenkom; *pst* nakam; *pres* nokem; *fut* yeenkom.
avenger נוקם *adj* nokem/-et.
avenue שדרה *nf* sder|ah/-ot (*+of:* -at).
(to) aver לאמת *inf* le'amet; *pst* eemet; *pres* me'amet; *fut* ye'amet.
average ממוצע *adj* memoots|a'/-a'at.
(to) average להתמצע *inf* leheetmatse'a'; *pst* heetmatsa'; *pres* meetmatse'a; *fut* yeetmatse'a.
averse שולל *adj* sholel/-et.
aversion סלידה *nf* sleed|ah/-ot (*+of:* -at).
(to) avert למנוע *inf* leemno'a'; *pst* mana'; *pres* mone'a'; *fut* yeemna'.
aviation תעופה *nf* te'oof|ah/-ot (*+of:* -at).
aviator טייס *nm* tayas/-eem (*pl+of:* -ey).
avocado אבוקדו *nm* avokado.
avocation 1. תחביב *nm* takhbeev/-eem; **2.** עיסוק צדדי *nm* 'eesook/-eem tsedadee/-yeem.
(to) avoid 1. לחמוק מפני *inf* lakhamok mee-peney; *pst* khamak *etc*; *pres* khomek *etc*; *fut* yakhamok *etc*; **2.** להימנע מ־ (abstain) *inf* leheemana' mee-; *pst & pres* neemna' mee-; *fut* yeemana' mee-.
(to) avow 1. להודות ברבים *inf* lehodot ba-rabeem; *pst* hodah *etc*; *pres* modeh *etc*; *fut* yodeh *etc*; **2.** להצהיר (declare) *inf* lehats'heer; *pst* heets'heer; *pres* mats'heer; *fut* yats'heer.
avowal הודאה *nf* hoda|'ah/-'ot (*+of:* -'at).
(to) await לצפות *inf* letsapot; *pst* tseepah; *pres* metsapeh; *fut* yetsapeh.
awake 1. ער *adj* 'er/-ah; **2.** פעיל (active) *adj* pa'eel/pe'eelah.
(wide) awake בעיניים פקוחות *adv* be-'eynayeem pekookhot.
(to) awake 1. להקיץ *inf* lehakeets; *pst* hekeets; *pres* mekeets; *fut* yakeets; **2.** להתעורר *inf* leheet'orer; *pst* heet'orer; *pres* meet'orer; *fut* yeet'orer.
(to) awaken לעורר *inf* le'orer; *pst* 'orer; *pres* me'orer; *fut* ye'orer.
award 1. פרס (prize) *nm* pras/-eem (*pl+of:* -ey); **2.** פסק־דין (judgment) *nm* pesak/peeskey deen.
(to) award 1. להעניק (grant) *inf* leha'aneek; *pst* he'eneek; *pres* ma'aneek; *fut* ya'aneek; **2.** לפסוק (adjudicate) *inf* leefsok; *pst* pasak (*p=f*); *pres* posek; *fut* yeefsok.
aware מודע *adj* mood|a'/-a'at.
away רחוק *adj* rakhok/rekhokah.
(right) away תיכף ומיד *adv* tekhef oo-meeyad.
(to give) away לתת במתנה *inf* latet bé-matanah; *pst* natan *etc*; *pres* noten *etc*; *fut* yeeten *etc*.
(to go) away 1. ללכת (leave) *inf* lalekhet; *pst* halakh; *pres* holekh; *fut* yelekh; **2.** לצאת לדרך (depart) *inf* latset le-derekh; *pst* yatsa *etc*; *pres* yotse *etc*; *fut* yetse *etc*.
(to take) away 1. לקחת *inf* lakakhat; *pst* lakakh; *pres* loke'akh; *fut* yeekakh; **2.** ליטול *inf* leetol; *pst* natal; *pres* notel; *fut* yeetol.
awe יראת כבוד *nf* yeer'at kavod.
awful איום *adv* ayom/ayoomah.
awfully 1. בפחד *adv* be-fakhad (*f=p*); **2.** מאוד *[colloq.] adv* me'od.
awhile לזמן מה *adv* lee-zman mah.
awkward 1. מביך (embarrasing) *adj* meveekh/-ah; **2.** מגושם (clumsy) *adj* megoosh|am/-emet.
awl 1. מרצע *nm* martse|'a'/-'eem (*pl+of:* -'ey); **2.** yanshoof/-eem (*pl+of:* -ey).
awning סוכך *nm* sokhekh.
ax, axe 1. גרזן *nm* garz|en-eeneem (*pl+of:* -eeney); **2.** קרדום kard|om/-oomeem (*pl+of:* -oomey).
axis ציר *nm* tseer/-eem (*pl+of:* -ey).
axle 1. סרן קדמי (front) *nm* seren keedmee; **2.** סרן אחורי (rear) *nm* seren akhoree.
azure תכול *adj* takhol/tekhoolah.

B.

B,b has ב (Bet) as its equivalent consonant in the Hebrew alphabet (בּ in dotted spelling).
babble 1. מלמול *nm* meelmool/-eem (*pl+of:* -ey); **2.** קשקוש (prattle) *nm* keeshkoosh/-eem (*pl+of:* -ey).
(to) babble למלמל *inf* lemalmel; *pst* meelmel; *pres* memalmel; *fut* yemalmel.
babe 1. תינוק *nm* teenok/-et (*pl:* -ot); **2.** בחורונת (girl) *nf* bakhooronet.
baboon בבון *nm* baboon/-eem (*pl+of:* -ey).
baby תינוק *nm* teenok/-et (*pl:* -ot).
baby carriage עגלת ילדים *nf* 'egl|at/-ot yeladeem.
baby grand פסנתר־כנף *nm* p'sant|er/-trey kanaf.
baby sitter 1. שומר טף *nmf* shomer/-et taf; **2.** שמרטף *[colloq.] nmf* shmartaf/-eet.
bachelor 1. רווק *nmf* ravak/-ah; **2.** בוגר אוניברסיטה (B.A.) *nmf* boger/-et ooneeverseetah.
bacillus חיידק *nm* khaydak/-eem (*pl+of:* -ey).
back 1. גב (hind part) *nm* gav/gab|eem (*b=v*; *pl+of:* -ey); **2.** חזרה (in return) *adv* khazarah; **3.** מגן (soccer) *nm* mag|en/-eeneem (*pl+of:* -eeney).

(to) back 1. לתת תימוכין *inf* latet teemookheen; *pst* natan *etc*; *pres* noten *etc*; *fut* yeeten *etc*; **2.** לתת גיבוי *[colloq.]* *inf* latet geebooy; *pst* natan *etc*; *pres* noten *etc*; *fut* yeeten *etc*.

(to pay) back 1. להחזיר *inf* lehakhzeer; *pst* hekhzeer; *pres* makhzeer; *fut* yakhzeer; **2.** לסלק (pay off) *inf* lesalek; *pst* seelek; *pres* mesalek; *fut* yesalek.

back ache כאב גב *nm* ke'ev/-ey gav.

back and forth הלוך וחזור *adv* halokh ve-khazor.

back-breaking מפרך *adj* mefarekh/-et.

(to) back down לסגת *inf* laseget; *pst & pres* nasog; *fut* yeesog.

(to) back out להתחמק *inf* leheetkhamek; *pst* heetkhamek; *pres* meetkhamek; *fut* yeetkhamek.

back pay פיגורי שכר *nm* peegoorey sakhar.

back seat מושב אחורי *nm* moshav akhoree.

back yard חצר אחורית *nf* khatser akhoreet.

backbone 1. חוט השדרה *nm* khoot ha-sheedrah; **2.** עמוד התווך (central pillar) *nm* 'amood/-ey ha-tavekh.

backer 1. פטרון *nmf* patron/-eet (*pl+of:* -ey); **2.** תומך (sponsor) *nmf* tomekh/-et (*pl+of:* tomkhey).

background רקע *nm* reka'.

backing 1. תימוכין *nm pl* teemookheen; **2.** גיבוי *[colloq.]* *nm* geebooy/-eem (*pl+of:* -ey).

backlash הילוך סרק *nm* heelookh/-ey srak

backlog הצטברות דברים *nf* heetstabroo|t/-yot dvareem.

backstage אחורי הקלעים *nm pl* akhorey ha-kla'eem.

backward מפגר *adj* mefager/-et.

backwardness פיגור *nm* peegoor/-eem (*pl+of:* -ey).

backwards אחורה *adv* akhorah.

bacon קותלי חזיר *nm pl* kotley khazeer.

bacteria 1. חיידקים *nm pl* khaydakeem (*sing:* khaydak; *pl+of:* -ey); **2.** מתגים (bacilli) *nm pl* metageem (*sing:* meteg; *pl+of:* meetgey).

bacteriology בקטריולוגיה *nf* bakteryologyah.

bad 1. רע *adj* ra'/-ah; **2.** לקוי (defective) *adj* lakooy/lekooyah.

(from) bad to worse מן הפח אל הפחת *adv* meen ha-pakh el ha-pakhat.

badge 1. תג *nm* tag/-eem (*pl+of:* -ey); **2.** סמל (emblem) *nm* semel/smaleem (*pl+of:* seemley).

(to) badger להטריד *inf* lehatreed; *pst* heetreed; *pres* matreed; *fut* yatreed.

badness רוע *nm* ro'a'.

(to) baffle לבלבל *inf* levalbel; *pst* beelbel (*b=v*); *pres* mevalbel; *fut* yevalbel.

bag 1. תיק (ladies') *nm* teek/-eem (*pl+of:* -ey); **2.** שקית (satchel) *nf* sakee|t/-yot.

baggage 1. מזוודות (suitcases) *nmf pl* meezvadot; **2.** מיטען (cargo) *nm* meet'an/-eem (*pl+of:* -ey).

baggage check תלוש מיטען *nm* tloosh/-ey meet'an.

bagpipe חמת חלילים *nf* khemat khaleeleem.

bail 1. ערבות *nf* 'arvoo|t/-yot; **2.** ערב *nm* 'arev/-eem.

(on) bail בערבות *adv* be-'arvoot.

(to) bail לשחרר בערבות *inf* leshakhrer be-'arvoot; *pst* sheekhrer *etc*; *pres* meshakhrer *etc*; *fut* yeshakhrer *etc*.

(to) bail out 1. לצנוח ממטוס (from plane) *inf* letsno'akh mee-matos; *pst* tsanakh *etc*; *pres* tsone'akh *etc*; *fut* yeetsnakh *etc*; **2.** לערוב לעציר (from arrest) *inf* la'arov le-'atseer; *pst* 'arav *etc*; *pres* 'arev *etc*; *fut* ya'arov *etc*.

bait פיתיון *nm* peet|ayon/-yonot (*+of:* -yon).

(to) bake לאפות *inf* le'efot; *pst* afah; *pres* ofeh; *fut* yofeh.

baker אופה *nm* of|eh/-eem (*pl+of:* -ey).

bakery מאפייה *nf* ma'afee|yah/-yot (*+of:* -yat).

baking powder אבקת אפייה avk|at/-ot afeeyah.

balance 1. מאזן ma'az|an/-aneem (*pl+of:* -ney); **2.** מאזניים (scale) *nm pl* mozn|ayeem (*pl+of:* -ney); **3.** איזון (levelling) *nm* eezoon/-eem (*pl+of:* -ey); **4.** שיווי משקל (balancing) *nm* sheevooy meeshkal.

(to) balance לאזן *inf* le'azen; *pst* eezen; *pres* me'azen; *fut* ye'azen.

balance of payments מאזן תשלומים *nm* ma'az|an/-ney tashloomeem.

balance of power מאזן כוחות *nm* ma'az|an/-ney kokhot.

balance of trade מאזן מסחרי *nm* ma'azan/-eem meeskharee/-yeem.

balcony 1. מרפסת *nf* meerp|eset/-asot (*pl+of:* -esot); **2.** גזוזטרה (verandah) *nf* gezooztra|h/-'ot; **3.** יציע (theater) *nm* yatsee'a'/yetsee'eem (*pl+of:* -ey).

bald קירח *adj* kere|'akh/-akhat.

bale חבילה גדולה *nf* khaveel|ah/-ot gedol|ah/-ot.

ball 1. כדור (toy) *nm* kadoor/-eem (*pl+of:* -ey); **2.** נשף ריקודים (dance) *nm* neshef/neeshpey reekoodeem.

ball bearing מסב כדורי *nm* meysa|v/-beem (*b=v*) kadooree/-yeem (*pl+of:* -bey).

ball game משחק בכדור *nm* meeskhak/-eem be-khadoor.

ballad בלדה *nf* balad|ah/-ot (*+of:* -at).

ballast 1. זבורית *nf* zvoreet; **2.** נטל (burden) *nm* netel.

ballet בלט *nm* balet/-eem.

balloon 1. כדור פורח *nm* kadoor/-eem por|e'akh/-kheem; **2.** בלון balon/-eem (*pl+of:* -ey).

ballot פתק הצבעה *nm* petek/peetkey hatsba'ah.

ballot box קלפי *nf* kalpee/-yot (*cpr* kalfee/-yot).

ballpoint pen עט כדורי *nm* 'et/-eem kadoree/-yeem.

balm צורי *nm* tsoree.

balmy מרגיע *adj* margee|'a'/-'ah.

balsam אפרסמון *nm* afarsemon/-eem (*pl+of:* -ey).

bamboo במבוק *nm* bambook.

ban 1. חרם kherem/kharamot; **2.** איסור (prohibition) *nm* eesoor/-eem (*pl+of:* -ey).

(to) ban 1. להחרים *inf* lehakhreem; *pst* hekhreem; *pres* makhareem; *fut* yakhreem; **2.** לאסור (prohibit) *inf* le'esor; *pst* asar; *pres* oser; *fut* ye'esor.

banana בננה *nf* banan|ah/-ot (*+of:* -at).

band 1. תזמורת (orchestra) *nf* teezmor|et/-ot; **2.** כנופיה (gang) *nf* knoof|yah/-yot (*+of:* -yat); **3.** סרט (strip) *nm* seret/srateem (*+of:* seertey).

(rubber) band גומייה *nf* goomee|yah/-yot (*+of:* -yat).

bandage תחבושת *nf* takhbosh|et/-ot.

bandit שודד *nm* shoded/-eem (*pl+of:* -ey).

bang קול חבטה *nm* kol/-ot khavatah.

(with a) bang ברעש גדול *adv* be-ra'ash gadol.
(to) bang the door לטרוק את הדלת *inf* leetrok et ha-delet; *pst* tarak *etc*; *pres* torek *etc*; *fut* yeetrok *etc*.
(to) banish 1. לגרש (expel) *inf* legaresh; *pst* geresh; *pres* megaresh; *fut* yegaresh; **2.** להגלות (exile) *inf* lehaglot; *pst* heeglah; *pres* magleh; *fut* yagleh.
(to) banish fear להפיג פחד *inf* lehafeeg pakhad; *pst* hefeeg *etc*; *pres* mefeeg *etc*; *fut* yafeeg *etc*.
banishment 1. גירוש (expulsion) *nm* geroosh/-eem (*pl+of:* -ey); **2.** הגליה (exile) *nf* hagla|yah/-yot (+*of:* -yat).
banister עמוד מעקה *nm* 'amood/-ey ma'akeh.
banjo בנג'ו *nm* banjo/-eem (*pl+of:* -ey).
bank 1. בנק *nm* bank/-eem; **2.** גדה (of river) *nf* gad|ah/-ot (+*of:* -at).
(mortgage) bank 1. בנק למשכנתאות *nm* bank/-eem le-mashkanta'ot; **2.** בנק אפותיקאי *nm* bank/-eem apoteka'ee/-yeem.
(the West) Bank 1. הגדה המערבית *nf* ha-gadah ha-ma'araveet; **2.** הגדה *(colloq. abbr.) nf* ha-gadah.
bank account חשבון בנק *nm* kheshbon/-ot bank.
(to) bank upon לסמוך על *inf* leesmokh 'al; *pst* samakh 'al; *pres* somekh 'al; *fut* yeesmokh 'al.
bankbook פנקס בנק peenkas/-ey bank
banker בנקאי *nm* banka|y/-'eem (*pl+of:* -'ey).
banking בנקאות *nf* banka'oot.
banknote 1. שטר כסף *nm* shetar/sheetrey kesef; **2.** בנקנוט *nm* banknot/-eem
bankrupt פושט רגל *nmf* posh|et/-etet (*pl:* -tey) regel.
(to go) bankrupt לפשוט את הרגל *inf* leefshot et ha-regel; *pst* pashat *(p=f) etc*; *pres* poshet *etc*; *fut* yeefshot *etc*.
bankruptcy פשיטת־רגל *nf* psheet|at/-ot regel.
(to go into) bankruptcy להכריז פשיטת־רגל *inf* lehakhreez pesheetat regel; *pst* heekhreez *etc*; makhreez *etc*; *fut* yakhreez *etc*.
banner דגל *nm* deg|el/-aleem (*pl+of:* deegley).
banquet 1. מסיבה *nf* meseeb|ah/-ot (+*of:* -at) **2.** בנקט *nm* banket/-eem.
baptism 1. טבילה לנצרות *nm* tveelah le-natsroot; **2.** טיהור (purge) *nm* teehoor/-eem (*pl+of:* -ey).
Baptist בפטיסט *nm* bapteest/-eem.
(to) baptize להטביל לנצרות *inf* lehatbeel le-natsroot; *pst* heetbeel *etc*; *pres* matbeel *etc*; *fut* yatbeel *etc*.
bar 1. מוט *nm* mot/-ot; **2.** דלפק (counter) *nm* delpek/-eem (*pl+of:* -ey)
bar, bar association לשכת עורכי הדין *nf* leeshkat 'orkhey ha-deen.
bar (saloon) באר *nm* bar/-eem.
barb 1. חוד *nm* khood; **2.** עוקץ (sting) *nm* 'ok|ets/-atseem (*pl+of:* 'ooktsey).
barbarian ברברי *nm* barbaree/-m.
barbarous 1. ברברי *adj* barbaree/-t; **2.** אכזרי (cruel) *adj* akhzaree/-t.
barbecue מסיבת צלי *nf* meseeb|at/-ot tsalee.
barbed wire תיל דוקרני *nm* tayeel dokranee.
barber ספר *nm* sapar/-eem (*pl+of:* -ey).
barbershop 1. מספרה *nf* meespar|ah/-ot (+*of:* meesperet); **2.** מספרה *cpr* masper|ah/-ot (+*of:* -at).
bard פייטן *nm* paytan/-eem (*pl+of:* -ey).
bare 1. חשוף *adj* khasoof/-ah; **2.** ערום (naked) *adj* 'arom/'aroomah.
(to lay) bare לערטל *inf* le'artel; *pst* 'eertel; *pres* me'artel; *fut* ye'artel.
barefoot יחף *adj* yakhef/yekhefah.
bareheaded גלוי ראש *adj* gloo|y/-yat rosh.
barelegged חשוף רגליים *adj* khasoof/-at raglayeem.
barely בקושי *adv* be-koshee.
bareness חשיפות *nf* khaseefoot.
bargain מציאה *nf* metsee|'ah/-'ot (+*of:* -'at).
(to) bargain להתמקח *inf* leheetmake'akh; *pst* heetmakakh; *pres* meetmake'akh; *fut* yeetmakakh.
barge דוברה *nf* dovr|ah/-ot (+*of:* -at).
baritone בריטון *nm* bareeton/-eem.
barium בריום *nm* baryoom.
bark 1. נביחה (dog's) *nf* neveekh|ah/-ot; **2.** קליפה (tree's) kleep|ah/-ot.
(to) bark לנבוח *inf* leenbo'akh; *pst* navakh *(v=b)*; *pres* nove'akh; *fut* yeenbakh.
barley שעורה *nf* se'or|ah/-eem.
barn אסם *nm* asam/-eem (*pl+of:* asmey).
barnacle טרדן *nmf* tardan/-eet.
barnyard 1. חצר משק *nm* khats|ar/-rot meshek; **2.** גורן (barn) *nm* goren/granot (*pl+of:* gornot).
barometer ברומטר *nm* baromet|er/-reem.
baron ברון *nmf* baron/-eet.
baroque ברוק *adj* barok.
barrage סכר *nm* sekh|er/-areem (*pl+of:* seekhrey).
barred 1. נעול *adj* na'ool/ne'oolah; **2.** מנוע (prevented) *adj* manoo'a/menoo'ah.
barrel חבית *nf* khavee|t/-yot.
barren 1. עקר *adj* 'akar/-ah; **2.** שומם *adj* shomem/-ah.
barrenness 1. עקרות *nf* 'akaroo|t/-yot; **2.** סטריליות *nf* stereeleeyoot.
barrette סיכת ראש *nf* seek|at/-ot rosh.
barricade 1. מתרס *nm* meetr|as/-aseem (*pl+of:* -esey); **2.** בריקדה *nf* bareekad|ah/-ot (+*of:* -at).
barrier 1. מחסום *nm* makhsom/-eem (*pl+of:* -ey); **2.** חיץ (partition) *nm* khayeets.
barter סחר חליפין *nm* sekhar khaleefeen.
base בסיס *nm* basees/beseeseem (+*of:* besees/-ey).
(to) base לבסס *inf* levases; *pst* beeses *(b=v)*; *pres* mevases; *fut* yevases.
baseball 1. כדור־בסיס *nm* kadoor basees; **2.** בייסבול *nm* beysbol.
baseless חסר־יסוד *adj* khas|ar/-rat yesod.
basement 1. קומת מרתף *nf* kom|at/-ot martef; **2.** מרתף (cellar) *nm* martef/-eem (*pl+of:* -ey)
baseness שיפלות *nf* sheefloo|t/-yot.
bashful ביישן *adj* bayshan/-eet.
bashfulness ביישנות *nf* bayshanoo|t/-yot.
basic 1. בסיסי *adj* beseesee/-t; **2.** תוכנת "בייסיק" (computer program) *nf* tokhnat/-ot "beysik".
basin כיור *nm* keeyor/-eem (*pl+of:* -ey).
basis בסיס *nm* basees (+*of:* besees).
(to) bask להתחמם *inf* leheetkhamem; *pst* heetkhamem; *pres* meetkhamem; *fut* yeetkhamem.

basket 1. סל *nm* sal/-eem (*pl+of:* -ey); **2.** סלסילה *nf* salseel|ah/-ot (+*of:* -at).

basketball כדורסל *nm* kadoorsal.

basketball player כדורסלן kadoorsalan/-eem (*pl+of:* -ey).

bass בס bas/-eem.

bastard 1. ממזר *nmf* mamzer/-et; **2.** ילד לא־חוקי *nmf* yeled/yaldah lo khookee/-t.

(to) baste 1. להכליב (stitches) *inf* lehakhleev; *pst* heekhleev; *pres* makhleev; *fut* yakhleev; **2.** לגדף (abuse) *inf* legadef; *pst* geedef; *pres* megadef; *fut* yegadef; **3.** לשמן בשר לטיגון (meat) *inf* leshamen basar le-teegoon; *pst* sheemen *etc*; *pres* meshamen *etc*; *fut* yeshamen *etc*.

bat 1. עטלף (mammal) *nm* 'atalef/-eem (*pl+of:* -ey); **2.** מחבט (paddle) *nm* makhbet/-eem (*pl+of:* -ey).

batch צרור *nm* tseror/-ot.

bath 1. אמבט (tub) *nm* ambat/-eem (*pl+of:* -ey); **2.** אמבטיה (taking bath) *nf* ambat|yah/-yot (+*of:* -yat); **3.** מרחץ (public bath) *nm* merkhats/-a'ot.

(to) bathe 1. להתרחץ *v rfl inf* leheetrakhets; *pst* heetrakhets; *pres* meetrakhets; *fut* yeetrakhets **2.** לרחוץ *vt inf* leerkhots; *pst* rakhats; *pres* rokhets; *fut* yeerkhats.

bathing suit בגד־ים *nm* beged/beegdey yam.

bathrobe חלוק רחצה *nm* khalook/-ey rakhatsah.

bathroom 1. חדר אמבטיה *nm* khad|ar/-rey ambatyah; **2.** אמבטיה *[colloq.] nf* ambat|yah/-yot (+*of:* -yat)

bathtub אמבט *nm* ambat/-eem (*pl+of:* -ey).

battalion גדוד *nm* gedood/-eem (*pl+of:* -ey).

(to) batter להלום קשה *inf* lahalom kasheh; *pst* halam *etc*; *pres* holem *etc*; *fut* yahalom *etc*.

battery 1. סוללה *nf* solel|ah/-ot (+*of:* -at); **2.** בטריה *[colloq.] nf* bater|yah/-yot (+*of:* -yat); **3.** מערכת *nf* ma'ar|ekhet/-akhot (*pl+of:* -khot).

battle קרב *nm* krav/-ot.

(to) battle ללחום *inf* leelkhom; *pst* lakham; *pres* lokhem; *fut* yeelkhom.

battlefield שדה־קרב *nm* sdeh/sdot krav.

battleship 1. אוניית קרב *nf* onee|yat/-yot krav; **2.** ספינת מלחמה (warship) *nf* sfeen|at/-ot meelkhamah.

bawl צריחה *nf* tsreekh|ah/-ot (+*of:* -at).

(to) bawl out לנזוף בקול רם *inf* leenzof be-kol ram; *pst* nazaf *etc*; *pres* nozef *etc*; *fut* yeenzof *etc*.

bay מפרץ *nm* meefr|ats/-atseem (*pl+of:* -etsey).

bayonet כידון *nm* keedon/-eem (*pl+of:* -ey).

bazaar 1. בזר *nm* bazar/-eem; **2.** שוק (market) *nm* shook/shvakeem (*pl+of:* shookey)

bazooka בזוקה *nf* bazook|ah/-ot (+*of:* -at).

(to) be להיות *inf* leehyot; *pst* hayah; *pres* heen|o/-ah; *fut* yeehyeh.

be what may יהיה אשר יהיה yeehyeh asher yeehyeh.

beach חוף *nm* khof/-eem (*pl+of:* -ey).

beachhead 1. ראש חוף *nm* rosh/rashey khof; **2.** דריסת רגל (foothold) *nf* dreesat regel.

beacon 1. משואה (fire-signal) *nf* masoo|'ah/-'ot (+*of:* -'at); **2.** מגדלור (lighthouse) *nm* meegdalor/-eem (*pl+of:* -ey).

bead חרוז *nm* kharooz/-eem (*pl+of:* -ey).

beak 1. מקור *nm* makor/-eem (*pl+of:* -ey); **2.** חרטום (bird's bill) *nm* khartom/-eem (*pl+of:* -ey).

beam 1. קורה *nf* kor|ah/-ot (+*of:* -at); **2.** אלומה (light) *nf* aloom|ah/-ot.

(radio) beam גל רדיו *nm* gal/-ey radyo.

(to) beam לקרון *inf* leekron; *pst* karan; *pres* koren; *fut* yeekran.

beaming קורן *adj* koren/-et.

bean 1. שעועית *nf* she'o'eet; **2.** פול *nm* pol/-eem (*pl+of:* -ey).

(coffee) beans פולי קפה *nm pl* poley kafeh

bear דוב *nm* dov/doob|eem (*pl+of:* -ey).

(to) bear 1. לשאת *inf* laset; *pst* nasa; *pres* nose; *fut* yeesa; **2.** להוביל (convey) *inf* lehoveel; *pst* hoveel; *pres* moveel; *fut* yoveel.

(to) bear a grudge לנטור *inf* leentor; *pst* natar; *pres* noter; *fut* yeentor.

(to) bear in mind לזכור *inf* leezkor; *pst* zakhar *(kh=k)*; *pres* zokher; *fut* yeezkor.

(to) bear out לאמת *inf* le'amet; *pst* eemet; *pres* me'amet; *fut* ye'amet.

bearable שאפשר לעמוד בו *adj* she-efshar la'amod bo/bah *(m/f)*.

beard זקן *nm* zakan/zekan|eem (*pl+of:* -ey).

bearded מזוקן *adj* mezook|an/-enet.

bearer 1. נושא הארון (of coffin) *nm* nos|e/-'ey he-aron; **2.** מוסר כתב זה (deliverer of this letter) *nmf* moser/-et ketav zeh; **3.** המוכ"ז (*acr of* 2) *nm* ha-mokaz; **4.** מוביל *nm* moveel/-eem (*pl+of:* -ey).

(the) bearer המוכ"ז (*acr of* 2, above) *nmf* ha-mokaz.

bearing 1. התנהגות *nf* heetnahagoo|t/-yot; **2.** יציבה (posture, carriage) *nf* yetseev|ah/-ot (+*of:* -at).

(ball) bearing מסב *nm* mesa|v/-beem (*pl+of:* -bey).

(fruit) bearing נושא פרי *adj* nose/-t pree.

beast חיה *nf* kha|yah/-yot (+*of:* -yat).

beat 1. מקצב *nm* meekts|av/-aveem (*pl+of:* -evey); **2.** מקוף (policeman's) *nm* makof/-eem (*pl+of:* -ey).

(to) beat להכות *inf* lehakot; *pst* heekah; *pres* makeh; *fut* yakeh.

(to) beat around the bush 1. להלך סחור־סחור *inf* lehalekh sekhor sekhor; *pst* heelekh *etc*; *pres* mehalekh *etc*; *fut* yehalekh *etc*; **2.** לברבר *[colloq.] inf* levarber; *pst* beerber *(b=v)*; *pres* mevarber; *fut* yevarber.

beaten מוכה *adj* mookeh/-ah.

beaten path שביל הרבים *nm* shveel ha-rabeem.

beater מקצף *nm* maktsef/-eem (*pl+of:* -ey).

(egg-)beater מקצף ביצים maktsef/-ey beytseem.

beating מכות *nf pl* makot.

beau מחזר *nm* mekhaz|er/-reem (*pl+of:* -rey).

beauteous יפהפה *adj* yefehf|eh/-yah.

beautiful יפה *adj* yaf|eh/-ah.

(to) beautify לייפות *inf* leyapot; *pst* yeepah; *pres* meyapeh; *fut* yeyapeh.

beauty יופי *nm* yofee.

beauty contest תחרות יופי *nf* takharoo|t/-yot yofee.

beauty parlor מכון יופי *nm* mekhon/-ey yofee.

beaver 1. בונה *nm* bon|eh/-eem *(pl+of: -ey)*; **2.** שקדן (diligent) *adj* shakdan/-eet.
became נהיה *v pst sing* neeh|yah/-yetah.
because 1. ־מפני ש *prep* meepney she-; **2.** ־בגלל ש (due to) *prep* beeglal she-; **3.** ־משום ש (for) *prep* mee-shoom she-; **4.** ־מכיוון ש (since) *prep* meekeyvan she-.
because of בגלל *prep* beeglal.
(to) beckon לאותת *inf* le'otet; *pst* otet; *pres* me'otet; *fut* ye'otet.
(to) become להיעשות *inf* lehe'asot; *pst* na'asah; *pres* na'aseh; *fut* ye'aseh.
(to) become angry 1. להתרגז *inf* leheetragez; *pst* heetragez; *pres* meetragez; *fut* yeetragez; **2.** להתקצף (get indignant) *inf* leheetkatsef; *pst* heetkatsef; *pres* meetkatsef; *fut* yeetkatsef.
(to) become frightened להיתקף פחד *inf* leheetakef pakhad; *pst & pres* neetkaf *etc*; *fut* yeetakef *etc*.
(to) become old להזדקן *inf* leheezdaken; *pst* heezdaken; *pres* meezdaken; *fut* yeezdaken.
(to) to become sick לחלות *inf* lakhalot; *pst* khalah; *pres* kholeh; *fut* yekheleh.
becoming הולם *adj* holem/-et.
bed מיטה *nf* meet|ah/-ot *(+of: -at)*.
(to go to) bed 1. לשכב לישון *inf* leeshkav leeshon; *pst* shakhav *(kh=k) etc*; *pres* shokhev *etc*; *fut* yeeshkav *etc*; **2.** לשכב עם (sex) *inf* leeshkav 'eem; *pst* shakhav *(kh=k) etc*; *pres* shokhev *etc*; *fut* yeeshkav *etc*.
(to put to) bed להשכיב לישון *inf* lehashkeev leeshon; *pst* heeshkeev *etc*; *pres* mashkeev *etc*; *fut* yashkeev *etc*.
bed and board לינה ואוכל leenah ve-okhel
bedbug פשפש *nm* peeshpesh/-eem *(pl+of: -ey)*.
bedclothes, bedding 1. כלי מיטה *nm pl* kley meetah; **2.** מצעים *nm pl* matsa'eem *(+of:* mats'ey*)*.
bedfellow 1. חבר למיטה *nmf* khaver/-ah le-meetah; **2.** בעל ברית *(figurat.) nmf* ba'al/-at breet.
bedlam בית משוגעים *nm* bet/batey meshooga'eem.
bedouin 1. בידואי *adj & nmf* bedoo'ee/-t; **2.** בדווי *adj & nmf* bedvee/-t.
bedpan סיר לילה *nm* seer/-ey laylah.
bedridden רתוק למיטה *adj* ratook/retookah le-meetah.
bedrock אבן יסוד *nf* even/avney yesod.
bedroom חדר שינה *nm* kheder/khadrey shenah.
bedside ליד המיטה *adv* le-yad ha-meetah.
bedside table שולחן לילה *nm* shoolkhan/-ot laylah.
bedspread ציפית *nf* tseepee|t/-yot.
bedtime שעת השינה *nf* she|'at/-'ot ha-shenah.
bee דבורה *nf* devor|ah/-eem *(+of: -at)*.
beech עץ אשור *nm* 'ets/'atsey ashoor.
beef בשר בקר *nm* besar bakar.
beefsteak אומצת בשר *nf* oomts|at/-ot basar.
beehive כוורת *nf* kav|eret/-arot.
beer בירה beer|ah/-ot.
beet סלק *nm* selek
beetle חיפושית kheepooshee|t/-yot.
(to) befall לקרות *inf* leekrot; *pst* karah; *pres* koreh; *fut* yeekreh.

(to) befit לתאום *inf* leet'om; *pst* ta'am; *pres* to'em; *fut* yeet'am.
before 1. לפני *adv* leefney; **2.** טרם *adv* terem.
beforehand מראש *adv* me-rosh.
(to) befriend להתיידד *inf* leheetyaded; *pst* heetyaded; *pres* meetyaded; *fut* yeetyaded.
(to) beg 1. לבקש (request) *inf* levakesh; *pst* beekesh *(b=v)*; *pres* mevakesh; *fut* yevakesh; **2.** להתחנן (implore) *inf* leheetkhanen; *pst* heetkhanen; *pres* meetkhanen; *fut* yeetkhanen; **3.** לפשוט יד (for alms) *inf* leefshot yad; *pst* pashat yad *(p=f)*; *pres* poshet yad; *fut* yeefshot yad.
(to) beget 1. להוליד *inf* leholeed; *pst* holeed; *pres* moleed; *fut* yoleed; **2.** לגרום *inf* leegrom; *pst* garam; *pres* gorem; *fut* yeegrom.
beggar 1. קבצן *nmf* kabtsan/-eet *(pl: -eem/-eeyot)*; **2.** פושט יד (mendicant) *nmf* posh|et/-etet *(pl: -tey/-tot)* yad.
(to) begin להתחיל *inf* lehatkheel; *pst* heetkheel; *pres* matkheel; *fut* yatkheel.
beginner מתחיל *nmf & adj* matkheel/-ah.
beginning 1. ראשית *nf* re'sheet; **2.** התחלה (start) *nf* hatkhalah/-ot *(+of: -at)*.
(to) begrudge לרטון *inf* leerton; *pst* ratan; *pres* roten; *fut* yeerton.
(in, on) behalf מטעם *adv* mee-ta'am
(to) behave להתנהג *inf* leheetnaheg; *pst* heetnaheg; *pres* meetnaheg; *fut* yeetnaheg.
behave yourself! !התנהג יפה *v imp sing m/f* heetna|heg/-hagee yafeh!
behavior התנהגות *nf* heetnahagoo|t/-yot.
(to) behead לערוף ראשים *inf* la'arof rasheem; *pst* 'araf *etc*; *pres* 'oref *etc*; *fut* ya'arof *etc*.
behind 1. מאחורי (in back of) *adv* me-akhorey; **2.** באיחור (late) *adv* be-'eekhoor **3.** מאחרי (in support of) *prep* me-akharey.
(from) behind מאחור *adv* me-akhor.
(to fall) behind לפגר *inf* lefager; *pst* peeger *(p=f)*; *pres* mefager; *fut* yefager.
behind one's back מאחורי הגב *adv* me-akhorey ha-gav.
behind time באיחור זמן *adv* be-'eekhoor zman.
(to) behold להסתכל *inf* leheestakel; *pst* heestakel; *pres* meestakel; *fut* yeestakel.
(to) behoove צריך היה *pst* tsareekh hayah; *pres* tsareekh; *fut* tsareekh yeehyeh.
being 1. הוויה *nf* hava|yah/-yot *(+of: -yat)*; **2.** מציאות *nf* metsee'oo|t/-yot.
(for the time) being בינתיים *adv* beynatayeem.
(human) being יצור אנוש *nm* yetsoor/-ey enosh.
belated מאוחר *adj* me'ookh|ar/-eret.
(to) belch לגהק *inf* legahek; *pst* geehek; *pres* megahek; *fut* yegahek.
(to) beleaguer לכתר *inf* lekhater; *pst* keeter *(k=kh)*; *pres* mekhater; *fut* yekhater.
Belgian בלגי *nmf & adj* belgee/-t.
Belgium בלגיה *nf* belgeeyah.
(to) belie להפריך *inf* lehafreekh; *pst* heefreekh; *pres* mafreekh; *fut* yafreekh.
belief אמונה *nf* emoon|ah/-ot *(+of: -at)*.
believable אמין *adj* ameen/-ah.

(to) believe להאמין *inf* leha'ameen; *pst* he'emeen; *pres* ma'ameen; *fut* ya'ameen.

(make) believe העמדת פנים *nf* ha'amad|at/-ot paneem.

believer מאמין *nmf* ma'ameen/-ah (*pl:* -eem; *+of:* -ey).

(to) belittle לזלזל *inf* lezalzel; *pst* zeelzel; *pres* mezalzel; *fut* yezalzel.

bell פעמון *nm* pa'amon/-eem (*pl+of:* -ey).

bellboy נער שליחויות *nm* na'ar/-ey shleekhooyot.

belle אישה יפה *nf* eeshah/nasheem yaf|ah/-ot.

belligerent 1. לוחם *nm* lokh|em/-ameem (*pl+of:* -amey); **2.** צד לוחם (belligerent party) *nm* tsad/tsedadeem lokh|em/-khameem.

bellow שאגה *nf* she'ag|ah/-ot (*+of:* sha'agat).

bellows מפוח *nm* mapoo|'akh/-kheem.

belly 1. בטן *nf* bet|en/-aneem (*pl+of:* beetney); **2.** כרס (abdomen) *nf* keres/kresot.

(on an empty) belly על קיבה ריקה *adv* 'al keyvah reykah.

belly dancer רקדנית בטן *nf* rakdanee|t/-yot beten.

bellyache כאב בטן *nm* ke'ev/-ey beten.

(to) belong להשתייך *inf* leheeshtayekh; *pst* heeshtayekh; *pres* meeshtayekh; *fut* yeeshtayekh.

belongings 1. חפצים אישיים *nm pl* khafatseem eesheeyeem; **2.** מטלטלים (chattels) *nm pl* meetalteleem.

beloved אהוב *adj* ahoov/-ah.

below למטה *adv* lematah.

(here) below כאן למטה *adv* kan lematah.

belt חגורה *nf* khagor|ah/-ot (*+of:* -at).

(to) bemoan לבכות *inf* levakot; *pst* beekah *(b=v)*; *pres* mevakeh; *fut* yevakeh.

bench 1. ספסל *nm* safsal/-eem (*pl+of:* safseley); **2.** כס המשפט (jurid.) *nm* kes ha-meeshpat.

(to) bend 1. לכופף *vt inf* lekhofef; *pst* kofef *(k=kh)*; *pres* mekhofef; *fut* yekhofef; **2.** להתכופף *v rfl inf* leheetkofef; *pst* heetkofef; *pres* meetkofef; *fut* yeetkofef.

beneath 1. למטה מ־ *adv* le-matah mee-; **2.** מתחת ל־ (under) *adv* mee-takhat le-.

benediction ברכה *nf* brakh|ah/-ot (*+of:* beerk|at/-ot).

benefactor מיטיב *nm* meyteev/-eem (*pl+of:* -ey).

beneficent מיטיב *adj* meyteev/-ah.

beneficial 1. מיטיב *adj* meyteev/-ah; **2.** מועיל (useful) *adj* mo'eel/-ah.

beneficiary 1. נהנה *adj* neheneh/-t; **2.** מוטב *nmf* moot|av/-evet (*pl:* -aveem/-avot; *+of:* -vey/-vot).

benefit 1. רווח *nm* revakh/-eem (*pl+of:* reevkhey); **2.** תועלת (use) to'elet; **3.** טובת הנאה (interest) *nf* tov|at/-ot hana'ah.

(to) benefit 1. להפיק תועלת *inf* lehafeek to'elet; *pst* hefeek *etc*; *pres* mefeek *etc*; *fut* yafeek *etc*; **2.** ליהנות (enjoy) *inf* lehanot; *pst* nehenah; *pres* neheneh; *fut* yehaneh.

benefit performance הצגת צדקה *nf* hatsag|at/-ot tsedakah.

benign 1. נוח *adj* no'akh/nokhah; **2.** שפיר (non-cancerous) *adj* shapeer/-ah.

benzine בנזין *nm* benzeen.

(to) bequeath 1. להנחיל *inf* lehankheel; *pst* heenkheel; *pres* mankheel; *fut* yankheel; **2.** להוריש (cause to inherit) *inf* lehoreesh; *pst* horeesh; *pres* moreesh; *fut* yoreesh.

bequest עיזבון *nm* 'eez|avon/-vonot (*+of:* -von).

(to) bereave לשלול *inf* leeshlol; *pst* shalal; *pres* sholel; *fut* yeeshlol.

bereaved, bereft שכול *adj* shakool/-ah.

(to be) bereaved לשכול *inf* leeshkol; *pst* shakhal *(kh=k)*; *pres* shokhel; *fut* yeeshkal.

bereavement 1. שכול *nm* shekhol; **2.** אבידה (loss) *nf* aved|ah/-ot (*+of:* -at).

berry גרגר *nm* garger/-eem (*pl+of:* -ey).

berth 1. מיטת תא (ship) *nf* meet|at/-ot ta; **2.** שטח עגינה (harbor) *nm* shetakh/sheetkhey 'ageenah.

(to) beseech להפציר *inf* lehaftseer; *pst* heeftseer; *pres* maftseer; *fut* yaftseer.

(to) beset להתקיף *inf* lehatkeef; *pst* heetkeef; *pres* matkeef; *fut* yatkeef.

beside 1. חוץ ל־ *adv* khoots le-; **2.** על יד (next to) *prep* 'al yad; **3.** אצל (near, at) *prep* etsel.

beside oneself לצאת מגדרו *inf* latset mee-geedro; *pst* yatsa *etc*; *pres* yotse *etc*; *fut* yetse *etc*.

beside the point שלא לעניין *adv* she-lo la-'eenyan.

besides בנוסף ל־ *prep* be-nosaf le-.

(to) besiege לצור על *inf* latsoor 'al; *pst & pres* tsar 'al; *fut* yatsoor 'al.

best 1. הכי טוב *adj* ha-khee tov/-ah; **2.** טוב ביותר *adj* tov/-ah be-yoter.

(at) best לכל היותר *adv* le-khol ha-yoter.

(one's) best מיטב היכולת *nm* meytav ha-yekholet.

bestial בהמי *adj* bahamee/-t.

(to) bestow להעניק *inf* leha'aneek; *pst* he'eneek; *pres* ma'aneek; *fut* ya'aneek.

bestseller רב־מכר *nm* rav/rabey *(b=v)* mekher.

bet הימור *nm* heemoor/-eem (*pl+of:* -ey).

(to) bet להמר *inf* lehamer; *pst* heemer; *pres* mehamer; *fut* yehamer.

(to) betake להתמסר *inf* leheetmaser; *pst* heetmaser; *pres* meetmaser; *fut* yeetmaser.

(to) betray לבגוד *inf* leevgod; *pst* bagad *(b=v)*; *pres* boged; *fut* yeevgod.

betrothal אירוסים *nm pl* eyroos|eem (*pl+of:* -ey).

betrothed ארוס *nmf* aroos/-ah.

better יותר טוב *adv* yoter tov.

(to) better לשפר *inf* leshaper; *pst* sheeper; *pres* meshaper; *fut* yeshaper.

(to get) better 1. להחלים *inf* lehakhaleem; *pst* hekheleem; *pres* makhaleem; *fut* yakhaleem; **2.** להבריא (recover) *inf* lehavree; *pst* heevree; *pres* mavree; *fut* yavree.

(so much the) better גם זו לטובה gam zo le-tovah.

better off כדאי יותר *adj* keda|y/-'eet yoter.

betterment שיפור *nm* sheepoor/-eem (*pl+of:* -ey).

between בין *prep* beyn.

(go) between מתווך *nm* metav|ekh/-kheem (*pl+of:* -khey).

(in) between 1. באמצע *adv* be-'emtsa'; **2.** בתוך *prep* be-tokh.

bevel שיפוע *nm* sheepoo|'a'/-'eem (*pl+of:* -'ey).

beverage משקה *nm* mashk|eh/-a'ot.

(to) bewail לבכות *inf* levakot; *pst* beekah *(b=v)*; *pres* mevakeh; *fut* yevakeh.
(to) beware להיזהר *inf* leheezaher; *pst & pres* neez'har; *fut* yeezaher.
beware! היזהר! *v imp nmf* heeza|her/-haree!
(to) bewilder להדהים *inf* lehad'heem; *pst* heed'heem; *pres* mad'heem; *fut* yad'heem.
bewildered נדהם *adj & pres* need'|ham/-hemet.
bewilderment תדהמה *nf* tad'hemah/-ot (*+of:* -at).
(to) bewitch להקסים *inf* lehakseem; *pst* heekseem; *pres* makseem; *fut* yakseem.
bewitched מוקסם *adj* mooks|am/-emet.
beyond 1. מעבר ל־ *adv* me-'ever le-; **2.** מעל ל־ (over) *adv* me-'al le-; **3.** יותר מ־ (more) *prep* yoter mee-.
beyond reach שאין להשיג *adv* she-'eyn lehaseeg.
bias 1. פנייה *nf* penee|yah/-yot (*+of:* -yat); **2.** דעה קדומה (prejudice) *f* de'ah/de'ot kedoom|ah/-ot.
bib סינר לתינוקות *nm* seenar/-eem le-teenokot.
Bible (תורה, נביאים, כתובים) תנ״ך *nm* tanakh (*acr of* Torah, Nevee'eem, Ketooveem).
biblical תנכי *adj* tanakhee/-t.
bibliography ביבליוגרפיה *nf* beebleeyograf|yah/-yot (*+of:* -yat).
bicarbonate דו־קרבונט *nm* doo-karbonat/-eem.
(to) bicker להתנצח *inf* leheetnatse'akh; *pst* heetnatse'akh; *pres* meetnatse'akh; *fut* yetnatse'akh.
bicycle אופניים *nm pl* ofan|ayeem (*pl+of:* -ey).
(to) bicycle לרכוב על אופניים *inf* leerkov 'al ofanayeem; *pst* rakhav *(kh=k) etc*; *pres* rokhev *etc*; *fut* yeerkav *etc*.
bid הצעת מחיר *nf* hatsa|'at/-'ot mekheer.
(fair) bid הצעה הוגנת *nf* hatsa|'ah/-'ot hog|enet/-not.
(to) bid להציע מחיר *inf* lehatsee'a' mekheer; *pst* heetsee'a' *etc*; *pres* matsee'a' *etc*; *fut* yatsee'a' *etc*.
(to) bid good-bye 1. לומר שלום *inf* lomar shalom; *pst* amar *etc*; *pres* omer *etc*; *fut* yomar *etc*; **2.** להיפרד (bid farewell) *inf* leheepared; *pst & pres* neefrad *(f=p)*; *fut* yeepared.
bidder משתתף במכרז *nmf* meeshtatef/-et be-meekhraz.
(to) bide one's time לחכות להזדמנות *inf* lekhakot le-heezdamnoot; *pst* kheekah *etc*; *pres* mekhakeh *etc*; *fut* yekhakeh *etc*.
biennial דו־שנתי *adj* doo-shnatee/-t.
bier עגלת קבורה *nf* 'egl|at/-ot kvoorah.
big גדול *adj* gadol/gedolah.
big brother, sister אח גדול *nmf* akh/-ot gadol/gedolah.
big-hearted נדיב־לב *adj* nedeev/-at lev.
big shot 1. אדם חשוב מאוד (VIP) *nm* adam khashoov me'od; **2.** אח״מ (*acr of* 1) *nm* akham/-eem (*pl+of:* -ey).
bigamy ביגמיה *nf* beegamyah.
bigot קנאי קיצוני *nm* kana|y/-'eem keetsonee/-yeem.
bigotry קנאות עיוורת *nf* kana'oot 'eeveret.
bikini ביקיני *nm* beekeenee.
bilateral דו־צדדי *adj* doo-tsedadee/-t.
bile מרה *nf* mar|ah (*+of:* -at).
bilingual דו־לשוני *adj* doo-leshonee/-t.
bill חשבון *nm* kheshbon/-ot.
(to) bill לחייב *inf* lekhayev; *pst* kheeyev; *pres* mekhayev; *fut* yekhayev.
bill of exchange שטר חליפין *nm* shtar/sheetrey khaleefeen.
bill of fare מפרט עלות לנסיעה *nm* meefr|at/-etey 'aloot lee-nesee'ah.
bill of lading תעודת מטען *nf* te'ood|at/-ot meet'an.
bill of rights כתב זכויות *nm* ktav/keetvey zekhooyot.
bill of sale שטר מכר *nm* shtar/sheetrey mekher.
billboard לוח מודעות *nm* loo|'akh/-khot moda'ot
billfold 1. ארנק (wallet) *m* arnak/-eem (*pl+of:* -ey); **2.** תיק (ladies bag) *nm* teek/-eem (*pl+of:* -ey).
billion מיליארד (1,000,000,000) *num nm* meelyard/-eem (*pl+of:* -ey).
billow נחשול *nm* nakhshol/-eem (*pl+of:* -ey).
bin 1. פח *nm* pakh/-eem (*pl+of:* -ey); **2.** פחית (tin) *nf* pakhee|t/-yot (*+of:* -yat); **3.** ארגז (box) arg|az/-azeem (*pl+of:* -ezey); **4.** מחסן (warehouse) *nm* makhs|an/-aneem (*pl+of:* -eney).
binary בינארי *adj* beenaree/-t.
(to) bind לכרוך *inf* leekhrokh; *pst* karakh *(k=kh)*; *pres* korekh; *fut* yeekhrokh.
binding 1. כריכה (of book) *nf* kreekhah/-ot (*+of:* -at); **2.** מחייב (obliging) *adj* mekhayev/-et.
(cloth) binding כריכת בד *nf* kreekh|at/-ot bad.
(paper) binding כריכת קרטון *nf* kreekh|at/-ot karton.
biography ביוגרפיה *nf* beeyograf|yah/-yot (*+of:* -yat).
biology ביולוגיה *nf* beeyologyah.
bipartisan 1. דו־מפלגתי *adj* doo-meeflagtee/-t **2.** דו־צדדי (bilateral) *adj* doo-tsedadee/-t.
birch עץ ליבנה *nm* 'ets/'atsey leevneh.
bird ציפור *nf* tseepor/-eem (*pl+of:* -ey).
bird of prey ציפור טרף *nf* tseepor/-ey teref.
bird's eye view מבט ממעוף הציפור *nm* mabat mee-me'oof ha-tseepor.
birth לידה *nf* leydah/-ot (*+of:* -at).
(to give) birth ללדת (*f* only) *inf* laledet; *pst* yaldah; *pres* yoledet; *fut* teled.
birth certificate תעודת־לידה *nf* te'ood|at/-ot leydah.
birth rate ילודה *nf* yelood|ah/-ot (*+of:* -at).
birthday יום הולדת *nm* yom/yemey hooledet.
birthmark סימן מלידה *nm* seeman/-eem mee-leydah.
birthplace מקום לידה *nm* mekom/-ot leydah
birthright זכות בכורה *nf* zekhoo|t/-yot bekhorah.
biscuit ביסקוויט *nm* beeskveet/-eem (*pl+of:* -ey).
bishop בישוף *nm* beeshof/-eem (*pl+of:* -ey).
bison 1. תאו *nm* te'o/-'eem (*pl+of:* -'ey); **2.** ג׳מוס *[colloq.] nm* djamoos/-eem (*pl+of:* -ey).
bit 1. קורטוב *nm* kortov; **2.** מקדח (drill) *nm* makde|'akh/-kheem (*pl+of:* -khey); **3.** רסן (horse) *nm* resen.
(not to care a) bit לא איכפת lo eekhpat.
bitch 1. כלבה *nf* kalbah/klavot (*+of:* kal|bah/-vot); **2.** כלבתה *[colloq.] figurat* klavt|eh/-ot.
bite נגיסה negees|ah/-ot (*+of:* -at).

(to) bite לנשוך *inf* leenshokh; *pst* nashakh; *pres* noshekh; *fut* yeeshokh.

(to) bite off לנגוס *inf* leengos; *pst* nagas; *pres* noges; *fut* yeengos.

bitter מר *adj* mar/-ah.

(to the) bitter end עד תום *adv* 'ad tom.

bitterness מרירות *nf* mereeroo|t/-yot.

biweekly דו־שבועון *nm* doo-shvoo'on/-eem (*pl+of:* -ey).

black שחור *adj* shakhor/shekhorah.

(to) blacken 1. להשחיר *inf* lehashkheer; *pst* heeshkheer; *pres* mashkheer; *fut* yashkheer **2.** להשמיץ (*figurat.*) *inf* lehashmeets; *pst* heeshmeets; *pres* mashmeets; *fut* yashmeets.

blackmail סחיטה *nf* sekheet|ah/-ot (*+of:* -at).

(to) blackmail לסחוט *v inf* leeskhot; *pst* sakhat; *pres* sokhet; *fut* yeeskhot.

blackness שחור *nm* shekhor.

blackout 1. איפול *nm* eepool/-eem (*pl+of:* -ey); **2.** האפלה (wartime) *nf* ha'afal|ah/-ot (*+of:* -at).

blacksmith נפח *nm* napakh/-eem (*pl+of:* -ey).

bladder שלפוחית השתן *nf* shalpookheet ha-sheten.

blade להב *nm* lahav/lehaveem (*pl+of:* -ey).

blame אשמה *nf* ashm|ah/-ot (*+of:* -at).

(to) blame 1. להאשים (accuse) *inf* leha'asheem; *pst* he'esheem; *pres* ma'asheem; *fut* ya'asheem; **2.** לתלות את הקולר ב־ (pin blame on) *inf* leetlot et ha-kolar be-; *pst* talah *etc*; *pres* toleh *etc*; *fut* yeetleh *etc*

blameless חף מאשמה *adj* khaf/khapah (*p=f*) me-ashmah.

(to) blanch להלבין *inf* lehalbeen; *pst* heelbeen; *pres* malbeen; *fut* yalbeen.

blank 1. חלק *adj* khalak/-ah; **2.** ריק (empty) *adj* reyk/-ah.

blank application טופס בקשה ריק *nm* tof|es/-sey bakashah reyk/-eem.

blank cartridge כדור סרק kadoor/-ey srak.

blank face פנים חסרות הבעה *nf pl* paneem khasrot haba'ah.

blank form טופס לא־ממולא *nm* tofes/tfaseem lo memoola/-'eem.

blank verse חרוז לבן *nm* kharooz/-eem lavan/levaneem.

blanket שמיכה *nf* smeekh|ah/-ot (*+of:* -at).

blare 1. תרועה *nf* troo|'ah/-'ot (*+of:* -'at); **2.** ברק (glare) *nm* barak/brakeem (*pl+of:* beerkey); **3.** רעם (thunder) ra'am/re'ameem (*pl+of:* ra'amey).

(to) blaspheme 1. לקלל (curse) *inf* lekalel; *pst* keelel; *pres* mekalel; *fut* yekalel; **2.** לנאץ (revile) *inf* lena'ets; *pst* nee'ets; *pres* mena'ets; *fut* yena'ets; **3.** לחלל שם שמיים (profane God's name) *inf* lekhalel shem shamayeem; *pst* kheelel *etc*; *pres* mekhalel *etc*; *fut* yekhalel *etc.*

blasphemy חילול השם *nm* kheelool ha-shem.

blast 1. נפץ (explosion) *nm* nef|ets/-atseem (*pl+of:* -atsey); **2.** הדף אוויר (blast of air) *nm* hedef aveer.

(to) blast לפוצץ *inf* lefotsets; *pst* potsets (*p=f*); *pres* mefotsets; *fut* yefotsets.

blaze להבה *nf* lehav|ah/-ot (*+of:* lahevet).

bleaching powder אבקת הלבנה *nf* avk|at/-ot halbanah.

bleak עגום *adj* 'agoom/-ah.

blear, bleary טרוט *adj* taroot/trootah.

(to) bleat לפעות *inf* leef'ot; *pst* pa'ah (*p=f*); *pres* po'eh; *fut* yeef'eh.

(to) bleed לדמם *inf* ledamem; *pst* deemem; *pres* medamem; *fut* yedamem.

blemish 1. כתם *nm* ket|em/-ameem (*pl+of:* keetmey); **2.** פסול (flaw) *nm* pesool; **3.** פגם (shortcoming) *nm* pegam/-eem (*pl+of:* -ey); **4.** מום (defect) moom/-eem (*pl+of:* -ey).

blend 1. תערובת *nf* ta'arov|et/-ot; **2.** מזיגה (mixture) *nf* mezeeg|ah/-ot (*+of:* -at).

(to) blend 1. לערבב (mix) *inf* le'arbev; *pst* 'eerbev; *pres* me'arbev; *fut* ye'arbev; **2.** למזג (mix) *inf* lemazeg; *pst* meezeg; *pres* memazeg; *fut* yemazeg.

(to) bless 1. לברך *inf* levarekh; *pst* berakh (*b=v*); *pres* mevarekh; *fut* yevarekh; **2.** לקדש (hallow) *inf* lekadesh; *pst* keedesh; *pres* mekadesh; *fut* yekadesh.

(God) bless you! 1. יברך אותך השם! yevarekh otkha/otakh (*m/f*) ha-shem! **2.** לבריאות! (Gesundheit!) lee-vree'oot! (*v=b; cpr* la-bree'oot!).

blessed מבורך *adj* mevor|akh/-ekhet.

blessing ברכה *nf* brakh|ah/-ot (*+of:* beer|kat/-khot)

blight כימשון *nm* keem|ashon/-shonot.

blind 1. עיוור *nmf & adj* 'eever/-et; **2.** וילון (curtain) *nm* veelon/-ot; **3.** תריס (shutter) *nm* trees/-eem (*pl+of:* -ey).

(to) blind לסנוור *inf* lesanver; *pst* seenver; *pres* mesanver; *fut* yesanver.

blind alley סימטה ללא מוצא *nf* seemta/-'ot le-lo motsa.

blind date פגישה עיוורת *nf* pegeeshah/-ot 'eev|eret/-rot.

blinded מסונוור *adj* mesoonv|ar-veret.

blinder מצמצם שדה הראייה *nm* metsamtsem sdeh ha-re'eeyah.

blindfold קשור עיניים *adj* keshoor/-at 'eynayeem.

blindly 1. בעיניים עצומות (blindfolded) *adv* be-'eynayeem 'atsoomot; **2.** כעיוור (like a blind man) *adv* ke-'eever.

blindness עיוורון *nm* eev|aron (*+of:* -ron).

blink מצמוץ *nm* meetsmoots/-eem (*pl+of:* -ey).

(to) blink למצמץ *inf* lematsmets; *pst* meetsmets; *pres* mematsmets; *fut* yematsmets.

blip צללית רדאר *nf* tslalee|t/-yot radar.

bliss אושר רב *nm* osher rav.

blister 1. חבורה (bruise) *nf* khaboor|ah/-ot (*+of:* -at); **2.** בועה (bubble) *nf* boo'ah/-ot (*+of:* -at).

blitz לוחמת בזק *nf* lokhm|at/-ot bazak.

blizzard סופת שלג *nf* soof|at/-ot sheleg.

(to) bloat לנפח *inf* lenape'akh; *pst* neepakh; *pres* menape'akh; *fut* yenape'akh.

blob בועה *nf* boo|'ah/-'ot (*+of:* -'at).

block 1. גוש *nm* goosh/-eem (*pl+of:* -ey); **2.** בלוק *nm* blok/-eem (*pl+of:* -ey); **3.** גלופה (cliché) *nf* gloof|ah/-ot (*+of:* -at).

(to) block out לסמן בקווים כלליים *inf* lesamen be-kaveem klaleeyeem; *pst* seemen *etc*; *pres* mesamen *etc*; *fut* yesamen *etc.*

blockade הסגר ימי *nm* hesger/-eem yamee/-yeem.
blood דם *nm* dam/-eem (*pl+of:* demey).
blood bank בנק הדם *nm* bank ha-dam.
blood libel עלילת דם *nf* 'aleel|at/-ot dam.
blood poisoning הרעלת דם *nf* har'alat/-ot dam.
blood pressure לחץ דם *nm* lakhats dam.
blood relative קרוב משפחה *nmf* krov/-at meeshpakhah.
blood test בדיקת דם *nf* bedeek|at/-ot dam.
blood transfusion עירוי דם *nm* 'eroo|y/-yey dam.
bloodshed 1. שפיכת דמים *nf* shfeekh|at/-ot dameem; **2.** שפיכות דמים *nf* shfeekhoot dameem.
bloodshot עקוב מדם *adj* 'akov/'akoobah *(b=v)* mee-dam.
bloodthirsty צמא דם *adj* tseme/-'at dam.
bloody 1. דמי *adj* damee/-t; **2.** עקוב מדם (bloodshot) *adj* 'akov/'akoobah *(b=v)* mee-dam; **3.** מגועל בדם (bloodstained) *adj* mego'al/-eem be-dam; **4.** ארור (*Brit. slang:* damned) *adj* aroor/-ah.
bloom פריחה *nf* preekh|ah/-ot (*+of:* -at).
(to) bloom לפרוח *inf* leefro'akh; *pst* parakh *(p=f)*; *pres* pore'akh; *fut* yeefrakh.
blooming פורח *adj* por|e'akh/-akhat.
blossom לבלוב *nm* leevloov/-eem (*pl+of:* -ey).
blot כתם *nm* ket|em/-ameem (*pl+of:* keetmey).
(to) blot out 1. למחוק עד תום *inf* leemkhok 'ad tom; *pst* makhak *etc*; *pres* mokhek *etc*; *fut* yeemkhok *etc*; **2.** להכחיד (destroy) *inf* lehakh'kheed (*cpr* lehak'kheed); *pst* heekh'kheed; *pres* makh'kheed; *fut* yakh'kheed.
blotch כתם גדול *nm* ket|em/-ameem gadol/gedoleem.
blouse חולצת נשים *nf* khoolts|at/-ot nasheem.
blow מהלומה *nf* mahaloom|ah/-ot (*+of:* -at).
(to) blow לנשוב *inf* leenshov; *pst* nashav; *pres* noshev; *fut* yeenshov.
(to) blow one's nose לגרוף את האף *inf* leegrof et ha-af; *pst* garaf *etc*; *pres* goref *etc*; *fut* yeegrof *etc*.
(to) blow open 1. לגלות ברבים *inf* legalot ba-rabeem; *pst* geelah *etc*; *pres* megaleh *etc*; *fut* yegaleh *etc*; **2.** לפוצץ *[slang]* *inf* lefotsets; *pst* potsets *(p=f)*; *pres* mefotsets; *fut* yefotsets.
(to) blow over להשתכח *inf* leheeshtake'akh; *pst* neeshtakakh; *pres* meeshtake'akh; *fut* yeeshtakakh.
(to) blow up לפוצץ *inf* lefotsets; *pst* potsets *(p=f)*; *pres* mefotsets; *fut* yefotsets.
blower מפוח *nm* mapoo|'akh/-kheem (*pl+of:* -khey).
blowout התפוצצות *nf* heetpotsetsoo|t/-yot
blowpipe מבער *nm* mav|'er/-'areem (*pl+of:* -'erey).
blowtorch מבער הלחמה mav'er/-ey halkhamah.
blue 1. כחול *adj* kakhol/kekhoolah; **2.** תכלת (light-blue) tekhelet.
bluebell פעמונית *nf* pa'amonee|t/-yot.
bluebird הציפור הכחולה *nf* ha-tseepor ha-kekhoolah.
(the) blues שירים נוגים *nm pl* sheereem noogeem
bluff 1. איום סרק *nm* eeyoom/-ey srak; **2.** תרמית (deceit) *nf* tarmee|t/-yot.
bluffer בלופר *nm* blofer/-eem.
bluing מכחיל *nm* makh'kheel (*cpr* mak'kheel)/-eem (*pl+of:* -ey).
bluish כחלחל *adj* kekhalkhal/-ah.
blunder 1. טעות גסה *nf* ta'oo|t/-yot gas|ah/-ot; **2.** מעשה שטות (stupidity) *nm* ma'as|eh/-ey shtoot.
blunt קהה *adj* keh|eh/-ah.
blur כתם מטשטש *nm* ket|em/-ameem metashtesh/-eem.
(to) blur לטשטש *inf* letashtesh; *pst* teeshtesh; *pres* metashtesh; *fut* yetashtesh.
blush סומק somek.
(to) blush להסמיק *inf* lehasmeek; *pst* heesmeek; *pres* masmeek; *fut* yasmeek.
(to) bluster להרעיש *inf* lehar'eesh; *pst* heer'eesh; *pres* mar'eesh; *fut* yar'eesh.
blustering מרעיש *adj* mar'eesh/-ah.
boar חזיר־בר *nm* khazeer/-ey bar.
board 1. ועד מנהל (committee) *nm* va'ad menahel; **2.** קרש (plank) *nm* keresh/krash|eem (*pl+of:* -ey).
(room and) board לינה ואוכל *nm pl* leenah ve-okhel.
(free on) board (*f.o.b.*) פו"ב *nm* fob.
board of directors 1. מועצת מנהלים *nf* mo'etset/mo'atsot menahaleem; **2.** מועצת דירקטורים *nf* mo'etset/mo'atsot deerektoreem.
boarder דייר־משנה *nm* dayar/-ey meeshneh
boarding house אכסניה *nf* akhsan|yah/-yot (*+of:* -yat).
boast התפארות *nf* heetpa'aroo|t/-yot.
(to) boast 1. להתפאר *inf* leheetpa'er; *pst* heetpa'er; *pres* meetpa'er; *fut* yeetpa'er; **2.** להתרברב (vaunt) *inf* leheetravrev; *pst* heetravrev; *pres* meetravrev; *fut* yeetravrev.
boastful רברבן *nmf & adj* ravrevan/-eet.
boastfulness רברבנות *nf* ravrevanoo|t/-yot.
boat 1. סירה *nf* seer|ah/-ot (*+of:* -at); **2.** ספינה *nf* sfeen|ah/-ot (*+of:* -at).
boathouse 1. בית סירות (shelter) *nm* bet seerot; **2.** ספינת מגורים (floating home) *nf* sfeenat/-ot megooreem.
boating שיט סירות *nm* sheyt seerot.
boatman סוור *nm* savar/-eem (*pl+of:* -ey).
bob תספורת קצרה *nf* teesporet ketsarah.
(to) bob one's hair להסתפר קצר *[colloq.]* *inf* leheestaper katsar; *pst* heestaper *etc*; *pres* meestaper *etc*; *fut* yeestaper *etc*.
bobbin סליל חוטים *nm* sleel/-ey khooteem.
bobwhite חוגלה *nf* khogl|ah/-ot (*+of:* -at).
bodice חזיית שרוכים *nf* khazee|yat/-yot srokheem.
bodily גופני *adj* goofanee/-t.
bodily harm פגיעה בגוף *nf* pegee|'ah/-'ot be-goof.
body 1. גוף *nm* goof/-eem (*pl+of:* -ey); **2.** קבוצה (group) *nf* kvoots|ah/-ot (*+of:* -at).
body and soul בלב ונפש *adv* be-lev va-nefesh.
body politic ישות מדינית *nm* yeshoo|t/-yot medeenee|t/-yot.
bodyguard שומר־ראש *nm* shom|er/-rey rosh.
bog 1. ביצה (swamp) *nf* beets|ah/-ot (*+of:* -at); **2.** מדמנה (dungpit) *nf* madmen|ah/-ot (*+of:* -at).
bohemian בוהמי *adj* bohemee/-t.

boil 1. בועה *nf* boo|'ah/-'ot (*+of:* -'at); **2.** חבורה *nf* khaboor|ah/-ot (*+of:* -at); **3.** פורונקול (furuncle) *[colloq.] nm* fooroonkool/-eem (*pl+of:* -ey).

(to) boil לרתוח *inf* leerto'akh; *pst* ratakh; *pres* rote'akh; *fut* yeertakh.

(to) boil down להסתכם *inf* leheestakem; *pst* heestakem; *pres* meestakem; *fut* yeestakem.

boiler דוד הרתחה *nm* dood/-ey hartakhah.

boiling point נקודת רתיחה *nf* nekoodat reteekhah.

boisterous צעקני *adj* tsa'akanee/-t.

bold נועז *adj* no|'az/-'ezet.

boldness תעוזה *nf* te'ooz|ah/-ot (*+of:* -at).

(to) bolster לתמוך *inf* leetmokh; *pst* tamakh; *pres* tomekh; *fut* yeetmokh.

bolt 1. לולב *nm* lol|av/-aveem (*pl+of:* -vey); **2.** בריח (locking bar) *nm* bree|'akh/-kheem (*pl+of:* -khey); **3.** בורג (screw) *nm* boreg/brageem (*pl+of:* borgey; *or:* beergey).

(to) bolt out להסתגר מפני *inf* leheestager mee-pney; *pst* heestager *etc*; *pres* meestager *etc*; *fut* yeestager *etc*.

bomb פצצה *nf* petsats|ah/-ot (*+of:* peetsets|at/-ot).

bomb shelter מקלט *nm* meeklat/-eem (*pl+of:* meekletey).

(to) bomb, bombard להפציץ *inf* lehaftseets; *pst* heeftseets; *pres* maftseets; *fut* yaftseets.

bombardment הפצצה *nf* haftsats|ah/-ot (*+of:* -at).

bombastic 1. בומבסטי *adj* bombastee/-t; **2.** מליצי *adj* meleetsee/-t.

bomber מפציץ *nm* maftseets/-eem (*pl+of:* -ey).

bonbon ממתק *nm* mamtak/-eem (*pl+of:* -ey).

bond 1. קשר *nm* kesh|er/-areem (*pl+of:* keeshrey); **2.** איגרת־חוב (debenture) *nf* eeg|eret/-rot khov; **3.** ערבות (bail) *nf* 'arvoo|t/-yot.

bondage עבדות *nf* 'avdoo|t/-yot.

bondsman עבד *nm* 'eved/'av|adeem (*pl+of:* -dey).

bone עצם *nf* 'etsem/'ats|amot (*pl+of:* -mot).

bonfire מדורה *nf* medoor|ah/-ot (*+of:* -at).

bonnet 1. מצנפת (headgear) *nf* meetsn|efet/-afot (*+of:* -efat); **2.** חיפת המנוע (engine hood) *nf* kheep|at/-ot ha-mano'a'.

bonus 1. בונוס *nm* bonoos/-eem (*pl+of:* -ey); **2.** מענק (grant) *nm* ma'an|ak/-akeem (*pl+of:* -key).

bony גרמי *adj* garmee/-t.

(to) boo לצעוק "בוז"! *inf* leets'ok "booz!"; *pst* tsa'ak *etc*; *pres* tso'ek *etc*; *fut* yeets'ak *etc*.

booby שוטה *nm* shot|eh/-eem (*pl+of:* -ey).

booby trap 1. מוקש (mine) *nm* mok|esh/-sheem (*pl+of:* -shey); **2.** מלכודת שוטים *nf* malkodet shoteem.

book ספר *nm* sefer/sfareem (*pl+of:* seefrey).

(cash) book פנקס הקופה *nm* peenk|as/-esey ha-koopah.

(The) Book 1. ספר התנ"ך *nm* sefer ha-tanakh; **2.** ספר הספרים (The Book of Books) *nm* sefer ha-sfareem.

(to) book passage להזמין כרטיס נסיעה *inf* lehazmeen kartees/-ey nesee'ah; *pst* heezmeen *etc*; *pres* mazmeen *etc*; *fut* yazmeen *etc*.

bookcase ארון ספרים *nm* aron/-ot sfareem.

bookend זוויתן למדף ספרים *nm* zaveetan/-eem le-mad|af/-fey sfareem.

bookkeeper פנקסן *nmf* peenk|asan/-esaneet.

bookkeeping פנקסנות *nf* peenkesanoo|t/-yot.

(double entry) bookkeeping פנקסנות כפולה *nf* peenkesanoot kefoolah.

booklet 1. ספרון *nm* seefron/-eem (*pl+of:* -ey); **2.** חוברת (brochure) *nf* khov|eret/-rot.

(to keep) books לנהל ספרים *inf* lenahel sfareem; *pst* neehel *etc*; *pres* menahel *etc*; *fut* yenahel *etc*.

bookseller מוכר ספרים *nm* mokh|er/-rey sfareem.

bookshelf מדף ספרים *nm* mad|af/-fey sfareem.

bookshop, bookstore חנות ספרים *nf* khanoo|t/-yot sfareem.

boom שגשוג פתע *nm* seegsoog/-ey peta'.

(to) boom לגעוש *inf* leeg'osh; *pst* ga'ash; *pres* go'esh; *fut* yeeg'ash.

boon הנאה *nf* hana|'ah/-'ot (*+of:* -'at).

boor בור *nm* boor/-eem (*pl+of:* -ey).

boorish 1. גס *adj* gas/-ah; **2.** מגושם *adj* megoosh|am/-emet.

boost עידוד *nm* 'eedood/-eem (*pl+of:* -ey).

(to) boost 1. להעלות *inf* leha'alot; *pst* he'elah; *pres* ma'aleh; *fut* ya'aleh; **2.** להגביר (intensify) *inf* lehagbeer; *pst* heegbeer; *pres* magbeer; *fut* yagbeer.

booster 1. העלאה *nf* ha'ala|'ah/-'ot (*+of:* -'at); **2.** הגברה (intensification) *nf* hagbar|ah/-ot (*+of:* -at).

boot 1. מגף *nm* mag|af/-afayeem (*pl+of:* -fey); **2.** נעל (shoe) *nf* na'al/-ayeem (*pl+of:* -ey).

bootblack מצחצח נעליים *nm* metsakhtse|'akh/-khey na'alayeem.

booth 1. תא *nm* ta/-'eem (*pl+of:* -ey); **2.** סוכה *nf* sook|ah/-ot (*+of:* -at).

bootlegger מבריח משקאות *nm* mavree|'akh/-khey mashka'ot.

bootlicker 1. מלחך פנכה *adj* melakhekh/-et peenkah; **2.** חנפן (flatterer) *adj* khanfan/-eet.

booty שלל *nm* shalal (*+of:* shlal).

booze משקה *nm* mashk|eh/-a'ot.

borax בורקס *nm* boraks.

border 1. גבול gvool/-ot; **2.** קצה (edge) *nm* katseh/ketsavot (*+of:* ketseh/katsvot).

(to) border on, upon לגבול עם *inf* leegbol 'eem; *pst* gaval 'eem *(v=b)*; *pres* govel 'eem; *fut* yeegbol 'eem.

bored משועמם *adj* mesho'am|am/-emet.

boredom שעמום *nm* shee'amoom/-eem (*pl+of:* -ey).

boric acid חומצת בור *nf* khoomtsat bor.

boring משעמם *adj* mesha'amem/-et.

born 1. יליד *adj* yeleed/-at; **2.** נולד *v pst 3rd pers* nol|ad/-dah *(m/f)*.

borough 1. פרוור *nm* parv|ar/-areem (*pl+of:* -erey); **2.** עיריית־משנה *nf* 'eeree|yat/-yot meeshneh.

(to) borrow 1. ללוות (money) *inf* leelvot; *pst* lavah; *pres* loveh; *fut* yeelveh; **2.** לשאול (things) *inf* leesh'ol; *pst* sha'al; *pres* sho'el; *fut* yeesh'al.

borrower 1. לווה *nm* lov|eh/-eem (*pl+of:* -ey); **2.** שואל (of things) *nm* sho|'el/-'aleem (*pl+of:* -'aley).

bosom 1. חיק *nm* kheyk/-eem (*pl+of:* -ey); **2.** חזה (chest) *nm* khaz|eh/-ot.

bosom friend ידיד נפש *nmf* yedeed/-at nefesh.
(in the) bosom of בחיק *adv* be-kheyk.
boss 1. בוס *nmf* bos/-eet; **2.** מעביד *nmf* ma'aveed/-ah.
bossy שתלטן *adj* shtaltan/-eet.
botany בוטניקה *nf* botaneekah.
botch 1. עבודה גרועה *nf* ‘avodah groo‘ah; **2.** עבודה פרטאצ׳ית *[slang] nf* ‘avod|ah/-ot partatchee|t/-yot.
bother מטרד *nm* meetr|ad/-adeem (+*of:* -edey).
(to) bother להטריד *inf* lehatreed; *pst* heetreed; *pres* matreed; *fut* yatreed.
bothersome 1. מדאיג *adj* mad'eeg/-ah; **2.** מטריד (annoying) *adj* matreed/-ah.
bottle בקבוק *nm* bakbook/-eem (*pl+of:* -ey).
bottle opener פותחן *nm* potkhan/-eem (*pl+of:* -ey).
bottleneck 1. צוואר בקבוק *nm* tsavar bakbook; **2.** פקק (traffic jam) *nm* pekak/-eem (*pl+of:* -ey).
bottom 1. תחתית *nf* takhtee|t/-yot; **2.** ישבן (buttocks) *nm* yashvan/-eem (*pl+of:* -ey).
(at the) bottom of ביסוד הכול *adv* bee-yesod hakol.
bottomless ללא תחתית *adj & adv* le-lo takhteet.
boudoir חדר הלבשה נשי *nm* khadar halbashah nashee.
bough ענף ‘anaf/-eem (*pl+of:* ‘anfey).
bouillon מרק בשר *nm* merak/meerkey basar;
boulder 1. סלע *nm* sela‘/sla‘eem (+*of:* sal‘ey); **2.** גוש אבן *nm* goosh/-ey even.
boulevard שדרה *nf* sder|ah/-ot (+*of:* -at).
(to) bounce 1. להעיף *inf* leha‘eef; *pst* he‘eef; *pres* me‘eef; *fut* ya‘eef; **2.** להתרברב (brag) *inf* leheetravrev; *pst* heetravrev; *pres* meetravrev; *fut* yeetravrev.
bouncer שומר־סף *nm* shom|er/-rey saf.
bound 1. קשור *adj* kashoor/keshoorah; **2.** כרוך (tied) *adj* karookh/krookhah; **3.** מחויב (obliged) *adj* mekhoo|yav/-yevet; **4.** תחום *nm* tekhoom/-eem (*pl+of:* -ey); **5.** גבול (border) *nm* gvool.
bound for שפניו אל *adj* she-pan|av/-ehah el.
bound to אלוץ *adj* aloots/-ah.
bound up מסור *adj* masoor/mesoorah.
boundary 1. גבול *nm* gvool/-ot; **2.** תחום (range) *nm* tekhoom/-eem (*pl+of:* -ey).
boundless ללא גבול *adj* le-lo gvool.
(out of) bounds מחוץ לתחום *adv* mee-khoots la-t'khoom.
bountiful נדיב *adj* nadeev/nedeevah.
bounty 1. נדיבות (generosity) *nf* nedeevoo|t/-yot; **2.** פרס (prize) *nm* pras/-eem (*pl+of:* -ey); **3.** מענק (grant) *nm* ma'an|ak/-akeem (+*of:* -key).
bouquet זר *nm* zer/-eem (*pl+of:* -ey).
bourgeois בורגני *nmf* boorganee/-t.
bout 1. סיבוב *nf* seevoov (*cpr* seeboov)/-eem (*pl+of:* -ey); **2.** נאגלה *[slang] nf* nagl|ah/-ot (+*of:* -at); **3.** התקף (of sickness) *nm* hetkef/-eem (*pl+of:* -ey).
bow קשת *nf* kesh|et/-atot.
(to) bow לקוד *inf* lakod; *pst & pres* kad; *fut* yeekod.
bow-tie עניבת־פרפר *nf* ‘aneev|at/-ot parpar.
bowels 1. מעיים *nm pl* me‘ayeem (*sing:* me‘ee; *pl+of:* me‘ey); **2.** קרביים (“innards”) *nm pl* kravayeem (*pl+of:* keervey).
bower סוכת ירק *nf* sook|at/-ot yerek.
bowl קערה *nf* ke‘ar|ah/-ot (+*of:* ka‘ar|at/-ot).
bowling כדורת *nf* kadoret.
box 1. קופסה *nf* koofs|ah/-a'ot (+*of:* -at); **2.** תא (jury, theater) *nm* ta/-'eem (*pl+of:* -'ey).
box office קופה *nf* koopah/-ot (+*of:* -at).
box seat מקום בתא makom/mekomot be-ta.
boxcar קרון מטען *nm* kron/-ot meet‘an.
boxer מתאגרף *nm* meet'agref/-eem (*pl+of:* -ey).
boxing אגרוף *nm* eegroof.
boy נער *nm* na‘ar/ne‘areem (*pl+of:* na‘arey).
boy scout צופה *nm* tsof|eh/-eem (*pl+of:* -ey).
boycott 1. חרם *nm* kherem/kharamot; **2.** בויקוט *nm* boykot/-eem.
boyhood נעורים *nm pl* ne‘oor|eem (*pl+of:* -ey).
boyish נערי *adj* na‘aree/-t.
(to) brace לחזק *inf* lekhazek; *pst* kheezek; *pres* mekhazek; *fut* yekhazek.
(to) brace (up) 1. להתאושש *inf* leheet'oshesh; *pst* heet'oshesh; *pres* meet'oshesh; *fut* yeet'oshesh; **2.** לאזור כוח (gather strength) *inf* le'ezor ko'akh; *pst* azar *etc*; *pres* ozer *etc*; *fut* ye'ezor *etc*.
bracelet צמיד *nm* tsameed/tsemeed|eem (*pl+of:* -ey).
braces כתפות *nf pl* ketefot.
bracket 1. תמך (support) *nm* temekh/tmakh|eem (*pl+of:* -ey); **2.** מדף (shelf) *nm* madaf/-eem (*pl+of:* -ey).
brackets סוגריים (punctuation) *nm pl* sograyeem.
brackish מלוח *adj* maloo'akh/melookhah.
brad מסמר *nm* masmer/-eem (*pl+of:* -ey).
(to) brag להתרברב *inf* leheetravrev; *pst* heetravrev; *pres* meetravrev; *fut* yeetravrev.
braggart רברבן *nm* ravrevan/-eet.
braid 1. צמה *nf* tsam|ah/-ot (+*of:* -at); **2.** מקלעת (plait) *nf* meekl|a‘at/-e‘ot.
(to) braid לקלוע *inf* leeklo‘a‘; *pst* kala‘; *pres* kole‘a‘; *fut* yeekla‘.
brain 1. מוח *nm* mo'akh/mokhot; **2.** שכל (wit) *nm* sekhel.
brain child פרי רוח *nm* pree roo'akh.
brain drain בריחת מוחות *nf* breekhat mokhot.
brain trust צוות מוחות *nm* tsevet mokhot.
brainwashing שטיפת מוח *nf* shteef|at/-ot mo'akh.
brain-wave הברקה *nf* havrak|ah/-ot (+*of:* -at).
brainy מחוכם *adj* mekhook|am/-emet.
brake 1. בלם *nm* belem/blameem (*pl+of:* -ey); **2.** מעצורים (restraints) *nm pl* ma'atsor|eem (*pl+of:* -ey).
brake band סרט־בלם *nm* seret/seertey belem/blameem.
brake drum תוף־בלם *nm* tof/toopey belem/blameem.
brake fluid נוזל בלמים *nm* nozel blameem.
brake lining רפידת־בלם *nm* refeed|at/-ot belem/blameem.
brake shoe גשיש בלם *nm* gesheesh/-ey belem/blameem.
(to apply the) brakes לבלום *inf* leevlom; *pst* balam (*b=v*); *pres* bolem; *fut* yeevlom.
bramble אטד *nm* atad/-eem (*pl+of:* atedey).

bran סובין *nm pl* soobeen.

branch 1. ענף *nm* 'anaf/-eem (*pl+of:* 'anfey); **2.** סניף (affiliate) *nm* sneef/-eem (*pl+of:* -ey).

branch office סניף *nm* sneef/-eem (*pl+of:* -ey).

brand 1. סוג *nm* soog/-eem (*pl+of:* -ey); **2.** תוצרת (produce) *nf* totseret; **3.** סימן מסחרי (trade mark) *nm* seeman/-eem meeskharee/-yeem.

(to) brand 1. לסמן (mark) *inf* lesamen; *pst* seemen; *pres* mesamen; *fut* yesamen; **2.** לצרוב (burn) *inf* leetsrov; *pst* tsarav; *pres* tsorev; *fut* yeetsrov.

brand-new חדיש *adj* khadeesh/-ah.

(to) brandish לנופף *inf* lenofef; *pst* nofef; *pres* menofef; *fut* yenofef.

brandy 1. קוניאק *[colloq.] nm* konyak/-eem; **2.** יין שרף *nm* yen-saraf; **3.** יי״ש (*acr of* 2) *nm* yash.

brash חצוף *adj* khatsoof/-ah.

brass פליז *nm* pleez.

brassband תזמורת כלי־נשיפה *nf* teezmor|et/-ot kley nesheefah.

brassiere חזייה *nf* khazee|yah/-yot (*+of:* -yat).

brat פרחח *nm* peerkhakh/-eem (*pl+of:* -ey).

bravado 1. התרברבות *nf* heetravrevoo|t/-yot; **2.** השוויצה *[slang]* hashvats|ah/-ot (*+of:* -at).

brave אמיץ *adj* ameets/-ah.

bravery 1. אומץ *nm* omets; **2.** אומץ־לב (courage) *nm* omets-lev.

brawl 1. תגרה (skirmish) *nf* teegr|ah/-ot (*+of:* -at); **2.** קטטה (quarrel) *nf* ketat|ah/-ot (*+of:* -at).

(to) brawl להתכתש *inf* leheetkatesh; *pst* heetkatesh; *pres* meetkatesh; *fut* yeetkatesh.

bray נעירה *nf* ne'eer|ah/-ot (*+of:* -at).

brazen 1. חצוף *adj* khatsoof/-ah; **2.** עשוי פליז (metallic) 'asooy/-ah pleez.

brazier 1. עובד בפליז *nm* 'oved/-eem bee-fleez (*f=p*); **2.** מנגל *[colloq.] nm* mangal/-eem.

breach הפרה *nf* hafar|ah/-ot (*+of:* -at).

breach of contract הפרת חוזה *nf* hafar|at/-ot khozeh.

breach of faith מעילה באימון *nf* me'eel|ah/-ot be-'eymoon.

breach of peace הפרת שלום *nf* hafar|at/-ot shalom.

breach of promise הפרת הבטחה לנישואין *nf* hafar|at/-ot havtakhah le-neesoo'eem.

bread לחם *nm* lekhem/lekhameem (*pl+of:* lakhamey).

breadbox תיבת הלחם *nf* teyv|at/-ot ha-lekhem.

breadline תור ללחם *nm* tor/-eem le-lekhem.

breadth רוחב *nm* rokhav/rekhaveem (*pl+of:* rakhvey).

breadwinner מפרנס *nmf* mefarnes/-et.

break 1. הפסקה (intermission) *nf* hafsak|ah/-ot (*+of:* -at); **2.** שבירה (breach) *nf* shveer|ah/-ot; **3.** הזדמנות (chance) *nf* heezdamnoo|t/-yot.

(to) break לשבור *inf* leeshbor; *pst* shavar (*v=b*); *pres* shover; *fut* yeeshbor.

(to) break away לחרוג *inf* lakhrog; *pst* kharag; *pres* khoreg; *fut* yakhrog.

(to) break even לאזן *inf* le'azen; *pst* eezen; *pres* me'azen; *fut* ye'azen.

(to) break into לפרוץ לתוך *inf* leefrots le-tokh; *pst* parats *etc*; *pres* porets *etc*; *fut* yeefrots *etc.*

(to) break out להימלט *inf* leheemalet; *pst & pres* neemlat; *fut* yeemalet.

(to) break up לשים קץ *inf* laseem kets; *pst & pres* sam kets; *fut* yaseem kets.

breakable שביר *adj* shaveer/shveerah.

breakage נזקי שבירה *nm pl* neezkey shveerah.

breakdown התמוטטות *nf* heetmotetoo|t/-yot.

breakfast ארוחת־בוקר *nf* arookh|at/-ot boker.

breakthrough פריצת־דרך *nf* preets|at/-ot derekh.

breakwater מזח *nm* mezakh/-eem (*pl+of:* meezkhey).

breast 1. חזה *nm* khaz|eh/-ot; **2.** שד (mammary) shad/-ayeem (*pl+of:* shedey)

(a clean) breast 1. הורדה מהלב *nf* horadah/-ot me-halev; **2.** וידוי (confession) *nm* veedoo|y/-yeem (*pl+of:* -yey)

breaststroke שחיית חזה *nf* sekhee|yat/-yot khazeh.

breath 1. נשימה *nf* nesheem|ah/-ot (*+of:* -at); **2.** שאיפת אוויר (of air) *nf* she'eef|at/-ot aveer.

(to) breathe 1. לנשום *inf* leenshom; *pst* nasham; *pres* noshem; *fut* yeenshom; **2.** לשאוף אוויר (air) *inf* leesh'of aveer; *pst* sha'af *etc*; *pres* sho'ef *etc*; *fut* yeesh'af *etc.*

(to) breathe a word לגלות דבר *inf* legalot davar; *pst* geelah *etc*; *pres* megaleh *etc*; *fut* yegaleh *etc.*

(to) breathe in לשאוף אוויר *inf* leesh'of aveer; *pst* sha'af *etc*; *pres* sho'ef *etc*; *fut* yeesh'af *etc.*

(to) breathe one's last לפחת נפשו *inf* lafakhat nafsh|o/-ah (*m/f*); *pst* nafakh *etc*; *pres* nofe'akh *etc*; *fut* yeepakh (*p=f*) *etc.*

(to) breathe out לנשוף *inf* leenshof; *pst* nashaf; *pres* noshef; *fut* yeenshof.

breathing נשימה *nf* nesheem|ah/-ot (*+of:* -at).

breathless ללא נשימה *adj & adv* le-lo nesheemah.

breathtaking עוצר־נשימה *adj* 'otser/-et nesheemah.

breeches מכנסיים *nm pl* meekhn|asayeem (*sing:* -as; *+of:* -esey).

(riding) breeches מכנסי רכיבה *nm pl* meekhnesey rekheevah.

breed גזע *nm* gez|a'/-a'eem (*pl+of:* geez'ey).

(to) breed לגדל *inf* legadel; *pst* geedel; *pres* megadel; *fut* yegadel.

breeder מגדל *nm* megad|el/-leem (*pl+of:* ley).

breeding 1. חינוך *nm* kheenookh; **2.** נימוסים (manners) *nm pl* neemoos|eem (*pl+of:* -ey); **3.** גידול (raising) *nm* geedool.

breeze משב־רוח *nm* mash|av/-vey roo'akh.

breezy רענן *adj* ra'anan/-ah.

brethren 1. אחים (familial) *nm pl* akheem; **2.** חברים (comrades) *nm pl* khavereem.

brevity קוצר *nm* kotser.

brew נזיד *nm* nazeed/nezeed|eem (*pl+of:* -ey).

(to) brew 1. לבשל *inf* levashel; *pst* beeshel (*b=v*); *pres* mevashel; *fut* yevashel; **2.** לזמום (intrigue) leezmom; *pst* zamam; *pres* zomem; *fut* yeezmom.

brewery מבשלת בירה *nf* meevshel|et/-ot beerah.

bribe שוחד *nm* shokhad/sheekhood|eem (*pl+of:* -ey).

(to) bribe לשחד *inf* leshakhed; *pst* sheekhed; *pres* meshakhed; *fut* yeshakhed.

bribery 1. שוחד *nm* shokhad; **2.** שלמונים (reward) *nm pl* shalmon|eem (*pl+of:* -ey).

brick לבנה *nf* levenah/-eem (*pl+of:* leevney).

brickbat הערה עוקצת *nf* he'arah/-ot 'ok|etset/-tsot.

bridal 1. של כלה (bride) shel kal|ah/-ot; **2.** של כלולות (wedding) shel kloolot.

bridal dress שמלת כלה *nf* seeml|at/-ot kalah.

bride כלה *nf* kalah/-ot (+*of:* -at).

bridegroom חתן *nm* khat|an/-aneem (*pl+of:* -ney).

bridge 1. גשר *nm* gesh|er/-areem (*pl+of:* geeshrey); **2.** ברידג׳ (game) *nm* breedj.

(suspension) bridge גשר תלוי *nm* gesher/gshareem talooy/tlooyeem.

(to) bridge לגשר *inf* legasher; *pst* geesher; *pres* megasher; *fut* yegasher.

(to) bridge a gap לגשר על פער *inf* legasher 'al pa'ar; *pst* geesher *etc; pres* megasher *etc; fut* yegasher *etc.*

bridle רסן *nm* resen/resaneem (*pl+of:* reesney).

(to) bridle לרסן *inf* lerasen; *pst* reesen; *pres* merasen; *fut* yerasen.

brief 1. קצר (short) *adj* katsar/ketsarah; **2.** תדריך (instructions) *nm* tadreekh/-eem (*pl+of:* -ey).

(to) brief לתדרך *inf* letadrekh; *pst* teedrekh; *pres* metadrekh; *fut* yetadrekh.

briefcase תיק *nm* teek/-eem (*pl+of:* -ey).

briefing תדרוך *nm* teedrookh/-eem (*pl+of:* -ey).

briefly בקיצור *adv* be-keetsoor.

brigade חטיבה *nf* khateev|ah/-ot (+*of:* -at).

(The Jewish) Brigade 1. הבריגדה היהודית *nf* ha-breegadah ha-yehoodeet; **2.** הבריגדה (*colloq. abbr.*) *nf* ha-breegadah.

brigadier תת־אלוף *nm* tat-aloof/-eem (*pl+of:* -ey).

brigadier-general אלוף *nm* aloof/-eem (*pl+of:* -ey).

bright 1. בהיר *adj* baheer/beheerah; **2.** מזהיר (brilliant) *adj* maz'heer/-ah.

(to) brighten 1. להאיר *inf* leha'eer; *pst* he'eer; *pres* me'eer; *fut* ya'eer; **2.** להבהיר *inf* lehav'heer; *pst* heev'heer; *pres* mav'heer; *fut* yav'heer.

brightness 1. זיו *nm* zeev; **2.** זוהר (shine) *nm* zohar/zehareem (*pl+of:* zohorey).

brilliant 1. מבריק *adj* mavreek/-ah; **2.** מזהיר (bright) *adj* maz'heer/-ah.

brimstone גופרית *nf* gofreet.

(to) bring להביא *inf* lehavee; *pst* hevee; *pres* mevee; *fut* yavee.

(to) bring about לגרום *inf* leegrom; *pst* garam; *pres* gorem; *fut* yeegrom.

(to) bring down להפיל *inf* lehapeel; *pst* heepeel; *pres* mapeel; *fut* yapeel.

(to) bring forth 1. ליילד (child) *inf* leyaled; *pst* yeeled; *pres* meyaled; *fut* yeyaled; **2.** להפיק (produce) *inf* lehafeek; *pst* hefeek; *pres* mefeek; *fut* yafeek; **3.** להוציא (take out) *inf* lehotsee; *pst* hotsee; *pres* motsee; *fut* yotsee.

(to) bring up 1. לגדל *inf* legadel; *pst* geedel; *pres* megadel; *fut* yegadel; **2.** לחנך (educate) *inf* lekhanekh; *pst* kheenekh; *pres* mekhanekh; *fut* yekhanekh.

brink סף *nm* saf/seep|eem (*pl+of:* -ey).

(on the) brink על סף *adv* 'al-saf.

brisk 1. תוסס *adj* toses/-et; **2.** זריז (quick) *adj* zareez/zreezah.

briskly לפתע *adv* le-feta'.

bristle זיף *nm* zeef/-eem (*pl+of:* -ey).

(to) bristle 1. להזדקר *inf* leheezdaker; *pst* heezdaker; *pres* meezdaker; *fut* yeezdaker; **2.** להתכסות זיפים (become covered with bristles) *inf* leheetkasot zeefeem; *pst* neetkasah *etc; pres* meetkaseh *etc; fut* yeetkaseh *etc.*

British 1. בריטי *nmf & adj* breetee/-t; **2.** אנגלי (English) *nmf* anglee/-yah; *adj* anglee/-t.

brittle 1. פריך *adj* pareekh/preekhah; **2.** שביר (fragile) *adj* shaveer/shveerah.

(to) broach 1. להרחיב פתח (enlarge opening) *inf* leharkheev petakh; *pst* heerkheev *etc; pres* markheev *etc; fut* yarkheev *etc;* **2.** להעלות לדיון (subject) *inf* leha'alot le-deeyoon; *pst* he'elah *etc; pst* ma'aleh *etc; fut* ya'aleh *etc.*

broad רחב *adj* rakhav/rekhavah.

(in) broad daylight לאור היום *adv* le-or ha-yom.

broad hint רמז ברור *nm* rem|ez/-azeem baroor/brooreem.

broad-minded 1. רחב אופקים *adj* rekhav/rakhavat ofakeem; **2.** סובלני (tolerant) *adj* sovlanee/-t.

broadcast שידור *nm* sheedoor/-eem (*pl+of:* -ey).

(to) broadcast לשדר *inf* leshader; *pst* sheeder; *pres* meshader; *fut* yeshader.

broadcasting station תחנת־שידור *nf* takhan|at/-ot sheedoor.

broadcloth 1. אריג צמר משובח (woolen) *nm* areeg/-ey tsemer meshoobakh/-eem; **2.** בד כותנה רחב (fabric) *nm* bad/-ey kootnah rakhav/rekhaveem.

(to) broaden להרחיב *inf* leharkheev; *pst* heerkheev; *pres* markheev; *fut* yarkheev.

broadside עלון פולמוס *nm* 'alon/-ey poolmoos.

brocade רקמה *nf* reekmah/rekamot (+*of:* reekm|at/-ot).

brochure 1. חוברת *nf* khov|eret/-rot; **2.** עלון (leaflet) *nm* 'alon/-eem (*pl+of:* -ey).

(to) broil לצלות *inf* leetslot; *pst* tsalah; *pres* tsoleh; *fut* yeetsleh.

broken שבור *adj* shavoor/shvoorah.

broken Hebrew עברית רצוצה *nf* 'eevreet retsootsah.

broker 1. ברוקר *nm* broker/-eem (*pl+of:* -ey); **2.** סוכן ניירות ערך (stockbroker) *m* sokh|en/-ney neyarot 'erekh.

bronchitis 1. דלקת הסימפונות *nf* daleket ha-seemponot; **2.** ברונכיט *nm* bronkheet.

bronze 1. ארד *nm* arad; **2.** ברונזה *nf* bronzah.

brooch סיכת קישוט *nf* seek|at/-ot keeshoot.

(to) brood 1. לדגור *inf* leedgor; *pst* dagar; *pres* doger; *fut* yeedgor; **2.** להרהר (keep thinking) *inf* leharher; *pst* heerher; *pres* meharher; *fut* yeharher.

(to) brood over לשקול מחדש *inf* leeshkol me-khadash; *pst* shakal *etc; pres* shokel *etc; fut* yeeshkol *etc.*

brook 1. פלג *nm* peleg/plageem (*pl+of:* palgey); **2.** נחל (stream) *nm* nakhal/nekhaleem (*pl+of:* nakhaley).

broom מטאטא *nm* mat'at|e/-'eem.

broomstick מקל למטאטא *nm* mak|el/-lot le-mat'at|e/-'eem.

broth 1. מרק בשר (meat soup) *m* merak/meerkey basar; **2.** מרק דגים (fish soup) *nm* merak/meerkey dageem.

brothel 1. בית בושת *nm* bet/batey boshet; **2.** בית זונות (whore-house) *nm* bet/batey zonot

brother אח *nm* akh/-eem (*pl+of:* -ey).

brother in-law גיס *nm* gees/-eem (*pl+of:* -ey).

brotherhood אחווה *nf* akhv|ah/-ot (*+of:* -at).

brotherly של אחווה *adj* shel akhvah.

brow גבה *nf* gab|ah/-ot (*+of:* -at).

brown חום *adj* khoom/-ah.

(to) browse 1. ללחך *inf* lelakhekh; *pst* leekhekh; *pres* melakhekh; *fut* yelakhekh; **2.** לדפדף (leaf) ledafdef; *pst* deefdef; *pres* medafdef; *fut* yedafdef.

bruise חבורה *nf* khaboor|ah/-ot (*+of:* -at).

(to) bruise 1. לחבול *vt inf* lakhbol; *pst* khaval (*v=b*); *pres* khovel; *fut* yakhbol; **2.** להכחיל ממכה (turn blue) *vi inf* lehakhekheel mee-makah; *cpr* lehak'kheel *etc*; *pst* heekhekheel *etc*; *pres* makhekheel *etc*; *fut* yakhekheel *etc*.

brunet, brunette 1. ברונט *adj* broonet/-eet; **2.** שחרחר (darkish) *adj* shekharkh|ar/-oret.

brunt הלם *nm* helem.

brunt of the battle נטל הקרב *nm* netel ha-krav.

brush 1. מברשת *nf* meevr|eshet/-ashot; **2.** מכחול (for painting) *nm* meekhekhol/-eem (*pl+of:* -ey).

(to) brush 1. להבריש *inf* lehavreesh; *pst* heevreesh; *pres* mavreesh; *fut* yavreesh; **2.** לצחצח (polish) *inf* letsakhtse'akh; *pst* tseekhtsakh; *pres* metsakhtse'akh; *fut* yetsakhtsakh.

(tooth)brush מברשת שיניים *nf* meevresh|et/-ot sheenayeem.

(to) brush aside לסלק הצידה *inf* lesalek ha-tseedah; *pst* seelek *etc*; *pres* mesalek *etc*; *fut* yesalek *etc*.

brush off סירוב *nm* seroov/-eem (*pl+of:* -ey).

(to) brush up לרענן *inf* lera'anen; *pst* ree'anen; *pres* mera'anen; *fut* yera'anen.

brushwood 1. גזרי עצים *nm pl* geezrey 'etseem; **2.** חורשה (thicket) *nf* khorsh|ah/-ot (*+of:* -at);

brusque 1. פתאומי (sudden) *adj* peet'omee/-t; **2.** גס (rude) *adj* gas/-ah.

brutal 1. ברוטלי *adj* brootalee/-t; **2.** אכזרי (cruel) *adj* akhzaree/-t.

brutality 1. ברוטליות *nf* brootaleeyoot; **2.** אכזריות (cruelty) *nf* akhzereeyoot.

brute 1. פרא־אדם *nm* pere'/peer'ey adam; **2.** יצור חייתי (savage creature) *nm* yetsoor/-eem khayatee/-yeem.

bubble בועה *nf* boo|'ah/-'ot (*+of:* -'at).

bubble gum גומי־לעיסה פמפם *nm* goomee-le'eesah pampam.

buck 1. צבי זכר (male deer) *nm* tsv|ee/-ayeem zakhar/zekhareem; **2.** דולר (US$) *nm* dol|ar/-areem (*pl+of:* -ey).

(to pass the) buck לגלגל אחריות על אחרים *inf* legalgel akhrayoot 'al akhereem; *pst* geelgel *etc*; *pres* megalgel *etc*; *fut* yegalgel *etc*.

buck private טוראי *nm* toora|y/-'eem (*pl+of:* -'ey).

bucket דלי *nm* dlee/dlay|eem (*pl+of:* -ey).

buckle אבזם *nm* avzem/-eem (*pl+of:* -ey).

(to) buckle down לגשת לעבודה במרץ *inf* lageshet la-'avodah be-merets; *pst & pres* neegash *etc*; *fut* yeegash *etc*.

(to) buckle under להתקפל *inf* leheetkapel; *pst* heetkapel; *pres* meetkapel; *fut* yeetkapel.

buckshot כדור עופרת *nm* kadoor/-ey 'oferet.

buckskin עור צבי *nm* 'or/-ot tsevee.

buckwheat כוסמת *nf* koosemet.

bud ניצן *nm* neetsan/-eem (*pl+of:* -ey).

buddy חבר *nm* khav|er/-ereem (*pl+of:* -rey).

(to) budge לזוז *inf* lazooz; *pst & pres* zaz; *fut* yazooz.

budget תקציב *nm* taktseev/-eem (*pl+of:* -ey).

buff 1. צהוב (color) *nm & adj* tsahov/tsehoobah (*b=v*); **2.** עירום (nude) *nm* 'eyrom; **3.** עור תאו (hide) *nm* 'or/-ot te'o.

(blindman's) buff מישחק בסנוורים *nm* mees'khak be-sanvereem.

buffalo תאו *nm* te'o.

buffer-state מדינת־חיץ *nf* medeen|at/-ot khayeets.

buffet מזנון *nm* meeznon/-eem (*pl+of:* -ey).

buffoon מוקיון *nm* mookyon/-eem (*pl+of:* -ey).

buggy 1. עגלה לסוס אחד (carriage) *nm* 'agalah le-soos ekhad; **2.** מלא פשפשים (full of bugs) *adj* male/mele'at peeshpesheem.

bugle חצוצרה *nf* khatsotsr|ah/-ot (*+of:* -at).

build 1. מבנה *nm* meevn|eh/-eem (*pl+of:* -ey); **2.** תבנית *nf* tavnee|t/-yot.

(to) build לבנות *inf* leevnot; *pst* banah (*b=v*); *pres* boneh; *fut* yeevneh.

build-up 1. הצטברות (accummulation) *nf* heetstabroo|t/-yot; **2.** פירסום אוהד (publicity) *nm* peersoom ohed.

(to) build up one's health להחזיר לאיתנו lehakhzeer le-eytan|o/-ah (*m/f*); *pst* hekhzeer *etc*; *pres* makhzeer *etc*; *fut* yakhzeer *etc*.

builder בונה *nmf* bon|eh/-ah.

building בניין *nm* been|yan/-yaneem (*pl+of:* -yeney).

bulb 1. בצל *nm* batsal/betsaleem; **2.** גלגל העין (eyeball) *nm* galgal ha-'ayeen

(electric) bulb נורת חשמל *nf* noor|at/-ot khashmal.

Bulgarian 1. בולגרי *nmf* boolgaree/-yah; **2.** בולגרי *adj* boolgaree/-t; **3.** בולגרית (language) *nf* boolgareet.

bulge בליטה *nf* bleet|ah/-ot (*+of:* -at).

bulgy נפוח *adj* nafoo'akh/nefookhah.

bulk 1. נפח *nm* nefakh/-eem (*pl+of:* neefkhey); **2.** מטען (cargo) *nm* meet'an/-eem (*pl+of:* -ey); **3.** החלק העיקרי (main part) *nm* ha-khelek ha-'eekree.

bulky 1. נפוח *adj* nafoo'akh/nefookhah; **2.** כבד (heavy) *adj* kaved/kvedah.

bull שור *nm* shor/shvareem (*pl+of:* shorey).

bulldog כלב בולדוג *nm* kelev/kalvey booldog.

bulldozer דחפור *nm* dakhpor/-eem (*pl+of:* -ey).

bullet כדור *nm* kadoor/-eem (*pl+of:* -ey).

bulletin בולטין *nm* booleteen/-eem (*pl+of:* -ey).

bulletproof חסין לכדורים *adj* khaseen/-ah le-khadooreem (*kh=k*).

bullfight מלחמת שוורים *nf* meelkh|emet/-amot shvareem.

bullfrog צפרדע קרקרנית *nf* tsefarde'a' karkeraneet.

bullion מטיל זהב *nm* meteel/-ey zahav.

bull's-eye לב המטרה (target) *nf* lev ha-matarah.
bullwark סוללה *nf* solel|ah/-ot (+*of:* -at).
bully בעל־זרוע *nm* ba'al/-ey zro'a'.
bum 1. בטלן *nm* batlan/-eem (*pl+of:* -ey); **2.** טפיל (parasite) *nm* tapeel/-eem (*pl+of:* -ey).
bumblebee דבורה *nf* dvor|ah/-eem (+*of:* -at).
bump 1. מכה (blow) *nf* mak|ah/-ot (+*of:* -at); **2.** בליטה (bulge) *nf* bleet|ah/-ot (+*of:* -at).
(to) bump להתנגש *inf* leheetnagesh; *pst* heetnagesh; *pres* meetnagesh; *fut* yeetnagesh.
(to) bump into להיתקל *inf* leheetakel; *pst & pres* neetkal; *fut* yeetakel.
(to) bump off להרוג *inf* laharog; *pst* harag; *pres* horeg; *fut* yaharog.
bumper 1. פגוש *nm* pagosh/-ot; **2.** טמבון *[colloq.]* *nm* tambon/-eem (*pl+of:* -ey).
bumpy road כביש מהמורות *nm* kveesh/-ey mahamorot.
bun 1. לחמנייה מתוקה (roll) *nf* lakhmanee|yah/-yot metook|ah/-ot; **2.** קוקו (hairdo) *nm* kookoo.
bunch 1. צרור *nm* tseror/-ot; **2.** חבורה (band) *nf* khavoor|ah/-ot (+*of:* -at).
bundle חבילה *nf* khaveel|ah/-ot (+*of:* -at).
bungalow בונגלו *nm* boongalo/-'ot.
bunion יבלת *nf* yab|elet/-alot.
bunk 1. שטויות! (nonsense) shtooyot! **2.** מיטת מדף (built-in bed) *nf* meet|at/-ot madaf.
buoy מצוף *nm* matsof/metsof|eem (*pl+of:* -ey).
(to) buoy up לעודד *inf* le'oded; *pst* 'oded; *pres* me'oded; *fut* ye'oded
buoyant 1. עליז *adj* 'aleez/-ah; **2.** מעודד (encouraging) *adj* me'oded/-et.
burden 1. מעמסה *nf* ma'am|asah/-asot (+*of:* -eset/-sot); **2.** נטל (load) *nm* netel.
burdensome מכביד *adj* makhbeed/-ah.
bureau 1. משרד (office) *nm* meesr|ad/-adeem (*pl+of:* -edey); **2.** לשכה (chamber) *nf* leeshkah/leshakhot (+*of:* leesh|kat/-khot).
(travel) bureau משרד נסיעות *nm* meesr|ad/-edey nesee'ot.
(weather) bureau חזאי מזג האוויר (weather forecaster) *nmf* khaza|y/-'eet mezeg ha-aveer.
burglar פורץ *nm* por|ets/-tseem (*pl+of:* -tsey).
burglary פריצה *nf* preets|ah/-ot (+*of:* -at).
burial קבורה *nf* kvoor|ah/-ot (+*of:* -at).
buried in thought שקוע במחשבות *adj* shakoo'a'/shkoo'ah be-makhshavot.
burlap בד יוטה *nm* bad/-ey yootah.
burly בעל־גוף *adj* ba'al/-ey goof.
burn כווייה *nf* kvee|yah/-yot (+*of:* -yat).
(to) burn 1. לבעור *vi inf* leev'or; *pst* ba'ar (*b=v*); *pres* bo'er; *fut* yeev'ar; **2.** לשרוף *vt inf* leesrof; *pst* saraf; *pres* soref; *fut* yeesrof.
burner מבער *nm* mav'er/-eem (*pl+of:* -ey).
(to) burnish 1. למרק (scrub) *inf* lemarek; *pst* merek; *pres* memarek; *fut* yemarek; **2.** לצחצח (polish) *inf* letsakhtse'akh; *pst* tseekhtsakh; *pres* metsakhtse'akh; *fut* yetsakhtsakh.
burrow 1. שוחה *nf* shookh|ah/-ot (+*of:* -at); **2.** מאורה (den) *nf* me'oor|ah/-ot (+*of:* -at).
(to) burrow 1. לחפור (dig) *vt* lakhpor; *pst* khafar (*f=p*); *pres* khofer; *fut* yakhpor; **2.** להתחפר (dig in) *v rfl inf* leheetkhaper; *pst* heetkhaper; *pres* meetkhaper.
burst פרץ *nm* perets/pratseem (+*of:* peertsey).
(to) burst להתפוצץ *inf* leheetpotsets; *pst* heetpotsets; *pres* meetpotsets; *fut* yeetpotsets.
(to) burst into tears לפרוץ בבכי *inf* leefrots bee-vekhee; *pst* parats *etc*; *pres* porets *etc*; *fut* yeefrots *etc.*
burst with laughter פרץ בצחוק *inf* leefrots bee-ts'khok; *pst* parats *etc*; *pres* porets *etc*; *fut* yeefrots *etc.*
(to) bury לקבור *inf* leekbor; *pst* kavar (*v=b*); *pres* kover; *fut* yeekbor.
bus אוטובוס *nm* otoboos/-eem (*pl+of:* -ey).
busboy עוזר למלצר *nm* 'oz|er/-reem le-meltsar.
bush 1. שיח *nm* see|'akh/-kheem (*pl+of:* -khey); **2.** סבך עצים (thicket) *nm* svakh 'etseem.
(to beat around the) bush לדבר סחור־סחור *inf* ledaber skhor-skhor; *pst* deeber *etc*; *pres* medaber *etc*; *fut* yedaber *etc.*
bushel בושל *nm* booshel/-eem.
bushing תותב מסב *nm* totav/-ey mesav.
bushy עבות *adj* 'av|ot/-ootah.
busily בזריזות *adv* bee-zreezoot.
business 1. עסק *nm* 'esek/'asakeem (*pl+of:* 'eeskey); **2.** עיסוק (occupation) *nm* 'eesook/-eem (*pl+of:* -ey); **3.** עסקים (deals) *nm pl* 'asakeem (+*of:* 'eeskey).
(doing) business לעשות עסקים *inf* la'asot 'asakeem; *pst* 'asah *etc*; *pres* 'oseh *etc*; *fut* ya'aseh *etc.*
(to have no) business לא מענייננו *adv* lo me-'eenyan|o/-ah (*m/f*).
business deal, transaction עיסקה *nf* 'eesk|ah/-a'ot (+*of:* -at/-ot).
businesslike 1. מעשי (practical) *adj* ma'asee/-t; **2.** מאורגן (organized) *adj* me'oorg|an/-enet.
businesswoman אשת עסקים *nf* eshet/neshot 'asakeem.
bust 1. חזה *nm* khaz|eh/-ot; **2.** שדיים (breasts) *nm pl* shadayeem; **3.** פסל ראש וחזה (sculpture) *nm* pesel/peesley rosh ve-khazeh.
(to) bust להתפוצץ *inf* leheetpotsets; *pst* heetpotsets; *pres* meetpotsets; *fut* yeetpotsets.
bustle המולה *nf* hamool|ah/-ot (+*of:* -at).
busy 1. עסוק *adj* 'asook/-ah; **2.** טרוד (occupied) *adj* tarood/troodah.
busy body מתערב בכול *adj* meet'arev/-et ba-kol.
busy street רחוב סואן *nm* rekhov/-ot so'en/so'aneem.
but 1. אבל *adv* aval; **2.** אולם *adv* oolam.
(not only) but לא זו בלבד אלא ש־ lo zo beelvad ela she-.
but for 1. מלבד *adv* meelvad; **2.** חוץ אשר (except for) *adv* khoots asher.
butcher קצב *nm* katsav/-eem (*pl+of:* -ey).
butcher's shop, butchery אטליז *nm* eetleez/-eem (*pl+of:* -ey).
butler משרת ראשי *nm* mesharet rashee.
butt 1. קצה (end) *nm* katseh/ketsavot (+*of:* kets|eh/-ot); **2.** קת (handle) *nf* kat/-ot.

(cigarette) butt בדל־סיגרייה *nm* bedal/beediey seegaree|yah/-yot.
(rifle) butt קת הרובה *nm* kat/-ey rov|eh/-eem.
(to) butt in לשסע *inf* leshase'a'; *pst* sheesa'; *pres* meshase'a'; *fut* yeshasa'.
(to) butt into להיתקל *inf* leheetakel; *pst & pres* neetkal; *fut* yeetakel.
butter חמאה *nf* khem|'ah/-'ot (+*of:* -'at).
buttercup נורית צהובה *nf* nooree|t/-yot tsehoob|ah/-ot.
butterfly פרפר *nm* parpar/-eem (*pl+of:* parperey).
buttermilk 1. חובץ *nm* khovets; **2.** חלב־חמאה *nm* khalev khem'ah.
buttocks 1. אחוריים *nf pl* akhor|ayeem (*pl+of:* -ey); **2.** עכוז (behind) *nm* 'akooz/-eem (*pl+of:* -ey).
button כפתור *nm* kaftor/-eem (*pl+of:* -ey).
buttonhole לולאה *nf* loola'|ah/-ot (+*of:* -at).
(to) buttonhole 1. לתפוס לשיחה *inf* leetpos le-seekhah; *pst* tafas *etc*; *pres* tofes *etc*; *fut* yeetpos (*f=p*) *etc*; **2.** לנדנד (*[slang]:* nag) *inf* lenadned; *pst* neadned; *pres* menadned; *fut* yenadned.
buttress 1. קיר תומך *nm* keer/-ot tom|ekh/-kheem; **2.** משען (support) *nm* meesh'an/-eem (*pl+of:* -ey).
(to) buttress 1. לחזק *inf* lekhazek; *pst* kheezek; *pres* mekhazek; *fut* yekhazek; **2.** לתמוך (support) *inf* leetmokh; *pst* tamakh; *pres* tomekh; *fut* yeetmokh.
buxom עם חזה לתפארת *adj* 'eem khazeh le-teef'eret.
buy קנייה *nf* kenee|yah/-yot (+*of:* -yat).
(to) buy לקנות *inf* leeknot; *pst* kanah; *pres* koneh; *fut* yeekneh.
(to) buy off 1. לשחד *inf* leshakhed; *pst* sheekhed; *pres* meshakhed; *fut* yeshakhed; **2.** לפדות (ransom) *inf* leefdot; *pst* padah (*p=f*); *pres* podeh; *fut* yeefdeh.
(to) buy up לרכוש בקנייה כוללת *inf* leerkhosh bee-kneeyah kolelet; *pst* rakhash *etc*; *pres* rokhesh *etc*; *fut* yeerkosh (*k=kh*) *etc*.
buyer 1. קונה *nm* kon|eh/-eem (*pl+of:* -ey); *nf* kon|ah/-ot (+*of:* -at); **2.** קניין (wholesale purchaser) *nmf* kanyan/-eet.
buzz זמזום zeemzoom/-eem (*pl+of:* -ey).
(to) buzz לזמזם *inf* lezamzem; *pst* zeemzem; *pres* mezamzem; *fut* yezamzem.
buzzard בז *nm* baz/-eem (*pl+of:* -ey).
buzzer זמזם *nm* zamzam/-eem (*pl+of:* -ey).
by 1. על ידי *prep* 'al-yedey; **2.** ע״י (initials of 1) *prep* 'al-yedey; **3.** מאת (authored by) me'et.
by and large בדרך כלל *adv* be-derekh klal.
by far בהרבה *adv* be-harbeh.
by night בלילה *adv* ba-laylah.
by-product תוצר־לוואי *nm* totsar/-ey levay.
by this time בינתיים *adv* beynatayeem.
bye-bye, (good) bye! !שלום shalom!
bygone שעבר *adj* she-'av|ar/-rah.
(let) bygones be bygones מה שהיה היה mah she-hayah hayah.
bylaw חוק־עזר *nm* khok/khookey 'ezer.
bypass 1. כביש עוקף *nm* kveesh/-eem 'ok|ef/-feem; **2.** השתלת מעקף (surgery) *nf* hashtal|at/-ot ma'akaf/-eem.
bypath שביל צדדי *nm* shveel/-e em tsedadee/-ye em.
bystander עומד מן הצד *nmf & adj* 'omed/-et meen ha-tsad.

C.

C,c 1. pronounced as in *ceiling* it is equivalent to Hebrew consonants Samekh (ס) or Seen (שׂ); **2.** pronounced as in *cab* it is equivalent to Hebrew consonants Kaf (כּ), if dotted, or Koof (ק); **3.** as ordinal numeral C. (third) its Hebrew equivalent is Geemel (ג׳).
cab מונית *nf* monee|t/-yot.
cab driver נהג מונית *nm* nahag/nehagey monee|t/-yot.
cabbage כרוב *nm* kroov.
cabin 1. תא באונייה (ship's) *nm* ta/-'eem bo-oneeyah; **2.** בקתה (in woods) *nf* beektah/bekatot (+*of:* beekt|at/-ot); **3.** ביתן (pavilion) *nm* beetan/-eem (*pl+of:* -ey).
cabinet 1. קבינט *nm* kabeenet/-eem; **2.** ממשלה (government) *nf* memshal|ah/-ot (+*of:* memshe|let/-lot).
cable 1. כבל *nm* kevel/kvaleem (*pl+of:* kavley); **2.** מברק (telegram) *nm* meevr|ak/-akeem (*pl+of:* -ekey).
(to) cable 1. להבריק *inf* lehavre ek; *pst* heevreek; *pres* mavreek; *fut* yavreek; **2.** לטלגרף (telegraph) *inf* letalgref; *pst* teelgref; *pres* metalgref; *fut* yetalgref.
cable address 1. כתובת טלגרפית *nf* ketovet telegrafeet; **2.** כתובת למברקים *nf* ketovet le-meevrakeem.
cablegram מברק *nm* meevr|ak/-akeem (*pl+of:* -ekey).
cabman 1. עגלון *nm* 'eglon/-eem (*pl+of:* -ey); **2.** רכב (coachman) *nm* rakav/-eem (*pl+of:* -ey).
cache מחבוא *nm* makhbo/-'eem (*pl+of:* -'ey)
(arms) cache סליק *nm* sleek/-eem (*pl+of:* -ey).
cackle 1. קרקור *nm* keerkoor/-eem (*pl+of:* -ey); **2.** פטפוט (prattle) *nm* peetpoot/-eem (*pl+of:* -ey).

(to) cackle לקשקש *inf* lekashkesh; *pst* keeshkesh; *pres* mekashkesh; *fut* yekashkesh.

cactus 1. צבר *nm* tsavar/-eem (*pl+of:* -ey; *cpr* tsab|ar/-reem; *pl+of:* -rey); **2.** קקטוס *nm* kaktoos/-eem (*pl+of:* -ey).

cad גס־רוח *nmf & adj* gas/-at roo'akh.

cadence 1. מקצב (rythm) *nm* meekts|av/-aveem (*pl+of:* -evey); **2.** מתכונת (proportion) *nf* matkon|et/-ot.

cadet 1. צוער *nm* tso'|er/-areem (*pl+of:* -arey); **2.** חניך (trainee) *nm* khaneekh/-eem (*pl+of:* -ey).

cadmium קדמיום *nm* kadmeeyoom.

cafe בית קפה *nm* bet/batey kafeh.

cafeteria 1. קפטריה *nf* kafeter|yah/-yot (*+of:* -yat); **2.** מסעדה בשירות עצמי (self-service) *nf* mees'adah/-ot be-sheroot 'atsmee.

caffein קפאין *nm* kafe'een.

cage כלוב *nm* kloov/-eem (*pl+of:* -ey).

cake 1. עוגה *nf* 'oog|ah/-ot (*+of:* -at); **2.** רקיק (wafer) *nm* rakeek/rekeek|eem (*pl+of:* -ey).

calamity אסון *nm* ason/-ot.

calcium סידן *nm* seedan/-eem (*pl+of:* -ey).

(to) calculate לחשב *inf* lekhashev; *pst* kheeshev; *pres* mekhashev; *fut* yekhashev.

(to) calculate on, upon לסמוך על *inf* leesmokh 'al; *pst* samakh 'al; *pres* somekh 'al; *fut* yeesmokh 'al.

calculated מחושב *adj* mekhoosh|av/-evet.

calculation 1. חישוב *nm* kheesho ov/-eem (*pl+of:* -ey); **2.** תחשיב (detailed evaluation) *nm* takhsheev/-eem (*pl+of:* -ey).

calculus 1. חשבון *nm* kheshbon; **2.** אבן בגוף (stone in the body) *nf* even/avaneem ba-goof.

calendar לוח שנה *nm* loo|'akh/-khot shanah.

calendar year 1. שנת לוח *nf* shnat/shnot loo'akh; **2.** שנה קלנדרית shan|ah/-eem kalendaree|t/-yot.

calf עגל *nm* 'egel/'agaleem (*pl+of:* 'egley).

calfskin עור עגל *nm* 'or/-orot 'egel/'agaleem.

caliber 1. קוטר *nm* koter/ketareem (*pl+of:* kotrey); **2.** קליבר *nm* kaleeb|er/-reem.

calico בד לבן *nm* bad lavan.

call 1. קריאה *nf* kree|'ah/-'ot (*+of:* -'at); **2.** ביקור (visit) *nm* beekoor/-eem (*pl+of:* -ey).

(on) call 1. כוננות *nf* koneno o|t/-yot; **2.** בכוננות *adv* be-khonenoot *(kh=k)*.

(phone) call 1. קריאה טלפונית *nf* kree|'ah/-'ot telefonee|t/-yot; **2.** שיחת טלפון *nf* seekh|at/-ot telefon.

(to) call לקרוא ל־ *inf* leekro le-; *pst* kara le-; *pres* kore le-; *fut* yeekra le-.

(to) call at לבקר אצל *inf* levaker etsel; *pst* beeker *etc*; *pres* mevaker *etc*; *fut* yevaker *etc*.

(to) call for להצריך *inf* lehatsreekh; *pst* heetsreekh; *pres* matsreekh; *fut* yatsreekh.

call girl נערת טלפון *nf* na'ar|at/-ot telefon.

(to) call on 1. לבקר אצל *inf* levaker etsel; *pst* beeker *etc*; *pres* mevaker *etc*; *fut* yevaker *etc*; **2.** לקרוא ל־ (appeal to) *inf* leekro le-; *pst* kara le-; *pres* kore le-; *fut* yeekra le-.

caller מבקר *nmf* mevaker/-et.

callous 1. נוקשה *adj* nooksh|eh/-ah; **2.** אדיש (indifferent) *adj* adeesh/-ah.

(to) call to order לקרוא לסדר *inf* leekro le-seder; *inf* kara *etc*; *pres* kore *etc*; *fut* yeekra *etc*.

(to) call together לכנס *inf* lekhanes; *pst* keenes *(k=kh)*; *pres* mekhanes; *fut* yekhanes.

(to) call up לטלפן *inf* letalpen; *pst* teelpen; *pres* metalpen; *fut* yetalpen

callus 1. יבלת *nf* yab|elet/-alot; **2.** צלקת *nf* tsal|eket/-akot.

calm 1. רגיעה *nf* regee'|ah/-ot (*+of:* -at); **2.** רגוע (relaxed) *adj* ragoo'a'/regoo'ah; **3.** רוגע (quiescent) *adj* rog|e'a'/-a'at.

(to) calm down 1. להירגע (oneself) *vi inf* leheraga'; *pst & pres* neerga'; *fut* yeraga'; **2.** להרגיע (others) *vt inf* lehargee'a'; *pst* heergee'a'; *pres* margee'a'; *fut* yarge e'a'.

calmly בקור־רוח be-kor-roo'akh.

calmness קור־רוח *nm* kor-roo'akh.

calorie קלוריה *nf* kalor|yah/-yot (*+of:* -yat).

calumny 1. דיבה *nf* deeb|ah/-ot (*+of:* -at); **2.** עלילה (frame-up) *nf* 'aleel|ah/-ot (*+of:* -at).

camel גמל *nm* gamal/gemal|eem (*pl+of:* -ey).

cameo קמיע *nm* kame'a'/kemel'ot (*pl+of:* -'ey).

camera מצלמה *nf* matslem|ah/-ot (*+of:* -at).

cameraman צלם *nm* tsalam/-eem (*pl+of:* -ey).

camerawoman צלמת *nf* tsal|emet/-amot.

camouflage הסוואה *nf* hasva|'ah/-'ot (*+of:* -'at).

(to) camouflage להסוות *inf* lehasvot; *pst* heesvah; *pres* masveh; *fut* yasveh.

camp 1. מחנה *nm* makhan|eh/-ot; **2.** מאהל (encampment) *nm* ma'ahal/-eem (*pl+of:* -ey);

(army) camp מחנה צבא *nm* makhan|eh/-ot tsava.

(political) camp מחנה תומכים *nm* makhan|eh/-ot tomkheem.

(summer) camp 1. קייטנה *nf* kayt|anah/-anot (*+of:* -anat/-not); **2.** מחנה קייט (*lit.*) *nm* makhan|eh/-ot kayeet.

(to) camp 1. לנטות אוהל (put up tent) *inf* leentot ohel; *pst* natah *etc*; *pres* noteh *etc*; *fut* yeeteh *etc*; **2.** לחנות (park) *inf* lakhanot; *pst* khanah; *pres* khoneh; *fut* yakhaneh.

campaign 1. מערכה *nf* ma'arakh|ah/-ot (*+of:* ma'ar|ekhet/-khot); **2.** מסע הסברה (persuasion drive) *nm* mas|a'/-'ot hasbarah.

camphor כופר *nm* kofer.

camping מחנאות *nf* makhna'oot.

camping ground 1. אתר מחנאות *nm* atar/-ey makhna'oot; **2.** חניון (parking lot) *nm* khanyon/-eem (*pl+of:* -ey).

campus קמפוס *nm* kampoos/-eem (*pl+of:* -ey).

can פחית *nf* pakhee|t/-yot.

can opener פותחן *nm* potkhan/-eem (*pl+of:* -ey).

Canada קנדה *nf* kanadah.

Canadian קנדי *nmf & adj* kanadee/-t.

canal תעלה *nf* te'al|ah/-ot (*+of:* -at).

(Suez) Canal תעלת סואץ *nf* te'alat soo'ets.

canalization 1. תיעול *nm* tee'ool/-eem (*pl+of:* -ey); **2.** ביוב (drainage) *nm* beeyoov/-eem (*pl+of:* -ey).

canary כנרית *nf* kanaree|t/-yot.

(to) cancel 1. לבטל *inf* levatel; *pst* beetel *(b=v)*; *pres* mevatel; *fut* yevatel; **2.** למחוק (wipe out) *inf* leemkhok; *pst* makhak; *pres* mokhek; *fut* yeemkhok.

cancellation ביטול *nm* beetool/-eem (*pl+of:* -ey).

cancer סרטן *nm* sartan.
cancerous סרטני *adj* sartanee/-t.
candid גלוי־לב *adj* glooy/-at lev.
candidacy מועמדות *nf* moo'amado|t/-yot.
candidate מועמד *nmf* mo'am|ad/-edet.
candle נר *nm* ner/-ot.
candlestick פמוט *nm* pamot/-ot.
candor גילוי־לב *nm* geelooy/-ey lev.
candy סוכרייה *nf* sookaree|yah/-yot (+*of:* -yat).
candy shop 1. חנות ממתקים khanoo|t/-yot mamtakeem; **2.** מגדניה *nf* meegdanee|yah/-yot (+*of:* -yat).
cane קנה *nm* kan|eh/-eem (+*of:* kene|h/-y).
(sugar) cane קנה סוכר *nm* kene|h/-y sookar.
(walking) cane מקל הליכה *nm* mak|el/-lot haleekhah.
cane chair כיסא קלוע *nm* kees|e/-'ot kaloo'a'/kloo'eem.
canine כלבי *adj* kalbee/-t.
canned משומר *adj* meshoom|ar/-eret.
cannery מפעל שימורים *nm* meef'al/-ey sheemooreem.
cannibal אוכל־אדם *nm* okh|el/-ley adam.
cannon תותח (artillery) *nm* totakh/-eem (*pl+of:* totkhey).
cannon fodder בשר תותחים *nm* besar totakheem.
cannonade הרעשת תותחים *nf* har'ash|at/-ot totakheem
canny חד־עין *adj* khad/-at 'ayeen.
canoe 1. בוצית *nf* bootsee|t/-yot; **2.** סירת קנו *nf* seer|at/-ot kanoo.
canon 1. חוק (law) *nm* khok/khook|eem (*pl+of:* -ey); **2.** כומר (priest) *m* komer/kemar|eem (*pl+of:* komrey).
canopy אפיריון *nf* apeeryon/-eem (*pl+of:* -ey).
(bridal) canopy חופה (in Yiddish: Chupeh) *nf* khoop|ah/-ot (+*of:* -at).
cantaloupe אבטיח צהוב *nm* avatee|'akh/-kheem tsahov/tsehoobeem *(b=v)*.
canteen 1. קנטינה *nf* kanteen|ah/-ot (+*of:* -at); **2.** שקם (in the army) *nm* shekem.
canton מחוז *nm* makhoz/mekhozot (+*of:* mekhoz).
canvas 1. בד (artist's) bad/-eem (*pl+of:* -ey); **2.** ברזנט (cloth) *nm* brezent/-eem.
canvass משאל *nm* meesh'al/-eem (*pl+of:* -ey).
(to) canvass לתשאל *inf* letash'el; *pst* teesh'el; *pres* metash'el; *fut* yetash'el.
canyon קניון *nm* kenyon/-eem (*pl+of:* -ey).
cap 1. כיפה (skullcap) *nf* keep|ah/-ot (+*of:* -at); **2.** כומתה (beret) *nf* koomt|ah/-ot (+*of:* -at).
(percussion) cap פיקת הקשה *nf* peek|at/-ot hakashah.
capability 1. יכולת *nf* yekholet; **2.** כושר (ability) *nm* kosher.
capable 1. מסוגל *adj* mesoog|al/-elet; **2.** כשיר (able) *adj* kasheer/kesheerah.
capacious מרווח *adj* meroovakh/-at.
capacity 1. כושר *nm* kosher; **2.** קיבול (displacement) *nm* keebool/-eem (*pl+of:* -ey).
(in the) capacity of בתורת *adj* be-torat.

cape 1. צוק (geogr.) *nm* tsook/-eem (*pl+of:* -ey); **2.** כף (geogr.) *nm* kef/-eem (*pl+of:* -ey); **3.** שכמייה (garment) *nf* sheekhmee|yah/-yot (+*of:* -yat).
capital 1. עיר בירה (town) *nf* 'eer/'arey beerah; **2.** הון (finance) *nm* hon; **3.** הוני *adj* honee/-t; **4.** כותרת עמוד (column's) *nf* kot|eret/-rot 'amood/-eem.
capital letter אות רישית (non-existent in Hebrew) *nf* ot/oteeyot reshee|t/-yot.
(to make) capital of לעשות הון מ־ *inf* la'asot hon mee-; *pst* 'asah *etc*; *pres* 'oseh *etc*; *fut* ya'aseh *etc*.
capital punishment עונש מוות *nm* 'onesh/'onshey mavet.
capitalism קפיטליזם *nm* kapeetaleezm.
capitalist 1. קפיטליסט *nmf & adj* kapeetaleest/-eet; **2.** בעל־הון (prospective investor) *nm* ba'al/-at hon.
capitalization צבירת הון *nf* tseveer|at/-ot hon.
(to) capitalize 1. לממן *inf* lemamen; *pst* meemen; *pres* memamen; *fut* yemamen; **2.** לכתוב באותיות רישיות (write in caps) *inf* leekhtov be-oteeyot resheeyot; *pst* katav *etc*; *pres* kotev *etc*; *fut* yeekhtov *etc*.
capitol קריית הממשלה *nf* keeryat ha-memshalah.
(to) capitulate להיכנע *inf* leheekana'; *pst & pres* neekhna'; *fut* yeekana' *(kh=k)*.
caprice קפריזה *nf* kapreez|ah/-ot (+*of:* -at).
capricious הפכפך *adj* hafakhp|akh/-ekhet.
(to) capsize להתהפך *inf* leheet'hapekh; *pst* heet'hapekh; *pres* meet'hapekh; *fut* yeet'hapekh.
capsule 1. כמוסה *nf* kemoos|ah/-ot (+*of:* -at); **2.** תא־לחץ (pressure-chamber) *nm* ta/-'ey lakhats.
captain 1. רב־חובל (sea) rav/rabey *(b=v)* khov|el/-leem; **2.** סרן (army) *nm* seren/sraneem (*pl+of:* sarney).
(to) captivate להקסים *inf* lehakseem; *pst* heekseem; *pres* makseem; *fut* yakseem.
captive שבוי *nmf* shavooy/shvoo|yah (+*of:* -ye em/-yot)
captivity שבי *nm* shvee (*also:* shevee).
captor שובה *nmf* shov|eh/-ah.
(to) capture 1. לקחת בשבי (prisoner) *inf* lakakhat ba-shevee; *pst* lakakh *etc*; *pres* loke'akh *etc*; *fut* yeekakh *etc*; **2.** לכבוש (conquer) *inf* leekhbosh; *pst* kavash *(v=b)*; *pres* kovesh; *fut* yeekhbosh; **3.** ללכוד (catch) *inf* leelkod; *pst* lakhad *(kh=k)*; *pres* lokhed; *fut* yeelkod.
car 1. מכונית *nf* mekhonee|t/-yot; **2.** קרון (wagon) *nm* karon/kronot (+*of:* kron); **3.** קרונית (wagonette) *nf* kronee|t/-yot.
(dining) car קרון־מסעדה *nf* kron/-ot mees'adah.
(freight) car קרון־משא *nf* kron/-ot masa.
caramel 1. קרמל *nm* karamel; **2.** סוכר שזוף *nf* sookar shazoof.
carat קרט *nm* karat/-eem.
caravan שיירה *nf* shay|arah/-arot (+*of:* -eret)
carbolic קרבולי *adj* karbolee/-t.
carbon פחמן *nm* pakhman/-eem (*pl+of:* -ey).
carbon dioxide פחמן דו־חמצני *nm* pakhman doo-khamtsanee.
carbon monoxide פחמן חד־חמצני *nm* pakhman khad-khamtsanee.

carbon paper 1. נייר עיתוק *nm* neyar 'eetook; **2.** נייר פחם *(lit., [colloq.])* *nm* neyar/-ot pekham.
carburetor מאייד me'ay|ed/-deem *(pl+of:* -dey).
carcass 1. פגר *nm* peg|er/-areem *(pl+of:* peegrey); **2.** נבלה *nf* nevel|ah/-ot *(+of:* neevl|at/-ot).
card כרטיס *nm* kartees/-eem *(pl+of:* -ey).
(file) card כרטיס בכרטסת *nm* kartees/-eem be-kharteset *(kh=k)*.
(identity) card תעודת־זהות *nf* te'ood|at/-ot zehoot.
(playing) card קלף *nm* klaf/-e em *(pl+of:* kalfey).
(post)card גלויה *nf* gloo|yah/-yot *(+of:* -yat).
(press) card תעודת־עיתונאי *nf* te'ood|at/-ot 'eetonay.
(visiting) card כרטיס־ביקור *nm* kartees/-ey beekoor.
card index כרטסת *nf* kart|eset/-asot.
cardboard קרטון *nm* karton/-eem *(pl+of:* -ey).
cardiac 1. קרדיאלי *adj* kardee'alee/-t; **2.** של חולי לב *adj* shel kholee lev.
cardinal 1. חשמן (church rank) *nm* khashman/-eem *(pl+of:* -ey); **2.** עיקרי (main) *adj* 'eekaree/-t.
cardinal number מספר יסודי *nm* meespar/-eem yesodee/-yeem.
(pack of) cards חבילת קלפים *nf* khaveel|at/-ot klafeem.
(to play) cards לשחק בקלפים *inf* lesakhek bee-klafeem; *pst* seekhek *etc*; *pres* mesakhek *etc*; *fut* yesakhek *etc*.
care 1. דאגה *nf* de'ag|ah/-ot *(+of:* da'g|at/-ot); **2.** טיפול (attendance) *nm* teepool/-eem *(pl+of:* -ey).
(not to) care לא אכפת lo eekhpat.
(to) care 1. לדאוג *inf* leed'og; *pst* da'ag; *pres* do'eg; *fut* yeed'ag; **2.** להיות אכפת לו (to be concerned) *inf* leehyot eekhpat lo/lah *(m/f)*; *pst* she-hayah *etc*; *pres* she- *etc*; she-yeehyeh *etc*.
(to take) care 1. להשגיח (supervise) *inf* lehashgee'akh; *pst* heeshgee'akh; *pres* mashgee'akh; *fut* yashgee'akh; **2.** להיזהר (be cautious) *inf* leheezaher; *pst & pres* neez'har; *fut* yeezaher.
career קריירה *nf* karyer|ah/-ot *(+of:* -at).
carefree חסר דאגות *adj* khas|ar/-rat de'agot.
careful זהיר *adj* zaheer/zeheerah.
(to be) careful להיזהר *inf* leheezaher; *pst & pres* neez'har; *fut* yeezaher.
carefully בזהירות bee-zeheeroot.
carefulness זהירות *nf* zeheeroot.
careless 1. חסר זהירות *adj* khas|ar/-rat zeheeroot; **2.** רשלן (negligent) *adj* rashlan/-eet.
carelessly 1. בפזיזות *adv* bee-fezeezo ot *(f=p)*; **2.** ברשלנות (negligently) *adv* be-rashlanoot.
carelessness 1. פזיזות *nf* pezeezoo|t/-yot; **2.** רשלנות (negligence) *nf* rashlanoo|t/-yot.
caress ליטוף *nm* leetoof/-eem *(pl+of:* -ey).
(to) caress ללטף *inf* lelatef; *pst* leetef; *pres* melatef; *fut* yelatef.
caretaker 1. משגיח *nmf* mashge e|'akh/-khah; **2.** ממלא מקום (deputy) *nmf* memale/-t makom.
carfare דמי נסיעה *nm pl* demey nesee'ah.
cargo מטען *nm* meet'an/-eem *(pl+of:* -ey).
cargo boat, ship אוניית משא *nf* onee|yat/-yot masa.
caricature קריקטורה *nf* kareekatoor|ah/-ot *(+of:* -at).
carload מלוא משאית *nm* melo/-'ot masa'eet.
carnal חושני *adj* khooshanee/-t.
carnation ציפורן *nm* tseepor|en/-neem *(pl+of:* -ney).
carnival קרנבל *nm* karnaval/-eem *(pl+of:* -ey).
carnivorous אוכל בשר *adj* okhel/-et basar.
carol מזמור *nm* meezmor/-eem *(pl+of:* -ey).
(to) carouse להשתכר *inf* leheeshtaker; *pst* heeshtaker; *pres* meeshtaker; *fut* yeeshtaker.
carpenter נגר *nm* nagar/-eem *(pl+of:* -ey).
carpentry נגרות *nf* nagaroot.
carpet שטיח *nm* shatee'akh/shteekh|eem *(pl+of:* -ey).
carriage כרכרה *nf* keerk|arah/-arot *(+of:* -eret/-erot)
carrier מוביל *nm* moveel/-eem *(pl+of:* -ey).
(aircraft) carrier נושאת מטוסים *nf* nos|et/-'ot metoseem.
(disease) carrier נושא מחלה *nm* nos|e/-'ey makhalah.
(mail) carrier 1. נושא מכתבים *nm* nos|e/-'ey meekhtaveem; **2.** דוור (postman) *nm* davar/-eem *(pl+of:* -ey).
carrot גזר *nm* gezer.
(to) carry לשאת *inf* laset; *pst* nasa; *pres* nose; *fut* yeesa.
(to) carry away ליטול *inf* leetol; *pst* natal; *pres* notel; *fut* yeetol.
(to) carry on 1. להמשיך (go on) *v inf* lehamsheekh; *pst* heemsheekh; *pres* mamsheekh; *fut* yamsheekh; **2.** להוסיף (continue) lehoseef; *pst* hoseef; *pres* moseef; *fut* yoseef.
(to) carry out לבצע *inf* levatse'a'; *pst* beetsa' *(b=v)*; *pres* mevatse'a'; *fut* yevatse'a'.
cart 1. עגלת־יד *nf* 'egl|at/-ot yad; **2.** דו־אופן (two-wheel cart) *nm* doo-ofan.
cartage דמי הובלה *nm pl* demey hovalah.
carter סבל עם הובלה *nm* sabal/-eem 'eem hovalah.
cartilage סחוס *nm* sekhoos.
carton תיבת קרטון *nf* teyv|at/-ot karton.
cartoon קריקטורה *nf* kareekatoor|ah/-ot *(+of:* -at).
cartoonist קריקטוריסט *nm* kareekatooreest/-eem.
cartridge 1. כדור *nm* kadoor/-eem *(pl+of:* -ey); **2.** מילוי (refill) *nm* meeloo|y/-yeem *(pl+of:* -yey).
cartridge belt חגורת כדורים *nf* khagor|at/-ot kadooreem.
cartridge box קופסת כדורים *nf* koofsa|t/-'ot kadooreem.
cartridge shell תרמיל *nm* tarmeel/-eem *(pl+of:* -ey).
(to) carve 1. לגלף *inf* legalef; *pst* geelef; *pres* megalef; *fut* yegalef; **2.** לחטוב (chop) *inf* lakhtov; *pst* khatav; *pres* khotev; *fut* yakhtov.
carver גלף *nm* galaf/-eem *(pl+of:* -ey).
carving גילוף *nm* geloof/-eem *(pl+of:* -ey).
carving knife 1. מאכלת *nf* ma'akhelet; **2.** סכין קצבים (butcher's knife) *nm* sakeen/-ey katsaveem.
cascade אשד מים *nm* eshed/ashdey mayeem.

case 1. מקרה *nm* meekr|eh/-reem (*pl+of:* -rey); **2.** תביעה משפטית (jurid.) *nf* tvee|'ah/-'ot meeshpatee|t/-yot.

(in any) case בכל מקרה be-khol meekreh.

(just in) case על כל צרה שלא תבוא 'al kol tsarah she-lo tavo.

(window) case מסגרת חלון *nf* meesger|et/-ot khalon/-ot.

(in) case that במקרה ש־ be-meekreh she-.

case work שיטת האירועים *nmf* sheetat ha-'eeroo'eem.

casement אגף חלון *nm* aga|f/-pey (*p=f*) khalon/-ot.

cash 1. מזומן (money) *nm* mezooman/-eem; **2.** קופה (box) *nf* koop|ah/-ot (*+of:* -at).

(to pay) cash לשלם במזומן *inf* leshalem bee-mezooman; *pst* sheelem *etc*; *pres* meshalem *etc*; *fut* yeshalem *etc*.

cash and carry שלם וקח shalem ve-kakh.

cash box קופה *nf* koop|ah/-ot (*+of:* -at).

cash on delivery מסירה נגד מזומנים *nf* meseerah neged mezoomaneem.

cash payment תשלום במזומנים *nm* tashloom/-eem bee-mezoomaneem.

cash register קופה רושמת *nf* koop|ah/-ot rosh|emet/-mot.

cashier 1. קופאי *nmf* koop|ay/-a'eet (*cpr* -a'ee); **2.** גזבר (treasurer) *nmf* geezbar/-eet.

cask 1. קסדה *nf* kasdah/kesadot (*+of:* kasdat); **2.** חבית (barrel) *nf* khavee|t/-yot.

casket ארון מתים *nf* aron/-ot meteem.

casserole 1. אלפס *nm* eelp|as/-aseem (*pl+of:* -esey); **2.** קדירה (pot) *nf* kedeyr|ah/-ot (*+of:* -at).

cassock גלימת כמרים *nf* gleem|at/-ot kemareem.

cast 1. להקה (theater) *nf* lahak|ah/-ot (*+of:* -at); **2.** תבנית גבס (mold) *nf* tavnee|t/-yot geves.

(to) cast לזרוק (throw) *inf* leezrok; *pst* zarak; *pres* zorek; *fut* yeezrok.

(to) cast a ballot להצביע בקלפי *inf* lehatsbee'a' be-kalpee; *pst* heetsbee'a' *etc*; *pres* matsbee'a' *etc*; *fut* yatsbee'a' *etc*.

(to) cast a statue לצקת פסל *inf* latseket pesel; *pst* yatsak *etc*; *pres* yotsek *etc*; *fut* yeetsok *etc*.

cast iron ברזל יציקה *nm* barzel yetseekah.

castanets קסטנייטות *nf pl* kastanyetot.

caste כת *nf* kat/keetot.

castle 1. טירה (fortress) *nf* teer|ah/-ot (*+of:* -at); **2.** ארמון (palace) *nm* armon/-ot.

castor oil שמן קיק *nm* shemen keek.

(to) castrate לסרס *inf* lesares; *pst* seres; *pres* mesares; *fut* yesares.

casual 1. לא מחייב *adj* lo mekhayev/-et; **2.** פשוט ונוח (simple) *adj* pashoot/peshootah ve-no|'akh/-khah.

casually כלאחר־יד kee-le-akhar-yad.

casualty נפגע *nm* neefg|a'/-a'eem (*pl+of:* -e'ey).

cat חתול *nm* khatool/-eem (*pl+of:* -ey).

catalogue 1. קטלוג *nm* katalog/-eem (*pl+of:* -ey); **2.** רשימה (list) *nf* resheem|ah/-ot (*+of:* -at).

cataract 1. מפל־מים *nm* map|al/-ley mayeem; **2.** ירוד (medic.) *nm* yarod.

catarrh נזלת *nf* nazelet.

catastrophe 1. קטסטרופה *nf* katastrof|ah/-ot (*+of:* -at); **2.** שואה (holocaust) *nf* sho|'ah/-'ot (*+of:* -'at).

catch 1. שלל *nm* shalal (*+of:* shelal); **2.** אחיזה (hold) *nf* akheez|ah/-ot (*+of:* -at).

(a good) catch שידוך מוצלח *nm* sheedookh mootslakh.

(to) catch לתפוס *nf inf* leetpos; *pst* tafas (*f=p*); *pres* tofes; *fut* yeetpos.

(to) catch a glimpse להציץ *inf* lehatseets; *pst* hetseets; *pres* metseets; *fut* yatseets.

(to) catch cold להצטנן *inf* leheetstanen; *pst* heetstanen; *pres* meetstanen; *fut* yeetstanen.

(to) catch on להתחיל להבין *inf* lehatkheel lehaveen; *pst* heetkheel *etc*; *pres* matkheel *etc*; *fut* yatkheel *etc*.

(to) catch one's eye למשוך תשומת לב *inf* leemshokh tesoomet-lev; *pst* mashakh *etc*; *pres* moshekh *etc*; *fut* yeemshokh *etc*.

catch phrase אימרת־כנף *nf* eemr|at/-ot kanaf.

catch question שאלת מלכודת *nf* she'el|at/-ot malkodet.

(to) catch up להשיג *inf* lehaseeg; *pst* heeseeg; *pres* maseeg; *fut* yaseeg.

catcher תופס *nm* tof|es/-seem (*pl+of:* -sey).

catching 1. תפיסה *nf* tfees|ah/-ot (*+of:* -at); **2.** מדביק (reaching) *adj* madbeek/-ah.

category סוג *nm* soog/-eem (*pl+of:* -ey).

(to) cater 1. לטפל *inf* letapel; *pst* teepel; *pres* metapel; *fut* yetapel; **2.** לספק שירותים *inf* lesapek sherooteem; *pst* seepek *etc*; *pres* mesapek *etc*; *fut* yesapek *etc*.

catering 1. קייטרינג *nm* keytereeng/-eem; **2.** שירותי אירוח (idem) *nf* sherootey eeroo'akh.

caterpillar זחל *nm* zakhal/zekhaleem (*pl+of:* zakhaley).

caterpillar tractor טרקטור זחל *nm* traktor/-ey zakhal.

cathedral קתדרלה *nf* katedral|ah/-ot (*+of:* -at).

cathode קתודה *nf* katod|ah/-ot (*+of:* -at).

cathode rays קרניים קתודיות *nf pl* karnayeem katodeeyot.

Catholic קתולי *adj & nmf* katolee/-t.

catsup 1. קצ'ופ *nm* ketchop; **2.** מיץ תבלין *nm* meets tavleen.

cattle בקר *nm* bakar.

cattle raising גידול בקר *nm* geedool bakar.

cattle ranch חוות בקר *nf* khav|at/-ot bakar.

cattleman בוקר *nm* bok|er/-reem (*pl+of:* -rey).

cattleraiser מגדל בקר *nm* megad|el/-ley bakar.

caucus כנס מפלגתי *nm* ken|es/-aseem meeflagtee/-yeem.

cauldron קלחת *nf* kalakh|at/-ot.

cauliflower כרובית *nf* krooveet.

cause 1. סיבה *nf* seeb|ah/-ot (*+of:* -at); **2.** מטרה (goal) *nf* matar|ah/-ot (*+of:* matr|at/-ot).

(to) cause לגרום *inf* leegrom; *pst* garam; *pres* gorem; *fut* yeegrom.

caustic 1. צורב *adj* tsorev/-et; **2.** עוקצני *adj* 'oktsanee/-t.

(to) cauterize לצרוב *inf* leetsrov; *pst* tsarav; *pres* tsorev; *fut* yeetsrov.

caution זהירות *nf* zeheeroo|t/-yot.

(to) caution להזהיר *inf* lehaz'heer; *pst* heez'heer; *pres* maz'heer; *fut* yaz'heer.

cautious זהיר *adj* zaheer/zeheerah.

cavalcade שיירת רוכבים *nf* shay|eret/-rot rokhveem.

cavalier 1. אביר *nm* abeer/-eem (*pl+of:* -ey); **2.** בן־לוויה (escort) *nmf* ben/bat levayah.

cavalry חיל פרשים *nm* kheyl/-ot parasheem.

cave מערה *nf* me'ar|ah/-ot (*+of:* -at).

cave in התמוטטות *nf* heetmotetoo|t/-yot.

(to) cave in להתמוטט *v inf* leheetmotet; *pst* heetmotet; *pres* meetmotet; *fut* yeetmotet.

cavern מערה גדולה *nf* me'ar|ah/-ot gedol|ah/-ot.

cavity 1. חור *nm* khor/-eem (*pl+of:* -ey); **2.** חלל *nm* khalal/-eem (*pl+of:* -ey).

caw צריחת עורב *nf* tsreekh|at/-ot 'or|ev/-veem.

(to) cease 1. לחדול *inf* lakhdol; *pst* khadal; *pres* khadel; *fut* yakhdol; **2.** להפסיק *inf* lehafseek; *pst* heefseek; *pres* mafseek; *fut* yafseek.

cease-fire הפסקת אש *nf* hafsak|at/-ot esh.

ceaseless בלתי פוסק *adj* beeltee posek/-et.

cedar ארז *nm* erez/arazeem (*pl+of:* arzey).

(to) cede לוותר *inf* levater; *pst* veeter; *pres* mevater; *fut* yevater.

ceiling תקרה *nf* teekr|ah/-ot (*+of:* -at).

ceiling price מחיר מרבי *nm* mekheer/-eem merabee/-yeem.

(to) celebrate לחוג *inf* lakhog; *pst* khagag; *pres* khogeg; *fut* yakhog.

celebrated 1. נודע *adj* nod|a'/-a'at; **2.** מפורסם (famed) *adj* mefoors|am/-emet

celebration 1. חגיגה (feast) *nf* khageeg|ah/-ot (*+of:* -at); **2.** טקס (ceremony) *nm* tek|es/-aseem (*pl+of:* teeksey).

celebrity אישיות מפורסמת *nf* eesheeyoot mefoorsemet (*nm & pl:* eesheem mefoorsameem).

celery 1. סלרי *nm* seleree; **2.** כרפס *nm* karpas.

celestial שמימי *adj* shmeymee/-t.

celibacy רווקות *nf* ravakoo|t/-yot.

cell 1. תא *nm* ta/-'eem (*pl+of:* -'ey); **2.** חדרון (room) *nm* khadron/-eem (*pl+of:* -ey).

cellar מרתף *nm* martef/-eem (*pl+of:* -ey).

celluloid צלולואיד *nm* tselooloyd.

cement 1. מלט (concrete) *nm* melet; **2.** צמנט *nm* tsement; **3.** דבק (glue) *nm* devek.

(to) cement 1. לחזק במלט (mortar) *inf* lekhazek be-melet; *pst* kheezek *etc*; *pres* mekhazek *etc*; *fut* yekhazek *etc*; **2.** לחזק בדבק (glue) *inf* lekhazek (*etc*) be-devek.

cemetery 1. בית עלמין *nm* bet/batey 'almeen; **2.** בית קברות (graveyard) *nm* bet/batey kvarot.

censor צנזור *nm* tsenzor/-eem (*pl+of:* -ey).

censorship צנזורה *nf* tsenzoor|ah (*+of:* -at).

censure גינוי *nm* geenoo|y/-yeem (*pl+of:* -yey).

(to) censure 1. לגנות *inf* leganot; *pst* geenah; *pres* meganeh; *fut* yeganeh; **2.** להוקיע (denounce) *inf* lehokee'a'; *pst* hokee'a'; *pres* mokee'a'; *fut* yokee'a'.

census 1. מיפקד *nm* meefk|ad/-adeem (*pl+of:* -edey); **2.** מיפקד אוכלוסים (population census) *nm* meefk|ad/-edey ookhlooseem.

cent סנט *nm* sent/-eem.

(per) cent 1. אחוז *nm* akhooz/-eem (*pl+of:* -ey); **2.** למאה (per hundred) le-me'ah.

centennial 1. יובל המאה *nm* yovel ha-me'ah; **2.** של יובל המאה *adj* shel yovel ha-me'ah.

center מרכז *nm* merk|az/-azeem (*pl+of:* -ezey).

centigrade מעלות צלסיוס *nf pl* ma'alot tselseeyoos.

centimeter 1. סנטימטר *nm* senteemet|er/-reem; **2.** ס"מ (*abbr.acr*) *nm* senteemet|er/-reem.

centipede 1. נדל *nm* nadal/nedaleem (*+of:* nedal/needley); **2.** מרבה־רגליים (*synon. of* 1) *nm* marbe|h/-y raglayeem.

central 1. מרכזי *adj* merkazee/-t; **2.** מרכזת (telephone exchange) *nf* meerk|ezet/-azot.

(to) centralize 1. למרכז *vt inf* lemarkez; *pst* meerkez; *pres* memarkez; *fut* yemarkez; **2.** להתמרכז *v rfl inf* leheetmarkez; *pst* heetmarkez; *pres* meetmarkez; *fut* yeetmarkez.

centrifugal צנטריפוגלי *adj* tsentreefoogalee/-t.

centripetal צנטריפטלי *adj* tsentreepetalee/-t.

century 1. מאת שנים *nf* me'at/me'ot shaneem; **2.** מאה *nf* me'ah/me'ot.

ceramic 1. קרמי *adj* keramee/-t; **2.** של חרס *adj* shel kheres.

ceramics קרמיקה *nf* kerameek|ah/-ot (*+of:* -at).

cereal 1. דגן *nm* dagan/deganeem (*pl+of:* degney); **2.** תבואה (grain) *nf* tvoo|'ah/-'ot (*+of:* -'at); **3.** דייסת גרגרי דגן (porridge) *nf* daysat/-ot gargerey dagan.

ceremonial 1. טקסי *adj* teeksee/-t; **2.** חגיגי festive *adj* khageegee/-t.

ceremonious טקסי *adj* teeksee/-t.

ceremony טקס *nm* tek|es/-aseem (*pl+of:* teeksey).

certain 1. מסוים (particular) *adj* mesoo|yam/-yemet; **2.** ודאי (sure) *adj* vada'ee/-t; **3.** בטוח (secure) *adj* batoo'akh/betookhah.

certainly 1. בוודאי (of course) *adv* be-vaday; **2.** בטח (surely) *[slang] adv* betakh.

certainty ודאות *nf* vada'oo|t/-yot.

certificate 1. אישור (confirmation) *nm* eeshoor/-eem (*pl+of:* -ey); **2.** תעודה (attestation) *nf* te'ood|ah/-ot (*+of:* -at).

certificate of birth תעודת לידה *nf* te'ood|at/-ot leydah.

certificate of death תעודת מוות *nf* te'ood|at/-ot mavet.

certificate of deposit תעודת פיקדון *nf* te'ood|at/-ot peekadon.

certification 1. אישור *nm* eeshoor/-eem (*pl+of:* -ey); **2.** הסמכה (graduation) *nf* hasmakh|ah/-ot (*+of:* -at).

certified public accountant רואה חשבון מוסמך *nm* ro'eh/ro'ey kheshbon moosmakh/-eem.

(to) certify לאשר *inf* le'asher; *pst* eesher; *pres* me'asher; *fut* ye'asher.

certitude 1. ודאות *nf* vada'oot; **2.** ביטחון (assurance) *nm* beet|akhon (*+of:* -khon).

cervix צוואר הרחם *nm* tsavar ha-rekhem.

cessation הפסקה *nf* hafsak|ah/-ot (*+of:* -at).

cesspool בור שופכים *nm* bor/-ot shofakheem.

chafe 1. שפשוף *nm* sheefshoof/-eem (*pl+of:* -ey); **2.** דלקת (inflammation) *nf* dal|eket/-akot.

chaff 1. מוץ *nm* mots; **2.** חמידת לצון (banter) *nf* khameedat/-ot latson

chagrin 1. דיכאון (depression) *nm* dee|ka'on/-kh'onot (*kh=k*; *+of:* deekh'on); **2.** אכזבה (disappointment) *nf* akhzav|ah/-ot (*+of:* -at).

chagrined 1. מדוכא *adj* medook|a/-et; **2.** מאוכזב (disappointed) *adj* me'ookhz|av/-evet

chain 1. שרשרת (ornament) *nf* sharsh|eret/-arot; **2.** שרשרת (for convicts) *nf* sharsher|et/-a'ot.

chain of generations שושלת הדורות *nf* shoshelet ha-dorot.

chain of mountains שרשרת הרים *nf* sharsher|et/-ot hareem.

chain reaction תגובת שרשרת *nf* tegoov|at/-ot sharsheret.

chain smoker מעשן בשרשרת *nmf* me'ashen/-et be-sharsheret.

chain store רשת חנויות *nf* reshet khanooyot.

chair כיסא *nm* kees|e/-'ot (*pl+of:* ot).

(arm)chair 1. כורסה *nf* koors|ah/-ot (*+of:* -at); **2.** כיסא־ידות *nm* keees|e/-'ot yadot.

(easy) chair כיסא מרגוע *nm* kees|e/-'ot margo'a'.

(folding) chair כיסא מתקפל *nm* kees|e/-'ot meetkap|el/-leem.

(rocking) chair כסנוע *nm* kesno|'a'/-'eem (*pl+of:* -'ey).

chair lift רכבל *nm* rakevel.

chairman 1. יושב־ראש *nmf* yoshev/-et rosh; **2.** יו"ר (*acr of* 1) yor/-eem (*pl+of:* -ey).

chairmanship ראשות *nf* rashoot.

chalice גביע *nm* gavee'a'/gvee|'eem (*pl+of:* -'ey).

chalk גיר *nm* geer/-eem (*pl+of:* -ey).

(to) chalk out 1. למחוק *inf* leemkhok; *pst* makhak; *pres* mokhek; *fut* yeemkhak; **2.** להוציא מכלל חשבון (exclude) *inf* lehotsee mee-klal kheshbon; *pst* hotsee *etc*; *pres* motsee *etc*; *fut* yotsee *etc*.

chalky 1. גירי *adj* geeree/-t; **2.** דמוי־גיר (chalklike) *adj* demoo|y/-yat geer.

challenge אתגר *nm* etg|ar/-areem (*pl+of:* -erey).

(to) challenge 1. להתמודד עם (compete) *inf* leheetmoded 'eem; *pst* heetmoded 'eem; *pst* meetmoded 'eem; *fut* yeetmoded 'eem; **2.** לחלוק על (contest) *inf* lakhalok 'al; khalak 'al; *pres* kholek 'al; *fut* yakhalok 'al.

chamber 1. לשכה *nf* leeshkah/leshakhot (*kh=k*; *+of:* leesh|kat/-khot); **2.** חדר (room) *nm* kheder/khadareem (*pl+of:* khadrey).

chamber music מוסיקה קמרית *nf* mooseekah kamereet.

chamber of commerce לשכת מסחר *nf* leesh|kat/-khot (*kh=k*) mees'khar.

chambermaid חדרנית *nf* khadranee|t/-yot.

chameleon זיקית *nf* zeekee|t/-yot.

chamois עור רך *nm* 'or rakh.

champagne שמפניה *nf* shampanyah.

champion 1. אלוף *nm* aloof/-eem (*pl+of:* -ey); **2.** לוחם למען (fighter for) *nm* lokh|em/-ameem le-ma'an.

championship אליפות *nf* aleefoo|t/-yot.

chance 1. מקרה *nm* meekreh/-eem (*pl+of:* -ey); **2.** הזדמנות (occasion) *nf* heezdamnoo|t/-yot; **3.** מזל (fortune) *nm* mazal.

(by) chance במקרה *adv* be-meekreh.

(game of) chance מישחק מזל *nm* meeskhak/-ey mazal.

(to run a) chance להסתכן *inf* leheestaken; *pst* heestaken; *pres* meestaken; *fut* yeestaken.

(to) chance לנסות מזל *inf* lenasot mazal; *pst* neesah *etc*; *pres* menaseh *etc*; *fut* yenaseh *etc*.

chancellor נגיד *nm* nageed/negeedeem.

chandelier נברשת *nf* neevr|eshet/-ashot.

change 1. שינוי (alteration) *nm* sheenoo|y/-yeem (*pl+of:* -yey); **2.** עודף (remainder money) *nm* 'od|ef/-feem (*pl+of:* -fey).

(small) change 1. כסף קטן *nm* kesef katan; **2.** פרוטרוט *nm* protrot.

(to) change 1. לשנות *inf* leshanot; *pst* sheenah; *pres* meshaneh; *fut* yeshaneh; **2.** לפרוט *inf* leefrot; *pst* parat (*p=f*); *pres* poret; *fut* yeefrot.

(to) change clothes 1. להחליף בגדים *inf* lehakhleef begadeem; *pst* hekhleef *etc*; *pres* makhleef *etc*; *fut* yakhleef *etc*; **2.** להתחלף *[colloq.] inf* leheetkhalef; *pst* heetkhalef; *pres* meetkhalef; *fut* yeetkhalef.

changeable עשוי להשתנות *adj* 'asoo|y/-yah leheeshtanot.

channel 1. ערוץ (radio, tv) *nm* 'aroots/-eem (*pl+of:* -ey); **2.** תעלה (maritime) *nf* te'al|ah/-ot (*+of:* -at); **3.** צינור (pipeline) *nm* tseenor/-ot.

chant 1. מזמור meezmor/-eem (*pl+of:* -ey); **2.** זמרה (singing) *nf* zeemr|ah/-ot (*+of:* -at).

(to) chant לזמר *inf* lezamer; *pst* zeemer; *pres* mezamer; *fut* yezamer.

chaos תוהו ובוהו *nm pl* tohoo va-vohoo.

chaotic מבולבל *adj* mevoolb|al/-elet.

chap 1. בחור (guy) *nm* bakhoor/-eem (*pl+of:* -ey); **2.** בקיע (crevice) *nm* bekee|'a'/-'eem (*pl+of:* -'ey).

(fine) chap בחור כהלכה *nm* bakhoor/-eem ka-halakhah.

chapel כנסייה קטנה *nf* knesee|yah/-yot ketan|ah/-ot.

chaperon בת־לוויה *nf* bat/benot levayah.

chaplain 1. איש דת *nm* eesh/anshey dat; **2.** קצין דת (army) *nm* ketseen/-ey dat.

chapter 1. פרק (of book) *nm* perek/prakeem (*pl+of:* peerkey); **2.** סניף (of organization) *nm* sneef/-eem (*pl+of:* -ey).

(to) char 1. לחרוך (scorch) *inf* lakhrokh; *pst* kharakh; *pres* khorekh; *fut* yakhrokh; **2.** לעבוד יומית (work) *inf* la'avod yomeet; *pst* 'avad *etc*; *pres* 'oved *etc*; *fut* ya'avod *etc*.

character 1. אופי (psych.) *nm* ofee; **2.** דמות (theater) *nf* demoo|t/-yot.

characteristic מאפיין *nm* me'afyen/-eem (*pl+of:* -ey); *adj* me'afyen/-et.

(to) characterize לאפיין *inf* le'afyen; *pst* eefyen; *pres* me'afyen; *fut* ye'afyen.

charcoal 1. פחם עץ *nm* pakham/pakhamey 'ets; **2.** פחם לציור *nm* pekham le-tseeyoor.

charcoal drawing ציור פחם *nm* tseeyoor/-ey pekham.

charge 1. מחיר (price) *nm* mekheer/-eem (*pl+of:* -ey); **2.** אישום (jurid.) *nm* eeshoom/-eem (*pl+of:* -ey); **3.** תפקיד (role) *nm* tafkeed/-eem (*pl+of:* -ey).

(to) charge 1. לגבות מחיר (price) *inf* leegbot mekheer; *pst* gavah *(v=b) etc; pres* goveh *etc; fut* yeegbeh *etc;* **2.** להאשים (indict) *inf* leha'asheem; *pst* he'esheem; *pres* ma'asheem; *fut* ya'asheem; **3.** להטיל תפקיד (role) *inf* lehateel tafkeed; *pst* heeteel *etc; pres* mateel *etc; fut* yateel *etc.*

(to be in) charge להיות ממונה על *inf* leehyot memoon|eh/-ah *(m/f)* 'al; *pst* hayah *etc; pres* hoo *etc; fut* yeehyeh *etc.*

charge account חשבון הקפה *nm* kheshbon/-ot hakafah.

(to) charge with murder להאשים ברצח *inf* leha'asheem be-retsakh; *pst* he'esheem *etc; pres* ma'asheem *etc; fut* ya'asheem *etc.*

charge d'affaires ממונה על שגרירות *nmf* memoon|eh/-ah 'al shagreeroot.

(battery) charger מטען סוללות *nm* mat'en/-ey solelot.

chariot מרכבה *nf* merkav|ah/-ot (*+of:* meerkevet).

charitable של צדקה *adj* shel tsedakah.

charity 1. צדקה *nf* tsedak|ah/-ot (*+of:* tseedkat); **2.** חסד (grace) *nm* khesed/khas|adeem (*pl+of:* -dey).

charlatan נוכל *nm* nokh|el/-leem (*pl+of:* -ley); *adj* nokhel/-et.

charm 1. חן *nm* khen; **2.** קמיע (amulet) *nm* kamey'a'/keme'|eem (*pl+of:* -'ey).

charming מקסים *adj* makseem/-ah.

chart סרטוט *nm* seertoot/-eem (*pl+of:* -ey).

(to) chart a course לתכנן מסלול *inf* letakhnen maslool; *pst* teekhnen *etc; pres* metakhnen *etc; fut* yetakhnen *etc.*

charter 1. תעודת רישום חברה *nf* te'ood|at/-ot reeshoom khevrah/khavarot; **2.** צ'רטר *nm* charter/-eem (*pl+of:* -ey).

charter member חבר מייסד mm khaver/-eem meyas|ed/-deem.

chase 1. מירוץ אחר *nm* merots/-eem akhar; **2.** רדיפה (pursuit) *nf* redeef|ah/-ot (*+of:* -at).

(to) chase away 1. לגרש (expel) *inf* legaresh; *pst* geresh; *pres* megaresh; *fut* yegaresh; **2.** לפזר (disperse) *inf* lefazer; *pst* peezer *(p=f); pres* mefazer; *fut* yefazer.

chasm תהום *nf* tehom/-ot.

chaste 1. צנוע (modest) *adj* tsanoo'a'/tsnoo'ah; **2.** בתול (virgin) *adj & nmf* batool/betoolah.

(to) chastise 1. לייסר *inf* leyaser; *pst* yeeser; *pres* meyaser; *fut* yeyaser; **2.** לנזוף (admonish) *inf* leenzof; *pst* nazaf; *pres* nozef; *fut* yeenzof.

chastisement 1. ענישה *nf* 'aneesh|ah/-ot (*+of:* -at); **2.** נזיפה (rebuke) *nf* nezeef|ah/-ot (*+of:* -at).

chastity 1. בתולים (virginity) *nm pl* betool|eem (*pl+of:* -ey); **2.** צניעות (modesty) *nf* tsnee'oot; **3.** פרישות מינית (sexual abstinence) *nf* preeshoot meeneet.

chat שיחה קלה *nf* seekh|ah/-ot kal|ah/-ot.

(to) chat לשוחח *inf* lesokhe'akh; *pst* sokhakh; *pres* mesokhe'akh; *fut* yesokhakh.

chattels מיטלטלים *nm pl* meetaltel|eem (*pl+of:* -ey).

chatter פטפוט *nm* peetpoot/-eem (*pl+of:* -ey).

(to) chatter 1. לקשקש *inf* lekashkesh; *pst* keeshkesh; *pres* mekashkesh; *fut* yekashkesh; **2.** לפטפט (prattle) *inf* lefatpet; *pst* peetpet *(f=p); pres* mefatpet; *fut* yefatpet.

chauffeur נהג *nm* nehag/-eem (*+of:* nahag/-ey).

cheap זול *adj* zol/-ah.

(dirt) cheap בזיל הזול *adv* be-zeel ha-zol.

(to feel) cheap להרגיש כנקלה *inf* lehargeesh ke-neekleh; *pst* heergeesh *etc; pres* margeesh *etc; fut* yargeesh *etc.*

(to) cheapen להוזיל *inf* lehozeel; *pst* hozeel; *pres* mozeel; *fut* yozeel.

cheaply בזול *adv* be-zol.

cheapness זולות *nf* zoloo|t/-yot.

(to) cheat 1. לרמות *inf* leramot; *pst* reemah; *pres* merameh; *fut* yerameh; **2.** להערים על (outsmart) *inf* leha'areem 'al; *pst* he'ereem 'al; *pres* ma'areem 'al; *fut* ya'areem 'al.

check 1. שיק *nm* shek/-eem (*cpr* chek/-eem); **2.** המחאה (*synon.* of 1) *nf* hamkha|'ah/-'ot (*+of:* -'at); **3.** ביקורת (control) *nf* beekor|et/-ot; **4.** בדיקה (test) *nf* bedeek|ah/-ot (*+of:* -at).

(to) check 1. לבדוק *inf* leevdok; *pst* badak *(b=v); pres* bodek; *fut* yeevdok; **2.** לרסן (restrain) *inf* lerasen; *pst* reesen; *pres* merasen; *fut* yerasen; **3.** לעצור (stop) *inf* la'atsor; *pst* 'atsar; *pres* 'otser; *fut* ya'atsor.

(to) check in לשכור חדר במלון *inf* leeskor kheder be-malon; *pst* sakhar *(kh=k) etc; pres* sokher *etc; fut* yeeskor *etc.*

(to) check out לפנות חדר במלון *inf* lefanot kheder be-malon; *pst* peenah *(p=f) etc; pres* mefaneh *etc; fut* yefaneh *etc.*

check point תחנת ביקורת *nf* takhn|at/-ot beekoret.

check-up בדיקת בריאות כללית *nf* bedeekat/-ot bree'oot klalee|t/-yot.

checkbook פנקס שיקים *nm* peenk|as/-esey shekeem.

checkerboard לוח "דמקה"*[colloq.] nm* loo|'akh/-khot "Damkah".

checkered 1. מתושבץ *adj* metooshb|ats/-etset; **2.** מגוון (variegated) *adj* megoovan/-enet.

checkers משחק "דמקה" *nm* mees'khak/-ey "Damkah".

checkmate מט בשחמט *nm* mat be-shakhmat.

checkroom מלתחה *nf* meltakh|ah/-ot (*+of:* -at).

cheek לחי *nf* lekh|ee/-ayayeem (*pl+of:* -yey).

cheekbone עצם הלחי *nm* 'etsem/'atsmot ha-lekh|ee/-ayayeem.

cheeky חצוף *adj* khatsoof/-ah.

cheer 1. עידוד *nm* 'eedood/-eem (*pl+of:* -ey); **2.** תרועה (shout) *nf* troo|'ah/-'ot (*+of:* -'at).

(to) cheer להריע ל־ *inf* leharee'a' le-; *pst* heree'a' le-; *pres* meree'a' le-; *fut* yaree'a' le-.

(to) cheer up 1. להתעודד *v rfl inf* leheet'oded; *pst* heet'oded; *pres* meet'oded; *fut* yeet'oded; **2.** לעודד (encourage) *vt inf* le'oded; *pst* 'oded; *pres* me'oded; *fut* ye'oded.

cheerful עליז *adj* 'aleez/-ah.

cheerfully ברוח טובה *adv* be-roo'akh tovah.

cheerfulnesss 1. שמחה *nf* seemkhah; **2.** עליצות (gaiety) *nf* 'aleetsoo|t/-yot.

cheerio! !היה שלום *v imp nmf* heyeh/heyee shalom!

cheerless קודר *adj* koder/-et.

cheers! !הידד *interj* heydad!

cheese גבינה *nf* gveen|ah/-ot (*+of:* -at).

(cottage) cheese גבינת קוטג׳ *nf* gveen|at/-ot kotej.

cheesecake 1. עוגת גבינה *nf* 'oog|at/-ot gveenah; **2.** תצלום נשי מושך (attractive female photo) tatsloom/-ey goof nashee moshekh.

chef 1. טבח ראשי (chief cook) *nm* tabakh/-eem rashee/-yeem; **2.** שף *nm* shef/-eem.

chemical 1. כימי *adj* keemee/-t; **2.** חומר כימי (chemical stuff) *nm* khom|er/-areem keemee/-yeem.

chemist 1. כימאי *nmf* keema|y (*cpr* keema'ee/-t); **2.** רוקח (pharmacist) *nmf* rok|e'akh/-akhat (*pl+of:* -khey).

chemistry כימיה *nf* keem|yah/-yot (*+of:* -yat).

(to) cherish להוקיר *inf* lehokeer; *pst* hokeer; *pres* mokeer; *fut* yokeer.

cherry דובדבן *nm* doovdevan/-eem (*pl+of:* -ey).

cherry tree עץ דובדבן *nm* 'ets/'atsey doovdevan.

chess שח *nm* shakh.

chessboard 1. לוח שח *nm* loo|'akh/-khot shakh; **2.** לוח ״דמקה״ (checkers) *nm* loo'akh/-khot "Damkah".

chest 1. חזה (part of body) *nm* khaz|eh/-ot; **2.** שידה (tallboy) *nf* sheed|ah/-ot (*+of:* -at); **3.** תיבה (box) *f* teyv|ah/-ot (*+of:* -at).

chestnut 1. ערמון *nm* 'armon/-eem (*pl+of:* -ey); **2.** ערמוני (color) *adj* 'armonee/-t.

chestnut tree עץ ערמון 'ets/'atsey 'armon.

(to) chew ללעוס *inf* leel'os; *pst* la'as; *pres* lo'es; *fut* yeeel'as.

chewing gum 1. מסטיק *[colloq.] nm* masteek/-eem; **2.** גומי־לעיסה *nm* goomee-le'eesah.

chic 1. שיק *nm & adj* sheek; **2.** אופנתי (fashionable) *adj* ofnatee/-t.

chicanery גניבת־דעת *nf* gneyv|at/-ot da'at.

chick 1. אפרוח (young bird) *nf* efro|'akh/-kheem (*pl+of:* -khey); **2.** בחורה (girl) *nf* bakhoor|ah/-ot (*+of:* -at); **3.** ״חתיכה״ (*[slang]:* "doll") *nf* khateekh|ah/-ot (*+of:* -at).

chick-pea חומוס *nm* khoomoos.

chicken תרנגולת *nf* tarnegol|et/-ot.

chicken coop לול *nm* lool/-eem (*pl+of:* -ey).

chicken-hearted מוג־לב *adj* moog/-at lev.

chicken pox אבעבועות־רוח *nf pl* ava'boo'ot roo'akh.

chicory עולש *nm* 'ol|esh/-asheem (*pl+of:* -shey).

(to) chide 1. להציק *inf* lehatseek; *pst* hetseek; *pres* metseek; *fut* yatseek; **2.** לגעור (scold) *inf* leeg'or; *pst* ga'ar; *pres* go'er; *fut* yeeg'ar.

chief 1. ראש (head) *nm* rosh/-eem (*pl+of:* -ey); **2.** מנהל (manager) *nm* mena|hel/-haleem (*pl+of:* -haley); **3.** מנהיג (leader) *nm* manheeg/-eem (*pl+of:* -ey).

(commander in) chief מפקד עליון *nm* mefaked 'elyon.

chief clerk פקיד ראשי *nmf* pakeed/pekeedah rashee/-t.

chief editor, (editor-in-)chief עורך ראשי *nmf* 'or|ekh/-et rashee/-t.

chief justice 1. זקן השופטים *nm* zekan ha-shofteem; **2.** נשיא בית המשפט העליון (in Israel: President of the Supreme Court) *nm* nesee bet-ha-meeshpat ha-'elyon.

chief of staff ראש מטה *nm* rosh mateh.

Chief of the General Staff 1. ראש המטה הכללי *nm* rosh ha-mateh ha-klalee; **2.** רמטכ״ל (*acr of* 1) *nm* ramatkal/-eem (*pl+of:* -ey).

chiefly בעיקר *adv* be-'eekar.

chieftain 1. ראש שבט *nm* rosh/-ey shevet/shvateem; **2.** ראש קבוצה (team captain) *nm* rosh/-ey kvoots|ah/-ot.

chiffon 1. אריג־משי *nm* areeg/-ey meshee; **2.** זהורית (rayon yarn) *nf* zehoreet.

chignon קוקו *[colloq.] nm* kookoo/-'eem.

child 1. ילד *nmf* yeled/yaldah (*pl:* yelad|eem/-ot; *pl+of:* yald|ey/-ot); **2.** תינוק (baby) *nmf* teenok/-et (*pl:* -ot); **3.** ולד (infant) *nm* vlad/-ot.

(with) child בהריון *adv* be-herayon.

child welfare טובת הילד *nf* tovat ha-yeled.

childbirth לידה *nf* leyd|ah/-ot (*+of:* -at).

childhood ילדות *nf* yaldoot.

childish ילדותי *adj* yaldootee/-t.

childless ערירי *adj* 'areeree/-t.

childlike כילד *adv* ke-yeled.

Children of Israel בני ישראל *nm pl* beney yeesra'el.

child's play משחק ילדים *nm* meeskhak/-ey yeladeem.

Chilean צ׳יליאני *nmf & adj* cheelyanee/-t.

chili פלפלת הגינה *nmf* peelpelet ha-geenah.

chill 1. קור *nm* kor; **2.** צינה (cold) *nf* tseen|ah/-ot (*+of:* -at); **3.** צמרמורת (shiver) *nf* tsmarmoret.

chilled מקורר *adj* mekor|ar/-eret.

chilly קריר *adj* kareer/kreerah.

chime צלצול פעמון *nm* tseeltsool/-ey pa'amon/-eem.

chimney ארובה *nf* aroob|ah/-ot (*+of:* -at).

chimpanzee קוף שימפנזה kof/-ey sheempanzeh.

chin סנטר *nm* santer/-eem (*pl+of:* -ey).

china חרסינה *nf* kharseen|ah/-ot.

chinaware כלי חרסינה *nm pl* kley kharseenah.

Chinese סיני *nm* seenee/-t.

chink 1. סדק *nm* sedek/sdakeem (*pl+of:* seedkey); **2.** נקישה (knock) *nf* nekeesh|ah/-ot (*+of:* -at).

chip 1. שבב *nm* shvav/-eem (*pl+of:* shvavey); **2.** אסימון־משחק (token) *nm* aseemon/-ey mees'khak.

(to) chip in להשתתף *inf* leheeshtatef; *pst* heeshtatef; *pres* meeshtatef; *fut* yeeshtatef.

chipmunk סנאי עקוד *nm* sna'ee/-m 'ak|od/-oodeem.

chiropodist 1. מומחה לטיפול ברגליים *nmf* moomkh|eh/-eet le-teepool be-raglayeem; **2.** פדיקוריסט *nmf* pedeekyooreest/-eet.

chiropractor מומחה לחילוץ עצמות *nmf* moomkh|eh/-eet le-kheeloots 'atsamot.

chirp ציוץ *nm* tseeyoots/-eem (*pl+of:* -ey).

(to) chirp לצייץ *inf* letsayets; *pst* tseeyets; *pres* metsayets; *fut* yetsayets.

chisel מפסלת *nf* mafs|elet/-alot (*pl+of:* -elot).

chivalrous אבירי *adj* abeeree/-t.
chivalry אבירות *nf* abeeroo|t/-yot.
chlorine כלור *nm* klor.
chloroform כלורופורם *nm* kloroform.
chockful גדוש *adj* gadoosh/gedooshah.
chocolate שוקולד *nm* shokol|ad/-adeem.
choice 1. מיבחר *nm* meevkhar/-eem (*pl+of:* -ey); **2.** ברירה (selection) *nf* brer|ah/-ot (*+of:* -at).
(with no) choice בלית ברירה *adv* be-let brerah.
choir מקהלה *nf* mak'hel|ah/-ot (*+of:* -at).
choke 1. חנק *nm* khenek; **2.** משנק (of a car) *nm* mashnek/-eem (*pl+of:* -ey)
(to) choke להחניק *inf* lehakhneek; *pst* hekhneek; *pres* makhneek; *fut* yakhneek.
cholera 1. חולירע *nf* kholeera'; **2.** כולירה *nf* kolerah.
cholestrol כולסטרול *nm* kolesterol.
(to) choose 1. לבחור *inf* leevkhor; *pst* bakhar *(b=v)*; *pres* bokher; *fut* yeevkhar; **2.** לברור (select) *inf* leevror; *pst* berar *(b=v)*; *pres* mevarer; *fut* yevarer.
chop 1. נתח *nm* netakh/-eem (*pl+of:* neetkhey); **2.** צלע (rib) *nf* tsela'/-ot (*pl+of:* tsal'ot).
chopper 1. מטחנת־בשר (meat mincer) *nf* matkhen|at/-ot basar; **2.** מסוק (helicopter) *nm* masok/-eem (*pl+of:* -ey).
choppy רוגש *adj* rogesh/-et.
chopsticks מקלות אכילה לאוכל סיני *nm pl* maklot akheelah le-okhel seenee.
choral 1. למקהלה *adj* le-mak'helah; **2.** הימנון דתי (relig. hymn) *nm* heemnon/-eem datee/-yeem.
chord מיתר *nm* meytar/-eem (*pl+of:* meytrey).
chore 1. עמל (toil) *nm* 'amal; **2.** טירחה (trouble) teerkh|ah/-ot (*+of:* -at).
choreography כוריאוגרפיה *nf* koreograf|yah/-yot (*+of:* -yat).
chorus 1. מקהלה *nf* mak'hel|ah/-ot (*+of:* -at); **2.** פזמון חוזר (refrain) *nm* peezmon khozer.
chosen נבחר *adj* neevkh|ar/-eret.
chowder מרק־דגים *nm* merak dageem.
(to) christen להטביל לנצרות *inf* lehatbeel le-natsroot; *pst* heetbeel *etc*; *pres* matbeel *etc*; *fut* yatbeel *etc*.
Christian נוצרי *nmf* notsree/-yah.
Christian name שם פרטי *nm* shem/-ot pratee/-yeem.
Christianity הנצרות *nf* ha-natsroot.
Christmas חג המולד *nm* khag ha-molad.
(Merry) Christmas! חג־מולד שמח! khag molad same'akh!
Christmas card כרטיס־ברכה לחג המולד *nm* kartees/-ey brakhah le-khag ha-molad.
Christmas Eve ערב חג המולד *nm* 'erev khag ha-molad.
Christmas tree עץ אשוח *nm* 'ets/'atsey ashoo'akh.
chrome, chromium כרום *nm* krom.
chromosome כרומוזום *nm* kromozom/-eem (*pl+of:* -ey).
chronic כרוני *adj* kronee/-t.
chronicle 1. סיפור תולדות *nm* seepoor/-ey toladot; **2.** העלאת זכרונות *nf* ha'ala|'at/-'ot zeekhronot.
(to) chronicle לרשום למזכרת *inf* leershom le-mazkeret; *pres* rasham *etc*; *pres* roshem *etc*; *fut* yeershom *etc*.
chronicler רושם קורות הימים *nm* roshem/-et korot ha-yameem.
chronological כרונולוגי *adj* kronologee|t/-yot.
chronology כרונולוגיה *nf* kronologyah/-ot (*+of:* -at).
chronometer שעון כרונומטרי *nm* sha'on/she'oneem kronometree/-yeem.
chrysanthemum חרצית *nf* khartsee|t/-yot.
chubby עגלגל ושמנמן *adj* 'agalgal/-ah oo-shmanman/-ah.
chuck טפיחה קלה *nf* tefeekh|ah/-ot kal|ah/-ot.
chuckle צחקוק *nm* tseekhkook/-eem (*pl+of:* -ey).
(to) chuckle לצחקק *inf* letsakhkek; *pst* tseekhkek; *pres* metsakhkek; *fut* yetsakhkek.
chug טרטור *nm* teertoor/-eem (*pl+of:* -ey).
chum ידיד *nmf* yedeed/-ah.
chunk 1. נתח *nm* netakh/-eem (*pl+of:* neetkhey); **2.** חתיכה (morsel) *nf* khateekh|ah/-ot (*+of:* -at).
church כנסייה *nf* knesee|yah/-yot (*+of:* -yat).
churchman 1. כומר *nm* komer/kemar|eem (*pl+of:* komrey); **2.** איש־כנסייה (clergyman) *nm* eesh/anshey kneseeyah.
churchyard חצר הכנסייה *nm* khatsar ha-kneseeyah.
churn מחבצה *nf* makhbets|ah/-ot (*+of:* -at).
(to) churn לבחוש *inf* leevkhosh; *pst* bakhash *(b=v)*; *pres* bokhesh; *fut* yeevkhosh.
chute 1. מגלש *nm* meegl|ash/-asheem (*pl+of:* -eshey); **2.** מפל (waterfall) *nm* map|al/-aleem (*pl+of:* -ley).
cider מיץ תפוחים *nm* meets tapookheem.
C.I.F. סי"ף *adv acr* seef.
cigar סיגר *nf* seegar/-eem (*pl+of:* -ey).
cigar store חנות סיגרים *nm* khanoo|t/-yot seegareem.
cigarette סיגרייה *nf* seegaree|yah/-yot (*+of:* -yat).
cigarette butt בדל סיגרייה *nm* bedal/beedley seegaree|yah/-yot.
cigarette case נרתיק סיגריות *nm* narteek/-ey seegareeyot.
cigarette holder קנה סיגרייה *nm* keneh seegareeyah.
cigarette lighter מצית *nm* matseet/-eem (*pl+of:* -ey).
cinch דבר בטוח *nm* davar batoo'akh.
cinder אוד *nm* ood/-eem (*pl+of:* -ey).
Cinderella לכלוכית *nf* leekhlookhee|t/-yot.
cinema 1. קולנוע (movie theater) *nm* kolno'a'/batey kolno'a'; **2.** ראינוע (silent) *nm* re'eeno'a'.
cinnabar קינובר (mineral) *nm* keenobar.
cinnamon קינמון *nm* keenamon.
cinnamon tree עץ קינמון *nm* 'ets/'atsey keenamon.
cipher צופן *nm* tsofen/tsefaneem (*pl+of:* tsofney).
cipher key מפתח הצופן *nm* mafte|'akh/-khot ha-tsofen.
circle חוג *nm* khoog/-eem (*pl+of:* -ey).
circuit 1. מעגל *nm* ma'ag|al/-aleem (*pl+of:* -ley); **2.** סיבוב (tour) seevoov/-eem (*pl+of:* -ey).
(short) circuit קצר חשמלי *nm* kets|er/-areem khashmalee/-yeem.

circuit breaker מתג *nm* meteg/metageem (*pl+of:* meetgey).

circular 1. חוזר *nm* khoz|er/-reem (*pl+of:* -rey); **2.** מעוגל *adj* me'oog|al/-elet.

(to) circulate 1. להפיץ *inf* lehafeets; *pst* hefeets; *pres* mefeets; *fut* yafeets; **2.** לנוע במעגל (move in circle) *inf* lanoo'a' be-ma'gal; *pst & pres* na' *etc*; *fut* yanoo'a' *etc*.

circulation 1. תפוצה (newspaper) *nf* tefoots|ah/-ot (*+of:* -at); **2.** מחזור (blood) *nm* makhzor/-eem (*pl+of:* -ey)

(to) circumcise למול *inf* lamool; *pst & pres* mal; *fut* yamool.

circumcision 1. מילה *nf* meelah; **2.** ברית מילה ("Brith") *nf* breet/-ot meelah.

circumference היקף *nm* hekef/-eem (*pl+of:* -ey).

circumflex תג *nm* tag/-eem (*pl+of:* -ey).

circumlocution גיבוב דברים *nm* geeboov/-ey dvareem.

(to) circumscribe 1. לתחום *inf* leetkhom; *pst* takham; *pres* tokhem; *fut* yeetkhom; **2.** להקיף במעגל (encircle) *inf* lehakeef be-ma'gal; *pst* heekeef *etc*; *pres* makeef *etc*; *fut* yakeef *etc*.

circumspect 1. זהיר *adj* zaheer/zeheerah; **2.** ערני (alert) *adj* 'eranee|t.

circumstance 1. נסיבה *nf* neseeb|ah/-ot (*+of:* -at); **2.** מסיבה (condition) *nf* meseeb|ah/-ot (*+of:* -at).

circumstantial נסיבתי *adj* neseebatee|t.

(to) circumvent לעקוף *inf* la'akof; *pst* 'akaf; *pres* 'okef; *fut* ya'akof.

circus 1. קרקס *nm* keerk|as/-aseem (*pl+of:* -esey); **2.** כיכר (plaza) *nf* keekar/-ot (*pl+of:* -rot).

cirrhosis שחמת *nf* shakhemet.

cistern מיכל מים *nm* mekhal/-ey mayeem.

citadel מצודה *nf* metsood|ah/-ot (*+of:* -at).

citation 1. ציון לשבח (commendation) *nm* tseeyoon/-eem le-shevakh; **2.** ציטוט (quotation) *nm* tseetoot/-eem (*pl+of:* -ey).

(to) cite 1. לצטט *inf* letsatet; *pst* tseetet; *pres* metsatet; *fut* yetsatet; **2.** לציין לשבח (commend) *inf* letsayen le-shevakh; *pst* tseeyen *etc*; *pres* metsayen *etc*; *fut* yetsayen *etc*.

citizen 1. אזרח *nmf* ezrakh/-eet; **2.** נתין (national) *nmf* nateen/neteenah (*+of:* neteen/-at).

citizenship 1. אזרחות *nf* ezrakhoo|t/-yot; **2.** נתינות (nationality) *nf* neteenoo|t/-yot.

citron אתרוג *nm* etrog/-eem (*pl+of:* -ey).

citrus פרי־הדר *nm* pree-hadar.

city 1. עיר *nf* 'eer/'ar|eem (*pl+of:* -ey); **2.** קריה (city) *nf* keeryah/krayot (*+of:* keer|yat/-yot).

city council מועצת העיר *nf* mo'etset ha-'eer.

city editor עורך חדשות מקומיות *nmf* 'orekh/-et khadashot mekomeeyot.

city hall בית העירייה *nm* bet ha-'eereeyah.

city plan תוכנית בניין עיר *nf* tokhnee|t/-yot beenyan 'eer.

city planner מתכנן ערים *nmf* metakhnen/-et 'areem.

civic 1. אזרחי *adj* ezrakhee|t; **2.** עירוני (municipal) *adj* 'eeronee|t.

civics תורת האזרחות *nf* torat ha-ezrakhoot.

civil 1. תרבותי *adj* tarbootee|t; **2.** מנומס (polite) *adj* menoom|as/-eset.

civil disobedience מרי אזרחי *nm* meree ezrakhee.

civil engineer מהנדס אזרחי *nmf* mehandes/-et ezrakhee/-t.

civil rights זכויות האזרח *nf pl* zekhooyot ha-'ezrakh.

civil servant 1. עובד מדינה *nmf* 'oved/-et (*pl:* 'ovd|ey/-ot) medeenah; **2.** פקיד ממשלתי (government officer) *nmf* pakeed/pekeedah memshaltee/-t.

civilian 1. אזרח *nmf* ezrakh/-eet (*pl:* -eem/-eeyot); **2.** אזרחי *adj* ezrakhee|t.

civilisation 1. ציביליזציה *nf* tseeveeleezats|yah/-yot; **2.** תרבות (culture) *nf* tarboo|t/-yot.

civility 1. אדיבות *nf* adeevoo|t/-yot; **2.** נימוס (politeness) *nm* neemoos/-eem (*pl+of:* -ey).

(to) civilize לתרבת *inf* letarbet; *pst* teerbet; *pres* metarbet; *fut* yetarbet.

civilized 1. מתורבת *adj* metoorb|at/-etet; **2.** תרבותי (cultured) *adj* tarbootee|t.

civvies לבוש אזרחי *nm* levoosh ezrakhee.

clad מלובש *adj* meloob|ash/-eshet.

claim 1. תביעה *nf* tvee|'ah/-'ot (*+of:* -'at); **2.** טענה (argument) *nf* ta'an|ah/-ot (*+of:* -at).

(to) claim 1. לתבוע (demand) *inf* leetbo'a'; *pst* tava' (*v=b*); *pres* tove'a'; *fut* yeetba'; **2.** לטעון (argue) *inf* leet'on; *pst* ta'an; *pres* to'en; *fut* yeet'an.

claim check אישור הפקדה *nm* eeshoor/-ey hafkadah.

(to) claim to be להתיימר *inf* leheetyamer; *pst* heetyamer; *pres* meetyamer; *fut* yeetyamer.

claimant תובע *nmf* tov|e'a'/-a'at (*pl:* -'eem/-'ot).

clairvoyant 1. חוזה עתידות *nmf* khoz|eh/-at 'ateedot; **2.** מגיד עתידות *nmf* mag|eed/-edet 'ateedot.

clam צדפה *nf* tseedpah/tsedafot (*f=p*).

clamber לטפס במאמץ *inf* letapes be-ma'amats; *pst* teepes *etc*; *pres* metapes *etc*; *fut* yetapes *etc*.

clammy לח וקר *adj* lakh/-ah ve-kar/-ah.

clamor 1. תביעה קולנית *nf* tvee'|ah/-ot kolanee|t/-yot; **2.** זעקה (outcry) *nf* ze'ak|ah/-ot (*+of:* za'ak|at/-ot).

clamorous קולני *adj* kolanee/-t.

clamp מלחצת *nf* malkh|etset/-atsot.

(to) clamp להדק במלחצת *inf* lehadek be-malkhetset; *pst* heedek *etc*; *pres* mehadek *etc*; *fut* yehadek *etc*.

clan 1. שבט (tribe) *nm* shev|et/-ateem (*pl+of:* sheevtey); **2.** חמולה *[colloq.] nf* khamool|ah/-ot (*+of:* -at).

clandestine 1. חשאי *adj* khasha'ee/-t; **2.** סודי (secret) *adj* sodee|t.

clang 1. הקשה *nf* hakash|ah/-ot (*+of:* -at); **2.** צלצול חזק *nm* tseeltsool/-eem khazak/-eem.

(to) clang להקיש חזק *inf* lehakeesh khazak; *pst* heekeesh *etc*; *pres* makeesh *etc*; *fut* yakeesh *etc*.

clannish 1. שבטי (tribal) *adj* sheevtee/-t; **2.** עדתי (communal) *adj* 'adatee/-t.

clap מחיאות כפיים *nf pl* mekhee'ot kapayeem.

clap of thunder קול רעם *nm* kol/-ot ra'am.

clapper ענבל *nm* 'eenb|al/-aleem (*pl+of:* -eley).

claret יין אדום *nm* yayeen adom.

(to) clarify 1. לברר *inf* levarer; *pst* berer *(b=v)*; *pres* mevarer; *fut* yevarer; **2.** להבהיר (make clear) *inf* lehavheer; *pst* heevheer; *pres* mavheer; *fut* yavheer.

clarinet קלרנית *nm* klarneet/-ot.

clarity בהירות *nf* beheeroot.

clash התנגשות *nf* heetnagshoo|t/-yot.

(to) clash להתנגש *inf* leheetnagesh; *pst* heetnagesh; *pres* meetnagesh; *fut* yeetnagesh.

(to) clasp לגפף *inf* legapef; *pst* geepef; *pres* megapef; *fut* yegapef.

class 1. כיתה (grade) *nf* keet|ah/-ot (*+of:* -at); **2.** שנתון (age group) *nm* shnaton/-eem (*pl+of:* -ey); **3.** מעמד (social standing) *nm* ma'amad/-ot.

class consciousness תודעה מעמדית *nf* toda'ah ma'amadeet.

classer, classeur עוקדן *nm* 'okdan/-eem (*pl+of:* -ey).

classic, classical 1. קלאסי *adj* klasee/-t; **2.** מופתי *adj* moftee|t.

classicism קלאסיציזם *nm* klaseetseezm/-eem.

classification סיווג *nm* seevoog/-eem (*pl+of:* -ey).

classified 1. מסווג *adj* mesoov|ag/-eget; **2.** סודי (secret) *adj* sodee/-t.

(to) classify לסווג *inf* lesaveg; *pst* seeveg; *pres* mesaveg; *fut* yesaveg.

classmate בן־כיתה *nmf* ben/bat keetah.

classroom חדר כיתה *nm* khad|ar/-rey keetah.

clatter קשקוש *nm* keeshkoosh/-eem (*pl+of:* -ey).

(to) clatter לקשקש *inf* lekashkesh; *pst* keeshkesh; *pres* mekashkesh; *fut* yekashkesh.

clause 1. התניה (stipulation) *nf* hatna|yah/-yot (*+of:* -yat); **2.** סעיף (article) *nm* se'eef/-eem (*pl+of:* -ey).

clavicle עצם הבריח *nm* 'etsem ha-bree'akh.

clavier מקלדת *nf* meekl|edet/-adot.

claw 1. טופר *nm* tofer/tfareem (*pl+of:* tofrey); **2.** ציפורן (nail) *nf* tseepor|en/-nayeem (*pl+of:* -ney).

claw hammer פטיש שסוע חרטום *nm* pateesh/-eem shesoo|'a'/-'ey khartom.

clay חומר *nm* khom|er-areem (*pl+of:* -rey).

(to) clean 1. לנקות *inf* lenakot; *pst* neekah; *pres* menakeh; *fut* yenakeh; **2.** לטהר (purify) *inf* letaher; *pst* teeher; *pres* metaher; *fut* yetaher.

clean-shaven מגולח למשעי *adj* megoolakh/-at le-meesh'ee.

(to) clean up לנקות כליל *inf* lenakot kaleel; *pst* neekah *etc*; *pres* menakeh *etc*; *fut* yenakeh *etc*.

cleancut 1. הגון *adj* hagoon/-ah; **2.** כיאות (proper) *adj* kaya'oot.

cleaner 1. מכון לניקוי יבש *nm* makhon/mekhoneem le-neekooy yavesh; **2.** חומר ניקוי (cleaning substance) *nm* khom|er/-rey neekooy.

cleaning woman 1. מנקה *nf* menak|ah/-ot; **2.** עוזרת (maid) *nf* 'oz|eret/-rot.

cleanliness ניקיון *nm* neekayon.

cleanly בצורה נקייה *adv* be-tsoorah nekeeyah.

cleanness 1. טוהר *nm* tohar; **2.** תום (candor) *nm* tom.

(to) cleanse 1. לנקות *inf* lenakot; *pst* neekah; *pres* menakeh; *fut* yenakeh; **2.** לטהר (purify) *inf* letaher; *pst* teeher; *pres* metaher; *fut* yetaher.

cleanser חומר ניקוי *nm* khom|er/-rey neekooy.

clear 1. ברור (unequivocal) *adj* baroor/broorah; **2.** פנוי (vacant) *adj* panooy/penooyah.

(in the) clear ללא דופי *adv* le-lo dofee.

(to) clear 1. לפנות (vacate) *inf* lefanot; *pst* peenah *(p=f)*; *pres* mefaneh; *fut* yefaneh; **2.** להסדיר (attend to) *inf* lehasdeer; *pst* heesdeer; *pres* masdeer; *fut* yasdeer.

clear profit רווח נקי *nm* revakh nakee.

clear-sighted בר־הבחנה *adj* bar/bat havkhanah;

(to) clear up 1. להתבהר (weather) *inf* leheetbaher; *pst* heetbaher; *pres* meetbaher; *fut* yeetbaher; **2.** להבהיר (clarify) *inf* lehavheer; *pst* heevheer; *pres* mavheer; *fut* yavheer.

clearance 1. אישור בטחוני (security) *nm* eeshoor/-eem beetkhonee/-yeem; **2.** סילוק חשבון (of account) *nm* seelook/-ey kheshbon/-ot.

clearance sale מכירת חיסול *nf* mekheer|at/-ot kheesool.

clearing 1. הסדר סילוקין (finance) *nm* hesder/-ey seelookeen; **2.** קורחת יער (forest) *nf* korkh|at/-ot ya'ar.

clearing house לשכת סילוקין *nf* leesh|kat/-khot seelookeen.

clearness 1. בהירות *nf* beheeroo|t/-yot; **2.** צלילות (lucidity) *nf* tseleeloo|t/-yot.

cleavage פילוג *nm* peeloog/-eem (*pl+of:* -ey).

cleaver קופיץ *nm* kofeets/-eem (*pl+of:* -ey).

clef מפתח במוסיקה *nm* mafte'akh be-mooseekah.

cleft 1. שסע *nm* shes|a'/-a'eem (*pl+of:* shees'ey); **2.** בקע (crack) *nm* bek|a'/-a'eem (*pl+of:* beek'ey).

clemency 1. חמלה (compassion) *nf* kheml|ah/-ot (*+of:* -at); **2.** רחמנות (pity) *nf* rakhmanoot; **3.** רכות (leniency) *nf* rakoot.

clement סלחן *adj* salkhan/-eet.

clench קמיצה *nf* kemeets|ah/-ot (*+of:* -at).

(to) clench 1. לסגור חזק leesgor khazak; *pst* sagar *etc*; *pres* soger *etc*; *fut* yeesgor *etc*; **2.** לקפוץ אגרוף (fist) *inf* leekpots egrof; *pst* kafats *(f=p) etc*; *pres* kofets *etc*; *fut* yeekpots *etc*.

clergy כמורה *nf* kemoor|ah/-ot (*+of:* -at).

clergyman כומר *nm* komer/kemareem (*pl+of:* komrey).

clerical משרדי *adj* meesradee/-t.

clerical work 1. עבודה משרדית *nf* 'avod|ah/-ot meesradee|t/-yot; **2.** פקידות (office work) *nf* pekeedoot.

clerk 1. פקיד *nmf* pakeed/pekeed|ah (*pl:* -eem/-ot); **2.** לבלר (scribe) *nm* lavlar/-eem (*pl+of:* -ey).

(law) clerk פקיד עורך־דין *nm* pekeed/-at 'orekh-deen.

clever 1. פיקח *adj* peek|e'akh/-'kheet; **2.** חכם (wise) *adj* khakham/-ah.

cleverly 1. בחוכמה *adv* be-khokhmah; **2.** בפיקחות (wisely) *adv* be-feek'khoot *(f=p)*.

cleverness 1. חוכמה *nf* khokhmah; **2.** פיקחות (wisdom) *nf* peek'khoot.

clew מפתח לפתרון *nm* mafte|'akh/-khot le-feetron *(f=p)*.

cliché 1. גלופה *nf* gloof|ah/-ot (*+of:* -at); **2.** קלישה *nm* kleeshe|h/-'ot; **3.** ביטוי נדוש (banality) *nm* beetooy/-eem nadosh/nedosheem.

click 1. נקישה *nf* nekeesh|ah/-ot (*+of:* -at); **2.** התאמה (fitting) *nf* hat'am|ah/-ot (*+of:* -at)

(to) click 1. לתאום (fit) *inf* leet'om; *pst* ta'am; *pres* to'em; *fut* yeet'am; **2.** לטקטק (tick) *inf* letaktek; *pst* teektek; *pres* metaktek; *fut* yetaktek.

client 1. לקוח *nmf* lako|'akh/-khah (*pl:* -khot); **2.** מרשה (legal) *nmf* marsh|eh/-ah (*+of:* -at).

clientele חוג לקוחות *nm* khoog lakokhot (*cpr* lekookhot).

cliff צוק *nm* tsook/-eem (*pl+of:* -ey).

climate אקלים *nm* akleem/-eem (*pl+of:* -ey).

climax שיא *nm* see/-'eem (*pl+of:* -'ey).

(to) climax להגיע לשיא *inf* lehagee'a' le-see; *pst* heegee'a' *etc; pres* magee'a' *etc; fut* yagee'a' *etc.*

climb 1. טיפוס *nm* teepoos/-eem (*pl+of:* -ey); **2.** עלייה *nf* 'alee|yah/-yot (*+of:* -yat).

(to) climb 1. לטפס *inf* letapes; *pst* teepes; *pres* metapes; *fut* yetapes; **2.** לעלות (go up) *inf* la'alot; *pst* 'alah; *pres* 'oleh; *fut* ya'aleh.

(to) climb down לרדת *inf* laredet; *pst* yarad; *pres* yored; *fut* yered.

climber מטפס *nm* metap|es/-seem (*pl+of:* -sey).

clime אקלים *nm* akleem/-eem (*pl+of:* -ey).

(to) clinch 1. לקבוע סופית *inf* leekbo'a' sofeet; *pst* kava' *(v=b) etc; pres* kove'a' *etc; fut* yeekba' *etc;* **2.** לקבוע מסמרות (establish principles) *inf* leekbo'a' masmerot; *pst* kava' *(v=b) etc; pres* kove'a' *etc; fut* yeekba' *etc.*

(to) cling להיצמד *inf* leheetsamed; *pst & pres* neetsmad; *fut* yeetsamed.

clinic 1. מרפאה *nf* meerp|a'ah/-a'ot (*+of:* -e'at/-e'ot); **2.** קליניקה *nf* kleeneek|ah/-ot (*+of:* -at).

clinician קליניקן *nmf* kleeneekan/-eet.

clink קול נקישה *nm* kol/-ot nekeeshah.

clip לגזוז *inf* leegzoz; *pst* gazaz; *pres* gozez; *fut* yeegzoz.

(paper) clip 1. מהדק *nm* mehad|ek/-keem (*pl+of:* -key); **2.** אטב *nm* etev/ataveem (*pl+of:* atvey).

(to) clip together להצמיד *inf* lehatsmeed; *pst* heetsmeed; *pres* matsmeed; *fut* yatsmeed.

clipper 1. מגזזיים (implement) *nm pl* meegz|azayeem (*+of:* -ezey); **2.** מפרשית מהירה (sailboat) *nf* meefrasee|t/-yot meheer|ah/-ot.

clipping גזיר *nm* gezeer/-eem (*pl+of:* -ey).

clique 1. חבר מרעים *nm* khever mere'eem; **2.** כנופיה (gang) *nf* knoof|yah/-yot (*+of:* -yat); **3.** קליקה *nf* kleek|ah/-ot (*+of:* -at).

cloak 1. מעיל *nm* me'eel/-eem (*pl+of:* -ey); **2.** גלימה (gown) *nf* gleem|ah/-ot (*+of:* -at).

cloak and dagger של ריגול *adj* shel reegool.

cloakroom מלתחה meltakh|ah/-ot (*+of:* -at).

clock 1. שעון (also watch) *nm* sha'on/she'on|eem (*pl+of:* -ey); **2.** שעון־קיר (wall) *nm* she'on/-ey keer.

(alarm) clock שעון מעורר *nm* sha'on/she'oneem me'orer/-eem.

(round the) clock יומם ולילה (day and night) *adv* yomam va-laylah.

clock tower מגדל שעון *nm* meegdal sha'on.

clockwise בכיוון השעון *adv* be-kheevoon ha-sha'on.

clockwork בדייקנות של שעון *adv* be-daykanoot shel sha'on.

(like) clockwork כמו שעון *adv* kemo sha'on.

clod 1. גוש אדמה (lump) *nm* goosh/-ey adamah; **2.** גולם (person) *nm* golem/glameem (*pl+of:* golmey).

clog קבקב *nm* kavka|v/-beem (*b=v; pl+of:* -bey).

(to) clog לסתום *inf* leestom; *pst* satam; *pres* sotem; *fut* yeestom.

clog dance ריקוד בקבקבים *nm* reekood be-kavkabeem.

cloister מנזר *nm* meenz|ar/-areem (*pl+of:* -erey).

close 1. קרוב *adj* karov/krovah; **2.** סמוך (neighboring) *adj* samookh/smookhah.

(to) close לסגור *inf* leesgor; *pst* sagar; *pres* soger; *fut* yeesgor.

(to a) close לידי גמר *adv* lee-yedey gemar.

(to) close an account לסגור חשבון *inf* leesgor kheshbon; *pst* sagar *etc; pres* soger *etc; fut* yeesgor *etc.*

close attention תשומת־לב קפדנית *nf* tesoomet-lev kapdaneet.

close-fisted קמוץ אגרופים *adj* kmoots/-at egrofeem.

close-fitting תואם בדקדקנות *adj* to'em/-et be-dakdekanoot.

(to) close in להתקרב *inf* leheetkarev; *pst* heetkarev; *pres* meetkarev; *fut* yeetkarev.

close-lipped שתקן *adj* shatkan/-eet.

(to) close out למכור את המלאי *inf* leemkor et ha-melay; *pst* makhar *(kh=k) etc; pres* mokher *etc; fut* yeemkor *etc.*

close quarters פנים אל פנים *adv* paneem el paneem.

close questioning תשאול מדוקדק *nm* teesh'ool/-eem medookdak/-eem.

(at a) close range מטווח קרוב *adv* mee-tvakh karov.

close translation תרגום מילולי *nm* teergoom/-eem meeloolee/-yeem.

closed chapter פרק סגור *nm* perek sagoor.

closed circuit מעגל סגור *nm* ma'agal/-eem sagoor/sgooreem.

closed season (hunting) עונת איסור הציד *nf* 'onat/-ot eesoor ha-tsayeed.

closed shop מקום עבודה מאורגן *nm* mekom/-ot 'avodah me'oorgan/-eem.

closely מקרוב *adv* mee-karov.

closeness קרבה *nf* keerv|ah/-ot (*+of:* -at).

closet 1. ארון (cupboard) *nm* aron/-ot; **2.** חדרון סגור (room) *nm* khadron sagoor.

(to) closet oneself/themselves להסתגר *inf* leheestager; *pst* heestager; *pres* meestager; *fut* yeestager.

close-up תצלום מקרוב *nm* tatsloom/-eem mee-karov.

closing prices 1. שער סגירה *nm* sha'ar/-ey sgeerah; **2.** שער נעילה *nm* sha'ar/-ey ne'eelah.

clot 1. גוש *nm* goosh/-eem (*pl+of:* -ey); **2.** קריש (blood) kareesh/kreesh|eem (*pl+of:* -ey).

cloth 1. בד *nm* bad/-eem (*pl+of:* -ey); **2.** אריג *nm* areeg/-eem (*pl+of:* -ey).

cloth binding כריכת־בד *nf* kreekh|at/-ot bad.

(to) clothe להלביש *inf* lehalbeesh; *pst* heelbeesh; *pres* malbeesh; *fut* yalbeesh.

clothes 1. בגדים *nm pl* begadeem (*+of:* beegdey); **2.** מלבושים (dresses) *nm pl* malboosh|eem (*+of:* -ey).

(suit of) clothes חליפת בגדים *nf* khaleef|at/-ot begadeem.

(to take off) clothes להתפשט *inf* leheetpashet; *pst* heetpashet; *pres* meetpashet; *fut* yeetpashet.

clothesline חבל כביסה *nm* khevel/khavley kveesah.

clothespin 1. הדק כביסה *nm* hedek/hadkey kveesah; **2.** אטב *nm* etev/ataveem (*pl+of:* atvey); **3.** מקל כביסה *[colloq.]* mak|el/-lot kveesah.

clothier 1. מוכר בגדי גברים *nm* mokher/-rey beegdey gvareem; **2.** סוחר קונפקציה *[colloq.]* sokh|er/-arey konfek'tsyah.

clothing לבוש *nm* levoosh.

cloud ענן *nm* 'anan/-eem (*pl+of:* 'aneney).

(to) cloud לערפל *inf* le'arpel; *pst* eerpel; *pres* me'arpel; *fut* ye'arpel.

cloudburst שבר־ענן *nm* shever 'anan.

cloudless 1. ללא ענן *adv* le-lo 'anan; **2.** בהיר (clear) *adj* baheer/beheerah.

cloudy מעונן *adj* me'oon|an/-enet.

clove ציפורן *nf* tseepor|en/-neem (*pl+of:* -ney).

cloven מפולג *adj* mefool|ag/-eget.

cloven hoof פרסה שסועה *nf* parsah shesoo'ah.

clover תלתן *nm* teeltan.

cloverleaf עלה תלתן *nm* 'ale|h/-y teeltan.

clown מוקיון *nm* mookyon/-eem (*pl+of:* -ey).

(to) cloy 1. לפטם עד לזרא *vt inf* lefatem 'ad le-zara; *pst* peetem (*p=f*) *etc*; *pres* mefatem *etc*; *fut* yefatem *etc*; **2.** להתפטם עד לזרא (overeat) *v rfl inf* leheetpatem 'ad le-zara; *pst* heetpatem *etc*; *pres* meetpatem *etc*; *fut* yeetpatem *etc*.

club 1. מועדון *nm* mo'adon/-eem (*pl+of:* -ey); **2.** אלה (stick) *nf* al|ah/-ot (*+of:* -at).

(to) club together להתכנס *inf* leheetkanes; *pst* heetkanes; *pres* meetkanes; *fut* yeetkanes.

clubhouse 1. בית ועד *nm* bet/batey va'ad; **2.** בית מועדון *nm* bet/batey mo'adon/-eem.

cluck קרקור *nm* keerkoor/-eem (*pl+of:* -ey).

clue מפתח לפתרון *nm* mafte'akh le-feetron (*f=p*).

clump סבך *nm* svakh.

(to) clump along לצעוד יחדיו *inf* leets'od yakhdav; *pst* tsa'ad *etc*; *pres* tso'ed *etc*; *fut* yeets'ad *etc*.

clump of bushes סבך שיחים *nm* svakh/seevkhey seekheem.

clump of trees סבך עצים *nm* svakh/seevkhey 'etseem.

clumsy 1. מסורבל *adj* mesoorb|al/-elet; **2.** מגושם (coarse) *adj* megoosh|am/-emet.

cluster 1. צרור *nm* tsror/-ot; **2.** אשכול (bunch) *nm* eshkol/-ot.

clutch מצמד *nm* matsmed/-eem (*pl+of:* -ey).

clutch pedal דוושת מצמד *nf* davsh|at/-ot matsmed.

clutter אי־סדר *nm* ee-seder.

Co. (*abbr.* **of Company**) **1.** חברה *nf* khevrah/khavarot (*+of:* khevrat); **2.** פלוגה (army) *nf* ploog|ah/-ot (*+of:* -at).

c/o 1. על ידי (care of) *prep* 'al yedey; **2.** אצל (at) *prep* etsel.

coach 1. קרון *nm* karon/kronot (*+of:* kron); **2.** כרכרה (carriage) *nf* keerkar|ah/-ot (*+of:* -at); **3.** טיולית (bus) *nf* teeyoolee|t/-yot; **4.** מאמן (trainer) *nm* me'am|en/-neem (*pl+of:* -ney).

(to) coach לאמן *inf* le'amen; *pst* eemen; *pres* me'amen; *fut* ye'amen.

coachman 1. עגלון *nm* 'eglon/-eem (*pl+of:* -ey); **2.** רכב (charioteer) *nm* rakav/-eem (*pl+of:* -ey).

(to) coagulate להתקרש *inf* leheetkaresh; *pst* heetkaresh; *pres* meetkaresh; *fut* yeetkaresh.

coal פחם *nm* pekham/-eem (*+of:* pakham/-ey).

coal mine מיכרה פחם *nm* meekhr|eh/-ot pekham.

coal tar עטרן *nm* 'eetran.

coalition קואליציה *nf* koaleets|yah/-yot (*+of:* -yat).

coalition government ממשלה קואליציונית *nf* memshalah/-ot koaleetsyonee|t/-yot.

coarse גס *adj* gas/-ah.

coarseness גסות *nf* gasoo|t/-yot.

coast חוף *nm* khof/khof|eem (*pl+of:* -ey).

coast guard משמר החופים *nm* meeshmar ha-khofeem.

coastal חופי khofee/-t.

coastal area אזור החוף *nm* ezor/azorey ha-khof.

coastline קו החוף *nm* kav/-ey ha-khof

coat מעיל *nm* me'eel/-eem (*pl+of:* -ey).

coat hanger 1. קשתית *nf* kashtee|t/-yot; **2.** קולב (clotheshanger) *nm* kolev/klaveem (*pl+of:* kolvey; *cpr* kolav/-eem).

coat of arms סמל מצויר *nm* semel/smaleem metsooyar/-eem.

coat of paint 1. מעטה צבע *nm* ma'at|eh/-ey tseva'; **2.** שכבת צבע (layer) *nf* sheekhv|at/-ot tseva'.

coated מצופה *adj* metsoop|eh/-ah.

coating ציפוי *nm* tseepooy/-eem (*pl+of:* -ey).

(to) coax לשדל *inf* leshadel; *pst* sheedel; *pres* meshadel; *fut* yeshadel.

coaxial cable כבל קואקסיאלי *nm* kevel/kvaleem ko'aksee'alee/-yeem.

cob אשבול *nm* eshbol/-eem (*pl+of:* -ey).

cobalt קובלט *nm* kobalt.

cobbler סנדלר *nmf* sandlar/-eet.

cobblestone חלוק־אבן *nm* khalook/-ey even.

cobweb קורי עכביש *nm pl* koorey 'akaveesh.

cocaine קוקאין *nm* koka'een.

cock תרנגול *nm* tarnegol/-eem (*pl+of:* -ey).

cock-a-doodle-doo קוקוריקו koo-koo-ree-koo.

cockeyed 1. פוזל *adj* pozel/-et; **2.** מסולף (distorted) *adj* mesool|af/-efet.

cockpit תא הטייס *nm* ta/-'ey ha-tayas/-eem.

cockroach 1. תיקן *nm* teekan/-eem (*pl+of:* -ey); **2.** ג'וק *[colloq.]* *nm* jook/-eem (*pl+of:* -ey).

cocksure מפריז בבטחונו העצמי *adj* mafreez/-ah be-veetkhon|o/-ah (*v=b*) ha-'atsmee.

cocktail קוקטייל *nm* kokteyl/-eem.

cocktail-party מסיבת קוקטייל *nf* meseeb|at/-ot kokteyl.

cocky 1. יהיר *adj* yaheer/yeheerah; **2.** רברבן (braggart) *adj* ravrevan/-eet.

cocoa קקאו *nm* kaka'o.

coconut אגוז קוקוס *nm* egoz/-ey kokos.

cocoon פקעת *nf* peka|'at/-'ot.
cod, codfish דג בקלה *nm* dag/degey bakalah.
cod-liver oil שמן דגים *nm* shemen dageem.
(to) coddle לפנק *inf* lefanek; *pst* peenek *(p=f)*; *pres* mefanek; *fut* yefanek.
code 1. ספר חוקים (law) *nm* sefer/seefrey khookeem; **2.** צופן (secret) *nm* tsofen/tsefaneem (*pl+of:* tsofney).
(to) code 1. לצפן *inf* letsapen; *pst* tseepen; *pres* metsapen; *fut* yetsapen; **2.** לקודד *inf* lekoded; *pst* koded; *pres* mekoded; *fut* yekoded.
code message מסר מוצפן *nm* mes|er/-areem mootspan/-eem.
code signal אות צופן *nf* ot/-ot tsofen.
codicil 1. סמפון צוואה *nm* seempon tsava'ah; **2.** נספח לצוואה (annex to will) *nm* neespakh/-eem le-tsava'ah.
(to) codify לכנס חוקים בקובץ *inf* lekhanes khookeem be-kovets; *pst* keenes *(k=kh) etc*; *pres* mekhanes *etc*; *fut* yekhanes *etc*.
co-ed סטודנטית *nf* stoodentee|t/-yot.
coeducation חינוך מעורב *nm* kheenookh me'orav.
(to) coerce 1. לאלץ *inf* le'alets; *pst* eelets; *pres* me'alets; *fut* ye'alets; **2.** לכפות (compel) *inf* leekhpot; *pst* kafah *(k=kh; f=p)*; *pres* kofeh; *fut* yeekhpeh.
coercion 1. אילוץ *nm* eeloots/-eem (*pl+of:* -ey); **2.** כפייה (compulsion) *nf* kfee|yah/-yot (*+of:* -yat).
coexistence דו־קיום *nm* doo-keeyoom.
coffee קפה *nm* kafeh.
(black) coffee קפה שחור *nm* kafeh shakhor.
coffee grinder, coffee mill מטחנת קפה *nf* matkhen|at/-ot kafeh.
coffee shop בית קפה *nm* bet/batey kafeh.
coffeepot קומקום קפה *nm* koomkoom/-ey kafeh.
coffer 1. תיבה *nf* teyv|ah/-ot (*+of:* -at); **2.** ארגז (box) *nm* argaz/-eem (*pl+of:* -ey).
coffin ארון מתים *nm* aron/-ot meteem.
cog שן בגלגל *nm* shen/sheenayeem be-galgal.
cognac קוניאק *nm* konyak.
cognate 1. קרוב משפחה *nmf* krov/-at meeshpakhah; **2.** שאר בשר (kin) *nm* she'er/-ey basar; **3.** מאותו מוצא (of same origin) *adj* me-oto motsá.
cognizance הכרה *nf* hakarah/-ot (*+of:* -at).
cogwheel גלגל שיניים *nm* galgal sheenayeem.
(to) cohabit לחיות כזוג *inf* leekhyot ke-zoog; *pst & pres* khay *etc*; *fut* yeekhyeh *etc*.
coherent הגיוני *adj* hegyonee/-t.
cohesion התלכדות *nf* heetlakdoo|t/-yot.
cohesive מתלכד *add* meetlaked/-et.
coif ברדס *nm* bardas/-eem (*pl+of:* -ey).
coiffeur ספר *nm* sapar/-eem (*pl+of:* -ey).
coiffure תסרוקת *nf* teesrok|et/-ot.
coil סליל *nm* sleel/-eem (*pl+of:* -ey).
(electric) coil סליל חשמלי *nm* sleel/-eem khashmalee/-yeem.
coin מטבע *nm* matbe|'a'/-'ot.
coinage טביעת מטבעות *nf* tvee|'at/-'ot matbe'ot.
(to) coincide 1. לחפוף *inf* lakhfof; *pst* khafaf; *pres* khofef; *fut* yakhfof; **2.** לתאום (match) *inf* leet'om; *pst* ta'am; *pres* to'em; *fut* yeet'am.
coincidence צירוף מקרים *nm* tseroof/-ey meekreem.
coincidental חופף *adj* khofef/-et.
coition, coitus הזדווגות *nf* heezdavgoo|t/-yot.
coke קוקס *nm* koks.
colander משמרת *nf* mesham|eret/-rot.
cold 1. קור *nm* kor; **2.** קר *adj* kar/-ah; **3.** הצטננות (catching cold) *nf* heetstanenoo|t/-yot.
(to be) cold להרגיש קור *inf* lehargeesh kor; *pst* heergeesh kor; *pres* margeesh kor; *fut* yargeesh kor.
(to catch a) cold להצטנן *inf* leheetstanen; *pst* heetstanen; *pres* meetstanen; *fut* yeetstanen.
cold feet מורך לב *nm* morekh-lev.
cold shoulder יחס צונן *nm* yakhas tsonen.
cold storage החסנה בקירור *nf* hakhsan|ah/-ot be-keroor.
(it is) cold today קר היום kar ha-yom.
cold war מלחמה קרה *nf* meelkhamah karah.
cold-blooded אכזרי *adj* akhzaree/-t.
coldness קרירות *nf* kreeroo|t/-yot.
colic כאב בטן *nm* ke'ev/-ey beten.
(to) collaborate לשתף פעולה *inf* leshatef pe'oolah; *pst* sheetef *etc*; *pres* meshatef *etc*; *fut* yeshatef *etc*.
collaboration שיתוף פעולה *nm* sheetoof pe'oolah.
collapse 1. מפולת *nf* mapol|et/-ot; **2.** התמוטטות (tottering) *nf* heetmotetoo|t/-yot.
(to) collapse להתמוטט *inf* leheetmotet; *pst* heetmotet; *pres* meetmotet; *fut* yeetmotet.
collapsible 1. מתקפל *adj* meetkapel/-et; **2.** עלול להתמוטט (liable to totter) *adj* 'alool/-ah leheetmotet.
collar צווארון *nm* tsav|aron/-roneem (*pl+of:* -roney).
(white) collar workers עובדי הצווארון הלבן *nm pl* 'ovdey ha-tsavaron ha-lavan.
collarbone עצם הבריח *nm* 'etsem ha-bree'akh.
(to) collate 1. ללקט *inf* lelaket; *pst* leeket; *pres* melaket; *fut* yelaket; **2.** להשוות (compare) *inf* lehashvot; *pst* heeshvah; *pres* mashveh; *fut* yashveh.
collateral 1. ערב (surety) *nm* arev/-eem (*pl+of:* -ey); **2.** מקביל (parallel) *adj* makbeel/-ah.
colleague עמית *nm* 'ameet/-eem (*pl+of:* -ey).
collect גוביינא *adv* goovayna.
(to) collect 1. לאסוף (assemble) *inf* le'esof; *pst* asaf; *pres* osef; *fut* ye'esof; **2.** לגבות (dues) *inf* leegbot; *pst* gavah *(v=b)*; *pres* goveh; *fut* yeegbeh.
collect cable מברק בגוביינא *nm* meevrak/-eem be-goovayna.
collect (telephone) call שיחת גוביינא *nf* seekh|at/-ot goovayna.
(to) collect oneself להירגע *inf* leheraga'; *pst & pres* neerga'; *fut* yeraga'.
collection 1. אוסף *nm* osef/osfeem (*pl+of:* osfey); **2.** גבייה *nf* gvee|yah/-yot (*+of:* -yat).
collective 1. קולקטיבי *adj* kolekteevee/-t; **2.** קיבוצי (common) *adj* keebootsee/-t; **3.** שיתופי (cooperative) *adj* sheetoofee/-t.
collective farm משק שיתופי *nm* meshek sheetoofee.
collectivism שתפנות *nf* shatfanoo|t/-yot
collector 1. אספן *nmf* asfan/-eet; **2.** גובה *nm* gov|eh/-eem (*pl+of:* -ey).

(tax) collector גובה מסים *nm* gov|eh/-ey meeseem.
college 1. מכללה (also: university) *nf* meekhl|alah/-alot (*+of:* -elet); **2.** מדרשה (also: academy) *nf* meedrashah/-ashot (*+of:* -eshet/-eshot); **3.** קולג׳ *nm* kolej/-eem.
college of engineering בית־ספר להנדסה *nm* bet/batey sefer le-handasah.
college of medicine בית־ספר לרפואה *nm* bet/batey sefer lee-refoo'ah.
(to) collide להתנגש *inf* leheetnagesh; *pst* heetnagesh; *pres* meetnagesh; *fut* yeetnagesh.
collie כלב רועה *nm* kelev/kalvey ro'eh/ro'eem.
collision התנגשות *nf* heetnagshoo|t/-yot.
colloquial 1. דיבורי *adj* deebooree/-t; **2.** מדובר (spoken) *adj* medoob|ar/-eret.
colloquial expression, colloquialism ביטוי בלשון המדוברת *nm* beetooy/-eem ba-lashon ha-medooberet.
collusion קשר להונאה *nm* kesher/kshareem le-hona'ah.
colon 1. נקודתיים (punctuation) *nf pl* nekoodatayeem; **2.** המעי הגס (anatomy) *nm* ha-me'ee ha-gas.
colonel אלוף־משנה *nm* aloof/-ey meeshneh.
colonial קולוניאלי *adj* kolonyalee/-t.
colonist 1. מתיישב *nmf* meetyash|ev/-evet (*pl:* -veem/-vot; *+of:* -vey); **2.** מתנחל (specifically: across the "Green Line") *nmf* meetnakh|el/-elet (*pl:* -aleem/-alot; *+of:* -aley).
colonization 1. התיישבות *nf* heetyashvoo|t/-yot; **2.** התנחלות (specifically: beyond the "Green Line") *nf* heetnakhaloo|t/-yot.
(to) colonize ליישב *inf* leyashev; *pst* yeeshev; *pres* meyashev; *fut* yeyashev.
colonnade 1. שדירת עמודים *nf* sdeyr|at/-ot 'amoodeem; **2.** סטו *nm* stav/-eem (*pl+of:* -ey).
colony מושבה (settlement) *nm* mosh|avah/-avot (*+of:* -evet/-vot).
color צבע *nm* tsev|a'/-a'eem (*pl+of:* tseev'ey).
color television טלוויזיה צבעונית *nf* teeleveez|yah/-yot tseev'onee|t/-yot.
colored 1. צבעוני *adj* tseev'onee/-t; **2.** מושפע (biased) mooshp|a'/-a'at.
colorful ססגוני *adj* sasgonee/-t.
coloring 1. מתן צבע *nm* matan tsev|a'/-a'eem; **2.** צביעה (painting) *nf* tsvee|'ah/-'ot (*+of:* -'at)
colorless חסר־צבע *adj* khas|ar/-rat tseva'.
colossal עצום *adj* 'atsoom/-ah.
colossus פסל ענק *nm* pesel/peesley 'anak.
colt סייח *nm* syakh/-eem (*pl+of:* -ey).
column 1. עמוד (structure) *nm* 'amood/-eem (*pl+of:* -ey); **2.** טור (newspaper) *nm* toor/-eem (*pl+of:* -ey).
coma 1. קומא *nf* koma; **2.** תרדמת *nf* tard|emet/-amot.
comb מסרק *nm* masrek/-eem (*pl+of:* -ey).
(to) comb 1. לסרק (hair) *inf* lesarek; *pst* serak; *pres* mesarek; *fut* yesarek; **2.** לסרוק (search) *inf* leesrok; *pst* sarak; *pres* sorek; *fut* yeesrok.
combat קרב *nm* krav/-ot.
combatant לוחם קרבי *nm* lokh|em/-ameem kravee/-yeem.
combination צירוף *nm* tseroof/-eem (*pl+of:* -ey).
(to) combine לצרף *inf* letsaref; *pst* tseraf; *pres* metsaref; *fut* yetsaref.
combo שלישיית ג׳ז *nf* shleesheey|at/-ot jaz.
combustible 1. דלק *nm* delek/dlakeem (*pl+of:* deelkey); **2.** דליק *adj* daleek/dleekah.
combustion בעירה *nf* be'er|ah/-ot (*+of:* -at).
(to) come לבוא *inf* lavo; *pst & pres* ba (*b=v*); *fut* yavo.
(to) come about להתרחש *inf* leheetrakhesh; *pst* heetrakhesh; *pres* meetrakhesh; *fut* yeetrakhesh.
(to) come back לחזור *inf* lakhzor; *pst* khazar; *pres* khozer; *fut* yakhzor.
(to) come between 1. לחצוץ *inf* lakhtsots; *pst* khatsats; *pres* khotsets; *fut* yakhtsots; **2.** להפריד בין (separate) *inf* lehafreed beyn; *pst* heefreed *etc*; *pres* mafreed *etc*; *fut* yafreed *etc*.
(to) come by להשיג (obtain) *inf* lehaseeg; *pst* heeseeg; *pres* maseeg; *fut* yaseeg.
(to) come forward להתנדב *inf* leheetnadev; *pst* heetnadev; *pres* meetnadev; *fut* yeetnadev.
(to) come in להיכנס *inf* leheekanes; *pst & pres* neekhnas (*kh=k*); *fut* yeekanes.
(to) come of age להגיע לפירקו *inf* lehagee'a' le-feerk|o/-ah (*m/f; f=p*); *pst* heegee'a' *etc*; *pres* magee'a' *etc*; *fut* yagee'a' *etc*.
(to) come off לצאת מזה *inf* latset mee-zeh; *pst* yatsa *etc*; *pres* yotse *etc*; *fut* yetse *etc*.
(to) come out 1. להתגלות (emerge) *inf* leheetgalot; *pst* neetgalah; *pres* meetgaleh; *fut* yeetgaleh; **2.** להופיע (appear) *inf* lehofee'a'; *pst* hofee'a'; *pres* mofee'a'; *fut* yofee'a'.
(to) come up לעלות *inf* la'alot; *pst* 'alah; *pres* 'oleh; *fut* ya'aleh.
comeback 1. שיבה *nf* sheevah/-ot (*+of:* -at) **2.** חזרה למצב קודם *nf* khazar|ah/-ot le-matsav kodem.
comedian 1. שחקן *nmf* sakhkan/-eet; **2.** בדרן (entertainer) *nmf* badran/-eet; **3.** ליצן (clown) *nm* leytsan/-eem (*pl+of:* -ey).
comedy 1. מחזה מבדר *nm* makhaz|eh/-ot mevad|er/-reem; **2.** קומדיה komedee|yah/-yot (*+of:* -yat).
comely 1. נאה *adj* na|'eh/-'ah; **2.** חינני (graceful) *adj* kheenanee/-t.
comet כוכב שביט *nm* kokh|av/-vey shaveet.
comfort 1. נוחות *nf* nokhoo|t/-yot; **2.** נחמה (consolation) *nf* nekham|ah/-ot (*+of:* -at).
comfortable 1. נוח *adj* no'akh/nokhah; **2.** נינוח (relaxed) *adj* neeno|'akh/-khah.
comfortably בנוחות *adv* be-nokhoot.
comforter מנחם *nm* menakh|em/-ameem (*pl+of:* -amey).
comfortless ללא נחמה *adj & adv* le-lonekhamah.
comic 1. קומי *adj* komee/-t; **2.** מצחיק (makes laugh) *adj* mats'kheek/-ah; **3.** קומיקאי *nmf* komeeka'ee/-t.
comic strip סדרה מצוירת *nf* seedrah metsooyeret.
comical קומי *adj* komee/-t.
coming בוא *nm* bo.
comma פסיק *nm* peseek/-eem (*pl+of:* -ey).

command 1. צו *nm* tsav/-eem (*pl+of:* -ey); **2.** פקודה (order) *nf* pekood|ah/-ot (+*of:* -at); **3.** פיקוד (act) *nm* peekood/-eem (*pl+of:* -ey).

(to) command 1. לצוות *inf* letsavot; *pst* tseevah; *pres* metsaveh; *fut* yetsaveh; **2.** לפקד *inf* lefaked; *pst* peeked (*p=f*); *pres* mefaked; *fut* yefaked.

command of Hebrew שליטה בעברית *nf* shleetah be-'eevreet.

(to) command respect לעורר כבוד le'orer kavod; *pst* 'orer *etc*; *pres* me'orer *etc*; *fut* ye'orer *etc*.

(to) commandeer לגייס לשירות (mobilize) *inf* legayes le-sheroot; *pst* geeyes *etc*; *pres* megayes *etc*.

commission 1. ועדה (sub-committee) *nf* ve'ad|ah/ve'adot (+*of:* -at/-ot); **2.** כתב־מינוי (letter of appointment) *nm* ketav/keetvey meenooy.

(out of) commission 1. לא תקין *adj* lo takeen/tekeenah; **2.** לא בר־שימוש (out of order) *adj* lo bar/bat sheemoosh.

commissioned מיופה־כוח *adj* meyoop|eh/-at ko'akh.

commissioned officer קצין מוסמך katseen/ketseeneem moosmakh/-eem.

(non-)commissioned officer 1. מפקד שאינו קצין *nm* mefak|ed/-deem she-eyn|o/-am katseen/ketseeneem; **2.** מש"ק (*acr.*) *nmf* mashak/-eet (*pl:* -eem/-eeyot).

commissioner נציב *nm* netseev/-eem (*pl+of:* -ey).

(high-)commissioner נציב עליון *nm* netseev 'elyon.

(police) commissioner ניצב משטרה *nm* neetsav/-ey meeshtarah.

(to) commit לבצע *inf* levatse'a'; *pst* beetsa' (*b=v*); *pres* mevatse'a'; *fut* yevatse'a'.

(to) commit to memory לשנן בעל פה *inf* leshanen be-'al peh; *pst* sheenen *etc*; *pres* meshanen *etc*; *fut* yeshanen *etc*.

(to) commit to prison לדון למאסר *inf* ladoon le-ma'asar; *pst & pres* dan *etc*; *fut* yadoon *etc*.

commitment התחייבות *nf* heetkhayvoo|t/-yot.

committal 1. כליאה *nf* kleee|'ah/-'ot (+*of:* -'at); **2.** נקיטת עמדה (taking position) *nf* nekeet|at/-ot 'emdah.

committee 1. ועד *nm* va'ad/ve'adeem (*pl+of:* -ey); **2.** ועדה (sub-committee) *nf* va'ad|ah/ve'adot (+*of:* va'ad|at/-ot).

(standing/steering) committee ועדה מתמדת *nf* va'adah matmedet.

committee of one מחליט יחיד *nm* makhleet yakheed.

commode שידה *nf* sheed|ah/-ot (+*of:* -at).

commodity מצרך *nm* meetsrakh/-akheem (*pl+of:* -ekhey).

common 1. כללי (general) *adj* klalee/-t; **2.** משותף (joint) *adj* meshoot|af/-efet; **3.** מצוי (ordinary) matsooy/metsooyah; **4.** ציבורי (public) *adj* tseebooree/-t; **5.** המוני (*vulgar*) hamonee/-t.

common carrier רכב ציבורי *nm* rekhev tseebooree.

common law המשפט המקובל *nm* ha-meeshpat ha-mekoobal.

common law marriage נישואים אזרחיים *nm pl* neesoo'eem ezrakhee'eem.

common market שוק משותף *nm* shook meshootaf.

common sense שכל ישר *nm* sekhel yashar.

common soldier חייל פשוט *nm* khayal/-eem pashoot/peshooteem

common stock מניה רגילה *nf* mena|yah/-yot regeel|ah/-ot.

commoner פשוט־עם *nm* peshoot/-ey 'am.

commonness המוניות *nf* hamoneeyoo|t/-yot.

commonplace 1. אמרה נדושה *nf* eemr|ah/-ot nedosh|ah/-ot; **2.** שגרתי (routine) *adj* sheegratee/-t.

(House of) Commons בית הנבחרים הבריטי *nm* bet ha-neevkhareem ha-breetee.

commonwealth קהילייה *nf* keheelee|yah/-yot (+*of:* -yat).

Commonwealth of Independent States (CIS) חבר המדינות העצמאיות (present name of former USSR) *nm* khever ha-medeenot ha-'atsma'eeyot.

commotion 1. מהומה *nf* mehoom|ah/-ot (+*of:* -at); **2.** תסיסה (unrest) *nf* tesees|ah/-ot (+*of:* -at).

commune קהילה *nf* keheel|ah/-ot (+*of:* -at).

(to) communicate 1. לקיים קשר (maintain touch) *inf* lekayem kesher; *pst* keeyem *etc*; *pres* mekayem *etc*; *fut* yekayem *etc*; **2.** ליצור קשר (contact) *inf* leetsor kesher; *pst* yatsar *etc*; *pres* yotser *etc*; *fut* yeetsor *etc*.

communication 1. הודעה *nf* hoda|'ah/-'ot (+*of:* -'at); **2.** התקשרות *nf* heetkashroo|t/-yot.

(means of) communication אמצעי תקשורת *nm pl* emtsa'ey teekshoret.

communications תקשורת *nf* teekshoret.

(minister of) communications שר התקשורת *nmf* sar/-at ha-teekshoret.

(ministry of) communications משרד התקשורת *nm* meesrad ha-teekshoret

communicative 1. נוח לשיחה *adj* no'akh/nokhah le-seekhah; **2.** פתוח להתקשרות (open for communication) *adj* patoo'akh/petookhah le-heetkashroot.

communion 1. השתתפות *nf* heeshtatfoo|t/-yot; **2.** הידברות (agreement) *nf* heedavroo|t/-yot; **3.** קהילה דתית (religious community) *nf* keheel|ah/-ot datee|t/-yot.

communiqué 1. הודעה רשמית *nf* hoda|'ah/-'ot reeshmee|t/-yot; **2.** קומוניקט *nm* komooneekat/-eem.

communism קומוניזם *nm* komooneezm.

communist קומוניסט *nmf* komooneest/-eet (+*of:* -eem/-eeyot).

community קהילה *nf* keheel|ah/-ot (+*of:* -at).

(to) communize 1. להפוך לקומוניסטי *vt inf* lahafokh le-komooneestee; *pst* hafakh *etc*; *pres* hofekh *etc*; *fut* yahafokh *etc*; **2.** להעביר לרשות הכלל (subject to common ownership) *vt inf* leha'aveer le-reshoot ha-klal; *pst* he'eveer *etc*; *pres* ma'aveer *etc*; *fut* ya'aveer *etc*.

commutation ticket כרטיסייה *nf* karteesee|yah/-yot (+*of:* -yat).

commutator 1. מחלף *nm* makhlef/-eem (*pl+of:* -ey); **2.** מתג (switch) *nm* meteg/-ageem (*pl+of:* meetgey).

(to) commute 1. ליומם *inf* leyomem; *pst & pres* yomem; *fut* yeyomem; **2.** להחליף (exchange) *vt inf* lehakhleef; *pst* hekhleef; *pres* makhleef; fur yakhleef; **3.** להמתיק (punishment) *vt pst* lehamteek; *pst* heemteek; *pres* mamteek; *fut* yamteek.

commuter יומם *nmf* yomem/-et.

compact 1. דחוס *adj* dakhoos/dekhoosah; **2.** תמציתי (summary) *adj* tamtseetee/-t; **3.** מצופף (crammed) *adj* metsof|af/-efet.

compactness דחיסות *nf* dekheesoo|t/-yot.

companion 1. בן־לוויה *nmf* ben/bat levayah; **2.** מדריך *nmf* madreekh/-ah.

companionship 1. חברות *nf* khaveroo|t/-yot; **2.** ידידות *nf* yedeedoo|t/-yot.

company 1. חברה *nf* khevrah/khavarot (*+of:* khevr|at/-ot); **2.** להקה (theatr.) *nf* lahakah/lehakot (*+of):* lahakat; **3.** פלוגה (army) *nf* ploog|ah/-ot (*+of:* -at).

(to keep) company להתרועע *inf* leheetro'e'a'; *pst* heetro'e'a'; *pres* meetro'e'a'; *fut* yeetro'e'a'.

(to part) company להיפרד *inf* leheepared; *pst & pres* neefrad; *fut* yeepared.

comparable משתווה *adj* meeshtav|eh/-ah.

comparative השוואתי *adj* hashva'atee/-t.

(to) compare להשוות *inf* lehashvot; *pst* heeshvah; *pres* mashveh; *fut* yashveh.

(beyond) compare ללא השוואה *adv* le-lo hashva'ah.

comparison השוואה *nf* hashva|'ah/-'ot (*+of:* -'at).

(beyond) comparison מעבר לכל השוואה *adv* me-'ever le-khol hashva'ah.

(in) comparison with בהשוואה עם *adv* be-hashva'ah 'eem.

compartment תא *nm* ta/ta'eem (*pl+of:* ta'ey)

compass 1. מצפן *nm* matspen/-eem (*pl+of:* -ey); **2.** היקף (extent) *nm* hekef/-eem (*pl+of:* -ey).

compassionate 1. רחום *adj* rakhoom/rekhoomah; **2.** חנון (commiserate) *adj* khanoon/-ah.

compatible מתיישב עם *adj* meetyashev/-et 'eem.

compatriot 1. בן־ארץ (landsman) *nmf* ben/bat erets; **2.** בן־עיר (townsman) *nmf* ben/bat 'eer.

(to) compel להכריח *inf* lehakhree'akh; *pst* heekhree'akh; *pres* makhree'akh; *fut* yakhree akh.

compendious 1. מקוצר *adj* mekoots|ar/-eret; **2.** מתומצת (summarized) *adj* metoomts|at/-etet.

(to) compensate לפצות *inf* lefatsot; *pst* peetsah (*p=f*); *pres* mefatseh; *fut* yefatseh.

compensation פיצוי *nm* peetsoo|y/-yeem (*pl+of:* -yey).

(to) compete 1. להתחרות *v rfl inf* leheetkharot; *pst* heetkharah; *pres* meetkhareh; *fut* yeetkhareh; **2.** לתחר (contest) *inf* letakher; *pst* teekher; *pres* metakher; *fut* yetakher.

competence סמכות *nf* samkhoo|t/-yot.

competent 1. מוסמך *adj* moosm|akh/-ekhet; **2.** בר־סמכא (qualified) *nmf* bar/bat samkha.

competition תחרות *nf* takharoo|t/-yot.

competitive בר־תחרות *adj* bar/bat takharoot.

competitive examination בחינה תחרותית *nf* bekheen|ah/-ot takhrootee|t/-yot.

competitor מתחרה *nmf* meetkhar|eh/-ah.

compilation 1. חיבור *nm* kheeboor/-eem (*pl+of:* -ey); **2.** לקט *nm* lek|et/-ateem (*pl+of:* leektey).

(to) compile 1. לחבר *inf* lekhaber; *pst* kheeber; *pres* mekhaber; *fut* yekhaber; **2.** ללקט *inf* lelaket; *pst* leeket; *pres* melaket; *fut* yelaket.

complacency שאננות *nf* sha'ananoo|t/-yot.

complacent שאנן *adj* sha'anan/-ah.

(to) complain להתלונן *inf* leheetlonen; *pst* heetlonen; *pres* meetlonen; *fut* yeetlonen.

complaint תלונה *nf* tloon|ah/-ot (*+of:* -at).

(to lodge a) complaint להגיש תלונה *inf* lehageesh tloonah; *pst* heegeesh *etc*; *pres* mageesh *etc*; *fut* yageesh *etc*.

complaisant 1. נעים *adj* na'eem/ne'eemah; **2.** אדיב *adj* adeev/-ah.

complement 1. השלמה *nf* hashlam|ah/-ot (*+of:* -at); **2.** משלים *adj* mashleem/-ah.

(to) complement להשלים *inf* lehashleem; *pst* heeshleem; *pres* mashleem; *fut* yashleem.

complete 1. שלם *adj* shalem/shlemah; **2.** גמור (finished) gamoor/gemoorah.

(to) complete להשלים *inf* lehashleem; *pst* heeshleem; *pres* mashleem; *fut* yashleem.

completely כליל *adv* kaleel.

completeness שלמות *nf* shlemoo|t/-yot.

completion 1. סיום *nm* seeyoom/-eem (*pl+of:* -ey); **2.** גמר *nm* gemer (*also:* gemar).

complex 1. מסובך *adj* mesoob|akh/-ekhet; **2.** תשלובת *nf* teeshlov|et/-ot.

complexion 1. מראה *nm* mar|'eh/-'ot (*pl+of:* -'ey); **2.** גון העור *nm* gon/-ey ha-'or.

complexity מורכבות *nf* moorkavoo|t/-yot.

compliance 1. ציות *nm* tseeyoot/-eem (*pl+of:* -ey); **2.** היענות *nf* he'anoo|t/-yot.

(in) compliance with בהתאם ל־ *adv* be-het'em le-.

(to) complicate לסבך *inf* lesabekh; *pst* seebekh; *pres* mesabekh; *fut* yesabekh.

complicated מסובך *adj* mesoob|akh/-ekhet.

complication 1. סיבוך *nm* seebookh/-eem (*pl+of:* -ey); **2.** תסבוכת (tangle) *nf* teesbokh|et/-ot.

complicity שותפות לדבר עבירה *nf* shootafoot lee-dvar 'averah.

compliment מחמאה *nf* makhma|'ah/-'ot (*+of:* -'at).

(to) compliment לחלוק מחמאה *inf* lakhlok makhma|'ah/-'ot; *pst* khalak *etc*; *pres* kholek *etc*; *fut* yakhlok *etc*.

complimentary copy עותק חינם *nm* 'ot|ek/-key kheenam.

complimentary ticket 1. כרטיס חינם (free) *nm* kartees/-ey kheenam; **2.** כרטיס הזמנה (invitation) *nm* kartees/-ey hazmanah.

(one's) compliments 1. דרישת שלום *nf* dreesh|at/-ot shalom; **2.** ד״ש (*acr of* 1) *nm* dash/-eem (*pl+of:* -ey).

(to) comply 1. למלא אחר *inf* lemale akhar; *pst* meele *etc*; *pres* memale *etc*; *fut* yemale *etc*; **2.** לציית (heed) *inf* letsayet; *pst* tseeyet; *pres* metsayet; *fut* yetsayet.

component 1. רכיב *nm* rekheev/-eem (*pl+of:* -ey); **2.** מרכיב *nm* markeev/-eem (*pl+of:* -ey).

(to) comport 1. לתאום *inf* leet'om; *pst* ta'am; *pres* to'em; *fut* yeet'am; **2.** לנהוג (behave) *inf* leenhog; *pst* nahag; *pres* noheg; *fut* yeenhag.

(to) compose 1. להרכיב (assemble) *inf* leharkeev; *pst* heerkeev; *pres* markeev; *fut* yarkeev; **2.** להלחין (music) *inf* lehalkheen; *pst* heelkheen; *pres* malkheen; *fut* yalkheen; **3.** לחבר (author) *inf* lekhaber; *pst* kheeber; *pres* mekhaber; *fut* yekhaber.

(to) compose oneself להירגע *inf* leheraga'; *pst & pres* neerga'; *fut* yeraga'.

composed רגוע *adj* ragoo'a'/regoo'ah.

composer מלחין *nm* malkheen/-eem (*pl+of:* -ey).

composite 1. מורכב *adj* moork|av/-evet; **2.** הרכב *nm* herkev/-eem (*pl+of:* -ey).

composition 1. מבנה (structure) *nm* meevn|eh/-eem (*pl+of:* -ey); **2.** יצירה מוסיקלית (music) *nf* yetseer|ah/-ot mooseekalee|t-yot.

composure 1. שלווה *nf* shalv|ah/-ot (*+of:* -at); **2.** רוגע *nm* rog|a'/rega'eem (*pl+of:* rog'ey); **3.** שליטה עצמית (self control) *nf* shleetah 'atsmeet.

compound 1. שטח מגודר (fenced area) *nm* shetakh/-eem megoodar/-eem; **2.** תרכובת (blend) *nf* teerkov|et/-ot; **3.** גוש בניינים (building complex) *nm* goosh/-ey beenyaneem.

compound interest ריבית דריבית *nf* reebeet de-reebeet.

(to) comprehend 1. להבין (understand) *v inf* lehaveen; *pst* heveen; *pres* meveen; *fut* yaveen; **2.** לתפוס (grasp) *inf* leetpos; *pst* tafas (*f=p*); *pres* tofes; *fut* yeetpos; **3.** לכלול (comprise) *inf* leekhlol; *pst* kalal (*k=kh*); *pres* kolel; *fut* yeekhlol.

comprehensible ניתן לתפיסה *adj* neet|an/-enet lee-tfeesah.

comprehension הבנה *nf* havan|ah/-ot (*+of:* -at).

comprehensive מקיף *adj* makeef/-ah.

compress 1. תחבושת *nf* takhbosh|et/-ot; **2.** אספלנית *nf* eespelanee|t/-yot.

(to) compress לדחוס *inf* leedkhos; *pst* dakhas; *pres* dokhes; *fut* yeedkhas.

compression דחיסות *nf* dekheesoo|t/-yot.

compressor מדחס *nm* madkh|es/-aseem (*pl+of:* -asey).

(to) comprise להכיל *inf* lehakheel; *pst* hekheel; *pres* mekheel; *fut* yakheel.

compromise פשרה *nf* peshar|ah/-ot (*+of:* -at).

(to) compromise 1. להתפשר (settle) *inf* leheetpasher; *pst* heetpasher; *pres* meetpasher; *fut* yeetpasher; **2.** לפגום בשם הטוב (hurt reputation) *inf* leefgom ba-shem ha-tov; *pst* pagam (*p=f*) *etc*; *pres* pogem *etc*; *fut* yeefgom *etc*.

compromising evidence עדות מחשידה *nf* 'edoo|t/-yot makhsheed|ah/-ot.

comptroller מפקח *nmf* mefak|e'akh/-akhat (*pl:* -'kheem/-'khot; *+of:* -'khey).

(state) comptroller מבקר המדינה *nm* mevaker ha-medeenah.

compulsion 1. אילוץ *nm* eeloots/-eem (*pl+of:* -ey); **2.** כפייה *nf* kfee|yah/-yot (*+of:* -yat).

compulsory 1. הכרחי *adj* hekhrekhee/-t; **2.** שבחובה *adj* she-be-khovah.

compunction 1. נקיפת מצפון *nf* nekeef|at/-ot matspoon; **2.** רגש אשמה (guilty feeling) *nm* regesh/reegshey ashmah.

computation חישוב *nm* kheeshoov/-eem (*pl+of:* -ey).

(to) compute לחשב *inf* lekhashev; *pst* kheeshev; *pres* mekhashev; *fut* yekhashev.

computer מחשב *nm* makhsh|ev/-aveem (*pl+of:* -avey).

(to) computerize למחשב *inf* lemakhshev; *pst* meekhshev; *pres* memakhshev; *fut* yemakhshev.

comrade חבר *nmf* khaver/-ah.

concave קעור *adj* ka'oor/ke'oorah.

(to) conceal 1. להסתיר (hide) *inf* lehasteer; *pst* heesteer; *pres* masteer; *fut* yasteer; **2.** לחפות על (cover-up) *inf* lekhapot 'al; *pst* kheepah 'al; *pres* mekhapeh 'al; *fut* yekhapeh 'al.

concealment 1. הסתרה *nf* hastar|ah/-ot (*+of:* -at); **2.** חיפוי על (cover up) *nm* kheepooy/-eem 'al.

(to) concede 1. להודות כי (confess) *inf* lehodot kee; *pst* hodah kee; *pres* modeh kee; *fut* yodeh kee; **2.** לוותר (give in) *inf* levater; *pst* veeter; *pres* mevater; *fut* yevater.

conceit 1. יהירות *nf* yeheeroot; **2.** גאוות שווא (false pride) *nf* ga'av|at/-ot shav.

conceited מתייהר *adj* meetyaher/-et.

conceivable מתקבל על הדעת *adj* meetkabel/-et 'al ha-da'at.

(to) conceive 1. להגות *inf* lahagot; *pst* hagah; *pres* hogeh; *fut* yehegeh; **2.** להרות (pregnancy) *inf* laharot; *pst* hartah; *pres* harah; *fut* tahareh.

concentrate תרכיז *nm* tarkeez/-eem (*pl+of:* -ey).

(to) concentrate 1. לרכז *vt inf* lerakez; *pst* reekez; *pres* merakez; *fut* yerakez; **2.** להתרכז *vi inf* leheetrakez; *pst* heetrakez; *pres* meetrakez; *fut* yeetrakez.

concentration 1. ריכוז (compulsory) *nm* reekooz/-eem (*pl+of:* -ey); **2.** התרכזות (voluntary) *nf* heetrakzoo|t/-yot.

concentration camp מחנה ריכוז *nm* makhn|eh/-ot reekooz.

concentric 1. בעל מרכז משותף *adj* ba'al/-at merkaz meshootaf; **2.** קונצנטרי *adj* kontsentree/-t.

concept 1. מושג *nm* moosag/-eem (*pl+of:* -ey); **2.** רעיון *nf* ra'ayon/-ot.

conception 1. קונצפציה *nf* kontsepts|yah/-yot; **2.** תפיסה *nf* tfees|ah/-ot (*+of:* -at); **3.** התעברות (pregnancy) *nf* heet'abroo|t/-yot.

concern 1. דאגה (worry) *nf* de'ag|ah/-ot (*+of:* da'ag|at/-ot); **2.** קונצרן (business) *nm* kontsern/-eem (*pl+of:* -ey).

(of no) concern לא איכפת *adv* lo eekhpat.

(to) concern 1. לנגוע ל- (regard) *inf* leengo'a' le-; *pst* naga' le-; *pres* noge'a' le-; *fut* yeega' le-; **2.** להעסיק (occupy) *inf* leha'aseek; *pst* he'eseek; *pres* ma'aseek; *fut* ya'aseek; **3.** להדאיג (worry) *inf* lehad'eeg; *pst* heed'eeg; *pres* mad'eeg; *fut* yad'eeg.

concerned 1. מודאג (worried) *adj* mood'|ag/-eget; **2.** נוגע בדבר (involved) *adj* nog|e'a'/-a'at be-davar,

(as far as I am) concerned ככל שזה נוגע לי *adv* ke-khol she-zeh noge'a' lee.

concerning בנוגע ל־ *adv* be-noge'a le-.

concert קונצרט *nm* kontsert/-eem (*pl+of:* -ey).

concerted מתוכנן במשותף *adj* metookhn|an/-enet bee-meshootaf.

concession 1. ויתור (yielding) *nm* veetoor/-eem (*pl+of:* -ey); **2.** זיכיון (privilege) *nm* zee|kayon/-khyonot (*+of:* -khyon).

concierge שוער *nmf* sho'er/-et.

(to) conciliate 1. לפייס (appease) *inf* lefayes; *pst* peeyes (*p=f*); *pres* mefayes; *fut* yefayes; **2.** להשכין שלום (settle dispute) *inf* lehashkeen shalom; *pst* heeshkeen *etc*; *pres* mashkeen *etc*; *fut* yashkeen *etc*.

concise תמציתי *adj* tamtseetee/-t.

conciseness תמציתיות *nf* tamtseeteeyoot.

(to) conclude 1. לסיים *v inf* lesayem; *pst* seeyem; *pres* mesayem; *fut* yesayem; **2.** לגמור (finish) *v inf* leegmor; *pst* gamar; *pres* gomer; *fut* yeegmor; **3.** לסכם (sum up) *inf* lesakem; *pst* seekem; *pres* mesakem; *fut* yesakem.

conclusion 1. סיכום (sum up) *nm* seekoom/-eem (*pl+of:* -ey); **2.** סיום (ending) *nm* seeyoom/-eem (*pl+of:* -ey).

conclusive 1. מכריע *adj* makhr|ee'a'/-a'at; **2.** חותך *adj* khotekh/-et.

conclusive evidence עדות מכרעת *nf* 'edoo|t/-yot makhr|a'at/-ee'ot.

(to) concoct 1. לבשל (cook up) *inf* levashel; *pst* beeshel (*b=v*); *pres* mevashel; *fut* yevashel; **2.** להמציא (invent) *inf* lehamtsee; *pst* heemtsee; *pres* mamtsee; *fut* yamtsee.

concoction תבשיל *nm* tavsheel/-eem (*pl+of:* -ey).

concomitant בו־זמני *adj* bo-zmanee/-t.

concomittantly בו־זמנית *adv* bo-zmaneet.

concord 1. הסכמה *nf* haskam|ah/-ot (*+of:* -at); **2.** התאמה (grammar) *nf* hat'am|ah/-ot (*+of:* -at).

concordance 1. קונקורדנציה *nf* konkordants|yah/-yot (*+of:* -yat); **2.** התאמה (agreement) *nf* hat'am|ah/-ot (*+of:* -at).

concourse 1. טיילת (promenade) *nf* tayelet/tayalot; **2.** רחבה (public square) *nf* rekhav|ah/-ot (*+of:* rakhav|at/-ot).

concrete 1. בטון *nm* beton/-eem (*pl+of:* -ey); **2.** מוחשי (actual) *adj* mookhashee/-t.

concrete block 1. בלוק *nm* blok/-eem (*pl+of:* -ey); **2.** בלוק בטון *nm* blok/-ey beton.

concrete mixer מערבל בטון *nm* me'arbel/-ey beton.

concubine 1. ידועה בציבור (common-law wife) *nf* yedoo'|ah/-ot ba-tseeboor; **2.** פילגש (mistress) *nf* peel|egesh/-agsh|eem (*pl+of:* -ey).

(to) concur 1. להסכים (agree) *inf* lehaskeem; *pst* heeskeem; *pres* maskeem; *fut* yaskeem; **2.** להצטרף לדיעה (second) *inf* leheetstaref la-de'ah; *pst* heetstaref *etc*; *pres* meetstaref *etc*; *fut* yeetstaref *etc*.

concurrence תמימות דעים *nf* temeemoo|t/-yot de'eem.

concurrent jurisdiction שיפוט מקביל *nm* sheefoot makbeel.

concurrent negligence התרשלות מקבילה *nf* heetrashloo|t/-yot makbeel|ah/-ot.

concurrent sentence עונש חופף *nm pl* 'on|esh/-sheem khofef/-eem.

concussion זעזוע *nm* za'azoo'|a/-eem (*pl+of:* -ey).

(to) condemn 1. לדון ל־ (sentence) *inf* ladoon le-; *pst & pres* dan le-; *fut* yadoon le-; **2.** לגנות (censure) *inf* leganot; *pst* geenah; *pres* meganeh; *fut* yeganeh; **3.** לפסול (rule out) *inf* leefsol; *pst* pasal (*p=f*); *pres* posel; *fut* yeefsol.

condemnation 1. גינוי (censure) *nm* geenooy/-eem (*pl+of:* -ey); **2.** הרשעה (conviction) *nf* harsha'|ah/-ot (*+of:* -at).

condensation 1. עיבוי *nm* 'eeboo|y/-yeem (*pl+of:* -yey); **2.** דחיסה *nf* dekhees|ah/-ot (*+of:* -at).

(to) condense 1. לעבות *inf* le'abot; *pst* 'eebah; *pres* me'abeh; *fut* ye'abeh; **2.** לצופף *inf* letsofef; *pst* tsofef; *pres* metsofef; *fut* yetsofef.

condensed milk חלב משומר *nm* khalav meshoomar.

(to) condescend להואיל *inf* leho'eel; *pst* ho'eel; *pres* mo'eel; *fut* yo'eel.

condescension מחילה על כבוד *nf* mekheel|ah/-ot 'al kavod.

condiment תבלין *nm* tavleen/-eem (*pl+of:* -ey).

condition 1. תנאי *nm* tena|y/-'eem (*pl+of:* -'ey); **2.** מצב (state) *nm* mats|av/-aveem (*pl+of:* -vey).

(air) condition מיזוג־אוויר *nm* meezoog/-ey aveer.

(on) condition that בתנאי ש־ *adv* bee-tnay she-.

conditional 1. מותנה *adj* mootneh/-t; **2.** על תנאי *adj* 'al tenay.

conditioned 1. מותאם *adj* moot|'am/-'emet; **2.** מוכשר *adj* mookhsh|ar/-eret.

(to) condole להביע תנחומים *inf* lehabee'a' *etc* tankhoomeem; *pst* heebee'a' *etc*; *pres* mabee'a' *etc*; *fut* yabee'a' *etc*.

condolence 1. ניחום *nm* neekhoom/-eem (*pl+of:* -ey); **2.** תנחומים *nm pl* tankhoom|eem (*+of:* -ey); **3.** השתתפות בצער (sympathy) *nf* heeshtatfoo|t/-yot be-tsa'ar.

condom 1. קונדום *nm* kondom (*cpr* kandon)/-eem (*pl+of:* -ey); **2.** כובעון *nm* kov|a'on/-'oneem (*pl+of:* -'oney).

(to) condone לקבל בסלחנות *inf* lekabel be-salkhanoot; *pst* keebel *etc*; *pres* mekabel *etc*; *fut* yekabel *etc*.

(to) conduce להוביל ל־ *inf* lehoveel le-; *pst* hoveel le-; *pres* moveel le-; *fut* yoveel le-.

conducive מביא לידי *adj* mevee/-'ah lee-yedey.

(to) conduct 1. לנהל (lead) *inf* lenahel; *pst* neehel; *pres* menahel; *fut* yenahel; **2.** לנצח (orchestra) *inf* lenatse'akh; *pst* neetsakh; *pres* menatse'akh; *fut* yenatse'akh; **3.** להוליך (electricity) *inf* leholeekh; *pst* holeekh; *pres* moleekh; *fut* yoleekh.

(to) conduct oneself להתנהג *inf* leheetnaheg; *pst* heetnaheg; *pres* meetnaheg; *fut* yeetnaheg.

conductor כרטיסן (train, bus, street-car) *nmf* karteesan/-eet.

(orchestra) conductor מנצח *nm* menats|e'akh/-kheem (*pl+of:* -khey).

(semi-)conductor מוליך למחצה *nm & adj* moleekh/-ah (*pl:* -eem/-ot) le-mekhetsah.

conduit 1. צינור (pipe) *nm* tseenor/-ot; **2.** תעלה (canal) *nf* te'al|ah/-ot (+*of:* -at).

cone 1. קונוס *nm* konoos/-eem (*pl+of:* -ey); **2.** חרוט *nm* kharoot/-eem (*pl+of:* -ey); **3.** אצטרובל (pine-) *nm* eetstroobal/-eem (*pl+of:* -ey).

confection ממתקים *nm pl* mamtakeem (*pl+of:* -ey).

confectionery מגדנייה *nf* meegdanee|yah/-yot (+*of:* -yat).

confederacy, confederation 1. קונפדרציה *nf* confederats|yah/-yot (+*of:* -yat); **2.** ברית (covenant) *nf* breet/-ot.

confederate 1. בעל־ברית *nm* ba'al/-ey breet; **2.** שותף לקשר *nmf* shootaf/-ah le-kesher.

(to) confer 1. להיוועץ (consult) *inf* leheeva'ets; *pst & pres* no'ats; *fut* yeeva'ets; **2.** להעניק (bestow) *inf* leha'aneek; *pst* he'eneek; *pres* ma'aneek; *fut* ya'aneek.

conference ועידה *nf* ve'eed|ah/-ot (+*of:* -at).

(to) confess 1. להתוודות *inf* leheetvadot; *pst* heetvadah; *pres* meetvadeh; *fut* yeetvadeh; **2.** להודות (admit) *inf* lehodot; *pst* hodah; *pres* modeh; *fut* yodeh.

confession 1. וידוי *nm* veedoo|y/-yeem (*pl+of:* -yey); **2.** הודאה (admission) *nf* hoda|'ah/-'ot (+*of:* -'at).

confession of faith הצהרת "אני מאמין" *nf* hats'har|at/-ot "anee ma'ameen".

confessional תא הווידוי *nf* ta/-'ey ha-veedooy.

confessor 1. מתוודה *nmf* meetvad|eh/-ah; **2.** כומר מוודה (father confessor) *nm* komer mevadeh.

(to) confide 1. לבטוח במישהו *inf* leevto'akh be-meeshe|hoo/-hee; *pst* batakh *(b=v) etc*; *pres* bote'akh *etc*; *fut* yeevtakh *etc*; **2.** לתת אימון (trust) *inf* latet emoon; *pst* natan *etc*; *pres* noten *etc*; *fut* yeeten *etc*.

confidence אימון *nm* eymoon.

confidence man רמאי *nm* rama|y/-'eem (*pl+of:* -'ey).

confident 1. בוטח בעצמו *adj* bot|e'akh/-akhat be-'atsm|o/-ah; **2.** בטוח (sure) *adj* batoo'akh/betookhah.

confidential 1. סודי (secret) *adj* sodee/-t; **2.** פנימי (inner) *adj* peneemee/-t.

confidently בביטחון *adv* be-veetakhon *(v=b)*.

(to) confine 1. להגביל (restrict) *inf* lehagbeel; *pst* heegbeel; *pres* magbeel; *fut* yagbeel; **2.** לכלוא (imprison) *inf* leekhlo; *pst* kala *(k=kh)*; *pres* kole; *fut* yeekhla.

(to) confine oneself להצטמצם *inf* leheetstamtsem; *pst* heetstamtsem; *pres* meetstamtsem; *fut* yeetstamtsem.

confined in bed רתוק למיטתו *adj* ratook/retookah le-meetat|o/-ah.

confinement 1. כליאה (imprisonment) *nf* klee|'ah/-'ot (+*of:* -'at); **2.** לידה (giving birth) *nf* leyd|ah/-ot (+*of:* -at).

(to) confirm לאשר *inf* le'asher; *pst* eesher; *pres* me'asher; *fut* ye'asher.

confirmation אישור *nm* eeshoor/-eem (*pl+of:* -ey).

(to) confiscate להחרים *inf* lehakhreem; *pst* hekhreem; *pres* makhreem; *fut* yakhreem.

confiscation החרמה *nf* hakhram|ah/-ot (+*of:* -at).

conflagration דליקת ענק *nf* dlek|at/-ot 'anak.

conflict סכסוך *nm* seekhsookh/-eem (*pl+of:* -ey).

conflicting סותר *adj* soter/-et.

confluence התמזגות *nf* heetmazgoo|t/-yot.

(to) conform 1. לתאום *inf* leet'om; *pst* ta'am; *pres* to'em; *fut* yeet'am; **2.** למלא אחר *inf* lemale akhar; *pst* meele *etc*; *pres* memale *etc*; *fut* yemale *etc*.

conformity התאמה *nf* hat'am|ah/-ot (+*of:* -at).

(to) confound 1. לבלבל (confuse) *inf* levalbel; *pst* beelbel; *pres* mevalbel *(v=b)*; *fut* yevalbel; **2.** לסכל (frustrate) *inf* lesakel; *pst* seekel; *pres* mesakel; *fut* yesakel.

(to) confront 1. לעמת *inf* le'amet; *pst* 'eemet; *pres* me'amet; *fut* ye'amet; **2.** לעמוד בפני (withstand) *inf* la'amod bee-fney; *pst* 'amad *etc*; *pres* 'omed *etc*; *fut* ya'amod *etc*.

(to) confuse 1. להביך *inf* lehaveekh; *pst* heveekh; *pres* meveekh; *fut* yaveekh; **2.** לבלבל (confound) *inf* levalbel; *pst* beelbel; *pres* mevalbel; *fut* yevalbel.

(to become) confused להתבלבל *inf* leheetbalbel; *pst* heetbalbel; *pres* meetbalbel; *fut* yeetbalbel.

confusing מביך *adj* meveekh/-ah.

confusion מבוכה *nf* mevookh|ah/-ot (+*of:* -at).

(to) congeal 1. להקריש *inf* lehakreesh; *pst* heekreesh; *pres* makreesh; *fut* yakreesh; **2.** להקפיא (freeze) *inf* lehakpee; *pst* heekpee; *pres* makpee; *fut* yakpee.

congenial נוח *adj* no'akh/nokhah.

congenital 1. מולד *adj* mool|ad/-edet; **2.** מלידה *adj* mee-leydah.

congestion 1. גודש *nm* godesh/gedasheem (*pl+of:* godshey); **2.** צפיפות־יתר (overcrowding) *nf* tsefeefoo|t/-yot yeter.

conglomeration גיבוב *nm* geeboov/-eem (*pl+of:* -ey).

(to) congratulate לברך *inf* levarekh; *pst* berakh *(b=v)*; *pres* mevarekh; *fut* yevarekh.

congratulations 1. ברכות *nf pl* brakhot (+*of:* beerkhot; *sing:* brakhah; +*of:* beerkat); **2.** איחולים (best wishes) *nm pl* eekhool|eem (+*of:* -ey).

(to) congregate לכנס *inf* lekhanes; *pst* keenes *(k=kh)*; *pres* mekhanes; *fut* yekhanes.

congregation קהילה דתית *nf* keheel|ah/-ot datee|t/-yot.

congress 1. קונגרס *nm* kongres/-eem (*pl+of:* -ey); **2.** ועידה (conference) *nf* ve'eed|ah/-ot (+*of:* -at).

(the U.S.) Congress 1. הקונגרס האמריקני *nm* ha-kongres ha-amereekanee; **2.** בית הנבחרים של ארצות־הברית *nm* bet/batey ha-neevkhareem shel artsot ha-breet.

(the Zionist) Congress הקונגרס הציוני ha-kongres ha-tseeyonee.

congressional של הקונגרס *adj* shel ha-kongres.

congressman, -woman חבר הקונגרס *nmf* khav|er/-rat ha-kongres.

conic, conical דמוי חרוט *adj* demoo|y/-yat kharoot.

conjecture השערה *nf* hash'ar|ah/-ot (+*of:* -at).

(to) conjecture לשער *inf* lesha'er; *pst* shee'er; *pres* mesha'er; *fut* yesha'er.

conjugal 1. של נישואים *adj* shel neesoo'eem; **2.** של בני זוג *adj* shel beney zoog.

(to) conjugate לנטות פועל *inf* leentot po'al; *pst* natah *etc; pres* noteh *etc; fut* yeeteh *etc.*
conjugation נטיית פעלים *nf* neteeǀyat/-yot pe'aleem.
conjunction 1. מלת חיבור (grammar) *nf* meelǀat/-ot kheeboor; **2.** חיבור (union) *nm* kheeboor/-eem (*pl+of:* -ey).
conjunctive 1. מחבר (joining) *adj* mekhaber/-et; **2.** מחובר (joined) *adj* mekhoobǀar/-eret.
(to) conjure 1. להשביע (swear in) *inf* lehashbee'a'; *pst* heeshbee'a'; *pres* mashhbee'a'; *fut* yashbee'a'; **2.** להעלות באוב (summon a spirit) *v inf* leha'alot be-ov; *pst* he'elah *etc; pres* ma'aleh *etc; fut* ya'aleh *etc.*
(to) connect 1. לקשר *inf* lekasher; *pst* keesher; *pres* mekasher; *fut* yekasher; **2.** לחבר (join) *inf* lekhaber; *pst* kheeber; *pres* mekhaber; *fut* yekhaber.
connecting rod טלטל *nm* taltal/-eem (*pl+of:* -ey).
connection, connexion 1. קשר *nm* keshǀer/-areem (*pl+of:* keeshrey); **2.** חיבור (joint) *nm* kheeboor/-eem (*pl+of:* -ey).
conniption התקף היסטריה *nm* hetkef/-ey heesteryah.
(to) connive 1. להתנכל *inf* leheetnakel; *pst* heetnakel; *pres* meetnakel; *fut* yeetnakel; **2.** לזום *inf* lazom; *pst* zamam; *pres* zomem; *fut* yazom.
connoisseur מבין דבר *nmf* meveen/-at davar.
connubial 1. של זוג נשוי *adj* shel zoog nasooy; **2.** של נישואים *adj* shel neesoo'eem.
(to) conquer 1. לכבוש *inf* leekhbosh; *pst* kavash (*k=kh; v=b*); *pres* kovesh; *fut* yeekhbosh; **2.** לנצח (vanquish) *inf* lenatse'akh; *pst* neetsakh; *pres* menatse'akh; *fut* yenatse'akh.
conqueror 1. כובש *adj* kovesh/-et; **2.** מנצח (victor) *nmf & adj* menatse'akh/-akhat.
conquest כיבוש *nm* keeboosh/-eem (*pl+of:* -ey).
conscience מצפון *nm* matspoon/-eem (*pl+of:* -ey).
conscientious 1. בעל מצפון *adj* ba'al/-at matspoon; **2.** דייקן (punctual) *adj* daykan/-eet.
conscious 1. מודע *adj* moodǀa'/-a'at; **2.** בהכרה (awake) *adv* be-hakarah.
consciousness 1. תודעה *nf* todaǀ'ah/-'ot (*+of:* -'at); **2.** הכרה (being awake) *nf* hakarǀah (*+of:* -at).
conscript מגויס לשירות חובה *nmf & adj* megooyǀas/-eset le-sheroot khovah.
(to) conscript לגייס לשירות חובה *inf* legayes le-sheroot khovah; *pst* geeyes *etc; pres* megayes *etc; fut* yegayes *etc.*
(to) consecrate להקדיש *inf* lehakdeesh; *pst* heekdeesh; *pres* makdeesh; *fut* yakdeesh.
consecration 1. הקדשה *nf* hakdashǀah/-ot (*+of:* -at); **2.** קידוש *nm* keedoosh/-eem (*pl+of:* -ey).
consecutive רצוף *adj* ratsoof/retsoofah.
consensus 1. קונסנסוס *nm* konsensoos (*cpr* kontsenzoos)/-eem; **2.** הסכמה כללית *nf* haskamah klaleet.
consent הסכמה *nf* haskamǀah/-ot (*+of:* -at).
(to) consent להסכים *inf* lehaskeem; *pst* heeskeem; *pres* maskeem; *fut* yaskeem.

consequence 1. תוצאה (result) *nf* totsǀa'ah/-a'ot (*+of:* -'at/-'ot); **2.** מסקנה (deduction) *nf* maskanǀah/-ot (*+of:* -at).
consequent שבא כתוצאה *adj* she-ba/-'ah ke-totsa'ah.
consequential 1. עיקבי *adj* 'eekvee/-t; **2.** בעל־חשיבות (important) *adj* ba'al/-at khasheevoot.
consequently 1. על כן *adv* al-ken; **2.** איפוא *adv* efo.
conservation שימור *nm* sheemoor.
conservatism שמרנות *nf* shamranooǀt/-yot.
conservative 1. שמרני *adj* shamranee/-t; **2.** קונסרבטיבי *adj* konservateevee/-t.
conservatory קונסרבטוריון *nm* konservatoryon/-eem (*pl+of:* -ey).
conserve, -s שימורים *nm pl* sheemoorǀeem (*pl+of:* -ey).
(to) conserve לשמר *inf* leshamer; *pst* sheemer; *pres* meshamer; *fut* yeshamer.
(to) consider 1. להתחשב ב־ *inf* leheetkhashev be-; *pst* heetkhashev be-; *pres* meetkhashev be-; *fut* yeetkhashev be-; **2.** לשקול (ponder) *inf* leeshkol; *pst* shakal; *pres* shokel; *fut* yeeshkol.
considerable 1. ניכר *adj* neekǀar/-eret; **2.** ראוי לציון (worth mentioning) *adj* ra'ooy/re'ooyah le-tseeyoon.
considerably במידה ניכרת *adv* be-meedah neekeret.
considerate מתחשב בזולת *adj* meetkhashev/-et ba-zoolat.
consideration 1. שיקול (argument) *nm* sheekool/-eem (*pl+of:* -ey); **2.** תמורה (counter-value) *nf* tmoorǀah/-ot (*+of:* -at).
(in) consideration of בתמורה ל־ *adv* bee-tmoorah le-.
considering בהתחשב עם *adv* be-heetkhashev 'eem.
(to) consign 1. לשלוח (send) *inf* leeshlo'akh; *pst* shalakh; *pres* shole'akh; *fut* yeeshlakh; **2.** להפקיד (entrust) *inf* lehafkeed; *pst* heefkeed; *pres* mafkeed; *fut* yafkeed.
consignee מקבל המשלוח *nmf* mekabel/-et ha-meeshlo'akh.
consignment משלוח *nm* meeshloǀ'akh/-kheem (*pl+of:* -khey).
(to) consist להיות מורכב מ־ (contain) *inf* leehyot moorkǀav/-evet mee-; *pst* hayah *etc; pres* hoo *etc; fut* yeehyeh *etc.*
consistency עיקביות *nf* 'eekveeyoot.
consistent 1. עיקבי *adj* 'eekvee/-t; **2.** תואם (fitting) *adj* to'em/-et; **3.** הגיוני (logical) *adj* hegyonee/-t.
consistory 1. קונסיסטוריה *nf* konseestorǀyah/-yot (*+of:* -yat); **2.** מועצה דתית (religious council) *nf* mo'atsǀah/-ot dateeǀt/-yot.
consolation 1. נחמה (solace) *nf* nekhamǀah/-ot (*+of:* -at); **2.** עידוד (encouragement) *nm* 'eedood/-eem (*pl+of:* -ey).
console 1. קונסול *[colloq.] nm* konsol/-eem (*pl+of:* -ey); **2.** לוח בקרה (control panel) *nm* looǀ'akh/-khot bakarah.
(to) console 1. לנחם (condole) *inf* lenakhem; *pst* neekhem; *pres* menakhem; *fut* yenakhem; **2.** לעודד (encourage) *inf* le'oded; *pst* 'oded; *pres* me'oded; *fut* ye'oded.

(to) consolidate 1. לחזק *inf* lekhazek; *pst* kheezek; *pres* mekhazek; *fut* yekhazek; **2.** ללכד (unify) *inf* lelaked; *pst* leeked; *pres* melaked; *fut* yelaked.

consolidation 1. ליכוד (unification) *nm* leekood/-eem (*pl+of:* -ey); **2.** חיזוק (strengthening) *nm* kheezook/-eem (*pl+of:* -ey).

consomme מרק־בשר *nm* merak/meerkey basar.

consonant 1. עיצור (grammar) *nm* 'eetsoor/-eem (*pl+of:* -ey); **2.** תואם (compatible) *adj* to'em/-et.

consort בן־זוג *nmf* ben/bat zoog.

(to) consort with להתרועע עם *inf* leheetro'e'a' 'eem; *pst* heetro'e'a' 'eem; *pres* meetro'e'a' 'eem; *fut* yeetro'e'a' 'eem.

consortium 1. קונסורציום *nm* konsortsyoom/-eem (*pl+of:* -ey); **2.** קבוצת חברות (group of companies) *nf* kvoots|at/-ot khavarot.

conspicuous 1. בולט (objectively) *adj* bolet/-et; **2.** מתבלט (standing out) *adj* meetbalet/-et.

conspiracy 1. קשר *nm* kesher; **2.** קנוניה (plot) *nf* kenoon|yah/-yot (+*of:* -yat).

conspirator קושר *nmf* kosh|er/-reem (*pl+of:* -rey).

(to) conspire לקשור קשר *inf* leekshor kesher; *pst* kashar *etc*; *pres* kosher *etc*; *fut* yeekshor *etc*.

constable שוטר *nmf* shoter/-et.

constabulary חיל שוטרים *nm* kheyl shotreem.

constancy 1. התמדה (persistence) *nf* hatmad|ah/-ot (+*of:* -at); **2.** יציבות (stability) *nf* yatseevoo|t/-yot; **3.** נאמנות (loyalty) *nf* ne'emanoo|t/-yot.

constant 1. יציב *adj* yatseev/-ah; **2.** מתמיד (persistent) *adj* matmeed/-ah; **3.** נאמן (loyal) *adj* ne'eman/-ah.

constantly 1. בקביעות *adv* bee-kvee'oot; **2.** תדיר (often) *adv* tadeer.

constellation 1. קונסטלאציה *nf* konstelats|yah/-yot (+*of:* -yat); **2.** קבוצת כוכבים (group of stars) *nf* kvoots|at/-ot kokhaveem.

consternation 1. מבוכה (dismay) *nf* mevookh|ah/-ot (+*of:* -at); **2.** תימהון (amazement) *nf nm* teem|ahon (+*of:* -hon).

(to) constipate לגרום לעצירות *inf* leegrom la-'atseeroot; *pst* garam *etc*; *pres* gorem *etc*; *fut* yeegrom *etc*.

constipation עצירות *nf* 'atseeroo|t/-yot.

constituency 1. אזור בחירה (voting area) *nm* eyzor/azorey bekheerah; **2.** ציבור בוחרים (electorate) *nm* tseeboor/-ey bokhareem.

constituent 1. בוחר (voter) *nmf* bokher/-et; **2.** מרכיב (component) *nm* markeev/-eem (*pl+of:* -ey).

(to) constitute 1. להוות *inf* lehavot; *pst* heevah; *pres* mehaveh; *fut* yehaveh; **2.** למנות (appoint) *inf* lemanot; *pst* meenah; *pres* memaneh; *fut* yemaneh; **3.** לכונן (establish) *inf* lekhonen; *pst* konen (*k=kh*); *pres* mekhonen; *fut* yekhonen.

constitution 1. חוקה (law) *nf* khook|ah/-ot (+*of:* -at); **2.** מבנה גופני (physical) *nm* meevneh goofanee; **3.** הרכב (structure) *nm* herkev/-eem (*pl+of:* -ey).

constitutional 1. קונסטיטוציוני *adj* konsteetootsyonee/-t; **2.** טיול בריאות יומי (daily walk) *nm* teeyool/-ey bree'oot yomee/-yeem.

(to) constrain להכריח *inf* lehakhree'akh; *pst* heekhree'akh; *pres* makhree'akh; *fut* yakhree'akh.

(to) construct לבנות *inf* leevnot; *pst* banah (*b=v*); *pres* boneh; *fut* yeevneh.

construction 1. בנייה (action) *nf* benee|yah/-yot (+*of:* -yat); **2.** מיבנה (structure) *nm* meevn|eh/-eem (*pl+of:* -ey); **3.** סדר מלים (syntax) *nm* seder meeleem.

constructive 1. קונסטרוקטיבי *adj* konstrookteevee/-t; **2.** מועיל (useful) *adj* mo'eel/-ah.

(to) construe להסיק *inf* lehaseek; *pst* heeseek; *pres* maseek; *fut* yaseek.

consul קונסול *nm* konsool/-eem (*pl+of:* -ey).

consulate קונסוליה konsool|yah/-yot (+*of:* -yat).

(to) consult להיוועץ ב־ *inf* leheeva'ets be-; *pst & pres* no'ats be-; *fut* yeeva'ets be-.

consultant יועץ *nmf* yo'ets/-et.

consultation ייעוץ *nm* ye'oots/-eem (*pl+of:* -ey).

(to) consume 1. לצרוך *inf* leetsrokh; *pst* tsarakh; *pres* tsorekh; *fut* yeetsrokh; **2.** לכלות (devour) *inf* lekhalot; *pst* keelah (*k=kh*); *pres* mekhaleh; *fut* yekhaleh.

consumer צרכן *nmf* tsarkhan/-eet (*pl:* -eem/-eeyot; +*of:* -ey).

consumer goods מצרכים *nm pl* meetsrakheem (*sing:* meetsr|akh; *pl+of:* -ekhey).

(to) consummate 1. לממש *inf* lemamesh; *pst* meemesh; *pres* memamesh; *fut* yemamesh; **2.** להשלים (complete) *inf* lehashleem; *pst* heeshleem; *pres* mashleem; *fut* yashleem.

consumption 1. צריכה *nf* tsreekh|ah/-ot (+*of:* -at); **2.** תצרוכת (of goods) *nf* teetsrokh|et/-ot; **3.** שחפת (tuberculosis) *nf* shakhefet.

consumptive 1. בזבזני *adj* bazbezanee/-t; **2.** שחפן (patient) *adj* shakhfan/-eet.

contact 1. מגע *nm* mag|a'/-a'eem (*pl+of:* -a'ey); **2.** קשר (connection) *nm* kesh|er/-areem (*pl+of:* keeshrey).

contact-lenses עדשות־מגע *nf pl* 'adshot-maga'.

contagion 1. הדבקה במחלה (contaminating) *nf* hadbak|ah/-ot be-makhal|ah/-ot; **2.** הידבקות במחלה (being contaminated) *nf* heedavkoo|t/-yot be-makhal|ah/-ot.

contagious 1. מדביק (contaminating) *adj* mad-b|eek/-ah; **2.** מידבק (being contaminated) *adj* meedabek/-et.

(to) contain 1. להכיל *inf* lehakheel; *pst* hekheel; *pres* mekheel; *fut* yakheel; **2.** לעצור (stop) *inf* la'atsor; *pst* 'atsar; *pres* 'otser; *fut* ya'atsor.

(to) contain oneself להתאפק *inf* leheet'apek; *pst* heet'apek; *pres* meet'apek; *fut* yeet'apek.

container מיכל *nm* mekh|al/-aleem (*pl+of:* -ley).

(to) contaminate 1. לזהם (pollute) *inf* lezahem; *pst* zeehem; *pres* mezahem; *fut* yezahem; **2.** ללכלך (dirty) *inf* lelakhlekh; *pst* leekhlekh; *pres* melakhlekh; *fut* yelakhlekh.

(to) contemplate 1. להתבונן *inf* leheetbonen; *pst* heetbonen; *pres* meetbonen; *fut* yeetbonen; **2.** לצפות (watch) *inf* leetspot; *pst* tsafah (*f=p*); *pres* tsofeh; *fut* yeetspeh.

contemplation 1. עיון *nm* 'eeyoon/-eem (*pl+of:* -ey); **2.** צפייה *nf* tsfee|yah/-yot (+*of:* -yat).

contemporary 1. בן־זמן (time) *nmf* ben/bat zman; **2.** בן־דור (generation) *nmf* ben/bat dor.
contempt 1. בוז *nm* booz; **2.** ביזיון (disgrace) *nm* beez|ayon/-yonot (+*of:* -yon).
contemptible בזוי *adj* bazooy/bezooyah.
contemptuous מבזה *adj* mevaz|eh/-ah.
(to) contend 1. לטעון (argue) *inf* leet'on; *pst* ta'an; *pres* to'en; *fut* yeet'an; **2.** להתחרות (compete) *inf* leheetkharot; *pst* heetkharah; *pst* meetkhareh; *fut* yeetkhareh.
content 1. מרוצה *adj* meroots|eh/-ah; **2.** תוכן *nm* tokhen/tekhaneem (*pl+of:* tokhney)
(to) content 1. לפייס (conciliate) *inf* lefayes; *pst* peeyes (*p=f*); *pres* mefayes; *fut* yefayes; **2.** לרצות (satisfy) *inf* leratsot; *pst* reetsah; *pres* meratseh; *fut* yeratseh.
(to one's heart's) content לשביעת רצון *adv* lee-svee'at ratson.
contented שבע־רצון *adj* sva'/sve'at ratson.
contention 1. מחלוקת *nf* makhalok|et/-ot; **2.** ריב *nm* reev/-eem (*pl+of:* -ey).
contentment שביעות־רצון *nf* svee'oot ratson.
contents 1. תוכן *nm* tokhen/tekhaneem (*pl+of:* tokhney); **2.** תכולה (capacity) *nf* tekhool|ah/-ot (+*of:* -at).
(table of) contents תוכן העניינים *nm* tokhen ha-'eenyaneem.
contest תחרות *nf* takharoo|t/-yot.
(to) contest לערער על *inf* le'ar'er 'al; *pst* 'eer'er 'al; *pres* me'ar'er 'al; *fut* ye'ar'er 'al.
(to) contest with להתחרות עם *inf* leheetkharot 'eem; *pst* heetkharah 'eem; *pres* meetkhareh 'eem; *fut* yeetkhareh 'eem.
context הקשר *nm* heksher/-eem (*pl+of:* -ey).
contiguous 1. גובל (bordering) govel/-et; **2.** סמוך (nearby) samookh/smookhah.
continent יבשת *nf* yab|eshet/-ashot.
continental 1. יבשתי *adj* yabashtee/-t; **2.** אירופי *adj* eyropee/-t.
contingency אפשרות *nf* efsharoo|t/-yot.
contingent 1. אפשרי *adj* efsharee/-t; **2.** מקרי *adj* meekree/-t.
continual 1. נמשך *adj* neemsh|akh/-ekhet; **2.** מתמיד *adj* matmeed/-ah.
continually 1. בתמידות *adv* bee-tmeedoot; **2.** ללא הפסק (uninterrupted) *adv* le-lo hefsek.
continuance 1. המשכיות *nf* hemshekheeyoo|t/-yot; **2.** התמשכות (duration) *nf* heetmashkhoo|t/-yot.
continuation 1. המשך *nm* hemshekh/-eem (*pl+of:* -ey); **2.** המשכה (prolongation) *nf* hamshakh|ah/-ot (+*of:* -at).
(to) continue להמשיך *inf* lehamsheekh; *pst* heemsheekh; *pres* mamsheekh; *fut* yamsheekh.
continuity 1. רציפות *nf* retseefoo|t/-yot; **2.** המשכיות *nf* hemshekheeyoo|t/-yot.
continuous 1. מתמיד *adj* matmeed/-ah; **2.** רצוף (consecutive) *adj* ratsoof/retsoofah; **3.** ללא הפסק (uninterrupted) *adj* le-lo hefsek.
contortion 1. עיקום *nm* 'eekoom/-eem (*pl+of:* -ey); **2.** עיוות *nm* 'eevoot/-eem (*pl+of:* -ey).
contour 1. קו גבול *nm* kav/-ey gvool; **2.** קו גובה *nm* kav/-ey govah.
contraband הברחה *nf* havrakh|ah/-ot (+*of:* -at).
contraband goods סחורה מוברחת *nf* sekhor|ah/-ot moovrakh|at/-ot.
contract חוזה *nm* khoz|eh/-eem (*pl+of:* -ey).
(marriage) contract כתובה (in Jewish ritual) ketoob|ah/-ot.
(to) contract 1. לכווץ (cause to shrink) *inf* lekhavets; *pst* keevets (*k=kh*); *pres* mekhavets; *fut* yekhavets; **2.** להתנות (stipulate) *inf* lehatnot; *pst* heetnah; *pres* matneh; *fut* yatneh; **3.** להתחייב (undertake) *inf* leheetkhayev; *pst* heetkhayev; *pres* meetkhayev; *fut* yeetkhayev.
(to) contract an illness להידבק במחלה *inf* leheedavek be-makhalah; *pst & pres* needbak (*b=v*) *etc*; *fut* yeedavek *etc.*
(to) contract marriage להתחתן *inf* leheetkhaten; *pst* heetkhaten; *pres* meetkhaten; *fut* yeetkhaten.
(to) contract the brows לקמט את המצח *inf* lekamet et ha-metsakh; *pst* keemet *etc*; *pres* mekamet *etc*; *fut* yekamet *etc.*
contraction התכווצות *nf* heetkavtsoo|t/-yot.
contractor קבלן *nm* kablan/-eem (*pl+of:* -ey).
(to) contradict לסתור *inf* leestor; *pst* satar; *pres* soter; *fut* yeestor.
contradiction סתירה *nf* steer|ah/-ot (+*of:* -at).
contradictory סותר *adj* soter.
contrary 1. נוגד (opposing) *adj* noged/-et; **2.** נגדי (opposite) *adj* negdee/-t; **3.** בניגוד (contrary to) *adv* be-neegood.
(on the) contrary להיפך *adv* le-hefekh.
contrast ניגוד *nm* neegood/-eem (*pl+of:* -ey).
(to) contrast להשוות זה לעומת זה *inf* lehashvot zeh le-'oomat zeh; *pst* heeshvah *etc*; *pres* mashveh *etc*; *fut* yashveh *etc.*
(to) contravene 1. להפר *inf* lehafer; *pst* hefer; *pres* mefer; *fut* yafer; **2.** לעבור על (transgress) *inf* la'avor 'al; *pst* 'avar 'al; *pres* 'over 'al; *fut* ya'vor 'al
(to) contribute לתרום *inf* leetrom; *pst* taram; *pres* torem; *fut* yeetrom.
contribution 1. תרומה (donation) *nf* troom|ah/-ot (+*of:* -at); **2.** השתתפות (participation) *nf* heeshtatfoo|t/-yot.
contributor 1. תורם (donor) *nm* tor|em/-et (*pl:* -meem/-mot); **2.** משתתף (participant) *nmf* meeshtatef/-et.
contrite 1. חוזר בתשובה (repentant) *nmf* khozer/-et bee-teshoovah; **2.** שבור לב (brokenhearted) *adj* shvoor/-at lev.
contrivance 1. תחבולה (scheme) *nf* takhbool|ah/-ot (+*of:* -at); **2.** מתקן (appliance) *nm* meetkan/-eem (*pl+of:* -ey).
(to) contrive לתחבל *inf* letakhbel; *pst* teekhbel; *pres* metakhbel; *fut* yetakhbel.
control 1. שליטה (rule) *nf* shleet|ah/-ot (+*of:* -at); **2.** בקרה (inspection) *nf* bakar|ah/-ot (+*of:* -at); **3.** פיקוח (supervision) *nm* peekoo|'akh/-kheem (*pl+of:* -khey).
(to lose) control לאבד שליטה *inf* le'abed shleetah; *pst* eebed *etc*; *pres* me'abed *etc*; *fut* ye'abed *etc.*
(to) control 1. לשלוט על (rule) *inf* leeshlot 'al; *pst* shalat 'al; *pres* sholet 'al; *fut* yeeshlot 'al; **2.** לפקח על

(supervise) *inf* lefake'akh 'al; *pst* peekakh 'al *(p=f)*; *pres* mefake'akh 'al; *fut* yefake'akh 'al.

(to) control oneself לשלוט ברוחו leeshlot be-rookh|o/-ah; *pst* shalat *etc*; *pres* sholet *etc*; *fut* yeeshlot *etc*.

control tower מגדל פיקוח *nm* meegd|al/-eley peekoo'akh.

controller מפקח mefak|e'akh/-'kheem (*pl+of*: -'khey).

controversy 1. מחלוקת (dispute) *nf* makhlok|et/-ot; **2.** חילוקי־דעות (dissensions) *nm pl* kheelookey de'ot.

contusion 1. חבורה *nf* khaboor|ah/-ot (*+of*: -at); **2.** חבלה *nf* khabal|ah/-ot (*+of*: -at).

conundrum חידה *nf* kheed|ah/-ot (*+of*: -at).

(to) convalesce 1. להחלים (recover) *inf* lehakhleem; *pst* hekhleem; *pres* makhleem; *fut* yakhleem; **2.** להבריא (recuperate) *inf* lehavree; *pst* heevree; *pres* mavree; *fut* yavree.

convalescence 1. החלמה (recovery) *nf* hakhlam|ah/-ot (*+of*: -at); **2.** הבראה (recuperation) *nf* havra|'ah/-'ot (*+of*: -'at).

convalescent 1. מחלים *adj* makhleem/-ah; **2.** מבריא *adj* mavree/-'ah.

(to) convene 1. לכנס *inf* lekhanes; *pst* keenes *(k=kh)*; *pres* mekhanes; *fut* yekhanes; **2.** לזמן (invite) *inf* lezamen; *pst* zeemen; *pres* mezamen; *fut* yezamen.

convenience נוחות *nf* nokhoot.

convenient נוח *adj* no'akh/nokhah.

conveniently בנוחות *adv* be-nokhoot.

convent מנזר לנזירות *nm* meenzar/-eem lee-nezeerot.

convention 1. ועידה (conference) *nf* ve'eed|ah/-ot (*+of*: -at); **2.** נוהג (custom) *nm* nohag/nohog|eem (*pl+of*: -ey).

conventional 1. מקובל *adj* mekoob|al/-elet; **2.** מוסכם (agreed) *adj* moosk|am/-emet.

(to) converge 1. להתכנס (convene) *inf* leheetkanes; *pst* heetkanes; *pres* meetkanes; *fut* yeetkanes; **2.** להתלכד (rally) *inf* leheetlaked; *pst* heetlaked; *pres* meetlaked; *fut* yeetlaked; **3.** להיפגש (meet) *v inf* leheepagesh; *pst & pres* neefgash *(f=p)*; *fut* yeepagesh.

conversant בקי *adj* bakee/bekee'ah.

conversation שיחה *nf* seekh|ah/-ot (*+of*: -at).

(to) converse 1. לשוחח (discuss) *inf* lesokhe'akh; *pst* sokhakh; *pres* mesokhe'akh; *fut* yesokhakh; **2.** לקיים קשרים (keep in touch) *inf* lekayem ksharеem; *pst* keeyem *etc*; *pres* mekayem *etc*; *fut* yekayem *etc*.

conversion המרה *nf* hamar|ah/-ot (*+of*: -at).

convert 1. גר־צדק (to Judaism) *nmf* ger/-at tsedek; **2.** גר (neophyte) *nm* ger/-eem (*pl+of*: -ey); **3.** מומר (to a non-Jewish faith) *nmf* moom|ar/-eret.

(to) convert 1. להמיר (exchange) *inf* lehameer; *pst* hemeer; *pres* memeer; *fut* yameer; **2.** לגייר (to Judaism) *inf* legayer; *pst* geeyer; *pres* megayer; *fut* yegayer; **3.** להתגייר (become Jewish) *v rfl inf* leheetgayer; *pst* heetgayer; *pres* meetgayer; *fut* yeetgayer; **4.** להפך ל־ (turn into) *inf* lehafekh le-; *pst & pres* nehefakh le-; *fut* yehafekh le-.

convertible 1. מכונית פתוחה (car) *nf* mekhonee|t-yot petookh|ah/-ot; **2.** בר־המרה (currency) *adj* bar/bat hamarah.

convex 1. קמור *adj* kamoor/kemoorah; **2.** מגובנן (hunched) *adj* megoovn|an/-enet.

(to) convey 1. להעביר (transmit) *inf* leha'aveer; *pst* he'eveer; *pres* ma'aveer; *fut* ya'aveer; **2.** למסור (pass) *inf* leemsor; *pst* masar; *pres* moser; *fut* yeemsor.

(to) convey thanks להביע תודה *inf* lehabee'a' tod|ah/-ot; *pst* heebee'a' *etc*; *pres* mabee'a' *etc*; *fut* yabee'a'.

conveyance 1. אמצעי תובלה (means of transport) *nm* emtsa|'ee/-'ey tovalah; **2.** הובלה (haulage) *nf* hoval|ah/-ot (*+of*: -at).

convict אסיר *nmf* aseer/-ah (*pl*: -eem/-ot; *+of*: -at/-ey).

(to) convict 1. להרשיע *inf* leharshee'a'; *pst* heershee'a'; *pres* marshee'a'; *fut* yarshee'a'; **2.** לחייב בדין (find guilty) *inf* lekhayev be-deen; *pst* kheeyev *etc*; *pres* mekhayev *etc*; *fut* yekhayev *etc*

conviction 1. הרשעה (for crime) *nf* harsha|'ah/-'ot (*+of*: -at); **2.** אמונה (belief) *nf* emooon|ah/-ot (*+of*: -at).

(to) convince לשכנע *inf* leshakhne'a'; *pst* sheekhna'; *pres* meshakhne'a'; *fut* yeshakhne'a'.

convincing משכנע *adj* meshakhn|e'a'/-a'at.

convivial עליז *adj* 'aleez/-ah.

convocation 1. כינוס *nm* keenoos/-eem (*pl+of*: -ey); **2.** עצרת (mass meeting) *nf* 'ats|eret/-arot.

(to) convoke 1. לכנס (call) *inf* lekhanes; *pst* keenes *(k=kh)*; *pres* mekhanes; *fut* yekhanes; **2.** לזמן (invite) *inf* lezamen; *pst* zeemen; *pres* mezamen; *fut* yezamen.

convoy 1. משמר ליווי (armed escort) *nm* meeshm|ar/-erey leevooy; **2.** שיירה (caravan) *nf* sha|yarah/-yarot (*+of*: -yeret).

(to) convulse לזעזע *inf* leza'ze'a'; *pst* zee'za'; *pres* meza'ze'a'; *fut* yeza'ze'a'.

convulsion פרפור *nm* peerpoor/-eem (*pl+of*: -ey).

coo המיה *nf* hem|yah/-yot (*+of*: -yat).

(to) coo להמות כיונה *inf* lahamot ke-yonah; *pst* hamah *etc*; *pres* homeh *etc*; *fut* yehemeh *etc*.

cook טבח *nmf* tabakh/-eet (*pl*: -eem/-eeyot; *+of*: -ey).

(to) cook לבשל *inf* levashel; *pst* beeshel *(b=v)*; *pres* mevashel; *fut* yevashel.

(to) cook up a plan לאלתר תוכנית *inf* le'alter tokhneet; *pst* eelter *etc*; *pres* me'alter *etc*; *fut* ye'alter *etc*.

cookbook ספר בישול *nm* sefer/seefrey beeshool.

cookery בישול *nm* beeshool/-eem (*pl+of*: -ey).

cookie, cooky עוגייה *nf* 'oogee|yah/-yot (*+of*: yat).

cooking בישול *nm* beeshool/-eem (*pl+of*: -ey).

cooking stove, cookstove תנור בישול *nm* tanoor/-ey beeshool.

cooking utensils כלי בישול *nm pl* kley beeshool.

cool 1. קריר *adj* kareer/kreerah; **2.** מתון (moderate) *adj* matoon/metoonah.

(to) cool לצנן *inf* letsanen; *pst* tseenen; *pres* metsanen; *fut* yetsanen.
(to) cool off להירגע *inf* leheraga'; *pst & pres* neerga'; *fut* yeraga'.
coolant חומר צינון *nm* khomer/khomrey tseenoon.
cooler 1. מצנן *nm* matsnen/-eem (*pl+of:* -ey); **2.** מקרר (refrigerator) *nm* mekarer/-eem (*pl+of:* -ey).
cool-headed קר־רוח *adj* kar/-at roo'akh.
coolness 1. קרירות *nf* kreeroo|t/-yot; **2.** אדישות (indifference) *nf* adeeshoo|t/-yot.
coon דביבון *nm* dveevon/-eem (*pl+of:* -ey).
(a) coon's age מזמן רב *adv* mee-zman rav.
co-op 1. קו־אופ *nm* ko-op; **2.** צרכנייה *nf* tsarkhanee|yah/-yot (+*of:* -yat).
coop 1. לול (for poultry) *nm* lool/-eem (*pl+of:* -ey); **2.** מכלאה (for cattle, detainees) *nf* meekhl|a'ah/-a'ot (+*of:* -a'at).
(chicken) coop לול תרנגולות *nm* lool/-ey tarnegolot.
(to) coop up לכלוא *inf* leekhlo; *pst* kala (*k=kh*); *pres* kole; *fut* yeekhla.
cooperate 1. לשתף פעולה *inf* leshatef pe'oolah; *pst* sheetef *pres* meshatef *etc*; *fut* yeshatef *etc*; **2.** לסייע (assist) *inf* lesaye'a'; *pst* seeya'; *pres* mesaye'a'; *fut* yesaye'a'.
cooperation שיתוף פעולה *nm* sheetoof pe'oolah.
cooperative 1. משתף פעולה *adj* meshatef/-et pe'oolah; **2.** קואופרטיב *nm* ko'operateev/-eem (*pl+of:* -ey);
(to) co-opt לצרף כחבר *inf* letsaref ke-khaver; *pst* tseraf *etc*; *pres* metsaref *etc*; *fut* yetsaref *etc*.
co-opted מצורף *adj* metsoraf/-efet.
coordinate 1. קואורדינטה *nf* ko'ordeenat|ah/-ot (+*of:* -at); **2.** תואם (fitting) *adj* to'em/-et.
(to) coordinate לתאם *inf* leta'em; *pst* te'em; *pres* meta'em; *fut* yeta'em.
coordination תיאום *nm* te'oom/-eem (*pl+of:* -ey).
co-owner שותף *nmf* shootaf/-ah (*pl:* -eem/-ot; *pl+of:* -ey).
cootie כינה *nf* keen|ah/-eem (+*of:* -at).
cop 1. שוטר *nmf* shot|er/-eret (*pl:* -reem/-rot); **2.** פקעת חוטים (yarn spindle) *nf* peka'at/pak'ot khooteem.
(to) cop 1. ללפף (spin) *inf* lelapef; *pst* leepef; *pres* melapef; *fut* yelapef; **2.** לתפוס (capture) *v inf* leetpos; *pst* tafas (*f=p*); *pres* tofes; *fut* yeetpos.
(to) cope לכסות *inf* lekhasot; *pst* keesah (*k=kh*); *pres* mekhaseh; *fut* yekhaseh.
(to) cope with 1. להתמודד עם *inf* leheetmoded 'eem; *pst* heetmoded 'eem; *pres* meetmoded 'eem; *fut* yeetmoded 'eem; **2.** להסתדר *v inf* leheestader; *pst* heestader; *pres* meestader; *fut* yeestader.
copier 1. מכונת העתקה (machine) *nm* mekhon|at/-ot ha'atakah; **2.** מעתיק (person) *nm* ma'ateek/-eem (*pl+of:* -ey).
copilot טייס משנה *nm* tayas/-ey meeshneh.
coping נדבך עליון *nm* needbakh/-eem 'elyon/-eem.
copious שופע *adj* shof|e'a'/-a'at.
copper נחושת *nf* nekhoshet.
copper coin מטבע נחושת *nm* matbe|'a'/-'ot nekhoshet.
copper kettle מחם *nm* mekham/-eem (*pl+of:* -ey).
coppersmith צורף נחושת *nm* tsor|ef/-fey nekhoshet.
(to) copulate 1. להזדווג *inf* leheezdaveg; *pst* heezdaveg; *pres* meezdaveg; *fut* yeezdaveg; **2.** לבעול (lay) *vt inf* leev'ol; *pst* ba'al (*b=v*); *pres* bo'el; *fut* yeev'al; **3.** להזדיין (obscene) *inf* leheezdayen; *pst* heezdayen; *pres* meezdayen; *fut* yeezdayen.
copy 1. העתק (letter) *nm* he'et|ek/-keem (*pl+of:* -key); **2.** עותק (book) *nm* 'ot|ek/-akeem (*pl+of:* -key).
(to) copy להעתיק *inf* leha'ateek; *pst* he'eteek; *pres* ma'ateek; *fut* ya'ateek.
copybook מחברת *nf* makhb|eret/-arot.
copyist 1. סופר סת"ם (Torah scribe) *nm* sof|er/-rey stam; **2.** מעתיק (transcriber) *nmf* ma'ateek/-ah; **3.** חקיין (immitator) *nmf* khakyan/-eet.
copyright 1. זכות יוצרים *nf* zekhoo|t/-yot yotsreem; **2.** קופירייט *nm* kopeerayt/-eem.
(to) copyright להבטיח זכות יוצרים *inf* lehavtee'akh zekhoot yotsreem; *pst* heevtee'akh *etc*; *pres* mavtee'akh *etc*; *fut* yavtee'akh *etc*.
copywriter 1. מהדיר *nmf* mahadeer/-ah; **2.** מנסח פרסומים (for advertising) *nmf* menas|e'akh/-akhat peersomeem.
coquetry 1. קוקטיות *nf* koketeeyoot; **2.** התחנחנות *nf* heetkhankhenoo|t/-yot.
coquette גנדרנית *nf & adj* gandranee|t-yot.
coral אלמוג *nm* almog/almoog|eem (*pl+of:* -ey).
coral reef שונית אלמוגים *nf* shoonee|t-yot almoogeem.
cord 1. מיתר (string) *nm* meytar/-eem (*pl+of:* meytrey); **2.** חוט חשמל (electr. cable) *nm* khoot/-ey khashmal; **3.** חבל (rope) *nm* khevel/khav|aleem (*pl+of:* -ley).
(spinal) cord חוט השדרה *nm* khoot ha-shedrah.
cordial לבבי *adj* levavee/-t.
cords מכנסי קורדרוי *nm pl* meekhnesey korderoy.
corduroy קורדרוי *nm* korderoy.
corduroy road כביש מוטות *nm* kveesh/-ey motot.
corduroys מכנסי קורדרוי *nm pl* meekhnesey korderoy.
core 1. ליבה *nf* leeb|ah/-ot (+*of:* -at); **2.** עיקר *nm* 'eek|ar/-areem (*pl+of:* -rey).
(to) core להוציא מהפרי את התווך *inf* lehotsee me-ha-pree et ha-tavekh; hotsee *etc*; *pres* motsee *etc*; *fut* yotsee *etc*.
co-respondent 1. נתבע נוסף *nmf* neetba'/-at nos|af/-efet (*pl:* -afeem/-afot); **2.** מאהב בתביעת גירושין (in divorces) *nmf* me'ahev/-et bee-tvee'at geroosheem.
cork 1. שעם *nm* sha'am; **2.** פקק (bottle) pekak/-eem (*pl+of:* -ey).
(to) cork 1. לסתום בפקק *inf* leestom bee-fekak (*f=p*); *pst* satam *etc*; *pres* sotem *etc*; *fut* yeestom *etc*; **2.** להשחיר בפקק שרוף (blacken) *inf* lehashkheer bee-fekak saroof; *pst* heeshkheer *etc*; *pres* mashkheer *etc*; *fut* yashkheer *etc*.
corkscrew 1. מחלץ *nm* makhlets/-eem (*pl+of:* -ey); **2.** חולץ פקקים *nm* khol|ets/-tsey pekakeem.

corn 1. תירס (maize) *nm* teeras; **2.** תבואה (grain) *nf* tvoo'|ah/-ot (*+of:* -at); **3.** יבלת (wart) *nf* yab|elet/-alot.

corn cure תרופה ליבלות *nf* troof|ah/-ot le-yabalot.

corn on the cob תירס על השיבולת *nm* teeras 'al ha-sheebolet.

cornbread לחם תירס *nm* lekhem/lakhmey teeras.

corncob שיבולת תירס *nf* sheebolet teeras.

cornea קרנית *nf* karnee|t/-yot.

corned beef 1. לוף *nm* loof; **2.** בוליביף *[slang] nm* booleebeef.

corner 1. פינה *nf* peen|ah/-ot; **2.** זווית *nf* zavee|t/-yot.

(to) corner ללחוץ אל הקיר *inf* leelkhots el ha-keer; *pst* lakhats *etc; pres* lokhets *etc; fut* yeelkhats *etc.*

corner bracket מדף פינתי *nm* madaf/-eem peenatee/-yeem.

corner cupboard ארון פינתי *nm* aron/-ot peenatee/-yeem.

corner shelf אצטבה פינתית *nf* eetstab|ah/-a'ot peenatee|t/-yot.

corner table שולחן פינתי *nm* shoolkhan/-ot peenatee/-yeem.

cornet 1. קורנית *nf* kornee|t/-yot; **2.** קרן *nm* keren/kranot (*pl+of:* karnot).

cornfield שדה תירס *nm* sdeh/sdot teeras.

cornflour, cornstarch 1. קמח תירס *nm* kemakh teeras; **2.** קורנפלור *[colloq.] nm* kornflor.

cornice כרכוב *nm* karkov/karkoob|eem (*b=v; pl+of:* -ey).

cornmeal קמח תירס *nm* kemakh teeras.

cornucopia קרן השפע *nf* keren ha-shefa'.

corny 1. נדוש *adj* nadosh/nedoshah; **2.** קלוקל (trite) *adj* klokel/-et.

corollary תולדה *nf* tolad|ah/-ot (*+of:* toledet).

coronation הכתרה *nf* hakhtar|ah/-ot (*+of:* -at).

coroner חוקר מקרי מוות *nmf* khoker/-et meekrey mavet.

coroner's inquest חקירת מקרה מוות *nf* khakeer|at/-ot meekreh mavet.

coronet עטרה *nf* 'at|arah/-arot (*+of:* -eret).

corporal 1. רב־טוראי *nmf* rav-toora|y/-'eet; **2.** רב"ט (*acr of* 1) *nmf* rabat/-eet (*pl:* -eem/-eeyot); **3.** גופני (bodily) *adj* goofanee|t.

corporation 1. תאגיד *nm* ta'ageed/-eem (*pl+of:* -ey); **2.** חברה (company) *nf* khevrah/khavarot (*+of:* khevr|at/-ot); **3.** איגוד (union) *nm* eegood/-eem (*pl+of:* -ey).

corps 1. סגל (staff) *nm* segel/sgaleem (*pl+of:* seegley); **2.** גייס (army) *nm* gayees/gyasot (*+of:* geys/-ot).

corps de ballet להקת באלט *nf* lahak|at/-ot balet.

(air) corps חיל אוויר *nm* kheyl/-ot aveer.

(diplomatic) corps סגל דיפלומטי *nm* segel deeplomatee.

corpse 1. גווייה *nf* gvee|yah/-yot (*+of:* -yat); **2.** גופה (body) *nf* goof|ah/-ot (*+of:* -at).

corpulent בעל־גוף *adj* ba'al/-at goof.

corpuscle גופיף *nm* goofeef/-eem (*pl+of:* -ey).

corral דיר *nm* deer/-eem (*pl+of:* -ey).

correct 1. נכון (right) *adj* nakhon/nekhonah; **2.** מדויק (exact) *adj* medoo|yak/-yeket; **3.** קורקטי (fair) *adj* korektee/-t.

correction 1. תיקון *nm* teekoon/-eem (*pl+of:* -ey); **2.** הגהה (proofreading) haga|hah/-hot (*+of:* -hat).

corrective מתקן *adj* metaken/-et.

correctly 1. כהלכה (properly) *adv* ka-halakhah; **2.** בצורה הנכונה (in the right manner) *adv* ba-tsoorah ha-nekhonah.

correctness 1. נכונות (truth) *nf* nekhonoot; **2.** קורקטיות *nf* korekteeyoot.

corrector מגיה *nm* mageeh|a/-eem (*pl+of:* -ey).

correlate קשור הדדית *adj* kashoor/keshoorah hadadeet.

(to) correlate לקשר הדדית *inf* lekasher hadadeet; *pst* keesher *etc; pres* mekasher *etc; fut* yekasher *etc.*

(to) correspond 1. להתכתב (exchange letters) *inf* leheetkatev; *pst* heetkatev; *pres* meetkatev; *fut* yeetkatev; **2.** להתאים (befit) *inf* lehat'eem; *pst* heet'eem; *pres* mat'eem; *fut* yat'eem.

correspondence 1. התכתבות *nf* heetkatvoo|t/-yot; **2.** תכתובת (exch. letters) *nf* teekhtov|et/-ot; **3.** התאמה (conformity) *nf* hat'am|ah/-ot (*+of:* -at).

correspondent 1. כתב (newsman) *nmf* kat|av/-evet (*pl:* -eem/-ot); **2.** מתכתב (letter writer) *nmf* meetkatev/-et.

corresponding מתאים *adj* mat'eem/-ah.

corridor 1. מסדרון *nm* meesderon/-ot; **2.** פרוזדור (anteroom) *nm* prozdor/-eem (*pl+of:* -ey).

(to) corroborate 1. לאשר (confirm) *v inf* le'asher; *pst* eesher; *pres* me'asher; *fut* ye'asher; **2.** לחזק (reinforce) *v inf* lekhazek; *pst* kheezek; *pres* mekhazek; *fut* yekhazek.

(to) corrode להחליד *inf* lehakhleed; *pst* hekhleed; *pres* makhleed; *fut* yakhleed.

corrugated iron ברזל גלי *nm* barz|el/-eeleem galee/-yeem.

corrupt מושחת *adj* mooshkh|at/-etet.

(to become) corrupt להיתפס לשחיתות *inf* leheetafes lee-sh'kheetoot; *pst & pres* neetpas (*p=f*) *etc; fut* yeetafes *etc.*

corruption שחיתות *nf* sh'kheetoo|t/-yot.

corsage 1. חזייה *nf* khazee|yah/-yot (*+of:* -yat); **2.** קישוט פרחים לאישה (bouquet) *nm* keeshoot prakheem le-eeshah.

corsair שודד־ים *nm* shoded/-ey yam.

corset מחוך *nm* makhokh/mekhokh|eem (*pl+of:* -ey).

cortex קליפה *nf* kleep|ah/-ot (*+of:* -at).

cortisone קורטיזון *nm* korteezon.

cosily, cozily 1. נוח *adv* no'akh; **2.** בנוחות (comfortably) *adv* be-nokhoot.

cosmetic קוסמטי *adj* kosmetee/-t.

cosmic קוסמי *adj* kosmee/-t.

cosmonaut 1. טייס־חלל *nmf* tayas/tayeset (*pl:* tayas|ey/-ot) khalal; **2.** קוסמונאוט *nmf* kosmonaut/-eet.

cosmopolitan קוסמופוליטי *adj* kosmopoleetee/-t.

cosmos 1. תבל *nf* tevel; **2.** הקוסמוס *nm* ha-kosmos.

cost עלות *nf* 'aloo|t/-yot.

(at) cost במחיר הקרן *adv* bee-mekheer ha-keren.

(to) cost לעלות *inf* la'alot; *pst* 'alah; *pres* 'oleh; *fut* ya'aleh.

cost accounting תמחיר *nm* tamkheer/-eem (*pl+of:* -ey).

cost, insurance and freight (CIF) סי״ף *adv* seef.

cost of living (CoL) יוקר המחיה *nm* yoker ha-meekhyah.

cost of living (CoL) index מדד יוקר המחיה *nm* madad/-ey yoker ha-meekhyah

costly ביוקר *adv* be-yoker.

(at all) costs בכל מחיר *adv* be-khol mekheer.

costume 1. תלבושת *nf* teelbosh|et/-ot; **2.** תחפושת (disguise) *nf* takhpos|et/-ot.

costume ball 1. נשף תלבושות *nm* neshef/neeshfey teelboshot; **2.** נשף מסיכות (masquerade) *nm* neshef/neeshfey masekhot.

costume jewellery תכשיטים מלאכותיים *nm* takhsheeteem mal'akhooteeyeem.

cot מיטת־שדה-f meet|at/-ot sadeh.

(folding) cot מיטה מתקפלת *nf* meet|ah/-ot meet-kap|elet/-lot.

cottage קוטג׳ *nm* kotej/-eem (*pl+of:* -ey).

cottage cheese גבינת קוטג׳ *nf* gveen|at/-ot kotej.

cotton כותנה kootn|ah/-ot.

cotton-gin מנפטה (plant) *nf* manp|etah/-etot (*+of:* -etet).

cotton seed 1. גרגרי כותנה *nm pl* gargerey kootnah; **2.** כוספה *nm* koosp|ah.

cotton wool 1. צמר־גפן *nm* tsemer-gefen; **2.** מוך *nm* mokh/-een.

cotton yarn 1. מטווה כותנה *nm* matv|eh/-ey kootnah; **2.** חוט כותנה (thread) *nm* khoot/-ey kootnah.

couch ספה sap|ah/-ot (*+of:* -at).

(to) couch 1. לבטא *inf* levate; *pst* beete (*b=v*); *pres* mevate; *fut* yevate; **2.** להביע *inf* lehabee'a'; *pst* heebee'a'; *pres* mabee'a'; *fut* yabee'a'.

cough שיעול *nm* shee'ool/-eem (*pl+of:* -ey).

(to) cough להשתעל *inf* leheeshta'el; *pst* heeshta'el; *pres* meeshta'el; *fut* yeeshta'el.

(whooping) cough שעלת *nf* sha'elet.

cough drop סוכרייה נגד שיעול *nf* sookaree|yah/-yot neged shee'ool.

(to) cough up ליאלץ לגלות *inf* leyalets legalot; *pst & pres* ne'elats *etc*; *fut* ye'alets *etc*.

council מועצה *nf* mo'ats|ah/-ot (*+of:* mo'etset).

councilman חבר מועצה עירונית *nmf* khav|er/-rat mo'atsah 'eeroneet.

councilor חבר מועצה *nmf* khav|er/-rat (*pl+of:* -rey) mo'atsah.

counsel 1. פרקליט *nmf* prakleet/-ah; **2.** עצה (advice) 'ets|ah/-ot (*+of:* 'atsat).

(to) counsel 1. לייעץ *inf* leya'ets; *pst* yee'ets; *pres* meya'ets; *fut* yeya'ets; **2.** להמליץ (recommend) *inf* lehamleets; *pst* heemleets; *pres* mamleets; *fut* yamleets.

counselor 1. יועץ משפטי (legal advisor) *nmf* yo'ets/-et meeshpatee/-t; **2.** פרקליט (lawyer) *nmf* prakleet/-ah (*+of:* -at; *pl+of:* -ey).

count 1. רוזן (title) *nmf* rozen/-et; **2.** חשבון (account) *nm* kheshbon/-ot; **3.** ספירה (numeration) *nf* sfeer|ah/-ot (*+of:* -at).

(to) count 1. לספור *vt inf* leespor; *pst* safar (*f=p*); *pres* sofer; *fut* yeespor; **2.** להיחשב (be considered) *vi inf* lehekhashev; *pst & pres* nekhshav; *fut* yekhashev.

(to) count on לסמוך על *inf* leesmokh 'al; *pst* samakh 'al; *pres* somekh 'al; *fut* yeesmokh 'al.

countdown ספירה לאחור *nf* sfeer|ah/-ot le-akhor.

countenance 1. פרצוף *nm* partsoof/-eem (*pl+of:* -ey); **2.** קלסתר (physiognomy) *nm* klaster/-eem (*pl+of:* -ey).

(to give) countenance to לעודד *inf* le'oded; *pst* 'oded; *pres* me'oded; *fut* ye'oded.

counter 1. דלפק *nm* delpek/-eem (*pl+of:* -ey); **2.** מונה (numerator) *nm* mon|eh/-eem (*pl+of:* -ey); **3.** נגדי (opposite) *adj* negdee/-t; **4.** נגד (against) *adv* neged.

(to run) counter לנגוד *inf* leengod; *pst* nagad; *pres* noged; *fut* yeengod.

(to) counter a blow להחזיר מכה *inf* lehakhzeer makah; *pst* hekhzeer *etc*; *pres* makhzeer *etc*; *fut* yakhzeer *etc*.

(to) counteract 1. לסתור *inf* leestor; *pst* satar; *pres* soter; *fut* yeestor; **2.** לסכל (frustrate) *inf* lesakel; *pst* seekel; *pres* mesakel; *fut* yesakel.

counterattack התקפת־נגד *nf* hatkaf|at/-ot neged.

counterbalance משקל־נגד *nm* meeshk|al/-eley neged.

counterclockwise נגד כיוון השעון *adv* neged keevoon ha-sha'on.

counterfeit 1. מזויף *adj* mezoo|yaf/-yefet; **2.** זיוף *nm* zeeyoof/-eem (*pl+of:* -ey).

counterfeit money כסף מזויף *nm* kesef mezooyaf.

countermand פקודת ביטול *nf* pekood|at/-ot beetool.

(to) countermand לבטל פקודה *inf* levatel pekoodah; *pst* beetel (*b=v*) *etc*; *pres* mevatel *etc*; *fut* yevatel *etc*.

counterpart 1. השלמה *nf* hashlam|ah/-ot (*+of:* -at); **2.** מקביל (parallel) *nm* makbeel/-eem (*pl+of:* -ey).

counterpoise 1. איזון *nm* eezoon; **2.** משקל נגדי (counterbalance) *nm* meeshkal negdee.

countersign חתימת־עזר *nf* khateem|at/-ot 'ezer.

countess רוזנת *nf* roz|enet/-not.

countless 1. בל־ייספר *adj* bal yeesafer/teesafer; **2.** לאין ספור *adv* le-eyn sfor.

country 1. ארץ (land) *nf* erets/aratsot (*pl+of:* artsot); **2.** איזור כפרי (rural area) *nm* ezor/azoreem kafree/-yeem; **3.** מולדת (fatherland) *nf* mol|edet/-adot (*pl+of:* -dot).

countryman 1. בן־ארץ ("landsman") *nmf* ben/bat (*pl:* ben|ey/-ot) erets; **2.** בן־כפר (peasant) *nmf* ben/bat kfar.

countryside נוף כפרי *nm* nof/-eem kafree/-yeem.

county מחוז *nm* makhoz/mekhozot (*+of:* mekhoz/-ot).

coup d'etat 1. הפיכת חצר *nf* hafeekh|at/-ot khatser; **2.** מהפיכת־פתע (sudden overthrow) *nf* mahapekh|at/-ot peta'.

coupé 1. חצי־תא *nm* khats|ee/-a'ey ta/-'eem; **2.** מכונית לזוג (two door car) *nf* mekhoneet le-zoog.

couple זוג *nm* zoog/-ot.

(to) couple 1. להצמיד *inf* lehatsmeed; *pst* heetsmeed; *pres* matsmeed; *fut* yatsmeed; **2.** לצרף (join) *inf* letsaref; *pst* tseraf; *pres* metsaref; *fut* yetsaref; **3.** לזווג (match) *inf* lezaveg; *pst* zeeveg; *pres* mezaveg; *fut* yezaveg.
couplet פזמון *nm* peezmon/-eem (*pl+of:* -ey).
coupling 1. מצמד *nm* matsmed/-eem (*pl+of:* -ey); **2.** צימוד (pairing) *nm* tseemood/-eem (*pl+of:* -ey); **3.** צירוף (juxtaposition) *nm* tseroof/-eem (*pl+of:* -ey).
coupon 1. תלוש *nm* tloosh/-eem (*pl+of:* -ey); **2.** שובר (voucher) *nm* shov|er/-reem (*pl+of:* -rey).
courage 1. עוז *nm* 'oz (*+of:* 'ooz); **2.** אומץ (bravery) *nm* omets.
courageous 1. אמיץ *adj* ameets/-ah; **2.** נועז (daring) *adj* no'az/no'ezet.
courier 1. בלדר *nmf* baldar/-eet; **2.** שליח (messenger) *nmf* shalee'akh/shleekhah (*+of:* shlee|akh/-khat/-khey).
course 1. קורס (lessons) *nm* koors/-eem (*pl+of:* -ey); **2.** מסלול (way) *nm* maslool/-eem (*pl+of:* -ey); **3.** מירוץ (race) *nm* merots/-eem (*pl+of:* -ey).
course of conduct התנהגות *nf* heetnahagoo|t/-yot.
(golf) course שדה גולף *nm* sdeh/-ot golf.
(in the) course of a... במהלך *adv* be-mahalakh.
(of) course כמובן ka-moovan.
(race) course מסלול מרוץ *nm* maslool/-ey merots.
(a straight) course מסלול ישיר *nm* maslool/-eem yasheer/yesheereem.
court 1. בית משפט (of law) *nm* bet/batey meeshpat; **2.** חצר (royal) *nf* khats|er/-erot (*+of:* -ar/-rot).
(tennis) court מגרש טניס *nm* meegr|ash/-eshey tenees.
(to) court לחזר *inf* lekhazer; *pst* kheezer; *pres* mekhazer; *fut* yekhazer.
(to pay) court לחזר *inf* lekhazer; *pst* kheezer; *pres* mekhazer; *fut* yekhazer.
(to) court danger להסתכן *inf* leheestaken; *pst* heestaken; *pres* meestaken; *fut* yeestaken.
court-martial בית־דין שדה bet/batey deen sadeh.
(to) court-martial להעמיד למשפט שדה *inf* leha'ameed le-meeshpat sadeh; *pst* he'emeed *etc*; *pres* ma'ameed *etc*; *fut* ya'ameed *etc*.
court plaster 1. פלסטרית (adhesive bandage) *nf* plastree|t/-yot; **2.** סלוואפלסט (*[colloq.]:* trade name for 1) *nm* salvaplast/-eem.
courteous 1. מנומס *adj* menoom|as/-eset; **2.** אדיב (polite) *adj* adeev/-ah.
courtesy 1. נימוס *nm* neemoos/-eem (*pl+of:* -ey); **2.** אדיבות (politeness) *nf* adeevoo|t/-yot.
courtier איש חצר *nm* eesh/anshey khatser.
courtship חיזור *nm* kheezoor/-eem (*pl+of:* -ey).
courtyard חצר *nf* khats|er/-erot (*+of:* -ar/-rot).
cousin 1. דודן *nmf* dodan/-eet (*pl:* -eem/-eeyot); **2.** בן־דוד *[colloq.]* ben/bat dod/-ah (*pl:* ben|ey/-ot dodeem).
cove מפרצון *nm* meefr|atson/-etsoneem (*+of:* -etson/-ey).
covenant 1. אמנה *nf* aman|ah/-ot (*+of:* -at); **2.** ברית (alliance) *nf* breet/-ot.
cover 1. כסוי *nm* kesoo|y/-yeem (*pl+of:* -yey); **2.** מיכסה (lid) *nm* meekhs|eh/-eem (*pl+of:* -ey).
(table) cover מפת שולחן *nf* map|at/-ot shoolkhan.
(to) cover 1. לכסות *inf* lekhasot; *pst* keesah (*k=kh*); *pres* mekhaseh; *fut* yekhaseh; **2.** לסקר (journalistic.) *inf* lesaker; *pst* seeker; *pres* mesaker; *fut* yesaker.
(under separate) cover 1. במעטפה נפרדת *adv* be-ma'atafah neefredet; **2.** במשלוח לחוד (separately dispatched) *adv* be-meeshlo'akh le-khood.
cover-charge דמי־שירות *nm pl* demey sheroot.
(to) cover distance לעבור מרחק *inf* la'avor merkhak/-eem; *pst* 'avar *etc*; *pres* 'over *etc*; *fut* ya'avor *etc*.
coverage 1. כיסוי *nm* keesooy/-eem (*pl+of:* -ey); **2.** סיקור (journalistic) seekoor/-eem (*pl+of:* -ey).
covering 1. מכסה (lid) *nm* meekhs|eh/-eem (*pl+of:* -ey); **2.** חיפוי (protection) *nm* kheepoo|y/-yeem (*pl+of:* -yey).
(to) covet לחמוד *inf* lakhmod; *pst* khamad; *pres* khomed; *fut* yakhmod.
covetous חמדני *adj* khamdanee/-t.
cow פרה *nf* par|ah/-ot (*+of:* -at).
coward 1. פחדן *nmf* pakhdan/-eet (*pl+of:* -ey); **2.** מוג־לב (faint-hearted) *adj* moog/-at lev.
cowardice, cowardliness 1. פחדנות *nf* pakhdanoo|t/-yot; **2.** שפלות (baseness) *nf* sheefloo|t/-yot.
cowardly פחדני *adj* pakhdanee/-t.
cowboy בוקר *nm* bok|er/-reem (*pl+of:* -rey).
(to) cower לרעוד מפחד *inf* leer'od mee-pakhad; *pst* ra'ad *etc*; *pres* ro'ed *etc*; *fut* yeer'ad *etc*.
cowhide עור פרה *nm* 'or/-ot par|ah/-ot.
cowl ברדס (hood) *nm* bard|as/-aseem (*pl+of:* -esey).
coxcomb כרבולת *nf* karbol|et/-ot.
coxswain ראש קבוצה בסירת־מירוץ *nm* rosh kvootsah be-seerat merots.
coy 1. ביישן (shy) *adj* bayshan/-eet; **2.** ענו (modest) *adj* 'anav/-ah.
coyote זאב ערבות *nm* ze'ev/-ey 'aravot.
cozy נעים ונוח *adj* na'eem/ne'eemah ve-no|'akh/-khah.
crab 1. סרטן *nm* sartan/-eem (*pl+of:* -ey); **2.** עגורן (construction) *nm* 'agooran/-eem (*pl+of:* -ey).
crack 1. בקיע *nm* bekee|'a'/-'eem (*pl+of:* -'ey); **2.** קול נפץ (explosion) *nm* kol/-ot nefets; **3.** הזדמנות (chance) *nf* heezdamnoo|t/-yot.
(to) crack a joke להשמיע בדיחה *inf* lehashmee'a' bedeekhah; *pst* heeshmee'a' *etc*; *pres* mashmee'a' *etc*; *fut* yashmee'a' *etc*.
(to) crack nuts לפצח אגוזים *inf* lefatse'akh egozeem; *pst* peetsakh (*p=f*) *etc*; *pres* mefatse'akh *etc*; *fut* yefatse'akh *etc*.
(at the) crack of dawn עם הנץ השחר *adv* 'eem hanets ha-shakhar.
crack up להתמוטט *inf* leheetmotet; *pst* heetmotet; *pres* meetmotet; *fut* yeetmotet.
crackdown מעבר לאמצעים חריפים *nm* ma'avar le-emtsa'eem khareefeem.
cracked 1. סדוק *adj* sadook/sdookah; **2.** פגום (defective) *adj* pagoom/pegoomah.

cracker 1. צנים *nm* tseneem/-eem (*pl+of:* -ey); **2.** זיקוק די־נור (firecracker) *nm* zeekook/-een dee-noor.

crackle קול נפץ חלש *nm* kol/-ot nefets khalash/-eem.

(to) crackle להיסדק לסדקים זעירים *inf* leheesadek lee-sdakeem ze'eereem; *pst & pres* neesdak *etc; fut* yeesadek *etc.*

cradle 1. עריסה (crib) *nf* 'arees|ah/-ot (+*of:* -at); **2.** ערש (bed) *nm* 'eres/'ar|asot (*pl+of:* -sot)

craft 1. מלאכה *nf* mel|akhah/-akhot (+*of:* -ekhet); **2.** אומנות (mechanic art) *nm* ooman|oot/-yot.

craftsman 1. בעל מלאכה (artisan) *nm* ba'al/-ey melakhah; **2.** בעל מקצוע (professional) *nmf* ba'al/-at meektso'a'.

crafty ערמומי *adj* 'armoomee/-t.

crag צוק *nm* tsook/-eem (*pl+of:* -ey).

(to) cram 1. להלעיט *inf* lehal'eet; *pst* heel'eet; *pres* mal'eet; *fut* yal'eet; **2.** לדחוס (compress) *inf* leedkhos; *pst* dakhas; *pres* dokhes; *fut* yeedkhas; **3.** לצופף (crowd in) *inf* letsofef; *pst* tsofef; *pres* metsofef; *fut* yetsofef.

cramp 1. עווית *nf* 'aveet/-ot; **2.** צבת (tongs) *nm* tsvat/-ot.

(to) cramp לדחוס *inf* leedkhos; *pst* dakhas; *pres* dokhes; *fut* yeedkhas.

cranberry חמוציות *nf* khamootsee|t/-yot.

crane 1. עגור (bird) *nm* 'agoor/-eem (*pl+of:* -ey); **2.** עגורן (machine) *nm* 'agooran/-eem (*pl+of:* -ey).

(to) crane one's neck למתוח את הצוואר *inf* leemto'akh et ha-tsavar; *pst* matakh *etc; pres* mote'akh *etc; fut* yeemtakh *etc.*

cranium גולגולת *nf* goolg|olet/-alot.

crank 1. ארכובה (of shaft) *nf* arkoob|ah/-ot (+*of:* -at); **2.** תמהוני (eccentric) *nmf & adj* teemhonee/-t; **3.** רופף (weak) *adj* rofef/-et.

crankcase בית הארכובה *nm* bet ha-arkoobah.

crankshaft גל הארכובה *nm* gal ha-arkoobah.

cranky כעסן *adj* ka'asan/-eet.

cranny 1. סדק *nm* sedek/sdakeem (*pl+of:* seedkey); **2.** סליק (colloq.: cache) *nm* sleek/-eem (*pl+of:* -ey).

crash 1. התרסקות (plane) *nf* heetraskoo|t/-yot; **2.** מפולת (financial) *nm* mapol|et/-ot; **3.** אריג גס (fabric) *nm* areeg/-eem gas/-eem.

(to) crash 1. להתרסק *v rfl inf* leheetrasek; *pst* heetrasek; *pres* meetrasek; *fut* yeetrasek; **2.** להתנפץ (smash) *inf* leheetnapets; *pst* heetnapets; *pres* meetnapets; *fut* yeetnapets; **3.** להתפרץ (break in) *inf* leheetparets; *pst* heetparets; *pres* meetparets; *fut* yeetparets.

crash-dive צלילת פתע *nf* tsleel|at/-ot peta'.

(to) crash into להתנפץ אל *inf* leheetnapets el; *pst* heetnapets el; *pres* meetnapets el; *fut* yeetnapets el.

crash landing נחיתת־אונס *nf* nekheet|at/-ot ones.

crash program תוכנית־חירום לייצור בזק *nf* tokhnee|t/-yot kheroom le-yeetsoor bazak.

crasher אורח לא־קרוא *nmf* ore'akh/orakhat lo karoo/kroo'ah.

crass גס *adj* gas/-ah.

crate תיבת אריזה *nf* teyv|at/-ot areezah.

(to) crate לארוז בתיבה *inf* le'eroz be-teyvah; *pst* araz *etc; pres* orez *etc; fut* ye'eroz *etc.*

crater 1. לוע *nm* lo|'a'/-'eem (*pl+of:* -'ey); **2.** מכתש (mortar) *nm* makhtesh/-eem (*pl+of:* -ey).

cravat עניבה *nf* 'aneev|ah/-ot (+*of:* -at).

(to) crave להשתוקק *inf* leheeshtokek; *pst* heeshtokek; *pres* meeshtokek; *fut* yeeshtokek.

(to) crave mercy לבקש רחמים *inf* levakesh rakhameem; *pst* beekesh *(b=v) etc; pres* mevakesh *etc; fut* yevakesh *etc.*

craven פחדני *adj* pakhdanee/-t.

craving תשוקה *nf* teshook|ah/-ot (+*of:* -at).

craw זפק *nm* zefek/zfakeem (*pl+of:* zeefkey).

crawl 1. זחילה *nf* zekheel|ah/-ot (+*of:* -at); **2.** שחיית חתירה (swimming) sekheeyat khateerah.

(to) crawl 1. לזחול *inf* leezkhol; *pst* zakhal; *pres* zokhel; *fut* yeezkhal; **2.** לשרוץ (swarm) *inf* leeshrots; *pst* sharats; *pres* shorets; *fut* yeeshrots.

(to) crawl with ants לשרוץ כבקרב נמלים *inf* leeshrots (*etc*) kee-ve-kerev nemaleem.

crayon עפרון־גיר *nm* 'efron/-ot geer.

craze 1. בולמוס *nm* boolmos/-eem (*pl+of:* -ey); **2.** שיגעון (madness) *nm* sheeg|a'on/-'onot (+*of:* -'on/-'onot).

(to) craze 1. לשגע *vt inf* leshage'a'; *pst* sheega'; *pres* meshage'a'; *fut* yeshage'a'; **2.** להשתגע *vi inf* leheeshtage'a'; *pst* heeshtaga'; *pres* meeshtage'a'; *fut* yeeshtage'a'.

crazy 1. משוגע *adj* meshoog|a'/-a'at; **2.** מטורף (mad) *adj* metor|af/-efet.

(to go) crazy להשתגע *vi inf* leheeshtage'a'; *pst* heeshtaga'; *pres* meeshtage'a'; *fut* yeeshtage'a'.

crazy about 1. מטורף ל־ (mad after) *adj* metor|af/-efet le-; **2.** להוט אחר (craving for) *adj* lahoot/lehootah akhar.

creak חריקה *nf* khareek|ah/-ot (+*of:* -at).

(to) creak 1. לחרוק *inf* lakhrok; *pst* kharak; *pres* khorek; *fut* yakhrok; **2.** לצרום (grate) *inf* leetsrom; *pst* tsaram; *pres* tsorem; *fut* yeetsrom.

cream 1. שמנת (milk-) *nf* sham|enet/-anot; **2.** משחה (paste) *nf* meesh'khah/meshakhot (+*of:* meesh'khat); **3.** מיטב (best) *nm* meytav; **4.** מצבע קרם (color) *adj* mee-tseva' krem.

(cold) cream קרם לפנים *nm* krem/-eem la-paneem.

(ice) cream גלידה *nf* gleed|ah/-ot (+*of:* -at).

(whipped) cream קצפת *nf* kats|efet/-afot.

cream of tomato soup מרק עגבניות *nm* merak/meerkey 'agvaneeyot.

cream puff תופין שמנת *nm* toofeen/-ey shamenet.

cream separator מחבצה *nf* makhbets|ah/-ot (+*of:* -at).

creamery 1. חנות לדברי חלב *nf* khanoo|t/-yot le-deevrey khalav; **2.** מחלבה (dairy) *nf* makhlav|ah/-ot (+*of:* makhlev|et/-ot).

creamy שמנוני *adj* shamnoonee/-t.

crease 1. קמט (wrinkle) *nm* kem|et/-ateem (*pl+of:* keemtey); **2.** פצע קל (slight wound) *nm* pets|a'/-a'eem kal/-eem.

(to) crease 1. לקמט *inf* lekamet; *pst* keemet; *pres* mekamet; *fut* yekamet; **2.** לפצוע קל (wound slightly) *inf* leeftso'a' kal; *pst* patsa' kal *(p=f); pres* potse'a' kal; *fut* yeeftsa' kal.

(to) create ליצור *inf* leetsor; *pst* yatsar; *pres* yotser; *fut* yeetsor.

creation יצירה *nf* yetseer|ah/-ot (*+of:* -at).

Creation 1. בריאת העולם *nf* bree'at ha-'olam; **2.** מעשה בראשית (works of Creation) *nm* ma'aseh bre'sheet.

creative יצירתי *adj* yetseeratee/-t.

creator 1. יוצר *nmf* yotser/-et; **2.** הבורא (the Creator) *nm* ha-bore.

creature יצור *nm* yetsoor/-eem (*pl+of:* -ey).

credence אמון *nm* emoon/-eem (*pl+of:* -ey).

credentials 1. מכתבי המלצה (recommendations) *nm pl* meekhtevey hamlatsah; **2.** כתבי האמנה (accreditations) *nm pl* keetvey ha'amanah.

credible אמין *adj* ameen/-ah.

credit 1. אשראי *nm* ashray; **2.** זכות (favor) *f* zekhoo|t/-yot; **3.** אמון (trust) *nm* emoon/-eem (*pl+of:* -ey).

(to) credit לזכות חשבון (account) *inf* lezakot kheshbon; *pst* zeekah *etc*; *pres* mezakeh *etc*; *fut* yezakeh *etc*.

(to do) credit להוסיף כבוד *inf* lehoseef kavod; *pst* hoseef *etc*; *pres* moseef *etc*; *fut* yoseef *etc*.

(to give) credit לתת אמון *inf* latet emoon; *pst* natan *etc*; *pres* noten *etc*; *fut* yeeten *etc*.

credit and debit זכות וחובה *nf & nf* zekhoot ve-khovah.

credit card כרטיס אשראי *nm* kartees/-ey ashray.

creditable 1. ראוי לשבח (praiseworthy) *adj* ra'ooy/re'ooyah le-shevakh; **2.** זכאי לאשראי (trustworthy) *adj* zaka|y/'eet le-ashray;

creditor 1. נושה *nmf* nosh|eh/-ah (*pl:* -eem/-ot; *+of:* -ey); **2.** מלווה (lender) *nmf* malv|eh/-ah (*pl:* -eem/-ot; *+of:* -ey).

credo "אני מאמין" *nm* "anee ma'ameen".

credulous מאמין לכל דבר *adj* ma'ameen/-ah le-khol davar.

creed אמונה *nf* emoon|ah/-ot (*+of:* -at).

creek יובל *nm* yooval/-eem (*pl+of:* -ey).

(to) creep 1. לזחול *inf* leezkhol; *pst* zakhal; *pres* zokhel; *fut* yeezkhal; **2.** להתרפס (ingratiate) *inf* leheetrapes; *pst* heetrapes; *pres* meetrapes; *fut* yeetrapes.

creeper 1. זוחל *nm* zokh|el/-aleem (*pl+of:* -aley); **2.** רמש (insect) *nm* rem|es/-aseem (*pl+of:* -asey); **3.** צמח מטפס (climbing plant) *nm* tsemakh/-eem metap|es/-seem.

(giving the) creeps מצמרר *adj* metsamrer/-et.

(to) cremate לשרוף לאפר *inf* leesrof le-'efer; *pst* saraf *etc*; *pres* soref *etc*; *fut* yeesrof *etc*.

cremation שריפת גופה לאפר *nf* sreyf|at/-ot goof|ah/-ot le-'efer.

crematory 1. משרפה *nf* meesraf|ah/-ot (*+of:* meesref|et/-ot); **2.** קרמטוריום *nm* krematoryoom/-eem (*pl+of:* -ey).

creme de menthe ליקר מינתה *nm* leeker/-eem meentah (*cpr* mentah).

creosote 1. קראוסוט *nm* kreosot; **2.** מישחת חיטוי לעצים *nf* meeshkh|at/-ot kheetooy le-'etseem.

crescent 1. סהרון *nm* saharon/-eem (*pl+of:* -ey); **2.** חצי־סהר *nm* khatsee sahar.

(Red) Crescent 1. "הסהרון האדום" *nm* "ha-saharon he-adom"; **2.** "חצי־הסהר האדום" *nm* "khatsee ha-sahar he-adom".

crest 1. שיא *nm* see/-'eem (*pl+of:* -'ey); **2.** פיסגה (summit) *nf* peesgah/pesagot (*+of:* peesg|at/-ot).

crestfallen מדוכא *adj* medook|a/-et.

Crete כרתים *nm* kreteem.

cretonne בד קרטון *nm* bad/-ey kreton.

crevice 1. סדק *nm* sedek/sdakeem (*pl+of:* seedkey); **2.** בקיע (crack) *nm* bekee|'a'/-'eem (*pl+of:* -'ey).

crew צוות *nm* tsevet/tsvateem (*pl+of:* tseevtey).

crew cut תספורת קצרה וחלקה *nf* teespor|et/-ot ketsar|ah/-ot ve-khalak|ah/-ot.

crib 1. אבוס (feed) *nm* evoos/-eem (*pl+of:* -ey); **2.** עריסה (sleep) *nf* 'arees|ah/-ot (*+of:* -at).

(to) crib להעתיק בלא רשות *inf* leha'ateek be-lo reshoot; *pst* he'eteek *etc*; *pres* ma'ateek *etc*; *fut* ya'ateek *etc*.

cricket 1. צרצר (insect) *nm* tsratsar/tseertsareem (*+of:* tseerts|ar/-erey); **2.** משחק קריקט (game) *nm* meeskhak/-ey kreeket.

crier כרוז *nm* karoz/-ot.

crime פשע *nm* pesha'/-eem (*pl+of:* peesh'ey).

criminal 1. פושע *nm* posh|e'a'/-'eem (*pl+of:* -'ey); **2.** פלילי *adj* pleelee/-t.

criminal code מערכת דיני העונשין *nf* ma'arekhet deeney ha-'onasheen.

criminal law חוק פלילי *nm* khok/khookeem pleelee/-yeem.

criminal negligence 1. רשלנות פלילית *nf* rashlanoot pleeleet; **2.** התרשלות נפשעת (guilty slackness) *nf* heetrashloo|t/-yot neefsha|'at/-'ot.

criminology קרימינולוגיה *nf* kreemenologyah.

crimp 1. מסולסל (hair) *adj* mesools|al/-elet; **2.** פריר (face) *adj* pareer/preerah.

crimson אדום כדם *adj* adom/adoomah ka-dam.

(to) cringe 1. להתכווץ מפחד *inf* leheetkavets mee-fakhad (*f=p*); *pst* heetkavets *etc*; *pres* meetkavets *etc*; *fut* yeetkavets *etc*; **2.** להתרפס (ingratiate) *inf* leheetrapes; *pst* heetrapes; *pres* meetrapes; *fut* yeetrapes.

crinkle קמט *nm* kem|et/-ateem (*pl+of:* keemtey).

cripple נכה *nmf* nakh|eh/-ah (*pl:* nekh|eem/-ot; *+of:* -at/-ey).

crisis משבר *nm* mashber/-eem (*pl+of:* -ey).

crisp 1. פריך *adj* pareekh/preekhah; **2.** פריר (crumby) *adj* pareer/preerah; **3.** מתולתל (curly) *adj* metoolt|al-elet.

crisp answer תשובה קולעת *nf* teshoov|ah/-ot kol|a'at/-'ot.

crisp wind רוח מרעננת *nf* roo'akh mera'anenet.

criterion 1. קריטריון *nm* kreeteryon/-eem (*pl+of:* -ey); **2.** אמת־מידה *nf* am|at/-ot meedah.

critic מבקר *nmf* mevak|er/-eret (*pl:* -reem/-rot; *+of:* -rey).

critical קריטי *adj* kreetee/-t.

criticism 1. ביקורת *nf* beekoret/-ot; **2.** גינוי *nm* geenooy/-eem (*pl+of:* -ey).

(to) criticize למתוח ביקורת *inf* leemto'akh beekoret; *pst* matakh *etc*; *pres* mote'akh *etc*; *fut* yeemtakh *etc*.

croak קרקור *nm* keerkoor/-eem (*pl+of:* -ey);

crochet צנירה *nf* tseneer|ah/-ot (+*of:* -at).

crochet hook אנקול צנירה *nm* ank|ol/-ey tseneerah.

crock כד חרס *nm* kad/-ey kheres.

crockery כלי חרס *nm* klee/kley kheres.

crocodile 1. תנין *nm* taneen/-eem (*pl+of:* -ey); **2.** תמסח (alligator) *nm* teems|akh/-akheem (*pl+of:* -ekhey).

crony ידיד ותיק *nm* yedeed/-ah vateek/-ah.

crook 1. רמאי *nm* ram|ay/-a'eem (*pl+of:* -a'ey); **2.** נוכל (swindler) *nmf* nokhel/-et.

crooked 1. עקום *adj* 'ak|om/-oomah **2.** שיקרי (false) *adj* sheekree/-t.

(to) croon לפזם *inf* lefazem; *pst* peezem *(p=f)*; *pres* mefazem; *fut* yefazem.

crooner זמר פזמונים *nmf* zam|ar/-eret peezmoneem.

crop יבול *nm* yevool/-eem (*pl+of:* -ey).

(to) crop 1. לכרות (ears) *vt inf* leekhrot; *pst* karat *(k=kh)*; *pres* koret; *fut* yeekhrot; **2.** לגזוז (hair) *vt inf* leegzoz; *pst* gazaz; *pres* gozez; *fut* yeegzoz; **3.** לקצור (harvest) *vt inf* leektsor; *pst* katsar; *pres* kotser; *fut* yeektsor; **4.** לגדל (plant, grow) *vt inf* legadel; *pst* geedel; *pres* megadel; *fut* yegadel.

crop dusting ריסוס מהאוויר *nm* reesoos/-eem me-ha-aveer.

crop of hair 1. בלורית *nf* bloreel|t/-yot; **2.** רעמה (mane) *nf* ra'am|ah/-ot (+*of:* -at).

(to) crop out (or up) 1. לצוץ *inf* latsoots; *pst & pres* tsats; *fut* yatsoots; **2.** לבצבץ (sprout) *inf* levatsbets; *pst* beetsbets *(b=v)*; *pres* mevatsbets; *fut* yevatsbets.

croquette 1. כופתה *nf* kooft|ah/-a'ot (+*of:* -at); **2.** כדור בשר (meat-ball) *nm* kadoor/-ey basar.

cross צלב *nm* tslav/-eem (*pl+of:* -ey).

(to) cross לחצות *inf* lakhatsot; *pst* khatsah; *pres* khotseh; *fut* yekhetseh.

crossbar מוט רוחב לדלתות *nm* mot/-ot rokhav lee-dlatot.

(to) crossbreed להכליא *inf* lehakhlee; *pst* heekhlee; *pres* makhlee; *fut* yakhlee.

cross-country דרך השדות *adv* derekh ha-sadot.

cross-examination חקירת שתי וערב *nf* khakeer|at/-ot shetee va-'erev.

(to) cross-examine לחקור חקירה נגדית *inf* lakhkor khakeerah negdeet; *pst* khakar *etc*; *pres* khoker *etc*; *fut* yakhkor *etc.*

cross-eyed פוזל *adj* pozel/-et.

cross section חתך *nm* khatakh/-eem (*pl+of:* -ey).

crossword puzzle תשבץ *nm* tashbets/-eem (*pl+of:* -ey).

crossing 1. צומת *nm* tsomet/tsemateem (*pl+of:* tsomtey); **2.** מעבר חצייה (pedestrian) *nm* ma'a|var/-vrey khatseeyah.

(railway) crossing מסעף מסילת הברזל *nm* mees'af/-ey meseel|at/-ot barzel.

(river) crossing צליחת נהר *nf* tsleekh|at/-ot nahar/neharot.

(road) crossing חציית כביש *nf* khatseey|at/-ot kveesh/-eem.

crossing gate מחסום רכבת (train) *nm* makhsom/-ey rakevet.

crossing point נקודת חצייה *nf* nekood|at/-ot khatseeyah.

crossroad(s) 1. הצטלבות *nf* heetstalvoo|t/-yot; **2.** צומת כבישים *nm* tsom|et/-tey kveesheem; **3.** פרשת דרכים *nf* parash|at/-ot drakheem.

crouch התכופפות *nf* heetkofefoo|t/-yot.

crow עורב *nm* 'or|ev/-veem (*pl+of:* -vey).

crow's nest נקודת תצפית *nf* nekood|at/-ot tatspeet.

crowbar מנוף *nm* manof/menof|eem (*pl+of:* -ey).

crowd המון *nm* hamon/-eem (*pl+of:* -ey).

crowded 1. צפוף *adj* tsafoof/tsefoofah; **2.** דחוס (compressed) *adj* dakhoos/dekhoosah.

crown 1. כתר *nm* ket|er/-areem (*pl+of:* keetrey); **2.** עטרה (diadem) *nf* 'atar|ah/-ot (+*of:* 'at|eret/-rot).

crown prince, -cess יורש עצר *nmf* yoresh/-et 'etser.

crowned מוכתר *adj* mookht|ar/-eret.

crucial 1. חיוני (vital) *adj* kheeyoonee/-t; **2.** מכריע (decisive) *adj* makhree|'a'/-'ah.

crucifix צלב *nm* tslav/-eem (*pl+of:* -ey).

(to) crucify לצלוב *inf* leetslov; *pst* tsalav; *pres* tsolev; *fut* yeetslov.

cruel אכזרי *adj* akhzaree/-t.

cruelty אכזריות *nf* akhzereeyoot.

cruet 1. צנצנת (flask) *nf* tseents|enet/-anot (*pl+of:* -enot); **2.** צלוחית (jar) *nf* tslokhee|t/-yot.

(oil) cruet 1. צנצנת שמן *nf* tseentsen|et/-ot shemen; **2.** צלוחית שמן *nf* tslokhee|t/-yot shemen.

(vinegar) cruet 1. צנצנת חומץ *nf* tseentsen|et/-ot khomets; **2.** צלוחית חומץ *nf* tslokhee|t/-yot khomets.

cruise שייט *nm* shayeet (+*of:* sheyt).

cruiser 1. שייטת (warship) *nf* sha|yetet/-yatot; **2.** ספינת טיולים (pleasure-boat) *nf* sfeen|at/-ot teeyooleem.

crumb פירור *nm* peroor/-eem (*pl+of:* -ey).

(to) crumb לפורר *inf* leforer; *pst* porer *(p=f)*; *pres* meforer; *fut* yeforer.

(to) crumble 1. להתמוטט *inf* leheetmotet; *pst* heetmotet; *pres* meetmotet; *fut* yeetmotet; **2.** להתפורר (disintegrate) *inf* leheetporer; *pst* heetporer; *pres* meetporer; *fut* yeetporer.

crummy 1. מלוכלך (dirty) *adj* melookhl|akh/-ekhet; **2.** שפל (base) *adj* shafal/shfalah.

(to) crumple 1. להתקמט *inf* leheetkamet; *pst* heetkamet; *pres* meetkamet; *fut* yeetkamet; **2.** להתכווץ (shrink) *inf* leheetkavets; *pst* heetkavets; *pres* meetkavets; *fut* yeetkavets.

(to) crunch לכרסם *inf* lekharsem; *pst* keersem *(k=kh)*; *pres* mekharsem; *fut* yekharsem.

crusade 1. מסע צלב *nm* mas|a'/-'ey tslav; **2.** מסע תעמולה (propaganda campaign) *nm* mas|a'/-'ey ta'amoolah; **3.** מסע הסברה (information campaign) *nf* mas|a'/-'ey hasbarah.

(to) crusade לנהל מאבק על *inf* lenahel ma'avak 'al; *pst* neehel *etc*; *pres* menahel *etc*; *fut* yenahel *etc.*

crusader 1. צלבן *nm* tsalvan/-eem (*pl+of:* -ey); **2.** לוחם למען רעיון (fighter for idea) *nf* lokhem/-et le-ma'an ra'ayon.

crush 1. התנגשות *nf* heetnagshoo|t/-yot; **2.** תשוקה (infatuation) *nf* teshook|ah/-ot (+*of:* -at).

(to) crush 1. למעוך *inf* leem'okh; *pst* ma'akh; *pres* mo'ekh; *fut* yeem'akh; **2.** לדכא (suppress) *inf* ledake; *pst* deeke; *pres* medake; *fut* yedake; **3.** להכריע (overwhelm) *inf* lehakhree'a'; *pst* heekhree'a'; *pres* makhree'a'; *fut* yakhree'a'.

(to) crush stone לכתוש אבנים *inf* leekhtosh avaneem; *pst* katash *(k=kh) etc; pres* kotesh *etc; fut* yeekhtosh *etc.*

crust 1. קרום *nm* kroom/-eem (*pl+of:* -ey); **2.** גלד (rind) *nm* geled/gladeem (*pl+of:* geeldey).

crusty נוקשה *adj* nooksh|eh/-ah.

crutch קב *nm* kav/kab|ayeem (*pl+of:* -ey).

crux עיקר *nm* 'eek|ar/-areem (*pl+of:* -rey).

cry 1. צעקה *nf* tse'ak|ah/-ot (+*of:* tsa'ak|at/-ot); **2.** בכייה (weeping) bekhee|yah/-yot (+*of:* -yat).

(to) cry 1. לבכות (weep) *inf* leevkot; *pst* bakhah *(kh=k); pres* bokheh; *fut* yeevkeh; **2.** לזעוק (protest) *inf* leez'ok; *pst* za'ak; *pres* zo'ek; *fut* yeez'ak; **3.** להתחנן (implore) *inf* leheetkhanen; *pres* heetkhanen; *pres* meetkhanen; *fut* yeetkhanen.

cry for help קריאה לעזרה *nf* kree|'ah/-'ot le-'ezrah.

(a far) cry from שונה בהרבה מ־ *adj* shoneh/-ah be-harbeh mee-.

(to) cry out 1. לצעוק (call out) *inf* leets'ok; *pst* tsa'ak; *pres* tso'ek; *fut* yeets'ak; **2.** לזעוק (lament) *inf* leez'ok; *pst* za'ak; *pres* zo'ek; *fut* yeez'ak; **3.** להתאונן (complain) *inf* leheet'onen; *pst* heet'onen; *pres* meet'onen; *fut* yeet'onen; **4.** לקונן (mourn) *inf* lekonen; *pst* konen; *pres* mekonen; *fut* yekonen.

crybaby בכיין *nmf* bakhyan/-eet.

cryptic מסתורי *adj* meestoree/-t.

crystal 1. גביש *nm* gaveesh/gveesh|eem (*pl+of:* -ey); **2.** בדולח (quartz) *nm* bedolakh; **3.** קריסטל *nm* kreestal/-eem (*pl+of:* -ey).

crystal clear ברור כשמש *adj & adv* baroor/broorah ka-shemesh.

crystalline 1. גבישי *adj* gveeshee/-t; **2.** בדולחי *adj* bedolkhee/-t.

(to) crystallize להתגבש *inf* leheetgabesh; *pst* heetgabesh; *pres* meetgabesh; *fut* yeetgabesh.

cub גור *nm* goor/-eem (*pl+of:* -ey).

cub reporter כתב מתחיל *nmf* kat|av/-evet matkheel/-ah.

cube קובייה *nm* koobee|yah/-yot (+*of:* -yat).

cube root שורש מעוקב *nm* shor|esh/-osheem me'ookav/-eem.

(ice) cube קוביית קרח *nf pl* koobee|yat/-yot kerakh.

cubic 1. מעוקב *adj* me'ook|av/-evet; **2.** בצורת קובייה (cube-like) *adj* be-tsoorat kooveeyah.

cubism קוביזם *nm* koobeezm.

cuckold מקורנן *adj* mekoornan.

cuckoo 1. קוקייה *nf* kookee|yah/-yot (+*of:* -yat); **2.** מטופש (fool) *adj* metoop|ash/-eshet.

cuckoo-clock שעון־קוקייה *nm* she'on/-ey kookeeyah.

cucumber מלפפון *nm* melafefon/-eem (*pl+of:* -ey).

cud גירה *nf* geyr|ah (+*of:* -at).

(to) cuddle 1. להתרפק *inf* leheetrapek; *pst* heetrapek; *pres* meetrapek; *fut* yeetrapek; **2.** ללטף (caress) *inf* lelatef; *pst* leetef; *pres* melatef; *fut* yelatef.

cudgel אלה *nf* al|ah/-ot (+*of:* -at).

(to) cudgel 1. לחבוט *inf* lakhbot; *pst* khavat *(v=b); pres* khovet; *fut* yakhbot; **2.** להרביץ (beat up) *inf* leharbeets; *pst* heerbeets; *pres* marbeets; *fut* yarbeets.

cue אות (hint) *nm* ot/-ot.

(to) cue 1. לתת אות *inf* latet ot; *pst* natan ot; *pres* noten ot; *fut* yeeten ot; **2.** לרמוז (hint) *v inf* leermoz; *pst* ramaz; *pres* romez; *fut* yeermoz.

cuff חפת *nm* khefet/khafateem (*pl+of:* kheftey).

cuisine 1. מטבח *nm* meetbakh; **2.** סגנון בישול (cooking style) *nm* seegnon/-ot beeshool.

(to) cull 1. לבחור *inf* leevkhor; *pst* bakhar *(b=v); pres* bokher; *fut* yeevkhar; **2.** לברור (select) *inf* leevror; *pst* barar *(b=v); pres* borer; *fut* yeevror.

(to) culminate להגיע לשיא *inf* lehagee'a' le-see; *pst* heegee'a' *etc; pres* magee'a' *etc; fut* yagee'a' *etc.*

culprit 1. עבריין *nmf* 'avaryan/-eet; **2.** נאשם (accused) *nmf* ne'esh|am/-emet.

cult פולחן *nm* poolkhan/-eem (*pl+of:* -ey).

(to) cultivate 1. לטפח (further) *inf* letape'akh; *pst* teepakh; *pres* metape'akh; *fut* yetape'akh; **2.** לעבד (land) *inf* le'abed; *pst* 'eebed; *pres* me'abed; *fut* ye'abed; **3.** לשכלל (improve) *inf* leshakhlel; *pst* sheekhlel; *pres* meshakhlel; *fut* yeshakhlel.

cultivated 1. מטופח (fostered) *adj* metoopakh/-at; **2.** מעובד (land) *adj* me'oob|ad/-edet.

cultivation 1. עיבוד (land) *nm* 'eebood; **2.** טיפוח (fostering) *nm* teepoo|'akh/-kheem (*pl+of:* -khey); **3.** פיתוח (development) *nm* peetoo'akh.

cultivator 1. עובד אדמה (farmer) 'ov|ed/-dey adamah; **2.** קלטרת (machine) *nf* kalt|eret/-arot (*pl+of:* -erot).

culture 1. תרבות *nf* tarboo|t/-yot; **2.** תרבית (microb.) *nf* tarbee|t/-yot.

cultured 1. תרבותי (educat.) *adj* tarbootee/-t; **2.** מתורבת (artific.) *adj* metoorb|at/-etet.

cumbersome 1. מגושם *adj* megoosh|am/-emet; **2.** מכביד (burden) *adj* makhbeed/-ah.

cunning 1. ערמומי *adj* 'armoomee/-t; **2.** שנון (sharp) *adj* shanoon/shnoonah.

cup 1. ספל *nm* sef|el/-aleem (*pl+of:* seefley); **2.** גביע (chalice, trophy) *nm* gavee'a'/gveel'eem (*pl+of:* -'ey).

cupboard ארון *nm* aron/-ot.

cur כלב כלאיים *nm* kelev/kalvey keel'ayeem.

curate כומר *nm* komer/kemareem (*pl+of:* komrey).

curator אוצר *nmf* otser/-et.

curb 1. רסן *nm* res|en/-aneem (*pl+of:* reesney); **2.** מחסום (check) *nm* makhsom/-eem (*pl+of:* -ey); **3.** בלם (brake) *nm* belem/blam|eem (*pl+of:* beelmey); **4.** אבן שפה (curbstone) *nf* even/avney safah.

(to) curb 1. לבלום *inf* leevlom; *pst* balam *(b=v); pres* bolem; *fut* yeevlom; **2.** לרסן (restrain) *inf* lerasen; *pst* reesen; *pres* merasen; *fut* yerasen; **3.** לעצור (stop) *inf* la'atsor; *pst* 'atsar; *pres* 'otser; *fut* ya'atsor.

curbstone אבן שפה *nf* even/avney safah.

curd קום *nm* kom.

(to) curd להקריש *inf* lehakreesh; *pst* heekreesh; *pres* makreesh; *fut* yakreesh.

(to) curdle להחמיץ *inf* lehakhmeets; *pst* hekhmeets; *pres* makhmeets; *fut* yakhmeets.

cure 1. תרופה *nf* troof|ah/-ot (*+of:* -at); **2.** ריפוי (healing) *nm* repooy/-eem (*pl+of:* -ey).

(to) cure לרפא *inf* lerape; *pst* reepe; *pres* merape; *fut* yerape.

cure-all תרופת־פלא *nf* troof|at/-ot pele.

curfew עוצר *nm* 'otser.

curio ממצא נדיר *nm* meemtsa/-'eem nadeer/ nedeereem.

curiosity סקרנות *nf* sakranoot.

curious סקרן *adj* sakran/-eet.

curl תלתל *nm* taltal/-eem (*pl+of:* -ey).

(to) curl להסתלסל *inf* leheestalsel; *pst* heestalsel; *pres* meestalsel; *fut* yeestalsel.

curly מתולתל *adj* metoolt|al/-elet.

currant דומדמנית *nf* doomdemanee|t/-yot.

currant bush שיח דומדמן *nm* see|'akh/-khey doomdeman.

currency מטבע *nm* matbe|'a'/-'ot.

(foreign) currency 1. מטבע זר *[colloq.]nm* matbe'a' zar; **2.** מטבע חוץ *nm* matbe'a' khoots.

(hard) currency מטבע קשה *nm* matbe'a' kasheh.

(paper) currency 1. כסף נייר *nm* kesef neyar; **2.** שטר כסף (banknote) *nm* shtar/sheetrey kesef.

current 1. זרם *nm* zerem/zrameem (*pl+of:* zeermey); **2.** נוכחי (present) *adj* nokhekhee/-t.

current account 1. חשבון עובר ושב *nm* kheshbon/ -ot 'over va-shav; **2.** חשבון עו"ש *nm* kheshbon/ -ot 'osh (*acr of* 1).

current events ענייני היום *nm pl* 'eenyeney ha-yom.

curriculum תוכנית לימודים *nf* tokhnee|t/-yot leemoodeem.

curriculum vitae תולדות חיים *nf pl* toldot khayeem.

curse 1. קללה *nf* klal|ah/-ot (*+of:* keelel|at/-ot); **2.** מארה (malediction) *nf* me'er|ah/-ot (*+of:* -at).

(to) curse לקלל *inf* lekalel; *pst* keelel; *pres* mekalel; *fut* yekalel.

cursed מקולל *adj* mekool|al/-elet.

cursive קורסיבי *adj* koorseevee/-t.

curt 1. קצר (brief) *adj* katsar/ketsarah; **2.** מקוצר (abbreviated) *adj* mekoots|ar/-eret.

(to) curtail 1. לקצץ *inf* lekatsets; *pst* keetsets; *pres* mekatsets; *fut* yekatsets; **2.** לקצר (shorten) *inf* lekatser; *pst* keetser; *pres* mekatser; *fut* yekatser.

curtain 1. וילון *nm* veelon/-ot; **2.** מסך (theater) *nm* masa|kh/-keem (*k=kh; pl+of:* -key).

(Iron) Curtain מסך הברזל *nm* masakh ha-barzel.

curvature 1. חמוק *nm* khamook/-eem (*pl+of:* -ey); **2.** עיקום (bend) *nm* 'eekoom/-eem (*pl+of:* -ey).

curve 1. עקומה *nf* 'akoom|ah/-ot (*+of:* -at); **2.** פיתול *nm* peetool/-eem (*pl+of:* -ey).

(to) curve 1. להתעקם *inf* leheet'akem; *pst* heet'akem; *pres* meet'akem; *fut* yeet'akem; **2.** להתעגל (become round) *inf* leheet'agel; *pst* heet'agel; *pres* meet'agel; *fut* yeet'agel.

curved 1. מעוקם *adj* me'ook|am/-emet; **2.** מעוגל (rounded) *adj* me'oog|al/-elet.

cushion כר *nm* kar/-eem (*pl+of:* -ey).

custard רפרפת ביצים *nf* rafref|et/-ot beytseem.

custodian אפוטרופוס *nmf* apotrop|os/-seet.

custody 1. השגחה *nf* hashgakhah; **2.** פיקוח (supervision) *nm* peekoo'akh.

(in) custody במעצר *adv* be-ma'atsar.

custom 1. נוהג *nm* nohag/nehageem (*pl+of:* nohogey); **2.** נוהל (procedure) *nm* nohal/nehaleem (*pl+of:* noholey); **3.** לפי הזמנה (to order) *adv* le-fee hazmanah.

custom built בנוי במיוחד *adj* banooy/benooyah bee-meyookhad.

custom made עשוי לפי הזמנה *adj* 'asoo|y/-yah le-fee hazman|ah/-ot.

custom regulations תקנות המכס *nf pl* takanot ha-mekhes.

custom tailor חייט לפי הזמנות *nm* khayat/-eem le-fee hazmanot.

customary מקובל *adj* mekoob|al/-elet.

customer לקוח *nmf* lako'akh/lekokh|ah (*pl:* -ot).

customhouse בית מכס *nm* bet/batey mekhes.

customhouse mark 1. תו מכס *nm* tav/-ey mekhes; **2.** גושפנקת מכס (seal) *nm* gooshpank|at/-ot mekhes.

customs מכס *nm* mekh|es/-aseem (*pl+of:* meekhsey).

customs clearance שחרור ממכס *nm* sheekhroor/ -eem mee-mekhes.

customs official, officer מוכס *nm* mokh|es/-seem (*pl+of:* -sey).

cut 1. חתך *nm* khatakh/-eem (*pl+of:* -ey); **2.** גיזרה (section) *nf* geezrah/gezarot (*+of:* geezr|at/-ot); **3.** חלק (share) khelek/khalakeem (*pl+of:* khelkey).

(short) cut קיצור־דרך *nm* keetsoor/-ey derekh.

(to) cut 1. לחתוך *inf* lakhtokh; *pst* khatakh; *pres* khotekh; *fut* yakhtokh; **2.** לגזור (fell) *inf* leegzor; *pst* gazar; *pres* gozer; *fut* yeegzor; **3.** לגזוז (hair) *inf* leegzoz; *pst* gazaz; *pres* gozez; *fut* yeegzoz.

(to) cut across לחתוך לרוחב *inf* lakhtokh la-rokhav; *pst* khatakh *etc*; *pres* khotekh *etc*; *fut* yakhtokh *etc*.

cut and dried קבוע מראש *adj* kavoo'a'/kevoo'ah me-rosh.

(to) cut capers להתנהג בצורה מוזרה *inf* leheetnaheg be-tsoorah moozarah; *pst* heetnaheg *etc*; *pres* meetnaheg *etc*; *fut* yeetnaheg *etc*.

(to) cut out 1. להפסיק *inf* lehafseek; *pst* heefseek; *pres* mafseek; *fut* yafseek; **2.** להסתלק (get out) *inf* leheestalek; *pst* heestalek; *pres* meestalek; *fut* yeestalek.

(to be) cut out for להיות מוכשר במיוחד ל־ *inf* leehyot mookhsh|ar/-eret bee-meyookhad le-.

cute 1. פיקח *adj* peek|e'akh/-'kheet; **2.** נחמד (delightful) *adj* nekhmad/-ah.

cuticle קרום העור בשולי הציפורניים *nm* kroom ha-'or be-shooley ha-tseepornayeem.

cutlery סכו"ם *nm* sakoom/-eem - *acr of* SAkeeneem, Kapot OO-Mazlegot סכינים, כפות ומזלגות (knives, spoons and forks)(*pl+of:* -ey).

cutlet קציצה *nf* ketseets|ah/-ot (*+of:* -at).

cutter 1. חותך *nm* khot|ekh/-kheem (*pl+of:* -khey); **2.** מקצץ (chopper) *nm* maktsets/-eem (*pl+of:* -ey).

(coast guard) cutter סירת משמר החופים *nf* seer|at/-ot meeshmar ha-khofeem.
(wood) cutter חוטב עצים *nm* khot|ev/-vey 'etseem.
cutthroat 1. רוצח (murderer) *nm* rots|e'akh/-kheem (*pl+of:* -khey); **2.** רצחני (homicidal) *adj* rats'khanee/-t.
cutting גזיר *nm* gezeer/-eem (*pl+of:* -ey).
cuttlefish דיונון *nm* dyonoon/-eem (*pl+of:* -ey).
cyanide ציאניד *nm* tsee'aneed/-eem.
cybernetics קיברנטיקה *nf* keeberneteekah.
cycle 1. מחזור *nm* makhzor/-eem (*pl+of:* -ey); **2.** גלגל (wheel) *nm* galgal/-eem (*pl+of:* -ey).
cyclist רוכב אופניים *nmf* rokhev/-et ofanayeem.
cyclone ציקלון *nm* tseeklon/-eem (*pl+of:* -ey).
cylinder 1. גליל *nm* galeel/gleel|eem (*pl+of:* -ey); **2.** צילינדר *nm* tseeleend|er/-reem (*pl+of:* -rey).
cylindrical 1. גלילי *adj* gleelee/-t; **2.** צילינדרי *adj* tseeleendree/-t.
cymbal מצלתיים *nm pl* metseeltayeem.
(to play the) cymbal לצלצל במצלתיים *inf* letsaltsel ba-metseeltayeem; *pst* tseeltsel *etc; pres* metsaltsel *etc; fut* yetsaltsel *etc.*
cynic ציניקן *nmf* tseeneekan/-eet; (*pl m:* -eem/-ey).
cynical ציני *adj* tseenee/-t.
cynicism ציניות *nf* tseeneeyoot.
cypress ברוש *nm* brosh/-eem (*pl+of:* -ey).
Cypriote 1. קפריסיני *nmf* kafreeseenee/-t; **2.** קפריסאי *[colloq.] nmf* kafreesa'ee/-t.
Cyprus 1. קפריסין (island) *nm* kafreeseen; **2.** קפריסין (country) *nf* kafreeseen.
Cyrillic קירילי *adj* keereelee/-t.
cyst 1. שלחוף *nm* shalkhoof/-eem (*pl+of:* -ey); **2.** כיסון *nm* keeson/-eem (*pl+of:* -ey).
Czech 1. צ׳כית (language) *nf* chekheet; **2.** צ׳כי *nmf & adj* chekhee/-t (*pl:* -m/-yot).
Czechoslovakia צ׳כוסלובקיה *nf* chekhoslovakyah.

D.

D musical note for which the equivalent in Hebrew is the continental רה (Re).
D,d consonant equivalent to the Hebrew letter ד (Daleth).
dab טפיחה *nf* tefeekh|ah/-ot (*+of:* -at).
(to) dab לטפוח *inf* leetpo'akh; *pst* tafakh *(f=p); pres* tofe'akh; *fut* yeetpakh.
(to) dabble לטבול *inf* leetbol; *pst* taval *(v=b); pres* tovel; *fut* yeetbol.
dabbler 1. טירון *nm* teeron/-eem (*pl+of:* -ey); **2.** דילטנט *nm* deeletant/-eem (*pl+of:* -ey).
dad אבא *nm* aba/avot *(b=v).*
daddy אבא׳לה *[colloq.] nm* abaleh.
daffodil נרקיס *nm* narkees/-eem (*pl+of:* -ey).
daft 1. שוטה *nmf & adj* shot|eh/-ah; **2.** משוגע *nmf adj* meshoog|a'/-a'at.
dagger פגיון *nm* peegyon/-ot.
dahlia דליה *nf* dal|yah/-yot (*+of:* -yat).
daily 1. יומי *adj* yomee/-t; **2.** יומית *adv* yomeet; **3.** מדי יום (every day) *adv* meedey yom; **4.** יומון (newspaper) *nm* yomon/-eem (*pl+of:* -ey).
daily newspaper עיתון יומי *nm* 'eeton/-eem yomee/-yeem
daily pay שכר יומי *nm* sakhar yomee.
daintily 1. ברוך *adv* be-rokh; **2.** בעדינות (delicately) *adv* ba-'adeenoot.
daintiness עדינות *nf* 'adeenoo|t/-yot.
dainty עדין *adj* 'adeen/-ah.
dais בימה *nf* beem|ah/-ot (*+of:* -at).
daisy 1. חרצית־בר *nf* khartsee|t/-yot bar; **2.** חיננית *nf* kheenanee|t/-yot.
dalliance 1. בזבוז זמן *nm* beezbooz/-ey zman; **2.** איחור (delay) *nm* eekhoor/-eem (*pl+of:* -ey).
(to) dally להשתהות *inf* leheeshtahot; *pst* heeshtahah; *pres* meeshtaheh; *fut* yeeshtaheh.
dam סכר *nm* sekh|er/-areem (*pl+of:* seekhrey).
damage נזק n nezek/nezakeem (*pl+of:* neezkey).
(to) damage להזיק *inf* lehazeek; *pst* heezeek; *pres* mazeek; *fut* yazeek.
dame 1. גבירה *nf* gveer|ah/-ot (*+of:* -at); **2.** נקבה *(slang: female) nf* nekeyv|ah/-ot (*+of:* -at).
damn ! לעזאזל *interj* la'azazel!
damnation 1. אבדון *nm* avadon; **2.** קללה (curse) *nf* klal|ah/-ot (*+of:* keelel|at/-ot).
damnatory מרשיע *adj* marshee|'a'/-'ah.
damnatory evidence עדות מרשיעה *nf* 'edoo|t/-yot marshee'|ah/-ot.
damned מקולל *adj* mekool|al/-elet.
damp 1. לח *adj* lakh/-ah; **2.** רטוב (wet) *adj* ratov/retoovah.
(to) dampen 1. להרטיב *inf* leharteev; *pst* heerteev; *pres* marteev; *fut* yarteev; **2.** לעכב (restrain) *inf* le'akev; *pst* 'eekev; *pres* me'akev; *fut* ye'akev.
dampness 1. לחות *nf* lakhoo|t/-yot; **2.** רטיבות (wetness) *nf* reteevoo|t/-yot.
damsel עלמה *nf* 'al|mah/-amot (*+of:* -mat/-mot).
dance 1. ריקוד *nm* reekood/-eem (*pl+of:* -ey); **2.** מחול (art) *nm* makhol/mekholot (*+of:* mekhol/-ot).
(folk) dance ריקוד־עם *nm* reekood/-ey 'am.
dance band תזמורת ריקודים *nf* teezmor|et/-ot reekoodeem.

dance hall אולם ריקודים *nm* oolam/-ey reekoodeem.

dancer 1. רקדן *nm* rakdan/-eem (*pl+of:* -ey); **2.** רקדנית (woman-dancer) *nf* rakdanee|t/-yot.

dancing ריקודים *nm pl* reekoodeem (*sing:* reekood; *pl+of:* -ey).

dancing partner בן־זוג לריקודים *nmf* ben/bat zoog le-reekoodeem.

dandruff קשקשים *nm pl* kaskas|eem (*pl+of:* -ey).

dandy 1. מצוין (excellent) *adj* metsooy|an/-enet; **2.** גנדרן (flirt) *nmf & adj* gandran/-eet; **3.** טרזן (fop) *nm* tarzan/-eem (*pl+of:* -ey).

Dane דני *nmf* denee/-t (*pl:* -m/-yot).

danger סכנה *nf* sakan|ah/-ot (*+of:* -at).

(mortal) danger סכנת מוות *nf* sakan|at/-ot mavet.

danger to life סכנת חיים *nf* sakan|at/-ot khayeem.

dangerous מסוכן *adj* mesook|an/-enet.

(to) dangle להיסחב *inf* leheesakhev; *pst & pres* neeskhav; *fut* yeesakhev.

Danish דני *adj* denee/-t (*pl:* -yeem/-yot).

dapper נקי *adj* nakee/nekeeyah.

dapple 1. מנומר *adj* menoom|ar/-eret; **2.** רבגוני (variegated) *adj* ravgonee/-t; **3.** רב־גוני (multi-colored) *cpr adj* ravgevanee/-t.

(to) dare להעז *inf* leha'ez; *pst* he'ez; *pres* me'ez; *fut* ya'ez.

daredevil 1. עז־נפש *adj* 'az/-at nefesh; **2.** פזיז (rash) *adj* pazeez/pezeezah.

daring 1. העזה *nf* he'az|ah/-ot (*+of:* -at); **2.** נועז (bold) *adj* no|'az/-'ezet.

dark (*adj.*) 1. חשוך *adj* khashookh/-ah; **2.** קודר (gloomy) *adj* koder/-et; **3.** אפל (dim) *adj* afel/-ah.

dark (n.) 1. חושך *nm* khoshekh; **2.** חשיכה (obscurity) *nf* khashekh|ah/-ot (*+of:* khesh'kh|at/-ot).

(after) dark עם חשיכה *adv* 'eem khashekhah.

(in the) dark 1. בחושך *adv* ba-khoshekh; **2.** ללא ידיעה (without knowledge) *adv* le-lo yedee'ah.

(to) darken 1. להחשיך *inf* lehakh'sheekh; *pst* hekh'sheekh; *pres* makh'sheekh; *fut* yakh'sheekh; **2.** להאפיל (black out) *inf* leha'afeel; *pst* he'efeel; *pres* ma'afeel; *fut* ya'afeel.

darkness חשיכה *nf* khashekh|ah/-ot (*+of:* khesh-kh|at/-ot).

darling 1. יקיר *nmf & adj* yakeer/-ah (*+of:* -at); **2.** חבוב *[colloq.] adj* khaboob/-ah.

(my) darling 1. יקירי *interj* yakeer|ee/-atee; **2.** חביבי *interj* khaveev|ee/-atee; **3.** חביבי *[slang] interj* khabeeb|ee/-tee (*m/f*).

(to) darn לתקן גרביים *inf* letaken garbayeem; *pst* teeken *etc*; *pres* metaken *etc*; *fut* yetaken *etc*.

dart חץ *nm* khets/kheets|eem (*pl+of:* -ey).

dash 1. מקף (-) *nm* mak|af/-afeem (*pl+of:* -fey); **2.** קו מפריד (-) *nm* kav/-eem mafreed/-eem.

(to) dash 1. לזנק *inf* lezanek; *pst* zeenek; *pres* mezanek; *fut* yezanek; **2.** לחוש (hasten) *inf* lakhoosh; *pst & pres* khash; *fut* yakhoosh.

dashing זוהר *adj* zoher/-et.

data נתונים *nm pl* netoon|eem (*pl+of:* -ey).

data processing עיבוד נתונים *nm* 'eebo od netooneem.

date 1. תאריך (time) *nm* ta'are ekh/-eem (*pl+of:* -ey); **2.** פגישה עם בן־זוג (meeting) *nf* pegeesh|ah/-ot 'eem ben/bat zoog; **3.** בן־זוג (partner) *nmf* ben/bat zoog kavoo'a'/kvoo'ah; **4.** תמר (fruit) *nm* tamar/temar|eem (*pl+of:* tamrey).

dateline תאריך משלוח *nm* ta'areekh/-ey meeshlo|akh/-kheem.

date-palm דקל *nm* dek|el/-aleem (*pl+of:* deekley).

date-plum אפרסמון *nm* afarsemon/-eem (*pl+of:* -ey).

daughter בת *nf* bat/banot (*pl+of:* bnot).

daughter in law כלה *nf* kal|ah/-ot (*+of:* -at).

(to) daunt להרתיע *inf* lehartee'a'; *pst* heertee'a'; *pres* martee'a'; *fut* yarte e'a'.

dauntless 1. עשוי לבלי־חת *adj* 'asoo|y/-yah lee-vlee khat; **2.** נועז (daring) *adj* no'|az/-ezet.

(to) dawdle להתבטל *inf* leheetbatel; *pst* heetbatel; *pres* meetbatel; *fut* yeetbatel.

dawn שחר *nm* shakhar.

(to) dawn להתחוור *inf* leheetkhaver; *pst* heetkhaver; *pres* meetkhaver; *fut* yeetkhaver.

day יום *nm* yom/yameem (*pl+of:* yemey).

day after tomorrow מחרתיים *nm* mokhoratayeem.

day before yesterday שלשום *nm* sheelshom.

day laborer שכיר־יום *nm* sekheer/-ey yom.

daybreak עלות השחר *nf* 'alot ha-shakhar.

daydream חלום בהקיץ *nm* khalom/-ot be-hakeets.

(to) daydream לחלום בהקיץ *inf* lakhalom be-hakeets; *pst* khalam *etc*; *pres* kholem *etc*; *fut* yakhalom *etc*.

daylight אור יום *nm* or yom.

(in broad) daylight לאור היום *adv* le-or ha-yom.

day-nursery מעון יום *nm* me'on/-ot yom.

(in) daytime בשעות היום *adv* bee-she'ot ha-yom.

(to) daze לסנוור *inf* lesanver; *pst* seenver; *pres* mesanver; *fut* yesanver.

(to) dazzle להמם *inf* lehamem; *pst* heemem; *pres* mehamem; *fut* yehamem.

dead 1. מת *adj* met/-ah; **2.** מת (corpse) *nm* met/-eem (*pl+of:* -ey).

dead certain במאה אחוז בטוח *adj* be-me'ah akhooz batoo'akh/betookhah.

dead tired מת מעייפות *adj* met/-ah me-'ayefoot.

(to) deaden להמית *inf* lehameet; *pst* hemeet; *pres* meme et; *fut* yameet.

deadline שעת האפס *nf* she|'at/-'ot ha-efes.

deadly 1. קטלני *adj* katlanee/-t; **2.** ממית *adj* meme et/-ah.

deaf חירש *nmf & adj* kheresh/-et.

deaf-mute חירש־אילם *nmf & adj* kheresh/-et eelem/-et.

deafening מחריש אוזניים *adj* makhreesh/-at oznayeem.

deafness חירשות *nf* khershoo|t/-yot.

deal עסקה *nf* 'eeskah/'asakot (*+of:* 'eesk|-at/-ot).

(fair) deal יחס הוגן *nm* yakhas hogen.

(make a) deal לעשות עסק *inf* la'asot 'esek/'asake em; *pst* 'asah *etc*; *pres* 'oseh *etc*; *fut* ya'aseh *etc*.

(square) deal עסקה הוגנת 'eeskah hogenet.

(to) deal cards לחלק קלפים *inf* lekhalek klafeem; *pst* kheelek *etc*; *pres* mekhalek *etc*; *fut* yekhalek *etc*.

(to) deal in לעסוק ב־ *inf* la'asok be-; *pst* 'asak be-; *pres* 'osek be-; *fut* ya'asok be-.
dealer עוסק *nmf* 'osek/-et.
(authorized) dealer עוסק מורשה *nm* 'os|ek/-keem moorsh|eh/-eem.
dean נשיא *nmf* nasee/nesee'ah (+*of:* nesee/-'at).
(university) dean דיקן *nm* dekan/-eem (*pl+of:* -ey).
dean's office דיקנאט *nm* dekanat/-eem (*pl+of:* -ey).
dear יקר *adj* yakar/yekarah.
(my) dear 1. יקירי *interj (m/f)* yakeer|ee/-atee; **2.** חביבי *interj (m/f)* khaveev|ee/-atee.
(oh) dear! אלי שבשמיים! *interj* elee she-ba-shamayeem!
dearly 1. מאוד *adv* me'od; **2.** ביוקר (expensively) *adv* be-yoker.
dearth מחסור *nm* makhsor/-eem (*pl+of:* -ey).
death מוות *nm* mavet (+*of:* mot).
death bed 1. מיטת גוסס *nf* meetat goses; **2.** ערש דווי *nf* 'eres dvay.
death blow מכת מוות *nf* mak|at/-ot mavet.
death certificate תעודת מוות *nf* te'ood|at/-ot mavet.
death penalty עונש מוות 'on|esh/-shey mavet.
death rate 1. תמותה *nf* temoot|ah/-ot (+*of:* -at); **2.** אחוז תמותה (percentage) *nm* akho oz/-ey temootah.
death warrant צו הוצאה להורג *nm* tsav/-ey hotsa'ah le-horeg.
deathless בן־אלמוות *nmf & adj* ben/-bat almavet.
debacle מפולת *nf* mapol|et/-ot.
(to) debar לשלול זכות *inf* leeshlol zekhoot; *pst* shalal *etc*; *pres* sholel *etc*; *fut* yeeshlol *etc*.
(to) debark לרדת לחוף *nf* laredet la-khof; *pst* yarad *etc*; *pres* yored *etc*; *fut* yered *etc*.
debarkation ירידה לחוף *nf* yereed|ah/-ot la-khof.
(to) debase להשחית *inf* lehash'kheet; *pst* heesh'kheet; *pres* mash'kheet; *fut* yash'khe et.
debasement השפלה *nf* hashpal|ah/-ot (+*of:* -at).
debatable נתון לוויכוח *adj* natoon/netoonah le-veekoo'akh.
debate ויכוח *nm* veekoo|'akh/-kheem (*pl+of:* -khey).
(futile) debate ויכוח סרק *nm* veeekoo|'akh/-khey srak.
(parliamentary) debate ויכוח פרלמנטרי *nm* veeko o|'akh/-kheem parlamentaree/-yeem.
(to) debate להתווכח *inf* leheetvake'akh; *pst* heetvakakh; *pres* meetvake'akh; *fut* yeetvakakh.
debauchery שחיתות *nf* shekheetoo|t/-yot.
debenture איגרת־חוב *nf* eeg|eret/-rot khov.
debil 1. דביל *nm* debeel/-eem (*pl+of:* -ey); **2.** דבילי *adj* debeelee/-t.
(to) debilitate להחליש *inf* lehakhleesh; *pst* hekhleesh; *pres* makhleesh; *fut* yakhleesh.
debility חולשה *nf* khoolsh|ah/-ot (+*of:* -at).
debit 1. דביט *nm* debeet/-eem; **2.** חוב (debt) *nm* khov/-ot; **3.** חובה *nf* khov|ah/-ot (+*of:* -at).
(to) debit לחייב *inf* lekhayev; *pst* kheeyev; *pres* mekhayev; *fut* yekhayev.
debonair עליז *adj* 'aleez/-ah.
(to) de-brief לתחקר *inf* letakhker; *pst* teekhker; *pres* metakhker; *fut* yetakhker.
de-briefing תחקיר *nm* takhkeer/-eem (*pl+of:* -ey).
debris חורבה kho|orbah/-rovot (+*of:* -orvat).
debt חוב *nm* khov/-ot.
(floating) debt חוב שוטף *nm* khov/-ot shot|ef/-feem.
(in) debt 1. בחובה *adv* be-khovah; **2.** שקוע בחובות *adj* shakoo'a'/shekoo'ah be-khovot.
(out of) debt לצאת מהחובות *inf* latset me-ha-khovot; *pst* yatsa *etc*; *pres* yotse *etc*; *fut* yetse *etc*.
(outstanding) debt 1. חוב תלוי ועומד *nm* khov/-ot talooy/tlooyeem ve-'om|ed/-deem; **2.** יתרת חוב (balance due) *nf* yeetr|at/-ot khov.
(to contract) debt להיכנס לחוב *inf* leheekanes le-khov; *pst & pres* neekhnas *(kh=k) etc*; *fut* yeekanes *etc*.
(to pay) debt לפרוע חוב *inf* leefro'a' khov; *pst* para' *(p=f) etc*; *pres* pore'a' *etc*; *fut* yeefra' *etc*.
debt collector גובה חובות *nm* gov|eh/-ey khovot.
debt of honor חובת כבוד *nf* khov|at/-ot kavod.
debtor 1. בעל־חוב *nmf* ba'al/-at (*pl* -ey) khov; **2.** חייב *nmf* kha|yav/-yevet.
(to) debunk לחשוף פרצוף *inf* lakhsof partsoof; *pst* khasaf *etc*; *pres* khosef *etc*; *fut* yakhsof *etc*.
debut הופעת בכורה *nf* hofa|'at/-'ot bekhorah.
debutante טירונית בהופעות בחברה *nf* teeronee|t/-yot be-hofa'ot ba-khevrah.
decade עשור *nm* 'asor/-eem (*pl+of:* -ey).
decadence ניוון *nm* neevoon/-eem (*pl+of:* -ey).
decadent מתנוון *adj* meetnaven/-et.
Decalogue עשרת הדיברות *nm pl* 'aseret ha-deebrot.
(to) decamp להסתלק *inf* leheestalek; *pst* heestalek; *pres* meestalek; *fut* yeestalek.
(to) decant למזוג *inf* leemzog; *pst* mazag; *pres* mozeg; *fut* yeemzog.
decanter בקבוק *nm* bakbook/-eem (*pl+of:* -ey).
(to) decapitate לערוף ראש *inf* la'arof rosh/rasheem; *pst* 'araf *etc*; *pres* 'oref *etc*; *fut* ya'arof *etc*.
decapitation עריפת ראש *nf* 'areef|at/-ot rosh/rasheem.
decay ריקבון *nm* reek|avon/-vonot (+*of:* -von).
decease פטירה *nf* peteer|ah/-ot (+*of:* -at).
(to) decease 1. למות (die) *inf* lamoot; *pst & pres* met; *fut* yamo ot; **2.** נפטר (passed away) *pst* neeft|ar/-erah; *pres* neeft|ar/-eret; (no *inf* or *fut*).
(the) deceased 1. הנפטר *nmf* ha-neeft|ar/-eret; **2.** המנוח (the late) *nmf* ha-mano'akh/menokhah.
deceit 1. רמאות *nf* rama'oo|t/-yot; **2.** מירמה (fraud) *nf* meerm|ah/-ot (+*of:* -at).
deceitful 1. כוזב *adj* kozev/-et; **2.** מתעה (misleading) *adj* mat|'eh/-'ah.
(to) deceive לרמות *inf* leramot; *pst* reemah; *pres* merameh; *fut* yerameh.
(to) decelerate להאט *inf* leha'et; *pst* he'et; *pres* me'et; *fut* ya'et.
December דצמבר *nm* detsember.
decency הגינות *nf* hageenoot.
decent הוגן *adj* hogen/-et.
decently בצורה הוגנת *adv* be-tsoorah hogenet.
decentralization ביזור *nm* beezoor/-eem (*pl+of:* -ey).

(to) decentralize לבזר *inf* levazer; *pst* beezer *(b=v); pres* mevazer; *fut* yevazer.
deception הונאה *nf* hona|'ah/-'ot (*+of:* -'at)
deceptive מטעה *adj* mat|'eh/-'ah.
(to) decide להחליט *inf* lehakhleet; *pst* hekhleet; *pres* makhleet; *fut* yakhleet.
decimal עשרוני *adj* 'esrone e/-t.
decimal point נקודת השבר העשרוני *nf* nekood|at/-ot ha-shever ha-'esronee.
(to) decimate לעשות שמות *inf* la'asot shamot; *pst* 'asah *etc*; *pres* 'oseh *etc*; *fut* ya'aseh *etc*.
(to) decipher לפענח *inf* lefa'ne'akh; *pst* pee'nakh *(p=f); pres* mefa'ne'akh; *fut* yefa'nakh.
decision החלטה *nf* hakhlat|ah/-ot (*+of:* -at).
decisive מכריע *adj* makhree|'a'/-'ah.
deck סיפון *nm* seepoon/-eem (*pl+of:* -ey)
deck chair כיסא מרגוע *nm* kees|e/-'ot margo'a'.
deck hand סיפונאי *nm* seepoona|y/-'eem (*pl+of:* -'ey).
deck of cards חפיסת קלפים *nm* khafees|at/-ot klafeem.
decking קישוט *nm* keeshoot/-eem (*pl+of:* -ey).
(to) declame לדקלם *inf* ledaklem; *pst* deeklem; *pres* medaklem; *fut* yedaklem.
declaration הצהרה *nf* hats'har|ah/-ot (*+of:* -at).
(the Balfour) Declaration הצהרת בלפור *nf* hats'harat balfoor.
declarative הצהרתי *adj* hats'haratee/-t.
declaratory judgment פסק-דין הצהרתי *nm* pesak/peeskey deen hats'haratee/-yeem.
(to) declare להצהיר *inf* lehats'heer; *pst* heets'heer; *pres* mats'heer; *fut* yats'heer.
(to) declare war להכריז מלחמה *inf* lehakhreez meelkham|ah/-ot; *pst* heekhreez *etc*; *pres* makhreez *etc*; *fut* yakhreez *etc*.
declension 1. נטייה במידרון *nf* netee|yah/-yot be-meedron; **2.** נטיית שם *(gram.) nf* netee|yat/-yot shem/-ot.
decline ירידה *nf* yereed|ah/-ot (*+of:* -at).
(to) decline 1. לסרב *inf* lesarev; *pst* serev; *pres* mesarev; *fut* yesarev; **2.** לדחות (reject) *inf* leedkhot; *pst* dakhah; *pres* dokheh; *fut* yeedkheh.
decode לפענח *inf* lefa'ne'akh; *pst* pee'nakh *(p=f); pres* mefa'ne'akh; *fut* yefa'nakh.
decoding פענוח pee'noo|'akh/-kheem (*pl+of:* -khey).
decolletage מחשוף *nm* makhsof/-eem (*pl+of:* -ey).
decolorant נוטל צבע *adj* notel/-et tseva'.
decomposable 1. פריק *adj* pare ek/preekah; **2.** רקיב (liable to rot) *adj* rakeev/rekeevah.
(to) decompose 1. לפרק *vt inf* lefarek; *pst* perak *(p=f); pres* mefarek; *fut* yefarek; **2.** להרקיב (rot) *vi inf* leharkeev; *pst* heerkeev; *pres* markeev; *fut* yarkeev.
decomposition הירקבות *nf* herakvoo|t/-yot
decompression ירידת לחץ *nf* yereed|at/-ot lakhats.
(to) decontaminate לחטא *inf* lekhate; *pst* kheete; *pres* mekhate; *fut* yekhate.
decontamination חיטוי *nm* kheetoo|y/-yeem (*pl+of:* -yey).
decontrol הסרת פיקוח *nf* hasar|at/-ot peekoo'akh.
(to) decontrol לבטל פיקוח *inf* levatel peekoo'akh; *pst* beetel *(b=v) etc; pres* mevatel *etc; fut* yevatel *etc*.
decor תפאורה *nf* taf'oor|ah/-ot (*+of:* -at).
(to) decorate 1. לקשט *inf* lekashet; *pst* keeshet; *pres* mekashet; *fut* yekashet; **2.** לעטר (adorn) *inf* le'ater; *pst* 'eeter; *pres* me'ater; *fut* ye'ater.
decorated מעוטר *adj* me'oot|ar/-eret.
decoration עיטור *nm* 'eetoor/-eem (*pl+of:* -ey).
decorative קישוטי *adj* keeshootee/-t.
decorator 1. תפאורן *nmf* taf'ooran/-eet; **2.** דקורטור *nm* dekorator/-eem (*pl+of:* -ey).
decoy פיתיון *nm* peet|ayon/-yonot (*+of:* -yon).
(to) decoy לפתות *inf* lefatot; *pst* peetah *(p=f); pres* mefateh; *fut* yefateh.
decrease ירידה *nf* yereed|ah/-ot (*+of:* -at).
(to) decrease 1. לקטון *inf* leekton; *pst* katan; *pres* katen; *fut* yeektan; **2.** לפחות (diminish) *inf* leefkhot; *pst* pakhat *(p=f); fut* pokhet; *fut* yeefkhat.
decreasing פוחת והולך *adj* pokhet/-et ve-holekh/-et.
decreasingly במידה פוחתת והולכת *adv* be-meedah pokhetet ve-holekhet.
decree צו *nm* tsav/-eem (*pl+of:* -ey).
(to) decree לצוות *inf* letsavot; *pst* tseevah; *pres* metsaveh; *fut* yetsaveh.
decrepit תשוש *adj* tashoosh/teshooshah.
decrepitude אפיסת כוחות *nf* afeesat kokhot.
(to) decry 1. לגנות (denounce) *inf* leganot; *pst* geenah; *pres* meganeh; *fut* yeganeh; **2.** לפסול (disqualify) *inf* leefsol; *pst* pasal *(p=f); pres* posel; *fut* yeefsol.
dedicate להקדיש *inf* lehakdeesh; *pst* heekdeesh; *pres* makdeesh; *fut* yakdeesh.
dedication הקדשה *nf* hakdash|ah/-ot (*+of:* -at).
(to) deduce להסיק *inf* lehaseek; *pst* heeseek; *pres* mase ek; *fut* yaseek.
deducible ניתן להסיק *adj* neet|an/-enet lehaseek.
(to) deduct 1. לנכות *inf* lenakot; *pst* neekah; *pres* menakeh; *fut* yenakeh; **2.** להפחית (reduce) *inf* lehafkheet; *pst* heefkheet; *pres* mafkheet; *fut* yafkheet.
deductible בר־ניכוי *adj* bar/bat neekooy.
(tax-)deductible מנוכה ממס *adj* menook|eh/-ah mee-mas.
deduction 1. ניכוי *nm* neekoo|y/-yeem (*pl+of:* -yey); **2.** מסקנה (conclusion) *nf* maskan|ah/-ot (*+of:* -at).
deductively מן הכלל אל הפרט *adv* meen ha-klal el ha-prat.
deed 1. מעשה *nm* ma'as|eh/-eem (*pl+of:* -ey); **2.** מסמך (document) *nm* meesmakh/-eem (*pl+of:* -ey).
(in word and) deed להלכה ולמעשה *adv* la-halakhah oo-le-ma'aseh.
(to) deem 1. לסבור *inf* leesbor; *pst* savar *(v=b); pres* sover; *fut* yeesbor; **2.** לחשוב (consider) *inf* lakhshov; *pst* khashav; *pres* khoshev; *fut* yakhshov.
deep 1. עמוק *adv* 'amok; **2.** עמוק *adj* 'am|ok/-ookah; **3.** עומק (depth) *nm* 'om|ek/-akeem (*pl+of:* -key).
deep-freeze הקפאה עמוקה *nf* hakpa|'ah/-'ot 'amook|ah/-ot.

(to) deep-freeze להקפיא הקפאה עמוקה *inf* lehakpe e hakpa'ah 'amookah; *pst* heekpee *etc*; *pres* makpe e *etc*; *fut* yakpee *etc*.

deep-laid מחוכם *adj* mekhook|am/-emet.

deep-rooted מושרש *adj* mooshr|ash/-eshet.

deep-sea שבלב־ים *adj* she-be-lev yam.

deep-seated תקוע איתן *adj* takoo'a'/tekoo'ah eytan.

(to) deepen להעמיק *inf* leha'ameek; *pst* he'emeek; *pres* ma'ameek; *fut* ya'ameek.

deeply 1. מאוד *adv* me'od; **2.** במידה רבה (to a large extent) *adv* be-meedah rabah.

deer צבי *nm* tsvee/tsva|yeem (*pl+of:* -yey).

deerskin עור צבי *nm* 'or/-ot tsev|ee/-aye em.

(to) deface להשחית פני *inf* lehashkheet peney; *pst* heeshkheet *etc*; *pres* mashkheet *etc*; *fut* yashkheet *etc*.

de-facto למעשה *adv* le-ma'aseh.

(to) defalcate למעול *inf* leem'ol; *pst* ma'al; *pres* mo'el; *fut* yeem'al.

defalcation מעילה *nf* me'eel|ah/-ot (*+of:* -at).

defamation השמצה *nf* hashmats|ah/-ot (*+of:* -at).

defamatory משמיץ *adj* mashmeets/-ah.

defamatory libel השמצה בכתב *nf* hashmats|ah/-ot bee-khtav.

(to) defame להשמיץ *inf* lehashmeets; *pst* heeshmeets; *pres* mashmeets; *fut* yashmeets.

default השתמטות *nf* heeshtamtoo|t/-yot.

(judged/tried by) default נידון שלא בפניו *nmf* needon/-ah she-lo be-fan|av/-eha *(f=p)*.

(to) default להשתמט *inf* leheeshtamet; *pst* heeshtamet; *pres* meeshtamet; *fut* yeeshtamet.

(in) default of בהיעדר *adv* be-he'ader.

defaulter משתמט *nmf* meeshtam|et/-etet (*pl:* -teem/-tot).

defeasible בר־ביטול *adj* bar/bat beetool

defeat תבוסה *nf* tvoos|ah/-ot (*+of:* -at).

(to) defeat 1. להביס *inf* lehavees; *pst* hevees; *pres* mevees; *fut* yavees; **2.** לנצח (vanquish) *inf* lenatse'akh; *pst* neetsakh; *pres* menatse'akh; *fut* yenatsakh.

defeatism תבוסנות *nf* tvoosanoo|t/-yot.

defeatist תבוסתן *nmf* tvoostan/-eet.

(to) defecate לעשות צרכים *inf* la'asot tsrakheem; *pst* 'asah *etc*; *pres* 'oseh *etc*; *fut* ya'aseh *etc*.

defecation עשיית צרכים *nf* 'aseeyat tsrakheem.

defect מגרעת *nf* meegr|a'at/-a'ot (*pl+of:* -e'ot).

defection בגידה *nf* begeed|ah/-ot (*+of:* -at).

defective לקוי *adj* lakooy/lekooyah.

(mentally) defective לקוי בשכלו *adj* lakooy/lekooyah be-seekhl|o/-ah.

defectiveness אי־תקינות *nm* ee-tekeenoo|t/-yot.

(to) defend להגן *inf* lehagen; *pst* hegen; *pres* megen; *fut* yagen.

defendable בר־הגנה *adj* bar/bat haganah.

defendant (in civil case) נתבע neetb|a'/-a'at (*pl:* -a'eem/-a'ot; *pl+of:* -e'ey).

defendant (in criminal case) נאשם *nmf* ne'esh|am/-emet (*pl:* -ameem/-amot; *pl+of:* -mey).

defender 1. סניגור *nmf* sanegor/-eet (*pl:* -eem/-eeyot; *pl+of:* -ey); **2.** מגן (protector) *nm* meg|en/-eeneem (*pl+of:* -eeney).

defense 1. הגנה *nf* hagan|ah/-ot (*+of:* -at); **2.** סניגוריה *nf* sanegor|yah/-yot (*+of:* -yat).

(counsel for the) defense סניגור *nmf* sanegor/-eet.

(Ministry of) Defense 1. משרד הביטחון (in Israel: Ministry of Security) *nm* meesrad/-edey ha-beetakhon; **2.** משרד ההגנה (in other countries) *nm* meesr|ad/-edey ha-haganah.

(self-)defense הגנה עצמית *nf* haganah 'atsmeet.

defense minister 1. שר הביטחון (in Israel: Minister of Security) *nm* sar/-ey ha-beetakhon; **2.** שר ההגנה (in other countries) *nm* sar/-ey ha-haganah.

defenseless חסר מגן *adj* khas|ar/-rat magen.

defensible בר־הגנה *adj* bar/bat haganah.

defensive 1. הגנתי *adj* haganatee/-t; **2.** דפנסיבי *adj* defenseevee/-t.

(on the) defensive בעמדת התגוננות *adv* be-'emd|at/-ot heetgonenoot.

defensive battle מגננה *nf* meegn|anah/-anot (*+of:* -enet).

defensive war מלחמת מגן *nf* meelkh|emet/-amot magen.

(to) defer 1. לדחות *inf* leedkhot; *pst* dakhah; *pres* dokheh; *fut* yeedkheh; **2.** לעכב (detain) *inf* le'akev; *pst* 'eekev; *pres* me'akev; *fut* ye'akev.

deference יראת כבוד *nf* yeer'at kavod.

(with all due) deference עם כל הכבוד *adv* 'eem kol ha-kavod.

(in) deference to מתוך יראת כבוד כלפי *adv* me-tokh yeer'at kavod kelapey.

deferentially ביראת כבוד *adv* be-yeer'at kavod.

deferment דחייה *nf* dekhee|yah/-yot (*+of:* -yat).

deferred דחוי *adj* dakhooy/dekhooyah.

deferred call שיחה דחויה *nf* seekhah/-ot dekhoo|yah/-yot.

deferred stock מניה נדחית *nf* mena|yah/-yot needkh|et/-ot.

defiance 1. התרסה *nf* hatras|ah/-ot (*+of:* -at); **2.** המריה (challenge) *nf* hamra|yah/-yot (*+of:* -yat).

(in) defiance of 1. למרות *adv* lamrot; **2.** על אף (in spite) 'al af.

defiant 1. ממרה *adj* mamr|eh/-ah; **2.** מתחצף (impertinent) *adj* meetkhatsef/-et.

defiantly בחוצפה *adv* be-khootspah.

deficiency 1. חסר *nm* kheser; **2.** חוסר *nm* khoser.

deficient 1. חסר *adj* khaser/-ah; **2.** פגום (faulty) *adj* pagoom/pegoomah.

deficit 1. גירעון *nm* ger|a'on/-'onot (*+of:* geer'on/-ot); **2.** דפיציט *nm* defeetseet/-eem (*pl+of:* -ey).

(to) defile לחלל *inf* lekhalel; *pst* kheelel; *pres* mekhalel; *fut* yekhalel.

defiled מחולל *adj* mekhool|al/-elet.

defilement חילול *nm* kheelool/-eem (*pl+of:* -ey)

(to) define להגדיר *inf* lehagdeer; *pst* heegdeer; *pres* magdeer; *fut* yagdeer.

defined מוגדר *adj* moogd|ar/-eret.

(well) defined מוגדר במפורש *adj* moogd|ar/-eret bee-meforash.

definite ברור *adj* baroor/broorah.

definite article ה״א הידיעה (Hebrew equivalent of "the") *(gram.) nf* he' ha-yedee'ah.

definitely בהחלט *adv* be-hekhlet.
definition הגדרה *nf* hagdar|ah/-ot (+*of:* -at).
definitive 1. סופי *adj* sofee/-t; **2.** מכריע (decisive) *adj* makhree|'a'/-'ah
definitively סופית *adv* sofeet.
(to) deflate 1. להוציא את האוויר *inf* lehotsee et ha-aveer; *pst* hotsee *etc; pres* motsee *etc; fut* yotsee *etc;* **2.** לכווץ (contract) *inf* lekhavets; *pst* keevets *(k=kh); pres* mekhavets; *fut* yekhavets.
deflation דפלציה *nf* deflats|yah/-yot (+*of:* -yat).
deflationary דפלציוני *adj* deflatsyonee/-t.
(to) deflect 1. להטות *inf* lehatot; *pst* heetah; *pres* mateh; *fut* yateh; **2.** להסיט (shift) *inf* lehaseet; *pst* heseet; *pres* meseet; *fut* yaseet.
deflection /deflexion 1. הסטה *nf* hasat|ah/-ot (+*of:* -at); **2.** סטייה (shift) *nf* stee|yah/-yot (+*of:* -yat).
defoliation שלכת *nf* shal|ekhet/-akhot.
(to) deform לעוות *inf* le'avet; *pst* 'eevet; *pres* me'avet; *fut* ye'avet.
deformation 1. עיוות *nm* 'eevoot/-eem (+*of:* -ey); **2.** השחתת צורה (defacing) *nf* hash'khat|at/-ot tsoorah.
deformed 1. מעוות *adj* me'oov|at/-etet; **2.** מושחת (defaced) *adj* mooshkh|at/-etet.
deformity מום *nm* moom/-eem (*pl+of:* -ey).
(to) defraud להונות *inf* lehonot; *pst* honah; *pres* merameh; *fut* yoneh.
defraudation הונאה *nf* hona|'ah/-'ot (+*of:* -'at).
(to) defray 1. לפרוע *inf* leefro'a'; *pst* para' *(p=f); pres* pore'a'; *fut* yeefra'; **2.** לשאת בהוצאות (reimbourse) *inf* laset be-hotsa'ot; *pst* nasa *etc; pres* nose *etc; fut* yeesa *etc.*
defrayal סילוק חשבון *nm* seelook/-ey kheshbon/-ot.
defroster מפשיר *nm* mafsheer/-eem (+*of:* -ey).
deft זריז *adj* zareez/zereezah.
deftly בזריזות *adv* bee-zereezoot.
deftness זריזות *nf* zereezoo|t/-yot.
defunct נפטר *nm* neeftar/-eem (*pl+of:* -ey).
(the) defunct 1. הנפטר *nmf* ha-neeft|ar/-eret; **2.** המנוח (late) *nmf* ha-mano'akh/menokhah.
(to) defy להתנגד בגלוי *inf* leheetnaged be-galooy; *pst* heetnaged *etc; pres* meetnaged *etc; fut* yeetnaged *etc.*
degenerate 1. מושחת *adj* mooshkh|at/-etet; **2.** דגנרט *nm* degenerat/-eem (*pl+of:* -ey).
(to) degenerate להתנוון *inf* leheetnaven; *pst* heetnaven; *pres* meetnaven; *fut* yeetnaven.
degeneration 1. ניוון *nm* neevoon/-eem (+*of:* -ey); **2.** דגנרציה *nf* degenerats|yah/-yot.
degenerative מנוון *adj* menoov|an/-enet.
degradation השפלה *nf* hashpal|ah/-ot (+*of:* -at).
(to) degrade 1. להוריד בדרגה *inf* lehoreed be-dargah; *pst* horeed *etc; pres* moreed *etc; fut* yoreed *etc;* **2.** להשפיל (debase) *inf* lehashpeel; *pst* heeshpeel; *pres* mashpeel; *fut* yashpeel.
degraded מושפל *adj* mooshp|al/-elet.
degrading משפיל *adj* mashpeel/-ah.
degree 1. מידה (measure) *nf* meed|ah/-ot (+*of:* -at); **2.** דרגה (standing) *nf* dargah/dragot (+*of:* dargat); **3.** מעלת חום (temperature) *nf* ma'al|at/-ot khom.
(academic) degree תואר אקדמי *nm* to'ar/te'areem akademee/-yeem.
(honorary) degree תואר כבוד *nm* to'ar/-ey kavod.
(third) degree חקירה בעינויים *nf* khakeer|ah/-ot be-'eenooyeem.
(to a) degree במידת־מה *adv* be-meedat mah.
(to take a) degree לקבל תואר אקדמי *inf* lekabel to'ar akademee; *pst* keebel *etc; pres* mekabel *etc; fut* yekabel *etc.*
degression 1. ירידה הדרגתית *nf* yereedah hadragateet; **2.** הורדת גובה המסים (tax-reduction) *nf* horadat govah ha-meeseem.
degressive פוחת והולך *adj* pokhet/-et ve-holekh/-et.
degustation טעימה *nf* te'eem|ah/-ot (+*of:* -at).
(to) dehumanize לשלול תכונות אנוש *inf* leeshlol tekhoonot enosh; *pst* shalal *etc; pres* sholel *etc; fut* yeeshlol *etc.*
(to) dehumidify להפיג לחות *inf* lehafeeg lakhoot; *pst* hefeeg *etc; pres* mefeeg *etc; fut* yafeeg *etc.*
(to) dehydrate לייבש *inf* leyabesh; *pst* yeebesh; *pres* meyabesh; *fut* yeyabesh.
dehydration 1. דהידראציה *nf* deheedrats|yah/-yot; **2.** צינום *nm* tseenoom/-eem (*pl+of:* -ey).
deification האלהה *nf* ha'ala|hah/-hot (+*of:* -hat).
(to) deify להאליל *inf* leha'aleel; *pst* he'eleel; *pres* ma'aleel; *fut* ya'aleel.
(to) deign להואיל *inf* leho'eel; *pst* ho'eel; *pres* mo'eel; *fut* yo'eel.
deity אלוהות *nf* elohoo|t/-yot.
(to) deject לדכדך *inf* ledakhdekh; *pst* deekhdekh; *pres* medakhdekh; *fut* yedakhdekh.
dejected מדוכדך *adj* medookhd|akh/-ekhet.
dejection דיכאון *nm* deek|a'on/-'onot (+*of:* -'on).
de jure דה־יורה *adv* deh yooreh.
(to) delate להלשין *inf* lehalsheen; *pst* heelsheen; *pres* malsheen; *fut* yalsheen.
delator מלשין *nm* malsheen/-eem (*pl+of:* -ey).
delay 1. עיכוב *nm* 'eekoov/-eem (*pl+of:* -ey); **2.** איחור (lateness) *nm* eekhoor/-eem (*pl+of:* -ey).
(to) delay להשהות *inf* lehash'hot; *pst* heesh'hah; *pres* mash'heh; *fut* yash'heh.
delayed מושהה *adj* moosh'heh/-t.
delayed action bomb 1. פצצת השהיה *nf* peetsets|at/-ot hash'hayah; **2.** פצצת שעון (time-bomb) *nf* peetsets|at/-ot sha'on.
delaying action פעולת השהיה *nf* pe'ool|at/-ot hash'hayah.
delectable 1. נעים *adj* na'eem/ne'eemah; **2.** משעשע (amusing) *adj* mesha'sh|e'a'/-a'at.
delectation 1. עינוג *nm* 'eenoog/-eem (*pl+of:* -ey); **2.** תענוג (pleasure) *nm* ta'anoog/-ot.
delegacy העברת סמכויות *nf* ha'avar|at/-ot samkhooyot.
delegate 1. ציר *nmf* tseer/-ah (*pl:* -eem/-ot; +*of:* -at/-ey); **2.** נציג (representative) *nmf* natseeg/netseeg|ah (*pl:* -eem/-ot; +*of:* -at/-ey).
(to) delegate 1. לאצול *inf* le'etsol; *pst* atsal; *pres* otsel; *fut* ye'etsol; **2.** למנות (appoint) *inf* lemanot; *pst* meenah; *pres* memaneh; *fut* yemaneh; **3.** לייפות

כוח (empower) *inf* leyapot ko'akh; *pst* yeepah *etc;* *pres* meyapeh *etc; fut* yeyapeh *etc.*

delegation משלחת *nf* meeshlakh|at/-ot.

delegation of power האצלת סמכויות *nf* ha'atsalat samkhooyot.

deletion מחיקה *nf* mekheek|ah/-ot (+*of:* -at).

deliberate 1. מחושב *adj* mekhoosh|av/-evet; **2.** מכוון (intended) *adj* mekhoov|an/-enet.

(to) deliberate 1. לדון *inf* ladoon; *pst & pres* dan; *fut* yadoon; **2.** לשקול (ponder) *inf* leeshkol; *pst* shakal; *pres* shokel; *fut* yeeshkol.

deliberately 1. במכוון *adv* bee-mekhoovan; **2.** במתכוון (intentionally) *adv* be-meetkaven; **3.** במזיד (willfully) *adv* be-mezeed.

deliberation 1. דיון *nm* deeyoon/-eem (*pl+of:* -ey); **2.** עיון (study) *nm* 'eeyoon/-eem (*pl+of:* -ey).

delicacy עדינות *nf* 'adeenoo|t/-yot.

delicate עדין *adj* 'adeen/-ah.

delicatessen store מעדנייה *nf* ma'adanee|yah/-yot (+*of:* -yat).

delicious 1. טעים *adj* ta'eem/te'eemah; **2.** נחמד (delightful) *adj* nekhmad/-ah.

deliciously בצורה ערבה *adv* be-tsoorah 'arevah.

delict 1. עבירה *nm* 'aver|ah/-ot (+*of:* -at); **2.** עוון (sin) *nm* 'avon/-ot.

delight 1. תענוג *nm* ta'anoog/-eem (*pl+of:* -ey); **2.** הנאה (enjoyment) *nf* hana|'ah/-'ot (+*of:* -'at).

(to) delight 1. ליהנות *inf* lehanot; *pst* nehenah; *pres* neheneh; *fut* yehaneh; **2.** להתענג (enjoy) *inf* leheet'aneg; *pst* heet'aneg; *pres* meet'aneg; *fut* yeet'aneg.

delighted נהנה *adj* neheneh/-t.

delightful מהנה *adj* mehan|eh/-ah.

delightfully בעונג רב *adv* be-'oneg rav.

delimitation 1. תחימה *nf* tekheem|ah/-ot (+*of:* -at); **2.** תיחום (demarcation) *nm* tekhoom/-eem (*pl+of:* -ey).

delinquency עבריינות *nf* 'avaryanoot.

(juvenile) delinquency עבריינות נוער *nf* 'avaryanoot no'ar.

delinquent 1. עבריין *nm* 'avaryan/-eem (*pl+of:* -ey); **2.** עברייני *adj* 'avaryanee/-t.

delirious 1. מטריף *adj* matreef/-ah; **2.** שגעוני (crazy) *adj* sheeg'onee/-t.

delirium טירוף *nm* teroof/-eem (*pl+of:* -ey).

(to) deliver 1. למסור *inf* leemsor; *pst* masar; *pres* moser; *fut* yeemsor; **2.** לספק (supply) *inf* lesapek; *pst* seepek; *pres* mesapek; *fut* yesapek; **3.** לגאול (redeem) *inf* leeg'ol; *pst* ga'al; *pres* go'el; *fut* yeeg'al.

deliverance 1. הצלה *nf* hatsal|ah/-ot (+*of:* -at); **2.** גאולה (redemption) *nf* ge'ool|ah/-ot (+*of:* -at).

delivery 1. מסירה *nf* meseer|ah/-ot (+*of:* -at); **2.** לידה (birth) *nf* leyd|ah/-ot (+*of:* -at).

delta דלתה *nf* delt|ah/-ot (+*of:* -at).

(to) delude 1. להונות *inf* lehonot; *pst* honah; *colloq.* *pres* merameh; *fut* yoneh; **2.** להוליך שולל (mislead) *inf* leholeekh sholal; *pst* holeekh *etc; pres* moleekh *etc; fut* yoleekh *etc.*

deluge 1. מבול *nm* mabool; **2.** הצפה (innundation) *nf* hatsaf|ah/-ot (+*of:* -at); **3.** שיטפון (flood) *nm* sheet|afon/-fonot (+*of:* -fon).

delusion אשליה *nf* ashla|yah/-yot (+*of:* -yat).

delusion of grandeur שגעון גדלות *nm* sheeg'on/-ot gadloot.

de luxe 1. דה-לוקס *adj* deh looks; **2.** של מותרות (luxurious) *adj* shel motarot.

(to) delve לחדור *inf* lakhdor; *pst* khadar; *pres* khoder; *fut* yakhdor.

demagogic /-ical דמגוגי *adj* demagogee/-t.

demagogically בצורה דמגוגית *adv* be-tsoorah demagogeet.

demagogue דמגוג *nm* demagog/-eem (*pl+of:* -ey).

demagoguery /demagogy דמגוגייה *nf* demagog|yah/-yot (+*of:* -yat).

demand 1. ביקוש *nm* beekoosh/-eem (*pl+of:* -ey); **2.** דרישה (requirement) *nf* dreesh|ah/-ot (+*of:* -at).

(in) demand מבוקש *adj* mevook|ash/-eshet.

(on) demand לפי דרישה *adv* lefee dreeshah.

(supply and) demand היצע וביקוש *nm & nm* hets|e'a'/-e'eem oo-veekoosh/-eem.

demandable שאפשר לדרוש *adj* she-'efshar leedrosh.

(to) demarcate לתחום *inf* leetkhom; *pst* takham; *pres* tokhem; *fut* yeetkham.

demarcation תיחום *nm* tekhoom/-eem (*pl+of:* -ey).

demarcation line קו תיחום *nm* kav/-ey tekhoom.

demarche צעד מדיני *nm* tsa'ad/tse'adeem medeenee/-yeem.

demeanor התנהגות *nf* heetnahagoo|t/-yot.

demented מטורף *adj* metor|af/-efet.

demilitarization פירוז *nm* perooz/-eem (*pl+of:* -ey).

(to) demilitarize לפרז *inf* lefarez; *pst* perez *(p=f);* *pres* mefarez; *fut* yefarez.

demilitarized מפורז *adj* mefor|az/-ezet.

demise 1. העברת בעלות (transfer of property) *nf* ha'avar|at/-ot ba'aloot; **2.** העברת שלטון (transfer of power) *nf* ha'avar|at/-ot sheelton.

demobilization שחרור *nm* sheekhroor/-eem (*pl+of:* -ey).

(to) demobilize 1. לשחרר משירות צבאי *inf* leshakhrer mee-sheroot tsva'ee; *pst* sheekhrer *etc; pres* meshakhrer *etc; fut* yeshakhrer *etc;* **2.** לפרק צבא (disband army) *inf* lefarek tsava; *pst* perek *(p=f) etc; pres* mefarek *etc; fut* yefarek *etc.*

democracy דמוקרטיה *f* demokrat|yah/-yot (+*of:* -yat).

democrat דמוקרט *nm* demokrat/-eem (*pl+of:* -ey).

democratic דמוקרטי *adj* demokratee/-t

(to) demolish להרוס *inf* laharos; *pst* haras; *pres* hores; *fut* yaharos.

demolition הריסה *nf* harees|ah/-ot (+*of:* -at).

demon 1. שד *nm* shed/-eem (*pl+of:* -ey); **2.** רוח רעה (evil spirit) *nf* roo|'akh/-khot ra|'ah/-'ot.

(to) demonstrate 1. להפגין (march) *inf* lehafgeen; *pst* heefgeen; *pres* mafgeen; *fut* yafgeen; **2.** להדגים (show) *inf* lehadgeem; *pst* heedgeem; *pres* madgeem; *fut* yadgeem; **3.** להוכיח (prove) *inf* lehokhee'akh; *pst* hokhee'akh; *pres* mokhee'akh; *fut* yokhee'akh.

demonstration 1. הפגנה (public) hafgan|ah/-ot (*+of:* -at); **2.** הדגמה (show) *nf* hadgam|ah/-ot (*+of:* -at).
demonstrative 1. הפגנתי *adj* hafganatee/-t; **2.** מדגים (illustrating) *adj* madgeem/-ah.
(to) demoralize לרפות ידיים *inf* lerapot yadayeem; *pst* reepah *etc; pres* merapeh *etc; fut* yerapeh *etc.*
(to) demote להוריד בדרגה *inf* lehoreed be-dargah; *pst* horeed *etc; pres* moreed *etc; fut* yoreed *etc.*
demotion הורדה בדרגה *nf* horad|ah/-ot be-dargah.
demurrage דמי השהיה *nm pl* dmey hash'hayah.
den 1. מאורה *nf* me'oor|ah/-ot/-et; **2.** גוב (pit) *nm* gov/goobeem (*pl+of:* goobey).
denial הכחשה *nf* hakh'khash|ah (*+of:* -at; *cpr* hak'khashah *etc*).
(self-)denial הקרבה עצמית *nf* hakravah 'atsmeet.
(to) denigrate 1. להשחיר *inf* lehash'kheer; *pst* heesh'kheer; *pres* mash'kheer; *fut* yash'kheer; **2.** להשמיץ (defame) *inf* lehashmeets; *pst* heeshmeets; *pres* mashmeets; *fut* yashmeets.
denim סרבל *nm* sarbal/-eem (*pl+of:* -ey).
denomination 1. כת דתית (faith) *nf* kat/keetot datee|t/-yot; **2.** סוג (class) *nf* soog/-eem (*pl+of:* -ey); **3.** ערך (value) *nm* 'erekh/'arakheem (*pl+of:* 'erkhey).
(to) denote 1. לסמן *inf* lesamen; *pst* seemen; *pres* mesamen; *fut* yesamen; **2.** לסמל (symbolize) *inf* lesamel; *pst* seemel; *pres* mesamel; *fut* yesamel.
(to) denounce 1. להוקיע *inf* lehokee'a'; *pst* hokee'a'; *pres* mokee'a'; *fut* yokee'a'; **2.** לנתק ברית (terminate alliance) *inf* lenatek breet; *pst* neetek *etc; pres* menatek *etc; fut* yenatek *etc.*
dense 1. סמיך *adj* sameekh/smeekhah; **2.** מטומטם (dull) *adj* metoomt|am/-emet.
density 1. צפיפות *nf* tsefeefoo|t/-yot; **2.** אטימות (opacity) *nf* ateemoo|t/-yot.
dent גומה *nf* goom|ah/-ot (*+of:* -at).
dental של שיניים *adj* shel sheenayeem.
dental floss חוט לניקוי שיניים *nm* khoot le-neekooy sheenayeem.
dentifrice תמרוק שיניים *nm* tamrook/-ey sheenayeem.
dentist רופא שיניים *nmf* rof|e/-'at (*pl:* -'ey/-'ot) sheenayeem.
dentistry רפואת שיניים *nf* refoo'at sheenayeem.
denunciation 1. גינוי *nm* geenooy/-eem (*pl+of:* -ey); **2.** ביטול (annulment) *nm* beetool/-eem (*pl+of:* -ey).
(to) deny 1. להכחיש *inf* lehakh'kheesh *pst* heekh'kheesh; *pres* makh'kheesh; *fut* yakh'kheesh; **2.** להכחיש *cpr* lehak'kheesh,heek'kheesh *etc;* **3.** לשלול (deprive) *inf* leeshlol; *pst* shalal; *pres* sholel; *fut* yeeshlol.
(to) depart 1. לצאת לדרך *inf* latset la-derekh; *pst* yatsa *etc; pres* yotse *etc; fut* yetse *etc;* **2.** להסתלק (go away) *inf* leheestalek; *pres* heestalek; *pres* meestalek; *fut* yeestalek.
departed שעזב *adj* she-'az|av/-vah.
department 1. מחלקה *nf* makhl|akah/-akot (*+of:* -eket/-ekot); **2.** אגף (wing) *nm* aga|f/-peem (*p=f; pl+of:* -pey); **3.** מיניסטריון (of state) *nm* meeneesteryon/-eem (*pl+of:* -ey).
departure 1. יציאה *nf* yetsee|'ah/-'ot (*+of:* -'at); **2.** הסתלקות (going away) *nf* heestalkoo|t/-yot.
(to) depend from להיות תלוי ב־ *inf* leehyot talooy be-; *pst* hayah *etc; pres* heeno *etc; fut* yeehyeh *etc.*
(to) depend on לסמוך על *inf* leesmokh 'al; *pst* samakh 'al; *pres* somekh 'al; *fut* yeesmokh 'al.
dependable אמין *adj* ameen/-ah
dependence תלות *nf* tloot.
dependency ארץ חסות *nf* erets/artsot khasoot.
dependent תלוי *nm* talooy/tlooy|eem (*pl+of:* -ey)
(to) depict לתאר *inf* leta'er; *pst* te'er; *pres* meta'er; *fut* yeta'er.
depilatory משיר שיער *nm* masheer/ ey se'ar.
(to) deplete 1. לרוקן (empty) *inf* leroken; *pst* roken; *pres* meroken; *fut* yeroken; **2.** לדלל (delute) *inf* ledalel; *pst* deelel; *pres* medalel; *fut* yedalel.
deplorable מצער *adj* metsa'er/-et.
(to) deplore לקבול על *inf* leekbol 'al; *pst* kaval 'al (*v=b*); *pres* kovel 'al; *fut* yeekbol 'al.
(to) deport להגלות *inf* lehaglot; *pst* heeglah; *pres* magleh; *fut* yagleh.
deportation הגליה *nf* hagla|yah/-yot (*+of:* -yat).
deportee 1. גולה *nmf* goleh/-ah; **2.** מגורש (expelled) *adj* megor|ash/-eshet.
deportment התנהגות *nf* heetnahagoo|t/-yot.
(to) depose להדיח *inf* lehadee'akh; *pst* heedee'akh; *pres* madee'akh; *fut* yadee'akh.
deposit 1. דמי־קדימה *nm pl* demey kedeemah; **2.** ערבות (surety) *nf* 'arevoo|t/-yot; **3.** פיקדון (guarantee) *nm* peek|adon/-donot (*+of:* -don); **4.** הפקדה (depositing) *nf* hafkad|ah/-ot (*+of:* -at).
(to) deposit 1. להפקיד *inf* lehafkeed; *pst* heefkeed; *pres* mafkeed; *fut* yafkeed; **2.** להשליש (with third party) *inf* lehashleesh; *pst* heeshleesh; *pres* mashleesh; *fut* yashleesh.
deposition עדות *nf* 'edoo|t/-yot.
depositor מפקיד *nm* mafkeed/-eem (*pl+of:* -ey).
depot 1. מחסן צבאי (army) *nm* makhsan/-eem tsva'ee/-yeem; **2.** תחנת רכבת (railroad) *nf* takhn|at/-ot rakevet.
(to) deprave 1. להשחית *inf* lehash'kheet; *pst* heesh'kheet; *pres* mash'kheet; *fut* yash'kheet; **2.** לקלקל (spoil) *inf* lekalkel; *pst* keelkel; *pres* mekalkel; *fut* yekalkel.
depraved מושחת *adj* moosh'kh|at/-etet.
(to) deprecate לגנות leganot; *pst* geenah; *pres* meganeh; *fut* yeganeh.
(to) depreciate 1. לפחת *inf* lefakhet; *pst* peekhet (*p=f*); *pres* mefakhet; *fut* yefakhet; **2.** להוריד ערך (reduce price) *inf* lehoreed 'erekh; *pst* horeed *etc; pres* moreed *etc; fut* yoreed *etc.*
(to) depress 1. ללחוץ *inf* leelkhots; *pst* lakhats; *pres* lokhets; *fut* yeelkhats; **2.** לדכא (oppress) *inf* ledake; *pst* deeka; *pres* medake; *fut* yedake; **3.** להחליש (weaken) *inf* lehakhleesh; *pst* hekhleesh; *pres* makhleesh; *fut* yakhleesh.
depressed מדוכא *adj* medooka/-'ah.
depressing מדכא *adj* medak|e/-'ah.
depression 1. שפלה (geograph.) *nf* shfel|ah/-ot (*+of:* -at); **2.** שפל כלכלי (economic) *nm* shefel

kalkalee; **3.** דיכאון (emotional) *nm* dee|ka'on (+*of:* deekh'on).

(to) deprive לשלול *inf* leeshlol; *pst* shalal; *pres* sholel; *fut* yeeshlol.

depth 1. עומק *nm* 'om|ek/-okeem (*pl+of:* -key); **2.** מעמקים *nm pl* ma'amak|eem (*pl+of:* -ey).

(in) depth לעומק *adv* la-'omek.

(in the) depth of the night באישון ליל *adv* be-eeshon layeel.

(in the) depth of winter בעיצומו של חורף *adv* be-'eetsoomo shel khoref.

deputation משלחת *nf* meeshlakh|at/-ot.

(to) depute לשגר *inf* leshager; *pst* sheeger; *pres* meshager; *fut* yeshager.

deputy 1. סגן *nmf* segan/-eet; **2.** ממלא מקום (replacement) *nmf* memale/-t makom.

(to) derail להוריד מהפסים *inf* lehoreed me-ha-paseem; *pst* horeed *etc*; *pres* moreed *etc*; *fut* yoreed *etc*.

(to) derange לשבש *inf* leshabesh; *pst* sheebesh; *pres* meshabesh; *fut* yeshabesh;

derby 1. כובע־לבד (hat) *nm* kov|a'/-'ey leved; **2.** תחרות (contest) *nf* takhroo|t/-yot.

derelict נטוש *adj* natoosh/netooshah.

(to) deride לעשות לצחוק *inf* la'asot lee-tsekhok; *pst* 'asah *etc*; *pres* 'oseh *etc*; *fut* ya'aseh *etc*.

derision 1. קלס (scorn) *nm* keles; **2.** לעג (mockery) *nm* la'ag.

(to) derive להפיק *inf* lehafeek; *pst* hefeek; *pres* mefeek; *fut* yafeek.

dermatology 1. חקר מחלות העור (study of skin diseases) *nm* kheker makhalot ha-'or; **2.** דרמטולוגיה *nf* dermatologyah.

derogatory 1. מזלזל *adj* mezalzel/-et; **2.** פוגם (hurting) *adj* pogem/-et.

derrick 1. מגדל־קידוח (drilling) *nm* meegd|al/-eley keedoo'akh; **2.** עגורן (construction) *nm* 'agooran/-eem (*pl+of:* -ey).

dervish דרוויש *nm* derveesh/-eem.

desalination המתקת מים *nf* hamtak|at/-ot mayeem.

(to) desalt, desalinate להמתיק מים *inf* lehamteek mayeem; *pst* heemteek *etc*; *pres* mamteek *etc*; *fut* yamteek *etc*.

(to) descend 1. לרדת *inf* laredet; *pst* yarad; *pres* yored; *fut* yered; **2.** להתנפל על (upon) *inf* leheetnapel 'al; *pst* heetnapel 'al; *pres* meetnapel 'al; *fut* yeetnapel 'al.

descendant צאצא *nm* tse'etsa/-'eem (*pl+of:* -'ey).

descent 1. ירידה *nf* yereed|ah/-ot (+*of:* -at); **2.** מוצא (ancestry) *nm* motsa.

(to) describe לתאר *inf* leta'er; *pst* te'er; *pres* meta'er; *fut* yeta'er.

description תיאור *nm* te'oor/-eem (*pl+of:* -ey).

descriptive תיאורי *adj* te'ooree/-t.

desegregation ביטול הפרדה גזעית *nm* beetool hafradah geez'eet.

desert מידבר *nm* meedbar/-eeyot.

deserter עריק *nmf* 'areek/-ah.

desertion עריקה *nf* 'areek|ah/-ot (+*of:* -at).

(to) deserve להיות ראוי *inf* leehyot ra'ooy/re'ooyah (*m/f*); *pst* hayah *etc*; *pres* hoo *etc*; *fut* yeehyeh *etc*.

deserving ראוי *adj* ra'ooy/re'ooyah.

design 1. סרטוט (sketch) *nm* seertoot/-eem (*pl+of:* -ey); **2.** תוכנית (plan) *nf* tokhnee|t/-yot. **3.** מזימה (scheme) *nf* mezeem|ah/-ot (+*of:* -at).

(to) designate לייעד *inf* leya'ed; *pst* yee'ed; *pres* meya'ed; *fut* yeya'ed.

designer 1. סרטט *nmf* sart|at/-etet; **2.** מתכנן (planner) *nmf* metakhnen/-et.

desirability רציות *nf* retseeyoot.

desirable רצוי *adj* ratsooy/retsooyah.

desire 1. תשוקה *nf* teshook|ah/-ot (+*of:* -at); **2.** רצון *nm* ratson/retsonot (+*of:* retson).

desirous 1. רוצה *adj* rots|eh/-ah; **2.** חפץ (willing) *adj* khafets/-ah.

(to) desist לחדול *inf* lakhdol; *pst* khadal; *pres* khadel; *fut* yekhdal.

desk 1. שולחן כתיבה *[colloq.] nm* shoolkhan/-ot keteevah; **2.** מכתבה *nf* meekht|avah/-avot (+*of:* evet).

desk clerk פקיד קבלה *nmf* pekeed/-at kabalah.

desk set מערכת כלי־כתיבה *nf* ma'ar|ekhet/-khot kley keteevah.

desolate שומם *adj* shomem/-et.

desolation 1. שיממון *nm* sheemamon; **2.** קדרות (gloom) *nf* kadroo|t/-yot.

despair ייאוש *nm* ye'oosh.

despairing 1. מייאש (exasperating) *adj* meya'esh/-et; **2.** מיואש (exasperated) *adj* meyoo|'ash/-'eshet.

desperate נואש *adj* no'ash/no'eshet.

desperation ייאוש *nm* ye'oosh.

despicable 1. נבזי *adj* neevzee/-t; **2.** מתועב (abominable) *adj* meto|'av/-'evet.

(to) despise לתעב *inf* leta'ev; *pst* tee'ev; *pres* meta'ev; *fut* yeta'ev.

despite 1. למרות *adv* lamrot; **2.** על אף *adv* 'al af.

(to) despoil לעשוק *inf* la'ashok; *pst* 'ashak; *pres* 'oshek; *fut* ya'ashok.

despondency דכדוך *nm* deekhdookh/-eem (*pl+of:* -ey).

despondent מדוכדך *adj* medookhd|akh/-ekhet.

despot עריץ *nmf* 'areets/-ah (+*of:* -at/-ey).

despotic 1. אכזרי *adj* akhzaree/-t; **2.** דספוטי *adj* despotee/-t.

despotism עריצות *nf* 'areetsoo|t/-yot.

dessert 1. מנה אחרונה *[colloq.] nf* man|ah/-ot akhron|ah/-ot; **2.** פרפרת *nf* parper|et/-a'ot.

destination יעד *nm* ya'ad/ye'ad|eem (*pl+of:* -ey).

(to) destine להועיד *inf* leho'eed; *pst* ho'eed; *pres* mo'eed; *fut* yo'eed.

destined מיועד *adj* meyoo|'ad/-'edet.

destiny גורל *nm* goral/-ot.

destitute חסר־כול *adj* khas|ar/-rat kol.

(to) destroy 1. להחריב *inf* lehakhreev; *pst* hekhreev; *pres* makhreev; *fut* yakhreev; **2.** להרוס (ruin) *inf* laharos; *pst* haras; *pres* hores; *fut* yaharos.

destroyer משחתת *nf* mash'kh|etet/-atot.

destruction חורבן *nm* khoorban/-ot.

detachable 1. ניתן להפרדה *adj* neet|an/-enet le-hafradah; **2.** מתנתק *adj* meetnatek/-et.

detached 1. מנותק *adj* menoot|ak/-eket; **2.** אדיש (indifferent) *adj* adeesh/-ah; **3.** אובייקטיבי (objective) *adj* obyekteevee/-t.

detachment פלוגה *nf* ploog|ah/-ot (*+of:* -at).

detail פרט *nm* prat/-eem (*pl+of:* -ey).

(to go into) detail להיכנס לפרטים *inf* leheekanes lee-frateem *(f=p)*; *pst & pres* neekhnas *(kh=k) etc*; *fut* yeekanes *etc*.

(to) detain 1. לעצור (stop) *inf* la'atsor; *pst* 'atsar; *pres* 'otser; *fut* ya'atsor; **2.** לעכב (delay) *inf* le'akev; *pst* 'eekev; *pres* me'akev; *fut* ye'akev.

(to) detect לגלות *inf* legalot; *pst* geelah; *pres* megaleh; *fut* yegaleh.

detective בלש *nm* balash/-eem (*pl+of:* -ey).

detective story רומן בלשי *nm* roman/-eem balashee/-yeem.

detention מעצר *nm* ma'ats|ar/-areem (*pl+of:* -rey).

detergent חומר ניקוי *nm* khom|er/-rey neekooy.

(to) deteriorate 1. להידרדר *inf* leheedarder; *pst* heedarder; *pres* meedarder; *fut* yeedarder; **2.** להתקלקל (get spoilt) *inf* leheetkalkel; *pst* heetkalkel; *pres* meetkalkel; *fut* yeetkalkel.

deterioration 1. הידרדרות *nf* heedarderoo|t/-yot; **2.** הרעה (worsening) *nf* hara|'ah/-'ot (*+of:* -'at).

determination נחרצות *nf* nekhratsoo|t/-yot.

(to) determine לחרוץ *inf* lakhrots; *pst* kharats; *pres* khorets; *fut* yakhrots.

determined נחרץ *adj* nekhr|ats/-etset.

deterrent מרתיע *nm* martee|'a'/-'eem (*pl+of:* -'ey).

deterrent factor גורם מרתיע *nm* gor|em/-meem martee|'a'/-'eem.

(to) detest לתעב *inf* leta'ev; *pst* tee'ev; *pres* meta'ev; *fut* yeta'ev.

(to) detonate לפוצץ *inf* lefotsets; *pst* potsets *(p=f)*; *pres* mefotsets; *fut* yefotsets.

detour מעקף *nm* ma'ak|af/-afeem (*pl+of:* -fey).

detrimental מזיק *adj* mazeek/-ah.

(to) devastate להחריב *inf* lehakhreev; *pst* hekhreev; *pres* makhreev; *fut* yakhreev.

(to) develop 1. להתפתח *vi* refl *inf* leheetpate'akh; *pst* heetpatakh; *pres* meetpate'akh; *fut* yeetpatakh; **2.** לפתח *vt inf* lefate'akh; *pst* peetakh *(p=f)*; *pres* mefate'akh; *fut* yefate'akh.

development 1. פיתוח (process) *nm* peetoo|'akh/-kheem (*pl+of:* -khey); **2.** התפתחות (result) *nf* heetpatkhoo|t/-yot.

(to) deviate לסטות *inf* leestot; *pst* satah; *pres* soteh; *fut* yeesteh.

deviation סטייה *nf* stee|yah/-yot (*+of:* -yat).

device 1. מתקן (mechanism) *nm* meetk|an/-aneem (*pl+of:* -eney); **2.** תחבולה (scheme) *nf* takhbool|ah/-ot (*+of:* -at).

(to one's own) devices לעזוב לנפשו *inf* la'azov le-nafsh|o/-ah; *pres* 'azav *etc*; *pres* 'ozev *etc*; *fut* ya'azov *etc*.

devil 1. שטן *nm* satan; **2.** שד *nm* shed/-eem (*pl+of:* -ey).

devilish שטני *adj* stanee/-t.

deviltry מעשה שטן *nm* ma'as|eh/-ey satan.

devious 1. עוקף (roundabout) *adj* 'okef/-et; **2.** סוטה (turning aside) *adj* sot|eh/-ah; **3.** מטעה (deceiving) *adj* mat'eh/-'ah.

(to) devise 1. לטכס *inf* letakes; *pst* teekes; *pres* metakes; *fut* yetakes; **2.** לזום (plot) *inf* lazom; *pst* zamam; *pres* zomem; *fut* yazom.

devoid משולל *adj* meshool|al/-elet.

(to) devote 1. להקדיש *inf* lehakdeesh; *pst* heekdeesh; *pres* makdeesh; *fut* yakdeesh; **2.** לייחד (assign) *inf* leyakhed; *pst* yeekhed; *pres* meyakhed; *fut* yeyakhed.

(to) devote oneself להתמסר *inf* leheetmaser; *pst* heetmaser; *pres* meetmaser; *fut* yeetmaser.

devoted מסור *adj* masoor/mesoorah.

devoted friend ידיד נאמן *nmf* yedeed/-ah ne'eman/-ah.

devotion מסירות *nf* meseeroo|t/-yot.

(to) devour 1. לטרוף *inf* leetrof; *pst* taraf; *pres* toref; *fut* yeetrof; **2.** לזלול (glut) *inf* leezlol; *pst* zalal; *pres* zolel; *fut* yeezlol.

devout אדוק *adj* adook/-ah.

dew טל *nm* tal/tlaleem (*pl+of:* taleley).

dewdrop אגל טל *nm* eg|el/-ley tal.

dewy רענן *adj* ra'anan/-ah.

dexterity 1. מיומנות *nf* meyoomanoo|t/-yot; **2.** זריזות (alertness) *nf* zreezoo|t/-yot.

dexterous 1. מיומן *adj* meyoom|an/-enet; **2.** זריז (alert) *adj* zareez/zreezah.

dextrose סוכר ענבים *nm* sookar 'anaveem.

diabetes סוכרת *nf* sookeret.

diabetic חולה סוכרת *nmf* khol|eh/-at sookeret.

diacritical 1. דיאקריטי *adj* dee'akreetee/-t; **2.** של ניקוד (of Hebrew's own system of under- and over-dotting for indicating vowels) *adj* shel neekood.

diadem 1. עטרה *nf* 'atar|ah/-ot (*+of:* 'ateret); **2.** נזר (coronet) *nm* nez|er/-areem (*pl+of:* neezrey).

(to) diagnose לאבחן *inf* le'avkhen; *pst* eevkhen; *pres* me'avkhen; *fut* ye'avkhen.

diagnosis 1. אבחון (action) *nm* eevkhoon/-eem (*pl+of:* -ey); **2.** אבחנה (result) *nf* avkhan|ah/-ot (*+of:* -at); **3.** דיאגנוזה *nf* dee'agnoz|ah/-ot (*+of:* -at).

diagonal 1. מלוכסן *adj* melookhs|an/-enet; **2.** אלכסוני (oblique) *adj* alakhsonee/-t.

diagram 1. תרשים *nm* tarsheem/-eem (*pl+of:* -ey); **2.** דיאגרמה *nf* dee'agram|ah/-ot (*+of:* -at).

dial 1. חוגה *nf* khoog|ah/-ot (*+of:* -at); **2.** לוחית מספרים (plate with numbers) *nf* lookhee|t/-yot meespareem.

dial tone צליל חיוג *nm* tsleel/-ey kheeyoog.

(to) dial לחייג *inf* lekhayeg; *pst* kheeyeg; *pres* mekhayeg; *fut* yekhayeg.

dialect 1. ניב *nm* neev/-eem (*pl+of:* -ey); **2.** עגה *[slang] nf* 'ag|ah/-ot (*+of:* -at).

dialogue 1. דו־שיח *nm* doo-see'akh; **2.** דיאלוג *nm* dee'alog/-eem (*pl+of:* -ey).

diameter קוטר *nm* koter/ketareem (*pl+of:* kotrey).

diamond יהלום *nm* yahalom/-eem (*pl+of:* -ey).

diaper חיתול *nm* kheetool/-eem (*pl+of:* -ey).

diaphragm סרעפת *nf* sar'efet.

diarrhea שילשול *nm* sheelshool/-eem (*pl+of:* -ey).

diary יומן *nm* yoman/-eem (*pl+of:* -ey).

Diaspora 1. הגולה *nf* ha-golah; **2.** התפוצות (lands of Jewish dispersion) *nf pl* ha-tfootsot.
dice קוביה *nf* koobee|yah/-yot (+*of:* -yat).
dichotomy התפצלות *nf* heetpatsloo|t/-yot.
dictate תכתיב *nm* takhteev/-eem (*pl+of:* -ey).
(to) dictate להכתיב *inf* lehakhteev; *pst* heekhteev; *pres* makhteev; *fut* yakhteev.
dictation הכתבה *nf* hakhtav|ah/-ot (+*of:* -at).
(at) dictation speed בקצב הכתבה *adv* be-ketsev hakhtavah.
(to take) dictation לקבל הכתבה *inf* lekabel hakhtavah; *pst* keebel *etc; pres* mekabel *etc; fut* yekabel *etc.*
dictator 1. רודן *nm* rodan/-eet; **2.** דיקטטור *nm* deektator/-eem (*pl+of:* -ey).
dictatorship 1. רודנות *nf* rodanoo|t/-yot; **2.** דיקטטורה *nf* deektatoor|ah/-ot (+*of:* -at).
diction 1. הגייה *nf* hagee|yah/-yot (+*of:* -yat); **2.** דיקציה *nf* deekts|yah/-yot (+*of:* -yat).
dictionary מילון *nm* meelon/-eem (*pl+of:* -ey).
die 1. מבלט *nm* mavlet/-eem (*pl+of:* -ey); **2.** מטריצה *nf* matreets|ah/-ot (+*of:* -at); **3.** קוביית משחק (dice cube) *nm* koobee|yat/-yot mees'khak.
(to) die 1. למות *inf* lamoot; *pst & pres* met; *fut* yamoot; **2.** לגווע (expire) *inf* leegvo'a'; *pst* gava'; *pres* gove'a'; *fut* yeegva'.
diehard קיצוני *adj* keetsonee/-t.
diet 1. תזונה *nf* tezoon|ah/-ot (+*of:* -at); **2.** דיאטה *nf* dee'et|ah/-ot (+*of:* -at).
(to) differ להיבדל *inf* leheebadel; *pst & pres* neevdal (*v=b*); *fut* yeebadel.
(to) differ with לחלוק על *inf* lakhlok 'al; *pst* khalak 'al; *pres* kholek 'al; *fut* yakhlok 'al.
difference 1. הבדל *nm* hevdel/-eem (*pl+of:* -ey); **2.** הפרש (remainder) *nm* hefresh/-eem (*pl+of:* -ey); **3.** שוני (variance) *nm* shonee.
(it makes no) difference אין חשיבות eyn khasheevoot.
different שונה *adj* shon|eh/-ah.
(to) differentiate 1. להבחין *inf* lehavkheen; *pst* heevkheen; *pres* mavkheen; *fut* yavkheen; **2.** להבדיל (distinguish) *inf* lehavdeel; *pst* heevdeel; *pres* mavdeel; *fut* yavdeel.
difficult 1. קשה *adj* kash|eh/-ah; **2.** מסובך (complex) *adj* mesoob|akh/-ekhet.
difficulty קושי *nm* koshee/kesha|yeem (*pl+of:* -yey).
diffidence 1. ביישנות (shyness) *nf* bayshanoo|t/-yot; **2.** חוסר־ביטחון (timidity) *nm* khoser beetakhon.
diffident 1. ביישן (shy) *adj* bayshan/-eet; **2.** חסר־ביטחון (timid) *adj* khas|ar/-rat beetakhon.
(to) diffuse 1. לפזר *inf* lefazer; *pst* peezer (*p=f*); *pres* mefazer; *fut* yefazer; **2.** להפיץ (disseminate) *inf* lehafeets; *pst* hefeets; *pres* mefeets; *fut* yafeets.
diffusion 1. פיזור *nm* peezoor/-eem (*pl+of:* -ey); **2.** התפזרות (dispersion) *nf* heetpazroo|t/-yot.
(to) dig לחפור *inf* lakhpor; *pst* khafar (*f=p*); *pres* khofer; *fut* yakhpor.
(to) dig under לכרות *inf* leekhrot; *pst* karah (*k=kh*); *pres* koreh; *fut* yeekhreh.
(to) dig up 1. לגלות *inf* legalot; *pst* geelah; *pres* megaleh; *fut* yegaleh; **2.** להשיג מידע (obtain information) *inf* lehaseeg meyda'; *pst* heeseeg *etc; pres* maseeg *etc; fut* yaseeg *etc.*
digest תקציר *nm* taktseer/-eem (*pl+of:* -ey).
digestible נוח לעיכול *adj* no'akh/nokhah le'eekool.
digestion עיכול *nm* 'eekool/-eem (*pl+of:* -ey).
digestive מעכל *adj* me'akel/-et.
dignified מכובד *adj* mekhoob|ad/-edet.
dignitary נושא משרה *nmf* nose/-t meesrah.
dignity 1. כבוד *nm* kavod; **2.** מעמד (status) *nm* ma'amad.
digraph דו־אות *nm* doo-'ot.
(to) digress לסטות *inf* leestot; *pst* satah; *pres* soteh; *fut* yeesteh.
digression 1. סטייה מהנושא *nf* stee|yah/-yot me-hanose; **2.** נטייה לצדדים *nf* netee|yah/-yot lee-tsedadeem.
dike סוללה *nf* solel|ah/-ot (+*of:* -at).
(to) dilate 1. להרחיב *inf* leharkheev; *pst* heerkheev; *pres* markheev; *fut* yarkheev; **2.** להתרחב (expand) *v rfl inf* leheetrakhev; *pst* heetrakhev; *pres* meetrakhev; *fut* yeetrakhev.
dilemma דילמה *nf* deelem|ah/-ot (+*of:* -at).
dilettante 1. חובבן *nmf* khovevan/-eet; **2.** שטחי (superficial) *adj* sheetkhee/-t.
diligence 1. שקידה *nf* shekeed|ah/-ot (+*of:* -at); **2.** התמדה (persistence) *nf* hatmad|ah/-ot (+*of:* -at).
(to) dilute 1. למהול (adulterate) *inf* leemhol; *pst* mahal; *pres* mohel; *fut* yeemhol; **2.** לדלל (thin) *inf* ledalel; *pst* deelel; *pres* medalel; *fut* yedalel.
dim עמום *adj* amoom/-ah.
dime עשרה סנטים (US coin) *nm pl* 'asarah senteem.
dimension 1. מימד *nm* memad/-eem (*pl+of:* -ey); **2.** גודל *nm* godel/gedaleem (*pl+of:* godley).
(to) diminish 1. לקטון *vi inf* leekton; *pst* katan; *pres* katen; *fut* yeektan; **2.** להפחית (reduce) *vt inf* lehafkheet; *pst* heefkheet; *pres* mafkheet; *fut* yafkheet.
diminution הקטנה *nf* haktan|ah/-ot (+*of:* -at).
diminutive 1. זעיר (tiny) *adj* za'eer/ze'eerah; **2.** שם חיבה מקוצר (affectionately shortened name) *nm* shem kheebah mekootsar.
dimness אפלוליות *nf* aflooleeyoot.
dimple גומת־חן *nf* goom|at/-ot khen.
din רעש *nm* ra'ash/re'ash|eem (*pl+of:* -ey).
(to) dine לסעוד *inf* lees'od; *pst* sa'ad; *pres* so'ed; *fut* yees'ad.
diner 1. קרון אוכל *nm* kron/-ot okhel; **2.** מסעדת דרכים *nf* mees|'edet/-'adot drakheem
dingy 1. כהה (dark) *adj* keheh/kehah; **2.** מלוכלך (dirty) *adj* melookhl|akh/-ekhet.
dining car קרון־מסעדה *nm* kron/-ot mees'adah.
dining room חדר אוכל *nm* khad|ar/-rey okhel.
dinner סעודה עיקרית *nf* se'oodah 'eekareet.
dinner coat, jacket 1. חליפת־ערב *nf* khaleef|at/-ot 'erev; **2.** סמוקינג *nm* smokeeng/-eem (*pl+of:* -ey).
dinner set מערכת כלי־אוכל *nf* ma'ar|ekhet/-khot kley okhel.
dinner time שעת ארוחת הערב *nf* she'at arookhat ha-'erev.

dint 1. עוצמה (force) *nf* 'otsm|ah/-ot (+*of:* -at); **2.** מהלומה (blow) mahaloom|ah/-ot (+*of:* -at)
(by) dint of מכוח *adv* mee-ko'akh.
diode דיודה *nf* dyod|ah/-ot (+*of:* -at).
dioxide דו־תחמוצת *nf* doo-takhmotset.
dip 1. שיפוע *nm* sheepoo|'a'/-'eem (*pl+of:* -'ey); **2.** טבילה (immersion) *nf* tveel|ah/-ot (+*of:* -at).
(to) dip 1. לטבול *inf* leetbol; *pst* taval *(v=b)*; *pres* tovel; *fut* yeetbol; **2.** לחדור (penetrate) *inf* lakhdor; *pst* khadar; *pres* khoder; *fut* yakhdor.
(to) dip out 1. להשתפך *inf* leheeshtapekh; *pst* heeshtapekh; *pres* meeshtapekh; *fut* yeeshtapekh; **2.** להתרוקן (empty) *v rfl inf* leheetroken; *pst* heetroken; *fut* meetroken; *fut* yeetroken.
diphtheria 1. אסכרה *nf* askarah; **2.** דיפתריה *nf* deefteryah.
diphthong דו־צליל *nm* doo-tsleel/-eem (*pl+of:* -ey).
diploma 1. תעודת־גמר *nf* te'ood|at/-ot gemar; **2.** דיפלומה *nf* deeplom|ah/-ot (+*of:* -at).
diplomacy דיפלומטיה *nf* deeplomatyah.
diplomat דיפלומט *nm* deeplomat/-eem (*pl+of:* -ey).
diplomatic דיפלומטי *adj* deeplomatee/-t
dipping טבילה *nf* tveel|ah/-ot (+*of:* -at).
dire מפחיד *adj* mafkheed/-ah.
direct 1. ישר *adj* yashar/yesharah; **2.** ישיר (straight) *adj* yasheer/yesheerah.
(to) direct 1. לכוון (address) *inf* lekhaven; *pst* keeven *(k=kh)*; *pres* mekhaven; *fut* yekhaven; **2.** להדריך (guide) *inf* lehadreekh; *pst* heedreekh; *pres* madreekh; *fut* yadreekh; **3.** לנהל (conduct) *vt inf* lenahel; *pst* neehel; *pres* menahel; *fut* yenahel.
direct current זרם ישר *nm* zerem yashar.
direct hit פגיעה ישירה *nf* pegee|'ah/-'ot yesheer|ah/-ot.
direct object מושא ישיר *nm* moosa/-'eem yasheer/yesheereem.
direction 1. כיוון (aiming) *nm* keevoon/-eem (*pl+of:* -ey); **2.** הוראה (instruction) *nf* hora|'ah/-'ot (+*of:* -'at); **3.** הנהלה (management) *nf* han'hal|ah/-ot (+*of:* -at).
directional antenna 1. משושה כיוונית *nf* meshosh|ah/-ot keevoonee|t/-yot; **2.** אנטנה כיוונית *nf* anten|ah/-ot keevoonee|t/-yot.
directional signal איתות מכוון *nm* eetoot/-eem mekhoovan/-eem.
directive הנחיה *nf* hankha|yah/-yot (+*of:* -yat).
directly ישירות *adv* yesheerot.
directness 1. יושר *nm* yosher; **2.** גילוי־לב (frankness) *nm* geelooy-lev.
director 1. מנהל (manager) *nmf* menahel/-et; **2.** דירקטור (board member) *nmf* deerek|tor/-toreet; **3.** בימאי (stage, screen) *nmf* beem|ay/-a'eet.
directory מדריך *nm* madreekh/-eem (+*of:* -ey).
(telephone) directory מדריך הטלפון *nm* madreekh/-ey ha-telefon.
dirigible 1. בר־כיוון *adj* bar/bat keevoon; **2.** ספינת־אוויר (airship) *nf* sfeen|at/-ot aveer.
dirt לכלוך *nm* leekhlookh/-eem (*pl+of:* -ey).
dirt cheap בזיל הזול *adv* be-zeel ha-zol.
dirt road דרך עפר *nf* derekh/darkhey 'afar.
dirty מלוכלך *adj* melookhl|akh/-ekhet.
dirty linen 1. כבסים מלוכלכים *nm pl* kvaseem melookhlakheem; **2.** כביסה מלוכלכת *[colloq.] nf* kveesah melookhlekhet.
dirty trick תחבולה שפלה *nf* takhbool|ah/-ot shfal|ah/-ot.
(to) disable 1. לשלול כושר *inf* leeshlol kosher; *pst* shalal *etc*; *pres* sholel *etc*; *fut* yeeshlol *etc*; **2.** להטיל מום (maim) *inf* lehateel moom; *pst* heeteel *etc*; *pres* mateel *etc*; *fut* yateel *etc*.
disadvantage 1. מכשול (handicap) *nm* meekh'shol/-eem (*pl+of:* -ey); **2.** נחיתות (inferiority) *nf* nekheetoo|t/-yot.
(at a) disadvantage 1. במצב נחות *adv* be-matsav nakhoot; **2.** כשידו על התחתונה (if bound to lose) *adv* ke-she-yado/-ah *(m/f)* 'al ha-takhtonah.
(to) disagree לחלוק על *inf* lakhlok 'al; *pst* khalak 'al; *pres* kholek 'al; *fut* yakhlok 'al.
disagreeable 1. לא־נוח *adj* lo-no'akh/nokhah; **2.** לא־נעים (unpleasant) *adj* lo na'eem/ne'eemah.
disagreement מחלוקת *nf* makhalok|et/-ot.
(to) disallow 1. לא להרשות *inf* lo leharshot; *pst* lo heershah; *pres* eyno marsheh; *fut* lo yarsheh; **2.** לאסור (forbid) *inf* le'esor; *pst* asar; *pres* oser; *fut* ye'esor.
(to) disappear להיעלם *inf* lehe'alem; *pst & pres* ne'elam; *fut* ye'alem.
disappearence היעלמות *nf* he'almoo|t/-yot.
(to) disappoint לאכזב *inf* le'akhzev; *pst* eekhzev; *pres* me'akhzev; *fut* ye'akhzev.
disappointing מאכזב *adj* me'akhzev/-et.
disappointment אכזבה *nf* akhzav|ah/-ot (+*of:* -at).
disapproval 1. מורת־רוח *nf* morat-roo'akh; **2.** שלילה (negation) *nf* shleel|ah/-ot (+*of:* -at).
(to) disapprove לשלול *inf* leeshlol; *pst* shalal; *pres* sholel; *fut* yeeshlol.
(to) disarm לפרק מנשק *inf* lefarek mee-neshek; *pst* perek *(p=f) etc*; *pres* mefarek *etc*; *fut* yefarek *etc*.
disarmament פירוק נשק *nm* perook neshek.
disarray 1. אי־סדר *nm* ee-seder; **2.** אנדרלמוסיה (chaos) *nf* andralamoos|yah/-yot (+*of:* -yat); **3.** לבוש מרושל (disorderly dress) *nm* levoosh merooshal.
(to) disarray 1. להביך *inf* lehaveekh; *pst* heveekh; *pres* meveekh; *fut* yaveekh; **2.** לבלבל (confuse) *inf* levalbel; *pst* beelbel *(b=v)*; *pres* mevalbel; *fut* yevalbel.
disaster אסון *nm* ason/-ot.
disastrous הרה אסון *adj* har|eh/-at ason.
(to) disband 1. לפזר *inf* lefazer; *pst* peezer *(p=f)*; *pres* mefazer; *fut* yefazer; **2.** לשחרר (release) *inf* leshakhrer; *pst* sheekhrer; *pres* meshakhrer; *fut* yeshakhrer.
(to) disbelieve לכפור *inf* leekhpor; *pst* kafar *(f=p)*; *pres* kofer; *fut* yeekhpor.
(to) disburse 1. לשלם *inf* leshalem; *pst* sheelem; *pres* meshalem; *fut* yeshalem; **2.** להוציא כספים (spend) *inf* lehotsee ksafeem; *pst* hotsee *etc*; *pres* motsee *etc*; *fut* yotsee *etc*.
disbursement 1. הוצאה *nf* hotsa|'ah/-'ot (+*of:* -'at); **2.** תשלום (payment) *nm* tashloom/-eem (*pl+of:* -ey).

(to) discard 1. להשליך הצידה *inf* lehashleekh hatseedah; *pst* heeshleekh *etc*; *pres* mashleekh *etc*; *fut* yashleekh *etc*; **2.** להיפטר מ־ (get rid of) *inf* leheepater mee-; *pst & pres* neeftar mee- *(f=p)*; *fut* yeepater mee-.

(to) discern להבחין *inf* lehavkheen; *pst* heevkheen; *pres* mavkheen; *fut* yavkheen.

discernment הבחנה *nf* havkhan|ah/-ot (+*of*: -at).

(to) discharge 1. לפרוק מטען (cargo) *inf* leefrok meet'an; *pst* parak *(p=f) etc*; *pres* porek *etc*; *fut* yeefrok *etc*; **2.** לשחרר (release) *inf* leshakhrer; *pst* sheekhrer; *pres* meshakhrer; *fut* yeshakhrer.

disciple 1. תלמיד *nmf* talmeed/-ah (+*of*: -at; *pl* -eem/-ot; +*of*: -ey); **2.** חסיד (adherent) *nm* khaseed/-eem (*pl+of*: -ey).

discipline משמעת *nf* meeshma'at.

(to) disclose לגלות *inf* legalot; *pst* geelah; *pres* megaleh; *fut* yegaleh.

(to) discolor 1. לשנות צבע (alter color) *vt inf* leshanot tseva'; *pst* sheenah *etc*; *pres* meshaneh *etc*; *fut* yeshaneh *etc*; **2.** לקלקל צבע (spoil color) *vt inf* lekalkel tseva'; *pst* keelkel *etc*; *pres* mekalkel *etc*; *fut* yekalkel *etc*.

discomfort מטרד *nm* meetr|ad/-adeem (*pl+of*: -edey).

(to) disconcert לבלבל *inf* levalbel; *pst* beelbel *(b=v)*; *pres* mevalbel; *fut* yevalbel.

(to) disconnect לנתק *inf* lenatek; *pst* neetek; *pres* menatek; *fut* yenatek.

disconnected מנותק *adj* menoot|ak/-eket.

disconsolate חסר־נוחם *adj* khas|ar/-rat nokham.

discontent אי שביעת רצון *nm* ee svee'at ratson.

(to) discontent לא להשביע רצון *inf* lo lehasbee'a' ratson; *pst* lo heesbee'a' *etc*; *pres* eyno masbee'a' *etc*; *fut* lo yasbee'a' *etc*.

discontented לא שבע רצון *adj* lo sva'/sve'at ratson.

(to) discontinue להפסיק *inf* lehafseek; *pst* heefseek; *pres* mafseek; *fut* yafseek.

discord 1. פילוג *nm* peeloog/-eem (*pl+of*: -ey); **2.** פירוד *nm* perood/-eem (*pl+of*: -ey).

discount 1. ניכיון *nm* neekayon/neekhyonot (*kh=k*; +*of*: neekhyon); **2.** הנחה (rebate) *nf* hanakh|ah/-ot (+*of*: -at).

discount rate שער ניכיון *nm* sha'ar/-ey neekayon.

(to) discourage לרפות ידיים *v inf* lerapot yadayeem; *pst* reepah *etc*; *pres* merapeh *etc*; *fut* yerapeh *etc*.

(to) discourage from לרפות ידיים מעשות *inf* lerapot yadayeem me-'asot; *pst* reepah *etc*; *pres* merapeh *etc*; *fut* yerapeh *etc*.

discouragement רפיון ידיים *nm* reefyon yadayeem

discourse 1. הרצאה (lecture) *nf* hartsa|'ah/-'ot (+*of*: -'at); **2.** שיחה (talk) *nf* seekh|ah/-ot (+*of*: -at).

(to) discourse 1. להרצות (lecture) *inf* lehartsot; *pst* heertsah; *pres* martseh; *fut* yartseh; **2.** לשוחח (hold talk) *inf* lesokhe'akh; *pst* sokhakh; *pres* mesokhe'akh; *fut* yesokhakh.

discourteous חסר אדיבות *adj* khas|ar/-rat adeevoot.

discourtesy חוסר נימוס *nm* khoser neemoos.

(to) discover לגלות *inf* legalot; *pst* geelah; *pres* megaleh; *fut* yegaleh.

discoverer מגלה תגליות *nmf* megal|eh/-at tagleeyot.

discovery תגלית *nf* taglee|t/-yot.

(to) discredit 1. להשמיץ (slander) *inf* lehashmeets; *pst* heeshmeets; *pres* mashmeets; *fut* yashmeets; **2.** לפגוע באמינות (undermine credibility) *v inf* leefgo'a' ba-ameenoot; *pst* paga' *(p=f) etc*; *pres* poge'a' *etc*; *fut* yeefga' *etc*.

discreet 1. דיסקרטי *adj* deeskretee/-t; **2.** שומר סוד (keeping secrecy) *adj* shomer/-et sod.

discrepancy אי־התאמה *nm* ee-hat'am|ah/-ot (+*of*: -at).

discretion 1. שיקול דעת *nm* sheekool/-ey da'at; **2.** שמירת סוד (keeping secrecy) *nf* shmeerat sod.

(to one's own) discretion להכרעתו שלו le-hakhra'at|o/-ah shel|o/-ah *(m/f)*.

(to) discriminate להפלות *inf* lehaflot; *pst* heeflah; *pres* mafleh; *fut* yafleh.

(to) discriminate against להפלות לרעה *inf* lehaflot le-ra'ah; *pst* heeflah *etc*; *pres* mafleh *etc*; *fut* yafleh *etc*.

discrimination אפליה *nf* afla|yah/-yot (+*of*: -yat).

(to) discuss 1. לדון *inf* ladoon; *pst & pres* dan; *fut* yadoon; **2.** לדסקס *[slang] inf* ledaskes; *pst* deeskes; *pres* medaskes; *fut* yedaskes.

discussion 1. דיון *nm* deeyoon/-eem (*pl+of*: -ey); **2.** ויכוח (argument) *nm* veekoo|'akh/-kheem (*pl+of*: -khey).

disdain בוז *nm* booz.

disdainful מלא בוז *adj* male/mele'at booz.

disease 1. חולי (sickness) *nm* khol|ee/-ayeem (*pl+of*: -yey); **2.** מחלה (illness) *nf* makhal|ah/-ot (+*of*: -at).

diseased נגוע חולי *adj* negoo|'a'/-'at kholee.

(to) disembark לרדת לחוף *inf* laredet la-khof; *pst* yarad *etc*; *pres* yored *etc*; *fut* yered *etc*.

(to) disentangle להוציא מסבך *inf* lehotsee mee-svakh; *pres* hotsee *etc*; *pres* motsee *etc*; *fut* yotsee *etc*.

(to) disfigure להשחית צורה *inf* lehash'kheet tsoorah; *pst* heesh'kheet *etc*; *pres* mash'kheet *etc*; *fut* yash'kheet *etc*.

(to) disfranchise לשלול זכות בחירה *inf* leeshlol zekhoot bekheerah; *pst* shalal *etc*; *pres* sholel *etc*; *fut* yeeshlol *etc*.

disgrace חרפה *nf* kherpah/kharafot (+*of*: kherpat).

(to) disgrace לעטות קלון *inf* la'atot kalon; *pst* 'atah *etc*; *pres* 'oteh *etc*; *fut* ya'ateh *etc*.

(to be in) disgrace להיות לגנאי *inf* leehyot lee-gnay; *pst* hayah *etc*; *pres* hoo *etc*; *fut* yeehyeh *etc*.

disgraceful מחפיר *adj* makhpeer/-ah.

disguise מסווה *nm* masv|eh/-eem (*pl+of*: -ey).

(to) disguise להסוות *inf* lehasvot; *pst* heesvah; *pres* masveh; *fut* yasveh.

disgust 1. גועל *nm* go'al; **2.** סלידה (revulsion) *nf* sleed|ah/-ot (+*of*: -at).

(to) disgust להגעיל *inf* lehag'eel; *pst* heeg'eel; *pres* mag'eel *etc* yag'eel.

disgusted נגעל *adj* neeg|'al/-'elet.

disgusting מגעיל *adj* mag'eel/-ah.

dish 1. צלחת (plate) *nf* tsalakh|at/-ot; **2.** תבשיל (cooked food) *nm* tavsheel/-eem (*pl+of:* -ey).

(to) dish לשים בצלחת *inf* laseem be-tsalakhat; *pst & pres* sam *etc; fut* yaseem *etc.*

dishcloth סמרטוט כלים *nm* smartoot/-ey keleem.

(to) dishearten לרפות ידיים *inf* lerapot yadayeem; *pst* reepah *etc; pres* merapeh *etc; fut* yerapeh *etc.*

disheveled 1. סתור שיער *adj* stoor/-at se'ar; **2.** לא מסודר (disorderly) *adj* lo mesood|ar/-eret; **3.** מרושל (slovenly) *adj* meroosh|al/-elet.

dishonest 1. לא ישר *adj* lo yashar/yesharah; **2.** נוכל (crook) *nmf* nokhel/-et.

dishonesty 1. חוסר יושר *nm* khoser yosher; **2.** חוסר הגינות (lack of fairness) *nm* khoser hageenoot.

dishonor חילול כבוד *nm* kheelool kavod.

(to) dishonor לחלל כבוד *inf* lekhalel kevod; *pst* kheelel *etc; pres* mekhalel *etc;* yekhalel *etc.*

dishonorable 1. מביש *adj* meveesh/-ah; **2.** מגונה (despicable) *adj* megoon|eh/-ah.

dishwasher מדיח כלים *nm* medee|'akh/-khey keleem.

disillusion התפכחות *nf* heetpak'khoo|t/-yot.

(to) disillusion לנפץ אשליות *inf* lenapets ashlayot; *pst* neepets *etc; pres* menapets *etc; fut* yenapets *etc.*

(to) disinfect לחטא *inf* lekhate; *pst* kheete; *pres* mekhate; *fut* yekhate.

disinfectant חומר חיטוי *nm* khom|er/-rey kheetooy.

disinfection חיטוי *nm* kheetoo|y/-yeem (*pl+of:* -yey).

(to) disinherit 1. לבטל ירושה *inf* levatel yerooshah; *pst* beetel (*b=v*) *etc; pres* mevatel *etc; fut* yevatel *etc;* **2.** להעביר מנחלתו (deprive of inheritance) *inf* leha'aveer mee-nakhlato; *pst* he'eveer *etc; pres* ma'aveer *etc; fut* ya'aveer *etc.*

(to) disintegrate להתפורר *inf* leheetporer; *pst* heetporer; *pres* meetporer; *fut* yeetporer.

disinterested 1. חסר עניין *adj* khas|ar/-rat 'eenyan; **2.** חסר פניות (impartial) *adj* khas|ar/-rat peneeyot.

disk 1. תקליט (record) *nm* takleet/-eem (*pl+of:* -ey); **2.** כונן (computer) *nm* konan; **3.** דיסקוס (sport) *nm* deeskoos/-eem (*pl+of:* -ey).

(compact) disk תקליטור *nm* takleetor/-eem (*pl+of:* -ey).

(hard) disk כונן קשיח *nm* konan kashee'akh.

diskbrakes בלמי דיסקיות *nm pl* beelmey deeskeeyot.

diskette דיסקית *nm* deeskee|t/-yot.

dislike 1. חוסר חיבה *nm* khoser kheebah; **2.** אנטיפתיה (antipathy) *nf* anteepatyah.

(to) dislike לא לחבב *inf* lo lekhabev; *pst* lo kheebev; *pres* eyno mekhabev; *fut* lo yekhabev.

(to) dislocate 1. להזיז *inf* lehazeez; *pst* hezeez; *pres* mezeez; *fut* yazeez; **2.** להסיט (shift) *inf* lehaseet; *pst* heseet; *pres* meseet; *fut* yaseet.

(to) dislodge לנשל *inf* lenashel; *pst* neeshel; *pres* menashel; *fut* yenashel.

disloyal 1. לא לויאלי *adj* lo loyalee/-t; **2.** לא־נאמן (unfaithful) *adj* lo ne'eman/-ah; **3.** בוגד (treacherous) *adj* boged/-et.

dismal עלוב *adj* 'aloov/-ah.

(to) dismantle לפרק *inf* lefarek; *pst* perek (*p=f*); *pres* mefarek; *fut* yefarek.

dismay אובדן עצות *nm* ovdan 'etsot.

(to) dismiss 1. לפטר (fire) *inf* lefater; *pst* peeter (*p=f*); *pres* mefater; *fut* yefater; **2.** לפטור (release) *inf* leeftor; *pst* patar (*p=f*); *pres* poter; *fut* yeeftor; **3.** לבטל (charges) levatel; *pst* beetel (*b=v*); *pres* mevatel; *fut* yevatel.

(to) dismiss the meeting לסגור את האסיפה *inf* leesgor et haasefah; *pst* sagar *etc; pres* soger *etc; fut* yeesgor *etc.*

dismissal 1. פיטורים *nm pl* peetoor|eem (*+of:* -ey); **2.** הדחה (impeachment) *nf* hadakh|ah/-ot (*+of:* -at).

(to) dismount 1. לרדת *vi inf* laredet; *pst* yarad; *pres* yored; *fut* yered; **2.** להוריד *vt inf* lehoreed; *pst* horeed; *pres* moreed; *fut* yoreed.

disobedience אי־ציות *nm* ee-tseeyoot/-eem (*pl+of:* -ey).

(civil) disobedience מרי אזרחי *nm* meree ezrakhee.

disobedient 1. לא מציית *adj* lo metsayet/-et; **2.** ממרה (unruly) *v pres & adj* mamr|eh/-ah.

(to) disobey להמרות *inf* lehamrot; *pst* heemrah; *pres* mamreh; *fut* yamreh.

disorder 1. אי־סדר *nm* ee-seder/sdareem; **2.** עירבוביה (confusion) *nf* 'eerboov|yah/-yot (*+of:* -yat).

disorderly פורע סדר *v pres & adj* por|e'a'/-a'at seder.

disorganization חוסר ארגון *nm* khoser eergoon.

(to) disown 1. להתנכר *inf* leheetnaker; *pst* heetnaker; *pres* meetnaker; *fut* yeetnaker; **2.** להתכחש (deny) *inf* leheetkakhesh; *pst* heetkakhesh; *pres* meetkakhesh; *fut* yeetkakhesh.

(to) disparage לזלזל *inf* lezalzel; *pst* zeelzel; *pres* mezalzel; *fut* yezalzel.

dispassionate 1. אובייקטיבי (objective) *adj* ob'yekteevee/-t; **2.** מיושב (calm) *adj* meyoosh|av/-evet; **3.** חסר פניות (impartial) *adj* khas|ar/-rat peneeyot.

dispatch 1. משלוח מהיר *nm* meeshlo|'akh/-kheem maheer/meheereem; **2.** איגרת (letter) *nf* eeg|eret/-rot.

(to) dispatch 1. לשגר בדחיפות *inf* leshager bee-d'kheefoot; *pst* sheeger *etc; pres* meshager *etc; fut* yeshager *etc;* **2.** לשלח (send off) *inf* leshale'akh; *pst* sheelakh; *pres* meshale'akh; *fut* yeshalakh.

(to) dispel 1. להניס *inf* lehanees; *pst* henees; *pres* menees; *fut* yanees; **2.** לפזר (disperse) *inf* lefazer; *pst* peezer (*p=f*); *pres* mefazer; *fut* yefazer.

dispensary מרפאה עממית *nf* meerpa|'ah/-'ot 'amamee|t/-yot.

dispensation 1. חלוקה *nf* khalook|ah/-ot (*+of:* -at); **2.** פטור (exemption) *nm* petor/-eem (*pl+of:* -ey).

(to) dispense 1. לחלק *inf* lekhalek; *pst* kheelek; *pres* mekhalek; *fut* yekhalek; **2.** לפטור (exempt) *inf* leeftor; *pst* patar (*p=f*); *pres* poter; *fut* yeeftor.

(to) dispense from לפטור מ־ *inf* leeftor (*etc*) mee-.

(to) dispense with לוותר על־ *inf* levater 'al; *pst* veeter 'al; *pres* mevater 'al; *fut* yevater 'al.

dispersal פיזור *nm* peezoor/-eem (*pl+of:* -ey).

(to) disperse להתפזר *inf* leheetpazer; *pst* heetpazer; *pres* meetpazer; *fut* yeetpazer.

(to) displace לסלק ממקומו *inf* lesalek mee-m'komo; *pst* seelek *etc;* *pres* mesalek *etc;* *fut* yesalek *etc.*

display הצגה לראווה *nf* hatsag|ah/-ot le-ra'avah.

(to) display להציג לראווה *inf* lehatseeg le-ra'avah; *pst* heetseeg *etc;* *pres* matseeg *etc;* *fut* yatseeg *etc.*

display cabinet 1. מזנון ראווה *nm* meeznon/-ey ra'avah; **2.** ויטרינה *[colloq.]* *nf* veetreen|ah/-ot (+*of:* -at).

display window חלון ראווה *nm* khalon/-ot ra'avah.

(to) displease לא למצוא חן *inf* lo leemtso khen; *pst* lo matsa *etc;* *pres* eyno motse *etc;* *fut* lo yeemtsa *etc.*

displeasure מורת רוח *nf* morat roo'akh.

disposal 1. סילוק (removal) *nm* seelook; **2.** רשות (control) *nf* reshoot.

(at the) disposal לרשות lee-reshoot.

(to) dispose 1. לערוך *inf* la'arokh; *pst* 'arakh; *pres* 'orekh; *fut* ya'arokh; **2.** להכין (prepare) *inf* lehakheen; *pst* hekheen; *pres* mekheen; *fut* yakheen; **3.** למקם (settle) *inf* lemakem; *pst* meekem; *pres* memakem; *fut* yemakem.

(to) dispose of לסלק *inf* lesalek; *pst* seelek; *pres* mesalek; *fut* yesalek.

disposition 1. הוראה *nf* hora|'ah/-'ot (+*of:* -'at); **2.** מצב־רוח (mood) *nm* mats|av/-vey roo'akh.

(bad) disposition מצב־רוח רע *nm* mats|av/-vey roo'akh ra'/ra'eem.

(good) disposition מצב־רוח טוב *nm* mats|av/-vey roo'akh tov/-eem.

(to) disprove להפריך *inf* lehafreekh; *pst* heefreekh; *pres* mafreekh; *fut* yafreekh.

dispute 1. ויכוח (argument) *nm* veekoo|'akh/-kheem (*pl+of:* -khey); **2.** מחלוקת (disagreement) *nf* makhalok|et/-ot.

(to) dispute 1. לערער *inf* le'ar'er; *pst* 'eer'er; *pres* me'ar'er; *fut* ye'ar'er; **2.** לחלוק על (contest) *inf* lakhlok 'al; *pst* khalak 'al; *pres* kholek 'al; *fut* yakhlok 'al.

(to) disqualify לפסול *inf* leefsol; *pst* pasal *(p=f);* *pres* posel; *fut* yeefsol.

disregard 1. חוסר התחשבות *nm* khoser heet'khashvoot; **2.** התעלמות (ignoring) *nf* heet'almoot.

(to) disregard להתעלם *inf* leheet'alem; *pst* heet'alem; *pres* meet'alem; *fut* yeet'alem.

disrepute שם רע *nm* shem ra'.

disrespect זלזול *nm* zeelzool/-eem (*pl+of:* -ey).

disrespectful מזלזל *v pres & adj* mezalzel/-et.

(to) disrobe 1. להתפשט (undress oneself) *v rfl inf* leheetpashet; *pst* heetpashet; *pres* meetpashet; *fut* yeetpashet; **2.** להפשיט (undress someone else) *vt inf* lehafsheet; *pst* heefsheet; *pres* mafsheet; *fut* yafsheet.

(to) disrupt לשבש *inf* leshabesh; *pst* sheebesh; *pres* meshabesh; *fut* yeshabesh.

(to) dissatisfy לא להשביע רצון *inf* lo lehasbee'a' ratson; *pst* lo heesbee'a' *etc;* *pres* eyno masbee'a' *etc;* *fut* lo yasbee'a' *etc.*

(to) dissect לבתר *inf* levater; *pst* veeter; *pres* mevater; *fut* yevater.

(to) dissemble 1. להתחפש *inf* leheetkhapes; *pst* heetkhapes; *pres* meetkhapes; *fut* yeetkhapes; **2.** להעמיד פנים (make believe) *inf* leha'ameed paneem; *pst* he'emeed *etc;* *pres* ma'ameed *etc;* *fut* ya'ameed *etc.*

dissension מחלוקת *nf* makhalok|et/-ot.

dissent חילוקי־דעות *nm pl* kheelookey de'ot.

(to) dissent לחלוק על *inf* lakhlok 'al; *pst* khalak 'al; *pres* kholek 'al; *fut* yakhlok 'al.

disservice שירות דוב *nm* sheroot/-ey dov.

dissidence פרישה מציבור *nf* preesh|ah/-ot mee-tseeboor.

dissident פורש *nmf* por|esh/-eshet (*pl:* -sheem; +*of:* -shey).

dissimulation 1. העמדת פנים *nf* ha'amadat paneem; **2.** התראות כאחר (make believe) *nf* heetra'oo|t/-yot ke-akher.

(to) dissipate לפזר *inf* lefazer; *pst* peezer *(p=f);* *pres* mefazer; *fut* yefazer.

dissipation 1. פיזור *nm* peezoor/-eem (*pl+of:* -ey); **2.** בזבוז (waste) *nm* beezbooz/-eem (*pl+of:* -ey).

dissolute 1. מופקר *adj* moofk|ar/-eret; **2.** מושחת (depraved) *adj* moosh'kh|at/-etet.

dissolution 1. התפרקות *nf* heetparkoo|t/-yot; **2.** הפרדה (separation) *nf* hafrad|ah/-ot (+*of:* -at).

(to) dissolve 1. להמס *vt inf* lehames; *pst* hemes; *pres* memes; *fut* yames; **2.** להימס (melt) *vi inf* leheemes; *pst & pres* names; *fut* yeemas.

(to) dissolve marriage לבטל נישואים *inf* levatel neesoo'eem; *pst* beetel *(b=v) etc;* *pres* mevatel *etc;* *fut* yevatel *etc.*

(to) dissolve parliament/knesset לפזר פרלמנט/כנסת *inf* lefaz|er parlament/knesset; *pst* peezer *(p=f) etc;* *pres* mefazer *etc;* *fut* yefazer *etc.*

(to) dissuade להניא מדעתו *inf* lehanee mee-da'ato; *pst* henee *etc;* *pres* menee *etc;* *fut* yanee *etc.*

distaff עסקי נשים *nm pl* 'eeskey nasheem.

distance מרחק *nm* merkhak/-eem (*pl+of:* -ey).

(at a) distance 1. ממרחק *adv* mee-merkhak; **2.** מנגד (afar) *adv* mee-neged.

distant 1. מרוחק *adj* merookh|ak/-eket; **2.** צונן (chilly) *adj* tsonen/-et.

(to be) distant from להתרחק *inf* leheetrakhek; *pst* heetrakhek; *pres* meetrakhek; *fut* yeetrakhek.

distant relative קרוב רחוק *nmf & adj* karov/krovah rakhok/rekhokah.

distantly בריחוק *adv* be-reekhook.

distaste גועל *nm* go'al.

distasteful 1. מאוס *adj* ma'oos/me'oosah; **2.** גועלי *adj* go'olee/-t (*cpr* go'alee/-t).

distemper 1. חולי *nm* khol|ee/-ayeem (*pl+of:* kholyey); **2.** מחלת כלבלבים (canine disease) *nf* makhalat klavlabeem.

(to) distend 1. להתמתח *inf* leheetmate'akh; *pst* heetmatakh; *pres* meetmate'akh; *fut* yeetmatakh; **2.** לנפח (inflate) *inf* lenape'akh; *pst* neepakh; *pres* menape'akh; *fut* yenapakh.

(to) distil לזקק *inf* lezakek; *pst* zeekek; *pres* mezakek; *fut* yezakek.

distillation זיקוק *nm* zeekook/-eem (*pl+of:* -ey).

distillery 1. בית זיקוק *nm* bet/batey zeekook; **2.** מזקקה *nf* meezk|akah/-akot (*pl+of:* -eket).

distinct 1. מובהק *adj* moov|hak/-heket; **2.** נפרד (separate) *adj* neefr|ad/-edet; **3.** שונה (different) *adj* shon|eh/-ah.

distinction 1. הצטיינות *nf* heetstaynoo|t/-yot; **2.** שוני (difference) *nm* shonee.

distinctive 1. ברור *adj* baroor/broorah; **2.** אופייני (typical) *adj* ofyanee/-t.

distinctly בבירור *adv* be-veyroor *(v=b)*.

(to) distinguish להבחין *inf* lehavkheen; *pst* heevkheen; *pres* mavkheen; *fut* yavkheen.

distinguished 1. מצטיין *adj* meetstayen/-et; **2.** בולט (outstanding) *adj* bolet/-et.

(to) distort לסרס *inf* lesares; *pst* seres; *pres* mesares; *fut* yesares.

distortion סירוס *nm* seroos/-eem (*pl+of:* -ey).

(to) distract להסיח דעת *inf* lehasee'akh da'at; *pst* heesee'akh *etc*; *pres* masee'akh *etc*; *fut* yasee'akh *etc*.

distracted 1. מפוזר *adj* mefooz|ar/-eret; **2.** מבולבל (mixed up) *adj* mevoolb|al/-elet.

distraction 1. הסחת דעת *nf* hasakh|at/-ot da'at; **2.** בידור (amusement) *adj* beedoor/-eem (*pl+of:* -ey).

distress מצוקה *nf* metsook|ah/-ot (*+of:* -at).

(in) distress 1. במצוקה *adv* bee-metsookah; **2.** בסכנה (ship) *adv* be-sakanah.

distressed נתון במצוקה *adj* natoon/netoonah bee-metsookah.

distressed area אזור מצוקה *nm* ezor/azorey metsookah.

(to) distribute 1. לחלק *inf* lekhalek; *pst* kheelek; *pres* mekhalek; *fut* yekhalek; **2.** להפיץ (disseminate) *inf* lehafeets; *pst* hefeets; *pres* mefeets; *fut* yafeets.

distribution 1. הפצה *nf* hafats|ah/-ot (*+of:* -at); **2.** חלוקה (partition) *nf* khalook|ah/-ot (*+of:* -at).

distributor 1. מפיץ *nmf* mefeets/-ah (*f+of:* -at; *nm pl+of:* -ey); **2.** מפלג (motor) mafleg/-eem (*pl+of:* -ey).

district 1. מחוז makhoz/mekhozot (*+of:* mekhoz/-ot); **2.** גליל (circuit) *nm* galeel/gleelot (*+of:* gleel); **3.** תחום (zone) *nm* tekhoom/-eem (*pl+of:* -ey).

district attorney תובע מחוזי *nmf* tov|e'a'/-a'at mekhozee/-t.

distrust חוסר אמון *nm* khoser emoon.

(to) distrust לא לתת אמון *inf* lo latet eymoon; *pst* lo natan *etc*; *pres* eyno noten *etc*; *fut* lo yeeten *etc*.

distrustful חשדן *adj* khashdan/-eet.

(to) disturb 1. להפריע *inf* lehafree'a'; *pst* heefree'a'; *pres* mafree'a'; *fut* yafree'a'; **2.** לבלבל (mix up) *inf* levalbel; *pst* beelbel *(b=v)*; *pres* mevalbel; *fut* yevalbel.

(don't) disturb yourself אל תטרח *v imp m/f* al teetr|akh/-ekhee.

disturbance 1. הפרעה *nf* hafra|'ah/-'ot (*+of:* -'at); **2.** הפרעת סדר (of the peace) *nf* hafra|'at/-'ot seder; **3.** מהומה (riot) *nf* mehoom|ah/-ot (*+of:* -at).

disturbed מופרע *adj* moofra'/-at.

disuse חוסר שימוש *nm* khoser sheemoosh.

(to fall into) disuse לצאת מכלל שימוש *inf* latset mee-klal sheemoosh; *pst* yatsa *etc*; *pres* yotse *etc*; *fut* yetse *etc*.

ditch 1. תעלה (canal) *nf* te'al|ah/-ot (*+of:* -at/-ot); **2.** חפירה (trench) *nf* khafeer|ah/-ot (*+of:* -at).

(irrigation) ditch תעלת השקיה *nf* te'al|at/-ot hashkayah.

(to) ditch להיפטר *inf* leheepater; *pst & pres* neeftar *(f=p)*; *fut* yeepater.

(to) ditch someone לזרוק מישהו לכלבים *inf* leezrok mee-she-hoo la-klaveem; *pst* zarak *etc*; *pres* zorek *etc*; *fut* yeezrok.

ditto 1. כנזכר לעיל (as mentioned above) ka-neezkar le-'eyl; **2.** כנ"ל (*acr of* 2) ka-nal.

diuretic משתן *nm* meshat|en/-neem (*pl+of:* -ney).

divan 1. אולם ישיבות מזרחי (oriental guestroom) *nm* oolam yesheevot meezrakhee; **2.** דרגש (couch) *nm* darg|ash/-asheem (*pl+of:* -eshey); **3.** דיואן *nm* deevan.

dive 1. צלילה *nf* tseleel|ah/-ot (*+of:* -at); **2.** מקום מפגש ידוע לשמצה (disreputable hangout) *nm* mekom meefgash yadoo'a' le-sheemtsah.

(to) dive לצלול *inf* leetslol; *pst* tsalal; *pres* tsolel; *fut* yeetslol.

dive bomber מפציץ צלילה *nm* maftseets/-ey tsleelah.

diver 1. אמודאי (professional) *nm* amod|ay/-a'eem (*pl+of:* -a'ey); **2.** צוללן (sportsman/woman) *nmf* tsolelan/-eet.

(to) diverge 1. לסטות (deviate) *inf* leestot; *pst* satah; *pres* soteh; *fut* yeesteh; **2.** להסתעף (branch out) *inf* leheesta'ef; *pst* heesta'ef; *pres* meesta'ef; *fut* yeesta'ef.

divergence 1. סטייה *nf* stee|yah/-yot (*+of:* -yat); **2.** ניגוד (contrast) *nm* neegood/-eem (*pl+of:* -ey).

divers 1. כמה kamah; **2.** אחדים (some) *pl* akhadeem.

diverse 1. שונה *adj* shon|eh/-ah; **2.** רב־צורני (multiform) *adj* rav-tsooranee/-t.

diversification גיוון *nm* geevoon/-eem (*pl+of:* -ey).

diversion פעולת הסחה *nf* pe'ool|at/-ot hasakhah.

diversity 1. רבגוניות *nf* ravgoneeyoo|t/-yot; **2.** שוני (variance) *nm* shonee.

(to) divert 1. להטות *inf* lehatot; *pst* heetah; *pres* mateh; *fut* yateh; **2.** להפנות (direct) *inf* lehafnot; *pst* heefnah; *pres* mafneh; *fut* yafneh.

(to) divide 1. לחלק *inf* lekhalek; *pst* kheelek; *pres* mekhalek; *fut* yekhalek; **2.** לפלג (split) *inf* lefaleg; *pst* peeleg *(f=p)*; *pres* mefaleg; *fut* yefaleg.

dividend 1. רווח *nm* revakh/-eem (*pl+of:* reevkhey); **2.** דיבידנד *nm* deeveedend/-eem.

divine אלוהי *adj* elohee/-t.

diving set מדי צלילה *nm pl* madey tsleelah.

divinity אלוהות *nf* elohoo|t/-yot.

division 1. חילוק (arithmetic) *nf* kheelook; **2.** אוגדה (army) *nf* oogd|ah/-ot (*+of:* -at); **3.** דיביזיה *nf* deeveez|yah/-yot (*+of:* -yat); **4.** חלוקה (partition) *nf* khalook|ah/-ot (*+of:* -at).

divorce 1. גירושים *nm pl* gerooshleem (*pl+of:* -ey); **2.** גט (rabbinical decree) *nm* get/geeteen; **3.** גט פיטורים (act) *nm* get-peetooreem.

(to) divorce להתגרש *inf* leheetgaresh; *pst* heetgaresh; *pres* meetgaresh; *fut* yeetgaresh.

dizziness סחרחורת *nf* sekharkhor|et/-ot.
dizzy סחרחר *adj* sekharkhar/-ah.
dizzy speed מהירות מסחררת *nf* meheeroo|t/-yot mesakhrer|et/-ot.
(hair-)do תסרוקת נשים *nf* teesrok|et/-ot nasheem.
(that will) do זה יספיק zeh yaspeek.
(that won't) do בכך לא יהיה די be-khakh lo yeehyeh day.
(to) do 1. לעשות *inf* la'asot; *pst* 'asah; *pres* 'oseh; *fut* ya'aseh; **2.** לפעול (act) *inf* leef'ol; *pst* pa'al; *pres* po'el; *fut* yeef'al.
(yes, I) do כן, אני מסכים ken, anee maskeem/-ah *(m/f)*.
(to) do a lesson לעשות שיעורים *inf* la'asot shee'ooreem; *pst* 'asah *etc*; *pres* 'oseh *etc*; *fut* ya'aseh *etc*.
(to) do away with להיפטר מ־ *inf* leheepater mee-; *pst & pres* neeftar mee- *(f=p)*; *fut* yeepater mee-.
do-it-yourself 1. עבודה עצמית *nf* 'avodah 'atsmeet; **2.** "עשה זאת בעצמך" "aseh zot be-'atsmekha".
(to) do one's hair 1. לסרק (comb) *vt inf* lesarek; *pst* serek; *pres* mesarek; *fut* yesarek; **2.** להסתרק (comb oneself) *v rfl inf* leheestarek; *pst* heestarek; *pres* meestarek; *fut* yeestarek.
(to) do the dishes להדיח כלים *inf* lehadee'akh keleem; *pst* hedee'akh *etc*; *pres* medee'akh *etc*; *fut* yadee'akh *etc*.
(to) do up 1. לתקן (mend) *inf* letaken; *pst* teeken; *pres* metaken; *fut* yetaken; **2.** לשפץ (overhaul) *inf* leshapets; *pst* sheepets; *pres* meshapets; *fut* yeshapets.
(to) do well in business לעשות חיל בעסקים *inf* la'asot khayeel ba-'asakeem; *pst* 'asah *etc*; *pres* 'oseh *etc*; *fut* ya'aseh *etc*;
(to have nothing to) do with 1. לא להיות מעוניין ב־ (not to be interested in) *inf* lo leehyot me'oonyan be-; *pst* lo hayah *etc*; *pres* eyno *etc*; *fut* lo yeehyeh *etc*; **2.** להימנע מכל קשר עם (refrain from contact with) *inf* leheemana' mee-kol kesher 'eem; *pst & pres* neemna' *etc*; *fut* yeemana' *etc*.
(to) do without 1. לוותר על *inf* levater 'al; *pst* veeter 'al; *pres* mevater 'al; *fut* yevater 'al; **2.** להסתדר בלי (get along without) *inf [colloq.]* leheestader blee; *pst* heestader *etc*; *pres* meestader *etc*; *fut* yeestader *etc*.
(how) do you do? מה שלומך? (greeting) mah shlom|kha/-ekh? *(m/f)*.
docile צייתן *adj* tsaytan/-eet.
dock מספנה *nf* meesp|anah/-anot (*+of:* -enet/-enot).
(dry) dock 1. מבדוק *nm* meevdok/-eem (*pl+of:* -ey); **2.** מספן יבש *nm* meespan/-eem yavesh/yevesheem.
(to) dock the wages לקצץ בשכר *inf* lekatsets ba-sakhar; *pst* keetsets *etc*; *pres* mekatsets *etc*; *fut* yekatsets *etc*.
doctor רופא *nmf* rof|e/-'ah (*pl:* -'eem/-'ot; *f+of:* -et).
doctoring oneself ריפוי עצמי *nm* reepooy 'atsmee.
doctrine 1. דוקטרינה *nf* doktreen|ah/-ot (*+of:* -at); **2.** מערכת עקרונות (set of principles) *nf* ma'arekhet 'ekronot.

document 1. מסמך *nm* meesm|akh/-akheem (*pl+of:* -ekhey); **2.** תעודה (certificate) *nf* te'ood|ah/-ot (*+of:* -at).
(to) document לתעד *inf* leta'ed; *pst* tee'ed; *pres* meta'ed; *fut* yeta'ed.
dodder כשות *nf* keshoot.
dodge 1. התחמקות *nf* heetkhamkoo|t/-yot; **2.** השתמטות (shirking) *nf* heeshtamtoo|t/-yot.
(to) dodge 1. לחמוק *inf* lakhmok; *pst* khamak; *pres* khomek; *fut* yakhmok; **2.** להשתמט (shirk) *inf* leheeshtamet; *pst* heeshtamet; *pres* meeshtamet; *fut* yeeshtamet.
(to) dodge around a corner לחמוק מאחורי פינה *inf* lakhmok me-akhorey peenah; *pst* khamak *etc*; *pres* khomek *etc*; *fut* yakhmok *etc*.
doe 1. איילה *nf* ayal|ah/-ot (*+of:* ayelet); **2.** צבייה (hind) *nf* tsvee|yah/-yot (*+of:* -yat).
dog כלב *nm* kelev/klaveem (*pl+of:* kalvey).
(hot) dog נקניקייה רתוחה *nf* nakneekee|yah/-yot retookh|ah/-ot.
dog-tired עייף ככלב *adj* 'ayef/-ah ke-khelev *(kh=k)*.
dogged עיקש *adj* 'eekesh/-et.
doghouse מלונה *nf* meloon|ah/-ot (*+of:* -at).
dogma 1. דוגמה *nf* dogm|ah/-ot (*+of:* -at); **2.** "אני מאמין"(credo of Judaism) *nm* "anee ma'ameen".
dogmatic דוגמתי *adj* dogmatee/-t.
doily מפית *nf* mapee|t/-yot.
doing 1. עשייה *nf* 'asee|yah/yot (*+of:* -yat); **2.** מעשה (deed) *nm* ma'as|eh/-eem (*pl+of:* -ey).
(great) doings גדולות ונצורות *nf pl* gedolot oo-netsoorot.
dole 1. גימלה *nf* geeml|ah/-a'ot (*+of:* -at); **2.** דמי אבטלה *nf* demey avtalah.
dolefish דג בקלה *nm* dag/degey bakalah.
doleful 1. עצוב *adj* 'atsoov/-ah; **2.** מדוכא (depressed) *adj* medook|a/-et.
doll בובה *nf* boob|ah/-ot (*+of:* -at).
(to) doll up להתקשט *inf* leheetkashet; *pst* heetkashet; *pres* meetkashet; *fut* yeetkashet.
dollar דולר *adj* dol|ar/-areem (*pl+of:* -arey).
dolly 1. בובונת *nf* boobonet; **2.** עגלת יד (mobile platform) *nf* 'egl|at/-ot yad.
dolphin דולפין *nm* dolfeen/-eem (*pl+of:* -ey).
domain 1. נחלה *nf* nakhl|ah/-a'ot (*+of:* -at/-ot); **2.** שטח פעולה (sphere of action) *nm* shetakh/sheetkhey pe'oolah.
dome כיפת בניין *nf* keep|at/-ot beenyan.
domestic 1. ביתי *adj* beytee/-t; **2.** מאולף (tamed) *adj* me'ool|af|-efet.
domicile 1. מגורים *nm pl* megoor|eem (*pl+of:* -ey); **2.** מקום מושב (abode) *nm* mekom/-ot moshav.
dominant 1. דומיננטי *adj* domeenantee/-t; **2.** חולש *v pres & adj* kholesh/-et.
(to) dominate לחלוש *inf* lakhlosh; *pst* khalash; *pres* kholesh; *fut* yakhlosh.
domination 1. שליטה *nf* shleet|ah/-ot; **2.** שררה (rule) *nf* srar|ah/-ot (*+of:* -at).
(to) domineer 1. להתנשא *inf* leheetnase; *pst* heetnase; *pres* meetnase; *fut* yeetnase; **2.** להשתלט (take control) *inf* leheeshtalet; *pst* heeshtalet; *pres* meeshtalet; *fut* yeeshtalet.

domineering 1. מתנשא *adj* meetnase/-t; **2.** שתלטני (overbearing) *adj* shtaltanee/-t.

dominion 1. דומיניון *nm* domeenyon/-eem (*pl+of:* -ey); **2.** ריבונות (sovereignty) *nf* reebonoo|t/-yot.

domino 1. מסיכה לעיניים *nf* masekh|ah/-ot la-'eynayeem; **2.** דומינו *nm* domeeno.

dominoes מישחק הדומינו *nm* mees'khak/-ey domeeno.

don 1. מרצה באוניברסיטה (university lecturer) *nmf* marts|eh/-ah be-ooneeverseetah; **2.** נכבד (notable) *nm* neekhb|ad/-adeem (*pl+of:* -edey).

(to) donate 1. לתרום *inf* leetrom; *pst* taram; *pres* torem; *fut* yeetrom; **2.** לתת במתנה (give as gift) *inf* latet be-matanah; *pst* natan *etc*; *pres* noten *etc*; *fut* yeeten *etc*.

donation תרומה *nf* troo|mah/-ot (+*of:* -at).

(the meat is well) done הבשר צלוי היטב ha-basar tsalooy heytev.

done in מותש עד מוות *adj* moot|ash/-eshet 'ad mavet.

donkey חמור *nm* khamor/-eem (+*of:* -ey).

doodad משהו כזה mashehoo kazeh.

doom 1. כליה *nf* klayah; **2.** גורל (fate) *nm* goral/-ot.

(the day of) doom 1. יום הדין *nm* yom ha-deen; **2.** אחרית הימים *nf* akhreet ha-yameem.

(to) doom לחרוץ גורל *inf* lakhrots goral; *pst* kharats *etc*; *pres* khorets *etc*; *fut* yakhrots *etc*.

doomed to failure 1. נדון לכישלון *v pres & adj* nadon/-ah le-kheeshalon *(kh=k)*; **2.** נדון לכליה nadon/-ah lee-khlayah *(kh=k)*.

doomsday 1. יום הדין *nm* yom ha-deen; **2.** אחרית הימים *nf* akhareet ha-yameem.

door דלת *nf* delet/dlatot (*pl+of:* daltot).

door latch בריח דלת *nm* bree|'akh/-khey delet/dlatot.

doorbell פעמון כניסה *nm* pa'amon/-ey keneesah.

doorknob ידית הדלת *nf* yadee|t/-yot ha-delet/dlatot.

doorman שוער *nm* sho|'er/-'areem (*pl+of:* -'arey).

doorstep מפתן *nm* meeft|an/-aneem (*pl+of:* -eney).

doorway פתח *nm* petakh/-eem (*pl+of:* peetkhey).

dope 1. סם (drug) *nm* sam/-eem (*pl+of:* -ey); **2.** מטומטם (imbecile) *nm* metoomt|am/-emet; **3.** מידע (information) *nm* meyda'.

(is a) dope מטומטם אחד *nmf* metoomt|am/-emet ekhad/akhat.

(to) dope לסמם *inf* lesamem; *pst* seemem; *pres* mesamem; *fut* yesamem.

dope fiend נרקומן *nmf* narkoman/-eet (*pl:* -eem/-eeyot; +*of:* -ey).

(to) dope oneself 1. להסתמם (get drugged) *v rfl inf* leheestamem; *pst* heestamem; *pres* meestamem; *fut* yeestamem; **2.** להשתכר (get drunk) *inf* leheeshtaker; *pst* heeshtaker; *pres* meeshtaker; *fut* yeeshtaker.

(to) dope out לנחש *inf* lenakhesh; *pst* neekhesh *pres* menakhesh; *fut* yenakhesh.

dormitory 1. אולם שינה *nm* oolam/-ey shenah; **2.** פנימייה (boarding school) *nf* peneemee|yah/-yot (+*of:* -yat).

dose מנה *nf* man|ah/-ot (+*of:* -at).

(to) dose oneself להתפטם בתרופות *inf* leheetpatem bee-troofot; *pst* heetpatem *etc*; *pres* meetpatem *etc*; *fut* yeetpatem *etc*.

dot 1. נקודה *nf* nekood|ah/-ot (+*of:* -at); **2.** דגש (accent modifying a Hebrew consonant) *nm* dagesh/degesheem; **3.** רבב (small stain) *nm* revav/-eem (*pl+of:* -ey).

(on the) dot בדיוק בזמן *adv* be-deeyook ba-zman.

(to) dot לנקד (in Hebrew script) *inf* lenaked; *pst* neeked; *pres* menaked; *fut* yenaked.

dotage סכלות זיקנה *nf* seekhloot zeeknah.

(to be in one's) dotage להיות עובר בטל leehyot 'over-batel; *pst* hayah *etc*; *pres* hoo *etc*; *fut* yeehyeh *etc*.

(to) dote 1. לגלות סימני זיקנה (show old age symptoms) *inf* legalot seemaney zeeknah; *pst* geelah *etc*; *pres* megaleh *etc*; *fut* yegaleh *etc*; **2.** להגזים בגילויי חיבה (exaggerate in showing affection) *inf* lehagzeem be-gelooyey kheebah; *pst* heegzeem *etc*; *pres* magzeem *etc*; *fut* yagzeem *etc*.

(to) dote on להשתגע על *inf* leheeshtage'a' 'al; *pst* heeshtage'a' 'al; *pres* meeshtage'a' 'al; *fut* yeeshtage'a' 'al.

double כפול *adj* kafool/kefoolah.

(to) double 1. להכפיל *inf* lehakhpeel; *pst* heekhpeel; *pres* makhpeel; *fut* yakhpeel; **2.** למלא מקום (substitute) *inf* lemale makom; *pst* meele *etc*; *pres* memale *etc*; *fut* yemale *etc*.

double bed 1. מיטה כפולה *nm* meet|ah/-ot kfool|ah/-ot; **2.** מיטה זוגית (twin bed) *nf* meet|ah/-ot zoogee|t/-yot.

double-breasted בעל פריפה כפולה *adj* ba'al/-at preef|ah/-ot kefool|ah/-ot.

double chin 1. פימה *nf* peem|ah/-ot (+*of:* -at); **2.** סנטר כפול *nm* santer/-eem kafool/kefooleem.

double entry פינקסנות כפולה *nf* peenkesanoot kefoolah.

double-faced דו־פרצופי *adj* doo-partsoofee/-t.

double feature שני סרטים בכרטיס אחד *nm pl* shney srateem be-khartees *(kh=k)* ekhad.

double standard איפה ואיפה *nf* eyfah ve-eyfah.

(to) double up 1. להשתתף בחצי (share fifty-fifty) *inf* leheeshtatef be-khetsee; *pst* heeshtatef *etc*; *pres* meeshtatef *etc*; *fut* yeeshtatef *etc*; **2.** לחלוק (equally share) *inf* lakhlok; *pst* khalak; *pres* kholek; *fut* yakhalok.

doublecross בגידה *nf* begeed|ah/-ot (+*of:* -at).

(to) doublecross לבגוד *inf* leevgod; *pst* bagad *(b=v)*; *pres* boged; *fut* yeevgod.

doubledeal מעשה הונאה *nm* ma'as|eh/-ey hona'ah.

doubles משחקי זוגות *nm pl* meeskhakey zoogot.

doubt ספק *nm* safek/sfekot.

doubtful מוטל בספק *adj* moot|al/-elet be-safek.

doubtless 1. ודאי *adj* vaday/-eet; **2.** ללא ספק *adv* le-lo safek.

douche מקלחת *nf* meeklakh|at/-ot.

dough 1. בצק *nm* batsek; **2.** עיסה *nf* 'ees|ah/-ot (+*of:* -at).

doughboy חייל פשוט *nm* khayal/-eem pashoot/peshooteem.

doughnut סופגנייה *nf* soofganee|yah/-yot (*+of:* -yat).
dove יונה *nf* yon|ah/-eem (*pl+of:* -ey).
"dovish" "יוני" *adj* yonee/-t.
down 1. למטה *adv* le-matah; **2.** ירוד (run down) *adj* yarood/yeroodah; **3.** מדוכא (depressed) *adj* medook|a/-et.
(pay) down לשלם טבין ותקילין *inf* leshalem taveen oo-tekeeleen; *pst* sheelem *etc; pres* meshalem *etc; fut* yeshalem *etc.*
(price is) down המחיר ירד *nm* ha-mekheer/-eem yar|ad/-doo.
(to put) down להוריד *inf* lehoreed; *pst* horeed; *pres* moreed; *fut* yoreed.
(to be) down on someone "לעלות" על מישהו *inf* "la'alot" 'al meeshehoo; *pst* 'alah *etc; pres* 'oleh *etc; fut* ya'aleh *etc.*
down payment 1. דמי קדימה *nm pl* demey kedeemah; **2.** תשלום התחלתי (starting payment) *nm* tashloom hatkhalatee.
(to cut) down prices להוריד מחירים *inf* lehoreed mekheereem; *pst* horeed *etc; pres* moreed *etc; fut* yoreed *etc.*
down the street במורד הרחוב *adv* be-morad ha-rekhov.
down to עד ל־ *adv* 'ad le-.
(to get) down to work לגשת לעבודה *inf* lageshet la-'avodah; *pst & pres* neegash *etc; fut* yeegash *etc.*
downcast 1. מושפל *adj* mooshp|al/-elet; **2.** מדוכדך (depressed) *adj* medookhd|akh/-ekhet.
(with) downcast eyes בעיניים מושפלות *adj* be-'eynayeem mooshpalot.
downfall מפלה *nf* map|alah/-alot (*+of:* -elet).
downgrade 1. מדרון (slope) *nm* meedron/-eem (*pl+of:* -ey); **2.** מורד (descent) *nm* mor|ad/-adot (*pl+of:* -dot).
(to) downgrade להוריד בדרגה *vt inf* lehoreed be-dargah; *pst* horeed *etc; pres* moreed *etc; fut* yoreed *etc.*
downpour גשם שוטף *nm* gesh|em/-ameem shot|ef/-feem.
downright 1. ברור (plain) *adj* baroor/broorah; **2.** מוחלט (absolute) *adj* mookhl|at/-etet; **3.** לגמרי (entirely) *adv* legamrey.
downright foolishness שטות מובהקת *nf* shtoot moovheket.
downstairs 1. למטה במדרגות *adv* le-matah ba-madregot; **2.** בקומה מתחת (floor below) *adv* ba-komah mee-takhat.
downstream במורד הנהר *adv* be-morad ha-nahar.
downtown 1. ברובע המסחרי (business quarter) *adv* ba-rova' ha-meeskharee; **2.** במרכז העיר (town center) *adv* be-merkaz ha-'eer.
downward, downwards כלפי מטה *adv* kelapey matah.
downy 1. מכוסה פלומה *adj* mekhoos|eh/-ah ploomah; **2.** מרגיע (calming) *adj* margee|'a'/-ah.
dowry 1. נדוניה *nf* nedoon|yah/-yot (*+of:* -yat); **2.** מוהר (payable by groom) *nm* mohar/-eem (*pl+of:* -ey).
doze נמנום *nm* neemnoom/-eem (*pl+of:* -ey).
(to) doze לנמנם *inf* lenamnem; *pst* neemnem; *pres* menamnem; *fut* yenamnem.
dozen תריסר *nm* treysar/-eem (*pl+of:* -ey).
drab 1. בצבע זית (olive-brown) *adj* be-tseva' zayeet; **2.** חסר ברק (dull) *adj* khas|ar/-rat barak.
draft 1. טיוטה (outline) *nf* tyoot|ah/-ot (*+of:* -at); **2.** סרטוט (sketch) *nm* seertoot/-eem (*pl+of:* -ey); **3.** המחאה (bank) *nf* hamkha|'ah/-'ot (*+of:* -'at); **4.** רוח פרצים (wind) *nm* roo|'akh/-khot pratseem; **5.** גיוס (military) *nm* geeyoos/-eem (*pl+of:* -ey).
(rough) draft טיוטה ראשונה *nf* tyoot|ah/-ot reeshon|ah/-ot.
draft age גיל גיוס *nm* geel geeyoos.
draft beer בירה מן החבית *nf* beerah meen he-khaveet.
draft call צו קריאה *nm* tsav/-ey kree'ah.
draft horse סוס משא *nm* soos/-ey masa.
draftee מחויל *nmf* mekhooyal/-yelet.
draftsman סרטט *nmf* sart|at/-etet.
drag 1. עיכוב *nm* 'eekoov/-eem (*pl+of:* -ey); **2.** סחבת (red-tape) *nf* sakhevet.
(to) drag on and on לסחוב עוד ועוד *inf* lees'khov 'od va-'od; *pst* sakhav *etc; pres* sokhev *etc; fut* yees'khav *etc.*
dragon דרקון *nm* drakon/-eem (*pl+of:* -ey).
drain 1. תעלת ניקוז *nf* ta'al|at/-ot neekooz; **2.** מעמסה כספית (financial burden) *nf* ma'amasah kaspeet.
(down the) drain על קרן הצבי *adv* 'al keren ha-tsvee.
(to) drain 1. לנקז *inf* lenakez; *pst* neekez; *pres* menakez; *fut* yenakez; **2.** לדלדל (deplete) *inf* ledaldel; *pst* deeldel; *pres* medaldel; *fut* yedaldel.
drainage ניקוז *nm* neekooz/-eem (*pl+of:* -ey).
drake ברווז *nm* barvaz/-eem (*pl+of:* -ey).
drama 1. מחזה (play) *nf* makhz|eh/-ot; **2.** דרמה *nf* dram|ah/-ot (*+of:* -at).
dramatic דרמתי *adj* dramatee/-t.
dramatist מחזאי *nmf* makhaz|ay/-a'eet.
(to) dramatize 1. להמחיז *inf* lehamkheez; *pst* heemkheez; *pres* mamkheez; *fut* yamkheez; **2.** להגזים (exaggerate) *inf* lehagzeem; *pst* heegzeem; *pres* magzeem; *fut* yagzeem.
drape 1. לקשט בבד *inf* lekashet be-vad; *pst* keeshet *etc; pres* mekashet *etc; fut* yekashet *etc;* **2.** לרפד (pad) *inf* leraped; *pst* reeped; *pres* meraped; *fut* yeraped; **3.** לתלות בקיפולים (hang in folds) *inf* leetlot be-keepooleem; *pst* talah *etc; pres* toleh *etc; fut* yeetleh *etc.*
drapery 1. ריפוד (upholstery) *nm* reepood/-eem (*pl+of:* -ey); **2.** מרפדייה (draper's workshop) *nf* marpedee|yah/-yot (*+of:* -yat).
drastic נמרץ *adj* neemr|ats/-etset.
drastic steps 1. צעדים נמרצים (energetic) *nm pl* tse'adeem neemratseem; **2.** אמצעים דרסטיים (means) emtsa'eem drasteeyeem.
draw תיקו (stalemate) *nm* teykoo.
(to) draw 1. למשוך (drag) *inf* leemshokh; *pst* mashakh; *pres* moshekh; *fut* yeemshokh; **2.** לצייר (sketch) *inf* letsayer; *pst* tseeyer; *pres* metsayer; *fut* yetsayer.

(to) draw a breath לשאוף אוויר *inf* leesh'of aveer; *pst* sha'af *etc*; *pres* sho'ef *etc*; *fut* yeesh'af *etc*.

(to) draw aside לקחת הצידה *inf* lakakhat ha-tseedah; *pst* lakakh *etc*; *pres* loke'akh *etc*; *fut* yeekakh *etc*.

(to) draw lots להטיל גורל *inf* lehateel goral; *pst* heteel *etc*; *pres* meteel *etc*; *fut* yateel *etc*.

(to) draw near 1. לקרב *vt inf* lekarev; *pst* kerev; *pres* mekarev; *fut* yekarev; **2.** להתקרב *v rfl inf* leheetkarev; *pst* heetkarev; *pres* meetkarev; *fut* yeetkarev.

(to) draw out 1. להאריך *inf* leha'areekh; *pst* he'ereekh; *pres* ma'areekh; *fut* ya'areekh; **2.** לדובב (induce to talk) *inf* leedovev; *pst* dovev *pres* medovev; *fut* yedovev.

(to) draw up לנסח *inf* lenase'akh; *pst* neesakh; *pres* menase'akh; *fut* yenasakh.

drawback 1. מגרעת *nf* meegra|'at/-'ot; **2.** עיכוב (hindrance) *nm* 'eekoov/-eem (*pl+of:* -ey).

drawbridge גשר זחיח *nm* gesh|er/-areem zakhee'akh/zekheekheem.

drawer 1. מגירה (compartment) *nf* meger|ah/-ot (*+of:* -at); **2.** מושך שיק (of a check) *nmf* moshekh/-et shek.

drawers תחתונים *nm pl* takhton|eem (*pl+of:* -ey).

drawing 1. רישום (sketch) *nm* reeshoom/-eem (*pl+of:* -ey); **2.** סרטוט (design) *nm* seertoot/-eem (*pl+of:* -ey).

drawing paper נייר סרטוט *nm* neyar/-ot seertoot.

drawing room חדר אורחים *nm* khad|ar/-rey orkheem.

dread חרדה kharad|ah/-ot (*+of:* kherd|at/-ot).

(to) dread לפחד *inf* lefakhed; *pst* pakhad (*p=f*); *pres* pokhed; *fut* mefakhed.

dreadful מבהיל *adj* mav|heel/-ah.

dream חלום *nm* khalom/-ot.

(to) dream לחלום *inf* lakhlom; *pst* khalam; *pres* kholem; *fut* yakhlom.

dreamer 1. חלמן *nmf* khalman/-eet; **2.** הוזה (visionary) *nmf* hoz|eh/-ah.

dreamland עולם הדמיון *nm* 'olam ha-deemyon.

(pleasant) dreams! חלומות נעימים! khalomot ne'eemeem!

dreamy חולמני *adj* kholmanee/-t.

dreary 1. מדכא (depressing) *adj* medak|e/-'et; **2.** עצוב (sad) *adj* 'atsoov/-ah.

dredge, dredger מחפר *nm* makhper/-eem (*pl+of:* -ey).

(to) dredge לנקות במחפר *inf* lenakot be-makhper; *pst* neekah *etc*; *pres* menakeh *etc*; *fut* yenakeh *etc*.

dregs 1. שיירים *nm pl* shyar|eem (*pl+of:* -ey); **2.** שיריים (from a Hassidic rebbe's table) *nm pl* sheerayeem.

(to) drench להרטיב *inf* leharteev; *pst* heerteev; *pres* marteev; *fut* yarteev.

drenching הרטבה *nf* hartav|ah/-ot (*+of:* -at).

dress 1. לבוש *nm* levoosh; **2.** שמלה (women's) *nf* seemlah/smalot (*+of:* seeml|at/-ot).

(to) dress 1. להתלבש *inf* leheetlabesh; *pst* heetlabesh; *pres* meetlabesh; *fut* yeetlabesh; **2.** ליישר (set straight) *inf* leyasher; *pst* yeesher; *pres* meyasher; *fut* yeyasher; **3.** לחבוש (bandage) *inf* lakhavosh; *pst* khavash; *pres* khovesh; *fut* yakhavosh.

(to) dress down 1. לנזוף (reprimand) *inf* leenzof; *pst* nazaf; *pres* nozef; *fut* yeenzof; **2.** להלקות (whip) *inf* lehalkot; *pst* heelkah; *pres* malkeh; *fut* yalkeh.

dress rehearsal חזרה כללית *nf* khazar|ah/-ot klalee|t/-yot.

dress suit לבוש רשמי *nm* levoosh reeshmee.

(to) dress up להתלבש יפה *inf* leheetlabesh yafeh; *pst* heetlabesh *etc*; *pres* meetlabesh *etc*; *fut* yeetlabesh *etc*.

dresser שידה *nf* sheed|ah/-ot (*+of:* -at).

(she is a good) dresser היא יודעת להתלבש *v f sing pres* hee yoda'at leheetlabesh.

dressing 1. רוטב (sauce) *nm* rotev/retaveem (*pl+of:* rotvey); **2.** תחבושת (bandage) *nf* takhbosh|et/-ot.

(a) dressing down נזיפה קשה *nf* nezeef|ah/-ot kash|ah/-ot.

dressing gown חלוק *nm* khalook/-eem (*pl+of:* -ey).

dressing room חדר הלבשה *nm* khad|ar/-rey halbashah.

dressing table שולחן תמרוקים *nm* shoolkhan/-ot tamrookeem.

dressmaker תופרת *nf* tof|eret/-rot.

dribble טפטוף *nm* teeftoof/-eem (*pl+of:* -ey).

(to) dribble 1. לטפטף *inf* letaftef; *pst* teeftef; *pres* metaftef; *fut* yetaftef; **2.** לכדרר (a ball) *inf* lekhadrer; *pst* keedrer (*k=kh*); *pres* mekhadrer; *fut* yekhadrer.

driblet 1. נטף *nm* netef/netafeem (*pl+of:* neetfey); **2.** קמצוץ (trifling amount) *nm* keemtsoots/-eem (*pl+of:* -ey).

dried מיובש *adj* meyoob|ash/-eshet.

dried fig תאנה מיובשת *nf* te'en|ah/-eem meyoob|eshet/-ashot.

drier, drier 1. מייבש *nm* meyab|esh/-sheem (*pl+of:* -shey); **2.** מכונת ייבוש (drying machine) *nf* mekhon|at/-ot yeeboosh.

(hair) drier מייבש שערות *nm* meyab|esh/-shey se'arot.

(laundry) drier מייבש כביסה *nm* meyab|esh/-shey kveesah.

drift דחיפה *nf* dekheef|ah/-ot (*+of:* -at).

(to get the) drift of לרדת לסודו של *inf* laredet le-sodo shel; *pst* yarad *etc*; *pres* yored *etc*; *fut* yered *etc*.

driftwood עצי סחף *nm pl* 'atsey sakhaf.

drill 1. מקדח (tool) *nm* makde|'akh/-kheem (*pl+of:* -khey); **2.** תרגיל־סדר (exercise) *nm* targeel/-ey seder.

(to) drill 1. לקדוח (bore) *inf* leekdo'akh; *pst* kadakh; *pres* kode'akh; *fut* yeekdakh; **2.** לתרגל (train) *inf* letargel; *pst* teergel; *pres* metargel; *fut* yetargel.

drily, dryly ביבשות *adv* bee-yeveshoot.

drink משקה *nm* mashk|eh/-a'ot.

(to) drink 1. לשתות *inf* leeshtot; *pst* shatah; *pres* shoteh; *fut* yeeshteh; **2.** לשתות לשוכרה (get drunk) *inf* leeshtot le-shokhrah; *pst* shatah *etc*; *pres* shoteh *etc*; *fut* yeeshteh.

(to) drink a toast להרים כוסית *inf* lehareem koseet; *pst* hereem *etc*; *pres* mereem *etc*; *fut* yareem *etc*.

(to) drink it down להטביע בשתייה *inf* lehatbee'a' bee-shteeyah; *pst* heetbee'a' *etc*; *pres* matbee'a' *etc*; *fut* yatbee'a' *etc*.

drinkable יפה לשתייה *adj* yaf|eh/-ah (*pl:* -eem/-ot) lee-shteeyah.

drip 1. נטף *nm* netef/netafeem (*pl+of:* neetfey); **2.** טפטוף (dribble) *nm* teeftoof/-eem (*pl+of:* -ey).

(to) drip לנטוף *inf* leentof; *pst* nataf; *pres* notef; *fut* yeetof.

drip-dry כבס ולבש *nm* kabes oo-levash.

drive 1. נסיעה ברכב (in a car) *nf* nesee|'ah/-'ot be-rekhev; **2.** מסע התרמה (campaign) *nm* mas|a'/-'ot hatramah.

(to) drive 1. לנהוג *inf* leenhog; *pst* nahag; *pres* noheg; *fut* yeenhag; **2.** להניע (move, force) *inf* lehanee'a'; *pst* henee'a'; *pres* menee'a'; *fut* yanee'a'.

(to) drive away להניס *inf* lehanees; *pst* henees; *pres* menees; *fut* yanees.

(to) drive a good bargain לעשות עסקה טובה *inf* la'asot 'eeskah tovah; *pst* 'asah *etc*; *pres* 'oseh *etc*; *fut* ya'aseh *etc*.

(to) drive mad לשגע *inf* leshagea; *pst* sheega'; *pres* meshage'a'; *fut* yeshage'a'.

drive-in movie theater קולנוע למכוניות *nm* kolno'a' lee-mekhoneeyot.

drive-in restaurant מסעדת רכב *nf* mees|'edet/-'adot rekhev.

drivel קשקוש *nm* keeshkoosh/-eem (*pl+of:* -ey).

(to) drivel לקשקש *inf* lekashkesh; *pst* keeshkesh; *pres* mekashkesh; *fut* yekashkesh.

driven נהוג *adj* nahoog/nehoogah.

driver נהג *nm* nehag/naheget (*pl:* nehag|eem/-ot; *+of:* -ey/-ot).

(pile) driver תוקע עמודים *nm* toke|'a'/-'ey 'amoodeem.

(slave) driver נוגש בעובדים *adj* nog|es/-et ba-'ovdeem.

(truck) driver נהג משאית *nm* nahag/nehagey masa'ee|t/-yot.

driveway כביש גישה *nm* kveesh/-ey geeshah.

(drunken) driving נהיגה בגילופין *nf* neheegah be-geeloofeen.

(what are you) driving at? מה כוונתך לרמוז? mah kavanat|kha/-ekh (*m/f*) leermoz?

driving school בית ספר לנהגות *nm* bet/batey sefer le-nehagoot.

drizzle 1. רביבים *nm pl* reveev|eem (*pl+of:* -ey); **2.** גשם דק (light rain) *nm* geshem dak.

drone 1. דבור (male honeybee) *nm* dvor/-eem; **2.** טפיל (parasite) *nmf* tapeel/-ah.

(to) drone 1. להתבטל *inf* leheetbatel; *pst* heetbatel; *pres* meetbatel; *fut* yeetbatel; **2.** להשמיע צליל חדגוני (produce monotonous sound) *inf* lehashmee'a' tsleel khadgonee; *pst* heeshmee'a' *etc*; *pres* mashmee'a' *etc*; *fut* yashmee'a' *etc*.

(to) droop 1. להשתופף *inf* leheeshtofef; *pst* heeshtofef; *pres* meeshtofef; *fut* yeeshtofef; **2.** לנבול (wither) *inf* leenbol; *pst* naval (*v=b*); *pres* novel; *fut* yeebol.

drooped shoulders כתפיים שחוחות *nf pl* ketefayeem shekhookhot.

drooping eyelids עפעפיים מושפלים *nm pl* 'af'apayeem mooshpaleem.

drop 1. טיפה *nf* teep|ah/-ot (*+of:* -at); **2.** נפילה (fall) *nf* nefeel|ah/-ot (*+of:* -at).

(to) drop 1. להפיל *vt* lehapeel; *pst* heepeel; *pres* mapeel; *fut* yapeel; **2.** ליפול (fall) *vi inf* leepol; *pst* nafal (*f=p*); *pres* nofel; *fut* yeepol.

(to) drop a line לכתוב כמה שורות *inf* leekhtov kamah shoorot; *pst* katav (*k=kh*) *etc*; *pres* kotev *etc*; *fut* yeekhtov *etc*.

(to) drop asleep להירדם מעייפות *inf* leheradem me-'ayefoot; *pst & pres* neerdam *etc*; *fut* yeradem *etc*.

(to) drop behind לפגר אחר *inf* lefager akhar; *pst* peeger (*p=f*) *etc*; *pres* mefager *etc*; *fut* yefager *etc*.

drop curtain מסך יורד *nm* masakh yored.

drop hammer קורנס *nm* koornas/-eem (*pl+of:* -ey).

(to) drop in לסור לביקור *inf* lasoor le-veekoor (*v=b*); *pst & pres* sar *etc*; *fut* yasoor *etc*.

(to) drop in a mailbox לזרוק לתיבת דואר *inf* leezrok le-teyvat do'ar; *pst* zarak *etc*; *pres* zorek *etc*; *fut* yeezrok *etc*.

drop out תלמיד שנשר *nmf* talmeed/-ah she-nash|ar/-rah.

(to) drop out 1. לנשור *inf* leenshor; *pst* nashar; *pres* nosher; *fut* yeenshor; **2.** להיפלט (unwillingly) *inf* leheepalet; *pst & pres* neeflat (*f=p*); *fut* yeepalet.

(to) drop the curtain להוריד מסך *inf* lehoreed masakh; *pst* horeed *etc*; *pres* moreed *etc*; *fut* yoreed *etc*.

(cough) drops טבליות נגד שיעול *nf pl* tavleeyot neged she'ool.

drought בצורת *nf* batsor|et/-ot.

drove 1. עדר (animals) *nm* 'eder/'adareem (*pl+of:* 'edrey); **2.** המון (people) *nm* hamon/-eem (*pl+of:* -ey).

(to) drown 1. לטבוע *vi inf* leetbo'a'; *pst* tava' (*v=b*); *pres* tove'a'; *fut* yeetba'; **2.** להטביע (someone else) *vt inf* lehatbee'a'; *pst* heetbee'a'; *pres* matbee'a'; *fut* yatbee'a'.

(to) drowse להתנמנם *inf* leheetnamnem; *pst* heetnamnem; *pres* meetnamnem; *fut* yeetnamnem.

drowsiness התנמנמות *nf* heetnamnemoo|t/-yot.

drowsy רדום *adj* radoom/redoomah.

(to become) drowsy להיתפס רדימות *inf* leheetafes redeemoot; *pst & pres* neetpas (*p=f*) *etc*; *fut* yeetafes *etc*.

(to) drudge לעבוד בפרך *inf* la'avod be-ferekh (*f=p*); *pst* 'avad *etc*; *pres* oved *etc*; *fut* ya'avod *etc*.

drug 1. תרופה (medicine) *nf* troof|ah/-ot (*+of:* -at); **2.** סם (narcotic) *nm* sam/-eem (*pl+of:* -ey).

(to) drug לסמם *inf* lesamem; *pst* seemem; *pres* mesamem; *fut* yesamem.

drug addict 1. מכור לסמים *nmf* makhoor/mekhoorah le-sameem; **2.** נרקומן *nmf* narkoman/-eet.

drug addiction התמכרות לסמים *nf* heetmakroot le-sameem.

(a) drug on the market סחורה ללא קופצים עליה sekhorah le-lo koftseem 'aleha.

druggist 1. רוקח (pharmacist) *nmf* rok|e'akh/-akhat; **2.** סוחר תרופות (druggist) *nm* sokh|er/-arey troofot.

drugstore 1. בית מרקחת (pharmacy - selling medicines only) *nm* bet/batey meerkakhat; **2.** חנות כלבו לתרופות (drugstore) *nf* khanoo|t/-yot kolbo lee-troofot.

drum תוף *nm* tof/toop|eem (*pl+of:* -ey).

(bass) drum טמבור *nm* tamboor/-eem (*pl+of:* -ey).

(to) drum לתופף *inf* letofef; *pst* tofef; *pres* metofef; *fut* yetofef.

(to) drum a lesson into someone 1. ללמד לקח *inf* lelamed lekakh et meeshe|hoo/hee (*m/f*); *pst* leemed *etc*; *pres* melamed *etc*; *fut* yelamed; **2.** להכניס למישהו לראש (get into one's head) *inf* lehakhnees le-meeshehoo la-rosh; *pst* heekhnees *etc*; *pres* makhnees *etc*; *fut* yakhnees *etc*.

drum major מנצח על תזמורת במצעד *nm* menatse'akh 'al teezmoret be-meets'ad.

(to) drum up trade להכניס רוח חיים במסחר *inf* lehakhnees roo'akh khayeem ba-meeskhar; *pst* heekhnees *etc*; *pres* makhnees *etc*; *fut* yakhnees *etc*.

drummer מתופף *nmf* metofef/-et.

drumstick מקל תיפוף *nm* mak|el-lot teefoof.

(to get) drunk להשתכר *inf* leheeshtaker; *pst* heeshtaker; *pres* meeshtaker; *fut* yeeshtaker.

drunkard שיכור *nmf* sheekor/-ah (*pl:* -eem/-ot; *+of:* -ey).

drunken שתוי *adj* shatooy/shtooyah.

drunkenness שכרות *nf* sheekhroot.

dry יבש *adj* yavesh/yeveshah.

(to) dry לייבש *inf* leyabesh; *pst* yeebesh; *pres* meyabesh; *fut* yeyabesh.

dry cleaner 1. חומר לניקוי יבש (substance) *nm* khom|er/-oreem le-neekooy yavesh; **2.** בעל מכון לניקוי יבש (dealer) *nmf* ba'al/-at makhon le-neekooy yavesh.

dry cleaning ניקוי יבש *nm* neekooy yavesh.

dry goods 1. אריגים (fabrics) *nm pl* areeg|eem (*pl+of:* -ey); **2.** בדים (textiles) *nm pl* bad|eem (*pl+of:* -ey).

dry measure מידות לשקילת מוצקים *nf pl* meedot lee-sh'keelat mootsakeem.

(to) dry up להתייבש *inf* leheetyabesh; *pst* heetyabesh; *pres* meetyabesh; *fut* yeetyabesh.

dryness יובש *nm* yovesh.

(to) dub להקליט פס־קול *inf* lehakleet pas-kol; *pst* heekleet; *pres* makleet *etc*; *fut* yakleet *etc*.

dubious מפוקפק *adj* mefookp|ak/-eket.

duchess דוכסית *nf* dookasee|t/-yot.

duck ברווז *nm* barv|az/-azeem (*pl+of:* -ey).

(lame) duck קנה רצוץ *nm* kaneh ratsoots.

duckling ברווזון *nm* barv|azon/-ezoneem (*pl+of:* ezon-ey).

dud 1. לא יוצלח *nmf [colloq.]* lo yootslakh/-eet; **2.** כישלון (failure) *nm* keesh|alon (*+of:* -lon).

dude גנדרן *nmf & adj* gandran/-eet.

due 1. מיועד *adj* meyo|'ad/-'edet; **2.** צפוי (expected) *adj* tsafooy/tsfooyah.

(the bill is) due השטר יגיע לפירעון ha-shtar yagee'a' le-fera'on (*f=p*).

(the train is) due at three o'clock הרכבת אמורה להגיע בשעה שלוש ha-rakevet amoorah lehagee'a' be-sha'ah shalosh.

due east שפניו מזרחה *adj* she-pan|av/-eha meezrakhah.

(in) due time ברגע הנכון *adv* ba-rega' ha-nakhon.

duel דו־קרב *nm* doo-krav.

(to) duel לצאת לדו־קרב *inf* latset le-doo-krav; *pst* yatsa *etc*; *pres* yotse *etc*; *fut* yetse *etc*.

dues מסי חבר *nm pl* meesey khaver.

duet זמרה בשניים *nf* zeemrah bee-shnayeem.

duke דוכס dookas/-eem (*pl+of:* -ey).

dukedom דוכסות *nf* dookasoo|t/-yot.

dull 1. משעמם (tedious) *adj* mesha'amem/-et; **2.** מטומטם (stupid) *adj* metoomt|am/-emet; **3.** עמום (dim) *adj* 'amoom/-ah.

dull pain כאב עמום *nm* ke'ev/-eem 'amoom/-eem.

dull sound צליל עמום *nm* tsleel/-eem 'amoom/-eem.

dullness, dulness 1. קהות *nf* kehoot; **2.** טמטום (stupidity) *nm* teemtoom.

duly 1. כדבעי *adv* keedeva'ey (*cpr* keedeba'ee); **2.** כנדרש (as required) *adv* ka-needrash; **3.** כיאות (properly) *adv* ka-ya'oot.

dumb אילם *nmf & adj* eelem/-et.

dumb creature 1. חיה אילמת *nf* kha|yah/-yot eel|emet/-mot; **2.** בהמה (animal) *nf* behem|ah/-ot.

dumbness אלם *nm* elem.

dummy 1. דמה *nm* demeh; **2.** גולם (robot, idiot) *nm* gol|em/-ameem (*pl+of:* -amey)

dump 1. מצבור אספקה (supplies) *nm* meetsbor/-ey aspakah; **2.** מצבור תחמושת (ammunition) *nm* meetsb|or/-ey takhmoshet.

(garbage) dump מזבלה *nf* meezb|al|ah/-alot (*+of:* -elet).

(to) dump 1. להשליך *inf* lehashleekh; *pst* heeshleekh; *pres* mashleekh; *fut* yashleekh; **2.** לזרוק (throw out) *inf* leezrok; *pst* zarak; *pres* zorek; *fut* yeezrok; **3.** לפרוק (unload) *inf* leefrok; *pst* parak (*p=f*); *pres* porek; *fut* yeefrok.

dumping 1. דמפינג *nm* dampeeng/-eem; **2.** הצפה בסחורה זולה (flooding with cheap merchandise) *nf* hatsafah bee-sekhorah zolah.

dumpling כופתה *nf* kooft|ah/-a'ot (*+of:* -at).

dunce 1. בער *nm* ba'ar/be'areem (*pl+of:* ba'arey); **2.** מפגר (dull-witted) *nmf* mefager/-et.

dune 1. דיונה *nf* dyoon|ah/-ot (*+of:* -at); **2.** חולית *nf* kholee|t/-yot.

dung זבל *nm* zevel/zvaleem (*pl+of:* zeevley).

dungarees סרבל *nm* sarbl|al/-aleem (*pl+of:* -eley).

dungeon צינוק *nm* tseenok/-eem (*pl+of:* -ey).

dunghill גל אשפה *nm* gal/-ey ashpah.

duodenum תריסריון *nm* treysaryon/-eem (*pl+of:* -ey).

dupe פתי *nmf* pet|ee/-ayah.

(to) dupe 1. לתעתע *inf* leta'te'a'; *pst* tee'ta'; *pres* meta'te'a'; *fut* yeta'ta'; **2.** להונות (deceive) *inf* lehonot; *pst* honah; *pres [colloq.]* merameh; *fut* yoneh.

duplicate 1. העתק (copy) *nm* he'tlek/-ekeem (*pl+of:* -key); **2.** זוגי (twofold) *adj* zoogee/-t; **3.** כפול (double) *adj* kafool/kefoolah.

(to) duplicate לשכפל *inf* lehshakhpel; *pst* sheekhpel; *pres* meshakhpel; *fut* yeshakhpel.

duplicity 1. דו־פרצופיות *nf* doo-partsoofeeyoot; **2.** צביעות (hypocrisy) *nf* tsvee'oot.

durable 1. בר־קיימא *adj* bar/bat kayama; **2.** מתמשך (continuous) *adj* meetmashekh/-et.

duration משך זמן *nm* meshekh zman.

during במשך *prep* be-meshekh.

dusk דמדומים *nm pl* deemdoom|eem (*pl+of:* -ey).

(at) dusk בין השמשות *adv* beyn ha-shmashot.

dusky 1. אפלולי *adj* afloolee/-t; **2.** קודר (gloomy) *adj* koder/-et.

dust אבק *nm* avak.

(cloud of) dust ענן אבק *nm* 'an|an/-eney avak.

(to) dust לנער אבק *inf* lena'er avak; *pst* nee'er *etc; pres* mena'er *etc; fut* yena'er *etc.*

dust jacket עטיפת ספר *nf* 'ateef|ah/-ot sefer/sfareem.

dust storm סופת חול *nf* soof|at/-ot khol.

duster מטלית *nf* matlee|t/-yot.

(feather) duster מטלית נוצות *nf* matleet notsot.

dusty מאובק *adj* me'oob|ak-eket.

Dutch 1. הולנדי *adj* holandee/-t; **2.** הולנדית (language) *nf* holandeet.

Dutch treat 1. כיבוד נוסח הולנד *nm* keebood noosakh holand; **2.** כל אחד משלם בעד עצמו (each one pays for himself) kol ekhad meshalem be'ad 'atsmo.

Dutchman הולנדי *nm* holandee/-m.

Dutchwoman הולנדית *nf* holandee|t/-yot.

duty 1. מכס (customs) *nm* mekh|es/-aseem (*pl+of:* meekhsey); **2.** חובה (obligation) *nf* khov|ah/-ot (*+of:* -at).

duty-free פטור ממכס *nm* petor/-eem mee-mekhes.

dwarf 1. גמד *nmf* gamad/-eem (*pl+of:* -ey); **2.** גמד *adj* gamad/-ah.

(to) dwarf לגמד *inf* legamed; *pst* geemed; *pres* megamed; *fut* yegamed.

(to) dwell 1. להתגורר *inf* leheetgorer; *pst* heetgorer; *pres* meetgorer; *fut* yeetgorer; **2.** להתעכב (elaborate) *inf* leheet'akev; *pst* heet'akev; *pres* meet'akev; *fut* yeet'akev.

(to) dwell on a subject להאריך בנושא *inf* leha'areekh ba-nose; *pst* he'ereekh *etc; pres* ma'areekh *etc; fut* ya'areekh *etc.*

dweller תושב *nmf* tosh|av/-evet.

dwelling מעון *nm* ma'on/me'onot (*+of:* me'on).

dwelling house בית מגורים *nm* bet/batey megooreem.

(to) dwindle 1. לקטון *inf* leekton; *pst* katan; *pres* katen; *fut* yeektan; **2.** להתמעט (decrease) *inf* leheetma'et; *pst* heetma'et; *pres* meetma'et; *fut* yeetma'et.

dye צבע *nm* tseva'/tsva'eem (*pl+of:* tseev'ey).

(to) dye לצבוע *inf* leetsbo'a'; *pst* tsava' *(v=b); pres* tsove'a'; *fut* yeetsba'.

dyeing צביעה *nf* tsvee|'ah/-'ot (*+of:* -'at).

dyer 1. צבע *nm* tsaba'/-'eem (*pl+of:* -'ey); **2.** צבעי *[colloq.] nmf* tsaba'ee/t.

dyer's shop חנות צבעים *nf* khanoo|t/-yot tsva'eem.

dynamic דינאמי *adj* deenamee/-t.

dynamics דינאמיקה *nf* deenameek|ah/-ot (*+of:* -at).

dynamite דינמיט *nm* deenameet.

dynamo דינמו *nm* deenamo.

dynasty שושלת *nf* shosh|elet/-alot.

dysentery 1. שלשול *nm* sheelshool/-eem (*pl+of:* -ey); **2.** דיזנטריה *nf* deezenteryah.

E.

E,e as a vowel in English, may be pronounced in several different ways, depending on the word or on whether it stands alone or in combination with other vowels or letters. In the transliteration we use in these dictionaries, however, *e* is invariably pronounced as in *edge*, when standing alone, and as in see when doubled.

each 1. כל kol; **2.** כל אחד (every) kol ekhad/akhat *(m/f).*

eager להוט *adj* lahoot/lehootah.

eagerness להיטות *nf* leheetoo|t/-yot.

eagle נשר *nm* nesh|er/-areem (*pl+of:* neeshrey).

ear 1. אוזן *nf* ozen/oznayeem (*pl+of:* ozney); **2.** ידית (handle) *nf* yadee|t/-yot.

(by) ear מתוך שמיעה *adv* mee-tokh shmee'ah.

ear muff כסוי אוזן *nm* kesoo|y/-yey ozen/oznayeem.

ear of corn קלח תירס *nm* kelakh/keelkhey teeras.

ear of wheat שיבולת *nf* sheebol|et/-eem (*pl+of:* -ey).

earache כאב אוזן *nm* ke'ev/-ey ozen.

eardrum תוף האוזן *nm* tof ha-ozen.

early riser משכים קום *adj* mashkeem/-ah koom

(at an) early date 1. במועד קרוב *adv* be-mo'ed karov; **2.** בהקדם (soon) *adv* be-hekdem.

(to) earmark לסמן *inf* lesamen; *pst* seemen; *pres* mesamen; *fut* yesamen.

(to) earn 1. להשתכר (money) *inf* leheestaker; *pst* heestaker; *pres* meestaker; *fut* yeestaker; **2.** להיות ראוי (deserve) *inf* leehyot ra'ooy; *pst* hayah *etc; pres* heeno *etc; fut* yeehyeh *etc.*

earnest רציני *adj* retseenee/-t.

(In) earnest, earnestly ברצינות *adv* bee-retseenoot.

earnestness רצינות *nf* retseenoo|t/-yot.

(in whole) earnestness בכל הרצינות *adv* be-khol *(kh=k)* ha-retseenoot.

earnings 1. שכר (wage) *nm* sakhar (*+of:* sekhar); **2.** הכנסות (income) *pl* hakhnasot.

earphone אוזנייה *nf* oznee|yah/-yot (*+of:* -yat).

earpiece אפרכסת טלפון *nf* afarkes|et/-ot telefon.

earring עגיל *nm* 'ageel/-eem (*pl+of:* -ey).

(within) earshot בתחום שמיעה *adv* bee-t'khoom shmee'ah.

earth 1. קרקע (ground) *nf* karka'; **2.** כדור הארץ (globe) kadoor ha-arets.

earthen עשוי עפר *adj* 'asoo|y/-yah 'afar.

earthenware כלי חומר *nm pl* kley khomer.

earthly 1. מעשי (practical) *adj* ma'asee/-t; **2.** חומרי (material) *adj* khomree/-t.

(of no) earthly use חסר שימוש מעשי *adj* khas|ar/-rat sheemoosh ma'asee.

earthquake רעידת אדמה *nf* re'eed|at/-ot adamah.

earthworm תולעת אדמה *nf* tol|a'at/-'ey adamah.

ease 1. קלות *nf* kaloo|t/-yot; **2.** הקלה (relief) *nf* hakal|ah/-ot (*+of:* -at).

(at) ease בנוח *adv* be-no'akh.

(to) ease להקל *inf* lehakel; *pst* hekel; *pres* mekel; *fut* yakel.

easel 1. חצובה *nf* khatsoov|ah/-ot (*+of:* -at); **2.** כנת ציירים (painters') *nf* kan|at/-ot tsayareem.

easily 1. בקלות *adv* be-kaloot; **2.** בנקל (lightly) *adv* be-nakel.

Easter חג הפסחא הנוצרי *nm* khag ha-paskha ha-notsree.

Easter Sunday יום ראשון של פסחא נוצרית *nm* yom reeshon shel paskha notsreet.

eastern מזרחי *adj* meezrakhee/-t.

eastward 1. מזרחה *adv* meezrakhah; **2.** מזרחי (E.) *adj* meezrakhee/-t.

easy קל *adj* kal/-ah.

easy chair 1. כיסא־נוח *nm* kees|e/-'ot no'akh; **2.** כורסה *nf* koors|ah/-a'ot (*+of:* -at)

easy money רווחים קלים *nm pl* revakheem kaleem.

(at an) easy pace בקצב מתון *adv* be-ketsev matoon.

(within) easy reach קל להשגה *adj* kal/-ah le-hasagah.

easygoing 1. נוח לבריות *adj* no'akh/nokhah la- bree'ot; **2.** מתון (moderate) *adj* matoon/metoonah.

(to) eat לאכול *inf* le'ekhol; *pst* akhal; *pres* okhel; *fut* yokhal.

(to) eat away לכרסם *inf* lekharsem; *pst* keersem *(k=kh); pres* mekharsem; *fut* yekharsem.

(to) eat one's words לחזור בו מדבריו *inf* lakhazor bo mee-dvarav; *pst* khazar *etc; pres* khozer *etc; fut* yakhazor *etc.*

(to) eat someone's heart out לגרום עגמת נפש *inf* leegrom 'agmat nefesh; *pst* garam *etc; pres* gorem *etc; fut* yeegrom *etc.*

eatable 1. אכיל *adj* akheel/-ah; **2.** ראוי למאכל אדם (worth eating) *adj* ra'ooy/re'ooyah le-ma'akhal adam.

(to) eavesdrop להאזין שלא ברשות *inf* leha'azeen shelo bee-reshoot; *pst* he'ezeen *etc; pres* ma'azeen *etc; fut* ya'azeen *etc.*

ebb שפל *nm* shefel.

(at a low) ebb בשיא השפל *adv* be-see ha-shefel.

ebb and flow גיאות ושפל *nm* ge'oot va-shefel.

ebb tide שפל המים *nm* shefel ha-mayeem.

ebony עץ הובנה *nm* 'ets/'atsey hovneh.

eccentric 1. תמהוני *adj* teemhonee/-t; **2.** מוזר (queer) *adj* mooz|ar/-ah; **3.** אקסצנטרי *adj* ekstsentree/-t.

ecclesiastic 1. כנסייתי *adj* keneseeyatee/-t; **2.** כומר (clergyman) *nm* komer/kemar|eem (*pl+of:* komrey).

echelon 1. דרג (level) *nm* dereg/drag|eem (*pl+of:* dargey); **2.** דירוג (system) *nm* deroog/-eem (*pl+of:* -ey).

(to) echelon לדרג *inf* ledareg; *pst* deereg; *pres* medareg; *fut* yedareg.

echo 1. הד *nm* hed/-eem (*pl+of:* -ey); **2.** בת־קול (rumor) *nf* bat-kol.

(to) echo 1. לשמש הד (reflect) *inf* leshamesh hed; *pst* sheemesh hed; *pres* meshamesh hed; *fut* yeshamesh hed; **2.** להדהד (sound) *inf* lehadhed; *pst* heedhed; *pres* mehadhed; *fut* yehadhed.

eclectic 1. ברירני *adj* bareranee/-t; **2.** אקלקטי *adj* eklektee/-t.

eclipse 1. ליקוי חמה (sun) leekoo|y/-yey khamah; **2.** ליקוי ירח (moon) *nm* leekoo|y/-yey yare'akh.

(to) eclipse להעמיד בצל *inf* leha'ameed ba-tsel; *pst* he'emeed *etc; pres* ma'ameed *etc; fut* ya'ameed *etc.*

ecologic, -al 1. אקולוגי *adj* ekologee/-t; **2.** סביבתי (environmental) *adj* sveevatee/-t.

ecology 1. איכות הסביבה (environment) *nf* eykhoot ha-sveevah; **2.** אקולוגיה *nf* ekologeeyah.

economic כלכלי *adj* kalkalee/-t.

economical חסכוני *adj* kheskhonee/-t.

economics כלכלה *nf* kalkal|ah/-ot (*+of:* -at).

economist כלכלן *nmf* kalkelan/-eet.

(to) economize 1. לקמץ *inf* lekamets; *pst* keemets; *pres* mekamets; *fut* yekamets; **2.** לחסוך (save) *inf* lakhsokh; *pst* khasakh; *pres* khosekh; *fut* yakhsokh.

economy 1. כלכלה *nf* kalkal|ah/-ot (*+of:* -at); **2.** חיסכון (saving) *nm* kheesakhon/kheskhonot (*+of:* kheskhon); **3.** משק (entire system) *nm* meshek.

ecstasy 1. אקסטזה *nf* ekstaz|ah/-ot (*+of:* -at); **2.** התפעלות (excited admiration) *nf* heetpa'aloo|t/-yot.

ecumenical 1. אקומני *adj* ekoomenee/-t; **2.** כלל־נוצרי (all-Christian) *adj* klal-notsree/-t.

eczema 1. גרב *nm* garav; **2.** אקזמה *nf* ekzem|ah/-ot (*+of:* -at).

eddy 1. מערבולת *nm* me'arbolet; **2.** שיבולת (rapids) *nf* sheebolet.

edelweiss חלבונה אצילה *nf* khelbonah atseelah.

Eden עדן *nm* 'eden.
(Garden of) Eden גן עדן *nm* gan 'eden.
edge 1. חוד (point) *nm* khod/khood|eem (*pl+of:* -ey); **2.** קצה (end) *nm* katseh/ketsavot (*+of:* ketseh/katsvot).
(to) edge 1. לחדד *inf* lekhaded; *pst* kheeded; *pres* mekhaded; *fut* yekhaded; **2.** להתקדם צעד צעד (advance gradually) *inf* leheetkadem tsa'ad tsa'ad; *pst* heetkadem *etc*; *pres* meetkadem *etc*; *fut* yeetkadem *etc*.
edgewise לצד החוד le-tsad ha-khood.
edging חידוד *nm* kheedood/-eem (*pl+of:* -ey).
edgy מעוצבן *adj* me'ootsb|an/-enet.
edible אכיל *adj* akheel/-ah.
edifice בניין לתפארת *nm* beenyan/-eem le-teef'eret.
(to) edify 1. להבהיר *inf* lehavheer; *pst* heevheer; *pres* mavheer; *fut* yavheer; **2.** לאלף דעת (improve mind) *inf* le'alef da'at; *pst* eelef *etc*; *pres* me'alef *etc*; *fut* ye'alef *etc*.
edifying מאלף *adj* me'alef/-et.
(to) edit לערוך *inf* la'arokh; *pst* 'arakh; *pres* 'orekh; *fut* ya'arokh.
edition 1. מהדורה *nf* mahadoor|ah/-ot (*+of:* -at); **2.** הוצאה (publication) *nf* hotsa|'ah/-'ot (*+of:* -'at).
editor עורך *nmf* 'orekh/-et.
editor in chief, (chief-)editor עורך ראשי *nmf* 'orekh/-et rashee/-t.
editorial 1. מאמר מערכת *nm* ma'am|ar/-rey ma'arekhet; **2.** מאמר ראשי (leading article) *nm* ma'amar/-eem rashee/-yeem.
editorial staff 1. מערכת (as a body) *nf* ma'ar|ekhet/-akhot (*pl+of:* -khot); **2.** צוות המערכת (as personnel) *nm* tsevet ha-ma'arekhet.
(to) editorialize להגניב דעות בדיווח *inf* lehagneev de'ot be-deevoo'akh; *pst* heegneev *etc*; *pres* magneev *etc*; *fut* yagneev *etc*.
(to) educate לחנך *inf* lekhanekh; *pst* kheenekh; *pres* mekhanekh; *fut* yekhanekh.
educated guess ניחוש אינטליגנטי *nm* neekhoosh/-eem eenteleegentee/-yeem.
education חינוך *nm* kheenookh.
educational חינוכי *adj* kheenookhee/-yeem.
educational institution מוסד חינוכי *nm* mosad/-ot kheenookhee/-yeem.
educator מחנך *nmf* mekhan|ekh/-ekhet (*pl:* -kheem/-ot; *+of:* -ey).
eel צלופח *nm* tslof|akh/-akheem (*pl+of:* -khey).
eerie 1. מוזר (weird) *adj* moozar/-ah; **2.** מבהיל (frightening) *adj* mavheel/-ah.
(to) efface 1. למחות (obliterate) *inf* leemkhot; *pst* makhah; *pres* mokheh; *fut* yeemkheh; **2.** למחוק (erase) *inf* leemkhok; *pst* makhak; *pres* mokhek; *fut* yeemkhok; **3.** להצניע (play down) *inf* lehatsnee'a'; *pst* heetsnee'a'; *pres* matsnee'a'; *fut* yatsnee'a'.
(self) effacing מצטנע *adj* meetstan|e'a'/-a'at.
effect 1. תוצאה (result) *nf* tots|a'ah/-a'ot (*+of:* -'at); **2.** השלכה (repercussion) *nf* hashlakh|ah/-ot (*+of:* -at).
(to) effect 1. להגשים (accomplish) *inf* lehagsheem; *pst* heegsheem; *pres* magsheem; *fut* yagsheem; **2.** להפעיל (activate, produce) *inf* lehaf'eel; *pst* heef'eel; *pres* maf'eel; *fut* yaf'eel.
(to go into) effect לקבל תוקף *inf* lekabel tokef; *pst* keebel *etc*; *pres* mekabel *etc*; *fut* yekabel *etc*.
effective 1. יעיל (efficient) *adj* ya'eel/ye'eelah; **2.** מרשים (impressive) *adj* marsheem/-ah.
effectively 1. בפועל *adv* be-fo'al; **2.** ממש (actually) *adv* mamash.
effects חפצים *nm pl* khafatseem (*pl+of:* kheftsey).
effectual 1. יעיל *adj* ya'eel/ye'eelah; **2.** מרשים (impressive) *adj* marsheem/-ah.
(to) effectuate לבצע *inf* levatse'a'; *pst* beetsa' *(b=v)*; *pres* mevatse'a'; *fut* yevatsa'.
effeminate נשי *adj* nashee/-t.
effete 1. תשוש (worn out) *adj* tashoosh/teshooshah; **2.** בלה (shabby) *adj* bal|eh/-ah.
efficacious תכליתי *adj* takhleetee/-t.
efficacy תכליתיות *nf* takhleeteeyoot.
efficiency יעילות *nf* ye'eeloo|t/-yot.
efficient יעיל *adj* ya'eel/ye'eelah.
effigy 1. דמות *nf* demoo|t/-yot; **2.** תבליט (relief) *nm* tavleet/-eem (*pl+of:* -ey).
(to burn in) effigy להעלות צלם באש *inf* leha'alot tselem ba-esh; *pst* he'elah *etc*; *pres* ma'aleh *etc*; *fut* ya'aleh *etc*.
effort מאמץ *nm* ma'amats/-eem (*pl+of:* -ey).
effrontery חוצפה *nf* khootsp|ah/-ot (*+of:* -at).
effusive משתפך *adj* meeshtapekh/-et.
e.g. 1. כגון kegon; **2.** למשל (for instance) le-mashal; **3.** דוגמת (like) doogmat.
egg ביצה *nf* beyts|ah/-eem (*+of:* -at/-ey).
(hard-boiled) egg 1. ביצה שלוקה *nf* beyts|ah shlook|ah/-ot; **2.** ביצה קשה *[colloq.] nf* beyts|ah/-eem kash|ah/-ot.
(soft-boiled) egg 1. ביצה מגולגלת *nf* beyts|ah/-eem megoolg|elet/-alot; **2.** ביצה רכה *[colloq.] nf* beyts|ah/-eem rak|ah/-ot.
(scrambled) egg ביצה טרופה *nf* beyts|ah/-eem troof|ah/-ot.
eggbeater מקצף *nm* maktsef/-eem (*pl+of:* -ey).
eggnog חלמונה *nf* khelmonah.
eggplant חציל *nm* khatseel/-eem (*pl+of:* -ey).
eggshell קליפת ביצה *nf* kleep|at/-ot beyts|ah/-eem.
ego ה"אני" *nm* ha-"anee".
egocentric 1. מרוכז בעצמו (self-centered) *adj* merook|az/-ezet be-'atsm|o/-ah; **2.** אגוצנטרי *adj* egotsentree/-t.
egotism 1. אנוכיות *nf* anokheeyoot; **2.** אגואיזם *nm* ego'eezm/-eem.
Egypt מצרים *nf* meetsrayeem.
Egyptian 1. מצרי *adj* meetsree/-t; **2.** מצרי *nmf* meetsree/-yah (*pl:* -m/-yot).
eider ברווז ים *nm* barv|az/-ezey yam.
eight 1. שמונה (8) *num m* shmonah; **2.** שמונה (8) *num f* shmoneh; **3.** ח' *num* khet (8 in *Hebr. num. sys.*).
eight hundred 1. שמונה מאות (800) *num* shmoneh me'ot; **2.** ת"ח *num* tat (800 in *Hebr. num. sys.*).
eight thousand 1. שמונת אלפים (8,000) *num* shmonat alafeem; **2.** ח' אלפים *num* khet alafeem (8,000 in *Hebr. num. sys.*).

eighteen 1. שמונה־עשר *num m* shmonah-'asar; **2.** שמונה־עשרה *num f* shmoneh-'esreh; **3.** י״ח *num* yod-khet (18 in *Hebr. num. sys.*).

eighteenth 1. השמונה־עשר *adj m* ha-shmonah-'asar; **2.** השמונה־עשרה *adj f* ha-shmoneh-'esreh; **3.** הי״ח *adj* ha-yod-khet (18th in *Hebr. num. sys.*).

eighth 1. שמיני (8th) *adj* shmeenee/-t; **2.** שמינית (1/8) *num f* shmeenee|t/-yot; **3.** ח׳ *adj* khet (8th in *Hebr. num. sys.*).

eightieth 1. השמונים *ord num* ha-shmoneem; **2.** הפ׳ *adj* ha-peh (80th in *Hebr. num. sys.*).

eighty 1. שמונים (80) *num* shmoneem; **2.** פ׳ *num* peh (80 in *Hebr. num. sys.*).

eighty-first 1. השמונים ואחד/ואחת *adj* ha-shmoneem ve-ekhad/ve-akhat *(m/f)*; **2.** הפ״א *adj* ha-peh-alef (81th in *Hebr. num. sys.*).

eighty-second 1. השמונים ושניים/ושתיים *adj num* ha-shmoneem oo-shnayeem/oo-shtayeem *(m/f)*; **2.** הפ״ב *adj* ha-peh-bet (82nd in *Hebr. num. sys.*).

eighty-third 1. השמונים ושלושה/ושלוש *ord num* ha-shmoneem oo-shloshah/ve-shalosh *(m/f)*; **2.** הפ״ג *adj* ha-peh-geemal (83rd in *Hebr. num. sys.*).

eighty-three 1. שמונים ושלושה/ושלוש *num* shmoneem oo-shloshah/ve-shalosh *(m/f)*; **2.** פ״ג *num* peh-geemal (83 in *Hebr. num. sys.*).

eighty-two 1. שמונים ושניים/ושתיים *num* shmoneem oo-shnayeem/oo-shtayeem *(m/f)*; **2.** פ״ב *num* peh-bet (82 in *Hebr. num. sys.*).

either 1. או ש־ *conj* o she-; **2.** גם לא (also not) *adv* gam lo.

(nor I) either אף אני לא af anee lo.

(in) either case בכל מקרה *adv* be-khol *(kh=k)* meekreh.

either of the two אחת מהשתיים *conj f* akhat me-ha-shtayeem.

(to) ejaculate 1. לפלוט *inf* leeflot; *pst* palat *(p=f)*; *pres* polet; *fut* yeeflot; **2.** להפליט זרע (sperm) *inf* lehafleet zera'; *pst* heefleet *etc*; *pres* mafleet *etc*; *fut* yafleet *etc*.

(to) eject 1. להפליט (oust) *inf* lehafleet; *pst* heefleet; *pres* mafleet; *fut* yafleet; **2.** לגרש (expel) *inf* legaresh; *pst* geresh; *pres* megaresh; *fut* yegaresh.

ejection 1. פליטה *nf* pleet|ah/-ot (*+of:* -at); **2.** גירוש (expulsion) *nm* geroosh/-eem (*pl+of:* -ey).

ejection seat כיסא חירום במטוס *nm* kees|e/-'ot kheroom be-matos.

elaborate 1. מדוקדק (meticulous) *adj* medookd|ak/-eket; **2.** משוכלל (sophisticated) *adj* meshookh-l|al/-elet.

(to) elaborate 1. לשכלל (perfect) *inf* leshakhlel; *pst* sheekhlel; *pres* meshakhlel; *fut* yeshakhlel; **2.** להשלים (complete) *inf* lehashleem; *pst* heeshleem; *pres* mashleem; *fut* yashleem; **3.** להרחיב את הדיבור (enlarge upon) *inf* leharkheev et ha-deeboor; *pst* heerkheev *etc*; *pres* markheev *etc*; *fut* yarkheev *etc*.

(to) elapse 1. לחלוף *inf* lakhlof; *pst* khalaf; *pres* kholef; *fut* yakhlof; **2.** לעבור (go by) *inf* la'avor; *pst* 'avar; *pres* 'over; *fut* ya'avor.

elastic גמיש *adj* gameesh/gemeeshah.

elasticity גמישות *nf* gemeeshoo|t/-yot.

elated 1. שמח *adj* same'akh/smekhah; **2.** מרומם (uplifted) *adj* merom|am/-emet.

elbow מרפק *nm* marpek/-eem (*pl+of:* -ey).

(to) elbow one's way through להבקיע דרך במרפקים *inf* lehavkee'a' derekh be-marpekeem; *pst* heevkee'a' *etc*; *pres* mavkee'a' *etc*; *fut* yavkee'a' *etc*.

elbow patch טלאי מרפק *nm* tla|y/-'ey marpek.

elbow rest מסעד זרוע *nm* mees'ad/-ey zro'a'.

(within) elbow reach בהישג יד *adv* be-heseg yad.

elbow room 1. מקום להתרווח *nm* makom leheetrave'akh; **2.** מרחב תימרון (manoeuvering space) *nm* merkhav/-ey teemroon.

elder 1. קשיש מ־ *adj* kasheesh/kesheeshah mee-; **2.** בכיר (senior) *adj* bakheer/bekheerah.

elder statesman מדינאי בכיר *nm* medeena|y/-'eem bakheer/bekheereem.

elderly מזדקן *adj* meezdaken/-et.

(our) elders אבותינו *nm pl* avoteynoo.

eldest בכיר ביותר *adj* bakheer be-yoter.

elect נבחר *nmf* neevkh|ar/-eret.

(to) elect 1. לבחור *inf* leevkhor; *pst* bakhar *(b=v)*; *pres* bokher; *fut* yeevkhar; **2.** לברור (select) *inf* leevror; *pst* barar *(b=v)*; *pres* borer; *fut* yeevror.

election 1. בחירה (choice) *nf* bekheer|ah/-ot (*+of:* -at); **2.** בחירות (elections) *nf pl* bekheerot.

elective מקצוע בחירה *nm* meeekts|o|'a'/'ot bekheerah.

elector בוחר *nm* bokh|er/-areem (*pl+of:* -arey).

electoral 1. של בחירות *adj* shel bekheerot; **2.** של בוחרים (of electorate) shel bokhareem.

electorate ציבור בוחרים *nm* tseeboor bokhareem.

electric חשמלי *adj* khashmalee/-t.

electric eye עין חשמלית *nf* 'ayeen khashmaleet.

electric fan מאוורר *nm* me'avrer/-eem (*pl+of:* -ey).

electric light תאורה חשמלית *nf* te'oorah khashmaleet.

electric meter שעון חשמל *nm* she'on/-ey khashmal.

electric percolator מסנן־קפה חשמלי *nm* masnen/-ey kafeh khashmalee/-yeem.

electric shaver מגלח חשמלי *nm* magle|'akh/-kheem khashmalee/-yeem.

electric storm סופת חשמל *nf* soof|at/-ot khashmal.

electric tape סרט בידוד *nm* seret/seertey beedood.

electrical חשמלי *adj* khashmalee/-t.

electrical engineer מהנדס חשמל *nmf* mehandes/-et (*pl:* -ey/-ot) khashmal.

electrical engineering הנדסת חשמל *nf* handasat khashmal.

electrician חשמלאי *nm* khashmal|ay/-a'eem (*pl+of:* -a'ey).

electricity חשמל khashmal.

electrification 1. חשמול *nm* kheeshmool/-eem (*pl+of:* -ey); **2.** אלקטריפיקאציה *nf* elektreefeekatseeyah.

(to) electrify לחשמל *inf* lekhashmel; *pst* kheeshmel; *pres* mekhashmel; *fut* yekhashmel.

electrocardiograph אלקטרו־קרדיוגרף *nm* elektro-kardyograf/-eem.

(to) electrocute לחשמל למוות *inf* lekhashmel la-mavet; *pst* kheeshmel *etc*; *pres* mekhashmel *etc*; *fut* yekhashmel *etc*.

electrode אלקטרודה *nf* elektrod|ah/-ot (+*of*: -at).

electrolysis אלקטרוליזה *nf* elektroleez|ah/-ot (+*of*: -at).

electromagnetic אלקטרו־מגנטי *adj* elektro-magnetee/-t

electron אלקטרון *nm* elektron/-eem (*pl+of*: -ey).

electronic אלקטרוני *adj* elektronee/-t.

electronics אלקטרוניקה *nf* elektroneekah.

electronics specialist אלקטרונאי *nm* elektron|ay/-a'eem (*pl+of*: -a'ey).

(to) electroplate לצפות במתכת *inf* letsapot be-matekhet; *pst* tseepah *etc*; *pres* metsapeh *etc*; *fut* yetsapeh *etc*.

electrostatic אלקטרו־סטאטי *adj* elektro-statee/-t.

elegance 1. הידור *nm* heedoor; **2.** אלגנטיות *nf* eleganteeyoot.

elegant 1. מהודר *adj* mehood|ar/-eret; **2.** אלגנטי *adj* elegantee/-t.

element 1. אלמנט *nm* element/-eem; **2.** יסוד (constituent part) *nm* yesod/-ot.

elemental, elementary 1. יסודי *adj* yesodee/-t; **2.** אלמנטרי *adj* elementaree/-t.

elementary school בית ספר יסודי *nm* bet/batey sefer yesodee/-yeem.

elephant פיל *nm* peel/-eem (*pl+of*: -ey).

(to) elevate 1. להעלות (lift) *inf* leha'alot; *pst* he'elah; *pres* ma'aleh; *fut* ya'aleh; **2.** להעלות במעמד (raise) *inf* leha'alot be-ma'amad; *pst* he'elah *etc*; *pres* ma'aleh *etc*; *fut* ya'aleh *etc*; **3.** להגביה (heighten) *inf* lehagbeeha; *pst* heegbeeha; *pres* magbeeha; *fut* yagbeeha.

elevation 1. רמה *nf* ram|ah/-ot (+*of*: -at); **2.** הגבהה (lift) *nf* hagba|hah/-hot (+*of*: -hat).

elevator מעלית *nf* ma'alee|t/-yot.

(grain) elevator ממגורה *nf* mamgoor|ah/-ot (+*of*: -at).

eleven 1. אחד־עשר *num m* akhad-'asar; **2.** אחת־עשרה *num f* akhat-'esreh; **3.** י״א *num* yod-alef (11 in *Hebr. num. sys.*).

eleven hundred אלף ומאה (thousand and one hundred) *num* elef oo-me'ah.

eleventh 1. האחד־עשר *ord num m* ha-akhad-'asar; **2.** האחת־עשרה *ord num f* ha-akhat-'esreh; **3.** הי״א *adj* ha-yod-alef (11th in *Hebr. num. sys.*).

elf שדון *nm* shedon/-eem (*pl+of*: -ey).

(to) elicit 1. לגלות *inf* legalot; *pst* geelah; *pres* megaleh; *fut* yegaleh; **2.** להפיק (extract) *inf* lehafeek; *pst* hefeek; *pres* mefeek; *fut* yafeek.

(to) elicit admiration לעורר התפעלות *inf* le'orer heetpa'aloot; *pst* 'orer *etc*; *pres* me'orer *etc*; *fut* ye'orer *etc*.

(to) elicit applause לקצור תשואות *inf* leektsor teshoo'ot; *pst* katsar *etc*; *pres* kotser *etc*; *fut* yeektsor *etc*.

eligible זכאי להיבחר *adj* zak|ay/-a'eet le-heebakher.

(to) eliminate לסלק *inf* lesalek; *pst* seelek; *pres* mesalek; *fut* yesalek.

elimination סילוק *nm* seelook/-eem (*pl+of*: -ey).

elite עילית *nf* 'eeleet/-ot (+*of*: -at).

elk דישון *nm* deeshon/-eem (*pl+of*: -ey).

elliptical אליפטי *adj* eleeptee/-t.

elm בוקיצה *nf* bookeets|ah/-ot (+*of*: -at).

(to) elope לברוח עם בן/בת זוג *inf* leevro'akh 'eem ben/bat zoog; *pst* barakh (*b=v*); *pres* bore'akh; *fut* yeevrakh.

elopement בריחה עם בן/בת זוג *nf* breekhah 'eem ben/bat zoog.

eloquence אמנות הדיבור *nf* omanoot ha-deeboor.

eloquent אמן הדיבור *adj* & *nmf* oman/-eet ha-deeboor.

else 1. אחרת akheret; **2.** ולא (otherwise) va-lo.

(nobody) else אף אחד אחר af ekhad/akhat akher/-et (*m/f*).

(nothing) else שום דבר חוץ מ־ shoom davar khoots mee-.

(or) else שאם לא כן she-'eem lo khen (*kh=k*).

(somebody) else, someone else מישהו אחר *nmf* meeshe|hoo/-hee akher/-et.

(what) else? ?וכי יש ברירה ve-khee yesh breyrah?.

elsewhere במקום אחר be-makom akher.

(to) elucidate 1. לברר *inf* levarer; *pst* berer (*b=v*); *pres* mevarer; *fut* yevarer; **2.** להבהיר (clear) *inf* lehavheer; *pst* heevheer; *pres* mavheer; *fut* yavheer.

elucidation הבהרה *nf* havhar|ah/-ot (+*of*: -at).

(to) elude 1. להתחמק (dodge) *inf* leheetkhamek; *pst* heetkhamek; *pres* meetkhamek; *fut* yeetkhamek; **2.** להשתמט (evade) *inf* leheeshtamet; *pst* heeshtamet; *pres* meeshtamet; *fut* yeeshtamet; **3.** להימנע (refrain) *inf* leheemana'; *pst* & *pres* neemna'; *fut* yeemana'.

elusive 1. חמקני *adj* khamkanee/-t; **2.** חמקמק (evasive) *adj* khamakmak/-ah.

emaciated תשוש *adj* tashoosh/teshooshah.

(to) emanate לנבוע *inf* leenbo'a'; *pst* nava' (*v=b*); *pres* nove'a'; *fut* yeenba'.

emanation נביעה *nf* nevee|'ah/-'ot (+*of*: -'at).

(to) emancipate 1. לשחרר *inf* leshakhrer; *pst* sheekhrer; *pres* meshakhrer; *fut* yeshakhrer; **2.** להשוות בזכויות (enfranchize) *inf* lehashvot bee-zekhooyot; *pst* heeshvah *etc*; *pres* mashveh *etc*; *fut* yashveh *etc*.

emancipation 1. שחרור (liberation) *nm* sheekhroor; **2.** שיווי זכויות (equal rights) *nm* sheevooy zekhooyot.

(to) embalm לחנוט *inf* lakhnot; *pst* khanat; *pres* khonet; *fut* yakhnot.

embankment סוללה *nf* solel|ah/-ot (+*of*: -at).

embargo 1. הסגר *nm* hesger/-eem (+*of*: -ey); **2.** אמברגו *nm* embargo.

(to put an) embargo on 1. להטיל הסגר (impose quarantine) *inf* lehateel hesger; *pst* heteel *etc*; *pres* meteel *etc*; *fut* yateel *etc*; **2.** להטיל אמברגו (impose embargo) *inf* lehateel embargo; *pst* heteel *etc*; *pres* meteel *etc*; *fut* yateel *etc*.

(to) embark 1. לעלות לסיפון (personally) *vi inf* la'alot le-seepoon; *pst* 'alah *etc*; *pres* 'oleh *etc*; *fut* ya'aleh *etc*; **2.** להטעין (goods) *vt inf* lehat'een; *pst* heet'een; *pres* mat'een; *fut* yat'een.

(to) embark upon לפתוח ב־ *inf* leefto'akh be-; *pst* patakh be-; *pres* pote'akh be-; *fut* yeeftakh be-.

embarkation 1. עלייה לסיפון (of passengers) *nf* 'aleelyah/-yot le-seepoon; **2.** הטענה (of goods) *nf* hat'an|ah/-ot (+*of:* -at).

(to) embarrass להביך *inf* lehaveekh; *pst* heveekh; *pres* meveekh; *fut* yaveekh.

(financially) embarrassed בקשיים כספיים *adv* bee-k'shayeem kaspeeyeem.

embarrasing מביך *adj* meveekh/-ah.

embarrassment מבוכה *nf* mevookh|ah/-ot (+*of:* -at).

embassy שגרירות *nf* shagreeroo|t/-yot.

(to) embellish 1. לייפות (beautify) *inf* leyapot; *pst* yeepah; *pres* meyapeh; *fut* yeyapeh; **2.** לקשט (adorn) *inf* lekashet; *pst* keeshet; *pres* mekashet; *fut* yekashet.

embers אודים *nm pl* ood|eem (*pl+of:* -ey).

(to) embezzle למעול *inf* leem'ol; *pst* ma'al; *pres* mo'el; *fut* yeem'al.

embezzlement מעילה *nf* me'eel|ah/-ot (+*of:* -at).

(to) embitter 1. למרר *inf* lemarer; *pst* merer; *pres* memarer; *fut* yemarer; **2.** להחריף (aggravate) *inf* lehakhreef; *pst* hekhreef; *pres* makhreef; *fut* yakhreef.

emblem סמל *nm* semel/smaleem (*pl+of:* seemley).

(to) embody 1. לגלם (incarnate) *inf* legalem; *pst* geelem; *pres* megalem; *fut* yegalem; **2.** להכליל (incorporate) *inf* lehakhleel; *pst* heekhleel; *pres* makhleel; *fut* yakhleel.

(to)embosom לאמץ ללב *inf* le'amets la-lev; *pst* eemets *etc*; *pres* me'amets *etc*; *fut* ye'amets *etc*.

(to) emboss להבליט *inf* lehavleet; *pst* heevleet; *pres* mavleet; *fut* yavleet.

embrace חיבוק *nm* kheebook/-eem (*pl+of:* -ey).

(to) embrace לחבק *inf* lekhabek; *pst* kheebek; *pres* mekhabek; *fut* yekhabek.

(to) embroider לרקום *inf* leerkom; *pst* rakam; *pres* rokem; *fut* yeerkom.

embroidery 1. רקימה (work) *nf* rekeem|ah/-ot (+*of:* -at); **2.** ריקמה (product) *nf* reekmah/rekamot (+*of:* reekm|at/-ot).

(to) embroil לסבך *inf* lesabekh; *pst* seebekh; *pres* mesabekh; *fut* yesabekh.

embryo עובר *nm* 'oob|ar/-areem (*pl+of:* -rey).

emerald 1. אזמרגד (smaragd) *nm* eezmaragd/-eem (*pl+of:* -ey); **2.** ברקת (agate) *nf* bareket; **3.** ירוק בהיר (color) *adj* yarok/yerookah baheer/beheerah.

(to) emerge 1. להתגלות (turn up) *inf* leheetgalot; *pst* heetgalah; *pres* meetgaleh; *fut* yeetgaleh; **2.** לצוף (pop up) *inf* latsoof; *pst & pres* tsaf; *fut* yatsoof.

emergency מצב חירום *nm* mats|av/-vey kheroom.

emergency landing נחיתת חירום *nf* nekheet|at/-ot kheroom.

Emergency Regulations תקנות לשעת חירום *nf pl* takanot lee-she'at kheroom.

emigrant 1. מהגר *nmf* mehag|er/-eret (*pl:* -reem/-rot; +*of:* -rey); **2.** יורד (from Israel) *nmf* yored/-et (*pl:* yord|eem; +*of:* -ey).

(to) emigrate 1. להגר *inf* lehager; *pst* heeger; *pres* mehager; *fut* yehager; **2.** לרדת (from Israel) *v inf* laredet; *pst* yarad; *pres* yored; *fut* yered.

emigration 1. הגירה *nf* hageer|ah/-ot (+*of:* -at); **2.** ירידה (from Israel) *nf* yereed|ah/-ot (+*of:* -at).

eminence רוממות *nf* romemoo|t/-yot.

eminent נודע *adj* noda'/-at.

(to) emit להפיק *inf* lehafeek; *pst* hefeek; *pres* mefeek; *fut* yafeek.

emotion התרגשות *nf* heetragshoo|t/-yot.

emotional רגשי *adj* reegshee/-t.

empathy אמפתיה *nf* empat|yah/-yot (+*of:* -yat).

emperor קיסר *nm* kesar/-eem (*pl+of:* -ey).

emphasis הדגשה *nf* hadgash|ah/-ot (+*of:* -at).

(to) emphasize להדגיש *inf* lehadgeesh; *pst* heedgeesh; *pres* madgeesh; *fut* yadgeesh.

emphatic 1. תקיף (forceful) *adj* takeef/-ah; **2.** מודגש (stressed) moodg|ash/-eshet.

emphatically בהדגשה *adv* be-hadgashah.

emphysema 1. נפחת *nf* napakhat; **2.** התנפחות (swelling) *nf* heetnapkhoo|t/-yot.

empire קיסרות *nf* kesaroo|t/-yot.

empirical 1. אמפירי *adj* empeeree/-t; **2.** נסיוני (experimental) *adj* neesyonee/-t.

(to) employ 1. להעסיק *inf* leha'aseek; *pst* he'eseek; *pres* ma'aseek; *fut* ya'aseek; **2.** להשתמש (use) *inf* leheeshtamesh; *pst* heeshtamesh; *pres* meesahtmesh; *fut* yeeshtamesh.

(to be in one's) employ להיות בשירותו של מישהו *inf* leehyot be-sheroot|o/-ah shel meeshe|hoo/-hee (*m/f*); *pst* hayah *etc*; *pres* heeno *etc*; *fut* yeehyeh *etc*.

employee שכיר *nmf* sakheer/sekheer|ah (*pl:* -eem/-ot; +*of:* -ey).

employer מעסיק *nm* ma'aseek/-eem (*pl+of:* -ey).

employment תעסוקה *nf* ta'asook|ah/-ot (+*of:* -at).

(to) empower 1. למלא את יד *inf* lemale et yad; *pst* meele *etc*; *pres* memale *etc*; *fut* yemale *etc*; **2.** לייפות כוח (empower) *inf* leyapot ko'akh; *pst* yeepah *etc*; *pres* meyapeh *etc*; *fut* yeyapeh *etc*.

empress קיסרית *nf* keysaree|t/-yot.

emptiness ריקנות *nf* reykanoo|t/-yot.

empty ריק *adj* reyk/-ah.

(to) empty 1. להריק *inf* lehareek; *pst* hereek; *pres* mereek; *fut* yareek; **2.** לרוקן (discharge) *inf* leroken; *pst* roken; *pres* meroken; *fut* yeroken

empty-handed בידיים ריקות *adv* be-yadayeem reykot.

empty-headed בור *nmf & adj* boor/-ah.

(to) emulate 1. ללכת בדרכי (follow) *inf* lalekhet be-darkhey; *pst* halakh *etc*; *pres* holekh *etc*; *fut* yelekh *etc*; **2.** לחקות בנאמנות (copy) *inf* lekhakot be-ne'emanoot; *pst* kheekah *etc*; *pres* mekhakeh *etc*; *fut* yekhakeh *etc*.

(to) enable לאפשר *inf* le'afsher; *pst* eefsher; *pres* me'afsher; *fut* ye'afsher.

(to) enact 1. לחוקק (legislate) *inf* lekhokek; *pst* khokek; *pres* mekhokek; *fut* yekhokek; **2.** להפעיל חוק (apply law) *inf* lehaf'eel khok; *pst* heef'eel khok; *pres* maf'eel khok; *fut* yaf'eel khok.

enamel אמייל *nm* emayl/-eem.

(to) enamor לעורר אהבה *inf* le'orer ahavah; *pst* 'orer *etc*; *pres* me'orer *etc*; *fut* ye'orer *etc*.

(to be) enamored להתאהב ב־ *inf* leheet'ahev be-; *pst* heet'ahev be-; *pres* meet'ahev be-; *fut* yeet'ahev be-.

enamored of מאוהב ב־ *adj* me'oo|hav/-hevet be-.

(to) encamp לתקוע אוהל *inf* leetko'a' ohel/ohaleem; *pst* taka' *etc*; *pres* toke'a' *etc*; *fut* yeetka' *etc*.

encampment מאהל *nm* ma'ahal/-eem (*pl+of*: -ey).

(to) enchant 1. להקסים *inf* lehakseem; *pst* heekseem; *pres* makseem; *fut* yakseem; **2.** לכשף (bewitch) *inf* lekhashef; *pst* keeshef *(k=kh)*; *pres* mekhashef; *fut* yekhashef.

enchanter קוסם *nm* kos|em/-meem (*pl+of*: -mey).

enchantment קסם *nm* kes|em/-ameem (*pl+of*: keesmey).

enchantress 1. קוסמת *nf* kos|emet/-mot; **2.** מקסימה (charming) *adj f* makseem|ah/-ot (*+of*: -at).

(to) encircle 1. לכתר *inf* lekhater; *pst* keeter *(k=kh)*; *pres* mekhater; *fut* yekhater; **2.** להקיף (surround) *inf* lehakeef; *pst* heekeef; *pres* makeef; *fut* yakeef

(to) enclose 1. לצרף *inf* letsaref; *pst* tseref; *pres* metsaref; *fut* yetsaref; **2.** לסגור מסביב על (close in on) *inf* leesgor mee-saveev 'al; *pst* sagar *etc*; *pres* soger *etc*; *fut* yeesgor *etc*.

enclosure 1. מתחם (ground) *nm* meetkham/-eem (*pl+of*: -ey); **2.** לוט (to a letter) *adj* loot/-ah.

(to) encompass 1. להקיף (surround) *inf* lehakeef; *pst* heekeef; *pres* makeef; *fut* yakeef; **2.** לכלול (comprise) *inf* leekhlol; *pst* kalal *(k=kh)*; *pres* kolel; *fut* yeekhlol.

encore הדרן *nm* hadran/-eem (*pl+of*: -ey).

encounter 1. מפגש *nm* meefg|ash/-asheem (*pl+of*: -eshey); **2.** היתקלות (bumping into) *nf* heetak-loo|t/-yot.

(to) encounter 1. לפגוש *inf* leefgosh; *pst* pagash *(p=f)*; *pres* pogesh; *fut* yeefgosh; **2.** להיתקל (bump into) *inf* leheetakel; *pst & pres* neetkal; *fut* yeetakel.

(to) encourage לעודד *inf* le'oded; *pst* 'oded; *pres* me'oded; *fut* ye'oded.

encouragement עידוד *nm* 'eedood/-eem (*pl+of*: -ey).

(to) encroach, (to) encroach upon 1. להסיג גבול (trespass) *inf* lehaseeg gvool; *pst* heeseeg *etc*; *pres* maseeg *etc*; *fut* yaseeg *etc*; **2.** לפלוש (invade, squat) *inf* leeflosh; *pst* palash *(p=f)*; *pres* polesh; *fut* yeeflosh.

(to) encumber להכביד *inf* lehakhbeed; *pst* heekhbeed; *pres* makhbeed; *fut* yakhbeed.

encyclopedia אנציקלופדיה *nf* entseeklopedl|yah/-yot (*+of*: -yat).

end 1. סוף *nm* sof/-eem (*pl+of*: -ey); **2.** סיום (termination) *nm* seeyoom/-eem (*pl+of*: -ey).

(on) end ללא הפסק *adv* le-lo hefsek.

(to) end לסיים *inf* lesayem; *pst* seeyem; *pres* mesayem; *fut* yesayem.

(to put an) end לשים קץ *inf* laseem kets; *pst & pres* sam kets; *fut* yaseem kets.

(no) end of things אין קץ לדברים eyn kets lee-dvareem.

(to) endanger לסכן *inf* lesaken; *pst* seeken; *pres* mesaken; *fut* yesaken.

(to) endear לחבב על־ *inf* lekhabev 'al; *pst* kheebev 'al; *pres* mekhabev 'al; *fut* yekhabev 'al.

(to) endear oneself להתחבב *inf* leheetkhabev; *pst* heetkhabev; *pres* meetkhabev; *fut* yeetkhabev.

endeavor מאמץ *nm* ma'amats/-eem (*pl+of*: -ey).

(to) endeavor 1. להשתדל *inf* leheeshtadel; *pst* heeshtadel; *pres* meeshtadel; *fut* yeeshtadel; **2.** להתאמץ (exert oneself) *inf* leheet'amets; *pst* heet'amets; *pres* meet'amets; *fut* yeet'amets.

endemic 1. מוגבל למקום (in area) *adj* moog-b|al/-elet le-makom; **2.** מוגבל לסוג אוכלוסייה (in sector of population) *adj* moogb|al/-elet le-soog ookhlooseeyah.

ending סיום *nm* seeyoom/-eem (*pl+of*: -ey).

endless ללא קץ *adv* le-lo kets.

(to) endorse 1. להסב (bill) *inf* lehasev; *pst* hesev; *pres* mesev; *fut* yasev; **2.** לתמוך (support) *inf* leetmokh; *pst* tamakh; *pres* tomekh; *fut* yeetmokh.

endorsement 1. הסבה (bill) *nf* hasav|ah/-ot (*+of*: -at); **2.** תמיכה (support) *nf* temeekhah/-ot (*+of*: -at).

endorser מסב *nmf* mesev/meseeb|ah (*b=v*; *pl*: -eem/-ot; *+of*: -ey).

(to) endow להעניק *inf* leha'aneek; *pst* he|'eneek; *pres* ma'aneek; *fut* ya'aneek.

endowment מענק *nm* ma'an|ak/-akeem (*pl+of*: -nkey).

(odds and) ends 1. שיריים *nm pl* sheerayeem; **2.** שונות (miscellaneous) *nf pl* shonot.

endurance כוח סבל *nm* ko'akh sevel.

(to) endure 1. לסבול (suffer) *inf* leesbol; *pst* saval *(v=b)*; *pres* sovel; *fut* yeesbol; **2.** לעמוד בסבל (hold out) *inf* la'amod ba-sevel; *pst* 'amad *etc*; *pres* 'omed *etc*; *fut* ya'amod *etc*.

enema חוקן *nm* khok|en/-aneem (*pl+of*: -ney).

enemy 1. אויב *nm* oyev/oyveem (*pl+of*: oyvey); **2.** שונא (foe) *nm* son|e/-'eem (*pl+of*: -'ey).

enemy alien נתין ארץ אויב *nmf* neteen/-at erets oyev.

energetic נמרץ *adj* neemr|ats/-etset.

energy 1. מרץ *nm* merets; **2.** אנרגיה *nf* energ|yah/-yot (*+of*: -yat).

(to) enervate להחליש *inf* lehakhleesh; *pst* hekhleesh; *pres* makhleesh; *fut* yakhleesh.

(to) enforce לאכוף *inf* le'ekhof; *pst* akhaf; *pres* okhef; *fut* ye'ekhof.

enforce law and order להשליט חוק וסדר *inf* lehashleet khok va-seder; *pst* heeshleet *etc*; *pres* mashleet *etc*; *fut* yashleet *etc*.

enforcement אכיפה *nf* akheef|ah/-ot (*+of*: -at).

(to) engage לעסוק ב־ *inf* la'asok be-; *pst* 'asak be-; *pres* 'osek be-; *fut* ya'asok be-.

(to) engage in battle להיכנס בקרב *inf* leheekanes bee-krav; *pst & pres* neekhnas *(kh=k) etc*; *fut* yeekanes *etc*.

(to) engage oneself to do לקבל על עצמו לעשות *inf* lekabel 'al 'atsmo la'asot; *pst* keebel *etc*; *pres* mekabel *etc*; *fut* yekabel *etc*.

engaged תפוס (telephone line) *adj* tafoos/tfoosah.

engaged in something עסוק במשהו *adj* 'asook/-ah be-mashehoo.

engaged to be married מאורס *adj* me'oor|as/-eset.

engagement אירוסים (betrothal) *nm pl* eyroos|eem (*pl+of:* -ey)

(previous) engagement התחייבות קודמת *nf* heetkhayvoo|t/-yot kod|emet/-mot.

(to) engender לגרום *inf* leegrom; *pst* garam; *pres* gorem; *fut* yeegrom.

engine מנוע *nm* mano'a'/meno|'eem (*pl+of:* -'ey).

engineer 1. מהנדס (in the continental sense, i.e. university trained) *nmf* mehandes/-et (*pl:* -eem/-ot; *pl+of:* -ey); **2.** הנדסאי (secondary school trained) *nmf* handas|ay/-a'eet (*pl+of:* -a'ey); **3.** מכונאי (operating an engine, locomotive *etc*) *nm* mekhon|ay/-a'eem (*pl+of:* -a'ey).

(to) engineer לתכנן *inf* letakhnen; *pst* teekhnen; *pres* metakhnen; *fut* yetakhnen.

engineering הנדסה *nf* handas|ah/-ot (*+of:* -at).

England אנגליה *nf* angleeyah.

English 1. אנגלי *adj* anglee/-t; **2.** אנגלית (language) *nf* angleet.

(the) English האנגלים *nm pl* ha-angleem.

Englishman, -woman אנגלי, ־יה *nmf* anglee/-yah.

(to) engrave לחרות *inf* lakhrot; *pst* kharat; *pres* khoret; *fut* yakhrot.

engraving חריתה *nf* khareet|ah/-ot (*+of:* -at).

(wood) engraving חריטה *nf* khareet|ah/-ot (*+of:* -at).

(to) engross לשקע כל כולו *inf* leshake'a' kol koolo; *pst* sheeka' *etc*; *pres* meshake'a' *etc*; *fut* yeshaka' *etc*

engrossed שקוע כל כולו *adj* shakoo'a'/shekoo'ah kol kool|o/-ah.

(to) engulf להציף *inf* lehatseef; *pst* hetseef; *pres* metseef; *fut* yatseef.

(to) enhance להגביר *inf* lehagbeer; *pst* heegbeer; *pres* magbeer; *fut* yagbeer.

enigma חידה *nf* kheed|ah/-ot (*+of:* -at).

(to) enjoin לחייב *inf* lekhayev; *pst* kheeyev; *pres* mekhayev; *fut* yekhayev.

(to) enjoin from לאסור *inf* le'esor; *pst* asar; *pres* oser; *fut* ye'esor.

(to) enjoy, (to) enjoy oneself ליהנות *inf* lehanot; *pst* nehenah; *pres* neheneh; *fut* yehaneh.

(to) enjoy the use of להיעזר ב־ *inf* lehe'azer be-; *pst & pres* ne'ezar be-; *fut* ye'azer be-.

enjoyable מהנה *adj* mehan|eh/-ah.

enjoyment הנאה *nf* hana|'ah/-'ot (*+of:* -'at).

(to) enlarge להגדיל *inf* lehagdeel; *pst* heegdeel; *pres* magdeel; *fut* yagdeel.

(to) enlarge upon להרחיב את הדיבור על *inf* leharkheev et ha-deeboor al; *pst* heerkheev *etc*; *pres* markheev *etc*; *fut* yarkheev *etc.*

enlargement הגדלה *nf* hagdal|ah/-ot (*+of:* -at).

(to) enlighten להשכיל מישהו להבין *inf* lehaskeel meeshe|hoo/-hee lehaveen; *pst* heeskeel *etc*; *pres* maskeel *etc*; *fut* yaskeel *etc.*

(to) enlist לגייס *inf* legayes; *pst* geeyes; *pres* megayes; *fut* yegayes.

enlistment התגייסות *nf* heetgaysoo|t/-yot.

(to) enliven להכניס רוח חיים *inf* lehakhnees roo'akh khayeem; *pst* heekhnees *etc*; *pres* makhnees *etc*; *fut* yakhnees *etc.*

enmity 1. איבה *nf* eyv|ah/-ot (*+of:* -at); **2.** עוינות (hostility) *f* 'oynoo|t/-yot.

(to) ennoble 1. לכבד *inf* lekhabed; *pst* keebed (*k=kh*); *pres* mekhabed; *fut* yekhabed; **2.** לרומם (raise) *inf* leromem; *pst* romem; *pres* meromem; *fut* yeromem.

enormous עצום *adj* 'atsoom/-ah.

enough 1. די *adv* day; **2.** מספיק (sufficient) *adj* masp|eek/-eket

(that is) enough! ! די, מספיק *interj* day, maspeek!

(to) enquire 1. לשאול (ask) *inf* leesh'ol; *pst* sha'al; *pres* sho'el; *fut* yeesh'al; **2.** לחקור (investigate) *inf* lakhkor; *pst* khakar; *pres* khoker; *fut* yakhkor.

(to) enrage להרגיז *inf* lehargeez; *pst* heergeez; *pres* margeez; *fut* yargeez.

(to) enrapture להקסים *inf* lehakseem; *pst* heekseem; *pres* makseem; *fut* yakseem.

(to) enrich להעשיר *inf* leha'asheer; *pst* he'esheer; *pres* ma'asheer; *fut* ya'asheer.

(to) enroll 1. לצרף *vt inf* letsaref; *pst* tseref; *pres* metsaref; *fut* yetsaref; **2.** להצטרף (join) *inf* leheetstaref; *pst* heetstaref; *pres* meetstaref; *fut* yeetstaref.

enrollment 1. צירוף *nm* tseroof/-eem (*pl+of:* -ey); **2.** הצטרפות (joining) *nf* heetstarfoo|t/-yot.

ensemble 1. צוות *nm* tsevet/tsvateem (*pl+of:* tseevtey); **2.** מכלול (sum total) *nm* meekhlol/-eem (*pl+of:* -ey).

ensign 1. דגל (flag) *nm* deg|el/-aleem (*pl+of:* deegley); **2.** תג (badge) *nm* tag/-eem (*pl+of:* -ey).

(to) enslave לשעבד *inf* lesha'bed; *pst* shee'bed; *pres* mesha'bed; *fut* yesha'bed.

enslavement שעבוד *nm* shee'bood/-eem (*pl+of:* -ey).

(to) ensnare ללכוד ברשת *inf* leelkod ba-reshet; *pst* lakhad *etc* (*kh=k*); *pres* lokhed *etc*; *fut* yeelkod *etc.*

(to) ensue לבוא בעיקבות *inf* lavo be-'eekvot; *pst & pres* ba (*b=v*) *etc*; *fut* yavo *etc.*

(to) ensure לבטח *inf* levate'akh; *pst* beetakh (*b=v*); *pres* mevate'akh; *fut* yevatakh.

(to) entail 1. לחייב *inf* lekhayev; *pst* kheeyev; *pres* mekhayev; *fut* yekhayev; **2.** לגרור (imply) *inf* leegror; *pst* garar; *pres* gorer; *fut* yeegror.

(to) entangle לסבך *inf* lesabekh; *pst* seebekh; *pres* mesabekh; *fut* yesabekh.

(to) enter להיכנס *inf* leheekanes; *pst & pres* neekhnas (*kh=k*); *fut* yeekanes.

enterprise 1. יוזמה *nf* yozm|ah/-ot (*+of:* -at); **2.** מיפעל (plant) *nm* meef'al/-eem (*pl+of:* -ey).

enterprising 1. מעז *adj* me'ez/me'eezah; **2.** נמרץ (energetic) *adj* neemr|ats/-etset.

(to) entertain 1. לבדר (amuse) *inf* levader; *pst* beeder (*b=v*); *pres* mevader; *fut* yevader; **2.** לארח (host) *inf* le'are'akh; *pst* eyrakh; *pres* me'are'akh; *fut* ye'arakh.

entertainer בדרן *nmf* badran/-eet.

entertaining משעשע *adj* mesha'sh|e'a'/-a'at.

entertainment בידור *nm* beedoor/-eem (*pl+of:* -ey).

(she) entertains a great deal מארחת די הרבה *pres 3rd pers sing f* me'arakhat dey harbeh.

enthusiasm התלהבות *nf* heetlahavoo|t/-yot.

enthusiast חסיד *nmf* khaseed/-ah (*f+of:* -at).

enthusiastic נלהב *adj* neel|hav/-hevet

(to be) enthusiastic להתלהב *inf* leheetlahev; *pst* heetlahev; *pres* meetlahev; *fut* yeetlahev.

(to) entice 1. לפתות (tempt) *inf* lefatot; *pst* peetah *(p=f)*; *pres* mefateh; *fut* yefateh; **2.** לשדל (talk into) *inf* leshadel; *pst* sheedel; *pres* meshadel; *fut* yeshadel.

enticement פיתוי *nm* peetoo|y/-yeem (*pl+of:* -yey).

entire שלם *adj* shalem/shlemah.

(the) entire world כל העולם *nm* kol ha-'olam.

entirely 1. לגמרי *adv* legamrey; **2.** כליל *adv* kaleel.

entirety 1. שלמות *nf* shlemoo|t/-yot; **2.** מלוא (full measure) melo.

(to) entitle להסמיך *inf* lehasmeekh; *pst* heesmeekh; *pres* masmeekh; *fut* yasmeekh.

entity ישות *nf* yeshoo|t/-yot.

entrails 1. מעיים (bowels) *nm pl* me'ayeem (*sing:* me'ee; *pl+of:* me'ey); **2.** קרביים (intestines) *nm pl* kravayeem (*pl+of:* keervey).

(to) entrain 1. לעלות לרכבת (board oneself) *vi inf* la'alot la-rakevet; *pst* 'alah *etc*; *pres* 'oleh *etc*; *fut* ya'aleh *etc*; **2.** להעלות לרכבת (put on) *vt inf* leha'alot le-rakevet; *pst* he'elah *etc*; *pres* ma'aleh *etc*; *fut* ya'aleh *etc*.

entrance כניסה *nf* kenees|ah/-ot (*+of:* -at).

entrance examination בחינת קבלה *nf* bekheen|at/-ot kabalah.

entrance fee דמי כניסה *nm pl* demey keneesah.

(to) entreat להפציר *inf* lehaftseer; *pst* heeftseer; *pres* maftseer; *fut* yaftseer.

entreaty הפצרה *nf* haftsar|ah/-ot (*+of:* -at).

entrée מנה ראשונה *nf* man|ah/-ot reeshon|ah/-ot.

(to) entrench להתחפר *inf* leheetkhaper; *pst* heetkhaper; *pres* meetkhaper; *fut* yeetkhaper.

(to) entrust 1. להפקיד *inf* lehafkeed; *pst* heefkeed; *pres* mafkeed; *fut* yafkeed; **2.** למסור למשמרת (consign) *inf* leemsor le-meeshmeret; *pst* masar *etc*; *pres* moser *etc*; *fut* yeemsor *etc*.

entry כניסה *nf* kenees|ah/-ot (*+of:* -at).

(double) entry רישום כפול *nm* reeshoom/-eem kafool/kfooleem.

(to) enumerate 1. לספור *inf* leespor; *pst* safar *(f=p)*; *pres* sofer; *fut* yeespor; **2.** למנות (count) *inf* leemnot; *pst* manah; *pres* moneh; *fut* yeemneh; **3.** לפרט (detail) *inf* lefaret; *pst* perat *(p=f)*; *pres* mefaret; *fut* yefaret.

(to) enunciate 1. לקבוע (pronounce) *inf* leekbo'a'; *pst* kava' *(v=b)*; *pres* kove'a'; *fut* yeekba'; **2.** להכריז (proclaim) *inf* lehakhreez; *pst* heekhreez; *pres* makhreez; *fut* yakhreez.

(to) envelop לעטוף *inf* la'atof; *pst* 'ataf; *pres* 'otef; *fut* ya'atof.

envelope מעטפה *nf* ma'at|afah/-afot (*+of:* -efet/-fot).

enviable ראוי לקנאה *adj* ra'ooy/re'ooyah le-keen'ah.

envious מתקנא *adj & v pres* meetkane/-t.

environment סביבה *nf* sveev|ah/-ot (*+of:* -at).

environs סביבות *nf pl* sveevot.

(to) envisage 1. לחזות מראש (foresee) *inf* lakhazot me-rosh; *pst* khazah *etc*; *pres* khozeh *etc*; *fut* yekhezeh *etc*; **2.** להביא בחשבון (take into account) *inf* lehavee be-kheshbon; *pst* hevee *etc*; *pres* mevee *etc*; *fut* yavee *etc*.

envoy 1. שליח (messenger) *nmf* shalee'akh/shleekh|ah (*+of:* shlee|'akh/-khat; *pl:* -kheem/-khot; *+of:* -khey/-khot); **2.** ציר (representative) *nmf* tseer/-ah (*pl:* -eem/-ot; *+of:* -at/-ey).

envy קנאה *nf* keen|'ah/-'ot (*+of:* -'at).

(to) envy לקנא *inf* lekane; *pst* keene; *pres* mekane; *fut* yekane.

enzyme אנזים *nm* enzeem/-eem (*pl+of:* -ey).

ephemeral 1. חולף (transitory) *adj* kholef/-et; **2.** בן־חלוף (short-lived) *adj* ben/bat khalof.

epic אפי *adj* epee/-t.

epidemic מגיפה *nf* magef|ah/-ot (*+of:* -at).

epilepsy 1. כפיון *nm* keefyon; **2.** אפילפסיה (medical term) *nf* epeelepsyah; **3.** מחלת הנפילה (traditional term) *nf* makhalat ha-nefeelah.

epileptic 1. נכפה *nmf* neekhp|eh/-ah; **2.** חולה נפילה *nmf* khol|eh/-at nefeelah

Epiphany חג ההתגלות הנוצרי *nm* khag ha-heetgaloot ha-notsree.

episode אפיזודה *nf* epeezod|ah/-ot (*+of:* -at).

epistle איגרת *nf* eeg|eret/-rot.

epitaph כתובת מצבה *nf* ketov|et/-ot matsevah.

epoch תקופה *nf* tekoof|ah/-ot (*+of:* -at).

equal שווה *adj* shav|eh/-ah

(to be) equal to a task להיות ראוי למשימה *inf* leehyot ra'ooy la-meseemah; *pst* hayah *etc*; *pres* heeno *etc*; *fut* yeehyeh *etc*.

equality שוויון *nm* sheevyon.

(to) equalize להשוות *inf* lehashvot; *pst* heeshvah; *pres* mashveh; *fut* yashveh.

equally 1. במידה שווה *adv* be-meedah shavah; **2.** באותה מידה (to same extent) *adv* be-otah meedah.

equation משוואה *nf* meeshv|a'ah/-a'ot (*+of:* -e'at/-e'ot).

equator קו המשווה *nm* kav ha-mashveh.

equilibrium שיווי משקל *nm* sheevooy meeshkal.

(to) equip לצייד *inf* letsayed; *pst* tseeyed; *pres* metsayed; *fut* yetsayed.

equipment ציוד *nm* tseeyood.

equitable צודק *adj* tsodek/-et.

equity צדק *nm* tsedek.

equivalent שווה־ערך *adj* shveh/shvat 'erekh.

equivocal דו־משמעי *adj* doo-mashma'ee/-t.

era עידן *nm* 'eedan/-eem (*pl+of:* -ey).

(to) eradicate לעקור מן השורש *inf* la'akor meen ha-shoresh; *pst* 'akar *etc*; *pres* 'oker *etc*; *fut* ya'akor *etc*.

(to) erase 1. למחוק *inf* leemkhok; *pst* makhak; *pres* mokhek; *fut* yeemkhak; **2.** למחות כליל (wipe out) *inf* leemkhot kaleel; *pst* makhah *etc*; *pres* mokheh *etc*; *fut* yeemkheh *etc*.

eraser מחק *nm* makhak/mekhakeem (*pl+of:* makhakey).

erasure מחיקה *nf* mekheek|ah/-ot (*+of:* -at)

ere לפני *prep* leefney.

erect 1. זקוף (upright) *adj* zakoof/zekoofah; **2.** תמיר (tall) *adj* tameer/temeerah.

(to) erect 1. לזקוף (raise) *inf* leezkof; *pst* zakaf; *pres* zokef; *fut* yeezkof; **2.** להקים (build) *inf* lehakeem; *pst* hekeem; *pres* mekeem; *fut* yakeem.

erection זיקפה *nf* zeekpah/zekafot (*f=p; +of:* zeekpat).

ermine סמור *nm* samoor/-eem (*pl+of:* -ey).

(to) erode לכרסם *inf* lekharsem; *pst* keersem (*k=kh*); *pres* mekharsem; *fut* yekharsem.

erosion סחף *nm* sakhaf.

erotic 1. עגבני (lusty) *adj* 'agvanee/-t; **2.** ארוטי *adj* erotee/-t.

(to) err 1. לטעות *inf* leet'ot; *pst* ta'ah; *pres* to'eh; *fut* yeet'eh; **2.** לשגות (make mistakes) *inf* leeshgot; *pst* shagah; *pres* shogeh; *fut* yeeshgeh.

errand שליחות *nf* shleekhoo|t/-yot.

errand boy נער שליחויות *nm* na'ar/-ey shleekhooyot.

errant 1. שוגה (straying) *adj* shog|eh/-ah; **2.** נע ונד (wandering) *adj* na'/na'ah va-nad/-ah.

erratic 1. מבולבל *adj* mevool|bal/-elet; **2.** משונה (queer) *adj* meshoon|eh/-ah.

erroneous שגוי *adj* shagooy/shgooyah.

error 1. שגיאה *nf* shgee|'ah/-'ot (*+of:* -'at); **2.** טעות (mistake) *nf* ta'oo|t/-yot.

erudition השכלה מעמיקה *nf* haskalah ma'ameekah.

(to) erupt להתפרץ *inf* leheetparets; *pst* heetparets; *pres* meetparets; *fut* yeetparets.

eruption התפרצות *nf* heetpartsoo|t/-yot.

(volcanic) eruption התפרצות הר־געש *nf* heetpartsoo|t/-yot har/-ey ga'ash.

(to) escalate להסלים *inf* lehasleem; *pst* heesleem; *pres* masleem; *fut* yasleem.

escalation הסלמה *nf* haslam|ah/-ot (*+of:* -at).

escapade הרפתקה *nf* harpatka|h/-'ot (*+of:* -t).

escape 1. היחלצות *nf* hekhaltsoo|t/-yot; **2.** בריחה (flight) *nf* breekh|ah/-ot.

(to) escape 1. להיחלץ *inf* lehekhalets; *pst & pres* nekhlats; *fut* yekhalets; **2.** להימלט (flee) *inf* leheemalet; *pst & pres* neemlat; *fut* yeemalet.

(it) escapes me נשמט מזכרוני *v pres* neeshm|at/-etah mee-zeekhronee.

escort מלווה *nmf* melav|eh/-ah.

(to) escort ללוות *inf* lelavot; *pst* leevah; *pres* melaveh; *fut* yelaveh.

escutcheon שלט סמל *nm* shelet/sheeltey semel.

especial מיוחד *adj* meyookh|ad/-edet.

especially במיוחד *adv* bee-meyookhad.

espionage ריגול *nm* reegool/-eem (*pl+of:* -ey).

essay מסה *nf* mas|ah/-ot (*+of:* -at).

essence 1. תמצית *nf* tamtsee|t/-yot; **2.** עיקר (core) *nm* 'eekar/-eem (*pl+of:* -ey).

essential 1. חיוני *adj* kheeyoonee/-t; **2.** עיקרי (main) *adj* 'eekaree/-t.

(to) establish להקים *inf* lehakeem; *pst* hekeem; *pres* mekeem; *fut* yakeem.

establishment הקמה *nf* hakam|ah/-ot (*+of:* -at).

(the) establishment הממסד *nm* ha-meemsad/-eem.

estate 1. מעמד (position) *nm* ma'amad/-ot; **2.** נכסים (properties) *pl* nekhaseem (*sing:* nekhes; *pl+of:* neekhsey).

(country) estate אחוזה מחוץ לעיר *nf* akhooz|ah/-ot mee-khoots la-'eer.

esteem כבוד *nm* kavod (*+of:* kevod).

(to) esteem לכבד *inf* lekhabed; *pst* keebed (*k=kh*); *pres* mekhabed; *fut* yekhabed.

estimable 1. ניתן להערכה *adj* neet|an/-enet le-ha'arakhah; **2.** ראוי להערכה (worthy of esteem) *adj* ra'ooy/re'ooyah le-ha'arakhah.

estimate 1. הערכה *nf* ha'arakh|ah/-ot (*+of:* -at); **2.** אומדן *nm* oomd|an/-aneem (*pl+of:* -eney).

(to) estimate 1. לאמוד *inf* le'emod; *pst* amad; *pres* omed; *fut* ye'emod; **2.** להעריך (value) *inf* leha'areekh; *pst* he'ereekh; *pres* ma'areekh; *fut* ya'areekh.

estimation 1. הערכה *nf* ha'arakh|ah/-ot (*+of:* -at); **2.** אומד (value) *nm* omed.

(to) estrange לנכר *inf* lenaker; *pst* neeker; *pres* menaker; *fut* yenaker.

estranged מנוכר *adj* menook|ar/-eret.

estrangement ניכור *nm* neekoor.

estuary שפך *nm* shefekh (*pl+of:* sheefkhey).

(to) etch 1. לחרוט (engrave) *inf* lakhrot; *pst* kharat; *pres* khoret; *fut* yakhrot; **2.** לגלף (carve) *inf* legalef; *pst* geelef; *pres* megalef; *fut* yegalef.

etching 1. חריטה (engraving) *nf* khareet|ah/-ot (*+of:* -at); **2.** גילוף (carving) *nm* geeloof/-eem (*pl+of:* -ey).

eternal נצחי *adj* neetskhee/-t.

eternity נצח *nm* netsakh/-eem.

ether אתר *nm* eter.

ethereal 1. שמיימי (heavenly) *adj* shmeymee/-t; **2.** רוחני (spiritual) *adj* rookhanee/-t.

ethical אתי *adj* etee/-t.

ethnic 1. אתני *adj* etnee/-t; **2.** לאומי (national) *adj* le'oomee/-t.

etiquette 1. טקס *nm* tek|es/-aseem (*pl+of:* teeksey); **2.** נימוסים (manners) *nm pl* neemooseem.

etymology אטימולוגיה *nf* eteemologyah.

eucalyptus אקליפטוס *nm* ekaleeptoos/-eem (*pl+of:* -ey).

euphemism 1. לשון נקייה *nf* lashon nekeeyah; **2.** לשון סגי נהור (meaning the opposite) *nf* leshon sagee nehor.

Europe אירופה *nf* eyropah.

European אירופי *adj* eyropee/-t.

(to) evacuate לפנות *inf* lefanot; *pst* peenah (*p=f*) *pres* mefaneh; *fut* yefaneh.

(to) evade 1. להימנע (refrain) *inf* leheemana'; *pst & pres* neemna'; *fut* yeemana'; **2.** להתחמק (shirk) *inf* leheetkhamek; *pst* heetkhamek; *pres* meetkhamek; *fut* yeetkhamek.

(to) evaluate להעריך *inf* leha'areekh; *pst* he'ereekh; *pres* ma'areekh; *fut* ya'areekh.

(to) evaporate להתאדות *inf* leheet'adot; *pst* heet'adah; *pres* meet'adeh; *fut* yeet'adeh.

evaporation התאדות *nf* heet'adoo|t/-yot.

evasion השתמטות *nf* heeshtamtoo|t/-yot.

evasive חמקני *adj* khamkanee/-t.

eve ערב *adv* 'erev.

(Christmas) Eve ערב חג־המולד *nm* 'erev khag ha-molad.

(New Year's) Eve 1. ערב השנה החדשה *nm* 'erev ha-shanah ha-khadashah; **2.** ליל סילבסטר *[colloq.]* (Sylvester Night) *nm* leyl/-ot seelvester.

(on the) eve of בערב *adv* be-'erev.
even 1. אפילו *conj* afeeloo; **2.** שווה (equal) *adj* shav|eh/-ah.
(not) even אף לא *conj* af lo.
(to be) even לסגור חשבון (close account) *inf* leesgor kheshbon; *pst* sagar *etc; pres* soger *etc; fut* yeesgor *etc.*
even dozen מלוא תריסר *nm* melo treysar.
even if 1. אפילו אם *[colloq.] conj* afeeloo eem; **2.** אף אם *conj* af eem.
even number מספר זוגי *nm* meespar/-eem zoogee/-yeem.
even so על אף אשר *conj* 'al af asher.
even temper אופי שקול *nm* ofee shakool.
even though אף על פי *conj* af 'al pee.
(to get) even with someone 1. להחזיר מידה כנגד מידה *inf* lehakhazeer meedah ke-neged meedah; *pst* hekhezeer *etc; pres* makhzeer *etc; fut* yakhzeer *etc;* **2.** לגמול מידה כנגד מידה *inf* leegmol meedah ke-neged meedah; *pst* gamal *etc; pres* gomel *etc; fut* yeegmol *etc.*
evening ערב *nm* 'erev/'ar|aveem *(pl+of: -vey)*
evening gown שמלת ערב *nf* seeml|at/-ot 'erev.
evening star 1. כוכב הערב *nm* kokhav ha-'erev; **2.** נוגה (Venus) *nm* nogah.
evenly 1. ביושר *adv* be-yosher; **2.** ללא משוא פנים (impartially) *adv* le-lo maso faneem *(f=p).*
evenness שוויונות *nf* sheevyonoo|t/-yot.
evenness of temper שלוות אופי *nf* shalvat ofee.
event 1. אירוע *nm* eeroo|'a'/-'eem *(pl+of: -'ey);* **2.** התרחשות *nf* heetrakhshoo|t/-yot.
(in any) event בכל מקרה *adv* be-khol meekreh *(kh=k).*
(in the) event of במקרה של *adv* be-meekreh shel.
eventful רב התרחשויות *adj* rav/rabat *(b=v)* heetrakhshooyot.
eventual הבא בעיקבות ha-ba/-'ah be-'eekvot.
eventually בסופו של דבר *adv* be-sofo shel davar.
ever אי־פעם *adv* ey pa'am.
(hardly) ever כמעט אף פעם *adv* keem'at af pa'am.
(if) ever אם אי־פעם *adv* eem ey pa'am.
(more than) ever יותר מאי־פעם *adv* yoter me-'ey pa'am.
(for) ever and ever לעולמי עד *adv* le-'olmey-'ad.
(best friend I) ever had הידיד הכי טוב שהיה לי אי־פעם ha-yadeed/yededah ha-khee tov/-ah she-ha|yah/-ytah lee ey-pa'am.
ever so much הרבה מאוד *adv* harbeh me'od.
evergreen 1. ירוק־עד *adj* yerok/yerookey 'ad; **2.** לא נשיר (coniferous) *adj* lo nasheer/nesheereem.
everlasting נצחי *adj* neetskhee/-t.
evermore 1. לתמיד (for always) *adv* le-tameed; **2.** לעולם (forever) *adv* le-'olam.
(for) evermore לעולמים (for ever and ever) *adv* le-'olameem.
every 1. כל (all) kol; **2.** כל אחד (each) *adj m/f* kol ekhad/akhat.
every bit of it על כולו ועל כרעיו *adv* 'al koolo ve-'al kra'av.
every day כל יום *adv* kol yom.
every now and then מדי פעם *adv* meedey pa'am.
every once in a while מפעם לפעם *adv* mee-pa'am le-fa'am *(f=p).*
every one of them כל אחד מהם *adj* kol ekhad/akhat mehem/mehen.
every other day אחת ליומיים *adv* akhat le-yomayeem
everybody 1. כל אדם *adv* kol adam; **2.** כל מן דהוא (anyone) *adv* kol man de-hoo.
everyone 1. כל אחד ואחד *adv nm* kol ekhad ve-ekhad; **2.** כל אחת ואחת *adv nf* kol akhat ve-akhat.
everything 1. הכול *nm* ha-kol; **2.** כל דבר (anything) *nm* kol davar.
everywhere בכל מקום *adv* be-khol *(kh=k)* makom.
(to) evict לפנות *inf* lefanot; *pst* peenah *(p=f); pres* mefaneh; *fut* yefaneh.
eviction פינוי *nm* peenoo|y/-yeem *(pl+of: -yey).*
evidence 1. עדות (testimony) *nf* 'edoo|t/-yot; **2.** הוכחה (proof) *nf* hokhakh|ah/-ot *(+of: -at).*
(to be in) evidence להוכיח *inf* lehokhee'akh; *pst* hokhee'akh; *pres* mokhee'akh; *fut* yokhee'akh.
evident 1. ברור (clear) *adj* baroor/broorah; **2.** גלוי (open) *adj* galooy/glooyah.
evil רע *adj* ra'/ra'ah.
(to cast the) evil eye להטיל "עין הרע" *inf* lehateel "'ayeen ha-ra'"; *pst* heteel *etc; pres* meteel *etc; fut* yateel *etc.*
(the) Evil One השטן *nm* ha-satan.
evildoer 1. רשע *nmf* rasha'/resha|'eet *(pl: -'eem/-'ot; +of:* reesh|'ey/-'ot); **2.** זד (villain) *nm* zed/-eem *(pl+of: -ey).*
(to) evoke להעלות זכר *inf* leha'alot zekher; *pst* he'elah *etc; pres* ma'aleh *etc; fut* ya'aleh *etc.*
(to) evoke laughter לעורר צחוק *inf* le'orer tsekhok; *pst* 'orer *etc; pres* me'orer *etc; fut* ye'orer *etc.*
(to) evoluate להתפתח *inf* leheetpate'akh; *pst* heetpatakh; *pres* meetpate'akh; *fut* yeetpatakh.
evolution 1. אבולוציה *nf* evoloots|yah/-yot *(+of: -yat)* **2.** התפתחות (development) *nf* heetpat-khoo|t/-yot.
(to) evolve 1. לפתח *vt inf* lefate'akh; *pst* peetakh *(p=f); pres* mefate'akh; *fut* yefatakh; **2.** התפתח (develop) *v rfl inf* leheetpate'akh; *pst* heetpate'akh; *pres* meetpate'akh; *fut* yeetpatakh.
ewe כבשה *nf* keevsah/kvasot *(+of:* keevs|at/-ot).
exact מדויק *adj* medoo|yak/-yeket.
exacting קפדני *adj* kapdanee/-t.
exactly בדיוק *adv* be-deeyook.
(to) exaggerate להגזים *inf* lehagzeem; *pst* heegzeem; *pres* magzeem; *fut* yagzeem.
exaggeration 1. הגזמה *nf* hagzam|ah/-ot *(+of: -at);* **2.** גוזמה (hyperbole) *nf* goozma|h/-'ot *(+of: -at).*
(to) exalt לשבח *inf* leshabe'akh; *pst* sheebakh; *pres* meshabe'akh; *fut* yeshabakh.
exaltation התפעלות *nf* heetpa'aloo|t/-yot.
examination 1. בחינה *nf* bekheen|ah/-ot *(+of: -at);* **2.** מבדק (test) *nm* meevd|ak/-akeem *(pl+of: -ekey).*
(to) examine 1. לבחון *inf* leevkhon; *pst* bakhan *(b=v); pres* bokhen; *fut* yeevkhan; **2.** לבדוק (test) *inf* leevdok; *pst* badak *(b=v); pres* bodek; *fut* yeevdok.
example דוגמה *nf* doogm|ah/-a'ot *(+of: -at).*

(to) exasperate 1. להוציא מגדרו *inf* lehotsee mee-geedro; *pst* hotsee *etc*; *pres* motsee *etc*; *fut* yotsee *etc*; **2.** לשגע (madden) *inf* leshage'a'; *pst* sheega'; *pres* meshage'a'; *fut* yeshaga'.

(to) excavate 1. לכרות *inf* leekhrot; *pst* karah *(k=kh)*; *pres* koreh; *fut* yeekhreh; **2.** לחפור (dig) *inf* lakhpor; *pst* khafar *(f=p)*; *pres* khofer; *fut* yakhpor.

(archeological) excavations חפירות ארכיאולוגיות *nf pl* khafeerot arkhe'ologeeyot (*sing:* khafeerah arkhe'ologeet).

(to) exceed 1. לחרוג *inf* lakhrog; *pst* kharag; *pres* khoreg; *fut* yakhrog; **2.** להפריז (exaggerate) *inf* lehafreez; *pst* heefreez; *pres* mafreez; *fut* yafreez.

exceedingly במידה יוצאת מן הכלל *adv* be-meedah yotset meen ha-klal.

exceedingly well טוב מאוד *adv* tov me'od.

(to) excel להצטיין *inf* leheetstayen; *pst* heetstayen; *pres* meetstayen; *fut* yeetstayen.

excellence הצטיינות *nf* heetstaynoo|t/-yot.

excellency הוד רוממות *nf* hod romemoot.

excellent מצוין *adj* metsoo|yan/-yenet.

except מלבד *prep* meelvad.

excepting להוציא *prep* lehotsee.

exception יוצא מן הכלל *adj* yotse/-t meen ha-klal.

(with the) exception of פרט ל־ *prep* prat le-.

(to take) exception to להסתייג *inf* leheestayeg; *pst* heestayeg; *pres* meestayeg; *fut* yeestayeg.

exceptional יוצא מגדר הרגיל *adj* yotse mee-geder ha-rageel.

excerpt 1. קטע *nm* ket|a'/-a'eem (*pl+of:* keet'ey); **2.** מובאה (citation) *nf* moova|'ah/-'ot (*+of:* -'at).

excess עודף *nm* 'od|ef/-ofeem (*pl+of:* -fey).

excess baggage עודף מטען *nm* 'od|ef/-fey meet'an.

excessive מופרז *adj* moofr|az/-ezet.

exchange 1. החלפה *nf* hakhlaf|ah/-ot (*+of:* -at); **2.** חליפין *adj* khaleefeen; **3.** חילופים (mutual) *nm pl* kheeloof|eem (*+of:* -ey).

(rate of) exchange שער חליפין *nm* sha'ar/-ey khaleefeen.

(telephone) exchange מרכזת טלפון *nf* meerkez|et/-ot telefon.

exchange of greetings חילופי ברכות *nf pl* kheeloofey brakhot.

(to) excite 1. לגרות *inf* legarot; *pst* gerah; *pres* megareh; *fut* yegareh; **2.** לשלהב (inflame) *vt inf* leshalhev; *pst* sheelhev; *pres* meshalhev; *fut* yeshalhev.

excited מרוגש *adj* meroog|ash/-eshet.

(to get) excited 1. להתרגש *inf* leheetragesh; *pst* heetragesh; *pres* meetragesh; *fut* yeetragesh; **2.** להשתלהב (to get inflamed) *v rfl inf* leheeshtalhev; *pst* heeshtalhev; *pres* meeshtalhev; *fut* yeeshtalhev.

excitement התרגשות *nf* heetragshoo|t/-yot.

exciting מרגש *adj* meragesh/-et.

(to) exclaim 1. לקרוא (call out) *inf* leekro; *pst* kara; *pres* kore; *fut* yeekra; **2.** לצעוק (cry out) *inf* leets'ok; *pst* tsa'ak; *pres* tso'ek; *fut* yeets'ak.

exclamation צעקה *nf* tse'ak|ah/-ot (*+of:* tsa'ak|at/-ot).

exclamation point סימן קריאה *nf* seeman/-ey kree'ah.

(to) exclude להוציא מכלל *inf* lehotsee mee-khlal *(kh=k)*; *pst* hotsee *etc*; *pres* motsee *etc*; *fut* yotsee *etc*.

exclusion הוצאה מכלל *nf* hotsa|'ah/-'ot mee-klal.

exclusive בלעדי *adj* beel'adee/-t.

exclusive of ... להוציא מכלל זה את... *adv* lehotsee mee-khlal *(kh=k)* zeh et.

(to) excommunicate 1. לנדות *inf* lenadot; *pst* needah; *pres* menadeh; *fut* yenadeh; **2.** להחרים (ban) *inf* lehakhreem; *pst* hekhreem; *pres* makhreem; *fut* yakhreem.

excommunication 1. נידוי *nm* needoo|y/-yeem (*pl+of:* -yey); **2.** חרם (boycott) *nm* kherem/kharamot.

excrement צואה *f* tso|'ah/-'ot (*+of:* -'at).

excursion טיול *nm* teeyool/-eem (*pl+of:* -ey).

excusable בר־צידוק *adj* bar/bat tseedook.

excuse צידוק *nm* tseedook/-eem (*pl+of:* -ey).

(to) excuse 1. להצטדק *v rfl inf* leheetstadek; *pst* heetstadek; *pres* meetstadek; *fut* yeetstadek; **2.** לסלוח (forgive) *vt inf* leeslo'akh; *pst* salakh; *pres* sole'akh; *fut* yeeslakh.

excuse me! 1. !סליחה (pardon) *interj* sleekhah! **2.** !סלח לי (pardon me!) *v imp* slakh/seelkhee *(m/f)* lee! **3.** !תסלח לי *[colloq.]* teesl|akh/-ekhee lee!

(to) execute 1. לבצע (carry out) *inf* levatse'a'; *pst* beetsa' *(b=v)*; *pres* mevatse'a'; *fut* yevatsa'; **2.** להוציא להורג (death sentence) *inf* lehotsee le-horeg; *pst* hotsee *etc*; *pres* motsee *etc*; *fut* yotsee *etc*.

execution 1. ביצוע (carrying out) beetsoo|'a'/'eem (*pl+of:* -'ey); **2.** הוצאה להורג (capital punishment) *nf* hotsa|'ah/-'ot le-horeg.

executioner תליין *nm* talyan/-eem (*pl+of:* -ey).

executive 1. מנהל (manager) *nmf* mena|hel/-helet (*pl:* -haleem/-halot; *+of:* -haley); **2.** הנהלה (management) *nf* hanhal|ah/-ot (*+of:* -at).

(the Histadrut) Executive הוועד הפועל של ההסתדרות *nm* ha-va'ad ha-po'el shel ha-heestadroot.

(the Zionist) Executive הוועד הפועל הציוני *nm* ha-va'ad ha-po'el ha-tseeyonee.

executor, -trix 1. מוציא לפועל *nm* motsee/-'ah la-po'al; **2.** אפיטרופוס (guardian) *nmf* epeetrop|os/-seet.

exemplary 1. מופתי *adj* moftee/-t; **2.** למופת (to be an example) *adj* le-mofet.

(to) exemplify להדגים *inf* lehadgeem; *pst* heedgeem; *pres* madgeem; *fut* yadgeem.

exempt פטור *adj* patoor/petoorah.

(to) exempt לפטור *inf* leeftor; *pst* patar *(p=f)*; *pres* poter; *fut* yeeftor.

exemption פטור *nm* petor/-eem (*pl+of:* -ey).

exercise 1. תרגיל *nm* targeel/-eem (*pl+of:* -ey); **2.** אימון (training) *nm* eemoon/-eem (*pl+of:* -ey); **3.** תפעול (activation) *nm* teef'ool/-eem (*pl+of:* -ey).

(to) exercise 1. להפעיל (activate) *inf* lehaf'eel; *pst* heef'eel; *pres* maf'eel; *fut* yaf'eel; **2.** לתרגל (train) *inf* letargel; *pst* teergel; *pres* metargel; *fut* yetargel;

3. ליישם (apply) *inf* leyasem; *pst* yeesem; *pres* meyasem; *fut* yeyasem.

exercised about something מתוח בשל משהו *adj* matoo'akh/metookhah be-shel mashehoo.

(to) exert 1. לאמץ *inf* le'amets; *pst* eemets; *pres* me'amets; *fut* ye'amets; **2.** להפעיל (activate) *inf* lehaf'eel; *pst* heef'eel; *pres* maf'eel; *fut* yaf'eel.

(to) exert oneself להתאמץ *inf* leheet'amets; *pst* heet'amets; *pres* meet'amets; *fut* yeet'amets.

exertion 1. מאמץ (effort) *nm* ma'amats/-eem (*pl+of:* -ey); **2.** הפעלה (activation) *nf* haf'al|ah/-ot (*+of:* -at).

(to) exhale לנשוף *inf* leenshof; *pst* nashaf; *pres* noshef; *fut* yeenshof.

exhaust מפלט *nm* maflet/-eem (*pl+of:* -ey).

exhaust manifold סעפת פליטה *nf* sa'efet pleetah.

exhaust pipe מפלט *nm* maflet/-eem (*pl+of:* -ey).

exhaust valve שסתום פליטה *nm* shastom/-ey pleetah.

exhausted מותש *adj* moot|ash/-eshet.

exhaustion 1. התשה (attrition) *f* hatash|ah/-ot (*+of:* -at); **2.** אפיסת כוחות (fatigue) *nf* afeesat kokhot.

exhaustive 1. ממצה *adj* memats|eh/-ah; **2.** מתיש (tiring) *adj* mateesh/-ah.

exhibit מוצג *nm* mootsag/-eem (*pl+of:* -ey).

(to) exhibit להציג לראווה *inf* lehatseeg le-ra'avah; *pst* heetseeg *etc*; *pres* matseeg *etc*; *fut* yatseeg *etc*.

exhibition 1. תצוגה (display) *nf* tetsoog|ah/-ot (*+of:* -at); **2.** תערוכה (exposition) *nf* ta'arookh|ah/-ot (*+of:* -at).

exhibitor מציג *nm* matseeg/-eem (*pl+of:* -ey).

(to) exhilarate 1. לשמח (gladden) *inf* lesame'akh; *pst* seemakh; *pres* mesame'akh; *fut* yesamakh; **2.** להרנין (cheer up) *inf* leharneen; *pst* heerneen; *pres* marneen; *fut* yarneen.

(to) exhort להפציר *inf* lehaftseer; *pst* heeftseer; *pres* maftseer; *fut* yaftseer.

(to) exhume להעלות מקבר *inf* leha'alot mee-kever; *pst* he'elah *etc*; *pres* ma'aleh *etc*; *fut* ya'aleh *etc*.

exigency דחיפות *nf* dekheefoo|t/-yot.

exigent דחוף *adj* dakhoof/dekhoofah.

exile 1. גירוש (expulsion) *nm* geroosh/-eem (*pl+of:* -ey); **2.** גולה (in Jewish context - diaspora; in other ones - deportation) *nf* gol|ah/-ot (*+of:* -at).

(to) exile 1. לגרש *inf* legaresh; *pst* geresh; *pres* megaresh; *fut* yegaresh; **2.** להגלות (deport) *inf* lehaglot; *pst* heeglah; *pres* magleh; *fut* yagleh.

(to) exist להתקיים *inf* leheetkayem; *pst* heetkayem; *pres* meetkayem; *fut* yeetkayem.

existence קיום *nm* keeyoom.

existent קיים *adj* kay|am/-emet.

exit יציאה *nf* yetsee|'ah/-'ot (*+of:* -'at).

(to) exit לצאת *inf* latset; *pst* yatsa; *pres* yotse; *fut* yetse.

exodus יציאה המונית *nf* yetsee'ah hamoneet.

(to) exonerate להסיר אשמה *inf* lehaseer ashmah; *pst* heseer *etc*; *pres* meseer *etc*; *fut* yaseer *etc*.

exorbitant 1. מופקע *adj* moofka'/-'at; **2.** מופרז (exaggerated) *adj* moofr|az/-ezet.

exotic אקזוטי *adj* ekzotee/-t.

(to) expand 1. להתרחב *inf* leheetrakhev; *pst* heetrakhev; *pres* meetrakhev; *fut* yeetrakhev; **2.** להרחיב (widen) *inf* leharkheev; *pst* heerkheev; *pres* markheev; *fut* yarkheev; **3.** להגדיל (enlarge) *inf* lehagdeel; *pst* heegdeel; *pres* magdeel; *fut* yagdeel.

expanse מרחב *nm* merkhav/-eem (*pl+of:* -ey).

expansion 1. התפשטות *nf* heetpashtoo|t/-yot; **2.** התרחבות (broadening) *nf* heetrakhavoo|t/-yot.

(to) expect 1. לסבור *inf* leesbor; *pst* savar (*v=b*); *pres* sover; *fut* yeesbor; **2.** לצפות (foresee) *inf* leetspot; *pst* tsafah (*f=p*); *pres* tsofeh; *fut* yeetspeh.

(I) expect so כך אני מניח kakh anee manee'akh.

expectation ציפייה *nf* tseepee|yah/-yot (*+of:* -yat).

expectorate ליחה *nf* leykh|ah/-ot (*+of:* -at).

expedient תכליתי *adj* takhleetee/-t.

(to) expedite לזרז *inf* lezarez; *pst* zeraz; *pres* mezarez; *fut* yezarez.

expedition 1. משלחת *nf* meeshl|akhat/-akhot (*pl+of:* -ekhot); **2.** מסע (voyage) *nm* masa'/-'ot.

(to) expend להוציא כספים *inf* lehotsee ksafeem; *pst* hotsee *etc*; *pres* motsee *etc*; *fut* yotsee *etc*.

expendable מיותר *adj* meyoot|ar/-eret.

expenditure הוצאה כוללת *nf* hotsa|'ah/-'ot kolel|et/-ot.

expense 1. הוצאה *nf* hotsa|'ah/-'ot (*+of:* -'at); **2.** תשלום (payment) *nm* tashloom/-eem (*pl+of:* -ey).

expensive יקר *adj* yakar/yekarah.

expensiveness יוקר *nm* yoker.

experience ניסיון *nm* nees|ayon/-yonot

(to) experience להתנסות *inf* leheetnasot; *pst* heetnasah; *pres* meetnaseh; *fut* yeetnaseh.

experienced 1. מנוסה *adj* menoos|eh/-ah; **2.** בעל ניסיון (with experience) *nmf* ba'al/-at neesayon.

experiment ניסוי *nm* neesoo|y/-yeem (*pl+of:* -yey).

experimental 1. נסיוני *adj* neesyonee/-t; **2.** ניסויי (trial) *adj* neesooyee/-t

expert 1. מומחה *nmf* moomkh|eh/-eet; **2.** מומחי (specialist) *adj* moomkhee/-t.

expertise מומחיות *nf* moomkheeyoo|t/-yot.

(to) expiate לכפר *inf* lekhaper; *pst* keeper (*k=kh*); *pres* mekhaper; *fut* yekhaper.

expiation 1. כיפור *nm* keepoor/-eem (*pl+of:* -ey); **2.** כפרה (absolution) *nf* kapar|ah/-ot (*+of:* -at).

expiration תפוגה *nf* tefoog|ah/-ot (*+of:* -at).

(to) expire לפוג *inf* lafoog; *pst & pres* pag (*p=f*); *fut* yafoog.

(to) explain 1. להסביר *inf* lehasbeer; *pst* heesbeer; *pres* masbeer; *fut* yaasbeer; **2.** לנמק (motivate) *inf* lenamek; *pst* neemek; *pres* menamek; *fut* yenamek.

explainable בר־הסברה *adj* bar/bat hasbarah.

explanation הסבר *nm* hesber/-eem (*pl+of:* -ey).

explanatory מסביר *adj* masbeer/-ah.

explicit מפורש *adj* mefor|ash/-eshet.

explicitly במפורש *adv* bee-meforash.

(to) explode 1. לפוצץ *vt* lefotsets; *pst* potsets (*p=f*); *pres* mefotsets; *fut* yefotsets; **2.** להתפוצץ *v rfl inf* leheetpotsets; *pst* heetpotsets; *pres* meetpotsets; *fut* yeetpotsets.

exploit עלילת גבורה *nf* 'aleel|at/-ot gvoorah.

exploitation ניצול *nm* neetsool/-eem (*pl+of:* -ey).
exploration חקר שטח *nm* kheker shetakh/shtakheem.
(to) explore לחקור שטח *inf* lakhkor shetakh; *pst* khakar *etc*; *pres* khoker *etc*; *fut* yakhkor *etc*.
explorer 1. חוקר *nmf* khoker/-et; **2.** נוסע (traveler) *nm* nos|e'a'/-'eem (*pl+of:* -'ey).
explosion התפוצצות *nf* heetpotsetsoo|t/-yot.
explosive חומר נפץ *nm* khom|er/-rey nefets.
export יצוא *nm* yetsoo.
(to) export לייצא *inf* leyatse; *pst* yeetse; *pres* meyatse; *fut* yeyatse.
exportation ייצוא *nm* yeetsoo.
(to) expose לחשוף (uncover) *inf* lakhsof; *pst* khasaf; *pres* khosef; *fut* yakhsof.
exposition תערוכה *nf* ta'arookh|ah/-ot (*+of:* -at).
exposure 1. חשיפה (stripping) *nf* khaseef|ah/-ot (*+of:* -at); **2.** הצגה לראווה (exhibition) *nf* hatsag|ah/-ot le-ra'avah.
(to die of) exposure לגווע מאפיסת כוחות *inf* leegvo'a' me-afeesat kokhot; *pst* gava' *etc*; *pres* gove'a' *etc*; *fut* yeegva' *etc*.
(to) expound להבהיר *inf* lehavheer; *pst* heevheer; *pres* mavheer; *fut* yavheer.
express 1. מהיר (fast) *adj* maheer/meheerah; **2.** ברור (distinct) *adj* baroor/broorah; **3.** מיוחד (special) *adj* meyookh|ad/-edet.
(to) express לבטא *inf* levate; *pst* beete (*b=v*); *pres* mevate; *fut* yevate.
express company חברה להובלה מהירה *nf* khevr|ah/-ot le-hovalah meheerah.
(in) express terms 1. במונחים מפורשים (in specified terms) *adv* be-moonakheem meforasheem; **2.** בתנאים ברורים (under clear conditions) *adv* bee-tna'eem brooreem.
express train רכבת מהירה *nf* rak|evet/-avot meheer|ah/-ot.
expression ביטוי *nm* beetoo|y/-yeem (*pl+of:* -yey).
expressive 1. עז־ביטוי *adj* 'az/-at beetooy; **2.** אקספרסיבי *adj* ekspreseevee/-t.
expressly במיוחד *adv* bee-meyookhad.
expressway כביש מהיר *nm* kveesh/-eem maheer/meheereem.
(to) expropriate להפקיע *inf* lehafkee'a'; *pst* heefkee'a'; *pres* mafkee'a'; *fut* yafkee'a'.
expropriation הפקעה *nf* hafka|'ah/-'ot (*+of:* -'at).
expulsion גירוש *nm* geroosh/-eem (*pl+of:* -ey).
exquisite 1. מעודן *adj* me'ood|an/-enet; **2.** מעולה (excellent) *adj* me'ool|eh/-ah.
exquisiteness עידון *nm* 'eedoon/-eem (*pl+of:* -ey).
extant קיים *adj* ka|yam/-yemet.
extemporaneous מאולתר *adj* me'oolt|ar/-eret.
(to) extend להעניק *inf* leha'aneek; *pst* he'eneek; *pres* ma'aneek; *fut* ya'aneek.
extended 1. מורחב (enlarged) *adj* moorkh|av/-evet; **2.** מוארך (prolonged) mo'or|akh-ekhet.
extension 1. הארכה (prolongation) ha'arakh|ah/-ot (*+of:* -at); **2.** שלוחה (telephone) *nf* shlookh|ah/-ot (*+of:* -at).
extensive רב־היקף *adj* rav/rabat (*b=v*) hekef.
extensively בהיקף גדול *adv* be-hekef gadol.
extensively used בשימוש מוגבר *adj* be-sheemoosh moogbar.
extent 1. מידה (measure) *nf* meed|ah/-ot (*+of:* -at); **2.** גודל (size) *nm* godel/gedaleem (*pl+of:* godley).
(to a great) extent במידה רבה *adv* be-meedah rabah.
(to some) extent במידה כלשהי *adv* be-meedah kolshehee.
(to the) extent of one's ability בגבולות היכולת *adv* bee-gvoolot ha-yekholet.
(to such an) extent that עד כדי כך ש־ *adv* 'ad kedey kakh she-.
(up to a certain) extent במידה מסוימת *adv* be-meedah mesooyemet.
(to) extenuate לרכך *inf* lerakekh; *pst* reekekh; *pres* merakekh; *fut* yerakekh.
exterior 1. חוץ *nm* khoots; **2.** חיצוני (exterior) *adj* kheetsonee/-t; **3.** חיצוניות (appearance) *nf* kheetsoneeyoo|t/-yot.
(to) exterminate להשמיד *inf* lehashmeed; *pst* heeshmeed; *pres* mashmeed; *fut* yashmeed.
extermination השמדה *nf* hashmad|ah/-ot (*+of:* -at).
external חיצוני *adj* kheetsonee/-t.
extinct 1. כבוי *adj* kavooy/kvooyah; **2.** נכחד (of species) *adj* neekhekh|ad/-edet.
extinction כיבוי *nm* keeboo|y/-yeem (*pl+of:* -yey).
(to) extinguish לכבות *inf* lekhabot; *pst* keebah (*k=kh*); *pres* mekhabeh; *fut* yekhabeh.
extinguisher מטפה *nm* matp|eh/-eem (*pl+of:* -ey).
(to) extirpate לעקור מן השורש *inf* la'akor meen ha-shoresh; *pst* 'akar *etc*; *pres* 'oker *etc*; *fut* ya'akor *etc*.
(to) extol לשבח *inf* leshabe'akh; *pst* sheebakh; *pres* meshabe'akh; *fut* yeshabakh.
(to) extort 1. לסחוט (to squeeze) *inf* leeskhot; *pst* sakhat; *pres* sokhet; *fut* yeeskhot; **2.** להוציא באיומים (blackmail) lehotsee be-eeyoomeem; *pst* hotsee *etc*; *pres* motsee *etc*; *fut* yotsee *etc*.
extortion סחיטה *nf* sekheet|ah/-ot (*+of:* -at).
extra 1. לחוד (separately) *adv* le-khood; **2.** כתוספת (as an addition) *adv* ke-tosefet.
extra fare תוספת דמי נסיעה *nf* tos|efet/-fot demey nesee'ah.
extra tire צמיג נוסף *nm* tsemeeg/-eem nosaf/-eem.
extra workman פועל נוסף *nm* po'el/po'aleem nosaf/-eem.
extract 1. תמצית *nf* tamtsee|t/-yot; **2.** קטע (excerpt) *nm* ket|a'/-a'eem (*pl+of:* keet'ey).
(to) extract להפיק *inf* lehafeek; *pst* hefeek; *pres* mefeek; *fut* yafeek.
extraction הפקה *nf* hafak|ah/-ot (*+of:* -at).
extracurricular שמחוץ לתוכנית *adj* she-mee-khoots la-tokhneet.
(to) extradite להסגיר *inf* lehasgeer; *pst* heesgeer; *pres* masgeer; *fut* yasgeer.
extradition הסגרה *nf* hasgar|ah/-ot (*+of:* -at).
extraordinarily באורח יוצא מן הרגיל *adj* be-orakh yotse mee-geder ha-rageel.
extraordinary יוצא מגדר הרגיל *adj* yotse/-t mee-geder ha-rageel.

(to) extrapolate לאמוד מלבר *inf* le'emod mee-levar; *pst* amad *etc; pres* omed *etc; fut* ye'emod *etc.*
extrapolation אומד מלבר *nm* omed mee-levar.
extravagance 1. בזבוז (waste) *nm* beezbooz/-eem (*pl+of:* -ey); **2.** הפרזה (exaggeration) *nf* hafraz|ah/-ot (*+of:* -at).
extravagant 1. יוצא דופן *adj* yotse/-t dofen; **2.** בזבזני (prodigal) *adj* bazbezanee/-t.
extravagant praise שבחים מוגזמים *nm pl* shvakheem moogzameem.
extravagant price מחיר מופרז *nm* mekheer/-eem moofraz/-eem.
extreme קיצוני *adj* keetsonee/-yeem.
extreme opinions דעות קיצוניות *nf pl* de'ot keetsoneeyot.
extremely ביותר *adv* be-yoter.
(to go to the) extremes להרחיק לכת *inf* leharkheek lekhet; *pst* heerkheek *etc; pres* markheek *etc; fut* yarkheek *etc.*
extremity קצה *nm* katseh/ketsavot (*+of:* ketseh/katsvot).
(in) extremity 1. במקרה סכנה (in case of danger) *adv* be-meekreh sakanah; **2.** בשעת דחק (in emergency) *adv* be-she'at dekhak.
(to) extricate לחלץ *inf* lekhalets; *pst* kheelets; *pres* mekhalets; *fut* yekhalets.
extrovert מחוצן *nmf* mekhoots|an/-enet.
exuberant שופע עליצות *adj* shof|e'a'/-a'at 'aleetsoot.
(to) exult 1. לשמוח (rejoice) *inf* leesmo'akh; *pst* samakh; *pres* same'akh; *fut* yeesmakh; **2.** לצהול (to be jubilant) *inf* leets'hol; *pst* tsahal; *pres* tssohel; *fut* yeets'hal.
eye עין *nf* 'ayeen/'eynayeem (*+of:* 'eyn/-ey).
(in a twinkling of an) eye כהרף עין *adv* ke-heref 'ayeen.
(hook and) eye וו ולולאה *m & f* vav ve-loola'ah.
(to) eye להעיף מבט *inf* leeha'eef mabat; *pst* he'eef *etc; pres* me'eef *etc; fut* ya'eef *etc.*
(to catch one's) eye לתפוש את עין *inf* leetpos et 'eyn; *pst* tafas *etc* (*f=p*); *pres* tofes *etc; fut* yeetfos *etc.*
(to keep an) eye לשים עין *inf* laseem 'ayeen; *pst & pres* sam *etc; fut* yaseem *etc.*
(to see) eye to eye לראות עין בעין *inf* leer'ot 'ayeen be-'ayeen; *pst* ra'ah *etc; pres* ro'eh *etc; fut* yeer'eh *etc.*
eye shade מצחייה *nf* meetskhee|yah/-yot (*+of:* -yat).
(to have before one's) eyes לשוות לנגד העיניים *inf* leshavot le-neged ha-'eynayeem; *pst* sheevah *etc; pres* meshaveh *etc; fut* yeshaveh *etc.*
eyeball גלגל העין *nm* galgal/-ey ha-'ayeen/'eynayeem.
eyebrow גבה *nf* gab|ah/-ot (*+of:* -at).
eyeful "חתיכה" *[slang] nf* khateekh|ah/-ot (*+of:* -at).
eyeglasses משקפיים *nm pl* meeshk|afayeem (*pl+of:* -efey).
eyelashes ריסים *nm pl* rees|eem (*pl+of:* -ey).
eyelet 1. לולאה (loop) *nf* lool|a'ah/-a'ot (*+of:* -'at/-'ot); **2.** חרך (loophole) *nm* khara|kh/-keem (*k=kh; pl+of:* -key).
eyelids עפעפיים *nm pl* 'af'ap|ayeem (*pl+of:* -ey).
(to have good) eyes להיות בעל ראייה טובה *inf* leehyot ba'al re'eeyah tovah; *pst* hayah *etc;* heeno *etc;* yeehyeh *etc.*
eyesight ראייה *nf* re'eeyah.
(poor) eyesight ראייה לקויה *nf* re'eeyah lekooyah.
eyesore מכאוב לעיניים *nm* makh'ov la-'eynayeem.
eyewash 1. תרחיץ לעיניים (medicated solution) tarkheets la-'eynayeem; **2.** שטויות (nonsense) *nf pl* shtooyot.
eyewitness עד ראייה *nm* 'ed/-at re'eeyah.

F.

F,f consonant to which the Hebrew alphabet equivalent is the letter Peh (פ), undotted. When so, it is referred to as Feh and reads f (or ph). Normally, however, texts being "unpointed", the reader has no way of knowing when it should read p or when f (i.e. ph) and must guess that by context. However, when it comes at the end of a word, it takes the form of a Final Letter (see *Introduction*, pages VI-VII) and is referred to as Feh Sofeet (ף) which always reads f (or ph).
fable 1. משל *nm* mashal/meshaleem (*pl+of:* meeshley); **2.** אגדה (legend) *nf* agad|ah/-ot (*+of:* -at).
fabric 1. אריג (cloth) *nm* areeg/-eem (*pl+of:* -ey); **2.** מארג (web) *nm* ma'ar|ag/-ageem (*pl+of:* -gey).
(to) fabricate 1. לייצר (produce) *inf* leyatser; *pst* yeetser; *pres* meyatser; *fut* yeyatser; **2.** לזייף (falsify) *inf* lezayef; *pst* zeeyef; *pres* mezayef; *fut* yezayef.
fabulous 1. נפלא *adj* neefla/-'ah; **2.** דמיוני (fantastic) *adj* deemyonee/-t.
facade חזית *nf* khazeet/-ot.
face 1. פנים *nm pl* paneem (*pl+of:* peney); **2.** פרצוף (physiognomy) *nm* partsoof/-eem (*pl+of:* -ey).

(brazen) face מצח נחושה *nm* metsakh nekhooshah.
(to) face להתייצב מול (confront) *inf* leheetyatsev mool; *pst* heetyatsev mool; *pres* meetyatsev mool; *fut* yeetyatsev mool.
(to lose) face 1. לנחול השפלה (be humiliated) *inf* leenkhol hashpalah; *pst* nakhal *etc*; *pres* nokhel *etc*; *fut* yeenkhal *etc*; **2.** לאבד יוקרה (lose prestige) *inf* le'abed yookrah; *pst* eebed *etc*; *pres* me'abed *etc*; *fut* ye'abed *etc*.
(to save one's) face להציל כבוד *inf* lehatseel kvod; *pst* heetseel *etc*; *pres* matseel *etc*; *fut* yatseel *etc*.
(to) face danger לעמוד בפני סכנה *inf* la'amod bee-fney sakanah; *pst* 'amad *etc*; *pres* 'omed; *fut* ya'amod.
face lift מתיחת פנים *nf* meteekh|at/-ot paneem.
(in the) face of נוכח *adv* nokhakh.
(on the) face of it לכאורה *adv* lee-khe-orah.
face to face פנים אל פנים *adv* paneem el paneem.
(to) face up to להתמודד עם *inf* leheetmoded 'eem; *pst* heetmoded 'eem; *pres* meetmoded 'eem; *fut* yeetmoded 'eem.
face value ערך נומינלי 'erekh/'arakheem nomeenalee/-yeem.
(to) face with marble לצפות בשיש *inf* letsapot be-shayeesh; *pst* tseepah *etc*; *pres* metsapeh *etc*; *fut* yetsapeh *etc*.
(to make) faces לעשות פרצופים *inf* la'asot partsoofeem; *pst* 'asah *etc*; *pres* 'oseh *etc*; *fut* ya'aseh *etc*.
(it) faces the street פונה לרחוב *adj* poneh/-ah la-rekhov.
(to) facilitate 1. לאפשר (make possible) *inf* le'afsher; *pst* eefsher; *pres* me'afsher; *fut* ye'afsher; **2.** להקל (ease) *inf* lehakel; *pst* hekel; *pres* mekel; *fut* yakel.
facility 1. אפשרות (possibility) *nf* efsharoo|t/-yot; **2.** מיומנות (skill) *nf* meyoomanoo|t/-yot; **3.** מיתקן (mechanism) *nm* meetk|an/-aneem (*pl+of:* -eney).
fact עובדה *nf* 'oovd|ah/-ot (*+of:* -at).
faction סיעה *nf* see|'ah/-'ot (*+of:* -'at).
factor 1. גורם *nm* gor|em/meem (*pl+of:* -mey); **2.** מתווך (mediator) *nmf* metav|ekh/-ekhet (*pl:* -kheem/-khot; *+of:* -khey).
factory 1. בית־חרושת *nm* bet/batey kharoshet; **2.** מפעל (plant) *nm* meef'al/-eem (*pl+of:* -ey).
faculty 1. כושר *nm* kosher; **2.** פקולטה (university) *nf* fakoolt|ah/-ot (*+of:* -at).
fad אופנה חולפת *nf* ofn|ah/-ot khol|efet/-fot.
(to) fade 1. לדהות *inf* leedhot; *pst* dahah; *pres* doheh; *fut* yeedheh; **2.** להימוג (disappear gradually) *inf* leheemog; *pst & pres* namog; *fut* yeemog.
(don't) fail 1. בל תאכזב! (don't disappoint!) *v fut imp* bal te'akhzev/-ee; **2.** בל תחמיץ! (don't miss!) *v fut imp* bal takhmeets/-eel (*m/f*).
(to) fail להיכשל *inf* leheekashel; *pst & pres* neekhshal (*kh=k*); *fut* yeekashel.
(without) fail ללא דיחוי *adv* le-lo deekhooy.
(to) fail a student 1. להכשיל תלמיד *inf* lehakh'sheel talmeed; *pst* heekh'sheel *etc*; *pres* makh'sheel *etc*; *fut* yakh'sheel *etc*; **2.** לנזוף בתלמיד (reprimand a student) *inf* leenzof be-talmeed; *pst* nazaf *etc*; *pres* nozef *etc*; *fut* yeenzof *etc*.
(to) fail in an examination להיכשל בבחינה *inf* leheekashel bee-vekheenah (*v=b*); *pst & pres* neekh'shal (*kh=k*) *etc*; *fut* yeekashel *etc*.
(to) fail to do it לא להשכיל לעשות זאת *inf* lo lehaskeel la'asot zot; *pst* lo heeskeel *etc*; *pres* eyno maskeel *etc*; *fut* lo yaskeel *etc*.
failure 1. כישלון *nm* keesh|alon/-lonot (*+of:* -lon); **2.** מחדל (omission) *nm* mekhdal/-eem (*pl+of:* -ey).
faint 1. חלש (weak) *adj* khalash/-ah; **2.** עמום (dim) *adj* 'amoom/-ah.
(to) faint להתעלף *inf* leheet'alef; *pst* heet'alef; *pres* meet'alef; *fut* yeet'alef.
(to feel) faint להרגיש סחרחורת *inf* lehargeesh skharkhoret; *pst* heergeesh *etc*; *pres* margeesh *etc*; *fut* yargeesh *etc*.
faint-hearted מוג לב *adj* moog/-at lev.
faintly במקצת *adv* be-meektsat.
faintness 1. חולשה (weakness) *nf* khoolsh|ah/-ot (*+of:* -at); **2.** רפיון (slackness) *nm* reefyon/-ot.
fair 1. יריד (exposition) *nm* yereed/-eem (*pl+of:* -ey); **2.** הוגן (just) *adj* hogen/-et; **3.** בהיר (blond) *adj* baheer/beheerah.
(to) fair להתבהר *inf* leheetbaher; *pst* heetbaher; *pres* meetbaher; *fut* yeetbaher.
(to act) fair לפעול בהגינות *inf* leef'ol ba-hageenoot; *pst* pa'al *etc*; *pres* po'el *etc*; *fut* yeef'al *etc* (*f=p*).
(to play) fair לנהוג בהגינות *inf* leenhog ba-hageenoot; *pst* nahag *etc*; *pres* noheg *etc*; *fut* yeen'hag *etc*.
(world) fair תערוכה עולמית *nf* ta'arookh|ah/-ot 'olamee|t/-yot.
fair chance סיכוי הוגן *nm* seekooy/-eem hog|en/-neem.
fair complection צבע עור בהיר *nm* tseva' 'or baheer.
fair hair שיער בהיר *nm* se'ar baheer.
fair name שם טוב *nm* shem tov.
fair play משחק הוגן *nm* meeskhak hogen.
fair weather מזג אוויר נאה *nm* mezeg aveer na'eh.
fairly 1. ביושר (justly) *adv* be-yosher; **2.** בהגינות (honestly) *adv* be-hageenoot; **3.** בערך (approximately) *adv* be-'erekh.
fairly difficult די קשה *adv* dey kasheh.
fairly well די טוב *adv* dey tov.
fairness 1. הגינות (honesty) *nf* hageenoot; **2.** בהירות (clarity) *nf* beheeroot.
fairy פיה *nf* feyah/feyot (*+of:* feyat).
fairy godmother 1. סנדקית טובה *nf* sandakeet tovah; **2.** תומך (sponsor) *nmf* tomekh/-et.
fairy tale סיפור בדים *nm* seepoor/-ey badeem.
fairyland ארץ האגדות *nf* erets ha-agadot.
faith 1. אמונה *nf* emoon|ah/-ot (*+of:* -at); **2.** דת (religion) *nf* dat/-ot.
(in good) faith בתום לב *adv* be-tom lev.
(to have) faith 1. להאמין (believe) *inf* leha'ameen; *pst* he'emeen; *pres* ma'ameen; *fut* ya'ameen; **2.** לתת אמון (trust) *inf* latet emoon; *pst* natan *etc*; *pres* noten *etc*; *fut* yeeten *etc*.

(to keep) faith לשמור אמונים *inf* leeshmor emooneem; *pst* shamar *etc*; *pres* shomer *etc*; *fut* yeeshmor.

(to lose) faith לאבד אמונה *inf* le'abed emoonah; *pst* eebed *etc*; *pres* me'abed *etc*; *fut* ye'abed *etc*.

faithful **1.** נאמן *adj* ne'eman/-ah; **2.** מסור (devoted) *adj* masoor/mesoorah.

faithfully בנאמנות *adv* be-ne'emanoot.

faithfully yours שלך בנאמנות *adv* shel|kha/-akh be-ne'emanoot.

faithfulness נאמנות *nf* ne'emanoo|t/-yot.

faithless **1.** חסר אמונה *adj* khas|ar/-rat emoonah; **2.** בוגד (traitor) *nmf & adj* boged/-et.

fake **1.** זיוף (act) *nm* zeeyoof/-eem (*pl+of:* -ey); **2.** נוכל (person) *nmf* nokhel/-et

(to) fake **1.** לזייף *inf* lezayef; *pst* zeeyef; *pres* mezayef; *fut* yezayef; **2.** להונות (deceive) *inf* lehonot; *pst* honah; *pres [colloq.]* merameh; *fut* yoneh.

falcon בז baz/-eem (*pl+of:* -ey).

fall **1.** נפילה (act) *nf* nefeel|ah/-ot (*+of:* -at); **2.** שלכת (season) shalekhet; **3.** סתיו (autumn) *nm* stav/-eem (*pl+of:* -ey).

(to) fall ליפול *inf* leepol; *pst* nafal *(f=p)*; *pres* nofel; *fut* yeepol.

(to) fall asleep להירדם *inf* leheradem; *pst & pres* neerdam; *fut* yeradem.

(to) fall back **1.** לסגת (retreat) *inf* laseget; *pst & pres* nasog; *fut* yeesog; **2.** לחזור בו (go back on) *inf* lakhzor bo; *pst* khazar bo; *pres* khozer bo; *fut* yakhzor bo.

(to) fall behind לפגר *inf* lefager; *pst* peeger *(p=f)*; *pres* mefager; *fut* yefager.

(to) fall in love להתאהב *inf* leheet'ahev; *pst* heet'ahev; *pres* meet'ahev; *fut* yeet'ahev.

(to) fall out with להסתכסך עם *inf* leheestakhsekh 'eem; *pst* heestakhsekh 'eem; *pres* meestakhsekh 'eem; *fut* yeestakhsekh 'eem.

(to) fall through **1.** לנחול מפלה (suffer defeat) *inf* leenkhol mapalah; *pst* nakhal *etc*; *pres* nokhel *etc*; *fut* yeenkhal *etc*; **2.** להיכשל (fail) *inf* leheekashel; *pst & pres* neekh'shal *(kh=k)*; *fut* yeekashel.

(to) fall to one ליפול לידיו של *inf* leepol le-yadav shel; *pst* nafal *(f=p) etc*; *pres* nofel *etc*; *fut* yeepol *etc*.

fallacy סברה מוטעית *nf* svar|ah/-ot moot|'et/-'ot.

fallen **1.** ירוד (low) *adj* yarood/yeroodah; **2.** נפול (lean) *adj* nafool/nefoolah.

fallout נשורת *nf* neshoret.

fallow שדה בור *nm* sdeh/sdot boor.

false **1.** לא נכון *adj* lo nakhon/nekhonah; **2.** כוזב (sham) *adj* kozev/-et; **3.** מזויף (counterfeit) *adj* mezoo|yaf/-yefet.

false return הצהרה כוזבת *nf* hats'har|ah/-ot koz|evet/-vot.

falsehood **1.** שקר (lie) *nm* sheker/shkareem (*pl+of:* sheekrey); **2.** רמאות (fraud) *nf* rama'oo|t/-yot.

falseness **1.** חוסר דיוק (inexactitude) *nm* khoser deeyook; **2.** בגידה (betrayal) *nf* begeed|ah/-ot (*+of:* -at).

(to) falsify **1.** לזייף *inf* lezayef; *pst* zeeyef; *pres* mezayef; *fut* yezayef; **2.** לסלף (distort) *inf* lesalef; *pst* seelef; *pres* mesalef; *fut* yesalef.

falsity **1.** כזב (lie) *nm* kazav/kezaveem (*pl+of:* keezvey); **2.** חוסר מהימנות (unreliability) *nm* khoser meheymanoot.

(to) falter להסס *inf* lehases; *pst* heeses; *pres* mehases; *fut* yehases.

(to) falter to an excuse להתנצל בהססנות leheetnatsel be-hasesanoot; *pst* heetnatsel *etc*; *pres* meetnatsel *etc*; *fut* yeetnatsel *etc*.

fame **1.** תהילה (glory) *nf* teheel|ah/-ot (*+of:* -at); **2.** מוניטין (reputation) *nm pl* moneeteen.

famed **1.** נודע (wellknown) *adj* nod|a'/-a'at; **2.** מפורסם (famous) *adj* mefoors|am/-emet.

familiar **1.** מוכר (known) *adj* mook|ar/-eret; **2.** מתמצא (versed in) *adj* meetmatse/-t; **3.** בקיא (expert) *adj* bakee/bekee'ah.

(to be) familiar with a subject לגלות בקיאות בנושא *inf* legalot bekee'oot be-nose; *pst* geelah *etc*; *pres* megaleh *etc*; *fut* yegaleh *etc*.

familiarity **1.** קירבה (closeness) *nf* keervah; **2.** חוסר רשמיות (informality) *nm* khoser reeshmeeyoot; **3.** בקיאות (expertise) *nf* bekee'oot; **4.** ידידות (cordiality) *nf* yedeedoo|t/-yot.

family משפחה *nf* meeshp|akh|ah/-akhot (*+of:* -akhat/-ekhot).

family name שם משפחה *nm* shem/shmot meeshpakhah.

family physician רופא משפחה *nmf* rofe/-t meeshpakhah.

family tree מגילת יוחסין *nf* megeel|at/-ot yookhaseen.

(to be in a) family way להיות בהריון *inf* leehyot be-herayon; *pst f* haytah *etc*; *pres f* heenah *etc*; *fut f* teehyeh *etc*.

famine **1.** רעב *nm* ra'av; **2.** רעבון *nm* re'avon (*+of:* ra'avon).

famished רעב *adj & v pres* ra'ev/re'evah.

famous **1.** ידוע (known) *adj* yadoo'a'/yedoo'ah; **2.** מפורסם (famed) *adj* mefoors|am/-emet.

fan **1.** מניפה *nf* meneef|ah/-ot (*+of:* -at); **2.** מאוורר (electric) *nm* me'avrer/-eem (*pl+of:* -ey); **3.** מעריץ (admirer) *nmf* ma'areets/-ah.

(to) fan **1.** לנשוף *inf* leenshof; *pst* nashaf; *pres* noshef; *fut* yeenshof; **2.** ללבות (stir) *inf* lelabot; *pst* leebah; *pres* melabeh; *fut* yelabeh.

(to) fan out להתפרס *inf* leheetpares; *pst* heetpares; *pres* meetpares; *fut* yeetpares.

fanatic קנאי *nmf & adj* kan|ay/-a'eet.

fanaticism **1.** קנאות *nf* kana'oot; **2.** פנטיות *nf* fanateeyoot.

fanciful **1.** הוזה *adj* hoz|eh/-ah; **2.** חולמני (dreamy) *adj* kholmanee/-t.

fancy **1.** דמיון (fantasy) *nm* deemyon/-ot; **2.** חיבה (liking) *nf* kheeb|ah/-ot (*+of:* -at); **3.** מקושט *adj* mekoosh|at/-etet.

(to) fancy **1.** לדמות (imagine) *inf* ledamot; *pst* deemah; *pres* medameh; *fut* yedameh; **2.** לחבב (like) *inf* lekhabev; *pst* kheebev; *pres* mekhabev; *fut* yekhabev.

(to have a) fancy לגלות חיבה *inf* legalot kheebah; *pst* geelah *etc*; *pres* megaleh *etc*; *fut* yegaleh *etc*.

(to strike a) fancy להשתוקק *inf* leheeshtokek; *pst* heeshtokek; *pres* meeshtokek; *fut* yeeshtokek.
fancy ball נשף מסיכות *nm* neshef/neeshfey masekhot.
fancy dress תחפושת *nf* takhpos|et/-ot.
fancy free בן־דרור *adj* ben/bat dror.
fancy goods סדקית *nf* seedkeet.
(to) fancy oneself לדמות עצמו *inf* ledamot 'atsmo; *pst* deemah *etc*; *pres* medameh *etc*; *fut* yedameh *etc*.
(to take a) fancy to לחשוק ב־ *inf* lakhshok be-; *pst* khashak be-; *pres* khoshek be-; *fut* yakhshok be-.
(I don't) fancy the idea לא לרוחי הרעיון lo le-rookhee ha-ra'yon.
(just) fancy the idea! היעלה על הדעת?! ha-ya'aleh 'al ha-da'at?!
fancywork 1. ריקמה (embroidery) *nf* reekmah/ rekamot (+*of:* reekm|at/-ot); **2.** סריגה עדינה (delicate knitting) *f* sreegah 'adeenah.
fang שן (tooth) *nf* shen/sheen|ayeem (*pl+of:* -ey).
fantastic 1. פנטסטי *adj* fantastee/-t; **2.** דמיוני (imaginary) *adj* deemyonee/-t.
fantasy 1. פנטסיה *nf* fantas|yah/-yot (+*of:* -yat); **2.** דמיון (imagination) *nm* deemyon/-ot.
far 1. רחוק *adj* rakhok/rekhokah; **2.** מרוחק (distant) *adj* merookh|ak/-eket.
(how) far? באיזה מרחק be-'eyzeh merkhak.
(so) far 1. עד כה *adv* 'ad koh; **2.** עד הלום (hither) *adv* 'ad halom.
far and wide מרוחק ורחב־ידיים *adj & adv* merookhak oo-rekhav yadayeem.
(as) far as במידה ש־ be-meedah she-.
(as) far as I know ככל שידוע לי *adv* ke-khol she-yadoo'a' lee.
far away הרחק *adv* harkhek.
far better טוב יותר פי כמה *adj* tov/-ah yoter pee khamah *(kh=k)*.
(it is a) far cry from עדיין רחוק מ־ 'adayeen rakhok mee-.
far journey מסע למרחקים *nm* mas|a'/-a'ot le-merkhakeem.
far-off מרחק רב *adv* merkhak rav.
far off הרחק מכאן *adv* harkhek mee-kan.
far-sighted מרחיק ראות *adj* markheek/-at re'ot.
faraway מרוחק *adj* merookh|ak/-eket.
farce 1. פרסה *nf* fars|ah/-ot (+*of:* -at); **2.** בדיחה (joke) *nf* bedeekh|ah/-ot (+*of:* -at).
fare דמי נסיעה *nm pl* demey nesee'ah.
(to) fare 1. להסתדר (get along) *inf* leheestader; *pst* heestader; *pres* meestader; *fut* yeestader; **2.** להתקדם (progess) *inf* leheetkadem; *pst* heetkadem; *pres* meetkadem; *fut* yeetkadem.
(to) fare forth לצאת לדרך *inf* latset le-derekh; *pst* yatsa *etc*; *pres* yotse *etc*; *fut* yetse *etc*.
farewell בירכת פרידה *nf* beer|kat/-khot *(kh=k)* preedah.
(to bid) farewell לבוא להיפרד *inf* lavo leheepared; *pst & pres* ba *etc*; *fut* yavo *etc*.
farewell party מסיבת פרידה *nf* meseeb|at/-ot preedah.
farfetched מרחיק לכת *adj* markheek/-at lekhet.
far-flung נרחב *adj* neerkh|av/-evet.

farm 1. משק חקלאי *nm* mesh|ek/-akeem khakla'ee/ -yeem; **2.** חווה (ranch) *nf* khav|ah/-ot (+*of:* -at).
farm produce תוצרת חקלאית *nf* totseret khakla'eet.
(to) farm לעבד אדמה *inf* le'abed adamah; *pst* 'eebed *etc*; *pres* me'abed *etc*; *fut* ye'abed *etc*.
(to) farm out להחכיר קרקע לקבלן משנה *inf* lehakhkeer karka' le-kablan meeshneh.
farmer 1. איכר (peasant) *nm* eekar/-eem (*pl+of:* -ey); **2.** חקלאי (agriculturer) *nm* khakl|ay/-a'eem (*pl+of:* -a'ey); **3.** חוואי (rancher) *nm* khav|ay/ -a'eem (*pl+of:* -a'ey).
Farmers Union התאחדות האיכרים *nf* heet'akhdoot ha-'eekareem.
farmhand פועל חקלאי *nm* po'el/po'aleem khakla'ee/-yeem.
farmhouse דירת משק *nf* deer|at/-ot meshek.
farming 1. חקלאות (agriculture) *nf* khakala'oot; **2.** חקלאי (agricultural) *adj* khakla'ee/-t.
farmyard חצר משק *nf* khats|ar/-rot meshek.
farther 1. הלאה *adv* hal'ah; **2.** הרחק *adv* harkhek.
farthest המרוחק ביותר *adj* ha-merookh|ak/-eket be-yoter.
(to) fascinate 1. לקסום (allure) *inf* leeksom; *pst* kasam; *pres* kosem; *fut* yeeksom; **2.** להקסים (charm) *inf* lehakseem; *pst* heekseem; *pres* makseem; *fut* yakseem; **3.** לצודד (captivate) *inf* letsoded; *pst* tsoded; *pres* metsoded; *fut* yetsoded.
fascination קסם *nm* kes|em/-ameem (*pl+of:* keesmey).
fashion אופנה *nf* ofn|ah/-ot (+*of:* -at).
(after a) fashion במידת מה *adv* be-meedat mah.
(out of) fashion לא אופנתי *adj* lo-ofnatee/-t.
(the latest) fashion הצעקה האחרונה ha-tse'akah ha-akhronah.
(to) fashion לעצב *inf* le'atsev; *pst* 'eetsev; *pres* me'atsev; *fut* ye'atsev.
(to be in) fashion להיות באופנה *inf* leehyot ba-ofnah; *pst* hayah *etc*; *pres* heeno *etc*; *fut* yeehyeh *etc*.
fashion plate גנדרן *nmf* gandran/-eet.
fashionable אופנתי *adj* ofnatee/-t.
fast 1. מהיר *adj* maheer/meheerah; **2.** עמיד (resistant) *adj* 'ameed/-ah.
(to) fast לצום *inf* latsoom; *pst & pres* tsam; *fut* yatsoom.
(watch is) fast השעון ממהר ha-sha'on memaher.
fast asleep אחוז תרדמה *adj* akhooz/-at tardemah.
fast color צבע עמיד *nm* tsev|a'/-a'eem 'ameed/ -eem.
(to) fasten להדק *inf* lehadek; *pst* heedek; *pres* mehadek; *fut* yehadek.
fastener 1. מהדק *nm* mehad|ek/-keem (*pl+of:* -key); **2.** אטב (paper-clip) *nm* etev/ataveem (*pl+of:* atvey); **3.** מחבר (clipping device) *nm* makhber/ -eem (*pl+of:* -ey).
fastidious 1. מפונק (spoilt) *adj* mefoon|ak/-eket; **2.** מדקדק (meticulous) *adj* medakdek/-et.
fat שמן *adj* shamen/shmenah.
(the) fat of the land חלב הארץ *nm* khelev ha-arets.
fat profits רווחים שמנים *nm pl* revakheem shmeneem.

fatal 1. אנוש *adj* (severe) anoosh/-ah; **2.** גורלי (fateful) *adj* goralee/-t.

fatal wounds פצעי מוות *nm pl* peets'ey mavet.

fatality 1. מקרה מוות *nm* meekr|eh/-ey mavet; **2.** גורל (fate) *nm* goral.

fate גורל *nm* goral.

father אב *nm* av/-ot (*+of:* avee).

father-in-law 1. חם *nm* kham/-eem (*+of:* -ee/-ey); **2.** חותן (wife's father) *m* khot|en/neem (*pl+of:* -ney).

fatherhood אבהות *nf* avahoot.

fatherland מולדת *nf* moledet.

fathom 1. אמה ימית (maritime "amah") *nf* am|ah/-ot yamee|t/-yot; **2.** כשני מטרים בים (about two meters of sea) kee-shney metreem ba-yam.

(to) fathom 1. למדוד לעומק *inf* leemdod la-'omek; *pst* madad *etc; pres* moded *etc; fut* yeemdod *etc;* **2.** לרדת לסוף דעת (follow one's thinking) *inf* laredet le-sof da'at; *pst* yarad *etc; pres* yored *etc; fut* yered *etc.*

fathomless עמוק לאין חקר *adj* 'am|ok/-ookah le-eyn kheker.

fatigue עייפות מצטברת *nf* 'ayefoot meetstaberet.

fatigues בגדי עבודה צבאיים *nm pl* beegdey 'avodah tsva'eeyeem.

fatness שומן *nm* shomen.

(to) fatten להשמין *inf* lehashmeen; *pst* heeshmeen; *pres* mashmeen; *fut* yashmeen.

faucet 1. ברז (tap) *m* berez/brazeem (*pl+of:* beerzey); **2.** מגופה (plug cork) *nf* megoof|ah/-ot (*+of:* -at).

(to a) fault יתר על המידה *adv* yater 'al ha-meedah.

(to be at) fault לשאת באשמה *inf* laset be-ashmah; *pst* nasa *etc; pres* nose *etc; fut* yeesa *etc.*

(to find) fault למצוא פגם *inf* leemtso pegam; *pst* matsa *etc; pres* motse *etc; fut* yeemtsa *etc.*

faultfinder מגלה פגמים *nmf* megal|eh/-at pegameem.

faultless ללא דופי *adv* le-lo dofee.

faulty 1. פגום (faulty) *adj* pagoom/pegoomah; **2.** לקוי (defective) *adj* lakooy/lekooyah.

favor 1. טובה (service) *nf* tov|ah/-ot (*+of:* -at); **2.** חסד (boon) *nm* khesed/khas|adeem (*pl+of:* -dey).

(to) favor 1. להעדיף (prefer) *inf* leha'adeef; *pst* he'edeef; *pres* ma'adeef; *fut* ya'adeef; **2.** לנטות חסד (to be partial to) *inf* leentot khesed; *pst* natah *etc; pres* noteh *etc; fut* yeeteh *etc.*

(your) favor of... מכתבכם מתאריך... meekhtavkhem mee-ta'areekh...

favorable חיובי *adj* kheeyoovee/-t.

favorably 1. בעין טובה *adv* be-'ayeen tovah; **2.** בחיוב (positively) *adv* be-kheeyoov

favorite 1. מועדף (preferred) *adj* mo'od|af/-efet; **2.** מבוכר (given priority) *adj* mevook|ar/-eret.

favoritism משוא פנים *nm* maso paneem.

fawn עופר *nm* 'of|er/-areem (*pl+of:* -rey).

fear פחד *nm* pakhad/pekhadeem (*pl+of:* pakhadey).

(to) fear 1. לפחד *inf* lefakhed; *pst* pakhad *(p=f); pres* pokhed; *fut* yefakhed; **2.** לחשוש (be apprehensive) *inf* lakhshosh; *pst* khashash; *pres* khoshesh; *fut* yakhshosh.

fearful 1. פחדן *nmf & adj* pakhdan/-eet; **2.** חששן (apprehensive) *adj* khasheshan/-eet.

fearless 1. עשוי לבלי חת *adj* 'asoo|y/-yah lee-vlee *(v=b)* khat; **2.** אמיץ (brave) *adj* ameets/-ah.

fearlessness אומץ לב *nm* omets lev.

feasibility מעשיות *nf* ma'aseeyoot.

feasible 1. בר־ביצוע *adj* bar/bat beetsoo'a'; **2.** אפשרי (possible) *adj* efsharee/-t.

feast חגיגה *nf* khageeg|ah/-ot (*+of:* -at).

(to) feast one's eyes on תאווה לעיניים *nf* ta'avah la-'eynayeem.

feat 1. מעלל *nm* ma'al|al/-aleem (*pl+of:* -eley); **2.** מעשה רב (great deed) *nm* ma'aseh rav.

feather נוצה *nf* nots|ah/-ot (*+of:* -at).

(to) feather לקשט בנוצות *inf* lekashet be-notsot; *pst* keeshet *etc; pres* mekashet *etc; fut* yekashet *etc.*

feathers נוצות (plumage) *nf pl* notsot.

feathers in one's cap 1. תהילה (glory) *nf* teheel|ah/-ot (*+of:* -at); **2.** הצטיינות (excellence) *nf* heetstaynoo|t/-yot.

featherweight משקל נוצה meeshkal notsah.

feathery קל כנוצה *adj* kal/-ah ka-notsah.

feature 1. חלק עיקרי *nm* khelek/khalakeem 'eek|aree/-reeyeem; **2.** דבר ראוי להבלטה (something deserving prominence) *nm* davar ra'ooy le-havlatah.

(to) feature להבליט *inf* lehavleet; *pst* heevleet; *pres* mavleet; *fut* yavleet.

feature article מאמר מובלט *nm* ma'amar/-eem moovlat/-eem.

features תווי פנים *nm pl* tavey paneem.

February פברואר *nm* febroo'ar.

(to be) fed up להרגיש שנמאס לו *inf* lehargeesh she-neem'as lo; *pst* heergeesh *etc; pres* margeesh *etc; fut* yargeesh *etc.*

federal 1. של ברית מדינות (of a federation of states) *adj* shel breet medeenot; **2.** פדרלי *adj* federalee/-t.

federation 1. התאגדות *nf* heet'agdoo|t/-yot; **2.** פדרציה *nf* federats|yah/-yot (*+of:* -yat).

Federation of Labor הסתדרות העובדים *nf* heestadroot ha-'ovdeem.

fee 1. תשלום (payment) *nm* tashloom/-eem; **2.** אגרה (tax) *nf* agr|ah/-ot (*+of:* -at).

(admission) fee דמי כניסה *nm pl* demey keneesah.

feeble 1. חלשלוש *adj* khalashloosh/-ah; **2.** רפה (weak) *adj* raf|eh/-ah.

feebly 1. מתוך חולשה *adv* mee-tokh khoolshah; **2.** ברפיון (weakly) *adv* be-reefyon.

feed מספוא (animal) *nm* meespo.

(to) feed 1. להאכיל *inf* leha'akheel; *pst* he'ekheel; *pres* ma'akheel; *fut* ya'akheel; **2.** להזין (supply food) *inf* lehazeen; *pst* hezeen; *pres* mezeen; *fut* yazeen; **3.** לספק חומר (supply material) *inf* lesapek khomer; *pst* seepek *etc; pres* mesapek *etc; fut* yesapek *etc.*

feedback 1. משוב *nm* mashov/meshov|eem (*pl+of:* -ey); **2.** היזון חוזר *nm [colloq.]* heezoon khozer.

feel 1. הרגשה *nf* hargash|ah/-ot (*+of:* -at); **2.** מרגש *[colloq.] nm* margash.

(has a nice) feel נותן הרגשה טובה *adj* noten/-et hargashah tovah.

(to) feel להרגיש *inf* lehargeesh; *pst* heergeesh; *pres* margeesh; *fut* yargeesh.

(to) feel better להרגיש יותר טוב *inf* lehargeesh yoter tov; *pst* heergeesh *etc*; *pres* margeesh *etc*; *fut* yargeesh *etc*.

(to) feel happy להרגיש מאושר *inf* lehargeesh me'ooshar; *pst* heergeesh *etc*; *pres* margeesh *etc*; *fut* yargeesh *etc*.

(to) feel one's way לגשש דרך *inf* legashesh derekh; *pst* geeshesh *etc*; *pres* megashesh *etc*; *fut* yegashesh.

(to) feel sad להתעצב *inf* leheet'atsev; *pst* heet'atsev; *pres* meet'atsev; *fut* yeet'atsev.

(to) feel sad for someone 1. לחמול על *inf* lakhmol 'al; *pst* khamal 'al; *pres* khomel 'al; *fut* yakhmol 'al; **2.** לרחם (pity) *inf* lerakhem; *pst* reekhem; *pres* merakhem; *fut* yerakhem.

feeler חיישן *nm* khayshan/-eem (*pl+of:* -ey).

feeling 1. הרגשה *nf* hargash|ah/-ot (*+of:* -at); **2.** רגש (sentiment) *nm* reg|esh/-ashot (*pl+of:* reegshot).

(to hurt someone's) feelings לפגוע ברגשות *inf* leefgo'a' be-reegshot; *pst* paga' *(p=f) etc*; *pres* poge'a' *etc*; *fut* yeepaga' *etc*.

(it) feels hot זה נראה חם zeh neer'eh kham.

(it) feels soft זה נראה רך zeh neer'eh rakh.

(to) feign להעמיד פנים *inf* leha'ameed paneem *pst* he'emeed *etc*; *pres* ma'ameed *etc*; *fut* ya'ameed *etc*.

(to) fell 1. לחטוב *inf* lakhtov; *pst* khatav; *pres* khotev; *fut* yakhtov; **2.** להפיל (knock down) *inf* lehapeel; *pst* heepeel; *pres* mapeel; *fut* yapeel.

fellow 1. בחור *nm* bakhoor/-eem (*pl+of:* -ey); **2.** חבר (comrade) *nm* khav|er/-ereem (*pl+of:* -rey); **3.** ידיד (friend) *nm adj* yedeed/-eem (*pl+of:* -ey).

fellow citizen 1. אזרח אותה ארץ ("landsman") *nmf* ezrakh/-eet otah erets; **2.** תושב אותה עיר (townsman) *nmf* tosh|av/-evet otah 'eer.

fellow man 1. הזולת (the other person) *nm* ha-zoolat; **2.** יצור אנוש (human being) *nm* yetsoor/-ey enosh.

fellow member 1. חבר לאגודה (association) *nmf* khaver/-ah la-agoodah; **2.** חבר למפלגה (party) *nmf* khaver/-ah le-meeflagah; **3.** חבר לצוות (staff) *nmf* khaver/-ah le-tsevet.

fellow student תלמיד אותו מוסד *nmf* talmeed/-at oto mosad.

fellow traveller 1. אוהד בסתר *nmf* ohed/-et be-seter; **2.** קומוניסט מוסווה (crypto-communist) *nmf* komooneest/-eet moosv|eh/-et.

fellowship 1. ידידות (comradeship) *nf* yedeedoo|t/-yot; **2.** מוסד למחקר (research foundation) *nm* mosad/-ot le-mekh'kar; **3.** חברות במוסד למחקר (membership in a fellowship) *nf* khaveroot be-mosad le-mekh'kar; **4.** מענק ממוסד למחקר (grant from a fellowship) *nm* ma'anak/-eem mee-mosad le-mekh'kar.

(to get a) fellowship לזכות במלגה *inf* leezkot be-meelgah; *pst* zakhah *(kh=k) etc*; *pres* zokheh *etc*; *fut* yeezkeh *etc*.

felony 1. עוון פלילי *nm* 'avon/-ot pleelee/-yeem; **2.** פשע חמור (serious crime) *nm* pesh|a'/-a'eem khamoor/-eem.

felt 1. לבד *nm* leved; **2.** עשוי לבד (felt made) *adj* 'asoo|y/-yat leved.

female 1. נקבה (impolite except as grammatical term) *nf* nekev|ah/-ot (*+of:* -at); **2.** אישה (woman) *nf* eeshah/nasheem (*+of:* eshet/neshey); **3.** נשי (womanly) *adj* nashee/-t.

female cat חתולה *nf* khatool|ah/-ot (*+of:* -at).

female dog כלבה *nf* kalbah/klavot (*v=b*; *+of:* kal|bat/-vot).

female screw אום *nm* om/oom|eem (*pl+of:* -ey).

female sex 1. המין הנשי *nm* ha-meen ha-nashee; **2.** המין היפה (beautiful sex) *nm* ha-meen ha-yafeh.

feminine נשי (womanly) *adj* nashee/-t.

feminine gender מין נקבה *nm* meen nekevah.

femininity נשיות *nf* nasheeyoot.

fence גדר *nf* ged|er/-erot (*pl+of:* geedrot).

(to sit on the) fence 1. לשבת על הגדר (literally) *inf* lashevet 'al hagader; *pst* yashav *etc*; *pres* yoshev *etc*; *fut* yeshev *etc*; **2.** לעמוד מן הצד (not to take sides) *inf* la'amod meen ha-tsad; *pst* 'amad *etc*; *pres* 'omed *etc*; *fut* ya'amod *etc*.

(to) fence 1. לסייף (exercise) *inf* lesayef; *pst* seeyef; *pres* mesayef; *fut* yesayef; **2.** לגדר (bar) *inf* legader; *pst* geeder; *pres* megader; *fut* yegader.

(to) fence in להתגדר *inf* leheetgader; *pst* heetgader; *pres* meetgader; *fut* yeetgader.

fencing 1. סיף (sport) *nm* sayeef; **2.** גידור (enclosing) *nm* geedoor/-eem.

fender כנף מכונית *nf* knaf/kanfey mekhoneet

ferment 1. תסיס *nm* tasees/tesees|eem (*pl+of:* -ey); **2.** פרמנט *nm* ferment/-eem (*pl+of:* -ey).

(to) ferment להתסיס *inf* lehat'sees; *pst* heet'sees; *pres* mat'sees; *fut* yat'sees.

fermentation תסיסה *nf* tesees|ah/-ot (*+of:* -at).

fern שרך *nm* sharakh.

ferocious 1. פראי (savage) *adj* peer'ee/-t; **2.** אכזרי (cruel) *adj* akhzaree/-t.

ferocity 1. פראיות (savagery) *nf* peer'eeyoot; **2.** אכזריות (cruelty) *nf* akhzereeyoot.

(to) ferret out 1. ללכוד (catch) *inf* leelkod; *pst* lakhad *(kh=k)*; *pres* lokhed; *fut* yeelkod; **2.** להחריד מרבצו (drive out) *inf* lehakhreed mee-reevtso; *pst* hekhreed *etc*; *pres* makhreed *etc*; *fut* yakhreed *etc*.

ferry מעבורת *nf* ma'bor|et/-ot.

(to) ferry להסיע במעבורת *inf* lehasee'a' be-ma'boret; *pst* heesee'a'; *pres* masee'a' *etc*; *fut* yasee'a' *etc*.

fertile פורה *adj* por|eh/-eeyah.

fertility פוריות *nf* poreeyoot.

(to) fertilize להפרות *inf* lehafrot; *pst* heefrah; *pres* mafreh; *fut* yafreh.

fertilizer דשן *nm* desh|en/-aneem (*pl+of:* deeshney).

fervent נלהב *adj* neel|hav/-hevet.

fervor התלהבות *nf* heetlahavoot.

fester מיגול *nm* meegool/-eem (*pl+of:* -ey).

(to) fester למגל *inf* lemagel; *pst inf* meegel; *pres* memagel; *fut* yemagel.

festival 1. פסטיבל *nm* festeeval/-eem (*pl+of:* -ey); **2.** חגיגה פומבית (celebration) *nf* khageeg|ah/-ot poombee|t/-yot.

festive חגיגי *adj* khageegee/-t.

festivity טקס חגיגי *nm* tek|es/-aseem khageegee/-yeem.

(to) fetch 1. להביא (bring) *inf* lehavee; *pst* hevee; *pres* mevee; *fut* yavee; **2.** להשיג (reach for) *inf* lehaseeg; *pst* heeseeg; *pres* maseeg; *fut* yaseeg.

fete מסיבה לכבוד *nf* meseeb|ah/-ot lee-khvod *(kh=k)*.

(to) fete לערוך מסיבה לכבוד *inf* la'arokh meseebah lee-khvod *(kh=k)*; *pst* 'arakh *etc*; *pres* 'orekh *etc*; *fut* ya'arokh *etc*.

fetid מבאיש *adj* mav'eesh/-ah.

fetish עצם נערץ *nm* 'etsem/'atsameem na'arats/-eem.

(to) fetter לכבול באזיקים *inf* leekhbol ba-azeekeem; *pst* kaval (*k=kh; v=b*) *etc*; *pres* kovel *etc*; *fut* yeekhbol *etc*.

fetters אזיקים *nm pl* azeek|eem (*pl+of:* -ey).

fetus עובר *nm* 'oob|ar/-areem (*pl+of:* -rey).

feud 1. ריב משפחות (quarrel between families) *nm* reev/-ey meeshpakhot; **2.** גאולת דם (vendetta) *nf* ge'oolat dam.

(old) feud סכסוך נושן *nm* seekhsookh/-eem noshan/-eem.

feudal פיאודלי *adj* fe'odalee/-t.

fever 1. קדחת *nf* kadakhat; **2.** חום (temperature) *nm* khom.

feverish קדחתני *adj* kadakhtanee/-t.

feverishness קדחתנות *nf* kadakhtanoot.

few 1. מעטים *adj pl* me'at|eem/-ot; **2.** אחדים (some) *num pl* akhad|eem/-ot.

fiance ארוס *nm* aroos/-eem (*pl+of:* -ey).

fiancée ארוסה *nf* aroos|ah/-ot (*+of:* -at).

fiasco כישלון מחפיר *nm* keesh|alon/-lonot makhpeer/-eem.

fib בדותה *nf* bedoot|ah/-ot (*+of:* -at).

(to) fib לספר בדותות *inf* lesaper bedootot; *pst* seeper *etc*; *pres* mesaper *etc*; *fut* yesaper *etc*.

fibber שקרן *nmf & adj* shakran/-eet

fiber סיב *nm* seev/-eem (*pl+of:* -ey).

fibrous סיבי seevee/-t.

fickle 1. הפכפך *adj* hafakhpakh/-ah; **2.** קל־דעת *adj* kal/-at da'at.

fiction 1. הנחה משפטית (legal) *nf* hanakh|ah/-ot meeshpatee|t/-yot; **2.** סיפורת (literary) *nf* seeporet.

fictional 1. דמיוני *adj* deemyonee/-t; **2.** בדוי (invented) *adj* badooy/bedooyah.

fictitious 1. מדומה (imaginary) *adj* medoom|eh/-ah; **2.** פיקטיבי *adj* feekteevee/-t.

fiddle כינור *nm* keenor/-ot.

(to) fiddle around לבזבז זמן *inf* levazbez zman; *pst* beezbez (*v=b*) *etc*; *pres* mevazbez *etc*; *fut* yevazbez *etc*.

fiddler כנר *nmf* kanar/-eet.

fidelity נאמנות *nf* ne'emanoo|t/-yot.

(to) fidget לנוע בעצבנות *inf* lanoo'a' be-'atsbanoot; *pst & pres* na *etc*; *fut* yanoo'a' *etc*.

field 1. שדה *nm* sad|eh/-ot (*+of:* sdeh/sdot); **2.** שטח (area) *nm* shetakh/shtakheem (*pl+of:* sheetkhey).

field artillery תותחנות שדה *nf* totkhanoot sadeh.

field glasses משקפת שדה *nf* meeshkef|et/-ot sadeh.

fieldwork 1. עבודת מחקר (researchwork) *nf* 'avod|at/-ot mekhkar; **2.** עבודה בשטח (case work) 'avod|ah/-ot ba-shetakh.

fiend 1. שטן *nm* satan/staneem (*+of:* stan/seetney); **2.** שד (demon) *nm* shed/eem (*pl+of:* -ey).

fiendish שטני *adj* stanee/-t.

fierce 1. אלים *adj* aleem/-ah; **2.** פראי (savage) *adj* peer'ee/-t.

fierceness 1. אלימות *f* aleemoot; **2.** פראות (savagery) *f* peer'oot.

fiery לוהט *adj* lohet/-et.

fife חליל *nm* khaleel/-eem (*pl+of:* -ey).

fifteen 1. חמישה־עשר *num m* khameeshah-'asar; **2.** חמש־עשרה *num f* khamesh-'esreh; **3.** ט"ו *num* tet-vav (15 in *Hebr. num. sys.*).

fifteen hundred אלף וחמש מאות (thousand five hundred) *num* elef va-khamesh-me'ot.

fifteenth 1. החמישה־עשר *adj m* ha-khameeshah-'asar; **2.** החמש־עשרה *adj f* ha-khamesh-'esreh; **3.** הט"ו *adj* ha-tet-vav (15th in *Hebr. num. sys.*).

fifth 1. חמישי *adj* khameeshee/-t; **2.** חמישית *nf* khameeshee|t/-yot; **3.** ה' *adj* heh (5th in *Hebr. num. sys.*).

fiftieth 1. החמישים *adj* ha-khameesheem; **2.** נ' *adj* noon (50th in *Hebr. num. sys.*).

fifty 1. חמישים *num* khameesheem; **2.** נ' *num* noon (50 in *Hebr. num. sys.*).

fifty-first 1. החמישים ואחד/ואחת *adj* ha-khameesheem ve-ekhad/ve-akhat *(m/f)*; **2.** הנ"א *adj* ha-noon-alef (51st in *Hebr. num. sys.*).

fifty-second 1. החמישים ושניים/ושתיים *adj* ha-khameesheem oo-shnayeem/oo-shtayeem *(m/f)*; **2.** הנ"ב *adj* ha-noon-bet (52nd in *Hebr. num. sys.*).

fifty-third 1. החמישים ושלושה/ושלוש *adj* ha-khameesheem oo-shloshah/ve-shalosh *(m/f)*; **2.** הנ"ג *adj* ha-noon-geemal (53rd in *Hebr. num. sys.*).

fifty-three 1. חמישים ושלושה/ושלוש *num* khameesheem oo-shloshah/ve-shalosh *(m/f)*; **2.** נ"ג *num* noon-geemal (53 in *Hebr. num. sys.*).

fifty-two 1. חמישים ושניים/ושתיים *num* khameesheem oo-shnayeem/oo-shtayeem *(m/f)*; **2.** נ"ב *num* noon-bet (52 in *Hebr. num. sys.*).

fig תאנה *nf* te'en|ah/-eem (*pl+of:* -ey).

fight 1. קטטה *nf* ketat|ah/-ot (*+of:* -at); **2.** מריבה (strife) *nf* mereev|ah/-ot (*+of:* -at).

(to) fight ללחום *inf* leelkhom; *pst* lakham; *pres* lokhem; *fut* yeelkhom.

(to) fight it out ללחום עד תום *inf* leelkhom 'ad tom; *pst* lakham *etc*; *pres* lokhem *etc*; *fut* yeelkhom *etc*.

(has a lot of) fight left עוד כוחו במותניו 'od kokho be-motnav.

(to) fight one's way through להבקיע דרך *inf* lehavkee'a' derekh; *pst* heevkee'a' *etc; pres* mavkee'a' *etc; fut* yavkee'a' *etc.*

fighter לוחם *nm* lokh|em/-ameem (*pl+of:* -amey).

fighter plane מטוס קרב *nm* metos/-ey krav.

fighting 1. לחימה *nf* lekheem|ah/-ot (*+of:* -at); **2.** לוחמה *nf* lokhm|ah/-ot (*+of:* -at).

(guerrilla) fighting לוחמת גרילה *nf* lokhmat/-ot gereelah.

figure 1. דמות (personality) *nf* demoo|t/-yot; **2.** פרצוף (face) *nm* partsoof/-eem (*pl+of:* -ey); **3.** גיזרה (body) *nf* geezrah/gzarot (*+of:* geezr|at/-ot); **4.** מיספר (number) *nm* meesp|ar/-areem (*pl+of:* -erey).

(to cut a poor) figure לעשות רושם עלוב *inf* la'asot roshem 'aloov; *pst* 'asah *etc; pres* 'oseh *etc; fut* ya'aseh *etc.*

figure of speech 1. מליצה *nf* meleets|ah/-ot (*+of:* -at); **2.** ביטוי ציורי (colorful expression) *nm* beetooy/-eem tseeyooree/-yeem.

(to) figure on 1. להביא בחשבון (take into account) *inf* lehavee be-kheshbon; *pst* hevee *etc; pres* mevee *etc; fut* yavee *etc;* **2.** לסמוך על (rely on) *inf* leesmokh 'al; *pst* samakh 'al; *pres* somekh 'al; *fut* yeesmokh 'al.

(to) figure out 1. לחשב (calculate) *inf* lekhashev; *pst* kheeshev; *pres* mekhashev; *fut* yekhashev; **2.** לחשבן (reckon) *inf* lekhashben; *pst* kheeshben; *pres* mekhashben; *fut* yekhashben.

figures מספרים *nm pl* meesp|areem (*pl+of:* -erey; *sing:* meespar).

(good at) figures יודע חשבון *adj* yod|e'a'/-a'at kheshbon.

filament 1. חוט דקיק (thin thread) *nm* khoot/-eem dakeek/-eem; **2.** נימה (string) *nf* neem|ah/-ot (*+of:* -at).

file תיק *nm* teek/-eem (*pl+of:* -ey).

(to) file 1. לתייק *inf* letayek; *pst* teeyek; *pres* metayek; *fut* yetayek; **2.** לרשום תביעה (claim) *inf* leershom tvee|'ah/-'ot; *pst* rasham *etc; pres* roshem *etc; fut* yeershom *etc;* **3.** להבריק כתבה (story) *inf* lehavreek katav|ah/-ot; *pst* heevreek *etc; pres* mavreek *etc; fut* yavreek *etc.*

filial של בן/בת *adj* shel ben/bat.

filigree עבודת פיליגרן ברקמה 'avod|at/-ot feeleegran be-reekmah.

(to) fill למלא *inf* lemale; *pst* meele; *pres* memale; *fut* yemale.

(to) fill out a blank למלא טופס (fill a form) *inf* lemale tofes/tfaseem; *pst* meele *etc; pres* memale *etc; fut* yemale *etc.*

(eyes) filled with tears עיניים מלאות דמעות 'eynayeem mele'ot dema'ot.

fillet 1. בשר פילה (meat) *nm* besar feeleh; **2.** בשר שוק (tendeloin) *nm* besar shok; **3.** דג פילה (tenderloin fish) *nm* dag feeleh; **4.** סרט לשיער (ribbon for the hair) *nm* seret/srateem la-se'ar.

filling סתימה (dental) *nf* steem|ah/-ot (*+of:* -at).

(gold) filling סתימת זהב *nf* steem|at/-ot zahav.

filly סוסה *nf* soos|ah/-ot (*+of:* -at).

film סרט *nm* seret/srateem (*pl+of:* seertey).

(to) film להסריט *inf* lehasreet; *pst* heesreet; *pres* masreet; *fut* yasreet.

film actor/actress שחקן בד *nmf* sakhkan/-eet bad.

film star כוכב קולנוע *nmf* kokh|av/-evet kolno'a'.

film test מבחן בד *nm* meevkhan/-ey bad.

filter מסנן *nm* masnen/-eem (*pl+of:* -ey).

filth 1. זוהמה (scum) *nf* zoohamah (*+of:* -at); **2.** לכלוך (dirt) *nm* leekhlookh/-eem (*pl+of:* -ey).

filthiness 1. זוהמה *nf* zoohamah; **2.** הזדהמות (infection) *nf* heezdahamoo|t/-yot.

filthy 1. מזוהם (polluted) *adj* mezo|ham/-hemet; **2.** מלוכלך (dirty) *adj* melookhl|akh/-ekhet.

fin סנפיר *nm* snapeer/-eem (*pl+of:* -ey).

final 1. סופי *adj* sofee/-t; **2.** מכריע (decisive) *adj* makhree|'a'/-'ah.

finally 1. סופית *adv* sofeet; **2.** סוף סוף (at last) *adv* sof sof.

financé 1. כספים (funds) *nm pl* kesafeem (*pl+of:* kaspey; *p=f*); **2.** פיננסים *nm pl* feenanseem.

(to) finance לממן *inf* lemamen; *pst* meemen; *pres* memamen; *fut* yemamen.

financial פיננסי *adj* feenansee/-t.

financier 1. איש כספים (moneyman) *nm* eesh/anshey kesafeem; **2.** מממן (investor) *nmf* memam|en/-enet (*pl* -neem; *+of:* -ney).

financing מימון *nm* meemoon/-eem (*pl+of:* -ey).

(to) find 1. למצוא *inf* leemtso; *pst* matsa; *pres* motse; *fut* yeemtsa; **2.** לגלות (discover) *inf* legalot; *pst* geelah; *pres* megaleh; *fut* yegaleh.

(to) find an occasion למצוא הזדמנות *inf* leemtso heezdamnoot; *pst* matsa *etc; pres* motse *etc; fut* yeemtsa *etc.*

(to) find fault with למצוא פגם *inf* leemtso pegam; *pst* matsa *etc; pres* motse *etc; fut* yeemtsa *etc.*

(to) find guilty למצוא אשם *inf* leemtso ashem; *pst* matsa *etc; pres* motse *etc; fut* yeemtsa *etc.*

(to) find oneself למצוא את עצמו *inf* leemtso et 'atsmo; *pst* matsa *etc; pres* motse *etc; fut* yeemtsa *etc.*

(to) find out לגלות *inf* legalot; *pst* geelah; *pres* megaleh; *fut* yegaleh.

finding 1. ממצא *nm* meemts|a/-a'eem (*pl+of:* -a'ey); **2.** מסקנה (judicial) *nf* maskan|ah/-ot (*+of:* -at); **3.** תגלית (discovery) *nf* taglee|t/-yot.

findings מסקנות *nf pl* mask|anot (*sing:* -anah; *pl+of:* -enot).

fine 1. זך *adj* zakh/zakah (*k=kh*); **2.** עדין (delicate) *adj* 'adeen/-ah; **3.** מעולה (excellent) *adj* me'ool|eh/-ah; **4.** מצוין (excellent) *adv* metsooyan.

fine קנס (penalty) *nm* kenas/-ot.

(in) fine 1. בסופו של דבר *adv* be-sofo shel davar; **2.** בקיצור (in short) *adv* be-keetsoor.

(to) fine 1. לקנוס *inf* leeknos; *pst* kanas; *pres* kones; *fut* yeeknos; **2.** להטיל קנס (impose fine) *inf* lehateel knas; *pst* heeteel *etc; pres* mateel *etc; fut* yateel *etc.*

(to feel) fine להרגיש מצוין *inf* lehargeesh metsooyan; *pst* heergeesh *etc; pres* margeesh *etc; fut* yargeesh *etc.*

fine arts האומנויות היפות *nf pl* he-omanooyot ha-yafot.

fine-looking נראה מצוין *adj* neer'eh/-t metsoo|yan/-yenet.
fine sand חול דק *nm* khol dak.
(to have a) fine time לבלות יפה *inf* levalot yafeh; *pst* beelah *(b=v) etc; pres* mevaleh; *fut* yevaleh *etc.*
fine weather מזג אוויר נאה *nm* mezeg aveer na'eh.
finely 1. יפה (subtly) *adv* yafeh; **2.** היטב (well) *adv* heytev.
fineness 1. עדינות *nf* 'adeenoot; **2.** דקות (delicacy) *nf* dakoot.
finery 1. קישוט *nm* keeshoot/-eem (*pl+of:* -ey); **2.** הידור *nm* heedoor.
finesse 1. תחכום (sophistication) *nm* teekhkoom/-eem (*pl+of:* -ey); **2.** דקות הביצוע *nf* dakoo|t/-yot ha-beetsoo'a'; **3.** מיומנות *nf* meyoomanoo|t/-yot.
finger אצבע *nf* etsb|a'/-a'ot (*pl+of:* -e'ot).
(the little) finger זרת *nf* zeret/zratot (*pl+of:* zeertot).
(middle) finger אמה *nf* am|ah/-ot (*+of:* -at).
(to) finger להצביע על *inf* lehatsbee'a' 'al; *pst* heetsbee'a' 'al; *pres* matsbee'a' 'al; *fut* yatsbee'a' 'al.
fingernail ציפורן *nf* tseepor|en/-nayeem (*pl+of:* -ney).
fingerprint טביעת אצבע *nf* tvee|'at/-'ot 'etsb|a'/-a'ot.
finicky 1. מדקדק *adj* medakdek/-et; **2.** קפדן (fastidious) *adj* kapdan/-eet.
finish 1. גמר (end) *nm* gemar; **2.** סיום (completion) *nm* seeyoom/-eem (*pl+of:* -ey); **3.** תגמיר (finishing touch) *nm* tagmeer/-eem (*pl+of:* -ey); **4.** גימור (*synon.* with 2 & 3) geemoor/-eem (*pl+of:* -ey).
(to) finish 1. לסיים (end) *inf* lesayem; *pst* seeyem; *pres* mesayem; *fut* yesayem; **2.** להשלים (complete) *inf* lehashleem; *pst* heeshleem; *pres* mashleem; *fut* yashleem.
(a rough) finish תגמיר גרוע *nm* tagmeer garoo'a'.
finished 1. מוגמר *adj* moogm|ar/-eret; **2.** שלם *adj* shalem/shlemah.
fir 1. אורן (pine) *nm* oren/oraneem (*pl+of:* oroney); **2.** אשוח (Christmas tree) *nm* ashoo'akh/-kheem (*pl+of:* -khey)
fire 1. אש (substance) *nf* esh; **2.** שריפה (occurrence) *nf* sref|ah/-ot (*+of:* -at); **3.** דליקה (conflagration) *nf* dlek|ah/-ot (*+of:* -at)
(to) fire לירות *inf* leerot; *pst* yarah; *pres* yoreh; *fut* yeereh.
(to be on) fire לעלות בלהבות *inf* la'alot be-lehavot; *pst* 'alah *etc; pres* 'oleh *etc; fut* ya'aleh *etc.*
(to catch) fire 1. להידלק (ignite) *inf* leheedalek; *pst & pres* needlak; *fut* yeedalek; **2.** לבעור (burn) *inf* leev'or; *pst* ba'ar *(b=v); pres* bo'er; *fut* yeev'ar.
(to set on) fire 1. להעלות באש *inf* leha'alot ba-'esh; *pst* he'elah *etc; pres* ma'aleh *etc; fut* ya'aleh *etc;* **2.** להצית (ignite) *inf* lehatseet; *pst* heetseet; *pres* matseet; *fut* yatseet
(under enemy) fire תחת אש אויב *adv* takhat esh oyev.
fire alarm אזעקת דליקה *nf* az'ak|at/-ot dlekah.
fire department מדור מכבי האש *nm* medor mekhabey ha-esh.
fire engine מכונית כיבוי *nf* mekhonee|t/-yot keebooy.
fire escape 1. מפלט דליקה *nm* meefl|at/-etey dlekah; **2.** יציאת חירום (emergency exit) *nf* yetsee|'at/-'ot kheroom
fire insurance ביטוח אש *nm* beetoo|'akh/-khey esh.
(to) fire an employee לפטר עובד *inf* lefater 'oved; *pst* peeter *(p=f) etc; pres* mefater *etc; fut* yefater *etc*
firearm 1. כלי ירייה *nm* klee/kley yereeyah; **2.** נשק חם *nm* neshek kham.
firebrand 1. אוד *nm* ood/-eem (*pl+of:* -ey); **2.** גחלת (ember) *nf* gakhelet/gekhaleem (*pl+of:* gakhaley).
firecracker פצצת רעש *nf* peetsets|at/-ot ra'ash.
firefly גחלילית *nf* gakhleelee|t/-yot.
fireman כבאי *nm* kab|ay/-a'eem (*pl+of:* -a'ey).
fireplace 1. אח *nf* akh/-eem; **2.** מוקד (hearth) *nm* moked.
fireproof חסין אש *adj* khaseen/-at esh.
(to) fireproof לחסן בפני אש *inf* lekhasen beefney esh; *pst* kheesen *etc; pres* mekhasen *etc; fut* yekhasen *etc.*
fireside 1. ליד האח המבוערת *adv* leyad ha-akh ha- mevo'eret; **2.** חיק המשפחה (home) *nm* khek ha-meeshpakhah.
firewood עצי הסקה *nm pl* 'atsey hasakah.
fireworks זיקוקין די נור *nm pl* zeekookeen dee noor.
firm *adj* **1.** איתן (steady) *adj* eytan/-ah; **2.** תקיף (vigorous) *adj* takeef/-ah; **3.** מוצק (solid) *adj* mootsak/-ah.
firm פירמה (business) *nf* feerm|ah/-ot (*+of:* -at).
firmament רקיע *nm* rakee'a'/rekee|'eem (*pl+of:* -'ey).
firmly בתוקף *adv* be-tokef
firmness תקיפות *nf* takeefoot.
first ראשון *adj* reeshon/-ah.
(at) first לכתחילה *adv* le-kha-t'kheelah.
(from the) first מההתחלה *adv* me-ha-hatkhalah.
first aid עזרה ראשונה *nf* 'ezrah reeshonah.
first aid kit ערכת עזרה ראשונה *nf* 'erk|at/-ot 'ezrah reeshonah.
first-born בכור *nmf & adj* bekhor/-ah.
first-class 1. מחלקה ראשונה (railcar) *nf* makhlakah reeshonah; **2.** סוג אל״ף *adj* (AA quality) soog alef.
first-cousin 1. דודן ראשון *nmf* dodan/-eet reeshon/-ah; **2.** בן־דוד ראשון *nmf* ben-dod/bat-dodah reeshon/-ah.
first floor קומה ראשונה *nf* komah reeshonah.
firsthand 1. מיד ראשונה *adj* mee-yad reeshonah; **2.** ממקור ראשון (1st class source) *adj* mee-makor reeshon.
first-rate ממדרגה ראשונה *adj* mee-medregah reeshonah.
fish דג *nm* dag/-eem (*pl+of:* dgey).
(to) fish לדוג *inf* ladoog; *pst & pres* dag; *fut* yadoog.
fish story 1. סיפור בדים *nm* seepoor/-ey badeem; **2.** צ׳יזבט *[slang] nm* cheezbat/-eem (*pl+of:* -ey).
fish market שוק הדגים *nm* shook ha-dageem.
(neither) fish nor fowl לא הא ולא דא lo ha ve-lo da.
fisher, fisherman דייג *nm* dayag/-eem (*pl+of:* -ey).
fishery מדגה *nm* meedg|eh/-eem (*pl+of:* -ey).
fishing דייג *nm* dayeeg (*+of:* deyg).

(to go) fishing לצאת לדיג *inf* latset le-dayeeg; *pst* yatsa *etc*; *pres* yotse *etc*; *fut* yetse *etc*.

fishing for compliments מחפש מחמאות *adj* mekhapes/-et makhma'ot

fishing rod חכה *nf* khak|ah/-ot (+*of*: -at).

fishing tackle 1. גלגלת חכה *nf* galgelet khakah; **2.** ציוד לדיג *nm* tseeyood le-dayeeg

fissure בקיע *nm* bekee|'a'/'eem (*pl+of*: -'ey).

fist אגרוף *nm* egrof/-eem (*pl+of*: -ey)

(to shake one's) fist לאיים באגרוף *inf* le'ayem be-'egrof; *pst* eeyem *etc*; *pres* me'ayem *etc*; *fut* ye'ayem *etc*.

fit 1. תואם (proper) *adj* to'em/-et; **2.** כשיר (health) *adj* kasheer/kesheerah.

(is a good) fit מידה תואמת *nm* meedah to'emet.

(to) fit 1. לתאום (suit) *inf* leet'om; *pst* ta'am; *pres* to'em; *fut* yeet'am; **2.** להתאים (adapt) *inf* lehat'eem; *pst* heet'eem; *pres* mat'eem; *fut* yat'eem.

fit of anger התקף זעם *nm* hetkef/-ey za'am.

(to) fit in with להשתלב עם *inf* leheeshtalev 'eem; *pst* heeshtalev 'eem; *pres* meeshtalev 'eem; *fut* yeeshtalev 'eem.

(to) fit out 1. לצייד (equip) letsayed; *pst* tseeyed; *pres* metsayed; *fut* yetsayed; **2.** לספק צרכים (supply) lesapek tsrakheem; *pst* seepek *etc*; *pres* mesapek *etc*; *fut* yesapek *etc*.

(it does not) fit the facts אינו תואם את העובדות eyno to'em et ha-'oovdot.

fit to be tied טעון קשירה *adj* ta'oon/te'oonah ksheerah.

(not to see) fit to do it לא למצוא לנכון לעשות זאת *inf* lo leemtso le-nakhon la'asot zot; *pst* lo matsa *etc*; *pres* eyno motse *etc*; *fut* lo yeemtsa.

fitness כושר *nm* kosher.

(physical) fitness כושר גופני *nm* kosher goofanee.

(by) fits and starts 1. בצורה לא־מסודרת (irregularly) *adv* be-tsoorah lo-mesooderet; **2.** לפי מצבי רוח (according to moods) *adv* lefee matsvey roo'akh.

fitting מדידה (measurement) *nf* medeed|ah/-ot (+*of*: -at).

fitting dress שמלה תואמת *nf* seemlah/smalot to'emet/to'amot.

five 1. חמישה *num m* khameeshah; **2.** חמש *num f* khamesh; **3.** ה' *num* heh (5 in *Hebr. num. sys.*).

five hundred 1. חמש מאות (500) *num* khamesh me'ot; **2.** ת״ק *num* tak (500 in *Hebr. num. sys.*).

five thousand 1. חמשת אלפים (5,000) *num* khameshet alafeem; **2.** ה' אלפים *num* heh alafeem (5,000 in *Hebr. num. sys.*).

fix 1. מבוכה (embarrassment) *nf* mevookh|ah/-ot (+*of*: -at); **2.** עסק ביש (mishap) 'es|ek/'eeskey beesh.

(to) fix 1. לתקן (mend) *inf* letaken; *pst* teeken; *pres* metaken; *fut* yetaken; **2.** להסדיר (arrange) *inf* lehasdeer; *pst* heesdeer; *pres* masdeer; *fut* yasdeer; **3.** לחזק (strengthen) *inf* lekhazek; *pst* kheezek; *pres* mekhazek; *fut* yekhazek.

(to) fix up לאכסן (lodge) *inf* le'akhsen; *pst* eekhsen; *pres* me'akhsen; *fut* ye'akhsen.

(to) fix up differences ליישב חילוקי דעות *inf* leyashev kheelookey de'ot; *pst* yeeshev *etc*; *pres* meyashev *etc*; *fut* yeyashev *etc*.

fixed 1. קבוע *adj* kavoo'a'/kvoo'ah; **2.** איתן *adj* eytan/-ah.

fixture קביעה *nf* kvee|'ah-/'ot (+*of*: -'at).

(electric light) fixtures אינסטלציה חשמלית *nf* eenstalatsyah khashmaleet.

flabby 1. רפה (feeble) *adj* raf|eh/-ah; **2.** חלש (weak) *adj* khalash/-ah; **3.** קלוש (scanty) *adj* kaloosh/klooshah.

flag דגל *nm* deg|el/-aleem (*pl+of*: deegley).

(to) flag 1. לדגל *inf* ledagel; *pst* deegel; *pres* medagel; *fut* yedagel; **2.** להיחלש (weaken) *inf* lehekhalesh; *pst & pres* nekhlash; *fut* yekhalesh.

flag lilly אירוס *nm* eeroos/-eem (*pl+of*: -ey).

flagrant 1. גלוי (open) *adj* galooy/glooyah; **2.** מחפיר (disgraceful) *adj* makhpeer/-ah.

flagstaff נס דגל *nm* nes/neesey deg|el/-aleem.

flagstone אבן מרצפת *nf* even/avney marts|efet/-afot.

flair 1. חוש ריח *nm* khoosh reyakh; **2.** טביעת עין (intuition) *nf* tvee'at 'ayeen.

flak אש נגד מטוסים *nf* esh neged metoseem.

flake פתית *nf* pateet/peteet|eem (*pl+of*: -ey).

(corn) flakes פתיתי תירס *nf pl* peteetey teeras.

flamboyant 1. מצועצע (ostentatious) *adj* metsoo'ts|a'/-a'at; **2.** רעשני (showy) *adj* ra'ashanee/-t.

flame להבה *nf* lehav|ah/-ot (+*of*: lahevet).

(to) flame 1. להתלקח (blaze) *inf* leheetlake'ah; *pst* heetlakakh; *pres* meetlake'akh; *fut* yeetlakakh; **2.** להשתלהב (get excited) *inf* leheeshtalhev; *pst* heeshtalhev; *pres* meeshtalhev; *fut* yeeshtalhev.

flame thrower להביור *nm* lehavyor/-eem (*pl+of*: -ey).

flaming לוהט *adj* lohet/-et.

flaming red בצבע אדום לוהט *adj* be-tseva' adom lohet.

flank אגף *nm* aga|f/-peem (*p=f*; *pl+of*: -pey).

(to) flank לאגף *inf* le'agef; *pst* eegef; *pres* me'agef; *fut* ye'agef.

flannel פלנל *nm* flanel/-eem.

flap 1. סטירה *nf* (slap) steer|ah/-ot (+*of*: -at); **2.** דש (of a suit) *nm* dash/-eem (*pl+of*: -ey).

(to) flap לסטור *inf* leestor; *pst* satar; *pres* soter; *fut* yeestor.

flare 1. התלקחות (blaze) *nf* heetlak'khoo|t/-yot; **2.** זיק (glow) *nm* zeek/-eem (*pl+of*: -ey).

(to) flare להתלקח *inf* leheetlake'ah; *pst* heetlakakh; *pres* meetlake'akh; *fut* yeetalakakh.

(to) flare up להתלקח מחדש *inf* leheetlake'ah me-khadash; *pst* heetlakakh *etc*; *pres* meetlake'akh *etc*; *fut* yeetalakakh *etc*.

(the illness) flared up המחלה החריפה מחדש ha-makhlah hekhreefah me-khadash.

flash הבזק *nm* hevzek/-eem (*pl+of*: -ey)

(in a) flash 1. כהרף עין (in a trice) *adv* ke-heref 'ayeen; **2.** בן־שנייה (in a second) *adv* been shneeyah; **3.** בן־רגע (in a moment) *adv* been-rega'.

(news) flash מבזק חדשות *nm* meevz|ak/-ekey khadashot.

(to) flash 1. להבזיק *inf* lehavzeek; *pst* heevzeek; *pres* mavzeek; *fut* yavzeek; **2.** לאותת (beacon) *inf* le'otet; *pst* otet; *pres* me'otet; *fut* ye'otet.

(to) flash by לחלוף במהירות הבזק *inf* lakhlof bee-meheeroot ha-bazak; *pst* khalaf *etc; pres* kholef *etc; fut* yakhlof *etc.*

flash bulb נורת הבזקה *nf* noor|at/-ot havzakah.

flash of hope זיק תקווה *nm* zeek/-ey teekvah.

flash of lightning נצנוץ ברק *nm* neetsnoots/-ey barak.

flash of wit הברקה *nf* havrak|ah/-ot (+*of:* -at).

flashing 1. מזרה אש *adj* mezar|eh/-at esh; **2.** משלהב *adj* meshalhev/-et; **3.** מדליק *[slang] adj* madleek/-ah.

flashlight 1. פנס כיס *nm* panas/-ey kees; **2.** מנורת הבזקה *nf* menor|at/-ot havzakah.

flashy 1. שטחי *adj* sheetkhee/-t; **2.** צעקני *adj* tsa'akanee/-t.

flask 1. מימייה *nf* meymee|yah/-yot (+*of:* -yat); **2.** צלוחית *nf* tslokhee|t/-yot.

flat 1. דירה (apartment) *nf* deer|ah/-ot (+*of:* -at); **2.** שטוח (level) *adj* shatoo'akh/shtookhah; **3.** מוחלט (absolute) *adj* mookhl|at/-etet.

(D) flat דו במול *nm* do bemol.

(to fall) flat לא לעורר כל התעניינות *inf* lo le'orer kol heet'anyenoot; *pst* lo 'orer *etc; pres* eyno me'orer *etc; fut* lo ye'orer *etc.*

(to *sing*) flat לשיר מזויף *[colloq.] inf* lasheer mezooyaf; *pst & pres* shar *etc; fut* yasheer *etc.*

flat broke חסר כל *adj* khas|ar/-rat kol.

flat denial הכחשה מכל וכל *nf* hakh'khash|ah/-ot mee-kol va-khol *(kh=k).*

flat rate מחיר אחיד *nm* mekheer/-eem akheed/-eem.

flatiron מגהץ *nm* mag|'hets/'hatseem (*pl+of:* 'hatsey).

flatly 1. במפורש *adv* bee-meforash; **2.** בצורה שטחית be-tsoorah sheetkheet.

(to refuse) flatly לסרב לחלוטין *inf* lesarev la-khalooteen; *pst* serev *etc; pres* mesarev *etc; fut* yesarev *etc.*

flatness 1. שטיחות *nf* shteekhoo|t/-yot; **2.** חוסר טעם *nm* khoser ta'am; **3.** תפלות *nf* tfeloo|t/-yot.

(to) flatten 1. לרדד *inf* leraded; *pst* reeded; *pres* meraded; *fut* yeraded; **2.** לשטח *inf* leshate'akh; *pst* sheetakh; *pres* meshate'akh; *fut* yeshatakh.

flatter פטיש ריקוע *nm* pateesh/-ey rekoo'a'.

flatterer חנפן *nmf & adj* khanfan/-eet

flattering מחניף *adj* makhneef/-ah;

flattery חנופה *nf* khanoop|ah/-ot (+*of:* -at).

flatulence 1. התנפחות *nf* heetnapkhoo|t/-yot; **2.** יומרנות (pretentiousness) *nf* yomranoo|t/-yot.

(to) flaunt להתגנדר *inf* leheetgander; *pst* heetgander; *pres* meetgander; *fut* yeetgander.

flavor 1. טעם *nm* ta'am/te'ameem (*pl+of:* ta'amey); **2.** ריח (smell) *nm* rey|akh/-khot.

flavorless 1. נטול ריח *adj* netool/-at reyakh; **2.** תפל *adj* tafel/tfelah.

flaw 1. פגם *nm* pegam/-eem (*pl+of:* -ey); **2.** ליקוי *nm* leekoo|y/-yeem (*pl+of:* -yey).

flawless 1. ללא פגם *adj* le-lo pegam; **2.** ללא רבב *adj* le-lo revav.

flax פישתן *nm* peeshtan.

(to) flay 1. לפשוט את העור *inf* leefshot et ha-'or; *pst* pashat *(p=f) etc; pres* poshet *etc; fut* yeefshot *etc;* **2.** לבקר בצורה קטלנית *inf* levaker be-tsoorah katlaneet; *pst* beeker *(b=v) etc; pres* mevaker *etc; fut* yevaker *etc.*

flea פרעוש *nm* par'osh/-eem (*pl+of:* -ey).

(to) flee 1. להימלט *inf* leheemalet; *pst & pres* neemlat; *fut* yeemalet; **2.** לברוח (run away) *inf* leevro'akh; *pst* barakh *(b=v); pres* bore'akh; *fut* yeevrakh.

fleece 1. גיזה *nf* geez|ah/-ot (+*of:* -at); **2.** צמר כבשה *nm* tsemer keevsah/kvaseem.

fleet 1. צי *nm* tsee/-yeem (*pl+of:* -yey); **2.** שייטת *nf* sha|yetet/-yatot.

fleeting 1. חולף *adj* kholef/-et; **2.** קצר מועד *adj* ketsar/keetsrat mo'ed.

flesh בשר *nm* basar/besareem (+*of:* besar/beesrey).

(in the) flesh בכבודו ובעצמו *adj* bee-khvod|o/-ah oo-ve-'atsm|o/-ah *(kh=k; v=b).*

flesh and blood בשר ודם *nm* basar va-dam.

flesh color צבע העור *nm* tseva' ha-'or

fleshy 1. בשרני *adj* basranee/-t; **2.** מגושם *adj* megoosh|am/-emet.

flexibility גמישות *nf* gemeeshoo|t/-yot.

flexible גמיש *adj* gameesh/gemeeshah.

flicker הבהוב *nm* heev'hoov/-eem (*pl+of:* -ey).

(to) flicker להבהב *inf* lehavhev; *pst* heevhev; *pres* mehavhev; *fut* yehavhev.

(to) flicker one's eyelash למצמץ בעפעף *inf* lematsmets be-'af'af; *pst* meetsmets *etc; pres* mematsmets *etc; fut* yematsmets *etc.*

flier טייס *nmf* tayas/tayeset (*pl:* tayaseem; +*of:* tayasey).

flight 1. טיסה (flying) *nf* tees|ah/-ot (+*of:* -at); **2.** מנוסה (fleeing) menoos|ah/-ot (+*of:* -at).

(to put to) flight להניס *inf* lehanees; *pst* henees; *pres* menees; *fut* yanees.

flight of stairs טור מדרגות *nm* toor madregot.

flimsy 1. מדובלל *adj* medoovl|al/-elet; **2.** בלתי־יעיל *adj* beeltee ya'eel/ye'eelah.

flimsy excuse הצטדקות סרק *nf* hetstadkoo|t/-yot srak.

fling 1. זריקה *nf* zreek|ah/-ot (+*of:* -at); **2.** הטלה *nf* hatal|ah/-ot (+*of:* -at).

(to) fling 1. לזרוק *inf* leezrok; *pst* zarak; *pres* zorek; *fut* yeezrok; **2.** להטיל *inf* lehateel; *pst* heteel; *pres* meteel; *fut* yateel.

(to go out on a) fling לצאת לבלות *inf* latset levalot; *pst* yatsa *etc; pres* yotse *etc; fut* yetse *etc.*

flint 1. אבן צור *nm* even/avney tsoor; **2.** חלמיש *nm* khalameesh.

(to) flip להצליף *inf* lehatsleef; *pst* heetsleef; *pres* matsleef; *fut* yatsleef.

flippancy התחצפות קלת ראש *nf* heetkhatsfoo|t/-yot kal|at/-ot rosh.

flippant פטפטני *adj* patpetanee/-t.

flirt 1. רודף אהבים *nmf & adj* rodef/-et ahaveem; **2.** עגבים *nm pl* 'agav|eem (*pl+of:* -ey).

(to) flirt 1. לפלרטט *inf* leflartet; *pst* fleertet; *pres* meflartet; *fut* yeflartet; **2.** לעגוב *inf* la'agov; *pst* 'agav; *pres* 'ogev; *fut* ya'agov.

(to carry on a) flirt להתנות אהבים *inf* lehatnot ahaveem; *pst* heetnah *etc*; *pres* matneh *etc*; *fut* yatneh *etc*.

flirtation 1. עגיבה *nf* 'ageev|ah/-ot (*+of:* -at); **2.** fleert/-eem (*pl+of:* -ey).

(to) flit לעבור דירה *inf* la'avor deerah; *pst* 'avar *etc*; *pres* 'over *etc*; *fut* ya'avor *etc*.

float 1. דוברה *nf* dovr|ah/-ot (*+of:* -at); **2.** מצוף *nm* matsof/metsof|eem (*pl+of:* -ey).

(to) float 1. לצוף *inf* latsoof; *pst & pres* tsaf; *fut* yatsoof; **2.** להשיט *inf* lehasheet; *pst* hesheet; *pres* mesheet; *fut* yasheet; **3.** להפיץ ניירות־ערך *inf* lehafeets neyarot-'erekh; *pst* hefeets *etc*; *pres* mefeets *etc*; *fut* yafeets *etc*.

flock 1. עדר *nm* 'eder/'adareem (*pl+of:* 'edrey); **2.** צאן מרעית (congregation) *nm pl* tson mar'eet.

(to) flock 1. להתכנס *inf* leheetkanes; *pst* heetkanes; *pres* meetkanes; *fut* yeetkanes; **2.** להתקהל *inf* leheetkahel; *pst* heetkahel; *pres* meetkahel; *fut* yeetkahel.

flock of people 1. קהל *nm* kahal (*+of:* kehal); **2.** התקהלות *nf* heetkahaloo|t/-yot.

(to) flock to לנהור אל *inf* leenhor el; *pst* nahar el; *pres* noher el; *fut* yeen'har el.

(to) flock together לצעוד שכם אחד *inf* leets'od sh'khem ekhad; *pst* tsa'ad *etc*; *pres* tso'ed *etc*; *fut* yeets'ad *etc*.

(to) flog להלקות *inf* lehalkot; *pst* heelkah; *pres* malkeh; *fut* yalkeh.

flogging 1. הלקאה *nf* halka|'ah/-'ot (*+of:* -'at); **2.** מלקות *nf pl* malkot.

flood 1. שיטפון sheet|afon/-fonot (*+of:* -fon); **2.** הצפה (innundation) *nf* hatsaf|ah/-ot (*+of:* -at); **3.** מבול (deluge) *nm* mabool.

(to) flood להציף *inf* lehatseef; *pst* hetseef; *pres* metseef; *fut* yatseef.

flood tide גיאות *nf* ge'oot.

floodgate סכר *nm* sekh|er/-areem (*pl+of:* seekhrey).

floodlight זרקור *nm* zarkor/-eem (*pl+of:* -ey).

floor 1. רצפה *nf* reetspah/retsafot (*+of:* reets|pat/-fot; *f=p*); **2.** קומה (story) *nf* kom|ah/-ot (*+of:* -at).

(to have the) floor לקבל רשות הדיבור *inf* lekabel reshoot ha-deeboor; *pst* keebel *etc*; *pres* mekabel *etc*; *fut* yekabel *etc*.

flop כישלון *nm* keesh|alon/-lonot (*+of:* -lon).

(to) flop להיכשל *inf* leheekashel; *pst & pres* neekhshal *(kh=k)*; *fut* yeekashel.

(to) flop down ליפול על הפנים *inf* leepol 'al ha-paneem; *pst* nafal (*f=p*) *etc*; *pres* nofel *etc*; *fut* yeepol *etc*.

(to) flop over להתהפך *inf* leheet'hapekh; *pst* leheet'hapekh; *pres* meet'hapekh; *fut* yeet'hapekh.

florist 1. בעל חנות פרחים *nmf* (shopkeeper) ba'al/-at khanoot prakheem; **2.** מגדל פרחים (grower) *nmf* megadel/-et prakheem.

florist's shop חנות פרחים *nf* khanoo|t/-yot prakheem.

floss חוט משי *nm* khoot/-ey meshee.

(dental) floss חוט דנטלי (לניקוי שיניים) *nm* khoot/-eem dentalee/-yeem (le-neekooy sheenayeeem).

flounder 1. פוטית *nf* pootee|t/-yot; **2.** דג סנדל *nm* dag/degey sandal.

(to) flounder 1. להתבלבל בדיבור *inf* leheetbalbel be-deeboor; *pst* heetbalbel *etc*; *pres* meetbalbel *etc*; *fut* yeetbalbel *etc*; **2.** להתנהל בכבידות *inf* leheetnahel bee-khvedoot; *pst* heetnahel *etc*; *pres* meetnahel *etc*; *fut* yeetnahel *etc* (*kh=k*).

flour קמח *nm* kemakh/-eem (*pl+of:* keemkhey).

flourish 1. קישוט *nm* keeshoot/-eem (*pl+of:* -ey); **2.** פאר pe'er.

(to) flourish 1. לפרוח (bloom) *inf* leefro'akh; *pst* parakh (*p=f*); *pres* pooreakh; *fut* yeefrakh; **2.** לשגשג (economically) *inf* lesagseg; *pst* seegseg; *pres* mesagseg; *fut* yesagseg.

floury קמחי *adj* keemkhee/-t.

flow זרימה *nf* zreem|ah/-ot (*+of:* -at).

(to) flow לזרום *inf* leezrom; *pst* zaram; *pres* zorem; *fut* yeezrom.

(to) flow into לזרום לתוך *inf* leezrom le-tokh; *pst* zaram *etc*; *pres* zorem *etc*; *fut* yeezrom *etc*.

flow of words שטף דיבור *nm* shetef deeboor.

flower פרח *nm* perakh/prakheem (*pl+of:* peerkhey).

flower bed ערוגת פרחים *nf* 'aroog|at/-ot prakheem.

flower vase אגרטל פרחים *nm* agartel/-ey prakheem.

flowering 1. פורח *adj* por|e'akh/-akhat; **2.** פריחה *nf* preekh|ah/-ot (*+of:* -at).

flowerpot עציץ *nm* 'atseets/-eem (*pl+of:* -ey).

flowery 1. נמלץ *adj* neeml|ats/-etset; **2.** מסולסל *adj* mesoolsal/-elet.

flowing 1. זורם *adj* zorem/-et; **2.** זרימה *nf* zreem|ah/-ot (*+of:* -at).

flowing with riches שופע עושר *adj* shof|e'a'/-a'at 'osher.

flown מוטס *adj* moot|as/-eset.

flu שפעת *nf* shapa'at.

fluctuate 1. להתנודד *inf* leheetnoded; *pst* heetnoded; *pres* meetnoded; *fut* yeetnoded; **2.** לעלות ולרדת *inf* la'alot ve-laredet; *pst* 'alah ve-yarad; *pres* 'oleh ve-yored; *fut* ya'aleh ve-yered.

fluctuation תנודה *nf* tenood|ah/-ot (*+of:* -at).

flue 1. ארובה *nf* aroob|ah/-ot (*+of:* -at); **2.** מעשנה *nf* ma'ashen|ah/-ot (*+of:* -at).

fluency 1. שטף *nm* shetef/shtafeem (*pl+of:* sheetfey); **2.** רהיטות *nf* reheetoo|t/-yot.

fluent שוטף *adj* shotef/-et.

fluently בשטף *adv* be-shetef.

(to speak Hebrew) fluently לדבר עברית שוטפת *inf* ledaber 'eevreet shotefet; *pst* deeber *etc*; *pres* medaber *etc*; *fut* yedaber *etc*.

fluff 1. מוך *nm* mokh; **2.** טעות בדקלום (error) *nf* ta'oo|t/-yot be-deekloom.

fluffy דמוי מוך *adj* dmooy/-at mokh.

fluffy hair שיער דמוי מוך *nm* sey'ar dmooy mokh.

fluid 1. נוזל *nm* noz|el/-leem (*pl+of:* -ley); **2.** נוזל *adj* nozel/-et; **3.** נזיל *adj* nazeel/nezeelah.

(to) flunk להיכשל *inf* leheekashel; *pst & pres* neekhshal *(kh=k)*; *fut* yeekashel.

(to) flunk out 1. לסלק מבית ספר *inf* lesalek mee-bet sefer; *pst* seelek *etc*; *pres* mesalek *etc*; *fut* yesalek *etc*; **2.** להסתלק מבית הספר *inf* leheestalek mee-bet ha-sefer; *pst* heestalek *etc*; *pres* meestalek *etc*; *fut* yeestalek *etc*.

flunky מלחך פנכה *adj* melakhekh/-et peenkah.

flurry 1. המולה *nf* hamool|ah/-ot (+*of*: -at); **2.** סערה *nf* se'ar|ah/-ot (+*of*: sa'arat).

flush (*adj*) **1.** שופע (abounding) *adj* shof|e'a'/-a'at; **2.** גדוש (full) *adj* gadoosh/gedooshah; **3.** סמוק (red) *adj* samook/smookah.

flush (n) משטף *nm* mashtef/-eem (*pl+of*: -ey).

(to) flush להסמיק *inf* lehasmeek; *pst* heesmeek; *pres* masmeek; *fut* yasmeek.

(to) flush out לשטוף החוצה *inf* leeshtof ha-khootsah; *pst* shataf *etc*; *pres* shotef *etc*; *fut* yeeshtof *etc*.

flute חליל *nm* khaleel/-eem (*pl+of*: -ey).

(to) flute לחלל *inf* lekhalel; *pst* kheelel; *pres* mekhalel; *fut* yekhalel.

flutter 1. נפנוף *nm* neefnoof/-eem (*pl+of*: -ey); **2.** רטט *nm* retet.

(to) flutter 1. לנפנף *inf* lenafnef; *pst* neefnef; *pres* menafnef; *fut* yenafnef; **2.** לרטט *inf* leratet; *pst* reetet; *pres* meratet; *fut* yeratet; **3.** לבוא במבוכה *inf* lavo bee-mevookhah; *pst & pres* ba (*b=v*) *etc*; *fut* yavo *etc*.

fly זבוב zvoov/-eem (*pl+of*: -ey).

(on the) fly באוויר *adv* ba-aveer

(to) fly 1. לעוף *inf* la'oof; *pst & pres* 'af *etc*; *fut* ya'oof; **2.** לטוס *inf* latoos; *pst & pres* tas; *fut* yatoos.

(to) fly at 1. לתקוף בחריפות *inf* leetkof be-khareefoot; *pst* takaf *etc*; *pres* tokef *etc*; *fut* yeetkof *etc*; **2.** להתפרץ באלימות *inf* leheetparets be-aleemoot; *pst* heetparets *etc*; *pres* meetparets *etc*; *fut* yeetparets *etc*.

(to) fly away להתעופף *inf* leheet'ofef; *pst* heet'ofef; *pres* meet'ofef; *fut* yeet'ofef.

(to) fly off the handle לצאת מן הכלים *inf* latset meen ha-keleem; *pst* yatsa *etc*; *pres* yotse *etc*; *fut* yetse *etc*.

(to) fly open להיפתח פתאום *inf* leheepatakh peet'om; *pst & pres* neeftakh (*f=p*) *etc*; *fut* yeepatakh *etc*.

(to) fly shut להיסגר פתאום *inf* leheesager peet'om; *pst & pres* neesgar *etc*; *fut* yeesager *etc*.

(to) fly up in anger להיתקף זעם *inf* leheetakef za'am; *pst & pres* neetkaf *etc*; *fut* yeetakef *etc*.

flyleaf דף חלק בספר *nm* daf/dapeem (*p=f*) khalak/-eem be-sefer.

foam קצף *nm* ketsef.

(to) foam להעלות קצף *inf* leha'alot ketsef; *pst* he'elah *etc*; *pres* ma'aleh *etc*; *fut* ya'aleh *etc*.

focus מוקד *nm* mok|ed/-deem (*pl+of*: -dey).

(to) focus 1. למקד *inf* lemaked; *pst* meeked; *pres* memaked; *fut* yemaked; **2.** להתמקד (concentrate on) *v rfl inf* leheetmaked; *pst* heetmaked; *pres* meetmaked; *fut* yeetmaked.

fodder 1. מספוא *nm* meespo; **2.** חציר *nm* khatseer/-eem (*pl+of*: -ey).

foe 1. אויב *nm* oyev/oyv|eem (*pl+of*: -ey); **2.** יריב (rival) *nmf* yareev/yereev|ah (*pl* -eem/-ot; *pl+of*: -ey).

fog ערפל *nm* 'ar|afel/-peleem (*p=f*; *pl+of*: -feeley).

(to) fog לערפל *inf* le'arpel; *pst* 'eerpel; *pres* me'arpel; *fut* ye'arpel.

foggy מעורפל *adj* me'oorp|al/-elet.

foghorn צופר ערפל *nm* tsof|ar/-rey 'arafel.

foil רדיד *nm* redeed/-eem (*pl+of*: -ey).

(tin) foil פח מרודד *nm* pakh/-eem meroodad/-eem.

(to) foil לסכל *inf* lesakel; *pst* seekel; *pres* mesakel; *fut* yesakel.

fold 1. קפל *nm* kefel/kfaleem (*pl+of*: keefley); **2.** קיפול *[colloq.] nm* keepool/-eem (*pl+of*: -ey).

(to) fold לקפל *inf* lekapel; *pst* keepel; *pres* mekapel; *fut* yekapel.

(to) fold one's arms להסתכל בחיבוק ידים *inf* leheestakel be-kheebook yadayeem; *pst* heestakel *etc*; *pres* meestakel *etc*; *fut* yeestakel *etc*.

(hundred)fold פי מאה *adv* pee me'ah.

(three)fold פי שלושה *adv* pee shloshah.

folder 1. תיק *nm* teek/-eem (*pl+of*: -ey); **2.** עוטפן *nm* 'otfan/-eem (*pl+of*: -ey).

folding מתקפל *adj* meetkapel/-et.

folding blinds תריסים מתקפלים *nm pl* treeseem meetkapleem.

folding door דלת מתקפלת *nf* delet/dlatot meetkap|elet/-lot.

folding machine מכונת קיפול *nf* mekhon|at/-ot keepool.

folding screen מסך מתקפל *nm* masakh meetkapel.

foliage עלווה *nf* 'alv|ah/-ot (+*of*: -at).

folio פוליו *nm* folyo.

folio edition מהדורת פוליו *nf* mahadoor|at/-ot folyo.

folk 1. עם *nm* am/amam|eem (*pl+of*: -ey); **2.** עממי *adj* 'amamee/-t; **3.** שבט (tribe) *nm* shevet/shvateem (*pl+of*: sheevtey).

folk dance 1. מחול עם *nm* mekhol/-ot 'am; **2.** ריקוד עם *nm* reekood/-ey 'am.

folk music מוסיקה עממית *nf* mooseekah 'amameet.

folklore פולקלור *nm* folklor/-eem.

folks קרובי משפחה *nm pl* krovey meeshpakhah

(to) follow 1. ללכת אחרי *inf* lalekhet akharey; *pst* halakh *etc*; *pres* holekh *etc*; *fut* yelekh *etc*; **2.** לצאת בעיקבות (in the steps) *inf* latset be-'eekvot; *pst* yatsa *etc*; *pres* yotse *etc*; *fut* yetse *etc*. **3.** לבוא בתוצאת *inf* lavo be-tots'at; *pst & pres* ba (*b=v*) *etc*; *fut* yavo *etc*.

(to) follow suit להמשיך באותה דרך *inf* lehamsheekh be-otah derekh; *pst* heemsheekh *etc*; *pres* mamsheekh *etc*; *fut* yamsheekh *etc*.

follower 1. תלמיד *nmf* talmeed/-ah (*pl*: -eem/-ot; +*of*: -at/-ey); **2.** חסיד (partisan) *nmf* khaseed/-ah (*pl*: -eem/-ot; +*of*: -at/-ey).

following 1. דלהלן *adj* deel'halan; **2.** קהל חסידים (flock of followers) *nm* kehal khaseedeem; **3.** ציבור מעריצים *nm* tseeboor ma'areetseem (admirers).

(as) follows כדלקמן ke-deelkaman.

folly 1. שיגעון *nm* sheeg|a'on/-'onot (+*of*: -'on); **2.** סיכלות (stupidity) *nf* seekhloo|t/-yot.

(to) foment 1. ללבות *inf* lelabot; *pst* leebah; *pres* melabeh; *fut* yelabeh; **2.** לחרחר (instigate) *inf* lekharkher; *pst* kheerkher; *pres* mekharkher; *fut* yekharkher.

fond 1. מחבב *v pres & adj* mekhabev/-et; **2.** כרוך אחרי *adj* karookh/krookhah akharey; **3.** מטופש *adj* metoop|ash/-eshet.

(to be) fond of לחבב *inf* lekhabev; *pst* kheebev; *pres* mekhabev; *fut* yekhabev.

(to) fondle ללטף *inf* lelatef; *pst* leetef; *pres* melatef; *fut* yelatef.

fondly 1. בחיבה *adv* be-kheebah; **2.** בטעות (erroneously) *adv* be-ta'oot.

fondness חיבה *nf* kheeb|ah/-ot (+*of:* -at).

font 1. מקור *nm* makor/mekorot (+*of:* mekor); **2.** סוג אותיות (type) *nm* soog/-ey oteeyot.

food 1. מזון *nm* ma|zon/mezonot (*pl+of:* mezon); **2.** מאכל (dish) *nm* ma'akhal/-eem (*pl+of:* -ey).

(frozen) food מאכל מוקפא *nm* ma'akhal/-eem mookpa/-'eem.

fool 1. שוטה *nmf* shot|eh/-ah; **2.** מטורף (madman) *nmf & adj* metor|af/-efet.

(to) fool 1. לשטות *inf* leshatot; *pst* sheetah; *pres* meshateh; *fut* yeshateh; **2.** לרמות (deceive) *inf* leramot; *pst* reemah; *pres* merameh; *fut* yerameh.

(to play the) fool להשתטות *inf* leheeshtatot; *pst* heeshtatah; *pres* meeshtateh; *fut* yeeshtateh.

(to) fool away the time להעביר זמן *inf* leha'aveer zman; *pst* he'eveer *etc*; *pres* ma'aveer *etc*; *fut* ya'aveer *etc*.

foolish טיפשי *adj* teepshee/-t.

foolishness טיפשות *nf* teepshoo|t/-yot.

foot 1. רגל *nf* regel/ragl|ayeem (*pl+of:* -ey); **2.** רגל *nf* (measure) regel.

(on) foot ברגל *adv* be-regel.

(to) foot 1. לפרוע *inf* leefro'a'; *pst* para' *(p=f)*; *pres* pore'a'; *fut* yeefra'; **2.** לסכם (sum up) *inf* lesakem; *pst* seekem; *pres* mesakem; *fut* yesakem.

(to put one's) foot in it לשגות משגה חמור *inf* leeshgot meeshgeh khamoor; *pst* shagah *etc*; *pres* shogeh *etc*; *fut* yeeshgeh *etc*.

foot soldier חייל רגלי *nm* khayal/-eem raglee/-yeem.

(to) foot the bill 1. לסלק חוב *inf* lesalek khov; *pst* seelek *etc*; *pres* mesalek *etc*; *fut* yesalek *etc*; **2.** לפרוע הוצאות (cover expenses) *inf* leefro'a' hotsa'ot; *pst* para' *(p=f) etc*; *pres* pore'a' *etc*; *fut* yeefra' *etc*.

football כדורגל (soccer) *nm* kadooregel.

footballer כדורגלן *nm* kadooraglan/-eem (*pl+of:* -ey).

foothold 1. מדרך כף רגל *nm* meedrakh kaf regel; **2.** דריסת רגל (access) *nm* drees|at/-ot regel.

footing 1. אחיזה *nf* akheez|ah/-ot (+*of:* -at); **2.** מעמד (standing) *nm* ma'amad/-ot.

(on a friendly) footing על רקע ידידותי *adv* 'al reka' yedeedootee.

(to lose one's) footing להפסיד מעמד *inf* lehafseed ma'amad; *pst* heefseed *etc*; *pst* mafseed *etc*; *fut* yafseed *etc*.

footlights אורות בימה *nm pl* orot beemah.

footman שמש במדים *nm* shamash/-eem be-madeem.

footnote הערת שוליים *nf* he'ar|at/-ot shoolayeem.

footpath שביל להולכי רגל *nm* shveel/-eem le-holkhey regel.

footprints עקבות *nm pl* 'akevot (*sing:* 'akev; *pl+of:* 'eekvot).

footstep צעד *nm* tsa'ad/tse'adeem (*pl+of:* tsa'adey).

(in the) footsteps of בעיקבות *adv* be-'eekvot.

footstool 1. שרפרף *nm* shrafra|f/-peem (*pl+of:* -pey); **2.** הדום *nm* hadom.

fop גנדרן *nm* gandran/-eem (*pl+of:* -ey).

for 1. בשביל *conj* beeshveel; **2.** בעבור *conj* ba-'avoor (*[colloq.]* 'avoor); **3.** למען *conj* lema'an; **4.** בעד *conj* be'ad.

(to pay one) for לשלם למישהו בעבור *inf* leshalem le-meeshehoo ba-'avoor; *pst* sheelem *etc*; *pres* meshalem *etc*; *fut* yeshalem *etc*.

(to thank one) for להודות בעבור *inf* lehodot ba-'avoor; *pst* hodah *etc*; *pres* modeh *etc*; *fut* yodeh *etc*.

(to know) for a fact לדעת בוודאות *inf* lada'at be-vada'oot; *pst* yada' *etc*; *pres* yode'a' *etc*; *fut* yeda' *etc*.

for all of one's intelligence עם כל חוכמתו 'eem kol khokhmat|o/-ah *(m/f)*.

for fear that מחשש פן *adv* me-khashash pen.

for good לעולמים *adv* le-'olameem.

(to take) for granted לקבל כמובן מאליו *inf* lekabel ke-moov|an/-enet me-'el|av/-eha *(m/f)*; *pst* keebel *etc*; *pres* mekabel *etc*; *fut* yekabel *etc*.

(as) for him/her אשר לו asher lo/lah.

for the present 1. בינתיים *adv* benatayeem; **2.** לעת עתה (meantime) *adv* le'et 'atah.

forage 1. מספוא *nm* meespo; **2.** חציר *nm* khatseer/-eem (*pl+of:* -ey).

(to) forage לחפש אחר מזון *inf* lekhapes akhar mazon; *pst* kheepes *etc*; *pres* mekhapes *etc*; *fut* yekhapes *etc*.

foray 1. פשיטה *nf* pesheet|ah/-ot (+*of:* -at); **2.** בזיזה (pillage) *nf* bezeez|ah/-ot (+*of:* -at).

(to) foray 1. לפשוט על *inf* leefshot 'al; *pst* pashat *(p=f)* 'al; *pres* poshet 'al; *fut* yeefshot 'al; **2.** לבוז (despoil) *inf* lavoz; *pst* bazaz *(b=v)*; *pres* bozez; *fut* yavoz.

forbear 1. אב קדמון *nm* av/-ot kadmon/-eem; **2.** אבי אבות (forefather) *nm* avee avot.

(to) forbear 1. לגלות סבלנות *inf* legalot savlanoot; *pst* geelah *etc*; *pres* megaleh *etc*; *fut* yegaleh *etc*; **2.** לחוס על (spare) *inf* lakhoos 'al; *pst pst & pres* khas 'al; *fut* yakhoos 'al; **3.** להימנע (abstain) *inf* leheemana'; *pst & pres* neemna'; *fut* yeemana'.

(to) forbid לאסור *inf* le'esor; *pst* asar; *pres* oser; *fut* ye'esor.

forbidden אסור *adj* asoor/-ah.

(it is) forbidden אסור *adv* asoor.

forbidding 1. דוחה *adj* dokh|eh/-ah; **2.** לא נעים (unpleasant) *adj* lo na'eem/ne'eemah.

force 1. כוח (power) *nm* ko'akh/kokhot; **2.** עוז (valor) *nm* 'oz; **3.** אלימות (violence) *nf* aleemoo|t/-yot.

(by) force 1. בכוח *adv* be-kho'akh *(kh=k)*; **2.** באונס (forcibly) *adv* be-'ones.

(in) force 1. בתוקף *adj* be-tokef; **2.** בר־תוקף (valid) *adj* bar/-at (+*of:* -at) tokef.

(to) force 1. להכריח (compel) lehakhree'akh; *pst* heekhree'akh; *pres* makhree'akh; *fut* yakhree'akh; **2.** לאכוף (enforce) le'ekhof; *pst* akhaf; *pres* okhef; *fut* ye'ekhof.

(to) force one's way להבקיע דרך *inf* lehavkee'a' derekh; *pst* heevkee'a' *etc*; *pres* mavkee'a' *etc*; *fut* yavkee'a' *etc*.

(to) force out לסלק בכוח *inf* lesalek be-kho'akh *(kh=k)*; *pst* seelek *etc*; *pres* mesalek *etc*; *fut* yesalek *etc*.

forced נאלץ *v pres & adj* ne'el|ats/-etset.

forceful 1. נמרץ *adj* neemr|ats/-etset; **2.** תקיף (firm) *adj* takeef/-ah.

forceps מלקחיים *nm pl* melk|akhayeem (*pl+of:* -ekhey)

(armed) forces כוחות מזוינים *nm pl* kokhot mezooyaneem.

forcible 1. חזק *adj* khazak/-ah; **2.** נמרץ (determined) *adj* neemr|ats/-etset.

ford 1. חציית נחל ברגל *nf* khatsee|yat/-yot nakhal ba-regel; **2.** מים רדודים (shallow waters) *nm pl* mayeem redoodeem.

(to) ford לחצות נחל ברגל *inf* lakhtsot nakhal ba-regel; *pst* khatsah *etc*; *pres* khotseh *etc*; *fut* yekhtseh *etc*

fore 1. קדמי *adj* keedmee/-t; **2.** קודם (previously) *adv* kodem; **3.** !הצידה (step aside!) *interj* hatseedah!

fore- (*prefix*) טרום (*prefix*) troom-.

forearm 1. אמת היד *nf* am|at/-ot ha-yad/-ayeem; **2.** זרוע *nf* zro|'a'/-'ot.

(to) forebode לנחש מראש *inf* lenakhesh me-rosh; *pst* neekhesh *etc*; *pres* menakhesh *etc*; *fut* yenakhesh *etc*.

foreboding רואה שחורות *adj* ro|'eh/-'ah sh'khorot.

forecast תחזית *nf* takhzee|t/-yot.

(to) forecast לחזות מראש *inf* lakhzot me-rosh; *pst* khazah *etc*; *pres* khozeh *etc*; ft yekhzeh *etc*.

(weather) forecast תחזית מזג אוויר *nf* takhzee|t/-yot mezeg aveer.

forecaster חזאי *nmf* khaz|ay/-'eet.

(to) foreclose לעקל *inf* le'akel; *pst* 'eekel; *pres* me'akel; *fut* ye'akel.

foreclosure עיקול 'eekool/-eem (*pl+of:* -ey).

forefather 1. אב קדמון *nm* av/-ot kadmon/-eem; **2.** אבי אבות *nm* avee/avot avot.

forefinger אצבע *nf* etsb|a'/-a'ot.

forefoot רגל קדמית *nf* regel/raglayeem keedmee|t/-yot.

(to) forego 1. לוותר *inf* levater; *pst* veeter; *pres* mevater; *fut* yevater; **2.** להתעלם מ־ (disregard) *inf* leheet'alem mee-; *pst* heet'alem mee-; *pres* meet'alem mee-; *fut* yeet'alem mee-; **3.** להימנע מ־ (abstain) *inf* leheemana' mee-; *pst & pres* neemna' mee-; *fut* yeemana' mee-.

foregone conclusion מסקנה בלתי־נמנעת *nf* maskan|ah/-ot beeltee neemn|a'at/-'ot.

foreground רקע קדמי *nm* reka' keedmee.

forehead מצח *nm* metsakh/-eem (*pl+of:* meetskhey).

foreign 1. נוכרי *adj* nokhree/-t; **2.** זר *adj* zar/-ah.

foreign-born 1. יליד נכר *nmf* yeleed/-at nekhar; **2.** יליד חוץ לארץ *nmf* yeleed/-at khoots-la-arets; **3.** יליד חו"ל *nmf* yeleed/-at khool (*acr of* 2).

foreign currency 1. מטבע חוץ *nm* matbe'a' khoots; **2.** מטבע זר *[colloq.] nm* matbe'a' zar.

foreign office משרד החוץ *nm* meesrad ha-khoots.

foreign to one's nature זר לרוחו *adj* zar/-ah le-rookh|o/-ah.

foreign trade סחר חוץ *nm* sekhar khoots.

foreigner 1. נוכרי *nmf* nokhree/-yah; **2.** זר (stranger) *nmf* zar/-ah (*pl:* -eem/-ot).

forelock 1. ציצת ראש *nf* tseets|at/-ot rosh; **2.** תלתל מצח *nm* taltal/-ey metsakh.

foreman 1. מנהל עבודה *nm* mena|hel/-haley 'avodah; **2.** משגיח (overseer) *nm* mashgee|'akh/-kheem (*pl+of:* -khey).

foremost 1. ראשי *adj* rashee/-t; **2.** חשוב ביותר (most important) *adj* khashoov/-ah be-yoter.

forenoon לפני הצהריים leefney ha-tsohorayeem.

forerunner 1. מבשר *nmf* mevaser/-et; **2.** חלוץ (pioneer) *nmf* khaloots/-ah.

foresaid 1. הנזכר לעיל *adj* ha-neezk|ar/-eret le-'eyl; **2.** הנ"ל *adj* hanal (*acr of* 1).

(to) foresee לחזות מראש *inf* lakhzot me-rosh; *pst* khazah *etc*; *pres* khozeh *etc*; *fut* yekhzeh *etc*.

foresight ראיית הנולד *nf* re'eeyat ha-nolad.

forest יער *nm* ya'ar/ye'arot (*pl+of:* ya'arot).

forest ranger שומר יער *nm* shom|er/-rey ya'ar.

(to) forestall לקדם פני *inf* lekadem peney; *pst* keedem *etc*; *pres* mekadem *etc*; *fut* yekadem *etc*.

forester יערן *nm* ya'aran/-eem (*pl+of:* -ey).

forestry יערנות *nf* ya'aranoot.

foretaste התענגות מראש *nf* heet'angoo|t/-yot me-rosh.

(to) foretell לנבא מראש *inf* lenabe me-rosh; *pst* neeba *etc*; *pres* menabe *etc*; *fut* yenabe *etc*.

foretooth שן קדמית *nf* shen/sheenayeem keedmee|t/-yot.

forever לנצח *adv* la-netsakh.

forfeit 1. קנס (fine) *nm* knas/-ot; **2.** כופר (ransom) *nm* kofer; **3.** משכון (pawn) *m* mashkon/-ot.

(to) forfeit 1. להפסיד זכות (right) *inf* lehafseed zekhoot; *pst* heefseed *etc*; *pres* mafseed *etc*; *fut* yafseed *etc*; **2.** לחלט (confiscate) *inf* lekhalet; *pst* kheelet; *pres* mekhalet; *fut* yekhalet.

(to) forge 1. לזייף (falsify) *inf* lezayef; *pst* zeeyef; *pres* mezayef; *fut* yezayef; **2.** לחשל (shape) *inf* lekhashel; *pst* kheeshel; *pres* mekhashel; *fut* yekhashel.

(to) forge ahead להתקדם *inf* leheetkadem; *pst* heetkadem; *pres* meetkadem; *fut* yeetkadem.

forgery זיוף *nm* zeeyoof/-eem (*pl+of:* -ey).

(to) forget לשכוח *inf* leeshko'akh; *pst* shakhakh; *pres* shokhe'akh; *fut* yeeshkakh *(kh=k)*.

forget-me-not 1. זכריה *nf* zeekhree|yah/-yot (+*of:* -yat); **2.** אל תשכחיני *nm* al teeshkakheenee.

(to) forget oneself 1. לאבד עשתונות *inf* le'abed 'eshtonot; *pst* eebed *etc*; *pres* me'abed *etc*; *fut* ye'abed *etc*; **2.** להתבלבל *inf* leheetbalbel; *pst* heetbalbel; *pres* meetbalbel; *fut* yeetbalbel.

(if I) forget thee, oh Jerusalem, let my right hand forget her cunning אם אשכחך, ירושלים,

תשכח ימיני eem eshkakhekh, yerooshalayeem, teeshkakh yemeenee!
forgetful שכחן *adj* shakhekhan/-eet.
forgetfulness שכחנות *nf* shakhekhanoot.
(to) forgive לסלוח *inf* leeslo'akh; *pst* salakh; *pres* sole'akh; *fut* yeeslakh.
(to) forgive a debt לוותר על חוב *inf* levater 'al khov; *pst* veeter *etc*; *pres* mevater *etc*; *fut* yevater *etc*.
(to) forgive a sin למחול עוון *inf* leemkhol 'avon/-ot; *pst* makhal *etc*; *pres* mokhel *etc*; *fut* yeemkhol *etc*.
forgiveness 1. סליחה *nf* sleekh|ah/-ot (+*of:* -at); **2.** מחילה *nf* mekheel|ah/-ot (+*of:* -at).
forgiving סלחני *adj* salkhanee/-t.
forgotten נשכח *adj* neeshkakh/-at.
fork 1. מזלג (eating) *m* mazleg/-ot; **2.** קילשון (pitchfork) *nm* keelshon/-eem (*pl+of:* -ey).
(to) fork 1. להסתעף *inf* leheesta'ef; *pst* heesta'ef; *pres* meesta'ef; *fut* yeesta'ef; **2.** להיפרד *inf* leheepared; *pst & pres* neefrad (*f=p*); *fut* yeepared.
forlorn 1. נטוש (derelict) *adj* natoosh/netooshah; **2.** עזוב (abandoned) *adj* 'azoov/-ah; **3.** חסר תקווה (hopeless) *adj* khas|ar/-rat teekvah.
form 1. צורה (shape) *nf* tsoor|ah/-ot (+*of:* -at); **2.** תבנית (mould) *nf* tavnee|t/-yot.
(blank) form טופס חלק *nm* tofes/tfaseem khalak/-eem.
(to) form 1. ליצור *inf* leetsor; *pst* yatsar; *pres* yotser; *fut* yeetsor; **2.** לעצב *inf* le'atsev; *pst* 'eetsev; *pres* me'atsev; *fut* ye'atsev; **3.** להוות (constitute) *inf* lehavot; *pst* heevah; *pres* mehaveh; *fut* yehaveh.
formal 1. פורמלי *adj* formalee/-t; **2.** מדויק (exact) *adj* medooy|ak/-yeket; **3.** רשמי (official) *adj* reeshmee/-t.
formal party מסיבה בתלבשות ערב *nf* meseebah be-teelbashot 'erev.
formality 1. פורמליות *nf* formaleeyoo|t/-yot; **2.** פרט פורמלי (detail) *nm* prat/-eem formalee/-yeem.
formally 1. רשמית *adv* reeshmeet; **2.** באורח רשמי (officially) *adv* be-orakh reeshmee.
format 1. גודל *nm* godel/gedaleem (*pl+of:* godley); **2.** צורה (shape) *nf* tsoor|ah/-ot (+*of:* -at); **3.** תבנית (mould) *nf* tavnee|t/-yot.
formation 1. מערך *nm* ma'ar|akh/-akheem (*pl+of:* -khey); **2.** תצורה *nf* tetsoor|ah/-ot (+*of:* -at).
formative צורני *adj* tsooranee/-t.
former לשעבר *adj* le-she-'avar.
(the) former 1. מי שהיה (ex) *adj* mee she-hay|ah/-tah; **2.** הנזכר לעיל (the above) *pron* ha-neezk|ar/-eret le-'eyl; **3.** הנ״ל *pron* ha-nal (*acr of* 2).
(in) former times בזמנים עברו bee-zmaneem 'avaroo.
formerly 1. לפנים *adv* lefaneem; **2.** לשעבר (onetime) *adv* le-she-'avar.
formidable 1. עצום *adj* 'atsoom/-ah; **2.** כביר (tremendous) *adj* kabeer/-ah.
formula 1. נוסחה *nf* nooskh|ah/-a'ot (+*of:* -at); **2.** נוסח (variation) *nm* noos|akh/-akheem (*pl+of:* -khey).
(to) formulate לנסח *inf* lenase'akh; *pst* neesakh; *pres* menase'akh; *fut* yenase'akh.
(to) forsake 1. לזנוח *inf* leezno'akh; *pst* zanakh; *pres* zone'akh; *fut* yeeznakh; **2.** לנטוש (abandon) *inf* leentosh; *pst* natash; *pres* notesh; *fut* yeentosh.
forsaken 1. זנוח *adj* zanoo'akh/znookhah; **2.** נטוש (abandoned) *adj* natoosh/netooshah.
(to) forswear 1. לוותר בשבועה (renounce) *inf* levater bee-shvoo'ah; *pst* veeter *etc*; *pres* mevater *etc*; *fut* yevater *etc*; **2.** להכחיש בשבועה (deny under oath) *inf* lehakh'kheesh bee-shvoo'ah; *pst* heekh'kheesh *etc*; *pres* makh'kheesh *etc*; *fut* yakh'kheesh *etc*; **3.** להישבע לשקר (perjure) *inf* leheeshava' la-sheker; *pst & pres* neeshba' (*b=v*) *etc*; *fut* yeeshava' *etc*.
fort 1. מצודה *nf* metsood|ah/-ot (+*of:* -at); **2.** מיבצר *nm* meevts|ar/-areem (*pl+of:* -erey).
forth 1. קדימה *adv* kadeemah; **2.** הלאה (further) *adv* hal'ah.
(and so) forth 1. וכן הלאה ve-khen (*kh=k*) hal'ah; **2.** וכולי (*etc*) ve-khooley; **3.** וכולי וכולי (*etc etc*) ve-khooley ve-khooley.
(back and) forth 1. הלוך ושוב *adv* halokh va-shoov; **2.** הנה והנה *adv* henah ve-henah.
(to go) forth לצאת *inf* latset; *pst* yatsa; *pres* yotse; *fut* yetse.
forthcoming ממשמש ובא *adj* memashmesh/-et oo-va/-'ah (*v=b*).
(will not be) forthcoming לא יבוא במהרה lo yavo bee-meherah.
forthright 1. ישר *adj* yashar/yesharah; **2.** מידי (immediate) meeyadee/-t.
forthright answer תשובה מידית *nf* teshoov|ah/-ot meeyadee|t/-yot.
forthwith 1. מיד *adv* meeyad; **2.** תיכף (presently) *adv* teykhef.
fortieth 1. הארבעים *adj* ha-arba'eem; **2.** מ׳ *adj* mem (40th in *Hebr. num. sys.*).
fortification ביצור *nm* beetsoor/-eem (*pl+of:* -ey).
(to) fortify 1. לבצר (reinforce) *inf* levatser; *pst* beetser (*b=v*); *pres* mevatser; *fut* yevatser; **2.** לחזק (strengthen) *inf* lekhazek; *pst* kheezek; *pres* mekhazek; *fut* yekhazek; **3.** לעודד (encourage) *inf* le'oded; *pst* 'oded; *pres* me'oded; *fut* ye'oded.
fortitude 1. חוזק *nm* khozek; **2.** עוז *nm* 'oz.
fortnight שבועיים *nm pl* shvoo'ayeem.
fortress 1. מבצר *nm* meevts|ar/-areem (*pl+of:* -erey); **2.** מעוז (stronghold) *nm* ma'oz/ma'ooz|eem (*pl+of:* -ey).
fortuitous 1. מקרי *adj* meekree/-t; **2.** ארעי (provisional) *adj* ara'ee/-t.
fortunate בר־מזל *adj* bar/bat mazal.
fortunately למרבה המזל *adv* le-marbeh ha-mazal.
fortune 1. הון (capital) *nm* hon; **2.** רכוש (property) *nm* rekhoosh; **3.** מזל (luck) *nm* mazal.
fortuneteller מגיד עתידות *nmf* mageed/-at ateedot.
forty 1. ארבעים *num* arba'eem; **2.** מ׳ *num* mem (40 in *Hebr. num. sys.*).
forty-first 1. הארבעים ואחד/ואחת *adj* ha-arba'eem ve-ekhad/ve-akhat (*m/f*); **2.** המ״א *adj* ha-mem-alef (41st in *Hebr. num. sys.*).
forty-second 1. הארבעים ושניים/ושתיים *adj num* ha-arba'eem oo-shnayeem/oo-shtayeem (*m/f*);

2. המ״ב *adj* ha-mem-bet (42nd in *Hebr. num. sys.*).

forty-third **1.** הארבעים ושלושה/ושלוש *ord num* ha-arba'eem oo-shloshah/ve-shalosh *(m/f)*; **2.** המ״ג *adj* ha-mem-geemal (43rd in *Hebr. num. sys.*).

forty-three **1.** ארבעים ושלושה/ושלוש *num* arba'eem oo-shloshah/ve-shalosh *(m/f)*; **2.** מ״ג *num* mem-geemal (43 in *Hebr. num. sys.*).

forty-two **1.** ארבעים ושניים/ושתיים *num* arba'eem oo-shnayeem/oo-shtayeem *(m/f)*; **2.** מ״ב *num* mem-bet (42 in *Hebr. num. sys.*).

forum **1.** פורום *nm* forum/-eem (*pl+of:* -ey); **2.** כיכר (plaza) *nm* keekar/-ot; **3.** בימה (platform) *nf* beem|ah/-ot (*+of:* -at).

forward **1.** קדימה *adv* kadeemah; **2.** קדמי *adj adj* keedmee/-t.

(to) forward **1.** לקדם *inf* lekadem; *pst* keedem; *pres* mekadem; *fut* yekadem; **2.** לשלוח (dispatch) *inf* leeshlo'akh; *pst* shalakh; *pres* shole'akh; *fut* yeeshlakh; **3.** להוביל (haul) *inf* lehoveel; *pst* hoveel; *pres* moveel; *fut* yoveel.

(to) forward a plan לקדם תוכנית *inf* lekadem tokhneet; *pst* keedem *etc*; *pres* mekadem *etc*; *fut* yekadem *etc*;

fossil מאובן *nm* me'oob|an/-eem (*pl+of:* -ney).

foster **1.** מאמץ *nm* me'am|ets/-tseem (*pl+of:* -tsey); **2.** אפיטרופוס (guardian) *nmf* epeetrop|os/-seet.

(to) foster **1.** לטפח *inf* letape'akh; *pst* teepakh; *pres* metape'akh; *fut* yetapakh; **2.** לכלכל (feed) *inf* lekhalkel; *pst* keelkel *(k=kh)*; *pres* mekhalkel; *fut* yekhalkel.

foul **1.** נתעב *adj* neet|'av/-'evet; **2.** מזוהם (dirty) *adj* mezo|ham/-hemet.

foul air אוויר מעופש *nm* aveer me'oopash.

foul language ניבול פה *nm* neebool/-ey peh.

foul linen **1.** לבנים צואים *nm pl* levaneem tso'eem; **2.** כבסים מלוכלכים (dirty linen) *nm pl* kvaseem melookhlakheem.

foul play **1.** מעשה בלתי הוגן (unfair act) ma'as|eh/-eem beeltee hog|en/-neem; **2.** מעשה פשע (crime) *nm* ma'as|eh/-ey pesha'.

foul weather מזג אוויר גרוע *nm* mezeg aveer garoo'a'.

foulmouthed מנבל פה *adj* menabel/-et peh.

(to) found לייסד *inf* leyased; *pst* yeesed; *pres* meyased; *fut* yeyased.

foundation **1.** יסוד *nm* yesod/-ot; **2.** קרן *nf* keren/ kranot (*pl+of:* karnot).

Foundation Fund קרן היסוד *nf* keren ha-yesod.

foundation stone אבן פינה *nf* even/avney peenah.

founder מייסד *nmf* meyased/-et.

(to) founder **1.** להתמוטט (collapse) *inf* leheetmotet; *pst* heetmotet; *pres* meetmotet; *fut* yeetmotet; **2.** לטבוע (ship) *inf* leetbo'a'; *pst* tava' *(v=b)*; *pres* tove'a'; *fut* yeetba'.

foundry בית יציקה *nm* bet/batey yetseekah.

fountain **1.** מזרקה *nf* meezr|akah/-akot (*+of:* -eket); **2.** מעיין (spring) *nm* ma'y|an/-ot (*pl+of:* ma'ayney).

fountain pen עט נובע *nm* 'et/-eem nov|e'a'/'eem.

four **1.** ארבעה *num m* arba'ah; **2.** ארבע *num f* arba'; **3.** ד׳ *num* dalet (four in *Hebr. num. sys.*).

four hundred **1.** ארבע מאות (400) *num* arba' me'ot; **2.** ת׳ *num* tav (400 in *Hebr. num. sys.*).

four thousand **1.** ארבעת אלפים (4,000) *num* arba'at alafeem; **2.** ה׳ אלפים *num* dalet alafeem (4,000 in *Hebr. num. sys.*).

fourscore שמונים (80) *num* shmoneem.

fourteen **1.** ארבעה־עשר *num m* arba'ah-'asar; **2.** ארבע־עשרה *num f* arba'-'esreh; **3.** י״ד *num* yod-dalet (14 in *Hebr. num. sys.*).

fourteen hundred אלף ארבע מאות (thousand four hundred) *num* elef arba' me'ot.

fourteenth **1.** הארבעה־עשר *adj m* ha-arba'ah-'asar; **2.** הארבע־עשרה *adj f* ha-arba' 'esreh; **3.** הי״ד *adj* ha-yod-dalet (14th in *Hebr. num. sys.*).

fourth רביעי *adj* reve'ee/-t.

Fourth of July ארבעה ביולי *nm* arba'ah be-yoolee.

fowl **1.** עוף *nm* 'of/-ot; **2.** בשר עוף *nm* besar 'of.

fox שועל *nm* shoo'al/-eem (*pl+of:* -ey).

foxy **1.** ערמומי *adj* 'armoomee/-t; **2.** חום־אדמדם (color) *adj* khoom/-ah adamdam/-ah.

fraction שבר מתמטי *nm* shever/shvareem matematee/-yeem.

fracture שבר בגוף *nm* shever/shvareem ba-goof.

(to) fracture לשבור עצם *inf* leeshbor 'etsem; *pst* shavar *(v=b) etc*; *pres* shover *etc*; *fut* yeeshbor *etc.*

fragile שביר *adj* shaveer/shveerah.

fragment **1.** שבר *nm* shever/shvareem; **2.** קטע (section) *nm* ket|a'/-a'eem (*pl+of:* keet'ey); **3.** רסיס (splinter) *nm* resees/-eem (*pl+of:* -ey).

fragrance ריח ניחוח *nm* rey|akh/-khot neekho|'akh.

fragrant **1.** ריחני *adj* reykhanee/-t; **2.** נעים *adj* na'eem/ne'eemah.

frail **1.** פריך *adj* pareekh/preekhah; **2.** שברירי *adj* shavreeree/-t.

frailty **1.** שבריריות *nf* shavreereeyoot; **2.** רפיון (weakness) *nm* reefyon.

frame **1.** מסגרת *nf* meesg|eret/-arot; **2.** מיבנה *nm* meevn|eh/-eem (*pl+of:* -ey); **3.** שלד (skeleton) *nm* sheled/shladeem (*pl+of:* sheeldey).

(embroidery) frame מסגרת לרקמה *nf* meesg|eret/ -arot le-reekmah.

(picture) frame מסגרת לתמונה *nf* meesg|eret/-arot lee-tmoon|ah/-ot.

(to) frame **1.** למסגר *inf* lemasger; *pst* meesger; *pres* memasger; *fut* yemasger; **2.** לעצב (mould) *inf* le'atsev; *pst* 'eetsev; *pres* me'atsev; *fut* ye'atsev.

(a) frame house צריף *nm* tsreef/-eem (*pl+of:* -ey).

(to) frame someone להעליל עלילה *inf* leha'aleel 'aleelah; *pst* he'eleel *etc*; *pres* ma'aleel *etc*; *fut* ya'aleel *etc.*

(to) frame up a charge לביים אשמה *inf* levayem ashmah; *pst* beeyem *(b=v) etc*; *pres* mevayem *etc*; *fut* yevayem *etc.*

framework **1.** מסגרת יסוד *nf* meesg|eret/-arot yesod; **2.** שלד (skeleton) *nm* sheled/shladeem (*pl+of:* sheeldey).

(French) Franc פרנק צרפתי *nm* frank/-eem tsarfatee/-yeem.

(Swiss) Franc פרנק שווייצי *nm* frank/-eem shvaytsee/-yeem (*[colloq.]* shveytsaree/-yeem).

franchise 1. זכות הצבעה (voting) *nf* zekhoo|t/-yot hatsba'ah; **2.** זכיון הפצה (distribution rights) *nm* zeekhyon/-ot hafatsah.

frank 1. גלוי לב *adj* glooy/-at lev; **2.** כן (honest) *adj* ken/-ah.

(to) frank ליהנות מפטור מבולי דואר *inf* lehanot mee-p'tor mee-booley do'ar; *pst* nehenah *etc*; *pres* neheneh *etc*; *fut* yehaneh *etc*.

(very) frank גלוי לב לחלוטין *adj* glooy/-at lev lakhalooteen.

frankfurter נקניקייה *nf* nakneekee|yah/-yot (*+of:* -yat).

frankness גילוי לב *nm* geelooy/-ey lev.

frantic מטורף *adj* metor|af/-efet.

frantically 1. בחמת רוגז *adv* ba-khamat rogez; **2.** בטירוף *adv* be-teroof.

fraternal של אחים *adj* shel akheem.

fraternity 1. אחווה *nf* akhv|ah/-ot (*+of:* -at); **2.** מיסדר אחווה (order) *nm* meesd|ar/-erey akhvah; **3.** קורפורציה *nf* korporatsy|ah/-ot.

(to) fraternize 1. להתרועע *inf* leheetro'e'a'; *pst* heetro'e'a'; *pres* meetro'e'a'; *fut* yeetro'e'a'; **2.** לנהוג כאח (treat like a brother) *inf* leenhog ke-akh; *pst* nahag *etc*; *pres* noheg *etc*; *fut* yeenhag *etc*.

fraud 1. הונאה *nf* hona'|ah/-'ot (*+of:* -'at); **2.** סילוף (distortion) *nm* seeloof/-eem (*pl+of:* -ey).

fraudulent 1. של רמאות *adj* shel rama'oot; **2.** של הונאה (swindle) *adj* shel hona'ah.

fray 1. מריבה *nf* mereev|ah/-ot (*+of:* -at); **2.** קטטה (brawl) *nf* ketat|ah/-ot (*+of:* -at).

(to) fray 1. לשפשף *inf* leshafshef; *pst* sheefshef; *pres* meshafshef; *fut* yeshafshef; **2.** לקרוע (tear) *inf* leekro'a'; *pst* kara'; *pres* kore'a'; *fut* yeekra'.

frayed בלוי *adj* balooy/blooyah.

freak 1. יוצא דופן *adj* yotse'/t dofen; **2.** מוזרות (queerness) *nf* moozaroo|t/-yot.

freckle נמש *nm* nem|esh/-asheem (*pl+of:* neemshey).

freckled, freckly מנומש *adj* menoom|ash/-eshet.

free 1. חופשי *adj* khofshee/-yah; **2.** חינם (of charge) *adj* kheenam.

(to) free לשחרר *inf* leshakhrer; *pst* sheekhrer; *pres* meshakhrer; *fut* yeshakhrer.

free advice עצת חינם *nf* 'ats|at/-ot kheenam.

(to give someone a) free hand להעניק יד חופשית *inf* leha'aneek yad khofsheet; *pst* he'eneek *etc*; *pres* ma'aneek *etc*; *fut* ya'aneek *etc*.

free hand drawing ציור יד חופשי *nm* tseeyoor/-ey yad khofshee/-yeem.

free of charge 1. חינם *adv* kheenam; **2.** ללא תשלום (without pay) *adv* le-lo tashloom.

free on board (f.o.b) 1. מחיר סחורה על הסיפון *nm* mekheer sekhorah 'al ha-seepoon; **2.** מחיר פו"ב *[colloq.] nm* mekheer/-ey fob.

free port נמל חופשי *nm* namel khofshee.

free press 1. עיתונות חופשית *nf* 'eetonoot khofsheet; **2.** חופש העיתונות (press freedom) *nm* khofesh ha-'eetonoot.

free speech חופש הדיבור *nm* khofesh ha-deeboor.

free thinker חופשי בדעותיו *adj* khofshee/-yah be-de'ot|av/-eha.

free translation תירגום חופשי *nm* teergoom/-eem khofshee/-yeem.

freedom 1. חופש *nm* khofesh; **2.** דרור (liberty) *nm* dror.

freeze 1. קיפאון (standstill) *nm* kee|pa'on (*+of:* -f'on; *f=p*); **2.** הקפאת מחירים (economic) *nf* hakpa|'at/-'ot mekheereem.

(to) freeze להקפיא *inf* lehakpee; *pst* heekpee; *pres* makpee; *fut* yakpee.

freezing קופא *adj* kofe/-t.

freezing point נקודת קיפאון *nf* nekood|at/-ot keepa'on.

freight 1. מטען (cargo) *nm* meet'an/-eem (*pl+of:* -ey); **2.** תובלה (carrying) *nf* toval|ah/-ot (*+of:* -at); **3.** דמי הובלה (payment) *nm pl* demey hovalah.

(by) freight ברכב הובלה *adv* be-rekhev hovalah.

freight car קרון משא *nm* kron/-ot masa.

freight ship, freighter אוניית משא *nf* onee|yat/-yot masa.

freight train רכבת משא *nf* rak|evet/-vot masa.

French 1. צרפתית (language) *nf* tsarfateet; **2.** צרפתי *adj* tsarfatee/-t.

French fries 1. טוגנים (potatoes) *nm pl* tooganeem (*sing* toogan); **2.** צ'יפס *[colloq.] nm pl* cheeps/-eem.

French leave 1. פרידה ללא גינונים *nf* preed|ah/-ot le-lo geenooneem; **2.** חופשה ללא רשות *nf* khoopsh|ah/-ot le'-lo reshoot.

Frenchman, Frenchwoman צרפתי *nmf* tsarfatee/-yah (*pl* -m/-yot).

frenzy 1. בולמוס *nm* boolmoos/-eem (*pl+of:* -ey); **2.** השתוללות heeshtoleloo|t/-yot.

frequency 1. תדר (electr.) *nm* teder/tedareem (*pl+of:* tedrey); **2.** תדירות *nf* tedeeroo|t/-yot; **3.** שכיחות *nf* shekheekhoo|t/-yot.

frequent 1. שכיח *adj* shakhee'akh/shkheekhah; **2.** תכוף *adj* takhoof/tkhoofah.

(to) frequent לבקר אצל *inf* levaker etsel; *pst* beeker *etc* (*b=v*); *pres* mevaker *etc*; *fut* yevaker *etc*.

frequently לעיתים קרובות *adv* le-'eeteem krovot.

fresh 1. טרי (not stale) *adj* taree/treeyah; **2.** חדיש (new) *adj* khadeesh/-ah; **3.** נועז (bold) *adj* no'az/no'ezet.

fresh water 1. מים מתוקים *nm pl* mayeem metookeem; **2.** מים חיים (bibl.) *nm pl* mayeem khayeem.

(to) freshen 1. לרענן *vt inf* lera'anen; *pst* ree'anen; *pres* mera'anen; *fut* yera'anen; **2.** להתרענן *v rfl inf* leheetra'anen; *pst* heetra'anen; *pres* meetra'anen; *fut* yeetra'anen.

freshly 1. מקרוב *adv* mee-karov; **2.** לאחרונה (lately) *adv* la-akhronah.

freshly painted צבוע טרי *adj* tsavoo'a'/tsvoo'ah taree.

freshman 1. טירון *nm* teeron/-eem (*pl+of:* -ey); **2.** סטודנט שנה א' *nmf* stoodent/-eet shanah alef.

freshness 1. טריות *nf* treeyoot; **2.** רעננות *nf* ra'ananoot.

fret 1. כרסום *nm* keersoom/-eem (*pl+of:* -ey); **2.** רוגז *nm* rogez.

(to) fret 1. להתרגז *inf* leheetragez; *pst* heetragez; *pres* meetragez; *fut* yeetragez; **2.** לקטר (*[slang]:*

grumble) *inf* lekater; *pst* keeter; *pres* mekater; *fut* yekater; **3.** לכרסם (gnaw) *inf* lekharsem; *pst* keersem *(k=kh)*; *pres* mekharsem; *fut* yekharsem; **4.** לשפשף (rub) *inf* leshafshef; *pst* sheefshef; *pres* meshafshef; *fut* yeshafshef.

fretful 1. מתמרמר *adj* meetmarmer/-et; **2.** מקטר *[slang] adj* mekater/-et.

fretwork עבודת קישוט *nf* ʻavod|at/-ot keeshoot.

friar נזיר *nm* nazeer/nezeer|eem *(pl+of: -ey)*.

friction חיכוך *nm* kheekookh/-eem *(pl+of: -ey)*.

Friday 1. יום שישי *nm* yom/yemey sheeshee; **2.** יום ו׳ *nm* yom/yemey vav.

fried מטוגן *adj* metoog|an/-enet.

friend 1. ידיד yedeed/-ah *(pl -eem/-ot; +of: -at/-ey)*; **2.** חבר (pal) *nm* khaver/-ah *(pl: -eem/-ot; sing+of: -at)*.

friendliness 1. יחס ידידותי *nm* yakhas yedeedootee; **2.** סבר פנים יפות (kind face) *nm* sever paneem yafot.

friendly 1. ידידותי *adj* yedeedootee/-t; **2.** מסביר פנים *adj* masbeer/-at paneem.

friendship ידידות *nf* yedeedoot.

frigate פריגטה *nf* freegat|ah/-ot *(+of: -at)*.

fright 1. פחד *nm* pakhad/pekhadeem *(pl+of: pakhdey)*; **2.** מורא *nm* mora/-'ot; **3.** בהלה (panic) *nf* behal|ah/-ot *(+of: -at)*.

(to) frighten 1. להפחיד *inf* lehafkheed; *pst* heefkheed; *pres* mafkheed; *fut* yafkheed; **2.** להבהיל (scare) *inf* lehavheel; *pst* heevheel; *pres* mavheel; *fut* yavheel.

(to) frighten away להטיל פחד *inf* lehateel pakhad; *pst* heeteel *etc*; *pres* mateel *etc*; *fut* yateel *etc*.

frightened 1. מבוהל *adj* mevo|hal/-helet; **2.** ניפחד *adj* neefkh|ad/-edet.

(to get) frightened 1. להיבהל *inf* leheebahel; *pst & pres* neevhal *(v=b)*; *fut* yeebahel; **2.** להיתקף פחד *inf* leheetakef pakhad; *pst & pres* neetkaf *etc*; *fut* yeetakef *etc*.

frightful 1. מפחיד *adj* mafkheed/-ah; **2.** מבהית (terrifying) *adj* mavheet/-ah.

frigid 1. צונן (cold) *adj* tsonen/-et; **2.** אדיש (indifferent) *adj* adeesh/-ah; **3.** פריג׳ידית (of a woman) *adj nf* freejeedee|t/-yot.

fringe 1. גדיל *nm* gadeel/gdeel|eem *(pl+of: -ey)*; **2.** ציצית ("tsitsess" - special fringes on garments worn by particularly observant Jews) *nf* tseetsee|t/-yot.

(to) fringe 1. לעטר *inf* leʻater; *pst* ʻeeter; *pres* meʻater; *fut* yeʻater; **2.** לקשט *inf* lekashet; *pst* keeshet; *pres* mekashet; *fut* yekashet.

fringe benefit הטבת שוליים *nf* hatav|at/-ot shoolayeem.

frippery לבוש צעקני *nm* levoosh tsaʻakanee.

frisk 1. פיזוז *nm* peezooz/-eem *(pl+of: -ey)*; **2.** דילוג *nm* deeloog/-eem *(pl+of: -ey)*; **3.** לערוך חיפוש על הגוף (search on body) *inf* laʻarokh kheepoos ʻal ha-goof; *pst* ʻarakh *etc*; *pres* ʻorekh *etc*; *fut* yaʻarokh *etc*

frisky 1. עליז ʻaleez/-ah; **2.** משתעשע (frolicsome) *adj* meeshtaʻsh|eʻa'/-aʻat.

fritter 1. כיסן בשר מטוגן *nm* keesan/-ey basar metoogan/-eem; **2.** סופגנייה (doughnut) *nf* soofganee|yah/-yot *(+of: -yat)*.

(to) fritter away לבזבז אחד לאחד *inf* levazbez ekhad le-'ekhad; *pst* beezbez *(b=v) etc*; *pres* mevazbez *etc*; *fut* yevazbez *etc*.

frivolity 1. קלות ראש *nm* kaloot rosh; **2.** הפקרות *nf* hefkeroot/-yot.

frivolous 1. קל־דעת *adj* kal/-at daʻat; **2.** שטותי (nonsensical) *adj* shtootee/-t.

(to and) fro הלוך ושוב *adv* halokh va-shov.

frock גלימה *nf* gleem|ah/-ot *(+of: -at)*.

frock coat פרק *nm* frak/-eem.

frog צפרדע *nm* tsfarde|ʻa'/-ʻeem *(pl+of: -ʻey)*.

frog in the throat 1. צרדת *nf* tsaredet; **2.** צרידות (hoarseness) *nf* tsreedoo|t/-yot.

frogman 1. צוללן *nm* tsolelan/-eem *(pl+of: -ey)*; **2.** איש צפרדע *nm* eesh/anshey tsfardeʻa'.

frolic משובה *nf* meshoov|ah/-ot *(+of: -at)*.

(to) frolic להשתובב *inf* leheeshtovev; *pst* heeshtovev; *pres* meeshtovev; *fut* yeeshtovev.

(to take away) from 1. ליטול ממישהו *inf* leetol mee-meeshehoo; *pst* natal *etc*; *pres* notel *etc*; *fut* yeetol *etc*; **2.** לקחת ממישהו *inf* lakahat mee-meeshehoo; *pst* lakakh *etc*; *pres* lokeʻakh *etc*; *fut* yeekakh *etc*.

front 1. חזית *nf* khazeet/-ot; **2.** קדמי *adj* keedmee/-t.

(in) front of 1. מול *adv* mool; **2.** בנוכחות (in presence of) *adv* be-nokhekhoot.

(to) front towards לפנות כלפי *inf* leefnot kelapey; *pst* panah *(p=f) etc*; *pres* poneh *etc*; *fut* yeefneh *etc*.

frost כפור *nm* kfor.

(to) frost 1. לזגג בסוכר (cake) *inf* lezageg be-sookar; *pst* zeegeg *etc*; *pres* mezageg *etc*; *fut* yezageg *etc*; **2.** לצפות בקרם *inf* letsapot bee-krem; *pst* tseepah *etc*; *pres* metsapeh *etc*; *fut* yetsapeh *etc*.

frosting ציפוי סוכרי לעוגה *nm* tseepooy sookaree le-ʻoogah.

frosty 1. קר רוח *adj* kar/-at rooʼakh; **2.** אדיש (indifferent) *adj* adeesh/-ah.

froth קצף *nm* ketsef.

(to) froth להקציף *inf* lehaktseef; *pst* heektseef; *pres* maktseef; *fut* yaktseef.

(to) froth at the mouth להעלות קצף על השפתיים *inf* lehaʻalot ketsef ʻal ha-sfatayeem; *pst* heʻelah *etc*; *pres* maʻaleh *etc*; *fut* yaʻaleh.

frown 1. פנים זועפות *nm pl* paneem zoʻafot; **2.** קימוט מצח *nm* keemoot/-ey metsakh.

(to) frown at להזעים פנים כלפי *inf* lehazʻeem paneem kelapey; *pst* heezʻeem *etc*; *pres* mazʻeem *etc*; *fut* yazʻeem *etc*.

frozen 1. קפוא (cold) *adj* kafoo/kefooʼah; **2.** מוקפא (foods; wages; funds) *adj* mookp|a/-et.

frozen foods מאכלים מוקפאים *nm pl* maʼakhaleem mookapaʼeem.

frugal 1. זול *adj* zol/-ah; **2.** חסכוני *adj* kheskhonee/-t.

fruit פרי *nm* pree/perot.

fruit salad סלט פירות *nm* salat perot

fruit tree עץ פרי *nm* ʻets/ʻatsey pree.

fruitful פורה *adj* por|eh/-eeyah.

fruitless 1. סרק *adj* srak; **2.** עקר *adj* ʻakar/-ah.

(to) frustrate 1. לסכל (obstruct) *inf* lesakel; *pst* seekel; *pres* mesakel; *fut* yesakel; **2.** לתסכל (disappoint) *inf* letaskel; *pst* teeskel; *pres* metaskel; *fut* yetaskel.

frustration 1. תסכול (disapointment) *nm* teeskool/-eem (*pl+of:* -ey); **2.** סיכול (counteraction) seekool/-eem (*pl+of:* -ey).

fry מאכל מטוגן *nm* ma'akhal/-eem metoogan/-eem.

(small) fry דגי רקק *nm pl* degey rekak.

(to) fry 1. לטגן *vt inf* letagen; *pst* teegen; *pres* metagen; *fut* yetagen; **2.** להיטגן *vi inf* leheetagen; *pst* neetagen; *pres* meetagen; *fut* yeetagen.

frying pan מחבת *nf* makhvat/-ot.

fudge 1. סוכרייה (candy) *nf* sookaree|yah/-yot (*+of:* -yat); **2.** שטויות (nonsense) *nf pl* shtooyot.

fuel דלק *nm* delek/dlakeem (*pl+of:* deelkey).

fugitive אסיר נמלט *nm* aseer/-eem neemlat/-eem.

(to) fulfill 1. להגשים *inf* lehagsheem; *pst* heegsheem; *pres* magsheem; *fut* yagsheem; **2.** למלא אחר *inf* lemale akhar; *pst* meele *etc; pres* memale *etc; fut* yemale *etc.*

fulfilment 1. הגשמה (materialization) *nf* hagsham|ah/-ot (*+of:* -at); **2.** מילוי *nm* meelooy.

(in) full 1. במלואו *adv* be-melo|'o/-'ah *(m/f)*; **2.** בשלימות *adv* bee-shlemoot.

(to the) full 1. במלואו *adv* bee-melo|'o/-'ah *(m/f)*; **2.** בשלמותbee-shlemoot.

full dress 1. לבוש רשמי (official) levoosh reeshmee; **2.** לבוש חגיגי (festive) levoosh khageegee.

full moon ירח מלא *nm* yare'akh male.

full of fun מאוד משעשע *adj* me'od mesha'sh|e'a'/-a'at.

full skirt חצאית באורך מלא *nf* khatsa'ee|t/-yot be-orekh male.

(at) full speed במלוא המהירות *adv* bee-melo ha-meheeroot.

(to know) full well לדעת ברורות *inf* lada'at broorot; *pst* yada' *etc; pres* yode'a' *etc; fut* yeda' *etc.*

full-blooded גזעי *adj* geez'ee/-t.

full-fledged בשל *adj* bashel/beshelah.

fullness 1. שפע *nm* shefa'; **2.** גודש *nm* godesh.

(to) fumble 1. לגשש *inf* legashesh; *pst* geeshesh; *pres* megashesh; *fut* yegashesh; **2.** להחטיא (miss) *inf* lehakhtee; *pst* hekhtee; *pres* makhtee; *fut* yakhtee.

(to) fume 1. להעלות עשן *inf* leha'alot 'ashan; *pst* he'elah *etc; pres* ma'aleh *etc; fut* ya'aleh *etc;* **2.** להתרגז (show anger) *inf* leheetragez; *pst* heetragez; *pres* meetragez; *fut* yeetragez.

fumes אדים *nm pl* ed|eem (*sing* ed) (*pl+of:* -ey).

(to) fumigate לגפר *inf* legaper; *pst* geeper; *pres* megaper; *fut* yegaper.

fun 1. בידור *nm* beedoor/-eem (*pl+of:* -ey); **2.** שעשועים *nm pl* (*sing* sha'shoo'a) sha'-shoo|'eem (*pl+of:* -'ey); **3.** כיף *[slang] (Arab.) nm* kef.

(for) fun לשם בידור *adv* le-shem beedoor.

(full of) fun 1. משעשע (amusing) *adj* mesha'-sh|e'a'/-a'at; **2.** מאוד מבדר (most entertaining) *adj* me'od mevader/-et.

(to have) fun 1. ליהנות (enjoy) *inf* lehanot; *pst* nehenah; *pres* neheneh; *fut* yehaneh; **2.** להתבדר (amuse oneself) *inf* leheetbader; *pst* heetbader; *pres* meetbader; *fut* yeetbader.

(to make) fun לעשות לצחוק *inf* la'asot lee-ts'khok; *pst* 'asah *etc; pres* 'oseh *etc; fut* ya'aseh *etc.*

function תפקיד *nm* tafkeed/-eem (*pl+of:* -ey).

(to) function לתפקד *inf* letafked; *pst* teefked; *pres* metafked; *fut* yetafked.

functional 1. תפקודי *adj* teefkoodee/-t; **2.** פונקציונלי *adj* foonktsyonalee/-t.

fund קרן *nf* keren/kranot (*pl+of:* karnot).

(Jewish National) Fund קרן קיימת לישראל *nf* keren kayemet le-yeesra'el.

(Foundation) Fund קרן היסוד *nf* keren ha-yesod.

(to) fund לממן *inf* lemamen; *pst* meemen; *pres* memamen; *fut* yemamen.

fundamental 1. יסודי *adj* yesodee/-t; **2.** יסוד (basis) *nm* yesod/-ot.

funds אמצעים *nm pl* emtsa|'eem (*pl+of:* -'ey).

funeral 1. הלוויה *nf* halva|yah/-yot (*+of:* -yat); **2.** של קבורה (of burial) *adj* shel kvoorah.

fungus פטרייה *nf* peetree|yah/-yot (*+of:* -yat).

funnel 1. משפך *nm* mashpekh/-eem (*pl+of:* -ey); **2.** אפרכסת (auricle) *nf* afark|eset/-asot.

(to) funnel לרכז *inf* lerakez; *pst* reekez; *pres* merakez; *fut* yerakez.

(the) funnies 1. ציורים מבדחים *nm pl* tseeyooreem mevadkheem; **2.** סדרות של קריקטורות (cartoon series) *nm pl* sdarot (*sing* seedrah) shel kareekatoorot.

funny 1. מצחיק (laughable) *adj* matskheek/-ah; **2.** מגוחך (ridiculous) *adj* megookh|akh/-ekhet.

fur פרווה *nf* parv|ah/-ot (*+of:* -at).

(to) fur לקשט בפרווה *inf* lekashet be-farvah *(f=p)*; *pst* keeshet *etc; pres* mekashet *etc; fut* yekashet *etc.*

fur coat מעיל פרווה *nm* me'eel/-ey parvah.

(to) furbish 1. לחדש *inf* lekhadesh; *pst* kheedesh; *pres* mekhadesh; *fut* yekhadesh; **2.** ללטש (polish) *inf* lelatesh; *pst* leetesh; *pres* melatesh; *fut* yelatesh.

furious 1. זועף (angry) *adj* zo'ef/-et; **2.** אחוז חימה (fierce) *adj* akhooz/-at kheymah.

(to) furl 1. לקפל (fold) *vt inf* lekapel; *pst* keepel; *pres* mekapel; *fut* yekapel; **2.** להתקפל (double up; *[slang]:* give in) *v rfl inf* leheetkapel; *pst* heetkapel; *pres* meetkapel; *fut* yeetkapel.

furlough חופשה *nf* khoofsh|ah/-ot (*+of:* -at).

furnace כבשן *nm* keevshan/-eem (*pl+of:* -ey).

(to) furnish 1. לצייד (equip) *inf* letsayed; *pst* tseeyed; *pres* metsayed; *fut* yetsayed; **2.** לספק (supply) *inf* lesapek; *pst* seepek; *pres* mesapek; *fut* yesapek.

(to) furnish a room לרהט חדר *inf* lerahet kheder; *pst* reehet *etc; pres* merahet *etc; fut* yerahet *etc.*

(to) furnish an apartment לרהט דירה *inf* lerahet deerah; *pst* reehet *etc; pres* merahet *etc; fut* yerahet *etc.*

furniture 1. ריהוט (generally) *nm* reehoot; **2.** רהיטים (as separate items) *nm pl* (*sing* raheet) raheet|eem (*pl+of:* -ey).

furniture store חנות רהיטים *nf* khanoo|t/-yot raheeteem.

furrow 1. תלם *nm* tel|em/-ameem (*pl+of:* talmey); **2.** קמט (wrinkle) *nm* kem|et/-ateem (*pl+of:* keemtey).

(to) furrow 1. לחרוש (plough) *inf* lakharosh; *pst* kharash; *pres* khoresh; *fut* yakharosh; **2.** לקמט (crease) *inf* lekamet; *pst* keemet; *pres* mekamet; *fut* yekamet.

further הלאה *adv* hal'ah.

(to) further לקדם *inf* lekadem; *pst* keedem; *pres* mekadem; *fut* yekadem.

furthermore יתר על כן *adv* yater 'al ken.

furthest מרוחק ביותר *adj* merookh|ak/-eket be-yoter.

furtive 1. גנוב *adj* ganoov/gnoovah; **2.** חמקני (evasive) *adj* khamkanee/-t.

fury 1. זעף (anger) *nm* za'af/ze'afeem (*pl+of:* za'afey); **2.** זעם (rage) *nm* za'am/ze'ameem (*pl+of:* za'amey).

fuse 1. נתיך (electr.) *nm* nateekh/neteekh|eem (*pl+of:* -ey); **2.** פקק ביטחון (safety) *nm* pekak/-ey beetakhon.

(to) fuse למזג *inf* lemazeg; *pst* meezeg; *pres* memazeg; *fut* yemazeg.

fuselage גוף מטוס *nm* goof/-ey matos/metoseem.

fusion 1. היתוך (melting) *nf* heetookh; **2.** מזיגה (lending) *nf* mezeeg|ah/-ot (*+of:* -at).

fuss התרוצצות *nf* heetrotsetsoo|t/-yot.

(to) fuss 1. לעשות עניין *inf inf* la'asot 'eenyan; *pst* 'asah *etc*; *pres* 'oseh *etc*; *fut* ya'aseh *etc*; **2.** להגזים (exaggerate) *inf* lehagzeem; *pst* heegzeem; *pres* magzeem; *fut* yagzeem.

(to make a) fuss over 1. לעשות עניינים בשל *inf* la'asot 'eenyaneem be-shel; *pst* 'asah *etc*; *pres* 'oseh *etc*; *fut* ya'aseh *etc*; **2.** לעשות בעיות בשל (make trouble over) *inf* la'asot be'ayot be-shel; *pst* 'asah *etc*; *pres* 'oseh *etc*; *fut* ya'aseh *etc*.

fussy נטפל לקטנות *adj* neetp|al/-elet lee-ktanot.

fussy dress לבוש קפדני *nm* levoosh kapdanee.

futile 1. שווא (vain) *adj* shav; **2.** חסר תועלת (useless) *adj* khas|ar/-rat to'elet.

future 1. עתיד *nm* 'ateed/-ot; **2.** עתידי *adj* 'ateedee/-t.

fuzz 1. נעורת *nf* ne'or|et/-ot; **2.** פלומה *nf* ploom|ah/-ot (*+of:* -at)

fuzzy מעורפל (vague) *adj* me'oorp|al/-elet.

G.

G,g equivalent to the Hebrew consonant ג (Gimal or *Gimel*). Wherever *G* is read as in *Geneva* or *gist*, it can still be transliterated into Hebrew by ג, with the addition of an apostrophe ג'.

(gift of) gab שטף דיבור *nm* shetef deeboor.

(to) gab לפטפט *inf* lefatpet; *pst* peetpet (*p=f*); *pres* mefatpet; *fut* yefatpet.

gabardine בד גברדין *nm* bad/-ey gabardeen.

gabble לקשקש *inf* lekashkesh; *pst* keeshkesh; *pres* mekashkesh; *fut* yekashkesh.

gable גמלון *nm* gamlon/-eem (*pl+of:* -ey).

gable window חלון בגג *nm* khalon/-ot ba-gag.

(to) gad לשוטט *inf* leshotet; *pst* shotet; *pres* meshotet; *fut* yeshotet.

gadget 1. מיתקן *nm* meetk|an/-aneem (*pl+of:* -eney); **2.** אמצאה (inventive contrivance) *nm* amtsa|'ah/-'ot (*+of:* -'at).

gag בדיחה (joke) *f* bedeekh|ah/-ot (*+of:* -at).

(to) gag להתבדח (joke) *inf* leheetbade'akh; *pst* heetbadakh; *pres* meetbade'akh; *fut* yeetbadakh.

gage (gauge) 1. מד *nm* mad/-eem (*pl+of:* -ey); **2.** מדיד (calibre) madeed/medeed|eem (*pl+of:* -ey).

gaiety עליצות *nf* 'aleetsoot.

gaily בשמחה *adv* be-seemkhah.

gain 1. רווח (profit) *nm* revakh/-eem (*pl+of:* reevkhey); **2.** הישג (achievement) *nm* heseg/-eem (*pl+of:* -ey).

(to) gain 1. להרוויח (profit) *inf* leharvee'akh; *pst* heervee'akh; *pres* marvee'akh; *fut* yarvee'akh; **2.** להשיג (achieve) *inf* lehaseeg; *pst* heeseeg; *pres* maseeg; *fut* yaseeg.

gainful 1. רווחי (profitable) *adj* reevkhee/-t; **2.** מכניס (lucrative) *adj* makhnees/-ah.

gait צורת הליכה *nf* tsoor|at/-ot haleekhah.

gala חגיגי *adj* khageegee/-t.

galaxy מערכת כוכבים *nf* ma'ar|ekhet/-khot kokhaveem.

gale סערה *nf* se'ar|ah/-ot (*+of:* sa'arat).

gale of laughter סערת צחוק *nf* sa'ar|at/-ot tsekhok.

gall 1. מרה (body organ) *nf* mar|ah/-ot (*+of:* -at); **2.** מרירות (bitterness) mereeroo|t/-yot.

gall bladder כיס המרה *nm* kees ha-marah.

gallant אבירי *adj* abeeree/-t.

gallantry 1. אבירות (chivalry) *nf* abeeroo|t/-yot; **2.** חיזור (courting) *nm* kheezoor/-eem (*pl+of:* -ey).

gallery 1. מסדרון (corridor) *nm* meesderon/-ot; **2.** מעבר (passage) *nm* ma'av|ar/-areem (*pl+of:* -rey); **3.** גלריה (art gallery) *nf* galer|yah/-yot (*+of:* -yat).

galley 1. יריעה (sheet) *nf* yereel'ah/-'ot (*+of:* -'at); **2.** אוניית משוטים עתיקה (ancient slave-propelled ship) *nf* oneeelyat/-yot meshoteem 'ateekah.

galley proof יריעת הגהה *nf* yereel'at/-'ot hagahah.

galley slave עבד באוניית משוטים *nm* 'eved/'avadeem be-oneeyat meshoteem.

gallon גלון *nm* galon/-eem (*pl+of:* -ey).

gallop דהירה *nf* deheerlah/-ot (*+of:* -at).

(to) gallop לדהור *inf* leedhor; *pst* dahar; *pres* doher; *fut* yeedhar.

gallows גרדום *nm* gardom/-eem (*pl+of:* -ey).

galosh ערדל *nm* 'ardlal/-alayeem (*pl+of:* -eley).

gamble הימור *nm* heemoor/-eem (*pl+of:* -ey).

(to) gamble להמר *inf* lehamer; *pst* heemer; *pres* mehamer; *fut* yehamer.

(to) gamble away להפסיד בהימורים *inf* lehafseed be-heemooreem; *pst* heefseed *etc*; *pres* mafseed *etc*; *fut* yafseed *etc*.

(to) gamble everything להמר על הכול *inf* lehamer 'al ha-kol; *pst* heemer *etc*; *pres* mehamer *etc*; *fut* yehamer *etc*.

gambol 1. דילוג (leap) *nm* deeloog/-eem (*pl+of:* -ey); **2.** ניתור (hopping) *nm* neetoor/-eem (*pl+of:* -ey).

(to) gambol 1. לדלג (leap) *inf* ledaleg; *pst* deeleg; *pres* medaleg; *fut* yedaleg; **2.** לנתר (hop) *inf* lenater; *pst* neeter; *pres* menater; *fut* yenater.

game 1. תחרות (competition) *nf* takharoolt/-yot; **2.** מישחק (play) *nm* mees'khak/-eem (*pl+of:* -ey); **3.** ציד (hunt) *nm* tsayeed (*+of:* tseyd).

gamebird ציפור־ציד *nf* tseepor/-ey tsayeed.

gamut סולם קולות *nm* soollam/-mey kolot.

gander אווז *nm* avlaz/-azeem (*pl+of:* -zey).

gang 1. חבורה (group) *nf* khavoorlah/-ot (*+of:* -at); **2.** כנופיה (of bandits) kenooflyah/-yot (*+of:* -yat).

(to) gang להתאגד בחבורה *inf* leheet'aged ba-khavoorah; *pst* heet'aged *etc*; *pres* meet'aged *etc*; *fut* yeet'aged *etc*.

(to) gang up against להתארגן בכנופיה נגד *inf* leheet'argen bee-knoofyah neged; *pst* heet'argen *etc*; *pres* meet'argen *etc*; *fut* yeet'argen *etc*.

gangplank כבש אונייה *nm* kevesh oneeyah.

gangrene 1. מק *nm* mak; **2.** נמק (rot) nemlek/-akeem (*pl+of:* neemkey).

gangster 1. איש כנופיה *nm* eesh/anshey kenooflyah/-yot; **2.** גנגסטר *nm* gangster/-eem (*pl+of:* -ey).

gangway 1. מעבר (passage) *nm* ma'avlar/-areem (*pl+of:* -rey); **2.** פרוזדור (corridor) *nm* prozdor/-eem (*pl+of:* -ey).

gantlet (gauntlet) כפפה *nf* kfaflah/-ot (*+of:* keefefat).

gap 1. פער *nm* pa'ar/pe'areem (*pl+of:* pa'arey); **2.** פירצה (break) *nf* peertsah/pratsot (*+of:* peertsat).

gape פעירת פה *nf* pe'eerlat/-ot peh.

(to) gape לפעור פה *inf* lef'or peh; *pst* pa'ar (*p=f*) peh; *pres* po'er peh; *fut* yeef'ar peh.

garage 1. מוסך *nm* moosalkh/-keem (*pl+of:* -key); **2.** גרז' *[colloq.] nm* garaj/-eem (*pl+of:* -ey).

(to)garage להחנות במוסך *inf* lehakhnot ba-moosakh; *pst* hekhnah *etc*; *pres* makhneh *etc*; *fut* yakhneh *etc*.

garb 1. לבוש *nm* levoosh; **2.** תלבושת (dress) *nf* teelboshlet/-ot.

garbage 1. זבל *nm* zevel; **2.** שפכים (sewage) *nm pl* shfakheem.

garden 1. גן *nm* gan/-eem (*pl+of:* -ey); **2.** גינה (small) *nf* geenlah/-ot (*+of:* -at).

garden-party מסיבת־גן *nf* meseeblat/-ot gan.

gardener גנן *nm* ganan/-eem (*pl+of:* -ey).

gardening גננות *nf* gananoot.

gargle גרגור *nm* geergoor/-eem (*pl+of:* -ey).

(to) gargle לגרגר *inf* legarger; *pst* geerger; *pres* megarger; *fut* yegarger.

gargoyle זרבובית *nf* zarbooveelt/-yot.

garland זר *nm* zer/-eem (*pl+of:* -ey).

garlic שום *nm* shoom.

garment לבוש *nm* levoosh.

garnish קישוט *nm* keeshoot/-eem (*pl+of:* -ey).

(to) garnish לקשט *inf* lekashet; *pst* keeshet; *pres* mekashet; *fut* yekashet.

garret עליית־גג *nf* 'aleelyat/-yot gag.

garrison חיל מצב *nm* kheyl/-ot matsav.

(to) garrison להציב חיל מצב *inf* lehatseev kheyl matsav; *pst* heetseev *etc*; *pres* matseev *etc*; *fut* yatseev *etc*.

garrulous פטפטן *adj & nmf* patpetan/-eet.

garter בירית *nf* beereelt/-yot (*+of:* -yat).

gas גז *nm* gaz/-eem (*pl+of:* -ey).

(cooking) gas גז בישול *nm* gaz beeshool.

(tear) gas גז מדמיע *nm* gaz madmee'a'.

(to) gas להמית בגז *inf* lehameet be-gaz; *pst* hemeet *etc*; *pres* memeet *etc*; *fut* yameet *etc*.

gas cooking range כיריים של גז *nf pl* keerayeem shel gaz.

gas cooking stove תנור גז *nm* tanoor/-ey gaz.

gas holder מיכל גז *nm* mekhal/-ey gaz.

gas meter מונה גז *nm* monleh/-ey gaz.

gasburner מבער גז *nm* mav'er/-ey gaz.

gaseous של אדי גזים *adj* shel edey gazeem.

gash 1. חתך (cut) *nm* khetekh/khatakhleem (*pl+of:* -ey); **2.** פצע (wound) petsa'/-eem (*pl+of:* peets'ey).

(to) gash 1. לחתוך (cut) *inf* lakhtokh; *pst* khatakh; *pres* khotekh; *fut* yakhtokh; **2.** לפצוע (wound) *inf* leeftso'a'; *pst* patsa' (*p=f*); *pres* potse'a'; *fut* yeeftsa'.

gasket אטם *nm* etem/atlameem (*pl+of:* -mey).

gaslight תאורת גז *nf* te'oorlat/-ot gaz.

gasoline בנזין *nm* benzeen.

gasp נשימה בכבדות *nf* nesheemah bee-khvedoot (*kh=k*).

(to) gasp לנשום בכבדות *inf* leenshom bee-khvedoot; *pst* nasham *etc*; *pres* noshem *etc*; *fut* yeenshom *etc* (*kh=k*).

gastric מן הקיבה *adj* meen ha-keyvah.

gastrointestinal מן הקיבה והמעיים *adj* meen ha-keyvah ve-ha-me'ayeem.

gate, gateway 1. שער (portal) sha'ar/she'areem (*pl+of:* sha'arey); **2.** פתח (doorway) *nm* petlakh/-akheem (*pl+of:* peetkhey).

(to) gather 1. לקבץ (collect) *inf* lekabets; *pst* keebets; *pres* mekabets; *fut* yekabets; **2.** לאסוף (rally) *inf* le'esof; *pst* asaf; *pres* osef; *fut* ye'esof;

3. לכנס (assemble) *inf* lekhanes; *pst* keenes *(k=kh)*; *pres* mekhanes; *fut* yekhanes.

(to) gather dust לספוג אבק *inf* leespog avak; *pst* safag *(f=p)* avak; *pres* sofeg avak; *fut* yeespog avak.

gathering 1. התקבצות *nf* heetkabtsoo|t/-yot; **2.** כנס (rally) *nm* ken|es/-as|eem (*pl+of:* keensey).

gaudy 1. מבריק *adj* mavreek/-ah; **2.** ראוותני (for show) *adj* ra'avtanee/-t.

gauge 1. מד *nm* mad/-eem (*pl+of:* -ey); **2.** מדיד (calibre) *nm* madeed/-eem (*pl+of:* -ey).

(to) gauge 1. למדוד (measure) *inf* leemdod; *pst* madad; *pres* moded; *fut* yeemdod; **2.** להעריך (estimate) *inf* leha'areekh; *pst* he'ereekh; *pres* ma'areekh; *fut* ya'areekh.

gaunt 1. מצומק (parched) *adj* metsoom|ak/-eket; **2.** זועף (angry) zo'ef/-et.

gauntlet כפפת שיריון *nf* keefef|at/-ot sheeryon.

(to throw down the) gauntlet להזמין לדו־קרב *inf* lehazmeen le-doo-krav; *pst* heezmeen *etc*; *pres* mazmeen *etc*; *fut* yazmeen *etc*.

gauze מלמלה *nf* malm|alah/-alot (*+of:* -elet/-elot).

gavel פטיש של יושב־ראש *nm* pateesh shel yoshev-rosh.

gawk גולם *nm* golem/glameem (*pl+of:* golmey).

gawky גולמי *adj* golmee/-t.

gay 1. עליז *adj* 'aleez/-ah; **2.** "עליז"("gay") *nm* 'aleez/-eem (*pl+of:* -ey); **3.** הומוסקסואל *nm* homoseksoo'al/-eem (*pl+of:* -ey); **4.** הומו *[colloq.]* *nm* homo/-'eem.

gaze מבט *nm* mab|at/-ateem (*pl+of:* -tey).

(to) gaze להסתכל *inf* leheestakel; *pst* heestakel; *pres* meestakel; *fut* yeestakel.

gazette עיתון רשמי *nm* 'eeton/-eem reeshmee/-yeem.

gazetteer אלמנך שמות *nm* almanakh shemot.

gear 1. לבוש (clothing) *nm* levoosh; **2.** מערכת גלגלי שיניים (toothed wheel system) *nf* ma'ar|ekhet/-khot galgaley sheenayeem.

(foot) gear צורכי הנעלה *nm pl* tsorkey han'alah.

(low) gear הילוך נמוך *nm* heelookh namookh.

(steering) gear מערכת היגוי *nf* ma'ar|ekhet/-khot heegooy.

(to be in) gear להיות במהלך *inf* leehyot be-mahalakh; *pst* hayah *etc*; *pres* heeno *etc*; *fut* yeehyeh *etc*.

(to shift) gear להחליף מהלך *inf* lehakhleef mahalakh; *pst* hekhleef *etc*; *pres* makhleef *etc*; *fut* yakhleef *etc*.

(to throw in) gear להכניס למהלך *inf* lehakhnees le-mahalakh; *pst* heekhnees *etc*; *pres* makhnees *etc*; *fut* yakhnees *etc*.

(to throw out of) gear להוציא ממהלך *inf* lehotsee mee-mahalakh; *pst* hotsee *etc*; *pres* motsee *etc*; *fut* yotsee *etc*.

gear box תיבת הילוכים *nf* teyv|at/-ot heelookheem.

gearshift lever ידית הילוכים *nf* yadee|t/-yot heelookheem.

geese (goose) ברווז *nm* barvaz/-eem (*pl+of:* -ey).

Geiger counter מונה גייגר *nm* mon|eh/-ey gayger.

gelatin, gelatine 1. מקפא *nm* meekp|a/-a'eem (*pl+of:* -e'ey); **2.** ג'לטין *nm* jelateen/-eem (*pl+of:* -ey).

gem אבן טובה *nf* even/avaneem tov|ah/-ot.

(to) geminate לכפול *inf* leekhpol; *pst* kafal *(k=kh; f=p)*; *pres* kofel; *fut* yeekhpol.

gender מין *nm* meen/-eem.

gene גן *nm* gen/-eem (*pl+of:* -ey).

general 1. כללי (common) *adj* klalee/-t; **2.** גנרל (army) *nm* general/-eem (*pl+of:* -ey); **3.** בכלל (in general) *adv* bee-khlal *(kh=k)*.

generality 1. הכללה *nf* hakhlal|ah/-ot (*+of:* -at); **2.** כלליות (applicability to all) *nf* klaleeyoot.

(to) generalize להכליל *inf* lehakhleel; *pst* heekhleel; *pres* makhleel; *fut* yakhleel.

(to) generate 1. להפיק *inf* lehafeek; *pst* hefeek; *pres* mefeek; *fut* yafeek; **2.** ליצור (produce) *inf* leetsor; *pst* yatsar; *pres* yotser; *fut* yeetsor; **3.** להוליד (give birth) *inf* leholeed; *pst* holeed; *pres* moleed; *fut* yoleed.

generation 1. דור *nm* dor/-ot (*pl+of:* -ey); **2.** הפקה (production) *nf* hafak|ah/-ot (*+of:* -at); **3.** יצירה (creation) *nf* yetseer|ah/-ot (*+of:* -at); **4.** הולדה (giving birth) *nf* holad|ah/-ot (*+of:* -at).

generator 1. מחולל *nm* mekholel/-eem (*pl+of:* -ey) khashmal; **2.** גנרטור *[colloq.]* *nm* gener|ator/-oreem.

generic 1. של מין (of kind) *adj* shel meen; **2.** של גזע (racial) *adj* shel geza'.

generosity נדיבות *nf* nedeevoo|t/-yot.

generous נדיב *adj* nadeev/nedeevah.

Genesis ספר בראשית *nm* sefer beresheet.

genetics 1. תורת התורשה *nf* torat ha-torashah; **2.** גנטיקה *nf* geneteekah.

Geneva ג'נבה *nf* jeneva.

genial 1. חביב *adj* khaveev/-ah; **2.** מסביר פנים *adj* masbeer/-at paneem.

genital של איברי המין *adj* shel evrey ha-meen.

genitals איברי מין *nm pl* evrey meen.

genitive 1. יחס הקניין (possessive case) *nm* yakhas ha-keenyan; **2.** סמיכות (construct case - see introduction) *nf* smeekhoot.

genius 1. גאון (person) ga'on/ge'on|eem (*pl+of:* -ey); **2.** כשרון מיוחד (talent for) *nm* keeshron/-ot meyookhad/-eem.

genocide השמדת עם *nf* hashmadat 'am.

genteel מנומס *adj* menoom|as/-eset.

gentile 1. לא־יהודי *nmf* lo-yehoodee/-yah; **2.** *adj* lo-yehoodee/-t.

gentle עדין *adj* 'adeen/-ah.

gentleman, -men ג'נטלמן *nm* jentel|men/-meneem.

gentlemanly 1. בצורה ג'נטלמנית *adv* be-tsoorah jentelmeneet; **2.** מנומס (well-mannered) *adj* menoom|as/-eset.

gentleman's ג'נטלמני *adj* jentelmenee/-t.

gentleness עדינות *nf* 'adeenoo|t/-yot.

gently בעדינות *adv* ba-'adeenoot.

genuine 1. אמיתי (true) *adj* ameetee/-t; **2.** ממשי (real) *adj* mamashee/-t.

geographical גיאוגרפי *adj* ge'ografee/-t.

geography גיאוגרפיה *nf* ge'ografyah.

geological גיאולוגי *adj* ge'ologee/-t

geologist גיאולוג *nm* ge'olog/-eem.

geology גיאולוגיה *nf* ge'ologyah.

geometric גיאומטרי *adj* ge'ometree/-t.
geometry גיאומטריה *adj* ge'ometreeyah
geophysicist גיאופיסיקאי *nmf* ge'ofeeseek|ay/-a'eet.
geophysics גיאופיסיקה *nf* ge'ofeeseekah.
geranium גרניון *nm* geranyon.
germ 1. חיידק *nm* khaydak/-eem (*pl+of:* -ey); **2.** מקור (of an idea) *nm* mekor/-ot.
germ carrier נושא חיידקים *nmf* nos|e/-'ey (*f:* -et/-'ot) khaydakeem.
germ cell תא חיידקים *nm* ta/ta'ey khaydakeem.
germ plasm פלסמת חיידקים *nf* plasm|at/-ot khaydakeem.
German 1. גרמני *nmf* germanee/-yah (*pl:* -m/-yot); **2.** גרמני *adj* germanee/-t; **3.** גרמנית (language) *nf* germaneet.
(East-)German 1. מזרח־גרמני *nmf* meezrakh-germanee/-yah; **2.** מזרח־גרמני *adj* meezrakh-germanee/-t.
(West-)German 1. מערב גרמני *nmf* ma'arav-germanee/-yah; **2.** *adj* ma'arav-germanee/-t.
germane 1. הולם *adj* holem/-et; **2.** קרוב משפחה (blood relative) *nmf* krov/-at meeshpakhah.
Germany גרמניה *nf* german|yah/-yot.
(former East-)Germany גרמניה המזרחית לשעבר *nf* germanyah ha-meezrakheet le-she'avar.
(former West-)Germany גרמניה המערבית לשעבר *nf* germanyah ha-ma'araveet le-she'avar.
germicide קוטל חיידקים *nm* kot|el/-ley khaydakeem.
(to) germinate לנבוט *inf* leenbot; *pst* navat (*v=b*); *pres* novet; *fut* yeenbot.
gerontology גרונטולוגיה *nf* gerontologyah.
gerund שם הפועל (grammar) *nm* shem ha-po'al.
gestation הריון *nm* her|ayon/-yonot (*+of:* -yon).
(to) gesticulate להרבות בתנועות ידיים *inf* leharbot bee-tnoo'ot yadayeem; *pst* heerbah *etc; pres* marbeh *etc; fut* yarbeh *etc.*
gesture מחווה *nf* mekhv|ah/-ot (*+of:* -at).
(a mere) gesture מחווה ותו לא mekhvah ve-too lo.
(to) get לקבל *inf* lekabel; *pst* keebel; *pres* mekabel; *fut* yekabel.
(to) get along לחיות בשלום *inf* leekhyot be-shalom; *pst & pres* khay *etc; fut* yeekhyeh *etc.*
(to) get angry 1. להיתקף כעס *inf* leheetakef ka'as; *pst & pres* neetkaf *etc; fut* yeetakef *etc;* **2.** להתרגז (become enraged) *v rfl inf* leheetragez; psat heetragez; *pres* meetragez; *fut* yeeragez.
(to) get away להסתלק *inf* leheestalek; *pst* heestalek; *pres* meestalek; *fut* yeestalek.
(to) get down 1. לרדת *inf* laredet; *pst* yarad; *pres* yored; *fut* yered; **2.** לגשת *inf* lageshet; *pst & pres* neegash; *fut* yeegash.
(to) get him to do it לאלץ אותו לעשות זאת *inf* le'alets oto la'asot zot; *pst* eelets *etc; pres* me'alets *etc; fut* ye'alets *etc.*
(to) get ill לחלות *inf* lakhlot; *pst* khalah; *pres* kholeh; *fut* yekhleh.
(to) get in להיכנס פנימה *inf* leheekanes peneemah; *pst & pres* neekhnas (*kh=k*) *etc; fut* yeekanes *etc.*
(I don't) get it לא אוכל להבין זאת lo ookhal lehaveen zot.
(to) get married 1. להינשא *inf* leheenase; *pst & pres* neesa; *fut* yeenase; **2.** להתחתן *inf* leheetkhaten; *pst* heetkhaten; *pres* meetkhaten; *fut* yeetkhaten.
(to) get off the train לרדת מהרכבת *inf* laredet me-ha-rakevet; *pst* yarad *etc; pres* yored *etc; fut* yered *etc.*
(to) get old להזדקן *inf* leheezdaken; *pst* heezdaken; *pres* meezdaken; *fut* yeezdaken.
(to) get on להמשיך *inf* lehamsheekh; *pst* heemsheekh; *pres* mamsheekh; *fut* yamsheekh.
(to) get out 1. להסתלק *inf* leheestalek; *pst* heestalek; *pres* meestalek; *fut* yeestalek. **2.** להיחלץ *inf* lehekhalets; *pst & pres* nekhlats; *fut* yekhalets.
(to) get over 1. להתגבר (overcome) *inf* leheetgaber; *pst* heetgaber; *pres* meetgaber; *fut* yeetgaber; **2.** לתת לעבור (let it pass) *inf* latet la'avor; *pst* natan *etc; pres* noten *etc; fut* yeeten *etc.*
(to) get ready להתכונן *inf* leheetkonen; *pst* heetkonen; *pres* meetkonen; *fut* yeetkonen.
(to) get rich להתעשר *inf* leheet'asher; *pst* heet'asher; *pres* meet'asher; *fut* yeet'asher.
(to) get rid of להיפטר מ־ *inf* leheepater mee-; *pst & pres* neeftar mee- (*f=p*); *fut* yeepater mee-.
(to) get through לפרוץ דרך *inf* leefrots derekh; *pst* parats *etc* (*p=f*); *pres* porets *etc; fut* yeefrots *etc.*
(to) get together 1. להתכנס (convene) *inf* leheetkanes; *pst* heetkanes; *pres* meetkanes; *fut* yeetkanes; **2.** להיפגש (meet) *inf* leheepagesh; *pst & pres* neefgash (*f=p*); *fut* yeepagesh.
(to) get up 1. להתעורר (from sleep) *inf* leheet'orer; *pst* heet'orer; *pres* meet'orer; *fut* yeet'orer; **2.** לקום על הרגליים (stand up) *inf* lakoom 'al ha-raglayeem; *pst & pres* kam *etc; fut* yakoom *etc.*
(I have) got to do it חייב אני לעשות זאת khayav anee la'asot zot.
(that's what) gets me, (that) gets my goat זה מה שמרגיז אותי zeh mah she-margeez otee.
ghastly מבעית *adj* mav'eet/-ah.
ghost רוח רפאים *nf* roo|'akh/-khot refa'eem.
ghost of a notion שמץ של מושג *nm* shemets shel moosag.
ghost writer סופר להשכיר *nmf* sofer/-et lehaskeer.
ghostly של רוחות רפאים *adj* shel rookhot refa'eem.
giant 1. ענק *nmf* 'anak/-eem (*pl+of:* -ey); **2.** ענקי *adj* 'an|akee/-t.
giddy קל דעת *adj* kal/-at da'at.
giddy speed מהירות מסחררת *nf* meheeroot mesakhreret.
gift מתנה *nf* mat|anah/-anot (*+of:* -nat/-not).
gifted מחונן *adj* mekhon|an/-enet.
gift of gab שטף דיבור *nm* shetef deeboor.
gigantic 1. עצום *adj* 'atsoom/-ah; **2.** ענקי (huge) *adj* 'anakee/-t.
(to) giggle לצחקק *inf* letsakhkek; *pst* tseekhkek; *pres* metsakhkek; *fut* yetsakhkek.
(to) gild להזהיב *inf* lehaz'heev; *pst* heez'heev; *pres* maz'heev; *fut* yaz'heev
gill זים *nm* zeem/-eem (*pl+of:* -ey).
gimmick תכסיס מחוכם *nm* takhsees/-eem mekhookam/-eem.

gin 1. מלכודת (trap) *nf* malkod|et/-ot; **2.** ג'ין (liquor) *nm* jeen.

(cotton) gin מנפטת כותנה *nf* manpet|at/-ot kootnah.

ginger זנגביל *nm* zangveel.

ginger ale משקה זנגביל *nm* mashkeh zangveel.

gingerbread עוגת זנגביל *nm* oog|at/-ot zangveel.

gingham כתונת פסים *nf* ketonet/kotnot paseem.

gipsy 1. צועני *nmf* tso'anee/-yah (*pl:* -m/-yot); **2.** *adj* tso'anee/-t.

giraffe ג'ירפה *nf* jeeraf|ah/-ot (*+of:* -at).

(to) gird לחגור *inf* lakhgor; *pst* khagar; *pres* khoger; *fut* yakhgor.

girdle חגורה *nf* khagor|ah/-ot (*+of:* -at).

girl 1. בחורה (young lady) *nf* bakhoor|ah/-ot (*+of:* -at); **2.** נערה (young girl) na'ar|ah/-ot (*+of:* -at); **3.** ילדה (small girl) *nf* yaldah/yeladot (*+of:* yald|at/-ot).

girlhood נערות *nf* na'aroot.

girlish כשל נערה צעירה *adj* ke-shel na'arah tse'eerah.

girth חגורה *nf* khagor|ah/-ot (*+of:* -at).

gist עיקר *nm* 'eekar/-eem (*pl+of:* -ey).

(to) give לתת *inf* latet; *pst* natan; *pres* noten; *fut* yeeten.

(to) give away 1. לתת במתנה *inf* latet be-matanah; *pst* natan *etc*; *pres* noten *etc*; *fut* yeeten *etc*; **2.** להוביל חתן או כלה לחופה (bridegroom or bride) *inf* lehoveel khatan o kalah la-khoopah.

(to) give back להחזיר *inf* lehakhzeer; *pst* hekhzeer; *pres* makhzeer; *fut* yakhzeer

(to) give birth ללדת *inf* laledet; *pst f* yaldah; *pres f* yoledet; *fut f* teled.

(to) give in להיכנע *inf* leheekana'; *pst & pres* neekhna' *(kh=k)*; *fut* yeekana'.

(to) give off לפלוט *inf* leeflot; *pst* palat *(p=f)*; *pres* polet; *fut* yeeflot.

(to) give out 1. לפרסם *inf* lefarsem; *pst* peersem *(p=f)*; *pres* mefarsem; *fut* yefarsem; **2.** להפיץ (spread) *inf* lehafeets; *pst* hefeets; *pres* mefeets; *fut* yafeets.

(to) give up 1. לוותר *inf* levater; *pst* veeter; *pres* mevater; *fut* yevater; **2.** להיכנע *inf* leheekana'; *pst & pres* neekhna' *(kh=k)*; *fut* yeekana'.

given נתון *nm* natoon/netoon|eem (*pl+of:* -ey).

given name שם נתון *nm* shem/-ot natoon/netooneem.

given that היות ש־ heyot she-.

given time שעה קבועה *nf* sha|'ah/-'ot kevoo|'ah/-'ot

giver נותן *nmf* noten/-et.

glacial קפוא *adj* kafoo/kefoo'ah.

glacier קרחון *nm* karkhon/-eem (*pl+of:* -ey).

glad שמח *adj* same'akh/smekhah.

(to) gladden לשמח *inf* lesame'akh; *pst* seemakh; *pres* mesame'akh; *fut* yesamakh.

glade מפער *nm* meef'ar/-eem (*pl+of:* -ey).

gladly בשמחה *adv* be-seemkhah.

gladness שמחה *nf* seemkhah/smakhot (*+of:* seemkh|at/-ot).

glamor 1. זוהר *nm* zohar; **2.** ברק *nm* (luster) barak.

glamorous זוהר *adj* zoher/-et.

glance מבט חטוף *nm* mabat/-eem khatoof/-eem.

(to) glance להעיף מבט *inf* leha'eef mabat; *pst* he'eef *etc*; *pres* me'eef *etc*; *fut* ya'eef *etc*.

gland בלוטה *nf* baloot|ah/-ot (*+of:* -at)

glare אור מסנוור *nm* or/-ot mesanver/-eem.

(to) glare at לסנוור *inf* lesanver; *pst* seenver; *pres* mesanver; *fut* yesanver.

glass זכוכית *nf* zekhookhee|t/-yot.

(looking) glass 1. מראה *nf* mar|'ah/-'ot (*+of:* at); **2.** ראי (mirror) *nm* re'ee.

glass blower מנפח זכוכית *nm* menap|e'akh/-khey zekhokheet.

glass case ארון זכוכית *nm* aron/-ot zekhookheet.

glasses משקפיים *nm pl* meeshk|afayeem (*pl+of:* -efey).

glassware כלי זכוכית *nm pl* kley zekhookheet.

glassy כעין הזכוכית *adj* ke-'eyn ha-zekhookheet.

glaze זיגוג *nm* zeegoog/-eem (*pl+of:* -ey).

(to) glaze לזגג *inf* lezageg; *pst* zeegeg; *pres* mezageg; *fut* yezageg.

glazier זגג *nm* zagag/-eem (*pl+of:* -ey).

gleam נצנוץ *nm* neetsnoots/-eem (*pl+of:* -ey).

(to) gleam 1. לנצנץ *inf* lenatsnets; *pst* neetsnets; *pres* menatsnets; *fut* yenatsnets; **2.** להבריק (glitter) *inf* lehavreek; *pst* heevreek; *pres* mavreek; *fut* yavreek.

glee 1. שמחה (joy) *nf* seemkhah/smakhot (*+of:* seemkh|at/-ot); **2.** עליצות (gaiety) *nf* 'aleetsoo|t/-yot.

glib 1. חלקלק *adj* khalaklak/-ah; **2.** פזיז (rash) *adj* pazeez/pezeezah.

glib excuse תירוץ חלקלק *nm* teroots/-eem khalaklak/-eem.

glib tongue נעים שיחה *adj* ne'eem/-at seekhah.

glide 1. גלישה *nf* gleesh|ah/-ot (*+of:* -at); **2.** דאייה (soaring) *nf* de'ee|yah/-yot (*+of:* -yat).

(to) glide 1. לגלוש *inf* leeglosh; *pst* galash; *pres* golesh; *fut* yeeglosh; **2.** לדאות (soar) *inf* leed'ot; *pst* da'ah; *pres* do'eh; *fut* yeed'eh.

glimmer ניצוץ *nm* neetsots/-ot.

glimmer of hope ניצוץ של תקווה *nm* neetsots shel teekvah.

glimpse מבט חטוף *nm* mabat/-eem khatoof/-eem.

(to catch a) glimpse להעיף מבט *inf* leha'eef mabat; *pst* he'eef *etc*; *pres* me'eef *etc*; *fut* ya'eef *etc*.

glint נצנוץ *nm* neetsnoots/-eem (*pl+of:* -ey).

(to) glisten לנצנץ *inf* lenatsnets; *pst* neetsnets; *pres* menatsnets; *fut* yenatsnets.

glitter ברק *nm* barak.

(to) gloat לבלוע בעיניים *inf* leevlo'a' be-'eynayeem; *pst* bala' *(b=v) etc*; *pres* bole'a' *etc*; *fut* yeevla' *etc*.

globe 1. כדור הארץ *nm* kadoor ha-arets; **2.** גלובוס *nm* globoos/-eem (*pl+of:* -ey).

gloom קדרות *nf* kadroo|t/-yot.

gloomy קודר *adj* koder/-et.

(to) glorify להלל *inf* lehalel; *pst* heelel; *pres* mehalel; *fut* yehalel.

glorious מהולל *adj* mehool|al/-elet.

glory תהילה *nf* teheel|ah/-ot (*+of:* -at).

gloss 1. הערה *nf* he'ar|ah/-ot (*+of:* -at); **2.** פירוש (commentary) *nm* peroosh/-eem (*pl+of:* -ey).

(to) gloss over לחפות על *inf* lekhapot 'al; *pst* kheepah 'al; *pres* mekhapeh 'al; *fut* yekhapeh 'al.

glossary לקט מלים *nm* leket/leektey meeleem.

glossy 1. חלק (smooth) *adj* khalak/-ah; **2.** נוצץ (shining) *adj* notsets/-et.

glove כפפה *nf* kfaf|ah/-ot (*+of:* keefef|at/-ot).

glow להט *nm* lahat.

(to) glow ללהוט *inf* leelhot; *pst* lahat; *pres* lohet; *fut* yeelhat.

glowing לוהט *adj* lohet/-et.

glow-worm גחלילית *nf* gakhleelee|t/-yot.

glue דבק *nm* devek/dvakeem (*pl+of:* deevkey).

glum 1. עצוב *adj* 'atsoov/-ah; **2.** מצוברח (moody) *adj* metsoovrakh/-at.

glutton 1. זולל וסובא *nmf & adj* zolel/-et ve-sove/-'t; **2.** גרגרן (gobbler) *nmf & adj* gargeran/-eet.

gluttonous רעבתן *adj* ra'avtan/-eet.

gluttony רעבתנות *nf* ra'avtanoo|t/-yot.

glycerin, glycerine גליצרין *nm* gleetsereen.

(to) gnarl 1. להתפתל *inf* leheetpatel; *pst* heetpatel; *pres* meetpatel; *fut* yeetpatel; **2.** לעוות (twist) *inf* le'avet; *pst* 'eevet; *pres* me'avet; *fut* ye'avet.

(to) gnash לחרוק שיניים *inf* lakhrok sheenayeem; *pst* kharak *etc*; *pres* khorek *etc*; *fut* yakhrok *etc*.

gnat 1. יבחוש *nm* yavkhoosh/-eem (*pl+of:* -ey); **2.** יתוש (mosquito) *nm* yatoosh/-eem (*pl+of:* -ey).

(to) gnaw לכרסם *inf* lekharsem; *pst* keersem (*k=kh*); *pres* mekharsem; *fut* yekharsem.

(it is a) go עשינו עסק 'aseenoo 'esek.

(to) go ללכת *inf* lalekhet; *pst* halakh; *pres* holekh; *fut* yelekh.

(to be on the) go לנוע ולנוד *inf* lanoo'a' ve-lanood; *pst & pres* na' ve-nad; *fut* yanoo'a' ve-yanood.

(to let) go להרפות *inf* leharpot; *pst* heerpah; *pres* marpeh; *fut* yarpeh.

(to) go around 1. ללכת מסביב *inf* lalekhet mee-saveev; *pst* halakh *etc*; *pres* holekh; *fut* yelekh *etc*; **2.** להקיף (encircle) *inf* lehakeef; *pst* heekeef; *pres* makeef; *fut* yakeef.

(not enough) to go around אין כדי להספיק לכולם en kedey lehaspeek le-khoolam (*kh=k*).

(to) go away להסתלק *inf* leheestalek; *pst* heestalek; *pres* meestalek; *fut* yeestalek.

(to) go back on one's word לחזור בו מדיבורו *inf* lakhzor bo mee-deebooro; *pst* khazar *etc*; *pres* khozer *etc*; *fut* yakhzor *etc*.

(to) go by לנהוג לפי *inf* leenhog lefee; *pst* nahag *etc*; *pres* noheg *etc*; *fut* yeenhag *etc*.

(to) go down 1. לרדת *inf* laredet; *pst* yarad; *pres* yored; *fut* yered; **2.** לצלול (dive) *inf* leetslol; *pst* tsalal; *pres* tsolel; *fut* yeetslol **3.** לטבוע (sink) leetbo'a'; *pst* tava' (*v=b*); *pres* tove'a'; *fut* yeetba'.

(to) go insane 1. לצאת מדעתו *inf* latset mee-da'ato; *pst* yatsa *etc*; *pres* yotse *etc*; *fut* yetse *etc*; **2.** להשתגע (go mad) *v refl* leheeshtage'a'; *pst* heeshtaga'; *pres* meeshtage'a'; *fut* yeeshtaga'.

(to) go into להיכנס לתוך *inf* leheekanes le-tokh; *pst & pres* neekhnas *etc* (*kh=k*); *fut* yeekanes *etc*.

(to) go off להתפוצץ (explode) *inf* leheetpotsets; *pst* heetpotsets; *pres* meetpotsets; *fut* yeetpotsets.

(to) go on להמשיך *inf* lehamsheekh; *pst* heemsheekh; *pres* mamsheekh; *fut* yamsheekh.

(to) go out 1. לצאת (outside) *inf* latset; *pst* yatsa; *pres* yotse; *fut* yetse; **2.** לצאת לבלות (have good time) *inf* latset levalot; *pst* yatsa *etc*; *pres* yotse *etc*; *fut* yetse *etc*.

(to) go over 1. לעבור על (peruse) *inf* la'avor 'al; *pst* 'avar 'al; *pres* 'over 'al; *fut* ya'avor 'al; **2.** לבדוק (check) *inf* leevdok; *pst* badak (*b=v*); *pres* bodek; *fut* yeevdok.

(to) go to sleep ללכת לישון *inf* lalekhet leeshon; *pst* halakh *etc*; *pres* holekh; *fut* yelekh *etc*.

(to) go under 1. לטבוע (drown) *inf* leetbo'a'; *pst* tava' (*v=b*); *pres* tove'a'; *fut* yeetba'; **2.** לפשוט רגל (go bankrupt) *inf* leefshot regel; *pst* pashat *etc* (*p=f*); *pres* poshet *etc*; *fut* yeefshot *etc*.

(to) go up לעלות *inf* la'alot; *pst* 'alah; *pres* 'oleh; *fut* ya'aleh.

goad מלמד *nm* malmed/-eem (*pl+of:* -ey).

goal 1. מטרה *nf* mat|arah/-ot (*+of:* -at); **2.** יעד (objective) *nm* ya'ad/ye'adeem (*pl+of:* ya'adey).

goat תיש *nm* tayeesh/tyash|eem (*pl+of:* -ey).

(male) goat תיש זכר tayeesh/tyasheem zakhar/zekhareem.

(scape-)goat שעיר לעזאזל *nm* sa'eer/se'eereem la'azazel.

goatie זקנקן *nm* zekankan/-eem (*pl+of:* -ey).

gobble קיעקוע *nm* kee'akoo|'a'/-'eem (*pl+of:* -'ey)

(to) gobble לזלול *inf* leezlol; *pst* zalal; *pres* zolel; *fut* yeezlol.

(to) gobble up לזלול עד תום *inf* leezlol 'ad tom; *pst* zalal *etc*; *pres* zolel *etc*; *fut* yeezlol *etc*.

go-between מתווך *nmf* metavekh/-et.

goblet גביע *nm* gavee'a'/gvee|'eem (*pl+of:* -'ey).

goblin שדון *nm* shedon/-eem (*pl+of:* -ey).

god אל *nm* el/-eem (*pl+of:* -ey).

God אלוהים *nm* eloheem.

godchild בן־חסות של סנדק *nm* ben/bat khasoot shel sandak.

goddamned ארור *adj* aroor/-ah.

goddess אלילה *nf* eleel|ah/-ot (*+of:* -at).

godfather סנדק *nm* sandak/-eem (*pl+of:* -ey).

godless כופר *nmf* kofer/-et.

godlike קדוש *adj* kadosh/kedoshah.

godly ירא שמיים *adj* yere/-'at shamayeem.

godmother סנדקית *nf* sandakee|t/-yot.

goggles משקפי מגן *nm pl* meeshkefey magen.

going to be עתיד להיות *adj* 'ateed/-ah leehyot.

(comings and) goings בואו וצאתו bo|'o/-'ah ve-tse't|o/-ah (*m/f*).

goiter זפקת *nf* zapeket.

gold זהב *nm* zahav.

golden עשוי זהב *adj* 'asoo|y/-yah zahav.

goldfinch חוחית *nf* khokhee|t/-yot.

goldfish דג זהב *nm* dag/degey zahav.

goldsmith צורף זהב *nm* tsor|ef/-fey zahav.

golf משחק גולף *nm* meeskhak golf.

gondola גונדולה *nf* gondol|ah/-ot (*+of:* -at).

gondola-car קרון תלוי *nm* kron/-ot talooy/tlooyeem.

(is) gone איננו *adj* eynen|oo/-ah.

(it is all) gone נעלם הכול ואיננו ne'elam ha-kol ve-eynenoo.

gone is, are הלך ואיננו halakh ve-eynenoo.

gong גונג *nm* gong/-eem.

good 1. טוב *adj* tov/-ah; **2.** *adv* tov.

(for) good לעולמים le-'olameem!

(to make) good 1. לפצות (compensate) *inf* lefatsot; *pst* peetsah *(p=f)*; *pres* mefatseh; *fut* yefatseh; **2.** להצליח (succeed) *inf* lehatslee'akh; *pst* heetslee'akh; *pres* matslee'akh; *fut* yatslee'akh.

(very) good טוב מאוד *adv* tov me'od.

good afternoon! צהריים טובים (greeting) tsohorayeem toveem!

good day כל טוב (greeting) kol toov!

good evening ערב טוב (greeting) 'erev tov!

Good Friday יום א׳ לפסחא הנוצרית *nm* yom alef la-paskha ha-notsreet.

good morning בוקר טוב (greeting) boker tov!

good night לילה טוב (greeting) laylah tov!

(to have a) good time לבלות בנעימים *inf* levalot bee-ne'eemeem; *pst* beelah *etc* *(b=v)*; *pres* mevaleh *etc*; *fut* yevaleh *etc*.

good-bye !שלום ולהתראות (greeting) shalom oo-leheetra'ot!

good-looking יפה תואר *adj* yef|eh/-at to'ar.

good-natured בעל מזג טוב *adj* ba'al/-at mezeg tov.

goodness טוב *nm* toov.

goody ממתק *nm* mamtak/-eem *(pl+of:* -ey).

goody-goody 1. מתחסד *adj* meetkhased/-et; **2.** צבוע (hypocrite) *nmf* tsavoo'a'/tsvoo'ah.

goof שוטה *nmf & adj* shot|eh/-ah.

goon בריון בעל זרוע *nm* beeryon/-eem ba'al/-ey zro'a.

goose אווזה *nf* avaz|ah/-ot (+*of:* avz|at/-ot).

gooseberry דומדמנית *nf* doomdemanee|t/-yot.

gooseflesh סמרור עור *nm* seemroor/-ey 'or.

gopher 1. צב (tortoise) *nm* tsa|v/-beem *(b=v; pl+of:* -bey); **2.** עץ גופר (tree) *nm* 'ets/'atsey gofer.

gore קריש דם *nm* kreesh/-ey dam.

(to) gore לנגח *inf* lenage'akh; *pst* neegakh; *pres* menage'akh; *fut* yenagakh.

gorge 1. גרון *nm* garon/gronot (+*of:* gron); **2.** ושט (gullet) *nm* veshet.

(to) gorge לזלול *inf* leezlol; *pst* zalal; *pres* zolel; *fut* yeezlol.

gorgeous נהדר *adj* nehed|ar/-eret.

gorilla 1. גורילה *nm* goreel|ah/-ot; **2.** שומר ראש (*[colloq.]*: bodyguard) *nm* shom|er/-rey rosh.

gory מגועל בדם *adj* mego|'al/-'elet be-dam.

gospel דברי אמת *nm pl* deevrey emet.

gospel truth תורה מסיני *nf* torah mee-seenay.

gossip רכילות *nf* rekheeloo|t/-yot.

(to) gossip לרכל *inf* lerakhel; *pst* reekhel; *pres* merakhel; *fut* yerakhel.

gossipy רכלני *adj* rakhlanee/-t.

(I have) got to do it חייב אני לעשות זאת kha|yav/-yevet anee la'asot zot.

Gothic גותי *adj* gotee/-t.

gouge 1. מפסלת *nf* mafs|elet/-alot; **2.** מירמה (swindle) *nf* meerm|ah/-ot (+*of:* -at).

(to) gouge 1. לפסל (sculp) *inf* lefasel; *pst* peesel *(p=f)*; *pres* mefasel *(f=p)*; *fut* yefasel; **2.** לרמות (swindle) *inf* leramot; *pst* reemah; *pres* merameh; *fut* yerameh.

(to) gouge someone's eyes out לעקור את העיניים למישהו *inf* la'akor et ha-'eynayeem le-meeshehoo; *pst* 'akar *etc*; *pres* 'oker *etc*; *fut* ya'akor *etc*.

goulash גולש *nm* goolash.

gourd דלעת *nf* dla|'at/-'ot.

gourmet מומחה למאכלים *nmf* moomkh|eh/-eet le-ma'akhaleem.

gout 1. צנית *nf* tseeneet; **2.** פודגרה *nf* podagrah.

(to) govern 1. למשול *inf* leemshol; *pst* mashal; *pres* moshel; *fut* yeemshol; **2.** לשלוט (dominate) *inf* leeshlot; *pst* shalat; *pres* sholet; *fut* yeeshlot.

governess אומנת *nf* omenet/omnot.

government ממשלה *nf* memsh|alah/-alot (+*of:* -elet).

governmental ממשלתי *adj* memshaltee/-t.

governor מושל *nm* mosh|el/-leem *(pl+of:* -ley)

gown שמלה *nf* seemlah/smalot (+*of:* seeml|at/-ot)

(dressing) gown חלוק *nm* khalook/-eem *(pl+of:* -ey).

grab 1. חטיפה (snatching) *nf* khateef|ah/-ot (+*of:* -at); **2.** תפיסה (catching) *nf* tfees|ah/-ot (+*of:* -at).

(to) grab 1. לחטוף (snatch) *inf* lakhtof; *pst* khataf; *pres* khotef; *fut* yakhtof; **2.** לתפוס (catch) leetpos; *pst* tafas *(f=p)*; *pres* tofes; *fut* yeetpos.

grace 1. חן *nm* khen; **2.** חסד (favor) *nm* khesed/ khas|adeem *(pl+of:* -dey)

(to say) grace לומר בירכת המזון *inf* lomar beerkat ha-mazon; *pst* amar *etc*; *pres* omer *etc*; *fut* yomar *etc*.

graceful חינני *adj* kheenanee/-t.

gracefully בחן *adv* be-khen.

gracefulness חינניות *nf* kheenaneeyoot.

(to be in the good) graces of לשאת חן בעיני *inf* laset khen be-'eyney; *pst* nasa *etc*; *pres* nose *etc*; *fut* yeesa *etc*.

gracious חינני *adj* kheenanee/-t.

gradation דירוג *nm* deroog/-eem *(pl+of:* -ey).

grade 1. דרג *nm* dereg/drageem *(pl+of:* deergey); **2.** דרגה (degree) *nf* dargah/dragot (+*of:* darg|at/ -ot).

(to) grade 1. לדרג *inf* ledareg; *pst* deereg; *pres* medareg; *fut* yedareg; **2.** לסווג (classify) lesaveg; *pst* seeveg; *pres* mesaveg; *fut* yesaveg.

grade crossing צומת חד־מפלסי *nm* tsomet/ tsemateem khad-meeflasee/-yeem.

(the) grades השכלה יסודית *nf* haskalah yesodeet.

gradual הדרגתי *adj* hadragatee/-t.

graduate בוגר *nmf* bog|er/-eret *(pl:* -reem; +*of:* -rey).

(university) graduate בוגר אוניברסיטה *nmf* boger/ -et ooneeverseetah.

(to do) graduate work להשתלם בעבודת גמר *inf* leheeshtalem ba-'avodat gemer; *pst* heeshtalem; *pres* meeshtalem; *fut* yeeshtalem.

graduation סיום חוק לימודים אוניברסיטאי *nm* seeyoom khok leemoodeem ooneeverseeta'ee.

graft 1. הרכבה (botany) *nf* harkav|ah/-ot (+*of:* -at); **2.** השתלה (skin *etc.*) *nf* hashtal|ah/-ot (+*of:* -at); **3.** שוחד (bribery) *nm* shokhad.

(to) graft 1. להשתיל (transplant) *inf* lehashteel; *pst* heeshteel; *pres* mashteel; *fut* yashteel; **2.** להרכיב

(botany) *inf* leharkeev; *pst* heerkeev; *pres* markeev; *fut* yarkeev.

grafter נוטל שוחד *nmf* notel/-et shokhad.

grain תבואה *nf* tvoo|'ah/-'ot (+*of:* -'at).

(against the) grain 1. למורת רוח *adv* le-morat roo'akh; **2.** מנוגד לטבעו (contrary to one's nature) *adj* menoog|ad/-edet le-teev'o.

gram גרם *nm* gram/-eem (*pl+of:* -ey).

grammar דקדוק *nm* deekdook.

grammar school בית ספר יסודי *nm* bet/batey sefer yesodee/-yeem.

grammatical דקדוקי *adj* deekdookee/-t.

granary אסם *nm* asam/-eem (*pl+of:* -ey).

grand 1. נהדר *adj* nehed|ar/-eret; **2.** מפואר (magnificent) *adj* mefo|'ar/-'eret.

grand piano פסנתר כנף *nm* pesant|er/-rey kanaf.

grandchild נכד *nmf* nekh|ed/-dah (*f+of:* -dat).

grandchildren נכדים *nmf pl* nekh|adeem/-adot (+*of:* -adey/-dot).

granddaughter נכדה *nf* nekh|dah/-adot.

grandeur גדולה *nf* gedoolah.

grandfather סב *nm* sav/-eem (*pl+of:* -ey).

grandiose כביר *adj* kabeer/-ah.

grandma, grandmother סבתא *nf* savt|a/-ot (*cpr* sabt|a/-ot).

grandness גדולה *nf* gedool|ah/-ot (+*of:* -at).

grandpa סבא *nm* sav|a/-eem (*pl+of:* -ey; *cpr* sab|a/-a'eem).

grandparent הורה־סב *nm* hor|eh/-eem sav/saveem.

grandson נכד *nm* nekh|ed/-adeem (*pl+of:* -adey).

grandstand בימת הצופים *nf* beemat ha-tsofeem.

grange חווה *nf* khav|ah/-ot (+*of:* -at).

granite שחם *nm* shakham.

granny סבתא *nf* savt|a/-ot (*cpr* sabt|a/-ot).

grant מענק *nm* ma'an|ak/-akeem (*pl+of:* -key).

(to) grant להעניק *inf* leha'aneek; *pst* he'eneek; *pres* ma'aneek; *fut* ya'aneek.

(to take for) granted לראות כמונח בקופסה *inf* leer'ot ke-moonakh be-koofsah; *pst* ra'ah *etc*; *pres* ro'eh *etc*; *fut* yeer'eh *etc*.

(to) granulate 1. לפורר *vt inf* leforer; *pst* porer *(p=f)*; *pres* meforer; *fut* yeforer; **2.** להתפורר (disintegrate) *v* refl leheetporer; *pst* heetporer; *pres* meetporer; *fut* yeetporer.

grapefruit אשכולית *nf* eshkolee|t/-yot.

grapes ענבים *nm pl* 'anaveem (*pl+of:* 'eenbey).

grapevine 1. גפן *nf* gef|en/-aneem (*pl+of:* gafney); **2.** מפי השמועה (rumors) *adv* mee-pee ha-shmoo'ah.

graph 1. עקומה *nf* 'akoom|ah/-ot (+*of:* -at); **2.** דיאגרמה *nf* dee'agram|ah/-ot (+*of:* -at).

(to) graph לסרטט עקומה *inf* lesartet 'akoomah; *pst* seertet *etc*; *pres* mesartet *etc*; *fut* yesartet *etc*.

graphic 1. ציורי *adj* tseeyooree/-t; **2.** גרפי *adj* grafee/-t.

graphite גרפית *nm* grafeet.

(to) grapple 1. לתפוס (catch) *inf* leetpos; *pst* tafas *(f=p)*; *pres* tofes; *fut* yeetpos; **2.** להיאבק *inf* lehe'avek; *pst & pres* ne'evak; *fut* ye'avek.

grasp תפיסה *nf* tfees|ah/-ot (+*of:* -at).

(to) grasp 1. לתפוס (comprehend) *inf* leetpos; *pst* tafas *(f=p)*; *pres* tofes; *fut* yeetpos; **2.** להבין (understand) *inf* lehaveen; *pst* heveen; *pres* meveen; *fut* yaveen.

(within one's) grasp בגבול היכולת לתפוס *adv* bee-gvool ha-yekholet leetpos.

(a good) grasp of a subject תפיסה נכונה של הנושא *nf* tfees|ah/-ot nekhon|ah/-ot shel ha-nose.

grass 1. עשב *nm* 'esev/'asabeem (*pl+of:* 'eesbey); **2.** דשא *nm* desh|e/-'a'eem.

grasshopper חגב *nm* khagav/-eem (*pl+of:* -ey).

grassroots שורשיות *nf* shorsheeyoot.

grassy מדשיא *adj* mad'shee/-'ah.

grate 1. סבכה *nf* svakh|ah/-ot (+*of:* -at); **2.** אח (fireplace) *nm* akh.

(to) grate 1. לרסק (food) *inf* lerasek; *pst* reesek; *pres* merasek; *fut* yerasek; **2.** לצרום (split ears) *inf* leetsrom; *pst* tsaram; *pres* tsorem; *fut* yeetsrom.

(to) grate on להרגיז *inf* lehargeez; *pst* heergeez; *pres* margeez; *fut* yargeez.

grateful אסיר תודה *adj* aseer/-at todah.

grater פומפייה *nf* poompee|yah/-yot (+*of:* -yat).

gratification 1. סיפוק *nm* seepook; **2.** שביעת רצון *nf* svee'at ratson.

(to) gratify 1. להשביע רצון *inf* lehasbee'a' ratson; *pst* heesbee'a' *etc*; *pres* masbee'a' *etc*; *fut* yasbee'a' *etc*; **2.** לתת סיפוק *inf* latet seepook; *pst* natan *etc*; *pres* noten *etc*; *fut* yeeten *etc*.

grating 1. סורג *nm* sor|eg/-geem (*pl+of:* -gey); **2.** סבכה *nf* svakh|ah/-ot (+*of:* seevkhat).

gratis חינם *adv* kheenam.

gratitude הכרת תודה *nf* hakar|at/-ot todah.

gratuitous 1. חינם *adj* kheenam; **2.** ללא סיבה (with no reason) *adj* le-lo seebah.

gratuitous statement אמירה חסרת שחר *nf* ameer|ah/-ot khasr|at/-ot shakhar.

gratuity 1. מענק *nm* ma'an|ak/-akeem (*pl+of:* -key); **2.** תשר (tip) *nf* tesh|er/-areem (*pl+of:* teeshrey).

grave 1. חמור *adj* khamoor/-ah; **2.** רציני (serious) *adj* retseenee/-t; **3.** קבר (tomb) *m* kever/kvareem (*pl+of:* keevrey).

gravel חצץ *nm* khatsats.

gravestone מצבה *nf* matsev|ah/-ot (+*of:* -at).

graveyard בית קברות *nm* bet/batey kvarot.

gravitation כוח הכובד *nm* ko'akh ha-koved.

gravity 1. חומרה *nf* khoomr|ah/-ot (+*of:* -at); **2.** רצינות (seriousness) *nf* retseenoot.

gravy רוטב צלי *nm* rotev tselee.

gray אפור *adj* afoor/-ah.

gray horse סוס אפור *nm* soos afor.

gray matter שכל *nm* sekhel.

gray-headed בעל ראש שיבה *nmf* ba'al/-at rosh seyvah.

grayish אפרפר *adj* afarpar/-ah.

grayish hair שיער מאפיר *nm* se'ar ma'afeer.

grayness אפרוריות *nf* afrooreeyoot.

graze מרעה *nm* meer'eh

(to) graze להוציא למרעה *inf* lehotsee le- meer'eh; *pst* hotsee; *pres* motsee *etc*; *fut* yotsee *etc*.

grease שמן סיכה *nm* shemen/sheemney seekhah.

(to) grease לסוך *inf* lasookh; *pst & pres* sakh; *fut* yasookh.

(to) grease the palm לשחד *inf* leshakhed; *pst* sheekhed; *pres* meshakhed; *fut* yeshakhed.

greasy 1. משומן *adj* meshoom|an/-enet; **2.** מלוכלך (dirty) *adj* melookhl|akh/-ekhet.

great 1. כביר *adj* kabeer/-ah; **2.** נעלה (sublime) *adj* na'al|eh/-ah.

(a) great deal במידה רבה *adv* be-meedah rabah.

great grandchild 1. נין *nmf* neen/-ah; **2.** שילש (3rd generation) *nmf* sheelesh/-ah.

great grandfather 1. אב שילש *nm* av/-ot sheelesh/-eem; **2.** אבי הסב *[colloq.]* (grandfather's *or grandmother's father) nm* avee ha-sav/-ta.

great grandmother 1. אם שילשה *nf* em/eemahot sheelesh|ah/-ot; **2.** אם הסב *[colloq.]* (grandfather's *or grandmother's father) nf* em ha-sav/-ta.

(a) great many די הרבה *adv* dey harbeh.

(a) great while שעה ארוכה *nf & adv* sha'ah arookah.

greatly בעיקר *adv* be-'eekar.

greatness גדולה *nf* gedoolah.

Grecian יווני *adj* yevanee/-t.

Greece יוון *nf* yavan.

(ancient) Greece יוון העתיקה *nf* yavan ha-'ateekah.

greed 1. חמדנות *nf* khamdanoo|t/-yot; **2.** גרגרנות *nf* gargeranoot.

greedily 1. בחמדה *adv* be-khemdah; **2.** בשקיקה *adv* bee-shkeekah.

greediness 1. חמדנות *nf* khamdanoo|t/-yot; **2.** להיטות *nf* leheetoo|t/-yot.

greedy 1. חמדן *adj* khamdan/-eet; **2.** תאוותן *adj* te'avtan/-eet.

Greek 1. יווני *adj* yevanee/-t; **2.** יווני *nmf* yevan|ee/-yah (*pl:* -m/-yot; *+of:* yevaney); **3.** יוונית (language) *nf* yevaneet.

green ירוק *adj* yarok/yerokah.

(to) green 1. להוריק *inf* lehoreek; *pst* horeek; *pres* moreek; *fut* yoreek; **2.** להתכסות דשא (to be covered with grass) *inf* leheetkasot deshe; *pst* heetkasah *etc*; *pres* meetkaseh *etc*; *fut* yeetkaseh *etc.*

(to grow) green להוריק *inf* lehoreek; *pst* horeek; *pres* moreek; *fut* yoreek.

(the fields look) green השדות מוריקים *nm pl* ha-sadot moreekeem.

greengrocer ירקן *nmf* yarkan/-eet.

greenhorn 1. טירון *nmf* teeron/-eet; **2.** חסר־ניסיון (inexperienced) *adj* khas|ar/-rat neesayon.

greenhouse חממה *nf* khamam|ah/-ot (*+of:* -at).

greenish ירקרק *adj* yerakr|ak/-eket.

greenness ירוקת *nf* yeroket.

(to) greet לקדם בברכה *inf* lekadem bee-vrakhah *(v=b)*; *pst* keedem *etc*; *pres* mekadem *etc*; *fut* yekadem *etc.*

greeting ברכה *nf* brakh|ah/-ot (*+of:* beer|kat/-khot; *kh=k*).

greetings! 1. ! ברכות *nf pl* brakhot! **2.** ! בירכותי (my best wishes!) *nf pl* beerkhotay!

grenade רימון *nm* reemon/-eem (*pl+of:* -ey).

(hand-)grenade רימון־יד *nm* reemon/-ey yad.

grey אפור *adj* afor/afoorah.

greyhound כלב־ציד *nm* kelev/kalvey tsayeed.

greyish אפרורי *adj* afrooree/-t.

greyness אפרוריות *nf* afrooreeyoot.

griddle מחתה *nf* makht|ah/-ot (*+of:* -at).

grief 1. צרה (sorrow) *nf* tsar|ah/-ot (*+of:* -at); **2.** אסון (calamity) *nm* ason/-ot; **3.** אבל (bereavement) evel.

grievance 1. תלונה (complaint) *nf* tloon|ah/-ot (*+of:* -at); **2.** התמרמרות (resentment) *nf* heetmarmeroo|t/-yot.

(to) grieve 1. להצטער *inf* leheetsta'er; *pst* heetsta'er; *pres* meetsta'er; *fut* yeetsta'er; **2.** להתאבל (mourn) *inf* leheet'abel; *pst* heet'abel; *pres* meet'abel; *fut* yeet'abel.

grievous חמור *adj* khamoor/-ah.

grill 1. מצלה *nm* meetsl|eh/-eem (*pl+of:* -ey); **2.** צלי (roast) *nm* tsalee.

(mixed) grill צלי מעורב *nm* tsalee me'orav.

(to) grill 1. לצלות (meat) *inf* leetslot; *pst* tsalah; *pres* tsoleh; *fut* yeetsleh; **2.** לחקור חשוד (interrogate suspect) *inf* lakhkor khashood; *pst* khakar *etc*; *pres* khoker *etc*; *fut* yakhkor *etc.*

grill-room מסעדת צלי *nf* mees|'edet/'adot tsalee.

grim קודר *adj* koder/-et.

grimace 1. העוויה *nf* ha'ava|yah/-yot (*+of:* -yat); **2.** פרצוף (*[colloq.]:* twisted expression) *nm* partsoof/-eem (*pl+of:* -ey).

(to) grimace 1. לעשות העוויות *inf* la'asot ha'avayot; *pst* 'asah *etc*; *pres* 'oseh *etc*; *fut* ya'aseh *etc*; **2.** לעשות פרצופים *inf* la'asot partsoofeem; *pst* 'asah *etc*; *pres* 'oseh *etc*; *fut* ya'aseh *etc.*

grime לכלוך *nm* leekhlookh/-eem (*pl+of:* -ey).

grimy מטונף *adj* metoon|af/-efet.

grin 1. חיוך *nm* kheeyookh/-eem (*pl+of:* -ey); **2.** בת־צחוק (smile) *nf* bat-tsekhok.

(to) grin לחייך *inf* lekhayekh; *pst* kheeyekh; *pres* mekhayekh; *fut* yekhayekh.

grind 1. טחינה *nf* tekheen|ah/-ot (*+of:* -at); **2.** עבודה קשה (hard work) *nf* 'avodah kashah.

(an axe to) grind קרדום לחפור בו kardom lakhpor bo.

(the daily) grind מטחנת השיגרה היומית *nf* matkhenat ha-sheegrah ha-yomeet.

(to) grind לטחון *inf* leet'khon; *pst* takhan; *pres* tokhen; *fut* yeetkhan.

(to) grind a hand organ לפרוט על אורגן *inf* lefrot 'al organ; *pst* parat *(p=f) etc*; *pres* poret *etc*; *fut* yeefrot *etc.*

(to) grind one's teeth לחרוק שיניים *inf* lakhrok sheenayeem; *pst* kharak *etc*; *pres* khorek *etc*; *fut* yakhrok *etc.*

grinder משחזה *nf* mash'kh|ezah/-ezot (*+of:* -ezat).

grindstone אבן משחזת *nf* even mashkhezet.

grip 1. תפס *nm* tefes/tfaseem (*pl+of:* teefsey); **2.** תפיסה (grasp) *nf* tfees|ah/-ot (*+of:* -at); **3.** אחיזה (hold) *nf* akheez|ah/-ot (*+of:* -at).

(to have a) grip on someone להיות בעל השפעה על מישהו *inf* leehyot ba'al/-at *(m/f)* hashpa'ah 'al meeshe|hoo/-hee *(m/f)*; *pst* hayah *etc*; *pres* heeno *etc*; *fut* yeehyeh *etc.*

grippe 1. שפעת *nf* shapa'at; **2.** גריפה *nf* greep|ah/-ot.

grit 1. חצץ *nm* khatsats; **2.** אומץ־לב (courage) *nm* omets-lev.

(to) grit לחרוק שיניים *inf* lakhrok sheenayeem; *pst* kharak *etc*; *pres* khorek *etc*; *fut* yakhrok *etc*.

grits 1. שיבולת־שועל *nf* sheebolet-shoo'al; **2.** גריסי שיפון (rye groats) *nm pl* greesey sheepon.

gritty אמיץ־לב (courageous) *adj* ameets/-at lev.

grizzly אפרורי *adj* afrooree/-t.

grizzly bear דוב אפור *nm* dov/doobeem *(b=v)* afor/afooreem.

groan 1. גניחה *nf* gneekh|ah/-ot (*+of:* -at); **2.** נאקה (moan) *nf* ne'ak|ah/-ot (*+of:* na'ak|at/-ot).

(to) groan 1. לגנוח *inf* leegno'akh; *pst* ganakh; *pres* gone'akh; *fut* yeegnakh; **2.** לרטון (grumble) *inf* leerton; *pst* ratan; *pres* roten; *fut* yeerton.

grocer בעל מכולת *nmf* ba'al/-at makolet.

groceries 1. דברי מכולת (grocery goods) *nm pl* deevrey makolet; **2.** סחורות מכולת (grocery merchandise) sekhorot makolet.

grocery מכולת *nf* makolet (*pl:* khanooyot makolet).

grocery store חנות מכולת *nf* khanoo|t/-yot makolet.

groom 1. חתן *nm* khatan/-eem (*pl+of:* -ey); **2.** סייס (horses) *nm* sayas/-eem (*pl+of:* -ey).

(to) groom 1. לטפל *inf* letapel; *pst* teepel; *pres* metapel; *fut* yetapel; **2.** לטפח (cultivate) *inf* letape'akh; *pst* teepakh; *pres* metape'akh; *fut* yetapakh.

(to) groom for a job לייעד לתפקיד *inf* leya'ed le-tafkeed; *pst* yee'ed *etc*; *pres* meya'ed *etc*; *fut* yeya'ed *etc*.

(to) groom oneself להכין עצמו *inf* lehakheen 'atsmo; *pst* hekheen *etc*; *pres* mekheen *etc*; *fut* yakheen *etc*.

(well) groomed מטופח כהלכה *adj* metoopakh/-at ka-halakhah.

groove 1. חריץ *nm* khareets/-eem (*pl+of:* -ey); **2.** נוהל (procedure) *nm* nohal/nehaleem (*pl+of:* noholey).

(to) groove לחרוץ *inf* lakhrots; *pst* kharats; *pres* khorets; *fut* yakhrots.

(to) grope לגשש *inf* legashesh; *pst* geeshesh; *pres* megashesh; *fut* yegashesh.

(to) grope for לגשש אחר *inf* legashesh akhar; *pst* geeshesh *etc*; *pres* megashesh *etc*; *fut* yegashesh *etc*.

gross 1. כולל *adj adj* kolel/-et; **2.** גולמי *adj* golmee/-t; **3.** כלל (total) *nm* klal.

(to) gross להרוויח ברוטו *inf* leharvee'akh brooto; *pst* heervee'akh *etc*; *pres* marvee'akh *etc*; *fut* yarvee'akh *etc*.

gross earnings 1. הכנסה כוללת *nf* hakhnasah kolelet; **2.** הכנסה גולמית *nf* hakhnasah golmeet.

gross ignorance בורות גסה *nf* booroot gasah.

gross weight משקל ברוטו *nm* meeshkal brooto.

grotesque 1. תמהוני *adj* teemhonee/-t; **2.** מוזר (strange) *adj* moozar/-ah.

grotto 1. מערה *nf* me'ar|ah/-ot (*+of:* -at); **2.** נקיק (ravine) *nm* nakeek/nekeek|eem (*pl+of:* -ey).

grouch 1. רטנונות *nf* ratnanoo|t/-yot; **2.** מצב רוח קודר (dark mood) *nm* mats|av/-vey roo'akh kod|er/-reem.

(to) grouch 1. לרטון *inf* leerton; *pst* ratan; *pres* roten; *fut* yeerton; **2.** להתמרמר (resent) *inf* leheetmarmer; *pst* heetmarmer; *pres* meetmarmer; *fut* yeetmarmer.

(to have a) grouch against לנצור טינה כלפי *inf* leentsor teenah kelapey; *pst* natsar *etc*; *pres* notser *etc*; *fut* yeentsor *etc*.

grouchy ממורמר *adj* memoorm|ar/-eret.

ground 1. קרקע *nf* kark|a'/-a'ot; **2.** שטח (space) *nm* shetakh/shtakheem (*pl+of:* sheetkhey).

(to) ground לקרקע *inf* lekarke'a'; *pst* keerka'; *pres* mekarke'a'; *fut* yekarka'.

(to break) ground 1. לחרוש קרקע בתולה *inf* lakhrosh karka' betoolah; *pst* kharash *etc*; *pres* khoresh *etc*; *fut* yakhrosh *etc*; **2.** לפתוח ב־ *inf* leefto'akh be-; *pst* patakh be- *(p=f)*; *pres* pote'akh be-; *fut* yeeftakh be-.

(to give) ground 1. לסגת (retreat) *inf* laseget; *pst & pres* nasog; *fut* yeesog; **2.** לנטוש (abandon) *inf* leentosh; *pst* natash; *pres* notesh; *fut* yeetosh.

(to hold one's) ground להחזיק מעמד *inf* lehakhzeek ma'amad; *pst* hekhzeek *etc*; *pres* makhzeek *etc*; *fut* yakhzeek *etc*.

ground crew צוות קרקע *nm* tsevet/tseevtey karka'.

ground floor קומת קרקע *nf* kom|at/-ot karka'.

grounded מקורקע *adj* mekoork|a'/-a'at.

(well) grounded מבוסס יפה *adj* mevoos|as/-eset yafeh.

groundless חסר בסיס *adj* khas|ar/-rat basees.

grounds נימוקים *nm pl* neemook|eem (*pl+of:* -ey).

group קבוצה *nf* kvoots|ah/-ot (*+of:* -at).

group insurance ביטוח קבוצתי *nm* beetoo|'akh/-kheem kvootsatee/-yeem.

group therapy ריפוי קבוצתי *nm* reepooy kvootsatee.

grove פרדס *nm* pardes/-eem (*pl+of:* -ey).

(citrus) grove 1. פרדס הדרים *nm* pardes/-ey hadareem; **2.** פרדס תפוזים (oranges) *nm* pardes/-ey tapoozeem.

(to) grow 1. לגדול *vi inf* leegdol; *pst* gadal; *pres* gadel; *fut* yeegdal; **2.** לצמוח (plant) *vi inf* leetsmo'akh; *pst* tsamakh; *pres* tsome'akh; *fut* yeetsmakh; **3.** לגדל *vt inf* legadel; *pst* geedel; *pres* megadel; *fut* yegadel.

(to) grow angry להיתקף זעם *inf* leheetakef za'am; *pst & pres* neetkaf *etc*; *fut* yeetakef *etc*.

(to) grow better להשתפר *inf* leheeshtaper; *pst* heeshtaper; *pres* meeshtaper; *fut* yeeshtaper.

(to) grow difficult 1. להסתבך (become complicated) *inf* leheestabekh; *pst* heestabekh; *pres* meestabekh; *fut* yeestabekh; **2.** לגלות נוקשות (become tough) *inf* legalot nookshoot; *pst* geelah *etc*; *pres* megaleh *etc*; *fut* yegaleh *etc*.

(to) grow late להיעשות מאוחר *inf* lehe'asot me'ookhar; *pst* na'asah *etc*; *pres* na'aseh *etc*; *fut* ye'aseh *etc*.

(to) grow old להזדקן *inf* leheezdaken; *pst* heezdaken; *pres* meezdaken; *fut* yeezdaken.

(to) grow out of a habit להשתחרר מהרגל *inf* leheeshtakhrer me-hergel; *pst* heeshtakhrer *etc*; *pres* meeshtakhrer *etc*; *fut* yeeshtakhrer *etc*.

(to) grow pale להחוויר *inf* lehakhveer; *pst* hekhveer; *pres* makhveer; *fut* yakhveer.

(to) grow tired להתעייף *inf* leheet'ayef; *pst* heet'ayef; *pres* meet'ayef; *fut* yeet'ayef.

growl 1. לרטון *inf* leerton; *pst* ratan; *pres* roten; *fut* yeerton; **2.** להתלונן (complain) *inf* leheetlonen; *pst* heetlonen; *pres* meetlonen; *fut* yeetlonen.

growler רטנן *nmf & adj* ratnan/-eet.

grown man אדם מבוגר *nm* ben adam/anasheem mevoogar/-eem.

grown with trees מגודל עצים *adj* megood|al/-elet 'etseem.

grown-up מבוגר *adj nmf* mevoog|ar/-eret.

growth 1. צמיחה *nf* tsmeekh|ah/-ot (+*of:* -at); **2.** גדילה *nf* gedeel|ah/-ot (+*of:* -at).

grubby 1. שורץ זחלים *adj* shorets/-et zekhaleem; **2.** מלוכלך (dirty) *adj* melookhl|akh/-ekhet.

grudge 1. טינה *nf* teen|ah/-ot (+*of:* -at); **2.** טרוניה (grievance) *nf* troon|yah/-yot (+*of:* -yat).

(to) grudge לרטון *inf* leerton; *pst* ratan; *pres* roten; *fut* yeerton.

gruff 1. זועף *adj* zo'ef/-et; **2.** ניחר (hoarse) *adj* neekh|ar/-eret.

grumble ריטון *nm* reetoon/-eem (*pl+of:* -ey).

(to) grumble לבוא בטרוניה *inf* lavo bee-troonyah; *pst & pres* ba *(b=v) etc; fut* yavo *etc.*

grumbler 1. רטנן *nmf* ratnan/-eet; **2.** מתלונן (complainant) *nmf* meetlonen/-et.

grumpy 1. כעוס (cross) *adj* ka'oos/ke'oosah; **2.** מצוברח (moody) metsoovrakh/-at.

grunt 1. צריחה *nf* tsreekh|ah/-ot (+*of:* -at); **2.** אנחה (sigh) *nf* anakh|ah/-ot (+*of:* ankh|at/-ot).

guarantee ערבות *nf* 'arvoo|t/-yot.

(to) guarantee לערוב *inf* la'arov; *pst* 'arav; *pres* 'arev; *fut* ya'arov.

guarantor ערב *nmf* 'arev/-ah.

guaranty 1. ערבות *nf* 'arvoo|t/-yot; **2.** ביטחון *nm* beet|akhon/-khonot (+*of:* -khon).

guard שומר *nm* shom|er/-reem (*pl+of:* -rey).

(to) guard לשמור *inf* leeshmor; *pst* shamar; *pres* shomer; *fut* yeeshmor.

(to) guard oneself against להישמר מפני *inf* leheeshamer mee-pney; *pst & pres* neeshmar *etc; fut* yeeshamer *etc.*

(to be on) guard, (to keep) guard לעמוד על המשמר *inf* la'amod 'al ha-meeshmar; *pst* 'amad *etc; pres* 'omed *etc; fut* ya'amod *etc.*

guardian 1. שומר (watchman) *nm* shom|er/-reem (*pl+of:* -rey); **2.** אפיטרופוס (custodian) *nmf* epeetrop|os/-seet.

guardian angel המלאך השומר *nm* ha-mal'akh ha-shomer.

guardianship אפיטרופסות *nf* epeetropsoo|t/-yot.

guardrail סורג מגן *nm* sor|eg/-gey magen.

guess ניחוש *nm* neekhoosh/-eem (*pl+of:* -ey).

(to) guess לנחש *inf* lenakhesh; *pst* neekhesh; *pres* menakhesh; *fut* yenakhesh.

guest אורח *nmf* ore'akh/orakhat (*pl:* orkh|eem/-ot; *pl+of:* -ey).

(to) guest להתארח *inf* leheet'are'akh; *pst* heet'arakh; *pres* meet'are'akh; *fut* yeet'arakh.

guffaw צחוק פרוע *nm* tsekhok paroo'a.

guidance 1. הדרכה *nf* hadrakh|ah/-ot (+*of:* -at); **2.** הכוונה (directive) *nf* hakhvan|ah/-ot (+*of:* -at).

guide 1. מדריך *nmf* madreekh/-ah (*f+of:* -at); **2.** מורה דרך *nm* mor|eh/-ey derekh.

guidebook 1. מדריך *nm* madreekh/-eem (*pl+of:* -ey); **2.** ספר הדרכה *nm* sefer/seefrey hadrakhah.

guideline קו מנחה *nm* kav/-eem mankh|eh/-eem.

guild אגודה מקצועית *nf* agood|ah/-ot meektso'ee|t/-yot.

guile 1. תחבולה *nf* takhbool|ah/-ot (+*of:* -at); **2.** רמאות (fraud) *nf* rama'oo|t/-yot.

guilt 1. אשמה *nf* ashm|ah/-ot (+*of:* -at); **2.** אשם *nm* asham.

guiltless חף מפשע *adj* kha|f/-pah *(p=f)* mee-pesha'.

guilty אשם *adj* ashem/-ah.

guise תחפושת *nf* takhpos|et/-ot.

(under the) guise of בתחפושת של *adv* be-takhposet shel.

guitar גיטרה *nf* geetar|ah/-ot (+*of:* -at).

gulf מפרץ *nm* meefr|ats/-atseem (*pl+of:* -etsey).

gull 1. שחף (bird) shakhaf/shekhafeem (*pl+of:* shakhfey); **2.** פתי (fool) *nmf* pet|ee/-ayah (*pl:* -ayeem/-ayot; +*of:* -ayey); **3.** רמאי (crook) ram|ay/-a'eet.

gullet ושט *nm* veshet.

gully 1. ערוץ *nm* 'aroots/-eem (*pl+of:* -ey); **2.** תעלה (canal) *nf* te'al|ah/-ot (*pl+of:* -at).

gulp 1. בליעה *nf* blee|'ah/-'ot (+*of:* -'at); **2.** שלוק *[slang] nm* shlook/-eem (*pl+of:* -ey).

(to) gulp down לרוקן כוסית *inf* leroken koseet; *pst* roken *etc; pres* meroken *etc; fut* yeroken *etc.*

gum 1. גומי (rubber) *nm* goomee; **2.** חניך (jaw-tissue) *nm* khaneekh/-ayeem (*pl+of:* -ey).

(chewing) gum 1. גומי לעיסה *nm* goomee le'eesah; **2.** מסטיק *[slang] nm* masteek/-eem.

gum tree עץ גומי *nm* 'ets/'atsey goomee.

gums חניכיים *nm pl* khaneekh/-ayeem (*pl+of:* -ey).

gun 1. תותח *nm* totakh/-eem (*pl+of:* totkhey); **2.** רובה (rifle) *nm* rov|eh/-eem (*pl+of:* -ey); **3.** אקדח *nm* ekd|akh/-okheem (*pl+of:* -okhey); **4.** כלי־ירייה (firearm) *nm* klee/kley yereeyah.

(a 21) gun salute הצדעה של 12 מתחי תותח *nf* hatsda'ah shel 21 matakhey totakh.

gunboat ספינת תותחים *nf* sfeen|at/-ot totakheem.

gunner תותחן *nm* totkhan/-eem (*pl+of:* -ey).

gunpowder אבק שריפה *nm* avak sreyfah.

gurgle גרגור *nm* geergoor/-eem (*pl+of:* -ey).

(to) gurgle לגרגר *inf* legarger; *pst* geerger; *pres* megarger; *fut* yegarger.

gush 1. שטף *nm* shetef/shtafeem (*pl+of:* sheetfey); **2.** זרם (stream) *nm* zerem/zrameem (*pl+of:* zeermey).

(to) gush 1. להשתפך *inf* leheeshtapekh; *pst* heeshtapekh; *pres* meeshtapekh; *fut* yeeshtapekh; **2.** לשפוע (flow) *inf* leeshpo'a'; *pst* shafa' *(f=p)*; *pres* shofe'a'; *fut* yeeshpa'.

gust 1. משב *nm* mash|av/-aveem (*pl+of:* -vey); **2.** טעם (taste) *nm* ta'am/te'ameem (*pl+of:* ta'amey).

gut מעי *nm* me'ee/me'ayeem (*pl+of:* me'ey).

guts 1. מעיים *nm pl* me'ayeem (*pl+of:* me'ey); **2.** קרביים *nm pl* kravayeem (*pl+of:* keervey); **3.** אומץ *nm* omets.

(to have) guts 1. להיות לו "דם" (be red-blooded) *inf* leehyot lo "dam"; *pst* hayah *etc; pres* yesh *etc; fut* yeehyeh *etc;* **2.** לגלות אומץ (prove the courage) *inf* legalot omets; *pst* geelah *etc; pres* megaleh *etc; fut* yegaleh *etc.*

gutter 1. מרזב *nm* marzev/-eem (*pl+of:* -ey); **2.** תעלת שופכין (sewer) te'al|at/-ot shofkheen.

guy 1. בחור *nm* bakhoor/-eem (*pl+of:* -ey); **2.** חברה'מן *[colloq.]* (fellow) *nmf* khevre|man/-eet; **3.** חבל-חיזוק (rope) *nm* khevel/khavley kheezook.

(to) guy 1. להרגיז *inf* lehargeez; *pst* heergeez; *pres* margeez; *fut* yargeez; **2.** להחזיק בחבל *inf* lehakhzeek be-khevel; *pst* hekhzeek *etc; pres* makhzeek *etc; fut* yakhzeek *etc.*

gymnasium אולם התעמלות *nm* oolam/-ey heet'amloot.

gymnastics התעמלות *nf* heet'amloot.

gypsy 1. צועני *nmf* tso'anee/-yah; **2.** צועני *adj* tso'anee/-t.

(to) gyrate 1. לסוב סביב צירו *inf* lasov sveev tseero; *pst & pres* sav *etc; fut* yasov *etc;* **2.** להסתובב סחור סחור (spin) *inf* leheestovev sekhor-sekhor; *pst* heestovev *etc; pres* meestovev *etc; fut* yeestovev *etc.*

gyroscope 1. גירוסקופ *nm* geeroskop/-eem; **2.** סביבון (spinning top) *nm* sveevon/-eem (*pl+of:* -ey).

H.

H,h semi-consonant of which, in the Hebrew alphabet, the equivalent is Heh (ה). However, when ending a word, the Heh is seldom pronounced. There, it indicates (mainly in the ordinary, unvowelled spelling), the presence of the vowels a (pronounced as in *mah*, *bar*) or, less often, e (pronounced as in *estuary, quest*). So it is in ילדה (yaldah), סוכה (sookah), or in משקה (mashkeh), צופה (tsofeh).

haberdashery 1. חנות סדקית *nf* khanoo|t/-yot seedkeet; **2.** דברי הלבשה (clothing articles) *nf pl* deevrey halbashah.

habit 1. הרגל *nm* hergel/-eem (*pl+of:* -ey); **2.** מנהג (custom) *nm* meenhag/-eem (*pl+of:* -ey).

(drinking) habit נטייה לשתיינות *nf* netee|yah/-yot le-shatyanoot.

habitable ראוי למגורים *adj* ra'ooy/re'ooyah lee-megooreem.

habitat מקום מגורים *nm* mekom/-ot megooreem.

habitual 1. רגיל *adj* rageel/regeelah; **2.** קבוע (permanent) *adj* kavoo'a'/kvoo'ah.

hack מהלומה (blow) *nf* mahaloom|ah/-ot (+*of:* -at).

(to) hack 1. להלום *inf* lahalom; *pst* halam; *pres* holem; *fut* yahalom; **2.** לבקע (split) *inf* levake'a'; *pst* beeka' *(b=v); pres* mevake'a' *fut* yevaka'.

hackneyed 1. נדוש *adj* nadosh/nedoshah; **2.** בנלי (banal) *adj* banalee/-t.

haft ידית *nf* yadee|t/-yot.

hag 1. זקנה בלה *nf* zeken|ah/-ot bal|ah/-ot; **2.** מרשעת זקנה (old shrew) *nf* meersha'at zekenah.

haggard כחוש *adj* kakhoosh/kekhooshah.

haggle מיקוח *nm* meekoo|'akh/-kheem (*pl+of:* -khey).

(to) haggle להתמקח *inf* leheetmake'akh; *pst* heetmakakh; *pres* meetmake'akh *fut* yeetmakakh.

hail ברד *nm* barad.

(to) hail לקדם בברכה *inf* lekadem bee-vrakhah *(v=b); pst* keedem *etc; pres* mekadem *etc fut* yekadem *etc.*

hail! יחי! *interj v fut* yekheel (*f* tekheel).

hailing from ממוצא *adj* mee-motsa.

hailstorm סופת ברד *nf* soof|at/-ot barad.

hair 1. שיער *nm* se'ar/-ot; **2.** שערה *nf* sa'arah/ se'arot (+*of:* sa'ar|at/-ot).

hair net רשת שיער *nf* reshet se'ar.

hair-raising מסמר שיער *adj* mesamer/-et se'ar.

hairbreadth חוט השערה *nm* khoot ha-sa'arah.

hairbrush מברשת שיער *nf* meevresh|et/-ot se'ar.

haircut תספורת *nf* teespor|et/-ot.

(to have a) haircut להסתפר *inf* leheestaper; *pst* heestaper; *pres* meestaper *fut* yeestaper.

hairdo תסרוקת *nf* teesrok|et/-ot.

hairdresser ספר *nmf* sapar/-eet.

hairdryer מייבש שיער *nm* meyab|esh/-shey se'ar.

hairless חסר שערות *adj* khas|ar/-rat se'arot.

hairpin סיכת ראש *nf* seek|at/-ot rosh.

hairy שעיר *adj* sa'eer/se'eerah.

half 1. חצי *nm* khats|ee/-a'eem (*pl+of:* -a'ey); **2.** מחצית *nf* makhatsee|t/-yot.

half an apple מחצית תפוח *nf* makhatseet tapoo'akh.

half-baked 1. אפוי למחצה *adj* afoo|y/-yah le-mekhetsah; **2.** מטומטם (stupid) *adj* metoom-t|am/-emet; **3.** לא רציני (not serious) *adj* lo'retseenee/-t.

half brother 1. אח למחצה (literally) *nm* akh/ -eem le-mekhetsah; **2.** אח חורג (step-brother) *nm* akh/-eem khor|eg/-geem.

half cooked 1. בלתי מבושל די *adj* beeltee mevoosh|al/-elet day/-ah; **2.** בלתי מוכן (not ready) *adj* beeltee mookhan/-ah.

half-breed בן תערובת *nmf* ben/bat ta'arovet.

half-hour 1. חצי־שעה *nm* khats|ee/-a'ey sha|'ah/-'ot; **2.** מחצית השעה *nf* makhatseet ha-sha'ah.

half-mast חצי התורן *nm* khatsee ha-toren.

half-open פתוח למחצה *adj* patoo'akh/petookhah le-mekhetsah.

half-past וחצי(...and a half) va-khetsee.

half-sister 1. אחות למחצה .1 (literally) *nf* akh|ot/-ayot le-mekhetsah; **2.** אח חורג (step-brother) *nm* akh|ot/-ayot khor|eget/-got.

half-truth 1. חצי־אמת *nm* khats|ee/-a'ey emet/ameetot; **2.** אמת חלקית (partial truth) emet/ameetot khelkee|t/-yot.

half-witted שוטה *nmf & adj* shot|eh/-ah.

halfway 1. במחצית בדרך *adv* be-makhatseet ha-derekh; **2.** באמצע (in the middle) be-'emtsa'.

(to do something) halfway לעשות חצי עבודה *inf* la'asot khatsee 'avodah; *pst* 'asah *etc; pres* 'oseh *etc fut* ya'aseh *etc.*

(to meet) halfway להתפשר (compromise) *inf* leheetpasher; *pst* heetpasher; *pres* meetpasher *fut* yeetpasher.

halfway between אמצע הדרך בין *nm* emtsa' ha-derekh beyn.

halfway finished גמור למחצה *adj* gamoor/gemoorah le-mekhetsah.

halibut דג פוטית *nm* dag/degey pooteet.

hall 1. אולם *nm* oolam/-ot (*pl+of:* -ey); **2.** פרוזדור *nm* (corridor) prozdor/-eem (*pl+of:* -ey).

(town-)hall בניין העירייה *nm* beenyan ha-'eereeyah.

hallmark תו מוצר *nm* tav/-ey mootsar.

(to) hallow לקדש *inf* lekadesh; *pst* keedesh; *pres* mekadesh *fut* yekadesh.

Halloween ליל "כל הקדושים" הנוצרי *nm* leyl "kol ha-kedosheem" ha-notsree.

hallway מיסדרון *nm* meesderon/-eem (*pl+of:* -ey).

halo הילה *nf* heel|ah/-ot (*+of:* -at).

halt הפסקה *nf* hafsak|ah/-ot (*+of:* -at).

(to) halt 1. לעצור *inf* la'atsor; *pst* 'atsar; *pres* 'otser *fut* ya'atsor; **2.** להפסיק (stop) *inf* lehafseek; *pst* heefseek; *pres* mafseek *fut* yafseek.

halt! 1. !עצור *imp interj* 'atsor! **2.** !עמוד (stop!) *imp interj* 'amod!

halter 1. אפסר (for horse) *nm* afs|ar/-areem (*pl+of:* -erey); **2.** לולאת תליה (for hanging) *nf* lool|'at/-'ot tleeyah.

halting 1. מהסס *adj* mehases/-et; **2.** צולע (limping) *adj* tsol|e'a'/-a'at.

haltingly בהיסוס *adv* be-heesoos.

(to) halve לחצות לשניים *inf* lakhtsot lee-shnayeem; *pst* khatsah *etc; pres* khotseh *etc; fut* yekhtseh *etc.*

(to go) halves לחלק חלק כחלק *inf* lekhalek khelek ke-khelek; *pst* kheelek *etc; pres* mekhalek *etc; fut* yekhalek *etc.*

ham 1. קותלי חזיר (meat) *nm pl* kotley khazeer; **2.** חובב אלחוט (amateur wireless operator) khovev/-ey alkhoot; **3.** שחקן חובב (amateur actor) *nmf* sakhkan/-eet khovev/-et.

ham and eggs ביציית קותלי חזיר *nf* beytsee|yat/-yot kotley khazeer.

hamburger אומצת המבורגר *nf* oomts|at/-ot hamboorger.

hamlet יישוב קטן *nm* yeeshoov/-eem katan/ketaneem.

hammer פטיש *nm* pateesh/-eem (*pl+of:* -ey).

(sledge) hammer קורנס *nm* koornas/-eem (*pl+of:* -ey).

(to) hammer 1. להלום *inf* lahalom; *pst* halam; *pres* holem *fut* yahalom; **2.** לחשל (forge) *inf* lekhashel; *pst* kheeshel; *pres* mekhashel *fut* yekhashel.

hammer and sickle פטיש ומגל *nm & nm* pateesh oo magal.

(to) hammer out 1. לגבש *inf* legabesh; *pst* geebesh; *pres* megabesh *fut* yegabesh; **2.** ליישר הדורים (straighten matters out) leyasher hadooreem; *pst* yeesher *etc; pres* meyasher *etc fut* yeyasher *etc.*

hammock ערסל *nm* 'ars|al/-aleem (*pl+of:* -eley).

hamper סל נצרים *nm* sal/-ey netsareem.

(to) hamper 1. לעכב *inf* le'akev; *pst* 'eekev; *pres* me'akev *fut* ye'akev; **2.** להפריע (stop) *inf* lehafree'a'; *pst* heefree'a'; *pres* mafree'a'; *fut* yafree'a'.

hand יד *nf* yad/-ayeem (*pl+of:* yedey).

(at) hand 1. מוכן לשימוש (ready for use) *adj* mookhan/-ah le-sheemoosh; **2.** ממשמש ובא (impending) *adj* memashmesh/-et oo-va/-'ah (*v=b*).

(first) hand ממקור ראשון *adj* mee-makor reeshon.

(made by) hand מעשה יד *nm & adj* ma'as|eh/-ey yad.

(on) hand עומד לרשות *adj* 'omed/-et lee-reshoot.

(on the other) hand מאידך me'eedakh.

(second) hand 1. יד שנייה *adj* yad shneeyah; **2.** משומש (used) *adj* meshoom|ash/-eshet.

hand and glove בצורה אינטימית *adv* be-tsoorah eenteemeet.

(to) hand down 1. לפסוק *inf* leefsok; *pst* pasak; *pres* posek (*p=f*); *fut* yeefsok; **2.** להוריש (bequeathe) *inf* lehoreesh; *pst* horeesh; *pres* moreesh *fut* yoreesh.

(to) hand in 1. למסור *inf* leemsor; *pst* masar; *pres* moser *fut* yeemsor; **2.** להגיש (submit) *inf* lehageesh; *pst* heegeesh; *pres* mageesh *fut* yageesh.

(to) hand over להסגיר *inf* lehasgeer; *pst* heesgeer; *pres* masgeer *fut* yasgeer.

handball כדור יד *nm* kadoor-yad.

handbill עלון פרסום *nm* 'alon/-ey peersoom.

hand in hand יד ביד *adv* yad be-yad.

(to) handcuff לשים באזיקים *inf* laseem ba-azeekeem; *pst & pres* sam *etc; fut* yaseem *etc.*

handcuffs אזיקים *nm pl* azeek|eem (*pl+of:* -ey).

handful קומץ *nm* komets.

handicap מכשול *nm* meekhshol/-eem (*pl+of:* -ey).

(to) handicap 1. להערים מכשולים *inf* leha'reem meekhsholeem; **2.** להכשיל (cause to fail) *inf* lehakhsheel; *pst* heekhsheel; *pres* makhsheel *fut* yakhsheel.

handicap race מרוץ מכשולים *nm* merots/-ey meekhsholeem.

handkerchief ממחטה *nf* meemkh|atah/-atot (*+of:* -etet)

handle ידית *nf* yadee|t/-yot.

handling טיפול *nm* teepool/-eem (*pl+of:* -ey).

(to) handle לטפל ב־ *inf* letapel be-; *pst* teepel be-; *pres* metapel be- *fut* yetapel be-.
handles easily קל לטיפול *adj* kal/-ah le-teepool.
handmade עבודת יד *nf* ʻavod|at/-ot yad.
handout דוגמת חינם *nf* doogm|at/-a'ot kheenam.
(to have one's) hands full כאשר הידיים מלאות עבודה ka-asher-ha-yadayeem mele'ot ʻavodah.
handsaw מסור־יד *nm* masor/-ey yad.
handshake לחיצת יד *nf* lekheets|at/-ot yad.
handsome יפה תואר *adj* yef|eh/-at to'ar.
(a) handsome sum סכום עתק *nm* sekhoom/-ey ʻatek.
handwork מלאכת יד *nf* melekhet yad.
handwriting כתב יד *nm* ketav-yad.
handy 1. שימושי *adj* sheemooshee/-t; **2.** נוח (convenient) *adj* noakh/nokhah.
(I don't care a) hang לא איכפת לי כלל lo eekhpat lee klal.
(to) hang לתלות *inf* leetlot; *pst* talah; *pres* toleh *fut* yeetleh.
(to) hang around להימצא בסביבה *inf* leheematse ba-sveevah; *pst & pres* neemtsa *etc; fut* yeematse *etc.*
(to) hang on להמשיך *inf* lehamsheekh; *pst* heemsheekh; *pres* mamsheekh; *fut* yamsheekh.
hang-over 1. צירי התפכחות *nm pl* tseerey heetpak'khoot; **2.** דכדוך שלאחר ליל הוללות (dejection felt the morning after) *nm* deekhdook she-le-akhar leyl holeloot.
(to) hang together לפעול מלוכדים *inf* leef'ol melookadeem; *pst pl* pa'aloo *etc (p=f); pres pl* po'aleem *etc; fut pl* yeef'aloo *etc.*
(to) hang up לטרוק טלפון *inf* leetrok telefon; *pst* tarak *etc; pres* torek *etc; fut* yeetrok *etc.*
hangar סככה לאווירונים *nf* sekhakh|ah/-ot la-aveeroneem.
hanger קולב *nm* kol|av/-eem *(pl+of: -vey).*
hanger-on נטפל *nmf* neetp|al/-elet.
hanging 1. תלייה *nf* tlee|yah/-yot *(+of: -yat);* **2.** תלוי ועומד (pending) *adj* talooy/tlooyah ve-ʻomed/-et.
hangings 1. וילונות תלייה *nm pl* veelonot tleeyah; **2.** שטיחי קיר (wall carpets) *nm pl* shteekhey keer.
hangman תליין *nm* talyan/-eem *(pl+of: -ey).*
hangnail דלדלת הציפורניים *nf* daldelet ha-tseepornayeem.
haphazard 1. מקרה *nm* meekr|eh/-eem *(pl+of: -ey);* **2.** מקרי (accidental) *adj* meekree/-t.
haphazardly 1. באקראי *adv* be-akray; **2.** שלא במתכוון (unintentionally) *adv* she-lo be-meetkaven.
hapless 1. ביש מזל *adj* beesh-mazal; **2.** אומלל (miserable) *adj* oomlal/-ah.
(to) happen לקרות *inf* leekrot; *pst* karah; *pres* koreh; *fut* yeekreh.
(to) happen to hear להזדמן לשמוע *inf* leheezdamen leeshmo'a'; *pst* heezdamen *etc; pres* meezdamen *etc; fut* yeezdamen *etc.*
(to) happen to meet לפגוש במקרה *inf* leefgosh be-meekreh; *pst* pagash *etc (p=f); pres* pogesh *etc; fut* yeefgosh *etc.*
(to) happen to pass by להזדמן לעבור *inf* leheezdamen la'avor; *pst* heezdamen *etc; pres* meezdamen *etc; fut* yeezdamen *etc.*
happening 1. אירוע *nm* eeroo|'a'/-'eem *(+of: -'ey);* **2.** הפנינג *nm* hepeneeng/-eem.
happily 1. למרבה המזל *adv* le-marbeh ha-mazal; **2.** באושר (in happiness) *adv* be-'osher.
happiness אושר *nm* osher.
happy מאושר *adj* me'oosh|ar/-eret.
(to be) happy להיות מאושר *inf* leehyot me'ooshar; *pst* hayah *etc; pres* heeno *etc; fut* yeehyeh *etc.*
harangue נאום משלהב *nm* ne'oom/-eem meshal|hev/-haveem.
(to) harangue לשלהב בנאום *inf* leshalhev bee-ne'oom; *pst* sheelhev *etc; pres* meshalhev *etc; fut* yeshalhev *etc.*
(to) harass 1. להציק *inf* lehatseek; *pst* heetseek; *pres* metseek; *fut* yatseek; **2.** להקניט (provoke) lehakneet; *pst* heekneet; *pres* makneet; *fut* yakneet.
harbor 1. נמל *nm* namel/nemaleem *(+of:* nemal/ neemley*);* **2.** מחסה (shelter) makhseh.
(to) harbor 1. לתת מחסה *inf* latet makhseh; *pst* natan *etc; pres* noten *etc; fut* yeeten *etc;* **2.** לנטור (bear grudge) *inf* leentor; *pst* natar; *pres* noter; *fut* yeetor.
hard 1. קשה (also: difficult) *adj* kash|eh/-ah; **2.** מוצק (solid) *adj* mootsak/-ah; **3.** חמור (serious) *adj* khamoor/-ah.
hard by קרוב מאוד *adj* karov/krovah me'od.
hard cash כסף מזומן *nm* kesef mezooman.
hard core גרעין נוקשה *nm* gar'een nooksheh.
hard currency מטבע קשה *nm* matbe'a' kasheh.
hard liquor משקה חריף *nm* mashkeh khareef.
hard luck ביש מזל *nm & adv* beesh mazal.
hard of hearing כבד שמיעה *adj* kvad/keevdat shmee'ah.
hard water מים קשים *nm pl* mayeem kasheem.
hard-working עובד קשה *adj* ʻoved/-et kasheh.
(to) harden להקשיח *inf* lehakshee'akh; *pst* heekshee'akh; *pres* makshee'akh; *fut* yakshee'akh.
hardening 1. קישוי *nm* keeshoo|y/-yeem *(pl+of: -yey);* **2.** חיסום (tempering) *nm* kheesoom/-eem *(pl+of: -ey).*
hardhearted קשוח לב *adj* keshoo|'akh/-khat lev.
hardly בקושי *adv* be-koshee.
hardness קשיות *nf* kashyoot.
hardship 1. קושי *nm* koshee/keshayeem *(+of:* keshee/koshyey*);* **2.** תלאה (suffering) *nf* tla|'ah/ -'ot *(+of: -'at).*
hardware 1. חומרי בניין *nm pl* khomrey beenyan; **2.** חומרה (in computers) *nf* khomr|ah/-ot *(+of: -at).*
hardware shop, store חנות לחומרי בניין *nf* khanoo|t/-yot le-khomrey beenyan.
hardy 1. אמיץ *adj* ameets/-ah; **2.** תקיף (firm) *adj* takeef/-ah.
hare ארנבת *nf* arn|evet/-avot.
harebrained 1. פזיז *adj* pazeez/pezeezah; **2.** קל דעת (fickle-minded) *adj* kal/-at da'at.
harelip שפה שסועה *nf* safah shesoo'ah.
harem הרמון *nm* harmon/-ot.
harlot זונה *nf* zon|ah/-ot *(+of: -at).*

harm 1. פגיעה *nf* pegee|'ah/-'ot (*+of:* -'at); **2.** נזק (damage) *nm* nez|ek/-akeem (*pl+of:* neezkey).

(to) harm 1. לפגוע (hurt) *vt inf* leefgo'a'; *pst* paga' *(p=f); pres* poge'a'; *fut* yeefga'; **2.** להזיק (damage) lehazeek; *pst* heezeek; *pres* mazeek; *fut* yazeek.; **3.** להרע (worsen) *inf* lehare'a'; *pst* hera'; *pres* mere'a'; *fut* yare'a'.

harmful 1. מזיק *adj* mazeek/-ah; **2.** מסוכן (dangerous) *adj* mesook|an/-enet.

harmless 1. בלתי מזיק *adj* beeltee mazeek/-ah; **2.** בלתי מסוכן (non-dangerous) *adj* beeltee mesook|an/-enet

harmonic הרמוני *adj* harmonee/-t.

harmonious 1. ערב *adj* 'arev/-ah; **2.** מתאים (fitting) *adj* mat'eem/-ah.

(to) harmonize למזג *inf* lemazeg; *pst* meezeg; *pres* memazeg; *fut* yemazeg.

harmony הרמוניה *nf* harmon|yah/-yot (*+of:* -yat).

harness ריתמה *nf* reetmah/retamot (*+of:* reetm|at/-ot).

(to) harness לרתום *vt* leertom; *pst* ratam; *pres* rotem; *fut* yeratem.

(to get back in) harness לחזור ולהירתם *inf* lakhzor oo-leheratem; *pst* khazar ve-neertam; *pres* khozer ve-neertam; *fut* yakhzor ve-yeratem.

harp נבל *nm* nevel/nevaleem (*pl+of:* neevley).

(to) harp לפרוט על נבל *inf* leefrot 'al nevel; *pst* parat *(p=f) etc; pres* poret *etc; fut* yeefrot *etc.*

(to) harp on לחזור על אותו פזמון *inf* lakhzor 'al oto peezmon; *pst* khazar *etc; pres* khozer *etc; fut* yakhzor *etc.*

harpoon צלצל *nm* tseelts|al/-aleem (*pl+of:* -eley).

harrow משדדה *nf* masded|ah/-ot (*+of:* -at).

harrowing 1. מחריד *adj* makhreed/-ah; **2.** מזעזע (shocking) *adj* meza'z|e'a'/-a'at.

(to) harry לקנטר *inf* lekanter; *pst* keenter; *pres* mekanter; *fut* yekanter.

harsh נוקשה *adj* nooksh|eh/-ah.

harshness נוקשות *nf* nookshoo|t/-yot.

harvest 1. קציר *nm* katseer/ketseer|eem (*pl+of:* -ey); **2.** תנובה (yield) *nf* tenoov|ah/-ot (*+of:* -at).

(to) harvest לקצור *inf* leektsor; *pst* katsar; *pres* kotser; *fut* yeektsor.

hash 1. תערובת *nf* ta'arov|et/-ot; **2.** חשיש (narcotic) *nm* khasheesh.

haste 1. חופזה *nf* khofz|ah/-ot (*+of:* -at); **2.** חיפזון (rush) *nm* kheepazon/khefzonot (*f=p; +of:* khefzon).

(in) haste בחופזה *adv* be-khofzah.

(to make) haste להזדרז *v rfl inf* leheezdarez; *pst* heezdarez; *pres* meezdarez; *fut* yeezdarez.

(to) hasten לזרז *vt inf* lezarez; *pst* zeraz; *pres* mezarez; *fut* yezarez.

hastily בחיפזון *adv* be-kheepazon.

hasty חפוז *adj* khafooz/-ah.

hat 1. כובע *nm* kov|a'/-a'eem (*pl+of:* -'ey); **2.** מגבעת (bonnet) *nf* meegb|a'at/-a'ot (*pl+of:* -e'ot).

hatch 1. דלת מעבר *nf* delet/daltot ma'avar; **2.** אפרוחים (fledglings) *nm pl* efrokh|eem (*pl+of:* -ey).

(to) hatch לדגור *inf* leedgor; *pst* dagar; *pres* doger; *fut* yeedgor.

hatchet 1. כילף *nf* kela|f/-pot *(p=f)*; **2.** קרדום (axe) *nm* kard|om/-oomeem (*pl+of:* -oomey).

(to bury the) hatchet 1. לעשות שלום *inf* la'asot shalom; *pst* 'asah *etc; pres* 'oseh *etc; fut* ya'aseh *etc;* **2.** לשים קץ לריב (end dispute) *inf* laseem kets le-reev; *pst & pres* sam *etc; fut* yaseem *etc.*

hatchway פתח מעבר *nm* petakh/peetkhey ma'avar.

hate שינאה *nf* seen|'ah/-'ot (*+of:* -at).

(to) hate לשנוא *inf* leesno; *pst & pres* sane; *fut* yeesna.

hateful שנוא *adj* sanoo'/snoo'ah.

hatred שינאה *nf* seen|'ah/-'ot (*+of:* -at).

haughthily ביהירות *adv* bee-yeheeroot.

haughtiness יהירות *nf* yeheeroo|t/-yot.

haughty 1. יהיר *adj* yaheer/yeheerah; **2.** רברבן (boaster) *nmf* ravrevan/-eet.

(to) haul 1. לגרור *inf* leegror; *pst* garar; *pres* gorer; *fut* yeegror; **2.** להוביל (transport) *inf* lehoveel; *pst* hoveel; *pres* moveel; *fut* yoveel.

(to) haul down the flag להוריד את הדגל *inf* lehoreed et ha-degel; *pst* horeed *etc; pres* moreed *etc; fut* yoreed *etc.*

haunch 1. ירך *nf* yarekh/yerekhayeem (*pl+of:* yarkhey); **2.** מותן *nm* mot|en/-nayeem (*pl+of:* -ney).

(to) haunt 1. להציק *inf* lehatseek; *pst* hetseek; *pres* metseek; *fut* yatseek; **2.** לפקוד בקביעות (visit regularly) *inf* leefkod bee-kvee'oot; *pst* pakad *(p=f) etc; pres* poked *etc; fut* yeefkod *etc.*

haunted house בית רדוף שדים ורוחות *nm* bayeet/bateem redoof/-ey shedeem ve-rookhot.

(that idea) haunts me רעיון זה אינו מרפה ממני ra'yon zeh eyno marpeh meemenee.

(to) have ־להיות ל (Note : Hebrew has no such verb. Instead, we say: to be at one's disposal, or: there is to one) *inf* leehyot le-; *pst* hayah le-; *pres* heeno le-; *fut* yeehyeh le-.

(to) have a look at להעיף מבט *inf* leha'eef mabat; *pst* he'eef *etc; pres* me'eef *etc; fut* ya'eef *etc.*

(to) have a suit made להזמין חליפה *inf* lehazmeen khaleefah; *pst* heezmeen *etc; pres* mazmeen *etc; fut* yazmeen *etc.*

(I'll not) have it so לא אסכים לכך lo askeem le-khakh *(kh=k).*

(what did she) have on במה היתה לבושה be-mah haytah levooshah.

(to) have to להיאלץ *inf* lehe'alets; *pst & pres* ne'elats; *fut* ye'alets.

haven 1. מקלט *nm* meekl|at/-ateem (*pl+of:* -etey); **2.** מעגן (anchorage) *nm* ma'ag|an/-aneem (*pl+of:* -ney).

(tax-)haven מקלט ממס *nm* meeklat/-eem mee-mas.

havoc 1. הרס *nm* heres; **2.** חורבן *nm* khoorban/-ot.

(to cause) havoc לגרום תהפוכה *inf* leegrom tahapookhah; *pst* garam *etc; pres* gorem *etc; fut* yeegrom.

hawk נץ *nm* nets/neets|eem (*pl+of:* -ey).

(to) hawk 1. לעוט על טרף *inf* la'oot 'al teref; *pst & pres* 'at *etc; fut* ya'oot *etc;* **2.** להשתעל (cough) leheeshta'el; *pst* heeshta'el; *pres* meeshta'el; *fut* yeeshta'el; **3.** לעסוק ברוכלות (peddle) *inf* la'asok be-rokhloot; *pst* 'asak *etc*; *pres* 'osek *etc*; *fut* ya'asok *etc*.

hawthorn 1. אטד *nm* atad; **2.** עוזרד *nm* 'oozrad.

hay 1. שחת *nf* shakhat; **2.** חציר (grass) *nm* khatseer/-eem (*pl+of:* -ey).

hay fever קדחת שחת *nf* kadakhat shakhat.

hayloft מתבן *nm* matben/-eem (*pl+of:* -ey).

haystack ערימת שחת *nf* 'arem|at/-ot shakhat.

(needle in a) haystack מחט בערימת שחת *nm* makhat be-'aremat shakhat.

hazard 1. מקרה *nm* meekr|eh/-eem (*pl+of:* -ey); **2.** סיכון (risk) *nm* seekoon/-eem (*pl+of:* -ey).

(to) hazard לסכן *inf* lesaken; *pst* seeken; *pres* mesaken; *fut* yesaken.

hazardous מסוכן *adj* mesook|an/-enet.

haze 1. אובך *nm* ovekh/ovakheem (*pl+of:* ovkhey); **2.** ערפל (fog) *nm* 'ar|afel/-peleem (*p=f; pl+of:* -peley).

hazel 1. לוז *nm* looz/-eem (*pl+of:* -ey); **2.** אגוז (nut) egoz/-eem (*pl+of:* -ey).

hazelnut 1. אילסר *nm* eels|ar/-areem (*pl+of:* -erey); **2.** חום־אדמדם (reddish-brown) khoom/-ah adamd|am/-emet.

hazy אביך *adj* aveekh/-ah.

he הוא *pron* hoo.

he who הוא אשר hoo asher.

he-goat תיש *nm* tayeesh/tyash|eem (*pl+of:* teyshey).

head 1. ראש *nm* rosh/-eem (*pl+of:* -ey); **2.** מנהיג (leader) *nmf* manheeg/-ah (*+of:* -at/-ey).

head of hair ראש מלא שערות *nm* rosh male se'arot.

head-on עם הראש קדימה *adv* 'eem ha-rosh kadeemah.

(it goes to one's) head עולה לו לראש *v pres* 'oleh/-ah lo la-rosh.

(out of one's) head ללא שכל *adv* le-lo sekhel.

(to) head 1. לעמוד בראש *inf* la'amod ba-rosh; *pst* 'amad *etc*; *pres* 'omed *etc*; *fut* ya'amod *etc*; **2.** להוביל (lead) *inf* lehoveel; *pst* hoveel; *pres* moveel; *fut* yoveel.

(to) head off למנוע *inf* leemno'a'; *pst* mana'; *pres* mone'a'; *fut* yeemna'.

(to) head towards להתקדם לקראת *v refl* leheetkadem leekrat; *pst* heetkadem *etc*; *pres* meetkadem *etc*; *fut* yeetkadem *etc*.

(to come to a) head לבוא עד משבר *inf* lavo 'ad mashber; *pst & pres* ba *(b=v) etc*; *fut* yavo *etc*.

(to keep one's) head 1. להחזיק מעמד *inf* lehakhzeek ma'amad; *pst* hekhzeek *etc*; *pres* makhzeek *etc*; *fut* yakhzeek *etc*; **2.** לשמור על צלילות *inf* leeshmor 'al tsleeloot; *pst* shamar *etc*; *pres* shomer *etc*; *fut* yeeshmor *etc*.

headache כאב ראש *nm* ke'ev/-ey rosh.

head-dress כסוי ראש *nm* kesooy/-ey rosh.

headgear 1. כסות ראש *nf* kesoot rosh; **2.** כובע *nm* kov|a'/-a'eem (*pl+of:* -'ey).

heading כותרת *nf* kot|eret/-rot.

headland 1. רצועת אדמה לא חרושה *nf* retsoo|'at/-'ot adamah lo kharooshlah/-ot; **2.** לשון יבשה (promontory) *nf* leshon/-ot yabashah.

headlight פנס קדמי *nm* panas/-eem keedmee/-yeem.

headline כותרת *nf* kot|eret/-arot.

headlong 1. עם הראש קדימה *adv* 'eem ha-rosh kadeemah; **2.** בקלות דעת (recklessly) *adv* be-kaloot da'at; **3.** קל־דעת (reckless) *adj* kal/-at da'at.

headquarters 1. מרכז (center) *nm* merk|az/-azeem (*pl+of:* -ezey); **2.** מפקדה (command) *nf* meef-k|adah/-adot (*+of:* -edet).

headset מערכת אוזניות *nf* ma'arekhet ozneeyot.

headstrong עיקש *adj* 'eekesh/-et.

headway התקדמות heetkadmoo|t/-yot.

(to make) headway להתקדם *inf* leheetkadem; *pst* heetkadem; *pres* meetkadem; *fut* yeetkadem.

(to) heal לרפא *inf* lerape; *pst* reepe; *pres* merape; *fut* yerape.

health בריאות *nf* bree'oot.

healthful 1. מבריא *adj* mavree/-'ah; **2.** בריא *adj* baree/bree'ah.

healthfulness, healthiness 1. בריאות *nf* bree'oot; **2.** חוסן (robustness) *nm* khosen.

healthy בריא *adj* baree/bree'ah.

heap ערימה *nf* 'arem|ah/-ot (*+of:* -at).

(to) heap לערום *inf* la'arom; *pst* 'aram; *pres* 'orem; *fut* ya'arom.

(to) hear לשמוע *inf* leeshmo'a'; *pst* shama'; *pres* shome'a'; *fut* yeeshma'.

(to) hear about someone לשמוע אודות מישהו *inf* leeshmo'a' odot meeshehoo; *pst* shama' *etc*; *pres* shome'a' *etc*; *fut* yeeshma' *etc*.

(to) hear of לשמוע ממישהו *inf* leeshmo'a' mee-meeshehoo; *pst* shama' *etc*; *pres* shome'a' *etc*; *fut* yeeshma' *etc*.

(I) heard that שמעתי כי *v pst* shama'tee kee.

hearing שמיעה *nf* shmee'ah.

(hard of) hearing כבד שמיעה *adj* kvad/keevdat shmee'ah.

(within) hearing בטווח שמיעה *adv* bee-tvakh shmee'ah.

hearing aid עזר שמיעה *nm* 'ez|er/-rey shmee'ah.

hearsay 1. שמועה (rumor) *nf* shmoo|'ah/-'ot (*+of:* -'at); **2.** רכילות (gossip) rekheeloo|t/-yot.

hearsay evidence עדות שמיעה *nf* 'edoo|t/-yot shmee'ah.

hearse רכב הלוויות *nm* rekhev halvayot.

heart לב *nm* lev/-avot.

(at) heart קרוב ללב *adj* karov/krovah la-lev.

(from the bottom of one's) heart מעומק לב *adv* me-'omek lev.

(to learn by) heart לשנן בעל פה *inf* leshanen be-'al peh; *pst* sheenen *etc*; *pres* meshanen *etc*; *fut* yeshanen *etc*.

(to take) heart לקוות *inf* lekavot; *pst* keevah; *pres* mekaveh; *fut* yekaveh.

(to take to) heart לקחת ללב *inf* lakakhat la-lev; *pst* lakakh *etc*; *pst* loke'akh *etc*; *fut* yeekakh *etc*.

heartache כאב לב *nm* ke'ev/-ey lev.

heart attack התקף לב *nm* hetkef/-ey lev.

heartbreak שברון לב *nm* sheevron/-ey lev.

(to) hearten לעודד (encourage) *inf* le'oded; *pst* 'oded; *pres* me'oded; *fut* ye'oded.

heartfelt יוצא מן הלב *adj* yotse/-t meen ha-lev.

heartfelt sympathy השתתפות מקרב לב *nf* heeshtatfoot mee-kerev lev.

hearth 1. אח *nm* akh; **2.** מוקד משפחתי (home) *nm* moked meeshpakhtee.

heartily מקרב לב *adv* mee-kerev lev.

(to eat) heartily לאכול בתיאבון *inf* le'ekhol be-te'avon; *pst* akhal *etc*; *pres* okhel *etc*; *fut* yokhal *etc*.

heartless חסר־לב *adj* khas|ar/-rat lev.

heart-rending שובר לב *adj* shover/-et lev.

hearty לבבי *adj* levavee/-t.

(a) hearty laugh צחוק מכל הלב *nm* tsekhok mee-kol ha-lev.

hearty meal ארוחה דשנה *nf* arookh|ah/-ot deshen|ah/-ot.

heat חום *nm* khom.

(to) heat לחמם *inf* lekhamem; *pst* kheemem; *pres* mekhamem; *fut* yekhamem.

heater 1. מיתקן חימום *nm* meetk|an/-eney kheemoom; **2.** תנור חימום (stove) *nm* tanoor/-ey kheemoom; **3.** דוד חימום (boiler) *nm* dood/-ey kheemoom.

heathen עובד אלילים *nmf* 'oved/-et (*pl:* 'ovd|ey/-ot) eleeleem.

heating הסקה *nf* hasak|ah/-ot (*+of:* -at).

(central) heating הסקה מרכזית *nf* hasakah merkazeet.

(to) heave להניף *inf* lehaneef; *pst* heneef; *pres* meneef; *fut* yaneef.

heaven 1. רקיע *nm* rakee'a'/rekee|'eem (*pl+of:* -'ey); **2.** שמיים (skies) *nm pl* shamayeem (*+of:* shmey).

heavenly משמיים *adv* mee-shamayeem.

heavily בכבדות *adv* bee-khvedoot *(kh=k)*.

heaviness כבדות *nf* kvedoot.

heavy כבד *adj* kaved/kvedah.

(with a) heavy heart בלב כבד *adv* be-lev kaved.

heavy rain גשם סוחף *nm* geshem sokhef.

heavyweight משקל כבד *nm & adj* meeshkal kaved.

hectic 1. סוער *adj* so'er/-et; **2.** קדחתני (feverish) *adj* kadakhtanee/-t.

hedge גדר חיה *nf* gader khayah.

(to) hedge 1. לגדור בשיחים *inf* leegdor be-seekheem; *pst* gadar *etc*; *pres* goder *etc*; *fut* yeegdor *etc*; **2.** לתחום (encircle) *inf* leetkhom; *pst* takham; *pres* tokhem; *fut* yeetkhom; **3.** להתחמק (dodge) *v* refl *inf* leheetkhamek; *pst* heetkhamek; *pres* meetkhamek; *fut* yeetkhamek.

hedgehog קיפוד *nm* keepod/-eem (*pl+of:* -ey).

hedonism אהבת תענוגות *nf* ahavat ta'anoogot.

(to) heed 1. לשים לב *inf* laseem lev; *pst&pres* sam *etc*; *fut* yaseem *etc*; **2.** להתחשב (show consideration) *inf* leheetkhashev; *pst* heetkhashev; *pres* meetkhashev; *fut* yeetkhashev.

(to pay) heed to 1. לשים לב לאזהרה *inf* laseem lev le-azharah; *pst&pres* sam *etc*; *fut* yaseem *etc*; **2.** להיזהר (take care) *inf* leheezaher; *pst&pres* neez'har; *fut* yeezaher.

heedless חסר התחשבות *adj* khas|ar/-rat heetkhashvoot.

heel 1. עקב *nm* 'akev/-eem (*pl+of:* 'eekvey); **2.** נבזה (scoundrel) *nm* neevz|eh/-eem (*pl+of:* -ey).

(to) heel 1. לנטות *vi inf* leentot; *pst* natah; *pres* noteh *etc*; *fut* yeeteh *etc.*; **2.** להטות *vt inf* lehatot; *pst* heetah; *pres* mateh; *fut* yateh.

(head over) heels 1. מעל לראש *adv* me-'al le-rosh; **2.** על פניו *adv* 'al panav.

hegemony 1. הגמוניה *nf* hegmon|yah/-yot (*+of:* -yat); **2.** שלטון (rule) sheelton/-ot.

heifer עגלה *nf* 'eglah/'agalot (*+of:* 'egl|at/-ot).

height 1. גובה *nm* govah/gvaheem (*pl+of:* govhey); **2.** קומה (stature) kom|ah/-ot (*+of:* -at).

height of folly שיא הסכלות *nm* see/-'ey ha-seekhloot.

(to) heighten 1. להגביה *inf* lehagbeeha; *pst* heegbeeha; *pres* magbeeha; *fut* yagbeeha; **2.** להעלות (lift) leha'alot; *pst* he'elah; *pres* ma'aleh; *fut* ya'aleh.

heinous מתועב *adj* meto|'av/-'evet.

heir יורש *nm* yoresh/yorsh|eem (*pl+of:* -ey).

heiress יורשת *nf* yor|eshet/-shot.

helicopter מסוק *nm* masok/-eem (*pl+of:* -ey).

helium הליום *nm* helyoom.

hell גיהינום *nm* geyheenom.

hello הלו! *interj* halo!

helm הגה *nm* hegeh/haga|heem (*pl+of:* -hey).

helmet קסדה *nf* kasdah/kesadot (*+of:* kasdat).

help עזרה *nf* 'ezr|ah (*+of:* -at).

(to) help 1. לעזור *inf* la'azor; *pst* 'azar; *pres* 'ozer; *fut* ya'azor; **2.** לסייע (assist) *inf* lesaye'a'; *pst* seeya'; *pres* mesaye'a'; *fut* yesaye'a'.

(he cannot) help but come לא יוכל שלא לבוא lo yookhal/tookhal *(m/f)* she-lo lavo.

(he cannot) help doing אינו יכול שלא לעשות eyn|o/-ah yakhol/yekholah *(m/f)* she-lo la'asot.

(to) help down לעזור לרדת *inf* la'azor laredet; *pst* 'azar *etc*; *pres* 'ozer *etc*; *fut* ya'azor *etc*

(he cannot) help it אין ביכולתו להימנע מכך eyn be-yekholt|o/-ah leheemana' mee-kakh.

(so) help me הריני נשבע לך *v pres* harenee neeshba'/-at lekha/lakh *(m/f)*.

helper עוזר *nmf* 'ozer/-et.

helpful רב־עזר *adj* rav/rabat *(m/f)* 'ezer.

helping 1. עזרה *nf* 'ezrah; **2.** מנה (portion) *nf* man|ah/-ot (*+of:* men|at/-ot)

helpless חסר אונים *adj* khas|ar/-rat oneem.

(a) helpless situation מצב ללא מוצא *nm* matsav/-eem le-lo motsa.

helplessness חוסר ישע *nm* khoser yesha'.

help yourself התכבד, בבקשה! *v imp sing* heetkab|ed/-dee *(m/f)*, bevakashah!

hem שפה *nf* saf|ah/-ot (*+of:* sf|at/-ot).

(to) hem לתפור מכפלת *inf* leetpor makhp|elet/-alot; *pst* tafar *(f=p) etc*; *pres* tofer *etc fut* yeetpor *etc.*

(to) hem and haw להשתמט מתשובה *inf* leheeshtamet mee-teshoovah; *pst* heeshtamet *etc*; *pres* meeshtamet *etc*; *fut* yeeshtamet *etc.*

(to) hem in להקיף בתפר *inf* lehakeef be-tefer; *pst* heekeef *etc*; *pres* makeef *etc*; *fut* yakeef *etc.*

hemisphere חצי כדור (הארץ) *nm* khatsee kadoor (ha-arets i.e. of the globe).

(Eastern) hemisphere חצי הכדור המזרחי *nm* khatsee ha-kadoor ha-meezrakhee.

(Western) hemisphere חצי הכדור המערבי *nm* khatsee ha-kadoor ha-ma'aravee.

hemlock רוש *nm* rosh.
hemoglobin המוגלובין *nm* hemoglobeen.
hemp קנבוס *nm* kanabos.
hemstitch תך מכפלת *nm* takh/takey makhpelet.
(to) hemstitch לתפור תך מכפלת *inf* leetpor takh/takey makhpelet; *pst* tafar *(f=p) etc; pres* tofer *etc; fut* yeetpor *etc.*
hen תרנגולת *nf* tarnegol|et/-ot.
hence 1. מכאן *adv* mee-kan; **2.** על כן (therefore) *adv* 'al ken.
(a week) hence בעוד שבוע *adv* be-'od shavoo'a'.
henceforth מכאן ואילך *adv* mee-kan ve-'eylakh.
hepatitis הפטיטיס *nf* hepateetees.
her 1. שלה (possessive case) *pron* shelah; **2.** אותה (accusative case) *pron* otah.
herald 1. כרוז *nm* karoz; **2.** מבשר (harbinger) mevas|er/-reem *(pl+of:* -rey).
(to) herald 1. להכריז (proclaim) *inf* lehakhreez; *pst* heekhreez; *pres* makhreez; *fut* yakhreez; **2.** לבשר (forebode) *inf* levaser; *pst* beeser *(b=v); pres* mevaser; *fut* yevaser.
herb עשב *nm* 'esev/'asaveem *(pl+of:* 'esvey).
herd עדר *nm* 'eder/'adareem *(pl+of:* 'edrey).
(the common) herd 1. ההמון *nm* he-hamon; **2.** האספסוף (rabble) ha-asafsoof.
(to) herd להתקבץ כעדר *inf* leheetkabets ke-'eder; *pst* heetkabets *etc; pres* meetkabets *etc; fut* yeetkabets *etc.*
(to) herdsman רועה *nm* ro'eh/ro'eem *(pl+of:* ro'ey).
here 1. כאן kan; **2.** פה (syn) poh.
here it is הרי זה כאן harey zeh kan.
(neither) here nor there אין זה נוגע לעניין eyn zeh noge'a' la-'eenyan.
hereafter 1. מכאן ואילך *adv* mee-kan ve-'eylakh; **2.** להבא (hereafter) *adv* lehaba.
(the) hereafter 1. העתיד לבוא *nm* he-'ateed lavo; **2.** העולם הבא (the world to come) *nm* ha-'olam ha-ba.
hereby בזה *adv m/f* ba-zeh/ba-zot.
hereditary תורשתי *adj* torashtee/-t.
heredity תורשה *nf* torash|ah/-ot.
herein בזאת *adv* ba-zot.
heresy כפירה kefeer|ah/-ot (+*of:* -at).
heretic כופר kofer/-et.
heretofore לפנים *adv* lefaneem.
herewith בזאת *adv* be-zot.
heritage מורשת *nf* mor|eshet/-ashot.
hermetic הרמטי *adj* hermetee/-t.
hermit 1. מתבודד *nmf* meetboded/-et; **2.** נזיר (monk/nun) *nmf* nazeer/nezeerah.
hernia שבר *nm* shever.
hero גיבור *nmf & adj* geebor|ah/-ot *(pl:* -eem/-ot; +*of:* -at/-ey).
heroic 1. של גבורה *adj* shel gvoorah; **2.** הרואי *adj* hero'ee/-t.
heroin הרואין hero'een.
heroine 1. גיבורה *nf* geebor|ah/-ot (+*of:* -at); **2.** דמות נשית מרכזית *nf* demoo|t/-yot nashee|t/-yot merkazee|t/-yot.
heroism גבורה *nf* gvoor|ah/-ot (+*of:* -at).
heron אנפה *nf* anaf|ah/-ot (+*of:* -at).
herring דג מלוח *nm* dag/-eem maloo'akh/melookheem.
hers שלה possess. *pron* shelah.
(a friend of) hers ידיד שלה *nmf* yedeed/-ah shelah.
herself היא עצמה hee 'atsmah.
(by) herself בעצמה *adv* be-'atsmah
(talking to) herself בדברה לעצמה *adv* be-dabrah le-'atsmah.
(she) herself did it היא עצמה עשתה זאת hee 'atsmah 'astah zot.
(to) hesitate להסס *inf* lehases; *pst* heeses *etc; pres* mehases *etc; fut* yehases.
hesitating, hesitant 1. מהסס *adj* mehases/-et; **2.** תוך היסוס (indeterminately) tokh heesoos.
hesitatingly בהיסוס *adv* be-heesoos.
hesitation היסוסים *nm pl* heesooseem.
(to) hew 1. לחטוב *inf* lakhtov; *pst* khatav; *pres* khotev; *fut* yakhtov; **2.** לדבוק ב־ (cling to) *inf* leedbok be-; *pst* davak *(v=b)* be-; *pres* davek be-; *fut* yeedbok be-.
heyday תקופת השיא *nf* tkoof|at/-ot ha-see.
(to) hibernate 1. לחרוף *inf* lakhrof; *pst* kharaf; *pres* khoref; *fut* yakhrof; **2.** להתבטל (loaf) *inf* leheetbatel; *pst* heetbatel; *pres* meetbatel; *fut* yeetbatel.
hiccup, hiccough שיהוק *nm* sheehook/-eem *(pl+of:* -ey).
(to) hiccup, (to) hiccough לשהק *inf* leshahek; *pst* sheehek; *pres* meshahek; *fut* yeshahek.
hickory היקוריה *nf* heekor|yah/-yot (+*of:* -yat).
hickory nut אגוז אמריקני *nm* egoz/-eem amereekanee/-yeem.
hidden מוסתר *adj* moost|ar/-eret.
(to) hide להסתיר *inf* lehasteer; *pst* heesteer; *pres* masteer; *fut* yasteer.
(to play) hide and seek לשחק במחבואים *inf* lesakhek be-makhbo'eem; *pst* seekhek *etc; pres* mesakhek *etc; fut* yesakhek *etc.*
(to) hide from להסתיר מפני *inf* lehasteer mee-pney; *pst* heesteer *etc; pres* masteer *etc; fut* yasteer *etc.*
hideous איום *adj* ayom/ayoomah.
hierarchy 1. סולם דרגות *nm* soolam deragot; **2.** הייררכיה heeyerarkh|yah/-yot (+*of:* -yat).
hieroglyph כתב חרטומים *nm* ketav khartoomeem.
high גבוה *adj* gavoha/gvohah.
(two feet) high בגובה שתי רגל be-govah shtey regel.
high and dry 1. עזוב ורצוץ *adj* 'azoov/-ah ve-ratsoos/oo-retsootsah; **2.** קצוץ כנפיים (with wings clipped) *adj* ketsoots/-at kenafayeem.
(to look) high and low לבדוק בכל מקום שרק אפשר *inf* leevdok be-khol *(kh=k)* makom she-rak efshar; *pst* badak *etc (b=v); pres* bodek *etc; fut* yeevdok *etc.*
high explosive חומר נפץ חזק *nm* khom|er/-rey nefets khazak/-eem.
(in) high gear בהילוך גבוה *adv* be-heelookh gavoha.
high priest, -ess כוהן גדול *nmf* kohen/-et gadol/-gedolah.

(in) high spirits במצב רוח מרומם *adv* be-matsav roo'akh meromam.

high tide גיאות *nf* ge'oot.

(it is) high time זה הרגע הנכון zeh ha-rega' ha-nakhon.

high wind רוח חזקה *nf* roo|'akh/-khot khazak|ah/-ot.

high-grade מסוג מעולה *adj* mee-soog me'ooleh.

high-handed בשרירות־לב bee-shreeroot lev.

high-minded אציל רוח *adj* atseel/-at roo'akh.

high-sounding יומרני *adj* yoomranee/-t.

high-strung עצבני *adj* 'atsbanee/-t.

highland רמה *nf* ram|ah/-ot (+*of:* -at).

highlight 1. גולת הכותרת (climax) *nf* goolat ha-koteret; **2.** שיא (peak) *nm* see/-'eem (*pl+of:* -'ey).

(to) highlight להבליט *inf* lehavleet; *pst* heevleet; *pres* mavleet; *fut* yavleet.

highly במידה רבה be-meedah rabah.

highly paid במשכורת גבוהה *adj* be-maskor|et/-ot gvo|hah/-hot.

highness הוד מעלה *nm* hod ma'al|ah (+*of:* -at).

highway כביש ראשי *nm* kveesh/-eem rashee/-yeem.

highwayman שודד דרכים *nm* shoded/-ey drakheem.

(to) hijack 1. לחטוף (kidnap) *inf* lakhtof; *pst* khataf; *pres* khotef; *fut* yakhtof; **2.** לגנוב (steal) *inf* leegnov; *pst* ganav; *pres* gonev; *fut* yeegnov.

hijacking חטיפה *nf* khateef|ah/-ot (+*of:* -at).

hike נסיעה ב״טרמפ״ *nf* nesee|'ah/-'ot bee-"tremp".

(to) hike לנסוע ב״טרמפים״ *inf* leenso'a' bee-"trempeem"; *pst* nasa' *etc*; *pres* nose'a' *etc*; *fut* yeesa' *etc*.

hiker 1. מטייל *nmf* metay|el/-leem (*pl+of:* -ley); **2.** ״טרמפיסט״ *[slang] nmf* "trempeest/-eet".

hill גבעה *nf* geev'ah/gva'ot (+*of:* geev|'at/-'ot).

(ant)hill גבעת נמלים *nf* geev|'at/-'ot nemaleem

(down)hill במורד גבעה *adv* be-morad geev'ah.

(up) hill במעלה גבעה *adv* be-ma'aleh geev'ah.

hillock 1. גבשושית *nf* gavshooshee|t/-yot; **2.** גבעה קטנה (small hill) *nf* geev'ah/gva'ot ketan|ah/-ot.

hillside 1. צלע הר *nf* tsela'/tsal'ot har/-eem; **2.** מדרון (slope) *nm* meedron/-eem (*pl+of:* -ey).

hilltop ראש גבעה *nm* rosh/-ey geev'ah/gva'ot.

hilly 1. הררי *adj* hararee/-t; **2.** משופע (slanting) *adj* meshoop|a'/-a'at.

hilt 1. ניצב *nm* neetsav/-eem (*pl+of:* -ey); **2.** ידית (handle) *nf* yadee|t/-yot.

him אותו *pron* oto.

himself הוא עצמו *pron* hoo 'atsmo.

hind 1. אחורי *adj* akhoree/-t; **2.** איילה (doe) *nf* ayal|ah/-ot (+*of:* ayelet).

(to) hinder 1. למנוע *inf* leemno'a'; *pst* mana'; *pres* mone'a'; *fut* yeemna'; **2.** להפריע (disturb) *inf* lehafree'a'; *pst* heefree'a'; *pres* mafree'a'; *fut* yafree'a'; **3.** לעכב (hold up) *inf* le'akev; *pst* 'eekev; *pres* me'akev; *fut* ye'akev.

hindmost 1. מרוחק (distant) *adj* merookh|ak/-eket; **2.** קיצוני (extreme) *adj* keetsonee/-t; **3.** אחרון (last) *adj* akhron/-ah.

hindrance 1. מניעה *nf* menee|'ah/-'ot (+*of:* -'at); **2.** מכשול (obstacle) *nm* meekhshol/-eem (*pl+of:* -ey).

hinge ציר *nm* tseer/-eem (*pl+of:* -ey).

(to) hinge 1. לתלות *vt inf* leetlot; *pst* talah; *pres* toleh; *fut* yeetleh; **2.** להיות תלוי (depend) *inf* leehyot talooy; *pst* hayah *etc*; *pres* heeno *etc*; *fut* yeehyeh *etc*.

(to) hinge on להיות תלוי ב־ *inf* leehyot talooy be-; *pst* hayah *etc*; *pres* heeno *etc*; *fut* yeehyeh *etc*.

hint רמז *nm* remez/remazeem (*pl+of:* reemzey).

(not to take the) hint לא לקלוט רמז *inf* lo leeklot remez; *pst* lo kalat *etc*; *pres* eyno kolet *etc*; *fut* lo yeeklot *etc*.

(to) hint לרמוז *inf* leermoz; *pst* ramaz; *pres* romez; *fut* yeermoz.

hip מותן *nm* mot|en/-nayeem (*pl+of:* -ney).

hippopotamus סוס יאור soos/-ey ye'or.

hire 1. השכרה (letting) *nf* haskar|ah/-ot (+*of:* -at); **2.** שכירה (renting) *nf* sekheer|ah/-ot (+*of:* -at).

(to) hire לשכור (rent) *inf* leeskor; *pst* sakhar *(kh=k)*; *pres* sokher; *fut* yeeskor.

(to) hire out להשכיר (let) *inf* lehaskeer; *pst* heeskeer; *pres* maskeer; *fut* yaskeer.

his שלו *pron* shelo.

(a friend of) his ידיד שלו *nmf* yedeed/-ah shelo.

hiss לחש *nm* lakhash/lekhasheem (*pl+of:* lakhshey).

(to) hiss ללחוש *inf* leelkhosh; *pst* lakhash; *pres* lokhesh; *fut* yeelkhash.

historian היסטוריון *nmf* heestoryon/-eem.

historic, historical היסטורי *adj* heestoree/-t.

history היסטוריה *nf* heestor|yah/-yot (+*of:* -yat).

histrionics 1. אמנות הבימה *nf* omanoo|t/-yot ha-beemah; **2.** מלאכותיות (artificiality) *nf* mal'akhooteeyoot.

hit 1. מהלומה (blow) *nf* mahaloom|ah/-ot (+*of:* -at); **2.** להיט (commercially) *nm* leheet/-eem (*pl+of:* -ey).

(to) hit 1. לפגוע *inf* leefgo'a'; *pst* paga' *(p=f)*; *pres* poge'a'; *fut* yeefga'; **2.** לקלוע (aim) *inf* leeklo'a'; *pst* kala'; *pres* kole'a'; *fut* yeekla'.

(they) hit it off well פתחו בצורה מוצלחת *v pst pl* patkhoo be-tsoorah mootslakhat.

(to) hit the mark 1. לקלוע למטרה *inf* leeklo'a' la-matarah; *pst* kala' *etc*; *pres* kole'a' *etc*; *fut* yeekla' *etc*; **2.** להגיע לרמה (attain level) *inf* lehagee'a' la-ramah; *pst* heegee'a' *etc*; *pres* magee'a' *etc*; *fut* yagee'a' *etc*.

(to) hit upon 1. להיתקל ב־ *inf* leheetakel be-; *pst & pres* neetkal be-; *fut* yeetakel be-; **2.** למצוא באקראי (happen to find) *inf* leemtso be-akray; *pst* matsa *etc*; *pres* motse *etc*; *fut* yeemtsa *etc*.

(to become a) hit להפוך ללהיט *inf* lahafokh le-laheet; *pst* hafakh *etc*; *pres* hofekh *etc*; *fut* yahafokh *etc*.

(to make a) hit with someone למצוא חן בעיני מישהו *inf* leemtso khen be-'eyney meeshehoo; *pst* matsa *etc*; *pres* motse *etc*; *fut* yeemtsa *etc*.

hitch 1. מכשול *nm* meekhshol/-eem (*pl+of:* -ey); **2.** עיכוב בלתי צפוי (unforeseen hindrance) *nm* 'eekoov/-eem beeltee tsafooy/tsfooyeem.

(to) hitch 1. לקשור *inf* leekshor; *pst* kashar; *pres* kosher; *fut* yeekshor; **2.** לבקש הסעה (ask for a free ride) *inf* levakesh hasa'ah; *pst* beekesh *(b=v) etc; pres* mevakesh *etc; fut* yevakesh *etc.*
hitchhike נסיעה ב״טרמפים״ *nf* nesee|'ah/-'ot bee-"trempeem".
hither הנה *adv* henah.
hither and thither הנה והנה *adv* henah va-henah.
hitherto עד כה 'ad koh.
hive כוורת *nf* kav|eret/-arot.
hives חרלת *nf* kharelet.
hoard 1. מאגר *nm* ma'ag|ar/-areem *(pl+of:* -rey); **2.** מצבור (dump) *nm* meetsbor/-eem *(pl+of:* -ey).
(to) hoard לאגור *inf* le'egor; *pst* agar; *pres* oger; *fut* ye'egor
hoarse צרוד *adj* tsarood/tsroodah.
hoarseness צרידות *nf* tsreedoo|t/-yot.
hoary 1. שב *adj* sav/-ah; **2.** בעל שער שיבה (gray-haired) *adj* ba'al/-at se'ar seyvah.
hoax תעלול רמייה *nm* ta'alool/-ey remeeyah.
hobble צליעה *nf* tslee|'ah/-'ot *(+of:* -'at).
(to) hobble 1. לדדות *inf* ledadot; *pst* deedah; *pres* medadeh; *fut* yedadeh; **2.** לצלוע (limp) leetslo'a'; *pst* tsala'; *pres* tsole'a'; *fut* yeetsla'.
hobby תחביב *nm* takhbeeb/-eem *(pl+of:* -ey).
hobo נווד *nm* navad/-eem *(pl+of:* -ey).
hodgepodge 1. בליל מאכלים *nm* bleel/-ey ma'akhaleem; **2.** ערבוביה (mixture) *nf* 'eerboov|yah/-yot *(+of:* -yat).
hoe מעדר *nm* ma'd|er/-reem *(pl+of:* -rey).
hog חזיר *nm* khazeer/-eem *(pl+of:* -ey).
hoist 1. מנוף הרמה *nm* menof/-ey haramah; **2.** מעלית (elevator) *nf* ma'alee|t/-yot.
(to) hoist 1. להניף *inf* lehaneef; *pst* heneef; *pres* meneef; *fut* yaneef; **2.** להרים (lift) lehareem; *pst* hereem; *pres* mereem; *fut* yareem.
hold אחיזה *nf* akheez|ah/-ot *(+of:* -at).
(how much does it) hold? כמה זה מכיל? kamah zeh mekheel?
(to) hold 1. לאחוז *inf* le'ekhoz; *pst* akhaz; *pres* okhez; *fut* yokhaz; **2.** להחזיק *inf* lehakhzeek; *pst* hekhzeek; *pres* makhzeek; *fut* yakhzeek.
(to) hold back someone 1. לעכב בעד מישהו *inf* le'akev be-'ad meeshehoo; *pst* 'eekev; *pres* me'akev *etc; fut* ye'akev; **2.** לעצור (stop) *inf* la'atsor; *pst* 'atsar; *pres* 'otser; *fut* ya'atsor.
(to) hold forth 1. להרצות (lecture) *inf* lehartsot; *pst* heertsah; *pres* martseh; *fut* yartseh; **2.** להציע (suggest) *inf* lehatsee'a'; *pst* heetsee'a'; *pres* matsee'a'; *fut* yatsee'a'.
(to) hold in place להחזיק במקום *inf* lehakhzeek ba-makom; *pst* hekhzeek *etc; pres* makhzeek *etc; fut* yakhzeek *etc.*
(to get) hold of 1. לשים יד על *inf* laseem yad 'al; *pst & pres* sam *etc; fut* yaseem *etc;* **2.** להשיג (reach) *inf* lehaseeg; *pst* heeseeg; *pres* maseeg; *fut* yaseeg.
(to take) hold of לקחת ליד *inf* lakakhat la-yad; *pst* lakakh *etc; pst* loke'akh *etc fut* yeekakh *etc.*
(to) hold off 1. לדחות *inf* leedkhot; *pst* dakhah; *pres* dokheh; *fut* yeedkheh; **2.** להרחיק (remove) *inf* leharkheek; *pst* heerkheek; *pres* markheek; *fut* yarkheek.
hold on! אל תרפה! (don't let loose!) *v imp* al tarp|eh!/-ee! *(pl:* -oo!).
(to) hold on 1. לדבוק ב־ (cling to) *inf* leedbok be-; *pst* davak be- *(v=b); pres* davek be-; *fut* yeedbok be-; **2.** להמשיך (continue) *inf* lehamsheekh; *pst* heemsheekh; *pres* mamsheekh; *fut* yamsheekh.
(to) hold one's own לעמוד על שלו *inf* la'amod 'al shelo; *pst* 'amad *etc; pres* 'omed *etc; fut* ya'amod *etc.*
(to) hold one's tongue לנצור לשונו *inf* leentsor leshono; *pst* natsar *etc; pres* notser *etc; fut* yeentsor *etc.*
(to) hold oneself erect לשמור על זקיפות *inf* leeshmor 'al zekeefoot; *pst* shamar *etc; pres* shomer *etc; fut* yeeshmor *etc.*
(to) hold out להחזיק מעמד *inf* lehakhzeek ma'amad; *pst* hekhzeek *etc; pres* makhzeek *etc; fut* yakhzeek *etc.*
(to) hold over 1. לדחות *inf* leedkhot; *pst* dakhah; *pres* dokheh; *fut* yeedkheh; **2.** להישאר (remain) *inf* leheesha'er; *pst & pres* neesh'ar; *fut* yeesha'er.
(to) hold someone responsible להטיל אחריות *inf* lehateel akhrayoot; *pst* heeteel *etc; pres* mateel *etc; fut* yateel *etc.*
(to) hold someone to his word לתבוע ממישהו לעמוד בדיבור *inf* leetbo'a' mee-meeshehoo la'amod be-deeboor; *pst* tava' *etc (b=v); pres* tove'a' *etc; fut* yeetba' *etc.*
(to) hold still 1. לשתוק *inf* leeshtok; *pst* shatak; *pres* shotek; *fut* yeeshtok; **2.** להישאר שקט ושותק (remain calm and silent) *inf* leheesha'er shaket/ sh'ketah ve-shotek/-et; *pst & pres* neesh'ar *etc; fut* yeesha'er *etc.*
(to) hold tight להחזיק חזק *[colloq.] inf* lehakhzeek khazak; *pst* hekhzeek *etc; pres* makhzeek *etc; fut* yakhzeek *etc.*
(to) hold to one's promise לתבוע שיעמוד בהבטחתו *inf* leetbo'a' she-ya'amod be-havtakhato; *pst* tava' *etc (b=v); pres* tove' *etc; fut* yeetba' *etc.*
hold-up שוד מזוין *nm* shod mezooyan.
(to) hold up 1. להרים (lift) *vt inf* lehareem; *pst* hereem; *pres* mereem; *fut* yareem; **2.** לעכב (delay) *inf* le'akev; *pst* 'eekev; *pres* me'akev; *fut* ye'akev; **3.** לבצע שוד (rob) *inf* levatse'a' shod; *pst* beetsa' *etc (b=v); pres* mevatse'a' *etc; fut* yevatse'a' *etc.*
holder מחזיק makhzeek/-eem *(pl+of:* -ey).
(cigarette) holder פייה לסיגריות *nf* pee|yah/-yot le-seegareeyot.
hole חור *nm* khor/-eem *(pl+of:* -ey).
(swimming) hole פינת שחייה *nf* peen|at/-ot sekheeyah.
(in a) hole 1. במצוקה *adv* bee-metsookah; **2.** שקוע בחובות (deep in debts) *adj* shakoo'a'/shkoo'ah be-khovot.
holiday 1. חג *nm* khag/-eem *(pl+of:* -ey); **2.** חופשה (vacation) *nf* khoofsh|ah/-ot *(+of:* -at).
holidays 1. חופשות החגים *nf pl* khoofshot ha-khageem; **2.** חופשות (vacations) *nf pl* khoofshot.
holiness קדושה *nf* kedoosh|ah *(+of:* -at).
hollow 1. חלול *adj* khalool/-ah; **2.** שקערורי (concave) *adj* shka'aroree/-t; **3.** לא כן *adj*

(insincere) lo ken/-ah; **4.** בלתי כנה (colloqial version of 3) *adj* beeltee ken|eh/-ah.

(to) hollow 1. לעשות חלול *inf* la'asot khalool; *pst* 'asah *etc; pres* 'oseh *etc fut* ya'aseh *etc;* **2.** לנקב (perforate) lenakev; *pst* neekev; *pres* menakev; *fut* yenakev.

holly צינית *nf* tseeneet.

holster נרתיק לאקדח *nm* narteek/-eem le-'ekd|akh/-okheem.

holy קדוש *adj* kadosh/kedoshah.

Holy Land ארץ הקודש *nf* erets ha-kodesh.

homage 1. כבוד *nm* kavod; **2.** כיבוד (honor) *nm* keebood/-eem (*pl+of:* -ey).

(to do) homage לחלוק כבוד *inf* lakhlok kavod; *pst* khalak *etc; pres* kholek *etc; fut* yakhlok *etc.*

home 1. קורת בית *nf* kor|at/-ot bayeet; **2.** הביתה (homeward) *adv* ha-baytah.

(at) home 1. בבית *adv* ba-bayeet; **2.** מסיבת בית (home-held party) *nf* meseeb|at/-ot bayeet.

(to strike) home לקלוע למטרה *inf* leeklo'a' la-matarah; *pst* kala' *etc; pres* kole'a' *etc; fut* yeekla' *etc.*

homeland מולדת *nf* mol|edet/-adot.

homeless חסר־בית *adj* khas|ar/-rat bayeet.

homelike 1. כמו בבית *adv* kemo ba-bayeet; **2.** ביתי (domestic) *adj* beytee/-t.

homely 1. פשוט *adj* pashoot/peshootah; **2.** חסר ברק (unpretentious) *adj* khas|ar/-rat barak.

home-made תוצרת בית *adj nf & adj* totseret bayeet

Home Office משרד הפנים *nm* meesr|ad/-edey ha-peneem.

home rule 1. שלטון בית *nm* sheelton-bayeet; **2.** אוטונומיה *nf* otonomee|yah/-yot (*+of:* -yat).

homesick מתגעגע הביתה *adj* meetga'g|e'a'/-a'at ha-baytah.

homesickness געגועים הביתה *nm pl* ga'agoo'eem ha-baytah.

homestead 1. חווה *nf* khav|ah/-ot (*+of:* -at); **2.** משק חקלאי (farm) *nm* meshek/-akeem khakla'ee/-yeem.

home stretch קטע הגמר במסלול *nm* keta' ha-gmar be-maslool.

homeward הביתה *adv* ha-baytah.

homeward voyage מסע הביתה *nm* masa' ha-baytah.

homework עבודת בית *nf* 'avod|at/-ot bayeet.

homicide רצח *nm* retsakh.

homogeneous הומוגני *adj* homogenee/-t.

(to) homogenize להמגן *inf* lehamgen; *pst* heemgen; *pres* mehamgen; *fut* yehamgen.

homosexual 1. הומוסקסואל *nm* homosexoo'al/-eem (*pl+of:* -ey); **2.** הומוסקסואלי *adj* homosexoo'alee/-t.

hone אבן משחזת *nf* even mashkhezet.

(to) hone להשחיז *inf* lehash'kheez; *pst* heesh'kheez; *pres* mash'kheez; *fut* yash'kheez.

honest 1. ישר *adj* yashar/yesharah; **2.** הגון (fair) hagoon/-ah; **3.** כן (sincere) *adj* ken/-ah.

honestly 1. ביושר *adv* be-yosher; **2.** באמת (truly) *adv* be-emet; **3.** באמונה (faithfully) be-emoonah.

honesty 1. יושר (equity) *nm* yosher; **2.** הגינות (fairness) *nf* hageenoo|t/-yot.

honey דבש *nm* dvash.

honeycomb חלת דבש *nf* khal|at/-ot dvash.

honeyed ממותק *adj* memoot|ak/-eket.

honeymoon ירח דבש *nm* yerakh/yarkhey dvash.

honeysuckle יערה *nf* ya'ar|ah/-ot (*+of:* -at).

honk 1. געגוע אווז *nm* ga'agoo|'a'/-'ey avaz; **2.** צפירת מכונית (of a car) *nf* tsfeer|at/-ot mekhonee|t/-yot.

(to) honk לצפור *inf* leetspor; *pst* tsafar *(f=p); pres* tsofer; *fut* yeetspor.

honor כבוד *nm* kavod.

(to) honor לכבד *inf* lekhabed; *pst* keebed *(k=kh); pres* mekhabed; *fut* yekhabed.

(upon my) honor על דיברתי כבוד 'al deevratee kavod.

honorable מכובד *adj* mekhoob|ad/-edet.

honorary 1. של כבוד *adj* shel kavod; **2.** שלא על מנת לקבל פרס *adj* she-lo 'al menat lekabel pras; **3.** בהתנדבות (voluntarily) *adj & adv* be-heetnadvoot.

hood מיכסה *nm* meekhs|eh/-eem (*pl+of:* -ey).

hoodlum 1. בריון *nm* beeryon/-eem (*pl+of:* -ey); **2.** פרחח (urchin) *nm* peerkhakh/-eem (*pl+of:* -ey).

hoof 1. פרסה *nf* pars|ah/prasot (*+of:* parsat); **2.** רגל (foot) *nf* regel.

hook 1. קרס *nm* keres/kraseem (*pl+of:* karsey); **2.** וו *nm* vav/-eem (*pl+of:* -ey).

(on his/her own) hook על אחריותו שלו *adv* 'al akhrayooto shel|o/-ah *(m/f).*

(by) hook *or* **by crook** בכל מחיר (whatever the cost) *adv* be-khol *(kh=k)* mekheer.

(to play) hooky להתחמק מבית הספר *inf* leheetkhamek mee-bet ha-sefer; *pst* heetkhamek *etc; pres* meetkhamek *etc; fut* yeetkhamek *etc.*

hooligan בריון מתפרע *nm* beeryon/-eem meet-par|e'a'/-'eem.

hoop חישוק *nm* kheeshook/-eem (*pl+of:* -ey); (Note: In Israeli politics the term is nowadays extensively used to signify prerequisites to peace process).

(to) hoop להדק בחישוקים *inf* lehadek be-kheeshookeem; *pst* heedek *etc; pres* mehadek; *fut* yehadek *etc.*

hoot צעקת לעג *nf* tsa'ak|at/-ot la'ag.

(to) hoot 1. לצעוק בלעג *inf* leets'ok be-la'ag; *pst* tsa'ak *etc; pres* tso'ek *etc; fut* yeets'ak *etc;* **2.** ליילל כינשוף (cry out like an owl) *inf* leyalel ke-yanshoof; *pst* yeelel *etc; pres* meyalel *etc; fut* yeyalel *etc.*

hooting צפצוף *nm* tseeftsoof/-eem (*pl+of:* -ey).

hop 1. קפיצה קצרה *nf* kfeets|ah/-ot ketsar|ah/-ot; **2.** ניתור *nm* neetoor/-eem (*pl+of:* -ey).

(to) hop לנתר *inf* lenater; *pst* neeter; *pres* menater; *fut* yenater.

hope תקווה *nf* teekv|ah/-ot (*+of:* -at).

(to) hope לקוות *inf* lekavot; *pst* keevah; *pres* mekaveh; *fut* yekaveh.

(to) hope against hope לקוות על אף הכל *inf* lekavot 'al af ha-kol; *pst* keevah *etc; pres* mekaveh *etc; fut* yekaveh *etc.*

(to) hope for לתלות תקווה *inf* leetlot teekvah/-ot; *pst* talah *etc; pres* toleh *etc; fut* yeetleh *etc.*

hopeful מקווה *adj* mekav|eh/-ah.

(a young) hopeful צעיר מבטיח *nm* tsa'eer/tse'eerah mavtee|'akh/-khah.

hopefully בתקווה *adv* be-teekvah.

hopeless חסר תקווה *adj* khas|ar/-rat teekvah.

(it is) hopeless אפסה כל תקווה afsah kol teekvah.

hopeless cause עניין אבוד *nm* 'eenyan avood.

hopeless illness מחלה חשוכת מרפא *nf* makhl|ah/-ot khasookh|at/-ot marpe.

hopelessly באין מוצא *adv* be-eyn motsa.

hopelessness חוסר מוצא *nm* khoser motsa.

horde 1. שבט נוודים *nm* shevet/sheevtey navadeem; **2.** המון *nm* hamon/-eem (*pl+of:* -ey).

horizon אופק *nm* of|ek/-akeem (*pl+of:* -key)

horizontal 1. אופקי *adj* ofkee/-t; **2.** מאוזן (*synon.* with 1) *adj* me'ooz|an/-enet.

horn 1. קרן *nf* keren/karn|ayeem (*pl+of:* -ey); **2.** צופר (car) *nm* tsofar/-eem (*pl+of:* -ey); **3.** שופר (blown in synagogue) *nm* shof|ar/-rot.

(to) horn 1. לנגח *inf* lenage'akh; *pst* neegakh; *pres* menage'akh; *fut* yenagakh; **2.** להצמיח קרניים (grow horns) *inf* lehatsmee'akh karnayeem; *pst* heetsmee'akh *etc*; *pres* matsmee'akh *etc*; *fut* yatsmee'akh *etc.*

(to blow one's own) horn 1. לשבח עצמו *inf* leshabe'akh 'atsmo; *pst* sheebakh *etc*; *pres* meshabe'akh *etc*; *fut* yeshabakh *etc*; **2.** להתרברב (brag) leheetravrev; *pst* heetravrev; *pres* meetravrev; *fut* yeetravrev.

(to) horn in 1. להתערב (interfere) *inf* leheet'arev; *pst* heet'arev; *pres* meet'arev; *fut* yeet'arev; **2.** להידחף *inf* leheedakhef; *pst & pres* needkhaf; *fut* yeedakhef.

horn of plenty קרן השפע *nf* keren ha-shefa'.

hornet 1. צרעה *nf* tseer'ah/tsera'ot (*+of:* tseer'at); **2.** דבור (wasp) *nm* daboor/-eem (*pl+of:* -ey).

hornet's nest קן צרעות *nm* ken/keeney ts|era'ot.

horoscope הורוסקופ *nm* horoskop/-eem (*pl+of:* -ey).

horrible נורא *adj* nora/-'ah.

horribly בצורה נוראה *adv* be-tsoorah nora'ah.

horrid מזוויע *adj* mazvee|'a'/-'ah.

(to) horrify 1. להבעית *inf* lehav'eet; *pst* heev'eet; *pres* mav'eet; *fut* yav'eet; **2.** להחריד (terrify) *inf* lahakhreed; *pst* hekhreed; *pres* makhreed; *fut* yakhreed.

horror זוועה *nf* zva|'ah/-'ot (*+of:* -'at).

hors d'oeuvre מנה ראשונה *nf* man|ah/-ot reeshon|ah/-ot.

horse סוס *nm* soos/-eem (*pl+of:* -ey).

(saddle) horse סוס רכיבה *nm* soos/-ey rekheevah.

horse dealer סוחר סוסים *nm* sokh|er/-arey sooseem.

horse race מרוץ סוסים *nm* merots/-ey sooseem.

horse sense שכל ישר *nm* sekhel yashar.

horseback 1. גב הסוס (liter.) *nm* gav ha-soos; **2.** ברכיבה (riding) *adv* bee-rekheevah.

(beggar on) horseback עבד כי ימלוך ("a slave when he becomes king" - Proverbs 30,22) 'eved kee yeemlokh.

(to ride) horseback לרכוב על סוס *inf* leerkov 'al soos; *pst* rakhav *etc* (*kh=k*); *pres* rokhev *etc*; *fut* yeerkav *etc.*

horsefly זבוב הסוסים *nm* zvoov/-ey ha-sooseem.

horselaugh צחוק פרוע *nm* tsekhok paroo'a'.

horseman פרש *nm* parash/-eem (*pl+of:* -ey).

horsemanship 1. פרשות (occupation) *nf* parashoot; **2.** אומנות הרכיבה (art) *nf* omanoot ha-rekheevah.

horsepower 1. כוח־סוס *nm* ko'akh/kokhot soos; **2.** כ"ס (*acr of* 1, equivalent to HP) *nm* ko'akh/kokhot soos.

horseradish חזרת *nf* khazeret.

horseshoe פרסת סוס *nf* pars|at/-ot soos/-eem.

hose 1. גרב (stocking) *nm* gerev/garb|ayeem (*pl+of:* -ey); **2.** זרנוק (rubber tube) *nm* zarnook/-eem (*pl+of:* -ey).

(half)hose גרב קצר *nm* gerev/garbayeem katsar/ketsareem.

(men's) hose גרבי גברים *nm pl* garbey gvareem.

hosiery 1. גרביים (socks) *nm pl* garb|ayeem (*pl+of:* -ey); **2.** לבנים (underwear) *nm pl* levaneem (*pl+of:* leevney); **3.** גופיות (vests) *nf* goofeeyot; **4.** תחתונים (underpants) *nf pl* takhton|eem (*pl+of:* -ey).

hosiery shop, store חנות ללבנים *nf* khanoot lee-levaneem.

hospitable מכניס אורחים *nmf & adj* makhnees/-at orkheem.

hospital בית חולים *nm* bet/batey kholeem.

hospitality הכנסת אורחים *nf* hakhnasat orkheem.

host מארח *nmf* me'ar|e'akh/-akhat.

hostage בן־ערובה *nmf* ben/bat 'aroobah.

hostel 1. אכסניה (inn) *nf* akhsan|yah/-yot (*+of:* -yat); **2.** מלון (hotel) *nm* malon/melonot.

(youth) hostel אכסניית נוער *nf* akhsan|yat/-yot no'ar.

hostess 1. מארחת *nf* me'ar|akhat/-khot; **2.** דיילת (stewardess) *nf* dayelet/dayalot.

hostile עוין *adj* 'oyen/-et.

hostility 1. עוינות *nf* 'oynoo|t/-yot; **2.** איבה (animosity) *nf* eyv|ah/-ot (*+of:* -at).

hot 1. חם *adj* kham/-ah; **2.** *adv* kham.

hotbed חממה *nf* khamam|ah/-ot (*+of:* -at).

hot-headed רתחן *adj* ratkhan/-eet.

hot house 1. חממה *nf* khamam|ah/-ot (*+of:* -at); **2.** גן־חורף (conservatory) *nm* gan/-ey khoref.

(it is) hot today חם היום kham ha-yom.

hotel מלון *nm* malon/melonot.

hotel keeper מלונאי *nmf* melon|ay/-a'eem (*pl+of:* -a'ey).

hotly 1. בחום *adv* be-khom; **2.** בהתלהבות (enthusiastically) *adv* be-heetlahavoot.

hound 1. כלב ציד *nm* kelev/kalvey tsayeed; **2.** נבל (scoundrel) *nm* naval/nevaleem.

hour שעה *nf* sha|'ah/-'ot (*+of:* she|'at/-'ot).

hour hand מחוג השעות *nm* mekhog ha-sha'ot.

hourly 1. מדי שעה *adv* meedey sha'ah; **2.** על השעה (on the hour) *adv* 'al ha-sha'ah.

house 1. בית *nm* bayeet/bat|eem (*pl+of:* -ey); **2.** שושלת (dynasty) *nf* shosh|elet/-alot.

(country) house בית כפרי *nm* bayeet/bateem kafree/-yeem.

(a full) house אולם מלא *nm* oolam/-ot male/ mele'eem.

(on the) house על חשבון ההנהלה *adv* 'al kheshbon ha-hanhalah.

household 1. משפחה *nf* meeshpakh|ah/-ot (+*of:* -at); **2.** משק הבית *nm* meshek ha-bayeet.

housekeeper 1. סוכנת בית (attendant) *nf* sokhenet bayeet; **2.** עקרת בית (housewife) *nf* 'ak|eret/-rot bayeet.

(a good) housekeeper עקרת בית טובה *nf* 'akeret bayeet tovah.

housekeeping 1. משק בית *nm* meshek bayeet; **2.** כלכלת הבית (expenses) *nf* kalkalat ha-bayeet.

housetop גג *nm* gag/-ot.

housewarming מסיבה לחנוכת בית *nf* meseebah la-khanookat bayeet.

housewife עקרת בית *nf* 'ak|eret/-rot bayeet.

housework עבודות משק הבית *nm* 'avodot meshek ha-bayeet.

housing שיכון *nm* sheekoon.

hovel 1. בקתה עלובה *nf* beekt|ah/-ot 'aloov|ah/-ot; **2.** דיר החסנה *nm* deer hakhsanah.

(to) hover לרחף *inf* lerakhef; *pst* reekhef; *pres* merakhef; *fut* yerakhef.

(to) hover around 1. לרפרף סביב *inf* lerafref saveev; *pst* reefref *etc; pres* merafref *etc; fut* yerafref *etc;* **2.** לפטרל (patrol) *inf* lefatrel; *pst* peetrel *(p=f); pres* mefatrel; *fut* yefatrel.

hovercraft רחפת *nf* rakh|efet/-afot.

how 1. איך eykh; **2.** כיצד keytsad.

how beautiful! מה יפה! *interj* mah yafeh!

how difficult it is מה קשה הדבר mah kasheh ha-davar.

how early! מה מאד מוקדם! *interj* mah me'od mookdam!.

how far is it? מה המרחק? mah ha- merkhak?

how long כמה זמן kamah zman?

how many כמה kamah.

(no matter) how much כמה שזה לא יהיה kamah she-zeh lo yeehyeh.

how much is it? 1. כמה זה עולה? kamah zeh 'oleh? **2.** מה זה עולה? *[colloq.]* mah zeh 'oleh?

how old are you? 1. בן כמה אתה? *nm* ben kamah atah? **2.** בת כמה את? *nf* bat kamah at?

however 1. אולם *conj* oolam; **2.** אבל (but) aval.

however difficult it may be כמה שלא יקשה הדבר kamah she-lo yeeksheh ha-davar.

however much ויעלה כמה שיעלה ve-ya'aleh kamah she-ya'aleh.

howl 1. יללה *nf* yelal|ah/-ot (+*of:* yeelelat/-ot); **2.** צריחה (scream) *nf* tsreekh|ah/-ot (+*of:* -at).

(to) howl 1. ליילל *inf* leyalel; *pst* yeelel; *pres* meyalel; *fut* yeyalel; **2.** לצרוח (yell) *inf* leetsro'akh; *pst* tsarakh; *pres* tsore'akh; *fut* yeetsrakh.

hub 1. טבור *nm* taboor/-eem (*pl+of:* -ey); **2.** מרכז (center) *nm* merk|az/-azeem (*pl+of:* -ezey).

hubbub 1. שאון *nm* sha'on (+*of:* she'on); **2.** המולה (turmoil) *nf* hamool|ah/-ot (+*of:* -at).

huckster 1. רוכל *nm* rokh|el/-leem (*pl+of:* -ley); **2.** רודף בצע (greedy) *adj* rodef/-et betsa'.

huddle 1. ערבוביה (mix) *nf* 'eerboov|yah/-yot (+*of:* -yat); **2.** המון (crowd) *nm* hamon/-eem (*pl+of:* -ey).

(to) huddle 1. לצופף יחדיו *inf* letsofef yakhdav; *pst* tsofef *etc; pres* metsofef *etc; fut* yetsofef *etc;* **2.** להצטופף (crowd) *v rfl inf* leheetstofef; *pst* heetstofef; *pres* meetstofef; *fut* yeetstofef.

(to go into a) huddle להסתודד *inf* leheestoded; *pst* heestoded; *pres* meestoded; *fut* yeestoded.

hue 1. גוון *nm* gaven/gvan|eem (+*of:* gon/-ey); **2.** צווחה (shriek) *nf* tsvakh|ah/-ot (+*of:* -at).

huff 1. טרוניה *nf* troon|yah/-yot (+*of:* -yat); **2.** תרעומת (grudge) *nf* tar'om|et/-ot.

(to) hug לחבק *inf* lekhabek; *pst* kheebek; *pres* mekhabek; *fut* yekhabek.

(to) hug the coast לשוט בקירבת החוף *inf* lashoot be-keervat ha-khof; *pst & pres* shat *etc; fut* yashoot *etc.*

huge 1. כביר *adj* kabeer/-ah; **2.** ענקי (giant) *adj* 'anakee/-t.

hull 1. קליפה (peel) *nf* kleep|ah/-ot (+*of:* -at); **2.** גוף אונייה (of a ship) *nm* goof oneeyah.

(to) hull לקלף *inf* lekalef; *pst* keelef; *pres* mekalef; *fut* yekalef.

hullabaloo מהומה *nf* mehoom|ah/-ot (+*of:* -at).

(to) hum לזמזם *inf* lezamzem; *pst* zeemzem; *pres* mezamzem; *fut* yezamzem.

(to) hum to sleep להרדים בזימזום מונוטוני *inf* lehardeem be-zeemzoom monotonee; *pst* heerdeem *etc; pres* mardeem *etc; fut* yardeem *etc.*

human 1. יצור אנוש *nm* yetsoor/-ey enosh; **2.** אנושי *adj* enooshee/-t.

humane הומני *adj* hoomanee/-t.

humanism 1. הומניות *nf* homaneeyoot; **2.** יחס אנושי (humane attitude) *nm* yakhas enooshee.

humanitarian הומניטרי *adj* hoomaneetaree/-t.

humanity האנושות *nf* ha-enoshoot.

humble 1. שפל־רוח *adj* shfal/sheeflat roo'akh; **2.** צנוע (modest) *adj* tsanoo'a'/tsenoo'ah.

humbleness צניעות *nf* tsenee'oot.

humbly בצניעות *adv* bee-tsenee'oot.

humid לח *adj* lakh/-ah.

humidify להגביר לחות *inf* lehagbeer lakhoot; *pst* heegbeer *etc; pres* magbeer *etc; fut* yagbeer *etc.*

humidity לחות *nf* lakhoo|t/-yot.

(to) humiliate להשפיל *inf* lehashpeel; *pst* heeshpeel; *pres* mashpeel; *fut* yashpeel.

humiliation השפלה *nf* hashpal|ah/-ot (+*of:* -at).

humility 1. ענווה *nf* 'anavah (+*of:* 'envat); **2.** צניעות (modesty) *nf* tsenee'oot.

hummingbird יונק דבש *nm* yon|ek/-key dvash.

humor 1. הומור *nm* hoomor; **2.** מצב־רוח (disposition) *nm* mats|av/-vey roo'akh.

(out of) humor מצוברח *adj* metsoovrakh/-at.

humorous 1. מבדח *adj* mevad|e'akh/-akhat; **2.** מצחיק (funny) *adj* matskheek/-ah.

hump 1. חטוטרת *nf* khatot|eret/-rot; **2.** דבשת (camel) *nf* dab|eshet/-ashot.

humpback גיבן *nmf & adj* geeben/-et.

hunch 1. חטוטרת *nf* khatot|eret/-rot; **2.** נבואת לב (premonition) *nf* nevoo|'at/-'ot lev.

hunchback גיבן *nmf* geeben/-et.

hundred מאה (100) *num* me'ah/-'ot.

hundred percent מאה אחוז *nm pl & adv* me'ah akhooz.

hundredth 1. המאה *adj* ha-me'ah; **2.** מאית (1/100; 0.01) *nf* me'ee|t-yot.

hunger רעב *nm* ra'av.

(to) hunger for 1. -לרעוב ל *inf* leer'ov le-; *pst* ra'av le-; *pres* ra'ev le-; *fut* yeer'av le-; **2.** -להשתוקק ל (crave for) *inf* leheeshtokek le-; *pst* heeshtokekle-; *pres* meeshtokek le-; *fut* yeeshtokek le-.

hungrily 1. ברעבתנות *adv* be-ra'avtanoot; **2.** בתאווה (craving) *adv* be-ta'avah.

hungry רעב *adj* ra'ev/re'evah.

(to go) hungry לרעוב ללחם *inf* leer'ov le-lekhem; *pst* ra'av *etc*; *pres* ra'ev *etc*; *fut* yeer'av *etc.*

hunk חתיכה גדולה *nm* khateekh|ah/-ot gedol|ah/-ot.

hunt ציד *nm* tsayeed.

(to) hunt לצוד *inf* latsood; *pst & pres* tsad; *fut* yatsood.

(to) hunt after, for לחפש אחר *inf* lekhapes akhar; *pst* kheepes *etc*; *pres* mekhapes *etc*; *fut* yekhapes *etc.*

(to) hunt down ללכוד *inf* leelkod; *pst* lakhad *(kh=k)*; *pres* lokhed; *fut* yeelkod.

hunter צייד *nmf* tsa|yad/-yedet.

huntsman 1. צייד *nm* tsayad/-eem (*pl+of:* -ey); **2.** ממונה על כלבי ציד *nm* memooneh 'al kalvey *(v=b)* tsayeed.

(to) hurl לזרוק *inf* leezrok; *pst* zarak; *pres* zorek; *fut* yeezrok.

(to) hurrah 1. לקרוא הידד *inf* leekro heydad; *pst* kara *etc*; *pres* kore *etc*; *fut* yeekra *etc*; **2.** להריע (cheer) *inf* leharee'a'; *pst* heree'a'; *pres* meree'a'; *fut* yaree'a'.

hurrah! 1. ! הידד *interj* heydad! **2.** ! יחי (long live!) *interj* yekheel/tekheel *(m/f)*; **3.** ! כיפך הי (milit. slang) *interj* keefak hey!

hurricane סופה *nf* soof|ah/-ot (*+of:* -at).

hurried 1. בהול *adj* bahool/behoolah; **2.** חפוז (hasty) *adj* khafooz/-ah.

hurriedly בחיפזון *adv* be-kheepazon.

(to) hurry 1. למהר *inf* lemaher; *pst* meeher; *pres* memaher; *fut* yemaher; **2.** להיחפז (hasten) *inf* lehekhafez; *pst & pres* nekhpaz *(p=f)*; *fut* yekhafez.

(to be in a) hurry להיות דחוק בזמן *inf* leehyot dakhook bee-zman; *pst* hayah *etc*; *pres* heeno *etc*; *fut* yeehyeh *etc.*

(to) hurry in להיחפז פנימה *inf* lehekhafez peneemah; *pst & pres* nekhpaz *etc (p=f)*; *fut* yekhafez *etc.*

(to) hurry out להיחפז החוצה *inf* lehekhafez ha-khootsah; *pst & pres* nekhpaz *etc (p=f)*; *fut* yekhafez *etc.*

(to) hurry up להזדרז *inf* leheezdarez; *pst* heezdarez; *pres* meezdarez; *fut* yeezdarez.

(to) hurt לפגוע *inf* leefgo'a'; *pst* paga' *(p=f)*; *pres* poge'a'; *fut* yeefga'.

(to) hurt one's feelings לפגוע ברגשות מישהו *inf* leefgo'a' be-reegshot meeshehoo; *pst* paga' *etc (p=f)*; *pres* poge'a' *etc*; *fut* yeefga' *etc.*

(my tooth) hurts כואבת לי שן ko'evet lee shen.

husband בעל *nm* ba'al/be'aleem (*pl+of:* ba'aley).

hush 1. שקט (quiet) *adj* shaket/sheketah; **2.** דומייה (silence) *nf* doomee|yah/-yot (*+of:* -yat); **3.** דממה (stillness) *nf* demamah (*+of:* deememat).

(to) hush להשתיק *inf* lehashteek; *pst* heeshteek; *pres* mashteek; *fut* yashteek.

hush! 1. ! הס *interj* has! **2.** ! שקט (quiet!) *interj* sheket!

hush money דמי לא יחרץ *nm pl* demey lo yekhrats.

(to) hush up a scandal להשתיק שערורייה *inf* lehashteek sha'arooree|yah/-yot; *pst* heeshteek *etc*; *pres* mashteek *etc*; *fut* yashteek *etc.*

husk קליפה *nf* kleep|ah/-ot (*+of:* -at).

(to) husk לקלף *inf* lekalef; *pst* keelef; *pres* mekalef; *fut* yekalef.

husky 1. חסון *adj* khas|on/-oonah; **2.** גדול גוף *adj* gedol/geedlat goof; **3.** צרוד (hoarse) *adj* tsarood/tseroodah.

hustle פעילות *nf* pe'eeloo|t/-yot.

(to) hustle 1. לדחוף (push) *inf* leedkhof; *pst* dakhaf; *pres* dokhef; *fut* yeedkhof; **2.** לזרז (hasten) *inf* lezarez; *pst* zerez; *pres* mezarez; *fut* yezarez; **3.** (hurry up) *v rfl inf* leheezdarez; *pst* heezdarez; *pres* meezdarez; *fut* yeezdarez.

hustle and bustle רעש והמולה *nm* ra'ash va-hamoolah.

hut 1. סוכה *nf* sook|ah/-ot (*+of:* -at); **2.** צריף (shack) tsreef/-eem (*pl+of:* -ey).

hyacinth יקינתון *nm* yakeenton/-eem (*pl+of:* -ey).

hybrid בן־כלאיים *nmf* ben/bat keel'ayeem.

hydraulic הידראולי *adj* heedraulee/-t.

hydro-electric הידרו־חשמלי *adj* heedro-khashmalee/-t.

hydrogen מימן *nm* meyman/-eem (*pl+of:* -ey).

hydrogen bomb פצצת מימן *nf* peetsets|at/-ot meyman.

hydrophobia 1. בעת מים *nf* ba'at/-ey mayeem; **2.** כלבת (rabies) *nf* kalevet.

hydroplane 1. מטוס ימי *nm* matos/metoseem yamee/-yeem; **2.** הידרופלן *nm* heedroplan/-eem (*pl+of:* -ey).

hygiene היגיינה *nf* heegyen|ah/-ot (*+of:* -at).

hymn 1. מזמור (song) *nm* meezmor/-eem (*pl+of:* -ey); **2.** המנון *nm* heemnon/-eem (*pl+of:* -ey).

hyphen 1. מקף (-) *nm* makaf/-eem (*pl+of:* -ey); **2.** קו־חיבור *nm* kav/-ey kheeboor.

hypnosis היפנוזה *nf* heepnoz|ah/-ot (*+of:* -at).

hypocrisy צביעות *nf* tsvee'oot.

hypocrite צבוע *nmf & adj* tsavoo'a'/tsvoo'ah.

hypocritical שיש בו צביעות *adj* she-yesh bo/bah *(m/f)* tsvee'oot.

hypothesis 1. השערה *nf* hash'ar|ah/-ot (*+of:* -at); **2.** היפותיזה *nf* heepotez|ah/-ot (*+of:* -at).

hysterical היסטרי *adj* heesteree/-t.

I.

I,i as a vowel, pronounced as in *mine* or *I*, it is transliterated איי (ay). However, when pronounced as in *this* or *give*, it has no exact equivalent in undotted Hebrew script.In the dotted script, on the other hand, the שווא נע (shva na') placed under a consonant x̣ might be regarded as the nearest thing to it. In these dictionaries, however, we use the short e for anything similar to that sound.

I 1. אני *pers pron* anee; **2.** אנוכי (more pretentious) pers *pron* anokhee.

ice קרח *nm* kerakh.

ice cream גלידה *nf* gleed|ah/-ot (*cpr* gleed|ah/-ot; *+of:* -at).

ice cream parlor סלון גלידה *nm* salon/-ey gleedah (*cpr* gleedah).

ice skates מחליקיים על קרח *nm pl* makhleekayeem 'al kerakh.

ice water מי קרח *nm pl* mey kerakh.

iceberg קרחון *nm* karkhon/-eem (*pl+of:* -ey).

icebox מקרר קרח (ice-cooled) *nm* mekarer/-ey kerakh.

iceman 1. מחלק קרח (distributor) *nm* mekhal|ek/-key kerakh; **2.** מוכר קרח (seller) *nm* mokh|er/-rey kerakh.

icicle נטיף קרח *nm* nateef/neteefey kerakh.

iconoclasm ניתוץ מוסכמות *nm* neetoots mooskamot.

icy קר כקרח *adj* kar/-ah ka-kerakh.

idea 1. רעיון *nm* ra'yon/-ot; **2.** אידיאה *nf* eede|'ah/-'ot (*+of:* -'at).

ideal 1. משאת־נפש *nf* mas|'at/-'ot nefesh; **2..** אידיאל *nm* eede'al/-eem (*pl+of:* -ey).

idealism אידיאליזם *nm* eede'aleezm.

idealist אידיאליסט *nmf* eede'aleest/-eet.

identical זהה *adj* ze|heh/-hah.

(to) identify לזהות *inf* lezahot; *pst* zeehah; *pres* mezaheh; *fut* yezaheh.

identity זהות *nf* zehoo|t/-yot.

ideology אידיאולוגיה *nf* eede'ologee|yah/-yot (*+of:* -yat).

IDF (*acr of* Israeli Defence Forces) צה"ל TSAHAL - official term for Israel's military forces (*acr of* צבא הגנה לישראל tsva haganah le-yeesra'el i.e. Israel's Defence Army).

idiom 1. ניב *nm* neev/-eem (*pl+of:* -ey); **2.** ביטוי מיוחד (specific expression) *nm* beetoo|y/-yeem meyookhad/-eem.

idiosyncrasy 1. רגישות מיוחדת *nf* regeeshoo|t/-yot meyookh|edet/-adot; **2.** אידיאוסינקרזיה *nf* eede'oseenkrazee|yah/-yot (*+of:* -yat).

idiot 1. אידיוט *nmf* eedee'ot/-eet; **2.** מטומטם (dullard) *adj* metoomt|am/-emet.

idiotic 1. אידיוטי *adj* eedee'otee/-t; **2.** טיפשי (stupid) *adj* teepshee/-t.

idle 1. בטל *adj* batel/betelah; **2.** עצל (lazy) *adj* 'atsel/-ah.

idleness 1. בטלה *nf* batal|ah/-ot (*+of:* -at); **2.** עצלות (laziness) 'atsloo|t/-yot.

idler 1. בטלן *nmf* batlan/-eet; **2.** עצלן (sluggard) *nmf* 'atslan/-eet.

idly בעצלתיים *adv* ba-'atsaltayeem.

idol אליל *nm* eleel/-eem (*pl+of:* -ey).

idolatry 1. עבודת אלילים *nf* 'avodat eleeleem; **2.** הערצה עיוורת (blind adoration) *nf* ha'aratsah 'eeveret.

(to) idolize 1. לאלל *inf* le'alel; *pst* eelel; *pres* me'alel *fut* ye'alel; **2.** להאליל *[colloq.] inf* leha'aleel; *pst* he'eleel; *pres* ma'aleel; *fut* ya'aleel; **3.** להעריץ בצורה עיוורת (adore blindly) *inf* leha'areets be-tsoorah 'eeveret; *pst* he'ereets *etc*; *pres* ma'areets *etc*; *fut* ya'areets *etc*.

idyl אידיליה *nf* eedeel|yah/-yot (*+of:* -yat).

if 1. אם eem; **2.** אילו eeloo.

(to) ignite 1. להדליק *inf* lehadleek; *pst* heedleek; *pres* madleek; *fut* yadleek; **2.** להצית (set fire) *inf* lehatseet; *pst* heetseet; *pres* matseet; *fut* yatseet.

ignition 1. הדלקה *nf* hadlak|ah/-ot (*+of:* -at); **2.** הצתה (car) *nf* hatsat|ah/-ot (*+of:* -at).

(electronic) ignition הצתה אלקטרונית *nf* hatsatah elektroneet.

ignition switch מתג הצתה *nm* meteg hatsatah.

ignoble נקלה *nm* neekl|eh/-eem (*pl+of:* -ey).

ignorance 1. בורות *nf* booroo|t/-yot; **2.** בערות (illiteracy) *nf* ba'aroo|t/-yot.

ignorant 1. בור *nmf & adj* boor/-ah; **2.** בער *nm* ba'ar/be'ar|eem (*pl+of:* ba'arey).

(to) ignore 1. לא לדעת *inf* lo lada'at; *pst* lo yada'; *pres* eyno yode'a'; *fut* lo yeda'; **2.** להתעלם *inf* leheet'alem; *pst* heet'alem; *pres* meet'alem; *fut* yeet'alem.

ill 1. חולה (sick) khol|eh/-ah; **2.** רע (bad) *adj* ra'/ra'ah; **3.** לא ידידותי (unfriendly) lo yedeedootee/-t.

ill-at-ease 1. נבוך *adj* navokh/nevokhah; **2.** לא נוח (uneasy) *adj* lo no|'akh/-khah.

ill nature אופי מרושע *nm* ofee meroosha'.

ill will רצון רע *nm* ratson ra'.

ill-advised לא חכם *adj* lo khakham/-ah.

ill-bred 1. בלתי מחונך *adj* beeltee mekhoon|akh/-ekhet; **2.** גס (rude) gas/-ah.

ill-clad מלובש גרוע *adj* meloob|ash/-eshet garoo'a'.

ill-humored מצוברח *adj* metsoovrakh/-at.

ill-mannered חסר נימוסים *adj* khas|ar/-rat neemooseem.

ill-natured רע לב *adj* ra'/ra'at lev.

illegal 1. בלתי חוקי *adj* beeltee khookee/-t; **2.** שלא כחוק (unlawful) *adj & adv* she-lo ka-khok.

illegitimate 1. בלתי חוקי *adj* beeltee khookee/-t; **2.** לא כשר (improper) lo kasher/kesherah.

illicit אסור (prohibited) *adj* asoor/-ah.

illiteracy 1. בערות *nf* ba'aroo|t/-yot; **2.** אי־ידיעת קרוא וכתוב (no knowledge of reading or writing) ee yedee'at kro oo-khetov *(kh=k)*.

illiterate 1. בער *nm* ba'ar; **2.** בור (ignorant) *nmf & adj* boor/-ah; **3.** אנאלפבית *nmf* analfabet/-eet.

illness מחלה *nf* makhl|ah/-ot (*+of:* -at).

(to) illuminate להאיר *inf* leha'eer; *pst* he'eer; *pres* me'eer; *fut* ya'eer.

illumination תאורה *nf* te'oor|ah/-ot (*+of:* -at).

illusion 1. אשליה *nf* ashla|yah/-yot (*+of:* -yat); **2.** אחיזת עיניים (jugglery) *nf* akheez|at/-ot 'eynayeem.

illusive 1. משלה *adj* mashl|eh/-ah; **2.** כוזב (false) *adj* kozev/-et.

illusory 1. משלה *adj* mashl|eh/-ah; **2.** מאחז עיניים (deceptive) *adj* me'akhez/-et 'eynayeem.

(to) illustrate לאייר *inf* le'ayer; *pst* eeyer; *pres* me'ayer; *fut* ye'ayer.

illustration איור *nm* eeyoor/-eem (*pl+of:* -ey).

illustrator מאייר *nmf* me'ayer/-et.

illustrious 1. מפורסם *adj* mefoors|am/-emet; **2.** מהולל (famed) *adj* mehool|al/-elet.

image 1. דמות *nf* demoo|t/-yot; **2.** דיוקן (portrait) *nm* dyok|an/-na'ot.

imaginary מדומה *adj* medoom|eh/-ah.

imagination דמיון *nm* deemyon/-ot.

imaginative עתיר דמיון *adj* 'ateer/-at deemyon.

(to) imagine 1. לדמות *inf* ledamot; *pst* deemah; *pres* medameh; *fut* yedameh; **2.** לדמיין (fantasize) *inf* ledamyen; *pst* deemyen; *pres* medamyen; *fut* yedamyen.

imbecile 1. גולם *nm* gol|em/-ameem (*pl+of:* mey); **2.** מטומטם (feebleminded) *nm* metoomtam/-eem (*pl+of:* -ey).

(to) imbibe 1. לספוג *inf* leespog; *pst* safag *(f=p)*; *pres* sofeg; *fut* yeespog; **2.** לשתות (drink) *inf* leeshtot; *pst* shatah; *pres* shoteh; *fut* yeeshteh; **3.** לקלוט (absorb) *inf* leeklot; *pst* kalat; *pres* kolet; *fut* yeeklot.

(to) imbue 1. להרטיב *inf* leharteev; *pst* heerteev; *pres* marteev; *fut* yarteev; **2.** לצבוע (paint) *inf* leetsbo'a'; *pst* tsava' *(v=b)*; *pres* tsove'a'; *fut* yeetsba'.

(to) imitate לחקות *inf* lekhakot; *pst* kheekah; *pres* mekhakeh; *fut* yekhakeh.

imitation חיקוי *nm* kheekoo|y/-yeem (*pl+of:* -yey).

imitator חקיין *nmf* khakyan/-eet.

immaculate 1. זך *adj* zakh/zakah; **2.** ללא דופי (irreproachable) *adj & adv* le-lo dofee.

immaterial חסר חשיבות *adj* khas|ar/-rat khasheevoot.

(it is) immaterial to me עבורי לא חשוב 'avooree lo khashoov.

immediate מידי *adj* meeyadee/-t.

immediately 1. תיכף *adv* tekhef; **2.** מיד (instantly) *adv* meeyad.

immense עצום *adj* 'atsoom/-ah.

immensity 1. עוצם *nm* 'otsem; **2.** גודל (vastness) *nm* godel.

(to) immerse 1. להטביל *vt inf* lehatbeel; *pst* heetbeel; *pres* matbeel; *fut* yatbeel; **2.** לטבול *vi* leetbol; *pst* taval *(v=b)*; *pres* tovel; *fut* yeetbol; **3.** לשקע (sink) *vt inf* leshake'a'; *pst* sheeka'; *pres* meshake'a'; *fut* yeshaka'; **4.** להשרות (dip) *inf* lehashrot; *pst* heeshrah; *pres* mashreh; *fut* yashreh.

immigrant 1. עולה (to Israel) *nmf* 'ol|eh/-ah (*pl:* -eem/-ot; *+of:* -ey); **2.** מהגר (to other countries) *nmf* mehag|er/-eret (*pl:* -reem/-rot; *+of:* -ey).

(to) immigrate 1. לעלות (to Israel) *inf* la'alot; *pst* 'alah; *pres* 'oleh; *fut* ya'aleh; **2.** להגר (to other countries) *inf* lehager; *pst* heeger; *pres* mehager; *fut* yehager.

immigration 1. עלייה (to Israel) *nf* 'alee|yah/-yot (*+of:* -yat); **2.** הגירה (to other countries) *nf* hageer|ah/-ot (*+of:* -at).

imminent ממשמש ובא *adj* memashmesh/-et oo-va/-'ah *(v=b)*.

immobile 1. דומם (motionless) *adj* domem/-et; **2.** יציב (stable) *adj* yatseev/-ah; **3.** בלתי־נייד (fixed) *adj* beeltee na|yad/-yedet.

immodest 1. חסר ענווה *adj* khas|ar/-rat 'anavah; **2.** בלתי צנוע (indecent) *adj* beeltee tsanoo'a'/-tsnoo'ah.

immoral 1. בלתי מוסרי *adj* beeltee moosaree/-t; **2.** מושחת (depraved) *adj* mooshkh|at/-etet.

immorality שחיתות *nf* shkheetoo|t/-yot.

immortal 1. בן־אלמוות *adj* ben/bat almavet; **2.** נצחי (eternal) *adj* neetskhee/-t.

immortality 1. אלמוות *nm* almavet; **2.** נצחיות (eternity) *nf* neetskheeyoot.

immovable 1. דלא ניידי *adj* de-la (*cpr* de-lo) naydey; **2.** מוצק (firm) *adj* mootsak/-ah.

immovable property נכסי דלא ניידי *nm pl* neekhsey de-la (*cpr* de-lo) naydee.

immovables מקרקעין *nm pl* mekarke'een.

immune 1. מחוסן (immunized) *adj* mekhoos|an/-enet; **2.** עמיד (resistant) *adj* 'ameed/-ah.

immunity חסינות *nf* khaseenoo|t/-yot.

(diplomatic) immunity חסינות דיפלומטית *nf* khassenoot deeplomateet.

(parliamentary) immunity חסינות פרלמנטרית *nf* khaseenoot parlamentareet.

immutable שאין להזיז *adj* she-'eyn lehazeez.

imp שדון *nm* shedon/-eem (*pl+of:* -ey).

(to) impair 1. לקלקל *inf* lekalkel; *pst* keelkel; *pres* mekalkel; *fut* yekalkel; **2.** להקטין (lessen) *inf* lehakteen; *pst* heekteen; *pres* makteen; *fut* yakteen; **3.** להטיל פגם (cause defect) *inf* lehateel pegam; *pst* heeteel *etc*; *pres* mateel *etc*; *fut* yateel *etc*.

impairment 1. פגם *nm* pegam/-eem (*pl+of:* -ey); **2.** קילקול *nm* keelkool/-eem (*pl+of:* -ey).

(to) impart 1. למסור (hand over) *inf* leemsor; *pst* masar; *pres* moser; *fut* yeemsor; **2.** לגלות (reveal) *inf* legalot; *pst* geelah; *pres* megaleh; *fut* yegaleh; **3.** להעניק (grant) *inf* leha'aneek; *pst* he'eneek; *pres* ma'aneek; *fut* ya'aneek.

impartial 1. חסר פניות *adj* khas|ar/-rat peneeyot; **2.** אובייקטיבי (objective) *adj* ob'yekteevee/-t.

impartiality 1. חוסר פניות *nm* khoser peneeyot; **2.** אובייקטיביות (objectiveness) *nf* ob'yekteeveyoot.

impassable בלתי עביר *adj* beeltee 'aveer/-ah.

impassioned נלהב *adj* neel|hav/-hevet.

impassive 1. אדיש *adj* adeesh/-ah; **2.** בלתי רגיש (insensitive) *adj* beeltee rageesh/regeeshah.

impatience 1. חוסר סבלנות *nm* khoser savlanoot; **2.** קוצר רוח (restlessness) *nm* kotser-roo'akh.

impatient 1. קצר רוח (restless) *adj* ketsar/keetsrat roo'akh; **2.** חסר סבלנות (irascible) *adj* khas|ar/-rat savlanoot.

(to) impeach 1. להאשים *inf* leha'asheem; *pst* he'esheem; *pres* ma'asheem; *fut* ya'asheem; **2.** להטיל דופי (defile) *inf* lehateel dofee; *pst* heeteel *etc*; *pres* mateel *etc*; *fut* yateel *etc*.

(to) impeach a person's honor לפגוע בכבוד אדם *inf* leefgo'a' bee-khvod *(kh=k)* adam.

impeachment 1. הדחה *nf* hadakh|ah/-ot (*+of:* -at); **2.** העמדה בספק (placing under doubt) *nf* ha'amadah be-safek.

impediment מכשול *nm* meekhshol/-eem (*pl+of:* -ey).

imperceptible בלתי מורגש *adj* beeltee moorg|ash/-eshet.

imperfect 1. בלתי מושלם *adj* beeltee mooshl|am/-emet; **2.** זמן עבר שלא נשלם *(gram.)* (continuous past tense) *nm* zman 'avar she-lo neeshlam.

imperial קיסרי *adj* kesaree/-t.

imperialism אימפריאליזם *nm* eemperyaleezm/-eem (*pl+of:* -ey).

(to) imperil לסכן *inf* lesaken; *pst* seeken; *pres* mesaken; *fut* yesaken.

imperious 1. הכרחי (imperative) *adj* hekhrekhee/-t; **2.** מתנשא (arrogant) *adj* meetnase'/-t.

impersonal 1. בלתי אישי *adj* beeltee eeshee/-t; **2.** סתמי (indefinite) *adj* stamee/-t.

(to) impersonate לגלם *inf* legalem; *pst* geelem; *pres* megalem; *fut* yegalem.

impertinence 1. חוסר שייכות (irrelevance) *nm* khoser shaykhoot **2.** חוצפה (insolence) *nf* khootsp|ah/-ot (*+of:* -at).

impertinent 1. שלא לעניין (irrelevant) *adj* she-lo la-'eenyan; **2.** חצוף (insolent) *adj* khatsoof/-ah.

impervious 1. אטום *adj* atoom/-ah; **2.** בלתי חדיר (impenetrable) *adj* beeltee khadeer/-ah.

impervious to reason נוגד כל היגיון *adj* noged/-et kol heegayon.

impetuous נמהר *adj* neem|har/-heret.

impetus דחף *nm* dakhaf/dekhafeem (*pl+of:* dakhafey).

impious 1. מחלל קודש *adj* mekhalel/-et kodesh; **2.** כופר (heretic) *nmf* kofer/-et.

implacable 1. חסר רחמים (pitiless) *adj* khas|ar/-rat rakhameem; **2.** נוקם ונוטר *adj* nokem/-et ve-noter/-et.

implant שתל *nm* shetel/shtaleem (*pl+of:* sheetley).

(to) implant להשתיל *inf* lehashteel; *pst* heeshteel; *pres* mashteel; *fut* yashteel.

implement 1. מכשיר (instrument) *nm* makhsheer/-eem (*pl+of:* -ey); **2.** כלי (tool) *nm* klee/keleem (*pl+of:* kley).

(to) implement 1. לבצע *inf* levatse'a'; *pst* beetsa' *(b=v)*; *pres* mevatse'a'; *fut* yevatsa'; **2.** להגשים (carry out) lehagsheem; *pst* heegsheem; *pres* magsheem; *fut* yagsheem.

implementation 1. ביצוע *nm* beetsoo|'a'/-'eem (*pl+of:* -'ey); **2.** הגשמה (realization) *nf* hagsham|ah/-ot (*+of:* -at).

implements כלים (tools) *nm* keleem (*pl+of:* kley).

(to) implicate 1. לסבך *inf* lesabekh; *pst* seebekh; *pres* mesabekh; *fut* yesabekh; **2.** להפליל (incriminate) *inf* lehafleel; *pst* heefleel; *pres* mafleel; *fut* yafleel.

implicit 1. ברור *adj* baroor/broorah; **2.** מובן מאליו (obvious) moov|an/-enet me-'el|av/-eha *(m/f)*.

implicitly כמובן *adv* ka-moovan.

(to) implore 1. להפציר *inf* lehaftseer; *pst* heeftseer; *pres* maftseer; *fut* yaftseer; **2.** להתחנן (beseech) *inf* leheetkhanen; *pst* heetkhanen; *pres* meetkhanen; *fut* yeetkhanen.

(to) imply 1. לכלול *inf* leekhlol; *pst* kalal *(k=kh)*; *pres* kolel; *fut* yeekhlol; **2.** לרמוז (intimate) *inf* leermoz; *pst* ramaz; *pres* romez; *fut* yeermoz.

impolite 1. חסר נימוס *adj* khas|ar/-rat neemoos; **2.** גס (rude) gas/-ah.

import יבוא *nm* yevoo.

(to) import לייבא *inf* leyabe; *pst* yeebe; *pres* meyabe; *fut* yeyabe.

import duty מכס mekh|es/-aseem (*pl+of:* meekhsey).

import license רשיון יבוא *nm* reeshyon/-ot yevoo.

import trade סחר יבוא *nm* sekhar yevoo.

importance חשיבות *nf* khasheevoo|t/-yot.

important חשוב *adj* khashoov/-ah.

importer יבואן *nmf* yevoo'an/-eet (*pl:* -eem/-eeyot; *+of:* -ey).

imports דברי יבוא *nm pl* deevrey yevoo.

(to) impose להטיל *inf* lehateel; *pst* heeteel; *pres* mateel; *fut* yateel.

(to) impose upon לכפות *inf* leekhpot; *pst* kafah *(k=kh)*; *pres* kofeh; *fut* yeekhpeh.

imposing מרשים *adj* marsheem/-ah

imposition 1. אכיפה *nf* akheef|ah/-ot (*+of:* -at); **2.** הטלה (tax) *nf* hatal|ah/-ot (*+of:* -at); **3.** רמאות (fraud) *nm* rama'oo|t/-yot.

impossibility 1. אי אפשרות *nf* ee efsharoot; **2.** חוסר יכולת *nm* khoser yekholet.

impossible 1. אי אפשר *adv* ee efshar; **2.** בלתי אפשרי (unfeasible) *adj* beeltee efsharee/-t; **3.** בלתי נסבל *adj* beeltee neesb|al/-elet.

impostor 1. מתחזה *nmf* meetkhaz|eh/-ah; **2.** נוכל (swindler) *nm* nokh|el/-leem (*pl+of:* -ley); **3.** רמאי (deceiver) *nmf* rama|y/-'eet.

imposture 1. התחזות *nf* heetkhazoo|t/-yot; **2.** הונאה (fraud) *nf* hona|'ah/-'ot (+*of:* -'at); **3.** גניבת דעת (deceit) *nf* gnev|at/-vot da'at.

impotence 1. אין־אונות (sexual) *nm* eyn-onoot; **2.** חולשה (weakness) *nf* khoolsh|ah/-ot (+*of:* -at).

impotent 1. חסר כוח גברא (sexually) *adj* khas|ar/-rat ko'akh gavra; **2.** חסר יכולת (unable) *adj* khas|ar/-rat yekholet; **3.** אימפוטנט *nmf* eempotent/-eet.

(to) impoverish לרושש *inf* leroshesh; *pst* roshesh; *pres* meroshesh; *fut* yeroshesh.

(to) impregnate 1. להיספג *inf* leheesafeg; *pst & pres* neespag (*p=f*); *fut* yeesafeg; **2.** לעבר (fecundate) *inf* le'aber; *pst* 'eeber; *pres* me'aber; *fut* ye'aber.

impress 1. חיקוק *nm* kheekook/-eem (*pl+of:* -ey); **2.** טביעה *nf* tvee|'ah/-'ot (+*of:* -'at).

(to) impress 1. להרשים (make impression) *inf* leharsheem; *pst* heersheem; *pres* marsheem; *fut* yarsheem; **2.** להחתים (make sign) *inf* lehakhteem; *pst* hekhteem; *pres* makhteem; *fut* yakhteem.

impression 1. רושם *nm* roshem/reshameem (*pl+of:* reeshmey); **2.** חותם (imprint) *nm* khotam/-ot.

impressive 1. מרשים *adj* marsheem/-ah; **2.** משכנע (convincing) *adj* meshakhn|e'a'/-a'at.

imprint 1. חקיקה *nf* khakeek|ah/-ot (+*of:* -at); **2.** חותם (impression) *nf* khotam.

(to) imprint 1. לחקוק *inf* lakhkok; *pst* khakak; *pres* khokek; *fut* yakhkok; **2.** לטבוע (impress) *inf* leetbo'a'; *pst* tava' (*v=b*); *pres* tove'a'; *fut* yeetba'.

(to) imprison 1. לכלוא (jail) *inf* leekhlo; *pst* kala (*k=kh*); *pres* kole; *fut* yeekhla; **2.** לאסור (arrest) *inf* le'esor; *pst* asar; *pres* oser; *fut* ye'esor.

imprisonment 1. כליאה (jailing) *nf* klee|'ah/-'ot (+*of:* -'at); **2.** מאסר (arrest) *nm* ma'as|ar/-areem (*pl+of:* -rey).

improbable בלתי סביר *adj* beeltee saveer/sveerah.

impromptu 1. מאולתר (improvised) *adj* me'oolt|ar/-eret; **2.** במאולתר (unexpectedly) *adv* bee-me'ooltar.

improper 1. לא נכון *adj* lo nakhon/nekhonah; **2.** בלתי מתאים (unfitting) *adj* beeltee mat'eem/-ah.

(to) improve 1. לשפר *inf* leshaper; *pst* sheeper; *pres* meshaper; *fut* yeshaper; **2.** להשביח (better) *inf* lehashbee'akh; *pst* heeshbee'akh; *pres* mashbee'akh; *fut* yashbee'akh; **3.** לשכלל (perfect) *vt inf* leshakhlel; *pst* sheekhlel; *pres* meshakhlel; *fut* yeshakhlel.

(to) improve one's time לצמצם הזמן הדרוש *inf* letsamtsem ha-zman ha-daroosh; *pst* tseemtsem *etc*; *pres* metsamtsem *etc*; *fut* yetsamtsem *etc.*

(to) improve upon לשפר לעומת *inf* leshaper le'oomat; *pst* sheeper *etc*; *pres* meshaper *etc*; *fut* yeshaper *etc.*

improvement 1. שיפור *nm* sheepoor/-eem (*pl+of:* -ey); **2.** השבחה (betterment) *nf* hashbakh|ah/-ot (+*of:* -at); **3.** שכלול (perfection) *nm* sheekhlool/-eem (*pl+of:* -ey).

improvisation אלתור *nm* eeltoor/-eem (*pl+of:* -ey).

(to) improvise לאלתר *inf* le'alter; *pst* eelter; *pres* me'alter; *fut* ye'alter.

imprudence 1. איוולת *nf* eevelet; **2.** חוסר זהירות (carelessness) *nm* khoser zeheeroot.

imprudent 1. בלתי נבון (unwise) beeltee navon/nevonah; **2.** בלתי זהיר (careless) *adj* beeltee zaheer/zeheerah.

impudence חוצפה *nf* khootsp|ah/-ot (+*of:* -at).

impudent חצוף *adj* khatsoof/-ah.

impulse דחף *nm* dakhaf/dekhafeem.

(to act on) impulse לפעול לפי דחף *inf* leef'ol lefee dakhaf; *pst* pa'al (*p=f*) *etc*; *pres* po'el *etc*; *fut* yeef'al *etc.*

impulsive אימפולסיבי *adj* eempoolseevee/-t.

impunity 1. אין עונש eyn 'onesh; **2.** לית דין ולית דיין (no justice, no judge) let deen ve-let dayan.

impure 1. מזוהם *adj* mezo|ham/-hemet; **2.** לא טהור (unclean) *adj* lo tahor/tehorah.

impurity 1. טומאה *nf* toom|'ah/-'ot (+*of:* -'at); **2.** זוהמה (filth) zooham|ah/-ot (+*of:* -at).

imputation 1. הטלת דופי *nf* hatal|at/-ot dofee; **2.** גינוי (censure) *nm* geenoo|y/-yeem (*pl+of:* -yey).

(to) impute 1. לייחס ל־ (ascribe) *inf* leyakhes le-; *pst* yeekhes le-; *pres* meyakhes le-; *fut* yeyakhes le-; **2.** לטפול על (attribute to) leetpol 'al; *pst* tafal 'al (*f=p*); *pres* tofel 'al; *fut* yeetpol 'al; **3.** להאשים (accuse) *inf* leha'asheem; *pst* he'esheem; *pres* ma'asheem; *fut* ya'asheem.

in 1. ב־ (prefixes) be-, bee-, ba-; **2.** בתוך (prep: inside) be-tokh; **3.** פנימה (into) *adv* peneemah.

(is the train) in? האם הגיעה הרכבת? ha-'eem heegee'ah ha-rakevet?

(to come) in להיכנס *inf* leheekanes; *pst & pres* neekhnas (*kh=k*); *fut* yeekanes.

(to put) in 1. להכניס *inf* lehakhnees; *pst* heekhnees; *pres* makhnees; *fut* yakhnees; **2.** להשקיע (invest) *inf* lehashkee'a'; *pst* heeshkee'a'; *pres* mashkee'a'; *fut* yashkee'a'.

in a week בעוד שבוע *adv* be-'od shavoo'a'.

(come) in a week *or* **two** תבוא בעוד שבוע שבועיים *v* (*fut as imp*) tavo/-'ee (*m/f*) be-'od shavoo'a' shvoo'ayeem.

(to be) in and out להיות יוצא ונכנס *inf* leehyot yotse ve-neekhnas; *pst* hayah *etc*; *pres* heeno *etc*; *fut* yeehyeh *etc.*

(to have it) in for someone לשמור טינה ל־ *inf* leeshmor teenah le-; *pst* shamar *etc*; *pres* shomer *etc*; *fut* yeeshmor *etc.*

in haste בחופזה *adv* be-khofzah.

(the tallest) in his class הגבוה מכולם בכיתה *adj* ha-gavoha/gvohah mee-koolam ba-keetah.

in the morning בבוקר *adv* ba-boker.

(at three) in the morning בשלוש לפנות בוקר be-shalosh leefnot boker.

(dressed) in white עוטה לבן *adj* 'ot|eh/-ah lavan.

(to be) in with someone להיות שותף למישהו ב־ *inf* leehyot shootaf le-meeshehoo be-; *pst* hayah *etc*; *pres* heeno *etc*; *fut* yeehyeh *etc.*

in writing בכתב *adv* bee-khtav (*kh=k*).

inability חוסר יכולת *nm* khoser yekholet.

inaccessible לא נגיש *adj* lo nageesh/negeeshah.

inaccurate לא מדויק *adj* lo-medoo|yak/-yeket.

inactive לא פעיל *adj* lo pa'eel/pe'eelah.
inactivity חוסר פעילות *nm* khoser pe'eeloot.
inadequate 1. לא מספיק (insufficient) *adj* lo maspeek/-ah; **2.** בלתי מתאים (unsuited) *adj* beeltee mat'eem/-ah.
inadvertent 1. שגוי *adj* shagooy/shgooyah; **2.** רשלן (negligent) *nmf & adj* rashlan/-eet.
inadvertently בשגגה *adv* bee-shgagah.
inadvisable 1. לא מעשי (not practical) *adj* lo ma'asee/-t; **2.** לא כדאי (not worthwhile) *adj* lo keday/kada'eet.
inanimate 1. ללא רוח חיים *adj* le-lo roo'akh khayeem; **2.** דומם (motionless) *adj* domem/-et.
inasmuch 1. הואיל (whereas) ho'eel; **2.** מאחר ש־ (since) me-akhar she-.
inasmuch as 1. הואיל ו־ (whereas) ho'eel ve-; **2.** מאחר־ש (since) me-akhar she-.
inattentive 1. רשלן (negligent) *adj* rashlan/-eet; **2.** שלא שם לב (paying no attention) *adj* she-lo sam/-ah lev.
(to) inaugurate 1. לחנוך *inf* lakhnokh; *pst* khanakh; *pres* khonekh; *fut* yakhnokh; **2.** לפתוח (open) *inf* leefto'akh; *pst* patakh *(p=f)*; *pres* pote'akh; *fut* yeeftakh.
inauguration 1. חנוכה *nf* khanook|ah/-ot (+*of:* -at); **2.** פתיחה (opening) *nf* peteekh|ah/-ot (+*of:* -at).
inboard בפנים אונייה *adv* bee-fneem *(f=p)* oneeyah.
inborn 1. מולד *adj* mool|ad/-edet; **2.** מלידה (from birth) *adv* mee-leydah.
incandescent 1. לוהט *adj* lohet/-et; **2.** יוקד (aglow) *adj* yoked/-et.
incapable 1. לא מסוגל (unfit) *adj* lo mesoog|al/-elet; **2.** חסר יכולת *adj* (unable) khas|ar/-rat yekholet.
(to) incapacitate 1. לשלול כושר *inf* leeshlol kosher; *pst* shalal *etc*; *pres* sholel *etc*; *fut* yeeshlol *etc*; **2.** לפסול (disqualify) *inf* leefsol; *pst* pasal *(p=f)*; *pres* posel; *fut* yeefsol.
incendiary 1. מבעיר *adj* mav'eer/-ah; **2.** מצית (arsonist) *adj* matseet/-ah; **3.** מסית (instigating) *adj* meseet/-ah.
incendiary bomb פצצת תבערה *nf* peetsets|at/-ot tav'erah.
incense קטורת *nf* ketoret.
incentive תמריץ *nm* tamreets/-eem (*pl+of:* -ey)
incessant בלתי פוסק *adj* beeltee posek/-et.
inch 1. אינץ' *nm* eench/-eem (*pl+of:* -ey); **2.** 2,54 ס"מ (2.54 cm) shnayeem peseek khameesheem ve-arba'ah senteemetreem.
(every) inch a man גבר מכף רגל ועד ראש *nm* gever mee-kaf regel ve-'ad rosh.
(within an) inch of לכדי אינץ אחד מ־ lee-khdey eench ekhad mee-.
(by) inches קמעה קמעה keem'ah keem'ah.
incidence התרחשות *nf* heetrakhshoo|t/-yot.
incident 1. מקרה *nm* meekr|eh/-eem (*pl+of:* -ey); **2.** אירוע (occurrence) *nm* eeroo|'a'/-'eem (*pl+of:* -'ey).
incidental מקרי *adj* meekree/-t.
incidentally באקראי *adv* be-akray.
incidentals הוצאות בלתי צפויות *nf pl* hotsa'ot beeltee tsfooyot.
incipient 1. התחלי *adj* hetkhelee/-t; **2.** מתחיל (initial) *adj* matkheel/-ah.
incision 1. חיתוך *nm* kheetookh/-eem (*pl+of:* -ey); **2.** חתך (cut) khetekh/khatakh|eem (*pl+of:* -ey).
(to) incite להסית *inf* lehaseet; *pst* heseet; *pres* meseet; *fut* yaseet.
incitement 1. הסתה *nf* hasat|ah/-ot (+*of:* -at). **2.** שיסוי (instigation) *nf* sheesoo|y/-yeem (*pl+of:* -yey)
inclement סגרירי *adj* sagreeree/-t.
inclination נטייה *nf* netee|yah/-yot (+*of:* -yat).
(to) incline לנטות *inf* leentot; *pst* natah; *pres* noteh; *fut* yeeteh.
(to) include לכלול *inf* leekhlol; *pst* kalal; *pres* kolel; *fut* yeekhlol *(k=kh)*.
inclusive 1. כולל *adj* kolel/-et; **2.** ועד בכלל (including) *adv* ve-'ad bee-khlal *(kh=k)*.
(from Sunday to Friday) inclusive 1. מיום א' ועד ו' כולל mee-yom alef ve-'ad vav kolel; **2.** מיום א' ועד ו' ועד בכלל mee-yom alef ve-'ad vav ve-'ad bee-khlal *(kh=k)*.
incoherent 1. חסר היגיון (senseless) *adj* khas|ar/-rat heegayon; **2.** מבולבל (mixed up) *adj* mevoolb|al/-elet.
income הכנסה *nf* hakhnas|ah/-ot (+*of:* -at).
income tax מס הכנסה *nm* mas hakhnasah.
income tax consultant יועץ מס *nm* yo'ets/yo'atsey mas.
incoming נכנס *adj* neekhn|as/-eset.
incomparable ללא השוואה *adj* le-lo hashva'ah.
incompatible 1. לא תואם (unfitting) *adj* lo to'em/-et; **2.** מנוגד (contrary) *adj* menoog|ad/-edet.
incompetent 1. לא מסוגל (incapable) *adj* lo mesoog|al/-elet; **2.** קצר־יד (powerless) *adj* ketsar/keetsrat yad.
incomplete לא מושלם *adj* lo mooshl|am/-emet.
incomprehensible 1. סתום *adj* satoom/stoomah; **2.** לא מובן (unintelligible) *adj* lo moov|an/-enet.
inconceivable לא מתקבל על הדעת *adj* lo meetkabel/-et 'al ha-da'at.
inconsiderate חסר התחשבות *adj* khas|ar/-rat heetkhashvoot.
inconsistency חוסר עיקביות *nm* khoser 'eekveeyoot.
inconsistent 1. לא עקיב *adj* lo 'akeev/-ah; **2.** לא עיקבי *adj* lo 'eekvee/-t.
inconspicuous 1. לא בולט *adj* lo bolet/-et; **2.** לא מורגש (not noticeable) *adj* lo moorg|ash/-eshet.
inconstancy 1. הפכפכנות *nf* hafakhpekhanoo|t/-yot; **2.** קלות דעת (lightheadedness) *nf* kaloot da'at.
inconstant 1. הפכפך *adj* hafakhpakh/-ah; **2.** לא יציב *adj* lo'yatseev/-ah.
incontestable שאין חולקים עליו *adj* she-'eyn kholkeen 'al|av/-eha.
inconvenience 1. אי־נוחות (discomfort) *nf* ee-nokhoo|t/-yot; **2.** אי־נעימות (unpleasantness) *f* ee-ne'eemoo|t/-yot.
inconvenient לא נוח *adj* lo no'akh/-khah.

incorporate 1. מאגד *adj* me'aged/-et; **2.** מחבר (uniting) *adj* mekhaber/-et.

(to) incorporate 1. לחבר (unite) *inf* lekhaber; *pst* kheeber; *pres* mekhaber; *fut* yekhaber; **2.** לאגד (organize) *inf* le'aged; *pst* eeged; *pres* me'aged; *fut* ye'aged.

incorrect 1. לא מדויק (inexact) *adj* lo medoo|yak/-yeket; **2.** לא נכון (inaccurate) *adj* lo nakhon/nekhonah; **3.** לקוי (faulty) *adj* lakooy/lekooyah.

incorrigible ללא תקנה *adj* le-lo takanah.

increase 1. גידול *nm* geedool/-eem (*pl+of:* -ey); **2.** תוספת (addition) *nf* tos|efet/-afot (*pl+of:* -fot).

(to) increase 1. להגדיל *inf* lehagdeel; *pst* heegdeel; *pres* magdeel; *fut* yagdeel; **2.** להגביר (intensify) *inf* lehagbeer; *pst* heegbeer; *pres* magbeer; *fut* yagbeer.

increasingly במידה גוברת והולכת *adv* be-meedah goveret ve-holekhet.

incredible 1. לא ייאמן (unbelievable) *adj* lo ye'amen/te'amen; **2.** פנטסטי (fantastic) *adj* fantastee/-t.

incredulity 1. חוסר אמונה *nm* khoser emoonah; **2.** ספקנות *nf* safkanoo|t/-yot.

incredulous ספקן *nmf* safkan/-eet.

increment 1. תוספת (supplement) *nf* tos|efet/-afot (*pl+of:* -fot); **2.** גידול (increase) *nm* geedool/-eem (*pl+of:* -ey).

(to) incriminate להפליל *inf* lehafleel; *pst* heefleel; *pres* mafleel; *fut* yafleel.

incubator 1. מדגרה *nf* madger|ah/-ot (*+of:* -at); **2.** אינקובטור *nm* eenkoobator/-eem (*pl+of:* -ey).

(to) inculcate להחדיר *inf* lehakhdeer; *pst* hekhdeer; *pres* makhdeer; *fut* yakhdeer.

(to) incur להיכנס להוצאות *inf* leheekanes le-hotsa'ot; *pst & pres* neekhnas *etc* (*kh=k*); *fut* yeekanes *etc.*

incurable חשוך מרפא *adj* khasookh/-at marpe.

indebted 1. חייב *adj* kha|yav/-yevet; **2.** אסיר תודה (grateful) *nmf & adj* aseer/-at todah.

indebtedness חבות *nf* khavoo|t/-yot.

indecency 1. חוסר הגינות (unfairness) *nm* khoser hageenoot; **2.** חוסר נימוס (impoliteness) *nm* khoser neemoos; **3.** גסות (rudeness) *nf* gasoo|t/-yot; **4.** אי־צניעות (immodesty) *nf* ee-tsnee'oot

indecent 1. לא הוגן (unfair) *adj* lo hogen/-et; **2.** לא מהוגן (irrespectable) *adj* lo mehoog|an/-enet; **3.** גס (coarse) *adj* gas/-ah; **4.** לא צנוע (immodest) *adj* lo tsanoo'a'/tsnoo'ah.

indecision 1. הססנות (hesitation) *nf* hasesanoo|t/-yot; **2.** חוסר החלטיות (irresolution) *nm* khoser hekhleteeyoot.

indeed באמת *adv* be-'emet.

indefensible 1. שאינו ניתן להגנה *adj* she-eyn|o/-ah neet|an/-enet le-haganah; **2.** לא מוצדק (unjustifiable) *adj* lo mootsd|ak/-eket.

indefinite 1. לא מוגדר *adj* lo moogd|ar/-eret; **2.** סתמי (vague) *adj* stamee/-t.

indelible לא מחיק *adj* lo makheek/mekheekah.

indelicate 1. לא מעודן *adj* lo me'ood|an/-enet; **2.** לא צנוע (immodest) *adj* lo tsanoo'a'/tsenoo'ah.

(to) indemnify 1. לשפות *inf* leshapot; *pst* sheepah; *pres* meshapeh; *fut* yeshapeh; **2.** לפצות (compensate) *inf* lefatsot; *pst* peetsah (*p=f*); *pres* mefatseh; *fut* yefatseh.

indemnity 1. שיפוי *nm* sheepoo|y/-yeem (*pl+of:* -yey); **2.** פיצוי (compensation) *nm* peetsoo|y/-yeem (*pl+of:* -yey).

(to) indent 1. לטבוע חותם *inf* leetbo'a' khotam; *pst* tava' (*v=b*) *etc*; *pres* tove'a' *etc*; *fut* yeetba' *etc*; **2.** להפנים (line) *inf* lehafneem; *pst* heefneem; *pres* mafneem; *fut* yafneem.

independence 1. עצמאות *nf* 'atsma'oot; **2.** אי־תלות (self-reliance) *nf* ee-tloot.

independent 1. עצמאי *nmf* atsma'ee/-t; **2.** לא תלוי (self-reliant) *adj* lo talooy/tlooyah.

indescribable שלא יתואר *adj* she-lo yeto'ar/teto'ar.

index 1. מפתח עניינים (table of contents) *nm* mafte'akh/-khot ha'eenyaneem; **2.** אינדקס *nm* eendeks/-eem (*pl+of:* -ey); **3.** מדד (measurement) *nm* madad/medad|eem (*pl+of:* -ey).

(alphabetic) index 1. אינדקס אלפביתי *nm* eendeks/-eem alefbetee/-yeem; **2.** אינדקס ערוך לפי אלף־בית *nm* eendeks 'arookh lefee alef-bet.

(building costs) index 1. מדד יוקר הבנייה *nm* madad/medadey yoker ha-beneeyah; **2.** אינדקס יוקר הבניה *nm* eendeks/-ey yoker ha-beneeyah.

(cost of living) index 1. מדד יוקר המחיה *nm* madad/medadey yoker ha-meekhyah; **2.** אינדקס יוקר המחיה *nm* eendeks/-ey yoker ha-meekhyah.

(to) index 1. למפתח *v inf* lemafte'akh; *pst* meeftakh; *pres* memafte'akh; *fut* yemafte'akh; **2.** לערוך בסדר אלף־בית (arrange in alphabetic order) *inf* la'arokh be-seder alef-bet; *pst* 'arakh *etc*; *pres* 'orekh *etc*; *fut* ya'arokh *etc.*

index finger אצבע *nf* etsb|a'/-a'ot (*cpr* etsba').

Indian 1. אינדיאני (American) *nmf & adj* eendee'anee/-t; **2.** הודי (from India) *nmf* hodee/-t; **3.** הודי *adj* hodee/-t.

(to) indicate 1. להצביע (point out) *inf* lehatsbee'a'; *pst* heetsbee'a'; *pres* matsbee'a'; *fut* yatsbee'a'; **2.** לציין (mark) *inf* letsayen; *pst* tseeyen; *pres* metsayen; *fut* yetsayen.

indication 1. ציון *nm* tseeyoon/-eem (*pl+of:* -ey); **2.** הצבעה *nf* (pointing out) hatsba|'ah/-'ot (*+of:* -'at); **3.** רמז (hint) *nm* remez/-azeem (*pl+of:* reemzey).

indicative 1. מצביע על *adj* matsbee|'a'/-'ah 'al; **2.** מציין *adj* (marking) metsayen/-et.

(to) indict להאשים כחוק *inf* leha'asheem ka-khok; *pst* he'esheem *etc*; *pres* ma'asheem *etc*; *fut* ya'asheem *etc.*

indictment אישום *nm* eeshoom/-eem (*pl+of:* -ey).

indifference 1. אדישות *nf* adeeshoo|t/-yot; **2.** שוויון נפש (nonchalance) *nm* sheevyon nefesh.

indifferent 1. אדיש *adj* adeesh/-ah; **2.** שווה נפש (unconcerned) *adj* shveh/shvat nefesh.

indigenous מקומי *adj* mekomee/-t.

indigent 1. דל *adj* dal/-ah; **2.** נצרך (needy) *adj* neetsr|akh/-ekhet.

indigestion קלקול קיבה *nm* keelkool/-ey keyvah.

indignant מתרעם *adj* meetra'em/-et.

indignantly בכעס *adv* be-kha'as (*kh=k*).

indignation 1. חרון *nm* kharon; **2.** כעס (anger) *nm* ka'as.

indignity 1. עלבון *nm* 'elbon/-ot; **2.** פגיעה בכבוד (disrespect) *nf* pegee|'ah/-'ot be-khavod *(kh=k)*.

indigo אינדיגו *nm* eendeego.

indigo blue כחול כהה *adj* kakhol/kekhoolah keheh/kehah.

indirect 1. לא ישיר *adj* lo yasheer/yesheerah; **2.** עקיף (roundabout) *adj* 'akeef/-ah.

indiscreet 1. שאינו שומר סוד *adj* she-'eyn|o/-ah shomer/-et sod; **2.** לא זהיר (careless) lo zaheer/zeheerah.

indiscretion 1. גילוי סוד *nm* geeloo|y/-yey sod/-ot; **2.** הדלפה (leak) *nf* hadlaf|ah/-ot (+*of:* -at).

indispensable 1. הכרחי *adj* hekhrekhee/-t; **2.** חיוני (vital) *adj* kheeyoonee/-t.

(to) indispose להחלות *vt* lehakhlot; *pst* hekhlah; *pres* makhleh; *fut* yakhleh.

indisposed 1. שלא בקו הבריאות *adj* she-lo be-kav ha-bree'oot; **2.** אינו נוטה (not inlined) *v pres & adj* eyn|o/-ah not|eh/-ah.

indisposition 1. מחלה קלה *nf* makhl|ah/-ot kal|ah/-ot; **2.** חולשה (weakness) *nf* khoolsh|ah/-ot (+*of:* -at).

indistinct 1. עמום *adj* 'amoom/-ah; **2.** מעורפל (obscured) *adj* me'oorp|al/-elet.

individual 1. בן־אדם (person) *nm* ben/beney adam; **2.** יחיד (private person) *nm* yakheed/yekheedeem.

individuality 1. אישיות (personality) *nf* eesheeyoot; **2.** פרטיות (privacy) *nf* prateeyoot.

indivisible לא מתחלק *adj* lo meetkhalek/-et.

(to) indoctrinate לשנן *inf* leshanen; *pst* sheenen; *pres* meshanen; *fut* yeshanen.

indolence 1. בטלה *nf* batal|ah/-ot (+*of:* -at); **2.** עצלות (laziness) *nf* 'atsloo|t/-yot.

indolent 1. עצל (lazy) *adj* 'atsel/-ah; **2.** מתבטל (loafer) *adj* meetbatel/-et.

indomitable 1. שאין להכניעו *adj* she-'eyn lehakhnee|'o/-'ah; **2.** עיקש (staunch) *adj* 'eekesh/-et.

indoor שבפנים הבית *adj* she-bee-fneem ha-bayeet *(f=p)*.

indoors 1. בבית *adv* ba-bayeet; **2.** בין כותלי הבית (inside the house) *adv* beyn kotley ha-bayeet.

(to go) indoors להיכנס הביתה *inf* leheekanes ha-baytah; *pst & pres* neekhnas *(kh=k) etc*; *fut* yeekanes *etc*.

(to) induce 1. לפתות (entice) *inf* lefatot; *pst* peetah; *pres* mefateh; *fut* yefateh; **2.** להמריץ (prod) *inf* lehamreets; *pst* heemreets; *pres* mamreets; *fut* yamreets.

inducement 1. פיתוי (enticement) *nm* peetoo|y/-yeem (*pl+of:* -yey); **2.** המרצה (goading) *nf* hamrats|ah/-ot (+*of:* -at).

(to) induct 1. לגייס (mobilize) *inf* legayes; *pst* geeyes; *pres* megayes; *fut* yegayes; **2.** להכניס לתפקיד *inf* lehakhnees le-tafkeed; *pst* heekhnees *etc*; *pres* makhnees *etc*; *fut* yakhnees *etc*.

induction 1. גיוס (military draft) *nm* geeyoos/-eem (*pl+of:* -ey); **2.** השראה (inspiration) *nf* hashra|'ah/-'ot (+*of:* -'at); **3.** הסקה מן הפרט על הכלל (method) *nf* hasakah meen ha-prat 'al ha-klal; **4.** אינדוקציה *nf* eendooktsee|yah/-yot (+*of:* -yat).

(to) indulge 1. להתמכר *v rfl inf* leheetmaker; *pst* heetmaker; *pres* meetmaker; *fut* yeetmaker; **2.** לפנק (pamper) *vt inf* lefanek; *pst* peenek *(p=f)*; *pres* mefanek; *fut* yefanek.

(to) indulge in לשגות ב־ *inf* leeshgot be-; *pst* shagah be-; *pres* shogeh be-; *fut* yeeshgeh be-.

indulgence 1. התמכרות *nf* heetmakroo|t/-yot; **2.** ותרנות (leniency) *nf* vatranoo|t/-yot; **3.** פינוק (spoiling) *nm* peenook/-eem (*pl+of:* -ey).

indulgent 1. ותרן *nmf & adj* vatran/-eet; **2.** נעתר (condescending) *adj* ne'et|ar/-eret.

industrial 1. חרושתי *adj* kharoshtee/-t; **2.** תעשייתי (manufacturing) *adj* ta'aseeyatee/-t.

industrialist 1. חרושתן *nmf* kharoshtan/-eet; **2.** תעשיין (manufacturer) *nmf* ta'aseeyan/-eet.

industrious חרוץ (diligent) *adj* kharoots/-ah.

industry 1. חרושת *nf* kharoshet; **2.** תעשייה (manufacture) *nf* ta'asee|yah/-yot (+*of:* -yat); **3.** חריצות (diligence) *nf* khareetsoo|t/-yot.

ineffable שאין לבטאו *adj* she-'eyn levat|'o/-'ah *(v=b)*.

ineffective חסר תוצאות *adj* khas|ar/-rat totsa'ot.

inefficient לא יעיל *adj* lo ya'eel/ye'eelah.

ineligible פסול להיבחר *adj* pasool/pesoolah leheebakher.

inequality חוסר שוויון *nm* khoser sheevyon.

inert 1. דומם *adj* domem/-et; **2.** חסר תנועה (motionless) *adj* khas|ar/-rat tenoo'ah.

inertia 1. התמד *nm* hetmed/-eem (*pl+of:* -ey); **2.** פיגור (lag) *nm* peegoor/-eem (*pl+of:* -ey).

inestimable לאין ערוך *adj* le-'eyn 'arokh

inevitable בלתי נמנע *adj* beeltee neemn|a'/a'at.

inexhaustible לא אכזב *adj* lo akhzav.

inexpedient 1. לא כדאי *adj* lo kada'ee/-t; **2.** לא יעיל (inefficient) *adj* lo ya'eel/ye'eelah.

inexpensive 1. לא יקר *adj* lo yakar/yekarah; **2.** זול (cheap) *adj* zol/-ah.

inexperience 1. חוסר ניסיון *nm* khoser neesayon; **2.** טירונות (novitiate) *nf* teeronoo|t/-yot.

inexperienced 1. חסר ניסיון *adj* khas|ar/-rat neesayon; **2.** טירון (novice) *nmf & adj* teeron/-eet.

inexplicable שאין להסבירו *adj* she-eyn lehasbeer|o/-ah *(m/f)*.

inexpressible שאינו בר־ביטוי *adj* she-eyn|o/-ah bar/bat beetooy *(m/f)*.

infallible שלעולם אינו טועה *adj* she-le-'olam eyn|o/-ah to|'eh/-'ah *(m/f)*.

infamous מביש *adj* meveesh/-ah.

infamy 1. ביזיון *nm* beez|ayon/-yonot (+*of:* -yon); **2.** קלון (shame) *nm* kalon/klonot (+*of:* klon).

infancy ינקות *nf* yankoo|t/-yot.

infant 1. יונק (suckling) *nmf* yonek/-et (*pl:* yonk|eem/-ot; *pl+of:* -ey); **2.** פעוט (small child) *nmf* pa'oot/-ah (+*of:* -at/-ey/-ot).

infantile 1. תינוקי *adj* teenokee/-t; **2.** ילדותי (childish) *adj* yaldootee/-t.

infantry 1. חיל רגלים *nm* kheyl/-ot ragleem; **2.** חי״ר (*acr of* 1) *nm* kheer.

(to) infect 1. לזהם *inf* lezahem; *pst* zeehem; *pres* mezahem; *fut* yezahem; **2.** להדביק (contaminate) *inf* lehadbeek; *pst* heedbeek; *pres* madbeek; *fut* yadbeek.

infection 1. זיהום *nm* zeehoom/-eem (*pl+of:* -ey); **2.** אילוח (contamination) *nm* eeloo|'akh/-kheem (*pl+of:* -khey).

infectious 1. מזהם *adj* mezahem/-et; **2.** מדביק (contagious) *adj* madbeek/-ah.

infectious disease מחלה מידבקת *nf* makhl|ah/-ot meedab|eket/-kot.

(to) infer להסיק (conclude) *inf* lehaseek; *pst* heeseek; *pres* maseek; *fut* yaseek.

inference מסקנה *nf* maskan|ah/-ot (*+of:* -at).

inferior נחות *adj* nakhoot/nekhootah.

inferiority נחיתות *nf* nekheetoo|t/-yot.

inferiority complex תסביך נחיתות *nm* tasbeekh/-ey nekheetoot.

infernal שטני *adj* stanee/-t.

infernal machine מכונת תופת *nf* mekhon|at/-ot tofet.

inferno תופת *nm* tofet.

(to) infest לשרוץ *inf* leeshrots; *pst* sharats; *pres* shorets; *fut* yeeshrots.

infidel 1. כופר (heretic) *nmf* kof|er/-eret (*pl:* -reem/-rot; *+of:* -rey); **2.** בוגד (traitor) *nmf & adj* bog|ed/-edet (*pl:* -deem/-dot; *+of:* -dey).

(to) infiltrate להסתנן *inf* leheestanen; *pst* heestanen; *pres* meestanen; *fut* yeestanen.

infinite אין־סופי *adj* en sofee/-t.

infinitive שורש הפועל *nm* shoresh ha-po'al.

infinity אין־סוף *nm* en sof/-eem (*pl+of:* -ey).

infirm 1. חולה *adj* khol|eh/-ah; **2.** מהסס (hesitant) *adj* mehases/-et.

infirmary מרפאה *nf* meerp|a'ah/-a'ot (*+of:* -e'at/-e'ot).

infirmity 1. מחלה *nf* makhl|ah/-ot (*+of:* -at); **2.** מיחוש (ache) *nm* mekhosh/-eem (*pl+of:* -ey).

(to) inflame לשלהב *inf* leshalhev; *pst* sheelhev; *pres* meshalhev; *fut* yeshalhev.

inflammation 1. דלקת *nf* dal|eket/-akot; **2.** קדחת (fever) *nf* kadakhat.

(to) inflate לנפח *inf* lenape'akh; *pst* neepakh; *pres* menape'akh; *fut* yenapakh.

inflation 1. ניפוח *nm* neepoo|'akh/-kheem (*pl+of:* -khey); **2.** הפקעת שערים (profiteering) *nf* hafka|'at/-'ot she'areem; **3.** אינפלציה *nf* eenflats|yah/-yot (*+of:* -yat).

inflationary אינפלציוני *adj* eenflatsyonee/-t.

inflection 1. נטייה *nf* netee|yah/-yot (*+of:* -yat); **2.** גיוון הקול (voice modulation) *nm* geevoon/-ey kol.

(to) inflict 1. להטיל על *inf* lehateel 'al; *pst* heeteel 'al; *pres* mateel 'al; *fut* yateel 'al; **2.** להנחית על (bring upon) *inf* lehankheet 'al; *pst* heenkheet 'al; *pres* mankheet 'al; *fut* yankheet 'al.

influence השפעה *nf* hashpa|'ah/-'ot (*+of:* -'at).

(to) influence להשפיע *inf* lehashpee'a'; *pst* heeshpee'a'; *pres* mashpee'a'; *fut* yashpee'a'.

influential בעל השפעה *nmf* ba'al/-at hashpa'ah.

influenza שפעת *nf* shapa'at.

influx 1. זרם *nm* zerem/zrameem (*pl+of:* zeermey); **2.** זרימה פנימה (inflow) *nf* zreem|ah/-ot peneemah.

(to) infold לעטוף *inf* la'atof; *pst* 'ataf; *pres* 'otef; *fut* ya'atof.

(to) inform 1. להודיע *inf* lehodee'a'; *pst* hodee'a'; *pres* modee'a'; *fut* yodee'a'; **2.** למסור (transmit) *inf* leemsor; *pst* masar; *pres* moser; *fut* yeemsor.

(to) inform against להלשין (denounce) *inf* lehalsheen; *pst* heelsheen; *pres* malsheen; *fut* yalsheen.

informal 1. לא רשמי (unofficial) *adj* lo reeshmee/-t (*cpr* lo rasmee/-t); **2.** ללא־גינונים (without ceremony) *adj & adv* le-lo geenooneem.

informal visit ביקור לא פורמלי *nm* beekoor/-eem lo formalee/-yeem.

informally באורח לא רשמי *adv* be-orakh lo reeshmee.

informant 1. מודיע *nm* modee|'a'/-'eem (*pl+of:* -'ey); **2.** מלשין (denouncer) *nmf* malsheen/-ah (*pl:* -eem/-ot; *+of:* -at/-ey).

information 1. מודיעין (service) *nm* modee'een; **2.** הסברה (propaganda) *nf* hasbar|ah/-ot (*+of:* -at); **3.** מידע (knowledge) *nm* meyda'.

(for your) information לידיעתך *adv m/f* lee-yedee'at|kha/-ekh (*m/f*).

infraction 1. הפרה *nf* hafar|ah/-ot (*+of:* -at); **2.** עבירה (contravention) 'aver|ah/-ot (*+of:* -at).

(to) infringe להפר *inf* lehafer; *pst* hefer; *pres* mefer; *fut* yafer.

(to) infringe upon 1. לעבור על (contravene) *inf* la'avor 'al; *pst* 'avar 'al; *pres* 'over 'al; *fut* ya'avor 'al; **2.** להסיג גבול (trespass) *inf* lehaseeg gvool; *pst* heeseeg *etc*; *pres* maseeg *etc* ; *fut* yaseeg *etc*.

(to) infuriate 1. לעורר זעם *inf* le'orer za'am; *pst* 'orer *etc*; *pres* me'orer *etc*; *fut* ye'orer *etc*; **2.** להרגיז (irritate) *inf* lehargeez; *pst* heergeez; *pres* margeez; *fut* yargeez.

(to) infuse 1. לצקת *inf* latseket; *pst* yatsak; *pres* yotsek; *fut* yeetsak; **2.** להחדיר (infiltrate) *inf* lehakhdeer; *pst* hekhdeer; *pres* makhdeer; *fut* yakhdeer.

ingenious מחוכם *adj* mekhook|am/-emet.

ingenuity 1. כושר המצאה *nm* kosher hamtsa'ah; **2.** חריפות (cleverness) *nf* khareefoo|t/-yot.

ingratitude כפיות טובה *nf* kfeeyoot tovah.

ingredient 1. מרכיב *nm* markeev/-eem (*pl+of:* -ey); **2.** סממן *nm* sameman/-eem (*pl+of:* -ey).

(to) inhabit לאכלס *inf* le'akhles; *pst* eekhles; *pres* me'akhles; *fut* ye'akhles.

inhabitant תושב *nmf* tosh|av/-evet (*pl:* -aveem; *+of:* -vey).

(to) inhale לשאוף (aspire) leesh'of; *pst* sha'af; *pres* sho'ef; *fut* yeesh'af.

inherent טבוע ב־ *adj* tavoo'a'/tvoo'ah be-.

(to) inherit לרשת *inf* lareshet; *pst* yarash; *pres* yoresh; *fut* yeerash.

inheritance ירושה *nf* yeroosh|ah/-ot (*+of:* -at).

(to) inhibit 1. לעכב *inf* le'akev; *pst* 'eekev; *pres* me'akev; *fut* ye'akev; **2.** לכבוש בלב *inf* leekhbosh ba-lev; *pst* kavash *etc* (*v=b*); *pres* kovesh *etc*; *fut* yeekhbosh *etc*.

inhibition 1. עכבה *nf* 'akav|ah/-ot (*+of:* -at); 2. מעצור נפשי *nm* ma'atsor/-eem nafshee/-yeem; 3. מנע *nm* men|a'/-a'eem (*pl+of:* -a'ey).

inhospitable שאינו מסביר פנים *adj* she-eyn|o/-ah masbeer/-ah paneem.

inhuman לא אנושי *adj* lo enooshee/-t.

inimitable שאינו ניתן לחיקוי *adj* she-eyn|o/-ah neet|an/-enet le-kheekooy.

iniquity 1. רשעות (wickedness) *nf* reesh'oo|t/-yot; 2. עוול (wrong) *nm* 'avel.

initial 1. ראש תיבה *nm* rosh/-ey teyv|ah/-ot; 2. התחלתי (beginning) *adj* hatkhalatee/-t.

(to) initial לחתום בראשי תיבות *inf* lakhtom be-rashey teyvot; *pst* khatam *etc*; *pres* khotem *etc*; *fut* yakhtom *etc*.

initials ראשי תיבות *nm pl* rashey teyvot.

(to) initiate 1. ליזום *inf* leezom; *pst* yazam; *pres* yozem; *fut* yeezom; 2. להתחיל (begin) lehatkheel; *pst* heetkheel; *pres* matkheel; *fut* yatkheel.

initiative יוזמה *nf* yozm|ah/-ot (*+of:* -at).

(to) inject 1. להזריק *inf* lehazreek; *pst* heezreek; *pres* mazreek; *fut* yazreek; 2. להכניס (introduce) *inf* lehakhnees; *pst* heekhnees; *pres* makhnees; *fut* yakhnees.

injection זריקה *nf* zreek|ah/-ot (*+of:* -at).

injunction 1. צו מניעה *nm* tsav/-ey menee'ah; 2. צו עשה (mandatory) *nm* tsav/-ey 'aseh; 3. צו לא תעשה (prohibitory) mj tsav/-ey lo ta'aseh.

(to) injure 1. לפצוע (wound) *inf* leeftso'a'; *pst* patsa' *(p=f)*; *pres* potse'a'; *fut* yeeftsa'; 2. לפגוע (hurt) *inf* leefgo'a'; *pst* paga' *(p=f)*; *pres* poge'a'; *fut* yeefga'; 3. להזיק (damage) *inf* lehazeek; *pst* heezeek; *pres* mazeek; *fut* yazeek.

injurious 1. פוגם *adj* pogem/-et; 2. מזיק (damaging) *adj* mazeek/-ah.

injury 1. פציעה (wound) *nf* petsee|'ah/-'ot (*+of:* -'at); 2. פגיעה (harm) *nf* pegee|'ah/-'ot (*+of:* -'at); 3. נזק (damage) *nm* nez|ek/-akeem (*pl+of:* neezkey).

injustice 1. אי־צדק (injustice) *nm* ee-tsedek; 2. עוול (wrong) *nm* 'avel.

ink דיו *nf* dyo.

inkling רמז *nm* rem|ez/-azeem (*pl+of:* reemzey).

inkstand קסת *nf* kes|et/-atot.

inkwell מיכל דיו *nm* meykhal/-ey dyo.

inlaid משובץ *adj* meshoob|ats/-etset.

inlaid work מעשה שיבוץ *nm* ma'aseh sheeboots.

inland פנים הארץ *nm* peneem ha-arets.

inlay 1. מילוי *nm* meeloo|y/-yeem (*pl+of:* -yey); 2. סתימה (tooth filling) *nf* steem|ah/-ot (*+of:* -at).

(to) inlay 1. לשבץ *inf* leshabets; *pst* sheebets; *pres* meshabets; *fut* yesahabets; 2. לקבוע (cement into) *inf* leekbo'a'; *pst* kava' *(v=b)*; *pres* kove'a'; *fut* yeekba'.

inmate 1. אסיר (of a prison) *nm* aseer/-ah (*pl:* -eem/-ot; *+of:* -at/-ey); 2. חוסה (of an institution) *nmf* khos|eh/-ah (*pl+of:* -ey).

inmost 1. פנימי ביותר *adj* peneemee/-t be-yoter; 2. חשאי (secret) *adj* khasha'ee/-t.

inn פונדק *nm* poond|ak/-akeem (*pl+of:* -ekey).

innate מולד *adj* mool|ad/-edet.

inner 1. חבוי *adj* khavoo|y/-yah; 2. פנימי (internal) *adj* peneemee/-t.

innermost, inmost שבתוך תוכו של *adj* she-be-tokh tokho shel.

inning 1. תור *nm* tor/-eem (*pl+of:* -ey); 2. הזדמנות (chance) *nf* heezdamnoo|t/-yot; 3. מחזור (baseball) *nm* makhzor/-eem (*pl+of:* -ey); 4. סיבוב (cricket) *nm* seevoov/-eem (*pl+of:* -ey).

innkeeper פונדקאי *nmf* poondek|ay/-a'ee/-t.

innocence 1. תמימות (candor) *nf* tmeemoo|t/-yot; 2. חפות (blamelessness) *nf* khapoo|t/-yot.

innocent 1. תמים (candid) tameem/tmeemah; 2. חף מפשע (not guilty) *adj* khaf/khapah *(p=f)* mee-pesha'.

innocuous לא מזיק *adj* lo mazeek/-ah.

innovation חידוש *nm* kheedoosh/-eem (*pl+of:* -ey).

innuendo רמיזה בעקיפין *nf* remeez|ah/-ot ba-'akeefeen.

innumerable לאין ספור *adj & adv* le'eyn sfor.

(to) inoculate 1. להרכיב *inf* leharkeev; *pst* heerkeev; *pres* markeev; *fut* yarkeev; 2. לחסן (immunize) *inf* lekhasen; *pst* kheesen; *pres* mekhasen; *fut* yekhasen.

inoffensive לא מזיק *adj* lo mazeek/-ah.

inopportune שלא בעיתו *adj* she-lo be-'eet|o/-ah.

input 1. כניסה (entry) kenees|ah/-ot (*+of:* -at); 2. הספק (capacity) *nm* hespek/-eem (*pl+of:* -ey).

(to) inquire 1. לחקור (investigate) *inf* lakhkor; *pst* khakar; *pres* khoker; *fut* yakhkor; 2. לבדוק (examine) *inf* leevdok; *pst* badak *(b=v)*; *pres* bodek; *fut* yeevdok.

(to) inquire about, after 1. לחקור אודות *inf* lakhkor odot; *pst* khakar *etc*; *pres* khoker *etc*; *fut* yakhkor *etc*; 2. לשאול לשלום (transmit regards) *inf* leesh'ol lee-shlom; *pst* sha'al *etc*; *pres* sho'el *etc*; *fut* yeesh'al *etc*.

(to) inquire into 1. לערוך חקירה לבירור *inf* la'arokh khakeerah le-veroor; *pst* 'arakh *etc*; *pres* 'orekh *etc*; *fut* ya'arokh *etc*. 2. לחקור (investigate) *vt inf* lakhkor; *pst* khakar; *pres* khoker; *fut* yakhkor.

inquiry חקירה ודרישה *nf* khakeerah oo-dreeshah.

inquisition אינקוויזיציה *nf* eenkveezeets|yah/-yot.

inquisitive 1. חקרני *adj* khakranee/-t; 2. סקרן (curious) *adj* sakran/-eet.

inroad 1. חדירה *nf* khadeer|ah/-ot (*+of:* -at); 2. פשיטה (incursion) *nf* pesheet|ah/-ot (*+of:* -at).

(to make) inroads upon 1. לחדור *inf* lakhdor; *pst* khadar; *pres* khoder; *fut* yakhdor; 2. לתקוף (attack) *inf* leetkof; *pst* takaf; *pres* tokef; *fut* yeetkof.

insane 1. משוגע *adj* meshoog|a'/-a'at; 2. (crazy) *nmf & adj* metoor|af/-efet.

insanity 1. שיגעון *nm* sheega'on/-'onot (*+of:* -'on); 2. טירוף (craze) *nm* teroof/-eem.

insatiable שאינו יודע שובעה *adj* she-'eyn|o/-ah yod|e'a'/-a'at sov'ah.

(to) inscribe 1. לחרות *inf* lakhrot; *pst* kharat; *pres* khoret; *fut* yakhrot; 2. לחקוק (engrave) *inf* lakhkok; *pst* khakak; *pres* khokek; *fut* yakhkok.

inscription כתובת *nf* ketov|et/-ot.

insect 1. חרק *nm* kherek/khar|akeem (*pl+of:* -key); 2. רמש (creeper) *nm* remes/-aseem (*pl+of:* reemsey).

insecure חסר ביטחון *adj* khas|ar/-rat beetakhon.

insensible חסר רגש *adj* khas|ar/-rat regesh.

insensitive חסר רגישות *adj* khas|ar/-rat regeeshoot.

inseparable שלא ניתן להפרדה *adj* she-lo neet|an/-enet le-hafradah.

insert 1. הבלעה *nf* havla|'ah/-'ot (+*of:* -'at); **2.** מודעה (ad) moda|'ah/-'ot (+*of:* -'at).

(to) insert לפרסם בעיתון *inf* lefarsem be-'eeton; *pst* peersem *etc* (*p=f*); *pres* mefarsem *etc*; *fut* yefarsem *etc*;.

insertion 1. הוספה (addition) *nf* hosaf|ah/-ot (+*of:* -at); **2.** קביעה (fixation) *nf* kvee|'ah/-'ot (+*of:* -'at).

inside בפנים *adv* bee-fneem.

(to turn) inside out להפוך עם הפנים החוצה *inf* lahafokh 'eem ha-paneem ha-khootsah; *pst* hafakh *etc*; *pres* hofekh *etc*; *fut* yahafokh *etc*.

insides קרביים *nm pl* krav|ayeem (*pl+of:* -ey).

insight 1. הבחנה *nf* havkhan|ah/-ot (+*of:* -at); **2.** הסתכלות (observation) *nf* heestakloo|t/-yot.

insignia 1. תג (badge) *nm* tag/-eem (*pl+of:* -ey); **2.** סימן (sign) *nm* seeman/-eem (*pl+of:* -ey); **3.** סמל (*symbol*) semel/smaleem (*pl+of:* seemley).

insignificant חסר־ערך *adj* khas|ar/-rat 'erekh.

(to) insinuate לרמוז בעקיפין *inf* leermoz ba-'akeefeen; *pst* ramaz *etc*; *pres* romez *etc*; *fut* yeermoz *etc*.

insinuation הטלת דופי בעקיפין *nf* hatal|at/-ot dofee ba-'akeefeen.

insipid תפל *adj* tafel/tfelah.

(to) insist 1. להפציר *inf* lehaftseer; *pst* heeftseer; *pres* maftseer; *fut* yaftseer; **2.** להתעקש *inf* leheet'akesh; *pst* heet'akesh; *pres* meet'akesh; *fut* yeet'akesh.

insistence 1. התמדה (persistence) *nf* hatmad|ah/-ot (+*of:* -at); **2.** עקשנות (obstinacy) *nf* 'akshanoo|t/-yot.

insistent מתעקש *adj* meet'akesh/-et.

insolence חוצפה *nf* khootsp|ah/-ot (+*of:* -at).

insolent חצוף *adj* khatsoof/-ah.

insoluble 1. שאינו נמס (cannot dissolve) *adj* she-'en|o/-ah names/nemasah; **2.** ללא פתרון (unsolvable) *adj* le-lo peetaron.

(to) inspect 1. לבקר (examine) *inf* levaker; *pst* beeker (*b=v*); *pres* mevaker; *fut* yevaker; **2.** לפקח (oversee) *inf* lefake'akh; *pst* peekakh (*p=f*); *pres* mefake'akh; *fut* yefakakh.

inspection ביקורת *nf* beekor|et/-ot.

inspector 1. מפקח *nm nmf* mefak|e'akh/-akhat (*pl:* -'kheem/-'khot; +*of:* -'khey); **2.** מבקר (comptroller) *nmf* mevaker/-et.

inspiration השראה *nf* hashra|'ah/-'ot (+*of:* -'at).

(to) inspire לתת השראה *inf* latet hashra'ah; *pst* natan *etc*; *pres* noten *etc*; *fut* yeeten *etc*.

(to) install להתקין (arrange) *inf* lehatkeen; *pst* heetkeen; *pres* matkeen; *fut* yatkeen.

installation 1. התקנה (installing) *nf* hatkan|ah/-ot (+*of:* -at); **2.** מתקן (apparatus) *nm* meetkan/-eem (*pl+of:* -ey).

installment, instalment תשלום לשיעורין *nm* tashloom/-eem le-sheeooreen.

(to pay in) instalments לפרוע בתשלומים *inf* leefro'a' be-tashloomeem; *pst* para' *etc* (*p=f*); *pres* pore'a' *etc*; *fut* yeefra' *etc*.

instance 1. דוגמה (example) *nf* doogm|ah/-a'ot (+*of:* -at); **2.** מקרה (occurrence) *nm* meekr|eh/-eem (+*of:* -ey); **3.** ערכאה (judicial) *nf* 'arka|'ah/-'ot (+*of:* -'at).

(for) instance 1. לדוגמה *adv* le-doogmah; **2.** למשל (e.g.) *adv* le-mashal.

instant 1. מידי (immediate) *adj* meeyadee/-t; **2.** לחודש זה (of this month) *adj* le-khodesh zeh.

(on the 10th) instant בעשרה לחודש זה *adv* ba-'asarah le-khodesh zeh.

instantaneous 1. חולף (fleeting) *adj* kholef/-et; **2.** רגעי (momentary) *adj* reeg'ee/-t.

instead במקום זאת *adv* bee-mekom zot.

instead of במקום *prep* bee-mekom.

instep קימור רגל *nm* keemoor/-ey regel/raglayeem.

(to) instigate להסית *inf* lehaseet; *pst* heseet; *pres* meseet; *fut* yaseet.

(to) instill להחדיר בהדרגה *inf* lehakhdeer be-hadragah; *pst* hekhdeer *etc*; *pres* makhdeer *etc*; *fut* yakhdeer *etc*.

instinct 1. יצר *nm* yets|er/-areem (*pl+of:* yeetsrey); **2.** אינסטינקט *nm* eensteenkt/-eem (*pl+of:* -ey).

instinctive אינסטינקטיבי *adj* eensteenkteevee/-t.

institute מכון *nm* makhon/mekhon|eem (*pl+of:* -ey).

(to) institute 1. לייסד (found) *inf* leyased; *pst* yeesed; *pres* meyased; *fut* yeyased; **2.** לקבוע (establish) *inf* leekbo'a'; *pst* kava' (*v=b*); *pres* kove'a'; *fut* yeekba'.

institution מוסד *nm* mos|ad/-adot (*pl+of:* -dot).

(to) instruct 1. להדריך (conduct) *inf* lehadreekh; *pst* heedreekh; *pres* madreekh; *fut* yadreekh; **2.** להורות (direct) *inf* lehorot; *pst* horah; *pres* moreh; *fut* yoreh.

instruction 1. הוראה *nf* (teaching) *nf* hora|'ah/-'ot (+*of:* -'at); **2.** חינוך (education) *nm* kheenookh.

(lack of) instruction חוסר חינוך *nm* khoser kheenookh.

instructions הנחיות *nf pl* hankha|yot (*sing:* -yah; +*of:* -yat).

instructive מאלף *adj* me'alef/-et.

instructor 1. מדריך *nmf* madreekh/-ah (*pl:* -eem/-ot; +*of:* -at/-ey); **2.** מורה (teacher) *nmf* mor|eh/-ah (*pl:* -eem/-ot; +*of:* -at/-ey).

instrument 1. מכשיר (device) *nm* makhsheer/-eem (*pl+of:* -ey); **2.** כלי (tool) *nm* klee/keleem (*pl+of:* kley).

instrumental יעיל *adj* ya'eel/ye'eelah.

(to be) instrumental in להיות לעזר *inf* leehyot le-'ezer; *pst* hayah *etc*; *pres* heeno *etc*; *fut* yeehyeh *etc*.

insubordinate לא ממושמע *adj* lo memooshm|a'/a'at.

insufferable בלתי נסבל *adj* beeltee neesb|al/-elet.

insufficiency אי־ספיקה *nf* ee-sfeek|ah/-ot (+*of:* -at).

insufficient לא מספיק *adj* lo maspl|eek/-eket.

(to) insulate לבודד *inf* levoded; *pst* boded (*b=v*); *pres* mevoded; *fut* yevoded.

insulation בידוד *nm* beedood/-eem (*pl+of:* -ey).

insulator 1. מבודד *nm* mevoded/-eem (*pl+of:* -ey); **2.** חומר בידוד (isolating stuff) *nm* khom|er/-rey beedood.

insult עלבון *nm* 'elbon/-ot.

(to) insult להעליב *inf* leha'aleev; *pst* he'eleev; *pres* ma'aleev; *fut* ya'aleev.

insurance ביטוח *nm* beetoo|'akh/-kheem (*pl+of:* -khey).

insurance agent סוכן ביטוח *nm* sokh|en/-enet (*pl:* -ney) beetoo'akh.

insurance company חברת ביטוח *nf* khevr|at/-ot beetoo'akh.

insurance policy פוליסת ביטוח *nf* polees|at/-ot beetoo'akh.

(accident) insurance ביטוח תאונות *nm* beetoo'akh te'oonot.

(fire) insurance ביטוח מאש *nm* beetoo'akh me-'esh.

(life) insurance ביטוח חיים *nm* beetoo'akh khayeem.

(to) insure לבטח *inf* levate'akh; *pst* beete'akh *(b=v)*; *pres* mevate'akh; *fut* yevate'akh.

insurgent מתקומם *nm* meetkomem/-eem (*pl+of:* -ey).

insurmountable שאין לגבור עליו *adj* she-'eyn leegvor 'al|av/-eha.

insurrection 1. מרידה *nf* mereed|ah/-ot (*+of:* -at); **2.** מרד (revolt) *nm* mered; **3.** התקוממות (uprising) *nf* heetkomemoo|t/-yot.

intact ללא פגע *adj* le-lo pega'.

integral אינטגרלי *adj* eentegralee/-t.

(to) integrate 1. למזג (blend) *inf* lemazeg; *pst* meezeg; *pres* memazeg; *fut* yemazeg; **2.** לבולל (assimilate) *inf* levolel; *pst* bolel *(b=v)*; *pres* mevolel; *fut* yevolel.

integration 1. היספגות (absorption) *nf* heesaf-goo|t/-yot; **2.** התבוללות (assimilation) *nf* heetboleloo|t/-yot; **3.** אינטגרציה *nf* eenteg-ratsy|ah/-ot.

integrity 1. שלמות *nf* shlemoo|t/-yot; **2.** יושר (honesty) *nm* yosher.

intellect שכל *nm* sekhel.

intellectual 1. איש רוח *nm* eesh/anshey roo'akh; **2.** משכיל *nmf* maskeel/-ah (*pl:* -eem/-ot; *+of:* -ey); **3.** אינטלקטואל *nmf* eentelektoo'al/-eet.

intelligence 1. תבונה *nf* tvoon|ah/-ot (*+of:* -at); **2.** מודיעין (military) *nm* modee'een; **3.** מודיעיני (of milit. intel.) *adj* mode'eenee/-t.

intelligent חכם *adj* khakham/-ah.

intelligentsia 1. השכבה המשכילה *nf* ha-sheekhvah/shekhavot ha-maskeel|ah/-ot; **2.** אינטליגנציה *nf* eenteleegentsyah.

intelligible 1. מובן *adj* moov|an/-enet; **2.** ברור (clear) *adj* baroor/broorah.

intemperance 1. אי התאפקות (lack of moderation) *nm* ee heet'apkoot; **2.** הפרזה בשתייה (excessive drinking) *nf* hafraz|ah/-ot bee-shteeyah.

(to) intend להתכוון *inf* leheetkaven; *pst* heetkaven; *pres* meetkaven; *fut* yeetkaven.

(to) intend to do it להתכוון ברצינות *inf* leheetkaven bee-retseenoot; *pst* heetkaven *etc*; *pres* meetkaven *etc*; *fut* yeetkaven *etc*.

intense עצום *adj* 'atsoom/-ah.

(to) intensify להגביר *inf* lehagbeer; *pst* heegbeer; *pres* magbeer; *fut* yagbeer.

intensity 1. עוצם *nm* 'otsem; **2.** עוצמה (strength) *nf* 'otsm|ah/-ot (*+of:* -at).

intensive אינטנסיבי *adj* eentenseevee/-t.

intent כוונה *nf* kavan|ah/-ot (*+of:* -at).

intent on 1. כשגמור עמו *adj* ke-she-gamoor 'eem|o/-ah; **2.** איתן בכוונתו (firmly decided) *adj* eytan/-ah be-khavanat|o/-ah *(kh=k)*.

intention כוונה *nf* kavan|ah/-ot (*+of:* -at).

intentional מכוון *adj* mekhoov|an/-enet.

intentionally במתכוון *adv* be-meetkaven.

(to all) intents and purposes מכל הבחינות *adv* mee-kol ha-bekheenot.

(to) inter לקבור *inf* leekbor; *pst* kavar *(b=v)*; *pres* kover; *fut* yeekbor.

(to) intercede 1. לפשר בין (between) *inf* lefasher beyn; *pst* peesher *(p=f)* beyn; *pres* mefasher beyn; *fut* yefasher beyn.; **2.** להשתדל בעד (for) *inf* leheeshtadel be'ad; *pst* heeshtadel *etc*; *pres* meeshtadel *etc*; *fut* yeeshtadel *etc*.

(to) intercept 1. ליירט (in the sky) *inf* leyaret; *pst* yeeret; *pres* meyaret; *fut* yeyaret; **2.** ללכוד בדרך (capture enroute) *inf* leelkod ba-derekh; *pst* lakhad *etc* *(kh=k)*; *pres* lokhed; *fut* yeelkod *etc*.

interception יירוט *nm* yeroot/-eem (*pl+of:* -ey).

intercession 1. פשרה (compromise) *nf* peshar|ah/-ot (*+of:* -at); **2.** השתדלות (lobbying) *nf* heeshtadloo|t/-yot.

interchange 1. המרה *nf* hamar|ah/-ot (*+of:* -at); **2.** חליפין (exchange) *nm pl* khaleefeen.

(to) interchange 1. להחליף זה בזה (one for one) *inf* lehakhleef zeh ba-zeh; *pst* hekhleef *etc*; *pres* makhleef *etc*; *fut* yakhleef *etc*; **2.** להמיר (convert) *inf* lehameer; *pst* hemeer; *pres* memeer; *fut* yameer.

(sexual) intercourse 1. מגע מיני *nm* mag|a'/-a'eem meenee/-yeem; **2.** מישגל (coitus) *nm* meeshgal/-eem (*pl+of:* -ey).

(to) intercross להצליב *inf* lehatsleev; *pst* heetsleev; *pres* matsleev; *fut* yatsleev.

interdental שבין שיניים *adj* she-beyn sheenayeem.

interest 1. עניין *nm* 'een|yan/-yaneem (*pl+of:* -yeney); **2.** ריבית (loan) *nf* reebeet.

(to) interest לעניין *inf* le'anyen; *pst* 'eenyen; *pres* me'anyen; *fut* 'eenyen.

interested מעוניין *adj* me'oon|yan/-yenet.

(to be, to become) interested in לגלות עניין ב־ *inf* legalot 'eenyan be-; *pst* geelah *etc*; *pres* megaleh *etc*; *fut* yegaleh *etc*.

interesting מעניין *adj* me'anyen/-et.

(to) interfere להתערב *inf* leheet'arev; *pst* heet'arev; *pres* meet'arev; *fut* yeet'arev.

(to) interfere with להפריע ל־ *inf* lehafree'a' le-; *pst* heefree'a' le-; *pres* mafree'a' le-; *fut* yafree'a' le-.

interference הפרעה *nf* hafra|'ah/-'ot (*+of:* -'at).

interior 1. פנימי *adj* peneemee/-t; **2.** פנים (interior) *nm* peneem.

interior designer אדריכל פנים *nmf* adreekhal/-eet peneem.

interjection מלת קריאה *nf* meel|at/-ot kree'ah.

(to) interlace 1. לשזור *inf* leeshzor; *pst* shazar; *pres* shozer; *fut* yeeshzor; **2.** לקלוע (weave) *inf* leeklo'a'; *pst* kala'; *pres* kole'a'; *fut* yeekla'.

(to) interlock 1. לשלב *inf* leshal<u>e</u>v; *pst* sheel<u>e</u>v; *pres* meshal<u>e</u>v; *fut* yeshal<u>e</u>v; **2.** לחבר (join) *inf* lekhab<u>e</u>r; *pst* kheeb<u>e</u>r; *pres* mekhab<u>e</u>r; *fut* yekhab<u>e</u>r.

interlude נגינת ביניים *nf* negeen|<u>a</u>t/-<u>o</u>t beyn<u>a</u>yeem.

intermediate 1. שבין לבין *adj* she-b<u>e</u>yn le-v<u>e</u>yn. **2.** מתווך (mediator) *nmf* metav<u>e</u>kh/-et.

(to) intermediate 1. לתווך (mediate) *inf* letav<u>e</u>kh; *pst* teev<u>e</u>kh; *pres* metav<u>e</u>kh; *fut* yetav<u>e</u>kh; **2.** לפשר (intercede) *inf* lefash<u>e</u>r; *pst* peesh<u>e</u>r *(p=f)*; *pres* mefash<u>e</u>r; *fut* yefash<u>e</u>r.

interminable ללא סוף *adj* le-l<u>o</u> sof.

(to) intermingle 1. לערבב *inf* le'arb<u>e</u>v; *pst* 'eerb<u>e</u>v; *pres* me'arb<u>e</u>v; *fut* ye'arb<u>e</u>v; **2.** לבולל (mix) *inf* levol<u>e</u>l; *pst* bol<u>e</u>l *(b=v)*; *pres* mevol<u>e</u>l; *fut* yevol<u>e</u>l.

intermission 1. הפסקה (pause) *nf* hafsak|<u>a</u>h/-<u>o</u>t (*+of:* -<u>a</u>t); **2.** הפסקת ביניים (interruption break) *nf* hafsak|<u>a</u>t/-<u>o</u>t beyn<u>a</u>yeem.

intermittent לסירוגין *adj* le-seroog<u>ee</u>n.

intermittent current זרם סירוגין *nm* z<u>e</u>rem seroog<u>ee</u>n.

intern רופא בית *nmf* rof<u>e</u>/-t b<u>a</u>yeet.

(to) intern 1. לכלוא (imprison) *inf* leekhl<u>o</u>; *pst* kal<u>a</u> *(k=kh)*; *pres* kol<u>e</u>; *fut* yeekhl<u>a</u> (imprison); **2.** לשמש רופא בית (serve as intern) *inf* leshamesh rof<u>e</u>/-t b<u>a</u>yeet; *pst* sheem<u>e</u>sh *etc*; *pres* meshamesh *etc*; *fut* yesham<u>e</u>sh *etc*.

internal פנימי *adj* peneem<u>ee</u>/-t.

international (בינלאומי) בין לאומי *adj* ben-le'oom<u>ee</u>/-t.

(to) interpose 1. לשים בין (place between) *inf* las<u>ee</u>m b<u>e</u>yn; *pst & pres* sam b<u>e</u>yn; *fut* yas<u>ee</u>m b<u>e</u>yn; **2.** לחצוץ (act as buffer) *inf* lakhts<u>o</u>ts; *pst* khats<u>a</u>ts; *pres* khots<u>e</u>ts; *fut* yakhts<u>o</u>ts.

(to) interpret 1. לפרש (comment) *inf* lefar<u>e</u>sh; *pst* per<u>a</u>sh *(p=f)*; *pres* mefar<u>e</u>sh; *fut* yefar<u>e</u>sh; **2.** לתרגם (translate) *inf* letarg<u>e</u>m; *pst* teerg<u>e</u>m; *pres* metarg<u>e</u>m; *fut* yetarg<u>e</u>m.

interpretation 1. פירוש *nm* per<u>oo</u>sh/-<u>ee</u>m (*pl+of:* -<u>e</u>y); **2.** פרשנות *nf* (commentary) *nf* parshan<u>oo</u>|t/-y<u>o</u>t.

interpreter 1. תורגמן (translator) *nmf* toorgem<u>a</u>n/-<u>ee</u>t; **2.** פרשן (commentator) *nmf* parsh<u>a</u>n/-<u>ee</u>t.

(to) interrogate לתשאל (question) *inf* letash'<u>e</u>l; *pst* teesh'<u>e</u>l; *pres* metash'<u>e</u>l; *fut* yetash'<u>e</u>l.

interrogation תשאול *nm* teesh'<u>oo</u>l/-<u>ee</u>m (*pl+of:* -<u>e</u>y).

interrogation mark, point, sign סימן שאלה *nm* seem<u>a</u>n/-<u>e</u>y she'el<u>a</u>h.

interrogative מתשאל *adj* metash'<u>e</u>l/-et.

(to) interrrupt להפסיק *inf* lehafs<u>ee</u>k; *pst* heefs<u>ee</u>k; *pres* mafs<u>ee</u>k; *fut* yafs<u>ee</u>k.

interruption הפסקה *nf* hafsak|<u>a</u>h/-<u>o</u>t (*+of:* -<u>a</u>t).

(to) intersect לחצות *inf* lakhts<u>o</u>t; *pst* khats<u>a</u>h; *pres* khots<u>e</u>h; *fut* yekhts<u>e</u>h.

intersection 1. חצייה *nf* khatsee|y<u>a</u>h/-y<u>o</u>t (*+of:* -y<u>a</u>t); **2.** הצטלבות (crossing) heetstalv<u>oo</u>|t/-y<u>o</u>t.

(street) intersection 1. הצטלבות רחובות *nf* heetstalv<u>oo</u>|t/-y<u>o</u>t rekhov<u>o</u>t; **2.** צומת (junction) *nm* ts<u>o</u>met/tsmat<u>ee</u>m (*pl+of:* tsomt<u>e</u>y).

(to) intersperse 1. לפזר (spread) *inf* lefaz<u>e</u>r; *pst* peez<u>e</u>r *(p=f)*; *pres* mefaz<u>e</u>r; *fut* yefaz<u>e</u>r; **2.** להפיץ (disseminate) *inf* lehaf<u>ee</u>ts; *pst* hef<u>ee</u>ts; *pres* mef<u>ee</u>ts; *fut* yaf<u>ee</u>ts.

(to) intertwine 1. לשלב (combine) *inf* leshal<u>e</u>v; *pst* sheel<u>e</u>v; *pres* meshal<u>e</u>v; *fut* yeshal<u>e</u>v; **2.** להשתלב (dovetail) *inf* leheeshtal<u>e</u>v; *pst* heeshtal<u>e</u>v; *pres* meeshtal<u>e</u>v; *fut* yeeshtal<u>e</u>v.

interurban בין עירוני *adj* b<u>e</u>yn 'eeron<u>ee</u>/-t.

interval 1. שהות *nf* sheh<u>oo</u>|t/-y<u>o</u>t; **2.** הפרש זמן *nm* hefr<u>e</u>sh/-<u>e</u>y zman.

(to) intervene להתערב (interfere) *inf* leheet'ar<u>e</u>v; *pst* heet'ar<u>e</u>v; *pres* meet'ar<u>e</u>v; *fut* yeet'ar<u>e</u>v.

intervention התערבות *nf* (interference) *nf* heet-'arv<u>oo</u>|t/-y<u>o</u>t.

interview 1. ראיון *nm* re'ay<u>o</u>n/ra'ayon<u>o</u>t (*+of:* ra-'ay<u>o</u>n); **2.** שיחה (talk) *nf* seekh|<u>a</u>h/-<u>o</u>t (*+of:* -<u>a</u>t).

(to) interview לראיין *inf* lera'y<u>e</u>n; *pst* ree'y<u>e</u>n; *pres* mera'y<u>e</u>n; *fut* yera'y<u>e</u>n.

intestate ללא צוואה *adj* le-l<u>o</u> tsava|'<u>a</u>h/-'<u>o</u>t.

intestinal של מעיים *adj* shel me'<u>a</u>yeem.

intestine מעי *nm* me'<u>ee</u>/ma'ayeem (*pl+of:* me'<u>e</u>y).

(large) intestine המעי הגס *nm* ha-me'<u>ee</u> ha-g<u>a</u>s.

intestines מעיים *nf pl* me'<u>a</u>yeem.

intimacy 1. קרבה (closeness) *nf* keerv|<u>a</u>h/-<u>o</u>t (*+of:* -<u>a</u>t); **2.** אינטימיות *nf* eent<u>ee</u>meeyoot.

intimate 1. סודי (clandestine) *adj* sod<u>ee</u>/-t; **2.** מקורב (closely befriended) *adj* mekor|<u>a</u>v/-<u>e</u>vet.

(to) intimate 1. להודיע (notify) *inf* lehod<u>ee</u>'a'; *pst* hod<u>ee</u>'a'; *pres* mod<u>ee</u>'a'; *fut* yod<u>ee</u>'a'; **2.** לרמוז בעקיפין (hint) *inf* leerm<u>o</u>z ba-'akeef<u>ee</u>n; *pst* ram<u>a</u>z *etc*; *pres* rom<u>e</u>z *etc*; *fut* yeerm<u>o</u>z *etc*.

intimation 1. הודעה *nf* hoda|'<u>a</u>h/-'<u>o</u>t (*+of:* -'<u>a</u>t); **2.** רמז (hint) *nm* r<u>e</u>m|ez/-az<u>ee</u>m (*pl+of:* reemz<u>e</u>y).

(to) intimidate 1. להפחיד (scare) *inf* lehafkh<u>ee</u>d; *pst* heefkh<u>ee</u>d; *pres* mafkh<u>ee</u>d; *fut* yafkh<u>ee</u>d; **2.** להרתיע (deter) lehart<u>ee</u>'a'; *pst* heert<u>ee</u>'a'; *pres* mart<u>ee</u>'a'; *fut* yart<u>ee</u>'a'.

intimidation 1. הפחדה *nf* hafkhad|<u>a</u>h/-<u>o</u>t (*+of:* -<u>a</u>t); **2.** איום (threat) *nm* eey<u>oo</u>m/-<u>ee</u>m (*pl+of:* -<u>e</u>y); **3.** הרתעה (deterrence) *nf* harta|'<u>a</u>h/-'<u>o</u>t (*+of:* -'<u>a</u>t).

into לתוך *prep* le-t<u>o</u>kh.

intolerable 1. לא נסבל *adj* lo neesb|<u>a</u>l/-<u>e</u>let; **2.** בלתי נסבל *[colloq.] adj* beelt<u>ee</u> neesb|<u>a</u>l/-<u>e</u>let.

intolerance 1. חוסר סובלנות *nm* kh<u>o</u>ser sovlan<u>oo</u>t; **2.** קנאות (fanaticism) *nf* kana'<u>oo</u>|t/-y<u>o</u>t.

intolerant 1. חסר סובלנות *adj* khas|<u>a</u>r/-rat sovlan<u>oo</u>t; **2.** קנאי (fanatic) *nmf & adj* kan|<u>a</u>y/-a'<u>ee</u>t.

intonation 1. הטעמה *nf* hat'am|<u>a</u>h/-<u>o</u>t (*+of:* -<u>a</u>t); **2.** הנגנה (voice modulation) *nf* hangan|<u>a</u>h/-<u>o</u>t (*+of:* -<u>a</u>t).

(to) intoxicate לשכר *inf* leshak<u>e</u>r; *pst* sheek<u>e</u>r; *pres* meshak<u>e</u>r; *fut* yeshak<u>e</u>r,

intoxicating liquors משקאות משכרים *nm pl* mashka'<u>o</u>t meshakr<u>ee</u>m.

intoxication 1. שיכרון (inebriation) *nm* shee|kar<u>o</u>n/-khron<u>o</u>t (*+of:* -khr<u>o</u>n); **2.** התלהבות (fervor) *nf* heetlahav<u>oo</u>|t/-y<u>o</u>t

intransigent ללא פשרות *adj* le-l<u>o</u> peshar<u>o</u>t.

intravenous תוך־ורידי *adj* tokh-vreed<u>ee</u>/-t.

(to) intrench להתחפר *inf* leheetkhap<u>e</u>r; *pst* heetkhap<u>e</u>r; *pres* meetkhap<u>e</u>r; *fut* yeetkhap<u>e</u>r.

(to) intrench oneself 1. להתחפר בעמדה *inf* leheetkhaper be-'emdah; *pst* heetkhaper *etc; pres* meetkhaper *etc; fut* yeetkhaper *etc;* **2.** להתעקש (stubbornly stick) *inf* leheet'akesh; *pst* heet'akesh; *pres* meet'akesh; *fut* yeet'akesh.

(to) intrench upon another's rights לפגוע בזכויות הזולת *inf* leefgo'a' bee-zekhooyot ha-zoolat; *pst* paga' *etc (p=f); pres* poge'a' *etc; fut* yeefga' *etc.*

(to be) intrenched לעמוד איתן (stand firm) *inf* la'amod eytan/-ah; *pst* 'amad; *pres* 'omed; *fut* ya'amod *etc.*

intrepid 1. אמיץ (brave) *adj* ameets/-ah; **2.** עשוי לבלי חת (fearless) *adj* 'asoo|y/-yah lee-vlee *(v=b)* khat.

intricate מסובך *adj* mesoob|akh/-ekhet.

intrigue 1. קנוניה *nf* kenoon|yah/-yot (*+of:* -yat); **2.** מזימה (plot) *nf* mezeem|ah/-ot (*+of:* -at).

(to) intrigue 1. לזמום (plot) *inf* leezmom; *pst* zamam; *pres* zomem; *fut* yeezmom. **2.** לחרחר ריב (stir quarrel) *inf* lekharkher reev; *pst* kheerkher *etc; pres* mekharkher *etc; fut* yekharkher *etc.*

intriguer 1. מחרחר ריב *adj* mekharkher/-et reev; **2.** סכסכן (quarrel-monger) *nmf & adj* sakhsekhan/-eet.

(to) introduce 1. להציג (present) *inf* lehatseeg; *pst* heetseeg; *pres* matseeg; *fut* yatseeg; **2.** להנהיג (institute) *inf* lehanheeg; *pst* heenheeg; *pres* manheeg; *fut* yanheeg; **3.** להכניס (bring in) *inf* lehakhnees; *pst* heekhnees; *pres* makhnees; *fut* yakhnees.

introduction 1. הקדמה (foreword) *nf* hakdam|ah/-ot (*+of:* -at); **2.** עשיית היכרות (presentation) *nf* 'aseeyat hekeroot.

introspection 1. הסתכלות פנימית (soul searching) *nf* heestakloot peneemeet; **2.** בחינה עצמית (self examination) *nf* bekheenah 'atsmeet.

introvert מופנם *adj* moofn|am/-emet.

(to) intrude 1. להידחק *inf* leheedakhek; *pst & pres* needkhak; *fut* yeedakhek; **2.** להתפרץ *inf* leheetparets; *pst* heetparets; *pres* meetparets; *fut* yeetparets.

intruder מתפרץ *nmf* meetpar|ets/-et.

intrusion התפרצות *nf* heetpartsoo|t/-yot.

intrusive שלא ברשות *adv* she-lo bee-reshoot.

intuition 1. כושר הבחנה (power of observation) *nm* kosher havkhanah; **2.** הסתכלות *nf* hees-takloo|t/-yot; **3.** אינטואיציה *nf* eentoo'eets|yah/-yot (*+of:* -at).

(to) inundate להציף *inf* lehatseef; *pst* hetseef; *pres* metseef; *fut* yatseef.

inundation הצפה *nf* hatsaf|ah/-ot (*+of:* -at).

(to) inure לתרגל *inf* letargel; *pst* teergel; *pres* metargel; *fut* yetargel.

(to) invade לפלוש *inf* leeflosh; *pst* palash *(p=f); pres* polesh; *fut* yeeflosh.

invader פולש *nm* pol|esh/sheem (*pl+of:* -shey).

invalid 1. חסר תוקף (not valid) *adj* khas|ar/-rat tokef; **2.** חולה (patient, sick) *nmf & adj* khol|eh/-ah **3.** נכה (disabled) *nmf & adj* nakh|eh/-ah (*pl:* -eem/-ot; *+of:* nekh|eh/-ey).

(enemy-action) invalid נכה פעולות אויב *nmf* nekh|eh/-at pe'oolot oyev.

(terrorist-action) invalid נכה פעולות טירור *nmf* nekh|eh/-at pe'oolot teror.

(war-)invalid נכה מלחמה *nm* nekh|eh/-at (*pl:* -ey/-ot) meelkhamah.

invalidity חוסר תוקף *nm* khoser tokef.

invaluable לא יסולא *adj* lo yesoola/tesoola.

invariable לא משתנה *adj* lo meeshtan|eh/-ah.

invariably ללא שינוי *adv* le-lo sheenooy.

invasion פלישה *nf* pleesh|ah/-ot (*+of:* -at).

(to) invent להמציא *inf* lehamtsee; *pst* heemtsee; *pres* mamtsee; *fut* yamtsee.

invention 1. המצאה *nf* hamtsa|'ah/-'ot (*+of:* -'at); **2.** בדותה (fabrication) *nf* bedoot|ah/-ot (*+of:* -at).

inventive בר כושר המצאה *adj* bar/bat kosher hamtsa'ah.

inventiveness כושר המצאה *nm* kosher hamtsa'ah

inventor ממציא *nmf* mamtsee/-'ah (*+of:* -'at; *pl+of:* -'ey).

inventory 1. רשימת מצאי *nf* resheem|at/-ot metsay; **2.** רשימת מלאי *[colloq.] nf* resheem|at/-ot melay; **3.** אינוונטר *nm* eenventar/-eem (*pl+of:* -ey).

inverse 1. הפוך *adj* hafookh/-ah; **2.** נגדי (opposite) *adj* negdee/-t.

(to) invert 1. להפוך (turn upside down) *inf* lahafokh; *pst* hafakh; *pres* hofekh; *fut* yahafokh; **2.** לשנות סדר (change order) *inf* leshanot seder; *pst* sheenah *etc; pres* meshaneh *etc; fut* yeshaneh *etc.*

(to) invest 1. להשקיע *inf* lehashkee'a'; *pst* heeshkee'a'; *pres* mashkee'a'; *fut* yashkee'a'; **2.** להטיל תפקיד *inf* lehateel tafkeed; *pst* heeteel *etc; pres* mateel *etc; fut* yateel *etc.*

(to) investigate 1. לחקור *vt inf* lakhkor; *pst* khakar; *pres* khoker; *fut* yakhkor; **2.** לבדוק (examine) *inf* leevdok; *pst* badak *(b=v); pres* bodek; *fut* yeevdok.

investigation חקירה ודרישה *nf & nf* khakeer|ah/-ot oo-dreesh|ah/-ot.

investigator חוקר *nmf* khoker/-et.

investment השקעה *nf* hashka|'ah/-'ot (*+of:* -'at).

investor משקיע *nm* mashkee|'a'/-'eem (*+of:* -'ey)

(to) invigorate 1. לחזק (strengthen) *inf* lekhazek; *pst* kheezek; *pres* mekhazek; *fut* yekhazek; **2.** לעודד (encourage) *inf* le'oded; *pst* 'oded; *pres* me'oded; *fut* ye'oded.

invincible לא מנוצח *adj* lo menootsakh/-at.

invisible 1. לא נראה *adj* lo neer|'eh/-'et; **2.** סמוי (unseen) *adj* samooy/smooyah.

invitation הזמנה *nf* hazman|ah/-ot (*+of:* -at).

(to) invite להזמין *inf* lehazmeen; *pst* heezmeen; *pres* mazmeen; *fut* yazmeen.

inviting 1. מפתה (enticing) *adj* mefat|eh/-ah; **2.** מושך (attractive) *adj* moshekh/-et.

invocation השבעה *nf* hashba|'ah/-'ot (*+of:* -'at).

invoice חשבונית *nf* kheshbonee|t/-yot.

(to) invoke 1. לקרוא לעזרה *inf* leekro le-'ezrah; *pst* kara *etc; pres* kore *etc; fut* yeekra *etc;* **2.** להשביע (incant) *inf* lehashbee'a'; *pst* heeshbee'a'; *pres* mashbee'a'; *fut* yashbee'a'.

involuntary שלא מרצון *adj* she-lo me-ratson.

(to) involve לסבך *inf* lesabekh; *pst* seebekh; *pres* mesabekh; *fut* yesabekh.

(to get) involved in difficulties להסתבך בקשיים *inf* leheestabekh bee-k'shayeem; *pst* heestabekh *etc; pres* meestabekh; *fut* yeestabekh.

involvement הסתבכות *nf* heestabkhoo|t/-yot.

inward פנימי *adj* peneemee/-t.

inwards פנימה *adv* peneemah.

iodine יוד *nm* yod.

ire כעס *nm* ka'as.

iridiscent 1. נוצץ (shining) *adj* notsets/-et; **2.** ססגוני (variegated) *adj* sasgonee/-t.

iris 1. קשתית (cornea) *nf* kashtee|t/-yot; **2.** קשת בענן (rainbow) *nf* kesh|et/-atot be-'anan; **3.** אירוס (Iridaceae) *nm* eeroos/-eem (*pl+of:* -ey).

Irish 1. אירלנדי *nm* eerlandee/-m; **2.** אירי *adj* eeree/-t.

(the) Irish האירים *nm pl* ha-eereem.

irksome 1. מייגע (tiring) *adj* meyag|e'a'/-a'at; **2.** משעמם (boring) *adj* mesha'mem/-et.

iron 1. ברזל (material) *nm* barzel/-eem (*pl+of:* -ey); **2.** מגהץ (utensil) *nm* mag'|hets/-hatseem (*pl+of:* -hatsey).

(to) iron לגהץ *inf* legahets; *pst* geehets; *pres* megahets; *fut* yegahets.

(to) iron out difficulties ליישר הדורים *inf* leyasher hadooreem; *pst* yeesher *etc; pres* meyasher *etc; fut* yeyasher *etc.*

ironical אירוני *adj* eeronee/-t.

ironing גיהוץ *nm* geehoots/-eem (*pl+of:* -ey).

ironwork ברזלנות *nf* barzelanoot.

ironworks מפעל לעיבוד ברזל *nm* meef'al/-eem le-'eebood barzel.

irony אירוניה *nf* eeron|yah/-yot (*+of:* -yat).

(to) irradiate להקרין *inf* lehakreen; *pst* heekreen; *pres* makreen; *fut* yakreen.

irrational 1. לא הגיוני (illogical) *adj* lo hegyonee/-t; **2.** לא רציונלי *adj* lo-ratsyonalee/-t.

irregular 1. לא סדיר (extraordinary) *adj* lo sadeer/sedeerah; **2.** חריג (exceptional) *adj* khareeg/-ah; **3.** לא רגיל (unusual) *adj* lo rageel/regeelah.

irrelevant לא רלוונטי *adj* lo relevantee/-t.

irreligious 1. לא דתי *adj* lo datee/-t; **2.** חילוני (agnostic) *adj* kheelonee/-t.

irremediable ללא תקנה *adj* le-lo takanah.

irreproachable ללא דופי *adj* le-lo dofee.

irresistible 1. שאין לעמוד בפניו *adj* she-eyn la'amod be-fan|av/-eha *(m/f)*; **2.** מצודד *adj* metsoded/-et.

irresolute 1. הססן (hesitant) *adj* hasesan/-eet; **2.** מפקפק (doubting) *adj* mefakpek/-et.

irreverence 1. חוסר דרך־ארץ (disrespect) *nm* khoser derekh erets; **2.** זלזול (scorn) *nm* zeelzool/-eem (*pl+of:* -ey)

irreverent 1. מזלזל (disrespectful) *adj* mezalzel/-et; **2.** חסר דרך ארץ (uncivil) *adj* khas|ar/-rat derekh erets.

(to) irrigate להשקות *inf* lehashkot; *pst* heeshkah; *pres* mashkeh; *fut* yashkeh.

irrigation השקיה *nf* hashka|yah/-yot (*+of:* -yat).

irrigation canal תעלת השקיה *nf* te'al|at/-ot hashkayah.

irritable רגזן *nmf & adj* ragzan/-eet.

(to) irritate 1. להרגיז *inf* lehargeez; *pst* heergeez; *pres* margeez; *fut* yargeez; **2.** להקניט (tease) *inf* lehakneet; *pst* heekneet; *pres* makneet; *fut* yakneet.

irritating מרגיז *adj* margeez/-ah.

irritation התרגזות *nf* heetragzoo|t/-yot.

(to) irrupt להתפרץ *inf* leheetparets; *pst* heetparets; *pres* meetparets; *fut* yeetparets.

island אי *nm* ee/-yeem (*pl+of:* -yey).

(traffic) island אי־תנועה *nm* ee/-yey tenoo'ah.

islander תושב אי *nm* toshav/-ey ee.

isle אי *nm* ee/-yeem (*pl+of:* -yey).

(to) isolate לבודד *inf* levoded; *pst* boded *(b=v)*; *pres* mevoded; *fut* yevoded.

isolation 1. בידוד *nm* beedood/-eem (*pl+of:* -ey); **2.** הסגר (quarantine) *nm* hesger/-eem (*pl+of:* -ey).

isolationism בדלנות *nf* badlanoo|t/-yot.

isometric איזומטרי *adj* eezometree/-t.

Israel ישראל *nf* yeesra'el.

Israeli 1. ישראלי *nmf* yeesre'elee/-t (*pl:* -m/-yot); **2.** *adj* yeesre'elee/-t (*pl:* -yeem/-yot).

Israeli Defence Forces צבא הגנה לישראל *nm* tsva haganah le-yeesra'el - Israel's military forces. Is mostly known by its *acr* TSAHAL צה"ל.

issue 1. בעיה (problem) *nf* be'a|yah/-yot (*+of:* -yat); **2.** נושא (subject) *nm* nos|e/-'eem (*pl+of:* -'ey); **3.** צאצא (descendant) *nm* tse'ets|a/-a'eem (*pl+of:* -a'ey).

(to) issue 1. להוציא *inf* lehotsee; *pst* hotsee; *pres* motsee; *fut* yotsee; **2.** להנפיק (shares) *inf* lehanpek; *pst* heenpeek; *pres* manpeek; *fut* yanpeek; **3.** לפרסם (publish) *inf* lefarsem; *pst* peersem *(p=f)*; *pres* mefarsem; *fut* yefarsem.

(without) issue ללא יורש *adv* le-lo yor|esh/-sheem.

(to take) issue with לחלוק על *inf* lakhlok 'al; *pst* khalak 'al; *pres* kholek 'al; *fut* yakhlok 'al.

isthmus מיצר יבשה *nm* meytsar/-ey yabashah.

it הוא/היא *m/f pron* hoo/hee (Hebrew has no neuter, only masculine and feminine).

it is I אני הוא אשר *m/f* anee hoo'/hee asher.

it is raining יורד גשם *pres* yored geshem; *pst* yarad *etc; fut* yered *etc.*

it is there שם זה אשר sham zeh asher.

it is three o'clock השעה שלוש ha-sha'ah shalosh.

(how goes) it? ?איך הולך eykh holekh?

(what time is) it? ?מה השעה mah ha-sha'ah?.

Italian 1. איטלקי *nmf* eetalkee/-yah (*pl:* -m/-yot); **2.** איטלקי *adj* eetalkee/-t; **3.** איטלקית (language) *nf* eetalkeet.

italic אות קורסיבית *nf* ot/-eeyot koorseevee|t/-yot.

(to) italicize להדגיש באותיות קורסיביות *inf* lehadgeesh be-oteeyot koorseeveeyot; *pst* heedgeesh *etc; pres* madgeesh *etc; fut* yadgeesh *etc.*

italics ((קורסיביות) אותיות מלוכסנות *nf pl* oteeyot koorseeveeyot (melookhsanot).

Italy איטליה *nf* eetaleeyah.

itch 1. עקצוץ *nm* 'eektsoots/-eem (*pl+of:* -ey); **2.** גירוד *[colloq.]* gerood/-eem (*pl+of:* -ey).;

(to) itch 1. לעקצץ *inf* le'aktsets; *pst* 'eektsets; *pres* me'aktsets; *fut* ye'aktsets; **2.** להשתוקק לגירוד

(need scratching) leheeshtokek le-gerood; *pst* heeshtokek *etc; pres* meeshtokek *etc; fut* yeeshtokek *etc.*

(to be) itching 1. להרגיש עקצוצים *inf* lehargeesh 'eektsootseem; *pst* heergeesh *etc; pres* margeesh *etc; fut* yargeesh *etc;* **2.** להרגיש גירוי לגרד *inf* lehargeesh gerooy legared; *pst* heergeesh *etc; pres* margeesh *etc; fut* yargeesh *etc.*

itchy מגורה *adj* megoor|eh/-ah.

(to feel) itchy לחוש מגורה *inf* lakhoosh megoreh *pst & pres* khash *etc; fut* yakhoosh *etc.*

item פריט *nm* preet/-eem (*pl+of:* -ey).

(to) itemize 1. לפרט *inf* lefaret; *pst* perat *(p=f); pres* mefaret; *fut* yefaret; **2.** לרשום פריט פריט *inf* leershom preet preet; *pst* rasham *etc; pres* roshem *etc; fut* yeershom *etc.*

itinerant 1. עובר אורח *nmf & adj* 'over/-et orakh; **2.** נייד (mobile) *adj* na|yad/-yedet.

itinerary 1. תוכנית נסיעות *nf* tokhnee|t/-yot nesee'ot; **2.** לוח זמנים *nm* loo|'akh/-khot zmaneem.

its שלו/שלה *pron m/f* (Hebrew having no neuter gender) shel|o/-ah.

itself הוא/היא עצמו/־ה *pron m/f* (Hebrew having no neuter gender) hoo/hee 'atsm|o/-ah.

(by) itself בעצמו/בעצמה *pron m/f* (Hebrew having no neuter gender) be-'atsm|o/-ah.

(in) itself עצמו / עצמה *pron m/f* (Hebrew having no neuter gender) 'atsm|o/-ah.

ivory שנהב *nm* shenhav.

ivory tower מגדל שן *nm* meegd|al/-eley shen.

ivy קיסוס *nm* keesos/-eem (*pl+of:* -ey).

J.

J,j has no equivalent consonant in Hebrew. It exists only in words of foreign origin, in which it is transliterated mostly by using a Geemal (ג׳) or, sometimes, a Zayeen (ז׳), each marked by an apostrophe.

(to) jab לתבוע *inf* leetbo'a'; *pst* tava' *(v=b); pres* tove'a'; *fut* yeetba'.

jabber פטפוט *nm* peetpoot/-eem (*pl+of:* -ey)

(to) jabber לפטפט *inf* lefatpet; *pst* peetpet *(p=f); pres* mefatpet; *fut* yefatpet.

jack 1. מנוף *nm* manof/-eem (*pl+of:* -ey); **2.** מגבה (lifting device) *nm* magbe|'ah/-heem (*pl+of:* -hey).

jack of all trades מומחה לכל *nm* moomkh|eh/-eet la-kol.

jack pot פרס עיקרי *nm* pras 'eekaree.

jack rabbit ארנב *nm* arn|av/-aveem (*pl+of:* -evey).

(to) jack up להרים במגבה *inf* lehareem be-magbe'ah; *pst* hereem *etc; pres* mereem *etc; fut* yareem *etc.*

jackal תן *nm* tan/-eem (*pl+of:* -ey).

jackass טיפש *nmf* teep|esh/-shah.

jacket 1. מקטורן *nm* meektoren/-neem (*pl+of:* -ney); **2.** ז׳אקט *nm* jacket/-eem.

(book) jacket עטיפה *nf* 'ateef|ah/-ot (*+of:* -at).

jackknife אולר גדול olar gadol.

Jaffa יפו *nf* yafo (*cpr* yafo).

jagged מחורץ *adj* mekhor|ats/-etset.

jail 1. כלא *nm* kele (*pl:* batey kele'); **2.** בית סוהר (prison) *nm* bet/batey sohar.

(to) jail 1. לכלוא *inf* leekhlo; *pst* kala *(k=kh); pres* kole; *fut* yeekhla; **2.** לאסור (arrest) *inf* le'esor; *pst* asar; *pres* oser; *fut* ye'esor.

jailer, jailor 1. כלאי *nm* kal|ay/-a'eem (*pl+of:* -a'ey); **2.** סוהר *nmf* soher/-et (*pl:* sohar|eem/-ot; *pl+of:* -ey).

jalopy טרנטה *[slang]* trant|eh/-ot.

jam 1. ריבה *nf* reeb|ah/-ot (*+of:* -at); **2.** צרה (trouble) tsar|ah/-ot (*+of:* -at).

(in a) jam בצרה *adv* be-tsarah.

(to) jam לדחוס *inf* leedkhos; *pst* dakhas; *pres* dokhes; *fut* yeedkhos.

(to) jam on the brakes ללחוץ על הבלמים leelkhots 'al ha-blameem; *pst* lakhats *etc; pres* lokhets *etc; fut* yeelkhats *etc.*

(to) jam one's fingers נתפסו לו האצבעות *v pst* neetpesoo lo ha-etsba'ot.

jam session מפגש מנגני ג׳אז *nm* meefgash menagney jaz.

(to) jam through לפרוץ בכוח *inf* leefrots be-kho'akh *(kh=k); pst* parats *etc (p=f); pres* porets *etc; fut* yeefrots *etc.*

(traffic) jam פקק תנועה pekak/-ey tnoo'ah.

jamming הפרעות לרדיו *nf pl* hafra'ot le-radyo.

janitor 1. שרת *nm* sharat/-eem (*pl+of:* -ey); **2.** שוער (porter) *nm* sho|'er/-'areem (*pl+of:* -'arey); **3.** חצרן (courtyard caretaker) *nm* khatsran/-eem (*pl+of:* -ey).

January ינואר *nm* yanoo'ar.

Japan יפן *nf* yapan.

Japanese 1. יפני *nmf & adj* yapanee/-t; **2.** יפנית (language) *nf* yapaneet.

jar צנצנת *nf* tseents|enet/-anot.

(large earthen) jar כד חרס גדול n kad/-ey kheres gadol/gedoleem.

(to) jar לצרום *inf* leetsrom; *pst* tsaram; *pres* tsorem; *fut* yeetsrom.

(to) jar one's nerves לעלות על העצבים *inf* la'alot 'al ha-'atsabeem; *pst* 'alah *etc;* *pres* 'oleh *etc;* *fut* ya'aleh *etc.*

jargon 1. עגה מקצועית *nf* 'ag|ah/-ot meektso'ee|t/-yot; **2.** ז'רגון *nm* jargon/-eem.

jasmine יסמין *nm* yasmeen/-eem (*pl+of:* -ey).

jasper יושפה *nm* yoshfeh.

jaundice צהבת *nf* tsahevet.

jaunt 1. טיול *nm* teeyool/-eem (*pl+of:* -ey); **2.** מסע (trip) mas|a'/-a'ot (*pl+of:* -'ey).

(to) jaunt לטייל *inf* letayel; *pst* teeyel; *pres* metayel; *fut* yetayel.

jaw 1. לסת *nf* les|et/-atot; **2.** סנטר (chin) *nm* sant|er/-ereem (*pl+of:* -trey); **3.** פה (mouth) *nm* peh/peeyot.

jawbone עצם הלסת *nf* 'etsem/'atsmot ha-leset.

jay עורב ביצות *nm* 'or|ev/-vey beetsot.

jaywalker הולך רגל שהוא עבריין תנועה *nmf* holekh/-et regel she-hoo/hee 'avaryan/-eet tenoo'ah.

jazz ג'אז *nm* jaz.

(to play) jazz לנגן ג'אז *inf* lenagen jaz; *pst* neegen jaz; *pres* menagen jaz; *fut* yenagen jaz.

(to) jazz up לעשות שמח *inf* la'asot same'akh; *pst* 'asah *etc;* *pres* 'oseh *etc;* *fut* ya'aseh *etc.*

jealous קנאי *nmf & adj* kan|ay/-a'eet.

(to be) jealous of someone לקנא במישהו *inf* lekane be-mee-she-hoo; *pst* keene *etc;* *pres* mekane *etc;* *fut* yekane *etc.*

jealousy קנאה *nf* keen|'ah/-'ot (*+of:* -'at).

jeans 1. מכנסי עבודה *nm pl* meekhnesey 'avodah; **2.** ג'ינס *nm* jeens/-eem (*pl+of:* -ey).

jeep ג'יפ *nm* jeep/-eem (*pl+of:* -ey).

jeer לעג *nm* la'ag.

(to) jeer ללעוג *inf* leel'og; *pst* la'ag; *pres* lo'eg; *fut* yeel'ag.

(to) jeer at לעשות ללעג *inf* la'asot le-la'ag; *pst* 'asah *etc;* *pres* 'oseh *etc;* *fut* ya'aseh *etc.*

jelly 1. קריש *nm* kareesh (*+of:* kreesh/-ey); **2.** מיקפא (frozen) *nm* meekp|a/-a'eem (*pl+of:* -e'ey); **3.** ג'לי *nm* jelee.

(to) jeopardize לסכן *inf* lesaken; *pst* seeken; *pres* mesaken; *fut* yesaken.

jeopardy סיכון *nm* seekoon/-eem (*pl+of:* -ey).

Jericho יריחו *nf* yereekho.

jerk 1. דחיפה (push) *nf* dekheef|ah/-ot (*+of:* -at); **2.** שוטה (fool) *nm* shot|eh/-eem (*pl+of:* -ey); **3.** תמהוני (queer) *nm* teemhon|ee/-eem (*pl+of:* -ey).

(to) jerk לסחוב לפתע *inf* leeskhov le-feta' *(f=p);* *pst* sakhav *etc;* *pres* sokhev *etc;* *fut* yeeskhav *etc.*

jerked beef בשר בקר מיובש *nm* besar bakar meyoobash.

jersey אפודת צמר *nf* afood|at/-ot tsemer.

Jerusalem ירושלים *nf* yerooshalayeem.

jest 1. בדיחה *nf* bedeekh|ah/-ot (*+of:* -at); **2.** הלצה (joke) *nf* halats|ah/-ot (*+of:* -at).

(to) jest להתבדח *inf* leheetbade'akh; *pst* heetbade'akh; *pres* meetbade'akh; *fut* yeetbade'akh.

jester 1. בדחן *nm* badkhan/-eem (*pl+of:* -ey); **2.** ליצן (clown) *nm* leytsan/-eem (*pl+of:* -ey).

jet סילון *nm* seelon/-eem (*pl+of:* -ey).

(gas) jet סילון גז *nm* seelon/-ey gaz.

jet airplane מטוס סילון *nm* metos/-ey seelon.

jet engine מנוע סילון *nm* meno|'a'/-'ey seelon.

jet-black שחור משחור *adj* shakhor mee-shkhor.

Jew יהודי *nm* yehood|ee/-eem (*pl+of:* -ey).

jewel אבן טובה *nf* even/avaneem tov|ah/-ot.

jewel box תיבת תכשיטים *nf* teyv|at/-ot takhsheeteem.

jeweler 1. צורף (goldsmith) *nm* tsor|ef/feem (*pl+of:* -fey); **2.** סוחר תכשיטים (storekeeper) *nm* sokh|er/-arey takhsheeteem.

jewelry תכשיטים *nm pl* takhsheet|eem (*pl+of:* -ey).

jewelry store חנות תכשיטים *nf* khanoo|t/-yot takhsheeeteem.

Jewess יהודייה *nf* yehoodee|yah/-yot (*+of:* -yat).

Jewish יהודי *adj* yehodee/-t.

Jewish Agency 1. הסוכנות היהודית *nf* ha-sokhnoot ha-yehoodeet; **2.** הסוכנות *[colloq.] abbr.* ha-sokhnoot.

Jewry היהדות *nf* ha-yahadoot.

(World) Jewry יהדות העולם *nf* yahadoot ha-'olam.

jiffy הרף עין *nm* heref 'ayeen.

(in a) jiffy כהרף עין *adv* ke-heref 'ayeen.

jig כרכור *nm* keerkoor/-eem (*pl+of:* -ey).

(to) jig לכרכר *inf* lekharker; *pst* keerker *(k=kh);* *pres* mekharker; *fut* yekharker.

jig saw מסור נימה *nm* masor/-ey neemah.

jiggle נענוע *nm* nee'noo|'a'/-'eem (*pl+of:* -'ey).

(to) jiggle 1. לנענע *vt inf* lena'ne'a'; *pst* nee'ne'a'; *pres* mena'ne'a'; *fut* yena'ne'a'; **2.** להתנועע *v rfl inf* leheetno'e'a'; *pst* heetno'a'; *pres* meetno'e'a'; *fut* yeetno'a'.

jigsaw puzzle 1. תצרף *nm* tatsref/-eem (*pl+of:* -'ey); **2.** חידת תחתיך *nf* kheed|at/-ot takhteekh; **3.** פאזל *[colloq.] m* pazel/-eem.

(to) jilt לנטוש אהוב *inf* leentosh ahoov/-ah; *pst* natash *etc;* *pres* notesh *etc;* *fut* yeetosh *etc.*

jingle צלצול *nm* tseeltsool/-eem (*pl+of:* -ey).

jingle-bell פעמון *nm* pa'amon/-eem (*pl+of:* -ey).

job 1. תפקיד *nm* tafkeed/-eem (*pl+of:* -ey); **2.** מישרה (function) *nf* meesr|ah/-ot (*+of:* -at); **3.** ג'וב *[colloq.] m* job/-eem (*pl+of:* -ey).

(out of a) job 1. ללא עבודה *adv* le-lo 'avodah; **2.** מובטל (unemployed) *adj* moovt|al/-elet.

jobber עובד בקבלנות *nmf* 'oved/-et be-kablanoot.

jockey רוכב מירוצים *nm* rokh|ev/-vey merotseem.

(to) jockey לתמרן *inf* letamren; *pst* teemren; *pres* metamren; *fut* yetamren.

(to) join 1. לצרף *vt inf* letsaref; *pst* tseraf; *pres* metsaref; *fut* yetsaref; **2.** להצטרף *v rfl inf* leheetstaref; *pst* heetstaref; *pres* meetstaref; *fut* yeetstaref.

joint 1. פרק *nm* perek/prakeem (*pl+of:* peerkey); **2.** מפרק (articulation) *nm* meefrak/-eem (*pl+of:* meefrekey); **3.** מאוחד (united) *adj* me'ookh|ad/-edet.

(out of) joint 1. שנשמט מפרקו *adj* she-neeshm|at/-etah mee-peerk|o/-ah; **2.** נקוע (dislocated) *adj* nakoo'a'/nekoo'ah; **3.** שלא כתקנו (out of order) *adj* she-lo ke-teekn|o/-ah.

joint account חשבון משותף *nm* kheshbon/-ot meshootaf/-eem.

joint action פעולה משותפת *nf* pe'ool|ah/-ot meshoot|efet/-afot.

joint committee ועד משותף *nm* va'ad/ve'adeem meshootaf/-eem.

joint creditor נושה משותף *nm* nosh|eh/-eem meshootaf/-eem.

Joint Distribution Committee הג׳וינט *nm* ha-joint.

joint heir יורש משותף *nm* yor|esh/-sheem meshootaf/-eem.

joint session ישיבה משותפת *nf* yesheev|ah/-ot meshoot|efet/-afot.

jointly במשותף *adv* bee-meshootaf.

joke 1. בדיחה *nf* bedeekh|ah/-ot (*+of:* -at); **2.** הלצה (jest) *nf* halats|ah/-ot (*+of:* -at).

(to) joke להתלוצץ *inf* leheetlotsets; *pst* heetlotsets; *pres* meetlotsets; *fut* yeetlotsets.

joker 1. ליצן *nm* leytsan/-eem (*pl+of:* -ey); **2.** קלף ליצן (card) klaf/kalfey leytsan.

jokingly 1. בהלצה *adv* ba-halatsah; **2.** בצחוק (jestingly) bee-tsekhok.

jolly 1. עליז *adj* 'aleez/-ah; **2.** משמח (gladdening) *adj* mesam|e'akh/-akhat; **3.** מאד (very) *adv* me'od.

jolt מכת פתע *nf* mak|at/-ot peta'.

(to) jolt 1. לטלטל *inf* letaltel; *pst* teeltel; *pres* metaltel; *fut* yetaltel; **2.** למשוך לפתע (snatch) *inf* leemshokh le-feta' *(f=p)*; *pst* mashakh *etc*; *pres* moshekh *etc*; *fut* yeemshokh *etc*.

jostle 1. היתקלות *nf* heetakloo|t/-yot; **2.** הידחקות (thrusting oneself) *nf* heedakhkoo|t/-yot.

(to) jostle 1. לדחוף *vt* leedkhof; *pst* dakhaf; *pres* dokhef; *fut* yeedkhof; **2.** להידחף (thrust oneself) *inf* leheedakhef; *pst & pres* needkhaf; *fut* yeedakhef.

jot נקודה *nf* nekood|ah/-ot (*+of:* -at).

(to) jot down לרשום בקצרה *inf* leershom bee-ketsarah; *pst* rasham *etc*; *pres* roshem *etc*; *fut* yeershom *etc*.

journal 1. עיתון *nm* 'eeton/-eem (*pl+of:* -ey); **2.** ז׳ורנאל *nm* joornal/-eem (*pl+of:* -ey); **3.** יומן (diary) *nm* yoman/-eem (*pl+of:* -ey).

journalism עיתונאות *nf* 'eetona'oot.

journalist עיתונאי *nmf* 'eeton|ay/-a'eet.

journalistic עיתונאי *adj* 'eetona'ee/-t.

journey מסע *nm* mas|a'/-a'ot (*pl+of:* -'ey).

(to) journey לנסוע *inf* leenso'a'; *pst* nasa'; *pres* nose'a'; *fut* yeesa'.

joy שמחה *nf* seemkhah/smakhot (*+of:* seemkh|at/-ot).

joyful 1. עליז *adj* 'aleez/-ah; **2.** מלא שימחה (joyous) *adj* mele/-'at seemkhah.

joyfully בשמחה *adv* be-seemkhah.

joyless עגום *adj* 'agoom/-ah.

joyous שמח *adj* same'akh/smekhah.

jubilant צוהל *adj* tsohel/-et.

jubilee יובל *nm* yov|el/-lot (*+of:* yovel ha-).

(diamond) jubilee יובל היהלום *nm* yovel ha-yahalom.

(golden) jubilee יובל הזהב *nm* yovel ha-zahav.

(silver) jubilee יובל הכסף *nm* yovel ha-kesef.

judge שופט *mf* shofet/-et.

(to) judge 1. לשפוט *inf* leeshpot; *pst* shafat *(f=p)*; *pres* shofet; *fut* yeeshpot; **2.** לדון (consider) *inf* ladoon; *pst & pres* dan; *fut* yadoon.

judge advocate קטיגור בבית־דין צבאי *mf* kategor/-eet be-vet-deen *(v=b)* tsva'ee.

judgment 1. שפיטה *nf* shfeet|ah/-ot (*+of:* -at); **2.** פסק דין (verdict) *nm* pesak/peeskey deen; **3.** הבנה (underestanding) havan|ah/-ot (*+of:* -at).

Judgment Day יום הדין *nm* yom ha-deen.

judicial משפטי *adj* meeshpatee/-t.

judicious 1. שקול *adj* shakool/shkoolah; **2.** מיושב (considerate) *adj* meyoosh|av/-evet.

jug 1. כד *nm* kad/-eem (*pl+of:* -ey); **2.** פח (can) *nm* pakh/-eem (*pl+of:* -ey).

(to) juggle 1. לבצע להטוטים *inf* levatse'a' lahatooteem; *pst* beetsa' *etc* (*b=v*); *pres* mevatse'a' *etc*; *fut* yevatsa' *etc*; **2.** לרמות (cheat) *inf* leramot; *pst* reemah; *pres* merameh; *fut* yerameh; **3.** לאחז עיניים (delude) *inf* le'akhez 'eynayeem; *pst* eekhez *etc*; *pres* me'akhez *etc*; *fut* ye'akhez *etc*.

(to) juggle accounts לזייף חשבונות *inf* lezayef kheshbonot; *pst* zeeyef *etc*; *pres* mezayef *etc*; *fut* yezayef *etc*.

juggler להטוטן *nmf* lahatootan/-eet.

juice 1. מיץ *nm* meets/-eem (*pl+of:* -ey); **2.** עסיס (essence) 'asees/-eem (*pl+of:* -ey).

(apple) juice מיץ תפוחים *nm* meets/-ey tapookheem.

(grapefruit) juice מיץ אשכוליות *nm* meets/-ey eshkoleeyot.

(orange) juice מיץ תפוזים *nm* meets/-ey tapoozeem.

juiciness עסיסיות *nf* 'aseeseeyoot.

juicy עסיסי *adj* 'aseesee/-t.

(a) juicy story סיפור פיקנטי *nm* seepoor/-eem peekantee/-yeem.

juke box מנגן תקליטים אוטומטי *nm* menag|en/-ney takleeteem otomatee/-yeem.

July יולי *nm* yoolee.

jumble בליל *nm* bleel/-eem (*pl+of:* -ey).

jump קפיצה *nf* kefeets|ah/-ot (*+of:* -at).

(always on the) jump תמיד עסוק מאוד *adj* tameed 'asook/-ah me'od.

(to) jump לקפוץ *inf* leekpots; *pst* kafats *(f=p)*; *pres* kofets; *fut* yeekpots.

(to) jump at the chance לקפוץ על הזדמנות *inf* leekpots 'al heezdamnoot; *pst* kafats *etc (f=p)*; *pres* kofets *etc*; *fut* yeekpots *etc*.

(to) jump bail להימלט תוך סיכון ערבות *inf* leheemalet tokh seekoon 'arevoot; *pst & pres* neemlat; *fut* yeemalet *etc*.

(to) jump over לדלג *inf* ledaleg; *pst* deeleg; *pres* medaleg; *fut* yedaleg.

(to) jump the track לרדת מן הפסים *inf* laredet meen ha-paseem; *pst* yarad *etc*; *pres* yored *etc*; *fut* yered *etc*.

(to) jump to conclusions להיחפז בהסקת מסקנות *inf* lehekhfez be-hasakat maskanot; *pst & pres* nekhpaz *etc*; *fut* yekhafez *etc (p=f)*.

jumper אפודה *nf* afood|ah/-ot (*+of:* -at).

jumpy עצבני *adj* 'atsbanee/-t.

junction 1. צומת *nm* tsomet/tsemateem (*pl+of:* tseemtey); **2.** התחברות (juncture) *nf* heetkhabroo|t/-yot.

juncture 1. מחבר *nm* makhber/-eem (*pl+of:* -ey); **2.** מיפנה (turnpoint) *nm* meefn|eh/-eem.

(at this) juncture בהזדמנות זו be-heezdamnoot zo.

June יוני *nm* yoonee.

jungle ג׳ונגל *nm* joongel/-eem (*pl+of:* -ey).

junior 1. זוטר *adj* zootar/-eet; **2.** צעיר (young) *adj* tsa'eer/tse'eerah.

juniper ערער *nm* 'ar'ar/-eem (*pl+of:* -ey).

junk 1. זבל *nm* zevel; **2.** גרוטה (scrap) *nf* groot|ah/-a'ot (*+of:* -at/-ot).

(Chinese) junk מפרשית סינית *nf* meefrasee|t/-yot seenee|t/-yot.

(to) junk להשליך כפסולת *inf* lehashleekh kee-fesolet (*f=p*); *pst* heeshleekh *etc*; *pres* mashleekh *etc*; *fut* yashleekh *etc*.

junket נסיעת־חינם בתפקיד *nf* nesee|'at/-'ot kheenam be-tafkeed.

junkie 1. נרקומן (addict) *nmf* narkoman/-eet; **2.** ספק סמים (dealer) *nmf* sapak/-eet sameem.

□ **Jupiter 1.** צדק (planet) *nm* tsedek; **2.** יופיטר (Roman god & planet) *nm* yoopeeter.

jurisdiction 1. סמכות שיפוט (competence) *nf* samkhoo|t/-yot sheefoot; **2.** תחום שיפוט (area) *nm* tekhoom/-ey sheefoot.

jurisprudence תורת המשפט *nf* torat ha-meeshpat.

jurist משפטן *nmf* meeshpetan/-eet.

juror מושבע *nm* mooshb|a'/-a'eem (*pl+of:* -e'ey).

jury חבר מושבעים *nm* khever mooshba'eem.

(grand) jury חבר מושבעים מיוחד *nm* khever mooshba'eem meyookhad.

just 1. צודק *adj* tsodek/-et; **2.** הוגן (fair) *adj* hogen/-et; **3.** רק *conj* rak; **4.** בדיוק (exactly) *adv* be-deeyook; **5.** בלבד (solely) *adv* bee-lvad.

(she is) just a little girl אינה אלא ילדונת eynah ela yaldonet.

just a minute! רגע אחד *interj* rega' ekhad!

just arrived רק הגיע *adj* rak heegee|'a'/-'ah.

just now זה עתה *adv* zeh 'atah.

(he) just left עזב אך הרגע *v pst* 'azav akh ha-rega'.

justice 1. צדק *nm* tsedek; **2.** יושר *nm* yosher.

(Chief) Justice נשיא בית המשפט העליון *nm* nesee bet ha-meeshpat ha-'elyon.

justification הצדקה *nf* hatsdak|ah/-ot (*+of:* -at).

(to) justify להצדיק *inf* lehatsdeek; *pst* heetsdeek; *pres* matsdeek; *fut* yatsdeek.

justly בצדק *adv* be-tsedek.

jut בליטה *nf* bleet|ah/-ot (*+of:* -at).

(to) jut 1. לבלוט *inf* leevlot; *pst* balat (*b=v*); *pres* bolet; *fut* yeevlot; **2.** להתבלט (stand out) *v rfl inf* leheetbalet; *pst* heetbalet; *pres* meetbalet; *fut* yeetbalet.

juvenile צעיר *adj* tsa'eer/tse'eerah.

juvenile court בית משפט לנוער *nm* bet/batey meeshpat le-no'ar.

juvenile delinquency עבריינות נוער *nf* 'avaryanoot no'ar.

juvenile delinquent עבריין צעיר *nmf* 'avaryan/-eet tsa'eer/tse'eerah.

K.

K,k consonant for which the Hebrew script has two equivalents: Koof (ק) and Kaf (כ). In this dictionary, both are transliterated k, since in the everyday speech of most people, no distinction can be detected between the way each of the two is pronounced. One is, however, advised to remember that, in Hebrew texts, while the Koof (ק) will invariably read k, the Kaf (כ) may often read kh (depending on whether, if that text were in "Pointed" script, it would be dotted (כּ) or not (כ,ך) (See Introduction)).

kangaroo קנגורו *nm* kengooroo.

Karaite קראי *nm* kara|'ee/-'eet (*pl:* -'eem; *+of:* -'ey).

keel שידרית אונייה *nf* sheedreet oneeyah.

(to) keel, (to) keel over להתהפך *inf* leheet'hapekh; *pst* heet'hapekh; *pres* meet'hapekh; *fut* yeet'hapekh.

keen 1. חריף *adj* khareef/-ah; **2.** להוט (eager) *adj* lahoot/lehootah.

keenness 1. חריפות *nf* khareefoot; **2.** מהירות תפיסה (acumen) *nf* meheeroo|t/-yot tefeesah.

keep 1. מחיה *nf* meekhyah; **2.** מבצר (fortress) *nm* meevtsar/-eem (*pl+of:* -ey).

(to) keep 1. להחזיק *inf* lehakhzeek; *pst* hekhzeek; *pres* makhzeek; *fut* yakhzeek; **2.** לקיים (preserve) *inf* lekayem; *pst* keeyem; *pres* mekayem; *fut* yekayem; **3.** לתחזק (maintain) *inf* letakhzek; *pst* teekhzek; *pres* metakhzek; *fut* yetakhzek; **4.** להמשיך (continue) *inf* lehamsheekh; *pst* heemsheekh; *pres* mamsheekh; *fut* yamsheekh.

(to) keep accounts לנהל חשבונות *inf* lenahel kheshbonot; *pst* neehel *etc*; *pres* menahel *etc*; *fut* yenahel *etc*.

(to) keep at it להתמיד *inf* lehatmeed; *pst* heetmeed; *pres* matmeed; *fut* yatmeed.

(to) keep away להתרחק מ־ *v rfl inf* leheetrakhek mee-; *pst* heetrakhek mee-; *pres* meetrakhek mee-; *fut* yeetrakhek mee-.

(to) keep back 1. למנוע (prevent) *inf* leemno'a'; *pst* mana'; *pres* mone'a'; *fut* yeemna'; **2.** לעצור (stop) *inf* la'atsor; *pst* 'atsar; *pres* 'otser; *fut* ya'atsor.

(to) keep from למנוע *inf* leemno'a'; *pst* mana'; *pres* mone'a'; *fut* yeemna'.

(to) keep going להמשיך ללכת *inf* lehamsheekh lalekhet; *pst* heemsheekh *etc*; *pres* mamsheekh *etc*; *fut* yamsheekh *etc*.

(to) keep off לשמור מרחק *inf* leeshmor merkhak; *pst* shamar *etc*; *pres* shomer *etc*; *fut* yeeshmor *etc*.

(to) keep one's hands off לא לגעת *inf* lo laga'at; *pst* lo naga'; *pres* eyno noge'a'; *fut* lo yeega'.

(to) keep one's temper לעצור ברוחו *inf* la'atsor be-rookho; *pst* 'atsar *etc*; *pres* 'otser *etc*; *fut* ya'atsor *etc*.

(to) keep quiet 1. לשתוק *inf* leeshtok; *pst* shatak; *pres* shotek; *fut* yeeshtok; **2.** לשקוט (rest) *inf* leeshkot; *pst* shakat; *pres* shaket; *fut* yeeshkot.

(to) keep something up 1. לתחזק (maintain) *inf* letakhzek; *pst* teekhzek; *pres* metakhzek; *fut* yetakhzek; **2.** לעדכן (update) *vt* le'adken; *pst* 'eedken; *pres* me'adken; *fut* ye'adken.

(to) keep to the right להקפיד על צד ימין *inf* lehakpeed 'al tsad yemeen; *pst* heekpeed *etc*; *pres* makpeed *etc*; *fut* yakpeed *etc*.

(to) keep track of לא לאבד קשר *inf* lo le'abed kesher; *pst* lo eebed; *pres* eyno me'abed *etc*; *fut* lo ye'abed *etc*.

keeper 1. שומר *nm* shom|er/-reem (*pl+of:* -rey); **2.** משגיח *nm* mashgee|'akh/-kheem (*pl+of:* -khey).

(jail) keeper 1. כלאי (warden) *nm* kal|ay/-a'eem (*pl+of:* -a'ey); **2.** סוהר (prison guard) *nmf* soher/-et (*pl:* sohar|eem/-ot; *+of:* -ey).

(Am I my brother's) keeper?! !?השומר אחי אנוכי (famous biblical quotation) ha-shomer akhee anokhee?!.

keeping 1. שמירה *nf* shmeer|ah/-ot (*+of:* -at); **2.** פרנוס *nm* (livelihood) peernoos; **3.** התאמה (adapting) *nf* hat'am|ah/-ot (*+of:* -at).

(in) keeping with -בהתאם ל be-het'em le-.

(for) keeps לתמיד *adv* le-tameed.

keepsake מזכרת *nf* mazk|eret/-arot.

keg חביונה *nf* khaveeyon|ah/-ot (*+of:* -at).

kennel 1. מלונה *nf* meloon|ah/-ot (*+of:* -at); **2.** בית גידול לכלבים *nm* bet/batey geedool lee-khlaveem (*kh=k*).

kerchief ממחטה *nf* meemkh|atah/-atot (*+of:* -etet).

kernel גרעין *nm* gar'een/-eem (*pl+of:* -ey).

kerosene נפט *nm* neft.

kettle 1. קומקום *nm* koomkoom/-eem (*pl+of:* -ey); **2.** דוד (boiler) *nm* dood/dvadeem (*pl+of:* doodey).

(tea) kettle קומקום תה *nm* koomkoom/-ey teh.

kettledrum תוף דוד *nm* tof/toopey (*p=f*) dood/dvadeem.

key מפתח *nm* mafte|'akh/-khot.

(in) key בראש אחד be-rosh ekhad.

(to) key 1. לנעול *inf* leen'ol; *pst* na'al; *pres* no'el; *fut* yeen'al; **2.** לכוון *inf* lekhaven; *pst* keeven; *pres* mekhaven; *fut* yekhaven.

key ring צרור מפתחות *nm* tsror maftekhot.

key word מלת מפתח *nf* meel|at/-ot mafte'akh.

(to) key up 1. להמריץ *inf* lehamreets; *pst* heemreets; *pres* mamreets; *fut* yamreets; **2.** לעודד (encourage) *inf* le'oded; *pst* 'oded; *pres* me'oded; *fut* ye'oded; **3.** לעורר (awaken) *inf* le'orer; *pst* 'orer; *pres* me'orer; *fut* ye'orer.

keyboard מקלדת *nf* meekl|edet/-adot.

keyed up 1. מתוח *adj* matoo'akh/metookhah; **2.** מעוצבן (nervous) *adj* me'ootsb|an/-enet.

keyhole חור המנעול *nm* khor ha-man'ool.

keynote צליל מוביל *nm* tsleel/-eem moveel/-eem.

keystone 1. עיקרון *nm* 'eekaron/'ekronot; **2.** אבן פינה (cornerstone) *nf* even/avney peenah.

khaki חקי *nm* khakee.

(to) kibbitz לייעץ מבלי שנתבקש *inf* leya'ets mee-blee she-neetbak|esh/-shah; *pst* yee'ets *etc*; *pres* meya'ets *etc*; *fut* yeya'ets *etc*.

kibbitzer 1. יועץ מבלי שנתבקש *nm* yo|'ets/'atseem mee-blee she-neetbak|esh/-shoo; **2.** קיביצר *nmf* keebeetser/-eet.

kick בעיטה *nf* be'eet|ah/-ot (*+of:* -at).

(to) kick לבעוט *inf* leev'ot; *pst* ba'at (*b=v*); *pres* bo'et; *fut* yeev'at.

(to have a) kick ליהנות *inf* lehanot; *pst* nehenah; *pres* neheneh; *fut* yehaneh.

(to) kick out להשליך החוצה *inf* lehashleekh ha-khootsah; *pst* heeshleekh *etc*; *pres* mashleekh *etc*; *fut* yashleekh *etc*.

(to) kick the bucket להתפגר *v rfl inf* leheetpager; *pst* heetpager; *pres* meetpager; *fut* yeetpager.

(to) kick up a lot of dust להקים מהומה רבה *inf* lehakeem mehoomah rabah; *pst* hekeem *etc*; *pres* mekeem *etc*; *fut* yakeem *etc*.

kickback 1. תשובה ניצחת *nf* teshoov|ah/-ot neetsakh|at/-ot; **2.** החזר מאונס *nm* hekhzer/-eem me-ones.

kickoff התחלה *nf* hatkhal|ah/-ot (*+of:* -at).

kid 1. ילד *nm* yel|ed/-adeem (*pl+of:* yaldey); **2.** גדי (young goat) *nm* ged|ee/-ayeem (*pl+of:* -ayey).

(to) kid 1. לקנטר *inf* lekanter; *pst* keenter; *pres* mekanter; *fut* yekanter; **2.** להתלוצץ (joke) *inf* leheetlotsets; *pst* heetlotsets; *pres* meetlotsets; *fut* yeetlotsets.

kid gloves כפפות משי *nf* keefefot meshee.

(to) kidnap לחטוף *inf* lakhtof; *pst* khataf; *pres* khotef; *fut* yakhtof.

kidnapper חוטף *nm* khot|ef/-feem (*pl+of:* -fey).

kidnapping חטיפה *nf* khateef|ah/-ot (*+of:* -at).

kidney כליה *nf* keelyah/klayot (*+of:* keel|yat/-yot).

kidney bean שעועית *nf* she'oo'eet.

kidney stones אבנים בכבד *nf pl* avaneem ba-kaved.

kill 1. הרג *nm* hereg; **2.** טרף *nm* teref.

(to) kill 1. להרוג *inf* laharog; *pst* harag; *pres* horeg; *fut* yaharog; **2.** לקטול (slay) *inf* leektol; *pst* katal; *pres* kotel; *fut* yeektol.

killer 1. רוצח *nmf* rotse'akh/-akhat; **2.** הורג *nmf* horeg/-et.

kiln 1. כבשן *nm* keevshan/-eem (*pl+of:* -ey); **2.** משרפה *nf* meesraf|ah/-ot.

kilo קילו *nm* keelo.

kilogram 1. קילוגרם *nm* keelogram/-eem; **2.** ק"ג (*acr* of 1) kgr.

kilometer 1. קילומטר *nm* keelometer; **2.** ק״מ (*acr of* 1) km.
kimono קימונו *nm* keemono.
kin 1. משפחה *nf* meeshp|akhah/-akhot (+*of:* -akhat/-ekhot); **2.** קרוב (relative) *nmf* karov/krov|ah (*pl:* -eem/-ot; +*of:* -at/-ey).
(nearest of) kin קרוב דם *nmf* krov/-at dam (*pl:* -ey).
(next of) kin בן־משפחה הקרוב ביותר *nmf* ben/bat meeshpakhah ha-karov/ha-krovah be-yoter.
kind 1. סוג *nm* soog/-eem (*pl+of:* -ey); **2.** טוב־לב *adj* tov/-at lev.
(pay in) kind 1. להחזיר מידה כנגד מידה *inf* lehakhzeer meedah ke-neged meedah; *pst* hekhzeer *etc; pres* makhzeer *etc; fut* yakhzeer *etc;* **2.** לשלם בסחורה (barter) *inf* leshalem bee-sekhorah; *pst* sheelem *etc; pres* meshalem *etc; fut* yeshalem *etc.*
kind of משהו כמו *nm* mashehoo kemo.
kind of tired עייף כלשהו *adj* 'ayef/-ah kolshehoo.
kind regards 1. דרישת שלום *nf* dreesh|at/-ot shalom; **2.** ד״ש חם *acr nm* dash kham.
kind-hearted טוב לב *adj* tov/-at lev.
(all) kinds of כל מיני kol meeney.
kindergarten גן ילדים *nm* gan/-ey yeladeem.
(to) kindle 1. להדליק *inf* lehadleek; *pst* heedleek; *pres* madleek; *fut* yadleek; **2.** לשלהב (inflame) *inf* leshalhev; *pst* sheelhev; *pres* meshalhev; *fut* yeshalhev.
kindling הדלקה *nf* hadlak|ah/-ot (+*of:* -at).
kindly באדיבות *adv* ba-adeevoot.
(not to take) kindly to criticism לא לסבול ביקורת *inf* lo leesbol beekoret; *pst* lo saval *etc* (*v=b*); *pres* eyno sovel *etc; fut* lo yeesbol *etc.*
kindness טוב לב *nm* toov lev.
kindred 1. משפחה *nf* meeshp|akhah/-akhot (+*of:* -akhat/-ekhot); **2.** קרובים *nm pl* krov|eem (*pl+of:* -ey).
kindred facts עובדות מתקשרות *nf pl* 'oovdot meetkashrot.
kindred spirits נשמות אחיות *nf pl* neshamot akhayot.
king מלך *nm* mel|ekh/-akheem (*pl+of:* malkhey).
kingdom 1. ממלכה *nf* maml|akhah/-akhot (+*of:* -ekhet/-ekhot); **2.** מלוכה (monarchy) *nf* melookh|ah/-ot (+*of:* -at); **3.** מלכות (royalty) *nf* malkhoo|t/-yot.
kingly 1. כיד המלך *adv* ke-yad ha-melekh; **2.** מלכותי (royal) *adj* malkhootee/-t.
kink 1. סלסול *nm* seelsool/-eem (*pl+of:* -ey); **2.** תלתול (twist) *nm* teeltool/-eem (*pl+of:* -ey).
kinky 1. מוזר *adj* moozar/-ah; **2.** לא חלק *adj* lo khalak/-ah.
kinship קרבת־משפחה *nf* keervat meeshpakhah.
kinsman קרוב משפחה *nm* krov/-ey meeshpakhah.
kipper דג מעושן *nm* dag/-eem me'ooshan/-eem.
kiss נשיקה *nf* nesheek|ah/-ot (+*of:* -at).
(to) kiss 1. לנשק *vt inf* lenashek; *pst* neeshek; *pres* menashek; *fut* yenashek; **2.** להתנשק *v refl* leheetnashek; *pst* heetnashek; *pres* meetnashek; *fut* yeetnashek

kit 1. זווד *nm* zvad/-eem (*pl+of:* -ey); **2.** תרמיל (bag) *nm* tarmeel/-eem (*pl+of:* -ey); **3.** ציוד (equipment) *nm* tseeyood.
(assembly) kit מערכת הרכבה *nf* ma'ar|ekhet/-khot harkavah.
(soldier's) kit, kitbag תרמיל חיילים *nm* tarmeel/-ey khayaleem.
kitchen מטבח *nm* meetb|akh/-akheem (*pl+of:* -ekhey).
kitchen range תנור מטבח *nm* tanoor/-ey meetbakh.
kitchen sink כיור מטבח *nm* keeyor/-ey meetbakh.
kitchenette מטבחון *nm* meetbekhon/-eem (*pl+of:* -ey).
kitchenware כלי מטבח *nm pl* kley meetbakh.
kite עפיפון *nm* 'afeefon/-eem (*pl+of:* -ey).
kitten חתלתולה *nf* khataltool|ah/-ot (*pl+of:* -at).
kitty 1. חתלתול *nm* khataltool/-eem (*pl+of:* -ey); **2.** קופת התערבויות (in games) *nf* koop|at/-ot heet'arvooyot.
knack 1. כשרון *nm* keeshron/-ot; **2.** מיומנות (dexterity) *nf* meyoomanoo|t/-yot.
knapsack תרמיל גב *nm* tarmeel/-ey gav.
knave 1. נוכל *nm* nokh|el/-leem (*pl+of:* -ey); **2.** נבל (scoundrel) *nm* naval/nevaleem.
(to) knead ללוש *inf* laloosh; *pst & pres* lash; *fut* yaloosh.
knee ברך *nf* berekh/beerk|ayeem (*k=kh; pl+of:* -ey).
knee-deep עד הברכיים *adv* 'ad ha-beerkayeem.
(to) kneel לכרוע ברך *inf* lekhro'a' berekh; *pst* kara' *etc* (*k=kh*); *pres* kore'a' *etc; fut* yeekhra' *etc.*
knell צלצול פעמונים *nm* tseeltsool/-ey pa'amoneem.
(to) knell להזעיק בפעמונים *inf* lehaz'eek be-fa'amoneem (*f=p*); *pst* heez'eek *etc; pres* maz'eek *etc; fut* yaz'eek *etc.*
knicknack 1. תכשיט *nm* takhsheet/-eem (*pl+of:* -ey); **2.** קישוט (ornament) *nm* keeshoot/-eem (*pl+of:* -ey).
knife סכין *nm* sakeen/-eem (*pl+of:* -ey).
(carving) knife 1. מאכלת *nf* ma'akhelet; **2.** סכין קצבים (butchers knife) *nm* sakeen/-ey katsaveem.
(pocket) knife אולר *nm* olar/-eem (*pl+of:* -ey).
knight אביר *nm* abeer/-eem (*pl+of:* -ey).
knight-errant 1. אביר נודד *nm* abeer noded; **2.** הרפתקן (adventurer) *nm* harpatkan/-eem (*pl+of:* -ey).
knighthood 1. אבירות *nf* abeeroo|t/-yot; **2.** תואר אבירות (title) *nm* to'ar/-ey abeeroot.
(to) knit לסרוג *inf* leesrog; *pst* sarag; *pres* soreg; *fut* yeesrog.
(to) knit one's brow להזעים גבות *inf* lehaz'eem gabot; *pst* heez'eem *etc; pres* maz'eem *etc; fut* yaz'eem *etc.*
knitting סריגה *nf* sreeg|ah/-ot (+*of:* -at).
knitting machine מכונת סריגה *nf* mekhon|at/-ot sreegah.
knitting needle מחט סריגה *nf* makhat/mekhatey sreegah.
knob 1. כפתור (button) *nm* kaftor/-eem (*pl+of:* -ey); **2.** גולה (ball-shaped) *nf* gool|ah/-ot (+*of:* at).
knock 1. דפיקה *nf* dfeek|ah/-ot (+*of:* -at); **2.** מכה *nf* mak|ah/-ot (+*of:* -at).

(to) knock 1. לדפוק *inf* leedpok; *pst* dafak *(f=p)*; *pres* dofek; *fut* yeedpok; **2.** להקיש (on door) *inf* lehakeesh; *pst* heekeesh; *pres* makeesh; *fut* yakeesh.

(to) knock down 1. להפיל ארצה *inf* lehapeel artsah; *pst* heepeel *etc*; *pres* mapeel *etc*; *fut* yapeel *etc*; **2.** להוריד מחיר (reduce price) *inf* lehoreed mekheer; *pst* horeed *etc*; *pres* moreed *etc*; *fut* yoreed *etc*.

(to) knock off 1. לחדול (cease) *inf* lakhadol; *pst* khadal; *pres* khadel; *fut* yekhdal; **2.** להפסיק עבודה (stop work) *inf* lehafseek 'avodah; *pst* heefseek *etc*; *pres* mafseek *etc*; *fut* yafseek *etc*.

(to) knock out לגבור במכה ניצחת *inf* leegbor be-makah neetsakhat; *pst* gavar *(v=b) etc*; *pres* gover *etc*; *fut* yeegbar *etc*.

knock-kneed כפוף ברכיים *adj* kefoof/-at beerkayeem.

knocker מקוש דלת *nm* makosh/-ey delet.

knoll 1. גבעה *nf* geev'ah/gva'ot (*+of:* geev|'at/-'ot); **2.** תל *nm* tel/teel|eem (*pl+of:* -ey).

knot 1. קשר *nm* kesh|er/-areem (*pl+of:* keeshrey); **2.** סיבוך (complication) *nm* seebookh/-eem (*pl+of:* -ey).

(to) knot לקשור *inf* leekshor; *pst* kashar; *pres* kosher; *fut* yeekshor.

knotty מסובך *adj* mesoob|akh/-ekhet.

(to) know לדעת *inf* lada'at; *pst* yada'; *pres* yode'a'; *fut* yeda'.

(to be in the) know להיות בסוד הדברים *inf* leehyot be-sod ha-dvareem; *pst* hayah *etc*; *pres* heen|o/-ah *etc*; *fut* yeehyeh *etc*.

know-how ידע מעשי *nm* yeda' ma'asee.

(to) know how to לדעת כיצד *inf* lada'at keytsad; *pst* yada' *etc*; *pres* yode'a' *etc*; *fut* yeda' *etc*.

(to) know of לדעת אודות *inf* lada'at odot; *pst* yada' *etc*; *pres* yode'a' *etc*; *fut* yeda' *etc*.

knowingly ביודעין *adv* be-yod'een.

knowledge ידיעה *nf* yedee|'ah/-'ot (*+of:* -'at).

(not to my) knowledge לא ככל שלי ידוע lo ke-khol she-lee yadoo'a'.

known ידוע *adj* yadoo'a'/yedoo'ah.

knuckle פרק אצבע *nm* perek/peerkey etsb|a'/-a'ot.

(to) knuckle להכות בפירקי אצבעות *inf* lehakot be-feerkey *(f=p)* etsba'ot.

(to) knuckle down להתמסר *inf* leheetmaser; *pst* heetmaser; *pres* meetmaser; *fut* yeetmaser.

knurl בליטה *nf* bleet|ah/-ot (*+of:* -at).

knurled מחורץ *adj* mekhor|ats/-etset.

Korea קוריאה *nf* kore'ah

Korean 1. קוריאני *adj & nmf* kore'anee/-t **2.** קוריאנית (language) *nf* kore'aneet.

kosher כשר *adj* kasher.

(to) kosher להכשיר *v inf* lehakh'sheer; *pst* heekh'sheer; *pres* makh'sheer; *fut* yakh'sheer.

K.W.H. 1. קילוואט־שעה (kilowatt-hour) *nm* keelovat/-eem sha'ah; **2.** קוו״ש (*acr of* 1).

L.

L,l is equivalent to the Hebrew consonant Lamed (ל).

"lab" מעבדה *nf* ma'ab|adah/-adot (*+of:* -edet).

label 1. תווית *nf* tavee|t/-yot; **2.** תו (mark) *nm* tav/-eem (*pl+of:* -ey).

(to) label 1. להדביק תוויות *inf* lehadbeek taveeyot; *pst* heedbeek *etc*; *pres* madbeek *etc*; *fut* yadbeek *etc*; **2.** לסווג (classify) *inf* lesaveg; *pst* seeveg; *pres* mesaveg; *fut* yesaveg.

labor 1. עמל (toil) *nm* 'amal; **2.** עבודה (work) 'avod|ah/-ot (*+of:* -at).

labor union ארגון עובדים *nm* eergoon/-ey 'ovdeem.

(in) labor בצירי לידה *adv* be-tseerey leydah.

(the General Federation of) Labor הסתדרות העובדים הכללית *nf* heestadroot ha-'ovdeem ha-klaleet.

(the Israel) Labor Party מפלגת העבודה הישראלית *nf* meefleget ha-'avodah ha-yeesre'eleet.

(to) labor לעמול *inf* la'amol; *pst* 'amal; *pres* 'amel; *fut* ya'amol.

laboratory מעבדה *nf* ma'ab|adah/-adot (*+of:* -edet).

laborer פועל *nm* po'el/po'aleem (*pl+of:* po'aley).

laborious מייגע *adj* meyag|e'a'/-a'at.

labyrinth 1. מבוך *nm* mavokh; **2.** לבירינת *nm* labeereent/-eem.

lace 1. שרוך *nm* srokh/-eem (*pl+of:* -ey); **2.** תחרה *nf* takhr|ah/-ot (*+of:* -at).

(gold) lace תחרת זהב *nm* takhr|at/-ot zahav.

(to) lace 1. לקשור בשרוך *inf* leekshor bee-srokh; *pst* kashar *etc*; *pres* kosher *etc*; *fut* yeekshor *etc*; **2.** לקשט בתחרה *inf* lekashet be-takhrah; *pst* keeshet *etc*; *pres* mekashet *etc*; *fut* yekashet *etc*.

lack חוסר *nm* khoser.

(to) lack לחסור *inf* lakhsor; *pst* khasar; *pres* khaser; *fut* yakhsor.

lackadaisical אדיש *adj* adeesh/-ah.

lackey משרת *nm* meshar|et/-teem (*pl+of:* -tey).

lacking חסר *adj* khas|ar/-rat.

lacks courage חסר תעוזה *adj* khas|ar/-rat te'oozah.

lacquer לכה *nf* lak|ah/-ot (*+of:* -at).

(to) lacquer ללכות *inf* lelakot; *pst* leekah; *pres* melakeh; *fut* yelakeh.

lad 1. בחור *nm* bakhoor/-eem (*pl+of:* -ey); **2.** צעיר (young fellow) *nm* tsa'eer/tse'eer|eem (*pl+of:* -ey).

ladder סולם *nm* soolam/-ot.
laden עמוס *adj* 'amoos/-ah.
ladies גברות *nf pl* gvarot.
ladle מצקת *nf* mats|eket/-akot.
(to) ladle לצקת *inf* latseket; *pst* yatsak; *pres* yotsek; *fut* yeetsok.
lady 1. גברת *nf* gveret/gvarot; **2.** ליידי *nf* leydee/-yot.
lady love אהובה *nf* ahoov|ah/-ot (+*of:* -at).
ladylike 1. כיאה לגברת *adv* ka-ya'eh lee-gveret; **2.** יאה לגברת *adj* ya'eh/ya'ah lee-gveret.
lag פיגור *nm* peegoor/-eem (*pl+of:* -ey).
(to) lag לפגר *inf* lefager; *pst* peeger *(p=f)*; *pres* mefager; *fut* yefager.
lagoon 1. בריכה *nf* breykh|ah/-ot (+*of:* -at); **2.** לגונה *nf* lagoon|ah/-ot (+*of:* -at).
lair מרבץ *nm* meerb|ats/-atseem (*pl+of:* -etsey).
lake אגם *nm* agam/-eem (*pl+of:* -ey).
lamb 1. כבש *nm* kev|es/-aseem (*pl+of:* keevsey); **2.** כבשה (sheep) *nf* keevs|ah/-ot (+*of:* -at).
lambskin עור כבש *nm* 'or/-ot kev|es/-aseem.
lame 1. חיגר *nmf & adj* kheeger/-et; **2.** נכה רגליים *adj* nekh|eh/-at raglayeem.
lame excuse התנצלות מזויפת *nf* heetnatsloo|t/-yot mezooy|efet/-afot.
(to) lame 1. לשתק *inf* leshatek; *pst* sheetek; *pres* meshatek; *fut* yeshatek; **2.** להטיל מום *inf* lehateel moom; *pst* heeteel moom; *pres* mateel moom; *fut* yateel moom.
lament קינה *nf* keen|ah/-ot (+*of:* -at).
(to) lament לקונן *inf* lekonen; *pst* konen; *pres* mekonen; *fut* yekonen.
lamentable מצער *adj* metsa'er/-et.
lamentation קינה *nf* keen|ah/-ot (+*of:* -at)
(to) laminate לפצל לירייעות דקיקות *v inf* lefatsel lee-yeree'ot dakeekot; *pst* peetsel *(f=p) etc*; *pres* mefatsel *etc*; *fut* yefatsel *etc.*
lamp מנורה *nf* menor|ah/-ot (+*of:* -at).
lamppost פנס רחוב *nm* panas/-ey rekhov/-ot.
lampshade סוכך *nm* sokhekh/-eem (*pl+of:* -ey).
lance רומח *nm* romakh/remakheem (*pl+of:* romkhey).
(to) lance 1. לדקור ברומח *inf* leedkor be-romakh; *pst* dakar *etc*; *pres* doker *etc*; *fut* yeedkor *etc*; **2.** לדקור באזמל (medical) *inf* leedkor be-eezmel; *pst* dakar *etc*; *pres* doker *etc*; *fut* yeedkor *etc*;
land 1. אדמה *nf* adam|ah/-ot (+*of:* adm|at/-ot); **2.** קרקע *nm* kark|a'/-a'ot.
(to) land לנחות *inf* leenkhot; *pst* nakhat; *pres* nokhet; *fut* yeenkhat.
(to) land a job להסתדר בג'וב *inf* leheestader be-job; *pst* heestader *etc*; *pres* meestader *etc*; *fut* yeestader *etc.*
land-grant הקצאת קרקע *nf* hakts|a'at/-a'ot karka'.
landholder 1. אריס *nm* arees/-eem (*pl+of:* -ey); **2.** חוכר (lessee) *nm* khokh|er/-eret (*pl:* -reem/-rot; +*of:* -ey); **3.** מחזיק בקרקע (tennant) *nm* makhzeek/-eem ba-karka'.
landing נחיתה *nf* nekheet|ah/-ot (+*of:* -at).
landing field, ground שדה נחיתה *nm* sdeh/sdot nekheetah.
landing strip מסלול נחיתה *nm* maslool/-ey nekheetah.
landlady בעלת־בית *nf* ba'al|at/-ot bayeet/bateem.
landlord בעל־בית *nm* ba'al/-ey bayeet/bateem.
landmark ציון דרך *nm* tseeyoon/-ey derekh.
landowner בעל קרקעות *nm* ba'al/-ey karka'ot.
landscape נוף nof/-eem (*pl+of:* -ey).
landslide 1. מפולת הרים *nf* mapolet hareem; **2.** מהפך (electoral) mahapakh/-eem (*pl+of:* -ey).
lane 1. סמטה צרה *nf* seemt|ah/-a'ot tsar|ah/-ot; **2.** שביל *nm* shveel/-eem (*pl+of:* -ey).
language 1. לשון *nf* lashon/leshonot (+*of:* leshon); **2.** שפה *nf* saf|ah/-ot (+*of:* sf|at/-ot).
languid 1. נרפה *adj* neerp|eh/-ah; **2.** חסר מרץ *adj* khas|ar/-rat merets.
(to) languish להימוק בגעגועים *inf* leheemok be-ga'goo'eem; *pst* namak *etc*; *pres* neemok *etc*; *fut* yeemak *etc.*
languor 1. חולשה *nf* khoolsh|ah/-ot (+*of:* -at); **2.** עייפות (fatigue) *nf* 'ayefoo|t/-yot.
lank כחוש וגבוה *adj* kakhoosh/kekhooshah ve-gavo'ah/oo-gevohah.
lanky גבוה ורזה *adj* gavo'ah/gevohah ve-raz|eh/-ah.
lantern 1. פנס *nm* panas/-eem (*pl+of:* -ey); **2.** פתח תאורה *nm* petakh/peetkhey te'oorah.
lap חיק *nm* kheyk/-eem (*pl+of:* -ey).
(to) lap 1. ללקק *inf* lelakek; *pst* leekek; *pres* melakek; *fut* yelakek; **2.** ללחך (lick) *inf* lelakhekh; *pst* leekhekh; *pres* melakhekh; *fut* yelakhekh.
(to) lap over לדלג על *inf* ledaleg 'al; *pst* deeleg 'al; *pres* medaleg 'al; *fut* yedaleg 'al.
lapel דש הבגד *nm* dash/-ey ha-beged/begadeem.
lapidary 1. לוטש *adj & v pres* lotesh/-et; **2.** סוחר באבנים טובות (dealer) *nm* sokher/areem ba-avaneem tovot.
lapse 1. שגיאה קלה (slight error) *nf* shgee|'ah/-'ot kal|ah/-ot; **2.** סטייה (deviation) *nf* stee|yah/-yot (+*of:* -yat); **3.** חלוף זמן (of time) *nm* khalof zman.
(to) lapse 1. לשגות (err) *inf* leeshgot; *pst* shagah; *pres* shogeh; *fut* yeeshgeh; **2.** להיכשל (fail) leheekashel; *pst & pres* neekhshal *(kh=k)*; *fut* yeekashel; **3.** לחלוף (pass) *inf* lakhlof; *pst* khalaf; *pres* kholef; *fut* yakhlof.
larboard צד שמאל של אונייה *nm* tsad smol shel oneeyah.
larceny גנבה *nf* gnev|ah/-ot (+*of:* -at).
lard שומן חזיר *nm* shooman khazeer.
larder מזווה *nm* mezav|eh/-eem (*pl+of:* -ey).
large גדול *adj* gadol/gedolah.
(at) large 1. מרחבי *adj* merkhavee/-t; **2.** נמלט ממאסר (escaped) *adj* neeml|at/-etet mee-ma'asar; **3.** חופשי (free) *adj* khofshee/-yah.
largely 1. ברובו *adv m/f* be-roob|o/-ah; **2.** בעיקר (mainly) *adv* be-'eekar.
large-scale בקנה־מידה גדול *adv & adj* bee-kneh meedah gadol.
lariat פלצור *nm* paltsoor/-eem (*pl+of:* -ey).
lark עפרוני *nm* 'efron|ee/-eem (*pl+of:* -ey).
larva זחל *nm* zakhal/zekhaleem (*pl+of:* zakhaley).
laryngitis דלקת גרון *nf* dal|eket/-akot garon.
larynx גרון *nm* garon/gronot (+*of:* gron).
lascivious תאוותני *adj* ta'avtanee/-t.

lash 1. שוט (whip) *nm* shot/-eem (*pl+of:* -ey); **2.** מלקות (whipping) *nf pl* malkot; **3.** עפעף (eyelashes) *nm* 'af'a|f/-payeem (*p=f; pl+of:* -pey).

(to) lash 1. להצליף *inf* lehatsleef; *pst* heetsleef; *pres* matsleef; *fut* yatsleef; **2.** להלקות *inf* lehalkot; *pst* heelkah; *pres* malkeh; *fut* yalkeh.

lass 1. נערה *nf* na'ar|ah/-ot (*+of:* -at); **2.** בחורה (girl) *nf* bakhoor|ah/-ot (*+of:* -at).

lassitude תשישות *nf* tesheeshoo|t/-yot.

last אחרון *adj* akhron/-ah (*pl:* -eem/-ot; *+of:* -ey).

last night אמש *nm* emesh.

last year אשתקד *adv* eshtakad.

(at) last סוף סוף *adv* sof sof.

(next to the) last שלפני האחרון *adj* she-leefney ha-akharon/-ah.

(to arrive) last להגיע אחרון *inf* lehagee'a' akharon; *pst* heegee'a' *etc*; *pres* magee'a' *etc*; *fut* yagee'a' *etc*.

(to) last 1. להתקיים (exist) *inf* leheetkayem; *pst* heetkayem; *pres* meetkayem; *fut* yeetkayem; **2.** להחזיק מעמד (hold out) lehakhzeek ma'amad; *pst* hekhzeek *etc*; *pres* makhzeek *etc*; *fut* yakhzeek *etc*.

lasting ממושך *adj* memoosh|akh/-ekhet.

lastly 1. לבסוף *adv* le-va-sof (*v=b*); **2.** לאחרונה (lately) *adv* la-akhronah.

latch 1. בריח *nm* bree|'akh/-kheem (*pl+of:* -khey); **2.** תפס מנעול *nm* tefes/teefsey man'ool.

(to) latch לסגור על בריח *inf* leesgor 'al bree'akh; *pst* sagar *etc*; *pres* soger *etc*; *fut* yeesgor *etc*.

late מאוחר *adj* me'ookh|ar/-eret.

late מאוחר *adv* me'ookhar.

late in the night מאוחר בלילה *adv* me'ookhar ba-laylah.

late in the week לקראת סוף השבוע *adv* leekrat sof ha-shavoo'a'.

late into the night מאוחר לתוך הלילה *adv* me'ookhar le-tokh ha-laylah.

(a) late hour שעה מאוחרת *nf* sha'ah me'ookheret.

(the) late Mr. X. מר פלוני המנוח mar plonee ha-mano'akh.

(the) late Mrs. X מרת פלונית המנוחה marat ploneet ha-menokhah.

(a) late supper ארוחת ערב מאוחרת *nf* arookh|at/-ot 'erev me'ookh|eret/-arot.

(of) late לאחרונה *adv* la-akhronah.

(ten minutes) late באיחור של עשר דקות *adv* be-'eekhoor shel 'eser dakot.

(to be) late לאחר *inf* le'akher; *pst* eekher; *pres* me'akher; *fut* ye'akher.

lately לאחרונה *adv* la-akharonah.

latent רדום *adj* radoom/redoomah.

later מאוחר יותר *adv* me'ookhar yoter.

lateral צדדי *adj* tsedadee/-t.

latest 1. הכי מאוחר *adj* ha-khee me'ookh|ar/-eret; **2.** *adv* ha-khee me'ookhar.

(at) latest 1. לכל המאוחר *adv* le-khol (*kh=k*) ha-me'ookhar; **2.** לא יאוחר מ־ (not later than) *adv* lo ye'ookhar mee-.

(the) latest fashion האופנה החדישה *nf* ha-ofn|ah/-ot ha-khadeesh|ah/-ot.

(the) latest news החדשה הטרייה ביותר *nf* ha-khadash|ah/-ot ha-tree|yah/-yot be-yoter.

lathe מחרטה *nf* makhret|ah/-ot (*+of:* -at).

lather קצף *nm* ketsef.

(to) lather להקציף *inf* lehaktseef; *pst* heektseef; *pres* maktseef; *fut* yaktseef.

Latin 1. לטיני *adj* lateenee/-t; **2.** לטינית (language) *nf* lateeneet.

Latin America 1. אמריקה הלטינית *nf* amereekah ha-lateeneet; **2.** אמל"ט (*acr of* 1) amlat.

latitude רוחב *nm* rokhav.

latter אחרון *nmf* akharon/-ah.

(towards the) latter part of the week לקראת סוף השבוע *adv* leekrat sof ha-shavoo'a'.

(the) latter זה האחרון *adj* zeh/zo ha-akhron/-ah.

lattice 1. רשת (net) *nf* resh|et/-atot (*pl+of:* reeshtot); **2.** סבכה (grill) *nf* svakh|ah/-ot (*+of:* seevkh|at/-ot).

(to) laud להלל *inf* lehalel; *pst* heelel; *pres* mehalel; *fut* yehalel.

laudable ראוי לשבח *adj* ra'ooy/re'ooyah le-shevakh.

laugh צחוק *nm* tsekhok/-eem (*pl+of:* -ey).

(to) laugh לצחוק *inf* leetskhok; *pst* tsakhak; *pres* tsokhek; *fut* yeetskhak.

(to) laugh at לצחוק מ־ *inf* leetskhok mee-; *pst* tsakhak mee-; *pres* tsokhek mee-; *fut* yeetskhak mee-.

(to) laugh loudly לצחוק בקול *inf* leetskhok be-kol; *pst* tsakhak *etc*; *pres* tsokhek *etc*; *fut* yeetskhak *etc*.

(to) laugh up one's sleeve לצחוק בסתר *inf* leetskhok ba-seter; *pst* tsakhak *etc*; *pres* tsokhek *etc*; *fut* yeetskhak *etc*.

(to) laugh in one's face לצחוק למישהו בפנים *inf* leetskhok le-meeshehoo ba-paneem; *pst* tsakhak *etc*; *pres* tsokhek *etc*; *fut* yeetskhak *etc*.

(loud) laugh צחוק קולני *nm* tsekhok kolanee.

laughable 1. מצחיק *adj* matskheek/-ah; **2.** מבדח (jesting) *adj* mevad|e'akh/-akhat.

laughter צחוק *nm* tsekhok/-eem (*pl+of:* -ey).

launch סירה גדולה *nf* seer|ah/-ot gedol|ah/-ot.

(to) launch 1. להשיק (put in water) *inf* lehasheek; *pst* heesheek; *pres* masheek; *fut* yasheek; **2.** לשגר (rocket) *inf* leshager; *pst* sheeger; *pres* meshager; *fut* yeshager; **3.** להתחיל (begin) *v inf* lehatkheel; *pst* heetkheel; *pres* matkheel; *fut* yatkheel.

(to) launch forth לשלח *inf* leshale'akh; *pst* sheelakh; *pres* meshale'akh; *fut* yeshalakh.

(to) launch forth on a journey לפתוח במסע *inf* leefto'akh be-masa'; *pst* patakh *etc* (*p=f*); *pres* pote'akh *etc*; *fut* yeeftakh *etc*.

(to) launder לכבס *inf* lekhabes; *pst* keebes (*k=kh*); *pres* mekhabes; *fut* yekhabes.

laundress כובסת *nf* kov|eset/-sot.

laundry מכבסה *nf* meekhb|asah/-asot (*+of:* -eset/-esot).

laurel עלה דפנה *nm* 'al|eh/-ey dafnah.

lava לבה *nf* lav|ah/-ot (*+of:* -at).

lavatory חדר רחצה *nm* khad|ar/-rey rakhtsah.

lavender 1. בושם (perfume) *nm* bosem/besameem (*pl+of:* bosmey); **2.** ארגמן־כחלחל (color) *adj* argaman-kekhalkhal/-ah.

lavish פזרני *adj* pazranee/-t.

(to) lavish 1. לבזבז *inf* levazbez; *pst* beezbez *(b=v)*; *pres* mevazbez; *fut* yevazbez; **2.** לפזר (squander) *inf* lefazer; *pst* peezer *(p=f)*; *pres* mefazer; *fut* yefazer.

(to) lavish praise upon להעריף שבחים על *inf* leha'areef shevakheem 'al; *pst* he'ereef *etc*; *pres* ma'areef *etc*; *fut* ya'areef *etc*.

lavishly בשפע *adv* be-shefa'.

law חוק *nm* khok/khook|eem (*pl+of:* -ey).

law-abiding שומר חוק *adj* shom|er/-rey khok.

law student סטודנט למשפטים *nmf* stoodent/-eet le-meeshpateem.

lawbreaker מפר חוק mefer/-at khok.

lawful חוקי *adj* khookee/-t.

lawless 1. פורע חוק *adj* por|e'a/-a'at khok; **2.** מופקר *nmf & adj* moofk|ar/-eret

lawmaker מחוקק *nm* mekhokek/-eem (*pl+of:* -ey).

lawn מדשאה *nf* meedsh|a'ah/-a'ot (*+of:* -e'at/-e'ot).

lawsuit תביעה משפטית *nf* tvee'ah/-'ot meesh-patee|t/-yot.

lawyer 1. עורך דין *nmf* orekh/-et (*pl:* 'orkh|ey/-ot) deen; **2.** עו"ד (*acr of* 1); **3.** פרקליט *nmf* prakleet/-ah (*+of:* -at); **4.** משפטן *nmf* meeshpetan/-eem.

lax 1. רופף *adj* rofef/-et; **2.** מרושל (negligent) *adj* meroosh|al/-elet.

laxative משלשל *nm* meshalshel/-eem (*pl+of:* -ey).

laxity 1. רשלנות (negligence) *nf* rashlanoo|t/-yot; **2.** רפיון (slackness) *nm* reefyon/-ot.

lay 1. חילוני *adj* kheelonee/-t; **2.** לא מקצועי (unprofessional) *adj* lo'-meektso'ee/-t.

(to) lay 1. להטיל *inf* lehateel; *pst* heeteel; *pres* mateel; *fut* yateel; **2.** לשים *inf* laseem; *pst & pres* sam; *fut* yaseem; **3.** להשכיב *inf* lehashkeev; *pst* heeshkeev; *pres* mashkeev; *fut* yashkeev.

(to) lay a wager להתערב *inf* leheet'arev; *pst* heet'arev; *pres* meet'arev; *fut* yeet'arev.

(to) lay aside להניח הצידה *inf* lehanee'akh ha-tseedah; *pst* heenee'akh *etc*; *pres* manee'akh; *fut* yanee'akh *etc*.

(to) lay away לשים בצד *inf* laseem ba-tsad; *pst & pres* sam *etc*; *fut* yaseem *etc*.

(to) lay by לחסוך *inf* lakhsokh; *pst* khasakh; *pres* khosekh; *fut* yakhsokh.

(to) lay bare לחשוף *inf* lakhsof; *pst* khasaf; *pres* khosef; *fut* yakhsof.

(to) lay down 1. לקבוע (assert) *inf* leekbo'a'; *pst* kava' *(v=b)*; *pres* kove'a'; *fut* yeekba'; **2.** להטיל (stake) *inf* lehateel; *pst* heeteel; *pres* mateel; *fut* yateel; **3.** לשים בצד (store) *inf* laseem ba-tsad; *pst & pres* sam *etc*; *fut* yaseem *etc*; **4.** להמר (wager) *inf* lehamer; *pst* heemer; *pres* mehamer; *fut* yehamer.

(to) lay down arms 1. להניח את הנשק *inf* lehanee'akh et ha-neshek; *pst* heenee'akh *etc*; *pres* manee'akh *etc*; *fut* yanee'akh *etc*; **2.** להיכנע (surrender) *inf* leheekana'; *pst & pres* neekhna' *(kh=k)*; *fut* yeekana'.

(to) lay hold of להחזיק ב־ lehakhzeek be-; *pst* hekhzeek be-; *pres* makhzeek be-; *fut* yakhzeek be-

(to) lay off a workman לפטר עובד *inf* lefater 'oved; *pst* peeter *etc* *(p=f)*; *pres* mefater *etc*; *fut* yefater *etc*.

(to) lay open 1. לגלות (uncover) *inf* legalot; *pst* geelah; *pres* megaleh; *fut* yegaleh; **2.** להסביר (explain) *inf* lehasbeer; *pst* heesbeer; *pres* masbeer; *fut* yasbeer.

(to) lay out 1. לסדר *inf* lesader; *pst* seeder; *pres* mesader; *fut* yesader; **2.** להוציא *inf* lehotsee; *pst* hotsee; *pres* motsee; *fut* yotsee.

(to) lay up לשמור לשימוש לאחר־כך *inf* leeshmor le-sheemoosh le-akhar-kakh; *pst* shamar *etc*; *pres* shomer *etc*; *fut* yeeshmor *etc*.

(to) lay waste 1. לשים לשממה *inf* laseem lee-shmamah; *pst & pres* sam *etc*; *fut* yaseem *etc*; **2.** להחריב (destroy) *inf* lehakhreev; *pst* hekhreev; *pres* makhreev; *fut* yakhreev.

layer 1. שכבה *nf* sheekhvah/shekhavot (*+of:* sheekhv|at/-ot); **2.** רובד (stratum) roved/revadeem (*pl+of:* rovdey); **3.** נדבך (course) *nm* needb|akh/-akheem (*pl+of:* -ekhey).

layman 1. הדיוט *nm* hedyot/-ot; **2.** לא־מקצוען (non-professional) *nm* lo meektso'an/-eem; **3.** חילוני (agnostic) *nmf* kheelonee/-t.

lazily בעצלתיים *adv* ba-'atsaltayeem.

laziness עצלות *nf* 'atsloo|t/-yot.

lazy עצל *nmf & adj* 'atsel/-ah.

lead עופרת *nf* 'oferet.

(to) lead 1. להוביל (guide) *inf* lehoveel; *pst* hoveel; *pres* moveel; *fut* yoveel; **2.** להקדים (precede) *inf* lehakdeem; *pst* heekdeem; *pres* makdeem; *fut* yakdeem; **3.** להנהיג (an army) *inf* lehanheeg; *pst* heenheeg; *pres* manheeg; *fut* yanheeg; **4.** לנצח על (conduct orchestra) *inf* lenatse'akh 'al; *pst* neetsakh 'al; *pres* menatse'akh 'al; *fut* yenatsakh 'al.

(to) lead astray להוליך שולל *inf* leholeekh sholal; *pst* holeekh *etc*; *pres* moleekh *etc*; *fut* yoleekh *etc*.

lead pencil עיפרון *nm* 'eeparon/'efronot (*f=p*; *+of:* 'efron).

(to) lead the way להראות דרך *inf* lehar'ot derekh; *pst* her'ah *etc*; *pres* mar'eh *etc*; *fut* yar'eh *etc*.

leaden יצוק עופרת *adj* yetsook/-at 'oferet.

leader 1. מנהיג *nmf* manheeg/-ah; **2.** מאמר ראשי (newspaper) *nm* ma'amar/-eem rashee/-yeem.

leadership מנהיגות *nf* manheegoo|t/-yot.

leading מוביל *adj* moveel/-ah.

leading man, lady שחקן ראשי *nm* sakhkan/-eet rashee/-t.

leading question שאלה מנחה *nf* she'el|ah/-ot mankh|ah/-ot.

leadoff 1. פתיחה *nf* peteekhah/-ot (*+of:* -at); **2.** הקדמה (foreword) *nf* hakdamah/-ot (*+of:* -at).

leaf עלה *nm* 'al|eh/-eem (*pl+of:* -ey)

(to) leaf לעלעל *inf* le'al'el; *pst* 'eel'el; *pres* me'al'el; *fut* ye'al'el.

(to) leaf through a booklet לדפדף בספרון *inf* ledafdef be-seefron; *pst* deefdef *etc*; *pres* medafdef *etc*; *fut* yedafdef *etc*.

leafless 1. חסר עלים *adj* khas|ar/-rat 'aleem; **2.** בשלכת *adj* be-shalekhet.

leaflet 1. עלון *nm* 'alon/-eem (*pl+of:* -ey); **2.** כרוז (pamphlet) *nm* krooz/-eem (*pl+of:* -ey).

leafy גדוש עלים *adj* gedoosh/-at 'aleem.

league 1. איגוד (alliance) *nm* eegood/-eem (*pl+of:* -ey); **2.** ליגה *nf* leegah/-ot (*+of:* -at).

(to) league 1. לכרות ברית *inf* leekhrot breet; *pst* karat *etc* (*k=kh*); *pres* koret *etc*; *fut* yeekhrot *etc*; **2.** להצטרף (join) *inf* leheetstaref; *pst* heetstaref; *pres* meetstaref; *fut* yeetstaref.

(the) League of Nations חבר הלאומים *nm* khever ha-le'oomeem.

leak 1. נזילה *nf* nezeelah/-ot (+*of:* -at); **2.** דליפה *nf* dleefah/-ot (+*of:* -at).

(to) leak 1. לדלוף *vi inf* leedlof; *pst* dalaf; *pres* dolef; *fut* yeedlof; **2.** להדליף *vt inf* lehadleef; *pst* heedleef; *pres* madleef; *fut* yadleef.

lean רזה *adj* razeh/-ah.

(to) lean להישען *inf* leheesha'en; *pst pres* neesh'an; *fut* yeesha'en.

(a) lean year שנה דלה *nf* shanah dalah.

leap 1. קפיצה *nf* kfeetsah/-ot (+*of:* -at); **2.** דילוג *nm* deeloog/-eem (*pl+of:* -ey).

leap year שנה מעוברת *nf* shan|ah/-eem me'oob|eret/-arot.

(to) learn 1. ללמוד *inf* leelmod; *pst* lamad; *pres* lomed; *fut* yeelmad; **2.** להיוודע *inf* leheevada'; *pst & pres* noda'; *fut* yeevada'.

learned מלומד *adj* meloom|ad/-edet.

learner 1. לומד *adj & v pres* lomed/-et; **2.** מתלמד *nmf* meetlamed/-et.

learning למידה *nf* lemeed|ah/-ot (+*of:* -at).

lease 1. שכירות *nf* sekheeroo|t/-yot; **2.** חכירה *nf* khakheer|ah/-ot (+*of:* -at).

(to) lease 1. לשכור *inf* leeskor; *pst* sakhar (*kh=k*); *pres* sokher; *fut* yeeskor; **2.** לחכור *inf* lakhkor; *pst* khakhar (*kh=k*); *pres* khokher; *fut* yakhkor; **3.** להחכיר *inf* lehakhkeer; *pst* hekhkeer; *pst* makhkeer; *fut* yakhkeer.

leash 1. רצועה *nf* retsoo|'ah/-'ot (+*of:* -'at); **2.** אפסר *nm* afs|ar/-areem (*pl+of:* -erey).

least 1. הכי פחות *adj* ha-khee pakhoot/pekhootah; **2.** פחות מכל *adv* pakhot mee-kol.

(at) least לפחות *adv* le-fakhot (*f=p*).

(the) least לכל הפחות *adv* le-khol (*kh=k*) ha-pakhot.

leather עור *nm* 'or/-ot.

leather strap רצועת עור *nf* retsoo|'at/-'ot 'or.

leave 1. חופשה (vacation) *nf* khoofsh|ah/-ot (+*of:* -at); **2.** רשות (permission) *nf* reshoot.

(to) leave לעזוב *inf* la'azov; *pst* 'azav; *pres* 'ozev; *fut* ya'azov.

(to take) leave of להיפרד *inf* leheepared; *pst & pres* neefrad (*f=p*); *fut* yeepared.

leave of absence חופשה *nf* khoofsh|ah/-ot (+*of:* -at).

(to) leave out להשמיט *inf* lehashmeet; *pst* heeshmeet; *pres* mashmeet; *fut* yashmeet.

leaven 1. שאור *nm* se'or; **2.** חמץ *nm* khamets.

leavings 1. שיירים *nm pl* shyar|eem (*pl+of:* -ey); **2.** פסולת *nf* psolet.

lecture הרצאה *nf* hartsa|'ah/-'ot (+*of:* -'at).

(to) lecture להרצות *inf* lehartsot; *pst* heertsah; *pres* martseh; *fut* yartseh.

lecturer מרצה *nmf* marts|eh/-ah (*pl:* -eem/-ot; +*of:* -ey).

ledge 1. זיז *nm* zeez/-eem (*pl+of:* -ey); **2.** לזבז *nm* lazbez/-eem (*pl+of:* -ey).

ledger פנקס חשבונות *nm* peenk|as/-esey kheshbonot.

leech עלוקה *nf* 'alook|ah/-ot (+*of:* -at).

leer מבט שלא בעין יפה *nm* mabat/-eem she-lo be-'ayeen yafah.

(to) leer להסתכל שלא בעין יפה *inf* leheestakel she-lo be-'ayeen yafah; *pst* heestakel *etc*; *pres* meestakel *etc*; *fut* yeestakel *etc*.

leeward 1. חסוי *adj* khasoo|y/-yah; **2.** מוגן מרוח *adj* moog|an/-enet me-roo'akh.

left שמאל *nm* smol.

(at, on the) left בצד שמאל *adv* be-tsad smol.

(I have two books) left נשארו לי שני ספרים בלבד neesh'aroo lee shney sfareem bee-levad.

lefthanded שמאלי *adj* smalee/-t.

lefthanded compliment מחמאה ברגל שמאל *nf* makhma|'ah/-'ot be-regel smol.

leftist שמאלני *adj* smolanee/-t.

leftover שארית *nf* she'eree|t/-yot.

left-wing אגף שמאלי *nm* aga|f/-peem (*p=f*) smalee/-yeem.

leg רגל *nf* regel/ragl|ayeem (*pl+of:* -ey).

legacy ירושה *nf* yeroosh|ah/-ot.

legal חוקי *adj* khookee/-t.

legal tender מטבע חוקי *nm* matbe'a' khookee.

(to) legalize 1. להכשיר lehakhsheer; *pst* heekhsheer; *pres* makhsheer; *fut* yakhsheer; **2.** לאשרר (authentify) *inf* le'ashrer; *pst* eeshrer; *pres* me'ashrer; *fut* ye'ashrer.

legate ציר *nm* tseer/-eem (*pl+of:* -ey).

legatee יורש *nmf* yor|esh/-eshet (*pl:* -sheem/-shot; +*of:* -shey).

legation צירות *nf* tseeroo|t/-yot.

legend אגדה *nf* agad|ah/-ot (+*of:* -at).

legendary אגדי *adj* agadee/-t.

leggings 1. מוקיים *nm pl* mook|ayeem (*pl+of:* -ey); **2.** חותלות *nf pl* khotlot.

legible קריא *adj* karee/kree'ah.

legion לגיון *nm* legyon/-ot.

(to) legislate לחוקק *inf* lekhokek; *pst* khokek; *pres* mekhokek; *fut* yekhokek.

legislation תחיקה *nf* tekheek|ah/-ot (+*of:* -at).

legislative תחיקתי *adj* tekheekatee/-t.

legislator מחוקק *nm* mekhokek/-eem (*pl+of:* -ey).

legislature בית מחוקקים *nm* bet/batey mekhokekeem.

legitimate חוקי *adj* khookee/-t.

(on one's last) legs על סף ההתמוטטות *adv* 'al saf ha-heetmotetoot.

leisure פנאי *nm* penay.

(at) leisure במצב נינוח *adv* be-matsav neeno'akh.

(at one's) leisure לכשיהיה נוח *adv* lee-khe-she-yeehyeh no'akh.

leisure hour שעת פנאי *nf* she'|at/-ot penay.

leisurely 1. מבוצע במתינות *adj* mevoots|a'/-a'at bee-meteenoot; **2.** במתינות *adv* bee-meteenoot.

lemon לימון *nm* leemon/-eem (*pl+of:* -ey).

lemon color צבע לימון *nm* tseva'/tseev'ey leemon.

lemon tree עץ לימון *nm* 'ets/'atsey leemon.

lemonade לימונדה *nf* leemonad|ah/-ot (+*of:* -at).

(to) lend 1. להשאיל (things) *inf* lehash'eel; *pst* heesh'eel; *pres* mash'eel; *fut* yash'eel; **2.** להלוות

(money) lehalvot; *pst* heelvah; *pres* malveh; *fut* yalveh.

lender 1. משאיל (things) *nm* mash'eel/-eem (*pl+of:* -ey); **2.** מלווה (money) *nmf* malv|eh/-ah.

(money) lender מלווה כספים *nmf* malv|eh/-at kesafeem.

length אורך *nm* or|ekh/-akheem (*pl+of:* -khey).

(at) length באריכות *adv* ba-areekhoot.

(to go to any) length לא לחסוך מאמץ *inf* lo lakhsokh ma'amats; *pst* lo khasakh *etc*; *pres* eyno khosekh *etc*; *fut* lo yakhsokh *etc*.

(to) lengthen להאריך *inf* leha'areekh; *pst* he'ereekh; *pres* ma'areekh; *fut* ya'areekh.

lengthwise 1. לאורכו *adj* le-ork|o/-ah (*m/f*); **2.** לאורך *adv* la-orekh.

lengthy 1. ארוך *adj* arokh/arookah; **2.** מאריך *adj* ma'areekh/-ah.

lenient 1. מקל *adj* mekel/-mekeelah; **2.** סובלן (tolerant) *adj* sovlan/-eet.

lens עדשה *nf* 'adash|ah/-ot (*+of:* 'adeshet).

lentils עדשים *nf pl* 'adash|eem (*pl+of:* -ey).

(pottage of) lentils נזיד עדשים *nm* nezeed 'adasheem.

leopard נמר *nm* namer/nemer|eem (*pl+of:* -ey).

leotard גרבוני ריקוד *nm* garboney reekood.

leper מצורע *nmf* metsor|a'/-a'at.

leprosy צרעת *nf* tsara'at.

less פחות *adv* pakhot.

less and less פחות ופחות *adv* pakhot oo-fakhot (*f=p*).

(to) lessen להפחית *inf* lehafkheet; *pst* heefkheet; *pst* mafkheet; *fut* yafkheet.

lesser פחות *adj* pakhoot/pekhootah.

lesson שיעור *nm* shee'oor/-eem (*pl+of:* -ey).

lest 1. לבל *conj* le-val (*v=b*); **2.** פן *conj* pen.

(to) let 1. להשכיר (lease) *inf* lehaskeer; *pst* heeskeer; *pres* maskeer; *fut* yaskeer; **2.** להרשות (allow) *inf* leharshot; *pst* heershah; *pres* marsheh; *fut* yarsheh; **3.** לאפשר (make possible) *inf* le'afsher; *pst* eefsher; *pres* me'afsher; *fut* ye'afsher.

let alone שלא לדבר על she-lo ledaber 'al.

(to) let down לאכזב *inf* le'akhzev; *pst* eekhzev; *pres* me'akhzev; *fut* ye'akhzev.

(to) let go לשחרר *inf* leshakhrer; *pst* sheekhrer; *pres* meshakhrer; *fut* yeshakhrer.

let him come ! שיבוא she-yavol

(to) let in להכניס *inf* lehakhnees; *pst* heekhnees; *pres* makhnees; *fut* yakhnees.

(to) let it be לא להפריע *inf* lo lehafree'a'; *pst* lo heefree'a'; *pres* eyno mafree'a'; *fut* lo yafree'a'.

(to) let know להודיע *inf* lehodee'a'; *pst* hodee'a'; *pres* modee'a'; *fut* yodee'a'.

(to) let loose לתת דרור ליצרים *inf* latet dror la-yetsareem; *pst* natan *etc*; *pres* noten *etc*; *fut* yeeten *etc*.

let my people go! ! שלח את עמי *v imp* shalakh et 'ameel

(to) let off לשחרר *inf* leshakhrer; *pst* sheekhrer; *pres* meshakhrer; *fut* yeshakhrer.

(to) let through לתת לעבור *inf* latet la'avor; *pst* natan *etc*; *pres* noten *etc*; *fut* yeeten *etc*.

(to) let up להאט קצב *inf* leha'et ketsev; *pst* he'et *etc*; *pres* me'et *etc*; *fut* ya'et *etc*.

letdown אכזבה *nf* akhzav|ah/-ot (*+of:* -at).

lethal קטלני *adj* katlanee/-t.

lethargy 1. רדמת *nf* rad|emet/-amot; **2.** אדישות (apathy) *nf* adeeshoo|t/-yot; **3.** ליאות (fatigue) *nf* le'oot; **4.** לתרגיה *nf* letarg|yah/-yot (*+of:* -yat).

(to fall into a) lethargy להיתקף תרדמה *inf* leheetakef tardemah; *pst & pres* neetkaf *etc*; *fut* yeetakef *etc*.

letter 1. מכתב *nm* meekht|av/-aveem (*pl+of:* -evey); **2.** איגרת (epistle) *nf* eeg|eret/-rot; **3.** אות (ABC unit) *nf* ot/-eeyot.

(air-)letter, airletter איגרת אוויר *nf* eeg|eret/-rot aveer.

(to the) letter כפשוטו *adv* kee-feshoot|o/-ah (*f=p*).

letter box תיבת מכתבים *nf* teyv|at/-ot meekhtaveem.

letter carrier 1. נושא מכתבים *nm* nos|e/-'ey meekhtaveem; **2.** דוור (postman) *nm* davar/-eem (*pl+of:* -ey).

letterhead כותרת נייר מכתבים *nf* kot|eret/-rot neyar meekhtaveem.

lettuce 1. חסה *nf* khas|ah/-ot (*+of:* -at); **2.** שטרי כסף (paper money) *nm pl* sheetrey kesef.

Levant 1. ארצות המזרח הקרוב *nf pl* artsot ha-meezrakh ha-karov; **2.** לבנט *nm* levant.

level 1. מישור (plain) *nm* meeshor/-eem (*pl+of:* -ey); **2.** משטח (flat ground) *nm* meesht|akh/-akheem (*pl+of:* -ekhey); **3.** רמה (degree) *nf* ram|ah/-ot (*+of:* -at); **4.** שווה *adj* shav|eh/-ah.

(on the) level בסדר *adv* be-seder.

(to) level 1. ליישר *inf* leyasher; *pst* yeesher; *pres* meyasher; *fut* yeyasher; **2.** להשוות (equalize) *inf* lehashvot; *pst* heeshvah; *pres* mashveh; *fut* yashveh.

level-headed מיושב בדעתו *adj* meyoosh|av/-evet be-da't|o/-ah.

(to) level to the ground להרוס עד היסוד *inf* laharos 'ad ha-yesod; *pst* haras *etc*; *pres* hores *etc*; *fut* yaharos *etc*.

lever 1. מוט *nm* mot/-ot; **2.** מנוף *nm* manof/menof|eem (*pl+of:* -ey).

(control) lever מוט ביקורת mot/-ot beekoret.

levity 1. קלות דעת *nf* kaloot da'at; **2.** קלות ראש (flippancy) *nf* kaloot rosh.

levy 1. מס *nm* mas/mees|eem (*pl+of:* -ey); **2.** היטל (tax) *nm* hetel/-eem (*pl+of:* -ey); **3.** גיוס (conscription) *nm* geeyoos/-eem (*pl+of:* -ey).

(to) levy 1. להטיל מס *inf* lehateel mas; *pst* heeteel mas; *pres* mateel mas; *fut* yateel mas; **2.** לגבות היטל (impose tax) *inf* leegbot hetel; *pst* gavah *etc* (*b=v*); *pres* goveh *etc*; *fut* yeegbeh *etc*.

lewd תאוותני *adj* ta'avtanee/-t.

lewdness 1. תאוותנות *nf* ta'avtanoot; **2.** זימה (licentiousness) *nf* zeem|ah (*+of:* -at).

lexicon 1. לקסיקון *nm* lekseekon/-eem (*pl+of:* -ey); **2.** מילון (dictionary) *nm* meelon/-eem (*pl+of:* -ey).

liabilities 1. מחויבויות *nf pl* mekhooyavooyot; **2.** חובות (duties) *nm pl* khovot.

liability 1. מחויבות *nf* mekhooyavoo|t/-yot; **2.** אחריות (responsibility) *nf* akhrayoot.

liable 1. עלול *adj* 'alool/-ah; **2.** אחראי (responsible) *adj* akhr|ay/-a'eet.
liaison 1. קשר *nm* kesh|er/-areem (*pl+of:* keeshrey); **2.** יחסי מין (sexual) *nm pl* yakhasey meen.
liar שקרן *nmf* shakran/-eet.
libel דיבה *nf* deeb|ah/-ot (*+of:* -at).
(to) libel להוציא דיבה *inf* lehotsee deebah; *pst* hotsee *etc*; *pst* motsee *etc*; *fut* yotsee *etc*.
liberal 1. חופשי בדעותיו (free thinker) *nm* khofshee/-t be-de'ot|av/-eha; **2.** נדיב *adj* nadeev/nedeevah (generous); **3.** ליברל *nm* leeberal/-eem (*pl+of:* -ey).
liberal arts מדעי הרוח *nm pl* mad'ey ha-roo'akh.
liberalism ליברליזם *nm* leeberaleezm.
liberality 1. נדיבות *nf* nedeevoo|t/-yot; **2.** מתנה (gift) *nf* matan|ah/-ot (*+of:* -at).
(to) liberalize להנהיג ליברליזציה *inf* lehanheeg leeberaleezatsyah; *pst* heenheeg *etc*; *pres* manheeg; *fut* yanheeg.
(to) liberate 1. לשחרר *inf* leshakhrer; *pst* sheekhrer; *pres* meshakhrer; *fut* yeshakhrer; **2.** לתת דרור (free) *inf* latet dror; *pst* natan *etc*; *pres* noten *etc*; *fut* yeeten *etc*.
liberation שחרור *nm* sheekhroor/-eem (*pl+of:* -ey).
liberator 1. משחרר *nm* meshakhrer/-eem (*pl+of:* -ey); **2.** גואל (redeemer) *nm* go|'el/-'aleem (*pl+of:* -ey).
libertine 1. פרוץ *adj* paroots/prootsah; **2.** תאוותן *nmf* ta'avtan/-eet.
liberty 1. דרור *nm* dror; **2.** חירות (freedom) *nf* kheroo|t/-yot; **3.** חופש *nm* khofesh.
librarian ספרן *nmf* safran/-eet.
library ספרייה *nf* seefree|yah/-yot (*+of:* -yat).
lice כינים *nf pl* keen|eem (*sing:* keenah; *pl+of:* -ey).
license, licence 1. רשיון *nm* reeshyon/-yonot (*+of:* -yon); **2.** רשות (permission) *nf* reshoo|t/-yot.
(driver's) license רשיון נהיגה *nm* reeshyon/-ot neheegah.
(to) license 1. להעניק רשיון *inf* leha'aneek reeshyon; *pst* he'eneek *etc*; *pres* ma'aneek *etc*; *fut* ya'aneek *etc*; **2.** להרשות (authorize) *inf* leharshot; *pst* heershah; *pres* marsheh; *fut* yarsheh.
license plate לוחית רישוי *nf* lookhee|t/-yot reeshooy.
licentious מופקר *nmf* moofk|ar/-eret.
lick 1. ליקוק *nm* leekook/-eem (*pl+of:* -ey); **2.** לקיקה *nf* lekeek|ah/-ot (*+of:* -at).
(to) lick 1. ללקק *inf* lelakek; *pst* leekek; *pres* melakek; *fut* yelakek; **2.** להביס (defeat) *inf* lehavees; *pst* hevees; *pres* mevees; *fut* yavees.
(not to do a) lick of work לא לעשות דבר *inf* lo la'asot davar; *pst* lo 'asah *etc*; *pres* eyno 'oseh *etc*; *fut* lo ya'aseh *etc*.
(to) lick someone's boot להתלקק אל *inf* leheetlakek el; *pst* heetlakek el; *pres* meetlakek el; *fut* yeetlakek el.
(to) lick the dust 1. ללחך עפר *inf* lelakhekh 'afar; *pst* leekhekh *etc*; *pres* melakhekh *etc*; *fut* yelakhekh *etc*; **2.** למות (die) *inf* lamoot; *pst & pres* met; *fut* yamoot; **3.** ליפול בקרב (fall in battle) *inf* leepol ba-krav; *pst* nafal *etc* (*f=p*); *pres* nofel *etc*; *fut* yeepol *etc*.
licking 1. ליקוק *nm* leekook/-eem (*pl+of:* -ey); **2.** הלקאה (flogging) *nf* halka|'ah/-'ot (*+of:* -'at); **3.** תבוסה (defeat) *nf* tvoos|ah/-ot (*+of:* -at).
lickspittle מלקק רוק *nm* melakek/-ey rok.
lid 1. עפעף (eye) *nm* 'af'a|f/-payeem (*pl+of:* -pey); **2.** מיכסה (cover) *nm* meekhs|eh/-eem (*pl+of:* -ey).
lie שקר *nm* shek|er/-areem (*pl+of:* sheekrey).
(to) lie לשקר *inf* leshaker; *pst* sheeker; *pres* meshaker; *fut* yeshaker.
(to) lie back לשכב על הגב *inf* leeshkav 'al ha-gav; *pst* shakhav *etc* (*kh=k*); *pres* shokhev *etc*; *fut* yeeshkav *etc*.
lie detector מכונת אמת *nf* mekhon|at/-ot emet.
(to) lie down 1. לשכב *inf* leeshkav; *pst* shakhav (*kh=k*); *pres* shokhev; *fut* yeeshkav; **2.** להישכב (put oneself down) *nf* leheeshakhev; *pst & pres* neeshkav (*k=kh*); *fut* yeeshakhev.
(to) lie in wait לארוב *inf* le'erov; *pst* arav; *pres* orev; *fut* ye'erov.
lieutenant 1. סגן *nm* seg|en/sganeem (*pl+of:* sganey); **2.** עוזר *nm* 'oz|er/-reem (*pl+of:* -rey).
(second) lieutenant 1. סגן משנה *nm* segen/sganey meeshneh; **2.** סג"מ (*acr of* 1) *nmf* sagam/-eet.
lieutenant colonel סגן אלוף *nm* sgan/-ey aloof/-eem.
lieutenant-general רב־אלוף *nm* ra|v/-bey (*b=v*) aloof/-eem.
life 1. חיים *nm pl* kha|yeem/-yey; **2.** נפש חיה (living soul) *nf* nefesh khayah; **3.** תולדות חיים (biography) *nf pl* toldot khayeem.
(from) life מהחיים *adv* me-ha-khayeem.
(still) life דומם *nm* domem/-eem (*pl+of:* -ey).
life belt, life preserver חגורת הצלה *nf* khagor|at/-ot hatsalah.
life-boat סירת הצלה *nf* seer|at/-ot hatsalah.
life expectancy תוחלת חיים *nf* tokhelet khayeem.
life imprisonment מאסר עולם *nm* ma'asar 'olam.
life insurance ביטוח חיים *nm* beetoo'akh khayeem
life pension קצבה לכל החיים *nf* keetsb|ah/-ot le-khol (*kh=k*) ha-khayeem.
lifeless חסר רוח חיים *adj* khas|ar/-rat roo'akh khayeem.
lifelessness היעדר רוח חיים *nm* he'ader roo'akh khayeem.
lifelike דומה למציאות *adj* dom|eh/-ah la-metsee'oot.
lifelong לכל החיים *adj* le-khol (*kh=k*) ha-khayeem.
lifetime 1. חלד *nm* kheled; **2.** לכל החיים *adj* le-khol (*kh=k*) ha-khayeem.
lift 1. מעלית *nf* ma'alee|t/-yot; **2.** הרמה (raising) *nf* haram|ah/-ot (*+of:* -at).
(to) lift להרים *inf* lehareem; *pst* hereem; *pres* mereem; *fut* yareem.
lift in a car 1. טרמפ *[slang] nm* tremp/-eem; **2.** הסעת חינם (free ride) *nf* hasa|'at/-'ot kheenam.
ligament 1. רצועה *nf* retsoo'ah/-'ot (*+of:* -'at); **2.** קישור (binding) *nm* keeshoor/-eem (*pl+of:* -ey).
ligature 1. תחבושת *nf* takhbosh|et/-ot; **2.** רצועה *nf* retsoo|'ah/-'ot (*+of:* -'at).

light 1. אור *nm* or/-ot; **2.** בהיר (in color) *adj* baheer/beheerah; **3.** קל (in weight) *adj* kal/-ah.

(to) light 1. להדליק *inf* lehadleek; *pst* heedleek; *pres* madleek; *fut* yadleek; **2.** להאיר *inf* leha'eer; *pst* he'eer; *pres* me'eer; *fut* ya'eer.

light drink משקה קל *nm* mashk|eh/-a'ot kal/-eem.

(to make) light of להקל ראש ב־ *inf* lehakel rosh be-; *pst* hekel rosh; *pres* mekel rosh; *fut* yakel rosh.

light opera אופרה קלה *nf* oper|ah/-ot kal|ah/-ot.

light sentence עונש קל *nm* 'on|esh/-sheem kal/-eem.

(to) lighten להקל *inf* lehakel; *pst* hekel; *pres* mekel; *fut* yakel.

lighter מצית *nm* matseet/-eem (*pl+of:* -ey).

lightheaded קל דעת *adj* kal/-at da'at.

lighthearted עליז *adj* 'aleez/-ah.

lighthouse מגדלור *nm* meegdalor/-eem (*pl+of:* -ey)

lighting תאורה *nf* te'oor|ah/-ot (*+of:* -at).

lightly בקלות *adv* be-kaloot.

lightness קלות *nf* kaloot.

lightning ברק *nm* barak/brakeem (*pl+of:* beerkey).

lightning rod 1. כליא־ברק *nm* kalee/-'ey barak; **2.** כליא־רעם (synon. with 1) *nm* kalee/-'ey ra'am.

lightweight משקל קל *nf* meeshkal kal.

like 1. בערך *adv* be-'erekh; **2.** כמעט (nearly) *adv* kee-me'at; **3.** כמו (as) *prep* kemo.

(do whatever you) like עשה כרצונך *v imp* 'as|eh/-ee kee-retson|kha/-ekh *(m/f)*.

(to) like לחבב *inf* lekhabev; *pst* kheebev; *pres* mekhabev; *fut* yekhabev.

(in) like manner בצורה דומה *adv* be-tsoorah domah.

(it looks) like rain הולך לרדת גשם holekh laredet geshem.

(to feel) like going בא לי ללכת ba lee lalekhet.

(to look) like someone להיראות כמישהו *inf* lehera'ot ke-meeshehoo; *pst* neer'ah *etc*; *pres* neer'eh *etc*; *fut* yera'eh *etc*.

likeable חביב *adj* khaveev/-ah.

likely 1. סביר *adj* saveer/sveerah; **2.** מתקבל על הדעת (reasonable) *adj* meetkabel/-et 'al ha-da'at.

likely place מקום מתאים *nm* makom mat'eem.

(it is) likely to happen עלול לקרות *adj* 'alool leekrot.

(to) liken להשוות *inf* lehashvot; *pst* heeshvah; *pres* mashveh; *fut* yashveh.

likeness 1. דמיון *nm* deemyon; **2.** דיוקן (portrait) *nm* dyok|an/-aneem (*pl+of:* -ney).

likes העדפות (preferences) *nf pl* ha'adafot.

likewise 1. גם כן *prep* gam ken; **2.** כמו כן (also) *prep* kemo khen *(kh=k)*.

liking חיבה *nf* kheeb|ah/-ot (*+of:* -at).

lilac 1. לילך *nm* leelakh; **2.** סגול (violet) *adj* sagol/segoolah.

lily חבצלת *nf* khavats|elet/-alot.

lily-white ללא רבב *adj* le-lo revav.

limb 1. איבר *nm* ev|ar/-areem (*pl+of:* -rey); **2.** כנף (wing) *nf* kanaf/kenafayeem (*pl+of:* kanfey); **3.** זרוע (arm) *nf* zro|a'/-'ot; **4.** רגל (leg) *nf* regel/ragl|ayeem (*pl+of:* -ey).

limber גמיש *adj* gameesh/gemeeshah.

(to) limber להגמיש *inf* lehagmeesh; *pst* heegmeesh; *pres* magmeesh; *fut* yagmeesh.

lime 1. תחמוצת סידן *nf* takhmotset seedan; **2.** סיד חי (unslacked) *nm* seed khay.

limelight 1. אלומת אור *nf* aloom|at/-ot or; **2.** מוקד התעניינות (focus of interest) *nm* mok|ed/-dey heet'anyenoot.

(in the) limelight באור הזרקורים *adv* be-or ha-zarkoreem.

limestone 1. אבן סיד *nf* even/avney seed; **2.** גיר (chalk) *nm* geer/-eem (*pl+of:* -ey).

limit 1. גבול *nm* gvool/-ot; **2.** סייג *nm* syag/-eem (*pl+of:* -ey).

(to) limit להגביל *inf* lehagbeel; *pst* heegbeel; *pres* magbeel; *fut* yagbeel.

limitation הגבלה *nf* hagbal|ah/-ot (*+of:* -at).

limited מוגבל *adj* moogb|al/-elet.

Limited 1. בעירבון מוגבל *adj* be-'eravon moogbal; **2.** בע"מ (Ltd.) be'am *or* B. M. (*acr of* 1).

limitless 1. ללא גבול *adj* le-lo gvool; **2.** ללא סייג *adj* le-lo syag.

limp 1. צליעה *nf* tslee|'ah/-'ot (*+of:* -'at); **2.** רפה *adj* raf|eh/-ah.

(to) limp לצלוע *inf* leetslo'a'; *pst* tsala'; *pres* tsole'a'; *fut* yeetsla'.

limpid 1. שקוף (transparent) *adj* shakoof/shekoofah; **2.** בהיר (clear) *adj* baheer/beheerah; **3.** זך (lucid) *adj* zakh/zakah *(k=kh)*; **4.** שליו (tranquil) *adj* shalev/shlevah.

line 1. קו *nm* kav/-eem (*pl+of:* -ey); **2.** שורה (row) *nf* shoor|ah/-ot (*+of:* -at); **3.** חבל (rope) *nm* khevel/khav|aleem (*pl+of:* -ley); **4.** משלח־יד (occupation) *nm* meeshlakh yad.

(pipe) line צינור *nm* tseenor/-ot.

(railway) line מסילת ברזל *nf* meseel|at/-ot barzel.

(to) line 1. לסרטט *inf* lesartet; *pst* seertet; *pres* mesartet; *fut* yesartet; **2.** להציב בשורה *inf* lehatseev be-shoorah; *pst* heetseev *etc*; *pres* matseev *etc*; *fut* yatseev *etc*.

line of goods שורת מצרכים *nf* shoor|at/-ot meetsrakheem.

(to) line up להסתדר בשורה *inf* leheestader be-shoorah; *pst* heestader *etc*; *pres* meestader *etc*; *fut* yeestader.

(to bring into) line 1. לסדר בשורה *inf* lesader be-shoorah; *pst* seeder *etc*; *pres* mesader *etc*; *fut* yesader *etc*; **2.** ליישר (straighten) *inf* leyasher; *pst* yeesher; *pres* meyasher; *fut* yeyasher.

(to get in) line להתייצב בשורה *inf* leheetyatsev be-shoorah; *pst* heetyatsev *etc*; *pres* meetyatsev; *fut* yeetyatsev *etc*.

lineage 1. ייחוס *nm* yeekhoos; **2.** שושלת יוחסין (family tree) *nf* shoshelet yookhaseen.

linear 1. ישר *adj* yashar/yesharah; **2.** קווי (ruled) *adj* kavee/-t.

lined מבוטן *adj* mevoot|an/-enet.

linen 1. פשתן *nm* peeshtan/-eem (*pl+of:* -ey); **2.** בד (cloth) *nm* bad/-eem (*pl+of:* -ey); **3.** לבנים (lingerie) *nm pl* levaneem (*pl+of:* leevney).

liner אוניית נוסעים *nf* onee|yat/-yot nos'eem.

lineup מערך *nm* ma'ar|akh/-akheem (*pl+of:* -khey).

(to) linger 1. להשתהות *inf* leheeshtahot; *pst* heeshtahah; *pres* meeshtaheh; *fut* yeeshtaheh; **2.** לשהות (tarry) *inf* leesh'hot; *pst* shahah; *pres* shoheh; *fut* yeesh'heh.

lingerie לבנים *nm pl* levaneem (*pl+of:* leevney).

linguistics בלשנות *nf* balshanoo|t/-yot.

lining בטנה *nf* beetnah/betanot (*+of:* beetn|at/-ot).

link 1. קשר *nm* kesh|er/-areem (*pl+of:* keeshrey); **2.** חוליה (ring) *nf* khool|yah/-yot (*+of:* -yat); **3.** פרק (joint) *nm* perek/prakeem (*pl+of:* peerkey).

(to) link 1. לקשר *inf* lekasher; *pst* keesher; *pres* mekasher; *fut* yekasher; **2.** לחבר (connect) *inf* lekhaber; *pst* kheeber; *pres* mekhaber; *fut* yekhaber.

(cuff) links 1. כפתור שרוול *nm* kaftor/-ey sharvool; **2.** רכס (buckle) *nm* rekh|es/-aseem (*pl+of:* reekhsey).

linnet פרוש *nm* paroosh/proosheem.

linoleum 1. שעמנית *nf* sha'amanee|t/-yot; **2.** לינוליאום *nm* leenole'oom.

linseed זרעי פשתן *nm pl* zar'ey peeshtan.

linseed oil שמן פשתן *nm* shemen/shmaney peeshtan.

lint מוך *nm* mokh.

lion 1. אריה *nm* aryeh/arayot; **2.** ארי *nm* aree/arayot; **3.** לביא *nm* lavee'/levee|'eem (*pl+of:* -'ey).

lion's share חלק הארי *nm* khelek ha-aree.

lioness לביאה *nf* levee|'ah/-'ot (*+of:* -'at).

lip שפה *nf* safah/sfatayeem (*pl+of:* seeftey).

lipstick 1. שפתון *nm* sfaton/-eem (*pl+of:* -ey); **2.** אודם *nm* odem; **3.** ליפסטיק *nm* leepsteek/-eem.

liquid 1. נוזל *nm* noz|el/-leem (*pl+of:* -ley); **2.** נוזלי *adj* nozlee/-t; **3.** נזיל (financially) *adj* nazeel/nezeelah.

liquid assets 1. נכסים נזילים *nm pl* nekhaseem nezeeleem; **2.** מזומנים (cash) *nm pl* mezoomaneem.

liquid measure מידת נוזלים *nf* meed|at/-ot nozleem.

(to) liquidate 1. לחסל *inf* lekhasel; *pst* kheesel; *pres* mekhasel; *fut* yekhasel; **2.** לפרוע חובות (pay off) *inf* leefro'a' khovot; *pst* para' *etc* (*p=f*); *pres* pore'a' *etc*; *fut* yeefra' *etc*.

liquidation חיסול *nm* kheesool/-eem (*pl+of:* -ey).

liquidity נזילות *nf* nezeeloot.

liquor 1. משקה חריף *nm* mashk|eh/-a'ot khareef/-eem; **2.** יין שרף (brandy) *nm* yeyn/-ot saraf; **3.** י״ש (*acr of* 2) yash.

lisp שנשון *nm* sheenshoon/-eem (*pl+of:* -ey).

(to) lisp לשנשן *inf* leshanshen; *pst* sheenshen; *pres* meshanshen; *fut* yeshanshen.

list רשימה *nf* resheem|ah/-ot (*+of:* -at).

(to) list 1. לפרט לפי הסדר *inf* lefaret lefee ha-seder; *pst* peret *etc* (*p=f*); *pres* mefaret *etc*; *fut* yefaret *etc*; **2.** לרשום ברשימה (enter) *inf* leershom ba-resheemah; *pst* rasham *etc*; *pres* roshem *etc*; *fut* yeershom *etc*.

listen ! שמע־נא *imp sing* shma'/sheem'ee na'!

(to) listen להאזין *inf* leha'azeen; *pst* he'ezeen; *pres* ma'azeen; *fut* ya'azeen.

(to) listen in להטות אוזן *inf* lehatot ozen; *pst* heetah *etc*; *pres* mateh *etc*; *fut* yateh *etc*.

listener מאזין *nm* ma'azeen/-eem (*pl+of:* -ey).

(radio) listener מאזין רדיו *nm* ma'azeen/-ey radyo.

listening post מוצב האזנה *nm* mootsav/-ey ha'azanah.

listless 1. חסר מרץ *adj* khas|ar/-rat merets; **2.** אדיש (apathetic) *adj* adeesh/-ah.

listlessness 1. חוסר הקשבה *nm* khoser hakshavah; **2.** אדישות (apathy) *nf* adeeshoot.

litany תחינה *nf* tekheen|ah/-ot (*+of:* -at).

literacy דעת קרוא וכתוב *nf* da'at kro oo-khetov (*kh=k*).

literal 1. מילולי *adj* meeloolee/-t; **2.** מדויק (exact) *adj* medoo|yak/-yeket.

literally 1. אות באות *adv* ot be-ot; **2.** מלה במלה (verbatim) *adv* meelah be-meelah.

literary ספרותי *adj* seefrootee/-t.

literate משכיל *nmf & adj* maskeel/-ah.

literature ספרות *nf* seefroot.

lithe גמיש *adj* gameesh/gemeeshah.

litigation 1. התדיינות *nf* heetdaynoo|t/-yot; **2.** ריב (dispute) *nm* reev/-eem (*pl+of:* -ey).

litter 1. גורים (young animals) *nm pl* goor|eem (*pl+of:* -ey); **2.** אלונקה (stretcher) *nf* aloonk|ah/-ot (*+of:* -at); **3.** אשפה (rubbish) *nf* ashp|ah/-ot (*+of:* -at).

(to) litter 1. להמליט (give birth) *inf* lehamleet; *pst* heemleet; *pres* mamleet; *fut* yamleet; **2.** ללכלך (make untidy) *inf* lelakhlekh; *pst* leekhlekh; *pres* melakhlekh; *fut* yelakhlekh.

little 1. מעט me'at; **2.** קצת (a bit) ketsat; **3.** קטן (small) *adj* katan/ketanah; **4.** פעוט (tiny) *adj* pa'oot/pe'ootah.

(a) little קצת ketsat.

little by little לאט לאט *adv* le'at le'at.

(a) little coffee קצת קפה ketsat kafeh.

(a) little while רגע קט *nm* rega' kat.

live חי *adj* khay/-ah.

(to) live לחיות *inf* leekhyot; *pst & pres* khay; *fut* yeekhyeh.

(long) live! יחי ! *interj* yekheel/tekheel (*m/f*).

live bomb פצצה חיה *nf* petsats|ah/-ot kha|yah/-yot.

live question בעיה אקטואלית *nf* be'a|yah/-yot aktoo'alee|t/-yot.

live wire 1. חוט טעון *nm* khoot ta'oon; **2.** פעלתן (active person) *nm* pe'altan/-eem (*pl+of:* -ey).

(to) live down להשכיח *inf* lehashkee'akh; *pst* heeshkee'akh; *pres* mashkee'akh; *fut* yashkee'akh.

(to) live up to לעמוד בציפיות *inf* la'amod be-tseepeeyot; *pst* 'amad *etc*; *pres* 'omed *etc*; *fut* ya'amod *etc*.

livelihood 1. מחיה *nf* meekh|yah/-yot (*+of:* -yat); **2.** פרנסה (subsistence) *nf* parnas|ah/-ot (*+of:* -at).

liveliness 1. עירנות *nf* 'eranoot; **2.** זריזות (agility) *nf* zreezoot.

lively 1. עירני *adj* 'eranee/-t; **2.** בזריזות (quickly) *adv* bee-zreezoot.

(to) liven 1. להפיח רוח חיים *inf* lehafee'akh roo'akh khayeem; *pst* hefee'akh *etc*; *pres* mefee'akh *etc*; *fut* yafee'akh *etc*; **2.** לעודד (encourage) *inf* le'oded; *pst* 'oded; *pres* me'oded; *fut* ye'oded.

liver כבד *nm* kaved/kvedeem (*pl+of:* -ey).

livery 1. בגדי שרד *nm pl* beegdey srad; **2.** מדים (uniform) *nm pl* mad|eem (*pl+of:* -ey).

livestock 1. מקנה *nm* meekneh; **2.** בהמות (cattle) *nf pl* behemot; **3.** צאן (young cattle) *nm* tson.

livid 1. כחלחל *adj* kekhalkhal/-ah; **2.** זועם (angry) *adj* zo'em/-et.

living 1. חי וקיים *adj* khay/-ah ve-ka|yam/-yemet; **2.** פעיל (active) *adj* pa'eel/pe'eelah.

(the) living אלה שבחיים *nm pl* eleh she-ba-khayeem.

living expenses הוצאות קיום *nf pl* hotsa'ot keeyoom.

living room 1. חדר מגורים *nm* khad|ar/-rey megooreem; **2.** חדר אורחים (drawing room) *nm* khad|ar/-rey orkheem.

lizard לטאה *nf* leta|'ah/-'ot (*+of:* -'at).

load 1. משא *nm* mas|a/-a'ot; **2.** נטל (burden) *nm* netel; **3.** עומס *nm* 'omes.

(to) load 1. להעמיס *inf* leha'amees; *pst* he'emees; *pres* ma'amees; *fut* ya'amees; **2.** להטעין (charge) *inf* lehat'een; *pst* heet'een; *pres* mat'een; *fut* yat'een.

(ship)load מיטען אונייה *nm* meet'an/-ey onee|yah/-yot.

loads of כמויות של *nf pl* kamooyot shel.

loaf כיכר *nf* keekar/-ot.

(sugar) loaf חרוט סוכר *nm* kharoot/-ey sookar.

loaf of bread כיכר לחם *nf pl* keek|ar/-krot lekhem.

loafer 1. בטלן *nm* batlan/-eem (*pl+of:* -ey); **2.** מתבטל (idler) meetbat|el/-leem (*pl+of:* -ley).

loan מלווה *nm* meelv|eh/-eem (*pl+of:* -ey).

loan shark מלווה בריבית קצוצה *nf* meelv|ah/-ot be-reebeet ketsootsah.

loan word מלה שאולה *nf* meel|ah/-eem she'ool|ah/-ot.

loath 1. מתעב *v pres & adj* meta'ev/-et; **2.** מסרב (refusing) *v pres & adj* mesarev/-et.

(to be) loath to לשנוא *inf* leesno; *pst* sane; *pres* sone; *fut* yeesna.

(to) loathe 1. לתעב *inf* leta'ev; *pst* te'av; *pres* meta'ev; *fut* yeta'ev; **2.** לשנוא (hate) *inf* leesno; *pst* sane; *pres* sone; *fut* yeesna.

loathsome 1. גועלי *adj* go'alee/-t; **2.** ניתעב (detestable) *adj* neet|'av/-'evet.

(to) lob לזרוק מעל לראש *inf* leezrok me-'al la-rosh; *pst* zarak *etc; pres* zorek *etc; fut* yeezrok *etc.*

lobby 1. אולם המתנה (waiting hall) *nm* oolam/-ey hamtanah; **2.** טרקלין (parlor) *nm* trakleen/-eem (*pl+of:* -ey); **3.** שדולה (lobbying group) *nf* shdool|ah/-ot (*+of:* -at).

(hotel) lobby אולם המתנה של מלון *nm* oolam/-ey hamtanah shel malon.

(to) lobby לשדל למען *inf* leshadel le-ma'an; *pst* sheedel *etc; pres* meshadel *etc; fut* yeshadel *etc.*

lobbying שתדלנות *nf* shtadlanoo|t/-yot.

lobe 1. תנוך *nm* tenookh/-eem (*pl+of:* -ey); **2.** בדל אוזן (earlap) *nm* bedal/beedley ozen; **3.** אונה (brain, lung) *nf* oon|ah/-ot (*+of:* -at).

lobster סרטן ים *nm* sart|an/-eney yam.

local 1. מקומי *adj* mekomee/-t; **2.** בית־ועד (club) *nm* bet/batey va'ad.

local train רכבת פרוורים *nf* rak|evet/-vot parvareem.

locality 1. אתר *nm* atar/-eem (*pl+of:* -ey); **2.** סביבה (neighborhood) *nf* sveev|ah/-ot (*+of:* -at).

localize 1. למקם *inf* lemakem; *pst* meekem; *pres* memakem; *fut* yemakem; **2.** להגביל למקום מסוים (restrict) *inf* lehagbeel le-makom mesooyam; *pst* heegbeel *etc; pres* magbeel *etc; fut* yagbeel *etc.*

(to) locate לאתר *inf* le'ater; *pst* eeter; *pres* me'ater; *fut* ye'ater.

location 1. אתר (place) *nm* atar/-eem (*pl+of:* -ey); **2.** מיקום (whereabout) *nm* meekoom/-eem (*pl+of:* -ey).

lock 1. מנעול (door) *nm* man'ool/-eem (*pl+of:* -ey); **2.** סכר (canal) *nm* sekh|er/-areem (*pl+of:* seekhrey); **3.** נצרה (firearm) *nf* neetsrah/netsarot (*+of:* neetsr|at/-ot).

(to) lock לנעול *inf* leen'ol; *pst* na'al; *pres* no'el; *fut* yeen'al.

(to) lock in לנעול בפנים *inf* leen'ol bee-fneem; *pst* na'al *etc; pres* no'el *etc; fut* yeen'al *etc.*

(to) lock out לנעול בפני *inf* leen'ol bee-fney; *pst* na'al *etc; pres* no'el *etc; fut* yeen'al *etc.*

lock, stock and barrel בכול מכל כל ba-kol mee-kol kol.

(to) lock up לכלוא *inf* leekhlo; *pst* kala *(k=kh); pres* kole; *fut* yeekhla.

locker ארון ננעל *nf* aron/-ot neen'al/-eem.

locket תליון *nm* teelyon/-eem (*pl+of:* -ey).

lockout השבתה *nf* hashbat|ah/-ot (*+of:* -at).

locksmith מסגר *nm* masger/-eem (*pl+of:* -ey).

locomotive קטר *nm* katar/-eem (*pl+of:* -ey).

locomotive engineer נהג קטר *nm* nahag/-ey katar/-eem.

locust ארבה *nm* arbeh.

locust tree רוביניה *nf* robeen|yah/-yot (*+of:* -yat).

lodge 1. בקתת־יער *nf* beekt|at/-ot ya'ar; **2.** צריף (hut) tsreef/-eem (*pl+of:* -ey); **3.** לשכה (chamber) *nf* leeshkah/leshakhot (*+of:* leesh|kat/-khot).

(to) lodge 1. לשכן *inf* leshaken; *pst* sheeken; *pres* meshaken; *fut* yeshaken; **2.** להלין (put up overnight) *inf* lehaleen; *pst* heleen; *pres* meleen; *fut* yaleen.

(to) lodge a complaint להגיש תלונה *inf* lehageesh tloonah; *pst* heegeesh *etc; pres* mageesh *etc; fut* yageesh *etc.*

lodger דייר־משנה *nm* dayar/-ey meeshneh.

lodging 1. חדר שכור *nm* kheder/khadareem sakhoor/skhooreem; **2.** דירה ארעית (provis. residence) *nf* deer|ah/-ot ara'ee|t/-yot.

loft עליית גג *nf* 'alee|yat/-yot gag.

(hay)loft מתבן *nm* matben/-eem (*pl+of:* -ey).

lofty 1. נישא *adj* nees|a/-a'ah; **2.** יהיר (haughty) *adj* yaheer/yeheerah.

log 1. קורה *nf* kor|ah/-ot (*+of:* -at); **2.** בול־עץ (blockhead) *nm* bool/-ey 'ets.

log cabin בקתת עץ *nf* beekt|at/-ot 'ets.

loggerhead מטומטם *nmf* metoomt|am/-emet.

(at) loggerheads בריב *adv* be-reev.

logic היגיון *nm* heegayon (*+of:* hegyon).

logical הגיוני *adj* hegyonee/-t.

logrolling 1. גלגול בולי־עצים *nm* geelgool booley 'etseem; **2.** העברת עודפי קולות (in elections) *nf* ha'avarat 'odfey kolot.

loin 1. ירך *nf* yarekh/yerekhayeem (*+of:* yerekh/ yarkhey); **2.** מותן (hip) *nf* mot|en/-nayeem (*pl+of:* -ney); **3.** חלציים (hip) *nm pl* khal|atsayeem (*pl+of:* -tsey).

(to) loiter 1. לשוטט *inf* leshotet; *pst* shotet; *pres* meshotet; *fut* yeshotet; **2.** להתבטל (loaf) *inf* leheetbatel; *pst* heetbatel; *pres* meetbatel; *fut* yeetbatel.

(to) loiter behind להשתהות מאחור *inf* leheeshtahot me-akhor; *pst* heeshtahah *etc*; *pres* meeshtaheh *etc*; *fut* yeeshtaheh *etc*.

loitering שוטטות *nf* shotetoo|t/-yot.

(to) loll 1. לשבת נוח *inf* lashevet no'akh; *pst* yashav *etc*; *pres* yoshev *etc*; *fut* yeshev *etc*. **2.** לשכב בעצלתיים (lounge) *inf* leeshkav ba-'atsaltayeem; *pst* shakhav *(kh=k)*; *pres* shokhev; *fut* yeeshkav.

lollipop סוכרייה על מקל *nf* sookaree|yah/-yot 'al makel.

lone 1. גלמוד *adj* galmood/-ah; **2.** בודד (solitary) *adj* boded/-et; **3.** ערירי (childless) *adj* 'areeree/-t.

loneliness בדידות *nf* bedeedoo|t/-yot.

lonely 1. בודד *adj* boded/-et; **2.** גלמוד (solitary) *adj* galmood/-ah.

lonesome 1. סובל מבדידות *v pres & adj* sovel/ -et mee-bedeedoot; **2.** עזוב לנפשו (forsaken) *adj* 'azoov/-ah le-nafsh|o/-ah.

long ארוך *adj* arokh/arookah *(k=kh)*.

(so) long ! היה שלום (greeting *m/f*) heyeh/hayee shalom!

(the whole day) long לאורך יום שלם *adv* le-orekh yom shalem.

(three feet) long שלוש רגל אורכו shalosh regel ork|o/-ah.

(to) long להשתוקק *inf* leheeshtokek; *pst* heeshtokek; *pres* meeshtokek; *fut* yeeshtokek.

long ago מזמן *adv* mee-zman.

(as) long as כל עוד *conj* kol 'od.

long-distance call שיחת חוץ *nf* seekh|at/-ot khoots.

(to) long for להתגעגע *inf* leheetga'ge'a'; *pst* heetga'ge'a'; *pres* meetga'ge'a'; *fut* yeetga'ge'a'.

(to be) long in coming לאחר לבוא *inf* le'akher lavo; *pst* eekher *etc*; *pres* me'akher *etc*; *fut* ye'akher *etc*.

(how) long is it since? ?כמה זמן חלף מאז... kamah zman khalaf me-az?

long-suffering 1. רב סבל *adj* rav/rabat *(b=v)* sevel; **2.** ארך אפיים (forbearing) *adj m* erekh apayeem.

long-term ארוך־מועד *adj* arokh/arook|at (*pl:* -ey/-ot) mo'ed.

long-winded ארכני *adj* arkanee/-t.

longer ארוך יותר *adj* yoter arokh/arookah.

(any) longer עוד יותר זמן *adv* 'od yoter zman.

(no) longer לא עוד *adv* lo 'od.

(not) longer לא יותר *adv* lo yoter.

longevity אריכות ימים *nf* areekhoot yameem.

longing געגועים *nm pl* ga'goo|'eem (*pl+of:* -'ey).

longingly בגעגועים *adv* be-ga'goo'eem.

longitude קו אורך *nm* kav/-ey orekh.

longshoreman סוור *nm* savar/-eem (*pl+of:* -ey).

look 1. מראה *nm* mar|'eh/-'ot; **2.** מבט (glance) *nm* mabat/-eem (*pl+of:* -ey).

(to) look 1. להביט *inf* lehabeet; *pst* heebeet; *pres* mabeet; *fut* yabeet; **2.** להסתכל (gaze) *inf* leheestakel; *pst* heestakel; *pres* meestakel; *fut* yeestakel; **3.** להיראות (appear) *inf* lehera'ot; *pst* neer'ah; *pres* neer'eh; *fut* yera'eh; **4.** לחפש (search) *inf* lekhapes; *pst* kheepes; *pres* mekhapes; *fut* yekhapes.

(to) look after 1. להשגיח *inf* lehashgee'akh; *pst* heeshgee'akh; *pres* mashgee'akh; *fut* yashgee'akh; **2.** לטפל ב־ (take care of) *inf* letapel be-; *pst* teepel be-; *pres* metapel be-; *fut* yetapel be-.

(to) look alike להיראות דומה *inf* lehera'ot domeh; *pst* neer'ah *etc*; *pres* neer'eh *etc*; *fut* yera'eh.

(to) look down on a person לבוז *inf* lavooz; *pst & pres* baz *(b=v)*; *fut* yavooz.

(to) look for לחפש *inf* lekhapes; *pst* kheepes; *pres* mekhapes; *fut* yekhapes.

(to) look forward לצפות קדימה *inf* leetspot kadeemah; *pst* tsafah *etc*; *pres* tsofeh *etc*; *fut* yeetspeh *etc*.

(to) look into 1. לחקור *inf* lakhkor; *pst* khakar; *pres* khoker; *fut* yakhkor; **2.** לבדוק (check) *inf* leevdok; *pst* badak *(b=v)*; *pres* bodek; *fut* yeevdok.

look out! ! היזהר heeza|her!/-haree!

(to) look out for להיזהר מפני *inf* leheezaher meepney; *pst & pres* neez'har *etc*; *fut* yeezaher *etc*.

(to) look over 1. לעבור ברפרוף *inf* la'avor be-reefroof; *pst* 'avar *etc*; *pres* 'over *etc*; *fut* ya'avor *etc*; **2.** לדפדף (peruse) *inf* ledafdef; *pst* deefdef; *pres* medafdef; *fut* yedafdef.

(to) look up 1. למצוא *inf* leemtso; *pst* matsa; *pres* motse; *fut* yeemtsa; **2.** לאתר (locate) *inf* le'ater; *pst* eeter; *pres* me'ater; *fut* ye'ater.

(to) look up to לכבד (respect) *inf* lekhabed; *pst* keebed *(k=kh)*; *pres* mekhabed; *fut* yekhabed.

looking glass מראה *nf* mar|'ah/-'ot (*+of:* -'at).

lookout 1. שמירה *nf* shmeer|ah/-ot (*+of:* -at); **2.** משמר (guard) *nm* meeshmar/-ot; **3.** מצפה שמירה (observation point) *nm* meetsp|eh/-ey shmeerah.

(to be on the) lookout לעמוד על המשמר *inf* la'amod 'al ha-meeshmar; *pst* 'amad *etc*; *pres* 'omed *etc*; *fut* ya'amod *etc*.

loom 1. נול *nm* nool/-eem (*pl+of:* -ey); **2.** מנור (weaver's beam) *nm* manor/-eem (*pl+of:* -ey).

(to) loom 1. להיראות ממרחק *inf* lehera'ot mee-merkhak; *pst* neer'ah *etc*; *pres* neer'eh *etc*; *fut* yera'eh *etc*; **2.** להזדקר (stand out) *inf* leheezdaker; *pst* heezdaker; *pres* meezdaker; *fut* yeezdaker.

loop 1. לולאה (closed) *f* loola|'ah/-'ot (*+of:* -'at); **2.** מעגל חשמלי (electric) *nm* ma'agal/ -eem khashmalee/-yeem; **3.** סיבוב (curve) *nm* seevoov/-eem (*pl+of:* -ey).

(to) loop להסתובב *inf* leheestovev; *pst* heestovev; *pres* meestovev; *fut* yeestovev.

loophole 1. חרך *nm* khara|kh/-keem *(kh=k; pl+of:* -key); **2.** חור בקיר (hole in wall) *nm* khor/-eem ba-keer/-ot; **3.** מנוס (escape) *nm* manos.

loose 1. רפה (slack) *adj* raf|eh/-ah; **2.** לא מוגבל (unfettered) *adj* lo moogb|al/-elet; **3.** פרוץ (unrestrained) *adj* paroots/prootsah.

(to) loose להתיר *inf* lehateer; *pst* heeteer; *pres* mateer; *fut* yateer.

(to let) loose לשחרר *inf* leshakhrer; *pst* sheekhrer; *pres* meshakhrer; *fut* yeshakhrer.

loose change 1. פרוטרוט *nm* protrot; **2.** מעות קטנות (small change) *nf pl* ma'ot ketanot; **3.** כסף קטן *[slang]* kesef katan.

loose jointed רפה פרקים *adj* ref|eh/-at prakeem.

loosely 1. בצורה רופפת *adv* be-tsoorah rofefet; **2.** ברשלנות (negligently) *adv* be-rashlanoot.

(to) loosen 1. להרפות *inf* leharpot; *pst* heerpah; *pres* marpeh; *fut* yarpeh; **2.** להתיר (untie) *inf* lehateer; *pst* heeteer; *pres* mateer; *fut* yateer.

(to) loosen one's hold לאבד שליטה *inf* le'abed shleetah; *pst* eebed *etc*; *pres* me'abed *etc*; *fut* ye'abed *etc.*

looseness 1. גמישות (limberness) *nf* gmeeshoo|t/-yot; **2.** רפיון (laxness) *nm* reefyon/-ot; **3.** שלשול (of bowels) *nm* sheelshool/-eem (*pl+of:* -ey).

loot 1. שלל *nm* shalal (*+of:* shlal); **2.** ביזה (plunder) *nf* beez|ah/-ot (*+of:* -at); **3.** מלקוח (booty) *nm* malko'akh.

(to) loot לבזוז *inf* leevzoz; *pst* bazaz *(b=v)*; *pres* bozez; *fut* yeevzoz.

(to) lop 1. לכרות *inf* leekhrot; *pst* karat *(k=kh)*; *pres* koret; *fut* yeekhrot; **2.** לחתוך (cut) *inf* lakhtokh; *pst* khatakh; *pres* khotekh; *fut* yakhtokh.

lopsided לא סימטרי *adj* lo seemetree/-t.

loquacious מכביר מלים *adj* makhbeer/-at meeleem.

lord 1. לורד *nm* lord/-eem (*pl+of:* -ey); **2.** אדון (master) *nm* adon/-eem (*pl+of:* -ey).

(the) Lord 1. אלוהים *nm* elo|heem (*+of:* -hey); **2.** אלוקים (as pronounced by observant Jews, except while in prayers, so as "not utter God's name in vain") elok|eem (*+of:* -key); **3.** אדוני *nm* adonay (not used at all by observant Jews, for above reason, except in prayers).

(to) lord לשלוט *inf* leeshlot; *pst* shalat; *pres* sholet; *fut* yeeshlot.

lordly 1. נהדר *adj* nehed|ar/-eret; **2.** בהתנשאות *adv* be-heetnas'oot.

lordship אדנות *nf* adnoot.

lorn עזוב *adj* 'azoov/-ah.

lorry משאית *nf* masa'ee|t/-yot.

(to) lose 1. לאבד *inf* le'abed; *pst* eebed; *pres* me'abed; *fut* ye'abed; **2.** להפסיד (financially) *inf* lehafseed; *pst* heefseed; *pres* mafseed; *fut* yafseed.

(to) lose sight of לאבד קשר עם *inf* le'abed kesher 'eem; *pst* eebed *etc*; *pres* me'abed *etc*; *fut* ye'abed *etc.*

loss 1. אבידה *nf* aveyd|ah/-ot (*+of:* -at); **2.** אובדן *nm* ovdan.

(at a) loss 1. בפחות מהמחיר *adv* be-fakhot me-ha-mekheer *(f=p)*; **2.** בהפסד *adv* be-hefsed.

(to sell at a) loss למכור בהפסד *inf* leemkor be-hefsed; *pst* makhar *etc* (*kh=k*); *pres* mokher *etc*; *fut* yeemkor *etc.*

lost אבוד *adj* avood/-ah.

(to get) lost ללכת לאיבוד *inf* lalekhet le-'eebood; *pst* halakh *etc*; *pres* holekh *etc*; *fut* yelekh *etc.*

lost in thought שקוע במחשבות *adj* shakoo'a'/shkoo'ah be-makhshavot.

lot 1. מגרש (land) *nm* meegrash/-eem (*pl+of:* -ey); **2.** מנה (section) *nf* man|ah/-ot (*+of:* men|at/-ot); **3.** מזל (luck) *nm* mazal/-ot.

(to fall to one's) lot ליפול בגורלו *inf* leepol be-goralo; *pst* nafal *(f=p) etc*; *pres* nofel *etc*; *fut* yeepol *etc.*

(a) lot better הרבה יותר טוב *adv* harbeh yoter tov.

(a) lot of חלק ניכר מ־ *nm* khelek neekar mee-.

lotion תרחיץ *nm* tarkheets/-eem (*pl+of:* -ey).

(to draw) lots להפיל גורל *inf* lehapeel goral; *pst* heepeel *etc*; *pres* mapeel *etc*; *fut* yapeel *etc.*

lots of כמויות של *nf pl* kamooyot shel.

lottery הגרלה *nf* hagral|ah/-ot (*+of:* -at).

loud 1. רם *adj* ram/-ah; **2.** בקול רם (aloud) *adv* be-kol ram.

loud-speaker רמקול *nm* ramkol/-eem (*pl+of:* -ey).

lounge 1. אולם המתנה (lobby) *nm* oolam/-ey hamtanah; **2.** דרגש (sofa) *nm* darg|ash/-asheem (*pl+of:* -eshey).

(to) lounge להתבטל *inf* leheetbatel; *pst* heetbatel; *pres* meetbatel; *fut* yeetbatel.

louse כינה *nf* keen|ah/-eem (*+of:* -at/-ey).

lousy 1. גרוע (bad) *adj* garoo'a'/groo'ah; **2.** נתעב (detestable) *adj* neet|'av/-'evet.

lovable 1. חביב *adj* khaveev/-ah; **2.** נחמד (pleasant) *adj* nekhmad/-ah.

love אהבה *nf* ahav|ah/-ot (*+of:* -at).

love affair פרשת אהבים *nf* parash|at/-eeyot ahaveem.

(to be in) love להיות מאוהב *inf* leehyot me'ohav; *pst* hayah *etc*; *pres* heeno *etc*; *fut* yeehyeh *etc.*

(to fall in) love with להתאהב *inf* leheet'ahev; *pst* heet'ahev; *pres* meet'ahev; *fut* yeet'ahev.

(to make) love להתעלס *inf* leheet'ales; *pst* heet'ales; *pres* meet'ales; *fut* yeet'ales.

(to make) love to להתנות אהבים עם *inf* lehatnot ahaveem 'eem; *pst* heetnah *etc*; *pres* matneh *etc*; *fut* yatneh *etc.*

(in) love with מאוהב ב־ *adj* me'o|hav/-hevet be-.

loveliness 1. חן *nm* khen; **2.** חינניות (charm) *nf* kheenaneeyoot.

lovely נחמד *adj* nekhmad/-ah.

lover מאהב *nmf* me'a|hev/-hevet (*pl:* -haveem; *+of:* havey).

loving אוהב *adj* ohev/-et.

lovingly באהבה *adv* be-ahavah.

low 1. נמוך *adj* namookh/nemookhah; **2.** שפל (base) *adj* shafal/shfalah.

(to) low לגעות *inf* leeg'ot; *pst* ga'ah; *pres* go'eh; *fut* yeeg'eh.

(to be) low לחסור *inf* lakhsor; *pst* khasar; *pres* khaser; *fut* yakhsor.

low gear הילוך נמוך *nm* heelookh namookh.

low key טון נמוך *nm* ton/-eem namookh/nemookheem.

low neck מחשוף נמוך *nm* makhsof/-eem namookh/nemookheem.

(in) low spirits במצב רוח קודר *adv* be-matsav roo'akh koder.
lower תחתון *adj* takhton/-ah
(to) lower 1. להנמיך *inf* lehanmeekh; *pst* heenmeekh; *pres* manmeekh; *fut* yanmeekh; **2.** להוריד (reduce) *inf* lehoreed; *pst* horeed; *pres* moreed; *fut* yoreed.
lower case letter 1. אות רגילה *nf* ot/-eeyot regeel|ah/-ot; **2.** אות קטנה (minuscule) *nf* ot/-eeyot ketan|ah/-ot.
lower classman תלמיד כיתה נמוכה *nmf* talmeed/-at keetah nemookhah.
lower house הבית התחתון *nm* ha-bayeet ha-takhton.
lowland שפלה *nf* shfel|ah/-ot (*+of:* -at).
lowliness 1. שיפלות *nf* sheefloo|t/-yot; **2.** עניות (poverty) *nf* 'aneeyoot; **3.** שפל *nm* shefel.
lowly 1. ענו *adj* 'anav/-ah; **2.** צנוע (modest) *adj* tsanoo'a'/tsenoo'ah.
lowness 1. שיפלות (baseness) *nf* sheefloo|t/-yot; **2.** נמיכות (shortness) *nf* nemeekhoo|t/-yot.
loyal נאמן *adj* ne'eman/-ah.
loyalty נאמנות *nf* ne'emanoo|t/-yot.
lubricant שמן סיכה *nm* shemen/shamney seekhah.
(to) lubricate 1. לסוך *inf* lasookh; *pst & pres* sakh; *fut* yasookh; **2.** לשמן (oil) *inf* leshamen; *pst* sheemen; *pres* meshamen; *fut* yeshamen.
lucid צלול *adj* tsalool/tsloolah.
lucidity צלילות הדעת *nf* tsleeloot ha-da'at.
luck 1. מזל *nm* mazal; **2.** הצלחה (success) *nf* hatslakh|ah/-ot (*+of:* -at).
(in) luck 1. במזל *adj* be-mazal; **2.** הולך לו *v pres* holekh lo/lah.
(in bad) luck 1. לא הולך לו/לה (going wrong) *v pres* lo holekh lo/lah *(m/f)*; **2.** ביש מזל (misfortune) *adj* beesh mazal.
luckily למרבה המזל *conj* le-marbeh ha-mazal.
lucky בר־מזל *adj* bar/bat mazal.
(to be) lucky שהמזל ישחק לו she-ha-mazal yesakhek lo.
lucrative מכניס *adj* makhnees/-ah.
ludicrous מגוחך *adj* megookh|akh/-ekhet.
lug אוזן כלי *nm* ozen/ozney klee.
(to) lug לסחוב *inf* leeskhov; *pst* sakhav; *pres* sokhev; *fut* yeeskhav.
(to) lug away לסחוב הצדה *inf* leeskhov ha-tseedah; *pst* sakhav *etc*; *pres* sokhev *etc*; *fut* yeeskhav *etc*.
luggage 1. מטען *nm* meet'an/-eem (*pl+of:* -ey); **2.** מזוודות (suitcases) *nf pl* meezvadot.
lugubrious 1. נוגה *adj* noog|eh/-ah; **2.** עצוב (sad) *adj* 'atsoov/-ah.
lukewarm 1. חמים *adj* khameem/-ah; **2.** פושר (tepid) *adj* posher/-et; **3.** אדיש (apathetic) *adj* adeesh/-ah.
lull הפוגה *nf* hafoog|ah/-ot (*+of:* -at).
(to) lull 1. להרגיע *inf* lehargee'a'; *pst* heergee'a'; *pres* margee'a'; *fut* yargee'a'; **2.** לשכך (soothe) *inf* leshakekh; *pst* sheekekh; *pres* meshakekh; *fut* yeshakekh.
lullaby שיר ערש *nm* sheer/-ey 'eres.
lumber 1. עצים *nm pl* 'etseem (*pl+of:* 'atsey); **2.** גרוטאות (scrap) *nf pl* groota'ot.
lumberjack חוטב עצים *nm* khot|ev/-vey 'etseem.
lumberman 1. סוחר עצים *nm* sokh|er/-arey 'etseem; **2.** סוחר גרוטאות (scrap dealer) *nm* sokh|er/-arey groota'ot.
lumberyard מחסן עצים *nm* makhs|an/-eney 'etseem.
luminary מאור *nm* ma'or/me'orot (*+of:* me'or).
luminous 1. מאיר *adj* me'eer/-ah; **2.** זוהר (shining) *adj* zoher/-et.
lump 1. גוש (mass) *nm* goosh/-eem (*pl+of:* -ey); **2.** נפיחות (swelling) *nf* nefeekhoo|t/-yot.
(to) lump 1. לגבב *inf* legabev; *pst* geebev; *pres* megabev; *fut* yegabev; **2.** לערום (grate) *inf* la'arom; *pst* 'aram; *pres* 'orem; *fut* ya'arom.
lump of sugar חפיסת סוכר *nf* khafees|at/-ot sookar.
lumpy 1. מלא קורות *adj* male/mele'ah korot; **2.** מטומטם (thickheaded) *adj* metoomt|am/-emet.
lunacy שיגעון *nm* sheeg|a'on/-'onot (*+of:* -'on).
lunatic 1. משוגע (madman) *nm* meshoog|a'/-a'eem (*pl+of:* -a'ey); **2.** משוגע (crazy) *adj* meshoog|a'/-a'at.
lunch ארוחת צהריים *nf* arookh|at/-ot tsohorayeem.
luncheon ארוחת צהריים חגיגית (festive) *nf* arookhat tsohorayeem khageegeet.
lunchroom מסעדת יום *nf* mees|'edet/-'adot yom.
lung ריאה *nf* re|'ah/-'ot (*+of:* -'at).
lurch 1. מבוכה *nf* mevookh|ah/-ot (*+of:* -at); **2.** מצוקה (distress) *nf* metsook|ah/-ot (*+of:* -at).
(to leave in the) lurch לנטוש לעת צרה *inf* leentosh le-'et tsarah; *pst* natash *etc*; *pres* notesh *etc*; *fut* yeetosh *etc*.
lure 1. פיתוי *nm* peetoo|y/-yeem (*pl+of:* -yey); **2.** משיכה (attraction) *nf* mesheekh|ah/-ot (*+of:* -at).
(to) lure לפתות *inf* lefatot; *pst* peetah *(p=f)*; *pres* mefateh; *fut* yefateh.
(to) lurk לארוב *inf* le'erov; *pst* arav; *pres* orev; *fut* ye'erov.
luscious 1. טעים *adj* ta'eem/te'eemah; **2.** מתוק (sweet) *adj* matok/metookah.
lust 1. תאווה *nf* ta'av|ah/-ot (*+of:* -at); **2.** חשק (desire) *nm* kheshek/khashakeem (*pl+of:* kheshkey).
(to) lust לחמוד (covet) *inf* lakhmod; *pst* khamad; *pres* khomed; *fut* yakhmod.
(to) lust after להתאוות *inf* leheet'avot; *pst* heet'avah; *pres* meet'aveh; *fut* yeet'aveh.
luster ברק *nm* barak.
lustrous 1. מבהיק *adj* mavheek/-ah; **2.** מבריק (brilliant) *adj* mavreek/-ah.
lusty 1. חזק *adj* khazak/-ah; **2.** בריא (sound) *adj* baree'/bree'ah.
lute עוד 'ood/-eem (*pl+of:* -ey).
luxuriance 1. שפע *nm* shefa'; **2.** מותרות (comfort) *nf pl* motarot.
luxuriant שופע *adj* shof|e'a'/-a'at.
luxurious 1. עשיר *adj* 'asheer/-ah; **2.** מפואר (resplendent) *adj* mefo|'ar/-'eret.
luxury 1. מותרות *nf pl* mot|arot (*+of:* -rot); **2.** לוקסוס *[colloq.] nm* looksoos.

lye 1. בורית *nf* boreet; **2.** אפר (ash) *nm* efer.
lying-in hospital בית־יולדות *nm* bet/batey yoldot.
lymph ליחה לבנה *nf* leykhah levanah.
lynch משפט לינץ׳ *nm* meeshp|at/-etey leench.
lynx חולדת בר *nf* khoold|at/-ot bar.

lyre נבל *nm* nevel.
lyric 1. שירה *nf* sheerah; **2.** לירי *adj* leeree/-t.
lyrical 1. לירי *adj* leeree/-t; **2.** שירי (poetical) *adj* sheeree/-t.
lyricism ליריות *nf* leereeyoot.

M.

M,m equivalent to the Hebrew consonant Mem (מ) which, when ending a word, takes a different shape : ם (called Mem sofeet) instead of מ.
macabre 1. מחריד *adj* makhreed/-ah; **2.** מקברי *adj* makabree/-t.
macadam 1. חצץ *nm* khatsats; **2.** זפזיף (gravel) *nm* zeefzeef.
macaroni אטריות *nf pl* eetree|yot (*sing:* -yah; *+of:* -yat).
macaroon שקדון *nm* shkedon/-eem (*pl+of:* -ey).
(the) Maccabeans המכבים *nm pl* ha-makabeem.
machination תחבולה *nf* takhbool|ah/-ot (*+of:* -at).
machine מכונה *nf* mekhon|ah/-ot (*+of:* -at)
(political) machine מנגנון מדיני *nm* manganon/-eem medeenee/-yeem.
(sewing) machine מכונת תפירה *nf* mekhon|at/-ot tfeerah.
machine-gun 1. מכונת ירייה *nf* mekhon|at/-ot yereeyah; **2.** מקלע *nm* makl|e'a'/-e'eem (*pl+of:* -e'ey)
(sub-)machine-gun תת־מקלע *nm* tat-makle|'a'/-'eem (*pl+of:* -e'ey).
machine-made עשוי במכונה *adj* 'asoo|y/-yah bee-mekhonah.
machinery 1. מנגנון (apparatus) *nm* mang|anon/-enoneem (*pl+of:* -enoney); **2.** מכונות (machines) *nf pl* mekhonot.
machinist מכונאי *nm* mekhon|ay/-'eem (*pl+of:* -a'ey).
mackerel 1. כופיה *nf* koof|yah/-yot (*+of:* -yat); **2.** מקרל *nm* makarel/-eem (*pl+of:* -ey).
mackintosh מעיל גשם *nm* me'eel/-ey geshem.
mad 1. משוגע (crazy) *adj* meshoog|a'/-a'at; **2.** מרוגז (irate) *adj* meroog|az/-ezet.
(to drive) mad לשגע *inf* leshage'a'; *pst* sheega'; *pres* meshage'a' *etc*; *fut* yeshaga'.
(to get) mad להתרגז *inf* leheetragez; *pst* heetragez; *pres* meetragez *etc*; *fut* yeetragez.
(to go) mad להשתגע *v rfl inf* leheeshtage'a'; *pst* heeshtage'a'; *pres* meeshtage'a'; *fut* yeeshtage'a'.
mad about משוגע ל־ *adj* meshoog|a'/-a'at le-.
(to be) mad about להשתגע על *v rfl inf* leheeshtage'a' 'al; *pst* heeshtage'a' 'al; *pres* meeshtage'a' 'al; *fut* yeeshtage'a' 'al.

madam, madame גברת *nf* gveret/gvarot.
madcap 1. פרא־אדם *nm* pere'/peer'ey adam; **2.** פוחז (reckless) *adj* pokhez/-et.
(to) madden לשגע *inf* leshage'a'; *pst* sheega'; *pres* meshage'a'; *fut* yeshaga'.
made עשוי *adj* 'asoo|y/-yah.
(home-)made תוצרת בית *adj* totseret bayeet.
(self-)made מתוצרת עצמית *adj* mee-totseret 'atsmeet.
(to have something) made להזמין *inf* lehazmeen; pat heezmeen; *pres* mazmeen *etc*; *fut* yazmeen.
made in Israel 1. תוצרת הארץ *nf* totseret ha-arets; **2.** כחול לבן (blue-white) *adj* kakhol-lavan.
made of עשוי מ־ *adj* 'assoo|y/-yah mee-.
made-up 1. מאופר *adj* me'oop|ar/-eret; **2.** בדוי (invented) *adj* badooy/bedooyah.
madly עד לשיגעון *adv* 'ad le-sheega'on.
madman מטורף *nmf* metor|af/-efet.
madness טירוף *nm* teroof.
magazine 1. מחסן *nm* makhs|an/-aneem (*pl+of:* -eney); **2.** ממגורה (silo) *nf* mamgoor|ah/-ot (*+of:* -at); **3.** תקופון (periodical) *nm* tekoofon/-eem (*pl+of:* -ey).
(powder) magazine מחסנית *nf* makhsanee|t/-yot.
magic 1. קסם *nm* kes|em/-ameem (*pl+of:* keesmey); **2.** מקסים *adj* (enchanting) *adj* makseem/-ah; **3.** כישוף (sorcery) keeshoof/-eem (*pl+of:* -ey).
magician קוסם *nm* kos|em/-meem (*pl+of:* -mey).
magistrate שופט *nmf* shof|et/-etet (*+of:* -tey/-tot).
magnanimous 1. רחב־לב *adj* rekhav/rakhavat lev; **2.** נדיב (generous) *adj* nadeev/nedeevah.
magnate איל הון *nm* eyl/-ey hon.
magnesium מגנזיום *nm* magnezyoom.
magnet מגנט *nm* magnet/-eem (*pl+of:* -ey).
magnetic מגנטי *adj* magnetee/-t.
magnetic pole קוטב מגנטי *nm* kotev magnetee.
magnetic tape סרט מגנטי *nm* seret/srateem magnetee/-yeem.
(to) magnetize למגנט *inf* lemagnet; *pst* meegnet; *pres* memagnet *etc*; *fut* yemagnet.
magnificence תפארת *nf* teef'eret.
magnificent 1. נפלא *adj* neefl|a/-a'ah; **2.** מפואר (resplendent) *adj* mefo|'ar/-'eret.
(to) magnify להגדיל *inf* lehagdeel; *pst* heegdeel; *pres* magdeel *etc*; *fut* yagdeel.

magnitude 1. גדולה *nf* gedool|ah (+*of:* -at); **2.** גדלות (greatness) *nf* gadloo|t/-yot; **3.** שיעור (size) *nm* shee'oor/-eem (*pl+of:* -ey).

magpie 1. לבני *nm* leevn|ee/-eem (*pl+of:* -ey); **2.** עורב נחל (crow) *nm* 'or|ev/-vey nakhal.

mahogany מהגוני *nm* mahagonee.

maid 1. עוזרת *nf* 'oz|eret/-rot; **2.** משרתת (housemaid) *nf* meshar|etet/-tot.

maid of honor 1. נערת הכלה *nf* na'ar|at/-ot ha-kalah; **2.** שושבינה (bridesmaid) *nf* shoshveen|ah/-ot (+*of:* -at).

(old) maid בתולה זקנה *nf* betool|ah/-ot zeken|ah/-ot.

maiden 1. בתולי *adj* betoolee/-t; **2.** ראשון (first) *adj* reeshon/-ah; **3.** טהור (pure) *adj* tahor/tehorah; **4.** חדש (new) *adj* khadash/-ah.

maiden lady גברת רווקה *nf* gveret ravakah.

maiden voyage מסע בכורה *nm* mas|a'/-'ey bekhorah.

mail דואר *nm* do'ar.

(air)mail דואר־אוויר *nm* do'ar aveer.

(Express) Mail מסירה מיוחדת *nf* meseerah meyookhedet.

(Special Delivery) Mail מסירה מיוחדת *nf* meseerah meyookhedet.

(registered) mail דואר רשום *nm* do'ar rashoom.

mailbag 1. שק דואר *nm* sak/-ey do'ar; **2.** מזוודה (valise) *nf* meezv|adah/-adot (+*of:* -edet/-edot).

mailbox תיבת דואר *nf* teyv|at/-ot do'ar.

mailman דוור *nm* davar/-eem (*pl+of:* -ey).

(to) maim 1. להטיל מום *inf* lehateel moom; *pst* heeteel moom; *pres* mateel moom; *fut* yateel moom. **2.** לגרום נכות (cripple) *inf* leegrom nakhoot; *pst* garam *etc*; *pres* gorem *etc*; *fut* yeegrom *etc.*

main ראשי *adj* rashee/-t.

(in the) main בעיקר *adv* be-'eekar.

main street רחוב ראשי *nm* rekhov/-ot rashee/-yeem.

mainland יבשת *nf* yab|eshet/-ashot.

mainly בעיקר *adv* be-'eekar.

mainspring 1. קפיץ ראשי *nm* kfeets/-eem rashee/-yeem; **2.** נימוק עיקרי (main argument) *nm* neemook/-eem 'eekaree/-yeem

(to) maintain 1. לקיים *inf* lekayem; *pst* keeyem; *pres* mekayem *etc*; *fut* yekayem; **2.** לטעון (claim) *inf* leet'on; *pst* ta'an; *pres* to'en; *fut* yeet'an; **3.** לתחזק (keep fit) *inf* letakhzek; *pst* teekhzek; *pres* metakhzek *etc*; *fut* yetakhzek.

maintenance תחזוקה *nf* takhzook|ah/-ot (+*of:* -at).

maize תירס *nm* teeras (*cpr* teeras).

majestic 1. מלכותי *adj* malkhootee/-t; **2.** נשגב (grand) *adj* neesg|av/-evet.

majesty הוד מלכות *nm* hod malkhoot.

major 1. רב־סרן (army rank) *nm* ra|v/-bey seren/sraneem; **2.** רס"ן (*acr of* 1); **3.** רבתי (greater) *adj* rabatee; **4.** בכיר (principal) *adj* bakheer/bekheerah; **5.** בגיר (senior) *adj* bageer/begeerah; **6.** עיקרי (main) *adj* 'eekaree/-t.

(to) major in להתמחות בלימודי *inf* leheetmakhot be-leemoodey; *pst* heetmakhah *etc*; *pres* meetmakheh *etc*; *fut* yeetmakheh *etc.*

major league ליגה בכירה בספורט המקצועני בארצות הברית *nf* leeg|ah/-ot bekheer|ah/-ot ba-sport ha-meektso'anee be-artsot ha-breet. (Note: In Israel, no sporting team is professional, at least officially. Many of the sportsmen, however, are professionals individually, e.g. in tennis, basketball and soccer).

majority 1. רוב *nm* rov; **2.** רוב דעות (major. vote) *nm* rov de'ot; **3.** בגרות משפטית (legal maturity) *nf* bagroot meeshpateet.

make תוצרת *nf* totseret.

(to) make 1. לעשות (do) *inf* la'asot; *pst* 'asah; *pres* 'oseh *etc*; *fut* ya'aseh; **2.** ליצור (create) *inf* leetsor; *pst* yatsar; *pres* yotser; *fut* yeetsor; **3.** לשאת (deliver) *inf* laset; *pst* nasa; *pres* nose; *fut* yeesa.

(to) make a clean breast להתוודות *inf* leheetvadot; *pst* heetvadah; *pres* meetvadeh; *fut* yeetvadeh.

(to) make a train להספיק לרכבת *inf* lehaspeek la-rakevet; *pst* heespeek *etc*; *pres* maspeek *etc*; *fut* yaspeek *etc.*

(to) make a turn לעשות סיבוב *inf* la'asot seevoov; *pst* 'asah *etc*; *pres* 'oseh *etc*; *fut* ya'aseh *etc.*

(to) make away with 1. לגנוב *inf* leegnov; *pst* ganav; *pres* gonev; *fut* yegnov; **2.** להיפטר מ־ *inf* leheepater mee-; *pst & pres* neeftar (*f=p*) mee-; *fut* yeepater mee-.

(to) make away with oneself להתאבד *inf* leheet'abed; *pst* heet'abed; *pres* meet'abed; *fut* yeet'abed.

(to) make headway להתקדם *inf* leheetkadem; *pst* heetkadem; *pres* meetkadem; *fut* yeetkadem.

(to) make much of להחשיב *inf* lehakhsheev; *pst* hekhsheev; *pres* makhsheev; *fut* yakhsheev.

(to) make neither head nor tail לא להבין בזה ולא כלום *inf* lo lehaveen ba-zeh ve-lo khloom (*kh=k*); *pst* lo heveen *etc*; *pres* eyno meveen *etc*; *fut* lo yaveen *etc.*

(to) make off 1. להימלט (escape) *inf* leheemalet; *pst & pres* neemlat *etc*; *fut* yeemalet; **2.** לברוח (flee) *inf* leevro'akh; *pst* barakh (*b=v*); *pres* bore'akh; *fut* yeevrakh.

(to) make out in the distance להבחין מרחוק *inf* lehavkheen me-rakhok; *pst* heevkheen *etc*; *pres* mavkheen *etc*; *fut* yavkheen *etc.*

(to) make over 1. לתת *inf* latet; *pst* natan; *pres* noten *etc*; *fut* yeeten; **2.** להעביר (transmit) *inf* leha'aveer; *pst* he'eveer; *pres* ma'aveer; *fut* ya'aveer.

(to) make sure להבטיח *inf* lehavtee'akh; *pst* heevtee'akh; *pres* mavtee'akh; *fut* yavtee'akh.

(to) make toward להתקדם לקראת *inf* leheetkadem leekrat; *pst* heetkadem *etc*; *pres* meetkadem *etc*; *fut* yeetkadem *etc.*

make-up 1. איפור (facial) *nm* eepoor/-eem (*pl+of:* -ey); **2.** תרכובת (composition) *nf* teerkov|et/-ot; **3.** אופי (character) *nm* ofee.

(facial) make-up איפור פנים *nm* eepoor paneem.

(to) make up 1. להשלים (reconcile) *inf* lehashleem; *pst* heeshleem; *pres* mashleem *etc*; *fut* yashleem; **2.** לפצות (compensate) *inf* lefatsot; *pst* peetsah (*p=f*); *pres* mefatseh *etc*; *fut* yefatseh.

(to) make up a story להמציא סיפור lehamtsee seepoor; *pst* heemtsee *etc*; *pres* mamtsee *etc*; *fut* yamtsee *etc*.

(to) make up after a quarrel להשלים לאחר ריב *inf* lehashleem le-akhar reev; *pst* heeshleem *etc*; *pres* mashleem *etc*; *fut* yashleem *etc*.

(to) make up for a loss לכסות הפסדים *inf* lekhasot hefsedeem; *pst* keesah *(k=kh) etc*; *pres* mekhaseh *etc*; *fut* yekhaseh *etc*.

(to) make up one's face להתאפר *inf* leheet'aper; *pst* heet'aper; *pres* meet'aper *etc*; *fut* yeet'aper.

(to) make up one's mind לקבל החלטה *inf* lekabel hakhlatah; *pst* keebel *etc*; *pres* mekabel *etc*; *fut* yekabel *etc*.

maker 1. עושה *nmf* 'os|eh/-ah; **2.** יוצר (author) *nm* yots|er/-reem (*pl+of:* -rey).

(the) Maker הבורא (the Creator) *nm* ha-bore.

makeshift 1. אמצעי ארעי *nm* emts|a'ee/-a'eem ara'ee/-yeem; **2.** תחליף (substitute) *nm* takhleef/-eem (*pl+of:* -ey).

malady 1. חולי *nm* kholee/kholayeem (*pl+of:* kholayey); **2.** מחלה (illness) *nf* makhl|ah/-ot (*+of:* -at).

malaria 1. קדחת *nf* kadakhat; **2.** מלריה *nf* malaryah.

malcontent 1. לא מרוצה (discontented) *adj* lo meroots|eh/-ah; **2.** נרגן (grumbling) *adj* neerg|an/-enet.

male 1. גבר *nm m* gever/gvareem (*pl+of:* gavrey); **2.** זכר (masculine) *nm* zakhar/zekhareem (*pl+of:* zeekhrey); **3.** גברי (manly) *adj* gavree/-t; **4.** זכרי (masculine) *adj* zekharee/-t.

malice 1. זדון *nm* zadon (*+of:* zdon); **2.** משטמה (hatred) *nf* mastem|ah/-ot (*+of:* -at).

malicious 1. זדוני *adj* zdonee/-t; **2.** שוטם (hating) *adj* sotem/-et.

malign 1. רע־לב (malicious) *adj* ra'/ra'at lev; **2.** מזיק (harmful) *adj* mazeek/-ah; **3.** ממאיר (cancerous) *adj* mam'eer/-ah; **4.** מליגני *[colloq.] adj* maleegnee/t.

(to) malign 1. לקטרג *inf* lekatreg; *pst* keetreg; *pres* mekatreg *etc*; *fut* yekatreg; **2.** להשמיץ (defame) *inf* lehashmeets; *pst* heeshmeets; *pres* mashmeets *etc*; *fut* yashmeets.

malignant 1. ממאיר *adj* mam'eer/-ah; **2.** מזיק (harmful) *adj* mazeek/-ah; **3.** מרושע (wicked) *adj* meroosh|a'/-a'at.

mallet 1. מקבת *nf* mak|evet/-avot (*pl+of:* -vot); **2.** פטיש (hammer) *nm* pateesh/-eem (*pl+of:* -ey).

malnutrition תת־תזונה *nf* tat-tezoonah.

malt לתת letet.

malted milk חלב מלותת *nm* khalav melootat.

mama, mamma אמא *nf* eema.

mammal יונק *nm* yon|ek/-keem (*pl+of:* key).

mammoth 1. ממותה *nf* mamoot|ah/-ot (*+of:* -at); **2.** ענקי (giant) *adj* 'anakee/-t.

mammy אמא'לה *nf* eemaleh.

man 1. איש *nm* eesh/anasheem (*pl+of:* anshey); **2.** בן־אדם (person) *nm* ben/-bney adam; **3.** גבר (male) *nm* gever/gvareem (*pl+of:* gavrey); **4.** אנוש (human) enosh/bney enosh.

(to) man 1. לאייש *inf* le'ayesh; *pst* eeyesh; *pres* me'ayesh; *fut* ye'ayesh; **2.** לתגבר (fortify) *inf* letagber; *pst* teegber; *pres* metagber *etc*; *fut* yetagber.

(to a) man 1. עד אחד *adv* 'ad ekhad; **2.** עד האחרון (to the last) *adv* 'ad ha-akhron/-ah *(m/f)*.

man and wife בעל ואישה *nm & nf* ba'al ve-eeshah.

man cook טבח *nm* tabakh/-eem (*pl+of:* -ey).

man-of-war אוניית מלחמה *nf* onee|yat/-yot meelkhamah.

(to) manage 1. לנהל *inf* lenahel; *pst* neehel; *pres* menahel; *fut* yenahel; **2.** לשלוט (control) *inf* leeshlot; *pst* shalat; *pres* sholet; *fut* yeeshlot; **3.** לאלף (tame) *inf* le'alef; *pst* eelef; *pres* me'alef *etc*; *fut* ye'alef; **4.** להסתדר (succeed) *inf* leheestader; *pst* heestader; *pres* meestader; *fut* yeestader.

(to) manage to do להצליח לעשות *inf* lehatslee'akh la'asot; *pst* heetslee'akh *etc*; *pres* matslee'akh *etc*; *fut* yatslee'akh *etc*.

manageable 1. נוח *adj* no'akh/nokhah; **2.** צייתן (obedient) *adj* tsaytan/-eet; **3.** נהיל (tractable) *adj* naheel/neheelah.

management 1. ניהול *nm* neehool/-eem (*pl+of:* -ey); **2.** הנהלה (executive board) *nf* hanhal|ah/-ot (*+of:* -at); **3.** מינהלה (administration) *nf* meen|halah/-halot (*+of:* -helet).

manager מנהל *nmf* mena|hel/-helet (*pl:* -haleem/-halot; *+of:* -haley).

(general) manager 1. מנהל כללי menahel/-et klalee/-t; **2.** מנכ״ל (*acr of* 1) mankal/-eet (*pl+of:* -ey).

mandate 1. הרשאה *nf* harsha|'ah/-'ot (*+of:* -'at); **2.** מינוי (appointment) *nm* meenoo|y/-yeem (*pl+of:* -yey); **3.** פקודה (order) *nf* pekood|ah/-ot (*+of:* -at); **4.** מנדט (in parliament) *nm* mandat/-eem (*pl+of:* -ey).

(British) Mandate המנדט הבריטי *nm* ha-mandat ha-breetee.

(to) mandate למסור לפי מנדט *inf* leemsor lefee mandat; *pst* masar *etc*; *pres* moser *etc*; *fut* yeemsor *etc*.

mandatory הכרחי *adj* hekhrekhee/-t.

mane רעמה *nf* ra'amah/re'amot (*+of:* ra'amat).

maneuver 1. תימרון *nm* teemron/-eem (*pl+of:* -ey); **2.** תכסיס (trick) *nm* takhsees/-eem (*pl+of:* -ey).

(to) maneuver 1. לתמרן *inf* letamren; *pst* teemren; *pres* metamren; *fut* yetamren; **2.** לתחבל (scheme) *inf* letakhbel; *pst* teekhbel; *pres* metakhbel; *fut* yetakhbel.

manful 1. נחוש *adj* nakhoosh/nekhooshah; **2.** אמיץ (brave) *adj* ameets/-ah.

manganese מנגן *nm* mangan.

mange שחין *nm* shekheen.

manger אבוס *nm* evoos/avoos|eem (*pl+of:* -ey).

mangle 1. מעגילה *nf* ma'geel|ah/-ot (*+of:* -at); **2.** מסחט (squeezer) *nm* maskh|et/-ateem (*pl+of:* -atey).

(to) mangle 1. לגהץ *inf* legahets; *pst* geehets; *pres* megahets; *fut* yegahets; **2.** להטיל מום (cripple) *inf* lehateel moom; *pst* heeteel moom; *pres* mateel moom; *fut* yateel moom; **3.** להשחית (desfigure) *inf* lehashkheet; *pst* heeshkheet; *pres* mashkheet; *fut* yashkheet.

mango מנגו *nm* mango.

mangy 1. מוכה שחין *adj* mook|eh/-at sh'kheen; **2.** מטונף (dirty) *adj* metoon|af/-efet.

manhood 1. גברות *nf* gavroot; **2.** בגרות (maturity) *nf* bagroo|t/-yot; **3.** אומץ (bravery) *nm* omets.

mania 1. שיגעון *nm* sheeg|a'on/-'onot (+*of:* -'on); **2.** תשוקה (desire) *nf* teshook|ah/-ot (+*of:* -at); **3.** מניה *nf* manee|yah/-yot (+*of:* -yat).

manicure מניקיור *nm* maneekyoor/-eem.

manifest -manifest 1. שטר מטען (cargo invoice) *nm* shtar/sheetrey meet'an; **2.** הצהרה (declaration) *nf* hats'har|ah/-ot (+*of:* -at); **3.** ברור *adj* baroor/brooranh; **4.** בולט לעין (conspicuous) *adj* bolet/-et la-'ayeen.

manifestation 1. הפגנה (demonstration) *nf* hafgan|ah/-ot (+*of:* -at); **2.** פירסום (display) *nm* peersoom/-eem (*pl+of:* -ey).

manifesto מנשר *nm* meensh|ar/-areem (*pl+of:* -erey).

manifold 1. משוכפל *adj* meshookhp|al/-elet; **2.** מגוון *adj* megoov|an/-enet.

manikin 1. ננס *nmf* nan|as/-eset; **2.** בובת הדגמה *nf* boob|at/-ot hadgamah.

manila paper נייר עטיפה חום *nm* neyar 'ateefah khoom.

(to) manipulate 1. לתפעל *inf* letaf'el; *pst* teef'el; *pres* metaf'el *etc*; *fut* yetaf'el; **2.** להשתמש ב־ (make use of) *inf* leheeshtamesh be-; *pst* heeshtamesh be-; *pres* meeshtamesh be-; *fut* yeeshtamesh be-.

manipulation 1. תפעול *nm* teef'ool/-eem (*pl+of:* -ey); **2.** שימוש (use) *nm* sheemoosh/-eem (*pl+of:* -ey).

mankind האנושות *nf* ha-enoshoot.

manly גברי *adj* gavree/-t.

mannequin דוגמן *nmf* doogman/-eet (*pl:* -eem/ -eeyot).

manner 1. דרך (way) *nf* derekh/drakheem (*pl+of:* darkhey); **2.** התנהגות (air) *nf* heetnahagoo|t/-yot.

(after this) manner בדרך זו *adv* be-derekh zo.

(by no) manner of means בשום פנים לא be-shoom paneem lo.

(in a) manner of speaking כביכול *adv* kee-v-yakhol.

mannerism 1. גינונים *nm pl* geenoon|eem (*pl+of:* -ey); **2.** הרגל (habit) *nm* hergel/-eem (*pl+of:* -ey).

manners נימוסים *nm pl* neemoos|eem (*pl+of:* -ey).

mannish 1. בצורה גברית *adv* be-tsoorah gavreet; **2.** בתוקף (strongly) *adv* be-tokef.

mansion בית מגורים לחוד *nm* bet/batey megooreem le-khood.

manslaughter הריגה *nf* hareeg|ah/-ot (+*of:* -at).

mantel רובד האח *nm* roved ha-akh.

mantle אדרת *nf* aderet/adarot (*pl+of:* adrot).

manual 1. מדריך *nm* madreekh/-eem (*pl+of:* -ey); **2.** ספר הוראות (instruction book) *nm* sefer/ seefrey hora'ot; **3.** ידני (hand-operated) *adj* yedanee/-t.

(training) manual מדריך תרגול *nm* madreekh/-ey teergool.

manufacture ייצור *nm* yeetsoor/-eem (*pl+of:* -ey).

(to) manufacture לייצר *inf* leyatser; *pst* yeetser; *pres* meyatser; *fut* yeyatser.

manufacturer 1. יצרן *nm* yatsran/-eem (*pl+of:* -ey); **2.** תעשיין (industrialist) *nm* ta'aseeyan/ -eem (*pl+of:* -ey).

manufacturing ייצור *nm* yeetsoor/-eem (*pl+of:* -ey).

manure זבל *nm* zevel/zvaleem (*pl+of:* zeevley).

manuscript 1. כתב־יד *nm* ketav/keetvey yad; **2.** בכתב־יד (handwritten) *adj* bee-khtav yad (*kh=k*).

many 1. הרבה *adj & adv* harbeh; **2.** רבים *adj pl* rab|eem/-ot (*m/f*).

(a great) many חלק ניכר מבין *nm* khelek neekar mee-beyn.

(too) many רבים מדי rabeem meeday.

(two guests too) many שני אורחים יותר מדי shney orkheem yoter meeday.

(how) many? ?כמה kamah?

many a time פעמים רבות *adv* pe'ameem rabot.

(as) many as רבים ככל *adj pl* rabeem ke-khol (*kh=k*).

(as) many as five עד כדי חמישה 'ad kedey khameeshah.

(a good) many of רבים מבין *nm pl* rabeem mee-beyn.

map מפה *nf* map|ah/-ot (+*of:* -at).

(to) map למפות *inf* lemapot; *pst* meepah; *pres* memapeh; *fut* yemapeh.

(to) map out לתכנן *inf* letakhnen; *pst* teekhnen; *pres* metakhnen; *fut* yetakhnen.

maple אדר *nm* eder

(to) mar 1. לחבל ב־ *inf* lekhabel be-; *pst* kheebel be-; *pres* mekhabel be-; *fut* yekhabel be-; **2.** לקלקל (spoil) *inf* lekalkel; *pst* keelkel; *pres* mekalkel; *fut* yekalkel.

marble שיש *nm* shayeesh.

(to play) marbles לשחק בגולות *inf* lesakhek be-goolot; *pst* seekhek *etc*; *pres* mesakhek; *fut* yesakhek *etc*.

March מרס *nm* mars.

march 1. צעדה *nf* tse'ad|ah/-ot (+*of:* tsa'ad|at/-ot); **2.** שיר לכת (song) *nm* sheer/-ey lekhet.

(to) march לצעוד *inf* leets'od; *pst* tsa'ad; *pres* tso'ed; *fut* yeets'ad.

(to) march in review לעבור בסך *inf* la'avor ba-sakh; *pst* 'avar *etc*; *pres* 'over *etc*; *fut* ya'avor *etc*.

(to) march out להתקדם לעבר *inf* leheetkadem le-'ever; *pst* heetkadem *etc*; *pres* meetkadem *etc*; *fut* yeetkadem *etc*.

mare 1. סוסה *nf* soos|ah/-ot (+*of:* -at); **2.** אתון (fem. donkey) *nf* aton/-ot.

margarine מרגרינה *nf* margareen|ah/-ot (+*of:* -at).

margin 1. שוליים *nm pl* shool|ayeem (*pl+of:* -ey); **2.** קצה (edge) *nm* katseh/ketsavot (+*of:* ketseh/ katsvot).

marginal שולי *adj* shoolee/-t.

marigold ציפורני חתול *nm* tseeporney khatool.

marijuana צמח קנבוס *nm* tsemakh/tseemkhey kanabos.

marina מעגן למפרשיות *nm* ma'agan/-eem le-meefraseeyot.

marine ימי *adj* yamee/-t.

(merchant) marine צי הסוחר *nm* tsee ha-sokher.
marine corps חיל נחתים *nm* kheyl/-ot nekhateem.
mariner 1. מלח *nm* malakh/-eem (*pl+of:* -ey); **2.** נווט (navigator) *nm* navat/-eem (*pl+of:* -ey).
maritime ימי *adj* yamee/-t.
mark 1. ציון *nm* tseeyoon/-eem (*pl+of:* -ey); **2.** אות (indication) *nm* ot/-ot; **3.** סימן (sign) *nm* seeman/-eem (*pl+of:* -ey).
(exclamation) mark סימן קריאה *nm* seeman/-ey kree'ah.
(German) Mark 1. מרק גרמני *nm* mark/-eem german|ee/-eem; **2.** מג״ר (*acr of* 1).
(question) mark סימן שאלה *nm* seeman/-ey she'elah.
(to) mark 1. לציין *inf* letsayen; *pst* tseeyen; *pres* metsayen; *fut* yetsayen; **2.** לסמן (indicate) *inf* lesamen; *pst* seemen; *pres* mesamen *etc; fut* yesamen.
(below the) mark 1. שלא בקו הבריאות *adv* she-lo be-kav ha-bree'oot; **2.** שלא לעניין (beside the point) *adv* she-lo la-'eenyan.
(bless the) mark בל נפתח פה לשטן bal neeftakh peh la-satan.
(to make one's) mark 1. להטביע חותם *inf* lehatbee'a' khotam; *pst* heetbee'a' *etc; pres* matbee'a' *etc; fut* yatbee'a' *etc;* **2.** לעשות רושם (impress) *inf* la'asot roshem; *pst* 'asah *etc; pres* 'oseh *etc; fut* ya'aseh *etc.*
(to miss the) mark להחטיא את המטרה *inf* lehakhtee et ha-matarah; *pst* hekhtee *etc; pres* makhtee *etc; fut* yakhtee *etc.*
(trade) mark סמל מסחרי *nm* semel/smaleem meeskharee/-yeem.
(to) mark down להפחית מחיר *inf* lehafkheet mekheer; *pst* heefkheet *etc; pres* mafkheet *etc; fut* yafkheet *etc.*
mark my word! שים לב לדבריי! *v imp* seem/-ee (*m/f*) lev lee-dvarayI
marked בולט *adj* bolet/-et.
marker סמן *nm* saman/-eem (*pl+of:* -ey).
market שוק *nm* shook/shvakeem (*pl+of:* shookey).
(black) market שוק שחור *nm* shook shakhor.
(stock) market שוק ניירות הערך *nm* shook (*pl+of:* -ey) neyarot ha-'erekh.
(to) market לשווק *inf* leshavek; *pst* sheevek; *pres* neshavek; *fut* yeshavek.
market place כיכר השוק *nf* keekar ha-shook.
market price מחיר השוק *nm* mekheer/-ey ha-shook.
market value שער השוק *nm* sh|a'ar/-ey ha-shook.
marketing שיווק *nm* sheevook/-eem (*pl+of:* -ey).
(quotation) marks 1. מרכאות *nf pl* merkha'ot; **2.** מרכאות כפולות (quotes) *nf pl* merkha'ot kfoolot.
(school) marks ציונים *nm pl* tseeyooneem (*pl+of:* -ey).
marksman 1. קלע *nm* kal|a'/-a'eem (*pl+of:* -'ey); **2.** צלף (sniper) *nm* tsalaf/-eem (*pl+of:* -ey).
marmalade ריבה *nf* reeb|ah/-ot (*+of:* -at).
maroon בצבע בורדו *adj* be-tseva' bordo.
marooned עזוב לנפשו *adj* 'azoov/-ah le-nafsh|o/-ah.
(to get) marooned להיעזב לנפשו *inf* lehe'azev le-nafsho; *pst & pres* ne'ezav *etc; fut* ye'azev *etc.*
marquis מרקיז *nm* markeez/-eem (*pl+of:* -ey).
marquise מרקיזה *nf* markeez|ah/-ot (*+of:* -at).
marriage נישואים *nm pl* neesoo|'eem (*pl+of:* -ey).
(civil) marriage נישואים אזרחיים *nm pl* neesoo'eem ezrakheeyeem.
marriage broker שדכן *nmf* shadkhan/-eet.
marriage contract כתובה *nf* ketoob|ah/-ot (*+of:* -at).
marriage license אישור לחיתון *nm* eeshoor le-kheetoon.
marriageable בר־חיתון *adj* bar/bat kheetoon.
married נשוי *adj* nasooy/nesoo'ah.
(to get) married 1. להינשא *inf* leheenase; *pst & pres* neesa; *fut* yeenase; **2.** להתחתן *inf* leheetkhaten; *pst* heetkhaten; *pres* metkhaten; *fut* yetkhaten.
married couple זוג נשוי *nm* zoog/-ot nasooy/nesoo'eem.
marrow 1. מוח עצמות *nm* mo'akh 'atsamot; **2.** לשד עצמות *nm* leshad 'atsamot.
(to) marry 1. לחתן (others) *vt inf* lekhaten; *pst* kheeten; *pres* mekhaten; *fut* yekhaten; **2.** לשאת אישה (a woman) *inf* lase't eeshah; *pst* nasa *etc; pres* nose *etc; fut* yeesa *etc.*
Mars מאדים (planet) *nm* ma'adeem.
marsh ביצה *nf* beets|ah/-ot (*+of:* -at).
marshal 1. מרשל *nm* marshal/-eem (*pl+of:* -ey); **2.** שליח בית המשפט *nm* shlee|'akh/-khey bet ha-meeshpat.
(fire) marshal ראש הכבאים *nm* rosh ha-kaba'eem.
(to) marshal 1. לערוך *inf* la'arokh; *pst* 'arakh; *pres* 'orekh; *fut* ya'arokh; **2.** לסדר *inf* lesader; *pst* seeder; *pres* mesader; *fut* yesader.
marshmalow חוטמית רפואית *nf* khotmeet refoo'eet.
marshy ביצתי *adj* beetsatee/-t.
mart 1. שוק *nm* shook/shvakeem (*pl+of:* shookey); **2.** מרכז סחר (trading center) *nm* merkaz/-ezey sakhar; **3.** יריד (fair) *nm* yereed/-eem (*pl+of:* -ey).
marten חולדה *nf* khoold|ah/-ot (*+of:* -at).
martial 1. צבאי (military) *nm* tsva'ee/-t.; **2.** מלחמתי (war) *adj* meelkhamtee/-t.
(court) martial 1. בית דין צבאי *nm* bet/batey deen tsva'ee/-yeem; **2.** משפט צבאי (trial) *nm* meeshpat/-eem tsva'ee/-yeem.
martial law משטר צבאי *nm* meeshtar tsva'ee.
martin סנונית *nf* snoonee|t/-yot.
martyr קדוש מעונה *nmf* kadosh/kedoshah me'oon|eh/-ah.
(to) martyr להקריב עצמו בעד מטרה *inf* lehakreev 'atsmo be'ad matarah; *pst* heekreev *etc; pres* makreev *etc; fut* yakreev *etc.*
martyrdom 1. קידוש השם *nm* keedoosh ha-shem; **2.** מות קדושים *nm* mot kedosheem.
marvel פלא *nm* pele'/pla'eem (*pl+of:* peel'ey).
(to) marvel להתפעל *inf* leheetpa'el; *pst* heetpa'el; *pres* meetpa'el *etc; fut* yeetpa'el.
marvelous 1. נפלא *adj* neefl|a'/-a'ah; **2.** נהדר *adj* nehed|ar/-eret.
mascot קמיע *nm* kame'a'/keme'ot.

masculine 1. ממין זכר *adj* mee-meen zakhar; **2.** זכר *adj* zakhar.

(to) mash 1. לרסק *inf* lerasek; *pst* reesek; *pres* merasek; *fut* yerasek; **2.** לקצוץ *inf* leektsots; *pst* katsats; *pres* kotsets *etc; fut* yeektsots.

mashed potatoes 1. רסק תפוחי אדמה *nm* resek tapookhey adamah; **2.** מחית (purée) *nf* mekhee|t/-yot; **3.** פירה (*synon.* with 2) *nm* peereh.

mask 1. מסכה *nf* masekh|ah/-ot (*+of:* -at); **2.** מסווה (disguise) *nm* masv|eh/-ot (*pl+of:* -ey).

(to) mask להסוות *inf* lehasvot; *pst* heesvah; *pres* masveh; *fut* yasveh.

masked ball נשף מסכות *nm* neshef/neeshfey masekhot.

mason בנאי *nm* ban|ay/-a'eem (*pl+of:* -a'ey).

(Free) Mason בונה חופשי *nm* bon|eh-eem khofsh|ee/-eem.

masonry 1. עבודת אבן (stonework) *nf* 'avod|at/-ot even; **2.** תנועת הבונים החופשיים (Free Masons Movement) *nf* tenoo'at ha-boneem he-khofsheeyeem.

masquerade הסוואה *nf* hasva|'ah/-'ot (*+of:* -'at).

(to) masquerade להתחפש *inf* leheetkhapes; *pst* heetkhapes; *pres* meetkhapes *etc; fut* yeetkhapes.

mass 1. אוסף *nm* os|ef/-afeem (*pl+of:* -fey); **2.** כמות גדולה (large quantity) *nf* kamoo|t/-yot gedol|ah/-ot; **3.** גוש (bloc) *nm* goosh/-eem (*pl+of:* -ey).

(to) mass להקהיל *inf* lehak'heel; *pst* heek'heel; *pres* mak'heel *etc; fut* yak'heel.

mass communications תקשורת המונים *nf* teekshoret hamoneem.

mass media אמצעי התקשורת *nm pl* emtsa'ey ha-teekshoret.

mass meeting אסיפת עם *nf* asef|at/-ot 'am.

(to) mass troops לרכז צבא *inf* lerakez tsava; *pst* reekez *etc; pres* merakez *etc; fut* yerakez *etc.*

massacre טבח *nm* tevakh.

(to) massacre 1. לטבוח *inf* leetbo'akh; *pst* tavakh *(v=b); pres* tove'akh *etc; fut* yeetbakh; **2.** להשמיד (exterminate) *inf* lehashmeed; *pst* heeshmeed; *pres* mashmeed *etc; fut* yashmeed.

massage עיסוי *nm* 'eesoo|y/-yeem (*pl+of:* -yey).

(to) massage לעסות *inf* le'asot; *pst* 'eesah; *pres* me'aseh *etc; fut* ye'aseh.

(the) masses המוני העמלים *nm pl* hamoney ha-'ameleem.

massive מסיבי *adj* maseevee/-t.

mast תורן *nm* toren/traneem (*pl+of:* torney).

master 1. ראש *nm* (head) rosh/rash|eem (*pl+of:* -ey); **2.** אומן (skill) *nm* ooman/-eem (*pl+of:* -ey).

(band) master ראש להקה *nm* rosh lahakah.

(to) master 1. להשתלט *inf* leheeshtalet; *pst* heeshtalet; *pres* meeshtalet *etc; fut* yeeshtalet; **2.** להתגבר על (overcome) *inf* leheetgaber 'al; *pst* heetgaber 'al; *pres* meetgaber 'al; *fut* yeetgaber 'al.

(to) master a language לרכוש שליטה בשפה *inf* leerkosh shleetah be-safah; *pst* rakhash *(kh=k) etc; pres* rokhesh *etc; fut* yeerkosh *etc.*

master builder 1. קבלן בניין (contractor) *nm* kablan/-ey beenyan; **2.** מהנדס אזרחי (civil engineer) *nmf* mehandes/-et ezrakhee/-t.

master key מפתח ראשי *nm* mafte|'akh/khot rashee/-yeem.

master of arts 1. מוסמך למדעי הרוח *nmf* moosm|akh/-ekhet le-mada'ey ha-roo'akh; **2.** מ.א. M.A.

master of science מוסמך למדעים *nmf* moosm|akh/-ekhet le-mada'eem.

masterful 1. מיומן *adj* meyoom|an/-enet; **2.** שתלטני (domineering) *adj* shtaltanee/-t.

masterly 1. מיומן *adj* meyoom|an/-enet; **2.** במיומנות *adv* bee-meyoomanoot.

masterpiece מעשה אמן *nm* ma'aseh oman.

master's degree תואר מאסטר *nm* to|'ar/-'orey master.

mastery 1. בקיאות *nf* bekee'oo|t/-yot; **2.** שליטה (control) *nf* shleet|ah/-ot (*+of:* -at).

mastiff כלב שמירה *nm* kelev/kalvey shmeerah.

(to) masturbate לאונן *inf* le'onen; *pst* onen; *pres* me'onen *etc; fut* ye'onen.

mat 1. מחצלת *nf* makhts|elet/-alot; **2.** מדרסה (doormat) *nf* meedr|asah/-asot (*+of:* -eset).

match 1. זיווג (pair) *nm* zeevoog/-eem (*pl+of:* -ey); **2.** תחרות (game) *nf* takhroo|t/-yot; **3.** גפרור (light) *nm* gafroor/-eem (*pl+of:* -ey).

(a good) match שידוך טוב *nm* sheedookh tov.

(does not) match אינו מתאים eyn|o/-ah mat'eem/-ah.

(has no) match אין שווה לו eyn shav|eh/-ah lo/lah *(m/f)*.

(to) match 1. להתאים *inf* lehat'eem; *pst* heet'eem; *pres* mat'eem *etc; fut* yat'eem; **2.** לשדך (pair) *inf* leshadekh; *pst* sheedekh; *pres* meshadekh *etc; fut* yeshadekh.

(to) match one's strength להתמודד שווה בשווה *inf* leheetmoded shaveh be-shaveh; *pst* heetmoded *etc; pres* meetmoded *etc; fut* yeetmoded *etc.*

(does not) match well אינו תואם יפה eyn|o/-ah to'em/-et yafeh.

matchbox קופסת גפרורים *nf* koofs|at/a'ot gafrooreem.

matchless שאין כמוהו *adj* she-eyn kamo|hoo'/-ha.

mate 1. בן־זוג (partner) *nm* ben/-ey zoog; **2.** חבר (companion) *nm* khav|er/-erah (*pl:* -ereem; *+of:* -rey); **3.** טייס משנה (co-pilot) *nm* tayas/-ey meeshneh.

(to) mate להזדווג *inf* leheezdaveg; *pst* heezdaveg; *pres* meezdaveg *etc; fut* yeezdaveg.

material חומר *nm* khom|er/-areem (*pl+of:* -rey).

(raw) material חומר־גלם *nm* khom|er/-rey gelem.

material to חשוב לעניין *adj* khashoov/-ah le-'eenyan.

maternal אמהי *adj* eemahee/-t.

maternity אמהות *nf* eemahoot.

mathematical מתמטי *adj* matematee/-t.

mathematician מתמטיקאי *nmf* matemateeka|y/-'eet.

mathematics מתמטיקה *nf* matemateekah.

matinee הצגה יומית *nf* hatsag|ah/-ot yomee|t/-yot.

matriarch 1. אם כראש משפחה em ke-rosh meeshpakhah; **2.** מטריארך *nm* matree'arkh.

(to) matriculate להירשם לאוניברסיטה *inf* leherashem la-ooneeverseetah; *pst & pres* neersham *etc; fut* yerashem *etc.*

matriculation בגרות *nf* bagroo|t/-yot.

matriculation certificate תעודת בגרות *nf* te'ood|at/-ot bagroot.

matriculation exams בחינות בגרות *nf* bekheen|at/-ot bagroot.

matrimony נישואים *nm pl* neesoo|'eem (*pl+of:* -'ey).

matrix מטריצה *nf* matreets|ah/-ot (*+of:* -at).

(dot) matrix printer מדפסת נקודות *nf* mad-pes|et/-ot nekoodot.

matron 1. אישה כבודה *nf* eeshah/nasheem kvood|ah/-ot; **2.** גברת נשואה (married lady) *nf* gveret/gvarot nesoo|'ah/-'ot; **3.** מנהלת משק (woman supervisor) *nf* mena|helet/-halot meshek.

matter 1. חומר (substance) *nm* khom|er/-areem (*pl+of:* -rey); **2.** עסק (affair) *nm* 'esek/'asakeem (*pl+of:* 'eeskey); **3.** מוגלה (pus) *nf* moogl|ah/-ot (*+of:* -at).

(a business) matter עניין עסקי *nm* 'eenyan 'eskee.

(it does not) matter אין זה חשוב eyn zeh khashoov.

(it is of no) matter אין זה משנה eyn zeh meshaneh.

(printed) matter דברי דפוס *nm pl* deevrey dfoos.

(serious) matter עניין רציני *nm* 'eenyan/-eem retseenee/-yeem.

(to) matter להיות בעל חשיבות *inf* leehyot ba'al khasheevoot; *pst* hayah *etc; pres* heeno *etc; fut* yeehyeh *etc.*

(what is the) matter? 1. ?מה העניין mah ha-'eenyan?; **2.** ?מה קרה (what happened?) mah karah?

matter for complaint נושא לתלונה *nm* nos|e/-'eem lee-tloonah.

matter of two minutes עניין של שתי דקות *nm* 'eenyan shel shtey dakot.

(in the) matter of 1. בנושא של be-nose shel; **2.** בעניין be-'eenyan.

(as a) matter of course כדבר המובן מאליו ke-davar ha-moovan me-elav.

(as a) matter of fact 1. לאמיתו של דבר *adv* la-ameeto shel davar; **2.** בעצם (actually) be-'etsem.

mattress מזרן *nm* meezr|an (*cpr* meezron)/-aneem (*pl+of:* -eney).

(spring) mattress מזרן קפיצי *nm* meezran/-eem kfeetsee/-yeem.

(rubberfoam) mattress מיזרן גומאוויר *nm* meez|ran/-eney goomaveer.

mature בוגר *adj* boger/-et.

(to) mature 1. להתבגר *inf* leheetbager; *pst* heetbager; *pres* meetbager *etc; fut* yeetbager; **2.** להבשיל (ripen) *inf* lehavsheel; *pst* heevsheel; *pres* mavsheel *etc; fut* yavsheel.

(a) mature note שטר בר־פירעון *nm* shtar/-ot bar/bney pera'on.

maturity 1. בגרות *nf* bagroo|t-yot; **2.** בשלות *nf* besheloo|t/-yot; **3.** מועד פירעון *nm* mo'ed/mo'adey (financial) pera'on.

(to) maul לפצוע *inf* leeftso'a'; *pst* patsa' *(p=f); pres* potse'a' *etc; fut* yeeftsa'.

maverick 1. חסר השתייכות *adj* khas|ar/-rat heeshtaykhoot; **2.** בלתי מפלגתי (non-partisan) *adj* beeltee meeflagtee/-t.

maxim 1. אימרה *nf* eemrah/amarot (*+of:* eemrat); **2.** פתגם (proverb) *nm* peetgam/-eem (*pl+of:* -ey).

maximum 1. מירב *nm* merav; **2.** מקסימום *nm* makseemoom.

may 1. מסוגל (able) *adj* mesoog|al/-elet; **2.** רשאי (permitted) *adj* rash|ay/-a'eet; **3.** יכול (can) *adj* yakhol/yekholah.

May מאי *nm* may.

(be what) may יהיה אשר יהיה yeeehyeh asher yeehyeh.

(she) may be late היא עלולה לאחר hee 'aloolah le'akher.

may be that ייתכן כי yeetakhen kee.

May Day אחד במאי *nm* ekhad be-may.

may I sit down? ?האוכל לשבת ha-ookhal lashevet?

May Queen מלכת יופי של חגיגות אחד במאי *nf* malk|at/-ot yofee shel khageegot ekhad be-may.

(it) may rain עלול לרדת גשם 'alool laredet geshem.

may you have a good time ! בילוי נעים beelooy na'eem!

maybe יתכן yeetakhen.

mayonnaise מיונית *nf* mayoneet.

mayor ראש עיר *nm* rosh/rashey 'eer.

mayoralty ראשות עיר *nf* rashoot 'eer.

maze 1. מבוך (labyrinth) *nm* mavokh; **2.** מבוכה (embarrassment) *nf* mevookh|ah/-ot (*+of:* -at); **3.** בלבול (confusion) *nm* beelbool/-eem (*pl+of:* -ey).

(in a) maze 1. במבוכה (embarrassed) *adv* bee-mevookhah; **2.** במצב של בלבול (in confusion) *adv* be-matsav shel beelbool.

me 1. אותי *pron* otee; **2.** לי (to me) *pron* lee; **3.** אני (I) *pron* anee; **4.** אנוכי (I) *pron* anokhee.

(give) me תן לי *v imp* ten/-ee *(m/f)* lee.

(for) me 1. בעדי *adv* ba'adee; **2.** עבורי (my behalf) *adv* 'avooree; **3.** בשבילי (my sake) *adv* bee-shveelee.

(with) me 1. אתי eetee; **2.** עמי *adv* 'eemee.

meadow 1. אחו *nm* akhoo; **2.** אדמת מרעה (grazing ground) *nf* adm|at/-ot meer'eh.

meadow lark עפרוני השדות *nm* 'efronee ha-sadot.

meager 1. דל *adj* dal/-ah; **2.** רזה (thin) *adj* raz|eh/-ah; **3.** זעום (scant) *adj* za'oom/ze'oomah.

meal 1. ארוחה *nf* arookh|ah/-ot (*+of:* -at); **2.** קמח גס (grain) *nm* kemakh gas.

(corn) meal תבשיל תירס *nm* tavsheel/-ey teeras.

mealtime 1. עת לסעוד *nf* 'et lees'od; **2.** עת צהריים (lunchtime) 'et tsohorayeem.

mean 1. שפל (malicious) *adj* shafal/shfalah; **2.** עלוב (miserable) 'aloov/-ah; **3.** קשה *adj* kash|eh/-ah; **4.** מסובך (difficult) *adj* mesoob|akh/-ekhet; **5.** חולני (sick) *adj* kholanee/-t; **6.** ממוצע (average) *adj* memoots|a'/-a'at.

(to) mean להתכוון *inf* leheetkaven; *pst* heetkaven; *pres* meetkaven *etc; fut* yeetkaven.

mean distance מרחק ממוצע *nm* merkhak/-eem memoots|a'/-a'eem.

meander 1. פיתול *nm* peetool/-eem (*pl+of:* -ey); **2.** דרך עקלקלה (crooked road) *nf* derekh/drakheem 'akalkal|ah/-ot.

(to) meander 1. להתפתל (wind) *inf* leheetpatel; *pst* heetpatel; *pres* meetpatel; *fut* yeetpatel; **2.** לשוטט (rove) *inf* leshotet; *pst* shotet; *pres* meshotet; *fut* yeshotet.

meaning 1. משמעות (sense) *nf* mashma'oo|t/-yot; **2.** כוונה (intent) *nf* kavan|ah/-ot (+*of:* -at).

(well) meaning בעל כוונות טובות *adj* ba'al/-at kavanot tovot.

meaningless חסר משמעות *adj* khas|ar/-rat mashma'oot.

meanness שפלות *nf* sheefloo|t/-yot.

means אמצעי *nm* emtsa|'ee/-'eem (*pl+of:* -'ey).

(a man of) means בעל אמצעים *nmf* ba'al/-at emtsa'eem.

(by all) means 1. בכל מחיר *adv* be-khol (*kh=k*) mekheer; **2.** בוודאי (certainly) *adv* be-vaday.

(by no) means 1. בשום פנים *adv* be-shoom paneem; **2.** בשום אופן (in no way) *adv* be-shoom ofen.

(by) means of באמצעות *adv* be-emtsa'oot.

(he) means well כוונתו טובה kavanato tovah.

meantime בינתיים *adv* beynatayeem.

(in the) meantime בינתיים *adv* beynatayeem.

meanwhile עד אז *adv* 'ad az.

measles חצבת *nf* khatsevet.

measurable מדיד *adj* madeed/medeedah.

measurably במידה מוגבלת *adv* be-meedah moogbelet.

measure 1. מידה *nf* meed|ah/-ot (+*of:* -at); **2.** אמת מידה (standard) *nf* amat/-amot meedah; **3.** אמצעי (means) *nm* emtsa|'ee/-'eem (*pl+of:* -'ey).

(beyond) measure מעבר לכל מידה *adv* me-'ever le-khol (*kh=k*) meedah.

(dry) measure מידת היבש *nf* meed|at/-ot ha-yavesh.

(in large) measure במידה רבה *adv* be-meedah rabah.

(to) measure למדוד *inf* leemdod; *pst* madad; *pres* moded *etc*; *fut* yeemdod.

measured מדוד *adj* madood/medoodah.

measurement 1. מדידה *nf* medeed|ah/-ot (+*of:* -at); **2.** מימד (extent) *nm* meymad/-eem (*pl+of:* -ey).

meat בשר *nm* basar/besareem (+*of:* besar).

(cold) meat נקניק *nm* nakneek/-eem (*pl+of:* -ey).

meat ball כדור בשר *nm* kadoor/-ey basar.

meat market שוק הבשר *nm* shook/-ey ha-basar.

meaty בשרני *adj* basranee/-t.

mechanic 1. מכונאי *nm* mekhon|ay/-a'eem (*pl+of:* -a'ey); **2.** מכאני *adj* mekhanee/-t.

mechanical מכאני *adj* mekhanee/-t.

mechanics 1. מכונאות *nf* mekhona'oot; **2.** מכאניקה *nf* mekhaneek|ah/-ot (+*of:* -at).

mechanism מנגנון *nm* manganon/mangenon|eem (*pl+of:* -ey).

medal 1. אות הצטיינות *nm* ot/-ot heetstaynoot; **2.** מדליה *nf* medal|yah/-yot (+*of:* -yat).

(to) meddle 1. להתערב (intervene) *inf* leheet'arev; *pst* heet'arev; *pres* meet'arev *etc*; *fut* yeet'arev; **2.** לבחוש (stir) *inf* leevkhosh; *pst* bakhash (*b=v*); *pres* bokhesh *etc*; *fut* yeevkhosh.

meddler, meddlesome בוחש בקדירה *nmf* bokhesh/-et ba-kdeyrah.

media כלי התקשורת *nm pl* kley ha-teekshoret.

median 1. תיכוני *adj* teekhonee/-t; **2.** ממוצע (medium) *nm* memoots|a'/-a'eem (*pl+of:* -a'ey).

median strip פס הפרדה *nm* pas/-ey hafradah.

mediation תיווך *nm* teevookh/-eem (*pl+of:* -ey).

mediator מתווך *nmf* metav|ekh/-ekhet (*pl:* -kheem/-khot; +*of:* -khey).

medical רפואי *adj* refoo'ee/-t.

medical school בית ספר לרפואה *nm* bet/batey sefer lee-refoo'ah.

medication תרופה *nf* troof|ah/-ot (+*of:* -at).

medicine 1. רפואה (science) *nf* refoo|'ah/-'ot (+*of:* -'at); **2.** תרופה (remedy) *nf* troof|ah/-ot (+*of:* -at).

medicine cabinet ארון תרופות *nm* aron/-ot troofot

medicine kit מערכת ציוד רפואי *nf* ma'arekhet tseeyood refoo'ee.

medicine man רופא אליל *nm* rof|e/-'ey eleel.

medieval של ימי הביניים *adj* shel yemey ha-beynayeem.

mediocre בינוני *adj* beynonee/-t.

mediocrity בינוניות *nf* beynoneeyoot.

(to) meditate 1. להרהר (muse) *inf* leharher; *pst* heerher; *pres* meharher *etc*; *fut* yeharher; **2.** לשקול (ponder) *inf* leeshkol; *pst* shakal; *pres* shokel *etc*; *fut* yeeshkol.

meditation הרהורים *nm pl* heerhoor|eem (*pl+of:* -ey).

Mediterranean ים־תיכוני *adj* yam-teekhonee/-t.

Mediterranean Sea הים התיכון *nm* ha-yam ha-teekhon.

medium 1. מדיום *nm* medyoom/-eem (*pl+of:* -ey); **2.** ממוצע (average) *adj* memoots|a'/-a'at.

medium of exchange אמצעי חליפין *nm* emtsa|'ee/-'ey khaleefeen.

medley 1. תערובת *nf* ta'arov|et/-ot; **2.** ערבוביה (mixture) *nf* 'eerboov|yah/-yot (+*of:* -yat).

meek 1. שפל־רוח *adj* shfal/sheeflat roo'akh; **2.** עניו (modest) *adj* 'anav/-ah.

meekness 1. שפלות־רוח *nf* sheefloot roo'akh; **2.** ענווה (modesty) *nf* 'an|avah (+*of:* -vat).

(to) meet 1. לפגוש *inf* leefgosh; *pst* pagash (*p=f*); *pres* pogesh *etc*; *fut* yeefgosh; **2.** להכיר (make acquaintance) *inf* lehakeer; *pst* heekeer; *pres* makeer *etc*; *fut* yakeer; **3.** להספיק ל־ (a train) *inf* lehaspeek le-; *pst* heespeek le-; *pres* maspeek le- *etc*; *fut* yaspeek le-; **4.** לספק (satisfy) *inf* lesapek; *pst* seepek; *pres* mesapek *etc*; *fut* yesapek; **5.** לפרוע (expenses) *inf* leefro'a'; *pst* para' (*p=f*); *pres* pore'a'; *fut* yeefra'; **6.** להשיב על אשמה (accusation) *inf* lehasheev 'al ashmah; *pst* hesheev *etc*; *pres* mesheev *etc*; *fut* yasheev *etc*.

(to) meet in battle להתמודד בקרב *inf* leheetmoded bee-krav; *pst* heetmoded *etc*; *pres* meetmoded *etc*; *fut* yeetmoded *etc*.

(to) meet with להיפגש עם *inf* leheepagesh 'eem; *pst & pres* neefgash (*p=f*) *etc*; *fut* yeepagesh *etc*.

meeting 1. אסיפה *nf* asef|ah/-ot (+*of:* -at); **2.** פגישה (rendez-vous) *nm* pegeesh|ah/-ot (+*of:* -at).
megaphone מגאפון *nm* megafon/-eem (*pl+of:* -ey).
melancholy 1. מרה שחורה (depression) *nf* marah shekhorah; **2.** מלנכוליה *nf* melankol|yah/-yot (+*of:* -yat); **3.** עצבות (sadness) *nf* 'atsvoo|t/-yot.
melee התכתשות *nf* heetkat'shoo|t/-yot.
mellow רך *adj* rakh/rakah *(k=kh)*.
(to) mellow 1. לרכך *inf* lerakekh; *pst* reekekh; *pres* merakekh *etc*; *fut* yerakekh; **2.** להתרכך (soften) *v refl* leheetrakekh; *pst* heetrakekh; *pres* meetrakekh *etc*; *fut* yeetrakekh.
melodious מלודי *adj* melodee/-t.
melodrama מלודרמה *nf* melodram|ah/-ot (+*of:* -at).
melody 1. לחן *nm* lakhan/lekhaneem (*pl+of:* lakhney); **2.** מלודיה *nf* melod|yah/-yot (+*of:* -yat).
melon מלון *nm* melon/-eem (*pl+of:* -ey).
(water)melon אבטיח *nm* avatee|'akh/-kheem (*pl+of:* -khey)
(to) melt להימס *inf* leheemes; *pst & pres* names; *fut* yeemas.
member 1. חבר *nm* khav|er/-ereem (*pl+of:* -rey); **2.** עמית (fellow) *nm* 'ameet/-eem (*pl+of:* -ey); **3.** איבר (organ) *nm* ev|er/-areem (*pl+of:* -rey).
membership 1. חברות *nf* khaveroo|t/-yot; **2.** ציבור החברים (body of members) *nm* tseeboor ha-khavereem.
membrane קרומית *nf* kroomee|t/-yot.
memento מזכרת *nf* mazk|eret/-arot.
memo 1. תזכורת *nf* teezkor|et/-ot; **2.** תרשומת (record) *nf* teershom|et/-ot.
memoirs זכרונות *nm pl* zeekhronot.
memorable 1. זכור *adj* zakhoor/zekhoorah; **2.** בלתי־נשכח (unforgettable) *adj* beeltee-neeshkakh/-at.
memorandum תזכיר *nm* tazkeer/-eem (*pl+of:* -ey).
memorandum book יומן פגישות *nm* yoman/-ey pegeeshot.
memorial 1. מצבת זיכרון (monument) *nf* matsev|et/-ot zeekaron; **2.** אזכרה (meeting) *nf* azkar|ah/-ot (+*of:* -at); **3.** של זיכרון (commemorative) *adj* shel zeekaron.
memories זכרונות *nm pl* zeekhronot.
(to) memorize לשנן *inf* leshanen; *pst* sheenen; *pres* meshanen *etc*; *fut* yeshanen.
memory זיכרון *nm* zee|karon/-khronot (*kh=k; +of:* -khron).
menace 1. איום *nm* eeyoom/-eem (*pl+of:* -ey); **2.** סכנה (danger) *nf* sakan|ah/-ot (+*of:* -at).
(to) menace לאיים *inf* le'ayem; *pst* eeyem; *pres* me'ayem *etc*; *fut* ye'ayem.
(is on the) mend משתפר והולך *v pres & adj* meeshtaper/-et ve-holekh/-et.
(to) mend לתקן *inf* letaken; *pst* teeken; *pres* metaken *etc*; *fut* yetaken.
(to) mend one's way לתקן דרכיו *inf* letaken drakhav; *pst* teeken *etc*; *pres* metaken *etc*; *fut* yetaken *etc*.
menial 1. משרת (servant) *nm* meshar|et/-teem (*pl+of:* -tey); **2.** מתרפס (subservient) *adj* meetrapes/-et.
menstruation וסת *nf* veset.
mensual חודשי *adj* khodshee/-t.
mental 1. שכלי (rational) *adj* seekhlee/-t; **2.** נפשי (psychic) *adj* nafshee/-t.
mentality מנטליות *nf* mentaleeyoot.
mention 1. ציון *nm* tseeyoon/-eem (*pl+of:* -ey); **2.** אזכור (reminder) *nm* eezkoor/-eem (*pl+of:* -ey).
(don't) mention it על לא דבר 'al lo davar.
menu תפריט *nm* tafreet/-eem (*pl+of:* -ey).
mercantile מסחרי *adj* meeskharee/-t.
mercenary שכיר חרב *nm* sekheer/-ey kherev.
merchandise סחורה *nf* sekhor|ah/-ot (+*of:* -at).
(piece of) merchandise פריט מסחרי *nm* preet/preeteem meeskharee/-yeem.
merchant סוחר *nm* sokh|er/-areem (*pl+of:* -arey).
merchant marine צי הסוחר *nm* tsee ha-sokher.
merciful 1. רב חסד *adj* rav/rabat *(b=v)* khesed; **2.** רחום (compassionate) *adj* rakhoom/rekhoomah; **3.** סלחני (forgiving) *adj* salkhanee/-t.
merciless 1. אכזרי (cruel) *adj* akhzaree/-t; **2.** חסר רחמים (pityless) *adj* khas|ar/-rat rakhameem.
mercury כספית *nf* kaspeet.
mercy 1. רחמים *nm pl* rakham|eem (*pl+of:* -ey); **2.** חנינה (pardon) *nf* khaneen|ah/-ot (+*of:* -at).
(at the) mercy נתון לחסדי *adj* natoon/netoonah le-khasdey.
mere 1. סתם *adv* stam; **2.** בלבד (solely) *adv* beelvad.
(a) mere formality פורמליות בלבד *nf* formaleeyoot beelvad.
(a) mere trifle שטות ותו לא *nf* shtoot ve-too lo.
merely 1. אך ורק *adv* akh ve-rak; **2.** בלבד (only) *adv* beelvad.
(to) merge למזג *inf* lemazeg; *pst* meezeg; *pres* memazeg *etc*; *fut* yemazeg.
merger מיזוג *nm* meezoog/-eem (*pl+of:* -ey).
meridian 1. קו אורך *nm* kav/-ey orekh; **2.** של צהריים (midday) *adj* shel tsohorayeem.
merit 1. זכות *nf* zekhoo|t/-yot; **2.** הצטיינות (distinction) *nf* heetstaynoo|t/-yot.
(to) merit 1. להיות ראוי *inf* leehyot ra'ooy; *pst* hayah *etc*; *pres* heeno *etc*; *fut* yeehyeh *etc*; **2.** להיות שווה (deserve) *inf* leehyot shaveh/-ah *etc*; *pres* heeno *etc*; *fut* yeehyeh *etc*.
meritorious בעל זכויות *adj* ba'al/-at zekhooyot.
mermaid בתולת ים *nf* betool|at/-ot yam.
merrily בשימחה *adv* be-seemkhah.
merriment 1. שימחה (joy) *nf* seemkhah/smakhot (+*of:* -seemkh/-at/-ot); **2.** עליצות (gladness) *nf* 'aleetsoot.
merry שמח *adj* same'akh/smekhah.
(to make) merry לעשות שמח *inf* la'asot same'akh; *pst* 'asah *etc*; *pres* 'oseh *etc*; *fut* ya'aseh *etc*.
Merry Christmas! !חג מולד שמח khag molad same'akh.
merry-go-round 1. סחרחרה *nf* skharkher|ah/-ot (+*of:* -at); **2.** קרוסלה (carousel) *nf* karoosel|ah/-ot (+*of:* -at).
merrymaker 1. בדחן *nmf* badkhan/-eet; **2.** ליצן (clown) *nm* leytsan/-eem (*pl+of:* -ey).
merrymaking 1. שימחה *nf* seemkhah/smakhot (+*of:* seemkh|at/-ot); **2.** עליזות *nf* 'aleezoo|t/-yot.

mesh 1. רשת *nf* resh|et/-atot (*pl+of:* reeshtot); **2.** מעשה רשת (network) *adj* ma'aseh reshet.

(to) mesh 1. ללכוד ברשת *vt inf* leelkod ba-reshet; *pst* lakhad *(kh=k) etc; pres* lokhed *etc; fut* yeelkod *etc;* **2.** להיתפש *vi inf* leheetafes; *pst & pres* neetfas; *fut* yeetafes; **3.** להשתלב (intertwine) *v rfl inf* leheeshtalev; *pst* heeshtalev; *pres* meeshtalev; *fut* yeeshtalev.

(to) mesh gears לשלב *inf* leshalev; *pst* sheelev; *pres* meshalev *etc; fut* yeshalev.

meshes רשת *nf* reshet.

mess 1. קנטינה (army canteen) *nf* kanteen|ah/-ot (*+of:* -at); **2.** בלבול (confusion) *nm* beelbool/-eem (*pl+of:* -ey); **3.** לכלוך (dirt) *nm* leekhlookh/-eem (*pl+of:* -ey). **4.** בלגן (jumble) *[slang] nm* balagan/ -eem.

(to) mess 1. לערבב *inf* le'arbev; *pst* 'eerbev; *pres* me'arbev *etc; fut* ye'arbev; **2.** ללכלך (dirty) *inf* lelakhlekh; *pst* leekhlekh; *pres* melakhlekh *etc; fut* yelakhlekh.

(to) mess around להסתובב בטל *inf* leheestovev batel; *pst* heestovev *etc; pres* meestovev *etc; fut* yeestovev.

(to make a) mess of לבלבל *inf* levalbel; *pst* beelbel *(b=v); pres* mevalbel; *fut* yevalbel.

mess of fish מנה דגים *nf* manah dageem.

(to) mess up לעשות מהפכות *inf* la'asot mahapekhot; *pst* 'asah *etc; pres* 'oseh *etc; fut* ya'aseh *etc.*

message 1. מסר *nm* mes|er/-areem (*pl+of:* meesrey); **2.** הודעה (notice) *nf* hoda|'ah/-'ot (*+of:* -'at); **3.** שליחות (mission) *nf* shleekhoo|t/-yot.

messenger שליח *nm* shalee'akh/shlee|khah (*pl:* -kheem/-khot; *+of:* shlee|akh/-khat/-khey).

Messiah משיח *nm* mashee'akh/mesheekheem (*+of:* meshee|'akh/-khey).

Messianic משיחי *adj* mesheekhee/-t.

messy 1. מבולבל *adj* mevoolb|al/-elet; **2.** פרוע *adj* paroo'a'/proo'ah.

metabolism חילוף חומרים *nm* kheeloof/-ey khomareem.

metal 1. מתכת *nf* mat|ekhet/-akhot; **2.** מתכתי *adj* matakhtee/-t.

metal cleaner משחת ניקוי למתכות *nf* meeshkh|at/ -ot neekooy le-matakhot.

metallic מתכתי *adj* matakhtee/-t.

metallurgy 1. תורת המתכות (technology) *nf* torat ha-matakhot; **2.** תעשיות המתכת (industries) *nf pl* ta'aseeyot ha-matekhet.

metaphor 1. מליצה *nf* meleets|ah/-ot (*+of:* -at); **2.** מטפורה *nf* metafor|ah/-ot (*+of:* -at).

metathesis סירוס אותיות *nm* seroos/-ey oteeyot.

meteor מטאור *nm* mete'or/-eem.

meteorite אבן מטאורית *nf* even/avaneem mete-'oree|t/-yot.

meteorological מטאורולוגי *adj* meteorologee/-t.

meteorology מטאורולוגיה meteorologyah.

meter מטר *nm* met|er/-reem.

method 1. שיטה *nf* sheet|ah/-ot (*+of:* -at); **2.** מתודה *nf* metod|ah/-ot (*+of:* -at).

methodical 1. שיטתי *adj* sheetatee/-t; **2.** מתודי *adj* metodee/-t.

metric מטרי *adj* metree/-t.

metric system השיטה המטרית *nf* ha-sheetah ha-metreet.

metropolis מטרופולין *nf* metropoleen.

metropolitan מטרופוליטני *adj* metropoleetanee/ -t.

mettle 1. מזג (temperament) *nm* mezeg; **2.** התלהבות (ardor) *nf* heetlahavoo|t/-yot.

mew יללת חתול *nf* yeelel|at/-ot khatool.

(to) mew ליילל *inf* leyalel; *pst* yeelel; *pres* meyalel; *fut* yeyalel.

Mexican 1. מקסיקני *adj & nmf* mekseekanee/-t; **2.** מקסיקאי *[colloq.] nmf* mekseeka'ee/-t.

Mexico מקסיקו *nf* mekseeko.

mezzanine קומת ביניים *nf* kom|at/-ot beynayeem.

mice עכברים *nm pl* 'akhb|areem (*sing:* 'akhbar; *pl+of:* -erey)

microbe חיידק *nm* khaydak/-eem (*pl+of:* -ey).

microfilm 1. סרט־זיעור *nm* seret/seertey zee'oor; **2.** מיקרופילם *nm* meekrofeelm/-eem (*pl+of:* -ey).

microphone מיקרופון *nm* meekrofon/-eem (*pl+of:* -ey).

microscope מיקרוסקופ *nm* meekroskop/-eem (*pl+of:* -ey).

microscopic מיקרוסקופי *adj* meekroskopee/-t.

mid 1. אמצעי *adj* emtsa'ee/-t; **2.** באמצע (amid) *adv* be-emtsa'.

(in) mid air במרומי האוויר *adv* bee-meromey ha-aveer.

midday חצי היום *nm* khatsee hayom.

middle 1. אמצע *nm* emtsa'; **2.** חצי (half) *nm* khatsee.

Middle Ages ימי הביניים *nm pl* yemey ha-beynayeem.

middle class מעמד בינוני *nm* ma'amad beynonee.

middle finger אמה *nf* am|ah/-ot (*+of:* -at).

(in the) middle of באמצע *adv* be-emtsa'.

(towards the) middle of the month לקראת מחצית החודש *adv* leekrat makhtseet ha-khodesh.

middle size גודל בינוני *nm* godel beynonee.

middle-aged בגיל העמידה *adj* be-geel ha-'ameedah.

middle-sized מגודל בינוני *adj* mee-godel beynonee.

middleman מתווך *nm* metav|ekh/-kheem (*pl+of:* -khey).

middy פרח קצונה בחיל־הים *nm* perakh/peerkhey ketsoonah be-kheyl ha-yam.

middy blouse חולצת פרח קצונה *nf* khoolts|at/-ot perakh ketsoonah.

midget 1. גמד *nm* gamad/-eem (*pl+of:* -ey); **2.** ננס *nm* nanas/-eem (*pl+of:* -ey).

midnight 1. חצות *nf* khatsot; **2.** חצות הלילה *nf* khatsot ha-laylah.

midnight blue כחול כהה (dark blue) *adj* kakhol keheh.

midriff סרעפת *nf* sar|'efet/-'afot.

midshipman פרח קצונה בצי *nm* perakh/peerkhey ketsoonah ba-tsee.

midst 1. אמצע *nm* emtsa'; **2.** תווך *nm* tavekh.

(in our) midst בקרבנו *adv* be-keerbenoo.

(in the) midst of 1. בלב *adv* be-l<u>e</u>v; **2.** בקרב *adv* be-k<u>e</u>rev.
midstream 1. באמצע הזרם *adv* be-emts<u>a</u>' ha-z<u>e</u>rem; **2.** בלב הנהר (midriver) *adv* be-l<u>e</u>v ha-nah<u>a</u>r
midsummer שלהי קיץ *nm pl* sheelh<u>e</u>y k<u>a</u>yeets.
midterm אמצע הסמסטר *nm* emts<u>a</u>' ha-sem<u>e</u>ster.
midterm examination בחינת חצי־סמסטר *nf* bekheen|<u>a</u>t/-<u>o</u>t khats<u>ee</u>-sem<u>e</u>ster.
midway 1. של מחצית הדרך *adj* shel makhts<u>ee</u>t ha-d<u>e</u>rekh; **2.** בחצי הדרך (halfway) *adv* ba-khats<u>ee</u> ha-d<u>e</u>rekh.
midweek אמצע השבוע *nm* <u>e</u>mtsa' ha-shav<u>oo</u>'a.
midwife מיילדת *nf* meyal|<u>e</u>det/-d<u>o</u>t.
mien 1. התנהגות *nf* heetnahagoo|t/-y<u>o</u>t; **2.** קלסתר (looks) *nm* klast<u>e</u>r/-<u>ee</u>m (*pl+of:* -<u>e</u>y).
mighty עצום *adj* 'ats<u>oo</u>m/-<u>a</u>h.
migrant 1. נווד *nm* nav<u>a</u>d/-<u>ee</u>m (*pl+of:* -<u>e</u>y); **2.** מהגר (emigrant) *nm* mehag|<u>e</u>r/-eret (*pl:* -r<u>ee</u>m; *+of:* -r<u>e</u>y).
(to) migrate 1. לנדוד *inf* leend<u>o</u>d; *pst* nad<u>a</u>d; *pres* nod<u>e</u>d; *fut* yeend<u>o</u>d; **2.** להגר (emigrate) lehag<u>e</u>r; *pst* heeg<u>e</u>r; *pres* mehag<u>e</u>r; *fut* yehag<u>e</u>r.
migration 1. נדידה *nf* nedeed|<u>a</u>h/-<u>o</u>t (*+of:* -<u>a</u>t); **2.** הגירה *nf* hageer|<u>a</u>h/-<u>o</u>t (*+of:* -<u>a</u>t).
mike מיקרופון *nm* meekrof<u>o</u>n/-eem (*pl+of:* -<u>e</u>y).
mild 1. עדין (gentle) *adj* 'ad<u>ee</u>n/-<u>a</u>h; **2.** מתון (moderate) *adj* mat<u>oo</u>n/metoon<u>a</u>h.
mildew עובש *nm* '<u>o</u>v|esh/-ash<u>ee</u>m (*pl+of:* -sh<u>e</u>y).
mildness 1. נחת *nf* n<u>a</u>khat; **2.** נועם (pleasantness) *nm* n<u>o</u>'am; **3.** רכות (softness) *nf* rak<u>oo</u>|t/-y<u>o</u>t.
mile 1. מיל *nm* meel; **2.** ק״מ 1,6 (1.6 kms) *nm* akh<u>a</u>t pes<u>ee</u>k shesh keelom<u>e</u>ter.
mileage 1. כמות נסיעות במילים *nf* kam<u>oo</u>t nesee'<u>o</u>t be-meel<u>ee</u>m; **2.** קילומטראז׳ (driving distance in kms) *nm* keelometr<u>a</u>j.
milestone אבן דרך *nf* <u>e</u>ven/avn<u>e</u>y d<u>e</u>rekh.
militancy מלחמתיות *nf* meelkhamteey<u>oo</u>t.
militant 1. לוחם (fighter) *nm* lokh|<u>e</u>m/-am<u>ee</u>m (*pl+of:* -am<u>e</u>y); **2.** *adj* lokh<u>e</u>m/et.
military צבאי *adj* tsva'<u>ee</u>/-t.
(the) military הצבא *nm* ha-tsav<u>a</u>.
military police משטרה צבאית *nf* meeshtar<u>a</u>h tsva'<u>ee</u>t
militia מיליציה *nf* meel<u>ee</u>ts|yah/-yot (*+of:* -yat).
milk חלב *nm* khal<u>a</u>v.
milk diet דיאטה חלבית *nf* dee'<u>e</u>t|ah/-ot khalav<u>ee</u>|t/-y<u>o</u>t.
milkmaid חלבנית *nf* khalvan<u>ee</u>|t/-yot.
milkman חלבן *nm* khalv<u>a</u>n/-<u>ee</u>m (*pl+of:* -<u>e</u>y).
milky חלבי *adj* khalav<u>ee</u>/-t.
Milky Way שביל החלב *nm* shv<u>ee</u>l he-khal<u>a</u>v.
mill 1. טחנה *nf* takhan|<u>a</u>h/-<u>o</u>t (*+of:* -<u>a</u>t); **2.** מטחנה (grinder) *nf* matkhen|<u>a</u>h/-<u>o</u>t (*+of:* -<u>a</u>t); **3.** בית חרושת (factory) *nm* bet/bat<u>e</u>y khar<u>o</u>shet.
(flour) mill טחנת קמח *nf* takhan|<u>a</u>t/-<u>o</u>t k<u>e</u>makh.
(saw)mill מנסרה *nf* meens|ar<u>a</u>h/-ar<u>o</u>t (*+of:* -<u>e</u>ret).
(spinning) mill מתווייה *nf* matvee|y<u>a</u>h/-y<u>o</u>t (*+of:* -y<u>a</u>t).
(sugar) mill בית חרושת לסוכר *nm* bet/bat<u>e</u>y khar<u>o</u>shet le-sook<u>a</u>r.
(textile) mill מפעל טקסטיל *nm* meef'<u>a</u>l/-<u>e</u>y takst<u>ee</u>l.
(to) mill לטחון *inf* leetkh<u>o</u>n; *pst* takh<u>a</u>n; *pres* tokh<u>e</u>n; *fut* yeetkh<u>a</u>n.
(to) mill around להתרוצץ סביב *inf* leheetrots<u>e</u>ts sav<u>ee</u>v; *pst* heetrots<u>e</u>ts *etc*; *pres* meetrots<u>e</u>ts *etc*; *fut* yeetrots<u>e</u>ts *etc*.
millenium תקופת אלף שנה *nf* tekoof|<u>a</u>t/-<u>o</u>t <u>e</u>lef shan<u>a</u>h.
miller טוחן *nm* tokh|<u>e</u>n/-an<u>ee</u>m (*pl+of:* -an<u>e</u>y).
milliner כובען נשים *nm* kova'<u>a</u>n/-<u>e</u>y n<u>a</u>sheem.
millinery כובענות נשים *nf* kov'an<u>oo</u>t nash<u>ee</u>m
millinery shop חנות לכובעי נשים *nf* khan<u>oo</u>|t/-y<u>o</u>t le-kov'<u>e</u>y nash<u>ee</u>m.
million מיליון (1,000,000) *num* meely<u>o</u>n/-eem (*pl+of:* -<u>e</u>y).
(a) million dollars מיליון דולר *nm* meely<u>o</u>n d<u>o</u>lar.
millionaire מיליונר *nmf & adj* meelyon<u>e</u>r/-eet.
millionth חלק המיליון (0.000001 or 1/1,000,000) *nm* khel|ek/-k<u>e</u>y ha-meely<u>o</u>n.
millstone אבן ריחיים *nf* even/avn<u>e</u>y reykh<u>a</u>yeem.
mimic מימיקה *nf* m<u>ee</u>meek|ah/-ot (*+of:* -at).
mimic battle קרב דמה *nm* krav/-<u>o</u>t d<u>e</u>meh.
mimicry חקיינות *nf* khakyan<u>oo</u>|t/-y<u>o</u>t.
(to) mince לטחון *inf* leetkh<u>o</u>n; *pst* takh<u>a</u>n; *pres* tokh<u>e</u>n; *fut* yeetkh<u>a</u>n.
(not to) mince words להתבטא בעדינות מעושה *inf* leheetbat<u>e</u> ba-'adeen<u>oo</u>t me'oos<u>a</u>h; *pst* heetbat<u>e</u> *etc*; *pres* meetbat<u>e</u> *etc*; *fut* yeetbat<u>e</u> *etc*.
mincemeat בשר טחון *nm* bas<u>a</u>r takh<u>oo</u>n.
mind 1. שכל (intelligence) *nm* s<u>e</u>khel; **2.** מחשבה (thought) *nf* makhsh|av<u>a</u>h/-av<u>o</u>t (*+of:* -<u>e</u>vet); **3.** רוח (spirit) *nf* r<u>oo</u>'akh; **4.** מטרה (purpose) *nf* matar|<u>a</u>h/-<u>o</u>t (*+of:* -<u>a</u>t); **5.** דעה (opinion) *nf* de|'<u>a</u>h/-'<u>o</u>t (*+of:* -'<u>a</u>t).
(I don't) mind לא איכפת לי lo eekhp<u>a</u>t lee.
(never) mind 1. אין דבר <u>e</u>n dav<u>a</u>r; **2.** לא איכפת (doesn't matter) lo eekhp<u>a</u>t; **3.** לא לשים לב (not to pay attention) *inf* lo las<u>ee</u>m lev; *pst & pres* lo sam lev; *fut* lo yas<u>ee</u>m lev.
(out of one's) mind יצא מדעתו *adj* yats<u>a</u> mee-da't<u>o</u>.
(to) mind 1. להשגיח *inf* lehashg<u>ee</u>'akh; *pst* heeshg<u>ee</u>'akh; *pres* mashg<u>ee</u>'akh; *fut* yashg<u>ee</u> akh; **2.** להתרעם (dislike) *inf* leheetra'<u>e</u>m; *pst* heetra'<u>e</u>m; *pres* meetra'<u>e</u>m; *fut* yeetra'<u>e</u>m.
(to change one's) mind 1. לשנות דעתו *inf* leshan<u>o</u>t da't<u>o</u>; *pst* sheen<u>a</u>h *etc*; *pres* meshan<u>e</u>h *etc*; *fut* yeshan<u>e</u>h *etc*; **2.** להתחרט (regret) *inf* leheetkhar<u>e</u>t; *pst* heetkhar<u>e</u>t; *pres* meetkhar<u>e</u>t; *fut* yeetkhar<u>e</u>t.
(to give someone a piece of one's) mind לומר לו את דעתי עליו *inf* lom<u>a</u>r lo et da't<u>ee</u> 'al<u>a</u>v; *pst* am<u>a</u>r *etc*; *pres* om<u>e</u>r *etc*; *fut* yom<u>a</u>r *etc*.
(to make up one's) mind לגמור אומר *inf* leegm<u>o</u>r <u>o</u>mer; *pst* gam<u>a</u>r <u>o</u>mer; *pres* gom<u>e</u>r <u>o</u>mer; *fut* yeegm<u>o</u>r <u>o</u>mer.
(to my) mind 1. לדעתי le-da't<u>ee</u>; **2.** לעניות דעתי (in my humble opinion) la-'aneey<u>oo</u>t da't<u>ee</u>.
(to speak one's) mind freely להביע דעה בגלוי *inf* lehab<u>ee</u>'a' de'<u>a</u>h be-gal<u>oo</u>y; *pst* heeb<u>ee</u>'a' *etc*; *pres* mab<u>ee</u>'a' *etc*; *fut* yab<u>ee</u>'a' *etc*.

(to) mind one's own business לא להתערב *inf* lo leheet'arev; *pst* lo heet'arev; *pres* eyno meet'arev; *fut* lo'yeet'arev.

(to have a) mind to -לרצות ל *inf* leertsot le-; *pst* ratsah le-; *pres* rotseh le-; *fut* yeertseh le-.

mindful 1. מקשיב *v pres & adj* maksheev/-ah; **2.** זהיר (careful) *adj* zaheer/zeheerah.

mine שלי possess. *pron* shelee.

(a book of) mine ספר שלי *nm* sefer/sfareem shelee.

mine 1. מוקש (explosive) *nm* mok|esh/-sheem (*pl+of:* -shey); **2.** מיכרה (ore) *nm* meekhr|eh/-ot.

(anti-personnel) mine מוקש נגד אדם *nm* mok|esh/-sheem neged adam.

(anti-tank) mine מוקש נגד טנקים *nm* mok|esh/-sheem neged tankeem.

(land)mine מוקש יבשתי *nm* mok|esh/-sheem yabeshtee/-yeem.

(side)-mine מוקש צד *nm* mok|esh/-shey tsad.

(to) mine 1. למקש (explosives) *inf* lemakesh; *pst* meekesh; *pres* memakesh; *fut* yemakesh; **2.** לכרות (ore) *inf* leekhrot; *pst* karah; *pres* koreh; *fut* yeekhreh.

minefield שדה מוקשים *nm* sdeh/sdot moksheem.

mine sweeper שולת מוקשים *nf* shol|at/-ot moksheem.

miner כורה *nm* kor|eh/-eem (*pl+of:* -ey).

mineral 1. מחצב *nm* makhts|av/-eveem (*pl+of:* -evey); **2.** מינרל *nm* meeneral/-eem (*pl+of:* -ey).

(to) mingle להתערבב *inf* leheet'arbev; *pres* heet'arbev; *pres* meet'arbev; *fut* yeet'arbev.

miniature 1. תמונה זוטא *nf* temoon|ah/-ot zoota; **2.** מזעור *nm* meez'oor/-eem (*pl+of:* -ey).

minimal 1. מזערי *adj* meez'aree/-t; **2.** מינימלי *adj* meeneemalee/-t.

(to) minimize 1. למזער *inf* lemaz'er; *pst* meez'er; *pres* memaz'er; *fut* yemaz'er; **2.** לזלזל (scorn) *inf* lezalzel; *pst* zeelzel; *pres* mezalzel; *fut* yezalzel.

minimum 1. מזער *nm* meez'ar; **2.** הכי פחות *adj* ha-khee pakhot; **3.** מינימום *nm & adv* meeneemoom.

mining 1. מיקוש (explosives) *nm* meekoosh/-eem (*pl+of:* -ey); **2.** הפעלת מיכרות (ore) *nf* haf'alat meekhrot; **3.** כרייה (digging) *nf* kree|yah/-yot (*+of:* -yat).

mining engineer מהנדס מיכרות *nm* mehandes/-ey meekhrot.

miniskirt חצאית מיני *nf* khatsa'ee|t/-yot meenee.

minister 1. שר (cabinet) *nmf* sar/-ah (*pl:* -eem/-ot; *+of:* -ey); **2.** ((באמריקה) כומר (clergy) *nm* komer (be-amereekah).

(to) minister 1. לספק (supply) *inf* lesapek; *pst* seepek; *pres* mesapek; *fut* yesapek; **2.** לנהל (conduct) *inf* lenahel; *pst* neehel; *pres* menahel; *fut* yenahel.

ministry משרד *nm* meesr|ad/-adeem (*pl+of:* -edey).

mink חורפן *nm* khorpan/-eem (*pl+of:* -ey).

minnow דגיג מים מתוקים *nm* degeeg/-ey mayeem metookeem.

minor 1. קטין (under-age) *nmf & adj* kateen/keteenah; **2.** זוטר (junior) *adj* zoot|ar/-eret.

minor key סולם מינורי *nm* soolam/-ot meenoree/-yeem.

minority מיעוט *nm* mee'oot/-eem (*pl+of:* -ey).

minstrel 1. בדרן *nm* badran/-eem (*pl+of:* -ey); **2.** זמר נודד (wandering singer) *nm* zamar/-eem noded/-eem; **3.** שחקן (comedian) *nm* sakhkan/-eem (*pl+of:* -ey).

mint 1. מנתה (flavor) *nf* mentah; **2.** סוכרייה (candy) *nf* sookaree|yah/-yot (*+of:* -yat); **3.** מטבע (money) matbe|'a'/-'ot.

(to) mint 1. לטבוע מטבעות (coin) *inf* leetbo'a' matbe'ot; *pst* tava' *etc*; *pres* tove'a' *etc*; *fut* yeetba' *etc*; **2.** לטבוע מושג (coin words) *inf* leetbo'a' moosag; *pst* tava' *etc*; *pres* tove'a' *etc*; *fut* yeetba' *etc*.

(a) mint of money המון כסף *nm* hamon kesef.

mintage שנת הטבעה *nf* shnat hatba'ah.

minuet מינואט *nm* meenoo'et/-eem.

minus 1. פחות pakhot; **2.** מינוס *nm* meenoos/-eem (*pl+of:* -ey).

(five) minus three חמש פחות שלוש khamesh pakhot shalosh.

minute 1. דקה *nf* dak|ah/-ot (*+of:* -at); **2.** מדוקדק (meticulous) *adj* medookd|ak/-eket.

minute hand מחוג הדקות *nm* mekhog/-ey ha-dakot.

minutes 1. פרטיכל *nm* prateykol/-eem (*pl+of:* -ey); **2.** פרוטוקול *nm* protokol/-eem (*pl+of:* -ey).

miracle 1. נס *nm* nes/nees|eem (*pl+of:* -ey); **2.** פלא (wonder) *nm* pele/pla'eem (*pl+of:* peel'ey).

miraculous פלאי *adj* pel'ee/-t.

mirage חזון תעתועים *nm* khazon/-ot ta'atoo'eem.

mire אדמת ביצה *nf* adm|at/-ot beetsah.

(to) mire לרפש *inf* lerapesh; *pres* reepesh; *pres* merapesh; *fut* yerapesh.

mirror 1. ראי *nm* re'ee; **2.** מראה *nf* mar|'ah/-'ot (*+of:* -'at).

(to) mirror לשקף *inf* leshakef; *pst* sheekef; *pres* meshakef; *fut* yeshakef.

mirth 1. עליזות *nf* 'aleezoo|t/-yot; **2.** עליצות (gaiety) *nf* 'aleetsoot.

mirthful מתהולל *adj* meet'holel/-et.

miry מרופש *adj* meroop|ash/-eshet.

misadventure מזל ביש *nm* mazal beesh.

(to) misbehave לנהוג שלא כשורה *inf* leenhog she-lo ka-shoorah; *pst* nahag *etc*; *pres* noheg *etc*; *fut* yeenhag *etc*.

miscarriage הפלה *nf* hapal|ah/-ot (*+of:* -at).

miscarriage of justice עיוות דין *nm* 'eevoot/-ey deen.

(to) miscarry 1. להיכשל (fail) *inf* leheekashel; *pst & pres* neekhshal *(kh=k)*; *fut* yeekashel; **2.** להפיל (abort) *inf* lehapeel; *pst f* heepeelah; *pres f* mapeelah; *fut f* tapeel.

miscellaneous שונות *nf pl* shonot.

mischief 1. תעלול *nm* ta'alool/-eem (*pl+of:* -ey); **2.** נזק (harm) nez|ek/-akeem (*pl+of:* neezkey).

mischievous 1. שובב *adj* shov|av/-evah; **2.** קנטרן (quarrelsome) *adj* kantran/-eet; **3.** מזיק (harmful) mazeek/-ah.

misconception מושג מוטעה *nm* moosag/-eem moot|'eh/-'eem.

misconduct התנהגות שלא כשורה *nf* heetnahagoot she-lo kashoorah.

(to) misconduct לנהוג שלא כשורה *inf* leenhog she-lo ka-shoorah; *pst* nahag *etc; pres* noheg *etc; fut* yeenhag *etc.*

(to) misconduct oneself להתנהג שלא כשורה *inf* leheetnaheg she-lo ka-shoorah; *pst* heetnaheg *etc; pres* meetnaheg *etc; fut* yeetnaheg *etc.*

misdeed חטא *nm* khet/khata|'eem (*pl+of:* -'ey)

misdemeanor עוון *nm* 'avon/-ot.

miser 1. קמצן *nmf & adj* kamtsan/-eet; **2.** כילי (stingy) *nm* keylay.

miserable 1. עלוב חיים *nmf & adj* 'aloov/-at khayeem; **2.** מיסכן (wretched) *adj* meesken/-ah.

miserably בצורה עלובה *adv* be tsoorah 'aloovah.

miserly 1. קמצן *adj* kamtsan/-eet; **2.** כילי (stingy) *nm* keylay.

misery 1. מצוקה *nf* metsook|ah/-ot (*+of:* -at); **2.** מחסור (shortage) *nm* makhsor/-eem (*pl+of:* -ey).

misfortune ביש מזל *adj* beesh mazal.

misgiving 1. חשש *nm* khashash/-ot; **2.** ספק (doubt) *nm* safek/sfekot.

misguided 1. תועה *adj* to'eh/to'ah; **2.** מולך שולל (misled) *adj* mool|akh/-ekhet sholal.

mishap 1. תקלה *nf* takal|ah/-ot (*+of:* -at); **2.** תקרית לא נעימה (unpleasant incident) *nf* takree|t/-yot lo ne'eem|ah/-ot.

(to) misjudge לשפוט לא נכון *inf* leeshpot lo nakhon; *pst* shafat *(f=p) etc; pres* shofet *etc; fut* yeeshpot *etc.*

mislaid מונח שלא במקום *adj* moonakh/-at she-lo ba-makom.

(to) mislay לשים שלא במקום *inf* laseem she-lo ba-makom; *pst & pres* sam *etc; fut* yaseem *etc.*

(to) mislead להוליך שולל *inf* leholeekh sholal; *pst* holeekh *etc; pres* moleekh *etc; fut* yoleekh *etc.*

misled שהולך שולל *adj* she-holekh/-et sholal.

mismanagement ניהול כושל *nm* neehool koshel.

(to) misplace לשים שלא במקום *inf* laseem she-lo ba-makom; *pst & pres* sam *etc; fut* yaseem *etc.*

misprint טעות דפוס *nf* ta'oo|t/-yot dfoos.

mispronunciation הגייה לא נכונה *nf* hagee|yah/-yot lo nekhon|ah/-ot.

(to) misquote לצטט לא נכון *inf* letsatet lo nakhon; *pst* tseetet *etc; pres* metsatet *etc; fut* yetsatet *etc.*

(to) misrepresent תיאור לא נכון *nm* te'oor/-eem lo nakhon/nekhoneem.

miss 1. עלמה (young woman) *nf* 'al|mah/-amot (*+of:* -mat); **2.** החטאה *nf* hakhta|'ah/-'ot (*+of:* -'at); **3.** כישלון (failure) *nm* keesh|alon/-lonot (*pl+of:* -lon).

(to) miss להחטיא *inf* lehakhtee; *pst* hekhtee; *pres* makhtee; *fut* yakhtee.

(just) missed being killed כמעט שנהרגתי kee-me'at she-neheragtee.

missile טיל *nm* teel/-eem (*pl+of:* -ey).

missing 1. נעדר *adj* ne'ed|ar/-eret; **2.** חסר (lacking) *adj* khaser/-ah.

mission 1. שליחות *nf* shleekhoo|t/-yot; **2.** משלחת (delegation) *nf* meeshlakhat/-ot.

missionary 1. מיסיונר *nmf* meesyoner/-eet; **2.** מיסיונרי *adj* meesyoneree/-t.

(to) misspell לשבש כתיב *inf* leshabesh keteev; *pst* sheebesh *etc; pres* meshabesh *etc; fut* yeshabesh *etc.*

mist 1. אד *nm* ed/-eem (*pl+of:* -ey); **2.** ערפל *nm* 'ar|afel/-feeleem (*+of:* -fel/-feeley).

(to) mist לערפל *inf* le'arpel; *pst* 'eerpel; *pres* me'arpel; *fut* ye'arpel.

mistake 1. שגיאה *nf* shgee|'ah/-'ot (*+of:* -'at) **2.** טעות (error) *nf* ta'oo|t/-yot.

(to) mistake לטעות *inf* leet'ot; *pst* ta'ah; *pres* to'eh; *fut* yeet'eh.

(to make a) mistake לעשות טעות *inf* la'asot ta'oot; *pst* 'asah *etc; pres* 'oseh *etc; fut* ya'aseh *etc.*

mistaken מוטעה *adj* moot'eh/-t.

(to be) mistaken לשגות *inf* leeshgot; *pst* shagah; *pres* shogeh; *fut* yeeshgeh.

mister 1. אדון *nm* adon; **2.** מר *nm* mar.

(to) mistreat להתייחס רע *inf* leheetyakhes ra'; *pst* heetyakhes ra'; *pres* meetyakhes ra'; *fut* yeetyakhes ra'.

mistress 1. גברת *nf* gveret/gvarot; **2.** בעלת בית (landlady) *nf* ba'al|at/-ot bayeet; **3.** פילגש (concubine) *nf* peel|egesh/-agsheem (*pl+of:* -agshey).

mistrial שפיטה שלא כדין *nm* shfeetah she-lo ka-deen.

mistrust אי־אמון *nm* ee-emoon.

(to) mistrust 1. לא להאמין *inf* lo leha'ameen; *pst* lo he'emeen; *pres* eyno ma'ameen; *fut* lo ya'ameen; **2.** לחשוד (suspect) *inf* lakhshod; *pst* khashad; *pres* khoshed; *fut* yakhshod.

mistrustful חשדן *nmf & adj* khashdan/-eet.

misty מעורפל *nf* me'oorp|al/-elet.

(to) misunderstand להבין לא נכון *inf* lehaveen lo nakhon; *pst* heveen *etc; pres* meveen *etc; fut* yaveen *etc.*

misunderstanding אי־הבנה *nf* ee-havan|ah/-ot.

(to) misuse להשתמש לרעה *inf* leheeshtamesh le-ra'ah; *pst* heeshtamesh *etc; pres* meeshtamesh *etc; fut* yeeshtamesh *etc.*

misuse (of funds) שימוש לרעה בכספים *nm* sheemoosh le-ra'ah bee-khesafeem *(kh=k).*

mite 1. פרוטה *nf* proot|ah/-ot (*+of:* -at); **2.** פצפון *[colloq.] adj* peetspon/-eet.

miter מחבר זווית *nm* makhber/-ey zaveet.

miter box מיתקן המדרה *nm* meetk|an/-eney hamdarah

(to) mitigate 1. להקל (alleviate) *inf* lehakel; *pst* hekel; *pres* mekel; *fut* yakel; **2.** לשכך (soothe) *inf* leshakekh; *pst* sheekekh; *pres* meshakekh; *fut* yeshakekh.

mitten כפפה ללא אצבעות *nf* kfaf|ah/-ot le-lo etsba'ot.

mix 1. ערבוב *nm* 'eerboov/-eem (*pl+of:* -ey); **2.** תערובת (mixture) *f* ta'arov|et/-ot.

(to) mix לערבב *inf* le'arbev; *pst* 'eerbev; *pres* me'arbev; *fut* ye'arbev.

(to) mix someone up לבלבל את מישהו *inf* levalbel et meeshehoo; *pst* beelbel *(b=v) etc; pres* mevalbel *etc; fut* yevalbel *etc.*

mix-up 1. תסבוכת *nf* teesbokh|et/-ot; **2.** בלבול (confusion) *nm* beelbool/-eem (*pl+of:* -ey).

mixture תערובת *nf* ta'arov|et/-ot.

moan 1. אנחה (sigh) *nf* anakh|ah/-ot (*+of:* ankh|at/-ot); **2.** אנקה (groan) *nf* anak|ah/-ot (*+of:* enk|at/-ot).

(to) moan 1. להיאנח (sigh) lehe'anakh; *pst & pres* ne'enakh; *fut* ye'anakh; **2.** להיאנק (groan) *inf* lehe'anek; *pst & pres* ne'enak; *fut* ye'anek.

moat תעלת מגן *nf* te'al|at/-ot magen.

mob 1. המון *nm* hamon/-eem (*pl+of:* -ey); **2.** אספסוף (rabble) *nm* asafsoof.

(to) mob 1. להתקהל *inf* leheetkahel; *pst* heetkahel; *pres* meetkahel; *fut* yeetkahel; **2.** להתפרע (go wild) *inf* leheetpare'a'; *pst* heetpare'a'; *pres* meetpare'a'; *fut* yeetpare'a'.

mobile נייד *adj* nayad/nayedet.

mobilization גיוס *nm* geeyoos/-eem (*pl+of:* -ey).

(to) mobilize לגייס *inf* legayes; *pst* geeyes; *pres* megayes; *fut* yegayes.

moccasin נעל מעור צבי רך *nf* na'al/-ayeem me-'or tsvee rakh.

mock 1. מדומה *adj* medoom|eh/-ah; **2.** מזויף (false) *adj* mezoo|yaf/-yefet; **3.** מבוים (staged) *adj* mevooy|am/-yemet.

(to) mock 1. לחקות (imitate) *inf* lekhakot; *pst* kheekah; *pres* mekhakeh; *fut* yekhakeh; **2.** לעשות ללעג (deride) *inf* la'asot le-la'ag; *pst* 'asah *etc*; *pres* 'oseh *etc*; *fut* ya'aseh *etc*.

(to) mock at ־ללעוג ל *inf* leel'og le-; *pst* la'ag le-; *pres* lo'eg le-; *fut* yeel'ag le-.

mock battle קרב דמה *nm* krav/-ot demeh.

mockery 1. חוכא וטלולא *nm pl* khookha ve-eetloola; **2.** לעג (derision) *nm* la'ag.

mockup דמה *nm* demeh.

mode אופן *nm* ofen/ofan|eem (*pl+of:* -ey).

model 1. דוגמה (sample) *nf* doogm|ah/a'ot; **2.** דגם (pattern) *nm* deg|em/-ameem (*pl+of:* deegmey); **3.** דוגמנית (mannequin) *nf* doogmanee|t/-yot; **4.** לדוגמה *adj* le-doogmah.

model school בית ספר לדוגמה *nm* bet/batey sefer le-doogmah.

modelling דוגמנות *nf* doogmanoot.

moderate מתון *adj* matoon/metoonah.

(to) moderate למתן *inf* lematen; *pst* meeten; *pres* mematen; *fut* yematen.

moderation מתינות *nf* meteenoo|t/-yot.

moderator מנחה *nmf* mankh|eh/-ah.

modern 1. חדיש *nf* khadeesh/-ah; **2.** מודרני *adj* modernee/-t.

(to) modernize לחדש *inf* lekhadesh; *pst* kheedesh; *pres* mekhadesh; *fut* yekhadesh.

modest צנוע *adj* tsanoo'a'/tsenoo'ah.

modesty 1. צניעות *nf* tsenee'oot; **2.** ענווה (humility) *nf* 'anavah.

modification שינוי פני *nm* sheenooy peney.

(to) modify לשנות פני *inf* leshanot peney; *pst* sheenah *etc*; *pres* meshaneh *etc*; *fut* yeshaneh *etc*.

modular מודולרי *adj* modoolaree/-t.

(to) modulate לסלסל בקול *inf* lesalsel ba-kol; *pst* seelsel *etc*; *pres* mesalsel *etc*; *fut* yesalsel *etc*.

module 1. מודד *nm* moded/-eem (*pl+of:* -ey); **2.** מודול *nm* modool/-eem (*pl+of:* -ey).

Mohammedan מוסלמי *adj* mooslemee/-t.

moist 1. לח *adj* lakh/-ah; **2.** רטוב (wet) *adj* ratoov/retoovah.

(to) moisten 1. להרטיב *inf* leharteev; *pst* heerteev; *pres* marteev; *fut* yarteev; **2.** ללחלח (dampen) *inf* lelakhle'akh; *pst* leekhlakh; *pres* melakhle'akh; *fut* yelakhlakh.

moisture 1. רטיבות *nf* reteevoo|t/-yot; **2.** טחב (dampness) *nm* takhav.

molar 1. שן טוחנת *nf* shen/sheenayeem tokh|enet/-anot; **2.** טוחן *adj* tokhen/-et.

molasses 1. דבשה *nf* deevshah; **2.** מולסה *nf* molasah.

mold 1. אימום (form) *nm* eemoom/-eem (*pl+of:* -ey); **2.** עובש (mildew) *nm* 'ovesh.

(to) mold 1. לעצב *inf* le'atsev; *pst* 'eetsev; *pres* me'atsev; *fut* ye'atsev; **2.** לצקת (cast) *inf* latseket; *pst* yatsak; *pres* yotsek; *fut* yeetsak.

(to) molder 1. להתפורר *inf* leheetporer; *pst* heetporer; *pres* meetporer; *fut* yeetporer; **2.** להרקיב (rot) *inf* leharkeev; *pst* heerkeev; *pres* markeev; *fut* yarkeev.

molding עיצוב *nm* 'eetsoov/-eem (*pl+of:* -ey).

moldy מעובש *adj* me'oob|ash/-eshet.

mole 1. שומה (spot) *nf* shoom|ah/-ot (*+of:* -at); **2.** חפרפרת (animal) khafarp|eret/-arot.

molecule 1. פרודה *nf* prood|ah/-ot (*+of:* -at); **2.** מולקולה *nf* molekool|ah/-ot (*+of:* -at).

(to) molest 1. לפגוע (hurt) *inf* leefgo'a'; *pst* paga' (*p=f*); *pres* poge'a'; *fut* yeefga'; **2.** להפריע (disturb) *inf* lehafree'a'; *pst* heefree'a'; *pres* mafree'a'; *fut* yafree'a'; **3.** לקנטר (annoy) lekanter; *pst* keenter; *pres* mekanter; *fut* yekanter.

(to) mollify לרכך *inf* lerakekh; *pst* reekekh; *pres* merakekh; *fut* yerakekh.

molten מותך *adj* moot|akh/-ekhet.

moment 1. רגע *nm* reg|a'/-a'eem (*pl+of:* reeg'ey); **2.** הרף עין (twinkle) *nm* heref 'ayeen.

momentary רגעי *adj* reeg'ee/-t.

momentous חשוב מאד *adj* khashoov/-ah me'od.

momentum תנופה *nf* tenoof|ah/-ot (*+of:* -at).

monarch מלך *nm* mel|ekh/-akheem (*pl+of:* malkhey).

monarchy ממלכה *nf* maml|akhah/-akhot (*pl+of:* -ekhet).

monastery מנזר *nm* meenzar/-eem (*pl+of:* -ey).

Monday 1. יום שני *nm* yom shenee; **2.** יום ב׳ *nm* yom bet.

monetary 1. כספי *adj* kaspee/-t; **2.** מוניטרי *adj* monetaree/-t.

money 1. כסף *nm* kes|ef/-afeem (*pl+of:* kaspey; *p=f*); **2.** ממון (capital) *nm* mamon.

(paper) money כסף נייר *nm* kesef neyar.

(silver) money מטבעות כסף *nm pl* matbe'ot kesef.

money changer חלפן *nm* khalfan/-eem (*pl+of:* -ey).

money order המחאת כסף *nf* hamkha|'at/-'ot kesef.

money-making 1. צבירת הון *nf* tsveerat hon. **2.** עשיית הון *nf* 'aseeyat hon.

monger 1. רוכל *nm* rokh|el/-leem (*pl+of:* -ley); **2.** תגר (trader) *nm* tagar/-eem (*pl+of:* -ey).

mongrel 1. כלב חוצות *nm* kelev/kalvey khootsot; **2.** בן כלאיים (crossbred) *nm* ben keel'ayeem.

monk נזיר *nm* nazeer/nezeer|eem (*pl+of:* -ey).

monkey קוף *nm* kof/-eem (*pl+of:* -ey).

(to) monkey with להתעסק עם *inf* leheet'asek 'eem; *pst* heet'asek 'eem; *pres* meet'asek 'eem; *fut* yeet'asek 'eem.

monkey wrench מפתח אנגלי *nm* mafte'akh anglee.

monkeyshine מעשה קונדס *nm* ma'aseh koondes.

monogram 1. משלבת *nf* meeshl|evet/-avot (*pl+of:* -evot); **2.** מונוגרמה *nf* monogram|ah/-ot (*+of:* -at).

monograph מונוגרפיה *nf* monograf|yah/-yot (*+of:* -yat).

monologue 1. חד־שיח *nm* khad see'akh; **2.** מונולוג monolog/-eem.

(to) monopolize לקבל מונופולין *inf* lekabel monopoleen; *pst* keebel *etc*; *pres* mekabel *etc*; *fut* yekabel *etc*.

monopoly מונופולין *nm* monopoleen.

monosyllable מלה חד־הברית *nf* meel|ah/-eem khad-havaree|t/-yot.

monotone 1. חדגוני *adj* khadgonee/-t; **2.** מונוטוני *adj* monotonee/-t.

monotonous 1. חד־צלילי *adj* khad-tsleelee/-t; **2.** מונוטוני *adj* monotonee/-t.

monotony מונוטוניות *nf* monotoneeyoot.

monster מפלצת *nf* meefl|etset/-atsot (*pl+of:* -etsot).

monstrosity דבר מפלצתי *nm* davar/dvareem meeflatstee/-yeem.

monstrous מפלצתי *adj* meeflatstee/-t.

month חודש *nm* khod|esh/-asheem (*pl+of:* -shey).

monthly 1. חודשי *adj* khodshee/-t; **2.** ירחון (magazine) *nm* yarkhon/-eem (*pl+of:* -ey); **3.** חודשית (per month) *adv* khodsheet.

monument מצבת זיכרון *nf* mats|evet/vot zeekaron

monumental מונומנטלי *adj* monoomentalee/-t.

moo געייה *nf* ge'ee|yah/-yot (*+of:* -yat).

mood מצב־רוח *nm* mats|av/-vey roo'akh.

(in a good) mood במצב־רוח טוב be-matsav roo'akh tov.

(in the) mood to במצב הרוח הנכון *adv* be-matsav ha-roo'akh ha-nakhon.

moody 1. מצוברח (changing) *adj* metsovrakh/-at; **2.** קודר (gloomy) *adj* koder/-et.

moon 1. ירח *nm* yare'akh; **2.** לבנה *nf* levan|ah/-ot (*+of:* -at).

(once in a blue) moon פעם ביובל *adv* pa'am be-yovel.

moonlight אור ירח *nm* or yare'akh.

moonlight dance מחול לאור ירח *nm* makhol le-'or yare'akh.

moonlit night ליל ירח *nm* leyl/-ot yare'akh.

moor 1. עגינה (anchorage) *nf* 'ageen|ah/-ot (*+of:* -at); **2.** מעגן (quayside) *nm* ma'agan/-eem (*pl+of:* -ey); **3.** אדמת בור (wasteland) adm|at/-ot boor.

(to) moor לקשור אונייה *inf* leekshor oneeyah; *pst* kashar *etc*; *pres* kosher *etc*; *fut* yeekshor *etc*.

mop סמרטוט *nm* smartoot/-eem (*pl+of:* -ey).

(dust) mop סמרטוט אבק *nm* smartoot/-ey avak.

mop of hair בלורית *nf* bloree|t/-yot.

moral 1. מוסרי *adj* moosaree/-t; **2.** מוסר (ethics) *nm* moosar.

moral philosophy 1. תורת המידות *nf* torat ha-meedot; **2.** אתיקה (ethics) *nf* eteek|ah/-ot (*+of:* -at).

morale 1. מוסר השכל (lesson to learn) *nm* moos|ar/-rey haskel; **2.** מורל (mental condition) *nm m* moral.

moralist מטיף מוסר *nmf* mateef/-at moosar.

morality מוסריות *nf* moosareeyoot.

(to) moralize להטיף מוסר *inf* lehateef moosar; *pst* heeteef *etc*; *pres* mateef *etc*; *fut* yateef *etc*.

morbid 1. מדוכא *adj* medook|a/-et; **2.** חולני (sickly) *adj* kholanee/-t.

mordant עוקצני *adj* 'oktsanee/-t.

more 1. עוד *adv* 'od; **2.** יותר (extra) *adj* yoter; **3.** נוסף (additional) *adj* nos|af/-sefet.

more and more 1. יותר ויותר *adv* yoter ve-yoter; **2.** עוד ועוד *adv* 'od va-'od.

(no) more 1. לא יותר lo yoter; **2.** לא עוד (never again) *adv* lo 'od.

(there is no) more 1. אין יותר eyn yoter; **2.** לא נשאר עוד (none left) lo neesh'ar 'od.

more *or* less פחות או יותר *adv* pakhot o yoter.

moreover יתר על כן *adv* yater 'al ken.

morning בוקר *nm* boker/bekareem (*pl+of:* bokrey).

morning-glory לפופית *nf* lefoofee|t/-yot.

morning paper עיתון בוקר *nm* 'eeton/-ey boker.

morning star שחר *nm* shakhar.

(good) morning! ! בוקר טוב boker tov!

(tomorrow) morning מחר בבוקר *adv* makhar ba-boker.

morphine מורפיום *nm* morfyoom.

morrow 1. מוחרת *nm* mokhorat; **2.** יום המוחרת *nm* yom/yemey ha-mokhorat.

(on the) morrow למוחרת *adv* la-mokhorat.

morsel 1. נתח *nm* netakh/netakheem (*pl+of:* neetkhey); **2.** פרוסה (slice) *nf* proos|ah/-ot (*+of:* -at).

mortal בן תמותה *nmf & adj* ben/bat tmootah.

mortality תמותה *nf* tmoot|ah/-ot (*+of:* -at).

mortar 1. טיט *nm* teet; **2.** טיח (plaster) *nm* tee'akh; **3.** מלט (cement) *nm* melet; **4.** מרגמה (cannon) *nf* margem|ah/-ot.

mortgage משכנתה *nf* mashkant|ah/-a'ot (*[colloq.]* mashkantah; *+of:* -at).

(to) mortgage למשכן *inf* lemashken; *pst* meeshken; *pres* memashken; *fut* yemashken.

(to) mortify 1. לסגף *vt* lesagef; *pst* seegef; *pres* mesagef; *fut* yesagef; **2.** להסתגף (the flesh) *v rfl inf* leheestagef; *pst* heestagef; *pres* meestagef; *fut* yeestagef; **3.** להשפיל (humiliate) *vt inf* lehashpeel; *pst* heeshpeel; *pres* mashpeel; *fut* yashpeel.

mosaic 1. פסיפס *nm* peseyfas/-eem (*pl+of:* -ey); **2.** מוזאיקה *nf* moza'eek|ah/-ot (*+of:* -at).

Moslem מוסלמי *adj & nmf* mooslemee/-t (*pl:* -eem/-eeyot).

mosquito יתוש *nm* yatoosh/-eem (*pl+of:* -ey).

mosquito net רשת נגד יתושים *nf* resh|et/-atot neged yeetoosheem.

moss חזזית *nf* khazazee|t/-yot.

mossy אכול אזוב *adj* akhool/-at ezov.

most 1. רוב *pron* rov; **2.** רובם *nmf* roob|am/-an.

(at the) most לכל היותר le-khol ha-yoter *(kh=k).*

(for the) most part לרוב *adv* la-rov.

most people רוב בני אדם *nm* rov bney adam.

(the) most that I can do כל שבידי *nm* kol she-be-yadee.

(the) most votes רוב קולות *nm* rov kolot.

mostly 1. על פי רוב ‘al pee rov; **2.** בעיקר (mainly) *adv* be-‘eekar.

moth עש *nm* ‘ash/-eem *(pl+of: -ey).*

mothball כדור נפתלין *nm* kadoor/-ey naftaleen.

moth-eaten אכול עש *adj* akhool/-at ‘ash.

mother אם *nf* em/eemahot.

mother country מולדת *nf* moledet.

mother tongue שפת אם *nf* sfat/sfot em.

mother-in-law 1. חותנת *nf* khot|enet/-not; **2.** חמות (in Bible texts: husband’s; nowadays: either) *nf* kham|ot/ayot.

mother-of-pearl צדף *nm* tsedef/tsdafeem *(pl+of:* tseedfey).

motherhood אמהות *nf* eemahoot.

motherly אמהי *adj* eemahee|t/-yot.

mother’s day יום האם *nm* yom ha-’em.

motif 1. רעיון מרכזי *nm* ra‘yon/-ot merkazee/-yeem; **2.** מניע *nm* menee|’a‘/-‘eem *(pl+of: -‘ey).*

motion 1. תנועה (movement) *nf* tnoo‘|ah/-‘ot *(+of:* -‘at); **2.** אות (signal) *nf* ot/-ot.

(to) motion לאותת *inf* le’otet; *pst* otet; *pres* me’otet; *fut* ye’otet.

motion picture סרט קולנוע *nm* seret/seertey kolno‘a.

motion sickness מחלת־ים *nf* makhlat yam.

motion-picture קולנועי *adj* kolno‘ee/-t.

motivation 1. תמריץ (incentive) *nm* tamreets/-eem *(pl+of: -ey)*; **2.** הנמקה (argumentation) *nf* hanmak|ah/-ot *(+of: -at)*; **3.** מוטיבציה *nf* moteevats|yah/-yot *(+of: -yat).*

motive מניע *nm* menee|’a‘/-‘eem *(pl+of: -‘ey).*

motley 1. מנומר *adj* menoom|ar/-eret; **2.** כותונת פסים (striped gown) *nf* kooton|et/-ot paseem; **3.** מגוון *adj* menoov|an/-enet.

motor מנוע *nm* mano’a‘/meno‘eem *(+of:* meno|’a‘/-‘ey).

(to) motor לנסוע במכונית *inf* leenso’a‘ bee-mekhoneet; *pst* nasa‘ *etc*; *pres* nose’a‘ *etc*; *fut* yeesa‘ *etc.*

motorbike קלנוע *nm* kalno|’a‘/-‘eem *(pl+of: -‘ey).*

motorboat סירת מנוע *nf* seer|at/-ot mano‘a.

motorcar מכונית *nf* mekhonee|t/-yot.

motorcoach אוטובוס *nm* otoboos/-eem *([colloq.]* otoboos; *pl+of: -ey).*

motorcycle אופנוע *nm* ofano|’a‘/-‘eem *(pl+of: -‘ey).*

motorist 1. נהג (male) *nf* nehag/-eem *(+of:* nahag/nehagey); **2.** נהגת (female) naheget/nehagot.

motorman 1. נהג קטר *nm* nahag/nehagey katar/-eem; **2.** נהג חשמלית (of streetcar) *nm* nahag/nehagey khashmalee|t/-yot.

motorscooter קטנוע *nm* katno|’a‘/-‘eem *(pl+of:* -‘ey).

mottled מנומר *adj* menoom|ar/-eret.

motto סיסמה *nf* seesm|ah/-a’ot *(+of: -at).*

mound 1. סוללה *nf* solel|ah/-ot *(+of: -at)*; **2.** תל (hillock) *nm* tel/teel|eem *(pl+of: -ey)*; **3.** גבעה (hill) *nf* geev‘ah/gva‘ot *(+of:* geev‘at/-‘ot).

mount 1. גבעה (hill) *nf* geev‘ah/gva‘ot *(+of:* geev‘at/-‘ot); **2.** רכיבה (riding) *nf* rekheev|ah/-ot *(+of: -at).*

(to) mount 1. לרכוב (ride) *inf* leerkov; *pst* rakhav *(kh=k); pres* rokhev; *fut* yeerkav; **2.** להציג (show) *inf* lehatseeg; *pst* heetseeg; *pres* matseeg; *fut* yatseeg.

mountain הר *nm* har/-eem *(pl+of: -ey).*

mountain goat יעל *nf* ya‘el/ye‘el|eem *(pl+of: -ey).*

mountain range שלשלת הרים *nf* shalshel|et/-ot hareem.

mountaineer מטפס הרים *nm* metap|es/-sey hareem.

mountainous הררי *adj* hararee/-t.

(to) mourn להתאבל *inf* leheet’abel; *pst* heet’abel; *pres* meet’abel; *fut* yeet’abel.

(to) mourn for 1. לאבול על *inf* le’evol ‘al; *pst & pres* avel ‘al; *fut* ye’eval; **2.** לבכות (cry over) *inf* levakot; *pst* beekah *(b=v); pres* mevakeh; *fut* yevakeh.

mourning אבל *nm* evel.

(in) mourning באבל *adv* be-’evel.

mouse עכבר *nm* ‘akhb|ar/-areem *(pl+of: -erey).*

mousetrap מלכודת עכברים *nf* malkod|et/-ot ‘akhbareem.

mouth פה *nm* peh/peeyot.

mouthful מלוא הפה *nm* melo ha-peh.

mouthpiece 1. פייה *nf* pee|yah/-yot *(+of: -yat)*; **2.** פומית *nf* poomee|t/-yot *(+of: -yat).*

movable 1. מיטלטל *adj* meetaltel/-elet; **2.** נייד *adj* nayad/-yedet.

movables 1. נכסי דניידי *nm pl* neekhsey de-naydey; **2.** מיטלטלים (chattels) *nm* meetalteleem.

move 1. מהלך (movement) *nm* mahal|akh/-akheem *(pl+of: -khey)*; **2.** מעבר דירה (apartment) *nm* ma‘av|ar/-rey deer|ah/-ot; **3.** תור (turn) *nm* tor/-eem *(pl+of: -ey).*

(to) move 1. לזוז *inf* lazooz; *pst & pres* zaz; *fut* yazooz; **2.** לעבור דירה (colloq.: change apartment) *inf* la‘avor deerah; *pst* ‘avar *etc*; *pres* ‘over *etc*; *fut* ya‘avor *etc*; **3.** להעלות הצעה (resolution) *inf* leha‘alot hatsa‘ah; *pst* he‘elah *etc*; *pres* ma‘aleh *etc*; *fut* ya‘aleh *etc*; **4.** לנקוט מהלך (in a game) *inf* leenkot mahalakh; *pst* nakat *etc*; *pres* noket *etc*; *fut* yeenkot *etc*; **5.** לרגש (emotionally) *inf* leragesh; *pst* reegesh; *pres* meragesh; *fut* yeragesh.

movement 1. תזוזה (motion) *nf* tezooz|ah/-ot *(+of: -at)*; **2.** מנגנון (mechanism) *nm* mang|anon/enoneem *(pl+of: -enoney)*; **3.** תנועה (political) *nf* tenoo|‘ah/-‘ot *(+of: -‘at)*; **4.** הרקת מעיים (bowels) *nf* harakat me‘ayeem.

movie סרט קולנוע *nm* sereet/seertey kolno‘a.

movies קולנוע *nm* kolno|’a‘/-‘eem *(pl+of: -‘ey).*

(to) mow 1. לקצור *inf* leektsor; *pst* katsar; *pres* kotser; *fut* yeektsor; **2.** לכסח דשא (cut off) *inf* lekhase’akh deshe; *pst* keesakh *etc (k=kh); pres* mekhase’akh *etc; fut* yekhasakh *etc.*

mower מקצרה *nf* maktser|ah/-ot *(+of: -at).*

(lawn) mower מכסחת דשא *nf* makhsekh|at/-ot deshe.

Mr. 1. מר *nm* mar; **2.** אדון *nm* adon.

Mrs. 1. מרת *nf* marat; **2.** גברת *nf* gveret.

much 1. רב *adj* rav/rabah *(b=v)*; **2.** הרבה *adv* harbeh.
(how) much? ?כמה kamah? (*[colloq.]*: kamah?).
(too) much יותר מדי *adv* yoter mee-day.
(very) much הרבה מאוד *adv* harbeh me'od.
(as) much as כאילו ke'eeloo.
much the same אותו דבר oto davar.
(not) much of לא רבים מתוך lo rab|eem/-ot *(m/f)* mee-tokh.
(to make) much of 1. להעריך *inf* leha'areekh; *pst* he'ereekh; *pres* ma'areekh; *fut* ya'areekh; **2.** להגזים בהערכה (over-value) *inf* lehagzeem be-ha'arakhah; *pst* heegzeem *etc*; *pres* magzeem *etc*; *fut* yagzeem *etc*.
(so) much that כה הרבה עד ש־ koh harbeh 'ad she-.
muck 1. מרעה (manure) *nm* meer'eh/-'eem (*pl+of*: -'ey); **2.** זבל (fertilizer) *nm* zevel/zvaleem (*pl+of*: zeevley); **3.** רקב (mire) *nm* rekev; **4.** חלאה (filth) *nf* khel|'ah/-'ot (*+of*: -'at).
mucous רירי *adj* reeree/-t.
mucous membrane קרומית רירית *nf* kroomee|t/-yot reeree|t/-yot.
mucus 1. ריר *nm* reer/-eem (*pl+of*: -ey); **2.** ליחה (discharge) *nf* leykh|ah/-ot (*+of*: -at).
mud בוץ *nm* bots.
muddle מבוכה *nf* mevookh|ah/-ot (*+of*: -at).
(to) muddle לבלבל *inf* levalbel; *pst* beelbel *(b=v)*; *pres* mevalbel; *fut* yevalbel.
(to) muddle through 1. לפלס דרך *inf* lefales derekh; *pst* peeles *(p=f) etc*; *pres* mefales *etc*; *fut* yefales *etc*; **2.** לצאת מן הסבך (disentangle oneself) *inf* latset meen ha-svakh; *pst* yatsa *etc*; *pres* yotse *etc*; *fut* yetse *etc*.
muddy 1. מרופש *adj* meroop|ash/-eshet; **2.** בוצי *adj* bootsee/-t; **3.** דלוח (dirty) *adj* daloo'akh/dlookhah.
muff רשלן *nmf & adj* rashlan/-eet.
(to) muff 1. להיכשל *inf* leheekashel; *pst & pres* neekhshal *(kh=k)*; *fut* yeekashel; **2.** לפספס *[colloq.]* lefasfes; *pst* feesfes; *pres* mefasfes; *fut* yefasfes.
muffin רקיק *nm* rakeek/rekeek|eem (*pl+of*: -ey).
(to) muffle להתכרבל *inf* leheetkarbel; *pst* heetkarbel; *pres* meetkarbel; *fut* yeetkarbel.
muffler סודר *nm* sood|ar/-areem (*pl+of*: -rey).
mufti לבוש אזרחי *nm* levoosh ezrakhee.
mug ספל *nm* sefel/sfaleem (*pl+of*: seefley).
mulberry תות *nm* toot/-eem (*pl+of*: -ey).
mulberry tree עץ תות *nm* 'et/'atsey toot.
mule 1. פרד *nm* pered/pradeem (*pl+of*: peerdey); **2.** פרדה (jennet) *nf* peerdah/pradot (*+of*: peerd|at/-ot).
(to) mull 1. לחמם יין *inf* lekhamem yayeen; *pst* kheemem *etc*; *pres* mekhamem *etc*; *fut* yekhamem *etc*; **2.** להרהר (muse) *v inf* leharher; *pst* heerher; *pres* meharher; *fut* yeharher.
multiple 1. מכופל *adj* mekhoop|al/-elet; **2.** רב־פנים (many-sided) *adj* rav/rabat paneem *(b=v)*; **3.** כפולה *nf* kefool|ah/-ot (*+of*: -at).
multiplication 1. כפל *nm* kefel; **2.** הכפלה (increase) *nf* hakhpal|ah/-ot (*+of*: -at).
multiplication table לוח הכפל *nm* loo'akh ha-kefel.
multiplicity ריבוי *nm* reebooly/-yeem (*pl+of*: -yey).
(to) multiply 1. להתרבות *v rfl inf* leheetrabot; *pst* heetrabah; *pres* meetrabeh; *fut* yeetrabeh; **2.** להכפיל (double) *vt inf* lehakhpeel; *pst* heekhpeel; *pres* makhpeel; *fut* yakhpeel; **3.** להרבות (increase) *vt inf* leharbot; *pst* heerbah; *pres* marbeh; *fut* yarbeh.
multitude המון *nm* hamon/-eem (*pl+of*: -ey).
mum דומם *adj* domem/-et.
(to keep) mum לשתוק *inf* leeshtok; *pst* shatak; *pres* shotek; *fut* yeeshtok.
mumble 1. מלמול *nm* meelmool/-eem (*pl+of*: -ey); **2.** ריטון *nm* reetoon/-eem (*pl+of*: -ey).
(to) mumble למלמל *inf* lemalmel; *pst* meelmel; *pres* memalmel; *fut* yemalmel.
(to talk in a) mumble לדבר מבין לשיניים *inf* ledaber mee-beyn la-sheenayeem; *pst* deeber *etc*; *pres* medaber *etc*; *fut* yedaber *etc*.
mummy 1. אמא (mother) *nm* eema; **2.** מומיה (enbalmed) *nf* moom|yah/-yot (*+of*: -yat).
mumps חזרת *nf* khazeret.
(to) munch לכרסם *inf* lekharsem; *pst* keersem *(k=kh)*; *pres* mekharsem; *fut* yekharsem.
mundane 1. יומיומי *adj* yomyomee/-t; **2.** רגיל (habitual) *adj* rageel/regeelah.
municipal עירוני *adj* 'eeronee/-t.
municipality עירייה *nf* 'eeree|yah/-yot (*+of*: -yat).
munition תחמושת *nf* takhmoshet.
(to) munition לחמש *inf* lekhamesh; *pst* kheemesh; *pres* mekhamesh; *fut* yekhamesh.
munition plant מפעל תחמושת *nm* meef'al/-ey takhmoshet.
mural 1. ציור קיר *nm* tseeyoor/-ey keer; **2.** שעל קיר *adj* she-'al keer.
murder 1. רצח *nm* retsakh; **2.** רציחה (killing) retseekh|ah/-ot (*+of*: -at).
(to) murder לרצוח *inf* leertso'akh; *pst* ratsakh; *pres* rotse'akh; *fut* yeertsakh.
murderer רוצח *nm* rots|e'akh/kheem (*pl+of*: -khey).
murderess רוצחת *nf* rotsakhat/-khot.
murderous רצחני *adj* ratskhanee/-t.
murky אפלולי *adj* afloolee/-t.
murmur 1. רחש (noise) *nm* rakhash/rekhasheem (*pl+of*: rakhshey); **2.** רינון (complaint) *nm* reenoon/-eem (*pl+of*: -ey).
(to) murmur 1. לרחוש *inf* leerkhosh; *pst* rakhash; *pres* rokhesh; *fut* yeerkhash; **2.** לרנן (slander) *inf* leranen; *pst* reenen; *pres* meranen; *fut* yeranen.
muscle שריר *nm* shreer/-eem (*pl+of*: -ey).
muscular שרירי *adj* shreeree/-t.
muse הרהור *nm* heerhoor/-eem (*pl+of*: -ey).
Muse 1. השראה *nf* hashra|'ah/-'ot (*+of*: -'at); **2.** מוזה *[colloq.] nf* mooz|ah/-ot (*+of*: -at).
(to) muse להרהר *inf* leharher; *pst* heerher; *pres* meharher; *fut* yeharher.
museum 1. בית נכות *nm* bet/batey nekhot; **2.** מוזיאון *nm* mooze'on/-eem (*pl+of*: -ey).
mush תבשיל תירס *nm* tavsheel/-ey teeras.
mushroom פטרייה *nf* peetree|yah/-yot (*+of*: -yat).
music 1. נגינה *nf* negeen|ah/-at; **2.** מוסיקה *nf* mooseek|ah (*+of*: -at).

music stand כן תווים *nm* kan/-ey taveem.

musical 1. מחזמר (comedy) *nm* makhzemer/makhzeemr|eem (*pl+of:* -ey); **2.** מוסיקלי *adj* mooseekalee/-t.

musical comedy 1. מחזה מוסיקלי *nm* makhaz|eh/-ot mooseekalee/-yeem; **2.** אופרטה *nf* operet|ah/-ot (*+of:* -at).

musician מוסיקאי *nmf* mooseeka|y/-'eet (*pl:* -'eem/-'eeyot; *+of:* -'ey).

muskmelon אבטיח צהוב *nm* avatee'akh/-kheem tsahov/tsehoobeem (*b=v).*

muskrat עכבר מושק *nm* 'akhb|ar/-erey mooshk.

muslin 1. מלמלה *nf* malmal|ah/-ot (*+of:* malmel|et/-ot); **2.** מוסלין *nm* moosleen.

(to) muss לערבב *inf* le'arbev; *pst* 'eerbev; *pres* me'arbev; *fut* ye'arbev.

must 1. מוכרח *adj & v pres* mookhrakh/-ah; **2.** נאלץ *adj & v pres* ne'el|ats/-etset.

mustache שפם *nm* safam/sfam|eem (*pl+of:* -ey).

mustard חרדל *nm* khardal.

mustard plaster אספלנית חרדל *nf* eespelanee|t/-yot khardal.

(to) muster לאסוף (collect) *inf* le'esof; *pst* asaf; *pres* osef; *fut* ye'esof.

(to pass) muster לעמוד בבדיקה *inf* la'amod bee-vdeekah (*v=b); pst* 'amad *etc*; *pres* 'omed *etc*; *fut* ya'amod *etc.*

(to) muster out לשחרר *inf* leshakhrer; *pst* sheekhrer; *pres* meshakhrer; *fut* yeshakhrer.

(to) muster up one's courage לאזור עוז *inf* le'ezor 'oz; *pst* azar 'oz; *pres* ozer 'oz; *fut* ye'ezor 'oz.

musty מעופש *adj* me'oop|ash/-eshet.

mute 1. אילם *adj* eelem/-et; **2.** אילם *nm* eel|em/-meem (*pl+of:* -mey).

(to) mutilate 1. לעוות *inf* le'avet; *pst* 'eevet; *pres* me'avet; *fut* ye'avet; **2.** להטיל מום (maim) *inf* lehateel moom; *pst* heeteel moom; *pres* mateel moom; *fut* yateel moom.

mutiny 1. התקוממות (uprising) *nf* heetkomemoo|t/-yot; **2.** התמרדות (rebellion) *nf* heetmardoo|t/-yot.

mutter מלמול *nm* meelmool/-eem (*pl+of:* -ey).

(to) mutter למלמל *inf* lemalmel; *pst* meelmel; *pres* memalmel; *fut* yemalmel.

mutton בשר כבש *nm* besar keves.

mutton chop נתח כבש לצלייה *nm* netakh/neetkhey keves lee-tsleeyah.

mutual הדדי *adj* hadadee/-t.

muzzle 1. מחסום *nm* makhsom/-eem (*pl+of:* -ey); **2.** לוע רובה (of rifle) *nm* lo'a'/lo'ey rov|eh/-eem.

(to) muzzle 1. לחסום *inf* lakhsom; *pst* khasam; *pres* khosem; *fut* yakhsom; **2.** להשתיק (silence) *inf* lehashteek; *pst* heeshteek; *pres* mashteek; *fut* yashteek.

my שלי possess. *pron* shelee.

myopia קוצר ראייה *nm* kotser re'eeyah.

myopic קצר־ראות *adj* ketsar/keetsrat re'oot.

myriad רבבה *nf* revav|ah/-ot (*+of:* reevevat).

myrtle הדס *nm* hadas/-eem (*pl+of:* -ey).

myself 1. בעצמי *pron* be-'atsmee; **2.** אני עצמי (I myself) *pron* anee 'atsmee.

(by) myself 1. בעצמי *pron nf* be-'atsmee; **2.** לבדי (myself alone) levadee.

(I talk to) myself מדבר אל עצמי medaber el 'atsmee.

(I) myself did so אני עצמי עשיתי כך anee 'atsmee 'aseetee kakh.

mysterious מסתורי *adj* meestoree/-t.

mystery 1. מסתורין *nm pl* meestor|een (*+of:* -ey); **2.** תעלומה (enigma) *nf* ta'aloom|ah/-ot (*+of:* -at); **3.** סוד (secret) *nm* sod/-ot.

mystic, mystical מיסטי *adj* meestee/-t.

myth 1. אגדה (legend) *nf* agad|ah/-ot (*+of:* -at); **2.** מיתוס *nm* meetos/-eem (*pl+of:* -ey).

mythology מיתולוגיה *nf* meetolog|yah/-yot (*+of:* -yat).

N.

N,n equivalent to the Hebrew consonant Noon (נ) which, when ending a word, takes a different shape : ן (called "Noon Sofeet") instead of נ.

(to) nab 1. לתפוס (seize) *inf* leetpos; *pst* tafas (*f=p*); *pres* tofes; *fut* yeetpos; **2.** לאסור (arrest) *inf* le'esor; *pst* asar; *pres* oser; *fut* ye'esor.

nag סייח *nm* syakh/-eem (*pl+of:* -ey).

(to) nag להציק *inf* lehatseek; *pst* hetseek; *pres* metseek; *fut* yatseek.

naiad נימפת ים *nf* neemf|at/-ot yam

nail 1. ציפורן (of finger or toe) *nf* tseepor|en/-nayeem (*pl+of:* -ney); **2.** מסמר (metal) *nm* masmer/-eem (*pl+of:* -ey).

(to) nail 1. לתפוס (seize) *inf* leetfos; *pst* tafas; *pres* tofes; *fut* yeetfos; **2.** להצמיד במסמרים (fasten) *inf* lehatsmeed be-masmereem; *pst* heetsmeed *etc*; *pres* matsmeed *etc*; *fut* yatsmeed *etc.*

(to) nail down לקבוע מסמרות *inf* leekbo'a' masmerot; *pst* kava' *etc* (*v=b*); *pres* kove'a' *etc*; *fut* yeekba' *etc.*

nail-file משוף ציפורניים *nm* mashof/meshofey tseepornayeem.

nail-polish לכה לציפורניים *nf* lak|ah/-ot le-tseepornayeem.
naive 1. תמים *adj* tameem/tmeemah; **2.** נאיבי *adj* na'eevee/-t.
naked 1. ערום *adj* 'arom/'aroomah; **2.** מרוקן (emptied) *adj* merook|an/-enet.
nakedness עירום *nm* 'erom/'eroom|eem (*pl+of:* -ey).
name שם *nm* shem/-ot (*pl+of:* shmot).
(family) name שם משפחה *nm* shem/shmot meeshpakhah.
(to) name 1. לקרוא בשם *inf* leekro be-shem; *pst* kara *etc; pres* kore *etc; fut* yeekra *etc;* **2.** לנקוב (specify) *inf* leenkov; *pst* nakav; *pres* nokev; *fut* yeenkov (*or:* yeekov).
(to make a) name for oneself לעשות שם לעצמו *inf* le'asot shem le-'atsmo; *pst* 'asah *etc; pres* 'oseh *etc; fut* ya'aseh *etc.*
(what is your) name? מה שמך? mah sheemkha?/ shmekh? *(m/f).*
nameless בן בלי שם *adj* ben/bat blee shem.
namely 1. כלומר kelomar; **2.** דהיינו (viz.) dehaynoo.
(to call) names לגדף *inf* legadef; *pst* geedef; *pres* megadef; *fut* yegadef.
namesake בעל אותו שם *nmf & adj* ba'al/-at oto shem.
nanny אומנת *nf* om|enet/-not.
nanny-goat עז 'ez/'eez|eem (*pl+of:* -ey).
nap נמנום *nm* neemnoom/-eem (*pl+of:* -ey).
(to take a) nap לחטוף נמנום *inf* lakhtof neemnoom; *pst* khataf *etc; pres* khotef *etc; fut* yakhtof *etc.*
nape עורף *nm* 'or|ef/-afeem (*pl+of:* -fey).
naphtha נפט *nm* neft.
napkin מפית *nf* mapee|t/-yot.
napkin ring טבעת למפיות *nf* taba'at le-mapeeyot.
Naples נפולי *nf* napolee.
narcosis 1. הרדמה *nf* hardam|ah/-ot (*+of:* -at); **2.** נרקוזה *nf* narkoz|ah/-ot (*+of:* -at).
narcotic 1. מרדים *adj* mardeem/-ah; **2.** סם (narcotic) *nm* sam/-eem (*pl+of:* -ey).
(to) narrate לספר *inf* lesaper; *pst* seeper; *pres* mesaper; *fut* yesaper.
narration 1. סיפור (story) *nm* seepoor/-eem (*pl+of:* -ey); **2.** הגדה (saga) *nf* hagad|ah/-ot (*+of:* -at).
narrative 1. סיפורי *adj* seepooree/-t; **2.** סיפור (story) *nm* seepoor/-eem (*pl+of:* -ey).
narrator מספר *nmf* mesaper/-et.
narrow 1. צר *adj* tsar/-ah; **2.** דחוק (sparse) *adj* dakhook/dekhookah.
(to) narrow 1. להצר *vt* lehatser; *pst* hetser; *pres* metser; *fut* yatser; **2.** לצמצם (restrict) *vt inf* letsamtsem; *pst* tseemtsem; *pres* metsamtsem; *fut* yetsamtsem; **3.** להצטמצם (confine oneself) *v rfl inf* leheetstamtsem; *pst* heetstamtsem; *pres* meetstamtsem; *fut* yeetstamtsem.
narrow escape היחלצות בנס *nf* heenatsloo|t/-yot be-nes.
narrow-gauge מסילת־ברזל צרה *nf* meseel|at/-ot barzel tsar|ah/-ot.
narrow-minded צר אופק *adj* tsar/-at ofek.

narrowness 1. צרות (cramped) *nf* tsaroo|t/-yot; **2.** חוסר סובלנות (intolerance) *nm* khoser sovlanoot.
nasal 1. חוטמי *adj* khotmee/-t; **2.** של אף *adj* shel af; **3.** מאונפף (phonetic) *adj* me'oonp|af/-efet.
nastiness 1. טינוף *nm* teenoof/-eem (*pl+of:* -ey); **2.** רישעות *nf* reesh'oo|t/-yot.
nasty 1. גס *adj* gas/-ah; **2.** גועלי (disgusting) *adj* go'olee/-t (*cpr* go'alee/-t).
nasty disposition מצב רוח מזופת *nm* mat|sav/-vey roo'akh mezoopat/-eem.
(a) nasty fall נפילה רצינית *nf* nefeel|ah/-ot retseenee|t/-yot.
natal מולד *adj* mool|ad/-edet.
nation 1. אומה *nf* oom|ah/-ot (*+of:* -at); **2.** לאום (ethnic) *nm* le'om/le'oom|eem (*pl+of:* -ey); **3.** מדינה (state) *nf* medeen|ah/-ot (*+of:* -at).
national 1. לאומי *adj* le'oomee/-t; **2.** נתין (subject) *nmf* nateen/neteen|ah (*pl:* -eem/-ot; *+of:* -at; *pl:* -ey); **3.** אזרח (citizen) *nmf* ezrakh/-eet (*pl:* -eem; *+of:* ezrekhey).
nationalism לאומנות *nf* le'oomanoo|t/-yot.
nationalist לאומני *nmf & adj* le'oomanee/-t.
nationality 1. נתינות *nf* neteenoo|t/-yot; **2.** אזרחות (citizenship) *nf* ezrakhoo|t/-yot; **3.** לאומיות (ethnic) *nf* le'oomeeyoo|t/-yot.
(to) nationalize להלאים *inf* lehal'eem; *pst* heel'eem; *pres* mal'eem; *fut* yal'eem.
native 1. יליד *nmf* yeleed/-ah (*+of:* -at; *pl+of:* -ey); **2.** מלידה (from birth) *adj* mee-leydah **3.** של לידה (of birth) *adj* shel leydah.
native land ארץ הלידה *nf* erets/artsot ha-leydah.
nativity מולד *nm* molad.
(Church of) Nativity כנסיית המולד (in Bethlehem) *nf* kneseeyat ha-molad.
N.A.T.O. 1. הברית הצפון אטלנטית (North Atlantic Treaty Organization) *nf* ha-breet ha-tsefon atlanteet; **2.** נאט״ו (non-Hebrew *acr of* 1 as pronounced) *nf* nato.
natty נקי ומסודר *adj* nakee/nekeeyah oo-mesoo-d|ar/-eret.
natural 1. טבעי *adj* teev'ee/-t; **2.** מצוין לתפקיד (ideally fit for the job) *adj* metsoo|yan/-yenet la-tafkeed.
naturalism נטורליזם natooraleezm/-eem.
naturalist חוקר טבע *nmf* khoker/-et teva'.
naturalization 1. אזרוח (of others) *nm* eezroo|'akh/-khee (*pl+of:* -khey); **2.** התאזרחות (of oneself) *nf* heet'azrekhoo|t/-yot.
Naturalization Certificate תעודת התאזרחות *nf* te'ood|at/-ot heet'azrekhoot.
(to) naturalize 1. להתאזרח (oneself) *v rfl inf* leheet'azre'akh; *pst* heet'azre'akh; *pres* meet'azre'akh; *fut* yeet'azre'akh; **2.** לאזרח (others) *vt inf* le'azre'akh; *pst* eezre'akh; *pres* me'azre'akh; *fut* ye'azre'akh.
naturally 1. באופן טבעי *adv* be-ofen teev'ee; **2.** כמובן (obviously) *adv* ka-moovan.
naturalness טבעיות *nf* teev'eeyoot.
nature 1. טבע *nm* teva'/tva'eem (*pl+of:* teev'ey); **2.** אופי (character) *nm* of|ee/-ayeem (*pl+of:* -yey).

naught 1. אפס *nm* efes/afaseem (*pl+of:* afsey); **2.** כישלון חרוץ (complete failure) *nm* keeshalon kharoots.

naughty שובב *adj* shov|av/-evah.

nausea 1. בחילה *nf* bekheel|ah/-ot (*+of:* -at); **2.** שאט נפש (disgust) *nm* she'at nefesh.

(to) nauseate 1. לעורר בחילה *vt inf* le'orer bekheelah; *pst* 'orer *etc; pres* me'orer *etc; fut* ye'orer *etc;* **2.** להיתקף בחילה *vi inf* leheetakef bekheelah; *pst & pres* neetkaf *etc; fut* yeetakef *etc.*

nauseating 1. מבחיל *adj* mavkheel/-ah; **2.** מגעיל (disgusting) *adj* mag'eel/-ah.

nauseous מבחיל *adj* mavkheel/-ah.

nautical ימי *adj* yamee/-t.

naval 1. של חיל הים (of Isr. navy) *adj* shel kheyl ha-yam; **2.** של הצי (of foreign navy) *adj* shel ha-tsee.

naval station תחנת שירות של חיל הים *nf* takhn|at/-ot sheroot shel kheyl ha-yam.

nave 1. תווך *nm* tavekh; **2.** אולם שבמרכז (central hall) oolam she-ba-merkaz.

navel 1. טבור *nm* taboor/-eem (*pl+of:* -ey); **2.** מרכז (center) *nm* merk|az/-eem (*pl+of:* -ezey).

navel orange תפוז ללא גרעינים *nm* tapooz/-eem le-lo gar'eeneem.

navigability כשירות לניווט *nf* kesheeroot le-neevoot.

navigable בר־ניווט *adj* bar/bat neevoot.

(to) navigate 1. לנווט *inf* lenavet; *pst* neevet; *pres* menavet; *fut* yenavet; **2.** לשוט (cruise) *inf* lashoot; *pst & pres* shat; *fut* yashoot.

navigation 1. ניווט neevoot/-eem (*pl+of:* -ey); **2.** שיט (sailing, rowing) *nm* shayeet.

navigator נווט *nm* navat/-eem (*pl+of:* -ey).

navy blue כחול כהה *adj* kakhol-keheh/ kekhoolah-kehah.

navy yard מספנת חיל הים *nf* meespen|et/-ot kheyl ha-yam.

nay 1. לא lo; **2.** לא זו בלבד ש־ (not only that) lo zo beelvad she-.

Nazarene 1. נוצרי קדום *nm* (early Christian) notsree/-m kadoom/kedoomeem; **2.** תושב נצרת (resident of Nazareth) *nmf* tosh|av/-evet (*pl+of:* -vey) Natsrat (*cpr* Natseret).

Nazareth נצרת (town) is pronounced Natsrat but, colloqially, is known as Natseret.

Nazi 1. נאצי *nm* natsee/-m; **2.** נאצי *adj* natsee/-t.

N.B. 1. נ.ב. noon-bet (*acr of* Latin *abbr.* nota bene); **2.** נ״ב noon-bet - *acr of* neezkartee be-davar נזכרתי בדבר - I just remembered; **3.** עיקר שכחתי (I forgot the main thing) 'eekar shakhakhtee.

neap tide גיאות נמוכה ביותר *nf* ge'oot nemookhah be-yoter.

near 1. קרוב *adj* karov/krovah; **2.** קרוב ל־ *adv* karov le-; **3.** כמעט (almost) *prep* keem'at.

Near East המזרח הקרוב *nm* ha-meezrakh ha-karov.

nearly כמעט *adv* keem'at.

nearness 1. קירבה *nf* keerv|ah/-ot (*+of:* -at); **2.** קירבת מקום (proximity) *nf* keervat makom.

nearsighted קצר רואי *adj* ketsar/keetsrat ro'ee.

nearsightedness קוצר ראות *nm* kotser re'oot.

neat 1. מסודר *adj* mesood|ar/-eret; **2.** יעיל (efficient) *adj* ya'eel/ye'eelah.

neatly בצורה מסודרת *adv* be-tsoorah mesooderet.

neatness 1. ניקיון *nm* neek|ayon/-yonot (*+of:* -yon); **2.** סדר (order) *nm* seder/sdareem (*pl+of:* seedrey); **3.** הופעה מסודרת (neat appearance) *nf* hofa'ah mesooderet.

nebula ערפילית *nf* 'arfeelee|t/-yot.

nebular ערפילי *adj* 'arfeelee/-t.

nebulous מעורפל *adj* me'oorp|al/-elet.

necessary 1. דרוש (required) *adj* daroosh/ drooshah; **2.** נחוץ (needed) *adj* nakhoots/ nekhootsah.

(to) necessitate להצריך *inf* lehatsreekh; *pst* heetsreekh; *pres* matsreekh; *fut* yatsreekh.

necessitous נצרך *nm* neetsr|akh/-akheem (*pl+of:* -ekhey).

necessity 1. הכרח *nm* hekhre'akh; **2.** צורך (need) tsorekh/tserakheem (*pl+of:* tsorkhey).

neck 1. צוואר *nm* tsav|ar/-arot (*pl+of:* -ey); **2.** גרון (throat) *nm* garon/gronot (*+of:* gron).

(to) neck 1. להתגפף *inf* leheetgapef; *pst* heetgapef; *pres* meetgapef; *fut* yeetgapef; **2.** להתמזמז (hug and, also, tarry) *[colloq.] v refl inf* leheetmazmez; *pst* heetmazmez; *pres* meetmazmez; *fut* yeetmazmez.

neckband צווארון *nm* tsav|aron/-roneem (*pl+of:* -roney).

necklace 1. רביד *nm* raveed/reveed|eem (*pl+of:* -ey); **2.** מחרוזת (beads *etc*) *nf* makhroz|et/-ot.

necktie עניבה *nf* 'aneev|ah/-ot (*+of:* -at).

necrology 1. רשימת נפטרים *nf* resheem|at/-ot neeftareem; **2.** נקרולוג (obituary) *nm* nekrolog/ -eem (*pl+of:* -ey).

necromancy דרישה אל המתים *nf* dreeshah el ha-meteem.

nee 1. מלידה *adj* mee-leydah; **2.** לבית *adj* le-vet (*v=b*).

need 1. צורך *nm* tsorekh/tsrakheem (*pl+of:* tsorkhey); **2.** מצוקה (poverty) *nf* metsook|ah/-ot (*+of:* -at).

(to) need 1. להצריך *vt inf* lehatsreekh; *pst* heetsreekh; *pres* matsreekh; *fut* yatsreekh; **2.** להזדקק (depend upon) *inf* leheezdakek; *pst* heezdakek; *pres* meezdakek; *fut* yeezdakek.

(if) need be 1. אם יהיה צורך eem yeehyeh tsorekh; **2.** בשעת הצורך (in case of need) be-she'at ha-tsorekh.

(for) need of 1. בשל צורך ב־ be-shel tsorekh be-; **2.** בגלל (for sake of) bee-glal.

needful נחוץ *adj* nakhoots/nekhootsah.

needle מחט *nf* makhat/mekhateem (*pl+of:* makhtey).

(to) needle 1. לתפור ביד *inf* leetpor ba-yad; *pst* tafar (*f=p*) *etc; pres* tofer *etc; fut* yeetpor *etc;* **2.** לעקוץ (annoy) *inf* la'akots; *pst* 'akats; *pres* 'okets; *fut* ya'akots.

needle-point חוד המחט *nm* khod ha-makhat.

needless ללא צורך *adv* le-lo tsorekh.

needlework 1. תפירה (sewing) *nf* tfeer|ah/-ot (*+of:* -at); **2.** מעשה רקמה *nm* ma'as|eh/-ey reekmah.

needy נצרך *nm* neetsr|akh/-eem (*pl+of:* -ekhey).

ne'er-do-well לא יוצלח *[colloq.] nmf* lo yootslakh/ -eet.

negation 1. שלילה *nf* shleel|ah/-ot (+*of:* -at); **2.** הכחשה (denial) *nf* hakh'khash|ah/-ot (+*of:* -at).
negative 1. שלילי *adj* shleelee/-t; **2.** שלילה (negation) *nf* shleel|ah/-ot (+*of:* -at); **3.** שלילי (army-slang for "no!") shleelee!
(to) negative לבטל *inf* levatel; *pst* beetel *(b=v)*; *pres* mevatel; *fut* yevatel.
negatively בשלילה *adv* bee-shleelah.
neglect הזנחה *nf* haznakh|ah/-ot (+*of:* -at).
(to) neglect to להתרשל ב־ *inf* leheetrashel be-; *pst* heetrashel be-; *pres* meetrashel be-; *fut* yeetrashel be-.
neglectful רשלני *adj* rashlanee/-t.
negligee 1. חלוק *nm* khalook/-eem (*pl+of:* -ey); **2.** לבוש שלא בקפידה (carelessly informal attire) *nm* levoosh she-lo bee-kfeedah.
negligence רשלנות *nf* rashlanoo|t/-yot.
negligent רשלני *nmf & adj* rashlanee/-t.
negligible חסר חשיבות *adj* khas|ar/-rat tarboot.
negotiable 1. סחיר *adj* sakheer/sekheerah; **2.** נתון למשא ומתן (open to negotiation) *adj* natoon/netoonah le-masa oo-matan.
(to) negotiate 1. לשאת ולתת *inf* laset ve-latet; *pst* nasa ve-natan; *pres* nose ve-noten; *fut* yeesa ve-yeeten; **2.** לנהל משא ומתן (conduct negotiatons) *inf* lenahel masa oo-matan; *pst* neehel *etc*; *pres* menahel *etc*; *fut* yebahel *etc*; **3.** לנהל מו"מ *inf* lenahel "moom" (*acr of* "masa oo-matan", *see 2*); *pres* menahel *etc*; *fut* yenahel *etc*.
negotiation 1. משא ומתן *nm & nm* masa oo-matan; **2.** מו"מ (*acr of* 1) *[colloq.]* moom/-eem (*pl+of:* -ey).
Negro כושי *nm* kooshee/-t (*cpr* kooshee/-t; *pl:* koosh|eem; *pl+of:* -ey).
negro של כושים *adj* shel koosheem.
neigh צהלה *nf* tsoholah/tsehalot (+*of:* -at).
(to) neigh לצהול *inf* leets'hol; *pst* tsahal; *pres* tsohel; *fut* yeets'hal.
neighbor שכן *nmf* shakhen/sh'khen|ah (*pl:* -eem/-ot; +*of:* -at/-ey).
neighborhood סביבה *nf* sveev|ah/-ot (+*of:* -at).
(in the) neighborhood of בסביבות *adv* bee-sveevot.
neighboring 1. שכן *adj* shakhen/sh'khen|ah (*pl:* -eem/-ot); **2.** בשכנות ל־ (next to) *adv* beesh'khenoot le-.
neighborly שבין שכנים *adj* she-beyn sh'kheneem.
neither 1. אף לא אחד *adj* af lo ekhad/akhat; **2.** אף אחד *[colloq.] adj* af ekhad/akhat.
neither... nor... לא... ולא... lo... va-lo...
neither of the two אף לא אחד מהשניים *adj* af lo ekhad/akhat me-ha-shnayeem/shtayeem.
neither one of us אף לא אחד משנינו *adj* af lo ekhad/akhat mee-shneynoo/shteynoo.
neither will I אף אני לא af anee lo'
neologism 1. תחדיש *nm* takhdeesh/-eem (*pl+of:* -ey); **2.** מלה חדשה (new word) *nf* meel|ah/-eem khadash|ah/-ot.
neomycin ניאומיצין *nm* ne'omeetseen.
neon ניאון *nm* ne'on/-eem (*pl+of:* -ey).
neophyte טירון *nmf & adj* teeron/-eet.
nephew אחיין *nm* akhyan/-eem (*pl+of:* -ey).
nepotism 1. העדפת קרובי משפחה *nf* ha'adafat krovey meeshpakhah; **2.** פרוטקציה לקרובי משפחה *[colloq.]* protektsee|yah/-yot lee-krovey meeshpakhah.
nerd מרובע *[colloq.] nm* meroob|a'/-a'at (*pl:* -a'eem/-a'ot; +*of:* -'ey).
nerve 1. עצב (anatomy) *nm* 'atsa|v/beem (+*of:* -bey); **2.** אומץ (courage) *nm* omets **3.** חוצפה (effrontery) *nf* khootsp|ah/-ot (+*of:* -at).
nerve-racking מורט עצבים *adj* moret/-et 'atsabeem.
nervous עצבני *adj* 'atsbanee/t.
nervous breakdown התמוטטות עצבים *nf* hetmotetoo|t/-yot 'atsabeem.
nervousness עצבנות *nf* 'atsbanoo|t/-yot.
nervy 1. אמיץ *adj* ameets/-ah; **2.** חצוף *adj* khatsoof/-ah.
nest קן *nm* ken/keen|eem (*pl+of:* -ey).
(wasp's) nest קן צרעות *nm* ken/keeney tsra'ot.
nest-egg חיסכון לעת צרה *nm* kheesakhon/kheskhonot le-'et tsarah.
(to) nestle להתרפק *inf* leheetrapek; *pst* heetrapek; *pres* meetrapek; *fut* yeetrapek.
net 1. רשת *nf* resh|et/-atot (*pl+of:* reeshtot); **2.** מכמורת (trawn) *nf* meekhmor|et/-ot; **3.** נטו (netto) *adj & adv* neto.
net price מחיר נטו *nm* mekheer/-ey neto.
net profit רווח נטו *nm* revakh/-eem neto.
(to) net 1. להרוויח נקי *[colloq.] vt inf* leharvee'akh nakee; *pst* heervee'akh *etc*; *pres* marvee'akh *etc*; *fut* yarvee'akh *etc* **2.** ללכוד ברשת (catch in one's net) *inf* leelkod ba-reshet; *pst* lakhad *etc* (*kh=k*); *pres* lokhed *etc*; *fut* yeelkod *etc*.
Netherlands הולנד *nf* holand.
netting רישות *nm* reeshoot/-eem (*pl+of:* -ey).
nettle סרפד *nm* seerp|ad/-adeem (*pl+of:* -edey).
(to) nettle לעקוץ *vt* la'akots; *pst* 'akats; *pres* 'okets; *fut* ya'akots.
network 1. רשת *nm* resh|et-atot (*pl+of:* reeshtot); **2.** הסתעפות *nf* heesta'afoot/-yot.
(radio) network רשת שידורי רדיו *nf* reshet/reeshtot sheedoorey radyo.
(television) network רשת שידורי טלוויזיה reshet/reeshtot sheedoorey televeezyah
neuralgia 1. כאב ראש (headache) *nm* ke'ev/-ey rosh; **2.** נירלגיה *nf* neyralg|yah/-yot (+*of:* -yat).
neurology 1. תורת העצבים *nf* torat ha-'atsabeem; **2.** נוירולוגיה *nf* neyrologyah.
neurosis 1. עצבת *nf* 'ats|evet/-avot; **2.** נירוזה *nf* neyroz|ah/-ot (+*of:* -at).
neurotic נירוטי *adj* neyrotee/-t.
neuter 1. סתמי *adj* stamee/-t; **2.** מין סתמי (gram. gender) *nm* meen stamee.
neutral 1. סתמי *adj* stamee/-t; **2.** ניטרלי *adj* neytralee/-t.
neutralism מדיניות ניטרלית *nf* medeeneeyoot neytraleet.
neutrality ניטרליות *adj* neytraleeyoot.

(to) neutralize לנטרל *inf* lenatrel; *pst* neetrel; *pres* menatrel; *fut* yenatrel.

neutron ניטרון *nm* neytron/-eem (*pl+of:* -ey).

never 1. לעולם לא (future) *adv* le-'olam lo; **2.** מעולם לא (past) *adv* me-'olam lo.

never ending שלעולם איננו נגמר *adj* she-le-'olam eynen|oo/-ah neegm|ar/-eret.

never mind 1. אל תשים לב *v imp* al taseem/-ee lev; **2.** מבלי שים לב (paying no attention) *adv* mee-blee seem lev.

nevermore לא עוד *adv* lo 'od.

nevertheless 1. אף על פי כן af 'al pee khen; **2.** בכל זאת (for all that) be-khol *(kh=k)* zot.

new חדש *adj* khadash/-ah.

new arrival פנים חדשות *nm pl* paneem khadashot.

new moon מולד הירח *nm* molad ha-yare'akh.

New Testament הברית החדשה *nf* ha-breet ha-khadashah.

New World העולם החדש *nm* ha-'olam he-khadash.

New Year's card כרטיס ברכה לשנה החדשה *nm* kartees/-ey brakhah la-shanah ha-khadashah.

New Year's day אחד בינואר *nm* ekhad be-yanoo'ar.

New Year's Eve 1. ליל 31 בדצמבר (the night of December 31) *nm* leyl shlosheem ve-'ekhad be-detsember; **2.** ערב ראש השנה האזרחית (eve of the secular new year) *nm* 'erev rosh ha-shanah ha-ezrakheet; **3.** סילבסטר (party) *nm* seelvester.

New Year's greetings! ברכות לשנה החדשה! *nf pl* brakhot la-shanah ha-khadashah!

New Yorker 1. ניו־יורקי *nmf* nyoo-yorkee/-t; **2.** תושב ניו־יורק (N.Y. resident) *nmf* tosh|av/-evet (*pl:* -vey) nyoo-york.

newborn 1. רך נולד *nm* rakh nolad; **2.** שזה עתה נולד (born just now) *adj* she-zeh 'atah nol|ad/-dah.

newcomer חדש מקרוב בא *adj* khadash/-ah mee-karov ba/-'ah.

newfangled חדיש *adj* khadeesh/-ah.

newly לאחרונה *adv* la-akhronah.

newly arrived שהגיע לאחרונה *adj* she-heegee|'a'/-'ah la-akhronah.

newlywed שזה עתה נישא *adj* she-zeh 'atah nees|a/-'ah (*pl:* -'oo').

newness חידוש *nm* kheedoosh.

news 1. חדשה *nf* khadash|ah/-ot (*+of:* khadsh|at/-ot); **2.** ידיעה (news report) *nf* yedee|'ah/-'ot (*+of:* -'at).

news agency סוכנות חדשות *nf* sokhnoo|t/-yot khadashot.

news beat שטח סיקור *nm* shetakh/sheetkhey seekoor.

news conference מסיבת עיתונאים *nf* meseeb|at/-ot 'eetona'eem.

news coverage סיקור חדשות *nm* seekoor/-ey khadashot.

news service שירות חדשות *nm* sheroot/-ey khadashot.

newsboy מוכר עיתונים *nm* mokh|er/-rey 'eetoneem.

newscast שידור חדשות *nm* sheedoor/-ey khadashot.

newscaster 1. קריין *nmf* karyan/-eet; **2.** שדרן (broadcaster) *nmf* shadran/-eet.

newsman עיתונאי *nmf* 'eeton|ay/-a'eet (*pl:* -a'eem/-a'eeyot; *+of:* -a'ey).

newspaper עיתון *nm* 'eeton/-eem (*pl+of:* -ey).

newspaperman עיתונאי *nmf* 'eeton|ay/-a'eet (*pl:* -a'eem/-a'eeyot; *+of:* -a'ey).

newsprint נייר עיתון *nm* nyar 'eeton.

newsreel יומן קולנוע *nm* yoman/-ey kolno'a'.

newsstand קיוסק עיתונים *nm* kyosk/-ey 'eetoneem.

newsworthy ראוי לפירסום *adj* ra'ooy/re'ooyah le-feersoom *(f=p)*.

newsy שופע חדשות *adj & v pres* shof|e'a'/-a'at khadashot.

next 1. הבא בתור (following) *adj* ha-ba/-'ah ba-tor; **2.** הקרוב (coming) *adj* ha-karov/krovah; **3.** העתיד (future) *adj* he-'ateed/ha-'ateedah.

next best הבא אחריו לטיב *adj* ha-ba/ba'ah akhrav le-teev.

next door בית סמוך *nm* bayeet/bateem samookh/smookheem.

next in turn הבא בתור *adj* ha-ba/-'ah ba-tor.

(in the) next life 1. בעולם הבא *adv* ba-'olam ha-ba; **2.** בגלגול הבא (reincarnation) *adv* ba-geelgool ha-ba.

next of kin שאר בשר *nmf* she'er/-at (*pl:* she'er|ey/-ot) basar.

next to 1. על יד al yad; **2.** ליד (adjacent to) *prep* le-yad; **3.** סמוך ל־ (near to) *adv* samookh le-.

next week 1. השבוע הבא *nm* ha-shavoo'a' ha-ba; **2.** בשבוע הבא *adv* ba-shavoo'a' ha-ba.

next year 1. השנה הבאה *nf* ha-shanah ha-ba/-'ah; **2.** בשנה הבאה *adv* ba-shanah ha-ba'ah.

nibble 1. כרסום *nm* keersoom/-eem (*pl+of:* -ey); **2.** "ביס" *[slang] nm* bees/-eem (*pl+of:* -ey).

(to) nibble 1. לכרסם *inf* lekharsem; *pst* keersem *(k=kh)*; *pres* mekharsem; *fut* yekharsem; **2.** לנגוס (bite) *vt inf* leengos; *pst* nagas; *pres* noges; *fut* yeengos.

nice 1. יפה (goodlooking) *adj* yaf|eh/-ah; **2.** נחמד (lovely) *adj* nekhmad/-ah; **3.** נעים (pleasant) *adj* na'eem/ne'eemah; **4.** טעים (tasty) *adj* ta'eem/te'eemah.

nice-looking יפה תואר *adj* yef|eh/-at to'ar.

nicely יפה *adv* yafeh.

(to get along) nicely with להסתדר יפה עם *inf* leheestader yafeh 'eem; *pst* heestader *etc*; *pres* meestader *etc*; *fut* yeestader *etc*.

nicety 1. דקות *nf* dakoo|t/-yot; **2.** עדינות (delicacy) *nf* 'adeenoo|t/-yot; **3.** אבחנה דקה (fine distinction) *nf* avkhan|ah/-ot dak|ah/-ot.

niche גומחה *nf* goomkh|ah/-ot (*+of:* -at).

nick 1. חריץ *nm* khareets/-eem (*pl+of:* -ey); **2.** חתך קטן (small groove) *nm* khatakh/-eem katan/ketaneem.

(to) nick 1. לחרוץ *inf* lakhrots; *pst* kharats; *pres* khorets; *fut* yakhrots; **2.** לבקע (chip) *inf* levake/a'; *pst* beekee'a'; *pres* mevake/a'; *fut* yevake'a'.

(in the) nick of time 1. ברגע הנכון *adv* ba-rega' ha-nakhon; **2.** בדקה התשעים (in the very last minute) *[colloq.] adv* ba-dakah ha-teesh'eem.

nickel ניקל *nm* neekel/-eem (*pl+of:* -ey).

nickel-plated מצופה ניקל *adj* metsoop|eh/-ah neekel.
nick-nack תכשיט זעיר *nm* takh'sheet/-eem za'eer/ze'eereem.
nickname 1. כינוי *nm* keenoo|y/-yeem (*pl+of:* -yey); **2.** שם לוואי (sobriquet) *nm* shem/shmot levay.
nicotine ניקוטין *nm* neekoteen.
niece אחיינית *nf* akhyanee|t/-yot.
nifty הדור *adj* hadoor/-ah.
niggardly בקמצנות *adv* be-kamtsanoot.
night 1. לילה *nf* laylah/leylot (*+of:* leyl); **2.** ליל (poetic) *nm* layeel (*+of:* leyl).
(Good) Night! לילה טוב! laylah tov!
(tomorrow) night מחר בלילה *adv* makhar ba-laylah.
night club מועדון לילה *nm* mo'adon/-ey laylah.
night letter מברק לילה *nm* meevr|ak/-ekey laylah.
(the) night of ליל ה־ *nm* leyl/-ot ha-.
night owl ציפור לילה *nf* tseepor/-ey laylah
night time בשעות הלילה *adv* bee-she'ot ha-laylah.
night walker 1. משוטט בלילות *nmf* meshotet/-et ba-leylot; **2.** סהרורי (somnambulist) *nmf* saharooree/-t.
night watchman שומר לילה *nm* shom|er/-rey laylah.
nightcap כוסית בטרם שינה *nf* kosee|t/-yot be-terem sheynah.
nightfall רדת הלילה *nm* redet ha-laylah.
nightgown כתונת לילה *nf* keton|et/-ot laylah.
nightingale זמיר *nm* zameer/zmeer|eem (*pl+of:* -ey).
nightlong שנמשך כל הלילה *adj* she-neemsh|akh/-ekhet kol ha-laylah.
nightly מדי לילה *adv* meedey laylah
nightmare סיוט *nm* seeyoot/-eem (*pl+of:* -ey).
nightshirt כתונת לילה *nf* keton|et/-ot laylah.
nihilism ניהיליזם *nm* neeheeleezm/-eem (*pl+of:* -ey).
nihilist ניהיליסט *nmf* neeheeleest/-eet.
nil 1. אפס *adj* efes; **2.** לא כלום lo kheloom.
Nile הנילוס *nm* ha-neeloos.
nimble 1. מהיר *adj* maheer/meheerah; **2.** זריז (alert) *adj* zareez/zereezah.
nimbus הילה *nf* heel|ah/-ot (*+of:* -at).
nincompoop שוטה *nmf* shot|eh/-ah.
nine 1. תשעה (9) *num m* teesh'ah; **2.** תשע (9) *num f* tesha; **3.** ט *num* tet (9 in *Hebr. num. sys.*).
nine hundred 1. תשע מאות (900) *num* tesha' me'ot; **2.** תת״ק *num* tatak (900 in *Hebr. num. sys.*).
nine thousand 1. תשעת אלפים (9,000) *num* teesh'at alafeem; **2.** ט' אלפים *num* tet alafeem (9,000 in *Hebr. num. sys.*).
nineteen 1. תשעה־עשר (19) *num m* teesh'ah-'asar; **2.** תשע־עשרה (19) *num f* tesha' 'esreh; **3.** י״ט *num* yod-tet (19 in *Hebr. num. sys.*).
nineteen hundred אלף תשע מאות (thousand nine hundred) *num* elef oo-tesha' me'ot.
nineteenth 1. התשעה־עשר (19th) *adj m* ha-teesh'ah 'asar; **2.** התשע־עשרה (19th) *adj f* ha-tesha' 'esreh; **3.** הי״ט *adj* ha-yod-tet (the 19th in *Hebr. num. sys.*).
ninetieth 1. התשעים (the 90th) *adj* ha-teesh'eem; **2.** הצ' *adj* ha-tsadee (90th in *Hebr. num. sys.*).
ninety 1. תשעים (90) *num* teesh'eem; **2.** צ' *num* tsadee (90 in *Hebr. num. sys.*).
ninety-first 1. התשעים ואחד/ואחת *adj* ha-teesh'eem ve-ekhad/ve-akhat (*m/f*); **2.** הצ״א *adj* ha-tsadee-alef (91st in *Hebr. num. sys.*).
ninety-second 1. התשעים ושניים/ושתיים *adj num* ha-teesh'eem oo-shnayeem/oo-shtayeem (*m/f*); **2.** הצ״ב *adj* ha-tsadee-bet (92nd in *Hebr. num. sys.*).
ninety-third 1. התשעים ושלושה/ושלוש *ord num* ha-teesh'eem oo-shloshah/ve-shalosh (*m/f*); **2.** הצ״ג *adj* ha-tsadee-geemal (93rd in *Hebr. num. sys.*).
ninety-three 1. תשעים ושלושה/ושלוש *num* teesh'eem oo-shloshah/ve-shalosh (*m/f*); **2.** צ״ג *num* tsadee-geemal (93 in *Hebr. num. sys.*).
ninety-two 1. תשעים ושניים/ושתיים *num* teesh'eem oo-shnayeem/oo-shtayeem (*m/f*); **2.** צ״ב *num* tsadee-bet (92 in *Hebr. num. sys.*).
ninth 1. תשיעי (9th) *adj* teshee'ee/-t; **2.** תשיעית (1/9) *num f* teshee'ee|t/-yot; **3.** ט' *adj* tet (9th in *Hebr. num. sys.*).
nip צביטה *nf* tsveet|ah/-ot (*+of:* -at).
(to) nip לצבוט *inf* leetsbot; *pst* tsavat (*b=v*); *pres* tsovet; *fut* yeetsbot.
(to) nip off להסתלק מהר *inf* leheestalek maher; *pst* heestalek *etc*; *pres* meestalek *etc*; *fut* yeestalek *etc*.
nipple פטמה *nf* peetmah/petamot (*+of:* peetmat).
nippy 1. זריז *adj* zareez/zreezah; **2.** חרוץ (diligent) *adj* kharoots/-ah.
nitrate 1. חנקה *nf* khank|ah/-ot (*+of:* -at); **2.** ניטרט *nm* neetrat/-eem (*pl+of:* -ey).
nitric acid חומצת חנקן *nf* khoomtsat khankan.
nitrogen חנקן *nm* khankan.
nitroglycerin, nitroglycerine ניטרוגליצרין *nm* neetrogleetsereen.
nitwit 1. טיפש *nmf* teep|esh/-shah; **2.** חסר שכל *adj* khas|ar/-rat sekhel.
no 1. לא lo; **2.** שאינו (un) -adj she-eyn|o/-ah; **3.** אל־ (non-) al-.
(I have) no friend אין לי אף ידיד eyn lee af yedeed.
no longer שוב לא *adv* shoov lo.
no matter how much כמה שזה לא יהיה *adj* kamah she-zeh lo yeehyeh.
no more 1. לא יותר (quantity) *adv* lo yoter; **2.** לא עוד (time) *adv* lo 'od.
no one 1. אף לא אחד *adj* af lo ekhad/akhat; **2.** אף אחד *[colloq.] adj* af ekhad/akhat.
no smoking! לא לעשן! lo le'ashen.
no use 1. לא יעזור lo ya'azor; **2.** אין תועלת eyn to'elet.
(of) no use 1. חסר שימוש *adj* khas|ar/-rat sheemoosh; **2.** ללא תועלת (uselessly) *adv* le-lo to'elet.
Noah's ark תיבת נוח *nf* teyvat no'akh.
nobby מפונדרק *slang adj* mefoondr|ak/-eket.

nobility 1. אצולה *nf* atsool|ah/-ot (*+of:* -at); **2.** אצילות *nf* atseeloo|t/-yot.
noble 1. אציל *nm* atseel/-eem; **2.** אציל נפש *adj* atseel/-at nefesh; **3.** אצילי *adj* atseelee/-t; **4.** נאצל (ennobled) *adj* ne'ets|al/-elet.
nobleman אציל *nm* atseel/-eem (*pl+of:* -ey).
nobody 1. שום איש shoom eesh; **2.** אף אדם (no person) af adam.
nocturnal לילי *adj* leylee/-t.
nod מנוד ראש *nm* menod rosh.
(to) nod להניד ראש *inf* lehaneed rosh; *pst* heneed *etc; pres* meneed *etc; fut* yaneed *etc.*
node 1. בליטה *nf* bleet|ah/-ot (*+of:* -at); **2.** כפתור (knob) *nm* kaftor/-eem (*pl+of:* -ey); **3.** קשר (contact) *nm* kesh|er/-areem (*pl+of:* keeshrey).
no-how בשום אופן *adv* be-shoom ofen.
noise רעש *nm* ra'ash/re'asheem (*pl+of:* ra'ashey).
(to) noise 1. להקים רעש *vt inf* lehakeem ra'ash; *pst* hekeem *etc; pres* mekeem *etc; fut* yakeem *etc;* **2.** לרעוש *vi inf* leer'osh; *pst* ra'ash; *pres* ro'esh; *fut* yeer'ash.
noiseless 1. לא רועש *adj* lo ro'esh/-et; **2.** שקט (quiet) *adj* shaket/sh'ketah.
noiselessly ללא רעש le-lo ra'ash.
noisily ברעש *adv* be-ra'ash.
noisy רועש *adj* ro'esh/-et.
nomad נווד *nm* navad/-eem (*pl+of:* -ey).
nomadic נודד *adj* noded/-et.
no man's land שטח הפקר *nm* shetakh/sheetkhey hefker.
nominal 1. שמי *adj* shemee/-t; **2.** על שם *adj* 'al shem; **3.** נומינלי *adj* nomeenalee/-t; **4.** שמני (grammar) *adj* shemanee/-t.
(to) nominate 1. להציע מועמד *inf* lehatsee'a' moo'am|ad/-edet; *pst* heetsee'a' *etc; pres* matsee'a' *etc; fut* yatsee'a' *etc;* **2.** למנות (appoint) *inf* lemanot; *pst* meenah; *pres* memaneh; *fut* yemaneh.
nomination בחירת מועמד *nf* bekheer|at/-ot moo'amad.
nominative 1. ממונה (appointed) *adj* memoon|eh/-ah; **2.** כולל שם (naming) *adj* kolel/-et shem/-ot; **3.** נומינטיב (grammar) *nm* nomeenateev/-eem.
nominee מיועד לתפקיד *nm* meyo|'ad/-'edet le-tafkeed.
non-belligerent שאינו צד לוחם *adj* she-en|o/-ah tsad lokhem.
nonchalance לא־אכפתיות *nf* lo-eekhpateeyoot.
nonchalant לא אכפתי *adj* lo eekhpatee/-t.
noncombatant שאינו צד לוחם *adj* she-eyno tsad lokhem.
noncommissioned officer 1. נגד *nm* nagad/-eem (*pl+of:* -ey); **2.** מפקד שאינו קצין (commander who is not an officer) *nm* mefaked she-'eyno katseen; **3.** מש"ק (*acr of* 2) *nmf* mashak/-eet (*pl:* -eem; *+of:* -ey).
noncommittal שאינו מחייב *adj* she-eyn|o/-ah mekhayev/-et.
nonconformist 1. מורד במוסכמות *nmf* mored/-et be-mooskamot; **2.** שאינו סתגלן *adj* she-eyn|o/-ah staglan/-eet.
nondescript קשה־תיאור *adj* kesh|eh/-at te'oor.
none 1. שום *nm* shoom; **2.** אף לא אחד (nobody) af lo ekhad/akhat.
none of his business אין זה עסקו eyn zeh 'eesk|o/-ah *(m/f).*
(we want) none of that זה לא ייתכן zeh lo yeetakhen.
none the happier that לא מאושר מזה ש־ lo me'oosh|ar/-eret *(m/f)* mee-zeh she-.
none the less על אף זאת 'al af zot.
nonentity 1. אפס *nm* efes/afaseem (*pl+of:* afsey). **2.** כלומ'ניק *[colloq.] nmf* kloomneek/-eet.
nonfiction ספרי עיון *nm pl* seefrey 'eeyoon.
nonfulfillment אי־ביצוע *nm* ee-beetsoo'a'.
nonintervention אי־התערבות *nf* ee heet'arvoot.
nonmetallic אל־מתכתי *adj* al-matakhtee/-t.
nonpartisan 1. בלתי מפלגתי *adj* beeltee meeflagtee/-t; **2.** בלתי מעורב (not involved) *adj* beeltee me'or|av/-evet.
(to) nonplus להביך *inf* lehaveekh; *pst* heveekh; *pres* meveekh; *fut* yaveekh.
nonprofit ללא רווח *adj* le-lo revakh.
nonresident לא־תושב *adj* lo toshav.
nonresidential שלא למגורים *adj* she-lo lee-megooreem.
nonscientific לא מדעי *adj* lo mada'ee/-t.
nonsectarian אל־כיתתי *adj* al-keetatee/-t.
nonsense 1. חוסר היגיון *nm* khoser heegayon; **2.** שטויות (trifles) *nf pl* shtooyot.
nonsensical לא הגיוני *adj* lo hegyonee/-t.
non-skid מונע החלקה *adj* mon|e'a'/-a'at hakhlakah.
nonstop 1. בלתי פוסק *adj* beeltee posek/-et; **2.** ישיר (direct) *adj* yasheer/yesheerah; **3.** ללא הפסק (ceaselessly) *adv* le-lo hefsek.
noodle אטרייה *nf* eetree|yah/-yot (*+of:* -yat).
nook 1. פינה *nf* peen|ah/-ot (*+of:* -at); **2.** פינה נידחת (forgotten corner) *nf* peenah needakhat.
noon 1. צהריים tsohorayeem; **2.** צהרי יום (noontime) *nm pl* tsohorey yom.
noonday צהרי יום *nm pl* tsohorey yom.
noonday meal ארוחת צהריים *nf* arookh|at/-ot tsohorayeem.
no-one אף אחד *adj* af ekhad/akhat.
noontide, noontime שעות צהריים *nf pl* she'ot tsohorayeem.
noose 1. לולאה *nf* loola|'ah/-'ot; **2.** עניבת תלייה (hanging loop) *nf* 'aneev|at/-ot teleeyah.
nor אף לא af lo.
Nordic צפוני tsefonee/-t.
norm 1. תקן *nm* teken/tekaneem (*pl+of:* teekney); **2.** נורמה *nf* norm|ah/-ot (*+of:* -at).
normal 1. תקין *adj* takeen/tekeenah; **2.** נורמלי *adj* normalee/-t.
north צפון *nm* tsafon.
North Africa צפון־אפריקה *nm* tsefon-afreekah.
North-African צפון־אפריקני *nmf & adj* tsefon-afreekanee/-t.
North America אמריקה צפון *nf* tsefon amereekah.
North American צפון־אמריקני *nm* tsefon-amereekanee/-t.
north wind רוח צפונית *nf* roo|'akh/-khot tsefonee|t/-yot.
northern צפוני *adj* tsefonee/-t.

northward צפונה *adv* tsafonah.
northwest צפון־מערב *nm* tsefon-ma'arav.
northwestern צפון־מערבי *adj* tsefon ma'aravee/-t.
Norway נורבגיה *nf* norvegyah.
Norwegian 1. נורבגי *adj* norvegee/-t (*pl:* -eeyeem/-eeyot); **2.** נורבגי (person) *nmf* norvegee/-t (*pl:* -eem/-eeyot); **3.** נורבגית (language) *nf* norvegeet.
nose 1. אף *nm* af/apeem (*p=f; pl+of:* apey); **2.** חוטם (synon. with 1) *nm* khot|em/-ameem (*pl+of:* -mey).
(to) nose 1. להביס בהפרש קטן (defeat by a narrow margin) *inf* lehavees be-hefresh katan; *pst* hevees *etc; pres* mevees *etc; fut* yavees *etc;* **2.** לחטט (pry) *inf* lekhatet; *pst* kheetet; *pres* mekhatet; *fut* yekhatet.
(to) nose around לרחרח *inf* lerakhre'akh; *pst* reekhre'akh; *pres* merakhre'akh; *fut* yerakhre'akh.
nosebag שק מספוא *nm* sak/-ey meespo.
nosebleed דימום מהאף *nm* deemoom/-eem me-ha-af.
nosedive צלילת מטוס *nf* tsleel|at/-ot matos/metoseem.
nosegay צרור פרחים *nm* tsror/-ot prakheem.
nose-ring נזם אף *nm* nezem/neezmey af.
nostalgia 1. געגועים לימים עברו *nm pl* ga'goo'eem le-yameem 'avaroo; **2.** נוסטלגיה *nf* nostalg|yah/-yot (*+of:* -yat).
nostalgic נוסטלגי *adj* nostalgee/-t.
nostril נחיר *nm* nekheer/-ayeem (*pl+of:* -ey).
nosy חטטני *adj* khatetanee/-t.
not לא lo.
not at all לגמרי לא *adv* le-gamrey lo.
not at all sure 1. לגמרי לא בטוח *adv* le-gamrey lo batoo'akh; **2.** לגמרי לא בטוח *adj* le-gamrey lo batoo'akh/betookhah.
not even a word אף לא מלה af lo meelah.
notable 1. ראוי לציון *adj* ra'ooy/re'ooyah le-tseeyoon; **2.** נכבד *nm* neekhb|ad/-adeem (*pl+of:* -edey).
(to) notarize 1. לקיים *vt inf* lekayem; *pst* keeyem; *pres* mekayem; *fut* yekayem; **2.** לאשר (authenticate) *inf* le'asher; *pst* eesher; *pres* me'asher; *fut* ye'asher.
notary נוטריון *nm* notaryon/-eem (*pl+of:* -ey).
(public) notary נוטריון ציבורי *nm* notaryon tseeboorее.
notch חריץ *nm* khareets/-eem (*pl+of:* -ey).
(to) notch לחרוץ *inf* lakhrots; *pst* kharats; *pres* khorets; *fut* yakhrots.
note 1. פתק *nm* pet|ek/-akeem (*pl+of:* peetkey); **2.** רשימה (memo) *nf* resheem|ah/-ot (*+of:* -at); **3.** צליל (musical) *nm* tsleel/-eem (*pl+of:* -ey).
(bank) note 1. שטר כסף *nm* shtar/sheetrey kesef; **2.** בנקנוטה *nf* banknot|ah/-ot (*+of:* -at).
(promissory) note שטר חוב *nm* shtar/sheetrey khov.
(to) note 1. לציין *inf* letsayen; *pst* tseeyen; *pres* metsayen; *fut* yetsayen; **2.** להבחין (distinguish) *inf* lehavkheen; *pst* heevkheen; *pres* mavkheen; *fut* yavkheen.
(to) note down לרשום *inf* leershom; *pst* rasham; *pres* roshem; *fut* yeershom.
notebook 1. מחברת *nf* makhb|eret/-arot; **2.** פנקס *nm* peenk|as/-aseem (*pl+of:* -esey).
noted מוכר *adj* mook|ar/-eret.
notepaper נייר מכתבים *nm* neyar meekhtaveem.
noteworthy ראוי לציון *adj* ra'ooy/re'ooyah le-tseeyoon.
nothing לא כלום lo khloom *(kh=k)*.
notice 1. הודעה מראש *nf* hoda|'ah/-'ot me-rosh. **2.** התראה *nf* hatra|'ah/-'ot (*+of:* -'at).
(short) notice הודעה ברגע האחרון *nf* hoda|'ah/-'ot ba-rega' ha-akhron.
(to) notice להבחין *inf* lehavkheen; *pst* heevkheen; *pres* mavkheen; *fut* yavkheen.
(to) take notice of לקבל לתשומת לב *inf* lekabel lee-tesoomet lev; *pst* keebel *etc; pres* mekabel *etc; fut* yekabel *etc.*
noticeable מורגש *adj* moorg|ash/-eshet.
(to) notify להודיע *inf* lehodee/a'; *pst* hodee/a'; *pres* modee/a'; *fut* yodee'a'.
notion מושג *nm* moosag/-eem (*pl+of:* -ey).
notoriety שם רע *nm* shem ra'.
notorious נודע לשמצה *adj* nod|a'/-a'at le-sheemtsah.
no-trump לא "מציאה" *[colloq.] adj* lo "metsee'ah".
notwithstanding 1. על אף *conj* 'al af; **2.** שלא בהתאם (not conform) *adv* she-lo be-het'em; **3.** בניגוד ל־ (contrary to) *adv* be-neegood le-.
nought אפס *nm* efes.
noun שם עצם *nm* shem/shmot 'etsem.
(to) nourish 1. להזין *inf* lehazeen; *pst* hezeen; *pres* mezeen; *fut* yazeen; **2.** לטפח (cultivate) *inf* letape'akh; *pst* teepakh; *pres* metape'akh; *fut* yetapakh.
nourishing מזין *adj* mezeen/-ah.
nourishment מזון *nm* mazon/mezonot (*+of:* mezon).
novel 1. רומן *nm* roman/-eem (*pl+of:* -ey); **2.** חדשני *adj* khadshanee/t.
novelist מחבר רומנים *nmf* mekhaber/-et romaneem.
novelty חידוש *nm* kheedoosh/-eem (*pl+of:* -ey).
November נובמבר *nm* november.
novice טירון *nmf* teeron/-eet.
novocaine נובוקאין *nm* novokayeen.
now 1. עכשיו *adv* 'akhshav; **2.** עתה *adv* 'atah; **3.** כעת (at this time) *adv* ka-'et.
(he left just) now רק הרגע יצא rak ha-rega' yatsa.
now and then מפעם לפעם *adv* mee-pa'am le-fa'am *(f=p)*.
now that עתה כאשר *adv* 'atah ka-asher
nowadays בימינו *adv* be-yameynoo.
noway, noways בשום דרך *adv* be-shoom derekh.
nowhere בשום מקום *adv* be-shoom makom.
noxious מזיק *adj* mazeek/-ah.
nozzle זרבובית *nf* zarboovee|t/-yot.
nuance גוון *nm* gaven/gvaneem (*+of:* gon/-ey).
nub בליטה *nf* bleet|ah/-ot (*+of:* -at).
nubile בשלה להינשא *adj f* beshel|ah/-ot leheenase.
nuclear גרעיני *adj* gar'eenee/-t.
nucleus גרעין *nm* gar'een/-eem (*pl+of:* -ey).
nude 1. עירום *nm* 'er|om/-oomeem (*pl+of:* -oomey); **2.** ערום (naked) *adj* 'ar|om/-oomah; **3.** מעורטל (undressed) *adj* me'oort|al/-elet.

nudge דחיפה קלה *nf* dekheef|ah/-ot kal|ah/-ot.
(to) nudge לנגוע קלות *inf* leengo'a' kalot; *pst* naga' *etc; pres* noge'a' *etc; fut* yeega' *etc.*
nugget גוש מתכת יקרה *nm* goosh/-ey matekhet yekarah.
nuisance מטרד *nm* meetr|ad/-adeem (*pl+of:* -edey).
null בטל *adj* batel/betelah.
(to) nullify לבטל *inf* levatel; *pst* beetel *(b=v); pres* mevatel; *fut* yevatel.
nullity 1. אפסות *nf* afsoo|t/-yot; **2.** ביטול (annulment) *nm* beetool/-eem (*pl+of:* -ey).
numb חסר תחושה *adj* khas|ar/-rat tekhooshah.
(to) numb להקהות חושים *inf* lehak'hot khoosheem; *pst* heek'hah *etc; pres* mak'heh *etc; fut* yak'heh *etc.*
number מספר *nm* meesp|ar/-areem (*pl+of:* -erey).
(to) number 1. למנות *vt inf* leemnot; *pst* manah; *pres* moneh; *fut* yeemneh; **2.** להימנות (count among) *vi inf* leheemanot 'eem; *pst* neemnah 'eem; *pres* neemneh 'eem; *fut* yeemaneh 'eem.
(to) number among לכלול בין *inf* lekhlol beyn; *pst* kalal *(k=kh) etc; pres* kolel *etc; fut* yeekhlol *etc (k=kh).*
numberless 1. לא ייספר *adj* lo yeesafer/teesafer; **2.** לאין ספור (countless) *adv* le-eyn sfor.
numeral 1. מספרי *adj* meesparee/-t; **2.** סיפרה (digit) *nf* seefrah/sefarot (*+of:* seefr|at/-ot).
numerical מספרי *adj* meesparee/-t.
numerous מרובה *adj* meroob|eh/-ah.
numskull טיפש *nm* teep|esh/-sheem (*pl+of:* -shey)
nun נזירה *nf* nezeer|ah/-ot (*+of:* -at).
nuptial של נישואים *adj* shel neesoo'eem.
nurse 1. אחות רחמנייה *nf* akh|ot/-ayot rakhmanee|yah/-yot; **2.** אחות *[colloq.] abbr. nf* akh|ot/-ayot (*pl+of:* -yot); **3.** מטפלת (nanny) *nf* metap|elet/-lot; **4.** אומנת (governess) *nf* om|enet/-not.
(to) nurse 1. לטפל *inf* letapel; *pst* teepel; *pres* metapel; *fut* yetapel; **2.** להניק *vt f inf* lehaneek; *pst* heneekah; *pres* meneekah; *fut* taneek.
(wet) nurse מינקת *nf* meyneket.
nursery 1. חדר תינוקות *nm* khad|ar/-rey teenokot; **2.** מעון לתינוקות *nm* ma'on/me'onot le-teenokot; **3.** גנון (pre-kindergarten) *nm* ganon/-eem (*pl+of:* -ey).
nursery school גן ילדים *nm* gan/-ey yeladeem.
nurseryman בעל משתלה *nm* ba'al/-ey meeshtal|ah/-ot (*cpr:* mashtel|ah/-ot).
nursing bottle בקבוק הנקה *nm* bakbook/-ey hanakah.
nursing home 1. בית־חולים פרטי *nm* bet/batey kholeem pratee/-yeem; **2.** בית אבות (old age home) *nm* bet/batey avot.
(to) nurture 1. לזון *inf* lazoon; *pst & pres* zan; *fut* yazoon; **2.** לכלכל (feed) *inf* lekhalkel; *pst* keelkel *(k=kh); pres* mekhalkel; *fut* yekhalkel.
nut 1. אגוז *nm* egoz/-eem (*pl+of:* -ey); **2.** אום (screw-nut) *nm* om/oomeem (*pl+of:* oomey); **3.** תמהוני (eccentric) *nmf* teemhonee/-t.
nutcracker מפצח אגוזים *nm* maftse|'akh/-khey egozeem.
nutmeg אגוז מוסקט *nm* egoz/-ey mooskat.
nutrient יסוד מזין *nm* yesod/-ot mezeen/-eem.
nutriment מזון *nm* mazon/mezonot (*+of:* mezon).
nutrition תזונה *nf* tezoon|ah/-ot (*+of:* -at).
nutritious מזין *adj* mezeen/-ah.
nuts מטורף (crazy) *nmf & adj* metor|af/-efet.
nutshell 1. קליפת אגוז *nf* kleep|at/-ot egoz; **2.** תמצית (gist) *nf* tamtsee|t/-yot.
nutty 1. מטורף *adj* metor|af/-efet; **2.** מלא אגוזים (full of nuts) *adj* male/mele'at egozeem.
(to) nuzzle לנבור באף *inf* leenbor ba-af; *pst* navar *etc (b=v); pres* nover *etc; fut* yeenbor *etc.*
nylon ניילון *nm* naylon/-eem (*pl+of:* -ey).
nymph 1. בתולת ים (mythological) *nf* betool|at/-ot yam; **2.** נימפה *nf* neemf|ah/-ot (*+of:* -at).

O.

O,o when pronounced as in *so, more* or *for*, is transliterated by ו (Vav). At the beginning of a word it will be preceded by א (Aleph) או.
oak 1. אלון *nm* alon/-eem (*pl+of:* -ey); **2.** עץ אלון (wood) *nm* 'ets alon.
oar משוט *nm* mashot/meshot|eem (*pl+of:* -ey).
oarsman משוטאי *nm* meshot|ay/-a'eem (*pl+of:* -a'ey).
oasis 1. נאות מדבר *nf* ne'ot meedbar; **2.** נווה מדבר (syn) *nm* neveh meedbar.
oat שיבולת־שועל *nf* sheebolet shoo'al.
oath שבועה *nf* shvoo|'ah/-'ot (*+of:* -'at).
oatmeal קמח שיבולת־שועל *nm* kemakh sheebolet shoo'al.
obedience 1. ציות *nm* tseeyoot/-eem (*pl+of:* -ey); **2.** צייתנות (submissiveness) *nf* tsaytanoo|t/-yot.
obedient צייתן *adj* tsaytan/-eet
obesity שומן גוף *nm* shomen goof.
(to) obey לציית *inf* letsayet; *pst* tseeyet; *pres* metsayet; *fut* yetsayet.
obituary 1. מודעת אבל *nf* mod|a'at/-'ot evel; **2.** נקרולוג *nm* nekrolog/-eem.

object 1. חפץ *nm* khefets/khafatseem *(pl+of:* kheftsey); **2.** תכלית (purpose) *nf* takhleet; **3.** מושא *(gram.) nm* moosa/-'eem *(pl+of:* -'ey).

(to) object 1. לערור *inf* la'aror; *pst* 'arar; *pres* 'orer; *fut* ya'aror; **2.** להתנגד (oppose) *inf* leheetnaged; *pst* heetnaged; *pres* meetnaged; *fut* yeetnaged.

objection הסתייגות *nf* heestaygoo|t/-yot.

objectionable מעורר הסתייגות *adj* me'orer/-et heestaygoot.

objective 1. מטרה *nf* matar|ah/-ot (+of: -at); **2.** חסר־פניות (unbiased) *adj* khas|ar/-rat peneeyot; **3.** אובייקטיבי *adj* obyekteevee/-t.

objectively באופן אובייקטיבי *adv* be-ofen obyekteevee.

obligation 1. חובה *nf* khov|ah/-ot (+of: -at); **2.** התחייבות (undertaking) *nf* heetkhayvoo|t/-yot.

(under) obligation to תוך התחייבות ל־ *adv* tokh heetkhayvoot le-.

obligatory מחייב *adj* mekhayev/-et.

(to) oblige 1. לחייב *inf* lekhayev; *pst* kheeyev; *pres* mekhayev; *fut* yekhayev; **2.** להכריח (coerce) *inf* lehakhree'akh; *pst* heekhree'akh; *pres* makhree'akh; *fut* yakhree'akh; **3.** לעשות טובה (do favor) *inf* la'asot tovah; *pst* 'asah *etc*; *pres* 'oseh *etc*; *fut* ya'aseh *etc*.

obliged 1. מחויב *adj* mekhoo|yav/-yevet; **2.** נאלץ (compelled) *adj* ne'el|ats/-etset.

(very much) obliged מאוד אסיר תודה *adj* me'od aseer/-at todah.

obliging 1. מיטיב *adj* meteev/-ah; **2.** גומל טובה (reciprocating) *adj* gomel/-et tovah.

oblique 1. אלכסון *adj* alakhson/-eet; **2.** משופע (inclined) *adj* meshoop|a'/-a'at.

(to) obliterate 1. למחות *inf* leemkhot; *pst* makhah; *pres* mokheh; *fut* yeemkheh; **2.** להכחיד (annihilate) *inf* lehakh'kheed; *pst* heekh'kheed; *pres* makh'kheed; *fut* yakh'kheed.

oblivion 1. שיכחה *nf* sheekhekh|ah/-ot (+of: -at); **2.** התעלמות (overlooking) *nf* heet'almoo|t/-yot.

oblivious 1. מתעלם *v pres & adj* meet'alem/-et; **2.** שאינו חש *adj* she-eyn|o/-ah khash/-ah.

oblong 1. מלבן *nm* malben/-eem *(pl+of:* -ey); **2.** מלבני (rectangular) *adj* malbenee/-t; **3.** מוארך (protracted) *adj* mo'or|akh/-ekhet.

obloquy לעז *nm* la'az.

obnoxious נתעב *adj* neet|'av/-'evet.

oboe אבוב *nm* aboov/-eem *(pl+of:* -ey).

obscene 1. מגונה *adj* megoon|eh/-ah; **2.** של זימה (lecherous) *adj* shel zeemah.

obscenity 1. תועבה *nf* to'ev|ah/-ot (+of: -at); **2.** ניבול פה (profanity) *nm* neebool/-ey peh.

obscure 1. אפל *adj* afel/-ah; **2.** מעורפל (foggy) *adj* me'oorp|al/-elet; **3.** סתום (not clear) *adj* satoom/stoomah.

(to) obscure 1. לערפל *inf* le'arpel; *pst* 'eerpel; *pres* me'arpel; *fut* ye'arpel; **2.** להסתיר (hide) *inf* lehasteer; *pst* heesteer; *pres* masteer; *fut* yasteer.

obscurity 1. אפילה *nf* afel|ah/-ot (+of: -at); **2.** אי־בהירות (vagueness) *nf* ee-beheeroo|t/-yot.

obsequies טקס קבורה *nm* tekes/teeksey kevoorah.

obsequious מתרפס *adj* meetrapes/-et.

observable 1. ניכר (noticeable) *adj* neek|ar/-eret; **2.** בולט (conspicuous) *adj* bolet/-et.

observance 1. קיום מצוות *nm* keeyoom meetsvot; **2.** שמירת חוק (law-abidance) *nf* shmeerat khok.

observant 1. שומר מצוות *nmf & adj* shomer/-et meetsvot; **2.** דתי *nmf & adj* datee/-t.

observation 1. הסתכלות *nf* heestakloo|t/-yot; **2.** הערה (remark) *nf* he'ar|ah/-ot (+of: -at).

observatory מצפה כוכבים *nm* meetsp|eh/-ey kokhaveem.

(to) observe 1. לקיים *inf* lekayem; *pst* keeyem; *pres* mekayem; *fut* yekayem; **2.** להעיר (remark) *inf* leha'eer; *pst* he'eer; *pres* me'eer; *fut* ya'eer; **3.** להבחין (distinguish) *inf* lehavkheen; *pst* heevkheen; *pres* mavkheen; *fut* yavkheen.

observer משקיף *nm* mashkeef/-eem *(pl+of:* -ey).

(to) obsess להשתלט על *inf* leheeshtalet 'al; *pst* heeshtalet 'al; *pres* meeshtalet 'al; *fut* yeeshtalet 'al.

obsession שיגעון לדבר אחד *nm* sheega'on le-davar ekhad.

obsolete 1. שיצא מכלל שימוש *adj* she-yats|a/-'ah mee-klal sheemoosh; **2.** מיושן (outmoded) *adj* meyoosh|an/-enet.

obstacle מכשול *nm* meekhshol/-eem *(pl+of:* -ey).

obstetrician רופא מיילד *nm* rof|e-'eem meyal|ed/-deem.

obstinacy עקשנות *nf* 'akshanoo|t/-yot.

obstinate 1. עיקש *adj* 'eekesh/-et; **2.** עקשני (stubborn) *adj* 'akshanee/-t.

obstreperous 1. רעשני *adj* ra'ashanee/-t; **2.** פרוע (unruly) *adj* paroo'a'/proo'ah.

(to) obstruct 1. להכשיל *inf* lehakh'sheel; *pst* heekh'sheel; *pres* makh'sheel; *fut* yakh'sheel; **2.** לחסום (block) *inf* lakhsom; *pst* khasam; *pres* khosem; *fut* yakhsom.

obstruction 1. הפרעה *nf* hafra|'ah/-'ot (+of: -'at); **2.** מניעה (hindrance) *nf* menee|'ah/-'ot (+of: -'at).

obstructive מפריע *adj* mafree|'a'/-'ah.

(to) obtain 1. להשיג (procure) *inf* lehaseeg; *pst* heeseeg; *pres* maseeg; *fut* yaseeg; **2.** לרכוש (acquire) leerkosh; *pst* rakhash *(k=kh)*; *pres* rokhesh; *fut* yeerkosh.

obtainable ניתן להשגה *adj* neet|an/-enet le-hasagah.

obtrusive קופץ בראש *adj* kofets/-et be-rosh.

obtuse קהה (blunt) keheh/kehah.

(to) obviate 1. למנוע *inf* leemno'a; *pst* mana'; *pres* mone'a; *fut* yeemna'; **2.** להרחיק (avert) *inf* leharkheek; *pst* heerkheek; *pres* markheek; *fut* yarkheek.

obvious 1. ברור *adj* baroor/broorah; **2.** מובהק (patent) *adj* moov|hak/-heket.

occasion 1. מועד (timely) *nm* mo'ed/mo'ad|eem *(pl+of:* -ey); **2.** סיבה (cause) *nf* seeb|ah/-ot (+of: -at); **3.** הזדמנות (chance) *nf* heezdamnoo|t/-yot; **4.** אירוע (event) *nm* eeroo|'a'/-'eem *(pl+of:* -'ey).

(to) occasion לזמן *inf* lezamen; *pst* zeemen; *pres* mezamen; *fut* yezamen.

occasional 1. מקרי *adj* meekree/-t; **2.** ארעי (provisional) *adj* ara'ee/-t.

occasionally לעתים מזומנות *adv* le-'eeteem mezoomanot.

occidental מערבי *adj* ma'aravee/-t.

occlusive 1. אוטם *adj* otem/-et; **2.** חוסם (blocking) *adj* khosem/-et.

occult מסתורי *adj* meestoree/-t.

occupancy 1. החזקה *nf* hakhzak|ah/-ot (*+of:* -at); **2.** תקופת דיור (length of tenancy) *nf* tekoof|at/-ot deeyoor.

occupant 1. מחזיק *nmf* makhzeek/-ah; **2.** דייר (tenant) *nmf* dayar/dayeret (*pl:* dayar|eem; *+of:* -ey).

occupation 1. משלח יד *nm* meeshlakh yad; **2.** כיבוש (military) *nm* keeboosh/-eem (*pl+of:* -ey); **3.** תפיסה (takeover) *nf* tfees|ah/-ot (*+of:* -at).

(to) occupy 1. לתפוס *inf* leetpos; *pst* tafas (*f=p*); *pres* tofes; *fut* yeetpos; **2.** להעסיק (preoccupy) *inf* leha'aseek; *pst* he'eseek; *pres* ma'aseek; *fut* ya'aseek.

(to) occur להתרחש *inf* leheetrakhesh; *pst* heetrakhesh; *pres* meetrakhesh; *fut* yeetrakhesh.

(to) occur to לקרות ל־ *inf* leekrot le-; *pst* karah le-; *pres* koreh le-; *fut* yeekreh le-.

occurrence התרחשות *nf* heetrakhshoo|t/-yot.

ocean אוקיינוס *nm* okyanos/-eem (*pl+of:* -ey).

o'clock לפי השעון lefee ha-sha'on.

octave אוקטבה *nf* oktav|ah/-ot (*+of:* -at).

October אוקטובר *nm* oktober.

octopus תמנון *nm* tmanoon (*cpr* tamnoon)/-eem (*pl+of:* -ey).

ocular של העין *adj* shel ha-'ayeen

oculist 1. רופא עיניים *nmf* rofe/-t 'eynayeem; **2.** אופטיקאי *nm* opteek|ay/-a'eem (*pl+of:* -a'ey).

odd 1. מוזר *adj* moozar/-ah; **2.** תמהוני (queer) *nm* teemhonee/-m; **3.** לא־זוגי (uneven) *adj* lo-zoogee/-t.

(thirty) odd שלושים ומעלה *num & adj* shlosheem va-ma'lah

odd change פרוטרוט *nm* protrot.

odd moments רגעי פנאי *nm pl* reeg'ey penay.

odd shoe נעל בודדת *nf* na'al/-ayeem boded|et/-ot.

odd volume כרך בודד *nm* kerekh/krakheem boded/-eem.

oddity 1. דבר מוזר *nm* davar/dvareem moozar/-eem; **2.** קוריוז (curiosity) *nm* kooryoz/-eem (*pl+of:* -ey).

oddly באורח מוזר *adv* be-orakh moozar.

odds 1. הסתברות *nf* heestabroo|t/-yot; **2.** יתרון (advantage) *nm* yeet|ron/-ot.

(against) odds מול חזקים ממנו *adv* mool khazakeem meemenoo.

odds and ends 1. פריטים שונים *nm pl* preeteem shoneem; **2.** שיירים (remnants) *nm pl* shyar|eem (*pl+of:* -ey).

(at) odds with חלוק על *adj* khalook/-ah 'al.

ode 1. שיר הלל *nm* sheer/-ey halel; **2.** אודה *nf* od|ah/-ot (*+of:* -at).

odious 1. שנוא *adj* sanoo/snoo'ah; **2.** גועלי (disgusting) *adj* go'alee/-t.

odor ריח *nm* rey|'akh/-khot.

(bad) odor ריח רע *nm* rey|'akh/-khot ra'/ra'eem.

odorous מדיף ריח *v pres & adj* madeef/-at rey'akh.

of 1. של *prep* shel; **2.** מן (from) *prep* meen; **3.** מ־ (abbr.of 2) mee-, me-.

(taste) of טעם של *nm* ta'am shel.

(to smell) of להדיף ריח *inf* lehadeef rey'akh; *pst* heedeef *etc*; *pres* madeef *etc*; *fut* yadeef *etc*.

of course כמובן *adv* ka-moovan.

of late לאחרונה *adv* la-akhronah.

off 1. מרוחק (distant) *adj* merookh|ak/-eket; **2.** בחופש (not tied up) *adv* be-khofesh.

(ten shekels) off עשרה שקלים פחות *num & adv* 'asarah shekaleem pakhot.

(ten kms off) במרחק עשרה קילומטרים *adv & num* be-merkhak 'asarah keelometreem.

(a day) off יום חופש *nm* yom khofesh.

(right) off מיד *adv* meeyad.

(to take) off 1. להסיר *inf* lehaseer; *pst* heseer; *pres* meseer; *fut* yaseer; **2.** להמריא (plane) *inf* lehamree; *pst* heemree; *pres* mamree; *fut* yamree.

(with his hat) off 1. כשהוא מסיר את הכובע ke-she-hoo meseer et ha-kova'; **2.** גלוי ראש (bareheaded) *adj* gloo|y/-yat rosh.

(the electricity is) off אין חשמל eyn khashmal.

(to be) off להסתלק *inf* leheestalek; *pst* heestalek; *pres* meestalek; *fut* yeestalek.

(well) off בעל אמצעים *nmf* ba'al/-at emtsa'eem.

off and on לסירוגין *adv* le-seroogeen.

off-color דהוי צבע *adj* dehoo|y/-yat tseva'.

off duty שלא בתפקיד *adv* she-lo be-tafkeed.

off the road במרחק מה מהכביש *adv* be-merkhak mah me-ha-kveesh.

(to be) off to war יצא למלחמה *v inf* latset la-meelkhamah; *pst* yatsa *etc*; *pres* yotse *etc*; *fut* yetse *etc*.

(to) offend 1. לפגוע ב־ *inf* leefgo'a' be-; *pst* paga' be- (*p=f*); *pres* poge'a' be-; *fut* yeefga' be-; **2.** לעלוב (insult) *inf* la'alov; *pst* 'alav; *pres* 'olev; *fut* ya'alov.

offender 1. עולב *nmf* 'olev/-et; **2.** עבריין (delinquent) *nmf* 'avaryan/-eet.

offense 1. עבירה *nf* 'aveyr|ah/-ot (*+of:* -at); **2.** עלבון (insult) 'elbon/-ot.

(weapon of) offense מכשיר הפגיעה *nm* makhsheer/-ey ha-pegee'ah.

(no) offense was meant לא היתה כוונה להעליב lo haytah kavanah leha'aleev.

offensive 1. פוגע *adj* pog|e'a'/-a'at; **2.** מעליב (insulting) *adj* ma'aleev/-ah; **3.** מתקפה *nf* meetk|afah/-afot (*+of:* -efet).

offer הצעה *nf* hatsa|'ah/-'ot (*+of:* -'at).

(to) offer להציע *inf* lehatsee'a; *pst* heetsee'a; *pres* matsee'a; *fut* yatsee'a'.

(to) offer to do ליטול על עצמו *inf* litol 'al 'atsmo; *pst* natal *etc*; *pres* notel *etc*; *fut* yeetol *etc*.

offering 1. קורבן (sacrifice) *nm* korban/-ot; **2.** תרומה (contribution) *nf* troom|ah/-ot (*+of:* -at).

offhand 1. מניה וביה *adv* meney oo-vey; **2.** בלא הכנה מוקדמת (without previous preparation) *adj* be-lo hakhanah mookdemet.

(in an) offhand manner כלאחר יד *adv* kee-le-akhar yad.

office 1. משרה (function) *nf* meesr|ah/-ot (*+of:* -at); **2.** משרד (place) *nm* meesr|ad/-eem (*pl+of:* -edey).

(box) office קופה *nf* koop|ah/-ot (*+of:* -at).

(post-)office דואר *nm* do'ar.

office boy נער שליח *nm* na'ar shalee'akh.

office building בניין משרדים *nm* been|yan/-yeney meesradeem.

officer 1. פקיד (official) *nmf* pakeed/pekeed|ah (*pl:* -eem/-ot; *+of:* -ey); **2.** שוטר (police) *nmf* shot|er/-eret (*pl:* -reem/-rot; *+of:* -rey); **3.** קצין (army) *nmf* katseen/ketseen|ah (*pl:* -eem/-ot; *+of:* ketseen/-at/-ey).

(to) officer 1. לפקד *inf* lefaked; *pst* peeked *(p=f)*; *pres* mefaked; *fut* yefaked; **2.** להדריך (instruct) *inf* lehadreekh; *pst* heedreekh; *pres* madreekh; *fut* yadreekh.

(through the good) offices of באדיבות *adv* ba-adeevoot.

official 1. פקיד *nmf* pakeed/pekeed|ah (*+of:* -at/-ey); **2.** רשמי *adj* reeshmee/-t.

(government) official פקיד ממשלתי *nmf* pakeed/pekeedah memshaltee/-t.

(to) officiate 1. לכהן *inf* lekhahen; *pst* keehen; *pres* mekhahen; *fut* yekhahen; **2.** לערוך (perform) *inf* la'arokh; *pst* 'arakh; *pres* 'orekh; *fut* ya'arokh.

officious 1. מתערב *v pres & adj* meet'arev/-et; **2.** תוחב אפו (meddlesome) *v pres & adj* tokhev/-et ap|o/-ah.

(to) offset 1. לפדות *inf* leefdot; *pst* padah *(p=f)*; *pres* podeh; *fut* yeefdeh; **2.** לקזז (compensate) *inf* lekazez; *pst* keezez; *pres* mekazez; *fut* yekazez.

offshore בריחוק מה מהחוף *adv* be-rekhook mah me-ha-khof.

offside 1. צד שמאל *nm* tsad smol; **2.** נבדל (soccer) *nm* neevdal.

offspring צאצא *nm* tse'etsa/-'eem (*pl+of:* -'ey).

offstage מאחורי הקלעים *adv* me-akhorey ha-kla'eem.

oft, often לעתים קרובות *adv* le-'eeteem krovot.

(how) often? באיזו תכיפות? be-eyzo tekheefoot?

oh! 1. אוי! *interj* oy! **2.** אויה! (poetical) *interj* oyah!

oil 1. שמן *nm* shemen/shmaneem (*pl+of:* sheemney); **2.** נפט (petroleum) *nm* neft.

(motor) oil שמן מנוע *nm* shemen/shamney mano'a'.

(to) oil לשמן *inf* leshamen; *pst* sheemen; *pres* meshamen; *fut* yeshamen.

oil can פחית שמן *nf* pakhee|t/-yot shemen.

oil painting ציור שמן *nm* tseeyoor/-ey shemen.

oil well באר נפט *nm* be'er/-ot neft.

oilcloth שעוונית *nf* sha'avanee|t/-yot.

oily שמנוני *adj* shamnoonee/-t.

old 1. זקן (when animate) *nmf & adj* zaken/zeken|ah (*pl:* -eem/-ot; *+of:* zekan/zeekney); **2.** ישן (when inanimate) *adj* yashan/yeshanah; **3.** עתיק (antique) *adj* 'ateek/-ah; **4.** קדום (ancient) *adj* kadoom/kedoomah.

(days of) old ימים עברו *nm pl* yameem 'avaroo.

(how) old are you? 1. בן כמה אתה? (addressing male) ben kamah atah? **2.** בת כמה את (addressing female) bat kamah at?

old enough to בוגר דיו כדי *adj* boger/-et da|yo/-yah kedey.

(an) old hand at בעל ניסיון ותיק ב־ *nmf* ba'al/-at neesayon vateek/-ah be-.

old maid בתולה זקנה *nf* betool|ah/-ot zken|ah/-ot.

old man זקן *nm* zaken/zekeneem (*pl+of:* zeekney).

Old Testament 1. הברית החדשה *nf* ha-breet ha-yeshanah; **2.** התנ"ך (the Bible) *nm* ha-tanakh.

old wine יין ישן *nm* yayeen yashan.

(an) old hand at 1. ותיק בנושא *adj* vateek/-ah ba-nose shel; **2.** בעל ניסיון (experienced) *adj* ba'al/-at neesayon.

olden עתיק יומין *adj* 'ateek/-at yomeen.

old-fashioned מיושן *adj* meyoosh|an/-enet.

old-timer ותיק *adj & nmf* vateek/-ah.

oleander הרדוף *nm* hardof/-eem (*pl+of:* -ey).

oligarchy 1. שלטון קבוצת לחץ *nm* sheelton kvoots|at/-ot lakhats; **2.** אוליגרכיה *nf* oleegarkh|yah/-yot (*+of:* -yat).

olive זית *nm* zayeet/zeyteem (*+of:* zeyt/-ey).

olive branch 1. ענף זית *nm* 'an|af/-fey zayeet; **2.** עלה זית (leaf) *nm* 'al|eh/-ey zayeet.

olive grove מטע זיתים *nm* mat|a'/-a'ey zeyteem.

olive oil שמן זית *nm* shemen/shamney zayeet/zeyteem.

olive tree עץ זית *nm* 'ets/'atsey zayeet/zeyteem.

Olympic אולימפי *adj* oleempee/-t.

omelet חביתה *nf* khaveet|ah/-ot (*+of:* -at).

omen אות לבאות *nm* ot/-ot la-ba'ot.

ominous מבשר רעות *adj* mevaser/-et ra'ot.

omission השמטה *nf* hashmat|ah/-ot (*+of:* -at).

(to) omit 1. להשמיט *inf* lehashmeet; *pst* heeshmeet; *pres* mashmeet; *fut* yashmeet; **2.** לדלג (skip) *inf* ledaleg; *pst* deeleg; *pres* medaleg; *fut* yedaleg.

omnibus אוטובוס *nm* otoboos/-eem (*+of:* -ey).

omnipotent כל־יכול *adj* kol yakhol/yekholah.

on 1. על 'al; **2.** קדימה (onward) kadeemah; **3.** ב־ (in) be-; **4.** ב־ (at) be-; **5.** אודות (about) *conj* odot; **6.** במשך (during) be-meshekh.

on all sides בכל הצדדים *adv* be-khol ha-tsedadeem *(kh=k)*.

on and on עד בוש *adv* 'ad bosh.

(farther) on 1. בהמשך הדרך *adv* be-hemshekh ha-derekh; **2.** יותר רחוק *adv* yoter rakhok.

(his hat is) on כובעו בראשו kova|'o/-'ah be-rosh|o/-ah.

(the light is) on האור דלוק ha-or/-ot dalook/dlookeem.

on arrival עם הגיע *adv* 'eem hagee'a'.

on board על סיפון *adv* 'al seepoon/-ey.

on condition that בתנאי ש־ bee-tnay she-.

on credit באשראי be-ashray.

on horseback ברכיבה *adv* bee-rekheevah.

on Monday 1. ביום שני *adv* be-yom shenee; **2.** ביום ב׳ *adv* be-yom bet.

on purpose בכוונה *adv* be-khavanah *(kh=k)*.

on sale למכירה *adv* lee-mekheerah.

on time בזמן *adv* ba-zman.

once פעם אחת *nf & adv* pa'am akhat.

(all at) once 1. בבת אחת *adv* be-vat akhat *(v=b)*; **2.** פתאום (suddenly) *adv* peet'om.

(at) once 1. מיד *adv* meeyad; **2.** בו בזמן (simultaneously) *adv* bo ba-zman.

(just this) once רק הפעם rak ha-pa'am.

once and for all 1. אחת ולתמיד akhat oo-le-tameed; **2.** סופית *adv* sofeet.

once in a while מפעם לפעם *adv* mee-pa'am le-fa'am *(f=p)*.

once upon a time לפני שנים רבות *adv* leefney shaneem rabot.

one 1. אחד *num m* ekhad; **2.** אחת *num f* akhat.

(the green) one זה הירוק *adj* zeh/zoo ha-yarok/yerokah.

(this) one 1. הזה *nm* ha-zeh; **2.** הזאת *nf* ha-zot.

(the) one and only האחד והיחיד *adj* ha-ekhad ve-ha-yakheed.

one another 1. זה את זה (masc) zeh et zeh; **2.** זו את זו (fem) zo et zo.

one by one 1. אחד־אחד *nm* ekhad-ekhad; **2.** אחת־אחת *nf* akhat-akhat.

(his) one chance האפשרות היחידה שלפניו ha-'efsharoot ha-yekheedah she-le-fanav *(f=p)*.

one hundred מאה (100) *num* me'ah/me'ot (*+of:* me'at).

one thousand אלף (1,000) *num* elef/alafeem (*pl+of:* alfey).

one who אחד אשר *nmf* ekhad/akhat asher.

one-armed גידם ידו האחת *nmf & adj* geedem/-et yad|o/-ah *(m/f)* ha-akhat.

one-eyed עיוור עינו האחת *nmf & adj* 'eever/-et 'eyn|o/-ah *(m/f)* ha-akhat.

one-sided חד־צדדי *adj* khad-tsedadee/-t.

one-way חד־כיווני *adj* khad-keevoonee/-t.

onerous 1. מעיק *adj* me'eek/-ah; **2.** כבד (heavy) *adj* kaved/kvedah.

oneself את עצמו et 'atsm|o/-ah *(m/f)*.

(by) oneself לבדו *adj* levad|o/-ah.

(to speak to) oneself לדבר אל עצמו *inf* ledaber el 'atsm|o/-ah *(m/f)*; *pst* deeber *etc*; *pres* medaber *etc*; *fut* yedaber *etc*.

ongoing מתרחש *adj* meetrakhesh/-et.

onion בצל *nm* batsal/betsaleem (*+of:* betsal/beetsley).

onlooker צופה *nmf* tsof|eh/-ah.

only 1. יחיד *adj* yakheed/yekheedah; **2.** לבד (alone) *adv* levad; **3.** רק (solely) *conj* rak.

onset 1. התחלה *nf* hatkhal|ah/-ot (*+of:* -at); **2.** ראשית (beginning) *nf* resheet.

onto 1. על פני 'ak peney; **2.** ־ממעל ל (over) *adv* mee-ma'al le-.

onward קדימה *adv* kadeemah.

onyx שוהם *nm* shoham.

(to) ooze 1. לטפטף *inf* letaftef; *pst* teeftef; *pres* metaftef; *fut* yetaftef; **2.** לדלוף (exude) *inf* leedlof; *pst* dalaf; *pres* dolef; *fut* yeedlof.

opal לשם *nm* leshem.

opaque אטום *adj* atoom/-ah.

open פתוח *adj* patoo'akh/petookhah.

(to) open לפתוח *inf* leefto'akh; *pst* patakh *(p=f)*; *pres* pote'akh; *fut* yeeftakh.

(into the) open air לאוויר הפתוח *adv* la-aveer ha-patoo'akh.

open country שדה פתוח *nm* sadeh patoo'akh.

(to) open eyes לפקוח עיניים *inf* leefko'akh 'eynayeem; *pst* pakakh *(p=f) etc*; *pres* poke'akh *etc*; *fut* yeefkakh *etc (p=f)*.

(to) open fire לפתוח באש *inf* leefto'akh be-'esh; *pst* patakh *(p=f) etc*; *pres* pote'akh *etc*; *fut* yeeftakh *etc*.

open house קבלת אורחים *nf* kabal|at/-ot orkheem.

open question שאלה פתוחה *nf* she'elah petookhah.

open-minded רחב אופקים *adj* rekhav/rakhavat ofakeem.

open to temptation חשוף לפיתויים *adj* khasoof/-ah le-feetooyeem *(f=p)*.

open winter חורף ללא כפור *nm* khoref le-lo kfor.

open-end ללא סייג *adj* le-lo syag.

opener פותחן *nm* potkhan/-eem (*pl+of:* -ey).

openhanded נדיב *adj* nadeev/nedeevah.

openmouthed פעור פה *adj* pe'oor/-at peh.

opening 1. פתיחה *nf* peteekh|ah/-ot (*+of:* -at); **2.** חור (hole) *nm* khor/-eem (*pl+of:* -ey); **3.** פתח (clearing) *nm* petakh/-eem (*pl+of:* peetkhey); **4.** מישרה פנויה (vacancy) *nf* meesr|ah/-ot penoo|yah/-yot.

opening night ערב בכורה *nm* 'erev/'arvey bekhorah.

(the) opening number המופע הפותח *nm* ha-mofa' ha-pote'akh.

opera אופרה *nf* oper|ah/-ot (*+of:* -at).

(comic) opera אופרה קומית *nf* oper|ah/-ot komee|t/-yot.

opera glasses משקפת לאופרה *nf* meeshk|efet/-afot le-operah.

opera house בניין האופרה *nm* beenyan ha-operah.

(to) operate 1. לתפעל (function) *inf* letaf'el; *pst* teef'el; *pres* metaf'el; *fut* yetaf'el; **2.** לנהל (manage) *inf* lenahel; *pst* neehel; *pres* menahel; *fut* yenahel.

(to) operate on a person לנתח מישהו (surgically) *inf* lenate'akh meeshehoo; *pst* neetakh *etc*; *pres* menate'akh *etc*; *fut* yenatakh *etc*.

operation 1. תפעול (function) *nm* teef'ool/-eem (*pl+of:* -ey); **2.** ניהול (management) *nm* neehool/-eem (*pl+of:* -ey); **3.** ניתוח (surgical) *nm* neetoo|'akh/-kheem (*pl+of:* -khey); **4.** עיסקה (business) *nf* 'eesk|ah/-a'ot (*+of:* 'eeskat).

(in) operation בפעולה *adv* bee-fe'oolah *(f=p)*.

operator 1. מפעיל *nm* maf'eel/-eem (*pl+of:* -ey); **2.** מכונאי (mechanic) *nm* mekhon|ay/-a'eem (*pl+of:* -a'ey); **3.** מנתח (surgery) *nm* menat|e'akh/-kheem (*pl+of:* -khey); **4.** איש עסקים ממולח (shrewd businessman/woman) *nmf* eesh/eshet 'asakeem memoolakh/-at (*pl:* anshey 'asakeem memoolakheem).

(mine) operator מנהל מיכרה *nm* mena|hel/-haley meekhr|eh/-ot.

(telegraph) operator טכנאי מברקה *nmf* tekhn|ay/-a'eet meevrakah.

(telephone) operator מרכזן *nmf* merk|azan/-ezaneet.

operetta אופרטה *nf* operet|ah/-ot (*+of:* -at).

ophthalmic של עיניים *adj* shel 'eynayeem.

opinion 1. דעה *nf* de'ah/de'ot (+*of:* da'at); **2.** חוות דעת (view) *nf* khav|at/-ot da'at; **3.** סברה (conjecture) *nf* svar|ah/-ot (+*of:* -at).

opium אופיום *nm* opyoom.

opponent בר־פלוגתא *nmf* bar/bat ploogta.

opportune 1. בעיתו *adj* be-'eet|o/-ah; **2.** מתאים (adequate) *adj* mat'eem/-ah.

opportunist סתגלן *nmf* staglan/-eet.

opportunity הזדמנות *nf* heezdamnoo|t/-yot.

(to) oppose להתנגד *inf* leheetnaged; *pst* heetnaged; *pres* meetnaged; *fut* yeetnaged.

opposing 1. מתנגד *nm* meetnag|ed-deem (*pl+of:* -dey); **2.** מנוגד (contrary) *adj* menoog|ad/-edet.

opposite 1. מול *adv* mool; **2.** מנגד (across) *adv* mee-neged.

(the) opposite ההפך *nm* ha-hefekh.

opposite to מול ה־ *adv* mool ha-.

opposition 1. התנגדות *nf* heetnagdoo|t/-yot; **2.** אופוזיציה *nf* opozeets|yah/-yot (+*of:* -yat).

(to) oppress לדכא *inf* ledake; *pst* deeka; *pres* medake; *fut* yedake.

oppression דיכוי *nm* deekoo|y/-yeem (*pl+of:* -yey).

oppressive 1. קשה (harsh) *adj* kash|eh/-ah; **2.** מעציב (distressing) *adj* ma'atseev/-ah.

oppressor 1. נוגש *nm* nog|es/-seem (*pl+of:* -sey); **2.** עריץ (tyrant) *nmf* 'areets/-ah.

optic 1. של העין *adj* shel ha-'ayeen; **2.** אופטי *adj* optee/-t.

optical אופטי *adj* optee/-t.

optician אופטיקאי *nm* opteek|ay/-a'eem (*pl+of:* -a'ey).

optimism אופטימיות *nf* opteemeeyoot.

optimist אופטימיסט *nmf* opteemeest/-eet (*pl+of:* -ey).

optimistic אופטימי *adj* opteemee/-t.

option 1. ברירה *nf* breyr|ah/-ot (+*of:* -at); **2.** אופציה *nf* optsee|yah/-yot (+*of:* -yat).

optional שברשות *adj* she-bee-reshoot.

optometrist אופטומטריסט *nm* optometreest/-eem (*pl+of:* -ey).

opulence שפע עושר *nm* shefa' 'osher.

opulent שופע עושר *adj* shof|e'a'/-a'at 'osher.

or או o.

oracle 1. אורים ותומים *nm pl* ooreem ve-toomeem; **2.** אורקל *nm* orakl.

oral 1. שבעל פה *adj* she-be-'al peh; **2.** בחינה בעל פה (exam) *nf* bekheen|ah/-ot be-'al peh.

orange 1. תפוז (fruit) *nm* tapooz/-eem (*pl+of:* -ey); **2.** כתום (color) *adj* katom/ketoomah.

orange blossom פריחת התפוזים *nf* preekhat ha-tapoozeem.

orange grove פרדס תפוזים *nm* pardes/-ey tapoozeem.

orangeade משקה פרי־הדר *nm* mashkeh pree hadar.

oration נאום חוצב להבות *nm* ne'oom/-eem khots|ev/-vey lehavot.

orator נואם *nm* no'em/no'am|eem (*pl+of:* -ey).

oratory אמנות הנאום *nf* omanoot ha-ne'oom.

orb 1. מסלול שמיימי (celestial sphere) *nm* maslool/-eem shmeymee/-yeem; **2.** כוכב kokhav/-eem (*pl+of:* -ey); **3.** גלגל העין (eyeball) *nm* galgal/-ey ha-'ayeen/'eynayeem.

orbit מסלול כוכבי *nm* maslool/-eem kokhavee/-yeem.

orbital 1. מסלולי *adj* masloolee/-t; **2.** דמוי ארובה demoo|y/-yat aroobah.

orchard 1. בוסתן *nm* boostan/-eem (*pl+of:* -ey); **2.** מטע (plantation) *nm* mat|a'/a'eem (*pl+of:* -a'ey); **3.** פרדס (grove) *nm* pardes/-eem (*pl+of:* -ey).

orchestra תזמורת *nf* teezmor|et/-ot.

(Israel Philarmonic) Orchestra 1. התזמורת הפילהרמונית הישראלית *nf* ha-teezmoret ha-feel-harmoneet ha-yeesre'eleet; **2.** הפילהרמונית *(colloq. abbr.) nf* ha-feelharmoneet.

orchestra seat מושב קדמי *nm* moshav/-eem keedmee/-yeem.

orchid סחלב *nm* sakhlav/-eem (*pl+of:* -ey).

(to) ordain להסמיך לכהונת דת *inf* lehasmeekh lee-khehoonat dat; *pst* heesmeekh *etc*; *pres* masmeekh *etc*; *fut* yasmeekh *etc*.

ordeal נתיב ייסורים *nm* neteev/-ey yesooreem.

order 1. פקודה (request) *nf* pekood|ah/-ot (+*of:* -at); **2.** מסדר (fraternity) *nm* meesdar/-eem (*pl+of:* -ey); **3.** הסדר (arrangement) *nm* hesder/-eem (*pl+of:* -ey).

(in) order בסדר *adv* be-seder.

(made to) order שהוכן בהזמנה *adj* she-hookh|an/-nah be-hazmanah.

(out of) order 1. מקולקל *adj* mekoolk|al/-elet; **2.** לא תקין (not functioning) *adj* lo takeen/tekeenah.

(to) order 1. לצוות *inf* letsavot; *pst* tseevah; *pres* metsaveh; *fut* yetsaveh; **2.** להזמין (request) *inf* lehazmeen; *pst* heezmeen; *pres* mazmeen; *fut* yazmeen.

(to) order away לגרש *inf* legaresh; *pst* gerash; *pres* megaresh; *fut* yegaresh.

(in) order that כדי ש־ kedey she-.

(in) order to למען אשר le-ma'an asher.

orderly 1. שומר סדר *adj* shomer/-et seder; **2.** מסודר (neatly arranged) *adj* mesood|ar/-eret.

ordinal סידורי *adj* seedooree/-t.

ordinal number מספר סידורי *nm* meespar/-eem seedooree/-yeem.

ordinance תקנה *nf* takan|ah/-ot (+*of:* -at).

ordinarily בדרך כלל *adv* be-derekh klal.

ordinary 1. שכיח *adj* shakhee'akh/shekheekhah; **2.** רגיל (regular) *adj* rageel/regeelah.

ordnance 1. תותחנים *nm pl* totkhan/-eem (*pl+of:* -ey); **2.** חימוש (armament) *nm* kheemoosh/-eem (*pl+of:* -ey).

ore עפרה *nf* 'afr|ah/-ot (+*of:* -at).

organ 1. איבר (of body) *nm* ever/evareem (*pl+of:* evrey); **2.** עוגב (mus.instrument) *nm* 'oogav/-eem (*pl+of:* -ey); **3.** אורגן *nm* organ/-eem (*pl+of:* -ey).

organic 1. אורגני *adj* organee/-t; **2.** חיוני (vital) *adj* kheeyoonee/-t.

organism 1. גוף חי *nm* goof/-eem kha|y/-yeem; **2.** מנגנון (mechanism) *nm* manganon/-eem (*pl+of:* -ey).

organist עוגבאי *nmf* 'oogav|ay/-a'eet.

organization 1. ארגון *nm* eergoon/-eem (*pl+of:* -ey); **2.** הסתדרות (union) *nf* heestadroo|t/-yot.
(to) organize לארגן *inf* le'argen; *pst* eergen; *pres* me'argen; *fut* ye'argen.
organizer מארגן *nmf* me'argen/-et (*pl+of:* -ey).
orgy אורגיה *nf* org|yah/-yot (*+of:* -yat).
orient מזרח *nm* meezrakh.
oriental מזרחי *adj* meezrakhee/-t.
(to) orientate לכוון *inf* lekhaven; *pst* keeven (*k=kh*); *pres* mekhaven; *fut* yekhaven.
orientation 1. התמצאות *nf* heetmats'oo|t/-yot; **2.** אוריינטציה *nf* oryentats|yah/-yot (*+of:* -at).
orifice 1. פייה *nf* pee|yah/-yot (*+of:* -yat); **2.** פתח (opening) *nm* petakh/-eem (*pl+of:* peetkhey).
origin 1. מקור makor/mekorot (*+of:* mekor) **2.** מוצא (source) *nm* motsa/-'eem (*pl+of:* -'ey).
original 1. מקורי *adj* mekoree/-t; **2.** תמהוני (queer) *nmf* teemhonee/-t.
originality מקוריות *nf* mekoreeyoot.
originally 1. במקורו *adv* bee-mekor|o/-ah (*m/f*); **2.** מתחילתו (from start) *adv* mee-tkheelat|o/-ah (*m/f*).
(to) originate 1. לצמוח (grow) *vi* leetsmo'akh; *pst* tsamakh; *pres* tsome'akh; *fut* yeetsmakh; **2.** להצמיח (produce) *vt inf* lehatsmee'akh; *pst* heetsmee'akh; *pres* matsmee'akh; *fut* yatsmee'akh; **3.** להמציא (invent) *vt inf* lehamtsee; *pst* heemtsee; *pres* mamtsee; *fut* yamtsee.
oriole זהבן *nm* zahavan/-eem (*pl+of:* -ey).
ornament קישוט *nm* keeshoot/-eem (*pl+of:* -ey).
(to) ornament לקשט *inf* lekashet; *pst* keeshet; *pres* mekashet; *fut* yekashet.
ornamental 1. קישוטי *adj* keeshootee/-t; **2.** אורנמנטלי *adj* ornamentalee/-t.
ornate 1. מקושט לראווה *adj* mekoosh|at/-etet le-ra'avah; **2.** בהידור מוגזם (dolled up) *adv* be-heedoor moogzam.
ornate style סגנון מליצי *nm* seegnon meleetsee.
orphan יתום *nmf* yatom/yetomah.
orphan asylum בית יתומים *nm* bet/batey yetomeem.
orphanage בית יתומים *nm* bet/batey yetomeem.
orthodox 1. שמרני *adj* shamranee/-t; **2.** אורתודוקסי *adj* ortodoksee/-t.
orthography 1. כתיב נכון *nm* keteev nakhon; **2.** אורתוגרפיה *nf* ortografee|yah/-yot (*+of:* -yat).
(to) oscillate 1. להתנודד *inf* leheetnoded; *pst* heetnoded; *pres* meetnoded; *fut* yeetnoded; **2.** לפקפק (doubt) *inf* lefakpek; *pst* peekpek (*p=f*); *pres* mefakpek; *fut* yefakpek.
ostentation התרברבות *nf* heetravrevoo|t/-yot.
ostentatious מתרברב *adj* meetravrev/-et.
ostrich 1. יען *nm* ya'en/ye'en|eem (*pl+of:* -ey); **2.** בת־יענה *nf* bat/benot ya'anah.
ostrich policy מדיניות בת היענה *nf* medeeneeyoot bat ha-ya'anah.
other אחר *adj* akher/-et.
(every) other day כל יומיים *adv* kol yomayeem.
(some) other day בפעם אחרת *adv* be-fa'am (*f=p*) akheret.
other than חוץ מאשר *adv* khoots me-asher.
otherwise אחרת *adv* akheret.
otter כלב מים *nm* kelev/kalbey mayeem.
(to) ought להיאלץ *inf* lehe'alets; *pst & pres* ne'elats; *fut* ye'alets.
ounce אונקייה *nf* oonkee|yah/-yot (*+of:* -yat).
our שלנו possess. *pron* shelanoo.
ours משלנו *poss. pron* mee-shelanoo.
(a friend of) ours אחד מידידינו *nm* ekhad mee-yedeedenoo.
ourselves אנו עצמנו *pron* anoo 'atsmenoo.
(by) ourselves בעצמנו *pron* be-'atsmenoo.
(we) ourselves אנו עצמנו *pron* anoo 'atsmenoo.
(to) oust 1. לגרש (expel) *inf* legaresh; *pst* gerash; *pres* megaresh; *fut* yegaresh; **2.** לעקור ממקומו (eradicate) *vt* la'akor mee-mekom|o/-ah; *pst* 'akar *etc*; *pres* 'oker *etc*; *fut* ya'akor *etc*.
out החוצה ha-khootsah.
(before the week is) out בטרם יחלוף השבוע *adv* be-terem yakhlof ha-shavoo'a'.
(the book is just) out הספר זה רק עתה הופיע *nm* ha-sefer zeh rak 'atah hofee'a'.
(the secret is) out נתגלה הסוד *v pst* neetgalah ha-sod.
(to fight it) out להיאבק עד הסוף *inf* lehe'avek 'ad ha-sof; *pst & pres* ne'evak *etc*; *fut* ye'avek *etc*.
(to have it) out ליישב סכסוך *inf* leyashev seekhsookh; *pst* yeeshev *etc*; *pres* meyashev *etc*; *fut* yeyashev *etc*.
(to speak) out 1. לומר גלויות (say openly) *inf* lomar glooyot; *pst* amar *etc*; *pres* omer *etc*; *fut* yomar *etc*; **2.** להרים קול (lift voice) *inf* lehareem kol; *pst* hereem kol; *pres* mereem kol; *fut* yareem kol.
out and out criminal פושע מושלם *nm* posh|e'a'/-a'at mooshl|am/-emet.
out and out refusal סירוב מוחלט *nm* seroov/-eem mookhlat/-eem.
out of מתוך mee-tokh.
(made) out of עשוי מ־ *adj* 'asoo|y/-yah mee-.
out-of-bounds מחוץ לתחום *adj* mee-khoots la-t'khoom.
out-of-date 1. שחלף מועדו *adj* she-khalaf mo'ad|o/-ah; **2.** שעבר זמנו *[colloq.] adj* she-'avar zman|o/-ah.
out of fear מפחד *adv* mee-pakhad.
out of humor במצב רוח רע *adj* be-matsav roo'akh ra'.
out of money ללא פרוטה *adj* le-lo prootah.
out of pocket הוצאות בפועל *nf pl* hotsa'ot be-fo'al.
out of print אזל azal/azlah.
out of touch with איבד כל קשר עם eebed/dah kol kesher 'eem.
out of town מחוץ לעיר *adv* mee-khoots la-'eer.
out of tune סלוף כיוונון *adj* sloof/-at keevnoon.
out of work 1. מחוסר עבודה *nmf* mekhoos|ar/-eret (*pl:* -rey/-rot) 'avodah; **2.** מובטל (unemployed) *m/f* moovt|al/-elet.
out patient חולה מן החוץ *nm* khol|eh/-ah meen ha-khoots.
outbreak 1. התפרצות (eruption) *nf* heetpartsoo|t/-yot; **2.** התקוממות (uprising) *nf* heetkomemoo|t/-yot; **3.** התקפה (attack) *nf* hatkaf|ah/-ot.

(at the) outbreak of the war בפרוץ המלחמה *adv* bee-frots *(f=p)* ha-meelkhamah.
outcast מנודה *nmf & adj* menood|eh/-ah.
outcome תוצאה *nf* tots|a'ah/-a'ot (+*of:* -'at).
outcry קריאה לעזרה *nf* kree|'ah/-'ot le-'ezrah.
outdoor תחת כיפת השמים *adv* takhat keepat ha-shamayeem.
outdoor games תחרויות תחת כיפת השמים *nf* takhrooyot takhat keepat ha-shamayeem.
outdoors בחוץ *adv* ba-khoots.
outer חיצון *adj* kheetson/-eet.
outer space החלל החיצון *nm* he-khalal ha-kheetson.
outfit ציוד tseeyood/-eem (*pl+of:* -ey).
(to) outfit לצייד *inf* letsayen; *pst* tseeyen; *pres* metsayen; *fut* yetsayen.
outgoing יוצא *adj* yotse/-t.
(to) outgrow להיגמל *inf* leheegamel; *pst & pres* neegmal; *fut* yeegamel.
(to) outguess 1. להתחכם ל- *inf* leheetkhakem le-; *pst* heetkhakem le-; *pres* meetkhakem le-; *fut* yeetkhakem le-; **2.** להערים על (outsmart) *inf* leha'areem 'al; *pst* he'ereem 'al; *pres* ma'areem 'al; *fut* ya'areem 'al.
outing טיול באוויר החופשי *nm* teeyool ba-aveer he-khofshee.
outlaw פורע חוק *nm* por|e'a'/-'ey khok.
(to) outlaw להוציא אל מחוץ לחוק *inf* lehotsee el mee-khoots la-khok; *pst* hotsee *etc*; *pres* motsee *etc*; *fut* yotsee *etc*.
outlay הוצאה *nf* hotsa|'ah/-'ot (+*of:* -'at).
(to) outlay להוציא כספים *inf* lehotsee kesafeem; *pst* hotsee *etc*; *pres* motsee *etc*; *fut* yotsee.
outlet 1. מוצא *nm* mots|a/-'a'eem (*pl+of:* -a'ey); **2.** סוכנות מכירה (sales agency) *nf* sokhnoo|t/-yot mekheerot.
outline 1. קווי יסוד *nm pl* kavey yesod; **2.** מיתאר (contour) *nm* meet'ar/-eem (*pl+of:* -ey).
(to) outline להתוות *inf* lehatvot; *pst* heetvah; *pres* matveh; *fut* yatveh.
(to) outlive להאריך ימים יותר *inf* leha'areekh yameem yoter; *pst* he'ereekh *etc*; *pres* ma'areekh *etc*; *fut* ya'areekh *etc*.
outlook סיכוי *nm* seekoo|y/-yeem (*pl+of:* -yey).
outlying מרוחק מהמרכז *adj* merookh|ak/-eket me-ha-merkaz.
outmoded 1. מיושן *adj* meyoosh|an/-enet; **2.** שיצא מהאופנה (out of fashion) *adj* she-yats|a/-'ah me-ha-ofnah.
outpost מוצב חיצוני *nm* mootsav/-eem kheetsonee/-yeem.
output 1. הספק *nm* hespek/-eem (*pl+of:* -ey); **2.** תפוקה (production) *nf* tefook|ah/-ot (+*of:* -at); **3.** תוצרת (produce) *nf* totseret.
outrage 1. נבלה *nf* neval|ah/-ot (+*of:* neevl|at/-ot); **2.** שערורייה (scandal) *nf* sha'arooree|yah/-yot (+*of:* -yat).
(to) outrage לעורר שערוריות *inf* le'orer sha'arooreeyot; *pst* 'orer *etc*; *pres* me'orer *etc*; *fut* ye'orer *etc*.
outrageous מזעזע *adj* meza'z|e'a'/-a'at.
outright 1. מוחלט *adj* mookhl|at/-etet; **2.** גמור (complete) *adj* gamoor/gemoorah.
(to) outrun לעבור בריצה *inf* la'avor be-reetsah; *pst* 'avar *etc*; *pres* 'over *etc*; *fut* ya'avor *etc*.
outset תחילת הדרך *nf* tekheelat ha-derekh.
(to) outshine 1. להבריק יותר *inf* lehavreek yoter; *pst* heevreek *etc*; *pres* mavreek *etc*; *fut* yavreek *etc*; **2.** לעלות על (surpass) *inf* la'alot 'al; *pst* 'alah 'al; *pres* 'oleh 'al; *fut* ya'aleh 'al.
outside 1. חיצוני (external) *adj* kheetsonee/-t; **2.** זר (foreign) *adj* zar/-ah.
outside בחוץ *adv* ba-khoots.
(at the) outside מבחוץ *adv* mee-ba-khoots.
(to close on the) outside לסגור מבחוץ *inf* leesgor mee-ba-khoots; *pst* sagar *etc*; *pres* soger *etc*; *fut* yeesgor *etc*.
outsider 1. מישהו מן החוץ *nmf* mee-she|hoo/-hee meen ha-khoots; **2.** זר (stranger) *nmf* zar/-ah.
outsize מידה גדולה מהרגיל *nf* meed|ah/-ot gedol|ah/-ot me-ha-rageel/regeelot.
outskirts סביבות *nm pl* sveevot.
outspoken גלוי לב *adj* gloo|y/-yat lev.
outstanding יוצא מן הכלל *adj* yotse/-t meen ha-klal.
outstanding bills שטרות שטרם נפרעו *nm pl* shtarot she-terem neefre'oo.
outstanding debts חובות לא מסולקים *nm pl* khovot lo mesoolakeem.
outstretched פרוש לרווחה *adj* paroos/proosah lee-revakhah.
(with) outstretched arms בזרועות פתוחות *adv* bee-zro'ot petookhot.
outward 1. חיצון (external) *adj* kheetson/-eet; **2.** בולט (apparent) *adj* bolet/-et.
outward bound עם הפנים החוצה *adv* 'eem ha-paneem ha-khootsah.
outwardly כלפי חוץ *adv* kelapey khoots
(to) outweigh לשקול יותר *inf* leeshkol yoter; *pst* shakal *etc*; *pres* shokel *etc*; *fut* yeeshkol *etc*.
oval סגלגל *adj* sgalgal/-ah.
ovary שחלה *nf* shakhl|ah/-ot (+*of:* -at).
ovation תשואות *nf pl* teshoo'ot.
oven תנור אפייה *nm* tanoor/-ey afeeyah.
over מעל *adv* me-'al.
(it is all) over הכול נגמר *nm* ha-kol neegmar.
(to do it) over לחזור שוב *inf* lakhzor shoov; *pst* khazar *etc*; *pres* khozer *etc*; *fut* yakhzor *etc*.
over again שוב *adv* shoov.
(all) over בכל כולו *adv* be-khol kool|o/-ah *(kh=k)*.
(all) over again פעם נוספת (once more) *nf & adv* pa'am/pe'ameem nos|efet/-afot.
over against לעומת *prep* le-'oomat.
over all מעל לכול *adv* me-'al la-kol
over and over שוב ושוב *adv* shoov va-shoov.
over here מעבר מזה *adv* me-'ever mee-zeh.
(all) over the city בכל העיר *adv* be-khol ha-'eer.
over there מהעבר ההוא *adv* me-ha-'ever ha-hoo.
over to נעבור עתה אל na'avor 'atah el.
overall 1. מקיף *adj* makeef/-ah; **2.** כולל (comprehensive) *adj* kolel/-et.
overalls סרבל *nm* sarbal/-eem (*pl+of:* -ey).

overboard 1. אל מעבר לסיפון *adv* el me-‘ever la-seepoon; **2.** לים (into the sea) *adv* la-yam.

overcast 1. קודר *adj* koder/-et; **2.** מעונן (clouded) *adj* me‘oon|an/-enet.

(to) overcharge 1. לגבות מחיר מוגזם (price) *inf* leegbot mekheer moogzam; *pst* gavah *etc* (*v=b*); *pres* goveh *etc*; *fut* yeegbeh; **2.** להעמיס עומס יתר (load) *inf* leha‘amees ‘omes yeter; *pst* he‘emees *etc*; *pres* ma‘amees *etc*; *fut* ya‘amees *etc*.

overcoat מעיל עליון *nm* me‘eel/-eem ‘elyon/-eem.

(to) overcome לגבור על *inf* leegbor ‘al; *pst* gavar ‘al; *pres* gover ‘al; *fut* yeegbar ‘al.

overcrowded 1. צפוף *adj* tsafoof/tsfoofah; **2.** מלא מפה אל פה (to capacity) *adj* male/mele‘ah mee-peh el peh.

overcurious סקרן יתר על המידה *adj* sakran/-eet yeter ‘al ha-meedah

overdraft 1. משיכת יתר *nf* mesheekh|at/-ot yeter; **2.** אוברדרפט *nm* overdraft/-eem.

overdue 1. שמועד פרעונו חלף *adj* she-mo‘ed peer‘on|o/-ah khalaf; **2.** שמשתהה מעל למותר (late) *v pres & adj* she-meeshtaheh me-‘al la-mootar.

(to) overeat לזלול *inf* leezlol; *pst* zalal; *pres* zolel; *fut* yeezlol.

(to) overexcite לרגש מעל לרצוי *inf* leragesh me-‘al la-ratsooy; *pst* reegesh *etc*; *pres* meragesh *etc*; *fut* yeragesh *etc*.

overexertion מאמץ יתר *nm* ma‘amats/-ey yeter.

overflow גודש *nm* godesh.

(to) overflow 1. לגדוש *inf* leegdosh; *pst* gadash; *pres* godesh; *fut* yeegdosh; **2.** לעבור על גדותיו (innundate) *inf* la‘avor ‘al gedot|av/-eha; *pst* ‘avar *etc*; *pres* ‘over *etc*; *fut* ya‘avor *etc*.

overgrown מגודל מדי *adj* megood|al/-elet meeday.

overgrown boy נער מגודל *nm* na‘ar/ne‘areem megoodal/-eem.

(to) overhang לבלוט החוצה *inf* leevlot ha-khootsah; *pst* balat *etc* (*b=v*); *pres* bolet *etc*; *fut* yeevlot *etc*.

overhaul שיפוץ כללי *nm* sheepoots/-eem klalee/-yeem.

(to) overhaul לשפץ *inf* leshapets; *pst* sheepets; *pres* meshapets; *fut* yeshapets.

overhead עילי *adj* ‘eelee/-t.

overhead expenses הוצאות עקיפות *nf pl* hotsa‘ot ‘akeefot.

(to) overhear לשמוע באקראי *inf* leeshmo‘a‘ be-akray; *pst* shama‘ *etc*; *pres* shome‘a‘ *etc*; *fut* yeeshma‘ *etc*.

(to) overheat לחמם מעל לדרוש *inf* lekhamem me‘al la-daroosh; *pst* kheemem *etc*; *pres* mekhamem *etc*; *fut* yekhamem *etc*.

overland 1. על פני האדמה *adv* ‘al peney ha-adamah; **2.** יבשתי *adj* yabeshtee/-t.

(to) overlap לחפוף *inf* lakhpof; *pst* khafaf (*f=p*); *pres* khofef; *fut* yakhpof.

(to) overlay 1. לפשוט על *inf* leefshot ‘al; *pst* pashat ‘al (*p=f*); *pres* poshet ‘al; *fut* yeefshot ‘al; **2.** לכסות (cover) *inf* lekhasot; *pst* keesah (*k=kh*); *pres* mekhaseh; *fut* yekhaseh.

overload מעמס יתר *nm* ma‘am|as/-sey yeter.

(to) overload להעמיס עומס יתר *inf* leha‘amees ‘omes yeter; *pst* he‘emees *etc*; *pres* ma‘amees *etc*; *fut* ya‘amees *etc*.

(to) overlook 1. להעלים עין *inf* leha‘aleem ‘ayeen; *pst* he‘eleem *etc*; *pres* ma‘aleem *etc*; *fut* ya‘aleem *etc*; **2.** לא להבחין (fail to notice) *inf* lo lehavkheen; *pst* lo heevkheen; *pres* eyno mavkheen; *fut* lo yavkheen; **3.** להתעלם (ignore) *v rfl inf* leheet‘alem; *pst* heet‘alem; *pres* meet‘alem; *fut* yeet‘alem.

overly יותר מדי *adv* yoter meeday.

overnight 1. בן־לילה *adv* been laylah; **2.** לילי (nocturnal) *adj* leylee/-t.

overnight bag שקית כלי שינה *nf* sakee|t/-yot kley sheynah.

overnight trip מסע לילי *nm* mas|a‘/-a‘ot leylee/-yeem.

overpass 1. מעבר עילי *nm* ma‘avar/-eem ‘eelee/-yeem; **2.** גשר (bridge) *nm* gesh|er/-areem (*pl+of:* geeshrey).

(to) overpower להכניע *inf* lehakhnee‘a‘; *pst* heekhnee‘a‘; *pres* makhnee‘a‘; *fut* yakhnee‘a‘.

(to) overrate להגזים בהערכה *inf* lehagzeem be-ha‘arakhah; *pst* heegzeem *etc*; *pres* magzeem *etc*; *fut* yagzeem *etc*.

(to) override 1. להכריע (prevail) *inf* lehakhree‘a‘; *pst* heekhree‘a‘; *pres* makhree‘a‘; *fut* yakhree‘a‘; **2.** לבטל (cancel) *inf* levatel; *pst* beetel (*b=v*); *pres* mevatel; *fut* yevatel.

(to) overrule 1. להשתלט *inf* leheeshtalet; *pst* heeshtalet; *pres* meeshtalet; *fut* yeeshtalet; **2.** לבטל (cancel) *inf* levatel; *pst* beetel (*b=v*); *pres* mevatel; *fut* yevatel.

(to) overrun 1. לפלוש *inf* leeflosh; *pst* palash (*p=f*); *pres* polesh; *fut* yeeflosh; **2.** לדרוס (trample) *inf* leedros; *pst* daras; *pres* dores; *fut* yeedros.

overseas מעבר לים *adv* me-‘ever la-yam.

(to) oversee לפקח *inf* lefake‘akh; *pst* peeke‘akh (*p=f*); *pres* mefake‘akh; *fut* yefake‘akh.

overseer מפקח *nmf* mefak|e‘akh/-akhat.

overshoe ערדל *nm* ‘ard|al/-alayeem (*pl+of:* -eley).

oversight 1. פיקוח (supervision) *nm* peekoo‘akh; **2.** טעות (error) *nf* ta‘oo|t/-yot; **3.** אי־הבחנה (failure to notice) *nf* ee-havkhan|ah/-ot (*+of:* -at).

(to) overstep לחרוג *inf* lakhrog; *pst* kharag; *pres* khoreg; *fut* yakhrog.

(to) overstep the bounds לחרוג מעבר למותר *inf* lakhrog me-‘ever la-mootar; *pst* kharag *etc*; *pres* khoreg *etc*; *fut* yakhrog *etc*.

(to) overtake לעבור על פני *inf* la‘avor ‘al peney; *pst* ‘avar *etc*; *pres* ‘over *etc*; *fut* ya‘avor *etc*.

overthrow 1. הפיכה *nf* hafeekh|ah/-ot (*+of:* -at); **2.** הפלה (overturn) *nf* hapal|ah/-ot (*+of:* -at).

(to) overthrow להפיל *inf* lehapeel; *pst* heepeel; *pres* mapeel; *fut* yapeel.

overtime שעות נוספות *nf pl* sha‘ot nosafot.

overtime pay תשלום שעות נוספות *nm* tashloom/-ey sha‘ot nosafot.

overture פתיחה *nf* peteekh|ah/-ot (*+of:* -at).

(to) overturn 1. למגר (cast down) *inf* lemager; *pst* meeger; *pres* memager; *fut* yemager; **2.** להפוך

(reverse) *inf* lahafokh; *pst* hafakh; *pres* hofekh; *fut* yahafokh.

(to) overwhelm 1. לדכא *inf* ledake; *pst* deeka; *pres* medake; *fut* yedake; **2.** להדביר (overcome) *inf* lehadbeer; *pst* heedbeer; *pres* madbeer; *fut* yadbeer.

overwhelming מכריע *adj* makhree|'a'/-'ah.

overwork עבודה מאומצת *nf* 'avodah me'oometset.

(to) overwork להעביד בפרך *inf* leha'aveed be-ferekh *(f=p)*; *pst* he'eveed *etc*; *pres* ma'aveed *etc*; *fut* ya'aveed *etc*.

(to) owe להיות חייב *inf* leehyot khayav; *pst* hayah *etc*; *pres* heeno *etc*; *fut* yeehyeh *etc*.

owing עקב *prep* 'ekev.

owl ינשוף *nm* yanshoof/-eem *(pl+of:* -ey).

own פרטי *adj* pratee/-t.

(a house of his) own בית משלו *nm* bayeet mee-shel|o/-ah *(m/f)*.

(on my) own על אחריותי שלי 'al akhrayootee shelee.

(into one's) own לקניינו שלו *adv* le-keenyan|o/-ah shel|o/-ah *(m/f)*.

(to) own להיות בעליו של *inf* leehyot be'alav shel; *pst* hayah *etc*; *pres* heeno *etc*; *fut* yeehyeh *etc*.

(to hold one's) own לעמוד על שלו *inf* la'amod 'al shel|o/-ah; *pst* 'amad *etc*; *pres* 'omed *etc*; *fut* ya'amod *etc*.

(his/her) own people 1. עמו שלו (nation) *nm* 'am|o/-ah shel|o/-ah *(m/f)*; **2.** משפחתו שלו (family) *nf* meeshpakht|o/-ah shel|o/-ah *(m/f)*.

(to) own to להיות חייב ל- *inf* leehyot khayav le-; *pst* hayah *etc*; *pres* heeno *etc*; *fut* yeehyeh *etc*.

(to) own up להודות (confess) *inf* lehodot; *pst* hodah; *pres* modeh; *fut* yodeh.

owner בעלים *nm pl* be'al|eem (*+of:* -av) shel.

ownership בעלות *nf* ba'aloo|t/-yot.

ox שור *nm* shor/shvareem *(pl+of:* shorey).

oxide תחמוצת *nf* takhmots|et/-ot.

(to) oxidize לחמצן *inf* lekhamtsen; *pst* kheemtsen; *pres* mekhamtsen; *fut* yekhamtsen.

oxygen חמצן *nm* khamtsan.

oyster צדף *nm* tsed|ef/-afeem *(pl+of:* tseedfey).

ozone אוזון *nm* ozon.

P.

P,p is transliterated as פ (Peh), even at the end of a word, e.g., ג'יפ *jeep*. (Note: פ is also used to transliterate "f" and "ph", e.g., פיליפ filip (Philip); in pointed Hebrew a dot is added within to distinguish p (פּ) from f (פ)).

pace 1. פסיעה *nf* pesee|'ah/-'ot (*+of:* -'at); **2.** צעד (step) *nm* tsa'ad/tse'adeem *(pl+of:* tsa'adey); **3.** קצב (rhythm) *nm* kets|ev/-aveem *(pl+of:* keetsvey).

pacemaker 1. קוצב *nm* kots|ev/-veem *(pl+of:* -vey); **2.** קוצב לב (for heart) *nm* kots|ev/-vey lev.

pacific 1. רודף שלום *adj* rodef/-et shalom; **2.** שליו (calm) *adj* shalev/shlevah.

Pacific Ocean האוקינוס השקט *nm* ha-okyanos ha-shaket.

pacifism 1. אהבת שלום *nf* ahavat shalom; **2.** פציפיזם *nm* patseefeezm.

(to) pacify להשכין שלום *inf* lehashkeen shalom; *pst* heeshkeen *etc*; *pres* mashkeen *etc*; *fut* yashkeen *etc.*.

pack 1. חפיסה *nf* khafees|ah/-ot (*+of:* -at); **2.** חבילה (parcel) *nf* khaveel|ah/-ot (*+of:* -at).

pack animal בהמת משא *nf* behemat/bahamot masa.

(to) pack off לשלח *inf* leshale'akh; *pst* sheelakh; *pst* meshale'akh; *fut* yeshalakh.

package 1. חבילה *nf* khaveel|ah/-ot (*+of:* -at); **2.** צרור (bundle) *nm* tsror/-ot.

packer אורז *nm* orez.

packet מעטפה *nf* ma'at|afah/-afot (*+of:* -efet).

packing אריזה *nf* areez|ah/-ot (*+of:* -at).

packing box תיבת אריזה *nf* teyv|at/-ot areezah (*+of:* -at).

packing house בית אריזה *nm* bet/batey areezah.

packing paper נייר אריזה *nm* neyar/-ot areezah.

pact 1. אמנה *nf* aman|ah/-ot (*+of:* -at); **2.** ברית *nf* breet/-ot.

pad 1. פנקס *nm* peenk|as/-aseem *(pl+of:* -esey); **2.** כרית (cushion) *nf* karee|t/-yot.

(to) pad לרפד *inf* leraped; *pst* reeped; *pres* meraped; *fut* yeraped.

padding ריפוד *nm* reepood/-eem *(pl+of:* -ey).

paddle משוט *nm* mashot/meshot|eem *(pl+of:* -ey).

(to) paddle לחתור *inf* lakhtor; *pst* khatar; *pres* khoter; *fut* yakhtor.

paddle wheel משוטה *nf* meshot|ah/-ot (*+of:* -at).

paddock דיר *nm* deer/-eem *(pl+of:* -ey).

padlock מנעול *nm* man'ool/-eem *(pl+of:* -ey).

pagan של עובדי אלילים *adj* shel 'ovdey eleeleem.

paganism עבודת אלילים *nf* 'avodat eleeleem.

page 1. עמוד (page) *nm* 'amood/-eem *(pl+of:* -ey); **2.** דף (leaf) *nm* daf/dapeem *(pl+of:* -ey; *p=f)*; **3.** נער משרת (boy) *nm* na'ar/ne'areem meshar|et/-teem.

(to) page לאתר על ידי קריאות בשם *inf* le'ater 'al yedey kree'ot be-shem.

pageant הצגת ראווה *nf* hatsag|at/-ot ra'avah.

paid משולם *adj* meshool|am/-emet.

pail דלי *nm* dlee/dla|yeem *(pl+of:* -yey).

pain כאב *nm* ke'ev/-eem *(pl+of:* -ey).

(in) pain בכאבים *adv* bee-khe'eveem *(kh=k)*.

(on) pain of תחת עונש *adv* takhat 'onesh.

painful מכאיב *adj* makh'eev/-ah.

painkiller גלולה נגד כאבים *nf* gool|ah/-ot neged ke'eveem.

painless ללא כאבים *adj & adv* le-lo ke'eveem.

pains כאבים *nm pl* ke'eveem.

(to take) pains להתאמץ *inf* leheet'amets; *pst* heet'amets; *pres* meet'amets; *fut* yeet'amets.

painstaking 1. מדוקדק *adj* medookd|ak/-eket; **2.** מקפיד *v pres & adj* makpeed/-ah.

paint 1. צבע (mixture) *nm* tseva'/tsva'eem (*pl+of:* tseev'ey); **2.** אודם (rouge) *nm* odem.

(to) paint 1. לצבוע (decorate) *inf* leetsbo'a'; *pst* tsava' *(v=b)*; *pres* tsove'a'; *fut* yeetsba'; **2.** לצייר (as art) *inf* letsayer; *pst* tseeyer; *pres* metsayer; *fut* yetsayer.

(to) paint the town red לערוך הילולא *inf* la'arokh heeloola; *pst* 'arakh *etc*; *pres* 'orekh *etc*; *fut* ya'arokh *etc*.

paintbrush מכחול *nm* meekh'khol/-eem (*pl+of:* -ey).

painter 1. צבע (artisan) *nm* tsaba'/-a'eem (*pl+of:* -a'ey); **2.** צייר (artist) tsa|yar/-yeret (*pl+of:* -yarey).

painting 1. צביעה (skill) *nf* tsvee|'ah/-'ot (*+of:* -'at); **2.** ציור (art) *nm* tseeyoor; **3.** תמונה (picture) *nf* temoon|ah/-ot (*+of:* -at).

pair 1. זוג *nm* zoog/-ot; **2.** צמד (couple) *nm* tsem|ed/-adeem (*pl+of:* tseemdey).

(a) pair of scissors זוג מספריים *nm* zoog/-ot meesparayeem.

(to) pair off לסדר בזוגות *inf* lesader be-zoogot; *pst* seeder *etc*; *pres* mesader *etc*; *fut* yesader *etc*.

pajamas פיג'מה *nf* peejam|ah/-ot (*+of:* -at).

pal 1. רע *nm* re'a'/re'eem (*pl+of:* re'ey); **2.** ידיד yadeed/yedeedeem (*+of:* yedeed/-ey).

palace ארמון *nm* armon/-ot.

palatial לתלפיות *adj* le-talpeeyot.

pale חיוור *adj* kheever/-et.

(to) pale להחוויר *inf* lehakhveer; *pst* hekhveer; *pres* makhveer; *fut* yakhveer.

paleness חיוורון *nm* kheev|aron (*+of:* -ron).

palisade גדר כלונסאות *nf* geder/geedrot kloonsa'ot.

(to) palisade לגדר *inf* legader; *pst* geeder; *pres* megader; *fut* yegader.

(to) pall לעייף *inf* le'ayef; *pst* 'eeyef; *pres* me'ayef; *fut* ye'ayef.

palliative 1. מקל *adj* mek|el/-eelah; **2.** הקלה (alleviation) *nf* hakal|ah/-ot (*+of:* -at).

pallid חיוור *adj* kheever/-et.

pallor חיוורון *nm* kheev|aron (*+of:* -ron).

palm 1. דקל *nm* dek|el/-aleem (*pl+of:* deekley); **2.** תמר (date-palm) *nm* tamar/temareem (*pl+of:* tamrey); **3.** כף היד (of the hand) *nf* kaf/kapot *(p=f)* ha-yad/-ayeem.

(to) palm something off on someone לתלות את הקולר במישהו *inf* leetlot et ha-kolar; *pst* talah *etc*; *pres* toleh *etc*; *fut* yeetleh *etc*.

palm tree 1. תומר *nm* tomer/temareem (*pl+of:* tomrey); **2.** עץ דקל *nm* 'ets/'atsey dek|el/-aleem.

palpable בר מישוש *adj* bar/bat meeshoosh.

(to) palpitate לפרפר *inf* lefarper; *pst* peerper *(p=f)*; *pres* mefarper; *fut* yefarper.

palpitation דפיקות לב *nf pl* defeekot lev.

paltry 1. חסר־ערך *adj* khas|ar/-rat 'erekh; **2.** מבוטל *adj* mevoot|al/-elet.

(to) pamper לפנק *inf* lefanek; *pst* peenek *(p=f)*; *pres* mefanek; *fut* yefanek.

pamphlet עלון *nm* 'alon/-eem (*pl+of:* -ey).

pan מחבת *nf* makhvat/-ot.

(dish) pan סיר להדחת צלחות *nm* seer/-eem la-hadakhat tsalakhot.

(frying) pan מחבת טיגון *nf* makhvat/-ot teegoon.

(to) pan out 1. להצליח *inf* lehatslee'akh; *pst* heetslee'akh; *pres* matslee'akh; *fut* yatslee'akh; **2.** להפיק זהב (gold) *inf* lehafeek zahav; *pst* hefeek *etc*; *pres* mefeek *etc*; *fut* yafeek *etc*.

pancake לביבה *nf* leveev|ah/-ot (*+of:* -at).

pander 1. סרסור *nm* seersoor/-eem (*pl+of:* -ey); **2.** מתווך (mediator) *nmf* metavekh/-et (*pl:* metavkh|eem/-ot; *pl+of:* -ey).

(to) pander 1. לסרסר *inf* lesarser; *pst* seerser; *pres* mesarser; *fut* yesarser; **2.** לתווך (mediate) *inf* letavekh; *pst* teevekh; *pres* metavekh; *fut* yetavekh.

pane שמשה *nf* sheemshah/shmashot (*+of:* sheemsh|at/-ot).

panel 1. צוות משיבים *nm* tsevet/tseevtot mesheeveem; **2.** חבר משתתפים *nm* khever meeshtatfeem.

(instrument) panel לוח מכשירים *nm* loo|'akh/-khot makhsheereem.

(jury) panel חבר מושבעים *nm* khever mooshba'eem.

(to) panel 1. למלא *inf* lemale; *pst* meele; *pres* memale; *fut* yemale; **2.** לקשט *inf* lekashet; *pst* keeshet; *pres* mekashet; *fut* yekashet.

panel door דלת מלואה *nf* delet/dlatot meloo|'ah/-'ot.

pang כאב פתאום *nm* ke'ev/-ey peet'om.

panhandle ידית של מחבת *nf* yadee|t/-yot shel makhvat.

(to) panhandle לחזר על הפתחים *inf* lekhazer 'al ha-p'takheem; *pst* kheezer *etc*; *pres* mekhazer *etc*; *fut* yekhazer *etc*.

panic 1. חרדה *nf* kharad|ah/-ot (*+of:* kherd|at/-ot); **2.** פניקה *nf* paneek|ah/-ot (*+of:* -at).

panic-stricken אחוז חרדה *adj* akhooz/-at kharadah.

panorama 1. נוף *nm* nof/-eem (*pl+of:* -ey); **2.** פנורמה *nf* panoram|ah/-ot (*+of:* -at).

pansy אמנון ותמר *nm* amnon ve-tamar.

(to) pant להתנשף *inf* leheetnashef; *pst* heetnashef; *pres* meetnashef; *fut* yeetnashef.

(to) pant for לערוג ל־ *inf* la'arog le-; *pst* 'arag le-; *pres* 'oreg le-; *fut* ya'arog le-.

panther 1. נמר *nm* namer/nemereem (*pl+of:* neemrey); **2.** פנתר *nm* panter/-eem (*pl+of:* -ey).

(the "Black) Panthers" movement תנועת הפנתרים השחורים *nf* tenoo'at ha-pantereem ha-shekhoreem.

panting בנשימה עצורה *adv* bee-nesheemah 'atsoorah.

pantomime פנטומימה *nf* pantomeem|ah/-ot (*+of:* -at).

pantry מזווה *nm* mezav|eh/-eem (*pl+of:* -ey).

pants 1. תחתונים (underwear) *nm pl* takhton|eem (*pl+of:* -ey); **2.** מכנסיים (trousers) *nm pl* meekhn|asayeem (*+of:* -esey).

papa אבא *nm* aba.

papacy אפיפיורות *nf* apeefyoroo|t/-yot.

papal אפיפיורי *adj* apeefyoree/-t.

paper 1. נייר (material) *nm* neyar/-ot; **2.** עיתון (daily) *nm* 'eeton/-eem (*pl+of:* -ey); **3.** עבודה בכתב (essay) *nf* avod|ah/-ot bee-khtav *(kh=k)*.

(on) paper בכתב *adv* bee-khtav *(kh=k)*.

paper doll בובת נייר *nf* boob|at/-ot neyar.

paper money שטר כסף *nm* shtar/sheetrey kesef.

paperweight אבן אכף *nf* even/avney ekhef.

paperback ספר בכריכה רכה *nm* sefer/sfareem bee-khreekhah rakah.

papers מסמכים *nm pl* meesm|akheem (*pl+of:* -ekhey).

(naturalization) papers מסמכי התאזרחות *nm pl* meesmekhey heet'azrekhoot.

par שווי *nm* shovee.

(above) par מעל לשווי *adv* me-'al la-shovee.

(at) par שווה בשווה *adv* shaveh be-shaveh.

(below) par מתחת לשווי me-takhat la-shovee.

parable משל *nm* mashal/meshaleem (*pl+of:* meeshley).

parachute 1. מצנח *nm* matsne|'akh/-kheem (*pl+of:* -khey); **2.** מיצנח *cpr nm* meetsn|akh/-akheem (*pl+of:* -ekhey).

parachutist צנחן *nm* tsankhan/-eem (*pl+of:* -ey).

parade 1. מסדר *nm* meesd|ar/-areem (*pl+of:* -erey); **2.** מצעד (march) *nm* meets'ad/-eem (*pl+of:* -ey).

parade ground כיכר מצעדים *nm* keekar meets'adeem.

(to make a) parade of 1. להציג לראווה *inf* lehatseeg le-ra'avah; *pst* heetseeg *etc*; *pres* matseeg *etc*; *fut* yatseeg *etc*; **2.** להתרברב (boast) *inf* leheetravrev; *pst* heetravrev; *pres* meetravrev; *fut* yeetravrev.

paradigm 1. מופת *nm* mof|et/-teem (*pl+of:* -tey); **2.** דוגמה (grammat.) *nf* doogm|ah/-a'ot (*+of:* -at).

paradise גן עדן *nm* gan/-ey 'eden.

paradox פרדוקס *nm* paradoks/-eem (*pl+of:* -ey).

paraffin פרפין *nm* parafeen.

paragraph 1. פיסקה *nf* peesk|ah/-a'ot (*pl+of:* -at); **2.** סעיף (article) *nm* se'eef/-eem (*pl+of:* -ey).

parallel מקביל *adj* makbeel/-ah.

(to) parallel להקביל *inf* lehakbeel; *pst* heekbeel; *pres* makbeel; *fut* yakbeel.

paralysis שיתוק *nm* sheetook/-eem (*pl+of:* -ey).

(to) paralyze לשתק *inf* leshatek; *pst* sheetek; *pres* meshatek; *fut* yeshatek.

paramount 1. ראשי *adj* rashee/-t; **2.** עליון *adj* 'elyon/-ah.

paranoia שגעון גדלות *nm* sheeg'on/-ot gadloot.

parapet מעקה *nm* ma'ak|eh/-ot.

(to) paraphrase לנסח זאת אחרת *inf* lenase'akh zot akheret; *pst* neese'akh *etc*; *pres* menase'akh *etc*; *fut* yenase'akh *etc*.

parasite טפיל *nm* tapeel/-eem (*pl+of:* -ey).

parasol שמשייה *nf* sheemshee|yah/-yot (*+of:* -yat).

paratroops חיל צנחנים *nm* kheyl/-ot tsankhaneem.

parcel חבילה *nf* khaveel|ah/-ot (*+of:* -at).

parcel post דואר חבילות *nm* do'ar khaveelot.

(to) parcel 1. לחלק *inf* lekhalek; *pst* kheelek; *pres* mekhalek; *fut* yekhalek; **2.** לעטוף *inf* la'atof; *pst* 'ataf; *pres* 'otef; *fut* ya'atof.

(to) parch להצמיא *inf* lehatsmee; *pst* heetsmee; *pres* matsmee; *fut* yatsmee.

parchment 1. קלף *nm* klaf/-eem (*pl+of:* -ey); **2.** גוויל (scroll) *nm* gveel/-eem (*pl+of:* -ey).

pardon 1. סליחה *nf* sleekh|ah/-ot (*+of:* -at); **2.** מחילה (forgiveness) *nf* mekheel|ah/-ot (*+of:* -at).

(I beg your) pardon 1. אבקש סליחה *v fut* avakesh sleekhah; **2.** סליחה! (more commonly used) *interj* sleekhah!

(to) pardon 1. לחון *inf* lakhon; *pst* khanan; *pres* khonen; *fut* yakhon; **2.** לסלוח (forgive) *inf* leeslo'akh; *pst* salakh; *pres* sole'akh; *fut* yeeslakh.

(to) pare 1. להפקיע *inf* lehafkheet; *pst* heefkheet; *pres* mafkheet; *fut* yafkheet; **2.** לקלף *inf* lekalef; *pst* keelef; *pres* mekalef; *fut* yekalef.

(to) pare down expenditures לצמצם הוצאות *inf* letsamtsem hotsa'ot; *pst* tseemtsem *etc*; *pres* metsamtsem *etc*; *fut* yetsamtsem *etc*.

parent הורה *nmf* hor|eh/-ah (*pl:* -eem/-ot; *+of:* -ey).

parentage הורות *nf* horoo|t/-yot.

parental של הורים *adj* shel horeem.

parenthesis סוגריים *nm pl* sogr|ayeem (*+of:* -ey).

parents הורים *nm pl* hor|eem (*+of:* -ey).

parish קהילה נוצרית *nf* keheel|ah/-ot notsree|t/-yot.

parishioner חבר קהילה *nmf* khaver/-at keheelah notsreet.

park 1. גן ציבורי *nm* gan/-eem tseebooree/-yeem; **2.** פרק *nm* park/-eem (*pl+of:* -ey).

(to) park להחנות *inf* lehakhnot; *pst* hekhnah; *pres* makhneh; *fut* yakhneh.

parking 1. חניה (ground) *nf* khana|yah/-yot (*+of:* -yat); **2.** חנייה (action) *nf* khanee|yah/-yot (*+of:* -yat).

(free) parking חניית חינם *nf* khaneeyat/-yot kheenam.

(no) parking! אין חנייה! *interj* eyn khaneeyah!

parking lot מיגרש חניה *nm* meegr|ash/-eshey khanayah.

parking space שטח חניה *nm* shetakh/sheetkhey khaneeyah.

parlance 1. דיון *nm* deeyoon/-eem (*pl+of:* -ey); **2.** שיחה (talk) *nf* seekh|ah/-ot (*+of:* -at).

parley 1. משא ומתן *nm* masa oo-matan; **2.** מו״מ (*acr of* 1) *nm* moom/-eem (*pl+of:* -ey).

parliament 1. בית נבחרים *nm* bet/batey neevkhareem; **2.** הכנסת (Isr. parliament) *nf* ha-kneset (*pl:* kenasot); **3.** פרלמנט *nm* parlament/-eem (*pl+of:* -ey).

parliamentary פרלמנטרי *adj* parlamentaree/-t.

parlor 1. טרקלין *nm* trakleen/-eem (*pl+of:* -ey); **2.** סלון (synon. with 1) *[colloq.] nm* salon/-eem (*pl+of:* -ey).

(beauty) parlor מכון יופי *nm* mekhon/-ey yofee.

parlor car קרון רכבת ייצוגי *nm* kron/-ot rakevet yeetsoogee/-yeem.
parochial 1. קרתני *adj* kartanee/-yeem; **2.** עדתי *adj* 'adatee/-t.
parody פרודיה *nf* parodee|yah/-yot (*+of:* -yat).
parole הן צדק *nm* hen tsedek.
(to) parole לשחרר על תנאי *inf* leshakhrer 'al tenay; *pst* sheekhrer *etc; pres* meshakhrer *etc; fut* yeshakhrer *etc.*
parrot תוכי *nm* tookee/-yeem (*pl+of:* -yey).
(to) parry להדוף *inf* lahadof; *pst* hadaf; *pres* hodef; *fut* yahadof.
parsley 1. פטרוסלינון *nm* petrosleenon/-eem (*pl+of:* -ey); **2.** פטרוזיליה *nf* petrozeel|yah/-yot (*+of:* -yat).
parsnip גזר לבן *nm* gezer lavan.
parson כומר *nm* komer/kemar|eem (*pl+of:* komrey).
part 1. חלק *nm* khelek/khalakeem (*pl+of:* khelkey); **2.** מנה (share) *nf* man|ah/-ot (*+of:* men|at/-ot); **3.** תפקיד (role) *nm* tafkeed/-eem (*pl+of:* -ey).
(do your) part עשה כמוטל עליך *v imp m/f* 'aseh/'asee ka-mootal 'alekha/'alayeekh.
(to) part 1. להיפרד *inf* leheepared; *pst & pres* neefrad *(f=p); fut* yeepared; **2.** לחלק (divide) *inf* lekhalek; *pst* kheelek; *pres* mekhalek; *fut* yekhalek.
part and parcel חלק בלתי נפרד *nm* khelek/khalakeem beeltee neefrad/-eem.
(to) part company להיפרד מ־ *inf* leheepared mee-; *pst & pres* neefrad mee-; *fut* yeepared mee-.
(to) part from להיפרד מעל *inf* leheepared me-'al-; *pst & pres* neefrad *(f=p) etc; fut* yeepared *etc.*
(to) part one's hair להפריד שיער בפסוקת *inf* lehafreed sey'ar bee-f'soket; *pst* heefreed *etc; pres* mafreed *etc; fut* yafreed *etc.*
part owner 1. שותף *nmf* shootaf/-ah (*pl:* -eem/-ot; *+of:* -ey); **2.** בעלים בחלק *nm* be'aleem be-khelek.
part time עבודה חלקית *nf* 'avod|ah/-ot khelkee|t/-yot.
(to) part with לוותר *inf* levater; *pst* veeter; *pres* mevater; *fut* yevater.
(to) partake ליטול חלק *inf* leetol khelek; *pst* natal *etc; pres* notel *etc; fut* yeetol *etc.*
partial 1. חלקי *adj* khelkee/-t; **2.** חד־צדדי (one-sided) *adj* khad tsdadee/-t.
partiality חד־צדדיות *nf* khad-tsdadeeyoot.
participant משתתף *nmf* meeshtat|ef/-efet (*pl:* -feem/-fot; *+of:* -fey).
(to) participate להשתתף *inf* leheeshtatef; *pst* heeshtatef; *pres* meeshtatef; *fut* yeeshtatef.
participation השתתפות *nf* heeshtatfoo|t/-yot.
participle בינוני (grammar) *nm* beynonee.
(passive) participle בינוני פעול (grammar) *nm* beynonee pa'ool.
(present) participle בינוני פועל (grammar) *nm* beynonee po'al.
particle 1. חלקיק *nm* khelkeek/-eem (*pl+of:* -ey); **2.** שמץ *nm* shemets.
particular 1. בודד (single) *adj* boded/-et; **2.** מיוחד (special) *adj* meyookh|ad/-edet; **3.** תובעני (demanding) *adj* tov'anee/-t.
particular (detail) פרט *nm* prat/-eem (*pl+of:* peertey).
(in) particular במיוחד *adv* bee-meyookhad.
particularly במיוחד *adv* bee-meyookhad.
parting 1. פרידה (departure) *nf* preed|ah/-ot (*+of:* -at); **2.** חלוקה (division) *nf* khalook|ah/-ot (*+of:* -at).
parting of the ways פרשת דרכים *nf* parash|at/-ot drakheem.
partisan 1. חד־צדדי *adj* khad-tsdadee/-t; **2.** פרטיזן *nm* parteezan/-eem (*pl+of:* -ey).
partition 1. חלוקה (division) *nf* khalook|ah/-ot (*+of:* -at); **2.** מחיצה (screen) *nf* mekheets|ah/-ot (*+of:* -at).
(to) partition 1. לחלק (divide) *inf* lekhalek; *pst* kheelek; *pres* mekhalek; *fut* yekhalek; **2.** להפריד במחיצה (separate) *inf* lehafreed bee-mekheetsah; *pst* heefreed *etc; pres* mafreed *etc; fut* yafreed *etc.*
partitive 1. חלקי *adj* khelkee/-t; **2.** מחלק (dividing) *adj* mekhalek/-et.
partly חלקית *adv* khelkeet.
partner 1. בן־זוג *nmf* ben/bat zoog; **2.** שותף *nmf* shootaf/-ah (*pl:* -eem/-ot; *+of:* -ey).
(business) partner שותף עסקי *nm* shootaf/-eem 'eskee/-yeem.
(dancing) partner בן־זוג לריקודים *nmf* ben/bat zoog le-reekoodeem.
partnership שותפות *nf* shoot|afoot/-fooyot.
partridge חוגלה *nf* khogl|ah/-ot (*+of:* -at).
(in foreign) parts בארצות נכר *adv* be-artsot nekhar.
(spare) parts חלקי חילוף *nm pl* khelkey kheeloof.
party 1. מסיבה (get-together) *nf* meseeb|ah/-ot (*+of:* -at); **2.** קבוצה (group) *nf* kvoots|ah/-ot (*+of:* -at); **3.** צד (in a dispute) *nm* tsad/tsedadeem (*pl+of:* tseedey).
(political) party מפלגה *nf* meefl|agah/-agot (*+of:* -eget/-ot).
pass מעבר *nm* ma'avar/-eem (*pl+of:* -rey).
(to) pass 1. לדון (sentence) *vt inf* ladoon; *pst & pres* dan; *fut* yadoon; **2.** לאשר (approve) *vt inf* le'asher; *pst* eesher; *pres* me'asher; *fut* ye'asher; **3.** לחוקק (law) *vt inf* lekhokek; *pst* khokek; *pres* mekhokek; *fut* yekhokek; **4.** לעבור (exam) *vt inf* la'avor; *pst* 'avar; *pres* 'over; *fut* ya'avor.
(to come to) pass לקרות *inf* leekrot; *pst* karah; *pres* koreh; *fut* yeekreh.
(to) pass away 1. למות (die) *inf* lamoot; *pst & pres* met; *fut* yamoot; **2.** להיעלם (disappear) *inf* lehe'alem; *pst & pres* ne'elam; *fut* ye'alem; **3.** להעביר את הזמן (time) *inf* leha'aveer et ha-zman; *pst* he'eveer *etc; pres* ma'aveer *etc; fut* ya'aveer *etc.*
(to) pass for להתחזות כ־ *vi (refl) inf* leheetkhazot ke-; *pst* heetkhazah ke-; *pres* meetkhazeh ke-; *fut* yeetkhazeh ke-.
pass key מפתח פתחכול *nm* mafte'akh/-khot petakhkol.
passable 1. חדיר (penetrable) *adj* khadeer/-ah; **2.** מתקבל על הדעת (acceptable) *adj* meetkabel/-et 'al ha-da'at.
passage 1. כרטיס נסיעה *nm* kartees/-ey nesee'ah; **2.** חלוף הזמן (of time) *nm* khalof ha-zman; **3.** קבלת החלטה (of resolution) kabalat

hakhlat|ah/-ot; **4.** חיקוק חוק (of law) *nm* kheekook/-ey khok.
passageway מסדרון *nm* meesderon/-ot.
passbook פנקס בנק *nm* peenkes/-ey bank.
passenger נוסע *nmf* nos|e'a'/-a'at (*pl:* -'eem/-'ot; *+of:* -'ey).
passer-by עובר אורח *nmf* 'over/-et (*pl+of:* 'ovrey) orakh.
passion 1. תאווה *nf* ta'av|ah/-ot (*+of:* -at); **2.** תשוקה (desire) *nf* teshook|ah/-ot (*+of:* -at).
passionate נלהב *adj* neel|'hav/-'hevet.
passive 1. סביל *adj* saveel/sveelah; **2.** פסיבי *adj* paseevee/-t.
Passover פסח *nm* pesakh/-eem (*pl+of:* peeskhey).
passport דרכון *nm* darkon/-eem (*pl+of:* -ey).
password סיסמה *nf* seesm|ah/-a'ot (*+of:* -at).
past 1. עבר *nm* 'avar; **2.** לשעבר (former) *adj* le-she-'avar.
(for some time) past כבר מכמה זמן *adv* kvar mee-kamah zman.
(lady with a) past אישה עם עבר *nf* eeshah 'eem 'avar.
past bearing מעל לכוח הסבל *prep* me-'al le-kho'akh ha-sevel.
(half) past four 1. ארבע וחצי arba' va-khetsee; **2.** ארבע ושלושים (four thirty) arba' oo-shlosheem.
past master אלוף לשעבר *nm & adj* aloof/-eem le-she-'avar.
(the) past president of נשיא לשעבר של *nm* nasee le-she-'avar shel.
past tense זמן עבר *nm* zman/-ey 'avar.
(to go) past the house לעבור על פני הבית *inf* la'avor 'al peney ha-bayeet; *pst* 'avar *etc*; *pres* 'over *etc*; *fut* ya'avor *etc*.
past understanding למעלה מבינת אנוש *prep* lema'lah mee-beenat enosh.
paste דבק *nm* devek/dvakeem (*pl+of:* deevkey).
(to) paste להדביק *inf* lehadbeek; *pst* heedbeek; *pres* madbeek; *fut* yadbeek.
pasteboard קרטון *nm* karton/-eem (*pl+of:* -ey).
pasteboard box תיבת קרטון *nf* teyv|at/-ot karton.
(to) pasteurize לפסטר *inf* lefaster; *pst* peester (*p=f*); *pres* mefaster; *fut* yefaster.
pastime בילוי זמן *nm* beeloo|y/-yey zman.
pastor כומר פרוטסטנטי *nm* komer/kemareem protestantee/-yeem.
pastoral 1. אידיליה *nf* eedeel|yah/-yot (*+of:* -yat); **2.** פסטורלי *adj* pastoralee/-t.
pastry עוגה *nf* 'oog|ah/-ot (*+of:* -at).
pastry cook אופה עוגות *nmf* ofeh/ofat oogot.
pasture מרעה *nm* meer|'eh/-'eem (*pl+of:* -'ey).
(to) pasture לרעות *inf* leer'ot; *pst* ra'ah; *pres* ro'eh; *fut* yeer'eh.
pat 1. טפיחה קלה *nf* tefeekh|ah/-ot kal|ah/-ot. **2.** כהלכה *adv* ka-halakhah.
(a lesson) pat שיעור כהלכה *nm* she'oor/-eem ka-halakhah.
(to) pat 1. לטפוח *inf* leetpo'akh; *pst* tafakh (*f=p*); *pres* tofe'akh; *fut* yeetpakh; **2.** ללטף (caress) *inf* lelatef; *pst* leetef; *pres* melatef; *fut* yelatef.
(to stand) pat לעמוד על דעתו *inf* la'amod 'al da'to; *pst* 'amad *etc*; *pres* 'omed *etc*; *fut* ya'amod *etc*.
pat of butter דבלול של חמאה *nm* davlool shel khem'ah.
patch 1. טלאי (repair) *nm* tla|y/-'eem (*pl+of:* -'ey); **2.** עלילה (plot) *nf* 'aleel|ah/-ot (*+of:* -at); **3.** מגרש (terrain) *nm* meegr|ash/-eem (*pl+of:* -ey).
(to) patch להטליא *inf* lehatlee; *pst* heetlee; *pres* matlee; *fut* yatlee.
(to) patch up a quarrel ליישב מריבה *inf* leyashev mereevah; *pst* yeeshev *etc*; *pres* meyashev *etc*; *fut* yeyashev *etc*.
pate 1. ראש *nm* rosh/-eem (*pl+of:* -ey); **2.** מוח (brain) *nm* mo'akh/mokhot.
(bald) pate ראש קירח *nm* rosh kere'akh.
patent 1. מוגן *adj adj* moog|an/-enet; **2.** פתוח (open) *adj* patoo'akh/petookhah; **3.** גלוי (manifest) *adj* galooy/glooyah.
patent פטנט *nm* patent/-eem (*pl+of:* -ey).
patent leather עור מבריק *nm* 'or/-ot mavreek/-eem.
patent medicine תרופה בדוקה *nf* troof|ah/-ot bedook|ah/-ot.
patent right 1. זכות יוצרים *nf* zekhoo|t/-yot yotsreem; **2.** זכות הפטנט *nf* zekhoo|t/-yot patent.
paternal אבהי *adj* avahee/-t.
paternity אבהות *nf* avahoo|t/-yot.
path 1. שביל *nm* shveel/-eem (*pl+of:* -ey); **2.** מסלול (trajectory) *nm* maslool/-eem (*pl+of:* -ey).
pathetic 1. מרגש *v pres & adj* meragesh/-et; **2.** פתטי *adj* patetee/-t.
pathology פתולוגיה *nf* patolog|yah/-yot (*+of:* -yat).
pathos פתוס *nm* patos/-eem (*pl+of:* -ey).
pathway נתיב *nm* nateev/neteev|eem (*pl+of:* -ey).
patience סבלנות *nf* savlanoo|t/-yot.
patient 1. סבלני *adj* savlanee/-t; **2.** חולה *nmf* khol|eh/-ah (*pl:* -eem/-ot; *+of:* -at/-ey); **3.** פציאנט *nmf* patsyent/-eet (*pl:* -eem/-eeyot; *+of:* -ey).
patriarch 1. אב קדמון *nm* av/-ot kadmon/-eem; **2.** פטריארך *nm* patree'arkh/-eem (*pl+of:* -ey).
patriarchal פטריארכלי *adj* patree'arkhalee/-t.
patrimony 1. נחלת אבות *nf* nakhl|at/-ot avot; **2.** מורשה (heritage) *nf* morash|ah/-ot (*+of:* -eshet)
patriot פטריוט *nmf* patree'ot/-eet.
patriotic פטריוטי *adj* patree'otee/-t.
patriotism 1. אהבת מולדת *nf* ahavat moledet; **2.** פטריוטיות *nf* patree'oteeyoot.
patrol משמר *nm* meeshmar/-ot.
(to) patrol לפטרל *inf* lefatrel; *pst* peetrel (*p=f*); *pres* mefatrel; *fut* yefatrel.
patron פטרון *nm* patron/-eem (*pl+of:* -ey).
patronage 1. חסות (protection) *nf* khasoo|t/-yot; **2.** ציבור לקוחות (clientele) *nm* tseeboor lekookhot; **3.** הסתכלות מגבוה (manner) *nf* heestakloot mee-gavoha.
patroness פטרונית *nf* patronee|t/-yot.
(to) patronize 1. להעניק חסות *inf* leha'aneek khasoot; *pst* he'eneek *etc*; *pres* ma'aneek *etc*; *fut* ya'aneek *etc*; **2.** להסתכל מגבוה (treat condescendingly) *inf* leheestakel mee-gavoha; *pst* heestakel *etc*; *pres* meestakel *etc*; *fut* yeestakel *etc*.

patter להג *nm* lahag/lehageem (*pl+of:* lahagey).

(to) patter ללהג *inf* lelaheg; *pst* leeheg; *pres* melaheg; *fut* yelaheg.

pattern 1. דגם (model) *nm* deg|em/-ameem (*pl+of:* deegmey). **2.** תבנית (mold) *nf* tav-nee|t/-yot; **3.** סרטוט (design) seertoot/-eem (*pl+of:* -ey).

(to) pattern oneself after להידמות ל־ *inf* leheedamot le-; *pst* heedamah le-; *pres* meedameh le-; *fut* yeedameh le-.

(to) pattern something after לתכנן דבר במתכונת *inf* letakhnen davar be-matkonet; *pst* teekhnen *etc*; *pres* metakhnen *etc*; *fut* yetakhnen *etc*.

paucity 1. דלות במיספר *nf* daloot be-meespar; **2.** מחסור (want) *nm* makhsor.

paunch 1. כרס *nm* keres/kresot; **2.** בטן (belly) bet|en/-aneem (*pl+of:* beetney).

pause 1. הפסקה *nf* hafsak|ah/-ot (*+of:* -at); **2.** אתנחתא *nf* etnakht|a/-'ot (*+of:* -at).

(to) pause להפסיק *inf* lehafseek; *pst* heefseek; *pres* mafseek; *fut* yafseek.

(to) pave לסלול *inf* leeslol; *pst* salal; *pres* solel; *fut* yeeslol.

(to) pave the way for לסלול דרך ל־ *inf* leeslol derekh le-; *pst* salal *etc*; *pres* solel *etc*; *fut* yeeslol *etc*.

(to) pave with bricks לרצף בלבנים *inf* leratsef bee-leveneem; *pst* reetsef *etc*; *pres* meratsef *etc*; *fut* yeratsef *etc*.

(to) pave with flagstones לרצף במרצפות גדולות *inf* leratsef be-martsafot gedolot; *pst* reetsef *etc*; *pres* meratsef *etc*; *fut* yeratsef *etc*.

pavement מדרכה *nf* meedrakh|ah/-ot (*+of:* meedrekh|et/-ot).

pavement brick לבנת מדרכה *nf* leevn|at/-ey meedrakhah.

pavilion ביתן *nm* beetan/-eem (*pl+of:* -ey).

paw רגל חיה *nf* regel/ragley kha|yah/-yot.

(to) paw 1. לתפוס בגסות *inf* leetpos be-gasoot; *pst* tafas *etc* (*f=p*); *pres* tofes *etc*; *fut* yeetpos *etc*; **2.** למשש בגסות *inf* (touch rudely) lemashesh be-gasoot; *pst* meeshesh *etc*; *pres* memashesh *etc*; *fut* yemashesh *etc*.

(to) paw the ground לבעוט בקרקע *inf* leev'ot ba-karka'; *pst* ba'at *etc* (*b=v*); *pres* bo'et *etc*; *fut* yeev'at *etc*.

pawn 1. עבוט *nm* 'avot/-eem (*pl+of:* -ey); **2.** משכון *nm* mashkon/-ot (*pl+of:* -ey).

(in) pawn ממושכן *adj* memooshk|an/-enet.

(to) pawn 1. למשכן *inf* lemashken; *pst* meeshken; *pres* memashken; *fut* yemashken; **2.** להלוות בעבוט *inf* lehalvot ba-'avot; *pst* heelvah *etc*; *pres* malveh *etc*; *fut* yalveh *etc*.

pawnbroker משכונאי *nm* mashkon|ay/-a'eem (*pl+of:* -a'ey).

pawnbroker's shop 1. בית משכון *nm* bet/batey mashkon; **2.** בית עבוט (*synon. of 1.*) *nm* bet/batey 'avot.

pay 1. משכורת *nf* maskor|et/-ot; **2.** שכר (remuneration) *nm* sakhar (*+of:* sekhar).

(to) pay 1. לשלם (remit) *inf* leshalem; *pst* sheelem; *pres* meshalem; *fut* yeshalem; **2.** לסלק (repay) *inf* lesalek; *pst* seelek; *pres* mesalek; *fut* yesalek; **3.** לתת רווחים (profit) *inf* latet revakheem; *pst* natan *etc*; *pres* noten *etc*; *fut* yeeten *etc*; **4.** להשתלם (worthwhile) *inf* leheeshtalem; *pst* heeshtalem; *pres* meeshtalem; *fut* yeeshtalem.

(to) pay a visit לערוך ביקור *inf* la'arokh beekoor; *pst* 'arakh *etc*; *pres* 'orekh *etc*; *fut* ya'arokh *etc*.

(to) pay attention לשים לב *inf* laseem lev; *pst & pres* sam lev; *fut* yaseem lev.

(to) pay back להחזיר כספים *inf* lehakhzeer ksafeem; *pst* hekhzeer *etc*; *pres* makhzeer *etc*; *fut* yakhzeer *etc*.

(to) pay court 1. לגלות חיבה *inf* legalot kheebah; *pst* geelah *etc*; *pres* megaleh *etc*; *fut* yegaleh *etc*; **2.** לחזר אחרי (court) *inf* lekhazer akharey; *pst* kheezer *etc*; *pres* mekhazer *etc*; *fut* yekhazer *etc*.

pay day יום תשלומים *nm* yom/yemey tashloomeem.

(to) pay down לשלם במזומן *inf* leshalem bee-mezooman; *pst* sheelem *etc*; *pres* meshalem *etc*; *fut* yeshalem *etc*;

(to) pay homage להשמיע דברי הוקרה *inf* lehashmee'a' deevrey hokarah; *pst* heeshmee'a' *etc*; *pres* mashmee'a'; *fut* yashmee'a' *etc*.

(to) pay one's respects להקביל פנים *inf* lehakbeel paneem; *pst* heekbeel *etc*; *pres* makbeel *etc*; *fut* yakbeel *etc*.

pay roll רשימת משכורת *nf* resheem|at/-ot maskorot.

payable בר־תשלום bar/bat (*pl:* bney/benot) tashloom.

paymaster שלם *nm* shalam/-eem (*pl+of:* -ey).

payment תשלום *nm* tashloom/-eem (*pl+of:* -ey).

payment in full תשלום במלואו *nm* tashloom/-eem bee-melo|'o/-'am,

payoff 1. סילוק מלא *nm* seelook male; **2.** חיסול חשבונות (settlement) *nm* kheesool kheshbonot.

pea אפונה *nf* afoon|ah/-eem (*pl+of:* -ey).

peace שלום *nm* shalom.

"Peace Now!" movement תנועת ״שלום עכשיו״! *nf* tenoo'at "shalom 'akhshav".

peaceable שקט *adj* shaket/shketah.

peaceful 1. שקט *adj* shaket/shketah; **2.** רגוע (calm) *adj* ragoo'a'/regoo'ah.

peach אפרסק *nm* afarsek/-eem (*pl+of:* -ey).

peach tree עץ אפרסק *nm* 'ets/'atsey afarsek/-eem.

peacock טווס *nm* tavas/-eem (*pl+of:* -ey).

(to act like a) peacock לנהוג מעשה טווס *inf* leenhog ma'aseh tavas; *pst* nahag *etc*; *pres* noheg *etc*; *fut* yeenhag *etc*.

peak 1. שיא *nm* see/-'eem (*pl+of:* -'ey); **2.** פסגה (summit) *nf* peesgah/psagot (*+of:* peesg|at/-ot).

peal צלצול פעמונים *nm* tseeltsool/-ey pa'amoneem.

(to) peal 1. להדהד *inf* lehadhed; *pst* heedhed; *pres* mehadhed; *fut* yehadhed; **2.** לרעום *inf* leer'om; *pst* ra'am; *pres* ro'em; *fut* yeer'am.

peal of laughter רעם צחוק *nm* ra'am/-ey tsekhok.

peal of thunder קול רעם *nm* kol/-ot ra'am.

peanut בוטן *nm* bot|en/-neem (*pl+of:* -ney).

pear אגס *nm* agas/-eem (*pl+of:* -ey).

pear tree עץ אגס *nm* 'ets/'atsey agas/-eem.

pearl פנינה *nf* peneen|ah/-eem (*pl+of:* -ey).

(mother-of-)pearl צדף *nm* tsed|ef/-afeem (*pl+of:* tseedfey).

pearl necklace ענק פנינים *nm* 'anak/-ey peneeneem.

pearly דמוי פנינה *adj* dmooy/-at peneenah.

peasant 1. איכר *nm* eekar/-eem (*pl+of:* -ey); **2.** של איכרים *adj* shel eekareem.

pebble אבן חצץ *nf* even/avney khatsats.

pecan אגוז פקאן *nm* egoz/-ey pekan.

peck 1. מידת יובש *nf* meed|at/-ot yovesh; **2.** תשעה ליטרים (nine litres) teesh'ah leetreem.

(to) peck לנקר *inf* lenaker; *pst* neeker; *pres* menaker; *fut* yenaker.

(a) peck of trouble מנה גדושה של צרות *nf* manah gedooshah shel tsarot.

peculiar 1. מיוחד *adj* meyookh|ad/-edet; **2.** מוזר (strange) *adj* moozar/-ah.

peculiarity ייחוד *nm* yeekhood/-eem (*pl+of:* -ey).

pedagogue פדגוג *nmf* pedagog/-eet.

pedagogy 1. חינוך *nm* kheenookh; **2.** פדגוגיה *nf* pedagog|yah/-yot (*+of:* -yat).

pedal דוושה *nf* davsh|ah/-ot (*+of:* -at).

(to) pedal 1. לדווש *inf* ledavesh; *pst* deevesh; *pres* medavesh; *fut* yedavesh; **2.** להריץ אופניים (speed bicycle) *inf* lehareets ofanayeem; *pst* hereets *etc*; *pres* mereets *etc*; *fut* yareets *etc*.

pedant קפדן *adj* kapdan/-eet.

pedantic 1. קפדני *adj* kapdanee/-t; **2.** פדנטי *adj* pedantee/-t.

(to) peddle לרכול *inf* leerkol; *pst* rakhal (*kh=k*); *pres* rokhel; *fut* yeerkol.

(to) peddle gossip לרכל *inf* lerakhel; *pst* reekhel; *pres* merakhel; *fut* yerakhel.

peddler רוכל *nm* rokh|el/-leem (*pl+of:* -ley).

pedestal 1. כן *nm* kan/-eem (*pl+of:* -ey); **2.** בסיס (base) *nm* basees/besees|eem (*pl+of:* -ey).

pedestrian 1. הולך רגל *nmf* holekh/-et (*pl:* holkhey) regel; **2.** רגלי *adj* raglee/-t.

pediatrician רופא ילדים *nmf* rofe/-t yeladeem.

pediatrics רפואת ילדים *nf* refoo'at yeladeem.

pedigree שושלת יוחסין *nf* shoshel|et/-ot yokhaseen.

peek הצצה *nf* hatsats|ah/-ot (*+of:* -at).

(to) peek להציץ *inf* lehatseets; *pst* hetseets; *pres* metseets; *fut* yatseets.

peel קליפה *nf* kleep|ah/-ot (*+of:* -at).

(to) peel לקלף *inf* lekalef; *pst* keelef; *pres* mekalef; *fut* yekalef.

(to keep one's eye) peeled לשים עין *inf* laseem 'ayeen; *pst & pres* sam *etc*; *fut* yaseem *etc*.

peep 1. הצצה *nf* hatsats|ah/-ot (*+of:* -at); **2.** צפצוף (whistle) *nm* tseeftsoof/-eem (*pl+of:* -ey).

(to) peep 1. להציץ *inf* lehatseets; *pst* hetseets; *pres* metseets; *fut* yatseets; **2.** לצפצף (whistle) *inf* letsaftsef; *pst* tseeftsef; *pres* metsaftsef; *fut* yetsaftsef.

peer 1. כערכו (equal) *nmf & adj* ke-'erk|o/-ah; **2.** אציל (noble) *nm* atseel/-eem (*pl+of:* -ey).

(to) peer להתבונן מקרוב *inf* leheetbonen mee-karov; *pst* heetbonen *etc*; *pres* meetbonen *etc*; *fut* yeetbonen *etc*.

peer group קבוצת שווים *nf* kvoots|at/-ot shaveem.

(to) peer into other people business לחטט בענייני אחרים *inf* lekhatet be-'eenyeney akhereem; *pst* kheetet *etc*; *pres* mekhatet *etc*; *fut* yekhatet *etc*.

peerless שאין שווה לו *adj* she-'eyn shav|eh/-ah lo/lah (*m/f*).

(to) peeve להרגיז *vt inf* lehargeez; *pst* heergeez; *pres* margeez; *fut* yargeez.

(to get) peeved להתרגז *vi (refl) inf* leheetragez; *pst* heetragez; *pres* meetragez; *fut* yeetragez.

peevish 1. רגזן *adj* ragzan/-eet; **2.** כעסן *adj* ka'asan/-eet.

peg 1. מסמר *nm* masmer/-eem (*pl+of:* -ey); **2.** יתד *nf* yated/yetedot (*+of:* yetad/yeetedot).

(to) peg 1. לתקוע *inf* leetko'a'; *pst* taka'; *pres* toke'a'; *fut* yeetka'; **2.** לחזק (strengthen) *inf* lekhazek; *pst* kheezek; *pres* mekhazek; *fut* yekhazek.

(to take a person down a) peg לקצץ כנפיים *inf* lekatsets kenafayeem; *pst* keetsets *etc*; *pres* mekatsets *etc*; *fut* yekatsets *etc*.

(to) peg along לעמול קשות *inf* la'amol kashot; *pst* 'amal *etc*; *pres* 'amel *etc*; *fut* ya'amol *etc*.

pejorative 1. גורע *adj* gor|e'a'/-a'at; **2.** הולך ורע (deteriorating) *v pres & adj* hol|ekh/-et va-ra'/ve-ra'ah.

pellet גלולה *nf* gool|ah/-ot (*+of:* -at).

pell-mell 1. מעורבב *adj adj* me'oorb|av/-evet; **2.** בערבוביה *adv* be-'eerboovyah.

pelt עור פרווה *nm* 'or/-ot parvah.

(to) pelt 1. לסקול *inf* leeskol; *pst* sakal; *pres* sokel; *fut* yeeskol; **2.** לרגום *inf* leergom; *pst* ragam; *pres* rogem; *fut* yeergom.

(to) pelt with stones לרגום באבנים *inf* leergom ba-avaneem; *pst* ragam *etc*; *pres* rogem *etc*; *fut* yeergom *etc*.

pelvis אגן הירכיים *nm* agan ha-yerekhayeem.

pen 1. עט (writing) *nm* 'et/-eem (*pl+of:* -ey); **2.** ציפורן (nib) *nm* tseeporen; **3.** דיר (for animals) *nm* deer/-eem (*pl+of:* -ey).

(fountain) pen עט נובע *nm* 'et/-eem nov|e'a'/-'eem.

(pig) pen דיר חזירים *nm* deer/-ey khazeereem.

(to) pen 1. לכתוב בעט (write) *inf* leekhtov be-'et; *pst* katav *etc* (*k=kh*); *pres* kotev *etc*; *fut* yeekhtov *etc*; **2.** לכלוא (enclose) *inf* leekhlo; *pst* kala (*k=kh*); *pres* kole; *fut* yeekhla.

penal פלילי *adj* pleelee/-t.

(to) penalize להעניש *inf* leha'aneesh; *pst* he'eneesh; *pres* ma'aneesh; *fut* ya'aneesh.

penalty עונש *nm* 'on|esh/-sheem (*pl+of:* -shey).

penance חרטה *nf* kharat|ah/-ot (*+of:* -at).

pencil עיפרון *nm* 'eeparon/'efronot (*f=p*; *+of:* 'efron).

pencil sharpener מחדד עפרונות *nm* mekhaded/-ey 'efronot.

pendant 1. נטיפה *nf* neteef|ah/-ot (*+of:* -at); **2.** עגיל (ear-ring) *nm* 'ageel/-eem (*pl+of:* -ey).

pending 1. תלוי ועומד *adj* talooy/tlooyah ve-'omed/-et; **2.** בעוד *prep* be-'od.

pendulum מטוטלת *nf* metoot|elet/-alot.

(to) penetrate לחדור *inf* lakhdor; *pst* khadar; *pres* khoder; *fut* yakhdor.

penetrating חודר *adj* khoder/-et.

penetration חדירה *nf* khadeer|ah/-ot (*+of:* -at).

penguin פינגווין *nm* peengveen/-eem (*pl+of:* -ey).

penholder קולמוס *nm* koolmos/-eem (*pl+of:* -ey).

penicillin פניצילין *nm* peneetseeleen/-eem (*pl+of:* -ey).

peninsula חצי־אי *nm* khats|ee/-a'ey ee/-yeem.

penitent 1. חוזר התשובה *nmf & adj* khozer/-et (*pl:* khozr|eem/-ot) bee-teshoovah; **2.** מתחרט *v pres & adj* meetkharet/-et.

penitentiary בית סוהר *nm* bet/batey sohar.

penknife אולר *nm* olar/-eem (*pl+of:* -ey).

penmanship כתיבה תמה *nf* keteevah tamah.

penname 1. כינוי ספרותי *nm* keenoo|y/-yeem seefrootee/-yeem; **2.** פסידונים *nm* pseydoneem/-eem (*pl+of:* -ey).

pennant 1. נס *nm* nes/nees|eem (*pl+of:* -ey); **2.** תליון (medallion) *nm* teelyon/-eem (*pl+of:* -ey); **3.** דגל (flag) *nm* deg|el/-aleem (*pl+of:* deegley).

penniless חסר פרוטה *adj* khas|ar/-rat prootah.

penny פרוטה *nf* proot|ah/-ot (*+of:* -at).

(to cost a pretty) penny לעלות הון *inf* la'alot hon; *pst* 'alah hon; *pres* 'oleh hon; *fut* ya'aleh hon.

pension 1. קצבה (legal term) *nf* keets|bah/-ba'ot (*+of:* -bat/-vot); **2.** גימלה *[colloq.] nf* geeml|ah/-a'ot (*+of:* -at); **3.** פנסיה pensee|yah/-yot (*+of:* -yat); **4.** פנסיון (boarding house) *nm* penseeyon/-eem (*pl+of:* -ey).

(old age) pension קיצבת זיקנה *nf* keetsb|at/-a'ot zeeknah.

(to) pension להעניק גימלה *inf* leha'aneek geemlah; *pst* he'eneek *etc*; *pres* ma'aneek *etc*; *fut* ya'aneek *etc*.

(to) pension off 1. להוציא לקצבה (legal term) *inf* lehotsee le-keetsbah; *pst* hotsee *etc*; *pres* motsee *etc*; *fut* yotsee *etc*; **2.** להוציא לגימלאות *[colloq.] inf* lehotsee le-geemla'ot; *pst* hotsee *etc*; *pres* motsee *etc*; *fut* yotsee *etc*.

pensionable בר־קצבה *nmf* bar/bat keetsbah.

pensionary, pensioner 1. קצבאי (legal term) *nmf* keetsb|ay/-a'eet; **2.** גימלאי *[colloq.] nm* geeml|ay/-a'eet (*pl:* -a'eem-/-a'eeyot; *+of:* -a'ey).

pensive שקוע במחשבות *adj* shakoo'a'/shekoo'ah be-makh'shavot.

pent מסוגר *adj nm adj* mesoog|ar/-eret.

pent-up emotions רגשות עצורים *nf pl* regashot 'atsooreem.

Pentecost שבועות *nm* shavoo'ot.

penthouse 1. דירת־פאר בקומת גג *nf* deer|at/-ot pe'er be-komat gag; **2.** פנטהאוז *nm* pent'ha'ooz/-eem (*pl+of:* -ey).

penult שלפני האחרון *adj* she-leefney ha-akhron/-ah.

people 1. אנשים *nm pl* anasheem (*+of:* anshey); **2.** אומה (nation) *nf* oom|ah/-ot (*+of:* -at).

pepper פלפל *nm* peelpel/-eem (*pl+of:* -ey).

(red) pepper פלפל אדום *nm* peelpel/-eem adom/adoomeem.

(to) pepper לפלפל *inf* lefalpel; *pst* peelpel (*p=f*); *pres* mefalpel; *fut* yefalpel.

pepper plant צמח הפלפל *nm* tsemakh/tseemkhey peelpel.

pepper shaker מבזקת פלפל *nf* mavzek|et/-ot peelpel.

(to) pepper with bullets לרסס בכדורים *inf* lerases be-khadooreem (*kh=k*); *pst* reeses *etc*; *pres* merases *etc*; *fut* yerases *etc*.

peppermint 1. נענה *nf* na'n|ah/-ot (*+of:* -at); **2.** מנתה (mint) *nf* meent|ah/-ot (*+of:* -at).

(green) peppers פלפלים ירוקים *nm pl* peelpeleem yerokeem.

per 1. ־ל le-; **2.** לכול le-khol (*kh=k*).

(as) per לפי lefee.

per capita לגולגולת *adv* le-goolgolet

per cent 1. למאה *adv* le-me'ah; **2.** אחוז (percent) *nm* akhooz/-eem (*pl+of:* -ey).

(one shekel) per dozen תריסר בשקל *num & adv* treysar be-shekel.

per year לשנה *adv* le-shanah.

percale בד סדינים *nm* bad sedeeneem.

(to) perceive 1. להבין *inf* lehaveen; *pst* heveen; *pres* meveen; *fut* yaveen; **2.** להבחין (notice) lehavkheen; *pst* heevkheen; *pres* mavkheen; *fut* yavkheen.

percentage אחוזים *nm pl* akhooz|eem (*pl+of:* -ey).

perceptible ניתן לתפיסה *adj* neet|an/-enet lee-tefeesah.

perception 1. תפיסה *nf* tfees|ah/-ot (*+of:* -at); **2.** תחושה (sense) *nf* tekhoosh|ah/-ot (*+of:* -at).

perceptive של תפיסה *adj* shel tfeesah.

perch אצטבת־לול לעופות *nf* eetstab|ah/-a'ot lool le-'ofot.

perchance אולי *adv* oolay.

percolate לבעבע *inf* leva'be'a'; *pst* bee'ba' (*v=b*); *pres* meva'be'a'; *fut* yeva'ba'.

percolator 1. חלחול *nm* khalkhool/-eem (*pl+of:* -ey); **2.** מסנן־הרתחה לקפה *nm* masnen/-ey hartakhah le-kafeh; **3.** פרקולטור *nm* perkoolator/-eem.

perdition 1. כליה *nf* klayah; **2.** אבדון (destruction) *nm* avadon.

perennial 1. רב־שנתי *adj* rav-shenatee/-t; **2.** נצחי (eternal) *adj* neetskhee/-t.

perfect מושלם *adj* mooshl|am/-emet.

(to) perfect לשכלל *inf* leshakhlel; *pst* sheekhlel; *pres* meshakhlel; *fut* yeshakhlel.

perfection שלמות *nf* shlemoo|t/-yot.

perfidious בוגדני *adj* bogdanee/-t.

perfidy בוגדנות *nf* bogdanoo|t/-yot.

(to) perforate לנקבב *inf* lenakbev; *pst* neekbev; *pres* menakbev; *fut* yenakbev.

perforation נקבוב *nm* neekboov/-eem (*pl+of:* -ey).

perforator 1. מנקב *nm* menak|ev/-veem (*pl+of:* -vey); **2.** מקב *nm* mak|ev/-veem (*pl+of:* -vey).

perforce מאונס *adj* me-'ones.

(to) perform לבצע *inf* levatse'a'; *pst* beetsa' (*b=v*); *pres* mevatse'a'; *fut* yevatsa'.

performance 1. הצגה (theater) *nf* hatsag|ah/-ot (*+of:* -at); **2.** ביצוע (achievement) *nm* beetsoo|'a'/-'eem (*pl+of:* -'ey).

perfume בושם *nm* bosem/besameem (*pl+of:* bosmey).

(to) perfume לבשם *inf* levasem; *pst* beesem (*b=v*); *pres* mevasem; *fut* yevasem.

perfumery 1. מיני בשמים *nm pl* meeney besameem; **2.** פרפומריה *nf* parfoomer|yah/-yot (*+of:* -yat).

perhaps 1. אולי (maybe) oolay; **2.** יתכן (possibly) *adv* yeetakhen; **3.** שמא (lest) *adv* shema.
peril סכנה *nf* sakan|ah/-ot (+*of:* -at).
perilous מסוכן *adj* mesook|an/-enet.
perimeter 1. היקף *nm* hekef/-eem (*pl+of:* -ey); **2.** פרימטר *nm* pereemet|er/-reem.
period 1. תקופה *nf* tekoof|ah/-ot (+*of:* -at); **2.** נקודה (full stop) nekood|ah/-ot (+*of:* -at).
periodic מעת לעת *adj* me-'et le-'et.
periodical כתב עת *nm* ketav/keetvey 'et.
periphery 1. היקף *nm* hekef/-eem (*pl+of:* -ey); **2.** פריפריה *nf* pereefer|yah/-yot (+*of:* -yat).
(to) perish לאבוד *inf* le'evod; *pst* avad; *pres* oved; *fut* yovad.
perishable מתכלה *adj* meetkal|eh/-et.
(to) perjure להישבע לשקר *inf* leheeshava' la-sheker; *pst & pres* neeshba' *etc* (*b=v*); *fut* yeeshava' *etc.*
perjury שבועת שווא *nf* shvoo|'at/-'ot shav.
permanence קביעות *nf* kvee'oot.
permanent קבוע *adj* kavoo'a'/kvoo'ah.
(to) permeate 1. לחלחל *inf* lekhalkhel; *pst* kheelkhel; *pres* mekhalkhel; *fut* yekhalkhel; **2.** להתפשט (spread) *inf* leheetpashet; *pst* heetpashet; *pres* meetpashet; *fut* yeetpashet.
permissible מותר *adj* moot|ar/-eret.
permission 1. רשות *nf* reshoot; **2.** היתר *nm* heter/-eem (*pl+of:* -ey).
permissive מתירני *adj* mateeranee/-t.
permit 1. רשיון *nm* reeshyon/-ot; **2.** היתר *nm* heter/-eem (*pl+of:* -ey).
(to) permit 1. להתיר *inf* lehateer; *pst* heeteer; *pres* mateer; *fut* yateer; **2.** להרשות (allow) *inf* leharshot; *pst* heershah; *pres* marsheh; *fut* yarsheh.
permutation חילוף ספרות *nm* kheeloof/-ey sfarot.
pernicious 1. ממאיר (cancerous) *adj* mam'eer/-ah; **2.** הרסני (destructive) *adj* harsanee/-t.
perpendicular 1. מאונך *adj* me'oon|akh/-ekhet. **2.** אנכי (vertical) anakhee/-t; **3.** ניצב (syn) *adj* neets|av/-evet.
(to) perpetrate לבצע *inf* levatse'a'; *pst* beetsa' (*b=v*); *pres* mevatse'a'; *fut* yevatse'a'.
perpetual נצחי *adj* neetskhee/-t.
(to) perpetuate להנציח *inf* lehantsee'akh; *pst* heentsee'akh; *pres* mantsee'akh; *fut* yantsee'akh.
(to) perplex 1. להדהים *inf* lehad'heem; *pst* heed'heem; *pres* mad'heem; *fut* yad'heem; **2.** להביך (confuse) *inf* lehaveekh; *pst* heveekh; *pres* meveekh; *fut* yaveekh.
perplexed 1. נדהם *adj* need|'ham/-'hemet; **2.** נבוך (confused) *adj* navokh/nevokhah.
perplexity 1. תסבוכת *nf* teesbokh|et/-ot; **2.** מבוכה (confusion) *nf* mevookh|ah/-ot (+*of:* -at).
(to) persecute לרדוף *inf* leerdof; *pst* radaf; *pres* rodef; *fut* yeerdof.
persecution רדיפה *nf* redeef|ah/-ot (+*of:* -at).
persecutor 1. רודף *nm* rod|ef/-feem (*pl+of:* -fey); **2.** נוגש *nm* nog|es/-seem (*pl+of:* -sey).
perseverance התמדה *nf* hatmad|ah/-ot (+*of:* -at).
(to) persevere להתמיד *inf* lehatmeed; *pst* heetmeed; *pres* matmeed; *fut* yatmeed.
(to) persist להתעקש *inf* leheet'akesh; *pst* heet'akesh; *pres* meet'akesh; *fut* yeet'akesh.
persistence התעקשות *nf* heet'akshoo|t/-yot.
persistent עיקש *adj* 'eekesh/-et.
person 1. אדם *nm* adam/beney-adam; **2.** אנוש (human) *nm* enosh/beney enosh; **3.** גוף (*gram.*) *nm* goof.
persona non grata אישיות לא־רצויה *nf* eesheeyoot lo retsooyah.
personable בעל אישיות *adj* ba'al/-at eesheeyoot.
personage דמות *nf* dmoo|t/-yot.
personal אישי *adj* eeshee/-t.
personality אישיות *nf* eesheeyoot.
personnel צוות *nm* tsevet/tsvateem (*pl+of:* tseevtey).
perspective 1. סיכוי *nm* seekoo|y/-yeem (*pl+of:* -yey); **2.** פרספקטיבה *nf* perspekteev|ah/-ot (+*of:* -at).
perspective drawing ציור בפרספקטיבה *nm* tseeyoor/-eem be-perspekteevah.
perspicacious בעל תפיסה חדה *adj* ba'al/-at tfeesah khadah.
perspicacity חדות תפיסה *nf* khadoo|t/-yot tfeesah.
perspiration הזעה *nf* haza|'ah/-'ot (+*of:* -'at).
(to) perspire להזיע *inf* lehazee'a'; *pst* heezee'a'; *pres* mazee'a'; *fut* yazee'a'.
(to) persuade לשכנע *inf* leshakhne'a'; *pst* sheekhna'; *pres* meshakhne'a'; *fut* yeshakhna'.
persuasion 1. שכנוע *nm* sheekhnoo|'a'/-'eem (*pl+of:* -'ey); **2.** אמונה (belief) *nf* emoon|ah/-ot (+*of:* -at).
persuasive משכנע *adj* meshakhn|e'a'/-a'at.
pert 1. מעיז *v pres & adj* me'eez/-ah; **2.** חצוף (impertinent) *adj* khatsoof/-ah.
(to) pertain להתייחס ל־ *inf* leheetyakhes le-; *pst* heetyakhes le-; *pres* meetyakhes le-; *fut* yeetyakhes le-.
pertinent נוגע לעניין *adj* nog|e'a'/-a'at la-'eenyan.
(to) perturb להדאיג *inf* lehad'eeg; *pst* heed'eeg; *pres* mad'eeg; *fut* yad'eeg.
perusal עיון *nm* 'eeyoon/-eem (*pl+of:* -ey).
(to) peruse לעיין *inf* le'ayen; *pst* 'eeyen; *pres* me'ayen; *fut* ye'ayen.
(to) pervade 1. לפעפע *inf* lefa'pe'a'; *pst* pee'pe'a' (*p=f*); *pres* mefa'pe'a'; *fut* yefa'pe'a'; **2.** להתפשט (spread) *inf* leheetpashet; *pst* heetpashet; *pres* meetpashet; *fut* yeetpashet.
perverse 1. נלוז *adj* naloz/nelozah; **2.** מושחת (corrupt) *adj* mooshkh|at/-etet.
pervert 1. מושחת (corrupt) *nm* moosh'khat/-eem (*pl+of:* -ey); **2.** סוטה (sexual) *nmf & adj* sot|eh/-ah; **3.** דגנרט (degenerate) *nm* degenerat/-eem (*pl+of:* -ey).
(to) pervert 1. לסלף *inf* lesalef; *pst* seelef; *pres* mesalef; *fut* yesalef; **2.** להשחית (destroy) *inf* lehashkheet; *pst* heeshkheet; *pres* mashkheet; *fut* yashkheet,
pessimism פסימיות *nf* peseemeeyoot.
pessimist 1. רואה שחורות *adj* ro'eh/ro'at shekhorot; **2.** פסימיסט *nm* peseemeest/-eem.
pest 1. מגיפה *nf* magef|ah/-ot (+*of:* -at); **2.** טרחן (nagger) *nm* tarkhan/-eem (*pl+of:* -ey); **3.** נודניק (nudnik) *nm* noodneek/-eet.

(to) pester 1. להציק *inf* lahatseek; *pst* hetseek; *pres* metseek; *fut* yatseek; **2.** לנדנד (nag) *inf* lenadned; *pst* needned; *pres* menadned; *fut* yenadned.

pesticide משמיד כנימות *adj nm* mashmeed/-at keneemot.

pestilence מגיפה *nf* magef|ah/-ot (*+of:* -at).

pet גור שעשועים *nm* goor/-ey sha'shoo'eem.

(to) pet 1. ללטף *inf* lelatef; *pst* leetef; *pres* melatef; *fut* yelatef; **2.** לפנק (pamper) *inf* lefanek; *pst* peenek *(p=f)*; *pres* mefanek; *fut* yefanek.

pet name כינוי חיבה *nm* keenoo|y/-yey kheebah.

petal עלה כותרת *nm* 'aleh/'aley koteret.

petcock שסתום קטן *nm* shastom/-eem katan/ ktaneem.

petition 1. בקשה *nf* bakash|ah/-ot (*+of:* -at); **2.** עתירה (plea) *nf* 'ateer|ah/-ot (*+of:* -at).

(to) petition לעתור *inf* la'ator; *pst* 'atar; *pres* 'oter; *fut* ya'ator.

(to) petrify 1. לאבן *vt inf* le'aben; *pst* eeben; *pres* me'aben; *fut* ye'aben; **2.** להתאבן *vi (refl) inf* leheet'aben; *pst* heet'aben; *pres* meet'aben; *fut* yeet'aben.

petrol דלק *nm* del|ek/-akeem (*pl+of:* deelkey).

petroleum נפט *nm* neft.

petticoat תחתונית *nf* takhtonee|t/-yot.

petty 1. פעוט *adj* pa'oot/pe'ootah; **2.** קל-ערך (trifling) *adj* kal/-at 'erekh.

petty cash קופה קטנה *nf* koopah ketanah.

petty larceny גניבה פעוטה *nf* genev|ah/-ot pe'oot|ah/-ot.

petty officer מש״ק בצי *nmf* mashak/-eet ba-tsee.

petty treason בגידה בזעיר אנפין *nf* begeed|ah/-ot bee-ze'eyr anpeen.

phalanx המון *nm* hamon/-eem (*pl+of:* -ey).

phantom 1. רוח רפאים *nf* roo|'akh/-khot refa'eem; **2.** דמיוני *adj* deemyonee/-t.

pharmacist רוקח *nmf* rok|e'akh/-akhat (*pl:* rok'kh|eem/-ot; *pl+of:* -ey).

pharmacy בית מרקחת *nm* bet/batey meerkakhat.

pharynx לוע *nm* lo'a'/lo'ot.

phase שלב *nm* shalav/shlabeem (*b=v*; *+of:* shla|v/ -bey)

pheasant פסיון *nm* pasyon/-eem (*pl+of:* -ey).

phenomenon תופעה *nf* tofa|'ah/-'ot (*+of:* -'at).

philanthropy 1. נדבנות *nf* nadvanoot; **2.** פילנתרופיה *nf* feelantrop|yah (*+of:* -yat).

philatelic בולאי *adj* bool|ay/-a'eet.

(Israel Post-Office) Philatelic Services השירות הבולאי *nm* ha-sheroot ha-boola'ee.

philately בולאות *nf* boola'oot.

philharmonic פילהרמוני *adj* feelharmonee/-t.

philharmonic orchestra תזמורת פילהרמונית *nf* teezmor|et/-ot feelharmonee|t/-yot.

(the Israel) Philharmonic Orchestra התזמורת הפילהרמונית הישראלית *nf* ha-teezmoret ha-feelharmoneet ha-yeesre'eleet.

Philistine פלשתי *nm* pleeshtee/-m

philology 1. בלשנות *nf* balshanoo|t/-yot; **2.** פילולוגיה *nf* feelolog|yah/-yot (*+of:* -yat).

philosophical פילוסופי *adj* feelosofee/-t.

philosophy פילוסופיה *nf* feelosof|yah/-yot (*+of:* -yat).

phlegm 1. ריר reer/-eem (*pl+of:* -ey); **2.** ליחה (mucus) *nf* leykh|ah/-ot (*+of:* -at).

phone טלפון *nm* telefon/-eem (*pl+of:* -ey).

phone טלפוני־ *adj* telefonee/-t.

(to) phone לטלפן *inf* letalpen; *pst* teelpen; *pres* metalpen; *fut* yetalpen.

phoneme פונמה *nf* fonem|ah/-ot (*+of:* -at).

phonetics 1. תורת ההגה *nf* torat ha-hegeh; **2.** פונטיקה *nf* foneteek|ah (*+of:* -at).

phonograph 1. מקול *nm* makol/-eem (*pl+of:* -ey); **2.** גרמופון *nm* gramofon/-eem (*pl+of:* -ey); **3.** פונוגרף *nm* fonograf/-eem (*pl+of:* -ey); **4.** פטיפון *nm* patefon/-eem (*pl+of:* -ey).

phonology 1. תורת הלשון *nf* torat ha-lashon; **2.** פונולוגיה *nf* fonolog|yah (*+of:* -yat).

phosphate פוספט *nm* fosfat/-eem (*pl+of:* -ey).

phosphorus זרחן *nm* zarkhan/-eem (*pl+of:* -ey).

photo, photograph 1. תצלום (product) *nm* tatsloom/-eem (*pl+of:* -ey); **2.** צילום (meaning action but colloquially used for product) *nm* tseeloom/-eem (*pl+of:* -ey).

photographer צלם *nmf* tsal|am/-emet (*pl:* tsa-lam|eem/-ot; *+of:* -ey)

(press) photographer צלם עיתונות *nmf* tsal|am/ -emet 'eetonoot (*pl:* -amey *etc*).

(television-)photographer צלם טלוויזיה *nm* tsalam/-ey televeezyah.

(video-)photographer צלם וידאו *nmf* tsal|am/ -emet veedyo.

photography 1. צילום (art) *nm* tseeloom; **2.** תורת הצילום (theory) *nf* torat ha-tseeloom.

phrase 1. משפט *nm* meeshpat/-ateem (*pl+of:* -etey); **2.** אימרה *nf* eemrah/amarot (*+of:* eemrat).

(to) phrase להביע במילים *inf* lehabee'a' be-meeleem; *pst* heebee'a' *etc*; *pres* mabee'a' *etc*; *fut* yabee'a' *etc*.

physic 1. תרופה *nf* troof|ah/-ot (*+of:* -at); **2.** סם משלשל (laxative) *nm* sam/-eem meshalshel/ -eem.

physical פיסי *adj* feesee/-t.

physician רופא *nmf* rof|e/-'ah (*pl:* -'eem/-'ot; *+of:* -et/-'ey).

physicist פיסיקאי *nmf* feeseekay/-'eet.

physics פיסיקה *nf* feeseek|ah/-ot (*+of:* -at).

physiological פיסיולוגי *adj* feesyologee/-t.

physiology פיסיולוגיה *nf* feesyolog|yah (*+of:* -yat).

physiotherapy פיסיותרפיה *nf* feesyoterap|yah/-yot (*+of:* -yat).

physique מבנה גוף *nm* meevneh goof.

pianist פסנתרן *nmf* p'santran/-eet.

piano פסנתר *nm* p'sant|er/-reem (*pl+of:* -rey).

piano bench ספסל לפסנתר *nm* safsal/-eem lee-p'santer.

piano stool כיסא פסנתרן *nm* kees|e/-'ot p'santran.

(grand) piano פסנתר כנף *nm* p'sant|er/-rey kanaf.

(upright) piano פסנתר זקוף *nm* p'sant|er/-reem zakoof/zkoofeem.

picaresque הרפתקני *adj* harpatkanee/-t.

pick 1. מכוש *nm* makosh/-eem (*pl+of:* -ey); **2.** קיסם (tooth) *nm* keys|am/-meem (*pl+of:* -mey); **3.** דורבן (spur) *nm* dorv|an/-aneem (*pl+of:* -eney).

(ice) pick בוקע קרח *nm* bok|e'a'/-'ey kerakh.
(to) pick 1. לברור (choose) *inf* leevror; *pst* barar *(b=v)*; *pres* borer; *fut* yeevror; **2.** לקטוף (flowers) *inf* leektof; *pst* kataf; *pres* kotef; *fut* yeektof; **3.** לצחצח (teeth) *inf* letsakhtse'akh; *pst* tseekhtsakh; *pres* metsakhtse'akh; *fut* yetsakhtsakh; **4.** למרוט (feathers) *inf* leemrot; *pst* marat; *pres* moret; *fut* yeemrot; **5.** לפתוח במריבה (quarrel) *inf* leefto'akh bee-mereevah; *pst* patakh *etc* *(p=f)*; *pres* pote'akh *etc*; *fut* yeeftakh *etc*.
(to) pick flaws לחפש מגרעות *inf* lekhapes meegra'ot; *pst* kheepes *etc*; *pres* mekhapes *etc*; *fut* yekhapes *etc*.
(to) pick out לבחור *inf* leevkhor; *pst* bakhar *(b=v)*; *pres* bokher; *fut* yeevkhar.
(to) pick pockets לכייס *inf* lekhayes; *pst* keeyes *(k=kh)*; *pres* mekhayes; *fut* yekhayes.
(to) pick up להרים *inf* lehareem; *pst* hereem; *pres* mereem; *fut* yareem.
(to) pick up speed להגביר מהירות *inf* lehagbeer meheeroot; *pst* heegbeer *etc*; *pres* magbeer *etc*; *fut* yagbeer *etc*.
pickaxe מכוש *nm* makosh/-eem *(pl+of:* -ey).
picket משמרת שובתים *nf* meeshmer|et/-ot shovteem.
(to) picket לקיים משמרות שובתים *inf* lekayem meeshmerot shovteem; *pst* keeyem *etc*; *pres* mekayem *etc*; *fut* yekayem *etc*.
(in a) pickle במצב ביש *adv* be-matsav beesh.
pickled כבוש *adj* kavoosh/kevooshah.
pickled fish דגים כבושים *nm* dag/-eem kavoosh/kevoosheem.
pickles 1. מחמצים *nm pl* makhmats|eem *(pl+of:* -ey); **2.** חמוצים *[colloq.] nm pl* khamoots|eem *(pl+of:* -ey).
pickpocket כייס *nm* kayas/-eem *(pl+of:* -ey).
picnic פיקניק *nm* peekneek/-eem *(pl+of:* -ey).
(to) picnic לערוך פיקניקים *inf* la'arokh peekneekeem; *pst* 'arakh *etc*; *pres* 'orekh *etc*; *fut* ya'arokh *etc*.
picture 1. תמונה *nf* temoon|ah/-ot (+*of:* -at); **2.** ציור (painting) *nm* tseeyoor/-eem *(pl+of:* -ey); **3.** דיוקן (portrait) *nm* dyok|an/-aneem *(pl+of:* -ney); **4.** תצלום (photo) *nm* tatsloom/-eem *(pl+of:* -ey); **5.** סרט (movie) *nm* seret/srateem *(pl+of:* seertey).
picture frame מסגרת תמונה *nf* meesger|et/-ot temoon|ah/-ot.
picture gallery גלריה לציורים *nf* galer|yah/-yot le-tseeyooreem.
(to) picture 1. לשקף *inf* leshakef; *pst* sheekef; *pres* meshakef; *fut* yeshakef; **2.** לצייר *inf* letsayer; *pst* tseeyer; *pres* metsayer; *fut* yetsayer.
picturesque ציורי *adj* tseeyooree/-t.
pie פשטידה *nf* pashteed|ah/-ot (+*of:* -at).
piece 1. חלק (part) *nm* khelek/khalakeem *(pl+of:* khelkey); **2.** קטע (segment) *nm* ket|a'/-a'eem *(pl+of:* keet'ey).
piece of advice עצה טובה *nf* 'etsah tovah.
piece of land שטח קרקע *nm* shetakh/sheetkhey karka'.
piece of money מטבע *nm* matbe|'a'/-'ot.
(to) piece 1. לחבר (join) *inf* lekhaber; *pst* kheeber; *pres* mekhaber; *fut* yekhaber; **2.** לאחות (stitch together) *inf* le'akhot; *pst* eekhah; *pres* me'akheh; *fut* ye'akheh.
(to) piece between meals לגשר בין ארוחות *inf* legasher beyn arookhot; *pst* geesher *etc*; *pres* megasher *etc*; *fut* yegasher *etc*.
piece of news חדשה *nf* khadash|ah/-ot (+*of:* -at).
piece of nonsense הבלים *nm pl* havaleem.
(to) piece together לצרף לתמונה שלימה *inf* letsaref lee-temoonah shelemah; *pst* tseraf *etc*; *pres* metsaref *etc*; *fut* yetsaref *etc*.
piecemeal 1. קמעא־קמעא *adv* keem'a-keem'a; **2.** בחלקים *adv* ba-khalakeem.
pier רציף *nm* ratseef/retseef|eem (+*of:* retseef/-ey).
(to) pierce 1. לחדור *inf* lakhdor; *pst* khadar; *pres* khoder; *fut* yakhdor; **2.** לנקב (bore) *inf* lenakev; *pst* neekev; *pres* menakev; *fut* yenakev.
piety אדיקות דתית *nf* adeekoot dateet.
pig חזיר *nm* khazeer/-eem *(pl+of:* -ey).
(guinea) pig שפן ניסיון *nm* shfan/-ey neesayon.
pig iron ברזל יציקה *nm* barzel/-ey yetseekah.
pigeon יונה *nf* yon|ah/-eem *(pl+of:* -ey).
pigeonhole תא למכתבים *nm* ta/-'eem le-meekhtaveem.
(to) pigeonhole לחלק בתאים *inf* lekhalek ba-ta'eem; *pst* kheelek *etc*; *pres* mekhalek *etc*; *fut* yekhalek *etc*.
pigheaded עקשן *adj* 'akshan/-eet.
pigment פיגמנט *nm* peegment/-eem *(pl+of:* -ey).
pigmy 1. ננס *nm* nanas/-eem *(pl+of:* -ey); **2.** גמד (dwarf) *nm nmf* gamad/-ah *(pl:* -eem; +*of:* -ey).
pile ערימה *nf* 'arem|ah/-ot (+*of:* -at).
(to) pile לערום *inf* la'arom; *pst* 'aram; *pres* 'orem; *fut* ya'arom.
(to) pile up לצבור *inf* leetsbor; *pst* tsavar *(v=b)*; *pres* tsover; *fut* yeetsbor.
piles טחורים (hemorrhoids) *nm pl* tekhor|eem *(pl+of:* -ey).
(to) pilfer 1. לגנוב (steal) *inf* leegnov; *pst* ganav; *pres* gonev; *fut* yeegnov; **2.** לסחוב *[slang] inf* leeskhov; *pst* sakhav; *pres* sokhev; *fut* yeeskhav.
pilferage סחיבה *nf* sekheev|ah/-ot (+*of:* -at).
pilgrim עולה רגל *nmf* 'ol|eh/-at regel.
pilgrimage עלייה לרגל *nf* 'alee|yah/-yot le-regel.
pill גלולה *nf* gloól|ah/-ot (+*of:* -at).
pillage ביזה *nf* beez|ah/-ot (+*of:* -at).
(to) pillage 1. לבוז *inf* lavoz; *pst* bazaz *(b=v)*; *pres* bozez; *fut* yavoz; **2.** לשדוד (rob) *inf* leeshdod; *pst* shadad; *pres* shoded; *fut* yeeshdod.
pillar עמוד תווך *nm* 'amood/-ey tavekh
(from) pillar to post ממקום למקום *adv* mee-makom le-makom.
pillory עמוד הקלון *nm* 'amood ha-kalon.
pillow כר *nm* kar/-eem *(pl+of:* -ey).
pillowcase ציפית *nf* tseepee|t/-yot.
pilot 1. נווט (boat) *nm* navat/-eem *(pl+of:* -ey); **2.** טייס (aircraft) *nm* tayas/-eem *(pl+of:* -ey).
(harbor) pilot נתב *nm* natav/-eem *(pl+of:* -ey).
pilot burner, pilot light מבער קטן *nm* mav'er/-eem katan/ketaneem.

pilot-plant מפעל נסיוני *nm* meef'al/-eem neesyonee/-yeem.

pimp 1. רועה זונות *nm* ro'e|h/-y zonot; **2.** סרסור לזנות (procurer) *nm* sarsoor/-eem lee-znoot.

pimple 1. פצעון *nm* peets'on/-eem (*pl+of:* -ey); **2.** חטט (papule) *nm* khatat/-eem (*pl+of:* -ey).

pin סיכה *nf* seek|ah/-ot (*+of:* -at).

(safety) pin 1. סיכת ביטחון *nf* seek|at/-ot beetakhon; **2.** פריפה *nf* preef|ah/-ot (*+of:* -at).

(tie) pin סיכת עניבה *nf* seek|at/-ot 'aneevah.

(to) pin להצמיד *inf* lehatsmeed; *pst* heetsmeed; *pres* matsmeed; *fut* yatsmeed.

(to) pin down לאלץ *inf* le'alets; *pst* eelets; *pres* me'alets; *fut* ye'alets.

pin money דמי כיס *nm pl* demey kees.

(to) pin one's hope to לתלות תקווה ב־ *inf* leetlot teekvah be-; *pst* talah *etc*; *pres* toleh *etc*; *fut* yeetleh *etc.*

(to) pin up לתלות מודעה *inf* leetlot moda'ah; *pst* talah *etc*; *pres* toleh *etc*; *fut* yeetleh *etc.*

pincer movement תנועת מלקחיים *nf* tenoo'at/-'ot melkakhayeem.

pincers מצבטיים *nm pl* meetsb|atayeem (*+of:* -etey).

(small) pincers מצבטיים קטנים *nm pl* meetsbatayeem ketaneem.

pinch 1. קורטוב *nm* kortov/-eem (*pl+of:* -ey); **2.** קמצוץ (grain) *nm* kamtsoots/-eem (*pl+of:* -ey); **3.** צביטה (squeeze) *nf* tsveet|ah/-ot (*+of:* -at).

(to) pinch לצבוט *inf* leetsbot; *pst* tsavat (*v=b*); *pres* tsovet; *fut* yeetsbot.

pinch hitter ממלא מקום (replacement) *nmf* memale/-t makom.

(fingers) pinched in the door אצבעות שנלכדו בדלת etsba'ot she-neelkedoo ba-delet.

pine אורן *nm* oren/oraneem (*pl+of:* orney).

(to) pine להשתוקק *inf* leheeshtokek; *pst* heeshtokek; *pres* meeshtokek; *fut* yeeshtokek.

(to) pine away להימוג *inf* leheemog; *pst & pres* namog; *fut* yeemog.

pine cone אצטרובל *nm* eetstroobal/-eem (*pl+of:* -ey).

(to) pine for לערוג ל־ *inf* la'arog le-; *pst* 'arag le-; *pres* 'oreg le-; *fut* ya'arog le-.

pine grove חורשת אורנים *nf* khorsh|at/-ot oraneem.

pine nut אגוז צנובר *nm* egoz/-ey tsnobar.

pineapple אננס *nm* ananas.

pinion סבבת *nf* sab|evet/-avot.

pink 1. ציפורן (flower) *nm* tseepor|en/-neem (*pl+of:* -ney); **2.** ורוד (color) *adj* varod/vroodah; **3.** שמאלן (leftist) *nmf* smolan/-eet.

(in the) pink of condition במיטבו *adv* be-metav|o/-ah (*m/f*).

pinnacle פסגה *nf* peesgah/pesagot (*+of:* peesg|at/-ot).

pint 1. חצי לוג *nm* khatsee log; **2.** פיינט *nm* paynt/-eem.

pioneer 1. חלוץ *nmf* khaloots/-ah (*pl:* -eem/-ot; *+of:* ey); **2.** חלוצי *adj* khalootsee/-t.

(to) pioneer לסלול דרך *inf* leeslol derekh; *pst* salal *etc*; *pres* solel *etc*; *fut* yeeslol *etc.*

pious אדוק בדתו *adj* adook/-ah be-dat|o/-ah.

pipe 1. מקטרת (smoking) *nf* meekt|eret/-arot; **2.** קנה עוגב (organ) *nm* ken|eh/-ey 'oogav; **3.** צינור (plumbing) *nm* tseenor/-ot.

(to) pipe 1. לחלל *inf* lekhalel; *pst* kheelel; *pres* mekhalel; *fut* yekhalel; **2.** לצפור (hoot) *inf* leetspor; *pst* tsafar (*f=p*); *pres* tsofer; *fut* yeetspor.

(to) pipe down 1. לשתוק (be silent) *inf* leeshtok; *pst* shatak; *pres* shotek; *fut* yeeshtok; **2.** לפטר (dismisss) *inf* lefater; *pst* peeter (*p=f*); *pres* mefater; *fut* yefater.

pipe line, pipeline 1. צינור (plumbing) *nm* tseenor/-ot; **2.** קו צינורות (conduit) kav/-ey tseenorot; **3.** צינור נפט (oil) *nm* tseenor/-ot neft.

pipe wrench מפתח צינורות *nm* mafte'akh tseenorot.

piper חלילן *nmf* khaleelan/-eet.

piping 1. צפירה *nf* tsefeer|ah/-ot (*+of:* -at); **2.** שריקה (whistle) *nf* shreek|ah/-ot (*+of:* -at).

piping hot לוהט *adj* lohet/-et.

pippin תפוח צהבהב *nm* tapoo|'akh/-kheem tsehavhav/-eem.

piquant פיקנטי *adj* peekantee/-t.

(to) pique להקניט *inf* lehakneet; *pst* heekneet; *pres* makneet; *fut* yakneet.

(to) pique oneself on להתגאות ב־ *inf* leheetga'ot; *pst* heetga'ah; *pres* meetga'eh; *fut* yeetga'eh.

pirate 1. שודד־ים (sea-robber) *m* shoded/-ey yam; **2.** גונב פטנטים (patent thief) *nm* gon|ev/-vey patenteem; **3.** גנב ספרותי (plagiarist) *nmf* gan|av/-evet seefrootee/-t **4.** פירט *nm* peerat/-eem (*pl+of:* -ey).

(to) pirate 1. לגנוב פטנטים *inf* leegnov patenteem; *pst* ganav *etc*; *pres* gonev *etc*; *fut* yeegnov *etc*; **2.** להשתמש ביצירות ללא רשות (unauthorized use) *inf* leheeshtamesh bee-yetseerot le-lo reshoot; *pst* heeshtamesh *etc*; *pres* meeshtamesh *etc*; *fut* yeeshtamesh *etc.*

pistol אקדח *nm* ekdakh/-eem (*pl+of:* ekdekhey).

piston בוכנה *nf* bookhn|ah/-ot (*pl+of:* -at).

piston ring טבעת בוכנה *nf* tab|a'at/-'ot bookhnah.

piston rod מוט הבוכנה *nm* mot/-ot ha-bookhn|ah/-ot.

pit 1. בור *nm* bor/-ot; **2.** זירה (arena) *nf* zeer|ah/-ot (*+of:* -at).

pitch 1. זפת *nm* zefet; **2.** גובה צליל (sound) *nm* govah tsleel; **3.** נטייה (inclination) *nf* netee|yah/-yot (*+of:* -yat).

(to) pitch 1. לנטות (tent) *inf* leentot; *pst* natah; *pres* noteh; *fut* yeeteh; **2.** לתפוס עמדה (take position) *inf* leetpos 'emdah; *pst* tafas *etc* (*f=p*); *pres* tofes *etc*; *fut* yeetpos *etc*; **3.** לזרוק (throw) *inf* leezrok; *pst* zarak; *pres* zorek; *fut* yeezrok.

pitch dark חושך ואפילה *nm & nf* khoshekh va-afelah.

(to) pitch in להתחיל בעבודה *inf* lehatkheel ba-'avodah; *pst* heetkheel *etc*; *pres* matkheel *etc*; *fut* yatkheel *etc.*

(to) pitch into להתקיף *inf* lehatkeef; *pst* heetkeef; *pres* matkeef; *fut* yatkeef.

pitcher 1. כד (vessel) *nm* kad/-eem (*pl+of:* -ey); **2.** זורק כדורים בבייסבול (baseball) *nm* zor|ek/-key kadooreem be-beysbol.

pitchfork קילשון *nm* keelshon/-eem (*pl+of:* -ey).

piteous מעורר רחמים *adj* me'orer/-et rakhameem.

pith עיקרו של דבר (gist) *nm* 'eekaro shel davar.

pitiful בזוי *adj* bazooy/bezooyah.

pitiless חסר רחמים *adj* khas|ar/-rat rakhameem.

pity 1. חמלה *nf* kheml|ah/-ot (*+of:* -at); **2.** רחמים (compassion) *nm pl* rakhameem.

(to) pity 1. לחמול *inf* lakhmol; *pst* khamal; *pres* khomel; *fut* yakhmol; **2.** לרחם (have mercy) *inf* lerakhem; *pst* reekhem; *pres* merakhem; *fut* yerakhem.

(what a) pity! ! מה חבל *interj* mah khavall

(for) pity's sake מתוך רחמנות *adv* mee-tokh rakhmanoot.

placard 1. כרזה *nf* kraz|ah/-ot (*+of:* -at) **2.** פלקט *nm* plakat/-eem (*pl+of:* -ey).

(to) placard להדביק כרזות *inf* lehadbeek krazot; *pst* heedbeek *etc; pres* madbeek *etc; fut* yadbeek *etc.*

place מקום *nm* makom/mekomot (*+of:* mekom)

(market) place כיכר השוק *nm* keekar ha-shook.

(in) place of במקום *adv* bee-m'kom.

place of business מקום עסק *nm* mekom/-ot 'esek.

place of worship מקום תפילה *nm* mekom/-ot tfeelah.

(it is not my) place to do it לא עלי המלאכה lo 'alay ha-melakhah.

placid 1. שקט *adj* shaket/shketah; **2.** שלוו (calm) shalev/shlevah.

plagiarism 1. גניבה ספרותית *nf* genev|ah/-ot seefrootee|t/-yot; **2.** פלגיאט *nm* plagyat/-eem (*pl+of:* -ey).

plague 1. מגיפה *nf* magef|ah/-ot (*+of:* -at); **2.** דבר (pestilence) *nm* dever.

(to) plague 1. להטריד *inf* lehatreed; *pst* heetreed; *pres* matreed; *fut* yatreed; **2.** להציק (pester) *inf* lehatseek; *pst* hetseek; *fut* metseek; *fut* yatseek.

plaid אריג מלוכסן *nm* areeg melookhsan.

plain (n.) 1. מישור (level country) *nm* meeshor/-eem (*pl+of:* -ey); **2.** ערבה (steppe) 'ar|avah/-avot (*+of:* -vat).

plain *adj* **1.** שטוח (flat) *adj* shatoo|'akh/shtookhah; **2.** פשוט (simple) *adj* pashoot/peshootah; **3.** גלוי לב (frank) *adj* gloo|y/-yat lev.

plain clothes man בלש בלבוש אזרחי *nm* balash/-eem bee-levoosh ezrakhee.

plain fool משוגע מושלם *nm* meshoog|a'/-a'eem mooshlam/-eem.

(in) plain sight לעיני כול *adv* le-'eyney kol.

plain-spoken אמור בפשטות *adj* amoor/-ah be-fashtoot *(f=p).*

plain stupid פשוט טיפשי *adj* pashoot teepshee/-t.

plain woman אישה ללא טיפת חן *nf* eeshah/nasheem le-lo teepat khen.

plaintiff 1. מתלונן *nmf* meetlonen/-et; **2.** תובע (claimant) *nmf* tov|e'a'/-a'at.

plaintive מביע תרעומת *adj* mabee|'a'/-'ah tar'omet.

plan 1. תוכנית *nf* tokhnee|t/-yot; **2.** תרשים (diagram) *nm* tarsheem/-eem (*pl+of:* -ey).

(to) plan לתכנן *inf* letakhnen; *pst* teekhnen; *pres* metakhnen; *fut* yetakhnen.

plane 1. מטוס (airplane) matos/metos|eem (*pl+of:* -ey); **2.** משטח (surface) *nm* meesht|akh/-akheem (*pl+of:* -ekhey); **3.** מקצעה (carpenter's) *nf* maktse|'ah/-'ot (*+of:* -'at).

plane tree דולב *nm* dolev/delaveem (*pl+of:* dolvey).

planet כוכב לכת *nm* kokh|av/-vey lekhet.

plank 1. קרש *nm* keresh/krasheem (*pl+of:* karshey); **2.** סעיף במצע מפלגתי (political platform) *nmf* se'eef/-eem be-matsa' meeflagtee.

(to) plank לצפות בקרשים *inf* letsapot bee-krasheem; *pst* tseepah *etc; pres* metsapeh *etc; fut* yetsapeh *etc.*

plant 1. צמח (vegetation) *nmf* tsemakh/-eem (*pl+of:* tseemkhey); **2.** מפעל (industry) *nmf* meef'al/-eem (*pl+of:* -ey).

(pilot) plant מפעל נסיוני *nmf* meef'al/-eem neesyonee/-yeem.

(to) plant 1. לשתול *inf* leeshtol; *pst* shatal; *pres* shotel; *fut* yeeshtol; **2.** להטמין אצל מישהו (hide) *inf* lehatmeen etsel meesheho; *pst* heetmeen *etc; pres* matmeen *etc; fut* yatmeen *etc.*

plantation מטע *nmf* mat|a'/-a'eem (*pl+of:* -a'ey).

(coffee) plantation מטע קפה *nmf* mat|a'/-a'ey kafeh.

(cotton) plantation מטע כותנה *nmf* mat|a'/-a'ey kootnah.

(rubber) plantation מטע גומי *nmf* mat|a'/-a'ey goomee.

(sugar) plantation מטע סוכר *nmf* mat|a'/-a'ey sookar.

planter נוטע *nmf* not|e'a'/-'eem (*pl+of:* -'ey).

plaque 1. לוח *nmf* loo|'akh/-khot; **2.** טבלה *nf* tavl|ah/-a'ot (*+of:* -at).

plasma פלסמה *nf* plasm|ah/-ot (*+of:* -at).

plaster 1. טיח *nmf* tee'akh; **2.** אספלנית (bandage) *nf* eespelanee|t/-yot; **3.** רטייה (patch) *nf* retee|yah/-yot (*+of:* -yat).

(mustard) plaster אספלנית חרדל *nf* eespelanee|t/-yot khardal.

(to) plaster 1. לטייח *inf* letaye'akh; *pst* teeye'akh; *pres* metaye'akh; *fut* yetaye'akh; **2.** להדביק *inf* lehadbeek; *pst* heedbeek; *pres* madbeek; *fut* yadbeek.

plaster of Paris גבס *nmf* geves.

plastic 1. פלסטי *adj* plastee/-t; **2.** חומר פלסטי (material) *nmf* khom|er/-areem plastee/-yeem.

plat 1. חלקה *nf* khelk|ah/-ot (*+of:* -at); **2.** תרשים (sketch) *nmf* tarsheem/-eem (*pl+of:* -ey).

(to) plat 1. לארוג *inf* le'erog; *pst* arag; *pres* oreg; *fut* ye'erog; **2.** לקלוע (twist) *inf* leeklo'a'; *pst* kala'; *pres* kole'a'; *fut* yeekla'.

plate 1. צלחת (eating) *nf* tsalakh|at/-ot; **2.** פלטה (metal) *nf* plat|ah/-ot (*pl+of:* -at).

(dental) plate שיניים תותבות *nf pl* sheenayeem totavot.

(to) plate לצפות *inf* letsapot; *pst* tseepah; *pres* metsapeh; *fut* yetsapeh.

plateau רמה *nf* ram|ah/-ot (*+of:* -at).

plated מצופה *adj* metsoop|eh/-ah.

plateful מלוא הצלחת *nmf* melo ha-tsalakhat.

platform 1. רציף *nmf* ratseef/retseef|eem (*+of:* retseef/-ey); **2.** פלטפורמה *nf* platform|ah/-ot (*+of:* -at).

(railway) platform רציף תחנת רכבת *nmf* retseef/-ey takhnat rakevet.

platinum פלטינה *nf* plateen|ah/-ot (*+of:* -at).

platitude אמת נדושה *nf* emet/ameetot nedosh|ah/-ot.

platter צלחת *nf* tsalakh|at/-ot.

play מחזה *nmf* makhz|eh/-ot.

(to) play 1. לשחק (drama or game) *inf* lesakhek; *pst* seekhek; *pres* mesakhek; *fut* yesakhek; **2.** לנגן (instrument) *inf* lenagen; *pst* neegen; *pres* menagen; *fut* yenagen.

(to) play a joke למתוח את מישהו *inf* leemto'akh et meeshehoo; *pst* matakh *etc; pres* mote'akh *etc; fut* yeemtakh *etc.*

(to) play cards לשחק בקלפים *inf* lesakhek bee-klafeem; *pst* seekhek *etc; pres* mesakhek *etc; fut* yesakhek *etc.*

(to) play havoc להפוך עולמות *inf* lahafokh 'olamot; *pst* hafakh *etc; pres* hofekh *etc; fut* yahafokh *etc.*

(to) play on words לשחק בלשון נופל על לשון *inf* lesakhek be-lashon nofel 'al lashon; *pst* seekhek *etc; pres* mesakhek *etc; fut* yesakhek *etc.*

(to) play tennis לשחק טניס *inf* lesakhek tenees; *pst* seekhek *etc; pres* mesakhek *etc; fut* yesakhek *etc.*

(to) play the fool להשתטות *inf* leheeshtatot; *pst* heeshtatah; *pres* meeshtateh; *fut* yeeshtateh.

(to give full) play to להבליט את *inf* lehavleet et; *pst* heevleet et; *pres* mavleet et; *fut* yavleet et.

player 1. שחקן (games or plays) *nmf* sakhkan/-eet (*pl:* -eem/-eeyot); **2.** נגן (music) *nmf* nagan/-eet (*pl:* -eem/-eeyot; *+of:* -ey).

(piano) player פסנתרן *nmf* pesantran/-eet (*pl+of:* -ey).

(violin) player כנר *nmf* kanar/-eet (*pl+of:* -ey).

player piano פסנתר אוטומטי *nmf* pesanter otomatee/-yeem.

playful אוהב שעשועים *adj* ohev/-et sha'ashoo'eem.

playground מגרש משחקים *nmf* meegr|ash/-eshey meeskhakeem.

playmate בן-זוג למשחקים *nmf* ben/bat zoog le-meeskhakeem.

plaything שעשוע *nmf* sha'ashoo|'a'/-'eem (*pl+of:* -'ey).

playwright מחזאי *nmf* makhza|y/-'eem (*pl+of:* -'ey).

plea 1. הודאה *nf* hoda|'ah/-'ot (*+of:* -'at); **2.** טענה *nf* ta'an|ah/-ot (*+of:* -at).

(on the) plea that בטענה ש- *adv* be-ta'anah she-.

(to) plead 1. לטעון *inf* leet'on; *pst* ta'an; *pres* to'en; *fut* yeet'an; **2.** להפציר (beg) *inf* lehaftseer; *pst* heeftseer; *pres* maftseer; *fut* yaftseer.

(to) plead guilty להודות באשמה *inf* lehodot ba-ashmah; *pst* hodah *etc; pres* modeh *etc; fut* yodeh *etc.*

pleasant נעים *adj* na'eem/ne'eemah.

pleasantry 1. הלצה *nf* halats|ah/-ot (*+of:* -at); **2.** בדיחה *nf* bedeekh|ah/-ot (*+of:* -at).

(to) please למצוא חן *inf* leemtso khen; *pst* matsa khen; *pres* motse khen; *fut* yeemtsa khen.

(as you) please כבקשתך *adv m/f* ke-vakashat|kha/-ekh (*v=b*).

(if you) please הואילה נא! ho'eelah na'!

please! 1. בבקשה! *interj* be-vakashah! (*v=b*); **2.** אנא! (syn) *interj* ana!

please do בבקשה, אנא! be-vakashah, ana! (*v=b*).

pleased מרוצה *adj* meroots|eh/-ah.

(to be) pleased להיות מרוצה *inf* leehyot merootseh; *pst* hayah *etc; pres* heeno *etc; fut* yeehyeh *etc.*

(to be) pleased with להיות שבע-רצון מ- *inf* leehyot sva' ratson mee-; *pst* hayah *etc; pres* heeno *etc; fut* yeehyeh *etc.*

pleasing מוצא חן *adj* motse/-t khen.

pleasure תענוג *nmf* ta'anoog/-ot.

pleasure trip מסע תענוגות *nmf* mas|a'/-'ey ta'anoogot.

(what is your) pleasure? מה רצונך? *m/f* mah retson|kha/-ekh?

pleat 1. קיפול *nmf* keepool/-eem (*pl+of:* -ey); **2.** קמט (crease) *nmf* kem|et/-ateem (*pl+of:* keemtey).

(to) pleat לקפל *inf* lekapel; *pst* keepel; *pres* mekapel; *fut* yekapel.

plebeian אחד העם *nmf* akha|d/-t ha-'am (*pl:* peshootey 'am).

pledge 1. הבטחה *nf* havtakh|ah/-ot (*+of:* -at); **2.** התחייבות (undertaking) *nf* heetkhayvoo|t-yot.

(to) pledge 1. להבטיח *inf* lehavtee'akh; *pst* heevtee'akh; *pres* mavtee'akh; *fut* yavtee'akh; **2.** לערוב (vouch) *inf* la'arov; *pst* 'arav; *pres* 'arev; *fut* ya'arov.

(as a) pledge of כעירבון ל- *adv* ke-'eravon le-.

(to) pledge one's word להתחייב על דברתו צדק *inf* leheetkhayev 'al deevrat|o/-ah (*m/f*) tsedek; *pst* heetkhayev *etc; pres* meetkhayev *etc; fut* yeetkhayev *etc.*

(to) pledge to secrecy להתחייב לשמירת סוד *inf* leheetkhayev lee-shmeerat sod; *pst* heetkhayev *etc; pres* meetkhayev *etc; fut* yeetkhayev *etc.*

plenary של מליאה *adj* shel melee'ah.

plenipotentiary מיופה כוח *nmf* meyoop|eh/-at ko'akh.

plentiful די והותר *adv* day ve-hoter.

plenty 1. למכביר *adv* le-makhbeer; **2.** מלוא *nmf* melo.

(that is) plenty זה די והותר zeh day ve-hoter.

plenty of time זמן למכביר *nmf* zman le-makhbeer.

pliable 1. כפיף *adj* kafeef/kefeefah; **2.** גמיש (flexible) *adj* gameesh/gemeeshah.

pliant 1. כפיף *adj* kafeef/kefeefah; **2.** נוח להשפעה *adj* no'akh/nokhah le-hashpa'ah.

pliers 1. מלקחת *nf* melk|akhat/-akhot (*pl+of:* -ekhot); **2.** צבת (tongs) *nf* tsvat/-ot; **3.** פלאייר *[colloq.]* *nmf* player/-eem.

plight 1. מצב גרוע *nmf* matsav garoo'a'; **2.** מצוקה *nf* metsook|ah/-ot (*+of:* -at).

(to) plod להלך בכבידות *inf* lehalekh bee-khvedoot; *pres* heelekh *etc; pres* mahalekh *etc; fut* yehalekh *etc.*

plosive סותם *adj* sotem/-et.

plot 1. עלילה (story) *nf* 'aleel|ah/-ot (*+of:* -at); **2.** קשר (conspiracy) *nmf* kesh|er/-areem (*pl+of:* keeshrey); **3.** חלקה (land) *nf* khelk|ah/-ot (*+of:* -at); **4.** תוכנית (plan) *nf* tokhnee|t/-yot.

(to) plot 1. לזום *inf* lazom; *pst* zamam; *pres* zomem; *fut* yazom; **2.** לתכנן (plan) *inf* letakhnen; *pst* teekhnen; *pres* metakhnen; *fut* yetakhnen.

plotter קושר kosh|er/-reem (*pl+of:* -rey).

plough, plow מחרשה *nf* makhresh|ah/-ot (+*of:* -at).

(to) plow 1. לחרוש *inf* lakhrosh; *pst* kharash; *pres* khoresh; *fut* yakhrosh; **2.** לפלס (pave way) *inf* lefales; *pst* peeles *(p=f)*; *pres* mefales; *fut* yefales.

plowshare את *nmf* et/-eem (*pl+of:* -ey).

(to) pluck 1. למרוט (feathers) *inf* leemrot; *pst* marat; *pres* moret; *fut* yeemrot; **2.** לפרוט על (guitar) *inf* leefrot 'al; *pst* parat *(p=f)* 'al; *pres* poret 'al; *fut* yeefrot 'al; **3.** לקטוף (flowers) *inf* leektof; *pst* kataf; *pres* kotef; *fut* yeektof.

plucky תקיף *adj* takeef/-ah.

plug 1. מסתם *nmf* mastem/-eem (*pl+of:* -ey); **2.** פקק (cork) *nmf* pekak/-eem (*pl+of:* -ey).

(electric) plug תקע חשמלי *nmf* tek|a'/-a'eem (*pl+of:* teek'ey).

(fire) plug מגופה *nf* megoof|ah/-ot (+*of:* -at).

(spark) plug מצת *nmf* matsat/-eem (*pl+of:* -ey).

(to) plug 1. לפקוק *inf* lefkok; *pst* pakak *(p=f)*; *pres* pokek; *fut* yeefkok; **2.** לסתום (stop) *inf* leestom; *pst* satam; *pres* sotem; *fut* yeestom.

(to) plug in לחבר לזרם *inf* lekhaber la-zerem; *pst* kheeber *etc*; *pres* mekhaber *etc*; *fut* yekhaber *etc.*

plug of tobacco גוש טבק *nmf* goosh/-ey tabak.

plum 1. שזיף (fruit) shezeef/-eem (*pl+of:* -ey); **2.** מבחר (choice) *nmf* meevkhar/-eem (*pl+of:* -ey).

plum pudding פודינג שזיפים *nmf* poodeeng shezeefeem.

plum tree עץ שזיפים *nmf* 'ets/'atsey shezeefeem.

plumage נוצות *nf pl* notsot.

plumb 1. בדיל *nmf* bedeel; **2.** משקולת (weight) *nf* meeshkol|et/-ot **3.** אנך (plummet) *nmf* anakh/-eem (*pl+of:* -ey).

(out of) plumb לא מאונך (non vertical) *adj* lo me'oon|akh/-ekhet.

(to) plumb 1. לרדת במאונך *inf* laredet bee-me'oonakh; *pst* yarad *etc*; *pres* yored *etc*; *fut* yered *etc*; **2.** לעבוד כשרברב (do plumber work) *inf* la'avod kee-shravrav; *pst* 'avad *etc*; *pres* 'oved *etc*; *fut* ya'avod *etc.*

plumb bob משקולת אנך *nf* meeshkol|et/-ot anakh.

plumb crazy משוגע על כל הראש *adj* meshoog|a'/-a'at 'al kol ha-rosh.

plumber 1. שרברב *nmf* shravrav/-eem (*pl+of:* -ey); **2.** אינסטלטור *nmf* eenstalator/-eem (*pl+of:* -ey).

plumbing 1. שרברבות *nf* shravravoot; **2.** צנרת (pipes) tsan|eret/-arot.

plume נוצה *nf* nots|ah/-ot (+*of:* -at).

(to) plume להתקשט בנוצות *inf* leheetkashet be-notsot; *pst* heetkashet *etc*; *pres* meetkashet *etc*; *fut* yeetkashet *etc.*

(to) plume oneself on להתפאר *inf* leheetpa'er; *pst* heetpa'er; *pres* meetpa'er; *fut* yeetpa'er.

plump 1. שמנמן *adj* shmanman/-ah; **2.** סגלגל *adj* sgalgal/-ah.

(to) plump down ליפול מטה בכבדות *inf* leepol matah bee-khvedoot; *pst* nafal *etc (f=p)*; *pres* nofel *etc*; *fut* yeepol *etc.*

plunder ביזה *nf* beez|ah/-ot (+*of:* -at).

(to) plunge לצלול *inf* leetslol; *pst* tsalal; *pres* tsolel; *fut* yeetslol.

(to) plunge headlong לצלול עם הראש קדימה *inf* leetslol 'eem ha-rosh kadeemah; *pst* tsalal *etc*; *pres* tsolel *etc*; *fut* yeetslol *etc.*

plunk 1. חבטה *nf* khavat|ah/-ot (+*of:* -at); **2.** בקול חבטה *adv* be-kol khavatah; **3.** בדיוק (exactly) *adv* be-deeyook.

(to) plunk לפרוט על (on instrument) *inf* leefrot 'al; *pst* parat 'al *(p=f)*; *pres* poret 'al; *fut* yeefrot 'al;

plural מספר רבים (grammar) *nmf* meespar rabeem.

plurality 1. ריבוי *nmf* reeboo|y/-yeem (*pl+of:* -yey); **2.** רוב קולות (voting) *nmf* rov kolot.

plus 1. ועוד ve-'od; **2.** פלוס ploos/-eem (*pl+of:* -ey).

(three) plus five שלוש ועוד חמש *num & num* shalosh ve-'od khamesh.

plus quantity כמות חיובית *nf* kamoo|t-yot kheeyoovee|t/-yot.

plush 1. קטיפה *nf* keteef|ah/-ot (+*of:* -at); **2.** פלוש *nmf* ploosh; **3.** מהודר (luxurious) *adj* mehood|ar/-eret.

plutocracy 1. שלטון העשירים *nmf* sheelton ha-'asheereem; **2.** פלוטוקרטיה *nf* plootokrat|yah/-yot (+*of:* -yat).

plutonium פלוטוניום *nmf* plootonyoom.

ply 1. עובי *nmf* 'ovee; **2.** לבד *nmf* leved.

(to) ply 1. לשקוד *inf* leeshkod; *pst* shakad; *pres* shoked; *fut* yeeshkod; **2.** לפלס דרך (pave way) *inf* lefales derekh; *pst* peeles *etc (p=f)*; *pres* mefales *etc*; *fut* yefales *etc.*

(to) ply a trade לעסוק במסחר *inf* la'asok be-meeskhar; *pst* 'asak *etc*; *pres* 'osek *etc*; *fut* ya'asok *etc.*

(to) ply oneself with לשבוע את *inf* leesbo'a' et; *pst* sava' et *(v=b)*; *pres* save'a' et; *fut* yeesba' et.

pneumatic פנימטי *adj* pneymatee/-t.

pneumonia דלקת ריאות *nf* daleket re'ot.

(to) poach לצוד ציד אסור *inf* latsood tsayeed asoor; *pst & pres* tsad *etc*; *fut* yatsood *etc.*

pocket כיס *nmf* kees/-eem (*pl+of:* -ey).

pocketbook ספר כיס *nmf* sefer/seefrey kees.

(woman's) pocketbook 1. פנקס כיס של אישה *nmf* peenkes/-ey kees shel eeshah; **2.** ארנק של אישה (handbag) *nmf* arnak/-eem shel eeshah/nasheeem.

pocketknife אולר *nmf* olar/-eem (*pl+of:* -ey).

pod 1. ארגז *nmf* argaz/-eem (*pl+of:* -ey); **2.** תרמיל *nmf* tarmeel/-eem (*pl+of:* -ey).

podium בימה *nf* beem|ah/-ot (+*of:* -at).

poem פואמה *nf* po'em|ah/-ot (+*of:* -at).

poet משורר *nmf* meshorer (*pl+of:* -ey).

poetess משוררת *nf* meshorer|et/-ot.

poetic שירה *nf* sheer|ah (+*of:* -at).

poetical פיוטי *adj* peeyootee/-t.

poetry 1. שירה *nf* sheerah (+*of:* at); **2.** פיוט *nmf* peeyoot (*pl+of:* -ey).

poignant מרשים *adj* marsheem/-ah.

point 1. נקודה *nf* nekood|ah/-ot (+*of:* -at); **2.** דגש (dot) *nmf* dagesh/degesh|eem (*pl+of:* -ey) **3.** עוקץ (sting) *nmf* 'ok|ets/-atseem (*pl+of:* 'ooktsey).

(not to the) point שלא לעניין *adv* she-lo la-'eenyan.
(not to see the) point לא להבחין במה מדובר lo le-havkheen ba-meh medoobar; *pst* lo heevkheen *etc*; *pres* eyno mavkheen *etc*; *fut* lo yavkheen *etc*.
(to) point להצביע *inf* lehatsbee'a'; *pst* heetsbee'a'; *pres* matsbee'a'; *fut* yatsbee'a'.
point blank 1. במטווח קצר *adv* be-meetvakh katsar; **2.** הישר למטרה (straight to the target) *adv* haysher la-matarah.
(on the) point of על סף *adv* 'al saf.
(to) point out 1. לציין *inf* letsayen; *pst* tseeyen; *pres* metsayen; *fut* yetsayen; **2.** להטעים (stress) *inf* lehat'eem; *pst* heet'eem; *pres* mat'eem; *fut* yat'eem.
pointed מחודד *adj* mekhood|ad/-edet.
pointed script כתב מנוקד *nmf* ketav menookad.
pointer 1. מחוג (indicator) *nmf* makhog/mekhog|eem (*pl+of:* -ey); **2.** כלב ציד (dog) *nmf* kelev/kalvey tsayeed **3.** עצה (advice) *nf* 'ets|ah/-ot (+*of:* 'ats|at/-ot).
poise 1. יציבה *nf* yatseev|ah/-ot (+*of:* -at); **2.** איזון (balance) *nmf* eezoon (*pl+of:* -ey).
(to) poise לאזן *inf* le'azen; *pst* eezen; *pres* me'azen; *fut* ye'azen.
poison רעל *nmf* ra'al/re'aleem (*pl+of:* ra'aley).
poisonous רעיל *adj* ra'eel/re'eelah.
poke 1. אמתחת כיס *nf* amt|akhat/-ekhot kees; **2.** מכת אגרוף *nf* mak|at/-ot egrof; **3.** דחיפה *nf* dekheef|ah/-ot (+*of:* -at).
(to) poke 1. לנקר *inf* lenaker; *pst* neeker; *pres* menaker; *fut* yenaker; **2.** לתחוב (thrust) *inf* leetkhov; *pst* takhav; *pres* tokhev; *fut* yeetkhav.
(to) poke around לחטט סביב *inf* lekhatet saveev; *pst* kheetet *etc*; *pres* mekhatet *etc*; *fut* yekhatet *etc*.
(to) poke fun at ללגלג *inf* lelagleg; *pst* leegleg; *pres* melagleg; *fut* yelagleg.
(to) poke into לתחוב את האף *inf* leetkhov et ha-af; *pst* takhav *etc*; *pres* tokhev *etc*; *fut* yeetkhav *etc*.
poker פוקר *nmf* poker.
polar קוטבי *adj* kotbee/-t.
polar bear דוב קרח *nmf* dov/doobey (*b=v*) kerakh.
polarity קוטביות *nf* kotbeeyoot.
polarization קיטוב *nmf* keetoov/-eem (*pl+of:* -ey).
Pole פולני *nmf* polanee/-yah (*pl:* -m/-yot).
pole 1. מוט *nmf* mot/-ot; **2.** עמוד (column) *nmf* 'amood/-eem (*pl+of:* -ey); **3.** קוטב (geogr.) kotev/ketaveem (*pl+of:* kotvey).
(North) Pole הקוטב הצפוני *nmf* ha-kotev ha-tsefonee.
(South) Pole הקוטב הדרומי *nmf* ha-kotev ha-dromee.
pole vault קפיצה במוט *nf* kefeetsah be-mot.
polemics פולמוס *nmf* poolmoos/-eem (*pl+of:* -ey).
police משטרה *nf* meesht|arah/-arot (+*of:* -eret/-erot).
(to) police לשטר *inf* leshater; *pst* sheeter; *pres* meshater; *fut* yeshater.
policeman שוטר *nmf* shot|er/-reem (*pl+of:* -rey).
policewoman שוטרת *nf* shot|eret/-rot.
policy מדיניות *nf* medeeneeyoot.
(insurance) policy פוליסת ביטוח *nf* polees|at/-ot beetoo'akh.
polio 1. שיתוק ילדים *nmf* sheetook yeladeem; **2.** פוליו *nmf* polyo.
Polish 1. פולני *nmf* polanee/-yah (*pl:* -m/-yot); **2.** פולני *adj* polanee/-t; **3.** פולנית (language) *nf* polaneet.
polish משחת הברקה *nf* meeshkh|at/-ot havrakah.
(shoe) polish משחת נעליים *nf* meeshkh|at/-ot na'alayeem.
(to) polish לצחצח *inf* letsakhtse'akh; *pst* tseekhtse'akh; *pres* metsakhtse'akh; *fut* yetsakhtse'akh.
polite מנומס *adj* menoom|as/-eset.
politeness 1. אדיבות *nf* adeevoo|t/-yot; **2.** נימוסים (manners) *nmf pl* neemoos|eem (*pl+of:* -ey).
politic 1. מחוכם *adj* mekhook|am/-emet; **2.** נבון (wise) *adj* navon/nevonah.
political 1. מדיני *adj* medeenee/-t; **2.** פוליטי *adj* poleetee/-t.
politician פוליטיקאי *nmf* poleeteek|ay/-a'eet.
politics 1. מדיניות *nf* medeeneeyoot; **2.** פוליטיקה *nf* poleeteek|ah/-ot (+*of:* -at).
poll 1. ספירת קולות *nf* sfeer|at/-ot kolot; **2.** הצבעה (voting) *nf* hatsb|'ah/-'ot (+*of:* -at).
(to) poll 1. לקבל קולות *inf* lekabel kolot; *pst* keebel *etc*; *pres* mekabel *etc*; *fut* yekabel *etc*; **2.** לערוך הצבעה (take vote) *inf* la'arokh hatsba'ah; *pst* 'arakh *etc*; *pres* 'orekh *etc*; *fut* ya'arokh *etc*.
poll tax מס גולגולת *nmf* mas/meesey goolgolet.
pollen 1. אבקית צמחים *nf* avakeet tsemakheem; **2.** פוליניום *nmf* poleenyoom.
(to) pollinate 1. להאביק *inf* leha'aveek; *pst* he'eveek; *pres* ma'aveek; *fut* ya'aveek; **2.** לאבק צמח (plant) *vt inf* le'abek tsemakh; *pst* eebek *etc*; *pres* me'abek *etc*; *fut* ye'abek *etc*.
polls קלפי *nf* kalpee/-yot.
polo פולו *nmf* polo.
polyglot 1. יודע שפות *nmf* yod|e'a'/-a'at safot; **2.** רב־לשוני (multilingual) *adj* rav-leshonee/-t.
pomegranate רימון *nmf* reemon/-eem (*pl+of:* -ey).
pomegranate tree עץ הרימון *nmf* 'ets/'atsey reemon.
pomp 1. הוד *nmf* hod; **2.** זוהר (glamor) *nmf* zohar.
pompous 1. מתגנדר *adj* meetgander/-et; **2.** מנופח (puffed up) *adj* menoopakh/-at.
pond בריכה *nf* brekh|ah/-ot (+*of:* -at).
(fish)pond בריכת דגים *nf* brekh|at/-ot dageem.
(to) ponder over 1. לשקול *inf* leeshkol; *pst* shakal; *pres* shokel; *fut* yeeshkol; **2.** להרהר (muse) *inf* leharher; *pst* heerher; *pres* meharher; *fut* yeharher.
ponderous כבד *adj* kaved/kvedah.
pontoon סירת גשרים *nf* seer|at/-ot gshareem.
pontoon bridge גשר סירות *nmf* gesher/geeshrey seerot.
pony 1. סוס קטן *nmf* soos/-eem katan/ketaneem; **2.** סייח *nmf* syakh/-eem (*pl+of:* -ey).
poodle כלב פודל *nmf* kelev/kalvey poodel.
pool בריכה *nf* brekh|ah/-ot (+*of:* -at).
(swimming) pool בריכת שחייה *nf* brekh|at/-ot sekheeyah.

(to) pool להפקיד בקרן משותפת *inf* kehafkeed be-keren meshootefet; *pst* heefkeed *etc; pres* mafkeed *etc; fut* yafkeed *etc.*

pool resources למזג משאבים *inf* lemazeg mash'abeem; *pst* meezeg *etc; pres* memazeg *etc; fut* yemazeg *etc.*

(to) pool together לצרף יחד *inf* letsaref yakhad; *pst* tseraf *etc; pres* metsaref *etc; fut* yetsaref *etc.*

poor 1. מסכן *adj* meesken/-ah; **2.** עני (pauper) *adj* 'anee/-yah; **3.** גרוע (bad) garoo'a'/groo'ah.

(the) poor העניים *nmf pl* ha-'aneeyeem.

poor little thing יצור מסכן *nmf* yetsoor meesken.

poor student סטודנט גרוע *nmf* stoodent/-eet garoo'a'/groo'ah.

poorhouse בית מחסה לעניים bet/batey makhseh la-'aneeyeem.

poorly 1. בצורה גרועה *adv* be-tsoorah groo'ah; **2.** מעט מאוד (very little) *adv* me'at me'od.

pop 1. קול נפץ (sound) *nmf* kol/-ot nefets; **2.** גזוז (drink) *nmf* gazoz/-eem; **3.** עממי (popular) *adj* 'amamee/-t.

(soda) pop גזוז *nmf* gazoz.

(to) pop להופיע לפתע *inf* lehofee'a' le-feta' *(f=p); pst* hofee'a' *etc; pres* mofee'a' *etc; fut* yofee'a' *etc.*

(to) pop the question להציע נישואים *inf* lehatsee'a' neesoo'eem; *pst* heetsee'a' *etc; pres* matsee'a' *etc; fut* yatsee'a' *etc.*

(to) pop in and out להתרוצץ יצוא וחזור *inf* leheetrotsets yatso ve-khazor; *pst* heetrotsets *etc; pres* meetrotsets *etc; fut* yeetrotsets *etc.*

pop music מוסיקת פופ *nf* mooseekat pop.

pop of a cork היחלצות פקק *nf* hekhaltsoot pekak.

(to) pop one's head out להוציא ראשו לרגע *inf* lehotsee rosh|o/-ah *(m/f)* le-rega'; *pst* hotsee *etc; pres* motsee; *fut* yotsee *etc.*

pop singer זמר פופ *nmf* zam|ar/-eret pop.

popcorn תירס קלוי *nmf* teeras kalooy.

(the) Pope האפיפיור *nmf* ha-apeefyor/-eem *(pl+of:* -ey).

popeyed פעור עיניים *adj* pe'oor/-at 'eynayeem.

poplar צפצפה *nf* tsaftsef|ah/-ot *(+of:* -at).

(black) poplar צפצפה שחורה *nf* tsaftsaf|ah/-ot shekhor|ah/-ot.

poplar grove חורשת צפצפות *nf* khorsh|at/-ot tsaftsafot.

poppy פרג *nmf* parag/prageem *(pl+of:* peergey).

populace 1. אספסוף *nmf* asafsoof; **2.** המון (crowd) *nmf* hamon/-eem *(pl+of:* -ey).

popular 1. עממי *adj* amamee/-t; **2.** מקובל (accepted) *adj* mekoob|al/-elet; **3.** פופולרי *adj* popoolaree/-t.

popularity 1. מוניטין *nmf pl* moneeteen; **2.** פופולריות *nf* popoolareeyoot.

(to) populate לאכלס *inf* le'akhles; *pst* eekhles; *pres* me'akhles; *fut* ye'akhles.

population אוכלוסייה *nf* ookhlooseelyah/-yot *(+of:* -yat).

populous רב אוכלוסין *adj* rav/rabat *(b=v)* ookhlooseen.

porcelain חרסינה *nf* kharseen|ah/-ot *(+of:* -at).

porch מרפסת *nmf* meerp|eset/-asot *(pl+of:* -esot).

porcupine קיפוד *nmf* keepod/-eem *(pl+of:* -ey).

pore נקבובית *nf* nakboovee|t/-yot.

(to) pore over a book לשקוע בספר *inf* leeshko'a' be-sefer; *pst* shaka' *etc; pres* shoke'a' *etc; fut* yeeshka' *etc.*

pork בשר חזיר *nmf* besar khazeer.

pork chop נתח בשר חזיר *nmf* netakh/neetkhey besar khazeer.

(salt) pork קותלי חזיר ממולחים *nmf pl* kotley khazeer memoolakheem.

pornography פורנוגרפיה *nf* pornografyah/-yot *(+of:* -yat).

porous נקבובי *adj* nakboovee/-t.

porridge דיסה *nf* days|ah/-ot *(+of:* -at).

port 1. נמל (harbor) *nmf* namel/nemeleem *(+of:* nemal/neemley); **2.** יין (wine) *nmf* yayeen/yeynot *(+of:* yeyn).

portable מיטלטל *adj* meetaltel/-et.

portal 1. דלת *nf* delet/dlatot *(pl+of:* daltot); **2.** שער (gate) *nmf* sha'ar/she'areem *(pl+of:* sha'arey).

portent אות לבאות *nmf* ot la-ba'ot.

portentous 1. מנבא *adj* menab|e/-'ah; **2.** מבשר (heralding) *adj* mevaser/-et.

porter 1. סבל *nmf* sabal/-eem *(pl+of:* -ey); **2.** שוער (doorkeeper) *nmf* sho'er/-et.

portfolio 1. תיק מסמכים *nmf* teek/-ey meesmakheem; **2.** תיק מיניסטריאלי (ministerial) *nmf* teek/-eem meeneesteryalee/-yeem.

porthole אשנב *nmf* eshna|v/-beem *(pl+of:* -bey; *b=v).*

portion 1. מנה *nf* man|ah/-ot *(+of:* men|at/-ot); **2.** חלק (share) *nmf* khelek/khalakeem *(pl+of:* khelkey); **3.** נדוניה (dowry) *nf* nedoon|yah/-yot *(+of:* -yat).

portly 1. כרסן *adj* kresan/-eet; **2.** שמנמן (fattish) *adj* shemanm|an/-enet.

portrait 1. דיוקן *nmf* dyok|an/-neem *(pl+of:* -ney); **2.** פורטרט *nmf* portret/-eem *(pl+of:* -ey).

(to) portray 1. לצייר (paint) *nf* letsayer; *pst* tseeyer; *pres* metsayer; *fut* yetsayer; **2.** לתאר (describe) *inf* leta'er; *pst* te'ar; *pres* meta'er; *fut* yeta'er.

portrayal תיאור *nmf* te'oor/-eem *(pl+of:* -ey).

pose 1. תנוחה (posture) *nf* tenookh|ah/-ot *(+of:* -at); **2.** העמדת פנים (affected attitude) *nf* ha'ama-d|at/-ot paneem; **3.** פוזה *nf* poz|ah/-ot *(+of:* -at).

(to) pose 1. לדגמן (as *m/f* model) *inf* ledagmen; *pst* deegmen/-ah; *pres* medagmen/-et; *fut* yedagmen/tedagmen; **2.** להעלות בעיה (a problem) *inf* leha'alot ba'yah; *pst* he'elah *etc; pres* ma'aleh *etc; fut* ya'aleh *etc.*

(to) pose as להתחזות ל- *v rfl inf* leheetkhazot le-; *pst* heetkhazah *etc; pres* meetkhazeh *etc; fut* yeetkhazeh *etc.*

position 1. מצב *nmf* matsav/-eem *(pl+of:* -ey); **2.** מוצב (military) *nmf* moots|av/-aveem *(pl+of:* -vey).

(to) position להציב בעמדה *inf* lehatseev be-'emdah; *pst* heetseev *etc; pres* matseev *etc; fut* yatseev *etc.*

positive חיובי *adj* kheeyoovee/-t.

(to) possess להחזיק *inf* lehakhzeek; *pst* hekhzeek; *pres* makhzeek; *fut* yakhzeek.

possession 1. חזקה *nf* khazak|ah/-ot (*+of:* khezk|at/-ot); **2.** בעלות (ownership) *nf* ba'aloo|t/-yot; **3.** רכוש (property) *nmf* rekhoosh.

possessive קנייני *adj* keenyanee/-t.

possessor מחזיק *nmf* makhzeek/-ah.

possibility אפשרות *nf* efsharoo|t/-yot.

possible אפשרי *adj* efsharee/-t.

possibly ייתכן *adv* yeetakhen.

post 1. עמוד (pole) *nmf* 'amood/-eem (*pl+of:* -ey); **2.** עמדה (position) *nf* 'emdah/'amadot (*+of:* 'emd|at/-ot).

(army) post מוצב צבאי *nmf* mootsav/-eem tseva'ee/-yeem.

(to) post להציב *inf* lehatseev; *pst* heetseev; *pres* matseev; *fut* yatseev.

post haste במהירות הבזק *adv* bee-meheeroot ha-bazak.

post office בית דואר *nmf* bet/batey do'ar.

post-office box תיבת דואר *nf* tev|at/-ot do'ar.

postage 1. ביול *nmf* beeyool/-eem (*pl+of:* -ey); **2.** דמי דואר (stamp fees) *nmf pl* demey do'ar.

postage stamp בול דואר *nmf* bool/-ey do'ar.

postal של דואר *adj* shel do'ar.

postal money order המחאת דואר *nf* hamkha|'at/-'ot do'ar.

postcard גלויה *nf* gloo|yah/-yot (*+of:* -yat).

(well) posted מדווח יפה *adj* medoovakh/-at yafeh.

poster 1. כרזה *nf* kraz|ah/-ot (*+of:* -at); **2.** פלקט *nmf* plakat/-eem (*pl+of:* -ey).

posterior אחוריים *nmf pl* akhor|ayeem (*pl+of:* -ey).

posterity הדורות הבאים *nmf pl* ha-dorot ha-ba'eem

posthumous שלאחר המוות *adj* she-le-akhar ha-mavet.

postman דוור *nmf* davar/-eem (*pl+of:* -ey).

postmaster מנהל דואר *nmf* menah|el/-aley do'ar.

postpaid עם ביול משולם *adv* 'eem beeyool meshoolam.

(to) postpone 1. לדחות *nf* leedkhot; *pst* dakhah; *pres* dokheh; *fut* yeedkheh; **2.** להשהות (delay) *inf* lehash'hot; *pst* heesh'hah; *pres* mash'heh; *fut* yash'heh.

postponement דחייה *nf* dekhee|yah/-yot (*+of:* -yat).

postscript 1. תוספת למכתב *nf* tos|efet/-afot le-meekhtav; **2.** עיקר שכחתי (I forgot the main point) 'eekar shakhakhtee; **3.** נ.ב. (Hebrew equivalent of N.B.) noon bet.

posture 1. תנוחה *nf* tenookh|ah/-ot (*+of:* -at); **2.** יציבה *nf* yetseev|ah/-ot (*+of:* -at).

(to) posture לאמץ לעצמו יציבה *inf* le'amets le-'atsmo yatseevah; *pst* eemets *etc*; *pres* me'mets *etc*; *fut* ye'amets *etc*.

postwar שלאחר המלחמה *adj* she-le-akhar ha-meelkhamah.

posy זר פרחים *nmf* zer/-ey prakheem.

pot סיר *nmf* seer/-eem (*pl+of:* -ey).

(flower) pot עציץ *nmf* 'atseets/-eem (*pl+of:* -ey).

pot hole נקב *nmf* nekev/-aveem (*pl+of:* neekvey).

potash אשלג *nmf* ashlag.

(Israel) Potash Works חברת האשלג *nf* khevrat ha-ashlag.

potassium אשלגן *nmf* ashlagan.

potato תפוח אדמה *nmf* tapoo|'akh/-khey adamah.

(sweet) potato 1. תפוד *nmf* tapood/-eem (*pl+of:* -ey); **2.** בטטה (syn) *nf* batat|ah/-ot (*+of:* -at).

potbellied כרסני *adj* kresanee/-t.

potency 1. עוצמה *nf* 'otsm|ah/-ot (*+of:* -at); **2.** כוח גברא (sexual) *nmf* ko'akh gavra.

potent 1. חזק *adj* khazak/-ah; **2.** בעל כוח גברא (sexually) *adj m* ba'al/-ey ko'akh gavra.

potential 1. בכוח *adj* be-khoakh (*kh=k*); **2.** פוטנציאל *nmf* potentsee'al/-eem (*pl+of:* -ey).

pottage 1. נזיד *nmf* nazeed/nezeed|eem (*pl+of:* -ey); **2.** מרק סמיך (thick soup) *nmf* marak/merakeem sameekh/smeekheem.

potter קדר *nmf* kadar/-eem (*pl+of:* -ey).

pottery 1. קדרות *nf* kadaroot; **2.** כלי חרס *nmf pl* kley kheres.

pouch 1. שקיק *nmf* sakeek/-eem (*pl+of:* -ey); **2.** כיס (pocket) *nmf* kees/-eem (*pl+of:* -ey).

(mail) pouch שק דואר *nmf* sak/-ey do'ar.

(tobacco) pouch שקית טבק *nf* sakee|t/-yot tabak.

poultice אספלנית מרוחה *nf* eespelanee|t/-yot merookh|ah/-ot.

poultry עופות בית *nf pl* 'ofot bayeet.

pounce זינוק *nmf* zeenook/-eem (*pl+of:* -ey).

(to) pounce into לזנק לתוך *inf* lezanek le-tokh; *pst* zeenek *etc*; *pres* mezanek *etc*; *fut* yezanek *etc*.

(to) pounce upon לעוט על *inf* la'oot 'al; *pst & pres* 'at 'al; *fut* ya'oot 'al.

pound ליטרה *nf* leetr|ah/-ot (*+of:* -at).

(to) pound 1. להכות *inf* lehakot; *pst* heekah; *pres* makeh; *fut* yakeh; **2.** להלום (hit) *inf* lahalom; *pst* halam; *pres* holem; *fut* yahalom.

pound of flesh ליטרת הבשר *nf* leetrat ha-basar.

pound sterling 1. לירה שטרלינג *nf* leer|ah/-ot shterleeng; **2.** לי״ש (*acr of* 1).

(to) pour 1. לשפוך *inf* leeshpokh; *pst* shafakh (*f=p*); *pres* shofekh; *fut* yeeshpokh; **2.** למזוג (fill) *inf* leemzog; *pst* mazag; *pres* mozeg; *fut* yeemzog.

(to) pout 1. לשרבט lesharbet; *pst* sheerbet; *pres* mesharbet; *fut* yesharbet; **2.** לכעוס (be angry) *inf* leekh'os; *pst* ka'as (*k=kh*); *pres* ko'es/-et; *fut* yeekh'as.

poverty עוני *nmf* 'onee.

powder 1. אבקה *nf* avak|ah/-akot (*+of:* -kat); **2.** אבק שריפה (explosive) *nmf* avak sreyfah; **3.** פודרה (beauty) *nf* poodr|ah/-ot (*+of:* -at).

powder compact פודרייה *nmf* poodree|yah/-yot (*+of:* -yat).

powder magazine מחסנית *nf* makhsanee|t/-yot.

(to) powder one's face לפדר פנים *inf* lefader; *pst* peeder (*p=f*); *pres* mefader; *fut* yefader.

powder puff כרית פודרה *nf* karee|t/-yot poodrah

power 1. כוח *nmf* ko'akh|kokhot; **2.** יכולת (capacity) *nf* yekholet.

(motive) power כוח מניע *nmf* ko'akh menee'a'.

power of attorney ייפוי־כוח *nmf* yeepoo|y/-yey ko'akh.

power plant תחנת כוח *nf* takhn|at/-ot ko'akh.

powerful 1. רב־כוח *adj* ra|v/-bat (*b=v*) ko'akh; **2.** עצום *adj* 'atsoom/-ah.

powerless חסר אונים *adj* khas|ar/-rat oneem.

practicable שמיש *adj* shameesh/shemeeshah.

practicable road דרך שמישה *nf* derekh/drakheem shmeesh|ah/-ot.

practical 1. מעשי *adj* ma'asee/-t; **2.** פרקטי *adj* praktee/-t.

practical joke מתיחה *nf* meteekh|ah/-ot (+*of:* -at).

practically למעשה *adv* le-ma'aseh.

practice 1. עיסוק במיקצוע (exercise of profession) *nmf* 'eesook/-eem be-meektso'a'; **2.** נוהל (procedure) *nmf* nohal/-eem (*pl+of:* -ey); **3.** נוהג (custom) *nmf* nohag/-eem (*pl+of:* -ey).

(to) practice, practise 1. לתרגל (exercise) *inf* letargel; *pst* teergel; *pres* metargel; *fut* yetargel; **2.** לעסוק במקצוע (exercise profession) *inf* la'asok be-meektso'a'; *pst* 'asak *etc*; *pres* 'osek *etc*; *fut* ya'asok *etc*.

practiced 1. בעל ניסיון *nmf* ba'al/-at neesyon; **2.** מנוסה (experienced) *adj* menoos|eh/-ah.

practitioner עוסק במקצוע *adj* 'osek/-et be-meektsoo'a'.

prairie ערבה *nf* 'arav|ah/-ot (+*of:* arv|at/-ot).

praise שבחים *nmf pl* shvakheem (*pl+of:* sheevkhey).

praiseworthy ראוי לשבח *adj* ra'ooy/re'ooyah le-shevakh.

(to) prance 1. לנתר *inf* lenater; *pst* neeter; *pres* menater; *fut* yenater; **2.** לרכוב בגאון (swagger) *inf* leerkov be-ga'on; *pst* rakhav *etc* (*kh=k*); *pst* rokhev *etc*; *fut* yeerkav *etc*.

prank מעשה קונדס *nmf* ma'as|eh/-ey koondes.

(to play) pranks לסדר מתיחות *inf* lesader meteekhot; *pst* seeder *etc*; *pres* mesader *etc*; *fut* yesader *etc*.

prate פטפוט *nmf* peetpoot/-eem (*pl+of:* -ey).

(to) prate לפטפט *inf* lefatpet; *pst* peetpet (*p=f*); *pres* mefatpet; *fut* yefatpet.

(to) prattle לקשקש *inf* lekashkesh; *pst* keeshkesh; *pres* mekashkesh; *fut* yekashkesh.

(to) pray 1. להתפלל *inf* leheetpalel; *pst* heetpalel; *pres* meetpalel; *fut* yeetpalel; **2.** להתחנן (besiege) *inf* leheetkhanen; *pst* heetkhanen; *pres* meetkhanen; *fut* yeetkhanen.

pray tell me אנא אמור לי *v imp (m/f)* ana, emor/eemree lee!

prayer תפילה *nf* tfeel|ah/-ot (+*of:* -at).

(Day of Atonement) prayer book מחזור ליום כיפור *nmf* makhzor le-yom keepoor.

(everyday) prayer book סידור תפילה *nmf* seedoor/-ey tfeelah.

(holiday) prayer book מחזור *nmf* makhzor/-eem (*pl+of:* -ey).

(Passover) prayer book מחזור לחג הפסח *nmf* makhzor le-khag ha-pesakh.

(Rosh-ha-Shanah) prayer book מחזור לראש השנה *nmf* makhzor le-rosh ha-shanah.

(Succot) prayer book מחזור לחג הסוכות *nmf* makhzor lekhag ha-sookot.

(Three Holidays) prayer book מחזור לשלוש רגלים (for Passover, Pentecost & Tabernacles) *nm* makhzor le-shalosh regaleem.

(to) preach להטיף *inf* lehateef; *pst* heeteef; *pres* mateef; *fut* yateef.

preacher 1. מטיף *nmf* mateef/-eem (*pl+of:* -ey); **2.** כומר (Christian) *nmf* komer/kemar|eem (*pl+of:* komrey).

preaching הטפה *nf* hataf|ah/-ot (+*of:* -at).

preamble מבוא *nmf* mavo/mevo'ot (+*of:* mevo).

prearranged מוסדר מראש *adj* moosd|ar/-eret me-rosh.

precarious 1. מסוכן *adj* mesook|an/-enet; **2.** רופף *adj* rofef/-et.

precaution אמצעי זהירות *nmf* emtsa|'ee/-'ey zeheeroot.

(to) precede להקדים *inf* lehakdeem; *pst* heekdeem; *pres* makdeem; *fut* yakdeem.

precedence דין קדימה *nmf* deen kedeemah.

precedent תקדים *nmf* takdeem/-eem (*pl+of:* -ey).

preceding קודם *adj* kodem/-et.

precept מצווה *nf* meetsv|ah/-ot (+*of:* -at).

precinct 1. אזור (area) *nmf* ezor/azor|eem (*pl+of:* -ey); **2.** סביבה (neighborhood) *nf* sveev|ah/-ot (+*of:* -at).

precious יקר־ערך *adj* yekar/yeekrat 'erekh.

precipice 1. תהום *nf* tehom/-ot; **2.** צוק (cliff) *nmf* tsook/-eem (*pl+of:* -ey).

precipitate נחפז *adj* nekhp|az/-ezet.

(to) precipitate 1. להחיש *inf* lehakheesh; *pst* hekheesh; *pres* mekheesh; *fut* yakheesh; **2.** לזרז (accelerate) *inf* lezarez; *pst* zerez; *pres* mezarez; *fut* yezarez; **3.** לשקע (chemistry) *inf* leshake'a'; *pst* sheeka'; *pres* meshake'a'; *fut* yeshaka'; **4.** לעבות (rain) *inf* le'abot; *pst* 'eebah; *pres* me'abeh; *fut* ye'abeh.

precipitation משקע *nmf* meeshk|a'/-a'eem (*pl+of:* -e'ey).

precipitous תלול *adj* talool/tloolah.

precise 1. מדויק *adj* medoo|yak/-yeket; **2.** מדוקדק *adj* medookd|ak/-eket.

precision 1. דיוק (exactness) *nmf* deeyook/-eem (*pl+of:* -ey); **2.** דייקנות (punctuality) *nf* dayka-noo|t/-yot.

(to) preclude להוציא מכלל חשבון *inf* lehotsee mee-khlal (*kh=k*) kheshbon; *pst* hotsee *etc*; *pres* motsee *etc*; *fut* yotsee *etc*.

precocious בשל בטרם עת *adj* bashel/beshelah be-terem 'et.

precursor 1. מקדים *nmf* makdeem/-ah; **2.** מבשר (herald) *nmf* mevaser/-et.

predecessor 1. קודם *adj* kodem/-et; **2.** זה שלפניו (the one before him/her) *adj* zeh/zoo she-le-fan|av/-eha.

(to) predestine להועיד מראש *inf* leho'eed me-rosh; *pst* ho'eed *etc*; *pres* mo'eed *etc*; *fut* yo'eed *etc*.

predicament מצב ביש *nmf* mats|av/-vey beesh.

predicate נשוא (grammar) *nmf* nasoo.

(to) predict לחזות מראש *inf* lakhzot me-rosh *inf* khazah *etc*; *pres* khozeh *etc*; *fut* yekhzeh *etc*.

prediction חיזוי מראש *nmf* kheezoo|y/-yeem me-rosh.

predilection העדפה *nf* ha'adaf|ah/-ot (+*of:* -at).

predisposed נוטה מראש *adj* not|eh/-ah me-rosh.

predominance השפעה מכרעת *nf* hashpa|'ah/-'ot makhr|a'at/-ee'ot.

predominant מכריע *adj* makhree|'a'/-'ah.

(to) predominate להכריע *inf* lehakhree'a'; *pst* heekhree'a'; *pst* makhree'a'; *fut* yakhree'a'.

preface הקדמה *nf* hakdam|ah/-ot (*+of:* -at).

(to) preface להקדים מבוא *inf* lehakdeem mavo; *pst* heekdeem *etc*; *pres* makdeem *etc*; *fut* yakdeem *etc*.

prefect ממונה על המחוז *nmf* memoon|eh/-eem 'al ha-makhoz/mekhozot.

(to) prefer 1. להעדיף *inf* leha'adeef; *pst* he'edeef; *pres* ma'adeef; *fut* ya'adeef; **2.** לבכר (give precedence) *inf* levaker; *pst* beeker *(b=v)*; *pres* mevaker; *fut* yavaker.

(to) prefer a claim להעלות תביעה *inf* leha'alot tvee'ah; *pst* he'elah *etc*; *pres* ma'aleh *etc*; *fut* ya'aleh *etc*.

preferable עדיף *adj* 'adeef/-ah.

preferably מוטב *adv* mootav.

preference 1. העדפה *nf* ha'adaf|ah/-ot (*+of:* -at); **2.** עדיפות (priority) *nf* 'adeefoo|t/-yot.

preferred מועדף *adj* mo'od|af/-efet.

preferred stock, share מניית בכורה *nf* mena|yat/-yot bekhorah.

prefix קידומת *nf* keedom|et/-ot.

(to) prefix להקדים קידומת *inf* lehakdeem keedomet; *pst* heekdeem *etc*; *pres* makdeem *etc*; *fut* yakdeem *etc*.

pregnancy הריון *nmf* her|ayon/-yonot (*+of:* -yon)

pregnant 1. הרה *adj f* har|ah/-ot; **2.** בהריון (in a family way) *adv* be-herayon.

prejudice 1. דעה קדומה (preconception) *nf* de'ah/de'ot kedoom|ah/-ot; **2.** פגיעה (harm) *nf* pegee|'ah/-'ot (*+of:* -'at).

(to) prejudice להזיק *inf* lehazeek; *pst* heezeek; *pres* mazeek; *fut* yazeek.

preliminaries הקדמות (introductions) *nf pl* hakdamot.

preliminary 1. מכין *adj* mekheen/-ah; **2.** מקדים (introductive) *adj* makdeem/-ah.

prelude 1. אקדמה *nf* akdam|ah/-ot (*+of:* -at); **2.** פרלודיה *nf* prelood|yah/-yot (*+of:* -yat).

(to) prelude לאקדם *inf* le'akdem; *pst* eekdem; *pres* me'akdem; *fut* ye'akdem.

premature שלפני זמנו *adj* she-leefney zman|o/-ah.

premature baby פג *nmf* pag/-eem (*pl+of:* -ey).

prematurely בטרם עת *adv* be-terem 'et.

premeditated בכוונה תחילה *adj* be-khavanah *(kh=k)* tekheelah.

premier 1. ראש ממשלה (prime-minister) *nmf* rosh/-ey memshal|ah/-ot; **2.** ראשי (chief) *adj* rashee/-t; **3.** ראשוני (earliest) *adj* reeshonee/-t.

premiere 1. הצגת בכורה *nf* hatsag|at/-ot bekhorah; **2.** פרמיירה *nf* premyer|ah/-ot (*+of:* -at).

premise הנחת יסוד *nmf* hanakh|at/-ot yesod.

premises חצרים (legal term) *nmf pl* khatsereem.

premium 1. דמי ביטוח *nmf pl* demey beetoo'akh; **2.** פרמיה *nf* prem|yah/-yot (*+of:* -yat).

(at a) premium במחיר גבוה יותר *adv* bee-mekheer gavoha yoter.

(insurance) premium פרמיית ביטוח *nf* prem|yat/-yot beetoo'akh.

prenatal שלפני הלידה *adj* she-leefney ha-leydah.

(to) preoccupy להעסיק *inf* leha'aseek; *pst* he'eseek; *pres* ma'aseek; *fut* ya'aseek.

prepaid משולם מראש *adj* meshool|am/-emet me-rosh.

(to send) prepaid לשלוח בתשלום מראש *inf* leeshlo'akh be-tashloom me-rosh; *pst* shalakh *etc*; *pres* shole'akh *etc*; *fut* yeeshlakh *etc*.

preparation הכנה *nf* hakhan|ah/-ot (*+of:* -at)

preparatory מכין *adj* mekheen/-ah.

(to) prepare להכין *inf* lehakheen; *pst* hekheen; *pres* mekheen; *fut* yakheen.

preparedness 1. נכונות *nf* nekhonoo|t/-yot; **2.** כוננות (readiness) *nf* konenoo|t/-yot.

preponderant מכריע *adj* makhree|'a'/-'ah.

preposition מלת יחס (grammar) meel|at/-ot yakhas.

(to) prepossess לעשות רושם טוב *inf* la'asot roshem tov; *pst* 'asah *etc*; *pres* 'oseh *etc*; *fut* ya'aseh *etc*.

prepossessing מלבב *adj* melabev/-et.

preposterous 1. מגוחך *adj* megookh|akh/-ekhet; **2.** טיפשי (stupid) *adj* teepshee/-t.

prerequisite 1. תנאי מוקדם *nmf* tena|y/-'eem mookdam/-eem; **2.** נדרש מראש *adj* needrash/-eshet me-rosh.

prerogative 1. זכות מיוחדת *nf* zekhoo|t/-yot meyookh|edet/-adot; **2.** סמכות מיוחדת (special authority) *nf* samkhoo|t/-yot meyookh|edet/-adot.

presage 1. בשורה *nf* besor|ah/-ot (*+of:* -at); **2.** חזון (vision) khazon/-ot.

(to) presage 1. לחזות מראש *inf* lakhzot me-rosh; *pst* khazah *etc*; *pres* khozeh *etc*; *fut* yekhzeh *etc*; **2.** לבשר (herald) levaser; *pst* beeser *(b=v)*; *pres* mevaser; *fut* yevaser.

(to) prescribe להורות *inf* lehorot; *pst* horah; *pres* moreh; *fut* yoreh.

prescription 1. מרשם (medical) *nmf* meersham/-eem (*pl+of:* -ey); **2.** מתכון (recipe) *nmf* matkon/-eem (*pl+of:* -ey); **3.** התיישנות (legal) *nf* heetyashnoo|t/-yot.

presence 1. נוכחות *nf* nokhekhoo|t/-yot; **2.** הופעה (appearance) *nf* hofa|'ah/-'ot (*+of:* -a) t.

presence of mind קור רוח *nmf* kor roo'akh.

present 1. זמן הווה (tense) *nmf* zman hoveh; **2.** מתנה (gift) *nf* mat|anah/-anot (*+of:* -nat/-not); **3.** שי (gift) *nmf* shay.

present נוכח *adj* nokhakh/-at.

(at) present כיום *adv* ka-yom.

(for the) present לפי שעה *adv* lefee sha'ah.

(to) present להציג *inf* lehatseeg; *pst* heetseeg; *pres* matseeg; *fut* yatseeg.

(to be) present להיות נוכח *inf* leehyot nokhe'akh; *pst* hayah *etc*; *pres* heeno *etc*; *fut* yeehyeh *etc*.

present company excepted למעט הנוכחים lema'et ha-nokhekheem.

present participle בינוני פועל (grammar) beynonee po'al.

presentation 1. הצגה *nf* hatsag|ah/-ot (*+of:* -at); **2.** הגשה (submitting) *nf* hagash|ah/-ot (*+of:* -at).

presentiment הרגשה מבשרת רעות *nf* hargash|ah/-ot mevas|eret/-rot ra'ot.

presently 1. מיד *adv* meeyad; **2.** עוד מעט *adv* 'od me'at.

preservation שימור *nmf* sheemoor.
preserve 1. שמורה *nf* shmoor|ah/-ot; **2.** שטח פרטי (private ground) shetakh pratee; **3.** ריבה (jam) *nf* reeb|ah/-ot (+*of:* -at).
(forest) preserve שמורת יער *nf* shmoor|at/-ot ya'ar.
(to) preserve לשמר *inf* leshamer; *pst* sheemer; *pres* meshamer; *fut* yeshamer.
(to) preside לשבת ראש *inf* lashevet rosh; *pst* yashav rosh; *pres* yoshev rosh; *fut* yeshev rosh.
(to) preside at, over לשבת ראש ב־ *inf* lashevet rosh be-; *pst* yashav *etc; pres* yoshev *etc; fut* yeshev *etc.*
presidency נשיאות *nf* nesee'oot.
president נשיא *nmf* nasee/nesee'ah (*pl:* -'eem/-'ot; +*of:* nesee/-'ey).
presidential נשיאותי *adj* nesee'ootee/-t.
press עיתונות *nf* 'eetonoot.
(daily) press עיתונות יומית *nf* 'eetonoot yomeet.
(foreign) press עיתונות חוץ *nf* 'eetonoot khoots.
(free) press עיתונות חופשית *nf* 'eetonoot khofsheet.
(printing) press בית דפוס *nmf* bet/batey dfoos.
(to) press 1. ללחוץ (bear down upon) *inf* leelkhots; *pst* lakhats; *pres* lokhets; *fut* yeelkhats; **2.** לגהץ (garment) *inf* legahets; *pst* geehets; *pres* megahets; *fut* yegahets; **3.** לכפות (compel) *inf* leekhpot; *pst* kafah (*k=kh; f=p*); *pres* kofeh; *fut* yeekhpeh.
(to) press forward לדרבן קדימה *inf* ledarben kadeemah; *pst* deerben *etc; pres* medarben *etc; fut* yedarben *etc.*
(to) press one's point לעמוד על שלו *inf* la'amod 'al shelo; *pst* 'amad *etc; pres* 'omed *etc; fut* ya'amod *etc.*
(to) press through the crowd להבקיע דרך בהמון *inf* lehavkee'a' derekh be-hamon; *pst* heevkee'a' *etc; pres* mavkee'a' *etc; fut* yavkee'a' *etc.*
(to be hard) pressed by work להיות לחוץ בעבודה *inf* leehyot lakhoots ba-'avodah; *pst* hayah *etc; pres* heeno *etc; fut* yeehyeh *etc.*
(hard) pressed for money דחוק לכסף *adj* dakhook/dekhookah be-kesef.
pressing דחוף *adj* dakhoof/dekhoofah.
pressure לחץ *nmf* lakhats/lekhatseem (*pl+of:* lakhtsey).
pressure cooker סיר־לחץ *nmf* seer/-ey lakhats.
pressure gauge מד־לחץ *nmf* mad/-ey lakhats.
(to) pressurize 1. להפעיל לחץ (exercize pressure) *inf* lehaf'eel lakhats; *pst* heef'eel *etc; pres* maf'eel *etc; fut* yaf'eel *etc;* **2.** לווסת לחץ (maintain pressure) *inf* levaset lakhats; *pst* veeset *etc; pres* mevaset *etc; fut* yevaset *etc.*
prestige יוקרה *nf* yookr|ah/-ot (+*of:* -at).
presumable 1. משוער *adj* mesho|'ar/-'eret; **2.** מסתבר (probable) *adj* meestaber/-et.
(to) presume 1. להניח *inf* lehanee'akh; *pst* heenee'akh; *pres* manee'akh; *fut* yanee'akh; **2.** להרשות לעצמו (permit oneself) *inf* leharshot le-'atsmo; *pst* heershah *etc; pres* marsheh *etc; fut* yarsheh *etc.*
(to) presume on לנצל לרעה *inf* lenatsel le-ra'ah; *pst* neetsel *etc; pres* menatsel *etc; fut* yenatsel *etc.*
(to) presume to להתחצף *inf* leheetkhatsef; *pst* heetkhatsef; *pres* meetkhatsef; *fut* yeetkhatsef.
presumption 1. הנחה (assumption) *nf* hanakh|ah/-ot (+*of:* -at); **2.** סברה (conjecture) *nf* svar|ah/-ot (+*of:* -at); **3.** חוצפה (audacity) *nf* khootsp|ah/-ot (+*of:* -at).
presumptious 1. עז פנים *adj* 'az/-at paneem; **2.** מתחצף *adj* meetkhatsef/-et.
(to) presuppose להניח מראש *inf* lehanee'akh me-rosh; *pst* heenee'akh *etc; pres* manee'akh *etc; fut* yanee'akh *etc.*
(to) pretend 1. להתיימר *v rfl inf* leheetyamer; *pst* heetyamer; *pres* meetyamer; *fut* yeetyamer; **2.** להעמיד פנים (feign) *inf* leha'ameed paneem; *pst* he'emeed *etc; pres* ma'ameed *etc; fut* ya'ameed *etc.*
pretense יומרה *nf* yoomr|ah/-ot (+*of:* -at).
(under) pretense of בתואנה כי be-to'anah kee.
pretension 1. טענה (claim) *nf* ta'anah/te'anot (+*of:* ta'an|at/-ot); **2.** יומרה (pretense) *nf* yoomr|ah/-ot (+*of:* -at); **3.** תואנה (unjustified claim) *nf* to'an|ah/-ot (+*of:* -at).
pretentious יומרני *adj* yoomr|anee/-t.
pretext אמתלה *nf* amatl|ah/-ot (+*of:* -at).
prettily 1. היטב *adv* heytev; **2.** יפה (beautifully) *adv* yafeh.
prettiness 1. חינניות (charm) *nf* kheenaneeyoot; **2.** יופי (beauty) *nmf* yofee.
pretty 1. חמוד *adj* khamood/-ah; **2.** יפה (beautiful) *adj* yaf|eh/-ah; **3.** למדי (quite) *adv* lemaday.
pretty well די טוב *adv* dey tov.
(to) prevail 1. לשרור *inf* leesror; *pst* sarar; *pres* sorer; *fut* yeesror; **2.** לגבור על *inf* leegbor 'al; *pst* gavar 'al (*v=b*); *pres* gover 'al; *fut* yeegbor 'al.
(to) prevail on (upon) להשפיע על *inf* lehashpee'a' 'al; *pst* heeshpee'a' 'al; *pres* mashpee'a' 'al; *fut* yashpee'a' 'al.
prevailing שורר *adj* sorer/-et.
prevalent נפוץ *adj* nafots/nefotsah.
(to) prevent למנוע *inf* leemno'a'; *pst* mana'; *pres* mone'a'; *fut* yeemna'.
prevention מניעה *nf* menee|'ah/-'ot (+*of:* -'at).
preventive מונע *adj* mon|e'a'/-a'at.
preview צפייה מוקדמת *nf* tsfee|yah/yot mookd|emet/-amot.
previous קודם *adj* kodem/-et.
previously מקודם *adv* mee-kodem.
prewar 1. שמלפני המלחמה *adj* she-mee-leefney ha-meelkhamah; **2.** קדם־מלחמתי *adj* kedam meelkhamtee/-t.
prey טרף *nmf* teref.
(bird of) prey ציפור טרף *nf* tseepor/-ey teref.
(to) prey on להציק *inf* lehatseek; *pst* heetseek; *pres* matseek; *fut* yatseek.
(it) preys upon my mind מנקר במוחי menaker/et be-mokhee.
price 1. מחיר *nmf* mekheer/-eem (*pl+of:* -ey); **2.** ערך (value) *nmf* 'erekh; **3.** פרס (reward) *nmf* pras/-eem (*pl+of:* -ey).
(at any) price בכל מחיר *adv* be-khol (*kh=k*) mekheer.

(to) price לקבוע מחיר *inf* leekbo'a' mekheer; *pst* kava' *(v=b) etc; pres* kove'a' *etc; fut* yeekba' *etc.*
priceless שאין לו מחיר *adj* she-eyn lo/lah mekheer.
(to) prick לדקור *inf* leedkor; *pst* dakar; *pres* doker; *fut* yeedkor.
(to) prick up one's ears לזקוף אוזניים *inf* leezkof oznayeem; *pst* zakaf *etc; pres* zokef *etc; fut* yeezkof *etc.*
prickly דוקרני *adj* dokranee/-t.
prickly heat 1. חררה *nf* khararah; **2.** גרדת (scabies) *nf* garedet.
prickly pear 1. צבר (cactus fruit) *nmf* tsavar/tsvareem (*pl+of:* tseevrey); **2.** צבר *cpr nmf* tsabar/-eet (native of Israel) *nmf* (*pl:* -eem/-eeyot; *+of:* -ey); **3.** סאברס (accepted slang) *nmf pl* sabres.
pride גאווה *nf* ga'av|ah/-ot (*+of:* -at).
(to) pride oneself on (upon) להתגאות ב־ *inf* leheetga'ot be-; *pst* heetga'ah be-; *pres* meetga'eh be-; *fut* yeetga'eh be-.
priest כוהן־דת *nmf* kohen/kohaney dat.
priesthood כהונה *nf* kehoon|ah/-ot (*+of:* -at).
prim 1. צנוע *adj* tsanoo'a'/tsenoo'ah; **2.** מעומלן *adj* (stiff) me'ooml|an/-enet.
primarily ראשית כל *adv* resheet kol.
primary 1. ראשוני (first) *adj* reeshonee/-t; **2.** בסיסי (basic) *adj* beseesee/-t.
primary color צבע יסוד *nmf* tseva'/tseev'ey yesod.
primary school בית ספר יסודי *nmf* bet/batey sefer yesodee/-yeem.
prime 1. ראשי (main) *adj* rashee/-t; **2.** מובחר (select) moovkh|ar/-eret.
(in one's) prime במיטבו *adv* be-meytav|o/-ah.
(to) prime 1. להפעיל *inf* lehaf'eel; *pst* heef'eel; *pres* maf'eel; *fut* yaf'eel; **2.** להכין ל־ (prepare for) *inf* lehakheen; *pst* hekheen le-; *pres* mekheen le-; *fut* yakheen le-.
prime minister ראש ממשלה *nmf* rosh/-ey memshal|ah/-ot.
prime number מספר ראשוני *nmf* meespar reeshonee.
primer אלפון *nmf* alfon/-eem (*pl+of:* -ey).
primeval קדמון *adj* kadmon/-ah.
primitive 1. ראשוני *adj* reeshonee/-t; **2.** פרימיטיבי *adj* preemeeteevee/-t.
primness 1. דיוק *nmf* deeyook/-eem (*pl+of:* -ey); **2.** דייקנות (punctuality) *nf* daykanoo|t/-yot.
(to) primp 1. לקשט *inf* lekashet; *pst* keeshet; *pres* mekashet; *fut* yekashet; **2.** להתגנדר *inf* leheetgander; *pst* heetgander; *pres* meetgander; *fut* yeetgander.
primrose רקפת *nf* rak|efet/-afot.
prince נסיך *nm* naseekh/neseekh|eem (*pl+of:* -ey).
princely כיד המלך *adv* ke-yad ha-melekh.
princess נסיכה *nf* neseekh|ah/-ot (*+of:* -at).
principal 1. ראשי *adj* rashee/-t; **2.** מנהל בית ספר *nmf* mena|hel/-helet (*pl:* -haley/-halot) bet/batey sefer.
principle עיקרון *nm* 'eekaron/'ekronot (*+of:* 'ekron).
print 1. אות (type) *nf* ot/-eeyot; **2.** הדפס (art) *nm* hedpes/-eem (*pl+of:* -ey); **3.** בד מודפס (fabric) *nm* bad/-eem moodpas/-eem.
(in) print בדפוס *adv* bee-defoos.
(out of) print אזל *v pst* azal/azlah.
(to) print להדפיס *inf* lehadpees; *pst* heedpees; *pres* madpees; *fut* yadpees.
printed fabric בד מודפס *nm* bad/-eem moodpas/-eem.
printer 1. מדפסת (computer's) *nf* madpes|et/-asot; **2.** מדפיס (artisan) *nm* madpees/-eem (*pl+of:* -ey).
printing 1. דפוס (art) *nm* defoos; **2.** הדפסה (action) *nf* hadpas|ah/-ot (*+of:* -at).
printing office משרד להדפסות *nf* meesrad/-eem le-hadpasot.
printing press בית דפוס *nm* bet/batey defoos.
prior קודם *adv* kodem.
prior to 1. טרם *adv* terem; **2.** קודם ל־ *adj* kodem/-et le-.
priority 1. דין קדימה *nm* deen kedeemah; **2.** זכות בכורה (seniority) zekhoo|t/-yot bekhorah.
prism 1. מנסרה *nf* meens|arah/-arot (*+of:* -eret); **2.** פריזמה *nf* preezm|ah/-ot (*+of:* -at).
prison 1. בית סוהר *nm* bet/batey sohar; **2.** כלא (jail) *nm* kele (*pl:* batey kele).
(to) prison לכלוא *inf* leekhlo; *pst* kala *(k=kh); pres* kole; *fut* yeekhla.
prisoner 1. אסיר *nmf* aseer/-ah (*pl:* -eem/-ot; *+of:* -ey); **2.** שבוי (war-) shavooy/shvoo|yeem (*pl+of:* -yey).
privacy 1. צנעת הפרט *nf* tseen'at ha-prat; **2.** פרטיות *nf* prateeyoot.
(no) privacy היעדר פרטיות *nm* he'ader prateeyoot.
private 1. פרטי *adj* pratee/-t; **2.** טוראי (soldier) *nm* toora|y/'eet (*pl:* -'eem/-'eeyot; *+of:* -'ey).
(in) private 1. ביחידות *adv* bee-yekheedoot; **2.** בארבע עיניים (between four eyes) *adv* be-arba' 'eynayeem; **3.** בחשאי (discreetly) ba-khashay.
private school בית ספר פרטי *nm* bet/batey sefer pratee/-yeem.
(a) private citizen אזרח פרטי *nm* ezrakh pratee.
privation מחסור *nm* makhsor/-eem (*pl+of:* -ey).
privilege 1. יתרון *nm* yeet|ron/-ronot (*+of:* -ron); **2.** זכות מיוחדת *nf* zekhoo|t/-yot meyookh|edet/-adot; **3.** פריבילגיה *nf* preeveeleg|yah/-yot (*+of:* -yat).
privileged 1. מועדף *adj* mo'od|af/-efet; **2.** בעל זכות מיוחדת *adj* ba'al/-at zekhoot meyookhedet.
(to be) privileged 1. ליהנות מזכות מיוחדת *inf* lehanot mee-zekhoot meyookhedet; *pst* nehenah *etc; pres* neheneh *etc; fut* yehaneh *etc;* **2.** להתכבד (be honored) *v* refl leheetkabed; heetkabed; *pres* meetkabed; *fut* yeetkabed.
privy 1. פרטי *adj* pratee/-t; **2.** סודי (secret) *adj* sodee/-t; **3.** אישי (personal) *adj* eeshee/-t; **4.** בית־שימוש (lavatory) *nm* bet/batey sheemoosh.
prize 1. פרס *nm* pras/-eem (*pl+of:* peersey); **2.** מעולה (excellent) me'ool|eh/-ah.
(to) prize להעריך מאוד *inf* leha'areekh me'od; *pst* he'ereekh *etc; pres* ma'areekh *etc; fut* ya'areekh *etc.*
prize fight תחרות אגרוף נושאת פרסים *nf* takhroo|t/-yot eegroof nos|e't/-'ot praseem.
prize fighter מתאגרף מקצועי *nm* meet'agref/-eem meektso'ee/-yeem.
prize medal מדליית פרס *nf* medal|yat/-yot pras.

probability סבירות *nf* sveeroo|t/-yot.
probable סביר *adj* saveer/sveerah.
probably מסתבר *adv* meestaber.
probation מבחן *nm* meevkhan/-eem (*pl+of:* -ey).
(on) probation במבחן *adv* be-meevkhan.
probe 1. מבדק *nm* meevd|ak/-akeem (*pl+of:* -ekey); **2.** בדיקה (check) *nf* bedeek|ah/-ot (*+of:* -at).
(to) probe לבחון *inf* leevkhon; *pst* bakhan (*b=v*); *pres* bokhen; *fut* yeevkhan.
problem בעיה *nf* ba'|yah/-yot (*+of:* be'ayat).
procedure 1. נוהל *nm* nohal/nehaleem (*pl+of:* noholey); **2.** הליך *nm* haleekh/-eem (*pl+of:* -ey).
(to) proceed 1. לעבור אל *inf* la'avor el; *pst* 'avar el; *pres* 'over el; *fut* ya'avor el; **2.** להתקדם (go ahead) *inf* leheetkadem; *pst* heetkadem; *pres* meetkadem; *fut* yeetkadem.
(to) proceed to להמשיך *inf* lehamsheekh; *pst* heemsheekh; *pres* mamsheekh; *fut* yamsheekh.
proceeding 1. הליך *nm* haleekh/-eem (*pl+of:* -ey); **2.** מהלך העניינים *nm* mahalakh ha-'eenyaneem.
proceedings דיונים *nm* deeyoon|eem (*pl+of:* -ey).
proceeds הכנסות *nf pl* hakhnasot.
process 1. סדרת פעולות (series) *nf* seedrat pe'oolot; **2.** תהליך (method) *nm* tahaleekh/-eem (*pl+of:* -ey).
(in the) process of being made בתהליך התבצעות be-tahaleekh heetbats'oot.
(in) process of time במרוצת הזמן *adv* bee-merootsat ha-zman.
procession תהלוכה *nf* tahalookh|ah/-ot (*+of:* -at).
(funeral) procession 1. הלוויה *nf* halva|yah/-yot (*+of:* -yat); **2.** תהלוכת אבל *nf* tahalookh|at/-ot evel.
(to) proclaim להכריז *inf* lehakhreez; *pst* heekhreez; *pres* makhreez; *fut* yakhreez.
proclamation הכרזה *nf* hakhraz|ah/-ot (*+of:* -at).
proclivity נטייה *nf* netee|yah/-yot (*+of:* -yat).
(to) procure 1. להשיג *inf* lehaseeg; *pst* heeseeg; *pres* maseeg; *fut* yaseeg; **2.** לסרסר זנות *inf* lesarser znoot; *pst* seerser *etc*; *pres* mesarser *etc*; *fut* yesarser *etc.*
(to) prod לדרבן *inf* ledarben; *pst* deerben; *pres* medarben; *fut* yedarben.
prodigal 1. בזבזן *nmf* bazbezan/-eet; **2.** בזבזני *adj* bazbezanee/-t.
prodigious 1. מפליא *adj* maflee/'ah; **2.** עצום (tremendous) *adj* 'atsoom/-ah.
prodigy 1. פלא *nm* pele/pla'eem (*pl+of:* peel'ey); **2.** נס (miracle) *nm* nes/nees|eem (*pl+of:* -ey).
(child) prodigy ילד־פלא *nm* yeled/yaldey pele.
produce תוצר *nm* totsar/-eem (*pl+of:* -ey).
(to) produce לייצר *inf* leyatser; *pst* yeetser; *pres* meyatser; *fut* yeyatser.
producer 1. יצרן *nm* yatsran/-eem (*pl+of:* -ey); **2.** מפיק *nm* mefeek/-eem (*pl+of:* -ey).
(theatrical) producer אמרגן *nm* amargan/-eem (*pl+of:* -ey).
product מוצר *nm* mootsar/-eem (*pl+of:* -ey).
production 1. תוצרת (product) *nf* totseret; **2.** ייצור (process) *nf* yeetsoor.
productive יצרני *adj* yatsranee/-t.
profanation חילול *nm* kheelool/-eem (*pl+of:* -ey).
profane 1. טמא *adj* tame/teme'ah; **2.** חילוני (agnostic) *adj* kheelonee/-t.
(to) profane לחלל *inf* lekhalel; *pst* kheelel; *pres* mekhalel; *fut* yekhalel.
(to) profess 1. להתיימר *inf* leheetyamer; *pst* heetyamer; *pres* meetyamer; *fut* yeetyamer; **2.** לטעון (claim) *inf* leet'on; *pst* ta'an; *pres* to'en; *fut* yeet'an.
profession מקצוע *nm* meektso|'a'/-'ot.
professional 1. מקצועי *adj adj* meektso'ee/-t; **2.** מקצוען (pro) *nmf* meektso'an/-eet.
professor פרופסור *nm* profes|or/-oreem (*pl+of:* -orey).
(to) proffer להציע *inf* lehatsee'a'; *pst* heetsee'a'; *pres* matsee'a'; *fut* yatsee'a'.
proficiency מיומנות *nf* meyoomanoo|t/-yot.
proficient מיומן *adj* meyoom|an/-enet.
profile 1. צדודית *nf* tsedoodee|t-yot; **2.** דיוקן (portrait) *nm* dyok|an/-neem (*pl+of:* -ney); **3.** פרופיל *nm* profeel/-eem (*pl+of:* -ey).
profit 1. רווח (gain) *nm* revakh/-eem (*pl+of:* reevkhey); **2.** תועלת (usefulness) *nf* to'elet.
(net) profit רווח נקי *nm* revakh nakee.
(to) profit 1. להרוויח *inf* leharvee'akh; *pst* heervee'akh; *pres* marvee'akh; *fut* yarvee'akh; **2.** לצאת נשכר (benefit) *inf* latset neeskar; *pst* yatsa *etc*; *pres* yotse *etc*; *fut* yetse *etc.*
profit and loss רווח והפסד *nm* revakh ve-hefsed.
(to) profit by 1. לצאת מורווח *inf* latset moorvakh; *pst* yatsa *etc*; *pres* yotse *etc*; *fut* yetse *etc*; **2.** להפיק תועלת (derive advantage) *inf* lehafeek to'elet; *pst* hefeek *etc*; *pres* mefeek *etc*; *fut* yafeek *etc.*
profitable רווחי *adj* reevkhee/-t.
profiteer ספסר *nm* safsar/-eem (*pl+of:* -ey).
(to) profiteer להפקיע מחירים *inf* lehafkee'a' mekheereem; *pst* heefkee'a' *etc*; *pres* mafkee'a' *etc*; *fut* yafkee'a' *etc.*
profound עמוק *adj* 'amok/-'amookah.
profuse שופע *adj* shof|e'a'/-a'at.
progeny צאצא *nm* tse'ets|a/-a'eem (*pl+of:* -a'ey).
prognosis פרוגנוזה *nf* prognoz|ah/-ot (*+of:* -at).
program תוכנית *nf* tokhnee|t/-yot.
progress 1. התקדמות *nf* heetkadmoo|t/-yot; **2.** קידמה *nf* keedm|ah/-ot (*+of:* -at).
(to) progress להתקדם *inf* leheetkadem; *pst* heetkadem; *pres* meetkadem; *fut* yeetkadem.
progressive 1. גדל והולך *adj* gadel/gedelah ve-holekh/-et; **2.** מתקדם *adj* meetkadem/-et; **3.** פרוגרסיבי *nmf & adj* progreseevee/-t.
(to) prohibit לאסור *inf* le'esor; *pst* asar; *pres* oser; *fut* ye'esor.
prohibition איסור *nm* eesoor/-eem (*pl+of:* -ey).
project 1. תוכנית *nf* tokhnee|t-yot; **2.** פרויקט *nm* proyekt/-eem.
(to) project להקרין *inf* lehakreen; *pst* heekreen; *pres* makreen; *fut* yakreen.
projectile 1. קליע *nm* kalee'a'/klee'eem (*pl+of:* klee'ey); **2.** טיל (missile) *nm* teel/-eem (*pl+of:* -ey).
projectile weapon נשק טילים *nm* neshek teeleem.
projection הקרנה *nf* hakran|ah/-ot (*+of:* -at).
projector 1. מטול *nm* matol/metol|eem (*pl+of:* -ey); **2.** מקרן *nm* makren/-eem (*pl+of:* -ey).

proletarian 1. פועל (worker) *nmf* po'el/po'al|eem (*pl+of:* -ey); **2.** בן/בת מעמד הפועלים (of the working class) ben/bat ma'amad ha-po'aleem; **3.** פרולטרי *adj* proletaree/-t.

proletariat 1. מעמד הפועלים (working class) *nm* ma'amad ha-po'aleem; **2.** פרולטריון *nm* proletaryon/-eem (*pl+of:* -ey).

prolific פורה *adj* por|eh/-ah.

prologue פרולוג *nm* prolog/-eem (*pl+of:* -ey).

(to) prolong 1. להאריך *inf* leha'areekh; *pst* he'ereekh; *pres* ma'areekh; *fut* ya'areekh; **2.** לחדש (renew) *inf* lekhadesh; *pst* kheedesh; *pres* mekhadesh; *fut* yekhadesh.

prolongation הארכה *nf* ha'arakh|ah/-ot (*+of:* -at).

promenade 1. טיילת *nf* tayelet/tayalot; **2.** טיול (excursion) teeyool/-eem (*pl+of:* -ey).

(to) promenade להוליך לראווה *inf* leholeekh le-ra'avah; *pst* holeekh *etc*; *pres* moleekh *etc*; *fut* yoleekh *etc*.

prominent בולט *adj* bolet/-et.

promiscuous 1. מופקר (licentious) *adj* moofk|ar/-eret; **2.** מזדווג ללא אבחנה (sexually) *adj* meezdaveg/-et le-lo avkhanah.

promise הבטחה *nf* havtakh|ah/-ot (*+of:* -at).

(to) promise להבטיח *inf* lehavtee'akh; *pst* heevtee'akh; *pres* mavtee'akh; *fut* yavtee'akh.

(the) Promised Land הארץ המובטחת *nf* ha-arets ha-moovtakhat.

promising מבטיח *adj* mavtee|'akh/-khah.

promissory מתחייב *adj* meetkhayev/-et.

promissory note שטר חוב *nm* shtar/sheetrey khov.

promontory צוק חוף *nm* tsook/-ey khof.

(to) promote 1. להעלות בדרגה *inf* leha'alot be-dargah; *pst* he'elah *etc*; *pres* ma'aleh *etc*; *fut* ya'aleh *etc*; **2.** לקדם (advance) *inf* lekadem; *pst* keedem; *pres* mekadem; *fut* yekadem.

promoter יזם *nm* yazam/-eem (*pl+of:* -ey).

promotion 1. קידום *nm* keedoom/-eem (*pl+of:* -ey); **2.** עלייה לכיתה (school) *nf* 'aleeyah le-keetah; **3.** העלאה בדרגה (rank, position) *nf* ha'ala|'ah/-'ot be-dargah.

prompt מהיר *adj* maheer/meheerah.

(to) prompt 1. להניע *inf* lehanee'a'; *pst* henee'a'; *pres* menee'a'; *fut* yanee'a'; **2.** לזרז (urge) *inf* lezarez; *pst* zerez; *pres* mezarez; *fut* yezarez.

promptly חיש *adv* kheesh.

promptness מידיות *adv* meeyadeeyoot.

(to) promulgate 1. לפרסם (publish) *inf* lefarsem; *pst* peersem *(p=f)*; *pres* mefarsem; *fut* yefarsem; **2.** להעביר (pass) *inf* leha'aveer; *pst* he'eveer; *pres* ma'aveer; *fut* ya'aveer.

prone 1. מועד ל־ *adj* moo|'ad/-'edet le-; **2.** שכוב על כרסו (prostrate) *adj* shakhoov/sh'khoovah 'al kres|o/-ah.

prong שן *nm* shen/sheenayeem (*pl+of:* sheeney).

pronoun כינוי השם (grammar) *nm* keenoo|y/-yey ha-shem.

(to) pronounce 1. לבטא *inf* levate; *pst* beete *(b=v)*; *pres* mevate; *fut* yevate; **2.** להכריז (declare) *inf* lehakhreez; *pst* heekhreez; *pres* makhreez; *fut* yakhreez.

pronounced מובהק *adj* moov|hak/-heket.

pronounced opinion דעה מובהקת *nf* de'ah moovheket.

pronouncement 1. קביעה *nf* kvee|'ah/-'ot (*+of:* -'at); **2.** הכרזה (announcement) *nf* hakhraz|ah/-ot (*+of:* -at).

pronunciation 1. היגוי *nm* heegoo|y/-yeem (*pl+of:* -yey); **2.** מבטא (accent) *nm* meevta/-'eem (*pl+of:* -'ey).

proof 1. הוכחה *nf* hokhakh|ah/-ot (*+of:* -at); **2.** ראיה (evidence) re'a|yah/-yot (*+of:* -yat); **3.** חסין (resistent) *adj* khaseen/-at.

proof against 1. הוכחה נגד *nf* hokhakh|ah/-ot neged; **2.** עמיד בפני (resistent to) *adj* 'ameed/-ah beefney.

(bomb)proof עמיד בפני פצצות *adj* 'ameed/-ah beefney petsatsot.

(fire)proof חסין אש *adj* khaseen/-at esh.

(galley) proof יריעת הגהה *nf* yeree|'at/-'ot hagahah.

(water)proof עמיד בפני מים *adj* 'ameed/-ah beefney mayeem.

proof sheet עלה הגהה *nm* 'al|eh/-ey haga|hah/-hot.

proofreader מגיה *nm* magee|'ah/-heem (*pl+of:* -hey).

prop משענת *nf* meesh|'enet/-'anot.

(to) prop 1. לתמוך *inf* leetmokh; *pst* tamakh; *pres* tomekh; *fut* yeetmokh; **2.** להישען (lean) *inf* leheesha'en; *pst & pres* neesh'an; *fut* yeesha'en.

propaganda תעמולה *nf* ta'amool|ah/-ot (*+of:* -at).

(to) propagate להפיץ *inf* lehafeets; *pst* hefeets; *pres* mefeets; *fut* yafeets.

propagation הפצה *nf* hafats|ah/-ot (*+of:* -at).

(to) propel 1. להניע *inf* lehanee'a'; *pst* heenee'a'; *pres* menee'a'; *fut* yanee'a'; **2.** לדחוף קדימה (push ahead) *inf* leedkhof kadeemah; *pst* dakhaf *etc*; *pres* dokhef *etc*; *fut* yeedkhaf *etc*.

propeller מדחף *nm* madkhef/-eem (*pl+of:* -ey).

proper 1. אמיתי *adj* ameetee/-t; **2.** נכון (right) *adj* nakhon/nekhonah.

proper noun שם עצם פרטי (grammar) *nm* shem/shmot 'etsem pratee/-yeem.

properly כיאות *adv* ka-ya'oot.

property 1. רכוש *nm* rekhoosh; **2.** נכס (asset) *nm* nekh|es/-aseem (*pl+of:* neekhsey).

prophecy נבואה *nf* nevoo|'ah/-'ot (*+of:* -'at).

(to) prophesy לנבא *inf* lenabe; *pst* neeba; *pres* menabe; *fut* yenabe.

prophet נביא *nmf* navee/nevee|'ah (*pl:* -'eem/-'ot; *+of:* -'at/-'ey)

prophetic נבואי *adj* nevoo'ee/-t.

propitious 1. מסייע *adj* mesa|ye'a'/-ya'at; **2.** מעודד (encouraging) *adj* me'oded/-et.

proportion 1. יחס *nm* yakhas/yekhaseem (*pl+of:* yakhsey); **2.** פרופורציה *nf* proportsee|yah/-yot (*+of:* -yat).

(out of) proportion מחוץ לכול פרופורציה mee-khoots le-khol *(kh=k)* proportsyah,

proportionate 1. יחסי *adj* yakhsee/-t; **2.** פרופורציונלי *adj* proportsyonalee/-t.

(well) proportioned בפרופורציות הנכונות ba-proportsyot ha-nekhonot.

proposal 1. הצעה *nf* hatsa|'ah/-'ot (*+of:* -at); **2.** הצעת נישואים (marriage) *nf* hatsa|'at/-'ot neesoo'eem.

(to) propose 1. להציע *inf* lehatsee'a'; *pst* heetsee'a'; *pres* matsee'a'; *fut* yatsee'a'; **2.** להציע נישואים (marriage) *inf* lehatsee'a' neesoo'eem; *pst* heetsee'a' *etc; pres* matsee'a' *etc; fut* yatsee'a' *etc.*

(to) propose to do something להתכונן לעשות דבר *inf* leheetkonen la'asot davar; *pst* heetkonen *etc; pres* meetkonen *etc; fut* yeetkonen *etc.*

proposition 1. הצעה *nf* hatsa'|ah/-'ot (*+of:* -'at); **2.** הנחה (supposition) *nf* hanakh|ah/-ot (*+of:* -at).

proprietor בעלים *nm pl* be'aleem (*+of:* be'alav shel).

propriety 1. הגינות *nf* hageenoo|t/-yot; **2.** התאמה (suitability) *nf* hat'am|ah/-ot (*+of:* -at); **3.** נימוסים (manners) *nm pl* neemoos/-eem (*pl+of:* -ey).

propulsion 1. הנעה *nf* hana|'ah/-'ot (*+of:* -'at); **2.** דחף (impulse) *nm* dakhaf/dekhafeem (*pl+of:* dakhfey).

(to) prorate לחלק לפי הערך *inf* lekhalek lefee ha-'erekh; *pst* kheelek *etc; pres* mekhalek *etc; fut* yekhalek *etc.*

prosaic 1. פרוזאי *adj* proza'ee/-t; **2.** שיגרתי (ordinary) *adj* sheegratee/-t.

prose פרוזה *nf* proz|ah/-ot (*+of:* -at).

(to) prosecute לתבוע לדין פלילי *inf* leetbo'a' le-deen pleelee; *pst* tava' *(v=b) etc; pres* tove'a' *etc; fut* yeetba' *etc.*

prosecution 1. תביעה *nf* tvee'ah/-'ot pleelee|t/-yot; **2.** קטגוריה *nf* kategor|yah/-yot (*+of:* -yat).

prosecutor 1. תובע *nmf* tov|e'a'/-a'at; **2.** קטגור *nm* kategor/-eem (*pl+of:* -ey).

prospect 1. סיכוי (chance) *nm* seekoo|y/-yeem (*pl+of:* -yey); **2.** תקווה (hope) *nf* teekv|ah/-ot (*+of:* -at); **3.** מועמד (candidate) *nmf* mo'am|ad/-edet.

(to) prospect לחפש מחצבים *inf* lekhapes makhtsaveem; *pst* kheepes *etc; pres* mekhapes *etc; fut* yekhapes *etc.*

prospective עתידי *adj* 'ateedee/-t.

prospector מחפש מחצבים *nm* mekhap|es/-sey makhtsaveem.

(to) prosper לשגשג *inf* lesagseg; *pst* seegseg; *pres* mesagseg; *fut* yesagseg.

prosperity שגשוג *nm* seegsoog/-eem (*pl+of:* -ey).

prosperous משגשג *adj* mesagseg/-et.

prostitute 1. זונה *nf* zon|ah/-ot (*+of:* -at); **2.** פרוצה *nf* prootsah/-ot.

(to) prostitute 1. לזנות *inf* leeznot; *pst f* zantah; *pres f* zonah; *fut f* teezneh; **2.** למכור עצמו *inf* leemkor *(m/f)* 'atsm|o/-ah; *pst* makhar *(kh=k) etc; pres* mokher *etc; fut* yeemkor *etc.*

prostrate 1. כנוע *adj* kanoo'a'/kenoo'ah; **2.** מתפלש *adj* meetpalesh/-et.

(to) prostrate להתפלש *inf* leheetpalesh; *pst* heetpalesh; *pres* meetpalesh; *fut* yeetpalesh.

protagonist 1. גיבור *nmf* geebor/-ah; **2.** דמות מובילה (leading figure) *nf* demoo|t/-yot moveel|ah/-ot.

(to) protect 1. להגן *inf* lehagen; *pst* hegen; *pres* megen; *fut* yagen; **2.** לשמור (guard) *inf* leeshmor; *pst* shamar; *pres* shomer; *fut* yeeshmor; **3.** לאבטח *inf* le'avte'akh; *pst* eevtakh; *pres* me'avte'akh; *fut* ye'avtakh.

protection 1. חסות *nf* khasoot; **2.** הגנה (defense) *nf* hagan|ah/-ot (*+of:* -at); **3.** איבטוח *nm* eevtoo|'akh/-kheem (*pl+of:* -khey).

"protection" 1. דמי חסות *nm pl* dmey khasoot; **2.** דמי סחיטה (blackmail) *nm* dmey skheetah.

protective נותן חסות *nmf* noten/-et khasoot.

protective tariff מכס מגן *nm* mekhes/meekhsey magen.

protector 1. מגן *nm* meg|en/-eeneem (*pl+of:* megeeney); **2.** תומך (supporter) *nm* tom|ekh/-kheem (*pl+of:* -khey).

protectorate ארץ חסות *nf* erets/artsot khasoot.

protege בן־חסות *nmf & adj* ben/bat khasoot.

protein פרוטאין *nm* prote'een/-eem (*pl+of:* -ey).

protest מחאה *nf* mekha|'ah/-'ot (*+of:* -'at).

(to) protest למחות *inf* leemkhot; *pst* makhah; *pres* mokheh; *fut* yeemkheh.

Protestant פרוטסטנטי *nmf* protestantee/-t.

protestation מחאה *nf* mekha|'ah/-'ot (*+of:* -'at).

protocol 1. פרטיכל (minutes) *nm* peerteykol/-eem (*pl+of:* -ey); **2.** פרוטוקול (rules) *nm* protokol/-eem (*pl+of:* -ey); **3.** טקס (ceremony) *nm* tek|es/-aseem (*pl+of:* teeksey).

protoplasm פרוטופלסמה *nf* protoplasm|ah/-ot (*+of:* -at).

prototype אב־טיפוס *nm* av/-ot teepoos/-eem.

(to) protract 1. למשוך *inf* leemshokh; *pst* mashakh; *pres* moshekh; *fut* yeemshokh; **2.** לסחוב (procrastinate) *inf* leeskhov; *pst* sakhav; *pres* sokhev; *fut* yeeskhov.

(to) protrude 1. להזדקר *inf* leheezdaker; *pst* heezdaker; *pres* meezdaker; *fut* yeezdaker; **2.** לבלוט (stand out) *inf* leevlot; *pst* balat *(b=v); pres* bolet; *fut* yeevlot.

protuberance 1. בליטה *nf* bleet|ah/-ot (*+of:* -at); **2.** תפיחה (swelling) *nf* tefeekh|ah/-ot (*+of:* -at).

proud גאה *adj* ge'eh/ge'ah.

(to) prove להוכיח *inf* lehokhee'akh; *pst* hokhee'akh; *pres* mokhee'akh; *fut* yokhee'akh.

proverb 1. משל (fable) *nm* mashal/meshaleem (*pl+of:* meeshley); **2.** פיתגם (saying) *nm* peetgam/eem (*pl+of:* -ey).

(to) provide 1. לספק (supply) *inf* lesapek; *pst* seepek; *pres* mesapek; *fut* yesapek; **2.** להעמיד לרשות (place at disposal) *inf* leha'ameed lee-reshoot; *pst* he'emeed *etc; pres* ma'ameed *etc; fut* ya'ameed *etc.*

(to) provide for לדאוג ל־ *inf* leed'og le-; *pst* da'ag le-; *pres* do'eg le-; *fut* yeed'ag le-.

(to) provide with להמציא *inf* lehamtsee; *pst* heemtsee; *pres* mamtsee; *fut* yamtsee.

provided 1. ובלבד *conj* oo-vee-levad *(v=b)*; **2.** בתנאי (on condition that) *conj* bee-tnay.

provided that בתנאי ש־ *conj* bee-tnay she-.

Providence ההשגחה העליונה *nf* ha-hashgakhah ha-'elyonah.

providential שבא משמיים she-ba/ba'ah mee-shamayeem.

provider מפרנס *nm* mefarnes/-eem (*pl+of:* -ey).
province 1. נפה *nf* naf|ah/-ot (+*of:* -at); **2.** פרובינציה *nf* proveentseeyah/-yot (+*of:* -yat).
(not within my) province לא בתחום שלי lo ba-tekhoom shelee.
provincial 1. פרובינציאל *nm* proveentsyal/-eem; **2.** קרתני (parochial) *adj* kartanee/-t; **3.** כפרי (villager) *nm* kafree/-yeem.
provision 1. אספקה (goods) *nf* aspak|ah/-ot (+*of:* -at); **2.** תוכנית (plan) *nf* tokhnee|t-yot.
provisional זמני *adj* zemanee/-t.
provisionally לפי שעה *adv* lefee sha'ah.
provisions 1. הוראות (instructions) *nf pl* hora'ot; **2.** אספקת מזון (food) *nf* aspakat mazon **3.** אספקה *[colloq.] nf* aspakah.
(to make the necessary) provisions לנקוט באמצעים הדרושים *inf* leenkot ba-'emtsa'eem ha-droosheem; *pst* nakat *etc*; *pres* noket *etc*; *fut* yeenkot *etc*.
proviso תנאי מיוחד *nm* tna|y/-'eem meyookhad/-eem.
provisory 1. זמני *adj* zmanee/-t; **2.** על תנאי (conditional) *adj* 'al tenay.
provocation 1. התגרות *nf* heetgaroo|t/-yot; **2.** פרובוקציה *nf* provokats|yah/-yot (+*of:* -yat).
(to) provoke לגרות *inf* legarot; *pst* gerah; *pres* megareh; *fut* yegareh.
prow חרטום *nm* khartom/-eem (*pl+of:* -ey).
prowess 1. גבורה *nf* gvoor|ah/-ot (+*of:* -at); **2.** אומץ לב (daring) *nm* omets lev.
(to) prowl לשחר לטרף *inf* leshakher le-teref; *pst* sheekher *etc*; *pres* meshakher *etc*; *fut* yeshakher *etc*.
proximity קירבה *nf* keerv|ah/-ot (+*of:* -at).
proxy 1. מורשה *nm* moorsh|eh/-eem (*pl+of:* -ey); **2.** שליח *nm* shalee'akh/shlee|kheem (+*of:* -'akh/-khey).
(by) proxy על ידי שליח 'al yedey shalee'akh.
prude 1. צנוע *adj* tsanoo'a'/tsenoo'ah; **2.** ענו (humble) *adj* 'anav/-ah; **3.** מצטנע (affectedly humble) *adj* meetstan|e'a'/-a'at.
prudence 1. תבונה *nf* tvoon|ah/-ot (+*of:* -at); **2.** זהירות (care) *nf* zeheeroo|t/-yot.
prudent 1. נבון *adj* navon/nevonah; **2.** זהיר (careful) *adj* zaheer/zeheerah.
prudery 1. צניעות *nf* tsenee'oo|t/-yot; **2.** הצטנעות (affected humbleness) *nf* heetstan'oo|t/-yot.
prudish 1. צנוע *adj* tsanoo'a'/tsenoo'ah; **2.** מצטנע (affectedly humble) *adj* meetstan|e'a'/-a'at.
prune 1. שזיף מיובש *nm* shezeef/-eem meyoobash/-eem; **2.** שוטה (fool) *nm* shot|eh/-eem (*pl+of:* -ey).
(to) prune 1. לגזום *inf* leegzom; *pst* gazam; *pres* gozem; *fut* yeegzom; **2.** לקצץ (curtail) *inf* lekatsets; *pst* keetsets; *pres* mekatsets; *fut* yekatsets.
(to) pry 1. לחטט *inf* lekhatet; *pst* kheetet; *pres* mekhatet; *fut* yeekhatet; **2.** להציץ (peep) *inf* lehatseets; *pst* hetseets; *pres* metseets; *fut* yatseets.
(to) pry a secret out לסחוט לגילוי סוד *inf* leeskhot le-geelooy sod; *pst* sakhat *etc*; *pres* sokhet *etc*; *fut* yeeskhat *etc*.
(to) pry apart להפריד בכוח *inf* lehafreed be-kho'akh *(kh=k)*; *pst* heefreed *etc*; *pres* mafreed *etc*; *fut* yafreed *etc*.
(to) pry into other people's affairs להתערב בעניינים לא לו *inf* leheet'arev be-'eenyaneem lo lo; *pst* heet'arev *etc*; *pres* meet'arev *etc*; *fut* yeet'arev.
(to) pry open לפרוץ לרווחה *inf* leefrots lee-revakhah; *pst* parats *etc*; *pres* porets *etc*; *fut* yeefrots *etc*.
(to) pry up להרים במנוף *inf* lehareem be-manof; *pst* hereem *etc*; *pres* mereem *etc*; *fut* yareem *etc*.
psalm מזמור *nm* meezmor/-eem (*pl+of:* -ey).
Psalms תהילים *nm pl* teheeleem.
pseudonym 1. שם ספרותי *nm* shem/-ot seefrootee/-yeem; **2.** פסידונים *nm* p'seydoneem/-eem (*pl+of:* -ey).
psychiatrist פסיכיאטר *nm* p'seekhee'atr/-eem (*pl+of:* -ey).
psychiatry פסיכיאטריה *nf* p'seekhee'atree|yah/-yot (+*of:* -yat).
psychoanalysis פסיכואנליזה *nf* p'seekho'ana-leez|ah/-ot (+*of:* -at).
psychological פסיכולוגי *adj* p'seekhologee/-t.
psychologist פסיכולוג *nm* p'seekholog/-eet.
psychosis פסיכוזה *nf* p'seekhoz|ah/-ot (+*of:* -at).
puberty התבגרות מינית *nf* heetbagroo|t/-yot meenee|t-yot.
public 1. קהל (audience) *nm* kahal/kehaleem (+*of:* kehal/kahaley); **2.** ציבור (community) *nm* tseeboor/-eem (*pl+of:* -ey); **3.** פומבי (open) *adj* poombee/-t; **4.** ציבורי (communal) *adj* tseebooree/-t.
(in) public 1. בפרהסיה *adv* be-farhesyah *(f=p)*; **2.** בגלוי (openly) *adv* be-galooy.
public health בריאות הציבור *nf* bree'oot ha-tseeboor.
public man איש ציבור *nm* eesh/-ey tseeboor.
public prosecutor 1. תובע כללי *nm* tove'a' klalee; **2.** נציג התביעה הכללית (prosecutor) *nm* netseeg/-at ha-tvee'ah ha-klaleet.
public relations 1. יחסי ציבור *nm pl* yakhasey tseeboor; **2.** יח"צ (*[slang]: acr of* 1) yakhats.
public relations man 1. איש יחסי ציבור *nm* eesh yakhsey tseeboor; **2.** יחצ"ן *nmf [slang] acr of* 1 yakhtsan/-eet.
public toilet בית־שימוש ציבורי *nm* bet/batey sheemoosh tseebooree/-yeem.
publication 1. פרסום *nm* peersoom/-eem (*pl+of:* -ey); **2.** הוצאה לאור *nf* hotsa|'ah/-'ot la-'or.
publicity פרסום *nm* peersoom/-eem (*pl+of:* -ey).
publicity man פרסומאי *nm* peersoom|ay/-a'eem (*pl+of:* -a'ey).
(to) publicize 1. לפרסם (make public) *inf* lefarsem; *pst* peersem *(p=f)*; *pres* mefarsem; *fut* yefarsem; **2.** לתת פירסום ל־ (give publicity to) *inf* latet peersoom le-; *pst* natan *etc*; *pres* noten *etc*; *fut* yeeten *etc*.
(to) publish להוציא לאור *inf* lehotsee la-or; *pst* hotsee *etc*; *pres* motsee *etc*; *fut* yotsee *etc*.
publisher 1. מוציא לאור *nm* motsee/-'eem la-'or; **2.** מו"ל (*acr of* 1) mol/-eem (*pl+of:* -ey).
publishing house 1. הוצאה לאור *nf* hotsa|'ah/-'ot la-'or; **2.** בית הוצאה *nm* bet/batey hotsa'ah.

(to) pucker 1. לקמט *vt inf* lekamet; *pst* keemet; *pres* mekamet; *fut* yekamet; **2.** להתקמט (wrinkle) *vi (refl) inf* leheetkamet; *pst* heetkamet; *pres* meetkamet; *fut* yeetkamet.

pudding 1. חביצה *nf* khaveets|ah/-ot (+*of:* -at); **2.** רפרפת *nf* rafr|efet/-afot (*pl+of:* -efot); **3.** פודינג *nm* poodeeng/-eem.

puddle שלולית *nf* shloolee|t/-yot.

puff משב *nm* mash|av/-veem (*pl+of:* -vey).

(cream)puff סופגנייה עם קצפת *nf* soofganee|yah/-yot 'eem katsefet.

(powder)puff כרית פודרה *nf* karee|t/-yot poodrah.

puff of wind משב רוח *nm* mash|av/-vey roo'akh.

puff pastry בצק עלים *nm* betsek 'aleem.

pug כלב בולדוג *nm* kelev/kalvey booldog.

pug nose אף סולד *nm* af soled.

pull משיכה *nf* mesheekh|ah/-ot (+*of:* -at).

(to) pull 1. למשוך *inf* leemshokh; *pst* mashakh; *pres* moshekh; *fut* yeemshokh; **2.** למתוח (stretch) *inf* leemto'akh; *pst* matakh; *pres* mote'akh; *fut* yeemtakh.

(to have) pull ליהנות מפרוטקציה *[colloq.] inf* lehanot mee-protektsyah; *pst* nehenah *etc*; *pres* neheneh *etc*; *fut* yehaneh *etc*.

(to) pull apart 1. לפרק (dismantle) *inf* lefarek; *pst* perek *(p=f)*; *pres* mefarek; *fut* yefarek; **2.** לגלות פגמים (reveal faults) *inf* legalot pegameem; *pst* geelah *etc*; *pres* megaleh *etc*; *fut* yegaleh *etc*; **3.** לבקר קשות (bitterly criticize) *inf* levaker kashot; *pst* beeker *(b=v) etc*; *pres* mevaker *etc*; *fut* yevaker *etc*.

(to) pull down the curtain להוריד מסך *inf* lehoreed masakh; *pst* horeed *etc*; *pres* moreed *etc*; *fut* yoreed *etc*.

(to) pull oneself together 1. להתאושש *inf* leheet'oshesh; *pst* heet'oshesh; *pres* meet'oshesh; *fut* yeet'oshesh; **2.** להתעודד (regained courage) *inf* leheet'oded; *pst* heet'oded; *pres* meet'oded; *fut* yeet'oded.

(to) pull through 1. להתגבר *inf* leheetgaber; *pst* heetgaber; *pres* meetgaber; *fut* yeetgaber; **2.** להיחלץ (overcome) *inf* lehekhalets; *pst & pres* nekhlats; *fut* yekhalets.

(to) pull up לעקור מן השורש *inf* la'akor meen ha-shoresh; *pst* 'akar *etc*; *pres* 'oker *etc*; *fut* ya'akor *etc*.

(the train) pulled into the station הרכבת נכנסה לתחנה ha-rakevet neekhnesah la-takhanah.

pullet פרגית *nf* pargee|t/-yot.

pulley גלגלת *nf* galg|elet/-alot.

pulp 1. ציפה *nf* tseef|ah/-ot (+*of:* -at); **2.** בשר הפרי (fruit's meat) *nm* besar ha-pree.

pulpit דוכן *nm* dookh|an/-aneem (*pl+of:* -ney).

(to) pulsate 1. לפעום *inf* leef'om; *pst* pa'am *(p=f)*; *pres* po'em; *fut* yeef'am; **2.** להלום (tick) *inf* lahalom; *pst* halam; *pres* holem; *fut* yahalom.

pulse דופק *nm* dofek.

(to) pulverize לאבק *inf* le'abek; *pst* eebek; *pres* me'abek; *fut* ye'abek.

pumice 1. אבן ספוגית *nf* even/avaneem sfogee|t/-yot; **2.** אבן נקבובית (porous stone) *nf* even/avaneem nakboovee|t/-yot.

pump משאבה *nf* mash'ev|ah/-ot (+*of:* -at).

(gasoline) pump משאבת דלק *nf* mash'ev|at/-ot delek.

(hand) pump משאבת יד *nf* mash'ev|at/-ot yad.

(tire) pump משאבת אוויר לצמיגים *nf* mash'ev|at/-ot aveer lee-tsmeegeem.

(water) pump משאבת מים *nf* mash'ev|at/-ot mayeem.

(to) pump לשאוב *inf* leesh'ov; *pst* sha'av; *pres* sho'ev; *fut* yeesh'av.

(to) pump someone לסחוט מידע ממישהו *inf* leeskhot meyda' mee-meeshhoo; *pst* sakhat *etc*; *pres* sokhet *etc*; *fut* yeeskhat *etc*.

pumpkin דלעת *nf* dla|'at/-'ot.

pun משחק מלים *nm* meeskhak/-ey meeleem.

(to) pun לשחק במלים *inf* lesakhek be-meeleem; *pst* seekhek *etc*; *pres* mesakhek *etc*; *fut* yesakhek *etc*.

punch 1. מכת אגרוף (blow) *nf* mak|at/-ot egrof; **2.** פונטש (drink) *nm* poonch; **3.** תקיפות (vitality) *nf* takeefoo|t/-yot.

(to) punch 1. לנקב (perforate) *inf* lenakev; *pst* neekev; *pres* menakev; *fut* yenakev; **2.** להלום באגרוף (with fist) *inf* lahalom be-egrof; *pst* halam *etc*; *pres* holem *etc*; *fut* yahalom *etc*.

(to) punch a hole לנקב חור *inf* lenakev khor; *pst* neekev *etc*; *pres* menakev *etc*; *fut* yenakev *etc*.

punch clock שעון נוכחות *nm* she'on/-ey nokhekhoot.

punchbowl קערת פונטש *nf* ka'ar|at/-ot poonch.

punchcard כרטיס ניקוב *nm* kartees/-ey neekoov.

punctual 1. מדויק *adj* medoo|yak/-yeket; **2.** דייקן (pedant) *nmf & adj* daykan/-eet.

punctuality דייקנות *nf* daykanoo|t/-yot.

(to) punctuate 1. לפסק *inf* lefasek; *pst* peesek *(p=f)*; *pres* mefasek; *fut* yefasek; **2.** לנקד (dot Hebrew script) *inf* lenaked; *pst* neeked; *pres* menaked; *fut* yenaked.

punctuation פיסוק *nm* peesook/-eem (*pl+of:* -ey).

puncture 1. נקר *nm* nek|er/-areem (*pl+of:* neekrey); **2.** תקר *[colloq.] nm* tek|er/-areem (*pl+of:* teekrey); **3.** פנצ'ר (colloquial mispronunciation of "puncture") *nm* pantcher/-eem (*pl+of:* -ey).

(tire) puncture 1. נקר בצמיג *nm* neker/nekareem ba-tsemeeg/-eem; **2.** תקר בצמיג *[colloq.] nm* tek|er/-areem ba-tsemeeg/-eem; **3.** פנצ'ר בצמיג *[slang] nm* pantcher/-eem ba-tsemeeg/-eem.

puncture proof 1. חסין נקרים *adj* khaseen/-at nekareem; **2.** חסין תקרים *[colloq.] adj* khaseen/-at tekareem.

punctured tire 1. צמיג נקור tsemeeg/-eem nakoor/nekooreem; **2.** צמיג מפונצ'ר *[colloq.] nm* tsemeeg/-eem mefoontchar/-eem.

(to) punish להעניש *inf* leha'aneesh; *pst* he'eneesh; *pres* ma'aneesh; *fut* ya'aneesh.

punishment עונש *nm* 'on|esh/-sheem (*pl+of:* -shey).

punt בעיטה *nf* be'eet|ah/-ot (+*of:* -at).

puny 1. פעוט *adj* pa'oot/pe'ootah; **2.** חסר־ערך (worthless) *adj* khas|ar/-rat 'erekh.

pup כלבלב *nm* klavlav/-eem (*pl+of:* -ey).

pupil תלמיד *nmf* talmeed/-ah (*pl:* -eem/-ot; +*of:* -at/-ey).

pupil of the eye אישון עין *nm* eeshon/-ey 'ayeen.

puppet בובה *nf* boob|ah/-ot (*+of:* -at).

puppet show תיאטרון בובות *nm* te'atron/-ey boobot.

puppy כלבלב *nm* klavlav/-eem (*pl+of:* -ey).

purchase קנייה *nf* kenee|yah/-yot (*+of:* -yat).

(to) purchase לקנות *inf* leeknot; *pst* kanah; *pres* koneh; *fut* yeekneh.

(to get a) purchase upon להשלים קנייה של *inf* lehashleem kenee|yah/-yot shel; *pst* heeshleem *etc; pres* mashleem *etc; fut* yashleem *etc.*

purchaser קונה *nmf* kon|eh/-ah (*pl:* -eem/-ot; *+of:* -at/-ey).

pure טהור *adj* tahor/tehorah.

puree 1. רסק *nm* res|ek/-akeem (*pl+of:* reeskey); **2.** *nf* mekhee|t/-yot; **3.** פיורה *nm* pyooreh.

purely אך ורק *conj* akh ve-rak.

purgative 1. משלשל *nm* meshalshel/-eem (*pl+of:* -ey); **2.** משלשל *adj* meshalshel/-et.

purgatory 1. כפרה *nf* kapar|ah/-ot (*+of:* -at); **2.** גיהינום (Hell) *nm* geyheenom.

purge טיהור *nm* tehoor/-eem (*pl+of:* -ey).

(to) purge 1. לטהר *inf* letaher; *pst* teeher; *pres* metaher; *fut* yetaher; **2.** לערוך "טיהור" (politically) *inf* la'arokh tehoor; *pst* 'arakh *etc; pres* 'orekh *etc; fut* ya'arokh *etc.*

(to) purify לזכך *inf* lezakekh; *pst* zeekekh; *pres* mezakekh; *fut* yezakekh.

Purim Carnival עדלאידע *nf* 'adloyad|ah/-ot (*+of:* -at).

Purim presents משלוח מנות *nm* meeshlo|'akh/-khey manot.

purist 1. טהרן *nm* taharan/-eem (*pl+of:* -ey); **2.** פוריסט *nm* pooreest/-eem (*pl+of:* -ey).

purity טוהר *nm* tohar.

purple 1. ארגמן *nm* argaman; **2.** בצבע ארגמן *adj* be-tseva' argaman.

purport 1. משמעות *nf* mashma'oo|t/-yot; **2.** כוונה (intention) kavan|ah/-ot (*+of:* -at).

(to) purport להתכוון *inf* leheetkaven; *pst* heetkaven; *pres* meetkaven; *fut* yeetkaven.

purpose 1. כוונה (intention) *nf* kavan|ah/-ot (*+of:* -at); **2.** מטרה (goal) *nf* matar|ah/-ot (*+of:* -at).

(for no) purpose ללא תועלת *adv* le-lo to'elet.

(on) purpose במתכוון *adv* be-meetkaven.

purposely 1. בזדון *adv* be-zadon; **2.** במזיד (willfully) *adv* be-mezeed.

purr 1. ימיום *nm* yeemyoom/-eem (*pl+of:* -ey).; **2.** נהימת חתול (cat's) *nf* neheem|at/-ot khatool.

(to) purr 1. לימיים *inf* leyamyem; *pst* yeemyem; *pres* meyamyem; *fut* yeyamyem; **2.** לנהום *inf* leenhom; *pst* naham; *pres* nohem; *fut* yeenhom.

purse ארנק *nm* arn|ak/-akeem (*pl+of:* -ekey).

(to) purse one's lips לכווץ שפתיים *inf* lekhavets sfatayeem; *pst* keevets *etc* (*k=kh*); *pres* mekhavets *etc; fut* yekhavets *etc.*

purser גזבר *nm* geezbar/-eem (*pl+of:* -ey).

pursuant בעיקבות *adv* be-'eekvot.

(to) pursue 1. לרדוף *inf* leerdof; *pst* radaf; *pres* rodef; *fut* yeerdof; **2.** ללכת בדרכי (follow) *inf* lalekhet be-darkhey; *pst* halakh *etc; pres* holekh *etc; fut* yelekh *etc;* **3.** לשקוד על (persevere) *inf* leeshkod 'al; *pst* shakad 'al; *pres* shoked 'al; *fut* yeeshkod 'al.

pursuer רודף *nm* rod|ef/-feem (*pl+of:* -fey).

pursuit 1. רדיפה *nf* redeef|ah/-ot (*+of:* -at); **2.** משלח יד (occupation) meeshl|akh/-ekhey yad.

(in) pursuit of ברדיפה אחר *adv* bee-redeefah akhar.

pus מוגלה *nf* moogl|ah/-ot (*+of:* -at).

push דחיפה *nf* dekheef|ah/-ot (*+of:* -at).

(to) push 1. לדחוף (shove) *inf* leedkhof; *pst* dakhaf; *pres* dokhef; *fut* yeedkhof; **2.** לקדם (promote) *inf* lekadem; *pst* keedem; *pres* mekadem; *fut* yekadem; **3.** לזרז (hurry) *inf* lezarez; *pst* zerez; *pres* mezarez; *fut* yezarez.

(to) push aside לדחוף הצידה *inf* leedkhof ha-tseedah; *pst* dakhaf *etc; pres* dokhef *etc; fut* yeedkhof *etc.*

(to) push forward לדחוף קדימה *inf* leedkhof kadeemah; *pst* dakhaf *etc; pres* dokhef *etc; fut* yeedkhof *etc.*

(to) push through לפרוץ קדימה *inf* leefrots kadeemah; *pst* parats *etc* (*p=f*); *pres* porets *etc; fut* yeefrots *etc.*

pushcart עגלת דחיפה *nf* 'egl|at/-ot dekheefah.

pussy חתולה *nf* khatool|ah/-ot (*+of:* -at).

(to) put לשים *inf* laseem; *pst & pres* sam; *fut* yaseem.

(to) put a question להציג שאלה *inf* lehatseeg she'elah; *pst* heetseeg *etc; pres* matseeg *etc; fut* yatseeg *etc.*

(to) put a stop to לשים קץ ל- *inf* laseem kets le-; *pst & pres* sam *etc; fut* yaseem *etc.*

(to) put across an idea לעשות נפשות לרעיון *inf* la'asot nefashot le-ra'yon; *pst* 'asah *etc; pres* 'oseh *etc; fut* ya'aseh *etc.*

(to) put away 1. לשים הצידה *inf* laseem ha-tseedah; *pst & pres* sam *etc; fut* yaseem *etc;* **2.** לזלול (eat greedily) *inf* leezlol; *pst* zalal; *pres* zolel; *fut* yeezlol.

(to) put before להציע *inf* lehatsee'a'; *pst* heetsee'a'; *pres* matsee'a'; *fut* yatsee'a'.

(to) put by money לחסוך כסף *inf* lakhsokh kesef; *pst* khasakh *etc; pres* khosekh *etc; fut* yakhsokh *etc.*

(to) put down 1. לדכא *inf* ledake; *pst* deeke; *pres* medake; *fut* yedake; **2.** להשפיל (humiliate) *inf* lehashpeel; *pst* heeshpeel; *pres* mashpeel; *fut* yashpeel.

(to) put in a word להמליץ על *inf* lehamleets 'al; *pst* heemleets 'al; *pres* mamleets 'al; *fut* yamleets 'al.

(to) put in writing לנסח בכתב *inf* lenase'akh bee-khtav (*kh=k*); *pst* neese'akh *etc; pres* menase'akh *etc; fut* yenase'akh *etc.*

(to) put off 1. לדחות *inf* leedkhot; *pst* dakhah; *pres* dokheh; *fut* yeedkheh; **2.** לפשוט (clothes) *inf* leefshot; *pst* pashat (*p=f*); *pres* poshet; *fut* yeefshot.

(to) put on להעמיד פנים *inf* leha'ameed paneem; *pst* he'emeed *etc; pres* ma'ameed *etc; fut* ya'ameed *etc.*

(to) put on airs להתרברב *inf* leheetravrev; *pst* heetravrev; *pres* meetravrev; *fut* yeetravrev.

(to) put on weight 1. להוסיף משקל *inf* lehoseef meeshkal; *pst* hoseef *etc; pres* moseef *etc; fut* yoseef *etc*; **2.** להשמין (fatten) *inf* lehashmeen; *pst* heeshmeen; *pres* mashmeen; *fut* yashmeen.

(to) put out 1. להוציא *inf* lehotsee; *pst* hotsee; *pres* motsee; *fut* yotsee; **2.** לכבות (fire) *inf* lekhabot; *pst* keebah *(k=kh)*; *pres* mekhabeh; *fut* yekhabeh; **3.** לנקר עין (eye) *inf* lenaker 'ayeen; *pst* neeker *etc*; *pres* menaker *etc*; *fut* yenaker *etc*.

(to) put to shame לבייש *inf* levayesh; *pst* beeyesh *(b=v)*; *pres* mevayesh; *fut* yevayesh.

(to) put up להציע מועמד *inf* lehatsee'a' moo'amad; *pst* heetsee'a' *etc*; *pres* matsee'a' *etc*; *fut* yatsee'a' *etc*.

(to) put up for sale להעמיד למכירה *inf* leha'ameed lee-mekheerah; *pst* he'emeed *etc*; *pres* ma'ameed *etc*; *fut* ya'ameed *etc*.

(to) put up with להשלים עם *inf* lehashleem 'eem; *pst* heeshleem *etc*; *pres* mashleem *etc*; *fut* yashleem *etc*.

(to) putrefy להרקיב *inf* leharkeev; *pst* heerkeev; *pres* markeev; *fut* yarkeev.

putrid רקוב *adj* rakoov/rekoovah.

(to) putter להתבטל *inf* leheetbatel; *pst* heetbatel; *pres* meetbatel; *fut* yeetbatel.

putty מרק *nm* mer|ek/-akeem (*pl+of:* meerkey).

(to) putty לסתום במרק *inf* leestom be-merek; *pst* satam *etc*; *pres* sotem *etc*; *fut* yeestom *etc*.

puzzle 1. חידה *nf* kheed|ah/-ot (*+of:* -at); **2.** מבוכה (confusion) *nf* mevookh|ah/-ot (*+of:* -at).

(crossword) puzzle חידת תשבץ *nf* kheed|at/-ot tashbets.

(to) puzzle 1. להתמיה *inf* lehatmee'ah; *pst* heetmee'ah; *pres* matmee'ah; *fut* yatmee'ah; **2.** להביא במבוכה (confuse) *inf* lehavee bee-mevookhah; *pst* hevee *etc*; *pres* mevee *etc*; *fut* yavee *etc*.

(to) puzzle out לפתור *inf* leeftor; *pst* patar *(p=f)*; *pres* poter; *fut* yeeftor.

(to) puzzle over להתעמק ב־ *inf* leheet'amek be-; *pst* heet'amek be-; *pres* meet'amek be-; *fut* yeet'amek be-.

(to be) puzzled לתמוה *inf* leetmo'ah; *pst* tamah; *pres* tame'ah; *fut* yeetmah.

pyramid פירמידה *nf* peerameed|ah/-ot (*+of:* -at).

Q.

Q,q is transliterated as ק (Kof). (Note: In English "q" is normally followed by "u" and pronounced as "qw". This is transliterated by קו (Kof Vav) or קוו (Kof Vav Vav), e.g., קווין (queen)).

quack 1. רופא־אליל *nm* rofe/ey eleel; **2.** רמאי *nm* ram|ay/-a'eem (*pl+of:* -a'ey).

(to) quack לקרקר *inf* lekarker; *pst* keerker; *pres* mekarker; *fut* yekarker.

quackery 1. רמאות *nf* rama'oo|t/-yot; **2.** הונאה (swindle) *nf* hona|'ah/-'ot (*+of:* -'at).

quadruped הולך על ארבע *nm* holekh/-khey 'al arba'.

quadruple כפול ארבע *adj* kafool/kefoolat arba'.

quadruplets רביעייה *nf* revee'ee|yah/-yot (*+of:* -yat).

quagmire 1. אדמת בוץ *nf* adm|at/-ot bots; **2.** תסבוכת (complication) *nf* teesbokh|et/-ot.

quail 1. שלו (bird) *nm* slav/-eem (*pl+of:* -ey); **2.** פחד (fear) *m* pakhad/pekhadeem (*pl+of:* pakhdey).

quaint 1. מוזר (queer) *adj* moozar/-ah; **2.** שונה (different) *adj* shon|eh/-ah.

quake רעידה *nf* re'eed|ah/-ot (*+of:* -at).

qualification כישור *nm* keeshoor/-eem (*pl+of:* -ey).

(to) qualify 1. להוכיח כישור *inf* lehokhee'akh keeshoor; *pst* hokhee'akh *etc*; *pres* mokhee'akh *etc*; *fut* yokhee'akh *etc*; **2.** להעריך *inf* leha'areekh me'od; *pst* he'ereekh; *pres* ma'areekh; *fut* ya'areekh; **3.** להסמיך *inf* lehasmeekh; *pst* heesmeekh; *pres* masmeekh; *fut* yasmeekh.

(to) qualify for a position להיות כשיר לתפקיד *inf* leehyot kasheer la-tafkeed; *pst* hayah *etc*; *pres* heeno *etc*; *fut* yeehyeh *etc*

(his studies) qualified him for the job לימודיו הכשירו אותו לתפקיד leemoodav heekhsheroo oto la-tafkeed.

quality 1. איכות *nf* eykhoo|t/-yot; **2.** טיב (nature) *nm* teev; **3.** תכונה (attribute) *nf* tekhoon|ah/-ot (*+of:* -at).

qualm 1. חולשה (weakness) *nf* khoolsh|ah/-ot (*+of:* -at); **2.** בחילה (nausea) *nf* bekheel|ah/-ot (*+of:* -at).

(to) quantify לקבוע כמות *inf* leekbo'a' kamoot; *pst* kava' *etc* *(v=b)*; *pres* kove'a' *etc*; *fut* yeekba' *etc*.

quantity 1. כמות *nf* kamoo|t/-yot; **2.** מספר (number) *nm* meespar/-eem (*pl+of:* -erey); **3.** גודל (size) *nm* godel/gedaleem (*pl+of:* godley).

quarantine 1. הסגר *nm* hesger; **2.** קרנטינה *nf* karanteen|ah/-ot (*+of:* -at).

(to) quarantine להחזיק בהסגר *inf* lehakhzeek be-hesger; *pst* hekhzeek *etc*; *pres* makhzeek *etc*; *fut* yakhzeek *etc*.

quarrel 1. מריבה *nf* mereev|ah/-ot (*+of:* -at); **2.** קטטה (fracas) *nf* ketat|ah/-ot (*+of:* -at).

(to) quarrel להתקוטט *inf* leheetkotet; *pst* heetkotet; *pres* meetkotet; *fut* yeetkotet.

quarrelsome מחפש ריב *adj* mekhapes/-et reev.

quarry מחצבה *nf* makhts|avah/-avot (*+of:* -evet).

(to) quarry 1. לחצוב *inf* lakhtsov; *pst* khatsav; *pres* khotsev; *fut* yakhtsov; **2.** לכרות (dig) *inf* leekhrot; *pst* karah *(k=kh); pres* koreh; *fut* yeekhreh.

quart רבע גלון *nm* reva'/reev'ey galon.

quarter 1. רבע (one fourth) *nm* rev|a'/-a'eem (*pl+of:* reev'ey); **2.** רובע (district) *nm* rova'/reva'eem (*pl+of:* rov'ey).

(to) quarter 1. לחלק לארבעה *inf* lekhalek le-arba'ah; *pst* kheelek *etc; pres* mekhalek *etc; fut* yekhalek *etc;* **2.** לשכן חיילים (billet) *inf* leshaken khayaleem; *pst* sheeken *etc; pres* meshaken *etc; fut* yeshaken *etc.*

quarter hour רבע שעה *nm* reva'/reev'ey sha'ah.

(a) quarter to רבע ל־ reva' le-.

(giving no) quarter to the enemy לבלי תת לאויב מנוח *adv* lee-vlee *(v=b)* tet la-oyev mano'akh.

quarterly 1. רבעון *nm* reev'on/-eem (*pl+of:* -ey); **2.** של רבע *adj* shel reva'; **3.** אחת לרבע שנה *adv* akhat le-reva' shanah.

quartermaster אפסנאי *nm* afsan|ay/-a'eem (*pl+of:* -a'ey).

quartet רביעייה *nf* revee'ee|yah/-yot (*+of:* -yat).

quartz קוורץ *nm* kvarts.

quaver 1. רעד *nm* ra'ad; **2.** סלסול *nm* seelsool/-eem (*pl+of:* -ey).

(to) quaver לרעוד *inf* leer'od; *pst* ra'ad; *pres* ro'ed; *fut* yeer'ad.

quay רציף *nm* ratseef/retseef|eem (*pl+of:* -ey).

queen מלכה *nf* malkah/melakhot *(kh=k)* (*+of:* mal|kat/-khot).

(beauty) queen מלכת יופי *nf* mal|kat/-khot yofee.

queer 1. מוזר *adj* moozar/-ah; **2.** תמוה (strange) *adj* tamooha/temoohah.

(to) queer 1. לקלקל *inf* lekalkel; *pst* keelkel; *pres* mekalkel; *fut* yekalkel; **2.** לשבש (disrupt) *inf* leshabesh; *pst* sheebesh; *pres* meshabesh; *fut* yeshabesh.

(to feel) queer להרגיש מוזר *inf* lehargeesh moozar; *pst* heergeesh *etc; pres* margeesh *etc; fut* yargeesh *etc.*

(to) queer oneself with להסתכסך עם *inf* leheestakhsekh 'eem; *pst* heestakhsekh 'eem; *pres* meestakhsekh 'eem; *fut* yeestakhsekh 'eem.

(to) quell 1. להדביר *inf* lehadbeer; *pst* heedbeer; *pres* madbeer; *fut* yadbeer; **2.** להשקיט (calm) *inf* lehashkeet; *pst* heeshkeet; *pres* mashkeet; *fut* yashkeet.

(to) quench 1. לרוות *inf* leravot; *pst* reevah; *pres* meraveh; *fut* yeraveh; **2.** לכבות (extinguish) *inf* lekhabot; *pst* keebah *(k=kh); pres* mekhabeh; *fut* yekhabeh.

query 1. תשאול (interrogation) *nm* teesh'ool/-eem (*pl+of:* -ey); **2.** ספק (doubt) *nm* safek/sfekot.

(to) query 1. לשאול (ask) *inf* leesh'ol; *pst* sha'al; *pres* sho'el; *fut* yeesh'al; **2.** לתמוה (wonder) *inf* leetmo'ah; *pst* tamah; *pres* tame'ah; *fut* yeetmah.

quest חיפוש *nm* kheepoos/-eem (*pl+of:* -ey).

question שאלה *nf* she'el|ah/-ot (*+of:* -at).

(beyond) question מעבר לכל ספק *adv* me-'ever le-khol *(kh=k)* safek.

(out of the) question לא בא בחשבון lo ba/ba'ah be-kheshbon.

(to) question 1. להטיל ספק (doubt) *inf* lehateel safek; *pst* heeteel *etc; pres* mateel *etc; fut* yateel *etc;* **2.** לתשאל (interrogate) *inf* letash'el; *pst* teesh'el; *pres* metash'el; *fut* yetash'el; **3.** לתחקר (investigate) *inf* letakhker; *pst* teekhker; *pres* metakhker; *fut* yetakhker; **4.** לערור על (dispute) *inf* la'aror 'al; *pres* 'arar 'al; *pres* 'orer 'al; *fut* ya'aror 'al.

question mark סימן שאלה *nm* seeman/-ey she'elah.

questionable מוטל בספק *adj* moot|al/-elet be-safek.

questioner מתשאל *nmf* metash'el/-et.

questioning תשאול *nm* teesh'ool/-eem.

questionnaire שאלון *nm* she'elon/-eem (*pl+of:* -ey).

quibble פלפול *nm* peelpool/-eem (*pl+of:* -ey).

(to) quibble להתפלפל *inf* leheetpalpel; *pst* heetpalpel; *pres* meetpalpel; *fut* yeetpalpel.

quick 1. מהיר (fast) *adj* maheer/meheerah; **2.** קרוב (near) *adj* karov/krovah; **3.** פיקח (smart) *adj* peek|e'akh/-kheet.

quick 1. מהר (fast) *adv* maher; **2.** חיש מהר (very fast) *adv* kheesh maher.

(to cut to the) quick 1. לחתוך בבשר החי *inf* lakhtokh ba-basar ha-khay; *pst* khatakh *etc; pres* khotekh *etc; fut* yakhtokh *etc;* **2.** לפגוע ברגשות (hurt feelings) *inf* leefgo'a' bee-rgashot; *pst* paga' *etc (p=f); pres* poge'a' *etc; fut* yeefga' *etc.*

quick assets נכסים קלי מימוש *nm pl* nekhaseem kaley meemoosh.

(to) quick freeze להקפיא בהקפאה מהירה *inf* lehakpee be-hakpa'ah meheerah; *pst* heekpee *etc; pres* makpee *etc; fut* yakpee *etc.*

quicktempered מהיר חימה *adj* meheer/-at kheymah.

quickwitted מהיר תפיסה *adj* meheer/-at tfeesah.

(to) quicken להחיש *inf* lehakheesh; *pst* hekheesh; *pres* mekheesh; *fut* yakheesh.

quickly מהר *adv* maher.

quickness 1. מהירות *nf* meheeroot; **2.** זריזות (agility) *nf* zreezoot.

quicksand חולות ביצה *nm pl* kholot beetsah.

quicksilver כספית *nf* kaspeet.

quiet 1. שקט *nm* sheket; **2.** שקט *adj* shaket/sheketah.

(to) quiet להרגיע *inf* lehargee'a'; *pst* heergee'a'; *pres* margee'a'; *fut* yargee'a'.

(to) quiet down להירגע *inf* leheraga'; *pst & pres* neerga'; *fut* yeraga'.

quietly בשקט *adv* be-sheket.

quietness 1. שלווה *nf* shalvah; **2.** שקט (quiet) *nm* sheket.

quill 1. נוצת כנף *nf* nots|at/-ot kanaf; **2.** קולמוס (pen) koolmos/-eem (*pl+of:* -ey).

quilt שמיכה חורפית *nf* smeekh|ah/-ot khorpee/t/-yot.

quince חבוש *nm* khavoosh/-eem (*pl+of:* -ey).

quinine כינין *or* חינין *nm* kheeneen.

quip 1. חידוד *nm* kheedood/-eem (*pl+of:* -ey); **2.** הערה שנונה *nf* he'ar|ah/-ot shenoon|ah/-ot.

quirk התנהגות מוזרה *nf* heetnahagoot moozarah.

(to) quit 1. לזנוח (abandon) *inf* leezno'akh; *pst* zanakh; *pres* zone'akh; *fut* yeeznakh; **2.** לחדול (cease) *inf* lakhdol; *pst* khadal; *pres* khadel; *fut* yekhdal; **3.** להתפטר (job) *v rfl inf* leheetpater; *pst* heetpater; *pres* meetpater; *fut* yeetpater.

(to) quit doing לחדול מעשות *inf* lakhdol me-'asot; *pst* khadal *etc*; *pres* khadel *etc*; *fut* yekhdal *etc*.

quite כמעט *adv* keem'at.

quite a few לא מעטים lo me'ateem.

quite a person אדם נהדר *nm* adam nehedar.

quite so אמת ויציב *adv* emet ve-yatseev.

quite the fashion מאוד אופנתי *adv & adj* me'od ofnatee/-t.

quits 1. שווה בשווה *adj* shaveh be-shaveh; **2.** מסולק (paid up) *adj* mesool|ak/-eket.

quittance 1. פטור *nm* petor/-eem (*pl+of:* -ey); **2.** פיצוי (compensation) *nm* peetsoo|y/-yeem (*pl+of:* -yey).

quitter 1. ותרן *nm* vatran/-eet; **2.** משתמט (shirker) *nm* meeshtam|et/-teem (*pl+of:* -tey).

quiver 1. רטט (movement) *nm* retet/retateem (*pl+of:* reetetey); **2.** אשפה (for arrows) *nf* ashp|ah/-ot (*+of:* -at).

(to) quiver לרטט *inf* laratet; *pst* reetet; *pres* meratet; *fut* yeratet.

quixotic דון־קישוטי *adj* don-keeshotee/-t.

quiz חידון *nm* kheedon/-eem (*pl+of:* -ey).

(to) quiz 1. להתלוצץ (ridicule) *inf* leheetlotsets; *pst* heetlotsets; *pres* meetlotsets; *fut* yeetlotsets; **2.** לבחון (test) *inf* leevkhon; *pst* bakhan *(b=v)*; *pres* bokhen; *fut* yeevkhon; **3.** לערוך חידון *inf* la'arokh kheedon; *pst* 'arakh *etc*; *pres* 'orekh *etc*; *fut* ya'arokh *etc*.

quizzical 1. ליצני *adj* leytsanee/-t; **2.** היתולי (comical) *adj* heetoolee/-t; **3.** מבלבל (confusing) *adj* mevalbel/-et.

quorum 1. מספר נוכחים מספיק *nm* meespar nokhekheem maspeek; **2.** קוורום *nm* kvoroom/-eem (*pl+of:* -ey).

quota מכסה *nf* meekhs|ah/-ot (*+of:* -at).

(import) quota מכסת יבוא *nf* meekhs|at/-ot yevoo.

quotation 1. הצעת מחיר (price) *nf* hatsa|'at/-'ot mekheer; **2.** ציטוט (citation) *nm* tseetoot/-eem (*pl+of:* -ey).

quotation marks 1. מרכאות *nm pl* merkha'ot; **2.** גרשיים (inverted commas) *nm pl* gershayeem.

quote 1. ציטטה *nf* tseetat|ah/-ot (*+of:* -at); **2.** ציטוט (citation) *nm* tseetoot/-eem (*pl+of:* -ey).

(to) quote 1. לצטט (cite) *inf* letsatet; *pst* tseetet; *pres* metsatet; *fut* yetsatet; **2.** לנקוב מחיר (state price) *inf* leenkov mekheer; *pst* nakav *etc*; *pres* nokev *etc*; *fut* yeenkov *etc*.

(to) quote from לצטט מתוך *inf* letsatet mee-tokh; *pst* tseetet *etc*; *pres* metsatet *etc*; *fut* yetsatet *etc*.

quotes מרכאות *nf pl* merkha'ot.

(in) quotes במרכאות *adv* be-merkha'ot.

quotient מנה *nf* man|ah/-ot (*+of:* men|at/-ot).

(intelligence) quotient מנת משכל *nf* men|at/-ot meeskal.

R.

R,r is transliterated as ר (Resh). Its sound is rolled in the throat.

rabbi (religious head of a group *or* **community)** רב *nm* rav/rabaneem (*pl+of:* rabaney).

(chief-)rabbi רב ראשי rav/rabaneem rashee/-yeem.

Rabbinate רבנות *nf* rabanoo|t/-yot.

(the Chief) Rabbinate הרבנות הראשית *nf* ha-rabanoot ha-rasheet.

rabbinic רבני *adj* rabanee/-t.

rabbi's wife רבנית rabanee|t/-yot.

rabbit 1. שפן (coney) *nm* shafan/shefaneem; **2.** ארנבת (hare) *nf* arn|evet/-avot.

rabble אספסוף *nm* asafsoof.

(to) rabble להתפרע *v inf* le-heetpare'a'; *pst* heetpara'; *pres* meetpare'a'; *fut* yeetpare'a'.

rabble-rouser מסית *nm* meseet/-eem (*pl+of:* -ey).

rabid משתולל *adj & v pres* meeshtolel/-et.

rabies כלבת *nf* kalevet.

race 1. מירוץ (running) *nm* merots/-eem (*pl+of:* -ey); **2.** תחרות (competition) *nf* takharoo|t/-yot; **3.** גזע (people) *nm* gez|a'/-a'eem (*pl+of:* geez'ey).

(horse) race מירוץ סוסים *nm* merots/-ey sooseem.

(the human) race הגזע האנושי *nm* ha-geza' ha-enooshee.

(to) race להתחרות *inf* le-heetkharot; *pst* heetkharah; *pres* meetkhareh; *fut* yeetkhareh.

race riot מהומה גזענית *nf* mehoom|ah/-ot geez'anee|t/-yot.

racecourse מסלול מירוץ *nm* maslool/-ey meroots.

rachitis רככת *nf* rakekhet.

racial גזעני *adj* geez'anee/-t.

racialism, racism גזענות *nf* geez'anoot.

racist גזען *nmf* geez'an/-eet.

rack 1. מסגרת *nf* meesg|eret/-arot; **2.** אצטבה (shelf) eetstab|ah/-a'ot.

racket 1. תרמית (fraud) *nf* tarmee|t/-yot; **2.** סחטנות (blackmail) sakhtanoo|t/-yot.

(tennis) racket מחבט *nm* makhbet/-eem (*pl+of:* -ey).

racketeer 1. סחטן (blackmailer) *nmf* sakhtan/-eet (*pl:* -eem; *+of:* -ey); **2.** נוכל (swindler) *nmf* nokh|el/-elet (*pl:* -leem; *+of:* -ley).

racketeering 1. סחטנות (blackmail) *nf* sakhta-noo|t/-yot; **2.** פשיעה (crime) *nf* peshee|'ah/-'ot (*+of:* -'at).

racquet מחבט *nm* makhbet/-eem (*pl+of:* -ey).

racy 1. תוסס *adj* toses/-et; **2.** עסיסי (juicy) *adj* 'aseesee/-t.

radar 1. מכ״ם *nm* makam (*acr of* Megaleh Keevoon oo-Makom i.e. direction and location exposer); **2.** ראדאר *nm* radar.

radar-proof חסין מכ״ם *adj* khaseen/-at makam.

radar screen מסך מכ״ם *nm* masa|kh/-key *(k=kh)* makam.

radial tire צמיג רדיאלי *nm* tsemeeg/-eem radyalee/-yeem.

radiance 1. זוהר *nm* zohar; **2.** זיו (brightness) *nm* zeev.

(to) radiate להקרין *inf* le-hakreen; *pst* heekreen; *pres* makreen; *fut* yakreen.

radiation קרינה *nf* kreen|ah/-ot.

radiator 1. מצנן (of a car) *nm* metsanen/-eem (*pl+of:* -ey); **2.** רדיאטור (of a car or of central heating) *[colloq.] nm* radyat|or/-oreem (*pl+of:* -orey).

radical 1. יסודי (thorough) *adj* yesodee/-t; **2.** קיצוני (extreme) *adj* keetsonee/-t; **3.** קיצוני (extremist) *nm* keetson|ee/-eeyeem (*pl+of:* -ey); **4.** רדיקלי *adj* radeekalee/-t.

radio 1. אלחוט (wireless) *nm* alkhoot; **2.** רדיו *nm* radyo.

radio act תסכית *nm* taskeet/-eem (*pl+of:* -ey).

radio receiver מקלט רדיו *nm* maklet/-ey radyo.

radio station 1. תחנת רדיו *nf* takhan|at/-ot radyo; **2.** תחנת שידור (broadcasting station) *nf* takhan|at/-ot sheedoor.

radio transmitter משדר *nm* mashder/-eem (*pl+of:* -ey).

radioactive רדיואקטיבי *adj* radyo-akteevee/-t.

radioactivity רדיואקטיביות *nf* radyo-akteeveeyoot.

radiotelegraph רדיו־טלגרף *nm* radyo-telegraf.

radiotelephone רדיו־טלפון *nm* radyo-telefon.

radiotelephone channel ערוץ רדיו־טלפוני *nm* 'aroots/-eem radyo-telefonee/-yeem.

radiotherapy 1. ריפוי בהקרנה *nm* reepooy be-hakranah; **2.** הקרנה (radiation) *nf* hakran|ah/-ot.

radius 1. רדיוס *nm* radyoos/-eem; **2.** קוטר *nm* koter (colloquial error since it actually means diameter and the correct term is therefore חצי־קוטר *nm* khatsee-koter i.e. half a diameter).

radix שורש *nm* shoresh/shar|asheem (*pl+of:* -shey).

raffia רפיה *nf* rafyah.

raft 1. דוברה *nf* dovr|ah/-ot (*+of:* -at); **2.** רפסודה (syn) *nf* rafsod|ah/-ot (*+of:* -at).

rag 1. סמרטוט *nm* smartoot/-eem (*pl+of:* -ey); **2.** סחבה *nf* sekhav|ah/-ot (*+of:* -at).

ragamuffin לבוש סחבות *nmf* levoosh/-at sekhavot.

rage 1. חימה *nf* kheymah; **2.** כעס (anger) *nm* ka'as.

(to) rage להתרגז *inf* le-heetragez; *pst* heetragez; *pres* meetragez; *fut* yeetragez.

ragged 1. בלוי (worn out) *adj* balooy/blooyah; **2.** קרוע (torn) *adj* karoo'a'/kroo'ah.

raging 1. מרוגז (vexed) *adj* meroog|az/-ezet; **2.** משתולל (running wild) *adj* meeshtolel/-et.

ragman, ragpicker סמרטוטר *nm* smartootar/-eem (*pl+of:* -ey).

(in) rags בלבוש סמרטוטים *adv* bee-levoosh smartooteem.

ragtag אספסוף *nm* asafsoof.

raid 1. פשיטה (attack) *nf* pesheet|ah/-ot (*+of:* -at); **2.** התנפלות (assault) *nf* heetnaploo|t/-yot.

(to) raid 1. לפשוט על *inf* lee-fshot 'al; *pst* pashat 'al *(p=f)*; *pres* poshet 'al; *fut* yeefshot 'al; **2.** לתקוף (attack) *inf* leetkof; *pst* takaf; *pres* tokef; *fut* yeetkof.

raider תוקף *nm* tok|ef/-feem (*pl+of:* -fey).

rail 1. פס (strip) *nm* pas/-eem (*pl+of:* -ey); **2.** מסילה (line) *nf* meseel|ah/-ot (*+of:* -at).

railing מעקה *nm* ma'ak|eh/-ot.

railroad, railway מסילת ברזל *nf* meseel|at/-ot barzel.

railway station תחנת רכבת *nf* takhan|at/-ot rakevet.

rain גשם *nm* geshem/geshameem (*pl+of:* geeshmey).

(to) rain 1. לרדת גשם *inf* laredet geshem; *pst* yarad *etc*; *pres* yored *etc*; *fut* yered *etc*; **2.** להגשים *[colloq.] inf* le-hagsheem; *pst* heegsheem; *pres* magsheem; *fut* yagsheem.

rainbow קשת בענן *nf* keshet be-'anan.

raincheck התחייבות על תנאי *nf* heet'khayvoo|t/-yot 'al tnay.

raincoat מעיל גשם *nm* me'eel/-ey geshem.

raindrop טיפת גשם *nf* teep|at/-ot geshem.

rainfall כמות הגשם *nf* kamoo|t/-yot ha-geshem.

rainproof עמיד לגשם *adj* 'ameed/-ah le-geshem.

rainstorm סופת גשמים *nf* soof|at/-ot geshameem.

rainwater מי גשם *nm pl* mey geshem.

rainy גשום *adj* gashoom/geshoomah.

rainy weather מזג אוויר גשום *nm* mezeg-aveer gashoom.

raise העלאה *nf* ha'ala|'ah/-'ot (*+of:* -'at).

(to) raise להעלות *inf* le-ha'alot; *pst* he'elah; *pres* ma'aleh; *fut* ya'aleh.

(to) raise children לגדל ילדים *inf* legadel yeladeem; *pst* geedel *etc*; *pres* megadel *etc*; *fut* yegadel *etc*.

(to) raise doubts לעורר ספקות *inf* le-'orer safek/sfekot; *pst* 'orer *etc*; *pres* me'orer *etc*; *fut* ye'orer *etc*.

(to) raise hell להפוך עולמות *inf* lahafokh 'olamot; *pst* hafakh *etc*; *pres* hofekh *etc*; *fut* yahafokh *etc*.

(to) raise prices 1. להעלות מחירים *inf* le-ha'alot mekheereem; *pst* he'elah *etc*; *pres* ma'aleh *etc*; *fut* ya'aleh *etc*; **2.** להפקיע שערים (profiteer) *inf* le-hafkee'a' she'areem; *pst* heefkee'a' *etc*; *pres* mafkee'a' *etc*; *fut* yafkee'a' *etc*.

(to) raise questions לעורר שאלות *inf* le-'orer she'elot; *pst* 'orer *etc*; *pres* me'orer *etc*; *fut* ye'orer *etc*.

(to) raise voice להרים קול *inf* le-hareem kol; *pst* hereem kol; *pres* mereem kol; *fut* yareem kol.

raised *adj* **1.** מורם moor|am/-emet; **2.** מובלט moovl|at/-etet.

raisin צימוק *nm* tseemook/-eem (*pl+of:* -ey).

rake 1. מגרפה (tool) *nf* magref|ah/-ot (*+of:* -at); **2.** הולל (debauched man) *nm* holel/-eem (*pl+of:* -ey).

rally 1. כינוס *nm* keenoos/-eem (*pl+of:* -ey); **2.** התקבצות (assembly) *nf* heetkabtsoo|t/-yot.

(to) rally 1. לכנס *inf* lekhanes; *pst* keenes *(k=kh)*; *pres* mekhanes; *fut* yekhanes. **2.** להזעיק (summon) *inf* lehaz'eek; *pst* heez'eek; *pres* maz'eek; *fut* yaz'eek.

ram איל *nm* ayeel/eyleem (*+of:* eyl/-ey).

(to) ram לנגח *inf* lenage'akh; *pst* neege'akh; *pres* menage'akh; *fut* yenage'akh.

ramble שוטטות *nf* shotetoo|t/-yot.

(to) ramble לשוטט *inf* leshotet; *pst* shotet; *pres* meshotet; *fut* yeshotet.

ramification הסתעפות *nf* heesta'afoot/-yot.

ramified מסועף *adj* meso|'af/-'efet.

(to) ramify להסתעף *inf* leheesta'ef; *pst* heesta'ef; *pres* meesta'ef; *fut* yeesta'ef.

ramp 1. כבש (gangplank) *nm* keves; **2.** רמפה (slope) *[colloq.] nf* ramp|ah/-ot.

(to) ramp לזנק *inf* lezanek; *pst* zeenek; *pres* mezanek; *fut* yezanek.

rampage השתוללות *nf* heeshtoleloot/-yot.

rampant 1. פרוע *adj* paroo'a'/proo'ah; **2.** ללא מעצור (unchecked) *adv* le-lo ma'atsor.

rampart סוללה *nf* solel|ah/-ot (*+of:* -at).

ramshackle 1. רעוע *adj* ra'oo'a'/re'oo'ah; **2.** נוטה ליפול (decrepit) *adj* not|eh/-ah leepol.

ranch חווה *nf* khav|ah/-ot (*+of:* -at).

rancor 1. איבה *nf* eyv|ah/-ot (*+of:* -at); **2.** שנאה (hate) *nf* seen|'ah/-'ot (*+of:* -'at).

random מקרי *adj* meekree/-t.

(at) random 1. במקרה *adv* be-meekreh; **2.** באקראי (by chance) *adv* be-akray.

range 1. טווח *nm* tvakh/-eem (*pl+of:* -ey); **2.** שורה (line) *nf* shoor|ah/-ot (*+of:* -at).

(long) range 1. ארוך־טווח *adj* arokh/arookat tvakh; **2.** לטווח ארוך *adv* lee-tvakh arokh.

(short) range 1. קצר־טווח *adj* ketsar/keetsrat tvakh; **2.** לטווח קצר *adv* lee-tvakh katsar.

(to) range 1. להתייצב *inf* leheetyatsev; *pst* heetyatsev; *pres* meetyatsev; *fut* yeetyatsev; **2.** להימנות עם (count among) *inf* leheemanot 'eem; *pst* neemnah *etc*; *pres* neemneh *etc*; *fut* yeemaneh *etc*.

range finder מד־מרחק *nm* mad/-ey merkhak.

rank דרגה *nf* dargah/dragot (*+of:* darg|at/-ot).

(to) rank להימנות עם *inf* leheemanot 'eem; *pst* neemnah *etc*; *pres* neemneh *etc*; *fut* yeemaneh *etc*.

(to) ransack 1. לחטט (search thoroughly) *inf* lekhatet; *pst* kheetet; *pres* mekhatet; *fut* yekhatet; **2.** לבוז (pillage) *inf* lavoz; *pst* bazaz *(b=v)*; *pres* bozez; *fut* yavoz; **3.** לשדוד (rob) *inf* leeshdod; *pst* shadad; *pres* shoded; *fut* yeeshdod.

ransom 1. כופר *nm* kofer; **2.** כופר־נפש (ransom per soul) *nm* kofer-nefesh.

(to) rant להתפרץ *inf* leheetparets; *pst* heetparets; *pres* meetparets; *fut* yeetparets.

(to) rap לבקר בחריפות *inf* levaker ba-khareefoot; *pst* beeker *(b=v) etc*; *pres* mevaker *etc*; *fut* yevaker *etc*.

rapacious חמסני *adj* khamsanee/-t.

(statutory) rape בעילת קטינה *nm* be'eelat keteenah.

rapid מהיר *adj* maheer/meheerah.

rapidity 1. מהירות (speed) *nf* meheeroo|t/-yot; **2.** שטף (fluency) *nm* shetef.

rapier סיף *nm* sayeef.

rapist אנס *nm* anas/-eem (*pl+of:* -ey).

rapt נלהב *adj* neel|hav/-hevet.

rapture 1. התפעלות *nf* heetpa'aloot; **2.** התלהבות (enthusiasm) *nf* heetlahavoot.

rare נדיר *adj* nadeer/nedeerah.

rarely לעיתים רחוקות *adv* le-'eeteem rekhokot.

rarity 1. נדירות (scarcity) *nf* nedeeroo|t/-yot; **2.** משהו נדיר (something rare) *nm* mashehoo nadeer.

rascal נבל *nm* naval/nevaleem.

rash 1. פריחה (skin) *nf* preekh|ah/-ot (*+of:* -at); **2.** בהול (hasty) *adj* bahool/behoolah; **3.** חפוז (rushed) *adj* khafooz/-ah.

rashness פזיזות *nf* pezeezoo|t/-yot.

rasp גירוד *nm* gerood/-eem (*pl+of:* -ey).

raspberry פטל *nm* petel.

rat חולדה *nf* khoold|ah/-ot (*+of:* -at).

rate 1. שיעור she'oor/-eem (*pl+of:* -ey); **2.** קצב (rhythm) *nm* kets|ev/-aveem (*pl+of:* keetsbey; *b=v*); **3.** שער (price) *nm* sha'ar/she'areem (*pl+of:* sha'arey).

(to) rate להיחשב *inf* lehekhashev; *pst & pres* nekhshav; *fut* yekhashev.

rate of exchange שער־חליפין *nm* sha'ar/-ey khaleefeen.

rather 1. במידת־מה (to some extent) *adv* be-meedat mah; **2.** אל נכון (probably) *adv* el nakhon.

ratification אישרור *nm* eeshroor/-eem.

(to) ratify לאשרר *inf* le'ashrer; *pst* eeshrer; *pres* me'ashrer; *fut* ye'ashrer.

rating 1. סיווג *nm* seevoog/-eem (*pl+of:* -ey); **2.** דירוג (grading) *nm* deroog/-eem (*pl+of:* -ey).

ratio יחס *nm* yakhas/yekhaseem (*pl+of:* -ey).

ration מנה קצובה *nf* man|ah/-ot ketsoov|ah/-ot.

rational 1. רציונלי *adj* ratsyonalee/t; **2.** הגיוני (logical) *adj* hegyonee/-t.

rationale טעם *nm* ta'am/te'ameem (*pl+of:* ta'amey).

(to) rationalize לחשב בצורה הגיונית *inf* lekhashev be-tsoorah hegyoneet; *pst* kheeshev *etc*; *pres* mekhashev *etc*; *fut* yekhashev *etc*.

rattle שקשוק *nm* sheekshook/-eem (*pl+of:* -ey).

(to) rattle 1. לשקשק *inf* leshakshek; *pst* sheekshek; *pres* meshakshek; *fut* yeshakshek; **2.** לקשקש (prattle) *inf* lekashkesh; *pst* keeshkesh; *pres* mekashkesh; *fut* yekashkesh.

rattlesnake נחש נקישה *nm* nekhash/nakhshey nekeeshah.

raucous צרוד *adj* tsarood/tseroodah.

(to) rave 1. התלהב *inf* leheetlahev; *pst* heetlahev; *pres* meetlahev; *fut* yeetlahev; **2.** להשתולל (rage) *inf* leheeshtolel; *pst* heeshtolel; *pres* meeshtolel; *fut* yeeshtolel.

raven עורב שחור *nm* 'or|ev/-veem shakhor/ shekhoreem.

ravenous רעב מאוד *adj* ra'ev/re'evah me'od.

ravine גיא *nm* gay/ge'ayot.

(to) ravish 1. לחטוף (food, pleasure) *inf* lakhtof; *pst* khataf; *pres* khotef; *fut* yakhtof; **2.** לזלול (devour) *inf* leezlol; *pst* zalal; *pres* zolel; *fut* yeezlol; **3.** לאנוס (rape) le'enos; past anas; *pres* ones; *fut* ye'enos.

ravishing מקסים *adj* makseem/-ah.

raw 1. גולמי *adj* golmee/-t; **2.** בוסר (not ripe) *adj* boser; **3.** גס (crude) *adj* gas/-ah; **4.** בלתי מבושל־ (not cooked) *adj* beeltee mevoosh|al/elet.

raw material חומר־גלם *nm* khom|er/-rey gelem.

ray קרן *nf* keren/karn|ayeem (*pl+of:* -ey).

ray of hope שביב של תקווה *nm* shveev/-eem shel teekvah.

rayon זהורית *nf* zehoreet.

(to) raze להרוס כליל *inf* laharos kaleel; *pst* haras *etc; pres* hores *etc; fut* yaharos *etc.*

razor 1. תער *nm* ta'ar/te'areem (*pl+of:* ta'arey); **2.** מכשיר גילוח (safety razor) *nm* makhsheer/ -ey geeloo'akh.

(electric) razor מכונת־גילוח חשמלית *nf* mekho-n|at/-ot geeloo'akh khashmalee|t/-yot.

razor blade סכין־גילוח *nm* sakeen/-ey geeloo'akh.

reach תחום השגה *nm* tekhoom hasagah.

(to) reach להשיג *inf* lehaseeg; *pst* heeseeg; *pres* maseeg; *fut* yaseeg.

(within) reach בתחום השגה *adv* bee-t'khoom hasagah.

(to) react להגיב *inf* lehageev; *pst* hegeev; *pres* megeev; *fut* yageev.

reaction תגובה *nf* tegoov|ah/-ot (*+of:* -at).

(to) read 1. לקרוא *vt inf* leekro; *pst* kara; *pres* kore; *fut* yeekra; **2.** להיקרא (be read) *vi inf* leheekare; *pst & pres* neekra; *fut* yeekare.

readable קריא *adj* karee/kree'ah.

reader 1. קורא *nm* kor|e/-'eem (*pl+of:* -'ey); **2.** מרצה (lecturer) *nmf* marts|eh/-ah (*pl:* -eem/-ot).

readership ציבור קוראים *nm* tseeboor kor|'eem/ -'ot.

readily 1. ברצון *adv* be-ratson; **2.** בקלות (easily) *adv* be-kaloot.

readiness נכונות *nf* nekhonoot.

reading 1. קריאה *nf* kree|'ah/-'ot (*+of:* -'at); **2.** גירסה (version) *nf* geers|ah/-ot (*+of:* -at).

ready מוכן *adj* mookhan/-ah.

real ממשי *adj* mamashee/-t.

real estate 1. מקרקעין *nm pl* mekarke'een; **2.** נכסי דלא ניידי (immovables) *nm pl* neekhsey de-lo naydee.

realism 1. חוש מציאות *nm* khoosh-metsee'oot; **2.** ריאליזם *nm* realeezm.

realist ריאליסט *nmf* realeest/-eet (*pl:* -eem/-eeyot).

reality מציאות *nf* metsee'oot.

realization 1. הגשמה *nf* hagsham|ah/-ot (*+of:* -at); **2.** מימוש *nm* meemoosh/-eem (*pl+of:* -ey).

(to) realize 1. להבין *inf* lehaveen; *pst* heveen; *pres* meveen; *fut* yaveen; **2.** להבחין (detect) *inf* le-havkheen; *pst* heevkheen; *pres* mavkheen; *fut* yavkheen; **3.** לממש (reap) *inf* lemamesh; *pst* meemesh; *pres* memamesh; *fut* yemamesh; **4.** להגשים (accomplish) *inf* lehagsheem; *pst* heegsheem; *pres* magsheem; *fut* yagsheem.

really 1. באמת *adv* be emet; **2.** בעצם (actually) *adv* be-'etsem.

realm 1. תחום *nm* t'khoom/-eem (*pl+of:* -ey); **2.** ממלכה (kingdom) *nf* maml|akhah/-akhot (*+of:* -ekhet/-ekhot).

realtor סוחר מקרקעין *nm* sokh|er/-arey mekarke'een.

(to) reap 1. לקצור *inf* leektsor; *pst* katsar; *pres* kotser; *fut* yeektsor. **2.** לאסוף (collect) *inf* le'esof; *pst* asaf; *pres* osef; *fut* ye'esof.

(to) reappear להופיע שוב *inf* lehofee'a' shoov; *pst* hofee'a' *etc; pres* mofee'a' *etc; fut* yofee'a' *etc.*

rear 1. עורף *nm* 'oref; **2.** עורפי *adj* 'orpee/-t; **3.** מאסף (rearguard) *nm* me'as|ef/-feem (*pl+of:* -fey); **4.** אחור *nm* akhor.

(to) rear לגדל *inf* legadel; *pst* geedel; *pres* megadel; *fut* yegadel.

rear-drive הינע אחורי *nm* hene'a' akhoree.

rearmament 1. חימוש *nm* kheemoosh; **2.** התחמשות *nf* (re-arming) *nf* heetkhamshoot.

reason 1. סיבה *nf* seeb|ah/-ot (*+of:* -at); **2.** היגיון (logic) *nm* heegayon (*+of:* hegyon).

(to) reason 1. לנמק (show cause) *inf* lenamek; *pst* neemek; *pres* menamek; *fut* yenamek; **2.** הסיק (conclude) *inf* lehaseek; *pst* heeseek; *pres* maseek; *fut* yaseek.

(with) reason בצדק *adv* be-tsedek.

(within) reason בגבול המתקבל על הדעת *adv* bee-gvool ha-meetkabel 'al ha-da'at.

(by) reason of 1. בגלל beeglal; **2.** בשל (on account of) be-shel.

reasonable 1. הגיוני *adj* hegyonee/-t; **2.** מתקבל על הדעת (stands to reason) *adj* meetkabel/-et 'al ha-da'at; **3.** זול (cheap) zol/-ah.

reasoning הנמקה *nf* hanmak|ah/-ot (*+of:* -at).

(to) reassure לעודד *inf* le'oded; *pst* 'oded; *pres* me'oded; *fut* ye'oded.

rebate הנחה *nf* hanakh|ah/-ot (*+of:* -at).

Rebbe(head of Chassidic sect) רבי rabee/ rabeeyeem.

rebel 1. מורד *nmf* mored/-et (*pl:* mord|eem/-ot); **2.** מרדן (mutineer) *adj* mardan/-eet.

(to) rebel 1. להתמרד (revolt) *inf* leheetmared; *pst* heetmared; *pres* meetmared; *fut* yeetmared; **2.** להתקומם (rise against) *inf* leheetkomem; *pst* heetkomem; *pres* meetkomem; *fut* yeetkomem.

rebellion 1. מרידה *nf* mereed|ah/-ot (*+of:* -at); **2.** התקוממות (uprising) *nf* heetkomemoo|t/-yot.

rebellious מרדני *adj* mardanee/-t.

rebuff סירוב *nm* seroov/-eem (*pl+of:* -ey).

(to) rebuff לדחות *inf* leedkhot; *pst* dakhah; *pres* dokheh; *fut* yeedkheh.

rebuke נזיפה *nf* nezeef|ah/-ot (*+of:* -at).

(to) rebuke לנזוף *inf* leenzof; *pst* nazaf; *pres* nozef; *fut* yeenzof.

recall 1. ביטול (cancellation) *nm* beetool/-eem (*pl+of:* -ey); **2.** קריאה בחזרה (call to return) *nf* kree'ah ba-khazarah.

(to) recall 1. להיזכר (remember) *inf* leheezakher; *pst & pres* neezkar *(k=kh)*; *fut* yeezakher; **2.** להחזיר (call back) *inf* lehakhzeer; *pst* hekhzeer; *pres* makhzeer; *fut* yakhzeer; **3.** לבטל (cancel) *inf* levatel; *pst* beetel *(b=v)*; *pres* mevatel; *fut* yevatel.

(to) recant לחזור בו *inf* lakhzor bo; *pst* khazar bo; *pres* khozer bo; *fut* yakhzor bo.

(to) recapitulate לסכם *inf* lesakem; *pst* seekem; *pres* mesakem; *fut* yesakem.

(to) recede לסגת *inf* laseget; *pst & pres* nasog; *fut* yeesog.

receipt 1. קבלה *nf* kabal|ah/-ot (*+of:* -at); **2.** תקבול (intake) *nm* takbool/-eem (*pl+of:* -ey).

(to) receive לקבל *inf* lekabel; *pst* keebel; *pres* mekabel; *fut* yekabel.

receiver 1. כונס נכסים (law) *nm* kon|es/-sey nekhaseem; **2.** קונה סחורה גנובה (buyer of stolen goods) *nm* koneh sekhorah gnoovah; **3.** מקלט (radio, TV) *nm* maklet/-eem (*pl+of:* -ey); **4.** שפופרת (telephone) *nf* shfof|eret/-arot.

recent 1. חדש *adj* khadash/-ah; **2.** מקרוב בא (lately arrived) *adj* mee-karov ba'/ba'ah.

recently 1. לאחרונה *adv* la-akhronah; **2.** מקרוב (lately) *adj* mee-karov.

receptacle בית קיבול *nm* bet/batey keebool;

reception 1. קבלת פנים (welcoming) *nf* kabal|at/-ot paneem; **2.** קבלת אורחים (hosting) *nf* kabal|at/-ot orkheem.

receptionist פקיד קבלה *nmf* pekeed/-at kabalah.

recess 1. הפסקה (interruption) *nf* hafsak|ah/-ot (*+of:* -at); **2.** פגרה (parliament, court) *nf* pagr|ah/-ot (*+of:* -at); **3.** גומחה (niche) *nf* goomkh|ah/-ot (*+of:* -at).

recipe 1. מתכון *nm* matkon/-eem (*pl+of:* -ey); **2.** מרשם (formula) *nm* meersh|am/-ameem (*pl+of:* -emey).

recipient מקבל *nm* mekab|el/-elet.

reciprocal הדדי *adj* hadadee/-t.

(to) reciprocate לגמול *inf* leegmol; *pst* gamal; *pres* gomel; *fut* yeegmol.

reciprocity הדדיות *nf* hadadeeyoot.

recital 1. רסיטל *nm* reseetal/-eem; **2.** דקלום (declamation) *nm* deekloom/-eem (*pl+of:* -ey)

(to) recite לדקלם *inf* ledaklem; *pst* deeklem; *pres* medaklem; *fut* yedaklem.

reckless חסר־מעצורים *adj* khas|ar/-rat ma'atsoreem.

(to) reckon 1. לחשב (calculate) *inf* lekhashev; *pst* kheeshev; *pres* mekhashev; *fut* yekhashev; **2.** לסבור (consider) *inf* leesbor; *pst* savar *(v=b)*; *pres* sover; *fut* yeesbor.

reckoning 1. חישוב *nm* kheeshoov/-eem (*pl+of:* -ey); **2.** התחשבנות *[colloq.]* (settling accounts) *nf* heetkhashbenoo|t/-yot.

(to) reclaim לטייב *inf* letayev; *pst* teeyev; *pres* metayev; *fut* yetayev.

reclamation 1. הכשרה לשימוש *nf* hakhsharah le-sheemoosh; **2.** טיוב (improvement of land) *nm* teeyoov/-eem (*pl+of:* -ey).

(to) recline להישען אחורה *inf* leheesha'en akhorah; *pst & pres* neesh'an *etc*; *fut* yeesha'en *etc.*

recluse מתבודד *nmf* meetboded/-et (*pl:* -eem/-ot).

recognition הכרה *nf* hakar|ah/-ot (*+of:* -at).

(to) recognize 1. להכיר *inf* lehakeer; *pst* heekeer; *pres* makeer; *fut* yakeer; **2.** להודות (admit) *inf* lehodot; *pst* hodah; *pres* modeh; *fut* yodeh.

recoil 1. רתע *nm* reta'; **2.** רתיעה (flinching) *nf* retee|'ah/-'ot (*+of:* -'at).

(to) recoil להירתע *inf* leherata'; *pst & pres* neerta'; *fut* yerata'.

recoilless ללא רתע *adj* le-lo reta'.

recoilless gun תותח לא־רתע *nm* tot|akh/-khey lo-reta'.

(to) recollect להיזכר *inf* leheezakher; *pst & pres* neezkar *(k=kh)*; *fut* yeezakher.

recollection 1. זכר *nm* zekher; **2.** זיכרון *nm* zeekaron/zeekhronot (*kh=k; +of:* zeekhron).

(to)recommend להמליץ *inf* lehamleets; *pst* heemleets; *pres* mamleets; *fut* yamleets.

recommendation המלצה *nf* hamlats|ah/-ot (*+of:* -at).

(to) recompense לפצות *inf* lefatsot; *pst* peetsah *(p=f)*; *pres* mefatseh; *fut* yefatseh.

(to) reconcile 1. ליישב (settle) *inf* leyashev; *pst* yeeshev; *pres* meyashev; *fut* yeyashev; **2.** לפייס (appease) *inf* lefayes; *pst* peeyes *(p=f)*; *pres* mefayes; *fut* yefayes; **3.** להשלים (make peace) *inf* lehashleem; *pst* heeshleem *etc*; *pres* mashleem *etc*; *fut* yashleem *etc.*

reconciliation התפייסות *nf* heetpaysoo|t/-yot.

reconnaissance סיור *nm* seeyoor/-eem (*pl+of:* -ey).

(to) reconsider לבחון מחדש *inf* leevkhon me-khadash; *pst* bakhan *(b=v) etc*; *pres* bokhen *etc*; *fut* yeevkhan *etc.*

(to) reconstitute 1. לשקם *inf* leshakem; *pst* sheekem; *pres* meshakem; *fut* yeshakem; **2.** להחזיר לקדמותו (restore) *inf* lehakhzeer le-kadmooto; *pst* hekhzeer *etc*; *pres* makhzeer *etc*; *fut* yakhzeer *etc.*

(to) reconstruct 1. לשחזר *inf* leshakhzer; *pst* sheekhzer; *pres* meshakhzer; *fut* yeshakhzer; **2.** לקומם (rebuild) *inf* lekomem; *pst* komem; *pres* mekomem; *fut* yekomem.

reconstruction 1. שחזור *nm* sheekhzoor/-eem (*+of:* -ey); **2.** בנייה מחדש (rebuilding) *nf* beneeyah me-khadash.

record 1. פרטיכל (minutes) *nm* prateykol/-eem; **2.** פרוטוקול *(syn.)* protokol/-eem; **3.** זיכרון דברים (memo) *nm* zeekhron-dvareem.

(gramophone) record תקליט *nm* takleet/-eem (*pl+of:* -ey).

(off the) record שלא לפירסום *adv* she-lo le-feersoom.

(on) record בפומבי *adv* be-foombee *(f=p)*.

(to) record 1. לרשום (in writing) *inf* leershom; *pst* rasham; *pres* roshem; *fut* yeershom; **2.** להקליט (electronically) *inf* lehakleet; *pst* heekleet; *pres* makleet; *fut* yakleet.

record-player 1. מקול *nm* makol/mekol|eem (*pl+of:* -ey); **2.** פטיפון *nm* pate|fon/-foneem.

recorder 1. רשם (registrar) *nm* rasham/-eem (*pl+of:* -ey); **2.** חליל (flute) *nm* khaleel/-eem (*pl+of:* -ey).

(cassette) recorder רשמקול קלטות *nm* reshamkol/-ey kalatot.

(tape) recorder רשמקול סלילים *nm* reshamkol/-ey sleeleem;

(video) recorder וידיאו רקורדר *nm* veedyo rekorder/-eem.

recount ספירה חוזרת *nf* sfeer|ah/-ot khoz|eret/-rot.

(to) recoup 1. לקבל חזרה *inf* lekabel khazarah; *pst* keebel *etc*; *pres* mekabel *etc*; *fut* yekabel *etc*; **2.** לפצות (compensate) *inf* lefatsot; *pst* peetsah (*p=f*); *pres* mefatseh; *fut* yefatseh.

recourse סעד *nm* sa'ad.

(to) recover (goods,rights) לקבל חזרה *inf* lekabel khazarah; *pst* keebel *etc*; *pres* mekabel *etc*; *fut* yekabel *etc*;

(to) recover (health) להתאושש *v rfl inf* leheet'oshesh; *pst* heet'oshesh; *pres* meet'oshesh; *fut* yeet'oshesh.

recovery 1. החלמה *nf* hakhlam|ah (*+of:* -at); **2.** התאוששות (pulling oneself together) *nf* heet'oshesh oo|t/-yot.

(to) recreate ליצור מחדש *inf* leetsor me-khadash; *pst* yatsar *etc*; *pres* yotser *etc*; *fut* yeetsor *etc*.

recreation נופש *nm* nofesh.

recruit 1. מגויס (draftee) *nmf* megoo|yas/-yeset; **2.** טירון (novice) *nmf* teeron/-eet.

(to) recruit לגייס *inf* legayes; *pst* geeyes; *pres* megayes; *fut* yegayes.

rectangle מלבן *nm* malben/-eem.

rectifier (electr.) מיישר־זרם *nm* meyash|er/-rey zerem.

(to) rectify ליישר *inf* leyasher; *pst* yeesher; *pres* meyasher; *fut* yeyasher.

rectitude יושר *nm* yosher.

rector רקטור *nm* rektor/-eem.

rectum 1. פי הטבעת *nm* pee ha-taba'at; **2.** תחת (vulg.) *nm* takhat.

(to) recuperate להחלים *inf* lehakhleem; *pst* hekhleem; *pres* makhleem; *fut* yakhleem.

(to) recur להישנות *inf* leheeshanot; *pst* neeshnah; *pres* neeshneh; *fut* yeeshaneh.

recurrence הישנות *nf* heeshanoo|t/-yot.

recurrent חוזר ונשנה *adj* khozer/-et ve-neeshn|eh/-et.

(to) recycle למחזר *inf* lemakhzer; *pst* meekhzer; *pres* memakhzer; *fut* yemakhzer.

red אדום *adj* adom/adoomah.

Red Sea ים־סוף *nm* yam-soof

(to) redden 1. להאדים *inf* leha'adeem; *pst* he'edeem; *pres* ma'adeem; *fut* ya'adeem; **2.** להסמיק (blush) *inf* lehasmeek; *pst* heesmeek; *pres* masmeek; *fut* yasmeek

reddish אדמדם *adj* adamd|am/-emet.

(to) redeem 1. לגאול *inf* leeg'ol; *pst* ga'al; *pres* go'el; *fut* yeeg'al; **2.** לפדות (ransom) *inf* leefdot; *pst* padah (*f=p*); *pres* podeh; *fut* yeefdeh.

redeemer 1. גואל *nm* go'|el/-aleem (*pl+of:* -aley); **2.** פודה ומציל (savior) *nm* podeh oo-matseel.

redemption גאולה *nf* ge'ool|ah (*+of:* -at).

redhead ג׳ינג׳ית *[colloq.] nmf* jeenjee/-t (*pl:* -m/-yot).

redness 1. אודם *nm* odem; **2.** אדמומיות (blush) *nf* admoomeeyoot.

(to) redouble להכפיל *inf* lehakhpeel; *pst* heekhpeel; *pres* makhpeel; *fut* yakhpeel.

redoubt מעוז *nm* ma'oz/ma'ooz|eem (*pl+of:* -ey).

redress פיצוי *nm* peetsooy/-eem (*pl+of:* -ey).

(to) redress 1. לפצות (compensate) *inf* lefatsot; *pst* peetsah (*p=f*); *pres* mefatseh; *fut* yefatseh; **2.** לתקן מעוות (make good) *inf* letaken me'oovat; *pst* teeken *etc*; *pres* metaken *etc*; *fut* yetaken *etc*.

redskin 1. אדום־עור *nm* adom/adoomey 'or; **2.** אינדיאני *nmf* eendyanee/-t.

(to) reduce 1. לצמצם *inf* letsamtsem; *pst* tseemtsem; *pres* metsamtsem; *fut* yetsamtsem; **2.** לרזות (slim) *inf* leerzot; *pst* razah; *pres* marzeh; *fut* yarzeh.

reduced 1. מוקטן (in size) *adj* mookt|an/-enet; **2.** מוזל (in price) *adj* mooz|al/-elet.

reducing exercises תרגילי הרזיה *nm pl* targeeley harzayah.

reduction 1. צמצום *nm* tseemtsoom/-eem (*pl+of:* -ey); **2.** הנחה (rebate) *nf* hanakh|ah/-ot (*+of:* -at).

redundent 1. עודף *adj* 'odef/-et; **2.** מיותר (superfluous) *adj* meyoot|ar/-eret.

reed 1. קנה *nm* kan|eh/-eem (*pl+of:* keney); **2.** סוף *nm* soof.

reef שונית *nf* shoonee|t/-yot.

(to) reek להסריח *inf* lehasree'akh; *pst* heesree'akh; *pres* masree'akh; *fut* yasree'akh.

reel 1. גלגל *nm* galgal/-eem (*pl+of:* -ey); **2.** סליל (spool) *nm* sleel/-eem (*pl+of:* -ey).

reel of film סליל צילום *nm* sleel/-ey tseeloom.

(to) re-elect לבחור מחדש *inf* leevkhor me-khadash; *pst* bakhar *etc*; *pres* bokher (*b=v*) *etc*; *fut* yeevkhar *etc*.

re-election בחירה מחדש *nf* bekheer|ah/-ot me-khadash.

re-entry כניסה מחדש *nf* keneesah me-khadash.

(to) re-establish לכונן מחדש *inf* lekhonen me-khadash; *pst* konen *etc* (*k=kh*); *pres* mekhonen *etc*; *fut* yekhonen *etc*.

(to) refer 1. להתייחס *inf* leheetyakhes; *pst* heetyakhes; *pres* meetyakhes; *fut* yeetyakhes; **2.** להעביר (transfer) *inf* leha'aveer; *pst* he'eveer; *pres* ma'aveer; *fut* ya'aveer.

referee 1. שופט *nm* shof|et/-teem (*pl+of:* -tey); **2.** בורר *nm* borer/-eem (*pl+of:* -ey).

reference 1. אסמכתה (authority) *nf* asmakht|ah/-a'ot (*+of:* -at); **2.** הסתמכות *nf* heestamkhoo|t/-yot.

(letter of) reference מכתב הסתמכות *nm* meekht|av/-evey heestamkhoot.

reference-book 1. ספר־יעץ (advisory) *nm* sefer/seefrey ya'ats; **2.** ספר מידע (informative) *nm* sefer/seefrey meyda'.

(with) reference to אשר ל־ asher le-

refill מילוי *nm* meelooy/-eem (*pl+of:* -ey).

(to) refill למלא מחדש *inf* lemale me-khadash; *pst* meele *etc*; *pres* memale *etc*; *fut* yemale *etc*.

(to) refine 1. לזקק (chemicals) *inf* lezakek; *pst* zeekek; *pres* mezakek; *fut* yezakek; **2.** לעדן (perfect) *inf* le'aden; *pst* 'eeden; *pres* me'aden; *fut* ye'aden.
refined 1. מזוקק (chemicals) *adj* mezook|ak/-eket; **2.** מעודן (taste) *adj* me'ood|an/enet.
refinement עידון *nm* 'eedoon/-eem (*pl+of:* -ey).
refinery בית־זיקוק *nm* bet/batey zeekook.
(to) reflect לשקף *inf* leshakef; *pst* sheekef; *pres* meshakef; *fut* yeshakef.
reflection 1. בבואה *nf* baboo|'ah/-'ot (+*of:* -'at); **2.** הרהור (thought) *nm* heerhoor/-eem (*pl+of:* -ey).
(on) reflection לאחר יישוב הדעת *adv* le-akhar yeeshoov ha-da'at.
reflex רפלקס *nm* refleks/-eem.
reform רפורמה *nf* reform|ah/-ot.
reformation תיקון *nm* teekoon/-eem (*pl+of:* -ey).
reformatory מוסד לעבריינים צעירים *nm* mosad/-ot le-'avaryaneem tse'eereem.
reformer רפורמטור *nm* reformat|or/-eem.
refraction השתברות *nf* heeshtabroo|t/-yot.
refractory עיקש *adj* 'eekesh/-et.
(to) refrain להימנע *inf* leheemana'; *pst & pres* neemna'; *fut* yeemana'.
(to) refresh לרענן *inf* lera'anen; *pst* ree'anen; *pres* mera'anen; *fut* yera'anen.
refreshing מרענן *adj* mera'anen/-et.
refreshment משקה מרענן *nm* mashk|eh/-a'ot mera'anen/-eem.
refrigeration קירור *nm* keroor.
refrigerator מקרר *nm* mekarer/-eem (*pl+of:* -ey).
refuge מפלט *nm* meefl|at/-ateem (*pl+of:* -etey).
refugee פליט *nmf* paleet/pleetah (*pl:* pleet|eem/-ot).
(to) refund לקבל החזר *inf* lekabel hekhzer; *pst* keebel *etc*; *pres* mekabel *etc*; *fut* yekabel *etc*.
(to) refurbish לחדש *inf* lekhadesh; *pst* kheedesh; *pres* mekhadesh; *fut* yekhadesh.
refusal סירוב *nm* seroov/-eem (*pl+of:* -ey).
refuse פסולת *nf* pesolet.
(to) refuse לסרב *inf* lesarev; *pst* serav; *pres* mesarev; *fut* yesarev.
(to) refute 1. להפריך *inf* lehafreekh; *pst* heefreekh; *pres* mafreekh; *fut* yafreekh; **2.** להזם (contradict) *inf* lehazem; *pst* hezem; *pres* mezem; *fut* yazem.
(to) regain 1. לחזור ל־ (come back to) *inf* lakhzor le-; *pst* khazar le-; *pres* khozer le-; *fut* yakhazor le-; **2.** למצוא שוב (once more find) *inf* leemtso shoov; *pst* matsa *etc*; *pres* motse *etc*; *fut* yeemtsa *etc*.
regard 1. שימת־לב *nf* seemat-lev; **2.** התחשבות *nf* heetkhashvoo|t/-yot.
(to) regard להחשיב *inf* lehakhsheev; *pst* hekhsheev; *pres* makhsheev; *fut* yakhsheev.
(with) regard to אשר ל־ *conj* asher le-.
regarding בנוגע ל־ *conj* be-noge'a' le-.
regardless מבלי להתחשב *adv* meevlee (*v=b*) leheetkhashev.
regards 1. דרישת שלום *nf* dreesh|at/-ot shalom; **2.** ד״ש (*acr of* 1) *nm* dash/-eem.
(as) regards בכל הנוגע ל־ be-khol ha-noge'a' le-
regent עוצר *nm* 'ots|er/-reem (*pl+of:* -rey).
regime משטר *nm* meesht|ar/-areem (*pl+of:* -erey).
regiment גדוד *nm* gedood/-eem (*pl+of:* -ey).
region אזור *nm* eyzor/azor|eem (*pl+of:* -ey).
regional אזורי *adj* eyzoree/-t.
register 1. פנקס הרשמה *nm* peeenk|as/-esey harshamah; **2.** משלב (music) meeshl|av/-aveem (*pl+of:* -evey).
registrar רשם *nm* rasham/-eem (*pl+of:* -ey).
registration הרשמה *nf* harsham|ah/-ot (+*of:* -at).
regret 1. צער tsa'ar; **2.** חרטה (repentance) *nf* kharat|ah/-ot (+*of:* -at).
(to) regret 1. להצטער (be sorry) *inf* leheets'ta'er; *pst* heets'ta'er; *pres* meets'ta'er; *fut* yeets'ta'er; **2.** להתחרט (repent) *inf* leheetkharet; *pst* heetkharet; *pres* meetkharet; *fut* yeetkharet.
regretful, regrettable מצער *adj* metsa'er/-et.
regular 1. סדיר *adj* sadeer/sedeerah; **2.** רגיל (standard) *adj* rageel/regeelah; **3.** קבוע (permanent) *adj* kavoo'a'/kvoo'ah.
regularity 1. סדירות *nf* sdeeroo|t/-yot **2.** קביעות (permanence) *adj* kvee'oo|t/-yot.
(to) regulate 1. להסדיר *inf* lehasdeer; *pres* heesdeer; *pres* masdeer; *fut* yasdeer; **2.** לכוון (attune) *inf* lekhaven; *pres* keeven (*k=kh*); *pres* mekhaven; *fut* yekhaven.
regulation 1. ויסות *nf* veesoot/-eem (*pl+of:* ey) **2.** תקנה (by-law) *nf* takan|ah/-ot (+*of:* -at).
regulator וסת *nf* vasat/-eem (*pl+of:* -ey).
(to) rehabilitate לשקם *inf* leshakem; *pst* sheekem; *pres* meshakem; *fut* yeshakem.
rehearsal חזרה *nf* khazar|ah/-ot (+*of:* -at).
reign ממלכת *nf* maml|akhah/-akhot (+*of:* -lekhet).
(to) reimburse להחזיר הוצאות *inf* lehakhzeer hotsa'ot; *pst* hekhzeer *etc*; *pres* makhzeer *etc*; *fut* yakhzeer *etc*.
reimbursement החזר *nm* hekhzer/-eem (*pl+of:* -ey).
rein מושכה *nf* moshkh|ah/-ot (+*of:* -at).
(to) reincarnate לגלם *inf* legalem; *pst* geelem; *pres* megalem; *fut* yegalem.
reincarnation 1. התגלמות *nf* heetgalmoot|t/-yot **2.** גלגול חדש (metamorphosis) *nm* geelgool/-eem khadash/-eem.
reindeer אייל *nm* ayal/-eem (*pl+of:* ayley).
(to) reinforce לתגבר *inf* letagber; *pst* teegber; *pres* metagber; *fut* yetagber.
reinforcement תגבורת *nf* teegbor|et/-ot.
(to) reiterate להדגיש שוב ושוב *inf* lehadgeesh shoov va-shoov; *pst* heedgeesh *etc*; *pres* madgeesh *etc*; *fut* yadgeesh *etc*.
(to) reject לדחות *inf* leedkhot; *pst* dakhah; *pres* dokheh; *fut* yeedkheh.
(to) rejoice לשמוח *inf* leesmo'akh; *pst* samakh; *pres* same'akh; *fut* yeesmakh.
rejoicing שמחה *nf* seemkhah/smakhot (+*of:* seemkhat).
(to) rejoin להצטרף מחדש *inf* leheetstaref me-khadash; *pst* heetstaref *etc*; *pres* meetstaref *etc*; *fut* yeetstaref *etc*.
(to) rejuvenate לחדש נעורים *inf* lekhadesh ne'ooreem; *pres* kheedesh *etc*; *pres* mekhadesh *etc*; *fut* yekhadesh *etc*.
relapse הישנות *nf* heeshanoo|t/-yot.

(to) relate 1. לייחס *inf* leyakhes; *pres* yeekhes; *pres* meyakhes; *fut* yeyakhes; **2.** לספר *inf* lesaper; *pres* seeper; *pres* mesaper; *fut* yesaper.

related 1. קרוב משפחה *nmf* krov/-at meeshpakhah (*pl:* -ey/-ot *etc*); **2.** מיוחס (attributed) *adj* meyoookh|as/-eset.

related by marriage מחותן *nm* mekhootan/-eem (*pl+of:* -ey).

relation 1. יחס *nm* yakhas/yekhaseem (*pl+of:* yakhsey); **2.** קשר (connection) *nm* kesh|er/-areem (*pl+of:* keeshrey).

(with) relation to בקשר ל־ *adv* be-kesher le-.

relationship 1. יחס (attitude) *nm* yakhas/ yekhaseem (*pl+of:* yakhsey); **2.** קרבה (family ties) *nf* keerv|ah/-ot **3.** שייכות (connection) *nf* sha-ykhoo|t/-yot.

relative 1. קרוב משפחה *nmf* krov/-at meeshpakhah (*pl:* -ey/-ot *etc*); **2.** יחסי *adj* yakhasee/-t.

relatively יחסית *adv* yakhseet.

(to) relax 1. להרפות מתח (relieve tension) *inf* leharpot metakh; *pst* heerpah *etc*; *pres* marpeh *etc*; *fut* yarpeh *etc*; **2.** להירגע (calm down) in leheraga'; *pst & pres* neerga'; *fut* yeraga'; **3.** לנוח (rest) *inf* lanoo'akh; *pst & pres* nakh; *fut* yanoo'akh.

relaxation 1. הרפיה *nf* harpa|yah/-yot (*+of:* -yat); **2.** נינוחות *nf* neenokhoot.

relay תמסיר *nm* tamseer/-eem (*pl+of:* -ey).

(electric) relay ממסר *nm* meemsar/-eem (*pl+of:* -ey)

(to) relay להעביר *inf* leha'aveer; *pst* he'eveer; *pres* ma'aveer; *fut* ya'aveer.

(to) release לשחרר *inf* leshakhrer; *pst* sheekhrer; *pres* meshakhrer; *fut* yeshakhrer.

(to) relegate לשלח *inf* leshale'akh; *pst* sheelakh; *pres* meshale'akh; *fut* yeshalakh.

(to) relent להרפות *inf* leharpot; *pst* heerpah; *pres* marpeh; *fut* yarpeh.

relentless ללא רחם *adv* le-lo rakhem.

relevant רלוונטי *adj* relevantee/-t.

reliability מהימנות *nf* mehemanoo|t/-yot.

reliable מהימן *adj* meheym|an/-enet.

reliance אמון *nm* emoon.

(self-)reliance ביטחון עצמי *nm* beetakhon 'atsmee.

relic 1. שריד (remnant) *nm* sareed/sreedeem (*pl+of:* sreedey); **2.** מזכרת (souvenir) *nf* maz-k|eret/-arot.

relief 1. הקלה *nf* hakal|ah/-ot (*+of:* -at); **2.** סעד (to needy) *nm* sa'ad.

(on) relief מקבל סעד *adj* mekabel/-et sa'ad.

(to) relieve 1. לשחרר (free) *inf* leshakhrer; *pst* sheekhrer; *pres* meshakhrer; *fut* yeshakhrer; **2.** להחליף (replace) *inf* lehakhleef; *pst* hekhleef; *pres* makhleef; *fut* yakhleef.

religion דת *nf* dat/-ot.

religious דתי *adj* datee/-yeem.

(to) relinquish לוותר *inf* levater; *pst* veeter; *pres* mevater; *fut* yevater.

relish 1. הנאה *nf* hana|'ah/-'ot (*+of:* -'at); **2.** טעם מיוחד (special taste) *nm* ta'am meyookhad.

(to) relocate לאתר מחדש *inf* le'ater me-khadash; *pst* eeter *etc*; *pres* me'ater *etc*; *fut* ye'ater *etc*.

reluctance אי־רצון *nm* ee-ratson.

reluctant חסר־רצון *adj* khas|ar/-rat ratson.

reluctantly בעל כורחו *adv* be'al korkh|o/-ah.

(to) rely לסמוך *inf* leesmokh; *pst* samakh; *pres* somekh; *fut* yeesmokh.

(to) remain להישאר *inf* leheesha'er; *pst & pres* neesh'ar; *fut* yeesha'er.

remainder שארית *nf* she'eree|t/-yot.

remains שרידים *nm pl* sreed|eem (*+of:* -ey).

remark הערה *nf* he'ar|ah/-ot (*+of:* -at).

(to) remark 1. להעיר *inf* leha'eer; *pst* he'eer; *pres* me'eer; *fut* ya'eer; **2.** להבחין *inf* lehavkheen; *pst* heevkheen; *pres* mavkheen; *fut* yavkheen.

remarkable בולט *adj* bolet/-et.

remarkably בצורה בולטת *adv* be-tsoorah boletet

remedy תרופה *nf* troof|ah/-ot (*+of:* -at).

(to) remedy לתקן מעוות *vt inf* letaken me'oovat; *pst* teeken *etc*; *pres* metaken *etc*; *fut* yetaken *etc*.

(to) remember 1. לזכור *vt inf* leezkor; *pst* zakhar (*kh=k*); *pres* zokher; *fut* yeezkor; **2.** להיזכר (recall) *vi inf* leheezakher; *pst & pres* neezkar (*k=kh*); *fut* yeezakher.

remembrance מזכרת *nf* mazk|eret/-arot.

(to) remind להזכיר *inf* lehazkeer; *pst* heezkeer; *pres* mazkeer; *fut* yazkeer.

reminder תזכורת *nf* teezkor|et/-ot.

reminiscence זכרונות *nm pl* zeekhronot.

remiss רשלני *adj* rashlanee/-t.

remission 1. פטור *nm* p'tor/-eem; **2.** ויתור (concession) *nm* veetoor/-eem.

(to) remit 1. לשלם (pay) *inf* leshalem; *pst* sheelem; *pres* meshalem; *fut* yeshalem; **2.** למסור (hand over) *inf* leemsor; *pst* masar; *pres* moser; *fut* yeemsor.

remittance 1. המחאה *nf* hamkha|'ah/-'ot (*pl+of:* -'at); **2.** העברת כסף (transfer) *nf* ha'avar|at/-ot kesef.

remnant שארית *nf* she'eree|t/-yot.

(to) remodel לעצב מחדש *inf* le'atsev me-khadash; *pst* 'eetsev *etc*; *pres* me'atsev *etc*; *fut* ye'atsev *etc*.

remorse 1. מוסר כליות *nm* moosar klayot; **2.** חרטה (repentance) *nf* kharat|ah/-ot (*+of:* -at).

remote מרוחק *adj* merookh|ak/-eket.

remote control שלט־רחוק *n* shlat-rakhok (*colloq. abbr.:* shlat).

removal סילוק *nm* seelook/-eem (*pl+of:* -ey).

(to) remove 1. לסלק (take away) *inf* lesalek; *pst* seelek; *pres* mesalek; *fut* yesalek; **2.** להסיר (take off) *inf* lehaseer; *pst* heseer; *pres* meseer; *fut* yaseer.

removed מרוחק *adj* merookh|ak/-eket.

(to) remunerate 1. לשלם *inf* leshalem; *pst* sheelem; *pres* meshalem; *fut* yeshalem; **2.** לפצות (compensate) *inf* lefatsot; *pst* peetsah (*p=f*); *pres* mefatseh; *fut* yefatseh.

remuneration 1. שכר (pay) *nm* sakhar (*+of:* sekhar); **2.** גמול (reward) *nm* gemool/-eem (*pl+of:* -ey).

renaissance, renascence תחייה *nf* tekhee|yah/-yot (*+of:* -yat).

(to) rend לקרוע (tear) *inf* leekro'a'; *pst* kara'; *pres* kore'a'; *fut* yeekra'.

(to) render 1. לגרום (cause) *inf* leegrom; *pst* garam; *pres* gorem; *fut* yeegrom; **2.** להפוך (turn) *inf* lahafokh; *pst* hafakh; *pres* hofekh; *fut* yahafokh.

(to) render account 1. למסור דין וחשבון *inf* leemsor deen ve-kheshbon; **2.** למסור דו״ח (*acr of* 1) *inf* leemsor doo'akh/dokhot; *pst* masar *etc; pres* moser *etc; fut* yeemsor *etc.*

(to) render homage לחלוק כבוד *inf* lakhlok kavod; *pst* khalak *etc; pres* kholek *etc; fut* yakhlok *etc.*

render useless לעשות לחסר תועלת *inf* la'asot le-khasar-to'elet; *pst* 'asah *etc; pres* 'oseh *etc; fut* ya'aseh *etc.*

rendition ביצוע *nm* beetsoo|'a/-'eem (*pl+of:* -'ey).

(to) renew לחדש *inf* lekhadesh; *pst* kheedesh; *pres* mekhadesh; *fut* yekhadesh.

renewal חידוש *nm* kheedoosh/-eem (*pl+of:* -ey).

(to) renounce 1. לבטל (cancel) *inf* levatel; *pst* beetel *(b=v)*; *pres* mevatel; *fut* yevatel; **2.** להסתלק מ־ (give up) *inf* leheestalek mee-; *pst* heestalek mee-; *pres* meestalek mee-; *fut* yeestalek mee-.

(to) renovate לשפץ *inf* leshapets; *pst* sheepets; *pres* meshapets; *fut* yeshapets.

renown מוניטין *nm pl* moneeteen.

renowned מפורסם *adj* mefoors|am/-emet.

rent שכירות *nf* sekheeroo|t/-yot.

(controlled) rent שכירות מוגנת *nf* sekheeroot moogenet.

(free) rent שכירות חופשית *nf* sekheeroot khofsheet.

(to) rent לשכור *inf* leeskor; *pst* sakhar *(kh=k)*; *pres* sokher; *fut* yeeskor.

rental דמי־שכירות *nm pl* demey-sekheeroot.

(to) reopen לפתוח מחדש *inf* leefto'akh me-khadash; *pst* patakh *(p=f) etc; pres* pote'akh *etc; fut* yeeftakh.

repair תיקון *nm* teekoon/-eem (*pl+of:* -ey).

(beyond) repair ללא תקנה *adv* le-lo takanah.

(to) repair לתקן *inf* letaken; *pst* teeken; *pres* metaken; *fut* yetaken.

reparation פיצוי *nm* peetsooy/-eem (*pl+of:* -ey).

repartee תשובה ניצחת *nf* teshoovah neetsakhat.

(to) repatriate 1. להחזיר למולדת (bring back to the fatherland, i.e. to Israel) *inf* lehakhzeer le-moledet; *pst* hekhzeer *etc; pres* makhzeer *etc; fut* yakhazeer *etc*; **2.** להעלות (assist in repatriation) *inf* leha'alot; *pst* he'elah; *pres* ma'aleh; *fut* ya'aleh.

repatriate 1. רפטריאנט *nm* repatree'ant/-eem; **2.** תושב חוזר (returning Israeli resident) *nm* toshav/-eem khoz|er/-reem.

(to) repay 1. לגמול (compensate) *inf* leegmol; *pst* gamal; *pres* gomel; *fut* yeegmol; **2.** לשלם בחזרה (pay back) *inf* leshalem ba-khazarah; *pst* sheelem *etc; pres* meshalem *etc; fut* yeshalem *etc.*

repayment 1. גמול *nm* gmool; **2.** החזר תשלום (reimbursement) *nm* hekhzer/-ey tashloom.

repeal 1. ביטול *nm* beetool/-eem (*pl+of:* -ey); **2.** ביטול תוקף (rescinder of validity) *nm* beetool/-ey tokef.

(to) repeal לבטל *inf* levatel; *pst* beetel *(b=v)*; *pres* mevatel; *fut* yevatel.

(to) repeat 1. לחזור על *inf* lakhzor 'al; *pst* khazar 'al; *pres* khozer 'al; *fut* yakhzor 'al; **2.** לשנן *inf* leshanen; *pst* sheenen; *pres* meshanen; *fut* yeshanen.

repeated חוזר *adj* khozer/-et.

repeatedly שוב ושוב *adv* shoov va-shoov.

(to) repel לדחות *inf* leedkhot; *pst* dakhah; *pres* dokheh; *fut* yeedkheh.

repellent 1. דוחה (repulsive) *adj* dokh|eh/-ah; **2.** אטים (airtight, waterproof) *adj* ateem/-ah.

(to) repent 1. להתחרט *inf* leheetkharet; *pst* heetkharet; *pres* meetkharet; *fut* yeetkharet; **2.** לחזור בתשובה (be a penitent) *inf* lakhzor bee-teshoovah; *pst* khazar *etc; pres* khozer *etc; fut* yakhzor *etc.*

repentance חרטה *nf* kharat|ah/-ot (*+of:* -at).

repentant 1. מתחרט *adj & v pres* meetkharet/-et; **2.** חוזר בתשובה (agnostic turned religious) *nmf & adj* khozer/-et bee-teshoovah.

repertoire רפרטואר *nm* repertoo'ar/-eem.

repetition 1. חזרה *nf* khazar|ah/-ot (*+of:* -at); **2.** שינון (memorizing) *nm* sheenoon/-eem (*pl+of:* -ey).

(to) replace להחליף *inf* lehakhleef; *pst* hekhleef; *pres* makhleef; *fut* yakhleef.

replaceable חליפי *adj* khaleefee/-t.

replacement 1. החלפה *nf* hakhlaf|ah/-ot (*+of:* -at); **2.** תחליף (substitute) *nm* takhleef/-eem (*pl+of:* -ey).

(to) replenish להשלים *inf* lehashleem; *pst* heeshleem; *pres* mashleem; *fut* yashleem.

replete גדוש *adj* gadoosh/gedooshah.

replica העתק *nm* he't|ek/-ekeem (*pl+of:* -key).

reply תשובה *nf* teshoov|ah/-ot (*+of:* -at).

(to reply) 1. להשיב *inf* lehasheev; *pst* hesheev; *pres* mesheev; *fut* yasheev; **2.** לענות (answer) *inf* la'anot; *pst* 'anah; *pres* 'oneh; *fut* ya'aneh.

report 1. דיווח (account) *nm* deevoo|'akh/-kheem (*pl+of:* -khey); **2.** דו״ח (*acr of* 1) *nm* doo|'akh/-khot (*cpr* dokh/-ot).

(news) report 1. ידיעה *nf* yedee'|ah/-ot (*+of:* -at); **2.** חדשה (news item) *nf* khadash|ah/-ot (*+of:* -at).

(to) report 1. לדווח (account) *inf* ledave'akh; *pst* deeve'akh; *pres* medave'akh; *fut* yedave'akh; **2.** להתייצב (present oneself) *inf* leheetyatsev; *pst* heetyatsev; *pres* meetyatsev; *fut* yeetyatsev.

reporter 1. רפורטר *nmf* reporter/-eet; **2.** כתב (correspondent) *nmf* kat|av/-evet; **3.** עיתונאי (journalist) *nmf* 'eeton|ay/-a'eet (*pl+of:* -a'ey).

(to) repose 1. לנוח *inf* lanoo'akh; *pst & pres* nakh; *fut* yanoo'akh; **2.** לסמוך (rely for support) *inf* leesmokh; *pst* samakh; *pres* somekh; *fut* yeesmokh.

repository בית קיבול *nm* bet/batey keebool.

(to) represent לייצג *inf* leyatseg; *pst* yeetseg; *pres* meyatseg; *fut* yeyatseg.

representation ייצוג *nm* yeetsoog/-eem (*pl+of:* -ey).

representative 1. נציג *nmf* natseeg/netseegah (*+of:* netseeg/-at; *pl:* -eem/-ot); **2.** בא־כוח (delegate) *nmf* ba/ba'at (*pl:* ba'ey/ba'ot) ko'akh.

(to) repress 1. לדכא (oppress) *inf* ledake; *pst* deeka; *pres* medake; *fut* yedake; **2.** להדחיק (exclude from consciousness) *inf* lehadkheek; *pst* heedkheek; *pres* madkheek; *fut* yadkheek.

repression 1. דיכוי (oppression) *nm* deekoo|y/-yeem (*pl+of:* -yey); **2.** הדחקה (exclusion from consciousness) *nf* hadkhak|ah/-ot (*+of:* -at).

reprieve ארכה *nf* ark|ah/-ot (*+of:* -at).

(to) reprieve 1. לדחות ביצוע עונש (postpone execution of punishment) *inf* leedkhot beetsoo'a' 'onesh; *pst* dakhah *etc; pres* dokheh *etc; fut* yeedkheh *etc;* **2.** להקל זמנית (relieve temporarily) *inf* lehakel zmaneet; *pst* hekel *etc; pres* mekel *etc; fut* yakel *etc.*

reprimand 1. נזיפה *nf* nezeef|ah/-ot (*+of:* -at); **2.** גערה (rebuke) *nf* ge'ar|ah/-ot (*+of:* ga'ar|at/-ot).

(to) reprimand לנזוף ב־ *inf* leenzof be-; *pst* nazaf be-; *pres* nozef be-; *fut* yeenzof be-.

reprint תדפיס *nm* tadpees/-eem (*pl+of:* -ey).

(to) reprint להדפיס מחדש *inf* lehadpees me-khadash; *pst* heedpees *etc; pres* madpees *etc; fut* yadpees *etc.*

reprisal פעולת תגמול *nf* pe'ool|at/-ot tagmool.

reproach 1. גערה *nf* ge'ar|ah/-ot (*+of:* ga'ar|at/-ot); **2.** דופי (blemish) *nm* dofee.

(to) reproach 1. לגעור (rebuke) *inf* leeg'or; *pst* ga'ar; *pres* go'er; *fut* yeeg'ar; **2.** להטיל דופי (blame) *inf* lehateel dofee; *pst* heteel *etc; pres* mateel *etc; fut* yateel *etc;* **3.** לנזוף *inf* leenzof; *pst* nazaf; *pres* nozef; *fut* yeenzof.

(to) reproduce 1. להעתיק (copy) *inf* leha'teek; *pst* he'teek; *pres* ma'teek; *fut* ya'teek; **2.** לשחזר (restore) *inf* leshakhzer; *pst* sheekhzer; *pres* meshakhzer; *fut* yeshakhzer.

reproduction 1. שחזור *nm* sheekhzoor/-eem (*pl+of:* -ey); **2.** רפרודוקציה *nf* reprodookts|yah/-yot (*+of:* -yat).

reproof תוכחה *nf* tokhakh|ah/-ot (*+of:* -at).

(to) reprove 1. לייסר *inf* leyaser; *pst* yeeser; *pres* meyaser; *fut* yeyaser; **2.** להוכיח (moralize) *inf* lehokhee'akh; *pst* hokhee'akh; *pres* mokhee'akh; *fut* yokhee'akh.

reptile 1. שרץ *nm* sherets/shrats|eem (*pl+of:* shertsey); **2.** רמש (worm) *nm* rem|es/-aseem (*pl+of:* reemsey); **3.** זוחל (creeper) *nm* zokh|el/-aleem (*pl+of:* -ley).

republic רפובליקה *nf* repoobleek|ah/-ot (*+of:* -at).

republican רפובליקני *nm & adj* repoobleekanee/-m.

repudiate 1. להכחיש (deny) *inf* lehakh'kheesh; *pst* heekh'kheesh; *pres* makh'kheesh; *fut* yakh'kheesh; **2.** לדחות (reject) *inf* leedkhot; *pst* dakhah; *pres* dokheh; *fut* yeedkheh.

repugnance סלידה *nf* sleed|ah/-ot (*+of:* -at).

repugnant מעורר סלידה *adj* me'orer/-et sleedah.

repulse דחייה *nf* dekhee|yah/-yot (*+of:* -yat).

(to) repulse לדחות בשאט נפש (reject in revulsion) *inf* leedkhot bee-she'at nefesh; *pst* dakhah *etc; pres* dokheh *etc; fut* yeedkheh *etc.*

repulsive מעורר גועל *adj* me'orer/-et go'al.

reputable בעל־שם *adj* ba'al/-at shem.

reputation מוניטין *nm pl* moneeteen.

repute פרסום *nm* peersoom/-eem (*pl+of:* -ey)

reputed אמור *adj* amoor/-ah.

reputedly לפי השמועה *adv* le-fee ha-shmoo'ah.

request בקשה *nf* bakash|ah/-ot (*+of:* -at).

(at the) request לבקשת *adv* le-vakashat *(v=b).*

(to) request 1. לבקש (ask) *inf* levakesh; *pst* beekesh *(b=v); pres* mevakesh; *fut* yevakesh; **2.** לתבוע (demand) *inf* leetbo'a'; *pst* tava' *(v=b); pres* tove'a'; *fut* yeetba'.

(to) require 1. לדרוש (demand) *inf* leedrosh; *pst* darash; *pres* doresh; *fut* yeedrosh; **2.** להצריך (necessitate) *inf* lehatsreekh; *pst* heetsreekh; *pres* matsreekh; *fut* yatsreekh.

requirement 1. צורך *nm* tsorekh/tserakheem (*pl+of:* tsorkey); **2.** דרישה (demand) *nf* dreesh|ah/-ot (*pl+of:* -at).

requisite נחוץ *adj* nakhoots/nekhootsah.

requisition דרישה *nf* dreesh|ah/-ot (*+of:* -at).

(to) rescind לבטל *inf* levatel; *pst* beetel *(b=v); pres* mevatel; *fut* yevatel.

rescue 1. הצלה (salvation) hatsal|ah/-ot (*+of:* -at); **2.** חילוץ (delivery) *nm* kheeloots/-eem (*pl+of:* -ey).

(to) rescue 1. להציל (save) *inf* lehatseel; *pst* heetseel; *pres* matseel; *fut* yatseel; **2.** לחלץ (deliver) *inf* lekhalets; *pst* kheelets; *pres* mekhalets; *fut* yekhalets.

research 1. מחקר *nm* mekh'k|ar/-areem (*pl+of:* -erey); **2.** חקר (search) *nm* kheker/khakareem (*pl+of:* kheekrey).

(to) research לחקור *inf* lakhkor; *pst* khakar; *pres* khoker; *fut* yakhkor.

resemblance דמיון *nm* deemyon/-ot.

(to) resemble לדמות *inf* leedmot; *pst* damah; *pres* domeh; *fut* yeedmeh.

(to) resent להתרעם *inf* leheetra'em; *pres* heetra'em; *pres* meetra'em; *fut* yeetra'em.

resentful שומר טינה *adj* shomer/-et teenah.

resentment תרעומת *nf* tar'om|et/-ot.

reservation 1. הסתייגות (taking exception) *nf* heestaygoo|t/-yot; **2.** איפוק (restraint) *nm* eepook/-eem (*pl+of:* -ey).

reserve 1. עתודה *nf* 'atood|ah/-ot (*+of:* -at); **2.** קרירות (chill) *nf* kreeroo|t/-yot.

(to) reserve 1. לשמור עבור *inf* leeshmor 'avoor; *pst* shamar *etc; pres* shomer *etc; fut* yeeshmor *etc;* **2.** לשים בצד (set aside) *inf* laseem; *pst & pres* sam *etc; fut* yaseem *etc.*

reserves כוחות מילואים (military) *nm pl* kokhot meeloo'eem

reservoir מאגר *nm* ma'agar/-areem (*pl+of:* -rey).

(water) reservoir מיכל מים *nm* meykhal/-ey mayeem.

(to) reside להתגורר *inf* leheetgorer; *pst* heetgorer; *pres* meetgorer; *fut* yeetgorer.

residence 1. מגורים (dwelling) *nm pl* megoor|eem (*pl+of:* -ey); **2.** מעון (home) *nm* ma'on/me'onot (*+of:* me'on).

resident תושב *nmf* tosh|av/-evet (*pl:* -aveem/-vot; *+of:* vey/-vot).

residential של מגורים *adj* shel megooreem.

residue 1. משקע *nm* meeshk|a'/-a'eem (*pl+of:* -e'ey); **2.** שארית (remainder) *nf* she'eree|t/-yot.

(to) resign להתפטר *inf* leheetpater; *pst* heetpater; *pres* meetpater; *fut* yeetpater.

(to) resign oneself to להסתפק ב־ *inf* leheestapek be-; *pst* heestapek be-; meestapek be-; *fut* yeestapek be-.

resignation 1. התפטרות *nf* heetpatroo|t/-yot; **2.** השלמה (giving in) *nf* hashlam|ah/-ot (+*of:* -at).

resilience גמישות *nf* gemeeshoo|t/-yot.

resin שרף *nm* sraf/-eem (*pl+of:* -ey).

(to) resist 1. להתנגד *inf* leheetnaged; *pst* heetnaged; *pres* meetnaged; *fut* yeetnaged; **2.** לעמוד בפני (withstand) *inf* la'amod beefney; *pst* 'amad *etc*; *pres* 'omed *etc*; *fut* ya'amod *etc*.

resistance התנגדות *nf* heetnagdoo|t/-yot.

resistant עמיד *adj* 'ameed/-ah.

resolute נחרץ *adj* nekhr|ats/-etset.

resolution החלטה *nf* hakhlat|ah/-ot (+*of:* -at).

(to) resolve להחליט *inf* lehakhleet; *pst* hekhleet; *pres* makhleet; *fut* yakhleet.

resonance תהודה *nf* tehood|ah/-ot (+*of:* -at).

resonant מהדהד *adj* mehadhed/-et.

resort מקום נופש *nm* mekom/-ot nofesh.

(to) resort לנקוט *inf* leenkot; *pres* nakat; *pres* noket; *fut* yeenkot.

(last) resort אמצעי אחרון *nm* emtsa'ee akharon.

(to) resound להדהד *inf* lehadhed; *pst* heedhed; *pres* mehadhed; *fut* yehadhed.

resource מקור *nm* makor/mekorot (+*of:* mekor).

(natural) resource אוצר טבע *nm* ots|ar/-rot teva'.

resourceful בעל תושייה *adj* ba'al/-at toosheeyah.

resourcefulness תושייה *nf* toosheeyah (+*of:* -yat).

(natural) resources משאבים *nm pl* mash'ab|eem (*pl+of:* -ey).

(to) respect לכבד *inf* lekhabed; *pst* keebed (*k=kh*); *pres* mekhabed; *fut* yekhabed.

(with) respect to אשר ל־ *conj* asher le-.

respectable מהוגן *adj* mehoog|an/-enet.

respecting בעניין be-eenyan.

respectively באותו סדר *adv* be-oto seder.

respiration נשימה *nf* nesheem|ah/-ot (+*of:* -at).

respite הפוגה *nf* hafoog|ah/-ot (+*of:* -at).

resplendent זוהר *adj* zoher/-et.

(to) respond 1. להשיב (reply) *inf* lehasheev; *pst* hesheev; *pres* mesheev; *fut* yasheev; **2.** לענות (answer) *inf* la'anot; *pst* 'anah; *pres* 'oneh; *fut* ya'aneh; **3.** להגיב (react) *inf* lehageev; *pst* hegeev; *pres* megeev; *fut* yageev.

response 1. היענות *nf* he'anoo|t/-yot; **2.** תגובה (reaction) *nf* tgoov|ah/-ot (+*of:* -at).

responsibility אחריות *nf* akhrayoo|t/-yot.

responsible אחראי *adj* akhra|y/-'eet.

responsive 1. נענה *adj & v pres* na'an|eh/-et. **2.** מגיב (reactive) *adj & v pres* megeev/-ah.

rest 1. מנוחה *nf* menookh|ah/-ot (+*of:* -at); **2.** שאר (remainder) *nm* she'ar; **3.** עודף (money) *[colloq.]* *nm* 'odef.

(at) rest רגוע *adj* ragoo'a'/regoo'ah.

(to) rest לנוח *inf* lanoo'akh; *pst & pres* nakh; *fut* yanoo'akh.

(to) rest in peace לנוח בשלום על משכבו (upon burial) *inf* lanoo'akh be-shalom 'al meeshkavo; *pst & pres* nakh *etc*; *fut* yanoo'akh *etc*.

restaurant מסעדה *nf* mees|'adah/-'adot (+*of:* -'edet).

restful נינוח *adj* neeno|'akh/-khah.

restitution החזרה *nf* hakhzar|ah/-ot (+*of:* -at).

restive קצר־רוח *adj* ketsar/keetsrat roo'akh.

restless חסר־מנוחה *adj* khas|ar/-rat menookhah.

restlessness עצבנות 'atsbanoo|t/-yot.

restoration שיקום *nm* sheekoom/-eem (*pl+of:* -ey).

(to) restore לשקם *inf* leshakem; *pst* sheekem; *pres* meshakem; *fut* yeshakem.

(to) restrain לבלום *inf* leevlom; *pst* balam (*b=v*); *pres* bolem; *fut* yeevlom.

restraint הבלגה *nf* havlag|ah/-ot (+*of:* -at).

(to) restrict לצמצם *inf* letsamtsem; *pst* tseemtsem; *pres* metsamtsem; *fut* yetsamtsem.

restricted מוגבל *adj* moogb|al/-elet.

restriction הגבלה *nf* hagbal|ah/-ot (+*of:* -at).

restroom חדר־נוחיות *nm* khad|ar/-rey nokheeyoot.

result תוצאה *nf* totsa|'ah/-'ot (+*of:* -'at).

(to) result 1. לנבוע (result from) *inf* leenbo'a'; *pst* nava' (*v=b*); *pres* nove'a'; *fut* yeenba'; **2.** נתן כתוצאה (result in) *pres* natan ke-totsa'ah; *pst* noten *etc*; *fut* yeeten *etc*.

resumé 1. סיכום *nm* seekoom/-eem (*pl+of:* -ey); **2.** סיכום ביוגרפי (job applicant's) *nm* seekoom/-eem beeyografee/-yeem.

(to) resume 1. לסכם (summarize); *pst* seekem; *pres* mesakem; *fut* yesakem; **2.** להתחיל מחדש (start anew) *inf* lehatkheel me-khadash; *pst* heetkheel *etc*; *pres* matkheel *etc*; *fut* yatkheel *etc*.

resurection תחייה *nf* tekhee|yah/-yot (+*of:* -yat).

resurgent מתעורר מחדש *adj & v pres* meet'orer/-et me-khadash.

(to) resuscitate להחזיר להכרה *inf* lehakhzeer le-hakarah; *pst* hekhzeer *etc*; *pres* makhzeer *etc*; *fut* yakhzeer *etc*.

retail 1. קמעונות *nf* keem'onoo|t/-yot; **2.** קמעוני *adj* keem'onee/-t.

retail merchant סוחר בקמעונות *nm pl* sokh|er/-areem be-keem'onoot.

retail price מחיר קמעוני *nm* mekheer/-eem keem'onee/-yeem.

retailer קמעונאי keem'ona|y/-'eet.

(to) retain להחזיק ב־ *inf* lehakhzeek be-; *pst* hekhzeek be-; *pres* makhzeek be-; *fut* yakhzeek be-.

retainer 1. שכר עורך־דין שכור (fee) *nm* sekhar 'orekh-deen sakhoor; **2.** משרת (servant) *nm* meshar|et/-teem (*pl+of:* -tey).

(to) retaliate לגמול *inf* leegmol; *pst* gamal; *pres* gomel; *fut* yeegmol.

retaliation תגמול *nm* tagmool/-eem (*pl+of:* -ey).

(to) retard להשהות *inf* lehash'hot; *pst* heesh'hah; *pres* mash'heh; *fut* yash'heh.

retarded מפגר *adj* mefager/-et.

retention 1. עצירה *nf* 'atseer|ah/-ot (+*of:* -at); **2.** זכירה (remembrance) *nf* zekheer|ah/-ot (+*of:* -at).

reticence שתקנות *nf* shatkanoo|t/-yot.

retinue פמליה *nf* pamal|yah/-yot (+*of:* -yat).

(to) retire 1. לפרוש *inf* leefrosh; *pst* parash (*p=f*); *pres* poresh; *fut* yeefrosh; **2.** לפרוש לקצבה (with a pension; legal term) *inf* leefrosh le-keetsbah; *pst* parash *etc* (*p=f*); *pres* poresh *etc*; *fut* yeefrosh *etc*; **3.** לצאת לגמלאות *(colloq. term) inf* latset le-geemla'ot; *pst* yatsa *etc; pres* yotse *etc; fut* yetse *etc.*

retired 1. בדימוס *adj* be-deemoos; **2.** (.מיל) (meel.) abbreviation of מילואים "meeloo'eem" i.e. "reserve" — an obligatory addition to any mention of an Israeli reserve-officer's military rank.

retirement 1. פרישה *nf* preesh|ah/-ot (+*of:* -at); **2.** יציאה לגימלאות (pensioning) *nf* yetsee'|ah/-ot le-geemla'ot.

(to) retort להשיב במקום *inf* lehasheev ba-makom; *pst* hesheev *etc; pres* mesheev *etc; fut* yasheev *etc.*

(to) retouch לשפר *inf* leshaper; *pst* sheeper; *pres* meshaper; *fut* yeshaper.

(to) retrace לשחזר *inf* leshakhzer; *pst* sheekhzer; *pres* meshakhzer; *fut* yeshakhzer.

(to) retract 1. לקחת חזרה (take back) *inf* lakakhat khazarah; *pst* lakakh *etc; pres* loke'akh *etc; fut* yeekakh *etc;* **2.** להתנצל (apologize) *inf* leheetnatsel; *pst* heetnatsel; *pres* meetnatsel; *fut* yeetnatsel.

retreat 1. נסיגה (withdrawal) *nf* neseeg|ah/-ot (+*of:* -at); **2.** מפלט (refuge) *nm* meefl|at/-ateem (*pl+of:* -etey).

(to) retreat לסגת *inf* laseget; *pst & pres* nasog; *fut* yeesog.

(to) retrench לקצץ *inf* lekatsets; *pst* keetsets; *pres* mekatsets; *fut* yekatsets.

retrial משפט חוזר *nm* meeshpat/-eem khoz|er/-reem.

(to) retrieve 1. להציל (save) *inf* lehatseel; *pst* heetseel; *pres* matseel; *fut* yatseel; **2.** להחזיר (recover) *inf* lehakhzeer; *pst* hekhzeer; *pres* makhzeer; *fut* yakhzeer.

retroactive רטרואקטיבי *adj* retro'akteevee/-t.

retroflex כפוף אחורה *adj* kafoof/kefoofah akhorah.

retrospect מבט אחורה *nm* mabat/-eem akhorah.

return 1. חזרה *nf* khazar|ah/-ot (+*of:* -at); **2.** תמורה (consideration) *nf* temoor|ah/-ot (+*of:* -at).

(to) return 1. לחזור *vi inf* lakhzor; *pst* khazar; *pres* khozer; *fut* yakhazor; **2.** להחזיר (give back) *vt inf* lehakhzeer; *pst* hekhzeer; *pres* makhzeer; *fut* yakhzeer.

(income-tax) return הצהרה למס־הכנסה *nf* hats'ha-r|ah/-ot le-mas hakhnasah.

return address כתובת השולח *nf* ktovet ha-shole'akh.

return ticket כרטיס הלוך וחזור *nm* kartees/-eem halokh ve-khazor.

(many happy) returns! !תזכה לשנים רבות *imp nmf* teezk|eh/-ee le-shaneem rabot!

reunion 1. כינוס *nm* keenoos/-eem (*pl+of:* -ey); **2.** איחוד מחדש (reunification) *nm* eekhood me-khadash.

(to) reunite 1. להתאחד מחדש *v rfl inf* leheet'akhed me-khadash; *pst* heet'akhed *etc; pres* meet'akhed *etc; fut* yeet'akhed *etc;* **2.** לאחד מחדש *vt inf* le'akhed me-khadash; *pst* eekhed *etc; pres* me'akhed *etc; fut* ye'akhed *etc.*

(to) reveal לגלות *inf* legalot; *pst* geelah; *pres* megaleh; *fut* yegaleh.

(to) revel להתהולל *inf* leheet'holel; *pst* heet'holel; *pres* meet'holel; *fut* yeet'holel.

revelation 1. גילוי *nm* geeloo|y/-yeem (*pl+of:* -yey); **2.** תגלית (discovery) *nf* tagleet/-yot.

revelry חנגה *nf* kheeng|ah/-ot (+*of:* -at).

revenge נקמה *nf* nekam|ah/-ot (+*of:* neekm|at/-ot).

(to) revenge לנקום *inf* leenkom; *pst* nakam; *pres* nokem; *fut* yeenkom.

revengeful נקמני *adj* nakmanee/-t.

revenue הכנסה hakhnas|ah/-ot (+*of:* -at).

revenue stamp בול הכנסה *nm* bool/-ey hakhnasah.

(to) revere להוקיר *inf* lehokeer; *pres* hokeer; *pres* mokeer; *fut* yokeer.

reverence יראת כבוד *nf* yeer'at kavod.

(the) Reverend כבוד הכומר *nm* kevod ha-komer/kemareem (*pl+of:* komrey).

reverent מעריץ *adj* ma'areets/-eem (*pl+of:* -ey).

reverie, revery הזיה *nf* haza|yah/-yot (+*of:* -yat).

reverse 1. הפך *nm* hefekh/hafakheem (*pl+of:* hafakhey); **2.** הילוך אחורי (reverse gear) *nm* heelookh akhoree.

(to) reverse להפוך *inf* lahafokh; *pst* hafakh; *pres* hofekh; *fut* yahafokh.

(to) revert לחזור *inf* lakhzor; *pst* khazar; *pres* khozer; *fut* yakhzor.

reversible הפיך *adj* hafeekh/-ah.

review סקירה *nf* skeer|ah/-ot (+*of:* -at).

(to) review לסקור *inf* leeskor; *pst* sakar; *pres* soker; *fut* yeeskor.

(to) revile לגדף *inf* legadef; *pst* geedef; *pres* megadef; *fut* yegadef.

(to) revise לבחון מחדש *inf* leevkhon me-khadash; *pst* bakhan *(b=v) etc; pres* bokhen *etc; fut* yeevkhan *etc.*

revision 1. רביזיה *nf* reveez|yah/-yot; **2.** בדיקה מחדש (re-examination) *nf* bedeek|ah/-ot me-khadash.

revisionist רביזיוניסט *nm* reveezyoneest/-eem (Note: In Israeli politics — oldtime member of a pre-State era right-wing Zionist faction of which the "Herut" party is now successor).

revival 1. החיאה (resuscitation) *nf* hakhya|'ah/-'ot (+*of:* -'at); **2.** תחייה (rebirth) *nf* tekhee|yah/-yot (+*of:* -yat).

(to) revive להחיות *inf* lehakhyot; *pst* hekhyah; *pres* mekhayeh; *fut* yekhayeh.

(to) revoke לבטל *inf* levatel; *pst* beetel *(b=v)*; *pres* mevatel; *fut* yevatel.

revolt 1. מרד *nm* mered; **2.** התקוממות (uprising) *nf* heetkomemoo|t/-yot.

(to) revolt 1. להתקומם *inf* leheetkomem; *pst* heetkomem; *pres* meetkomem; *fut* yeetkomem; **2.** להתמרד (rise against) *v rfl inf* leheetmared; *pst* heetmared; *pres* meetmared; *fut* yeetmared.

revolting מבחיל *adj* mavkheel/-ah.

revolution מהפכה *nf* mahp|ekhah/-ekhot (+*of:* -ekhet).

revolutionary מהפכני *adj* mahpekhanee/-t.

revolutionist מהפכן *nm* mahpekhan/-eem (*pl+of:* -ey).

(to) revolve להסתובב *inf* leheestovev; *pres* heestovev; *pst* meestovev; *fut* yeestovev.
revolver אקדח *nm* ekd|akh/-akheem (*pl+of:* -ekhey).
reward פרס *nm* pras/-eem (*pl+of:* -ey).
(to) reward 1. לגמול *inf* leegmol; *pst* gamal; *pres* gomel; *fut* yeegmol; **2.** להעניק פרס (grant prize, bonus) *inf* leha'aneek pras; *pst* he'eneek *etc*; *pres* ma'aneek *etc*; *fut* ya'aneek *etc*.
(to) rewrite לשכתב *inf* leshakhtev; *pst* sheekhtev; *pres* meshakhtev; *fut* yeshakhtev.
rhapsody רפסודיה *nf* rapsod|yah/-yot (*+of:* -yat).
rhetoric 1. מליצה (figure of speech) *nf* melee-ts|ah/-ot (*+of:* -at); **2.** רטוריקה *nf* retoreek|ah/-ot (*+of:* -at).
rheumatism שיגרון *nm* sheeg|aron (*+of:* -ron).
rhinoceros קרנף *nm* karna|f/-peem (*p=f*; *pl+of:* -pey).
rhubarb ריבס *nm* reebas.
rhyme חרוז *nm* kharooz/-eem (*pl+of:* -ey).
rhythm 1. קצב *nm* kets|ev/-aveem (*pl+of:* keetsbey); **2.** ריתמיקה *nf* reetmeek|ah/-ot (*+of:* -at).
rhythmical 1. ריתמי *adj* reetmee/-t; **2.** קיצבי *adj* keetsbee/-t.
rib צלע *nf* tsel|a'/-a'ot (*pl+of:* tsal'ot).
ribbon סרט *nm* seret/srateem (*pl+of:* seertey).
rice אורז *nm* orez.
riches עושר *nm* 'osher.
rickety רופף *adj* rofef/-et.
(to) rid לפטור *inf* leeftor; *pst* patar *(p=f)*; *pres* poter; *fut* yeeftor.
(to get) rid of להיפטר מ־ *inf* leheepater mee-; *pst & pres* neeftar mee- *(f=p)*; *fut* yeepater mee-.
riddle חידה *nf* kheed|ah/-ot (*+of:* -at).
(to) riddle לנקב ככברה *inf* lenakev kee-khvarah *(kh=k)*; *pst* neekev *etc*; *pres* menakev *etc*; *fut* yenakev *etc*.
(to) ride לרכוב *inf* leerkov; *pst* rakhav *(kh=k)*; *pres* rokhev; *fut* yeerkav.
rider 1. רוכב *nmf & v pres* rokh|ev/-evet (*pl:* -veem/-vot; *pl+of:* -vey) **2.** פרש (horseman) *nm* parash/-eem (*pl+of:* -ey).
ridge רכס *nm* rekh|es/-aseem (*pl+of:* reekhsey).
ridicule לעג *nm* la'ag/le'ageem (*pl+of:* -ey).
(to) ridicule ללעוג *inf* leel'og; *pst* la'ag; *pres* lo'eg; *fut* yeel'ag.
ridiculous מגוחך *adj* megokh|akh/-ekhet.
rifle רובה *nm* rov|eh/-eem (*pl+of:* -ey).
rift קרע *nm* kera'/kra'eem (*pl+of:* keer'ey).
(to) rig להרכיב *inf* leharkeev; *pst* heerkeev; *pres* markeev; *fut* yarkeev.
right 1. זכות (privilege) *nf* zekhoo|t/-yot; **2.** ימין (political conservatives) *nm* yameen (*+of:* yemeen).
(to the) right ימינה *adv* yemeenah.
(is it) right? 1. ?הנכון הדבר ha-nakhon ha-davar?; **2.** ?האם זה צודק ha'eem zeh tsodek?
right angle זווית ישרה *nf* zavee|t/-yot yeshar|ah/-ot.
right hand יד ימין *nf* yad yameen.
right-hand drive הגה ימני *nm* hegeh yemanee.
right side 1. צד ימין *nm* tsad yameen; **2.** הצד הנכון (morally) *nm* ha-tsad ha-nakhon.
(from) right to left מימין לשמאל *adv* mee-yameen lee-smol.
righteous צדיק *nm* tsadeek/-eem (*pl+of:* -ey).
righteousness צדק *nm* tsedek.
rightful הוגן *adj* hogen/-et.
rightist ימני *adj* yemanee/-t.
rigid נוקשה *adj* nooksh|eh/-ah.
rigidity קשיחות *nf* kesheekhoot.
rigor חומרה *nf* khoomr|ah/-ot (*+of:* -at).
rigorous קפדני *adj* kapdanee/t.
rim מסגרת *nf* meesg|eret/-arot (*pl+of:* -erot).
rind 1. קליפה *nf* kleep|ah/-ot (*+of:* -at); **2.** קרום (crust) *nm* kroom/-eem (*pl+of:* -ey).
ring 1. טבעת *nf* taba|'at/-a'ot; **2.** זירה (arena) *nf* zeer|ah/-ot (*+of:* -at).
(to) ring לצלצל *inf* letsaltsel; *pst* tseeltsel; *pres* metsaltsel; *fut* yetsaltsel.
ringleader ראש הכנופיה *nm* rosh/-ey ha-kenoo-f|yah/-yot.
ringlet תלתל *nm* taltal/-eem (*pl+of:* -ey).
rinse לשטוף *inf* leeshtof; *pst* shataf; *pres* shotef; *fut* yeeshtof.
riot 1. מהומה *nf* mehoom|ah/-ot (*+of:* -at); **2.** התפרעות (disturbance) *nf* heetpar'oo|t/-yot.
(to) riot להתפרע *inf* leheetpare'a'; *pst* heetpara'; *pres* meetpare'a'; *fut* yeetpara'.
(to) rip 1. לקרוע (tear) *inf* leekro'a'; *pst* kara'; *pres* kore'a'; *fut* yeekra'; **2.** לפרום (open stitches) *inf* leefrom; *pst* param *(p=f)*; *pres* porem; *fut* yeefrom.
ripe בשל *adj* bashel/beshelah.
(to) ripen להבשיל *inf* lehavsheel; *pst* heevsheel; *pres* mavsheel; *fut* yavsheel.
ripeness בשלות *nf* besheloot.
ripple אדווה *nf* adv|ah/-ot (*+of:* -at).
rise 1. עלייה (ascent) *nf* 'alee|yah/-yot (*+of:* -yat); **2.** העלאה (raise of salary, prices, rank) *nf* ha'ala|'ah/-'ot (*+of:* -'at).
(to) rise 1. לעלות *inf* la'alot; *pst* 'alah; *pres* 'oleh; *fut* ya'aleh; **2.** להתרומם (ascend) *nf* leheetromem; *pst* heetromem; *pres* meetromem; *fut* yeetromem.
risk סיכון *nm* seekoon/-eem (*pl+of:* -ey).
(to) risk 1. לסכן (endanger) *vt inf* lesaken; *pst* seeken; *pres* mesaken; *fut* yesaken; **2.** להסתכן (endanger oneself) *v rfl inf* leheestaken; *pst* heestaken; *pres* meestaken; *fut* leheestaken.
risky מסוכן *adj* mesok|an/-enet.
rite 1. טקס *nm* tek|es/-aseem (*pl+of:* teeksey); **2.** נוסח (version) *nm* nosakh/nesakheem (*pl+of:* nooskhey).
ritual 1. פולחן *nm* poolkhan/-eem (*pl+of:* -ey); **2.** טקסי *adj* teeksee/-t.
rival מתחרה *adj & nmf* meetkhar|eh/-ah.
(to) rival להתחרות *inf* leheetkharot; *pst* heetkharah; *pres* meetkhareh; *fut* yeetkhareh.
rivalry תחרות *nf* takhroo|t/-yot.
river נהר *nm* nahar/neharot (*+of:* nehar).
rivet מסמרת masm|eret/-arot.
road 1. דרך *nf* derekh/drakheem (*pl+of:* darkhey; *k=kh*); **2.** כביש (highway) *nm* kveesh/-eem (*pl+of:* -ey).

road-house פונדק *nm* poond|ak/-akeem (*pl+of:* -ekey).

roadside שולי הכביש *nm pl* shooley ha-kveesh.

(to) roam לשוטט *inf* leshotet; *pst* shotet; *pres* meshotet; *fut* yeshotet.

roar שאגה *nf* she'ag|ah/-ot (*+of:* sha'agat).

(to) roar לשאוג *inf* leesh'og; *pst* sha'ag; *pres* sho'eg; *fut* yeesh'ag.

(to) roar with laughter להתפוצץ מצחוק *inf* leheetpotsets mee-ts'khok; *pst* heetpotsets *etc*; *pres* meetpotsets *etc*; *fut* yeetpotsets *etc*.

roast צלי *nm* tsalee (*+of:* tselee).

(to) roast לצלות *inf* leetslot; *pst* tsalah; *pres* tsoleh; *fut* yeetsleh.

roastbeef צלי־בקר *nm* tselee-bakar.

(to) rob לשדוד *inf* leeshdod; *pst* shadad; *pres* shoded; *fut* yeeshdod.

robber שודד *nm* shoded/-eem (*pl+of:* -ey).

robbery שוד *nm* shod (*pl:* מקרי שוד meekrey shod).

robe 1. חלוק *nm* khalook/-eem (*pl+of:* -ey); **2.** גלימה (dressing gown) *nf* gleem|ah/-ot (*+of:* -at).

robin אדום־החזה *nm* adom/adoomey he-khazeh.

robust חסון *adj* khas|on/-oonah.

rock סלע *nm* sela'/sla'eem (*pl+of:* sal'ey).

(to) rock 1. לנענע (shake) *vt inf* lena'ne'a'; *pst* nee'ne'a'; *pres* mena'ne'a'; *fut* yena'ne'a'; **2.** להתנענע (sway) *vi inf* leheetna'ne'a'; *pst* heetna'ne'a'; *pres* meetna'ne'a'; *fut* yeetna'ne'a

rocker 1. כסנוע *nm* kesno|'a'/-'eem (*pl+of:* -'ey); **2.** כיסא־נדנדה (rocking chair) *nm* kees|e/-'ot nadnedah.

rocket טיל *nm* teel/-eem (*pl+of:* -ey).

rocking מתנועע *adj* meetno|'e'a'/-'a'at.

rocky סלעי *adj* sal'ee/-t.

rod מוט *nm* mot/-ot.

rodent מכרסם mekharsem/-eem (*pl+of:* -ey).

rogue נוכל (swindler) *adj & nmf* nokh|el/-leem (*pl+of:* -ley).

roguish קונדסי *adj* koondesee/-t.

role תפקיד *nm* tafkeed/-eem (*pl+of:* -ey).

roll גליל *nm* galeel/gleeleem (*+of:* -gleel/-ey).

(to) roll להתגלגל *inf* leheetgalgel; *pst* heetgalgel; *pres* meetgalgel; *fut* yeetgalgel.

roll of bread לחמנייה *nf* lakhmanee|yah/-yot (*+of:* -yat).

roll of film סליל צילום *nm* sleel/-ey tseeloom.

roller 1. מכבש (press) *nm* makhbesh/-eem (*pl+of:* -ey); **2.** מעגילה (mangle) *nf* ma'ageel|ah/-ot (*+of:* -at).

rollerskate גלגלית *nf* galgalee|t/-yot.

Roman 1. רומי *adj* romee/-t; **2.** רומאי *nm* roma|'ee/-'eem (*pl+of:* -'ey).

romance סיפור אהבים *nm* seepoor/-ey ahaveem.

romantic רומנטי *adj* romantee/-t.

romanticism רומנטיקה *nf* romanteek|ah/-ot (*+of:* -at).

romanticist נפש רומנטית *nf* nef|esh/-ashot romantee|t/-yot.

Rome רומא *nf* roma.

roof גג *nm* gag/-ot.

roof of the mouth חך (palate) *nm* khekh/kheek|eem (*k=kh; pl+of:* -ey).

room 1. חדר (chamber) *nm* kheder/khad|areem (*pl+of:* -rey); **2.** מקום (place) *nm* makom/mekomot (*+of:* mekom/-ot).

roomer דייר לחדר *nmf* dayar/dayeret le-kheder.

roominess מרחב *nm* merkhav/-eem (*pl+of:* -ey).

roomy מרווח *adj* meroovakh/-at.

roost לול *nm* lool/-eem (*pl+of:* -ey).

rooster תרנגול *nm* tarnegol/-eem (*pl+of:* -ey).

root שורש *nm* shor|esh/-asheem (*pl+of:* -shey).

(to) root להכות שורשים *inf* lehakot shorasheem; *pst* heekah *etc*; *pres* makeh *etc*; yakeh *etc*.

rooted מושרש *adj* mooshr|ash/-eshet.

rootless חסר שורשים *adj* khas|ar/-rat shorasheem.

rope חבל *nm* khevel/khav|aleem (*pl+of:* -ley).

rose 1. שושנה *nf* shoshan|ah/-eem (*pl+of:* -ey); **2.** ורד (synon. with 1) *nm* vered/vradeem (*pl+of:* vardey).

rosebud ניצת ורד *nf* neets|at/-ot vered/vradeem.

roster לוח תורנויות *nm* loo'akh toranooyot.

rostrum בימה *nf* beem|ah/-ot (*+of:* -at).

rosy ורדרד *adj* vradrad/-ah.

(to) rot להרקיב *inf* leharkeev; *pst* heerkeev; *pres* markeev; *fut* yarkeev.

rotary סיבובי *adj* seevoovee/-t.

(to) rotate 1. לסובב (circle) *vt inf* lesovev; *pst* sovev; *pres* mesovev; *fut* yesovev; **2.** להסתובב (revolve) *v rfl inf* leheestovev; *pst* heestovev; *pres* meestovev; *fut* yeestovev; **3.** להתחלף לפי תור (exchange positions) *inf* leheetkhalef lefee tor; *pst* heetkhalef *etc*; *pres* meetkhalef *etc*; *fut* yeetkhalef *etc*.

rotation 1. סיבוב *nm* seeboov/-eem (*pl+of:* -ey); **2.** רוטציה (political) *nf* rotats|yah/-yot (*+of:* -yat).

rotten 1. קלוקל *adj* klokel/-et; **2.** מזופת *[colloq.] adj* mezoop|at/-etet; **3.** רקוב (decayed) *adj* rakoov/rekoovah.

rough 1. גס (coarse) *adj* gas/-ah; **2.** מחוספס (scaled) *adj* mekhoosp|as/-eset.

rough estimate הערכה גסה *nf* ha'arakhah gasah.

rough ground 1. שטח מבותר (cleft) *nm* shetakh mevootar; **2.** שטח קשה (difficult) *nm* shetakh kasheh.

rough sea ים סוער *nm* yam so'er.

rough weather מזג אוויר קשה *nm* mezeg-aveer kasheh.

roughly 1. בערך *adv* be-'erekh; **2.** בקושי (hardly) be-koshee.

round 1. עגול *adj* 'ag|ol/-oolah; **2.** שלם (complete) *adj* shalem/shlemah; **3.** סביב ל־ *adv* saveev le-.

round סיבוב (in sports) *nm* seevoov/-eem (*pl+of:* -ey).

(to) round 1. לעגל (round off sum) *inf* le'agel; *pst* 'eegel; *pres* me'agel; *fut* ye'agel; **2.** להשלים (complete) *inf* lehashleem; *pst* heeshleem; *pres* mashleem; *fut* yashleem.

round of ammunition 1. ירייה (shot) *nf* yeree|yah/-yot (*+of:* -yat); **2.** כדור (bullet) kadoor/-eem (*pl+of:* -ey).

round trip הלוך ושוב *adv* halokh va-shov.

(to) round up לאסוף *inf* le'esof; *pst* asaf; *pres* osef; *fut* ye'esof.

roundabout עקיף *adj* 'akeef/-ah.
(to) rouse 1. לעורר *inf* le'orer; *pst* 'orer; *pres* me'orer; *fut* ye'orer; **2.** לשלהב (incite) *inf* leshalhev; *pst* sheelhev; *pres* meshalhev; *fut* yeshalhev.
rout תבוסה מוחצת *nf* tvoos|ah/-ot mokh|etset/-atsot.
(to) rout להביס *inf* lehavees; *pst* hevees; *pres* mevees; *fut* yavees.
route 1. נתיב (path) *nm* nateev/neteeveem (+*of:* neteev/-ey); **2.** דרך (way) *nf* derekh/drakheem (*pl+of:* darkhey).
(to) route לנתב *inf* lenatev; *pst* neetev; *pres* menatev; *fut* yenatev.
routine 1. שגרה *nf* sheegr|ah/-ot (+*of:* -at); **2.** נוהג (usage) *nm* nohag/-eem (*pl+of:* -ey).
(to) rove לשוטט *inf* leshotet; *pst* shotet; *pres* meshotet; *fut* yeshotet.
rover משוטט *nm* meshotet/-eem (*pl+of:* -ey).
row 1. שורה (line) *nf* shoor|ah/-ot (+*of:* -at); **2.** מריבה (quarrel) *nf* mereev|ah/-ot (+*of:* -at).
(to) row לחתור *inf* lakhtor; *pst* khatar; *pres* khoter; *fut* yakhtor.
rowboat סירת משוטים *nf* seer|at/-ot meshoteem.
rower חותר *nm* khot|er/-reem (*pl+of:* -rey)
royal מלכותי *adj* malkhootee/-t.
royalist מלוכני *adj* melookhanee/-t.
royalties תמלוגים *nm pl* tamloog/-eem (*pl+of:* -ey)
royalty מלכות *nf* malkhoo|t/-yot.
rub שפשוף *nm* sheefshoof/-eem (*pl+of:* -ey).
(to) rub 1. לשפשף *vt inf* leshafshef; *pst* sheefshef; *pres* meshafshef; *fut* yeshafshef; **2.** להשתפשף (wear out) *v rfl inf* leheeshtafshef; *pst* heshtafshef; *pres* meeshtafshef; *fut* yeeshtafshef.
rubber גומי *nm* goomee.
rubber band גומייה *nf* goomee|yah/-yot (+*of:* -yat).
rubber stamp חותמת גומי *nf* khot|emet/-mot goomee.
rubbish 1. זבל (garbage) *nm* zevel; **2.** שטויות (nonsense) *nf pl* shtooyot.
rubble שברי אבן *nm pl* sheevrey even.
rubric 1. רובריקה *nf* roobreek|ah/-ot (+*of:* -at); **2.** מדור (section) *nm* mador/medorot (+*of:* medor).
ruby 1. אבן אודם *nf* even/avney odem; **2.** רובין *nm* roobeen/-eem (*pl+of:* -ey).
rudder הגה *nm* hegeh/hagal'eem (*pl+of:* -'ey).
ruddy אדמדם *adj* adamd|am/-emet.
rude גס *adj* gas/-ah.
rudeness גסות *nf* gasoot.
rueful נוגה *adj* noog|eh/-ah.
ruffle מקבץ *nm* meekb|ats/-atseem (*pl+of:* -etsey).
(to) ruffle 1. להפריע *inf* lehafree'a'; *pst* heefree'a'; *pres* mefree'a'; *fut* yafree'a'; **2.** לטרוף קלפים (cards) *inf* leetrof klafeem; *pst* taraf *etc*; *pres* toref *etc*; *fut* yeetrof *etc*.
rug שטיח *nm* shatee'akh/sheteekh|eem (*pl+of:* -ey).
rugged 1. מקומט *adj* mekoom|at/-etet; **2.** קשוח (hard) *adj* kashoo'akh/keshookhah.
ruin חורבה *nf* khoorb|ah/khoravot (+*of:* khoorbat/khorvot).
(to) ruin 1. לרושש (impoverish) *inf* leroshesh; *pst* roshesh; *pres* meroshesh; *fut* yeroshesh; **2.** להחריב (destroy) *inf* lehakhreev; *pst* hekhreev; *pres* makhreev; *fut* yakhreev.
ruinous חרב *adj* kharev/-ah.
rule 1. כלל *nm* klal/-eem (*pl+of:* -ey); **2.** סרגל (straight edge) *nm* sargel/-eem (*pl+of:* -ey).
(as a) rule בדרך כלל *adv* be-derekh klal.
(to) rule 1. לשלוט *inf* leeshlot; *pst* shalat; *pres* sholet; *fut* yeeshlot; **2.** לקבוע *inf* leekbo'a'; *pst* kava' (*v=b*); *pres* kove'a'; *fut* yeekba'.
(to) rule out להוציא מכלל אפשרות *inf* lehotsee mee-klal efsharoot; *pst* hotsee *etc*; *pres* motsee *etc*; *fut* yotsee *etc*
ruler שליט *nm* shaleet/-eem (*pl+of:* -ey).
ruling פסק *nm* pesak/-eem (*pl+of:* peeskey).
rum רום *nm* room.
rumble 1. המיה (low rolling sound) *nf* hem|yah/-yot (+*of:* -yat); **2.** תגרת־רחוב (street fight) *nf* teegr|at/-ot rekhov.
(to) ruminate 1. להרהר (meditate) *inf* leharher; *pst* heerher; *pres* meharher; *fut* yeharher; **2.** להעלות גירה (chew cud) *inf* leha'alot geyrah; *pst* he'elah *etc*; *pres* ma'aleh *etc*; *fut* ya'aleh *etc*.
(to) rummage לחטט *inf* lekhatet; *pst* kheetet; *pres* mekhatet; *fut* yekhatet.
rumor שמועה *nf* shemoo|'ah/-'ot (+*of:* -'at).
(it is) rumored שמועה אומרת *nf* shmoo|'ah/-'ot omeret/omrot.
rump עכוז *nm* 'akooz/-eem (*pl+of:* -ey).
(to) rumple לקמט *inf* lekamet; *pst* keemet; *pres* mekamet; *fut* yekamet.
rumpus מהומה *nf* mehoom|ah/-ot (+*of:* -at).
run 1. ריצה *nf* reets|ah/-ot (+*of:* -at); **2.** מהלך (move) *nm* mahal|akh/-akheem (*pl+of:* -khey)
(in the long) run בסופו של דבר *adv* be-sofo shel davar.
(to) run 1. לרוץ *inf* laroots; *pst* & *v pres* rats; *fut* yaroots; **2.** לנהל (to conduct, manage) *inf* lenahel; *pst* neehel; *pres* menahel; *fut* yenahel.
(to) run a fever לקבל חום *inf* lekabel khom; *pst* keebel *etc*; *pres* mekabel *etc*; *fut* yekabel *etc*.
(to) run away לברוח *inf* leevro'akh; *pst* barakh (*b=v*); *pres* bore'akh; *fut* yeevrakh.
run down מדוכדך *adj* medookhd|akh/-ekhet.
(to) run over לדרוס *inf* leedros; *pst* daras; *pres* dores; *fut* yeedros.
runaway 1. בריחה (flight) *nf* breekh|ah/-ot (+*of:* -at); **2.** בורח (fugitive) *nmf* & *adj* bor|e'akh/akhat.
runner רץ *nm* rats/-eem (*pl+of:* -ey).
running 1. במרוצה *adv* bee-mrootsah; **2.** ריצה *nf* reets|ah/-ot (+*of:* -at); **3.** מירוץ (race) *nm* merots/-eem (*pl+of:* -ey).
(in) running condition במצב תקין *adv* be-matsav takeen.
running expenses 1. הוצאות שוטפות *nf pl* hotsa'ot shotfot; **2.** הוצאות תחזוקה (overhead) *nf pl* hotsa'ot takhzookah.
running water מים זורמים *nm pl* mayeem zormeem.
runt ננס *nmf* nan|as/-eset.
runway 1. מסלול המראה masl|ool/-ey hamra'ah; **2.** מסלול (course) *nm* maslool/-eem (*pl+of:* -ey).

rupture 1. שבר *nm* shever/shvareem (*pl+of:* sheevrey); **2.** ניתוק (cutting off) *nm* neetook/-eem (*pl+of:* -ey).

(to) rupture 1. לנתק (cut off) *vt inf* lenatek; *pst* neetek; *pres* menatek; *fut* yenatek; **2.** להינתק (be severed) *vi inf* leheenatek; *inf* neetak; *pres* menootak; *fut* yenootak.

rush חיפזון *nm* kheepazon (*+of:* khefzon; *f=p*).

(to) rush למהר *inf* lemaher; *pst* meeher; *pres* memaher; *fut* yemaher.

rush hour שעת עומס *nf* she|'at/-'ot 'omes.

Russia רוסיה *nf* roosyah.

Russian 1. רוסי *nmf* roosee/-yah; **2.** רוסי *adj* roosee/-t; **3.** רוסית (language) *nf* rooseet.

rust חלודה *nf* khalood|ah/-ot (*+of:* -at).

(to) rust להחליד *inf* lehakhleed; *pst* hekhleed; *pres* makhleed; *fut* yakhleed.

rustic כפרי *adj* kafree/-t.

(to) rustle לרשרש *inf* lerashresh; *pst* reeshresh; *pres* merashresh; *fut* yerashresh.

rut 1. תלם (furrow) *nm* telem/tlameem (*pl+of:* talmey); **2.** חריץ (groove) *nm* khareets/-eem (*pl+of:* -ey); **3.** שגרה (routine) *nf* sheegr|ah/-ot (*pl+of:* -at).

ruthless אכזרי *adj* akhzaree/-t.

ruthlessness אכזריות *nf* akhzareeyoot.

rye 1. שיפון *nm* sheefon (*cpr* sheepon); **2.** ויסקי שיפון (whisky) *nm* veeskee sheefon (*cpr* sheepon).

S.

S,s Constant having several different equivalents in the Hebrew alphabet, depending on how it is pronounced in English. In these dictionaries it is used in only one way as pronounced in *so, soft* or *plus.* As such it transliterates two identical-sounding (see *Introduction*, p. v) Hebrew consonants samekh (ס) and seen (שׂ).

Sabbath שבת *nf* shabat/-ot.

sabbatical year שנת שבתון *nf* shn|at/-ot shabaton.

saber חרב *nf* kherev/kharavot.

sabotage חבלה *nf* khabal|ah/-ot (*+of:* -at).

(to) sabotage לחבל *inf* lekhabel; *pst* kheebel; *pres* mekhabel; *fut* yekhabel.

sack 1. תרמיל (bag) *nm* tarmeel/-eem (*pl+of:* -ey); **2.** ביזה (looting) *nf* beez|ah/-ot (*+of:* -at).

(to) sack לפטר (terminate employment) *inf* lefater; *pst* peeter (*p=f*); *pres* mefater; *fut* yefater.

sacred 1. קדוש (holy) *adj* kadosh/kedoshah; **2.** מקודש (regarded as sacred) *adj* mekood|ash/-eshet.

sacredness קדושה *nf* kdoosh|ah (*+of:* -at).

sacrifice 1. קורבן (object) *nm* korban/-ot; **2.** הקרבה (action) *nf* hakarav|ah/-ot (*+of:* -at).

sacrifice sale מכירה בהפסד *nf* mekheer|ah/-ot be-hefsed.

(to) sacrifice להקריב *inf* lehakreev; *pst* heekreev; *pres* makreev; *fut* yakreev.

sacrilege חילול קודש *nm* kheelool kodesh.

sacrilegious מחלל קודש *adj* mekhalel/-et kodesh.

sacrosanct מקודש יותר מכול *adj* mekood|ash/-eshet yoter mee-kol.

sad עצוב *adj* 'atsoov/-ah.

(to) sadden 1. להעציב (others) *inf* leha'atseev; *pst* he'etseev; *pres* ma'atseev; *fut* ya'atseev; **2.** להתעצב (oneself) *inf* leheet'atsev; *pst* heet'atsev; *pres* meet'atsev; *fut* yeet'atsev.

saddle 1. אוכף (horse) *nm* ook|af/-afeem (*pl+of:* -fey); **2.** מושב (bicycle) moshav/-eem (*pl+of:* -ey).

saddle horse סוס רכיבה *nm* soos/-ey rekheevah.

(to) saddle 1. לאכוף *inf* le'ekhof; *pst* akhaf; *pres* okhef; *fut* ye'ekhof; **2.** להשתלט (prevail) *inf* leheeshtalet; *pst* heeshtalet; *pres* meeshtalet; *fut* yeeshtalet.

(to) saddle with responsibilities להטיל אחריות *inf* lehateel akhrayoot; *pst* heeteel *etc*; *pres* mateel *etc*; *fut* yateel *etc.*

saddlebag אמתחת *nf* amtakh|at/-ot.

saddletree מסגרת אוכף *nf* meesger|et/-ot ookaf.

sadistic סדיסטי *adj* sadeestee/-t.

sadness 1. עצב *nm* 'etsev; **2.** עצבות *nf* 'atsvoo|t/-yot.

safe 1. בטוח (secure) *adj* batoo'akh/betookhah; **2.** אמין (trustworthy) *adj* ameen/-ah.

safe and sound בריא ושלם *adj* baree ve-shalem/bree'ah oo-shlemah.

(to play) safe לנהוג זהירות *inf* leenhog zeheeroot; *pst* nahag *etc*; *pres* noheg *etc*; *fut* yeenhag *etc.*

safe-conduct תעודת מעבר *nf* te'ood|at/-ot ma'avar.

safe-deposit כספת *nf* kas|efet/-afot.

safe-deposit box כספת בנק *nf* kas|efet/-fot bank.

safeguard 1. סייג (limitation) *nm* syag/-eem (*pl+of:* -ey); **2.** אמצעי ביטחון (means) *nm* emtsa|'ee/-'ey beetakhon

(to) safeguard לאבטח *inf* le'avte'akh; *pst* eevte'akh; *pres* me'avte'akh; *fut* ye'avte'akh.

safely בשלום *adv* be-shalom.

(to arrive) safely להגיע בשלום *inf* lehagee'a' be-shalom; *pst* heegee'a' *etc*; *pres* magee'a' *etc*; *fut* yagee'a' *etc.*

safety בטיחות *nf* beteekhoo|t/-yot.
safety razor סכין גילוח *nm* sakeen/-ey geeloo'akh.
safety pin סיכת ביטחון *nf* seek|at/-ot beetakhon.
safety valve שסתום ביטחון *nm* shastom/-ey beetakhon.
(in) safety בבטחה *adv* be-veetkhah *(v=b)*.
saffron 1. זעפרן *nm* ze'afran; **2.** צהוב (yellow) *adj* tsahov/tsehoobah *(b=v)*.
sag 1. שקיעה *nf* shekee|'ah/-'ot (*+of:* -'at); **2.** ירידה (descent) *nf* yereed|ah/-ot (*+of:* -at).
(to) sag לשקוע *inf* leeshko'a'; *pst* shaka'; *pres* shoke'a'; *fut* yeeshka'.
(his shoulders) sag כתפיו שחו *nm & v* ketefav shakhoo.
sagacious נבון *adj* navon/nevonah.
sagacity 1. שנינות *nf* shneenoo|t/-yot; **2.** תושייה (resourcefulness) *nf* tooshee|yah/-yot (*+of:* -at).
sage 1. חכם *adj* khakham/-ah; **2.** חכם *nm* kha-kh|am/-ameem (*pl+of:* -mey); **3.** לענה *nf* (plant)la'an|ah/-ot (*+of:* -at).
(it is) said that אומרים כי *v pl pres* omreem kee.
sail 1. מפרש (canvas) *nm* meefr|as/-aseem (*pl+of:* -esey); **2.** שיט (trip) *nm* shayeet (*+of:* sheyt).
(to) sail להפליג *inf* lehafleeg; *pst* heefleeg; *pres* mafleeg; *fut* yafleeg.
(to) sail a kite להניף עפיפון *inf* lehaneef 'afeefon; *pst* heneef *etc*; *pres* meneef *etc*; *fut* yaneef *etc*.
(to) sail along the coast לשייט לאורך החוף *inf* leshayet le-'orekh ha-khof; *pst* sheeyet *etc*; *pres* meshayet *etc*; *fut* yeshayet *etc*.
(to set) sail להפליג *inf* lehafleeg; *pst* heefleeg; *pres* mafleeg; *fut* yafleeg.
(under full) sail במפרשים פרושים *adv* be-meefraseem prooseem.
sailboat מפרשית *nf* meefrasee|t/-yot.
sailor מלח *nm* malakh/-eem (*pl+of:* -ey).
saint קדוש *nmf* kadosh/kedosh|ah (*pl:* -eem/-ot; *+of:* kdosh/-ey).
saintly של קדוש *adj* shel kadosh/kedoshah.
sake סיבה *nf* seeb|ah/-ot (*+of:* -at).
(for my) sake למעני *adv* le-ma'anee.
(for pity's) sake למען השם *adv* le-ma'an ha-shem.
(for the) sake of למען le-ma'an.
(for the) sake of argument לשם ויכוח בלבד *adv* le-shem veekoo'akh beelvad.
Samaria שומרון *nm* shomron.
Samaritan שומרוני *nmf* shomronee/-t (*pl:* -eem; *+of:* -ey).
salacious 1. של זימה *adj* shel zeemah; **2.** פורנוגרפי *adj* pornografee/-t.
salad סלט *nm* salat/-eem (*pl+of:* -ey).
(fruit) salad סלט פירות *nm* salat/-ey perot.
(green) salad סלט ירקות *nm* salat/-ey yerakot.
salad dressing רוטב לסלט *nm* rotev/retaveem le-salat.
salary משכורת *nf* maskor|et/-ot.
sale 1. מכירה *nf* mekheer|ah/-ot (*+of:* -at); **2.** מכר *nm* mekher.
(for) sale, (on) sale למכירה *adv* lee-mekheerah.
sale by auction מכירה פומבית *nf* mekheer|ah/-ot poombee|t/-yot.
sales tax מס קנייה (*lit.:* purchase tax) *nm* mas/meesey kneeyah.
salesman 1. זבן *nm* zaban/-eem (*pl+of:* -ey); **2.** מוכר (colloq) *nm* mokh|er/-reem (*pl+of:* -rey).
(travelling) salesman סוכן מכירות נוסע *nm* so-kh|en/-ney mekheerot nos|e'a'/-'eem.
saleswoman 1. זבנית *nf* zabanee|t/-yot; **2.** מוכרת *[colloq.] nf* mokh|eret/-rot.
salient 1. בליטה *nf* bleet|ah/-ot (*+of:* -at); **2.** בולט *adj* bolet/-et.
saline מלוח *adj* maloo'akh/melookhah.
saliva 1. ריר *nm* reer/-eem (*pl+of:* -ey); **2.** רוק (spittle) *nm* rok.
sallow צהבהב *adj* tsehavha|v/-bah *(b=v)*.
sally 1. גיחה *nf* geekh|ah/-ot (*+of:* -at); **2.** טיול (outing) *nm* teeyool/-eem (*pl+of:* -ey).
(to) sally להגיח *inf* lehagee'akh; *pst* heegee'akh; *pres* megee'akh; *fut* yagee'akh.
(to) sally forth לצאת *inf* latset; *pst* yatsa; *pres* yotse; *fut* yetse.
salmon 1. אלתית *nf* eeltee|t/-yot; **2.** סלמון *nm* salmon.
saloon 1. מסבאה (bar) *nf* meesba|'ah/-'ot; **2.** טרקלין (social hall) *nm* trakleen/-eem (*pl+of:* -ey).
salpeter מלחת *nf* melakhat.
salt 1. מלח (sodium chloride) *nm* melakh/-eem (*pl+of:* meelkhey); **2.** ממולח (wit) *adj* memoolakh/-at.
(to) salt להמליח *inf* lehamlee'akh; *pst* heemlee'akh; *pres* mamlee'akh; *fut* yamlee'akh.
salt mine מכרה מלח *nm* meekhr|eh/-ot melakh.
(the) salt of the earth 1. מלח הארץ *nm* melakh ha-arets; **2.** בני עלייה (aristocracy) *nm pl* beney 'aleeyah.
(to) salt one's money away 1. לחסוך (save) *inf* lakhsokh; *pst* khasakh; *pres* khosekh; *fut* yakhsokh; **2.** להשקיע במשהו בטוח (invest) *inf* lehashkee'a' be-mashehoo batoo'akh; *pst* heeshkee'a' *etc*; *pres* mashkee'a' *etc*; *fut* yashkee'a' *etc*.
salt pork בשר חזיר ממולח *nm* besar khazeer memoolakh.
salt shaker ממלחה *nf* meeml|akhah/-akhot (*+of:* -akhat).
salt water מי מלח *nm pl* mey melakh.
saltcellar ממלחה *nf* meeml|akhah/-akhot (*+of:* -akhat).
(smelling) salts מלחי הרחה *nm pl* meelkhey harakhah.
salty מלוח *adj* maloo'akh/mlookhah.
salutary 1. מבריא *adj* mavree/-'ah; **2.** מועיל (useful) *adj* mo'eel/-ah.
salute הצדעה *nf* hatsda|'ah/-'ot (*+of:* -'at).
(gun) salute מטח הצדעה *nm* matakh/matkhey hatsda'ah.
(to) salute 1. להצדיע *inf* lehatsdee'a'; *pst* heetsdee'a'; *pres* matsdee'a'; *fut* yatsdee'a';. **2.** לקדם בברכה (welcome) *inf* lekadem bee-vrakhah *(v=b)*; *pst* keedem *etc*; *pres* mekadem *etc*; *f ut* yekadem *etc*.
sanitation תברואה *nf* tavroo'ah.

salvage 1. הצלה *nf* hatsal|ah/-ot (+*of:* -at); **2.** חילוץ *nm* kheeloots/-eem (*pl+of:* -ey).

(to) salvage לחלץ *inf* lekhalets; *pst* kheelets; *pres* mekhalets; *fut* yekhalets.

salvation הצלה *nf* hatsal|ah/-ot (+*of:* -at).

salve משחה *nf* meeshkh|ah/-ot (+*of:* -at).

(to) salve להביא מזור *inf* lehavee mazor; *pst* hevee *etc; pres* mevee *etc; fut* yavee *etc.*

salvo מטח matakh/-eem (*pl+of:* matkhey).

same 1. אותו *pron* oto/otah; **2.** זהה (identical) *adj* zeheh/zehah.

(the) same אותו הדבר oto ha-davar.

(it is all the) same to me אחת היא לי akhat hee lee.

sample דוגמה *nf* doogm|ah/-a'ot (+*of:* -at).

(to) sample לבחון לפי דוגמאות *inf* leevkhon lefee doogma'ot; *pst* bakhan *etc; pres* bokhen *etc; fut* yeevkhan *etc.*

(book of) samples פנקס דגמים *nm* peenk|as/-esey degameem

sanatorium בית הבראה *nm* bet/batey havra'ah.

(to) sanctify לקדש *inf* lekadesh; *pst* keedesh; *pres* mekadesh; *fut* yekadesh.

sanctimonious מתחסד *adj* meetkhased/-et.

sanction 1. אשרור *nm* eeshroor/-eem (+*of:* -ey); **2.** אמצעי ענישה (punitive measures) *nm* emtsa|'ee/-'ey 'aneeshah.

(to) sanction 1. לאשרר *inf* le'ashrer; *pst* eeshrer; *pres* me'ashrer; *fut* ye'ashrer; **2.** לתת תוקף (validate) *inf* latet tokef; *pst* natan *etc; pres* noten *etc; fut* yeetan *etc.*

sanctions 1. עיצומים (in labor disputes) *nm pl* 'eetsoom|eem (*pl+of:* -ey); **2.** סנקציות *nf pl* sanktsyot.

sanctity קדושה *nf* kedoosh|ah/-ot (+*of:* -at).

sanctuary מיקלט *nm* meekl|at/-ateem (*pl+of:* -etey).

sand חול *nm* khol/-ot.

sandal סנדל *nm* sand|al/-aleem (*pl+of:* -eley).

sandbag שק חול *nm* sak/-ey khol.

sandpaper נייר זכוכית *nm* neyar zekhookheet.

sandstone אבן חול *nmf* even/avney khol-.

sandwich כריך *nm* kareekh/kreekh|eem (+*of:* -ey).

(to) sandwich לחסום מלפנים ומאחור *inf* lakhsom mee-lefaneem oo-me-akhor.

sandy חולי *adj* kholee/-t.

sandy haired צהוב־אדמדם *adj* tsahov-adamdam/tsehoobah-adamdemet *(b=v).*

sane שפוי *adj* shafooy/shefooyah.

sanitarium בית הבראה *nm* bet/batey havra'ah.

sanitary תברואי *adj* tavroo'ee/-t.

sanitation תברואה *nf* tavroo|'ah/-'ot (+*of:* -'at).

sanity שפיות *nf* shefeeyoo|t/-yot.

sap מיץ *nm* meets/-eem (*pl+of:* -ey).

(to) sap למצוץ *inf* leemtsots; *pst* matsats; *pres* motsets; *fut* yeemtsots.

sapling שתיל *nm* shteel/-eem (*pl+of:* -ey).

sapphire ספיר *nm* sapeer.

sarcasm 1. לגלוג עוקצני (derision) *nm* leegloog/-eem 'oktsanee/-yeem; **2.** סרקזם *nm* sarkazm (*pl+of:* -ey).

sarcastic 1. עוקצני (mordant) *adj* 'oktsanee/-t; **2.** לגלגני (derisive) *adj* laglegane e/-t; **3.** סרקסטי *adj* sarkastee/-t.

sardines סרדינים *nm pl* sardeen|eem (*pl+of:* -ey).

sardonic 1. עוקצני *adj* 'oktsanee/-t; **2.** של לעג מר (mocking) *adj* shel la'ag mar.

sash אבנט *nm* avnet/-eem (*pl+of:* -ey).

(window) sash מסגרת חלון *nf* meesger|et/-ot khalon/-ot.

satchel ילקוט *nm* yalkoot/-eem (*pl+of:* -ey).

(to) sate להשביע *inf* lehasbee'a'; *pst* heesbee'a'; *pres* masbee'a'; *fut* yasbee'a'.

sateen סטין *nm* sateen.

satellite לוויין *nm* lavyan/-eem (*pl+of:* -ey).

(to) satiate 1. לפטם *inf* lefatem; *pst* peetem *(p=f); pres* mefatem; *fut* yefatem; **2.** להשביע מעל ומעבר *inf* lehasbee'a' me-'al oo me-'ever; *pst* heesbee'a' *etc; pres* masbee'a' *etc; fut* yasbee'a' *etc.*

satin 1. אטלס *nm* atlas; **2.** סטן *nm* saten.

satire סטירה *nf* sateer|ah/-ot (+*of:* -at).

satirical סטירי *adj* sateeree/-t.

(to) satirize לעשות לצחוק *inf* la'asot lee-ts'khok; *pst* 'asah *etc; pres* 'oseh *etc; fut* ya'aseh *etc.*

satisfaction סיפוק *nm* seepook/-eem (*pl+of:* -ey).

satisfactorily כדי הנחת הדעת *adv* kedey hanakhat ha-da'at.

satisfactory מניח את הדעת *adj* manee|'akh/-khah et ha-da'at.

satisfied 1. מרוצה (pleased) *adj* meroots|eh/-ah; **2.** שבע רצון (contented) *adj* sva'/sve'at ratson; **3.** משוכנע (convinced) *adj* meshookhn|a'/-a'at.

(to) satisfy 1. להשביע רצון *inf* lehasbee'a' ratson; *pst* heesbee'a' *etc; pres* masbee'a' *etc; fut* yasbee'a' *etc;* **2.** לספק (content) *inf* lesapek; *pst* seepek; *pres* mesapek; *fut* yesapek; **3.** לשכנע (convince) *inf* leshakhne'a'; *pst* sheekhne'a'; *pres* meshakhne'a'; *fut* yeshakhne'a'.

(to) saturate להרוות *inf* leharvot; *pst* heervah; *pres* marveh; *fut* yarveh.

Saturday 1. שבת *nf* shabat/-ot; **2.** יום שבת (day of the Sabbath) *nm* yom/yemey shabat.

sauce רוטב *nm* rotev/retaveem (*pl+of:* rotvey).

sauce dish כלי לרוטב *nm* klee/keleem le-rotev.

saucepan אילפס *nm* eelp|as/-aseem (*pl+of:* -esey).

saucer 1. צלחת *nf* tsalakh|at/-ot; **2.** תחתית (plate) *nf* takhtee|t/-yot.

(flying) saucer צלחת מעופפת *nf* tsalakh|at/-ot me'ofef|et/-ot.

sauciness עסיסיות *nf* 'aseeseeyoot.

saucy 1. עסיסי *adj* 'aseesee/-t; **2.** חצוף (cheeky) *adj* khatsoof/-ah.

(to) saunter לטייל להנאה *inf* letayel le-hana'ah; *pst* teeyel *etc; pres* metayel *etc; fut* yetayel *etc.*

sausage 1. נקניק *nm* nakneek/-eem (*pl+of:* -ey); **2.** נקניקייה (hot dog) *nf* nakneekee|yah/-yot (+*of:* -yat).

savage 1. פראי *adj* pra'ee/-t; **2.** פרא־אדם *nm* pere/peer'ey adam.

savagery פראות *nf* pra'oot.

savant מלומד *nm* meloomad/-eem (*pl+of:* -ey).

(to) save 1. להציל(rescue) *inf* lehatseel; *pst* heetseel; *pres* matseel; *fut* yatseel; **2.** לחסוך(hoard) *inf* lakhsokh; *pst* khasakh; *pres* khosekh; *fut*

yakhsokh; **3.** לשמור על(guard) *inf* leeshmor al; *pst* shamar al; *pres* shomer al; *fut* yeeshmor al.
(to) save from לשמור מפני *inf* leeshmor mee-pney; *pst* shamar *etc*; *pres* shomer *etc*; *fut* yeeshmor *etc*.
(to) save one's face להציל כבוד *inf* lehatseel kevod; *pst* heetseel *etc*; *pres* matseel *etc*; *fut* yatseel *etc*.
saver מושיע *nm* moshee'a'/-'eem (*pl+of:* -'ey)
(life) saver מציל *nm* matseel/-eem (*pl+of:* -ey).
saving 1. מושיע *adj* moshee|'a'/-'ah; **2.** מציל (rescuing) *adj* matseel/-ah; **3.** חוסך (economizing) *adj* khosekh/-et.
saving 1. מלבד *prep* meelvad **2.** -פרט ל *prep* prat le-.
savings חסכונות *nm pl* kheskhonot.
savings bank בנק לחיסכון *nm* bank/-eem le-kheesakhon.
savior מושיע *nm* moshee'a'/-'eem (*pl+of:* -'ey)
savor 1. טעם (taste) *nm* ta'am/te'ameem (*pl+of:* ta'amey); **2.** סממן (ingredient) *nm* sameman/-eem (*pl+of:* -ey); **3.** תבלין (spice) *nm* tavleen/-eem (*pl+of:* -ey).
(to) savor of לטעום *inf* leet'om; *pst* ta'am; *pres* to'em; *fut* yeet'am.
(it) savors of treason מריח לבגידה *v pres* meree|'akh/-khah lee-vgeedah *(v=b)*.
savory 1. טעים *adj* ta'eem/te'eemah; **2.** מבושם (perfumed) *adj* mevoos|am/-emet.
saw מסור *nm* masor/-eem (*pl+of:* -ey).
(to) saw לנסר *inf* lenaser; *pst* neeser; *pres* menaser; *fut* yenaser.
sawdust נסורת *nf* nesor|et/-ot.
sawmill מנסרה *nf* meens|arah/-arot (*+of:* -eret).
sawhorse משענת לניסור *nf* meesh'enet le-neesoor.
(it) saws easily מתנסר בקלות *v pres* meetnaser be-kaloot.
(Anglo-)Saxon אנגלוסקסי *adj* anglosaksee/-t.
saxophone סקסופון *nm* saksofon/-eem (*pl+of:* -ey).
(that is to) say כלומר *prep* kelomar.
(the final) say ההכרעה הסופית *nf* ha-hakhra'ah ha-sofeet.
(to) say לומר *inf* lomar; *pst* amar; *pres* omer; *fut* yomar.
(to have one's) say לומר דברו *inf* lomar dvaro; *pst* amar *etc*; *pres* omer *etc*; *fut* yomar *etc*.
(has a) say in the matter יש לו מה לומר בנידון yesh lo mah lomar ba-needon.
(to) say the least לפחות *prep* le-fakhot *(f=p)*.
saying 1. אמירה *nf* ameer|ah/-ot (*+of:* -at); **2.** אימרה (dictum) *nf* eemrah/amarot (*+of:* eemrat).
(as the) saying goes כדבר הפתגם kee-dvar ha-peetgam.
scab 1. מפר שביתה (in a strike) *nm* mefer/-at shveetah; **2.** גלד (crust) *nm* geled/gladeem (*pl+of:* geeldey).
(to) scab 1. להפר שביתה (in a strike) *inf* lehafer shveetah; *pst* hefer *etc*; *pres* mefer *etc*; *fut* yafer *etc*; **2.** להגליד (encrust) *inf* lehagleed; *pst* heegleed; *pres* magleed; *pres* yagleed.
scabbard נדן *nm* nadan/nedaneem (*pl+of:* nedaney).
scabby עם פצעים שהגלידו *adj* 'eem petsa'eem she-heegleedoo.
scabrous 1. מלא קשקשים *adj* male/mele'at kaskaseem; **2.** מסובך (complex) *adj* mesoob|akh/-ekhet.
scaffold גרדום *nm* gardom/-eem (*pl+of:* -ey).
scaffolding פיגומים *nm pl* peegoom/-eem (*sing:* peegoom; *pl+of:* -ey).
scald כווייה ברותחים *nf* kvee|yah/-yot be-rotkheem.
(to) scald לגרום כוויות *inf* leegrom kveeyot; *pst* garam *etc*; *pres* gorem *etc*; *fut* yeegrom *etc*.
(to) scald milk להרתיח חלב *inf* lehartee'akh khalav; *pst* heertee'akh *etc*; *pres* martee'akh *etc*; *fut* yartee'akh *etc*.
scale 1. קנה מידה *nm* kneh meedah; **2.** דירוג (grading) *nm* deroog/-eem (*pl+of:* -ey); **3.** סולם (ladder) *nm* soolam/-ot.
(platform) scale מאזני גשר *nm pl* mozney gesher.
(to) scale לדרג *inf* ledareg; *pst* dereg; *pres* medareg; *fut* yedareg.
(to) scale down prices להוזיל מחירים *inf* lehozeel mekheereem; *pst* hozeel *etc*; *pres* mozeel *etc*; *fut* yozeel *etc*.
(pair of) scales מאזני כפות *nm pl* mozney kapot.
scallop צידפה *nf* tseedpah/tsedafot (*f=p*; *+of:* tseed|pat/-fot).
(to) scallop לגזור סלסולים *inf* leegzor seelsooleem; *pst* gazar *etc*; *pres* gozer *etc*; *fut* yeegzor *etc*.
scalp קרקפת *nf* kark|efet/-afot.
(to) scalp לקרקף *inf* lekarkef; *pst* keerkef; *pres* mekarkef; *fut* yekarkef.
scalpel אזמל מנתחים *nm* eezmel/-ey menatkheem.
scaly מכוסה קשקשים *adj* mekhoos|eh/-at kaskaseem.
scaly with rust מכוסה חלודה *adj* mekhoos|eh/-at khaloodah.
scamp מנוול *nmf* menoov|al/-elet.
scamper בריחה מבוהלת *nf* breekh|ah/-ot mevo|helet/-halot.
(to) scamper לברוח בבהלה *inf* leevro'akh be-vehalah *(v=b)*; *pst* barakh*(b=v) etc*; *pres* bore'akh *etc*; *fut* yeevrakh *etc*.
(to) scan לבחון ברפרוף *inf* leevkhon be-reefroof; *pst* bakhan *(b=v) etc*; *pres* bokhen *etc*; *fut* yeevkhan *etc*.
scandal 1. שערורייה *nf* sha'arooree|yah/-yot (*+of:* -yat); **2.** סקנדל *[slang] nm* skandal/-eem.
(to) scandalize לגרום שערורייה *inf* leegrom sha'arooreeyah; *pst* garam *etc*; *pres* gorem *etc*; *fut* yeegrom *etc*.
scandalous 1. מחפיר *adj* makhpeer/-ah; **2.** שערורייתי *adj* sha'arooreeyatee/-t.
scant 1. זעום *adj* za'oom/ze'oomah; **2.** דל (poor) dal/-ah.
(to) scant 1. לצמצם *inf* letsamtsem; *pst* tseemtsem; *pres* metsamtsem; *fut* yetsamtsem; **2.** להתקמצן *[colloq.] inf* leheetkamtsen; *pst* heetkamtsen; *pres* meetkamtsen; *fut* yeetkamtsen.
scanty 1. זעום *adj* za'oom/ze'oomah; **2.** דל (poor) dal/-ah.
scapegoat שעיר לעזאזל *nm* sa'eer la-'aza'zel.
scar 1. צלקת (skin blemish) *nf* tsal|eket/-akot; **2.** שרטת (mark) *nf* sar|etet/-atot.

(to) scar לצלק *inf* letsalek; *pst* tseelek; *pres* metsalek; *fut* yetsalek.

scarce נדיר *adj* nadeer/nedeerah.

scarcely לא מספיק *adj* lo masp|eek/-eket.

scarcity נדירות *nf* nedeeroo|t/-yot.

scare בהלה *nf* behal|ah/-ot (+*of:* -at).

(to) scare להבהיל *inf* lehav'heel; *pst* heev'heel; *pres* mav'heel; *fut* yav'heel.

(to) scare away להרתיע *inf* lehartee'a'; *pst* heertee'a'; *pres* martee'a'; *fut* yartee'a'.

scarecrow דחליל *nm* dakhleel/-eem (*pl+of:* -ey).

scares easily נבהל בקלות *adj* neev|hal/-helet be-kaloot.

scarf 1. צעיף *nm* tsa'eef/tse'eef|eem (*pl+of:* -ey); **2.** סודר (shawl) *nm* sood|ar/-areem (*pl+of:* -rey).

scarlet 1. אדום־בהיר (light-red) *adj* adom-baheer/ adoomah-beheerah; **2.** שני (crimson) *nm* shanee.

scarlet fever שנית *nf* shaneet.

scary 1. מפחיד (frightening) *adj* mafkheed/-ah; **2.** ניפחד (frightened) *adj* neefkh|ad/-edet.

scat! !הסתלק intj *v imp* heestal|ek!/keel *(m/f)*.

(to) scatter לפזר *inf* lefazer; *pst* peezer *(p=f)*; *pres* mefazer; *fut* yefazer.

scatterbrained 1. פזור נפש *adj* pezoor/-at nefesh; **2.** מפוזר *[colloq.] adj* mefooz|ar/-eret.

scattered מפוזר *adj* mefooz|ar/-eret.

scene 1. חיזיון *nf* kheezayon/khezyonot (+*of:* khezyon); **2.** מראה (view) *nm* mar|'eh/-'ot; **3.** התפרצות מביכה (outburst) *nf* heetpar-tsoo|t/-yot meveekh|ah/-ot.

(to make a) scene 1. לעורר שערורייה *inf* le'orer sha'arooreeyah; *pst* 'orer *etc*; *pres* me'orer *etc*; *fut* ye'orer *etc*; **2.** לעשות סצינות *[colloq.] inf* la'asot s'tsenot; *pst* 'asah *etc*; *pres* 'oseh *etc*; *fut* ya'aseh *etc*.

scenery 1. נוף *nm* nof/-eem (*pl+of:* -ey); **2.** מראה (view) *nm* mar|'eh/-'ot.

(stage) scenery תפאורה *nf* taf'oor|ah/-ot (+*of:* -at).

(behind the) scenes מאחורי הקלעים *adv* me-akhorey ha-kla'eem.

scent 1. ריח (odor) rey|'akh/-khot; **2.** בושם (perfume) *nm* bosem; **3.** עקבות (traces) *nf pl* 'akavot (+*of:* 'eekvot).

(a keen) scent חוש ריח רגיש *nm* khoosh rey'akh rageesh.

(to) scent להריח *inf* leharee'akh; *pst* heree'akh; *pres* meree'akh; *fut* yaree'akh.

(to be on the) scent לעלות על עקבות *inf* la'alot 'al 'eekvot; *pst* 'alah *etc*; *pres* 'oleh *etc*; *fut* ya'aleh *etc*.

scepter שרביט *nm* sharveet/-eem (*pl+of:* -ey).

sceptic 1. ספקני *adj* safkanee/-t; **2.** סקפטי *adj* skeptee/-t.

scepticism 1. ספקנות *nf* safkanoo|t/-yot; **2.** סקפטיות *nf* skepteeyoo|t/-yot.

schedule 1. טבלה *nf* tavl|ah/-a'ot (+*of:* -at); **2.** תוספת (annex) *nm* tos|efet/-afot.

(on) schedule בזמן ba-zman.

(time) schedule לוח זמנים loo|'akh/-khot zmaneem;

(to) schedule 1. לשבץ *inf* leshabets; *pst* sheebets; *pres* meshabets; *fut* yeshabets; **2.** לתכנן (plan) *inf* letakhnen; *pst* teekhnen; *pres* metakhnen; *fut* yetakhnen.

scheme 1. תוכנית (plan) tokhnee|t/-yot; **2.** קנוניה (plot) *nf* knoon|yah/-yot (+*of:* -yat).

(color) scheme צירוף צבעים *nm* tseroof/-ey tsva'eem.

(to) scheme לזום *inf* lazom; *pst* zamam; *pres* zomem; *fut* yazom.

schemer 1. זומם *nmf* zomem/-et; **2.** חורש מזימות *nm* khor|esh/-shey mezeemot.

scheming 1. תכנון (planning) *nm* teekhnoon/-eem (*pl+of:* -ey); **2.** חיבול תחבולות (intriguing) *nm* kheebool takhboolot.

schism פילוג *nm* peeloog/-eem (*pl+of:* -ey).

schizophrenia סכיזופרניה *nf* skheezofren|yah/-yot (+*of:* -yat).

scholar 1. מלומד *nmf* meloom|ad/-edet; **2.** תלמיד חכם *nm* talmeed/-ey khakham/-eem.

scholarly למדני *adj* lamdanee/-t.

scholarship 1. למדנות (learning) *nf* lamdanoot; **2.** מלגה (grant) *nf* meelg|ah/-ot (+*of:* -at).

(to have a) scholarship לזכות במענק *inf* leezkot be-ma'anak; *pst* zakhah *(kh=k) etc*; *pres* zokheh *etc*; *fut* yeezkeh *etc*.

scholastic 1. של בתי־ספר *adj* shel batey-sefer; **2.** חינוכי (educational) *adj* kheenookhee/-t.

school בית־ספר *nm* bet/batey-sefer.

school board הנהלת בית־ספר *nf* hanhal|at/-ot bet/ batey sefer.

school day יום לימודים *nm* yom/yemey leemoodeem.

school of fish להקת דגים *nf* lahak|at/-ot dageem.

schoolboy תלמיד בית־ספר *nm* talmeed/-ey bet-sefer.

schoolgirl תלמידת בית־ספר *nf* talmeed|at/-ot bet-sefer.

schoolhouse בניין בית ספר *nm* been|yan/-yeney bet/batey sefer.

schooling חינוך *nm* kheenookh.

schoolmaster מנהל בית־ספר *nm* mena|hel/-haley bet/batey sefer.

schoolmate 1. חבר לכיתה *nm* khaver/-ah la-keetah; **2.** בן־כיתה *nmf* ben/bat keetah.

schoolroom 1. חדר־לימודים *nm* khad|ar/-rey leemoodeem; **2.** כיתה *nf* keet|ah/-ot (+*of:* -at).

schoolteacher מורה *nmf* mor|eh/-ah (*pl:* -eem/-ot; +*of:* -at/-ey).

schooner מפרשית *nf* meefrasee|t/-yot.

science מדע *nm* mad|a'/-a'eem (*pl+of:* -'ey).

scientific מדעי *adj* mada'ee/-t.

scientifically באופן מדעי be-ofen mada'ee.

scientist מדען *nm* mad'an/-eet (*pl:* -eem/-eeyot; +*of:* -ey).

(to) scintillate להבריק *inf* lehavreek; *pst* heevreek; *pres* mavreek; *fut* yavreek.

scion 1. נצר *nm* netser; **2.** חוטר (twig) *nm* khoter.

scissors מספריים *nm pl* meesp|arayeem (*pl+of:* -erey).

sclerosis 1. טרשת *nf* tareshet; **2.** הסתיידות העורקים (artery calcification) *nf* heestaydoot ha-'orkeem.

scoff 1. בוז *nm* booz; **2.** לעג (mockery) *nm* la'ag.

(to) scoff ללעוג *inf* leel'og; *pst* la'ag; *pres* lo'eg; *fut* yeel'ag.

(to) scoff at לזלזל ב־ *inf* lezalzel be-; *pst* zeelzel be-; *pres* mezalzel be-; *fut* yezalzel be-.

scold 1. נזיפה *nf* nezeef|ah/-ot (+*of:* -at); **2.** מרשעת (shrew) *nf* meersha'at.

(to) scold 1. לנזוף *inf* leenzof; *pst* nazaf; *pres* nozef; *fut* yeenzof; **2.** לגעור (rebuke) *inf* leeg'or; *pst* ga'ar; *pres* go'er; *fut* yeeg'ar.

scolding 1. נזיפה *nf* nezeef|ah/-ot (+*of:* -at); **2.** גערה (rebuke) *nf* ge'ar|ah/-ot (+*of:* ga'ar|at/-ot).

scoop 1. מחתה (tool) *nf* makht|ah/-ot (+*of:* -at); **2.** כמות (quantity) *nf* kamoo|t/-yot; **3.** רווח תועפות (winnings) *nm* revakh/reevkhey to'afot.

(newspaper) scoop 1. ידיעה בלעדית בעיתון *nf* yedee'ah/-'ot beel'adee|t/-yot be-'eeton; **2.** סקופ *nm* skoop/-eem (*pl+of:* -ey).

(to) scoop 1. לגרוף *inf* leegrof; *pst* garaf; *pres* goref; *fut* yeegrof; **2.** לדלות (heave up) *inf* leedlot; *pst* dalah; *pres* doleh; *fut* yeedleh.

(to) scoop in a good profit לגרוף רווחים *inf* leegrof revakheem; *pst* garaf *etc*; *pres* goref *etc*; *fut* yeegrof *etc*.

scoot! ברח ! *v imp sing* brakh!/beerkhee! (*m/f*).

(to) scoot לזנק ולרוץ *inf* lezanek ve-laroots; *pst* zeenek ve-rats; *pres* mezanek ve-rats; *fut* yezanek ve-yaroots.

scooter קטנוע *nm* katno|'a'/-'eem (*pl+of:* -'ey).

scope 1. היקף *nm* hekef/-eem (*pl+of:* -ey); **2.** מרחב (expanse) *nm* merkhav/-eem (*pl+of:* -ey).

scorch כווייה קלה *nf* kvee|yah/-yot kal|ah/-ot.

(to) scorch 1. לחרוך *inf* lakhrokh; *pst* kharakh; *pres* khorekh; *fut* yakhrokh; **2.** לצרוב (scald) *inf* leetsrov; *pst* tsarav; *pres* tsorev; *fut* yeetsrov.

score 1. מניין *nm* meen|yan/-yaneem (*pl+of:* -yeney); **2.** מצב נקודות בתחרות (in competition) *nm* matsav nekoodot be-takharoot; **3.** חריץ אזכור (marking notch) *nm* khareets/-ey eezkoor.

(musical) score 1. תכליל *nm* takhleel/-eem (*pl+of:* -ey); **2.** פרטיטורה *nf* parteetoor|ah/-ot (+*of:* -at).

(on that) score בהקשר זה be-heksher zeh.

(to) score 1. לסמן *inf* lesamen; *pst* seemen; *pres* mesamen; *fut* yesamen; **2.** לרשום לזכות (points) *inf* leershom lee-zekhoot; *pst* rasham *etc*; *pres* roshem *etc*; *fut* yeershom *etc*.

(to keep the) score למנות *inf* leemnot; *pst* manah; *pres* moneh; *fut* yeemneh.

(to) score a success לזכות בהצלחה *inf* leezkot be-hatslakhah; *pst* zakhah *etc* (*kh=k*); *pres* zokheh *etc*; *fut* yeezkeh *etc*.

(on the) score of 1. בגלל *prep* bee-glal; **2.** על יסוד *prep* 'al yesod.

(to) score points לרשום נקודות *inf* leershom nekoodot; *pst* rasham *etc*; *pres* roshem *etc*; *fut* yeershom *etc*.

(to settle old) scores לחסל חשבונות *inf* lekhasel kheshbonot; *pst* kheesel *etc*; *pres* mekhasel *etc*; *fut* yekhasel *etc*.

scorn בוז *nm* booz.

(to) scorn 1. לרחוש בוז *inf* leerkhosh booz; *pst* rakhash booz; *pres* rokhesh booz; *fut* yeerkhash booz; **2.** לבוז (disdain) *inf* lavooz; *pst & pres* baz (*b=v*); *fut* yavooz.

scorpion עקרב *nm* 'akra|v/-beem (*b=v*; *pl+of:* -bey).

Scotch 1. סקוטי *nmf & adj* skotee/-t; **2.** ויסקי *nm* veeskee.

scoundrel 1. נוכל *nm* nokh|el/-leem (*pl+of:* -ley); **2.** נבל (villain) *nm* naval/nevaleem.

(to) scour 1. למרק *inf* lemarek; *pst* merek; *pres* memarek; *fut* yemarek; **2.** לנקות (cleanse) *inf* lenakot; *pst* neekah; *pres* menakeh; *fut* yenakeh.

(to) scour the country להפוך את הארץ בחיפוש אחר *inf* lahafokh et ha-arets be-kheepoos akhar; *pst* hafakh *etc*; *pres* hofekh *etc*; *fut* yahafokh *etc*.

scourge 1. פרגול (lash) *nm* pargol/-eem (*pl+of:* -ey); **2.** נגע (plague) *nm* neg|a'/-a'eem (*pl+of:* neeg'ey).

(to) scourge 1. להביא פורענות על *inf* lehavee poor'anoot 'al; *pst* hevee *etc*; *pres* mevee *etc*; *fut* yavee *etc*; **2.** לייסר (punish) *inf* leyaser; *pst* yeeser; *pres* meyaser; *fut* yeyaser.

scout סייר *nm* sayar/-eem (*pl+of:* -ey).

(a good) scout צופה נאמן *nm* tsofeh ne'eman.

(boy)scout צופה *nm* tsof|eh/-eem (*pl+of:* -ey).

scoutmaster מדריך צופים *nmf* madreekh/-at tsofeem.

scowl מבט זועף *nm* mabat/-eem zo'ef/zo'afeem.

(to) scowl להזעים פנים *inf* lehaz'eem paneem; *pst* heez'eem *etc*; *pres* maz'eem *etc*; *fut* yaz'eem *etc*.

scramble 1. הידחקות *nf* heedakhakoo|t/-yot; **2.** ערבוביה *nf* 'eerboov|yah/-yot (+*of:* -yat).

(to) scramble 1. להידחק (move) *inf* leheedakhek; *pst & pres* needkhak; *fut* yeedakhek; **2.** לטרוף (eggs) *inf* leetrof; *pst* taraf; *pres* toref; *fut* yeetrof; **3.** לערבב (mix up) *inf* le'arbev; *pst* 'eerbev; *pres* me'arbev; *fut* ye'arbev.

(to) scramble for להיאבק על *inf* lehe'avek 'al; *pst & pres* ne'evak 'al; *fut* ye'avek 'al.

(to) scramble up להשיג *inf* lehaseeg; *pst* heeseeg; *pres* maseeg; *fut* yaseeg.

scrambled egg ביצה טרופה *nf* beyts|ah/-eem troof|ah/-ot.

scrap 1. פיסה (fragment) *nf* pees|ah/-ot (+*of:* -at); **2.** מריבה (fight) *nf* mereev|ah/-ot (+*of:* -at).

(to) scrap לזרוק *inf* leezrok; *pst* zarak; *pres* zorek; *fut* yeezrok.

scrap iron גרוטאות *nf pl* groota'ot (*sing:* grootah).

scrap paper נייר טיוטה *nm* neyar/-ot tyootah.

scrapbook 1. פנקס הדבקות *nm* peenk|as/-esey hadbakot. **2.** תלקיט *nm* talkeet/-eem (*pl+of:* -ey).

scrape 1. גירוד *nm* gerood/-eem (*pl+of:* -ey); **2.** מצב ביש (a fix) *nm* mats|av/-vey beesh.

(to) scrape 1. לשייף (abrasively) *inf* leshayef; *pst* sheeyef; *pres* meshayef; *fut* yeshayef; **2.** לגרד (rub) *inf* legared; *pst* gered; *pres* megared; *fut* yegared.

(to bow and) scrape להתרפס *inf* leheetrapes; *pst* heetrapes; *pres* meetrapes; *fut* yeetrapes.

(to) scrape along להסתדר *inf* leheestader; *pst* heestader; *pres* meestader; *fut* yeestader.

(to) scrape together לקבץ יחד *inf* lekabets yakhad; *pst* keebets *etc*; *pres* mekabets *etc*; *fut* yekabets *etc*.

scraper 1. מגרד (tool) magred/-eem (*pl+of:* -ey); **2.** כילי (miser) *nmf* keel|ay/-a'eet.

(sky)scraper גורד שחקים *nm* gor|ed/-dey shekhakeem.

scraps שאריות *nf pl* she'ereeyot.

scratch 1. שריטה *nf* sreet|ah/-ot (+*of:* -at); **2.** גירוד (itch) *nm* gerood/-eem (*pl+of:* -ey); **3.** שרטת (mark) *nf* sar|etet/-atot.

(to) scratch 1. לשרוט (rub) *inf* leesrot; *pst* sarat; *pres* soret; *fut* yeesrot; **2.** לשרבט (write badly) *inf* lesharbet; *pst* sheerbet; *pres* mesharbet; *fut* yesharbet.

(to start from) scratch להתחיל מבראשית *inf* lehatkheel mee-beresheet; *pst* heetkheel *etc; pres* matkheel *etc; fut* yatkheel *etc.*

(to) scratch out לגרד מהיכן שהוא *[colloq.] inf* legared me-heykhan shehoo; *pst* gered *etc; pres* megared *etc; fut* yegared *etc.*

scrawl 1. שרבוט *nm* sheerboot/-eem (*pl+of:* -ey); **2.** קשקוש *[slang] nm* keeshkoosh/-eem (*pl+of:* -ey).

(to) scrawl 1. לשרבט *inf* lesharbet; *pst* sheerbet; *pres* mesharbet; *fut* yesharbet; **2.** לכתוב בכתב מרושל (write carelessly) *inf* leekhtov bee-khtav merooshal; *pst* katav *etc; pres* kotev *etc; fut* yeekhtov *etc* (*kh=k*).

scrawny דק בשר *adj* dak/-at basar.

scream 1. צווחה *nf* tsevakh|ah/-ot (+*of:* tseevkhat); **2.** צריחה *nf* tsereekh|ah/-ot (+*of:* -at).

(he's a) scream הוא "משגע" *[slang]* hoo "meshage'a"

(to) scream 1. לצרוח *inf* leetsro'akh; *pst* tsarakh; *pres* tsore'akh; *fut* yeetsrakh; **2.** לצווח (yell) *inf* leetsvo'akh; *pst* tsavakh; *pres* tsove'akh; *fut* yeetsvakh.

screech צווחה *nf* tsvakh|ah/-ot (+*of:* -at).

(to) screech 1. לצרוח *inf* leetsro'akh; *pst* tsarakh; *pres* tsore'akh; *fut* yeetsrakh; **2.** לצווח (yell) *inf* leetsvo'akh; *pst* tsavakh; *pres* tsove'akh; *fut* yeetsvakh.

screech owl תנשמת *nf* teensh|emet/-amot.

screen 1. מסך הקרנה (projection) *nm* masa|kh/-key hakranah; **2.** מסך חוצה (divider) *nm* masakh khotseh; **3.** רשת (sifter) *nf* resh|et/-atot (*pl+of:* reeshtot).

(motion picture) screen מסך קולנוע *nm* masa|kh/-key kolno'a'.

(to) screen לבדוק אחד לאחד *inf* leevdok ekhad le-'ekhad; *pst* badak (*b=v*) *etc; pres* bodek *etc; fut* yeevdok *etc.*

screen door דלת רשת *nf* delet/daltot reshet.

screen play תסריט *nm* tasreet/-eem (*pl+of:* -ey).

(to) screen windows להאפיל חלונות *inf* leha'afeel khalonot; *pst* he'efeel *etc; pres* ma'afeel *etc; fut* ya'afeel *etc.*

(wire) screen 1. מסך רשת *nm* masa|kh/-key reshet; **2.** רשת (net) *nf* reshet/-atot (*pl+of:* reeshtot).

screw בורג *nm* boreg/brageem (*pl+of:* borgey).

(to) screw 1. לברג *inf* levareg; *pst* bereg; *pres* mevareg; *fut* yevareg; **2.** להבריג (join with screws) *inf* lehavreeg; *pst* heevreeg; *pres* mavreeg; *fut* yavreeg; **3.** לזיין (obscene slang) *inf* lezayen; *pst* zeeyen; *pres* mezayen; *fut* yezayen.

(to) screw a lid on להבריג מכסה *inf* lehavreeg meekhseh; *pst* heevreeg *etc; pres* mavreeg *etc; fut* yavreeg *etc.*

screw eye בורג בעל אוזן boreg/brageem ba'al/-ey ozen.

screw nut אום *nm* om/oom|eem (*pl+of:* -ey).

screw propeller מדחף בורגי *nm* madkhef/-eem borgee/-yeem.

screw thread תבריג *nm* tavreeg/-eem (*pl+of:* -ey).

(to) screw up one's courage להרהיב עוז *inf* leharheev 'oz; *pst* heerheev 'oz; *pres* marheev 'oz; *fut* yarheev 'oz.

screwball תמהוני *nmf* teemhonee/-t.

screwdriver מברג *nm* mavreg/-eem (*pl+of:* -ey).

scribble 1. כתב מרושל *nm* ketav merooshal; **2.** קשקוש (doodle) *[slang] nm* keeshkoosh/-eem (*pl+of:* -ey).

(to) scribble 1. לשרבט *inf* lesharbet; *pst* sheerbet; *pres* mesharbet; *fut* yesharbet; **2.** לקשקש (doodle) *[colloq.] inf* lekashkesh; *pst* keeshkesh; *pres* mekashkesh; *fut* yekashkesh.

scribe סופר *nmf* sof|er/-eret (*pl:* -reem; +*of:* -rey).

script 1. כתב *nm* ketav; **2.** אותיות כתב (letters) oteeyot ketav; **3.** תסריט (text of play, movie) *nm* tasreet/-eem (*pl+of:* -ey)

script writer 1. תסריטאי *nmf* tasreet|ay/-a'eet; **2.** תסריטן *nmf* tasreetan/-eem (*pl+of:* -ey).

scripture copyist סופר סת"ם *nm* sof|er/-rey stam.

(the) Scriptures כתבי הקודש *nm pl* keetvey ha-kodesh.

scroll מגילה *nf* megeel|ah/-ot (+*of:* -at).

Scroll of the Law ספר תורה *nm* sefer/seefrey torah.

scrub 1. קרצוף *nm* keertsoof/-eem (*pl+of:* -ey); **2.** מדרגה שנייה *adj* mee-dargah shneeyah.

scrub oak אלון ננסי *nm* alon/-eem nanasee/-yeem.

scrub pine אורן ננסי *nm* oren/oraneem nanasee/-yeem.

scrubwoman עובדת ניקיון *nf* 'ov|edet/-dot neekayon.

scruple 1. נקיפת מצפון *nf* nekeef|at/-ot matspoon; **2.** היסוס (hesitation) *nm* heesoos/-eem (*pl+of:* -ey).

(to) scruple להתענות בנקיפות מצפון *inf* leheet'anot bee-nekeefot matspoon; *pst* heet'anah *etc; pres* meet'aneh *etc; fut* yeet'aneh *etc.*

scrupulous 1. בעל מצפון *adj* ba'al/-at matspoon; **2.** מדקדק *adj v pres* medakdek/-et.

(to) scrutinize 1. לבדוק *inf* leevdok; *pst* badak; *pres* bodek; *fut* yeevdok; **2.** לבחון (examine) *inf* leevkhon; *pst* bakhan (*b=v*); *pres* bokhen; *fut* yeevkhan.

scrutiny בדיקה מדוקדקת *nf* bdeek|ah/-ot medookd|eket/-akot.

(to) scuff לגרור רגליים *inf* leegror raglayeem; *pst* garar *etc; pres* gorer *etc; fut* yeegror *etc.*

scuffle תגרה מבולבלת *nf* teegr|ah/-ot mevoolb|elet/-alot.

(to) scuffle להשתתף בתגרה *inf* leheeshtatef be-teegrah; *pst* heeshtatef *etc; pres* meeshtatef *etc; fut* yeeshtatef *etc.*

sculptor פסל *nm* pasal/-eem (*pl+of:* -ey).

sculptress פסלת *nf* pas|elet/-alot.

sculpture פיסול *nm* peesool/-eem (*pl+of:* -ey).

(to) sculpture לפסל *inf* lefasel; *pst* peesel *(p=f)*; *pres* mefasel; *fut* yefasel.

scum חלאה *nf* khel|'ah (*+of:* -'at).

(to) scum להסיר זוהמה *inf* lehaseer zoohamah; *pst* heseer *etc*; *pres* meseer *etc*; *fut* yaseer *etc*.

(to) scurry לאוץ *inf* la'oots; *pst & pres* ats; *fut* ya'oots.

(to) scuttle 1. לאוץ (hurry) *inf* la'oots; *pst & pres* ats; *fut* ya'oots; **2.** להטביע (vessel) *inf* lehatbee'a'; *pst* heetbee'a'; *pres* matbee'a'; *fut* yatbee'a'.

scythe חרמש *nm* khermesh/-eem (*pl+of:* -ey).

sea ים *nm* yam/-eem (*pl+of:* -ey).

(at) sea 1. בלב־ים *adv* be-lev yam; **2.** באובדן עצות (at loss) *adv* be-ovdan 'etsot.

(to put to) sea להפליג *inf* lehafleeg; *pst* heefleeg; *pres* mafleeg; *fut* yafleeg.

sea ימי *adj* yamee/-t.

sea biscuit צנים של מלחים *nm* tseneem/-eem shel malakheem.

sea green 1. ירוק צהבהב (yellow-green) *adj* yarok/yerookah tsehav|hav/-hevet; **2.** ירוק כחלחל (bluish green) *adj* yarok/yerookah kekhalkhal/-ah.

sea level גובה פני הים *nm* govah pney ha-yam.

sea lion ארי ים *nm* aree/aryot yam.

sea power מעצמה ימית *nf* ma'atsam|ah/-ot yamee|t/-yot.

seaboard 1. שפת הים *nm* sfat ha-yam; **2.** חופי *adj* khofee/-t.

seacoast חוף ים *nm* khof/-ey yam

seagull שחף *nm* shakhaf/shekhafeem (*pl+of:* shakhafey).

seal 1. חותם (stamp) *nm* khotam/-ot; **2.** כלב ים (animal) *nm* kelev/kalvey yam.

(to set one's) seal to להטביע חותם *inf* lehatbee'a' khotam; *pst* heetbee'a' *etc*; *pres* matbee'a'; *fut* yatbee'a' *etc*.

(to) seal with sealing wax לחתום בשעווה *inf* lakhtom be-sha'avah; *pst* khatam *etc*; *pres* khotem *etc*; *fut* yakhtom *etc*.

sealing wax שעווה לחותמות *nf* sha'avah le-khotamot.

seam 1. תפר *nm* tef|er/-areem (*pl+of:* teefrey); **2.** סדק *nm* sed|ek/-akeem (*pl+of:* seedkey).

(to) seam לחבר בתפרים *inf* lekhaber bee-tfareem; *pst* kheeber *etc*; *pres* mekhaber *etc*; *fut* yekhaber *etc*.

seaman ימאי *nm* yam|ay/-a'eem (*pl+of:* -'ey).

seamstress תופרת *nf* tof|eret/-rot.

seaplane מטוס ימי *nm* mat|os/-ooseem yamee/-yeem.

seaport נמל ימי *nm* namel/nemeleem yamee/-yeem.

sear 1. קמל *adj* kamel/kemelah; **2.** יבש (dry) *adj* yavesh/yeveshah.

(to) sear לצרוב בברזל מלובן *inf* leetsrov be-varzel *(v=b)* melooban; *pst* tsarav *etc*; *pres* tsorev *etc*; *fut* yeetsrov *etc*.

search חיפוש *nm* kheepoos/-eem (*pl+of:* -ey).

(to) search 1. לחפש *inf* lekhapes; *pst* kheepes; *pres* mekhapes; *fut* yekhapes; **2.** לערוך חיפוש (carry out search) *inf* la'arokh kheepoos; *pst* 'arakh *etc*; *pres* 'orekh *etc*; *fut* ya'arokh *etc*.

(to) search a prisoner לערוך חיפוש אצל אסיר *inf* la'arokh kheepoos etsel aseer; *pst* 'arakh *etc*; *pres* 'orekh *etc*; *fut* ya'arokh *etc*.

(to) search for לחפש אחר *inf* lekhapes akhar; *pst* kheepes *etc*; *pres* mekhapes *etc*; *fut* yekhapes *etc*.

(to) search into לחקור *inf* lakhkor; *pst* khakar; *pres* khoker; *fut* yakhkor.

(in) search of בחיפוש אחר *adv* be-kheepoos akhar.

search warrant צו חיפוש *nm* tsav/-ey kheepoos.

searchlight זרקור *nm* zarkor/-eem (*pl+of:* -ey).

seashore חוף ים *nm* khof/-ey yam.

seasick חולה ים *adj* khol|eh/-at yam.

seasickness מחלת ים *nf* makhalat yam.

seaside שפת הים *nf* sfat ha-yam.

season עונה *nf* 'on|ah/-ot (*+of:* -at).

(Christmas) season עונת חג המולד *nf* 'on|at/-ot khag ha-molad.

(harvest) season עונת הקציר *nf* 'on|at/-ot ha-katseer.

(to) season 1. להבשיל (ripen) *inf* lehavsheel; *pst* heevsheel; *pres* mavsheel; *fut* yavsheel; **2.** לתבל (spice) letabel; *pst* teebel; *pres* metabel; *fut* yetabel.

(to arrive in good) season להגיע בהקדם *inf* lehagee'a' be-hekdem; *pst* heegee'a' *etc*; *pres* magee'a' *etc*; *fut* yagee'a' *etc*.

season ticket כרטיס עונתי *nm* kartees/-eem 'onatee/-yeem.

seasoning 1. תבלין (spice) *nm* tavleen/-eem (*pl+of:* -ey); **2.** תיבול (spicing) *nm* teebool/-eem (*pl+of:* -ey).

seat 1. כיסא (chair) *nm* kees|e/-a'ot (*pl+of:* -'ot); **2.** מושב (site) *nm* mosh|av/-aveem (*pl+of:* -vey); **3.** מרכז (headquarters) merk|az/-azeem (*pl+of:* -ezey); **4.** עכוז (body) *nm* 'akooz/-eem (*pl+of:* -ey).

(to) seat להושיב *inf* lehosheev; *pst* hosheev; *pres* mosheev; *fut* yosheev.

seat of learning מרכז למידה *nm* merk|az/-ezey lemeedah.

(to) seat oneself להתיישב *v rfl inf* leheetyashev; *pst* heetyashev; *pres* meetyashev; *fut* yeetyashev.

(it) seats in a thousand people מכיל מקומות ישיבה לאלף איש mekheel mekomot yesheevah le-'elef eesh.

seaweed אצת ים *nf* ats|at/-ot yam.

(to) secede לפרוש *inf* leefrosh; *pst* parash *(p=f)*; *pres* poresh; *fut* yeefrosh.

(to) seclude 1. לבודד (isolate) *inf* levoded; *pst* boded *(b=v)*; *pres* mevoded; *fut* yevoded; **2.** להדיר מן (prohibit) *inf* lehadeer meen; *pst* heedeer meen; *pres* madeer meen; *fut* yadeer meen.

(to) seclude oneself לבודד עצמו *inf* levoded 'atsmo; *pst* boded *(b=v) etc*; *pres* mevoded *etc*; *fut* yevoded *etc*;

secluded מבודד *adj* mevood|ad/-edet.

seclusion 1. בידוד *nm* beedood/-eem (*pl+of:* -ey); **2.** הסתגרות (self-imposed) *nf* heestagroo|t/-yot.

second 1. שני *ord num* shenee/shneeyah *(m/f)* **2.** משנה (deputy) *nm* meeshn|eh/-eem (*pl+of:* -ey); **3.** עוזר (assistant) *nmf* 'ozer/-et; **4.** שושבין (best man) shoshveen/-eem (*pl+of:* -ey).

(to) second 1. לתמוך ב־ *inf* leetmokh be-; *pst* tamakh be-; *pres* tomekh be-; *fut* yeetmokh be-; **2.** להצטרף אל *inf* leheetstaref el; *pst* heetstaref el; *pres* meetstaref el; *fut* yeetstaref el.

secondary 1. משני (in importance) *adj* meeshnee/-t; **2.** תיכוני (learning) *adj* teekhonee/-t.

secondary education השכלה תיכונית *nf* haskalah teekhoneet.

secondary school בית ספר תיכון *nm* bet/batey sefer teekhon/-eem.

second lieutenant סגן משנה *nm* segen/seegney meeshneh.

(on) second thought בהרהור שני *adv* be-heerhoor shenee.

second-hand 1. משומש *adj* meshoom|ash/-eshet; **2.** מיד שנייה *adj & adv* mee-yad shneeyah.

secondly שנית *adv* sheneet.

second-rate 1. מדרגה שניה *adj* mee-dargah shneeyah; **2.** סוג ב (B quality) *adj* soog bet.

secrecy 1. סודיות *nf* sodeeyoot; **2.** חשאיות *nf* khasha'eeyoot.

secret 1. סוד *nm* sod/-ot; **2.** סודי *adj* sodee/-t.

secret service שירות חשאי *nm* sheroot/-eem khasha'ee/-yeem.

secretariat מזכירות *nf* mazkeeroo|t/-yot.

secretary 1. מזכיר *nmf* mazkeer/-ah (*+of:* -at; *pl+of:* -ey); **2.** שר (minister) *nmf* sar/-ah (*pl:* -eem; *+of:* -at/-ey).

Secretary of State 1. מזכיר המדינה *nm* mazkeer/-ey ha-medeenah; **2.** שר החוץ (Israeli and European equivalent) *nmf* sar/-at ha-khoots.

(general) secretary 1. מזכיר כללי *nm* mazkeer/-eem klalee/-yeem; **2.** מזכ״ל (*acr of* 1) *nmf* mazkal/-eet (*pl+of:* -ey).

(private) secretary מזכיר אישי *nm* mazkeer/-ah eeshee/-t.

(to) secrete להפריש *inf* lehafreesh; *pst* heefreesh; *pres* mafreesh; *fut* yafreesh.

secretion הפרשה *nf* hafrash|ah/-ot (*+of:* -at).

secretive עוטה סודיות *adj* 'oteh/'otah sodeeyoot.

secretive gland בלוטת הפרשה *nf* baloot|at/-ot hafrashah.

secretly 1. בסוד *adv* be-sod; **2.** בחשאי *adv* ba-khashay.

sect כת *nf* kat/keetot.

section 1. מחלקה *nf* makhl|akah/-akot (*+of:* -eket); **2.** חלק (part) *nm* khelek/khalakeem (*pl+of:* khelkey); **3.** סעיף (article) *nm* se'eef/-eem (*pl+of:* -ey).

(to) section לחלק *inf* lekhalek; *pst* kheelek; *pres* mekhalek; *fut* yekhalek.

secular חילוני *adj* kheelonee/-t.

secure בטוח *adj* batoo'akh/betookhah.

(to) secure 1. להבטיח *inf* lehavtee'akh; *pst* heevtee'akh; *pres* mavtee'akh; *fut* yavtee'akh; **2.** לבצר (reinforce) *inf* levatser; *pst* beetser *(b=v)*; *pres* mevatser; *fut* yevatser.

securely בבטחה *adv* be-veetkhah *(v=b)*.

securities ניירות ערך *nm pl* neyarot 'erekh (*sing:* neyar 'erekh).

security 1. ביטחון *nm* beet|akhon/-khonot (*+of:* -khon); **2.** ערבות (bond) *nf* 'arvoo|t/-yot.

Security Council מועצת הביטחון *nm* mo'etset ha-beetakhon.

sedan מכונית סגורה *nf* mekhoneet segoorah.

sedate מיושב בדעתו *adj* meyoosh|av/-evet be-da'a|to/-tah.

sedation שיכוך *nm* sheekookh/-eem (*pl+of:* -ey).

sedative 1. משכך כאבים *nm m* meshak|ekh/-'khey ke'eveem; **2.** משכך (soothing) *adj* meshakekh/-et; **3.** גלולת הרגעה (pill) *nf* glool|at/-ot harga'ah.

sedentary של ישיבה *adj* shel yesheevah.

sediment משקע *nm* meeshk|a'/-a'eem (*pl+of:* -e'ey).

sedition הסתה למרד *nf* hasatah le-mered.

seditious מסית למרד *nm* meseet/-eem le-mered.

(to) seduce לפתות *inf* lefatot; *pst* peetah *(p=f)*; *pres* mefateh; *fut* yefateh.

seduction 1. פיתוי *nm* peetoo|y/-yeem (*pl+of:* -yey); **2.** הדחה (abetting) *nf* hadakh|ah/-ot (*+of:* -at).

see 1. כס *nm* kes; **2.** מעמד (standing) *nm* ma'amad/-ot.

(Holy) See הכס הקדוש *nm* ha-kes ha-kadosh.

(let me) see הבה נבדוק *v fut pl* havah neevdok.

(to) see - לראות *inf* leer'ot; *pst* ra'ah; *pres* ro'eh; *fut* yeer'eh.

(to) see a person home ללוות מישהו לביתו *inf* lelavot meeshehoo le-veyto *(v=b)*; *pst* leevah *etc*; *pres* melaveh *etc*; *fut* yelaveh *etc*.

(to) see a person off להיפרד מיוצא לדרך *inf* leheepared mee-yotse le-derekh; *pst & pres* neefrad *(f=p) etc*; *fut* yeepared *etc*.

(to) see a person through a difficulty לסייע לאדם בדחקו lesaye'a' le-adam bee-dakhko; *pst* seea' *etc etc*; *pres* mesaye'a' *etc*; *fut* yesaya' *etc*.

see that you do it דאג לעשות זאת *v imp* de'ag/da'agee la'asot zot *(m/f)*.

(to) see through a person לראות אדם כאילו שקוף היה *inf* leer'ot adam ke'eeloo shakoof hayah; *pst* ra'ah *etc*; *pres* ro'eh *etc*; *fut* yeer'eh *etc*.

(to) see to it לדאוג לכך *v inf* leed'og le-khakh *(kh=k)*; *pst* da'ag *etc*; *pres* do'eg *etc fut* yeed'ag *etc*.

(to) see to one's affairs לעסוק בענייניו שלו *inf* la'asok be-'eenyan|av/-eha shel|o/-ah *(m/f)*.

seed 1. גרעין (grain) *nm* gar'een/-eem (*pl+of:* -ey); **2.** זרע (semen) *nm* zera'/zra'eem (*pl+of:* zar'ey); **3.** פרי (fruit) *nm* pree.

(to go to) seed להתבלות *v rfl inf* leheetbalot; *pst* heetbalah; *pres* meetbaleh; *fut* yeetbaleh.

seedling שתיל *nm* shteel/-eem (*pl+of:* -ey).

seedy 1. מלא גרעינים *adj* male/mele'at gar'eeneem **2.** מרושל (untidy) *adj* merooshl|al/-elet.

(hide and) seek משחק מחבואים *nm* meeskhak/-ey makhbo'eem.

(to) seek לחפש *inf* lekhapes; *pst* kheepes; *pres* mekhapes; *fut* yekhapes.

(to) seek after לחפש אחר *inf* lekhapes (*etc*) akhar.

(to) seek to לנסות *inf* lenasot; *pst* neesah; *pres* menaseh; *fut* yenaseh.

(to) seem להיראות *inf* lehera'ot; *pst* neer'ah; *pres* neer'eh; *fut* yera'eh.

seemingly לכאורה *adv* leekh'orah.

seemly 1. הולם *adj* holem/-et; **2.** הגון *adj* hagoon/-ah.

(it) seems to me נראה לי *v pres* neer'eh lee.
(who has) seen military service ששירת בצבא *adj* she-sher|et/tah ba-tsava.
(to) seep 1. לחלחל *inf* lekhalkhel; *pst* kheelkhel; *pres* kheelkhel; *fut* yekhalkhel; **2.** להסתנן (infiltrate) *inf* leheestanen; *pst* heestanen; *pres* meestanen; *fut* yeestanen.
seer חוזה *nm* khoz|eh/-ah.
seesaw נדנדת קורה *nf* nadnedat korah.
(to) seethe לרתוח *inf* leerto'akh; *pst* ratakh; *pres* rote'akh; *fut* yeertakh.
segment 1. קטע *nm* ket|a'/-a'eem (*pl+of:* keet'ey); **2.** פלח (fruit) *nm* pelakh/plakheem (*pl+of:* peelkhey)
(to) segregate להפריד *inf* lehafreed; *pst* heefreed; *pres* mafreed; *fut* yafreed.
segregation הפרדה *nf* hafrad|ah/-ot (*+of:* -at).
(racial) segregation הפרדה גזעית hafradah geez'eet.
(to) seize 1. ללכוד (catch) *inf* leelkod; *pst* lakhad (*kh=k*); *pres* lokhed; *fut* yeelkod; **2.** לעצור (arrest) *inf* la'atsor; *pst* 'atsar; *pres* 'otser; *fut* ya'atsor; **3.** לחטוף (grasp) lakhtof; *pst* khataf; *pres* khotef; *fut* yakhtof; **4.** לתפוס (capture) *inf* leetpos; *pst* tafas (*f=p*); *pres* tofes; *fut* yeetpos.
(to) seize upon ללכוד *inf* leelkod; *pst* lakhad (*kh=k*); *pres* lokhed; *fut* yeelkod.
(to become) seized with fear להיתפש לפחד *inf* leheetafes le-fakhad (*f=p*); *pst & pres* neetfas *etc*; *fut* yeetafes *etc*
seizure 1. תפישה (of possessions) *nf* tefees|ah/-ot (*+of:* -at); **2.** לכידה (of a criminal) *nf* lekheed|ah/-ot (*+of:* -at); **3.** התקף (illness) *nm* hetkef/-eem (*pl+of:* -ey).
seldom לעיתים נדירות *adv* le-'eeteem nedeerot.
select מובחר *adj* moovkh|ar/-eret.
(to) select 1. לבחור *inf* leevkhor; *pst* bakhar (*b=v*); *pres* bokher; *fut* yeevkhar; **2.** לברור *inf* leevror; *pst* barar (*b=v*); *pres* borer; *fut* yeevror.
selection 1. בחירה *nf* bekheer|ah/-ot (*+of:* -at); **2.** סלקציה *nf* selekts|yah/-yot.
self עצמו *pers pron* 'atsm|o/-ah (*m/f*).
(by one)self בעצמו *pers pron* be-'atsm|o/-ah (*m/f*).
(for one)self לעצמו *pers pron* le-'atsm|o/-ah (*m/f*).
(his wife and) self הוא ואשתו hoo ve-'eeshto.
(her)self בעצמה *pers pron nf* be-'atsmah
(him)self בעצמו *pers pron nm* be-'atsmo.
(one's other) self ה"אני" האחר שלו *nm* ha-anee ha-akher shel|o/-ah (*m/f*).
self-centered 1. מרוכז בעצמו *adj* merook|az/-ezet be-'atsm|o/-ah; **2.** אגוצנטרי *adj* egotsentree/-t.
self-conscious 1. מודע לעצמו *adj* mood|a'/-a'at le-'atsm|o/-ah; **2.** נבוך בחברה *adj* navokh/nevookhah be-khevrah.
self-control שליטה עצמית *nf* shleetah 'atsmeet.
self-defence הגנה עצמית *nf* haganah 'atsmeet.
self-denial התנזרות *nf* heetnazroo|t/-yot.
self-esteem כבוד עצמי *nm* kavod 'atsmee.
self-evident ברור מעצמו *adj* baroor/broorah me-'atsm|o/-ah.
self-government ממשל עצמי *nm* meemshal/-eem 'atsmee/-yeem.
self-interest טובת עצמו *nf* tovat 'atsm|o/-ah (*m/f*).
self-love אהבת עצמו *nf* ahavat 'atsm|o/-ah (*m/f*).
self-possessed מושל ברוחו *adj* moshel/-et be-rookh|o/-ah.
self-sacrifice הקרבה עצמית *nf* hakravah 'atsmeet.
self-satisfied מרוצה מעצמו *adj* meroots|eh/-ah me-'atsm|o/-ah.
selfish אנוכיי *adj* anokheyee/-t.
selfishly באנוכיות *adv* be-anokheeyoot.
selfishness אנוכיות *nf* anokheeyoot.
selfsame 1. זהה *adj* zeheh/zehah; **2.** אותו עצמו *pers pron* oto/otah 'atsm|o/-ah.
(to) sell למכור *inf* leemkor; *pst* makhar (*kh=k*); *pres* mokher; *fut* yeemkor.
(to) sell at auction למכור במיכרז *inf* leemkor (*etc*) be-meekhraz.
(to) sell out לחסל עסק *inf* lekhasel 'esek; *pst* kheesel *etc*; *pres* mekhasel *etc*; *fut* yekhasel *etc*.
seller מוכר *nmf* mokh|er/-eret (*pl:* -reem/-rot; *+of:* -rey).
(our)selves בעצמנו *pers pron* be-'atsmenoo.
(them)selves בעצמם *pers pron* be-'atsm|am/-an (*m/f*).
semblance מראית עין *nf* mar'eet 'ayeen.
semicircle חצי עיגול *nm* khats|ee/-a'ey 'eegool/-eem.
semicolon נקודה ופסיק *nf & nm* nekoodah oo-fseek (*f=p*).
seminar סמינריון *nm* semeenaryon/-eem (*pl+of:* -ey).
seminary סמינר *nm* semeenar/-eem (*pl+of:* -ey).
Semite 1. בן שם *nm* ben/-ey shem; **2.** שמי *nmf & adj* shemee/-t.
Semitic שמי *adj* shemee/-t.
semi-trailer גורר למחצה *nm* gorer/-eem le-mekhtsah.
senate סינט *nm* senat/-eem.
senator סינטור *nm* senator/-eem (*pl+of:* -ey).
(to) send לשלוח *inf* leeshlo'akh; *pst* shalakh; *pres* shole'akh; *fut* yeeshlakh.
(to) send away 1. לשלח *inf* leshale'akh; *pst* sheele'akh; *pres* meshale'akh; *fut* yashale'akh; **2.** לפטר (fire) *inf* lefater; *pst* peeter (*p=f*); *pres* mefater; *fut* yefater.
(to) send forth 1. לפרסם *inf* lefarsem; *pst* peersem (*p=f*); *pres* mefarsem; *fut* yefarsem; **2.** להוציא החוצה *inf* lehotsee ha-khootsah; *pst* hotsee *etc*; *pres* motsee *etc*; *fut* yotsee *etc*.
(to) send someone up for 12 years לשלוח ל־12 שנות מאסר *inf* leeshlo'akh lee-shteym-'esreh shnot ma'asar; *pst* shalakh *etc*; *pres* shole'akh *etc*; *fut* yeeshlakh *etc*.
(to) send word 1. להודיע *inf* lehodee'a'; *pst* hodee'a'; *pres* modee'a'; *fut* yodee'a'; **2.** להעביר הודעה (transmit notice) *inf* leha'aveer hoda'ah; *pst* he'eveer *etc*; *pres* ma'aveer *etc*; *fut* ya'aveer *etc*.
sender 1. שולח *nmf* shol|e'akh/-akhat; **2.** ממען *nm* mema|'en/-'aneem (*pl+of:* -'aney).
senile סנילי *adj* seneelee/-t.
senility 1. תשישות זיקנה *nf* tesheeshoot zeeknah; **2.** סניליות *nf* seneeleeyoot.

senior 1. בגיר (older) *adj* bageer/-begeerah; **2.** בכיר (superior) *adj* bakheer/bekheerah.

(somebody's) senior הממונה עליו *nmf* ha-memoon|eh/-ah 'alav/'aleha *(m/f)*.

senior citizen אזרח ותיק *nmf* ezrakh/-eet vateek/-ah.

senior class כיתה בכירה *nf* keet|ah/-ot bekhee-r|ah/-ot.

sensation 1. תחושה (feeling) *nf* tekhoosh|ah/-ot (+*of:* -at); **2.** סנסציה (excitement) *nf* sensats|yah/-yot (+*of:* -yat).

sensational סנסציוני *adj* sensatsyonee/-t.

sense 1. חוש (function) *nm* khoosh/-eem (*pl+of:* -ey); **2.** רגש (sentiment) *nm* regesh/regashot (*pl+of:* reegshot); **3.** תבונה (judgment) *nf* tevoo-n|ah/-ot (+*of:* -at); **4.** מובן (meaning) *nm* moovan/-eem (*pl+of:* -ey).

(common) sense שכל ישר *nm* sekhel yashar.

(to) sense לחוש *inf* lakhoosh *pst & pres* khash; *fut* yakhoosh.

senseless חסר טעם madj khas|ar/-rat ta'am.

sensibility רגישות *nf* regeeshoo|t/-yot.

sensible 1. הגיוני (reasonable) *adj* hegyonee/-t; **2.** מורגש (appreciable) *adj* moorg|ash/-eshet.

sensibly בהיגיון *adv* be-heegayon.

sensitive רגיש *adj* rageesh/regeeshah.

sensitiveness רגישות *nf* regeeshoo|t/-yot.

(to) sensitize 1. לרגש *inf* leragesh; *pst* reegesh; *pres* meragesh; *fut* yeragesh; **2.** ליצור רגישות *inf* leetsor regeeshoot; *pst* yatsar *etc*; *pres* yotser *etc*; *fut* yeetsor *etc*.

sensual חושני *adj* khooshanee/-t.

sensuality חושניות *nf* khoshaneeyoo|t/-yot.

sentence 1. משפט (grammatical) *nm* meeshp|at/-ateem (*pl+of:* -etey); **2.** גזר־דין (by a court) *nm* gezar/geezrey deen.

(death) sentence גזר־דין מוות *nm* gzar/geezrey deen mavet.

sentiment רגש *nm* regesh/regashot (*pl+of:* reegshey).

sentimental 1. רגשי *adj* reegshee/-t; **2.** רגשני *adj* ragshanee/-t; **3.** סנטימנטלי *adj* senteementalee/-t.

sentimentality 1. רגשנות *nf* ragshanoot; **2.** סנטימנטליות *nf* senteementaleeyoot.

sentinel, sentry זקיף *nm* zakeef/zekeef|eem (*pl+of:* -ey).

sentinel, sentry זקיף *nm* zakeef/zekeef|eem (*pl+of:* -ey).

separate 1. נפרד (apart) *adj* neefr|ad/-edet; **2.** שונה (different) *adj* shon|eh/-ah.

(to) separate להפריד *inf* lehafreed; *pst* heefreed; *pres* mafreed; *fut* yafreed.

separately 1. לחוד *adv* lekhood; **2.** בניפרד *adv* be-neefrad.

separation 1. פירוד (state) *nm* perood/-eem (*pl+of:* -ey); **2.** הפרדה (act) hafrad|ah/-ot (+*of:* -at).

sepulcher 1. קבורה *nf* kevoor|ah/-ot (+*of:* -at); **2.** קבר (grave) *nm* kev|er/-areem (*pl+of:* keevrey).

sequel המשך *nm* hemshekh/-eem (*pl+of:* -ey).

sequence 1. רצף (continuity) *nm* rets|ef/-afeem (*pl+of:* reetsfey); **2.** תוצאה (result) *nf* totsa|'ah/-'ot (+*of:* -'at).

serenade סרנדה *nf* serenad|ah/-ot (+*of:* -at).

serene 1. רוגע *adj* rog|e'a'/-a'at; **2.** רם־מעלה (high-ranking) *adj* ram/-at ma'alah.

serenity רוגע *nm* roga'.

sergeant סמל *nmf* sam|al/-elet (*pl+of:* -aley).

sergeant-at-arms קצין טקס *nm* ketseen/-ey tekes.

sergeant-major רב־סמל *nm* rav-samal/rabey *(b=v)* samaleem.

serial סדרה בהמשכים *nf* seedrah/sdarot be-hemshekheem.

serial novel רומן בהמשכים *nm* roman/-eem be-hemshekheem.

serial number מספר סידורי *nm* meespar/-eem seedooree/-yeem.

serious רציני *adj* retseenee/-t.

seriously ברצינות *adv* bee-retseenoot.

seriousness רצינות *nf* retseenoot.

sermon דרשה *nf* drash|ah/-ot (+*of:* -at).

serpent נחש *nm* nakhash/nekhash|eem (*pl+of:* -ey)

serum נסיוב *nm* nasyoov/-eem (*pl+of:* -ey).

servant משרת *nmf* meshar|et/-etet (*pl:* -teem/-tot; +*of:* -tey).

(to) serve 1. לשרת *inf* lesharet; *pst* sheret; *pres* mesharet; *fut* yesharet; **2.** לשמש (wait on) *inf* leshamesh; *pst* sheemesh; *pres* meshamesh; *fut* yeshamesh; **3.** להגיש (supply) *inf* lehageesh; *pst* heegeesh; *pres* mageesh; *fut* yageesh.

(to) serve a term in prison לשבת תקופה בכלא *inf* lashevet tekoofah ba-kele; *pst* yashav *etc*; *pres* yoshev *etc*; *fut* yeshev *etc*.

(to) serve as לשמש בתור *inf* leshamesh be-tor; *pst* sheemesh *etc*; *pres* meshamesh *etc*; *fut* yeshamesh *etc*;

(to) serve for לשמש ל־ *inf* leshamesh le-; *pst* sheemesh le-; *pres* meshamesh le-; *fut* yeshamesh le-;

(to) serve notice on 1. למסור הזמנה לדין *inf* leemsor hazmanah le-deen; *pst* masar *etc*; *pres* moser *etc*; *fut* yeemsor *etc*; **2.** לשגר התראה *inf* leshager hatra'ah; *pst* sheeger *etc*; *pres* meshager *etc*; *fut* yeshager *etc*.

(to) serve one's purpose למלא את שליחותו *inf* lemale et shleekhooto; *pst* meele *etc*; *pres* memale *etc*; *fut* yemale *etc*.

server 1. שמש (servant) *nm* shamash/-eem (*pl+of:* -ey); **2.** חובט ראשונה (tennis) *nmf* khovet/-et reeshonah.

serves you right מגיע לך magee'a' lekha/lakh *(m/f)*.

service 1. שירות *nm* sheroot/-eem (*pl+of:* -ey); **2.** מסירה (citation) *nf* meseer|ah/-ot (+*of:* -at); **3.** חבטת פתיחה (tennis) *nf* khavat|at/-ot p'teekhah.

(at your) service לשירותך le-sheroot|kha/-ekh *(m/f)*.

(funeral) service הלוויה *nf* halva|yah/-yot (+*of:* -yat).

(mail) service שירות דואר *nm* sheroot/-ey do'ar.

(table) service מערכת שולחן *nf* ma'ar|ekhet/-khot shoolkhan.

(tea) service מערכת תה *nf* ma'ar|ekhet/-khot teh.
(to) service לתחזק (maintain) *inf* letakhzek; *pst* teekhzek; *pres* metakhzek; *fut* yetakhzek.
service entrance כניסה לעובדים *nf* keneesah la-'ovdeem.
service man 1. איש שירות *nm* eesh/anshey sheroot; **2.** שרת *nm* sharat/-eem (*pl+of:* -ey).
service station תחנת שירות *nf* takhan|at/-ot sheroot.
serviceable 1. שמיש *adj* shameesh/shemeeshah; **2.** תכליתי (purposeful) *adj* takhleetee/-t.
servile מתרפס *adj* meetrapes/-et.
servitude עבדות *nf* 'avdoo|t/-yot.
session ישיבה *nf* yesheev|ah/-ot (*+of:* -at).
set 1. מערכת *nf* ma'ar|ekhet/-akhot (*pl+of:* -khot); **2.** מערכת כלים (dishes) ma'ar|ekhet/-khot keleem; **3.** צרור מפתחות (keys) *nm* tseror/-ot maftekhot; **4.** מערכת שיניים (teeth) *nf* ma'ar|ekhet/-khot sheenayeem.
set 1. איתן (firm) *adj.* eytan/-ah; **2.** מבוסס (established) *adj* mevoos|as/-eset.
(radio) set מקלט רדיו *nm* maklet/-ey radyo.
(TV) set מקלט טלוויזיה *nm* maklet/-ey televeezyah.
(to) set 1. להציב *inf* lehatseev; *pst* heetseev; *pres* matseev; *fut* yatseev; **2.** לקבוע (fix) *inf* leekbo'a'; *pst* kava' (*v=b*); *pres* kove'a'; *fut* yeekba'; **3.** לשחרר (free) *inf* leshakhrer; *pst* sheekhrer; *pres* meshakhrer; *fut* yeshakhrer; **4.** לשבץ (precious stones) *inf* leshabets; *pst* sheebets; *pres* meshabets; *fut* yeshabets; **5.** לשקוע (go down) *inf* leeshko'a'; *pst* shaka'; *pres* shoke'a'; *fut* yeeshka'; **6.** להתקשות (harden) *inf* leheetkashot; *pst* heetkashah; *pres* meetkasheh; *fut* yeetkasheh.
(to) set a bone לקבע עצם *inf* lekabe'a' 'etsem; *pst* keeba' *etc*; *pres* mekabe'a' *etc*; *fut* yekaba' *etc*.
(to) set a trap לטמון מלכודת *inf* leetmon malkodet; *pst* taman *etc*; *pres* tomen *etc*; *fut* yeetmon *etc*.
(to) set an example לשמש דוגמה *inf* leshamesh doogmah; *pst* sheemesh *etc*; *pres* meshamesh *etc*; *fut* yeshamesh *etc*;
(to) set aside לדחות הצידה *inf* leedkhot ha-tseedah; *pst* dakhah *etc*; *pres* dokheh *etc*; *fut* yeedkheh *etc*.
(to) set back לעכב *inf* le'akev; *pst* 'eekev; *pres* me'akev; *fut* ye'akev.
(to) set forth on a journey לצאת למסע *inf* latset le-masa'; *pst* yatsa *etc*; *pres* yotse *etc*; *fut* yetse *etc*.
(to) set on fire להעלות באש *inf* leha'alot ba-'esh; *pst* he'elah *etc*; *pres* ma'aleh *etc*; *fut* ya'aleh *etc*.
(to) set one's heart on להשתוקק *inf* leheeshtokek; *pst* heeshtokek; *pres* meeshtokek; *fut* yeeshtokek.
(to) set one's mind לגמור אומר *inf* leegmor omer; *pst* gamar *etc*; *pres* gomer *etc*; *fut* yeegmor *etc*.
(to) set out to -לפתוח ב *inf* leefto'akh be-; *pst* patakh (*p=f*) be-; *pres* pote'akh be-; *fut* yeeftakh be-.
(to) set right לתקן *inf* letaken; *pst* teeken; *pres* metaken; *fut* yetaken.
(to) set up 1. להתקין (install) *inf* lehatkeen; *pst* heetkeen; *pres* matkeen; *fut* yatkeen; **2.** לסדר בדפוס (in type, print) *inf* lesader bee-dfoos; *pst* seeder *etc*; *pres* mesader *etc*; *fut* yesader *etc*; **3.** להקים (erect) *inf* lehakeem; *pst inf* hekeem; *pres* mekeem; *fut* yakeem.
(to) set upon someone "לעלות" על מישהו *inf* la'alot 'al meeshehoo; *pst* 'alah *etc*; *pres* 'oleh *etc*; *fut* ya'aleh *etc*.
setback 1. היעצרות *nf* he'atsroo|t/-yot; **2.** בלימה *nf* bleem|ah/-ot (*+of:* -at).
settee ספה *nf* sap|ah/-ot (*+of:* -at).
setting 1. תמונה (scene) *nf* temoon|ah/-ot (*+of:* -at); **2.** תסריט (scenario) *nm* tasreet/-eem (*pl+of:* -ey); **3.** שקיעה (sun, moon) *nf* shekee|'ah/-'ot (*+of:* -'at);
(to) settle 1. ליישב (colonize, settle dispute) *inf* leyashev; *pst* yeeshev; *pres* meyashev; *fut* yeyashev; **2.** לפתור (solve) *inf* leeftor; *pst* patar (*p=f*); *pres* poter; *fut* yeeftor; **3.** להסדיר (put in order) *inf* lehasdeer; *pst* heesdeer; *pres* masdeer; *fut* yasdeer.
(to) settle down 1. להשתקע *inf* leheeshtake'a'; *pst* heeshtaka'; *pres* meeshtake'a'; *fut* yeeshtaka'; **2.** להירגע (relax) *inf* leheraga'; *pst & pres* neerga'; *fut* yeraga'.
(to) settle on a date לקבוע תאריך *inf* leekbo'a' ta'areekh; *pst* kava' (*v=b*) *etc*; *pres* kove'a' *etc*; *fut* yeekba' *etc*;
(to) settle property להקנות נכסים *inf* lehaknot nekhaseem; *pst* heeknah *etc*; *pres* makneh *etc*; *fut* yakneh *etc*
(to) settle the matter להסדיר את העניין *inf* lehasdeer et ha-'eenyan; *pst* heesdeer *etc*; *pres* masdeer *etc*; *fut* yasdeer *etc*.
settlement 1. יישוב (community) *nm* yeeshoov/-eem (*pl+of:* -ey); **2.** הסדר (arrangement) *nm* hesder/-eem (*pl+of:* -ey); **3.** הורשה (property) *nf* horash|ah/-ot (*+of:* -at).
(marriage) settlement נדוניה *nf* nedoon|yah/-yot (*+of:* -yat).
settler 1. מתיישב *nm* meet'yash|ev/-veem; **2.** מתנחל (in West Bank) *nm* meetnakh|el/-aleem (*pl+of:* -aley).
settler of disputes מיישב סיכסוכים *nm* meyash|ev/-vey seekhsookheem.
setup 1. מבנה *nm* meevn|eh/-eem (*pl+of:* -ey); **2.** צורת ארגון (organization) *nf* tsoor|at/-ot eergoon.
seven 1. שבעה *num* sheev'ah/sheva' (*m/f*); **2.** 'ז*num* zayeen (7 in *Hebr. num. sys.*).
seven hundred 1. שבע מאות *num* shva' me'ot; **2.** ת"ש*num* tash (700 in *Hebr. num. sys.*).
seventeen 1. שבעה עשר *num nm* sheev'ah-'asar; **2.** שבע עשרה *num nf* shva'-'esreh; **3.** י"ז *num* yod-zayeen (17 in *Hebr. num. sys.*).
seventeenth 1. השבעה עשר *adj m* ha-sheev'ah-'asar; **2.** השבע-עשרה *adj f* ha-shva'-'esreh; **3.** הי"ז *adj* ha-yod-zayeen (17th in *Hebr. num. sys.*).
seventh שביעי *adj* shevee'ee/-t; **2.** 'ז*adj* zayeen (7th in *Hebr. num. sys.*).
seventieth 1. השבעים *adj* ha-sheev'eem; **2.** 'ע*adj* 'ayeen (70th in *Hebr. num. sys.*).
seventy 1. שבעים *num* sheev'eem **2.** 'ע*num* 'ayeen (70 in *Hebr. num. sys.*).
(to) sever לנתק *inf* lenatek; *pst* neetek; *pres* menatek; *fut* yenatek.

several 1. אחדים (some) akhadeem; **2.** רבים (many) rabeem.

severance pay פיצויי פיטורין *nm pl* peetsooyey peetooreen.

severe חמור *nm* khamor/-eem (*pl+of:* -ey).

severity חומרה *nf* khoomr|ah/-ot (*+of:* -at).

(to) sew לתפור *inf* leetpor; *pst* tafar *(f=p)*; *pres* tofer; *fut* yeetpor.

sewage 1. מי שופכין *nm pl* mey shofkheen; **2.** מי ביוב *nm pl* mey beeyoov.

sewer 1. תעלת ביוב *nf* te'al|at/-ot beeyoov; **2.** תעלת שופכין (syn) *nf* te'al|at/-ot shofkheen.

sewing תפירה *nf* tfeer|ah/-ot (*+of:* -at).

sewing machine מכונת תפירה *nf* mekhon|at/-ot tfeerah.

sex מין *nm* meen/-eem (*pl+of:* -ey).

sex-appeal 1. משיכה מינית *nf* mesheekhah meeneet. **2.** סקס־אפיל *nm* seksapeel.

sextant סקסטנט *nm* sekstant.

sextet שישייה *nf* sheeshee|yah/-yot (*+of:* -yat).

sexton שמש *nm* shamash/-eem (*pl+of:* -ey).

sexual 1. מיני *adj* meenee/-t; **2.** סקסואלי *adj* seksoo'alee/-t.

sexy 1. מגרה מינית *adj* megar|eh/-ah meeneet; **2.** סקסי *adj* seksee/-t.

shabbily בבלויי סחבות *adv* bee-vloyey *(v=b)* sekhavot.

shabby מרופט *adj* meroop|at/-etet.

shack בקתה *nf* beektah/bekatot (*+of:* beektat).

shackles אזיקים *nm pl* azeek|eem (*pl+of:* -ey).

shade 1. צל (shadow) *nm* tsel/-aleem (*pl+of:* tseeleley); **2.** גוון (nuance) *nm* gaven/gvaneem (*pl+of:* gon/-ey); **3.** כסוי (cover) *nm* kesoo|y/-yeem (*pl+of:* -yey); **4.** מצחון (visor) *nf* meets'khon/-eem (*pl+of:* -ey); **5.** אהיל (lampshade) *nm* aheel/-eem (*pl+of:* -ey).

(in the) shade of בצלו של *adv* be-tseelo shel.

shade of meaning גוון של מובן *nm* gaven shel moovan.

shadow 1. צד חשוך (dark side) *nm* tsad khashookh; **2.** רוח רפאים (phantom) *nm* roo|'akh/-khot refa'eem.

(under the) shadow of בצל *adv* be-tsel.

shadow of doubt צל של ספק *nm* tsel shel safek.

(to) shadow someone לעקוב אחר מישהו *inf* la'akov akhar meeshe|hoo/-hee.

shadowy 1. קלוש *adj* kaloosh/klooshah; **2.** מעורפל (foggy) me'oorpl|al/-elet.

shady 1. מצל (giving shade) *adj* mets|el/-eelah; **2.** מוצל (shaded) *adj* moots|al/-elet; **3.** מפוקפק (of questionable character) *adj* mefookp|ak/-eket.

shady business עסק מפוקפק *nm* 'esek/'asakeem mefookpak/-eem.

shady character טיפוס מפוקפק *nm* teepoos/-eem mefookpak/-eem.

shaft 1. מוט *nm* mot/-ot; **2.** כלונס (stilt) *nm* klon|as/-sa'ot; **3.** פיר (narrow space) *nm* peer/-eem (*pl+of:* -ey).

shaggy 1. שעיר *adj* sa'eer/se'eerah; **2.** מדובלל (sparse) *adj* medoovl|al/-elet.

(to) shake 1. לנענע *inf* lena'ne'a'; *pst* nee'na'; *pres* mena'ne'a'; *fut* yena'na'; **2.** להניע *inf* lehanee'a'; *pst* henee'a'; *pres* menee'a'; *fut* yanee'a'.

(to) shake hands ללחוץ ידיים *inf* leelkhots yadayeem; *pst* lakhats *etc*; *pres* lokhets *etc*; *fut* yeelkhats *etc*.

(to) shake one's head להניד ראש *inf* lehaneed rosh; *pst* heneed *etc*; *pres* meneed *etc*; *fut* yaneed *etc*.

(to) shake with cold לרעוד מקור *inf* leer'od mee-kor; *pst* ra'ad *etc*; *pres* ro'ed *etc*; *fut* yeer'ad *etc*.

(to) shake with fear להתחלחל מפחד *inf* leheetkhalkhel mee-pakhad; *pst* heetkhalkhel *etc*; *pres* meetkhalkhel *etc*; *fut* yeetkhalkhel *etc*.

shake-up שידוד מערכות *nm* sheedood/-ey ma'arakhot.

shaky רעוע *adj* ra'oo'a'/re'oo'ah.

shallow 1. רדוד *adj* radood/redoodah; **2.** שטחי (superficial) sheetkhee/-t.

shallowness 1. רדידות *nf* redeedoo|t/-yot; **2.** שטחיות *nf* sheetkheeyoot.

sham 1. העמדת פנים *nf* ha'amad|at/-ot paneem; **2.** מדומה *adj* medoom|eh/-ah.

(to) sham להעמיד פנים *inf* leha'ameed paneem; *pst* he'emeed *etc*; *pres* ma'ameed *etc*; *fut* ya'ameed *etc*.

sham battle תרגיל קרב *nm* targeel/-ey krav.

shambles 1. שדה קטל *nm* sed|eh/-ot ketel; **2.** בית מטבחיים (slaughterhouse) bet/batey meetbakhayeem; **3.** בלגן (confusion) *(slang) nm* balagan/-eem.

shame 1. בושה *nf* boosh|ah/-ot (*+of:* -at); **2.** חרפה *nf* kherp|ah (*+of:* -at).

(it is a) shame חרפה ובושה *interj* kherpah oo-vooshah *(v=b)* !

shame on you! בושה לך ! *interj* booshah lekha!/lakh! *(m/f)*.

(to bring) shame upon להמיט קלון על *inf* lehameet kalon 'al; *pst* hemeet *etc*; *pres* memeet *etc*; *fut* yameet *etc*.

shameful 1. מביש *adj* meveesh/-ah; **2.** מחפיר *adj* makhpeer/-ah.

shameless 1. חסר בושה *adj* khas|ar/-rat booshah; **2.** מחוצף *adj* mekhoots|af/-efet.

shamelessness חוצפה *nf* khootsp|ah/-ot (*+of:* -at).

shampoo שמפו *[colloq.] nm* shampo/-'eem.

shamrock תלתן *nm* teeltan/-eem (*+of:* -ey).

shank 1. שוק *nf* shok/-ayeem (*pl+of:* -ey); **2.** רגל *nf* regel/ragl|ayeem (*pl+of:* -ey).

shanty 1. בקתה *nf* beektah/bekatot (*+of:* beektat); **2.** צריף *nm* ts'reef/-eem (*pl+of:* -ey).

shape 1. צורה (form) *nf* tsoor|ah/-ot (*+of:* -at); **2.** גיזרה (figure) *nf* geezrah/gezarot (*+of:* geezr|at/-ot); **3.** מצב (condition) mats|av/-aveem (*pl+of:* -vey).

(in bad) shape במצב עלוב be-matsav 'aloov.

(to) shape 1. לצור *inf* latsoor; *pst & pres* tsar; *fut* yatsoor; **2.** לעצב (form) *inf* le'atsev; *pst* 'eetsev; *pres* me'atsev; *fut* ye'atsev; **3.** לגבש (consolidate) *inf* legabesh; *pst* geebesh; *pres* megabesh; *fut* yegabesh.

(to put into) shape לתת צורה לדברים *inf* latet tsoorah lee-dvareem; *pst* natan *etc*; *pres* noten *etc*; *fut* yeeten *etc*.

(to) shape one's life לעצב את חייו שלו *inf* le'atsev et kha|yav/-yeha shel|o/-ah; *pst* 'eetsev *etc*; *pres* me'atsev *etc*; *fut* ye'atsev *etc*.

shapeless 1. חסר־צורה *adj* khas|ar/-rat tsoorah; **2.** מרושל (slack) *adj* meroosh|al/-elet.

(the plan is) shaping up התוכנית מקבלת צורה ha-tokhneet mekabelet tsoorah.

share 1. חלק (participation) *nm* khelek/khalakeem (*pl+of:* khelkey); **2.** מנייה (of stock) *nf* menayah/-yot (*+of:* -yat).

(to) share 1. לקחת חלק *inf* lakakhat khelek; *pst* lakakh *etc*; *pres* loke'akh *etc*; *fut* yeekakh; **2.** לחלוק עם (partake) *inf* lakhlok 'eem; *pst* khalak 'eem; *pres* kholek 'eem; *fut* yakhlok 'eem.

(to) share a thing with לחלוק עם *inf* lakhlok 'eem; *pst* khalak 'eem; *pres* kholek 'eem; *fut* yakhlok 'eem.

(to) share in להתחלק ב־ *inf* leheetkhalek be-; *pst* heetkhalek be-; *pres* meetkhalek be-; *fut* yeetkhalek be-.

shareholder בעל מניה *nmf* ba'al/-at mena|yah/-yot (*pl:* ba'aley).

shark 1. כריש (fish) *nm* kareesh/kreesh|eem (*pl+of:* -ey); **2.** נוכל *nm* nokh|el/-leem (*pl+of:* -ley); **3.** מומחה (expert) moomkh|eh/-eet.

(loan) shark מלווה בריבית קצוצה *nm* malv|eh/-eem be-reebeet ketsootsah.

sharp 1. חד *adj* khad/-ah; **2.** שנון (biting) *adj* shanoon/shnoonah; **3.** חריף (acute) *adj* khareef/-ah; **4.** מזהיר (bright) *adj* maz'heer/-ah; **5.** פתאומי (sudden) *adj* peet'omee/-t.

(at ten o'clock) sharp בשעה עשר בדיוק *adv* be-sha'ah 'eser be-deeyook.

sharp criticism בקורת נוקבת *nf* beekor|et/-ot nok|evet/-vot.

sharp curve סיבוב חד *nm* seevoov/-eem khad/-eem.

sharp ear אוזן חדה *nf* ozen/oznayeem khad|ah/-ot.

sharp features תווי פנים חדים *nm pl* tavey paneem khadeem.

sharp struggle מאבק מר *nm* ma'avak/-eem mar/-eem.

sharp turn פנייה חדה *nf* pnee|yah/-yot khad|ah/-ot.

(to) sharpen 1. לחדד *inf* lekhaded; *pst* kheeded; *pres* mekhaded; *fut* yekhaded; **2.** להשחיז *inf* lehashkheez; *pst* heeshkheez; *pres* mashkheez; *fut* yashkheez.

(pencil) sharpener מחדד עפרונות *nm* mekhaded/-ey 'efronot.

sharply 1. בחריפות *adv* ba-khareefoot; **2.** בדיוק בזמן (arrive) *adv* be-deeyook ba-zman.

sharpness 1. שנינות *nf* shneenoo|t/-yot; **2.** חדות *nf* khadoo|t/-yot.

(to) shatter לנפץ *inf* lenapets; *pst* neepets; *pres* menapets; *fut* yenapets.

(to) shatter hopes לנפץ תיקוות *inf* lenapets (*etc*) teekvot.

(his health was) shattered בריאותו נתערערה *nf* bree'oot|o/-ah (*m/f*) neet'ar'erah.

shave תגלחת *nf* teeglakh|at/-ot.

(a close) shave הינצלות בנס *nf* heenatsloo|t/-yot be-nes.

(to) shave 1. לגלח *vt inf* legale'akh; *pst inf* geele'akh; *pres* megale'akh; *fut* yegale'akh; **2.** להתגלח (oneself) *v rfl inf* leheetgale'akh; *pst* heetgale'akh; *pres* meetgale'akh; *fut* yeetgale'akh.

(clean) shaven מגולח למשעי *adj* megoolakh/-at le-meesh'ee.

shaving גילוח *nm* geeloo|'akh/-kheem (*pl+of:* -khey).

shaving brush מברשת גילוח *nf* meevresh|et/-ot geeloo'akh.

shaving cream משחת גילוח *nf* meeshkh|at/-ot geeloo'akh.

shaving soap סבון גילוח *nm* sabon/-ey geeloo'akh.

shaving spray תרסיס גילוח *nm* tarsees/-ey geeloo'akh.

shawl סודר *nm* sood|ar/-areem (*pl+of:* -rey).

she היא *nf pron* hee.

she who היא היא אשר hee hee asher.

she-bear דובה *nf* doob|ah/-ot (*+of:* -at).

she-goat עיזה *nf* 'eez|ah/-ot (*+of:* -at).

sheaf אלומה *nf* aloom|ah/-ot (*+of:* -at).

(to) sheaf לאלם אלומות *inf* le'alem aloomot; *pst* eelem *etc*; *pres* me'alem *etc*; *fut* ye'alem *etc*.

(to) shear לגזוז *inf* leegzoz; *pst* gazaz; *pres* gozez; *fut* yeegzoz.

shearing גז *nm* gez.

shears 1. מגזזה *nf* magzez|ah/-ot (*+of:* -at); **2.** מספריים *nm pl* meespl|arayeem (*+of:* -erey).

sheath 1. נדן *nm* nedan/-eem (*pl+of:* -ey); **2.** נרתיק *nm* narteek/-eem (*pl+of:* -ey).

(to) sheathe להחזיר לנדן *inf* lehakhzeer lee-nedan; *pst* hekhzeer *etc*; *pres* makhzeer *etc*; *fut* yakhzeer *etc*.

shed 1. להזיל (tears) *inf* lehazeel; *pst* heezeel; *pres* mazeel; *fut* yazeel; **2.** להפיץ (light) lehafeets; *pst* hefeets; *pres* mefeets; *fut* yafeets; **3.** לשפוך (blood) *inf* leeshpokh; *pst* shafakh (*f=p*); *pres* shofekh; *fut* yeeshpokh.

(to) shed leaves להשיר עלים *inf* lehasheer 'aleem; *pst* heesheer *etc*; *pres* masheer; *fut* yasheer *etc*.

sheen 1. ברק *nm* barak/brakeem (*pl+of:* beerkey); **2.** זוהר *nm* zohar.

sheep 1. צאן *nf pl* tson; **2.** כבשים *nf pl* kvaseem.

sheepdog כלב רועים *nm* kelev/kalvey ro'eem

sheepfold דיר צאן *nm* deer/-ey tson.

sheepskin 1. עור כבש *nm* 'or/-ot keves/kvaseem; **2.** קלף (parchment) *nm* klaf.

sheer 1. טהור (pure) *adj* tahor/tehorah; **2.** דק (thin) *adj* dak/-ah; **3.** תלול (steep) *adj* talool/teloolah.

(by) sheer force בכוח הזרוע בלבד *adv* be-khoa'akh (*kh=k*) ha-zro'a' bee-lvad.

sheet 1. סדין (bed) *m* sadeen/sdeen|eem (*pl+of:* -ey); **2.** גיליון (paper) *nm* geel|ayon/-yonot (*+of:* -yon); **3.** לוח (metal) *nm* loo|'akh/-khot.

sheet lightning ברק יריעה *nm* brak/beerkey yeree'ah.

shelf 1. מדף *nm* madaf/-eem (*pl+of:* -ey); **2.** אצטבה (ledge) *nf* eetstab|ah/-a'ot (*+of:* -at).

shell 1. פגז (artillery) *nm* pagaz/pegazeem (*+of:* pegaz/peegzey); **2.** קונכייה (of snail) *nf* konkheelyah/-yot (*+of:* -yat); **3.** קליפה (peel) *nf* kleep|ah/-ot (*+of:* -at).

(to) shell להפגיז *inf* lehafgeez; *pst* heefgeez; *pres* mafgeez; *fut* yafgeez.

shellac לכה מזוקקת *nf* lakah mezookeket.

shellfish רכיכה *nf* rakeekh|ah/-ot (*+of:* -at).

shelter 1. מקלט (refuge) *nm* meekl|at/-ateem (*pl+of:* -etey); **2.** מחסה (protection) *nm* makhas|eh/-eem (*pl+of:* -ey).

(air-raid) shelter מקלט *nm* meekl|at/-ateem (*pl+of:* -etey).

(to take) shelter למצוא מחסה *inf* leemtso makhaseh; *pst* matsa *etc*; *pres* motse *etc*; *fut* yeemtsa *etc*.

(to) shelve 1. למדף *inf* lemadef; *pst* meedef; *pres* memadef; *fut* yemadef; **2.** לגנוז (defer) *inf* leegnoz; *pst* ganaz; *pres* gonez; *fut* yeegnoz.

shepherd רועה *nm* ro|'eh/-'eem (*pl+of:* -'ey).

sherbet 1. שרבת *nm* sherbet; **2.** מרק פירות (fruit soup) *nm* merak/meerkey perot; **3.** גלידת פירות (fruit ice-cream) *nf* gleed|at/-ot perot.

sheriff 1. שריף *nm* shereef/-eem (*pl+of:* -ey); **2.** ראש המשטרה המקומית *nm* rosh ha-meeshtarah ha-mekomeet.

sherry שרי *nm* sheree.

shield מגן *nm* mag|en/-eeneem (*pl+of:* -eeney).

(to) shield 1. להגן על *inf* lehagen 'al; *pst* hegen 'al; *pres* megen 'al; *fut* yagen 'al; **2.** להסתיר (conceal) *inf* lehasteer; *pst* heesteer; *pres* masteer; *fut* yasteer.

(Red) Shield of David מגן דוד אדום *nm* magen daveed adom.

shift 1. העתקה *nf* ha'atak|ah/-ot (*+of:* -at); **2.** החלפה (change) *nf* hakhlaf|ah/-ot (*+of:* -at); **3.** העברה (transfer) *nf* ha'avar|ah/-ot (*+of:* -at).

(gear) shift מערכת הילוכים *nf* ma'ar|ekhet/-khot heelookheem.

(to) shift 1. להזיז *inf* lehazeez; *pst* hezeez; *pres* mazeez; *fut* yazeez; **2.** להעתיק *inf* leha'ateek; *pst* he'eteek; *pres* ma'ateek; *fut* ya'ateek.

(to) shift for oneself להסתדר בכוח עצמו *v rfl inf* leheestader be-kho'akh 'atsm|o/-ah (*m/f*); *pst* heestader *etc*; *pres* meestader *etc*; *fut* yeestader *etc*.

(to) shift gears להחליף הילוכים *inf* lehakhleef heelookheem; *pst* hekhleef *etc*; *pres* makhleef *etc*; *fut* yakhleef *etc*.

(to) shift the blame להעביר אשמה *inf* leha'aveer ashmah; *pst* he'eveer *etc*; *pres* ma'aveer *etc*; *fut* ya'aveer *etc*.

shiftless 1. רפה רצון *adj* ref|eh/-at ratson; **2.** רשלן (careless) *nmf* rashl|an/-eet.

shilling שילינג *nm* sheeleeng/-eem.

shimmy 1. ריקוד השימי (dance) *nm* reekood ha-sheemee; **2.** זוע (vibration) *nm* zoo'a'.

shin שוק *nf* shok|ah/-ot (*+of:* -at).

(to) shin up לטפס *inf* letapes; *pst* teepes; *pres* metapes; *fut* yetapes.

shine 1. זוהר (beam) *nm* zohar/zehareem (*pl+of:* zohorey); **2.** ברק (polish) *nm* barak.

(rain or) shine בכל מזג אוויר שהוא *adv* be-khol (*kh=k*) mezeg aveer she-hoo.

(to) shine 1. לזהור *inf* leez'hor; *pst* zahar; *pres* zoher; *fut* yeez'har; **2.** לצחצח (polish) *inf* letskhtse'akh; *pst* tseekhtse'akh; *pres* metsakhtse'akh; *fut* yetsakhtse'akh.

(to give a shoe)shine לצחצח נעליים *inf* letskhtse'akh (*etc*) na'alayeem.

shingle רעף *nm* ra'af/re'afeem (*pl+of:* ra'afey).

(to) shingle 1. לרעף *inf* lera'ef; *pst* ree'ef; *pres* mera'ef; *fut* yera'ef; **2.** לכסות ברעפים *inf* lekhasot bee-re'afeem; *pst* keesah (*k=kh*) *etc*; *pres* mekhaseh *etc*; *fut* yekhaseh *etc*.

shingles שלבקת חוגרת (disease) *nf* shalbeket khogeret.

shining זוהר *adj* zoher/-et.

shiny מבריק *adj* mavreek/-ah.

ship 1. אונייה *nf* onee|yah/-yot (*+of:* -yat); **2.** ספינה (boat) *nf* sfeen|ah/-ot (*+of:* -at); **3.** אווירון (air) *nm* aveeron/-eem (*pl+of:* -ey).

(to) ship 1. להטעין באונייה *inf* lehat'een bo-oneeyah; *pst* heet'een *etc*; *pres* mat'een *etc*; *fut* yat'een *etc*; **2.** לשגר (dispatch) *inf* leshager; *pst* sheeger; *pres* meshager; *fut* yeshager.

(on) shipboard על סיפון אונייה *adv* 'al seepoon oneeyah.

shipbuilder 1. בונה־אוניות *nm* bon|eh/-ey oneeyot; **2.** בעל מספנות (shipyard owner) *nm* ba'al/-at meespan|ah/-ot.

shipmate מלח חבר *nm* malakh/-eem khaver/-eem.

shipment 1. הטענה *nf* hat'an|ah/-ot (*+of:* -at); **2.** משלוח (consignment) *nm* meeshlo|'akh/-kheem (*pl+of:* -khey).

shipper קבלן הובלה *nm* kablan/-ey hovalah.

shipping ספנות *nf* sapanoo|t/-yot.

shipping charges הוצאות משלוח *nf pl* hotsa'ot meeshlo'akh.

shipping clerk פקיד משלוח *nmf* pekeed/-at meeshlo'akh.

shipwreck היטרפות אונייה *nf* heetarfoot oneeyah.

(to) shipwreck 1. להיות באונייה שנטרפה *inf* leehyot bo-oneeyah she-neetarfah; *pst* hayah *etc*; *pres* heeno *etc*; *fut* yeehyeh *etc*; **2.** להטביע אונייה (sink ship) *inf* lehatbee'a' oneeyah; *pst* heetbee'a'; *pres* matbee'a' *etc*; *fut* yatbee'a' *etc* **3.** לנחול כישלון (fail) *inf* leenkhol keeshalon; *pst* nakhal *etc*; nokhel *etc*; *fut* yeenkhal *etc*.

shipyard מספנה *nf* meesp|anah/-anot (*+of:* -enet/-enot).

(to) shirk להשתמט *inf* leheeshtamet; *pst* heeshtamet; *pres* meeshtamet; *fut* yeeshtamet.

shirker משתמט *nm* meeshtam|et/-teem (*pl+of:* -ey) t.

shirt 1. כותונת *nf* kooton|et/-ot (*+of:* ketonet/kotnot); **2.** חולצה *nf* khoolts|ah/-ot (*+of:* -at).

shirtsleeves שרוולי כותונת *nm pl* sharvooley kootonet.

shirtwaist חולצת נשים *nf* khoolts|at/-ot nasheem.

shiver רעדה *nf* re'ad|ah/-ot (*+of:* ra'ad|at/-ot)

(to) shiver 1. לרעוד *inf* leer'od; *pst* ra'ad; *pres* ro'ed; *fut* yeer'ad; **2.** להתחלחל *inf* leheetkhalkhel; *pst* heetkhalkhel; *pres* meetkhalkhel; *fut* yeetkhalkhel.

shoal 1. שרטון *nm* seerton/-eem (*pl+of:* -ey); **2.** מים רדודים (water) *nm pl* mayeem redoodeem.

shock 1. הלם *nm* helem; **2.** אפתעה (surprise) *nm* afta|'ah/-'ot (+*of:* -'at); **3.** זעזוע (blow) *nm* za'azoo|'a'/-'eem (*pl+of:* -'ey).
(to) shock 1. להדהים (scandalize) *inf* lehadheem; *pst* heedheem; *pres* madheem; *fut* yadheem; **2.** להרשים (impress) *inf* leharsheem; *pst* heersheem; *pres* marsheem; *fut* yarsheem.
shock absorber בולם זעזועים *nm* bol|em/-mey za'azoo'eem.
shock troops פלוגות מחץ *nf* ploogot makhats.
shocking 1. מדהים *adj* mad'heem/-ah; **2.** מזעזע *adj* (perturbing) meza'z|e'a'/-a'at.
shoe נעל *nf* na'al/-ayeem (*pl+of:* -ey).
(brake) shoe סנדל בלם *nm* sandal/-ey belem.
(horse)shoe פרסה *nf* pars|ah/-ot (+*of:* -at).
shoe blacking צחצוח נעליים *nm* tseekhtsoo'akh na'alayeem.
shoe polish משחת נעליים *nf* meeshkh|at/-ot na'alayeem.
shoe store חנות נעליים *nf* khanoo|t/-yot na'alayeem.
shoeblack מצחצח נעליים *nm* metsakhtse|'akh/-khey na'alayeem.
shoehorn כף לנעליים *nf* kaf le-na'alayeem.
shoelace שרוך נעל *nm* srokh/-ey na'al/-ayeem.
shoemaker סנדלר *nm* sandlar/-eem (*pl+of:* -ey).
shoestring 1. שרוך נעל *nm* srokh/-ey na'al; **2.** סכום פעוט *nm* skhoom/-eem pa'oot/pe'ooteem.
shoot 1. ירי *nm* yeree; **2.** ציד tsayeed (+*of:* tseyd); **3.** תחרות קליעה *nf* takharoo|t/-yot klee'ah.
(to) shoot 1. לירות (firearm) *inf* leerot; *pst* yarah; *pres* yoreh; *fut* yeerah; **2.** לזרוק (throw) *inf* leezrok; *pst* zarak; *pres* zorek; *fut* yeezrok; **3.** לצלם (photograph) *inf* letsalem; *pst* tseelem; *pres* metsalem; *fut* yetsalem.
(to) shoot it out with someone להחליף ירויות עם מישהו *inf* lehakhleef yereeyot 'eem meeshehoo; *pst* hekhleef *etc*; *pres* makhleef *etc*; *fut* yakhleef *etc*.
(to) shoot up a place להמטיר יריות ללא אבחנה *inf* lehamteer yereeyot le-lo avkhanah; *pst* heemteer *etc*; *pres* mamteer *etc*; *fut* yamteer.
shooter 1. קלע *nm* kala'/-'eem (*pl+of:* -'ey); **2.** צלף (sniper) *nm* tsalaf/-eem (*pl+of:* -'ey).
shooting יריות *nf pl* yereeyot.
shooting match תחרות יריות *nf* takharoo|t/-yot yereeyot.
shooting pain כאב פתאומי חד *nm* ke'ev peet'omee khad.
shooting star 1. כוכב נופל *nm* kokhav/-eem nof|el/-leem; **2.** מטאור *nm* mete'or/-eem (*pl+of:* -ey).
shop 1. בית מלאכה (workshop) *nm* bet/batey melakhah; **2.** חנות (store) *nf* khanoo|t/-yot.
(barber)shop מספרה *nf* meespar|ah/-ot (+*of:* -eret).
(beauty) shop מכון יופי *nm* mekhon/-ey yofee.
(to) shop 1. לערוך קניות *inf* la'arokh keneeyot; *pst* 'arakh *etc*; *pres* 'orekh *etc*; *fut* ya'arokh *etc*; **2.** לעשות קניות (syn) *[colloq.] inf* la'asot keneeyot; *pst* 'asah *etc*; *pres* 'oseh *etc*; *fut* ya'aseh *etc*.
(to talk) shop לשוחח בעניני עסקים *inf* lesokhe'akh be-'eenyeney 'asakeem; *pst* sokhakh *etc*; *pres* mesokhe'akh *etc*; *fut* yesokhakh *etc*.
shop window חלון ראווה *nm* khalon/-ot ra'avah.
shopgirl זבנית *nf* zabanee|t/-yot.
shopkeeper חנווני *nmf* khenvan|ee/-eet (*pl:* -eem/-eeyot; *pl+of:* -ey).
shopper 1. קונה *nm* kon|eh/-ah (*pl:* -eem/-ot; +*of:* -at/-ey); **2.** עורך קניות *nm* 'or|ekh/khey kneeyot.
shopping עריכת קניות *nf* 'areekhat kneeyot.
(to go) shopping לצאת לקניות *inf* latset lee-kneeyot; *pst* yatsa *etc*; *pres* yotse *etc*; *fut* yetse *etc*.
shore חוף *nm* khof/-eem (*pl+of:* -ey).
(ten miles off) shore במרחק עשרה מילין מהחוף be-merkhak 'asarah meeleen me-ha-khof.
shore patrol משמר חופים *nm* meeshmar khofeem.
shorn גזוז *adj* gazooz/gezoozah.
short 1. קצר (length) *adj* katsar/ketsarah; **2.** נמוך (height) *adj* namookh/nemookhah.
(for) short 1. בקיצור *adv* be-keetsoor; **2.** לשם קיצור *adv* le-shem keetsoor.
(in) short 1. בקצרה *adv* bee-ketsarah; **2.** לשם סיכום *adv* le-shem seekoom.
(to cut) short 1. להפסיק פתאום *inf* lehafseek peet'om; *pst* heefseek *etc*; *pres* mafseek *etc*; *fut* yafseek *etc*; **2.** לקצר (shorten) *inf* lekatser; *pst* keetser; *pres* mekatser; *fut* yekatser.
(to stop) short לעצור לפתע *inf* la'atsor le-feta' (*f=p*) *etc*; *pst* 'atsar; *pres* 'otser *etc*; *fut* ya'atsor *etc*.
short circuit קצר חשמלי *nm* kets|er/-areem khashmalee/-yeem.
short cut קיצור דרך *nm* keetsoor/-ey derekh.
short-legged קצר רגליים *adj* ketsar/keetsrat raglayeem.
short loan 1. גמילות חסד *nf* gemeeloo|t/-yot khesed; **2.** הלוואה לזמן קצר (term) *nf* halva|'ah/-'ot lee-zman katsar.
short notice שהות קצרה מדי *nf* shehoot ketsarah meeday.
(to be) short of לחסור *inf* lakhsor; *pst* khasar; *pres* khaser; *fut* yekhsar.
(to run) short of something לחסור *inf* lakhsor; *pst* khasar; *pres* khaser; *fut* yekhsar.
(in) short order מיד *adv* meeyad.
short story סיפור קצר *nm* seepoor/-eem katsar/ketsareem.
short term קצר מועד *adj* ketsar/keetsrat mo'ed.
(in a) short time בתוך זמן מועט *adv* be-tokh zman moo'at.
short wave גלים קצרים *nm pl* galeem ketsareem.
shortage מחסור *nm* makhsor/-eem (*pl+of:* -ey).
shortcoming מגרעת *nf* meegr|a'at/-a'ot (*pl+of:* -e'ot).
(to) shorten לקצר *inf* lekatser; *pst* keetser; *pres* mekatser; *fut* yekatser.
shortening 1. קיצור (length) *nm* keetsoor/-eem (*pl+of:* -ey); **2.** שומן אפייה (baking) *nm* shooman/-ey afeeyah.
shorthand קצרנות *nf* katsranoo|t/-yot.
shorthand-typist קצרן *nmf* katsran/-eet (*pl:* -eem/-eeyot; +*of:* -ey).
shortly בקרוב *adv* be-karov.
shortness קוצר *nm* kotser.

shorts מכנסיים קצרים *nm pl* meekhnasayeem ketsareem.

shortsighted קצר ראייה *adj* ketsar/keetsrat re'eeyah.

shot 1. ירייה (discharge) *nf* yeree|yah/-yot (*+of:* -yat); **2.** כדורית (pellet) *nf* kadooree|t/-yot; **3.** זריקה (injection) *nf* zreek|ah/-ot (*+of:* -at); **4.** יידוי (throw) *nm* yeedoo|y/-yeem (*pl+of:* -yey).

(a good) shot קלע טוב *nmf* kala'/-'eet tov/-ah.

(big) shot 1. גברא רבא *nm* gavra raba; **2.** "מאכר" גדול *[slang] nm* makher gadol.

(not by a long) shot לא בא בחשבון lo ba/ba'ah be-kheshbon.

(within rifle) shot בטווח ירי רובה *adv* bee-tvakh yeree roveh.

(to take a) shot at לנסות לירות על *inf* lenasot leerot 'al; *pst* neesah *etc*; *pres* menaseh *etc*; *fut* yenaseh *etc.*

shotgun רובה ציד *nm* rov|eh/-ey tsayeed.

shoulder 1. שכם (person) *nm* shekh|em/-ameem (*+of:* shekhem/sheekhmey); **2.** גב (animal) *nm* gav/gabeem (*+of:* gev/gabey).

(straight from the) shoulder בגילוי לב (frankly) be-geelooy lev.

(to) shoulder להעמיס על הגב *inf* leha'amees 'al ha-gav; *pst* he'emees *etc*; *pres* ma'amees *etc*; *fut* ya'amees 'etc.

shoulder blade עצם השכם *nm* 'etsem ha-shekhem.

shoulder strip רצועת כתף *nf* retsoo|'at/-'ot katef.

(to turn a cold) shoulder to לפנות עורף *inf* leefnot 'oref; *pst* panah *(p=f) etc*; *pres* poneh *etc*; *fut* yeefneh *etc.*

shoulders כתפיים *nf pl* ketefayeem (*pl+of:* keetfey).

shout 1. צעקה *nf* tse'ak|ah/-ot (*+of:* tsa'ak|at/-ot); **2.** צווחה *nf* tsvakh|ah/-ot (*+of:* tseevkhat).

(to) shout לצעוק *inf* leets'ok; *pst* tsa'ak; *pres* tso'ek; *fut* yeets'ak.

shove דחיפה *nf* dekheef|ah/-ot (*+of:* -at).

(to) shove 1. לדחוף *inf* leedkhof; *pst* dakhaf; *pres* dokhef; *fut* yeedkhof; **2.** להדוף *inf* lahadof; *pst* hadaf; *pres* hodef; *fut* yahadof.

(to) shove aside להדוף הצידה *inf* lahadof ha-tseedah; *pst* hadaf *etc*; *pres* hodef *etc*; *fut* yahadof *etc.*

(to) shove off להסתלק *inf* leheestalek; *pst* heestalek; *pres* meestalek; *fut* yeestalek.

shovel 1. יעה *nm* ya'eh/ya'eem (*pl+of:* ye'ey); **2.** את *nm* et/eet|eem (*pl+of:* -ey).

show 1. תצוגה (exhibition) *nf* tetsoog|ah/-ot (*+of:* -at); **2.** הפגנה (demonstration) *nf* hafgan|ah/-ot (*+of:* -at); **3.** הצגה (spectacle) *nf* hatsag|ah/-ot (*+of:* -at).

(to) show 1. להציג (exhibit) *inf* lehatseeg; *pst* heetseeg; *pres* matseeg; *fut* yatseeg; **2.** להוכיח (prove) *inf* lehokhee'akh; *pst* hokhee'akh; *pres* mokhee'akh; *fut* yokhee'akh; **3.** להופיע (appear) *inf* lehofee'a'; *pst* hofee'a'; *pres* mofee'a'; *fut* yofee'a'.

(to a) show להצגה *adv* le-hatsagah.

(to make a) show of oneself לעשות עצמו לראווה *inf* la'asot 'atsmo le-ra'avah; *pst* 'asah *etc*; *pres* 'oseh *etc*; *fut* ya'aseh *etc.*

(to) show off להתהדר *v rfl inf* leheet'hader; *pst* heet'hader; *pres* meet'hader; *fut* yeet'hader.

show place אתר ראווה *nm* atar/-ey ra'avah.

(to) show someone in להזמין פנימה *inf* lehazmeen peneemah; *pst* heezmeen *etc*; *pres* mazmeen *etc*; *fut* yazmeen *etc.*

(to) show up להופיע *inf* lehofee'a'; *pst* hofee'a'; *pres* mofee'a'; *fut* yofee'a'.

show window חלון ראווה *nm* khalon/-ot ra'avah.

showcase תיבת ראווה *nf* teyv|at/-ot ra'avah.

showdown חשיפת קלפים *nf* khaseef|at/-ot klafeem

shower מקלחת *nf* meeklakh|at/-ot.

(bridal) shower 1. מסיבת כלה *nf* meseeb|at/-ot kalah; **2.** מטר מתנות (of gifts) *nm* metar matanot.

showpiece פאר התוצרת *nm* pe'er ha-totseret.

showroom אתר תצוגה *nm* atar/-ey tetsoogah.

showy ראוותני *adj* re'avtanee/-t.

shred 1. רסיס *nm* resees/-eem (*pl+of:* -ey); **2.** קרע *nm* kera'/kra'eem (*pl+of:* keer'ey).

(to tear to) shreds לקרוע לגזרים *inf* leekro'a' lee-gzareem; *pst* kara' *etc*; *pres* kore'a' *etc*; *fut* yeekra' *etc.*

shrew מרשעת *nf* meersha|'at/-ot.

shrewd 1. פיקח *adj* peek|e'akh/-akhat; **2.** שנון (keen) *adj* shanoon/shnoonah.

shriek צריחה *nf* tsereekh|ah/-ot (*+of:* -at).

(to) shriek לצרוח *inf* leetsro'akh; *pst* tsarakh; *pres* tsore'akh; *fut* yeetsrakh.

shrill צרחני *adj* tsarkhanee/-t.

shrimp חסילון *nm* khaseelon/-eem (*pl+of:* -ey).

shrine 1. אתר מקודש *nm* atar/-eem mekoodash/-eem; **2.** ארון קודש (holy ark) *nm* aron/-ot kodesh.

(to) shrink להתכווץ *inf* leheetkavets; *pst* heetkavets; *pres* meetkavets; *fut* yeetkavets.

(to) shrink back לסגת אחור *inf* laseget akhor; *pst & pres* nasog *etc*; *fut* yeesog *etc*

(to) shrink from להירתע מ־ *inf* leherata' mee-; *pst & pres* neerta' mee-; *fut* yerata' mee-.

shrinkage התכווצות *nf* heetkavtsoo|t/-yot.

(to) shrivel 1. לכמוש *vi* leekhmosh; *pst* kamash *(k=kh)*; *pres* kamesh; *fut* yeekhmosh; **2.** להכמיש *vt inf* lehakhmeesh; *pst* heekhmeesh; *pres* makhmeesh; *fut* yakhmeesh.

shroud תכריכים *nm pl* takhreekh|eem (*pl+of:* -ey).

(to) shroud לעטוף בתכריכים *inf* la'atof be-takhreekheem; *pst* 'ataf *etc*; *pres* 'otef *etc*; *fut* ya'atof *etc.*

shrub שיח *nm* see|'akh/-kheem (*pl+of:* -khey).

shrubbery שיחים *nm pl* seekh|eem (*pl+of:* -ey).

shrug משיכת כתפיים *nf* mesheekh|at/-ot ketefayeem.

(to) shrug למשוך בכתפיים *inf* leemshokh ba-ketefayeem; *pst* mashakh *etc*; *pres* moshekh *etc*; *fut* yeemshokh *etc.*

shudder 1. רעד *nm* ra'ad/re'adeem (*pl+of:* ra'adey); **2.** חלחלה *nf* khalkhal|ah/-ot (*+of:* -at).

(to) shudder 1. להתחלחל *inf* leheetkhalkhel; *pst* heetkhalkhel; *pres* meetkhalkhel; *fut* yeethhalkhel; **2.** לרעוד (tremble) *inf* leer'od; *pst* ra'ad; *pres* ro'ed; *fut* yeer'ad.

shuffle 1. גרירת רגליים *nf* greer|at/-ot raglayeem; **2.** טריפת קלפים (cards) *nf* treef|at/-ot klafeem.

(it is your) shuffle תורך לטרוף קלפים tor|kha/-ekh *(m/f)* leetrof klafeem.

(to) shuffle 1. לטרוף קלפים (cards) *inf* leetrof klafeem; *pst* taraf *etc*; *pres* toref *etc*; *fut* yeetrof *etc*; **2.** לבלבל (confuse) *inf* levalbel; *pst* beelbel *(b=v)*; *pres* mevalbel; *fut* yevalbel.

shuffle board לוח החלקה *nm* loo|'akh/-khot hakhlakah.

(to) shun להתרחק מ־ *v* refl leheetrakhek mee-; *pst* heetrakhek mee-; *pres* meetrakhek mee-; *fut* yeetrakhek mee-.

(to) shut לסגור *inf* leesgor; *pst* sagar; *pres* soger; *fut* yeesgor.

(to) shut down 1. לסגור כליל *inf* leesgor kaleel; *pst* sagar *etc*; *pres* soger *etc*; *fut* yeesgor *etc*; **2.** להשבית (factory *etc*) *inf* lehashbeet (lock out); *pst* heeshbeet; *pres* mashbeet; *fut* yashbeet.

(to) shut in 1. לכלוא *inf* leekhlo; *pst* kala *(k=kh)*; *pres* kole; *fut* yeekhla; **2.** לעצור (arrest) *inf* la'atsor; *pst* 'atsar; *pres* 'otser; *fut* ya'atsor.

(to) shut off 1. להפסיק (water, gas) *inf* lehafseek; *pst* heefseek; *pres* mafseek; *fut* yafseek **2.** לנתק (electricity, telephone) *inf* lenatek; *pst* neetek; *pres* menatek; *fut* yenatek.

(to) shut off from להסתגר מפני *v rfl inf* leheestager meepney; *pst & pres* meestager *etc*; *fut* yeestager *etc*.

(to) shut out 1. להסתגר *v* refl leheestager; *pst* heestager; *pres* meestager; *fut* yeestager; **2.** לסגור בפני (deny entry) *inf* leesgor beefney; *pst* sagar *etc*; *pres* soger *etc*; *fut* yeesgor *etc*.

shut the door! סגור את הדלת! *v imp* segor/seegree *(m/f)* et ha-delet.

shut up! 1. בלום פיך! *v imp* blom peekha/ beelmee peekh! *(m/f)*; **2.** תשתוק (keep silent) *v fut* teesht|ok!/-ekee-! *(m/f)*.

(to) shut up 1. להשתתק *inf* leheeshtatek; *pst* heeshtatek; *pres* meeshtatek; **2.** לסתום (clog) *inf* leestom; *pst* satam; *pres* sotem; *fut* yeestom.

shutter 1. תריס *nm* trees/-eem *(pl+of:* -ey); **2.** סגר (lock) *nm* seg|er/-areem *(pl+of:* seegrey). **3.** צמצם (camera) *nm* tsamtsam/-eem *(pl+of:* -ey).

(to) shutter לסגור תריסים *inf* leesgor treeseem; *pst* sagar *etc*; *pres* soger *etc*; *fut* yeesgor *etc*.

shuttle סליל אריגה *nm* sleel/-ey areegah.

(to) shuttle לנוע הלוך ושוב *inf* lanoo'a' halokh va-shov *pst & pres* na' *etc*; *fut* yanoo'a' *etc*.

shuttle service שירות הסעה הלוך ושוב *nf* sheroot/ -ey hasa'ah halokh va-shov.

shy ביישן *nmf* bayshan/-eet.

(to) shy 1. להירתע *inf* leherata'; *pst & pres* neerta'; *fut* yerata'; **2.** להתבייש (feel ashamed) *v* refl leheetbayesh; *pst* heetbayesh; *pres* meetbayesh; *fut* yeetbayesh.

(to) shy away לסגת לפתע *inf* laseget le-feta'; *pst & pres* nasog *etc*; *fut* yeesog *etc*.

shyster עורך־דין נוכל *nm* orekh-deen nokhel.

sibilant שורק *adj* shorek/-et.

Sicily סיציליה *nf* seetseelyah.

sick חולה *adj* khol|eh/-ah.

(to make) sick להגעיל *inf* lehag'eel; *pst* heeg'eel; *pres* mag'eel; *fut* yag'eel.

(to be) sick for להתגעגע *inf* leheetga'ge'a'; *pst* heetga'ga'; *pres* meetga'ge'a'; *fut* yeetga'ga'.

sick leave חופשת מחלה *nf* khoofsh|at/-ot makhalah.

(to be) sick of להתעייף מ־ *inf* leheet'ayef mee-; *pst* heet'ayef mee-; *pres* meet'ayef mee-; *fut* yeet'ayef mee-.

(to) sicken להחלות *inf* lehakhlot; *pst* hekhlah; *pres* makhleh; *fut* yakhleh.

sickening מחליא *adj* makhlee/-'ah.

sickle חרמש *nm* khermesh/-eem *(pl+of:* -ey).

sickly חולני *adj* kholanee/-t.

sickness מחלה *nf* makhl|ah/-ot *(+of:* -at).

side 1. צד (faction) *nm* tsad/tsedadeem *(pl+of:* tseedey); **2.** עבר (surface) *nm* 'ever/'avareem *(pl+of:* 'evrey); **3.** צלע (hillside) *nf* tsel|a'/-a'ot *(pl+of:* tsal'ot).

(by his/her) side לצידו/־ה *adv* le-tseed|o/-ah.

(by the) side of על יד *prep* 'al yad

side arms נשק צד *nm* neshek tsad.

side by side זה ליד זה *adj* zeh/zo le-yad zeh/zo.

side car 1. רכב צד *nm* rekhev tsad; **2.** סירת אופנוע (of motorcycle) *nf* seer|at/-ot ofano'a';

side effect תוצאת לוואי *nf* tots|'at/-'ot levay.

side glance מבט מלוכסן *nm* mabat/-eem melookhsan/-eem.

side issue עניין צדדי *nm* 'eenyan tsedadee.

side light 1. פרט לוואי (detail) *nm* prat/-ey levay; **2.** מנורת צד (lantern) *nf* menor|at/-ot tsad.

side mine מיטען צד *nm* meet'an/-ey tsad.

side whiskers זקן לחיים *nm* zekan lekhayayeem.

(to) side with לצדד ב־ *inf* letsaded be-; *pst* tseeded be-; *pres* metsaded be-; *fut* yetsaded be-.

sideboard מזנון *nm* meeznon/-eem *(pl+of:* -ey).

sideburns זקן לחיים *nm* zkan/-ey lekhayayeem.

sideline תעסוקה צדדית *nf* ta'asook|ah/-ot tseda-dee|t/-yot.

(on all) sides מכל צד mee-kol tsad.

(to take) sides with להזדהות עם *inf* leheezdahot 'eem; *pst* heezdahah 'eem; *pres* meezdaheh 'eem; *fut* yeezdaheh 'eem.

sideslip התחלקות לצד *nf* heetkhalkoo|t/-yot la-tsad.

sidetrack מסלול צדדי *nm* maslool/-eem tsedadee/ -yeem.

(to) sidetrack להעביר הצידה *inf* leha'aveer ha-tseedah; *pst* he'eveer *etc*; *pres* ma'aveer *etc*; *fut* ya'aveer *etc*.

sideview מראה צדדי *nm* mar|'eh/-'ot tsedadee/ -yeem.

sidewalk מדרכה *nf* meedr|akhah/-akhot *(+of:* -ekhet).

sideways הצידה *adv* ha-tseedah.

siege מצור *nm* matsor.

(to lay) siege להטיל מצור *inf* lehateel matsor; *pst* heeteel *etc*; *pres* mateel *etc*; *fut* yateel *etc*.

(to) sift לסנן *inf* lesanen; *pst* seenen; *pres* mesanen; *fut* yesanen.

sigh אנחה *nf* anakh|ah/-ot *(+of:* enkhat).

(to) sigh להתאנח *inf v* refl leheet'aneakh; *pst* heet'anakh; *pres* meet'ane'akh; *fut* yeet'anakh.

sight 1. ראייה (sense) *nf* re'eeyah (*+of:* -yat); **2.** מראה (view) *nf* mar|'eh/-'ot; **3.** כוונת (gun) *nf* kav|enet/-anot.

(at first) sight ממבט ראשון *adv* mee-mabat reeshon.

(he is a) sight הוא נראה איום hoo neer'eh ayom.

(payable at) sight לתשלום מיד עם הצגתו le-tashloom meeyad 'eem hatsaga|to/-tah.

(this room is a) sight החדר הוא זוועה ha-kheder hoo zva'ah.

(to) sight 1. לראות *inf* leer'ot; *pst* ra'ah; *pres* ro'eh; *fut* yeer'eh; **2.** לכוון *inf* lekhaven; *pst* keeven *(k=kh)*; *pres* mekhaven; *fut* yekhaven.

(to know by) sight להכיר מראייה *inf* lehakeer me-re'eeyah; *pst* heekeer *etc*; *pres* makeer *etc*; *fut* yakeer *etc.*

(to lose) sight לאבד קשר *inf* le'abed kesher; *pst* eebed *etc*; *pres* me'abed *etc*; *fut* ye'abed *etc.*

(in) sight of 1. מול *adv* mool; **2.** בקרבת (near) be-keervat.

(to catch) sight of להבחין ב־ *inf* lehavkheen be-; *pst* heevkheen be-; *pres* mavkheen be-; *fut* yavkheen be-.

sightseeing תיור באתרים *nm* teeyoor ba-atareem.

sightseeing tour סיור לאתרים *nm* seeyoor/-eem la-atareem

sign 1. אות (signal) *nm* ot/-ot; **2.** סימן (indication) *nm* seeman/-eem (*pl+of:* -ey); **3.** שלט (placard) *nm* shelet/shlateem (*pl+of:* sheeltey).

(to) sign לחתום *inf* lakhtom; *pst* khatam; *pres* khotem; *fut* yakhtom.

(to) sign off לנעול שידור leen'ol sheedoor; *pst* na'al *etc*; *pres* no'el *etc*; *fut* yeen'al *etc.*

(to) sign on 1. להעסיק (employ) *inf* leha'aseek; *pst* he'eseek; *pres* ma'aseek; *fut* ya'aseek; **2.** לקבל עבודה (accept employment) *inf* lekabel 'avodah; *pst* keebel *etc*; *pres* mekabel *etc*; *fut* yekabel *etc.*

(to) sign over property להעביר רכוש *inf* leha'aveer rekhoosh; *pst* he'eveer *etc*; *pres* ma'aveer *etc*; *fut* ya'aveer *etc.*

(to) sign up 1. להתגייס; *pst* leheetgayes; *pst* heetgayes; *pres* meetgayes; *fut* yeetgayes; **2.** להצטרף (join) leheetstaref; *pst* heetstaref; *pres* meetstaref; *fut* yeetstaref.

signal 1. איתות *nm* eetoot/-eem (*pl+of:* -ey); **2.** בולט *adj* bolet/-et.

(alarm) signal אות אזעקה *nm* ot/-ot az'akah.

(distress) signal קריאה לעזרה *nf* kree|'ah/-'ot le-'ezrah.

(time) signal אות זמן ברדיו *nm* ot/-ot zman ba-radyo.

(to) signal לאותת *inf* le'otet; *pst* otet; *pres* me'otet; *fut* ye'otet.

signal center מרכז קשר *nm* merk|az/-ezey kesher.

signal code קוד איתותים *nm* kod/-ey eetooteem.

signal corps חיל קשר *nm* kheyl/-ot kesher.

signal tower מגדל איתות *nm* meegd|al/-eley eetoot.

signatory חותם *nmf* khotem/-et.

signature חתימה *nf* khateem|ah/-ot (*+of:* -at).

signboard שלט *nm* shelet/shlateem (*pl+of:* sheeltey).

signer חותם *nm* khot|em/-meem (*pl+of:* -mey).

significance 1. משמעות *nf* mashma'oo|t/-yot; **2.** חשיבות (importance) *nf* khasheevoo|t/-yot.

significant 1. משמעותי *adj* mashma'ootee/-t; **2.** בולט (outstanding) bolet/-et.

(to) signify 1. להורות *inf* lehorot; *pst* horah; *pres* moreh; *fut* yoreh; **2.** לציין (mark) *inf* letsayen; *pst* tseeyen; *pres* metsayen; *fut* yetsayen; **3.** לרמוז (intimate) leermoz; *pst* ramaz; *pres* romez; *fut* yeermoz.

signpost תמרור *nm* tamroor/-eem (*pl+of:* -ey).

silence שתיקה *nf* shteek|ah/-ot (*+of:* -at).

(to) silence 1. להשתיק *inf* lehashteek; *pst* heeshteek; *pres* mashteek; *fut* yashteek; **2.** להסות (still) lehasot; *pst* heesah; *pres* mehaseh; *fut* yehaseh.

silent 1. שותק *adj* shotek/-et; **2.** שתקן *nmf* shatkan/-eet.

silent partner שותף לא פעיל *nmf* shootaf/-ah lo pa'eel/pe'eelah.

silhouette צללית *nf* tselalee|t/-yot.

(to) silhouette להצטלל *inf* leheetstalel; *pst* heetstalel; *pres* meetstalel; *fut* yeetstalel.

silouhetted against מצטלל על רקע *adj* meetstalel/-et 'al reka'.

silk משי *nm* meshee.

silk industry תעשית המשי *nf* ta'aseeyat/-yot ha-meshee.

silk ribbon סרט משי *nm* seret/seertey meshee.

silken עשוי משי *adj* 'asoo|y/-yah meshee.

silkworm תולעת משי *nf* tol|a'at/-'ey meshee.

silky 1. רך *adj* rakh/rakah *(k=kh)*; **2.** מבריק (glittering) mavreek/-ah.

sill 1. סף *nm* saf/seep|eem (*p=f*; *pl+of:* -ey); **2.** מפתן (threshold) *nm* meeft|an/-aneem (*pl+of:* -eney).

(window) sill אדן חלון *nm* eden/adney khalon/-ot.

silly 1. טיפשי *adj* teepshee/-t; **2.** טיפש *nmf* teep|esh/-shah.

silt סחופת *nf* sekhofet.

silver 1. כסף (metal) *nm* kesef; **2.** כלי כסף (dishes) *nm pl* kley-kesef; **3.** סכו״ם (tableware) *nm* sakoom/-eem (*pl+of:* -ey); **4.** בצבע הכסף (color) *adj* be-tseva' kesef.

silver עשוי כסף *adj* 'asoo|y/-yah kesef.

(to) silver להכסיף *inf* lehakhseef; *pst* heekhseef; *pres* makhseef; *fut* yakhseef.

silver-plated מוכסף *adj* mookhs|af/-efet.

silver wedding חתונת כסף *nf* khatoon|at/-ot kesef.

(to) silver a mirror לצפות מראה בכסף *inf* letsapot mar'ah be-khesef *(kh=k)*; *pst* tseepah *etc*; *pres* metsapeh *etc*; *fut* yetsapeh *etc.*

silvery כספי *adj* kaspee/-t

similar דומה *adj* dom|eh/-ah.

similarity דמיון *nm* deemyon/-ot.

simile 1. דימוי *nm* deemoo|y/-yeem (*pl+of:* -yey); **2.** משל (fable) *nm* mashal/meshaleem (*pl+of:* meeshley).

(to) simmer לרתוח לאט *inf* leerto'akh le-'eet|o/-ah *(m/f)*; *pst* ratakh *etc*; *pres* rote'akh *etc*; *fut* yeertakh *etc.*

simple פשוט *adj* pashoot/peshootah.

simple-minded 1. גלוי־לב *adj* gloo|y/-yat lev; **2.** שוטה (fool) *nmf* shot|eh/-ah.
simpleton בור *nm* boor/-eem *(pl+of:* -ey).
simplicity פשטות *nf* pashtoo|t/-yot.
(to) simplify לפשט *inf* lefashet; *pst* peeshet *(p=f)*; *pres* mefashet; *fut* yefashet.
simply בפשטות *adv* be-fashtoot *(f=p)*.
(to) simulate 1. לחקות *inf* lekhakot; *pst* kheekah; *pres* mekhakeh; *fut* yekhakeh; **2.** להתחפש (disguise) *v rfl* leheetkhapes; *pst* heetkhapes; *pres* meetkhapes; *fut* yeetkhapes.
simultaneous בו־זמני bo-zmanee/-t.
sin חטא *nm* khet/khata|'eem *(pl+of:* -'ey).
since 1. מאז (from) *conj* me-az; **2.** מאחר ו־ (because) *prep* me-'akhar ve- **3.** החל ב־ (as from) *adv* hakhel be-.
(ever) since מאז ועד הלום *adv* me-az ve-'ad ha-lom.
(long) since זמן רב מאז *adv* zman rav me-az.
(we have been here) since five אנו כאן משעה חמש anoo kan mee-sha'ah khamesh.
sincere 1. כן *adj* ken/-ah; **2.** לבבי (hearty) levavee/-t.
sincerity כנות *nf* kenoo|t/-yot.
sinecure 1. משרה נוחה ומשתלמת *nf* meesr|ah/-ot nokh|ah/-ot oo-meeshtal|emet/-mot; **2.** ג׳וב *[slang] nm* job/-eem.
sinew 1. גיד *nm* geed/-eem *(pl+of:* -ey); **2.** מיתר (chord) *nm* meytar/-eem *(pl+of:* -ey).
sinewy 1. חזק *adj* khazak/-ah; **2.** קשוח (hard-hearted) *adj* kashoo'akh/keshookhah.
sinful חוטא *adj* khote/-t.
(to) sing - 1. לשיר (also poetry) *inf* lasheer; *pst & pres* shar; *fut* yasheer; **2.** לזמר (melodies) *inf* lezamer; *pst* zeemer; *pres* mezamer; *fut* yezamer.
(to) sing out of tune לזייף בזמרה *inf* lezayef be-zeemrah; *pst* zeeyef *etc*; *pres* mezayef *etc*; *fut* yazayef *etc.*
(to) sing to sleep להרדים בשירי ערש *inf* lehardeem be-sheerey 'eres; *pst* heerdeem *etc*; *pres* mardeem *etc*; *fut* yardeem *etc.*
singe חריכה *nf* khareekh|ah/-ot (+*of:* -at).
(to) singe לחרוך *inf* lakhrokh; *pst* kharakh; *pres* khorekh; *fut* yakhrokh.
singer זמר *nmf* zam|ar/-eret *(pl+of:* -arey).
single 1. יחיד (unique) *adj* yakheed/yekheedah; **2.** מיוחד (distinct) *adj* meyookh|ad/-edet; **3.** רווק (unmarried) *nmf & adj* ravak/-ah.
single-entry bookkeeping 1. פנקסנות פשוטה *nf* peenkesanoot peshoootah; **2.** פנקסנות חד־צדדית *adj* peenkesanoot khad-tsedadeet.
(to) single out 1. לייחד *inf* leyakhed; *pst* yeekhed; *pres* meyakhed; *fut* yeyakhed; **2.** לברור לו (select) *inf* leevror lo; *pst* barar *(b=v)* lo; *pres* borer lo; *fut* yeevror lo.
single room חדר בודד *nm* kheder/khadareem boded/-eem.
single woman 1. רווקה *nf* ravak|ah/-ot (+*of:* -at); **2.** אישה בודדה (lone) *nf* eeshah/nasheem bode-d|ah/-ot.
(not a) single word אף לא מלה af lo meelah.
singlehanded ללא עזרה *adv* le-lo 'ezrah.
singsong נעימה מונוטונית *nf* ne'eem|ah/-ot monotonee|t/-yot.
singular 1. יחיד במינו *adj* yakheed/yekheedah be-meen|o/-ah; **2.** מספר יחיד (grammar) *nm* meespar yakheed.
sinister מבשר רעות *adj* mevaser/-et ra'ot.
sink 1. כיור *nm* keeyor/-eem *(pl+of:* -ey); **2.** קערת שופכין *nf* ka'ar|at/-ot shofkheen.
(to) sink 1. לשקוע *inf* leeshko'a'; *pst* shaka'; *pres* shoke'a'; *fut* yeeshka'; **2.** לטבע (vessel) *inf* letabe'a'; *pst* teebe'a'; *pres* metabe'a'; *fut* yetabe'a'.
(to) sink into one's mind להיחרט במוח *inf* lehekharet ba-mo'akh; *pst & pres* nekhrat *etc*; *fut* yekharet *etc.*
(to) sink one's teeth into להתמודד עם *inf* leheetmoded 'eem; *pst* heetmoded 'eem; *pres* meetmoded 'eem; *fut* yeetmoded 'eem.
(to) sink to sleep לשקוע בשינה *inf* leeshko'a' be-sheynah; *pst* shaka' *etc*; *pres* shoke'a' *etc*; *fut* yeeshka' *etc.*
sinner חוטא *nmf* khote/-t.
sinuous מתפתל *adj* meetpatel/-et.
sinus 1. גת *nf* gat/-ot; **2.** סינוס *nm* seenoos/-eem *(pl+of:* -ey).
(frontal) sinus סינוס קידמי *nm* seenoos/-eem keedmee/-yeem.
sip לגימה *nf* legeem|ah/-ot (+*of:* -at).
(to) sip ללגום *inf* leelgom; *pst* lagam; *pres* logem; *fut* yeelgom.
siphon סיפון *nm* seefon/-eem *(pl+of:* -ey).
(to) siphon לשאוב *inf* leesh'ov; *pst* sha'av; *pres* sho'ev; *fut* yeesh'av.
sir 1. אדון *nm* adon/-eem; **2.** אדוני/רבותיי (vocatively) *nm* adonee/rabotay.
siren 1. בתולת־ים *nf* betool|at/-ot yam; **2.** אישה מפתה (seductress) eeshah/nasheem mefat|ah/-ot; **3.** סירנה (warning) *nf* seerenah/-ot (+*of:* -at).
sirloin בשר מותן *nm* besar moten.
sirup 1. עסיס *nm* 'asees/-eem *(pl+of:* -ey); **2.** סירופ *nm* seerop/-eem *(pl+of:* -ey).
sissy 1. רכרוכי *adj* rakhrookhee/-t; **2.** גבר רכרוכי *nm* gever/gvareem rakhrookhee/-yeem.
sister-in-law גיסה *nf* gees|ah/-ot (+*of:* -at).
(to) sit down 1. לשבת *inf* lashevet; *pst* yashav; *pres* yoshev; *fut* yeshev; **2.** להתיישב (for more time) *v rfl inf* leheetyashev; *pst* heetyashev; *pres* meetyashev; *fut* yeetyashev
sit-down strike שביתת שבת *nf* shveet|at/-ot shevet.
(to) sit out לשבת בחיבוק ידיים *inf* lashevet be-kheebook yadayeem; *pst* yashav *etc*; *pres* yoshev *etc*; *fut* yeshev *etc.*
(to) sit still לשבת בשקט *inf* lashevet be-sheket; *pst* yashav *etc*; *pres* yoshev *etc*; *fut* yeshev *etc.*
(to) sit tight 1. לשמור על מעמדו *inf* leeshmor 'al ma'amado; *pst* shamar *etc*; *pres* shomer *etc*; *fut* yeeshmor *etc*; **2.** לשתוק *inf* leeshtok; *pst* shatak; *pres* shotek; *fut* yeeshtok.
(to) sit up להמתין בציפייה *inf* lehamteen be-tseepeeyah; *pst* heemteen *etc*; *pres* mamteen *etc*; *fut* yamteen *etc.*

(to) sit up all night להיות ער כל הלילה *inf* leehyot 'er/-ah kol ha-laylah; *pst* hayah *etc*; *pres* heeno *etc*; *fut* yeehyeh *etc*.

(to) sit up and take notice לגלות ענין רב *v inf* legalot 'eenyan rav; *pst* geelah *etc*; *pres* megaleh *etc*; *fut* yegaleh *etc*.

site 1. מקום *nm* makom/mekomot (+*of:* mekom); **2.** אתר *nm* atar/-eem (*pl+of:* -ey).

(baby)sitter שמרטף *[colloq.] nmf* shmartaf/-eet.

sitting מושב *nm* mosh|av/-aveem (*pl+of:* -vey).

sitting duck מטרה נוחה *nf* matarah nokhah.

sitting room טרקלין *nm* trakleen/-eem (*pl+of:* -ey).

situated 1. ממוקם *adj* memook|am/-emet; **2.** נמצא (located) *adj* neemts|a/-et.

situation 1. מצב (position) *nm* mats|av/-aveem (*pl+of:* -vey); **2.** מיקום (location) *nm* meekoom/-eem (*pl+of:* -ey); **3.** תעסוקה (employment) *nf* ta'asook|ah/-ot (+*of:* -at); **4.** מעמד (status) *nm* ma'amad; **5.** סיטואציה *nf* seetoo'ats|yah/-yot (+*of:* -yat).

six 1. שישה *num m* sheeshah (+*of:* sheshet); **2.** שש *num f* shesh; **3.** ו' *num* vav (6 in *Hebr. num. sys.*).

six hundred 1. שש מאות *num* shesh me'ot **2.** תר' *num* tar (600 in *Hebr. num. sys.*).

sixteen 1. שישה־עשר *num m* sheeshah-'asar **2.** שש־עשרה *num f* shesh-'esreh; **3.** ט"ז *num* tet-zayeen (16 in *Hebr. num. sys.*).

sixteenth 1. השישה־עשר *adj m* ha-sheeshah-'asar; **2.** השש־עשרה *adj f* ha-shesh-'esreh; **3.** הט"ז *adj* ha-tet-zayeen (16th in *Hebr. num. sys.*).

sixth 1. שישי *adj* sheeshee/-t; **2.** ו' *adj* vav (6th in *Hebr. num. sys.*).

sixtieth 1. השישים *adj* ha-sheesheem; **2.** ס' *adj* samekh (60th in *Hebr. num. sys.*).

sixty 1. שישים (60) *num* sheesheem; **2.** ס' *num* samekh (60 in *Hebr. num. sys.*).

size 1. גודל *nm* godel/gedaleem (*pl+of:* godley); **2.** מידה (measure) *nf* meed|ah/-ot (+*of:* -at); **3.** שיעור (quantity) *nm* she'oor/-eem (*pl+of:* -ey).

(to) size למיין *inf* lemayen; *pst* meeyen; *pres* memayen; *fut* yemayen.

(to) size up 1. לאמוד *inf* le'emod; *pst* amad; *pres* omed; *fut* ye'emod; **2.** להעריך (evaluate) *inf* leha'areekh; *pst* he'ereekh; *pres* ma'areekh; *fut* ya'areekh.

sizzle רחישה *nf* rekheesh|ah/-ot (+*of:* -at).

(to) sizzle לרחוש *inf* leerkhosh; *pst* rakhash; *pres* rokhesh; *fut* yeerkhash.

skate גלגילית *nf* galgeelee|t/-yot.

(ice) skate מחליקיים על קרח *nm pl* makhaleekayeem 'al kerakh.

(roller) skates גלגיליות *nf pl* galgeeleeyot.

skein כריכה של חוטים *nf* kreekh|ah/-ot shel khooteem.

skeleton שלד *nm* sheled/shladeem (*pl+of:* sheeldey).

skeleton key מפתח פתחכל *nm* mafte|'akh/-khot petakhkol.

skeptic 1. ספקני *adj* safkanee/-t; **2.** סקפטי *adj* skeptee/-t.

sketch 1. רישום (drawing) *nm* reeshoom/-eem (*pl+of:* -ey); **2.** תרשים (outline) *nm* tarsheem/-eem (*pl+of:* -ey).

(to) sketch 1. לרשום *inf* leershom; *pst* rasham; *pres* roshem; *fut* yeershom; **2.** להתוות (outline) *inf* lehatvot; *pst* heetvah; *pres* matveh; *fut* yatveh.

ski סקי *nm* skee.

(to) ski לגלוש *inf* leeglosh; *pst* galash; *pres* golesh; *fut* yeeglosh.

skid החלקה *nf* hakhlak|ah/-ot (+*of:* -at).

(to) skid להחליק הצידה (car) *inf* lehakhleek ha-tseedah; *pst* hekhleek *etc*; *pres* makhleek *etc*; *fut* yakhleek *etc*.

skiing גלישה *nf* gleesh|ah/-ot (+*of:* -at).

skill מיומנות *nf* meyoomanoo|t/-yot.

skilled מיומן *adj* meyoom|an/-enet.

skillet אלפס *nm* eelp|as/-eseem (*pl+of:* -esey).

skillful, skilful מיומן *adj* meyoom|an/-enet.

(to) skim 1. להסיר קרום (remove layer) *inf* lehaseer kroom; *pst* heseer *etc*; *pres* meseer *etc*; *fut* yaseer *etc*; **2.** לדפדף ב־ *inf* ledafdef be-; *pst* deefdef be-; *pres* medafdef be-; *fut* yedafdef be-.

skim milk חלב רזה *nm* khalav razeh.

(to) skimp לתת בצמצום *inf* latet be-tseemtsoom; *pst* natan *etc*; *pres* noten *etc*; *fut* yeeten *etc*.

skimpy קמצני *adj* kamtsanee/-t.

skin עור *nm* 'or/-ot.

(to save one's) skin להציל את עורו *inf* lehatseel et 'or|o/-ah *(m/f)*.

skin-deep שטחי *adj* sheetkhee/-t.

(to) skin someone להוריד למישהו את העור *inf* lehoreed le-meeshe|hoo/-hee et ha-'or; *pst* horeed *etc*; *pres* moreed *etc*; *fut* yoreed *etc*.

skinny 1. כחוש *adj* kakhoosh/kekhooshah; **2.** רזה (thin) *adj* raz|eh/-ah.

skip דילוג *nm* deeloog/-eem (*pl+of:* -ey).

(to) skip 1. לדלג *inf* ledaleg; *pst* deeleg; *pres* medaleg; *fut* yedaleg; **2.** להשמיט (omit) *vt inf* lehashmeet; *pst* heeshmeet; *pres* mashmeet; *fut* yashmeet.

(to) skip out להסתלק במהירות *inf* leheestalek bee-meheeroot; *pst* heestalek *etc*; *pres* meestalek *etc*; *fut* yeestalek *etc*.

skipper רב־חובל *nm* rav/rabey khov|el/-leem.

skirmish תגרה *nf* teegr|ah/-ot (+*of:* -at).

(to) skirmish להתכתש *inf* leheetkatesh; *pst* heetkatesh; *pres* meetkatesh; *fut* yeetkatesh.

skirt חצאית *nf* khatsa'ee|t/-yot

(to) skirt להקיף בשוליים *inf* lehakeef ba-shoolayeem; *pst* heekeef *etc*; *pres* makeef *etc*; *fut* yakeef *etc*.

(to) skirt along a coast לשייט לאורך חוף *inf* leshayet le-'orekh ha-khof; *pst* sheeyet *etc*; *pres* meshayet *etc*; *fut* yeshayet *etc*.

skit מהתלה *nf* mahatal|ah/-ot (+*of:* -at).

skunk מצחין *adj* matskheen/-ah.

sky 1. שמיים *nm pl* shamayeem (*pl+of:* shmey); **2.** רקיע (syn) *nm* rakee'a/rekee|'eem (*pl+of:* -ey).

(blue) sky שמיים כחולים *nm pl* shamayeem kekhooleem.

sky-blue תכלת *nf* tekhelet.

skylark עפרוני *nm* 'efron|ee/-eem (*pl+of:* -ey).

skylight צוהר בתקרה *nm* tsohar/tsehareem ba-teekrah.

skyrocket 1. זיקוק אש *nm* zeekook/-ey esh; **2.** רקיטה *nf* raket|ah/-ot (+*of:* -at).

skyscraper גורד שחקים *nm* gor|ed/-dey shekhakeem.

slab 1. לוח *nm* loo|'akh/-khot; **2.** טבלה *nf* tavl|ah/-a'ot (+*of:* -at).

(marble) slab לוח שיש *nm* loo|'akh/-khot shayeesh.

slack 1. רפוי *adj* rafooy/refooyah; **2.** מרושל (neglectful) *adj* meroosh|al/-elet.

(to take up the) slack 1. למתוח (stretch) *inf* leemto'akh; *pst* matakh; *pres* mote'akh; *fut* yeemtakh; **2.** ללחוץ (press) *inf* leelkhots; *pst* lakhats; *pres* lokhets; *fut* yeelkhats.

slack season עונת המלפפונים *nf* 'on|at/-ot ha-melafefoneem.

(to) slacken להחליש *inf* lehakhleesh; *pst* hekhleesh; *pres* makhleesh; *fut* yakhleesh.

slacks מכנסיים נוחים *nm pl* meekhnasayeem nokheem.

slag סיגים *nm pl* seeg|eem (*pl+of:* -ey).

slam טריקה *nf* treek|ah/-ot (+*of:* -at).

(grand) slam זכייה בברידג *nf* zekheee|yah/-yot bee-breedj.

(to) slam לטרוק *inf* leetrok; *pst* tarak; *pres* torek; *fut* yeetrok.

slam of a door טריקת דלת *nf* treek|at/-ot delet/dlatot.

(to) slam someone להטיח מלים כדרבונות *inf* lehatee'akh meeleem ka-dorvonot.

slander דיבה *nf* deeb|ah/-ot (+*of:* -at).

(to) slander להוציא דיבה *inf* lehotsee deebah; *pst* hotsee *etc*; *pres* motsee *etc*; *fut* yotsee *etc.*

slanderous מוציא דיבה *adj* motsee/-'ah deebah.

slang 1. עגה *nf* 'ag|ah/-ot (+*of:* -at); **2.** סלנג *nm* slang/-eem.

slant 1. נטייה *nf* netee|yah/-yot (+*of:* -yat); **2.** עיוות (distortion) *nm* 'eevoot/-eem (*pl+of:* -ey); **3.** שיפוע (slope) *nm* sheepoo|'a/-'eem (*pl+of:* -'ey).

(to) slant 1. להטות *inf* lehatot; *pst* heetah; *pres* mateh; *fut* yateh; **2.** לעוות (distort) *inf* le'avet; *pst* 'eevet; *pres* me'avet; *fut* ye'avet.

slap סטירה *nf* steer|ah/-ot (+*of:* -at).

(to) slap לסטור *inf* leestor; *pst* satar; *pres* soter; *fut* yeestor.

slapstick מעשה ליצנות *nm* ma'as|eh/-ey leytsanoot.

slash חתך *nm* khat|akh/-akheem (*pl+of:* -khey).

(to) slash לחתוך רצועות *inf* lakhtokh retsoo'ot; *pst* khatakh *etc*; *pres* khotekh *etc*; *fut* yakhtokh *etc.*

slat 1. פס עץ (wooden) *nm* pas/-ey 'ets; **2.** לוחית אבן (stony) *nf* lookhee|t/-yot even.

slate 1. רעף *nm* ra'af/re'afeem (*pl+of:* ra'afey); **2.** אריח (tile) *nm* aree|'akh/-kheem (*pl+of:* -khey); **3.** רשימת מועמדים (list of candidates) *nf* resheem|at/-ot mo'omadeem.

slate pencil עפרון גיר *nm* efron/-ey geer.

slated מיועד *adj* meyo|'ad/-'edet.

slaughter טבח *nm* tevakh.

slaughterhouse בית מטבחיים *nm* bet/batey meetbakhayeem.

Slav 1. סלבי *nmf* slavee/-t; **2.** סלבי *adj* slavee/-yeem.

slave עבד *nm* 'eved/'avadeem (*pl+of:* 'avdey).

(to) slave לעמול בפרך *inf* la'amol be-ferekh; *pst* 'amal *etc*; *pres* 'amel *etc*; *fut* ya'amol *etc.*

slave driver 1. נוגש *nmf* noges/-et; **2.** מעביד בפרך (*figurat.*) *nmf* ma'aveed/-ah be-ferekh.

slave labor עבודת ניצול *nf* 'avod|at/-ot neetsool.

slaver 1. סוחר עבדים *nm* sokh|er/-arey 'avadeem; **2.** סוחר בנשים לזנות *nm* sokher/-areem be-nasheem lee-znoot.

(to) slaver להחניף עד לזרא *inf* lehakhneef 'ad le-zara; *pst* hekhneef *etc*; *pres* makhneef *etc*; *fut* yakhneef *etc.*

slavery עבדות *nf* 'avdoo|t/-yot.

Slavic סלבי *adj* slavee/-t.

slavish 1. צייתני *adj* tsaytanee/-t; **2.** עיוור (blind) *adj* 'eever/-et.

(to) slay 1. להרוג (kill) laharog; *pst* harag; *pres* horeg; *fut* yaharog; **2.** לטבוח *inf* leetbo'akh; *pst* tavakh (*v=b*); *pres* tove'akh; *fut* yeetbakh.

sled מזחלת *nf* meezkh|elet/-alot.

sleek 1. חלק *adj* khalak/-ah; **2.** מלוטש (honed) *adj* meloot|ash/-eshet.

(to) sleek להחליק *inf* lehakhleek; *pst* hekhleek; *pres* makhleek; *fut* yakhleek.

sleep שינה *nf* sheynah (+*of:* shnat).

(to) sleep לישון *inf* leeshon; *pst & pres* yashen; *fut* yeeshan.

(to go to) sleep ללכת לישון *inf* lalekhet leeshon; *pst* halakh *etc*; *pres* holekh *etc*; *fut* yelekh *etc.*

(to put to) sleep להשכיב לישון *inf* lehashkeev leeshon; *pst* heeshkeev *etc*; *pres* mashkeev *etc*; *fut* yashkeev *etc.*

(to) sleep it off לישון עד שיחלוף *inf* leeshon 'ad she-yakhlof; *pst & pres* yashen; *fut* yeeshan.

(to) sleep off a headache לישון שיחלוף כאב הראש *inf* leeshon she-yakhlof ke'ev ha-rosh; *pst & pres* yashen *etc*; *fut* yeeshan *etc.*

(to) sleep on it להימלך עד למוחרת *inf* leheemalekh 'ad la-mokhorat; *pst & pres* neemlakh *etc*; *fut* yeemalekh *etc.*

sleeper 1. קרון שינה *nm* kron/-ot sheynah; **2.** תא שינה *nm* ta/ta'ey sheynah.

sleepily מתוך שינה *adv* mee-tokh sheynah.

sleepiness רדימות *nf* redeemoo|t/-yot.

sleeping 1. רדום *adj* radoom/redoomah; **2.** נרדם *adj* neerd|am/-emet; **3.** ישן (asleep) *adj* yashen/yeshenah.

sleeping car קרון שינה *nm* kron/-ot sheynah.

sleeping partner שותף לא־פעיל *nm* shootaf/-ah lo'-pa'eel/pe'eelah.

sleeping pill גלולת שינה *nf* glool|at/-ot sheynah.

sleeping sickness מחלת השינה *nf* makhlat ha-sheynah.

sleepless חסר שינה *adj* khas|ar/-rat sheynah.

sleepy 1. רדום *adj* radoom/redoomah; **2.** ישנוני *adj* yashnoonee/-t.

(to be) sleepy להיות רדום *inf* leehyot radoom; *pst* hayah *etc*; *pres* heeno *etc*; *fut* yehyeh *etc.*

sleet גשם עם פיתות קרח *nm* geshem 'eem peetot kerakh.

sleeve שרוול *nm* sharvool/-eem (*pl+of:* -ey).

sleigh 1. מגררה *nf* meegr|arah/-arot (*+of:* -eret/-erot); **2.** עגלת חורף (winter carriage) *nf* 'egl|at/-ot khoref.

sleigh bells פעמוני מגררה *nm pl* pa'amoney meegrarah.

sleight להטוט *nm* lahatoot/-eem (*pl+of:* -ey).

sleight of hand 1. זריזות ידיים *nf* zereezoot yadayeem; **2.** אחיזת עיניים (trick) *nf* akheez|at/-ot 'eynayeem.

slender 1. דק גו *adj* dak/-at gev; **2.** עדין (delicate) *adj* 'adeen/-ah.

sleuth 1. בלש *nm* balash/-eem (*pl+of:* -ey); **2.** כלב משטרה (police-dog) *nm* kelev/kalvey meeshtarah.

slice 1. פרוסה *nf* proos|ah/-ot (*+of:* -at); **2.** נתח (cut) *nm* netakh/-eem (*pl+of:* neetkhey).

(to) slice 1. לפרוס *inf* leefros; *pst* paras (*p=f*); *pres* pores; *fut* yeefros; **2.** לחתוך נתח (cut) *inf* lakhtokh netakh; *pst* khatakh *etc*; *pres* khotekh *etc*; *fut* yakhtokh *etc*.

slick 1. זריז *adj* zareez/zreezah; **2.** חלקלק (smooth) *adj* khalaklak/-ah.

slicker מעיל גשם אטים *nm* me'eel/-ey geshem ateem/-eem.

slide שקופית (photographic) *nf* shekoofee|t/-yot.

(land)slide מהפך *nm* mahp|akh/-kheem (*pl+of:* -khey).

(microscope) slide שקופית למיקרוסקופ *nf* shekofee|t/-yot le-meekroskop.

(to) slide 1. להחליק *inf* lehakhleek; *pst* hekhleek; *pres* makhleek; *fut* yakhleek; **2.** לגלוש *inf* leeglosh; *pst* galash; *pres* golesh; *fut* yeeglosh.

(to let something) slide להזניח *inf* lehaznee'akh; *pst* heeznee'akh; *pres* maznee'akh; *fut* yaznee'akh.

slide cover כסוי לשקופית *nm* kesoo|y/-yeem lee-shekoofee|t/-yot.

slide frame מסגרת לשקופית *nf* meesg|eret/-arot lee-shekoofee|t/-yot.

(to) slide into להשתחל *inf* leheeshtakhel; *pst* heeshtakhel; *pres* meesahtakhel; *fut* yeeshtakhel.

(to) slide out להשתחל החוצה *inf* leheeshtakhel (*etc*) ha-khootsah.

slide rule סרגל חישוב *nm* sargel/-ey kheeshoov.

slight 1. הזנחה (neglect) *nf* haznakh|ah/-ot (*+of:* -at); **2.** קל (small) *adj* kal/-ah; **3.** זילזול (insult) *nm* zeelzool/-eem (*pl+of:* -ey).

slightly 1. כלשהו *adv* kolshehoo; **2.** במידה מצומצמת *adv* be-meedah metsoomtsemet.

slim 1. דק *adj* dak/-ah; **2.** רזה (lean) *adj* raz|eh/-ah.

slime 1. טיט *nm* teet; **2.** יוון (mud) *nm* yaven (*+of:* yeven).

slimy 1. שפל *adj* shafal/shefelah; **2.** מכוסה טיט (mud-covered) *adj* mekhoos|eh/-ah teet.

sling 1. מקלעת *nf* meekla'at/-'ot; **2.** קלע *nm* kel|a'/-a'eem (*pl+of:* kal'ey).

(to) sling לקלוע *inf* leeklo'a'; *pst* kala'; *pres* kole'a'; *fut* yeekla'.

sling arms! תלה נשק! *v imp* teleh neshek!

slingshot 1. קלע kela'/kla'eem (*pl+of:* kal'ey); **2.** מקלעת *nf* meekla|'at/-'ot.

(to) slink להתגנב *inf* leheetganev; *pst* heetganev; *pres* meetganev; *fut* yeetganev.

(to) slink away לחמוק חרש *inf* lakhmok kheresh; *pst* khamak *etc*; *pres* khomek *etc*; *fut* yakhmok *etc*.

slip 1. התחלקות *nf* heetkhalkoo|t/-yot; **2.** מישגה (mistake) *nm* meeshg|eh/-eem (*pl+of:* -ey); **3.** מעידה (toppling) *nf* me'eed|ah/-ot (*+of:* -at).

(to) slip 1. להחליק (slide) *inf* lehakhleek; *pst* hekhleek; *pres* makhleek; *fut* yakhleek; **2.** לשגות (err) *inf* leeshgot; *pst* shagah; *pres* shogeh; *fut* yeeshgeh.

(to let an opportunity) slip להחמיץ הזדמנות *inf* lehakhmeets heezdamnoot; *pst* hekhmeets *etc*; *pres* makhmeets *etc*; *fut* yakhmeets *etc*

(to) slip away להתחמק *inf* leheetkhamek; *pst* heetkhamek; *pres* meetkhamek; *fut* yeetkhamek.

(to) slip in להתגנב *inf* leheetganev; *pst* heetganev; *pres* meetganev; *fut* yeetganev.

slip of paper פיסת נייר *nf* pees|at/-ot neyar.

slip of the pen פליטת קולמוס *nf* pleet|at/-ot koolmos.

slip of the tongue פליטת פה *nf* pleet|at/-ot peh.

(to) slip one's dress on להתלבש בחיפזון *inf* leheetlabesh be-kheepazon; *pst* heetlabesh *etc*; *pres* meetlabesh *etc*; *fut* yeetlabesh *etc*.

(to) slip out of joint לנקוע *inf* leenko'a'; *pst* naka'; *pres* noke'a'; *fut* yeeka'.

(to) slip something off להפשיט *inf* lehafsheet; *pst* heefsheet; *pres* mafsheet; *fut* yafsheet.

(it) slipped my mind נשמט מזכרוני *v pst* neeshmat mee-zeekhronee.

slipper נעל בית *nf* na'al/-ey bayeet.

slippery 1. חלקלק *adj* khalaklak/-ah; **2.** חמקמק (evasive) *adj* khamakmak/-ah.

(to) slit לחתוך לאורך *inf* lakhtokh le-'orekh; *pst* khatakh *etc*; *pres* khotekh *etc*; *fut* yakhtokh *etc*.

(to) slit into strips לחתוך לרצועות *inf* lakhtokh lee-retsoo'ot; *pst* khatakh *etc*; *pres* khotekh *etc*; *fut* yakhtokh *etc*.

slobber 1. ריר *nm* reer; **2.** דברי הבאי (vain talk) *nm pl* deevrey havay.

(to) slobber להזיל ריר *inf* lehazeel reer; *pst* heezeel *etc*; *pres* mazeel *etc*; *fut* yazeel *etc*.

slobbering 1. פטפטן *adj* patpetan/-eet; **2.** מדבר הבלים (talking nonsense) *adj* medaber/-et havaleem.

slogan סיסמה *nm nf* seesm|ah/-a'ot (*+of:* -at).

slop 1. מי שפכים *nm pl* mey shefakheem; **2.** טיט *nm* teet.

(to) slop 1. לשפוך (spill) *inf* leeshpokh; *pst* shafakh (*f=p*); *pres* shofekh; *fut* yeeshpokh; **2.** להתיז (splash) *inf* lehateez; *pst* heeteez; *pres* mateez; *fut* yateez.

slope 1. מדרון *nm* meedron/-eem (*pl+of:* -ey); **2.** שיפוע (tilt) *nm* sheepoo|'a/-'eem (*pl+of:* -'ey).

(to) slope להטות באלכסון *inf* lehatot ba-alakhson; *pst* heetah *etc*; *pres* mateh *etc*; *fut* yateh *etc*.

sloppy מרושל *adj* meroosh|al/-elet.

slops מי שופכין *nm pl* mey shofkheen.

slot 1. סדק (opening) *nm* sed|ek/-akeem (*pl+of:* seedkey); **2.** חריץ למטבעות (for coins) *nm* khareets/-eem le-matbe'ot.

slot machine מיתקן למכירה אוטומטית *nm* meetkan/-eem lee-mekheerah otomateet.

sloth 1. עצלות (laziness) *nf* 'atsloo|t/-yot; **2.** עצלן (animal) *nm* 'atslan/-eem (*pl+of:* -ey).

slouch 1. רישול (posture) *nm* reeshool; **2.** רשלן (person) *nmf* rashlan/-eet.

(to) slouch לעמוד ברישול *inf* la'amod be-reeshool; *pst* 'amad *etc; pres* 'omed *etc; fut* ya'amod *etc.*

(to walk with a) slouch להתהלך ברישול *inf* leheet'halekh be-reeshool; *pst* heet'halekh *etc; pres* meet'halekh *etc; fut* yeet'halekh *etc.*

slouch hat מגבעת מושפלת שוליים *nf* meegba'at mooshpelet shoolayeem.

slovenliness רשלנות *nf* rashlanoo|t/-yot.

slovenly 1. מוזנח *adj* mooznakh/-at; **2.** מרושל *adj* merooshl|al/-elet.

slow 1. איטי (low speed) *adj* eetee/-t; **2.** מאוחר (late) *adj* me'ookh|ar/-eret; **3.** עצלני (sluggish) *adj* 'atslanee/-t.

(to) slow down להאט *inf* leha'et; *pst* he'et; *pres* me'et; *fut* ya'et.

slowness איטיות *nf* eeteeyoot.

slug 1. חילזון ערום *nm* kheelazon/khelzonot 'arom/aroomeem; **2.** רכיכה חסרת קונכייה *nf* rakeekh|ah/-ot khasr|at/-ot konkhee|yah/-yot.

(to) slug 1. להרביץ *inf* leharbeets; *pst* heerbeets; *pres* marbeets; *fut* yarbeets; **2.** להכות (beat-up) *inf* lehakot; *pst* heekah; *pres* makeh; *fut* yakeh.

sluggard עצלן *nmf* 'atslan/-eet.

sluggish 1. עצלני *adj* 'atslanee/-t; **2.** איטי *adj* eetee/-t.

sluice מנוף *nm* manof/menof/-eem (*pl+of:* -ey).

sluicegate שערי סכר *nm pl* sha'arey sekher.

(to) slum לסייר במשכנות עוני *inf* lesayer be-meeshkenot 'onee; *pst* seeyer *etc; pres* mesayer *etc; fut* yesayer *etc.*

slumber תנומה *nf* tenoom|ah/-ot (*+of:* -at).

(to) slumber 1. לנום *inf* lanoom; *pst & pres* nam; *fut* yanoom; **2.** לנמנם *inf* lenamnem; *pst* neemnem; *pres* menamnem; *fut* yenamnem.

slump מפולת *nf* mapol|et/-ot.

(to) slump להידרדר *inf* leheedarder; *pst* heedarder; *pres* meedarder; *fut* yeedarder.

slums מישכנות עוני *nf pl* meeshkenot 'onee.

slush 1. תמיסת שלג (snow) *nf* tmees|at/-ot sheleg; **2.** מי רפש (mud) *nm pl* mey refesh; **3.** מי שופכין (refuse) *nm pl* mey shofkheen; **4.** דברים בטלים (drivel) *nm pl* dvareem beteleem.

sly 1. ערמומי *adj* 'armoomee/-t; **2.** חשאי (secret) *adj* khasha'ee/-t; **3.** שנון (crafty) *adj* shanoon/shnoonah.

(on the) sly בחשאי *adv* ba-khashay.

slyness ערמומיות *nf* 'armoomeeyoot.

smack 1. טעימה (taste) *nf* te'eem|ah/-ot (*+of:* -at); **2.** נשיקה מצלצלת (kiss) nesheek|ah/-ot metsaltsel|et/-ot; **3.** הצלפה (crack) *nf* hatslaf|ah/-ot (*+of:* -at); **4.** סטירה מצלצלת (slap) *nf* steer|ah/-ot metsaltsel|et/-ot.

smack הישר *adv* haysher.

(to) smack 1. לנשק בנשיקה מצלצלת *inf* lenashek bee-nesheekah metsaltselet; *pst* neeshek *etc; pres* menashek *etc; fut* yenashek *etc;* **2.** לסטור (slap) *inf* leestor; *pst* satar; *pres* soter; *fut* yeestor.

(to) smack of להדיף ריח של *inf* lehadeef rey'akh shel; *pst* heedeef *etc; pres* madeef *etc; fut* yadeef *etc.*

(a) smack of something שמץ דבר *nm* shemets davar.

(to) smack one's lips ללקק שפתיים *inf* lelakek sefatayeem; *pst* leekek *etc; pres* melakek *etc; fut* yelakek *etc.*

small 1. קטן (size) *adj* katan/ketanah; **2.** זעיר (tiny) *adj* za'eer/ze'eerah; **3.** מבוטל (insignificant) *adj* mevoot|al/-elet.

(to feel) small להרגיש בושה *inf* lehargeesh booshah; *pst* heergeesh *etc; pres* margeesh *etc; fut* yargeesh *etc.*

small arms נשק קל *nm* neshek kal.

small change 1. כסף קטן *nm* kesef katan; **2.** פרוטרוט *nm* protrot.

small fry דגי רקק *nm pl* degey rekak.

small hours השעות הקטנות *nf pl* ha-sha'ot ha-ktanot.

small letters 1. אותיות קטנות *nf pl* oteeyot ketanot; **2.** אותיות רגילות (non-capital) *nf pl* oteeyot regeelot.

small talk 1. פטפוט *nm* peetpoot/-eem (*pl+of:* -ey); **2.** שיחה קלה *nf* seekhah kalah.

small time קל ערך *adj* kal/-at 'erekh.

small town קרתני *adj* kartanee/-t.

small voice קול רך ומתוק *nm* kol rakh oo-matok.

smallness קטנות *nf* katnoo|t/-yot.

smallpox אבעבועות *nf pl* ava'boo'ot.

smart 1. פיקח (intelligent) *adj* peek|e'akh/-'kheet; **2.** נמרץ (astute) *adj* neemr|ats/-etset; **3.** נוצץ (stylish) *adj* notsets/-et.

(to) smart 1. לכאוב *vi inf* leekh'ov; *pst* ka'av *(k=kh); pres* ko'ev; *fut* yeekh'av; **2.** להכאיב *vt inf* lehakh'eev; *pst* heekh'eev; *pres* makh'eev; *fut* yakh'eev.

(to out)smart להערים על *inf* leha'areem 'al; *pst* he'ereem 'al; *pres* ma'areem 'al; *fut* ya'areem 'al.

smart remark הערה קולעת *nf* he'ar|ah/-ot kol|a'at/-'ot.

smart set חוג נוצץ *nm* khoog notsets.

smash 1. מכה (blow) *nf* mak|ah/-ot (*+of:* -at); **2.** התנפצות (shattering) *nf* heetnaptsoo|t/-yot.

smash hit 1. להיט *nm* laheet/leheet|eem (*pl+of:* -ey); **2.** מסמר העונה (of the season) *nm* masmer/-ey ha-'onah.

smashup התנגשות *nf* heetnagshoo|t/-yot.

smattering ידיעה שטחית *nf* yedee'|ah/-'ot sheetkhee|t/-yot.

smear מריחה *nf* mereekh|ah/-ot (*+of:* -at).

(to) smear למרוח *inf* leemro'akh; *pst* marakh; *pres* more'akh; *fut* yeemrakh.

(to) smear with paint ללכלך בצבע *inf* lelakhlekh be-tseva'; *pst* leekhlekh *etc; pres* melakhlekh *etc.*

smell ריח *nm* rey|'akh/-khot.

(to) smell להריח *inf* leharee'akh; *pst* heree'akh; *pres* meree'akh; *fut* yaree'akh.

(to take a) smell לרחרח *inf* lerakhre'akh; *pst* reekhree'akh; *pres* merakhre'akh; *fut* yerakhre'akh.

smell of ריח של *nm* rey|'akh/-khot shel.

(to) smell of להדיף ריח של *inf* lehadeef rey'akh shel; *pst* heedeef *etc; pres* madeef *etc; fut* yadeef *etc.*

smelling salts מלחי הרחה *nm pl* meelkhey harakhah.
smelly מסריח *adj* masree|'akh/-khah.
(to) smelt להתיך *inf* lehateekh; *pst* heeteekh; *pres* mateekh; *fut* yateekh.
smelting furnace כור היתוך *nm* koor/-ey heetookh.
smile חיוך *nm* kheeyookh/-eem (*pl+of:* -ey).
(to) smile לחייך *inf* lekhayekh; *pst* kheeyekh; *pres* mekhayekh; *fut* yekhayekh.
smiling חייכני *adj* khaykhanee/-t.
smilingly בחיוך *adv* be-kheeyookh.
(to) smite להכות *inf* lehakot; *pst* heekah; *pres* makeh; *fut* yakeh.
smith 1. נפח *nm* napakh/-eem (*pl+of:* -ey); **2.** חרש־ברזל *nm* kharash/-ey barzel.
(black)smith נפח *nm* napakh/-eem (*pl+of:* -ey).
(gold)smith צורף זהב *nm* tsor|ef/-fey zahav.
(silver)smith צורף כסף *nm* tsor|ef/-fey kesef.
smithy מפחה *nf* map|akhah/-akhot (*+of:* -akhat/-khot).
(to be) smitten with להיתקף ב־ *inf* leheetakef be-; *pst & pres* neetkaf be-; *fut* yeetakef be-.
smock מפחה *nf* map|akhah/-akhot (*+of:* -akhat/-khot).
smoke עשן *nm* ‘ashan.
(cloud of) smoke ענן עשן *nm* ‘an|an/-eney ‘ashan.
(to have a) smoke לעשן סיגרייה *inf* le‘ashen seegareeyah; *pst* ‘eeshen *etc*; *pres* me‘ashen *etc*; *fut* ye‘ashen *etc*.
(to) smoke לעשן *inf* le‘ashen; *pst* ‘eeshen; *pres* me‘ashen; *fut* ye‘ashen.
smoke screen מסך עשן *nm* masa|kh/-key *(k=kh)* ‘ashan.
(to) smoke out להוציא ממאורתו *inf* lehotsee mee-me’oorato; *pst* hotsee *etc*; *pres* motsee *etc*; *fut* yotsee *etc*.
smoker מעשן *nm* me‘ash|en/-neem (*pl+of:* -ney).
smokestack ארובה *nf* aroob|ah/-ot (*+of:* -at).
smoking עישון *nm* ‘eeshoon/-eem (*pl+of:* -ey).
smoking car קרון מעשנים *nm* kron/-ot me‘ashneem.
smoking compartment תא מעשנים *nm* ta/ta'ey me‘ashneem.
smoking room חדר עישון *nm* khad|ar/-rey ‘eeshoon.
smoky אפוף עשן *adj* afoof/-at ‘ashan.
smooth 1. חלק (even) *adj* khalak/-ah; **2.** שקט (serene) *adj* shaket/sheketah; **3.** נעים (pleasant) *adj* na‘eem/ne‘eemah; **4.** נבון (wise) *adj* navon/nevonah.
(to) smooth 1. להחליק *inf* lehakhleek; *pst* hekhleek; *pres* makhleek; *fut* yakhleek; **2.** ליישר (straighten) *inf* leyasher; *pst* yeesher; *pres* meyasher; *fut* yeyasher.
smooth disposition מצב רוח אדיב *nm* matsav roo'akh adeev.
smooth manners נימוסי אדיבות *nm pl* neemoosey adeevoot.
(to) smooth over ליישר הדורים *inf* leyasher hadooreem; *pst* yeesher *etc*; *pres* meyasher *etc*; *fut* yeyasher *etc*.
smooth style סגנון קליל *nm* seegnon kaleel.
smooth talker פטפטן חלקלק *nm* patpetan khalaklak.
smoothly 1. בקלות *adv* be-kaloot; **2.** ללא בעיות (without problems) *adv* le-lo ba‘yot.
smoothness 1. שוויון (evenness) *nm* sheevyon/-ot; **2.** נעימות (pleasantness) *nf* ne‘eemoo|t/-yot.
(to) smother 1. לחנוק (throttle) *vt inf* lakhnok; *pst* khanak; *pres* khonek; *fut* yakhnok; **2.** להחניק (suffocate) *inf* lehakhneek; *pst* hekhneek; *pres* makhneek; *fut* yakhneek; **3.** לדעוך (fade) *inf* leed‘okh; *pst* da‘akh; *pres* do‘ekh; *fut* yeed‘akh.
smudge 1. כתם *nm* ket|em/-ameem (*pl+of:* keetmey); **2.** רבב (blemish) *nm* revav/-eem (*pl+of:* -ey).
(to) smudge 1. לטשטש *inf* letashtesh; *pst* teeshtesh; *pres* metashtesh; *fut* yetashtesh; **2.** למרוח (smear) *inf* leemro'akh; *pst* marakh; *pres* more'akh; *fut* yeemrakh.
(to) smuggle להבריח *inf* lehavree'akh; *pst* heevree'akh; *pres* mavree'akh; *fut* yavree'akh.
(to) smuggle in להבריח ארצה *inf* lehavree'akh artsah; *pst* heevree'akh; *pres* mavree'akh; *fut* yavree'akh.
(to) smuggle out להבריח לחו"ל *inf* lehavree'akh le-khool; *pst* heevree'akh; *pres* mavree'akh; *fut* yavree'akh.
smuggler מבריח *nm* mavree|'akh/-kheem (*pl+of:* -khey).
smutty 1. של ניבול פה *adj* shel neebool peh; **2.** מזוהם (dirty) *adj* mezo|ham/-hemet; **3.** גס (coarse) *adj* gas/-ah.
snack 1. חטיף *nm* khateef/-eem (*pl+of:* -ey); **2.** ארוחה קלה (light meal) *nf* arookh|ah/-ot kal|ah/-ot.
snag 1. בליטה *nf* (protuberance) *nf* bleet|ah/-ot (*+of:* -at); **2.** תקלה (obstacle) *nf* takal|ah/-ot (*+of:* -at).
(to hit a) snag להיתקל במכשול *inf* leheetakel be-meekhshol; *pst & pres* neetkal *etc*; *fut* yeetakel *etc*.
(to) snag 1. להשחית *inf* lehash'kheet; *pst* heesh'kheet; *pres* mash'kheet; *fut* yash'kheet; **2.** לקלקל (spoil) *inf* lekalkel; *pst* keelkel; *pres* mekalkel; *fut* yekalkel.
snail 1. חילזון (gastropod) *nm* kheelazon/khelzonot (*+of:* khelzon); **2.** שבלול (cochlear) *nm* shablool/-eem (*pl+of:* -ey).
snake נחש *nm* nakhash/nekhasheem (*+of:* nekhash/nakhashey).
(to) snake 1. להתפתל *inf* leheetpatel; *pst* heetpatel; *pres* meetpatel; *fut* yeetpatel; **2.** להתגנב *inf* leheetganev; *pst* heetganev, *pres* meetganev; *fut* yeetganev.
(cold) snap גל קור *nm* gal/-ey kor.
(doesn't care a) snap לא אכפת לו lo eekhpat lo/lah *(m/f)*.
(to) snap 1. לסגור בקולי קולות (close noisily) *inf* leesgor be-koley kolot; *pst* sagar *etc*; *pres* soger *etc*; *fut* yeesgor *etc*; **2.** לצלם (photograph) *inf* letsalem; *pst* tseelem; *pres* metsalem; *fut* yetsalem; **3.** להישבר (break) *inf* leheeshaver; *pst & pres* neeshbar *(b=v)*; *fut* yeeshaver.

(to) snap at לקפוץ על *inf* leekpots ʻal; *pst* kafats *(f=p)* ʻal; *pres* kofets ʻal; *fut* yeekpots ʻal.

(to) snap back at להחזיר עקיצה *inf* lehakhzeer ʻakeetsah; *pst* hekhzeer *etc*; *pres* makhzeer *etc*; *fut* yakhzeer *etc*.

snap fastener פריפת לחץ *nmf* preef|at/-ot lakhats.

snap judgment החלטה חפוזה *nf* hakhlat|ah/-ot khafooz|ah/-ot.

snap lock מנעול לחיצה *nm* manʻool/-ey lekheetsah.

(to) snap off להשתחרר *inf* leheeshtakhrer; *pst* heeshtakhrer; *pres* meeshtakhrer; *fut* yeeshtakhrer.

(to) snap one's fingers לנקוף אצבע *inf* leenkof etsbaʻ; *pst* nakaf *etc*; *pres* nokef *etc*; *fut* yeenkof *etc*.

(to) snap shut לסגור לפתע *inf* leesgor le-fetaʻ *(f=p)*; *pst* sagar *etc*; *pres* soger *etc*; *fut* yeesgor *etc*.

(to) snap together לכפתר *inf* lekhafter; *pst* keefter *(k=kh)*; *pres* mekhafter; *fut* yekhafter.

(to) snap up לקטוע בגסות *inf* leektoʻaʻ be-gasoot; *pst* kataʻ *etc*; *pres* koteʻaʻ *etc*; *fut* yeektaʻ *etc*.

snappy 1. מהיר תגובה *adj* meheer/-at tegoovah; **2.** זריז (quick) *adj* zareez/zereezah.

snappy cheese גבינה פיקנטית חמצמצה *nf* gveen|ah/-ot peekantee|t/-yot khamatsmats|ah/-ot.

snappy eyes עיניים זריזות *nf pl* ʻeynayeem zereezot.

snapshot תצלום בזק *nm* tatsloom/-ey bazak.

(to) snapshot לצלם צילומי בזק *inf* letsalem tseeloomey bazak; *pst* tseelem *etc*; *pres* metsalem *etc*; *fut* yetsalem *etc*.

snare 1. מלכודת (trap) *nf* malkod|et/-ot; **2.** מארב (ambush) *nm* maʼar|av/-aveem (*pl+of:* -vey).

snarl 1. נהימה *nf* neheem|ah/-ot (*+of:* -at); **2.** תרעומת (murmur) *nf* tarʻom|et/-ot.

(to) snarl 1. נהם *inf* leenhom; *pst* naham; *pres* nohem; *fut* yeenham; **2.** לרטון (murmur) *inf* leerton; *pst* ratan; *pres* roten; *fut* yeerton.

snatch חטיפה *nf* khateef|ah/-ot (*+of:* -at).

(to) snatch 1. לחטוף *inf* lakhtof; *pst* khataf; *pres* khotef; *fut* yakhtof; **2.** לתפוס (catch) *inf* leetpos; *pst* tafas *(f=p)*; *pres* tofes; *fut* yeetpos.

(to) snatch at לקפוץ על *inf* leekpots ʻal; *pst* kafats *(f=p)* ʻal; *pres* kofets ʻal; *fut* yeekpots ʻal.

sneak 1. בדוי *adj* badooy/bedooyah; **2.** מלשין (informer) *nmf* malsheen/-ah.

(to) sneak לחמוק *inf* lakhmok; *pst* khamak; *pres* khomek; *fut* yakhmok.

(to) sneak in 1. להתגנב *inf* leheetganev; *pst* heetganev; *pres* meetganev; *fut* yeetganev; **2.** להלשין (inform on) *inf* lehalsheen; *pst* heelsheen; *pres* malsheen; *fut* yalsheen.

(to) sneak out לחמוק החוצה בגניבה *inf* lakhmok ha-khootsah bee-gnevah; *pst* khamak *etc*; *pres* khomek *etc*; *fut* yakhmok *etc*.

sneaky מתגנב *adj* meetganev/-et.

sneer 1. לעג *nm* laʻag; **2.** בוז (contempt) *nm* booz.

(to) sneer 1. ללגלג *inf* lelagleg; *pst* leegleg; *pres* melagleg; *fut* yelagleg; **2.** לחייך בלעג (smile) *inf* lekhayekh be-laʻag; *pst* kheeyekh *etc*; *pres* mekhayekh *etc*; *fut* yekhayekh *etc*; **3.** להתקלס ב־ (gesture) *inf* leheetkales be-; *pst* heetkales be-; *pres* meetkales be-; *fut* yeetkales be-.

(to) sneer at ללעוג ל־ *inf* leelʻog le-; *pst* laʻag le-; *pres* loʻeg le-; *fut* yeelʻag le-.

sneeze התעטשות *nf* heetʻatʼshoo|t/-yot.

(to) sneeze להתעטש *inf* leheetʻatesh; *pst* heetʻatesh; *pres* meetʻatesh; *fut* yeetʻatesh.

sniff ריחרוח *nm* reekhroo|ʼakh/-kheem (*pl+of:* -khey).

(to) sniff לרחרח *inf* lerakhreʼakh; *pst* reekhrakh; *pres* merakhreʼakh; *fut* yerakhrakh.

(to) sniff at לבוז *inf* lavooz; *pst & pres* baz; *fut* yavooz.

sniffle נזלת *nf* naz|elet/-alot.

snip חתיכה גזורה *nf* khateekh|ah/-ot gzoor|ah/-ot.

(to) snip לגזור במיספריים *inf* leegzor be-meesparayeem.

(to) snip off לכרות *inf* leekhrot; *pst* karat *(k=kh)*; *pres* koret; *fut* yeekhrot.

(to) snipe לצלוף *inf* leetslof; *pst* tsalaf; *pres* tsolef; *fut* yeetslof.

sniper צלף *nm* tsalaf/-eem (*pl+of:* -ey).

(to) snitch לחטוף *inf* lakhtof; *pst* khataf; *pres* khotef; *fut* yakhtof.

(to) snivel להתבכיין *inf* leheetbakhyen; *pst* heetbakhyen; *pres* meetbakhyen; *fut* yeetbakhyen.

snob 1. שחצן *nf* shakhtsan/-eet; **2.** סנוב *nmf* snob/-eet (*pl:* -eem/-eeyot).

snobbery סנוביות *nf* snobeeyoot.

snoop חיטוט *nm* kheetoot/-eem (*pl+of:* -ey).

(to) snoop לחטט *inf* lekhatet; *pst* kheetet; *pres* mekhatet; *fut* yekhatet.

snooze תנומה קלה *nf* tnoomah kalah.

(to take a) snooze לחטוף תנומה קלה *inf* lakhtof tnoomah kalah; *pst* khataf *etc*; *pres* khotef *etc*; *fut* yakhtof *etc*.

snore נחירה *nf* nekheer|ah/-ot (*+of:* -at).

(to) snore לנחור *inf* leenkhor; *pst* nakhar; *pres* nokher; *fut* yeenkhor.

snorkel צינור שנורקל *nm* tseenor/-ot shnorkel.

snort חירחור *nm* kheerkhoor/-eem (*pl+of:* -ey).

(to) snort לחרחר *inf* lekharkher; *pst* kheerkher; *pres* mekharkher; *fut* yekharkher.

snot הפרשה מהאף *nf* hafrash|ah/-ot me-ha-af.

(to) snot להפריש מהאף *inf* lehafreesh me-ha-af; *pst* heefreesh *etc*; *pres* mafreesh *etc*; *fut* yafreesh *etc*.

snotty בזוי *adj* bazooy/bzooyah.

snout חרטום *nm* khartom/-eem (*pl+of:* -ey).

snow שלג *nm* sheleg/shlageem (*pl+of:* shalgey).

snowball כדור שלג *nm* kadoor/-ey sheleg.

snowdrift סחף שלג *nm* sakhaf/-ey sheleg.

snowfall ירידת שלג *nf* yereed|at/-ot sheleg.

snowflakes פתיתי שלג *nf pl* pteetey sheleg.

snowstorm סופת שלגים *nf* soof|at/-ot shlageem.

snowy מושלג *nf* mooshl|ag/-eget.

snub 1. זילזול *nm* zeelzool/-eem (*pl+of:* -ey); **2.** השפלה (humiliation) *nf* hashpal|ah/-ot (*+of:* -at).

(to) snub לזלזל *inf* lezalzel; *pst* zeelzel; *pres* mezalzel; *fut* yezalzel.

snub nose אף סולד *nm* af/apeem sol|ed/-deem.

snuff טבק הרחה *nm* tabak harakhah.

(to) snuff at 1. לרחרח *inf* lerakhreʼakh; *pst* reekhrakh; *pres* merakhreʼakh; *fut* yerakhrakh.

2. להריח *inf* leharee'akh; *pst* heree'akh; *pres* meree'akh; *fut* yaree'akh.

(to) snuff out 1. לכבות *inf* lekhabot; *pst* keebah; *pres* mekhabeh; *fut* yekhabeh; **2.** להשמיד *inf* lehashmeed; *pst* heeshmeed; *pres* mashmeed; *fut* yashmeed.

snug 1. לחוץ (squeezed) *adj* lakhoots/lekhootsah; **2.** נינוח (comfortable) neeno|'akh/-khah.

so כך *conj* kakh.

(is that) so ? האמנם כך ? ha-omnam kakh ?

(ten minutes or) so עשר דקות בערך 'eser dakot be-'erekh.

so-and-so כך וכך kakh ve-khakh *(kh=k)*.

so as to למען אשר le-ma'an asher.

so-called המכונה ha-mekhoon|eh/-ah.

so far עד כה *adv* 'ad koh.

(and) so forth וכך הלאה ve-khakh hal'ah.

so many כה רבים koh rabeem.

so much כה רבות koh rabot.

so much for that נסתפק בכך *v pres pl* neestapek be-khakh *(kh=k)*.

so much that עד כדי כך ש־ 'ad kdey kakh she-.

so much the better מוטב שכך mootav she-khakh.

so that כדי ש־ kdey she-.

so-so ככה־ככה kakhah-kakhah.

so then ובכן oo-ve-khen.

(I believe) so כך אני סבור kakh anee savoor/svoorah *(m/f)*.

soak שרייה *nf* shree|yah/-yot (*+of:* -yat).

(to) soak להשרות *inf* lehashrot; *pst* heeshrah; *pres* mashreh; *fut* yashreh.

(to) soak up לספוג *inf* leespog; *pst* safag *(f=p)*; *pres* sofeg; *fut* yeespog.

soaked through רטוב עד העצם *adj* ratoov/retoovah 'ad ha-'etsem.

soap סבון *nm* sabon/-eem (*pl+of:* -ey).

(soft) soap 1. סבון נוזלי (liquid) *nm* sabon/-eem nozlee/-yeem; **2.** חנופה (flattery) *nf* khanoop|ah (*+of:* -at).

(to) soap לסבן *inf* lesaben; *pst* seeben; *pres* mesaben; *fut* yesaben.

soap bubble בועת סבון *nf* boo|'at/-'ot sabon.

soap dish סבונייה *nf* sabonee|yah/-yot (*+of:* -yat).

soap flakes פתיתי סבון *nf pl* pteetey sabon.

soap opera סידרה משודרת *nf* seedrah/sdarot meshood|eret/-arot.

soapy מכיל סבון *adj* mekheel/-at sabon.

(to) soar 1. להתרומם *inf* leheetromem; *pst* heetromem; *pres* meetromem; *fut* yeetromem; **2.** להמריא (take off) *inf* lehamree; *pst* heemree; *pres* mamree; *fut* yamree'.

sob 1. בכי *nm* bkhee/beekhyot; **2.** התיפחות *nf* heetyapkhoo|t/-yot.

(to) sob 1. לבכות *inf* leevkot; *pst* bakhah (b=v; kh=k); *pres* bokheh; *fut* yeevkeh; **2.** להתיפח *inf* leheetyape'akh; *pst* heetyapakh; *pres* meetyape'akh; *fut* yeetyapakh.

sober 1. מפוכח *adj* mefookakh/-at; **2.** מתון (temperate) *adj* matoon/metoonah; **3.** רציני (serious) *adj* retseenee/-t; **4.** שפוי (sane) shafooy/shfooyah; **5.** נינוח (calm) *adj* neeno|akh/-khah.

(to be) sober לא להשתכר *inf* lo leheeshtaker; *pst* lo heeshtaker; *pres* eyno meeshtaker; *fut* lo yeeshtaker.

(to) sober down להירגע *inf* leheraga'; *pst & pres* neerga'; *fut* yeraga'.

(to) sober up להתפכח *inf* leheetpake'akh; *pst* heetpakakh; *pres* meetpake'akh; *fut* yeetpakakh.

soberly בצורה מפוכחת *adv* be-tsoorah mefookakhat.

soberness פיכחון *nm* peekakhon.

sobriety 1. פיכחון *nm* peekakhon; **2.** מתינות (moderation) *nf* meteenoot.

soccer כדורגל *nm* kadooregel.

soccer match תחרות כדורגל *nf* takhroo|t/-yot kadooregel.

soccer player כדורגלן *nm* kadooraglan/-eem (*pl+of:* -ey).

sociable חברותי *adj* khavrootee/-t.

social 1. חברתי *adj* khevratee/-t; **2.** סוציאלי *adj* sotsee'alee/-t.

social aid סעד *nm* sa'ad.

social assistance עזרה סוציאלית *nf* 'ezrah sotsee'aleet.

social work עבודה סוציאלית *nf* 'avodah sotsee'aleet.

social worker עובד סוציאלי *nmf* 'oved/-et sootsee'alee/-t (*pl:* 'ovdeem sotsee'aleeyeem).

socialism סוציאליזם *nm* sotsee'aleezm/-eem.

socialist 1. סוציאליסט *nmf* sotsee'aleest/-eet; **2.** סוציאליסטי *adj* sotsee'aleestee/-t.

socialite איש חברה *nmf* eesh/'eshet khevrah.

(to) socialize לטפח יחסי חברות *inf* letape'akh yakhsey khaveroot; *pst* teepakh *etc*; *pres* metape'akh *etc*; *fut* yetapakh *etc.*

society 1. חברה (company) *nf* khevrah/khavarot (*+of:* khevr|at/-ot); **2.** אגודה (association) *nf* agood|ah/-ot (*+of:* -at); **3.** החברה הגבוהה (high society) *nf* ha-khevrah ha-gvohah.

sociology סוציולוגיה *nf* sotsyologee|yah/-yot (*+of:* -yat).

sock 1. גרב (garment) *nm* gerev/garb|ayeem (*pl+of:* -ey); **2.** מהלומה (blow) *nf* mahaloom|ah/-ot (*+of:* -at).

(to) sock להרביץ *inf* leharbeets; *pst* heerbeets; *pres* marbeets; *fut* yarbeets.

socket 1. שקע *nm* shek|a'/-a'eem (*pl+of:* sheek'ey); **2.** תושבת (for tube) *nf* tosh|evet/-avot (*pl+of:* -vot); **3.** בית־נורה (for bulb) *nm* bet/batey noor|ah/-ot.

sod רובד רגבים מודשאים *nm* roved/ravdey regaveem moodsha'eem.

(to) sod לכסות ברובד רגבים מודשאים *inf* lekhasot be-roved regaveem moodsha'eem; *pst* keesah *(k=kh) etc*; *pres* mekhaseh *etc*; *fut* yekhaseh *etc.*

soda סודה *nf* sodah.

(baking) soda סודה לאפייה *nf* sodah le-afeeyah.

soda fountain קיוסק לגזוז *nm* kyosk/-eem le-gazoz.

soda water 1. גזוז *nm* gazoz; **2.** מי סודה *nm pl* mey sodah.

sodium נתרן *nm* natran/-eem (*pl+of:* -ey).

sofa ספה *nf* sap|ah/-ot (*+of:* -at).

soft 1. רך (not hard) *adj* rakh/rakah; **2.** עדין (gentle) *adj* 'adeen/-ah.

soft-boiled egg ביצה רכה *adj nf* beyts|ah/-eem rak|ah/-ot.

soft coal פחם חימר *nm* pakh|am/-mey kheymar.

soft drink משקה קל *nm* mashk|eh/-a'ot kal/-eem.

soft-hearted טוב לב *adj* tov/-at lev.

(to) soft pedal לטשטש *inf* letashtesh; *pst* teeshtesh; *pres* metashtesh; *fut* yetashtesh.

soft soap 1. סבון נוזלי *nm* sabon/-eem nozlee/-yeem; **2.** חנופה (flattery) *nf* khanoop|ah (+*of:* -at).

soft water מים רכים *nm pl* mayeem rakeem.

(to) soften לרכך *inf* lerakekh; *pst* reekekh; *pres* merakekh; *fut* yerakekh.

(to) soften one's voice להנמיך את הקול *inf* heenmeekh et ha-kol; *pst* heenmeekh *etc*; *pres* manmeekh *etc*; *fut* yanmeekh *etc*.

softly בעדינות *adv* ba-'adeenoot.

softness רכות *nf* rakoo|t/-yot.

soggy לח *adj* lakh/-ah;

soil 1. קרקע *nf* kark|a'/-a'ot; **2.** עפר *nm* 'af|ar/-areem (*pl+of:* -arey).

(to) soil 1. ללכלך *vt inf* lelakhlekh; *pst* leekhlekh; *pres* melakhlekh; *fut* yelakhlekh; **2.** להתלכלך *v rfl inf* leheetlakhlekh; *pst* heetlakhlekh; *pres* meetlakhlekh; *fut* yeetlakhekh.

soiree 1. נשף *nm* nesh|ef/-afeem (*pl+of:* neeshpey); **2.** נישפייה (party) *nf* neeshfee|yah/-yot (+*of:* -yat).

sojourn שהייה *nf* shehee|yah/-yot (+*of:* -yat).

(to) sojourn לשהות *inf* leesh'hot; *pst* shahah; *pres* shoheh; *fut* yeesh'heh.

solace נחמה *nf* nekham|ah/-ot (+*of:* -at).

(to) solace לנחם *inf* lenakhem; *pst* neekhem; *pres* menakhem; *fut* yenakhem.

solar 1. שימשי *adj* sheemshee/-t; **2.** סולרי *adj* solaree/-t.

solar battery סוללת שמש *nf* solel|at/-ot shemesh.

solar energy אנרגיית השמש *nf* energeeyat ha-shemesh.

solar plexus מיקלעת השמש *nf* meekla'at ha-shemesh.

solar system מערכת השמש *nf* ma'arekhet ha-shemesh.

sold מכור *adj* makhoor/mekhoorah.

sold on an idea מכור לרעיון *adj* makhoor/mekhoorah le-ra'yon.

solder 1. לחם *nm* lakham; **2.** חומר הלחמה (material) *nm* khom|er/-rey halkhamah.

(to) solder להלחים *inf* lehalkheem; *pst* heelkheem; *pres* malkheem; *fut* yalkheem.

soldering iron מלחם *nm* malkh|em/-ameem (*pl+of:* -amey).

soldier חייל khayal/-eem (*pl+of:* -ey).

(Israel Defence Forces — IDF) soldier חייל צה"ל *nm* khayal/-ey tsahal.

(Israeli) soldier חייל ישראלי *nm*khayal/-eem yeesre'elee/-yeem.

(woman-)soldier חיילת *nf* khay|elet/-alot.

soldier of fortune הרפתקן צבאי harpatkan/-eem tsva'ee/-yeem.

sole סולייה *nf* sool|yah/-yot (+*of:* -yat).

(to) sole להתקין סוליות *inf* lehatkeen soolyot; *pst* heetkeen *etc*; *pres* matkeen *etc*; *fut* yatkeen *etc*.

solely אך ורק *prep* akh ve-rak.

solemn 1. חגיגי (festive) *adj* khageegee/-t; **2.** טיקסי (ceremonial) *adj* teeksee/-t; **3.** רציני (serious) *adj* retseenee/-t.

solemnity 1. חגיגיות *nf* khageegeeyoot; **2.** טיקסיות (ceremonial) *nf* teekseeyoot.

(to) solicit 1. לבקש (entreat) *inf* levakesh; *pst* beekesh (*v=b*); *pres* mevakesh; *fut* yevakesh; **2.** לתבוע (request) *inf* leetbo'a'; *pst* tava'; *pres* tove'a'; *fut* yeetba'; **3.** לפתות (tempt) *inf* lefatot; *pst* peetah (*p=f*); *pres* mefateh; *fut* yefateh.

solicitor עורך דין בריטי *nm* 'or|ekh/-khey deen breetee/-yeem.

solicitous 1. חרד *adj* khared/-ah; **2.** דואג *adj* do'eg/-et.

solicitude דאגה *nf* de'ag|ah/-ot (+*of:* da'ag|at/-ot).

solid 1. מוצק *nm* mootsak/-eem (*pl+of:* -ey); **2.** יציב (stable) *adj* yatseev/yetseev|ah; **3.** מבוסס (founded) *adj* mevoos|as/-eset.

solid blue כחול כולו *adj* kakhol/kekhoolah kool|o/-ah.

(the country is) solid for הארץ עומדת איתנה אחרי ha-arets 'omedet eytanah akhrey.

solid gold זהב טהור *nm* zahav tahor.

(for one) solid hour במשך שעה שלימה *adv* be-meshekh sha'ah shleymah.

solid-state מוצק *adj* mootsak/-ah.

solidarity סולידריות *nf* soleedareeyoot.

(to) solidify 1. למצק *inf* lematsek; *pst* meetsek; *pres* mematsek; *fut* yematsek; **2.** לגבש (crystallize) *inf* legabesh; *pst* geebesh; *pres* megabesh; *fut* yegabesh; **3.** לבסס (base) *inf* levases; *pst* beeses (*b=v*); *pres* mevases; *fut* yevases.

solidity 1. מוצקות *nf* mootsakoo|t/-yot; **2.** מיקשה (hardness) meeksh|ah/-ot (+*of:* -at).

soliloquy חד־שיח *nm* khad-see'akh.

solitaire אבן טובה משופצת *nf* even tovah meshoobetset.

solitary 1. בודד *adj* boded/-et; **2.** גלמוד *adj* galmood/-ah.

solitary confinement צינוק *nm* tseenok.

solitude בדידות *nf* bdeedoo|t/-yot.

solo סולו *nm & adj* solo.

soloist סולן *nmf* solan/-eet (*pl+of:* -ey).

soluble 1. מסיס *adj* masees/meseesah; **2.** פתיר (problem) pateer/pteerah.

solution 1. פיתרון (problem) *nm* peetron/-ot; **2.** תמיסה (liquid) *nf* tmees|ah/-ot (+*of:* -at).

(to) solve 1. לפתור (problem) *inf* leeftor; *pst* patar (*p=f*); *pres* poter; *fut* yeeftor; **2.** להמיס (solid) *inf* lehamees; *pst* hemees; *pres* memees; *fut* yamees.

solvent ממוסס *nm* memoses/-eem (*pl+of:* -ey).

somber קודר *adj* koder/-et.

some 1. כמה kamah; **2.** אי־אלה ee-'eleh.

some twenty people כעשרים איש ke-'esreem eesh.

somebody מישהו *nmf* meeshe|hoo/-hee.

(a) somebody אישיות eesheeyoot.

somehow איכשהו *adv* eykhshehoo.

somehow *or* **other** כך או אחרת *adv* kakh o akheret.

someone מישהו *nmf* meeshe|hoo/-hee.

somersault 1. קפיצת התהפכות באוויר *nf* kfeets|at/-ot heet'hapkhoot ba-aveer; **2.** סלטה *nf* salt|ah/-ot (*+of:* -at).

something משהו *nm* mashehoo.

something else משהו אחר *nm* mashehoo akher.

sometime 1. אי־פעם *adv* ey-fa'am; **2.** בזמן מן הזמנים *adv* bee-zman meen ha-zmaneem.

sometimes לפעמים *adv* lee-fe'ameem.

somewhat כלשהו *adj* kolshe|hoo/-hee.

somewhere אי שם *adv* ey-sham.

somewhere else במקום אחר be-makom akher.

somnambulant סהרורי *nmf* saharooree/-t.

son בן *nm* ben/baneem (*pl+of:* bney).

son-in-law חתן *nm* khat|an/-neem (*pl+of:* -ney).

song 1. שיר (also poetical) *nm* sheer/-eem (*pl+of:* -ey); **2.** זמר (only melodious) *nm* zemer/zmareem (*pl+of:* zeemrey).

(to buy something for a) song לקנות בפרוטות leeknot bee-frootot; *pst* kanah *etc*; *pres* koneh *etc*; *fut* yeekneh *etc*.

song bird ציפור שיר *nm* tseepor/-ey sheer.

(the) Song of Songs שיר השירים *nm* sheer ha-sheereem.

songster 1. זמר *nmf* zam|ar/-eret (*pl:* -areem/-arot; *+of:* -arey); **2.** מלחין (composer) *nmf* malkheen/-ah (*+of:* -at/-ey).

sonic קולי *adj* kolee/-t.

sonic barrier מחסום הקול *nm* makhsom ha-kol.

sonic boom בום על־קולי *nm* boom/-eem 'al-kolee/-yeem.

sonnet סונטה *nf* sonat|ah/-ot (*+of:* -at).

sonorous מצלצל *adj* metsaltsel/-et.

soon בקרוב *adv* be-karov.

(how) soon ? בעוד כמה זמן ? be-'od kamah zman?

soon after זמן קצר אחרי *adv* zman katsar akhrey.

soon as 1. משרק *adv* mee-she-rak; **2.** מיד כאשר *adv* meeyad ka-asher.

soot פיח *nm* pee'akh.

(to) soothe 1. להרגיע *inf* lehargee'a'; *pst* heergee'a'; *pres* margee'a'; *fut* yargee'a'; **2.** לרכך *inf* lerakekh; *pst* reekekh; *pres* merakekh; *fut* yerakekh.

soothsayer מגיד עתידות *nmf* mageed/-at 'ateedot.

sooty מפוייח *adj* mefooyakh/-at.

sop 1. שוחד *nm* shokhad; **2.** דמי "לא יחרץ" (blackmail) *nm pl* dmey "lo yekhrats".

(to) sop 1. להרטיב *vt inf* leharteev; *pst* heerteev; *pres* marteev; *fut* yarteev; **2.** להתרטב *v rfl inf* leheetratev; *pst* heetratev; *pres* meetratev; *fut* yeetratev.

(to) sop up לספוג (absorb) *inf* leespog; *pst* safag (*f=p*); *pres* sofeg; *fut* yeespog (*f=p*).

sophisticated מתוחכם *adj* metookhk|am/-emet.

sophomore סטודנט שנה ב' בקולג' *nmf* stoodent/-eet shanah bet be-koledj.

sopping wet רטוב עד העצמות *adj* ratoov/retoovah 'ad ha-'atsamot.

soprano 1. סופרנו *nmf* soprano; **2.** זמרת סופרנו (singer) *nf* zam|eret/-rot soprano.

(high) soprano קול סופרנו גבוה *nm* kol/-ot soprano gavoha/gvoheem.

soprano voice קול סופרנו *nm* kol/-ot soprano.

sorcerer 1. אשף *nmf* ashaf/-eet; **2.** קוסם (magician) *nmf* kosem/-et.

sordid 1. שפל (vile) *adj* shafel/shfalah; **2.** מזוהם (filthy) *adj* mezo|ham/-hemet.

sore 1. כאוב (painful) *adj* ka'oov/ke'oovah; **2.** מכאיב (grievous) *adj* makh'eev/-ah; **3.** פגוע (injured) pagoo'ah/pegoo'ah; **4.** ניפגע (offended) *adj* neef-g|a'/-a'at.

(to be) sore at להתרעם על *inf* leheetra'em 'al; *pst* heetra'em 'al; *pres* meetra'em 'al; *fut* yeetra'em 'al.

(a sight for) sore eyes מחזה מרנין *nm* makhz|eh/-ot marneen/-ey lev.

sore throat כאב גרון *nm* ke'ev/-ey garon

sorely אנושות *adv* anooshot.

sorely in need of זקוק עד מאד ל־ *adj* zakook/zkookah 'ad me'od le-.

soreness 1. כאב *nm* ke'ev/-eem (*pl+of:* -ey); **2.** דלקת *nf* dal|eket/-akot.

sorghum דורה *nf* doorah.

sorrel 1. חומעה (herb) *nf* khoom'ah; **2.** חום־אדמדם (reddish-brown) *adj* khoom/-ah adamd|am/-emet.

sorrow 1. עצב (sadness) *nm* 'etsev; **2.** יגון (grief) *nm* yagon/yegonot (*+of:* yegon); **3.** חרטה (repentance) *nf* kharat|ah/-ot (*+of:* -at).

(to) sorrow 1. להצטער (regret) *inf* leheetsta'er; *pst* heetsta'er; *pres* meetsta'er; *fut* yeetsta'er; **2.** להתחרט (repent) *inf* leheetkharet; *pst* heetkharet; *pres* meetkharet; *fut* yeetkharet.

sorrowful 1. עצוב *adj* 'atsoov/-ah; **2.** עגום (sad) 'agoom/-ah.

sorrowfully בצער *adv* be-tsa'ar.

sorry מצטער *adj* meetsta'er/-et.

sorry! סליחה ! *interj* sleekhah!

(I am) sorry 1. אני מצטער anee metsta'er/-et! (*m/f*); **2.** סליחה ! *interj* sleekhah!

(I am) sorry for him/her אני מרחם עליו anee merakhem/-et 'alav/'aleha (*m/f*).

sort 1. סוג *nm* soog/-eem (*pl+of:* -ey); **2.** מין (kind) *nm* meen/-eem (*pl+of:* -ey); **3.** טיפוס (type) *nm* teepoos/-eem (*pl+of:* -ey).

(to) sort 1. לסווג *inf* lesaveg; *pst* seeveg; *pres* mesaveg; *fut* yesaveg; **2.** למיין (classify) *inf* lemayen; *pst* meeyen; *pres* memayen; *fut* yemayen.

sort of tired עייף כלשהו *adj* 'ayef/-ah kolshehoo.

(to) sort out לברור *inf* leevror; *pst* barar (*b=v*); *pres* borer; *fut* yeevror (*b=v*).

sortie גיחה *nf* geekh|ah/-ot (*+of:* -at).

(all) sorts כל מיני kol meeney.

(of) sorts מסוג נחות *adj* mee-soog nakhoot.

so-so ככה־ככה *adv* kakhah-kakhah.

soul 1. נפש *nm* nef|esh/-ashot; **2.** נשמה *nf* nesham|ah/-ot (*+of:* neeshm|at/-ot).

(not a) soul אף נפש חיה af nefesh khayah.

sound 1. צליל *nm m* tsleel/-eem (*pl+of:* -ey); **2.** קול (voice) *nm* kol/-ot; **3.** רעש (noise) *nm* ra'ash/re'asheem (*pl+of:* ra'ashey).

sound 1. בריא (healthy) *adj* baree/bree'ah; **2.** איתן (firm) *adj* eytan/-ah.

(safe and) sound בריא ושלם *adj* baree/bree'ah ve-shalem/shlemah.

(to) sound להישמע *inf* leheeshama‘; *pst & pres* neeshma‘; *fut* yeeshama‘.
(a) sound beating הצלפה כהלכה *nf* hatslaf|ah/-ot ka-halakhah.
sound business עסק טוב *nm* ‘esek tov.
sound of mind בריא בשיכלו *adj* baree/bree'ah be-seekhl|o/-ah.
(to) sound out 1. לבחון *inf* leevkhon; *pst* bakhan *(b=v); pres* bokhen; *fut* yeevkhon; **2.** לבדוק (check) *inf* leevdok; *pst* badak *(b=v); pres* bodek; *fut* yeevdok.
sound reasoning הגיון בריא *nm* heegayon baree.
sound sleep שינה בריאה *nf* sheynah bree'ah.
sound title תואר מבוסס *nm* to'ar mevoosas.
sound wave גל קולי *nm* gal/-eem kolee/-yeem.
soundly 1. כהלכה *adv* ka-halakhah; **2.** ביעילות (efficiently) *adv* be-ye‘eeloot.
soundness 1. איתנות (firmness) *nf* eytanoot; **2.** בריאות (healthiness) *nf* bree'oot; **3.** תוקף (validity) *nm* tokef.
soundness of body בריאות הגוף *nf* bree'oot ha-goof.
soundproof אטום לרעש *adj* atoom/-ah le-ra‘ash.
soup מרק *nm* marak/merakeem *(pl+of:* meerkey).
soup kitchen בית תמחוי *nm* bet/batey tamkhooy.
sour 1. חמוץ (acid-like) *adj* khamoots/-ah; **2.** זועף (peevish) *adj* zo‘ef/-et.
sour 1. מחמצת *nf* makhm|etset/-atsot; **2.** בוסר *nm* boser.
(to) sour להחמיץ *inf* lehakhmeets; *pst* hekhmeets; *pres* makhmeets; *fut* yakhmeets.
sour milk לבן *nm* leben.
source מקור *nm* makor/mekorot *(+of:* mekor).
sourness חמיצות *nf* khameetsoo|t/-yot.
souse בשר כבוש *nm* basar kavoosh.
south 1. דרום *nm* darom; **2.** דרומית *adv* dromeet.
South Africa 1. דרום־אפריקה *nf* drom-afreekah; **2.** דרא״פ *nm* drap *(acr of* 1).
South African 1. דרום־אפריקאי *nmf* drom-afreeka'ee/-t; **2.** דרום־אפריקני *adj* drom-afrekanee/-t.
South America דרום־אמריקה *nf* drom-amereekah.
South American 1. דרום־אמריקאי *nmf* drom-amereeka'ee/-t; **2.** דרום־אמריקני *adj* drom-amereekanee/-t.
south pole ציר דרומי *nm* tseer dromee.
southeast דרום־מזרח *nm* drom-meezrakh.
southeast of דרום־מזרחית ל־ *adv* dromeet-meezrakheet le-.
southeastern דרום־מזרחי *adj* drom-meezrakhee/-t.
southern דרומי *adj* dromee/-t.
Southern Cross הצלב הדרומי *nm* ha-tslav ha-dromee.
southerner תושב הדרום *nmf* tosh|av/-evet *(pl:* -vey/-vot) ha-darom.
southward דרומה *adv* daromah.
southwest דרום־מערב *nm* drom-ma‘rav.
southwest of דרום מערבית ל־ *adv* dromeet-ma‘araveet le-.
southwestern דרום־מערבי *adj* drom-ma‘aravee/-t.
souvenir מזכרת *nf* mazk|eret/-arot.
sovereign 1. מלך *nm* mel|ekh/-akheem *(pl+of:* malkhey); **2.** ריבון *nm* reebon/-eem *(pl+of:* -ey).
sovereignty ריבונות *nf* reebonoo|t/-yot.
soviet סובייטי *adj* sovyetee/-t.
(the) Soviets הסובייטים *nm pl* ha-sovyeteem.
(to) sow לזרוע *inf* leezro'a‘; *pst* zara‘; *pres* zore'a‘; *fut* yeezra‘.
sown זרוע *adj* zaroo'a‘/zroo‘ah.
soybean פול סויה *nm* pol/-ey soyah.
spa אתר נופש *nm* atar/-ey nofesh.
space 1. חלל *nm* khalal/-eem *(pl+of:* -ey); **2.** שטח (area) *nm* shetakh/-eem *(pl+of:* sheetkhey); **3.** רווח (interval) *nm* revakh/-eem *(pl+of:* reevkhey).
space sciences מדעי החלל *nm pl* mad‘ey he-khalal.
space station תחנת חלל *nf* takhn|at/-ot khalal.
space suit תלבושת חלל *nf* teelbosh|et/-ot khalal.
spacecraft חללית *nf* khalalee|t/-yot.
spaceman איש חלל *nm* eesh/anshey khalal.
spacious מרווח *adj* meroovakh/-at.
spade 1. את חפירה *nm* et/-ey khafeerah; **2.** עלה בקלפים (cards) *nm* ‘aleh bee-klafeem.
(to) spade לחפור *inf* lakhpor; *pst* khafar *(f=p); pres* khofer; *fut* yakhpor.
(to call a) spade a spade לקרוא לדבר בשמו *inf* leekro la-davar bee-shmo; *pst* kara *etc*; *pres* kore *etc*; *fut* yeekra *etc.*
Spain ספרד *nf* sfarad.
span 1. אורך *nm* orekh/orakheem *(pl+of:* orkhey); **2.** רוחק (distance) *nm* rokhak/rekhakeem *(pl+of:* rokhokey); **3.** משך (length) meshekh.
(to) span 1. להימתח על פני *inf* leheematakh ‘al pney; *pst & pres* neemtakh *etc*; *fut* yeematakh *etc*; **2.** להשתרע (extend) *inf* leheestare'a‘; *pst* heestara‘; *pres* meestare'a‘; *fut* yeestara‘.
span of life 1. אורך חיים *nm* orekh khayeem; **2.** תוחלת חיים (life expectancy) *nf* tokh|elet/-alot khayeem.
spangle לוחית נוצצת *nf* lookhee|t/-yot notsets|et/-ot.
(to) spangle לכסות בנקודות כסף *inf* lekhasot bee-nekoodot kesef; *pst* keesah *(k=kh) etc*; *pres* mekhaseh *etc*; *fut* yekhaseh *etc.*
spangled with stars זרוע כוכבים *adj* zaroo'a‘/zroo‘ah kokhaveem.
Spaniard ספרדי *nmf* sfaradee/-yah *(pl:* sfaradee|m/-yot).
spaniel כלב ספנייל *nm* kelev/kalvey spaneeyel.
Spanish 1. ספרדי *adj* sfaradee/-t; **2.** ספרדית (language) sfaradeet.
Spanish Jew 1. יהודי ספרדי *nm* yehoodee/-m sfaradee/-m; **2.** ספרדי *nmf* sfaradee/-yah.
Spanish Rite נוסח ספרד *nm* noosakh sfarad.
spank הצלפה בישבן *nf* hatslaf|ah/-ot ba-yashvan.
(to) spank להצליף בישבן *inf* lehatsleef ba-yashvan; *pst* heetsleef *etc*; *pres* matsleef *etc*; *fut* yatsleef *etc.*
spanking הצלפה בישבן *nf* hatslaf|ah/-ot ba-yashvan.
spanner 1. מפתח לברגים (for screws) *nm* mafte|'akh/-khot lee-vrageem *(v=b)*; **2.** מפתח לאומים (for screw-nuts) *nm* mafte|'akh/-khot le'-'oomeem.

(to) spar להתאגרף על פי הספר *inf* leheet'agref 'al pee ha-sefer; *pst* heet'agref *etc*; *pres* meet'agref *etc*; *fut* yeet'agref.

spare 1. מיותר *adj* meyoot|ar/-eret; **2.** עודף *adj* 'odef/-et.

(time to) spare שעות פנאי *nf pl* she'ot pnay.

(to) spare 1. לחסוך *inf* lakhsokh; *pst* khasakh; *pres* khosekh; *fut* yakhsokh; **2.** לקמץ (economize) *inf* lekamets; *pst* keemets; *pres* mekamets; *fut* yekamets.

(I cannot) spare another shekel אף שקל אחד נוסף אין לי להפריש af shekel ekhad nosaf eyn lee lehafreesh.

spare cash 1. כסף מיותר *nm* kesef meyootar; **2.** עודף מזומנים *nm* 'od|ef/-fey mezoomaneem.

(to) spare no expense לא לחוס על הוצאות *inf* lo lakhoos 'al hotsa'ot; *pst & pres* lo khas *etc*; *fut* lo yakhoos *etc*.

(I cannot) spare the car today אין ביכולתי להסתדר בלי הרכב היום eyn bee-yekholtee leheestader blee ha-rekhev hayom.

(to) spare the enemy לחוס על האויב *inf* lakhoos 'al ha-oyev; *pst & pres* khas *etc*; *fut* yakhoos *etc*.

spare tire צמיג חילוף *nm* tsemeeg kheeloof.

sparetime פנאי *nm* penay.

spark 1. ניצוץ *nm* neetsots/-ot; **2.** הברקה *nf* havrak|ah/-ot (+*of:* -at).

(to) spark להתיז ניצוצות *inf* lehateez neetsotsot; *pst* heeteez *etc*; *pres* mateez *etc*; *fut* yateez *etc*.

spark plug 1. מצת *nm* mats|et/-'teem (*pl+of:* -'tey); **2.** פלאג *[colloq.] nm* plag/-eem (*pl+of:* -ey).

sparkle 1. ניצוץ (flash) *nm* neetsots/-ot; **2.** הברקה (spiritual) *nf* havrak|ah/-ot (+*of:* -at).

(to) sparkle 1. לנצנץ *inf* lenatsnets; *pst* neetsnets; *pres* menatsnets; *fut* yenatsnets; **2.** לתסוס (seethe) *inf* leet'sos; *pst* tasas; *pres* toses; *fut* yeet'sos.

sparkling תוסס *adj* toses/-et.

sparkling wine יין נתזים *nm* yeyn/-ot netazeem.

sparrow דרור *nm* dror/-eem (*pl+of:* -ey).

sparse 1. דליל *adj* daleel/dleelah; **2.** מועט (little) *adj* moo|'at/-'etet.

sparse hair שיער דליל *nm* sey'ar daleel.

spasm עווית *nf* 'aveet/-ot.

spastic 1. עוויתי *adj* 'aveetee/-t; **2.** חולה עווית *adj* khol|eh/-at 'aveet.

spats עוטפי רגליים *nm pl* 'otfey raglayeem.

spatter 1. זילוף *nm* zeeloof/-eem (*pl+of:* -ey); **2.** כתם (stain) *nm* ket|em/-ameem (*pl+of:* keetmey).

(to) spatter להתיז *inf* lehateez; *pst* heeteez; *pres* mateez; *fut* yateez.

(so to) speak כביכול keevyakhol.

(to) speak לדבר *inf* ledaber; *pst* deeber; *pres* medaber; *fut* yedaber.

(to) speak for לדבר בשם *inf* ledaber be-shem; *pst* deeber *etc*; *pres* medaber *etc*; *fut* yedaber *etc*.

(to) speak one's mind להביע דעתו *inf* lehabee'a' da'to; *pst* heebee'a' *etc*; *pres* mabee'a' *etc*; *fut* yabee'a' *etc*.

(to) speak out, (to) speak up לומר דברו *inf* lomar dvaro; *pst* amar *etc*; *pres* omer *etc*; *fut* yomar *etc*.

speak to the point! ! דבר לעניין *v imp sing* dab|er/ree (*m/f*) la-'eenyan!

speaker 1. נואם *nmf* no'em/-et (*pl:* no'am|eem; +*of:* -ey); **2.** דובר *nmf* dover/-et.

(loud)speaker רמקול *nm* ramkol/-eem (*pl+of:* -ey).

speaker of the Knesset יושב ראש הכנסת *nm* yoshev-rosh ha-kneset.

spear 1. חנית *nf* khaneet/-ot; **2.** כידון (bayonet) *nm* keedon/-eem (*pl+of:* -ey); **3.** רומח (lance) *nm* romakh/remakheem (*pl+of:* romkhey).

(to) spear 1. לדקור בחנית *inf* leedkor be-khaneet; *pst* dakar *etc*; *pres* doker *etc*; *fut* yeedkor *etc*; **2.** לשפד (pierce) *inf* leshaped; *pst* sheeped; *pres* meshaped; *fut* yeshaped.

spearmint נענע *nm* na'na'.

special מיוחד *adj* meyookh|ad/-edet.

special delivery 1. מסירה מיוחדת *nf* meseeerah meyookhedet; **2.** אקספרס *[colloq.] adv* ekspres.

specialist מומחה *nmf* moomkh|eh/-eet.

specialization התמחות *nf* heetmakhoo|t/-yot.

(to) specialize להתמחות *inf* leheetmakhot; *pst* heetmakhah; *pres* meetmakheh; *fut* yeetmakheh.

specially במיוחד *adv* bee-meyookhad.

specialty 1. ייחוד *nm* yeekhood/-eem (*pl+of:* -ey); **2.** תחום התמחות (specialization field) *nm* tkhoom/-ey heetmakhoot.

species 1. מינים *nm pl* meen|eem (+*of:* -ey); **2.** זן (variety) *nm* zan/-eem (*pl+of:* -ey); **3.** סוג (sort) *nm* soog/-eem (*pl+of:* -ey).

specific 1. מסוים *adj* mesoo|yam/-yemet; **2.** מוגדר (defined) *adj* moogd|ar/-eret; **3.** ספציפי *adj* spetseefee/-t.

specific gravity משקל סגולי *nm* meshkal/-eem segolee/-yeem.

specifically 1. במיוחד *adv* bee-meyookhad; **2.** באופן ספציפי *adv* be-'ofen spetseefee.

(to) specify 1. להגדיר *inf* lehagdeer; *pst* heegdeer; *pres* magdeer; *fut* yagdeer; **2.** לפרט (detail) *inf* lefaret; *pst* perat *(p=f)*; *pres* mefaret; *fut* yefaret.

specimen דוגמה *nf* doogm|ah/-a'ot (+*of:* -at).

speck 1. רבב *nm* revav/-eem (*pl+of:* -ey); **2.** כתם (stain) *nm* ket|em/-ameem (*pl+of:* keetmey).

(not a) speck ללא רבב *adv* le-lo revav.

speckle נקודה *nf* nekood|ah/-ot (+*of:* -at).

(to) speckle לנמר *inf* lenamer; *pst* neemer; *pres* menamer; *fut* yenamer.

speckled מנומר *adj* menoom|ar/-eret.

speckled with freckles זרוע בהרות קיץ *adj* zaroo'a'/zroo'ah beharot kayeets.

spectacle 1. חיזיון *nm* kheezayon/khezyonot (+*of:* khezyon); **2.** הצגה (show) *nf* hatsag|ah/-ot (+*of:* -at).

(to make a) spectacle of oneself לעשות עצמו לצחוק *inf* la'asot 'atsm|o/-ah *(m/f)* lee-ts'khok.

spectacles משקפיים *nm pl* meeshk|afayeem (*pl+of:* -efey).

spectacular ראוותני *adj* re'avtanee/-t.

spectator צופה *nm* tsof|eh/-ah.

specter רוח רפאים *nf* roo|'akh/-khot refa'eem.

spectrograph 1. רושם תחזית *nm* rosh|em/-mey takhzee|t/-yot; **2.** ספקטרוגרף *nm* spektrograf/-eem (*pl+of:* -ey).

spectrum ספקטרום *nm* spektroom/-eem (*pl+of:* -ey).

(to) speculate 1. להרהר (muse) *inf* leharher; *pst* heerher; *pres* meharher; *fut* yeharher; **2.** לספסר (market) *inf* lesafser; *pst* seefser; *pres* mesafser; *fut* yesafser.

speculation 1. השערה (supposition) hash'ar|ah/-ot (+*of:* -at); **2.** ספסרות (market) *nf* safsaroo|t/-yot.

speculative 1. עיוני (theoretical) *adj* 'eeyoonee/-t; **2.** ספקולטיבי (profiteering) *adj* spekoolateevee/-t.

speculator 1. ספסר *nmf* safsar/-eem (*pl+of:* -ey); **2.** ספקולנט *nm* spekoolant/-eet.

speech 1. נאום (address) *nm* ne'oom/-eem (*pl+of:* -ey); **2.** דיבור (talking) *nm* deeboor/-eem (*pl+of:* -ey).

(to make a) speech לנאום *inf* leen'om; *pst* na'am; *pres* no'em; *fut* yeen'am.

speechless מוכה אלם *adj* mook|eh/-at elem.

speed מהירות *nf* meheeroo|t/-yot.

(at full) speed במלוא המהירות *adv* bee-mlo ha-meheeroot.

(to) speed להאיץ *inf* leha'eets; *pst* he'eets; *pres* me'eets; *fut* ya'eets.

speed limit סייג מהירות *nm* syag/-ey meheeroot.

speedily מהר *adv* maher.

speedometer 1. מד־מהירות *nm* mad/-ey meheeroot; **2.** ספידומטר *nm* speedomet|er/-reem.

speedy מהיר *adj* maheer/meheerah.

spell 1. קסם (charm) *nm* kes|em/-ameem (*pl+of:* keesmey); **2.** פרק זמן (period) *nm* perek/peerkey zman; **3.** התקף (sickness attack) *nm* hetkef/-eem (*pl+of:* -ey).

(under a) spell מוקסם *adj* mooks|am/-emet.

(to) spell 1. לאיית *inf* le'ayet; *pst* eeyet; *pres* me'ayet; *fut* ye'ayet; **2.** משמעותו (meaning that) mashma'oot|o/-ah (*m/f*).

(how is it) spelled? איך לאיית זאת? eykh le'ayet zot?

speller 1. מאיית *nm* me'ay|et/-eem (*pl+of:* -ey); **2.** מילון כתיב (dictionary) *nm* meelon/-ey keteev.

(electronic) speller מאיית אלקטרוני *nm* me'ay|et/-teem elektronee/-yeem.

spelling כתיב *nm* keteev/-eem.

("deficient") spelling כתיב חסר *nm* keteev khaser.

("plene") spelling כתיב מלא *nm* keteev male.

spelling book ספר לימוד הכתיב *nm* sefer/seefrey leemood ha-k'teev.

(to) spend להוציא כספים *inf* lehotsee ksafeem; *pst* hotsee *etc*; *pres* motsee *etc*; *fut* yotsee *etc*.

(to) spend time להעביר זמן *inf* leha'aveer zman; *pst* he'eveer zman; *pres* ma|'aveer zman; *fut* ya'aveer zman.

spendthrift 1. בזבזן *nm* bazbezan/-eet; **2.** פזרן (prodigal) pazran/-eet.

sperm זרע *nm* zera'.

sphere 1. כדור *nm* kadoor/-eem (*pl+of:* -ey); **2.** תחום (field) *nm* tekhoom/-eem (*pl+of:* -ey); **3.** ספירה *nf* sfer|ah/-ot (+*of:* -at).

spherical כדורי *adj* kadooree/-t.

sphynx ספינקס *nm* sfeenks/-eem (*pl+of:* -ey).

spice תבלין *nm* tavleen/-eem (*pl+of:* -ey).

(to) spice לתבל *inf* letabel; *pst* teebel; *pres* metabel; *fut* yetabel.

spicy 1. מתובל *adj* metoob|al-elet; **2.** מפולפל (peppered) *adj* mefoolp|al/-elet.

spider עכביש *nm* 'akaveesh/-eem (*pl+of:* -ey).

spider web קורי עכביש *nm* koorey 'akaveesh.

spigot 1. מגופה *nf* megoof|ah/-ot (+*of:* -at); **2.** ברז (tap) *nm* berez/brazeem (*pl+of:* beerzey).

spike 1. חידוד *nm* kheedood/-eem (*pl+of:* -ey); **2.** דורבן *nm* dorvan/-ot.

(to) spike להוציא מכלל שימוש *inf* lehotsee mee-khlal sheemoosh; *pst* hotsee *etc*; *pres* motsee *etc*; *fut* yotsee *etc*.

spill 1. הישפכות *nf* heeshafkhoo|t/-yot; **2.** גלישה (overflow) *nf* gleesh|ah/-ot (+*of:* -at).

(to) spill 1. לשפוך *inf* leeshpokh; *pst* shafakh (*f=p*); *pres* shofekh; *fut* yeeshpokh; **2.** לגלוש (overflow) *inf* leeglosh; *pst* galash; *pres* golesh; *fut* yeeglosh.

spin 1. סחרור *nm* seekhroor/-eem (*pl+of:* -ey); **2.** סיבוב (rotation) *nm* seevoov/-eem (*pl+of:* -ey).

(to) spin 1. לטוות (thread) *inf* leetvot; *pst* tavah; *pres* toveh; *fut* yeetveh; **2.** לסובב (rotate) *vt inf* lesovev; *pst* sovev; *pres* mesovev; *fut* yesovev; **3.** להסתובב (turn round) *v.rfl inf* leheestovev; *pst* heestovev; *pres* meestovev; *fut* yeestovev.

(to) spin out להאריך את הדיבור *inf* leha'areekh et ha-deeboor; *pst* he'ereekh *etc*; *pres* ma'areekh *etc*; *fut* ya'areekh *etc*.

(to) spin yarns לספר סיפורים *inf* lesaper seepooreem; *pst* seeper *etc*; *pres* mesaper *etc*; *fut* yesaper *etc*.

spinach תרד *nm* tered.

spinal של השידרה shel ha-sheedrah.

spinal column עמוד השידרה *nm* 'amood/-ey ha-sheedrah.

spinal cord חוט השידרה *nm* khoot ha-sheedrah.

spindle 1. פלך *nm* pelekh/plakheem (*pl+of:* peelkhey); **2.** כישור *nm* keeshor/-eem (*pl+of:* -ey).

spine 1. שידרה *nf* sheedr|ah/-ot (+*of:* -at); **2.** גב (back) *nm* gav/gab|eem (*b=v*) (*pl+of:* -ey); **3.** עוקץ (thorn) *nm* 'okets/'ookts|eem (*pl+of:* -ey).

spinner מטווייה *nf* matvee|yah/-yot (+*of:* -yat).

spinning טווייה (thread) *nf* tvee|yah/-yot (+*of:* -yat).

spinning machine מכונת טווייה *nf* mekhon|at/-ot tveeyah.

spinning mill מטווייה *nf* matvee|yah/-yot (+*of:* -yat).

spinning wheel גלגל טווייה *nm* galgal/-ey tveeyah.

spinster רווקה *nm* ravak|ah/-ot (+*of:* -at).

spiral 1. סלילי *adj* sleelee/-t; **2.** לולייני (twisted) *adj* loolyanee/-t.

spiral staircase מדרגות לולייניות *nf pl* madregot loolyaneeyot.

spire 1. פיתול *nm* peetool/-eem (*pl+of:* -ey); **2.** תורן מגדל *nm* tor|en/-ney meegdal/-eem.

spirit 1. כוהל (alcohol) *nm* kohal; **2.** רוח (soul) *nm* roo|'akh/-khot.

(to) spirit away לחטוף *inf* lakhtof; *pst* khataf; *pres* khotef; *fut* yakhtof.

spirited מלא מרץ *adj* male/mele'at merets.

(in low) spirits בדכדוך *adv* be-deekhdookh.

(in high) spirits במצב־רוח מרומם *adv* be-matsav roo'akh meromam.

(out of) spirits 1. עצוב 'atsoov/-ah; **2.** נדכא (depressed) *adj* needk|a/-et.

spiritual 1. רוחני *adj* rookhanee/-t; **2.** שיר דתי (music) *nm* sheer/-eem datee/-yeem.

spite 1. רשעות *nf* reesh'oo|t/yot; **2.** טינה *nf* (grudge) teen|ah/-ot (+*of:* -at); **3.** קנטור (annoyance) *nm* keentoor/-eem (*pl+of:* -ey).

(out of) spite לשם קנטור *adv* le-shem keentoor.

(to) spite 1. לקנטר *inf* lekanter; *pst* keenter; *pres* mekanter; *fut* yekanter; **2.** להכעיס (anger) *inf* lehakh'ees; *pst* heekh'ees; *pres* makh'ees; *fut* yakh'ees.

(in) spite of 1. למרות *adv* lamrot; **2.** על אף (notwithstanding) *conj* 'al af.

spiteful קנטרני *adj* kantranee/-t.

splash 1. נתז *nm* net|ez/-azeem (*pl+of:* neetzey); **2.** כתם (stain) *nm* ket|em/-ameem (*pl+of:* keetmey).

(to) splash להתיז *inf* lehateez; *pst* heeteez; *pres* mateez; *fut* yateez.

spleen 1. טחול *nm* tekhol/-eem (*pl+of:* -ey); **2.** מרירות (bitterness) *nf* mereeroo|t/-yot.

splendid מצוין *adj* metsoo|yan/-yenet.

splendor 1. פאר *nm* pe'er; **2.** הוד *nm* hod.

splice 1. איחוי *nm* eekhoo|y/-yeem (*pl+of:* -yey); **2.** חיבור (joint) *nm* kheeboor/-eem (*pl+of:* -ey).

(to) splice 1. לאחות *inf* le'akhot; *pst* eekhah; *pres* me'akheh; *fut* ye'akheh; **2.** לחבר (join) *inf* lekhaber; *pst* kheeber; *pres* mekhaber; *fut* yekhaber

splicer מחבר *nm* makhber/-eem (*pl+of:* -ey).

splint 1. קישושת *nf* keeshosh|et/-ot; **2.** קנה חיזוק *nm* (strengthening strip) *nm* ken|eh/-ey kheezook.

(to) splint לשים בקישושת *inf* laseem be-keeshoshet; *pst & pres* sam *etc; fut* yaseem *etc.*

splinter 1. רסיס *nm* rasees/resees|eem (*pl+of:* -ey); **2.** שבב *nm* shvav/-eem (*pl+of:* -ey).

(to) splinter לנפץ לרסיסים *inf* lenapets lee-reseeseem; *pst* neepets *etc; pres* menapets *etc; fut* yenapets *etc.*

split 1. התפצלות *nf* heetpatsloo|t/-yot; **2.** מפוצל *adj* mefoots|al/-elet.

(to) split לפצל *inf* lefatsel; *pst* peetsel *(p=f); pres* mefatsel; *fut* yefatsel.

(to) split hairs להתפלפל *inf* leheetpalpel; *pst* heetpalpel; *pres* meetpalpel; *fut* yeetpalpel.

(to) split one's side with laughter להתפוצץ מצחוק *inf* leheetpotsets mee-tskhok; *pst* heetpotsets *etc; pres* meetpotsets *etc;* yeetpotsets *etc.*

split personality אישיות מפוצלת *nf* eesheeyoot mefootselet.

(to) split the difference להתחלק בהפרש *inf* leheetkhalek ba-hefresh; *pst* heetkhalek *etc; pres* meetkhalek *etc; fut* yeetkhalek *etc.*

splurge פעלתנות ראווה *nf* pe'altanoo|t/-yot ra'avah.

spoil שלל shalal (+*of:* shelal).

(to) spoil 1. לקלקל (decay) *inf* lekalkel; *pst* keelkel; *pres* mekalkel; *fut* yekalkel; **2.** להזיק (harm) *inf* lehazeek; *pst* heezeek; *pres* mazeek; *fut* yazeek; **3.** לפנק (pamper) *inf* lefanek; *pst* peenek *(p=f); pres* mefanek; *fut* yefanek.

spoils of war שלל מלחמה *nm* shelal meelkhamah.

spoken 1. נאמר *adj* ne'em|ar/-eret; **2.** אמור (said) *adj* amoor/-ah.

spokesman דובר *nmf* dover/et.

sponge 1. ספוג (absorbent) sfog/-eem (*pl+of:* -ey); **2.** טפיל (dependent person) *nm* tapeel/-eem (*pl+of:* -ey).

(to) sponge 1. להספיג *inf* lehaspeeg; *pst* heespeeg; *pres* maspeeg; *fut* yaspeeg; **2.** לנקות בספוג *inf* lenakot bee-sfog; *pst* neekah *etc; pres* menakeh *etc; fut* yenakeh *etc.*

(to) sponge up להספיג בספוג *inf* lehaspeeg bee-sfog; *pst* heespeeg *etc; pres* maspeeg *etc; fut* yaspeeg *etc.*

spongecake לובנן *nm* loovnan/-eem (*pl+of:* -ey).

sponger 1. סחטן *nmf* sakhtan/-eet; **2.** טפיל (parasite) tapeel/-eem (*pl+of:* -ey).

spongy ספוגי *adj* sfogee/-t.

sponsor 1. פטרון *nm* patron/-eet; **2.** תומך *nmf* tomekh/-et.

(to) sponsor לתמוך *inf* leetmokh; *pst* tamakh; *pres* tomekh; *fut* yeetmokh.

sponsored נתמך *adj* neetm|akh/-ekhet.

sponsorship 1. חסות *nf* khasoo|t/-yot; **2.** פטרונות *nf* patronoo|t/-yot.

spontaneity 1. מידיות *nf* meeyadeeyoot; **2.** ספונטניות *nf* spontaneeyoot.

spontaneous 1. מידי *adj* meeyadee/-t; **2.** ספונטני *adj* spontanee/-t.

spook רוח רפאים *nf* roo|'akh/-khot refa'eem.

spool סליל sleel/-eem (*pl+of:* -ey).

(to) spool לכרוך על סליל *inf* leekhrokh 'al sleel; *pst* karakh *(k=kh) etc; pres* korekh *etc; fut* yeekhrokh *etc.*

spoon 1. כף *nf* kaf/kapot *(p=f)*; **2.** כפית (teaspoon) *nf* kapee|t/-yot.

(to) spoon 1. לגרוף *inf* leegrof; *pst* garaf; *pres* goref; *fut* yeegrof; **2.** לשכב צמוד (lie next) *inf* leeshkav tsamood; *pst* shakhav *etc; pres* shokhev *etc; fut* yeeshkav *etc;* **3.** להתעלס (make love) *inf* leheet'ales; *pst* heet'ales; *pres* meet'ales; *fut* yeet'ales.

spoonful מלוא הכף *nm* melo ha-kaf.

sporadic 1. מתרחש מזמן לזמן *adj* meetrakhesh/-et mee-zman lee-zman; **2.** ספורדי *adj* sporadee/-t.

sport 1. ספורט *nm* sport/-eem; **2.** שעשוע (fun) *nm* sha'ashoo|'a'/-eem (*pl+of:* -'ey); **3.** ליצנות (jesting) *nf* leytsanoo|t/-yot.

(a good) sport בחור כהלכה *nm* bakhoor/-ah ka-halakhah.

(in) sport לשם בידור *adv* le-shem beedoor.

(to) sport 1. לבדר *inf* levader; *pst* beeder *(b=v); pres* mevader; *fut* yevader; **2.** להתגנדר *inf* leheetgander; *pst* heetgander; *pres* meetgander; *fut* yeetgander.

(to) sport a new dress להתהדר בשמלה חדשה *inf* leheet'hader ba-seemlah khadashah; heet'hader *etc; pres* meet'hader *etc; fut* yeet'hader *etc.*

(to make) sport of להתלוצץ *inf* leheetlotsets; *pst* heetlotsets; *pres* meetlotsets; *fut* yeetlotsets.

sporting chance סיכוי שקול *nm* seekoo|y/-yeem shakool/sh'kooleem.

sporting goods צורכי ספורט *nm pl* tsorkhey sport.

sports של ספורט *adj* shel sport.
sports car מכונית ספורט *nf* mekhoneeֽ|t/-yot sport.
sports clothes בגדי ספורט *nm pl* beegdey sport.
sports fan חובב ספורט *nm* khovev/-ey sport.
sportsman ספורטאי *nmf* sport|ay/-'eet (*pl:* -a'eem; *+of:* -'ey).
spot 1. כתם (blemish) *nm* ket|em/-ameem (*pl+of:* keetmey); **2.** מקום (place) *nm* makom/mekomot (*+of:* mekom).
(on the) spot בו במקום *adv* bo ba-makom.
(to) spot 1. לגלות *inf* legalot; *pst* geelah; *pres* megaleh; *fut* yegaleh; **2.** לזהות (identify) *inf* lezahot; *pst* zeehah; *pres* mezaheh; *fut* yezaheh; **3.** להכתים (soil) lehakhteem; *pst* heekhteem; *pst* makhteem; *fut* yakhteem.
spot cash מזומנים *nm pl* mezoomaneem.
spot news חדשות אחרונות *nf pl* khadashot akharonot.
spot remover מוציא כתמים *nm* motsee/-'ey ketameem.
spotless ללא רבב *adj* le-lo revav.
spotlight 1. זרקור ממקד *nm* zarkor/-eem mema-k|ed/-deem; **2.** זרקור (searchlight) *nm* zarkor/-eem (*pl+of:* -ey).
spotter משגיח חשאי *nmf* mashgee|'akh/-khah khasha'ee/-t.
spouse בן־זוג *nmf* ben/bat zoog.
spout 1. זרבובית *nf* zarboovee|t/-yot; **2.** צינור (pipe) *nm* tseenor/-ot.
(to) spout להתיז *inf* lehateez; *pst* heeteez; *pres* mateez; *fut* yateez.
sprain נקע *nm* nek|a'/-a'eem (*pl+of:* neek'ey).
(to) sprain לנקוע *inf* leenko'a'; *pst* naka'; *pres* noke'a'; *fut* yeeka'.
(to) sprain one's ankle לנקוע קרסול *inf* leenko'a' (*etc*) karsol.
sprawl הסתרחות *nf* heestarkhoo|t/-yot.
(to) sprawl להסתרח *inf* leheestare'akh; *pst* heestare'akh; *pres* meestare'akh; *fut* yeestare'akh.
spray 1. תרסיס (liquid) *nm* tarsees/-eem (*pl+of:* -ey); **2.** ענף (branch) *nm* 'anaf/-eem (*pl+of:* 'anfey).
(to) spray לרסס *inf* lerases; *pst* reeses; *pres* merases; *fut* yerases.
sprayer מרסס *nm* marses/-eem (*pl+of:* -ey).
spread 1. שיעור *nm* shee'oor/-eem (*pl+of:* -ey); **2.** היקף (extent) *nm* hekef/-eem (*pl+of:* -ey).
(to) spread 1. להפיץ *inf* lehafeets; *pst* hefeets; *pres* mefeets; *fut* yafeets; **2.** לפזר (scatter) *inf* lefazer; *pst* peezer (*p=f*); *pres* mefazer; *fut* yefazer.
(to) spread apart להתפזר כל אחד לחוד *v rfl inf* leheetpazer kol ekhad le-khood; *pst* heetpazer *etc*; *pres* meetpazer *etc*; *fut* yeetpazer *etc*.
(to) spread butter למרוח חמאה *inf* leemro'akh khem'ah; *pst* marakh *etc*; *pres* more'akh *etc*; *fut* yeemrakh *etc*.
(to) spread out the table-cloth לפרוש מפה *inf* leefros mapah; *pst* paras (*p=f*) *etc*; *pres* pores *etc*; *fut* yeefros *etc*.
(to) spread paint on לשים שכבת צבע על *inf* laseem sheekhvat tseva' 'al; *pst & pres* sam *etc*; *fut* yaseem *etc*.
(to) spread with לכסות עם *inf* lekhasot 'eem; *pst* keesah (*k=kh*) 'eem; *pres* mekhaseh 'eem; *fut* yekhaseh 'eem.
spree בולמוס *nm* boolmoos/-eem (*pl+of:* -ey).
(shopping) spree בולמוס קניות *nm* boolmoos/-ey keneeyot.
sprig 1. נצר *nm* nets|er/-areem (*pl+of:* -arey); **2.** חוטר (scion) *nm* khot|er/-areem (*pl+of:* -rey); **3.** נערון (stripling) *nm* na'aron/-eem (*pl+of:* -ey).
sprightly מלא חיים *adj* male/mele'at khayeem.
spring 1. אביב (season) aveev/-eem (*pl+of:* -ey); **2.** מעיין (source) *nm* ma'ayan/-ot; **3.** קפיץ (coil) *nm* kefeets/-eem (*pl+of:* -ey).
(to) spring 1. לקפוץ *inf* leekpots; *pst* kafats (*f=p*); *pres* kofets; *fut* yeekpots; **2.** לצוץ (pop up) *inf* latsoots; *pst & pres* tsats; *fut* yatsoots; **3.** לנבוע (originate) *inf* leenbo'a'; *pst* nava' (*v=b*); *pres* nove'a'; *fut* yeenba'.
(to) spring at לקפוץ על *inf* leekpots 'al; *pst* kafats (*f=p*) 'al; *pres* kofets 'al; *fut* yeekpots 'al.
spring board 1. קרש קפיצה *nm* keresh/karshey kefeetsah; **2.** מקפצה (take-off board) *nf* makpe-ts|ah/-ot (*+of:* -at).
spring fever בולמוס אהבה *nm* boolmoos/-ey ahavah.
(to) spring from לצוץ מתוך *inf* latsoots mee-tokh; *pst & pres* tsats *etc*; *fut* yatsoots *etc*.
spring mattress מזרן קפיצי *nm* meezran/-eem kefeetsee/-yeem.
(to) spring something open לפתוח בכוח *inf* leefto'akh be-kho'akh; *pst* patakh (*p=f*) *etc*; *pres* pote'akh *etc*; *fut* yeeftakh *etc*.
(to) spring to one's feet לקפוץ על רגליו *inf* leekpots 'al raglav; *pst* kafats (*f=p*) *etc*; *pres* kofets *etc*; *fut* yeekpots *etc*.
(to) spring up להתפרץ *inf* leheetparets; *pst* heetparets; *pres* meetparets; *fut* yeetparets.
spring water מי מעיין *nm pl* mey ma'ayan.
springtime עונת האביב *nf* 'on|at/-ot he-aveev.
sprinkle 1. זילוף *nm* zeeloof/-eem (*pl+of:* -ey); **2.** גשם קל *nm* gesh|em/-ameem kal/-eem.
(to) sprinkle להתיז *inf* lehateez; *pst* heeteez; *pres* mateez; *fut* yateez.
sprinkle of salt קמצוץ מלח *nm* keemtsoots/-ey melakh.
sprint מרוץ קצר־מסלול *nm* merots/-eem ketsar/keetsrey maslool.
(to) sprint לרוץ למרחק קצר *inf* laroots le-merkhak katsar; *pst & pres* rats *etc*; *fut* yaroots *etc*.
sprout נבט *nm* nev|et/-ateem (*pl+of:* neevtey).
(to) sprout לנבוט *inf* leenbot; *pst* navat (*v=b*); *pres* novet; *fut* yeenbot.
spruce 1. מהדר בלבושו (neat) *adj* mehader/-et bee-levoosh|o/-ah; **2.** אשוחית (tree) *nf* ashoo-khee|t/-yot.
(to) spruce up להדר בהופעתו *inf* lehader be-hofa'ato; *pst* heeder *etc*; *pres* mehader *etc*; *fut* yehader *etc*.
spur 1. דורבן *nm* dorv|an/-anot (*pl+of:* -enot); **2.** תמריץ (incentive) *nm* tamreets/-eem (*pl+of:* -ey).

(to) spur לדרבן *inf* ledarben; *pst* deerben; *pres* medarben; *fut* yedarben.

(on the) spur of the moment על רגל אחת *adv* 'al regel akhat.

(to) spur on לדרבן להתקדם *inf* ledarben leheetkadem; *pst* deerben *etc*; *pres* medarben *etc*; *fut* yedarben *etc*.

spur track מסעף קצר *nm* mees'af/-eem katsar/ketsareem.

spurious מזויף *adj* mezoo|yaf/-yefet.

spurn דחייה בבוז *nf* dekhey|ah/-yot be-vooz *(v=b)*.

(to) spurn לדחות בבוז *inf* leedkhot be-vooz *(v=b)*; *pst* dakhah *etc*; *pres* dokheh *etc*; *fut* yeedkheh *etc*.

spurt פרץ *nm* perets/pratseem *(pl+of:* peertsey).

(to) spurt לפרוץ לפתע *inf* leefrots le-feta' *(f=p)*; *pst* parats *(p=f) etc*; *pres* porets *etc*; *fut* yeefrots *etc*.

spurt of anger התפרצות זעם *nf* heetpartsoo|t/-yot za'am.

spurts of flame התפרצויות להבה *nf pl* heetpartsooyot lehavah.

sputter פרץ דיבורים *nm* perets/peertsey deebooreem.

(to) sputter להתיז מהפה *inf* lehateez rok me-ha-peh; *pst* heeteez *etc*; *pres* mateez *etc*; *fut* yateez *etc*.

sputum 1. כיח *nm* kee'akh; **2.** רוק (spit) *nm* rok.

spy מרגל *nmf* meragel/-et.

(to) spy לרגל *inf* leragel; *pst* reegel; *pres* meragel; *fut* yeragel.

(to) spy on לרגל אחרי *inf* leragel akharey; *pst* reegel *etc*; *pres* meragel *etc*; *fut* yeragel *etc*.

spyglass משקפת *nf* meeshk|efet/-afot.

squab 1. גוזל *nm* goz|al/-aleem *(pl+of:* -ley); **2.** שמנמן (plump) *adj* shmanman/-ah; **3.** חסר ניסיון (inexperienced) *adj* khas|ar/-rat neesayon.

squabble ריב על לא דבר *nm* reev/-eem 'al lo davar.

squad, squadron 1. פלוגה *nf* ploog|ah/-ot *(+of:* -at); **2.** חוליה *nf* khool|yah/-yot *(+of:* -yat).

squad car ניידת משטרה *nf* nayedet/naydot meeshtarah.

squalid 1. עלוב *adj* 'aloov/-ah; **2.** מטונף (filthy) *adj* metoon|af/-efet.

squall סופת פתע *nf* soof|at/-ot peta'.

(to) squall לצווח *inf* leetsvo'akh; *pst* tsavakh; *pres* tsove'akh; *fut* yeetsvakh.

(to) squander לבזבז *inf* levazbez; *pst* beezbez *(b=v)*; *pres* mevazbez; *fut* yevazbez.

square 1. ריבוע (rectangle) *nm* reeboo|'a'/-'eem *(pl+of:* -'ey); **2.** פרק מרכזי (central park) *nm* park/-eem merkazee/-yeem; **3.** גוש (block) *nm* goosh/-eem *(pl+of:* -ey).

square מרובע *adj* meroob|a'/-a'at.

(a) "square" מרובע *[slang] nmf* meroob|a'/-a'at.

(on the) square 1. הוגן (fair) *adj* hogen/-et; **2.** כן (sincere) *adj* ken/-ah.

(to) square 1. לרבע *inf* lerabe'a'; *pst* reebe'a'; *pres* merabe'a'; *fut* yerabe'a'; **2.** ליישר (straighten) *inf* leyasher; *pst inf* yeesher; *pres* meyasher; *fut* yeyasher; **3.** לאזן (balance) *inf* le'azen; *pst* eezen; *pres* me'azen; *fut* ye'azen.

(to) square a person with another להתאים אדם לאדם *inf* lehat'eem adam le-adam; *pst* heet'eem *etc*; *pres* mat'eem *etc*; *fut* yat'eem *etc*.

square corner זווית ישרה *nm* zavee|t/-yot yeshar|ah/-ot.

square dance ריקוד לארבעה זוגות *nf* reekood le-arba'ah zoogot.

square deal עסקה הוגנת *nf* 'eeskah hogenet.

square meal ארוחה משביעה *nf* arookh|ah/-ot masbee|'ah/-'ot.

square mile מיל רבוע *nm* meel/-eem ravoo'a'/revoo'eem

(to) square one's shoulders ליישר כתפיים *inf* leyasher ketefayeem; *pst inf* yeesher *etc*; *pres* meyasher *etc*; *fut* yeyasher *etc*.

(to) square oneself with להצדיק עצמו בפני *inf* lehatsdeek 'atsmo beefney; *pst* heetsdeek *etc*; *pres* matsdeek *etc*; *fut* yatsdeek *etc*.

square root שורש מרובע *nm* shor|esh/-osheem meroob|a'/-a'eem.

squarely ביושר *adv* be-yosher.

squash 1. דלעת (pumpkin) *nf* dla|'at/-'ot; **2.** המון דחוס (dense crowd) *nm* hamon dakhoos; **3.** משחק דומה לטניס (tennis-like game) *nm* meeskhak domeh le-tenees.

(to) squash 1. למעוך *inf* leem'okh; *pst* ma'akh; *pres* mo'ekh; *fut* yeem'akh; **2.** להידחק (push ahead) *inf* leheedakhek; *pst & pres* needkhak; *fut* yeedakhek.

squat גוץ ורחב *adj* goots/-ah ve/oo rakhav/rekhavah.

(to) squat 1. לשבת *vi inf* lashevet; *pst* yashav; *pres* yoshev; *fut* yeshev; **2.** להושיב בכפיפה אחת *vt inf* lehosheev bee-khefeefah akhat; *pst* hosheev *etc*; *pres* mosheev *etc*; *fut* yosheev *etc*.

squatter פולש לקרקע לא לו *nmf* polesh/-et le-karka' lo lo/lah.

squawk צווחה *nf* tsevakh|ah/-ot *(+of:* tseevkhat).

(to) squawk 1. לצווח (yell) leetsvo'akh; *pst* tsavakh; *pres* tsove'akh; *fut* yeetsvakh; **2.** להתלונן (complain) *inf* leheetlonen; *pst* heetlkonen; *pres* meetlonen; *fut* yeetlonen.

squeak 1. ציוץ *nm* tseeyoots/-eem *(pl+of:* -ey); **2.** חריקה (grating) *nf* khareek|ah/-ot *(+of:* -at).

(to) squeak לצייץ *inf* letsayets; *pst* tseeyets; *pres* metsayets; *fut* yetsayets.

squeal 1. צווחה *nf* tsevakh|ah/-ot *(+of:* tseevkhat); **2.** יבבה (wailing) *nf* yevav|ah/-ot *(+of:* yeevev|at/-ot).

(to) squeal 1. לצווח *inf* leetsvo'akh; *pst* tsavakh; *pres* tsove'akh; *fut* yeetsvakh; **2.** לייבב (wail) *inf* leyabev; *pst* yeebev; *pres* meyabev; *fut* yeyabev; **3.** להלשין (denounce) *inf* lehalsheen; *pst* heelsheen; *pres* malsheen; *fut* yalsheen.

squeamish 1. יפה נפש *nmf* yef|eh/-at nefesh; **2.** איסטניס (fastidious) *nmf* eestenees/-eet.

squeeze 1. לחיצה *nf* lekheets|ah/-ot *(+of:* -at); **2.** סחיטה (wringing) *nf* sekheet|ah/-ot *(+of:* -at).

(to) squeeze 1. ללחוץ (press) *inf* leelkhots; *pst* lakhats; *pres* lokhets; *fut* yeelkhats; **2.** לסחוט (wring, extort) *inf* leeskhot; *pst* sakhat; *pres* sokhet; *fut* yeeskhat.

(to) squeeze into לדחוס לתוך *inf* leedkhos le-tokh; *pst* dakhas *etc*; *pres* dokhes *etc*; *fut* yeedkhos *etc*.

(to) squeeze out the juice להוציא את המיץ *inf* lehotsee et ha-meets; *pst* hotsee *etc; pres* motsee *etc; fut* yotsee *etc.*

(to) squeeze through a crowd להידחק דרך המון *inf* leheedakhek derekh hamon; *pst & pres* needkhak *etc; fut* yeedakhek *etc.*

(to) squelch 1. לרמוס *inf* leermos; *pst* ramas; *pres* romes; *fut* yeermos; **2.** לדרוס (trample) *inf* leedros; *pst* daras; *pres* dores; *fut* yeedros.

(to) squelch a revolt לדכא מרד *inf* ledake mered; *pst* deeka *etc; pres* medake *etc; fut* yedake *etc.*

squid דיונון *nm* dyonoon/-eem (*pl+of:* -ey).

squint פזילה *nf* pezeel|ah/-ot (*+of:* -at).

(to) squint 1. לפזול *inf* leefzol; *pst* pazal (*p=f*); *pres* pozel; *fut* yeefzol; **2.** ללכסן מבט (glance sideways) *inf* lelakhsen mabat; *pst* leekhsen *etc; pres* melakhsen *etc; fut* yelakhsen *etc.*

squint-eyed 1. פוזל *adj* pozel/-et; **2.** צר־עין (envious) *adj* tsar/-at- 'ayeen.

squire בעל אחוזה *nm* ba'al/-ey akhooz|ah/-ot.

(to) squire ללוות אישה *inf* lelavot eeshah; *pst* leevah *etc; pres* melaveh *etc; fut* yelaveh *etc.*

(to) squirm להתפתל *inf* leheetpatel; *pst* heetpatel; *pres* meetpatel; *fut* yeetpatel.

(to) squirm out of a difficulty להיחלץ מקושי *inf* lehekhalets mee-koshee; *pst & pres* nekhlats *etc; fut* yekhalets *etc.*

squirrel סנאי *nm* sna|'ee/-'eem (*pl+of:* -'ey).

squirt זילוף *nm* zeeloof/-eem (*pl+of:* -ey).

(to) squirt לזלף *inf* lezalef; *pst* zeelef; *pres* mezalef; *fut* yezalef.

stab דקירה *nf* dekeer|ah/-ot (*+of:* -at).

(to) stab לדקור *inf* leedkor; *pst* dakar; *pres* doker; *fut* yeedkor.

stability יציבות *inf* yatseevoo|t/-yot.

stable 1. אורווה *nf* oor|vah/-avot (*+of:* -vat/-vot); **2.** יציב *adj adj* yatseev/yetseevah.

stack ערימה *nf* 'arem|ah/-ot (*+of:* -at).

(to) stack לערום *inf* la'arom; *pst* 'aram; *pres* 'orem; *fut* ya'arom.

(library) stacks ערימות ספרים *nf* 'aremot sfareem.

stadium איצטדיון *nm* eetstadyon/-eem (*pl+of:* -ey).

staff 1. מטה (command) *nm* mat|eh/-ot; **2.** מוט (pole) *nm* mot/-ot; **3.** צוות (personnel) *nm* tsevet/tsvateem (*pl+of:* tseevtey).

(army) staff מטה צבאי *nm* mat|eh/-ot tseva'ee/-yeem.

(editorial) staff חברי מערכת *nm pl* khavrey ma'arekhet.

(musical) staff הרכב נגנים *nm* herkev/-ey naganeem.

(teaching) staff חבר מורים *nm* khever moreem.

(to) staff לאייש *inf* le'ayesh; *pst* eeyesh; *pres* me'ayesh; *fut* ye'ayesh.

staff of life לחם *nm* lekh|em/-ameem (*pl+of:* lakhamey).

staff officer קצין מטה *nm* ketseen/-ey mateh.

stag צבי *nm* tsev|ee/-yeem (*pl+of:* -yey).

stag dinner סעודת רווקים *nf* se'ood|at/-ot ravakeem.

stage 1. במה (platform) *nf* bam|ah/-ot (*+of:* -at); **2.** בימה (theater) *nf* beem|ah/-ot (*+of:* -at) **3.** שלב (period) *nm* shalav/shlab|eem (*b=v; pl+of:* -ey).

(to) stage לביים *inf* levayem; *pst* beeyem (*b=v*); *pres* mevayem; *fut* yevayem.

(to) stage a hold-up לבצע שוד *inf* levatse'a' shod; *pst* beetsa' (*b=v*) *etc; pres* mevatse'a' *etc; fut* yevatsa' *etc.*

(to) stage a surprise לגרום אפתעה *inf* leegrom afta'ah; *pst* garam *etc; pres* gorem *etc; fut* yeegrom *etc.*

stage hand פועל במה *nm* po'el/po'aley beemah.

stagecoach מרכבת נוסעים בקו קבוע *nf* meerkev|et/-ot nos'eem be-kav kavoo'a'.

(by easy) stages בהדרגה *adv* be-hadragah.

stagger התנודדות heetonodedoo|t/-yot.

(to) stagger 1. להתנודד *inf* leheetnoded; *pst* heetnoded; *pres* meetnoded; *fut* yeetnoded. **2.** להתמיה (astonish) *inf* lehatmee'ah; *pst* heetmee'ah; *pres* matmee'ah; *fut* yatmee'ah.

(to) stagger working hours לסדר שעות עבודה לסירוגין *inf* lesader she'ot 'avodah le-seroogeen; *pst* seeder *etc; pres* mesader *etc; fut* yesader *etc.*

stagnant קופא על שמריו *adj* kofe/-t 'al shmar|av/-eha.

staid מיושב *adj* meyoosh|av/-evet.

stain כתם *nm* ket|em/-ameem (*pl+of:* keetmey).

(to) stain להכתים *inf* lehakhteem; *pst* hekhteem; *pres* makhteem; *fut* yakhteem.

stained-glass window ויטרינה *nf* veetreen|ah/-ot (*+of:* -at).

stainless 1. ללא רבב *adj* le-lo revav; **2.** ללא דופי (flawless) *adj* le-lo dofee; **3.** אלחלד (rustproof) *adj* alkheled.

stainless steel פלדת אל־חלד *nf* peeldat al-kheled.

stair מדרגה *nf* madreg|ah/-ot (*+of:* -at).

stairs מדרגות *nf pl* madregot.

stairway מערכת מדרגות *nf* ma'arekhet madregot.

stake 1. יתד *nf* yated/yetedot (*+of:* yated); **2.** חבל ונחלה (share) *nm & nf* khevel ve-nakhlah; **3.** עמוד מוקד (burning post) *nm* 'amood/-ey moked.

(has much at) stake יש לו הרבה מה להפסיד *[colloq.]* yesh lo/lah harbeh mah lehafseed.

(his future is at) stake עתידו תלוי בכך 'ateed|o/-ah talooy be-khakh (*kh=k*).

(to) stake 1. לסמן *inf* lesamen; *pst* seemen; *pres* mesamen; *fut* yesamen; **2.** לבסס (secure) *inf* levases; *pst* beeses (*b=v*); *fut* mevases; *fut* yevases; **3.** להטיל על כף המאזניים (wager) *inf* lehateel 'al kaf ha-moznayeem; *pst* heeteel *etc; pres* mateel *etc; fut* yateel *etc.*

(to die at the) stake לעלות על המוקד *inf* la'alot 'al ha-moked; *pst* 'alah *etc; pres* 'oleh *etc; fut* ya'aleh *etc.*

(a) stake in the future of חלק בעתידו של *nm* khelek ba-'ateed|o/-ah shel.

(to) stake off לסמן ביתדות *inf* lesamen bee-yetedot; *pst* seemen *etc; pres* mesamen *etc; fut* yesamen *etc.*

stale 1. מיושן *adj* meyoosh|an/-enet; **2.** חסר־טעם (tasteless) *adj* khas|ar/-rat ta'am; **3.** נדוש (trite) *adj* nadosh/nedoshah.

stalemate קיפאון *nm* keepa'on (*+of:* keef'on; *f=p*).

stalk 1. גבעול *nm* geev'o̲l/-e̲em (*pl+of:* -e̲y); **2.** קנה (stem) *nm* kan|e̲h/-e̲em (*pl+of:* kene̲y).

stall 1. תא באורווה (stable compartment) *nm* ta/-'e̲em be-'oorva̲h; **2.** דוכן מכירה (counter) *nm* dookh|a̲n/-ne̲y mekheera̲h.

(to) stall להשתתק (auto motor) *inf* leheeshtate̲k; *pst* heeshtate̲k; *pres* meeshtate̲k; *fut* yeeshtate̲k.

stalling השתתקות מנוע *nf* heeshtatkoo̲|t/-yo̲t mano̲'a'.

stallion סוס רביעה *nm* soos/-e̲y revee'a̲h.

stalwart 1. איתן *adj* eyta̲n/-a̲h; **2.** נאמן (faithful) *adj* ne'ema̲n/-a̲h.

stamina כוח עמידה *nm* ko̲'akh 'ameeda̲h.

stammer גמגום *nm* geemgo̲om/-e̲em (*pl+of:* -e̲y).

(to) stammer לגמגם *inf* legamge̲m; *pst* geemge̲m; *pres* megamge̲m; *fut* yegamge̲m.

stammerer מגמגם *nmf & adj* megamge̲m/-et.

stammering גימגום *nm* geemgo̲om/-e̲em (*pl+of:* -e̲y).

stamp 1. בול *nm* bool/-e̲em (*pl+of:* -e̲y); **2.** תווית (label) *nf* tave̲e|t-yot; **3.** חותמת (seal) *nf* khot|e̲met/-amo̲t (*pl+of:* -mo̲t).

(postage) stamp בול דואר *nm* bool/-e̲y do̲'ar.

(revenue) stamp בול הכנסה *nm* bool/-e̲y hakhnasa̲h.

(to) stamp 1. להדביק בולים (affix) *inf* lehadbe̲ek boole̲em; *pst* heedbe̲ek *etc*; *pres* madbe̲ek *etc*; *fut* yadbe̲ek *etc*; **2.** לסמן (mark) *inf* lesame̲n; *pst* seeme̲n; *pres* mesame̲n; *fut* yesame̲n.

(to) stamp one's foot 1. להטביע עקבות (imprint) *inf* lehatbe̲e'a' 'akevo̲t; *pst* heetbe̲e'a' *etc*; *pres* matbe̲e'a' *etc*; *fut* yatbe̲e'a' *etc*; **2.** לרקוע (strike forcibly) *inf* leerko̲'a'; *pst* raka̲'; *pres* roke̲'a'; *fut* yeerka̲'; **3.** לדרוך (tread) *inf* leedro̲kh; *pst* dara̲kh; *pres* dore̲kh; *fut* yeedro̲kh.

(to) stamp out לעקור מן השורש *inf* la'ako̲r meen ha-sho̲resh; *pst* 'aka̲r *etc*; *pres* 'oke̲r *etc*; *fut* ya'ako̲r *etc*.

stampede מנוסת בהלה *nf* menoos|a̲t/-o̲t behala̲h.

(to) stampede להניס מנוסת בהלה *inf* lehane̲es menoosa̲t behala̲h; *pst* hene̲es *etc*; *pres* mene̲es *etc*; *fut* yane̲es *etc*.

stanch 1. עצירה *nf* 'atseer|a̲h/-o̲t; **2.** נאמן (faithful) *adj* ne'ema̲n/-a̲h; **3.** מסור (devoted) *adj* maso̲or/mesoora̲h.

(to) stanch 1. לעצור *inf* la'atso̲r; *pst* 'atsa̲r; *pres* 'otse̲r; *fut* ya'atso̲r; **2.** להיעצר (be stopped) *inf* lehe'atse̲r; *pst & adj* ne'etsa̲r; *fut* ye'atse̲r.

stand 1. דוכן (shop) *nm* dookh|a̲n/-ane̲em (*pl+of:* -ne̲y); **2.** עמדה (position) *nf* 'emda̲h/'amado̲t (*+of:* 'emd|a̲t/-o̲t); **3.** עמידה (standing) *nf* 'ameed|a̲h/-o̲t (*+of:* -a̲t).

(grand)stand יציע ראשי באצטדיון *nm* yatse̲e'a' rashe̲e ba-'eetstadyo̲n.

(music) stand דוכן לתווים *nm* dookha̲n/-e̲em le-tave̲em.

(to) stand 1. לקום (rise) *inf* lako̲om; *pst & adj* kam; *fut* yako̲om; **2.** לעמוד (be up) *inf* la'amo̲d; *pst* 'ama̲d; *pres* 'ome̲d; *fut* ya'amo̲d; **3.** לעמוד בפני (withstand) *inf* la'amo̲d beefne̲y; *pst* 'ama̲d; *pres* 'ome̲d *etc*; *fut* ya'amo̲d *etc*.

(umbrella) stand מיתקן למטריות *nm* meetka̲n/-e̲em le-meetreeyo̲t.

(to) stand a chance להיות בר־סיכוי *inf* leehyo̲t bar-seekoo̲y; *pst* haya̲h *etc*; *pres* heeno̲ *etc*; *fut* yeehye̲h *etc*.

(to) stand an expense לעמוד בהוצאה *inf* la'amo̲d be-hotsa'a̲h; *pst* 'ama̲d; *pres* 'ome̲d *etc*; *fut* ya'amo̲d *etc*.

(to) stand aside לעמוד בצד *inf* la'amo̲d ba-tsa̲d; *pst* 'ama̲d; *pres* 'ome̲d *etc*; *fut* ya'amo̲d *etc*.

(to) stand back of להתייצב מאחורי *inf* leheetyatse̲v me-akhore̲y; *pst* heetyatse̲v *etc*; *pres* meetyatse̲v *etc*; *fut* yeetyatse̲v *etc*.

(to) stand by לעמוד הכן *inf* la'amo̲d hakhe̲n; *pst* 'ama̲d; *pres* 'ome̲d *etc*; *fut* ya'amo̲d *etc*.

(to) stand for להעמיד עצמו *inf* leha'ame̲ed 'atsm|o̲/-a̲h (*m/f*); *pst* he'eme̲ed *etc*; *pres* ma'ame̲ed *etc*; *fut* ya'ame̲ed *etc*.

stand-in מחליף *nmf* makhle̲ef/-a̲h.

(to) stand in the way לעמוד למכשול *inf* la'amo̲d le-meekhsho̲l; *pst* 'ama̲d; *pres* 'ome̲d *etc*; *fut* ya'amo̲d *etc*.

(to) stand on end להסתתר *inf* leheestate̲r; *pst* heestate̲r; *pres* meestate̲r; *fut* yeestate̲r.

(to) stand one's ground לעמוד על שלו *inf* la'amo̲d 'al shelo̲; *pst* 'ama̲d; *pres* 'ome̲d *etc*; *fut* ya'amo̲d *etc*.

(to) stand out לבלוט *inf* leevlo̲t; *pst* bala̲t (*b=v*); *pres* bole̲t; *fut* yeevlo̲t.

(to) stand up for לעמוד על המשמר *inf* la'amo̲d 'al ha-meeshma̲r; *pst* 'ama̲d; *pres* 'ome̲d *etc*; *fut* ya'amo̲d *etc*.

standard 1. תקן (norm) *nm* te̲k|en/-ane̲em (*pl+of:* teekne̲y); **2.** דגם (model) *nm* de̲g|em/-ame̲em (*pl+of:* deegme̲y); **3.** בסיס (base) *nm* base̲es/besees|e̲em (*pl+of:* -e̲y); **4.** צורה (manner) *nf* tsoor|a̲h/-o̲t (*+of:* -a̲t).

(gold) standard בסיס הזהב *nm* bse̲es ha-zaha̲v.

(to be up to) standard לעמוד בתקנים *inf* la'amo̲d ba-tekane̲em; *pst* 'ama̲d; *pres* 'ome̲d *etc*; *fut* ya'amo̲d *etc*.

standard-bearer דגלן *nm* dagla̲n/-e̲em (*pl+of:* -e̲y).

standardization 1. תקינה *nf* tekeen|a̲h/-o̲t (*+of:* -a̲t); **2.** סטנדרדיזציה *nf* standardeeza̲ts|yah/-yot (*+of:* -yat).

(to) standardize לקבוע תקנים *inf* leekbo̲'a' tekane̲em; *pst* kava̲' (*v=b*) *etc*; *pres* kove̲'a' *etc*; *fut* yeekba̲' *etc*.

standby מצב הכן *nm* mats|a̲v/-ve̲y hakhe̲n.

standing 1. מעמד (position) *nm* ma'ama̲d/-e̲em (*pl+of:* -e̲y); **2.** מוניטין (fame) *nm pl* moneete̲en.

standing קבוע *adj* kavo̲o'a'/kvoo'a̲h.

(of long) standing מקדמת דנא *adv* mee-kadma̲t dena̲.

standing army צבא קבע *nm* tseva̲ ke̲va'.

standing water מים עומדים *nm pl* ma̲yeem 'omde̲em.

standing room only מקומות עמידה בלבד *nm pl* mekomo̲t 'ameeda̲h bee-lva̲d.

standstill 1. קיפאון *nm* kee|pa'o̲n (*+of:* -f'o̲n; *f=p*); **2.** הפסקה (intermission) *nf* hafsak|a̲h/-o̲t (*+of:* -a̲t).

(to come to a) standstill להשתתק *inf* leheeshtatek; *pst* heeshtatek; *pres* meeshtatek; *fut* yeeshtatek.

stanza בית בשיר *nm* bayeet/bateem be-sheer.

staple 1. כליב (pin) *nm* kleev/-eem (*pl+of:* -ey); **2.** סחורה עיקרית (main merchandise) *nf* skhorah 'eekreet.

(to) staple להכליבה *inf* lehakhleev; *pst* heekhleev; *pres* makhleev; *fut* yakhleev.

stapler 1. מכלב *nm* makhlev/-eem (*pl+of:* -ey); **2.** שדכן *[slang] nm* shadkhan/-eem (*pl+of:* -ey).

staples מצרכים חיוניים *nm pl* meetsrakheem kheeyooneeyeem.

star 1. כוכב *nm* kokh|av/-eem (*pl+of:* -vey); **2.** מזל (luck) *nm* mazal/-ot.

(movie) star כוכב קולנוע *nmf* kokh|av/-evet (*pl:* kokhv|ey/-ot) kolno'a'.

(television) star כוכב טלוויזיה *nmf* kokh|av/-evet (*pl:* kokhv|ey/-ot) televeezyah.

(to) star 1. לככב *inf* lekhakev; *pst* keekev *(k=kh)*; *pres* mekhakev; *fut* yekhakev; **2.** *cpr inf* lekakhev; *pst* keekhev; *pres* mekakhev; *fut* yekakhev.

Star of David מגן־דוד *nm* mag|en/-eeney daveed.

star spangled זרוע כוכבים *adj* zaroo'a'/zroo'ah kokhaveem.

starboard, starboard side צד ימין באונייה *nm* tsad yemeen bo-oneeyah.

starch עמילן *nm* 'ameelan/-eem (*pl+of:* ey).

(to) starch לעמלן *inf* le'amlen; *pst* 'eemlen; *pres* me'amlen; *fut* ye'amlen.

stare מבט *nm* mabat/-eem (*pl+of:* -ey).

(to) stare לתקוע מבט *inf* leetko'a' mabat; *pst* taka' *etc*; *pres* toke'a' *etc*; *fut* yeetka' *etc*.

starfish כוכב־ים *nm* kokh|av/-vey yam.

stark 1. מוחלט (complete) *adj* mookhl|at/-etet; **2.** קודר (grim) *adj* koder/-et.

stark folly שטות מוחלטת *nf* shtoot mookhletet.

stark mad משוגע על כל הראש *adj* meshoog|a'/-a'at 'al kol ha-rosh.

stark naked ערום לחלוטין *adj* 'arom/'aroomah la-khalooteen.

stark narrative סיפור ללא כחל וסרק *nm* seepoor/-eem le-lo kakhal oo-srak.

starlight אור כוכבים *nm* or kokhaveem.

starry זוהר ככוכב *adj* zoher/-et ka-kokhaveem.

start 1. התחלה (beginning) *nf* hatkhal|ah/-ot (*+of:* -at); **2.** זינוק (in sports) *nm* zeenook/-eem (*pl+of:* -ey).

(to) start 1. להתחיל (begin) *inf* lehatkheel; *pst* heetkheel; *pres* matkheel; *fut* yatkheel; **2.** להתניע (engine) *inf* lehatnee'a'; *pst* heetnee'a'; *pres* matnee'a'; *fut* yatnee'a'; **3.** להפעיל (activate) *inf* lehaf'eel; *pst* heef'eel; *pres* maf'eel; *fut* yaf'eel.

(to) start after someone לצאת בעיקבות מישהו *inf* latset be-'eekvot meeshehoo; *pst* yatsa *etc*; *pres* yotse *etc*; *fut* yetse *etc*.

(to) start off לפתוח ב־ *inf* leefto'akh be-; *pst* patakh be-; *pres* pote'akh be-; *fut* yeeftakh be-.

(to) start out on a trip לצאת למסע *inf* latset le-masa'; *pst* yatsa *etc*; *pres* yotse *etc*; *fut* yetse *etc*.

(to) start the motor להתניע מנוע *inf* lehatnee'a' mano'a'; *pst* heetnee'a' *etc*; *pres* matnee'a' *etc*; *fut* yatnee'a' *etc*.

starter 1. מתנע (automobile) *nm* matne|'a'/-'eem (*pl+of:* -'ey); **2.** יזם (initiator) *nm* yazam/-eem (*pl+of:* -ey); **3.** ראשון (first) *nmf* reeshon/-ah.

(self-)starter מתניע מעצמו *nm* matnee|'a'/-'eem me-'atsm|o/-am.

(to) startle 1. להחריד *inf* lehakhreed; *pst* hekhreed; *pres* makhreed; *fut* yakhreed; **2.** להפתיע *inf* lehaftee'a'; *pst* heeftee'a'; *pres* maftee'a'; *fut* yaftee'a'.

startling מדהים *adj* mad'heem/-ah.

starvation רעב *nm* ra'av.

starvation wages משכורת רעב *nf* maskor|et/-ot ra'av.

(to) starve 1. להרעיב *vt inf* lehar'eev; *pst* heer'eev; *pres* mar'eev; *fut* yar'eev; **2.** לרעוב *vi inf* leer'ov; *pst* ra'av; *pres* ra'ev; *fut* yeer'av.

state 1. מצב (condition) *nm* matsav/-eem (*pl+of:* -ey); **2.** ממשלה (government) *nf* memsh|alah/-alot (*+of:* -elet/-elot); **3.** מדינה (country) medee-n|ah/-ot (*+of:* -at).

(in great) state ברעש גדול *adv* be-ra'ash gadol.

(to) state 1. להצהיר *inf* lehats'heer; *pst* heets'heer; *pres* mats'heer; *fut* yats'heer; **2.** לקבוע (fix) *inf* leekbo'a'; *pst* kava' *(v=b)*; *pres* kove'a'; *fut* yeekba'.

State Department 1. מחלקת המדינה *nf* makhleket ha-medeenah; **2.** משרד החוץ של ארצות הברית (U.S. foreign office) *nm* meesrad ha-khoots shel artsot ha-breet.

State of Israel מדינת ישראל *nf* medeenat yeesra'el.

stately מלא הוד *adj* male/mele'at hod.

statement 1. הצהרה (declaration) *nf* hats'har|ah/-ot (*+of:* -at); **2.** הודעה (announcement) *nf* hoda|'ah/-'ot (*+of:* -'at); **3.** חשבון (bill) *nm* kheshbon/-ot.

stateroom אולם פאר *nm* oolam/-ot pe'er.

statesman מדינאי *nm* medeen|ay/-a'eem (*pl+of:* -a'ey).

static 1. סטטיקה *nf* stateek|ah/-ot (*+of:* -at); **2.** סטטי *adj* statee/-t.

station 1. בסיס (operations point) *nm* basees/besees|eem (*pl+of:* -ey); **2.** מעמד (condition) *nm* ma'amad/-ot; **3.** תחנה (post) *nf* takhan|ah/-ot (*+of:* -at).

(broadcasting) station תחנת שידור *nf* takhan|at/-ot sheedoor.

(to) station 1. להציב *inf* lehatseev; *pst* heetseev; *pres* matseev; *fut* yatseev; **2.** לשכן (house) *inf* leshaken; *pst* sheeken; *pres* meshaken; *fut* yeshaken.

station wagon מכונית סטיישן *nf* mekhonee|t-yot steyshen.

stationary נייח *adj* nayakh/nayekhet.

stationery צורכי כתיבה *nm pl* tsorkhey keteevah.

statistics סטטיסטיקה *nf* stateesteek|ah/-ot (*+of:* -at).

statuary אוסף פסלים *nm* osef/osfey pesaleem.

statue 1. פסל *nm* pes|el/-aleem (*pl+of:* peesley); **2.** אנדרטה (monument) *nf* andart|ah/-a'ot (*+of:* -at).

stature שיעור קומה *nm* she'oor komah.

status 1. מעמד *nm* ma'amad/-ot; **2.** סטטוס *nm* statoos/-eem (*pl+of:* -ey).

statute חוק *nm* khok/khook|eem (*pl+of:* -ey).

statutes תקנון *nm* takanon/-eem (*pl+of:* -ey).

staunch 1. איתן *adj* eytan/-ah; **2.** נאמן (faithful) *adj* ne'eman/-ah.

stave לוח של חבית *nm* loo|'akh/-khot shel khaveet.

(to) stave 1. לנפץ *inf* lenapets; *pst* neepets; *pres* menapets; *fut* yenapets; **2.** להרחיק (drive away) *inf* leharkheek; *pst* heerkheek; *pres* markheek; *fut* yarkheek.

(to) stave off 1. להדוף *inf* lahadof; *pst* hadaf; *pres* hodef; *fut* yahadof; **2.** לדחוף (push) *inf* leedkhof; *pst* dakhaf; *pres* dokhef; *fut* yeedkhof.

stay 1. שהייה (sojourn) *nf* shehee|yah/-yot (*+of:* -yat); **2.** עצירה (halt) *nf* 'atseer|ah/-ot (*+of:* -at); **3.** עיכוב (stoppage) *nm* 'eekoov/-eem (*pl+of:* -ey).

(to grant a) stay להעניק ארכה *inf* leha'aneek arkah; *pst* he'eneek *etc*; *pres* ma'aneek *etc*; *fut* ya'aneek *etc*.

(to) stay 1. להישאר (remain) *inf* leheesha'er; *pst & adj* neesh'ar; *fut* yeesha'er; **2.** לשהות (sojourn) *inf* leesh'hot; *pst* shahah; *pres* shoheh; *fut* yeesh'heh; **3.** לעצור (check) *inf* la'atsor; *pst* 'atsar; *pres* 'otser; *fut* ya'atsor.

stay of execution עיכוב הוצאה להורג *nm* 'eekoov/-ey hotsa'ah lehoreg.

stay of proceedings 1. הפסקת דיון (of hearing) *nf* hafsak|at/-ot deyoon; **2.** עיכוב פעולות (of steps) *nm* 'eekoov/-ey pe'oolot.

(to) stay up all night להישאר ער כל הלילה *inf* leheesha'er 'er kol ha-laylah; *pst & adj* neesh'ar *etc*; *fut* yeesha'er *etc*.

stead מקום *nm* makom/mekomot (*+of:* mekom).

(in his/her) stead במקומו *adv* bee-mekom|o/-ah (*m/f*).

(in good) stead לתועלת *adv* le-to'elet.

steadfast 1. יציב *adj* yatseev/-ah; **2.** איתן (firm) *adj* eytan/-ah.

steadily בהתמדה *adv* be-hatmadah.

steadiness 1. התמדה *nf* hatmad|ah/-ot (*+of:* -at); **2.** קביעות (permanence) *nf* kvee'oot.

steady 1. סדיר *adj* sadeer/sedeerah; **2.** יציב (stable) *adj* yatseev/-ah.

(to) steady 1. להתייצב *inf* leheetyatsev; *pst* heetyatsev; *pres* meetyatsev; *fut* yeetyatsev; **2.** לייצב (stabilize) *inf* leyatsev; *pst* yeetsev; *pres* meyatsev; *fut* yeyatsev.

steak 1. אומצת בשר *nf* oomts|at/-ot basar; **2.** סטייק *nm* steyk/-eem (*pl+of:* -ey).

(to) steal 1. לגנוב *inf* leegnov; *pst* ganav; *pres* gonev; *fut* yeegnov; **2.** להתגנב (stalk) *v rfl inf* leheetganev; *pst* heetganev; *fut* meetganev; *fut* yeetganev.

(to) steal away להתגנב *inf* leheetganev; *pst* heetganev; *fut* meetganev; *fut* yeetganev.

(to) steal into a room להתגנב לחדר *inf* leheetganev la-kheder; *pst* heetganev *etc*; *fut* meetganev *etc*; *fut* yeetganev *etc*.

(to) steal out of a room להתחמק מהחדר *inf* leheetkhamek me-ha-kheder; *pst* heetkhamek *etc*; *pres* meetkhamek *etc*; *fut* yeetkhamek *etc*.

(to enter by) stealth להתגנב *inf* leheetganev; *pst* heetganev; *pres* meetganev; *fut* yeetganev

stealthy 1. חשאי *adj* khasha'ee/-t; **2.** מתחמק *adj* meetkhamek/-et.

steam 1. קיטור *nm* keetor; **2.** אדי קיטור *nm* edey keetor.

(to) steam 1. לאדות *inf* le'adot; *pst* eedah; *pres* me'adeh; *fut* ye'adeh; **2.** לפלוט אדים (vapor) *inf* leeflot edeem; *pst* palat *(p=f) etc*; *pres* polet *etc*; *fut* yeeflot *etc*.

steam engine מנוע קיטור *nm* meno|'a'/-'ey keetor.

steam heat חימום בקיטור *nm* kheemoom be-keetor.

(to) steam into port לעשות דרכה לתוך נמל (of a ship) *inf* la'asot darkah le-tokh namel; *pst nf* 'astah *etc*; *pres nf* 'osah *etc*; *fut nf* ta'aseh *etc*.

steam roller מכבש *nm* makhbesh/-eem (*pl+of:* -ey).

steamboat ספינת קיטור *nf* sfeen|at/-ot keetor.

steamer, steamship אוניית קיטור *nf* onee|yat/-yot keetor.

steed סוס *nm* soos/-eem (*pl+of:* -ey).

steel 1. פלדה *nf* plad|ah/-ot (*+of:* peeldat); **2.** עשוי פלדה *adj* 'asoo|y/-yah pladah.

(stainless) steel פלדת אל־חלד *nf* peeld|at/-ot al-kheled.

(to) steel להקשיח לבו *inf* lehakshee'akh leebo; *pst* heekshee'akh *etc*; *pres* makshee'akh *etc*; *fut* yakshee'akh *etc*.

(to) steel one's heart לאמץ לבו *inf* le'amets leebo; *pst* eemets *etc*; *pres* me'amets *etc*; *fut* ye'amets *etc*.

steel wool צמר פלדה *nm* tsemer pladah.

steep תלול *adj* talool/teloolah.

(to) steep להשרות *inf* lehashrot; *pst* heeshrah; *pres* mashreh; *fut* yashreh.

steep price מחיר מופרז *nm* mekheer/-eem moofraz/-eem.

steeple צריח *nm* tseree'akh/-kheem (*pl+of:* -khey).

steepness תלילות *nf* tleeloo|t/-yot.

steer שור בן־בקר *nm* shor/shvareem ben/-ey bakar.

(to) steer 1. לנווט *inf* lenavet; *pst* neevet; *pres* menavet; *fut* yenavet; **2.** לנהוג (drive) *inf* leenhog; *pst* nahag; *pres* noheg; *fut* yeenhag.

(to) steer a course לנווט מסלול *inf* lenavet maslool; *pst* neevet *etc*; *pres* menavet *etc*; *fut* yenavet *etc*.

steering easily קל להיגוי *adj* kal/-ah le-heegooy.

steering wheel גלגל הגה *nm* galgal/-ey hegeh.

stellar כוכבי *adj* kokhavee/-t.

stem 1. גבעול *nm* geev'ol/-eem (*pl+of:* -ey); **2.** גזע (trunk) *nm* gez|a'/-a'eem (*pl+of:* geez'ey).

(to) stem 1. לעצור *inf* la'atsor; *pst* 'atsar; *pres* 'otser; *fut* ya'atsor; **2.** לסכור (dam) *inf* leeskor; *pst* sakhar *(kh=k)*; *pres* sokher; *fut* yeeskor.

(to) stem from לנבוע מתוך *inf* leenbo'a' mee-tokh; *pst* nava' *(v=b) etc*; *pres* nove'a' *etc*; *fut* yeenba' *etc*.

stench סרחון *nm* seerkhon/-eem (*pl+of:* -ey).

stencil 1. שעווית *nf* sha'avee|t-yot; **2.** סטנסיל *nm* stenseel/-eem (*pl+of:* -ey).

(to) stencil לשכפל *inf* leshakhpel; *pst* sheekhpel; *pres* meshakhpel; *fut* yeshakhpel.

stenographer 1. קצרן *nmf* katsran/-eet; **2.** סטינוגרפיסט *nmf* stenografeest/-eet.

stenography 1. קצרנות *nf* katsranoo|t/-yot; **2.** סטינוגרפיה *nf* stenograf|yah/-yot (*+of:* -yat).

step 1. צעד (pace) *nm* tsa'ad/tse'adeem (*pl+of:* tsa'adey); **2.** מדרגה (staircase) *nf* madreg|ah/-ot (+*of:* -at); **3.** שלב (degree) *nm* shalav/shlab|eem (*pl+of:* -ey); **4.** מאמץ (effort) *nm* ma'amats/-eem (*pl+of:* -ey).

(to) step 1. לצעוד *inf* leets'od; *pst* tsa'ad; *pres* tso'ed; *fut* yeets'ad; **2.** לפסוע (pace) *inf* leefso'a'; *pst* pasa' *(p=f)*; *pres* pose'a'; *fut* yeefsa'.

(to) step aside לזוז הצידה *inf* lazooz ha-tseedah; *pst & adj* zaz *etc*; *fut* yazooz *etc*.

(to) step back לזוז אחורה *inf* lazooz akhorah; *pst & adj* zaz *etc*; *fut* yazooz *etc*.

step by step צעד צעד *adv* tsa'ad tsa'ad.

(to) step down לרדת מעל *inf* laredet me-'al; *pst* yarad *etc*; *pres* yored *etc*; *fut* yered *etc*.

(to) step off a distance למדוד מרחק בצעדים *inf* leemdod merkhak bee-tse'adeem; *pst* madad *etc*; *pres* moded *etc*; *fut* yeemdod *etc*.

(to) step on it, (to) step on the gas להזדרז *inf* lehheezdarez; *pst* heezdarez; *pres* meezdarez; *fut* yeezdarez.

(to) step out לצאת החוצה לרגע *inf* latset ha-khootsah le-rega'; *pst* yatsa *etc*; *pres* yotse *etc*; *fut* yetse *etc*.

(to) step up 1. להגביר *inf* lehagbeer; *pst* heegbeer; *pres* magbeer; *fut* yagbeer; **2.** לזרז (hurry) *inf* lezarez; *pst* zerez; *pres* mezarez; *fut* yezarez.

(to be in) step with לצעוד צעד בצעד עם *inf* leets'od tsa'ad be-tsa'ad 'eem; *pst* tsa'ad *etc*; *pres* tso'ed *etc*; *fut* yeets'ad *etc*.

stepfather אב חורג *nm* av/-ot khor|eg/-geem.

stepmother אם חורגת *nf* em/'eemahot khor|eget/-got.

steppe ערבה *nf* 'arav|ah/-ot (+*of:* -at).

stepping stone 1. אבן מדרך *nf* even/avney meedrakh; **2.** קרש קפיצה (spring board) *nm* keresh/karshey kefeetsah.

(to take) steps לנקוט צעדים *inf* leenkot tse'adeem; *pst* nakat *etc*; *pres* noket *etc*; *fut* yeenkot *etc*.

stereotype 1. הטפס *nm* hetpes/-eem (*pl+of:* -ey); **2.** סטריאוטיפ *nm* stereoteep/-eem (*pl+of:* -ey).

sterile 1. מעוקר *adj* me'ook|ar/-eret; **2.** סטרילי *adj* stereelee/-t.

sterility 1. עקרות *nf* 'akaroo|t/-yot; **2.** סטריליות *nf* stereeleeyoot.

sterilization 1. עיקור *nm* 'eekoor/-eem (*pl+of:* -ey); **2.** סירוס (castration) *nm* seroos/-eem (*pl+of:* -ey); **3.** סטריליזציה *nf* stereeleezats|yah/-yot (+*of:* -yat).

(to) sterilize 1. לעקר *inf* le'aker; *pst* 'eeker; *pres* me'aker; *fut* ye'aker; **2.** לחטא (disinfect) *inf* lekhate; *pst* kheete; *pres* mekhate; *fut* yekhate; **3.** לסרס (castrate) *inf* lesares; *pst* seras; *pres* mesares; *fut* yesares.

sterling שטרלינג *nm* shterleeng/-eem (*pl+of:* -ey).

sterling pound 1. לירה שטרלינג *nf* leer|ah/-ot shterling; **2.** לי״ש (*acr of* 1) *nm* leesh.

sterling silver כסף טהור *nm* kesef tahor.

stern 1. חמור *adj* khamoor/-ah; **2.** מחמיר (severe) *adj* makhmeer/-ah; **3.** קשוח (austere) *adj* kashoo'akh/keshookhah.

stern ירכתי אונייה (ship) *nm pl* yarketey oneeyah.

sternness 1. קפדנות *nf* kapdanoot; **2.** צנע (austerity) *nm* tsena'.

stethoscope 1. מסכת *nm* masket/-eem (*pl+of:* -ey); **2.** סטתוסקופ *nm* stetoskop/-eem (*pl+of:* -ey).

stevedore סוור *nm* savar/-eem (*pl+of:* -ey).

stew 1. נזיד *nm* nazeed/nezeed|eem (*pl+of:* -ey); **2.** תבשיל (cooked food) *nm* tavsheel/-eem (*pl+of:* -ey).

(to) stew להתבשל *inf* leheetbashel; *pst* heetbashel; *pres* meetbashel; *fut* yeetbashel.

(in a) stew 1. טרוד *adj* tarood/troodah; **2.** מוטרד (annoyed) *adj* mootr|ad/-edet.

steward 1. כלכל *nm* kalkal/-eem (*pl+of:* -ey); **2.** מנהל משק בית (housekeeper) menahel meshek bayeet; **3.** דייל (flight) *nm* dayal/-eem (*pl+of:* -ey).

stewardess דיילת *nf* day|elet/-alot.

stick 1. מקל *nm* mak|el/-lot; **2.** מוט (pole) *nm* mot/-ot.

(control) stick מוט היגוי *nm* mot/-ot heegooy.

(walking) stick מקל הליכה *nm* mak|el/-lot haleekhah.

stick of dynamite מקל דינמיט *nm* mak|el/-lot deenameet.

(to) stick out one's hand להושיט יד *inf* lehosheet yad; *pst* hosheet yad; *pres* mosheet yad; *fut* yosheet yad.

(to) stick out one's tongue לחרוץ לשון *inf* lakhrots lashon; *pst* kharats *etc*; *pres* khorets *etc*; *fut* yakhrots *etc*.

(to) stick someone up לשדוד מישהו *inf* leeshdod meeshe|hoo/-hee *(m/f)*; *pst* shadad *etc*; *pres* shoded *etc*; *fut* yeeshdod *etc*.

(to) stick something in לתחוב לתוך *inf* leetkhov le-tokh; *pst* takhav *etc*; *pres* tokhev *etc*; *fut* yeetkhov *etc*.

(to) stick to a job לדבוק בתפקיד *inf* leedbok ba-tafkeed; *pst* davak *(v=b) etc*; *pres* davek *etc*; *fut* yeedbok *etc*.

stick-up שוד *nm* shod.

sticker 1. מדבקה *nf* madbek|ah/-ot (+*of:* -at); **2.** תווית *nf* tavee|t/-yot.

sticky 1. דביק *adj* daveek/dveekah; **2.** צמוג *adj* tsamog/tsmoogah.

stiff 1. נוקשה *adj* nooksh|eh/-ah; **2.** קשיח (hard) *adj* kashee'akh/kesheekhah.

stiff גווייה (corpse) *nf* gvee|yah/-yot (+*of:* -yat).

(scared) stiff מפוחד עד מוות *adj* mefookh|ad/-edet 'ad mavet.

stiff climb עלייה קשה *nf* 'alee|yah/-yot kash|ah/-ot.

stiff collar צווארון קשה *nm* tsav|aron/-roneem kash|eh/-eem.

stiff-necked קשה עורף *adj* kesheh/keshat 'oref.

stiff price מחיר גבוה מדי *nm* mekheer/-eem gavoha/gvoheem meeday.

(to) stiffen 1. להקשיח *inf* lehakshee'akh; *pst* heekshee'akh; *pres* makshee'akh; *fut* yakshee'akh; **2.** להתקשות (harden) *inf* leheetkashot; *pst* heetkashah; *pres* meetkasheh; *fut* yeetkasheh.

stiffness קשיחות *nf* kesheekhoot.

(to) stifle להחניק *inf* lehakhneek; *pst* hekhneek; *pres* makhneek; *fut* yakhneek.

stigma אות קלון *nm* ot/-ot kalon.

(to) stigmatize להדביק אות קלון *inf* lehadbeek ot kalon; *pst* heedbeek *etc*; *pres* madbeek *etc*; *fut* yadbeek *etc*.

still 1. שקט (quiet) *adj* shaket/sheketah; **2.** נוח (at ease) *adj* no'akh/nokhah; **3.** דומם *adj* domem/-et.

still תצלום דומם (photograph) *nm* tatsloom/-eem domem/-eem.

still 1. עוד *adv* 'od; **2.** עדיין *adv* 'adayeen; **3.** אף על פי כן (nevertheless) af 'al pee khen.

(to) still 1. להשקיט (calm) *inf* lehashkeet; *pst* heeshkeet; *pres* mashkeet; *fut* yashkeet; **2.** להשתיק (silence) *inf* lehashteek; *pst* heeshteek; *pres* mashteek; *fut* yashteek.

still-life דומם *nm* domem/-eem (*pl+of:* -ey).

stillborn מת מולד *adj* met/-ah mool|ad/-edet.

stillness 1. דומייה *nf* doomee|yah/-yot (*+of:* -yat); **2.** שקט (quiet) *nm* sheket.

stilt קב הגבהה *nm* kav/kabey *(b=v)* hagbahah.

stilted 1. מוגבה *adj* moogb|ah/-ahat; **2.** מנופח (exaggerated) *adj* menoopakh/-at.

stimulant 1. ממריץ *nm* mamreets/-eem (*pl+of:* -ey); **2.** מגרה *adj* megar|eh/-ah.

(to) stimulate 1. להמריץ *inf* lehamreets; *pst* heemreets; *pres* mamreets; *fut* yamreets; **2.** לגרות (excite) *inf* legarot; *pst* gerah; *pres* megareh; *fut* yegareh.

stimulation 1. המרצה *nf* hamrats|ah/-ot (*+of:* -at); **2.** עידוד (encouragement) *nm* 'eedood/-eem (*pl+of:* -ey).

stimulus תמריץ *nm* tamreets/-eem (*pl+of:* -ey).

sting 1. עוקץ *nm* 'okets/'ookts|eem (*pl+of:* -ey); **2.** עקיצה (bite) *nf* 'akeets|ah/-ot (*+of:* -at).

(to) sting 1. לעקוץ *inf* la'akots; *pst* 'akats; *pres* 'okets; *fut* ya'akots; **2.** להכאיב (cause pain) *inf* lehakh'eev; *pst* heekh'eev; *pres* makh'eev; *fut* yakh'eev.

sting of remorse מוסר כליות *nm* moosar klayot.

stinginess קמצנות *nf* kamtsanoot.

stingy קמצן *nmf & adj* kamtsan/-eet.

stink 1. סרחון *nm* seerkhon/-ot; **2.** שערורייה (scandal) *nf* sha'arooree|yah/-yot (*+of:* -yat).

(to) stink להסריח *inf* lehasree'akh; *pst* heesree'akh; *pres* masree'akh; *fut* yasree'akh.

stint 1. מכסה *nf* meekhs|ah/-ot (*+of:* -at); **2.** מגבלה (limitation) *f* meegb|alah/-alot (*+of:* -elet).

(to) stint לקמץ ב־ *inf* lekamets be-; *pst* keemets be-; *pres* mekamets be-; *fut* yekamets be-.

(without) stint ללא מגבלה *adv* le-lo meegbalah.

(to) stint oneself להגביל עצמו *inf* lehagbeel 'atsmo; *pst* heegbeel *etc*; *pres* magbeel *etc*; *fut* yagbeel *etc*.

(to) stipulate להתנות *inf* lehatnot; *pst* heetnah; *pres* matneh; *fut* yatneh.

stipulation התניה *nf* hatna|yah/-yot (*+of:* -yat).

stir 1. רעש *nm* ra'ash/re'asheem (*pl+of:* ra'ashey); **2.** התרגשות (emotion) *nf* heetragshoo|t/-yot.

(to) stir 1. לבחוש (mix) *inf* leevkhosh; *pst* bakhash *(b=v)*; *pres* bokhesh; *fut* yeevkhash; **2.** לעורר (awaken) *inf* le'orer; *pst* 'orer; *pres* me'orer; *fut* ye'orer.; **3.** להניע (move) *inf* lehanee'a'; *pst* henee'a'; *pres* menee'a'; *fut* yanee'a'; **4.** להלהיב (inflame) *inf* lehalheev; *pst* heelheev; *pres* malheev; *fut* yalheev.

(to) stir up 1. לחרחר (instigate) *inf* lekharkher; *pst* kheerkher; *pres* mekharkher; *fut* yekharkher; **2.** לדרבן (bolster) *inf* ledarben; *pst* deerben; *pres* medarben; *fut* yedarben.

stirring 1. בחישה (mixing) *nf* bekheesh|ah/-ot (*+of:* -at); **2.** פעיל (active) *adj* pa'eel/pe'eelah.

stirrup משוורת *nf* meeshv|eret/-arot.

stitch 1. תפר *nm* tef|er/-areem (*pl+of:* teefrey); **2.** לולאה (loop) *nf* loola|'ah/-'ot (*+of:* -'at).

(to) stitch 1. לתפר *inf* letaper; *pst* teeper; *pres* metaper; *fut* yetaper; **2.** לאחות *inf* le'akhot; *pst* eekhah; *pres* me'akheh; *fut* ye'akheh.

(in) stitches מתפקע מצחוק *adj* meetpak|e'a'/-a'at mee-ts'khok.

stock 1. מלאי (supply) *nm* melay; **2.** בקר (cattle) *nm* bakar; **3.** מוצא (lineage) *nm* motsa; **4.** מניה (share) *nf* mena|yah/-yot (*+of:* -yat).

(in) stock במלאי *adv* ba-m'lay.

(meat) stock רוטב בשר *nm* rotev basar.

(to) stock 1. לצייד *inf* letsayed; *pst* tseeyed; *pres* metsayed; *fut* yetsayed; **2.** להצטייד (equip oneself) *inf* leheetstayed; *pst* heetstayed; *pres* meetstayed; *fut* yeetstayed.

(to) stock a farm לצייד משק במלאי *inf* letsayed meshek bee-m'lay; *pst* tseeyed; *pres* metsayed; *fut* yetsayed.

stock answer טענה שגרתית *nf* ta'an|ah/-ot sheegratee|t-yot.

stock breeder מגדל בקר *nm* megad|el/-ley bakar.

stock company חברת מניות *nf* khevr|at/-ot menayot.

stock exchange בורסה *nf* boors|ah/-ot (*+of:* -at).

stock farm חווה לגידול בקר *nf* khav|ah/-ot le-geedool bakar.

stock market שוק המניות *nm* shook/-ey ha-menayot.

stock size גודל רגיל *nm* godel/gedaleem rageel/regeeleem.

(to) stock up with להצטייד ב־ *inf* leheetstayed be-; *pst* heetstayed be-; *pres* meetstayed be-; *fut* yeetstayed be-.

stockade 1. מכלאה *nf* meekhla|'ah/-'ot (*+of:* meekhle|'at/-'ot); **2.** שטח מגודר (fenced enclosure) *nm* shet|akh/-akheem megoodar/-eem.

stockbrocker 1. מתווך מניות metav|ekh/-khey menayot; **2.** ברוקר *nm* broker/-eem (*pl+of:* -ey).

stockholder בעל מניות *nmf* ba'al/-at (*pl:* -ey) menayot.

stocking גרב *nm* gerev/garb|ayeem (*pl+of:* -ey).

stocky גוץ וחסון *adj* goots/-ah ve/va khas|on/-oonah.

stockyard מכלאת מעבר *nf* meekhle|'at/-'ot ma'avar.

stoic 1. שולט ברגשותיו *adj adj* sholet/-et be-reegshot|av/-eha; **2.** סטואי *adj* sto'ee/-t.

stolen גנוב *adj* ganoov/genoovah.

stolid 1. חסר הבעה *adj* khas|ar/-rat haba'ah; **2.** חסר רגישות (insensitive) *adj* khas|ar/-rat regeeshoot.

stomach 1. בטן *nf* bet|en/-aneem (*pl+of:* beetney); **2.** קיבה *nf* keyv|ah/-ot (*+of:* -at).
(to) stomp לרמוס *inf* leermos; *pst* ramas; *pres* romes; *fut* yeermos.
stone 1. אבן *nf* even/avaneem (*pl+of:* avney); **2.** גלעין (kernel) *nm* gal'een/-eem (*pl+of:* -ey).
(to) stone 1. לסקול *inf* leeskol; *pst* sakal; *pres* sokel; *fut* yeeskol; **2.** לרגום (cast stones at) *inf* leergom; *pst* ragam; *pres* rogem; *fut* yeergom.
Stone Age תקופת האבן *nf* tekoofat ha-even.
stone-deaf חירש לחלוטין *nmf & adj* kheresh/-et la-khalooteen.
(within a) stone's throw בטווח יידוי אבן *adv* bee-tvakh yeedooy even.
stony 1. אבני *adj* avnee/-t; **2.** סלעי (rocky) *adj* sal'ee/-t.
stool 1. שרפרף *nm* shrafra|f/-peem (*p=f; pl+of:* -pey); **2.** פעולת קיבה (fecal discharge) *nf* pe'ool|at/-ot keyvah; **3.** הלשנה (informing) *nf* halshan|ah/-ot (*+of:* -at).
stool pigeon מלשין *nmf* malsheen/-ah.
stoop 1. כפיפת גו *nf* kfeef|at/-ot gev; **2.** מרפסת (porch) *nf* meerp|eset/-asot.
(to) stoop 1. להתכופף *inf* leheetkofef; *pst* heetkofef; *pres* meetkofef; *fut* yeetkofef; **2.** להיכנע (give in) *inf* leheekana'; *pst & adj* neekhna' *(kh=k)*; *fut* yeekana'.
(to walk with a) stoop ללכת שחוח *inf* lalekhet shekho'akh; *pst* halakh *etc*; *pres* holekh *etc*; *fut* yelekh *etc*.
stoop-shouldered שחוח *adj* shakho'akh/ shekhokhah.
stop 1. עצירה *nf* 'atseer|ah/-ot (*+of:* -at); **2.** תחנה (station) *nf* takhan|ah/-ot (*+of:* -at); **3.** קץ (ending) *nm* kets/keets|eem (*pl+of:* -ey).
(to) stop 1. לעצור (pause) *inf* la'atsor; *pst* 'atsar; *pres* 'otser; *fut* ya'atsor; **2.** לחסום (block) *inf* lakhasom; *pst* khasam; *pres* khosem; *fut* yakhasom.
(to) stop at a hotel להתאכסן במלון *inf* leheet'akhsen be-malon; *pst* heet'akhsen *etc*; *pres* meet'akhsen *etc*; *fut* yeet'akhsen *etc*.
(to) stop at nothing לא להירתע משום דבר *inf* lo leherata' mee-shoom davar; *pst & adj* lo neerta' *etc*; *fut* lo yerata' *etc*.
(to) stop from למנוע leemno'a'; *pst* mana'; *pres* mone'a'; *fut* yeemna'.
(to) stop over לעצור ללינה *inf* la'atsor le-leenah; *pst* 'atsar *etc*; *pres* 'otser *etc*; *fut* ya'atsor *etc*.
(to) stop short להיעצר לפתע *inf* lehe'atser le-feta'; *pst & adj* ne'etsar *etc*; *fut* ye'atser *etc*.
(to) stop up לסתום *inf* leestom; *pst* satam; *pres* sotem; *fut* yeestom.
stopover שהיית ביניים *nf* shehee|yat/-yot beynayeem.
stoppage 1. עצירה *nf* 'atseer|ah/-ot (*+of:* -at); **2.** סתימה (blockage) *nf* steem|ah/-ot (*+of:* -at); **3.** היפסקות (cessation) *nf* heepaskoo|t/-yot.
(work) stoppage הפסקת עבודה *nf* hafsak|at/-ot 'avodah.
stopper 1. פקק *nm* pekak/-eem (*pl+of:* -ey); **2.** שעון־עצר (stop-watch) *nm* she'on/-ey 'etser.
storage החסנה *nf* hakhsan|ah/-ot (*+of:* -at).
(to keep in) storage להחזיק בהחסנה *inf* lehakhzeek be-hakhsanah; *pst* hekhzeek *etc*; *pres* makhzeek *etc*; *fut* yakhzeek *etc*.
storage battery סוללת מצברים *nf* solel|at/-ot matsbereem.
store 1. חנות (shop) *nf* khanoo|t/-yot; **2.** מחסן (depot) *nm* makhsan/-eem (*pl+of:* -ey).
(department) store חנות כלבו *nf* khanoo|t/-yot kolbo.
(dry-goods) store 1. חנות סדקית *nf* khanoo|t/ -yot seedkeet; **2.** חנות גלנטריה *nf* khanoo|t/-yot galanteryah.
(electronics) store חנות לצורכי אלקטרוניקה *nf* khanoo|t/-yot le-tsorkhey elektroneekah.
(fashion goods) store חנות לדברי אופנה *nf* khanoo|t/-yot le-deevrey ofnah.
(fruit) store חנות ירקן (greengrocer's) *nf* khanoo|t/ -yot yarkan/-eem.
(grocery) store חנות מכולת *nf* khanoo|t/-yot makolet.
(hardware) store חנות לחומרי בניין *nf* khanoo|t/ -ot le-khomrey beenyan.
(hat) store חנות כובעים *nf* khanoo|t/-yot kova'eem.
(in) store צפוי *adj* tsafooy/tsefooyah.
(photo) store חנות לצורכי צילום *nf* khanoo|t/-yot le-tsorkhey tseeloom.
(shoe) store חנות נעליים *nf* khanoo|t/-yot na'alayeem.
(stationery) store חנות לצורכי כתיבה *nf* khanoo|t/ -yot le-tsorkhey keteevah.
(to) store 1. להחסין *v inf* lehakhseen; *pst* hekhseen; *pres* makhseen; *fut* yakhseen; **2.** לאחסן *[colloq.]* *inf* le'akhsen; *pst* eekhsen; *pres* me'akhsen; *fut* ye'akhsen; **3.** לצבור (accummulate) *inf* leetsbor; *pst* tsavar *(v=b)*; *pres* tsover; *fut* yeetsbor.
(to have in) store לשמור במלאי *inf* leeshmor ba-m'lay; *pst* shamar *etc*; *pres* shomer *etc*; *fut* yeeshmor *etc*.
(to) store up לאגור (hoard) *inf* le'egor; *pst* agar; *pres* oger; *fut* ye'egor.
storehouse מחסן *nm* makhsan/-eem (*pl+of:* -ey).
storekeeper 1. חנווני *nmf* khenvan|ee/-eet (*pl:* -eem; *+of:* -ey); **2.** מחסנאי (warehouse-man) *nm* makhsena|y/-'eem.
storeroom מזווה *nm* mezav|eh/-eem (*pl+of:* -ey).
stores מלאי *nm* melay.
stork 1. חסידה *nf* khaseed|ah/-ot (*+of:* -at); **2.** עגור (crane) *nm* 'agoor/-eem (*pl+of:* -ey).
storm 1. סערה (weather) *nf* se'ar|ah/-ot (*+of:* sa'ar|at/-ot); **2.** מהומה (disturbance) *nf* mehoom|ah/-ot (*+of:* -at).
(hail) storm סופת ברד *nf* soof|at/-ot barad.
(snow)storm סופת שלג *nf* soof|at/-ot sheleg.
(to) storm להסתער *inf* leheesta'er; *pst* heesta'er; *pres* meesta'er; *fut* yeesta'er.
(wind)storm סופת רוח *nf* soof|at/-ot roo'akh.
storm troops פלוגות סער *nf pl* ploogot sa'ar.
stormy סוער *adj* so'er/-et.
story 1. סיפור (tale) *m* seepoor/-eem (*pl+of:* -ey); **2.** רינון (gossip) *nm* reenoon/-eem (*pl+of:* -ey); **3.** עלילה (plot) *nf* 'aleel|ah/-ot (*+of:* -at); **4.** קומה (floor) *nf* kom|ah/-ot (*+of:* -at).

(newspaper) story כתבה בעיתון *nf* katav|'ah/-'ot ba-'eeton.

storyteller מספר *nm* mesap|er/-reem (*pl+of:* -rey).

stout 1. נאמן *adj* ne'eman/-ah; **2.** אמיץ (brave) *adj* ameets/-ah; **3.** עקשני (stubborn) *adj* 'akshanee/-t.

stove 1. תנור *nm* tanoor/-eem (*pl+of:* -ey); **2.** כיריים (range) *nm pl* keerayeem.

(electric) stove 1. תנור חשמלי *nm* tanoor/-eem khashmalee/-yeem; **2.** כיריים חשמליים (electric range) *nm* keerayeem khashmaleeyeem.

(gas) stove כיריים של גז *nm pl* keerayeem shel gaz.

(to) stow 1. לארוז לשם הסתרה (pack to hide) *inf* le'eroz le-shem hastarah; *pst* araz *etc; pres* orez *etc; fut* ye'eroz *etc;* **2.** לצופף (close up) *inf* letsofef; *pst* tsofef; *pres* metsofef; *fut* yetsofef.

stowaway נוסע סמוי *nmf* nose'a'/-a'at samooy/smooyah.

(to) straddle לעמוד בפישוק רגליים *inf* la'amod be-feesook raglayeem; *pst* 'amad; *pres* 'omed *etc; fut* ya'amod *etc.*

(to) strafe להפציץ מגובה נמוך *inf* lehaftseets mee-govah namookh; *pst* heeftseets *etc; pres* maftseets *etc; fut* yaftseets *etc.*

(to) straggle 1. לפגר *inf* lefager; *pst* peeger *(p=f); pres* mefager; *fut* yefager; **2.** להתפזר (disperse) *v refl* leheetpazer; *pst* heetpazer; *pres* meetpazer; *fut* yeetpazer.

(to) straggle behind להזדנב מאחור *inf* leheezdanev me-akhor; *pst* heezdanev *etc; pres* meezdanev *etc; fut* yeezdanev *etc.*

straight ישירות *adv* yesheerot.

straight 1. ישיר (direction) *adj* yasheer/yesheerah; **2.** הוגן (fair) *adj* hogen/-et.

(for two hours) straight במשך שעתיים רצופות *adv* be-meshekh sha'atayeem retsoofot.

(to set a person) straight להעמיד את מישהו על *inf* leha'ameed et meeshe|hoo/-hee *(m/f)* 'al; *pst* he'emeed *etc; pres* ma'ameed *etc; fut* ya'ameed *etc.*

straight away תיכף ומיד *adv* teykhef oo-meeyad.

straight face הבעת־פנים רצינית *nf* haba'at paneem retseeneet.

straight from the shoulder בגילוי לב *adv* be-geelooy lev.

straight hair שיער חלק *nm* sey'ar khalak.

straight off ללא שהיות *adv* le-lo sheheeyot.

straight rum רום טהור *nm* room tahor.

(to) straighten 1. להתיישר *inf* leheetyasher; *pst* heetyasher; *pres* meetyasher; *fut* yeetyasher. **2.** ליישר (rectify) *inf* leyasher; *pst* yeesher; *pres* meyasher; *fut* yeyasher.

straightforward 1. כן *adj* ken/-ah; **2.** במישרין (directly) *adv* be-meyshareen.

straightness יושר *nm* yosher.

straightway מיד *adv* meeyad.

strain 1. מתח *nm* metakh/-eem (*pl+of:* -ey); **2.** גזע (ancestry) *nm* gez|a'/-a'eem (*pl+of:* geez'ey); **3.** נימה (tone) *nf* neem|ah/-ot (*+of:* -at).

(to) strain 1. למתוח *inf* leemto'akh; *pst* matakh; *pres* mote'akh; *fut* yeemtakh; **2.** לסנן (filter) *inf* lesanen; *pst* seenen; *pres* mesanen; *fut* yesanen; **3.** לאמץ (exert) *inf* le'amets; *pst* eemets; *pres* me'amets; *fut* ye'amets; **4.** להתאמץ (strive) *inf inf* leheet'amets; *pst* heet'amets; *pres* meet'amets; *fut* yeet'amets.

(to) strain one's wrist לכופף זרוע למישהו *inf* lekhofef zro'a' le-meeshehoo; *pst* kofef *(k=kh) etc; pres* mekhofef *etc; fut* yekhofef *etc.*

strainer מסננת *nf* meesn|enet/-anot.

strait 1. מיצר *nm* meytsar/-eem (*pl+of:* -ey); **2.** מצוקה (distress) *f* metsook|ah/-ot (*+of:* -at).

straitjacket כתונת משוגעים *nf* ketonet/kotnot meshooga'eem.

straitlaced 1. טהרני *adj* taharanee/-t; **2.** פוריטני *adj* pooreetanee/-t.

straits מיצרים *nm pl* meytsar|eem (*pl+of:* -ey).

strand 1. גדה *nf* gad|ah/-ot (*+of:* -at); **2.** גדיל (tuft) *nm* gedeel/-eem (*pl+of:* -ey); **3.** נימה (fiber) *nf* neem|ah/-ot (*+of:* -at).

(to) strand להפקיר לנפשו *inf* lehafkeer le-nafsho; *pst* heefkeer *etc; pres* mafkeer *etc; fut* yafkeer *etc.*

strand of hair ציצת ראש *nf* tseets|at/-ot rosh.

strand of pearls מחרוזת פנינים *nf* makhroz|et/-ot pneeneem.

stranded 1. נעזב *adj* ne'ez|av/-evet; **2.** תקוע (stuck) *adj* takoo'a'/tekoo'ah.

strange 1. זר *adj* zar/-ah; **2.** מוזר (queer) *adj* moozar/-ah.

strangeness 1. זרות *nf* zaroo|t/-yot; **2.** ניכור (alienation) *nm* neekoor/-eem (*pl+of:* -ey).

stranger 1. זר *nmf & adj* zar/-ah; **2.** נוכרי (alien) *nmf* nokhree/-yah.

(to) strangle לחנוק *inf* lakhnok; *pst* khanak; *pres* khonek; *fut* yakhnok.

strap רצועה *nf* retsoo|'ah/-'ot (*+of:* -'at).

(metal) strap פס מתכת *nm* pas/-ey matekhet.

(to) strap לקשור ברצועות *inf* leekshor bee-retsoo'ot; *pst* kashar *etc; pres* kosher *etc; fut* yeekshor *etc.*

stratagem תכסיס *nm* takhsees/-eem (*pl+of:* -ey).

strategic 1. אסטרטגי *adj* astrategee/-t; **2.** סטרטגי *adj* strategee/-t.

strategy אסטרטגיה *nf* astrategee|yah/-yot (*+of:* -yat).

stratosphere סטרטוספירה *nf* stratosfer|ah/-ot (*+of:* -at).

straw קש *nm* kash.

(doesn't care a) straw לא אכפת לו כהוא זה lo eekhpat lo ke-hoo zeh.

straw-colored בצבע הקש *adj* be-tseva' ha-kash.

straw hat כובע קש *nm* kov|a'/-'ey kash.

straw man 1. איש קש *nm* eesh/anshey kash; **2.** דחליל (scarecrow) *nm* dakhleel/-eem (*pl+of:* -ey).

straw vote הצבעת סרק *nf* hatsba|'at/-'ot srak.

straw widow אלמנת קש *nf* almen|at/-ot kash.

straw widower אלמן קש *nm* alm|an/-eney kash.

strawberry תות־שדה *nm* toot/-ey sadeh.

stray 1. חיית בית תועה *nf* kha|yat/-yot bayeet to'ah/to'ot; **2.** נודד *adj* noded/-et.

(to) stray לתעות *inf* leet'ot; *pst* ta'ah; *pres* to'eh; *fut* yeet'eh.

stray remark הערה בודדת *nf* he'ar|ah/-ot boded|et/-ot.

streak 1. פס (stripe) *nm* pas/-eem (*pl+of:* -ey); **2.** עורק (artery) *nm* 'or|ek/-keem (*pl+of:* -ey); **3.** עקבות *nf* (traces) *pl* 'akevot (+*of:* 'eekvot); **4.** קרן אור (beam) *nf* keren/karney or.

(to) streak לסמן בפסים *inf* lesamen be-faseem (*f=p*); *pst* seemen *etc*; *pres* mesamen *etc*; *fut* yesamen *etc*.

streak of lightning נצנוץ ברק *nm* neetsnoots/-ey barak

stream 1. זרם *nm* zerem/zrameem (*pl+of:* zeermey); **2.** נחל (brook) *nm* nakhal/nekhaleem (*pl+of:* nakhley).

(down)stream עם הזרם *adv* 'eem ha-zerem.

(up)stream נגד הזרם *adv* neged ha-zerem.

(to) stream 1. לנהור (flock) *inf* leenhor; *pst* nahar; *pres* noher; *fut* yeenhar; **2.** לזרום (flow) *inf* leezrom; *pst* zaram; *pres* zorem; *fut* yeezrom; **3.** לזלוג (drip) *inf* leezlog; *pst* zalag; *pres* zoleg; *fut* yeezlog.

stream of cars נחשול כלי רכב *nm* nakhshol/-ey kley rekhev.

(to) stream out of לפרוץ מתוך *inf* leefrots mee-tokh; *pst* parats (*p=f*) *etc*; *pres* porets *etc*; *fut* yeefrots *etc*.

streamer 1. נס *nm* nes/nees|eem (*pl+of:* -ey); **2.** דגל (flag) *nm* deg|el/-aleem (*pl+of:* degley); **3.** טרנספרנט *nm* transparant/-eem (*pl+of:* -ey).

streamlined זרים *adj* zareem/zreemah.

street רחוב *nm* rekhov/-ot.

streetcar חשמלית *nf* khashmalee|t-yot.

streetfloor קומת קרקע *nf* kom|at/-ot karka'.

streetwalker 1. זונת־רחוב *nf* zon|at/-ot rekhov; **2.** יצאנית (prostitute) *nf* yats'anee|t-yot.

strength 1. כוח *nm* ko'akh/-khot; **2.** עוצמה (might) *nf* 'otsm|ah/-ot (+*of:* -at).

(on the) strength of בהסתמך על *adv* be-heestamekh (*pl+of:* 'al).

(to) strengthen 1. לחזק (reinforce) *vt inf* lekhazek; *pst* kheezek; *pres* mekhazek; *fut* yekhazek; **2.** להתחזק *v rfl inf* leheetkhazek; *pst* heetkhazek; *pres* meetkhazek; *fut* yeetkhazek.

strenuous 1. מפרך *adj* mefarekh/-et; **2.** נמרץ (vigorous) *adj* neemr|ats/-etset.

streptomycin סטרפטומיצין *nm* streptomeetseen/-eem.

stress 1. עומס *nm* 'omes; **2.** עוצמה (force) *nf* 'otsm|ah/-ot (+*of:* -at); **3.** דחיפות (urgency) *nf* dekheefoo|t/-yot; **4.** הדגשה (intensity) *nf* hadgash|ah/-ot (+*of:* -at); **5.** הטעמה (phonetic) *nf* hat'am|ah/-ot (*pl+of:* -at).

(to) stress להדגיש *inf* lehadgeesh; *pst* heedgeesh; *pres* madgeesh; *fut* yadgeesh.

stretch 1. כברת דרך (distance) *nf* keevr|at/-ot derekh; **2.** משך זמן (time) *nm* meshekh zman; **3.** תקופת מאסר (prison term) *nf* tekoof|at/-ot ma'asar.

(home) stretch קטע אחרון במירוץ *nm* keta' akharon be-merots.

(to) stretch למתוח *inf* leemto'akh; *pst* matakh; *pres* mote'akh; *fut* yeemtakh.

stretch of imagination אימוץ כוח הדמיון *nm* eemoots ko'akh ha-deemyon.

(to) stretch oneself להתאמץ *inf* leheet'amets; *pst* heet'amets; *pres* meet'amets; *fut* yeet'amets.

(to) stretch out one's hand להושיט יד *inf* lehosheet yad; *pst* hosheet yad; *pres* mosheet yad; *fut* yosheet yad.

stretcher אלונקה *nf* aloonk|ah/-ot (+*of:* -at).

(to) strew לפזר *inf* lefazer; *pst* peezer (*p=f*); *pres* mefazer; *fut* yefazer.

strewn מפוזר *adj* mefooz|ar/-eret.

stricken נגוע *adj* nagoo'a'/negoo'ah.

strict 1. חמור *adj* khamoor/-ah; **2.** קפדני (rigorous) *adj* kapdanee/-t.

(in) strict confidence בסוד גמור *adv* be-sod gamoor.

stride 1. מאמץ (effort) *nm* ma'amats/-eem (*pl+of:* -ey); **2.** צעד (step) *nm* tsa'ad/tse'adeem (*pl+of:* tsa'adey).

(to) stride להתאמץ *inf* leheet'amets; *pst* heet'amets; *pres* meet'amets; *fut* yeet'amets.

strife 1. מריבה *nf* mereev|ah/-ot (+*of:* -at); **2.** מחלוקת (dispute) *nf* makhlok|et/-ot.

strike 1. שביתה (work stoppage) *nf* shveet|ah/-ot (+*of:* -at); **2.** מכה (blow) *nf* mak|ah/-ot (+*of:* -at); **3.** התקפה (attack) *nf* hatkaf|ah/-ot (+*of:* -at); **4.** גילוי (discovery) *nm* geeloo|y/-yeem (*pl+of:* -yey).

(hunger) strike שביתת רעב *nf* shveet|at/-ot ra'av.

(sit down) strike שביתת שבת *nf* shveet|at/-ot shevet.

(to) strike 1. לשבות (cease work) *inf* leeshbot; *pst* shavat (*v=b*); *pres* shovet; *fut* yeeshbot; **2.** להיתקל (collide) *inf* leheetakel; *pst & adj* neetkal; *fut* yeetakel; **3.** להדליק גפרור (a match) *inf* lehadleek gafroor; *pst* heedleek *etc*; *pres* madleek *etc*; *fut* yadleek *etc*.

(to) strike at להלום *inf* lahalom; *pst* halam; *pres* holem; *fut* yahalom.

(to) strike off למחוק *inf* leemkhok; *pst* makhak; *pres* mokhek; *fut* yeemkhok.

(to) strike one's attention לעורר תשומת לב *inf* le'orer tesoomet lev; *pst* 'orer *etc*; *pres* me'orer *etc*; *fut* ye'orer *etc*.

(to) strike one's head against להטיח ראש ב־ *inf* lehatee'akh rosh be-; *pst* heetee'akh *etc*; *pres* matee'akh *etc*; *fut* yatee'akh *etc*.

(to) strike out in a certain direction לפנות לכיוון מסויים *inf* leefnot le-keevoon mesooyam; *pst* panah (*p=f*) *etc*; *pres* poneh *etc*; *fut* yeefneh *etc*.

(to) strike someone for a loan לסחוט ממישהו הלוואה *inf* leeskhot mee-meeshehoo halva'ah; *pst* sakhat *etc*; *pres* sokhet *etc*; *fut* yeeskhat *etc*.

(to) strike up a friendship לקשור ידידות *inf* leekshor yedeedoot; *pst* kashar *etc*; *pres* kosher *etc*; *fut* yeekshor *etc*.

(to) strike with terror להטיל פחד *inf* lehateel pakhad; *pst* heeteel *etc*; *pres* mateel *etc*; *fut* yateel *etc*.

(how does he/she) strike you? ?איך הוא נראה לך eykh hoo/hee (*m/f*) neer|'eh/-'et (*m/f*) lekha/lakh (*m/f*)?

strikebreaker מפיר שביתה *nmf* mefeer/-at (*pl:* -ey) shveetah.
striker שובת *nmf* shov|et/-etet (*pl:* -teem; *+of:* -tey).
striking מרשים (impressive) *adj* marsheem/-ah.
string 1. מיתר *nm* meytar/-eem (*pl+of:* -ey); **2.** חוט (thread) *nm* khoot/-eem (*pl+of:* -ey).
(to) string 1. לקשור *inf* leekshor; *pst* kashar; *pres* kosher; *fut* yeekshor; **2.** למתוח (stretch) *inf* leemto'akh; *pst* matakh; *pres* mote'akh; *fut* yeemtakh.
string bean שעועית *nf* she'oo'ee|t/-yot.
string of lies מסכת שקרים *nf* masekhet shekareem.
(to) string out להתמשך *inf* leheetmashekh; *pst* heetmashekh; *pres* meetmashekh; *fut* yeetmashekh.
(to) string up 1. לתלות *inf* leetlot; *pst* talah; *pres* toleh; *fut* yeetleh; **2.** לעצבן (enervate) *inf* le'atsben; *pst* 'eetsben; *pres* me'atsben; *fut* ye'atsben.
(pulling) strings פרוטקציה *[colloq.]* *nf* protekts|yah/-yot.
sringstrip רצועה *nf* retsoo|'ah/-'ot (*+of:* -'at).
(the Gaza) Strip 1. רצועת עזה *nf* retsoo'at 'azah; **2.** הרצועה *[colloq.]* ha-retsoo'ah.
(to) strip naked להפשיט ערום *inf* lehafsheet 'arom; *pst* heefsheet *etc*; *pres* mafsheet *etc*; *fut* yafsheet *etc*.
strip of land רצועת אדמה *nf* retsoo|'at/-'ot adamah.
(to) strip the gears להרוס את המהלכים *inf* laharos et ha-mahalakheem; *pst* haras *etc*; *pres* hores *etc*; *fut* yaharos *etc*.
(to) strip the skin from לפשוט את העור מעל *inf* leefshot et ha-'or me-'al; *pst* pashat *(p=f) etc*; *pres* poshet *etc*; *fut* yeefshot *etc*.
stripe 1. סרט (band) *nm* seret/srateem (*pl+of:* seertey); **2.** סימן דרגה (rank *symbol*) *nm* seeman/-ey dargah; **3.** סוג (kind) *nm* soog/-eem (*pl+of:* -ey).
(to) stripe לסמן בפסים *inf* lesamen be-faseem *(f=p)*; *pst* seemen *etc*; *pres* mesamen *etc*; *fut* yesamen *etc*.
striped מסומן בפסים *adj* mesoom|an/-enet be-faseem *(f=p)*.
(to) strive להתאמץ *inf* leheet'amets; *pst* heet'amets; *pres* meet'amets; *fut* yeet'amets.
(to) strive to לשאוף אל *inf* leesh'of el; *pst* sha'af el; *pres* sho'ef el; *fut* yeesh'af el.
stroke 1. חבטה (blow) *nf* khavat|ah/-ot (*+of:* -at); **2.** צלצול (sound) *nm* tseeltsool/-eem (*pl+of:* -ey).
(apoplectic) stroke מכת שבץ *nf* mak|at/-ot shavats.
(breast) stroke שחיית חזה *nf* sekheeyat khazeh.
(to) stroke ללטף *inf* lelatef; *pst* leetef; *pres* melatef; *fut* yelatef.
stroke of a bell צלצול פעמון *nm* tseeltsool/-ey pa'amon.
stroke of a painter's brush משיחת מיכחול *nf* mesheekh|at/-ot meekhekhol.
(at the) stroke of five משיצלצל השעון חמש mee-she-yetsaltsel ha-sha'on khamesh.
stroke of lightning מכת ברק *nf* mak|at/-ot barak.
stroke of the hand מחי יד *nm* mekhee yad.
stroke of the pen מחי עט *nm* mekhee 'et.
stroll טיול נינוח ברגל *nm* teeyool/-eem neeno|'akh/-kheem be-regel.
(to) stroll לשוטט רגלי *inf* leshotet raglee; *pst* shotet *etc*; *pres* meshotet *etc*; *fut* yeshotet *etc*.
(to) stroll the streets לשוטט ברחובות *inf* leshotet ba-rekhovot; *pst* shotet *etc*; *pres* meshotet *etc*; *fut* yeshotet *etc*.
strong חזק *adj* khazak/-ah.
strong chance סיכוי מובהק *nm* seekooy moovhak.
strong coffee קפה חריף *nm* kafeh khareef.
strong market שוק איתן *nm* shook eytan.
strong-willed בעל רצון איתן *adj* ba'al/-at ratson eytan.
strong arm זרוע איתנה *nf* zro'a' eytanah.
stronghold מעוז *nm* ma'oz/ma'ooz|eem (*pl+of:* -ey).
strop רצועת השחזה *nf* retsoo|'at/-'ot hashkhazah.
(to) strop להשחיז ברצועה *inf* lehashkheez bee-retsoo'ah; *pst* heeshkheez *etc*; *pres* mashkheez *etc*; *fut* yashkheez *etc*.
struck with disease נגוע במחלה *adj* nagoo'a'/negoo'ah be-makhalah.
struck with terror מוכה פחדים *adj* mook|eh/-at pekhadeem.
structural מיבני *adj* meevnee/-t.
structure מיבנה *nm* meevn|eh/-eem (*pl+of:* -ey).
struggle מאבק *nm* ma'avak/-eem (*pl+of:* -ey).
(to) struggle להיאבק *inf* lehe'avek; *pst & pres* ne'evak; *fut* ye'avek.
stub 1. גדם *nm* ged|em/-ameem (*pl+of:* geedmey); **2.** תלוש (coupon) *nm* teloosh/-eem (*pl+of:* -ey).
stub book פינקס תלושים *nm* peenkes/-ey telooshеem.
stub of a cigarette בדל סיגריה *nm* bedal/beedley seegaree|yah/-yot.
stubble 1. שלף (corn, grain) *nm* shelef/shlafeem (*pl+of:* sheelfey); **2.** זיפי זקן (beard) *nm pl* zeefey zakan.
stubborn עיקש *adj* 'eekesh/-et.
stubborness 1. עקשנות *nf* 'akshanoo|t/-yot; **2.** עיקשות (obstinacy) *nf* 'eekshoo|t/-yot.
stucco 1. טיח חוץ *nm* tee'akh khoots; **2.** שפריץ *[colloq.]* shpreets/-eem.
stuck on משוגע אחרי *adj* meshoog|a'/-a'at akharey.
stuck up 1. מתייהר *adj* meetyaher/-et; **2.** משתחץ *[colloq.]* *adj* meeshtakhets/-et.
stud 1. גולה (knob) *nf* gool|ah/-ot (*+of:* -at); **2.** בורג (bolt) *nm* boreg/brageem (*pl+of:* borgey); **3.** כפתור (button) *nm* kaftor/-eem (*pl+of:* -ey).
student 1. סטודנט (university) *nmf* stoodent/-eet (*pl:* -eem/-eeyot); **2.** תלמיד (pupil) *nm* talmeed/-ah (*pl:* -eem/-ot; *+of:* -at).
studhorse סוס הרבעה *nm* soos/-ey harba'ah.
studied מלומד *adj* meloom|ad/-edet.
studio 1. אולפן *nm* oolpan/-eem (*pl+of:* -ey); **2.** סטודיו *nm* stoodyo.
studious חרוץ *adj* kharoots/-ah.
study 1. מחקר (research) *nm* mekhkar/-eem (*pl+of:* -ey); **2.** חדר עבודה (room) *nm* khad|ar/-rey 'avodah.
(to) study 1. ללמוד *inf* leelmod; *pst* lamad; *pres* lomed; *fut* yeelmad; **2.** לחקור (research) *inf* lakhkor; *pst* khakar; *fut* khoker; *fut* yakhkor.

stuff 1. חומר (material) *m* khom|er/-oreem (*pl+of:* -rey); **2.** אריג (cloth) *nm* areeg/-eem (*pl+of:* -ey); **3.** דבר (thing) *nm* davar/dvareem (*pl+of:* deevrey); **4.** תרופה (medicine) *nf* troof|ah/-ot (*+of:* -at); **5.** פסולת (junk) *nf* pesolet.

(of good) stuff מאריג משובח *adj* me-areeg meshoobakh.

(to) stuff להלעיט *inf* lehal'eet; *pst* heel'eet; *pres* mal'eet; *fut* yal'eet.

stuffing פיטום *nm* peetoom/-eem (*pl+of:* -ey).

(to) stumble 1. להיכשל (fail) *inf* leheekashel; *pst & adj* neekhshal *(kh=k)*; *fut* yeekashel; **2.** למעוד (slip) *inf* leem'od; *pst* ma'ad; *pres* mo'ed; *fut* yeem'ad.

(to) stumble upon להיתקל ב־ *inf* leheetakel be-; *pst & adj* neetkal be-; *fut* yeetakel be-.

stump 1. גדם *nm* gedem/gdameem (*pl+of:* geedmey); **2.** נאום בחירות (elections speech) *nm* ne'oom/-ey bekheerot.

(to) stump לגדוע *inf* leegdo'a'; *pst* gada'; *pres* gode'a'; *fut* yeegda'.

stump of a tail גדם זנב *nm* gedem/geedmey zanav/znavot.

(to) stump the country לצאת למסע נאומים *inf* latset be-masa' ne'oomeem; *pst* yatsa *etc*; *pres* yotse *etc*; *fut* yetse *etc*.

stumpy גוץ ושמן *adj* goots/-ah ve/'oo shamen/shmenah.

(to) stun להדהים *inf* lehadheem; *pst* heedheem; *pres* madheem; *fut* yadheem.

stunning 1. מדהים *adj* madheem/-ah; **2.** נפלא (marvelous) *adj* neefla/-'ah.

stunt 1. מעשה נועז *nm* ma'as|eh/-eem no'az/-eem; **2.** קונץ *[colloq.] nm* koonts/-eem (*pl+of:* -ey).

(to) stunt להפליא לעשות *inf* lehaflee' la'asot; *pst* heeflee *etc*; *pres* maflee *etc*; *fut* yaflee *etc*.

stupefaction טמטום *nm* teemtoom/-eem (*pl+of:* -ey).

(to) stupefy לטמטם *inf* letamtem; *pst* teemtem; *pres* metamtem; *fut* yetamtem.

stupendous 1. כביר *adj* kabeer/-ah; **2.** עצום (great) *adj* 'atsoom/-ah.

stupid טיפשי *adj* teepshee/-t.

stupidity טיפשות *nf* teepshoo|t/-yot.

stupor הלם *nm* helem.

(in a) stupor בהלם *adv* be-helem.

sturdy 1. איתן *adj* eytan/-ah; **2.** תקיף (resolute) *adj* takeef/-ah.

stutter גמגום *nm* geemgoom/-eem (*pl+of:* -ey).

(to) stutter לגמגם *inf* legamgem; *pst* geemgem; *pres* megamgem; *fut* yegamgem.

stutterer גמגמן *nmf* gamgeman/-eet.

stuttering 1. גמגום *nm* geemgoom/-eem (*pl+of:* -ey); **2.** מגמגם *adj* megamgem/-et.

style סגנון *nm* seegnon/-ot.

(in) style במיטב האופנה *adv* be-meytav ha-ofnah.

(to) style 1. לכנות (name) *inf* lekhanot; *pst* keenah *(k=kh)*; *pres* mekhaneh; *fut* yekhaneh; **2.** לעצב (design) *inf* le'atsev; *pst* 'eetsev; *pres* me'atsev; *fut* ye'atsev.

(to) style a dress לגזור לבוש אופנתי *inf* leegzor levoosh ofnatee; *pst* gazar *etc*; *pres* gozer *etc*; *fut* yeegzor *etc*.

stylish 1. מסוגנן *adj* mesoogn|an/-enet; **2.** אופנתי (fashionable) *adj* ofnatee/-t.

(hair) stylist מעצב שיער *nmf* me'atsev/-et se'ar.

(to) stylize לסגנן *inf* lesagnen; *pst* seegnen; *pres* mesagnen; *fut* yesagnen.

subdivision חלוקת משנה *nf* khalook|at/-ot meeshneh.

(to) subdue להדביר *inf* lehadbeer; *pst* heedbeer; *pres* madbeer; *fut* yadbeer.

subdued מרוכך *adj* merook|akh/-ekhet.

subdued light תאורה מעומעמת *nf* te'oorah me'oom'emet.

subject 1. נושא (grammar: topic) *nm* nos|e/-'eem **2.** נתין (national) *nmf* nateen/neteen|ah (*pl:* -eem; *+of:* -ey); **3.** מקצוע לימוד (study) meektso|'a'/-'ot leemood.

subject 1. מותנה *adj* mootn|eh/-eyt; **2.** כפוף *adj* kafoof/kefoofah.

(to) subject 1. לחשוף ל־ *inf* lakhsof; *pst* khasaf; *pres* khosef; *fut* yakhsof; **2.** להכניע *inf* lehakhnee'a'; *pst* heekhnee'a'; *pres* makhnee'a'; *fut* yakhnee'a'.

subjection 1. חישוף *nm* kheesoof/-eem (*pl+of:* -ey); **2.** הכנעה *nf* hakhna|'ah/-'ot (*+of:* -at).

subjective 1. אישי *adj* eeshee/-t; **2.** סובייקטיבי *adj* soobyekteevee/-t.

(to) subjugate לשעבד *inf* lesha'bed; *pst* shee'bed; *pres* mesha'bed; *fut* yesha'bed.

(to) sublet להשכיר בשכירות־משנה *inf* lehaskeer bee-s'kheeroot meeshneh; *pst* heeskeer *etc*; *pres* maskeer *etc*; *fut* yaskeer *etc*.

(to) sublimate 1. לזכך *inf* lezakekh; *pst* zeekekh; *pres* mezakekh; *fut* yezakekh; **2.** לזקק (refine) *inf* lezakek; *pst* zeekek; *pres* mezakek; *fut* yezakek.

sublime נשגב *adj* neesgav/-ah.

submachine-gun תת־מקלע *nm* tat-makle|'a'/-'eem (*pl+of:* -'ey).

submarine 1. צוללת *nf* tsolel|et/-ot; **2.** תת־ימי *adj* tat-yamee/-t.

(to) submerge לצלול *inf* leetslol; *pst* tsalal; *pres* tsolel; *fut* yeetslol.

submission 1. כניעה (yielding) *nf* kenee|'ah/-'ot (*+of:* -'at); **2.** הגשה (presenting) *nf* hagash|ah/-ot (*+of:* -at).

submissive צייתני *adj* tsaytanee/-t.

(to) submit 1. להיכנע (surrender) *inf* leheekana'; *pst & pres* neekhna' *(kh=k)*; *fut* yeekana'; **2.** להגיש (put forward) *inf* lehageesh; *pst* heegeesh; *pres* mageesh; *fut* yageesh; **3.** לטעון (claim) *inf* leet'on; *pst* ta'an; *pres* to'en; *fut* yeet'an.

(to) submit a report להגיש דו״ח *inf* lehageesh doo'akh; *pst* heegeesh *etc*; *pres* mageesh *etc*; *fut* yageesh *etc*.

(to) submit to punishment לקבל את הדין *inf* lekabel et ha-deen; *pst* keebel *etc*; *pres* mekabel *etc*; *fut* yekabel *etc*.

subordinate 1. פקוד *nmf* pakood/pekood|ah (*pl:* -eem/-ot; *pl+of:* -ey); **2.** נחות (inferior) *adj* nakhoot/nekhootah.

subpoena הזמנה לבית משפט *nf* hazman|ah/-ot le-vet *(v=b)* meeshpat.

(to) subpoena להזמין להתייצב בבית משפט *inf* lehazmeen leheetyatsev be-vet *(v=b)* meeshpat; *pst* heezmeen; *pres* mazmeen *etc; fut* yazmeen *etc.*

(to) subscribe 1. לחתום *inf* lakhtom; *pst* khatam; *pres* khotem; *fut* yakhtom; **2.** לחתום כמנוי *inf* lakhtom ke-manooy; *pst* khatam *etc; pres* khotem *etc; fut* yakhtom *etc.*

(to) subscribe ten shekels לתרום עשרה שקלים *inf* leetrom 'asarah shekaleem; *pst* taram *etc; pres* torem *etc; fut* yeetrom *etc.*

subscriber מנוי *nmf* manooy/menoo|yah (*pl:* -yeem; *pl+of:* -yey).

subscription 1. דמי חתימה *nm pl* demey khatee-m|ah/-ot; **2.** דמי מנוי *nm pl* dmey manooy/menooyeem.

subsequent הבא אחריו *adj* ha-ba/-'ah akhr|av/-eha.

subsequently לאחר כך *adv* le-akhar kakh.

subservient מתרפס *adj* meetrapes/-et.

(to) subside 1. לשכוך *inf* leeshkokh; *pst* shakhakh *(kh=k); pres* shokhekh; *fut* yeeshkakh; **2.** לשקוע *inf* leeshko'a'; *pst* shaka'; *pres* shoke'a'; *fut* yeeshka'.

(to) subsidize לסבסד *inf* lesabsed; *pst* seebsed; *pres* mesabsed; *fut* yesabsed.

subsidy סובסידיה *nf* soobseed|yah/-yot (*+of:* -yat).

(to) subsist 1. להתקיים *v rfl inf* leheetkayem; *pst* heetkayem; *pres* meetkayem; *fut* yeetkayem; **2.** להחזיק מעמד (hold on) *inf* lehakhzeek ma'mad; *pst* hekhzeek *etc; pres* makhzeek *etc; fut* yakhzeek *etc.*

subsistence 1. קיום *nm* keeyoom/-eem (*pl+of:* -ey); **2.** מחיה (sustenance) *nf* meekh|yah (*+of:* -yat).

substantial מהותי *adj* mahootee/-t.

(in) substantial agreement תוך הסכמה עקרונית *adv* tokh haskamah 'ekroneet.

(to) substantiate 1. לאמת *inf* le'amet; *pst* eemet; *pres* me'amet; *fut* ye'amet; **2.** לבסס (establish) *inf* levases; *pst* beeses *(b=v); pres* mevases; *fut* yevases.

substantive 1. שם עצם (grammar) *nm* shem/shmot 'etsem; **2.** מהותי (substantial) *adj* mahootee/-t.

substitute 1. תחליף *nm* takhleef/-eem (*pl+of:* -ey); **2.** ממלא מקום (replacement) *nmf* memal|e/-et makom.

(to) substitute 1. להחליף *inf* lehakhleef; *pst* hekhleef; *pres* makhleef; *fut* yakhleef; **2.** לשים במקום (replace) *inf* laseem bee-m'kom; *pst & pres* sam *etc; fut* yaseem *etc.*

substitution 1. החלפה *nf* hakhlaf|ah/-ot (*+of:* -at); **2.** המרה (exchange) *nf* hamar|ah/-ot (*+of:* -at).

substratum שיכבת יסוד *nf* sheekhv|at/-ot yesod.

subterfuge תחבולה *nf* takhbool|ah/-ot (*+of:* -at).

subterranean תת־קרקעי *adj* tat-karka'ee/-t.

subtitle כותרת משנה *nf* kot|eret/-rot meeshneh.

subtitles 1. כתוביות (film, tv) *nf pl* ketooveeyot (*sing:* ketooveet); **2.** תרגום בגוף הסרט *[colloq.] nm* teergoom/-eem be-goof ha-seret.

subtle שנון *adj* shanoon/shnoonah.

subtlety 1. שנינות *nf* shneenoo|t/-yot; **2.** אבחנה דקה (refined distinction) *nf* avkhan|ah/-ot dak|ah/-ot.

(to) subtract לחסר *inf* lekhaser; *pst* kheeser; *pres* mekhaser; *fut* yekhaser.

subtraction חיסור *nm* kheesoor/-eem (*pl+of:* -ey).

suburb פרבר *nm* parbar/-eem (*pl+of:* -ey).

suburban פרברי *adj* parbaree/-t.

suburbia הפרברים *nm pl* ha-parbareem.

subvention 1. מענק *nm* ma'an|ak/-akeem (*pl+of:* -key); **2.** סובסידיה *nf* soobseed|yah/-yot (*+of:* -at).

subversive חתרני *adj* khatranee/-t.

subway 1. רכבת תחתית (train) *nf* rak|evet/-avot takhteet; **2.** מעבר תת־קרקעי (passage) *nm* ma'avar/-eem tat-karka'ee/-yeem.

(to) succeed 1. להצליח *inf* lehatslee'akh; *pst* heetslee'akh; *pres* matslee'akh; *fut* yatslee'akh; **2.** לבוא במקום (follow, replace) *inf* lavo bee-m'kom; *pst & pres* ba *etc; fut* yavo *etc.*

success הצלחה *nf* hatslakh|ah/-ot (*+of:* -at).

successful 1. מצליח *adj* matslee|'akh/-khah; **2.** מוצלח (fortunate) *adj* mootslakh/-at.

successfully בהצלחה *adv* be-hatslakhah.

succession 1. רצף (sequence) *nm* rets|ef/-afeem (*pl+of:* retsfey); **2.** ירושה (heritage) *nf* yeroo-sh|ah/-ot (*+of:* -at).

successive רצוף *adj* ratsoof/retsoofah.

successor יורש *nmf* yor|esh/-eshet (*pl:* -sheem; *+of:* -shey).

succor 1. תמיכה *nf* temeekh|ah/-ot (*+of:* -at); **2.** עזרה (aid) 'ezr|ah (*+of:* -at).

(to) succor לסייע *inf* lesaye'a'; *pst* seeya'; *pres* mesaye'a'; *fut* yesaya'.

(to) succumb 1. להיכנע *inf* leheekana'; *pst & pres* neekhna' *(kh=k); fut* yeekana'; **2.** למות (die) lamoot; *pst & pres* met; *fut* yamoot.

such 1. כזה *adj* ka-zeh/-zot; **2.** כזאתי *[colloq.] adj nf* kazotee.

such a 1. שכזה *adj* she-ka-zeh/-zot; **2.** שכזאתי *[colloq.] adj nf* she-ka-zotee.

such a good man כזה אדם טוב *[colloq.]* ka-zeh adam tov.

(at) such an hour בשעה שכזאת *adv* be-sha'ah she-ka-zot.

(at) such and such place במקום זה וזה *adv* be-makom zeh va-zeh.

such as 1. כגון ke-gon; **2.** דוגמת *adj* doogmat

suck 1. מציצה *nf* metseets|ah/-ot (*+of:* -at); **2.** יניקה (mother's milk) *nf* yeneek|ah/-ot (*+of:* -at).

(to) suck 1. למצוץ *inf* leemtsots; *pst* matsats; *pres* motsets; *fut* yeemtsots; **2.** לינוק (mother's milk) *inf* leenok; *pst* yanak; *pres* yonek; *fut* yeenok.

(to) suck up למצוץ עד תום *inf* leemtsots 'ad tom; *pst* matsats *etc; pres* motsets *etc; fut* yeemtsots *etc;*

sucker 1. ינוקא *nm* yanooka; **2.** יונק *nmf* yon|ek/-eket (*pl:* -keem; *+of:* -key); **3.** פראייר *[slang] nmf* frayer/-eet (*pl:* -eem; *+of:* -ey).

(to) suckle להניק *inf* lehaneek; *pst (f)* heneekah; *pres (f)* meneekah; *fut (f)* taneek.

suction 1. מציצה (with lips) *nf* metseets|ah/-ot (*+of:* -at); **2.** שאיבה (with pump) *nf* she'eev|ah/-ot (*+of:* -at).

sudden פתאומי *adj* peet'omee/-t.

(all of a) sudden לפתע פיתאום *adv* le-feta' *(f=p)* peet'om.

suddenly לפתע *adv* le-feta' *(f=p).*
suddenness פתאומיות *nf* peet'omeeyoot.
suds קצף סבון *nm* ketsef sabon.
(to) sue לתבוע לדין *inf* leetbo'a' le-deen; *pst* tava' *(v=b) etc; pres* tove'a' *etc; fut* yeetba' *etc.*
(to) sue for damages לתבוע נזקים *inf* leetbo'a' nezakeem; *pst* tava' *(v=b) etc; pres* tove'a' *etc; fut* yeetba' *etc.*
(to) sue for peace לבקש שלום *inf* levakesh shalom; *pst* beekesh *(b=v) etc; pres* mevakesh *etc; fut* yevakesh *etc.*
suet 1. חלב בהמות *nm* khelev behemot; **2.** שומן כליות (kidney fat) *nm* shooman klayot.
(to) suffer 1. לסבול *inf* leesbol; *pst* saval *(v=b); pres* sovel; *fut* yeesbol; **2.** לגלות סובלנות (tolerate) *inf* legalot sovlanoot; *pst* geelah *etc; pres* megaleh *etc; fut* yegaleh *etc.*
sufferer סובל *nmf & adj* sovel/-et (*pl:* sovl|eem; *+of:* -ey).
suffering 1. ייסורים *nm pl* yeesoor|eem (*pl+of:* -ey); **2.** סבל (pain) *nm* sev|el/-alot (*pl+of:* seevlot); **3.** סובל *adj* sovel/-et.
(to) suffice להספיק *inf* lehaspeek; *pst* heespeek; *pres* maspeek; *fut* yaspeek.
sufficient מספיק *adj* masp|eek/-eket.
sufficiently במידה מספקת be-meedah maspeket.
suffix סיומת *nf* seeyom|et/-ot.
(to) suffocate 1. לחנוק *vt* lakhnok; *pst* khanak; *pres* khonek; *fut* yakhnok; **2.** להיחנק *vi* lehekhanek; *pst & pres* nekhnak; *fut* yekhanek.
suffocation מחנק *nm* makhnak/-eem (*pl+of:* -ey).
suffrage זכות הצבעה *nf* zekhoo|t/-yot hatsba'ah.
sugar סוכר *nm* sookar/-eem (*pl+of:* -ey).
(lump of) sugar חפיסת סוכר *nf* khafees|at/-ot sookar.
(to) sugar להמתיק *inf* lehamteek; *pst* heemteek; *pres* mamteek; *fut* yamteek.
sugar bowl מסכרת *nf* meesk|eret/-arot.
sugar cane קנה סוכר *nm* keneh sookar.
(to) suggest 1. להציע (propose) *inf* lehatsee'a'; *pst* heetsee'a'; *pres* matsee'a'; *fut* yatsee'a'; **2.** לרמוז (hint) *inf* leermoz; *pst* ramaz; *pres* romez; *fut* yeermoz.
suggestion הצעה *nf* hatsa|'ah/-'ot (*+of:* -'at).
suggestive מרמז *adj* meramez/-et.
suicide התאבדות *nf* heet'abdoo|t/-yot.
(to commit) suicide להתאבד *inf* leheet'abed; *pst* heet'abed; *pres* meet'abed; *fut* yeet'abed.
suit 1. חליפה (clothing) *nf* khaleef|ah/-ot (*+of:* -at); **2.** תביעה (law) *nf* tvee|'ah/-'ot (*+of:* -'at); **3.** סדרה (cards) *nf* seedrah/sdarot (*+of:* seedrat).
(to) suit 1. להלום *nf* lahalom; *pst* halam; *pres* holem; *fut* yahalom; **2.** להתאים (fit) *inf* lehat'eem; *pst* heet'eem; *pres* mat'eem; *fut* yat'eem.
suit yourself עשה כטוב בעיניך *v imp sing* 'aseh/'asee ka-tov be-'eyn|ekha/-ayeekh *(m/f).*
suitable 1. הולם *adj* holem/-et; **2.** מתאים (befitting) *adj* mat'eem/-ah.
suitably בצורה הולמת *adv* be-tsoorah holemet.
suitcase מזוודה *nf* meezv|adah/-adot (*+of:* -edet).
suite פמליה *nf* pamal|yah/-yot (*+of:* -yat).
(bedroom) suite מערכת חדרי שינה ma'arekhet khadrey sheynah.
suite of rooms מערכת חדרים *nf* ma'arekhet khadareem.
suitor מחזר *nm* mekhaz|er/-reem (*pl+of:* -rey).
sulfa drug תרופת סולפה *nf* troof|at/-ot soolfah.
sulfate to **sulfuric** see **sulphate** to **sulphuric**.
sulk שתיקה רועמת *nf* sheteek|ah/-ot ro'emet/ro'amot.
(to) sulk לשתוק בזעם *inf* leeshtok be-za'am; *pst* shatak *etc; pres* shotek *etc; fut* yeeshtok *etc.*
sulky מצוברח *adj* metsoovrakh/-at.
sullen קודר ועוין *adj* koder/-et ve-'oyen/-et.
(to) sully 1. להכתים *inf* lehakhteem; *pst* heekhteem; *pres* makhteem; *fut* yakhteem; **2.** לטמא (profane) *inf* letame; *pst* teeme; *pres* metame; *fut* yetame.
sulphate גופרה *nf* gofr|ah/-ot (*+of:* -at).
sulphur גופרית *nf* gofreet.
sulphuric גופרתי *adj* gofratee/-t.
sulphuric acid חומצה גופרתית *nf* khoomts|ah/-ot gofratee|t/-yot.
sultan שולטן *nm* sooltan/-eem (*+of:* -ey).
sultry 1. לוהט ולח *adj* lohet/-et ve-lakh/-ah; **2.** חמסיני (weather) *adj* khamseenee/-t.
sultry heat 1. חום לוהט *nm* khom lohet; **2.** חמסין (weather) *nm* khamseen/-eem (*pl+of:* -ey).
sum 1. סכום *nm* sekhoom/-eem (*pl+of:* -ey); **2.** סך הכול (total) *nm* sakh ha-kol.
(total) sum סכום כולל *nm* skhoom/-eem kolel/-eem.
(to) sum up לסכם *inf* lesakem; *pst* seekem; *pres* mesakem; *fut* yesakem.
(to) summarize 1. לתמצת *inf* letamtset; *pst* teemtset; *pres* metamtset; *fut* yetamtset; **2.** לסכם (sum up) *inf* lesakem; *pst* seekem; *pres* mesakem; *fut* yesakem.
summary 1. תקציר *nm* taktseer/-eem (*pl+of:* -ey); **2.** מסכם בקיצור (covering briefly) *adj* mesakem/-et be-keetsoor.
summer קיץ *nm* kayeets/keyts|eem (*+of:* -ey).
summer resort נווה קיט *nm* neveh kayeet.
summer school לימודי קיץ *nm pl* leemoodey kayeets.
summersault 1. סבב כפול *nm* sevev kafool; **2.** סלטה *nf* salt|ah/-ot (*+of:* -at).
summit פסגה *nf* peesgah/pesagot (*+of:* peesg|at/-ot).
summit meeting מפגש פסגה *nm* meefg|ash/-eshey peesgah
(to) summon לצוות להתייצב letsavot leheetyatsev; *pst* tseevah *etc; pres* metsaveh *etc; fut* yetsaveh *etc.*
summons הזמנה לבית־משפט *nf* hazman|ah/-ot le-vet *(v=b)* meeshpat.
sumptuous 1. הדור *adj* hadoor/-ah; **2.** מפואר (luxurious) *adj* mefo|'ar/-'eret.
sun שמש *nf* shemesh/shmashot (*pl+of:* sheemshot).
sun bath אמבט שמש *nm* ambat/ambetey shemesh.
sun lamp מנורה כחולה *nf* menorah kekhoolah.
(to) sun oneself להשתזף *inf* leheeshtazef; *pst* heeshtazef; *pres* meeshtazef; *fut* yeeshtazef.
sunbeam קרן שמש *nf* keren/karney shemesh.
sunburn כוויית שמש *nf* kvee|yat/-yot shemesh.

(to) sunburn לקבל כוויות מהשמש *inf* lekabel kveeyot shemesh; *pst* keebel *etc*; *pres* mekabel *etc*; *fut* yekabel *etc*.
sundae גלידת פירות *nf* gleed|at/-ot perot.
Sunday 1. יום ראשון *nm* yom/yemey reeshon; **2.** יום א׳ *nm* yom/yemey alef.
Sunday best בגדי שבת *nm pl* beegdey shabat.
sundial שעון שמש *nm* she'on/-ey shemesh.
sundown שקיעת החמה *nf* shekee|'at/'ot ha-khamah.
sundry שונות *nf pl* shonot.
sunflower חמנית *nf* khamanee|t/-yot.
sunglasses משקפי שמש *nm pl* meeshkefey shemesh.
sunken שקוע *adj* shakoo'a'/shekoo'ah.
sunlight אור השמש *nm* or ha-shemesh.
sunny 1. מוצף שמש *adj* moots|af/-efet shemesh; **2.** בהיר (bright) *adj* baheer/beheerah.
sunny day יום שמש *nm* yom/yemey shemesh.
sunrise זריחת השמש *nf* zreekh|at/-ot ha-shemesh.
sunset שקיעת השמש *nf* shekee|'at/-ot ha-shemesh.
sunshine אור שמש *nm* or shemesh.
sunstroke מכת שמש *nf* mak|at/-ot shemesh.
suntan שיזוף *nm* sheezoof/-eem (*pl+of:* -ey).
(to) suntan להשתזף *inf* leheeshtazef; *pst* heeshtazef; *pres* meeshtazef; *fut* yeeshtazef.
(to) sup לסעוד סעודת ערב *inf* lees'od se'oodat 'erev.; *pst* sa'ad *etc*; *pres* so'ed *etc*; *fut* yees'ad *etc*.
superb נפלא *adj* neefla/-'ah.
superficial שטחי *adj* sheetkhee/-t.
superfluous מיותר *adj* meyoot|ar/-eret.
superhuman על-אנושי *adj* 'al-'enooshee/-t.
(to) superintend לפקח *inf* lefake'akh; *pst* peeke'akh (*p=f*); *pres* mefake'akh; *fut* yefake'akh.
superintendent 1. מפקח *nm* mefak|e'akh/-'kheem (*pl+of:* -'khey); **2.** רב-פקד (of police) *nm* rav/rabey (*b=v*) pakad/-eem.
superior 1. עולה על *adj* 'ol|eh/-ah 'al; **2.** ממונה על (in charge of) *nmf* memoon|eh/-ah 'al.
superiority 1. עדיפות (preference) *nf* 'adeefoo|t/-yot; **2.** עליונות (prominence) *nf* 'elyonoo|t/-yot.
superiority complex תסביך עליונות *nm* tasbeekh/-ey 'elyonoot.
superlative 1. עילאי *adj* 'eela'ee/-t; **2.** ערך ההפלגה (grammar) *nm* 'erekh ha-haflagah.
superman אדם עליון *nm* adam 'elyon.
supermarket 1. מרכול *nm* markol/-eem (*pl+of:* -ey); **2.** סופרמרקט *nm* soopermarket/-eem (*pl+of:* -ey).
supernatural על-טבעי *adj* 'al-teev'ee/-t.
(the) supernatural דברים שמחוץ לגדר הטבע *nm pl* dvareem she-mee-khoots le-geder ha-teva'.
(to) supersede לבוא במקום *inf* lavo bee-m'kom; *pst & pres* ba *etc*; *fut* yavo *etc*.
supersonic על-קולי *adj* 'al-kolee/-t.
superstition אמונה טפלה *nf* emoon|ah/-ot tefe-l|ah/-ot.
superstitious מאמין באמונות טפלות *adj* ma'ameen/-ah be-emoonot tefelot.
(to) supervise 1. להשגיח *inf* lehashgee'akh; *pst* heeshgee'akh; *pres* mashgee'akh; *fut* yashgee'akh; **2.** לפקח (superintend) *inf* lefake'akh; *pst* peekakh (*p=f*); *pres* mefake'akh; *fut* yefakakh.
supervision פיקוח *nm* peekoo|'akh/-kheem (*pl+of:* -khey).
supervisor משגיח *nm* mashgee'akh/-kheem-(*pl+of:* -khey).
supper ארוחת ערב *nf* arookh|at/-ot 'erev.
(to) supplant 1. לבוא במקום *inf* lavo bee-m'kom; *pst & pres* ba (*b=v*) *etc*; *fut* yavo *etc*; **2.** לשמש תחליף (substitute) *inf* leshamesh takhleef; *pst* sheemesh *etc*; *pres* meshamesh *etc*; *fut* yeshamesh *etc*.
supple 1. כפוף *adj* kafoof/kefoofah; **2.** גמיש (elastic) *adj* gameesh/gemeeshah.
supplement 1. תוספת *nf* tos|efet/-afot (*+of:* -fot); **2.** מוסף (newspaper) *nm* moosaf/-eem (*pl+of:* -ey).
(to) supplement 1. להשלים *inf* lehashleem; *pst* heeshleem; *pres* mashleem; *fut* yashleem; **2.** להוסיף (add) *inf* lehoseef; *pst* hoseef; *pres* moseef; *fut* yoseef.
suppliant, supplicant עותר *nm* 'ot|er/-eret (*pl:* -reem; *+of:* -rey).
supplication תחינה *nf* tekheen|ah/-ot (*+of:* -at).
supply 1. היצע *nm* hetse|'a'/-'eem (*pl+of:* -'ey); **2.** מלאי *nm* melay.
(to) supply 1. לספק *inf* lesapek; *pst* seepek; *pres* mesapek; *fut* yesapek; **2.** לצייד (equip) *inf* letsayed; *pst* tseeyed; *pres* metsayed; *fut* yetsayed.
supply and demand היצע וביקוש *nm & nm* hetse'a' oo- veekoosh (*v=b*).
supply pipe צינור הספקה *nm* tseenor/-ot haspakah.
supplies מלאי *nm* melay.
support 1. תמיכה *nf* temeekh|ah/-ot (*+of:* -at); **2.** סיוע (aid) *nm* seeyoo'a'.
(to) support 1. לתמוך (keep from falling) *inf* leetmokh; *pst* tamakh; *pres* tomekh; *fut* yeetmokh; **2.** לפרנס (provide for) *inf* lefarnes; *pst* peernes (*p=f*); *pres* mefarnes; *fut* yefarnes; **3.** לשאת (bear) *inf* laset; *pst* nasa; *pres* nose; *fut* yeesa.
supporter תומך *nmf* tom|ekh/-ekhet (*pl:* -kheem/-khot; *+of:* -khey).
(to) suppose 1. לשער *inf* lesha'er; *pst* shee'er; *pres* mesha'er; *fut* yesha'er; **2.** לסבור (assume) *inf* leesbor; *pst* savar (*v=b*); *pres* sover; *fut* yeesbor.
supposed 1. חייב (required) *adj* kha|yav-yevet; **2.** אמור (believed) *adj* amoor/-ah.
supposedly כמשוער *adv* ka-mesho'ar.
supposition השערה *nf* hash'ar|ah/-ot (*+of:* -at).
suppository פתילה *nf* peteel|ah/-ot (*+of:* -at).
(to) suppress לשים קץ *inf* laseem kets; *pst & pres* sam *etc*; *fut* yaseem *etc*.
(to) suppress 1. לדכא (revolt) *inf* ledake; *pst* deeka; *pres* medake; *fut* yedake; **2.** לסגור (newspaper) *inf* leesgor; *pst* sagar; *pres* soger; *fut* yeesgor; **3.** להדחיק (feelings) *inf* lehadkheek; *pst* heedkheek; *pres* madkheek; *fut* yadkheek; **4.** להעלים (information) *inf* leha'aleem; *pst* he'eleem; *pres* ma'aleem; *fut* ya'aleem.
suppression 1. דיכוי *nm* deekoo|y/-yeem (*pl+of:* -yey); **2.** סגירה (newspaper) *nf* segeer|ah/-ot (*+of:* -at); **3.** הדחקה (of feelings) *nf* hadkhak|ah/

-ot (+*of:* -at); **4.** העלמה (of information) *nf* ha'alam|ah/-ot (+*of:* -at).

supremacy עליונות *nf* 'elyonoo|t/-yot.

supreme עליון *adj* 'elyon/-ah.

sure 1. בטוח *adj* batoo'akh/betookhah; **2.** ודאי (certain) *adj* vada'ee/-t.

(be) sure to do it תדאג שזה ייעשה *[colloq.]* teed'ag/-ee *(m/f)* she-zeh yee'aseh.

surely 1. בטח *adv* betakh; **2.** בוודאי (certainly) *adv* be-vaday.

surety 1. ערבות (bail) *nf* 'arvoo|t/-yot; **2.** ערב (bailsman) *nmf* 'arev/-ah (*pl:* -eem; +*of:* -ey).

surf 1. דוכי *nm* dokhee/dekha|yeem (+*of:* dekh|ee/-ayey); **2.** קצף גלים (foam on waves) *nm* ketsef galeem.

surface פני השטח *nf* peney ha-shetakh.

surfboard מיגררת גלים *nf* meegrer|et/-ot galeem.

surfeit 1. זלילה *nf* zleel|ah/-ot (+*of:* -at); **2.** הפרזה (excess) *nf* hafraz|ah/-ot (+*of:* -at)

(to) surfeit 1. לזלול *inf* leezlol; *pst* zalal; *pres* zolel; *fut* yeezlol; **2.** להפריז (overindulge) *inf* lehafreez; *pst* heefreez; *pres* mafreez; *fut* yafreez.

surge התפרצות גלים *nf* heetpartsoo|t/-yot galeem.

(to) surge 1. לגעוש *inf* leeg'osh; *pst* ga'ash; *pres* go'esh; *fut* yeeg'ash; **2.** להתפרץ (erupt) leheetparets; *pst* heetparets; *pres* meetparets; *fut* yeetparets.

surgeon 1. מנתח *nm* menat|e'akh/-kheem (*pl+of:* khey); **2.** כירורג *nm* keeroorg/-eem (*pl+of:* -ey).

(dental) surgeon רופא שיניים *nmf* rofe/-t sheenayeem.

surgery כירורגיה *nf* keeroorgee|yah/-yot (+*of:* -yat).

surgical כירורגי *adj* keeroorgee/-t.

surly 1. חמוץ פנים *adj* khamoots/-at paneem; **2.** קודר (morose) *adj* koder/-et.

surmise 1. ניחוש *nm* neekhoosh/-eem (*pl+of:* -ey); **2.** סברה *nf* svar|ah/-ot (+*of:* -at).

(to) surmise לנחש *inf* lenakhesh; *pst* neekhesh; *pres* menakhesh; *fut* yenakhesh.

(to) surmount לגבור על *inf* leegbor 'al; *pst* gavar 'al *(v=b)*; *pres* gover 'al; *fut* yeegbor 'al.

surname 1. שם משפחה *nm* shem/-ot meeshpakhah; **2.** כינוי (nickname) *nm* kee-noo|y/-yeem (*pl+of:* -yey).

(to) surname לכנות *inf* lekhanot; *pst* keenah *(k=kh)*; *pres* mekhaneh; *fut* yekhaneh.

(to) surpass לעלות על *inf* la'alot 'al; *pst* 'alah 'al; *pres* 'oleh 'al; *fut* ya'aleh 'al.

surpassing עולה על *adj* 'ol|eh/-ah 'al.

surplus 1. עודף *nm* 'od|ef/-afeem (*pl+of:* -fey). **2.** עודף *adj* 'odef/-et.

surprise 1. אפתעה *nf* afta|'ah/-'ot (+*of:* -'at). **2.** תמיהה (bewilderment) *nf* temee|hah/-hot (+*of:* -hat).

(to) surprise להפתיע *inf* lehaftee'a'; *pst* heeftee'a'; *pres* maftee'a'; *fut* yaftee'a'.

surprising מפתיע *adj* maftee|'a'/-'ah.

surrender כניעה *nf* kenee|'ah/-'ot (+*of:* -'at).

(to) surrender להיכנע *inf* leheekana'; *pst & pres* neekhna' *(kh=k)*; *fut* yeekana'.

(to) surround 1. להקיף *inf* lehakeef; *pst* heekeef; *pres* makeef; *fut* yakeef; **2.** לכתר (encircle) *inf* lekhater; *pst* keeter *(k=kh)*; *pres* mekhater; *fut* yekhater.

surrounding מקיף *adj* makeef/-ah.

surroundings סביבה *nf* sveev|ah/-ot (+*of:* -at).

surtax מס יסף *nm* mas/meesey yesef.

survey 1. סקר (review) *nm* sek|er/-areem (*pl+of:* seekrey); **2.** מדידה (measure) *nf* medeed|ah/-ot (+*of:* -at); **3.** תכנון (plan) *nm* teekhnoon/-eem (*pl+of:* -ey).

survey course קורס כללי כולל *nm* koors klalee kolel.

(public opinion) survey סקר דעת קהל *nm* seker/seekrey da'at kahal.

(to) survey 1. לסקור *inf* leeskor; *pst* sakar; *pres* soker; *fut* yeeskor; **2.** למדוד (measure) *inf* leemdod; *pst* madad; *pres* moded; *fut* yeemdod.

surveyor מודד *nm* moded/-eem (*pl+of:* -ey).

survival הישרדות *nf* heesardoot.

(to) survive 1. לשרוד *inf* leesrod; *pst* sarad; *pres* sored; *fut* yeesrod; **2.** להישאר בחיים (remain alive) *inf* leheesha'er ba-khayeem; *pst & pres* neesh'ar etc; *fut* yeesha'er *etc.*

survivor שריד *nmf* sareed/sreed|ah (*pl:* -eem; *pl+of:* -ey).

susceptible 1. ניתן *adj* neet|an/-enet; **2.** רגיש *adj* rageesh/regeeshah.

susceptible of proof ניתן להוכחה *adj* neet|an/-enet le-hokhakhah.

susceptible to עלול *adj* 'alool/-ah.

suspect חשוד *nmf & adj* khashood/-ah (*pl:* -eem; +*of:* -ey).

(to) suspect לחשוד *inf* lakhshod; *pst* khashad; *pres* khoshed; *fut* yakhshod.

(to) suspend 1. להפסיק זמנית *inf* lehafseek zmaneet; *pst* heefseek *etc*; *pres* mafseek *etc*; *fut* yafseek *etc*; **2.** להתלות (defer) *inf* lehatlot; *pst* heetlah; *pres* matleh; *fut* yatleh; **3.** להשעות (debar) *inf* lehash'ot; *pst* heesh'ah; *pres* mash'eh; *fut* yash'eh.

suspenders כתפות *nf pl* ketefot.

suspense מתח *nm* metakh/-eem (*pl+of:* -ey).

(in) suspense בחוסר ודאות *adv* be-khoser vada'oot.

suspension התלייה *nf* hatla|yah/-yot (+*of:* -yat).

suspension bridge גשר תלוי *nm* gesh|er/-areem talooy/telooyeem.

suspicion חשד *nm* khashad/-ot.

suspicious חשדן *nmf adj* khashdan/-eet.

(to) sustain 1. להאריך (prolong) *inf* leha'areekh; *pst* he'ereekh; *pres* ma'areekh; *fut* ya'areekh; **2.** לתמוך (support) *inf* leetmokh; *pst* tamakh; *pres* tomekh; *fut* yeetmokh; **3.** לשאת (bear) *inf* laset; *pst* nasa; *pres* nose; *fut* yeesa; **4.** לאמת (confirm) *inf* le'amet; *pst* eemet; *pres* me'amet; *fut* ye'amet.

sustenance אמצעי מחיה *nm pl* emtse'ey meekhyah.

swagger הילוך מתרברב *nm* heelookh meetravrev.

(to) swagger להתרברב *inf* leheetravrev; *pst* heetravrev; *pres* meetravrev; *fut* yeetravrev.

swain מאהב בן כפר *nm* me'a|hev/-haveem ben/-ey kefar.

swallow 1. בליעה *nf* blee|'ah/-'ot (+*of:* -'at); **2.** לגימה (liquid) *nf* legeem|ah/-ot (+*of:* -at); **3.** סנונית (bird) snoonee|t/-yot.

swamp ביצה *nf* beets|ah/-ot (+*of:* -at).

(to) swamp להציף *inf* lehatseef; *pst* hetseef; *pres* metseef; *fut* yatseef.

swamp land אדמת ביצה *nf* adm|at/-ot beetsah.

swamped with work מוצף עבודה *adj* moots|af/-efet 'avodah.

swampy 1. ביצתי *adj* beetsatee/-t; **2.** טובעני (marshy) *adj* tov'anee/-t.

swan ברבור *nm* barboor/-eem (*pl+of:* -ey).

swap חילופין *nm pl* kheeloof|een (*pl+of:* -ey).

(to) swap להתחלף ב־ *inf* leheetkhalef be-; *pst* heetkhalef be-; *pres* meetkhalef be-; *fut* yeetkhalef be-.

swarm נחיל *nm* nekheel/-eem (*pl+of:* -ey).

(to) swarm לשרוץ *inf* leeshrots; *pst* sharats; *pres* shorets; *fut* yeeshrots.

swarthy שחרחר *inf* shkharkhar/-ah.

swastika צלב קרס *nm* tslav/-ey keres.

(to) swat לחבוט *inf* lakhbot; *pst* khavat *(v=b)*; *pres* khovet; *fut* yakhbot.

sway 1. נענוע *nm* na'anoo|'a'/-'eem (*pl+of:* -'ey); **2.** שליטה (rule) *nf* shleet|ah/-ot (+*of:* -at).

(to) sway 1. להתנועע (move) *inf* leheetno'e'a'; *pst* heetno'a'; *pres* meetno'e'a'; *fut* yeetno'a'; **2.** לשלוט (rule) *inf* leeshlot; *pst* shalat; *pres* sholet; *fut* yeeshlot.

(to) swear 1. להישבע *vi inf* leheeshava'; *pst & pres* neeshba' *(b=v)*; *fut* yeeshava'; **2.** להשביע (administer oath) *vt inf* lehashbee'a'; *pst* heeshbee'a'; *pres* mashbee'a'; *fut* yashbee'a'; **3.** לקלל (revile) *inf* lekalel; *pst* keelel; *pres* mekalel; *fut* yekalel.

(to) swear by 1. להישבע ב־ *inf* leheeshava' be-; *pst & pres* neeshba' *(b=v)* be-; *fut* yeeshava' be-; **2.** לתת כל אימונו ב־ (fully confide in) *inf* latet kol emoono/-ah be-; *pst* natan *etc*; *pres* noten *etc*; *fut* yeeten *etc.*

(to) swear off smoking להישבע להפסיק לעשן *inf* leheeshava' lehafseek le'ashen; *pst & pres* neeshba' *(b=v) etc*; *fut* yeeshava' *etc.*

sweat זיעה *nf* ze|'ah/-'ot (+*of:* -'at).

(to) sweat להזיע *inf* lehazee'a'; *pst* heezee'a'; *pres* mazee'a'; *fut* yazee'a'.

sweater 1. אפודה *nf* afood|ah/-ot (+*of:* -at); **2.** סוודר *[colloq.] nm* sveder/-eem (*pl+of:* -ey).

sweaty 1. גורם להזעה *adj* gorem/-et le-haza'ah; **2.** רווי זיעה *adj* revoo|y/-yat ze'ah.

Swede שוודי *nmf & adj* shvedee/-t.

Sweden שוודיה *nf* shvedeeyah.

Swedish שוודית (language) *nf* shvedeet.

sweep 1. גריפה *nf* greef|ah/-ot (+*of:* -at); **2.** תנופה (momentum) *nf* tenoof|ah/-ot (+*of:* -at).

(a clean) sweep טיהור יסודי *nm* teehoor/-eem yesodee/-yeem.

(to) sweep לטאטא *inf* leta'te; *pst* tee'ta; *pres* meta'te; *fut* yeta'te.

(to) sweep down upon להחריב *inf* lehakhreev; *pst* hekhreev; *pres* makhreev; *fut* yakhreev.

(to) sweep everything away לטאטא במאטא השמד *inf* leta'te'be-mat'ate hashmed; *pst* tee'ta *etc*; *pres* meta'te; *fut* yeta'te.

sweeper מטאטא *nm* mat'at|e/-'eem (*pl+of:* -'ey).

(carpet) sweeper מבריש שטיחים *nm* mavreesh/-ey sheteekheem.

sweeping סוחף *adj* sokhef/-et.

sweeping victory נצחון סוחף *nm* neets|akhon/-khonot sokh|ef/-afeem.

sweepings פסולת *nf* pesolet.

sweepstake פיס *nm* payees.

sweet 1. מתוק *adj* matok/metookah; **2.** ממתק (candy) *nm* mamtak/-eem (*pl+of:* -ey)

(my) sweet! מותק שלי! motek shelee!

sweet butter חמאה ללא מלח *nf* khem'ah le-lo melakh.

sweet corn תירס ירוק *nm* teeras yarok.

sweet dreams! חלומות נעימים! khalomot ne'eemee'm!

sweet milk חלב טרי *nm* khalav taree.

sweet pea אפונה ריחנית *nf* afoonah reykhaneet.

sweet potato בטטה *nf* batat|ah/-ot (+*of:* -at).

(a) sweet tooth חולשה לדברי מתיקה *nf* khoolshah le-deevrey meteekah.

(to) sweeten להמתיק *inf* lehamteek; *pst* heemteek; *pres* mamteek; *fut* yamteek.

sweetheart 1. אהוב (lover) *nmf* ahoov/-ah (+*of:* -at; *pl:* -eem/-ot); **2.** אהובי! (my darling!) *nmf* ahoov|ee!/-atee! **3.** מותק שלי (my sweet) *nmf* motek shelee!

sweetmeat סוכרייה *nf* sookaree|yah/-yot (+*of:* -yat).

sweetness מתיקות *nf* meteekoo|t/-yot.

swell 1. מצוין (fine) *adj* metsoo|yan/-yenet; **2.** חשוב (important) *adj* khashoov/-ah; **3.** תפיחות (bulge) *nf* tefeekhoo|t/-yot.

(to) swell 1. לתפוח *inf* leetpo'akh; *pst* tafakh *(f=p)*; *pres* tofe'akh; *fut* yeetpakh; **2.** לגאות (rise) *inf* leeg'ot; *pst* ga'ah; *pres* go'eh; *fut* yeeg'eh.

(a) swell head הגזמה בערך עצמו *nf* hagzamah be-'erekh 'atsmo.

swelling תפיחה *nf* tefeekh|ah/-ot (+*of:* -at).

(to) swelter להיחלש מחום *inf* lehekhalesh me-khom; *pst & pres* nekhlash *etc*; *fut* yekhalesh *etc.*

swerve סטייה *nf* stee|yah/-yot (+*of:* -yat).

(to) swerve לסטות *inf* leestot; *pst* satah; *pres* soteh; *fut* yeesteh.

(a) swerve to the right פניית־פתע ימינה *nf* pnee|yat/-yot peta' yemeenah.

swift מהיר *adj* maheer/meheerah.

swiftness מהירות *nf* meheeroo|t/-yot.

swim שחייה *nf* sekhee|yah/-yot (+*of:* -yat).

(to) swim across לחצות בשחייה *inf* lakhtsot bee-s'kheeyah; *pst* khatsah *etc*; *pres* khotseh *etc*; *fut* yekhtseh *etc.*

swim suit בגד ים *nm* beged/beegdey yam.

swimmer שחיין *nmf* sakhyan/-eet.

swindle הונאה *nf* hona|'ah/-'ot (+*of:* -'at).

(to) swindle להונות *inf* lehonot; *pst* honah; *pres* *[colloq.]* merameh; *fut* yoneh.

swine חזיר *nm* khazeer/-eem (*pl+of:* -ey).

swing 1. נדנדה *nf* nadned|ah/-ot (*+of:* -at); **2.** חופש פעולה (freedom of action) *nm* khofesh pe'oolah; **3.** מוסיקת ג'ז קצבית (music) *nf* mooseekat jaz keetsbeet.

(in full) swing במלוא התנופה *adv* bee-m'lo ha-tenoofah.

(to) swing 1. להניף *inf* lehaneef; *pst* heneef; *pres* meneef; *fut* yaneef; **2.** לארגן (organize) *inf* le'argen; *pst* eergen; *pres* me'argen; *fut* ye'argen.

(to give someone full) swing לתת למישהו חופש פעולה מלא *inf* latet le-meeshehoo khofesh pe'oolah male; *pst* natan *etc*; *pres* noten *etc*; *fut* yeeten *etc*.

(to) swing a deal לארגן עסקה *inf* le'argen 'eeskah; *pst* eergen *etc*; *pres* me'argen *etc*; *fut* ye'argen *etc*.

(to) swing around לסובב *inf* lesovev; *pst* sovev; *pres* mesovev; *fut* yesovev.

(to) swing open לפתוח לרווחה *inf* leefto'akh lee-revakhah; *pst* patakh *(p=f) etc*; *pres* pote'akh *etc*; *fut* yeeftakh *etc*.

swinger מתפרפר *[slang] nmf* meetparper/-et.

swinging door דלת הנפתחת לשני הצדדים *nf* del|et/-atot ha-neeftakh|at/-ot lee-shney ha-tsdadeem.

(to) swipe 1. לחבוט *inf* lakhbot; *pst* khavat *(v=b)*; *pres* khovet; *fut* yakhbot; **2.** להכות (hit) *inf* lehakot; *pst* heekah; *pres* makeh; *fut* yakeh.

swirl סחרחורת *nf* sekharkhor|et/-ot.

(to) swirl להסתחרר *inf* leheestakhrer; *pst* heestakhrer; *pres* meestakhrer; *fut* yeestakhrer.

Swiss 1. שווייצי *adj & nmf* shvaytsee/-t; **2.** שווייצרי *[colloq.] adj & nmf* shveytsaree/-t.

switch 1. החלפה (change) *nf* hakhlaf|ah/-ot (*+of:* -at); **2.** שוט (whip) *nm* shot/-eem (*pl+of:* -ey); **3.** הלקאה (blow) *nf* halka|'ah/-'ot (*+of:* -'at).

(electric) switch מתג חשמלי *nm* met|eg/-ageem khashmalee/-yeem.

(railway) switch מסוט *nm* masot/mesot|eem (*pl+of:* ey).

(to) switch 1. להחליף כיוון *inf* lehakhleef keevoon; *pst* hekhleef *etc*; *pres* makhleef *etc*; *fut* yakhleef *etc*; **2.** למתג *inf* lemateg; *pst* meeteg; *pres* memateg; *fut* yemateg.

(to) switch off לכבות *inf* lekhabot; *pst* keebah *(k=kh)*; *pres* mekhabeh; *fut* yekhabeh.

(to) switch on להדליק *inf* lehadleek; *pst* heedleek; *pres* madleek; *fut* yadleek.

switchboard 1. לוח מתגים *nm* loo'akh/-khot metageem; **2.** מרכזת (telephone exchange) *nf* meerk|ezet/-azot.

Switzerland 1. שווייץ *nf* shvayts; **2.** שווייצרייה *[colloq.] nf* shveytsaryah.

swivel סביבול *nm* sveevol/-eem (*pl+of:* -ey).

swivel chair כסא מסתובב *nm* kees|e/-ot meestovev/-eem.

swoon עילפון *nm* 'eelafon (*+of:* 'elfon).

(to) swoon להתמוגג עד לעילפון *inf* leheetmogeg 'ad le-'eelafon; *pst* heetmogeg *etc*; *pres* meetmogeg *etc*; *fut* yeetmogeg *etc*.

swoop חטיפה במחי יד khateef|ah/-ot bee-mekhee yad.

(at one) swoop בבת אחת *adv* be-vat akhat.

(to) swoop down upon לעוט לפתע על *inf* la'oot le-feta' 'al; *pst & pres* 'at *etc*; *fut* ya'oot *etc*.

(to) swoop off להרפות לפתע *inf* leharpot le-feta'; *pst* heerpah *etc*; *pres* marpeh *etc*; *fut* yarpeh *etc*.

(to) swoop up לתפוס *inf* leetpos; *pst* tafas *(f=p)*; *pres* tofes; *fut* yeetpos.

sword חרב *nmf* kherev/khar|avot (*pl+of:* -vot).

sword belt אזן חרב *nm* az|en/-ney kherev.

sword rattling צחצוח חרבות *nm* tseekhtsoo|'akh/-khey kharavot.

syllable הברה *nf* havar|ah/-ot (*+of:* -at).

syllabus תוכנית לימודים *nf* tokhnee|t/-yot leemoodeem.

symbol סמל *nm* semel/smaleem (*pl+of:* seemley).

symbolic סמלי *adj* seemlee/-t.

symbolism 1. סמליות *nf* seemleeyoot; **2.** סימבוליזם *nm* seemboleezm/-eem (*pl+of:* -ey).

symmetrical סימטרי *adj* seemetree/-t.

symmetry סימטריה *nf* seemetr|yah/-yot (*+of:* -yat).

sympathetic 1. אוהד *adj* ohed/-et; **2.** מסמפט *[colloq.] adj* mesampet/-et.

sympathetic towards מגלה אהדה כלפי *adj & v pres* megal|eh/-ah ahadah kelapey.

(to) sympathize 1. לאהוד *inf* le'ehod; *pst* ahad; *pres* ohed; *fut* ye'ehad; **2.** לסמפט *inf* lesampet; *pst* seempet; *pres* mesampet; *fut* yesampet.

sympathy 1. אהדה *nf* ahad|ah/-ot (*+of:* -at); **2.** סימפתיה *nf* seempat|yah/-yot (*+of:* -yat).

(extend one's) sympathy להביע תנחומים *inf* lehabee'a' tankhoomeem; *pst* heebee'a' *etc*; *pres* mabee'a' *etc*; *fut* yabee'a' *etc*.

symphony סימפוניה *nf* seemfon|yah/-yot (*+of:* -yat).

symphony orchestra תזמורת סימפונית *nf* teezmo-r|et/-ot seemfonee|t/-yot.

symposium 1. רב־שיח *nm* rav/rabey *(b=v)* see'akh; **2.** סימפוזיון *nm* seempozyon/-eem (*pl+of:* -ey).

symptom 1. סימן מחלה *nm* seeman/-ey makhlah; **2.** סימפטום *nm* seemptom/-eem (*pl+of:* -ey).

syndicate 1. התאגדות *nf* heet'agdoo|t/-yot; **2.** סינדיקט *nm* seendeekat/-eem (*pl+of:* -ey).

(to) syndicate 1. להתאגד *inf* leheet'aged; *pst* heet'aged; *pres* meet'aged; *fut* yeet'aged; **2.** למכור במאוגד *inf* leemkor bee-me'oogad; *pst* makhar *(kh=k) etc*; *pres* mokher *etc*; *fut* yeemkor *etc*.

syndrome 1. תסמונת *nf* teesmon|et/-ot; **2.** סינדרום *nm* seendrom/-eem (*pl+of:* -ey).

synedrion, synedrium סנהדרין *nf* sanhedreen/-eem.

synonym 1. מלה נרדפת *nf* meel|ah/-eem neer-d|efet/-afot; **2.** סינונים *nm* seenoneem/-eem (*pl+of:* -ey).

synonymous 1. נירדף ל־ *adj* neerd|af/-efet le-; **2.** סינונימי *adj* seenoneemee/-t.

synopsis תקציר *nm* taktseer/-eem (*pl+of:* -ey).

syntax תחביר *nm* takhbeer/-eem (*pl+of:* -ey).

synthesis 1. מיזוג *nm* meezoog/-eem (*pl+of:* -ey); **2.** סינתזה *nf* seentez|ah/-ot (*+of:* -at).

(to) synthesize 1. למזג *inf* lemazeg; *pst* meezeg; *pres* memazeg; *fut* yemazeg; **2.** לסנתז *inf* lesantez; *pst* seentez; *pres* mesantez; *fut* yesantez.

synthesizer סינתסייזר *nm* seentesayzer/-eem (*pl+of:* -ey).

synthetic 1. מלאכותי *adj* mal'akhootee/-t; **2.** סינתטי *adj* seentetee/-t.

syphilis עגבת *nf* 'agevet.

syringe מזרק *nm* mazrek/-eem (*pl+of:* -ey).

syrup סירופ *nm* seerop/-eem (*pl+of:* -pey).

system 1. שיטה *nf* sheet|ah/-ot (*+of:* -at); **2.** מערכת (set) *nf* ma'ar|ekhet/-akhot (*pl+of:* -khot); **3.** סיסטמה *nf* seestem|ah/-ot (*+of:* -at).

systematic 1. שטתי *adj* sheetatee/-t; **2.** סיסטמטי *adj* seestematee/-t.

systole התכווצות לב *nf* heetkavtsoo|t/-yot lev.

T.

T,t consonant for which the Hebrew alphabet provides two identically pronounced equivalents: Tet (ט) and Tav (ת). Under the Official Transliteration Rules prescribed by the Hebrew Language Academy for personal and geographical names, Tav (ת) is also used to transliterate th, which is a sound unknown to Hebrew.

tab 1. דש (flap) *nm* dash/-eem (*pl+of:* -ey); **2.** חשבון (bill) *nm* kheshbon/-ot.

tabernacle סוכה *nf* sook|ah/-ot (*+of:* -at).

(the Feast of) Tabernacles חג הסוכות *nm* khag ha-sookot.

table 1. שולחן *nm* shoolkhan/-ot; **2.** לוח (list) *nm* loo|'akh/-khot; **3.** טבלה (data list) *nf* tavl|ah/-a'ot (*+of:* -at).

(to) table להוריד מסדר היום *inf* lehoreed mee-seder ha-yom; *pst* horeed *etc; pres* moreed *etc; fut* yoreed *etc.*

table cover כסוי שולחן *nm* kesoo|y/-yey shoolkhan.

table d'hote ארוחה אחידה *nf* arookh|ah/-ot akhee-d|ah/-ot.

table manners נימוסי שולחן *nm pl* neemoosey shoolkhan

tablecloth מפת שולחן *nf* map|at/-ot shoolkhan.

Tables of the Covenant לוחות הברית *nm pl* lookhot ha-breet.

tablespoon כף מרק *nf* kaf/kapot (*p=f*) marak.

tablespoonful מלוא הכף *nm* melo ha-kaf.

tableware כלי שולחן *nm pl* kley shoolkhan.

tabloid עיתון סנסציות *nm* 'eeton/-ey sensatsyot.

taboo 1. אסור *adj* asoor/-ah; **2.** טאבו *adj & adv* taboo.

(to) tabulate לערוך בטבלאות *inf* la'arokh be-tavla'ot; *pst* 'arakh *etc; pres* 'orekh *etc; fut* ya'arokh *etc.*

tacit 1. משתמע *adj* meeshtam|e'a'/-a'at; **2.** מובן מאליו (implied) *adj* moov|an/-enet me-'el|av/-eha (*m/f*).

taciturn שתקן *adj* shatkan/-eet.

tack 1. נעץ *nm* na'ats/ne'atseem (*pl+of:* na'atsey); **2.** שינוי עמדה *nm* sheenoo|y/-yey 'emdah.

(to) tack 1. להדק בנעצים *inf* lehadek bee-ne'atseem; *pst* heedek *etc; pres* mehadek *etc; fut* yehadek *etc;* **2.** לשנות עמדה *inf* leshanot 'emdah; *pst* sheenah *etc; pres* meshaneh *etc; fut* yeshaneh *etc.*

(to change) tack לשנות כיוון *inf* leshanot keevoon; *pst* sheenah *etc; pres* meshaneh *etc; fut* yeshaneh *etc.*

tackle 1. גלגלת (pulley) *nf* galg|elet/-alot; **2.** ציוד (equipment) *nm* tseeyood.

(fishing) tackle גלגלת דיג *nf* galg|elet/-alot dayeeg.

(to) tackle 1. לטפל *inf* letapel; *pst* teepel; *pres* metapel; *fut* yetapel; **2.** להתמודד *inf* leheetmoded; *pst* heetmoded; *pres* meetmoded; *fut* yeetmoded.

tact 1. חוש מידה *nm* khoosh meedah; **2.** טקט *nm* takt.

tactful בעל טקט *adj* ba'al/-at takt.

tactical 1. מבצעי *adj* meevtsa'ee/-t; **2.** תכסיסי (strategic) *adj* takhseesee/-t; **3.** טקטי *adj* taktee/-t.

tactics 1. תכסיסים (methods) *nm pl* takhseeseem (*sing:* takhsees; *pl+of:* -ey); **2.** טקטיקה (military) *nf* takteek|ah/-ot (*+of:* -at).

tactless חסר טקט *adj* khas|ar/-rat takt.

taffeta טפטה *nf* taftah.

tag 1. תווית (label) *nf* tavee|t/-yot; **2.** קצה שרוך פרום (loose end) *nm* ketseh srokh paroom.

(to) tag להדביק תו *inf* lehadbeek tav; *pst* heedbeek tav; *pres* madbeek tav; *fut* yadbeek tav.

(to) tag after לעקוב מקרוב אחר *inf* la'akov mee-karov akhar *inf* 'akav *etc; pres* 'okev *etc; fut* ya'akov *etc.*

tail 1. זנב (animal) zanav/znavot (*+of:* znav/zanvot); **2.** קצה (of object) *nm* katseh/ketsavot (*+of:* ketseh/katsvot).

(to) tail 1. לבלוש אחר *inf* leevlosh akhar; *pst* balash (*b=v*) *etc; pres* bolesh *etc; fut* yeevlosh *etc;* **2.** לעקוב אחרי (track) *inf* la'akov akhrey; *pst* 'akav *etc; pres* 'okev *etc; fut* ya'akov *etc.*

taillight פנס אחורי *nm* panas/-eem akhoree/-yeem.

tailor חייט *nm* khayat/-eem (*pl+of:* -ey).

(to) tailor לתפור לפי מידה *inf* leetpor lefee meedah; *pst* tafar (*f=p*) *etc; pres* tofer *etc; fut* yeetpor *etc.*

taint כתם ket|em/-ameem (*pl+of:* keetmey).

(to) taint 1. להכתים *inf* lehakhteem; *pst* heekhteem; *pres* makhteem; *fut* yakhteem; **2.** לזהם (pollute) lezahem; *pst* zeehem; *pres* mezahem; *fut* yezahem.

take 1. לקיחה *nf* lekeekh|ah/-ot (+*of:* -at); **2.** פדיון (proceeds) *nm* peedyon/-ot; **3.** קטע מוסרט (of movie) *nm* ket|a'/-a'eem moosrat/-eem.

(to) take לקחת *inf* lakakhat; *pst* lakakh; *pres* loke'akh; *fut* yeekakh.

(to) take a chance לקפוץ על הזדמנות *inf* leekpots 'al heezdamnoot; *pst* kafats *(f=p) etc; pres* kofets *etc; fut* yeekpots *etc.*

(to) take a fancy to להתחיל לחבב *inf* lehatkheel lekhabev; *pst* heetkheel *etc; pres* matkheel *etc; fut* yatkheel *etc.*

(to) take a look at להעיף מבט על *inf* leha'eef mabat 'al; *pst* he'eef *etc; pst* me'eef *etc; fut* ya'eef *etc.*

(to) take after לחקות *inf* lekhakot; *pst* kheekah; *pres* mekhakeh; *fut* yekhakeh.

(to) take amiss להבין לא נכון *inf* lehaveen lo nakhon; *pst* heveen *etc; pres* meveen *etc; fut* yaveen *etc.*

(to) take an oath 1. להישבע *vi inf* leheeshava'; *pst etc pres* neeshba' *(b=v); fut* yeeshava'; **2.** להשביע (administer oath) *vt inf* lehashbee'a'; *pst* heeshbee'a'; *pres* mashbee'a'; *fut* yashbee'a'.

(to) take apart לפרק לחתיכות *inf* lefarek la-khateekhot; *pst* perek *(p=f) etc; pres* mefarek *etc; fut* yefarek *etc.*

(to) take away להסיר *inf* lehaseer; *pst* heseer; *pres* meseer; *fut* yaseer.

(to) take back לחזור בו *inf* lakhazor bo/bah *(m/f); pst* khazar *etc; pres* khozer *etc; fut* yakhazor *etc.*

(to) take back to להחזיר *inf* lehakhzeer; *pst* hekhzeer; *pres* makhzeer; *fut* yakhzeer.

(to) take by surprise להפתיע *inf* lehaftee'a'; *pst* heeftee'a'; *pres* maftee'a'; *fut* yaftee'a'.

(to) take care of 1. לדאוג ל- *inf* leed'og le-; *pst* da'ag le-; *pres* do'eg le-; *fut* yeed'ag le-; **2.** לשמור על *inf* leeshmor 'al; *pst* shamar 'al; *pres* shomer 'al; *fut* yeeshmor 'al.

(to) take charge of לקבל לאחריותו *inf* lekabel le-akhrayooto; *pst* keebel *etc; pres* mekabel *etc; fut* yekabel *etc.*

(to) take cold להצטנן *inf* leheets'tanen; *pst* heets'tanen; *pres* meets'tanen; *fut* yeets'tanen.

(to) take down in writing 1. להעלות על הכתב *inf* leha'alot 'al ha-ktav; *pst* he'elah *etc; pres* ma'aleh *etc; fut* ya'aleh *etc;* **2.** לרשום (note) *inf* leershom; *pst* rasham; *pres* roshem; *fut* yeershom.

(to) take effect לקבל תוקף *inf* lekabel tokef; *pst* keebel *etc; pres* mekabel *etc; fut* yekabel *etc.*

(to) take in 1. לכלול *inf* leekhlol; *pst* kalal *(k=kh); pres* kolel; *fut* yeekhlol; **2.** לקצר (shorten) *inf* lekatser; *pst* keetser; *pres* mekatser; *fut* yekatser; **3.** להבין (understand) *inf* lehaveen; *pst* heveen; *pres* meveen; *fut* yaveen; **4.** להאזין (listen) *inf* leha'azeen; *pst* he'ezeen; *pres* ma'azeen; *fut* ya'azeen.

(I) take it that עלי להבין כי 'alay lehaveen kee.

(to) take leave 1. להיפרד *inf* leheepared; *pst & pres* neefrad *(f=p); fut* yeepared; **2.** להסתלק (make off) *inf* leehstalek; *pst* heestalek; *pres* meestalek; *fut* yeestalek.

take-off המראה *nf* hamra|'ah/-'ot (+*of:* -'at).

(to) take off 1. לפשוט (undress) *inf* leefshot; *pst* pashat *(p=f); pres* poshet; *fut* yeefshot; **2.** להמריא (airplane) *inf* lehamree; *pst* heemree; *pres* mamree; *fut* yamree.

(to) take offense להיעלב *inf* lehe'alev; *pst & pres* ne'elav; *fut* ye'alev.

(to) take on a responsibility לקבל אחריות *inf* lekabel akhrayoot; *pst* keebel *etc; pres* mekabel *etc; fut* yekabel *etc.*

(to) take out 1. להוציא lehotsee; *pst* hotsee; *pres* motsee; *fut* yotsee; **2.** לצאת לבילויים יחדיו (go out together) *inf* latset le-veeloo'eem *(v=b)* yakhdav; *pst* yatsa *etc; pres* yotse *etc; fut* yetse *etc.*

(to) take place להתרחש *inf* leheetrakhesh; *pst* heetrakhesh; *pres* meetrakhesh; *fut* yeetrakhesh.

(to) take stock להעריך *inf* leha'areekh; *pst* he'ereekh; *pres* ma'areekh; *fut* ya'areekh.

(to) take the floor לקבל רשות הדיבור *inf* lekabel reshoot ha-deeboor; *pst* keebel *etc; pres* mekabel *etc; fut* yekabel *etc.*

(to) take to heart לקחת ללב *inf* lakakhat la-lev; *pst* lakakh *etc; pres* loke'akh *etc; fut* yeekakh *etc.*

(to) take to task לנזוף *inf* leenzof; *pst* nazaf; *pres* nozef; *fut* yeenzof.

(to) take up space לתפוס מקום *inf* leetpos makom; *pst* tafas *(f=p) etc; pres* tofes *etc; fut* yeetpos *etc.*

(to) take up the matter לדון בעניין *inf* ladoon ba-'eenyan; *pst & pres* dan *etc; fut* yadoon *etc.*

(to be) taken ill ליפול למשכב *inf* leepol le-meeshkav; *pst* nafal *(f=p) etc; pres* nofel *etc; fut* yeepol *etc.*

talcum טלק *nm* talk.

talcum powder אבקת טלק *nf* avk|at/-ot talk.

tale סיפור *nm* seepoor/-eem (*pl*+*of:* -ey).

talebearer מלשין *nmf* malsheen/-ah.

talent כשרון *nm* keeshron/-ot.

talented כשרוני *adj* keeshronee/-t.

(to tell) tales לספר מעשיות *inf* lesaper ma'aseeyot; *pst* seeper *etc; pres* mesaper *etc; fut* yesaper *etc.*

talk שיחה *nf* seekh|ah/-ot (+*of:* -at).

(to) talk 1. לדבר *inf* ledaber; *pst* deeber; *pres* medaber; *fut* yedaber; **2.** לשוחח (chat) *inf* lesokhe'akh; *pst* sokhakh; *pres* mesokhe'akh; *fut* yesokhakh.

(to) talk into לשכנע ל- *inf* leshakhne'a' le-; *pst* sheekhna' le-; *pres* meshakhne'a' le-; *fut* yeshakhna' le-.

(to) talk nonsense לדבר שטויות *inf* ledaber shtooyot; *pst* deeber *etc; pres* medaber *etc; fut* yedaber *etc.*

talk of the town 1. שיחת העיר *nf* seekhat ha-'eer; **2.** שיחת היום (topic of the day) *nf* seekhat ha-yom.

(to) talk out of לשכנע לחזור בו *inf* leshakhne'a' lakhzor bo; *pst* sheekhna' *etc; pres* meshakhne'a' *etc; fut* yeshakhna' *etc.*

(to) talk over לדון מחדש *inf* ladoon me-khadash; *pst & pres* dan *etc; fut* yadoon *etc.*

(to) talk up לעורר התענינות *inf* le'orer heet'anyenoot; *pst* 'orer *etc; pres* me'orer *etc; fut* ye'orer *etc.*

talkative 1. מרבה דברים *adj* marb|eh/-ah (*pl+of:* -ey) dvareem; **2.** פטפטן (chatterer) *nmf & adj* patpetan/-eet.

talker 1. דברן *nm* dabran/-eet; **2.** פטפטן *adj* patpetan/-eet.

tall גבה קומה *adj* gvah/geevhat komah.

(six feet) tall כשני מטר גובה *adj* kee-shney meter govah.

tall tale גוזמה רבה *nf* goozmah rabah.

tallow חלב *nm* khelev.

tally 1. חשבון *nm* kheshbon/-ot; **2.** שובר (voucher) *nm* shovar/-eem (*pl+of:* -ey).

(to) tally 1. לחשב (reckon) *inf* lekhashev; *pst* kheeshev; *pres* mekhashev; *fut* yekhashev; **2.** לתאם חשבונות (match accounts) *inf* leta'em kheshbonot; *pst* te'em *etc*; *pres* meta'em *etc*; *fut* yeta'em *etc*.

tally sheet תעודת סיכום *nf* te'ood|at/-ot seekoom.

(to) tally up להסתכם *inf* leheestakem; *pst* heestakem; *pres* meestakem; *fut* yeestakem.

(to) tally with ־להתאים ל (adjust to) *inf* lehat'eem le-; *pst* heet'eem le-; *pres* mat'eem le-; *fut* yat'eem le-.

Talmud תלמוד *nm* talmood.

tame 1. מבויית *adj* mevoo|yat/-yetet; **2.** מאולף (trained) *adj* meo'ool|af/-efet.

(to) tame 1. לאלף (train) *inf* le'alef; *pst* eelef; *pres* me'alef; *fut* ye'alef; **2.** לרסן (rein) *inf* lerasen; *pst* reesen; *pres* merasen; *fut* yerasen; **3.** לביית (domesticate) *inf* levayet; *pst* beeyet *(b=v)*; *pres* mevayet; *fut* yevayet.

(to) tamper 1. להתערב *inf* leheet'arev; *pst* heet'arev; *pres* meet'arev; *fut* yeet'arev; **2.** להתעסק שלא ביודעין (deal underhand) *inf* leheet'asek she-lo be-yod'een; *pst* heet'asek *etc*; *pres* meet'asek *etc*; *fut* yeet'asek *etc*.

(to) tamper with a lock להתעסק עם מנעול *inf* leheet'asek 'eem man'ool; *pst* heet'asek *etc*; *pres* meet'asek *etc*; *fut* yeet'asek *etc*.

tampon טמפון *nm* tampon/-eem (*pl+of:* -ey).

tan 1. קליפת אלון (tanbark) *nf* kleep|at/-ot alon; **2.** חומר לעיבוד עורות (tanning material) *nm* khomer le-'eebood 'orot; **3.** שיזפון (suntan) *nm* sheez|afon (*+of:* -fon); **4.** חום־צהבהב (color) *adj* khoom/-ah tsehav|hav/-hevet.

(to) tan 1. לעבד לעור (hide into leather) *inf* le'abed le-'or; *pst* 'eebed *etc*; *pres* me'abed *etc* *fut* ye'abed *etc*; **2.** להלקות (whip) *inf* lehalkot; *pst* heelkah; *pres* malkeh; *fut* yalkeh; **3.** להשתזף (suntan) *v rfl inf* leheeshtazef; *pst* heeshtazef; *pres* meeshtazef; *fut* yeeshtazef.

tang 1. לשון אזמל *nf* leshon/-ot eezmel; **2.** ריח חריף *nm* re'akh/rekhot khareef/-eem.

tangent משיק *adj* masheek/-ah.

tangerine מנדרינה *nf* mandareen|ah/-ot (*+of:* -at).

tangible מוחשי *adj* mookhashee/-t.

tangle 1. סבך *nm* svakh; **2.** פקעת *nf* peka|'at/-'ot.

(to) tangle 1. לסבך *inf* lesabekh; *pst* seebekh; *pres* mesabekh; *fut* yesabekh; **2.** להתבלבל (get confused) *inf* leheetbalbel; *pst* heetbalbel; *pres* meetbalbel; *fut* yeetbalbel.

tank 1. מיכל (container) *nm* meykhal/-eem (*pl+of:* -ey); **2.** טנק (military) *nm* tank/-eem (*pl+of:* -ey).

(swimming) tank בריכה *nf* breykh|ah/-ot (*+of:* -at).

tanker מכלית *nf* mekhalee|t/-yot.

tanner בורסקאי *nm* boorska|'ee/-'eem (*pl+of:* -'ey).

tannery 1. בורסקי *nm* boorskee; **2.** בית חרושת לעורות *nm* bet/batey kharoshet le-'orot.

tannic acid טנין *nm* taneen.

(to) tantalize להפיח תקוות שווא *inf* lehafee'akh teekvot shav; *pst* hefee'akh *etc*; *pres* mefee'akh *etc*; *fut* yafee'akh *etc*.

tantamount ־כמוהו כ kamo|hoo/hah ke-.

tantrum התפרצות זעם *nf* heetpartsoo|t/-yot za'am.

tap 1. ברז (faucet) *nm* berez/brazeem (*pl+of:* beerzey); **2.** טפיחה (knock) *nf* tefeekh|ah/-ot (*+of:* -at).

(beer on) tap בירה מחבית *nf* beerah me-khaveet.

(to) tap לשאוב נוזל *inf* leesh'ov nozel; *pst* sha'av *etc*; *pres* sho'ev *etc*; *fut* yeesh'av *etc*.

tap dance ריקוד טפ *nm* reeekood/-ey tep.

tape סרט *nm* seret/srateem (*pl+of:* seertey).

(adhesive) tape סרט הדבקה *nm* seret/seertey hadbakah.

(recording) tape סרט הקלטה *nm* seret/seertey haklatah.

(to) tape 1. להקליט בסרט (record) *inf* lehakleet be-seret; *pst* heekleet *etc*; *pres* makleet *etc*; *fut* yakleet *etc*; **2.** למדוד בסרט (measure) *inf* leemdod be-seret; *pst* madad *etc*; *pres* moded *etc*; *fut* yeemdod *etc*.

tape measure סרט מדידה *nm* seret/seertey medeedah.

tape recorder רשמקול *nm* reshamkol/-eem (*pl+of:* -ey).

taper 1. נר שעווה דקיק (candle) *nm* ner/-ot sha'avah dakeek/-eem; **2.** התחדדות הדרגתית (gradual thinning) *nf* heetkhadedoo|t/-yot hadragatee|t/-yot.

(to) taper להפחית בהדרגה lehafkheet be-hadragah; *pst* heefkheet *etc*; *pres* mafkheet *etc*; *fut* yafkheet *etc*.

tapestry טפיט *nm* tapet/-eem (*pl+of:* -ey).

tapeworm תולעת סרט *nf* tola|'at/-'ey seret.

taproom מסבאה *nf* meesb|a'ah/-a'ot (*pl+of:* -e'at/-e'ot).

tar זפת *nf* zefet.

(to) tar לזפת *inf* lezapet; *pst* zeepet; *pres* mezapet; *fut* yezapet.

tardy 1. מאחר *adj* me'akher/-et; **2.** מפגר *adj* mefager/-et.

(to be) tardy לאחר *inf* le'akher; *pst* eekher; *pres* me'akher; *fut* ye'akher.

target מטרה *nf* matar|ah/-ot (*pl+of:* -at).

target area מטווח *nm* meetv|akh/-akheem (*pl+of:* -ekhey).

target practice אימוני קליעה *nm pl* eemooney klee'ah.

tariff תעריף *nm* ta'areef/-eem (*pl+of:* -ey).

tarnish השחרה *nf* hashkhar|ah/-ot (*+of:* -at).

(to) tarnish להשחיר *inf* lehash'kheer; *pst* heesh'kheer; *pres* mash'kheer; *fut* yash'kheer.

(to) tarry להתמהמה *inf* leheetmahme'ah; *pst* heetmahme'ah; *pres* meetmahme'ah; *fut* yeetmahme'ah.
tart 1. עוגת פירות (pie) *nf* 'oog|at/-ot perot; **2.** יצאנית (prostitute) *nf* yats'anee|t/-yot.
tart 1. חמוץ *adj adj* khamoots/-ah; **2.** שנון *adj* shanoon/shnoonah; **3.** חריף (sharp) khareef/-ah.
tart reply מענה שנון *nm* ma'aneh shanoon.
task 1. משימה *nf* meseem|ah/-ot (*+of:* -at); **2.** תפקיד (role) *nm* tafkeed/-eem (*pl+of:* -ey).
(to take to) task לייסר *inf* leyaser; *pst* yeeser; *pres* meyaser; *fut* yeyaser.
task force כוח משימה *nm* ko'akh meseemah.
tassel גדיל *nm* gedeel/-eem (*pl+of:* -ey).
taste טעם *nm* ta'am/te'ameem (*pl+of:* ta'amey).
(after)taste טעם לוואי *nm* ta'am levay.
(in good) taste במיטב הטעם *adv* be-meytav ha-ta'am.
(to) taste לטעום *inf* leet'om; *pst* ta'am; *pres* to'em; *fut* yeet'am.
taste of onion טעם בצל *nm* ta'am batsal.
tasteless 1. חסר טעם *adj* khas|ar/-rat ta'am; **2.** תפל (insipid) *adj* tafel/tefelah.
tasty טעים *adj* ta'eem/te'eemah.
tatter 1. קרע *nm* kera'/kra'eem (*pl+of:* keer'ey); **2.** סחבה *nf* sekhav|ah/-ot (*+of:* -at).
tattered קרוע ובלוי *adj & adj* karoo'a'/kroo'ah oo-balooy/blooyah.
tattle ברבור *nm* beerboor/-eem (*pl+of:* -ey).
(to) tattle 1. לברבר *inf* levarber; *pst* beerber (*b=v*); *pres* mevarber; *fut* yevarber; **2.** לגלות סודות (divulge secrets) *inf* legalot sodot; *pst* geelah *etc*; *pres* megaleh *etc*; *fut* yegaleh *etc*.
tattletale 1. רכילות *nf* rekheeloo|t/-yot; **2.** רכלן *adj* rakhlan/-eet.
tattoo כתובת קעקע *nf* ketov|et/-ot ka'aka'.
taunt לגלוג פוגע *nm* leegloog/-eem pog|e'a'/-'eem.
(to) taunt -ללעוג ל *inf* leel'og le-; *pst* la'ag le-; *pres* lo'eg le-; *fut* yeel'ag le-.
tavern 1. אכסניה *nf* akhsan|yah/-yot (*+of:* -yat); **2.** פונדק (inn) *nm* poond|ak/-akeem (*pl+of:* -ekey)
tax מס *nm* mas/mees|eem (*pl+of:* -ey).
(income) tax מס הכנסה *nm* mas hakhnasah.
(property) tax מס רכוש *nm* mas rekhoosh.
(purchase) tax מס קנייה *nm* mas keneeyah.
(to) tax להטיל מס *inf* lehateel mas; *pst* heeteel mas; *pres* mateel mas; *fut* yateel mas.
(value-added) tax 1. מס ערך מוסף *nm* mas 'erekh moosaf; **2.** מע״מ *nm* (widely used *acr of* 1.) ma'am.
tax collector גובה מסים *nm* gov|eh/-ey meeseem.
tax cut קיצוץ במסים *nm* keetsoots/-eem be-meeseem.
tax evasion השתמטות ממס *nf* heeshtamtoo|t/-yot mee-mas.
tax exempt פטור ממס *adj* patoor/petoorah mee-mas.
tax-free חופשי ממס *adj* khofshee/-t mee-mas.
(to) tax one's patience להפקיע סבלנותו של *inf* lehafkee'a' savlanooto shel; *pst* heefkee'a' *etc*; *pres* mafkee'a' *etc*; *fut* yafkee'a' *etc*.

taxable בר־מיסוי *adj* bar/bat meesooy.
taxation מיסוי *nm* meesoo|y/-yeem (*pl+of:* -yey).
taxi 1. מונית *nf* monee|t/-yot; **2.** טקסי *nm* taksee.
(to) taxi לקחת מונית *[colloq.] inf* lakakhat moneet; *pst* lakakh *etc*; *pres* loke'akh; *fut* yeekakh *etc*.
taxicab 1. מונית *nf* monee|t/-yot; **2.** טקסי *nm* taksee.
taxidermy ייצור פוחלצים *nm* yeetsoor pookhlatseem.
taxidriver נהג מונית *nm* nahag/nehagey monee|t/-yot.
taxpayer משלם מסים *nm* meshal|em/-mey meeseem.
tea תה *nm* teh.
(to) teach ללמד *inf* lelamed; *pst* leemed; *pres* melamed; *fut* yelamed.
teacher מורה *nmf* mor|eh/-ah (*f+of:* -at; *pl:* -eem/-ot; *+of:* -ey).
teaching הוראה *nf* hora|'ah (*+of:* -'at).
teacup ספל תה *nm* sefel/seefley teh.
teakettle קומקום תה *nm* koomkoom/-ey teh.
team צוות *nm* tsev|et/-ateem (*pl+of:* tseevtey).
(to) team 1. להיצמד leheetsamed; *pst & pres* neetsmad; *fut* yeetsamed; **2.** להתחבר (join) leheetkhaber; *pst* heetkhaber; *pres* meetkhaber; *fut* yeetkhaber.
(to) team up להוות צוות *inf* lehavot tsevet; *pst* heevah *etc*; *pres* mehaveh *etc*; *fut* yehaveh *etc*.
team work עבודת צוות *f* 'avod|at/-ot tsevet.
teamster 1. עגלון (carter) *nm* 'eglon/-eem (*pl+of:* -ey); **2.** נהג משאית *nm* (truck driver) nahag/nehagey masa'ee|t/-yot.
teapot קומקום תה *nm* koomkoom/-ey teh.
tear דמעה (from eye) *nf* deem'ah/dema'ot (*+of:* deem|'at/-'ot).
tear gas גז מדמיע *nm* gaz/-eem madmee|'a'/-'eem.
(to) tear לקרוע *inf* leekro'a'; *pst* kara'; *pres* kore'a'; *fut* yeekra'.
(wear and) tear בלאי *nm* blay.
(to) tear apart לקרוע לגזרים *inf* leekro'a' lee-gzareem; *pst* kara' *etc*; *pres* kore'a' *etc*; *fut* yeekra' *etc*.
(to) tear away לעקור *inf* la'akor; *pst* 'akar; *pres* 'oker; *fut* ya'akor.
(to) tear down להרוס *inf* laharos; *pst* haras; *pres* hores; *fut* yaharos.
(to) tear off in a hurry להסתלק בחיפזון *inf* leheestalek be-kheepazon; *pst* heestalek *etc*; *pres* meestalek *etc*; *fut* yeestalek *etc*.
(to) tear one's hair למרוט שערות ראשו *inf* leemrot sa'arot rosho; *pst* marat *etc*; *pres* moret *etc*; *fut* yeemrot *etc*.
tearful דומע *adj* dom|e'a'/-a'at.
(to burst into) tears לפרוץ בדמעות *inf* leefrots bee-dma'ot; *pst* parats (*p=f*) *etc*; *pres* porets *etc*; *fut* yeefrots *etc*.
(to) tease להקניט *inf* lehakneet; *pst* heekneet; *pres* makneet; *fut* yakneet.
teaspoon כפית *nf* kapee|t/-yot.
teaspoonful מלוא כפית *nm* melo kapeet.
teat פטמה *nf* peetm|ah/-ot (*+of:* -at).
technical טכני *adj* tekhnee/-t.

technician טכנאי *nm* tekhn|ay/-a'eem (*pl+of:* -a'ey).
technique טכניקה *nf* tekhneek|ah/-ot (+*of:* -at).
technology טכנולוגיה *nf* tekhnolog|yah/-yot (+*of:* -yat).
teddy bear דובון *nm* doobon/-eem (*pl+of:* -ey).
tedious 1. מייגע *adj* meyag|e'a'/-a'at; **2.** משעמם (boring) *adj* mesha'mem/-et.
tediousness שעמום *nm* shee'amoom/-eem (*pl+of:* -ey).
(to) teem לרחוש *inf* leerkhosh; *pst* rakhash; *pres* rokhesh; *fut* yeerkhash.
(to) teem with לשרוץ *inf* leeshrots; *pst* sharats; *pres* shorets; *fut* yeeshrots.
teen-ager בן טיפש־עשרה *nmf* ben/bat teepesh-'esreh.
teens גיל העשרה *nm* geel/-ey ha-'esreh.
(in one's) teens בשנות העשרה שלו *adv* be-shnot ha-'esreh shel|o/-ah *(m/f)*.
teeth שיניים *nf pl* sheen|ayeem (*pl+of:* -ey).
(by the skin of his) teeth בעור שיניו *adv* be-'or sheen|av/-eha *(m/f)*.
telecast שידור *nm* sheedoor/-eem (*pl+of:* -ey).
telegram 1. מברק *nm* meevr|ak/-akeem (*pl+of:* -ekey); **2.** טלגרמה *nf* telegram|ah/-ot (+*of:* -at).
telegraph 1. מברקה *nf* meevrak|ah/-ot (+*of:* meevrek|et/-ot); **2.** טלגרף *nm* telegraf.
telegraphic 1. מוברק *adj* moovr|ak/-eket; **2.** טלגרפי *adj* telegrafee/-t.
telegraphy טלגרפיה *nf* telegraf|yah/-yot (+*of:* -yat).
telepathy טלפתיה *nf* telepat|yah/-yot (+*of:* -yat).
telephone טלפון *nm* telefon/-eem (*pl+of:* -ey).
(push-button) telephone טלפון לחיצים *nm* telefon/-ey lekheetseem.
(to) telephone לטלפן *inf* letalpen; *pst* teelpen; *pres* metalpen; *fut* yetalpen.
telephone booth תא טלפון *nm* ta/-'ey telefon.
telephone call שיחת טלפון *nf* seekh|at/-ot telefon.
telephone directory מדריך טלפון *nm* madreekh/-ey telefon.
telephone operator טלפונאי *nmf* telefon|ay/-a'eet.
telephone receiver מכשיר טלפון *nm* makhsheer/-ey telefon.
telephone token אסימון *nm* aseemon/-eem (*pl+of:* -ey).
teleprinter, teletype טלפר *nm* talpar/-eem (*pl+of:* -ey).
telescope טלסקופ *nm* teleskop/-eem (*pl+of:* -ey).
television טלוויזיה *nf* televeez|yah/-yot (+*of:* -yat).
(black and white) television טלוויזיה בשחור־לבן *nf* televeez|yah/-yot be-shakhor-lavan.
(cable) television טלוויזיה בכבלים *nf* televeezyah bee-khvaleem *(kh=k)*.
(color) television טלוויזיה צבעונית *nf* televeez|yah/-yot tseev'onee|t/-yot.
television broadcast שידור טלוויזיה *nm* sheedoor/-ey televeezyah.
television program תוכנית טלוויזיה *nf* tokhnee|t/-yot televeezyah.
television receiver מקלט טלוויזיה *nm* maklet/-ey televeezyah.
television recorder 1. מקלט חוזי *nm* maklet/-ey khozee; **2.** מכשיר וידיאו *[colloq.] nm* makh'sheer/-ey veede'o.
television set מקלט טלוויזיה *nm* maklet/-ey televeezyah.
(to) tell 1. לספר (recount) *inf* lesaper; *pst* seeper; *pres* mesaper; *fut* yesaper; **2.** לזהות (identify) *inf* lezahot; *pst* zeehah; *pres* mezaheh; *fut* yezaheh.
(his/her age is beginning to) tell הגיל נותן אותותיו בו ha-geel noten ototav bo/bah *(m/f)*.
(to) tell on someone להלשין על מישהו *inf* lehalsheen 'al meeshehoo; *pst* heelsheen *etc*; *pres* malsheen *etc*; *fut* yalsheen *etc*.
(to) tell someone off לנזוף במישהו *inf* leenzof be-meeshe|hoo/-hee *(m/f)*; *pst* nazaf *etc*; *pres* nozef *etc*; *fut* yeenzof *etc*.
teller 1. פקיד קהל *nmf* pekeed/-at kahal; **2.** קופאי בבנק (bank) *nmf* koopa|y (*cpr* koopa|'ee)/-'eet be-bank; **3.** כספר *(syn. of 2) nmf* kaspar/-eet (*pl+of:* -ey); **4.** מספר (story) *nmf* mesaper/-et.
temerity 1. תעוזה *nf* te'ooz|ah/-ot (+*of:* -at); **2.** פזיזות (rashness) *nf* pezeezoo|t/-yot.
temper 1. מזג *nm* mezeg/mezageem (*pl+of:* meezgey); **2.** אופי (character) *nm* of|ee/-ayeem (*pl+of:* -yey).
(to) temper 1. למתן (moderate) *inf* lematen; *pst* meeten; *pres* mematen; *fut* yematen; **2.** לרכך (soften) *inf* lerakekh; *pst* reekekh; *pres* merakekh; *fut* yerakekh; **3.** לחסם (metal) *vt inf* lekhasem; *pst* kheesem; *pres* mekhasem; *fut* yekhasem.
(to keep one's) temper לשלוט ברוחו *inf* leeshlot be-rookh|o/-ah *(m/f)*; *pst* shalat *etc*; *pres* sholet *etc*; *fut* yeeshlot *etc*.
(to lose one's) temper לאבד את קור רוחו *inf* le'abed et kor rookh|o/-ah *(m/f)*; *pst* eebed *etc*; *pres* me'abed *etc*; *fut* ye'abed *etc*.
temperament 1. מזג *nm* mezeg/mezageem (*pl+of:* meezgey); **2.** אופי (character) *nm* ofee/ofa|yeem (*pl+of:* -yey); **3.** טמפרמנט *nm* temperament/-eem (*pl+of:* -ey).
temperamental 1. הפכפך *adj* hafakhpakh/-ah; **2.** ניסער *adj* nees'ar/-'eret; **3.** בעל טמפרמנט *adj* ba'al/-at temperament.
temperance הינזרות ממשקאות *nf* heenazroo|t/-yot mee-mashka'ot.
temperate 1. ממוזג *adj* memooz|ag/-eget; **2.** מתון (moderate) *adj* matoon/metoonah.
temperature 1. מידות החום *nf* opl meedot ha-khom; **2.** טמפרטורה *nf* temperatoor|ah/-ot (+*of:* -at).
(has a) temperature יש לו חום yesh lo/lah *(m/f)* khom.
tempest סערה *nf* se'ar|ah/-ot (+*of:* sa'ar|at/-ot).
tempestuous סוער *adj* so'er.
temple 1. היכל (palace) *nm* heykhal/-eem (*pl+of:* -ey); **2.** בית־כנסת (synagogue) *nm* bet/batey keneset; **3.** מקדש (sacred worshiping edifice) *nm* meekd|ash/-asheem (*pl+of:* -eshey).
(the First) Temple בית ראשון *nm* bayeet reeshon.
(the Second) Temple בית שני *nm* bayeet shenee.
tempo 1. קצב *nm* ketsev; **2.** טמפו *nm* tempo.
temporal זמני *adj* zmanee/-t.
temporarily זמנית *adv* zmaneet.

temporary ארעי *adj* ara'ee/-t.
(to) tempt לפתות *inf* lefatot; *pst* peetah *(p=f)*; *pres* mefateh; *fut* yefateh.
temptation פיתוי *nm* peetoo|y/-yeem (*pl+of:* -yey).
tempter מפתה *nmf* mefat|eh.
tempting 1. מפתה *adj* mefat|eh/-ah; **2.** מגרה (exciting) *adj* megar|eh/-ah.
ten 1. עשרה *num m* 'asarah; **2.** עשר *num f* 'eser; **3.** י' *num* yod (10 in *Hebr. num. sys.*).
(the) Ten Commandments עשרת הדיברות *nm pl* 'aseret ha-deebrot.
tenable עמיד *adj* 'ameed/-ah.
tenacious 1. עקשן *adj* 'akshan/-eet; **2.** מחזיק בחוזקה *adj* makhzeek/-ah be-khozkah.
tenacity 1. כוח עמידה *nf* ko'akh ameedah; **2.** דביקות (devotion) *nf* dvekoo|t/-yot.
tenant דייר *nmf* dayar/dayeret (*pl:* dayar|eem; *+of:* -ey).
(to) tend 1. לעבד *inf* le'abed; *pst* 'eebed; *pres* me'abed; *fut* ye'abed; **2.** לטפל (handle) *inf* letapel; *pst* teepel; *pres* metapel; *fut* yetapel; **3.** לנטות (incline) *inf* leentot; *pst* natah; *pres* noteh; *fut* yeeteh.
tendency נטייה *nf* netee|yah/-yot (*+of:* -yat).
tender 1. הצעה מחייבת (binding offer) *nf* hatsa|'ah/-'ot mekha|yevet/-yvot; **2.** הצעת תשלום (payment offer) *nf* hatsa|'at/-'ot tashloom; **3.** מטענית (vehicle) *nf* meet'an'ee|t/-yot; **4.** טנדר *(colloq. syn. of 3) nm* tender/-eem.
tender 1. רחום *adj* rakhoom/rekhoomah; **2.** רגיש (sensitive) *adj* rageesh/regeeshah; **3.** ענוג (delicate) *adj* 'anog/'anoogah.
(legal) tender עובר לסוחר *adj* 'over/-et la-sokher.
tender-hearted רחמן *adj* rakhman/-eet.
tenderloin בשר אחוריים *nm* besar akhorayeem.
tenderness 1. נועם *nm* no'am; **2.** רוך (delicacy) *nm* rokh.
tendon 1. גיד *nm* geed/-eem (*pl+of:* -ey); **2.** מיתר (cord) *nm* meytar/-eem (*pl+of:* -ey).
tendril קנוקנת *nf* kenok|enet/-anot (*pl+of:* -not)
tenement משכנות עוני בהשכרה *nm pl* meeshkenot 'onee be-haskarah.
tennis טניס *nm* tenees.
tenor טנור *nm* tenor/-eem (*pl+of:* -ey).
tenor voice קול טנור *nm* kol/-ot tenor.
tense 1. דרוך *adj* darookh/drookhah; **2.** מתוח (strained) *adj* matoo'akh/metookhah; **3.** זמן (grammar) *nm* zman/-ee (*pl+of:* -ey).
tension מתח *nm* metakh/-eem (*pl+of:* meetkhey).
tent אוהל *nm* ohel/ohol|eem (*pl+of:* -ey).
(to) tent לנטות אוהל *inf* leentot ohel; *pst* natah *etc*; *pres* noteh *etc*; *fut* yeeteh *etc*.
tentacle איבר מישוש *nm* eyv|ar/-rey meeshoosh.
tentative נסיוני *adj* neesyonee/-t.
tenth עשירי *adj* 'aseeree/-t.
tenuous 1. קלוש *adj* kaloosh/klooshah; **2.** רפה (flimsy) *adj* raf|eh/-ah.
tenure 1. תקופת כהונה *nf* tekoof|at/-ot kehoonah; **2.** קביעות (permanence) *nf* kvee'oot.
tepid פושר *adj* posher/-et.

term 1. מועד *nm* mo'ed/mo'ad|eem (*pl+of:* -ey); **2.** מונח (word) *nm* moonakh/-eem (*pl+of:* -ey); **3.** תנאי (provision) *nm* tena|y/-'eem (*pl+of:* -'ey).
(to) term להגדיר *inf* lehagdeer; *pst* heegdeer; *pres* magdeer; *fut* yagdeer.
terminable הולך להיגמר *adj* holekh/-et leheegamer.
terminal 1. מסוף *nm* masof/mesof|eem (*pl+of:* -ey); **2.** סופי (final) *adj* sofee/-t.
(electric) terminal 1. מסוף זרם *nm* mesof/-ey zerem; **2.** פקק (plug) *nm* pekak/-eem (*pl+of:* -ey).
(to) terminate להביא לסיום *inf* lehavee le-seeyoom.
termination 1. סוף *nm* sof; **2.** סיום (conclusion) *nm* seeyoom/-eem (*pl+of:* -ey).
termite נמלה לבנה *nf* nemal|ah/-eem levan|ah/-ot.
terms תנאים *nm pl* tna|'eem (*pl+of:* -'ey).
(on good) terms ביחסים טובים *adv* bee-yekhaseem toveem.
(not on speaking) terms ברוגז *adv* be-rogez.
(to come to) terms להגיע לכלל הסכמה *inf* lehagee'a' lee-khlal haskamah; *pst* heegee'a' *etc*; *pres* magee'a' *etc*; *fut* yagee'a' *etc*.
terrace 1. משטח מדורג *nm* meeshtakh/-eem medoorag/-eem; **2.** גג שטוח (flat roof) *nm* gag/-ot shatoo'akh/shetookheem; **3.** טרסה *nf* teras|ah/-ot (*+of:* -at).
terrestrial 1. יבשתי *adj* yabashtee/-t; **2.** של כדור הארץ *adj* shel kadoor ha-arets.
terrible נורא *adj* nora/-'ah.
terrier 1. שפלן *nm* shaflan/-eem (*pl+of:* -ey); **2.** כלב טרייר *nm* kelev/kalbey *(b=v)* teryer.
terrific עצום *adj* 'atsoom/-ah.
(to) terrify להבעית *inf* lehav'eet; *pst* heev'eet; *pres* mav'eet; *fut* yav'eet.
territory 1. חבל ארץ *nm* khevel erets; **2.** טריטוריה *nf* tereetor|yah/-yot (*+of:* -yat).
terror 1. אימה *nf* eym|ah/-ot (*+of:* -at); **2.** טרור *nm* teror.
terrorist 1. מחבל *nmf* mekhab|el/-elet (*pl:* -leem/-lot; *+of:* -ley); **2.** טרוריסט *nmf* teroreest/-eet (*pl:* -eem; *pl+of:* -ey).
test 1. מבחן *nm* meevkhan/-eem (*pl+of:* -ey); **2.** בדיקה (checking) *nf* bedeek|ah/-ot (*+of:* -at); **3.** ניסוי (experiment) *nm* neesoo|y/-yeem (*pl+of:* yey).
(to undergo a) test לעמוד למבחן *inf* la'amod le-meevkhan; *pst* 'amad *etc*; *pres* 'omed *etc*; *fut* ya'amod *etc*.
test pilot טייס ניסוי *nm* tayas/-ey neesooy.
test tube מבחנה *nf* mavkhen|ah/-ot (*+of:* -at).
test-tube baby תינוק מבחנה *nm* teenok/-ot mavkhenah.
testament צוואה *nf* tsava|'ah/-'ot (*+of:* -'at).
(the New) Testament הברית החדשה *nf* ha-breet ha-khadashah.
(the Old) Testament 1. התנ"ך *m* ha-tanakh (*acr of* Torah, Nevee'eem, Ketooveem תורה,נביאים כתובים).
(to) testify להעיד *inf* leha'eed; *pst* he'eed; *pres* me'eed; *fut* ya'eed.
testimony עדות *nf* 'edoo|t/-yot.

tetanus 1. צפדת *nf* tsapedet; **2.** טטנוס *nm* tetanoos/-eem.

text 1. נוסח *nm* noos|akh/-akheem (*pl+of:* -'khey); **2.** טקסט *nm* tekst/-eem (*pl+of:* -ey).

textbook ספר לימוד *nm* sefer/seefrey leemood.

textile 1. אריג *nm* areeg/-eem (*pl+of:* -ey); **2.** טקסטיל *nm* teksteel/-eem (*pl+of:* -ey).

textile mill בית חרושת לטקסטיל *nm* bet/batey kharoshet le-teksteel.

textually מלה במלה *adv* meelah be-meelah.

texture 1. מרקם *nm* meerk|am/-ameem (*pl+of:* -emey); **2.** מארג (weave) *nm* ma'ar|ag/-ageem (*pl+of:* -gey).

than 1. -מ, -מ , (*prefix*) me-, mee-; **2.** מאשר me-asher.

(more) than he/she knows יותר משהוא עצמו יודע yoter mee-she-hoo/hee (*m/f*) 'atsm|o/-ah yod|e'a'/-a'at.

(more) than once יותר מפעם *adv* yoter mee-pa'am.

(to) thank להודות *inf* lehodot; *pst* hodah; *pres* modeh; *fut* yodeh.

(has oneself to) thank for הודות לו עצמו hodot lo 'atsmo.

thank heaven ! תודה לאל! todah la-el!

thank you תודה *nf* tod|ah/-ot (*+of:* -at).

thankful אסיר תודה *adj* aseer/-at todah.

thankfully בהכרת תודה *adv* be-hakarat todah.

thankfulness הכרת תודה *nf* hakarat todah.

thankless כפוי טובה *adj* kefoo|y/-yat tovah.

thankless task תפקיד כפוי טובה *nm* tafkeed/-eem kefoo|y/-yey tovah.

thanks! ! תודה todah!

thanksgiving הודייה *nf* hoda|yah/-yot (*+of:* -yat).

Thanksgiving Day חג ההודיה *nm* khag ha-hodayah.

that ההוא *adj* ha-hoo/hee.

that אשר *pron* asher.

(so) that 1. -כך ש kakh she-; **2.** -כדי ש (in order that) kedey she-.

that far עד כדי כך *adv* 'ad kedey kakh.

that is כלומר *conj* kelomar.

that long זמן כה רב *nm* zman koh rav.

that of -ההוא מ *adj* ha-hoo/hee mee-.

that which ההוא אשר *adj* ha-hoo/hee asher.

thatch 1. סכך *nm* sekhakh; **2.** קש (straw) *nm* kash.

(to) thatch לסוכך *inf* lesokhekh; *pst* sokhekh; *pres* mesokhekh; *fut* yesokhekh.

thatched roof גג קש *nm* gag/-ot kash.

thaw הפשרה *nf* hafshar|ah/-ot (*+of:* -at).

(to) thaw להפשיר *inf* lehafsheer; *pst* heefsheer; *pres* mafsheer; *fut* yafsheer.

the 1. -הָ, -הַ ha- — definite article prefixing all nouns and adjectives except those specified in 2; **2.** -הֶ he- — definite article prefixing some of the nouns and adjectives of which the opening syllable begins with ח (khet) pronounced kha, which in *"pointed"* Hebrew would have been under-dotted with a *"big kamats"* (קמץ גדול).

the more...the less... ...ככל שיותר... כן פחות ke-khol she-yoter... ken pakhot...

theater 1. תיאטרון *nm* te'atron/-eem (*pl+of:* -ey); **2.** זירה (arena) *nf* zeer|ah/-ot (*+of:* -at).

theater of war זירת הקרב *nf* zeer|at/-ot ha-krav.

theatrical תיאטרלי *adj* te'atralee/-t.

thee לך *pron* lekha/lakh (*m/f*).

theft גניבה *nf* gneyv|ah/-ot (*+of:* -at).

their, theirs שלהם possessive *pron* shelahe|m/-n (*m/f*).

(a friend of) theirs ידיד משלהם *m/f* yedeed/-ah mee-shelahe|m/-n.

them אותם *pron* ota|m/-n (*m/f*).

(to) them להם *pron* lahe|m/-n (*m/f*).

thematic של נושא *adj* shel nose.

theme 1. נושא *nm* nos|e/-'eem (*pl+of:* -'ey); **2.** רעיון יסוד (basic idea) *nm* ra'yon/-ot yesod.

theme song פזמון חוזר *nm* peezmon/-ot khoz|er/-reem.

themselves הם עצמם *pron* hem/hen 'atsma|m/-n (*m/f*).

(to) themselves להם עצמם *pron* lahe|m/-n 'atsma|m/-n (*m/f*).

then 1. אז *adv* az; **2.** אחרי כן (thereafter) *adv* akhrey khen; **3.** לכן (therefore) *conj* lakhen; **4.** כאשר (when) *prep* ka-asher.

(now and) then מזמן לזמן *adv* mee-zman lee-zman.

(very well) then ובכן oo-ve-khen.

thence מאז *adv* me-az.

thenceforth מאז ואילך *adv* me-az ve-'eylakh.

theological תיאולוגי *adj* te'ologee/-t.

theology תיאולוגיה *nf* te'olog|yah/-yot (*+of:* -yat).

theoretical 1. עיוני *adj* 'eeyoonee/-t; **2.** תיאורטי *adj* te'oretee/-t.

theory תיאוריה *nf* te'oree|yah/-yot (*+of:* -yat).

therapeutic 1. ריפויי *adj* repooyee/-t; **2.** תרפויטי *adj* terapevtee/-t.

therapy 1. ריפוי *nm* reepoo|y/-yeem (*pl+of:* -yey); **2.** תרפיה *nf* terap|yah/-yot (*+of:* -yat).

there שם *adv* sham.

there are 1. יש yesh; **2.** ישנם (more specific) *pl* yeshna|m/-n (*m/f*).

there followed an argument התפתח ויכוח heetpatakh veekoo'akh.

there is 1. יש yesh; **2.** ישנו (more specific) yesh-n|o/-ah (*m/f*).

thereabout, thereabouts 1. בערך שם *adv* be-'erekh sham; **2.** -בסמוך ל (next to) *adv* be-samookh le-.

thereafter מאז ואילך *adv* me-az ve-'eylakh.

thereby בכך bekhakh.

therefor לפיכך lefeekhakh.

therefore לכן lakhen.

therefrom 1. מכאן mee-kan; **2.** משם (from there) *adv* mee-sham.

therein בזה ba-zeh/zot (*m/f*).

thereof של זה shel zeh/zot (*m/f*).

thereon על זה 'al zeh/zot (*m/f*).

thereupon 1. מיד לאחר מכן *adv* meyad le-akhar meeken; **2.** עקב זאת (consequently) 'ekev zot.

thermal 1. חם *adj* kham/-ah; **2.** תרמי *adj* termee/-t.

thermometer מדחום *nm* madkh|om/-oomeem (*pl+of:* -oomey).

thermonuclear גרעיני *adj* gar'eenee/-t.

thermos 1. שמרחום *nm* shmarkh|om/-oomeem (*pl+of:* -oomey); **2.** תרמוס *nm* termos/-eem (*pl+of:* -ey).

thermos bottle בקבוק תרמוס *nm* bakbook/-ey termos.

thermostat תרמוסטט *nm* termostat/-eem (*pl+of:* -ey).

these 1. אלה *pron* eleh/eloo *(m/f)*; **2.** הללו *pron* halaloo.

thesis 1. הנחה *nf* hanakh|ah/-ot (*+of:* -at); **2.** מחקר (research) mekhkar/-eem (*pl+of:* -ey); **3.** דיסרטציה *nf* disertats|yah/-yot (*+of:* -yat).

they הם *pron* hem/hen *(m/f)*.

thick 1. עבות *adj* 'avot/'avootah; **2.** סמיך (dense) *adj* sameekh/smeekhah; **3.** קשה הבנה (stupid) kesh|eh/-at havanah.

(one inch) thick 1. בעובי של אינץ be-'ovee shel eench; **2.** בעובי של שני סנטימטר וחצי be-'ovee shel shney senteemeter va-khetsee.

(through) thick and thin באש ובמים *adv* ba-'esh oo-va-mayeem.

thick-headed 1. מטומטם *adj* metoomt|am/-emet; **2.** מטופש (silly) *adj* metoop|ash/-eshet.

(in the) thick of the crowd בלב ההמון *adv* be-lev he-hamon.

(in the) thick of the fighting בעיצומו של הקרב *adv* be-'eetsoomo shel ha-krav.

thick-set 1. עבה *adj* 'aveh/'avah; **2.** רחב־גרם (broad-shouldered) *adj* rekhav/rakhavat gerem.

thick-skinned בעל עור עבה *adj* ba'al/-at 'or 'aveh.

thick voice קול צרוד *nm* kol/-ot tsarood/tsroodeem.

(to) thicken 1. לעבות *vt inf* le'abot; *pst* 'eebah; *pres* me'abeh; *fut* ye'abeh; **2.** להתעבות *v rfl inf* leheet'abot; *pst* heet'abah; *pres* meet'abeh; *fut* yeet'abeh.

(the plot) thickens העלילה מסתבכת ha-'aleelah meestabekhet.

thicket חורשה *nf* khoorsh|ah/-ot (*+of:* -at).

thickly בצפיפות *adv* bee-tsfeefoot.

thickness עובי *nm* 'ovee.

thief גנב *nmf* ganav/-ah (*pl:* -eem; *pl+of:* -ey).

(to) thieve לגנוב *inf* leegnov; *pst* ganav; *pres* gonev; *fut* yeegnov.

thigh ירך *nf* yarekh/yerekhayeem (*pl+of:* yarkhey).

thimble אצבעון *nm* etsb|a'on/'-e'oneem (*+of:* -e'on/-e'oney).

thin 1. דק *adj* dak/-ah; **2.** רזה (slim) *adj* raz|eh/-ah; **3.** דליל (sparse) *adj* daleel/dleelah; **4.** עדין (fine) *adj* 'adeen/-ah; **5.** רפה (weak) *adj* raf|eh/-ah.

(to) thin 1. לדלל (dilute) *inf* ledalel; *pst* deelel; *pres* medalel; *fut* yedalel; **2.** לרזות (slim) *inf* leerzot; *pst* razah; *pres* razeh (*[colloq.]* marzeh); *fut* yeerzeh.

thin broth מרק דליל *nm* marak/merakeem daleel/deleeleem.

thin excuse תירוץ קלוש *nm* teroots/-eem kaloosh/klooshheem.

thin hair שיער דליל *nm* se'ar daleel.

thine שלך *poss. pron* shel|kha/-akh *(m/f)*.

thing 1. דבר *nm* davar/dvareem (*+of:* dvar/deevrey); **2.** חפץ (object) *nm* khefets/khafatseem (*pl+of:* kheftsey).

(no such) thing לא קיים משהו כזה lo kayam mashehoo kazeh.

(this is the) thing to do זה מה שיש לעשות zeh mah she-yesh la'asot.

(to) think לחשוב *inf* lakhshov; *pst* khashav; *pres* khoshev; *fut* yakhshov.

(to) think it over לעיין בדבר *inf* le'ayen ba-davar; *pst* 'eeyen *etc*; *pres* me'ayen *etc*; *fut* ye'ayen *etc*.

(to) think nothing of 1. שלא להתחשב ב־ *adv* she-lo leheet'khashev be-; **2.** שלא לדבר על (not to speak of) *adv* she-lo ledaber 'al.

(to) think of לחשוב אודות *inf* lakhshov odot; *pst* khashav *etc*; *pres* khoshev *etc*; *fut* yakhshov *etc*.

(what do you) think of her? מה אתה חושב עליה? mah atah/at khoshev/-et 'aleha?

(to) think up an excuse להמציא תירוץ *inf* lehamtsee teroots; *pst* heemtsee *etc*; *pres* mamtsee *etc*; *fut* yamtsee *etc*.

(to) think well of לחשוב טובות על *inf* lakhshov tovot 'al; *pst* khashav *etc*; *pres* khoshev; *fut* yakhshov *etc*.

thinker הוגה דעות *nm* hog|eh/-ey de'ot.

(to my way of) thinking לדעתי *adv* le-da'tee.

thinly בצורה דלילה *adv* be-tsoorah deleelah.

thinness דקות *nf* dak|ah/-ot.

third שלישי *adj* shleeshee/-t

third degree חקירה בעינויים *nf* khakeerah be-'eenooyeem.

third party צד שלישי *nm* tsad shleeshee.

thirst 1. צמא *nm* tsama; **2.** צימאון *nm* tseem|a'on (*+of:* -'on).

(to) thirst לצמוא *inf* leetsmo; *pst* tsama; *pres* tsame; *fut* yeetsma.

(to) thirst for להשתוקק ל־ *inf* leheeshtokek le-; *pst* heeshtokek le-; *pres* meeshtokek le-; *fut* yeeshtokek le-.

thirsty צמא *adj* tsame/tsme'ah.

(to be) thirsty לצמוא *inf* leetsmo; *pst* tsama; *pres* tsame; *fut* yeetsma.

thirteen 1. שלושה־עשר (13) *num (m)* shloshah-'asar; **2.** שלוש־עשרה(13) *num (f)* shlosh-'esreh; **3.** י״ג *num* yod-geemel (13 in *Hebr. num. syst.*).

thirteenth 1. השלושה־עשר (13) *adj (m)* ha-shloshah-'asar; **2.** השלוש־עשרה(13) *adj (f)* ha-shlosh-'esreh; **3.** הי״ג *adj* ha-yod-geemel (13 in *Hebr. num. syst.*).

thirtieth 1. השלושים (30th) *adj* ha-shlosheem; **2.** הל׳ *adj* ha-lamed (30th in *Hebr. num. syst.*).

thirty 1. שלושים (30) *num* shlosheem; **2.** ל׳ *num* lamed (30 in *Hebr. num. syst.*).

this, this one 1. הזה *pron nm* ha-zeh; **2.** הזאת *pron nf* ha-zot; **3.** הזאתי *[slang] pron f* ha-zotee.

thistle דרדר *nm* dard|ar/-areem (*pl+of:* -erey).

thither 1. לשם *adv* le-sham **2.** שמה (thereto) shamah.

thong רצועת עור *nf* retsoo|'at/-'ot 'or.

thorn קוץ *nm* kots/-eem (*pl+of:* -ey).

thorny דוקרני *adj* dokranee/-t.

thorough 1. מוגמר (finished) *adj* moogm|ar/-eret; **2.** יסודי (radical) *adj* yesodee/-t; **3.** מקיף (comprehensive) *adj* makeef/-ah.

thoroughbred גזעי *adj* geez'ee/-t.
thoroughfare 1. רחוב סואן *nm* rekhov/-ot so'en/so'aneem; **2.** דרך ראשית (main road) *nf* derekh/drakheem rashee|t/-yot.
those 1. ההם *pron* ha-he|m/-n *(m/f)*; **2.** אותם *pron* otam/-n *(m/f)*.
those of אלה מ־ el|eh/-oo mee- *(m/f)*.
those which, those who אלה אשר eleh/eloo *(m/f)* asher.
thou 1. אתה *pron m* atah; **2.** את *pron f* at.
though 1. אם כי eem kee. **2.** על אף אשר 'al af asher.
(as) though כאילו ke'eeloo.
thought 1. מחשבה *nf* makhshav|ah/-ot (+*of:* makhshevet); **2.** חשיבה (cogitation) *nf* khashee-v|ah/-ot (+*of:* -at); **3.** רעיון (idea) *nm* ra'yon/-ot; **4.** דאגה (concern) *nf* de'ag|ah/-ot (+*of:* da'g|at/-ot).
(lost in) thought שקוע במחשבות *adj* shakoo'a'/shkoo'ah be-makhshavot.
(to give no) thought לא לשים לב *inf* lo laseem lev; *pst & pres* lo sam lev; *fut* lo yaseem lev.
thoughtful 1. זהיר (careful) *adj* zaheer/zeheerah; **2.** מתחשב (considerate) *adj* meetkhashev/-et.
thoughtful of others מתחשב בזולת *adj* meetkhashev/-et ba-zoolat.
thoughtfully תוך התחשבות *adv* tokh heetkhashvoot.
thoughtfulness התחשבות *nf* heetkhashvoo|t/-yot.
thoughtless חסר התחשבות *adj* khas|ar/-rat heetkhashvoot.
thoughtlessly ללא כל התחשבות *adv* le-lo kol heetkhashvoot.
thoughtlessness 1. פזיזות (rashness) *nf* pezee-zoo|t/-yot; **2.** חוסר התחשבות (inconsiderateness) *nm* khoser heetkhashvoot.
thousand אלף *num* elef.
(two) thousand אלפיים *num* (2,000) alpayeem.
(one) thousandth אלפית (fraction) *nf* alpee|t/-yot.
(the) thousandth האלף *adj* ha-'elef.
(to) thrash להרביץ מכות נמרצות *inf* leharbeets makot neemratsot; *pst* heerbeets *etc*; *pres* marbeets *etc*; *fut* yarbeets *etc*.
(to) thrash out a matter ללבן דברים עד תום *inf* lelaben dvareem 'ad tom; *pst* leeben *etc*; *pres* melaben *etc*; *fut* yelaben.
thread 1. חוט *nm* khoot/-eem (*pl+of:* -ey); **2.** פתיל *nm* peteel/-eem (*pl+of:* -ey).
(screw) thread תבריג *nm* tavreeg/-eem (*pl+of:* -ey).
(to) thread להשחיל *inf* lehashkheel; *pst* heeshkheel; *pres* mashkheel; *fut* yashkheel.
(to) thread a screw לתברג בורג *inf* letavreg boreg; *pst* teevreg *etc*; *pres* metavreg *etc*; *fut* yetavreg *etc*.
(to) thread one's way through a crowd לגשש דרך בתוך המון *inf* legashesh derekh be-tokh hamon; *pst* geeshesh *etc*; *pres* megashesh *etc*; *fut* yegashesh *etc*.
threadbare 1. מרופט *adj* meroop|at/-etet; **2.** בלוי *adj* balooy/blooyah.
threat איום *adj* ayom/ayoomah.
(to) threaten לאיים *inf* leayem; *pst* eeyem; *pres* me'ayem; *fut* ye'ayem.

threatening מאיים *adj* me'ayem/-et.
three 1. שלושה (3) *num m* shloshah; **2.** שלוש (3) *num f* shalosh; **3.** ג' *num* geemel (3 in *Hebr. num. syst.*).
three-cornered בעל שלושה קצוות *adj* ba'al/-at shloshah ketsavot.
three hundred 1. שלוש מאות (300) *num* shlosh me'ot; **2.** ש' *num* sheen (300 in *Hebr. num. syst.*.)
three ply תלת־רובדי *adj* telat rovdee/-t.
three score שישים (60) *num* sheesheem.
three thousand 1. שלושת אלפים (3,000) *num* shloshet alafeem; **2.** ג' אלפים *num* geemel alafeem (3,000 in *Hebr. num. syst.*.)
threefold פי שלושה *adv* pee shloshah.
threshing machine מכונת דיש *nf* mekhon|at/-ot dayeesh.
threshold 1. סף saf/sap|oom (*p=f; pl+of:* -ey); **2.** מפתן *nm* meeftan/-eem (*pl+of:* -ey).
thrice 1. פי שלושה *adv* pee shloshah; **2.** שלוש פעמים (three times) shalosh pe'ameem.
thrift חיסכון *nm* kheesakhon/khes|khonot (+*of:* -khon).
thrifty 1. חסכוני *adj* kheskhonee/-t; **2.** חוסך (saving) *adj* khosekh/-et.
thrill 1. רטט *nm* ret|et/-ateem (*pl+of:* reetetey); **2.** התרגשות (excitement) *nf* heetragshoo|t/-yot.
(to) thrill להרטיט *inf* leharteet; *pst* heerteet; *pres* marteet; *fut* yarteet.
thriller מותחן *nm* motkhan/-eem (*pl+of:* -ey).
(to) thrive לשגשג *inf* lesagseg; *pst* seegseg; *pres* mesagseg; *fut* yesagseg.
throat גרון *nm* garon/gronot (+*of:* gron).
throb פעימה *nf* pe'eem|ah/-ot (+*of:* -at).
(to) throb לפעום *inf* leef'om; *pst* pa'am *(p=f)*; *pres* po'em; *fut* yeef'am.
throe 1. כאב *nm* ke'ev/-eem (*pl+of:* -ey); **2.** ייסורים *nm pl* yeesoor/-eem (*pl+of:* -ey).
throes 1. צירים *nm pl* tseer|eem (*pl+of:* -ey); **2.** חבלי לידה (birth pangs) *nm pl* khevley leydah.
thrombosis 1. קריש בדם *nm* kareesh/kreesheem ba-dam; **2.** תרומבוזה *nm* trombozah/-ot (*pl+of:* -at).
throne כס מלכות *nm* kes malkhoot.
throng המון *nm* hamon/-eem (*pl+of:* -ey).
(to) throng 1. להתקהל *inf* leheetkahel; *pst* heetkahel; *pres* meetkahel; *fut* yeetkahel; **2.** למלא עד אפס מקום (fill to capacity) *inf* lemale 'ad efes makom; *pst* meele *etc*; *pres* memale *etc*; *fut* yemale *etc*.
throttle משנק *nm* mashnek/-eem (*pl+of:* -ey).
(to) throttle 1. לשנק *inf* leshanek; *pst* sheenek; *pres* meshanek; *fut* yeshanek; **2.** להחניק (suffocate) *inf* lehakhneek; *pst* hekhneek; *pres* makhneek; *fut* yakhneek.
(to) throttle down להקטין מהירות *inf* lehakteen meheeroot; *pst* heekteen *etc*; *pres* makteen *etc*; *fut* yakteen *etc*.
throttle lever ידית המשנק *nf* yadeet ha-mashnek.
through 1. דרך *adv* derekh; **2.** מבעד (by way of) *prep* mee-be'ad; **3.** בגלל (on account of) bee-glal; **4.** במשך (during) be-meshekh; **5.** באמצעות (by means of) *adv* be-'emtsa'oot.

(to carry a plan) through להוציא תוכנית אל הפועל *inf* lehotsee tokhneet el ha-po'al; *pst* hotsee *etc*; *pres* motsee *etc*; *fut* yotsee *etc*.

(to go) through 1. להתנסות (attempt) *inf* leheetnasot; *pst* heetnasah; *pres* meetnaseh; *fut* yeetnaseh; **2.** לעבור (pass) *inf* la'avor; *pst* 'avar; *pres* 'over; *fut* ya'avor.

(wet) through רטוב לגמרי *adj* ratov/retoobah *(b=v)* legamrey.

through bus אוטובוס ישיר *nm* otoboos/-eem yasheer/yesheereem.

through ticket כרטיס ישיר *nm* kartees/-eem yasheer/yesheereem.

through train רכבת ישירה *nf* rak|evet/-avot yesheer|ah/-ot.

(to be) through with לגמור עם *inf* leegmor 'eem; *pst* gamar 'eem; *pres* gomer 'eem; *fut* yeegmor 'eem.

throughout 1. כל כולו (all through) *adj* kol kool|o/-ah; **2.** לכל אורך (during) *adv* le-khol orekh; **3.** מכל הבחינות (from all aspects) *adv* mee-kol ha-bekheenot.

throughout the year במשך כל השנה *adv* be-meshekh kol ha-shanah.

(to) throw 1. לזרוק *inf* leezrok; *pst* zarak; *pres* zorek; *fut* yeezrok; **2.** ליידות (stones) *inf* leyadot; *pst* yeedah; *pres* meyadeh; *fut* yeyadeh.

(to) throw away 1. לזרוק *inf* leezrok; *pst* zarak; *pres* zorek; *fut* yeezrok; **2.** להיפטר מ־ (get rid of) *inf* leheepater mee-; *pst & pres* neeftar *(f=p)* mee-; *fut* yeepater mee-; **3.** לבזבז (squander) levazbez; *pst* beezbez *(b=v)*; *pres* mevazbez; *fut* yevazbez.

(to) throw down להפיל *inf* lehapeel; *pst* heepeel; *pres* mapeel; *fut* yapeel.

(to) throw dust לזרות חול בעיניים *inf* leezrot khol ba-'eynayeem; *pst* zarah *etc*; *pres* zoreh *etc*; *fut* yeezreh *etc*.

(to) throw good money after bad לזרוק את החבל אחרי הדלי *inf* leezrok et ha-khevel akharey ha-dlee; *pst* zarak *etc*; *pres* zorek *etc*; *fut* yeezrok *etc*.

(to) throw off a burden להיפטר ממעמסה *inf* leheepater mee-ma'amasah; *pst & pres* neeftar *(f=p) etc*; *fut* yeepater *etc*.

(to) throw out 1. לדחות *inf* leedkhot; *pst* dakhah; *pres* dokheh; *fut* yeedkheh; **2.** לפלוט (ejaculate) *inf* leeflot; *pst* palat *(p=f)*; *pres* polet; *fut* yeeflot.

(to) throw out of gear להפריע לפעולה מסודרת *inf* lehafree'a' lee-fe'oolah *(f=p)* mesooderet; *pst* heefree'a' *etc*; *pres* mafree'a' *etc*; *fut* yafree'a' *etc*.

(to) throw out of work לפטר מעבודה *inf* lefater me-'avodah; *pst* peeter *(p=f) etc*; *pres* mefater *etc*; *fut* yefater *etc*.

(to) throw overboard להטיל לים *inf* lehateel la-yam; *pst* heeteel *etc*; *pres* mateel *etc*; *fut* yateel *etc*.

(to) throw up 1. להקיא (vomit) *inf* lehakee; *pst* hekee; *pres* mekee; *fut* yakee; **2.** לוותר (give in) levater; *pst* veeter; *pres* mevater; *fut* yevater.

thrush קיכלי מזמר *nm* keekhlee mezamer.

thrust 1. נעיצה *nf* ne'eets|ah/-ot (+*of*: -at); **2.** דחיפה (push) *nf* dekheef|ah/-ot (+*of*: -at).

(to) thrust 1. לנעוץ (stab) *inf* leen'ots; *pst* na'ats; *pres* no'ets; *fut* yeen'ats; **2.** לתחוב (insert) *inf* leetkhov; *pst* takhav; *pres* tokhev; *fut* yeetkhav; **3.** לתקוע (plug) *inf* leetko'a'; *pst* taka'; *pres* toke'a'; *fut* yeetka'; **4.** לבתק (pierce) *inf* levatek; *pst* beetek *(b=v)*; *pres* mevatek; *fut* yevatek.

(to) thrust a task upon someone לכפות משימה על מישהו *inf* leekhpot meseemah 'al meeshe|hoo/-hee *(m/f)*; *pst* kafah *(k=kh; f=p) etc*; *pres* kofeh *etc*; *fut* yeekhpeh *etc*.

(to) thrust aside לדחוף הצידה *inf* leedkhof hatseedah; *pst* dakhaf *etc*; *pres* dokhef *etc*; *fut* yeedkhaf *etc*.

(to) thrust one's way לפלס לעצמו דרך *inf* lefales le-'atsm|o/-ah *(m/f)* derekh; *pst* peeles *(p=f) etc*; *pres* mefales *etc*; *fut* yefales *etc*.

(to) thrust out 1. לטרוד *inf* leetrod; *pst* tarad; *pres* tored; *fut* yeetrod; **2.** לשרבב (stick out) *inf* lesharbev; *pst* sheerbev; *pres* mesharbev; *fut* yesharbev.

thud חבטה *nf* khavat|ah/-ot (+*of*: -at).

thug 1. סכינאי *nm* sakeen|ay/-a'eem (*pl+of*: -a'ey); **2.** רוצח (assassin) rots|e'akh/-kheem (*pl+of*: -khey).

thumb 1. אגודל *nm* agoodal/-eem (*pl+of*: -ey); **2.** בוהן (syn) *nm* bohen/behonot.

(under the) thumb of תחת השפעתו של takhat hashpa'ato shel.

thumbtack נעץ *nm* na'ats/ne'atseem (*pl+of*: na'atsey).

thump 1. חבטה *nf* khavat|ah/-ot (+*of*: -at); **2.** הקשה (sound of blow) *nf* hakash|ah/-ot (+*of*: -at).

(to) thump 1. לחבוט *inf* lakhbot; *pst* khavat *(v=b)*; *pres* khovet; *fut* yakhbot; **2.** להקיש (knock) *inf* lehakeesh; *pst* heekeesh; *pres* makeesh; *fut* yakeesh.

thunder רעם *nm* ra'am/re'ameem (*pl+of*: ra'amey).

(to) thunder לרעום *inf* leer'om; *pst* ra'am; *pres* ro'em; *fut* yeer'am.

thunderbolt 1. ברק *nm* barak/brakeem (*pl+of*: beerkey); **2.** ברק ורעם *nm* barak va-ra'am.

thundering בקולות וברקים *adv* be-kolot oo-vrakeem.

thunderous רועם *adj* ro'em/-et.

thunderstorm סופת רעמים *nf* soof|at/-ot re'ameem.

Thursday 1. יום חמישי *nm* yom/yemey khameeshee; **2.** יום ה׳ yom/yemey heh.

thus 1. כך kakh; **2.** לפיכך (consequently) lefeekhakh.

thus far עד כה *adv* 'ad koh.

(to) thwart 1. לסכל *inf* lesakel; *pst* seekel; *pres* mesakel; *fut* yesakel; **2.** לשים לאל (frustrate) *inf* laseem le-al; *pst & pres* sam *etc*; *fut* yaseem *etc*.

thy שלך *poss. pron* shel|kha/-akh *(m/f)*.

thyme קורנית *nf* koranee|t/-yot.

thyroid gland בלוטת התריס *nf* baloot|at/-ot ha-trees.

thyself בעצמך (yourself) be-'atsm|ekha/-ekh *(m/f)*.

tick 1. תקתוק *nm* teektook/-eem (*pl+of*: -ey); **2.** קרצית (insect) *nf* kartsee|t/-yot.

(to) tick 1. לסמן *inf* lesamen; *pst* seemen; *pres* mesamen; *fut* yesamen; **2.** לטקטק (type) *inf* letaktek; *pst* teektek; *pres* metaktek; *fut* yetaktek.

ticket 1. כרטיס *nm* kartees/-eem (*pl+of:* -ey); **2.** רשימת מועמדים (list of candidates) *nf* reshee-m|at/-ot moo'amadeem.

ticket collector כרטיסן *nmf* karteesan/-eet.

ticket office משרד כרטיסים *nm* meesr|ad/-edey karteeseem.

ticket window אשנב כרטיסים *nm* eshn|av/-abey *(b=v)* karteeseem.

tickle דגדוג *nm* deegdoog/-eem (*pl+of:* -ey).

(to) tickle 1. למצוא חן (please) leemtso khen; *pst* matsa *etc*; *pres* motse *etc*; *fut* yeemtsa *etc*; **2.** לדגדג (touch) *inf* ledagdeg; *pst* deegdeg; *pres* medagdeg; *fut* yedagdeg; **3.** לשעשע (amuse) *inf* lesha'she'a'; *pst* shee'she'a'; *pres* mesha'she'a'; *fut* yesha'she'a'.

tickled to death משועשע עד אין קץ *adj* meshoo'-sh|a'/-a'at 'ad eyn kets.

ticklish רגיש לדגדוג *adj* rageesh/regeeshah le-deegdoog.

tidal wave נחשול *nm* nakhshol/-eem (*pl+of:* -ey).

tidbit חתיכה הראויה להתכבד בה *nf* khateekhakh ha-re'ooyah leheetkabed bah.

tide 1. גאות ושפל *nf & nm* ge'oot va-shefel; **2.** מגמה (trend) megam|ah/-ot (*+of:* -at).

(to) tide over a difficulty להתגבר על קושי *inf* leheetgaber 'al koshee; *pst* heetgaber *etc*; *pres* meetgaber *etc*; *fut* yeetgaber *etc*.

tidewater 1. מי גאות *nm pl* mey ge'oot; **2.** מי שטפונות (floodwater) *nm pl* mey sheetfonot.

tidings בשורות חדשות *nf pl* besorot khadashot.

tidy 1. מסודר *adj* mesood|ar/-eret; **2.** נקי *adj* nakee/nekeeyah

(to) tidy 1. לסדר *inf* lesader; *pst* seeder; *pres* mesader; *fut* yesader; **2.** לנקות (clean) *inf* lenakot; *pst* neekah; *pres* menakeh; *fut* yenakeh.

(to) tidy oneself up להתנקות *v rfl inf* leheetnakot; *pst* heetnakah; *pres* meetnakeh; *fut* yeetnakeh.

(a) tidy sum סכום ניכר *nm* skhoom/-eem neekar/-eem.

tie 1. עניבה (garment) *nf* 'aneev|ah/-ot (*+of:* -at); **2.** קשר (connection) *nm* kesh|er/-areem (*pl+of:* keeshrey); **3.** לולאה (loop) *nf* loola'|ah/-'ot (*+of:* -'at); **4.** תיקו (even score) *nm* teykoo.

(railway) tie קרש מחבר בין הפסים *nf* keresh mekhaber beyn ha-paseem.

(to) tie 1. לקשור (bind) *inf* leekshor; *pst* kashar; *pres* kosher; *fut* yeekshor; **2.** להדק (fasten) *inf* lehadek; *pst* heedek; *pres* mehadek; *fut* yehadek; **3.** לחבר (unite) *inf* lekhaber; *pst* kheeber; *pres* mekhaber; *fut* yekhaber; **4.** לקשר (connect) *inf* lekasher; *pst* keesher; *pres* mekasher; *fut* yekasher.

(the result was a) tie התוצאה הייתה תיקו ha-totsa'ah haytah teykoo.

(to) tie tight לקשור חזק *inf* leekshor khazak; *pst* kashar *etc*; *pres* kosher *etc*; *fut* yeekshor.

(to) tie up the traffic לחסום את התעבורה *inf* lakhsom et ha-ta'avoorah; *pst* khasam *etc*; *pres* khosem *etc*; *fut* yakhsom *etc*.

tier 1. נדבך *nm* needb|akh/-akheem (*pl+of:* -ekhey); **2.** טור (row) *nm* toor/-eem (*pl+of:* -ey).

(close) ties קשרים הדוקים *nm pl* keshareem hadookeem.

tiger נמר *nm* namer/nemer|eem (*pl+of:* -ey).

tiger cat חתול נמרי *nm* khatool/-eem nemeree/-yeem.

tight 1. לחוץ (squeezed) *adj* lakhoots/lekhootsah; **2.** חתום (sealed) *adj* khatoom/-ah; **3.** איתן (firm) *adj* eytan/-ah; **4.** קמצן (stingy) *adj* kamtsan/-eet; **5.** שיכור (drunk) *adj* sheekor/-ah.

(it fits) tight תואם במדוקדק *adj* to'em/-et bee-medookdak.

(sit) tight! !שב ואל תזוז *v imp sing* shev/shvee ve-al tazooz/-eel *(m/f)*.

(sleep) tight! !ליל מנוחה leyl menookhah!

(to close) tight לסגור היטב *inf* leesgor heytev; *pst* sagar *etc*; *pres* soger *etc*; *fut* yeesgor *etc*.

(to hold on) tight להיצמד בחוזקה *inf* leheetsamed be-khozkah; *pst & pres* neetsmad *etc*; *fut* yeetsamed *etc*.

tight control פיקוח חמור *nm* peekoo'akh khamoor.

tight corner מצב חמור *nm* matsav/-eem khamoor/-eem.

tight market שוק דחוק *nm* shook/shvakeem dakhook/dkhookeem.

(in a) tight spot במיצר ba-meytsar.

(to) tighten להדק *inf* lehadek; *pst* heedek; *pres* mehadek; *fut* yehadek.

tight turn פנייה חדה *nf* pnee|yah/-yot khad|ah/-ot.

tightfisted קמצן *nmf* kamtsan/-eet.

tightlipped שומר סוד *adj* shomer/-et sod.

tightness 1. צפיפות (denseness) *nf* tsefeefoo|t/-yot; **2.** דחיסות (compressibility) *nf* dekheesoo|t/-yot; **3.** מתיחות (tenseness) *nf* meteekhoo|t/-yot.

tightrope חבל מתוח *nm* khevel matoo'akh.

tights 1. גרבונים (for women) *nm pl* garvon|eem (*+of:* -ey); **2.** לבוש הדוק לגוף (for dancers) *nm* levoosh hadook la-goof.

tightwad קמצן *nmf* kamtsan/-eet.

tigress נמרה *nf* nemer|ah/-ot (*+of:* -at).

tile 1. מרצפת *nf* martsef|et/-ot; **2.** חרסינה (on walls) *nf* kharseen|ah/-ot (*+of:* -at); **3.** לבנה (brick) *nf* leven|ah/-eem (*+of:* -at/-ey); **4.** בלטה (of floor) *[colloq.] nf* balat|ah/-ot (*+of:* -at).

(roof) tile רעף *nm* ra'af/re'afeem (*pl+of:* ra'fey).

(to) tile 1. לרצף (floor, walls) *inf* leratsef; *pst* reetsef; *pres* meratsef; *fut* yeratsef; **2.** לרעף (roof) *inf* lera'ef; *pst* ree'ef; *pres* mera'ef; *fut* yera'ef.

till 1. עד *prep* 'ad; **2.** עד אשר (until) *conj* 'ad asher; **3.** -עד ש (*abbr.* of 2) 'ad she-.

till 1. מגירה לכסף *nm* megeyr|ah/-ot le-kesef; **2.** אדמת חרס (clay ground) *nf* adm|at/-ot kheres.

(to) till 1. לעבד אדמה *inf* le'abed adamah; *pst* 'eebed *etc*; *pres* me'abed *etc*; *fut* ye'abed *etc*; **2.** לחרוש (plough) *inf* lakhrosh; *pst* kharash; *pres* khoresh; *fut* yakhrosh.

tillage 1. עבודת אדמה *nf* 'avodat adamah; **2.** יבול *nm* yevool/-eem (*pl+of:* -ey).

tilt 1. הטיה *nf* hata|yah/-yot (*+of:* -yat); **2.** לכסון (slant) *nm* leekhsoon/-eem (*pl+of:* -ey).

(at full) tilt במלוא הקיטור *adv* bee-mlo ha-keetor.

(to) tilt 1. להטות *inf* lehatot; *pst* heetah; *pres* mateh; *fut* yateh; **2.** ללכסן (veer) *inf* lelakhsen; *pst* leekhsen; *pres* melakhsen; *fut* yelakhsen.

timber 1. עצי בניין *nm* 'atsey beenyan; **2.** קורה (beam) *nf* kor|ah/-ot (+*of:* -at).

time 1. זמן *nm* zman/-eem (*pl+of:* -ey); **2.** שעה (hour) *nf* sha|'ah/-'ot (+*of:* she|'at/-'ot); **3.** פעם (instances) *nf* pa'am/pe'ameem (*pl+of:* pa'amey).

(at one) time פעם *adv* pa'am.

(at one and the same) time בו זמנית *adv* bo-zmaneet.

(at the same) time בו בזמן *adv* bo ba-zman.

(at this) time 1. בימים אלה *adv* be-yameem eleh; **2.** כעת (now) *adv* ka'et.

(behind) time באיחור זמן *adv* be-'eekhoor zman.

(in) time במועד ba-mo'ed.

(on) time בדיוק בזמן (exactly) *adv* be-deeyook ba-zman.

(to) time 1. למדוד זמן *inf* leemdod zman; *pst* madad *etc*; *pres* moded *etc*; *fut* yeemdod *etc*; **2.** להתאים קצב (adjust pace) *inf* lehat'eem ketsev; *pst* heet'eem *etc*; *pres* mat'eem *etc*; *fut* yat'eem *etc*; **3.** לווסת (regulate) *inf* levaset; *pst* veeset; *pres* mevaset; *fut* yevaset; **4.** לתזמן (with stopwatch) *inf* letazmen; *pst* teezmen; *pres* metazmen; *fut* yetazmen.

(to beat) time להקיש קצב *inf* lehakeesh ketsev; *pst* heekeesh *etc*; *pres* makeesh *etc*; *fut* yakeesh *etc*.

(to buy on) time לקנות בתשלומים *inf* leeknot be-tashloomeem; *pst* kanah *etc*; *pres* koneh *etc*; *fut* yeekneh *etc*.

(to have a good) time לבלות יפה *inf* levalot yafeh; *pst* beelah *(b=v) etc*; *pres* mevaleh *etc*; *fut* yevaleh *etc*.

time-out פסק־זמן *nm* pesek/peeskey zman.

(from) time to time 1. מזמן לזמן *adv* mee-zman lee-zman; **2.** לפעמים (occasionally) *adv* lee-fe'ameem *(f=p)*.

(what) time is it? ?מה השעה mah ha-sha'ah?

timeless נצחי *adj* neetskhee/-t.

timely 1. בעתו *adv* be-'eet|o/-ah *(m/f)*; **2.** מוקדם (early) *adv & adj* mookd|am/-emet.

timepiece שעון *nm* sha'on/she'on|eem (*pl+of:* -ey).

times 1. פעם *prep* pa'am; **2.** כפול (multiplied by) kafool.

(at) times לפעמים *adv* lee-fe'ameem *(f=p)*.

(several) times פעמים רבות *nf pl* pe'ameem rabot.

timetable לוח זמנים *nm* loo|'akh/-khot zmaneem

timid 1. הססן *nmf & adj* hasesan/-eet; **2.** ביישן (bashful) *nmf & adj* bayshan/-eet.

timidity 1. הססנות *nf* hasesanoo|t/-yot; **2.** ביישנות (bashfulness) *nf* bayshanoo|t/-yot.

timing 1. תזמון (stopwatch) *nm* teezmoon/-eem (*pl+of:* -ey); **2.** עיתוי (choosing right time) *nm* 'eetoo|y/-yeem (*pl+of:* -yey).

timorous 1. מפוחד *adj* mefookh|ad/-edet; **2.** חששן (apprehensive) *nmf adj* khasheshan/-eet.

tin 1. פח *nm* pakh/-eem (*pl+of:* -ey); **2.** בדיל (chemical) *nm* bedeel.

tin can 1. פחית *nf* pakhee|t/-yot; **2.** קופסה (box) *nf* koofs|ah/-a'ot (+*of:* -at).

tin foil 1. ריקוע פח *nm* reekoo|'a'/-'ey pakh; **2.** נייר כסף (food wrapping) *nm* neyar/-ot kesef.

tincture 1. צבע *nm* tseva'/tsva'eem (*pl+of:* tseev'ey); **2.** גוון (shade) *nm* gaven/gevaneem (+*of:* gon/-ey).

tincture of iodine תמיסת יוד *nf* temees|at/-ot yod.

tinder חומר הצתה *nm* khom|er/-rey hatsatah.

tinge שמץ *nm* shemets.

(to) tinge לגוון *inf* legaven; *pst* geeven; *pres* megaven; *fut* yegaven

tingle רטט *nm* ret|et/-ateem (*pl+of:* reetetey).

(to) tingle with excitement לרטוט מהתרגשות *inf* leertot me-heetragshoot; *pst* ratat *etc*; *pres* rotet *etc*; *fut* yeertot *etc*.

tinker פחח (repairman) *nm* pekhakh/-eem (*pl+of:* -ey).

tinkle צלצול *nm* tseeltsool/-eem (*pl+of:* -ey).

(to) tinkle לצלצל *inf* letsaltsel; *pst* tseeltsel; *pres* metsaltsel; *fut* yetsaltsel.

tinsel 1. לוחית מבריקה *nf* lookhee|t/-yot mav-reek|ah/-ot; **2.** ראוותני וזול *adj* ra'avtanee/-t ve-zol/-ah.

tint 1. צבע *nm* tsev|a'/-a'eem (*pl+of:* tseev'ey); **2.** גוון *nm* gaven/gvaneem (+*of:* gon/-ey).

(to) tint לצבוע *inf* leetsbo'a'; *pst* tsava' *(v=b)*; *pres* tsove'a'; *fut* yeetsba'.

tiny 1. זעיר *adj* za'eer/ze'eerah; **2.** קטנטן *adj* ketant|an/-onet.

tip 1. חוד (point) *nm* khood/-eem (*pl+of:* -ey); **2.** תשר (money) *nm* tesh|er/-areem (*pl+of:* teeshrey); **3.** רמז (hint) *nm* remez/-azeem (*pl+of:* reemzey).

(to) tip לתשור *inf* leet'shor; *pst* tashar; *pres* tosher; *fut* yeetshor.

(to) tip off להזהיר *inf* lehaz'heer; *pst* heezheer; *pres* maz'heer; *fut* yaz'heer.

(from) tip to toe על פרטי פרטיו *adv* 'al pratey pratav.

tipsy מבוסם *adj* mevoos|am/-emet.

tiptoe בהונות הרגליים *nm* behonot ha-raglayeem

(to) tiptoe לפסוע על בהונות הרגלים *inf* leefso'a' 'al behonot ha-raglayeem; *pst* pasa' *(p=f) etc*; *pres* pose'a' *etc*; *fut* yeefsa' *etc*.

tiptop שופרא דשופרא *nm* shoofra de-shoofra.

tirade השתפכות מילולית *nf* heeshtapkhoo|t/-yot meelooleе|t/-yot.

tire צמיג (auto) *nm* tsmeeg/-eem (*pl+of:* -ey).

(flat) tire 1. נקר בצמיג *nm* nek|er/-areem ba-tsemeeg/-eem; **2.** תקר בצמיג *[colloq.]* *nm* teker/tkareem ba-tsmeeg/-eem; **3.** פנצ'ר (colloquial rendering of "puncture") *nm* pantcher/-eem (*pl+of:* -ey).

(to) tire להתעייף *inf* leheet'ayef; *pst* heet'ayef; *pres* meet'ayef; *fut* yeet'ayef.

tired 1. עייף *adj* 'ayef/-ah; **2.** משועמם (bored) *adj* meshoo'm|am/-emet.

tired out באפיסת כוחות *adv* ba-afeesat kokhot.

tireless שאינו יודע לאות *adj* she-'eyn|o/-ah yod|e'a'/-a'at le'oot.

tiresome מייגע *adj* meyag|e'a'/-a'at.

tissue 1. רקמה (web) *nf* reekmah/-rekamot (+*of:* reekm|at/-ot); **2.** מלמלית (disposable) *nf* malma-lee|t/-yot.

titanic ענקי *adj* 'anakee/-t.

titanium טיטניום *nm* teetaneeyoom.
tithe מעשר *nm* ma'aser (*+of:* ma'sar).
title 1. תואר *nm* to'ar/to'or|eem (*pl+of:* -ey); **2.** כותרת (heading) *nf* kot|eret/-arot (*pl+of:* -rot).
title page שער ספר *nm* sha'ar/-ey sefer/sfareem.
to 1. אל *prep* el; **2.** -לְ, -לַ, -לִ la-, le-, lee- (abbreviated forms of 1. The pronunciation depends on the vowel in the following syllable e.g., le-bayeet, le-soos, but lee-zman).
to עד *adv* 'ad.
(near) to -קרוב ל *adv* karov le-
to and fro הנה והנה *adv* henah va-henah
(bills) to be paid 1. חשבונות לפירעון *nm pl* kheshbonot le-fera'on (*f=p*); **2.** שטרות לפרעון (promissory notes) *nm pl* shtarot le-fera'on (*f=p*).
(frightened) to death מפוחד עד מוות *adj* mefookh|ad/-edet 'ad mavet.
(he has) to go עליו ללכת 'alav/'aleha (*m/f*) lalekhet.
(from house) to house מבית לבית mee-bayeet le-vayeet (*v=b*).
(not) to my knowledge לא עד כמה שלי ידוע lo 'ad kamah she-lee yadoo'a'.
to the 1. -אל ה *prep & definite article* el ha-; **2.** la- (abbreviated form of 1. e.g. la-bayeet, la-soos, la-zman).
(a quarter) to two רבע לשתיים *nm* reva' lee-shtayeem.
toad 1. קרפדה *nm* karp|ad/-ah/-ot (*+of:* -edet/-edot); **2.** גועל (disgust) go'al.
toast 1. לחם קלוי (bread) *nm* lekhem kalooy; **2.** הרמת כוסית *nf* (drink) haram|at/-ot koseet.
(to) toast להרים כוס לחיי (drink to) *inf* lehareem kos le-khayey; *pst* hereem *etc*; *pres* mereem *etc*; *fut* yareem *etc*.
toaster מצנם *nm* matsnem/-eem (*pl+of:* -ey).
tobacco טבק *nm* tabak.
today היום *adv* ha-yom
toe אצבע הרגל *nf* etsb|a'/-e'ot ha-regel/-raglayeem.
(big) toe בוהן הרגל *nm* bohen/behonot ha-regel/ raglayeem.
(to) toe in להתכנס *inf* leheetkanes; *pst* heetkanes; *pres* meetkanes; *fut* yeetkanes.
toenail ציפורן רגל *nf* tseepor|en/-ney regel/ raglayeem.
together 1. יחדיו *adv* yakhdav; **2.** ביחד (jointly) *adv* be-yakhad.
(all) together בסך הכול *adv* be-sakh ha-kol
(to call) together לכנס *inf* lekhanes; *pst* keenes (*k=kh*); *pres* mekhanes; *fut* yekhanes.
(to come) together להתכנס *inf* leheetkanes; *pst* heetkanes; *pres* meetkanes; *fut* yeetkanes.
(to walk) together לצעוד יחדיו *inf* leets'od yakhdav; *pst* tsa'ad *etc*; *pres* tso'ed *etc*; *fut* yeets'ad *etc*.
together with ביחד עם *adv* be-yakhad 'eem.
toil 1. עמל *nm* 'amal; **2.** יגע (labor) *nm* yega'.
(to) toil לעמול קשה *inf* la'amol kasheh; *pst* 'amal *etc*; *pres* 'amel *etc*; *fut* ya'amol *etc*.
toilet 1. בית־שימוש (lavatory) *nm* bet/batey sheemoosh; **2.** אסלה (bowl) *nf* as|lah/-alot (*+of:* -lat).
toilet articles כלי איפור *nm* klee/-kley eepoor.
toilet case תיבת איפור *nf* teyv|at/-ot eepoor.
toilet paper נייר טואלט *nm* neyar too'alet.
token 1. אסימון (coin) *nm* aseemon/-eem (*pl+of:* -ey); **2.** סמל(*symbol*) *nm* semel/smaleem (*pl+of:* seemley).
token payment תשלום סמלי *nm* tashloom/-eem seemlee/-yeem.
tolerance סובלנות *nf* sovlanoot.
tolerant סובלני *adj* sovlanee/-t.
(to) tolerate 1. לסבול (suffer) *inf* leesbol; *pst* saval (*v=b*); *pres* sovel; *fut* yeesbol; **2.** להתיר (allow) *inf* lehateer; *pst* heeteer; *pres* mateer; *fut* yateer.
toleration סובלנות *nf* sovlanoo|t/-yot.
toll 1. אגרת מעבר (payment) *nf* agr|at/-ot ma'avar; **2.** צלצול (ring) *nm* teeltsool/-eem (*pl+of:* -ey).
(to) toll לצלצל בפעמונים *inf* letsaltsel ba-pa'amoneem; *pst* tseeltsel *etc*; *pres* metsaltsel *etc*; *fut* yetsaltsel *etc*.
toll bridge גשר אגרה *nm* gesher/geeshrey agrah.
toll call שיחה בין־עירונית *nf* seekh|ah/-ot been-'eeronee|t/-yot.
toll gate כניסה לכביש אגרה *nf* kenees|ah/-ot lee-khveesh (*kh=k*) agrah.
toll road כביש אגרה *nm* kveesh/-ey agrah.
tomato עגבנייה *nf* 'agvanee|yah/-yot (*+of:* -yat).
tomb קבר *nm* kev|er/-areem (*pl+of:* keevrey).
tomboy בת המתנהגת כבן *nf* bat ha-meetnahegeт ke-ven (*v=b*).
tombstone מצבה *nf* mats|evah/-evot (*+of:* -vat/ -vot).
tomcat חתול *nm* khatool/-eem (*pl+of:* -ey).
tome כרך עב־כרס *nm* kerekh/krakheem 'av/-ey kares (*cpr* keres).
tommy-gun תת־מקלע *nm* tat-makl|e'a'/-e'eem (*pl+of:* -e'ey).
tomorrow מחר *nm & adv* makhar.
(day after) tomorrow מחרתיים *nm & adv* mokhrotayeem.
tomorrow morning מחר בבוקר *adv* makhar ba-boker.
tomorrow noon מחר בצהריים *adv* makhar ba-tsohorayeem.
ton טונה *nf* ton|ah/-ot (*+of:* -at).
tone 1. גובה הצליל (pitch) *nm* govah ha-tseleel; **2.** צליל (sound) *nm* tseleel/-eem (*pl+of:* -ey).
(to) tone 1. לכוון צליל (sound) *inf* lekhaven tsleel; *pst* keeven (*k=kh*) *etc*; *pres* mekhaven *etc*; *fut* yekhaven *etc*; **2.** לשוות גוון (color) *inf* leshavot gaven; *pst* sheevah *etc*; *pres* meshaveh *etc*; *fut* yeshaveh *etc*.
(to) tone down לרכך *inf* lerakekh; *pst* reekekh; *pres* merakekh; *fut* yerakekh.
(to) tone down one's voice להנמיך קול *inf* lehanmeekh kol; *pst* heenmeekh kol; *pres* manmeekh kol; *fut* yanmeekh kol.
(to) tone in with להתאים עם *inf* lehat'eem 'eem; *pst* heet'eem 'eem; *pres* mat'eem 'eem; *fut* yat'eem 'eem.
(to) tone up לחזק *inf* lekhazek; *pst* kheezek; *pres* mekhazek; *fut* yekhazek.

tongs 1. מלקחיים *nm pl* melk|akhayeem (*+of:* -ekhey); **2.** צבת (pliers) *nf* tsevat/-ot.
tongue לשון *nf* lashon/leshonot (*+of:* leshon).
tongue-tied כבד פה *adj* kevad/keevdat peh.
tonic 1. תרופת מרץ *nf* troof|at/-ot merets; **2.** מי־סודה (soda) *nm pl* mey sodah.
tonight הלילה *adv* ha-laylah.
tonnage 1. תפוסה *nf* tefoos|ah/-ot (*+of:* -at); **2.** טונאז' *nm* tonaj.
tonsilitis דלקת שקדים *nf* dal|eket/-akot sh'kedeem.
tonsils שקדים *nm pl* sh'ked|eem (*pl+of:* -ey).
too 1. אף *prep* af; **2.** גם (also) *prep* gam; **3.** מדי (than required) *prep* meeday.
(it is) too bad! צר מאד *adj* tsar me'od.
too many רבים מדי *adj pl* rab|eem/-ot meeday.
too much יותר מדי *adv* yoter meeday.
tool 1. כלי *nm* klee/keleem (*pl+of:* kley); **2.** מכשיר (instrument) *nm* makhsheer/-eem (*pl+of:* -ey).
tool box ארגז כלים *nm* arg|az/-ezey keleem.
toot צפירה *nf* tsefeer|ah/-ot (*+of:* -at).
(to) toot לצפור *inf* letspor; *pst* tsafar *(f=p)*; *pres* tsofer; *fut* yeetspor.
(to) toot one's own horn לעשות פרסומת לעצמו *inf* la'asot persomet le-'atsm|o/-ah *(m/f)*; *pst* 'asah *etc*; *pres* 'oseh *etc*; *fut* ya'aseh *etc*.
(to have a sweet) tooth לעוט אחר דברי מתיקה *inf* la'oot akhar deevrey meteekah; *pst & pres* 'at *etc*; *fut* ya'oot *etc*.
(to fight) tooth and nail להיאבק בחירוף נפש *inf* lehe'avek be-kheroof nefesh; *pst & pres* ne'evak *etc*; *fut* ye'avek *etc*.
tooth mark מנשך *nm* meensh|akh/-akheem (*pl+of:* -ekhey).
toothache כאב שיניים *nm* ke'ev/-ey sheenayeem.
toothbrush מברשת שיניים *nf* meevresh|et/-ot sheenayeem.
toothed 1. משונן *adj* meshoon|an/-enet; **2.** בעל שיניים *nmf* ba'al/-at sheenayeem.
toothless חסר שיניים *adj* khas|ar/-rat sheenayeem.
toothpaste משחת שיניים *nf* meeshkh|at/-ot sheenayeem.
toothpick 1. קיסם שיניים *nm* kees|em/-mey sheenayeem; **2.** מחצצה *nf* makhts|etsah/-ot (*+of:* -at).
top 1. פסגה (peak) *nf* peesgah/psagot (*+of:* peesg|at/-ot); **2.** צד עליון (upper surface) *nm* tsad 'elyon; **3.** צמרת (treetop) *nm* tsam|eret/-arot (*pl+of:* -rot); **4.** מכסה (cover) *nm* meekhs|eh/-eem (*pl+of:* -ey).
(filled up to the) top מלא עד למעלה *adj* male/ mle'ah 'ad le-ma'lah.
top billing הופעה בראש רשימה *nf* hofa'ah be-rosh resheemah.
top-heavy כבד יותר בחלקו העליון *adj* kaved/ kevedah yoter be-khelk|o/-ah *(m/f)* ha-'elyon.
(on) top of בנוסף ל־ (in addition to) *adv* be-nosaf le-.
(at the) top of his class בראש הכיתה *adv* be-rosh ha-keetah.
(to) top off להשלים עד הסוף *inf* lehashleem 'ad ha-sof; *pst* heeshleem *etc*; *pres* mashleem *etc*; *fut* yashleem *etc*.
(at the) top of one's voice בקול רם *adv* be-kol ram.
top priority עדיפות עליונה *nf* 'adeefoo|t/-yot 'elyon|ah/-ot.
(at) top speed במהירות מרבית *adv* bee-meheeroot meyrabeet.
(from) top to bottom מלמעלה עד למטה *adv* mee-le-ma'lah 'ad le-matah.
topaz 1. פטדה *nf* peeted|ah/-ot (*+of:* -at); **2.** טופז *nm* topaz/-eem (*pl+of:* -ey).
toper שיכור מועד *nm* sheekor moo'ad.
topic נושא *nm* nos|e/-'eem (*pl+of:* -'ey).
topmost עליון *adj* 'elyon/-ah.
topography טופוגרפיה *nf* topograf|yah/-yot (*+of:* -yat).
(to) topple 1. להתמוטט *v rfl inf* leheetmotet; *pst* heetmotet; *pres* meetmotet; *fut* yeetmotet; **2.** למוטט *vt* lemotet; *pst* motet; *pres* memotet; *fut* yemotet.
(to) topple over להתהפך *inf* leheet'hapekh; *pst* heet'hapekh; *pres* meet'hapekh; *fut* yeet'hapekh.
topsy-turvy 1. מבולבל *adj* mevoolb|al/-elet; **2.** בערבוביה *adv* be-'eerboovyah.
torch לפיד *nm* lapeed/-eem (*pl+of:* -ey).
torch song שיר אהבה נכזבת *nm* sheer/-ey ahavah neekhzevet.
torment ייסורים *nm pl* yeesoor|eem/-ey.
(to) torment לייסר *inf* leyaser; *pst* yeeser; *pres* meyaser; *fut* yeyaser.
tornado 1. סערה *nf* se'ar|ah/-ot (*+of:* sa'ar|at/-ot); **2.** סופת טורנדו *nf* soof|at/-ot tornado.
torpedo טורפדו *nm* torped|o/-ot (*+of:* -at).
(to) torpedo לטרפד *inf* letarped; *pst* teerped; *pres* metarped; *fut* yetarped.
torpedo boat סירת טורפדו *nf* seer|at/-ot torpedo.
torque פיתול *nm* peetool/-eem (*pl+of:* -ey).
torrent שיטפון *nm* sheet|afon/-fonot (*+of:* -fon).
torrid 1. לוהט *adj* lohet/-et; **2.** צחיח *adj* tsakhee'akh/tskheekhah.
torsion 1. עיקום *nm* 'eekoom/-eem (*pl+of:* -ey); **2.** פיתול *nm* peetool/-eem (*pl+of:* -ey).
tortoise צב יבשה *nm* tsa|v/-bey *(b=v)* yabashah.
tortuous עקלקל *adj* 'akalkal/-ah.
torture עינוי *nm* 'eenoo|y/yeem (*pl+of:* -yey).
(to) torture לענות *inf* le'anot; *pst* 'eenah; *pres* me'aneh; *fut* ye'aneh.
toss 1. זריקה *nf* zreek|ah/-ot (*+of:* -at); **2.** הטלה (casting) *nf* hatal|ah/-ot (*+of:* -at).
(to) toss 1. לזרוק *inf* leezrok; *pst* zarak; *pres* zorek; *fut* yeezrok; **2.** להטיל (cast) *inf* lehateel; *pst* heeteel; *pres* mateel; *fut* yateel.
(to) toss aside להשליך *inf* lehashleekh; *pst* heeshleekh; *pres* mashleekh; *fut* yashleekh.
toss-up הטלת גורל *nf* hatal|at/-ot goral.
tot פעוט *nmf* pa'ot/-ah.
total 1. סך הכול *nm* sakh ha-kol; **2.** שלם (entire) *adj* shalem/shlemah.
totalitarian 1. רודני *adj* rodanee/-t; **2.** טוטליטרי *adj* totaleetaree/-t.
(to) totter 1. לדדות *inf* ledadot; *pst* deedah; *pres* medadeh; *fut* yedadeh; **2.** להתנודד (oscillate) *inf*

leheetnoded; *pst* heetnoded; *pres* meetnoded; *fut* yeetnoded.

touch 1. נגיעה *nf* negee|'ah/-'ot (+*of:* -'at); **2.** מגע (contact) *nm* mag|a'/-a'eem (*pl+of:* -a'ey).

(magic) touch מגע קסמים *nm* maga' kesameem.

(to) touch לנגוע *inf* leengo'a'; *pst* naga'; *pres* noge'a'; *fut* yeega'.

touch-and-go 1. חולף *adj* kholef/-et; **2.** לא בטוח (uncertain) *adj* lo batoo'akh/betookhah.

(to) touch at a port לעגון בנמל *inf* la'agon ba-namel; *pst* 'agan *etc*; *pres* 'ogen; *fut* ya'agon *etc*.

(a) touch of fever טיפה חום גבוה *[colloq.]* teepah khom gavoha.

(to) touch off an explosive לפוצץ *inf* lefotsets; *pst* potsets *(p=f)*; *pres* mefotsets; *fut* yefotsets.

(to) touch up לשפר כלשהו *inf* leshaper kolshehoo; *pst* sheeper *etc*; *pres* meshaper *etc*; *fut* yeshaper *etc*.

(to keep in) touch with לקיים קשר עם *inf* lekayem kesher 'eem; *pst* keeyem *etc*; *pres* mekayem *etc*; *fut* yekayem *etc*.

touchstone אבן בוחן *nf* even/avney bokhan.

touching נוגע ללב *adj* nog|e'a'/-a'at la-lev.

touchy 1. רגיש *adj* rageesh/regeeshah; **2.** פגיע (vulnerable) *adj* pagee'a'/pegee'ah.

tough 1. קשוח *adj* kashoo'akh/keshookhah; **2.** אלים (violent) *adj* aleem/-ah; **3.** בריון (ruffian) *nm* beeryon/-eem (*pl+of:* -ey).

(to) toughen להקשיח *inf* lehakshee'akh; *pst* heekshee'akh; *pres* makshee'akh; *fut* yakshee'akh.

toughness קשיחות *nf* kesheekhoo|t/-yot.

toupee פאה גברית *nf* pe|'ah/-'ot gavree|t/-yot.

tour סיור *nm* seeyoor/-eem.

(to) tour לסייר *inf* lesayer; *pst* seeyer; *pres* mesayer; *fut* yesayer.

touring car מכונית תיור *nf* mekhonee|t/-yot teeyoor.

tourism תיירות *nf* tayaroo|t/-yot.

tourist תייר *nmf* tayar/tayeret (*pl:* tayar|eem/-ot; *pl+of:* -ey).

tournament תחרות *nf* takhroo|t/-yot.

tourniquet חוסם עורקים *nm* khos|em/-mey 'orkeem.

(to) tow לגרור *inf* leegror; *pst* garar; *pres* gorer; *fut* yeegror.

(to take in) tow לגרור *inf* leegror; *pst* garar; *pres* gorer; *fut* yeegror.

towboat 1. סירת גרר *nf* seer|at/-ot grar; **2.** גוררת *nf* gorer|et/-ot.

toward four o'clock קרוב לשעה ארבע *adv* karov le-sha'ah arba'.

toward, towards 1. לקראת *adv* leekrat; **2.** לעבר *adv* le-'ever.

towel מגבת *nf* mag|evet/-avot (*pl+of:* -vot).

tower מגדל *nm* meegd|al/-aleem (*pl+of:* -eley).

(to) tower להתנשא *inf* leheetnase; *pst* heetnase; *pres* meetnase; *fut* yeetnase.

towering מתנשא *adj* meetnas|e/-et.

town 1. עיר (center) *nf* 'eer/'ar|eem (*pl+of:* -ey); **2.** עירוני (municipal) *adj* 'eeronee|t/-yot.

town hall בניין העירייה *nm* beenyan ha-'eereeyah.

township עיירה *nf* 'ayar|ah/-ot (+*of:* 'ayeret).

townsman בן עיר *nm* ben/-ey 'eer.

towrope חבל גרירה *nm* khevel/khavley greerah.

toxic רעיל *adj* ra'eel/re'eelah.

toy צעצוע *nm* tsa'atsoo|'a'/-'eem (*pl+of:* -'ey).

(to) toy 1. להשתעשע *inf* leheeshta'ashe'a'; *pst* heeshta'ashe'a'; *pres* meeshta'ashe'a'; *fut* yeeshta'ashe'a'; **2.** לשחק (play) *inf* lesakhek; *pst* seekhek; *pres* mesakhek; *fut* yesakhek.

trace 1. סימן *nm* seeman/-eem (*pl+of:* -ey); **2.** שריד (remnant) *nm* sareed/sreed|eem (*pl+of:* -ey); **3.** עקבות *nf pl* 'eekvot.

(to) trace להתחקות אחר *inf* leheetkhakot akhar; *pst* heetkhakah *etc*; *pres* meetkhakeh *etc*; *fut* yeetkhakeh *etc*.

(to) trace the source of לאתר את המקור *inf* le'ater et ha-makor; *pst* eeter *etc*; *pres* me'ater *etc*; *fut* ye'ater *etc*.

trachea קנה *nm* kan|eh/-eem (*pl+of:* keney).

trachoma 1. גרענת *nf* gar'enet; **2.** טרכומה *[colloq.]* *nf* trakhomah/-ot (+*of:* -at).

track 1. מסלול *nm* maslool/-eem (*pl+of:* -ey); **2.** פסים (railroad) *nm pl* pas|eem (+*of:* -ey).

(off the) track שלא במסלול הנכון *adv* she-lo ba-maslool ha-nakhon.

(race) track מסלול מירוץ *nm* masIool/-ey merots.

(railroad) track מסילת ברזל *nf* meseel|at/-ot barzel.

(to) track לעקוב *inf* la'akov; *pst* 'akav; *pres* 'okev; *fut* ya'akov.

(to) track down ללכוד *inf* leelkod; *pst* lakhad *(kh=k)*; *pres* lokhed; *fut* yeelkod.

(one) track mind משוגע לדבר אחד *nmf* meshoo-g|a'/-a'at le-davar ekhad.

(on the) track of בעיקבות *adv* be-'eekvot.

(to keep) track of לעקוב אחר *inf* la'akov akhar; *pst* 'akav *etc*; *pres* 'okev *etc*; *fut* ya'akov *etc*.

track sports התעמלויות מסלול *nf pl* heet'amlooyot maslool.

tract 1. אזור *nm* ezor/azor|eem (*pl+of:* -ey); **2.** חוברת (pamphlet) *nf* khov|eret/-rot; **3.** מרחב (area) *nm* merkhav/-eem (*pl+of:* -ey).

traction 1. גרירה *nf* greer|ah/-ot (+*of:* -at); **2.** מתיחה (stretching) *nf* meteekh|ah/-ot (+*of:* -at).

tractor טרקטור *nm* traktor/-eem (*pl+of:* -ey).

trade 1. מסחר *nm* meeskhar; **2.** אומנות (craft) *nf* oomanoo|t/-yot.

(free) trade סחר חופשי *nm* sakhar khofshee.

(to) trade 1. לסחור *inf* leeskhor; *pst* sakhar; *pres* sokher; *fut* yeeskhar; **2.** להחליף (exchange) *inf* lehakhleef; *pst* hekhleef; *pres* makhleef; *fut* yakhleef.

trade agreement 1. הסכם סחר (commerce) *nm* heskem/-ey sakhar; **2.** הסכם עבודה (labor) heskem/-ey 'avodah.

trade school בית ספר מקצועי *nm* bet/batey sefer meektso'ee/-yeem.

trade union איגוד מקצועי *nm* 'eegood/-eem meektso'ee/-yeem.

(free) trade zone איזור סחר חופשי *nm* ezor/azorey sakhar khofshee/-yeem.

trademark סמל מסחרי *nm* semel/smaleem meeskharee/-yeem.

trader אוניית סוחר (boat) *nf* oneeyat/-yot sokher.

tradesman סוחר *nm* sokh|er/-areem (*pl+of:* -arey).
tradition מסורת *nf* masor|et/-ot.
traditional מסורתי *adj* masortee/-t.
traffic 1. תעבורה *nf* ta'avoor|ah/-ot (*+of:* -at); **2.** סחר (trade) *nm* sakhar.
(to) traffic לסחור *inf* leeskhor; *pst* sakhar; *pres* sokher; *fut* yeeskhar.
tragedy טרגדיה *nf* traged|yah/-yot (*+of:* -yat).
tragic טרגי *adj* tragee/-t.
trail 1. עקב (trace) *nm* 'akev/-ot (*pl+of:* 'eekvot); **2.** שביל (path) *nm* shveel/-eem (*pl+of:* -ey).
(to) trail 1. לגרור (pull) *inf* leegror; *pst* garar; *pres* gorer; *fut* yeegror; **2.** ללכת בעיקבות (follow) *inf* lalekhet be-'eekvot; *pst* halakh *etc; pres* holekh *etc; fut* yelekh *etc.*
(to) trail behind 1. להיסחב מאחור *inf* leheesakhev me-akhor; *pst & pres* neeskhav *etc; fut* yeesakhev *etc;* **2.** להזדנב (queue) *inf* leheezdanev; *pst* heezdanev; *pres* meezdanev; *fut* yeezdanev.
train 1. רכבת (railroad) *nf* rak|evet/-avot; **2.** שובל (dress) *nm* shovel/shvaleem (*pl+of:* shovley); **3.** שובל (*cpr* of 2) *nm* shoval/-eem (*pl+of:* -ey); **4.** כבודה (retinue) *nf* kevood|ah/-ot (*+of:* -at).
(freight) train רכבת משא *nf* rak|evet/-vot masa.
(to) train 1. לאמן *inf* le'amen; *pst* eemen; *pres* me'amen; *fut* ye'amen; **2.** להדריך (instruct) *inf* lehadreekh; *pst* heedreekh; *pres* madreekh; *fut* yadreekh.
trainer 1. מאמן (coach) *nmf* me'am|en/-enet (*pl* -neem; *+of:* -ney); **2.** מדריך (instructor) *nmf* madreekh/-ah.
training 1. הכשרה *nf* hakhshar|ah/-ot (*+of:* -at); **2.** הדרכה (coaching) *nf* hadrakh|ah/-ot (*+of:* -at).
(pioneer) training הכשרה חלוצית *nf* hakhsharah khalootseet.
training camp 1. מחנה אימונים *nm* makhan|eh/-ot emooneem; **2.** מחנה הכשרה *nf* makhan|eh/-ot hakh'sharah.
trait 1. תכונה *nf* tekhoon|ah/-ot (*+of:* -at); **2.** טבע (nature) *nm* teva'.
traitor בוגד *nmf* bog|ed/-edet (*pl:* -deem; *pl+of:* -dey).
tram חשמלית *nf* khashmalee|t/-yot.
tramp 1. נווד (wanderer) *nm* navad/-eem (*pl+of:* -ey) **2.** אישה מופקרת (licentious woman) *nf* eeshah/nasheem moofk|eret/-arot; **3.** אוניית משא משוטטת (ship) *nf* onee|yat masa meshotetet.
(to) tramp 1. לשוטט *inf* leshotet; *pst* shotet; *pres* meshotet; *fut* yeshotet; **2.** לצעוד בכבדות *inf* leets'od bee-khvedoot; *pst* tsa'ad *etc; pres* tso'ed *etc; fut* yeets'ad *etc.*
(to) trample 1. לדרוך *inf* leedrokh; *pst* darakh; *pres* dorekh; *fut* yeedrokh; **2.** לרמוס (tread) *inf* leermos; *pst* ramas; *pres* romes; *fut* yeermos.
(to) trample on לדרוך על *inf* leedrokh 'al; *pst* darakh 'al; *pres* dorekh 'al; *fut* yeedrokh 'al.
trance 1. מצב היפנוטי *nm* matsav/-eem heepnotee/-yeem; **2.** טראנס *nm* trans/-eem.
(in a) trance בטראנס *adv* bee-trans.
tranquil 1. שלו *adj* shalev/-shlevah; **2.** רגוע (relaxed) *adj* ragoo'a'/regoo'ah.
tranquility, tranquillity שלווה *nf* shalv|ah (*+of:* -at).
tranquilizer, tranquillizer סם הרגעה *nm* sam/-ey harga'ah.
(to) transact 1. לנהל *inf* lenahel; *pst* neehel; *pres* menahel; *fut* yenahel; **2.** לבצע (carry out) *inf* levatse'a'; *pst* beetsa' *(b=v); pres* mevatse'a'; *fut* yevatsa'.
transaction עסקה *nf* 'eeskah/'asakot (*+of:* 'eesk|at/-ot).
transatlantic טרנסאטלנטי *adj* transatlantee/-t.
(to) transcend 1. לחרוג (overstep) *inf* lakhrog; *pst* kharag; *pres* khoreg; *fut* yakhrog; **2.** לעלות על (surpass) *inf* la'alot 'al; *pst* 'alah 'al; *pres* 'oleh 'al; *fut* ya'aleh 'al.
transcontinental 1. עבר־יבשתי *adj* 'ever-yabeshtee/-t; **2.** טראנסקונטיננטלי *adj* trans-konteenentalee/-t.
(to) transcribe לתעתק *inf* leta'tek; *pst* tee'tek; *pres* meta'tek; *fut* yeta'tek.
transcript תעתיק *nm* ta'teek/-eem (*pl+of:* -ey).
transfer 1. העברה *nf* ha'avar|ah/-ot (*+of:* -at); **2.** מסירה (delivery) *nf* meseer|ah/-ot (*+of:* -at).
transfer of ownership העברת בעלות *nf* ha'avar|at/-ot ba'aloot.
(to) transfigure לשנות מראה *inf* leshanot mar'eh; *pst* sheenah *etc; pres* meshaneh *etc; fut* yeshaneh *etc.*
(to) transform 1. לשנות צורה *inf* leshanot tsoorah; *pst* sheenah *etc; pres* meshaneh *etc; fut* yeshaneh *etc;* **2.** להפוך ל־ *vt inf* lahafokh le-; *pst* hafakh le-; *pres* hofekh le-; *fut* yahafokh le-.
transformation שינוי צורה *nm* sheenoo|y/-yey tsoorah.
transformer שנאי *nm* shan|ay/-a'eem (*pl+of:* -a'ey).
(to) transgress 1. לחרוג *inf* lakhrog; *pst* kharag; *pres* khoreg; *fut* yakhrog; **2.** להפר חוק *inf* lehafer khok; *pst* hefer *etc; pres* mefer *etc; fut* yafer *etc.*
(to) transgress the bounds of לחרוג מגבולות *inf* lakhrog mee-gvoolot; *pst* kharag *etc; pres* khoreg *etc; fut* yakhrog *etc.*
transgression 1. חריגה *nf* khareeg|ah/-ot (*+of:* -at); **2.** פריצת גדר (excess) *nf* preets|at/-ot gader.
transgressor פורץ גדר *nmf & adj* porets/-et (*pl:* portsey) gader.
transient 1. עובר אורח *nmf* 'over/-et (*pl:* 'ovrey) orakh; **2.** בן חלוף *adj* ben/bat khalof.
transistor טרנזיסטור *nm* tranzeestor/-eem (*pl+of:* -ey).
transit מעבר *nm* ma'av|ar/-areem (*pl+of:* -rey).
transition 1. חילוף *nm* kheeloof/-eem (*pl+of:* -ey); **2.** שינוי (change) *nm* sheenoo|y/-yeem (*pl+of:* -yey).
transitive 1. חולף *adj* kholef/-et; **2.** זמני (provisional) *adj* zmanee/-t.
transitive verb פועל יוצא (gram) *nm* po'al/pe'aleem yots|e/-'eem
transitory קצר *adj* katsar/ketsarah.
Transjordan עבר הירדן (officially called Jordan now) *nm* (area) *nf* (state) 'ever ha-yarden.
(to) translate לתרגם *inf* letargem; *pst* teergem; *pres* metargem; *fut* yetargem.

translation תרגום *nm* teergoom/-eem (*pl+of:* -ey).

translator 1. מתרגם *nm* metargem/-eem (*pl+of:* -ey); **2.** מתורגמן (interpreter) *nmf* metoorgeman/-eet (*pl+of:* -ey).

translucent 1. מעביר אור *adj* ma'aveer/-at or. **2.** עמום (dim) *adj* 'amoom/-ah.

transmission 1. העברה *nf* ha'avar|ah/-ot (+*of:* -at); **2.** שידור (broadcast) *nm* sheedoor/-eem (*pl+of:* -ey).

(to) transmit 1. להעביר *inf* leha'aveer; *pst* he'eveer; *pres* ma'aveer; *fut* ya'aveer; **2.** למסור (deliver) *inf* leemsor; *pst* masar; *pres* moser; *fut* yeemsor; **3.** לשדר (broadcast) *inf* leshader; *pst* sheeder; *pres* meshader; *fut* yeshader.

transmitter משדר *nm* mashder/-eem (*pl+of:* -ey).

transparent שקוף *adj* shakoof/shkoofah.

transplant 1. השתלה (operation) *nf* hashtal|ah/-ot (+*of:* -at); **2.** שתל (organ) *nm* shetel/shtaleem (*pl+of:* sheetley).

(to) transplant להשתיל *inf* lehashteel; *pst* heeshteel; *pres* mashteel; *fut* yashteel.

transport 1. תובלה (moving) *nf* toval|ah/-ot (+*of:* -at); **2.** קסם (rapture) *nm* kesem/ksameem (*pl+of:* keesmey).

(to) transport 1. להעביר *inf* leha'aveer; *pst* he'eveer; *pres* ma'aveer; *fut* ya'aveer; **2.** להוביל (cart) *inf* lehoveel; *pst* hoveel; *pres* moveel; *fut* yoveel; **3.** להקסים (enrapture) lehakseem; *pst* heekseem; *pres* makseem; *fut* yakseem.

transport plane מטוס תובלה *nm* metos/-ey tovalah.

transportation 1. הובלה (goods) *nf* hoval|ah/-ot (+*of:* -at); **2.** הסעה (passengers) *nf* hasa|'ah/-'ot (+*of:* -'at); **3.** ריגוש עילאי (enrapture) *nm* reegoosh/-eem 'eel|a'ee/-a'eeyeem.

transported with joy שאינו יודע נפשו מאושר *adj* she-'eyn|o/-ah yod|e'a'/-a'at nafsh|o/-ah me-'osher.

(to) transpose להחליף סדר *inf* lehakhleef seder; *pst* hekhleef *etc*; *pres* makhleef *etc*; *fut* yakhleef *etc*.

transverse 1. רוחבי (lateral) *adj* rokhbee/-t; **2.** אלכסוני (diagonal) *adj* alakhsonee/-t.

trap מלכודת *nf* malkod|et/-ot.

(mouse)trap מלכודת עכברים *nf* malkod|et/-ot 'akhbareem.

trapeze 1. מתח נע *nm* metakh na'; **2.** טרפז *nm* trapez/-eem (*pl+of:* -ey).

trapezoid טרפזי *adj* trapezee/-t.

trappings קישוטי לבוש *nm pl* keeshootey levoosh.

trash 1. אשפה *nf* ashp|ah/-ot (+*of:* -at); **2.** אספסוף (mob) *nm* asafsoof.

trash-can פח אשפה *nm* pakh/-ey ashpah.

travel 1. מסע *nm* mas|a'/-a'ot (*pl+of:* -'ey); **2.** נסיעה (trip) *nf* nesee|'ah/-'ot (+*of:* -'at).

(to) travel לנסוע *inf* leenso'a'; *pst* nasa'; *pres* nose'a'; *fut* yeesa'.

travel agency סוכנות נסיעות *nf* sokhnoo|t/-yot nesee'ot.

travel bureau משרד נסיעות *nm* meesr|ad/-edey nesee'ot.

traveler נוסע *nmf* nos|e'a'/-a'at (*pl:* -'eem; +*of:* -'ey).

traveler's check המחאת נוסעים *nf* hamkha|'at/-'ot nos'eem.

traveling תיור *nm* teeyoor/-eem (*pl+of:* -ey).

traveling expenses הוצאות נסיעה *nf pl* hots'ot nesee'ah.

traveling salesman סוכן נודד *nm* sokh|en/-neem noded/-eem.

travelogue 1. סרט מסע *nm* seret/seertey masa'; **2.** רשמי מסע (travel notes) *nm pl* reeshmey masa'.

(to) traverse 1. לחצות *inf* lakhtsot; *pst* khatsah; *pres* khotseh; *fut* yekhtseh; **2.** לעבור *inf* la'avor; *pst* 'avar; *pres* 'over; *fut* ya'avor.

travesty חיקוי נלעג *nm* kheekoo|y/-yeem neel'ag/-eem.

tray 1. מגש *nm* magash/-eem (*pl+of:* -ey); **2.** מגירה (drawer) *nf* meger|ah/-ot (+*of:* -at).

treacherous בוגדני *adj* bogdanee/-t.

treachery בגידה *nf* begeed|ah/-ot (+*of:* -at).

tread מדרך כף רגל *nm* meedrakh kaf regel.

(to) tread 1. לרמוס (trample) *inf* leermos; *pst* ramas; *pres* romes; *fut* yeermos; **2.** לדרוך (walk) *inf* leedrokh; *pst* darakh; *pres* dorekh; *fut* yeedrokh.

(tire) tread סוליית צמיג *nf* sool|yat/-yot tsemeeg/-eem.

treadmill 1. מכשיר דיווש *nm* makh'sheer/-ey deevoosh; **2.** שגרה מייגעת (tiring routine) *nf* sheegrah meyaga'at.

treason בגידה *nf* begeed|ah/-ot (+*of:* -at).

treasonable בוגדני *adj* bogdanee/-t.

treasure אוצר *nm* ots|ar/-arot (*pl+of:* -rot).

treasurer גזבר *nmf* geezbar/-eet.

treasury משרד האוצר *nm* meesrad ha-otsar.

(Secretary of the) Treasury שר האוצר (בארצות הברית) *nm* sar ha-otsar (be-artsot ha-breet).

treat 1. תענוג *nm* ta'anoog/-ot; **2.** הזמנת עינוגים (invitation) *nf* hazman|at/-ot 'eenoogeem.

(to) treat 1. להתיחס אל (consider) *inf* leheetyakhes el; *pst* heetyakhes el; *pres* meetyakhes el; *fut* yeetyakhes el; **2.** לכבד ב־ (offer food) *inf* lekhabed be-; *pst* keebed *(k=kh)* be-; *pres* mekhabed be-; *fut* yekhabed be-; **3.** לטפל ב־ (medically) *inf* letapel be-; *pst* teepel be-; *pres* metapel be-; *fut* yetapel be-.

treatise 1. חיבור (compilation) *nm* kheeboor/-eem (*pl+of:* -ey); **2.** מונוגרפיה *nf* monograf|yah/-yot (+*of:* -yat); **3.** מפה (map) *nf* map|ah/-ot (+*of:* -at).

treatment טיפול *nm* teepool/-eem (*pl+of:* -ey).

(medical) treatment טיפול רפואי *nm* teepool/-eem refoo'ee/-yeem.

treaty 1. ברית (covenant) *nf* breet/-ot; **2.** אמנה (pact) *nf* aman|ah/-ot (+*of:* -at); **3.** חוזה (contract) *nm* khoz|'eh/-eem (*pl+of:* -ey).

treble 1. סופרנו *nmf* soprano; **2.** פי שלושה (threefold) *adv* pee shloshah.

treble voice קול סופרנו *nm* kol/-ot soprano.

tree 1. עץ *nm* 'ets/-eem (*pl+of:* 'atsey); **2.** אילן (syn) *nm* eelan/-ot.

(apple) tree עץ תפוח *nm* 'ets/'atsey tapoo'akh.

(family) tree מגילת יוחסין *nf* megeel|at/-ot yookhaseen.

(shoe) tree אימום של נעל *nm* eemoom/-eem shel na'al/-ayeem.

(up a) tree אובד עצות *adj* oved/-et 'etsot.
treeless שומם מעצים *adj* shomem/-et me-'etseem.
treetop צמרת *nf* tsam|eret/-arot (*pl+of:* -rot).
trellis שבכה *nf* svakh|ah/-ot (*+of:* -at).
tremble רעד *nm* ra'ad/re'adeem (*pl+of:* ra'adey).
(to) tremble 1. לרעוד *inf* leer'od; *pst* ra'ad; *pres* ro'ed; *fut* yeer'ad; **2.** לחרוד (fear) lakhrod; *pst* kharad; *pres* khared; *fut* yekhrad.
tremendous 1. עצום *adj* 'atsoom/-ah; **2.** נורא (terrific) *adj* nora/-'ah.
tremor 1. רעידה *nf* re'eed|ah/-ot (*+of:* -at); **2.** רטט *nm* retet/retateem (*pl+of:* reetetey).
tremulous 1. רועד *adj* ro'ed/-et; **2.** רוטט (quivering) *adj* rotet/-et.
trench 1. חפירה *nf* khafeer|ah/-ot (*+of:* -at); **2.** תעלה (canal) *nf* te'al|ah/-ot (*+of:* -at/-ot).
trend 1. מגמה *nf* megam|ah/-ot (*+of:* -at); **2.** כיוון (direction) *nm* keevoon/-eem (*pl+of:* -ey).
trespass 1. הסגת גבול *nf* hasag|at/-ot gvool; **2.** חטא (sin) khet/khata|'eem (*pl+of:* -'ey).
(to) trespass 1. להסיג גבול *inf* lehaseeg gvool; *pst* heeseeg *etc*; *pres* maseeg *etc*; *fut* yaseeg *etc*; **2.** לחטוא (sin) *inf* lakhto; *pst* khata; *pres* khote; *fut* yekhta.
(to) trespass on property להסיג גבול רכוש *inf* lehaseeg gvool rekhoosh; *pst* heeseeg *etc*; *pres* maseeg *etc*; *fut* yaseeg *etc*.
(no) trespassing! ! אין מעבר eyn ma'avar!
tress תלתל ארוך *nm* taltal/-eem arokh/arookeem (*k=kh).*
trestle 1. חמור עבודה (table legs) *nm* khamor/-ey 'avodah; **2.** פיגום (scaffolding) *nm* peegoom/-eem (*pl+of:* -ey).
trial 1. ניסיון (attempt) *nm* nees|ayon/-yonot (*+of:* -yon); **2.** שפיטה (by court) *nf* shfeetah/-ot (*+of:* -at) **3.** משפט (hearing) *nm* meeshp|at/-ateem (*pl+of:* -etey); **4.** מאמץ (effort) *nm* ma'amats/-eem (*pl+of:* -ey).
trial flight טיסת ניסיון *nf* tees|at/-ot neesayon.
triangle משולש *nm* meshoolash/-eem (*pl+of:* -ey).
triangular בעל שלושה קצוות *adj* ba'al/-at shloshah ketsavot.
tribe שבט *nm* shevet/shvateem (*pl+of:* sheevtey).
tribulation 1. תלאה *nf* tla|'ah/-'ot (*+of:* -'at); **2.** נגע (affliction) *nm* neg|a'/-a'eem (*pl+of:* neeg'ey).
tribunal בית דין *nm* bet/batey deen.
tribune 1. במה *nmf* bam|ah/-ot (*+of:* -at); **2.** דוכן (platform) *nm* dookhan/-eem (*pl+of:* -ey).
tributary 1. יובל (stream) *nm* yooval/-eem (*pl+of:* -ey); **2.** מעלה מס (paying) *adj* ma'al|eh/-ah mas.
tribute 1. שלמי תודה (thank offering) *nm pl* shalmey todah; **2.** מס (payment) *nm* mas/mees|eem (*pl+of:* -ey).
trice הרף עין *nm* heref 'ayeen.
trick תחבולה *nf* takhbool|ah/-ot (*+of:* -at).
(to) trick 1. להונות *inf* lehonot; *pst* honah; *pres* *[colloq.]* merameh; *fut* yoneh; **2.** לרמות (cheat) *inf* leramot; *pst* reemah; *pres* merameh; *fut* yerameh.
(to) trick oneself up להתלבש חגיגית *inf* leheetlabesh khageegeet; *pst* heetlabesh *etc*; *pres* meetlabesh *etc*; *fut* yeetlabesh *etc*.
trickery 1. גניבת דעת *nf* genev|at/-ot da'at; **2.** רמאות (cheating) *nf* rama'oo|t/-yot.
trickle 1. זרימה טיפין טיפין *nf* zreem|ah tepeen teepeen; **2.** טפטוף (dripping) *nm* teeftoof/-eem (*pl+of:* -ey).
(to) trickle לטפטף *inf* letaftef; *pst* teeftef; *pres* metaftef; *fut* yetaftef.
tricky 1. מטעה *adj* mat|'eh/-'ah; **2.** ערמומי (sly) *adj* 'armoomee/-t.
trifle דבר חסר ערך *nm* davar/dvareem khas|ar/-rey 'erekh.
(to) trifle 1. לנהוג בקלות ראש *inf* leenhog be-kaloot rosh; *pst* nahag *etc*; *pres* noheg *etc*; *fut* yeenhag *etc*; **2.** להשתעשע *inf* leheeshta'ashe'a'; *pst* heeshta'ashe'a'; *pres* meeshta'ashe'a'; *fut* yeeshta'ashe'a'.
trigger הדק *nm* hedek/had|akeem (*pl+of:* -key).
trill סלסול קול *nm* seelsool/-ey kol.
(to) trill the "r" להרטיט את הרי"ש *inf* leharteet et ha-resh; *pst* heerteet *etc*; *pres* marteet *etc*; *fut* yarteet *etc*.
trilogy טרילוגיה *nf* treelog|yah/-yot (*+of:* -yat).
trim 1. מסודר יפה *adj* mesood|ar/-eret yafeh; **2.** תקינות (regularity) *nf* tekeenoot.
(to) trim 1. לסדר יפה arrange *inf* lesader yafeh; *pst* seeder *etc*; *pres* mesader *etc*; *fut* yesader *etc*; **2.** לגזוז (beard) *inf* leegzoz; *pst* gazaz; *pres* gozez; *fut* yeegzoz.
(in) trim for במיטבו לקראת *adv* be-meytav|o/-ah leekrat.
(to) trim up לקשט *inf* lekashet; *pst* keeshet; *pres* mekashet; *fut* yekashet.
trimming 1. קישוט *nm* keeshoot/-eem (*pl+of:* -ey); **2.** גיזום (pruning) *nm* geezoom/-eem (*pl+of:* -ey).
trimmings תוספות *nf pl* tosafot.
trinity שלישייה (trio) *nf* shleeshee|yah/-yot (*+of:* -yat).
(Holy) Trinity השילוש הקדוש *nm* ha-sheeloosh ha-kadosh.
trinket תכשיט זול *nm* takhsheet/-eem zol/-eem.
trip 1. מסע *nm* mas|a'/-a'ot (*pl+of:* -'ey); **2.** נסיעה (journey) *nf* nesee|'ah/-'ot (*+of:* -'at); **3.** טיול (excursion) *nm* teeyool/-eem (*pl+of:* -ey); **4.** מעידה (fall) *nf* me'eed|ah/-ot (*+of:* -at).
(to) trip 1. למעוד *inf* leem'od; *pst* ma'ad; *pres* mo'ed; *fut* yeem'ad; **2.** להכשיל (cause to fail) *vt* lehakhsheel; *pst* heekhsheel; *pres* makhsheel; *fut* yakhsheel.
triphthong תלת־תנועה *nf* telat-tenoo|'ah/-'ot (*+of:* -'at).
triple משולש *adj* meshool|ash/-eshet.
(to) triple לשלש *inf* leshalesh; *pst* sheelesh; *pres* meshalesh; *fut* yeshalesh.
triplicate בשלושה עותקים *adj* bee-shloshah 'otakeem.
tripod חצובה *nf* khatsoov|ah/-ot (*+of:* -at).
trite נדוש *adj* nadosh/nedoshah.
triumph ניצחון *nm* neets|akhon/-khonot (*+of:* -khon)
(to) triumph 1. לנצח *inf* lenatse'akh; *pst* neetse'akh; *pres* menatse'akh; *fut* yenatse'akh; **2.** לנחול ניצחון (score victory) *inf* leenkhol neetsahon; *pst* nakhal *etc*; *pres* nokhel *etc*; *fut* yeenkhal *etc*.

triumphal של ניצחון *adj* shel neetskhon.
triumphant מנצח *adj* menats|e'akh/-akhat.
triumphantly בתרועת ניצחון *adv* bee-troo|'at/-'ot neetsakhon.
trivial 1. קל ערך *adj* kal/-at 'erekh; **2.** של מה בכך (insignificant) *adj* shel mah-be-khakh; **3.** טריוויאלי *adj* treevyalee/-t.
triviality עניין פעוט *nm* 'eenyan/-eem pa'oot/pe'ooteem.
trolley חשמלית *nf* khashmalee|t/-yot.
trombone טרומבון *nm* trombon/-eem (*pl+of:* -ey).
troop 1. צבא *nm* tsava/tsva'ot (+*of:* tsva/tseev'ot); **2.** גדוד (batallion) *nm* gedood/-eem (*pl+of:* -ey); **3.** פלוגה (company) *nf* ploog|ah/-ot (+*of:* -at).
troop carrier נושא גייסות *nm* nos|e/-'ey gyasot.
trooper 1. פרש *nm* parash/-eem (*pl+of:* -ey); **2.** שוטר רוכב (mounted policeman) *nm* shot|er/-reem rokh|ev/-veem.
trophy מזכרת ניצחון *nmf* mazker|et/-ot neetsakhon.
Tropic of Cancer חוג הסרטן *nm* khoog ha-sartan.
Tropic of Capricorn חוג הגדי *nm* khoog ha-gedee.
tropical טרופי *adj* tropee/-t.
trot ריצה קלה *nf* reets|ah/-ot kal|ah/-ot.
(to) trot 1. להצעיד מהר *vt inf* lehats'eed maher; *pst* heets'eed *etc; pres* mats'eed *etc; fut* yats'eed *etc;* **2.** לצעוד מהר *vi inf* leets'od maher; *pst* tsa'ad *etc; pres* tso'ed *etc; fut* yeets'ad *etc.*
troubadour טרובדור *nm* troobadoor/-eem (*pl+of:* -ey).
trouble 1. צרה *nf* tsar|ah/-ot (+*of:* -at); **2.** דאגה (worry) *nf* de'ag|ah/-ot (+*of:* da'ag|at/-ot); **3.** טרדה (bother) *nf* teerdah/tradot (+*of:* teerd|at/-ot).
(heart) trouble מיחושי לב *nm pl* mekhooshey lev.
(in) trouble בצרה *adv* be-tsarah.
(not worth the) trouble לא שווה את המאמץ *[colloq.]* lo shav|eh/-ah et ha-ma'amats.
(to) trouble 1. להטריח *inf* lehatree'akh; *pst* heetree'akh; *pres* matree'akh; *fut* yatree'akh; **2.** להטריד (bother) *inf* lehatreed; *pst* heetreed; *pres* matreed; *fut* yatreed.
(don't) trouble! אל תטרח ! *v imp sing* al teetr|akh/-ekhee!
trouble shooter מתמחה בפתרון בעיות *nmf* moomkh|eh/-eet be-feetron (*f=p*) ba'yot.
trouble spot 1. אתר סכסוך *nm* atar/-ey seekhsookh; **2.** מוקד צרות (focus) *nm* moked tsarot.
troublemaker עושה צרות *nmf* 'os|eh/-ah (*pl:* -ey) tsarot.
troublesome 1. מטריד *adj* matreed/-ah; **2.** מדאיג (worrying) *adj* mad'eeg/-ah.
trough 1. אבוס *nm* evoos/avoos|eem (*pl+of:* -ey); **2.** שוקת (drinking-) *nf* shoket.
troupe להקה *nf* lahak|ah/lehakot (+*of:* lahak|at/-ot).
trousers מכנסיים *nm pl* meekhn|asayeem (*pl+of:* -esey).
trousseau 1. מערכת מלבושים וכלי־בית לכלה (bride's set of utensils and dresses) *nf* ma'arekhet malboosheem oo-khley (*kh=k*) bayeet la-kalah; **2.** נדוניה (dowry) *nf* nedoon|yah/-yot (+*of:* -yat); **3.** נכסי מלוג (legal term) *nm pl* neekhsey mlog.
trout טרוטה *nf* troot|ah/-ot (+*of:* -at).
trowel כף סיידים (whitewasher's) *nf* kaf/kapot (*p=f*) sayadeem.
truant 1. משתמט *nm* meestam|et/-teem (*pl+of:* tey); **2.** נעדר שלא ברשות (AWOL) *nm* ne'edar/-eem she-lo bee-reshoot.
(to play) truant להתחמק מבית הספר *inf* leheetkhamek mee-bet ha-sefer; *pst* heetkhamek *etc; pres* meetkhamek *etc; fut* yeetkhamek *etc.*
truce 1. הפוגה *nf* hafoog|ah/-ot (+*of:* -at); **2.** שביתת נשק (armistice) *nf* shveet|at/-ot neshek.
truck משאית *nf* masa'ee|t/-yot.
(to) truck להוביל משאית *inf* lehoveel masa'eet; *pst* hoveel *etc; pres* moveel *etc; fut* yoveel *etc*
truck driver נהג משאית *nm* nahag/nehagey masa'ee|t/-yot.
trudge הליכה בכבדות *nf* haleekhah bee-khvedoot (*kh=k*).
(to) trudge לשרך דרכו *inf* lesarekh dark|o/-ah (*m/f*); *pst* serakh *etc; pres* mesarekh *etc; fut* yesarekh *etc.*
true 1. אמיתי (not false) *adj* ameetee/-t; **2.** מדויק (exact) *adj* medoo|yak/-yeket.
true copy העתק נאמן *nm* he'etek/-eem ne'eman/-eem.
truly 1. באמת (not falsely) *adv* be-'emet; **2.** בדיוק (exactly) *adv* be-deeyook.
(very) truly yours 1. שלך בנאמנות shel|kha/-akh (*m/f*) be-ne'emanoot; **2.** בכבוד רב (more widely used: respectfully yours) be-khavod (*kh=k*) rav.
trump קלף עדיפות *nm* klaf/-ey 'adeefoot.
(to) trump up an excuse 1. לבדות הצדקה *inf* leevdot hatsdakah; *pst* badah (*b=v*) *etc; pres* bodeh *etc; fut* yeevdeh *etc;* **2.** לגרד תירוץ *[colloq.] inf* legared teroots; *pst* gered *etc; pres* megared *etc; fut* yegared *etc.*
trumpet חצוצרה *nf* khatsotsr|ah/-ot (+*of:* -at).
(ear) trumpet חצוצרת השמע *nf* khatsotsr|at/-ot ha-shema'.
(to) trumpet 1. לחצצר *inf* lekhatsetser; *pst* kheetsetser; *pres* mekhatsetser; *fut* yekhatsetser; **2.** לחצרץ *[colloq.] inf* lekhatsrets; *pst* kheetsrets; *pres* mekhatsrets; *fut* yekhatsrets.
truncheon אלה *nf* al|ah/-ot (+*of:* -at).
trunk 1. ארגז מזוודה (box) *nm* arg|az/-ezey meezvadah; **2.** גזע (stem) *nm* gez|a'/-a'eem (*pl+of:* geez'ey).
trunk call שיחה בין־עירונית *nf* seekh|ah/-ot ben-'eeronee/-t.
trunk line קו בין־עירוני *nm* kav ben-'eeronee/-t.
trunks תחתונים קצרים *nm pl* takhtoneem ketsareem.
trust 1. מהימנות (reliance) *nf* meheymanoo|t/-yot; **2.** אשראי (credit) *nm* ashray; **3.** הקפה (charge) *nf* hakaf|ah/-ot (+*of:* -at); **4.** איגוד חברות (firms) *nm* eegood/-ey khavarot.
(to) trust לתת אמון *inf* latet emoon; *pst* natan *etc; pres* noten *etc; fut* yeeten *etc.*
trust company חברת נאמנות *nf* khevr|at/-ot ne'emanoot.

trustee 1. נאמן *nm* ne'eman/-eem *(pl+of:* -ey); **2.** אפוטרופוס (guardian) *nm* epeetrop|os/-seem *(pl+of:* sey).

(board of) trustees מועצת נאמנים *nf* mo'etset ne'emaneem.

(university) trustees נאמנים של האוניברסיטה *nm pl* ne'emaneem shel ha-ooneeverseetah.

trusteeship נאמנות *nf* ne'emanoo|t/-yot.

trustful, trusting 1. מאמין *adj* ma'ameen/-ah; **2.** בוטח *adj* bot|e'akh/-akhat.

trustworthy, trusty מהימן *adj* meheyman/-ah.

truth אמת *nf* emet/ameetot.

truthful 1. דובר אמת *adj* dover/-et emet; **2.** כן (sincere) *adj* ken/-ah.

truthfulness כנות *nf* kenoot.

try 1. ניסיון *nm* nees|ayon/-yonot *(+of:* -yon); **2.** השתדלות *nf* heeshtadloo|t/-yot.

(to) try 1. לנסות *inf* lenasot; *pst* neesah; *pres* menaseh; *fut* yenaseh; **2.** להשתדל *inf* leheeshtadel; *pst* heeshtadel; *pres* meeshtadel; *fut* yeeshtadel; **3.** לשפוט (judge) *inf* leeshpot; *pst* shafat *(f=p)*; *pres* shofet; *fut* yeeshpot.

(to) try on a suit למדוד חליפה *inf* leemdod khaleef|ah/-ot; *pst* madad *etc*; *pres* moded *etc*; *fut* yeemdod *etc*.

(to) try one's luck לנסות מזלו *inf* lenasot mazalo; *pst* neesah *etc*; *pres* menaseh *etc*; *fut* yenaseh *etc*.

(to) try someone's patience להעמיד במבחן סבלנות של מישהו *inf* leha'ameed be-meevkhan savlanoot shel meeshe|hoo/-hee *(m/f)*; *pst* he'emeed *etc*; *pres* ma'ameed *etc*; *fut* ya'ameed *etc*.

(to) try to לעשות ניסיון *inf* la'asot neesayon; *pst* 'asah *etc*; *pres* 'oseh *etc*; *fut* ya'aseh *etc*.

trying 1. מכביד *adj* makhbeed/-ah; **2.** מרגיז (irritating) *adj* margeez/-ah.

tub 1. אמבט *nm* amb|at/-ateem *(pl+of:* -etey); **2.** גיגית (wash-) *nf* geegee|t/-yot.

(to) tub לעשות אמבטיה *inf* la'asot ambatyah; *pst* 'asah *etc*; *pres* 'oseh *etc*; *fut* ya'aseh *etc*.

tuba טובה *nf* toob|ah/-ot *(+of:* -at).

tube 1. אבוב (tire) *nm* aboov/-eem *(pl+of:* -ey); **2.** צינור (pipe) *nm* tseenor/-ot.

(inner) tube פנימי *nm* pneemee/-yeem.

(radio) tube נורת רדיו *nf* noor|at/-ot radyo.

tubercular שחוף *adj* shakhoof/shekhoofah.

tuberculosis שחפת *nf* shakhefet.

tuck קפל *nm* kef|el/-aleem *(pl+of:* keefley).

(to) tuck 1. להפשיל *inf* lehafsheel; *pst* heefsheel; *pres* mafsheel; *fut* yafsheel; **2.** לתחוב (stick in) *inf* leetkhov; *pst* takhav; *pres* tokhev; *fut* yeetkhav.

(to) tuck in לזלול לשובע *inf* leezlol la-sova'; *pst* zalal *etc*; *pres* zolel *etc*; *fut* yeezlol *etc*.

(to) tuck up one's sleeves להפשיל שרוולים *inf* lehafsheel sharvooleem; *pst* heefsheel *etc*; *pres* mafsheel *etc*; *fut* yafsheel *etc*.

Tuesday 1. יום שלישי *nm* yom/yemey shleeshee; **2.** יום ג' *nm* yom/yemey geemel.

tuft 1. פקעת (cluster) peka|'at/-'ot *(pl+of:* pak'ot); **2.** חתימת זקן (trace of beard) *nf* khateem|at/-ot zakan.

tug 1. משיכה *nf* mesheekh|ah/-ot *(+of:* -at); **2.** גרירה (tow) *nf* greer|ah/-ot *(+of:* -at).

tug of war 1. משיכת חבל *nf* mesheekh|at khevel; **2.** מאבק קשה (bitter struggle) *nm* ma'avak/-eem kash|eh/-eem.

(to) tug לגרור *inf* leegror; *pst* garar; *pres* gorer; *fut* yeegror.

tugboat ספינת גרר *nf* sfeen|at/-ot grar.

tuition שכר לימוד *nm* sekhar leemood.

tulip צבעוני *nm* tseev'on|ee/-eem *(pl+of:* -ey).

tumble אנדרלמוסיה *nf* andralmoos|yah/-yot *(+of:* -yat).

(to) tumble להתהפך *inf* leheet'hapekh; *pst* heet'hapekh; *pres* meet'hapekh; *fut* yeet'hapekh.

(to) tumble down ליפול *inf* leepol; *pst* nafal *(f=p)*; *pres* nofel; *fut* yeepol.

(to) tumble into ליפול תוך היתקלות ב־ *v inf* leepol tokh heetakloot be-; *pst* nafal *(f=p) etc*; *pres* nofel *etc*; *fut* yeepol *etc*.

(to) tumble over להתהפך *inf* leheet'hapekh; *pst* heet'hapekh; *pres* meet'hapekh; *fut* yeet'hapekh.

tumbler 1. לוליין *nm* loolyan/-eem *(pl+of:* -ey); **2.** נחום תקום (humpty dumpty) *nm* nakhoom takoom; **3.** כוס (drinking glass) *nf* kos/-ot.

tumor 1. גידול *nm* geedool/-eem *(pl+of:* -ey); **2.** תפיחה (swelling) *nf* tefeekh|ah/-ot *(+of:* -at).

tumult 1. המולה *nf* hamool|ah/-ot *(+of:* -at); **2.** התרגשות (commotion) *nf* heetragshoo|t/-yot.

tumultuous רעשני *adj* ra'ashanee/-t.

tuna 1. טונה *nf* toon|ah/-ot *(+of:* -at); **2.** דג טונה (tuna fish) *nm* dag/degey toonah.

tune 1. לחן (melody) *nm* lakhan/lekhaneem *(pl+of:* lakhaney); **2.** גובה צליל (pitch) *nm* govah tseleel.

(in) tune 1. בעצה אחת עם *adv* be-'etsah akhat 'eem; **2.** מכוון (directed) *adj* mekhoov|an/-enet.

(out of) tune סלוף כוונון *adj* sloof/-at keevnoon.

(to) tune 1. לכוונן *inf* lekhavnen; *pst* keevnen *(k=kh)*; *pres* mekhavnen; *fut* yekhavnen; **2.** להרמן (harmonize) *inf* leharmen; *pst* heermen; *pres* meharmen; *fut* yeharmen.

(to) tune up the motor לכוונן מנוע *inf* lekhavnen mano'a; *pst* keevnen *(k=kh) etc*; *pres* mekhavnen *etc*; *fut* yekhavnen *etc*.

tunic 1. איצטלה *nf* eetstal|ah/-ot *(+of:* -at); **2.** מעיל קצר (short overcoat) *nm* me'eel/-eem katsar/ketsareem.

tunnel מנהרה *nf* meen|harah/-harot *(+of:* -heret).

(to) tunnel לכרות מנהרה *inf* leekhrot meenharah; *pst* karah *(k=kh) etc*; *pres* koreh *etc*; *fut* yeekhreh *etc*.

turban 1. מצנפת *nf* meetsn|efet/-afot; **2.** טורבן *nm* toorban/-eem *(pl+of:* -ey).

turbine טורבינה *nf* toorbeen|ah/-ot *(+of:* -at).

turbulent 1. גועש *adj* go'esh/-et; **2.** מופרע (disturbed) *adj* moofr|a'/-a'at.

turf 1. שכבת עשבים *nf* sheekhv|at/-ot 'asabeem; **2.** תחום שליטה (control area) *nm* tekhoom/-ey shleetah.

Turk טורקי *nmf* toorkee/-yah.

turkey תרנגול הודו n tarnegol/-ey hodoo.

Turkey טורקיה *nf* toorkeeyah.

Turkish 1. טורקית (language) *nf* toork<u>ee</u>t; **2.** טורקי *adj* toork<u>ee</u>/-t.

turmoil מהומה *nf* mehoom|<u>a</u>h/-<u>o</u>t (*+of:* -<u>a</u>t).

turn תור *nm* tor/-<u>ee</u>m (*pl+of:* -<u>e</u>y).

(at every) turn על כל צעד *adv* ‘al kol ts<u>a</u>‘ad.

(it is my) turn תורי שלי הפעם tor<u>ee</u> shel<u>ee</u> ha-p<u>a</u>‘am.

(to) turn 1. לסובב (rotate) *inf* lesov<u>e</u>v; *pst* sov<u>e</u>v; *pres* mesov<u>e</u>v; *fut* yesov<u>e</u>v; **2.** לחרוט (shape) *inf* lakhr<u>o</u>t; *pst* khar<u>a</u>t; *pres* khor<u>e</u>t; *fut* yakhr<u>o</u>t; **3.** להיעשות (become) *inf* lehe‘as<u>o</u>t; *pst inf* na‘as<u>a</u>h; *pres* na‘as<u>e</u>h; *fut* ye‘as<u>e</u>h.

(to do a good) turn לעשות טובה *inf* la‘as<u>o</u>t tov<u>a</u>h; *pst* ‘as<u>a</u>h *etc*; *pres* ‘os<u>e</u>h *etc*; *fut* ya‘as<u>e</u>h *etc*.

(to) turn back לחזור *inf* lakhz<u>o</u>r; *pst* khaz<u>a</u>r; *pres* khoz<u>e</u>r; *fut* yakhz<u>o</u>r.

(to) turn down an offer לדחות הצעה *inf* leedkh<u>o</u>t hatsa‘<u>a</u>h; *pst* dakh<u>a</u>h *etc*; *pres* dokh<u>e</u>h *etc*; *fut* yeedkh<u>e</u>h *etc*.

(to) turn in 1. למסור *inf* leems<u>o</u>r; *pst* mas<u>a</u>r; *pres* mos<u>e</u>r; *fut* yeems<u>o</u>r; **2.** לשכב לישון (go to bed) *inf* leeshk<u>a</u>v leesh<u>o</u>n; *pst* shakh<u>a</u>v *(kh=k) etc*; *pres* shokh<u>e</u>v *etc*; *fut* yeeshk<u>a</u>v *etc*.

(to) turn inside out להפוך על פיו *inf* lahaf<u>o</u>kh ‘al p<u>ee</u>|v/-<u>a</u>h *(m/f)*; *pst* haf<u>a</u>kh *etc*; *pres* hof<u>e</u>kh *etc*; *fut* yahaf<u>o</u>kh *etc*.

(to) turn into להפוך ל- *inf* lahaf<u>o</u>kh le-; *pst* haf<u>a</u>kh le-; *pres* hof<u>e</u>kh le-; *fut* yahaf<u>o</u>kh le-.

turn of mind יחס שכלי *nm* y<u>a</u>khas seekhl<u>ee</u>.

(to) turn off 1. לכבות *inf* lekhab<u>o</u>t; *pst* keeb<u>a</u>h *(k=kh)*; *pres* mekhab<u>e</u>h; *fut* yekhab<u>e</u>h; **2.** לסגור (shut) *inf* leesg<u>o</u>r; *pst* sag<u>a</u>r; *pres* sog<u>e</u>r; *fut* yeesg<u>o</u>r.

(to) turn off the main road לסטות מהכביש הראשי *inf* leest<u>o</u>t me-ha-kv<u>ee</u>sh ha-rash<u>ee</u>; *pst* sat<u>a</u>h *etc*; *pres* sot<u>e</u>h *etc*; *fut* yeest<u>e</u>h *etc*.

(to) turn on להדליק *inf* lehadl<u>ee</u>k; *pst* heedl<u>ee</u>k; *pres* madl<u>ee</u>k; *fut* yadl<u>ee</u>k.

(to) turn on someone לעורר חשק אצל מישהו *inf* le‘or<u>e</u>r kh<u>e</u>shek ’<u>e</u>tsel m<u>ee</u>shehoo’.

(to) turn out להתברר *inf* leheetbar<u>e</u>r; *pst* heetbar<u>e</u>r; *pres* meetbar<u>e</u>r; *fut* yeetbar<u>e</u>r.

(to) turn out well להסתיים לטובה *inf* leheestay<u>e</u>m le-tov<u>a</u>h; *pst* heestay<u>e</u>m *etc*; *pres* meestay<u>e</u>m *etc*; *fut* yeestay<u>e</u>m *etc*.

(to) turn over להתהפך *v rfl inf* leheet’hap<u>e</u>kh; *pst* heet’hap<u>e</u>kh; *pres* meet’hap<u>e</u>kh; *fut* yeet’hap<u>e</u>kh.

(to) turn over and over להתהפך שוב ושוב *inf* lehee’hap<u>e</u>kh shoov va-sh<u>oo</u>v; *pst* heet’hap<u>e</u>kh *etc*; *pres* meet’hapekh *etc*; *fut* yeet’hap<u>e</u>kh *etc*.

(to) turn sour להחמיץ *inf* lehakhm<u>ee</u>ts; *pst* hekhm<u>ee</u>ts; *pres* makhm<u>ee</u>ts; *fut* yakhm<u>ee</u>ts.

(to) turn to 1. לפנות אל *inf* leefn<u>o</u>t el; *pst* pan<u>a</u>h ’el *(p=f)*; *pres* pon<u>e</u>h ’el; *fut* yeefn<u>e</u>h ’el; **2.** לפנות לעזרה (for aid) *inf* leefn<u>o</u>t le-‘ezr<u>a</u>h; *pst* pan<u>a</u>h *(p=f) etc*; *pres* pon<u>e</u>h *etc*; *fut* yeefn<u>e</u>h *etc*.

(to) turn to the left לפנות שמאלה *inf* leefn<u>o</u>t sm<u>o</u>lah; *pst* pan<u>a</u>h *etc*; *pres* pon<u>e</u>h *(p=f) etc*; *fut* yeefn<u>e</u>h *etc*.

(to) turn up 1. להופיע *inf* lehof<u>ee</u>‘a; *pst* hof<u>ee</u>‘a; *pres* mof<u>ee</u>‘a; *fut* yof<u>ee</u>‘a; **2.** לקפל (fold) *inf* lekap<u>e</u>l; *pst* keep<u>e</u>l; *pres* mekap<u>e</u>l; *fut* yekap<u>e</u>l.

(to) turn up one’s nose at לבוז *inf* lav<u>oo</u>z; *pst & pres* baz *(b=v)*; *fut* yav<u>oo</u>z.

(to) turn up one’s toes להתפגר *[colloq.] inf* leheetpag<u>e</u>r; *pst* heetpag<u>e</u>r; *pres* meetpag<u>e</u>r; *fut* yeetpag<u>e</u>r.

(to) turn upside down להפוך על פיו *inf* lahaf<u>o</u>kh ‘al p<u>ee</u>v; *pst* haf<u>a</u>kh *etc*; *pres* hof<u>e</u>kh *etc*; *fut* yahaf<u>o</u>kh *etc*.

turncoat בוגד *nmf* bog<u>e</u>d/-et.

turning point נקודת מפנה *nf* nekood|<u>a</u>t/-<u>o</u>t meefn<u>e</u>h.

turnip לפת *nm* l<u>e</u>fet.

turnover מחזור *nm* makhz<u>o</u>r/-<u>ee</u>m (*pl+of:* -<u>e</u>y).

turnover collar צווארון מתקפל *nm* tsav|ar<u>o</u>n/-ron<u>ee</u>m meetkap|<u>e</u>l/-l<u>ee</u>m

(annual) turnover מחזור שנתי *nm* makhz<u>o</u>r/-<u>ee</u>m shnat<u>ee</u>/-y<u>ee</u>m.

(business) turnover מחזור עסקי *nm* makhz<u>o</u>r/-<u>ee</u>m ‘esk<u>ee</u>/-y<u>ee</u>m.

(labor) turnover תחלופת עובדים *nf* takhloof|<u>a</u>t/-<u>o</u>t ‘ovd<u>ee</u>m.

turnpike כביש אגרה *nm* kev<u>ee</u>sh/-<u>e</u>y agr<u>a</u>h.

(it) turns my stomach מרירתי מתהפכת mereyrat<u>ee</u> meet’hap<u>e</u>khet.

(to take) turns לפעול לפי תור *inf* leef‘<u>o</u>l lef<u>ee</u> tor; *pst* pa‘<u>a</u>l *(p=f) etc*; *pres* po‘<u>e</u>l *etc*; *fut* yeef‘<u>a</u>l *etc*.

turntable 1. דיסקת התקליט *nf* deesk<u>a</u>t ha-takl<u>ee</u>t; **2.** בימה מסתובבת (rotating stage) *nf* beem<u>a</u>h meestov<u>e</u>vet.

turpentine טרפנטין *nm* terpent<u>ee</u>n.

turpitude שחיתות *nf* sh’kheet<u>oo</u>|t/-y<u>o</u>t.

turquoise טורקיז *nm* toork<u>ee</u>z.

turret צריח *nm* tser<u>ee</u>|’akh/-kh<u>ee</u>m (*pl+of:* -kh<u>e</u>y).

turtle צב *nm* ts<u>a</u>|v/-b<u>ee</u>m (*pl+of:* -b<u>e</u>y).

turtledove תור *nm* tor/-<u>ee</u>m (*pl+of:* -<u>e</u>y).

tusk שנהב *nm* shenh<u>a</u>|v/-b<u>ee</u>m (*b=v; pl+of:* -b<u>e</u>y).

tussle 1. תגרה *nf* teegr|<u>a</u>h/-<u>o</u>t (*+of:* -<u>a</u>t); **2.** התגוששות (wrestling) *nf* heetgoshesh<u>oo</u>|t/-y<u>o</u>t

tutor מורה פרטי *nmf* mor|<u>e</u>h/-<u>a</u>h prat<u>ee</u>/-t.

(to) tutor ללמד באורח פרטי *inf* lelam<u>e</u>d be-<u>o</u>fen prat<u>ee</u>; *pst* leem<u>e</u>d *etc*; *pres* melam<u>e</u>d *etc*; *fut* yelam<u>e</u>d *etc*.

tuxedo 1. חליפת ערב *nf* khaleef|<u>a</u>t/-<u>o</u>t ‘<u>e</u>rev; **2.** סמוקינג *nm* sm<u>o</u>keeng/-eem (*pl+of:* -ey).

twangy מאנפף *adj* me’anp<u>e</u>f/-et.

tweed טוויד *nm* tv<u>ee</u>d.

tweezers מלקט *nm* malk<u>e</u>t/-<u>ee</u>m (*pl+of:* -<u>e</u>y).

twelfth 1. השנים עשר *adj m* ha-shn<u>e</u>ym-‘as<u>a</u>r; **2.** השתים עשרה *adj f* ha-sht<u>e</u>ym-‘esr<u>e</u>h; **3.** הי״ב *adj* ha-yod-b<u>e</u>t (12th in *Hebr. num. sys.*).

twelve 1. שנים עשר (12) *num m* shn<u>e</u>ym-‘as<u>a</u>r; **2.** שתים עשרה *num f* sht<u>e</u>ym-‘esr<u>e</u>h; **3.** י״ב *num* yod-b<u>e</u>t (12 in *Hebr. num. sys.*).

twentieth 1. העשרים *adj* ha-‘esr<u>ee</u>m; **2.** הכ׳ *adj* ha-k<u>a</u>f (20th in *Hebr. num. sys.*).

twenty 1. עשרים (20) *num* ‘esr<u>ee</u>m; **2.** כ׳ *num* kaf (20 in *Hebr. num. sys.*).

twice 1. פעמיים *nf pl* pa‘am<u>a</u>yeem; **2.** כפליים (double) *adv* keefl<u>a</u>yeem.

twig זלזל *nm* zalz<u>a</u>l/-<u>ee</u>m (*pl+of:* -<u>e</u>y).

twilight 1. דמדומים *nm pl* deemdoom|eem (*pl+of:* -ey); **2.** בין השמשות (dawn, dusk) *adj* beyn ha-shmashot.

twin 1. תאום *nmf* te'om/-ah (*pl:* -eem/-ot; *+of:* -ey); **2.** זוגי (even) *adj* zoogee/-t.

twine חוט שזור *nm* khoot/-eem shazoor/ shezooreem.

(to) twine 1. לשזור *inf* leesh'zor; *pst* shazar; *pres* shozer; *fut* yeeshzor; **2.** לכרוך (wrap) *inf* leekhrokh; *pst* karakh *(k=kh)*; *pres* korekh; *fut* yeekhrokh.

twinge מדקרת כאב *nf* madker|et/-ot ke'ev.

(to) twinge לגרום מדקרות כאב *inf* leegrom madkerot ke'ev; *pst* garam *etc*; *pres* gorem; *fut* yeegrom *etc*.

twinkle 1. הרף עין *nm* heref 'ayeen; **2.** נצנוץ (flicker) *nm* neetsnoots/-eem (*pl+of:* -ey).

(in the) twinkle of an eye כהרף עין *adv* ke-heref 'ayeen.

(to) twinkle 1. לנצנץ *inf* lenatsnets; *pst* neetsnets; *pres* menatsnets; *fut* yenatsnets; **2.** להבליח (flicker) *inf* lehavlee'akh; *pst* heevlee'akh; *pres* mavlee'akh; *fut* yavlee'akh.

twirl סיבוב מהיר *nm* seevoov/-eem maheer/ meheereem.

(to) twirl להסתובב מהר *inf* leheestovev maher; *pst* heestovev *etc*; *pres* meestovev *etc*; *fut* yeestovev *etc*.

twist 1. שזירה *nf* shezeer|ah/-ot (*+of:* -at); **2.** נטייה (inclination) *nf* netee|yah/-yot (*+of:* -yat); **3.** עיוות (irregularity) *nf* 'eevoot/-eem (*pl+of:* -ey).

(mental) twist עיוות שכלי *nm* 'eevoot/-eem seekhlee/-yeem.

(to) twist 1. לסובב (turn) *inf* lesovev; *pst* sovev; *pres* mesovev; *fut* yesovev; **2.** ללפף (coil) *inf* lelapef; *pst* leepef; *pres* melapef; *fut* yelapef.

twitch 1. פרכוס *nm* peerkoos/-eem (*pl+of:* -ey); **2.** התכווצות (convulsion) heetkavtsoo|t/-yot; **3.** עווית (spasm) *nf* 'avee|t/-ot.

(to) twitch לפרכס *inf* lefarkes; *pst* peerkes *(p=f)*; *pres* mefarkes; *fut* yefarkes.

twitter ציוץ *nm* tseeyoots/-eem (*pl+of:* -ey)

(to) twitter לצייץ *inf* letsayets; *pst* tseeyets; *pres* metsayets; *fut* yetsayets.

two 1. שניים *num m* shnayeem (*+of:* shney); **2.** שתיים *num f* shtayeem (*+of:* shtey); **3.** ב' *num* bet (2 in *Hebr. num. sys.*).

two-cylinder 1. דו־בוכנתי *adj* doo-bookhnatee/-t; **2.** דו־צילינדרי *adj* doo-tseeleendree/-t.

two-faced דו־פרצופי *adj* doo-partsoofee/-t.

two-fisted גברתן *adj* gvartan/-eet.

twofold כפול *adj* kafool/kefoolah.

two hundred 1. מאתיים (200) *num* matayeem; **2.** ר' *num* resh (200 in *Hebr. num. sys.*).

two thousand 1. אלפיים (2,000) *num* alpayeem; **2.** ב' אלפים *num* bet alafeem (2,000 in *Hebr. num. sys.*).

two-way דו־מסלולי *adj* doo-masloolee/-t.

type 1. טיפוס *nm* teepoos/-eem (*pl+of:* -ey); **2.** דגם (model) *nm* deg|em/-ameem (*pl+of:* degmey); **3.** סדר אותיות (print) *nm* sedar oteeyot.

(to) type לתקתק *inf* letaktek; *pst* teektek; *pres* metaktek; *fut* yetaktek.

typesetter סדר *nm* sadar/-eem (*pl+of:* -ey).

(electronic) typesetting סדר אלקטרוני sedar elektronee.

(photo-)typesetting סדר צילום *nm* sedar tseeloom.

(to) typewrite לכתוב במכונה *inf* leekhtov bee-mekhonah; *pst* katav *(k=kh) etc*; *pres* kotev *etc*; *fut* yeekhtov *etc*.

(to touch-)typewrite לכתוב בשיטה עיוורת *inf* leekhtov be-sheetah 'eeveret; *pst* katav *(k=kh) etc*; *pres* kotev *etc*; *fut* yeekhtov *etc*.

typewriter מכונת־כתיבה *nf* mekhon|at/-ot keteevah.

(electronic) typewriter מכונת כתיבה אלקטרונית *nf* mekhon|at/-ot keteevah elektronee|t/-yot

(Hebrew) typewriter מכונת כתיבה עברית *nf* mekhon|at/-ot keteevah 'eevree|t/-yot.

(Latin) typewriter מכונת כתיבה לטינית *nf* mekhon|at/-ot keteevah lateeneet.

typewriting כתיבה במכונה *nf* keteevah bee-mekhonah.

typewritten כתוב במכונה *adj* katoov/ketoovah bee-mekhonah.

typhoid טיפוס המעיים *nm* teefoos ha-me'ayeem.

typhus טיפוס הבהרות *nm* teefoos ha-beharot.

typical טיפוסי *adj* teepoosee/-t.

typist כתבן במכונה *nmf* katvan/-eet bee-mekhonah.

typographical של דפוס *adj* shel defoos.

typographical error שגיאת דפוס *nf* shegee|'at/-'ot defoos.

tyrannical רודני *adj* rodanee/-t.

tyranny 1. רודנות *nf* rodanoo|t/-yot; **2.** עריצות (despotism) *nf* 'areetsoo|t/-yot.

tyrant רודן *nm* rodan/-eet.

U.

U,u when pronounced as in *use*, is transliterated as יו (Yod Vav). Hebrew has no equivalent for *u* pronounced as in *but*. Whenever sounding as the *u* in *super*, it is transliterated oo.

ubiquitous נמצא בכל מקום *adj* neemts|a/-et be-khol *(kh=k)* makom.

udder עטין *nm* 'ateen/-eem *(pl+of:* -ey).

ugliness כיעור *nm* kee'oor.

ugly מכוער *adj* mekho|'ar/-'eret.

ulcer 1. כיב *nm* keev/-eem *(pl+of:* -ey); **2.** מורסה (pus) *nf* moors|ah/-ot (+*of:* -at); **3.** אולקוס *nm* oolkoos/-eem *(pl+of:* -ey).

ulterior 1. עתידי (future) *adj* 'ateedee/-t; **2.** שלאחר מכן (subsequent) *adj* she-le-akhar mee-ken; **3.** כמוס (undisclosed) *adj* kamoos/kemoosah.

ultimate 1. סופי *adj* sofee/-t; **2.** אחרון (last) *adj* akhron/-ah.

ultimately בסופו של דבר *adv* be-sofo shel davar.

ultimatum 1. התראה אחרונה *nf* hatra'ah akhronah; **2.** אולטימטום *nm* oolteematoom/-eem *(pl+of:* -ey).

ultramodern 1. מודרני ביותר *adj* modernee/-t be-yoter; **2.** אולטרה־מודרני *adj* ooltra-modernee/-t.

ultraviolet אולטרה־סגול *adj* ooltra sagol/sgoolah.

umbilical cord חבל הטבור *nm* khevel ha-taboor.

umbrella מטרייה *nf* meetree|yah/-yot (+*of:* -yat).

umpire 1. בורר *nm* borer/-eem *(pl+of:* -ey); **2.** שופט (referee) *nm* shof|et-teem *(pl+of:* -tey); **3.** פוסק (arbiter) *nm* pos|ek/-keem *(pl+of:* -ey).

un 1. לא lo'-; **2.** אל al-; **3.** בלתי beeltee-.

unable חסר יכולת *adj* khas|ar/-rat yekholet.

unabridged לא מקוצר *adj* lo mekoots|ar/-eret.

unable to come אין ביכולתו להגיע eyn bee-yekholt|o/-ah *(m/f)* lehagee'a.

unaccented לא מודגש *adj* lo moodg|ash/-eshet.

unaccustomed לא מורגל *adj* lo moorg|al/-elet.

unaffected לא נפגע *adj* lo neefg|a'/-a'at.

unafraid לא מפחד *adj* lo mefakhed/-et.

unalterable לא ניתן לשינוי *adj* lo neet|an/-enet le-sheenooy.

unanimity תמימות דעים *nf* temeemoot de'eem.

unanimous פה אחד *adj* peh ekhad.

unarmed 1. לא חמוש *adj* lo khamoosh/-ah; **2.** בלתי מזוין *[colloq.] adj* beeltee mezoo|yan/-yenet.

unassuming בלתי מתיימר *adj* beeltee meetyamer/-et.

unattached 1. לא נשוי *adj* lo nasooy/nesoo'ah; **2.** לא משתייך *adj* lo meeshtayekh/-et.

unavoidable בלתי נמנע *adj* beeltee neemn|a'/-a'at.

unaware 1. לא מודע *adj* lo mood|a'/-a'at; **2.** בלא יודעים *adv & adj* be-lo yod'eem.

unbalanced 1. לא מאוזן *adj* lo me'ooz|an/-enet; **2.** לא שפוי (mentally) *adj* lo shafooy/shefooyah.

unbalanced account חשבון לא מאוזן *nm* kheshbon/-ot lo me'oozan/-eem.

unbearable בלתי נסבל *adj* beeltee neesb|al/-elet.

unbeatable שאין להדבירו *adj* she-eyn lehadbeer|o/-ah.

unbecoming בלתי הולם *adj* beeltee holem/-et.

(an) unbecoming dress שמלה בלתי הולמת *nf* seemlah beeltee holemet.

unbelief חוסר אמונה *nm* khoser emoonah.

unbelievable לא ייאמן *adj* lo ye'amen/te'amen.

unbeliever כופר *nmf* kofer/-et.

unbelieving ספקן *adj* safkan/-eet.

unbending 1. לא מתכופף *adj* lo meetkofef/-et; **2.** תקיף (determined) *adj* takeef/-ah.

unbiased לא משוחד *adj* lo meshookh|ad/-edet.

(to) unbosom לשפוך לבו *inf* leeshpokh leeb|o/-ah *(m/f)*; *pst* shafakh *(f=p) etc*; *pres* shofekh *etc*; *fut* yeeshpokh *etc.*

unbound 1. מכורך (book) *adj* mekhor|akh/-ekhet; **2.** לא קשור (unattached) *adj* lo kashoor/keshoorah.

unbreakable בלתי שביר *adj* beeltee shaveer/shveerah.

unbroken שלם *adj* shalem/shlemah.

(to) unbutton להתיר כפתורים *inf* lehateer kaftoreem; *pst* heeteer *etc*; *pres* mateer *etc*; *fut* yateer *etc.*

uncanny שלא כדרך הטבע *adj* she-lo ke-derekh ha-teva'.

unceasing בלתי פוסק *adj* beeltee posek/-et.

uncertain 1. לא ודאי *adj* lo vada'ee/-t; **2.** מעורפל *adj* me'oorp|al/-elet.

uncertainty חוסר ודאות *nm* khoser vada'oot.

unchangeable שאינו ניתן לשינוי *adj* she-eyn|o/-ah neet|an/-enet le-sheenooy.

unchanged ללא שינוי *adv & adj* le-lo sheenooy.

uncharitable 1. קפדן *adj* kapdan/-eet; **2.** מחמיר (severe) *adj* makhmeer/-ah.

uncivilized חסר תרבות *adj* khas|ar/-rat tarboot.

uncle דוד *nm* dod/-eem *(pl+of:* -ey).

Uncle Sam הדוד סם *nm* ha-dod sem.

Uncle Tom הדוד תום *nm* ha-dod tom.

unclean 1. לא נקי *adj* lo nakee/nekeeyah; **2.** מלוכלך (dirty) *adj* melookhl|akh/-ekhet.

uncomfortable לא נוח *adj* lo no'akh/nokhah.

uncommon לא רגיל *adj* lo rageel/regeelah.

uncompromising חסר פשרות *adj* khas|ar/-rat pesharot.

unconcerned חסר התעניינות *adj* khas|ar/-rat heet'anyenoot.

unconditional ללא תנאים *adj* le-lo tena'eem.

uncongenial לא נעים *adj* lo na'eem/ne'eemah.

unconquerable שאינו ניתן לכיבוש *adj* she-eyn|o/-ah neet|an/-enet le-kheeboosh *(kh=k)*.

unconquered שלא נכבש *adj* she-lo neekhb|ash/-eshah.

unconscious חסר הכרה *adj* khas|ar/-rat hakarah.

unconsciousness חוסר הכרה *nm* khoser hakarah.

unconstitutional נוגד את החוקה *adj* noged/-et et ha-khookah.

uncontrollable שאין שליטה עליו *adj* she-eyn shleetah 'alav.

unconventional לא קונבנציונלי *adj* lo konventsyonalee/-t.

uncouth 1. מגושם *adj* megoosh|am/-emet; **2.** גס (rude) *adj* gas/-ah.

(to) uncover 1. לחשוף *inf* lakhsof; *pst* khasaf; *pres* khosef; *fut* yakhsof; **2.** לגלות (reveal) *inf* legalot; *pst* geelah; *pres* megaleh; *fut* yegaleh.

unction משחה *nf* meeshkh|ah/-ot (*+of:* -at).

unctuous דמוי משחה *adj* demoo|y/-yat meeshkhah.

uncultivated 1. לא מעובד *adj* lo me'oob|ad/-edet; **2.** בור (fallow) *adj* boor/-ah.

uncultured חסר תרבות *adj* khas|ar/-rat tarboot.

undaunted עשוי לבלי חת *adj* 'asoo|y/-yah lee-vlee *(v=b)* khat.

undecided לא שלם בדעתו *adj* lo shalem/shlemah be-da't|o/-ah.

undeniable 1. שאין להפריכו *adj* she-eyn lehafreekh|o/-ah; **2.** שאין לסרב לו (one cannot refuse) *adj* she-eyn lesarev lo/lah.

under 1. תחת *adv* takhat; **2.** מתחת ל־ *prep* mee-takhat le-; **3.** פחות מ־ (less than) *prep* pakhot mee-.

under age, underage קטין *adj* kateen/keteenah

under cover, undercover 1. חשאי *adj* khasha'ee/-t; **2.** סודי (secret) *adj* sodee/-t.

under obligation to מחוייב כלפי *adj* mekhoo|yav/-yevet kelapey.

under secretary 1. תת־מזכיר *nm* tat-mazkeer/-eem (*pl+of:* -ey); **2.** סגן שר (in U.S. administration) *nm* segan/-eet sar.

under side, underside שטח תחתי *nm* shetakh takhtee.

under the cover of במסווה של *adv* be-masveh shel.

under the pretense of באמתלה של *adv* ba-amatlah shel.

under twelve מתחת לגיל שתים־עשרה *adv* mee-takhat le-geel shteym-'esreh.

(to) underbid להציע פחות מדי *inf* lehatsee'a pakhot meeday; *pst* heetsee'a *etc*; *pres* matsee'a *etc*; *fut* yatsee'a *etc*.

underbrush שיח נמוך *nm* see|'akh/-kheem namookh/nemookheem.

underclothes 1. תחתונים *nm pl* takhtoneem (*pl+of:* -ey); **2.** לבנים (underwear) *nm pl* levaneem (*pl+of:* leevney).

underdog מקופח *nmf* mekoop|akh/-akhat (*pl:* -akheem; *+of:* -khey)

underdose מנה לא מספקת *nf* man|ah/-ot lo masp|eket/-eekot.

underdeveloped טעון פיתוח *adj* te'oon/-at peetoo'akh.

(to) underestimate למעט בערך של *inf* lema'et ba-'erekh shel; *pst* mee'et *etc*; *pres* mema'et *etc*; *fut* yema'et *etc*.

underfed 1. סובל מתת תזונה *adj* sovel/-et mee-tat tezoonah; **2.** מורעב (starved) *adj* moor|'av/-'evet.

(to) undergo להתנסות *inf* leheetnasot; *pst* heetnasah; *pres* meetnaseh; *fut* yeetnaseh.

undergraduate סטודנט לתואר ראשון *nmf* stoodent/-eet le-to'ar reeshon

underground 1. מחתרת makht|eret/-arot; **2.** תת־קרקעי *adj* tat-karka'ee/-t.

underhanded 1. חשאי *adj* khasha'ee/-t; **2.** מוסווה (camouflaged) *adj* moosv|eh/-et.

(to) underline 1. למתוח קו מתחת *inf* leemto'akh kav mee-takhat; *pst* matakh *etc*; *pres* mote'akh *etc*; *fut* yeemtakh *etc*; **2.** להדגיש (underscore) *inf* lehadgeesh; *pst* heedgeesh; *pres* madgeesh; *fut* yadgeesh.

underlying 1. יסודי *adj* yesodee/-t; **2.** נסתר (hidden) *adj* neest|ar/-eret.

(to) undermine לחתור תחת *inf* lakhtor takhat; *pst* khatar *etc*; *pres* khoter *etc*; *fut* yakhtor *etc*.

underneath מתחת *adv* mee-takhat.

undernourishment תת־תזונה *nf* tat-tezoonah.

(to) underpay לשלם שכר ירוד *inf* leshalem sakhar yarood; *pst* sheelem *etc*; *pres* meshalem *etc*; *fut* yeshalem *etc*.

underpinning מושען מלמטה *adj* moosh|'an/-'enet mee-le-matah

(to) underscore להדגיש בקו מתחת *inf* lehadgeesh be-kav mee-takhat; *pst* heedgeesh *etc*; *pres* madgeesh *etc*; *fut* yadgeesh *etc*.

(to) undersell למכור בפחות *inf* leemkor be-fakhot *(f=p)*; *pst* makhar *(kh=k) etc*; *pres* mokher *etc*; *fut* yeemkor *etc*.

undershirt גופייה *nf* goofee|yah/-yot (*+of:* -yat).

undersigned חתום מלמטה *adj* khatoom/-ah mee-le-matah.

(the) undersigned 1. החתום מטה *nmf* hekhatoom/ha-khatoomah matah; **2.** הח"מ (*acr of* 1) *nmf* hekhatoom/ha-khatoomah matah.

undersized 1. גמוד *adj* gamood/gemoodah; **2.** נמוך (short) *adj* namookh/nemookhah.

underskirt תחתונית *nf* takhtonee|t/-yot.

understaffed בצוות שאינו מספיק *adj* be-tsevet she-eyno maspeek.

(to) understand להבין *inf* lehaveen; *pst* heveen; *pres* meveen; *fut* yaveen.

understandable ניתן להבנה *adj* neet|an/-enet la-havanah.

understood מובן *adj* moov|an/-enet.

understudy שחקן מחליף *nmf* sakhkan/-eet makhleef/-ah.

(to) understudy למלא מקום שחקן *inf* lemale mekom sakhkan; *pst* meele *etc*; *pres* memale'; *fut* yemale *etc*.

(to) undertake ליטול על עצמו *inf* leetol 'al 'atsmo; *pst* natal *etc*; *pres* notel *etc*; *fut* yeetol *etc*.

undertaker קברן *nm* kabran/-eem (*pl+of:* -ey).

undertaking 1. משימה *nf* meseem|ah/-ot (+*of:* -at); **2.** התחייבות (commitment) *nf* heetkhayvoo|t/-yot.

undertow זרם נגד חופי *nm* zerem/zrameem neged-khoopee/-yeem.

underwater תת־מימי *adj* tat maymee/-t.

under way מתקדם בדרכו *adj* meetkadem/-et be-dark|o/-ah.

underwear 1. תחתונים *nm pl* takhton|eem (*pl+of:* -ey); **2.** לבנים (underclothing) *nm pl* levaneem (*pl+of:* leevney).

underworld עולם תחתון *nm* 'olam takhton.

(to) underwrite 1. לבטח *inf* levate'akh; *pst* beete'akh *(b=v)*; *pres* mevate'akh; *fut* yevate'akh; **2.** לערוב (vouch) *inf* la'arov; *pst* 'arav; *pres* 'arev; *fut* ya'arov.

undesirable לא רצוי *adj* lo ratsooy/retsooyah.

undisturbed ללא הפרעות *adv & adj* le-lo hafra'ot.

(to) undo 1. לפרוע leefro'a; *pst* para' *(p=f)*; *pres* pore'a; *fut* yeefra'; **2.** לבטל (cancel) *inf* levatel; *pst* beetel *(b=v)*; *pres* mevatel; *fut* yevatel; **3.** לשחרר (release) *inf* leshakhrer; *pst* sheekhrer; *pres* meshakhrer; *fut* yeshakhrer.

(to) undo her hair לפרוע שערותיה leefro'a sa'aroteha; *pst* para' *(p=f) etc*; *pres* pore'a *etc*; *fut* yeefra' *etc*.

undone לא עשוי *adj* lo 'asoo|y/-yah.

(still) undone שטרם נעשה *adj* she-terem na'asah/ne'estah.

undoubtedly ללא ספק *adv* le-lo safek.

(to) undress להתפשט *inf* leheetpashet; *pst* heetpashet; *pres* meetpashet; *fut* yeetpashet.

undue 1. מופרז *adj* moofr|az/-ezet; **2.** לא הוגן (unfair) lo hogen/-et.

(to) undulate להתנחשל *inf* leheetnakh'shel; *pst* heetnakh'shel; *pres* meetnakh'shel; *fut* yeetnakh'shel.

unduly 1. שלא כדין *adv* she-lo ka-deen; **2.** בצורה מופרזת (excessively) *adv* be-tsoorah moofrezet.

undying נצחי *adj* neetskhee/-t.

(to) unearth 1. לחשוף *inf* lakhsof; *pst* khasaf; *pres* khosef; *fut* yakhsof; **2.** לגלות (uncover) *inf* legalot; *pst* geelah; *pres* megaleh; *fut* yegaleh.

uneasily 1. בעצבנות *adv* be-'atsbanoot; **2.** בחוסר מנוחה (restlessly) *adv* be-khoser menookhah.

uneasiness מבוכה *nf* mevookh|ah/-ot (+*of:* -at).

uneasy 1. מתוח *adj* matoo'akh/metookhah; **2.** מודאג (worried) *adj* mood|'ag/-'eget.

uneducated לא מחונך *adj* lo mekhoon|akh/-ekhet.

unemployed מובטל *nmf* moovt|al/-elet (*pl:* -aleem; +*of:* -aley).

unemployed funds קרן אבטלה *nf* keren/karnot avtalah.

unemployment אבטלה *nf* avtal|ah/-ot (+*of:* -at).

unending ללא קץ *adj* le-lo kets.

unequal לא שווה *adj* lo shav|eh/-ah.

unequivocal חד משמעי *adj* khad mashma'ee/-t.

unerring 1. שאינו טועה *adj* she-eyn|o/-ah to'eh/to'ah; **2.** מדויק (exact) *adj* medoo|yak/-yeket.

unessential לא הכרחי *adj* lo hekhrekhee/-t.

uneven 1. לא חלק *adj* lo khalak/-ah; **2.** לא ישר (not straight) *adj* lo yashar/yesharah.

uneven number מספר לא־זוגי *nm* meespar/-eem lo zoogee/-yeem.

unevenness חיספוס *nm* kheespoos/-eem (*pl+of:* -ey).

uneventful שגרתי *adj* sheegratee/-t.

unexpected לא צפוי *adj* lo tsafooy/tsfooyah.

unexpectedly באורח לא צפוי *adv* be-orakh lo tsafooy.

unexpressive חסר רגש *adj* khasar/-rat regesh.

unfailing 1. לא אכזב *adj* lo akhzav; **2.** נאמן (reliable) *adj* ne'eman/-ah.

unfair לא הוגן *adj* lo hogen/-et.

unfairly שלא בצורה הוגנת *adv* she-lo be-tsoorah hogenet.

unfaithful 1. לא נאמן *adj* lo ne'eman/-ah; **2.** בוגד (adulterous) *adj* boged/-et.

unfamiliar 1. לא בקי *adj* lo bakee/bekee'ah; **2.** זר (foreign) *adj* zar/-ah.

unfamiliar with שאינו מתמצא ב־ *adj* she-eyn|o/-ah meetmats|e/-et be-

(to) unfasten להתיר *inf* lehateer; *pst* heeteer; *pres* mateer; *fut* yateer.

unfavorable 1. לא נוח *adj* lo no'akh/nokhah; **2.** שלילי (negative) *adj* shleelee/-t.

unfeeling נטול רגש *adj* netool/-at regesh.

unfinished לא גמור *adj* lo gamoor/gemoorah,

unfit לא כשיר *adj* lo kasheer/kesheerah.

(to) unfold 1. לגולל *inf* legolel; *pst* golel; *pres* megolel; *fut* yegolel; **2.** לפתוח (open) *inf* leefto'akh; *pst* patakh *(p=f)*; *pres* pote'akh; *fut* yeeftakh.

unforeseen לא צפוי *adj* lo tsafooy/tsefooyah.

unforgettable בלתי נשכח *adj* beeltee neeshkakh/-at.

unfortunate 1. ביש מזל *adj* beesh mazal; **2.** אומלל (miserable) *adj* oomlal/-ah.

unfortunately למרבה הצער *adv* le-marbeh ha-tsa'ar.

unfounded חסר יסוד *adj* khas|ar/-rat yesod.

unfrequent לא שכיח *adj* lo shakhee'akh/sh'kheekhah.

unfriendly לא ידידותי *adj* lo yedeedootee/-t.

unfruitful עקר *adj* 'akar/-ah.

(to) unfurl 1. לפרוש *inf* leefros; *pst* paras *(p=f)*; *pres* pores; *fut* yeefros; **2.** לגולל (unfold) *inf* legolel; *pst* golel; *pres* megolel; *fut* yegolel.

unfurnished לא מרוהט *adj* lo mero|hat/-hetet.

ungainly 1. מגושם *adj* megoosh|am/-emet; **2.** מסורבל (clumsy) *adj* mesoorb|al/-elet.

ungrateful כפוי טובה *adj* kefoo|y/-yat tovah.

unguarded 1. לא שמור *adj* lo shamoor/shmoorah; **2.** לא זהיר *adj* lo zaheer/zeheerah.

unhappy 1. לא מאושר *adj* lo me'oosh|ar/-eret; **2.** אומלל (miserable) *adj* oomlal/-ah.

unharmed 1. לא ניזוק *adj* lo neezok/-ah; **2.** לא נפגע (unhurt) lo neefg|a'/-a'at.

unhealthy 1. לא בריא *adj* lo baree/bree'ah; **2.** מזיק לבריאות (detrimental to health) *adj* mazeek/-ah la-bree'oot.

unheard of שלא נשמע כמותו *adj* she-lo neeshm|a'/-e'ah kemot|o/-ah.

(to) unhitch 1. להתיר *inf* lehateer; *pst* heeteer; *pres* mateer; *fut* yateer; **2.** לשחרר (untie) *inf* leshakhrer; *pst* sheekhrer; *pres* meshakhrer; *fut* yeshakhrer.

unholy 1. חושני (sensual) *adj* khooshanee/-t; **2.** טמא (profane) *adj* tame/teme'ah.

(to) unhook 1. להוריד מאנקול *inf* lehoreed me-ankol; *pst* horeed *etc*; *pres* moreed *etc*; *fut* yoreed *etc*; **2.** לפתוח (open) *inf* leefto'akh; *pst* patakh *(p=f)*; *pres* pote'akh; *fut* yeeftakh.

unhurt ללא פגיעה *adj* le-lo pgee'ah.

uniform 1. אחיד *adj* akheed/-ah; **2.** מדים (dress) *nm pl* mad|eem (*pl+of:* -ey).

uniformity אחידות *nf* akheedoo|t/-yot.

(to) unify לאחד *inf* le'akhed; *pst* eekhed; *pres* me'akhed; *fut* ye'akhed.

unilateral חד־צדדי *adj* khad tsedadee/-t.

unimportant לא חשוב *adj* lo khashoov/-ah.

uninhibited חסר מנעים *adj* khas|ar/-rat mena'eem.

uninterested לא מעוניין *adj* lo me'oon|yan/-yenet.

uninteresting לא מעניין *adj* lo me'anyen/-et.

union 1. איגוד *nm* eegood/-eem (*pl+of:* -ey); **2.** התאחדות (association) *nf* heet'akhdoo|t/-yot.

Union of Socialist Soviet Republics 1. ברית המועצות *nf* breet ha-mo'atsot; **2.** ברה״מ (*acr of* 1) *nf* breet ha-mo'atsot.

unison הרמוניה של קולות *nf* harmoneeyah shel kolot.

(in) unison 1. בהרמוניה עם *adv* be-harmoneeyah 'eem; **2.** יחד עם *adv* yakhad 'eem.

unit יחידה *nf* yekheed|ah/-ot (*+of:* -at).

(to) unite 1. לאחד *vt inf* le'akhed; *pst* eekhed; *pres* me'akhed; *fut* ye'akhed; **2.** להתאחד (merge with) *v rfl* leheet'akhed; *pst* heet'akhed; *pres* meet'akhed; *fut* yeet'akhed.

united מאוחד *adj* me'ookh|ad/-edet.

United Kingdom הממלכה המאוחדת *nf* ha-mamlakhah ha-me'ookhedet.

United Nations 1. האומות המאוחדות *nf pl* ha-'oomot ha-me'ookhadot; **2.** האו״ם (*acr of* 1) *nm* ha-oom.

United States of America 1. ארצות הברית *nf pl* artsot ha-breet; **2.** ארה״ב (*acr of* 1) *nf* arhab.

unity אחדות *nf* akhdoo|t/-yot.

universal 1. כללי *adj* klalee/-t; **2.** אוניברסלי *adj* ooneeversalee/-t.

universe 1. יקום *nm* yekoom; **2.** עולם (world) *nm* 'olam/-ot.

university 1. אוניברסיטה *nf* ooneeverseet|ah/-a'ot (*+of:* -at); **2.** מכללה (conferring B.A. only) meekhl|alah/-alot (*+of:* -elet/-elot).

unjust לא צודק *adj* lo tsodek/-et.

unjustifiable שאין להצדיקו *adj* she-eyn lehatsdeek|o/-ah.

unkempt 1. לא מסורק *adj* lo mesor|ak/-eket; **2.** פרוע (disheveled) *adj* paroo'a/proo'ah.

unkind 1. רע לב *adj* ra'/ra'at lev; **2.** נוקשה (harsh) *adj* nooksh|eh/-ah.

unknown לא ידוע *adj* lo yadoo'a/yedoo'ah.

unknown quantity נעלם *nm* ne'elam/-eem (*pl+of:* -ey).

(it is) unknown אין יודעים eyn yod'eem.

unlawful 1. שלא כדין *adj* she-lo ka-deen; **2.** בלתי חוקי (illegal) *adj* beeltee khookee/-t.

(to) unleash להתיר את הרצועה *inf* lehateer et ha-retsoo'ah; *pst* heeteer *etc*; *pres* mateer *etc*; *fut* yateer *etc*.

unless 1. אלא אם כן *cnj* ela eem ken; **2.** עד שלא 'ad she-lo'.

unlicensed 1. ללא רשיון (without permit) *adv & adj* le-lo reeshyon; **2.** שלא ברשות (unauthorized) *adj* she-lo bee-reshoot.

unlike שלא כמו she-lo kemo'.

unlikely לא מתקבל על הדעת *adj* lo meetkabel/-et 'al ha-da'at.

unlimited בלתי מוגבל *adj* beeltee moogb|al/-elet.

(to) unload לפרוק *inf* leefrok; *pst* parak *(p=f)*; *pres* porek; *fut* yeefrok.

(to) unlock לפתוח במפתח *inf* leefto'akh be-mafte'akh; *pst* patakh *(p=f) etc*; *pres* pote'akh *etc*; *fut* yeeftakh *etc*.

(to) unloose 1. לשחרר *inf* leshakhrer; *pst* sheekhrer; *pres* meshakhrer; *fut* yeshakhrer; **2.** להרפות (let loose) *inf* leharpot; *pst* heerpah; *pres* marpeh; *fut* yarpeh.

unlucky 1. ביש מזל (unfortunate) *adj* beesh-mazal; **2.** אומלל (of bad omen) *adj* oomlal/-ah.

(an) unlucky number מיספר ביש מזל *nm* meespar beesh mazal.

unmanageable שאין לרסנו *adj* she-eyn lerasn|o/-ah.

unmanned 1. לא מאוייש *adj* lo me'oo|yash/-yeshet; **2.** שהותש כוחו (exhausted) *adj* she-hootash kokh|o/-ah.

unmarked לא מסומן *adj* lo mesoom|an/-enet.

unmarried 1. לא נשוי *adj* lo nasooy/nesoo'ah; **2.** רווק (bachelor) *nmf & adj* ravak/-ah.

(to) unmask 1. להסיר מסווה *inf* lehaseer masveh; *pst* heseer *etc*; *pres* meseer *etc*; *fut* yaseer *etc*; **2.** לגלות פרצוף אמיתי (reveal true face) *inf* legalot partsoof ameetee; *pst* geelah *etc*; *pres* megaleh *etc*; *fut* yegaleh *etc*.

unmerciful חסר רחמים *adj* khas|ar/-rat rakhameem.

unmistakable שאין לטעות בו *adj* she-'eyn leet'ot bo/bah.

unmoved 1. אדיש *adj* adeesh/-ah; **2.** לא מושפע (uninfluenced) lo mooshp|a'/-a'at.

unnatural לא טיבעי *adj* lo teev'ee/-t.

(an) unnatural mother אם שאינה אמא em she-eynah eema'.

unnecessary לא נחוץ *adj* lo nakhoots/nekhootsah.

unnoticed לא מורגש *adj* lo moorg|ash/-eshet.

unobliging שאינו עוזר לזולת *adj* she-eyn|o/-ah 'ozer/-et la-zoolat.

unobserved שלא הבחינו בו *adj* she-lo heevkheenoo bo/bah.

unobtainable שאין להשיגו *adj* she-eyn lehaseeg|o/-ah.

unobtrusive נחבא אל הכלים *adj* nekhb|a/-et el ha-keleem.

unoccupied 1. פנוי *adj* panooy/pnooyah; **2.** לא מועסק (unemployed) *adj* lo moo'as|ak/-eket.

unofficial 1. לא רשמי lo reeshmee/-t; **2.** בלתי רשמי *(incorrect colloquial pronounciation) adj* beeltee rasmee/-t.

unorganized לא מאורגן *adj* lo me'oorg|an/-enet.

unoriginal לא מקורי *adj* lo mekoree/-t.

unorthodox 1. לא מקובל *adj* lo'mekoob|al/-elet; **2.** חדשני (innovative) *adj* khadshanee/-t.

(to) unpack לפרוק *inf* leefrok; *pst* parak *(p=f); pres* porek; *fut* yeefrok.

unpaid 1. לא משולם *adj* lo'meshool|am/-emet; **2.** חינם (free) *adj & adv* kheenam.

unpaid bills 1. חשבונות שלא נפרעו *nm pl* kheshbonot she-lo neefre'oo; **2.** שטרות שלא כובדו (promissory notes) *nm pl* shtarot she-lo koobdoo.

unpleasant 1. לא נעים *adj* lo na'eem/-ah; **2.** לא נעים *adv* lo na'eem.

unpleasantness אי נעימות *nf* ee ne'eemoo|t/-yot.

unpleasantness of a situation אי הנעימות שבמצב *nf* ee ha-ne'eemoot she-ba-matsav.

(an) unpleasantness with אי נעימות בקשר ל- *nf* ee ne'eemoo|t/-yot be-kesher le-.

unprecedented חסר תקדים *adj* khas|ar/-rat takdeem.

unpremeditated שלא בכוונה תחילה *adj* she-lo be-khavanah *(kh=k)* tkheelah.

unprepared לא מוכן *adj* lo mookhan/-ah.

unpretentious חסר יומרות *adj* khas|ar/-rat yoomrot.

unprintable לא ראוי לדפוס *adj* lo ra'ooy/re'ooyah lee-dfoos.

unproductive 1. לא יעיל *adj* lo ya'eel/-ye'eelah; **2.** ללא תוצאות (with no results) *adv & adj* le-lo totsa'ot.

unprofessional 1. לא מיקצועי *adj* lo meektso'ee/-t; **2.** חובבני (amateurish) *adj* khovevanee/-t.

unprofitable לא ריווחי *adj* lo reevkhee/-t.

unpublished שטרם פורסם *adj* she-terem poors|am/-emah.

unqualified 1. לא מוסמך *adj* lo moosm|akh/-ekhet; **2.** מוחלט (with no reservations) *adj* mookhl|at/-etet.

unquenchable לא ניתן לכיבוי *adj* lo neet|an/-enet le-kheebooy *(kh=k)*.

unquestionable שאין להעמידו בספק *adj* she-eyn leha'ameed|o/-ah be-safek.

(to) unravel 1. להתיר *inf* lehateer; *pst* heeteer; *pres* mateer; *fut* yateer; **2.** להבהיר (clarify) *inf* lehavheer; *pst* heevheer; *pres* mavheer; *fut* yavheer; **3.** לפתור (solve) leeftor; *pst* patar *(p=f); pres* poter; *fut* yeeftor.

unreal 1. לא ממשי lo mamashee/-t; **2.** לא ריאלי *adj* lo re'alee/-t.

unreasonable 1. חסר היגיון *adj* khas|ar/-rat heegayon; **2.** לא סביר (implausible) *adj* lo saveer/sveerah.

unrecognizable שאין להכירו *adj* she-eyn lehakeer|o/-ah.

unrefined 1. גולמי (crude) *adj* golmee/-t; **2.** לא מזוקק (unpurified) *adj* lo mezook|ak/-eket; **3.** גס (rough) *adj* gas/-ah; **4.** לא מעודן (not subtle) lo me'ood|an/-enet.

unreliable לא מהימן *adj* lo meheym|an/-enet.

unrest אי־שקט *nm* ee-sheket.

(to) unroll לגולל *inf* legolel; *pst* golel; *pres* megolel; *fut* yegolel.

unruly פרוע *adj* paroo'a/proo'ah.

unsafe 1. לא בטוח *adj* lo batoo'akh/betookhah; **2.** מסוכן (dangerous) *adj* mesook|an/-enet.

unsalable לא למכירה *adj* lo lee-mekheerah.

unsatisfactory 1. שאינו מניח את הדעת *adj* she-eyn|o/-ah manee|'akh/-khah et ha-da'at; **2.** בלתי מספיק (insufficient) *adj* beeltee maspeek/-ah.

unscrupulous חסר מצפון *adj* khas|ar/-rat matspoon.

unseasonable שלא בעונה *adj* she-lo ba-'onah.

(to) unseat 1. להדיח מתפקיד *inf* lehadee'akh mee-tafkeed; *pst* heedee'akh; *pres* madee'akh; *fut* yadee'akh; **2.** לפטר (fire) *inf* lefater; *pst* peeter *(p=f); pres* mefater; *fut* yefater.

unseen לא נראה *adj* lo neer|'eh/-'et.

unselfish 1. לא אנוכיי *adj* lo anokheyee/-t; **2.** לא אגואיסטי (non-egotist) *adj* lo ego'eestee/-t;. **3.** נדיב (generous) *adj* nadeev/nedeevah.

unselfishness 1. חוסר פניות אישיות *nm* khoser peneeyot eesheeyot; **2.** אלטרואיזם *nm* altroo'eezm.

unsettled 1. לא מיושב (unpopulated) *adj* lo meyoosh|av/-evet; **2.** לא יציב (unstable) *adj* lo yatseev/-ah; **3.** מופרע (disturbed) *adj* moofr|a'/-a'at.

unsettled bills חשבונות שלא נפרעו *nm pl* kheshbonot she-lo neefre'oo.

unsettled weather מזג אוויר לא־יציב *nm* mezeg aveer lo yatseev.

(an) unsettled liquid נוזל דלוח *nm* nozel daloo'akh.

unshaken לא מעורער *adj* lo me'oor|'ar/-'eret.

unsightly לא נעים למראה *adj* lo na'eem/ne'eemah le-mar'eh.

unskilled לא מאומן *adj* lo me'oom|an/-enet.

unskilled laborer פועל פשוט *nm* po'el/pa'aleem pashoot/pshooteem.

unskillful לא מיומן *adj* lo meyoom|an/-enet.

unsociable לא חברותי *adj* lo khevrootee/-t.

unsophisticated לא מתוחכם *adj* lo metookhk|am/-emet.

unsound 1. לא בריא (unhealthy) *adj* lo baree/bree'ah; **2.** פגום (defective) *adj* pagoom/pegoomah; **3.** לקוי (faulty) *adj* lakooy/lekooyah.

unspeakable שאין להעלותו על השפתיים *adj* she-eyn leha'alot|o/-ah 'al ha-sfatayeem.

unstable לא יציב *adj* lo yatseev/-ah.

unsteady 1. הפכפך (fickle) *adj* hafakhpakh/-ah; **2.** לא יציב (unstable) lo yatseev/-ah.

unsuccessful לא מוצלח *adj* lo mootslakh/-at.

unsuccessfully ללא תוצאות *adj* le-lo totsa'ot.

unsuitable לא מתאים *adj* lo mat'eem/-ah.

unsuspected 1. לא חשוד *adj* lo khashood/-ah; **2.** שלא חשבו עליו (not thought of) *adj* she-lo khashvoo 'al|av/-eha.

untenable בלתי ניתן להגנה *adj* beeltee neet|an/-enet le-haganah.
unthinkable שאין להעלותו על הדעת *adj* she-eyn leha'alot|o/-ah 'al ha-da'at.
untidy 1. לא מסודר *adj* lo mesood|ar/-eret; **2.** מרושל (negligent) *adj* meroosh|al/-elet.
(to) untie להתיר קשר *inf* lehateer kesher; *pst* heeteer *etc*; *pres* mateer *etc*; *fut* yateer *etc*.
until 1. עד אשר *prep* 'ad asher; **2.** עד (till) *prep* 'ad
untimely שלא בזמן הנכון *adv* she-lo ba-zman ha-nakhon.
untiring ללא ליאות *adj* le-lo le'oot.
untold לאין ספור *adj* le-eyn sfor.
untouched 1. ללא פגע (unscathed) *adj* le-lo pega'; **2.** אדיש (impassive) *adj* adeesh/-ah.
(left) untouched שיצא בשלום *adj* she-yats|a/-'ah be-shalom.
untrained לא מאומן *adj* lo me'oom|an/-enet.
untried שטרם נוסה *adj* she-terem noosah.
untried law case משפט שטרם נתברר *nm* meeshpat/-eem she-terem neetbarer/-oo'.
untroubled 1. רגוע *adj* ragoo'a/regoo'ah; **2.** לא מוטרד (not bothered) *adj* lo mootr|ad/-edet.
untrue 1. כוזב *adj* kozev/-et; **2.** לא נכון (incorrect) *adj* lo nakhon/nekhonah.
untruth 1. שקר *nm* shek|er/-areem (*pl+of:* sheekrey); **2.** כזב (falsehood) *nm* kazav/kezaveem (*+of:* kezav/keezvey).
untutored 1. בור *adj* boor; **2.** לא מחונך *adj* lo mekhoon|akh/-ekhet.
unused 1. לא מורגל *adj* lo moorg|al/-elet; **2.** שלא היה בשימוש *adj* she-lo hay|ah/-tah be-sheemoosh.
unusual לא רגיל *adj* lo rageel/regeelah.
unusually שלא כרגיל *adv* she-lo ka-rageel.
unvarnished לא מצוחצח *adj* lo metsookhtsakh/-at.
(to) unveil 1. להסיר לוט *inf* lehaseer lot; *pst* heseer lot; *pres* meseer lot; *fut* yaseer lot; **2.** להוריד צעיף (remove veil) *inf* lehoreed tse'eef; *pst* horeed *etc*; *pres* moreed *etc*; *fut* yoreed *etc*.
unwarranted 1. לא מוצדק *adj* lo mootsd|ak/-eket. **2.** לא מוסמך (unauthorized) *adj* lo moosm|akh/-ekhet.
unwary 1. נמהר *adj* neem|har/-heret; **2.** לא זהיר (careless) *adj* lo zaheer/zeheerah
unwashed לא רחוץ *adj* lo rakhoots/rekhootsah.
unwelcome לא רצוי *adj* lo ratsooy/retsooyah.
unwholesome 1. לא בריא *adj* lo baree/bree'ah; **2.** מזיק (harmful) mazeek/-ah.
unwieldy 1. מגושם *adj* megoosh|am/-emet; **2.** קשה לשימוש (hard to use) *adj* kash|eh/-ah le-sheemoosh.
unwilling 1. סרבן *adj* sarvan/-eet; **2.** בוחל (abhorring) *adj* bokhel/-et.
(to be) unwilling to לסרב *inf* lesarev; *pst* serev; *pres* mesarev; *fut* yesarev.
unwillingly באי רצון *adv* be-ee ratson.
unwillingness חוסר רצון *nm* khoser ratson.
unwise לא נבון *adj* lo navon/nevonah.
unwonted 1. לא רגיל (unusual) *adj* lo rageel/regeelah; **2.** לא מקובל (uncustomary) *adj* lo mekoob|al/-elet.
unworthy לא ראוי *adj* lo ra'ooy/re'ooyah.
(to) unwrap 1. לגולל *inf* legolel; *pst* golel; *pres* megolel; *fut* yegolel; **2.** לפתוח *inf* leefto'akh; *pst* patakh (*p=f*); *pres* pote'akh; *fut* yeeftakh.
unwritten 1. לא כתוב *adj* lo katoov/ketoovah; **2.** שלא בכתב *adj* she-lo bee-khtav.
up 1. על (above) *adv* 'al; **2.** עד (till) *prep* 'ad; **3.** זקוף (standing) *adj* zakoof/zekoofah; **4.** גמור (finished) *adj* gamoor/gemoorah.
up against 1. פנים אל פנים *adv* paneem el paneem; **2.** מול (facing) *adv* mool.
up and coming 1. מבטיח *adj* mavtee|'akh/-khah; **2.** בעל סיכויים (having chances) *nmf & adj* ba'al/-at seekooyeem.
up and down 1. פה ושם *adv* poh va-sham; **2.** ללא תיכנון (without a plan) *adv* le-lo teekhnoon.
up on the news מעודכן בחדשות היום *adj* me'oodk|an/-enet be-khadashot ha-yom.
up the river במעלה הנהר *adv* be-ma'aleh ha-nahar.
up to now עד כה *'ad koh*.
up to one's old tricks חוזר לסורו *adj* khozer/-et le-soor|o/-ah.
(his time is) up זמנו תם zman|o/-ah tam.
(prices are) up המחירים עולים ha-mekheereem 'oleem.
(that is) up to you הדבר הוא להכרעתך ha-davar hoo le-hakhra'at|kha/-ekh (*m/f*).
(to) up להעלות *inf* leha'alot; *pst* he'elah; *pres* ma'aleh; *fut* ya'aleh.
(what's) up? מה קורה? mah koreh?
(to) upbraid 1. לנזוף *inf* leenzof; *pst* nazaf; *pres* nozef; *fut* yeenzof; **2.** להוכיח (reprove) *inf* lehokhee'akh; *pst* hokhee'akh; *pres* mokhee'akh; *fut* yokhee'akh.
(to) update לעדכן *inf* le'adken; *pst* 'eedken; *pres* me'adken; *fut* ye'adken.
(to) upgrade 1. לשפר *inf* leshaper; *pst* sheeper; *pres* meshaper; *fut* yeshaper; **2.** להעלות מחיר *inf* leha'alot mekheer; *pst* he'elah *etc*; *pres* ma'aleh *etc*; *fut* ya'aleh *etc*.
upheaval תהפוכה *nf* tahapookh|ah/-ot (*+of:* -at).
uphill 1. במעלה ההר (ascending) *adv* be-ma'aleh ha-har; **2.** כרוך במאמץ (laborious) *adj* karookh/krookhah be-ma'amats.
(to) uphold 1. להחזיק *inf* lehakhzeek; *pst* hekhzeek; *pres* makhzeek; *fut* yakhzeek; **2.** לחזק (strengthen) *vt inf* lekhazek; *pst* kheezek; *pres* mekhazek; *fut* yekhazek.
(to) upholster לרפד *inf* leraped; *pst* reeped; *pres* meraped; *fut* yeraped.
upholstery 1. ריפוד (material) *nm* reepood/-eem (*pl+of:* -ey); **2.** מרפדייה (workshop) *nf* marpedee|yah/-yot (*+of:* -yat).
upkeep אחזקה *nf* akhzak|ah/-ot (*+of:* -at).
upland 1. רמה *nf* ram|ah/-ot (*+of:* -at); **2.** רמתי *adj* ramatee/-t.
uplift 1. הרמה *nf* haram|ah/-ot (*+of:* -at); **2.** התעלות (spiritual) *nf* heet'aloo|t/-yot.
(to) uplift 1. להרים *inf* lehareem; *pst* hereem; *pres* mereem; *fut* yareem; **2.** לגרום להתעלות

(spiritually) *inf* leegrom le-heet'aloot; *pst* garam *etc; pres* gorem *etc; fut* yeegrom *etc.*

upon 1. על *prep* 'al; **2.** על פני (over) *prep* 'al peney.

upon arriving עם בוא *adv* 'eem bo'.

upper 1. עליון *adj* 'elyon/-ah; **2.** עילי (upmost) *adj* 'eelee/-t.

upper berth מיטה עילית *nf* meet|ah/-ot 'eelee|t/-yot.

upper hand 1. יתרון (advantage) *nm* yeetron/-not; **2.** עדיפות (priority) *nf* 'adeefoo|t/-yot; **3.** שליטה (control) *nf* shleet|ah/-ot (*+of:* -at).

upper middle class מעמד בינוני גבוה *nm* ma'amad beynonee gavoha.

upright 1. זקוף *adj* zakoof/zekoofah; **2.** ישר דרך (straightforward) *adj* yeshar/yeeshrat derekh.

upright piano פסנתר זקוף *nm* p'santer/-eem zakoof/zekoofeem.

uprightness 1. זקיפות קומה *nf* zekeefoot komah; **2.** כנות (honesty) *nf* kenoo|t/-yot.

uprising התקוממות *nf* heetkomemoo|t/-yot.

uproar 1. שאון *nm* sha'on (*+of:* she'on); **2.** רעש (noise) ra'ash/re'asheem (*pl+of:* ra'ashey).

uproarious 1. הומה *adj* hom|eh/-ah; **2.** רועש (noisy) *adj* ro'esh/-et.

(to) uproot לעקור מן השורש *inf* la'akor meen ha-shoresh; *pst* 'akar *etc; pres* 'oker *etc; fut* ya'akor *etc.*

ups and downs עליות ומורדות *nf & nm pl* 'aleeyot oo-moradot.

upset 1. עצוב (sad) *adj* 'atsoov/-ah; **2.** הפוך (overturned) *adj* hafookh/-ah.

(to) upset 1. להפוך (capsize) *inf* lahafokh; *pst* hafakh; *pres* hofekh; *fut* yahafokh; **2.** להעציב (sadden) *vt* leha'atseev; *pst* he'etseev; *pres* ma'atseev; *fut* ya'atseev.

(to become) upset להיתקף צער *inf* leheetakef tsa'ar; *pst & pres* neetkaf *etc; fut* yeetakef *etc.*

upshot 1. תוצאה (result) *nf* tots|a'ah/-a'ot (*+of:* -a'at/-'ot); **2.** פועל יוצא (consequence) *nm* po'al yotse'.

upside בצד העליון *adv* ba-tsad ha-'elyon.

upside down 1. הפוך *adj* hafookh/-ah; **2.** תוהו ובוהו (disorder) *nm & nm* tohoo va-vohoo.

upstage בירכתי הבימה *adv* be-yarketey ha-beemah.

(to) upstage להסתיר פנים מהקהל *inf* lehasteer paneem me-ha-kahal; *pst* heesteer *etc; pres* masteer *etc; fut* yasteer *etc.*

upstairs 1. למעלה *adv* le-ma'lah; **2.** של קומה מעלינו *adj* shel komah me'alenoo.

upstart 1. הדיוט שעלה לגדולה (parvenu) *nm* hedyot she-'alah lee-gedoolah; **2.** קבצן שנתעשר (nouveau riche) *nm* kabtsan she-neet'asher.

up-to-date מעודכן *adj* me'oodk|an/-enet.

uptown 1. במעלה העיר *adv* be-ma'aleh ha-'eer; **2.** בחלק העליון של העיר (in upper part) *adv* ba-khelek ha-'elyon shel ha-'eer.

upturn 1. סיבוב כלפי מעלה *nm* seeboov/-eem kelapey ma'lah; **2.** מפנה לטובה (turn for the better) *nm* meefneh le-tovah.

(to) upturn להפוך כלפי מעלה *inf* lahafokh kelapey ma'lah; *pst* hafakh *etc; pres* hofekh *etc; fut* yahafokh *etc.*

upward 1. אל על *adv* el 'al; **2.** מופנה למעלה *adj* moofn|eh/-et le-ma'lah.

upward of יותר מאשר *adv* yoter me-asher.

upwards כלפי מעלה *adv* kelapey ma'lah.

uranium אורניום *nm* ooranyoom.

urban עירוני *adj* 'eeronee/-t.

urchin 1. פרחח (mischievous) *nm* peerkhakh/-eem (*pl+of:* -ey); **2.** ילד מסכן (poor) *nm* yel|ed/-adeem meesken/-eem.

(sea) urchin קיפוד ים *nm* keepod/-ey yam.

urge 1. דחף *nm* dakhaf/dekhafeem (*pl+of:* dakhfey); **2.** כמיהה (longing) *nf* kemee|hah/-hot (*+of:* -hat).

(to) urge 1. לדחוף *inf* leedkhof; *pst* dakhaf; *pres* dokhef; *fut* yeedkhof; **2.** לתבוע במפגיע (demand) *inf* leetbo'a' be-mafgee'a'; *pst* tava' (*v=b*) *etc; pres* tove'a' *etc; fut* yeetba' *etc.*

urgency דחיפות *nf* dekheefoo|t/-yot.

urgent דחוף *adj* dakhoof/dekhoofah.

urinal 1. כלי שתן (receptacle) *nm* klee/kley sheten; **2.** משתנה (place) *nf* meesht|anah/-anot (*+of:* -enet).

(to) urinate להשתין *inf* lehashteen; *pst* heeshteen; *pres* mashteen; *fut* yashteen.

urine שתן *nm* sheten/shtaneem (*pl+of:* sheetney).

urn 1. כד *nm* kad/-eem (*pl+of:* -ey); **2.** צנצנת (jar) *nf* tseents|enet/-anot.

us 1. לנו (dative) *pron* lanoo; **2.** אותנו (accusative) *pron* otanoo.

usage 1. נוהג *nm* nohag/nehageem (*pl+of:* nohogey); **2.** מנהג (custom) *nm* meenhag/-eem (*pl+of:* -ey); **3.** שימוש (use) *nm* sheemoosh/-eem (*pl+of:* -ey).

(hard) usage נוהג מקובל nohag/nehageem mekoobal/-eem.

use 1. שימוש *nm* sheemoosh/-eem (*pl+of:* -ey); **2.** ניצול (application) *nm* neetsool/-eem (*pl+of:* -ey); **3.** תועלת (advantage) *nf* to'elet.

(of no) use ללא תועלת *adj* le-lo to'elet.

(out of) use שיצא מכלל שימוש *adj* she-yats|a/-'ah mee-khlal (*kh=k*) sheemoosh.

(to) use 1. להשתמש *inf* leheeshtamesh; *pst* heeshtamesh; *pres* meeshtamesh; *fut* yeeshtamesh; **2.** לנצל (employ) *inf* lenatsel; *pst* neetsel; *pres* menatsel; *fut* yenatsel.

(no further) use for אין תועלת יותר ב־ eyn to'elet yoter be-.

(what is the) use of it? מה בצע ב־? mah betsa' be-?

(to) use up 1. לצרוך (consume) *inf* leetsrokh; *pst* tsarakh; *pres* tsorekh; *fut* yeetsrokh; **2.** לנצל עד תום (exhaust) *inf* lenatsel 'ad tom; *pst* neetsel *etc; pres* menatsel *etc; fut* yenatsel *etc.*

use your judgment עשה כרצונך *v imp (m/f)* 'aseh/'asee kee-retson|kha/-ekh.

used משומש *adj* meshoom|ash/-eshet.

(to be) used to להיות רגיל ל־ *inf* leehyot rageel le-; *pst* hayah *etc; pres* heeno *etc; fut* yehyeh *etc.*

(he) used to do it הוא נהג לעשות זאת hoo nahag la'asot zot.

useful 1. מועיל *adj* mo'eel/-ah; **2.** שימושי (practical) *adj* sheemooshee/-t.

usefulness תועלת *nf* to'elet.

useless חסר תועלת *adj* khas|ar/-rat to'elet.
uselessness חוסר תועלת *nm* khoser to'elet.
usher 1. סדרן *nm* sadran/-eem (*pl+of:* -ey); **2.** שמש (in court) *nm* shamash/-eem (*pl+of:* -ey).
(to) usher 1. להכניס פנימה *inf* lehakhnees peneemah; *pst* heekhnees *etc*; *pres* makhnees *etc*; *fut* yakhnees *etc*; **2.** להושיב במקום (seat) *inf* lehosheev ba-makom; *pst* hosheev *etc*; *pres* mosheev *etc*; *fut* yosheev *etc*.
usual 1. רגיל *adj* rageel/regeelah; **2.** שכיח (common) *adj* shakhee'akh/shekheekhah.
usually 1. כרגיל *adv* ka-rageel; **2.** בדרך כלל (generally) *adv* be-derekh klal.
usurer מלווה בריבית קצוצה *nm* malv|eh/-eem be-reebeet ketsootsah.
(to) usurp 1. ליטול בכוח *inf* leetol be-kho'akh (*kh=k*); *pst* natal *etc*; *pres* notel *etc*; *fut* yeetol *etc*; **2.** להסיג גבול (trespass) *inf* lehaseeg gvool; *pst* heeseeg *etc*; *pres* maseeg *etc*; *fut* yaseeg *etc*.
usury ריבית קצוצה *nf* reebeet ketsootsah.
utensil 1. כלי *nm* klee/keleem (*pl+of:* kley); **2.** מכשיר (tool) *nm* makhsheer/-eem (*pl+of:* -ey).
uterus רחם *nm* rekh|em/-ameem (*pl+of:* rakhmey).
utilitarian 1. תועלתן *nmf* to'altan/-eet; **2.** תועלתני *adj* to'altanee/-t.
utility 1. דבר מועיל *nm* davar/dvareem mo'eel/-eem; **2.** תועלת (use) *nf* to'elet.
(public) utility שירות ציבורי *nm* sheroot/-eem tseebooree/-yeem.
(to) utilize לנצל *inf* lenatsel; *pst* neetsel; *pres* menatsel; *fut* yenatsel.
utmost 1. ביותר *adv* be-yoter; **2.** מלוא (full extent) *nm* melo מיטב (the best) *nm* meytav.
(he/she did his/her) utmost עשה כמיטב יכולתו 'as|ah/-tah ke-meytav yekholt|o/-ah (*m/f*).
(to the) utmost עד קצה גבול היכולת *adv* 'ad ketseh gvool ha-yekholet.
utter 1. מוחלט *adj* mookhl|at/-etet; **2.** גמור (complete) *adj* gamoor/gemoorah.
(to) utter 1. לבטא *inf* levate; *pst* beete (*b=v*); *pres* mevate; *fut* yevate; **2.** להביע (express) *inf* lehabee'a'; *pst* heebee'a'; *pres* mabee'a'; *fut* yabee'a'.
(to) utter a cry להשמיע זעקה *inf* lehashmee'a' ze'akah; *pst* heeshmee'a' *etc*; *pres* mashmee'a' *etc*; *fut* yashmee'a' *etc*.
utterance ביטוי *nm* beetoo|y/-yeem (*pl+of:* -yey).
uttermost 1. מיטב *nm* meytav; **2.** מלוא (full extent) *nm* melo.
uvula ענבל *nm* 'eenbal/-eem (*pl+of:* -ey).
uvular ענבלי *adj* 'eenbalee/-t.

V.

V,v consonant for which the Hebrew alphabet offers two equivalents. One is ב (the unpointed "Bet" called "Vet"), used in words like רובה (roveh), הביס (hevees), or תגובה (tegoovah). The other is ו (Vav, which, when in the middle of a word, is doubled as וו in the unpointed spelling).
vacancy 1. חלל ריק (space) *nm* khalal/-eem reyk/-eem; **2.** משרה פנויה (job) *nf* meesr|ah/-ot penoo|yah/-yot; **3.** פער (gap) *nm* pa'ar/pe'areem (*pl+of:* pa'arey).
vacant פנוי *adj* panooy/penooyah.
(to) vacate לפנות *inf* lefanot; *pst* peenah (*p=f*); *pres* mefaneh; *fut* yefaneh.
vacation 1. פגרה *nf* pagr|ah/-ot (*+of:* -at); **2.** חופשה (leave) *nf* khoofsh|ah/-ot (*+of:* -at).
(to) vaccinate 1. להרכיב (inoculate) *inf* leharkeev; *pst* heerkeev; *pres* markeev; *fut* yarkeev; **2.** לחסן (immunize) *inf* lekhasen; *pst* kheesen; *pres* mekhasen; *fut* yekhasen.
vaccination 1. הרכבה (inoculation) *nf* harkav|ah/-ot (*+of:* -at); **2.** חיסון (immunization) *nm* kheesoon/-eem (*pl+of:* -ey).
vaccine תרכיב חיסון *nf* tarkeev/-ey kheesoon.
(to) vacillate לפסוח על שתי הסעיפים *inf* leefso'akh 'al shtey ha-se'eepeem; *pst* pasakh (*p=f*) *etc*; *pres* pose'akh *etc*; *fut* yeefsakh *etc*.
vacuum 1. ריק *nm* reek; **2.** חלל ריק (empty space) *nm* khalal/-eem reyk/-eem.
vacuum cleaner 1. שואב אבק *nm* sho'ev/sho'avey avak; **2.** שואבק (*abbr. synon.*) *nm* sho'av|ak/-akeem (*pl+of:* -key).
vagabond 1. נע ונד (wanderer) *nm* na' va-nad; **2.** בטלן (idler) *nm* batlan/-eem (*pl+of:* -ey).
vagrancy נוודות *nf* navadoo|t/-yot.
vagrant 1. נווד *nm* navad/-eem (*pl+of:* -ey); **2.** הלך (wanderer) *nm* helekh.
vague 1. לא ברור *adj* lo baroor/broorah; **2.** מעורפל (foggy) *adj* me'oorp|al/-elet.
vain 1. מתנשא (arrogant) *adj* meetnas|e/-et; **2.** חסר משמעות (meaningless) *adj* khas|ar/-rat mashma'oot.
vainglory שחץ *nm* shakhats.
vale עמק *nm* 'emek/'amakeem (*pl+of:* 'eemkey).
valedictory נאום פרידה *nm* ne'oom/-ey predah.
valentine מזכרת אהבה *nf* mazk|eret/-erot ahavah.
valet 1. משרת אישי *nm* meshar|et/-teem eeshee/-yeem; **2.** שמש (attendant) *nm* shamash/-eem (*pl+of:* -ey).

valiant אמיץ *adj* ameets/-ah.
valid בר תוקף *adj* bar/bat tokef.
validity 1. תוקף *nm* tokef; **2.** תקיפות (vigor) *f* tekeefoo|t/-yot.
valise מיזוודת יד *nf* meezved|et/-ot yad
valley 1. עמק *nm* 'emek/'amakeem (*pl+of:* 'eemkey). **2.** בקעה *nf* beek'ah/beka'ot (*+of:* beek|'at/-ot).
valor אומץ *nm* omets.
valorous אמיץ לב *adj* ameets/-at lev.
valuable בעל ערך *adj* ba'al/-at 'erekh.
valuables דברי ערך *nm pl* deevrey 'erekh.
valuation הערכה *nf* ha'arakh|ah/-ot (*+of:* -at).
value 1. שווי (worth) *nm* shovee; **2.** ערך (price) *nm* 'erech/'arakheem (*pl+of:* 'erkhey); **3.** אומד (estimation) *nm* omed.
(to) value 1. להעריך *inf* leha'areekh; *pst* he'ereekh; *pres* ma'areekh; *fut* ya'areekh; **2.** להוקיר (esteem) *inf* lehokeer; *pst* hokeer; *pres* mokeer; *fut* yokeer.
valueless חסר־ערך *adj* khas|ar/-rat 'erekh.
valve שסתום *nm* shastom/-eem (*pl+of:* -ey).
(safety) valve שסתום ביטחון *nm* shastom/-ey beetakhon.
vampire ערפד *nm* 'arp|ad/-adeem (*pl+of:* -edey).
van 1. משאית סגורה *nf* masa'ee|t/-yot segoor|ah/-ot; **2.** חלוץ (vanguard) *nmf* khaloots/-ah (*+of:* -at; *pl:* -eem; *+of:* -ey).
vandalism 1. פראות *nf* pra'oo|t/-yot; **2.** ונדליזם *nm* vandaleezm/-eem (*pl+of:* -ey).
vane שבשבת *nf* shavsh|evet/-avot.
vanguard חלוץ *nm* khaloots/-eem (*pl+of:* -ey).
vanilla 1. שנף *nm* shenef; **2.** וניל *nm* vaneel.
(to) vanish להיעלם *inf* lehe'alem; *pst & pres* ne'elam; *fut* ye'alem.
vanity 1. הבל *nm* hevel/hav|aleem (*pl+of:* -ley); **2.** רהב (boasting) *nm* rahav.
vanity case פודרייה *nf* poodree|yah/-yot (*+of:* -yat).
vanity table שולחן טואלט *nm* shoolkhan/-ot too'alet.
(to) vanquish להביס *inf* lehavees; *pst* hevees; *pres* mevees; *fut* yavees.
vantage יתרון *nm* yeet|aron/-ronot (*+of:* -ron).
(point of) vantage 1. נקודת תצפית *nf* nekood|at/-ot tatspeet; **2.** עמדת יתרון (advantage) *nf* 'emd|at/-ot yeetaron.
vapor 1. אדים *nm pl* ed/-eem (*pl+of:* -ey); **2.** קיטור (steam) *nm* keetor.
(to) vaporize 1. לאייד *vt inf* le'ayed; *pst* eeyed; *pres* me'ayed; *fut* ye'ayed; **2.** להתאדות *v rfl inf* leheet'adot; *pst* heet'adah; *pres* meet'adeh; *fut* yeet'adeh.
variable 1. משתנה *adj* meeshtan|eh/-ah; **2.** הפכפך (fickle) *adj* hafakhpakh.
variance שוני *nm* shonee.
(at) variance חולק על *adj* kholek/-et 'al.
variant גרסה שונה *nf* geers|ah/-a'ot shon|ah/-ot.
variation שינוי *nm* sheenoo|y/-yeem (*pl+of:* -yey).
varied שונה *adj* shon|eh/-ah (*pl:* -eem/-ot).
variegated מגוון *adj* megoov|an/-enet.
variety מיגוון *nm* meegvan/-eem (*pl+of:* -ey).
variety show הצגת קברט *nf* hatsag|at/-ot kabaret.
various שונים *adj pl* shon|eem/-ot.

varnish משחת הברקה *nf* meesh'kh|at/-ot havrakah.
(to) varnish לצחצח *inf* letsakhtse'akh; *pst* tseekhtse'akh; *pres* metsakhtse'akh; *fut* yetsakhtse'akh.
(to) vary לגוון *inf* legaven; *pst* geeven; *pres* megaven; *fut* yegaven.
vase אגרטל *nm* agartel/-eem (*pl+of:* -ey).
Vaseline וזלין *nm* vazeleen/-eem (*pl+of:* -ey).
vassal 1. צמית *nm* tsameet/tsmeet|eem (*pl+of:* -ey); **2.** וסל *nm* vasal/-eem (*pl+of:* -ey).
vast נרחב *adj* neerkh|av/-evet.
vastly במידה רבה *adv* be-meedah rabah.
vastness רוחב *nm* rokhav/rekhaveem (*pl+of:* rokhvey).
vat מיכל גדול *nm* meykhal/-eem gadol/gedoleem.
vaudeville 1. מחזה קומי *nm* makhz|eh/-ot komee/-yeem; **2.** וודביל *nm* vodeveel/-eem (*pl+of:* -ey).
vault 1. קמרון *nm* keemron/-eem (*pl+of:* -ey); **2.** כיפה (dome) *nf* keep|ah/-ot (*+of:* -at).
(bank) vault כספת *nf* kas|efet/afot (*pl+of:* -fot).
(pole) vault קפיצה במוט *nf* kefeets|ah/-ot be-mot.
(to) vault לקפוץ *inf* leekpots; *pst* kafats *(f=p)*; *pres* kofets; *fut* yeekpots.
vaunt התרברבות *nf* heetravrevoo|t/-yot.
(to) vaunt להתרברב *inf* leheetravrev; *pst* heetravrev; *pres* meetravrev; *fut* yeetravrev.
veal בשר עגל *nm* besar 'egel.
veal cutlet אומצת עגל *nf* oomts|at/-ot 'egel.
(to) veer 1. לחוג *inf* lakhoog; *pst & pres* khag; *fut* yakhoog; **2.** לשנות כיוון (switch direction) *inf* leshanot keevoon; *pst* sheenah *etc*; *pres* meshaneh *etc*; *fut* yeshaneh *etc*.
vegetable ירק yarak/yerakot (*+of:* yerak/yarkot).
vegetable garden גן ירק *nm* gan/-ey yarak.
vegetables ירקות *nm pl* yerakot.
(fresh) vegetables ירקות טריים *nm pl* yerakot treeyeem.
vegetarian צמחוני *nmf* tseemkhonee/-t.
(to) vegetate לחיות חיים ללא טעם *inf* leekhyot khayeem le-lo ta'am; *pst & pres* khay *etc*; *fut* yeekhyeh *etc*.
vegetation צמחייה *nf* tseemkhee|yah/-yot (*+of:* -yat).
vehemence 1. להט *nm* lahat; **2.** אלימות (violence) *nf* aleemoo|t/-yot.
vehement 1. עז *adj* 'az/-ah; **2.** נסער (stormy) *adj* nees|'ar/-'eret.
vehicle רכב *nm* rekhev/kley rekhev (*[colloq.] pl:* rekhaveem).
vehicular traffic תנועת כלי רכב *nf* tenoo'at kley rekhev
veil צעיף *nm* tse'eef/-eem (*pl+of:* -ey).
(to) veil להליט *inf* lehaleet; *pst* heleet; *pres* meleet; *fut* yaleet.
vein 1. וריד *nm* vreed/-eem (*pl+of:* -ey); **2.** נימה (tone) *nf* neem|ah/-ot (*+of:* -at).
veined מגויד *adj* megoo|yad/-yedet.
velocity מהירות *nf* meheeroo|t/-yot.
velvet קטיפה *nf* keteef|ah/-ot (*+of:* -at).
velvety קטיפני *adj* keteefanee/-t.
vendor 1. מוכר *nmf* mokher/-et; **2.** זבן zaban/-eet **3.** מזבנת (vending machine) *nf* mezab|enet/-not.

veneer לביד *nm* leveed/-eem (*pl+of:* -ey).
venerable מכובד *adj* mekhoob|ad/-edet.
(to) venerate 1. לכבד (respect) *inf* lekhabed; *pst* keebed *(k=kh)*; *pres* mekhabed; *fut* yekhabed; **2.** להוקיר (esteem) *inf* lehokeer; *pst* hokeer; *pres* mokeer; *fut* yokeer.
veneration הוקרה *nf* hokar|ah/-ot (*+of:* -at).
venereal 1. של מחלת מין *adj* shel makhal|at/-ot meen; **2.** ונרי *adj* veneree/-t.
Venetian blinds תריס רפפות *nm* trees/-ey refafot.
Venezuelan ונצואליאני *nmf & adj* venetsoo'elyanee/-t.
vengeance נקמה *nf* nekam|ah/-ot (*+of:* neekm|at/-ot).
(with a) vengeance בחמת נקם *adv* ba-khamat nakam.
venison בשר צבי *nm* besar tsevee.
venom ארס *nm* eres.
venomous ארסי *adj* arsee/-t.
vent 1. פתח (opening) *nm* petakh/-eem (*pl+of:* peetkhey); **2.** מוצא (escape) *nm* motsa; **3.** פורקן (relief) *nm* poorkan.
(to) vent 1. להתקין פתח *inf* lehatkeen petakh; *pst* heetkeen *etc*; *pres* matkeen *etc*; *fut* yatkeen *etc*; **2.** לתת ביטוי (give expression) *inf* latet beetooy; *pst* natan *etc*; *pres* noten *etc*; *fut* yeeten *etc*.
(to give) vent לתת פורקן *inf* latet poorkan; *pst* natan *etc*; *pres* noten *etc*; *fut* yeeten *etc*.
(to) ventilate לאוורר *inf* le'avrer; *pst* eevrer; *pres* me'avrer; *fut* ye'avrer.
ventilation אוורור *nm* eevroor/-eem (*pl+of:* -ey).
ventilator מאוורר *nm* me'avrer/-eem (*pl+of:* -ey).
venture 1. מעפל *nm* ma'apal/-eem (*pl+of:* -ey); **2.** פעולה נועזת (daring affair) *nf* pe'ool|ah/-ot no'ezet/no'azot.
(business) venture עסקה נועזת *nf* 'eesk|ah/'asakot no'ezet/no'azot.
(to) venture להעז *inf* leha'ez; *pst* he'ez; *pres* me'ez; *fut* ya'ez.
(to) venture outside להסתכן לצאת *inf* leheestaken latset; *pst* heestaken *etc*; *pres* meestaken *etc*; *fut* yeestaken *etc*.
(to) venture to להסתכן ב־ *inf* leheestaken be-; *pst* heestaken be-; *pres* meestaken be-; *fut* yeestaken be-.
venturous מסתכן *adj* meestaken/-et.
veranda מרפסת *nf* meerp|eset/-asot (*pl+of:* -esot).
verb פועל *nm* po'al/pe'aleem (*pl+of:* po'oley)
verbal מילולי *adj* meeloolee/-t.
verbatim מלה במלה *adv* meelah be-meelah.
verbose מגבב מלים *adj* megabev/-et meeleem.
verdict 1. פסק דין *nm* psak/peeskey deen; **2.** החלטה (decision) *nf* hakhlat|ah/-ot (*+of:* -at).
verdict of "not guilty" זיכוי בדין *nm* zeekooly/-yeem be-deen.
verdure ירקות *nm pl* yerakot.
verge 1. קצה (edge) *nm* katseh/ketsavot (*+of:* kets|eh/-ot); **2.** גבול (border) *nm* gvool/-ot.
(on the) verge of על גבול *adv* 'al gvool.
(to) verge on לגבול עם *inf* leegbol 'eem; *pst* gaval *(v=b)* 'eem; *pres* govel 'eem; *fut* yeegbol 'eem.
(to) verge toward לנטות לצד *inf* leentot le-tsad; *pst* natah *etc*; *pres* noteh *etc*; *fut* yeeteh *etc*.
(to) verify לוודא *inf* levade; *pst* veede; *pres* mevade; *fut* yevade.
verily באמת *adv* be-emet.
veritable 1. אמיתי *adj* ameetee/-t; **2.** מוחשי (real) *adj* mookhashee/-t.
vermillon ששר *nm* shashar.
vernacular עגה מקומית *nf* 'ag|ah/-ot mekomee|t/-yot.
versatile רב־שימושי *adj* rav sheemooshee/-t.
verse 1. בית בשיר *nm* bayeet/bateem be-sheer; **2.** חרוז (rhyme) *nm* kharooz/-eem (*pl+of:* -ey).
versed 1. מיומן *adj* meyoom|an-enet. **2.** מנוסה (experienced) *adj* menoos|eh/-ah.
version גרסה *nf* geers|ah/-a'ot (*+of:* -at).
vertebra חוליה *nf* khool|yah/-yot (*+of:* -yat).
vertebrate בעל חוליות *nmf & adj* ba'al/-at khoolyot.
vertical מאונך *adj* me'oon|akh-ekhet.
vertigo סחרחורת *nf* sekharkhor|et/-ot.
very מאוד *adv* me'od.
(it is) very hot today חם מאד היום kham me'od ha-yom.
(the) very man אותו אדם אשר oto adam asher.
very many רבים מאוד *adj pl* rab|eem/-ot me'od.
very much הרבה מאוד *adv* harbeh me'od.
(the) very thought of עצם המחשבה אודות 'etsem ha-makhshavah odot.
vessel כלי (receptacle) *nm* klee/keleem (*pl+of:* kley).
(blood) vessel כלי דם *nm* klee/kley dam.
vest 1. חזייה (brassiere) *nf* khazee|yah/-yot (*+of:* -yat); **2.** גופייה (undershirt) *nf* goofee|yah/-yot (*+of:* -yat); **3.** לסוטה (waistcoat) *nf* lesoot|ah/-ot (*+of:* -at).
(to) vest 1. להעטות *inf* leha'atot; *pst* he'etah; *pres* ma'ateh; *fut* ya'ateh; **2.** להקנות (grant) *inf* lehaknot; *pst* heeknah; *pres* makneh; *fut* yakneh.
(to) vest with power להקנות סמכות *inf* lehaknot samkhoot; *pst* heeknah *etc*; *pres* makneh *etc*; *fut* yakneh *etc*.
vestibule פרוזדור *nm* prozdor/-eem (*pl+of:* -ey).
vestige 1. שריד *nm* sareed/sreedeem (*+of:* sreed/-ey); **2.** סימן (sign) *nm* seeman/-eem (*pl+of:* -ey).
vestment 1. לבוש *nm* levoosh; **2.** גלימה (cloak) *nf* gleem|ah/-ot (*+of:* -at).
veteran 1. חייל משוחרר *nm* khayal/-eem meshookhrar/-eem; **2.** ותיק (oldtimer) *nm* vateek/-eem (*pl+of:* -ey).
veterinary 1. רופא וטרינר *nm* rof|e/-'eem vetereenaree/-yeem; **2.** וטרינרי *adj* vetereenaree/-t.
veto 1. איסור *nm* eesoor/-eem (*pl+of:* -ey); **2.** וטו *nm* veto.
(to) veto 1. להטיל וטו *inf* lehateel veto; *pst* heeteel *etc*; *pres* mateel *etc*; *fut* yateel *etc*; **2.** לאסור (forbid) *inf* le'esor; *pst* asar; *pres* oser; *fut* ye'esor.
(to) vex 1. לצער *inf* letsa'er; *pst* tsee'er; *pres* metsa'er; *fut* yetsa'er; **2.** להרגיז (annoy) *inf* lehargeez; *pst* heergeez; *pres* margeez; *fut* yargeez.
vexation רוגז *nm* rogez.
via 1. דרך *adv* derekh; **2.** על ידי (c/o) *adv* 'al yedey; **3.** באמצעות (by means of) *adv* be-emtsa'oot.
viable בר קיימא *adj* bar/bat kayama.

viaduct גשר יבשתי *nm* gesh|er/-areem yabeshtee/-yeem.
vial צלוחית *nf* tselokhee|t/-yot.
(small) vial צלוחית קטנה *nf* tselokhee|t/-yot ketan|ah/-ot.
viand מזון *nm* mazon/mezonot (+*of:* mezon).
(to) vibrate לרטוט *inf* leertot; *pst* ratat; *pres* rotet; *fut* yeertot.
vibration 1. רטט *nm* ret|et/-ateem (*pl+of:* reetetey); **2.** תנודה (oscillation) *nf* tnood|ah/-ot (+*of:* -at).
vicarious 1. חליפי *adj* khaleefee/-t; **2.** שבא במקום (replacing) *adj* she-ba/-'ah bee-mekom.
vice 1. פריצות (licentiousness) *nf* preetsoo|t/-yot; **2.** משנה (deputy) *nm* meeshn|eh/-eem (*pl+of:* -ey); **3.** סגן (assistant) *nmf* segan/-eet.
vice-president סגן נשיא *nm* segan/-ey nasee/nesee'eem.
vice-versa להיפך *prep* le-hefekh.
viceroy משנה למלך *nm* meeshneh le-melekh
vicinity שכנות *nf* seekhenoo|t/-yot.
vicious מושחת *adj* moosh'kh|at/-etet.
vicious dog כלב נושך *nm* kelev/klaveem nosh|ekh/-kheem.
vicissitude תהפוכה *nf* tahapookh|ah/-ot (+*of:* -at).
victim קורבן *nm* korban/-ot.
(to) victimize לעשות מישהו לקורבן la'asot meeshehoo le-korban; *pst* 'asah *etc*; *pres* 'oseh *etc*; *fut* ya'aseh *etc*.
victor מנצח *nmf* menats|e'akh/-akhat.
victorious מנצח *adj* menats|e'akh/-akhat.
victory ניצחון *nm* neets|akhon/khonot (+*of:* -khon)
victuals צורכי מזון *nm pl* tsorkhey mazon.
video, video recorder וידיאו *nm* veede'o.
(to) vie להתחרות *inf* leheetkharot; *pst* heetkharah; *pres* meetkhareh; *fut* yeetkhareh.
Vienna וינה *nf* veenah.
Viennese וינאי *nmf & adj* veena'ee/-t.
view 1. שדה ראייה (field of vision) *nm* sedeh/sedot re'eeyah; **2.** השקפה (opinion) *nf* hash-kaf|ah/-ot (+*of:* -at); **3.** מבט (inspection) *nm* mab|at/-ateem (*pl+of:* -tey); **4.** תכלית (aim) *nf* takhlee|t/-yot.
(on) view מוצג לראווה *adj* moots|ag/-eget le-ra'avah.
(within) view בתחום ראייה *adv* bee-tkhoom re'eeyah.
(in) view of לאור *conj* le-or.
(with a) view to בצפייה ל־ *adv* bee-tsfeeyah le-.
viewpoint נקודת השקפה *nf* nekood|at/-ot hashkafah.
vigil ערות *nf* 'eroo|t/-yot.
(to keep) vigil להשגיח *inf* lehashgee'akh; *pst* heeshgee'akh; *pres* mashgee'akh; *fut* yashgee'akh.
vigilance ערנות *nf* 'eranoo|t/-yot.
vigilant 1. משגיח בדריכות *adj* mashgee|'akh/-khah bee-dreekhoot; **2.** ער (alert) *adj* 'er/-ah.
vigor עוז *nm* 'oz.
vigorous 1. עז *adj* 'az/-ah; **2.** נמרץ (determined) *adj* neemr|ats/-etset.
vile 1. נתעב *adj* neet|'av/-'evet; **2.** שפל (mean) *adj* shafal/shefalah.

villa 1. חווילה *nf* khaveel|ah/-ot (+*of:* -at); **2.** וילה (*colloq.*) *nf* veel|ah/-ot (+*of:* -at).
village 1. כפר *nm* kefar/-eem (*pl+of:* -ey); **2.** מושב (coop. settlement) *nm* moshav/-eem (*pl+of:* -ey).
villager 1. כפרי *nm* kafree/-yeem (*pl+of:* -yey); **2.** מושבניק (*[slang]:* moshav-member) *nm* moshavneek/-eet.
villain נבל *nm* naval/neval|eem (*pl+of:* -ey).
villainous מרושע *adj* meroosh|a'/-a'at.
villainy שפלות *nf* sheefloo|t/-yot.
vim 1. עוצמה *nf* 'otsm|ah/-ot (+*of:* -at); **2.** מרץ (energy) *nm* merets.
(to) vindicate 1. לסנגר *inf* lesanger; *pst* seenger; *pres* mesanger; *fut* yesanger; **2.** לנקות מאשמה (clear) *inf* lenakot me-ashmah; *pst* neekah *etc*; *pres* menakeh *etc*; *fut* yenakeh *etc*.
vindictive נקמני *adj* nakmanee/-t.
vine 1. גפן *nf* gef|en/-aneem (*pl+of:* gafney); **2.** מטפס (climbing plant) *nm* metap|es/-seem (*pl+of:* -sey)
vinegar חומץ *nm* khomets.
vineyard כרם *nm* kerem/krameem (*pl+of:* karmey).
vintage 1. בציר (season) *nm* batseer (+*of:* betseer); **2.** שנת בציר (year) *nf* shn|at/-ot batseer.
(to) violate 1. להפר *inf* lehafer; *pst* hefer; *pres* mefer; *fut* yafer; **2.** לחלל (desecrate) *inf* lekhalel; *pst* kheelel; *pres* mekhalel; *fut* yekhalel.
violation הפרה *nf* hafar|ah/-ot (+*of:* -at).
violence אלימות *nf* aleemoo|t/-yot.
violent אלים *adj* aleem/-ah.
violet 1. סיגלית (flower) *nf* seegalee|t/-yot; **2.** סגול (color) *adj* sagol/segoolah.
violin כינור *nm* keenor/-ot.
violinist כנר *nmf* kanar/-eet (*pl:* -eem/-ot).
viper צפע *nm* tsefa'/tsefa'eem (*pl+of:* tseef'ey).
virgin 1. בתולה *nf* betool|ah/-ot; **2.** בתול *adj* batool/betoolah.
virginal בתולי *adj* betoolee/-t.
virile גברי *adj* gavree/-t.
virtual ממשי *adj* mamashee/-t.
virtually למעשה *adv* le-ma'aseh.
virtue סגולה *nf* segool|ah/-ot (+*of:* -at).
virtuous מוסרי *adj* moosaree/-t.
virulent קטלני *adj* katlanee/-t.
virus 1. נגיף *nm* nageef/negeef|eem (*pl+of:* -ey); **2.** וירוס *nm* veeroos/-eem (*pl+of:* -ey).
visa 1. אשרה *nf* ashr|ah/-ot (+*of:* -at); **2.** ויזה *nf* veez|ah/-ot (+*of:* -at).
vis-a-vis אל מול *adv* el mool.
(to) visa להעניק אשרה *inf* leha'aneek ashrah; *pst* he'eneek *etc*; *pst* ma'aneek *etc*; *fut* ya'aneek *etc*.
visage קלסתר *nm* klaster/-eem (*pl+of:* -ey).
viscera קרביים *nf* krav|ayeem (*pl+of:* -ey).
vise מלחציים *nm pl* melkhats|ayeem (*pl+of:* -ey).
visible 1. נראה לעין *adj* neer|'eh/-'et la-'ayeen; **2.** גלוי (open) *adj* galooy/glooyah.
vision 1. ראייה *nf* re'ee|yah/-yat; **2.** חזון (foresight) *nm* khazon/-ot.
visionary 1. חוזה *nmf* khoz|eh/-ah (+*of:* -at/-ey); **2.** הוזה (dreamer) *adj* hoz|eh/-ah (+*of:* -at/-ey).
visit ביקור *nm* beekoor/-eem (*pl+of:* -ey).
(to) visit לבקר *inf* levaker; *pst* beeker (*b=v*); *pres* mevaker; *fut* yevaker.

(to) visit punishment upon להביא על עונשו את *inf* lehavee 'al 'onsh|o/-ah et.

visitation 1. ביקור *nm* beekoor/-eem (*pl+of:* -ey); **2.** עונש משמיים (punishment) *nm* 'onesh mee-shamayeem.

visiting card כרטיס ביקור *nm* kartees/-ey beekoor.

visitor 1. מבקר *nm* mevaker/-et; **2.** אורח (guest) *nmf* ore'akh/orakhat (*pl+of:* orkhey).

visor 1. מצחייה *nf* meetskhee|yah/-yot (*+of:* -yat); **2.** מצחת קסדה (of helmet) *nf* meetskh|at/-ot kasdah.

vista 1. מראה *nm* mar|'eh/-'ot; **2.** נוף (scenery) *nm* nof/-eem (*pl+of:* -ey).

visual 1. חזותי *adj* khazootee/-t; **2.** של ראייה (of sight) *adj* shel re'eeyah.

(to) visualize לשוות לנגד העיניים *inf* leshavot le-neged ha-'eynayeem; *pst* sheevah *etc; pres* meshaveh *etc; fut* yeshaveh *etc.*

vital חיוני *adj* kheeyoonee/-t.

vitality חיוניות *nf* kheeyooneeyoot.

(to) vitalize להפיח חיים ב־ *inf* lehafee'akh khayeem be-; *pst* hefee'akh *etc; pres* mefee'akh *etc; fut* yafee'akh *etc.*

vitamin ויטמין *nm* veetameen/-eem (*pl+of:* -ey).

vivacious 1. עירני *adj* 'eranee/-t; **2.** מלא חיים (lively) *adj* mele/-'at khayeem.

vivacity עירנות *nf* 'eranoo|t/-yot.

vivid מלא חיים *adj* mele/-'at khayeem.

(to) vivify להחיות *inf* lehakhyot; *pst* hekhyah; *pres* mekhayeh; *fut* yekhayeh.

vivisection נתיחת גוף חי *nf* neteekh|at/-ot goof khay.

vocabulary אוצר מלים *nm* otsar meeleem.

vocal קולי *adj* kolee/-t.

vocal cords מיתרי הקול *nm pl* meytarey ha-kol.

vocation 1. משלח יד *nm* meeshlakh yad; **2.** ייעוד (mission) *nm* ye'ood/-eem (*pl+of:* -ey).

vogue אופנה *nf* ofn|ah/-ot (*+of:* -at).

(in) vogue אופנתי *adj* ofnatee/-t.

voice 1. קול *nm* kol/-ot; **2.** זכות דיבור (right to speak) *nf* zekhoo|t/-yot deeboor.

voiced consonant עיצור מונע *nm* 'eetsoor/-eem moon|a'/-a'eem.

voiceless חסר קול *adj* khas|ar/-rat kol.

voiceless consonant עיצור בלתי־מונע *nm* 'eetsoor/-eem beeltee moon|a'/-'eem.

void 1. בטל *adj* batel/betelah; **2.** חסר תוקף (invalid) *adj* khas|ar/-rat tokef.

(to) void 1. לפסול *inf* leefsol; *pst* pasal *(p=f); pres* posel; *fut* yeefsol; **2.** לבטל (annul) *inf* levatel; *pst* beetel *(b=v); pres* mevatel; *fut* yevatel.

void of חסר *adj* khaser/-ah.

volatile 1. נדיף *adj* nadeef/nedeefah; **2.** הפכפך (fickle) *adj adj* hafakhpakh/-ah.

volcanic 1. של הר געש *adj* shel har ga'ash; **2.** וולקני *adj* voolkanee/-t.

volcano הר געש *nm* har/-ey ga'ash.

volition רצייה *nf* retsee|yah/-yot (*+of:* -yat).

volley מטח *nm* matakh/-eem (*pl+of:* -ey).

volley ball כדור עף *nm* kadoor 'af.

volt וולט *nm* volt/-eem (*pl+of:* -ey).

voltage 1. מתח *nm* metakh/-eem (*pl+of:* -ey); **2.** וולטאז *nm* voltaj/-eem (*pl+of:* -ey).

voluble קולח מילים *adj* kol|e'akh/-akhat meeleem.

volume 1. נפח (capacity) *nm* nefakh/-eem (*pl+of:* neefkhey); **2.** כמות (quantity) *nf* kamoo|t/-yot; **3.** כרך (tome) *nm* kerekh/krakheem (*pl+of:* keerkhey).

voluminous רב ממדים *adj* rav/rabat memadeem *(b=v).*

voluntary 1. רצוני *adj* retsonee/-t; **2.** בהתנדבות *adv* be-heetnadvoot.

volunteer מתנדב *nm* meetnad|ev/-veem (*pl+of:* -vey).

(to) volunteer להתנדב *inf* leheetnadev; *pst* heetnaadev; *pres* meetnadev; *fut* yeetnadev.

voluptuous חושני *adj* khooshanee/-t.

vomit קיא *nm* kee.

(to) vomit להקיא *inf* lehakee; *pst* hekee; *pres* mekee; *fut* yakee.

voracious רעבתני *adj* ra'avtanee/-t.

vortex מערבולת *nf* me'arbol|et/-ot,

vote 1. קול *nm* kol/-ot; **2.** הצבעה (voting) *nf* hatsba|'ah/-'ot (*+of:* -'at).

(to) vote להצביע *inf* lehatsbee'a'; *pst* heetsbee'a'; *pres* matsbee'a'; *fut* yatsbee'a'.

voter 1. מצביע *nm* matsbee|'a'/-'eem (*pl+of:* -'ey); **2.** בוחר (elector) *nm* bokh|er/-areem (*pl+of:* arey).

(to) vouch 1. לאשר *inf* le'asher; *pst* eesher; *pres* me'asher; *fut* ye'asher; **2.** להעיד (attest) *inf* leha'eed; *pst* he'eed; *pres* me'eed; *fut* ya'eed.

(to) vouch for לערוב ל־ *inf* la'arov le-; *pst* 'arav le-; *pres* 'arev le-; *fut* ya'arov le-.

voucher 1. שובר *nm* shov|er/-reem (*pl+of:* -rey); **2.** ערב (guarantor) *nm* 'arev/-eem (*pl+of:* -ey).

(to) vouchsafe להעניק *inf* leha'aneek; *pst* he'eneek; *pres* ma'aneek; *fut* ya'aneek.

vow נדר *nm* ned|er/-areem (*pl+of:* needrey).

(to) vow 1. לנדור *inf* leendor; *pst* nadar; *pres* noder; *fut* yeendor; **2.** להבטיח (promise) *inf* lehavtee'akh; *pst* heevtee'akh; *pres* mavtee'akh; *fut* yavtee'akh.

vowel תנועה *nf* tenoo|'ah/-'ot (*+of:* -'at).

voyage 1. מסע *nm* mas|a'/-a'ot (*pl+of:* -'ot); **2.** נסיעה (trip) *nf* nesee|'ah/-'ot (*+of:* -'at).

(to) voyage 1. לנסוע *inf* leenso'a'; *pst* nasa'; *pres* nose'a'; *fut* yeesa'; **2.** לערוך מסע (travel) *inf* la'arokh masa'; *pst* 'arakh *etc; pres* 'orekh *etc; fut* ya'arokh *etc.*

vulgar 1. גס *adj* gas/-ah; **2.** המוני (common) *adj* hamonee/-t.

vulnerable פגיע *adj* pagee'a'/pegee'ah.

vulture 1. עוזנייה *nf* 'oznee|yah/-yot (*+of:* -yat); **2.** נשר (eagle) *nm* nesh|er/-areem (*pl+of:* neeshrey).

W.

W,w semi-consonant for which the Hebrew alphabet has no equivalent. Hebrew makes no distinction, in fact, between *W* and *V*; most Israelis pronounce *Washington* as *Vashington*, using ו and וו for the transliteration of both W and V.

wad מוך *nm* mokh.

wad of money צרור שטרי כסף *nm* tseror/-ot sheetrey kesef.

waddle הילוך כשל ברווז *nm* heelookh ke-shel barvaz.

(to) waddle להלך כברווז *inf* lehalekh ke-barvaz.

(to) wade להתקדם בעצלתיים *inf* leheetkadem ba-'atsaltayeem; *pst* heetkadem *etc; pres* meetkadem *etc; fut* yeetkadem *etc.*

wafer, waffle 1. אפיפית *nf* afeefee|t/-yot; **2.** ופל *[colloq.] nm* vaf|el/-leem (*pl+of:* -ley).

waft 1. משב *nm* mash|av/-aveem (*pl+of:* -vey); **2.** זרם (current) *nm* zerem/zrameem (*pl+of:* zeermey).

(to) waft להיגרף בזרם *inf* leheegaref be-zerem; *pst & pres* neegraf *etc; fut* yeegaref *etc.*

wag נענוע *nm* nee'noo|'a'/-'eem (*pl+of:* -'ey).

(to) wag לנענע *inf* lena'ne'a'; *pst* nee'na'; *pres* mena'ne'a'; *fut* yena'na'.

wag the tail לכשכש בזנב *inf* lekhashkesh ba-zanav; *pst* keeshkesh *(k=kh) etc; pres* mekhashkesh *etc; fut* yekhashkesh *etc.*

wage, wages 1. שכר *nm* sakhar (*+of:* sekhar); **2.** משכורת (salary) *nf* maskor|et/-ot.

(to) wage לנהל מלחמה *inf* lenahel meelkhamah; *pst* neehel *etc; pres* menahel *etc; fut* yenahel *etc.*

wage earner שכיר *nmf* sakheer/sekheerah (*+of:* -at; *pl+of:* -ey).

wage scale סולם משכורות *nm* soolam maskorot.

wager 1. התערבות *nf* heet'arvoo|t/-yot; **2.** הימור (bet) *nm* heemoor/-eem (*pl+of:* -ey).

(to) wager 1. להתערב *inf* leheet'arev; *pst* heet'arev; *pres* meet'arev; *fut* yeet'arev; **2.** להמר (bet) *inf* lehamer; *pst* heemer; *pres* mehamer; *fut* yehamer.

wagon 1. עגלה (cart) *nf* 'agal|ah/-ot (*+of:* 'egl|at/-ot); **2.** קרון מטען (railroad) *nm* kron/-ot meet'an.

(on the) wagon בהתנזרות ממשקאות חריפים *adv* be-heetnazroot mee-mashka'ot khareefeem.

wail יבבה *nf* yevav|ah/-ot (*+of:* yeevev|at/-ot).

(to) wail לייבב *inf* leyabev; *pst* yeebev; *pres* meyabev; *fut* yeyabev.

waist מותן *nm* mot|en/-nayeem (*pl+of:* -ney).

waistband חגורת מותניים *nf* khagor|at/-ot motnayeem.

waistcoat 1. חזייה *nf* khazee|yah/-yot (*+of:* -yat); **2.** לסוטה (vest) *nf* lesoot|ah/-ot (*+of:* -at).

waistline קו המותניים *nm* kav ha-motnayeem.

wait המתנה *nf* hamtan|ah/-ot (*+of:* -at).

(to) wait 1. לחכות *inf* lekhakot; *pst* kheekah; *pres* mekhakeh; *fut* yekhakeh; **2.** להמתין *inf* lehamteen; *pst* heemteen; *pres* mamteen; *fut* yamteen.

(to lie in) wait לארוב *inf* le'erov; *pst* arav; *pres* orev; *fut* ye'erov.

(to) wait for לחכות ל־ *inf* lekhakot le-; *pst* kheekah le-; *pres* mekhakeh le-; *fut* yekhakeh le-.

(to) wait on לשמש את *inf* leshamesh et; *pst* sheemesh et; *pres* meshamesh et; *fut* yeshamesh et.

(to) wait table לשמש מלצר *inf* leshamesh meltsar; *pst* sheemesh *etc; pres* meshamesh *etc; fut* yeshamesh *etc.*

waiter מלצר *nm* meltsar/-eem (*pl+of:* -ey).

waiting המתנה *nf* hamtan|ah/-ot (*+of:* -at).

waiting room חדר המתנה *nm* khad|ar/-rey hamtanah.

waitress מלצרית *nf* meltsaree|t/-yot.

(to) waive לוותר על *inf* levater 'al; *pst* veeter 'al; *pres* mevater 'al; *fut* yevater 'al.

(to) waive one's right להסתלק מזכות *inf* lehheestalek mee-zekhoot; *pst* heestalek *etc; pres* meestalek *etc; fut* yeestalek *etc*

waiver 1. ויתור *nm* veetoor/-eem (*pl+of:* -ey); **2.** ויתרון (legal term) *nm* veet|aron/-ronot (*+of:* -ron).

wake 1. שובל (in water) *nm* shov|el/-oleem (*pl+of:* -ley); **2.** עקבות (traces) *nm pl* 'akevot (*+of:* 'eekvot); **3.** עירנות (alertness) *nf* 'eranoo|t/-yot.

(to) wake לעורר *vt inf* le'orer; *pst* 'orer; *pres* me'orer; *fut* ye'orer.

(in the) wake of בעיקבות *adv* be-'eekvot.

(to) wake up להתעורר *v rfl inf* leheet'orer; *pst* heet'orer; *pres* meet'orer; *fut* yeet'orer.

wakeful 1. ער *adj* 'er/-ah; **2.** עירני (alert) *adj* 'eranee/-t.

(to) waken לעורר *vt inf* le'orer; *pst* 'orer; *pres* me'orer; *fut* ye'orer.

walk 1. צעידה *nf* tse'eed|ah/-ot (*+of:* -at); **2.** הליכה ברגל (marching) *nf* haleekh|ah/-ot ba-regel; **3.** טיול (promenade) *nm* teeyool/-eem (*pl+of:* -ey).

(a ten minute) walk עשר דקות הליכה ברגל *nf pl* 'eser dakot haleekhah be-regel.

(to) walk להלך ברגל *inf* lehalekh ba-regel; *pst* heelekh *etc; pres* mehalekh *etc; fut* yehalekh *etc.*

(to) walk away להתרחק *inf* leheetrakhek; *pst* heetrakhek; *pres* meetrakhek; *fut* yeetrakhek.

(to) walk back home לחזור הביתה *inf* lakhzor ha-baytah; *pst* khazar *etc; pres* khozer *etc; fut* yakhzor *etc.*

(to) walk down לרדת *inf* laredet; *pst* yarad; *pres* yored; *fut* yered.

(to) walk in להיכנס *inf* leheekanes; *pst & pres* neekhnas *(kh=k); fut* yeekanes.

walk of life אורח חיים *nm* orakh/orkhot khayeem.

(to) walk out לצאת *inf* latset; *pst* yatsa; *pres* yotse; *fut* yetse.

walkaway תחרות שקל לנצח בה *nf* takhroo|t/-yot she-kal lenatse'akh bah.

walking הליכה ברגל *nf* haleekh|ah/-ot ba-regel.

wall 1. קיר *nm* keer/-ot; **2.** כותל (from inside) *nm* kotel/ketaleem (*pl+of:* kotley); **3.** חומה (fort) *nf* khom|ah/-ot (*+of:* -at); **4.** דופן (side) *nm* dofen/defaneem (*pl+of:* dofnot).

(the Wailing) Wall הכותל המערבי *nm* ha-kotel ha-ma'aravee.

(to drive to the) wall ללחוץ לקיר *inf* leelkhots la-keer; *pst* lakhats *etc; pres* lokhets *etc; fut* yeelkhats *etc.*

wall newspaper עיתון קיר *nm* 'eeton/-ey keer.

wallet ארנק *nm* arn|ak/-akeem (*pl+of:* -ekey).

wallflower פרח קיר *nm* perakh/peerkhey keer.

wallop מהלומה *nf* mahaloom|ah/-ot (*+of:* -at).

(to) wallop 1. להלום *inf* lahalom; *pst* halam; *pres* holem; *fut* yahalom; **2.** להלקות (whip) *inf* lehalkot; *pst* heelkah; *pres* malkeh; *fut* yalkeh.

(to) wallow להתפלש *inf* leheetpalesh; *pst* heetpalesh; *pres* meetpalesh; *fut* yeetpalesh.

wallpaper טפיט *nm* tapet/-eem (*pl+of:* -ey).

walnut 1. אגוז (fruit) egoz/-eem (*pl+of:* -ey); **2.** עץ אגוז (tree) *nm* 'ets/'atsey egoz/-eem; **3.** עשוי עץ אגוז (of walnut wood) *adj* 'asoo|y/-yah 'ets egoz.

waltz ולס *nm* vals/-eem (*pl+of:* -ey).

wan 1. חולני *adj* kholanee/-t; **2.** חיוור (pale) *adj* kheever/-et.

wand 1. מטה *nm* mat|eh/-ot; **2.** מקל (baton) *nm* mak|el/-lot.

(magic) wand מטה קסמים *nm* mateh kesameem.

(to) wander 1. לשוטט *inf* leshotet; *pst* shotet; *pres* meshotet; *fut* yeshotet; **2.** לנדוד (roam) *inf* leendod; *pst* nadad; *pres* noded; *fut* yeendod.

(to) wander away להרחיק נדוד *inf* leharkheek nedod; *pst* heerkheek *etc; pres* markheek *etc; fut* yarkheek *etc.*

(to) wander away from להסתלק מ־ *inf* leheestalek mee-; *pst* heestalek mee; *pres* meestalek mee-; *fut* yeestalek mee-.

wanderer נע ונד *nm* na' va-nad.

wane 1. ירידה *nf* yereed|ah/-ot (*+of:* -at); **2.** התמעטות (dwindling) *f* heetma'atoo|t/-yot.

(on the) wane בקו ירידה *adv* be-kav yereedah.

(to) wane להתמעט *inf* leheetma'et; *pst* heetma'et; *pres* meetma'et; *fut* yeetma'et.

want 1. מחסור *nm* makhsor/-eem (*pl+of:* -ey); **2.** צורך (need) *nm* tsorekh/tserakheem (*pl+of:* tsorkhey); **3.** עוני (poverty) *nm* 'onee.

(in) want בחוסר כל *adv* be-khoser kol.

(to) want 1. לרצות (desire) *inf* leertsot; *pst* ratsah; *pres* rotseh; *fut* yeertseh; **2.** לחסור (lack) *inf* lakhsor; *pst* khasar; *pres* khaser; *fut* yakhsor.

wanting חסר *adj* khaser/-ah.

wanton 1. אכזרי *adj* akhzaree/-t; **2.** זדוני (malign) *adj* zdonee/-t; **3.** חסר מצפון (immoral) *adj* khas|ar/-rat matspoon.

war מלחמה *nf* meelkh|amah/-amot (*+of:* -emet).

(Second World) War מלחמת העולם השנייה *nf* meelkhemet ha-'olam ha-shneeyah.

(state of) war מצב מלחמה *nm* matsav meelkhamah.

(to) war להילחם *inf* leheelakhem; *pst & pres* neelkham; *fut* yeelakhem.

(to declare) war להכריז מלחמה *inf* leahkhreez meelkhamah; *pst* heekhreez *etc; pres* makhreez *etc; fut* yakhreez *etc.*

(the Lebanon) War מלחמת לבנון (1982) *nf* meelkhemet levanon.

(the Sinai) War 1. מלחמת סיני (1956) *nf* melkhemet seenay; **2.** מבצע קדש (*synon. of* "the Sinai Campaign") *nm* meevtsa' kadesh.

(the Six Day) War מלחמת ששת הימים (1967) *nf* meelkhemet sheshet ha-yameem.

war cemetery בית קברות צבאי *nm* bet/batey kvarot tseva'ee/-yeem.

war crimes פשעי מלחמה *nm* peesh'ey meelkhamah.

war disabled נכה מלחמה *nm* nekhe|h/-y meelkhamah.

war effort מאמץ מלחמתי *nm* ma'amats meelkhamtee.

war loan מלווה מלחמה *nm* meelv|eh/-ot meelkhamah.

war memorial אנדרטה לנופלים *nf* andart|ah/-ot la-nofleem.

(Israel's) War of Independance מלחמת העצמאות (1948) *nf* meelkhemet ha-'atsma'oot.

(Israel's) War of Liberation מלחמת השיחרור *(synon. with prec.) nf* meelkhemet ha-sheekhroor.

war veteran חייל משוחרר *nm* khayal/-eem meshookhrar/-eem.

warble סלסול קול *nm* seelsool/-ey kol.

(to) warble לסלסל בקול *inf* lesalsel be-kol; *pst* seelsel *etc; pres* mesalsel *etc; fut* yesalsel *etc.*

warbler סבכי מזמר *nm* seebkhee/-m mezam|er/-reem.

ward 1. מחלקה בבית חולים (in hospital) *nf* makhlak|ah/-ot be-vet *(v=b)* kholeem; **2.** אגף בבית סוהר (in prison) *nm* aga|f/-peem *(p=f)* be-vet *(v=b)* sohar; **3.** קטין בפיקוח אפוטרופוס (under custody) *nmf* kateen/keteenah be-feekoo'akh *(f=p)* epeetropos.

(to) ward off למנוע *inf* leemno'a'; *pst* mana'; *pres* mone'a'; *fut* yeemna'.

warden סוהר *nm* soher/sohar|ee (*pl+of:* -ey).

(prison) warden מפקד בית סוהר *nm* mefak|ed/-dey bet sohar.

wardrobe 1. ארון בגדים (closet) *nm* aron/-ot begadeem; **2.** מלתחה (garments) *nf* meltakh|ah/-ot (*+of:* -at).

warehouse 1. מחסן סחורות *nm* makhsan/-ey sekhorot; **2.** מחסן לממכר סחורות (store) makhsan/-eem le-meemkar sekhorot.

wares סחורות *nf pl* sekhorot.

warfare לוחמה *nf* lokhm|ah/-ot (*+of:* -at).

warhead ראש חץ *nm* rosh/-ey khets.

warlike מלחמתי *adj* meelkhamtee/-t.

warm 1. חם (temperature) *adj* kham/-ah; **2.** נלהב (enthusiastic) *adj* neel|hav/-hevet; **3.** טרי (fresh) *adj* taree/treeyah.

(he is) warm יש לו חום yesh lo khom

(to) warm לחמם *inf* lekhamem; *pst* kheemem; *pres* mekhamem; *fut* yekhamem.

warm blooded חמום מוח *adj* khamoom/-at mo'akh.

warm hearted בעל לב חם *adj* ba'al/-at lev kham.

(to) warm over 1. לחמם מחדש *inf* lekhamem me-khadash; *pst* kheemem *etc*; *pres* mekhamem *etc*; *fut* yekhamem *etc*; **2.** לחמם יתר על המידה (overheat) *inf* lekhamem yater 'al ha-meedah; *pst* kheemem *etc*; *pres* mekhamem *etc*; *fut* yekhamem *etc*.

(it is) warm today חם היום kham ha-yom.

(to) warm up להתחמם *inf* leheetkhamem; *pst* heetkhamem; *pres* meetkhamem; *fut* yeetkhamem.

warmonger מחרחר מלחמה *nm* mekharkher/-ey meelkhamah.

warmth 1. חום (heat) *nm* khom; **2.** חמימות (friendship) *nf* khameemoo|t/-yot.

(to) warn להזהיר *inf* lehaz'heer; *pst* heez'heer; *pres* maz'heer; *fut* yaz'heer.

warning אזהרה *nf* az'har|ah/-ot (*+of:* -at).

(let that be a) warning to you ישמש לך הדבר כאזהרה yeshamesh lekha/lakh *(m/f)* ha-davar ke-azharah.

warp 1. עיקול *nm* 'eekool/-eem (*pl+of:* -ey); **2.** עיוות (twist) *nm* 'eevoot/-eem (*pl+of:* -ey).

(to) warp 1. לעקל *inf* le'akel; *pst* 'eekel; *pres* me'akel; *fut* ye'akel; **2.** לעוות (twist) *inf* le'avet; *pst* 'eevet; *pres* me'avet; *fut* ye'avet.

warrant 1. הצדקה (sanction) *nf* hatsdak|ah/-ot (*+of:* -at); **2.** כתב מינוי (writ) *nm* ketav/keetvey meenooy.

(search) warrant צו חיפוש *nm* tsav/-ey kheepoos.

(to) warrant 1. לאשר *inf* le'asher; *pst* eesher; *pres* me'asher; *fut* ye'asher; **2.** להצדיק (justify) *inf* lehatsdeek; *pst* heetsdeek; *pres* matsdeek; *fut* yatsdeek; **3.** לערוב (guarantee) *inf* la'arov; *pst* 'arav; *pres* 'arev; *fut* ya'arov; **4.** להבטיח (promise) *inf* lehavtee'akh; *pst* heevtee'akh; *pres* mavtee'akh; *fut* yavtee'akh.

warrant of arrest 1. צו מאסר *nm* tsav/-ey ma'asar; **2.** צו מעצר (detention) *nm* tsav/-ey ma'atsar.

warrant of attachment צו עיקול *nm* tsav/-ey 'eekool.

warrior לוחם *nm* lokh|em/-ameem (*pl+of:* -amey).

Warsaw ורשה *nf* varshah.

warship אוניית מלחמה *nf* oneel|yat/-yot meelkhamah.

wart יבלת *nf* yab|elet/-alot.

wary 1. זהיר *adj* zaheer/zeheerah; **2.** עירני (alert) 'eranee/-t.

wary of חשדן *adj* khashdan/-eet.

wash 1. רחצה *nf* rakhts|ah/-ot (*+of:* -at); **2.** כביסה (laundry) *nf* kvees|ah/-ot (*+of:* -at).

(car) wash רחיצת רכב *nf* rekheets|at/-ot rekhev.

(mouth)wash שטיפת פה *nf* shteef|at/-ot rekhev.

(to) wash 1. לרחוץ *vt inf* leerkhots; *pst* rakhats; *pres* rokhets; *fut* yeerkhats; **2.** להתרחץ (oneself) *v rfl inf* leheetrakhets; *pst* heetrakhets; *pres* meetrakhets; *fut* yeetrakhets; **3.** לכבס (launder) *inf* lekhabes; *pst* keebes *(k=kh)*; *pres* mekhabes; *fut* yekhabes.

wash and wear כבס ולבש kabes oo-levash.

(to) wash away לשטוף *inf* leeshtof; *pst inf* shataf; *pres* shotef; *fut* yeeshtof.

washable רחיץ *adj* rakheets/rekheetsah.

washbowl קערת רחצה *nf* ka'ar|at/-ot rakhtsah.

washcloth מטלית רחיצה *nf* matlee|t/-yot rekheetsah.

washed away by the waves נסחף בגלי הים *adj* neeskh|af/-efet be-galey ha-yam.

washed out 1. דהוי *adj* dahooy/dehooyah; **2.** עייף (tired) *adj* 'ayef/-ah.

washed up 1. נסחף *adj* neeskh|af/-efet; **2.** גמור (finished) *adj* gamoor/gemoorah.

washer 1. דסקית (for screw-bolt) *nf* deeskee|t/-yot; **2.** שייבה (colloquial *synon. of* 1) *nf* shayb|ah/-ot (*+of:* -at); **3.** כובס (launderer) *nmf* koves/-et.

washerwoman כובסת *nf* kov|eset/-sot.

washing 1. כביסה (action) *nf* kvees|ah/-ot (*+of:* -at); **2.** כבסים (material) *nm pl* kvas|eem (*pl+of:* -ey).

washing machine מכונת כביסה *nf* mekhon|at/-ot kveesah.

washout כישלון *nm* keesh|alon/-lonot (*+of:* -lon).

wasp צרעה *nf* tseer'ah/tsera'ot (*+of:* tseer|'at/-'ot)

waste 1. ביזבוז *nm* beezbooz/-eem (*pl+of:* -ey); **2.** פסולת (refuse) *nf* pesol|et/-ot.

(to) waste לבזבז *inf* levazbez; *pst* beezbez *(b=v)*; *pres* mevazbez; *fut* yevazbez.

(to go) waste להתבזבז *inf* leheetbazbez; *pst* heetbazbez; *pres* meetbazbez; *fut* yeetbazbez.

(to lay) waste 1. להשמים *inf* lehashmeem; *pst* heshmeem; *pres* mashmeem; *fut* yashmeem; **2.** להחריב (devastate) *inf* lehakhreev; *pst* hekhreev; *pres* makhreev; *fut* yakhreev.

(to) waste away לפזר לריק *inf* lefazer la-reek; *pst* peezer *(p=f) etc*; *pres* mefazer *etc*; *fut* yefazer *etc*.

waste basket סל פסולת *nm* sal/-ey pesolet.

waste of time איבוד זמן *nm* eebood zman.

waste land 1. אדמת בור *nf* adm|at/-ot boor; **2.** שממה (desert) *nf* shmamah/-ot (*+of:* sheemem|at/-ot).

waste paper פסולת נייר *nf* pesol|et/-ot neyar.

wasteful 1. בזבזני *adj* bazbezanee/-t; **2.** הרסני (destructive) *adj* harsanee/-t.

watch 1. שעון (timepiece) *nm* sha'on/she'on|eem (*pl+of:* -ey); **2.** משמרת (guard) *nf* meeshm|eret/-arot.

(on the) watch על המשמר *adv* 'al ha-meeshmar.

(digital) watch שעון דיגיטלי *nm* sha'on/she'oneem degeetalee/-yeem.

(to) watch 1. לצפות (look) *inf* leetspot; *pst* tsafah *(f=p)*; *pres* tsofeh; *fut* yeetspeh; **2.** להשגיח (observe) *inf* lehashgee'akh; *pst* heeshgee'akh; *pres* mashgee'akh; *fut* yashgee'akh.

(to keep) watch לשמור *inf* leeshmor; *pst* shamar; *pres* shomer; *fut* yeeshmor.

(wrist) watch שעון יד *nm* she'on/-ey yad.

watch chain שרשרת שעון sharsher|et/-ot sha'on.
(to) watch out for להיזהר מפני *inf* leheezaher meepney; *pst & pres* neez'har *etc*; *fut* yeezaher *etc*.
watchful עירני *adj* 'eranee/-t.
watchmaker שען *nm* she'an/-eem (*pl+of:* -ey).
watchman שומר *nm* shom|er/-reem (*pl+of:* -rey).
watchtower מגדל שמירה *nm* meegd|al/-eley shmeerah.
watchword סיסמה *nf* seesm|ah/-a'ot (*+of:* -at).
water מים *nm pl* mayeem (*+of:* mey).
(my eyes) water עיניי זולגות מים 'eynay zolgot mayeem.
(to) water 1. להשקות *inf* lehashkot; *pst* heeshkah; *pres* mashkeh; *fut* yashkeh; **2.** לרסס במים (sprinkle) *inf* lerases be-mayeem; *pst* reeses *etc*; *pres* merases *etc*; *fut* yerases *etc*.
water color 1. צבעי מים *nm pl* tseev'ey mayeem; **2.** ציור בצבעי מים (painting) *nm* tseeyoor/-eem be-tseev'ey mayeem.
water power כוח מפל המים *nm* ko'akh mapal ha-mayeem.
water ski סקי מים *nm* skee mayeem.
water sports ספורט מים *nm* sport mayeem.
water supply אספקת מים *nf* aspakat mayeem.
waterfall מפל מים *nm* map|al/-ley mayeem.
waterfront 1. שפת הים *nf* sfat ha-yam; **2.** שטח הנמל (harbor area) *nm* shetakh ha-namel.
watermelon אבטיח *nm* avatee'akh/-kheem (*pl+of:* -khey).
waterpower כוח הידראולי *nm* ko'akh heedraulee.
waterproof אטים מים *adj* ateem/-at mayeem.
(my mouth) waters פי מתמלא רוק pee meetmale' rok.
waterspout שבר ענן *nm* shever/sheevrey 'anan.
watertight 1. בלתי חדיר למים *adj* beeltee-khadeer/-ah le-mayeem; **2.** חסין לפרשנויות (impossible to misinterpret) *adj* khaseen/-ah le-farshanooyot *(f=p)*.
waterway 1. נתיב מים *nm* neteev/-ey mayeem; **2.** תעלה (canal) *nf* te'al|ah/-ot (*+of:* -at).
watery מימי *adj* meymee/-t.
wave גל *nm* gal/-eem (*pl+of:* -ey).
(permanent) wave סלסול תמידי *nm* seelsool temeedee.
(to) wave 1. לנופף *inf* lenofef; *pst* nofef; *pres* menofef; *fut* yenofef; **2.** להתנוסס (be hoisted) *inf* leheetnoses; *pst* heetnoses; *pres* meetnoses; *fut* yeetnoses.
(to) wave aside לנופף הצידה *inf* lenofef ha-tseedah; *pst* nofef *etc*; *pres* menofef *etc*; *fut* yenofef *etc*.
(to) wave good-bye לנפנף לשלום *inf* lenafnef le-shalom; *pst* neefnef *etc*; *pres* menafef *etc*; *fut* yenafnef *etc*.
(to) wave hair לסלסל שיער *inf* lesalsel sey'ar; *pst* seelsel *etc*; *pres* mesalsel *etc*; *fut* yesalsel *etc*.
wave of the hand הינף יד *nm* henef yad.
(to) wave one's hand לנפנף ביד *inf* lenafnef ba-yad; *pst* neefnef *etc*; *pres* menafef *etc*; *fut* yenafnef *etc*.
wavelength אורך גל *nm* orekh/orkhey gal/-eem.
waver 1. פיקפוק *nf* peekpook/-eem (*pl+of:* -ey); **2.** היסוס (hesitation) *nm* heesoos/-eem (*pl+of:* -ey).
(to) waver 1. להתנודד *inf* leheetnoded; *pst* heetnoded; *pres* meetnoded; *fut* yeetnoded; **2.** להסס (hesitate) *inf* lehases; *pst* heeses; *pres* mehases; *fut* yehases.
wavy 1. גלי *adj* galee/-t; **2.** מסולסל (curly) *adj* mesoolsal/-elet.
wax שעווה *nf* sha'av|ah/-ot (*+of:* -at).
wax candle נר שעווה *nm* ner/-ot sha'avah.
wax paper נייר שעווה *nm* neyar/-ot sha'avah.
way 1. דרך *nf* derekh/drakheem (*pl+of:* darkhey); **2.** הרגל (custom) *nm* hergel/-eem (*pl+of:* -ey); **3.** אופן (manner) *nm* of|en/-aneem (*pl+of:* -ney).
(by the) way דרך אגב *prep & adv* derekh agav.
(in a family) way בהריון *adv* be-herayon.
(in no) way בשום אופן *adv* be-shoom ofen.
(out of the) way 1. מסולק (disposed of) *adj* mesoolak/-eket; **2.** שלא בדרך הזאת (remote) *adv* she-lo ba-derekh ha-zot.
(to give) way להיכנע *inf* leheekana'; *pst & pres* neekhna' *(kh=k)*; *fut* yeekana' *etc*.
(to have one's) way לעשות כרצונו *inf* la'asot kee-retsono; *pst* 'asah *etc*; *pres* 'oseh *etc*; *fut* ya'aseh *etc*.
(well under) way בשלב מתקדם *adv* be-shalav meetkadem.
(to make) way for לפנות דרך ל־ *inf* lefanot derekh le-; *pst* peenah *(p=f) etc*; *pres* mefaneh *etc*; *fut* yefaneh *etc*.
way in כניסה *nf* kenees|ah/-ot (*+of:* -at).
(by) way of 1. בדרך של *adv* be-derekh shel; **2.** באמצעות (by means of) *adv* be-emtsa'oot.
(by) way of comparison על דרך ההשוואה *adv* 'al derekh ha-hashva'ah.
(a long) way off עוד רחוקה הדרך 'od rekhokah ha-derekh.
way out יציאה *nf* yetsee|'ah/-'ot (*+of:* -'at).
way through דרך מעבר *nf* derekh/darkhey ma'avar.
(on the) way to בדרך אל *adv* ba-derekh el.
wayfarer עובר אורח *nmf* over/-et (*pl:* ovrey) orakh.
(to) waylay לארוב ולשדוד *inf* le'erov ve-leeshdod; *pst* arav ve-shadad; *pres* orev ve-shoded; *fut* ye'erov ve-yeeshdod.
wayside על אם הדרך *adv* 'al em ha-derekh.
wayside inn פונדק דרכים *nm* poond|ak/-ekey drakheem.
wayward 1. סורר ומורה *adj* sorer/-et oo-mor|eh/-ah; **2.** הפכפך (fickle) *adj* hafakhpakh/-ah.
we 1. אנחנו *pron* anakhnoo; **2.** אנו (*synon. of* 1) *pron* anoo.
weak 1. חלש *adj* khalash/-ah; **2.** רופף (slack) *adj* rofef/-et.
weak market שוק חלש *nm* shook khalash.
weak minded רפה שכל *adj* ref|eh/-ey sekhel.
weak tea תה רפה *nm* teh rafeh.
(to) weaken להחליש *inf* lehakhleesh; *pst* hekhleesh; *pres* makhleesh; *fut* yakhleesh.
weakly 1. תשוש *adj* tashoosh/teshooshah; **2.** רפה (slack) *adj* raf|eh/-ah.
weakness חולשה *nf* khoolsh|ah/-ot (*+of:* -at).

wealth 1. עושר *nm* 'osher; **2.** שפע (abundance) *nm* shefa'.

wealthy עשיר *adj* 'asheer/-ah.

(to) wean לגמול *inf* leegmol; *pst* gamal; *pres* gomel; *fut* yeegmol.

weapon נשק *nm* neshek.

wear לבוש *nm* levoosh.

(clothes for summer) wear בגדי קיץ *nm pl* beegdey kayeets.

(men's) wear הלבשת גברים *nf* halbashat gvareem.

(to) wear 1. לשאת (carry) *inf* laset; *pst* nasa; *pres* nose; *fut* yeesa; **2.** ללבוש (dress in) *inf* leelbosh; *pst* lavash *(v=b)*; *pres* lovesh; *fut* yeelbash.

wear and tear בלאי *nm* blay.

(to) wear away 1. לשחוק (grind to powder) *vt inf* leeshkhok; *pst* shakhak; *pres* shokhek; *fut* yeeshkhak; **2.** להשתחק (be rubbed away) *v rfl inf* leheeshtakhek; *pst* heeshtakhek; *pres* meeshtakhek; *fut* yeeshtakhek; **3.** לבזבז (waste) *inf* levazbez; *pst* beezbez *(b=v)*; *pres* mevazbez; *fut* yevazbez; **4.** לכלות (finish off) *inf* lekhalot; *pst* keelah *(k=kh)*; *pres* mekhaleh; *fut* yekhaleh.

(to) wear off 1. להיעלם *inf* lehe'alem; *pst & pres* ne'elam; *fut* ye'alem; **2.** לפוג (expire) *inf* lafoog; *pst & pres* pag *(p=f)*; *fut* yafoog.

(to) wear out 1. להוגיע (tire) *inf* lehogee'a'; *pst* hogee'a'; *pres* mogee'a'; *fut* yogee'a'; **2.** לקלקל מרוב שימוש (use up) *inf* lekalkel me-rov sheemoosh; *pst* keelkel *etc*; *pres* mekalkel *etc*; *fut* yekalkel *etc*; **3.** לעייף (weary) *vt inf* le'ayef; *pst* 'eeyef; *pres* me'ayef; *fut* ye'ayef.

wearily תוך עייפות *adv* tokh 'ayefoot.

weariness עייפות *f* 'ayefoot.

wearing 1. של הלבשה *adj* shel halbashah; **2.** מייגע (tiring) *adj* meyage'a'/-a'at.

wearisome מעייף *adj* me'ayef/-et.

(it) wears well מחזיק מעמד יפה makhzeek/-ah ma'amad yafeh.

weary עייף (tired) *adj* 'ayef/-ah.

weasel 1. סמור ms samoor/-eem *(pl+of: -ey)*; **2.** נוכל (scoundrel) *nm* nokh|el/-leem *(pl+of: -ley)*.

weather מזג אוויר *nm* mezeg aveer.

(fine) weather מזג אוויר נאה *nm* mezeg aveer na'eh.

(to) weather 1. לייבש באוויר הפתוח *inf* leyabesh ba-aveer ha-patoo'akh; *pst* yeebesh *etc*; *pres* meyabesh *etc*; *fut* yeyabesh *etc*; **2.** להחזיק מעמד (hold out) *inf* lehakhzeek ma'amad; *pst* hekhzeek *etc*; *pres* makhzeek *etc*; *fut* yakhzeek *etc*.

(to) weather a storm לעמוד מול הסערה *inf* la'amod mool ha-se'arah; *pst* 'amad *etc*; *pres* 'omed *etc*; *fut* ya'amod *etc*.

weather-beaten מחושל *adj* mekhoosh|al/-elet.

weather bureau השירות המטאורולוגי *nm* ha-sheroot ha-mete'orologee.

weather conditions תנאי מזג האוויר *nm pl* tena'ey mezeg ha-aveer.

weather report תחזית מזג האוויר *nf* takhzee|t/-yot mezeg ha-aveer.

weather vane שבשבת *nf* shavsh|evet/-avot.

(to) weave 1. לארוג (cloth) *inf* le'erog; *pst* arag; *pres* oreg; *fut* ye'erog; **2.** לטוות תוכניות (to plan) *inf* leetvot tokhneeyot; *pst* tavah *etc*; *pres* toveh *etc*; *fut* yeetveh *etc*.

weaver אורג *nm* oreg/-et *(pl:* org|eem/-ot; *+of:* -ey).

web 1. מארג *nm* ma'ar|ag/-ageem *(pl+of: -gey)*; **2.** מסכת (weaving) *nf* mas|ekhet-akhot.

(spider's) web קורי עכביש *nm pl* koorey 'akaveesh.

(to) wed 1. לשאת אישה (take a wife) *inf* laset eeshah; *pst* nasa *etc*; *pres* nose *etc*; *fut* yeesa *etc*; **2.** להינשא לאיש (marry a man) *inf f* leheenase le-eesh; *pst* nees'ah *etc*; *pres* neeset *etc*; *fut* teenase *etc*; **3.** להתחתן (get married) *inf* leheetkhaten; *pst* heetkhaten; *pres* meetkhaten; *fut* yeetkhaten.

wedded נשוי *adj* nasooy/nesoo'ah.

wedded to an idea מכור לרעיון *adj* makhoor/mekhoorah le-ra'yon.

wedding חתונה *nf* khatoon|ah/-ot *(+of: -at)*.

(silver) wedding חתונת הכסף *nf* khatoon|at/-ot ha-kesef.

wedding day יום נישואים *nm* yom/yemey neesoo'eem.

wedding trip מסע ירח הדבש (honeymoon) *nm* masa' yerakh ha-dvash.

wedge 1. טריז *nm* treez/-eem *(pl+of: -ey)*; **2.** יתד (peg) *nm* yated/yetedot; **3.** משולש (triangle) *nm* meshoolash/-eem *(pl+of: -ey)*.

(to) wedge להכניס טריז *inf* lehakhnees treez; *pst* heekhnees *etc*; *pres* makhnees *etc*; *fut* yakhnees *etc*.

Wednesday 1. יום רביעי *nm* yom/yemey revee'ee; **2.** יום ד' *nm* yom/yemey dalet.

wee זערער *adj* ze'ar'ar/-ah.

weed עשב שוטה *nm* 'esev/'asaveem shot|eh/-eem.

(to) weed a garden לנכש עשבים בגן *inf* lenakesh 'asaveem ba-gan; *pst* neekesh *etc*; *pres* menakesh *etc*; *fut* yenakesh *etc*.

(to) weed out לעקור מן השורש *inf* la'akor meen ha-shoresh; *pst* 'akar *etc*; *pres* 'oker *etc*; *fut* ya'akor *etc*.

weedy מלא עשבים שוטים *adj* male/mele'at 'asaveem shoteem.

week שבוע *nm* shavoo|'a'/-'ot.

week end סוף שבוע *nm* sof/-ey shavoo'a'.

(a) week from today בעוד שבוע מהיום *adv* be-'od shavoo'a' me-ha-yom.

weekday יום חול *nm* yom/yemey khol.

weekly 1. שבועון (periodical) *nm* shvoo'on/-eem *(pl+of: -ey)*; **2.** שבועי (of a week) *adj* shvoo'ee/-t; **3.** אחת לשבוע (once a week) *adv* akhat le-shavoo'a'.

(to) weep לבכות *inf* leevkot; *pst* bakhah *(b=v; kh=k)*; *pres* bokheh; *fut* yeevkeh.

weeping בכייה *nf* bekhee|yah/-yot *(+of: -yat)*.

weeping willow ערבת בבל 'arv|at/-ot bavel.

weevil תולעת זיפית *nf* tola|'at/-'ey zeefeet.

(to) weigh 1. לשקול *inf* leeshkol; *pst* shakal; *pres* shokel; *fut* yeeshkol; **2.** להכביד (burden) *inf* lehakhbeed; *pst* heekhbeed; *pres* makhbeed; *fut* yakhbeed.

(to) weigh anchor להרים עוגן *adj inf* lehareem 'ogen; *pst* hereem *etc*; *pres* mereem *etc*; *fut* yareem *etc*.

(to) weigh down להעיק *inf* leha'eek; *pst* he'eek; *pres* me'eek; *fut* ya'eek.

(to) weigh on one's conscience להכביד על המצפון *inf* lehakhbeed 'al ha-matspoon; *pst* heekhbeed *etc*; *pres* makhbeed *etc*; *fut* yakhbeed *etc*.

weight 1. משקל *nm* meeshkal/-eem (*pl+of:* -ey); **2.** כובד (heaviness) *nm* koved.

(paper) weight משקולת לניירות *nf* meeshkol|et/-ot lee-neyarot.

(to) weight 1. להעיק *inf* leha'eek; *pst* he'eek; *pres* me'eek; *fut* ya'eek; **2.** להכביד (burden) *inf* lehakhbeed; *pst* heekhbeed; *pres* makhbeed; *fut* yakhbeed.

weighty 1. רב־משקל *adj* rav/rabat *(b=v)* meeshkal; **2.** מעיק (oppressive) *adj* me'eek/-ah.

weird 1. מוזר *adj* moozar/-ah; **2.** שלא מעלמא הדן (out of this world) she-lo me-'alma haden.

welcome קבלת פנים *nf* kabal|at/-ot paneem.

(you are) welcome הינך מוזמן heen|kha/-ekh moozm|an/-enet *(m/f)*.

welcome guest אורח רצוי *nm* ore'akh/orkheem ratsooy/retsooyeem.

(you are) welcome here בואך לשלום בקרבנו bo'akha/bo'ekh *(m/f)* le-shalom be-keerbenoo.

welcome home! 1. ! ברוך הבא (greeting) barookh/brookhah *(m/f)* ha-ba/-'ah! (*pl:* brookheem ha-ba'eem!); **2.** ! ברוך הנמצא (return greeting) barookh/brookhah ha-neemts|a/-et! (*pl:* brookheem ha-neemtsa'eem!).

welcome news משמחת חדשה *nf* khadash|ah/-ot mesam|akhat/-khot.

welcome rest מנוחה מבורכת *nf* menookhah mevorekhet.

(you are) welcome to use it נא לעשות בו שימוש na la'asot bo/bah *(m/f)* sheemoosh.

weld 1. ריתוך (action) *m* reetookh/-eem (*pl+of:* -ey); **2.** חלק מרותך (part) *nm* khelek/khalakeem merootakh/-eem.

(to) weld 1. לרתך *inf* leratekh; *pst* reetekh; *pres* meratekh; *fut* yeratekh; **2.** להלחים *nf* lehalkheem; *pst* heelkheem; *pres* malkheem; *fut* yalkheem.

welfare 1. סעד *nm* sa'ad; **2.** רווחה (relief) *nf* revakhah (*+of:* ravkhat).

welfare work עבודה סוציאלית *nf* 'avodah sotsyaleet.

well 1. באר (shaft) *nf* be'er/-ot; **2.** בור (cistern) *nm* bor/-ot; **3.** מעיין (spring) *nm* ma'ayan/-ot.

well 1. היטב *adv* heytev; **2.** במידה ניכרת (considerably) *adv* be-meedah neekeret.

(all is) well הכול טוב ויפה ha-kol tov ve-yafeh.

(artesian) well באר ארטזיאנית *nf* be'er/-ot artezyanee|t/-yot.

(to) well לנבוע *inf* leenbo'a'; *pst* nava' *(v=b)*; *pres* nove'a'; *fut* yeenba'.

well-being 1. רווחה *nf* revakhah (*+of:* ravkhat); **2.** קיום נאה (comfortable existence) *nm* keeyoom na'eh.

well-bred מחונך יפה *adj* mekhoon|akh/-ekhet yafeh.

well fixed מסודר יפה *adj* mesood|ar/-eret yafeh.

well-groomed לבוש בקפידה *adj* lavoosh/levooshah bee-kfeedah.

well-known 1. ידוע *adj* yadoo'a'/yedoo'ah; **2.** נודע (famous) *adj* noda'/-at.

well-meaning בעל כוונות טובות *adj* ba'al/-at kavanot tovot.

well-nigh כמעט *adv* kee-me'at.

well-off 1. אמיד *adj* ameed/-ah; **2.** במצב כלכלי טוב (economically well) *adv & adj* be-matsav kalkalee tov.

well over forty מעל לארבעים ויותר me-'al le-arba'eem ve-yoter.

well then הבה איפוא havah eyfo.

well-to-do עשיר *adj* 'asheer/-ah.

(it is) well to do it כדאי לעשות זאת keday la'asot zot.

welt 1. חבורה *nf* khaboor|ah/-ot (*+of:* -at); **2.** פס־עור בנעל (shoe's basic leather strip) *nm* pas/-ey 'or ba-na'al/-ayeem.

west 1. מערב *nm* ma'arav; **2.** מערבי *adj* ma'aravee/-t.

(the) West-Bank הגדה המערבית *nf* ha-gadah ha-ma'araveet.

western 1. מערבי *adj* ma'aravee/-t; **2.** מערבון (movie) *nm* ma'arvon/-eem (*pl+of:* -ey).

(the) Western Wall הכותל המערבי *nm* ha-kotel ha-ma'aravee.

westerner איש המערב *nm* eesh/anshey ha-ma'arav.

(to) westernize להחדיר תרבות המערב *inf* lehakhdeer tarboot ha-ma'arav; *pest* hekhdeer *etc*; *pres* makhdeer; *fut* yakhdeer *etc*.

westward 1. מערבה *adv* ma'aravah; **2.** הנע מערבה *adj* ha-na'/na'ah ma'aravah.

wet רטוב *adj adj* ratoov/retoovah.

wetback גונב גבול *nm* gon|ev/-vey gvool.

wetness רטיבות *nf* reteevoo|t/-yot.

wetnurse מינקת *nf* meyneket.

whack 1. מהלומה (blow) *nf* mahaloom|ah/-ot (*+of:* -at); **2.** הלקאה (flogging) *nf* halka|'ah/-'ot (*+of:* -'at).

(to) whack 1. להלום *inf* lahalom; pest halam; *pres* holem; *fut* yahalom; **2.** להלקות (flog) *inf* lehalkot; pest heelkah; *pres* malkeh; *fut* yalkeh.

whale לווייתן *nm* leev|yatan/-yetaneem (*pl+of:* -yetaney).

(to) whale לצוד לווייתנים *inf* latsood leevyetaneem; *pst & pres* tsad *etc*; *fut* yatsood *etc*.

wharf רציף *nm* ratseef/retseef|eem (*pl+of:* -ey).

what מה mah?

what a man! ! איזה בן־אדם eyzeh ben adam!

what book? ? איזה ספר eyzeh sefer?

(take) what books you need קח כל הספרים שיידרשו לך kah/kekhee kol ha-sfareem she-yeedarshoo lekha/lakh *(m/f)*.

what do you mean? ? מה כוונתך mah kavanat|kha/-ekh? *(m/f)*.

what for? ? לשם מה le-shem mah?

what happy children! ! איזה ילדים מאושרים eyzeh yeladeem me'ooshareem!

whatever, whatsoever 1. כל מה kol mah; **2.** כלשהו (any) kolshe|hoo/-hee *(m/f)*.

(any person) whatever כל אדם שהוא kol adam she-hoo.

(no money) whatever ! אף פרוטה af prootah!
(do it) whatever happens עשה זאת ויהיה אשר יהיה 'aseh/'asee *(m/f)* zot ve-yeehyeh asher yeehyeh.
wheat חיטה *nf* kheet|ah/-eem *(pl+of:* -ey).
(to) wheedle 1. לנסות *inf* lenasot; *pst* neesah; *pres* menaseh; *fut* yenaseh; **2.** להחניף (flatter) *inf* lehakhneef; *pst* hekhneef; *pres* makhneef; *fut* yakhneef.
wheel 1. אופן *nm* ofan/-eem *(pl+of:* -ey); **2.** גלגל (*synon. of* 1) *nm* galgal/-eem *(pl+of:* -ey).
(steering) wheel הגה *nm* hegeh/haga|'eem *(pl+of:* -'ey).
(to) wheel להסיע *inf* lehasee'a'; *pst* heesee'a'; *pres* masee'a'; *fut* yasee'a'.
(to) wheel around להסתובב *v rfl inf* leheestovev; *pst* heestovev; *pres* meestovev; *fut* yeestovev.
wheel chair כיסא גלגלים *nm* kees|e/-'ot galgaleem.
(to) wheel the baby להסיע תינוק *inf* lehasee'a' teenok; *pst* heesee'a' *etc; pres* masee'a' *etc; fut* yasee'a' *etc.*
wheelbarrow מריצה *nf* mereets|ah/-ot *(+of:* -at).
wheeze שריקה *nf* shreek|ah/-ot *(+of:* -at).
when 1. ?מתי matay? **2.** אימתי (also: whenever) eymatay? **3.** כאשר (as) *adv* ka-asher.
whence 1. מהיכן ש־ me-heykhan she-; **2.** מהמקום אשר (from where) me-ha-makom asher.
whenever 1. אימתי eymatay; **2.** כל אימת (each time) *adv* kol eymat.
where 1. ?איפה *adv* eyfo? **2.** היכן heykhan?
whereabouts 1. מקום הימצא mekom heematse; **2.** סביבה (neighborhood) *nf* sveev|ah/-ot *(+of:* -at).
whereas 1. היות heyot; **2.** מאחר ש־ (since) me-akhar she-; **3.** בעוד ש־ (while) be-'od she-.
whereby 1. שעל ידי כך she-'al yedey kakh; **2.** שבכך she-be-khakh *(kh=k).*
wherefore שלפיכך she-lefee-khakh.
wherein שבו she-bo/bah *(m/f).*
whereof שבגינו she-be-geen|o/-ah *(m/f).*
whereto לאן *adv* le'an.
whereupon 1. שכתוצאה ממנו (as result of which) she-ke-totsa'ah meemen|oo/-ah *(m/f);* **2.** שמיד לאחריו (whereafter) she-meeyad le-akhr|av/-eha *(m/f).*
wherever 1. היכן שלא heykhan he-lo; **2.** בכל אשר (any place where) be-khol *(kh=k)* asher.
wherewithal 1. אמצעים (means) *nm pl* emts|a'eem *(pl+of:* -e'ey); **2.** כסף (money) *nm* kes|ef/-afeem *(pl+of:* kaspey; *p=f).*
(to) whet 1. להשחיז (sharpen) *inf* lehashkheez; *pst* heeshkheez; *pres* mashkheez; *fut* yashkheez; **2.** לגרות (stimulate) *inf* legarot; *pst* gerah; *pres* megareh; *fut* yegareh.
whether 1. אם eem; **2.** אם אכן (if indeed) eem akhen.
(I doubt) whether אני מסופק אם anee mesoop|ak/-eket *(m/f)* eem.
whether we escape *or* **not** אם נינצל ואם לאו eem neenatsel ve-'eem lav.
which 1. אשר *pron* asher; **2.** ?איזה eyz|eh/-o? *(m/f);* **3.** ?לאיזה le-'eyz|eh/-o? *(m/f).*
which boy has it? ?אצל מי מהילדים זה נמצא etsel mee me-ha-yeladeem zeh neemtsa?
(during) which time כאשר אותה שעה עצמה ka-asher otah sha'ah 'atsmah.
which way did he go? ?לאיזה כיוון פנה le-'eyzeh keevoon panah?
whichever 1. איזשהו *pron* eyzeh-she-hoo/'eyzo-she-hee *(m/f);* **2.** כל אשר *adj* kol asher.
whichever road you take כל דרך שתיראה לך kol derekh she-tera'eh lekha/lakh *(m/f).*
whiff 1. משב רוח קל (waft) *nm* mash|av/-vey roo'akh kal/-eem; **2.** ריח קלוש (odor) *nm* rey|'akh/-khot kaloosh/klooshеem.
(to) whiff לנשוב קלות *inf* leenshov kalot; *pst* nashav *etc; pres* noshev *etc; fut* yeenshov *etc.*
while 1. בעוד be-'od; **2.** תקופה קצרה (short period) *nf* tekoof|ah/-ot ketsar|ah/-ot; **3.** פרק זמן (*synon. of* 2) *nm* perek/peerkey zman.
(a short) while שעה קלה *nf* sha|'ah/-'ot kal|ah/-ot.
(worth one's) while כדאי *adj* kedai/kada'eet.
(a short) while ago לפני שעה קלה *adv* leefney sha'ah kalah.
(to) while away the time להעביר את הזמן *inf* leha'aveer et ha-zman; *pst* he'eveer *etc; pres* ma'aveer *etc; fut* ya'aveer *etc.*
whilst בעוד be-'od.
whim קפריזה *nf* kapreez|ah/-ot *(+of:* -at).
whimper יבבה חרישית *nf* yevav|ah/-ot khareeshee|t/-yot.
(to) whimper לייבב חרש *inf* leyabev kheresh; *pst* yeebev *etc; pres* meyabev; *fut* yeyabev *etc.*
whimsical 1. הפכפך *adj* hafakhpakh/-ah; **2.** קפריזי (capricious) *adj* kapreezee/-t.
whine יללה *nf* yelal|ah/-ot *(+of:* yeelel|at/-ot).
(to) whine ליילל *inf* leyalel; *pst* yeelel; *pres* meyalel; *fut* yeyalel.
whiner יללן *nmf* yalelan/-eet.
whip שוט *nm* shot/-eem *(pl+of:* -ey).
(to) whip להצליף בשוט *inf* lehatsleef be-shot; *pst* heetsleef *etc; pres* matsleef *etc; fut* yatsleef *etc.*
(to) whip up 1. להזדרז להכין *inf* leheezdarez lehakheen; *pst* heezdarez *etc; pres* meezdarez *etc; fut* yeezdarez *etc;* **2.** לשסות (instigate) *inf* leshasot; *pst* sheesah; *pres* meshaseh; *pres* yeshaseh.
whipping 1. הצלפה *nf* hatslaf|ah/-ot *(+of:* -at); **2.** הלקאה (flogging) *nf* halka|'ah/-'ot *(+of:* -'at).
whipping boy שעיר לעזאזל (scapegoat) *nm* sa'eer/se'eereem la-'azazel.
whipping (whipped) cream קצפת *nf* kats|efet/-afot.
whir זמזום אווירון *nm* zeemzoom/-ey aveeron.
(to) whir לזמזם כאווירון *inf* lezamzem ka-aveeron; *pst* zeemzem *etc; pres* mezamzem *etc; fut* yezamzem *etc.*
whirl 1. ערבול *nm* 'eerbool/-eem *(pl+of:* -ey); **2.** סיבוב (spin) *nm* seevoov/-eem *(pl+of:* -ey).
(to) whirl להסתובב סחור סחור *inf* leheestovev sekhor sekhor; *pst* heestovev *etc; pres* meestovev *etc; fut* yeestovev *etc.*
whirlpool מערבולת *nf* me'arbol|et/-ot.

(my head) whirls 1. מסתחרר לי הראש meestakhrer lee ha-rosh; **2.** ראשי עלי סחרחר (literary biblical equivalent) roshee 'alay skharkhar.

whirlwind סופה *nf* soof|ah/-ot (+*of:* -at).

whisk מקצף (kitchen tool) *nm* maktsef/-eem (*pl+of:* -ey).

(to) whisk לטאטא *inf* leta'te; *pst* tee'ta; *pres* meta'te; *fut* yeta'te.

(to) whisk away לטאטא הצידה *inf* leta'te ha-tseedah; *pst* tee'ta *etc*; *pres* meta'te *etc*; *fut* yeta'te *etc*.

(with a) whisk of the broom בהנפת מטאטא אחת *adv* ba-hanafat mat'ate akhat.

whiskbroom מטאטא *nm* mat'at|e/-'eem (*pl+of:* -'ey).

whiskers זקן לחיים *nm* zekan lekhayayeem.

whiskey ויסקי *nm* veeskee.

whisper לחישה *nf* lekheesh|ah/-ot (+*of:* -at).

(to) whisper ללחוש *inf* leelkhosh; *pst* lakhash; *pres* lokhesh; *fut* yeelkhash.

(to talk in a) whisper לדבר בלחש *inf* ledaber be-lakhash; *pst* deeber *etc*; *pres* medaber *etc*; *fut* yedaber *etc*.

(it is) whispered that מלחשים כי melakhsheem kee.

whistle 1. שריקה *nf* shreek|ah/-ot (+*of:* -at); **2.** צפצוף *nm* tseeftsoof/-eem (*pl+of:* -ey).

(to) whistle 1. לשרוק *inf* leeshrok; *pst* sharak; *pres* shorek; *fut* yeeshrok; **2.** לצפצף *inf* letsaftsef; *pst* tseeftsef; *pres* metsaftsef; *fut* yetsaftsef

(to) whistle for someone לשרוק למישהו *inf* leeshrok le-meeshehoo; *pst* sharak *etc*; *pres* shorek *etc*; *fut* yeeshrok *etc*.

whit קורטוב *nm* kortov.

white 1. לבן (color) *adj* lavan/levanah; **2.** צחור (pure) *adj* tsakhor/tsekhorah; **3.** חיוור (pale) *adj* kheever/-et.

white color צבע לבן *nm* tseva' lavan.

(to show the) white feather לגלות פחד *inf* legalot pakhad; *pst* geelah *etc*; *pres* megaleh *etc*; *fut* yegaleh *etc*.

white lie שקר מתוך נימוס *nm* sheker mee-tokh neemoos.

white-livered 1. מוג לב *adj* moog/-at lev; **2.** חולני (sickly) *adj* kholanee/-t.

white tie חליפת ערב *nf* khaleef|at/-ot 'erev.

(to) whiten להלבין *inf* lehalbeen; *pst* heelbeen; *pres* malbeen; *fut* yalbeen.

whiteness לובן *nm* loven.

whitewash תמיסת סיד *nf* temees|at/-ot seed.

(to) whitewash 1. לסייד *inf* lesayed; *pst* seeyed; *pres* mesayed; *fut* yesayed; **2.** לטהר (cleanse) *inf* letaher; *pst* teeher; *pres* metaher; *fut* yetaher.

whither 1. לאן (whereto) le'an; **2.** ? לשם מה (what for) le-shem mah?

(to) whittle לגלף *inf* legalef; *pst* geelef; *pres* megalef; *fut* yegalef.

(to) whittle down expenses לצמצם *inf* letsamtsem; *pst* tseemtsem; *pres* metsamtsem; *fut* yetsamtsem.

(to) whiz לזמזם *inf* lezamzem; *pst* zeemzem; *pres* mezamzem; *fut* yezamzem.

(to be a) whiz להצטיין *inf v refl inf* leheetstayen; *pst* heetstayen; *pres* meetstayen; *fut* yeetstayen.

who? 1. ?מי interr. *pron* mee? **2.** אשר relat. *pron* asher; **3.** -ש (*prefix, abbr.* of 2) she-.

(he) who 1. הוא אשר hoo asher; **2.** -כל מי ש (each one who) kol mee she-

who is it? 1. ?מי זה mee zeh? **2.** ?מי שם (who's there) mee sham?

whoever -כל מי ש kol mee she-.

whole 1. כל kol; **2.** כולו (all of it) kool|o/-ah (*m/f*).

(as a) whole במלואו *adj* bee-mlo|'o/-'ah (*m/f*).

(on the) whole בסך הכול be-sakh ha-kol.

(the) whole day 1. כל היום *adv* kol ha-yom **2.** היום כולו ha-yom koolo.

wholehearted בכל לב *adv* be-khol (*kh=k*) lev.

wholeheartedly עם כל הלב *adv* 'eem kol ha-lev.

wholesale 1. מכירה סיטונית *nf* mekheer|ah/-ot seetonee|t/-yot; **2.** בסיטונות *adv* be-seetonoot.

(by) wholesale בסיטונות *adv* be-seetonoot.

(to) wholesale למכור בסיטונות *inf* leemkor be-seetonoot; *pst* makhar (*kh=k*) *etc*; *pres* mokher *etc*; *fut* yeemkor *etc*.

wholesale dealer סיטונאי *nm* seetona|y/-'eem (*pl+of:* -'ey).

wholesale slaughter טבח ללא הבחנה *nm* tevakh le-lo havkhanah.

wholesale trade מסחר סיטונאי *nm* meeskhar seetona'ee.

wholesome 1. בריא (healthy) *adj* baree/bree'ah; **2.** מבריא (healthful) *adj* mavree/-'ah; **3.** מיטיב (beneficial) *adj* meyteev/-ah.

wholesome man אדם טוב *nm* adam/beney-adam tov/-eem.

wholly לגמרי *adv* legamrey.

whom אשר אותו asher ot|o/-ah (*pl:* ota|m/-n).

(for) whom אשר לו asher lo/lah (*pl* lahe|m/-n)

whoop 1. צעקה (shout) *nf* tse'ak|ah/-ot (+*of:* -tsa'ak|at/-ot); **2.** גניחה (groan) *nf* geneekh|ah/-ot (+*of:* -at).

(to) whoop 1. לגנוח *inf* leegno'akh; *pst* ganakh; *pres* gone'akh; *fut* yeegnakh; **2.** לצעוק (shout) *inf* leets'ok; *pst* tsa'ak; *pres* tso'ek; *fut* yeets'ak.

(to) whoop it up להקים זעקה *inf* lehakeem ze'akah; *pst* hekeem *etc*; *pres* mekeem *etc*; *fut* yakeem *etc*.

whooping cough שעלת *nf* sha'elet.

whore 1. פרוצה *nf* proots|ah/-ot (+*of:* -at); **2.** זונה (prostitute) *nf* zon|ah/-ot (+*of:* -at).

whose 1. אשר... שלו (of his) asher... shelo; **2.** אשר... שלה (of hers) asher... shelah; **3.** אשר... שלהם (of theirs - masc.) asher... shelahem; **4.** אשר... שלהן (of theirs - fem.) asher... shelahen.

why 1. ?למה lamah? **2.** ?מדוע madoo'a'?

(the reason) why -הסיבה לכך ש ha-seebah le-khakh (*kh=k*) she-.

why, of course 1. אדרבה adrabah; **2.** כמובן (certainly) ka-moovan.

why, that is not true אבל, זה לא נכון aval, zeh lo nakhon.

wick פתילה *nf* peteel|ah/-ot (+*of:* -at).

wicked 1. מרושע *adj* meroosh|a'/-a'at; **2.** רע (bad) *adj* ra'/ra'ah.

wickedness רשעות *nf* reesh'oot.
wicker 1. נצר *nm* nets|er/-areem (*pl+of:* neetsrey); **2.** קלוע (plaited) *adj* kaloo'a'/kloo'ah.
wicket 1. פשפש (door) *nm* peeshp|ash/-asheem (*pl+of:* -eshey); **2.** אשנב (window) *nm* eshna|v/-beem (*b=v; pl+of:* -bey); **3.** שער (cricket) *nm* sha'ar/she'areem (*pl+of:* sha'arey).
wide 1. רחב *adj* rakhav/rekhavah; **2.** ברוחב של (of ... width) *adv* be-rokhav shel...
(far and) wide בארצות רבות ושונות *adv* ba-aratsot rabot ve-shonot.
(to open) wide 1. לפקוח לרווחה (eyes) *inf* leefko'akh lee-revakhah; *pst* pakakh (*p=f*) *etc*; *pres* poke'akh *etc*; *fut* yeefkakh *etc*; **2.** לפתוח לרווחה (doors) *inf* leefto'akh lee-revakhah; *pst* patakh (*p=f*) *etc*; *pres* pote'akh *etc*; *fut* yeeftakh *etc*.
(two feet) wide שישים ס״מ רוחב (60 cms wide) sheeshheem senteemeter rokhav.
wide apart רחוקים זה מזה *adj pl* rekhokeem zeh mee-zeh.
wide-awake ער לחלוטין *adj* 'er/-ah la-khalooteen.
wide of the mark הרחק מהיעד *adv* harkhek me-ha-ya'ad.
wide open פעור *adj* pa'oor/pe'oorah.
widely 1. על פני שטח רחב *adv* 'al peney shetakh rakhav; **2.** בהרבה (considerably) *adv* be-harbeh.
(to) widen להרחיב *inf* leharkheev; *pst* heerkheev; *pres* markheev; *fut* yarkheev.
widespread נפוץ מאוד *adj* nafots/nefotsah me'od.
widow אלמנה *nf* alm|anah/-anot (*+of:* -enat/-enot).
widower אלמן *nm* alm|an/-aneem (*pl+of:* -eney).
width רוחב *nm* rokhav/rekhaveem (*pl+of:* rokhvey).
(to) wield 1. להיטיב להשתמש *inf* leheyteev leheeshtamesh; *pst* heyteev *etc*; *pres* meyteev *etc*; *fut* yeyteev *etc*; **2.** להפעיל (exercise) *inf* lehaf'eel; *pst* heef'eel; *pres* maf'eel; *fut* yaf'eel.
wife 1. רעיה *nf* ra'yah/re'ayot (*+of:* ra'yat); **2.** אישה (also means: woman) *nf* eeshah/nasheem (*+of:* eshet/neshey).
wig 1. פיאה נוכרית *nf* pe'|ah/-'ot nokhree|t/-yot; **2.** קפלט (literary) *nm* kaflet/-eem (*pl+of:* -ey)
(to) wiggle לכשכש *inf* lekhashkesh; *pst* keeshkesh (*k=kh*); *pres* mekhashkesh; *fut* yekhashkesh.
wigwam 1. בית אינדיאני *nm* bayeet/bateem eendyanee/-yeem; **2.** ויגוואם *nm* veegvam/-eem (*pl+of:* -ey).
wild 1. פרא (animal) *adj* pere/pra'eet; **2.** בר (plant) bar.
(to drive) wild לשגע *inf* leshage'a'; *pst* sheege'a'; *pres* meshage'a'; *fut* yeshage'a'.
wild-eyed מבוהל *adj* mevo|hal/-helet.
wildcat חתול בר *nm* khatool/-ey bar.
wildcat scheme תוכנית דמיונית *nf* tokhnee|t/-yot deemyonee|t/-yot.
wilderness שממה *nf* shmam|ah/-ot (*+of:* sheemem|at/-ot).
wildness פראות *nf* pra'oot.
wile 1. עורמה *nf* 'orm|ah/-ot (*+of:* -at); **2.** תחבולה (stratagem) *nf* takhbool|ah/-ot (*+of:* -at).
wilful, willful זדוני *adj* zedonee/-t.

will 1. רצון (wish) *nm* ratson/retsonot (*+of:* retson); **2.** צוואה (testament) *nf* tsava|'ah/-'ot (*+of:* -'at).
(free) will רצון חופשי *nm* ratson khofshee.
(ill) will רצון רע *nm* ratson ra'.
(to) will 1. לחפוץ (desire) *inf* lakhpots; *pst & pres* khafets (*f=p*); *fut* yakhpots; **2.** לצוות (dispose of by testament) *inf* letsavot; *pst* tseevah; *pres* metsaveh; *fut* yetsaveh.
(I) will not do it זאת לא אעשה zot lo e'eseh.
willing רוצה *adj* rots|eh/-ah.
willingly ברצון *adv* be-ratson.
willingness נכונות *nf* nekhonoot.
willow ערבה *nf* 'arav|ah/-ot (*+of:* -at).
(weeping) willow ערבה בוכייה *nf* 'arav|ah/-ot bokhee|yah/-yot.
(to) wilt 1. לקמול *inf* leekmol; *pst & pres* kamel; *fut* yeekmol; **2.** לנבול (wither) *inf* leenbol; *pst* naval (*v=b*); *pres* novel; *fut* yeenbol.
wily ערום *adj* 'aroom/-ah.
(to) win 1. לזכות *inf* leezkot; *pst* zakhah (*kh=k*); *pres* zokheh; *fut* yeezkeh; **2.** לנצח (vanquish) *inf* lenatse'akh; *pst* neetse'akh; *pres* menatse'akh; *fut* yenatse'akh.
(to) win out להצליח *inf* lehatslee'akh; *pst* heetslee'akh; *pres* matslee'akh; *fut* yatslee'akh.
(to) win over להעביר לצידו *inf* leha'aveer le-tseed|o/-ah (*m/f*); *pst* he'eveer *etc*; *pres* ma'aveer *etc*; *fut* ya'aveer *etc*.
(to) wince 1. לעוות פנים *inf* le'avet paneem; *pst* 'eevet *etc*; *pres* me'avet *etc*; *fut* ye'avet *etc*; **2.** להירתע כמו מכאב (flinch) *inf* leherata' kemo mee-ke'ev; *pst & pres* neerta' *etc*; *fut* yerata' *etc*;
winch מנוף *nm* manof/menofeem (*+of:* menof/-ey).
wind 1. רוח *nm* roo|'akh/-khot; **2.** ליפוף (coiling) *nm* leepoof/-eem (*pl+of:* -ey).
(to) wind 1. לסובב *inf* lesovev; *pst* sovev; *pres* mesovev; *fut* yesovev; **2.** ללפף (coil) *inf* lelapef; *pst* leepef; *pres* melapef; *fut* yelapef *etc*.
(got) wind of גונב אליו goonav elav/'eleha (*m/f*).
(to) wind someone around one's finger לסובב על אצבעו הקטנה *inf* lesovev 'al etsba|'o/-'ah ha-ktanah; *pst* sovev; *pres* mesovev; *fut* yesovev.
(to) wind up one's affairs לחסל עסקיו *inf* lekhasel 'asak|av/-eha; *pst* kheesel *etc*; *pres* mekhasel *etc*; *fut* yekhasel.
windbag 1. פטפטן *nmf* patpetan/-eet; **2.** חמת חלילים (bagpipes) *nf* khemat khaleeleem.
windfall מתנה משמיים *nf* matanah mee-shamayeem.
winding ליפוף *nm* leepoof/-eem (*pl+of:* -ey).
winding staircase גרם מדרגות לוליני *nm* gerem madregot loolyanee.
windmill טחנת רוח *nf* takhn|at/-ot roo'akh.
window חלון *nf* khalon/-ot.
window shade 1. תריס בד *nm* trees/-ey bad; **2.** וילון *nm* veelon/-ot.
window sill אדן חלון *nm* eden/adney khalon/-ot.
(show) window חלון ראווה *nm* khalon/-ot ra'avah.
windowpane 1. שמשה sheemshah/shmashot (*+of:* sheemsh|at/-ot); **2.** זגוגית *nf* zgoogee|t/-yot.
windpipe 1. קנה *nm* kane (*+of:* ken|eh/-ey); **2.** גרגרת *nf* garg|eret/-arot.
windshield מגן רוח *nm* mag|en/-eeney roo'akh.

windy 1. סוער *adj* so'er/-et; **2.** פטפטן (verbose) *adj* patpetan/-eet.
(it is) windy רוחות מנשבות בחוץ ba-khoots menashvot rookhot.
wine יין *nm* yayeen/yeynot (*+of:* yeyn).
wine cellar מרתף יינות *nm* martef/-ey yeeynot.
wing 1. כנף *nf* kanaf/kenafayeem (*+of:* kenaf/kanfey); **2.** אגף (building) *nm* aga|f/-peem (*p=f; pl+of:* -pey).
(to take) wing להסתלק *inf* leheestalek; *pst* heestalek; *pres* meestalek; *fut* yeestalek.
(under the) wing of 1. בחסות (auspices) *adv* be-khasoot; **2.** בפיקוח (supervision) be-feekoo'akh (*f=p*).
winged 1. מכונף *adj* mekhoon|af/-efet; **2.** מעופף (flying) *adj* me'ofef/-et.
wingspread מוטת כנפיים *nf* moot|at/-ot kenafayeem.
wink 1. רמיזה *nf* remeez|ah/-ot (*+of:* -at); **2.** קריצה (blink) *nf* kreets|ah/-ot (*+of:* -at).
(I didn't sleep a) wink לא עצמתי עין lo 'atsamtee 'ayeen.
(to) wink 1. לקרוץ (blink) *inf* leekrots; *pst* karats; *pres* korets; *fut* yeekrots; **2.** לרמוז (hint) *inf* leermoz; *pst* ramaz; *pres* romez; *fut* yeermoz.
winner זוכה *nmf* zokh|eh/-ah.
winner of a prize 1. חתן פרס *nm* khat|an/-ney pras; **2.** כלת פרס *nf* kal|at/-ot pras.
winning 1. מצליח (successful) *adj* matslee'|akh/-khah; **2.** מקסים (charming) *adj* makseem/-ah.
winnings זכייות *nf* zekheeyot.
winsome מלבב *adj* melabev/-et.
winter חורף *nm* khor|ef/-ofeem (*pl+of:* -pey; *p=f*).
winter clothes בגדי חורף *nm pl* beegdey khoref.
wintry חורפי *adj* khorpee/-t.
(to) wipe לנגב *inf* lenagev; *pst* neegev; *pres* menagev; *fut* yenagev.
(to) wipe away tears למחות דמעות *inf* leemkhot dema'ot; *pst* makhah; *pres* mokheh; *fut* yeemkheh.
(to) wipe off למחוק *inf* leemkhok; *pst* makhak; *pres* mokhek; *fut* yeemkhok.
(to) wipe out להשמיד *inf* lehashmeed; *pst* heeshmeed; *pres* mashmeed; *fut* yashmeed.
wire 1. חוט מתכת *nm* khoot/-ey matekhet; **2.** תיל (iron wire) *nm* tayeel (*+of:* teyl); **3.** מיברק (telegram) *nm* meevr|ak/-akeem (*pl+of:* -ekey).
(barbed) wire תיל דוקרני *nm* tayeel dokranee.
wire fence גדר תיל *nf* geder/geedrot tayeel.
wire netting גדר רשת *nf* geder/geedrot reshet.
wire-pulling משיכה בחוטים *nf* mesheekh|ah/-ot ba-khooteem.
wire tapping ציתות־סתר *nm* tseetoot/-ey seter.
wireless 1. אלחוט *nm* alkhoot; **2.** אלחוטי *adj* alkhootee/-t; **3.** רדיו *nm* radyo.
wireless telegraphy טלגרף אלחוטי *nm* telegraf alkhootee.
wiry 1. תילי *adj* teylee/-t; **2.** רזה וחזק (slim and strong) raz|eh/-ah ve-khazak/-ah.
wisdom 1. בינה *nf* been|ah/-ot (*+of:* -at); **2.** תבונה (prudence) *nf* tvoon|ah/-ot (*+of:* -at).
wisdom tooth שן בינה *nm* shen/sheeney beenah.
wise 1. חכם (clever) *adj* khakham/-ah; **2.** נבון (prudent) *adj* navon/nevonah; **3.** מיושב (judicious) *adj* meyoosh|av/-evet
(in no) wise בשום פנים *adv* be-shoom paneem.
(to get) wise to להבחין *inf* lehavkheen; *pst* heevkheen; *pres* mavkheen; *fut* yavkheen.
wisecrack הערה מחוכמת *nf* he'ar|ah/-ot mekhook|emet/-amot.
wish 1. חפץ *nm* khefets; **2.** משאלה (request) *nf* meesh|'alah/-'alot (*+of:* -elet).
(to) wish 1. לחפוץ *inf* lakhpots; *pst & pres* khafets (*f=p*); *fut* yakhpots; **2.** לרצות *inf* leertsot; *pst* ratsah; *pres* rotseh; *fut* yeertseh.
(to) wish for לייחל *inf* leyakhel; *pst inf* yeekhel; *pres* meyakhel; *fut* yeyakhel.
(I) wish it were true הלואי והיה זה אמת halevay ve-hayah zeh emet.
wishful thinking משאלת לב *nf* meesh|'elet/-'alot lev.
wistful משתוקק *adj* meeshtokek/-et.
wit 1. שכל *nm* sekhel; **2.** שנינות (sarcasm) *f* shneenoo|t/-yot.
witch מכשפה *nf* mekhashef|ah/-ot (*+of:* -at).
witchcraft כישוף *nm* keeshoof/-eem (*pl+of:* -ey).
with עם 'eem.
(filled) with ממולא ב־ *adj* memool|a/-et be-.
(the one) with... ההוא עם... ha-hoo/hee (*m/f*) 'eem.
(to) withdraw לסגת *inf* laseget; *pst & pres* nasog; *fut* yeesog.
(to) withdraw a statememt לבטל הודעה *inf* levatel hoda'ah; *pst* beetel (*b=v*) *etc*; *pres* mevatel *etc*; *fut* yevatel *etc*.
withdrawal נסיגה *nf* neseeg|ah/-ot (*+of:* -at).
(to) wither לקמול *inf* leekmol; *pst & pres* kamel; *fut* yeekmol.
(to) withhold 1. למנוע *inf* leemno'a'; *pst* mana'; *pres* mone'a'; *fut* yeemna'; **2.** לעצור (stop) *inf* la'atsor; *pst* 'atsar; *pres* 'otser; *fut* ya'atsor.
(to) withhold one's consent להימנע מתת הסכמתו *inf* leheemana' mee-tet haskamat|o/-ah (*m/f*); *pst & pres* neemna' *etc*; *fut* yeemana' *etc*.
within בתוך *adv* be-tokh.
within five miles כשמונה קילומטר בערך (approx. eight kms) *adv* kee-shmonah keelometreem be-'erekh.
(it is) within my power בכוחי הוא be-khokhee hoo (*kh=k*).
without 1. בלי *adv* blee; **2.** מבלי (condition) mee-blee; **3.** בלעדי (except) beel'adey.
without my seeing him מבלי שאראה אותו mee-blee she-'er'eh oto.
(to) withstand לעמוד מול *inf* la'amod mool; *pst* 'amad mool; *pres* 'omed mool; *fut* ya'amod mool.
witness עד *nmf* 'ed/-ah (*pl:* -eem/-ot; *+of:* -at/-ey).
(to) witness להיות עד ל... *inf* leehyot 'ed le-; *pst* hayah *etc*; *pres* heeno *etc*; *fut* yeehyeh *etc*.
(at one's) wit's end אובד עצות *adj* oved/-et 'etsot.
(out of one's) wits מטורף *adj* metor|af/-efet.
(to lose one's) wits לאבד עשתונותיו *inf* le'abed 'eshtonot|av/-eha (*m/f*); *pst* eebed *etc*; *pres* me'abed *etc*; *fut* ye'abed *etc*.

(to use one's) wits לעשות שימוש בשיכלו *inf* la'asot sheemoosh be-seekhl|o/-a; *pst* 'asah *etc; pres* 'oseh *etc; fut* ya'aseh *etc.*

witticism 1. חידוד *nm* kheedood/-eem (*pl+of:* -ey); **2.** אמרה שנונה (sarcastic remark) *nf* eemr|ah/-ot shnoon|ah/-ot.

witty 1. שנון *adj* shanoon/shnoonah; **2.** חריף (pungent) *adj* khareef/-ah.

witty remark הערה שנונה *nf* he'ar|ah/-ot shnoon|ah/-ot.

wives 1. רעיות *nf* re'ayot (*+of:* ra'yot); **2.** נשים (also: women) *nf pl* nasheem (*pl+of:* neshey).

wizard 1. אשף *nm* ashaf/-eet (*pl:* -eem; *+of:* -ey); **2.** קוסם (magician) *nm* kos|em/-meem (*pl+of:* -mey).

(to) wobble לפקפק *inf* lefakpek; *pst* peekpek *(p=f); pres* mefakpek; *fut* yefakpek.

woe צער *nm* tsa'ar.

woe is me ! !אוי לי *interj* oy lee !

woeful כולו יגון *adj* kool|o/-ah yagon.

wolf זאב *nm* ze'ev/-eem (*pl+of:* -ey).

woman אישה *nf* eeshah/nasheem (*+of:* eshet/neshey).

woman writer סופרת *nf* sof|eret/rot.

womanhood נשיות *nf* nasheeyoot.

womankind המין הנשי *nf* ha-meen ha-nashee.

womanly נשי *adj* nashee/-t.

womb רחם *nf* rekh|em/-ameem (*pl+of:* rakhamey).

wonder 1. פלא *nm* pele/pla'eem (*pl+of:* peel'ey). **2.** תמיהה (amazement) *f* temee|hah/-hot (*+of:* -hat).

(in) wonder בתמיהה *adv* bee-tmeehah.

(to) wonder להתפלא *inf* leheetpale; *pst* heetpale; *pres* meetpale; *fut* yeetpale.

(to) wonder at לתמוה על *inf* leetmoha 'al; *pst* tamah 'al; *pres* tame'ah 'al; *fut* yeetmah 'al.

(I should not) wonder if לא אתפלא אם lo etpale eem.

(no) wonder that מה פלא אם mah pele eem.

(I) wonder what time it is השאלה היא מה השעה עכשיו ha-she'elah hee mah ha-sha'ah 'akhshav.

(I) wonder when he came השאלה היא מתי הגיע ha-she'elah hee matay heegee'a'.

wonderful נפלא *adj* neefl|a/-'ah.

wonderfully להפליא *adv* lehaflee.

wonderfully well טוב להפליא *adj & adv* tov/-ah lehaflee.

wondrous באופן מתמיה *adv* be-ofen matmee'ah.

wont 1. הרגל *nm* hergel/-eem (*pl+of:* -ey); **2.** נוהג *v pres & adj* noheg/-et.

(to be) wont to -להיות רגיל ל *inf* leehyot rageel le-; *pst* hayah *etc; pres* heeno *etc; fut* yehyeh *etc.*

(to) woo 1. לחזר אחר (court) *inf* lekhazer akhar; *pst* kheezer *etc; pres* mekhazer; *fut* yekhazer *etc;* **2.** להפציר (entreat) *inf* lehaftseer; *pst* heeftseer; *pres* maftseer; *fut* yaftseer.

wood 1. עץ (material) *nm* 'ets; **2.** יער (forest) *nm* ya'ar/ye'arot (*pl+of:* ya'arot); **3.** עצי הסקה (firewood) *nm pl* 'atsey hasakah.

(fire)wood עצי הסקה *nm pl* 'atsey hasakah.

(piece of fire)wood בול עץ להסקה *nm* bool/-ey 'ets le-hasakah.

(touch) wood! !בלי עין הרע *interj* blee 'ayeen ha-ra'!

wood engraving חריטה בעץ *nf* khareetah be-'ets.

woodshed צריף עץ *nm* tsereef/-ey 'ets.

woodcut גלופת עץ *nf* gloof|at/-ot 'ets.

woodcutter חוטב עצים *nm* khot|ev/-vey 'etseem.

wooded מיוער *adj* meyo|'ar/-'eret.

wooden עשוי עץ 'asoo|y/-yat 'ets.

woodland אדמת יער *nf* adm|at/-ot ya'ar.

woodman יערן *nm* ya'aran/-eem (*pl+of:* -ey).

woodpecker נקר *nm* nakar/-eem (*pl+of:* -ey).

woodwork עבודת עץ *nf* 'avod|at/-ot 'ets.

woof 1. אריג *nm* areeg/-eem (*pl+of:* -ey); **2.** ערב (transverse threads) *nm* 'erev.

wool צמר *nm* tsemer.

wool-bearing מניב צמר *adj* meneev/-at tsemer.

wool dress שמלת צמר *nf* seeml|at/-ot tsemer.

woolen עשוי צמר *adj* 'asoo|y/-yat tsemer.

woolen mill בית חרושת לעיבוד לצמר bet/batey kharoshet le-'eebood tsemer.

wooly צמיר *adj* tsameer/tsemeerah.

word 1. מלה (vocable) *nf* meel|ah/-eem (*+of:* -at/-ot); **2.** שמועה (rumor) *nf* shmoo|'ah/-'ot (*+of:* -'at); **3.** צו (order) *nm* tsav/-eem (*pl+of:* -ey).

(pass)word סיסמה *nf* seesm|ah/-ot.

(by) word of mouth בדיבור פה *adv* be-deeboor peh.

wording ניסוח *nm* neesoo|'akh/kheem (*pl+of:* -khey).

wordy רב־מלל *adj* rav/rabat melel.

work 1. עבודה (labor) *nf* 'avod|ah/-ot (*+of:* -at); **2.** מלאכה (craft) *nf* melakh|ah/-ot (*+of:* mele'khet/mal'akhot); **3.** מאמץ (effort) *nm* ma'amats/-eem (*pl+of:* -ey); **4.** משימה (task) *nf* meseem|ah/-ot (*+of:* -at);**5.** תעסוקה (employment) *nf* ta'asook|ah/-ot (*+of:*-at); **6.** יצירה (creation) *nf* yetseer|ah/-ot (*+of:* -at).

(at) work בעבודה *adv* ba-'avodah.

(to) work 1. לעבוד (labor) *inf* la'avod; *pst* 'avad; *pres* 'oved; *fut* ya'avod; **2.** לעמול (toil) *inf* la'amol; *pst* 'amal; *pres* 'amel; *fut* ya'amol; **3.** לפעול (act) *inf* leef'ol; *pst* pa'al *(p=f); pres* po'el; *fut* yeef'al; **4.** להפעיל (activate) *inf* lehaf'eel; *pst* heef'eel; *pres* maf'eel; *fut* yaf'eel.

(to) work havoc להסב נזק *inf* lehasev nezek; *pst* hesev *etc; pres* mesev *etc; fut* yasev *etc.*

(to) work loose לשחרר *inf* leshakhrer; *pst* sheekhrer; *pres* meshakhrer; *fut* yeshakhrer.

(to) work one's way through college לקיים עצמו בבית ספר גבוה lekayem 'atsmo/-ah *(m/f)* be-vet *(v=b)* sefer gavoha.

(to) work one's way up להתקדם בעבודה *inf* leheetkadem ba'avodah; *pst* heetkadem *etc; pres* meetkadem *etc; fut* yeetkadem *etc.*

(it did not) work out לא נסתייע הדבר lo neestaye'a' ha-davar.

(to) work out a plan לעבד תוכנית *inf* le'abed tokhneet; *pst* 'eebed *etc; pres* me'abed *etc; fut* ye'abed *etc.*

workable בר־ביצוע *adj* bar/bat beetsoo'a'.

(all) worked up כולו מוסת ומרוגז *adj* koolo/-ah moos|at/-etet oo-meroog|az/-ezet.
(the plan) worked well התוכנית פעלה יפה ha-tokhneet pa'alah yafeh.
worker 1. פועל *nmf* po'el/-et (*pl:* po'al|eem/-ot; *pl+of:* -ey); **2.** עובד *nmf* 'ov|ed/-edet (*pl:* -deem/-dot; *+of:* -dey).
working 1. עובד (functioning) *adj* 'oved/-et; **2.** פעיל (active) *adj* pa'eel/pe'eelah; **3.** יעיל (efficient) *adj* ya'eel/ye'eelah.
working class 1. מעמד העמלים *nm* ma'amad ha-'ameleem; **2.** מעמד הפועלים (accepted colloquial *synon. of* 1) *nm* ma'amad ha-po'aleem.
working hours שעות עבודה *nf pl* she'ot 'avodah.
(a hard-)working man אדם עמל *nm* adam 'amel.
workingman איש עמל eesh/anshey 'amal.
workman פועל *nm* po'el/po'al/-eem (*pl+of:* -ey).
workmanship מלאכה *nf* melakh|ah/-ot (*+of:* mele'khet/mal'akhot).
works 1. מפעל (plant) *nm* meef'al/-eem (*pl+of:* -ey); **2.** כתבים (writings) *nm pl* ketaveem (*+of:* keetvey).
workshop בית מלאכה *nm* bet/batey melakhah.
world עולם *nm* 'olam/-ot.
world war מלחמת עולם *nf* meelkhemet 'olam.
world-shaking מרעיש עולמות *adj* mar'eesh/-at 'olamot.
worldly 1. גשמי *adj* gashmee/-t; **2.** חילוני (secularistic) *adj* kheelonee/-t; **3.** מתוחכם (sophisticated) *adj* metookhk|am/-emet.
worm תולעת *nf* tol|a'at/-a'eem (*pl+of:* -'ey).
(to) worm a secret out לסחוט סוד *inf* leeskhot sod; *pst* sakhat sod; *pres* sokhet sod; *fut* yeeskhat sod.
worm-eaten אכול תולעים *adj* akhool/-at tola'eem.
(to) worm oneself into להסתנן *inf* leheestanen; *pst* heestanen; *pres* meestanen; *fut* yeestanen.
worry דאגה *nf* de'ag|ah/-ot (*+of:* da'ag|at/-ot).
(to) worry לדאוג *inf* leed'og; *pst* da'ag; *pres* do'eg; *fut* yeed'ag.
worse גרוע *adj* garoo'a'/groo'ah.
(from bad to) worse מן הפח אל הפחת *adv* meen ha-pakh el ha-pakhat.
(to change for the) worse להשתנות לרעה *inf* leheeshtanot le-ra'ah; *pst* heeshtanah *etc; pres* meeshtaneh *etc; fut* yeeshtaneh *etc.*
(to get) worse להחמיר *inf* lehakhmeer; *pst* hekhmeer; *pres* makhmeer; *fut* yakhmeer.
worse and worse יותר ויותר גרוע *adv* yoter ve-yoter garoo'a'.
worse off גרוע יותר *adj* garoo'a'/groo'ah yoter.
worse than ever גרוע מאי־פעם *adv* garoo'a' me-'ey pa'am.
worship 1. סגידה *nf* segeed|ah/-ot (*+of:* -at); **2.** פולחן (cult) *nm* poolkhan/-eem (*pl+of:* -ey).
(to) worship 1. לסגוד *inf* leesgod; *pst* sagad; *pres* soged; *fut* yeesgod; **2.** להעריץ (idolize) *inf* leha'areets; *pst* he'ereets; *pres* ma'areets; *fut* ya'areets.
worshipper 1. חסיד *nm* khaseed/-eem (*pl+of:* -ey); **2.** מעריץ *adj* ma'areets (*pl+of:* -ey).
(the) worshipers המתפללים ha-meetpaleleem.
worst גרוע מכול *adj* garoo'a'/groo'ah mee-kol.
(the) worst הכי גרוע *adj* ha-khee garoo'a'/groo'ah.
worth 1. שווי *nm* shovee; **2.** ערך (value) *nm* 'erekh/'arakheem (*pl+of:* 'erkey); **3.** כדאי (worthy) *adj* keda|y/-'eet.
(to get one's money's) worth לקבל תמורה לכספו *inf* lekabel temoorah le-kasp|o/-ah; *pst* keebel *etc; pres* mekabel *etc; fut* yekabel *etc.*
worth doing שכדאי לעשותו *adj* she-keday la'asot|o/-ah.
worth hearing שכדאי לשמעו *adj* she-keday le-shom|'o/-'ah (*m/f*).
(one shekel's) worth of בשווי שקל אחד *adv* be-shovee shekel ekhad.
worth while כדאי *adj* keda'ee/-t.
worthless חסר ערך *adj* khas|ar/-rat 'erekh.
worthy 1. בר ערך *adj* bar/bat 'erekh; **2.** מכובד (honored) *adj* mekhoob|ad/-edet.
wound פצע *nm* pets|a'/-a'eem (*pl+of:* peets'ey).
(to) wound לפצוע *inf* leeftso'a'; *pst* patsa' (*p=f*); *pres* potse'a'; *fut* yeeftsa'.
(to) wow להלהיב *inf* lehalheev; *pst* heelheev; *pres* malheev; *fut* yalheev.
wrangle 1. מריבה *nf* mereev|ah/-ot (*+of:* -at); **2.** התכתשות (fight) *nf* heetkat'shoo|t/-yot.
(to) wrangle 1. לריב (quarrel) *inf* lareev; *pst & pres* rav; *fut* yareev; **2.** להתכתש (fight) *inf* leheetkatesh; *pst* heetkatesh; *pres* meetkatesh; *fut* yeetkatesh.
wrap עטיפה *nf* 'ateef|ah/-ot (*+of:* -at).
(to) wrap לעטוף *inf* la'atof; *pst* 'ataf; *pres* 'otef; *fut* ya'atof.
(to) wrap oneself up להתעטף *v rfl inf* lehee'atef; *pst* heet'atef; *pres* meet'atef; *fut* yeet'atef.
wrapped up 1. שקוע ב־ *adj* shakoo'a'/shekoo'ah be-; **2.** קשור ב־ (tied with) *adj* kashoor/keshoorah be-.
wrapper 1. עטיפה *nf* 'ateef|ah/-ot (*+of:* -at); **2.** אורז (packer) *nmf* orez/-et.
(woman's) wrapper חלוק *nm* khalook/-eem (*pl+of:* -ey).
wrapping חומר עיטוף *nm* khom|er/-rey 'eetoof.
wrapping paper נייר עטיפה *nm* neyar 'ateefah.
wrath זעם *nm* za'am.
wrathful זועם *adj* zo'em/-et.
wreath 1. זר *nm* zer/-eem (*pl+of:* -ey); **2.** עטרה *nf* 'at|arah/-arot (*+of:* -eret/-rot).
wreath of smoke תימרות עשן *nf pl* teemrot 'ashan
wreck 1. חורבן (destruction) *nm* khoorban/-ot; **2.** אונייה טרופה (shipwreck) *nf* onee|yah/-yot troof|ah/-ot; **3.** שבר כלי (wreckage) *nm* shever/sheevrey klee.
(a nervous) wreck אדם שבור *nm* adam/beney-adam shavoor/shvooreem.
(to) wreck 1. לשבור *inf* leeshbor; *pst* shavar (*v=b*); *pres* shover; *fut* yeeshbor; **2.** לנפץ (smash) *inf* lenapets; *pst* neepets; *pres* menapets; *fut* yenapets.
(to) wreck a train להוריד רכבת מן הפסים *inf* lehoreed rakevet meen ha-paseem; *pst* horeed *etc; pres* moreed *etc; fut* yoreed *etc.*
wrench מפתח ברגים *nm* mafte|'akh/-khot brageem.

(monkey) wrench 1. מפתח מתכוונן *nm* mafte'akh/-khot meetkavnen/-eem; **2.** מפתח אנגלי *nm* mafte'akh/-khot anglee/-yeem.

(to) wrench 1. לפתל *inf* lefatel; *pst* peetel *(p=f)*; *pres* mefatel; *fut* yefatel; **2.** לעקם בכוח (bend by force) *inf* le'akem be-kho'akh *(kh=k)*; *pst* 'eekem *etc*; *pres* me'akem *etc*; *fut* ye'akem *etc*; **3.** לנקוע (injure) *inf* leenko'a'; *pst* naka'; *pres* noke'a'; *fut* yeka'.

(to) wrest להוציא בכוח *inf* lehotsee be-kho'akh *(kh=k)*; *pst* hotsee *etc*; *pres* motsee *etc*; *fut* yotsee *etc*.

wrestle מאבק *nm* ma'av|ak/-akeem (*pl+of:* -key).

(to) wrestle להיאבק *inf* lehe'avek; *pst & pres* ne'evak; *fut* ye'avek.

wrestler מתאבק *nm* meet'av|ek/-keem (*pl+of:* -key).

wrestling היאבקות *nf* he'avkoo|t/-yot.

wretch עלוב *adj* 'aloov/-ah.

wretched 1. עלוב־חיים (miserable) *nmf* 'aloov/-at khayeem; **2.** ביש מזל (unfortunate) *nm* beesh-mazal; **3.** רע (bad) *adj* ra'/ra'ah.

(a) wretched piece of work דוגמה של עבודה גרועה *nf* doogmah shel 'avodah groo'ah.

(to) wriggle 1. להתפתל *inf* leheetpatel; *pst* heetpatel; *pres* meetpatel; *fut* yeetpatel; **2.** להתעקם (bend) *inf* leheet'akem; *pst* heet'akem; *pres* meet'akem; *fut* yeet'akem.

(to) wriggle out להיחלץ איכשהו (somehow) *inf* lehekhalets eykh-she-hoo; *pst & pres* nekhlats *etc*; *fut* yekhalets *etc*.

(to) wring לסחוט *inf* leeskhot; *pst* sakhat; *pres* sokhet; *fut* yeeskhat.

(to) wring money from someone לסחוט כספים ממישהו *inf* leeskhot kesafeem mee-mee-she|hoo/-hee *(m/f)*; *pst* sakhat *etc*; *pres* sokhet *etc*; *fut* yeeskhat.

(to) wring out לסחוט עד תום *inf* leeskhot 'ad tom; *pst* sakhat *etc*; *pres* sokhet *etc*; *fut* yeeskhat *etc*.

wrinkle קמט *nm* kem|et/-ateem (*pl+of:* keemtey).

(to) wrinkle לקמט *inf* lekamet; *pst* keemet; *pres* mekamet; *fut* yekamet.

(the latest) wrinkle in style הצעקה האחרונה באופנה ha-tse'akah ha-akhronah ba-ofnah.

wrist פרק כף היד *nm* perek/peerkey kaf ha-yad.

wrist watch שעון יד *nm* she'on/-ey yad.

writ כתב *nm* ketav/-eem (*pl+of:* keetvey).

(the Holy) Writ כתבי הקודש *nm pl* keetvey ha-kodesh.

(to) write לכתוב *inf* leekhtov; *pst* katav *(k=kh)*; *pres* kotev; *fut* yeekhtov.

(to) write back לענות על מכתב *inf* la'anot 'al meekhtav; *pst* 'anah *etc*; *pres* 'oneh *etc*; *fut* ya'aneh *etc*.

(to) write down לרשום *inf* leershom; *pst* rasham; *pres* roshem; *fut* yeershom.

(to) write off למחוק *inf* leemkhok; *pst* makhak; *pres* mokhek; *fut* yeemkhok.

(to) write out 1. להעלות על הכתב *inf* leha'alot 'al ha-ktav; *pst* he'elah *etc*; *pres* ma'aleh *etc*; *fut* ya'aleh *etc*; **2.** לרשום בשלמות *inf* leershom bee-shlemoot; *pst* rasham *etc*; *pres* roshem *etc*; *fut* yeershom *etc*.

(to) write up 1. לתאר בכתב *inf* leta'er bee-khtav *(kh=k)*; *pst* te'er *etc*; *pst* meta'er *etc*; *fut* yeta'er *etc*; **2.** להלל בכתב *inf* lehalel (laudably) bee-khtav *(kh=k)*; *pst* heelel *etc*; *pres* mehalel *etc*; *fut* yehalel *etc*.

writer 1. כותב *nmf* kotev/-et; **2.** סופר (author) *nm* sof|er/-reem (*pl+of:* -rey).

(to) writhe להתפתל *inf* leheetpatel; *pst* heetpatel; *pres* meetpatel; *fut* yeetpatel.

writing כתיבה *nf* keteev|ah/-ot (*+of:* -at).

(hand)writing כתב היד *nm* ketav ha-yad.

writing desk שולחן כתיבה *nm* shoolkhan/-ot keteevah.

writing paper נייר כתיבה *nm* neyar keteevah.

written כתוב *adj* katoov/ketoovah.

wrong 1. לא נכון (incorrect) *adj* lo nakhon/nekhonah; **2.** מסולף (wicked) *adj* mesool|af/-efet; **3.** שלא במקומו (misplaced) *adj* she-lo bee-mekom|o/-ah.

(to be in the) wrong לטעות *inf* leet'ot; *pst* ta'ah; *pres* to'eh; *fut* yeet'eh.

(to do) wrong לעשות עוול *inf* la'asot 'avel; *pst* 'asah *etc*; *pres* 'oseh *etc*; *fut* ya'aseh *etc*.

(to go) wrong להשתבש *inf* leheeshtabesh; *pst* heeshtabesh; *pres* meeshtabesh; *fut* yeeshtabesh.

(the) wrong book לא הספר הנכון lo ha-sefer ha-nakhon.

(in the) wrong place במקום הלא נכון *adv* ba-makom ha-lo nakhon.

(the) wrong side of a fabric הצד ההפוך של הבד *nm* ha-tsad he-hafookh shel ha-bad.

(the) wrong side of the road צידו הלא נכון של הכביש *nm* tseed|o/-ah *(m/f)* ha-lo nakhon shel ha-kveesh.

wrought 1. מעובד *adj* me'oob|ad/-edet; **2.** מחושל (hammered) *adj* mekhoosh|al/-elet.

wrought iron ברזל חשיל *nm* barzel khasheel.

wrought silver כסף חשיל *nm* kesef khasheel.

wrought up מרוגש *adj* meroog|ash/-eshet.

wry מעוות *adj* me'oov|at/-etet.

wry face פרצוף מעוות *nm* partsoof/-eem me'oovat/-eem.

X.

X,x has no equivalent in the Hebrew alphabet. In the Hellenistic Era (2,300 years ago), it was transliterated כס (Kaf Samekh). In recent years, however, the Hebrew Language Academy has ruled that קס (Kof Samekh) would be more appropriate.

x איקס (algebraic letter, *etc*) *nm* eeks/-eem.

xenophobe שונא זרים *nmf & adj* sone/-t zareem.

xenophobia שנאת זרים *nf* seen'at zareem.

xerography קסירוגרפיה *nf* kserografeeyah.

(to) xerox לעשות העתקים מצולמים *inf* la'asot he'tekeem metsoolameem; *pst* 'asah *etc*; *pres* 'oseh *etc*; *fut* ya'aseh *etc*.

Xerox copy העתק מצולם *nm* he'et|ek/-keem metsoolam/-eem.

X-mas חג המולד *nm* khag ha-molad.

X-ray 1. קרני רנטגן (rays) *nm pl* karney rentgen; **2.** צילום רנטגן (photo) *nm* tseeloom/-ey rentgen.

(to) X-ray להקרין ברנטגן *inf* lehakreen be-rentgen; *pst* heekreen *etc*; *pres* makreen *etc*; *fut* yakreen *etc*.

xylophone קסילופון *nm* kseelofon/-eem (*pl+of:* -ey).

Y.

Y,y semi-consonant which, whenever pronounced as in *yard, young* or *year*, has the Hebrew letter י (yod) as its equivalent. (Indeed, that is how y is used in our transliteration.) Its capacity as a vowel (as in *why, cloudy, myrtle*) - is not used in our transliteration at all.

yacht יאכטה *nf* yakht|ah/-ot (*+of:* -at).

(to) yacht לשייט ביאכטה *inf* leshayet be-yakhtah; *pst* sheeyet *etc*; *pres* meshayet *etc*; *fut* yashayet *etc*.

Yankee יאנקי *nm* yankee/-m.

yard 1. 92,4 סנטימטרים (92.4 cms) teesh'eem oo-shnayeem peseek arba'ah senteemetreem; **2.** בניין עזר (enclosure) *nm* been|yan/-yeney 'ezer. **3.** חצר (space) *nf* khats|er/-erot (*+of:* -ar/-rot).

(back) yard חצר אחורית *nf* khatser akhoreet.

(barn)yard חצר משק *nf* khatsar meshek.

(ship)yard מספנה *nf* meesp|anah/-anot (*+of:* -enet/-enot).

yardstick קנה מידה *nm* ken|eh/-ey meedah.

yarn 1. חוט *nm* khoot/-eem (*pl+of:* -ey); **2.** סיפור בדים *nm* seepoor/-ey badeem.

yawn פיהוק *nm* peehook/-eem (*pl+of:* -ey).

(to) yawn לפהק *inf* lefahek; *pst* peehek (*p=f*); *pres* mefahek; *fut* yefahek.

yeah 1. כן ken; **2.** אמנם כן (indeed so) omnam ken; **3.** יתר על כן *adv* yater 'al ken.

year שנה *nm* shan|ah/-eem (*+of:* shn|at/-ot).

(by the) year לפי שנים *adv* lefee shaneem.

(last) year 1. השנה שעברה *nf* ha-shanah she-'avrah; **2.** אשתקד *adv* eshtakad.

(leap) year שנה מעוברת *nf* shan|ah/-eem me'oob|eret/-arot.

(next) year 1. השנה הבאה *nf* ha-shanah ha-ba'ah; **2.** בשנה הבאה *adv* ba-shanah haba'ah.

(this) year השנה *adv* ha-shanah.

(Happy New) Year to you! 1. !לשנה טובה *interj* le-shanah tovah! **2.** !לשנה טובה תכתבו (traditional well-wishing some weeks before and during Rosh-hashana) *interj* le-shanah tovah teekatevoo! **3.** !גמר טוב (traditional well-wishing from the day after Rosh-hashana through Yom-Kippur inclusive) *interj* gemar tov!

year's income הכנסה שנתית *nf* hakhnas|ah/-o shnatee|t/-yot.

(New) Year's Eve 1. ערב ראש השנה האזרחית 'erev rosh ha-shanah ha-'ezrakheet; **2.** ליל סילבסטר *nm* leyl/-ot seelvester.

yearbook 1. ספר שנה *nm* sefer/seefrey shanah; **2.** שנתון *nm* shnaton/-eem (*pl+of:* -ey).

yearling בן שנתו *nmf* ben/bat shna|to/-ah.

yearly 1. שנתי *adj adj* shnatee/-t; **2.** אחת לשנה *adv* akhat le-shanah.

(to) yearn לערוג *inf* la'arog; *pst* 'arag; *pres* 'oreg; *fut* ya'arog.

(to) yearn for להשתוקק ל־ *inf* leheeshtokek; *pst* heeshtokek; *pres* meeshtokek; *fut* yeeshtokek.

yearning 1. כמיהה *nf* kemee|hah/-hot (*+of:* -hat); **2.** כיסופים (longing) *nm pl* keesoofeem (*pl+of:* -ey).

yeast שמרים *nm pl* shmar|eem (*pl+of:* -ey).

yell צעקה *nf* tse'ak|ah/-ot (*+of:* tsa'ak|at/-ot).

(to) yell לצעוק *inf* leets'ok; *pst* tsa'ak; *pres* tso'ek; *fut* yeets'ak.

yellow 1. צבע צהוב *nm* tseva' tsahov; **2.** צהוב *adj* tsahov/tsehoobah *(b=v)*.

yellow fever קדחת צהובה *nf* kadakhat tsehoobah.

yellowish צהבהב tsehav|hav/-hevet.

yelp 1. יללה *nf* yelal|ah/-ot (*+of:* yeelel|at/-ot); **2.** נביחה (bark) *nf* neveekh|ah/-ot (*+of:* -at).

(to) yelp 1. ליילל *inf* leyalel; *pst* yeelel; *pres* meyalel; *fut* yeyalel; **2.** לנבוח *inf* leenbo'akh; *pst* navakh *(v=b)*; *pres* nove'akh; *fut* yeenbakh.

Yemen תימן *nm* teyman.

Yemenite 1. תימני *nmf* teymanee/-yah (*pl:* -m/ -yot). **2.** תימני *adj* teymanee/-t.

yes 1. כן ken; **2.** הן (literary) hen.

yesman אומר הן *nm* omer/omrey hen.

yesterday אתמול *nm* etmol.

(the day before) yesterday שלשום *nm* sheelshom.

yet 1. טרם *adv* terem; **2.** עוד *conj* 'od.

(as) yet בינתיים *adv* beynatayeem.

(not) yet עוד לא *adv* 'od lo.

Yiddish 1. אידיש (language) *nf* eedeesh; **2.** אידישאי *adj* eedeesha'ee/-t; **3.** אידי *[colloq.] adj* eedee/-t; **4.** אידישי (derogatory) *adj* eedeeshee/-t.

(in) Yiddish 1. באידיש *adv* be-'eedeesh; **2.** בלשון האידית (language) *adv* ba-lashon ha-'eedeet.

Yiddish joke 1. בדיחה אידית *nf* bedeekh|ah/ -ot eedee|/-yot; **2.** בדיחה באידיש (syn) *nf* bedeekh|ah/-ot be-'eedeesh.

Yiddish theater תיאטרון אידי *nm* te'atron/-eem eedee/-yeem.

"Yiddishe mamma" "אימא יהודייה" *[colloq.] nf* eema yehoodeeyah.

Yiddishist 1. חובב אידיש (amateur) *nmf* khovev/ -et (*pl:* -ey) eedeesh; **2.** ידען אידיש (connoisseur) *nm* yad'an/-ey eedeesh; **3.** אידישיסט (devotee) *nmf* eedeesheest/-eet.

Yiddishism 1. ביטוי אידישאי (idiom) *nm* beetoo|y/-yeem eedeesha'ee/-yeem; **2.** אידישיזמוס (ideology) *nm* eedeesheezmoos.

yield 1. תנובה *nf* tenoov|ah/-ot (*+of:* -at); **2.** יבול (crop) *nm* yevool/-eem (*pl+of:* -ey).

(to) yield 1. להניב (produce) *inf* lehaneev; *pst* heneev; *pres* meneev; *fut* yaneev; **2.** להיכנע (surrender) *inf* leheekana'; *pst & pres* neekhna' *(kh=k)*; *fut* yeekana'.

(to) yield five percent להניב חמישה אחוזים *inf* lehaneev khameeshah akhoozeem; *pst* heneev *etc*; *pres* meneev *etc*; *fut* yaneev *etc*.

yodel ידלול *nm* yeedlool/-eem (*pl+of:* -ey).

(to) yodel ליידלל *inf* leyadlel; *pst* yeedlel; *pres* meyadlel; *fut* leyadlel.

yoke עול *nm* 'ol.

(to) yoke 1. להכביד עול *inf* lehakhbeed 'ol; *pst* heekhbeed 'ol; *pres* makhbeed 'ol; *fut* yakhbeed 'ol; **2.** לשעבד (subdue) *inf* lesha'bed; *pst* sheee'bed; *pres* mesha'bed; *fut* yesha'bed.

yolk חלמון *nm* khelmon/-eem (*pl+of:* -ey).

yonder 1. ההוא *adj* ha-hoo/hee *(m/f)*; **2.** שם *adv* sham.

you 1. אתה *pron m sing* atah; **2.** את *pron f sing* at; **3.** אתם *pron m pl* atem; **4.** אתן *pron f pl* aten.

(to) you 1. לך *m sing* lekha; **2.** לך *f sing* lakh; **3.** לכם *m pl* lakhem; **4.** לכן *f pl* lakhen.

you yourself 1. אתה עצמך *m sing* atah 'atsmekha; **2.** את עצמך *f sing* at 'atsmekh.

you yourselves 1. אתם עצמכם *m pl* atem 'atsmekhem; **2.** אתן עצמכן *f pl* aten 'atsmekhen.

young צעיר *adj* tsa'eer/tse'eerah.

(the) young הנוער *nm* ha-no'ar.

(the) young generation הדור הצעיר *nm* ha-dor ha-tsa'eer.

young leaf עלה רך *nm* 'al|eh/-eem rakh/rakeem *(k=kh)*.

young man 1. בחור *nm* bakhoor/-eem (*pl+of:* -ey); **2.** עלם (literary) *nm* 'elem/'alameem (*pl+of:* 'almey).

(her) young ones ילדיה הרכים *nm pl* yeladeha ha-rakeem.

young woman 1. בחורה *nf* bakhoor|ah/-ot (*+of:* -at); **2.** עלמה *nf* 'al|mah/-amot (*+of:* -mat/-mot).

youngster נער *nm* na'ar/ne'areem (*pl+of:* na'arey).

your, yours 1. שלך possess. *pron m sing* shelkha; **2.** שלך *possess. pron f sing* shelakh; **3.** שלכם possess. *pron m pl* shelakhem; **4.** שלכן possess. *pron f pl* shelakhen.

(a friend of) yours ידיד שלך *nmf* yedeed/-ah shel|kha/-akh *(m/f)*.

yourself 1. אתה עצמך *m sing* atah 'atsmekha; **2.** את עצמך *f sing* at 'atsmekh.

(to) yourself 1. לעצמך *m sing* le-'atsmekha; **2.** לעצמך *f sing* le-'atsmekh.

(you) yourself 1. אתה עצמך *m sing* atah 'atsmekha; **2.** את עצמך *f sing* at 'atsmekh.

yourselves 1. בעצמכם *m pl* be-'atsmekhem; **2.** בעצמכן *f pl* be-'atsmekhen

(to) yourselves 1. לעצמכם *m pl* le-'atsmekhem; **2.** לעצמכן *f pl* le-'atsmekhen.

youth 1. נעורים *nm pl* ne'oor|eem (*pl+of:* -ey); **2.** נוער (young persons) *nm* no'ar; **3.** נער (boy) na'ar/ne'areem (*pl+of:* na'arey).

youthful צעיר *adj* tsa'eer/tse'eerah.

Yuletide עונת חג המולד *nf* 'onat khag ha-molad.

Z.

Z,z consonant for which the Hebrew letter ז (zayeen) is the equivalent.
zeal 1. להט *nm* lahat/lehateem (*pl+of:* lahatey); **2.** קנאות (fanaticism) *nf* kana'oot.
zealot קנאי *nmf* kan|ay/-a'eet.
zealous 1. נלהב *adj* neel|hav/-hevet; **2.** להוט (eager) *adj* lahoot/lehootah.
zenith 1. פסגה *nf* peesg|ah/psagot (*+of:* peesg|at/-ot); **2.** זנית zeneet.
zephyr 1. צפריר *nm* tsafreer/-eem (*pl+of:* -ey); **2.** רוח קלה *nf* (gentle breeze) *nf* roo'akh kalah.
zero אפס *nm* efes/afaseem (*pl+of:* afsey).
zest 1. טעם נעים *nm* ta'am na'eem; **2.** חשק (relish) *nm* kheshek/khashakeem (*pl+of:* kheshkey).
zigzag זיגזג *nm* zeegzag.
(to) zigzag לזגזג *inf* lezagzeg; *pst* zeegzeg; *pres* mezagzeg; *fut* yezagzeg.
zinc אבץ *nm* avats.
zip code מיקוד *nm* meekood/-eem (*pl+of:* -ey).
zipper 1. רוכסן *nm* rokhsan/-eem (*pl+of:* -ey); **2.** ריץ'-רץ' *[colloq.] nm* reetchratch/-eem (*pl+of:* -ey).
zodiac גלגל המזלות *nm* galgal ha-mazalot.
(sign of the) zodiac מזל *nm* mazal/-ot.
zone איזור *nm* eyzor/azor|eem (*pl+of:* -ey).
(to) zone לחלק לאזורים *inf* lekhalek le-azoreem; *pst* kheelek *etc; pres* mekhalek *etc; fut* yekhalek *etc.*
zoo גן חיות *nm* gan/-ey khayot.
zoological זואולוגי *adj* zo'ologee/-t.
zoology זואולוגיה *nf* zo'olog|yah (*+of:* -yat).